TRAVELING WITH YOUR PET
THE AAA PETBOOK®

The AAA guide to more than 14,000
pet-friendly, AAA Approved® hotels
and campgrounds across the
United States and Canada.

15th Edition

AAA PUBLISHING

AAA thanks the following organization for its assistance:
Veterinary Emergency & Critical Care Society

Cover Photos

Front: Editors' Pick - Cody Bear at Seven Springs Resort, Champion, Pennsylvania
Submitted by owner Kathy Havey
Back: 1st place Photo Contest Winner: Jack Ryan at Shaver Lake, California
Submitted by owner Susan K. Robinson
Spine: 2nd place Photo Contest Winner: Mandie at Mammoth Lakes, California
Submitted by owners Gisenyi and Jeremy Wansor

Published by AAA Publishing
1000 AAA Drive, Heathrow, Florida 32746

Fifteenth Edition Copyright © 2013 AAA Publishing. All rights reserved.
ISBN: 978-1-59508-530-6 Stock Number 552213
Printed in the USA by Quad/Graphics, Inc.

This book was printed on third-party certified sustainably forested paper.

ABOUT THIS BOOK

Welcome to the 15th edition of *Traveling With Your Pet: The AAA PetBook®*, an indispensable, easy-to-use resource for travelers with pets. This comprehensive book provides all the information needed to take a four-legged friend on the road, from activity planning to trip preparation to finding a place to stay.

Recreational Resources

- Dog parks where you and your furry friends can play, exercise or just relax.
- A roundup of attractions that allow pets or offer kennel service.
- Recreation information for U.S. and Canadian national public lands that allow pets.

Practical Considerations

- An extensive list of emergency animal clinics for unexpected situations en route and at your destination, compiled by the Veterinary Emergency & Critical Care Society.
- Procedures and tips for crossing the U.S./Canadian border in either direction with pets.
- Policies pertaining to service animals.

Detailed Accommodation Listings

- Specific pet policy details: deposits and fees (rounded to the nearest dollar), size restrictions, housekeeping and pet care services, designated rooms and other stipulations.
- Listings for more than 13,000 AAA Approved hotels which include AAA's trustworthy Diamond Ratings, the traveler's assurance of quality accommodations and reliable decision making information, plus facility details including rates, highway directions, amenities, recreation, dining and accessibility.
- Listings for more than 700 top-rated campgrounds, including pet policies, facility details and AAA member discounts.

About the AAA PetBook Photo Contest

Have some great pictures from traveling with your pet? The annual AAA PetBook Photo Contest sponsored by Best Western gives you a chance to win great prizes and see your pet pictured on a cover of the next edition. Turn the page to read about the current contest winners, and turn to the photo gallery insert to see some irresistible photos of finalists. For contest requirements and an entry form, visit AAA.com/PetBook.

Picture Your Pet as the Next AAA PetBook® Cover Model!

For a chance to see your pet on a cover of the next edition of **Traveling With Your Pet: The AAA PetBook®,** enter the AAA PetBook Photo Contest Sponsored by Best Western, open yearly from May 1 to Nov. 30. Visit **AAA.com/PetBook** for contest rules, an entry form, prize listings and photos of previous winners and finalists.

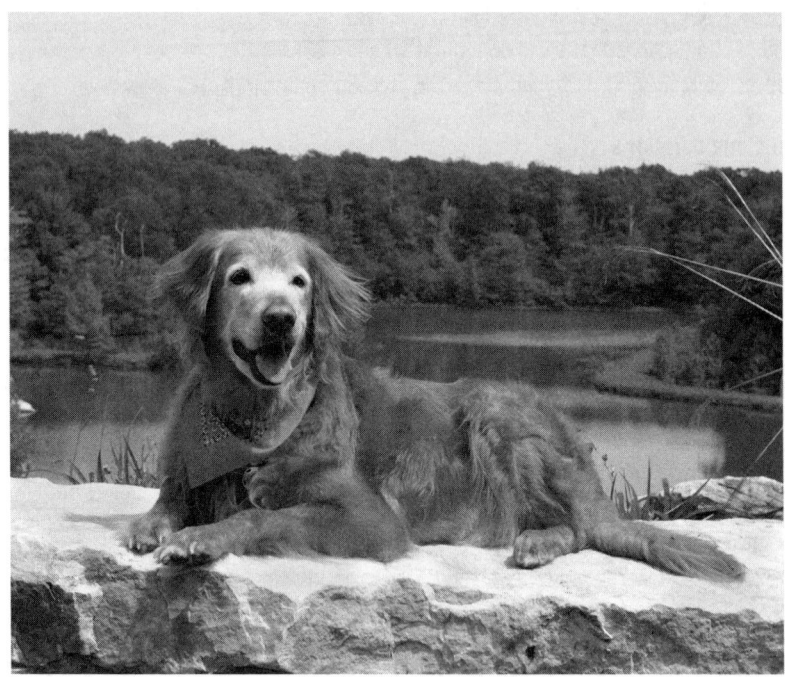

Editors' Pick — Cody Bear

Every so often, we get a photo contest entry that's so compelling our editors elect to use it on the book's front cover — separate from the placements designated for our first- and second-place contest winners. This year we awarded the honor to Cody Bear, a frequent traveler and running enthusiast from Pennsylvania.

This amiable golden retriever is shown here vacationing at Seven Springs Resort in Champion, Penn. His family says they wouldn't dream of leaving Cody Bear at home when they travel. They especially enjoy bringing Cody Bear and his sister Ginger to Seven Springs so the dogs can run all they want.

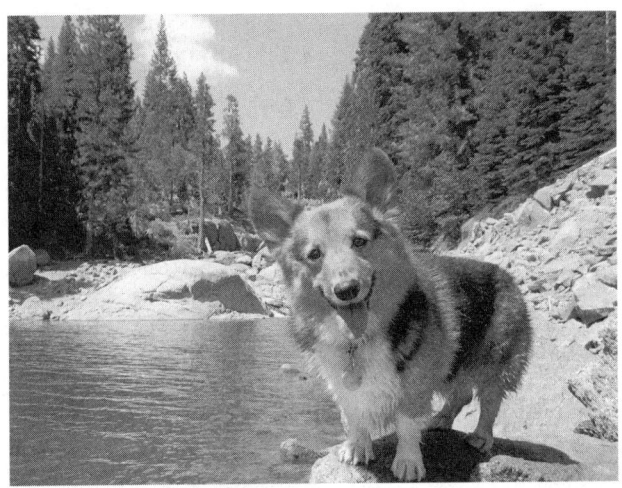

1st place winner — Jack Ryan

Jack Ryan, a joyful Pembroke Welsh corgi from California, is pictured enjoying a family camping trip at Shaver Lake, Calif. Chock-full of contagious enthusiasm for every sight, sound and scent of nature, Jack Ryan is a welcome travel companion and eager explorer. He and his family especially enjoy visiting beautiful Shaver Lake, surrounded by pine trees, fern grottos and hiking trails.

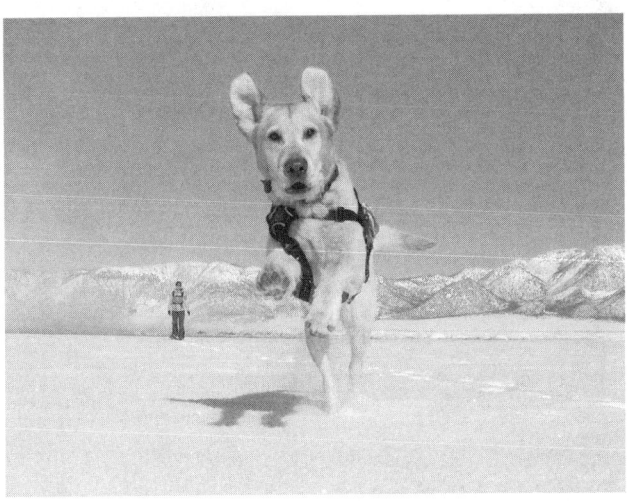

2nd place winner — Mandie

Mandie, an enthusiastic Labrador retriever from California, loves outdoor activities. She's pictured enjoying a romp in the snow at Mammoth Lakes, Calif. Mandie brings her family great joy with her spontaneity and fun, keeping them warm at night and on the go. She carries her own backpack when enjoying favorite activities — camping and hiking.

Turn to Page 353 to view a sampling of more highlights from the last photo contest.

TABLE OF CONTENTS

AAA PetBook® Photo Contest

Traveling With Pets

Pet-Friendly Places

Pet-Friendly Lodgings

U.S. Lodgings

Canadian Lodgings

Pet-Friendly Campgrounds

Many people view their pets as full-fledged members of the family. Spot and Snowball often have their own beds, premium-quality foods, a basketful of toys and a special place in their humans' hearts.

Until it's time to go on vacation, that is. Then the family dog or cat is consigned to "watching the fort" at home while everyone else experiences the joy of traveling. Many animal lovers hesitate to take their pet with them because they don't think they'll be able to find accommodations that accept four-legged guests. Others aren't sure how — or if — their furry friends will adapt.

The truth is, including a pet in the family vacation is fairly easy, so long as you plan ahead. Most pets respond well to travel, a fact that isn't lost on the tourism industry. More than 14,000 AAA Approved hotels and campgrounds from coast to coast are pet-friendly, and airline bookings for pet passengers are on the rise. Great companions at home, pets are earning their stripes on the road, too.

So if you've been longing to hit the trail with a canine or feline companion, read the tips on the following pages. You may find that a getaway can be far more enjoyable with than without your pet.

Should Your Pet Travel?

Before you make reservations, determine if your pet is able to travel. Most animals can and do make the most of the experience, but a small percentage simply are not cut out for traveling. Illness, physical condition and temperament are important factors, as is your pet's ability to adjust to such stresses as changes to his environment and routine. When in doubt, check with your veterinarian. If you feel your pet isn't up to the trip, it's better for everyone if he stays home.

❧ **Rule 1: Pets who are very young, very old, pregnant, sick, injured, prone to biting or excessive vocalizing, or who cannot follow basic obedience commands should not travel.**

Even if Spot and Snowball are seasoned travelers, take into account the type of vacation and activities you have planned. No pet is going to be happy (or safe) cooped up in a car or hotel room. Likewise, the family dog may love camping and hiking, but the family cat may not. Putting a little thought toward your animal's needs and safety will pay off in a more enjoyable vacation for everyone.

❧ **Rule 2: If your pet can't actively participate in the trip, she should stay home.**

Most of the information in this book pertains to cats and dogs. If you own a bird, hamster, pig, ferret, lizard or other exotic creature, remember that unusual animals are not always accepted as readily as more conventional pets. Always specify the type of pet you have when making arrangements.

Also check states' animal policies. **Hawaii** imposes a 120-day quarantine for all imported dogs, cats and other carnivores to prevent the importation of rabies. In some cases, the quarantine period may be reduced to 5 days or less if a pet meets various pre- and post-arrival requirements. Guide dogs and service dogs are exempt from the quarantine provided they have: a standard health certificate issued within 30 days prior to arrival; a current rabies vaccination with documentation of the product name, lot number and lot expiration date; a successful result of an OIE-FAVN rabies blood test conducted after 1 year of age; and an electronic identification microchip implanted and operational. Upon arrival, guide dogs and service dogs still must be examined for external parasites. For additional details, obtain the Hawaii Rabies Quarantine Information Brochure from the Hawaii Department of Agriculture, Animal Quarantine Station, 99-951 Halawa Valley St., Aiea, HI 96701-5602; phone (808) 483-7151, e-mail rabiesfree@hawaii.gov. Further information also is available from the department's web site: www.hawaii.gov/hdoa/ai/aqs/info.

North Carolina has stringent restrictions regarding pets in lodgings. Make certain you understand an accommodation's specific policies before making reservations.

❧ **Rule 3: Be specific when making travel plans that include your pet. Nobody wants unpleasant surprises on vacation.**

If Spot and Snowball stay behind, leave them in good hands while you're gone. **Family, friends and neighbors** make good sitters (provided they're willing), especially if they know your pet and can care for him in your home. Provide detailed instructions for feeding, exercise and medication, as well as phone numbers for your destination, your veterinarian and your local animal emergency clinic.

Professional pet sitters offer a range of services, from feeding and walking your pet daily to full-time house sitting while you are gone. Interview several candidates, and always check credentials and references. For additional information, contact the National Association of Professional Pet Sitters or Pet Sitters International. *(See sidebars on p. 8 and p. 9.)*

Kennels board many animals simultaneously and generally are run by professionals who will provide food and exercise according to your instructions. Pets usually are kept in a run (dogs) or cage (cats and small dogs) and may not get the same level of human interaction as at home. Veterinary clinics also board pets and may be the best choice if yours is sick, injured or needs special medical care.

Veterinarians, fellow pet owners and professional associations are a good source of referrals for sitters and kennels.

❧ **Rule 4: Never leave your pet with someone you don't trust.**

Travelers Who Have Disabilities

Individuals with disabilities who own service animals to assist them with everyday activities undoubtedly face challenges, but traveling should not be one of them. Service animals (the accepted term for animals trained to help people with disabilities) are not pets and thus are not subject to many of the laws or policies pertaining to pets.

The Americans With Disabilities Act (ADA) defines a service animal as "any guide dog, signal dog or other animal individually trained to provide assistance to an individual with a disability." ADA regulations stipulate that public accommodations are required to modify policies, practices and procedures to permit the use of a service animal by an individual with a disability.

The purpose of these regulations is to provide equal access opportunities for people with disabilities and to ensure that they are not separated from their service animals. A tow truck operator, for example, must allow a service animal to ride in the truck with her owner rather than in the towed vehicle.

Public accommodations may charge a fee or deposit to an individual who has a disability — provided that fee or deposit is required of all customers — but no fees or deposits may be charged for the service animal, even those normally charged for pets.

The handler/owner is responsible for the animal's care and behavior; if the dog creates an altercation or poses a direct threat, the handler may be required to remove it from the premises and pay for any resulting damages.

CHOOSING A PET SITTER

Before hiring a pet sitter, ask:
- Is he or she insured (for commercial liability) and bonded?
- What is included in the fee?
- Does the sitter require that your pet have a current vaccination?
- What kind of animals does the sitter typically care for?
- How will a medical, weather or home emergency be handled?
- Does he or she fully understand your pet's medical or dietary needs?
- How much time will be spent with your pet?

The pet sitter should:
- Have a polished, professional attitude.
- Provide references.
- Have a standard contract outlining terms of service.
- Have experience in caring for animals.
- Insist on current vaccinations.
- Ask about your pet's health, temperament, schedule and needs.
- Visit and interact with your pet before you leave.
- Devote time and attention to your pet.
- Be affiliated with pet care organizations.

Be sure you:
- Explain your pet's personality — favorite toys, good and bad habits, hiding spots, general health, etc.
- Leave care instructions, keys, food and water dishes, extra supplies (food, medication, etc.), and phone numbers for your veterinarian and an emergency contact.
- Bring pets inside before leaving.

CHOOSING A KENNEL

Before reserving a kennel, ask:
- What is included in the fee?
- Are current vaccinations required?
- What kind of animals do they board?
- How will a medical or weather emergency be handled?
- Will your pet be kept in a cage or run?
- Will your pet receive daily exercise?
- Does the kennel fully understand your pet's medical or dietary needs?
- How and how often will staff interact with your pet?

The kennel should:
- Require proof of current vaccinations.
- Be clean, well-ventilated and offer adequate protection from the elements.
- Have separate areas for dogs, cats and other animals, with secure fencing and caging.
- Clean and disinfect facilities daily.
- Give your pet his regular food on his regular schedule.
- Provide soft bedding in runs/cages.
- Understand your pet's medical needs.
- Provide or obtain veterinary care if necessary.
- Offer sufficient supervision.
- Have a friendly, animal-loving staff.

Be sure you:
- Notify staff of behavior quirks (dislike of other animals, children, etc.).
- Provide food and medication.
- Leave a familiar object with your pet.
- Leave phone numbers for your veterinarian and an emergency contact.
- Spend time with your pet before boarding him.

Pet Partners, an organization devoted to companion and service animals, has information about laws that affect people and service animals in public accommodations. Phone (425) 679-5500 for more information, or visit www.petpartners.org.

Preparing Your Pet for Travel

Happily, many vacations can be planned to include fun activities for pets. Trips to parks, nature trails, the ocean or lakes offer exposure to the world beyond the window or fence at home, as well as the chance to explore new sights and sounds. Even the streets of an unfamiliar city can provide a smorgasbord of discoveries for your animal friend to enjoy.

Once you decide Spot and Snowball are ready to hit the road, plan accordingly:

❧ **Get a clean bill of health from the veterinarian.** Update your pet's vaccinations, check his general physical condition and obtain a health certificate showing proof of up-to-date inoculations, particularly rabies, distemper and kennel cough. Such documentation will be necessary if you cross state or country lines, and also may come in handy in the unlikely event your pet gets lost and must be retrieved from the local shelter. Don't forget to ask the doctor about potential health risks at your destination (Lyme disease, heartworm infection) and the necessary preventive measures.

If your pet is taking prescribed medicine, pack a sufficient supply plus a few days' extra. Also take the prescription in case you need a refill. Be prepared for emergencies by getting the names and numbers of clinics or doctors at your destination from your veterinarian or the American Animal Hospital Association. **Hint:** Obtain these references before you leave and keep them handy throughout the trip.

Make sure your pet is in good physical shape overall, especially if you are planning an active vacation. If your animal is primarily sedentary or overweight, he may not be up to lengthy hikes through the woods.

Note: Some owners believe a sedated animal will travel more easily than one that is fully aware, but this is rarely the case. In fact, tranquilizing an animal can make travel much more stressful. Always consult a veterinarian about what is best for your pet, and administer sedatives only under the doctor's direction. In addition, never give an animal medication that is specifically prescribed for humans. The dosage may be too high for an animal's much smaller body mass, or may cause dangerous side effects.

❧ **Acclimate your pet to car travel.** Even if you're flying, your pet will have to ride in the car to get to the airport or terminal, and you don't want any unpleasant surprises before departure.

Some animals are used to riding in the car and even enjoy it. But most associate the inside of the carrier or the car with one thing only: the annual visit to the V-E-T. Considering that these visits usually end with a jab from a sharp needle, it's no wonder that some pets forget their training and act up in the car. If this is your situation, you

CONTACT INFORMATION

The following organizations offer information, tips, brochures and other travel materials designed to help you and your pet enjoy a happy and safe vacation.

American Animal Hospital Association
12575 W. Bayaud Ave., Lakewood, CO 80228
(303) 986-2800 — www.healthypet.com

American Society for the Prevention of Cruelty to Animals
424 E. 92nd St., New York, NY 10128-6804
(212) 876-7700 — www.aspca.org

American Veterinary Medical Association
1931 N. Meacham Rd., Suite 100
Schaumburg, IL 60173-4360
(800) 248-2862 — www.avma.org

The Humane Society of the United States
2100 L St. N.W., Washington, DC 20037
(202) 452-1100 — www.humanesociety.org

National Association of Professional Pet Sitters
15000 Commerce Pkwy., Suite C
Mt. Laurel, NJ 08054
(856) 439-0324 — www.petsitters.org

PetGroomer.com
P.O. Box 2489
Yelm, WA 98597
(360) 446-5348 — www.petgroomer.com

Pet Sitters International
201 E. King St., King, NC 27021
(336) 983-9222 — www.petsit.com

USDA-APHIS
USDA-APHIS-Animal Care
4700 River Rd., Unit 84
Riverdale, MD 20737-1234
(301) 734-7833 —
www.aphis.usda.gov/animal_welfare/index.shtml

will have to re-train your animal to view a drive as a reward, not a punishment.

Begin by allowing your pet to become used to the car without actually going anywhere. Then take short trips to places that are fun for animals, such as the park or the drive-through window at a fast-food restaurant. (Keep those indulgent snacks to a minimum!) Be sure to praise her for good behavior with words, petting and healthy treats. It shouldn't take long before you and your furry friend are enjoying leisurely drives without incident. *(See Traveling by Car, p. 12.)*

❧ **Brush up on behavior.** Will Snowball make a good travel companion? Or will he be an absolute terror on the road? Don't wait until the vacation is already under way to find out; review general behavioral guidelines with respect to your animal, keeping in mind that the unfamiliarity of travel situations may test the temperament of even the most well-behaved pet.

It's a good idea to socialize Spot by exposing her to other people and animals (especially if she normally stays inside). You're likely to encounter both on your trip, and it is important that she learns to behave properly in the company of strangers. Make her introduction to the outside world gradual, such as a walk in a new neighborhood or taking her along while you run errands. Exposure to new situations will help reduce fear of the unknown and result in more socially acceptable behavior.

Is your pet housebroken? How is he around children? Does he obey vocal commands? Be honest about your animal's ability to cope in unfamiliar surroundings. Depending on the length and nature of the trip and your pet's level of command response, an obedience refresher course might be a good idea.

❧ **Learn about your destination.** Check into quarantines or other restrictions well in advance, and make follow-up calls as your departure date approaches. Find out what types of documentation will be required — not just en route, but on the way home as well.

Be aware of potential safety or health risks where you're going, and plan accordingly. For example, the southeastern United States — particularly Florida — is home to alligators and heartworm-carrying mosquitoes, and many mountainous and wooded areas may harbor ticks that transmit Lyme disease.

Confirm all travel plans within a few days of your departure, especially with lodgings and airlines; their policies may have changed after you made the reservations. If you plan to visit state parks or attractions that accept pets on the premises, obtain their animal regulations in advance.

❧ **Determine the best mode of transportation.** Most people traveling with pets drive. Many airlines do accept animals in the passenger cabin or cargo hold, and as more people choose to fly with their pet airlines are becoming more pet-conscious. Restrictions vary as to the type and number of pets an airline will carry, however, so inquire about animal shipping and welfare policies before making reservations. If your pet must travel in the cargo

WHAT TO TAKE

❑ Carrier or crate. *(See Selecting a Carrier or Crate, p. 11, for specifications.)*

❑ Nylon or leather collar or harness, license tag, ID tag(s) and leash. All should be sturdy and should fit your pet properly.

❑ Food and water dishes.

❑ Can opener and spoon (for canned food).

❑ An ample supply of food, plus a few days' extra.

❑ Bottled water from home. (Many animals are finicky about their drinking water.)

❑ Cooler with ice.

❑ Healthy treats.

❑ Medications, if necessary.

❑ Health certificate and other required documents.

❑ A blanket or other bedding. (If your pet is used to sleeping on the furniture, bring an old blanket or sheet to place on top of the hotel's bedding.)

❑ Litter supplies (for cats or other small animals), a scooper and plastic bags (for dogs).

❑ Favorite toys.

❑ Carpet deodorizer.

❑ Chewing preventative.

❑ A recent photograph and a written description including name, breed, gender, height, weight, coloring and distinctive markings.

❑ Grooming supplies:
comb/brush
nail clippers
shampoo
cloth and paper towels
cotton balls/tissues

❑ First-aid kit:
gauze, bandages and adhesive tape
hydrogen peroxide
rubbing alcohol
ointment
muzzle
scissors
tweezers (for removing ticks, burrs, splinters, etc.)
local emergency phone numbers
first-aid guide (such as *Pet First Aid: Cats & Dogs*, published by The Humane Society of the United States and the American Red Cross)

hold, heed the cautionary advice in the Traveling by Air section. *(See p. 13.)*

Flying is really the only major alternative to car travel. Amtrak, as well as Greyhound and other interstate bus lines, do not accept pets. **Note:** Seeing-eye dogs and other service animals are exempt from the regulations prohibiting pets on Amtrak and interstate bus lines. Local rail and bus companies may allow pets in small carriers, but this is an exception rather than a rule.

The only cruise ship that currently permits pets is the Cunard Line's *Queen Mary 2* (on trans-Atlantic crossings only); kennels are provided, but animals are accepted on a very limited basis. Some small charter and sightseeing boat companies permit pets onboard, however.

A word of advice: Never try to sneak your pet onto any mode of public transportation where she is not permitted. You may face legal action or fines, and the animal may be confiscated if discovered.

❧ **Pack as carefully for your pet as you do for yourself.** *(See What To Take, p. 10.)* Make sure she has a collar with a license tag and ID tag(s) listing her name and yours, along with your address and phone number. As an added precaution, some owners outfit their dog with a second tag listing the name and number of a contact person at home. Popular backup identification methods are to have your animal tattooed with an ID number (usually a social security number) or to implant a microchip under her skin.

If your pet requires medication, make sure that is specified on his tag. This helps others understand your animal's needs and also may prevent people from keeping a found pet or from stealing one to sell.

Note: Choke chains, collars that tighten when they are pulled, may be useful during training sessions, but they do not make good full-time collars. If the chain catches on something, your pet could choke herself trying to pull free. For regular wear, use a harness or a conventional collar made of nylon or leather.

Selecting a Carrier or Crate

This is one of the most important steps in ensuring your pet's safety when traveling. A good-quality carrier not only contains your pet during transit, it also gives him a safe, reassuring place to stay when confinement is necessary at your destination. Acclimate the animal before the trip so he views the crate as a cozy den, not a place of exile.

If you plan to travel by car, a carrier will confine your pet en route, and also may come in handy if Spot or Snowball must stay in the room unsupervised. A secured crate will prevent your pet from escaping from the room when the cleaning staff arrives, or at night if camping in the open. *(See At Your Destination, p. 15.)*

Some airlines allow small pets to travel in the passenger cabin as carry-on luggage. There are no laws dictating

the type of carrier to use, but remember that it must be small enough to fit under a standard airplane seat and should not exceed 45 linear inches (length + width + height), or roughly **22 by 14 by 9 inches.** Depending on the airline, carrier size limits may be even smaller. If your pet will be flying in the cargo hold, you must use a carrier that meets U.S. Department of Agriculture Animal and Plant Health Inspection Service (USDA-APHIS) specifications. *(See Traveling by Air, p. 13.)*

Crates are available at pet supply stores; some airlines also sell carriers. Soft-sided travel bags are handy for flyers with small pets. Before you make the investment, make sure your carrier is airline-approved.

Even if you never take to the skies, these common-sense guidelines provide a good rule of thumb in selecting a crate for other uses. USDA-APHIS rules stipulate the following:

❧ The crate must be enclosed, but with ventilation openings occupying at least 14 percent of total wall space, at least one-third of which must be located on the top half of the kennel. A three-quarter-inch lip or rim must surround the exterior to prevent air holes from being blocked.

❧ The crate must open easily, but must be sufficiently strong to hold up during normal cargo transit procedures (loading, unloading, etc.).

❧ The floor must be solid and leakproof, and must be covered with an absorbent lining or material (such as an old towel or litter).

❧ The crate must be just large enough to allow the animal to turn freely while standing, and to have a full range of normal movement while standing or lying down.

❧ The crate must offer exterior grips or handles so that handlers do not have to place their hands or fingers inside.

❧ Food and water dishes must be securely attached and accessible without opening the kennel.

Ventilation openings

Live animal label

Spacer bar

Name and address label

Food and water dishes

HEATSTROKE AND HYPOTHERMIA

The best way to treat heatstroke or hypothermia is to prevent it. Do not leave pets unattended in a car, even if only for a few minutes. Also heed airlines' restrictions on pet travel, and carefully investigate animal welfare policies to make certain the airline has safeguards to protect your pet from both conditions.

Other preventive measures are to avoid strenuous exercise — including such activities as hiking and "fetch" — when the sun is strongest (10 a.m.-2 p.m.), and to provide your pet access to clean, fresh drinking water at all times.

Following are the warning signs and basic first aid for heatstroke and hypothermia. Always be alert to your pet's physical condition and watch for symptoms — immediate attention to the situation may mean the difference between life and death. If your pet is struck with either disorder, take him to an animal hospital or veterinarian as fast as safely possible.

HEATSTROKE

Symptoms
- rapid, shallow breathing
- excessive salivation
- heavy panting
- hot to the touch
- glazed eyes
- unsteadiness, dizziness
- deep red or purple tongue or gums
- vomiting
- body temperature of 104 F or higher

First Aid
- place pet in the shade
- quickly dampen with cool water, especially on the head and neck
- give small amounts of water

HYPOTHERMIA

Symptoms
- shivering
- weakness
- lethargy
- cold to the touch
- body temperature of 95 F or lower

First Aid
- place in a warm area
- wrap in towels or a blanket
- quickly warm by gently massaging the head, chest and extremities

---

- If the carrier has wheels, they must be removed or immobilized prior to loading.

- One-inch lettering stating "Live Animals" must be placed visibly on the exterior and must be accompanied by directional arrows showing the crate's proper orientation. It also is a good idea to label the crate with your name, home address and home phone number, as well as an address and phone number where you can be reached during the trip. **Hint:** Use an adhesive label or an indelible marker and write directly on the crate, as paper may be ripped off accidentally in transit.

- Attach a list of care instructions (feeding, watering, etc.) for a 24-hour period to the exterior of the carrier. This will help airport workers care for your pet if he is sent to the wrong destination.

- If you are traveling with multiple pets, note that crates may contain only one animal whose weight exceeds 20 pounds. Smaller animals may travel together under the following guidelines: one species to a crate, except compatible dogs and cats of similar size; two puppies or kittens under 6 months of age; 15 guinea pigs or rabbits; 50 hamsters. **Note:** These are federal limits; airlines may impose more stringent regulations.

Traveling by Car

The first step in ensuring your pet's well-being during a vacation is to train her to ride in the car. For safety reasons, pets should be confined to the back seat, either in a carrier or a harness attached to the car's seat belt. This keeps the animal from interfering with or distracting the driver, and also may save her life in the event of an accident. And a restrained animal will not be able to break free and run away the second the car door is opened.

To help prevent car sickness, feed your pet a light meal 4 to 6 hours before departing. Do not give an animal food or water in a moving vehicle.

Never allow your pet to ride in the bed of a pickup truck. It's illegal in some states; he also can jump out or be thrown, endangering himself and others on the road. Harnessing or leashing him to the truck bed is not advisable either: If he tries to jump out, he could be dragged along the road or the restraint could become a noose. Avoid placing animals in campers or trailers as well. **If your pet cannot ride in the car with you, leave him at home.**

Don't let your dog stick her head out the window, no matter how enjoyable it seems. Road debris and other flying objects can injure delicate eyes and ears, and the animal is at greater risk for severe injury if the vehicle should stop suddenly or be struck. If it is hot outside, run the air conditioner instead of opening the windows, and be sure that the air flow is reaching your pet.

AAA recommends that drivers stop every 2 hours to stretch their legs and take a quick break from driving. Your pet will appreciate the same break. Plan to visit a rest stop every 4 hours or so to let him have a drink and a chance to answer the call of nature. (Cat owners should bring along a litter box; dog owners should clean up afterward.)

Be sure your pet is leashed before opening the car door. This is not merely a courtesy to fellow travelers; it will prevent her from unexpectedly breaking free and running away. Keep in mind that even the most obedient pet may become disoriented during travel or in strange places and set off for home. **Hint:** If your pet is not used to traveling, use a harness instead of a collar; it is more difficult for an animal to wriggle out of a harness.

NEVER leave an animal in a parked car, even if the windows are partially open. Even on pleasant days the temperature inside a car can soar to well over 100 degrees in less than 10 minutes, placing your pet at risk for heatstroke and possibly death. On very cold days, hypothermia is a risk. Also, animals left unattended in parked cars frequently are stolen.

Traveling by Air

(Service animals are normally exempt from most of the regulations and fees specified in this section. Check policies with the airline when making reservations.)

Opinion is divided as to whether air travel is truly safe for pets. Statistically, it is less dangerous than being a passenger in a car, but some experts warn of potentially deadly conditions for animals. The truth lies somewhere in between: Most pets arrive at their destination in fine condition, but death or injury is always a possibility. Before you decide to fly, know the risk factors and the necessary precautions to keep your pet safe.

❧ **Determine whether your pet is fit to fly.** The Animal Welfare Act (AWA), administered by USDA-APHIS, specifies that dogs and cats must be at least 8 weeks old and weaned at least 5 days before air travel. Animals that are very young, very old, pregnant, ill or injured should not fly at all. Cats, snub-nosed dogs (pugs, boxers, etc.) and long-nosed dogs (shelties, collies, etc.) are prone to severe respiratory difficulties in an airplane's poorly ventilated cargo hold and should travel only in the passenger cabin (if size allows) with their owner. Some airlines will not accept snub-nosed breeds if the temperature exceeds 75 degrees anywhere in the routing. A few airlines may not allow snub-nosed breeds in the cargo hold at any time of year.

❧ **Decide where your pet will fly.** Most animals fly in the hold as checked baggage when traveling with their owners, or as cargo when they are unaccompanied. The AWA was enacted to ensure animals traveling in this manner are treated humanely and are not subjected to dangerous or life-threatening conditions. For specific requirements pertaining to your animal, check with the airline in advance, as policies vary. Some airlines will not ship dogs as checked baggage, and others will only accept dogs shipped as cargo from "known shippers"; i.e., commercial shippers or licensed pet breeders.

Items classified as "dangerous goods" (dry ice or toxic chemicals, for example) must be transported in a different part of the hold from where live animals are carried. Some planes are designed to have separate hold areas, but so-called "people mover" airlines that are primarily interested in getting human passengers from one point to another as quickly as possible may not give priority to this feature. Check your airline's specific baggage policies so you know exactly where in the hold your pet will be traveling.

Small pets may be taken into the passenger cabin with you as carry-on luggage on most airlines. This places the animal's welfare squarely in your hands but is feasible only if he is very well-behaved and fits comfortably in a container that meets standard carry-on regulations. *(See Selecting a Carrier or Crate, p. 11.)* Keep in mind that the carrier — with the animal inside — must be kept under the seat in front of you throughout the flight. Most airlines charge a fee (anywhere from $50-$125 each way) for carry-on pets. **Note:** AWA regulations do not apply to animals traveling in the cabin.

AIRLINE CONTACT INFORMATION

Following is a list of the major North American airlines and their toll-free reservation numbers.

Web site addresses include information about flying with animals. **Hint:** Look under links for baggage, cargo or special travel needs, or do a site search for "pets."

Air Canada . . . .(888) 247-2262
www.aircanada.com

AirTran Airways . . . .(800) 247-8726
www.airtran.com

Alaska Airlines . . . .(800) 252-7522
www.alaskaair.com

American Airlines . . . .(800) 433-7300
www.aa.com

Delta Air Lines . . . .(800) 221-1212
www.delta.com

JetBlue Airways . . . .(800) 538-2583
www.jetblue.com

Southwest Airlines . . . .(800) 435-9792
www.southwest.com

United Airlines . . . .(800) 864-8331
www.united.com

❧ **Do your homework.** Investigate the airline's animal transport and welfare policies, especially if you are flying with a small or commuter airline. All airlines are subject to basic AWA regulations, but specific standards of care vary greatly from one company to another. Do your research well in advance and confirm the information 24-48 hours before departing.

The more information an airline provides, the better care your pet is likely to receive. Beware of companies that have vague animal welfare guidelines, or none at all. All major airlines provide information about pet transport on their Web sites. Also talk to fellow travelers and pet owners about their experiences. Finally, keep in mind that airlines are not required to transport live animals and can refuse to carry them for any reason.

❧ **Protect your investment.** Most people think of their pets as part of the family, but the legal system assigns them the same value as a piece of luggage. Inquire about insurance — an airline that won't insure animals in its care may not be the right one for your pet. (Always read the fine print before purchasing any insurance policy.) Also ask if the airline's workers are trained to handle animals. Few are, but it doesn't hurt to check.

PET INSURANCE

Just like their owners, pets can experience major medical problems at some point in their lifetime — even those that live indoors. And if illness strikes while you're on the road, it may be necessary to obtain care quickly. As a result, more and more people who travel with their devoted companion are considering pet health insurance.

Insurance plans run the gamut from basic coverage and routine care for illness and injury to comprehensive health maintenance, vaccinations and exams. Annual premiums range from less than $100 to more than $350, depending on the type of pet and plan. When choosing your plan, consider the following:

- What are the enrollment guidelines (age, breed, specific restrictions, etc.)?

- Which expenses are covered and which are excluded?

- What is the plan's policy concerning existing health problems?

- Does the plan allow you to use your own veterinarian?

- How are veterinary fees paid?

- Is a multiple pet discount offered?

Remember, it's up to you to choose an airline that values pets and will treat yours with care.

❧ **Understand the potential hazards.** Because a plane's cargo hold is neither cooled nor heated until take-off, the most dangerous time for your pet is that spent on the ground in this unventilated compartment. In summer the space absorbs heat while the plane sits on the tarmac; the reverse is true in winter, when it is no warmer inside the hold than outside. Both instances expose pets to the possibility of serious injury or death from heatstroke or hypothermia. **Note:** The latter also may be a concern during flight if the hold's heater is disabled or turned off, allowing the temperature to drop to near-freezing levels.

To minimize these risks, USDA-APHIS rules prohibit animals from being kept in the hold or on the tarmac for more than 45 minutes when temperatures are above 85 F or below 45 F. Some airlines impose even tighter temperature restrictions and may not permit animals to fly on planes going to cities where the ground temperatures may exceed these limits during certain months of the year. (Exceptions may be made for animals whose veterinarians certify they are acclimated to colder temperatures, but never warmer.)

❧ **Make stress-free travel arrangements.** Once you decide to fly, reserve space for Spot or Snowball when you arrange your own tickets, preferably well in advance of your travel date. Airlines accept only a limited number of animals per flight — usually two to four in the passenger cabin and one pet per passenger — on a first-come, first-served basis. More animals are generally allowed in the cargo hold.

Prepare to pay a fee each way; the cost is often greater for large animals traveling on a flight without their owner. Always reconfirm your reservations and flight information 24-48 hours before departure.

If your pet will be flying in the hold, travel on the same plane and reserve a nonstop flight. This not only reduces the danger of heatstroke or hypothermia during layovers, it also eliminates the possibility that she will be placed on the wrong connecting flight. In summer, fly during the early morning or late evening when temperatures are cooler. Because of large crowds and the chance of heavy air traffic causing delays, avoid holiday travel whenever possible.

Additional precautions may be necessary when traveling outside the United States and Canada. Other countries may impose lengthy quarantines, and airline workers outside North America may not be bound by animal welfare laws. (See International Travel, p. 17.)

❧ **Play an active role in your pet's well-being.** Flying safely with your pet requires careful planning and attention to his welfare. See the veterinarian within 10 days of departure for a health certificate (required by most airlines) and a pre-flight check-up.

Address any concerns you have about your pet traveling by air, especially if you are considering tranquilization. Sedation usually is not recommended for cats and dogs, regardless of whether they fly in the cabin or in the hold. Exposure to increased altitude pressure can create respiratory and cardiovascular problems; animals with short, wide heads are particularly susceptible to disorientation and possible injury. Sedation should never be administered without your veterinarian's approval.

Obtain an airline-approved carrier and acclimate your pet to its presence by leaving it open with a familiar object inside. A sturdy, well-ventilated crate adds an additional measure of protection.

Because animals are classified as luggage, they may be loaded on the plane via conveyor belt. If the crate falls off the belt, your pet could be injured or released. Ask that she be hand-carried on and off the plane, and that you be permitted to watch both procedures. Also ask about "counter-to-counter" shipping, in which the animal is loaded immediately before departure and unloaded immediately after arrival. There usually is an additional fee for this service.

Make sure you will have access to your pet if there is a lengthy layover or delay. Think twice about flying on an airline that won't allow you to check on your animal under such circumstances.

❧ **Prepare for the flight.** Keep in mind that traveling with an animal will require additional pre-flight time and preparation on your part. Exercise your pet before the flight, and arrive at least 2 but not more than 4 hours before departure. If he is traveling as carry-on luggage, check-in is normally at the passenger terminal; if he is traveling as checked baggage or as cargo in the cargo hold, proceed to the airline's cargo terminal, which is often in a different location. Find this out when making reservations and again when confirming flight information.

Make sure your animal's crate is properly labeled and secured, but do not lock it in case airline personnel have to provide emergency care. Include an ice pack for extra comfort on a hot day or a hot water bottle on a cold day. **Hint:** Wrap in a towel to prevent leaking.

Do not feed your pet less than 4 hours before departure, but provide water up until boarding. **Hint:** Freeze water in the bowl so that it melts throughout the trip, providing a constant drinking source.

Spot or Snowball should wear a sturdy collar (breakaway collars are recommended for cats) and two identification tags marked with your name, home address and phone number, and travel address and phone number. It's also a good idea to clip your pet's nails before departure so they won't accidentally get caught on any part of the carrier.

Note: You may be required to take your pet out of the carrier as you pass through security on your way to the gate. Make sure the animal is wearing a collar and leash or harness.

Attach food and water dishes inside the carrier so that airline workers can reach them without opening the door. If the trip will take longer than 12 hours, also attach a plastic bag with at least one meal's worth of dry food. Animals under 16 weeks of age must be fed every 12 hours, adult animals every 24 hours. Water must be provided at least every 12 hours, regardless of the animal's age.

Allow your pet to answer the call of nature before boarding, but do not take her out of the carrier while in the terminal. As a courtesy, wait until you are outside and away from fellow travelers. Keep her leash with you — do not leave it inside or attached to the kennel.

If your pet is traveling as carry-on luggage, let the passenger sitting next to you know. Someone with allergies may want to change seats.

Perhaps the most important precaution is to alert the flight crew and the captain that your pet is aboard. The pilot must activate the heater for the cargo hold; make sure this is done once you are in the air. If there are layovers or delays, ask the flight crew to be sure your pet has adequate shelter and/or ventilation; better yet, ask them to allow you to check in-person.

If you have arranged to watch your pet being unloaded, ask a flight attendant to call the baggage handlers and let them know you are on the way. Above all, do not hesitate to voice any concerns you have for your pet's welfare — it is your responsibility to do so.

❧ **Be prepared for emergencies.** In the unlikely event your pet gets lost en route, contact the airline, local humane shelters, animal control agencies or USDA-APHIS. Many airlines can trace a pet that was transferred to the wrong flight. If your pet is injured in transit, proceed to the nearest animal hospital; register any complaints with USDA-APHIS. **Hint:** Carry a list of emergency contact numbers and a current photograph of your pet in your wallet or purse, just in case.

At Your Destination

How well you and your companion behave on the road directly affects the way future furry travelers will be treated. Always clean up after your pet and keep him under your control. This is not only a courtesy to fellow human travelers; it's the surest way to enjoy a safe and happy vacation.

Inquire about pet policies before making lodging reservations. Properties may impose restrictions on the type or size of pet allowed, or they may designate only certain rooms, such as smoking rooms, for travelers with animals. If you have a dog, get a room on the first floor with direct access outside, preferably near a walking area; keep her leashed on any excursion.

Lodgings may have supervision policies requiring that pets be crated when unattended or that they may not be left alone at all. Allow your pet only in designated exercise or animal-approved areas; never take him into such off-limits places as the lobby, pool area, patio or restaurant. Prepare to receive limited housekeeping service, or none at all.

Expect to pay some type of additional charge, which may be per room or per pet and may include any of the following: refundable deposit, non-refundable deposit, daily fee, weekly fee.

If staying with friends or relatives, make certain your pet is a welcome guest. Know and respect their "house rules," especially if they have small children or pets of their own.

Once in the room, check for such hazards as chemically treated toilet water, hiding spaces and electrical cords before freeing your pet. Give her time to adjust to her new surroundings under your supervision.

Above all, practice good "petiquette":

🐾 Try not to leave your pet alone, but if you must, crate or otherwise confine her.

🐾 Crate at night as well.

🐾 To keep your pet and the housekeeper from having an unexpected encounter, leave the "Do Not Disturb" sign on the door when you go out without him.

🐾 Barking dogs make poor hotel neighbors — keep your pet quiet.

🐾 Don't allow your pet on the furniture. If she insists on sleeping on the bed, bring a bedspread or sheet from home and place that on top of the hotel bedding.

🐾 Clean up after your pet immediately — inside the room and out — and leave no trace of him behind when checking out.

🐾 Dispose of litter and other "accidents" properly — check with housekeeping.

🐾 Notify the management immediately if something is damaged, and be ready to pay for repairs.

🐾 Add a little extra to the housekeeping tip.

🐾 When you take your pet out of the room, keep her leashed, especially in wilderness areas and around small children. No matter how obedient she is at home, new stimuli and distractions may cause her to forget or ignore vocal commands. Know and obey animal policies at parks, beaches and other public areas. Check before arriving to make certain animals still are welcome, even if you've been there before — the rules may have changed.

🐾 Look for outdoor cafes when selecting restaurants. For health reasons, pets are not permitted inside eating establishments, but many restaurants allow animals to sit quietly with their owners at outdoor tables. Drive-through restaurants are another alternative.

In Case of Emergency

Be prepared for any turn of events by knowing how to get to the nearest animal hospital. (See Emergency Animal Clinics, p. 56.) Also have the name and number of a local animal shelter and a local veterinarian handy — ask your veterinarian for a recommendation. Take first-aid supplies with you and know how to use them. An animal in pain may become aggressive, so exercise caution at all times.

Emergency evacuation shelters do not accept pets, and domesticated animals do not fare well if left to weather an emergency on their own, especially when far from home. Avert a potential tragedy by planning in advance where you will go with your pet in case of evacuation. Use the listings in this book to find other lodgings willing to take you and your pet. Above all, don't wait for disaster to strike. Leave as soon as the evacuation order is announced, and take your animal with you.

The Great Outdoors

Travelers planning an active or camping vacation should make some additional preparations. Check in advance to be sure your pet is permitted at campgrounds, parks, beaches, trails and anywhere else you will be visiting. If there are restrictions — and there usually are — follow them. Remember that pets other than service animals usually are not allowed in public buildings.

Note: It is not advisable to take animals other than dogs into wilderness areas. For example, bringing a pet is not recommended at some national parks in Alaska. Also keep in mind that rural areas often have few veterinarians and even fewer boarding kennels.

Use common sense. Clean up after your pet, do not allow excessive vocalizing and keep her under your control. If the property requires your pet to be leashed or crated at all times, do so. Few parks or natural areas will allow a pet to be unattended, even when chained — the risk of disagreeable encounters with other travelers or wildlife is too great. The National Park Service may confiscate pets that harm wildlife or other visitors.

If camping, crate your pet at night to protect him from the elements and predators. (Chaining confines the animal but won't keep him from becoming a midnight snack.)

When hiking, stick to the trail and keep your pet on a short leash. It is all too easy for an unleashed pet to wander off and get lost or fall prey to a larger animal. Keep an eye out for such wildlife as alligators, bears, big cats, porcupines and skunks, and avoid other dogs and small children. Be aware of indigenous poisonous plants, such as English ivy and oleander, or those causing physical injury, such as cactus, poison ivy or stinging nettle. Your veterinarian or local poison control center should be able to give you a full list of hazardous flora.

Before setting out on the trail, make sure both of you are in good physical shape. An animal that rarely exercises at home will not suddenly be ready for a 10-mile trek across uneven terrain. Plan a hike well within the limits of your pet's endurance, and don't push — remember, if Spot gets too tired to make it back on her own, you'll have to carry her.

Carry basic first-aid supplies, including a first-aid guide. *(See What To Take, p. 10.)* Also carry fresh drinking water for both of you — "found" water may contain harmful germs or toxins. Drink often, not just when thirst strikes, and have your pet do the same. Watch for signs of dehydration, leg or foot injuries, heat exhaustion or heatstroke. Stop immediately and return home or to camp if any of these occur.

Note: Dogs can carry their own backpacks (check your local pet store for specially designed packs), but should never carry more than one-third of their body weight. Train the dog to accept the pack beforehand, and only use it with a strong, healthy animal in excellent physical condition.

No matter where or how you spend your vacation, visit the veterinarian when you return home to check for injuries, parasites and general health.

Traveling Between the United States and Canada

Traveling across the international border with your pet — either from the United States into Canada or from Canada into the United States — should prove largely hassle-free, although some basic regulations need to be kept in mind. All U.S. and Canadian citizens traveling between the United States and Canada are required to show a passport or other accepted secure document. For additional information about secure documents visit www.travel.state.gov or phone (877) 487-2778.

U.S. Customs grants returning U.S. citizens who stay in Canada more than 48 hours an individual $800 duty-free exemption (if not used within the prior 30 days). Any amount over the $800 exemption is subject to duty.

The exemption is based on fair retail value and applies to goods acquired for personal or household use or as gifts but not intended for sale. All items for which the exemption is claimed must accompany you upon return.

A 5 percent goods and services tax (GST) is levied on most items sold and most services rendered in Canada. A 12 to 15 percent harmonized sales tax (HST), which includes the GST, is charged on goods and services in British Columbia, Ontario, New Brunswick, Nova Scotia and Newfoundland and Labrador.

U.S. citizens taking pet cats and dogs 3 months of age and older into Canada must carry a rabies vaccination certificate signed by a licensed veterinarian that describes the animal, provides proof of rabies vaccination and includes documentation of the product name, lot number and lot expiration date. Collar tags are not sufficient proof of immunization. The certificate also is needed to bring a pet dog back into the United States; make sure the vaccination doesn't expire while you're in Canada. **Note:** Pit bulls are not permitted to be taken into Ontario.

Service animals are exempt from import restrictions. Also exempt are puppies and kittens under 3 months old; obtain a certificate of health from your veterinarian indicating that the animal is too young to vaccinate. **Note:** For details on pet imports, contact the Canadian Embassy; 501 Pennsylvania Ave. N.W., Washington, DC 20001; phone (202) 682-1740. The Web site address is www.canadianembassy.org.

The Canadian Food Inspection Agency (CFIA) provides additional pet information; phone (800) 442-2342 or visit the Web site at www.inspection.gc.ca. If you need assistance while in Canada, contact the U.S. Embassy, P.O. Box 866/Station B, Ottawa, ON, Canada K1P 5T1; phone (613) 688-5335.

Canadian Customs allows Canadian citizens to bring back from the United States, duty and tax free, goods valued up to $800 any number of times per year, provided the visit is 48 hours or more. A $200 exemption, excluding alcoholic beverages and tobacco products, may be claimed if the visit is 24 hours or more and no other exemption is being used. If returning from a visit of 7 days or more (not counting the day of departure from Canada), the exemption goes up to $800.

Canadian travelers may take pet cats and dogs into the United States with no restrictions, but U.S. Customs requires that dogs have proof of rabies vaccination no less than 30 days before arrival. For additional information on U.S. regulations, contact the USDA-APHIS National Center for Import and Export, (301) 734-8364.

International Travel

If you plan to travel abroad with Spot or Snowball, prepare for a lengthy flight and at least a short quarantine period. Be aware that airline and animal workers in other countries may not be bound by the same animal welfare laws that exist in the United States and Canada. Contact the embassy or consulate at your destination for information about documentation and quarantine requirements, animal control laws and animal welfare regulations.

As with any trip, have your pet checked by your regular veterinarian within 10 days of departure to obtain a health certificate showing proof of rabies and other inoculations. If you are traveling with an animal other than a domesticated dog or cat, check with USDA-APHIS for restrictions or additional documentation required.

The booklet "Pets and Wildlife: Licensing and Health Requirements" has general information about traveling abroad with animals; write U.S. Customs & Border Protection, 1300 Pennsylvania Ave. N.W., Washington, DC 20229, or visit www.cbp.gov.

Note: Island nations such as Australia and the United Kingdom, which are rabies-free, have adopted the Pet Travel Scheme (PETS) to allow entry for dogs, cats and ferrets from the U.S. and Canada without the usual 6-month quarantine. Pets must be tested and vaccinated for rabies at least 21 days prior to travel, be implanted with microchip identification and receive a certificate of treatment from an official government veterinarian. For information, visit the U.K. Web site for the Department for Environment, Food and Rural Affairs (DEFRA) at www.defra.gov.uk. Hawaii, which has a standard 120-day quarantine for all imported animals except guide dogs, has adopted a similar expedited program of 5 days or less; a pet must have been vaccinated at least *twice* for rabies in its lifetime.

Loss Prevention Tips

Searching the woods or an unfamiliar town for a missing pet is easily prevented by following these helpful tips:

❧ Have your pet wear a sturdy nylon or leather collar with current ID and rabies tags firmly attached. Be sure the ID tag includes the phone number of an emergency contact. Consider having your pet implanted with microchip identification; it's a simple procedure similar to a vaccination.

❧ Keep your pet on a leash or harness. Even trained animals can become agitated or disoriented in unfamiliar surroundings and fail to obey vocal commands.

❧ Attach the leash or harness while your pet is still inside the closed car or crate.

❧ Do not leave your pet unattended at any time, anywhere. A stolen pet is extremely difficult to recover.

❧ Escape-proof your hotel room by crating your pet and asking hotel management to make certain no one enters your room while you are gone. (Inform the property that you're traveling with an animal when making reservations.)

❧ Take along a recent picture and a detailed written description of your pet.

If your pet gets lost these steps will improve your chances of recovery:

❧ If your pet is lost in transit, contact the airline immediately. Ask to trace the animal via the airline's automated baggage tracking system.

❧ Contact local police, animal control, animal shelters, humane organizations and veterinary clinics with a description and a recent photograph. Stay in contact until your pet is found, and provide your home and destination phone numbers.

❧ Post signs and place an ad in the local newspaper so that anyone who comes across your pet knows she is lost and how to reach you.

The Last Word

You are ultimately responsible for your pet's welfare and behavior while traveling. Since animals cannot speak for themselves, it is up to you to focus on your pet's well-being every step of the way. It also is important to make sure he conducts himself properly so that other pets will be welcome visitors in the future. Following the common-sense information in this book will help ensure that both you and your animal companion have a safe and happy trip.

Pet-Friendly Places

in the United States and Canada

Dog Parks
Attractions
National Public Lands
Emergency Animal Clinics

DOG PARKS

A dog park is a place where people and their dogs can play together. These places offer dogs an area to play, exercise and socialize with other dogs while their owners enjoy the park-like setting. Dog park size and features vary greatly from location to location, from several hundred square feet in urban areas to several hundred acres in the suburbs and rural locations. Dog owners should remember to always keep their animal leashed until they reach the dog park entrance, to maintain voice control of their animal at all times, to bring their own supply of bags for picking up after their pet (and to be diligent in doing so), and to always have fresh water available for their dog. Please observe all dog park rules. The dog parks listed here welcome people who travel with their dogs; private parks or parks requiring local residency are not included. **Note:** Fence types and heights vary, and some areas have no fencing at all, requiring that the dog be under firm voice control.

United States

ARIZONA

Lewis Kingman Park - Kingman
parks.cityofkingman.gov
2201 E. Andy Devine Ave.
Daily 6 a.m.-10 p.m.
Fenced, 9 acres, double-gated entry, trees, shade, benches, shelter, picnic area and grills, multi-purpose field, separate areas for large and small dogs, water, disposal bags, parking, lights, restrooms, access for the disabled.

Lions' Dog Park - Lake Havasu City
lhcaz.gov
1340 McCulloch Blvd., within London Bridge Beach
Daily dawn-10:30 p.m.
Fenced, 2 acres, grass, trees.

S.A.R.A. Dog Park - Lake Havasu City
lhcaz.gov
7260 S. SARA Park Way, within S.A.R.A. Park.
Daily dawn-10:30 p.m.
Fenced, 2 acres, grass, walking paths, benches.

Countryside Park - Mesa
mesaaz.gov/parksrec
3130 E. Southern Ave., in Countryside Park.
Wed.-Mon. dawn to 10:00 p.m.
Fenced, 1.2 acres, park benches, separate areas for timid and active dogs, water fountains for both people and dogs, parking, disposal bags, trash cans.

Quail Run Park - Mesa
mesaaz.gov/parksrec
4155 E. Virginia, in Quail Run Park north of McDowell Road and off Greenfield
Daily dawn-10 p.m.; closed Thursdays for maintenance.
More than 3 acres, fenced, park benches, separate areas for active and timid dogs, water fountains for people and dogs, parking, disposal bags, trash cans.

Echo Mountain Off Leash Area - Phoenix
phoenix.gov, (602) 262-6696 (wet weather)
2302 W. Grovers Ave. (located in Grovers Basin on 20th Street at Cave Creek Road)
Daily 6:30 a.m.-10 p.m.
Fenced, double-gated entry, 2.3 acres with grass surface, disposal bags, drinking fountains, trash cans, separate areas for large and small dogs.

PETsMART Dog Park at Washington Park - Phoenix
phoenix.gov, (602) 262-6971 (wet weather)
21st Avenue north of Maryland, between Bethany Home and Glendale roads
Daily 6:30 a.m.-10 p.m.
Fenced, 2.65 acres with grass surface, double-gated entries, benches, water fountain, two dog-watering stations, disposal bags, trash cans, separate areas for large and small dogs. Access for the disabled.

RJ Dog Park at Pecos Park - Phoenix
phoenix.gov, (602) 262-6111
48th Street and Pecos Parkway (enter from 48th Street via Chandler Boulevard)
Daily 6 a.m.-11 p.m.; closed temporarily after heavy rains
Fenced, 2 acres with grass surface, double-gated entry, benches, water fountain, separate areas for large and small dogs. Access for the disabled.

Rose Mofford Sports Complex - Phoenix
phoenix.gov, (602) 261-8011
9833 N. 25th Ave. (north of Dunlap)
Daily 6:30 a.m.-10 p.m.
Fenced, 2.5 acres with grass surface, double-gated entries, benches, trees, water fountain, disposal bags, trash cans, separate areas for large and small dogs. Access for the disabled.

Steele Indian School Park - Phoenix
phoenix.gov
West side of 7th Street, just north of Indian School Road
Daily 6 a.m.-10 p.m.
Fenced, 1.83 acres with granite surface, double-gated entries, disposal bags, trash cans, separate areas for large and small dogs. Access for the disabled.

Chaparral Park - Scottsdale
scottsdaleaz.gov
5401 N. Hayden Rd. at McDonald Drive
Daily 5:30 a.m.-10 p.m., May-Oct.; 6 a.m.-10 p.m., rest of year. Closed for maintenance Tues. and Fri. 8-noon and in wet conditions. Phone (480) 312-2353 for status.
Fenced, 4 acres, benches, shade, restroom, water, lighted, separate areas for large and small dogs.

Horizon Park - Scottsdale
scottsdaleaz.gov
15444 N. 100th St. at Thompson Peak Parkway (east of SR 101 off Frank Lloyd Wright Boulevard)
Daily dawn-dusk. Closed Thursdays 9:30 a.m.-12:30 p.m. for maintenance.
Fenced, less than 1 acre, benches, shade structure, tables, disposal bags, trash cans, parking, phones, restrooms, people/dog drinking fountains.

Vista del Camino Park - Scottsdale
scottsdaleaz.gov
7800 E. Pierce St. (take Pierce Street heading west from Hayden Road)
Daily 5:30 a.m.-10 p.m.
Fenced, less than 1 acre, double-gated entry, lighted, grass turf, benches, restrooms nearby, water fountains for dogs and people, mutt mitt stations.

Creamery Park - Tempe
tempe.gov, (480) 350-5200
8th Street and Una Avenue (just south of University Drive near Rural Road)
Daily 6 a.m.-10 p.m.
Fenced, lighted, benches, disposal bags, trash cans, parking, water.

Jaycee Park - Tempe
tempe.gov, (480) 350-5200
5th Street and Hardy Drive
Daily 6 a.m.-10 p.m.
Fenced, lighted, trees, benches, disposal bags, trash cans, parking, water. Access for the disabled.

Mitchell Park - Tempe
tempe.gov, (480) 350-5200
Mitchell Drive and 9th Street
Daily 6 a.m.-10 p.m.; closed Mondays for maintenance.
Fenced, lighted, trees, benches, disposal bags, trash cans, parking, water. Access for the disabled.

Papago Park - Tempe
tempe.gov, (480) 350-5200
Curry Road and College Avenue
Fri.-Wed. 6 a.m.-10 p.m.
Fenced, lighted, trees, disposal bags, trash cans, parking, water.

P. Ben Arrendondo Sports Complex - Tempe
tempe.gov, (480) 350-5200
Warner Road and Hardy Drive
Daily 6 a.m.-10 p.m.
Fenced, lighted, trees, disposal bags, trash cans, parking, water.

Christopher Columbus Park - Tucson
tucsonaz.gov, (520) 791-4873
4600 N. Silverbell Rd.
Daily dawn-dusk.
Fenced, less than 1 acre, water fountain for dogs, scrambling area, shaded area with ramada, scooper dispenser.

Reid Park - Miko's Corner Playground - Tucson
tucsonaz.gov, (520) 791-4873
Country Club Road and 22nd Street (use Picnic Place or Concert Place entrances off Country Club Road)
Daily 7 a.m.-10 p.m.
Fenced, lighted, three double-entry gates, large turf areas, divided 2-acre site for large and small dogs, dog-friendly potable water fountains, scooper dispenser, ramada with tables. Named after Miko, a Tucson police dog that lost its life in the line of duty.

Jacobs Park - Tucson
tucsonaz.gov, (520) 791-4873
3300 N. Fairview Ave. on the west side of Jacobs Park
Daily dawn-dusk.
Fenced, turf area, walkway, picnic table, double-entry gate.

Palo Verde Park - Tucson
tucsonaz.gov, (520) 791-5930
300 S. Mann Ave. (south of Broadway Boulevard, west of Kolb Road)
Daily 6 a.m.-10:30 p.m.
Fenced, less than 1 acre, separate areas for large and small dogs, both with separate double-entry gates; entire facility lighted; DG/pea gravel surface, no turf; picnic tables; trash cans; water fountains for dogs on each side; scooper dispensers.

Purple Heart - Rita Ranch Dog Park - Tucson
tucsonaz.gov, (520) 791-4873
10050 Rita Rd. (near Rees Loop)
Daily 7 a.m.-10 p.m.
Fenced, 1 acre, separate large and small dog areas, benches, trees, lights, dog-friendly drinking fountains.

Sixth Avenue Dog Park - Tucson
tucsonaz.gov, (520) 791-4873
2075 N. Sixth Ave. (east side of Sixth Avenue across from Northwest Center and Mansfield Park)
Daily dawn-dusk.
Fenced, ramada, tables, wash area, double-entry gate.

Udall Park - Tucson
tucsonaz.gov, (520) 791-4931
7290 E. Tanque Verde Rd.
Daily 6 a.m.-10 p.m.
Fenced, 1 acre, trash cans, seating, water for dogs.

CALIFORNIA

Calabasas Bark Park - Calabasas
cityofcalabasas.com
4232 Las Virgenes Rd. (approximately 2 miles west of US 101 on the south side)
Daily 5 a.m.-9 p.m.
Fenced, lighted, trees, benches, scoops, trash cans, paved parking, water fountain for dogs, separate areas for large and small dogs.

Canine Corral - Carmichael
carmichaelpark.com
5750 Grant Ave. at Fair Oaks Blvd.
Daily dawn-10 p.m.
Fenced, 1 acre, double-gated entry, trees, benches, shade, small dog area, disposal bags, trash cans, water, parking, lights. Access for the disabled.

Costa Mesa Bark Park - Costa Mesa
cmbarkpark.org, (949) 733-4101
890 Arlington Ave. at Newport Boulevard (across from the Orange County Fairgrounds Equestrian Center)
Wed.-Mon. dawn-9 p.m.
Fenced, 2.1 acres, night lights dusk-9 p.m., grass turf, trees, benches, tables, disposal bags, trash cans, parking, restrooms, water fountains, water for dogs, separate small dog area. Access for the disabled.

Elk Grove Dog Park - Elk Grove
yourcsd.com, (916) 405-5355
9950 Elk Grove-Florin Rd.
Daily dawn-dusk.
Fenced, grass, 1.2 acres.

Laguna Community Dog Park - Elk Grove
yourcsd.com, (916) 405-5355
9014 Brucevillle Rd.
Daily dawn-dusk.
Fenced, grass, less than 1 acre.

Morse Community Dog Park - Elk Grove
yourcsd.com, (916) 405-5355
5540 Bellaterra Dr.
Daily dawn-dusk.
Fenced, grass, 1.3 acres, separate small dog area, disposal bags, water.

Ernie Smith Dog Park - El Verano
sonoma-county.org
18776 Gilman Dr.
Daily dawn-dusk.
Fenced, less than 1 acre, double-gated entry, water fountain for dogs, picnic tables, disposal bags, trash can, free parking.

Elizabeth Anne Perrone Dog Park - Glen Ellen
sonoma-county.org
13630 Sonoma Hwy. in Sonoma Valley Regional Park (SR 12 between Arnold Drive and Madrone Road)
Daily dawn-dusk. Parking fee $5 or annual park pass.
Fenced, 1 acre, double-gated entry, covered gazebo, shade trees, water fountain for dogs, disposal bags, trash can.

Badger Dog Park - Healdsburg
ci.healdsburg.ca.us
Heron Drive in Badger Park
Daily 6 a.m.-dusk.
Fenced, dog run best suited to small dogs, water, picnic table, shade.

Villa Chanticleer Dog Park - Healdsburg
ci.healdsburg.ca.us
1248 N. Fitch Mountain Rd.
Daily 6 a.m.-dusk.
Fenced, 1.5 acres, water, picnic table, shade, footpath.

Huntington Dog Beach - Huntington Beach
dogbeach.org
Pacific Coast Highway between 21st and Seapoint streets
Daily 5 a.m.-10 p.m.; metered parking lots close at 10 p.m.
Unfenced, benches and tables on the bluffs above the beach,
disposal bags, trash cans, metered parking, restrooms. Dogs
may be off leash anywhere within dog beach boundaries while
under an owner's supervision. Access for the disabled to the
sand.

Laguna Niguel Pooch Park - Laguna Niguel
cityoflagunaniguel.org
31461 Golden Lantern near Fire Station #49
Tues.-Thurs. and Sat. 7 a.m.-dusk, Sun. 8 a.m.-dusk, Mon. and
Fri. noon-dusk.
Fenced, 1 acre, wood chip ground cover, picnic tables,
shelters, disposal bag dispenser, parking opposite the fire
station, restroom, water faucet with hose, separate fenced area
for small dogs. Access for the disabled.

Downtown Dog Park - Long Beach
longbeach.gov
Lincoln Park at Broadway and Pacific Avenue
Daily dawn-dusk.
Fenced, double-gated entry, separate small dog area, benches,
disposal bags, trash cans, water.

K-9 Corner Dog Park - Long Beach
longbeach.gov
9th Street and Pacific Avenue
Daily 6 a.m.-10 p.m.
Fenced, less than 1 acre, double-gated entry, separate small
dog area, benches, disposal bags, trash cans, water, lights.

Recreation Dog Park - Long Beach
longbeach.gov
5201 E. 7th St. at Park Avenue
Daily 6 a.m.-10 p.m.; closed Mondays until noon for
maintenance
Fenced, 2 acres, lighted, trees, crushed-granite surface,
benches, tables, disposal bags, trash cans, parking, water,
separate fenced area for small dogs. Access for the disabled.

Rosie's Dog Beach - Long Beach
longbeach.gov
Ocean Boulevard between Roycroft and Argonne avenues;
metered parking in lot on Bennett Avenue.
Daily 6 a.m.-8 p.m.
Unfenced, 2.9 acres; bring disposal bags.

Uptown Dog Park - Long Beach
longbeach.gov
4600 Long Beach Blvd., on west side of Scherer Park.
Daily dawn-dusk.
Fenced, double-gated entry, separate small dog area, benches,
disposal bags, trash cans, water, parking.

Wrigley Heights Dog Park - Long Beach
longbeach.gov
3401 Golden Ave.
Daily 6 a.m.-10 p.m.; closed Mon. 6 a.m.-noon for
maintenance.
Fenced, 1.9 acres, double-gated entry, separate small dog
area, benches, disposal bags, trash cans, water, trees.

Barrington Dog Park - Los Angeles
laparks.org
333 S. Barrington Ave.
Daily dawn-dusk.
Fenced, 1.5 acres, separate small and big dog areas, benches,
water, scoops, parking.

Hermon Dog Park - Los Angeles
hermondogpark.org
5566 Via Marisol, between Monterey Road and Arroyo Seco
Parkway
Daily dawn-dusk.
Fenced, 1 acre, double-gated entry, separate small and big
dog areas, decomposed granite surface, trees, benches, water,
disposal bags.

Mill Valley Dog Park - Mill Valley
millvalleydogpark.org
Camino Alto and Sycamore Ave.
Daily dawn-dusk.
Partially fenced, 3 acres, trees, shade, disposal bags, agility
stations, trash cans, water. The park fronts Richardson Bay
and is fenced on the land sides only. Parking is available about
350 feet from the park; dogs must be leashed from the parking
areas to the park. Access for the disabled.

Morgan Hill Dog Park - Morgan Hill
morganhilldog.org
Edmundson Avenue and Monterey Road (entrance is shared
with Centennial Recreation Center)
Daily dawn-dusk; closed Wednesday morning for maintenance.
Fenced, between 2 and 3 acres, separate small dog area,
natural grass, trees, tables, parking, water, double-gated entry,
bulletin board, disposal bags, trash cans.

Palm Springs Dog Park - Palm Springs
palmspringsca.gov
3200 E. Tahquitz Canyon Way, behind City Hall
Daily 24 hours.
Fenced, 1.6 acres, lighted, double-gated entry, trees, benches,
tables, shelter, disposal bags, trash cans, parking, phones,
dual-level water fountains, separate areas for large and small
dogs, antique fire hydrants, unusual iron fence created by
sculptor Phill Evans. Access for the disabled.

Alice's Dog Park - Pasadena
pasadenapooch.org
3026 E. Orange Grove (located within Vina Vieja Park, east of
Sierra Madre Boulevard)
Daily dawn-dusk.
Fenced, 2.5 acres for large dogs, 1 acre for small dogs,
double-gated entry, grass, trees, benches, water, shelter,
disposal bags, trash cans, parking. Access for the disabled.

Rocky Memorial Park - Petaluma
cityofpetaluma.net
2204 W. Casa Grande Rd., southwest of Lakeville Hwy.
Daily 6 a.m. to 10 p.m.
Partially fenced, 7.8 acres, parking.

Redondo Beach Dog Park - Redondo Beach
rbdogpark.com
Southeast corner of 190th Street and Flagler Lane
Daily dawn-dusk; closed Wed. dawn-noon for maintenance.
Fenced, trees, benches, disposal bags, trash cans, parking,
phones, water, separate fenced area for small dogs. Access for
the disabled.

Bannon Creek Park - Sacramento
cityofsacramento.org
2780 Azevedo Dr., near West El Camino Avenue
Daily 5 a.m.-10 p.m.
Fenced, less than 1 acre, double-gated entry, benches,
disposal bag dispensers, water fountain/faucet for dogs.

Glenbrook Dog Park - Sacramento
cityofsacramento.org
8500 La Riviera Dr. in Glenbrook Park, behind the little league
fields
Daily 5 a.m.-10 p.m.
Fenced, 1 acre, double-gated entry, water fountain for dogs,
shade, trees, seating, picnic tables.

Granite Dog Park - Sacramento
cityofsacramento.org
8200 Ramona Ave., off Power Inn Road in Granite Regional Park
Daily 5 a.m.-10 p.m.
Fenced, 2 acres, double-gated entry, lights, bench, disposal bags, trash cans, water spigot for dogs. Access for the disabled.

North Natomas Regional Park Dog Park - Sacramento
cityofsacramento.org
2501 New Market Dr.
Daily dawn-dusk.
Fenced, 2.5 acres, separate small dog area, grass and crushed granite surface, benches, trash cans, water.

Partner Park - Sacramento
cityofsacramento.org
5699 South Land Park Dr. at Fruitridge Road, behind the Belle Cooledge Community Center. Parking available behind community center.
Daily 5 a.m.-10 p.m.
Fenced, 2 acres, lighted, double-gated entry, landscaped with turf and mature trees, bench, disposal bags, trash cans, water spigot for dogs. Access for the disabled.

Regency Community Park - Dog Park - Sacramento
cityofsacramento.org
5500 Honor Pkwy. in North Natomas
Daily 5 a.m.-10 p.m.
Fenced, 2 acres, double-gated entry, water fountain for dogs, turf and decomposed granite areas, trees, benches.

Sutters Landing Dog Park - Sacramento
cityofsacramento.org
20 28th St. (cross street is B Street)
Daily dawn-dusk.
Fenced, 2.5 acres, separate small dog area, trash cans, water.

Tanzanite Community Park - Sacramento
cityofsacramento.org
2220 Tanzanite Way in Tanzanite Community Park
Daily 5 a.m.-10 p.m.
Fenced, 2 acres, double-gated entry, landscaped with turf and native grass, trees, benches, disposal bags, trash cans, water fountain for dogs.

Balboa Park - San Diego
sandiego.gov
Daily 24 hours.
Unfenced, large field.
Two off-leash areas:
(1) Nate's Point at El Prado, on the south side of Cabrillo Bridge
(2) Morley Field, northwest of the tennis courts.

Cadman Community Park - San Diego
sandiego.gov
4280 Avati Dr.
Daily 7-9:30 a.m. and 5-7:30 p.m., in summer; 7:30-10 a.m. and 4:30-7 p.m., rest of year.
Unfenced; observe off-leash boundaries.

Capehart Park (Pacific Beach) - San Diego
sandiego.gov
Soledad Mountain Road and Feldspar Street
Daily 24 hours.
Fenced, 1 acre, picnic tables, benches, parking, separate grass-turf areas for large and small dogs, areas to provide water to dogs, water fountain.

Dog Beach - San Diego
sandiego.gov
Voltaire Street in Ocean Beach (enter the parking lot at the west end of Voltaire Street)
Daily 24 hours.
Unfenced, disposal bags, trash cans, water, restrooms nearby. Access for the disabled.

Doyle Community Park - San Diego
sandiego.gov
8175 Regents Rd. (behind the Doyle Recreation Center)
Daily 24 hours.
Fenced, no lights, separate grass-turf areas for large and small dogs.

Fiesta Island - San Diego
sandiego.gov
Part of Mission Bay Park
Daily 6 a.m.-10 p.m.
This island allows dogs anywhere outside the fenced areas.

Grape Street Park - San Diego
sandiego.gov
Grape Street and Granada Avenue
Mon.-Fri. 7:30 a.m.-9 p.m., Sat.-Sun. and holidays 9-9.
Unfenced, 5 acres, lighted, trees, benches, tables, trash cans, parking, restrooms, water.

Kearny Mesa Community Park - San Diego
sandiego.gov
3170 Armstrong St.
Daily 6:30 a.m.-10 p.m.
Unfenced, 1 acre, lights, water.

Rancho Peñasquitos Park - San Diego
sandiego.gov
Salmon River Road at Fairgrove Lane
Daily dawn-dusk. Fenced, 1 acre, double-gated entry, benches, parking, separate large and small dog areas.

San Dimas Dog Park - San Dimas
sandimasdogpark.org
301 Horsethief Canyon Rd. (cross streets are Sycamore and San Dimas Canyon Road)
Daily dawn-dusk; closed alternating Wednesdays from noon-2 for maintenance.
Fenced, 1 acre, double-gated entry, trees, grass, benches, shelter, tables, separate small dog area, disposal bags, trash cans, water, parking. Access for the disabled.

San Francisco
San Francisco regularly reviews its off-leash ("dog play area") policies. Refer to sfrecpark.org/documents/DogBrochure.pdf for the most recent information on dog parks.

Alta Plaza Park - San Francisco
sfgov.org Clay Street between Scott and Steiner streets on the second terrace of the park
Daily 6 a.m.-10 p.m.
Unfenced, less than 1 acre; dogs must be under firm voice control.

Bernal Heights - San Francisco
sfgov.org
Bernal Heights Boulevard at the top of the hill
Daily 6 a.m.-10 p.m.
Unfenced; dogs must be under firm voice control.

Buena Vista Park - San Francisco
sfgov.org
Buena Vista West Avenue at Central Avenue
Daily 6 a.m.-10 p.m.
Unfenced; dogs must be under firm voice control.

Corona Heights - San Francisco
sfgov.org
Roosevelt Way and Museum Way in the field next to the Randall Museum
Daily 6 a.m.-10 p.m.
Fenced.

Dolores Park - San Francisco
sfgov.org
Between Church and Dolores streets, south of the tennis courts and soccer field
Daily 6 a.m.-10 p.m.
Unfenced; dogs must be under firm voice control.

Douglass Park - San Francisco
sfgov.org
27th and Douglass streets, upper field
Daily 6 a.m.-10 p.m.
Unfenced; dogs must be under firm voice control.

Eureka Valley Recreation Center - San Francisco
sfgov.org
Collingwood Street, adjacent to the tennis courts and east of the baseball diamond
Daily 6 a.m.-10 p.m.
Fenced.

Golden Gate Park - San Francisco
sfgov.org
Four off-leash areas:
(1) Southeast section bounded by Lincoln Way, King Drive and 5th and 7th avenues
(2) Northeast section at Stanyan and Grove streets
(3) South-central area bounded by King Drive, Middle Drive and 34th and 38th avenues
(4) Fenced dog-training area near 38th Avenue and Fulton Street.

Lafayette Park - San Francisco
sfgov.org
Near Sacramento Street between Octavia and Gough streets
Daily 6 a.m.-10 p.m.
Unfenced; dogs must be under firm voice control.

Lake Merced - San Francisco
sfgov.org
Lake Merced Boulevard and Middlefield Drive, northern lake area
Daily 6 a.m.-10 p.m.
Unfenced; dogs must be under firm voice control.

McKinley Square - San Francisco
sfgov.org
San Bruno Avenue and 20th Street, on the west slope
Daily 6 a.m.-10 p.m.
Unfenced; dogs must be under firm voice control.

McLaren Park - San Francisco
sfgov.org
Daily 6 a.m.-10 p.m.
Two off-leash areas:
(1) Top of hill at Shelly Drive and Mansell Street
(2) South entrance at 1600 block of Geneva Avenue, exclusive of habitat area (the open area fenced on roadway)

Mountain Lake Park - San Francisco
sfgov.org
North of Lake Street at 8th Avenue, east end of the park
Daily 6 a.m.-10 p.m.
Unfenced; dogs must be under firm voice control.

Potrero Hill Mini Park - San Francisco
sfgov.org
22nd Street between Arkansas and Connecticut streets
Daily 6 a.m.-10 p.m.
Unfenced; dogs must be under firm voice control.

St. Mary's Park - San Francisco
sfgov.org
Justin and Benton streets, lower terrace of the park
Daily 6 a.m.-10 p.m.
Fenced.

Stern Grove - San Francisco
sfgov.org
Wawona Street between 21st and 23rd avenues, north side
Daily 6 a.m.-10 p.m.
Unfenced; dogs must be under firm voice control.

Upper Noe Recreation Center - San Francisco
sfgov.org
30th Street between Church and Sanchez streets, behind and along the baseball field
Daily 6 a.m.-10 p.m.
Fenced.

Field of Dogs - San Rafael
fieldofdogs.org
3540 Civic Center Dr. (near the intersection of US 101 and North San Pedro Road)
Daily dawn-dusk.
Fenced, double-gated entry, trees, benches, tables, shelter, disposal bags, trash cans, parking, water. Access for the disabled.

DeTurk Roundbarn Park - Santa Rosa
ci.santa-rosa.ca.us
819 Donahue St. (between West 8th and 9th streets)
Daily dawn-dusk (in winter, large dog area is closed; all dogs use the small dog area).
Fenced, less than 1 acre, water.

Doyle Park Dog Park - Santa Rosa
ci.santa-rosa.ca.us
700 Hoen Ave. in Doyle Park (go west on Sonoma Avenue, turn left on Hoen Avenue and then turn right into the parking lot; the fenced dog park is behind the stadium)
Daily dawn-dusk (in winter, large dog area is closed; all dogs use the small dog area).
Fenced, less than 1 acre, bench, disposal bags, water, restrooms, separate areas for large and small dogs.

Galvin Dog Park - Santa Rosa
ci.santa-rosa.ca.us
3330 Yulupa Ave. in Don Galvin Park (next to Bennet Valley Golf Course)
Daily dawn-dusk (in winter, large dog area is closed; all dogs use the small dog area).
Fenced, less than 1 acre, double-gated entry, trees, trash cans, parking, water, picnic tables, restrooms. Access for the disabled.

Harvest Park Dog Park - Santa Rosa
ci.santa-rosa.ca.us
231 Burt St.
Daily dawn-dusk.
Fenced, less than 1 acre, double-gated entry; bring water and disposal bags.

Northwest Community Dog Park - Santa Rosa
ci.santa-rosa.ca.us
2620 W. Steele Ln. in Northwest Community Park (go west on Gurneville Road, turn right on Marlow Road and then turn right at the first traffic light into the park's parking lot; walk east along the path to the dog park on the left)
Daily dawn-dusk (in winter, large dog area is closed; all dogs use the small dog area).
Fenced, less than 1 acre, benches, disposal bags, trash cans, restrooms nearby, water, separate area for small dogs.

Place to Play Dog Park - Santa Rosa
ci.santa-rosa.ca.us
2375 W. 3rd St.
Daily 6 a.m.-9 p.m.
Fenced, less than 1 acre, double-gated entry, benches, water.

Rincon Valley Dog Park - Santa Rosa
ci.santa-rosa.ca.us
5108 Badger Rd. in Rincon Valley Community Park
Daily dawn-dusk (in winter, large dog area is closed; all dogs use the small dog area).
Fenced, less than 1 acre, trees, benches, tables, disposal bags, trash cans, parking, phones, restrooms, water, separate fenced areas for large and small dogs (area for large dogs closed during the winter), fenced pond area for dogs (open year-round). Monitors are present during peak hours to enforce rules. Access for the disabled.

Off-leash, unfenced, under voice control areas:

700 Doyle Park Drive - Santa Rosa
ci.santa-rosa.ca.us
700 Doyle Park Dr. (go west on Sonoma Avenue, turn left on Hoen Avenue and then turn right into the parking lot; the unfenced, off-leash area is to the right of the fenced dog park)
Daily 6-8 a.m.

Franklin Park - Santa Rosa
ci.santa-rosa.ca.us
2095 Franklin Ave.
Daily 6-8 a.m.

Southwest Community - Santa Rosa
ci.santa-rosa.ca.us
1698 Hearn Ave.
Daily 6-8 a.m.

Youth Community - Santa Rosa
ci.santa-rosa.ca.us
1725 Fulton Rd.
Daily 6-8 a.m.

Remington Dog Park - Sausalito
sausalitodogpark.org
Ebbtide Avenue at Bridgeway Boulevard
Mon.-Fri. 7-7, Sat.-Sun. 8-7
Fenced, lighted, safety-gated entry, picnic tables, benches, tents for shelter, scoops and scooper cleaning station, trash cans, parking, water, tennis balls and racquets provided.

Animal Care Center Dog Park - Sebastopol
sonoma-county.org
500 Ragle Rd.
Daily dawn-dusk. Small dogs only Mon.-Fri. 11-noon, Sat.-Sun. 3-4. Parking fee $5 or annual park pass.
Fenced, less than 1 acre, double-gated entry, disposal bags, trash can, parking, shade, water fountain for dogs. Access for the disabled.

Arbor Dog Park - Seal Beach
ci.seal-beach.ca.us
4665 Lampson Ave., between Valley View Street and Los Alamitos Boulevard off Lampson Avenue
Daily dawn-dusk; closed Thursday 8 a.m.-noon for maintenance. Non-resident user license available for a $12 annual fee; see Web site.
Fenced, 2.2 acres, double-gated entry, trees, benches, disposal bags, trash cans, water, parking. Access for the disabled.

Jacinto Creek Park Dog Park - South Sacramento
cityofsacramento.org
8600 W. Stockton Blvd., South Sacramento
Daily 5 a.m.-10 p.m.
Fenced, 2 acres, double-gated entry, drinking fountain for dogs, turf and decomposed granite areas, trees, obstacle course for dogs, benches.

Baldy View Dog Park - Upland
uplandpl.lib.ca.us
11th Street between Mountain Avenue and San Antonio Avenue
Daily dawn-dusk. Annual family membership $25.
Fenced, 5 acres, double-gated entry and exit, grass turf, shade trees, benches, free parking, separate areas for large and small dogs, water stations for dogs.

Heather Farms Dog Park - Walnut Creek
walnut-creek.org
550 N. San Carlos Dr. in Heather Farms Park
Mon.-Fri. 7 a.m.-8 p.m., Sat.-Sun. and holidays 8-8. Park closed Tues. 7 a.m.-noon for maintenance and during rainy weather; phone the Turf Hotline at (925) 256-3574 for status.
Fenced, double-gated entry, separate areas for large and small dogs, grass, trees, benches, tables, disposal bags, water, trash cans, parking. Access for the disabled.

COLORADO

Grandview Off-Leash Dog Park - Aurora
auroragov.org
17900 E. Quincy Ave. (just east of Pitkin Street, adjacent to Quincy Reservoir on the lake's west side)
Daily dawn-dusk.
Fenced, trash cans, parking, water.

East Boulder Community - Boulder City
bouldercolorado.gov
5660 Sioux Dr.
Daily dawn-dusk.
Fenced, 2.75 acres, separate areas for large and small dogs, disposal bags, trash cans, parking, water, fenced-off swimming area. Access for the disabled.

Foothills Community Park - Boulder City
bouldercolorado.gov
Locust Avenue and Lee Hill Road, west of Broadway Street
Daily dawn-dusk.
Fenced, 2 acres, separate areas for large and small dogs, disposal bags, trash cans, parking, water. Access for the disabled.

Howard H. Hueston Park - Boulder City
bouldercolorado.gov
34th Street near O'Neal Parkway
Daily dawn-dusk.
Unfenced, trees, benches, tables, trash cans, parking. Dogs must be under voice control and kept in sight at all times. Access for the disabled.

Valmont Dog Park - Boulder City
bouldercolorado.gov
5275 Valmont Rd. at Airport Road
Daily dawn-dusk.
Fenced, 3 acres, separate areas for large and small dogs, disposal bags, trash cans, parking, water (available seasonally). Access for the disabled.

Carter Park Dog Park - Breckenridge
townofbreckenridge.com
South end of High Street
Daily 24 hours.
Fenced, less than 1 acre, grass, trees, benches, tables, disposal bags, trash cans, water, parking. Please note there is no lighting. Access for the disabled.

Palmer Park - Colorado Springs
springsgov.com
Maizeland Road and Academy Boulevard
Daily 5 a.m.-11 p.m., May-Oct.; 5 a.m.-9 p.m., rest of year.
Fenced, benches, tables, disposal bags, trash cans, parking, restrooms, water. Access for the disabled.

Rampart Dog Park - Colorado Springs
springsgov.com
8270 Lexington Dr. (from the intersection of Lexington Drive
and North Union Boulevard, go north on Lexington, then turn
left into the park entrance)
Daily 5 a.m.-11 p.m., May-Oct.; 5 a.m.-9 p.m., rest of year.
Fenced, trees, benches, disposal bags, trash cans, parking,
water. Access for the disabled.

Barnum Park - Denver
denvergov.org
Hooker Street and West 5th Avenue
Daily dawn-dusk.
Natural barriers (turf with split-rail fencing to delineate
boundaries), 3 acres, trees, disposal bags, trash cans, parking,
restroom, bulletin board.

Berkeley Park - Denver
denvergov.org
Sheridan Boulevard and West 46th Avenue, west of the lake
Daily dawn-dusk.
Fenced, 2 acres, turf, double-gated entry, trees, disposal bags,
trash cans, parking, bulletin board.

Fuller Park - Denver
denvergov.org
Franklin Street and East 29th Avenue, northwest section (enter
from 29th Avenue)
Daily dawn-dusk.
Fenced, 1 acre, turf, double-gated entry, disposal bags, trash
cans, bulletin board, on-street neighborhood parking only.

Green Valley Ranch East Park - Denver
denvergov.org
Jebel Street and East 45th Avenue, southwest section (dog
park accessible from parking lot)
Daily dawn-dusk.
Natural barriers (native vegetation and split-rail fencing to
delineate boundaries), 2 acres, disposal bags, trash cans,
parking.

Josephine Dog Park - Denver
denvergov.org
Josephine and 16th Avenue
Daily dawn-dusk.
Fenced, disposal bags, trash cans, benches.

Kennedy Park - Denver
denvergov.org
Hampden Avenue and South Dayton Street, southwest section
Daily dawn-dusk.
Natural barriers (native vegetation and split-rail fencing to
delineate boundaries), 3 acres, disposal bags, trash cans,
bulletin board, very limited parking (complex parking lot not
open to dog park visitors).

Stapleton Dog Park - Denver
denvergov.org
E. 24th Avenue and Syracuse Street
Daily dawn-dusk.
Fenced, 3 acres, double-gated entry, shade structures, trees,
street parking, bulletin board, dog-friendly drinking fountains,
disposal bags, trash cans.

Railyard Dog Park - Denver
denvergov.org
19th Avenue and Little Raven Street
Daily dawn-dusk.
Fenced, separate small dog area, water, shade, trees, disposal
bags, trash cans.

City Bark at City Park - Pueblo
pueblo.us
800 Goodnight Ave.
Daily 6 a.m.-10 p.m.
Fenced, 2.3 acres, double-gated entry, trees, benches, shade,
tables, disposal bags, trash cans, water, parking. Access for
the disabled.

Westminster Dog Park - Westminster
ci.westminster.co.us
105th Avenue and Simms Street
Daily dawn-dusk.
Partially fenced, 420-acre open space, trees, benches, shelter,
shade, disposal bags, trash cans, water, parking. Access for
the disabled.

Little Dry Creek Dog Park - Westminster
ci.westminster.co.us
3655 W. 69th Pl.
Daily dawn-dusk.
Fenced, 1.75 acres, trees, benches, disposal bags, trash cans,
water.

CONNECTICUT
Southbury Dog Park - Southbury
southbury-ct.org
Roxbury Road (Route 67), next to Red Sable Horse Farm
Daily dawn-dusk.
Fenced, double-gated entry, benches, tables, separate small
dog area, disposal bags, trash cans, water, parking, onsite
stream accessed by a staircase.

DELAWARE
Levels Road Park - Middletown
middletownde.org
900 Levels Road (Route 15), within Levels Road Park
Daily 7 a.m.-dusk.
Fenced, 5-acre large dog area, 3-acre small dog area,
double-gated entry, trees, benches, shade, grass, disposal
bags, trash cans, water available spring-fall, parking.

Rockford Park Off-Leash Area - Wilmington
destateparks.com
Park Drive and Red Oak Road
Daily 8 a.m.-dusk.
Unfenced, more than 5 acres, trees, benches, shade, disposal
bags, trash cans, water.

FLORIDA
Canine Cove at South County Regional Park - Boca Raton
pbcgov.com
12551 Glades Rd., west of Boca Raton in South County
Regional Park
Daily dawn-dusk; closed Wednesday noon-3 for maintenance.
Fenced, 4 acres, paved pathways, shaded sitting areas,
disposal bag dispensers and receptacles, trash cans,
restrooms and parking nearby, gazebos, separate areas for
large and small dogs, canine drinking stations, dog wash area.

Happy Tails Canine Park - Bradenton
mymanatee.org
51st Street West at G.T. Bray Park, about halfway between
Manatee Avenue and Cortez Road
Daily dawn-dusk. Closed Thurs. 7-10 and last Fri. of the month
2-dusk for maintenance.
Eight-foot fence, 3 acres, separate area for small dogs, trees,
benches, tables, disposal bags, trash cans, parking, restrooms
nearby, water.

Dr. Paul's Memorial Dog Park - Coral Springs
toppetcare.com/petutopiawelcome.html
2915 Sportsplex Dr. in the Sportsplex Regional Park Complex
(park off Sportsplex Drive at the west pedestrian entrance)
Daily dawn - 9:30 p.m.
Enclosed, lighted, trees, shaded area, paved running path,
picnic table, gazebo, disposal bag dispensers, trash cans,
indoor restroom, separate areas for large and small dogs,
water fountains for dogs and people, dog shower, dog statues,
weatherproof dog agility equipment.

Dog Park at Lake Ida - Delray Beach
pbcgov.com
1455 Lake Ida Rd. (take the Atlantic Avenue West exit off I-95, proceed west to Congress Avenue, go north on Congress for 1 mile, turn right onto Lake Ida Road and proceed east under I-95; park entrance is on the left)
Daily dawn-dusk; closed Thurs. noon-3 for maintenance.
Fenced, 2.5 acres, partial paved pathway, eight shaded sitting areas, disposal bag dispensers and receptacles, restrooms and parking nearby, separate fenced areas for large and small dogs, two canine drinking stations, dog washing area, information kiosk.

Pooch Pines Dog Park at Okeeheelee Park - Delray Beach
pbcgov.com
7715 Forest Hill Blvd. (off I-95 exit Forest Hill Boulevard, west to the main Okeeheelee Park entrance on the north side of the road; follow the park road to the Pooch Pines sign, turn right and continue to the top of the hill)
Daily dawn-dusk; closed Wed. noon-3 for maintenance.
Fenced, 5 acres, paved pathways, shaded sitting areas, disposal bag dispensers and receptacles, trash cans, restrooms and parking nearby, separate areas for large and small dogs, canine drinking stations, dog washing area.

Bark Park at Snyder Park - Fort Lauderdale
fortlauderdale.gov
3299 S.W. 4th Ave.
Daily 7 a.m.-7 p.m.; closed Thurs. 8-11 for maintenance.
Closed Jan. 1 and Dec. 25.
Entry fee varies; canine beach $7.
Fenced, two open-air pavilions, benches, disposal bags, trash cans, parking, restrooms, water, separate area for small dogs, two hose stations, water fountains, agility equipment, small nature area with more than 20 labeled native trees, canine swimming in East Lake, canine beach (Fri.-Sun. only). Access for the disabled. Note: Dogs must remain in the car until arrival at Bark Park and are not permitted in the remainder of Snyder Park.

P.E.A.R. Park Dog Park - Leesburg
lakecountyfl.gov
5336 University Ave., within Palatlakaha Environmental and Agricultural Reserve Park
Daily 6:30 a.m.-7 p.m.
Fenced, separate small/big dog areas.

Millennium Dog Park - Ocala
millenniumdogpark.com
2513 S.E. 32nd Ave.
Mon.-Wed. and Sat.-Sun. 8 a.m.-7 p.m., in summer; 8-6, in winter.
Fenced, 4.5 acres, double-gated entry, grass, trees, benches, shelter, shade, small dog area, disposal bags, trash cans, water, parking. Access for the disabled.

Dog Leg Canine Park - Palmetto
mymanatee.org
7550 69th St. E.
Daily dawn-dusk. Closed Thurs. 7 a.m.-10 a.m. and last Fri. of the month 2-dusk for maintenance.
Fenced, 3 acres, trees, separate small dog area, disposal bags, doggie drinking fountains, shelter.

Paw Park of Historic Sanford - Sanford
pawparksanford.org
427 French Ave. (US 17/92) in Sanford's Historic District, 20 minutes north of downtown Orlando. From I-4, take the SR 46 exit (exit 101C, Sanford/Mount Dora), proceed east on SR 46 approximately 4 miles to French Ave., turn right (southbound) and get into the left thru-lane; the Paw Park is on the left just past the Burger King.
Daily 7:30 a.m.-8 p.m.
Fenced, double-gated entry, shaded with mature oak trees, historic lighting, paved walkway, benches, tables, disposal bag dispensers, parking, self-watering bowls, water misting station, dog showers, separate area for small dogs, community bulletin board. Access for the disabled.

17th Street Paw Park - Sarasota
scgov.net
4570-4730 17th St.
Daily dawn-dusk.
Fenced, separate areas for large and small dogs, tables, benches, shade, drinking fountain for dogs, disposal bags, trash cans.

Lakeview Paw Park - Sarasota
scgov.net
7150 Lago St.
Daily dawn-dusk.
Fenced, separate areas for large and small dogs, water, disposal bags, trash cans.

Davis Islands Dog Park - Tampa
tampagov.net
1002 Severn St.
Daily dawn-dusk.
Fenced, with two areas at the south end of the island: a 1-acre dry area and a 1.5-acre beach with more than 200 feet of waterfront. Both areas have double-gated entries, disposal bags, trash cans and water. Designated off-leash area on the beach.

Gadsden Park - Tampa
tampagov.net
6901 S. MacDill Ave., southwest corner of the grounds.
Daily dawn-dusk.
Fenced, 1 acre, double-gated entry, water, disposal bags, trash cans, benches, tables, shade trees.

Giddens Park - Tampa
tampagov.net
5202 N. 12th St.
Daily dawn-dusk.
Fenced, 1 acre, double-gated entry, drinking fountains for dogs and people, disposal bags, trash cans, benches, tables, shade trees.

James Urbanski Dog Park at Al Lopez Park - Tampa
tampagov.net
4810 N. Himes Ave.
Daily dawn-dusk.
Fenced, 1.5 acres, separate area for small dogs, double-gated entry, disposal bags, trash cans, benches, tables, shade trees.

Palma Ceia Park - Tampa
tampagov.net
2200 Marti St.
Mon.-Fri. 8 a.m.-dusk or 7:15 p.m. (whichever is earlier), Sat.-Sun. 9 a.m.-dusk or 7:15 p.m. (whichever is earlier).
Fenced, less than 1 acre, double-gated entry, disposal bags, trash cans, benches, tables, shade trees.

Picnic Island Park - Tampa
tampagov.net
7409 Picnic Island Blvd.
Daily dawn-dusk.
Fenced, double-gated entry, disposal bags, trash cans, benches, tables, shade trees. Designated off-leash area on beach.

Rowlett Park - Tampa
tampagov.net
2401 E. Yukon St.
Daily dawn-dusk.
Fenced, 1.75 acre, double-gated entry, disposal bags, trash cans, benches, tables, shade trees, separate areas for large and small dogs, agility equipment.

Lake Idamere Dog Park - Tavares
lakecountyfl.gov
12335 County Rd. 448, within Lake Idamere Park
Daily dawn-dusk.
Fenced, separate small-dog area, trees, benches, shade, disposal bags, water, trash cans.

North Lake Community Park Dog Park - Umatilla
lakecountyfl.gov
40730 Roger Giles Rd., within North Lake Community Park
Daily 6:30 a.m.-10 p.m.
Fenced, double-gated entry, trees, benches, shelter, shade, disposal bags, grass, trash cans, water, parking, lights. Access for the disabled.

Brohard Beach & Paw Park - Venice
venicegov.com
1600 Harbor Dr. S.
Daily 7 a.m.-dusk.
Six-foot fence, trees, benches, tables, shelter, disposal bags, trash cans, parking, water, dog shower, separate area for small dogs, community bulletin board. Dog Beach is accessed by a boardwalk from Paw Park. Dogs are permitted in a restricted area along Brohard Beach as indicated by beach signs. Access for the disabled.

Woodmere Park & Woodmere Paw Park - Venice
scgov.net
3951 Woodmere Park Blvd. (2 blocks north of US 41 on Jacaranda Boulevard)
Daily dawn-dusk.
Fenced, 2.5 acres, double-gated entry, trees, benches, tables, disposal bags, trash cans, parking, restrooms, water, double-gated section for small dogs near the front gate, dog shower, community bulletin board.

IDAHO

Moscow Dog Park - Moscow
dogparkfriends.org
2019 White Ave. (next to the Humane Society of the Palouse)
Daily dawn-dusk; closed Wed. 7 a.m.-9 a.m. for maintenance.
Fenced, 1 acre, grass, two double-gated entries, trees, shade, tables, benches, disposal bags, trash cans, water, parking, large tire structures for dogs to climb on or run through. Access for the disabled.

Nampa Dog Park - Nampa
nampaparks.org
East Amity Avenue and 2nd Street South, near the Kings Road overpass
Daily half an hour before dawn to half an hour after dusk.
Fenced, 6 acres, grass, double-gated entry, trees, benches, walking trails, shelter, shade, tables, separate small dog area, disposal bags, trash cans, water, parking. Access for the disabled.

ILLINOIS

Rover's Run Dog Park - Homewood
hfparks.com, (708) 957-0300
Near 191st Street and Center Avenue in Apollo Park
Daily dawn-dusk.
Annual membership fee $25 (non-residents); $15 (residents). A list of current vaccinations is required.
Fenced, 3 acres, double-gated entry, separate training area and entrance, benches, covered picnic tables, free parking, walking path, water fountain for dogs and people.

Bradley Dog Park - Peoria
peoriaparks.org
1314 N. Park Rd. (cross street is Farmington Road)
Daily dawn-dusk.
Fenced, 5 acres, double-gated entry, trees, benches, shade, tables, separate small dog area, disposal bags, trash cans, water, parking, grass and wood mulch. Access for the disabled.

East Side Sports Complex Dog Park - St. Charles
st-charlesparks.org
3565 Legacy Blvd. (east of Kirk Road and about 1 mile south of Rt. 64)
Daily 9 a.m.-dusk (weather permitting).
Fenced, less than 1 acre, separate small dog area, interactive play equipment, water.

James O. Breen Community Park Dog Park - St. Charles
st-charlesparks.org
Corner of Campton Hills and Peck Road
Daily 9 a.m.-dusk (weather permitting).
Fenced, 2.5 acres, double-gated entry, trees, benches, activity stations, disposal bags, trash cans, parking, dog water fountain.

River Bend Community Park Dog Park - St. Charles
st-charlesparks.org
Courier and Geneva avenues
Daily 9 a.m.-dusk (weather permitting).
Fenced, less than 1 acre, double-gated entry, disposal bags, trash cans, parking, dog water fountain.

IOWA

Rita's Ranch Off Leash Dog Park - Iowa City
jcdogpac.org
Scott Boulevard between E. Court and Muscatine Avenue
Daily dawn-dusk.
Day pass $5, yearly tag $25 ($5 discount for spayed/neutered dogs)
Fenced, approximately 3 acres, double-gated entry, disposal bags, trash cans, parking.

Thornberry Off Leash Dog Park - Iowa City
jcdogpac.org
End of Foster Road; closest cross street is Canton Street
Daily dawn-dusk.
Day pass $5, yearly tag $25 ($5 discount for spayed/neutered dogs)
Fenced, 10 acres, four separately fenced areas (all dogs, small dogs, training area and a pond for dog swimming and wading), grass, trees, disposal bags, trash cans, asphalt walking path, parking. Water is trucked in except during winter; bring your own container. Access for the disabled.

Lewis and Clark Dog Park - Sioux City
sioux-city.org
5100 Correctionville Rd., within Bacon Creek Park
Daily 7 a.m.-dusk.
Fenced, 4 acres for larger dogs, 1 acre for small dogs, double-gated entry, trees, grass, benches, trash cans, water, parking, disposal bags. Access for the disabled.

KANSAS

El Dorado Dog Park - El Dorado
visiteldoradoks.com
400 E. Locust Ave.
Daily dawn-dusk.
Fenced, less than 1 acre, double-gated entry, trees, grass, benches, water, disposal bags, trash cans, parking. Access for the disabled.

KENTUCKY

Kenton Paw Park - Covington
kentoncounty.org
3951 Madison Pike (Rt. 17) at Pioneer Park
Daily dawn-dusk.
Fenced, 2 acres, double-gated entry, trees, grass, benches, tables, separate areas for large and small dogs, disposal bags. Beautiful creekside setting with additional area for agility (not always available).

Judy Rains Memorial Dog Park - Richmond
parks.richmond.ky.us
299 Lake Reba Dr., within Lake Reba Park
Daily 8 a.m.-dusk.
Fenced, less than 1 acre, double-gated entry, trees, grass, benches, tables, separate small dog area, disposal bags, trash cans, water, parking, lights.

MASSACHUSETTS

The South Boston Bark Park - Boston
sbbarkpark.org
Columbia Road and Day Boulevard
Daily 6 a.m.-8 p.m.
Fenced, less than 1 acre, double-gated entry, trees, benches, separate small dog area, trash cans, water, pea stone with cement walkways, street parking. Access for the disabled.

Pilgrim Bark Park - Provincetown
provincetowndogpark.org
Shank Painter Road at Rt. 6. Do not park on Shank Painter Road; park on the east side of Rt. 6.
Daily dawn-dusk.
Fenced, nearly 1 acre, separate small dog area, disposal bags, trash cans. Many features, like the custom benches and welcome sign, have been made by local artists.

MICHIGAN

Pet Supplies "Plus" Dog Park at Hillcrest Park - Grand Rapids
grcity.us
1415 Lyon St. N.E. and Benjamin Street N.E. at Hillcrest Park
Daily dawn-dusk.
Fenced, 1 acre, double-gated entry, separate small dog area, shade, water, disposal bags. Street parking is available, or park at Fuller Park and walk to Hillcrest.

Orion Oaks Bark Park - Lake Orion
destinationoakland.com
South of Clarkston Road on Joslyn Road (park at the north Joslyn Road entrance and follow the signs)
Daily 8 a.m. to half-hour after dusk, or as posted.
A park pass is required; a daily pass is available at the Lake Orion Township office (open Mon.-Fri.) on Joslyn Road south of the park; or at the Independence Oaks County Park (open daily) on Sashabaw Road, 2.5 miles north of I-75.
Day pass per private vehicle $10 (non-resident); $5 (resident); $4 (ages 63+). Annual pass per private vehicle $46 (non-resident); $30 (ages 63+ and resident).
Fenced, 7 acres, trees, benches, tables, disposal bags, trash cans, parking, portable toilet, water. A portion of Lake Sixteen is reserved for canine swimming. Access for the disabled.

Soldan Dog Park at Hawk Island County Park - Lansing
pk.ingham.org
1601 E. Cavanaugh Rd., just north of Hawk Island County Park; the dog park main entrance is through the park. The dog park also can be accessed from the west off the River Trail in Scott Woods; drive to the very north end of the Hawk Island parking area, then walk a short distance (with your dog or dogs on-leash) past the Hawk Island Maintenance Building to the main dog park entrance.
Daily 8 a.m.-dusk. Key fob required for entry; see Web site for details.
Fenced, 17 acres, double-gated entry, diverse natural area with trails, a large pond and an open field, disposal bags, parking, dog and human drinking fountains. Access for the disabled.

Lyon Oaks Bark Park - Lyon Township
destinationoakland.com
Pontiac Trail between Wixom and Old Plank roads
Daily 8 a.m. to half-hour after dusk, or as posted.
A park pass is required and is available at the park.
Day pass per private vehicle $10 (non-resident); $5 (resident); $4 (ages 63+). Annual pass per private vehicle $46 (non-resident); $30 (ages 63+ and resident).
Fenced, 13 acres of open fields, benches, tables, disposal bags, trash cans, parking, restrooms, water pump.

Red Oaks Dog Park - Madison Heights
destinationoakland.com
Dequindre Road, adjacent to Red Oaks Waterpark
Daily 8 a.m. to 9 p.m., or as posted.
Fenced, 5.2 acres, 3 separate large and small dog areas, shelter, water, tables, benches, disposal bags, trash cans, paved parking.

MINNESOTA

Note: In the greater Minneapolis area there are multiple off-leash sites within a 15-minute drive of downtown Minneapolis/St. Paul. There are additional sites in rural/suburban areas of the seven-county metropolitan area. Some parks require a permit for use. Please read descriptions carefully.

Alimagnet Dog Park - Burnsville (south metro suburb)
alimagnetdogpark.org
1200 Alimagnet Pkwy. (from central St. Paul, go south on I-35E to the CR 42 exit, east to CR 11, then north on CR 11 to Alimagnet Parkway and turn right; the dog park is on the right)
Daily 5 a.m.-10 p.m. Permit required; for more information visit the Web site or phone the Recreation Department at (952) 895-4500.
Fenced, 7 acres, double-gated entry, wooded areas, open fields, mowed prairie-grass trail, benches, tables, disposal bags, trash cans, lights, parking, phones, restrooms, water, pond.

Dakota Woods Dog Park (south metro rural)
co.dakota.mn.us
16470 Blaine Ave. south of CR 46 (160th Street East) in the center of Dakota County near Coates Daily 5 a.m.-10 p.m.
Pass required.
Fenced, 16 acres of wooded and open spaces with a walking trail loop, tables, disposal bag dispensers, trash cans, parking, portable toilets, no surface water; bring your own water.

Elm Creek Park Reserve - Dayton (northwest metro rural)
threeriversparkdistrict.org
13080 Territorial Rd.
Daily 5 a.m.-10 p.m. Permit required; day permits are available at the site. Annual special-use permits may be obtained online.
Fenced, 30 acres with a mowed trail, trees, tables, trash cans, parking, restrooms.

Battle Creek Off-Leash Site - Maplewood (east central metro)
co.ramsey.mn.us
Lower Afton and McKnight roads
Daily dawn-dusk except as posted seasonally. No permit required.
Partially fenced, 35 acres, tables, trash cans, parking.

Franklin Terrace - Minneapolis
minneapolisparks.org
925 Franklin Terr. and 30th Avenue South
Daily 6 a.m.-10 p.m. Permit required.
Fully fenced, 1.3 acres, double-gated entry at the east and west ends of the site, bench, disposal bag dispensers, on-street parking.

Lake of the Isles Park - Minneapolis
minneapolisparks.org
2845 Lake of the Isles Pkwy. W. at West 28th Street
Daily 6 a.m.-10 p.m. Permit required.
Fully fenced, 1.8 acres, double-gated entry at the northern end of the site, separate small dog area, lighted at the southern end, benches, disposal bag dispensers.

Loring Park - Minneapolis
minneapolisparks.org
132 Willow St. at Maple Street and Harmon Place
Daily 6 a.m.-10 p.m. Permit required.
Fenced, less than 1 acre, disposal bag dispensers, limestone boulders for climbing and sitting, crushed limestone surface.

Minnehaha Park - Minneapolis
minneapolisparks.org
5399 S. Minnehaha Park Dr. and East 54th Street
Daily 6 a.m.-10 p.m. Permit required.
Partially fenced, 7.4 acres along the Mississippi River (where dogs can swim), disposal bag dispensers, lighted parking area (parking permit required), portable toilet in parking area.

Victory Prairie Park - Minneapolis
minneapolisparks.org
4701 Russell Ave. N.
Daily 6 a.m.-10 p.m. Permit required.
Fenced, 2.6 acres.

Plymouth Dog Park - Plymouth
ci.plymouth.mn.us
CR 47 in northwest Plymouth, about 2 blocks west of Dunkirk Lane on the south side of CR 47
Daily dawn-dusk. No permit required.
Unfenced, 10 acres, separate area for small dogs, trash cans; bring your own water and disposal bags.

Cleary Lake Regional Park - Prior Lake (south metro rural)
threeriversparkdistrict.org
18106 Texas Ave.
Daily 5 a.m.-10 p.m. Permit required; day permits are available at the site. Annual special-use permits may be obtained online.
Fenced, 28 acres, tables, trash cans, parking, restrooms, pond. Trails are mowed in summer, packed in winter.

Crow-Hassan Park Reserve - Rogers (northwest metro rural)
threeriversparkdistrict.org
Sylvan Lake Road west of Rogers (from I-94, take the Rogers exit and go south through town to the T intersection, turn right on CR 116 and proceed to CR 203, turn left and follow CR 203 to the park entrance)
Daily 5 a.m.-10 p.m. Permit required; day permits are available at the site. Annual special-use permits may be obtained online.
Unfenced, 40 acres with a mowed trail, trees, tables, trash cans, parking, restrooms.

Woodview Dog Park - Roseville (central)
co.ramsey.mn.us
Larpenteur Avenue, just east of Dale Street (access gate to main off-leash area is about 100 yards down the bike trail)
Daily dawn-dusk; small dog play times posted online. No permit required.
Partially fenced (along bike trail only), 4 acres, trees, tables, disposal bags, trash cans, parking, water, separate fenced area for small dogs. Access for the disabled during all open hours regardless of dog size.

Arlington Off Leash Dog Area - St. Paul
stpaul.gov
Arkwright Street at Arlington Avenue (from I-35E, take the Maryland Avenue exit east to Arkwright Street, then go north; the park is on the right)
Daily dawn-dusk. No permit required.
Fenced, 4.5 acres with trails and woods, tables, disposal bags, trash cans, parking. Park users sometimes leave gates open; keep your dog under voice control to prevent escapes, bring your own water.

High Bridge Dog Park - St. Paul
stpaul.gov
59 Randolph Ave., entrance on w. end of dog park.
Daily dawn-dusk. No permit required.
Fenced, 7 acres with trail and woods, tables, disposal bags, trash cans, parking. Park users sometimes leave gates open; keep your dog under voice control to prevent escapes, bring your own water.

Rice Creek Off-Leash Site - Shoreview (northeast metro)
co.ramsey.mn.us
Lexington Avenue, just south of CR J
Daily dawn-dusk. No permit required.
Unfenced, 13 acres of flat prairie vegetation, tables, trash cans, parking, small pond.

Otter Lake Dog Park - White Bear Township (northeast suburban)
co.ramsey.mn.us
Otter Lake Road (take I-35E to the CR J exit, then CR J east to Otter Lake Road, following it south to the dog park; the entrance is next to the boat launch)
Daily dawn-dusk except as posted seasonally. No permit required.
Partially fenced, 10 acres of rolling hills with wooded and open prairie vegetation, separate 1-acre fenced area for small dogs. The park is fenced adjacent to Otter Lake Road and along most of the south boundary, bounded on the east by a large wetland and on the north by Otter Lake.

NEBRASKA

Hanscom Dog Park - Omaha
omahadogparks.org
32nd and Woolworth avenues, within Hanscom Park
Daily dawn-dusk.
Fenced, double-gated entry, separate small dog area, trees, benches, shade, tables, disposal bags, trash cans, parking.

Hefflinger Dog Park - Omaha
omahadogpark.org
11111 W. Maple Rd. (Old Maple Road and N. 112th Avenue)
Daily dawn-dusk.
Fenced, 7.5 acres, double-gated entry, separate small dog area, trees, benches, shade, tables, disposal bags, trash cans, parking. Water is available Memorial Day through Labor Day. The off-leash area is inside the dog park gates; a leash is required in all other areas.

NEVADA

Note: All Clark County/Las Vegas dog park areas include water, seating and waste receptacles.

Desert Breeze Park Dog Park - Clark County/Las Vegas (NW)
clarkcountynv.gov
8425 W. Spring Mountain Rd. at Durango Drive
Daily 6 a.m. - 11 p.m.
Three runs, trees.

Desert Inn Dog Park - Clark County/Las Vegas (SE)
clarkcountynv.gov
3570 Vista del Monte Dr. (near Lamb Boulevard and Boulder Highway)
Daily 6 a.m.-11 p.m.

Dog Fancier's Park - Clark County/Las Vegas (SE)
clarkcountynv.gov, (702) 455-8200
5800 E. Flamingo Rd. at Jimmy Durante Boulevard
Daily 6 a.m.-11 p.m. Since this 12-acre park also is used for dog shows and training, phone ahead to confirm schedule.

Molasky Park Dog Park - Clark County/Las Vegas (SE)
clarkcountynv.gov
1065 E. Twain Ave. (west of Maryland Parkway; dog run is south of Twain Avenue)
Daily 6 a.m.-11 p.m.
10 acres.

Shadow Rock Dog Park - Clark County/Las Vegas (NE)
clarkcountynv.gov
2650 Los Feliz St. at Lake Mead Boulevard (east of Hollywood Boulevard; dog run is east of the park area)
Daily 6 a.m.-11 p.m.
Tree, two shade shelters.

Silverado Ranch Park Dog Park - Clark County/Las Vegas (SE)
clarkcountynv.gov
9855 S. Gillespie St.
Daily 6 a.m.-11 p.m.
Two runs, one for dogs under 30 pounds and another for dogs over 29 pounds; lights.

Spring Valley Dog Park - Clark County/Las Vegas (SW)
clarkcountynv.gov
7600 W. Flamingo Rd.
Daily 6 a.m.-11 p.m.
Three runs, lights.

Sunset Park - Clark County/Las Vegas (SE)
clarkcountynv.gov
2601 E. Sunset Rd. (closest parking is off Eastern Avenue between Sunset and Warm Springs roads)
Daily 6 a.m.-11 p.m.
Two runs for large and small dogs.

NEW HAMPSHIRE

Derry Dog Park - Derry
derry.nh.us
45 Fordway St.
Daily dawn-dusk.
Fenced, less than 1 acre, double-gated entry, gazebo, picnic tables, separate area for small dogs, bone-shaped dog pool (open in summer only). Tunnel, seesaw, tire jump and other agility items are provided. Children under 9 are not permitted. Rules are posted on fence inside and out. Parking is free but somewhat limited after 25 vehicles.

Dog Park at South Mill Pond - Portsmouth
cityofportsmouth.com
South Mill Pond at Junkins Avenue and South Street
Daily dawn-dusk.
Fenced, double-gated entry, separate large and small dog areas, stone and grass surface, benches, shelter, tables, disposal bags, trash cans, water, parking.

NEW MEXICO

Canine Skyline Dog Park - Albuquerque
cabq.gov
12700 Montgomery Blvd. N.E.
Daily 6 a.m.-10 p.m.
Fenced, double-gated entry, water in non-winter months.

Coronado Dog Park - Albuquerque
cabq.gov
301 McKnight Ave. N.W.
Daily 6 a.m.-10 p.m.
Fenced, double-gated entry, no water.

Los Altos Dog Park - Albuquerque
cabq.gov
821 Eubank Blvd. N.E.
Daily 6 a.m.-10 p.m.
Fenced, double-gated entry, no water, lights.

Montessa Dog Park - Albuquerque
cabq.gov
3615 Los Picaros Rd. S.E.
Daily 6 a.m.-10 p.m.
Fenced, double-gated entry, no water.

North Domingo Baca Dog Park - Albuquerque
cabq.gov
7520 Corona Ave. N.E.
Daily 6 a.m.-10 p.m.
Fenced, double-gated entry, no water, lights.

Ouray Dog Park - Albuquerque
cabq.gov
7500 Ouray Rd. N.W.
Daily 6 a.m.-10 p.m.
Fenced, double-gated entry, water in non-winter months. Access for the disabled.

Rio Grande Triangle Dog Park - Albuquerque
cabq.gov
1451 Kit Carson Ave. S.E.
Daily 6 a.m.-10 p.m.
Fenced, double-gated entry, no water, lights.

Roosevelt Dog Park - Albuquerque
cabq.gov
500 Spruce St. S.E.
Mon.-Fri 6 a.m.-10 a.m. Apr.-Sept.; Mon.-Fri. 6 a.m.-11 a.m., rest of year. Closed holidays.
Fenced, double-gated entry, no water.

Santa Fe Village Dog Park - Albuquerque
cabq.gov
5700 Bogart St. N.W.
Daily 6 a.m.-10 p.m.
Fenced, double-gated entry, trees, benches, shade, disposal bags, trash cans, water in non-winter months. Access for the disabled.

Tom Bolak Urban Forest Dog Park - Albuquerque
cabq.gov
2000 Dakota St. N.E.
Daily 6 a.m.-10 p.m.
Fenced, double-gated entry, water in non-winter months.

Tower Pond Dog Park - Albuquerque
cabq.gov
Tower Road S.W. and 86th Street S.W.
Daily 6 a.m.-10 p.m.
Fenced, double-gated entry, no water.

USS Bullhead Dog Park - Albuquerque
cabq.gov
1606 San Pedro Dr. S.E.
Daily 6 a.m.-10 p.m.
Fenced, double-gated entry, no water, lights.

Westgate Community Dog Park - Albuquerque
cabq.gov
Cartagena Avenue and Valley View Drive
Daily 6 a.m.-10 p.m.
Fenced, double-gated entry, no water, lights.

NEW YORK

Barkyard-LaSalle Off-Leash Dog Park - Buffalo
thebarkyard.org
101-397 Dar Dr.
Daily dawn-dusk. Small dog hours: Tues. 4-6, Sun. 1-3.
Fenced, 1.6 acres, double-gated entry, benches, trash cans.
Access for the disabled.

Wegmans Good Dog Park - Liverpool
onondagacountyparks.com
49 Cold Springs Tr., within Onondaga Lake Park
Daily dawn-dusk.
Fenced, 1 acre, double-gated entry, playground quality pea
gravel and grass, trees, separate small dog area, agility
equipment, benches, water (May-Oct.), disposal bags, trash
cans, parking.

New York City (Manhattan and boroughs)
urbanhound.com
nycgovparks.org

Canine Court, Van Cortlandt Park - Bronx
West 252nd Street and Broadway (enter on the path on 252nd
and follow it about 100 feet to the left)
Daily dawn-dusk.
Fenced with two large runs: a basic dog run and a canine
agility playground with teeter-totter, hurdles, ladder, three chutes
and a hanging tire.

Ewen Park ("John's Run") - Bronx (Riverdale)
Riverdale to Johnson avenues, south of West 232nd Street
and down the steps in the clearing on the right
Daily dawn-dusk.
Unfenced, plastic lawn furniture, scenic views.

Seton Park - Bronx (Riverdale)
West 235th Street and Independence Avenue (west of
Independence on 235th Street, near the Spuyten Duyvil
Library)
Daily dawn-dusk.

Prospect Park - Brooklyn
fidobrooklyn.org
Grand Army Plaza and Flatbush; off-leash areas may be
accessed from all park entrances
Daily 9 p.m.-1 a.m. and 5-9 a.m. At all other times dogs must
be on a leash; minimum fine for non-compliance $100.
Off-leash areas are the Long Meadow, Nethermead and
Peninsula open meadows. Ball fields are off-limits to dogs at all
times. **Note:** Use of the park is at the owner's risk. Dogs may
be off-leash with appropriate supervision in the three large
meadows at the hours specified above; please observe all
off-leash rules. Rules are posted online and at park entrances.
Dogs must be on a leash at all other places and times.

Owl's Head Park - Brooklyn (Bay Ridge)
68th Street and Shore Road
Tree, grass surface, disposal bags.

Hillside Park - Brooklyn Heights
Columbia Heights and Middagh Street
Daily 24 hours.
Fenced.

Palmetto Playground - Brooklyn Heights
Columbia Place and State Street (in the corner by the
Brooklyn-Queens Expressway)
Daily 24 hours.
Benches, one park light, water.

Tompkins Square Park - Manhattan (East Village)
East 9th Street at Avenue B
Daily 6 a.m.-midnight.
Benches, picnic tables, water, a canine memorial. Access for
the disabled.

Madison Square Park - Manhattan (Gramercy/Flatiron/Union Square)
East 24th Street at Fifth Avenue
Daily 6 a.m.-midnight. Trees, benches, disposal bags, water.

Thomas Jefferson Park - Manhattan (Harlem)
East 112th Street at First Avenue
Daily 24 hours.
Benches, wood chip surface.

J. Hood Wright Park - Manhattan (Inwood/Ft. George/Washington Heights)
West 173rd Street between Fort Washington Avenue and
Haven Avenue

Fishbridge Park - Manhattan (Lower East Side)
Dover Street at Pearl Street, just south of the Brooklyn Bridge
Daily dawn-dusk.
Benches, water hose, wading pool (open in summer only),
lockbox for toys, lockbox with newspapers for picking up after
your dog.

Peter Detmold Park - Manhattan (Midtown East)
East 49th Street at FDR Drive (behind Beekman Place)
Daily dawn-9 p.m., June-Sept.; dawn-8 p.m., Mar.-May and
Oct.-Nov.; dawn-7 p.m., rest of year.
Trees, benches, historical lamps, disposal bags.

Carl Schurz Park - Manhattan (Upper East Side)
East 86th Street at East End Avenue
Daily dawn-1 a.m.
Benches, scoops, pea gravel surface. A second run for small
dogs (past the main run, toward the East River) has a scenic
view of the river and the 59th Street Bridge.

Riverside Park at 72nd Street - Manhattan (Upper West Side/Morningside Heights)
West 72nd Street
Daily 6 a.m.-1 a.m.
Bench, hanging flowerpots, disposal bags, scoopers.

Riverside Park at 87th Street - Manhattan (Upper West Side/Morningside Heights)
West 87th Street
Daily dawn-dusk.
Separate areas for large and small dogs, water fountain and
hose.

Riverside Park at 105th Street - Manhattan (Upper West Side/Morningside Heights)
riversidedog.org
West 105th Street, Riverside Park Central Promenade
Daily dawn-dusk.
Trees, crushed granite surface, benches, disposal bag
dispensers, water fountain, water faucet for dogs, separate
area for small dogs.

Theodore Roosevelt Park - Manhattan (Upper West Side/Morningside Heights)
West 81st Street at Columbus Avenue
Daily 8 a.m.-10 p.m.
Shade trees, benches, dog water faucet, separate run for small
dogs.

Washington Square Park - Manhattan (West Village)
West 4th Street at Thompson Street
Daily 6 a.m.-midnight.
Trees, pea gravel surface, benches, scoopers, water hose,
water bowls.

Freeway Dog Park - Queens (Rockaway Beach)
arfarfrockaway.org
Rockaway Freeway between Beach 83rd and Beach 81st streets
Daily 8 a.m.-9 p.m.
Fenced, double-gated entry, trees, separate small dog area, benches, disposal bags. Access for the disabled.

Doughboy Plaza - Queens (Woodside)
Woodside Avenue from 54th to 56th streets (also south of Woodside at 56th Street) at Windmuller Park
Daily dawn-dusk.
Fenced, trash can.

Peekskill Dog Park - Peekskill
cityofpeekskill.com
1795 Main St.
Daily dawn-dusk.
Fenced, double-gated entry, trees, benches, shade, tables, separate small and large dog area, disposal bags, trash cans, parking.

NORTH CAROLINA

Poston Dog Park - Gastonia Co.
gaston.nc.us
1101 Lowell Spencer Mountain Rd.
Daily 7 a.m.-dusk.
Fenced, 5 acres, double-gated entry, separate small dog area, trees, benches, grass, disposal bags, trash cans, water, parking.

Down East Dog Park - New Bern
newbern-nc.org
332 Glenburnie Dr. in Glenburnie Park
Daily dawn-dusk.
Annual fee $35-$43 for the first dog, $20-$28 for each additional dog. Weekend pass $15. Proof of current rabies vaccination is required. Phone (252) 639-2901 for more information.
Fenced. The main 1-acre area is for large dogs over 25 pounds, but dogs of any size may use it; a separate area is set aside for puppies and small dogs.

OHIO

Park 4 Paws - Avon Lake
avonlake.org
33401 Weber Rd. at Weiss Field
Daily 7 a.m.-9 p.m.
Fenced, double-gated entry, trees, benches, shade, separate small dog area, disposal bags, trash cans, water, parking. Access for the disabled.

Armleder Park Dog Park - Cincinnati
greatparks.org
5057 Wooster Pl.
Daily dawn-dusk.
Fenced, trees, shelter, parking, separate large and small dog areas, canine showers and drinking fountains, paved walking trail.

Mt. Airy Dog Park - Cincinnati
cincyparks.com
Westwood Northern Boulevard in Mt. Airy Forest's Highpoint Picnic Area, between Montana Avenue and North Bend Road
Daily dawn-dusk.
Fenced, 2 acres, trees, benches, tables, shelter, trash cans, parking, restrooms, water. Access for the disabled.

Washington Dog Park - Cincinnati
washingtonpark.org
1230 Elm St.
Daily 6 a.m.-11 p.m.
Fenced, less than 1 acre, water creek for dog play, dog-friendly water fountain, benches.

Big Walnut Dog Park - Columbus
parks.columbus.gov
5000 E. Livingston Ave. in Big Walnut Park (across from Walnut Ridge High School)
Daily 7 a.m.-11 p.m.
Fenced, 3 acres, two double-gated entries, separate small dog area, swimming pond, shade trees, picnic tables, paved parking, lights.

Three Creeks Dog Park - Columbus
parks.columbus.gov
2748 Spangler Rd.
Daily 8 a.m.-dusk.
Fenced, 5 acres, separate small dog area, walking paths, water.

Wheeler Dog Park - Columbus
parks.columbus.gov
725 Thurber Dr. W.
Daily 7 a.m.-11 p.m.
Fenced, 1.5 acres, benches, lights, walking paths, water, street parking.

Montgomery County Bark Park - Dayton
mcohio.org
6794 Webster St., corner of Webster Street and Wyse Road
Daily dawn-dusk.
Fenced, 6 acres, canine agility equipment, tables, chairs, water, gazebo, trash cans. Access for the disabled.

Pooch Playground - Gahanna
gahanna.gov
940 Pizzurro Pkwy. From I-270 South, take exit 37 to Hamilton Road. Turn right (south) onto Hamilton and immediately get in the left lane to turn left into Pizzurro Park.
Daily dawn-dusk.
Fenced, 4 acres, double-gated entry, trees, benches, separate small dog area, agility area, disposal bags, trash cans, water (spring through fall), parking. Access for the disabled. There are trees along the perimeter and in the small dog area. Dogs may swim in the creek outside the fenced enclosure.

Mentor Dog Park - Mentor
cityofmentor.com
6647 Hopkins Rd.
Daily dawn-dusk.
Fenced, less than 1 acre, double-gated entry, benches, shelter, agility equipment, shade, tables, separate small dog area, disposal bags, trash cans, dog water fountain, parking. Access for the disabled.

OKLAHOMA

Biscuit Acres Park - Tulsa
biscuitacres.com
91st Street between Sheridan Road and Yale Avenue in Hunter Park
Wed.-Sun. 5 a.m.-9 p.m., May 1-first week of Nov.; Thurs.-Sun., second week of Nov.-Dec. 31; Fri.-Sun., rest of year.
Fenced, double-gated entry, 2.5 acres, separate small dog area, water, trees, shade, benches, tables, water fountain.

Joe Station Bark Park - Tulsa
cityoftulsa.org
2279 Charles Page Blvd.
Daily 5 a.m.-11 p.m., in summer; 5 a.m.-9 p.m., in winter. Closed Mon. 5 a.m.-9 a.m. for maintenance.
Fenced, separate small dog area, water, shade, parking, lights. Located at a former baseball field and named for one of the trolley stops along the historic Interurban Line that once connected Tulsa and Sand Springs.

OREGON

Awbrey Reservoir - Bend
DogPAC.org
N.W. 10th and Trenton
Daily dawn-dusk.
Unfenced 5-acre area with access to trails, parking.

Big Sky - Bend
DogPAC.org
21690 Neff Rd.
Daily dawn-dusk.
5 fenced acres, 6 unfenced acres.

Gooddog! Offleash Area - Bend
DogPAC.org
Century Drive, west of Entrada Lodge
Daily dawn-dusk.
Unfenced, several miles of trails with river access.

Hollinshead Dog Park - Bend
DogPAC.org
1235 N.E. Jones Rd.
Daily dawn-dusk.
3 partially unfenced acres.

Overturf Butte Reservoir - Bend
DogPAC.org
Skyliner Summit Loop
Daily dawn-dusk.
4 partially fenced acres.

Pine Nursery - Bend
DogPAC.org
Deschutes Market Road and Yeoman Road (entrance on
Yeoman Road)
Daily dawn-dusk.
18 fenced acres with an open area.

Ponderosa Dog Park - Bend
DogPAC.org
225 S.E. 15th St., south of Bear Creek Road
Daily dawn-dusk.
4 fenced acres.

Riverbend Beach - Bend
DogPAC.org
799 N.W. Columbia St.
Daily dawn-dusk.
Fenced, double-gated entry, benches, disposal bags, trash
cans, water, swimming access.

Alton Baker Park - Eugene
eugene-or.gov
South of Leo Harris Parkway (park in the lot south of Autzen
Stadium and cross the pedestrian bridge to the dog park)
Daily 6 a.m.-11 p.m.
Fenced, benches, tables, simple shelters for protection from
sun and rain, disposal bag receptacles, water.

Amazon Park - Eugene
eugene-or.gov
East of 29th Street and Amazon Parkway
Daily 6 a.m.-11 p.m.
Fenced, separate small dog area, benches, tables, simple
shelters for protection from sun and rain, disposal bag
receptacles, water, parking nearby.

Candlelight Park - Eugene
eugene-or.gov
Royal Avenue and Throne Drive
Daily 6 a.m.-11 p.m.
Fenced, benches, tables, disposal bag receptacles.

Wayne Morse Family Farm - Eugene
eugene-or.gov
Crest Drive and Lincoln Street (park in the main parking area
at 595 Crest Dr. and take the trail east)
Daily 6 a.m.-11 p.m.
Fenced, benches, tables, simple shelters for protection from
sun and rain, disposal bag receptacles, water.

Brentwood Park - Portland
portlandonline.com
Southeast 60th Avenue and Duke Street
Daily 5 a.m.-midnight.
Fenced.

Chimney Park - Portland
portlandonline.com
9360 N. Columbia Blvd.
Daily 5 a.m.-midnight.
Fenced, 6 acres of off-leash meadow and trails. Dogs should
be under excellent voice command.

Delta Park - Portland
portlandonline.com
North Denver Avenue and Martin Luther King Jr. Boulevard (off
I-5 exit 307 across from the East Delta Sports Complex)
Daily 6 a.m.-midnight, May-Oct. (open during dry season only).
Fenced, 5 acres of off-leash field, trees, benches; bring your
own water. Dogs are not allowed on the sports fields.

Gabriel Park - Portland
portlandonline.com
Southwest 45th Avenue and Vermont Street
Daily 5 a.m.-midnight, May-Oct. (open during dry season only).
Fenced, off-leash area, trees, picnic tables, water. Dogs must
remain leashed when not in the off-leash area.

Normandale Park - Portland
portlandonline.com
Northeast 57th Avenue and Halsey Street
Daily 5 a.m.-midnight.
Fenced.

Sacajawea Park - Portland
portlandonline.com
Northeast 75th Ave. and Roselawn Street
Daily 5 a.m.-midnight.
Fenced.

Wallace Park - Portland
portlandonline.com
Northwest 25th Avenue and Raleigh Street
Daily 5 a.m.-midnight.
Fenced.

PENNSYLVANIA

Conneaut Lake Bark Park - Conneaut Lake
conneautlakebarkpark.com
12810 Foust Rd.
Membership required, ranges from $4 (Mon.-Fri.), $8
(Sat.-Sun.) through annual plan. Proof of current vaccinations
required. Contact (814) 382-2478 for more information.
Daily dawn-dusk (weather permitting).
Four fenced areas within 35 acres, water stations, swimming
pond and regulation dock diving platform, walking trail,
parking, picnic tables, portable restroom, disposal bags, trash
cans.

Canine Meadows Off-Leash Dog Area - York
yorkcountyparks.org
400 Mundis Race Rd., within John C. Rudy Park
Daily 8 a.m.-dusk. Area is closed during wet conditions; phone
(717) 840-7440 for information.
Fenced, 13.5 acres, double-gated entry, three separate dog
areas, information kiosk, disposal bags, water, trash cans,
parking.

TEXAS

White Rock Lake Dog Park - Dallas
whiterockdogpark.org
8000 Mockingbird Point, within White Rock Lake Park
Daily 5 a.m.-11 p.m. (weather permitting); closed for maintenance second and fourth Mon. of the month.
Fenced, 2.5 acres, trees, benches, disposal bags, trash cans, parking, restrooms, water fountains, separate fenced areas for large and small dogs, fenced swimming area for dogs in White Rock Lake.

Independence Dog Park - Pearland
pearlandparks.com
3919 Liberty Dr.
Daily 6 a.m.-10 p.m.
Fenced, separate small dog area, agility equipment, covered picnic area, disposal bags, water.

Southdown Dog Park - Pearland
pearlandparks.com
2150 Countryplace Pkwy., within Southdown Park near the Westside Event Center
Daily 6 a.m.-10 p.m.
Fenced, separate small dog area, agility equipment, shade, disposal bags, water.

Jack Carter Park - Plano
plano.gov
Pleasant Valley Drive and Spring Creek Parkway (less than one block north of the intersection on Pleasant Valley Drive)
Daily dawn-dusk (weather permitting); closed for maintenance first and third Tues. of the month.
Fenced, 2 acres, double-gated entry, benches, disposal bags, trash cans, parking, water fountains for dogs and people.

Round Rock Dog Depot - Round Rock
roundrocktexas.gov
800 Deerfoot Dr.
Daily 6 a.m.-8 p.m., Apr. 1-Oct. 1; daily 6-6, rest of year.
Fenced, approximately 2 acres, grass, agility equipment, double-gated entry, disposal bags, separate areas for large and small dogs, has a train depot theme with a windmill and a water tower that acts as a mister for hot dogs in summer.

VERMONT

Watson Dog Park - Hartford
watsondogpark.org
Maple Street and Rt. 14 N., between Rt. 5 N. and Christian Street
Daily dawn-9 p.m., May-Nov.; weather permitting, Dec.-Apr.
Fenced, 1 acre, double-gated entry, trees, benches, separate small dog area, disposal bags, water, parking. Access for disabled.

VIRGINIA

Note: Disposal bag receptacles are provided at Alexandria parks; patrons must provide their own bags.

Ben Brenman Park - Alexandria
alexandriava.gov
Cameron Station along Backlick Creek
Daily 6 a.m.-10 p.m.
Fenced, disposal bag receptacles, trash cans, parking.

Dog Park - Alexandria
alexandriava.gov
5000 block of Duke Street east of the Charles E. Beatley Jr. Library
Daily 6 a.m.-10 p.m.
Fenced, disposal bag receptacles, trash cans, parking.

Dog Run at Carlyle - Alexandria
alexandriava.gov
450 Andrews Ln.
Daily 6 a.m.-10 p.m.
Fenced, disposal bag receptacles, trash cans, parking.

Montgomery Park - Alexandria
alexandriava.gov
Fairfax and 1st streets
Daily 6 a.m.-10 p.m.
Fenced, disposal bag receptacles, trash cans, parking.

Simpson Stadium Park - Alexandria
alexandriava.gov
Monroe Avenue
Daily 6 a.m.-10 p.m.
Fenced, disposal bag receptacles, trash cans, parking, water fountains for dogs.

Off-leash, unfenced, under voice control areas:

Braddock Road - Alexandria
alexandriava.gov
Southeast corner of Braddock Road and Commonwealth Avenue
Daily 6 a.m.-10 p.m.
Unfenced.

Chambliss Street - Alexandria
alexandriava.gov
Chambliss Street at Grigsby Avenue, south of the tennis courts
Daily 6 a.m.-10 p.m.
Unfenced; area is marked by traffic barriers.

Chinquapin Park - Alexandria
alexandriava.gov
King Street at the east end of the loop road
Daily 6 a.m.-10 p.m.
Unfenced; area is marked by traffic barriers.

Edison Street - Alexandria
alexandriava.gov
Edison Street, west of the cul-de-sac between the bike trail and Berkey Photo Processing
Daily 6 a.m.-10 p.m.
Unfenced; area is marked by traffic barriers.

Ft. Williams - Alexandria
alexandriava.gov
Ft. Williams and New Ft. Williams Parkway
Daily 6 a.m.-10 p.m.
Unfenced; area is marked by traffic barriers.

Founders Park - Alexandria
alexandriava.gov
Oronoco Street and Union Street, northeast corner
Daily 6 a.m.-10 p.m.
Unfenced; 100-by-100-foot area is marked by traffic barriers.

Hooff's Run - Alexandria
alexandriava.gov
East of Commonwealth Avenue between Oak and Chapman streets
Daily 6 a.m.-10 p.m.
Unfenced; area is marked by traffic barriers.

Monticello Park - Alexandria
alexandriava.gov
Beverly Drive, east of the entrance
Daily 6 a.m.-10 p.m.
Unfenced; 50-by-200-foot area is marked by traffic barriers.

North Fort Ward Park - Alexandria
alexandriava.gov
Braddock Road, east side of entrance
Daily 6 a.m.-10 p.m.
Unfenced; 100-by-100-foot area is marked by traffic barriers.

Tarleton Park - Alexandria
alexandriava.gov
Mill Run west of Gordon Street
Daily 6 a.m.-10 p.m.
Unfenced.

Timberbranch Parkway - Alexandria
alexandriava.gov
Median to Timberbranch Parkway between Braddock Road
and Oakley Place
Daily 6 a.m.-10 p.m.
Unfenced; area is marked by traffic barriers.

Windmill Hill Park - Alexandria
alexandriava.gov
Gibbon and Union streets
Daily 6 a.m.-10 p.m.
Unfenced.

W&OD Railroad - Alexandria
alexandriava.gov
Raymond Avenue (200 feet of the W&OD Railroad
right-of-way south of Raymond)
Daily 6 a.m.-10 p.m.
Unfenced; area is marked by traffic barriers.

Benjamin Banneker Park - Arlington County
arlingtonva.us
1701 N. Sycamore St. (take I-66 west to Sycamore Street/exit
69, turn left on Sycamore and proceed past the East Falls
Church Metro Station, turn right onto North 16th Street and
take the first right, which dead-ends at the dog exercise area)
Daily dawn to half-hour after dusk.
Fully fenced, 11 acres, picnic table, benches, lights until 8 p.m.,
water.

Fort Barnard Park - Arlington County
arlingtonva.us
South Pollard Street and South Walter Reed Drive (from Rt.
50, take Glebe Road south, turn right on South Walter Reed
Drive and proceed to Pollard Street; the park is on the right)
Daily dawn to half-hour after dusk.
Fully fenced, picnic table, benches, lights until 9 p.m., water.

Glencarlyn Park - Arlington County
arlingtonva.us
301 S. Harrison St. (from Rt. 50, head west to Carlin Springs
Road, exit right and then turn left at the stop sign, pass under
Rt. 50 and follow Carlin Springs to 4th Street, turn left on 4th
Street and proceed 5 blocks until the road ends at the
Glencarlyn Park sign, the park road until it ends; park
and walk over a small bridge and stream to the exercise area)
Daily dawn to half-hour after dusk.
Unfenced area near a creek and woods, picnic table, benches.

Shirlington Park - Arlington County
arlingtonva.us
2601 S. Arlington Mill Dr., bordering South Four Mile Run
between Shirlington Road and South Walter Reed Drive along
the bicycle path between a storage facility and the water, near
but not in Jennie Dean Park (from South Four Mile Run, turn
south onto Nelson and park behind the storage facility; there
are no signs indicating the dog park)
Daily dawn to half-hour after dusk.
Partially fenced, picnic table, benches, water.

Towers Park - Arlington County
arlingtonva.us
801 S. Scott St., behind the tennis courts
Daily dawn to half-hour after dusk.
Fully fenced, 3.5 acres, separate small dog area, lights,
parking.

The Hanover Dog Park - Ashland
co.hanover.va.us
13017 Taylor Complex Ln.
Daily dawn-dusk.
Fenced, grass, dog agility equipment, water, disposal bags,
benches, parking.

Red Wing Park - Virginia Beach
vbgov.com
1398 General Booth Blvd.
Daily 7:30 a.m.-dusk.
Annual fee for first-time visitors $15; owners must register at
the park office, show proof of pet's rabies shot and vaccines,
and obtain a city dog license.
Fenced, benches, disposal bags, parking, restrooms, water.
Access for the disabled.

Woodstock Community Park - Virginia Beach
vbgov.com
5709 Providence Rd.
Daily 7:30 a.m.-dusk.
Annual fee for first-time visitors $15; owners must register at
the park office, show proof of pet's rabies shot and vaccines,
and obtain a city dog license.
Fenced, benches, disposal bags, restrooms, parking. Access
for the disabled.

WASHINGTON

Cedar River Dog Park - Renton
ci.renton.wa.us
1500 Houser Way S., next to Cedar River Trail
Daily dawn-dusk.
Fenced, 3.5 acres with 8,000 square feet reserved for
small/shy dogs, short grass, mulch, gravel, water, benches,
trees, shelter, tables, parking.

I-5 Colonnade Park - Seattle
coladog.org
Lakeview Boulevard and Franklin Avenue East in the Eastlake
neighborhood beneath I-5, south of East Howe Street
Daily 6 a.m.-11 p.m.
Fenced, 1.2 acres, double-gated entry, water fountain for dogs;
the I-5 freeway deck provides shelter from the elements.

I-90 "Blue Dog Pond" - Seattle
coladog.org
Martin Luther King Jr. Way and South Massachusetts Street,
on the northwest corner
Daily 6 a.m.-11 p.m.
Fenced, 1 acre, parking, water fountain for dogs, Blue Dog
sculpture. No off-leash areas in I-90 Lid Park, just east of Blue
Dog Pond.

Dr. Jose Rizal Park - Seattle
coladog.org
1008 12th Ave. S. on North Beacon Hill; off-leash area is in
the lower portion of the park
Daily 6 a.m.-11 p.m.
Fenced, 4 acres, double-gated entry, parking, water fountain for
dogs, scenic view of downtown.

Genesee Park - Seattle
coladog.org
46th Avenue South and South Genesee Street
Daily 6 a.m.-11 p.m.
Fenced, 3 acres, double-gated entry, parking, water fountain for
dogs.

Golden Gardens Park - Seattle
coladog.org
8498 Seaview Pl. N.W. in Ballard
Daily 6 a.m.-11 p.m.
Fenced, 1 acre, lighted, parking, water fountain for dogs. The
off-leash area is in the upper (eastern) portion of the park;
dogs are not allowed on the lower beach area.

Northacres Park - Seattle
coladog.org
North 130th Street, west of I-5; off-leash area is in the
northeast corner of the park at 12530 Third Ave. N.E., north of
the ball field. Parking is available on the west side of the park
along 1st Street Northeast and on the south side along North
125th Street
Daily 6 a.m.-11 p.m.
Fenced, double-gated entry, parking, water fountain for dogs.

Plymouth Pillars Park - Seattle
coladog.org
Boren Avenue and Pike Street on Capitol Hill above I-5
Daily 6 a.m.-11 p.m.
Fenced, 9,800 square feet, double-gated entry, water fountain
for dogs, scenic view of downtown Seattle.

Regrade Park - Seattle
coladog.org
3rd Avenue and Bell Street, downtown
Fenced, 13,000 square feet, double-gated entry, water fountain
for dogs.

Westcrest Park - Seattle
coladog.org
8806 8th Ave. S.W. in West Seattle
Daily 6 a.m.-11 p.m.
Fenced, 5 acres, shelters, lights, separate area for small dogs,
parking, water fountain for dogs. The off-leash area is along
the east side of the reservoir.

Woodland Park - Seattle
coladog.org
West Green Lake Way North, west of the tennis courts
Daily 6 a.m.-11 p.m.
Fenced, 1 acre, double-gated entry, parking, water fountain for
dogs.

Patricia Simonet Laughing Dog Park - Spokane
spokanecounty.org
26715 E. Spokane Bridge Rd. in Gateway Park
Daily dawn-dusk.
Fenced, 3.5 acres, grass and wooded walking area,
double-gated entry, parking, water fountain for dogs (not
available in winter), restrooms, disposal bags, trash cans.
Access for the disabled.

Canada

ALBERTA

Buena Vista Great Meadow - Edmonton
edmonton.ca, (780) 496-1475
North of Laurier Park and Buena Vista Drive and south of
Melton Ravine in the vicinity of 88 Avenue
Unfenced; area does not include the pedestrian bridge access
trail, Yorath property or the trail north to McKenzie Ravine.
This is a hot-air balloon site, so please leash your dog during
balloon launches.

Hermitage Park North - Edmonton
edmonton.ca, (780) 496-1475
129 Avenue to 137 Avenue; also 22 Street along the riverbank
where signs designate an off-leash area.
Unfenced. This is a multiuse area in the valley north of the
park's fishing pond and picnic area.

Jackie Parker Park - Edmonton
edmonton.ca, (780) 496-1475
Whitemud Freeway and 50th Street
Unfenced. Includes the area south of the 44 Avenue entrance;
dogs are not allowed on the golf course or north of the service
road playground.

Keehewin Blackmud - Edmonton
edmonton.ca, (780) 496-1475
Pipeline corridor, 104 Street and 20 Avenue to the south end
of 109 Street (excludes Bearspaw Drive West and Blackmud
Creek and Ravine)
Unfenced.

Kennedale - Edmonton
edmonton.ca, (780) 496-1475
Ravine west of the 40 Street loop, west to 47 Street and the
top of the bank
Unfenced.

Lauderdale - Edmonton
edmonton.ca, (780) 496-1475
South end of Grand Trunk Park, from 127 to 129 Avenue and
113A to 109 Street
Unfenced.

Mill Creek Ravine North - Edmonton
edmonton.ca, (780) 496-1475
68 Avenue and 93 Street, accessible from the west or north
sides of Argyll Park
Unfenced. A granular trail along the bottom of the ravine leads
to the Whyte (82) Avenue overpass.

Terwillegar Park - Edmonton
edmonton.ca, (780) 496-1475
Rabbit Hill Road
Unfenced. This is a multiuse area.

MANITOBA

Bourkevale Park - Winnipeg
winnipeg.ca
100 Ferry Rd., south of the dike along the riverbank
Daily 6 a.m.-10 p.m.
Unfenced, trash cans, parking; bring your own disposal bags.

Juba Park & Pioneer Avenue - Winnipeg
winnipeg.ca
Pioneer Avenue, all vacant land west of the walkway to Juba
Park
Daily 6 a.m.-10 p.m.
Unfenced, trash cans, parking; bring your own disposal bags.

Kil-Cona Park - Winnipeg
winnipeg.ca
Lagimodiere Boulevard in the area north of the west parking
lot. Parking available near McIvor entrance.
Daily 6 a.m.-10 p.m.
Unfenced, trash cans, parking; bring your own disposal bags.

King's Park - Winnipeg
winnipeg.ca
Kilkenny Drive and King's Drive, northeast of the retention
pond.
Daily 6 a.m.-10 p.m.
Unfenced, trash cans, parking; bring your own disposal bags.

Little Mountain Park - Winnipeg
winnipeg.ca
Northwest corner of the park adjacent to Klimpike Road and
Farmer Avenue
Daily 6 a.m.-10 p.m.
Unfenced, trash cans, parking; bring your own disposal bags.

Maple Grove Park - Winnipeg
winnipeg.ca
Frobisher Road, north area of the park
Daily 6 a.m.-10 p.m.
Unfenced, separate fenced area for puppies, trash cans,
parking; bring your own disposal bags.

Mazenod Park - Winnipeg
winnipeg.ca
Area surrounding retention pond, bordered by Mazenod Road,
Camiel Sys Street and Beghin Street
Daily 6 a.m.-10 p.m.
Unfenced, trash cans, parking; bring your own disposal bags.

Westview Park - Winnipeg
winnipeg.ca
Midland Street and Saskatchewan Avenue; entire park is an
off-leash area
Daily 6 a.m.-10 p.m.
Unfenced, trash cans, parking; bring your own disposal bags.

Woodsworth Park - Winnipeg
winnipeg.ca
West of Hekla off Keewatin Street, northeast of King Edward
Avenue and Park Lane
Daily 6 a.m.-10 p.m.
Unfenced, trash cans, parking; bring your own disposal bags.

United States

CALIFORNIA

 Disneyland® Resort

(714) 781-4400, 1313 Harbor Blvd., is off I-5 Disneyland Dr. and Disney Way exits at 1313 Harbor Blvd., Anaheim
Disneyland® Resort consists of two family-oriented theme parks—Disneyland® Park and Disney California Adventure® Park—and the shops, restaurants and entertainment of Downtown Disney® District. Indoor kennel facilities are available on a first-come, first-served basis at Disneyland Kennel Club, located to the right of the main entrance of Disneyland® park; overnight boarding is not available. Pets are permitted to ride on Disneyland® Resort trams but are not permitted on buses running to and from Toy Story Parking Lot. Both theme parks are open daily with extended hours during the summer, on some holidays and on weekends. Cost: One-day, one-park ticket $87; $81 (ages 3-9). Two-day $170; $158 (ages 3-9). Three-day $220; $205 (ages 3-9). Four-day $245; $225 (ages 3-9). Five-day $260; $240 (ages 3-9). One-day Park Hopper® ticket $125; $119 (ages 3-9). Two-day $200; $188 (ages 3-9). Three-day $250; $235 (ages 3-9). Four-day $275; $255 (ages 3-9). Five-day $290; $270 (ages 3-9). Validity periods for Park Hopper® tickets vary according to ticket type. Select theme park tickets are available at participating AAA/CAA Travel offices. Pets can be left at the resort's kennel for a fee. Parking: $15 (autos or motorcycles); $20 (RVs). Disneyland.com

LEGOLAND California

(760) 918-5346, One LEGOLAND Dr., off I-5 exit Cannon Road E. at LEGOLAND Dr., Carlsbad
The more than 60 rides—including three roller coasters—shows and attractions in this 128-acre family theme park are geared for kids ages 2 to 12. Free kennel services are unavailable until summer 2013; phone ahead to confirm schedule. Open daily mid-May to Labor Day and holidays. Open Thurs.-Mon. rest of year. Days closed and closing times may be extended in the off-season. Cost: One-day admission $75; $65 (ages 3-12 and 60+). Resort Hopper (1-day admission includes LEGOLAND, LEGOLAND Water Park and SEA LIFE Carlsbad Aquarium) $95; $85 (ages 3-12 and 60+); $9 (ages 1-2). Water Park Hopper (1-day admission includes LEGOLAND and LEGOLAND Water Park) or SEA LIFE Hopper (1-day admission includes LEGOLAND and SEA LIFE Carlsbad Aquarium) $89; $79 (ages 3-12 and 60+); $11 (ages 1-2). Two-day admission tickets also are available. Parking: $12; $15 (campers or RVs); $5 (motorcycles). california.legoland.com

SeaWorld San Diego

(800) 257-4268, 500 SeaWorld Dr., 500 SeaWorld Dr., off I-5 on Mission Bay's south shore, San Diego
SeaWorld San Diego offers animal shows, rides and exhibits featuring marine creatures from around the world, including killer whales, sharks, penguins and sea lions. Talented dolphins, pilot whales, birds and humans perform in the Blue Horizons show. Pet facility provided for a nominal charge on a first-come, first-served basis. Opens daily at 9 or 10; closing times vary. Hours vary and may be extended during summer and holiday periods. Phone ahead for show schedules. Cost: $73; $65 (ages 3-9). Kennel $10. Rates may vary; phone ahead. Parking: $15; $11 (motorcycles); $20 (RVs); $25 (preferred). seaworldparks.com/en/seaworld-sandiego

Six Flags Magic Mountain

(661) 255-4111, 26101 Magic Mountain Pkwy., 26101 Magic Mountain Pkwy., Valencia
Thrill rides, Looney Tunes characters, action shows—there is something here to amuse almost everyone. Free kennel facilities are available in the main parking lot. Opens daily at 10:30, late Mar.-Labor Day; Fri.-Sun. at 10:30, day after Labor Day-Oct. 31; Sat.-Sun. and holidays at 10:30, rest of year. Closing times vary. Cost: $64.99; $39.99 (under 48 inches tall); free (ages 0-2). Prices may vary; phone ahead. Parking: $15; $20 (RVs and buses). www.sixflags.com

Universal Studios Hollywood

(800) 864-8377, 100 Universal Dr., 100 Universal City Plaza. For guests arriving by Metro, a free shuttle across the street from the station provides transportation to the gate entrance, Universal City
In addition to thrill rides and attractions, Universal Studios gives visitors a behind-the-scenes look at the workings of a major film and TV studio. Complimentary kennel service. Daily 9-9, in summer; 10-6, rest of year. The Studio Tour is offered continuously; last tour departs 2 hours, 45 minutes before closing during summer. Cost: $80; $72 (under 48 inches tall). Front of Line passes are available; details are available at the front gate. Rates and availability of attractions may vary; phone ahead. Members save 10 percent on select dining and souvenirs at Universal Studios Hollywood and Universal CityWalk Hollywood. Parking: $15 (per private vehicle); $10 (per private vehicle after 3 p.m.); $17 (RVs); $20 (preferred). www.universalstudios.com

DISTRICT OF COLUMBIA

 Washington Monument

(202) 426-6841, 15th St. & Constitution Ave. N.W., near the center of the National Mall; the grounds extend from 14th to 17th sts. and from Constitution to Independence aves. N.W., Washington, D.C.

This instantly recognizable 555-foot marble obelisk commemorates our nation's first president and is surrounded by expansive grounds. Pets on leash. Daily 9-5 (also 5-10, Memorial Day-Labor Day). Phone ahead for updates regarding tours to the observation room. Cost: Advance ticket reservations $2 per ticket. www.nps.gov/wamo

FLORIDA

 Busch Gardens Tampa Bay

(888) 800-5447, 3000 E. Busch Blvd. (SR 580), 2 mi. e. of jct. I-275 exit 50 or 2 mi. w. of I-75 exit 265, Tampa

This family entertainment park combines world-class thrill rides, live entertainment and one of North America's largest zoos, providing an adventure for the entire family. Indoor kennel facilities. Generally opens daily between 9 and 10; closing times vary. Cost: $81.99; $73.99 (ages 3-9). Admission includes a second visit within 7 days of first visit. There is an additional fee for the Serengeti Safari Tour. The Length of Stay ticket, a 14-day combination ticket with Adventure Island, is $99.99; $91.99 (ages 3-9). Parking: $13; $15 (RVs); $18 (preferred). www.buschgardens.com

 SeaWorld Orlando

(800) 327-2420, 7007 SeaWorld Dr., at jct. I-4 and SR 528 (Beachline Expwy.), Orlando

This marine life adventure park presents crowd-pleasing animal shows starring a family of performing killer whales. SeaWorld also features numerous attractions and rides, including Manta, a flying coaster, as well as a penguin encounter area and simulated helicopter rides. Air-conditioned kennels. Opens daily at 9; closing times vary. Last admission is 1 hour before closing. Cost: $81.99; $73.99 (ages 3-9). For an additional $10 per ticket, guests can enjoy a second visit within 7 days of their first visit; stop at the Information and Reservations Center during your first visit for details. Fourteen-day combination ticket with Aquatica $119.99; $111.99 (ages 3-9). There is an additional fee for VIP tours. AAA members save on the Makahiki Luau and Dine with Shamu. Reservations are required for these dining experiences; visit Guest Relations for details. Parking: $14; $15 (RVs); $20 (preferred). www.seaworld.com/orlando

 Universal Orlando Resort

(407) 363-8000, 1000 Universal Studios Plaza, off I-4 exit 75A (eastbound) or 74B (westbound), following signs to the parking garages at 6000 Universal Blvd., Orlando

At Universal Orlando you can "ride the movies" at the Universal Studios® theme park, cavort with superheroes and cartoon characters at Universal's Islands of Adventure® theme park, or visit the specialty shops, themed restaurants and entertainment venues at Universal CityWalk®. Air-conditioned kennels. The theme parks generally open daily at 9; closing times vary by season. Universal CityWalk open daily 11 a.m.-2 a.m. Theme park and CityWalk hours may vary; phone ahead. Cost: A 1-day Base ticket to either Universal Studios Florida or Universal's Islands of Adventure is $88; $82 (ages 3-9). A 1-day Park-to-Park ticket, which allows same-day access to both Universal Studios Florida and Universal's Islands of Adventure, is $123; $117 (ages 3-9). A 2-day Base ticket, which allows access to one park per day, is $119.99; $109.99 (ages 3-9). A 2-day Park-to-Park ticket, which allows same-day access to both parks, is $139.99; $129.99 (ages 3-9). Tickets are also available for 3-, 4- and 7-day access to parks. Multiday tickets include admission to select live entertainment venues at Universal CityWalk. Special advance purchase discount tickets are available at participating AAA offices. Members can show their AAA/CAA card and save 10 percent at select merchandise and restaurant locations within the resort (excluding food or merchandise carts, tobacco, candy, film, collectibles, and clearance and sundry items). Parking: $15; $3 (6-10 p.m.); free (after 10 p.m.). Valet parking $15-$40.

 Walt Disney World® Resort

(407) 824-4321, 3111 World Dr., accessible from Florida's Tpke., US 192, Osceola Pkwy. and several exits off I-4 s. of Orlando, Lake Buena Vista

The sprawling complex includes Magic Kingdom® Park, Epcot®, Disney's Hollywood Studios™, Disney's Animal Kingdom® Theme Park, family water parks and numerous entertainment, shopping and dining facilities.

With the exception of service dogs for guests with disabilities, pets are not permitted in the Theme Parks or Disney Resort hotels, or on Disney buses. Best Friends Pet Care boarding facility offers air-conditioned accommodations for pets across from Disney's Port Orleans Resort at 2510 Bonnet Creek Pkwy. Reservations at Best Friends Pet Care are not required but are suggested. Disney Resort hotel reservations do not guarantee space for pets. Phone (877) 4 WDW-PETS for information and reservations. WDW.BestFriendsPetCare.com

Theme parks open daily generally at 9; closing times vary. Cost: One-day, one-park admission $89; $83 (ages 3-9). Ticket options for additional fees include admission to other entertainment areas and "hopping" between theme parks. Select theme park tickets are available at participating AAA/CAA Travel offices. Parking: $14; $15 (camper or trailer); free (Disney resort guests with valid resort ID). The fee allows parking at any of the theme parks for that entire day. Disneyworld.com

GEORGIA

 Six Flags Over Georgia

(770) 948-9290, 275 Riverside Pkwy., 275 Riverside Pkwy. S.W., Austell
Six Flags offers rides, attractions and live shows. Kennel facilities are available. Opens daily at 10:30, late May-early Aug.; Sat.-Sun. at 10:30, early Mar.-late May and early Aug.-late Sept. Closing times vary. The park also is open select days in Oct. for Fright Fest. Cost: All-inclusive 1-day $54.99; $39.99 (children under 48 inches tall); free (ages 0-2). AAA members save on select services and merchandise. See Guest Relations for details. Parking: $16. www.sixflags.com/parks/overgeorgia/index.asp

ILLINOIS

 Six Flags Great America

(847) 249-4636, 542 SR 21N, 1 mi. e. of I-94 on Grand Ave. (SR 132), Gurnee
Six Flags Great America offers 14 coasters, a water park, shows, parades, rides and attractions for the whole family. Kennel facilities are available. Theme park open daily at 10, mid-May to late Aug.; Sat.-Sun. at 10, first three weeks in Sept.; Fri. at 5, Sat.-Sun. at 11, in Oct. Closing times vary. Water park days and hours vary. Cost: (Includes Six Flags Hurricane Harbor) $61.99; $41.99 (children under 48 inches tall); free (ages 0-2). Prices may vary; phone ahead. AAA members save on select services and merchandise. See guest relations for details. Parking: $22. www.sixflags.com/greatamerica/index.aspx

IOWA

 Pella Historical Village

(641) 628-4311, jct. E. First and Franklin sts., Pella
A country store, log cabin, grist mill, windmill, smithy and other buildings (including Wyatt Earp's boyhood home) are reminders of this town's Dutch heritage. Leashed pets are permitted but are not allowed in the windmill. Mon.-Sat. 9-4, mid-Mar. through Dec. 31. Cost: $10; $6 (ages 12+ and students with ID); $2 (ages 5-11). www.pellatuliptime.com

MASSACHUSETTS

 Bunker Hill Monument

(617) 242-5641, in Monument Square in Charlestown (T: Community College), Boston
Part of Boston National Historical Park, this 221-foot-tall granite obelisk commemorates the site of the Battle of Bunker Hill, which occurred on June 17, 1775. Leashed pets are permitted on the grounds but not inside the monument. Daily 9-5 (also 5-6, July-Aug.). Last admission 30 minutes before closing. Cost: Free. www.nps.gov/bost/historyculture/bhm.htm

MISSOURI

 The Gateway Arch

(877) 982-1410, Memorial Dr. and Market St. within Jefferson National Expansion Memorial park, St. Louis
This curved, stainless steel monument soars 630 feet high and symbolizes the gateway to the West. A tram ride takes visitors to an observation deck. Pets on leashes are permitted on the grounds. Ticket center open daily 8 a.m.-10 p.m., Memorial Day-Labor Day; 9-6, rest of year. Last tram departs 50 minutes before closing. Cost: $3 (ages 16+). Tram ride $7; $5 (ages 3-15). Individual movie admission $4; $2.50 (ages 3-15). www.nps.gov/jeff

 Six Flags St. Louis

(636) 938-5300, I-44 & Allenton Rd., off I-44 at 4900 Six Flags Rd., Eureka
Themed areas showcase a variety of shows, rides and attractions; kids will have a ball exploring Bugs Bunny National Park. Air-conditioned kennel facilities are at the parking lot entrance. Pets cannot be kept overnight, and must have current vaccinations and registration tags. Park open early Apr.-Oct. 28; days and hours vary. Hurricane Harbor open Memorial Day weekend-Labor Day; days and hours vary. Cost: (Includes Hurricane Harbor) $49.99; $36.99 (children under 48 inches tall); free (ages 0-2). Prices may vary; phone ahead. AAA members save on select services and merchandise. See guest relations for details. Parking: $18. www.sixflags.com/parks/stlouis/parkinfo/index.asp

NORTH CAROLINA

 Carowinds

(704) 588-2600, 14523 Carowinds Blvd., 10 mi. s. on I-77 to exit 90, Charlotte
Depicting the past and present of the Carolinas, the themed areas at this park offer roller coasters, water rides, children's play areas and other family entertainment. Air-conditioned kennels are available. Park opens daily at 10, late May to mid-Aug.; Sat.-Sun. at 10, late Mar. to late May, mid-Aug. through Labor Day and in Oct.; Sat. at 10, Sun. at noon, weekend after Labor Day-Sept. 30. Closing times vary. Cost: Park (all-inclusive) $54.99; $36.99 (ages 62+ and under 48 inches tall); $29.99 (after 4 p.m.); free (ages 0-2). Two-day pass $59.99. Parking: $12. www.carowinds.com

OHIO

 Kings Island

(513) 754-5700, 6300 Kings Island Dr., 6300 Kings Island Dr., Mason
Kings Island is a family entertainment park featuring 14 hair-raising roller coasters; Soak City Waterpark, the park's 33-acre water playground; costumed Peanuts cartoon characters; and a variety of live shows. A day-use pet kennel is available for a fee. Park opens daily at 10 a.m., late May-late Aug.; Fri.-Sun. at 11, in Oct.; Sat.-Sun. at 10 a.m., late Apr. to late May and first weekend in Sept. Closing times vary. Soak City Waterpark daily 11-7, late May-late Aug. Cost: (includes Soak City Waterpark) $54.99; $33.99 (ages 3-6, ages 62+ and children under 48 inches tall). Dinosaurs Alive! $5. Prices vary throughout the season; phone ahead to confirm. Parking: $12. www.visitkingsisland.com

PENNSYLVANIA

 Hersheypark

(800) 437-7439, 100 W. Hersheypark Dr., just off SR 743 and US 422, Hershey
Hersheypark has more than 65 rides and attractions— including 12 roller coasters—plus live entertainment. Visitors can enjoy a marine mammal show, song and dance reviews and concerts highlighting big-name performers. ZooAmerica North American Wildlife Park covers 11 acres. Open daily at 10, Memorial Day-Labor Day; Sat.-Sun. at 10, in May; Sat.-Sun. at 10, select weekends in Sept. after Labor Day. Closing times vary; phone ahead. Phone for Springtime and Halloween schedules. Cost: (includes ZooAmerica North American Wildlife Park) $56.95; $35.95 (ages 3-8 and 55-69); $22.95 (ages 70+). Sunset admission (after 3 when park closes at 6, after 4 when park closes at 8, after 5 when park closes at 10 and 11) $28.95; $24.95 (ages 3-8 and 55-69); $17.95 (ages 70+). Other admission packages, including multiday options, are available. www.hersheypark.com

TEXAS

 SeaWorld San Antonio

(800) 700-7786, 10500 SeaWorld Dr., 10500 SeaWorld Dr., San Antonio
A 250-acre marine life adventure park, SeaWorld San Antonio entertains and educates with shark exhibits, a penguin habitat, the "Believe" show starring world-famous killer whale Shamu, and a high-energy whale and dolphin show. Such thrill rides as Journey to Atlantis, the Steel Eel and Great White coasters, and the Rio Loco and Texas splashdown water rides add to the excitement. Outdoor kennel facilities (owner must provide food). Opens daily at 9 or 10, late May-Aug. 31; days and hours vary rest of year. Cost: $59.99; $49.99 (ages 3-9). Combination ticket with Aquatica $79.99; $69.99 (ages 3-9). Admission and parking prices may vary; phone ahead. Parking: $15; $20 (preferred). seaworldparks.com/en/seaworld-sanantonio

Six Flags Fiesta Texas

(210) 697-5050, 17000 I-10W, 17000 I-10W, San Antonio
Housed in a former rock quarry, the park celebrates Texas and the Southwest with thrill and family-style rides, live entertainment and themed areas. Kennel facilities are located to the right of the main entrance. Pets cannot be kept overnight and must have current vaccinations and registration tags. Park open daily, Memorial Day-Aug. 26 (also in mid-Mar. for spring break); open Sat.-Sun. and some weekdays, Mar. 1-day before Memorial Day; open select days, Sept. 1-early Jan. Park hours vary. Water park opens daily at noon, June 2-late Aug.; opens select days at noon in May and Sept. Water park closing times vary. Cost: $59.99; $44.99 (under 48 inches tall); free (ages 0-2). Rates may vary; phone ahead. AAA members save on select services and merchandise. See guest relations for details. Parking: $17. www.sixflags.com

Six Flags Over Texas

(817) 530-6000, 2201 Road to Six Flags, 2201 Road to Six Flags, Arlington
Themed areas, each featuring thrill rides, food and entertainment, depict Texas under six different flags: Spain, France, Mexico, the Republic of Texas, the Confederate States of America and the United States. Air-conditioned kennels (fee). Daily late May-early Aug.; Sat.-Sun., Mar. 1-late May, mid-Aug. through Oct. 31 and day after Thanksgiving-Dec. 31. Hours vary. Cost: $59.99; $42.99 (under 48 inches tall); free (ages 0-2). Rates may vary; phone ahead. AAA members save on select services and merchandise. See guest relations for details. Parking: $17; $22 (preferred). www.sixflags.com

VIRGINIA

Busch Gardens Williamsburg

(800) 343-7946, 1 Busch Gardens Blvd., 1 Busch Gardens Blvd., Williamsburg
This European-themed adventure park offers something for the entire family, from thrill rides to entertaining shows to villages representing England, Germany, France and other nations. Kennel facilities (England parking lot); fee $10 per pet per day. Open Mar.-Dec.; days and hours vary. Cost: $69.99; $59.99 (ages 3-9). Multiday and combination tickets with Water Country USA are available. Parking: $13. www.buschgardens.com/bgw/default.aspx

Kings Dominion

(804) 876-5000, 16000 Theme Park Dr., .5 mi. e. off I-95 exit 98 on SR 30, Doswell
The 400-acre park features a water park, thrill rides, children's play areas, costumed characters, live shows and specialty shopping. Kennels are available. Parks open daily, Memorial Day-Labor Day. Schedules vary rest of year; phone ahead. Cost: (includes WaterWorks in season) $59.99; $37.99 (ages 62+ and under 48 inches tall); free (ages 0-2). Prices may vary. Parking: $15.
www.kingsdominion.com

WASHINGTON

 Hovander Homestead Park

(360) 384-3444, 1 mi. s. via Hovander Rd. to 5299 Nielsen Ave., Ferndale
This restored house, dating from 1903 and furnished with antiques, is within a large park encompassing gardens, picnic sites and a children's farm area. Dogs are allowed in on-leash areas of the park. Grounds open daily 8 a.m.-dusk. House open Thurs.-Sun. 12:30-4:30, Memorial Day-Labor Day. The house is not always open during scheduled times; phone ahead to confirm. The boardwalk may be closed during designated hunting season. Cost: House $1; 50c (ages 0-12).
www.co.whatcom.wa.us/parks/hovander/index.jsp

Canada

ONTARIO

 Canada's Wonderland

(905) 832-7000, off Hwy. 400, Rutherford Rd. exit northbound or Major MacKenzie Dr. E. exit southbound at 9580 Jane St., Vaughan
Thrill rides at this theme park include the hair-raising Behemoth rollercoaster and the Backlot Stunt Coaster, while Nickelodeon Central and Hanna-Barbera Land will entertain little ones. Air-conditioned kennels are available for a fee. Daily late May-Labour Day; open some weekends early May-late May and day after Labour Day-late Oct. Gates open at 10; closing time varies. Phone to verify schedule and admission. Cost: Passport for grounds and most rides $39.99; $32.99 (ages 3-6 and 60+). Concerts are available at an extra charge. Height restrictions apply to some rides. Parking: $15. www.canadaswonderland.com

 Upper Canada Village

(613) 543-4328, 13740 CR 2, 11 km (7 mi.) e. on CR 2 off Hwy. 401, Morrisburg
Upper Canada Village re-creates life during the 1860s through a working community of artisans and costumed interpreters who perform chores typical of the era. Seeing eye and hearing aid dogs are welcome. All other pets must be kept on a leash and may not enter historic buildings. Daily 9:30-5, Victoria Day weekend-Labour Day; Wed.-Sun. 9:30-5, day after Labour Day-Thanksgiving. Cost: Village $15; $12 (ages 6-18 and 65+); free (ages 0-5). Rates may vary; phone ahead. www.uppercanadavillage.com

The National Public Lands listed below permit pets on a leash. Keep in mind that animals may be prohibited from entering public buildings and even some areas outdoors, particularly those that are ecologically sensitive. Where swimming is permitted, there are usually no lifeguards on duty; people and pets swim at their own risk. Specific pet policies vary from park to park and are subject to change. Always check in advance regarding any applicable regulations and to confirm that pets are still permitted where you are going.

Be aware of dangers to your pet in natural areas, including snakes, ticks and fast-moving currents in rivers and streams. An unleashed dog may chase after a wild animal and become separated from its owner, increasing the risk of loss or injury. Never leave your pet unattended. Keep him leashed or crated at all times. Follow park guidelines faithfully, and monitor your pet's behavior; the National Park Service may confiscate pets that harm wildlife or other visitors. *For additional information on outdoor vacations, see The Great Outdoors, p. 16.*

United States

ALABAMA

Conecuh National Forest
On the Alabama-Florida border.
(334) 222-2555
🚴 ⛺ 🥾 🧺 🏊

Horseshoe Bend National Military Park
12 mi. n. of Dadeville on SR 49.
(256) 234-7111
🥾 🧺 🏊 🏛

Talladega National Forest
In central Alabama.
(256) 362-2909
⛺ 🥾 🧺 🏊

Tuskegee National Forest
Northeast of Tuskegee.
(334) 727-2652
🚴 ⛺ 🥾 🧺

William B. Bankhead National Forest
In northwestern Alabama.
(205) 489-5111
🚴 ⛺ 🥾 🧺 🏊

ALASKA

Chugach National Forest
Along the Gulf of Alaska from Cape Suckling to Seward.
(907) 743-9500
🚴 ⛺ 🥾 🧺 🏛

Denali National Park and Preserve
In south-central Alaska.
(907) 683-2294
⛺ 🥾 🧺 🏛 🍽

Glacier Bay National Park and Preserve
North of Cross Sound to the Canadian border.
(907) 697-2230
⛺ 🥾 🏛 🍽

Kenai Fjords National Park
Southeastern side of the Kenai Peninsula.
(907) 224-7500 or (907) 224-2132
⛺ 🥾 🧺 🏛

Lake Clark National Park and Preserve
In southern Alaska.
(907) 644-3626
⛺ 🏛

Tongass National Forest
In southeastern Alaska.
(907) 228-6220
⛺ 🥾 🧺 🏛

Wrangell-St. Elias National Park and Preserve
In southeastern Alaska, northwest of Tongass National Forest.
(907) 822-7250
⛺ 🥾 🧺 🏛

ARIZONA

Apache-Sitgreaves National Forests
In east-central Arizona.
(928) 333-4301
🚴 ⛺ 🥾 🧺 🏛 🍽

Coconino National Forest
In north-central Arizona.
(928) 527-3600
⛺ 🥾 🧺 🏊 🍽

Coronado National Forest
In southeastern Arizona and southwestern New Mexico.
(520) 388-8300
🚴 ⛺ 🥾 🧺 🏛

Glen Canyon National Recreation Area
In northern Arizona and Southern Utah.
(928) 608-6200
⛺ 🥾 🧺 🏊 🏛 🍽

Grand Canyon National Park
In northwestern Arizona.
(928) 638-2901
⛺ 🥾 🧺 🏛 🍽

Kaibab National Forest
In north-central Arizona.
(928) 643-7298
🚴 ⛺ 🥾 🧺 🏛 🍽

🚴 Bicycling Trails　⛺ Camping　🥾 Hiking Trails　🧺 Picnic Facilities
🏊 Swimming　🏛 Visitor Center　🍽 Food Service

Petrified Forest National Park
In east-central Arizona, east of Holbrook.
(928) 524-6228
🚶 ⛱ 👥 🍴

Prescott National Forest
In central Arizona.
(928) 443-8000
⛺ 🚶 ⛱ 🍴

Saguaro National Park
Two districts, 15 mi. east and west of Tucson.
(520) 733-5153
🚲 ⛺ 🚶 ⛱ 👥

Tonto National Forest
In central Arizona.
(602) 225-5200
🚲 ⛺ 🚶 ⛱ 🛶 🍴

ARKANSAS

Buffalo National River
In northwestern Arkansas.
(870) 439-2502
⛺ 🚶 ⛱ 🛶 👥 🍴

Hot Springs National Park
In western Arkansas.
(501) 620-6701
⛺ 🚶 ⛱ 👥

Ouachita National Forest
In west-central Arkansas and southeastern Oklahoma.
(501) 321-5202
🚲 ⛺ 🚶 ⛱ 🛶 👥

Ozark National Forest
In northwestern Arkansas.
(479) 964-7200
🚲 ⛺ 🚶 ⛱ 🛶 👥

St. Francis National Forest
In east-central Arkansas.
(479) 964-7200
⛺ 🚶 ⛱ 🛶

CALIFORNIA

Angeles National Forest
In southern California.
(626) 574-5200
🚲 ⛺ 🚶 ⛱ 🛶 👥 🍴

Cleveland National Forest
In southwestern California.
(858) 673-6180
🚲 ⛺ 🚶 ⛱ 👥 🍴

Death Valley National Park
Along the Nevada border in east-central California.
(760) 786-3200
⛺ 🚶 ⛱ 🛶 👥

Eldorado National Forest
In central California.
(530) 644-6048
🚲 ⛺ 🚶 ⛱ 🛶 👥 🍴

Golden Gate National Recreation Area
North of the Golden Gate Bridge and in northern and western San Francisco.
(415) 561-4700
🚲 ⛺ 🚶 ⛱ 🛶 👥 🍴

Inyo National Forest
In east-central California.
(760) 873-2400
🚲 ⛺ 🚶 ⛱ 🛶 👥 🍴

Joshua Tree National Park
East of Desert Hot Springs.
(760) 367-5500
⛺ 🚶 ⛱ 👥

King Range National Conservation Area
In northwestern California.
(707) 825-2300
🚲 ⛺ 🚶 ⛱ 🛶 👥 🍴

Klamath National Forest
In northern California.
(530) 842-6131
🚲 ⛺ 🚶 ⛱ 🛶 👥

Lassen National Forest
In northeastern California.
(530) 257-2151
🚲 ⛺ 🚶 ⛱ 🛶 👥 🍴

Lassen Volcanic National Park
In northeastern California.
(530) 595-4444
⛺ 🚶 ⛱ 🛶 👥 🍴

Los Padres National Forest
In southern California.
(805) 968-6640
🚲 ⛺ 🚶 ⛱ 🛶 👥

Mendocino National Forest
In northwestern California.
(530) 934-2350
🚲 ⛺ 🚶 ⛱ 🛶 👥 🍴

Modoc National Forest
In northeastern California.
(530) 233-5811
🚲 ⛺ 🚶 ⛱ 🛶 👥

Mojave National Preserve
Between I-15 and I-40 in southeastern California.
(760) 252-6108
⛺ 🚶 ⛱ 👥 🍴

Plumas National Forest
In northern California.
(530) 283-2050
🚲 ⛺ 🚶 ⛱ 🛶 👥 🍴

Point Reyes National Seashore
Along the California coast just north of San Francisco.
(415) 464-5100
🚲 ⛺ 🚶 ⛱ 👥 🍴

Redwood National and State Parks
On the northern California coast.
(707) 465-7765
🚲 ⛺ 🥾 🌳 🏊 🏛 🍴

San Bernardino National Forest
In southern California.
(909) 382-2600
🚲 ⛺ 🥾 🌳 🏊 🏛 🍴

Santa Monica Mountains National Recreation Area
West from Griffith Park in Los Angeles past the Ventura County line.
(805) 370-2301
⛺ 🥾 🌳 🏊 🏛 🍴

Sequoia and Kings Canyon National Parks
In east-central California.
(559) 565-3341
⛺ 🥾 🌳 🏛

Sequoia National Forest
In south-central California.
(559) 784-1500
🚲 ⛺ 🥾 🌳 🏊 🏛 🍴

Shasta-Trinity National Forests
In northern California.
(530) 226-2500
🚲 ⛺ 🥾 🌳 🏊 🏛 🍴

Sierra National Forest
In central California.
(559) 297-0706
🚲 ⛺ 🥾 🌳 🏊 🏛 🍴

Six Rivers National Forest
In northwestern California.
(707) 442-1721
🚲 ⛺ 🥾 🌳 🏊 🏛 🍴

Smith River National Recreation Area
Within Six Rivers National Forest in northwestern California.
(707) 457-3131
🚲 ⛺ 🥾 🌳 🏊

Stanislaus National Forest
Within Six Rivers National Forest in northwestern California.
(707) 457-3131
🚲 ⛺ 🥾 🌳 🏊 🍴

Tahoe National Forest
In north-central California.
(530) 265-4531
⛺ 🥾 🌳 🏊 🏛 🍴

Whiskeytown-Shasta-Trinity National Recreation Area
North and west of Redding.
(530) 242-3400
🚲 ⛺ 🥾 🌳 🏊 🏛 🍴

Yosemite National Park
In central California.
(209) 372-0200
🚲 ⛺ 🥾 🌳 🏊 🏛 🍴

COLORADO

Arapaho and Roosevelt National Forests and Pawnee National Grassland
In north-central Colorado.
(970) 295-6700
🚲 ⛺ 🥾 🌳 🏊 🏛

Arapaho National Recreation Area
In north-central Colorado.
(970) 887-4100
🚲 ⛺ 🥾 🌳 🏊 🏛

Black Canyon of The Gunnison National Park
In western Colorado.
(970) 249-1914
⛺ 🥾 🌳 🏛

Curecanti National Recreation Area
In south-central Colorado between Gunnison and Montrose, paralleling US 50.
(970) 641-2337
⛺ 🥾 🌳 🏊 🏛 🍴

Dinosaur National Monument
In northeast Utah and northwest Colorado.
(435) 781-7700
🚲 ⛺ 🥾 🌳 🏛

Grand Mesa—Uncompahgre—Gunnison National Forests
In west-central Colorado.
(970) 874-6600
🚲 ⛺ 🥾 🌳 🏛 🍴

Great Sand Dunes National Park and Preserve
Northeast of Alamosa.
(719) 378-6399
⛺ 🥾 🌳 🏛

Mesa Verde National Park
In southwestern Colorado.
(970) 529-4465
⛺ 🥾 🌳 🏛

Pikes Peak and Pike National Forest
In south-central Colorado.
(719) 553-1400
🚲 ⛺ 🥾 🌳 🏛 🍴

Rio Grande National Forest
In south-central Colorado.
(719) 852-5941
🚲 ⛺ 🥾 🌳 🏊 🏛

Rocky Mountain National Park
In north-central Colorado.
(970) 586-1206
⛺ 🥾 🌳 🏛

🚲 Bicycling Trails   ⛺ Camping   🥾 Hiking Trails   🌳 Picnic Facilities
🏊 Swimming   🏛 Visitor Center   🍴 Food Service

Routt National Forest
In northwestern Colorado.
(970) 638-4516
♿ ⛺ 🚶 ⛱ ⛵ 🏕

San Isabel National Forest
In central Colorado.
(719) 553-1400
♿ ⛺ 🚶 ⛱ 🏕 🍽

San Juan National Forest
In southwestern Colorado.
(970) 247-4874
♿ ⛺ 🚶 ⛱ ⛵ 🏕 🍽

White River National Forest
In west-central Colorado.
(970) 945-2521
♿ ⛺ 🚶 ⛱ ⛵ 🏕 🍽

FLORIDA
Apalachicola National Forest
In northwestern Florida.
(850) 926-3561
♿ ⛺ 🚶 ⛱ ⛵

Biscayne National Park
In southeast Florida.
(305) 230-7275
⛺ 🚶 ⛱ ⛵ 🏕 🍽

Ocala National Forest
In north-central Florida.
(352) 236-0288
♿ ⛺ 🚶 ⛱ ⛵ 🏕 🍽

Osceola National Forest
Near the Georgia border.
(386) 752-2577
♿ ⛺ 🚶 ⛱ ⛵

GEORGIA
Chattahoochee River National Recreation Area
North of Atlanta.
(678) 538-1200
♿ 🚶 ⛱ ⛵ 🏕

Chattahoochee and Oconee National Forests
In central and northern Georgia.
(770) 297-3000
♿ ⛺ 🚶 ⛱ ⛵ 🏕

Cumberland Island National Seashore
On Cumberland Island in southeastern Georgia.
(912) 882-4336
♿ ⛺ 🚶 ⛱ ⛵ 🏕

IDAHO
Boise National Forest
In southwestern Idaho.
(208) 373-4007
♿ ⛺ 🚶 ⛱ ⛵ 🏕

Caribou-Targhee National Forest
In southeastern Idaho.
(208) 524-7500
⛺ 🚶 ⛱ ⛵ 🏕

Clearwater National Forest
In northeastern Idaho.
(208) 476-4541
⛺ 🚶 ⛱ ⛵ 🏕

Idaho Panhandle National Forests
In northern and northwestern Idaho.
(208) 765-7223
♿ ⛺ 🚶 ⛱ ⛵

Nez Perce National Forest
In northwestern Idaho.
(208) 983-1950
♿ ⛺ 🚶 ⛱ ⛵ 🏕

Payette National Forest
In west-central Idaho.
(208) 634-0700
♿ ⛺ 🚶 ⛱ ⛵ 🏕

Salmon-Challis National Forest
In east-central Idaho.
(208) 756-5100
⛺ 🚶 ⛱ ⛵ 🍽

Sawtooth National Forest
In south-central Idaho.
(208) 737-3200
♿ ⛺ 🚶 ⛱ ⛵ 🏕 🍽

Sawtooth National Recreation Area
In south-central Idaho.
(208) 727-5013
♿ ⛺ 🚶 ⛱ ⛵ 🏕 🍽

ILLINOIS
Shawnee National Forest
In southern Illinois.
(618) 253-7114
⛺ 🚶 ⛱ ⛵ 🏕

INDIANA
Hoosier National Forest
In southern Indiana.
(812) 275-5987
♿ ⛺ 🚶 ⛱ ⛵

Indiana Dunes National Lakeshore
On the southern shore of Lake Michigan.
(219) 926-7561
⛺ 🚶 ⛱ ⛵ 🏕

KENTUCKY
Daniel Boone National Forest
Five districts in eastern and southeastern Kentucky.
(859) 745-3100
♿ ⛺ 🚶 ⛱ 🏕 🍽

Daniel Boone National Forest (Laurel River Lake)
Off I-75 west of Corbin.
(606) 864-4163
♿ ⛺ 🚶 ⛱ ⛵

Daniel Boone National Forest (Red River Gorge Geological Area)
Off SR 15.
(606) 663-8100
🔺 🏕 ⛱ 👥

Daniel Boone National Forest (Rockcastle)
22 mi. southwest of London via SR 192/3497.
(606) 864-4163
🔺 🏕 ⛱ 🏊

Daniel Boone National Forest (Sawyer)
5 mi. west of Cumberland Falls on SR 90, then 7 mi. north on SR 896 following signs.
(606) 376-5323
🔺 🏕 ⛱

Daniel Boone National Forest (S-Tree)
.5 mi. west of McKee on US 421, 3 mi. south on SR 89, 1 mi. west on FR 43, then south on FR 20 following signs.
(606) 864-4163
🔺 🏕 ⛱

Daniel Boone National Forest (Turkey Foot)
3 mi. north of McKee on SR 89, then east on FR 4 following signs for 3 mi.
(606) 864-4163
🔺 🏕 ⛱

Land Between The Lakes National Recreation Area
In western Kentucky and Tennessee.
(270) 924-2000
🚲 🔺 🏕 ⛱ 🏊 👥

Mammoth Cave National Park
In south-central Kentucky 10 mi. west of Cave City.
(270) 758-2180
🚲 🔺 🏕 ⛱ 👥

LOUISIANA
Bayou Sauvage National Wildlife Refuge
Within the New Orleans city limits.
(985) 882-2000
🚲 🏕 ⛱

Kisatchie National Forest
In central and northern Louisiana.
(318) 473-7160
🔺 🏕 ⛱ 🏊

Sabine National Wildlife Refuge
In southwestern Louisiana.
(337) 762-3816
🏕

MAINE
Acadia National Park
Along the Atlantic coast southeast of Bangor.
(207) 288-3338
🚲 🔺 🏕 ⛱ 🏊 👥 🍽

MICHIGAN
Hiawatha National Forest
In Michigan's Upper Peninsula.
(906) 786-4062
🚲 🔺 🏕 ⛱ 🏊 👥

Huron-Manistee National Forests
In the northern part of the Lower Peninsula.
(231) 775-2421
🚲 🔺 🏕 ⛱ 🏊 👥

Ottawa National Forest
In Michigan's Upper Peninsula.
(906) 932-1330
🚲 🔺 🏕 ⛱ 🏊 👥

Pictured Rocks National Lakeshore
Along Lake Superior in Michigan's Upper Peninsula.
906-387-3700
🔺 🏕 ⛱ 🏊 👥

Sleeping Bear Dunes National Lakeshore
Along Lake Michigan in the northwestern part of the Lower Peninsula.
(231) 326-5134
🔺 🏕 ⛱ 🏊 👥

MINNESOTA
Chippewa National Forest
In north-central Minnesota.
(218) 335-8600
🚲 🔺 🏕 ⛱ 🏊 👥 🍽

Superior National Forest
In northeastern Minnesota.
(218) 626-4300
🚲 🔺 🏕 ⛱ 🏊 👥 🍽

MISSISSIPPI
Bienville National Forest
In central Mississippi.
(601) 469-3811
🔺 🏕 ⛱ 🏊 👥

Delta National Forest
In west-central Mississippi.
(662) 873-6256
🚲 🔺 🏕 ⛱ 👥

De Soto National Forest
In southeastern Mississippi.
(601) 528-6160
🚲 🔺 🏕 ⛱ 🏊 👥

Gulf Islands National Seashore
Along the Gulf of Mexico in southern Mississippi.
(228) 875-9057
🔺 🏕 ⛱ 👥

Holly Springs National Forest
In north-central Mississippi.
(662) 236-6550
🔺 🏕 ⛱ 🏊 👥

🚲 Bicycling Trails   🔺 Camping   🏕 Hiking Trails   ⛱ Picnic Facilities
🏊 Swimming   👥 Visitor Center   🍽 Food Service

Homochitto National Forest
In the southwestern corner of Mississippi.
(601) 384-5876
🐾 ⛺ 🚶 🍴 🚤 🏕

Tombigbee National Forest
In east-central Mississippi.
(662) 285-3264
🐾 ⛺ 🚶 🍴 🚤 🏕

MISSOURI
Mark Twain National Forest
Southern Missouri.
(573) 364-4621
🐾 ⛺ 🚶 🍴 🚤

Mark Twain National Forest (Big Bay)
1 mi. southeast of Shell Knob on SR 39, then 3 mi.
southeast on CR YY.
(573) 364-4621
⛺ 🍴 🚤

Mark Twain National Forest (Crane Lake)
12 mi. south of Ironton off SR 49 and CR E.
(573) 364-4621
🐾 🚶 🍴 🚤

Mark Twain National Forest (Fourche Lake)
18 mi. west of Doniphan on US 160.
(573) 364-4621
🚶 🍴

Mark Twain National Forest (Noblett Lake)
8 mi. west of Willow Springs on SR 76, then 1.4 mi. south
on SR 181, 3 mi. southeast on CR AP and 1 mi.
southwest on CR 857.
(573) 364-4621
🐾 ⛺ 🚶 🍴

Mark Twain National Forest (Pinewoods Lake)
2 mi. west of Ellsinore on SR 60.
(573) 364-4621
🐾 🚶 🍴 🚤

Mark Twain National Forest (Red Bluff)
1 mi. east of Davisville on CR V, then 1 mi. north on FR
2011.
(573) 364-4621
⛺ 🚶 🍴 🚤

Ozarks and Ozark National Scenic Riverways
In southeastern Missouri.
(573) 323-4236
⛺ 🚶 🍴 🚤 🏕 🍽

MONTANA
Beaverhead-Deerlodge National Forest
In southwestern Montana.
(406) 683-3900
🐾 ⛺ 🚶 🍴 🚤

Bighorn Canyon National Recreation Area
In southern Montana and northern Wyoming.
(406) 666-2412
⛺ 🚶 🍴 🚤 🏕 🍽

Bitterroot National Forest
In western Montana.
(406) 363-7100
🐾 ⛺ 🚶 🍴 🚤 🏕

Custer National Forest
In southeastern Montana.
(406) 255-1400
🐾 ⛺ 🚶 🍴 🚤 🍽

Flathead National Forest
In northwestern Montana.
(406) 758-5204
🐾 ⛺ 🚶 🍴 🚤 🏕

Gallatin National Forest
In south-central Montana.
(406) 522-2520
🐾 ⛺ 🚶 🍴 🚤 🏕 🍽

Glacier National Park
In northwestern Montana.
(406) 888-7800
⛺ 🚶 🍴 🚤 🏕 🍽

Helena National Forest
In west-central Montana.
(406) 449-5201
⛺ 🚶 🍴 🚤

Kootenai National Forest
In northwestern Montana.
(406) 293-6211
🐾 ⛺ 🚶 🍴 🚤 🏕 🍽

Lewis and Clark National Forest
In central Montana.
(406) 791-7700
⛺ 🚶 🍴 🚤

NEVADA
Great Basin National Park
In central Nevada, 5 mi. west of Baker near the
Nevada-Utah border.
(775) 234-7331
⛺ 🚶 🍴 🏕 🍽

Humboldt-Toiyabe National Forest
In central, western, northern and southern Nevada and
eastern California.
(775) 331-6444
🐾 ⛺ 🚶 🍴

Lake Mead National Recreation Area
In northwestern Arizona and southeastern Nevada.
(702) 293-8990
🐾 ⛺ 🚶 🍴 🚤 🏕 🍽

NEW HAMPSHIRE
White Mountains and White Mountain National Forest
In northern New Hampshire.
(603) 528-8721
🐾 ⛺ 🚶 🍴 🚤 🏕

NEW JERSEY
Gateway National Recreation Area (Sandy Hook Unit)
In northeastern New Jersey.
(732) 872-5970
🚴 🚶 🏕 ⛱ 🏢 🍴

NEW MEXICO
Carson National Forest
In north-central New Mexico.
(575) 758-6200
🚴 ⛺ 🚶 🏕 🏢

Chaco Culture National Historical Park
In northwestern New Mexico.
(505) 786-7014
🚴 ⛺ 🚶 🏕 🏢

Cibola National Forest
In central New Mexico.
(505) 856-7325
🚴 ⛺ 🚶 🏕 ⛱ 🏢

El Malpais National Monument and National Conservation Area
23 mi. south of I-40 via SRs 53 and 117.
(505) 783-4774
🚴 ⛺ 🚶 🏕 🏢

Gila National Forest
In southwestern New Mexico.
(575) 388-8201
🚴 ⛺ 🚶 🏕 ⛱ 🏢

Lincoln National Forest
In south-central New Mexico.
(575) 434-7200
🚴 ⛺ 🚶 🏕 🍴

Santa Fe National Forest
In north-central New Mexico between the Jemez Mountains and the Sangre de Cristo Mountains.
(505) 438-5300
🚴 ⛺ 🚶 🏕 🏢

NEW YORK
Finger Lakes National Forest
In south-central New York on a ridge between Seneca and Cayuga lakes, via I-90, I-81 and SR 17.
(607) 546-4470
🚴 ⛺ 🚶 🏕 🏢

Gateway National Recreation Area (Jamaica Bay Unit)
In Brooklyn and Queens boroughs in New York City.
(718) 338-3799
🚴 ⛺ 🚶 🏕 ⛱ 🏢 🍴

Gateway National Recreation Area (Staten Island Unit)
On Staten Island borough in New York City.
(718) 354-4500
🚴 🚶 🏕 ⛱ 🏢 🍴

NORTH CAROLINA
Cape Hatteras National Seashore
In eastern North Carolina along the Outer Banks.
(252) 473-2111
⛺ 🚶 🏕 ⛱ 🏢

Croatan National Forest
In southeastern North Carolina.
(252) 638-5628
🚴 ⛺ 🚶 🏕 ⛱

Croatan National Forest (Cedar Point)
1.25 mi. north jct. SRs 24 and 58, 3 mi. southeast of Swansboro.
(252) 638-5628
⛺ 🚶 🏕

Nantahala National Forest
At North Carolina's southwestern tip.
(828) 257-4200
🚴 ⛺ 🚶 🏕 ⛱

Nantahala National Forest (Hanging Dog)
21 acres 5 mi. northwest of Murphy on SR 1326.
(828) 837-5152
⛺ 🚶 🏕

Nantahala National Forest (Jackrabbit Mountain)
10 mi. northeast of Hayesville via US 64, SR 175 and SR 1155.
(828) 524-6441
⛺ 🚶 🏕 ⛱

Nantahala National Forest (Standing Indian Mountain)
9 mi. west of Franklin on US 64, 2 mi. east on old US 64, then 2 mi. south on FR 67.
(828) 524-6441
⛺ 🚶 🏕

Pisgah National Forest
In western North Carolina.
(828) 257-4200
🚴 ⛺ 🚶 🏕 ⛱ 🏢

Pisgah National Forest (Lake Powhatan)
7 mi. southwest of Asheville on SR 191 and FR 3484.
(828) 670-5627
🚴 ⛺ 🚶 🏕 ⛱

Pisgah National Forest (Rocky Bluff)
3 mi. south of Hot Springs on SR 209.
(828) 682-6146
⛺ 🚶 🏕

Uwharrie National Forest
In central North Carolina.
(910) 576-6391
🚴 ⛺ 🚶 🏕 ⛱

Uwharrie National Forest (Badin Lake)
10 mi. north of Troy on SR 109.
(910) 576-6391
⛺ 🚶 🏕 ⛱

🚴 Bicycling Trails   ⛺ Camping   🚶 Hiking Trails   🏕 Picnic Facilities
⛱ Swimming   🏢 Visitor Center   🍴 Food Service

NORTH DAKOTA
Theodore Roosevelt National Park (North Unit)
In western North Dakota.
(701) 842-2333
🔺 🏕 🚻 👫

Theodore Roosevelt National Park (South Unit)
In western North Dakota.
(701) 623-4466
🔺 🏕 🚻 👫

OHIO
Cuyahoga Valley National Park
In northeastern Ohio.
(800) 257-9477
♿ 🔺 🏕 🚻 👫 🍴

OKLAHOMA
Black Kettle National Grasslands
Off SR 283 in Cheyenne.
(580) 497-2143
🔺 🏕 🚻 🚣 🍴

Chickasaw National Recreation Area
In south-central Oklahoma.
(580) 622-3161
♿ 🔺 🏕 🚻 🚣 👫

OREGON
Crater Lake National Park
On the crest of the Cascade Range off SR 62.
(541) 594-3100
♿ 🔺 🏕 🚻 👫 🍴

Deschutes National Forest
In central Oregon 6 mi. south of Bend via US 97.
(541) 383-5300
♿ 🔺 🏕 🚻 🚣 👫 🍴

Fremont-Winema National Forests
In south-central Oregon.
(541) 947-2151
♿ 🔺 🏕 🚻 🚣 👫 🍴

Hells Canyon National Recreation Area
In northeastern Oregon and western Idaho.
(509) 758-0616
🔺 🏕 🚻 👫

Malheur National Forest
In eastern Oregon.
(541) 575-3000
♿ 🔺 🏕 🚻 🚣

Mt. Hood and Mt. Hood National Forest
In northwestern Oregon.
(888) 622-4822
♿ 🔺 🏕 🚻 🚣 👫 🍴

Ochoco National Forest
In central Oregon off US 26.
(541) 416-6500
♿ 🔺 🏕 🚻 🚣

Oregon Dunes National Recreation Area
Between North Bend and Florence.
(541) 750-7000
🔺 🏕 🚻 🚣 👫

Rogue River–Siskiyou National Forest
In southwestern Oregon off I-5 from Medford.
(541) 858-2200
♿ 🔺 🏕 🚻 🚣 👫

Siuslaw National Forest
In western Oregon.
(541) 750-7000
♿ 🔺 🏕 🚻 🚣 👫

Umatilla National Forest
In northeastern Oregon.
(541) 278-3716
♿ 🔺 🏕 🚻 🚣 👫

Umpqua National Forest
In southwestern Oregon 33 mi. east of Roseburg on SR 138.
(541) 672-6601
♿ 🔺 🏕 🚻 🚣 👫 🍴

Wallowa-Whitman National Forest
In northeastern Oregon.
(541) 523-6391
🔺 🏕 🚻 🚣

Willamette National Forest
In western Oregon.
(541) 225-6300
♿ 🔺 🏕 🚻 🚣 🍴

PENNSYLVANIA
Allegheny National Forest
In northwestern Pennsylvania.
(814) 723-5150
♿ 🔺 🏕 🚻 🚣 👫 🍴

Delaware Water Gap National Recreation Area
In eastern Pennsylvania and northwestern New Jersey.
(570) 426-2457
🔺 🏕 🚻 🚣 👫

SOUTH CAROLINA
Congaree National Park
Southeast of Hopkins.
(803) 776-4396
🔺 🏕 🚻 👫

Francis Marion National Forest
On the Coastal Plain north of Charleston.
(803) 561-4000
♿ 🔺 🏕 🚻 👫

Sumter National Forest
In western South Carolina.
(803) 561-4000
♿ 🔺 🏕 🚻 🚣

SOUTH DAKOTA
Badlands National Park
In southwestern South Dakota.
(605) 433-5361

⬛ 🏃 🪑 👥 🍴

Black Hills National Forest
In southwestern South Dakota.
(605) 673-9200
🚲 ⬛ 🏃 🪑 🏊 👥 🍴

Wind Cave National Park
In southwestern South Dakota.
(605) 745-4600
🚲 ⬛ 🏃 🪑 👥 🍴

TENNESSEE

Big South Fork National River and Recreation Area
In northeastern Tennessee and southeastern Kentucky.
(423) 286-7275
🚲 ⬛ 🏃 🪑 🏊 👥 🍴

Cherokee National Forest
In eastern Tennessee.
(423) 476-9700
🚲 ⬛ 🏃 🪑 🏊 👥

TEXAS

Amistad National Recreation Area
Northwest of Del Rio via US 90.
(830) 775-7491
⬛ 🏃 🪑 🏊

Angelina National Forest
In east Texas.
(936) 897-1068
⬛ 🏃 🪑 🏊

Big Bend National Park
In southwest Texas.
(432) 477-2251
⬛ 🏃 🪑 👥 🍴

Davy Crockett National Forest
In east Texas.
(936) 655-2299
⬛ 🏃 🪑 🏊

Guadalupe Mountains National Park
110 mi. east of El Paso on US 62/180.
(915) 828-3251
⬛ 🏃 🪑 👥

Lake Meredith National Recreation Area
45 mi. northeast of Amarillo and 9 mi. west of Borger via SR 136.
(806) 857-3151
⬛ 🪑 🏊

Padre Island National Seashore
On Padre Island near Corpus Christi.
(361) 949-8068
⬛ 🏃 🪑 🏊 👥 🍴

Sabine National Forest
In east Texas.
(409) 625-1940
⬛ 🏃 🪑 🏊

Sam Houston National Forest
40 mi. north of Houston in east Texas.
(936) 344-6205
🚲 ⬛ 🏃 🪑 🏊

UTAH

Arches National Park
In eastern Utah.
(435) 719-2100
⬛ 🏃 🪑 👥

Ashley National Forest
In northeastern Utah.
(435) 789-1181
🚲 ⬛ 🏃 🪑 🏊 👥 🍴

Bryce Canyon National Park
In southwestern Utah.
(435) 834-5322
⬛ 🏃 🪑 👥 🍴

Canyonlands National Park
In southeastern Utah.
(435) 719-2313
⬛ 🏃 🪑 👥

Capitol Reef National Park
10 mi. east of Torrey on SR 24.
(435) 425-3791
🚲 ⬛ 🏃 🪑 👥

Dixie National Forest
In southwestern Utah.
(435) 865-3700
🚲 ⬛ 🏃 🪑 🏊 👥 🍴

Fishlake National Forest
In south-central Utah.
(435) 896-9233
🚲 ⬛ 🏃 🪑 👥 🍴

Flaming Gorge National Recreation Area
In northeastern Utah on the Wyoming-Utah border.
(435) 784-3445
🚲 ⬛ 🏃 🪑 🏊 👥 🍴

Manti-La Sal National Forest
In southeastern Utah.
(435) 637-2817
🚲 ⬛ 🏃 🪑 🍴

Uinta National Forest
In north-central, central and northeastern Utah.
(801) 342-5100
🚲 ⬛ 🏃 🪑 🏊 👥

Wasatch-Cache National Forest
In northeastern and north-central Utah.
(801) 342-5100
🚲 ⬛ 🏃 🪑 🏊 👥

Zion National Park
In southwestern Utah.
(435) 772-3256
🚲 ⬛ 🏃 🪑 👥 🍴

🚲 Bicycling Trails   ⬛ Camping   🏃 Hiking Trails   🪑 Picnic Facilities
🏊 Swimming   👥 Visitor Center   🍴 Food Service

VERMONT

Green Mountains and Green Mountain National Forest
In south-central Vermont.
(802) 747-6700
🎿 ⛺ 🚶 🔆 🛶

VIRGINIA

George Washington and Jefferson National Forests
In western Virginia and the eastern edge of West Virginia.
(540) 265-5100
🎿 ⛺ 🚶 🔆 🛶 🛖

Mount Rogers National Recreation Area
In southwestern Virginia.
(276) 783-5196
🎿 ⛺ 🚶 🔆 🛶 🛖

Shenandoah National Park
In northwestern Virginia.
(540) 999-3500
⛺ 🚶 🔆 🛖 🍴

WASHINGTON

Colville National Forest
In northeastern Washington.
(509) 684-7000
🎿 ⛺ 🚶 🔆 🛶

Gifford Pinchot National Forest
In southwestern Washington.
(360) 891-5000
🎿 ⛺ 🚶 🔆 🛶 🛖 🍴

Gifford Pinchot National Forest (Goose Lake)
13 mi. west of Trout Lake via SR 141, FR 24 and FR 60.
(509) 395-3400
⛺ 🔆 🛶

Gifford Pinchot National Forest (Takhlakh Lake)
32 mi. southeast of Randle via SR 131, FR 23 and FR 2329.
(360) 497-1100
⛺ 🚶 🔆 🛶

Lake Chelan National Recreation Area
In north-central Washington.
(509) 682-1900
⛺ 🚶 🔆 🛖 🍴

Lake Roosevelt National Recreation Area
In northeastern Washington.
(509) 633-9441
⛺ 🔆 🛶 🛖 🍴

Mount Baker-Snoqualmie National Forest
2 mi. east of Glacier on SR 542.
(425) 783-6000
🎿 ⛺ 🚶 🔆 🛶 🛖 🍴

Mount Baker-Snoqualmie National Forest (Douglas Fir)
2 mi. east of Glacier on SR 542.
(425) 783-6000
⛺ 🚶 🔆

Mount Baker-Snoqualmie National Forest (Horseshoe Cove)
14 mi. north of Concrete on Baker Lake.
(360) 599-2714
⛺ 🚶 🛶

Mount Baker-Snoqualmie National Forest (Shannon Creek)
24 mi. north of Concrete on Baker Lake.
(360) 599-2714
⛺ 🚶 🔆 🛶

Mount Rainier National Park
In west-central Washington.
(360) 569-2211
🎿 ⛺ 🚶 🔆 🛖 🍴

Okanogan-Wenatchee National Forest
In north-central Washington.
(509) 826-3275
🎿 ⛺ 🚶 🔆 🛶 🛖 🍴

Okanogan-Wenatchee National Forest (Bonaparte Lake)
7 mi. northwest of Wauconda via SR 20 and CR 4953.
(509) 664-9200
⛺ 🔆 🛶

Okanogan-Wenatchee National Forest (Bumping Lake)
3 mi. south of Goose Prairie.
(509) 664-9200
⛺ 🔆 🛶

Okanogan-Wenatchee National Forest (Kachess)
15 mi. north of Easton via I-90 and FR 49.
(509) 852-1100
🎿 ⛺ 🚶 🔆 🛶

Okanogan-Wenatchee National Forest (Lost Lake)
17 mi. northwest of Wauconda via SR 20, CR 4953, FR 32 and FR 33.
(509) 852-1100
⛺ 🔆 🛶

Okanogan-Wenatchee National Forest (Rimrock Lake Area)
At Rimrock off US 12.
(509) 653-1401
⛺ 🔆 🛶

Olympic National Forest
In northwestern Washington.
(360) 956-2402
🎿 ⛺ 🚶 🔆 🛶 🛖 🍴

Olympic National Forest (Falls Creek)
3 mi. east of US 101 on Quinault Lake.
(360) 956-2402
⛺ 🚶 🔆 🛶

Olympic National Forest (Willaby)
2 mi. east of US 101 on Quinault Lake.
(360) 956-2402
⛺ 🚶 🔆 🛶

Olympic National Forest (Wynoochee Lake-Coho)
1 mi. west of Montesano on US 12, then 37 mi. north on
FR 22 (Old Wynoochee Valley Rd.).
(360) 956-2402
🚲 ▲ 🚶 ⛱ ⛴

Olympic National Park
In the Olympic peninsula in northwestern Washington.
(360) 565-3130
▲ 🚶 ⛱ ⛴ 👫 🍴

Ross Lake National Recreation Area
Between the north and south sections of North Cascades
National Park.
(360) 854-7200
▲ 🚶 ⛱ 👫 🍴

WEST VIRGINIA
Monongahela National Forest
In eastern West Virginia.
(304) 636-1800
🚲 ▲ 🚶 ⛱ ⛴ 👫 🍴

Monongahela National Forest (Lake Sherwood)
11 mi. northeast of Neola on SR 14.
(304) 636-1800
🚲 ▲ 🚶 ⛱ ⛴

New River Gorge National River
Between Fayetteville and Hinton.
(304) 465-0508
🚲 🚶 ⛱ ⛴ 👫

Spruce Knob-Seneca Rocks National Recreation Area
In east-central West Virginia.
(304) 257-4488
▲ 🚶 ⛱ ⛴ 👫

WISCONSIN
Apostle Islands National Lakeshore
Off northern Wisconsin's Bayfield Peninsula in Lake
Superior.
(715) 779-3397

▲ 🚶 ⛱ ⛴ 👫

Chequamegon-Nicolet National Forest
In north-central and northeastern Wisconsin.
(715) 362-1300
🚲 ▲ 🚶 ⛱ ⛴ 🍴

St. Croix National Scenic Riverway
Running 252 mi. from Cable to Prescott.
(715) 483-2274
▲ 🚶 ⛱ ⛴ 👫

WYOMING
Bighorn National Forest
In north-central Wyoming.
(307) 674-2600
▲ 🚶 ⛱ 🍴

Devils Tower National Monument
Between Sundance and Hulett.
(307) 467-5283
▲ 🚶 ⛱ ⛴ 👫

Grand Teton National Park
In northwestern Wyoming.
(307) 739-3300
🚲 ▲ 🚶 ⛱ ⛴ 👫 🍴

Medicine Bow National Forest
In southeastern Wyoming.
(307) 745-2300
🚲 ▲ 🚶 ⛱ ⛴ 👫

Shoshone National Forest
In northwestern Wyoming.
(307) 527-6241
🚲 ▲ 🚶 ⛱ ⛴ 👫 🍴

Yellowstone National Park
In northwestern Wyoming.
(307) 344-7381
▲ 🚶 ⛱ 👫 🍴

Canada

ALBERTA
Banff National Park
In southwestern Alberta, west of Calgary.
(403) 762-1550
🚲 ▲ 🚶 ⛱ ⛴ 👫 🍴

Elk Island National Park
In central Alberta, east of Edmonton.
(780) 992-2950
▲ 🚶 ⛱ 👫 🍴

Jasper National Park
In west-central Alberta along the British Columbia border.
(780) 852-3858
🚲 ▲ 🚶 ⛱ ⛴ 👫 🍴

Waterton Lakes National Park
In Alberta's southwestern corner.
(403) 859-2224
🚲 ▲ 🚶 ⛱ ⛴ 👫 🍴

BRITISH COLUMBIA
Glacier National Park
In southeastern British Columbia.
(250) 837-7500
▲ 🚶 ⛱ 👫 🍴

Gulf Islands National Park Reserve
Off the southeast coast of Vancouver Island.
(250) 654-4000
▲ 🚶 ⛱ ⛴

🚲 Bicycling Trails   ▲ Camping   🚶 Hiking Trails   ⛱ Picnic Facilities
⛴ Swimming   👫 Visitor Center   🍴 Food Service

Kootenay National Park
In southeastern British Columbia.
(250) 343-6783
[icons]

Mount Revelstoke National Park
In southeastern British Columbia.
(250) 837-7500
[icons]

Pacific Rim National Park Reserve
On the southwestern coast of Vancouver Island.
(250) 726-7721
[icons]

Yoho National Park
On the British Columbia-Alberta border.
(250) 343-6783
[icons]

MANITOBA
Riding Mountain National Park
In southwestern Manitoba.
(204) 848-7275
[icons]

NEW BRUNSWICK
Fundy National Park
On Hwy. 114, 130 km. southwest of Moncton.
(506) 887-6000
[icons]

Kouchibouguac National Park
On Hwy. 134, north of Moncton.
(506) 876-2443
[icons]

NEWFOUNDLAND AND LABRADOR
Gros Morne National Park
On Newfoundland's western coast.
(709) 458-2417
[icons]

Terra Nova National Park
In eastern Newfoundland.
(709) 533-2801
[icons]

NORTHWEST TERRITORIES
Wood Buffalo National Park
On the Northwest Territories-Alberta border.
(867) 872-7900
[icons]

NOVA SCOTIA
Cape Breton Highlands National Park
5 km. northeast of Che´ticamp on Cabot Tr.
(902) 224-2306
[icons]

Kejimkujik National Park and National Historic Site
In southwestern Nova Scotia off Hwy. 8 at Maitland Bridge.
(902) 682-2772
[icons]

ONTARIO
Bruce Peninsula National Park
In southwestern Ontario.
(519) 596-2233
[icons]

Fathom Five National Marine Park
Off the northern tip of the Bruce Peninsula in southern Ontario.
(519) 596-2233
[icons]

Georgian Bay Islands National Park
Along the southeastern portion of Georgian Bay.
(705) 526-9804
[icons]

Point Pelee National Park
South of Leamington.
(519) 322-2365
[icons]

Pukaskwa National Park
On the north shore of Lake Superior.
(807) 229-0801
[icons]

St. Lawrence Islands National Park
In the St. Lawrence River between Kingston and Brockville.
(613) 923-5261
[icons]

PRINCE EDWARD ISLAND
Prince Edward Island National Park
Along the island's northern shore.
(902) 672-6350
[icons]

QUEBEC
Forillon National Park
20 km. northeast of Gaspe´ via Hwy. 132.
(418) 368-5505
[icons]

La Mauricie National Park
North of Trois-Rivie´res via Hwy. 55.
(819) 538-3232
[icons]

SASKATCHEWAN
Grasslands National Park
Between Val Marie and Killdeer in southern Saskatchewan.
(306) 298-2257
[icons]

Prince Albert National Park
In central Saskatchewan.
(306) 663-4522
[icons]

This list of emergency animal clinics in the United States and Canada is provided by the Veterinary Emergency & Critical Care Society (VECCS) as a service to the community for information purposes only. This is not to be construed as a certification or an endorsement of any clinic listed. For further information, contact the society at (210) 698-5575 or online at www.veccs.org. Note: Hours frequently change, and not all clinics are open 24 hours or in the evening. In addition, not all facilities listed here are emergency clinics. In non-emergency situations, it's best to call first.

If you are traveling to an area not covered in this list, be prepared for an emergency by asking your regular veterinarian to recommend a clinic or veterinarian at your destination. The American Animal Hospital Association also can recommend veterinary clinics that meet the association's high standards for veterinary care. For additional information contact the association at (303) 986-2800.

United States

ALABAMA

Animal Medical Center
2864 Acton Rd., Birmingham
(205) 967-7389

Emergency Pet Care
4524 Southlake Pkwy., Suite 28, Birmingham
(205) 988-5988

Southern Regional Veterinary Emergency Services
301 Westgate Pkwy., Dothan
(334) 699-7787

Animal Emergency Clinic of North Alabama
2112 Memorial Pkwy. S.W., Huntsville
(256) 533-7600

Animal Emergency & Referral Center of Mobile
2573 Government Blvd., Mobile
(251) 706-0890

ALASKA

Pet Emergency Treatment, Inc.
2320 E. Dowling Rd., Anchorage
(907) 274-5636

After Hours Veterinary Emergency Clinic
8 Bonnie Ave., Fairbanks
(907) 479-2700

ARIZONA

Animal Health Services
37555 N. Cave Creek Rd., Cave Creek
(480) 488-6181

First Regional Animal Hospital
1233 W. Warner Rd., Chandler
(480) 732-0335

Emergency Animal Clinic, PLC
86 W. Juniper, Gilbert
(480) 497-0222

1st Emergency Pet Care
1423 S. Highley Rd., #102, Mesa
(408) 924-1123

Emergency Animal Clinic
1235 S. Gilbert Rd., Suite 24, Mesa
(480) 497-0222

Mesa Veterinary Hospital
858 N. Country Club Dr., Mesa
(480) 833-7330

Emergency Animal Clinic
9875 W. Peoria Ave., Peoria
(623) 974-1520

Emergency Animal Clinic, PLC
2260 W. Glendale Ave., Phoenix
(602) 995-3757

North Valley Animal Emergency Center
3134 W. Carefree Hwy., Suite A-2, Phoenix
(623) 516-8571

Sonora Veterinary Specialists
4015 E. Cactus Rd., Phoenix
(602) 765-3700

Ironwood Animal Hospital
85 W. Combs Rd., Suite 116, San Tan Valley
(480) 888-2299

Emergency Animal Clinic
14202 N. Scottsdale Rd., Suite 163, Scottsdale
(480) 949-8001

Paradise Valley Emergency Animal Clinic
6969 E. Shea Blvd., Suite 225, Scottsdale
(480) 991-1848

Arizona Veterinary Surgery
4131 E. Speedway Blvd., Tucson
(520) 795-9955

Ina Road Animal Hospital
7320 N. La Cholla Blvd., Suite 114, Tucson
(520) 544-7700

Pima Pet Clinic / Animal Emergency Service
4832 E. Speedway Blvd., Tucson
(520) 327-5624

Southern Arizona Veterinary Specialty and Emergency Center
141 E. Fort Lowell Rd., Tucson
(520) 888-3177

Southern Arizona Veterinary Specialty and Emergency Center
7474 E. Broadway Blvd., Tucson
(520) 888-3177

Valley Animal Hospital, P.C.
4984 E. 22nd St., Tucson
(520) 748-0331

Veterinary Specialty Center of Tucson
4909 N. La Canada Dr., Tucson
(520) 795-9955

ARKANSAS
Ft. Smith Animal Emergency Clinic
4301 Regions Park Dr., Suite 3, Fort Smith
(479) 649-3100

Pulaski County Veterinary Emergency Clinic
801 John Barrow #6, Little Rock
(501) 224-3784

After Hour Animal Hospital
290 Smokey Ln., North Little Rock
(501) 955-0911

Animal Emergency & Specialty Clinic
8735 Sheltie Dr., Suite G, North Little Rock
(501) 224-3784

Animal Emergency Clinic of Northwest Arkansas
1110 Mathias Dr., Suite E, Springdale
(501) 927-0007

CALIFORNIA
East Bay Veterinary Emergency
1312 Sunset Dr., Antioch
(925) 754-5001

Central Coast Pet Emergency Clinic
1558 W. Branch St., Arroyo Grande
(805) 489-6573

Atascadero Pet Hospital and Emergency Center
9575 El Camino Real, Atascadero
(805) 466-3880

Animal Emergency & Urgent Care
4300 Easton Dr., Suite 1, Bakersfield
(661) 322-6019

Pet Emergency Treatment and Specialty (PETS) Referral Center
1048 University Ave., Berkeley
(510) 548-6684

East of the River Veterinary Emergency Clinic
222 Boston Tpke., Bolton
(860) 646-6134

United Emergency Animal Clinic
1657 S. Bascom Ave., Campbell
(408) 371-6282

Pacific Veterinary Specialists and Emergency Critical Care Center
1980 41st Ave., Capitola
(831) 476-2584

North Valley Emergency Veterinary Clinic
2500 Zanella Way, Suite A, Chico
(530) 899-1720

Contra Costa Veterinary Emergency Center
1410 Monument Blvd., Suite 108, Concord
(925) 798-2900

VCA Aacacia Animal Hospital
939 W. 6th St., Corona
(951) 371-1002

Advanced Critical Care of Los Angeles
9599 Jefferson Blvd., Culver City
(310) 558-6100

UC Davis Veterinary Medical Teaching Hospital - Small Animal Clinic
1 Garrod Dr., Davis
(530) 752-1393

Pet Specialists of Monterey
451 Canyon Del Rey Blvd., Del Rey Oaks
(831) 899-7387

Tri-Valley Animal Emergency Center
7111 Amador Plaza Rd., Dublin
(925) 771-5630

Vetcare Emergency & Specialty Care Center
7660 Amador Valley Blvd., Dublin
(925) 556-1234

Emergency Pet Clinic of San Gabriel Valley
3254 Santa Anita Ave., El Monte
(626) 579-4550

North Coast Veterinary and Emergency
414 Encinitas Blvd., Encinitas
(760) 632-1072

Animal Urgent Care
2430 S. Escondido Blvd., Escondido
(760) 738-9600

Animal Emergency Center
3954 A Jacobs Ave., Eureka
(707) 443-2776

Solano-Napa Pet Emergency Clinic
4437 Central Pl., Fairfield
(707) 864-1444

VCA All-Care Animal Referral Center
18440 Amistad St., Suite E, Fountain Valley
(714) 963-0909

Ohlone Veterinary Emergency Clinic
1618 Washington Blvd., Fremont
(510) 657-6620

Central California Veterinary Specialty Center
6606 N. Blackstone Ave., Fresno
(559) 451-0800

Fresno Pet Emergency & Referral Center, Inc.
7375 N. Palm Bluffs Ave., Fresno
(559) 437-3766

Veterinary Emergency Service, Inc.
1639 N. Fresno St., Fresno
(559) 486-0520

Orange County Emergency Pet Clinic
12750 Garden Grove Blvd., Garden Grove
(714) 537-3032

eMash, Inc. Emergency & Mobile Animal Services Hospital
10825 Watsonville Rd., Gilroy
(408) 847-1122

Animal Emergency Clinic
12022 La Crosse Ave., Grand Terrace
(909) 825-9350

Irvine Regional Animal Emergency Hospital
1371 Reynolds Ave., Irvine
(949) 833-9020

North Orange County Emergency Pet Clinic
1474 S. Harbor Blvd., La Habra
(714) 441-2925

Pet Emergency & Specialty Center
5232 Jackson Dr., Suite 105, La Mesa
(619) 462-4800

Animal Emergency Clinic
1055 W. Avenue M, Suite 101, Lancaster
(661) 723-3959

Animal Specialty Group
4641 Colorado Blvd., Los Angeles
(818) 244-7977

Animal Surgical & Emergency Center
1535 S. Sepulveda Blvd., Los Angeles
(310) 473-5906

Animal Surgical and Emergency Center (ASEC)
1535 S. Sepulveda Blvd., Los Angeles
(310) 473-1561

Eagle Rock Emergency Pet Clinic
4254 Eagle Rock Blvd., Los Angeles
(323) 254-7382

VCA West Los Angeles Animal Hospital
1818 S. Sepulveda Blvd., Los Angeles
(310) 473-2951

Animal Urgent Care
2805 Hillcrest, Mission Viejo
(949) 364-6228

Portola Plaza Veterinary Hospital
27752 Santa Margarita Pkwy., Mission Viejo
(949) 859-2101

Modesto Veterinary Emergency Clinic
1800 Prescott Rd., Suite E, Modesto
(209) 527-8844

Monterey Peninsula Veterinary Emergency & Specialty Center
20 Lower Ragsdale Dr., Suite 150, Monterey
(831) 373-7374

All Creatures Emergency Center
22722 Lyons Ave., #5, Newhall
(661) 291-1121

Central Orange County Emergency Animal Clinic
3720 Campus Drive, Suite D, Newport Beach
(949) 261-7979

Crossroads Animal Emergency and Referral Clinic
11057 E. Rosecrans Ave., Norwalk
(562) 863-2522

Orange Veterinary Hospital
1100 W. Chapman Ave., Orange
(714) 997-8200

Extraordinary Veterinary Services
5714 Los Coyotes Dr., Palm Springs
(760) 202-8710

South Peninsula Veterinary Emergency Clinic
3045 Middlefield Rd., Palo Alto
(650) 494-1461

Animal Emergency Clinic of Pasadena
2121 E. Foothill Blvd., Pasadena
(626) 564-0704

Animal Emergency Clinic of San Diego
12775 Poway Rd., Poway
(858) 748-7387

Animal Care Center
6470 Redwood Dr., Rohnert Park
(707) 584-4343

Atlantic St. Veterinary Hospital and Pet Emergency Center, Inc.
1100 Atlantic St., Roseville
(916) 783-4655

El Camino Veterinary Hospital
4000 El Camino Ave., Sacramento
(916) 488-6878

Mueller Animal Hospital
6420 Freeport Blvd., Sacramento
(916) 428-9202

Northern California Veterinary Specialists
7425 Greenhaven Dr., Sacramento
(916) 231-0696

VCA Sacramento Veterinary Referral Center
9801 Old Winery Pl., Sacramento
(916) 362-3111

San Carlos Pet Emergency Hospital
718 El Camino Real, San Carlos
(650) 591-5718

Animal ER of San Diego
5610 Kearny Mesa Rd., Suite A, San Diego
(858) 569-0600

VCA Emergency Animal Hospital and Referral Center
2317 Hotel Cir. S., San Diego
(619) 299-2400

Veterinary Specialty Hospital
10435 Sorrento Valley Rd., San Diego
(858) 875-7500

All Animals Emergency Hospital
1333 Ninth Ave., San Francisco
(415) 566-0531

Pets Unlimited
2343 Fillmore St., San Francisco
(415) 563-6700

San Francisco Veterinary Specialists
600 Alabama St., San Francisco
(415) 401-9200

Emergency Animal Clinic of South San Jose
5440 Thornwood Dr., Suite E, San Jose
(408) 578-5622

Bay Area Veterinary Emergency Clinic
14790 Washington Ave., San Leandro
(510) 352-6080

California Veterinary Specialists
100 N. Rancho Santa Fe Rd., San Marcos
(760) 734-4433

North Peninsula Veterinary Emergency Clinic, Inc.
227 N. Amphlett Blvd., San Mateo
(650) 348-2575

The Pet Emergency and Specialty Center of Marin
901 E. Francisco Blvd., Suite C, San Rafael
(415) 456-7372

California Animal Referral & Emergency Hospital
301 E. Haley St., Santa Barbara
(805) 899-2273

Pacific Emergency Pet Hospital, Inc.
2963 State St., Santa Barbara
(805) 682-5120

Santa Cruz Veterinary Hospital
2585 Soquel Dr., Santa Cruz
(831) 475-5400

North Bay Animal Emergency Hospital
1304 Wilshire Blvd., Santa Monica
(310) 451-8962

Emergency Animal Hospital of Santa Rosa
1946 Santa Rosa Ave., Santa Rosa
(707) 544-1647

PetCare East Veterinary Hospital
2425 Mendocino Ave., Santa Rosa
(707) 579-3900

PetCare West Veterinary Hospital
1370 Fulton Rd., Santa Rosa
(707) 579-5900

Beverly Oaks Animal Hospital and Emergency Animal Clinic
14302 Ventura Blvd., Sherman Oaks
(818) 788-7860

TLC Pet Medical Centers - South Pasadena
1412 Huntington Dr., South Pasadena
(626) 441-8555

Associated Veterinary Emergency Services
3008 E. Hammer Ln., #115, Stockton
(209) 952-8387

Animal Emergency Centre
11730 Ventura Blvd., Studio City
(818) 760-3882

Emergency Pet Clinic of Temecula
27443 Jefferson Ave., Temecula
(951) 695-5044

Conejo Valley Veterinary Hospital
1850 E. Thousand Oaks Blvd., Thousand Oaks
(805) 495-4671

Pet Emergency Clinic
2967 N. Moorepark Rd., Thousand Oaks
(805) 492-2436

Animal Emergency Referral Center
3511 Pacific Coast Hwy., Suite A, Torrance
(310) 325-3000

Emergency Pet Clinic of South Bay
2325 Torrance Blvd., Torrance
(310) 320-8300

Monte Vista Small Animal Hospital
901 E. Monte Vista Ave., Turlock
(209) 634-0023

Advanced Critical Care & Internal Medicine
2965 Edinger Ave., Tustin
(949) 654-8950

Inland Valley Emergency Pet Clinic
10 W. 7th St., Upland
(909) 931-7871

Pet Emergency Clinic
2301 S. Victoria Ave., Ventura
(805) 642-8562

Veterinary Medical and Surgical Group
2199 Sperry Ave., Ventura
(805) 339-2290

Animal Emergency Clinic
15532 Bear Valley Rd., Victorville
(760) 962-1122

Pinnacle Veterinary Service, Inc.
2300 S. Divisadero St., Visalia
(559) 732-8000

Tulare-Kings Veterinary Emergency Service
4240 W. Mineral King, Visalia
(559) 739-7054

Coastal Emergency Animal Hospital
1900 Hacienda Dr., Vista
(760) 630-6343

TLC Pet Medical Centers - West Hollywood
8725 Santa Monica Blvd., West Hollywood
(310) 859-4852

COLORADO

Animal Urgent Care
7851 Indiana St., Arvada
(303) 420-7387

Aurora Veterinary Emergency Center
18511 E. Hampden Ave., Aurora
(303) 699-1665

Valley Emergency Pet Care
180 Fiou Ln., Suite 101, Basalt
(970) 927-5066

Alpenglow Veterinary Specialty & Emergency Center
3640 Walnut St., Boulder
(303) 443-4569

Animal Emergency & Referral Center
1480 W. Midway Blvd., Boulder
(303) 464-7744

Boulder Emergency Pet Clinic
1658 30th St., Boulder
(303) 440-7722

VCA Douglas County Animal Hospital
531 Jerry St., Castle Rock
(303) 688-2480

Animal Emergency Care Centers - North
5520 N. Nevada Ave., Colorado Springs
(719) 260-7141

Animal Emergency Care Centers- South
3775 Airport Rd., Colorado Springs
(719) 578-9300

Animal Emergency Care, Inc.
5752 N. Academy Blvd., Colorado Springs
(719) 260-7141

VCA Alameda East Veterinary Hospital
9770 E. Alameda Ave., Denver
(303) 366-2639

Central Veterinary Emergency Services
3550 S. Jason St., Englewood
(303) 874-7387

Pets of Northern Colorado
3629 23rd Ave., Evans
(970) 339-8700

Fort Collins Veterinary Emergency Hospital
816 S. Lemay Ave., Fort Collins
(970) 484-8080

James L. Voss Veterinary Teaching Hospital Colorado State University
300 W. Drake Rd., Fort Collins
(970) 221-4535

Grand Valley Veterinary Emergency Center
1660 North Ave., Grand Junction
(970) 255-1911

Animal Hospital Specialty Center
5640 County Line Pl., Suite 1, Highlands Ranch
(303) 740-9595

Animal Critical Care & Emergency Services, Inc.
1597 Wadsworth Blvd., Lakewood
(303) 239-1200

Animal E.R.
221 W. County Line Rd., Littleton
(720) 283-9348

Columbine Animal Hospital & Emergency Clinic
5546 W. Canyon Tr., Littleton
(303) 929-4040

Animal Emergency & Critical Care
230 S. Main St., Longmont
(303) 678-8844

Animal Emergency Services of Northern Colorado
201 W. 67th Ct., Loveland
(970) 663-5760

Animal Emergency & Urgent Care
17701 Cottonwood Dr., Parker
(720) 842-5050

Emergency Animal Hospital of Pueblo
472 S. Joe Martinez Blvd., Pueblo
(719) 229-7030

Pueblo Area Pet Emergency Hospital
712 Fortino Blvd., Pueblo
(719) 544-7788

Community Pet Hospital
12311 Washington St., Thornton
(303) 451-1333

Northside Emergency Pet Clinic, P.C.
945 W. 124th Ave., Westminster
(303) 252-7722

Wheat Ridge Animal Hospital / Wheat Ridge Veterinary Specialists
3695 Kipling St., Wheat Ridge
(303) 424-3325

CONNECTICUT
Farmington Valley Veterinary Emergency Hospital
9 Avonwood Rd., Avon
(860) 674-1886

VCA Cheshire Veterinary Hospital
1572 S. Main St., Cheshire
(203) 271-1577

New Haven Hospital for Veterinary Medicine, Inc.
843 State St., New Haven
(203) 865-0878

VCA Veterinary Referral & Emergency Center
123 W. Cedar St., Norwalk
(203) 854-9960

V-E-T-S (Veterinary Emergency Treatment Services)
8 Enterprise Ln., Oakdale
(860) 444-8870

Animal Emergency Hospital Of Central Connecticut
588 Cromwell Ave., Rocky Hill
(860) 563-4447

Cornell University Veterinary Specialists
880 Canal St., Stamford
(203) 595-2777

Shoreline Animal Emergency Clinic
7365 Main St., Stratford
(203) 375-6500

Connecticut Veterinary Center
470 Oakwood Ave., West Hartford
(860) 233-8564

DELAWARE
VCA Newark Animal Hospital
1360 Marrows Rd., Newark
(302) 737-8100

Veterinary Emergency Center of Delaware
1212 E. Newport Pike, Wilmington
(302) 691-3647

Windcrest Animal Emergency Hospital
3705 Lancaster Pike, Wilmington
(302) 998-2995

DISTRICT OF COLUMBIA
Friendship Hospital for Animals
4105 Brandywine St., Washington
(202) 363-7300

FLORIDA

Calusa Veterinary Center
6900 Congress Ave., Boca Raton
(561) 999-3000

Southwest Florida Veterinary Specialists & 24 Hour Emergency Hospital
28400 Old 41 Rd., Suite 1, Bonita Springs
(239) 992-8387

PetPB Animal Emergency & Referral Center
2246 N. Congress Ave., Boynton Beach
(561) 752-3232

Veterinary Emergency Center
3915 Cortez Rd. W., Bradenton
(941) 896-9420

Animal Emergency Clinic of Brandon
693 W. Lumsden Rd., Brandon
(813) 684-3013

Animal ER of SW Florida
1327 N.E. Pine Island Rd., Suite 110, Cape Coral
(239) 673-7426

Veterinary Emergency Clinic of Central Florida - Casselberry
195 Concord Dr., Casselberry
(407) 644-4449

Animal Emergency and Critical Care Services of S. Florida
9410 Stirling Rd., Cooper City
(954) 432-5611

Coral Springs Animal Hospital
2160 N. University Dr., Coral Springs
(954) 753-1800

Florida Veterinary Referral Center & 24 Hour Emergency & Critical Care
9220 Estero Park Commons Blvd., Suite 7, Estero
(239) 992-8878

Animal Emergency Trauma Center
2200 W. Oakland Park Blvd., Fort Lauderdale
(954) 731-4228

Pet Emergency Center
921 E. Cypress Creek Rd., Fort Lauderdale
(954) 772-0420

Emergency Veterinary Clinic, Inc.
2045 Collier Ave., Fort Myers
(239) 939-5542

Animal Emergency and Referral Center
3984 S. US 1, Fort Pierce
(772) 466-3441

Affiliated Pet Emergency Services
7314 W. University Ave., Gainesville
(352) 373-4444

Hollywood Animal Hospital
2864 Hollywood Blvd., Hollywood
(954) 920-3556

Animal ER
3444 Southside Blvd., Suite 101, Jacksonville
(904) 642-4357

Emergency Pet Care, LLC
14185 Beach Blvd., Suite 7, Jacksonville
(904) 223-8000

Emergency Pet Care of Jupiter
300 Central Blvd., Jupiter
(561) 746-0555

Tampa Bay Veterinary Emergency Service
1501-A Belcher Rd., Suite 1A, Largo
(727) 531-5752

Veterinary Emergency Clinic of Central Florida - Leesburg
33040 Professional Dr., Leesburg
(352) 728-4440

Animal Emergency and Critical Care Center of Brevard
2281 W. Eau Gallie Blvd., Melbourne
(321) 725-5365

AEC-Animal Emergency Clinic South
8429 S.W. 132nd St., Miami
(305) 251-2096

Doral Centre Animal Clinic
9589 N.W. 41st St., Miami
(305) 598-1234

Knowles Animal Clinic - Snapper Creek Emergency Clinic
9933 Sunset Dr., Miami
(305) 279-2323

Miami Pet Emergency
11774 S.W. 88th St., Miami
(305) 273-8100

Miami Veterinary Specialists
8601 Sunset Dr., Miami
(305) 665-2820

The Pet Emergency Room
6394 S. Dixie Hwy., Miami
(305) 666-4142

Animal Specialty Hospital of Florida (ASH)
10130 Market St., Suite 1, Naples
(239) 263-0480

Emergency Pet Hospital of Collier Co.
6530 Dudley Dr., Naples
(941) 263-8010

Ocala Animal Emergency Hospital
1815 N.E. Jacksonville Rd., Ocala
(352) 840-0044

Clay-Duval Pet Emergency Clinic
275 Corporate Way, Suite 200, Orange Park
(904) 264-8281

Veterinary Emergency Clinic of Central Florida - South Orlando
2080 Principal Row, Orlando
(407) 438-4449

Pet Emergency and Critical Care Clinic
3816 Northlake Blvd., Palm Beach Gardens
(561) 691-9999

A.A.Animal ER Center, LLC
36401 US 19N, Palm Harbor
(727) 787-5402

Animal Emergency of Countryside, Inc.
30610 US 19N, Palm Harbor
(727) 786-5755

St. Francis Emergency Animal Hospital
6602 Pines Blvd., Pembroke Pines
(954) 962-0300

Veterinary Emergency Referral Center
4800 N. Davis Hwy., Pensacola
(850) 477-3914

The Veterinary Emergency Clinic
17829 Murdock Cir., Port Charlotte
(941) 255-5222

Animal Specialty and Emergency Hospital
5775 Schenck Ave., Rockledge
(321) 752-7600

Critical Care & Veterinary Specialists of Sarasota
4937 S. Tamiami Tr., Sarasota
(941) 929-1818

Sarasota Veterinary Emergency Hospital
7515-7517 S. Tamiami Tr., Sarasota
(941) 923-7260

Animal Emergency Clinic of St. Petersburg
3165 22nd Ave. N., St. Petersburg
(727) 323-1311

Noahs Animal Hospital and 24 Hour Emergency
2050 62nd Ave. N., St. Petersburg
(727) 522-6640

Pet Emergency & Critical Care Clinic, Inc.
2239 S. Kanner Hwy., Stuart
(772) 781-3302

Allied Veterinary Emergency Hospital
2324 Centerville Rd., Tallahassee
(850) 222-0123

FVS (Florida Veterinary Specialists)
3000 Busch Lake Blvd., Tampa
(813) 933-8944

Tampa Bay Veterinary Emergency Service
238 E. Bearss Ave., Tampa
(813) 265-4043

Animal E.R.
8237 Cooper Creek Blvd., University Park
(941) 355-2884

Animal Emergency Clinic
3425 Forest Hill Blvd., West Palm Beach
(561) 433-2244

Palm Beach Veterinary Specialists
3884 Forest Hill Blvd., West Palm Beach
(561) 434-5700

VCA Cabrera Animal Hospital
6390 S.W. 8th St., West Miami
(305) 261-2374

GEORGIA

All Pets Emergency and Referral Center, P.C.
6460 Highway 9N, Alpharetta
(678) 366-2125

University of Georgia - Vet. Teaching Hospital
College of Veterinary Medicine, Athens
(706) 542-3221

Animal Emergency Center of Sandy Springs
228 Sandy Springs Pl. N.E., Atlanta
(404) 252-7881

Georgia Veterinary Specialists & Emergency Care
455 Abernathy Rd. N.E., Atlanta
(404) 459-0963

North Georgia Veterinary Specialists
1328 Buford Hwy., Building 200, Buford
(678) 835-3300

East Metro Animal Emergency Clinic, LLC
6225 Hwy. 278 N.W., Covington
(678) 212-0300

PetFirst 24 Hour Animal Hospital
4075 Pleasant Hill Rd., Duluth
(678) 745-1262

Southern Crescent Animal Emergency Clinic
1270 Hwy. 54 E., Fayetteville
(770) 460-8166

An-Emerge Animal Emergency Clinic
275 Pearl Nix Pkwy., Suite 3, Gainesville
(770) 534-2911

Eastside Animal Medical Center
1835 Grayson Hwy., Grayson
(678) 958-5530

Animal Emergency Center of Gwinnett
1956 Lawrenceville-Suwanee Rd., Lawrenceville
(770) 277-3220

Cobb Emergency Veterinary Clinic
630 Cobb Pkwy. N., Suite C, Marietta
(770) 424-9157

Animal Emergency Center of North Fulton
900 Mansell Rd., Suite 19, Roswell
(770) 594-2266

Savannah Veterinary Emergency Clinic
317 Eisenhower Dr., Savannah
(912) 355-6113

DeKalb-Gwinnett Animal Emergency Clinic
6430 Lawrenceville Hwy., Tucker
(770) 491-0661

Cherokee Emergency Veterinary Clinic
7800 Hwy. 92, Woodstock
(678) 238-0700

HAWAII

Veterinary Emergency & Referral Center of Hawaii
1347 Kapiolani Blvd., Suite 103, Honolulu
(808) 735-7735

IDAHO

Mountain View Animal Hospital / Pet ER
3435 N. Cole Rd., Boise
(208) 375-0251

WestVet Animal Emergency & Specialty Center
5019 N. Sawyer Ave., Garden City
(208) 375-1600

Idaho Falls Veterinary Emergency Clinic
3151 McNeil Dr., Idaho Falls
(208) 552-0662

All Valley Animal Care Center
2326 E. Cinema Dr., Meridian
(208) 888-0818

WestVet Animal Emergency
3085 E. Magic View Dr., Suite. 110, Meridian
(208) 288-0400

North Idaho Pet Emergency
2700 E. Seltice Way, Suite 12, Post Falls
(208) 777-2707

ILLINOIS

Animal E.R. of Arlington Heights
1195 E. Palatine Rd., Arlington Heights
(847) 394-6049

VCA Aurora Animal Hospital
2600 W. Galena Blvd., Aurora
(630) 896-8541

Animal Emergency Clinic of McLean County
2505 E. Oakland Ave., Bloomington
(309) 665-5020

Veterinary Specialty Center
1515 Busch Pkwy., Buffalo Grove
(847) 459-7535

Animal Emergency Clinic of Champaign County
1713 S. State St., Unit 4, Champaign
(217) 359-1977

Chicago Veterinary Emergency & Specialty Center
3123 N. Clybourne Ave., Chicago
(773) 281-7110

Animal Emergency Center
2005 Mall St., Collinsville
(618) 346-1898

Emergency Veterinary Care South
13715 S. Cicero Ave., Crestwood
(708) 388-3771

Animal Emergency of McHenry County
1095 Pingree Rd., Suite 120, Crystal Lake
(815) 479-9119

Arboretum View Animal Hospital
2551 Warrenville Rd., Downers Grove
(630) 963-0424

Dundee Animal Hospital
199 Penny Ave., Dundee
(847) 428-6114

Midwest Animal Emergency Hospital
7510 W. North Ave., Elmwood Park
(708) 453-4755

VCA Franklin Park Animal Hospital
9846 W. Grand Ave., Franklin Park
(847) 455-4922

Hawthorne Animal Hospital
5 Cougar Dr., Glen Carbon
(618) 288-3971

Animal Emergency & Treatment Center
1810 E. Belvidere Rd., Grayslake
(847) 548-5300

Emergency Veterinary Services
820 Ogden Ave., Lisle
(630) 960-2900

Animal Emergency of Mokena
19110 S. 88th Ave., Mokena
(708) 326-4800

Animal Emergency & Critical Care Center
1810 Frontage Rd., Northbrook
(847) 564-5775

Tri-County Animal Emergency Clinic
1800 N. Sterling Ave., Peoria
(309) 672-1565

Animal Emergency Clinic of Rockford
4236 Maray Dr., Rockford
(815) 229-7791

Animal 911
3735 W. Dempster St., Skokie
(847) 673-9110

Animal Emergency Clinic of Springfield
1333 W. Wabash Ave., Springfield
(617) 698-0870

Emergency Veterinary Services of St. Charles
530 Dunham Rd., St. Charles
(630) 584-7447

ASPCA Animal Poison Control Center
1717 S. Philo Rd., Suite 36, Urbana
(217) 337-5030

University of Illinois College of Veterinary Medicine
1008 W. Hazelwood Dr., Urbana
(217) 333-5300

INDIANA

VCA Northwood Animal Hospital
3255 N. SR 9, Anderson
(765) 649-5218

St. Francis Family Pet Health Care
822 W. Plymouth St., Bremen
(574) 546-9005

Circle City Veterinary Specialty & Emergency Hospital
9650 Mayflower Park Dr., Carmel
(317) 872-8387

Northeast Indiana Veterinary Emergency & Specialty Hospital
5818 Maplecrest Rd., Fort Wayne
(260) 426-1062

Airport Animal Emergi-Center, P.C.
5235 W. Washington St., Indianapolis
(317) 248-0832

Indianapolis Veterinary Emergency Center
5425 Victory Dr., Indianapolis
(317) 782-4484

Noah's Animal Hospital & 24 Hour Emergency Center
5510 Millersville Rd., Indianapolis
(317) 253-1327

VCA Indiana Veterinary Specialists & Emergency Center
8250 Bash St., Indianapolis
(317) 849-4925

Animal Emergency Clinic of Tippecanoe County
1343 Sagamore Pkwy. N., Lafayette
(765) 449-2001

Animal Emergency Clinic
2324 Grape Rd., Mishawaka
(574) 259-8387

Calumet Emergency Veterinary Clinic
216 W. Lincoln Hwy., Schererville
(219) 865-0970

North Central Veterinary Emergency Center
1645 S. US 421, Westville
(219) 785-7300

IOWA
Iowa State University Veterinary Clinical Sciences Teaching Hospital
1600 S. 16th St., Ames
(515) 294-4900

Animal Emergency Center of the Quad Cities
1510 State St., Bettendorf
(563) 344-9599

Eastern Iowa Veterinary Specialty Center
755 Capital Dr. S.W., Cedar Rapids
(319) 841-5161

Animal Emergency & Referral Center of Central Iowa
6110 Creston Ave., Des Moines
(515) 280-3051

KANSAS
Kansas State University Vet. Med. Teaching Hospital
1800 Denison Ave., Manhattan
(785) 532-4100

VCA Mission Animal Referral & Emergency Center
5914 Johnson Dr., Mission
(913) 722-5566

BluePearl Veterinary Partners
11950 W. 110th St., Overland Park
(913) 642-9563

Central Kansas Veterinary Center
515 W. Blanchard Ave., South Hutchinson
(620) 663-8387

Emergency Animal Clinic of Topeka
839 S.W. Fairlawn Rd., Topeka
(785) 272-2926

Veterinary Emergency & Specialty Hospital of Wichita
727 S. Washington St., Wichita
(316) 262-5321

KENTUCKY
AA Small Animal Emergency Service
150 Dennis Dr., Lexington
(859) 276-2505

Jefferson Animal Hospital & Regional Emergency Center
4504 Outer Loop, Louisville
(502) 966-4104

Louisville Veterinary Specialty & Emergency Services
13160 Magisterial Dr., Louisville
(502) 244-3036

Greater Cincinnati Veterinary Specialists & Emergency Services
11 Beacon Dr., Wilder
(859) 572-0560

LOUISIANA
Animal Emergency Clinic of Baton Rouge
7353 Jefferson Hwy., Baton Rouge
(225) 927-8800

Baton Rouge Pet Emergency Hospital
1514 Cottondale Dr., Baton Rouge
(225) 925-5566

Sherwood South Animal Emergency & Critical Care Care Center
3803 S. Sherwood Forest Blvd., Baton Rouge
(225) 293-6440

Louisiana Veterinary Referral Center
2611 Florida St., Mandeville
(985) 626-4862

Southeast Veterinary Emergency & Critical Care
3409 Division St., Metairie
(504) 219-0444

MAINE
Eastern Maine Emergency Veterinary Clinic
15 Dirigo Dr., Brewer
(207) 989-6267

Animal Emergency Clinic of Mid-Maine
37 Strawberry Ave., Lewiston
(207) 777-1110

Animal Emergency Clinic
739 Warren Ave., Portland
(207) 878-3121

Maine Veterinary Referral Center
1500 Technology Way, Enterprise Business Park
Scarborough
(207) 885-1290

MARYLAND

Anne Arundel Veterinary Emergency Clinic (AAVEC)
808 Bestgate Rd., Annapolis
(410) 224-0331

Emergency Veterinary Clinic
32 Mellor Ave., Baltimore
(410) 788-7040

Falls Road Animal Hospital
6314 Falls Rd., Baltimore
(410) 825-9100

Animal Emergency Hospital
807B Belair Rd., Bel Air
(410) 420-7297

Harford Emergency Veterinary Services
526 Underwood Ln., Bel Air
(410) 420-8000

Emergency Veterinary Clinic, Inc.
32 Mellor Ave., Catonsville
(410) 788-7042

Emergency Animal Hospital of Ellicott City
10270 Baltimore National Pike (US 40W), Ellicott City
(410) 750-1177

Crossroads Animal Referral and Emergency (CARE)
1080 W. Patrick St., Frederick
(301) 662-2273

Frederick Emergency Animal Hospital
434 Prospect Blvd., Frederick
(301) 662-6622

VCA Veterinary Referral Associates
500 Perry Pkwy., Gaithersburg
(301) 926-3300, ext. 140

Mountain View Animal Emergency
17747 Virginia Ave., Hagerstown
(301) 733-7339

Metropolitan Emergency Animal Clinic
12106 Nebel St., Rockville
(301) 770-5226

Pets ER Gateway Crossing
329 Tilghman Rd., Suite 100, Salisbury
(410) 543-8400

PET ER
1209 Cromwell Bridge Rd., Towson
(410) 252-8387

Southern Maryland Veterinary Referral Center
3485 Rockefeller Ct., Waldorf
(301) 638-0988

Central Carroll Animal Emergency
1030 Baltimore Blvd., Suite 180, Westminster
(410) 871-9001

Westminster Veterinary Hospital & Emergency / Trauma Center
269 W. Main St., Westminster
(410) 848-3363

MASSACHUSETTS

Animal Emergency Care
164 Great Rd., Acton
(978) 263-1742

Angell Memorial Animal Hospital
350 S. Huntington Ave., Boston
(617) 522-7282

Cape Cod Veterinary Specialists Emergency Service
230 Main St., Buzzards Bay
(508) 759-5125

Wignall Animal Hospital
1837 Bridge St., Dracut
(978) 454-8272

Fall River Animal Hospital, Inc.
33 18th St., Fall River
(508) 675-6374

Essex County Veterinary Emergency Hospital
247 Chickering Rd., North Andover
(978) 725-5544

Tufts University School of Veterinary Medicine
200 Westboro Rd., North Grafton
(508) 839-7826

Animal ER
1634 W. Housatonic St., Pittsfield
(413) 997-3425

Veterinary Emergency & Specialty Hospital
141 Greenfield Rd., South Deerfield
(413) 665-4911

Cape Animal Referral & Emergency Center
79 Theophilus Smith Rd., South Dennis
(508) 398-7575

VCA South Shore Animal Hospital
595 Columbian St., South Weymouth
(781) 337-6622

Angell Animal Medical Center - Western New England
171 Union St., Springfield
(413) 785-1221

Boston Road Animal Hospital
1235 Boston Rd., Springfield
(413) 783-1203

Mass-RI Veterinary ER
477 Milford Rd., Swansea
(508) 730-1112

Tufts Veterinary Emergency Treatment and Specialties (Tufts VETS)
525 South St., Walpole
(508) 668-5454

Vetcision Hospitals
293 Second Ave., Waltham
(781) 810-1010

Veterinary Emergency & Specialty Center of New England
180 Bear Hill Rd., Waltham
(781) 684-8387

New England Animal Medical Center
595 W. Center St., West Bridgewater
(508) 580-2515

Massachusetts Veterinary Referral Hospital
20 Cabot Rd., Woburn
(781) 932-5802

Woburn Animal Hospital
373 Russell St., Woburn
(718) 933-0170

MICHIGAN

Affiliated Veterinary Emergency Service, P.C.
15220 Southfield Rd., Allen Park
(313) 389-1700

Animal Emergency Clinic
4126 Packard Rd., Ann Arbor
(734) 971-8774

Ann Arbor Animal Hospital
2150 W. Liberty St., Ann Arbor
(734) 662-4474

Emergency Veterinary Hospital
5245 Jackson Rd., Ann Arbor
(734) 369-6446

Michigan Veterinary Specialists
3412 E. Walton Blvd., Auburn Hills
(248) 371-3713

Oakland Veterinary Emergency & Critical Care
1400 Telegraph Rd., Bloomfield Hills
(248) 334-6877

Oakland Veterinary Emergency Group
1948 Telegraph Rd., Bloomfield Hills
(248) 334-1555

Animal Emergency Hospital of Macomb
43731 N. Gratiot Ave., Clinton Township
(586) 307-3730

Animal ER Center
1120 Welch Rd., Commerce
(248) 960-7200

Veterinary Emergency Service - West
24400 Ford Rd., Dearborn Heights
(313) 274-3300

Michigan State University Veterinary Teaching Hospital
736 Wilson Rd., East Lansing
(517) 353-5420

Animal Emergency Hospital
1007 S. Ballenger Hwy., Flint
(810) 238-7557

Animal Emergency Hospital
3260 Plainfield Ave. N.E., Grand Rapids
(616) 361-9911

Michigan Veterinary Specialists
1425 Michigan St. N.E., Suite F, Grand Rapids
(616) 284-5300

Southwest Michigan Animal Emergency Hospital
3301 S. Burdick St., Kalamazoo
(616) 381-5228

Lansing Veterinary Urgent Care
3276 E. Jolly Rd., Lansing
(517) 393-9200

Veterinary Emergency Service - East
28223 John R Rd., Madison Heights
(248) 547-4677

Veterinary Care Specialists
205 Rowe Rd., Milford
(248) 684-0468

Animal Emergency Center
24360 Novi Rd., Novi
(248) 348-1788

Veterinary Emergency Service - West
40850 Ann Arbor Rd., Plymouth
(734) 207-8500

Animal Emergency Center
265 E. 2nd St., Rochester
(248) 651-1788

Great Lakes Pet Emergencies
1221 Tittabawassee Rd., Saginaw
(989) 752-1960

Michigan Veterinary Specialists
29080 Inkster Rd., Southfield
(248) 354-6660

MINNESOTA

South Metro Animal Emergency Care
14690 Pennock Ave., Apple Valley
(952) 953-3737

Affiliated Emergency Veterinary Service
11850 Aberdeen St. N.E., Blaine
(763) 754-5000

Affiliated Emergency Veterinary Hospital
1615 Coon Rapids Blvd., Coon Rapids
(763) 754-9434

Affiliated Emergency Veterinary Service
2314 W. Michigan St., Duluth
(218) 302-8000

Affiliated Emergency Veterinary Service
7717 Flying Cloud Dr., Eden Prairie
(952) 942-8272

Affiliated Emergency Veterinary Service
4708 Hwy. 55, Golden Valley
(763) 529-6560

Animal Emergency Clinic
1163 Helmo Ave. N., Oakdale
(651) 501-3766

Affiliated Emergency Veterinary Service
121 23rd Ave. S.W., Rochester
(507) 424-3976

Affiliated Emergency Veterinary Service
4180 Thielman Ln., Suite 120, St. Cloud
(320) 258-3481

Animal Emergency Clinic
301 University Ave., St. Paul
(651) 293-1800

University of Minnesota, College of Veterinary
Medicine - Veterinary Medical Center
1365 Gortner Ave., St. Paul
(612) 626-8387

MISSISSIPPI
Gulf Coast Veterinary Emergency Hospital
13095 Hwy. 67, Biloxi
(228) 392-7474

MISSOURI
Animal Emergency Clinic
7095 Metropolitan Blvd., Suite G, Barnhart
(636) 464-2846

Animal Emergency Clinic
12501 Natural Bridge Rd., Bridgeton
(314) 739-1500

University of Missouri - Veterinary Med. Teaching
Hospital
900 E. Campus Dr., Columbia
(573) 882-7821

Animal Emergency Center
8141 N. Oak Trfy., Kansas City
(816) 455-5430

Animal Emergency & Referral Hospital
3495 N.E. Ralph Powell Rd., Lee's Summit
(816) 554-4990

VSS Emergency Center
1021 Howard George Dr., Manchester
(636) 227-6100

Animal Emergency Clinic
334 Fort Zumwalt Sq., O'Fallon
(636) 240-5496

Emergency Veterinary Clinic of Southwest Missouri
400 S. Glenstone Ave., Springfield
(417) 890-1600

Animal Emergency Clinic
9937 Big Bend Blvd., St. Louis
(314) 822-7600

Animal Emergency & Referral Center
16457 Village Plaza View Dr., Wildwood
(636) 458-1777

MONTANA
Pet Emergency Center
1914 S. Reserve St., Missoula
(406) 829-9300

NEBRASKA
United Vet Emergency Treatment Services
3700 S. 9th St., Lincoln
(402) 489-6800

Animal Emergency Clinic
9664 Mockingbird Dr., Omaha
(402) 339-6232

NEVADA
Animal Emergency Center of Las Vegas
3340 E. Patrick Ln., Las Vegas
(702) 457-8050

Las Vegas Animal Emergency Hospital
5231 W. Charleston Blvd., Las Vegas
(702) 822-1045

Veterinary Emergency and Critical Care Center
8650 W. Tropicana Ave., Suite B-104, Las Vegas
(702) 262-7070

Warm Springs Veterinary Emergency Clinic
2500 W. Warm Springs Rd., Las Vegas
(702) 614-5454

Animal Emergency Center of Reno
6425 S. Virginia St., Reno
(775) 851-3600

NEW HAMPSHIRE
Capital Area Veterinary Emergency Service
1 Intervale Rd., Concord
(603) 227-1199

Small Animal Veterinary Emergency Service
63 Evans Dr., Lebanon
(603) 306-0007

Veterinary Emergency Center of Manchester
336 Abby Rd., Manchester
(603) 666-6677

Winnipesaukee Veterinary Emergency Center
8 Maple Street, Suite 2, Meredith
(603) 279-1117

The Animal Hospital of Nashua
168 Main Dunstable Rd., Nashua
(603) 880-3034

Animal Medical Center of New England
168 Main Dunstable Rd., Nashua
(603) 821-7222

The Veterinary Emergency, Critical Care & Cancer
Center of New Hampshire
15 Piscataqua Dr., Portsmouth
(603) 431-3600

Port City Veterinary Referral Hospital
215 Commerce Way, Suite 100, Portsmouth
(603) 433-0056

Rockingham Emergency Veterinary Hospital
3 Cobbetts Pond Rd., Windham
(603) 870-9770

NEW JERSEY
Animal Emergency & Referral Associates
1237 Bloomfield Ave., Fairfield
(973) 226-3282

Central Jersey Veterinary Emergency Service
643 Rt. 27, Iselin
(732) 283-3535

Jersey Shore Veterinary Emergency Service
1000 Rt. 70, Lakewood
(732) 363-3200

Crown Veterinary Specialists
23 Blossom Hill Rd., Lebanon
(908) 236-4120

Red Bank Veterinary Hospital Linwood
535 Maple Ave., Linwood
(609) 926-5300

North Jersey Veterinary Emergency Services
724 Ridge Rd., Lyndhurst
(201) 438-7122

Animal Emergency Service of South Jersey
220 Moorestown-Mount Laurel Rd., Mount Laurel
(856) 727-1332

Newton Veterinary Hospital
116 Hampton House Rd., Newton
(973) 383-4321

Oradell Animal Hospital
580 Winters Ave., Paramus
(201) 262-0010

Alliance Emergency Veterinary Clinic
540 Rt. 10 W., Randolph
(973) 328-2844

Animerge
21 Rt. 206 N., Raritan
(908) 707-9077

NorthStar VETS
315 Robbinsville-Allentown Rd., Robbinsville
(609) 259-8300

Garden State Veterinary Specialists
1 Pine St., Tinton Falls
(732) 922-0011

Red Bank Veterinary Hospital
197 Hance Ave., Tinton Falls
(732) 747-3636

Regional Veterinary Emergency & Specialty Center
4250 Rt. 42, Turnersville
(856) 728-1400

NEW MEXICO

Staley's Veterinary Medical Clinic
1407 Indian Wells Rd., Alamogordo
(505) 437-3063

Veterinary Emergency & Specialty Center of New Mexico
4000 Montgomery Blvd. N.E., Albuquerque
(505) 884-3433

ABQ PetCare Hospital
9032 Montgomery Blvd. N.E., Albuquerque
(505) 299-8387

Veterinary Emergency & Specialty Center of Santa Fe
2001 Vivigen Way, Santa Fe
(505) 984-0625

NEW YORK

Greater Buffalo Veterinary Emergency Clinic
4949 Main St., Amherst
(716) 839-4044

Veterinary Emergency & Critical Care Center
2115 Downer Street Rd., Baldwinsville
(315) 638-3500

Katonah Bedford Veterinary Center
546 N. Bedford Rd., Bedford Hills
(914) 241-7700

Atlantic Coast Veterinary Specialists
3250 Veterans Memorial Hwy., Bohemia
(631) 285-7780

Veterinary Emergency & Referral Group
318 Warren St., Brooklyn
(718) 522-9400

Animal Emergency Service
6230-C Jericho Tpke., Commack
(631) 462-6044

Veterinary Medical Center of Central New York
5841 Bridge St., Suite 200, East Syracuse
(315) 446-7933

New York Veterinary Specialty & Emergency Center
2233 Broadhollow Rd., Farmingdale
(631) 694-3400

Natural Vet For Pets, P.C.
585 Warburton Ave., Hastings-on-Hudson
(914) 478-4100

Animal Emergency Clinic of the Hudson Valley
1112 Morton Blvd., Kingston
(845) 336-0713

Capital District Animal Emergency Clinic
222 Troy Schenectady Rd., Latham
(518) 785-1094

Orange County Animal Emergency Service
517 Rt. 211 E., Middletown
(845) 692-0260

Ultravet Diagnostics
220 E. Jericho Tpke., Mineola
(516) 294-6680

Flannery Animal Hospital
789 Little Britain Rd., New Windsor
(845) 565-7387

BluePearl - Manhattan
410 W. 55th St., New York
(212) 767-0099

Fifth Avenue Veterinary Specialists
1 W. 15th St., New York
(212) 924-3311

Manhattan Veterinary Group
240 E. 80th St., New York
(212) 988-1000

Orchard Park Veterinary Medical Center
3930 N. Buffalo Rd., Orchard Park
(716) 662-6660

Long Island Veterinary Specialists / Animal Emergency & Critical Care Center
163 S. Service Rd., Plainview
(516) 501-1700

Animal Emergency Clinic of the Hudson Valley
84 Patrick Ln., Poughkeepsie
(845) 471-8242

East End Veterinary Emergency Center
67 Commerce Dr., Riverhead
(631) 369-4513

Animal Hospital of Pittsford
2816 Monroe Ave., Rochester
(716) 271-7700

Veterinary Specialists & Emergency Service
825 White Spruce Blvd., Rochester
(585) 424-1277

Animal Hospital of the Rockaways
114-10 Beach Channel Dr., Rockaway Park
(718) 474-0500

Animal Emergency Service
280-L Middle Country Rd., Selden
(631) 698-2225

Valley Cottage Animal Hospital
202 Rt. 303, Valley Cottage
(845) 268-9263

Central Veterinary Associates
73 W. Merrick Rd., Valley Stream
(516) 825-3066

VCA Veterinary Referral & Emergency Center of Westbury
609-5 Cantiague Rock Rd., Westbury
(516) 420-0000

Nassau Animal Emergency Hospital
740 Old Country Rd., Westbury
(516) 333-6262

The Veterinary Emergency Group
193 Tarrytown Rd., White Plains
(914) 949-8779

Animal Specialty Center
9 Odell Plaza, Yonkers
(914) 457-4000

NORTH CAROLINA

Small Animal Emergency Services
1335 N. Sandhills Blvd., Aberdeen
(910) 944-0405

Regional Emergency Animal Care Hospital (REACH)
677 Brevard Rd., Asheville
(828) 665-4399

Animal Emergency Clinic of the High Country
1126 Blowing Rock Rd., Suite A, Boone
(828) 268-2833

Animal Emergency Clinic of Cary
220 High House Rd., Cary
(919) 462-8989

Veterinary Specialty Hospital of the Carolinas
6405 Tryon Rd., Cary
(919) 233-4911

Animal Medical Hospital
3832 Monroe Rd., Charlotte
(704) 334-4684

Carolina Veterinary Specialists - Animal Emergency & Trauma Center
2225 Township Rd., Charlotte
(704) 504-9608

Triangle Veterinary Referral Hospital
608 Morreene Rd., Durham
(919) 489-0615

After Hours Veterinary Emergency Clinic
5505 W. Friendly Ave., Greensboro
(336) 851-1990

Carolina Veterinary Specialists - Animal Emergency & Trauma Center
501 Nicholas Rd., Greensboro
(336) 632-0605

Happy Tails Veterinary Emergency Clinic
2936 Battleground Ave., Greensboro
(336) 288-2688

Pet Emergency Clinic of Pitt County
2207-A Evans St., Greenville
(252) 321-1521

Veterinary Referral Hospital of Hickory
126 Hwy. 321 S.W., Hickory
(828) 328-2660

Carolina Veterinary Specialists - Animal Emergency & Trauma Center
12117 Statesville Rd., Huntersville
(704) 949-1100

Cabarrus Emergency Veterinary Clinic
1317 S. Cannon Blvd., Kannapolis
(704) 932-1182

Charlotte Veterinary Emergency & Trauma Services
2440 Plantation Center Dr., Matthews
(704) 844-6440

After Hours Animal Emergency Clinic
409 Vick Ave., Raleigh
(919) 781-5145

North Carolina State University Small Animal Emergency Service
4700 Hillsborough St., Raleigh
(919) 513-6130

Quail Corners Animal Hospital & 24 Hour Emergency Care
1613 E. Millbrook Rd., Raleigh
(919) 876-0739

Thomasville Veterinary Hospital, P.A.
303 National Hwy., Thomasville
(336) 475-9119

Eastern Carolina Veterinary Emergency Treatment Services
4909-D Expressway Dr., Wilson
(252) 265-9920

Animal Emergency Services of Forsyth County
7781 North Point Blvd., Winston-Salem
(336) 377-2866

Carolina Veterinary Specialists - Animal Emergency & Trauma Center
1600 Hanes Mall Blvd., Winston-Salem
336-896-0902

NORTH DAKOTA
Red River Animal Emergency Clinic
1401 Oak Manor Ave. S., Suite 2, Fargo
701-478-9299

OHIO
Akron Veterinary Referral & Emergency Center
1321 Centerview Cir., Akron
(330) 665-4996

Animal Emergency Clinic West
2101 N. Cleveland-Massillon Rd., Akron
(216) 362-6001

Metropolitan Veterinary Hospital
1053 S. Cleveland-Massillon Rd., Akron
(330) 666-2976

VCA Great Lakes Veterinary Specialists
5035 Richmond Rd., Bedford Heights
(216) 831-6789

Animal Emergency Clinic West
5320 W. 140th St., Brook Park
(216) 362-6000

Stark County Veterinary Emergency Clinic, LLC
2705 Fulton Dr. N.W., Canton
(330) 452-5117

Cincinnati Animal Referral and Emergency (CARE) Care Center
6995 E. Kemper Rd., Cincinnati
(513) 530-0911

Capital Veterinary Referral & Emergency Center
5230 Renner Rd., Columbus
(614) 870-0480

Ohio State University Veterinary Medical Center
601 Vernon Tharp St., Columbus
(614) 292-3551

Dayton Care Center
6405 Clyo Rd., Dayton
(937) 428-0911

Dayton Emergency Veterinary Clinic
2714 Springboro W., Dayton
(937) 293-2714

After Hours Animal Emergency Clinic, Inc.
2680 W. Liberty St., Girard
(330) 530-8387

Animal Emergency & Specialty Center
5152 Grove Ave., Lorain
(440) 240-1400

Aaron Animal Clinic and Emergency Hospital
7640 Broadview Rd., Parma
(216) 901-9980

Animal Emergency & Critical Care Center of Toledo, Inc.
2785 W. Central Ave., Toledo
(419) 473-0328

VCA Green Animal Medical Center
1620 Corporate Woods Cir., Uniontown
(330) 896-4040

Cleveland Road Animal Hospital
2752 Cleveland Rd., Wooster
(330) 345-6063

MedVet Associates, Ltd.
300 E. Wilson Bridge Rd., Worthington
(614) 846-5800

OKLAHOMA
Animal Emergency Center
931 S.W. 74th St., Oklahoma City
(405) 631-7828

Neel Veterinary Hospital
2700 N. MacArthur Blvd., Oklahoma City
(405) 947-8387

Veterinary Emergency and Critical Care Hospital
1800 W. Memorial Rd., Oklahoma City
(405) 749-6989

Animal Emergency Center, Inc.
4055 S. 102nd E. Ave., Tulsa
(918) 665-0508

OREGON
Animal Emergency Center of Central Oregon
1245 S.E. 3rd St., Suite C3, Bend
(541) 385-9110

Northwest Veterinary Specialists Emergency Service
16756 S.E. 82nd Dr., Clackamas
(503) 656-3999

Southern Oregon Veterinary Specialty Center
3265 Biddle Rd., Medford
(541) 282-7711

Dove Lewis Emergency Animal Hospital
1945 N.W. Pettygrove St., Portland
(503) 228-7281

VCA Southeast Portland Animal Hospital
13830 S.E. Stark St., Portland
(503) 255-8139

Salem Veterinary Emergency Clinic
3215 Market St. N.E., Salem
(503) 588-8082

Emergency Veterinary Hospital
103 W. Q St., Springfield
(541) 746-0112

Emergency Veterinary Clinic of Tualatin
19314 S.W. Mohave Ct., Tualatin
(503) 691-7922

PENNSYLVANIA

Veterinary Referral and Emergency Center
318 Northern Blvd., Clarks Summit
(570) 587-7777

Northwest Pennsylvania Pet Emergency Center
429 W. 38th St., Erie
(814) 866-5920

Keystone Veterinary Emergency and Referral
1200 W. Chester Pike, Havertown
(484) 454-5412

Center for Animal Referral and Emergency Services (CARES)
2010 Cabot Blvd. W., Suite D, Langhorne
(215) 750-2774

Gwynedd Veterinary Hospital and Emergency Service
1615 W. Point Pike, Lansdale
(215) 699-9294

Veterinary Specialty & Emergency Center
301 Veterans Hwy., Levittown
(215) 750-7884

Allegheny Veterinary Emergency Trauma & Specialty (AVETS)
4224 Northern Pike, Monroeville
(412) 373-4200

Metropolitan Veterinary Associates
2626 Van Buren Ave., Norristown
(610) 666-1050

Matthew J. Ryan Hospital for Small Animals - University of Pennsylvania
3900 Spruce St., Philadelphia
(215) 746-8911

Pittsburgh Veterinary Specialty & Emergency Center
807 Camp Horn Rd., Pittsburgh
(412) 366-3400

VCA Castle Shannon Animal Hospital Service
3610 Library Rd., Pittsburgh
(412) 885-2500

Hickory Veterinary Hospital
2303 Hickory Rd., Plymouth Meeting
(610) 828-3054

Creature Comforts Veterinary Service
Old Route 115, Saylorsburg
(570) 992-0400

Central Pennsylvania Veterinary Emergency Treatment Services
1522 Martin St., State College
(814) 237-4670

Bucks County Veterinary Emergency Trauma Service
978 Easton Rd., Warrington
(215) 918-2200

Animal Emergency Center
395 Susquehanna Tr., Watsontown
(570) 742-7400

Valley Central Emergency Veterinary Hospital
210 Fullerton Ave., Whitehall
(610) 435-5588

Animal Emergency and Referral Center of York
1640 S. Queen St., York
(717) 767-5355

RHODE ISLAND

Ocean State Veterinary Specialists
1480 S. County Tr., East Greenwich
(401) 886-6787

SOUTH CAROLINA

Charleston Veterinary Referral Center
3484 Shelby Ray Ct., Charleston
(843) 614-8387

Palmetto Regional Emergency Hospital for Animals
10298 Two Notch Rd., Columbia
(803) 865-1418

South Carolina Veterinary Emergency Care
3924 Fernandina Rd., Columbia
(803) 798-3837

Animal Emergency Clinic
393 Woods Lake Rd., Greenville
(864) 232-1878

Mt. Pleasant Emergency Veterinary Hospital
930-B Pine Hollow Rd., Mt. Pleasant
(843) 216-7554

Animal Emergency Hospital of the Strand
303 Hwy. 15, Suite 1, Myrtle Beach
(843) 445-9797

Coastal Carolina Veterinary Specialists
3163 W. Montague Ave., North Charleston
(843) 744-3372

Care Animal Regional Emergency Clinic of Spartanburg
1291 Asheville Hwy., Spartanburg
(864) 591-1923

SOUTH DAKOTA

Veterinary Emergency Hospital
3508 S. Minnesota Ave., Suite 104, Sioux Falls
(605) 977-6200

TENNESSEE

Midland Pet Emergency Center, Inc.
235 Calderwood St., Alcoa
(865) 982-1007

Airport Pet Emergency Clinic
2436 Hwy. 75, Blountville
(423) 279-0574

Affiliated Veterinary Specialists
1668 Mallory Ln., Brentwood
(615) 333-1212

Regional Institute for Veterinary Emergencies & Referrals
2132 Amnicola Hwy., Chattanooga
(423) 698-4612

Animal Emergency Clinic of Maury County, LLC
1900B Shady Brook St., Columbia
(931) 380-1929

PetMed Emergency Center, LLC
830 N. Germantown Pkwy., Suite 105, Cordova
(901) 624-9002

Jackson Pet Emergency Clinic, LLC
2815-D N. Highland, Jackson
(731) 660-4343

Knoxville Pet Emergency Clinic
1819 Ailor Ave., Knoxville
(865) 637-0114

University of Tennessee Veterinary Teaching Hospital
2407 River Dr., Knoxville
(865) 974-8387

Animal Medical Center
234 River Rock Blvd., Murfreesboro
(615) 867-7575

Nashville Pet Emergency Clinic
2000 12th Ave. S., Nashville
(615) 383-2600

Nashville Veterinary Specialists & Animal Emergency
2971 Sidco Dr., Nashville
(615) 386-0107

TEXAS

I-20 Animal Medical Center
5820 W. I-20, Arlington
(817) 478-9238

AM/PM Animal Hospital
2239 S. Lamar Blvd., Austin
(512) 448-2676

Austin Vet Care - Central
4106 N. Lamar Blvd., Austin
(512) 459-4336

Emergency Animal Hospital of Northwest Austin - North Branch
12034 Research Blvd., Suite 8, Austin
(512) 331-6121

Emergency Animal Hospital of Northwest Austin - South Branch
4434 Frontier Tr., Austin
(512) 899-0955

White Angel Animal Hospital
1901 RR 620 N., Austin
(512) 266-7838

Southeast Texas Animal Emergency Clinic
3420 W. Cardinal Dr., Beaumont
(409) 842-3239

Burleson Animal Emergency Hospital
805 N.E. Alsbury Blvd., Burleson
(817) 447-9194

North Texas Emergency Pet Clinic
1712 W. Frankford Rd., Suite 108, Carrolton
(972) 323-1310

Texas A&M University Veterinary Teaching Hospital
4475 TAMU, College Station
(979) 845-3541

Heritage Veterinary Hospital
3930 Glade Rd., Suite 120, Colleyville
(817) 358-0404

Emergency Animal Clinic
12101 Greenville Ave., Suite 118, Dallas
(972) 994-9110

The E-Clinic, Inc.
3337 Fitzhugh Ave., Dallas
(214) 520-8388

Grayson County Animal Emergency Clinic
3301 Woodlawn Blvd., Denison
(903) 337-0898

Denton County Animal Emergency Room
4145 S. I-35E, Suite 101, Denton
(940) 271-1200

El Paso Animal Emergency Center
1220 Airway Blvd., El Paso
(915) 203-0818

Airport Freeway Animal Emergency Clinic
411 N. Main St., Euless
(817) 571-2088

DFW North Emergency Veterinary Clinic
2311 Cross Timbers, Suite 319, Flower Mound
(469) 464-2964

Metro West Emergency Veterinary Center
3201 Hulen St., Fort Worth
(817) 731-3734

Animal Emergency Hospital of North Texas
2700 W. Hwy. 114, Grapevine
(817) 410-2273

Animal Emergency Center of West Houston
4823 Hwy. 6N, Houston
(832) 593-8387

Animal Emergency Clinic SH 249
18707 SH 249, Houston
(281) 890-8875

Animal Emergency Clinic Southeast
10331 Gulf Frwy., Houston
(713) 941-8460

Houston Veterinary Services, Inc.
111 West Loop S., #200, Houston
(713) 693-1100

Veterinary Emergency Referral Group, Inc.
8921 Katy Frwy., Houston
(713) 932-9589

Animal Emergency Clinic North East
10205 Birchridge Dr., Humble
(281) 446-4900

VCA Metroplex Animal Hospital & Pet Lodge
700 W. Airport Frwy., Irving
(972) 438-7113

After Hours Veterinary Services
2501 S. W.S. Young, Suite 413, Killeen
(254) 628-5017

VCA Animal Emergency Hospital Southeast Calder Road
1108 Gulf Frwy. S., Suite 280, League City
(281) 332-1678

Lake Ray Hubbard Emergency Pet Care Center
4651 N. Belt Line Rd., Mesquite
(972) 226-3377

Emergency Pet Care of Round Rock
301 Chisholm Tr., Round Rock
(512) 961-5200

Angel of Mercy Animal Critical Care, Inc.
8734 Grissom Rd., San Antonio
(210) 684-2105

Animal Emergency Room
4315 Fredericksburg Rd., Suite 2, San Antonio
(210) 737-7380

Emergency Pet Center
8503 Broadway #105, San Antonio
(210) 822-2873

Emergency Pet Center
280 I-35, Suite 100, San Antonio
(830) 609-2873

Emergency Pet Center
503 E. Sonterra Blvd., Suite 103, San Antonio
(210) 404-2873

I-10 Pet Emergency
10822 Fredericksburg Rd., San Antonio
(210) 691-0900

Northeast Emergency Animal Clinic
8365 Perrin Beitel, San Antonio
(210) 650-3141

Animal Emergency Clinic - Sugar Land
9920 Hwy. 90A, Suite 100C, Sugar Land
(281) 340-8387

Southwest Freeway Animal Hospital & Emergency Center
15575 Southwest Frwy., Sugar Land
(281) 491-8387

Sugar Land Veterinary Specialists & Emergency Center
1515 Lake Pointe Pkwy., Sugar Land
(281) 491-7800

Texas Animal Medical Center
4900 Steinbeck Bend, Waco
(254) 753-0901

Animal Emergency & Urgent Care Center of the Woodlands
27870 I-45 N., The Woodlands
(281) 367-5444

UTAH
Central Emergency Animal Hospital
55 E. Miller Ave., Salt Lake City
(801) 487-1325

Pet E.R. - The Pet Emergency Room
6360 S. Highland Dr., Salt Lake City
(801) 278-3367

Animal Emergency Center
2465 N. Main St., Suite 5, Sunset
(801) 776-8118

VERMONT
Burlington Emergency & Veterinary Specialists
200 Commerce St., Williston
(802) 863-2387

VIRGINIA
Alexandria Veterinary Emergency Service
2660 Duke St., Alexandria
(703) 823-3601

Greenbrier Emergency Animal Hospital
370 Greenbrier Dr., Suite A-2, Charlottesville
(434) 202-1616

Veterinary Emergency Treatment Service & Specialty
1540 Airport Rd., Charlottesville
(434) 973-3519

Greenbrier Veterinary Emergency Center
1100 Eden Way N., Suite 101B, Chesapeake
(757) 366-9000

SouthPaws Veterinary Referral Center
8500 Arlington Blvd., Fairfax
(703) 752-9100

Fredericksburg Regional Veterinary Emergency Center, LLC
2301 1/2 Jefferson Davis Hwy., Fredericksburg
(540) 372-3470

Animal Emergency Critical Care Associates
165 Fort Evans Rd. N.E., Leesburg
(703) 777-5755

Animal Emergency & Critical Care of Lynchburg
3432 Odd Fellows Rd., Lynchburg
(434) 846-1504

Veterinary Referral & Critical Care (VRCC)
1596 Hockett Rd., Manakin Sabot
(804) 784-8722

Prince William Emergency Veterinary Clinic
8610 Centreville Rd., Manassas
(703) 361-8287

Veterinary Emergency & Specialty Center - Midlothian
2460 Colony Crossing Pl., Midlothian
(804) 744-9800

Blue Ridge Veterinary Associates
120 E. Cornwell Ln., Purcellville
(540) 338-7387

Veterinary Emergency & Specialty Center - Carytown
3312 W. Cary St., Richmond
(804) 353-9000

Emergency Veterinary Services of Roanoke
4902 Frontage Rd. N.W., Roanoke
(540) 563-8575

Regional Veterinary Referral Center
6651 Backlick Rd., Springfield
(703) 451-8900

The Cove Center of Veterinary Expertise
6550 Hampton Roads Pkwy., Suite 113, Suffolk
(757) 935-9111

The Hope Center for Advanced Veterinary Medicine
140 Park St. S.E., Vienna
(703) 242-4732

Beach Veterinary Emergency Clinic
1124 Lynnhaven Pkwy., Virginia Beach
(757) 468-4900

Tidewater Veterinary Emergency & Critical Care Center
364 S. Independence Blvd., Virginia Beach
(757) 499-5463

Valley Emergency Veterinary Clinic, LLC
164-4 Garber Ln., Winchester
(540) 662-7811

Woodbridge Animal Hospital
2703 Caton Hill Rd., Woodbridge
(703) 897-5665

Animal Emergency Center
5007 Victory Blvd., Yorktown
(757) 234-0461

Peninsula Emergency Veterinary Clinic
1120 George Washington Memorial Hwy., Yorktown
(757) 874-8115

WASHINGTON

After Hours Animal Emergency Clinic
718 Auburn Way N., Auburn
(253) 939-6272

Animal Emergency Care
317 Telegraph Rd., Bellingham
(360) 758-2200

Animal Emergency Clinic of Everett
3625 Rucker Ave., Everett
(425) 258-4466

VCA Alpine Animal Hospital
888 N.W. Sammamish Rd., Issaquah
(425) 392-8888

Animal Emergency Service, East
636 7th Ave., Kirkland
(425) 827-8727

Seattle Veterinary Specialists
11814 115th Ave. N.E., Suite 102, Kirkland
(425) 823-9111

Agape Pet Emergency Center
16418 7th Pl. W., Lynnwood
(425) 741-2688

VCA Veterinary Specialty Center of Seattle
20115 44th Ave. W., Lynnwood
(425) 697-6106

Pet Emergency Center
14434 Avon Allen Rd., Mount Vernon
(360) 848-5911

Mid-Columbia Pet Emergency Services
8913 Sandifur Pkwy., Pasco
(509) 547-3577

Animal Emergency & Trauma Center
320 Lindvig Way, Poulsbo
(360) 697-7771

VCA Central Kitsap Animal Hospital
10310 Central Valley Rd. N.E., Poulsbo
(360) 692-6162

Washington State University
Veterinary Teaching Hospital, 100 Grimes Way, Pullman
(509) 335-0711

Animal Emergency Hospital of Redmond
16421 Cleveland St., Suite H, Redmond
(425) 250-7090

Animal Critical Care & Emergency Services (ACCES)
11536 Lake City Way, N.E., Seattle
(206) 364-1660

Emerald City Emergency Clinic
4102 Stone Way N., Seattle
(206) 634-9000

Five Corners Veterinary Hospital
15707 1st Ave. S., Seattle
(206) 243-2982

Animal Medical Center Of Seattle
14810 15th Ave N.E., Shoreline
(206) 204-3366

PSCVM Small Animal Emergency and Critical Care Center
11308 92nd St. S.E., Snohomish
(360) 563-5300

Pet Emergency Clinic
21 E. Mission Ave., Spokane
(509) 326-6670

Puget Sound Veterinary Referral Center - The Animal Emergency Clinic
5608 S. Durango St., Tacoma
(253) 474-0791

Summit Veterinary Referral Center
2505 S. 80th St., Tacoma
(253) 983-1114

Columbia River Veterinary Specialists
6818 N.E. Fourth Plain Blvd., Suite C, Vancouver
(360) 694-3007

St. Francis 24 Hr. Animal Hospital
12010 N.E. 65th St., Vancouver
(360) 253-5446

Yakima Pet Emergency Service
510 W. Chestnut Ave., Yakima
(509) 452-4138

WEST VIRGINIA

Kanawha Valley Animal Emergency Clinic
5304 MacCorkle Ave. S.W., Charleston
(304) 768-2911

Animal Urgent Care, Inc.
4201 Wood St., Wheeling
(304) 233-0002

WISCONSIN

Fox Valley Animal Referral Center
4706 New Horizons Blvd., Appleton
(920) 993-9193

Animal Emergency Center
2100 W. Silver Spring Dr., Glendale
(414) 540-6710

Green Bay Animal Emergency Center
933 Anderson Dr., Suite F, Green Bay
(920) 494-9400

Crawford Animal Hospital
4607 S. 108th St., Greenfield
(414) 543-3499

Emergency Clinic for Animals
229 W. Beltline Hwy., Madison
(608) 274-7772

University of Wisconsin Veterinary Teaching Hospital
2015 Linden Dr., Madison
(608) 263-7600

Veterinary Emergency Service
4902 E. Broadway, Madison
(608) 222-2455

Veterinary Emergency Service
1612 N. High Point Rd., Suite 100, Middleton
(608) 831-1101

Central Wisconsin Animal Emergency Center
1420 Kronenwetter Dr., Mosinee
(715) 693-6934

Lakeshore Veterinary Specialists & Emergency Hospital
207 W. Seven Hills Rd., Port Washington
(262) 268-7800

Animal ER / Critical Care of Southeast Wisconsin
4333 S. Green Bay Rd., Racine
(262) 553-9223

Wisconsin Veterinary Referral Center
360 Bluemound Rd., Waukesha
(262) 542-3241

Canada

ALBERTA

Calgary Animal Referral and Emergency Centre
7140 12th St. S.E., Calgary
(403) 520-8387

Calgary North Veterinary Hospital and Emergency Service
4204 4th St. N.W., Calgary
(403) 277-0135

McKnight 24 Hour Veterinary Hospital
34-5010 4th St. N.E., Calgary
(403) 457-0911

Western Veterinary Specialist & Emergency Centre
1802 10th Ave. S.W., Calgary
(403) 770-1340

Animal Emergency Hospital South, Ltd.
3823 99 St., Edmonton
(780) 436-5880

Edmonton Veterinarians Emergency Clinic
11104 102nd Ave., Edmonton
(780) 433-9505

BRITISH COLUMBIA

Animal Critical Care Group
1410 Boundary Rd., Burnaby
(604) 473-4882

Central Animal Emergency Clinic
812 Roderick Ave., Coquitlam
(604) 931-1911

Animal Emergency Clinic of the Fraser Valley
306-6325 204th St., Langley
(604) 514-1711

Mainland Animal Emergency Clinic
15338 Fraser Hwy., Surrey
(604) 588-4000

Vancouver Animal Emergency Clinic, Ltd.
1590 W. 4th St., Vancouver
(604) 734-5104

Central Victoria Veterinary Hospital
760 Roderick St., Victoria
(250) 475-2495

MANITOBA

Winnipeg Animal Emergency Clinic
400 Pembina Hwy., Winnipeg
(204) 452-9427

NOVA SCOTIA

Metro Animal Emergency Clinic
201 Brownlow Ave., Unit 32, Dartmouth
(902) 468-0674

ONTARIO

Veterinary Emergency Clinic of York Region
14879 Yonge St., Aurora
(905) 713-2323

Huronia Veterinary Emergency Clinic
115 Bell Farm Rd., Unit 110, Barrie
(705) 722-0377

Pet Hospital of Prince Edward and Hastings Counties
5529 Hwy. 62 S., Belleville
(613) 968-9956

Emergency Veterinary Clinic
#1 Wexford Rd., Brampton
(905) 495-9907

North Town Veterinary Hospital
496 Main St. N., Brampton
(905) 451-2000

Burgess Veterinary Emergency Clinic
775 Woodview Rd., Burlington
(905) 637-8111

Alta Vista Animal Health
2616 Bank St., Gloucester
(613) 731-9911

Halton-Wentworth Emergency Vet Clinic
505 King St. W., Hamilton
(905) 529-1004

London Veterinary Emergency Clinic
41 Adelaide St. N., Unit 43, London
(519) 432-7341

Mississauga-Oakville Veterinary Emergency Hospital
2285 Bristol Cir., Oakville
(905) 829-9444

Vaughan-Richmond Hill Veterinary Emergency Clinic
10303 Yonge St., Richmond Hill
(905) 884-1832

Niagara Veterinary Emergency Clinic
2F Tremont Dr., Unit 1, St. Catharines
(905) 641-3185

Toronto Veterinary Emergency Hospital
21 Rolark Dr., Scarborough
(416) 247-8387

Veterinary Emergency Clinic
920 Yonge St., #117, Toronto
(416) 920-2002

Veterinary Emergency Hospital of West Toronto
150 Norseman St., Toronto
(416) 239-3453

Animal Emergency Clinic
1910 Dundas St. E., Unit 122, Whitby
(905) 576-3031

QUEBEC

DMV Veterinary Centre
2300 54e Ave., Montreal
(514) 633-8888

Daubigny Veterinary Hospital
3349 Wilfrid-Hamel Blvd., Québec
(418) 872-5355

University of Montreal / Companion Animal Clinic
3200 Sicotte St., St.-Hyacinthe
(450) 778-8111

Pet-Friendly Lodgings

How to Use the Listings

U.S. Lodgings

Canadian Lodgings

Campground Listings

Some 14,000 AAA Approved hotels and campgrounds across North America accept traveling pets. This guide provides listings for those lodgings in the United States and Canada that roll out the welcome mat for pets as well as the people who love them.

For the purpose of this book, "pets" are domestic cats or dogs. If you are planning to travel with any other kind of animal — particularly such exotic pets as birds or reptiles — check with the property before making definite plans. Expect to keep nontraditional pets crated at all times.

Note: Always inform the management that you are traveling with an animal; you may be fined if you do not declare your pet. Many properties require guests with pets to sign a waiver or release form and to pay for the room with a credit card. Of course, whether you pay in cash or by credit card, you will be held liable for any damages caused by your pet, even if the property does not charge a deposit or pet fee. It is not a good idea to leave your pet unattended in the room, but if you must, crate him and notify management. When in public areas, keep your pet leashed and do not allow him to disturb other guests.

About the Listings

Geographic listings are used for accuracy and consistency; lodgings are listed under the city or town in which they physically are located — or in some cases under the nearest recognized city or town. For a complete list of all cities within a state or province, see the comprehensive City Index at the beginning of the corresponding section.

U.S. properties are shown first, followed by Canadian properties. Most listings are alphabetically organized by state or province, city and establishment name. Reflecting contemporary travel patterns, properties in some cities or towns may instead be listed within destination cities or areas. Such "vicinity cities" and their listings will be shown alphabetically in the destination city or area, and the vicinity city also will appear in alphabetical order in the City Index, along with the page number on which the listings begin.

Each listing provides the following information (see sample listing, next page):

❶ Symbol denoting Official Appointment (OA) properties. The OA program permits properties to display and advertise the ⒶⒶⒶ or ⒶⒶ logo. OAs have a special interest in serving AAA/CAA members. Ask if they offer special member amenities such as free breakfast, early check-in/late check-out, free room upgrade, free local phone calls, etc.

❷ Diamond Rating

❸ Property name

❹ Lodging classification
(see next page for descriptions)

❺ Special amenities offered. These properties provide an additional benefit to pets, such as treats, toys or gifts, pet sitting and/or walking, a pet menu, food/water dishes, pet sheets or pillows, pet beds or other extras.

❻ Telephone number

❼ Two-person (2P) rate year-round, and cancellation notice validity period (if more than 48 hours). Rates listed are daily. **Note:** Most establishments accept credit cards, but a small number require cash, so please call ahead to verify. "Call for rates" indicates rates were not available at time of printing. Please contact property for current rate information.

❽ Physical address and/or highway location, if available

❾ Exterior or interior corridors

❿ Pet policies. If the phrase "pets accepted" appears, the property does accept pets but specific information was unavailable at press time. Otherwise, pet-specific policies are denoted as follows:

Size. "Very small" denotes pets weighing up to 10 pounds; "small," up to 25 pounds; "medium," up to 50 pounds; and "large," up to 100 pounds. If no size is specified, the property accepts pets of all sizes.

Species. "Other" indicates the property accepts animals other than dogs and cats. Always call ahead and specify the type of pet you plan to bring.

Deposits and fees. Includes the dollar amount, the type of charge (refundable deposit or nonrefundable fee), the frequency of the charge and whether the charge is per pet or per room.

Designated rooms. Guests with pets are placed in certain rooms, often smoking rooms or those on the ground floor.

Housekeeping service. The phrase "service with restrictions" denotes properties that require the pet to be crated, removed or attended by the owner during housekeeping service.

Supervision. The pet is required to be supervised at all times.

Crate. The pet must be crated when the owner is not present.

⓫ Member values, services and facilities:

ECO Indicates lodgings that have been certified by well-established government and/or private eco-certification organizations. For more information about these organizations and their programs, visit AAA.com/eco.

🔌 Electric vehicle charging station on premises. Station locations are provided by Department of Energy.

SAVE Discounted standard room rate or lowest public rate available at time of booking for dates of stay

📶 Wireless Internet service on premises

⊠ Smoke-free premises

♿M Accessible features
(call property for available
services and amenities)

📶 Refrigerator

📟 Coffee maker

🍴 Restaurant on premises

🏊 Pool

☒ Recreational activities

📵 No air conditioning

📺 No TV

☎ No telephones

Please note: Some in-room amenities represented by the icons in the listings may be available only in selected rooms, and may incur an extra fee. Please inquire when making your reservations.

It is important to remember that animal policies do change; always confirm policies, restrictions and fees with the lodging when making reservations and again 1-2 days before departure.

Listing information is subject to change. All listing information was accurate at press time. However, lodging rates and policies change and the publisher cannot be held liable for changes occurring after publication. AAA cannot guarantee the safety of guests or their pets at any facility.

AAA Diamond Ratings

Before a property is listed by AAA, it must satisfy a set of minimum standards regarding basic lodging needs as identified by AAA members. If a property meets those requirements (determined during an unannounced evaluation by a AAA inspector), it is assigned a Diamond Rating.

Once an establishment becomes AAA Approved, it is then assigned a rating of one to five Diamonds, indicat-

ing the extensiveness of its facilities, amenities and services, from basic to moderate to luxury. The Diamond Ratings guide members in selecting establishments appropriately matched to their needs and expectations.

▽ Budget-oriented, offering basic comfort and hospitality.

▽▽ Affordable, with modestly enhanced facilities, décor and amenities.

▽▽▽ Distinguished, multi-faceted with enhanced physical attributes, amenities and guest comforts.

▽▽▽▽ Refined, stylish with upscale physical attributes, extensive amenities and a high degree of hospitality, service and attention to detail.

▽▽▽▽▽ Ultimate luxury, sophistication and comfort with extraordinary physical attributes, meticulous personalized service, extensive amenities and impeccable standard of excellence.

Lodging Classifications

BB **Bed & Breakfast:** Typically small-scale, emphasizing personal touches. Individually decorated units may not include televisions, telephones or private bathrooms. Usually a common room and continental or full, hot breakfast.

CA **Cabin/Cottage:** Vacation-oriented, typically small-scale, free-standing units with simple construction, homey design and basic décor. Often in wooded, rural or waterfront location. Cleaning supplies, utensils and bath linens provided. Check-in may be off site.

CO **Condominium:** Vacation-oriented, commonly for extended stays. Routinely rented through a management company. Generally one or more bedrooms, living room, full kitchen and eating area. Studio units combine sleeping and living areas. Cleaning supplies, utensils and linens provided. Check-in may be off site.

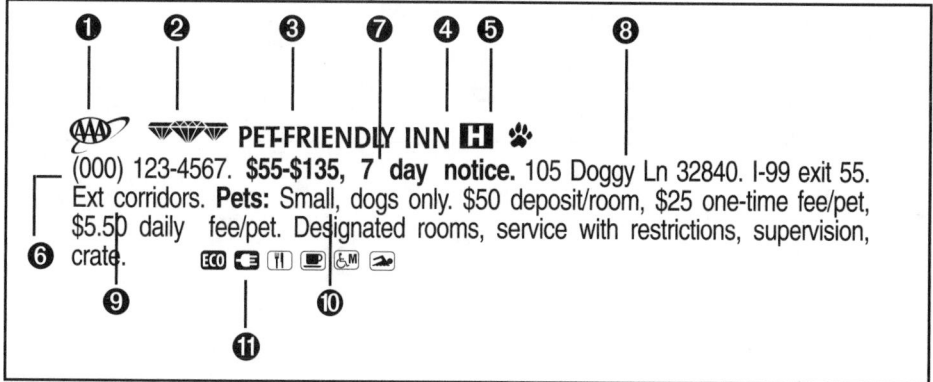

CI Country Inn: Similar to bed and breakfasts but larger scale with spacious public areas and dining facility that serves, at a minimum, breakfast and dinner.

H Hotel: Commonly multistory with interior room entrances. Unit styles vary. Public areas determined by overall theme, location and service level, but may include restaurant, shops, fitness center, spa, business center and meeting rooms.

M Motel: Commonly one- or two-story with exterior room entrances and drive-up parking. Typically one bedroom with bathroom. Limited public areas and facilities.

RA Ranch: Typically a working ranch with rustic, Western theme, equestrian activities and various unit styles.

VH Vacation Rental House: Commonly for extended stays. Typically large scale, freestanding and of varying design. Routinely rented through a management company. Often two or more bedrooms, living room, full kitchen, dining room and multiple bathrooms. Cleaning supplies, utensils and linens supplied. Check-in may be off site.

Campground Listings

Camping information provided by Woodall's®

Geographic listings are used for accuracy and consistency. Campgrounds are listed under the city or town in which they physically are located — or in some cases under the nearest recognized city or town. Not all listings include physical addresses. U.S. campgrounds are listed first, followed by Canadian campgrounds. Listings are alphabetically organized by state or province, city and campground name.

Note: Call first before taking your pet on a camping trip, as campground policies regarding pets may change, including any possible fees that may be assessed.

Each listing provides the following information (see sample listing):

❶ Location

❷ Campground name

❸ Symbol denoting Official Appointment (OA) campgrounds. The OA program permits privately operated Campgrounds to display and advertise the AAA or CAA logo. OAs have a special interest in serving AAA/CAA members.

❹ Telephone number

❺ Two-person rates are listed as minimum to maximum and include any additional fees that may typically be found at the site such as air conditioning, TV service and heating. Rates and discounts are subject to change. "Call for rates" indicates rates were not available at time of printing. Please contact property for current rate information.

❻ Most campgrounds accept any or all of the major credit cards, including American Express, MasterCard and Visa. If a campground accepts only cash, the phrase "(no credit cards)" appears.

❼ Physical address and/or highway location and mailing address (if available).

❽ Member values, services and facilities:

🚫 No Tents

🏊 Pool

🎯 Recreational activities

♿ Accessible features
(call property for available services and amenities)

United States Lodgings

ALABAMA

ABBEVILLE

BEST WESTERN-Abbeville Inn M

(334) 585-5060. **$65-$80.** 1237 US Hwy 431 S 36310. Jct SR 27. Ext corridors. **Pets:** Accepted. SAVE

ALBERTVILLE

Microtel Inn & Suites by Wyndham Albertville H

(256) 894-4000. **$69-$79.** 220 Hwy 75 N 35951. Jct US 431 and SR 75, just ne. Int corridors. **Pets:** Accepted.

Quality Inn H

(256) 891-2600. **$80.** 315 Martling Rd 35950. On US 431, just e of SR 75. Ext corridors. **Pets:** Accepted.

ALEXANDER CITY

Baymont Inn & Suites Alexander City H

(256) 234-7099. **$79-$99.** 4335 US Hwy 280 35010. US 280, just s of jct SR 22; just w of jct SR 63. Ext corridors. **Pets:** Accepted.

ANDALUSIA

Econo Lodge M

(334) 222-7511. **Call for rates.** 1421 Dr MLK Jr Expwy 36420. On US 84 Bypass. Ext corridors. **Pets:** Small. $10 daily fee/pet. No service, supervision. SAVE

ARAB

Quality Inn H

(256) 586-5777. **$89-$99.** 706 N Brindlee Mountain Pkwy 35016. On US 231, 0.5 mi n of jct SR 69. Ext corridors. **Pets:** Small. $15 daily fee/pet. Service with restrictions, supervision.

ATHENS

BEST WESTERN Athens Inn H

(256) 233-4030. **$70-$100, 3 day notice.** 1329 Hwy 72 35611. I-65 exit 351, just w. Ext corridors. **Pets:** Medium. $20 daily fee/pet. Designated rooms, service with restrictions, supervision. SAVE

Quality Inn Athens H

(256) 232-0030. **Call for rates.** 1488 Thrasher Blvd 35611. I-65 exit 351, just ne. Ext corridors. **Pets:** Accepted.

Sleep Inn Athens H

(256) 232-4700. **$60-$100.** 1115 Audubon Ln 35611. I-65 exit 351, just nw. Int corridors. **Pets:** Accepted.

ATMORE

Holiday Inn Express H

(251) 368-1585. **$99-$139.** 111 Lakeview Cir 36504. I-65 exit 57, just s. Int corridors. **Pets:** Other species. $50 deposit/pet. Service with restrictions, supervision.

Muskogee Inn H

(251) 368-8182. **$89-$128, 3 day notice.** 6141 Hwy 21 36502. I-65 exit 57, just e. Int corridors. **Pets:** Medium. $30 deposit/pet. Designated rooms, no service, supervision.

AUBURN

The Crenshaw Guest House BB

(334) 821-1131. **Call for rates.** 371 N College St 36830. Just w of downtown. Ext/int corridors. **Pets:** Accepted.

The Hotel at Auburn University & Dixon Conference Center H

(334) 821-8200. **$119-$329.** 241 S College St 36830. Just e of downtown. Int corridors. **Pets:** $250 deposit/room. Designated rooms, service with restrictions, supervision.

Lexington Hotel University Convention Center H

(334) 821-7001. **Call for rates.** 1577 S College St 36832. I-85 exit 51, 1.4 mi w on US 29/SR 147. Ext corridors. **Pets:** Accepted. SAVE

Quality Inn H

(334) 821-6699. **$56-$70.** 2283 S College St 36832. I-85 exit 51, just ne. Int corridors. **Pets:** Accepted.

Quality Inn M

(334) 502-5020. **Call for rates.** 1212 Mall Pkwy 36831. Adjacent to Colonial Mall. Ext corridors. **Pets:** Accepted.

BIRMINGHAM METROPOLITAN AREA

BESSEMER

BEST WESTERN PLUS Bessemer Hotel & Suites H

(205) 481-1950. **$99-$139.** 5041 Academy Ln 35022. I-20/59 exit 108, just sw. Int corridors. **Pets:** Small. $20 daily fee/pet. Designated rooms, service with restrictions, supervision. SAVE

Quality Inn H

(205) 428-3194. **$79-$99.** 5021 Academy Ln 35022. I-20/59 exit 108, just sw. Ext corridors. **Pets:** Small. $15 daily fee/room. Service with restrictions, crate.

Sleep Inn H

(205) 424-0000. **$69-$190.** 1259 Greenmor Dr 35022. I-459 exit 6, just s, then just w. Int corridors. **Pets:** Other species. $20 daily fee/pet. Designated rooms, service with restrictions, supervision.

BIRMINGHAM

▼▼▼▼ Comfort Inn Birmingham Airport 🅷
(205) 957-0084. **$85-$150.** 4965 Montevallo Rd 35210. I-20 exit 132B, just s. Int corridors. **Pets:** Other species. $20 daily fee/pet. Designated rooms, service with restrictions. 🛜 🕭 🛏 💻 ➳

▼▼ Days Inn 🅷
(205) 324-4510. **$65-$140.** 905 11th Ct W 35204. I-20/59 exit 123, just sw. Ext/int corridors. **Pets:** Medium. $10 daily fee/pet. Service with restrictions, supervision. 🛜 🛏 💻 ➳

▼▼▼▼ Days Inn Highway 280 Ⓜ
(205) 991-9977. **$70-$150.** 4627 Hwy 280 E 35242. I-459 exit 19 (US 280), 1.4 mi e. Ext corridors. **Pets:** Other species. $20 daily fee/pet. Service with restrictions, crate. 🛜 🛏 💻 ➳ ✕

▼▼▼▼ Drury Inn & Suites-Birmingham Southeast 🅷
(205) 967-2450. **$94-$174.** 3510 Grandview Pkwy 35243. I-459 exit 19 (US 280), just e; in Grandview. Int corridors. **Pets:** Service with restrictions, supervision. 🛜 🛏 💻 ➳

▼▼▼▼ Embassy Suites Birmingham 🅷
(205) 879-7400. **$129-$169.** 2300 Woodcrest Pl 35209. Just n of jct US 31 and 280 exit 21st Ave southbound, 0.3 mi s. Int corridors.
Pets: Accepted. 🛜 🕭 🛏 💻 🍽 ➳

▼▼ Homestead Studio Suites-Birmingham Perimeter Park South 🅷
(205) 967-3800. **$60-$110.** 12 Perimeter Park S 35243. I-459 exit 19 (US 280), 0.5 mi e, then just s. Ext corridors. **Pets:** $25 daily fee/pet. Designated rooms, service with restrictions. 🛜 🛏 💻

▼▼▼▼ The Hotel Highland at Five Points South, an Ascend Collection hotel 🅷
(205) 933-9555. **$119-$299.** 1023 20th St S 35205. 1.5 mi s; in Five Points South. Int corridors. **Pets:** Small. $35 one-time fee/room. Designated rooms, service with restrictions, supervision. 🛜 ✕ 🛏 💻

▼▼ La Quinta Inn Birmingham / Cahaba Park South 🅷
(205) 995-9990. **$59-$111.** 513 Cahaba Park Cir 35242. I-459 exit 19 (US 280), 1.2 mi e. Int corridors. **Pets:** Service with restrictions, supervision. 🛜 🛏 🛏

▼▼▼▼ Residence Inn by Marriott Birmingham 🅷
(205) 991-8686. **$99-$139.** 3 Greenhill Pkwy 35242. I-459 exit 19 (US 280), 2 mi e. Ext corridors. **Pets:** Large, other species. $100 one-time fee/room. Service with restrictions, crate. 🛜 ✕ 🛏 💻 ➳ ✕

🅰🅰🅰 ▼▼▼▼ Residence Inn by Marriott Birmingham Downtown @ UAB 🅷
(205) 731-9595. **$103-$169.** 821 20th St S 35205. Jct University Blvd, just s; corner of 8th Ct S. Int corridors. **Pets:** Medium. $100 one-time fee/room. Designated rooms, service with restrictions, crate.
ⓈⒶⓋⒺ 🛜 ✕ 🕭 🛏 💻 ➳

🅰🅰🅰 ▼▼▼▼ Sheraton Birmingham Hotel 🅷
(205) 324-5000. **$89-$299.** 2101 Richard Arrington Jr Blvd N 35203. I-20/59 exit 22nd St. Int corridors. **Pets:** Accepted.
ⓈⒶⓋⒺ 🛜 ✕ 🛏 💻 🍽 ➳ ✕

CALERA

▼▼ Quality Inn 🅷
(205) 668-3641. **Call for rates.** 357 Hwy 304 35040. I-65 exit 231, just se. Ext corridors. **Pets:** Other species. $20 daily fee/room. Service with restrictions, supervision. 🛜 🛏 💻 ➳

FULTONDALE

▼▼▼▼ Holiday Inn Express Fultondale 🅷
(205) 439-6300. **$89-$149.** 1733 Fulton Rd 35068. I-65 exit 267, just e. Int corridors. **Pets:** Accepted. 🛜 ✕ 🛏 💻 ➳

GARDENDALE

▼▼ ▼▼ Microtel Inn & Suites by Wyndham Gardendale 🅷
(205) 631-6320. **$74-$109.** 850 Odum Rd 35071. I-65 exit 271, just e, then just s. Int corridors. **Pets:** Medium. $25 one-time fee/room. Designated rooms, service with restrictions. 🛜 🛏 💻 ➳

HOMEWOOD

🅰🅰🅰 ▼▼▼▼ Aloft Birmingham Soho Square 🅷 🐾
(205) 874-8055. **$109-$229.** 1903 29th Ave S 35209. I-59 exit 126A, 3.5 mi s on US 31, then just w; corner of 19th St S; downtown. Int corridors. **Pets:** Medium. Service with restrictions, crate.
ⓈⒶⓋⒺ 🛜 ✕ 🕭 🛏 💻 🍽 ➳

🅰🅰🅰 ▼▼▼▼ BEST WESTERN PLUS Carlton Suites 🅷
(205) 940-9990. **$109-$189.** 140 State Farm Pkwy 35209. I-65 exit 255, just w to Wildwood Pkwy, then just n. Int corridors. **Pets:** Medium, dogs only. $20 daily fee/pet. No service, supervision.
ⓈⒶⓋⒺ 🛜 🛏 💻 ➳

▼▼▼ Drury Inn & Suites-Birmingham Southwest 🅷
(205) 940-9500. **$104-$179.** 160 State Farm Pkwy 35209. I-65 exit 255, 0.5 mi on northwest frontage road. Int corridors. **Pets:** Service with restrictions, supervision. 🛜 🛏 💻 ➳

▼▼▼▼ La Quinta Inn & Suites Birmingham (Homewood) 🅷
(205) 290-0150. **$71-$144.** 60 State Farm Pkwy 35209. I-65 exit 255, 0.9 mi on northwest frontage road. Int corridors. **Pets:** Service with restrictions, supervision. 🛜 🛏 💻 ➳

▼▼▼▼ Quality Inn 🅷
(205) 945-9600. **$55-$80.** 155 Vulcan Rd 35209. I-65 exit 256 northbound; exit 256A southbound, just nw. Ext/int corridors. **Pets:** $25 daily fee/pet. Designated rooms, service with restrictions, crate.
🛜 🕭 🛏 💻 ➳

🅰🅰🅰 ▼▼▼▼ Residence Inn by Marriott Birmingham Homewood 🅷
(205) 943-0044. **$109-$179.** 50 State Farm Pkwy 35209. I-65 exit 255, 1 mi on northwest frontage road. Int corridors. **Pets:** Accepted.
ⓈⒶⓋⒺ 🛜 ✕ 🕭 🛏 💻 ➳ ✕

▼▼▼ Super 8 🅷
(205) 945-9888. **$55-$116, 3 day notice.** 140 Vulcan Rd 35209. I-65 exit 256 northbound; exit 256A southbound, just nw. Int corridors. **Pets:** Small. $5 daily fee/pet. Service with restrictions, crate.
🛜 🛏 💻

▼▼▼▼ TownePlace Suites by Marriott Birmingham Homewood 🅷
(205) 943-0114. **$79-$129.** 500 Wildwood Cir 35209. I-65 exit 255, 0.6 mi w, then just n. Int corridors. **Pets:** Accepted.
ⒺⒸⓄ 🛜 ✕ 🕭 🛏 💻 ➳

HOOVER

▼▼▼▼ Days Inn at the Galleria 🅷
(205) 985-7500. **$69-$119.** 1800 Riverchase Dr 35244. I-459 exit 13, 0.5 mi s on US 31, then 0.4 mi w on SR 150. Ext corridors. **Pets:** Accepted.
🛜 🛏 💻 ➳

🅰🅰🅰 ▼▼▼▼ Homewood Suites Birmingham-SW/Riverchase Galleria 🅷
(205) 637-2900. **$99-$299.** 121 Riverchase Pkwy E 35244. I-65 exit 247, just sw on Valleydale Rd, then just n. Int corridors. **Pets:** Medium, dogs only. $75 one-time fee/pet. Service with restrictions, crate.
ⓈⒶⓋⒺ 🛜 🕭 🛏 💻 ➳ ✕

▼▼▼▼ Homewood Suites by Hilton 🅷
(205) 995-9823. **$99-$159.** 215 Inverness Center Dr 35242. I-459 exit 19 (US 280), 1.8 mi e, then just s. Int corridors. **Pets:** Accepted.
🛜 🛏 💻 ➳ ✕

▼▼ La Quinta Inn & Suites Birmingham Hoover 🏨
(205) 403-0096. **$59-$129.** 120 Riverchase Pkwy E 35244. I-65 exit 247, just sw on Valleydale Rd, then just n. Int corridors. **Pets:** Service with restrictions, supervision. 🛜 ⌨ 🍴 🖥 🏊

▼▼▼ Residence Inn by Marriott Birmingham/Hoover 🏨
(205) 733-1655. **$102-$149.** 2725 John Hawkins Pkwy 35244. I-459 exit 13A (Galleria Blvd/SR 50), 0.5 mi se to SR 150, then 1.5 mi s. Int corridors. **Pets:** Other species. $100 one-time fee/room. Service with restrictions. 🛜 ⌨ 🍴 🖥 🏊

▼▼▼ The Wynfrey Hotel 🏨
(205) 987-1600. **$129-$1200.** 1000 Riverchase Galleria 35244. I-459 exit 13. Int corridors. **Pets:** Small. $50 daily fee/room. Service with restrictions. 🛜 ⌨ 🖥 🍴 🏊 ⌨

IRONDALE

▼▼▼ Holiday Inn Express Hotel & Suites Birmingham East 🏨
(205) 957-0555. **$89-$169.** 811 Old Grants Mill Rd 35210. I-20 exit 133, just sw on Crescent Blvd, then just s. Int corridors. **Pets:** Accepted. 🛜 🍴 🖥 🏊

▼▼ Quality Inn Birmingham East 🏨
(205) 956-4100. **$75-$150.** 3910 Kilgore Memorial Dr 35210. I-20 exit 133, just e. Ext corridors. **Pets:** Accepted. 🛜 🍴 🖥 🏊

LEEDS

🅰 ▼▼▼ BEST WESTERN PLUS Bass Hotel & Suites 🏨
(205) 640-5300. **$86-$256.** 1949 Village Dr 35094. I-20 exit 144A westbound; exit 144B eastbound, just ne. Int corridors. **Pets:** Very small. $10 daily fee/pet. Service with restrictions, supervision.
SAVE 🛜 🍴 🖥 🏊

▼▼ Days Inn of Leeds Ⓜ
(205) 699-9833. **$75-$256.** 1838 Ashville Rd 35094. I-20 exit 144A eastbound; exit 144B westbound, just s. Ext corridors. **Pets:** Accepted. 🛜 🍴 🖥 🏊

PELHAM

🅰 ▼▼▼ BEST WESTERN PLUS Oak Mountain Inn 🏨
(205) 982-1113. **$70-$150.** 100 Bishop Cir 35124. I-65 exit 246, just sw, then just s on State Park Rd. Int corridors. **Pets:** Accepted. SAVE 🛜 🍴 🖥 🏊

▼▼ Quality Inn 🏨
(205) 444-9200. **Call for rates.** 110 Cahaba Valley Pkwy 35124. I-65 exit 246, just nw. Ext corridors. **Pets:** Medium, other species. $40 daily fee/pet. Designated rooms, service with restrictions, supervision. 🛜 🍴 🖥 🏊

PELL CITY

▼▼▼ Holiday Inn Express Pell City 🏨 🐾
(205) 884-0047. **Call for rates.** 240 Vaughan Ln 35125. I-20 exit 158 eastbound; exit 158A westbound, just ne. Int corridors. **Pets:** Small. $50 one-time fee/room. Service with restrictions, supervision. 🛜 🍴 🖥 🏊

TRUSSVILLE

▼▼ Quality Inn 🏨
(205) 661-9323. **Call for rates.** 4730 Norrell Dr 35173. I-59 exit 141, just e on Chalkville Rd, then just n. Ext corridors. **Pets:** Accepted. 🛜 🍴 🖥 🏊

END METROPOLITAN AREA

CLANTON

🅰 ▼▼ BEST WESTERN Inn 🏨
(205) 280-1006. **$65-$100.** 801 Bradberry Ln 35046. I-65 exit 205, 0.5 mi e. Ext corridors. **Pets:** Small, dogs only. $10 daily fee/pet. Designated rooms, service with restrictions, supervision. SAVE 🛜 🍴 🖥 🏊

CULLMAN

🅰 ▼▼ BEST WESTERN Fairwinds Inn 🏨
(256) 737-5009. **$63-$140.** 1917 Commerce Ave NW 35055. I-65 exit 310, just e. Ext corridors. **Pets:** Large, dogs only. $20 daily fee/pet. Service with restrictions, supervision. SAVE 🛜 🍴 🖥 🏊

▼▼ Sleep Inn & Suites 🏨
(256) 734-6166. **$60-$120.** 2050 Old Hwy 157 35057. I-65 exit 310, just ne. Int corridors. **Pets:** Accepted. 🛜 🍴 🖥 🏊

DAPHNE

▼▼▼ Homewood Suites by Hilton Mobile East Bay/Daphne 🏨
(251) 621-0100. **$149-$249.** 29474 N Main St 36526. I-10 exit 35A eastbound; exit 35 westbound, just s. Int corridors. **Pets:** Accepted. 🛜 ⌨ 🍴 🖥 🏊

DECATUR

🅰 ▼▼▼ BEST WESTERN River City Hotel 🏨
(256) 301-1388. **$80-$90, 3 day notice.** 1305 Front Ave 35603. I-65 exit 334, 8 mi n. Int corridors. **Pets:** Small. $20 daily fee/room. Service with restrictions, supervision. SAVE 🛜 ⌨ 🍴 🖥 🏊

▼▼ Comfort Inn & Suites 🏨
(256) 355-1999. **Call for rates.** 2212 Danville Rd SW 35601. SR 67, jct Beltline Rd SW. Int corridors. **Pets:** Medium, other species. $10 daily fee/room. Service with restrictions. 🛜 🍴 🖥 🏊

▼▼▼ Holiday Inn Hotel & Suites 🏨
(256) 355-3150. **$79-$139.** 1101 6th Ave NE 35601. Just w of jct US 31, 72A and SR 20. Ext/int corridors. **Pets:** Small. $15 one-time fee/room. Designated rooms, service with restrictions, crate. 🛜 ⌨ 🍴 🖥 🍴 🏊

▼▼ Microtel Inn & Suites by Wyndham Decatur 🏨 🐾
(256) 301-9995. **$59-$69, 3 day notice.** 2226 Beltline Rd SW 35601. On SR 67, 4 mi w of jct US 31. Int corridors. **Pets:** $20 one-time fee/pet. Service with restrictions, supervision. 🛜 ⌨ 🍴 🖥 🏊

▼▼ Quality Inn 🏨
(256) 355-2229. **Call for rates.** 2120 Jameson Pl SW 35603. SR 67, 1.6 mi s of jct US 72A; 3.9 mi n of jct US 31. Ext corridors. **Pets:** Accepted. 🛜 🍴 🖥 🏊

DEMOPOLIS

🅰 ▼▼▼ BEST WESTERN PLUS Two Rivers Hotel & Suites 🏨 🐾
(334) 289-2611. **$110.** 662 US Hwy 80 W 36732. Jct US 43, 0.8 mi w. Int corridors. **Pets:** Large. $50 deposit/room. Service with restrictions, supervision. SAVE 🛜 ⌨ 🍴 🖥 🏊

DOTHAN

▼▼▼ Comfort Suites 🏨 🐾
(334) 792-9000. **$90-$111.** 1650 Westgate Pkwy 36303. 0.7 mi n of jct US 231 and 431, just e. Int corridors. **Pets:** Small, other species. $45 one-time fee/room. Service with restrictions, supervision. 🛜 ⌨ ⌨ 🍴 🖥 🏊

🅰 ▼▼ Days Inn Ⓜ
(334) 671-3700. **$65.** 3071 Ross Clark Cir 36301. Just s of jct US 84; west end of town. Ext corridors. **Pets:** Small, dogs only. $15 deposit/pet. Service with restrictions, supervision. SAVE 🛜 ⌨ 🍴 🖥

▼▼ ▼▼ Howard Johnson Inn M
(334) 792-3339. **$55-$145.** 2244 Ross Clark Cir 36301. 1.4 mi s of jct SR 52; west end of town. Ext corridors. **Pets:** Dogs only. $15 daily fee/pet. Service with restrictions, supervision. 🛜 🛁 💻 ≈

▼▼▼▼ La Quinta Inn & Suites-Dothan H
(334) 793-9090. **$93-$156.** 3593 Ross Clark Cir 36303. Just w of jct US 231; northwest part of town. Int corridors. **Pets:** Service with restrictions, supervision. 🛜 ᴹ 🛁 💻 ≈

ENTERPRISE
▼▼ ▼▼ Americas Best Value Inn & Suites M
(334) 348-2378. **$60-$70.** 101 Access Dr 36330. Jct US 84 and SR 167, 0.5 mi w. Ext corridors. **Pets:** $10 daily fee/pet. No service.
🛜 🛁 💻 ≈

▼▼ ▼▼ Quality Inn M
(334) 393-2304. **Call for rates.** 615 Boll Weevil Cir 36330. On US 84 Bypass. Ext corridors. **Pets:** Accepted. 🛜 🛁 💻 ≈

EUFAULA
▼▼ ▼▼ Baymont Inn & Suites Eufaula M
(334) 687-7747. **Call for rates.** 136 Towne Center Blvd 36027. On US 431, 1 mi s of US 82 E. Ext corridors. **Pets:** Accepted.
🛜 🛁 💻 ≈

▼▼▼▼ Eufaula Comfort Suites H
(334) 616-0114. **Call for rates.** 12 Paul Lee Pkwy 36027. 1.7 mi s on US 431 from jct US 82 E, then just e. Int corridors. **Pets:** Medium. $25 daily fee/pet. Service with restrictions, supervision.
🛜 ✕ ᴹ 🛁 💻 ≈ ✕

EVERGREEN
AAA ▼▼ ▼▼ Comfort Inn M
(251) 578-4701. **$64-$71.** 1571 Ted Bates Rd 36401. I-65 exit 96, just w. Ext corridors. **Pets:** Other species. $10 daily fee/pet. Designated rooms, service with restrictions, supervision. SAVE 🛜 🛁 💻 ≈

▼▼ ▼▼ Econo Lodge Inn & Suites M
(251) 578-2100. **Call for rates.** 215 Hwy 83 36401. I-65 exit 96, just w. Ext corridors. **Pets:** Accepted. 🛜 🛁 💻

▼▼▼▼ Sleep Inn & Suites H 🐾
(251) 578-9590. **Call for rates.** 78 Liberty Hill Pl 36401. I-65 exit 96, just ne. Int corridors. **Pets:** Small, dogs only. $10 deposit/pet, $10 daily fee/pet. Designated rooms, no service. 🛜 ᴹ 🛁 💻 ≈

FAIRHOPE
▼▼ ▼▼ Key West Inn M
(251) 990-7373. **$59-$109.** 231 S Greeno Rd 36532. On US 98, 1.9 mi s of jct SR 104. Ext corridors. **Pets:** Medium. $15 daily fee/pet. Service with restrictions, crate. 🛜 🛁 💻 ≈

FLORENCE
▼▼▼▼ Baymont Inn & Suites Florence/Muscle Shoals M
(256) 764-5326. **$69-$84.** 115 Ana Dr 35630. On US 43/72, just nw of jct SR 133 (Cox Creek Pkwy). Ext corridors. **Pets:** Accepted.
🛜 🛁 💻 ≈

AAA ▼▼▼▼▼▼ Marriott Shoals Hotel and Spa H
(256) 246-3600. **$131-$195.** 800 Cox Creek Pkwy S 35630. Jct US 43/72 and SR 133 (Cox Creek Pkwy), 1.5 mi s; at Wilson Dam. Int corridors. **Pets:** $75 one-time fee/pet. Service with restrictions, crate.
SAVE 🛜 ✕ ᴹ 🛁 💻 🍽 ≈ ✕

AAA ▼▼ ▼▼ Quality Inn H
(256) 740-0444. **$70-$79.** 150 Etta Gray St 35630. US 43/72, just se of jct SR 133 (Cox Creek Pkwy). Int corridors. **Pets:** Medium. $10 daily fee/pet. Designated rooms, service with restrictions, supervision.
SAVE 🛜 ✕ 🛁 💻 ≈

FOLEY
AAA ▼▼ ▼▼ Econo Lodge & Suites H
(251) 943-9100. **$70-$120.** 2682 S McKenzie St 36535. On SR 59, 1.9 mi s of jct US 98. Ext corridors. **Pets:** Medium. $20 one-time fee/pet. Service with restrictions, crate. SAVE 🛜 ᴹ 🛁 💻 ≈

GENEVA
▼▼ ▼▼ Briarwood Inn of Geneva M
(334) 684-7715. **$75-$104.** 1503 W Magnolia Ave 36340. On SR 52, 0.3 mi w of jct SR 196. Ext corridors. **Pets:** Small, dogs only. $10 daily fee/pet. Designated rooms, service with restrictions, supervision.
🛜 🛁 ≈

GREENVILLE
▼▼ ▼▼ Baymont Inn & Suites Greenville/At I-65 M
(334) 382-6300. **Call for rates.** 71 Jameson Ln 36037. I-65 exit 130, just n on SR 185, then just w on Cahaba Rd. Ext corridors.
Pets: Accepted. 🛜 🛁 💻 ≈

AAA ▼▼ ▼▼ BEST WESTERN Inn M
(334) 382-9200. **$60-$95.** 56 Cahaba Rd 36037. I-65 exit 130, just n on SR 185. Ext corridors. **Pets:** Very small. $20 daily fee/pet. Service with restrictions, supervision. SAVE 🛜 🛁 💻 ≈

AAA ▼▼ ▼▼ Comfort Inn H
(334) 383-9595. **$60-$95.** 1029 Fort Dale Rd 36037. I-65 exit 130, just n on SR 185. Int corridors. **Pets:** Accepted.
SAVE 🛜 ᴹ 🛁 💻 ≈

AAA ▼▼ ▼▼ Days Inn M
(334) 382-3118. **$68-$75.** 946 Fort Dale Rd 36037. I-65 exit 130, just s on SR 185. Ext corridors. **Pets:** Very small. $10 daily fee/pet. No service.
SAVE 🛜 🛁 💻 ≈

GULF SHORES
▼▼▼▼ Staybridge Suites- Gulf Shores H
(251) 975-1030. **$99-$179.** 3947 Hwy 59 36542. On Gulf Shores Pkwy, 3.1 mi n of jct SR 180. Int corridors. **Pets:** Accepted.
🛜 ᴹ 🛁 💻 ≈ ✕

GUNTERSVILLE
AAA ▼▼▼▼ BEST WESTERN PLUS Lake Guntersville Hotel H
(256) 582-2220. **$80-$190.** 2140 Gunter Ave 35976. Jct US 431 (Gunter Ave) and SR 79. Ext corridors. **Pets:** Accepted.
SAVE 🛜 ᴹ 🛁 💻 🍽 ≈ ✕

HAMILTON
▼▼ ▼▼ Days Inn H
(205) 921-1790. **$50-$165.** 1849 Military St S 35570. US 78 exit 14, 1 mi n, then 1 mi w on US 43. Ext corridors. **Pets:** Medium. $10 daily fee/pet. Designated rooms, service with restrictions, supervision.
🛜 🛁 💻 ≈

HOPE HULL
▼▼▼▼ Hampton Inn Airport H
(334) 280-9592. **$89-$109.** 60 Wasden Rd 36043. I-65 exit 164, just w. Int corridors. **Pets:** Accepted. 🛜 🛁 💻 ≈

HUNTSVILLE
▼▼ ▼▼ Extended StayAmerica Huntsville-U.S. Space and Rocket Center H
(256) 830-9110. **$65-$100.** 4751 Governors House Dr 35805. I-565 exit 17A, just s, then 0.5 mi w. Ext corridors. **Pets:** $25 daily fee/pet. Designated rooms, service with restrictions. 🛜 ᴹ 🛁 💻

▼▼▼▼ Holiday Inn Express Hotel & Suites H
(256) 721-1000. **$69-$135.** 3808 University Dr 35816. I-565 exit 17A, just e. Int corridors. **Pets:** Small. $50 one-time fee/room. Designated rooms, service with restrictions, supervision. 🛜 🛁 💻 ≈

Holiday Inn Huntsville Downtown 🅷

(256) 533-1400. **Call for rates.** 401 Williams Ave SW 35801. Just w of Church St; downtown. Int corridors. **Pets:** Medium, other species. $30 one-time fee/pet. Designated rooms, service with restrictions, crate.

La Quinta Inn & Suites Huntsville Madison Square 🅷

(256) 830-8999. **$66-$129.** 4890 University Dr NW 35816. I-565 exit 14B, 2.6 mi n on SR 255 (Research Park Blvd), then 0.9 mi e on US 72. Int corridors. **Pets:** Service with restrictions, supervision.

La Quinta Inn Huntsville (Research Park) 🅷

(256) 830-2070. **$59-$118.** 4870 University Dr NW 35816. I-565 exit 14B, 2.6 mi n on SR 255 (Research Park Blvd), then 1.1 mi e on US 72. Ext corridors. **Pets:** Service with restrictions, supervision.

La Quinta Inn Huntsville (Space Center) 🅷

(256) 533-0756. **$59-$115.** 3141 University Dr NW 35816. I-565 exit 17A, 1.1 mi n on SR 53 (Jordan Ln), then 0.6 mi e on US 72. Ext corridors. **Pets:** Service with restrictions, supervision.

Microtel Inn & Suites by Wyndham Huntsville 🅷

(256) 859-6655. **$59-$78.** 1820 Chase Creek Row 35811. Jct US 72 and Shields Rd, just n, then just w. Int corridors. **Pets:** Accepted.

TownePlace Suites by Marriott Huntsville 🅷

(256) 971-5277. **$94-$174.** 1125 McMurtrie Dr 35806. I-565 exit 14B, 2.6 mi n on SR 255 (Research Park Blvd), 0.8 mi w on US 72, then just s. Int corridors. **Pets:** Other species. $100 one-time fee/room. Designated rooms, service with restrictions, crate.

The Westin Huntsville 🅷 ❀

(256) 428-2000. **$129-$299.** 6800 Governors West NW 35806. I-565 exit 14A, 0.5 mi n on SR 255 (Research Park Blvd), just w on Old Madison Pike, then 0.5 mi n. Int corridors. **Pets:** Medium, dogs only. $50 one-time fee/room. Service with restrictions, supervision.

JASPER

Quality Inn 🅷

(205) 387-7710. **$74-$94.** 1100 Hwy 78/118 E 35501. SR 118, 1.8 mi w of jct SR 69. Ext corridors. **Pets:** Accepted.

LINCOLN

Comfort Inn 🅷

(205) 763-9777. **$69-$89.** 850/A Speedway Industrial Dr 35096. I-20 exit 168, just se. Int corridors. **Pets:** Medium. $10 daily fee/pet. Service with restrictions, supervision.

LUVERNE

GuestHouse Inn & Suites 🅷

(334) 335-3050. **$65-$75.** 1701 Montgomery Hwy 36049. Jct US 331 and SR 10. Int corridors. **Pets:** Other species. $20 one-time fee/room. Supervision.

MADISON

Country Inn & Suites By Carlson 🅷

(256) 325-0007. **$75-$200.** 101 Westchester Dr 35758. I-565 exit 8, just n, then just w. Int corridors. **Pets:** Medium. $15 daily fee/pet. Designated rooms, service with restrictions, supervision.

MILLBROOK

Key West Inn 🅜

(334) 309-2004. **$69-$120.** 2275 Cobbs Ford Rd 36054. I-65 exit 179, just e. Ext corridors. **Pets:** Accepted.

MOBILE

Battleship Inn Resort 🅜

(251) 432-2703. **$89-$109.** 2701 Battleship Pkwy 36602. I-10 exit 27, just e. Ext corridors. **Pets:** Accepted.

Candlewood Suites Downtown 🅷 ❀

(251) 690-7818. **$119-$129.** 121 N Royal St 36602. Corner of St. Louis St; downtown; parking and rear entrance on St. Joseph St. Int corridors. **Pets:** Large. $75 one-time fee/pet. Service with restrictions, crate.

Drury Inn-Mobile 🅷

(251) 344-7700. **$99-$149.** 824 W I-65 Service Rd S 36609. I-65 exit 3 (Airport Blvd), just w, then just s on service road. Int corridors. **Pets:** Service with restrictions, supervision.

Holiday Inn Mobile West I-10 🅷

(251) 666-5600. **$109-$139.** 5465 Hwy 90 W 36619. I-10 exit 15B, just e on US 90, then just s on Coca Cola Rd. Int corridors. **Pets:** Accepted.

La Quinta Inn Mobile 🅜

(251) 343-4051. **$59-$133.** 816 W I-65 Service Rd S 36609. I-65 exit 3 (Airport Blvd), just w, then just s. Ext/int corridors. **Pets:** Service with restrictions, supervision.

Renaissance-The Battle House Mobile Hotel & Spa 🅷

(251) 338-2000. **$149-$249.** 26 N Royal St 36602. I-10 exit 26B (Water St) eastbound, w on Government St, then just n. Int corridors. **Pets:** Other species. $75 one-time fee/room. Designated rooms, service with restrictions.

Residence Inn by Marriott Mobile 🅷

(251) 304-0570. **$119-$189.** 950 W I-65 Service Rd S 36609. I-65 exit 3 (Airport Blvd), just w, then 0.4 mi s. Int corridors. **Pets:** Accepted.

TownePlace Suites by Marriott Mobile 🅷

(251) 345-9588. **$109-$199.** 1075 Montlimar Dr 36609. I-65 exit 3 (Airport Blvd), 0.5 mi w, then 0.5 mi s. Int corridors. **Pets:** Other species. $75 one-time fee/pet. Supervision.

MONROEVILLE

BEST WESTERN of Monroeville 🅜

(251) 575-9999. **$69-$76.** 4419 S Alabama Ave 36460. On SR 21, 0.5 mi n of jct US 84. Ext corridors. **Pets:** Accepted.

Holiday Inn Express 🅷

(251) 743-3333. **Call for rates.** 120 Hwy 21 S 36460. On SR 21, just s of jct US 84. Int corridors. **Pets:** Medium, other species. $20 daily fee/pet. Service with restrictions.

Mockingbird Inn & Suites 🅜

(251) 743-3297. **$68-$120.** 4389 S Alabama Ave 36460. On SR 21, 0.5 mi n of jct US 84. Ext corridors. **Pets:** Accepted.

MONTGOMERY

Baymont Inn & Suites 🅜

(334) 277-4442. **$60-$70.** 5837 Monticello Dr 36117. I-85 exit 6, just n, then just e. Ext corridors. **Pets:** Accepted.

Candlewood Suites at Eastchase 🅷

(334) 277-0677. **$70-$119.** 9151 Boyd Cooper Pkwy 36117. I-85 exit 11, just sw. Int corridors. **Pets:** Medium. $50 one-time fee/room. Service with restrictions, supervision.

Drury Inn & Suites-Montgomery 🅷

(334) 273-1101. **$99-$174.** 1124 Eastern Blvd 36117. I-85 exit 6, just n. Int corridors. **Pets:** Service with restrictions, supervision.

▼▼▼▼ Embassy Suites Montgomery Conference Center 🅷

(334) 269-5055. **$124-$194.** 300 Tallapoosa St 36104. Between Molton and Commerce sts; in historic downtown. Int corridors. **Pets:** Small, other species. $100 one-time fee/pet. Service with restrictions, crate.

▼▼▼▼ Holiday Inn Express Hotel & Suites 🅷

(334) 288-8844. **$72-$99.** 4273 Troy Hwy 36116. 1 mi s of jct US 80 and 231 (Troy Hwy). Int corridors. **Pets:** Accepted.

▼▼▼▼ Homewood Suites by Hilton 🅷

(334) 272-3010. **$99-$189.** 1800 Interstate Park Dr 36109. I-85 exit 4, just n on Perry Hill, then just e. Int corridors. **Pets:** Large. $100 one-time fee/room. Service with restrictions, crate.

▼▼ ◆ La Quinta Inn & Suites Montgomery Carmichael Road 🅷

(334) 277-6000. **$59-$118.** 5225 Carmichael Rd 36106. I-85 exit 6, just s on Eastern Blvd, then just w. Int corridors. **Pets:** Service with restrictions, supervision.

▼▼ La Quinta Inn Montgomery Eastern Bypass Ⓜ

(334) 271-1620. **$59-$111.** 1280 East Blvd 36117. I-85 exit 6, just s. Ext corridors. **Pets:** Service with restrictions, supervision.

▼▼ Motel 6 #4263 Ⓜ

(334) 280-1866. **$46-$60.** 7760 Slade Plaza Blvd 36105. I-65 exit 164, just s. Int corridors. **Pets:** Other species. Service with restrictions, supervision.

▼▼▼▼ Residence Inn by Marriott Montgomery 🅷

(334) 270-3300. **$89-$139.** 1200 Hilmar Ct 36117. I-85 exit 6, just s on Eastern Blvd, then just e. Ext/int corridors. **Pets:** Accepted.

▼▼▼▼ Sleep Inn & Suites 🅷

(334) 387-1004. **$70-$90.** 5005 Carmichael Rd 36106. I-85 exit 6, just s. Int corridors. **Pets:** Medium. $10 daily fee/pet. Service with restrictions, supervision.

▼▼▼▼ Staybridge Suites-EastChase 🅷

(334) 277-9383. **$114-$134.** 7800 EastChase Pkwy 36117. I-85 exit 9 (Taylor Rd), just s, then 1 mi e; in The Shoppes of EastChase. Int corridors. **Pets:** Other species. $50 one-time fee/room. Service with restrictions.

▼▼▼▼ TownePlace Suites by Marriott Montgomery 🅷

(334) 396-5505. **$85-$104.** 5047 Towneplace Dr 36106. I-85 exit 6, just s on Eastern Blvd, then just w on Carmichael Rd. Int corridors. **Pets:** Accepted.

OXFORD

▼▼ Comfort Inn Ⓜ

(256) 831-0860. **$65-$75.** 138 Elm St 36203. I-20 exit 185, just s. Ext corridors. **Pets:** Other species. $25 one-time fee/room. Service with restrictions.

◉◉◉ ▼▼▼▼ Hampton Inn & Suites 🅷

(256) 831-8958. **$69-$139.** 210 Colonial Dr 36203. I-20 exit 188, just n, then w. Int corridors. **Pets:** Medium, other species. Designated rooms, service with restrictions, supervision.

◉◉◉ ▼▼▼▼ Holiday Inn Express & Suites Anniston/Oxford 🅷

(256) 835-8768. **$89-$144.** 160 Colonial Dr 36203. I-20 exit 188, just n, then w. Int corridors. **Pets:** Medium, other species. $25 daily fee/pet. Service with restrictions, supervision.

▼▼ ▼ Quality Inn Ⓜ

(256) 835-2170. **Call for rates.** 161 Colonial Dr 36203. I-20 exit 188, just n, then w. Ext corridors. **Pets:** Accepted.

▼▼ ▼ Super 8 Oxford Ⓜ

(256) 241-3210. **$50-$200.** 1600 Hwy 21 S 36203. I-20 exit 185, just s. Ext corridors. **Pets:** Accepted.

OZARK

▼▼ ▼ Baymont Inn & Suites Ozark Ⓜ

(334) 774-0233. **Call for rates.** 1360 S US Hwy 231 36360. 0.3 mi s of jct SR 249. Ext corridors. **Pets:** Accepted.

PRATTVILLE

▼▼ ▼ Baymont Inn & Suites Prattville 🅷

(334) 361-6463. **Call for rates.** 104 Jameson Ct 36067. I-65 exit 179, 1 mi w. Ext corridors. **Pets:** Small. $15 daily fee/pet. Service with restrictions.

▼▼ ▼ La Quinta Inn & Suites 🅷

(334) 358-5454. **$75-$155.** 261 Interstate Commercial Park Loop 36066. I-65 exit 181, just w. Int corridors. **Pets:** Service with restrictions, supervision.

▼▼ ▼ Quality Inn 🅷

(334) 365-6003. **$70-$80.** 797 Business Park Dr 36066. I-65 exit 181, just sw, then just n. Int corridors. **Pets:** Medium. $10 daily fee/pet. Designated rooms, service with restrictions, supervision.

PRICEVILLE

▼▼ ▼ Comfort Inn 🅷

(256) 355-1037. **$80-$125.** 3239 Point Mallard Pkwy 35601. I-65 exit 334, just w. Int corridors. **Pets:** Accepted.

▼▼ ▼ Super 8 - Decatur Ⓜ

(256) 355-2525. **$58-$65.** 70 Marco Dr 35603. I-65 exit 334, just e. Ext corridors. **Pets:** Small, dogs only. $8 daily fee/room. Designated rooms, service with restrictions, supervision.

SARALAND

▼▼ ▼ Microtel Inn & Suites by Wyndham Saraland/North Mobile 🅷

(251) 675-5045. **$70-$90.** 1124 Shelton Beach Rd 36571. I-65 exit 13, just e, then just n. Int corridors. **Pets:** Small, other species. $25 one-time fee/pet. Designated rooms, service with restrictions, supervision.

SCOTTSBORO

▼▼ ▼ Quality Inn 🅷 🐾

(256) 574-6666. **Call for rates.** 208 Micah Way 35768. On US 72, just s of jct SR 35. Ext corridors. **Pets:** Small. $15 daily fee/pet. Service with restrictions, crate.

SELMA

▼▼ ▼ Quality Inn Ⓜ

(334) 874-8600. **Call for rates.** 2420 Broad St 36701. On SR 22, just n of jct US 80. Ext corridors. **Pets:** Accepted.

▼▼ ▼ Selma Hotel 🅷

(334) 872-0461. **$50-$60, 3 day notice.** 1710 W Highland Ave 36701. On US 80. Ext corridors. **Pets:** Accepted.

SHEFFIELD

▼▼▼▼ Emerald River Hotel 🅷

(256) 381-4710. **$65.** 4900 Hatch Blvd 35660. 4 mi n on US 43 from jct US 72. Ext/int corridors. **Pets:** Accepted.

SYLACAUGA
▼▼ Quality Inn **H**

(256) 245-4141. **Call for rates.** 89 Gene Stewart Blvd 35151. Off US 280, just s. Ext corridors. **Pets:** Accepted. 🛜 🛄 🖵 🏊

TROY
🆔 ▼▼▼ Econo Lodge of Troy **M**

(334) 566-7799. **$54-$59.** 811 Hwy 231 S 36081. On US 231, 1.5 mi s of jct US 29. Ext corridors. **Pets:** Accepted. [SAVE] 🛜 🛄 🖵 🏊

TUSCALOOSA
▼▼ Baymont Inn & Suites Tuscaloosa **H**

(205) 345-5018. **Call for rates.** 5021 Oscar Baxter Dr 35403. I-59/20 exit 71A, just s. Ext corridors. **Pets:** Accepted. 🛜 🛄 🖵 🏊

🆔 ▼▼▼ BEST WESTERN Park Plaza Motor
Inn **H** 🐾

(205) 556-9690. **$72-$89.** 3801 McFarland Blvd 35405. I-59/20 exit 73, just ne on US 82. Ext corridors. **Pets:** Medium, other species. $10 one-time fee/room. Designated rooms, service with restrictions, supervision. [SAVE] 🛜 🛄 🖵 🏊

🆔 ▼▼▼ Centerstone Inn **H**

(205) 556-3232. **$90-$105.** 4700 Doris Pate Dr 35405. I-59/20 exit 76, just n. Int corridors. **Pets:** Large, other species. $25 one-time fee/pet. Service with restrictions, crate. [SAVE] 🛜 🛄 🖵 🏊

▼▼ La Quinta Inn Tuscaloosa **M**

(205) 349-3270. **$59-$115.** 4122 McFarland Blvd E 35405. I-59/20 exit 73, just sw on US 82. Ext corridors. **Pets:** Service with restrictions, supervision. 🛜 🛄 🖵 🏊

🆔 ▼▼▼ Rodeway Inn **H**

(205) 556-5696. **$66-$90.** 4300 Skyland Blvd E 35405. I-59/20 exit 76, 0.4 mi s. Int corridors. **Pets:** Service with restrictions, supervision.
[SAVE] 🛜 🛄 🖵 🏊

▼▼▼ Wingate by Wyndham Tuscaloosa **H**

(205) 553-5400. **$102-$429.** 4918 Skyland Blvd E 35405. I-59/20 exit 76, just n. Int corridors. **Pets:** Other species. $20 daily fee/room. Service with restrictions, crate. 🛜 ✕ ♿ 🛄 🖵 🏊

TUSCUMBIA
▼▼ Microtel Inn & Suites by Wyndham Tuscumbia/Muscle
Shoals **H**

(256) 248-0055. **$69-$140.** 1852 Hwy 72 E 35674. Just w of jct US 72 and 43. Int corridors. **Pets:** Small. $15 daily fee/pet. Service with restrictions, supervision. 🛜 ✕ ♿ 🛄 🖵 🏊

ALASKA

CITY INDEX

ANCHORAGE
🆔 ▼▼▼▼ Clarion Suites Downtown **H**

(907) 222-5005. **$89-$259, 3 day notice.** 1110 W 8th Ave 99501. Corner of L St and W 8th Ave. Int corridors. **Pets:** Dogs only. $150 one-time fee/room. Service with restrictions, supervision.
[SAVE] 🛜 ✕ ♿ 🛄 🖵 🏊

▼▼▼▼ Hilton Anchorage **H**

(907) 272-7411. **$100-$350.** 500 W 3rd Ave 99501. Corner of E St. Int corridors. **Pets:** Accepted. 🛜 ♿ 🛄 🖵 🍴 🏊 ✕

▼▼ Microtel Inn & Suites by Wyndham Anchorage
Airport **M**

(907) 245-5002. **$85-$170.** 5205 Northwood Dr 99517. Jct International Airport Rd, just n. Int corridors. **Pets:** $10 daily fee/pet. Service with restrictions, crate. 🛜 ♿ 🛄 🖵

🆔 ▼▼▼ Millennium Alaskan Hotel Anchorage **H**

(907) 243-2300. **$129-$299, 3 day notice.** 4800 Spenard Rd 99517. Jct International Airport Rd, just n. Int corridors. **Pets:** Accepted.
[SAVE] 🛜 ✕ ♿ 🛄 🖵 🍴

▼▼ Motel 6-4216 **M**

(907) 677-8000. **Call for rates.** 5000 A St 99503. Jct C St, just n on A St, then just n. Int corridors. **Pets:** Other species. Service with restrictions, supervision. 🛜 ♿

▼▼▼▼ Residence Inn by Marriott **H**

(907) 563-9844. **$129-$269.** 1025 E 35th Ave 99508. Corner of SR 1 (Seward Hwy) and 36th Ave. Int corridors. **Pets:** Accepted.
🛜 ✕ ♿ 🛄 🖵 🏊 ✕

🆔 ▼▼▼▼ Sheraton Anchorage Hotel & SPA **H** 🐾

(907) 276-8700. **$219-$369.** 401 E 6th Ave 99501. 6th Ave and Denali St. Int corridors. **Pets:** Medium, dogs only. Service with restrictions, supervision. [SAVE] 🛜 ✕ ♿ 🛄 🖵 🍴

CANTWELL
🆔 ▼▼ Backwoods Lodge **M**

(907) 768-2232. **$90-$170, 10 day notice.** Denali Hwy MM 133.8 99729. Parks Hwy (Milepost 210), just e. Ext corridors. **Pets:** Medium. Service with restrictions, supervision. [SAVE] 🛜 ✕ 🛄 🖵 🐾

DENALI NATIONAL PARK AND PRESERVE
▼▼ McKinley Chalet Resort **H**

(907) 683-8200. **Call for rates.** Milepost 238.5 Parks Hwy 99755. Milepost 238.5 on SR 3 (Parks Hwy). Ext/int corridors. **Pets:** Accepted.
🛜 ✕ ♿ 🖵 🍴 🐾

FAIRBANKS
🆔 ▼▼▼▼ Pike's Waterfront Lodge **H** 🐾

(907) 456-4500. **$89-$450.** 1850 Hoselton Dr 99709. Jct Airport Way and Hoselton Dr. Ext/int corridors. **Pets:** Other species. $25 daily fee/pet. Designated rooms, service with restrictions, crate.
[SAVE] 🛜 ✕ ♿ 🛄 🖵 🍴 ✕

▼▼▼ Westmark Fairbanks Hotel & Conference Center **H**

(907) 456-7722. **$79-$239.** 813 Noble St 99701. Just n of Airport Way at 10th Ave; just w of SR 2; downtown. Int corridors. **Pets:** Other species. $10 daily fee/room. Designated rooms, service with restrictions, supervision. 🛜 ✕ ♿ 🛄 🖵 🍴

HAINES

◆◆◆ ▼ Captain's Choice Motel **M**

(907) 766-3111. **$137-$184.** 108 2nd Ave N 99827. Jct 2nd Ave and Dalton St. Ext corridors. **Pets:** Other species. $25 one-time fee/room. Service with restrictions, supervision. [SAVE] [📶] [🛏] [💻] [AC]

HOMER

◆◆◆ ▼▼ BEST WESTERN PLUS Bidarka Inn **H** 🐾

(907) 235-8148. **$79-$219.** 575 Sterling Hwy 99603. Just n of Pioneer Ave on Sterling Hwy (SR 1). Ext/int corridors. **Pets:** Large, other species. $15 daily fee/pet. Designated rooms, service with restrictions, supervision. [SAVE] [📶] [♿M] [🛏] [💻] [🍽]

JUNEAU

▼▼ Westmark Baranof Hotel **H** 🐾

(907) 586-2660. **$125-$239.** 127 N Franklin St 99801. At 2nd and Franklin sts; downtown. Int corridors. **Pets:** Small, dogs only. Designated rooms, service with restrictions, supervision.

[📶] [✕] [🛏] [💻] [🍽] [AC]

KETCHIKAN

◆◆ ▼▼▼ BEST WESTERN PLUS Landing Hotel **H** 🐾

(907) 225-5166. **$145-$246.** 3434 Tongass Ave 99901. Across from Alaska Marine Hwy ferry terminal. Ext/int corridors. **Pets:** Large, other species. $10 daily fee/pet. Designated rooms, service with restrictions, crate. [SAVE] [📶] [✕] [♿M] [🛏] [💻] [🍽]

◆◆◆ ▼▼ Cape Fox Lodge **H**

(907) 225-8001. **$99-$210.** 800 Venetia Way 99901. Above Creek St (tramway from Creek St). Ext/int corridors. **Pets:** Dogs only. $10 daily fee/pet. Designated rooms, service with restrictions, supervision. [SAVE] [📶] [♿M] [🛏] [💻] [🍽] [AC]

KODIAK

◆◆◆ ▼▼▼ BEST WESTERN Kodiak Inn & Convention Center **H**

(907) 486-5712. **$105-$206.** 236 W Rezanof Dr 99615. 0.3 mi w of ferry terminal; center. Ext/int corridors. **Pets:** Accepted. [SAVE] [📶] [♿M] [🛏] [💻] [🍽] [AC]

▼▼ Comfort Inn Kodiak **H**

(907) 487-2700. **$110-$190.** 1395 Airport Way 99615. Adjacent to Kodiak Airport. Int corridors. **Pets:** Medium, dogs only. $15 daily fee/pet. Designated rooms, service with restrictions, supervision. [📶] [♿M] [🛏] [💻] [AC]

SEWARD

◆◆◆ ▼▼ Hotel Seward **H** 🐾

(907) 224-8001. **$59-$379, 3 day notice.** 221 Fifth Ave 99664. Just n of Alaska SeaLife Center; downtown. Int corridors. **Pets:** Medium, dogs only. $25 daily fee/pet. Designated rooms, supervision. [SAVE] [📶] [✕] [♿M] [🛏] [💻] [🍽] [AC]

SITKA

◆◆◆ ▼▼ Shee Atika Totem Square Inn **H**

(907) 747-3693. **$149-$229.** 201 Katlian St 99835. In Totem Square Complex near Municipal Office. Int corridors. **Pets:** Small, other species. $50 deposit/room, $10 daily fee/pet. Service with restrictions, supervision. [SAVE] [📶] [✕] [♿M] [🛏] [💻] [🍽] [AC]

▼▼ Super 8-Sitka **H**

(907) 747-8804. **$99-$139.** 404 Sawmill Creek Rd 99835. Just e from corner of Lake St and Halibut Point/Sawmill Creek Rd; center. Int corridors. **Pets:** Medium, other species. $15 daily fee/pet. Designated rooms, service with restrictions, supervision. [📶] [♿M] [🛏] [💻]

▼▼ Westmark Sitka **H**

(907) 747-6241. **$99-$299.** 330 Seward St 99835. Center. Int corridors. **Pets:** Accepted. [📶] [✕] [♿M] [🛏] [💻] [🍽] [AC]

SKAGWAY

▼▼ Westmark Inn Skagway **M**

(907) 983-6000. **$108-$145.** 3rd Ave & Spring St 99840. Jct 3rd and Broadway sts; downtown. Ext/int corridors. **Pets:** Accepted. [📶] [✕] [♿M] [🛏] [💻] [🍽] [AC]

TOK

▼▼ Cleft of the Rock Bed & Breakfast **BB**

(907) 883-4219. **$110-$165, 3 day notice.** 0.5 Sundog Tr 99780. Jct SR 1 and 2 (Alaskan Hwy), 2.5 mi w on SR 2 (Alaskan Hwy) to Sundog Tr, then 0.5 mi n. Ext/int corridors. **Pets:** Accepted. [📶] [✕] [🛏] [💻] [AC]

▼▼ Westmark Inn Tok **M**

(907) 883-5174. **$99-$199.** Jct Alaska & Glenn Hwys 99780. On SR 1; jct SR 2 (Alaskan Hwy). Ext corridors. **Pets:** Accepted. [📶] [✕] [♿M] [💻] [🍽]

TRAPPER CREEK

▼▼ Gate Creek Cabins **CA**

(907) 733-1393. **$150-$590, 10 day notice.** Mile 10.5 Petersville Rd 99683. Milepost 114 (Parks Hwy), 10.5 mi w at Petersville Rd. Ext corridors. **Pets:** Accepted. [📶] [✕] [🛏] [💻] [✕] [AC] [🚭]

▼▼ Trapper Creek Inn & RV Park **M**

(907) 733-2302. **$99-$139, 10 day notice.** Mile 114.6 Parks Hwy 99683. George Parks Hwy (SR 3), Milepost 114. Ext corridors. **Pets:** $50 deposit/pet. Service with restrictions, supervision. [📶] [✕] [🛏] [💻] [🍽] [AC] [🚭]

VALDEZ

◆◆◆ ▼▼ BEST WESTERN Valdez Harbor Inn **H**

(907) 835-3434. **$100-$180.** 100 N Harbor Dr 99686. Just s at Meals Ave. Int corridors. **Pets:** Medium, dogs only. $250 deposit/room, $10 daily fee/pet. Designated rooms, service with restrictions, supervision. [SAVE] [📶] [♿M] [🛏] [💻] [🍽] [AC]

WASILLA

◆◆◆ ▼▼▼ BEST WESTERN Lake Lucille Inn **H**

(907) 373-1776. **$99-$199.** 1300 W Lake Lucille Dr 99654. SR 3 (George Parks Hwy), just w on Hallea Ln; center. Int corridors. **Pets:** $20 daily fee/pet. Service with restrictions. [SAVE] [📶] [✕] [♿M] [🛏] [💻] [✕] [AC]

ARIZONA

AJO

▼ La Siesta Motel **M**

(520) 387-6569. **$60-$65.** 2561 N Ajo-Gila Bend Hwy 85321. On SR 85, 1.8 mi n of town plaza. Ext corridors. **Pets:** Other species. Service with restrictions, supervision.

AMADO

▼▼▼ Amado Territory Inn **BB**

(520) 398-8684. **$129-$139, 7 day notice.** 3001 E Frontage Rd 85645. I-19 exit 48, just e, then just s. Int corridors. **Pets:** Accepted.

BENSON

AAA ▼ ▼▼▼ BEST WESTERN Quail Hollow Inn **H**

(520) 586-3646. **$80-$130.** 699 N Ocotillo Rd 85602. I-10 exit 304 (Ocotillo Rd), just s. Ext corridors. **Pets:** Other species. $20 daily fee/pet. Designated rooms, service with restrictions, supervision.

BISBEE

AAA ▼ ▼▼ Americas Best Value Inn & Suites **M**

(520) 432-2293. **$80-$375.** 1372 Hwy 92 85603. 0.8 mi w of jct Naco Hwy; southwest of downtown. Ext corridors. **Pets:** Medium, dogs only. $10 daily fee/pet. Designated rooms, no service, supervision.

▼▼▼▼ Audrey's Inn **CO**

(520) 227-6120. **$105-$145.** 20 Brewery Ave 85603. Just ne of Main St; in historic district. Int corridors. **Pets:** Dogs only. $100 deposit/room. No service.

AAA ▼ ▼▼ San Jose Lodge **M**

(520) 432-5761. **$55-$180.** 2102 Naco Hwy 85603. SR 92 W, 1.5 mi s. Ext corridors. **Pets:** Other species. $10 daily fee/pet. Designated rooms, no service, supervision.

BULLHEAD CITY

AAA ▼ ▼▼ BEST WESTERN Bullhead City Inn **H**

(928) 754-3000. **$70-$80.** 1126 Hwy 95 86429. 1.8 mi s of Laughlin Bridge. Ext corridors. **Pets:** Medium. $20 one-time fee/pet. Service with restrictions, supervision.

▼▼ Lake Mohave Resort Motel **M**

(928) 754-3245. **$95-$170, 3 day notice.** 2690 E Katherine Spur Rd 86429. Jct SR 95, 1.5 mi e on SR 68, 1 mi n, then 5.4 mi e; at Katherine Landing; in Lake Mead National Recreation area. Ext corridors. **Pets:** $50 deposit/room, $10 daily fee/pet. Service with restrictions, crate.

CAMERON

AAA ▼ ▼▼ Cameron Trading Post Motel, Restaurant & Gift Shop **M**

(928) 679-2231. **$59-$109.** 466 N Hwy 89 86020. 1 mi from east gate turn off. Ext corridors. **Pets:** Other species. $15 daily fee/room.

CAMP VERDE

AAA ▼ ▼▼ Cliff Castle Casino Hotel **H**

(928) 567-6611. **$69-$199.** 333 Middle Verde Rd 86322. I-17 exit 289, 0.4 mi se. Ext corridors. **Pets:** Accepted.

▼▼ Comfort Inn-Camp Verde **H** ❀

(928) 567-9000. **$70-$120.** 340 N Goswick Way 86322. I-17 exit 287, just e, then just s. Int corridors. **Pets:** Other species. $15 daily fee/room. Designated rooms, service with restrictions.

▼ Super 8-Camp Verde **M**

(928) 567-2622. **$60-$100.** 1550 W Hwy 260 86322. I-17 exit 287, just e. Int corridors. **Pets:** Accepted.

CASA GRANDE

AAA ▼ ▼▼ Holiday Inn Express & Suites Casa Grande **H**

(520) 509-6333. **$89-$129.** 805 N Cacheries Ct 85122. I-10 exit 194 (SR 287), 0.6 mi w. Int corridors. **Pets:** $20 daily fee/pet. Service with restrictions, crate.

AAA ▼ ▼▼▼ Holiday Inn Hotel Casa Grande **H**

(520) 426-3500. **$79-$139.** 777 N Pinal Ave 85122. I-10 exit 194 (SR 287), 3.9 mi w. Int corridors. **Pets:** Medium. $20 one-time fee/pet. Service with restrictions, supervision.

AAA ▼ ▼▼ Super 8 **H**

(520) 836-8800. **$60-$99.** 2066 E Florence Blvd 85222. I-10 exit 194 (SR 287), 0.6 mi w. Int corridors. **Pets:** $10 daily fee/pet. Service with restrictions, supervision.

COTTONWOOD

AAA ▼ ▼▼▼ BEST WESTERN Cottonwood Inn **H**

(928) 634-5575. **$80-$135.** 993 S Main St 86326. On SR 89A, at SR 260. Ext corridors. **Pets:** Very small, dogs only. $15 daily fee/pet. Designated rooms, service with restrictions, supervision.

▼▼ Motel 6 Ⓜ

(928) 634-3678. **$55-$99.** 1089 S SR 260 86326. On SR 260, just e of jct SR 89A. Ext corridors. **Pets:** Other species. Service with restrictions. supervision. 🛰 ☒ 📱

▼▼ Pines Motel Ⓜ

(928) 634-9975. **$59-$99.** 920 S Camino Real 86326. Jct SR 260, just nw on SR 89A, then just s. Ext corridors. **Pets:** $20 one-time fee/pet. Designated rooms, service with restrictions, supervision.

ECO 🛰 ☒ 📱 🏊

▲▲▲ ▼ The View Motel Ⓜ

(928) 634-7581. **$58-$110.** 818 S Main St 86326. On SR 89A, 0.4 mi nw of jct SR 260. Ext corridors. **Pets:** Dogs only. $10 daily fee/pet. Service with restrictions, supervision. SAVE 🛰 📱 🏊

EAGAR

▲▲▲ ▼▼ BEST WESTERN Sunrise Inn Ⓜ

(928) 333-2540. **$86-$124.** 128 N Main St 85925. Jct SR 260, just n; jct US 60, 1.5 mi s. Ext corridors. **Pets:** Other species. $10 one-time fee/pet. Service with restrictions, crate. SAVE 🛰 📱

EHRENBERG

▲▲▲ ▼▼ BEST WESTERN Desert Oasis Ⓗ

(928) 923-9711. **$75-$150.** S Frontage Rd 85334. I-10 exit 1, just s; 0.5 mi e of Colorado River. Int corridors. **Pets:** Medium, other species. Crate.

SAVE 🛰 📱 🏊

ELOY

▼ Motel 6-1263 Ⓜ

(520) 836-3323. **$45-$61.** 4965 S Sunland Gin Rd 85231. I-10 exit 200, just w. Ext corridors. **Pets:** Other species. Service with restrictions, supervision. 🛰 📱 🏊

FLAGSTAFF

▲▲▲ ▼▼ BEST WESTERN Pony Soldier Inn & Suites Ⓗ

(928) 526-2388. **$70-$150.** 3030 E Route 66 86004. I-40 exit 201, just n, then 1 mi w. Int corridors. **Pets:** Other species. $20 one-time fee/room. Designated rooms, service with restrictions, supervision.

SAVE 🛰 ☒ 📱 🏊

▼▼▼ Comfort Inn I-17/I-40 Ⓗ

(928) 774-2225. **$80-$130.** 2355 S Beulah Blvd 86001. I-40 exit 195, just n to Forest Meadows St, then 1 blk w. Int corridors. **Pets:** Large, other species. $20 daily fee/room. Service with restrictions, supervision.

🛰 📱 🏊

▲▲▲ ▼▼ Days Inn & Suites Ⓗ

(928) 527-1477. **$70-$160.** 3601 E Lockett Rd 86004. I-40 exit 201, 0.5 mi w on I-40 business loop, then just n on Fanning Dr. Int corridors. **Pets:** Other species. $25 one-time fee/room, $5 daily fee/room. Designated rooms, service with restrictions, supervision.

SAVE 🛰 ☒ 📱 🏊

▼▼▼ Drury Inn & Suites-Flagstaff Ⓗ

(928) 773-4900. **$149-$239.** 300 S Milton Rd 86001. I-40 exit 195, 1.8 mi n on SR 89A (Milton Rd). Int corridors. **Pets:** Service with restrictions, supervision. ECO 🛰 ☒ ♿ 📱 🏊

▲▲▲ ▼ Econo Lodge-University Ⓜ

(928) 774-7326. **$39-$149.** 914 S Milton Rd 86001. I-40 exit 195, 1.2 mi n on SR 89A (Milton Rd). Ext corridors. **Pets:** Small. $10 daily fee/pet. Service with restrictions, supervision. SAVE 🛰 📱 🏊

▼ Motel 6-Flagstaff West #1000 Ⓜ

(928) 779-3757. **$45-$69.** 2745 S Woodlands Village Blvd 86001. I-40 exit 195, just n to Forest Meadows St, w to Beulah Blvd, just s, then just w. Ext corridors. **Pets:** Other species. Service with restrictions, supervision. 🛰 ♿ 📱 🏊

▼▼ Quality Inn University Ⓗ

(928) 774-8771. **$50-$170.** 2000 S Milton Rd 86001. I-40 exit 195, just n to Forest Meadows St, then right. Int corridors. **Pets:** Other species. $10 daily fee/room. Service with restrictions, supervision.

🛰 ☒ 📱 🏊

▲▲▲ ▼▼▼ Radisson Woodlands Hotel Flagstaff Ⓗ

(928) 773-8888. **$99-$209, 3 day notice.** 1175 W Route 66 86001. I-40 exit 195, 1.5 mi n on SR 89A (Milton Rd), then 0.5 mi w. Int corridors. **Pets:** Medium. $50 one-time fee/room. Designated rooms, service with restrictions. SAVE 🛰 ☒ ♿ 📱 🍽 🏊 ☒

▼▼ Ramada Inn-Lucky Lane Ⓗ

(928) 779-3614. **$50-$210.** 2350 E Lucky Ln 86004. I-40 exit 198 (Butler Ave), just n, then just e. Ext corridors. **Pets:** Accepted.

🛰 📱 🏊

▲▲▲ ▼▼▼ Sonesta ES Suites Flagstaff Ⓗ 🐾

(928) 526-5555. **$89-$229.** 3440 N Country Club Dr 86004. I-40 exit 201, 0.5 mi s. Ext/int corridors. **Pets:** $50 one-time fee/room. Designated rooms, service with restrictions, crate.

SAVE 🛰 ☒ 📱 🏊

▲▲▲ ▼▼▼ Super 8-Flagstaff Mall Ⓜ

(928) 526-0818. **$49-$190.** 3725 N Kasper Ave 86004. I-40 exit 201, just n, 0.5 mi w on I-40 business loop, then just n. Int corridors. **Pets:** Accepted. SAVE 🛰 📱

FLORENCE

▼▼◆ Holiday Inn Express & Suites Ⓗ 🐾

(520) 868-9900. **$69-$349, 3 day notice.** 240 W Hwy 287 85132. Just w of jct SR 79 and 287. Int corridors. **Pets:** Large. $15 daily fee/room. Service with restrictions, supervision. 🛰 ☒ 📱 🏊

▼▼▼ Rancho Sonora Inn Ⓒ

(520) 868-8000. **$79-$225, 3 day notice.** 9198 N Hwy 79 85232. On SR 79, 5 mi s of SR 287. Ext corridors. **Pets:** $10 daily fee/room. Designated rooms, service with restrictions, crate. 🛰 ☒ 📱 🏊

FOREST LAKES

▲▲▲ ▼ Forest Lakes Lodge Ⓜ

(928) 535-4727. **$64-$89.** 2823 SR 260 85931. On SR 260; between MM 288 and 289. Ext corridors. **Pets:** Small, dogs only. $15 one-time fee/room. Service with restrictions, supervision. SAVE 🛰 📱 ☒ ♿

GILA BEND

▼ America's Choice Inn & Suites Ⓗ

(928) 683-6311. **$75-$105.** 2888 Butterfield Tr 85337. I-8 exit 119, just nw. Int corridors. **Pets:** $10 one-time fee/room. Service with restrictions, supervision. 🛰 📱 🏊

▲▲▲ ▼▼▼ BEST WESTERN Space Age Lodge Ⓜ

(928) 683-2273. **$99-$189.** 401 E Pima St 85337. Business Loop I-8; center. Ext corridors. **Pets:** Medium. $20 one-time fee/pet. Designated rooms, service with restrictions, supervision.

SAVE 🛰 ☒ 📱 🍽 🏊

GLOBE

▼▼ Quality Inn Ⓗ

(928) 425-7575. **$60-$180.** 1565 E South St 85501. On US 60, 1 mi e of town. Ext corridors. **Pets:** Accepted. 🛰 ☒ 📱 🏊

GRAND CANYON NATIONAL PARK AREA

GRAND CANYON NATIONAL PARK - SOUTH RIM

Canyon Plaza Resort Grand Canyon H ❖
(928) 638-2673. **$83-$268.** 406 Canyon Plaza Ln 86023. On SR 64; 2 mi s of South Rim entrance. Ext/int corridors. **Pets:** Small, other species. $50 one-time fee/room. Service with restrictions, crate.

The Grand Hotel H
(928) 638-3333. **$119-$259, 3 day notice.** Hwy 64 86023. On SR 64; 2 mi s of South Rim entrance. Int corridors. **Pets:** Medium, other species. $25 one-time fee/pet. Designated rooms, service with restrictions, supervision.

Red Feather Lodge H
(928) 638-2414. **$75-$290.** 300 SR 64 86023. On SR 64; 2 mi s of South Rim entrance. Ext/int corridors. **Pets:** Medium, dogs only. $50 deposit/room, $25 one-time fee/room. Designated rooms, service with restrictions, supervision.

END AREA

HEBER

BEST WESTERN Sawmill Inn M
(928) 535-5053. **$55-$85.** 1877 Hwy 260 85928. 0.5 mi e of center. Ext corridors. **Pets:** Dogs only. $10 daily fee/pet. Designated rooms, service with restrictions, supervision.

HOLBROOK

BEST WESTERN Arizonian Inn H
(928) 524-2611. **$90-$136.** 2508 Navajo Blvd 86025. I-40 exit 289, 0.5 mi w. Ext corridors. **Pets:** Large. $10 daily fee/pet. Designated rooms, supervision.

Comfort Inn H
(928) 524-6131. **$70-$99.** 2602 E Navajo Blvd 86025. I-40 exit 289, just w. Ext corridors. **Pets:** Accepted.

Days Inn M
(928) 524-6949. **$60-$85.** 2601 Navajo Blvd 86025. I-40 exit 289, 0.3 mi w. Ext corridors. **Pets:** Medium. $15 daily fee/pet. Designated rooms, service with restrictions, supervision.

Magnuson Hotel Adobe Inn M ❖
(928) 524-3948. **$59-$109.** 615 W Hopi Dr 86025. I-40 exit 285, 1 mi e on US 180 (Hopi Dr). Ext corridors. **Pets:** Medium. $10 daily fee/pet. Designated rooms, service with restrictions, supervision.

Ramada Limited H
(928) 524-2566. **$57-$63.** 2608 E Navajo Blvd 86025. I-40 exit 289, just w. Ext corridors. **Pets:** Accepted.

JEROME

Connor Hotel of Jerome H
(928) 634-5006. **Call for rates.** 160 S Main St 86331. Center. Int corridors. **Pets:** Accepted.

KAYENTA

Hampton Inn of Kayenta H ❖
(928) 697-3170. **Call for rates.** Hwy 160 86033. Just w of US 163. Int corridors. **Pets:** Small. Supervision.

KINGMAN

BEST WESTERN PLUS A Wayfarer's Inn & Suites H
(928) 753-6271. **$103-$128.** 2815 E Andy Devine Ave 86401. I-40 exit 53, 0.5 mi w on Route 66. Ext corridors. **Pets:** Medium, dogs only. $10 daily fee/pet. Service with restrictions, supervision.

BEST WESTERN PLUS King's Inn & Suites H
(928) 753-6101. **$92-$109.** 2930 E Andy Devine Ave 86401. I-40 exit 53, just w on Route 66. Ext corridors. **Pets:** Other species. $8 one-time fee/room. Designated rooms, service with restrictions, supervision.

Comfort Inn H
(928) 718-1717. **$85-$115.** 3129 E Andy Devine Ave 86401. I-40 exit 53, just w on Route 66. Int corridors. **Pets:** Small, dogs only. $20 one-time fee/room. Designated rooms, service with restrictions, supervision.

Days Inn West M
(928) 753-7500. **$70-$260.** 3023 E Andy Devine Ave 86401. I-40 exit 53, just w on Route 66. Ext corridors. **Pets:** Other species. $10 daily fee/pet. Service with restrictions, supervision.

Holiday Inn Express Hotel & Suites H
(928) 718-4343. **$109-$129.** 3031 E Andy Devine Ave 86401. I-40 exit 53, just w on Route 66. Int corridors. **Pets:** Other species. $20 one-time fee/pet. Designated rooms, service with restrictions.

SpringHill Suites by Marriott H
(928) 753-8766. **$98-$169.** 3101 E Andy Devine Ave 86401. I-40 exit 53, just w on Route 66. Int corridors. **Pets:** Small, other species. $20 one-time fee/pet. Designated rooms, service with restrictions, supervision.

Travelodge Kingman M
(928) 757-1188. **$50-$90.** 3275 E Andy Devine Ave 86401. I-40 exit 53, just e on Route 66. Ext corridors. **Pets:** Medium. $10 one-time fee/room. Service with restrictions, supervision.

KOHLS RANCH

Kohl's Ranch Lodge CO
(928) 478-4211. **$109-$483.** 202 S Kohl's Ranch Lodge Rd 85541. SR 87, 16.6 mi e on US 260, MM 238-239. Ext/int corridors. **Pets:** Accepted.

LAKE HAVASU CITY

Days Inn Lake Havasu M
(928) 855-7841. **$65-$144.** 1700 McCulloch Blvd N 86403. Just ne of Lake Havasu Ave; center. Ext corridors. **Pets:** Accepted.

Hampton Inn Lake Havasu H
(928) 855-4071. **$119-$149.** 245 London Bridge Rd 86403. 0.5 mi n of London Bridge. Ext/int corridors. **Pets:** Other species. Designated rooms, service with restrictions, supervision.

Havasu Travelodge M

(928) 680-9202. **$69-$193, 3 day notice.** 480 London Bridge Rd 86403. 1 mi n of London Bridge. Int corridors. **Pets:** Medium. $10 daily fee/pet. Designated rooms, service with restrictions, supervision.

SAVE 🛜 ✕ 🛗 💻

Island Suites H

(928) 855-7333. **Call for rates.** 236 S Lake Havasu Ave 86403. Just s of jct McCulloch Blvd. Int corridors. **Pets:** Accepted.

🛜 🛗 💻 ⊇ ✕

Motel 6 Lakeside - #4067 M

(928) 855-3200. **Call for rates.** 111 London Bridge Rd 86403. 0.3 mi n of London Bridge. Int corridors. **Pets:** Other species. Service with restrictions, supervision. 🛜

The Nautical Beachfront Resort H ❧

(928) 855-2141. **$69-$550, 3 day notice.** 1000 McCulloch Blvd N 86403. 1.4 mi w of London Bridge/SR 95, follow signs. Ext corridors. **Pets:** Other species. $20 daily fee/pet. Designated rooms, service with restrictions, supervision. SAVE 🛜 ✕ 🛗 💻 🍴 ⊇ ✕

Quality Inn & Suites M

(928) 855-1111. **$60-$160.** 271 S Lake Havasu Ave 86403. SR 95, just e on Swanson Ave, then just s. Ext corridors. **Pets:** Other species. $20 one-time fee/room. Service with restrictions, crate.

🛜 🛗 💻 🍴 ⊇

NOGALES

Candlewood Suites H

(520) 281-1111. **$99-$159, 3 day notice.** 875 N Frank Reed Rd 85621. I-19 exit 4, just w to Frank Reed Rd, then just nw. Int corridors. **Pets:** Accepted. 🛜 ✕ 🛗 💻

Holiday Inn Express Hotel Nogales H

(520) 281-0123. **$99-$159, 3 day notice.** 850 W Shell Rd 85621. I-19 exit 4, just w to Frank Reed Rd, then just nw. Int corridors. **Pets:** Accepted. 🛜 ✕ 🛗 💻 ⊇

Siesta Motel M

(520) 287-4671. **$60-$80.** 673 N Grand Ave 85621. On Business Loop I-19, 1 mi n of International border. Ext corridors. **Pets:** $10 daily fee/pet. No service, supervision. SAVE 🛜 🛗 ⊇

PAGE

Lake Powell Days Inn & Suites H

(928) 645-2800. **$70-$240.** 961 N Hwy 89 86040. On US 89, just s. Int corridors. **Pets:** $25 daily fee/pet. Designated rooms, service with restrictions, supervision. 🛜 ✕ 🛗 💻 ⊇

Lake Powell Resort and Marina H

(928) 645-2433. **$109-$229.** 100 Lakeshore Dr 86040. 4 mi n of Glen Canyon Dam via US 89. Int corridors. **Pets:** Accepted.

SAVE 🛜 ✕ 🛗 💻 🍴 ⊇ ✕

PARKER

BEST WESTERN Parker Inn H

(928) 669-6060. **$80-$130.** 1012 Geronimo Ave 85344. Jct SR 95, just e. Int corridors. **Pets:** Large, other species. Designated rooms, service with restrictions, supervision. SAVE 🛜 ✕ 🛗 💻

Blue Water Resort & Casino H

(928) 669-7000. **$60-$190, 3 day notice.** 11300 Resort Dr 85344. Jct SR 62, 1.3 mi nw on SR 95. Ext corridors. **Pets:** Medium, dogs only. Designated rooms, service with restrictions, supervision.

SAVE 🛜 🛗 💻 🍴 ⊇ ✕

PAYSON

Americas Best Value Inn M

(928) 474-2283. **$50-$121.** 811 S Beeline Hwy 85541. SR 87, 0.7 mi s of SR 260. Ext/int corridors. **Pets:** Small, dogs only. $15 daily fee/pet. Designated rooms, service with restrictions, supervision.

SAVE 🛜 🛗 💻

BEST WESTERN Payson Inn H ❧

(928) 474-3241. **$70-$160.** 801 N Beeline Hwy 85541. SR 87, 0.6 mi n of SR 260. Ext corridors. **Pets:** Other species. $20 daily fee/room. Designated rooms, service with restrictions, crate. SAVE 🛜 🛗 💻 ⊇

Motel 6 Payson #4794 M

(928) 474-2382. **Call for rates.** 1005 S Beeline Hwy 85541. SR 87, 0.9 mi s of SR 260. Ext corridors. **Pets:** Accepted. 🛜 🛗 💻 ⊇

Wooden Nickel Cabins CA

(928) 478-4519. **$120-$139, 30 day notice.** 165 Hunter Creek Dr 85541. SR 87, 22 mi e on SR 260, then 0.7 mi n; just w of MM 275, follow signs. Ext corridors. **Pets:** Accepted. ✕ 🛗 💻 ✕ 🖼

PEACH SPRINGS

Hualapai Lodge H

(928) 769-2230. **$100-$120, 3 day notice.** 900 Historic Route 66 86434. Center. Int corridors. **Pets:** Small. $25 daily fee/pet. Designated rooms, service with restrictions, crate.

SAVE 🛜 ♿ 🛗 💻 🍴 ⊇

PHOENIX METROPOLITAN AREA

APACHE JUNCTION

Apache Junction Motel M

(480) 982-7702. **$49-$89, 3 day notice.** 1680 W Apache Tr 85120. US 60 exit 195, 2 mi n, then just w. Ext corridors. **Pets:** Very small, dogs only. $15 one-time fee/pet. Designated rooms, service with restrictions, supervision. SAVE 🛜 🛗 💻

BUCKEYE

Days Inn-Buckeye H

(623) 386-5400. **$80-$170.** 25205 W Yuma Rd 85326. I-10 exit 114 (Miller Rd), just sw. Ext corridors. **Pets:** Other species. $15 deposit/pet. Service with restrictions, supervision. SAVE 🛜 🛗 💻 ⊇

CAREFREE

The Boulders, A Waldorf Astoria Resort H ❧

(480) 488-9009. **$129-$329.** 34631 N Tom Darlington Dr 85377. Jct Scottsdale and Bell rds, 11 mi n. Ext corridors. **Pets:** Large. $100 one-time fee/room. Supervision. SAVE 🛜 ✕ 🛗 💻 🍴 ⊇ ✕

Carefree Resort & Conference Center H

(480) 488-5300. **$59-$870, 3 day notice.** 37220 Mule Train Rd 85377. SR 101 exit 36 (Pima Rd), 12.2 mi n to Cave Creek Rd, 1 mi w, then 0.4 mi n. Ext/int corridors. **Pets:** Accepted.

SAVE 🛜 ✕ 🛗 💻 🍴 ⊇ ✕

CHANDLER

Chandler Super 8 H ❧

(480) 961-3888. **$48-$120.** 7171 W Chandler Blvd 85226. I-10 exit 160 (Chandler Blvd), just e. Int corridors. **Pets:** Medium, other species. $5 daily fee/pet. Designated rooms, service with restrictions, crate.

🛜 🛗 💻 ⊇

Comfort Inn Chandler H

(480) 857-4969. **$75-$135.** 7400 W Boston St 85226. I-10 exit 160 (Chandler Blvd), just e, then just s on Southgate Dr. Int corridors. **Pets:** Medium, other species. $20 daily fee/pet. Designated rooms, service with restrictions, supervision. SAVE 🛜 ♿ 🛗 ⊇

Crowne Plaza San Marcos Golf Resort 🅷
(480) 812-0900. **$79-$199.** 1 San Marcos Pl 85225. Jct Chandler Blvd, just s on Arizona Ave, then just w on Buffalo St; in historic downtown. Ext corridors. **Pets:** Small. $50 one-time fee/pet. Designated rooms, service with restrictions, supervision. [SAVE] 🛜 🗔 🖥 🍴 ⊃ ⊗

Hawthorn Suites by Wyndham-Chandler 🅷
(480) 705-8881. **$79-$219.** 5858 W Chandler Blvd 85226. I-10 exit 160 (Chandler Blvd), 1.5 mi e. Int corridors. **Pets:** Accepted.
[SAVE] 🛜 🗔 🖥 ⊃

Hilton Phoenix Chandler 🅷
(480) 899-7400. **$99-$249.** 2929 W Frye Rd 85224. SR 202 exit 50B (Price Rd), 0.4 mi n, then just w. Int corridors. **Pets:** Accepted.
🛜 🗔 🖥 🍴 ⊃

Homewood Suites by Hilton Phoenix-Chandler 🅷
(480) 753-6200. **$99-$279.** 7373 W Detroit St 85226. I-10 exit 160 (Chandler Blvd), 0.4 mi e, n on 54th St, then just w. Int corridors.
Pets: Accepted. 🛜 ♿ 🗔 🖥 ⊃ ⊗

Homewood Suites by Hilton-Phoenix/Chandler Fashion Center 🅷
(480) 963-5700. **$119-$209.** 1221 S Spectrum Blvd 85286. SR 202 exit 50B (Price Rd), just s. Int corridors. **Pets:** Accepted.
🛜 ♿ 🗔 🖥 ⊃ ⊗

Quality Inn 🅷
(480) 705-0922. **$63-$130.** 255 N Kyrene Rd 85226. I-10 exit 160 (Chandler Blvd), 1.5 mi e, then just n. Int corridors. **Pets:** Accepted.
[SAVE] 🛜 ⊗ ♿ 🗔 🖥 ⊃

Residence Inn by Marriott-Chandler Fashion Center 🅷 ✿
(480) 782-1551. **$109-$259.** 200 N Federal St 85226. I-10 exit 160 (Chandler Blvd), 4.2 mi e, just n on N Metro Blvd, then just e. Int corridors. **Pets:** Medium, other species. $100 one-time fee/pet. Service with restrictions, crate. 🛜 ⊗ ♿ 🗔 🖥 ⊃

Sheraton Wild Horse Pass Resort & Spa 🅷
(602) 225-0100. **$149-$299, 3 day notice.** 5594 W Wild Horse Pass Blvd 85226. I-10 exit 162, 2.4 mi w. Int corridors. **Pets:** Accepted.
[SAVE] 🛜 ⊗ 🗔 🖥 🍴 ⊃ ⊗

Windmill Suites of Chandler 🅷
(480) 812-9600. **$79-$225.** 3535 W Chandler Blvd 85226. I-10 exit 160 (Chandler Blvd), 4 mi e. Int corridors. **Pets:** Accepted.
[SAVE] 🛜 ⊗ 🗔 🖥 ⊃ ⊗

FOUNTAIN HILLS

Comfort Inn Fountain Hills 🅷
(480) 837-5343. **$40-$150.** 17105 E Shea Blvd 85268. 0.5 mi w of SR 87 (Beeline Hwy). Int corridors. **Pets:** Small, other species. $15 daily fee/pet. Designated rooms, service with restrictions, supervision.
[SAVE] 🛜 🗔 🖥 ⊃

Holiday Inn Hotel & Suites-Fountain Hills/North Scottsdale 🅷
(480) 837-6565. **Call for rates.** 12800 N Saguaro Blvd 85268. Jct Shea Blvd, 2.2 mi n; center. Int corridors. **Pets:** Accepted.
🛜 ⊗ ♿ 🗔 🖥 🍴 ⊃ ⊗

GLENDALE

Comfort Suites Glendale University of Phoenix Stadium Area 🅷
(623) 271-9005. **$89-$299.** 9824 W Camelback Rd 85305. Loop 101 exit 5 (Camelback Rd), just w to 99th St, then just n. Int corridors.
Pets: Large. $25 one-time fee/room. Designated rooms, service with restrictions, supervision. 🛜 ⊗ ♿ 🗔 🖥 ⊃

Residence Inn by Marriott Phoenix Glendale Sports & Entertainment District 🅷
(623) 772-8900. **$76-$229.** 7350 W Zanjero Blvd 85305. Loop 101 exit 7 (Glendale Ave), then e. Int corridors. **Pets:** Accepted.
🛜 ⊗ ♿ 🗔 🖥 ⊃ ⊗

Staybridge Suites 🅷
(623) 842-0000. **$79-$229.** 9340 W Cabela Dr 85305. Loop 101 exit 7 (Glendale Ave), e on Zanjero Blvd, then left. Int corridors. **Pets:** Medium. $150 one-time fee/pet. Service with restrictions, supervision.
🛜 ⊗ ♿ 🗔 🖥 ⊃

GOODYEAR

BEST WESTERN PLUS Phoenix Goodyear Inn 🅷
(623) 932-3210. **$90-$170.** 55 N Litchfield Rd 85338. I-10 exit 128, 0.8 mi s. Ext/int corridors. **Pets:** $15 daily fee/room. Service with restrictions, crate. [SAVE] 🛜 ⊗ 🗔 🖥 🍴 ⊃

Comfort Suites Goodyear 🅷 ✿
(623) 266-2884. **$79-$159.** 15575 W Roosevelt St 85338. I-10 exit 126, just s on Estrella Pkwy, then just w. Int corridors. **Pets:** Medium. $25 one-time fee/pet. Designated rooms, service with restrictions, supervision.
🛜 ⊗ 🗔 🖥 ⊃

Hampton Inn & Suites Goodyear 🅷
(623) 536-1313. **$135-$229.** 2000 N Litchfield Rd 85395. I-10 exit 128, 0.5 mi n. Int corridors. **Pets:** Accepted. 🛜 ♿ 🗔 🖥 ⊃ ⊗

Holiday Inn & Suites Goodyear 🅷 ✿
(623) 547-1313. **$129-$209.** 1188 N Dysart Rd 85395. I-10 exit 129 (Dysart Rd), just n. Int corridors. **Pets:** Medium. $35 one-time fee/room. Service with restrictions, crate. 🛜 🗔 🖥 ⊃

Holiday Inn Express West Phoenix/Goodyear 🅷
(623) 535-1313. **$109-$199.** 1313 N Litchfield Rd 85395. I-10 exit 128, just n. Int corridors. **Pets:** Accepted.
🛜 ⊗ ♿ 🗔 🖥 ⊃ ⊗

Quality Inn & Suites Goodyear 🅷
(623) 932-9191. **$60-$129.** 950 N Dysart Rd 85338. I-10 exit 129 (Dysart Rd), just s. Ext corridors. **Pets:** $50 deposit/room, $15 daily fee/pet. Service with restrictions, crate. 🛜 🗔 🖥 ⊃

Residence Inn by Marriott 🅷
(623) 866-1313. **$125-$299.** 2020 N Litchfield Rd 85395. I-10 exit 128, 0.6 mi n. Int corridors. **Pets:** Accepted. 🛜 ⊗ ♿ 🗔 🖥 ⊃ ⊗

TownePlace Suites by Marriott Phoenix/Goodyear 🅷 ✿
(623) 535-5009. **$119-$299.** 13971 W Fillmore St 85338. I-10 exit 128, just s, then just w. Int corridors. **Pets:** Other species. $100 one-time fee/room. Service with restrictions, supervision.
🛜 ⊗ ♿ 🗔 🖥 ⊃

LITCHFIELD PARK

The Wigwam 🅷
(623) 935-3811. **Call for rates.** 300 Wigwam Blvd 85340. I-10 exit 128 (Litchfield Rd), 2.4 mi n, then 0.4 mi e. Ext corridors. **Pets:** Medium, dogs only. $15 daily fee/room. Service with restrictions, supervision.
[SAVE] 🛜 ⊗ 🗔 🖥 🍴 ⊃ ⊗

MESA

Arizona Golf Resort & Conference Center 🅷
(480) 832-3202. **$89-$209.** 425 S Power Rd 85206. 1.3 mi n of US 60 (Superstition Frwy) exit 188 (Power Rd); southeast corner of Broadway and Power rds; entrance on Broadway Rd. Ext corridors. **Pets:** Accepted.
[SAVE] 🛜 ⊗ 🗔 🖥 🍴 ⊃ ⊗

(AAA) ▼▼▼ BEST WESTERN Mezona Inn H ❀

(480) 834-9233. **$75-$175.** 250 W Main St 85201. Just e of Country Club Dr; downtown. Ext corridors. **Pets:** $20 one-time fee/room. Designated rooms, service with restrictions, supervision.

SAVE 🛜 ✕ 🔌 💻 🍴 ⊃~

(AAA) ▼▼▼ BEST WESTERN Superstition
Springs H ❀

(480) 641-1164. **$79-$125.** 1342 S Power Rd 85206. Just n of US 60 (Superstition Frwy) exit 188 (Power Rd); northwest corner of Power Rd and Hampton Ave. Ext corridors. **Pets:** Large. $10 daily fee/pet. Designated rooms, service with restrictions, supervision.

SAVE 🛜 🔌 💻 ⊃~

▼▼▼▼ Days Hotel Mesa Country Club H

(480) 844-8900. **$66-$140.** 333 W Juanita Ave 85210. US 60 (Superstition Frwy) exit 179 (Country Club Dr), just s, then just e. Int corridors. **Pets:** Other species. $5 daily fee/pet. Service with restrictions, crate.

🛜 ✕ 🔌 💻 ⊃~

▼▼▼ Days Inn-East Mesa H

(480) 981-8111. **$58-$120.** 5531 E Main St 85205. 0.4 mi e of Higley Rd. Ext corridors. **Pets:** Small, dogs only. $10 daily fee/pet. Designated rooms, service with restrictions, crate. 🛜 🔌 💻 ⊃~

▼▼▼▼ Dobson Ranch Inn & Suites H ❀

(480) 831-7000. **$72-$165.** 1666 S Dobson Rd 85202. Just s of US 60 (Superstition Frwy) exit 177 (Dobson Rd). Ext/int corridors. **Pets:** Medium. $10 daily fee/pet. Designated rooms, service with restrictions, supervision.

🛜 ✕ 🔌 💻 🍴 ⊃~

(AAA) ▼▼▼▼ Hilton Phoenix East/Mesa H

(480) 833-5555. **$79-$189.** 1011 W Holmes Ave 85210. US 60 (Superstition Frwy) exit 178 (Alma School Rd), just n, then just e. Int corridors. **Pets:** Accepted. SAVE 🛜 🔌 💻 🍴 ⊃~ ✕

▼▼▼ Holiday Inn & Suites Phoenix-Mesa/Chandler H

(480) 964-7000. **$99-$209.** 1600 S Country Club Dr 85210. US 60 (Superstition Frwy) exit 179 (Country Club Dr), just s. Ext/int corridors. **Pets:** Small. $50 one-time fee/room. Designated rooms, service with restrictions, supervision. 🛜 ✕ ♿M 🔌 💻 🍴 ⊃~

▼▼▼ Homestead Studio Suites Hotel Phoenix-Mesa H

(480) 752-2266. **$70-$80.** 1920 W Isabella Ave 85202. Just s of US 60 (Superstition Frwy) exit 177 (Dobson Rd). Ext corridors. **Pets:** $25 daily fee/pet. Designated rooms, service with restrictions. 🛜 🔌 💻

▼▼▼▼ La Quinta Inn & Suites Mesa Superstition
Springs H

(480) 654-1970. **$71-$155.** 6530 E Superstition Springs Blvd 85206. US 60 (Superstition Frwy) exit 187 (Superstition Springs Blvd) eastbound, just se; exit 188 (Power Rd) westbound, just sw. Int corridors. **Pets:** Service with restrictions, supervision. 🛜 ♿M 🔌 💻 ⊃~

▼▼▼▼ La Quinta Inn & Suites Phoenix Mesa West H

(480) 844-8747. **$59-$133.** 902 W Grove Ave 85210. US 60 (Superstition Frwy) exit 178 (Alma School Rd), just n, then just e. Int corridors. **Pets:** Service with restrictions, supervision. 🛜 🔌 💻 ⊃~

▼▼ Motel 6-Mesa South #1030 M

(480) 834-0066. **$45-$65.** 1511 S Country Club Dr 85210. US 60 (Superstition Frwy) exit 179 (Country Club Dr), northeast corner. Ext corridors. **Pets:** Other species. Service with restrictions, supervision.

🛜 ♿M 🔌 ⊃~

▼▼ Quality Inn & Suites Mesa/Phoenix H ❀

(480) 964-2897. **$50-$110.** 1410 S Country Club Dr 85210. US 60 (Superstition Frwy) exit 179 (Country Club Dr), just n. Ext corridors. **Pets:** Medium, dogs only. $10 daily fee/pet. Service with restrictions, supervision. 🛜 🔌 💻 ⊃~

▼▼▼▼ Residence Inn by Marriott Phoenix Mesa H

(480) 610-0100. **$79-$249.** 941 W Grove Ave 85210. US 60 (Superstition Frwy) exit 178 (Alma School Rd), just n, then just e. Int corridors. **Pets:** Medium. $100 one-time fee/room. Service with restrictions.

🛜 ✕ ♿M 🔌 💻 ⊃~ ✕

▼▼▼ Sleep Inn of Mesa H

(480) 807-7760. **Call for rates.** 6347 E Southern Ave 85206. US 60 (Superstition Frwy) exit 188 (Power Rd), 0.8 mi n, then 0.4 mi w to mall entrance. Int corridors. **Pets:** Medium, other species. $25 one-time fee/pet, $10 daily fee/pet. Supervision. 🛜 🔌 💻 ⊃~

PARADISE VALLEY

▼▼▼ Hermosa Inn H

(602) 955-8614. **$199-$624, 7 day notice.** 5532 N Palo Cristi Rd 85253. 1 mi s of Lincoln Dr; corner of Stanford Dr. Ext corridors.
Pets: Accepted. 🛜 ✕ 🔌 💻 🍴 ⊃~ ✕

(AAA) ▼▼▼ ▼▼▼ Montelucia Resort & Spa H ❀

(480) 627-3200. **$139-$369, 3 day notice.** 4949 E Lincoln Dr 85253. Southeast corner of Lincoln Dr and Tatum Blvd, enter from Lincoln Dr. Ext/int corridors. **Pets:** Medium. $100 deposit/room. Service with restrictions, supervision. SAVE 🛜 ✕ 🔌 💻 🍴 ⊃~ ✕

(AAA) ▼▼▼ ▼▼▼ Sanctuary on Camelback
Mountain H ❀

(480) 948-2100. **$279-$719, 7 day notice.** 5700 E McDonald Dr 85253. SR 101 exit McDonald Dr, 3.9 mi w; 1.8 mi w of jct Scottsdale Rd. Ext corridors. **Pets:** Medium, other species. $100 one-time fee/room. Designated rooms, service with restrictions, supervision.

SAVE 🛜 ✕ 🔌 💻 🍴 ⊃~ ✕

PEORIA

▼▼ Comfort Suites by Choice Hotels/Peoria Sports
Complex H

(623) 334-3993. **$59-$199.** 8473 W Paradise Ln 85382. Loop 101 exit 14 (Bell Rd), just e to 83rd Ave, just s, then just w. Int corridors.
Pets: Accepted. 🛜 ✕ 🔌 💻 ⊃~

▼▼▼ Extended StayAmerica Peoria H

(623) 487-0020. **$70-$80.** 7345 W Bell Rd 85382. Loop 101 exit 14 (Bell Rd), 1.2 mi e. Int corridors. **Pets:** $25 daily fee/pet. Designated rooms, service with restrictions. 🛜 🔌 💻

▼▼▼ Hampton Inn H

(623) 486-9918. **$69-$259.** 8408 W Paradise Ln 85382. Loop 101 exit 14 (Bell Rd), just e to 83rd Ave, just s, then just w. Int corridors.
Pets: Accepted. 🛜 ✕ 🔌 💻 ⊃~

▼▼▼ Holiday Inn Express Hotel & Suites Peoria
North-Glendale H

(623) 853-1313. **$89-$169.** 16771 N 84th Ave 85382. Loop 101 exit 14 (Bell Rd), just w, then just s. Int corridors. **Pets:** $25 daily fee/room. Service with restrictions. 🛜 ♿M 🔌 💻 ⊃~

▼▼▼ La Quinta Inn & Suites Phoenix West Peoria H

(623) 487-1900. **$59-$184.** 16321 N 83rd Ave 85382. Loop 101 exit 14 (Bell Rd), just e, then just s. Int corridors. **Pets:** Service with restrictions, supervision. 🛜 ✕ 🔌 💻 ⊃~

▼▼▼ Ramada Peoria Convention Center H

(623) 979-7200. **$46-$125.** 8955 W Grand Ave 85345. Loop 101 N exit 11 (Grand Ave), 0.5 mi e. Int corridors. **Pets:** Medium. $10 daily fee/pet. Designated rooms, service with restrictions, crate.

🛜 ✕ 🔌 💻 🍴 ⊃~

▼▼▼ Residence Inn by Marriott H ❀

(623) 979-2074. **$200-$370.** 8435 W Paradise Ln 85382. Loop 101 exit 14 (Bell Rd), just e to 83rd Ave, just s, then just w. Int corridors.
Pets: $100 one-time fee/room. Service with restrictions, crate.
🛜 ✕ 🔌 💻 ⊃~ ✕

PHOENIX

(AAA) ▼▼▼ Aloft Phoenix Airport Hotel H

(602) 275-6300. **$79-$229.** 4450 E Washington St 85034. SR 143 exit Washington St, just w. Int corridors. **Pets:** Accepted.

SAVE 🛜 ✕ ♿M 🔌 💻 ⊃~

Arizona Biltmore Resort & Spa, A Waldorf Astoria Hotel 🅷

(602) 955-6600. **$109-$255.** 2400 E Missouri Ave 85016. Jct Camelback Rd, 0.5 mi n on 24th St, then 0.4 mi e. Ext/int corridors. **Pets:** Accepted.

BEST WESTERN Phoenix I-17 MetroCenter Inn 🅷 ❀

(602) 864-6233. **$80-$129.** 8101 N Black Canyon Hwy 85021. I-17 exit 206 (Northern Ave), just e, then just n; on east side of freeway. Ext corridors. **Pets:** Other species. $20 daily fee/pet. Designated rooms, service with restrictions, supervision.

BEST WESTERN PLUS InnSuites Phoenix Hotel & Suites 🅷 ❀

(602) 997-6285. **$69-$169.** 1615 E Northern Ave 85020. SR 51 exit 7, 0.6 mi w. Ext corridors. **Pets:** Medium. $25 one-time fee/room. Designated rooms, service with restrictions, crate.

Candlewood Suites Phoenix 🅷

(602) 861-4900. **$69-$139.** 11411 N Black Canyon Hwy 85029. I-17 exit 208 (Peoria Ave), just e, then 0.4 mi n. Int corridors. **Pets:** Large, other species. $15 daily fee/pet. Service with restrictions, crate.

Clarion Hotel @ Phoenix Tech Center 🅷

(480) 893-3900. **$60-$110.** 5121 E La Puenta Ave 85044. I-10 exit 157 (Elliot Rd), just w, just n on 51st St, then just e. Ext corridors. **Pets:** Accepted.

Coast Phoenix Sky Harbor Hotel 🅷

(602) 273-7778. **Call for rates.** 4300 E Washington St 85034. SR 202 exit 2 (44th St), 0.7 mi s. Int corridors. **Pets:** Accepted.

Comfort Inn-Phoenix North 🅷

(602) 978-2222. **$81-$99.** 2641 W Union Hills Dr 85027. I-17 exit 214A (Union Hills Dr), just w. Int corridors. **Pets:** Accepted.

Comfort Suites Metrocenter 🅷 ❀

(602) 861-3900. **$59-$159.** 10210 N 26th Dr 85021. I-17 exit 208 (Peoria Ave), just e, just s on 25th Ave, then 0.3 mi w on W Beryl Ave. Int corridors. **Pets:** $25 one-time fee/room. Service with restrictions, supervision.

Crowne Plaza Phoenix 🅷

(602) 943-2341. **$79-$159.** 2532 W Peoria Ave 85029. I-17 exit 208 (Peoria Ave), just e, then just n on 25th Ave. Int corridors. **Pets:** Accepted.

Drury Inn & Suites Phoenix Airport 🅷

(602) 437-8400. **$119-$184.** 3333 E University Dr 85034. I-10 exit 151 (University Dr), just e, then just s on Elwood St. Int corridors. **Pets:** Service with restrictions, supervision.

Drury Inn & Suites Phoenix Happy Valley 🅷

(623) 879-8800. **$139-$204.** 2335 W Pinnacle Peak Rd 85027. I-17 exit 217 (Pinnacle Peak Rd), just e. Int corridors. **Pets:** Service with restrictions, supervision.

Econo Lodge Airport 🅼

(602) 273-1601. **Call for rates.** 3037 E Van Buren St 85008. SR 202 exit 1C (32nd St), 0.6 mi s, then just w. Ext corridors. **Pets:** Accepted.

Embassy Suites Phoenix Airport at 24th St 🅷 ❀

(602) 957-1910. **$89-$239.** 2333 E Thomas Rd 85016. SR 51 exit 2 (44th St), just e. Ext corridors. **Pets:** Small. $20 one-time fee/room. Service with restrictions, supervision.

Embassy Suites Phoenix-Biltmore 🅷

(602) 955-3992. **$94-$249.** 2630 E Camelback Rd 85016. Just n of Camelback Rd, on 26th St. Int corridors. **Pets:** Small. $40 one-time fee/room. Service with restrictions.

Embassy Suites Phoenix North 🅷

(602) 375-1777. **$73-$189.** 2577 W Greenway Rd 85023. I-17 exit 211, just e. Ext corridors. **Pets:** Other species. $50 one-time fee/room. Service with restrictions, crate.

Extended StayAmerica-Phoenix-Chandler 🅷

(480) 785-0464. **Call for rates.** 14245 S 50th St 85044. I-10 exit 159, just w on Ray Rd, just s, then just e. Int corridors. **Pets:** $25 daily fee/pet. Designated rooms, service with restrictions.

Extended StayAmerica Phoenix-Chandler-E Chandler Blvd 🅷

(480) 753-6700. **$80-$90.** 5035 E Chandler Blvd 85048. I-10 exit 160 (Chandler Blvd), just w. Ext corridors. **Pets:** $25 daily fee/pet. Designated rooms, service with restrictions.

Extended StayAmerica Phoenix-Deer Valley 🅷

(623) 879-6609. **$65-$75.** 20827 N 27th Ave 85027. I-10 exit 215 (Rose Garden Ln) northbound, just w; exit 215B southbound, just w, then 0.4 mi s. Int corridors. **Pets:** $25 daily fee/pet. Designated rooms, service with restrictions.

Extended Stay Deluxe Phoenix-Biltmore 🅷

(602) 265-6800. **$95-$105.** 5235 N 16th St 85016. Jct SR 51, just w on Camelback Rd, then just n. Int corridors. **Pets:** $25 daily fee/pet. Designated rooms, service with restrictions.

Extended Stay Deluxe (Phoenix/Midtown) 🅷

(602) 279-9000. **$85-$95.** 217 W Osborn Rd 85013. Just w of Central Ave; between Indian School and Thomas rds. Int corridors. **Pets:** $25 daily fee/pet. Designated rooms, service with restrictions.

Hampton Inn Phoenix Biltmore 🅷

(602) 956-5221. **$69-$199.** 2310 E Highland Ave 85016. Just sw of Camelback Rd and 24th St. Int corridors. **Pets:** Accepted.

Hilton Phoenix Airport 🅷

(480) 894-1600. **$109-$209.** 2435 S 47th St 85034. I-10 exit 151 (University Dr), 2 mi n, then just w. Int corridors. **Pets:** Accepted.

Hilton Phoenix Suites 🅷

(602) 222-1111. **$89-$269.** 10 E Thomas Rd 85012. Just e of Central Ave; in Phoenix Plaza. Int corridors. **Pets:** Accepted.

Homewood Suites by Hilton Phoenix-Biltmore 🅷

(602) 508-0937. **$79-$159.** 2001 E Highland Ave 85016. Just e of 20th St. Int corridors. **Pets:** Accepted.

Homewood Suites by Hilton Phoenix Metrocenter 🅷

(602) 674-8900. **$70-$159.** 2536 W Beryl Ave 85021. I-17 exit 208 (Peoria Ave), just e, just s on 25th Ave, then just w. Int corridors. **Pets:** Accepted.

Homewood Suites Phoenix North/Happy Valley 🅷

(623) 580-1800. **Call for rates.** 2470 W Charlotte Dr 85085. I-17 exit 217 (Pinnacle Peak Rd), 0.6 mi n on Frontage Rd. Int corridors. **Pets:** Accepted.

La Quinta Inn & Suites Phoenix Chandler 🅷

(480) 961-7700. **$71-$144.** 15241 S 50th St 85044. I-10 exit 160 (Chandler Blvd), just w, then just n. Int corridors. **Pets:** Service with restrictions, supervision.

La Quinta Inn & Suites Phoenix I-10 West 🄷
(602) 595-7601. **$59-$155.** 4929 W McDowell Rd 85035. I-10 exit 139 (51st Ave), just n, then just e. Int corridors. **Pets:** Service with restrictions, supervision. 🛜 ⊠ 🛢 💻 ⊃

La Quinta Inn Phoenix-Arcadia 🄷
(602) 956-6500. **$60-$145.** 4727 E Thomas Rd 85018. Just w of 48th St. Ext/int corridors. **Pets:** Service with restrictions, supervision.
🛜 ⊠ 🛢 💻 ⊃

La Quinta Inn Phoenix North 🄷
(602) 993-0800. **$59-$118.** 2510 W Greenway Rd 85023. I-17 exit 211, just e. Ext corridors. **Pets:** Service with restrictions, supervision.
🛜 🛢 💻 ⊃ ⊠

La Quinta Inn Phoenix Thomas Road 🄼
(602) 258-6271. **$59-$111.** 2725 N Black Canyon Hwy 85009. I-17 exit 201 (Thomas Rd), just e, then just s; on east side of freeway. Ext corridors. **Pets:** Service with restrictions, supervision.
🛜 ♿ 🛢 💻 ⊃

Motel 6 Phoenix-North #344 🄼
(602) 993-2353. **$45-$55.** 2330 W Bell Rd 85023. I-17 exit 212, just e. Ext corridors. **Pets:** Other species. Service with restrictions, supervision.
🛜 ⊃

Motel 6 Phoenix West #696 🄼
(602) 272-0220. **$45-$55.** 1530 N 52nd Dr 85043. I-10 exit 139 (51st Ave), just n to McDowell Rd, just w, then just s. Ext corridors.
Pets: Other species. Service with restrictions, supervision. 🛜 🛢 ⊃

Phoenix Residence Inn by Marriott Desert View 🄷
(480) 563-1500. **$109-$289, 3 day notice.** 5665 E Mayo Blvd 85054. SR 101 exit 32 (56th St), just s, then just e. Int corridors. **Pets:** Other species. $100 one-time fee/room. Designated rooms, service with restrictions, crate. 🛜 ⊠ ♿ 🛢 💻 ⊃

🅰🅰🅰 **Pointe Hilton Squaw Peak Resort** 🄷 🐾
(602) 997-2626. **$99-$259.** 7677 N 16th St 85020. SR 51 exit Glendale Ave, 0.4 mi w, then 0.6 mi n. Ext corridors. **Pets:** Large, other species. $75 one-time fee/room. Service with restrictions.
SAVE 🛜 ⊠ 🛢 💻 🍽 ⊃ ⊠

🅰🅰🅰 **Pointe Hilton Tapatio Cliffs Resort** 🄷
(602) 866-7500. **$99-$259.** 11111 N 7th St 85020. I-17 exit 207 (Dunlap Ave), 3 mi e, then 2 mi n. Ext corridors. **Pets:** Accepted.
ECO SAVE 🛜 ♿ 🛢 💻 🍽 ⊃ ⊠

🅰🅰🅰 **Red Roof Inn Phoenix West** 🄷
(602) 233-8004. **$50-$126.** 5215 W Willetta St 85043. I-10 exit 139 (51st Ave), just n, just e on McDowell Rd, then just s. Int corridors. **Pets:** Large, other species. Service with restrictions, supervision.
SAVE 🛜 ♿ 🛢 💻 ⊃

Residence Inn by Marriott Phoenix 🄷
(602) 864-1900. **$99-$169.** 8242 N Black Canyon Hwy 85051. I-17 exit 207 (Dunlap Ave), just w, then 0.8 mi s; on frontage road. Ext/int corridors. **Pets:** Large, other species. $100 one-time fee/room. Service with restrictions. 🛜 ⊠ 🛢 💻 ⊃ ⊠

Residence Inn by Marriott Phoenix Airport 🄷 🐾
(602) 273-9220. **$99-$209.** 801 N 44th St 85008. SR 202 exit 2 (44th St), just s. Int corridors. **Pets:** Medium. $75 one-time fee/room. Service with restrictions. ECO 🛜 ⊠ ♿ 🛢 💻 ⊃ ⊠

Residence Inn by Marriott Phoenix North/Happy Valley 🄷 🐾
(623) 580-8833. **$99-$189.** 2035 W Whispering Wind Dr 85085. I-17 exit 128 (Happy Valley Rd), 0.4 mi e to 23rd Ave, just s, then just e. Int corridors. **Pets:** Medium, other species. $100 one-time fee/room. Service with restrictions. 🛜 ⊠ 🛢 💻 ⊃ ⊠

The Ritz-Carlton, Phoenix 🄷
(602) 468-0700. **$229-$439.** 2401 E Camelback Rd 85016. Southeast corner of Camelback Rd and 24th St. Int corridors. **Pets:** Accepted.
🛜 ⊠ 🛢 💻 🍽 ⊃ ⊠

🅰🅰🅰 **Royal Palms Resort and Spa** 🄷 🐾
(602) 840-3610. **$149-$599, 7 day notice.** 5200 E Camelback Rd 85018. Just e of 52nd St. Ext/int corridors. **Pets:** Medium, dogs only. $100 one-time fee/room. Designated rooms, service with restrictions, supervision. ECO ⛅ SAVE 🛜 ⊠ 🛢 💻 🍽 ⊃ ⊠

🅰🅰🅰 **Sheraton Crescent Hotel** 🄷
(602) 943-8200. **$125-$635.** 2620 W Dunlap Ave 85021. I-17 exit 207 (Dunlap Ave), just e. Int corridors. **Pets:** Accepted.
SAVE 🛜 ⊠ ♿ 🛢 💻 🍽 ⊃ ⊠

🅰🅰🅰 **Sheraton Phoenix Downtown Hotel** 🄷
(602) 262-2500. **$299-$729.** 340 N 3rd St 85004. I-10 exit 145A (7th St), 0.5 mi s to Fillmore St, just w, then just s. Int corridors. **Pets:** Accepted.
ECO SAVE 🛜 ⊠ ♿ 🛢 💻 🍽 ⊃ ⊠

🅰🅰🅰 **Sleep Inn Airport** 🄷
(480) 967-7100. **$60-$150.** 2621 S 47th Pl 85034. I-10 exit 151 (University Dr), 2 mi n, then just w. Int corridors. **Pets:** Accepted.
SAVE 🛜 🛢 💻 ⊃

🅰🅰🅰 **Sleep Inn Phoenix North** 🄷
(602) 504-1200. **$54-$159.** 18235 N 27th Ave 85053. I-17 exit 214A (Union Hills Dr), just w, then just s. Int corridors. **Pets:** Small. $15 daily fee/pet. Designated rooms, service with restrictions, supervision.
SAVE 🛜 ♿ 🛢 💻 ⊃

🅰🅰🅰 **Super 8-Downtown Phoenix/Convention Center** 🄼
(602) 252-6823. **$65-$145.** 965 E Van Buren St 85006. I-10 exit 145 (7th St), just s, then just e. Ext corridors. **Pets:** Medium. $25 one-time fee/room. Designated rooms, service with restrictions, supervision.
SAVE 🛜 ⊠ 🛢 💻 ⊃

🅰🅰🅰 **Super 8 Phoenix Metro North** 🄼
(602) 995-8451. **$36-$59.** 8130 N Black Canyon Hwy 85051. I-17 exit 206 (Northern Ave), just w, then just n on west side of freeway. Ext corridors. **Pets:** Small. $10 daily fee/pet. Service with restrictions, supervision.
SAVE 🛜 🛢 💻 ⊃

Super 8-Phoenix West 🄷
(602) 415-0888. **$50-$79.** 1242 N 53rd Ave 85043. I-10 exit 139 (51st Ave), just s to Latham Rd, then just w. Int corridors. **Pets:** Accepted.
🛜 🛢 💻 ⊃

TownePlace Suites by Marriott Phoenix North 🄷
(602) 943-9510. **$62-$126.** 9425 N Black Canyon Frwy 85021. I-17 exit 207 (Dunlap Ave), just e, then 0.3 mi n. Int corridors. **Pets:** Accepted.
🛜 ⊠ ♿ 🛢 💻

🅰🅰🅰 **The Westin Phoenix Downtown** 🄷
(602) 429-3500. **$369-$589, 3 day notice.** 333 N Central Ave 85004. Northeast corner of Central Ave and Van Buren St. Int corridors.
Pets: Accepted. SAVE 🛜 ⊠ ♿ 🛢 💻 🍽 ⊃

SCOTTSDALE

🅰🅰🅰 **BEST WESTERN PLUS Sundial** 🄷 🐾
(480) 994-4170. **$100-$259.** 7320 E Camelback Rd 85251. Just e of Scottsdale Rd. Ext corridors. **Pets:** Other species. $25 daily fee/pet. Service with restrictions, supervision. SAVE 🛜 ⊠ ♿ 🛢 💻 ⊃

🅰🅰🅰 **The Canyon Suites at The Phoenician** 🄷
(480) 423-2880. **$299-$2500, 7 day notice.** 6000 E Camelback Rd 85251. 0.5 mi w of 64th St; in The Phoenician. Int corridors.
Pets: Accepted. ⛅ SAVE 🛜 ♿ 🍽 ⊃ ⊠

Chaparral Suites Scottsdale H ❖
(480) 949-1414. **$99-$279.** 5001 N Scottsdale Rd 85250. At Chaparral Rd. Ext corridors. **Pets:** Dogs only. $25 one-time fee/pet. Service with restrictions, supervision. SAVE 🛰 &M 📶 📟 ❙❙ ➥ ⊠

Clarion Hotel Scottsdale H
(480) 945-4392. **$59-$209.** 5101 N Scottsdale Rd 85250. Just n of Chaparral Rd. Ext corridors. **Pets:** Dogs only. $250 deposit/room. Service with restrictions. SAVE 🛰 ⊠ &M 📶 📟 ❙❙ ➥

Comfort Suites by Choice Hotels-Old Town H
(480) 946-1111. **$70-$170.** 3275 N Drinkwater Blvd 85250. North of Thomas Rd; just e of Scottsdale Rd. Int corridors. **Pets:** Medium, other species. $25 one-time fee/room. Service with restrictions, crate. 🛰 ⊠ &M 📶 📟 ➥

Country Inn & Suites By Carlson H ❖
(480) 314-1200. **$59-$209, 3 day notice.** 10801 N 89th Pl 85260. SR 101 exit 41 (Shea Blvd), just e, then just n. Int corridors. **Pets:** Small. $15 daily fee/room. Designated rooms, service with restrictions, supervision. 🛰 ⊠ 📶 📟 ➥

Courtyard by Marriott Scottsdale at Mayo Clinic H ❖
(480) 860-4000. **$69-$229.** 13444 E Shea Blvd 85259. SR 101 exit 41 (Shea Blvd), 5.8 mi e. Int corridors. **Pets:** Small, other species. $50 one-time fee/room. Service with restrictions. ECO SAVE 🛰 ⊠ &M 📶 📟 ❙❙ ➥

Days Inn & Suites Scottsdale CO ❖
(480) 948-3800. **$79-$229.** 7330 N Pima Rd 85258. 0.4 mi n of Indian Bend Rd; on west side of Pima Rd. Ext/int corridors. **Pets:** Other species. $20 daily fee/pet. Designated rooms, service with restrictions. 🛰 ⊠ 📶 📟 ➥ ⊠

DoubleTree Resort by Hilton Paradise Valley - Scottsdale H
(480) 947-5400. **$79-$249.** 5401 N Scottsdale Rd 85250. Just n of Chaparral Rd; on east side of Scottsdale Rd. Ext corridors. **Pets:** Large. $50 one-time fee/room. Service with restrictions, supervision. SAVE 🛰 📶 📟 ❙❙ ➥ ⊠

Extended StayAmerica-Phoenix-Scottsdale H
(480) 607-3767. **$85-$95.** 15501 N Scottsdale Rd 85254. SR 101 exit 38 (Frank Lloyd Wright Blvd), 2 mi w, 0.5 mi s on Scottsdale Rd, then just e on Tierra Buena Ln. Ext corridors. **Pets:** $25 daily fee/pet. Designated rooms, service with restrictions. 🛰 📶 📟

Extended Stay Deluxe Phoenix-Scottsdale H
(480) 483-1333. **$100-$110.** 10660 N 69th St 85254. Jct Scottsdale Rd, just w on Shea Blvd, then just n. Int corridors. **Pets:** $25 daily fee/pet. Designated rooms, service with restrictions. 🛰 📶 📟 ➥

Fairmont Scottsdale Princess H
(480) 585-4848. **$159-$2659, 7 day notice.** 7575 E Princess Dr 85255. SR 101 exit 34 (Scottsdale Rd), 0.8 mi s, then just e; 0.6 mi n of Bell Rd. Ext/int corridors. **Pets:** Accepted. ECO SAVE 🛰 &M 📶 📟 ❙❙ ➥ ⊠

FireSky Resort & Spa, A Kimpton Hotel H ❖
(480) 945-7666. **$115-$469, 3 day notice.** 4925 N Scottsdale Rd 85251. Southeast corner of Scottsdale and Chaparral rds. Int corridors. **Pets:** Other species. Designated rooms, service with restrictions, supervision. ECO ⊕ SAVE 🛰 ⊠ &M 📟 ❙❙ ➥ ⊠

Four Seasons Resort Scottsdale at Troon North H
(480) 515-5700. **$149-$839, 7 day notice.** 10600 E Crescent Moon Dr 85262. SR 101 exit 36 (Pima Rd), 4.7 mi n, 2 mi e on Happy Valley Rd, then 1.5 mi n on Alma School Rd. Ext corridors. **Pets:** Accepted. SAVE 🛰 ⊠ &M 📶 📟 ❙❙ ➥ ⊠

Gainey Suites Hotel H
(480) 922-6969. **$129-$239.** 7300 E Gainey Suites Dr 85258. Just e of Scottsdale Rd. Int corridors. **Pets:** Medium, dogs only. $100 deposit/room. Service with restrictions, crate. SAVE 🛰 ⊠ 📶 📟 ➥ ⊠

Hampton Inn & Suites Scottsdale Riverwalk H
(480) 270-5393. **$79-$209.** 9550 E Indian Bend Rd 85256. SR 101 exit 44 (Indian Bend Rd), just e. Int corridors. **Pets:** Medium, other species. $150 deposit/room. Designated rooms, supervision. SAVE 🛰 ⊠ &M 📶 📟 ➥

Hampton Inn Scottsdale H
(480) 443-3233. **$69-$229.** 10101 N Scottsdale Rd 85253. Just s of Shea Blvd. Int corridors. **Pets:** Accepted. 🛰 ⊠ &M 📶 📟 ➥

Hilton Scottsdale Resort & Villas H
(480) 948-7750. **$89-$259.** 6333 N Scottsdale Rd 85250. SR 101 exit 45, 2.1 mi w on McDonald Dr, then 0.3 mi n. Int corridors. **Pets:** Large, dogs only. $50 one-time fee/room. Service with restrictions, crate. SAVE 🛰 📶 📟 ❙❙ ➥ ⊠

Holiday Inn Express Hotel & Suites-Scottsdale H
(480) 675-7665. **$69-$229.** 3131 N Scottsdale Rd 85251. Northeast corner of Scottsdale Rd and Earll Dr. Int corridors. **Pets:** Accepted. 🛰 ⊠ &M 📶 📟 ➥

Holiday Inn Express Scottsdale North H ❖
(480) 596-6559. **$119-$249.** 7350 E Gold Dust Ave 85258. Just e of Scottsdale Rd; just s of Shea Blvd; on north side of Gold Dust Ave. Int corridors. **Pets:** Other species. $20 daily fee/room. Designated rooms, service with restrictions. 🛰 ⊠ &M 📶 📟 ➥

Homestead Studio Suites Hotel-Phoenix-Scottsdale M
(480) 994-0297. **$75-$85.** 3560 N Marshall Way 85251. Just w of Scottsdale Rd on Goldwater, just s. Ext corridors. **Pets:** $25 daily fee/pet. Designated rooms, service with restrictions. 🛰 &M 📶 📟 ➥

Homewood Suites by Hilton Phoenix/Scottsdale H
(480) 368-8705. **$99-$299.** 9880 N Scottsdale Rd 85253. 0.5 mi s of Shea Blvd. Int corridors. **Pets:** Other species. $75 one-time fee/room. Service with restrictions, crate. 🛰 📶 📟 ➥ ⊠

Hospitality Suite Resort H 🐾
(480) 949-5115. **$47-$144.** 409 N Scottsdale Rd 85257. Just n of McKellips Rd; on east side of Scottsdale Rd. Ext corridors. **Pets:** Medium, dogs only. Designated rooms, service with restrictions, crate. 🛰 ⊠ 📶 📟 ❙❙ ➥ ⊠

Hotel Indigo Scottsdale H
(480) 941-9400. **$79-$150, 3 day notice.** 4415 N Civic Center Plaza 85251. Scottsdale Rd, just e on Camelback Rd, just s on 75th St. Ext/int corridors. **Pets:** Accepted. SAVE 🛰 ⊠ &M 📶 📟 ➥

Hotel Valley Ho H ❖
(480) 248-2000. **$89-$359.** 6850 E Main St 85251. 0.4 mi w of Scottsdale Rd, just s of Indian School Rd; on north side of Main St. Ext/int corridors. **Pets:** Medium, other species. Service with restrictions, supervision. ECO SAVE 🛰 ⊠ 📶 📟 ❙❙ ➥ ⊠

Hyatt house Scottsdale/Old Town H
(480) 946-7700. **$89-$499.** 4245 N Drinkwater Blvd 85251. 0.3 mi e of Scottsdale Rd. Ext corridors. **Pets:** Accepted. SAVE 🛰 ⊠ 📶 📟 ➥

Hyatt Regency Scottsdale Resort & Spa at Gainey Ranch H ❖
(480) 444-1234. **$117-$545, 3 day notice.** 7500 E Doubletree Ranch Rd 85258. SR 101 exit 43, 2.6 mi w on Via de Ventura. Ext/int corridors. **Pets:** Medium, other species. $50 daily fee/pet. Designated rooms, service with restrictions. ECO SAVE 🛰 📶 📟 ❙❙ ➥ ⊠

◈ ▼▼ ▼▼ **JW Marriott Camelback Inn Resort & Spa** H
(480) 948-1700. **$109-$529, 3 day notice.** 5402 E Lincoln Dr 85253. 0.5 mi e of Tatum Blvd; on north side of Lincoln Dr. Ext corridors. **Pets:** $75 one-time fee/room. Service with restrictions, supervision.
SAVE 🤶 ✕ 🖥 🛢 💻 🍽 ⚊ ✕

▼▼ ▼▼ **La Quinta Inn & Suites Phoenix Scottsdale** H
(480) 614-5300. **$59-$144.** 8888 E Shea Blvd 85260. SR 101 exit 41 (Shea Blvd); northeast corner. Int corridors. **Pets:** Service with restrictions, supervision. 🤶 🖥 🛢 💻 ⚊

◈ ▼▼ ▼▼ **Marriott Scottsdale McDowell Mountain** H
(480) 502-3836. **$99-$349.** 16770 N Perimeter Dr 85260. SR 101 exit 36 (Princess Dr/Pima Rd), just w to N Perimeter Dr, then 0.6 mi s. Int corridors. **Pets:** Small, dogs only. $50 one-time fee/room. Service with restrictions. SAVE 🤶 ✕ 🖥 🛢 💻 🍽 ⚊

▼▼ ▼▼ **Millennium Scottsdale Resort & Villas** H
(480) 948-5050. **$59-$339, 3 day notice.** 7401 N Scottsdale Rd 85253. 0.8 mi n of Indian Bend Rd. Int corridors. **Pets:** Medium, dogs only. $50 one-time fee/room. Designated rooms, service with restrictions.
🤶 ✕ 🛢 💻 🍽 ⚊ ✕

▼▼ **Motel 6 Scottsdale #29** M
(480) 946-2280. **$55-$85.** 6848 E Camelback Rd 85251. Just w of Scottsdale Rd. Ext corridors. **Pets:** Other species. Service with restrictions, supervision. 🤶 🛢 ⚊

◈ ▼▼ ▼▼ **The Phoenician** H
(480) 941-8200. **$199-$2500, 7 day notice.** 6000 E Camelback Rd 85251. 0.5 mi w of 64th St. Ext/int corridors. **Pets:** Accepted.
ECO ⊂⊃ SAVE 🤶 ✕ 🛢 💻 🍽 ⚊ ✕

◈ ▼▼ ▼▼ **Radisson Fort McDowell Resort & Casino** H
(480) 789-5300. **Call for rates.** 10438 N Ft. McDowell Rd 85264. Jct Shea Blvd, 1.6 mi ne on SR 87. Int corridors. **Pets:** Accepted.
SAVE 🤶 ✕ 🖥 🛢 💻 🍽 ⚊ ✕

▼▼ ▼▼ **Residence Inn by Marriott Scottsdale North** H
(480) 563-4120. **$109-$269.** 17011 N Scottsdale Rd 85255. SR 101 exit 34 (Scottsdale Rd), 1.1 mi s; northeast corner of Frank Lloyd Wright Blvd and Scottsdale Rd. Int corridors. **Pets:** Accepted.
🤶 ✕ 🛢 💻 ⚊ ✕

◈ ▼▼ ▼▼ **Residence Inn by Marriott, Scottsdale/ Paradise Valley** H
(480) 948-8666. **$69-$269.** 6040 N Scottsdale Rd 85253. Just n of McDonald Dr. Ext/int corridors. **Pets:** Other species. $100 one-time fee/room. Service with restrictions, crate.
SAVE 🤶 ✕ 🖥 🛢 💻 ⚊ ✕

◈ ▼▼ ▼▼ **Scottsdale Cottonwoods Resort** H
(480) 991-1414. **Call for rates.** 6160 N Scottsdale Rd 85253. Just n of McDonald Dr. Ext corridors. **Pets:** Medium. $75 one-time fee/room. Designated rooms, service with restrictions, supervision.
SAVE 🤶 ✕ 🛢 💻 ⚊ ✕

▼▼ ▼▼ **Scottsdale Resort & Athletic Club** H
(480) 344-0600. **$89-$609.** 8235 E Indian Bend Rd 85250. 1.5 mi e of Scottsdale Rd. Ext corridors. **Pets:** Medium, dogs only. $35 one-time fee/room. Designated rooms, service with restrictions, supervision.
🤶 ✕ 🛢 💻 🍽 ⚊ ✕

◈ ▼▼ ▼▼ **Scottsdale Resort & Conference Center** H
(480) 991-9000. **$79-$359, 3 day notice.** 7700 E McCormick Pkwy 85258. Just w of Hayden Rd; 0.7 mi e of Scottsdale Rd. Ext/int corridors. **Pets:** $150 deposit/room. Designated rooms, service with restrictions, crate. ECO SAVE 🤶 ✕ 🛢 💻 🍽 ⚊ ✕

▼▼ ▼▼ **Scottsdale Thunderbird Suites** H
(480) 951-4000. **$59-$229.** 7515 E Butherus Dr 85260. 0.8 mi n of Thunderbird Rd; 0.5 mi e of Scottsdale Rd. Ext/int corridors. **Pets:** Other species. $15 daily fee/pet. Service with restrictions, crate.
🤶 ✕ 🖥 🛢 💻 🍽 ⚊

▼▼ ▼▼ **SpringHill Suites by Marriott-Scottsdale North** H
(480) 922-8700. **$59-$249.** 17020 N Scottsdale Rd 85255. Just n of Frank Lloyd Wright Blvd. Int corridors. **Pets:** Accepted.
🤶 ✕ 🖥 🛢 💻 ⚊ ✕

◈ ▼▼ ▼▼ **TownePlace Suites by Marriott Scottsdale** H
(480) 551-1100. **$66-$199.** 10740 N 90th St 85260. SR 101 exit 41 (Shea Blvd), just e to 90th St, then just n. Int corridors. **Pets:** Accepted.
ECO SAVE 🤶 ✕ 🖥 🛢 💻 ⚊

◈ ▼▼ ▼▼ ▼▼ **The Westin Kierland Resort & Spa** H ❀
(480) 624-1000. **$139-$709, 7 day notice.** 6902 E Greenway Pkwy 85254. 0.5 mi w of Scottsdale Rd. Int corridors. **Pets:** Designated rooms, service with restrictions, crate.
ECO ⊂⊃ SAVE 🤶 ✕ 🛢 💻 🍽 ⚊ ✕

◈ ▼▼ ▼▼ ▼▼ **W Scottsdale** H ❀
(480) 970-2100. **$119-$709.** 7277 E Camelback Rd 85251. Just e of Scottsdale Rd. Int corridors. **Pets:** Medium. $100 one-time fee/room, $25 daily fee/room. Service with restrictions, supervision.
SAVE 🤶 🖥 🛢 💻 🍽 ⚊

▼▼ ▼▼ **Zona Hotel & Suites Scottsdale** H
(480) 585-1234. **$129-$209.** 7677 E Princess Blvd 85255. SR 101 exit 34 (Scottsdale Rd), 0.8 mi s, then just e. Ext corridors. **Pets:** Medium. $75 one-time fee/room. Designated rooms, service with restrictions, crate.
🤶 ✕ 🛢 💻 🍽 ⚊ ✕

SURPRISE

◈ ▼▼ ▼▼ **Comfort Inn & Suites of Surprise** H
(623) 544-6874. **$59-$109.** 13337 W Grand Ave 85374. Jct Bell Rd, 0.4 mi se. Int corridors. **Pets:** Accepted.
SAVE 🤶 ✕ 🖥 🛢 💻 ⚊

◈ ▼▼ ▼▼ **Hampton Inn & Suites Surprise** H
(623) 537-9122. **$89-$209.** 14783 W Grand Ave 85374. Jct Bell Rd, 2 mi nw. Int corridors. **Pets:** Accepted. SAVE 🤶 ✕ 🖥 🛢 💻 ⚊

▼▼ ▼▼ **Quality Inn & Suites** H
(623) 583-3500. **$59-$215.** 16741 N Greasewood St 85374. US 60 (Grand Ave), 1.1 mi e on Bell Rd, then just s. Int corridors. **Pets:** Accepted. 🤶 ✕ 🛢 💻 ⚊

▼▼ ▼▼ **Residence Inn by Marriott Phoenix NW Surprise** H
(623) 249-6333. **$119-$299.** 16418 N Bullard Ave 85374. Jct US 60 (Grand Ave), 1.4 mi w on Bell Rd, then just s. Int corridors. **Pets:** Accepted. 🤶 ✕ 🖥 🛢 💻 ⚊ ✕

◈ ▼▼ ▼▼ **Windmill Suites in Surprise** H ❀
(623) 583-0133. **$69-$224.** 12545 W Bell Rd 85378. US 60 (Grand Ave), 1 mi e. Int corridors. **Pets:** Other species. Designated rooms, service with restrictions, crate. SAVE 🤶 ✕ 🛢 💻 ⚊ ✕

TEMPE

◈ ▼▼ ▼▼ **Aloft Hotel Tempe** H
(480) 621-3300. **$99-$279.** 951 E Playa Del Norte Dr 85281. SR 202 Loop (Red Mountain Frwy) exit 7 (Rural Rd), just s on Scottsdale Rd, then just e. Int corridors. **Pets:** Accepted.
ECO SAVE 🤶 ✕ 🖥 🛢 💻

◈ ▼▼ ▼▼ **BEST WESTERN Inn of Tempe** H
(480) 784-2233. **$70-$150.** 670 N Scottsdale Rd 85281. SR 202 Loop (Red Mountain Frwy) exit 7 (Rural Rd S), just s. Int corridors. **Pets:** Large, dogs only. $10 daily fee/pet. Designated rooms, service with restrictions, crate. SAVE 🤶 ✕ 🛢 💻

BEST WESTERN PLUS Tempe by the Mall [H]
(480) 820-7500. **$80-$175.** 5300 S Priest Dr 85283. I-10 exit 155 (Baseline Rd), 0.4 mi e, then just s. Int corridors. **Pets:** Accepted.

Country Inn & Suites By Carlson, Phoenix Airport at Tempe [H]
(480) 858-9898. **$79-$199.** 808 N Scottsdale Rd 85281. SR 202 Loop (Red Mountain Frwy) exit 7 (Rural Rd S), just n. Int corridors. **Pets:** Accepted.

Days Inn & Suites [H]
(480) 345-8585. **$49-$84.** 1660 W Elliot Rd 85284. I-10 exit 157, just e. Ext corridors. **Pets:** Accepted.

Fiesta Resort Conference Center [H]
(480) 967-1441. **$79-$159.** 2100 S Priest Dr 85282. I-10 exit 153 (Broadway Rd), 0.5 mi e. Ext corridors. **Pets:** Medium. $50 one-time fee/room. Designated rooms, service with restrictions, crate.

Four Points by Sheraton Tempe [H]
(480) 968-3451. **$79-$199.** 1333 S Rural Rd 85281. US 60 (Superstition Frwy) exit 174 (Rural Rd), 2 mi n. Int corridors. **Pets:** Medium, other species. $25 daily fee/pet. Service with restrictions, crate.

Hampton Inn & Suites-Tempe/ASU [H]
(480) 675-9799. **$79-$159.** 1429 N Scottsdale Rd 85281. SR 202 Loop (Red Mountain Frwy) exit 7 (Rural Rd S), 0.5 mi n. Ext corridors. **Pets:** Medium, other species. Service with restrictions, supervision.

Hawthorn Suites by Wyndham [H]
(480) 633-2744. **$70-$135.** 2301 E Southern Ave 85282. Loop 101 exit 54 (Southern Ave/Baseline Rd); at southeast corner. Int corridors. **Pets:** Small, dogs only. $50 one-time fee/pet. Designated rooms, service with restrictions, supervision.

Homestead Studio Suites Hotel-Phoenix/Airport/Tempe [H]
(480) 557-8880. **$65-$75.** 2165 W 15th St 85281. I-10 exit 153 (Broadway Rd), 0.3 mi ne, just nw on S 52nd St, then just w. Int corridors. **Pets:** $25 daily fee/pet. Designated rooms, service with restrictions.

Hotel Tempe Phoenix Airport InnSuites Hotel & Suites [H]
(480) 897-7900. **$75-$179.** 1651 W Baseline Rd 85283. I-10 exit 155 (Baseline Rd), just e. Ext corridors. **Pets:** Accepted.

La Quinta Inn Phoenix Sky Harbor Airport South [H]
(480) 967-4465. **$59-$140.** 911 S 48th St 85281. I-10 exit 153 (Broadway Rd) eastbound; exit 153A (University Dr) westbound, 0.8 mi n; on south side of University Dr; east side of SR 143 (Hohokam Expwy). Ext/int corridors. **Pets:** Service with restrictions, supervision.

Ramada Limited Tempe ASU [M]
(480) 736-1700. **$49-$129.** 1915 E Apache Blvd 85281. US 60 (Superstition Frwy) exit 175, 1.9 mi n on McClintock Dr, then 0.3 mi e. Ext corridors. **Pets:** Medium. $50 deposit/pet, $15 daily fee/pet. Service with restrictions, crate.

Red Roof Inn Phoenix Airport [H]
(480) 449-3205. **$49-$118.** 2135 W 15th St 85281. I-10 exit 153 (Broadway Rd), just nw on S 52nd St, then just w. Int corridors. **Pets:** Large, other species. Service with restrictions, supervision.

Residence Inn by Marriott Tempe [H]
(480) 756-2122. **$129-$229.** 5075 S Priest Dr 85282. I-10 exit 155 (Baseline Rd), 0.4 mi e, then just n. Ext/int corridors. **Pets:** Accepted.

Rodeway Inn-ASU-Tempe [M]
(480) 393-3090. **$40-$75.** 2101 E Apache Blvd 85281. Loop 101 exit University Blvd, just w to Price Rd; exit southbound, 0.9 mi s, then 0.5 mi w. Ext corridors. **Pets:** Small. $50 deposit/pet, $20 one-time fee/pet, $20 daily fee/pet. Designated rooms, service with restrictions, supervision.

Sheraton Phoenix Airport Hotel-Tempe [H]
(480) 967-6600. **$79-$359, 3 day notice.** 1600 S 52nd St 85281. I-10 exit 153B (Broadway Rd) westbound; exit 153A (48th St) eastbound, 0.3 mi ne. Int corridors. **Pets:** Large. $70 one-time fee/room. Service with restrictions, crate.

Super 8 Tempe/ASU [M]
(480) 967-8891. **$49-$143.** 1020 E Apache Blvd 85281. Just e of Rural Rd; just e of ASU main campus. Ext corridors. **Pets:** Small, dogs only. $10 daily fee/pet. Designated rooms, service with restrictions, supervision.

Tempe Mission Palms Hotel [H]
(480) 894-1400. **$99-$319.** 60 E 5th St 85281. Jct University Dr, just n on Mill Ave, then just e; downtown. Int corridors. **Pets:** $75 deposit/room, $25 one-time fee/pet. Service with restrictions, supervision.

TownePlace Suites by Marriott Tempe at Arizona Mills Mall [H]
(480) 345-7889. **$89-$152.** 5223 S Priest Dr 85283. I-10 exit 155 (Baseline Rd), southeast corner of Baseline Rd and Priest Dr. Int corridors. **Pets:** Accepted.

TOLLESON

Premier Inns [H]
(623) 533-4660. **Call for rates.** 8399 W Lynwood St 85353. I-10 exit 135 (83rd Ave), just n, then just w. Ext corridors. **Pets:** Accepted.

YOUNGTOWN

BEST WESTERN Inn & Suites of Sun City [H] ✿
(623) 933-8211. **Call for rates.** 11201 Grand Ave 85363. On US 60, just se of 113th Ave. Ext/int corridors. **Pets:** Medium. $10 daily fee/pet. Designated rooms, service with restrictions, supervision.

END METROPOLITAN AREA

PINETOP-LAKESIDE

BEST WESTERN Inn of Pinetop [M]
(928) 367-6667. **$75-$139.** 404 E White Mountain Blvd 85935. On SR 260. Ext corridors. **Pets:** Large. $10 daily fee/pet. Service with restrictions, supervision.

Econo Lodge Inn & Suites [M]
(928) 367-3636. **$74-$169, 3 day notice.** 458 E White Mountain Blvd 85935. On SR 260; east end of town. Ext corridors. **Pets:** $10 daily fee/pet. Service with restrictions, supervision.

Executive Inn & Suites M

(928) 367-4146. **$49-$89.** 1023 E White Mountain Blvd 85935. On SR 260; east end of town. Ext corridors. **Pets:** Small, dogs only. $10 daily fee/pet. Designated rooms, service with restrictions, supervision.

 Hon-Dah Resort Casino & Conference Center H

(928) 369-0299. **$114-$200.** 777 Hwy 260 85935. Jct SR 260 and 73; east end of town. Int corridors. **Pets:** $50 one-time fee/room. Service with restrictions, supervision.

Northwoods Resort CA

(928) 367-2966. **Call for rates.** 165 E White Mountain Blvd 85935. On SR 260, MM 352. Ext corridors. **Pets:** Accepted.

Super 8 H

(928) 367-3161. **$60-$109.** 1202 E White Mountain Blvd 85935. On SR 260; east end of town. Int corridors. **Pets:** Accepted.

TimberLodge Inn M

(928) 367-4463. **$45-$99.** 1078 E White Mountain Blvd 85935. On SR 260; east end of town. Ext corridors. **Pets:** Other species. $10 daily fee/pet. Designated rooms, service with restrictions, crate.

PRESCOTT

BEST WESTERN Prescottonian M

(928) 445-3096. **$85-$130.** 1317 E Gurley St 86301. On SR 89, just s of jct SR 69. Ext corridors. **Pets:** Large, dogs only. $15 daily fee/room. Service with restrictions, supervision.

Forest Villas Hotel H

(928) 717-1200. **$87-$109.** 3645 Lee Cir 86301. Jct SR 69, just n on Lee Blvd, then just e. Int corridors. **Pets:** Very small. $35 one-time fee/pet. Designated rooms, service with restrictions, supervision.

Hassayampa Inn H

(928) 778-9434. **$89-$219.** 122 E Gurley St 86301. Jct Marina St; downtown. Int corridors. **Pets:** Accepted.

Prescott Cabin Rentals-Lynx Creek Farm CA

(928) 778-9573. **$87-$309, 31 day notice.** 5555 Onyx Dr 86303. Jct SR 89, 5 mi e on SR 69, 0.4 mi s on dirt/gravel road. Ext corridors. **Pets:** Other species. $10 daily fee/pet. No service, crate.

Quality Inn M

(928) 776-1282. **Call for rates.** 1105 E Sheldon St 86301. 0.4 mi e of jct SR 89. Int corridors. **Pets:** Small. $25 daily fee/pet. Supervision.

Residence Inn by Marriott H

(928) 775-2232. **$113-$209.** 3599 Lee Cir 86301. Jct SR 69, just n on Lee Blvd, then just e. Int corridors. **Pets:** Other species. $50 one-time fee/room. Service with restrictions, crate.

SpringHill Suites by Marriott H

(928) 776-0998. **$109-$219.** 200 E Sheldon St 86301. On SR 89; at Marina St. Int corridors. **Pets:** Accepted.

Wyndham Garden Hotel Prescott H

(928) 777-0770. **$79-$169.** 4499 E SR 69 86301. On SR 69, 3.6 mi e of jct SR 89. Int corridors. **Pets:** Medium. $50 one-time fee/pet. Designated rooms, service with restrictions, supervision.

PRESCOTT VALLEY

Americas Best Value Inn H

(928) 772-2200. **$59-$155.** 8383 E SR 69 86314. On SR 69, just w of N Navajo Dr. Int corridors. **Pets:** $6 one-time fee/pet. Designated rooms, service with restrictions, supervision.

Arizona Inn of Prescott Valley H

(928) 772-8600. **$69-$125.** 7875 E Hwy 69 86314. On SR 69; corner of Windsong Rd. Ext corridors. **Pets:** Other species. $50 deposit/room. Service with restrictions.

Comfort Suites Prescott Valley H

(928) 771-2100. **$79-$129.** 2601 N Crownpointe Dr 86314. Just w on SR 69, then n on Market St. Int corridors. **Pets:** Medium. $40 one-time fee/room. Designated rooms, service with restrictions, supervision.

QUARTZSITE

Super 8-Quartzsite M

(928) 927-8080. **$70-$140, 3 day notice.** 2050 Dome Rock Rd 85359. I-10 exit 17, just s to Frontage Rd, then 0.6 mi w. Int corridors. **Pets:** Other species. $10 daily fee/pet. Service with restrictions, supervision.

SAFFORD

BEST WESTERN Desert Inn M

(928) 428-0521. **$85.** 1391 W Thatcher Blvd 85546. US 191, 1 mi w on US 70. Ext corridors. **Pets:** Large, other species. $15 daily fee/room. Service with restrictions, crate.

Days Inn M

(928) 428-5000. **$70-$73.** 520 E Hwy 70 85546. US 191, 0.5 mi e. Ext corridors. **Pets:** Accepted.

ST. MICHAELS

Navajoland Inn & Suites H

(928) 871-5690. **$75-$175, 14 day notice.** 392 W Hwy 264 86511. Jct SR 12, 1.5 mi w. Ext corridors. **Pets:** Accepted.

ST. JOHNS

Days Inn M

(928) 337-4422. **$71-$86.** 125 E Commercial St 85936. On US 191/SR 61; center. Ext corridors. **Pets:** Accepted.

SEDONA

Amara Hotel, Restaurant & Spa H

(928) 282-4828. **$129-$299, 3 day notice.** 100 Amara Ln 86336. Jct SR 179, 0.4 mi ne; center. Int corridors. **Pets:** Medium, dogs only. $40 one-time fee/pet. Designated rooms, service with restrictions, crate.

BEST WESTERN PLUS Arroyo Roble Hotel & Creekside Villas H

(928) 282-4001. **$169-$269.** 400 N SR 89A 86336. Jct SR 179, 0.5 mi ne. Ext corridors. **Pets:** Medium. $50 deposit/room, $20 daily fee/room. Designated rooms, service with restrictions, supervision.

BEST WESTERN PLUS Inn of Sedona H

(928) 282-3072. **$119-$229.** 1200 W SR 89A 86336. Jct SR 179, 1.2 mi w. Ext corridors. **Pets:** Other species. $20 one-time fee/room. Designated rooms, service with restrictions, supervision.

Casa Sedona Bed and Breakfast Inn BB
(928) 282-2938. **$159-$279, 7 day notice.** 55 Hozoni Dr 86336. Jct SR 179, 3 mi w on SR 89A, then 3 blks nw via Tortilla, Southwest and Hozoni drs. Ext/int corridors. **Pets:** Small. $25 daily fee/room. Designated rooms, service with restrictions, supervision.

El Portal Sedona Hotel H
(928) 203-9405. **$199-$399, 15 day notice.** 95 Portal Ln 86336. Jct SR 89A, just s on SR 179, then just w. Ext/int corridors. **Pets:** Other species. Service with restrictions, supervision.

Hilton Sedona Resort & Spa H
(928) 284-4040. **$169-$329.** 90 Ridge Trail Dr 86351. Jct SR 89A, 7.3 mi s on SR 179. Int corridors. **Pets:** Medium, other species. $50 one-time fee/room. Designated rooms, service with restrictions, supervision.

King's Ransom Sedona Hotel H
(928) 282-7151. **Call for rates.** 771 SR 179 86336. 0.7 mi s of jct SR 89A. Ext/int corridors. **Pets:** Accepted.

La Quinta Inn Sedona/Village of Oak Creek H
(928) 284-0711. **$83-$188.** 6176 SR 179 86351. Jct Bell Rock Blvd, just s. Int corridors. **Pets:** Service with restrictions, supervision.

L'Auberge de Sedona Inn and Spa H
(928) 282-1661. **Call for rates.** 301 L'Auberge Ln 86336. Jct SR 179, just n on SR 89A, then ne; down the hill. Ext/int corridors. **Pets:** Dogs only. $5 daily fee/pet. Designated rooms, service with restrictions, supervision.

The Lodge at Sedona BB
(928) 204-1942. **$189-$349, 14 day notice.** 125 Kallof Pl 86336. Jct SR 179, 1.8 mi w on SR 89A, then just s. Ext/int corridors. **Pets:** Medium, dogs only. $35 daily fee/pet. Designated rooms, supervision.

Matterhorn Inn M
(928) 282-7176. **$99-$189.** 230 Apple Ave 86336. Jct SR 179, just ne on SR 89A; uptown. Ext corridors. **Pets:** Medium. $15 daily fee/pet. Designated rooms, service with restrictions, crate.

Orchards Inn of Sedona H
(928) 282-2405. **$124-$259, 7 day notice.** 254 N SR 89A 86336. Jct SR 179, just ne on SR 89A. Ext corridors. **Pets:** Accepted.

Poco Diablo Resort H
(928) 282-7333. **$89-$289.** 1752 State Route 179 86336. Jct SR 179, 2 mi s of SR 89A. Ext corridors. **Pets:** Dogs only. $25 daily fee/pet. Designated rooms, service with restrictions.

Sedona Real Inn & Suites H
(928) 282-1414. **$95-$340.** 95 Arroyo Piñon Dr 86336. Jct SR 179, 3.4 mi w on SR 89A, just sw. Ext corridors. **Pets:** Medium, other species. $30 one-time fee/pet. Designated rooms, service with restrictions, supervision.

Sedona Rouge Hotel & Spa H
(928) 203-4111. **$209-$279, 3 day notice.** 2250 W Hwy 89A 86336. Jct SR 179, 2 mi w. Ext/int corridors. **Pets:** Medium, dogs only. $100 deposit/room, $50 one-time fee/pet. Designated rooms, service with restrictions, supervision.

Sedona Super 8 H
(928) 282-1533. **$80-$129.** 2545 W Hwy 89A 86336. Jct SR 179, 2.4 mi w. Int corridors. **Pets:** Medium, other species. $25 one-time fee/pet. Designated rooms, service with restrictions, supervision.

Sky Ranch Lodge M
(928) 282-6400. **$80-$250.** 1105 Airport Rd 86336. Jct SR 179, 1 mi w on SR 89A, then 1 mi s. Ext corridors. **Pets:** Large, other species. $10 daily fee/pet. Service with restrictions, supervision.

Southwest Inn at Sedona H
(928) 282-3344. **Call for rates.** 3250 W Hwy 89A 86336. Jct SR 179, 3.5 mi w. Ext corridors. **Pets:** Accepted.

Village Lodge M
(928) 284-3626. **$49-$89, 3 day notice.** 105 Bell Rock Plaza 86351. Jct SR 179, just w. Ext/int corridors. **Pets:** Small, dogs only. Designated rooms, service with restrictions, supervision.

SELIGMAN

Canyon Lodge M
(928) 422-3255. **$58-$68.** 22340 Old Hwy 66 86337. I-40 exit 121, 1 mi n, then 0.7 mi e. Ext corridors. **Pets:** Medium. $25 daily fee/pet. Designated rooms, service with restrictions, crate.

Deluxe Inn Motel M
(928) 422-3244. **$57-$67.** 22295 Old Hwy 66 86337. I-40 exit 121 eastbound, 1 mi n, then 0.7 mi e; exit 123 westbound, just ne on I-40 business loop, then 2.4 mi w. Ext corridors. **Pets:** Small. $15 one-time fee/pet. Service with restrictions, supervision.

SHOW LOW

BEST WESTERN Paint Pony Lodge M
(928) 537-5773. **$79-$119.** 581 W Deuce of Clubs Ave 85901. On US 60 and SR 260. Ext corridors. **Pets:** Small, other species. $100 deposit/room, $15 daily fee/pet. Service with restrictions, supervision.

Days Inn M
(928) 537-4356. **$64-$95, 3 day notice.** 480 W Deuce of Clubs Ave 85901. On US 60 and SR 260. Ext/int corridors. **Pets:** Small. $10 one-time fee/pet. Service with restrictions.

K C Motel M
(928) 537-4433. **$59-$79.** 60 W Deuce of Clubs Ave 85901. On US 60 and SR 260. Ext corridors. **Pets:** Large, dogs only. $10 daily fee/pet. Service with restrictions, supervision.

Kiva Motel M
(928) 537-4542. **$58-$68, 3 day notice.** 261 E Deuce of Clubs Ave 85901. On US 60 and SR 260; center. Ext corridors. **Pets:** Small, dogs only. $5 daily fee/pet. Service with restrictions, supervision.

Super 8 H
(928) 532-7323. **$70-$76.** 1751 W Deuce of Clubs Ave 85901. 2 mi w of jct US 60 and SR 260, south side. Int corridors. **Pets:** Other species. $15 daily fee/room. Supervision.

SIERRA VISTA

Americas Best Value Inn M
(520) 459-5380. **$60-$85.** 100 Fab Ave 85635. Jct Business SR 90 and Fry Blvd, then just e of main gate to Fort Huachuca. Ext corridors. **Pets:** Dogs only. $10 daily fee/pet. Designated rooms, service with restrictions, supervision.

Candlewood Suites H
(520) 439-8200. **$119-$169, 3 day notice.** 1904 S Hwy 92 85635. Jct SR 90 and 92, 1.4 mi s. Int corridors. **Pets:** Other species. $30 one-time fee/room. Service with restrictions, crate.

ⒶⒶⒶ ▼▼▼ Days Inn Ⓗ
(520) 458-8500. **$69-$129.** 3460 E Fry Blvd 85635. Just w of jct SR 90 and 92. Ext corridors. **Pets:** Medium, other species. $10 daily fee/pet. Service with restrictions, supervision.
[SAVE] 🛜 ✕ 🔧 🛏 💻 ⊶

▼▼▼▼ Holiday Inn Express Ⓗ
(520) 439-8800. **$99-$149, 3 day notice.** 1902 S Hwy 92 85635. Jct SR 90 and 92, 1.4 mi s. Int corridors. **Pets:** Accepted.
🛜 ✕ 🔧 🛏 💻 ⊶

ⒶⒶⒶ ▼▼▼ Quality Inn Ⓗ
(520) 458-7900. **$62-$69.** 1631 S Hwy 92 85635. On SR 92, 1 mi s of jct SR 90. Int corridors. **Pets:** Large. $10 daily fee/pet. Designated rooms, service with restrictions, crate. [SAVE] 🛜 🔧 🛏 💻 ⊶

ⒶⒶⒶ ▼▼▼ Sun Canyon Inn Ⓗ
(520) 459-0610. **Call for rates.** 260 N Garden Ave 85635. Just n of Fry Blvd; just e of main gate to Fort Huachuca. Int corridors. **Pets:** Dogs only. $20 daily fee/pet. Service with restrictions, supervision.
[SAVE] 🛜 🔧 🛏 💻 ⑂ ⊶

▼▼▼▼ TownePlace Suites by Marriott Ⓗ
(520) 515-9900. **$99-$189.** 3399 Rodeo Dr 85635. Jct SR 90, 1.5 mi s on SR 92, just w on Avenida Cochise, just s on Oakmont Dr, then just e. Int corridors. **Pets:** Other species. $100 one-time fee/room. Service with restrictions. 🛜 ✕ 🔧 🛏 💻 ⊶

SNOWFLAKE
▼▼ Comfort Inn Ⓗ
(928) 536-3888. **$60-$120.** 2055 S Main St 85937. SR 77, just s of town. Int corridors. **Pets:** Other species. $15 daily fee/pet. Service with restrictions, supervision. 🛜 🔧 🛏 ⊶

TAYLOR
ⒶⒶⒶ ▼▼▼ Rodeway Inn-Silver Creek Inn Ⓜ
(928) 536-2600. **$60-$70.** 825 N Main St 85939. On SR 77. Ext corridors. **Pets:** Other species. $10 daily fee/pet. Supervision.
[SAVE] 🛜 🔧 🛏 💻

TOMBSTONE
▼▼ ◆ Landmark Lookout Lodge Ⓗ
(520) 457-2223. **$99-$130.** 781 N Hwy 80 85638. On SR 80, 1 mi n. Ext corridors. **Pets:** Accepted. [SAVE] 🛜 ✕ 🔧 🛏 💻 ⊶

TUBAC
ⒶⒶⒶ ▼▼▼▼ Tubac Golf Resort & Spa Ⓗ ❀
(520) 398-2211. **$109-$339, 3 day notice.** 1 Otero Rd 85646. I-19 exit 40 (Chavez Siding Rd), on east side, then 2 mi s. Ext corridors. **Pets:** Medium. $25 daily fee/pet. Designated rooms, no service, supervision. [ECO] [SAVE] 🛜 ✕ 🔧 🛏 💻 ⑂ ⊶ ⊠

TUBA CITY
ⒶⒶⒶ ▼▼▼ Quality Inn Navajo Nation Ⓗ
(928) 283-4545. **$103-$168.** 10 N Main St 86045. 1 mi n of US 160. Int corridors. **Pets:** Medium. $10 daily fee/pet. Service with restrictions, supervision. [SAVE] 🛜 🔧 🛏 💻 ⑂

Tucson Metropolitan Area

CATALINA
ⒶⒶⒶ ▼▼▼ BEST WESTERN Catalina Inn Ⓗ
(520) 818-9500. **$78-$120.** 15691 N Oracle Rd 85739. 4.6 mi n of Tangerine Rd. Ext/int corridors. **Pets:** Accepted.
[SAVE] 🛜 ✕ 🔧 🛏 💻 ⊶

GREEN VALLEY
ⒶⒶⒶ ▼▼▼ BEST WESTERN Green Valley Inn Ⓗ
(520) 625-2250. **$89-$109.** 111 S La Canada Dr 85614. I-19 exit 65, just w, then just s. Int corridors. **Pets:** Medium. $20 daily fee/pet. Service with restrictions, crate. [SAVE] 🛜 ✕ 🔧 🛏 💻 ⑂ ⊶

ⒶⒶⒶ ▼▼▼▼ Comfort Inn Ⓗ
(520) 399-3736. **$90-$129.** 90 W Esperanza Blvd 85614. I-19 exit 65, just w. Int corridors. **Pets:** $20 deposit/pet, $20 daily fee/pet. Designated rooms, service with restrictions, supervision. [SAVE] 🛜 🔧 🛏 💻 ⊶

▼▼ Holiday Inn Express Ⓗ
(520) 625-0900. **Call for rates.** 19200 S I-19 Frontage Rd 85614. I-19 exit 69 (Duval Mine Rd), west side of interstate, then just s. Int corridors. **Pets:** Accepted. 🛜 🔧 🛏 💻 ⊶

MARANA
▼▼ La Quinta Inn & Suites NW Tucson Marana Ⓗ
(520) 572-4235. **$71-$166.** 6020 W Hospitality Rd 85743. I-10 exit 246 (Cortaro Rd), just w, then just n. Int corridors. **Pets:** Service with restrictions, supervision. 🛜 ✕ 🔧 🛏 💻 ⊶

ⒶⒶⒶ ▼▼▼ Red Roof Inn Tucson North Ⓗ
(520) 744-8199. **$41-$125.** 4940 W Ina Rd 85743. I-10 exit 248 (Ina Rd), just w. Int corridors. **Pets:** Large, other species. Service with restrictions, supervision. [SAVE] 🛜 🔧 🛏 💻 ⊶

ⒶⒶⒶ ▼▼▼ ▼▼▼ The Ritz-Carlton, Dove Mountain Ⓗ ❀
(520) 572-3000. **Call for rates.** 15000 N Secret Springs Dr 85658. I-10 exit 240 (Tangerine Rd), 5 mi e to Dove Mountain Dr, then 4.5 mi n, follow signs. Int corridors. **Pets:** Small, dogs only. $125 one-time fee/room.
[SAVE] 🛜 ✕ 🔧 🛏 💻 ⑂ ⊶ ⊠

ORO VALLEY
ⒶⒶⒶ ▼▼▼ ▼▼▼ Hilton Tucson El Conquistador Golf & Tennis Resort Ⓗ ❀
(520) 544-5000. **$89-$279.** 10000 N Oracle Rd 85704. I-10 exit 248 (Ina Rd); jct Ina Rd, 4.4 mi n. Ext/int corridors. **Pets:** Large, other species. $50 one-time fee/room. Service with restrictions.
[ECO] [SAVE] 🛜 🔧 🛏 💻 ⑂ ⊶ ⊠

TUCSON
ⒶⒶⒶ ▼▼▼ Americas Best Value Inn-Tucson Ⓗ
(520) 884-5800. **Call for rates.** 810 E Benson Hwy 85713. I-10 exit 262, just s. Ext corridors. **Pets:** Medium. $25 deposit/pet. Service with restrictions, supervision. [SAVE] 🛜 🔧 🛏 ⊶

ⒶⒶⒶ ▼▼▼▼ Arizona Riverpark Inn Ⓗ
(520) 239-2300. **$69-$299.** 350 S Freeway 85745. I-10 exit 258 (Broadway Blvd/Congress St), just w, then 0.4 mi s. Ext/int corridors. **Pets:** Medium. $36 one-time fee/room. Service with restrictions, crate.
[SAVE] 🛜 🔧 🛏 💻 ⑂ ⊶ ⊠

ⒶⒶⒶ ▼▼▼▼ BEST WESTERN PLUS InnSuites Tucson Foothills Hotel & Suites Ⓗ
(520) 297-8111. **$69-$179.** 6201 N Oracle Rd 85704. I-10 exit 250 (Orange Grove Rd), 4 mi e, then just s. Ext corridors. **Pets:** $20 one-time fee/room. Designated rooms, service with restrictions.
[SAVE] 🛜 🔧 🛏 💻 ⊶ ⊠

BEST WESTERN PLUS Royal Sun Inn & Suites H ❖
(520) 622-8871. **$69-$299.** 1015 N Stone Ave 85705. I-10 exit 257 (Speedway Blvd), 0.8 mi e, then just s. Ext corridors. **Pets:** Medium. $20 daily fee/room. Service with restrictions, supervision.
ECO SAVE 📶 ✕ 🛗 💻 🍴 ➥

Catalina Park Inn Bed and Breakfast BB
(520) 792-4541. **$109-$189, 14 day notice.** 309 E 1st St 85705. I-10 exit 257 (Speedway Blvd), 1 mi e to 5th Ave, just s, then just e. Ext/int corridors. **Pets:** Small, dogs only. Designated rooms, supervision.
📶 ✕

Comfort Suites at Sabino Canyon H
(520) 298-2300. **Call for rates.** 7007 E Tanque Verde Rd 85715. Jct Grand Rd, 0.4 mi ne. Ext corridors. **Pets:** Medium. $25 daily fee/pet. Designated rooms, service with restrictions, supervision.
📶 ✕ 🛗 💻 ➥

Comfort Suites at Tucson Mall H
(520) 888-6676. **$90-$180.** 515 W Auto Mall Dr 85705. I-10 exit 254 (Prince Rd), 1.9 mi e, then 1.2 mi n. Int corridors. **Pets:** Other species. $10 one-time fee/pet. Designated rooms, service with restrictions, crate.
📶 ✕ 🛗 💻 ➥ ✕

Comfort Suites Tucson Airport H
(520) 295-4400. **$69-$169.** 6935 S Tucson Blvd 85756. Just n of Tucson International Airport. Int corridors. **Pets:** Accepted.
📶 ✕ 🛗 💻 ➥

Country Inn & Suites By Carlson, Tucson-Airport H
(520) 741-9000. **$79-$169.** 6681 S Tucson Blvd 85756. 0.4 mi n of Tucson International Airport entrance. Int corridors. **Pets:** Dogs only. $25 one-time fee/room. Designated rooms, service with restrictions, supervision.
SAVE 📶 ♨ 🛗 💻 ➥

Country Inn & Suites By Carlson-Tucson City Center H ❖
(520) 867-6200. **$89-$199.** 705 N Freeway 85745. I-10 exit 257 (Speedway Blvd), just w, then just s. Int corridors. **Pets:** $25 one-time fee/room. Designated rooms, service with restrictions, supervision.
SAVE 📶 ✕ 🛗 💻 ➥

Crossland Economy Studios-Tucson-Butterfield Dr H
(520) 745-3612. **$60-$70.** 4800 S Butterfield Dr 85714. I-10 exit 264B eastbound, just n to Irvington Rd, just e to Hotel Dr, then just n; exit 264 westbound, just n. Ext corridors. **Pets:** $25 daily fee/pet. Designated rooms, service with restrictions. 📶 🛗 💻

Desert Diamond Casino & Hotel H
(520) 342-3100. **$99-$209.** 7350 S Nogales Hwy 85756. I-19 exit 95 (Valencia Rd), 1.4 mi e, then 1 mi s. Int corridors. **Pets:** $500 deposit/room. Service with restrictions, crate.
SAVE 📶 ✕ ♨ 🛗 💻 🍴 ➥

DoubleTree by Hilton Tucson-Reid Park H
(520) 881-4200. **$99-$329.** 445 S Alvernon Way 85711. I-10 exit 259 (22nd St), 4 mi e, then just n. Ext/int corridors. **Pets:** Medium, other species. $50 one-time fee/room. Designated rooms, service with restrictions, supervision. SAVE 📶 ✕ 🛗 💻 🍴 ➥ ✕

DoubleTree Suites by Hilton Tucson Airport H
(520) 225-0800. **$89-$189.** 7051 S Tucson Blvd 85756. At entrance to Tucson International Airport. Ext corridors. **Pets:** Medium. $50 one-time fee/pet. Service with restrictions. 📶 ♨ 🛗 💻 🍴 ➥

Econo Lodge M
(520) 622-6714. **Call for rates.** 1136 N Stone Ave 85705. I-10 exit 257 (Speedway Blvd), 0.8 mi e, then just n. Ext corridors. **Pets:** Medium, dogs only. $10 deposit/pet, $10 one-time fee/pet. Designated rooms, service with restrictions, crate. 📶 🛗 ➥

Extended StayAmerica-Tucson-Grant Rd H
(520) 795-9510. **$70-$80.** 5050 E Grant Rd 85712. 0.5 mi e of Swan Rd. Ext corridors. **Pets:** $25 daily fee/pet. Designated rooms, service with restrictions. 📶 🛗 💻

Four Points by Sheraton Tucson Airport H ❖
(520) 746-0271. **$79-$219.** 7060 S Tucson Blvd 85756. At entrance to Tucson International Airport. Int corridors. **Pets:** Medium, dogs only. $25 daily fee/room. Designated rooms, service with restrictions, supervision.
SAVE 📶 ✕ 🛗 💻 ➥

Hampton Inn Tucson North H ❖
(520) 206-0602. **$89-$179.** 1375 W Grant Rd 85745. I-10 exit 256 (Grant Rd), just w. Int corridors. **Pets:** Other species. Designated rooms, service with restrictions, supervision. 📶 ✕ ♨ 🛗 💻 ➥

Hilton Tucson East H ❖
(520) 721-5600. **$69-$149.** 7600 E Broadway Blvd 85710. 0.5 mi e of Kolb Rd. Int corridors. **Pets:** Large, other species. $50 one-time fee/room. Designated rooms, service with restrictions, supervision.
SAVE 📶 ♨ 🛗 💻 🍴 ➥ ✕

Holiday Inn Express Tucson Airport H
(520) 889-6600. **$79-$189.** 2548 E Medina Rd 85756. 0.5 mi n of Tucson International Airport entrance. Int corridors. **Pets:** Accepted.
SAVE 📶 ♨ 🛗 💻 ➥

Holiday Inn Hotel & Suites-Tucson Airport North H
(520) 746-1161. **$49-$109.** 4550 S Palo Verde Blvd 85714. I-10 exit 264 westbound; exit 264B eastbound, 0.5 mi n. Ext/int corridors.
Pets: Accepted. 📶 ♨ 🛗 💻 🍴 ➥

La Posada Lodge & Casitas H
(520) 887-4800. **Call for rates.** 5900 N Oracle Rd 85704. 0.5 mi s of Orange Grove Rd. Ext corridors. **Pets:** Accepted.
📶 ✕ 🛗 💻 🍴 ➥

La Quinta Inn & Suites Tucson Airport H
(520) 573-3333. **$71-$133.** 7001 S Tucson Blvd 85706. Just n of Tucson International Airport. Int corridors. **Pets:** Service with restrictions, supervision. 📶 ♨ 🛗 💻 ➥

La Quinta Inn Tucson East H
(520) 747-1414. **$59-$133.** 6404 E Broadway Blvd 85710. Just e of Wilmot Rd. Ext corridors. **Pets:** Service with restrictions, supervision.
📶 🛗 💻 ➥

The Lodge @ Ventana Canyon H ❖
(520) 577-1400. **$99-$799, 21 day notice.** 6200 N Clubhouse Ln 85750. I-10 exit 256 (Grant Rd), 8.6 mi e, 0.6 mi e on Tanque Verde Rd, 2 mi n on Sabino Canyon Rd, then 3.2 mi n on Kolb Rd. Ext/int corridors. **Pets:** Dogs only. $100 one-time fee/room. Service with restrictions.
SAVE 📶 ✕ 🛗 💻 ➥ ✕

Lodge on the Desert H
(520) 320-2000. **$109-$429, 3 day notice.** 306 N Alvernon Way 85711. I-10 exit 258 (Broadway Blvd/Congress St), 4 mi e, then just n. Ext corridors. **Pets:** Small, dogs only. $25 daily fee/room. Designated rooms, service with restrictions, supervision. SAVE 📶 ✕ 🛗 💻 🍴 ➥

Loews Ventana Canyon H ❖
(520) 299-2020. **$129-$349, 3 day notice.** 7000 N Resort Dr 85750. I-10 exit 256 (Grant Rd), 8.6 mi e, 0.6 mi e on Tanque Verde Rd, 2 mi n on Sabino Canyon Rd, then 3.5 mi n on Kolb Rd. Ext/int corridors. **Pets:** Other species. $25 one-time fee/room. Service with restrictions, supervision. ECO SAVE 📶 ✕ ♨ 🛗 💻 🍴 ➥ ✕

Motel 6 Tucson North #1127 H
(520) 744-9300. **$45-$61.** 4630 W Ina Rd 85741. I-10 exit 248 (Ina Rd), just e to Camino de Oeste, then just n. Int corridors. **Pets:** Other species. Service with restrictions, supervision. 📶 🛗 ➥

(AAA) ▼▼▼ ▼▼▼ Omni Tucson National Resort �H
(520) 297-2271. **$109-$459, 3 day notice.** 2727 W Club Dr 85742. I-10 exit 246 (Cortaro Rd), 3.5 mi e, then just n on Shannon Rd. Ext corridors. **Pets:** Accepted. 〔SAVE〕 📶 ✖ 🛗 🖥 🐾 ✖

(AAA) ▼▼▼ ▼▼▼ Quality Inn & Suites Oracle Foothills �H
(520) 575-9255. **$69-$199.** 7411 N Oracle Rd 85704. SR 77 (Oracle Rd), just n of Ina Rd. Ext corridors. **Pets:** Small. $10 daily fee/pet. Service with restrictions, crate. 〔SAVE〕 📶 ✖ 🛗 🖥 🐾 ✖

(AAA) ▼▼▼ Quality Inn Tucson Airport �H
(520) 294-2500. **$59-$139.** 2803 E Valencia Rd 85706. 1 mi ne of Tucson International Airport; just e of Tucson Blvd. Ext/int corridors. **Pets:** Medium. $10 daily fee/pet. Service with restrictions, supervision. 〔SAVE〕 📶 🛗 🖥 🐾

(AAA) ▼▼▼ ▼▼▼ Radisson Suites Tucson �H
(520) 721-7100. **$76-$269.** 6555 E Speedway Blvd 85710. Just e of Wilmot Rd. Ext corridors. **Pets:** Medium. $25 one-time fee/pet. Designated rooms, service with restrictions, supervision.
〔SAVE〕 📶 🛗 🖥 🍴 🐾 ✖

(AAA) ▼▼▼ ▼▼▼ Ramada Foothills Inn & Suites �H
(520) 886-9595. **$65-$170.** 6944 E Tanque Verde Rd 85715. Jct Campbell Ave, 5.5 mi e on Grant Rd, then just ne. Ext corridors. **Pets:** Small. $25 one-time fee/pet. Designated rooms, service with restrictions, crate.
〔SAVE〕 📶 🛗 🖥 🐾

(AAA) ▼▼▼ ▼▼▼ Red Roof Inn-Tucson South �H
(520) 571-1400. **$39-$120.** 3704 E Irvington Rd 85714. I-10 exit 264 westbound; exit 264B eastbound. Ext corridors. **Pets:** Large, other species. Service with restrictions, supervision. 〔SAVE〕 📶 🛗 🐾

▼▼▼ ▼▼▼ Residence Inn by Marriott-Tucson �H 🐾
(520) 721-0991. **$79-$200.** 6477 E Speedway Blvd 85710. Just e of Wilmot Rd. Ext corridors. **Pets:** Medium, other species. $100 one-time fee/room. Service with restrictions. 📶 ✖ 🛗 🖥 🐾 ✖

▼▼▼ ▼▼▼ Residence Inn by Marriott Tucson Airport �H 🐾
(520) 294-5522. **$76-$169.** 2660 E Medina Rd 85756. 0.5 mi n of airport entrance on Tucson Blvd, just e. Int corridors. **Pets:** $100 one-time fee/room. Service with restrictions. 📶 ✖ 🛗 🖥 🐾 ✖

▼▼▼ ▼▼▼ Residence Inn by Marriott Williams Centre �H
(520) 790-6100. **$129-$229.** 5400 E Williams Cir 85711. Jct Campbell Ave, 3.8 mi e on Broadway Blvd, then just s and just e on Williams Blvd. Int corridors. **Pets:** Other species. $100 one-time fee/room. Service with restrictions. 📶 ✖ 🛗 🛗 🖥 🐾 ✖

(AAA) ▼▼▼ Rodeway Inn-University of AZ M
(520) 622-6446. **$43-$120.** 1248 N Stone Ave 85705. I-10 exit 257 (Speedway Blvd) eastbound, just e, then just n. Ext corridors. **Pets:** Small. $10 daily fee/pet. Service with restrictions, crate.
〔SAVE〕 📶 🛗 🐾

(AAA) ▼▼▼ ▼▼▼ Sheraton Tucson Hotel & Suites �H
(520) 323-6262. **$79-$279.** 5151 E Grant Rd 85712. Jct Campbell Ave, 3.6 mi e. Ext/int corridors. **Pets:** Accepted.
〔SAVE〕 📶 ✖ 🛗 🛗 🖥 🍴 🐾 ✖

▼▼▼ ▼▼▼ Staybridge Suites Tucson Airport �H
(520) 807-1004. **$99-$249.** 2705 E Executive Dr 85756. 0.7 mi n of Tucson International Airport. Int corridors. **Pets:** Accepted.
📶 ✖ 🛗 🛗 🖥 🐾

▼▼▼ ▼▼▼ Studio 6 Extended Stay #6002 M
(520) 746-0030. **$43-$63.** 4950 S Outlet Center Dr 85706. I-10 exit 264A eastbound; exit 264B westbound, just s, then just nw on Julian Dr. Ext corridors. **Pets:** Other species. $10 daily fee/room. Service with restrictions, supervision. 📶 🛗 🖥 🐾

▼▼▼ ▼▼▼ TownePlace Suites by Marriott �H
(520) 292-9697. **$84-$109.** 405 W Rudasill Rd 85704. Jct Orange Grove Rd, 0.5 mi s on Oracle Rd, then just e. Int corridors. **Pets:** $75 one-time fee/room. Service with restrictions, crate. 📶 ✖ 🛗 🖥 🐾

(AAA) ▼▼▼ ▼▼▼ TownePlace Suites by Marriott Tucson Airport �H
(520) 294-6677. **$109-$164.** 6595 S Bay Colony Dr 85756. 0.7 mi n of Tucson International Airport. Int corridors. **Pets:** Accepted.
〔SAVE〕 📶 ✖ 🛗 🛗 🖥 🐾

▼▼▼ ▼▼▼ TownePlace Suites by Marriott Tucson Williams Centre �H 🐾
(520) 747-0720. **$77-$149.** 384 S Williams Blvd 85711. Jct Campbell Ave, 3.8 mi e on Broadway Blvd, just s. Int corridors. **Pets:** Other species. $100 one-time fee/room. Service with restrictions, crate.
📶 ✖ 🛗 🛗 🖥 🐾

(AAA) ▼▼▼ ▼▼▼ The Westin La Paloma Resort & Spa �H
(520) 742-6000. **$99-$539, 7 day notice.** 3800 E Sunrise Dr 85718. SR 77 (Oracle Rd), 4.6 mi e on Ina Rd via Skyline and Sunrise drs, then just s on Via Palomita. Ext corridors. **Pets:** Accepted.
〔ECO〕 〔SAVE〕 📶 ✖ 🛗 🖥 🐾 ✖

(AAA) ▼▼▼ ▼▼▼ Westward Look Wyndham Grand Resort & Spa �H
(520) 297-1151. **$99-$250, 7 day notice.** 245 E Ina Rd 85704. I-10 exit 248 (Ina Rd), 6 mi e, then just n on Westward Look Dr. Ext corridors. **Pets:** Other species. $75 one-time fee/room. Designated rooms, service with restrictions, supervision.
〔ECO〕 〔SAVE〕 📶 ✖ 🛗 🖥 🍴 🐾 ✖

(AAA) ▼▼▼ ▼▼▼ Windmill Suites at St. Philip's Plaza �H
(520) 577-0007. **$75-$300.** 4250 N Campbell Ave 85718. I-10 exit 254 (Prince Rd), 4 mi e, then 1 mi n. Int corridors. **Pets:** Accepted.
〔SAVE〕 📶 ✖ 🛗 🖥 🐾 ✖

END METROPOLITAN AREA

WELLTON

▼▼ Microtel Inn & Suites by Wyndham Wellton �H
(928) 785-3777. **$67-$95.** 28784 Commerce Way 85356. I-8 exit 30, just s. Int corridors. **Pets:** Accepted. 📶 ✖ 🛗 🖥 🐾

WICKENBURG

(AAA) ▼▼▼ BEST WESTERN Rancho Grande �H 🐾
(928) 684-5445. **$68-$86.** 293 E Wickenburg Way 85390. On US 60; center. Ext corridors. **Pets:** Other species. $8 daily fee/room. Service with restrictions, supervision. 〔SAVE〕 📶 🛗 🖥 🐾 ✖

▼▼ Quality Inn Wickenburg �H
(928) 684-5461. **$69-$95, 5 day notice.** 850 E Wickenburg Way 85390. 1.3 mi se on US 60. Int corridors. **Pets:** Small. $15 daily fee/pet. Designated rooms, service with restrictions, supervision.
📶 ✖ 🛗 🖥 🐾

(AAA) ▼▼▼ Super 8 Wickenburg M 🐾
(928) 684-0808. **$59-$99.** 1021 N Tegner St 85390. 1 mi n of jct US 60 and 93. Ext/int corridors. **Pets:** Small. $10 daily fee/pet. Designated rooms, service with restrictions, supervision. 〔SAVE〕 📶 🛗 🖥

WILLCOX

🔺 ▼▼▼ Days Inn M
(520) 384-4222. **$50-$55.** 724 N Bisbee Ave 85643. I-10 exit 340, just s. Ext corridors. **Pets:** Medium, dogs only. $7 daily fee/pet. Service with restrictions, supervision. (SAVE) 🛜 🖥 💻 🏊

▼▼▼ Holiday Inn Express & Suites Willcox H
(520) 384-3333. **$81-$101.** 1251 N Virginia Ave 85643. I-10 exit 340, just n. Int corridors. **Pets:** Medium. $20 daily fee/pet. Designated rooms, service with restrictions, supervision. 🛜 ♿M 🖥 💻 🏊

WILLIAMS

🔺 ▼▼▼▼ BEST WESTERN PLUS Inn of Williams H
(928) 635-4400. **$80-$250.** 2600 W Route 66 86046. I-40 exit 161, just e. Int corridors. **Pets:** Other species. $25 daily fee/pet. Designated rooms, service with restrictions, supervision.
(SAVE) 🛜 ✕ 🖥 💻 🍴 🏊

🔺 ▼▼▼ Days Inn of Williams M
(928) 635-4051. **$59-$179.** 2488 W Route 66 86046. I-40 exit 161, just e. Int corridors. **Pets:** Medium. $20 daily fee/room. Designated rooms, no service, supervision. (SAVE) 🛜 ✕ 🖥 💻 🏊

▼▼▼ Holiday Inn Williams H
(928) 635-4114. **$110-$160.** 950 N Grand Canyon Blvd 86046. I-40 exit 163, just s. Int corridors. **Pets:** Other species. Service with restrictions. 🛜 ♿M 🖥 💻 🍴 🏊

🔺 ▼▼▼ Mountain Ranch Resort at Beacon Hill H
(928) 635-2693. **$89-$189.** 6701 E Mountain Ranch Rd 86046. I-40 exit 171 (Deer Farm Rd), just s. Ext corridors. **Pets:** Medium. $45 one-time fee/room. Designated rooms, service with restrictions, supervision.
(SAVE) 🛜 ✕ 🖥 💻 🍴 🏊 ✕

🔺 ▼ Travelodge Williams M
(928) 635-2651. **$60-$145.** 430 E Route 66 86046. I-40 exit 163, 0.5 mi s, then just e. Ext corridors. **Pets:** Dogs only. $10 daily fee/pet. Designated rooms, supervision. (SAVE) 🛜 🖥 💻 🏊

WINDOW ROCK

🔺 ▼▼▼ Quality Inn Navajo Nation Capital H
(928) 871-4108. **$99-$119.** 48 W Hwy 264 86515. Center. Ext corridors. **Pets:** Medium. $50 deposit/room. Service with restrictions, crate.
(SAVE) 🛜 🖥 💻 🍴

WINSLOW

🔺 ▼▼▼▼ BEST WESTERN PLUS Winslow Inn H
(928) 289-2960. **$100-$150.** 816 Transcon Ln 86047. I-40 exit 255, just n. Int corridors. **Pets:** Medium, dogs only. $10 daily fee/pet. Service with restrictions, supervision. (SAVE) 🛜 ✕ ♿M 🖥 💻 🏊

▼▼▼▼ La Posada Hotel H
(928) 289-4366. **$109-$169, 7 day notice.** 303 E 2nd St 86047. I-40 exit 253, 1 mi s to Route 66 (2nd St), then just e; in historic downtown. Int corridors. **Pets:** Accepted. 🛜 ✕ ♿M 🖥 🍴 🏊

YUMA

🔺 ▼▼▼ BEST WESTERN Coronado Motor Hotel H
(928) 783-4453. **$79-$159.** 233 4th Ave 85364. I-8 exit 172 (4th Ave) eastbound, 0.5 mi s; exit 1 (Harold C. Giss Pkwy) westbound, 1 mi w. Ext corridors. **Pets:** Medium. $10 one-time fee/pet. Designated rooms, service with restrictions, crate. (SAVE) 🛜 ✕ 🖥 💻 🍴 🏊

🔺 ▼▼▼ BEST WESTERN PLUS InnSuites Yuma Mall Hotel & Suites H
(928) 783-8341. **$69-$179.** 1450 Castle Dome Ave 85365. I-8 exit 2 (16th St/US 95), just e to Yuma Palms Pkwy, just n, then just w. Ext corridors. **Pets:** Accepted. (SAVE) 🛜 🖥 💻 🍴 🏊

▼▼▼ Candlewood Suites H
(928) 726-2800. **$90-$129.** 2036 S Ave 3 E 85365. I-8 exit 3, just n, then just w on Frontage Rd. Int corridors. **Pets:** Accepted.
🛜 ✕ ♿M 🖥 💻

▼▼▼ Clarion Suites H
(928) 726-4830. **$53-$143.** 2600 S 4th Ave 85364. I-8 exit 2 (16th St/US 95) eastbound, 1 mi w, then 1.3 mi s; exit 3 (SR 280) westbound, 0.5 mi s, then 2 mi w. Ext corridors. **Pets:** Small, dogs only. $25 daily fee/pet. Service with restrictions, supervision. 🛜 ✕ 🖥 💻 🏊

▼▼ Comfort Inn H
(928) 782-1200. **$65-$110.** 1691 S Riley Ave 85365. I-8 exit 2 (16th St/US 95), just w. Int corridors. **Pets:** Large. $5 daily fee/room. Service with restrictions, crate. 🛜 ♿M 🖥 💻 🏊

🔺 ▼▼▼ Holiday Inn H
(928) 782-9300. **$99-$169.** 1901 E 18th St 85365. I-8 exit 2 (16th St/US 95), 0.4 mi e on 16th St, just s on Pacific Ave, then just w. Int corridors. **Pets:** Large. $15 daily fee/pet. Service with restrictions, supervision. (SAVE) 🛜 ✕ ♿M 🖥 💻 🍴 🏊

▼▼▼ Holiday Inn Express & Suites H
(928) 317-1400. **$89-$129.** 2044 S Ave 3 E 85365. I-8 exit 3, just n, then just w on Frontage Rd. Int corridors. **Pets:** Accepted.
🛜 ✕ ♿M 🖥 💻 🏊

▼▼▼ Homewood Suites by Hilton H
(928) 782-4100. **$116-$134.** 1955 E 16th St 85365. I-8 exit 2 (16th St/US 95), 0.4 mi e. Int corridors. **Pets:** Accepted.
🛜 ♿M 🖥 💻 🏊 ✕

🔺 ▼▼▼ La Fuente Inn & Suites H
(928) 329-1814. **$80-$179.** 1513 E 16th St 85365. I-8 exit 2 (16th St/US 95), just e. Ext corridors. **Pets:** Medium. $25 one-time fee/room. Designated rooms, service with restrictions, supervision.
(SAVE) 🛜 🖥 💻 🏊 ✕

▼▼ Microtel Inn & Suites by Wyndham Yuma H
(928) 345-1777. **$70-$85.** 11274 S Fortuna Rd 85367. I-8 exit 12 (Fortuna Rd), just s, then w on frontage road. Int corridors. **Pets:** Small. $10 daily fee/pet. Service with restrictions, supervision.
🛜 ✕ 🖥 💻 🏊

▼▼ Oak Tree Inn H
(928) 539-9000. **$69-$99, 3 day notice.** 1731 Sunridge Dr 85365. I-8 exit 2 (16th St/US 95), just e, then just s. Ext/int corridors. **Pets:** Accepted. 🛜 ✕ 🖥 💻 🏊

▼▼▼ Radisson Hotel Yuma H
(928) 783-8000. **$99-$180.** 1501 S Redondo Center Dr 85365. I-8 exit 2 (16th St/US 95), just w, then just n. Int corridors. **Pets:** Small, dogs only. $25 daily fee/pet. Designated rooms, service with restrictions, supervision. (ECO) 🛜 ✕ 🖥 💻 🍴 🏊

▼▼ Shilo Inn Hotel & Suites-Yuma H
(928) 782-9511. **$70-$180.** 1550 S Castle Dome Ave 85365. I-8 exit 2 (16th St/US 95), just e to Yuma Palms Pkwy, just n, then just w. Int corridors. **Pets:** Dogs only. $25 one-time fee/room. Designated rooms, service with restrictions, supervision. 🛜 ✕ ♿M 🖥 💻 🏊 ✕

▼▼▼ TownePlace Suites by Marriott H
(928) 783-6900. **$89-$189.** 1726 S Sunridge Dr 85365. I-8 exit 2 (16th St/US 95), just e to Sunridge Dr, then just s. Int corridors. **Pets:** Accepted. 🛜 ✕ ♿M 🖥 💻 🏊

🔺 ▼▼▼ Yuma Cabana Motel M
(928) 783-8311. **$46-$130, 3 day notice.** 2151 S 4th Ave 85364. I-8 exit 2 (16th St/US 95), 1 mi w, then 0.5 mi s. Int corridors. **Pets:** Medium, dogs only. $6 daily fee/pet. Designated rooms, service with restrictions, supervision. (SAVE) 🛜 ✕ 🖥 💻 🏊

ARKANSAS

ALMA

▽▽ Comfort Inn & Suites H
(479) 632-4141. **Call for rates.** 439 Hwy 71 N 72921. I-40 exit 13, just n. Ext/int corridors. **Pets:** Accepted. 🛰 🍴 💻

ARKADELPHIA

◇◇◇ ▽▽◇ BEST WESTERN Continental Inn H
(870) 246-5592. **$69-$79.** 136 Valley St 71923. I-30 exit 78, just e. Ext corridors. **Pets:** Large. $10 daily fee/pet. Service with restrictions.
SAVE 🛰 🍴 💻 🏊

▽▽◇ Hampton Inn H
(870) 403-0800. **$79-$129.** 108 Malvern Rd 71923. I-30 exit 78, just ne. Int corridors. **Pets:** Small. Designated rooms, service with restrictions, supervision. 🛰 ♿ 🍴 💻 🏊

BATESVILLE

▽▽ Ramada H
(870) 698-1800. **$75-$100.** 1325 N St. Louis St 72501. 1 mi n on US 167. Ext corridors. **Pets:** Small. $20 daily fee/pet. Service with restrictions, crate. 🛰 🍴 💻 🍴 🏊

▽ Super 8-Batesville M
(870) 793-5888. **$55-$59.** 1287 N St. Louis St 72501. 1 mi n on US 167. Int corridors. **Pets:** Accepted. 🛰 🍴 💻

BENTON

◇◇◇ ▽▽◇ BEST WESTERN Benton Inn H 🐾
(501) 778-9695. **$76-$81.** 17036 I-30 72019. I-30 exit 117 southbound; exit 118 northbound, just w. Ext corridors. **Pets:** Large. $10 daily fee/pet. Service with restrictions, crate. SAVE 🛰 🍴 💻 🏊

BENTONVILLE

◇◇◇ ▽▽▽◇ Comfort Suites Bentonville/Rogers H
(479) 715-0335. **$69-$119.** 2011 SE Walton Blvd 72712. I-540 exit 85, just w. Int corridors. **Pets:** Accepted.
SAVE 🛰 ✕ 🍴 💻 🏊 ✕

▽▽◇ Courtyard by Marriott H
(479) 273-3333. **$75-$179.** 1001 McClain Rd 72712. I-540 exit 88, just e. Int corridors. **Pets:** Accepted. 🛰 ✕ ♿ 🍴 💻 🏊 ✕

▽▽◇ La Quinta Inn & Suites Bentonville H
(479) 271-7555. **$75-$166.** 1001 SE Walton Blvd 72712. I-540 exit 85, 0.7 mi w. Int corridors. **Pets:** Service with restrictions, supervision.
🛰 ♿ 🍴 💻 🏊 ✕

▽▽ Suburban Extended Stay Hotel H
(479) 268-4400. **$50-$85.** 200 SW Suburban Ln 72712. I-540 exit 85, 1.6 mi w. Int corridors. **Pets:** Accepted. 🛰 🍴 💻

▽▽▽ TownePlace Suites by Marriott
Bentonville/Rogers H 🐾
(479) 621-0202. **$79-$129.** 3100 SE 14th St 72712. I-540 exit 86, just e. Int corridors. **Pets:** Other species. $50 one-time fee/room. Service with restrictions, crate. 🛰 ✕ ♿ 🍴 💻 🏊

▽▽▽ Wingate by Wyndham H
(479) 418-5400. **$74-$129.** 7400 SW Old Farm Blvd 72712. 7.4 mi w of jct Walton and SW Regional Airport blvds. Int corridors. **Pets:** Other species. $50 one-time fee/room. Designated rooms, no service, crate.
🛰 ✕ ♿ 🍴 💻 🏊 ✕

BLYTHEVILLE

◇◇◇ ▽▽◇ BEST WESTERN Blytheville Inn H
(870) 762-5200. **$60-$80.** 1101 Kari Ln 72315. I-55 exit 63, just nw. Ext corridors. **Pets:** Accepted. SAVE 🛰 🍴 💻 🏊

▽▽▽ Comfort Inn & Suites H
(870) 763-0900. **$97-$104.** 1510 E Main St 72315. I-55 exit 67, just w. Int corridors. **Pets:** Large, other species. $15 one-time fee/room. Designated rooms, service with restrictions. 🛰 ✕ ♿ 🍴 💻 🏊

▽▽▽ Holiday Inn H
(870) 763-5800. **$95-$119.** 1121 E Main St 72315. I-55 exit 67, just w. Ext/int corridors. **Pets:** Accepted. 🛰 ✕ 🍴 💻 🍴 🏊

▽▽ Quality Inn H
(870) 763-7081. **$72.** 1520 E Main St 72315. I-55 exit 67, just w. Ext corridors. **Pets:** Accepted. 🛰 🍴 💻 🍴 🏊

BRYANT

▽▽ Americas Best Value Inn M
(501) 653-7800. **$55-$90.** 407 W Commerce St 72022. I-30 exit 123, just sw. Ext corridors. **Pets:** Small, dogs only. $10 daily fee/pet. Service with restrictions, supervision. 🛰 🍴 💻

◇◇◇ ▽▽▽ Berkshire Inn & Suites H
(501) 847-7120. **$59-$84, 7 day notice.** 210 Office Park Dr 72022. I-30 exit 123, just w. Ext corridors. **Pets:** Small, dogs only. $15 daily fee/pet. Service with restrictions, crate. SAVE 🛰 🍴 💻 🏊

▽▽ Comfort Inn & Suites H
(501) 653-4000. **$80-$130.** 209 W Commerce St 72022. I-30 exit 123, just w. Int corridors. **Pets:** Small, other species. $10 daily fee/pet. Designated rooms, service with restrictions, supervision.
🛰 🍴 💻 🏊 ✕

◇◇◇ ▽▽▽ Holiday Inn Express H
(501) 847-0900. **$79-$109.** 2915 Main St 72022. I-30 exit 123, just n on west service road. Int corridors. **Pets:** Small, dogs only. $25 one-time fee/pet. Service with restrictions, supervision.
SAVE 🛰 ♿ 🍴 💻 🏊

◇◇◇ ▽▽▽ Hometown Hotel.com H
(501) 653-0123. **$59-$84.** 2921 Main St 72022. I-30 exit 123, just nw. Ext/int corridors. **Pets:** Small, dogs only. $15 one-time fee/pet. Service with restrictions, supervision. SAVE 🛰 ✕ ♿ 🍴 💻

▽▽▽ La Quinta Inn & Suites Bryant H
(501) 847-9494. **$78-$166.** 408 W Commerce St 72022. I-30 exit 123, just sw. Int corridors. **Pets:** Service with restrictions, supervision.
🛰 ✕ 🍴 💻 🏊

▼▼ ▼▼ Super 8 Ⓜ
(501) 847-7888. **$50-$70.** 201 Dell Dr 72022. I-30 exit 123, just e. Ext corridors. **Pets:** Medium, dogs only. $20 deposit/pet, $10 one-time fee/pet. Designated rooms, service with restrictions, supervision. 🛜 🚪 💻

CABOT
▼▼ ▼▼ Days Inn & Suites - Cabot Ⓗ
(501) 605-1810. **$80-$110.** 1302 W Locust St 72023. US 67/167 exit 19, just ne. Int corridors. **Pets:** Medium. $10 daily fee/pet. Service with restrictions, crate. 🛜 ✖ 🚪 💻 ⌁

CLARKSVILLE
ⒶⒶⒶ ▼▼ ▼▼ BEST WESTERN Sherwood Inn Ⓗ 🐾
(479) 754-7900. **$67-$82.** 1207 S Rogers Ave 72830. I-40 exit 58, just n. Ext corridors. **Pets:** $10 one-time fee/room. Service with restrictions, supervision. 🆂🅰🆅🅴 🛜 🚪 💻 ⌁

CLINTON
ⒶⒶⒶ ▼▼ ▼▼ BEST WESTERN Hillside Inn Ⓗ
(501) 745-4700. **Call for rates.** 1025 Hwy 65 B 72031. Just w of jct US 62. Ext corridors. **Pets:** Large, other species. $8 daily fee/room. Supervision. 🆂🅰🆅🅴 🛜 ✖ 🚪 💻 ⌁

CONWAY
ⒶⒶⒶ ▼▼ ▼▼ BEST WESTERN Conway Ⓗ
(501) 329-9855. **$65-$70.** 816 E Oak St 72032. I-40 exit 127, just n. Ext corridors. **Pets:** Other species. Service with restrictions, supervision. 🆂🅰🆅🅴 🛜 🚪 💻 ⌁

ⒶⒶⒶ ▼▼▼▼ Candlewood Suites Ⓗ
(501) 329-8551. **$82-$109.** 2360 Sanders St 72033. I-40 exit 125, just se. Int corridors. **Pets:** Large, other species. $75 one-time fee/room. Service with restrictions, supervision. 🆂🅰🆅🅴 🛜 🚪 💻

▼▼▼▼ La Quinta Inn & Suites Ⓗ
(501) 328-5100. **$90-$173.** 2350 Sanders St 72032. I-40 exit 125, just se. Int corridors. **Pets:** Service with restrictions, supervision. 🛜 ✖ 🅼 🚪 💻 ⌁

▼▼ ▼▼ Microtel Inn & Suites by Wyndham Conway Ⓗ
(501) 327-0898. **$60-$105.** 2475 Sanders St 72032. I-40 exit 125, just se. Int corridors. **Pets:** Accepted. 🛜 🚪 💻

▼▼ ▼▼ Quality Inn Ⓗ
(501) 329-0300. **Call for rates.** 150 Skyline Dr N 72032. I-40 exit 125, just n. Ext corridors. **Pets:** Accepted. 🛜 🚪 💻 ⌁

EL DORADO
▼▼ ▼▼ La Quinta Inn El Dorado Ⓗ
(870) 863-6677. **$72-$134.** 2303 Junction City Rd 71730. Just e of jct US 167 and 82 business route. Int corridors. **Pets:** Service with restrictions, supervision. 🛜 🚪 💻 ⌁

EUREKA SPRINGS
▼▼▼▼ 1886 Crescent Hotel & Spa Ⓗ
(479) 253-9766. **$169-$219, 3 day notice.** 75 Prospect Ave 72632. 1.3 mi n of jct SR 23 on US 62B Historic Loop. Int corridors. **Pets:** $25 daily fee/room. Service with restrictions, crate. 🛜 ✖ 🚪 💻 🍴 ⌁

▼▼▼▼ Arsenic & Old Lace B&B 🅱🅱 🐾
(479) 253-5454. **$159-$329, 15 day notice.** 60 Hillside Ave 72632. 1.2 mi n on SR 23, just sw; downtown. Ext/int corridors. **Pets:** Dogs only. $30 one-time fee/room. Designated rooms, service with restrictions, crate. 🛜 ✖ 🚪

▼▼ ▼▼ Basin Park Hotel - A Magnuson Grand Hotel Ⓗ
(479) 253-7837. **$89-$164, 3 day notice.** 12 Spring St 72632. 0.7 mi n of jct US 62 via SR 23 N; downtown. Int corridors. **Pets:** $25 daily fee/room. Service with restrictions, crate. 🛜 ✖ 🚪 💻 🍴

ⒶⒶⒶ ▼▼ ▼▼ BEST WESTERN Eureka Inn Ⓗ
(479) 253-9551. **$70-$130.** 101 E Van Buren St 72632. Just w of jct US 62 and SR 23. Ext/int corridors. **Pets:** Accepted.
🆂🅰🆅🅴 🛜 ✖ 🚪 💻 ⌁ ✖

ⒶⒶⒶ ▼▼ ▼▼ BEST WESTERN Inn of the Ozarks Ⓗ 🐾
(479) 253-9768. **$59-$109, 3 day notice.** 207 W Van Buren St 72632. 0.5 mi w of jct US 62 and SR 23. Ext corridors. **Pets:** Dogs only. $10 daily fee/pet. Designated rooms, service with restrictions, supervision.
🆂🅰🆅🅴 🛜 🚪 💻 🍴 ⌁ ✖

▼▼ ▼▼ Days Inn Ⓜ
(479) 253-8863. **$60-$160, 3 day notice.** 120 W Van Buren St 72632. Just w of jct US 62 and SR 23. Ext corridors. **Pets:** Small, dogs only. $15 daily fee/room. Service with restrictions, supervision.
🛜 🚪 💻 ⌁

FAYETTEVILLE
ⒶⒶⒶ ▼▼ ▼▼ BEST WESTERN Windsor Suites Ⓗ 🐾
(479) 587-1400. **$85-$95.** 1122 S Futrall Dr 72701. I-540 exit 62, just se. Ext corridors. **Pets:** Medium. $15 daily fee/pet. Designated rooms, service with restrictions, crate. 🆂🅰🆅🅴 🛜 🚪 💻 ⌁

▼▼▼▼ Comfort Inn & Suites Ⓗ
(479) 571-5177. **Call for rates.** 1234 Steamboat Dr 72704. I-540 exit 64, just nw. Int corridors. **Pets:** Medium. $100 deposit/room, $25 daily fee/pet. Designated rooms, service with restrictions, crate. 🛜 🚪 💻 ⌁

▼▼ ▼▼ Sleep Inn by Choice Hotels Ⓗ
(479) 587-8700. **$84-$120.** 728 E Millsap Rd 72703. I-540 exit 67, 1.6 mi e, then just s on US 71B. Int corridors. **Pets:** Other species. $25 one-time fee/room. Service with restrictions, crate. 🛜 🚪 💻

▼▼▼▼ Staybridge Suites Ⓗ
(479) 695-2400. **$109-$209.** 1577 W 15th St 72701. Just w of jct Razorback Rd. Int corridors. **Pets:** Other species. $15 one-time fee/room, $10 daily fee/room. Service with restrictions, crate. 🛜 🅼 🚪 💻 ⌁

FORDYCE
▼▼ ▼▼ Days Inn Ⓗ
(870) 352-2400. **$77-$110.** 2500 W 4th St 71742. US 79/167, 1 mi w. Ext/int corridors. **Pets:** Medium. $10 daily fee/pet. Designated rooms, service with restrictions, crate. 🛜 🚪 💻 ⌁

FORREST CITY
ⒶⒶⒶ ▼▼ ▼▼ BEST WESTERN Colony Inn Ⓗ 🐾
(870) 633-0870. **Call for rates.** 2333 N Washington St 72335. I-40 exit 241A, just s. Ext corridors. **Pets:** Large, other species. $20 daily fee/room. Designated rooms, service with restrictions, supervision.
🆂🅰🆅🅴 🛜 🚪 💻 ⌁

▼▼ ▼▼ Days Inn Forrest City Ⓗ
(870) 633-6300. **$80.** 200 Holiday Dr 72335. I-40 exit 241B, just n. Ext corridors. **Pets:** Accepted. 🛜 🚪 💻 🍴 ⌁

FORT SMITH
▼▼ ▼▼ AmericInn of Fort Smith Ⓗ
(479) 484-0227. **$79-$89.** 2120 Burnham Rd 72903. I-540 exit 8A (Rogers Ave), just w. Int corridors. **Pets:** Other species. Service with restrictions, crate. 🛜 🚪 💻 ⌁ ✖

▼▼▼▼ Aspen Hotel & Suites Ⓗ 🐾
(479) 452-9000. **Call for rates.** 2900 S 68th St 72903. I-540 exit 8B (Rogers Ave), just e. Int corridors. **Pets:** Other species. Service with restrictions, crate. 🛜 ✖ 🚪 💻 ⌁

▼▼ ▼▼ Baymont Inn & Suites Fort Smith Ⓗ
(479) 484-5770. **$55-$79.** 2123 Burnham Rd 72903. I-540 exit 8A (Rogers Ave), just w. Int corridors. **Pets:** Other species. Service with restrictions, supervision. 🛜 🚪 💻 ⌁

Beland Manor Bed & Breakfast BB
(479) 782-3300. **$99-$185, 5 day notice.** 1320 S Albert Pike 72903. I-540 exit 8A (Rogers Ave), 1.3 mi w. Int corridors. **Pets:** Accepted.

Courtyard by Marriott Downtown Fort Smith H
(479) 783-2100. **$99-$159.** 900 Rogers Ave 72901. Just s of US 64 (Garrison Ave); downtown. Int corridors. **Pets:** Accepted.

GuestHouse Inn H
(479) 646-5100. **$65-$80.** 3600 Grinnell Ave 72908. I-540 exit 12, 0.5 mi se. Int corridors. **Pets:** Accepted.

Holiday Inn City Center Fort Smith H
(479) 783-1000. **$99-$169.** 700 Rogers Ave 72901. Just s of US 64 (Garrison Ave); downtown. Int corridors. **Pets:** $50 one-time fee/pet. Service with restrictions, crate.

Holiday Inn Express H
(479) 452-7500. **Call for rates.** 6813 Phoenix Ave 72903. I-540 exit 8B (Rogers Ave), 0.6 mi e, then 0.5 mi s. Int corridors. **Pets:** Accepted.

Residence Inn by Marriott H
(479) 478-8300. **$98-$161.** 3005 S 74th St 72903. I-540 exit 8A (Rogers Ave), 0.8 mi e. Int corridors. **Pets:** $75 one-time fee/room. Service with restrictions, crate.

HARDY

BEST WESTERN Village Inn M
(870) 856-2176. **$68-$75, 7 day notice.** 3587 Hwy 62/412 72542. On US 62/412, 2 mi sw. Ext corridors. **Pets:** Small, dogs only. $25 daily fee/pet. Designated rooms, service with restrictions, crate.

HARRISON

Holiday Inn Express Hotel & Suites H
(870) 741-3636. **$96-$116.** 117 Hwy 43 E 72601. Just e of jct US 62/65/412 and SR 43. Int corridors. **Pets:** Small. $25 one-time fee/pet. Service with restrictions, supervision.

Quality Inn H
(870) 741-7676. **$70-$99.** 1210 Hwy 62/65 N 72601. On US 62/65/412, 1 mi e. Ext/int corridors. **Pets:** Small. $25 one-time fee/pet. Service with restrictions, supervision.

HELENA-WEST HELENA

BEST WESTERN Inn H
(870) 572-2592. **Call for rates.** 1053 Hwy 49 W 72390. US 49, 3 mi w. Ext corridors. **Pets:** Medium, other species. $20 daily fee/room. Designated rooms, service with restrictions, supervision.

HOPE

BEST WESTERN of Hope H
(870) 777-9222. **$78.** 1800 Holiday Dr 71801. I-30 exit 30, just nw. Ext corridors. **Pets:** Other species. $10 daily fee/room. Service with restrictions, supervision.

HOT SPRINGS

BEST WESTERN Winner's Circle Inn H
(501) 624-2531. **$90-$140, 7 day notice.** 2520 Central Ave 71901. 1.3 mi n of jct US 270 and SR 7. Ext corridors. **Pets:** Medium, dogs only. $25 one-time fee/room. Designated rooms, service with restrictions, crate.

Clarion Resort H
(501) 525-1391. **$89-$165.** 4813 Central Ave 71913. 5.5 mi s of jct US 270 and SR 7. Int corridors. **Pets:** Accepted.

Embassy Suites Hot Springs-Hotel & Spa H
(501) 624-9200. **$119-$229.** 400 Convention Blvd 71901. Just w of jct US 70. Int corridors. **Pets:** Large, other species. $50 one-time fee/room. Designated rooms, service with restrictions, supervision.

Staybridge Suites H
(501) 525-6500. **$99-$199.** 103 Lookout Cir 71913. 3.5 mi s of jct US 270 and SR 7. Int corridors. **Pets:** Large, other species. $75 one-time fee/room. Designated rooms, service with restrictions.

JACKSONVILLE

Super 8 H
(501) 982-9219. **$65.** 1850 John Harden Dr 72076. US 67/167 exit 10B southbound; exit 11 northbound. Ext corridors. **Pets:** Dogs only. $10 daily fee/pet. Service with restrictions, supervision.

JOHNSON

Inn at the Mill, an Ascend Collection hotel H
(479) 443-1800. **Call for rates.** 3906 Greathouse Springs Rd 72741. I-540 exit 69, just e. Int corridors. **Pets:** Accepted.

TownePlace Suites by Marriott Fayetteville North/Springdale H
(479) 439-1905. **$70-$150.** 5437 S 48th St 72741. I-540 exit 69, just se. Int corridors. **Pets:** Accepted.

JONESBORO

Candlewood Suites H
(870) 336-6500. **$80-$150.** 2906 Kazi St 72401. Just ne of jct US 63 and Caraway Rd. Int corridors. **Pets:** Large, other species. $75 one-time fee/pet. Designated rooms, service with restrictions, crate.

Fairfield Inn & Suites by Marriott Jonesboro H
(870) 277-1870. **$85-$140.** 3408 Access Rd 72401. 0.7 mi e of jct Stadium Blvd and Phillips Dr. Int corridors. **Pets:** Other species. $75 one-time fee/room. Designated rooms, service with restrictions, crate.

Holiday Inn of Jonesboro H
(870) 935-2030. **$89-$129.** 3006 S Caraway Rd 72401. Just n of jct US 63. Ext/int corridors. **Pets:** Medium. $15 one-time fee/pet. Designated rooms, service with restrictions, supervision.

LITTLE ROCK

Clarion Hotel Medical Center H
(501) 664-5020. **$89-$169.** 925 S University Ave 72204. I-630 exit 5, just s. Int corridors. **Pets:** Accepted.

Comfort Inn & Suites, Downtown Little Rock @ The Clinton Library H
(501) 687-7700. **$89-$100.** 707 I-30 72202. I-30 exit 140A, just e. Int corridors. **Pets:** Other species. $50 one-time fee/room. Service with restrictions, supervision.

Comfort Inn & Suites Little Rock Airport H
(501) 376-2466. **$84-$105.** 4301 E Roosevelt Rd 72206. I-440 exit 3, just n. Int corridors. **Pets:** Other species. $25 one-time fee/room. Designated rooms, service with restrictions, supervision.

Embassy Suites Hotel Little Rock H
(501) 312-9000. **$119-$259.** 11301 Financial Centre Pkwy 72211. Jct I-430 and 630, just w. Int corridors. **Pets:** Accepted.

▼▼▼ **Holiday Inn Airport Conference Center** 🄷
(501) 490-1000. **$89-$139.** 3201 Bankhead Dr 72206. I-440 exit 3, just s.
Int corridors. **Pets:** Accepted. 🛰 ✕ ⌖ 🛏 💻 🍴 🏊

▼▼▼ **Holiday Inn Express Airport** 🄷
(501) 490-4000. **$85-$108.** 3121 Bankhead Dr 72206. I-440 exit 3, just s.
Ext/int corridors. **Pets:** Small. $25 one-time fee/room. Designated rooms,
service with restrictions, supervision. 🛰 🛏 💻 🏊

▼▼▼ **Residence Inn by Marriott** 🄷
(501) 312-0200. **$99-$119.** 1401 S Shackleford Rd 72211. I-430 exit 5,
just n. Int corridors. **Pets:** Medium. $100 one-time fee/room. Service with
restrictions. 🛰 ✕ 🛏 💻 🏊 ✕

▼▼▼ **TownePlace Suites by Marriott - Little Rock** 🄷
(501) 708-1917. **$89-$129.** 12 Crossings Ct 72205. I-430 exit 5, 0.6 mi e.
Int corridors. **Pets:** Medium. $100 one-time fee/room. Service with restric-
tions. 🛰 ✕ ⌖ 🛏 💻 🏊

LONOKE

🄰🄰🄰 ▼▼▼ **BEST WESTERN PLUS Lonoke**
Hotel 🄷 ❀
(501) 676-8880. **Call for rates.** 102 Dee Dee Ln 72086. I-40 exit 175,
just n. Int corridors. **Pets:** Medium, dogs only. $50 deposit/pet, $16 daily
fee/pet. Service with restrictions, supervision. SAVE 🛰 🛏 💻 🏊

🄰🄰🄰 ▼▼ **Days Inn** 🄷
(501) 676-5138. **$65-$80.** 105 Dee Dee Ln 72086. I-40 exit 175, just n.
Ext corridors. **Pets:** Medium, other species. $10 one-time fee/pet. Service
with restrictions. SAVE 🛰 🛏 💻 🏊

🄰🄰🄰 ▼▼▼ **Holiday Inn Express Hotel & Suites** 🄷
(501) 676-7800. **$114-$124.** 104 Dee Dee Ln 72086. I-40 exit 175, just
n. Int corridors. **Pets:** Medium. $25 daily fee/pet. Service with restrictions,
supervision. SAVE 🛰 ⌖ 🛏 💻 🏊

MARION

🄰🄰🄰 ▼▼▼ **BEST WESTERN Regency Motor Inn** 🄷
(870) 739-3278. **$69-$75.** 3635 I-55 72364. I-55 exit 10, just nw. Ext
corridors. **Pets:** Medium. $10 one-time fee/room. Service with restrictions,
crate. SAVE 🛰 🛏 💻 🏊

MAUMELLE

🄰🄰🄰 ▼▼▼ **Holiday Inn Express & Suites-Maumelle** 🄷
(501) 851-4422. **Call for rates.** 200 Holiday Dr 72113. I-40 exit 142, just
s. Int corridors. **Pets:** Accepted. SAVE 🛰 ✕ ⌖ 🛏 💻 🏊

MCGEHEE

🄰🄰🄰 ▼▼▼ **BEST WESTERN McGehee** 🄼
(870) 222-3564. **$79-$83.** 1202 Hwy 65 N 71654. Center. Ext corridors.
Pets: Medium, dogs only. $20 daily fee/pet. Designated rooms, service
with restrictions, supervision. SAVE 🛰 🛏 💻 🏊

MOUNTAIN HOME

🄰🄰🄰 ▼▼▼ **Comfort Inn** 🄷 ❀
(870) 424-9000. **$89-$165.** 1031 Highland Cir 72653. 1.5 mi e on US
62B. Ext/int corridors. **Pets:** Small, dogs only. $25 one-time fee/room.
Designated rooms, service with restrictions, supervision.
SAVE 🛰 ⌖ 🛏 💻 🏊

▼▼ **Days Inn** 🄷
(870) 425-1010. **$73-$89.** 1746 E Hwy 62B 72653. On US 62B, 2.3 mi
e. Int corridors. **Pets:** Accepted. 🛰 ⌖ 🛏 💻 🏊

▼▼▼ **Holiday Inn Express** 🄷
(870) 425-6200. **$125-$135.** 1005 Coley Dr 72653. 1.4 mi e on US 62B.
Int corridors. **Pets:** $35 one-time fee/pet. Service with restrictions, crate.
🛰 ⌖ 🛏 💻 🏊

▼ **Super 8-Mountain Home** 🄼
(870) 424-5600. **$65-$70.** 865 Hwy 62 E 72653. On US 62B, 1.3 mi e.
Int corridors. **Pets:** $10 daily fee/pet. Designated rooms, no service,
supervision. 🛰 🛏 💻

🄰🄰🄰 ▼▼▼ **Teal Point Resort** 🄲🄰
(870) 492-5145. **$80-$410,** 60 day notice. 715 Teal Point Rd 72653.
3.5 mi e of jct US 62 and 62 business route, 0.6 mi n on CR 406, follow
signs. Ext corridors. **Pets:** $10 daily fee/pet. Designated rooms, no ser-
vice, supervision. SAVE 🛰 ✕ 🛏 🏊 ✕ 🖼

MOUNTAIN VIEW

🄰🄰🄰 ▼▼ **BEST WESTERN Fiddlers Inn** 🄼 ❀
(870) 269-2828. **Call for rates.** 601 Sylamore Ave 72560. 1 mi n on SR
5, 9 and 14. Ext corridors. **Pets:** Medium, dogs only. $15 daily fee/pet.
Service with restrictions, crate. SAVE 🛰 🛏 💻 🏊

NORTH LITTLE ROCK

▼▼▼ **Holiday Inn-North** 🄷
(501) 758-1851. **$89-$99.** 120 W Pershing Blvd 72114. I-40 exit 152
westbound; exit 153A eastbound. Int corridors. **Pets:** Other species. $30
one-time fee/room. Designated rooms, service with restrictions, crate.
🛰 🛏 💻 🍴 🏊

▼▼ **La Quinta Inn & Suites North Little Rock-McCain**
Mall 🄷
(501) 945-0808. **$63-$144.** 4311 Warden Rd 72116. US 67/167 exit 1B
northbound; exit 1 southbound. Int corridors. **Pets:** Service with restrictions, supervision. 🛰 🛏 💻 🏊

▼▼ **La Quinta Inn Little Rock North Landers Road** 🄷
(501) 758-8888. **$59-$133.** 4100 E McCain Blvd 72117. US 67/167 exit
1A northbound; exit 1 southbound. Ext corridors. **Pets:** Service with
restrictions, supervision. 🛰 🛏 💻 🏊

🄰🄰🄰 ▼▼ **Red Roof Inn** 🄷
(501) 945-0080. **$49-$90.** 5711 Pritchard Dr 72117. I-40 exit 157, just sw.
Int corridors. **Pets:** Large, other species. Service with restrictions, supervision. SAVE 🛰 🛏 🏊

▼▼▼ **Residence Inn by Marriott-North** 🄷
(501) 945-7777. **$109-$129.** 4110 Healthcare Dr 72117. I-40 exit 156,
just nw. Int corridors. **Pets:** Accepted. 🛰 ✕ 🛏 💻 🏊 ✕

PINE BLUFF

🄰🄰🄰 ▼▼ **BEST WESTERN PLUS Presidential Hotel &**
Suites 🄷
(870) 535-6300. **$80-$140.** 3104 Market St 71601. I-530 exit 46, just n.
Int corridors. **Pets:** Accepted. SAVE 🛰 🛏 💻 🏊

▼▼ **Comfort Inn** 🄷
(870) 535-5300. **$55-$99.** 2809 Pines Mall Dr 71601. I-530 exit 46, just
n. Int corridors. **Pets:** Service with restrictions, supervision.
🛰 🛏 💻 🏊

▼▼▼ **Holiday Inn Express Hotel & Suites** 🄷
(870) 879-3800. **Call for rates.** 3620 Camden Rd 71603. I-530 exit 39,
just sw. Int corridors. **Pets:** Other species. $15 daily fee/pet. Service with
restrictions, crate. 🛰 ⌖ 🛏 💻 🏊

POCAHONTAS

▼▼ **Days Inn & Suites** 🄷
(870) 892-9500. **$86-$172.** 2805 Hwy 67 S 72455. 1.7 mi s. Int corridors.
Pets: $10 daily fee/pet. Designated rooms, service with restrictions,
supervision. 🛰 🛏 💻

ROGERS

🄰🄰🄰 ▼▼▼ **Aloft Rogers-Bentonville** 🄷 ❀
(479) 268-6799. **$90-$170, 3 day notice.** 1103 S 52nd St 72758. I-540
exit 83, just nw. Int corridors. **Pets:** Medium. $40 deposit/pet. Designated
rooms, service with restrictions, supervision.
SAVE 🛰 ✕ 🛏 💻 🏊

▼▼▼ **Candlewood Suites** H

(479) 636-2783. **$89-$99.** 4601 W Rozell St 72757. I-540 exit 85, 0.5 mi n on 46th St. Int corridors. **Pets:** Large, other species. $75 one-time fee/room, $5 daily fee/room. Service with restrictions, crate.

🛜 🛋 💻 🏊

▼▼▼ **Country Inn & Suites By Carlson** H

(479) 633-0055. **$89.** 4304 W Walnut St 72756. I-540 exit 85, just e. Int corridors. **Pets:** Accepted. 🛜 🛋 💻 🏊

▼▼▼ **Embassy Suites Northwest Arkansas** H 🐾

(479) 254-8400. **$119-$259.** 3303 Pinnacle Hills Pkwy 72758. I-540 exit 83, just w, then 0.6 mi s. Int corridors. **Pets:** Large. $50 one-time fee/room. Designated rooms, service with restrictions, crate.

🛜 ♿ 🛋 💻 🍴 🏊 ✂

▼▼ **Microtel Inn & Suites by Wyndham Rogers** H

(479) 636-5551. **$50-$60.** 909 S 8th St 72756. 0.5 mi s of jct Walnut St. Int corridors. **Pets:** Small, dogs only. $10 daily fee/pet. Service with restrictions, supervision. 🛜 🛋 💻

(AAA) ▼▼▼ **Residence Inn by Marriott** H

(479) 636-5900. **$99-$159.** 4611 W Locust St 72756. I-540 exit 85, 0.4 mi n on 46th St. Int corridors. **Pets:** Other species. $75 one-time fee/room. Service with restrictions, crate.

[SAVE] 🛜 ✂ ♿ 🛋 💻 🏊 ✂

▼▼▼ **Staybridge Suites Rogers-Bentonville** H

(479) 845-5701. **Call for rates.** 1801 S 52nd St 72758. I-540 exit 83, just nw. Int corridors. **Pets:** Large. $15 one-time fee/room, $10 daily fee/room. Service with restrictions, crate. 🛜 ✂ ♿ 🛋 💻

RUSSELLVILLE

▼▼▼ **La Quinta Inn & Suites** H

(479) 967-2299. **$90-$155.** 111 E Harrell Dr 72802. I-40 exit 81, just se. Int corridors. **Pets:** Service with restrictions, supervision.

🛜 ✂ 🛋 💻 🏊 ✂

▼▼ **Quality Inn** H

(479) 967-7500. **$62-$79.** 3019 E Parkway Dr 72802. I-40 exit 84, just s. Ext corridors. **Pets:** Medium. $10 daily fee/pet. Service with restrictions, supervision. 🛜 🛋 💻 🏊

SEARCY

▼▼ **Microtel Inn & Suites by Wyndham Searcy** H

(501) 268-1555. **$55-$95.** 3668 Ferren Tr 72143. US 67/167 exit 46, just ne. Int corridors. **Pets:** Accepted. 🛜 🛋 💻

SPRINGDALE

▼▼▼ **Hampton Inn & Suites** H

(479) 756-3500. **$89-$199.** 1700 S 48th St 72762. I-540 exit 72, just e. Int corridors. **Pets:** Small, other species. Service with restrictions, crate.

🛜 ♿ 🛋 💻 🏊

▼▼▼ **Holiday Inn Northwest AR Hotel & Convention Center** H

(479) 751-8300. **$89-$169.** 1500 S 48th St 72762. I-540 exit 72, just e. Int corridors. **Pets:** Small. $35 one-time fee/pet. Service with restrictions, supervision. 🛜 ✂ 🛋 💻 🍴 🏊 ✂

▼▼▼ **La Quinta Inn & Suites Springdale** H

(479) 751-2626. **$66-$188.** 1300 S 48th St 72764. I-540 exit 72, just e. Int corridors. **Pets:** Service with restrictions, supervision.

🛜 ♿ 🛋 💻 🏊 ✂

(AAA) ▼▼▼ **Residence Inn by Marriott** H 🐾

(479) 872-9100. **$71-$160.** 1740 S 48th St 72762. I-540 exit 72, just e to 48th St, then just s. Int corridors. **Pets:** Other species. $75 one-time fee/room. Service with restrictions. [SAVE] 🛜 ✂ 🛋 💻 🏊 ✂

STAR CITY

▼▼ ▼ **Star City Inn & Suites** H

(870) 628-6883. **$57-$95.** 1308 N Lincoln Ave 71667. Just n on US 425. Int corridors. **Pets:** Small, dogs only. $5 daily fee/pet. Service with restrictions, supervision. 🛜 🛋 💻 🏊

TEXARKANA

▼▼ **La Quinta Inn & Suites Texarkana** H

(870) 773-1000. **$75-$144.** 5102 N State Line Ave 71854. I-30 exit 223B, just n. Int corridors. **Pets:** Service with restrictions, supervision.

🛜 🛋 💻 🏊

VAN BUREN

(AAA) ▼▼ **BEST WESTERN Van Buren Inn** H

(479) 474-8100. **$81-$90.** 1903 N 6th St 72956. I-40 exit 5, just n. Ext corridors. **Pets:** Other species. $20 daily fee/pet. Designated rooms, service with restrictions, supervision. [SAVE] 🛜 💻 🏊

▼▼▼ **Sleep Inn & Suites** H 🐾

(479) 262-6776. **$60-$100.** 1633 N 12th Ct 72956. 0.6 mi e of jct SR 59. Int corridors. **Pets:** Medium, other species. $15 deposit/room. Supervision.

🛜 ✂ ♿ 🛋 💻 🏊

CALIFORNIA

CITY INDEX

AGOURA HILLS

AAA ▼▼▼ Sheraton Agoura Hills Hotel **H**

(818) 707-1220. **$99-$229.** 30100 Agoura Rd 91301. US 101 exit 38 (Reyes Adobe Rd), just w, then just s. Int corridors. **Pets:** Accepted.
SAVE 📶 ✕ ♿ 🛏 💻 ▮▮ 🏊

ALPINE

▼▼▼ Ayres Lodge Alpine **M**

(619) 445-5800. **$99-$139.** 1251 Tavern Rd 91901. I-8 exit 30 (Tavern Rd), just s. Ext corridors. **Pets:** Medium, dogs only. $45 one-time fee/room. Designated rooms, service with restrictions, supervision.
📶 ✕ 🛏 💻 🏊

ALTURAS

AAA ▼▼▼ BEST WESTERN Trailside Inn **M**

(530) 233-4111. **$85-$100.** 343 N Main St 96101. Just s of jct SR 299/US 395 and Main St; jct W 4th St; center. Ext corridors. **Pets:** Dogs only. $10 daily fee/pet. Designated rooms, service with restrictions, supervision. SAVE 📶 ✕ ♿ 🛏 💻 🏊

AAA ▼▼ Super 8 **M**

(530) 233-3545. **$65-$75.** 511 N Main St 96101. Jct SR 299 and US 395, 0.4 mi s on US 395; at W 5th St. Ext corridors. **Pets:** Medium, dogs only. $10 one-time fee/pet. Designated rooms, supervision.
SAVE 📶 🛏 💻

ANAHEIM

AAA ▼▼▼ Anaheim Plaza Hotel & Suites **H**

(714) 772-5900. **$89-$218.** 1700 S Harbor Blvd 92802. I-5 exit 110 (Harbor Blvd/Ball Rd) northbound; exit 110A (Harbor Blvd) southbound, 0.6 mi s. Ext corridors. **Pets:** Accepted. SAVE 📶 ♿ 🛏 💻 ▮▮ 🏊

AAA ▼▼▼ Clarion Hotel Anaheim Resort **H**

(714) 750-3131. **$69-$199.** 616 Convention Way 92802. I-5 exit 109 (Katella Ave/Disney Way) northbound; exit 109A (Katella Ave/Orangewood Ave) southbound, 0.8 mi w to Harbor Blvd, just s, then just w. Int corridors. **Pets:** Small, other species. $25 one-time fee/room, $10 daily fee/pet. Designated rooms, service with restrictions, crate.
SAVE 📶 ✕ ♿ 🛏 💻 ▮▮ 🏊

▼▼▼ Embassy Suites Hotel Anaheim-North **H**

(714) 632-1221. **$119-$199.** 3100 E Frontera St 92806. SR 91 exit 31 (Kramer Blvd/Glasset St) eastbound; exit 32 westbound, just s, then just e. Int corridors. **Pets:** Accepted. ECO 📶 🛏 💻 ▮▮ 🏊 ✕

▼▼▼ Extended StayAmerica-Orange County-Anaheim Convention Center **M**

(714) 502-9988. **$59-$89.** 1742 S Clementine St 92802. I-5 exit 109 (Katella Ave/Disney Way) northbound; exit 109A (Katella Ave/Orangewood Ave) southbound, just w, then just n. Int corridors. **Pets:** $25 daily fee/pet. Designated rooms, service with restrictions. 📶 🛏 💻 🏊

▼▼▼ Hotel Menage **H**

(714) 758-0900. **$89-$199, 3 day notice.** 1221 S Harbor Blvd 92805. I-5 exit 110 (Harbor Blvd/Ball Rd) northbound; exit 110A (Harbor Blvd) southbound, just n. Ext corridors. **Pets:** Small. $25 daily fee/room. Designated rooms, service with restrictions, supervision.
📶 ✕ 🛏 💻 ▮▮ 🏊

▼▼▼ Motel 6 Anaheim-Maingate #1066 **M**

(714) 520-9696. **$59-$85.** 100 W Disney Way 92802. I-5 exit 109 (Katella Ave/Disney Way) northbound; exit 109B (Disney Way/Anaheim Blvd) southbound, just w, just n on Anaheim Blvd, then just w. Ext corridors. **Pets:** Other species. Service with restrictions, supervision. 📶 🛏 🏊

▼▼▼ Red Lion Hotel Anaheim **H**

(714) 750-2801. **$99-$250, 3 day notice.** 1850 S Harbor Blvd 92802. I-5 exit 109 (Katella Ave/Disney Way) northbound; exit 109A (Katella Ave/Orangewood Ave) southbound, 0.8 mi w, then just s. Int corridors. **Pets:** Other species. $15 one-time fee/room. Service with restrictions, crate. 📶 ✕ ♿ 🛏 💻 ▮▮ 🏊

▼▼▼ Residence Inn by Marriott Anaheim Maingate **H**

(714) 533-3555. **$113-$239.** 1700 S Clementine St 92802. I-5 exit 109 (Katella Ave/Disney Way) northbound; exit 110A (Katella Ave/Orangewood Ave) southbound, just w, then just n. Ext corridors. **Pets:** Small. $100 one-time fee/room. Designated rooms, service with restrictions, crate.
📶 ✕ ♿ 🛏 💻 🏊 ✕

AAA ▼▼▼ Sheraton Anaheim Hotel **H** 🐾

(714) 778-1700. **$139-$229.** 900 S Disneyland Dr 92802. I-5 exit 110 (Harbor Blvd/Ball Rd) northbound; exit 110A (Harbor Blvd) southbound, just n, just w on Ball Rd, then just n. Int corridors. **Pets:** Other species. $25 one-time fee/room. Service with restrictions, supervision.
SAVE 📶 ✕ ♿ 🛏 💻 ▮▮ 🏊 ✕

AAA ▼▼▼ Sheraton Park Hotel at the Anaheim Resort **H** 🐾

(714) 750-1811. **$129-$295, 3 day notice.** 1855 S Harbor Blvd 92802. I-5 exit 109 (Katella Ave/Disney Way) northbound; exit 109A (Katella Ave/Orangewood Ave) southbound, 0.8 mi w, then just s. Int corridors. **Pets:** Medium. Designated rooms, service with restrictions, crate.
SAVE 📶 ✕ 🛏 💻 ▮▮ 🏊

▼▼▼ Staybridge Suites-Anaheim Resort **H**

(714) 748-7700. **$89-$149.** 1855 S Manchester Ave 92802. I-5 exit 109 (Katella Ave/Disney Way) northbound; exit 109A (Katella Ave/Orangewood Ave) southbound, just n, 0.3 mi s; adjacent to west side of freeway. Int corridors. **Pets:** Accepted. 📶 ♿ 🛏 💻 🏊

▼▼▼ TownePlace Suites by Marriott Anaheim Maingate Near Angel Stadium **M**

(714) 939-9700. **$89-$189.** 1730 S State College Blvd 92806. I-5 exit 109 (Katella Ave/Disney Way) northbound; exit 109A (Katella Ave/Orangewood Ave) southbound, 0.7 mi e, then just n. Int corridors. **Pets:** Accepted. 📶 ✕ 🛏 💻 🏊

ANDERSON

AAA ▼▼▼ BEST WESTERN PLUS Anderson Inn **H** 🐾

(530) 365-2753. **$85-$150.** 2688 Gateway Dr 96007. I-5 exit 668 (Central Anderson/Lassen Nat'l Park) northbound, just ne on Balls Ferry Rd, then just se; exit southbound, just e, just s on McMurry Dr, then just e. Ext corridors. **Pets:** Other species. $20 daily fee/room. Designated rooms, service with restrictions, supervision. SAVE 📶 ♿ 🛏 💻 🏊

▼▼▼ Gaia Hotel & Spa Shasta **H**

(530) 365-7077. **$96-$129.** 4125 Riverside Pl 96007. I-5 exit 670 (Riverside Ave), just e, then just n. Ext corridors. **Pets:** Medium. $50 one-time fee/pet. Designated rooms, service with restrictions, supervision.
ECO 📶 ✕ 🛏 💻 ▮▮ 🏊 ✕

ANGELS CAMP

AAA ▼▼▼ BEST WESTERN PLUS Cedar Inn & Suites **H**

(209) 736-4000. **$69-$199, 3 day notice.** 444 S Main St 95222. On SR 49; center. Ext/int corridors. **Pets:** Accepted.
SAVE 📶 ✕ ♿ 🛏 💻 🏊

AAA ▼▼ Jumping Frog Motel **M**

(209) 736-2191. **$70-$165, 3 day notice.** 330 Murphys Grade Rd 95222. Just e of jct SR 49; center. Ext corridors. **Pets:** Small, dogs only. $12 one-time fee/pet, $12 daily fee/pet. Designated rooms, service with restrictions, supervision. SAVE 📶 🛏 💻

▼▼ Travelodge **H**

(209) 736-4242. **$69-$189.** 600 N Main St 95221. On SR 49; north end of town. Ext corridors. **Pets:** Dogs only. $50 deposit/room, $10 daily fee/pet. Service with restrictions, supervision. 📶 ✕ ♿ 🛏 💻 🏊

ANTIOCH

▼▼▼ Comfort Suites Antioch-Oakley **H**

(925) 755-1222. **$89-$139.** 5549 Bridgehead Rd 94561. In Oakley; just e of SR 160 and 4; just n of Main St. Int corridors. **Pets:** Medium, dogs only. $25 daily fee/pet. Designated rooms, service with restrictions, supervision. 📶 ✕ ♿ 🛏 💻 🏊

ARCATA

▼ Arcata Super 8 🅷
(707) 822-8888. **$58-$180.** 4887 Valley West Blvd 95521. US 101 exit Giuntoli Ln/Janes Rd, just e, then just s. Int corridors. **Pets:** Accepted.
🛜 🚪 🖵

ⒶⒶⒶ ▼ BEST WESTERN Arcata Inn Ⓜ ❖
(707) 826-0313. **$81-$186.** 4827 Valley West Blvd 95521. US 101 exit Giuntoli Ln/Janes Rd, just e, then just s. Ext corridors. **Pets:** Dogs only. $20 one-time fee/room. Designated rooms, service with restrictions, supervision. 〔SAVE〕 🛜 🚪 🖵 ⤳

ⒶⒶⒶ ▼▼▼ Days Inn & Suites Arcata Ⓜ
(707) 826-2827. **$90-$120.** 4701 Valley West Blvd 95521. US 101 exit Giuntoli Ln/Janes Rd, just e, then just s. Ext corridors. **Pets:** Dogs only. $15 daily fee/pet. Designated rooms, service with restrictions, supervision. 〔SAVE〕 🛜 ⌕ 🚪 🖵 ⤳

▼▼ Hotel Arcata 🅷
(707) 826-0217. **Call for rates.** 708 9th St 95521. Corner of G St; downtown; in Plaza. Int corridors. **Pets:** Accepted. 🛜 🖵 🍴 ⒶⒸ

ⒶⒶⒶ ▼▼▼ Quality Inn Arcata 🅷
(707) 822-0409. **$84-$129.** 3535 Janes Rd 95521. US 101 exit Giuntoli Ln/Janes Rd, just w. Int corridors. **Pets:** $10 daily fee/pet. Service with restrictions, supervision. 〔SAVE〕 🛜 🚪 🖵 ⤳

ARNOLD

ⒶⒶⒶ ▼▼▼ Arnold Meadowmont Lodge Ⓜ
(209) 795-1394. **$84-$175.** 2011 Hwy 4 95223. On SR 4; west end of town. Ext corridors. **Pets:** Medium, dogs only. $20 daily fee/pet. Designated rooms, service with restrictions, supervision.
〔SAVE〕 🛜 ⌕ ⌕ 🚪 🖵 ⒶⒸ

ARROYO GRANDE

ⒶⒶⒶ ▼▼▼▼ BEST WESTERN Casa Grande Inn Ⓜ ❖
(805) 481-7398. **$59-$189.** 850 Oak Park Rd 93420. US 101 exit 188 (Oak Park Rd), just e. Ext/int corridors. **Pets:** Large, other species. $20 daily fee/room. Designated rooms, service with restrictions, supervision.
〔SAVE〕 🛜 🚪 🖵 ⤳ ⌕

AUBURN

ⒶⒶⒶ ▼▼▼▼ BEST WESTERN Golden Key 🅷 ❖
(530) 885-8611. **$89-$169.** 13450 Lincoln Way 95603. I-80 exit 121 (Foresthill Rd/Auburn Ravine Rd), just e, then n. Ext corridors. **Pets:** $15 one-time fee/pet. Designated rooms, service with restrictions, supervision.
〔SAVE〕 🛜 ⌕ 🚪 🖵 ⤳

▼▼▼ Holiday Inn-Auburn 🅷 ❖
(530) 887-8787. **$109-$209.** 120 Grass Valley Hwy 95603. I-80 exit SR 49, just nw. Int corridors. **Pets:** Medium, dogs only. $30 one-time fee/room. Service with restrictions, crate.
ⒺⒸⓄ 🛜 ⌕ 🚪 🖵 🍴 ⤳

ⒶⒶⒶ ▼▼▼ Quality Inn Gold Country Ⓜ
(530) 885-7025. **$55-$75.** 13490 Lincoln Way 95603. I-80 exit 121 (Foresthill Rd/Auburn Ravine Rd), just e, then just n. Ext/int corridors. **Pets:** Medium. $15 daily fee/room. Service with restrictions, supervision.
〔SAVE〕 🛜 ⌕ 🚪 🖵 ⤳

BAKERSFIELD

ⒶⒶⒶ ▼ Americas Best Value Inn Ⓜ
(661) 366-1630. **$50-$85.** 8230 E Brundage Ln 93307. SR 99 exit 24 (SR 58 E), 7 mi e, exit 117 (SR 184/Weedpatch Hwy), just n, then just e. Ext/int corridors. **Pets:** Medium, other species. $5 daily fee/pet. Service with restrictions, supervision. 〔SAVE〕 🛜 🚪 🖵 ⤳

ⒶⒶⒶ ▼ BEST WESTERN Heritage Inn Ⓜ
(661) 764-6268. **$85-$90.** 253 Trask St 93314. I-5 exit 253 (Stockdale Hwy), just e. Ext corridors. **Pets:** Very small. $10 daily fee/pet. Designated rooms, service with restrictions, supervision.
〔SAVE〕 🛜 ⌕ 🚪 🖵 ⤳

ⒶⒶⒶ ▼▼▼▼ BEST WESTERN PLUS Hill House 🅷
(661) 327-4064. **$84-$139.** 700 Truxton Ave 93301. SR 99 exit 25 (California Ave), 1.2 mi e, 0.4 mi n on Chester Ave, then 0.4 mi e. Int corridors. **Pets:** Medium. $15 daily fee/pet. Designated rooms, service with restrictions, supervision. 〔SAVE〕 🛜 🚪 🖵 🍴 ⤳

▼▼▼ California Best Inn Ⓜ
(661) 834-3377. **Call for rates.** 1030 Wible Rd 93304. SR 99 exit 23 (Ming Ave), just e, then 0.7 mi n. Ext corridors. **Pets:** Accepted.
🛜 🚪 🖵 ⤳

▼▼▼ DoubleTree by Hilton Hotel Bakersfield 🅷
(661) 323-7111. **$89-$119.** 3100 Camino Del Rio Ct 93308. SR 99 exit 26 (SR 58 W/Rosedale Hwy), just w, then just s. Int corridors.
Pets: Accepted. ⒺⒸⓄ 🛜 ⌕ 🚪 🖵 ⤳

▼▼▼ Extended Stay Deluxe Bakersfield-Chester Lane 🅷
(661) 328-8181. **$84-$139.** 3600 Chester Ln 93309. SR 99 exit 25 (California Ave), just w to Real Rd, just s, then just w. Int corridors. **Pets:** $25 daily fee/pet. Designated rooms, service with restrictions. 🛜 🚪 🖵

ⒶⒶⒶ ▼▼▼ Garden Suites Inn 🅷 ❖
(661) 833-6066. **$55-$99.** 2310 Wible Rd 93304. SR 99 exit 23 (Ming Ave), just e. Int corridors. **Pets:** $10 daily fee/pet. Designated rooms, service with restrictions, supervision. 〔SAVE〕 🛜 🚪 🖵 ⤳

▼▼▼ Hampton Inn & Suites Bakersfield North/Airport 🅷
(661) 391-0600. **Call for rates.** 8818 Spectrum Park Way 93308. SR 99 exit 30 (SR 65) northbound, just e to Merle Haggard Dr, just n to Spectrum Park Way, then just s; exit 31 (7th Standard Rd) southbound, 0.5 mi e, then just s. Int corridors. **Pets:** Medium. Service with restrictions, crate.
🛜 🚪 🖵 ⤳

▼▼▼ Homewood Suites 🅷
(661) 664-0400. **Call for rates.** 1505 Mill Rock Way 93311. SR 99 exit 23 (Ming Ave), 4 mi w, then just n. Int corridors. **Pets:** Accepted.
🛜 🚪 🖵 ⤳

▼▼▼ Howard Johnson Inn 🅷
(661) 396-1425. **$49-$64.** 2700 White Ln 93304. SR 99 exit 21 (White Ln), just e. Ext corridors. **Pets:** Large. $10 daily fee/pet. Designated rooms, service with restrictions, supervision. 🛜 🚪 🖵 ⤳

▼▼▼ La Quinta Inn & Suites Bakersfield North 🅷
(661) 393-7775. **$99-$159.** 8858 Spectrum Park Way 93308. SR 99 exit 30 (SR 65) northbound, just e to Merle Haggard Dr, just n to Spectrum Park Way, then just s; exit 31 (7th Standard Rd) southbound, just e, then just s. Int corridors. **Pets:** Service with restrictions, supervision.
🛜 ⌕ 🚪 🖵 ⤳

▼▼▼ La Quinta Inn Bakersfield South Ⓜ
(661) 325-7400. **$59-$188.** 3232 Riverside Dr 93308. SR 99 exit 26A (SR 58 W/Rosedale Hwy) southbound, just e, then just n; exit 26B (Buck Owens Blvd) northbound, just s. Ext corridors. **Pets:** Service with restrictions, supervision. 🛜 ⌕ 🚪 🖵 ⤳

▼▼▼ The Padre Hotel 🅷 ❖
(661) 427-4900. **$109-$139.** 1702 18th St 93301. SR 58 exit 26A (Rosedale Hwy), 1.5 mi e, 0.3 mi s on F St, then 0.3 mi s. Int corridors. **Pets:** Small, other species. $100 one-time fee/room. Service with restrictions, supervision. 🛜 ⌕ 🚪 🖵 🍴

▼▼▼ Residence Inn by Marriott 🅷 ❖
(661) 321-9800. **$109-$179.** 4241 Chester Ln 93309. SR 99 exit 25 (California Ave), 0.5 mi w, then just n. Int corridors. **Pets:** Large. $100 one-time fee/room. Service with restrictions.
ⒺⒸⓄ 🛜 ⌕ 🚪 🖵 ⤳ ⌕

▼▼ Sleep Inn Ⓜ
(661) 399-2100. **$49-$169.** 6257 Knudson Dr 93308. SR 99 exit 28 (Olive Dr), just w, then just n. Int corridors. **Pets:** Accepted.
🛜 ⌕ ⌕ 🚪 🖵

(AAA) ▼▼▼ Super 8 M
(661) 833-1000. **$59-$75.** 3620 Wible Rd 93309. SR 99 exit 21 (White Ln), just w, then 0.3 mi n. Ext corridors. **Pets:** Medium, other species. $5 daily fee/pet. Service with restrictions, supervision.
[SAVE] 🛰 🖶 🖵 🏊

(AAA) ▼▼▼ Super 8 Bakersfield M
(661) 322-1012. **$60-$80.** 901 Real Rd 93309. SR 99 exit 25 (California Ave), just w, then just s. Ext corridors. **Pets:** Very small. $10 daily fee/pet. Designated rooms, service with restrictions, supervision.
[SAVE] 🛰 🖶 🖵 🏊

(AAA) ▼▼▼ Travelodge of Bakersfield M
(661) 325-0772. **$56-$80.** 1011 Oak St 93304. SR 99 exit 25 (California Ave), just e, then just s. Ext/int corridors. **Pets:** $15 daily fee/pet. Designated rooms, service with restrictions, supervision.
[SAVE] 🛰 🖶 🖵 🏊

▼▼ Vagabond Inn South M
(661) 831-9200. **Call for rates.** 6501 Colony St 93307. SR 99 exit 20 (Panama Ln), just e, then just s. Ext corridors. **Pets:** Accepted.
🛰 🖶 🖵 🏊

BANNING

▼▼▼ Banning Travelodge M
(951) 849-1000. **$65-$120.** 1700 W Ramsey St 92220. I-10 exit 99 (22nd St), just n, then 0.4 mi e. Ext corridors. **Pets:** Medium, dogs only. $10 daily fee/pet. Designated rooms, service with restrictions, supervision.
🛰 🖶 🖵 🏊

(AAA) ▼▼▼ Days Inn M
(951) 849-0092. **$70-$160.** 2320 W Ramsey St 92220. I-10 exit 99 (22nd St), just n, then just w. Ext corridors. **Pets:** Dogs only. $10 daily fee/pet. Service with restrictions, crate. [SAVE] 🛰 🖶 🖵 🏊

▼▼▼ Hampton Inn & Suites H
(951) 922-1000. **$79-$239.** 6071 Joshua Palmer Way 92220. I-10 exit 96 (Highland Springs Ave), just n, then just e. Int corridors. **Pets:** Small. $25 daily fee/pet. Designated rooms, service with restrictions, crate.
🛰 🖶 🖵 🏊

▼▼ Super 8 M
(951) 849-8888. **$60-$120.** 1690 W Ramsey St 92220. I-10 exit 99 (22nd St), just n, then 0.4 mi e. Int corridors. **Pets:** Medium, dogs only. $10 daily fee/pet. Designated rooms, service with restrictions, supervision.
🛰 ⊠ 🖶 🖵 🏊

BARSTOW

▼▼▼ Comfort Suites H ❀
(760) 253-3600. **$99-$149.** 2571 Fisher Blvd 92311. I-15 exit 178 (Lenwood Rd), just ne; n of Barstow Outlets. Int corridors. **Pets:** $25 one-time fee/pet. Designated rooms, service with restrictions, crate.
🛰 ⊠ 🖵ᴹ 🖶 🖵 🏊

▼▼▼ Country Inn & Suites By Carlson H ❀
(760) 307-3121. **$99-$199.** 2812 Lenwood Rd 92311. I-15 exit 178 (Lenwood Rd), just se, then just s. Int corridors. **Pets:** $20 daily fee/pet. Designated rooms, service with restrictions, supervision.
🛰 ⊠ 🖶 🖵 🏊

(AAA) ▼▼▼ Days Inn South at Lenwood M
(760) 253-2121. **$80-$100.** 2551 Commerce Pkwy 92311. I-15 exit 178 (Lenwood Rd), just w, then just n; 8 mi s of town. Ext corridors. **Pets:** Medium. $10 one-time fee/pet. Service with restrictions, crate.
[SAVE] 🛰 🖶 🖵 🏊

(AAA) ▼▼▼ Econo Lodge M
(760) 256-2133. **$49-$59.** 1230 E Main St 92311. I-15 exit 184B (E Main St) northbound; exit 184 (E Main St/I-40 E/Needles) southbound; 0.9 mi w. Ext corridors. **Pets:** Accepted. [SAVE] 🛰 🖶 🖵 🏊

▼▼▼ Hampton Inn & Suites H
(760) 253-2600. **$99-$229.** 2710 Lenwood Rd 92311. I-15 exit 178 (Lenwood Rd), just se, then 0.5 mi s. Int corridors. **Pets:** Other species. Service with restrictions, crate. 🛰 🖵ᴹ 🖶 🖵 🏊

▼▼ Holiday Inn Express, Barstow-Historic Route 66 H
(760) 256-1300. **$89-$149.** 1861 W Main St 92311. I-15 exit 181 (L St), 0.5 mi n, then just e. Int corridors. **Pets:** $25 one-time fee/room. Service with restrictions, supervision. 🛰 🖶 🖵 🏊

▼▼▼▼ Holiday Inn Express Hotel & Suites H
(760) 253-9200. **$129-$199.** 2700 Lenwood Rd 92311. I-15 exit 178 (Lenwood Rd), just se, then 0.5 mi s. Int corridors. **Pets:** $50 one-time fee/room. Designated rooms, service with restrictions, supervision.
🛰 🖵ᴹ 🖶 🖵 🏊

▼▼▼ Quality Inn M 🐾
(760) 256-6891. **$79-$159.** 1520 E Main St 92311. I-15 exit 184B (E Main St) northbound; exit 184 (E Main St/I-40 E/Needles) southbound, 0.3 mi w. Ext corridors. **Pets:** Small, dogs only. $100 deposit/room. Designated rooms, service with restrictions. 🛰 🖶 🖵 🍴 🏊

▼▼ Rodeway Inn M
(760) 256-7581. **Call for rates.** 1261 E Main St 92311. I-15 exit 184B (E Main St) northbound; exit 184 (E Main St/I-40 E/Needles) southbound, 0.8 mi w. Ext corridors. **Pets:** Accepted. 🛰 ⊠ 🖶 🖵 🏊

(AAA) ▼▼▼ Stardust Inn M
(760) 256-7116. **$40-$60.** 901 E Main St 92311. I-15 exit 183 (Barstow Rd), 0.8 mi n, then 0.4 mi e. Ext corridors. **Pets:** Very small, dogs only. $8 daily fee/pet. Designated rooms, service with restrictions, supervision.
[SAVE] 🛰 🖶 🖵 🏊

BASS LAKE

(AAA) ▼▼▼ The Pines Resort Chalets CA
(559) 642-3121. **Call for rates.** 54449 Rd 432 93604. 6 mi e of SR 41 exit CR 222, e on CR 274, then s on CR 434. Ext corridors.
Pets: Accepted. [SAVE] ⊠ 🖶 🖵 🍴 🏊 ⊠

BEAUMONT

(AAA) ▼▼▼ BEST WESTERN El Rancho Motor Inn M
(951) 845-2176. **$62-$190.** 480 E 5th St 92223. I-10 exit 94 (SR 79/Beaumont Ave), just n, then just e. Ext corridors. **Pets:** Other species. $10 daily fee/pet. Designated rooms, service with restrictions.
[SAVE] 🛰 🖶 🖵 🏊

▼▼ Rodeway Inn M
(951) 845-1436. **$60-$300.** 1265 E 6th St 92223. I-10 exit 94 (SR 79/Beaumont Ave), just n, then 0.7 mi e. Ext corridors. **Pets:** Medium, dogs only. $10 daily fee/pet. Designated rooms, service with restrictions, supervision. 🛰 ⊠ 🖶 🖵 🏊

BENICIA

(AAA) ▼▼▼ BEST WESTERN PLUS Heritage Inn H ❀
(707) 746-0401. **$100-$190.** 1955 E 2nd St 94510. I-780 exit Central Benicia/E 2nd St, just e. Ext/int corridors. **Pets:** Medium. $20 daily fee/room. Designated rooms, service with restrictions, supervision.
[SAVE] 🛰 🖶 🖵 🏊

BERKELEY

(AAA) ▼▼ Americas Best Value Golden Bear Inn M 🐾
(510) 525-6770. **$80-$160.** 1620 San Pablo Ave 94702. I-80 exit 12 (Gilman St), 0.5 mi e, then just s. Ext corridors. **Pets:** Other species. $15 one-time fee/room. Service with restrictions, supervision.
[SAVE] 🛰 ⊠ 🖶 🖵 🎦

(AAA) ▼▼▼ ▼▼ Claremont Hotel Club & Spa H
(510) 843-3000. **$189-$499.** 41 Tunnel Rd 94705. SR 13 and 24 exit SR 24 (Claremont Ave) eastbound, 1 mi n; I-80 exit 11 (University Ave E), just e, then 1.5 mi s on San Pablo Ave, 2.6 mi e on Ashby Ave, then just e. Int corridors. **Pets:** Medium, dogs only. $99 one-time fee/room. Designated rooms, service with restrictions, supervision.
[SAVE] 🛰 ⊠ 🖵ᴹ 🖵 🍴 🏊 ⊠

(AAA) ▼▼▼▼ DoubleTree by Hilton Berkeley Marina H
(510) 548-7920. **$129-$269.** 200 Marina Blvd 94710. I-80 exit 11 (University Ave), 0.5 mi w; on Berkeley Marina. Int corridors. **Pets:** Accepted.
[ECO] [SAVE] 🛰 ⊠ 🖵ᴹ 🖶 🖵 🍴 🏊 ⊠

Hotel Durant, a Joie de Vivre hotel H
(510) 845-8981. **Call for rates.** 2600 Durant Ave 94704. I-80 exit 11
(University Ave E), 2 mi e to Oxford St, 0.3 mi s, then 0.5 mi e; jct
Bowditch St. Int corridors. **Pets:** Accepted. 🖂 🛜 ✕ 🖵 🍴

BIG BEAR LAKE

Bay Meadows Resort CA
(909) 866-4666. **$79-$369, 3 day notice.** 39756 Big Bear Blvd 92315.
SR 18, 1 mi w of Village. Ext corridors. **Pets:** Dogs only. $10 one-time
fee/pet. Designated rooms, service with restrictions, supervision.
🛜 ✕ 🖬 🖵 🏊 ⓧ

**BEST WESTERN PLUS Big Bear
Chateau** H
(909) 866-6666. **$190-$259, 3 day notice.** 42200 Moonridge Rd 92315.
SR 18, 1.5 mi e of Pine Knot Ave, 0.5 mi s. Int corridors. **Pets:** $30 one-
time fee/room. Designated rooms, service with restrictions, supervision.
🆂🅰🆅🅴 🛜 ✕ 🖬 🖵 🏊 ⓧ ⓧ

Big Bear Lake Front Lodge M
(909) 866-8271. **$78-$300, 3 day notice.** 40360 Lakeview Dr 92315.
SR 18, 1 mi w of Pine Knot Ave. Ext/int corridors. **Pets:** $30 daily fee/pet.
Designated rooms, service with restrictions, supervision.
🛜 ✕ 🖬 🖵 ⓧ ⓧ 🕾

Eagle's Nest Bed & Breakfast BB �というわけ
(909) 866-6465. **$115-$185, 5 day notice.** 41675 Big Bear Blvd 92315.
SR 18, 1 mi e of Pine Knot Ave. Ext/int corridors. **Pets:** Other species.
$10 daily fee/pet. Designated rooms, service with restrictions, supervision.
🛜 ✕ 🖬 🖵

Golden Bear Cottages CA
(909) 866-2010. **$99-$169, 90 day notice.** 39367 Big Bear Blvd 92315.
SR 18, 2 mi w of village. Ext corridors. **Pets:** Accepted.
🛜 ✕ 🖬 🖵 🏊 ⓧ ⓧ

Grey Squirrel Resort CA
(909) 866-4335. **$79-$450, 30 day notice.** 39372 Big Bear Blvd 92315.
SR 18, 2 mi w of village. Ext corridors. **Pets:** Other species. $10 daily
fee/pet. Service with restrictions, crate.
🆂🅰🆅🅴 🛜 ✕ 🖬 🖵 🏊 ⓧ ⓧ

Pine Knot Guest Ranch CA 🐾
(909) 866-6500. **$99-$199, 7 day notice.** 908 Pine Knot Ave 92315.
Just s of SR 18 and downtown area. Ext corridors. **Pets:** Other species.
$10 daily fee/pet. Service with restrictions. 🛜 ✕ 🖬 🖵

Sleepy Forest Cottages CA
(909) 866-7444. **$79-$299, 15 day notice.** 426 Eureka Dr 92315. SR
18, 0.7 mi e of Pine Knot Ave, just n. Ext corridors. **Pets:** Accepted.
🛜 ✕ 🖬 🖵

Timber Haven Lodge CA 🐾
(909) 866-7207. **$113-$340, 7 day notice.** 877 Tulip Ln 92315. SR 18,
1.8 mi w of Pine Knot Ave, 0.4 mi s. Ext corridors. **Pets:** Medium, other
species. $30 daily fee/pet. Service with restrictions, supervision.
🛜 ✕ 🖬 🖵 ⓧ ⓧ

BIG PINE

Big Pine Motel M
(760) 938-2282. **Call for rates.** 370 S Main St 93513. On US 395. Ext
corridors. **Pets:** Accepted. 🛜 ✕ 🖬 🖵

Bristlecone Motel M
(760) 938-2067. **$55-$80.** 101 N Main St 93513. On US 395. Ext corridors. **Pets:** Other species. Service with restrictions, supervision.
🆂🅰🆅🅴 🛜 ✕ 🖬 🖵

BISHOP

Americas Best Value Inn M
(760) 873-4912. **$65-$195.** 192 Short St 93514. US 395 to Short St, just
e. Ext corridors. **Pets:** Other species. $10 daily fee/pet. Designated
rooms, service with restrictions, supervision. 🆂🅰🆅🅴 🛜 🖬 🖵

**BEST WESTERN PLUS Bishop Holiday Spa
Lodge** M 🐾
(760) 873-3543. **$90-$300.** 1025 N Main St 93514. On US 395. Ext corridors. **Pets:** Small, dogs only. $20 daily fee/pet. Designated rooms, ser-
vice with restrictions, supervision. 🆂🅰🆅🅴 🛜 🖬 🖬 🖵 🏊

Chalfant House Bed & Breakfast BB
(760) 872-1790. **$85-$115.** 213 Academy St 93514. On US 395, just w.
Ext/int corridors. **Pets:** Accepted. 🛜 ✕ 🕾

Comfort Inn M
(760) 873-4284. **$85-$250.** 805 N Main St 93514. On US 395. Ext corridors. **Pets:** Small. $15 daily fee/room. Designated rooms, service with
restrictions, supervision. 🆂🅰🆅🅴 🛜 🖬 🖬 🖵 🏊

Holiday Inn Express Hotel & Suites H
(760) 872-2423. **$119-$299.** 636 N Main St 93514. On US 395. Int corridors. **Pets:** Medium, dogs only. $25 daily fee/pet. Designated rooms,
service with restrictions, supervision.
🆂🅰🆅🅴 🛜 ✕ 🖬 🖬 🖵 ⓧ

Joseph House Inn BB
(760) 872-3389. **$148-$178, 14 day notice.** 376 W Yaney St 93514. 0.3
mi w of US 395. Int corridors. **Pets:** Dogs only. Service with restrictions, service with restrictions, supervision. 🛜 ✕ 🕾

La Quinta Inn Bishop - Mammoth Lakes H
(760) 873-6380. **$83-$183.** 651 N Main St 93514. On US 395. Int corridors. **Pets:** Service with restrictions, supervision.
🛜 ✕ 🖬 🖬 🖵

Ramada Limited M
(760) 872-1771. **$75-$250.** 155 E Elm St 93514. On US 395, just e. Ext
corridors. **Pets:** Other species. $15 daily fee/pet. Designated rooms, ser-
vice with restrictions, supervision. 🆂🅰🆅🅴 🛜 🖬 🖬 🖵 🏊

Super 8 M
(760) 872-1386. **$65-$180.** 535 S Main St 93514. On US 395. Ext corridors. **Pets:** Other species. $10 deposit/pet, $10 daily fee/pet. Supervision.
🛜 🖬 🖵 🏊

Vagabond Inn M 🐾
(760) 873-6351. **$80-$295.** 1030 N Main St 93514. On US 395. Ext corridors. **Pets:** Dogs only. $15 daily fee/pet. Designated rooms, service with
restrictions, supervision. 🛜 🖬 🖬 🖵 🏊

BLYTHE

BEST WESTERN Sahara M
(760) 922-7105. **$99-$189.** 825 W Hobsonway 92225. I-10 exit 239
(Lovekin Blvd), just n, then just w. Ext corridors. **Pets:** Medium. $10 daily
fee/room. Service with restrictions, supervision. 🆂🅰🆅🅴 🛜 🖬 🖵 🏊

Clarion Inn M
(760) 922-9000. **$79-$129.** 900 W Hobsonway 92225. I-10 exit 239
(Lovekin Blvd), just n, then just w. Ext corridors. **Pets:** Small. $20 daily
fee/pet. Designated rooms, service with restrictions, supervision.
🛜 🖬 🖵 🏊

BRAWLEY

BEST WESTERN PLUS Main Street Inn M
(760) 351-9800. **$115.** 1562 E Main St 92227. On SR 78 and 111. Ext/int
corridors. **Pets:** Medium. $20 daily fee/pet. Service with restrictions, crate.
🆂🅰🆅🅴 🛜 🖬 🖵 🏊

BREA

Chase Suite Hotels M
(714) 579-3200. **$109-$299.** 3100 E Imperial Hwy 92821. SR 57 exit 9
(SR 90), 1.5 mi e. Ext corridors. **Pets:** Medium. $150 deposit/room, $10
daily fee/pet. Designated rooms, service with restrictions, supervision.
🛜 ✕ 🖬 🖵 🏊

Embassy Suites Hotel 🄷 ✻
(714) 990-6000. **Call for rates.** 900 E Birch St 92821. SR 57 exit 9 (SR 90), 0.5 mi w on Imperial Hwy, 0.3 mi n on Randolph Ave, then just e. Int corridors. **Pets:** Medium, other species. $40 daily fee/room. Service with restrictions, supervision. 🛜 🗗 💻 🍴 ⊶

BRIDGEPORT

Redwood Motel 🎟
(760) 932-7060. **$59-$250.** 425 Main St 93517. On US 395; on north side of town. Ext corridors. **Pets:** $10 daily fee/pet. Designated rooms, service with restrictions, supervision. 🆂🅰🆅🅴 🛜 🗗 💻

Ruby Inn 🎟 ✻
(760) 932-7241. **$100-$225.** 333 Main St 93517. On US 395; center of town. Ext corridors. **Pets:** Service with restrictions, supervision.
🆂🅰🆅🅴 🛜 ✕ 🗗 💻

Silver Maple Inn 🎟
(760) 932-7383. **$80-$140.** 310 Main St 93517. On US 395; center of town. Ext corridors. **Pets:** Other species. Supervision.
🆂🅰🆅🅴 🛜 ✕ 🗗 💻 🐾

Walker River Lodge 🎟
(760) 932-7021. **$85-$220.** 100 Main St 93517. On US 395; at south end of town. Ext corridors. **Pets:** Other species. Supervision.
🆂🅰🆅🅴 🛜 🗗 💻 ⊶

BUELLTON

Quality Inn Santa Ynez Valley 🎟
(805) 688-0022. **$71-$89.** 630 Ave of the Flags 93427. US 101 exit 140B (Ave of the Flags) southbound, just s; exit 140A (SR 246) northbound, just w, then just n. Ext/int corridors. **Pets:** Other species. $25 one-time fee/pet. Designated rooms, service with restrictions, supervision.
🆂🅰🆅🅴 🛜 ✕ 🗗 💻

Santa Ynez Valley Marriott 🄷 ✻
(805) 688-1000. **$149-$259.** 555 McMurray Rd 93427. US 101 exit 140A (SR 246), just e, then just n. Int corridors. **Pets:** Other species. $80 one-time fee/room. Service with restrictions.
🆂🅰🆅🅴 🛜 ✕ 🗗 💻 🍴 ⊶ ✕

BUENA PARK

The Buena Park Hotel & Suites 🎟
(714) 522-7360. **$89-$159.** 7555 Beach Blvd 90620. SR 91 exit 23B (Beach Blvd/SR 39), just s. Ext corridors. **Pets:** Small, dogs only. $25 daily fee/pet. Designated rooms, service with restrictions, crate.
🛜 🗗 💻 ⊶ ✕

BURNEY

Charm Motel 🎟 ✻
(530) 335-3300. **$65-$185.** 37363 Main St 96013. 0.5 mi ne on SR 299; jct Roff Way. Ext corridors. **Pets:** Other species. $20 daily fee/pet. Designated rooms, service with restrictions, supervision.
🆂🅰🆅🅴 🛜 ✕ 🗗 💻

Green Gables Motel 🎟 ✻
(530) 335-3300. **$65-$155.** 37385 Main St 96013. 0.5 mi ne on SR 299; jct Roff Way and SR 299. Ext corridors. **Pets:** Other species. $20 daily fee/pet. Service with restrictions, supervision. 🆂🅰🆅🅴 🛜 ✕ 🗗 💻

CALEXICO

BEST WESTERN John Jay Inn 🎟
(760) 768-0442. **$68-$76.** 2421 Scaroni Ave 92231. I-8 exit 118A (SR 111 S), 5.5 mi s, just w on W Cole Rd, then just n. Int corridors.
Pets: Accepted. 🆂🅰🆅🅴 🛜 🗗 💻 ⊶

CALIMESA

Calimesa Inn Motel 🎟
(909) 795-2536. **$60-$110.** 1205 Calimesa Blvd 92320. I-10 exit 88 (Calimesa Blvd), just ne. Ext corridors. **Pets:** $10 daily fee/pet. Designated rooms, service with restrictions, supervision. 🆂🅰🆅🅴 🛜 🗗 ⊶

CAMARILLO

BEST WESTERN Camarillo Inn 🎟 ✻
(805) 987-4991. **$87-$140.** 295 E Daily Dr 93010. US 101 exit 55 (Las Posas Rd), just n, then just e. Ext corridors. **Pets:** $20 daily fee/room. Designated rooms, service with restrictions, supervision.
🆂🅰🆅🅴 🛜 🗗 💻 ⊶

Camarillo Residence Inn by Marriott 🄷
(805) 388-7997. **$129-$239.** 2912 Petit St 93012. US 101 exit 53A (Flynn Rd) northbound, 0.8 mi n, then just w; exit Dawson Dr southbound, just w. Int corridors. **Pets:** $100 one-time fee/room. Service with restrictions, supervision. 🛜 ✕ 🗗 💻 ⊶ ✕

CAMBRIA

BEST WESTERN PLUS Fireside Inn On Moonstone Beach 🎟 ✻
(805) 927-8661. **$109-$379, 7 day notice.** 6700 Moonstone Beach Dr 93428. SR 1 exit Moonstone Beach Dr, just w, then 0.5 mi s. Ext corridors. **Pets:** Medium. $20 daily fee/room. Designated rooms, service with restrictions, supervision. 🆂🅰🆅🅴 🛜 ✕ 🄼 🗗 💻 ⊶ 🐾

Blue Dolphin Inn 🄷 ✻
(805) 927-3300. **$159-$369.** 6470 Moonstone Beach Dr 93428. SR 1 exit Moonstone Beach Dr, just w, then 0.7 mi n. Int corridors. **Pets:** Small, dogs only. $25 daily fee/pet. Designated rooms, service with restrictions, supervision. 🛜 ✕ 🗗 💻 🐾

Blue Whale Inn Bed & Breakfast 🄱🄱
(805) 927-4647. **$347-$470, 10 day notice.** 6736 Moonstone Beach Dr 93428. SR 1 exit Moonstone Beach Dr, just w, then 0.5 mi s. Ext corridors. **Pets:** Accepted. 🆂🅰🆅🅴 🛜 ✕ 🗗 💻 🐾

Cambria Shores Inn 🎟 ✻
(805) 927-8644. **$169-$350, 7 day notice.** 6276 Moonstone Beach Dr 93428. SR 1 exit Moonstone Beach Dr, just w, then 0.8 mi s. Ext corridors. **Pets:** Dogs only. $25 daily fee/pet. Supervision.
🛜 ✕ 🗗 💻

Castle Inn by the Sea 🎟 ✻
(805) 927-8605. **$109-$209.** 6620 Moonstone Beach Dr 93428. SR 1 exit Moonstone Beach Dr, just w, then 0.5 mi s. Ext corridors. **Pets:** Small, dogs only. $25 daily fee/pet. Designated rooms, service with restrictions, supervision. 🛜 ✕ 🗗 💻 ⊶ 🐾

Fog Catcher Inn 🎟
(805) 927-1400. **$139-$500.** 6400 Moonstone Beach Dr 93428. SR 1 exit Moonstone Beach Dr, just w, then 0.7 mi s. Ext corridors. **Pets:** Accepted.
🛜 ✕ 🗗 💻 ⊶ 🐾

Pelican Inn & Suites 🄷
(805) 927-1500. **Call for rates.** 6316 Moonstone Beach Dr 93428. SR 1 exit Moonstone Beach Dr, just w, then 0.8 mi s. Ext/int corridors.
Pets: Accepted. 🛜 ✕ 🄼 🗗 💻 ⊶ 🐾

Sand Pebbles Inn 🄷
(805) 927-5600. **$124-$314.** 6252 Moonstone Beach Dr 93428. SR 1 exit Moonstone Beach Dr, just w, then 0.9 mi s. Int corridors. **Pets:** Accepted.
🛜 ✕ 🗗 💻 🐾

Sea Otter Inn 🎟
(805) 927-5888. **$99-$329, 3 day notice.** 6656 Moonstone Beach Dr 93428. SR 1 exit Moonstone Beach Dr, just w, then 0.5 mi s. Ext corridors. **Pets:** Medium. $25 daily fee/pet. Designated rooms, service with restrictions, supervision. 🛜 ✕ 🗗 💻 ⊶ 🐾

White Water Inn 🎟
(805) 927-1066. **$129-$289, 7 day notice.** 6790 Moonstone Beach Dr 93428. SR 1 exit Moonstone Beach Dr, just w, then 0.4 mi s. Ext corridors. **Pets:** Accepted. 🛜 ✕ 🗗 🐾

CAMPBELL

▼▼▼▼ **Larkspur Landing Campbell** 🅗 ❖
(408) 364-1514. **Call for rates.** 550 W Hamilton Ave 95008. SR 17 exit Hamilton Ave, 1 mi w. Int corridors. **Pets:** Medium. $75 one-time fee/room. Designated rooms, service with restrictions, supervision.
[ECO] 🛜 ✕ Ⓜ 🛄 💻

▼▼▼▼ **The PruneYard Plaza Hotel** 🅗 ❖
(408) 559-4300. **$209-$269.** 1995 S Bascom Ave 95008. SR 17 exit Hamilton Ave, 0.3 mi e, then s. Int corridors. **Pets:** Large. $75 one-time fee/room. Designated rooms, service with restrictions, supervision.
[ECO] 🛜 ✕ Ⓜ 🛄 💻

▼▼▼▼ **Residence Inn by Marriott-San Jose** 🅗
(408) 559-1551. **$113-$199.** 2761 S Bascom Ave 95008. SR 17 exit Camden Ave E, just n. Ext corridors. **Pets:** Accepted.
🛜 ✕ Ⓜ 🛄 💻 🏊

▼▼▼▼ **TownePlace Suites by Marriott-San Jose/Campbell** 🅗 ❖
(408) 370-4510. **$129-$249.** 700 E Campbell Ave 95008. SR 17 exit Hamilton Ave E, 0.3 mi to Bascom Ave, 0.3 mi s, then 0.3 mi w. Int corridors. **Pets:** Other species. $75 one-time fee/room. Designated rooms, service with restrictions, crate. 🛜 ✕ Ⓜ 🛄 💻

CARDIFF-BY-THE-SEA

▼▼▼▼ **Holiday Inn Express Encinitas Cardiff By The Sea** 🅗
(760) 944-0427. **Call for rates.** 1661 Villa Cardiff Dr 92007. I-5 exit 40 (Birmingham Dr), just e, then just n. Int corridors. **Pets:** Medium. $50 one-time fee/pet. Service with restrictions, crate.
🛜 ✕ Ⓜ 🛄 💻 🏊

CARLSBAD

▼▼▼▼ **Carlsbad by the Sea Resort** 🅗
(760) 438-7880. **$109-$279.** 850 Palomar Airport Rd 92011. I-5 exit 47 (Palomar Airport Rd), just e. Ext corridors. **Pets:** Accepted.
🛜 Ⓜ 🛄 💻 🍴 🏊

▼▼▼▼ **Homewood Suites by Hilton Carlsbad-North San Diego County** 🅗
(760) 431-2266. **$133-$269.** 2223 Palomar Airport Rd 92011. I-5 exit 47 (Palomar Airport Rd), 3.1 mi e. Int corridors. **Pets:** Accepted.
🛜 ✕ Ⓜ 🛄 💻 🏊 ✕

𝔸𝔸𝔸 ▼▼▼▼ **Hyatt house San Diego/Carlsbad** 🅗
(760) 929-8200. **$109-$269.** 5010 Avenida Encinas 92008. I-5 exit 48 (Cannon Rd), just w, then just s. Int corridors. **Pets:** Medium. $150 one-time fee/room. Service with restrictions, supervision.
[SAVE] 🛜 ✕ Ⓜ 🛄 💻 🏊

▼▼▼▼ **La Quinta Inn & Suites San Diego Carlsbad** 🅜
(760) 438-2828. **$95-$320.** 760 Macadamia Dr 92011. I-5 exit 45 (Poinsettia Ln/Aviara Pkwy), just w to Ave Encinas, just n, then just e. Ext corridors. **Pets:** Service with restrictions, supervision.
🛜 ✕ 🛄 💻 🏊

𝔸𝔸𝔸 ▼◆▼◆▼ **Park Hyatt Aviara Resort, Golf Club & Spa** 🅗
(760) 448-1234. **$225-$518, 7 day notice.** 7100 Aviara Resort Dr 92011. I-5 exit 45 (Poinsettia Ln/Aviara Pkwy), 1 mi e on Poinsettia Ln, 1 mi s on Aviara Pkwy, then just sw. Int corridors. **Pets:** Accepted.
[SAVE] 🛜 ✕ 🛄 💻 🍴 🏊 ✕

▼▼▼ **Ramada Inn & Suites** 🅜
(760) 438-2285. **$79-$259.** 751 Macadamia Dr 92011. I-5 exit 45 (Poinsettia Ln/Aviara Pkwy), just w to Ave Encinas, then 0.3 mi n. Ext corridors. **Pets:** Small, other species. Designated rooms, service with restrictions, crate. 🛜 ✕ 🛄 💻 🏊

▼◆▼◆▼ **West Inn & Suites** 🅗 ❖
(760) 448-4500. **$159-$399, 3 day notice.** 4970 Avenida Encinas 92008. I-5 exit 48 (Cannon Rd), just w, then just n. Int corridors. **Pets:** Other species. $150 one-time fee/room. Designated rooms, service with restrictions, supervision. 🛜 ✕ Ⓜ 🛄 💻 🍴 🏊

CARPINTERIA

▼◆▼◆▼ **Holiday Inn Express & Suites** 🅗
(805) 566-9499. **$109-$249.** 5606 Carpinteria Ave 93013. US 101 exit 86A (Casitas Pass Rd), just s, then just e. Int corridors. **Pets:** Other species. $15 daily fee/room. Designated rooms, service with restrictions, supervision. 🛜 ✕ Ⓜ 🛄 💻 🏊

CASTRO VALLEY

▼◆▼◆▼ **Quality Inn** 🅗
(510) 538-9501. **$79-$189.** 2532 Castro Valley Blvd 94546. I-580 exit Castro Valley Blvd, 0.3 mi n. Int corridors. **Pets:** Small. $10 daily fee/pet. Service with restrictions, supervision. 🛜 Ⓜ 🛄 💻 🏊

CAYUCOS

▼◆▼◆▼ **Beachwalker Inn** 🅜
(805) 995-2133. **Call for rates.** 501 S Ocean Ave 93430. On SR 1 business route. Ext corridors. **Pets:** Accepted. 🛜 ✕ 🛄 💻 🕮

▼◆▼◆▼ **Cayucos Beach Inn** 🅜 ❖
(805) 995-2828. **$85-$195, 3 day notice.** 333 S Ocean Ave 93430. On SR 1 business route. Ext corridors. **Pets:** Medium, dogs only. $10 daily fee/pet. Designated rooms, service with restrictions, supervision.
🛜 ✕ Ⓜ 🛄 💻

𝔸𝔸𝔸 ▼◆▼ **Cypress Tree Motel** 🅜
(805) 995-3917. **$50-$132.** 125 S Ocean Ave 93430. On SR 1 business route. Ext corridors. **Pets:** Other species. Service with restrictions, supervision. [SAVE] 🛜 ✕ 🛄 💻 🕮

𝔸𝔸𝔸 ▼◆▼◆▼ **Shoreline Inn On The Beach** 🅜 ❖
(805) 995-3681. **$105-$225, 3 day notice.** 1 N Ocean Ave 93430. On SR 1 business route. Ext corridors. **Pets:** Other species. $25 one-time fee/pet. Service with restrictions, supervision.
[SAVE] 🛜 ✕ 🛄 💻 🕮

CEDARVILLE

𝔸𝔸𝔸 ▼◆▼◆▼ **Sunrise Motel** 🅜
(530) 279-2161. **$69-$79, 7 day notice.** 62271 Hwy 299 W 96104. Jct SR 299 and CR 1, 0.6 mi w on CR 1. Ext corridors. **Pets:** Medium. $10 daily fee/pet. Designated rooms, service with restrictions, supervision.
[SAVE] 🛜 ✕ 🛄 💻 ☎

CHESTER

𝔸𝔸𝔸 ▼▼▼ **BEST WESTERN Rose Quartz Inn** 🅗
(530) 258-2002. **$116-$151.** 306 Main St 96020. 0.3 mi w of center on SR 36. Int corridors. **Pets:** Medium, other species. $15 daily fee/pet. Designated rooms, service with restrictions, supervision.
[SAVE] 🛜 ✕ Ⓜ 🛄 💻

CHICO

𝔸𝔸𝔸 ▼◆▼◆▼ **BEST WESTERN PLUS Heritage Inn - Chico** 🅗 ❖
(530) 894-8600. **$95-$120.** 25 Heritage Ln 95926. Just e of SR 99, via Cohasset Rd. Int corridors. **Pets:** $30 one-time fee/room. Designated rooms, service with restrictions, supervision.
[SAVE] 🛜 Ⓜ 🛄 💻 🏊

𝔸𝔸𝔸 ▼▼▼▼ **Holiday Inn Chico & Conference Center** 🅗
(530) 345-2491. **Call for rates.** 685 Manzanita Ct 95926. SR 99 exit 387A (Mangrove Ave/Cohasset Rd), follow Mangrove Ave, just sw. Int corridors. **Pets:** $30 one-time fee/pet. Designated rooms, no service, supervision. [SAVE] 🛜 Ⓜ 🛄 💻 🍴 🏊

AAA ▽▽▽▽ Oxford Suites **H** ❀
(530) 899-9090. **$99-$179.** 2035 Business Ln 95928. SR 99 exit 384 (E 20th St), just e, then just s. Int corridors. **Pets:** $35 one-time fee/room. Designated rooms, service with restrictions, supervision.
SAVE 🛜 📶M 🔌 💻 ➰ ✕

AAA ▽▽▽▽ Residence Inn by Marriott Chico **H**
(530) 894-5500. **$134-$189.** 2485 Carmichael Dr 95928. SR 99 exit 383 (Skyway/Park Ave), just w, then just n. Int corridors. **Pets:** Accepted.
SAVE 🛜 ✕ 🔌 💻 ➰ ✕

AAA ▽▽ Super 8 **H**
(530) 345-2533. **$57-$317.** 655 Manzanita Ct 95926. SR 99 exit 387A (Mangrove Ave/Cohasset Rd), follow Mangrove Ave, then just se. Int corridors. **Pets:** Medium. $10 daily fee/pet. Service with restrictions, supervision. SAVE 🛜 🔌 💻 ➰

CHOWCHILLA

▽▽▽ Days Inn Gateway to Yosemite **M**
(559) 665-4821. **$60-$100.** 220 E Robertson Blvd 93610. SR 99 exit Robertson Blvd, just w. Ext corridors. **Pets:** Large, other species. $10 daily fee/pet. Service with restrictions, crate. 🛜 🔌 💻 ➰

▽▽▽ Holiday Inn Express & Suites Gateway to Yosemite **H**
(559) 665-3300. **$79-$169.** 309 Prosperity Blvd 93610. SR 99 exit Robertson Blvd, just w. Int corridors. **Pets:** Other species. $25 daily fee/pet. Service with restrictions, crate. 🛜 ✕ 📶M 🔌 💻 ➰

CLOVIS

▽▽▽ Comfort Suites **H**
(559) 299-9992. **$89-$119.** 143 Clovis Ave 93612. SR 168 exit Herndon Ave E, just s. Int corridors. **Pets:** Other species. $35 one-time fee/room. Crate. 🛜 ✕ 📶M 🔌 💻 ➰

COALINGA

AAA ▽▽▽▽ BEST WESTERN Big Country Inn **M** ❀
(559) 935-0866. **Call for rates.** 25020 W Dorris Ave 93210. I-5 exit SR 198/Hanford-Lemoore, just w. Ext corridors. **Pets:** Medium. $20 daily fee/pet. Designated rooms, service with restrictions, supervision.
SAVE 🛜 📶M 🔌 💻 ➰

AAA ▽▽▽▽ The Inn at Harris Ranch **H**
(559) 935-0717. **$159-$350.** 24505 W Dorris Ave 93210. I-5 exit SR 198/Hanford-Lemoore, just e. Ext/int corridors. **Pets:** Other species. $20 one-time fee/pet. Designated rooms, service with restrictions, supervision.
SAVE 🛜 ✕ 📶M 🔌 💻 🍴 ➰

COLTON

AAA ▽▽▽▽ Holiday Inn Express **H**
(951) 788-9900. **$79-$109.** 2830 S Iowa Ave 92324. I-215 exit 37 (La Cadena Dr) northbound; exit 37 (Iowa Ave) southbound, just se. Int corridors. **Pets:** Medium. $25 one-time fee/room. Designated rooms, service with restrictions, crate. SAVE 🛜 🔌 💻 ➰

COLUMBIA

▽ Columbia Gem Motel **M**
(209) 532-4508. **$99-$159.** 22131 Parrotts Ferry Rd 95370. 3 mi n of Sonora; 1 mi from Columbia State Historic Park. Ext corridors. **Pets:** Dogs only. Service with restrictions, supervision.
✕ 🔌 💻 🎵

CONCORD

AAA ▽▽▽▽ BEST WESTERN PLUS Heritage Inn **H**
(925) 686-4466. **$87-$90.** 4600 Clayton Rd 94521. I-680 exit Treat Blvd/Geary Rd, 4.8 mi ne, then 0.4 mi e. Ext corridors. **Pets:** Accepted.
SAVE 🛜 📶M 🔌 💻 ➰

AAA ▽▽▽▽ Crowne Plaza Hotel Concord/Walnut Creek **H** ❀
(925) 825-7700. **$119-$189.** 45 John Glenn Dr 94520. I-680 exit Concord Ave, just e. Int corridors. **Pets:** Large. $35 one-time fee/pet. Service with restrictions, crate. SAVE 🛜 ✕ 📶M 🔌 💻 🍴 ➰ ✕

AAA ▽▽▽ Days Inn Concord **H**
(925) 674-9400. **$59-$110.** 5370 Clayton Rd 94521. 6.5 mi e of jct I-680 and SR 24; I-680 exit SR 242 to Clayton Rd, 5.5 mi e. Ext corridors. **Pets:** Medium. $75 deposit/room. Crate. SAVE 🛜 📶M 🔌 💻

AAA ▽▽▽▽ Hilton Concord **H** ❀
(925) 827-2000. **Call for rates.** 1970 Diamond Blvd 94520. I-680 exit Willow Pass Rd, just e. Int corridors. **Pets:** Other species. $150 deposit/room, $50 one-time fee/room. Service with restrictions, crate.
ECO SAVE 🛜 ✕ 📶M 🔌 💻 🍴 ➰ ✕

CORNING

AAA ▽▽▽▽ BEST WESTERN PLUS Corning Inn **H** ❀
(530) 824-5200. **$89-$159.** 910 Hwy 99 W 96021. I-5 exit 631 (Central Corning), just e. Int corridors. **Pets:** $15 daily fee/pet. Designated rooms, service with restrictions, supervision. SAVE 🛜 🔌 💻 ➰

AAA ▽▽▽ Days Inn **H**
(530) 824-2000. **$54-$135.** 3475 Hwy 99 W 96021. I-5 exit 630 (South Ave), just e, then just s. Int corridors. **Pets:** Medium. $10 daily fee/pet. Designated rooms, service with restrictions, supervision.
SAVE 🛜 📶M 🔌 💻 ➰

▽▽▽ Holiday Inn Express Hotel & Suites **H** ❀
(530) 824-6400. **$104-$119.** 3350 Sunrise Way 96021. I-5 exit 630 (South Ave), just e, then just s. Int corridors. **Pets:** Other species. $10 daily fee/pet. Designated rooms, service with restrictions, supervision.
🛜 🔌 💻 ➰

AAA ▽▽▽ Super 8 Corning **M** ❀
(530) 824-2468. **$66-$124.** 2165 Solano St 96021. I-5 exit 631 (Central Corning), just e. Ext corridors. **Pets:** Medium. $15 daily fee/pet. Designated rooms, service with restrictions, supervision.
SAVE 🛜 📶M 🔌 💻 ➰

CORONA

▽▽▽ Ayres Suites Corona West **H**
(951) 738-9113. **$89-$169.** 1900 Frontage Rd 92882. SR 91 exit 48 (Maple St/W 6th St) eastbound; exit Maple St westbound, just sw. Ext/int corridors. **Pets:** Accepted. 🛜 🔌 💻 ➰

AAA ▽▽▽▽ BEST WESTERN Kings Inn **M** ❀
(951) 734-4241. **$69-$99.** 1084 Pomona Rd 92882. SR 91 exit 49 (Lincoln Ave), just ne. Ext corridors. **Pets:** Medium, dogs only. $10 daily fee/room. Designated rooms, service with restrictions, crate.
SAVE 🛜 🔌 💻 ➰

▽▽▽ Hotel Paseo **M**
(951) 371-7185. **$92-$155.** 1805 W 6th St 92882. SR 91 exit 48 (Maple St/W 6th St) eastbound; exit Maple St westbound, just se. Ext corridors. **Pets:** Accepted. 🛜 ✕ 🔌 💻 ➰ ✕

▽▽▽▽ Residence Inn by Marriott Corona **H**
(951) 371-0107. **$98-$129.** 1015 Montecito Dr 92879. I-15 exit 95 (Magnolia Ave), just e, just n on El Camino, just w on Carly Way, then just n. Int corridors. **Pets:** Large, other species. $100 one-time fee/room.
🛜 ✕ 📶M 🔌 💻 ➰ ✕

COSTA MESA

▽▽▽▽ Costa Mesa Marriott **H**
(714) 957-1100. **$99-$299.** 500 Anton Blvd 92626. I-405 exit 9B (Bristol St), just n, then 0.3 mi e. Int corridors. **Pets:** Accepted.
ECO 🛜 ✕ 📶M 🔌 💻 🍴 ➰

▼▼▼▼ **Crowne Plaza Costa Mesa Orange County** 🅷 ❖
(714) 557-3000. **$109-$299.** 3131 S Bristol St 92626. I-405 exit 9B (Bristol St), just s. Int corridors. **Pets:** Small, dogs only. $20 daily fee/pet. Service with restrictions, supervision. 🛜 ⊠ 🛏 💻 🍽 ⛱

▼▼▼▼ **Hilton Orange County/Costa Mesa** 🅷
(714) 540-7000. **$109-$189.** 3050 Bristol St 92626. I-405 exit 9B (Bristol St), just s. Int corridors. **Pets:** Accepted.
🅴🅲🅾 🛜 ⊠ 🄼 🛏 💻 🍽 ⛱

🄰🄰🄰 ▼▼▼ **Residence Inn by Marriott** 🅷 ❖
(714) 241-8800. **$109-$359.** 881 W Baker St 92626. SR 73 exit 17B (Bear St); SR 55 exit 5B (Baker St). Ext corridors. **Pets:** Large, other species. $100 one-time fee/room. Designated rooms, service with restrictions, crate. 🅴🅲🅾 🆂🅰🆅🅴 🛜 ⊠ 🛏 💻 ⛱ ⊠

🄰🄰🄰 ▼▼▼ **Travelodge-Orange County Airport** 🅼
(714) 557-8700. **$85-$159.** 1400 Bristol St 92626. I-405 exit 9B (Bristol St), 2 mi se. Ext corridors. **Pets:** Small. $50 one-time fee/pet. Designated rooms, service with restrictions, supervision. 🆂🅰🆅🅴 🛜 🛏 💻 ⛱

🄰🄰🄰 ▼▼▼ **The Westin South Coast Plaza Hotel** 🅷
(714) 540-2500. **$129-$375.** 686 Anton Blvd 92626. I-405 exit 9B (Bristol St), just n, then just e. Int corridors. **Pets:** Accepted.
🅴🅲🅾 🆂🅰🆅🅴 🛜 ⊠ 🄼 💻 🍽 ⛱ ⊠

CRESCENT CITY
🄰🄰🄰 ▼ **Americas Best Value Inn** 🅼 ❖
(707) 464-4141. **$50-$125.** 440 Hwy 101 N 95531. Between Cooper and 9th sts; across from Del Norte County Fairground. Ext corridors. **Pets:** Small, other species. $10 daily fee/room. Designated rooms, service with restrictions, supervision. 🆂🅰🆅🅴 🛜 🛏 💻 🅺

🄰🄰🄰 ▼▼▼ **Econo Lodge Crescent City** 🅼
(707) 464-6106. **$59-$99, 3 day notice.** 725 Hwy 101 N 95531. On US 101, jct Northcrest St. Ext corridors. **Pets:** Dogs only. $12 daily fee/pet. Designated rooms, no service, supervision. 🆂🅰🆅🅴 🛜 🛏 💻 🅺

▼ **Hiouchi Motel** 🅼
(707) 458-3041. **$61-$66.** 2097 Hwy 199 95531. On US 199, 5.5 mi e of jct US 101. Ext corridors. **Pets:** Accepted.
🛜 ⊠ 🛏 💻 🅺 🔒

🄰🄰🄰 ▼▼▼ **Super 8** 🅼
(707) 464-4111. **$55-$130.** 685 Hwy 101 S/Redwood Hwy 95531. On US 101. Ext corridors. **Pets:** Small, dogs only. $15 daily fee/pet. Designated rooms, service with restrictions, supervision. 🆂🅰🆅🅴 🛜 🛏 💻 🅺

CUPERTINO
🄰🄰🄰 ▼▼▼▼ **Cypress Hotel** 🅷
(408) 253-8900. **$84-$319.** 10050 S De Anza Blvd 95014. I-280 exit De Anza Blvd, 0.7 mi s. Int corridors. **Pets:** Accepted.
🅴🅲🅾 🆂🅰🆅🅴 🛜 ⊠ 🄼 🍽 ⛱

CYPRESS
🄰🄰🄰 ▼▼▼ **Hyatt house Cypress/Anaheim** 🅷
(714) 828-4000. **$114-$229.** 5905 Corporate Ave 90630. I-605 exit 1D (Katella Ave) southbound; exit 1B (Katella Ave/Willow St) northbound, 3 mi e, 0.4 mi n on Valley View Ave, then just w. Int corridors. **Pets:** Medium. $150 one-time fee/pet. Designated rooms, service with restrictions, crate. 🆂🅰🆅🅴 🛜 ⊠ 🛏 💻 ⛱

DANA POINT
🄰🄰🄰 ▼▼▼ **BEST WESTERN PLUS Marina Shores Hotel** 🅷
(949) 248-1000. **Call for rates.** 34280 Pacific Coast Hwy 92629. I-5 exit 79 (Pacific Coast Hwy) southbound; exit 79 (Beach Cities Dr) northbound, 0.6 mi w, then 0.5 mi n. Ext/int corridors. **Pets:** $15 daily fee. Service with restrictions, crate. 🆂🅰🆅🅴 🛜 ⊠ 🄼 🛏 💻 ⛱

▼▼▼▼ **Blue Lantern Inn** 🅱🅱
(949) 661-1304. **$200-$610, 7 day notice.** 34343 Street of Blue Lantern 92629. I-5 exit 79 (Pacific Coast Hwy) southbound; exit 79 (Beach Cities Dr) northbound, 1.5 mi n on Pacific Coast Hwy, then just w. Int corridors. **Pets:** Dogs only. $65 one-time fee/room. Designated rooms, service with restrictions, supervision. 🛜 ⊠ 🛏 💻 ⊠

▼▼▼▼ **The Ritz-Carlton, Laguna Niguel** 🅷 ❖
(949) 240-2000. **$455-$635, 3 day notice.** One Ritz-Carlton Dr 92629. I-5 exit 79 (Pacific Coast Hwy) northbound, 3 mi n, then just w; exit 86 (Crown Valley Pkwy) southbound, 3 mi w, 1 mi s on Pacific Coast Hwy, then just w. Int corridors. **Pets:** $150 one-time fee/room, $50 daily fee/room. Designated rooms, service with restrictions. 🛜 ⊠ 🄼 🛏 💻 🍽 ⛱

🄰🄰🄰 ▼▼▼ **St. Regis Resort, Monarch Beach** 🅷 ❖
(949) 234-3200. **$375-$6000, 7 day notice.** One Monarch Beach Resort 92629. I-5 exit 79 (Pacific Coast Hwy) northbound, 3 mi n, then 0.5 mi e on Niguel Rd; exit 86 (Crown Valley Pkwy) southbound, 3 mi w, 1 mi s on Pacific Coast Hwy, then 0.5 mi e on Niguel Rd. Int corridors. **Pets:** Medium. $150 one-time fee/pet. Designated rooms, service with restrictions, supervision. 🆂🅰🆅🅴 🛜 ⊠ 🄼 🛏 💻 🍽 ⛱ ⊠

DANVILLE
🄰🄰🄰 ▼▼▼ **BEST WESTERN PLUS Danville Sycamore Inn** 🅷 ❖
(925) 855-8888. **$85-$150, 3 day notice.** 803 Camino Ramon 94526. I-680 exit Sycamore Valley Rd, just e, then just s. Ext/int corridors. **Pets:** Medium. $15 daily fee/pet. Designated rooms, service with restrictions, crate. 🆂🅰🆅🅴 🛜 🄼 🛏 💻 ⛱

DAVIS
🄰🄰🄰 ▼▼▼ **BEST WESTERN University Lodge** 🅼
(530) 756-7890. **$99-$120.** 123 B St 95616. I-80 exit 72B (Richards Blvd) westbound, just nw to 1st St, just w to B St, then just n; exit 72 (Richards Blvd) eastbound, just nw to 1st St, just w to B St, then just n; at 2nd and B sts. Ext corridors. **Pets:** Other species. $15 daily fee/pet. Service with restrictions, supervision. 🆂🅰🆅🅴 🛜 🛏 💻 ⊠

🄰🄰🄰 ▼▼▼ **University Park Inn & Suites** 🅷
(530) 756-0910. **$88-$199.** 1111 Richards Blvd 95616. I-80 exit 72B (Richards Blvd) westbound; exit 72 (Richards Blvd) eastbound, just nw. Ext corridors. **Pets:** $15 daily fee/pet. Designated rooms, supervision. 🆂🅰🆅🅴 🛜 🄼 🛏 💻 ⛱

DEATH VALLEY NATIONAL PARK
▼▼ **Stovepipe Wells Village** 🅼
(760) 786-2387. **$100-$155.** 360 SR 190 92328. On SR 190; 24 mi nw of visitor center. Ext corridors. **Pets:** Supervision.
🛜 ⊠ 🄼 🛏 💻 🍽 ⛱

DELANO
🄰🄰🄰 ▼▼▼ **BEST WESTERN Liberty Inn** 🅼
(661) 725-0976. **$75-$200.** 14394 County Line Rd 93215. SR 99 exit 58 (County Line Rd), just e, then just n on Girard St. Int corridors. **Pets:** Medium, dogs only. $20 daily fee/room. Service with restrictions, supervision. 🆂🅰🆅🅴 🛜 🛏 💻 ⛱

🄰🄰🄰 ▼▼▼ **Rodeway Inn** 🅼
(661) 725-1022. **$70-$129.** 2211 Girard St 93215. SR 99 exit 58 (County Line Rd), just e, then just s. Ext corridors. **Pets:** Medium. $10 daily fee/pet. Service with restrictions, supervision. 🆂🅰🆅🅴 🛜 🛏 💻 ⛱

DINUBA
▼▼▼ **Reedley Country Inn Bed & Breakfast** 🅱🅱
(559) 638-2585. **$85-$95, 3 day notice.** 43137 Rd 52 93618. SR 99 exit 121 (Manning Ave), 10 mi e, then 1 mi s. Ext/int corridors.
Pets: Accepted. ⊠

DIXON

BEST WESTERN PLUS Inn Dixon
(707) 678-1400. **$89-$155, 3 day notice.** 1345 Commercial Way 95620. I-80 exit 64 (Pitt School Rd), just s, then just e. Ext/int corridors. **Pets:** Medium. $20 daily fee/room. Designated rooms, service with restrictions, supervision.

Comfort Suites - West of UC Davis
(707) 676-5000. **$75-$250.** 155 Dorset Dr 95620. I-80 exit 66A (Currey Rd) westbound, follow SR 113 S; exit 66 (Currey Rd) eastbound, just s on SR 113. **Pets:** Medium. $25 daily fee/pet. Designated rooms, service with restrictions, supervision.

DORRIS

Golden Eagle Motel
(530) 397-3114. **$39-$99.** 100 W 1st St 96023. US 97; center. Ext corridors. **Pets:** $5 daily fee/pet. Designated rooms, service with restrictions, supervision.

DOUGLAS CITY

Indian Creek Lodge
(530) 623-6294. **$69-$89, 3 day notice.** 59741 Hwy 299 W 96024. On SR 299, 1.5 mi w of jct SR 299 and CR 3. Ext corridors. **Pets:** Dogs only. $150 deposit/room, $10 daily fee/pet. Designated rooms, supervision.

DOWNIEVILLE

Riverside Inn
(530) 289-1000. **$88-$180, 3 day notice.** 206 Commercial St (SR 49) 95936. On SR 49; center. Ext corridors. **Pets:** Other species. $15 one-time fee/pet. Service with restrictions, supervision.

DUBLIN

Holiday Inn Dublin
(925) 828-7750. **$69-$149.** 6680 Regional St 94568. At northwest quadrant of I-580 and 680. Int corridors. **Pets:** $35 one-time fee/room. Designated rooms, service with restrictions, supervision.

La Quinta Inn & Suites Dublin - Pleasanton
(925) 828-9393. **$60-$210.** 6275 Dublin Blvd 94568. I-580 exit Hopyard/Dougherty Rd, just n. Int corridors. **Pets:** Service with restrictions, supervision.

DUNSMUIR

Oak Tree Inn
(530) 235-4100. **Call for rates.** 4000 Siskiyou Ave 96025. I-5 exit 732 (Siskiyou Ave), just e. Int corridors. **Pets:** Other species. Service with restrictions, supervision.

EAST PALO ALTO

Four Seasons Hotel Silicon Valley at East Palo Alto
(650) 566-1200. **$525-$645.** 2050 University Ave 94303. US 101 exit University Ave. Int corridors. **Pets:** Accepted.

EL CENTRO

TownePlace Suites by Marriott
(760) 370-3800. **$99-$139.** 3003 S Dogwood Rd 92243. I-8 exit 116 (Dogwood Rd), 0.5 mi s. Int corridors. **Pets:** Accepted.

ELK GROVE

Extended StayAmerica-Sacramento-Elk Grove
(916) 683-3753. **$79-$94.** 2201 Longport Ct 95758. I-5 exit 508 (Laguna Blvd), 0.5 mi e, just s on Harbour Point Dr, then just w. Int corridors. **Pets:** $25 daily fee/pet. Designated rooms, service with restrictions.

Fairfield Inn & Suites by Marriott Sacramento Elk Grove
(916) 681-5400. **$99-$159.** 8058 Orchard Loop Ln 95624. SR 99 exit 289 (Cosumnes River Blvd/Calvine Rd), just e to Calvine Rd, then just s. Int corridors. **Pets:** Accepted.

Holiday Inn Express & Suites
(916) 478-4000. **$89-$120.** 2460 Maritime Dr 95758. I-5 exit 506 (Elk Grove Blvd), just e to Harbour Point Dr, just n, then just w; SR 99 exit Elk Grove Blvd, 5 mi w, just n on Harbour Point Dr, then just w. Int corridors. **Pets:** Medium. $35 one-time fee/pet. Service with restrictions, crate.

Holiday Inn Express Hotel & Suites
(916) 478-9000. **$116-$152.** 9175 W Stockton Blvd 95758. SR 99 exit 287 (Laguna Blvd), just w, then just n; in Laguna Gateway Shopping Center. Int corridors. **Pets:** Medium. $60 one-time fee/pet. Designated rooms, service with restrictions, supervision.

EL PORTAL

Yosemite View Lodge
(209) 379-2681. **$95-$499, 7 day notice.** 11136 Hwy 140 95318. Just w of Yosemite National Park West Gate. Ext corridors. **Pets:** Accepted.

EMERYVILLE

Hyatt house Emeryville/San Francisco Bay Area
(510) 601-5880. **$139-$259.** 5800 Shellmound St 94608. I-80 exit Powell St, just e. Int corridors. **Pets:** Medium. $150 one-time fee/pet. Designated rooms, service with restrictions.

ENCINITAS

BEST WESTERN Encinitas Inn & Suites at Moonlight Beach
(760) 942-7455. **Call for rates.** 85 Encinitas Blvd 92024. I-5 exit 41B (Encinitas Blvd), just w. Ext corridors. **Pets:** Other species. $20 daily fee/room. Designated rooms, service with restrictions, supervision.

Econo Lodge Moonlight Beach Encinitas
(760) 436-4999. **$69-$199.** 410 N Coast Hwy 101 92024. I-5 exit 41B (Encinitas Blvd), 0.6 mi w, then 0.6 mi n. Ext/int corridors. **Pets:** Small, other species. $25 daily fee/pet. Designated rooms, service with restrictions, crate.

Howard Johnson-Encinitas
(760) 944-3800. **$63-$160.** 607 Leucadia Blvd 92024. I-5 exit 43 (Leucadia Blvd), just e. Ext corridors. **Pets:** Accepted.

ESCONDIDO

BEST WESTERN Escondido Hotel
(760) 740-1700. **$100-$150.** 1700 Seven Oakes Rd 92026. I-15 exit 33 (El Norte Pkwy), just e, then just n. Int corridors. **Pets:** Other species. $25 one-time fee/pet. Service with restrictions, crate.

Comfort Inn San Diego/Escondido
(760) 489-1010. **$80-$139.** 1290 W Valley Pkwy 92029. I-15 exit 31 (Valley Pkwy), just w. Int corridors. **Pets:** Small. $15 daily fee/pet. Designated rooms, service with restrictions, supervision.

Escondido Lodge
(760) 743-9733. **Call for rates.** 2650 S Escondido Blvd 92025. I-15 exit 29 (Felicita Rd/Citracado Pkwy), 0.8 mi e on Citracado Pkwy, then just s. Ext corridors. **Pets:** Small. $25 one-time fee/pet. Service with restrictions, supervision.

AAA ▼▼ Rodeway Inn **M**
(760) 746-0441. **$54-$78.** 250 W El Norte Pkwy 92026. I-15 exit 33 (El Norte Pkwy), 1 mi e. Ext corridors. **Pets:** Medium. $25 daily fee/pet. Designated rooms, service with restrictions, supervision. SAVE 🛜 🛗 💻

EUREKA

AAA ▼▼▼ BEST WESTERN PLUS Bayshore Inn **H** ❀
(707) 268-8005. **$80-$230.** 3500 Broadway 95503. US 101; south end of town. Ext corridors. **Pets:** Dogs only. $20 daily fee/room. Designated rooms, service with restrictions, supervision.
SAVE 🛜 🛗 💻 🍽 🏊 🐾

▼▼▼▼ Carter House Inns **CI** ❀
(707) 444-8062. **$159-$595, 3 day notice.** 301 L St 95501. Just w of US 101 S. Int corridors. **Pets:** Dogs only. $50 one-time fee/room. Designated rooms, service with restrictions, supervision.
🛜 🚫 🍽 🍴 🐾

AAA ▼▼ Clarion Hotel **H**
(707) 442-1601. **$100-$160.** 2223 4th St 95501. US 101 exit V St northbound; exit W St southbound. Ext/int corridors. **Pets:** Small. $10 daily fee/pet. Designated rooms, service with restrictions, supervision.
SAVE 🛜 🛗 💻 🏊

AAA ▼▼ Eureka Town House Motel **M**
(707) 443-4536. **$55-$150.** 933 4th St 95501. On US 101 southbound; corner of K St. Ext corridors. **Pets:** Medium, dogs only. $10 daily fee/room. Service with restrictions, supervision. SAVE 🛜 🛗 💻 🐾

AAA ▼▼ Quality Inn Eureka **M**
(707) 443-1601. **Call for rates.** 1209 4th St 95501. On US 101 southbound; between M and N sts. Ext corridors. **Pets:** Accepted.
SAVE 🛜 🛗 💻 🐾 🐾

AAA ▼▼▼ Red Lion Hotel Eureka **H**
(707) 445-0844. **$99-$189.** 1929 4th St 95501. On US 101 southbound; between T and V sts. Int corridors. **Pets:** Other species. $15 one-time fee/room. Service with restrictions, crate.
SAVE 🛜 🚫 🛗 💻 🍴 🐾

FAIRFIELD

▼▼ Extended StayAmerica-Fairfield-Napa Valley **H**
(707) 438-0932. **$94-$109.** 1019 Oliver Rd 94534. I-80 exit Texas St, just w. Int corridors. **Pets:** $25 daily fee/pet. Designated rooms, service with restrictions. 🛜 🐾 🛗 💻

▼▼▼▼ Homewood Suites Fairfield-Napa Valley Area **H**
(707) 863-0300. **$129-$189.** 4755 Business Center Dr 94534. I-80 exit Green Valley Rd/Suisun Valley Rd, n on Green Valley Rd, then just e. Int corridors. **Pets:** Medium, dogs only. $75 one-time fee/pet. Designated rooms, service with restrictions, supervision.
🛜 🐾 🛗 💻 🐾 🐾

▼▼▼▼ Staybridge Suites Fairfield-Napa Valley Area **H**
(707) 863-0900. **Call for rates.** 4775 Business Center Dr 94534. I-80 exit Green Valley Rd/Suisun Valley Rd, n on Green Valley Rd, then just e. Int corridors. **Pets:** Accepted. 🛜 🚫 🐾 🛗 💻 🐾

FALLBROOK

AAA ▼▼▼▼ Pala Mesa Resort **H**
(760) 728-5881. **$119-$269.** 2001 Old Hwy 395 92028. I-15 exit 46 (SR 76/Pala Rd/Oceanside), just w, then 2 mi n. Ext corridors.
Pets: Accepted. SAVE 🛜 🛗 💻 🍴 🐾 🐾

FALL RIVER MILLS

AAA ▼▼ Hi-Mont Motel **M** ❀
(530) 336-5541. **$69-$104.** 43021 Bridge St 96028. 0.4 mi sw on SR 299; jct SR 299 E and Bridge St. Ext corridors. **Pets:** Other species. $20 daily fee/pet. Service with restrictions, supervision.
SAVE 🛜 🚫 🛗 💻

FERNDALE

▼▼▼ Shaw House Inn **BB**
(707) 786-9958. **$125-$275, 15 day notice.** 703 Main St 95536. Center. Ext/int corridors. **Pets:** Accepted. 🛜 🚫 🍴 🐾

FIREBAUGH

AAA ▼▼▼ BEST WESTERN Apricot Inn **M**
(559) 659-1444. **$80-$110.** 46290 W Panoche Rd 93622. I-5 exit W Panoche Rd, just w. Ext corridors. **Pets:** Medium, other species. $20 daily fee/room. Service with restrictions, supervision.
SAVE 🛜 🐾 🛗 💻 🏊

FISH CAMP

AAA ▼▼▼▼ The Cottages at Tenaya Lodge **H** ❀
(559) 683-6555. **$149-$425, 7 day notice.** 1122 Hwy 41 93623. 2 mi from Yosemite National Park South Gate. Ext corridors. **Pets:** Dogs only. $75 one-time fee/room. Designated rooms, supervision.
SAVE 🛜 🚫 🐾 🛗 💻 🐾 🐾

▼▼ The Narrow Gauge Inn **H** ❀
(559) 683-7720. **$79-$250, 4 day notice.** 48571 Hwy 41 93623. 4 mi from Yosemite National Park South Gate. Ext corridors. **Pets:** Other species. $25 one-time fee/pet. Service with restrictions, crate. 🛜 🚫 💻 🐾

AAA ▼▼▼▼ Tenaya Lodge at Yosemite **H** ❀
(559) 683-6555. **$129-$425, 7 day notice.** 1122 Hwy 41 93623. 2 mi from Yosemite National Park South Gate. Int corridors. **Pets:** Dogs only. $75 one-time fee/room. Designated rooms, supervision.
SAVE 🛜 🚫 🐾 🛗 💻 🍴 🐾 🐾

FOLSOM

AAA ▼▼▼ Lake Natoma Inn Hotel & Conference Center **H** ❀
(916) 351-1500. **$89-$169.** 702 Gold Lake Dr 95630. US 50 exit Folsom Blvd, 3 mi n, then 0.5 mi e on Riley St; behind The Lakes Specialty Shopping Center. Int corridors. **Pets:** Other species. $45 one-time fee/room, $15 daily fee/pet. Service with restrictions.
SAVE 🛜 🐾 🛗 💻 🍴 🐾 🐾

▼▼▼ Larkspur Landing Home Suite Hotels Folsom **H**
(916) 355-1616. **Call for rates.** 121 Iron Point Rd 95630. US 50 exit Folsom Blvd, 0.5 mi n to Iron Point Rd, then 0.3 mi e. Int corridors. **Pets:** Medium. $75 one-time fee/room. Designated rooms, service with restrictions, crate. ECO 🛜 🚫 🐾 🛗 💻 🐾

▼▼▼ Residence Inn by Marriott **H**
(916) 983-7289. **$119-$179.** 2555 Iron Point Rd 95630. US 50 exit E Bidwell St, just n, then just w. Int corridors. **Pets:** Other species. $100 one-time fee/room. Service with restrictions, supervision.
🛜 🚫 🐾 🛗 💻 🐾 🐾

FORTUNA

AAA ▼▼▼ BEST WESTERN Country Inn **M** ❀
(707) 725-6822. **$70-$139.** 2025 Riverwalk Dr 95540. US 101 exit 687 (Kenmar Rd), just w. Ext corridors. **Pets:** Medium, dogs only. $20 one-time fee/pet. Service with restrictions, supervision.
SAVE 🛜 🐾 🛗 💻 🏊

AAA ▼▼▼ Fortuna Super 8 **M**
(707) 725-2888. **$80-$230.** 1805 Alamar Way 95540. US 101 exit 687 (Kenmar Rd), 0.3 mi w on Riverwalk Dr. Ext corridors. **Pets:** Dogs only. $15 daily fee/pet. Designated rooms, service with restrictions, supervision.
SAVE 🛜 🛗 💻

▼▼▼ Holiday Inn Express **H**
(707) 725-5500. **Call for rates.** 1859 Alamar Way 95540. US 101 exit 687 (Kenmar Rd), 0.3 mi w on Riverwalk Dr. Ext corridors. **Pets:** Medium, dogs only. $20 daily fee/pet. Designated rooms, service with restrictions, supervision. 🛜 🚫 🛗 💻 🏊

FOUNTAIN VALLEY

▼▼▼ Residence Inn by Marriott 🅷
(714) 965-8000. **$169-$319.** 9930 Slater Ave 92708. I-405 exit 14 (Brookhurst St), just n, then just w. Ext corridors. **Pets:** Accepted.
📶 ⊠ 🛏 💻 ➿ ⊠

FREMONT

AAA ▼▼▼ BEST WESTERN PLUS Garden Court Inn 🅷
(510) 792-4300. **$110-$130.** 5400 Mowry Ave 94538. I-880 exit Mowry Ave, just e. Int corridors. **Pets:** Large. $20 daily fee/room. Designated rooms, service with restrictions, supervision.
SAVE 📶 ♿ 🛏 💻 ➿

▼▼▼ La Quinta Inn & Suites Fremont 🅷
(510) 445-0808. **$66-$184.** 46200 Landing Pkwy 94538. I-880 exit Fremont Blvd/Cushing Pkwy, just w. Int corridors. **Pets:** Service with restrictions, supervision. 📶 ♿ 🛏 💻 ➿

▼▼▼ Residence Inn by Marriott 🅷
(510) 794-5900. **$89-$149.** 5400 Farwell Pl 94536. I-880 exit Mowry Ave, just e. Ext corridors. **Pets:** Accepted.
📶 ⊠ ♿ 🛏 💻 ➿ ⊠

FRESNO

AAA ▼▼ Ambassador Inn & Suites 🅼
(559) 442-1082. **$55-$80.** 1804 W Olive Ave 93728. SR 99 exit Olive Ave, just w. Ext corridors. **Pets:** $25 deposit/pet. Designated rooms, service with restrictions, supervision. SAVE 📶 🛏 💻 ➿

AAA ▼▼▼ BEST WESTERN PLUS Village Inn 🅷
(559) 226-2110. **Call for rates.** 3110 N Blackstone Ave 93703. SR 41 exit Shields Ave, 0.3 mi w. Int corridors. **Pets:** Large. $20 one-time fee/room. Designated rooms, service with restrictions, supervision.
SAVE 📶 ⊠ 🛏 💻 ➿

▼▼ Extended StayAmerica Fresno-North 🅷
(559) 438-7105. **$79-$94.** 7135 N Fresno St 93720. SR 41 exit Herndon Ave E, just n. Ext corridors. **Pets:** $25 daily fee/pet. Designated rooms, service with restrictions. 📶 ♿ 🛏 💻 ➿

AAA ▼▼▼ La Quinta Inn & Suites Fresno Northwest 🅷
(559) 275-3700. **$89-$166.** 5077 N Cornelia Ave 93722. SR 99 exit Shaw Ave E, just n. Int corridors. **Pets:** Service with restrictions, supervision. SAVE 📶 ⊠ ♿ 🛏 💻 ➿

AAA ▼▼▼ La Quinta Inn & Suites Fresno Riverpark 🅷
(559) 449-0928. **$119-$188.** 330 E Fir Ave 93720. SR 41 exit Herndon Ave, just e. Int corridors. **Pets:** Service with restrictions, supervision. SAVE 📶 ⊠ ♿ 🛏 💻 ➿

▼▼▼ La Quinta Inn Fresno Yosemite 🅷
(559) 442-1110. **$63-$133.** 2926 Tulare St 93721. SR 99 exit Fresno St, 1 mi e to R St, then s, then just e. Ext/int corridors. **Pets:** Service with restrictions, supervision. 📶 ♿ 🛏 💻 ➿

▼▼ Motel 6 Fresno #4390 🅼
(559) 276-1910. **$50-$80, 14 day notice.** 5021 N Barcus Ave 93722. SR 99 exit Shaw Ave, just e. Ext corridors. **Pets:** Other species. Service with restrictions, supervision. 📶 🛏 💻

AAA ▼▼▼ Park Inn by Radisson Fresno 🅷
(559) 226-2200. **$120-$185.** 3737 N Blackstone Ave 93726. SR 41 exit Shields Ave, 0.3 mi w, then just n. Int corridors. **Pets:** Accepted.
SAVE 📶 ⊠ ♿ 🛏 💻 ▯▮ ➿

▼▼ Red Roof Inn Fresno-Yosemite Gateway 🅷
(559) 222-4445. **$69-$99.** 4141 N Blackstone Ave 93726. SR 41 exit Ashlan Ave, 0.3 mi w. Int corridors. **Pets:** Large, other species. Service with restrictions, supervision. 📶 ♿ 🛏 💻 ➿

▼▼▼ Residence Inn by Marriott 🅷
(559) 222-8900. **$98-$149.** 5322 N Diana St 93710. SR 41 exit Shaw Ave, 0.3 mi w, n on Blackstone Ave, then e on Barstow Ave. Int corridors. **Pets:** Small. $100 one-time fee/room. Service with restrictions, supervision. ECO 📶 ⊠ 🛏 💻 ➿ ⊠

▼▼ Rodeway Inn 🅷
(559) 431-3557. **Call for rates.** 6730 N Blackstone Ave 93710. SR 41 exit Herndon Ave W, then s. Ext corridors. **Pets:** Accepted.
📶 🛏 💻 ➿

▼▼▼ TownePlace Suites by Marriott 🅷 🐾
(559) 435-4600. **$89-$169.** 7127 N Fresno St 93720. SR 41 exit Herndon Ave E, then just n. Int corridors. **Pets:** Other species. $100 one-time fee/room. Designated rooms, service with restrictions, crate.
📶 ⊠ ♿ 🛏 💻 ➿

FULLERTON

▼▼▼ Fullerton Marriott Hotel at California State University 🅷
(714) 738-7800. **$79-$169.** 2701 E Nutwood Ave 92831. SR 57 exit 7 (Nutwood Ave) northbound; exit 7 (Nutwood Ave/Chapman Ave) southbound, just w. Int corridors. **Pets:** Accepted.
ECO 📶 ⊠ ♿ 🛏 💻 ➿ ⊠

GARBERVILLE

AAA ▼▼▼ Benbow Inn 🅷
(707) 923-2124. **$110-$595, 5 day notice.** 445 Lake Benbow Dr 95542. US 101 exit Benbow Lake Rd, just w; 2 mi s of downtown. Int corridors. **Pets:** Accepted. SAVE 📶 ⊠ 🛏 💻 ▯▮ ➿ ⊠

AAA ▼▼▼ BEST WESTERN PLUS Humboldt House Inn 🅼 🐾
(707) 923-2771. **$110-$140.** 701 Redwood Dr 95542. US 101 exit Garberville, just e. Ext corridors. **Pets:** Medium, dogs only. $15 one-time fee/pet. Designated rooms, service with restrictions, supervision.
SAVE 📶 🛏 💻 ➿

GARDEN GROVE

▼▼▼ Anaheim Marriott Suites 🅷
(714) 750-1000. **$125-$233.** 12015 Harbor Blvd 92840. I-5 exit 107B (Chapman Ave) northbound, 1.5 mi w, then just s; exit 107C (State College/The City Dr) southbound, just s on State College Blvd, 1.5 mi w on Chapman Ave, then just s. Int corridors. **Pets:** Accepted.
📶 ⊠ ♿ 🛏 💻 ▯▮ ➿ ⊠

▼▼ Candlewood Suites Anaheim-South 🅷
(714) 539-4200. **$79-$149.** 12901 Garden Grove Blvd 92843. SR 22 exit 13 (Haster St) westbound; exit 13 (Fairview St) eastbound, just n, then just w. Int corridors. **Pets:** Medium. $15 daily fee/room. Service with restrictions, supervision. 📶 ♿ 🛏 💻

▼▼▼ Residence Inn by Marriott Anaheim Resort Area 🅷
(714) 591-4000. **$119-$189.** 11931 Harbor Blvd 92840. I-5 exit 107B (Chapman Ave) northbound, 1.5 mi w, then just n; exit 107C (State College Blvd/The City Dr) southbound, just s on State College Blvd, 1.5 mi w on Chapman Ave, then just n. Int corridors. **Pets:** Medium. $100 one-time fee/room. Designated rooms, service with restrictions.
📶 ⊠ ♿ 🛏 💻 ➿ ⊠

AAA ▼▼▼ Sheraton Garden Grove Anaheim South 🅷 🐾
(714) 703-8400. **$99-$249.** 12221 Harbor Blvd 92840. I-5 exit 110 (Harbor Blvd/Ball Rd), 2.2 mi s. Int corridors. **Pets:** Medium, other species. $150 one-time fee/room. Service with restrictions, crate.
SAVE 📶 ⊠ 🛏 💻 ▯▮ ➿

GILROY

BEST WESTERN PLUS Forest Park Inn H ❀

(408) 848-5144. **$109-$239.** 375 Leavesley Rd 95020. US 101 exit Leavesley Rd, just w. Int corridors. **Pets:** Medium. $20 daily fee/pet. Designated rooms, service with restrictions, supervision.

SAVE 🛜 ✕ 🕭M 🖪 🖵 ⊇ ⊠

Quality Inn & Suites H

(408) 847-5500. **$79-$249.** 8430 Murray Ave 95020. US 101 exit Leavesley Rd, just w. Ext corridors. **Pets:** Large. $10 daily fee/pet. Service with restrictions, supervision. SAVE 🛜 🖪 🖵 ⊇

GLENNVILLE

The Bunkhouse Motel M

(661) 536-9100. **$65-$75, 3 day notice.** 12044 Hwy 155 93226. On SR 155, at Granite Rd. Ext corridors. **Pets:** Accepted.

🛜 ✕ 🖪 🖵 🍴

GRAEAGLE

Chalet View Lodge H

(530) 832-5528. **$89-$315, 7 day notice.** 72056 Hwy 70 96103. Jct SR 70 and 89, 5.7 mi e on SR 70. Ext corridors. **Pets:** Other species. $25 daily fee/room. Designated rooms, service with restrictions, supervision.

🛜 ✕ 🖪 🖵 🍴 ⊇ ⊠

GRASS VALLEY

BEST WESTERN Gold Country Inn M

(530) 273-1393. **$89-$189.** 972 Sutton Way 95945. SR 20 and 49 exit 183 (Brunswick Rd), just e, then just n; midway between Grass Valley and Nevada City. Ext corridors. **Pets:** Other species. $20 one-time fee/pet. Service with restrictions, supervision. SAVE 🛜 🖪 🖵 ⊇

The Gold Miners Inn Holiday Inn Express & Suites H ❀

(530) 477-1700. **$109-$199.** 121 Bank St 95945. SR 49 exit 182A (SR 174/Colfax Ave) northbound, just n on Auburn St, then just e; exit 182B (SR 174/Colfax Ave) southbound, just n on Auburn St, then just e. Int corridors. **Pets:** Large, other species. $50 one-time fee/pet. Service with restrictions, crate. 🛜 ✕ 🕭M 🖪 🖵

Grass Valley Courtyard Suites Spa & Conference Center H ❀

(530) 272-7696. **$160-$360, 3 day notice.** 210 N Auburn St 95945. SR 49 exit 182A (Colfax/SR 174) northbound, just w to S Auburn St, then just n; exit 182B (E Main St/Grass Valley) southbound, just n to E Main St, just w to S Auburn St, then just n; just n of jct Richardson St. Ext corridors. **Pets:** Dogs only. $50 one-time fee/pet. Supervision.

SAVE 🛜 🕭M 🖵 ⊇ ⊠

GROVELAND

Groveland Hotel at Yosemite National Park CI ❀

(209) 962-4000. **$145-$345.** 18767 Main St 95321. Center. Int corridors. **Pets:** Other species. $20 daily fee/pet. Service with restrictions, crate.

SAVE 🛜 ✕ 🖵 🍴

HANFORD

Sequoia Inn H

(559) 582-0338. **$81-$89.** 1655 Mall Dr 93230. SR 198 exit 12th Ave N, just e. Int corridors. **Pets:** $30 one-time fee/room. Service with restrictions, supervision. SAVE 🛜 ✕ 🖪 🖵 ⊇

HAWAIIAN GARDENS

La Quinta Inn & Suites Hawaiian Gardens H

(562) 860-2500. **$87-$161.** 12441 Carson St 90716. I-605 exit 3 (Carson St), 1 mi e. Int corridors. **Pets:** Service with restrictions, supervision.

🛜 ✕ 🕭M 🖪 🖵

HAYWARD

La Quinta Inn & Suites Hayward Oakland Airport H

(510) 732-6300. **$83-$188.** 20777 Hesperian Blvd 94541. I-880 exit A St, 0.5 mi w. Int corridors. **Pets:** Service with restrictions, supervision.

SAVE 🛜 ✕ 🕭M 🖪 🖵 ⊇

HEMET

Quality Inn M

(951) 766-1902. **$79-$99.** 1201 W Florida Ave 92543. 1.5 mi w of SR 79 N (San Jacinto St) on SR 74/79. Ext corridors. **Pets:** Small. $20 daily fee/pet. Designated rooms, service with restrictions, supervision.

ECO SAVE 🛜 🕭M 🖪 🖵 ⊇

Travelodge Inn of Hemet M

(951) 925-6605. **$60-$79.** 2625 W Florida Ave 92545. 2.4 mi w of SR 79 N (San Jacinto St) on SR 74/79. Ext corridors. **Pets:** Small. $10 daily fee/pet. Designated rooms, service with restrictions, supervision.

SAVE 🛜 🖪 🖵 ⊇

HESPERIA

Econo Lodge M

(760) 949-1515. **$55-$125.** 11976 Mariposa Rd 92345. I-15 exit 147 (Bear Valley Rd), just e, then just s. Ext corridors. **Pets:** Small, dogs only. $10 daily fee/pet. Service with restrictions, supervision. 🛜 🖪 🖵

Holiday Inn Express Hotel & Suites H

(760) 244-7674. **$65-$99, 3 day notice.** 9750 Key Pointe Dr 92345. I-15 exit 143 (Hesperia/Main St), just w on Main St, then just n. Int corridors. **Pets:** Medium. $25 daily fee/room. Crate.

SAVE 🛜 ✕ 🕭M 🖪 🖵 ⊇

HUNTINGTON BEACH

BEST WESTERN Harbour Inn & Suites H ❀

(562) 592-4770. **Call for rates.** 16912 Pacific Coast Hwy 90742. I-405 exit 15 (Magnolia St/Warner Ave W), 6 mi s, then 0.5 mi n. Int corridors. **Pets:** Very small. $45 daily fee/pet. Designated rooms, service with restrictions, supervision. SAVE 🛜 ✕ 🖪 🖵

Hyatt Regency Huntington Beach Resort & Spa H

(714) 698-1234. **$162-$450, 7 day notice.** 21500 Pacific Coast Hwy 92648. I-405 exit 16 (Beach Blvd), 6.5 mi s, then just w. Int corridors. **Pets:** Accepted. ECO SAVE 🛜 🕭M 🖪 🖵 🍴 ⊇ ⊠

The Waterfront Beach Resort A Hilton Hotel H ❀

(714) 845-8000. **$188-$449.** 21100 Pacific Coast Hwy 92648. I-405 exit 16 (Beach Blvd), 6.5 mi s, then just w. Int corridors. **Pets:** Large. $50 one-time fee/pet. Designated rooms, service with restrictions, crate.

ECO 🔄 SAVE 🛜 ✕ 🕭M 🖪 🖵 🍴 ⊇ ⊠

IDYLLWILD

Quiet Creek Inn CA ❀

(951) 468-4208. **$89-$165, 14 day notice.** 26345 Delano Dr 92549. SR 243, 0.8 mi sw of town center, 0.4 mi w on Toll Gate Rd, then just n. Ext corridors. **Pets:** Large, other species. $35 one-time fee/room. Supervision.

🛜 ✕ 🖪 🖵 ⊠ ⊠

Woodland Park Manor CA

(951) 659-2657. **$99-$205, 10 day notice.** 55350 S Circle Dr 92549. From SR 243 and town center, 1.5 mi ne. Ext corridors. **Pets:** $15 one-time fee/pet. Supervision. 🛜 ✕ 🖪 🖵 ⊇ ⊠

INDIAN WELLS

Hyatt Regency Indian Wells Resort & Spa H ❀
(760) 341-1000. **$81-$387, 7 day notice.** 44-600 Indian Wells Ln 92210. I-10 exit 134 (Cook St), 4.4 mi s, 1.5 mi e on SR 111, then just n. Ext/int corridors. **Pets:** Medium, dogs only. $100 one-time fee/room. Designated rooms, service with restrictions.

Miramonte Resort and Spa H
(760) 341-2200. **$99-$499, 3 day notice.** 45-000 Indian Wells Ln 92210. I-10 exit 134 (Cook St), 4.4 mi s, 1.5 mi e on SR 111, then just s. Ext/int corridors. **Pets:** Accepted.

INDIO

BEST WESTERN Date Tree Hotel M ❀
(760) 347-3421. **$70-$451.** 81-909 Indio Blvd 92201. I-10 exit 139 (Jefferson St/Indio Blvd), 2.5 mi se. Int corridors. **Pets:** Other species. $15 daily fee/pet. Service with restrictions.

Indian Palms Country Club & Resort H
(760) 775-4444. **$84-$209.** 48-630 Monroe St 92201. I-10 exit 142 (Monroe St), 3 mi s. Ext corridors. **Pets:** Medium. $15 daily fee/room. Service with restrictions, crate.

IRVINE

Hilton Irvine/Orange County Airport H
(949) 833-9999. **$69-$200.** 18800 MacArthur Blvd 92612. I-405 exit 8 (MacArthur Blvd/John Wayne Airport), 0.5 mi s. Int corridors.
Pets: Accepted.

Hyatt Regency Irvine H ❀
(949) 975-1234. **$81-$297.** 17900 Jamboree Rd 92614. I-405 exit 7 (Jamboree Rd), just ne. Int corridors. **Pets:** $50 daily fee/pet. Service with restrictions, supervision.

Residence Inn by Marriott Irvine John Wayne Airport H
(949) 261-2020. **$94-$349.** 2855 Main St 92614. I-405 exit 7 (Jamboree Rd), just n, then just e. Int corridors. **Pets:** Accepted.

Residence Inn by Marriott-Irvine Spectrum H
(949) 380-3000. **$99-$379.** 10 Morgan St 92618. I-5 exit 94 (Alton Pkwy) southbound; exit 94B (Alton Pkwy) northbound, 2 mi e. Ext corridors. **Pets:** Other species. $100 one-time fee/room. Service with restrictions.

JACKSON

BEST WESTERN Amador Inn H ❀
(209) 223-0211. **$79-$89.** 200 S Hwy 49 95642. Just se of jct SR 49 and 88. Int corridors. **Pets:** Large, other species. $15 daily fee/pet. Service with restrictions, supervision.

The Jackson Lodge M
(209) 223-0486. **$65-$135.** 850 N Hwy 49 95642. On SR 49 and 88, 0.5 mi w. Ext corridors. **Pets:** Medium. $15 deposit/pet. Designated rooms, service with restrictions, supervision.

JAMESTOWN

1859 Historic National Hotel, A Country Inn CI ❀
(209) 984-3446. **$140-$160, 3 day notice.** 18183 Main St 95327. In historic downtown. Int corridors. **Pets:** Medium. $25 daily fee/room. Designated rooms, service with restrictions, supervision.

Country Inn Sonora M
(209) 984-0315. **$59-$289.** 18730 Hwy 108 95327. SR 108 and 49, 1 mi e of town. Ext corridors. **Pets:** Medium. $10 daily fee/pet. Designated rooms, service with restrictions, supervision.

Jamestown Railtown Motel M
(209) 984-3332. **Call for rates.** 10301 Willow St 95327. Center. Ext corridors. **Pets:** Accepted.

Victorian Gold Bed & Breakfast BB
(209) 984-3429. **$115-$185, 5 day notice.** 10382 Willow St 95327. Center; in historic downtown. Int corridors. **Pets:** Accepted.

JULIAN

Julian Lodge B & B Mountain Inn M ❀
(760) 765-1420. **$80-$200.** 2720 C St 92036. Just s of Main St on SR 78 and 79. Ext/int corridors. **Pets:** $30 one-time fee/room. Supervision.

JUNE LAKE

Double Eagle Resort/Spa CA
(760) 648-7004. **$169-$400, 30 day notice.** 5587 Hwy 158 93529. On SR 158; 3 mi w of village. Ext corridors. **Pets:** $50 one-time fee/room. Designated rooms, service with restrictions, supervision.

Gull Lake Lodge M
(760) 648-7516. **$79-$204, 7 day notice.** 132 Leonard Ave 93529. 0.3 mi n on Knoll St, then 0.3 mi e on Bruce St; in village. Ext corridors. **Pets:** Other species. Designated rooms, service with restrictions, supervision.

KERNVILLE

Barewood Inn & Suites M
(760) 376-1910. **$75-$195.** 7013 Wofford Blvd 93285. In Wofford Heights. Ext corridors. **Pets:** Accepted.

River View Lodge M
(760) 376-6019. **Call for rates.** 2 Sirretta St 93238. On Kernville Rd; at the bridge. Ext corridors. **Pets:** Accepted.

KETTLEMAN CITY

BEST WESTERN Kettleman Inn & Suites M
(559) 386-0804. **$108-$160.** 33410 Powers Dr 93239. E of and adjacent to I-5 exit SR 41 N, 0.3 mi to Bernard Dr, then 0.3 mi n. Ext corridors. **Pets:** Small, other species. $10 daily fee/pet. Supervision.

Super 8 M
(559) 386-9530. **$69-$75.** 33415 Powers Dr 93239. E of and adjacent to I-5 exit SR 41 N, 0.3 mi to Bernard Dr, then 0.3 mi n. Ext corridors. **Pets:** Accepted.

KLAMATH

Motel Trees M
(707) 482-3152. **$70-$145.** 15495 Hwy 101 N 95548. On US 101, 4.5 mi n of Klamath. Ext corridors. **Pets:** $10 daily fee/pet. Designated rooms, supervision.

LAGUNA BEACH

Art Hotel-Laguna Beach M
(949) 494-6464. **$99-$199, 3 day notice.** 1404 N Coast Hwy 92651. SR 133 to Coast Hwy, then 1.1 mi n on SR 1. **Pets:** Designated rooms.

Casa Laguna Inn & Spa BB ❀
(949) 494-2996. **$150-$650, 5 day notice.** 2510 S Coast Hwy 92651. SR 133 to Coast Hwy, then 1.3 mi s on SR 1. Ext corridors. **Pets:** Medium, dogs only. $25 daily fee/pet. Service with restrictions, supervision.

▼▼▼▼ Holiday Inn Laguna Beach H
(949) 494-1001. **$129-$399.** 696 S Coast Hwy 92651. SR 133 to Coast Hwy, then 0.5 mi s on SR 1. Ext corridors. **Pets:** Accepted.
🛜 ⊠ ⊟ 💻 🍴 ⇌

▼▼▼▼ Inn at Laguna Beach H ❀
(949) 497-9722. **$279-$485, 7 day notice.** 211 N Coast Hwy 92651. SR 133 to Coast Hwy, then just n on SR 1. Ext/int corridors. **Pets:** Medium, dogs only. Crate. 🛜 ⊠ ⊟ 💻 ⇌

▼▼▼▼ Laguna Cliffs Inn M
(949) 497-6645. **Call for rates.** 475 N Coast Hwy 92651. SR 133 to Coast Hwy, then 0.5 mi n on SR 1. Ext corridors. **Pets:** Accepted.
🛜 ⊠ ⊟ 💻 ⇌

AAA ▼▼▼▼▼ Montage Laguna Beach H
(949) 715-6000. **Call for rates.** 30801 S Coast Hwy 92651. SR 133 to Coast Hwy, then 3 mi s on SR 1. Ext/int corridors. **Pets:** Accepted.
ECO SAVE 🛜 ⊠ ⊟ 💻 🍴 ⇌ ⊠

AAA ▼▼▼▼▼ Surf & Sand Resort H ❀
(949) 497-4477. **Call for rates.** 1555 S Coast Hwy 92651. SR 133, 1 mi s. Ext corridors. **Pets:** Small. $100 one-time fee/room. Service with restrictions, supervision. SAVE 🛜 ⊠ ⊟M ⊟ 💻 🍴 ⇌ ⊠

▼▼▼ The Tides Laguna Beach M ❀
(949) 494-2494. **$109-$315, 3 day notice.** 460 N Coast Hwy 92651. SR 133 to Coast Hwy, then 0.5 mi n on SR 1. Ext corridors. **Pets:** $40 daily fee/pet. Designated rooms, service with restrictions, supervision.
🛜 ⊠ ⊟ 💻 ⇌

LAKE ARROWHEAD

▼▼▼▼ Arrowhead Saddleback Inn CI
(909) 336-3571. **$137-$648, 7 day notice.** 300 S SR 173 92352. On SR 173, jct SR 189. Ext/int corridors. **Pets:** Other species. $10 daily fee/pet. Designated rooms, service with restrictions, crate.
🛜 ⊠ ⊟ 💻 🍴

AAA ▼▼▼▼ Arrowhead Tree Top Lodge M
(909) 337-2311. **$89-$189, 7 day notice.** 27992 Rainbow Dr 92352. 0.3 mi s of Lake Arrowhead Village on SR 173. Ext corridors. **Pets:** Medium, dogs only. $25 daily fee/pet. Designated rooms, service with restrictions, supervision. SAVE 🛜 ⊠ ⊟ 💻 ⇌ ⊠ ⊠

AAA ▼▼▼▼▼ Lake Arrowhead Resort and Spa H
(909) 336-1511. **$169-$449, 3 day notice.** 27984 Hwy 189 92352. Just w of SR 173; in Lake Arrowhead Village. Int corridors. **Pets:** Dogs only. $25 daily fee/pet. Designated rooms, service with restrictions, crate.
SAVE 🛜 ⊠ ⊟M ⊟ 💻 🍴 ⇌ ⊠

LAKE ELSINORE

▼▼▼▼ Holiday Inn Express Hotel & Suites H
(951) 674-4333. **$89-$109.** 31573 Canyon Estates Dr 92532. I-15 exit 73 (Diamond Dr/Railroad Canyon Rd), just e, just ne on Summerhill Dr, then just n. Int corridors. **Pets:** Accepted. 🛜 ⊠ ⊟M ⊟ 💻 ⇌

LAKE FOREST

AAA ▼▼▼▼ The Prominence Hotel and Suites H
(949) 900-1288. **$89-$199.** 20768 Lake Forest Dr 92630. I-5 exit 92A (Lake Forest Dr) northbound; exit 92 (Bake Pkwy/Lake Forest Dr) southbound, 4 mi e. Int corridors. **Pets:** Accepted.
SAVE 🛜 ⊠ ⊟M ⊟ 💻 ⇌

AAA ▼▼▼▼ Quality Inn & Suites Irvine Spectrum H
(949) 458-1900. **$89-$209.** 23702 Rockfield Blvd 92630. I-5 exit 92A (Lake Forest Dr) northbound; exit 92 (Bake Pkwy/Lake Forest Dr) southbound, 0.5 mi e on Lake Forest Dr, then just s. Int corridors. **Pets:** Accepted. SAVE 🛜 ⊟ 💻 🍴 ⇌

▼▼▼▼ Staybridge Suites Irvine East/Lake Forest H
(949) 462-9500. **$119-$189.** 2 Orchard Rd 92630. I-5 exit 92B (Bake Pkwy) northbound; exit 92 (Bake Pkwy/Lake Forest Dr) southbound, 4.7 mi e on Bake Pkwy, just n on Rancho Pkwy S, then just w. Int corridors. **Pets:** Large, other species. $75 one-time fee/pet. Service with restrictions, supervision. 🛜 ⊟M ⊟ 💻 ⇌ ⊠

LAKE TAHOE AREA

OLYMPIC VALLEY

▼▼▼▼ PlumpJack Squaw Valley Inn H ❀
(530) 583-1576. **Call for rates.** 1920 Squaw Valley Rd 96146. I-80 exit SR 89, 8.3 mi s, then 2.2 mi sw. Int corridors. **Pets:** Dogs only. $150 one-time fee/pet. Service with restrictions.
🛜 ⊠ ⊟M ⊟ 💻 🍴 ⇌ ⊠ ⊠

SOUTH LAKE TAHOE

▼▼▼ Alpenrose Inn M ❀
(530) 544-2985. **$69-$199, 7 day notice.** 4074 Pine Blvd 96150. Just s of casino area to Stateline Ave, 0.3 mi w to Pine Blvd, then just s. Ext corridors. **Pets:** $50 deposit/pet, $15 daily fee/pet. Designated rooms, service with restrictions, crate. 🛜 ⊠ ⊟ 💻

AAA ▼▼▼ BEST WESTERN PLUS Timber Cove Lodge H
(530) 541-6722. **$139-$269.** 3411 Lake Tahoe Blvd 96150. 1.8 mi s of casino area on US 50. Ext corridors. **Pets:** Accepted.
SAVE 🛜 ⊠ ⊟M ⊟ 💻 ⇌ ⊠

▼▼▼ Big Pines Mountain House of Tahoe M
(530) 541-5155. **$55-$65.** 4083 Cedar Ave 96150. Just s of casino area to Stateline Ave, just w, then just s. Ext corridors. **Pets:** $15 daily fee/pet. Service with restrictions, supervision. 🛜 ⊠ ⊟M ⊟ 💻 ⇌

AAA ▼▼ Capri Motel M
(530) 544-3665. **$40-$300, 3 day notice.** 932 Stateline Ave 96150. Just s of casino area to Stateline Ave, then just w. Ext corridors. **Pets:** Designated rooms, service with restrictions, supervision.
SAVE 🛜 ⊟ 💻 ⇌ ⊠

▼ Econo Lodge M
(530) 544-3959. **$55-$65.** 2659 Lake Tahoe Blvd 96150. 0.8 mi e of jct US 50 and SR 89. Ext corridors. **Pets:** Accepted. 🛜 ⊟ 💻

AAA ▼▼▼ Fireside Lodge - An All Inclusive Premier Bed & Breakfast BB ❀
(530) 544-5515. **$119-$325, 7 day notice.** 515 Emerald Bay Rd 96150. 1.3 mi n of jct US 50 and SR 89. Ext corridors. **Pets:** Other species. $25 daily fee/pet. SAVE 🛜 ⊠ ⊟ 💻 ⊠ ⊠

▼▼▼ Heavenly Valley Lodge BB ❀
(530) 564-1500. **$125-$290.** 1261 Ski Run Blvd 96150. US 50 exit Ski Run Blvd, then 0.5 mi se; jct Pioneer Tr. Ext corridors. **Pets:** Dogs only. $25 daily fee/pet. Designated rooms, service with restrictions, crate.
🛜 ⊠ ⊟ 💻 ⊠ ⊠

▼▼▼ Highland Inn M
(530) 544-3862. **$69-$299, 3 day notice.** 3979 Lake Tahoe Blvd 96150. 0.4 mi sw of casino area; near Heavenly Village. Ext corridors. **Pets:** Dogs only. $20 daily fee/pet. Designated rooms, service with restrictions, supervision. 🛜 ⊠ ⊟

▼ Howard Johnson Inn M
(530) 541-4000. **$49-$229.** 3489 Lake Tahoe Blvd 96150. 1.5 mi s of casino area. Ext corridors. **Pets:** Accepted. 🛜 ⊟ 💻 ⇌

AAA ▼▼▼▼ Inn By The Lake H ❀
(530) 542-0330. **$130-$680, 3 day notice.** 3300 Lake Tahoe Blvd 96150. 2.2 mi sw of casino area on US 50. Int corridors. **Pets:** Medium, dogs only. $25 daily fee/pet. Designated rooms, service with restrictions, supervision. SAVE 🛜 ⊠ ⊟M ⊟ 💻 🍴 ⇌ ⊠

▼▼ Lake Tahoe Ambassador Lodge M
(530) 544-6461. **$95-$145, 3 day notice.** 4130 Manzanita Ave 96150. Just s of casino area, just w on Stateline Ave to Manzanita Ave, then just s. Ext corridors. **Pets:** Other species. $10 daily fee/room. Service with restrictions, crate. 🛜 ✕ 🛏 💻 🏊 ⚿

▼▼ Park Tahoe Inn M
(530) 544-6000. **Call for rates.** 4011 Lake Tahoe Blvd 96150. 0.4 mi sw of casino area; at Park Ave and Lake Tahoe Blvd (US 50); across from Heavenly Village. Ext corridors. **Pets:** Accepted.
🛜 ✕ 🛏 💻 🏊

◀◀▷ ▼▼▼ Rodeway Inn Casino Center M ❀
(530) 541-7150. **$49-$249, 3 day notice.** 4127 Pine Blvd 96150. 0.3 mi w on Stateline Ave, just s on Pine Blvd. Ext/int corridors. **Pets:** $15 one-time fee/pet. Designated rooms, supervision.
[SAVE] 🛜 ✕ 🛏 💻 🏊

◀◀▷ ▼▼▼ Tahoe Chalet Inn-The Theme Inn M
(530) 544-3311. **Call for rates.** 3860 Lake Tahoe Blvd 96150. 0.7 mi s of casino area on US 50. Ext corridors. **Pets:** Accepted.
[SAVE] 🛜 ✕ 🛏 💻 🏊

◀◀▷ ▼▼▼ Tahoe Keys Resort CO ❀
(530) 544-5397. **$112-$1700.** 599 Tahoe Keys Blvd 96150. 0.5 mi e of jct US 50 and SR 89, 1 mi n. Ext corridors. **Pets:** Dogs only. $25 one-time fee/pet. Designated rooms, service with restrictions, crate.
[SAVE] 🛜 🛏 💻 🏊 ✕ ⚿

◀◀▷ ▼▼▼ Tahoe Valley Lodge & Spa M
(530) 541-0353. **$125-$495, 7 day notice.** 2241 Lake Tahoe Blvd 96150. 0.5 mi e of jct US 50 and SR 89. Ext corridors. **Pets:** Very small, dogs only. $15 daily fee/pet. Designated rooms, service with restrictions, supervision. [SAVE] 🛜 ✕ 🛏 💻 🏊

TAHOE CITY

▼▼ Mother Nature's Inn M ❀
(530) 581-4278. **$65-$149, 7 day notice.** 551 N Lake Blvd 96145. SR 28 (N Lake Blvd), 0.5 mi e of jct SR 89; behind Mother Nature's Store. Int corridors. **Pets:** Other species. $15 daily fee/pet. Service with restrictions. 🛜 ✕ 🛏 💻

▼▼ River Ranch Lodge M
(530) 583-4264. **Call for rates.** 2285 River Rd 96145. I-80 exit SR 89, 11 mi s; 3.5 mi n from city center. Ext/int corridors. **Pets:** Dogs only. $15 daily fee/pet. Designated rooms, service with restrictions, supervision.
🛜 ✕ 🛗 🍴 ⚿

TAHOE VISTA

▼▼ Cedar Glen Lodge M
(530) 546-4281. **$99-$216, 10 day notice.** 6589 N Lake Blvd 96148. SR 28, 1.5 mi w of SR 267. Ext corridors. **Pets:** Accepted.
🛜 ✕ 🛗 🛏 💻 🏊 ✕ ⚿

▼▼ Holiday House M ❀
(530) 546-2369. **$125-$225.** 7276 N Lake Blvd 96148. SR 28, 1 mi w of SR 267. Ext corridors. **Pets:** Other species. $30 one-time fee/pet. Supervision. 🛜 ✕ 🛗 🛏 💻 ⚿

TRUCKEE

▼▼▼▼ The Cedar House Sport Hotel H ❀
(530) 582-5655. **$170-$390, 3 day notice.** 10918 Brockway Rd 96161. I-80 exit 188 (SR 267) westbound; exit 188B (SR 267) eastbound, 1.5 mi s, then 0.8 mi nw. Int corridors. **Pets:** Large, dogs only. $100 one-time fee/pet. Designated rooms, service with restrictions, supervision.
🛜 ✕ 🛏 💻 🍴

◀◀▷ ▼▼▼▼ Larkspur Hotel Truckee-Tahoe H ❀
(530) 587-4525. **$136-$212.** 11331 Brockway Rd 96161. I-80 exit 188 (SR 267) westbound; exit 188B (SR 267) eastbound, 1.5 mi se, then just w. Int corridors. **Pets:** Dogs only. $35 daily fee/pet. Service with restrictions, crate. [SAVE] 🛜 ✕ 🛗 💻 🍴 🏊 ✕

◀◀▷ ▼▼▼▼ The Ritz-Carlton, Lake Tahoe H ❀
(530) 562-3000. **$249-$899, 7 day notice.** 13031 Ritz-Carlton Highlands Ct 96161. I-80 exit 188 (SR 267) westbound; exit 188B (SR 267) eastbound, 6.5 mi se, then 2.8 mi w. Int corridors. **Pets:** $125 one-time fee/room. Designated rooms, service with restrictions, supervision.
[ECO] [SAVE] 🛜 ✕ 🛗 💻 🍴 🏊 ✕

END AREA

LANCASTER

◀◀▷ ▼▼▼ Comfort Inn & Suites H ❀
(661) 723-2001. **$96-$125.** 1825 W Ave J-12 93534. SR 14 exit 43 (Ave J) northbound; exit 20th St southbound, just s, then just e. Int corridors. **Pets:** Medium, other species. $200 deposit/pet, $25 daily fee/pet. Service with restrictions, supervision. [SAVE] 🛜 🛗 🛏 💻 🏊 ✕

◀◀▷ ▼▼▼ Holiday Inn Express H
(661) 951-8848. **$99-$149.** 43719 17th St W 93534. SR 14 exit 42 (Ave K), just e, then just n. Int corridors. **Pets:** Dogs only. $100 deposit/pet, $10 daily fee/pet. Designated rooms, service with restrictions, supervision.
[SAVE] 🛜 🛗 🛏 💻 🏊

▼▼▼▼ Homewood Suites Lancaster H ❀
(661) 723-8040. **$139-$159.** 2320 W Double Play Way 93536. SR 14 exit 44 (Ave I), just w, s on Valley Central Way, then just e. Int corridors. **Pets:** Medium. $200 one-time fee/room. Service with restrictions, crate. 🛜 🛗 🛏 💻 🏊 ✕

◀◀▷ ▼▼▼ Inn of Lancaster M ❀
(661) 945-8771. **$69-$89.** 44131 Sierra Hwy 93534. SR 14 exit 42 (Ave K), 2 mi e, then just n. Ext corridors. **Pets:** Medium. $35 deposit/room. Service with restrictions, crate. [SAVE] 🛜 🛏 💻 🏊 ✕

◀◀▷ ▼▼▼▼ Oxford Inn & Suites M
(661) 949-3423. **$79-$139.** 1651 W Ave K 93534. SR 14 exit 42 (Ave K), just w. Int corridors. **Pets:** Accepted. [SAVE] 🛜 🛗 🛏 💻 🏊

LA PALMA

▼▼▼▼ La Quinta Inn & Suites Buena Park H
(714) 670-1400. **$83-$151.** 3 Centerpointe Dr 90623. SR 91 exit 21 (Orangethorpe Ave/Valley View St) eastbound; exit 22 (Orangethorpe Ave/Valley View St) westbound, just n. Int corridors. **Pets:** Service with restrictions, supervision. 🛜 🛏 💻 🏊

LA QUINTA

▼▼▼▼ La Quinta Resort & Club, A Waldorf Astoria Resort H
(760) 564-4111. **$109-$539.** 49-499 Eisenhower Dr 92253. I-10 exit 137 (Washington St), 4.7 mi s, then 1 mi w. Ext corridors. **Pets:** Accepted.
🛜 ✕ 🛏 💻 🍴 🏊 ✕

LATHROP

▼▼▼ Comfort Inn H
(209) 983-1177. **$90-$170.** 14730 S Harlan Rd 95330. I-5 exit Lathrop Rd, just e. Int corridors. **Pets:** Accepted. 🛜 🛗 🛏 💻 🏊 ✕

▼▼ Days Inn H
(209) 982-1959. **$55-$90.** 14750 S Harlan Rd 95330. I-5 exit Lathrop Rd, just e. Int corridors. **Pets:** Accepted. 🛜 🛗 🛏 💻 🏊

▼▼▼ Quality Inn & Suites H
(209) 858-1234. **$70-$100.** 16855 Harlan Rd 95330. I-5 exit Louise Ave, just e. Ext corridors. **Pets:** $20 daily fee/pet. Service with restrictions, supervision. 🛜 🛗 🛏 💻 🏊

LEBEC

 Holiday Inn Express Frazier Park/Lebec **H**

(661) 248-1600. **$105-$139, 3 day notice.** 612 Wainright Ct 93243. I-5 exit 205 (Frazer Mountain Rd), just n. Int corridors. **Pets:** Accepted.

Ramada Limited Grapevine **M**

(661) 248-1530. **$74-$94.** 9000 Country Side Ct 93243. I-5 exit 215 (Grapevine Rd), just w. Ext corridors. **Pets:** Medium, dogs only. $20 daily fee/pet. Designated rooms, service with restrictions, supervision.

LEE VINING

 Murphey's Motel **M**

(760) 647-6316. **$58-$128.** 51493 Hwy 395 93541. On US 395; in town. Ext corridors. **Pets:** Medium. $5 daily fee/room. Designated rooms, service with restrictions, supervision.

LINCOLN

Holiday Inn Express Hotel & Suites **H**

(916) 644-3440. **$109-$159.** 155 Ferrari Ranch Rd 95648. SR 65 exit Ferrari Ranch Rd, 0.9 mi sw, then just s on Groveland Ln. Int corridors. **Pets:** Medium. $35 daily fee/pet. Designated rooms, service with restrictions, supervision.

LINDSAY

Super 8 **M**

(559) 562-5188. **$65-$175.** 390 N Hwy 65 93247. On SR 65. Ext corridors. **Pets:** Accepted.

LIVERMORE

Holiday Inn Express Hotel & Suites-Livermore **H**

(925) 961-9600. **$99-$139.** 3000 Constitution Dr 94551. I-580 exit Airway Blvd/Collier Canyon Rd, just n. Int corridors. **Pets:** Accepted.

La Quinta Inn Livermore **H**

(925) 373-9600. **$65-$155.** 7700 Southfront Rd 94551. I-580 exit Greenville Rd, just s. Int corridors. **Pets:** Service with restrictions, supervision.

Residence Inn by Marriott **H**

(925) 373-1800. **$94-$208.** 1000 Airway Blvd 94551. I-580 exit Airway Blvd/Collier Canyon Rd, just n. Ext corridors. **Pets:** Other species. $75 one-time fee/room. Service with restrictions.

LODI

BEST WESTERN Royal Host Inn **H** ✿

(209) 369-8484. **$90-$120.** 710 S Cherokee Ln 95240. 0.8 mi s on SR 99 business route. Ext corridors. **Pets:** Medium. $20 one-time fee/room. Designated rooms, service with restrictions.

Holiday Inn Express **H**

(209) 210-0150. **$109-$199.** 1337 E Kettleman Ln 95240. SR 99 exit Kettleman Ln, 0.4 mi e. Int corridors. **Pets:** Accepted.

Microtel Inn & Suites by Wyndham **H**

(209) 367-9700. **$69-$79.** 6428 W Banner St 95242. I-5 exit SR 12, just e. Int corridors. **Pets:** Large. $10 daily fee/pet. Service with restrictions, supervision.

Motel 6 Lodi **H**

(209) 334-6422. **Call for rates.** 1140 S Cherokee Ln 95240. SR 99 exit Kettleman Ln W, just n. Ext corridors. **Pets:** Other species. Service with restrictions, supervision.

Wine & Roses Hotel Spa and Restaurant **CI**

(209) 334-6988. **$239-$495.** 2505 W Turner Rd 95242. I-5 exit Turner Rd, 5 mi e; SR 99 exit Turner Rd, 2.4 mi w. Ext corridors. **Pets:** Medium. $45 daily fee/pet. Designated rooms, service with restrictions, crate.

LOMA LINDA

Loma Linda Inn **M**

(909) 583-2500. **$75-$85, 10 day notice.** 24532 University Ave 92354. I-10 exit 74 (Tippecanoe Ave), 1 mi s, just w on Stewart St, just s on Campus, then just w. Ext corridors. **Pets:** Accepted.

LOMPOC

Comfort Inn & Suites **H**

(805) 735-8555. **$89-$149.** 1621 N H St 93436. SR 1, 1.8 mi n of Ocean Ave. Int corridors. **Pets:** Medium. $25 one-time fee/pet. Service with restrictions, supervision.

Days Inn **M**

(805) 735-7744. **$80-$140.** 1122 N H St 93436. SR 1, 1.2 mi n of Ocean Ave. Ext/int corridors. **Pets:** Medium. $25 one-time fee/room. Service with restrictions, supervision.

LONE PINE

BEST WESTERN PLUS Frontier Motel **H**

(760) 876-5571. **$95-$128.** 1008 S Main St 93545. US 395; south end of town. Ext corridors. **Pets:** Designated rooms, supervision.

Comfort Inn **H**

(760) 876-8700. **$79-$215.** 1920 S Main St 93545. US 395, 1.5 mi s of town. Int corridors. **Pets:** Medium. $20 daily fee/pet. Designated rooms, service with restrictions, supervision.

Dow Villa Motel **M**

(760) 876-5521. **$80-$165.** 310 S Main St 93545. US 395; center of town. **Pets:** Medium, other species. $100 deposit/room. Designated rooms, service with restrictions, supervision.

Timberline Motel **M**

(760) 876-4555. **$45-$99, 3 day notice.** 215 E Post St 93545. US 395, just e. Ext corridors. **Pets:** Small, dogs only. $10 daily fee/pet. Designated rooms, service with restrictions, crate.

LOS ALAMITOS

Residence Inn by Marriott-Cypress/Los Alamitos **H**

(714) 484-5700. **$118-$239.** 4931 Katella Ave 90720. I-605 exit 1D (Katella Ave) southbound; exit 1B (Katella Ave/Willow St) northbound, 1.9 mi e. Int corridors. **Pets:** Medium, other species. $100 one-time fee/room. Service with restrictions, crate.

LOS ALTOS

Residence Inn by Marriott-Palo Alto/Los Altos **H**

(650) 559-7890. **$149-$289.** 4460 El Camino Real 94022. US 101 exit San Antonio Rd, 2 mi w to SR 82, then just n. Int corridors. **Pets:** Accepted.

LOS ANGELES METROPOLITAN AREA

ALHAMBRA

AAA ▼▼▼ Super 8 Los Angeles/Alhambra

(323) 225-2310. **$65-$130.** 5350 S Huntington Dr 90032. I-10 exit 22 (Fremont Ave), 2.5 mi n, then 0.5 mi w. Ext corridors. **Pets:** $20 deposit/ pet. Designated rooms, service with restrictions.

SAVE 🛜 🗟M 🛏 🖵

ARCADIA

▼▼ Extended StayAmerica-Los Angeles-Arcadia 🅷

(626) 446-6422. **$89-$149.** 401 E Santa Clara St 91006. I-210 exit 33 (Huntington Dr), just w to 5th Ave, just n, then just w. Int corridors. **Pets:** $25 daily fee/pet. Designated rooms, service with restrictions.

🛜 🗟M 🛏 🖵

▼▼▼ Residence Inn by Marriott 🅷

(626) 446-6500. **$139-$219.** 321 E Huntington Dr 91006. I-210 exit 33 (Huntington Dr), 0.5 mi w, then just n on Gateway Dr. Ext corridors. **Pets:** Medium, other species. $100 one-time fee/room. Service with restrictions, crate. ECO 🛜 ☒ 🗟M 🛏 🖵 ⊅ ☒

BEVERLY HILLS

▼▼▼ Avalon Hotel 🅷

(310) 277-5221. **$250-$370.** 9400 W Olympic Blvd 90212. I-10 exit 6 (Robertson Blvd), 1.7 mi n, then 0.8 mi w. Ext/int corridors. **Pets:** Medium, dogs only. $100 one-time fee/pet. Designated rooms, service with restrictions, supervision. ECO 🛜 🛏 🖵 ⊅⊅

▼▼◆▼▼ The Beverly Hills Hotel and Bungalows 🅷

(310) 276-2251. **$510-$710.** 9641 Sunset Blvd 90210. I-405 exit 57 (Sunset Blvd), 3.7 mi e. Ext/int corridors. **Pets:** Accepted.

🛜 ☒ 🗟M 🛏 🖵 🍴 ⊅ ☒

▼▼◆▼▼ The Beverly Hilton 🅷

(310) 274-7777. **$229-$379.** 9876 Wilshire Blvd 90210. I-405 exit 55 (Wilshire Blvd), 2.2 mi e. Int corridors. **Pets:** Accepted.

ECO 🛜 ☒ 🛏 🖵 🍴 ⊅ ☒

AAA ▼▼◆▼▼ Beverly Wilshire A Four Seasons Hotel 🅷 ✿

(310) 275-5200. **$545-$1625.** 9500 Wilshire Blvd 90212. I-405 exit 55 (Wilshire Blvd), 4.5 mi e. Int corridors. **Pets:** Small, dogs only. Service with restrictions, supervision.

SAVE 🛜 ☒ 🛏 🖵 🍴 ⊅ ☒

AAA ▼▼◆▼▼ L'Ermitage Beverly Hills 🅷 ✿

(310) 278-3344. **$385-$1700.** 9291 Burton Way 90210. I-10 exit 6 (Robertson Blvd), 3.1 mi n, then just w. Int corridors. **Pets:** Medium. $35 daily fee/pet. Service with restrictions, crate.

SAVE 🛜 ☒ 🗟M 🛏 🖵 🍴 ⊅ ☒

AAA ▼▼◆▼▼ Montage Beverly Hills 🅷

(310) 860-7800. **$495-$700.** 225 N Canon Dr 90210. I-405 exit 55A (Santa Monica Blvd), 3.4 mi e, then 0.4 mi s. Int corridors. **Pets:** Accepted. ECO SAVE 🛜 ☒ 🗟M 🛏 🖵 🍴 ⊅ ☒

AAA ▼▼◆▼▼ The Peninsula Beverly Hills 🅷 ✿

(310) 551-2888. **$515-$8000.** 9882 S Santa Monica Blvd 90212. I-405 exit 55A (Santa Monica Blvd), 2.2 mi e, at Wilshire Blvd. Int corridors. **Pets:** Other species. $35 daily fee/pet.

SAVE 🛜 ☒ 🗟M 🛏 🖵 🍴 ⊅ ☒

AAA ▼▼◆▼▼ SLS Hotel at Beverly Hills 🅷

(310) 247-0400. **$599-$7000.** 465 S La Cienega Blvd 90048. I-10 exit 7A (La Cienega Blvd), 2.5 mi n. Int corridors. **Pets:** Accepted.

🛏 SAVE 🛜 ☒ 🗟M 🛏 🖵 🍴 ⊅ ☒

BURBANK

▼▼▼ Holiday Inn-Burbank 🅷

(818) 841-4770. **Call for rates.** 150 E Angeleno Ave 91502. I-5 exit 146A (Olive Ave) northbound; exit 146A (Verdugo Ave) southbound, just e. Int corridors. **Pets:** Accepted. 🛜 🗟M 🛏 🖵 🍴 ⊅ ☒

AAA ▼▼▼ ▼▼ Hotel Amarano Burbank 🅷

(818) 842-8887. **$159-$585.** 322 N Pass Ave 91505. SR 134 exit 2 (Hollywood Way) westbound, just w on Alameda Ave, then 0.5 mi n; exit 2 (Pass Ave) eastbound, 0.5 mi n. Int corridors. **Pets:** Accepted.

SAVE 🛜 ☒ 🗟M 🛏 🖵 🍴 ⊅ ☒

AAA ▼▼▼ Los Angeles Marriott Burbank Airport Hotel 🅷

(818) 843-6000. **$99-$229.** 2500 Hollywood Way 91505. I-5 exit 149 (Hollywood Way), 1 mi s. Int corridors. **Pets:** Small, dogs only. $75 one-time fee/pet. Designated rooms, service with restrictions, supervision.

ECO SAVE 🛜 ☒ 🗟M 🛏 🖵 🍴 ⊅

▼▼▼ Residence Inn by Marriott Burbank Downtown 🅷

(818) 260-8787. **$118-$135.** 321 S 1st St 91502. I-5 exit 146A (Olive Ave) northbound, just e on Angeleno Ave, then just s; exit 146A (Verdugo Ave) southbound, just s on Front St, just e on Verdugo Ave, then just n. Int corridors. **Pets:** Accepted. 🛜 ☒ 🛏 🖵 ⊅

CALABASAS

AAA ▼▼▼ The Anza - A Calabasas Hotel 🅷

(818) 222-5300. **$109-$189.** 23627 Calabasas Rd 91302. US 101 exit 29 (Valley Cir/Mulholland Dr), just w, then 0.6 mi n. Int corridors. **Pets:** Medium, dogs only. $75 deposit/room, $20 daily fee/room. Designated rooms, service with restrictions, supervision.

SAVE 🛜 ☒ 🛏 🖵 ⊅

CARSON

▼▼ Extended StayAmerica-Los Angeles/Carson 🅷

(310) 323-2080. **$64-$94.** 401 E Albertoni St 90746. SR 91 exit 7B (Avalon Blvd), just s, then just w. Int corridors. **Pets:** $25 daily fee/pet. Designated rooms, service with restrictions. 🛜 🗟M 🛏 🖵

CERRITOS

AAA ▼▼▼ Sheraton Cerritos Hotel at Towne Center 🅷 ✿

(562) 809-1500. **$99-$219, 7 day notice.** 12725 Center Court Dr 90703. SR 91 exit 19B (Artesia/Bloomfield Dr), just s to Town Center Dr, just e, then just s. Int corridors. **Pets:** Medium, dogs only. $25 one-time fee/ room. Service with restrictions, supervision. SAVE 🛜 ☒ 🖵 🖵 ⊅

CHATSWORTH

AAA ▼▼ Ramada 🅷

(818) 998-5289. **$94-$109.** 21340 Devonshire St 91311. SR 118 exit 35 (De Soto Ave), 1.5 mi s, then 0.5 mi w. Int corridors. **Pets:** Small. $75 deposit/room, $10 daily fee/pet. Designated rooms, supervision.

SAVE 🛜 🛏 🖵 ⊅

▼▼ Staybridge Suites 🅷

(818) 773-0707. **$155-$166.** 21902 Lassen St 91311. SR 118 exit 34 (Topanga Canyon Blvd), 2 mi s, then just e. Ext/int corridors. **Pets:** Accepted. 🛜 ☒ 🗟M 🛏 🖵 ⊅

CLAREMONT

▼▼▼ Hotel Casa 425 🅷

(909) 624-2272. **$195-$400, 3 day notice.** 425 W First St 91711. I-10 exit 47 (Indian Hill Blvd N), 1.2 mi n, then just w. Ext corridors. **Pets:** Dogs only. $65 one-time fee/room. Designated rooms, service with restrictions, supervision. 🛜 ☒ 🗟M 🛏 🖵

▼▼ ▼▼ Hotel Claremont & Tennis Club M

(909) 621-4831. **$59-$69.** 840 S Indian Hill Blvd 91711. I-10 exit 47 (Indian Hill Blvd), just s; enter on Auto Center Dr. Ext corridors. **Pets:** Other species. Service with restrictions, crate.

🛰 ⬛ℳ 🖥 🖳 🗷 ⌦

COMMERCE

▼▼▼ DoubleTree by Hilton Hotel Los Angeles - Commerce H

(323) 887-8100. **$109-$249.** 5757 Telegraph Rd 90040. I-5 exit 128B (Washington Blvd), just e, then just s. Int corridors. **Pets:** Accepted.

🛰 ⬛ℳ 🖥 🖳 🍴 ⌦

COVINA

▼▼ ▼▼ Park Inn by Radisson Covina H

(626) 915-3441. **Call for rates.** 1211 E Garvey St 91724. I-10 exit 38B (Holt Ave), just n, then just w. Ext corridors. **Pets:** Accepted.

ⒺⒸⓄ 🛰 ⬛ℳ 🖥 🖳 🍴 ⌦

CULVER CITY

ⒶⒶⒶ ▼▼▼ ▼▼ Four Points by Sheraton LA Westside H ❀

(310) 641-7740. **$99-$229.** 5990 Green Valley Cir 90230. I-405 exit 49 (Slauson Ave/Sepulveda Blvd), just ne to Green Valley Cir. Int corridors. **Pets:** Medium. $25 daily fee/room. Designated rooms, service with restrictions, supervision. ⓈⒶⓋⒺ 🛰 🗷 ⬛ℳ 🖥 🖳 🍴 ⌦

DIAMOND BAR

▼▼▼ Ayres Suites Diamond Bar H

(909) 860-6290. **$99-$159.** 21951 Golden Springs Dr 91765. SR 57/60 exit 24B (Grand Ave), just s, then 0.5 mi w. Int corridors. **Pets:** Accepted.

🛰 🗷 🖥 🖳 ⌦ 🗷

DOWNEY

▼▼▼ Embassy Suites Hotel H ❀

(562) 861-1900. **$135-$209.** 8425 Firestone Blvd 90241. I-605 exit 10 (Firestone Blvd), 2 mi w. Int corridors. **Pets:** Large, other species. $25 daily fee/room. Designated rooms, service with restrictions, supervision.

🛰 ⬛ℳ 🖥 🖳 🍴 ⌦

EL MONTE

▼▼ ▼▼ Americas Best Value Inn & Suites M

(626) 442-8354. **$77-$98.** 12040 Garvey Ave 91732. I-10 exit 30 (Garvey Ave) westbound, just w; exit 29A (Peck Rd) eastbound, just s to Garvey Ave, then 0.6 mi e. Ext corridors. **Pets:** Medium. $15 daily fee/pet. Designated rooms, service with restrictions, supervision. 🛰 🖥 🖳 ⌦

EL SEGUNDO

▼▼ ▼▼ Embassy Suites-LAX South H

(310) 640-3600. **$109-$249.** 1440 E Imperial Ave 90245. I-405 exit 45B (Imperial Hwy), 1.6 mi w. Int corridors. **Pets:** Medium. $35 daily fee/pet. Designated rooms, service with restrictions, supervision.

⬛⬛ 🛰 ⬛ℳ 🖥 🖳 🍴 ⌦

▼▼ ▼▼ Extended StayAmerica-Los Angeles-LAX Airport-El Segundo M

(310) 607-4000. **$84-$119.** 1910 E Mariposa Ave 90245. I-105 exit 1B (Sepulveda Blvd), 1 mi s. Ext corridors. **Pets:** $25 daily fee/pet. Designated rooms, service with restrictions. 🛰 ⬛ℳ 🖥 🖳

ⒶⒶⒶ ▼▼▼ ▼▼ Hyatt house Los Angeles LAX/El Segundo H

(310) 725-0100. **$139-$199.** 810 S Douglas St 90245. I-405 exit 43 (Rosecrans Ave), 0.5 mi e, then just n. Ext corridors. **Pets:** Accepted.

ⓈⒶⓋⒺ 🛰 🗷 ⬛ℳ 🖥 🖳 ⌦ 🗷

▼▼▼ ▼▼ Residence Inn by Marriott-LAX/El Segundo H

(310) 333-0888. **$159-$229.** 2135 E El Segundo Blvd 90245. I-405 exit 44 (El Segundo Blvd), 1.4 mi w. Int corridors. **Pets:** Accepted.

🛰 🗷 ⬛ℳ 🖥 🖳 ⌦ 🗷

GLENDALE

ⒶⒶⒶ ▼▼▼ ▼▼ Hilton Los Angeles North/Glendale & Executive Meeting Center H

(818) 956-5466. **$139-$229.** 100 W Glenoaks Blvd 91202. SR 134 exit 7B (Brand Blvd), just n, then just w. Int corridors. **Pets:** Accepted.

ⒺⒸⓄ ⓈⒶⓋⒺ 🛰 ⬛ℳ 🖥 🖳 🍴 ⌦

▼▼ ▼▼ Los Angeles Days Inn-Glendale H

(818) 956-0202. **$94-$169.** 450 W Pioneer Dr 91203. SR 134 exit 7A (Pacific Ave), just s, then just e. Int corridors. **Pets:** Medium. $50 deposit/room. Designated rooms, service with restrictions, supervision.

🛰 🖥 🖳 🍴 ⌦

▼▼ ▼▼ Vagabond Inn Glendale M

(818) 240-1700. **Call for rates.** 120 W Colorado St 91204. SR 134 exit 7B (Brand Blvd), 1 mi s, then just w. Ext corridors. **Pets:** Accepted.

🛰 🗷 🖥 🖳 ⌦

HACIENDA HEIGHTS

▼▼ ▼▼ Vagabond Inn M

(626) 820-6888. **Call for rates.** 1239 S Hacienda Blvd 91745. SR 60 exit 16 (Hacienda Blvd), just n. Ext corridors. **Pets:** Accepted. 🛰 🖥

HAWTHORNE

▼▼▼ Candlewood Suites LAX Hawthorne H

(310) 973-3331. **$99-$129.** 11410 Hawthorne Blvd 90250. I-105 exit 3 (Hawthorne Blvd/Prairie Ave), 0.6 mi s. Int corridors. **Pets:** Small, other species. $75 one-time fee/pet. Designated rooms, service with restrictions, crate. 🛰 🗷 🖥 🖳 ⌦

▼▼ ▼▼ TownePlace Suites by Marriott M

(310) 725-9696. **$159-$179.** 14400 Aviation Blvd 90250. I-405 exit 43 (Rosecrans Ave), 0.4 mi w. Int corridors. **Pets:** Large. $100 one-time fee/room. Service with restrictions. ⒺⒸⓄ 🛰 🗷 🖥 🖳 ⌦

HERMOSA BEACH

▼▼▼ Quality Inn & Suites H

(310) 374-2666. **$89-$159.** 901 Aviation Blvd 90254. SR 1 (Pacific Coast Hwy), just e. Ext/int corridors. **Pets:** $20 daily fee/room. Designated rooms, service with restrictions, supervision. 🛰 🗷 🖥 🖳

HOLLYWOOD

▼▼ ▼▼ Hilton Garden Inn Los Angeles/Hollywood H

(323) 876-8600. **$129-$369.** 2005 N Highland Ave 90068. US 101 exit Highland Ave, just s. Int corridors. **Pets:** Accepted.

🛰 🗷 ⬛ℳ 🖥 🖳 🍴 ⌦

ⒶⒶⒶ ▼▼▼ ▼▼ Hollywood Hotel H

(323) 315-1800. **$99-$249.** 1160 N Vermont Ave 90029. US 101 exit 6A (Vermont Ave), 0.5 mi n. Int corridors. **Pets:** Medium. $35 daily fee/pet. Service with restrictions, supervision.

⬛⬛ ⓈⒶⓋⒺ 🛰 🗷 ⬛ℳ 🖥 🖳 ⌦

ⒶⒶⒶ ▼▼ ▼▼ Motel 6 Los Angeles - Hollywood #4044 M

(323) 464-6006. **$75-$150.** 1738 N Whitley Ave 90028. US 101 exit 9C southbound, just s, just w, then just s. Int corridors. **Pets:** Other species. Service with restrictions, supervision. ⓈⒶⓋⒺ 🛰 🗷 🖥

ⒶⒶⒶ ▼▼▼ ▼▼ W Hollywood H ❀

(323) 798-1300. **$639-$10000.** 6250 Hollywood Blvd 90028. US 101 exit 8B (Hollywood Blvd), 0.5 mi w. Int corridors. **Pets:** Large, dogs only. $100 one-time fee/room, $25 daily fee/pet. Service with restrictions, supervision.

ⒺⒸⓄ ⓈⒶⓋⒺ 🛰 🗷 ⬛ℳ 🖥 🖳 🍴 ⌦

INDUSTRY

▼▼▼ ▼▼ Pacific Palms Resort H

(626) 810-4455. **Call for rates.** One Industry Hills Pkwy 91744. SR 60 exit 18 (Azusa Ave), 1.3 mi n, 0.5 mi w. Int corridors. **Pets:** Dogs only. $35 daily fee/pet. Service with restrictions, supervision.

🛰 ⬛ℳ 🖳 🍴 ⌦ 🗷

LA MIRADA

▼▼▼ Residence Inn by Marriott 🅷

(714) 523-2800. **$129-$219.** 14419 Firestone Blvd 90638. I-5 exit 118 (Valley View Ave), just n, then 0.5 mi e. Ext corridors. **Pets:** Accepted.

🛜 ✕ 🕭M 🛏 🖵 🐾 🖾

LONG BEACH

▼▼ Extended StayAmerica-Los Angeles-Long Beach Airport 🅷

(562) 989-4601. **$69-$99.** 4105 E Willow St 90815. I-405 exit 27 (Lakewood Blvd), 0.3 mi sw. Int corridors. **Pets:** $25 daily fee/pet. Designated rooms, service with restrictions. 🛜 🕭M 🛏 🖵

▼▼▼ Hilton Long Beach 🅷

(562) 983-3400. **$99-$329.** 701 W Ocean Blvd 90831. I-710 exit Downtown/Broadway, just e to Daisy Ave, just s to Ocean Blvd, then just w. Int corridors. **Pets:** Accepted.

🌲 🔌 🛜 ✕ 🕭M 🛏 🖵 🍽 🐾

▼▼▼ Hotel Current 🅼 🐾

(562) 597-1341. **$119-$199.** 5325 E Pacific Coast Hwy 90804. I-405 exit 23 (SR 22/Long Beach) northbound, 2 mi nw; exit 27 (Lakewood Blvd) southbound, 2 mi se on SR 1. Ext corridors. **Pets:** $50 one-time fee/pet. Designated rooms, service with restrictions, crate.

🌲 🛜 ✕ 🛏 🖵 🐾

▼▼▼▼ Hotel Maya - a DoubleTree by Hilton 🅷

(562) 435-7676. **$139-$299.** 700 Queensway Dr 90802. I-710 exit 1A (Harbor Scenic Dr/Queen Mary), 1.3 mi s, then just e. Ext corridors. **Pets:** Accepted. 🛜 ✕ 🛏 🖵 🍽 🐾 🖾

▼▼▼ Renaissance Long Beach Hotel 🅷

(562) 437-5900. **$128-$229.** 111 E Ocean Blvd 90802. I-710 exit Downtown/Broadway, 0.8 mi e to Long Beach Blvd, just s, then just w. Int corridors. **Pets:** Accepted.

🌲 🛜 ✕ 🕭M 🛏 🖵 🍽 🐾 🖾

▼▼▼ Residence Inn by Marriott Long Beach 🅷

(562) 595-0909. **$142-$219.** 4111 E Willow St 90815. I-405 exit 27 (Lakewood Blvd), just s, then just w. Ext corridors. **Pets:** Accepted.

🌲 🛜 ✕ 🕭M 🛏 🖵 🐾 🖾

▼▼▼ Residence Inn by Marriott Long Beach Downtown South Waterfront 🅷 🐾

(562) 495-0700. **$132-$259.** 600 Queensway Dr 90802. I-710 exit 1A (Harbor Scenic Dr/Queen Mary), 1.3 mi s, then just w. Int corridors. **Pets:** Large, other species. $100 one-time fee/room. Service with restrictions. 🛜 ✕ 🛏 🖵 🐾

LOS ANGELES

𝔸𝔸𝔸 ▼▼▼ BEST WESTERN PLUS Dragon Gate Inn 🅷 🐾

(213) 617-3077. **$119-$199.** 818 N Hill St 90012. US 101 exit 2C (Broadway), 0.6 mi n to Alpine St, just e, then just n. Ext corridors. **Pets:** Medium, other species. $20 daily fee/pet. Designated rooms, service with restrictions, supervision. 🆂🅰🆅🅴 🛜 ✕ 🛏 🖵

𝔸𝔸𝔸 ▼▼ Beverly Laurel Motor Hotel 🅼

(323) 651-2441. **$114-$155.** 8018 Beverly Blvd 90048. I-10 exit 7B (Fairfax Ave), 2.8 mi n, then just w. Ext corridors. **Pets:** Small. $50 daily fee/pet. Designated rooms, service with restrictions, supervision.

🆂🅰🆅🅴 🛜 🛏 🍽 🐾

▼▼ Extended StayAmerica-Los Angeles/LAX Airport 🅷

(310) 568-9337. **$99-$129.** 6531 S Sepulveda Blvd 90045. I-405 exit 49 (Howard Hughes Pkwy), 0.9 mi w, then just n. Int corridors. **Pets:** $25 daily fee/pet. Designated rooms, service with restrictions.

🛜 🕭M 🛏 🖵

𝔸𝔸𝔸 ▼▼▼ Four Points by Sheraton LAX 🅷 🐾

(310) 645-4600. **$99-$299.** 9750 Airport Blvd 90045. I-405 exit 46 (Century Blvd), 1.5 mi w, then just n. Int corridors. **Pets:** Medium, dogs only. $25 daily fee/room. Designated rooms, service with restrictions, supervision. 🆂🅰🆅🅴 🛜 ✕ 🛏 🖵 🍽 🐾

▼▼▼ ▼▼▼ Four Seasons Hotel Los Angeles at Beverly Hills 🅷 🐾

(310) 273-2222. **$505-$10500.** 300 S Doheny Dr 90048. I-10 exit 6 (Robertson Blvd), 3 mi n to Burton Way, then just w. Int corridors. **Pets:** Very small. Service with restrictions.

🛜 ✕ 🕭M 🛏 🖵 🍽 🐾 🖾

𝔸𝔸𝔸 ▼▼▼▼ Hilton Checkers Los Angeles 🅷 🐾

(213) 624-0000. **$169-$289.** 535 S Grand Ave 90071. SR 110 exit 6th St, just w to Olive St, just n to 5th St, then just s. Int corridors. **Pets:** Medium, dogs only. $50 one-time fee/pet. Service with restrictions, crate. 🆂🅰🆅🅴 🛜 ✕ 🛏 🖵

▼▼▼ Hilton Los Angeles Airport 🅷

(310) 410-4000. **$99-$239.** 5711 W Century Blvd 90045. I-405 exit 46 (Century Blvd), 0.8 mi w. Int corridors. **Pets:** $50 one-time fee/room. Designated rooms, service with restrictions, crate.

🌲 🔌 🛜 🛏 🖵 🍽 🐾

𝔸𝔸𝔸 ▼▼▼▼ Hotel Bel-Air 🅷 🐾

(310) 472-1211. **$530-$760.** 701 Stone Canyon Rd 90077. I-405 exit 57 (Sunset Blvd), 1.7 mi e, then 0.7 mi n. Ext corridors. **Pets:** Medium. $200 one-time fee/room. 🆂🅰🆅🅴 🛜 ✕ 🛏 🖵 🍽 🐾 🖾

𝔸𝔸𝔸 ▼▼▼▼ Hotel Palomar LA Westwood 🅷

(310) 475-8711. **Call for rates.** 10740 Wilshire Blvd 90024. I-405 exit 55B (Wilshire Blvd), 1 mi w; in Westwood. Int corridors. **Pets:** Accepted.

🌲 🔌 🆂🅰🆅🅴 🛜 ✕ 🛏 🖵 🍽 🐾

𝔸𝔸𝔸 ▼▼▼▼ Hyatt Regency Century Plaza 🅷 🐾

(310) 228-1234. **$162-$450.** 2025 Avenue of the Stars 90067. I-10 exit 6 (Robertson Blvd), 2.7 mi n to Olympic Blvd, 1.9 mi w, then just n. Int corridors. **Pets:** $30 daily fee/pet. Service with restrictions, supervision.

🆂🅰🆅🅴 🛜 🕭M 🛏 🖵 🍽 🐾 🖾

𝔸𝔸𝔸 ▼▼▼▼ InterContinental Los Angeles Century City 🅷

(310) 284-6500. **$229-$399.** 2151 Avenue of the Stars 90067. I-10 exit 6 (Robertson Blvd), 2.7 mi n to Olympic Blvd, 1.9 mi w, then just n. Int corridors. **Pets:** Accepted. 🆂🅰🆅🅴 🛜 ✕ 🛏 🖵 🍽 🐾 🖾

▼▼▼▼ JW Marriott Los Angeles L.A. LIVE 🅷

(213) 765-8600. **$209-$499.** 900 W Olympic Blvd 90015. I-110 exit 9th St, s on Flower St, then just w. Int corridors. **Pets:** Accepted.

🔌 🛜 ✕ 🕭M 🛏 🖵 🍽 🐾 🖾

▼▼▼ La Quinta Inn & Suites LAX 🅷

(310) 645-2200. **$78-$210.** 5249 W Century Blvd 90045. I-405 exit 46 (Century Blvd), just w. Int corridors. **Pets:** Service with restrictions, supervision. 🛜 🛏 🖵 🐾

▼▼▼ Luxe City Center Hotel 🅷

(213) 748-1291. **$189-$499.** 1020 S Figueroa St 90015. SR 110 exit Olympic southbound, just e; exit 9th St northbound, just e to Flower St, just s to 11th St, just w, then just n. Int corridors. **Pets:** Accepted.

🛜 🕭M 🛏 🖵 🍽

▼▼▼ Luxe Sunset Boulevard Hotel 🅷

(310) 476-6571. **$209-$490.** 11461 Sunset Blvd 90049. I-405 exit 57 (Sunset Blvd), just w. Int corridors. **Pets:** Accepted.

🛜 ✕ 🕭M 🖵 🍽 🐾 🖾

𝔸𝔸𝔸 ▼▼▼▼ Omni Los Angeles Hotel at California Plaza 🅷 🐾

(213) 617-3300. **Call for rates.** 251 S Olive St 90012. SR 110 exit 4th St southbound; exit 6th St northbound, just e, then just n. Int corridors. **Pets:** Small, other species. $50 one-time fee/room. Designated rooms, service with restrictions, supervision.

🆂🅰🆅🅴 🛜 ✕ 🛏 🖵 🍽 🐾

▼▼▼ The Orlando Hotel 🅷

(323) 658-6600. **$249-$1500.** 8384 W 3rd St 90048. I-10 exit 7A (La Cienega Blvd), 2.3 mi n, then just e. Int corridors. **Pets:** Small. $50 daily fee/pet. Designated rooms, service with restrictions, supervision.

🛜 ✕ 🛏 🖵 🍽 🐾 🖾

▼▼▼ **Radisson Hotel at Los Angeles Airport** H ❀
(310) 670-9000. **Call for rates.** 6225 W Century Blvd at Sepulveda Blvd 90045. I-405 exit 46 (Century Blvd), 1.6 mi w. Int corridors.
Pets: Medium. $150 deposit/room, $25 one-time fee/pet. Service with restrictions. ECO 🛜 ✕ 🗐 ⬛ 🛏 ➳

▼▼▼ **Radisson Hotel Midtown Los Angeles at USC** H
(213) 748-4141. **Call for rates.** 3540 S Figueroa St 90007. SR 110 exit Exposition Blvd, just w, then just n. Int corridors. **Pets:** Accepted.
🛜 ✕ 🔎M 🗐 ⬛ 🛏 ➳

▼▼▼ **Residence Inn by Marriott-Beverly Hills** H ❀
(310) 228-4100. **$170-$226.** 1177 S Beverly Dr 90035. I-10 exit 6 (Robertson Blvd), 1.6 mi n to Pico Blvd, then 0.6 mi w. Int corridors.
Pets: $100 one-time fee/pet, $10 daily fee/pet. Designated rooms, service with restrictions, supervision. 🛜 ✕ 🔎M 🗐 ⬛

▲▲▲ ▼▼▼▼ **Sheraton Gateway, Los Angeles** H ❀
(310) 642-1111. **$339-$409.** 6101 W Century Blvd 90045. I-405 exit 46 (Century Blvd), 1.3 mi w. Int corridors. **Pets:** Medium, dogs only. $50 one-time fee/room. Service with restrictions, supervision.
ECO SAVE 🛜 ✕ 🔎M 🗐 ⬛ 🛏 ➳

▲▲▲ ▼▼▼▼ **Sheraton Los Angeles Downtown Hotel** H
(213) 488-3500. **$139-$359, 7 day notice.** 711 S Hope St 90017. SR 110 exit 6th St southbound, just e, then just s. Int corridors.
Pets: Accepted. SAVE 🛜 ✕ 🔎M 🗐 ⬛ 🛏

▲▲▲ ▼▼▼▼ **Sofitel Los Angeles** H
(310) 278-5444. **Call for rates.** 8555 Beverly Blvd 90048. I-10 exit 7A (La Cienega Blvd), 2.5 mi n. Int corridors. **Pets:** Accepted.
ECO ⬅ SAVE 🛜 ✕ 🛏 ➳ ✕

▲▲▲ ▼▼▼ **Travelodge Hotel at Lax** H
(310) 649-4000. **$100-$229.** 5547 W Century Blvd 90045. I-405 exit 46 (Century Blvd), 0.5 mi w. Ext/int corridors. **Pets:** Other species. $20 daily fee/pet. Designated rooms, service with restrictions, crate.
SAVE 🛜 🗐 ⬛ 🛏 ➳

▲▲▲ ▼▼▼▼ **The Westin Bonaventure Hotel & Suites** H
(213) 624-1000. **$159-$2500.** 404 S Figueroa St 90071. SR 110 exit 6th St, just n, e on 4th St, then s on Flower St. Int corridors. **Pets:** Accepted.
ECO SAVE 🛜 ✕ 🔎M 🗐 ⬛ 🛏 ➳

▲▲▲ ▼▼▼▼ **The Westin Hotel-Los Angeles Airport** H
(310) 216-5858. **$124-$324.** 5400 W Century Blvd 90045. I-405 exit 46 (Century Blvd), just w. Int corridors. **Pets:** Accepted.
ECO SAVE 🛜 ✕ 🔎M ⬛ 🛏 ➳ ✕

MANHATTAN BEACH
▼▼▼ **Belamar Hotel** H
(310) 750-0300. **$179-$499.** 3501 N Sepulveda Blvd 90266. I-405 exit 43 (Rosecrans Ave), 1.5 mi w, then just s. Int corridors. **Pets:** Accepted.
ECO 🛜 ✕ 🔎M 🗐 ⬛ 🛏 ➳ ✕

▼▼▼ **Manhattan Beach Marriott** H
(310) 546-7511. **$249-$269.** 1400 Parkview Ave 90266. I-405 exit 43 (Rosecrans Ave), 1 mi w, then just s. Int corridors. **Pets:** Medium, dogs only. $200 one-time fee/pet. Designated rooms, service with restrictions, supervision. ECO 🛜 ✕ ⬛ 🛏 ➳ ✕

▼▼▼ **Residence Inn by Marriott** H
(310) 421-3100. **$149-$299.** 1700 N Sepulveda Blvd 90266. I-405 exit 43B (Rosecrans Ave), 1.5 mi w, then 1 mi s on SR 1. Ext corridors. **Pets:** $100 one-time fee/room. Service with restrictions, crate.
🛜 ✕ 🔎M 🗐 ⬛ 🛏 ✕

MARINA DEL REY
▲▲▲ ▼▼▼▼▼ **The Ritz-Carlton, Marina del Rey** H ❀
(310) 823-1700. **$299-$699.** 4375 Admiralty Way 90292. SR 90 (Marina Frwy), just s on Lincoln Blvd (SR 1), then just w on Bali Way. Int corridors. **Pets:** Small, other species. $125 one-time fee/room. Service with restrictions, supervision. SAVE 🛜 ✕ 🔎M ⬛ 🛏 ➳ ✕

MONROVIA
▼▼▼ **DoubleTree by Hilton Hotel Monrovia - Pasadena Area** H
(626) 357-1900. **$149-$249.** 924 W Huntington Dr 91016. I-210 exit 33 (Huntington Dr), just s. Int corridors. **Pets:** Accepted.
🛜 🔎M 🗐 ⬛ 🛏 ➳

▼▼▼ **Extended StayAmerica-Los Angeles-Monrovia** H
(626) 256-6999. **$89-$149.** 930 S Fifth Ave 91016. I-210 exit 33 (Huntington Dr), just w, then just n. Int corridors. **Pets:** $25 daily fee/pet. Designated rooms, service with restrictions. 🛜 🗐 ⬛

MONTEREY PARK
▼▼ **Floral Inn** H
(323) 263-9888. **$67-$76.** 1560 Monterey Pass Rd 91754. I-60 exit 20C (Cesar Chavez Ave), 1.5 mi s. Ext corridors. **Pets:** Other species. $50 deposit/room, $5 daily fee/pet. Service with restrictions, supervision.
🛜 🗐 ➳

NORTH HOLLYWOOD
▲▲▲ ▼▼▼ **Colony Inn** M
(818) 763-2787. **$80-$150.** 4917 Vineland Ave 91601. US 101 exit 12C (Vineland Ave), 1 mi n. Ext corridors. **Pets:** Medium, other species. $35 one-time fee/pet. Designated rooms, service with restrictions, supervision.
SAVE 🛜 🗐

NORTHRIDGE
▼▼ **Extended StayAmerica-Los Angeles/Northridge** H
(818) 734-1787. **$89-$139.** 19325 Londelius St 91324. SR 118 exit 37 (Tampa Ave), 3 mi s. Int corridors. **Pets:** $25 daily fee/pet. Designated rooms, service with restrictions. 🛜 🔎M 🗐 ⬛

PASADENA
▼▼▼ **Hilton Pasadena** H
(626) 577-1000. **$99-$329.** 168 S Los Robles Ave 91101. I-210 exit 26B (Lake Ave), 0.3 mi s to Colorado Blvd, then 0.4 mi w. Int corridors.
Pets: Accepted. ⬅ 🛜 ✕ 🔎M 🗐 ⬛ 🛏 ➳

▼▼▼ **Howard Johnson Pasadena** M
(626) 304-9678. **$85-$160.** 1599 E Colorado Blvd 91106. I-210 exit 27B (Allen Ave) westbound; exit 27 (Hill Ave) eastbound, 0.8 mi s. Ext corridors. **Pets:** Accepted. 🛜 ✕ 🗐 ⬛ ➳

▼▼▼ **Quality Inn Pasadena** M
(626) 796-9291. **$84-$109.** 3321 E Colorado Blvd 91107. I-210 exit 29B (Madre St), just s, then 0.3 mi w. Ext corridors. **Pets:** $20 daily fee/pet. Service with restrictions, supervision. 🛜 ✕ 🗐 ⬛ 🛏 ✕

▲▲▲ ▼▼▼ **Saga Motor Hotel** M
(626) 795-0431. **$105-$115.** 1633 E Colorado Blvd 91106. I-210 exit 27 (Hill Ave), just s, then just e. Ext/int corridors. **Pets:** Small, dogs only. $35 one-time fee/room. Designated rooms, service with restrictions, supervision. SAVE 🛜 ✕ 🗐 ➳

▲▲▲ ▼▼▼ **Sheraton Pasadena Hotel** H ❀
(626) 449-4000. **$139-$379.** 303 E Cordova St 91101. I-210 exit 26B (Lake Ave), 0.7 mi s, then just w. Int corridors. **Pets:** Dogs only. $75 deposit/pet. Designated rooms, service with restrictions, supervision.
ECO SAVE 🛜 ✕ 🔎M 🗐 ⬛ 🛏 ➳

▲▲▲ ▼▼▼ **Super 8** M
(626) 449-3020. **$69-$220.** 2863 E Colorado Blvd 91107. I-210 exit 29A (San Gabriel Blvd), 0.3 mi s, then just e. Ext corridors. **Pets:** Small. $20 daily fee/pet. Designated rooms, no service, supervision.
SAVE 🛜 🗐 ⬛ ➳

▲▲▲ ▼▼▼ **Vagabond Inn Executive** M
(626) 449-3170. **$90-$500.** 1203 E Colorado Blvd 91106. I-210 exit 27A (Hill Ave), just s, then just w. Ext/int corridors. **Pets:** $25 daily fee/pet. Service with restrictions. SAVE 🛜 🔎M 🗐 ⬛ ➳

(AAA) ▼▼▼ ▼▼▼ The Westin-Pasadena ⊞
(626) 792-2727. **$149-$399.** 191 N Los Robles Ave 91101. I-210 exit Los Robles Ave, just s; in Plaza Las Fuentes. Int corridors. **Pets:** Accepted.
[SAVE] 🛜 ✕ 🛠M 🍴 🖵 🛗 ⊁ 🏊

POMONA

(AAA) ▼▼▼ Sheraton Fairplex ⊞ ❄
(909) 622-2220. **$119-$259.** 601 W McKinley Ave 91768. I-10 exit 45A (White Ave) eastbound, 0.5 mi n, then just w; exit 43 (Fairplex Dr) westbound, 1 mi n, then 0.7 mi e. Int corridors. **Pets:** Large. $200 deposit/room. Designated rooms, service with restrictions, supervision.
[SAVE] 🛜 ✕ 🛠M 🍴 🖵 🛗 ⊁ 🏊

▼▼▼ Shilo Inn Suites Hotel - Pomona Hilltop ⊞
(909) 598-7666. **Call for rates.** 3101 Temple Ave 91768. SR 57 exit 20 (Temple Ave), just w. Int corridors. **Pets:** Dogs only. $25 one-time fee/room. Designated rooms, service with restrictions, supervision.
🛜 ✕ 🍴 🖵 🛗 ⊁ 🏊

RANCHO PALOS VERDES

▼▼▼ ▼▼▼ Terranea Resort ⊞
(310) 265-2800. **$245-$4600, 7 day notice.** 100 Terranea Way 90275. I-110 exit Gaffey St, 1.5 mi s, 6.5 mi w on 25th St (which becomes Palos Verdes Dr S), then just w. Ext/int corridors. **Pets:** Accepted.
🛜 ✕ 🍴 🖵 🛗 ⊁ 🏊

REDONDO BEACH

(AAA) ▼▼▼ BEST WESTERN PLUS Sunrise Hotel at Redondo Beach Marina ⊞
(310) 376-0746. **$149-$400.** 400 N Harbor Dr 90277. I-405 exit 40A (Artesia Blvd) northbound; exit 40B (Redondo Beach Blvd) southbound, 0.5 mi w to Artesia Blvd, 1.5 mi w to Aviation Blvd, 1.2 mi sw to Pacific Coast Hwy, 1 mi s to Beryl St, then 0.4 mi w. Int corridors.
Pets: Accepted. [SAVE] 🛜 ✕ 🍴 🖵 ⊁ 🏊

(AAA) ▼▼▼ Ramada Limited ⚄
(310) 540-5998. **$64-$144.** 435 S Pacific Coast Hwy 90277. I-405 exit 38B (Western Ave) northbound; exit 40 (Artesia Blvd/Redondo Beach) southbound, 0.6 mi w on Artesia Blvd (SR 91), s on Hawthorn Blvd (SR 107), 1.7 mi s, w on Del Amo Blvd, 1.4 mi s on N Prospect Ave, 0.7 mi w on Torrance Blvd, 0.5 mi, then just s. Ext corridors. **Pets:** Very small, dogs only. $50 one-time fee/pet. Designated rooms, no service, supervision. [SAVE] 🛜 🍴 🖵

SAN GABRIEL

(AAA) ▼▼▼ ▼▼▼ Hilton Los Angeles/San Gabriel ⊞ ❄
(626) 270-2700. **$159-$229.** 225 W Valley Blvd 91776. I-10 exit 24 (New Ave), 0.6 mi n, then 0.3 mi e. Int corridors. **Pets:** Large. $50 deposit/room. Service with restrictions, supervision.
[SAVE] 🛜 🛠M 🍴 🖵 🛗 ⊁ 🏊

SAN PEDRO

(AAA) ▼▼▼ DoubleTree Hotel San Pedro-Port of Los Angeles ⊞
(310) 514-3344. **$99-$229.** 2800 Via Cabrillo Marina 90731. I-110 exit Gaffey St, 1.8 mi s, 0.5 mi e on 22nd St, then 0.4 mi s. Int corridors.
Pets: Accepted. [SAVE] 🛜 🍴 🖵 🛗 ⊁ 🏊

SANTA CLARITA

(AAA) ▼▼▼ BEST WESTERN Valencia Inn ⚄
(661) 255-0555. **$90-$250.** 27413 Wayne Mills Pl 91355. I-5 exit 170 (Magic Mountain Pkwy), just e. Ext corridors. **Pets:** Other species. $10 daily fee/pet. Designated rooms. [SAVE] 🛜 🍴 🖵 🏊

▼▼▼ Embassy Suites Valencia ⊞
(661) 257-3111. **$109-$169.** 28508 Westinghouse Pl 91355. I-5 exit 172 (SR 126/Newhall Ranch Rd), just se, just e on Vanderbilt Way, then just n. Int corridors. **Pets:** Accepted. 🛜 🍴 🖵 🛗 ⊁

▼▼ Extended StayAmerica Los Angeles-Valencia ⊞
(661) 255-1044. **$100-$110.** 24940 W Pico Canyon Rd 91381. I-5 exit 167 (Lyons Ave), just w. Int corridors. **Pets:** $25 daily fee/pet. Designated rooms, service with restrictions. 🛜 🍴 🖵

▼▼▼ Fairfield Inn by Marriott ⚄
(661) 290-2828. **$89-$129.** 25340 The Old Rd 91381. I-5 exit 167 (Lyons Ave), just w. Ext/int corridors. **Pets:** Accepted. 🛜 ✕ 🍴 🖵 🏊

▼▼▼ La Quinta Inn & Suites Santa Clarita-Valencia ⊞
(661) 286-1111. **$102-$188.** 25201 The Old Rd 91381. I-5 exit 167 (Lyons Ave), just w to Chiquella Ln, just s, then just sw. Int corridors.
Pets: Service with restrictions, supervision. 🛜 ✕ 🍴 🖵 🏊

▼▼▼ Residence Inn by Marriott ⊞
(661) 290-2800. **$119-$249.** 25320 The Old Rd 91381. I-5 exit 167 (Lyons Ave), just w. Int corridors. **Pets:** Other species. $75 one-time fee/room. Service with restrictions. 🛜 ✕ 🛠M 🍴 🖵 🏊 ⊁

(AAA) ▼▼▼ Super 8-Santa Clarita ⚄
(661) 252-1722. **$65-$107.** 17901 Sierra Hwy 91351. SR 14 exit 6A (Sierra Hwy/Via Princessa), 1.5 mi n. Int corridors. **Pets:** Medium, dogs only. $15 daily fee/pet. Service with restrictions, supervision.
[SAVE] 🛜 🍴 🖵 ⊁

SANTA MONICA

▼▼▼ Channel Road Inn 🅱🅱
(310) 459-1920. **$175-$425, 7 day notice.** 219 W Channel Rd 90402. SR 1 (Pacific Coast Hwy), just e. Ext/int corridors. **Pets:** Small, dogs only. $65 one-time fee/pet. Designated rooms, service with restrictions, supervision. 🛜 ✕

(AAA) ▼▼▼ ▼▼▼ The Fairmont Miramar Hotel & Bungalows ⊞ ❄
(310) 576-7777. **$309-$2199.** 101 Wilshire Blvd 90401. I-10 exit 1B (Lincoln Blvd), 0.6 mi n, then 0.6 mi w. Ext/int corridors. **Pets:** Service with restrictions, supervision. [ECO] [SAVE] 🛜 ✕ 🛠M 🖵 🍴 ⊁ 🏊

▼▼▼ The Georgian Hotel ⊞ ❄
(310) 395-9945. **$252-$528.** 1415 Ocean Ave 90401. I-10 exit 1B (Lincoln Blvd), just n, then 0.5 mi w on Broadway. Int corridors.
Pets: Medium. $100 one-time fee/room. Service with restrictions, supervision. 🛜 ✕ 🍴 🖵 🛗

(AAA) ▼▼▼ ▼▼▼ JW Marriott Santa Monica Le Merigot ⊞
(310) 395-9700. **$440-$460.** 1740 Ocean Ave 90401. I-10 exit 1B (Lincoln Blvd), 0.3 mi s, 0.6 mi w on Pico Blvd, then just n. Int corridors.
Pets: Accepted. [SAVE] 🛜 ✕ 🛠M 🖵 🛗 ⊁ 🏊

▼▼▼ ▼▼▼ Loews Santa Monica Beach Hotel ⊞
(310) 458-6700. **Call for rates.** 1700 Ocean Ave 90401. I-10 exit 1B (Lincoln Blvd), 0.3 mi s, 0.6 mi w on Pico Blvd, then just n. Int corridors.
Pets: Accepted. 🍴 🛜 ✕ 🛠M 🖵 🛗 ⊁ 🏊

(AAA) ▼▼▼ ▼▼ Sheraton Delfina Santa Monica ⊞ ❄
(310) 399-9344. **$249-$599.** 530 Pico Blvd 90405. I-10 exit 1B (Lincoln Blvd), just s. Int corridors. **Pets:** Medium, dogs only. $75 one-time fee/room. Supervision. [SAVE] 🛜 ✕ 🍴 🖵 🛗 🏊

(AAA) ▼▼▼ Travelodge-Santa Monica/Pico Blvd ⚄
(310) 450-5766. **$129-$209.** 3102 Pico Blvd 90405. I-10 exit 2 (Centinela Ave), just s, then just w. Ext corridors. **Pets:** Small. Designated rooms, service with restrictions, supervision. [SAVE] 🛜 ✕ 🍴 🖵

▼▼▼ Viceroy Santa Monica ⊞
(310) 260-7500. **Call for rates.** 1819 Ocean Ave 90401. I-10 exit 1B (Lincoln Blvd), 0.3 mi s, 0.6 mi w on Pico Blvd, then just n. Int corridors.
Pets: Accepted. 🛜 ✕ 🛠M 🍴 ⊁

SEAL BEACH

(AAA) ▼▼▼ The Pacific Inn ⚄
(562) 493-7501. **$119-$199.** 600 Marina Dr 90740. I-405 exit 22 (Seal Beach Blvd/Los Alamitos Blvd), 2.6 mi s, 0.5 mi w on Pacific Coast Hwy, then just sw. Ext/int corridors. **Pets:** $50 one-time fee/room. Designated rooms, service with restrictions, supervision.
[SAVE] 🛜 ✕ 🛠M 🍴 🖵 ⊁ 🏊

SHERMAN OAKS

AAA ▼▼▼▼ BEST WESTERN PLUS Carriage Inn **M**
(818) 787-2300. **$109-$239.** 5525 Sepulveda Blvd 91411. I-405 exit 64 (Burbank Blvd), just e, then just s. Ext/int corridors. **Pets:** Accepted.
(SAVE) 🛜 🖺 🖥 🍴 🐾

SOUTH PASADENA

▼▼▼▼ Arroyo Vista Inn **BB**
(323) 478-7300. **$150-$300, 14 day notice.** 335 Monterey Rd 91030. SR 110 exit 64 (Marmion Way) northbound, 0.8 mi e, then just n; exit 31A (Orange Grove Ave) southbound, 0.3 mi e, 0.6 mi s, then just n. Int corridors. **Pets:** Accepted. 🛜 ✕ ☎

STUDIO CITY

▼▼▼▼ Sportsmen's Lodge Hotel **H**
(818) 769-4700. **$99-$249.** 12825 Ventura Blvd 91604. US 101 exit 15 (Coldwater Canyon Ave), 0.8 mi s, then just e. Int corridors.
Pets: Accepted. 🛜 🖺 🖥 🍴 🐾

TARZANA

AAA ▼▼ St. George Inn & Suites **M**
(818) 345-6911. **$68-$105.** 19454 Ventura Blvd 91356. US 101 exit 24 (Tampa Ave), just s, then just w. Ext corridors. **Pets:** Medium. $150 deposit/room, $25 one-time fee/room. Service with restrictions, supervision. (SAVE) 🛜 🖺 🐾

TORRANCE

AAA ▼▼▼ Ramada Torrance **M** 🐾
(310) 325-0660. **$85-$139.** 2888 Pacific Coast Hwy 90505. I-405 exit 39 (Crenshaw Blvd), 5.2 mi s, then just w. Ext corridors. **Pets:** Medium. $20 daily fee/pet. Designated rooms, service with restrictions, supervision.
(SAVE) 🛜 🖺 🖥

▼▼▼▼ Residence Inn by Marriott **H**
(310) 543-4566. **$132-$219.** 3701 Torrance Blvd 90503. I-405 exit 42A (Hawthorne Blvd), 3.2 mi s, then just e. Ext corridors. **Pets:** Medium, other species. $100 one-time fee/room. Service with restrictions, supervision. (ECO) 🛜 ✕ 🖺 🖥 🐾 ✕

▼▼▼▼ Staybridge Suites **M**
(310) 371-8525. **$99-$189.** 19901 Prairie Ave 90503. I-405 exit 39 (Crenshaw Blvd), 0.4 mi s to 190th St, 0.9 mi w, then 0.4 mi s. Ext corridors. **Pets:** Large. $15 daily fee/pet. Service with restrictions, crate.
🛜 🖺 🖥 🐾

UNIVERSAL CITY

AAA ▼▼▼▼ Hilton Los Angeles/Universal
City **H** 🐾
(818) 506-2500. **$169-$199.** 555 Universal Hollywood Dr 91608. US 101 exit 12A (Lankershim Blvd), just n, then just e. Int corridors. **Pets:** Large, dogs only. $50 one-time fee/room. Designated rooms, service with restrictions, supervision. (ECO) 📧 (SAVE) 🛜 🖺 🖥 🍴 🐾

AAA ▼▼▼▼ Sheraton Universal Hotel, at Universal
Studios **H**
(818) 980-1212. **$189-$409.** 333 Universal Hollywood Dr 91608. US 101 exit 12A (Lankershim Blvd), just n, then just e. Int corridors.
Pets: Accepted. (SAVE) 🛜 ✕ 🖺 🖥 🍴 🐾

WALNUT

▼▼▼ Quality Inn & Suites **H**
(909) 594-9999. **$85-$120.** 1170 Fairway Dr 91789. SR 60 exit 21 (Fairway Dr), 0.3 mi s. Int corridors. **Pets:** Small. $200 deposit/room, $35 daily fee/room. Designated rooms, service with restrictions, crate.
🛜 🖺 🖥 🐾

WEST HOLLYWOOD

AAA ▼▼▼▼ Andaz West Hollywood **H**
(323) 656-1234. **$171-$491, 3 day notice.** 8401 Sunset Blvd 90069. I-10 exit 7A (La Cienega Blvd), 4.4 mi n, then just e. Int corridors.
Pets: Accepted. (ECO) (SAVE) 🛜 🖺 🐾

AAA ▼▼▼▼ Chamberlain West Hollywood **H** 🐾
(310) 657-7400. **$289-$475.** 1000 Westmount Dr 90069. I-10 exit 7A (La Cienega Blvd), 4 mi n to Santa Monica Blvd, just w, then just n. Int corridors. **Pets:** Medium, dogs only. $125 one-time fee/pet. Supervision.
(SAVE) 🛜 ✕ 🖺 🖥 🍴 🐾

AAA ▼▼▼▼ The Grafton on Sunset **H**
(323) 654-4600. **$189-$429.** 8462 Sunset Blvd 90069. I-10 exit 7A (La Cienega Blvd), 4.4 mi n, then just e. Int corridors. **Pets:** Accepted.
(SAVE) 🛜 🐾

▼▼▼▼ Le Montrose Suite Hotel **H**
(310) 855-1115. **$209-$599, 3 day notice.** 900 Hammond St at Cynthia St 90069. I-10 exit 7A (La Cienega Blvd), 2.6 mi n to San Vicente Blvd, 1.3 mi nw, then just w. Int corridors. **Pets:** Accepted.
🛜 ✕ 🖺 🖥 🍴 🐾 ✕

▼▼▼▼ Le Parc Suite Hotel **H**
(310) 855-8888. **$275-$499.** 733 N West Knoll Dr 90069. I-10 exit 7A (La Cienega Blvd), 3.5 mi n, just w on Melrose Ave, then just n. Int corridors.
Pets: Accepted. 🛜 🖺 🖥 🍴 🐾 ✕

AAA ▼▼▼▼ The London West Hollywood **H** 🐾
(310) 854-1111. **$249-$999.** 1020 N San Vicente Blvd 90069. I-10 exit 7A (La Cienega Blvd), 2.6 mi n, then 1.5 mi nw. Int corridors. **Pets:** Small, dogs only. $100 one-time fee/room, $25 daily fee/room. Designated rooms, service with restrictions, supervision.
(SAVE) 🛜 🖺 🖥 🍴 🐾

AAA ▼▼▼▼ Sunset Marquis Hotel & Villas **H**
(310) 657-1333. **$250-$850.** 1200 N Alta Loma Rd 90069. I-10 exit 7A (La Cienega Blvd), 4.5 mi n to Holloway Dr, just w, then just n. Int corridors. **Pets:** Accepted. (SAVE) 🛜 🖺 🖥 🍴 🐾

WHITTIER

AAA ▼▼▼ Vagabond Inn **M**
(562) 698-9701. **$70-$120.** 14125 E Whittier Blvd 90605. I-605 exit 15 (Whittier Blvd), 3.5 mi e. Ext corridors. **Pets:** $15 daily fee/pet. Designated rooms, service with restrictions, supervision.
(SAVE) 🛜 🖺 🖥 🐾

WOODLAND HILLS

▼▼▼▼ Hilton Woodland Hills/Los Angeles **H**
(818) 595-1000. **$109-$229.** 6360 Canoga Ave 91367. US 101 exit 26B (Canoga Ave), 1 mi n. Int corridors. **Pets:** Accepted.
🛜 ✕ 🖺 🖥 🍴

▼▼▼▼ Holiday Inn Express & Suites **H**
(818) 222-2299. **$99-$109.** 22617 Ventura Blvd 91364. US 101 exit 28 (Fallbrook) southbound, n to Ventura Blvd, just e; exit 27C northbound, just w. Ext/int corridors. **Pets:** Accepted. 🛜 ✕ 🖺 🖥

AAA ▼▼▼▼ Warner Center Marriott Hotel **H**
(818) 887-4800. **$109-$470.** 21850 Oxnard St 91367. US 101 exit 27A (Topanga Canyon Blvd N), 0.6 mi n, then just e. Int corridors.
Pets: Small, dogs only. $75 one-time fee/room. Designated rooms, service with restrictions, supervision.
(SAVE) 🛜 ✕ 🖺 🖥 🍴 🐾 ✕

END METROPOLITAN AREA

LOS BAÑOS

Americas Best Value Inn M
(209) 826-5002. **$62-$82.** 330 W Pacheco Blvd 93635. On SR 152; center. Ext corridors. **Pets:** Small. $12 daily fee/pet. Service with restrictions, supervision.

BEST WESTERN Executive Inn H
(209) 827-0954. **$78-$99.** 301 W Pacheco Blvd 93635. On SR 152; center. Int corridors. **Pets:** Medium, dogs only. $20 daily fee/pet. Designated rooms, service with restrictions, supervision.

Vagabond Inn Executive H ❖
(209) 827-4677. **Call for rates.** 20 W Pacheco Blvd 93635. On SR 152; center. Int corridors. **Pets:** Dogs only. $20 daily fee/pet. Designated rooms, service with restrictions, supervision.

LOS GATOS

Los Gatos Lodge H
(408) 354-3300. **$109-$229.** 50 Los Gatos Saratoga Rd 95032. SR 17 exit E Los Gatos, just e. Ext/int corridors. **Pets:** Medium, dogs only. $10 daily fee/room. Designated rooms, service with restrictions, supervision.

MADERA

Quality Inn Madera H
(559) 664-0100. **$59-$169.** 317 North G St 93637. SR 99 exit Central Madera, just e. Int corridors. **Pets:** Accepted.

MAMMOTH LAKES

BEST WESTERN PLUS High Sierra Hotel H ❖
(760) 924-1234. **$102-$270.** 3228 Main St 93546. On SR 203, just w of jct Old Mammoth Rd. Int corridors. **Pets:** Large, dogs only. $20 daily fee/room. Designated rooms, service with restrictions, supervision.

Mammoth Mountain Inn H ❖
(760) 934-2581. **$129-$239, 14 day notice.** 1 Minaret Rd 93546. 5 mi w of town on SR 203. Int corridors. **Pets:** $200 deposit/room, $50 daily fee/room. Service with restrictions, crate.

Shilo Inn Suites-Mammoth Lakes H
(760) 934-4500. **$110-$240.** 2963 Main St 93546. On SR 203, just e of Old Mammoth Rd. Int corridors. **Pets:** Dogs only. $25 one-time fee/room. Designated rooms, service with restrictions, supervision.

Sierra Lodge H
(760) 934-8881. **$69-$199.** 3540 Main St 93546. On SR 203, 0.6 mi w of Old Mammoth Rd. Int corridors. **Pets:** Other species. $10 daily fee/pet. Designated rooms, service with restrictions, supervision.

Sierra Nevada Lodge H ❖
(760) 934-2515. **$139-$999, 14 day notice.** 164 Old Mammoth Rd 93546. Just s of SR 203. Ext/int corridors. **Pets:** Dogs only. $20 daily fee/pet. Designated rooms, service with restrictions, supervision.

The Westin Monache Resort H ❖
(760) 934-0400. **$169-$1399.** 50 Hillside Dr 93546. SR 203, 1 mi w to Minaret Rd, 0.3 mi n to Forest Tr, just w, then just nw. Int corridors. **Pets:** Medium, dogs only. Designated rooms, service with restrictions, supervision.

MANTECA

BEST WESTERN PLUS Executive Inn & Suites H
(209) 825-1415. **$79-$99.** 1415 E Yosemite Ave 95336. Jct SR 99 and 120 exit E Yosemite Ave, just w. Ext corridors. **Pets:** Accepted.

MARIPOSA

BEST WESTERN Yosemite Way Station Motel H
(209) 966-7545. **$59-$229.** 4999 Hwy 140 95338. SR 140 at SR 49 S. Ext corridors. **Pets:** Medium. $20 daily fee/pet. Designated rooms, service with restrictions, supervision.

Comfort Inn Yosemite Valley Gateway H
(209) 966-4344. **$90-$170.** 4994 Bullion St 95338. Jct SR 140 and 49 S, just e. Ext corridors. **Pets:** Small, other species. $75 deposit/room, $15 daily fee/pet. Designated rooms, service with restrictions, supervision.

The Mariposa Lodge H
(209) 966-3607. **$69-$159.** 5052 Hwy 140 95338. Center. Ext corridors. **Pets:** Medium. $15 daily fee/pet. Designated rooms, supervision.

Miners Inn Motel M
(209) 742-7777. **$69-$249.** 5181 Hwy 49 N 95338. On SR 49, n at SR 140. Ext/int corridors. **Pets:** Other species. $25 daily fee/pet. Designated rooms, service with restrictions, supervision.

MARTINEZ

BEST WESTERN PLUS John Muir Inn H
(925) 229-1010. **$112-$116.** 445 Muir Station Rd 94553. Jct I-680 and SR 4, 2.3 mi w on SR 4 to Pine/Center Ave exit, then just s. Int corridors. **Pets:** Accepted.

MARYSVILLE

Comfort Suites H
(530) 742-9200. **$77-$144.** 1034 N Beale Rd 95901. SR 70 exit 20A (Feather River Blvd/Yuba College) northbound, just e, then just n; exit 20B (N Beale Rd) southbound, just e, then just s. Int corridors. **Pets:** Medium. $150 deposit/room, $10 daily fee/pet. Designated rooms, service with restrictions, supervision.

Motel 6 (South) H
(530) 742-2700. **$89-$109.** 1111 N Beale Rd 95901. SR 70 exit 20A (Feather River Blvd/Yuba College) northbound, just e; exit 20B (N Beale Rd) southbound, just e, just s, then just e; jct Feather River Blvd. Int corridors. **Pets:** Other species. Service with restrictions, supervision.

MCCLOUD

McCloud Dance Country RV Resort CA
(530) 964-2252. **Call for rates.** 480 Hwy 89 96057. Jct SR 89 and Squaw Valley Rd, just s; behind big red barn. Ext corridors. **Pets:** Accepted.

McCloud Hotel BB ❖
(530) 964-2822. **$125-$215, 10 day notice.** 408 Main St 96057. I-5 exit 736 (SR 89/McCloud), 9 mi e; jct SR 89 and W Minnesota Ave, 0.3 mi se on W Minnesota to Main St, then just n. Int corridors. **Pets:** Other species. $25 one-time fee/room. Designated rooms, service with restrictions, supervision.

McCloud Mercantile Hotel H
(530) 964-2330. **Call for rates.** 241 Main St 96057. I-5 exit 736 (SR 89/McCloud), 9 mi e; jct SR 89 and W Minnesota Ave, 0.3 mi se on W Minnesota Ave to Main St, then just n. Int corridors. **Pets:** Accepted.

MENLO PARK

Red Cottage Inn & Suites M
(650) 326-9010. **$129-$219.** 1704 El Camino Real 94025. US 101 exit 406 (Marsh Rd), 0.4 mi s on Middlefield Rd, 0.6 mi w on Encinal Rd, then just n. Ext corridors. **Pets:** Accepted.

MERCED

BEST WESTERN PLUS Inn H
(209) 723-2163. **$86-$95.** 1033 Motel Dr 95341. SR 99 exit E Childs Ave or SR 140, just e. Ext corridors. **Pets:** $15 daily fee/room. Designated rooms, service with restrictions, supervision.

Comfort Inn Merced H
(209) 383-0333. **$69-$79.** 730 Motel Dr 95341. SR 99 exit SR 140, just e. Ext corridors. **Pets:** Small, other species. $15 one-time fee/pet. Designated rooms, service with restrictions, crate.

Ramada Inn H
(209) 723-3121. **$79-$99.** 2010 E Childs Ave 95340. SR 99 exit E Childs Ave, just e. Ext/int corridors. **Pets:** Accepted.

MILPITAS

BEST WESTERN PLUS Brookside Inn H
(408) 263-5566. **$99-$169.** 400 Valley Way 95035. I-880 exit Calaveras Blvd (SR 237), just e. Ext/int corridors. **Pets:** Small. $20 daily fee/pet. Service with restrictions, supervision.

Beverly Heritage Hotel H
(408) 943-9080. **$69-$239.** 1820 Barber Ln 95035. Northwest quadrant of I-880 and Montague Expwy. Int corridors. **Pets:** Accepted.

Larkspur Landing Milpitas/San Jose H
(408) 719-1212. **$99-$269.** 40 Ranch Dr 95035. SR 237 exit McCarthy Blvd, just n. Int corridors. **Pets:** Accepted.

Residence Inn by Marriott H
(408) 941-9222. **$109-$249.** 1501 California Cir 95035. I-880 exit Dixon Landing Rd E, just s. Int corridors. **Pets:** Accepted.

Sheraton San Jose Hotel H
(408) 943-0600. **$99-$269.** 1801 Barber Ln 95035. 4 mi n of San Jose International Airport; 0.3 mi nw of I-880 and Montague Expwy. Ext/int corridors. **Pets:** Medium, other species. Service with restrictions, supervision.

TownePlace Suites by Marriott H
(408) 719-1959. **$109-$249.** 1428 Falcon Dr 95035. I-680 exit Montague Expwy W, then just n. Int corridors. **Pets:** Other species. $100 one-time fee/room. Service with restrictions.

MIRANDA

Miranda Gardens Resort CA
(707) 943-3011. **$105-$265, 7 day notice.** 6766 Ave of the Giants 95553. US 101 exit 650, 0.3 mi s on Maple Hills Rd, then 1.5 mi e. Ext corridors. **Pets:** Medium. $150 deposit/room, $15 daily fee/pet. Designated rooms, service with restrictions, supervision.

MI-WUK VILLAGE

Christmas Tree Inn H
(209) 586-1005. **$89-$129, 3 day notice.** 24685 Hwy 108 95346. On SR 108, 15 mi e of Sonora. Ext corridors. **Pets:** Medium, dogs only. $15 daily fee/room. Designated rooms, service with restrictions, supervision.

MODESTO

BEST WESTERN Town House Lodge H
(209) 524-7261. **$70-$81.** 909 16th St 95354. SR 99 exit Central Modesto, 1 mi e; at I St. Ext corridors. **Pets:** $20 one-time fee/pet. Service with restrictions, crate.

Comfort Inn H
(209) 544-2000. **$69-$82.** 2025 W Orangeburg Ave 95350. SR 99 exit Briggsmore Ave E, then just s. Int corridors. **Pets:** Accepted.

Courtyard by Marriott H
(209) 577-3825. **$104-$114.** 1720 Sisk Rd 95350. SR 99 exit Briggsmore Ave, 0.3 mi n. Int corridors. **Pets:** Small. $35 one-time fee/pet. Service with restrictions, supervision.

DoubleTree by Hilton Hotel Modesto H
(209) 526-6000. **$99-$259.** 1150 9th St 95354. SR 99 exit Central Modesto northbound; exit Maze Blvd southbound, just e. Int corridors. **Pets:** Accepted.

Microtel Inn & Suites by Wyndham Modesto Ceres H
(209) 538-6466. **$65-$89.** 1760 Herndon Rd 95307. SR 99 exit Hatch Rd E, just s. Int corridors. **Pets:** Other species. $50 deposit/room. Designated rooms, service with restrictions, crate.

Quality Inn H
(209) 578-5400. **$55-$105.** 500 Kansas Ave 95351. SR 99 exit Kansas Ave, just e. Int corridors. **Pets:** $50 deposit/room, $20 daily fee/room. Service with restrictions.

MOJAVE

BEST WESTERN PLUS Desert Winds M
(661) 824-3601. **$92-$102.** 16200 Sierra Hwy 93501. On SR 14 and 58; center. Ext corridors. **Pets:** Medium. $20 one-time fee/room. Service with restrictions, supervision.

Days Inn-Mojave M
(661) 824-2421. **$55-$110.** 16100 Sierra Hwy 93501. On SR 14; center. Ext corridors. **Pets:** Medium, dogs only. $10 daily fee/pet. Service with restrictions, supervision.

Desert Inn M
(661) 824-2518. **$49-$69.** 1954 Hwy 58 93501. Just e of SR 14. Ext corridors. **Pets:** Medium, dogs only. Service with restrictions, crate.

Mariah Country Inn & Suites H
(661) 824-4980. **$89-$139.** 1385 Hwy 58 93501. SR 14 exit 172 (SR 58), 1.5 mi e. Int corridors. **Pets:** Medium. $20 one-time fee/pet. Service with restrictions, supervision.

MONTEREY PENINSULA AREA

CARMEL-BY-THE-SEA

Briarwood Inn 🅱🅱 ❀
(831) 626-9056. **Call for rates.** San Carlos St 93921. 3 blks n of Ocean Ave; at 4th Ave. Ext corridors. **Pets:** Small, dogs only. $25 deposit/pet. Designated rooms, service with restrictions, supervision.
[SAVE] 🛜 ⊠ 🛏 💻 🅰

Carmel Country Inn 🅱🅱 ❀
(831) 625-3263. **$275-$425, 7 day notice.** Dolores St & 3rd Ave 93921. 4 blks n of Ocean Ave. Ext corridors. **Pets:** Other species. $20 daily fee/pet. Service with restrictions, supervision. 🛜 ⊠ 🛏 💻 🅰

Carmel Fireplace Inn Bed & Breakfast 🅱🅱 ❀
(831) 624-4862. **Call for rates.** San Carlos St & 4th Ave 93921. 3 blks n of Ocean Ave. Ext corridors. **Pets:** Small, dogs only. $25 deposit/pet. Designated rooms, service with restrictions, supervision.
[SAVE] 🛜 ⊠ 🛏 💻 🅰

Carmel Garden Court 🅱🅱
(831) 624-6926. **$150-$245, 7 day notice.** 4th Ave & Torres St 93923. 3 blks n of Ocean Ave. Ext corridors. **Pets:** $50 one-time fee/pet. Service with restrictions, supervision. ⊠ 🛏 💻 🅰

Carmel Lodge 🅷 ❀
(831) 624-1255. **Call for rates.** San Carlos St & 5th Ave 93921. 2 blks n of Ocean Ave. Ext/int corridors. **Pets:** Dogs only. $35 daily fee/pet. Designated rooms, service with restrictions.
[SAVE] 🛜 ⊠ 🛏 💻 🍴 🅰

Carmel Mission Inn 🅷
(831) 624-1841. **$99-$529.** 3665 Rio Rd 93923. 1 mi s on SR 1. Ext/int corridors. **Pets:** Large. $35 one-time fee/pet. Designated rooms, service with restrictions, supervision. 🛜 ⊠ ⓜ 🛏 💻 🍴 🌥

Carmel Resort Inn 🅜
(831) 293-8390. **$79-$289, 3 day notice.** Carpenter St & 1st Ave 93923. SR 1 exit Carpenter St, 0.5 mi w. Ext corridors. **Pets:** Accepted.
🛜 ⊠ 🛏 💻 🅰

Coachman's Inn 🅷
(831) 624-6421. **$145-$435, 3 day notice.** San Carlos St at 7th Ave 93921. Just s of Ocean Ave on San Carlos St; between 7th and 8th aves. Ext corridors. **Pets:** $25 daily fee/pet. Designated rooms, supervision. [SAVE] 🛜 ⊠ ⓜ 🛏 💻 ⊠ 🅰

Cypress Inn 🅷
(831) 624-3871. **Call for rates.** Lincoln & 7th Ave 93922. Just s off Ocean Ave. Ext/int corridors. **Pets:** Accepted. 🛜 ⊠ 🛏 🍴 🅰

Hofsas House 🅷 ❀
(831) 624-2745. **$90-$400, 3 day notice.** San Carlos St 93921. 3 blks n off Ocean Ave; between 3rd and 4th aves. Ext corridors. **Pets:** Dogs only. $25 daily fee/pet. Designated rooms, service with restrictions, supervision.
[SAVE] 🛜 ⊠ 🛏 💻 🌥 🅰

Horizon Inn & Ocean View Lodge 🅷 ❀
(831) 624-5327. **$106-$390, 3 day notice.** 3rd Ave & Junipero Ave 93921. 4 blks n off Ocean Ave. Ext corridors. **Pets:** Large, dogs only. $20 daily fee/pet. Designated rooms, service with restrictions, supervision.
[SAVE] 🛜 ⊠ ⓜ 🛏 💻 🅰

Svendsgaard's 🅷 ❀
(831) 624-1511. **$149-$259, 3 day notice.** 4th Ave & San Carlos St 93921. 3 blks n off Ocean Ave. Ext corridors. **Pets:** $25 daily fee/pet. Designated rooms, service with restrictions, supervision.
[SAVE] 🛜 ⊠ 🛏 💻 🌥 🅰

CARMEL VALLEY

Bernardus Lodge 🅷 ❀
(831) 658-3400. **$315-$2030, 7 day notice.** 415 W Carmel Valley Rd 93924. 9.5 mi e of SR 1; just e of Los Laureles Grade. Ext corridors. **Pets:** Large, dogs only. $75 one-time fee/room. Service with restrictions, supervision. [SAVE] 🛜 ⊠ ⓜ 🛏 💻 🍴 🌥

Carmel Valley Ranch 🅷 ❀
(831) 625-9500. **$300-$1200, 7 day notice.** One Old Ranch Rd 93923. 6.3 mi e of SR 1 via Carmel Valley Rd to Robinson Canyon Rd exit, follow signs. Ext corridors. **Pets:** Other species. $100 one-time fee/room. 🛜 ⊠ ⓜ 🛏 💻 🍴 🌥 ⊠

MARINA

The Sanctuary Beach Resort 🅷
(831) 883-9478. **$169-$550, 3 day notice.** 3295 Dunes Dr 93933. SR 1 exit Reservation Rd, just w. Ext corridors. **Pets:** Accepted.
🛜 ⊠ ⓜ 🛏 💻 🍴 🌥 🅰

MONTEREY

Bay Park Hotel 🅷
(831) 649-1020. **$99-$350.** 1425 Munras Ave 93940. SR 1 exit Soledad Dr/Munras Ave, just w. Int corridors. **Pets:** Medium. $20 daily fee/pet. Designated rooms, service with restrictions, supervision.
[SAVE] 🛜 ⊠ ⓜ 🛏 💻 🍴 🌥

BEST WESTERN PLUS Beach Resort Monterey 🅷
(831) 394-3321. **Call for rates.** 2600 Sand Dunes Dr 93940. SR 1 exit Del Rey Oaks, just w. Ext corridors. **Pets:** Accepted.
[SAVE] 🛜 ⊠ ⓜ 🛏 💻 🍴 🌥

BEST WESTERN PLUS Victorian Inn 🅷 ❀
(831) 373-8000. **$119-$700, 3 day notice.** 487 Foam St 93940. SR 1 exit Monterey, 3.4 mi w. Ext/int corridors. **Pets:** Other species. $30 daily fee/pet. Designated rooms, service with restrictions, crate.
[SAVE] 🛜 ⊠ ⓜ 🛏 💻 🅰

Casa Munras, A Larkspur Collection Hotel 🅷 ❀
(831) 375-2411. **Call for rates.** 700 Munras Ave 93940. SR 1 exit Soledad Dr/Munras Ave, 0.8 mi w. Ext/int corridors. **Pets:** $50 one-time fee/room. Designated rooms, service with restrictions, supervision.
[ECO] 🛜 ⊠ 🛏 💻 🍴 🌥 🅰

Comfort Inn-Monterey Bay 🅷
(831) 373-3081. **$59-$189.** 2050 N Fremont St 93940. SR 1 exit Fremont St or Casa Verde Way, 0.3 mi e. Ext corridors. **Pets:** Small. $25 daily fee/pet. Designated rooms, service with restrictions, supervision.
[SAVE] 🛜 ⊠ ⓜ 🛏 💻

Comfort Inn-Monterey by the Sea 🅷
(831) 372-2908. **$65-$189.** 1252 Munras Ave 93940. SR 1 exit Soledad Dr/Munras Ave, just s. Ext corridors. **Pets:** Accepted.
[ECO] [SAVE] 🛜 ⊠ ⓜ 🛏 💻 🌥

El Adobe Inn 🅜
(831) 372-5409. **$49-$299, 3 day notice.** 936 Munras Ave 93940. SR 1 exit Soledad Dr/Munras Ave, 0.6 mi w. Ext corridors. **Pets:** Dogs only. $15 daily fee/pet. Designated rooms, service with restrictions, supervision.
[SAVE] 🛜 ⊠ 🛏 💻 🅰

Hotel Abrego 🅷 ❀
(831) 372-7551. **$119-$600, 3 day notice.** 755 Abrego St 93940. SR 1 exit Fremont St, 0.8 mi w. Ext/int corridors. **Pets:** Dogs only. $30 daily fee/pet. Designated rooms, service with restrictions, supervision.
[SAVE] 🛜 ⊠ ⓜ 🛏 💻 🌥

▼▼▼▼ Hotel Pacific 🏨 ❖
(831) 373-5700. **Call for rates.** 300 Pacific St 93940. SR 1 exit Del Monte Ave, 2.2 mi w. Ext/int corridors. **Pets:** Medium. $50 one-time fee/room. Designated rooms. 📶 ✕ 👤M 🛏 💻 🚖

✦ ▼▼▼▼ Hyatt Regency Monterey Hotel & Spa 🏨 ❖
(831) 372-1234. **$99-$450, 3 day notice.** 1 Old Golf Course Rd 93940. SR 1 exit Aguajito Rd northbound; exit Monterey southbound, just e. Int corridors. **Pets:** Medium, dogs only. $75 one-time fee/room. Service with restrictions, crate.
🌿 SAVE 📶 ✕ 👤M 🛏 💻 🍴 🚖 ✕ 🚗

✦ ▼▼▼▼ InterContinental The Clement Monterey 🏨
(831) 375-4500. **$179-$399.** 750 Cannery Row 93940. Between Prescott and David aves. Int corridors. **Pets:** Accepted.
SAVE 📶 ✕ 👤M 💻 🍴 🚖 ✕

▼▼▼▼ Mariposa Inn & Suites 🏨
(831) 649-1414. **Call for rates.** 1386 Munras Ave 93940. SR 1 exit Soledad Dr/Munras Ave, just w. Ext/int corridors. **Pets:** Small, dogs only. $40 daily fee/pet. Service with restrictions, supervision.
📶 ✕ 👤M 🛏 💻 🚖

✦ ▼▼▼ Monterey Bay Lodge 🏨
(831) 372-8057. **$79-$349.** 55 Camino Aguajito 93940. SR 1 exit Aguajito Rd, just w. Ext corridors. **Pets:** Medium, dogs only. $15 daily fee/pet. Service with restrictions, supervision.
SAVE 📶 ✕ 👤M 🛏 💻 🍴 🚖

✦ ▼▼▼ Monterey Fireside Lodge 🅼
(831) 373-4172. **$69-$599, 3 day notice.** 1131 10th St 93940. SR 1 exit Aguajito Rd or Monterey, just w. Ext corridors. **Pets:** Other species. $20 daily fee/pet. Designated rooms, no service, supervision.
SAVE 📶 ✕ 🚗

✦ ▼▼▼▼ Old Monterey Inn 🅱🅱 ❖
(831) 375-8284. **$199-$499, 14 day notice.** 500 Martin St 93940. SR 1 exit Soledad Dr/Munras Ave, 1 mi w; from Fisherman's Wharf, 1 mi s on Pacific St to Martin St, 2 blks w. Ext/int corridors. **Pets:** Small, dogs only. $30 daily fee/pet. Designated rooms, service with restrictions, supervision.
SAVE 📶 ✕

✦ ▼▼▼▼ Portola Hotel & Spa 🏨 ❖
(831) 649-4511. **$179-$525.** 2 Portola Plaza 93940. 2 mi w of SR 1 exit Del Monte or Munras aves; near Fisherman's Wharf; downtown. Int corridors. **Pets:** Other species. $50 one-time fee/room. Supervision.
🌿 SAVE 📶 ✕ 👤M 🛏 💻 🍴 🚖 ✕

PACIFIC GROVE

✦ ▼▼▼ Bide-A-Wee Inn & Cottages 🅼 ❖
(831) 372-2330. **$79-$429, 3 day notice.** 221 Asilomar Ave 93950. 1 mi n of SR 68. Ext corridors. **Pets:** Medium, dogs only. $25 daily fee/pet. Designated rooms, service with restrictions, supervision.
SAVE 📶 ✕ 🛏 💻 🚗

▼▼▼ The Centrella Bed & Breakfast Inn 🅱🅱 ❖
(831) 372-3372. **$119-$299, 7 day notice.** 612 Central Ave 93950. At 17th St; center. Ext/int corridors. **Pets:** Medium, dogs only. $50 one-time fee/pet. Designated rooms, service with restrictions, crate.
📶 ✕ 👤M 💻 🚗

▼▼ Deer Haven Inn 🅼
(831) 373-7784. **$59-$249, 3 day notice.** 750 Crocker Ave 93950. Just e of SR 68 via Sinex Ave. Ext corridors. **Pets:** Medium, dogs only. $25 daily fee/pet. Designated rooms, service with restrictions, supervision.
📶 ✕ 🛏 💻 🚗

▼▼▼ Gosby House Inn 🅱🅱
(831) 375-1287. **$135-$310, 7 day notice.** 643 Lighthouse Ave 93950. Downtown. Ext/int corridors. **Pets:** Accepted. 📶 ✕ 🛏 💻 🚗

▼▼▼ Green Gables Inn 🅱🅱
(831) 375-2095. **$155-$325, 7 day notice.** 301 Ocean View Blvd 93950. At 5th St. Ext/int corridors. **Pets:** Dogs only. $65 one-time fee/pet. Designated rooms, service with restrictions, supervision. 📶 ✕ 💻 🚗

▼▼▼▼ Lighthouse Lodge & Cottages 🏨 ❖
(831) 655-2111. **$99-$895, 3 day notice.** 1150 Lighthouse Ave 93950. 0.5 mi w of Seventeen Mile Dr. Ext corridors. **Pets:** Other species. $50 one-time fee/room. Designated rooms, service with restrictions.
📶 ✕ 👤M 🛏 💻 🚖 🚗

▼▼▼ Pacific Gardens Inn 🏨
(831) 646-9414. **$99-$203, 7 day notice.** 701 Asilomar Blvd 93950. Just n of SR 68. Ext corridors. **Pets:** Accepted. 📶 ✕ 🛏 💻 🚗

▼▼▼ Sea Breeze Inn and Cottages 🏨 ❖
(831) 372-7771. **$79-$499.** 1100 Lighthouse Ave 93950. Just w of Seventeen Mile Dr; jct Lighthouse and Grove Acre aves. Ext/int corridors. **Pets:** Other species. $25 one-time fee/pet. Designated rooms, service with restrictions, crate. 📶 ✕ 🛏 💻 🍴 🚗

▼▼▼ Sea Breeze Lodge 🅼 ❖
(831) 372-3431. **$79-$499.** 1101 Lighthouse Ave 93950. Just w of Seventeen Mile Dr. Ext corridors. **Pets:** Other species. $25 one-time fee/pet. Designated rooms, service with restrictions, crate.
📶 ✕ 🛏 💻 🚖 🚗

PEBBLE BEACH

▼▼▼ The Lodge at Pebble Beach 🏨
(831) 624-3811. **Call for rates.** 1700 Seventeen Mile Dr 93953. Off SR 1. Ext/int corridors. **Pets:** Accepted.
📶 ✕ 👤M 💻 🍴 🚖 ✕ 🚗

SEASIDE

✦ ▼▼▼ Thunderbird Motel 🅼
(831) 394-6797. **$39-$249, 3 day notice.** 1933 Fremont Blvd 93955. SR 1 business route, 0.3 mi n. Ext corridors. **Pets:** Small. $50 deposit/pet. Designated rooms, service with restrictions, supervision.
SAVE 📶 🛏 🚗

END AREA

MORENO VALLEY

✦ ▼▼▼▼ BEST WESTERN Moreno Hotel & Suites 🅼 ❖
(951) 924-4546. **$89-$149.** 24840 Elder Ave 92557. SR 60 exit 62 (Perris Blvd) westbound, just n, then just w; exit eastbound, just e on Sunnymead Blvd, just n on Perris Blvd, then just w. Ext corridors. **Pets:** Large. $20 daily fee/pet. Designated rooms, service with restrictions, supervision. SAVE 📶 🛏 💻 🚖

✦ ▼▼▼ La Quinta Inn & Suites 🏨
(951) 486-9000. **$95-$177.** 23090 Sunnymead Blvd 92553. SR 60 exit 60 (Frederick St/Pigeon Pass Rd), just s, then just e. Int corridors. **Pets:** Service with restrictions, supervision.
SAVE 📶 ✕ 👤M 🛏 💻 🚖

MORGAN HILL

▼▼▼ Residence Inn by Marriott 🏨 ❖
(408) 782-8311. **$109-$259.** 18620 Madrone Pkwy 95037. US 101 exit Cochrane W, just n. Int corridors. **Pets:** Medium, other species. $100 one-time fee/room. Service with restrictions.
📶 ✕ 👤M 🛏 💻 🚖

MORRO BAY

▼▼▼ Beach Bungalow Inn & Suites [M] ❀

(805) 772-9700. **$109-$269, 3 day notice.** 1050 Morro Ave 93442. SR 1 exit Morro Bay Blvd, 0.8 mi w, then just n. Ext corridors. **Pets:** Medium, dogs only. $20 daily fee/pet. Designated rooms, crate.

🛰 ✕ 🛎 💻 🎬

✦ ▼▼▼ BEST WESTERN El Rancho [M] ❀

(805) 772-2212. **$69-$269, 3 day notice.** 2460 Main St 93442. SR 1 exit Morro Bay Blvd, 0.5 mi n. Ext corridors. **Pets:** Large. $12 daily fee/pet. Service with restrictions, crate. (SAVE) 🛰 🕭M 🛎 💻 ⇲ 🎬

▼▼ Days Inn [M]

(805) 772-2711. **$79-$224.** 1095 Main St 93442. SR 1 exit Morro Bay Blvd, 0.7 mi w, then just n. Ext corridors. **Pets:** Dogs only. $22 daily fee/pet. Designated rooms, service with restrictions, supervision.

🛰 ✕ 🛎 💻 🎬

▼▼ Econo Lodge [M]

(805) 772-5609. **$99-$250, 3 day notice.** 1100 Main St 93442. SR 1 exit Morro Bay Blvd, 0.7 mi w, then just n. Ext corridors. **Pets:** Small, dogs only. $25 daily fee/pet. Designated rooms, service with restrictions, supervision. 🛰 ✕ 🛎 💻

✦ ▼▼▼ The Inn at Morro Bay [H]

(805) 772-5651. **$99-$425.** 60 State Park Rd 93442. SR 1 exit Morro Bay Blvd, 0.7 mi w, then 1 mi s on Main St. Ext corridors.
Pets: Accepted. (SAVE) 🛰 ✕ 🕭M 🛎 💻 🍴 ⇲ 🛇 🎬

✦ ▼▼▼ Morro Bay Sandpiper Inn [M]

(805) 772-7503. **$55-$199, 3 day notice.** 540 Main St 93442. SR 1 exit Morro Bay Blvd, 0.7 mi w, then 0.4 mi s. Ext corridors. **Pets:** Accepted.
(SAVE) 🛰 ✕ 🛎 💻 🎬

▼▼▼ Sea Pines Golf Resort [H]

(805) 528-5252. **$124-$219.** 1945 Solano St 93402. SR 1 exit Los Osos/Baywood Park, 4 mi s on S Bay Blvd, 1.6 mi w on Los Osos Valley Rd, 0.3 mi. n on Pecho Rd, then just w on Skyline Dr; in Los Osos. Ext corridors. **Pets:** Dogs only. $25 daily fee/room. Designated rooms, service with restrictions. 🛰 ✕ 🛎 💻 🍴 🛇

MOUNTAIN VIEW

▼▼▼ Extended StayAmerica-San Jose, Mountain View [H]

(650) 962-1500. **$119-$134.** 190 E El Camino Real 94040. SR 82, just w of SR 85. Ext corridors. **Pets:** $25 daily fee/pet. Designated rooms, service with restrictions. 🛰 🕭M 🛎 💻

▼▼▼ Hotel Avante, a Joie de Vivre hotel [H] ❀

(650) 940-1000. **$89-$499.** 860 E El Camino Real 94040. US 101 exit 398B (SR 85/Cupertino); exit SR 82 S (Sunnyvale), 0.5 mi e. Int corridors. **Pets:** Medium, dogs only. $20 daily fee/room. Designated rooms, service with restrictions, supervision.
(ECO) 🛰 ✕ 🕭M 🛎 💻 ⇲

▼▼▼ Residence Inn by Marriott - Palo Alto/Mountain View [H]

(650) 940-1300. **$119-$289.** 1854 W El Camino Real 94040. US 101 exit 399 (Shoreline Blvd/Mountain View), 2 mi to SR 82, then 0.5 mi n. Ext corridors. **Pets:** Accepted. 🛰 ✕ 🕭M 🛎 💻 ⇲ 🛇

MOUNT SHASTA

✦ ▼▼▼ BEST WESTERN PLUS Tree House [H]

(530) 926-3101. **$99-$199.** 111 Morgan Way 96067. I-5 exit 738 (Central Mount Shasta), just e. Ext/int corridors. **Pets:** Other species. $15 one-time fee/pet. Service with restrictions, supervision.
(SAVE) 🛰 ✕ 🛎 💻 🍴 ⇲

✦ ▼▼ Cold Creek Inn [M] ❀

(530) 926-9851. **$69-$155.** 724 N Mount Shasta Blvd 96067. I-5 exit 738 (Central Mount Shasta), 0.5 mi ne on W Lake St, then 0.5 mi nw. Ext corridors. **Pets:** Other species. $20 daily fee/pet. Designated rooms, service with restrictions, supervision. (SAVE) 🛰 ✕ 🛎 💻

MYERS FLAT

✦ ▼▼▼ Myers Inn [BB]

(707) 943-3259. **$161-$203, 14 day notice.** 12913 Ave of the Giants 95554. US 101 exit Myers Flat, just w. Int corridors. **Pets:** Accepted.
(SAVE) 🛰 ✕ 🎬 🖨

NEEDLES

▼▼▼ Americas Best Value Inn [M] ❀

(760) 326-4501. **$49-$199, 3 day notice.** 1102 E Broadway 92363. I-40 exit 144 (US 95/E Broadway), just sw. Ext corridors. **Pets:** Other species. $10 daily fee/pet. Designated rooms. 🛰 🛎 💻 ⇲

✦ ▼▼▼ BEST WESTERN Colorado River Inn [M] ❀

(760) 326-4552. **$79-$109.** 2371 W Broadway 92363. I-40 exit 141 (W Broadway/River Rd), 0.3 mi se; on Business Loop I-40. Ext corridors. **Pets:** Other species. $15 daily fee/room. Designated rooms, service with restrictions, supervision. (SAVE) 🛰 ✕ 🛎 💻 ⇲

✦ ▼▼▼ Rio del Sol Inn [M]

(760) 326-5660. **$50-$85.** 1111 Pashard St 92363. I-40 exit 141 (W Broadway/River Rd), just sw. Ext corridors. **Pets:** Other species. $10 daily fee/room. Service with restrictions, supervision. (SAVE) 🛰 🛎 💻 ⇲

NEWARK

▼▼▼ Chase Suite Hotel [H]

(510) 795-1200. **Call for rates.** 39150 Cedar Blvd 94560. I-880 exit Mowry Ave, just w, then 0.3 mi s. Ext corridors. **Pets:** Accepted.

🛰 ✕ 🛎 💻 ⇲

▼▼▼ Hilton Newark/Fremont [H] ❀

(510) 490-8390. **$109-$209.** 39900 Balentine Dr 94560. I-880 exit Stevenson Blvd, just w. Int corridors. **Pets:** Medium, other species. $50 one-time fee/room. Designated rooms, service with restrictions, supervision.
🛰 🕭M 🛎 💻 🍴 ⇲

▼▼▼ Homewood Suites by Hilton [H]

(510) 791-7700. **$109-$169.** 39270 Cedar Blvd 94560. I-880 exit Mowry Ave, w to Cedar Blvd, then 0.3 mi s. Int corridors. **Pets:** Accepted.
🛰 🕭M 🛎 💻 ⇲ 🛇

✦ ▼▼▼ Residence Inn by Marriott Newark/Silicon Valley [H]

(510) 739-6000. **$85-$299.** 35466 Dumbarton Ct 94560. SR 84 exit Newark Blvd, just s. Int corridors. **Pets:** Accepted.
(ECO) (SAVE) 🛰 ✕ 🕭M 🛎 💻 ⇲ 🛇

▼▼▼ W Silicon Valley [H]

(510) 494-8800. **Call for rates.** 8200 Gateway Blvd 94560. SR 84 exit Thornton Ave, just s. Int corridors. **Pets:** Accepted.
🛰 ✕ 🕭M 🛎 💻 🍴 ⇲

NEWPORT BEACH

✦ ▼▼▼▼ Balboa Bay Resort [H]

(949) 645-5000. **$199-$529.** 1221 W Coast Hwy 92663. SR 73 exit 15 (Jamboree Rd), 3.5 mi s, then just w. Int corridors. **Pets:** Accepted.
(SAVE) 🛰 🕭M 🛎 💻 🍴 ⇲ 🛇

▼▼ Extended StayAmerica-Orange County/John Wayne Airport [H]

(949) 851-2711. **$69-$104.** 4881 Birch St 92660. I-405 exit 8 (MacArthur Blvd), 0.8 mi s, then just e. Int corridors. **Pets:** $25 daily fee/pet. Designated rooms, service with restrictions. 🛰 🕭M 🛎 💻

✦ ▼▼▼▼ Fairmont Newport Beach [H]

(949) 476-2001. **$119-$299.** 4500 MacArthur Blvd 92660. I-405 exit 8 (MacArthur Blvd), 1 mi s. Int corridors. **Pets:** Accepted.
(ECO) (SAVE) 🛰 🛎 💻 🍴 ⇲ 🛇

✦ ▼▼▼▼ Hyatt Regency Newport Beach [H] ❀

(949) 729-1234. **$90-$261.** 1107 Jamboree Rd 92660. SR 73 exit 15 (Jamboree Rd), 3 mi s. Ext/int corridors. **Pets:** Medium, dogs only. $50 daily fee/pet. Designated rooms, service with restrictions, supervision.
(ECO) (SAVE) 🛰 🕭M 🛎 💻 🍴 ⇲ 🛇

AAA ◈◈◈◈ Island Hotel Newport Beach H
(949) 759-0808. **$219-$5000.** 690 Newport Center Dr 92660. SR 73 exit 14 (MacArthur Blvd) northbound, 3 mi s to San Joaquin Hills Rd, then 0.5 mi w; exit 15 (Jamboree Rd) southbound, 2.5 mi s to San Joaquin Hills Rd, then 0.5 mi e. Int corridors. **Pets:** Accepted.
[SAVE] [icons]

◈◈◈◈ Newport Beach Marriott Bayview Hotel H
(949) 854-4500. **$149-$239.** 500 Bayview Cir 92660. SR 73 exit 15 (Jamboree Rd), just s, just w on Bayview Pl, then just n. Int corridors. **Pets:** Accepted. [icons]

NIPOMO

◈◈ Kaleidoscope Inn & Gardens B&B BB
(805) 929-5444. **$125-$160, 7 day notice.** 130 E Dana St 93444. US 101 exit 179 (Tefft St), 0.7 mi e, just s on Thompson Rd, then just e. Ext/int corridors. **Pets:** Other species. Designated rooms, no service, supervision. [icons]

NOVATO

AAA ◈◈◈◈ Inn Marin M ☀
(415) 883-5952. **$119-$329.** 250 Entrada Dr 94949. US 101 exit Ignacio Blvd, just w, just n on Enfrente Rd, then just e. Ext corridors. **Pets:** Large, other species. $20 one-time fee/pet. Service with restrictions, supervision. [icons]

OAKHURST

AAA ◈◈◈◈ BEST WESTERN PLUS Yosemite Gateway Inn H
(559) 683-2378. **$85-$199.** 40530 Hwy 41 93644. SR 49, 0.8 mi n. Ext corridors. **Pets:** Medium, dogs only. $50 deposit/room, $20 daily fee/room. Service with restrictions, supervision.
[SAVE] [icons]

AAA ◈◈◈◈ Château du Sureau CI
(559) 683-6860. **$385-$585, 14 day notice.** 48688 Victoria Ln 93644. Just w of jct SR 41 and 49. Ext/int corridors. **Pets:** Small, dogs only. $75 one-time fee/room. Crate. [SAVE] [icons]

AAA ◈◈ Comfort Inn Yosemite Area H
(559) 683-8282. **$70-$200.** 40489 Hwy 41 93644. SR 49, 0.5 mi n. Ext corridors. **Pets:** Other species. $20 daily fee/room. Designated rooms, service with restrictions, supervision. [SAVE] [icons]

OAKLAND

◈◈◈◈ Hilton Oakland Airport H
(510) 635-5000. **$129-$199.** 1 Hegenberger Rd 94621. I-880 exit Hegenberger Rd, 1 mi w; 1.3 mi e of Metropolitan Oakland International Airport. Int corridors. **Pets:** Accepted. [icons]

◈◈◈◈ Homewood Suites by Hilton H
(510) 663-2700. **$129-$219.** 1103 Embarcadero 94606. I-880 exit 16th Ave/Embarcadero southbound; exit 5th Ave/Embarcadero northbound, just w. Int corridors. **Pets:** Accepted. [icons]

AAA ◈◈◈◈ La Quinta Inn Oakland Airport Coliseum H
(510) 632-8900. **$71-$155.** 8465 Enterprise Way 94621. I-880 exit Hegenberger Rd, just e. Int corridors. **Pets:** Service with restrictions, supervision. [SAVE] [icons]

AAA ◈◈◈ Quality Inn H
(510) 562-4888. **$69-$149.** 8471 Enterprise Way 94621. I-880 exit Hegenberger Rd, just e. Ext corridors. **Pets:** Small. $100 deposit/room, $10 daily fee/room. Designated rooms, service with restrictions, supervision. [SAVE] [icons]

AAA ◈◈◈◈ Red Lion Hotel Oakland International Airport H
(510) 635-5300. **Call for rates.** 150 Hegenberger Rd 94621. I-880 exit Hegenberger Rd, 0.8 mi w. Int corridors. **Pets:** Other species. $15 one-time fee/room. Service with restrictions, crate. [SAVE] [icons]

AAA ◈◈◈ Waterfront Hotel, a Joie de Vivre hotel H ☀
(510) 836-3800. **$105-$279.** 10 Washington St 94607. I-880 exit Broadway, 0.5 mi w. Int corridors. **Pets:** Supervision.
[ECO] [SAVE] [icons]

OCEANO

◈◈ Oceano Inn M
(805) 473-0032. **$69-$219, 3 day notice.** 1252 Pacific Blvd 93445. On SR 1. Ext corridors. **Pets:** Small, dogs only. $15 daily fee/pet. Service with restrictions, supervision. [icons]

OCEANSIDE

◈◈ La Quinta Inn San Diego Oceanside H
(760) 450-0730. **$83-$221.** 937 N Coast Hwy 92054. I-5 exit 54B (Coast Hwy/Oceanside) southbound; exit 54B (Camp Pendleton) northbound, just w. Int corridors. **Pets:** Service with restrictions, supervision.
[icons]

◈◈ Motel 6 #4208 M
(760) 721-1543. **$55-$129.** 909 N Coast Hwy 92054. I-5 exit 54B (Coast Hwy/Oceanside) southbound; exit 54B (Camp Pendleton) northbound, just w. Int corridors. **Pets:** Other species. Service with restrictions, supervision.
[ECO] [icons]

◈◈◈ Residence Inn by Marriott San Diego/Oceanside H ☀
(760) 722-9600. **$109-$209.** 3603 Ocean Ranch Blvd 92056. I-5 exit 52 (Oceanside Blvd), 3.3 mi e, 0.5 mi n on Rancho del Oro Rd, then just e. Int corridors. **Pets:** Other species. $100 one-time fee/room. Service with restrictions. [icons]

AAA ◈◈◈ Super 8 Oceanside M
(760) 757-7700. **$55-$154.** 3240 Mission Ave 92058. I-5 exit 53 (Mission Ave), 2 mi e. Ext/int corridors. **Pets:** Small, dogs only. $10 daily fee/pet. Designated rooms, service with restrictions, supervision.
[SAVE] [icons]

OJAI

◈◈◈ Blue Iguana Inn M ☀
(805) 646-5277. **$119-$299, 7 day notice.** 11794 N Ventura Ave 93023. 2.5 mi w of town on SR 33. Ext corridors. **Pets:** Medium, dogs only. $20 daily fee/pet. Service with restrictions, supervision.
[icons]

◈◈◈ Casa Ojai Inn M
(805) 646-8175. **$99-$199.** 1302 E Ojai Ave 93023. 0.8 mi e on SR 150. Ext corridors. **Pets:** Medium. $25 daily fee/pet. Designated rooms, service with restrictions, crate. [ECO] [icons]

AAA ◈◈◈ Oakridge Inn M
(805) 649-4018. **$55-$160, 3 day notice.** 780 N Ventura Ave 93022. 4 mi s on SR 33; 2 mi e of Lake Casitas; in Oak View. Ext corridors. **Pets:** Medium. $15 one-time fee/pet. Designated rooms, service with restrictions, supervision. [SAVE] [icons]

AAA ◈◈◈◈ Ojai Valley Inn & Spa H ☀
(805) 646-1111. **$309-$409, 3 day notice.** 905 Country Club Rd 93023. 1 mi w on SR 150, 0.3 mi s. Ext/int corridors. **Pets:** Medium, dogs only. $125 one-time fee/pet. Service with restrictions, supervision.
[SAVE] [icons]

ONTARIO

◈◈◈ Ayres Boutique Suites Ontario Airport H ☀
(909) 937-9700. **$89-$169.** 204 N Vineyard Ave 91764. I-10 exit 54 (Vineyard Ave), 0.3 mi s. Int corridors. **Pets:** Other species. $45 one-time fee/room. Designated rooms, service with restrictions.
[icons]

BEST WESTERN PLUS InnSuites Airpark Ontario Hotel & Suites **H** ❀

(909) 466-9600. **$69-$179.** 3400 Shelby St 91764. I-10 exit 56 (Haven Ave), just n to Inland Empire Blvd, just w, then just se. Ext corridors. **Pets:** Medium. $20 one-time fee/pet. Designated rooms, service with restrictions, crate. SAVE 🛜 🛢 💻 🏊 🏋

DoubleTree by Hilton Hotel Ontario Airport **H**

(909) 937-0900. **$89-$159.** 222 N Vineyard Ave 91764. I-10 exit 54 (Vineyard Ave), 0.4 mi s. Int corridors. **Pets:** Medium. $50 one-time fee/room. Service with restrictions, crate. ECO 🛜 🛢 💻 🍽 🏊

Hilton Ontario Airport **H**

(909) 980-0400. **$79-$179.** 700 N Haven Ave 91764. I-10 exit 56 (Haven Ave), just n. Int corridors. **Pets:** $50 one-time fee/pet. Service with restrictions. ECO 🛜 🛜 🏋 🛢 💻 🍽 🏊

La Quinta Inn & Suites Ontario Airport **H**

(909) 476-1112. **$63-$144.** 3555 Inland Empire Blvd 91764. I-10 exit 56 (Haven Ave), just n, then just e. Int corridors. **Pets:** Service with restrictions, supervision. 🛜 🛢 💻 🏊

Quality Inn Ontario Airport **M** ❀

(909) 937-2999. **$79-$119.** 514 N Vineyard Ave 91764. I-10 exit 54 (Vineyard Ave), just s. Ext corridors. **Pets:** Small. $20 daily fee/pet. Designated rooms, service with restrictions, supervision.

SAVE 🛜 🛢 💻 🏊

Residence Inn by Marriott Ontario-Airport **H**

(909) 937-6788. **$149-$199.** 2025 Convention Center Way 91764. I-10 exit 54 (Vineyard Ave), just s, then 1 blk e. Ext corridors. **Pets:** Accepted.

🛜 🏋 🛢 💻 🏊 🏋

Sheraton Ontario Airport Hotel **H** ❀

(909) 937-8000. **$89-$259.** 429 N Vineyard Ave 91764. I-10 exit 54 (Vineyard Ave), just s. Int corridors. **Pets:** Medium. Designated rooms, service with restrictions, supervision.

SAVE 🛜 🏋 🛢 💻 🍽 🏊

ORANGE

Ayres Inn Orange **H**

(714) 978-9168. **$99-$139.** 3737 W Chapman Ave 92868. I-5 exit 107B (Chapman Ave) northbound, just w; exit 107C (State College/The City Dr) southbound, just s on State College Blvd, then just w. Int corridors.

Pets: Accepted. 🛜 🏋 🛢 💻 🍽 🏊

DoubleTree by Hilton Hotel Anaheim - Orange County **H**

(714) 634-4500. **$99-$199.** 100 The City Dr 92868. I-5 exit 107B (Chapman Ave) northbound, just w; exit 107C (State College Blvd/The City Dr) southbound, just s on State College Blvd, then just w. Int corridors. **Pets:** Large, dogs only. $75 one-time fee/pet. Service with restrictions, supervision. 🛜 🏋 🛢 💻 🏊 🏋

ORICK

Elk Meadow Cabins **CA**

(707) 488-2222. **$200-$300, 21 day notice.** 7 Valley Green Camp Rd 95555. US 101, milepost 124. Ext corridors. **Pets:** Medium, dogs only. $16 daily fee/room. Designated rooms, no service, supervision.

SAVE 🛜 🏋 🛢 💻 🏋 🏋

ORLAND

Orland Inn **M**

(530) 865-7632. **$59-$89.** 1052 South St 95963. I-5 exit 618 (CR 16/South St), just ne; in Stony Creek Shopping Center. Ext corridors. **Pets:** Large, other species. $6 daily fee/pet. Service with restrictions, crate. SAVE 🛜 🏋 🛢 🏊

OROVILLE

Americas Best Value Inn & Suites **M**

(530) 533-7070. **$65-$95.** 580 Oro Dam Blvd 95965. SR 70 exit SR 162 (Oro Dam Blvd), 0.3 mi e. Ext corridors. **Pets:** Medium, dogs only. $10 daily fee/pet. Designated rooms, service with restrictions, supervision. SAVE 🛜 🏋 🛢 💻

Super 8 Oroville **H**

(530) 533-9673. **$70-$90.** 1470 Feather River Blvd 95965. SR 70 exit 47 (Montgomery St), just ne, then s. Int corridors. **Pets:** Dogs only. $15 daily fee/pet. Designated rooms, service with restrictions.

🛜 🏋 🛢 💻 🏊 🏋

OXNARD

BEST WESTERN PLUS Oxnard Inn **M** ❀

(805) 483-9581. **$90-$249.** 1156 S Oxnard Blvd 93030. US 101 exit 61 (Rose Ave) northbound, 3 mi s, then 1 mi se; exit 62B (Oxnard Blvd) southbound, 3.5 mi s. Ext corridors. **Pets:** Small, dogs only. $40 one-time fee/pet. Designated rooms, service with restrictions, supervision.

SAVE 🛜 🏋 🛢 💻 🏊

Comfort Inn-Oxnard/Camarillo **M**

(805) 201-6000. **$89-$249.** 1001 E Channel Islands Blvd 93033. US 101 exit 61 (Rose Ave), 3.5 mi s, then 1.5 mi w. Ext corridors. **Pets:** Small, dogs only. $35 one-time fee/pet. Service with restrictions, supervision.

SAVE 🛜 🏋 🛢 💻 🏊 🏋

Embassy Suites Mandalay Beach Resort **H**

(805) 984-2500. **$149-$369.** 2101 Mandalay Beach Rd 93035. US 101 exit 64 (Victoria Ave), 5.5 mi s to Channel Islands Blvd, 0.5 mi w to Harbor Blvd, 0.3 mi n to Costa De Oro, then just w. Ext/int corridors.

Pets: Accepted. 🛜 🏋 🛢 💻 🍽 🏊

GrandStay Residential Suites Hotel **H**

(805) 983-6808. **$110-$150.** 2211 E Gonzales Rd 93036. US 101 exit Santa Clara Ave to Rice Ave, 0.4 mi w, then just n. Int corridors.

Pets: Accepted. SAVE 🛜 🏋 🛢 💻 🏊 🏋

Residence Inn by Marriott at River Ridge **H** ❀

(805) 278-2200. **$107-$217.** 2101 W Vineyard Ave 93036. US 101 exit 62A (Vineyard Ave), 1.8 mi w. Ext corridors. **Pets:** Small, other species. $100 one-time fee/room. Service with restrictions, crate.

SAVE 🛜 🏋 🏋 🛢 💻 🏊 🏋

PALMDALE

Embassy Suites **H**

(661) 266-3756. **$89-$259.** 39375 5th St W 93551. SR 14 exit 37 (Rancho Vista Blvd/Ave P), just w, just s to Trade Center Dr, then just e. Int corridors. **Pets:** Accepted. 🛜 🏋 🛢 💻 🍽 🏊

Holiday Inn Palmdale-Lancaster **H**

(661) 947-8055. **$99-$149.** 38630 5th St W 93551. SR 14 exit 35 (Palmdale Blvd), 0.5 mi w. Int corridors. **Pets:** Other species. $75 one-time fee/room. Service with restrictions, supervision.

🛜 🏋 🏋 🛢 💻 🍽 🏊 🏋

Residence Inn by Marriott **H**

(661) 947-4204. **$109-$199.** 514 W Ave P 93551. SR 14 exit 37 (Rancho Vista Blvd/Ave P), just e. Int corridors. **Pets:** Small. $100 one-time fee/room. Service with restrictions, crate.

🛜 🏋 🏋 🛢 💻 🏊 🏋

Staybridge Suites **H** ❀

(661) 947-9300. **$149-$200.** 420 W Park Dr 93551. SR 14 exit 35 (Palmdale Blvd), 0.5 mi w. Int corridors. **Pets:** Medium, other species. $75 deposit/room. Designated rooms, service with restrictions, crate.

🛜 🏋 🏋 🛢 💻 🏊 🏋

PALM DESERT

BEST WESTERN PLUS Palm Desert Resort **M**

(760) 340-4441. **$90-$250.** 74-695 Hwy 111 92260. I-10 exit 134 (Cook St), 4.4 mi s, then 0.3 mi w. Ext corridors. **Pets:** Other species. $10 daily fee/room. Service with restrictions, supervision.

SAVE 🛜 🏋 🏋 🛢 💻 🏊 🏋

WWW Comfort Suites M
(760) 360-3337. **$79-$109.** 39585 Washington St 92211. I-10 exit 137 (Washington St), just n. Int corridors. **Pets:** Other species. $20 daily fee/room. Service with restrictions, supervision.

ECO 🛜 ✕ 🏃M 🛏 🖥 �ↄ 🐾

WWW Embassy Suites Hotel H
(760) 340-6600. **$89-$449.** 74-700 Hwy 111 92260. I-10 exit 134 (Cook St), 4.4 mi s, then 0.3 mi w. Ext corridors. **Pets:** Medium. $50 one-time fee/room. Designated rooms, service with restrictions.

ECO 🛜 🛏 🖥 🍴 �ↄ 🐾

AAA WWW Homewood Suites by Hilton-Palm Desert H 🐾
(760) 568-1600. **$89-$289.** 36-999 Cook St 92211. I-10 exit 134 (Cook St), 0.5 mi s; in The Village at University Park. Int corridors. **Pets:** Medium, other species. $75 one-time fee/room. Service with restrictions, supervision. SAVE 🛜 🏃M 🖥 🐾

AAA WWW The Inn at Deep Canyon M
(760) 346-8061. **$106-$229, 3 day notice.** 74470 Abronia Tr 92260. I-10 exit 134 (Cook St), 4.4 mi s to SR 111, 0.5 mi w, then just s on Deep Canyon Rd. Ext corridors. **Pets:** Other species. $10 daily fee/pet. Service with restrictions. SAVE 🛜 🛏 🖥 �ↄ

AAA WWW Residence Inn by Marriott H 🐾
(760) 776-0050. **$119-$299.** 38-305 Cook St 92211. I-10 exit 134 (Cook St), 0.8 mi s. Ext corridors. **Pets:** Small, other species. $75 one-time fee/room. Service with restrictions, supervision.

SAVE 🛜 ✕ 🛏 🖥 �ↄ 🐾

PALM SPRINGS

WW A Place In The Sun M
(760) 325-0254. **$119-$379, 7 day notice.** 754 E San Lorenzo Rd 92264. Just e of Palm Canyon Dr on Mesquite Ave, just n on Random Rd, then just e. Ext corridors. **Pets:** Other species. $15 daily fee/pet. Service with restrictions. 🛜 ✕ 🛏 🖥 �ↄ

AAA WW BEST WESTERN Inn At Palm Springs M
(760) 325-9177. **$70-$250.** 1633 S Palm Canyon Dr 92264. 1.3 mi s of Tahquitz Canyon Way. Ext corridors. **Pets:** Accepted.

SAVE 🛜 ✕ 🛏 🖥 ở

WWW Hilton Palm Springs H
(760) 320-6868. **$100-$365.** 400 E Tahquitz Canyon Way 92262. Just e of Indian Canyon Dr. Int corridors. **Pets:** Accepted.

🖿 🛜 🛏 🖥 🍴 ở 🐾

AAA WWWW Hyatt Regency Suites Palm Springs H 🐾
(760) 322-9000. **$68-$387, 3 day notice.** 285 N Palm Canyon Dr 92262. Downtown. Ext/int corridors. **Pets:** Medium. $25 daily fee/pet. Designated rooms, service with restrictions, crate.

SAVE 🛜 🏃M 🛏 🖥 🍴 ở 🐾

WWW Renaissance Palm Springs Hotel H
(760) 322-6000. **$99-$299, 3 day notice.** 888 Tahquitz Canyon Way 92262. 0.4 mi e of Indian Canyon Dr. Int corridors. **Pets:** Accepted.

🛜 ✕ 🏃M 🛏 🖥 🍴 ở 🐾

WWW Villa Royale Inn CI 🐾
(760) 327-2314. **$99-$500, 3 day notice.** 1620 S Indian Tr 92264. 2 mi se of Tahquitz Canyon Way on Palm Canyon Dr, then just n. Ext corridors. **Pets:** Small, dogs only. $75 deposit/pet. Designated rooms, service with restrictions, supervision. 🛜 ✕ 🛏 🖥 🍴 ở 🐾

PALO ALTO

AAA WWW Comfort Inn Palo Alto/Stanford Area M
(650) 493-3141. **$85-$280.** 3945 El Camino Real 94306. US 101 exit Oregon Expwy/Page Mill Rd, 1 mi s. Ext corridors. **Pets:** Medium, dogs only. $20 daily fee/pet. Designated rooms, service with restrictions, supervision. SAVE 🛜 ✕ 🏃M 🛏 🖥

AAA WWWW Crowne Plaza Cabana Hotel H
(650) 857-0787. **$109-$529.** 4290 El Camino Real 94306. US 101 exit San Antonio Rd, 0.4 mi n. Ext/int corridors. **Pets:** Accepted.

ECO SAVE 🛜 ✕ 🏃M 🛏 🖥 🍴 ở

AAA WWWW Dinah's Garden Hotel H
(650) 493-2844. **$99-$750.** 4261 El Camino Real 94306. US 101 exit San Antonio Rd S, 0.4 mi n on SR 82. Ext/int corridors. **Pets:** Accepted.

ECO SAVE 🛜 ✕ 🏃M 🛏 🖥 🍴 ở

AAA WWWW Quality Inn Palo Alto/Stanford Area M
(650) 493-2760. **$85-$280.** 3901 El Camino Real 94306. US 101 exit Oregon Expwy/Page Mill Rd, 2 mi w to SR 82, then se to Ventura Ave. Ext corridors. **Pets:** Medium, dogs only. $20 daily fee/pet. Designated rooms, service with restrictions, supervision.

SAVE 🛜 ✕ 🏃M 🛏 🖥

AAA WWWW Sheraton Palo Alto Hotel H 🐾
(650) 328-2800. **$109-$509, 3 day notice.** 625 El Camino Real 94301. US 101 exit 402 (Embarcadero Rd/Oregon Expwy), 1.8 mi w, then just n on SR 82. Int corridors. **Pets:** Large, other species. Service with restrictions, supervision. ECO SAVE 🛜 ✕ 🏃M 🛏 🖥 🍴 ở

WWW Stanford Terrace Inn H
(650) 857-0333. **Call for rates.** 531 Stanford Ave 94306. US 101 exit Oregon Expwy, 0.4 mi n on SR 82, then just w. Ext corridors. **Pets:** Accepted. ECO 🛜 🏃M 🖥 ở

AAA WWWW The Westin Palo Alto H 🐾
(650) 321-4422. **$129-$559, 3 day notice.** 675 El Camino Real 94301. US 101 exit 402 (Embarcadero Rd), 1.8 mi w, then just n on SR 82. Int corridors. **Pets:** Large, other species. Service with restrictions, supervision.

ECO 🖿 SAVE 🛜 ✕ 🏃M 🖥 🍴 ở 🐾

PARADISE

AAA WWW Comfort Inn H
(530) 876-0191. **$80-$120.** 5475 Clark Rd 95969. SR 191 (Skyway Rd), 1.1 mi e on Pearson Rd, 0.3 mi s. Int corridors. **Pets:** Dogs only. $10 daily fee/pet. Designated rooms, service with restrictions, supervision. SAVE 🛜 🛏 🖥 ở

AAA WW Lantern Inn M
(530) 877-5553. **$55-$82.** 5799 Wildwood Ln 95969. Just n of jct Pearson and Skyway rds, then 1 blk w off Skyway Rd. Ext corridors. **Pets:** Accepted. SAVE 🛜 🛏 🖥 ở

WWW Ponderosa Gardens Motel M 🐾
(530) 872-9094. **$89-$139.** 7010 Skyway 95969. 2 blks e; center. Ext corridors. **Pets:** Other species. $200 deposit/room, $10 daily fee/pet. Designated rooms, service with restrictions, supervision.

🛜 🏃M 🛏 🖥 ở

PASO ROBLES

WWWW Holiday Inn Express Hotel & Suites H 🐾
(805) 238-6500. **$109-$249.** 2455 Riverside Ave 93446. US 101 exit 231B (SR 46 E), just w, then just n. Int corridors. **Pets:** Dogs only. $35 one-time fee/room. Designated rooms, service with restrictions, supervision. 🛜 ✕ 🏃M 🛏 🖥 ở

WWW La Quinta Inn & Suites Paso Robles H
(805) 239-3004. **$107-$331.** 2615 Buena Vista Dr 93446. US 101 exit 234 northbound; exit 231B (SR 46 E) southbound, 0.3 mi e, then just n. Int corridors. **Pets:** Service with restrictions, supervision.

🛜 ✕ 🛏 🖥 ở

AAA WWW Paso Robles Inn H 🐾
(805) 238-2660. **$95-$330, 3 day notice.** 1103 Spring St 93446. US 101 exit 232 (Spring St) northbound, 0.8 mi n; exit 231A (16th St) southbound, just w, then just s. Ext/int corridors. **Pets:** Dogs only. $25 daily fee/room. Designated rooms, service with restrictions, supervision.

SAVE 🛜 ✕ 🛏 🖥 🍴 ở

PATTERSON

 BEST WESTERN PLUS Villa Del Lago Inn 🅷

(209) 892-5300. **$80-$140.** 2959 Speno Dr 95363. I-5 exit Sperry Rd, just e. Int corridors. **Pets:** Accepted.

PHELAN

BEST WESTERN Cajon Pass **M**

(760) 249-6777. **Call for rates.** 8317 Hwy 138 92371. I-15 exit 131 (SR 138/Palmdale), just w. Ext corridors. **Pets:** Accepted.

PISMO BEACH

BEST WESTERN PLUS Shelter Cove Lodge **M** ❖

(805) 773-3511. **$109-$329, 3 day notice.** 2651 Price St 93449. US 101 exit 191B (Shell Beach Rd) northbound, just w, then 0.3 mi n; exit 191B (Price St) southbound, just w, then 0.4 mi n. Ext corridors. **Pets:** Dogs only. $20 daily fee/room. Designated rooms, service with restrictions, supervision.

BEST WESTERN PLUS Shore Cliff Lodge 🅷 ❖

(805) 773-4671. **$109-$399, 3 day notice.** 2555 Price St 93449. US 101 exit 191B (Shell Beach Rd) northbound; exit 191B (Price St) southbound, just w. Ext/int corridors. **Pets:** Dogs only. $20 daily fee/room. Designated rooms, service with restrictions, supervision.

Cliffs Resort 🅷 ❖

(805) 773-5000. **$149-$475, 3 day notice.** 2757 Shell Beach Rd 93449. US 101 exit 193 (Spyglass Dr) northbound; exit 193 (Shell Beach Rd) southbound, just w, then just n. Int corridors. **Pets:** Dogs only. $55 one-time fee/room. Designated rooms, service with restrictions.

Cottage Inn by the Sea **M** ❖

(805) 773-4617. **$109-$399, 7 day notice.** 2351 Price St 93449. US 101 exit 191B (Shell Beach Rd) northbound, just w, then 0.5 mi s; exit 191B (Price St) southbound, just w, then just s. Ext corridors. **Pets:** Medium, other species. $75 one-time fee/room. Designated rooms, service with restrictions, supervision.

Dolphin Bay Resort & Spa 🄲🄾 ❖

(805) 773-4300. **$345-$1160.** 2727 Shell Beach Rd 93449. US 101 exit 193 (Spyglass Dr) northbound; exit 193 (Shell Beach Rd) southbound, just w, then just n; in Shell Beach area. Ext corridors. **Pets:** Other species. $65 daily fee/room. Designated rooms, service with restrictions.

Edgewater Inn & Suites **M**

(805) 773-4811. **$99-$269.** 280 Wadsworth Ave 93449. US 101 exit 191A (Wadsworth Ave) northbound, just w; exit 191B (Price St) southbound, just w, then 0.4 mi s on Dolliver St. Ext corridors. **Pets:** Service with restrictions, supervision.

Oxford Suites 🅷 ❖

(805) 773-3773. **$95-$229.** 651 Five Cities Dr 93449. US 101 exit 189 (4th St), just w, then just s. Ext corridors. **Pets:** Medium, other species. $25 one-time fee/room. Designated rooms, service with restrictions, supervision.

Pismo Lighthouse Suites **M** ❖

(805) 773-2411. **$179-$499, 3 day notice.** 2411 Price St 93449. US 101 exit 191B (Shell Beach Rd) northbound, just w, then 0.5 mi s; exit 191B (Price St) southbound, just w, then just s. Ext corridors. **Pets:** Dogs only. $25 daily fee/room. Designated rooms, service with restrictions, supervision.

Sandcastle Inn **M** ❖

(805) 773-2422. **$145-$509.** 100 Stimson Ave 93449. US 101 exit 190 (Price St) northbound, 0.3 mi s, then just w; exit 190B (Hinds Ave) southbound, just w, then just s. Ext/int corridors. **Pets:** Medium. $75 one-time fee/room. Designated rooms, service with restrictions, supervision.

SeaCrest OceanFront Hotel **M** ❖

(805) 773-4608. **$119-$429.** 2241 Price St 93449. US 101 exit 191B (Shell Beach Rd) northbound, just w, then 0.5 mi s; exit 191B (Price St) southbound, just w, then just s. Ext/int corridors. **Pets:** Other species. Designated rooms, service with restrictions, supervision.

Sea Gypsy Motel **M**

(805) 773-1801. **$65-$275.** 1020 Cypress St 93449. US 101 exit 191A (Wadsworth Ave) northbound, 0.3 mi w to Cypress St, then just s; exit 191A (SR 1) southbound, just w on Wadsworth Ave, then just s. Ext/int corridors. **Pets:** Other species. $15 daily fee/pet. Service with restrictions, supervision.

Shell Beach Inn **M**

(805) 773-4373. **$65-$225.** 653 Shell Beach Rd 93449. US 101 exit 191B (Shell Beach Rd) northbound, just w, then 1.2 mi s; exit 191B (Price St) southbound, just w, then 1 mi n; in Shell Beach area. Ext corridors. **Pets:** Small, dogs only. $20 one-time fee/pet. Service with restrictions, supervision.

Spyglass Inn 🅷

(805) 773-4855. **$99-$379.** 2705 Spyglass Dr 93449. US 101 exit 193 (Spyglass Dr) northbound; exit 193 (Shell Beach Rd) southbound, just w, then just n. Ext corridors. **Pets:** Accepted.

PLACENTIA

Fairfield Inn by Marriott 🅷

(714) 996-4410. **$79-$99.** 710 W Kimberly Ave 92870. SR 57 exit 6 (Orangethorpe Ave) southbound; exit 6A (Orangethorpe Ave) northbound, just w, just n on Placentia Ave, then just e. Ext/int corridors. **Pets:** Accepted.

Residence Inn by Marriott 🅷

(714) 996-0555. **$132-$219.** 700 W Kimberly Ave 92870. SR 57 exit 6 (Orangethorpe Ave) southbound; exit 6A (Orangethorpe Ave) northbound, just w, just n on Placentia Ave, then just e. Ext corridors. **Pets:** $100 one-time fee/room. Designated rooms, service with restrictions, crate.

PLACERVILLE

BEST WESTERN PLUS Placerville Inn 🅷

(530) 622-9100. **Call for rates.** 6850 Green Leaf Dr 95667. US 50 exit 44A (Missouri Flat Rd S), just e. Int corridors. **Pets:** Other species. $20 daily fee/pet. Designated rooms, service with restrictions, supervision.

PLEASANT HILL

Extended StayAmerica-Pleasant Hill-Buskirk Ave 🅷

(925) 945-6788. **$99-$114.** 3220 Buskirk Ave 94523. I-680 exit Treat Blvd/Geary Rd E, just n. Int corridors. **Pets:** $25 daily fee/pet. Designated rooms, service with restrictions.

Hyatt house Pleasant Hill 🅷 ❖

(925) 934-3343. **$99-$219.** 2611 Contra Costa Blvd 94523. I-680 exit Contra Costa Blvd, then w. Int corridors. **Pets:** Medium, other species. $150 one-time fee/room. Designated rooms, service with restrictions, crate.

Residence Inn by Marriott-Pleasant Hill 🅷

(925) 689-1010. **$109-$259.** 700 Ellinwood Way 94523. I-680 exit Willow Pass Rd W to S Contra Costa Blvd, e on Ellinwood Dr, then n. Ext/int corridors. **Pets:** Accepted.

PLEASANTON

AAA ▼▼▼▼ BEST WESTERN PLUS Pleasanton Inn 🅗
(925) 463-1300. **$110-$130.** 5375 Owens Ct 94588. I-580 exit Hopyard Rd, just s. Ext corridors. **Pets:** Large. $35 daily fee/pet. Designated rooms, service with restrictions, supervision.
SAVE 📶 👤M 🛗 💻 ➿

▼▼▼▼ Hilton Pleasanton at the Club 🅗
(925) 463-8000. **$109-$249.** 7050 Johnson Dr 94588. In southeast quadrant of jct I-580 and 680. Int corridors. **Pets:** $50 deposit/pet. Service with restrictions, crate. 📶 👤M 🛗 💻 🍴 ➿ ⊠

▼▼▼▼ Larkspur Landing Pleasanton 🅗
(925) 463-1212. **Call for rates.** 5535 Johnson Dr 94588. I-580 exit Hopyard Rd S, w on Owen. Int corridors. **Pets:** Accepted.
ECO 📶 ⊠ 👤M 🛗 💻

AAA ▼▼▼▼ Pleasanton Marriott 🅗
(925) 847-6000. **$99-$359.** 11950 Dublin Canyon Rd 94588. I-580 exit Foothill Rd, 0.3 mi s. Int corridors. **Pets:** Accepted.
SAVE 📶 ⊠ 👤M 🛗 💻 🍴 ➿ ⊠

▼▼▼▼ Residence Inn by Marriott 🅗 🐾
(925) 227-0500. **$89-$189.** 11920 Dublin Canyon Rd 94588. I-580 exit Foothill Rd S, then w. Int corridors. **Pets:** Other species. $100 one-time fee/room. Service with restrictions, supervision.
📶 ⊠ 👤M 🛗 💻 ➿ ⊠

AAA ▼▼▼▼ Sheraton Pleasanton Hotel 🅗
(925) 463-3330. **$89-$219.** 5990 Stoneridge Mall Rd 94588. Jct I-580 and 680, 0.5 mi sw; I-580 exit Foothill Rd, 0.3 mi s, then 0.3 mi e on Canyon Way. Int corridors. **Pets:** Accepted.
SAVE 📶 ⊠ 👤M 🛗 💻 🍴 ➿

PLYMOUTH

AAA ▼▼▼▼ Shenandoah Inn 🅗
(209) 245-4491. **$99-$149, 3 day notice.** 17674 Village Dr 95669. On SR 49, south end of town. Ext corridors. **Pets:** $10 daily fee/pet. Designated rooms, service with restrictions, supervision.
SAVE 📶 ⊠ 🛗 💻 ➿ 🅩

POLLOCK PINES

AAA ▼▼▼▼ BEST WESTERN Stagecoach Inn 🅜
(530) 644-2029. **$99-$139.** 5940 Pony Express Tr 95726. US 50 exit 57 (Pollock Pines) eastbound, just n, then 1 mi e; exit Sly Park Rd westbound, just n, then 1 mi w. Ext corridors. **Pets:** Accepted.
SAVE 📶 👤M 🛗 💻 ➿

PORTERVILLE

AAA ▼▼▼▼ BEST WESTERN PLUS Porterville Inn 🅗
(559) 781-7411. **$99-$109.** 350 W Montgomery Ave 93257. SR 65, 0.8 mi e on SR 190, just s on Jaye St, then just e. Int corridors.
Pets: Accepted. SAVE 📶 ⊠ 👤M 🛗 💻 ➿

PORT HUENEME

▼▼▼▼ Holiday Inn Express & Suites 🅗 🐾
(805) 986-5353. **$117-$229.** 350 E Port Hueneme Rd 93041. US 101 exit 62A (Vineyard Rd), just s to Oxnard Blvd, 2 mi s to Wooley Rd, 1 mi w to Ventura Rd, then 3 mi s. Int corridors. **Pets:** Small, dogs only. $75 one-time fee/room, $20 daily fee/pet. Designated rooms, service with restrictions, crate. 📶 ⊠ 🛗 💻 ➿

PORTOLA

▼▼▼ Sleepy Pines Motel 🅜
(530) 832-4291. **$67-$140, 3 day notice.** 74631 Hwy 70 96122. 1 mi w of center on SR 70. Ext corridors. **Pets:** Small, dogs only. Service with restrictions, supervision. 📶 🛗 💻

RAMONA

AAA ▼▼▼ Ramona Valley Inn 🅜
(760) 789-6433. **$68-$125.** 416 Main St 92065. SR 78, 0.5 mi e of jct SR 67. Ext corridors. **Pets:** $15 one-time fee/room. Service with restrictions, supervision. SAVE 📶 🛗 ➿ 🅩

RANCHO CORDOVA

▼▼▼ Extended StayAmerica-Sacramento-White Rock Rd 🅗
(916) 635-2363. **$69-$84.** 10721 White Rock Rd 95670. US 50 exit Zinfandel Dr, just s. Ext corridors. **Pets:** $25 daily fee/pet. Designated rooms, service with restrictions. 📶 👤M 🛗 💻

▼▼▼▼ Fairfield Inn & Suites by Marriott 🅗
(916) 858-8680. **$69-$139.** 10745 Gold Center Dr 95670. US 50 exit Zinfandel Dr, just s to White Rock Rd, just e, then just n; jct Gold Center Dr. Int corridors. **Pets:** Accepted. 📶 ⊠ 👤M 🛗 💻 ➿

▼▼▼▼ Holiday Inn Rancho Cordova 🅗 🐾
(916) 635-4040. **$99-$149.** 11269 Point East Dr 95742. US 50 exit Sunrise Blvd S, e on Folsom Blvd, then just n. Int corridors. **Pets:** Medium. $50 one-time fee/pet. Designated rooms, service with restrictions, supervision. ECO 📶 ⊠ 👤M 🛗 💻 🍴 ➿ ⊠

AAA ▼▼▼▼ Hyatt Place Sacramento/Rancho Cordova 🅗
(916) 635-4799. **$89-$219.** 10744 Gold Center Dr 95670. US 50 exit Zinfandel Dr, just s on Zinfandel Dr, just e on White Rock Rd, just n on Prospect Park Dr, then just w. Int corridors. **Pets:** Dogs only. $50 one-time fee/room. Designated rooms, service with restrictions, supervision.
SAVE 📶 ⊠ 🛗 💻 ➿

▼▼▼▼ La Quinta Inn & Suites Sacramento Rancho Cordova 🅗
(916) 638-1111. **$59-$151.** 11131 Folsom Blvd 95670. US 50 exit Sunrise Blvd, just s, then just w. Int corridors. **Pets:** Service with restrictions, supervision. 📶 👤M 🛗 💻 ➿

▼▼▼ Red Lion Inn 🅗
(916) 631-7500. **Call for rates.** 10713 White Rock Rd 95670. US 50 exit Zinfandel Dr, just s, then just w. Ext/int corridors. **Pets:** Other species. $15 one-time fee/room. Service with restrictions, crate.
📶 👤M 🛗 💻 ➿

▼▼▼▼ Residence Inn by Marriott 🅗
(916) 851-1550. **$90-$250.** 2779 Prospect Park Dr 95670. US 50 exit Zinfandel Dr, just s to White Rock Rd, just e, then just n; jct Gold Center Dr. Int corridors. **Pets:** Accepted. 📶 ⊠ 🛗 💻 ➿ ⊠

RANCHO CUCAMONGA

AAA ▼▼▼▼ Aloft Ontario-Rancho Cucamonga 🅗
(909) 484-2018. **$94-$294, 7 day notice.** 10480 4th St 91730. I-10 exit 59 (Haven Ave), 0.3 m n, then just w. Int corridors. **Pets:** Accepted.
SAVE 📶 ⊠ 👤M 🛗 💻 ➿

AAA ▼▼▼▼ Four Points by Sheraton Ontario Rancho Cucamonga 🅗
(909) 204-6100. **$85-$299.** 11960 Foothill Blvd 91739. I-15 exit 112 (Foothill Blvd), 0.8 mi w. Int corridors. **Pets:** Medium. $75 deposit/room. Designated rooms, service with restrictions, supervision.
SAVE 📶 ⊠ 🛗 💻 ➿

▼▼▼▼ Homewood Suites 🅗
(909) 481-6480. **$89-$159.** 11433 Mission Vista Dr 91730. I-15 exit 110 (4th St), just w to Richmond Pl, just n, then just w. Int corridors. **Pets:** Medium. $75 one-time fee/room. Supervision.
📶 👤M 🛗 💻 ⊠

▼▼▼▼ TownePlace Suites by Marriott 🅗
(909) 466-1100. **$79-$159.** 9625 Milliken Ave 91730. I-10 exit 57 (Milliken Ave), 0.6 mi n. Int corridors. **Pets:** Accepted.
📶 ⊠ 👤M 🛗 💻 ➿

RANCHO MIRAGE

Agua Caliente Casino Resort Spa H ❀

(760) 321-2000. **$99-$599, 3 day notice.** 32-250 Bob Hope Dr 92270. I-10 exit 130 (Ramon Rd/Bob Hope Dr), just s. Int corridors. **Pets:** Small, dogs only. $60 one-time fee/pet. Designated rooms, service with restrictions, supervision. SAVE

The Westin Mission Hills Resort & Spa H ❀

(760) 328-5955. **$89-$1499, 3 day notice.** 71-333 Dinah Shore Dr 92270. I-10 exit 130 (Ramon Rd/Bob Hope Dr), 1 mi s on Bob Hope Dr, then 0.6 mi w. Ext corridors. **Pets:** Medium, dogs only. Designated rooms, no service, supervision. SAVE

RED BLUFF

BEST WESTERN PLUS Antelope Inn H

(530) 527-8882. **$92-$150.** 203 Antelope Blvd 96080. I-5 exit 649 (SR 36), just e. Int corridors. **Pets:** Large, other species. $14 daily fee/pet. Service with restrictions, supervision. SAVE

Comfort Inn H

(530) 529-7060. **$80-$155.** 90 Sale Ln 96080. I-5 exit 649 (SR 36), 0.3 mi e. Int corridors. **Pets:** Dogs only. $15 daily fee/pet. Service with restrictions, supervision. SAVE

Sportsman Lodge M

(530) 527-2888. **$55-$150, 3 day notice.** 768 Antelope Blvd 96080. I-5 exit 649 (SR 36), 1.5 mi e. Ext corridors. **Pets:** $7 one-time fee/pet, $7 daily fee/pet. Designated rooms, no service, supervision.

SAVE

REDCREST

Redcrest Resort CA ❀

(707) 722-4208. **$80-$275, 14 day notice.** 26459 Ave of the Giants 95569. US 101 exit Redcrest southbound; exit Redcrest/Holmes northbound, just e, then just n. Ext corridors. **Pets:** Large. $10 daily fee/pet. Designated rooms, service with restrictions, supervision.

SAVE

REDDING

Baymont Inn & Suites Redding H

(530) 722-9100. **$84-$140.** 2600 Larkspur Ln 96002. I-5 exit 677 (Cypress Ave), just e, then just s. Int corridors. **Pets:** Dogs only. $20 daily fee/pet. Designated rooms, service with restrictions, supervision.

SAVE

BEST WESTERN PLUS Hilltop Inn H ❀

(530) 221-6100. **$129-$169.** 2300 Hilltop Dr 96002. I-5 exit 677 (Cypress Ave), just e, then just n. Ext corridors. **Pets:** Medium. $20 daily fee/room. Designated rooms, service with restrictions, supervision.

SAVE

BEST WESTERN PLUS Twin View Inn & Suites H

(530) 241-5500. **$89-$149.** 1080 Twin View Blvd 96003. I-5 exit 681 (Twin View Blvd), just w. Int corridors. **Pets:** $20 one-time fee/pet. Designated rooms, service with restrictions, supervision.

SAVE

Bridge Bay Resort M

(530) 275-3021. **$85-$190, 3 day notice.** 10300 Bridge Bay Rd 96003. I-5 exit 690, just w. Ext corridors. **Pets:** $50 deposit/pet, $10 daily fee/pet. Service with restrictions, supervision. SAVE

Comfort Inn H

(530) 221-4472. **$90-$145.** 850 Mistletoe Ln 96002. I-5 exit 677 (Cypress Ave), 0.8 mi n on Hilltop Dr, then just e. Int corridors. **Pets:** Medium, other species. $10 daily fee/pet. Designated rooms, service with restrictions, supervision. SAVE

Fairfield Inn & Suites by Marriott H ❀

(530) 243-3200. **$109-$159.** 5164 Caterpillar Rd 96003. I-5 exit 681 (Twin View Blvd) northbound; exit 681B southbound, just w, then just n. Int corridors. **Pets:** $25 daily fee/room. Designated rooms, service with restrictions, supervision.

Fawndale Lodge & RV Resort M

(530) 275-8000. **Call for rates.** 15215 Fawndale Rd 96003. I-5 exit 689 (Fawndale Rd), just e, then 0.3 mi s; 10 mi n of town; 1 mi s of Shasta Lake. Ext corridors. **Pets:** Accepted.

Holiday Inn H

(530) 221-7500. **$115-$185.** 1900 Hilltop Dr 96002. I-5 exit 677 (Cypress Ave), just e, then 0.8 mi n. Int corridors. **Pets:** Dogs only. $100 deposit/room, $10 daily fee/pet. Service with restrictions, supervision.

SAVE

Oxford Suites H ❀

(530) 221-0100. **$99-$159.** 1967 Hilltop Dr 96002. I-5 exit 677 (Cypress Ave), just e, then just n. Ext/int corridors. **Pets:** Small, other species. $25 one-time fee/room. Designated rooms, service with restrictions, supervision. SAVE

Redding Travelodge H

(530) 243-5291. **$85-$209.** 540 N Market St 96003. I-5 exit 680 (Lake Blvd) northbound, 0.5 mi w to Market St, then 0.5 mi s; exit Market St southbound, 2 mi s. Ext corridors. **Pets:** Accepted.

SAVE

Red Lion Hotel Redding H

(530) 221-8700. **$109-$189.** 1830 Hilltop Dr 96002. I-5 exit SR 44 (Hilltop Dr) southbound, just e, then just s; exit 677 (Cypress Ave) northbound, just e, then 0.6 mi n. Int corridors. **Pets:** Other species. $15 one-time fee/room. Service with restrictions, crate.

REDLANDS

Ayres Hotel Redlands H ❀

(909) 335-9024. **$99-$169.** 1015 W Colton Ave 92374. I-10 exit 77B (Tennessee St) westbound; exit 77C (Tennessee St) eastbound, just s, then just e. Ext corridors. **Pets:** Other species. $45 one-time fee/room. Designated rooms, service with restrictions.

ECO

Dynasty Suites-Redlands M ❀

(909) 793-6648. **$79-$149.** 1235 W Colton Ave 92374. I-10 exit 77C (Tennessee St) eastbound; exit 77B (Tennessee St) westbound, just s, then just w. Ext corridors. **Pets:** Small, dogs only. $15 daily fee/pet. Designated rooms, service with restrictions, supervision.

ECO SAVE

REDWOOD CITY

Sofitel San Francisco Bay H

(650) 598-9000. **$110-$315, 7 day notice.** 223 Twin Dolphin Dr 94065. US 101 exit Marine Pkwy E, 0.5 mi s. Int corridors. **Pets:** Accepted.

ECO SAVE

TownePlace Suites by Marriott H

(650) 593-4100. **$149-$249.** 1000 Twin Dolphin Dr 94065. US 101 exit Redwood Shores Pkwy, 0.3 mi e, then just s. Int corridors. **Pets:** Accepted.

REEDLEY

Edgewater Inn M

(559) 637-7777. **$75-$79.** 1977 W Manning Ave 93654. 12 mi e of SR 99 via Manning Ave. Ext corridors. **Pets:** Other species. $8 deposit/pet. Designated rooms, supervision. SAVE

RIDGECREST

BEST WESTERN PLUS China Lake Inn M

(760) 371-2300. **$90-$100.** 400 S China Lake Blvd 93555. On US 395 business route. Ext corridors. **Pets:** Large. $25 daily fee/pet. Designated rooms, service with restrictions, supervision.

SAVE

▼▼ Budget Inn & Suites M
(760) 375-1351. **$55-$75.** 831 N China Lake Blvd 93555. On US 395 business route; near center of town. Ext corridors. **Pets:** Very small. $50 deposit/room. Designated rooms, service with restrictions, supervision.
🛜 ✕ 🖨

∞ ▼▼▼ Carriage Inn M
(760) 446-7910. **$79-$149.** 901 N China Lake Blvd 93555. On SR 178 and US 395 business route; center. Ext corridors. **Pets:** Accepted.
[SAVE] 🛜 🕭ᴹ 🖨 🖵 🍴 ⇻ ✕

∞ ▼▼▼ Econo Lodge Inn & Suites M
(760) 446-2551. **$65-$85.** 201 Inyokern Rd 93555. SR 178 and US 395 business route, just w of China Lake Blvd. Ext corridors. **Pets:** Small, dogs only. $10 one-time fee/pet. Service with restrictions, supervision.
[SAVE] 🛜 🕭ᴹ 🖨 🖵 ⇻

∞ ▼▼▼ Heritage Inn & Suites H
(760) 446-6543. **$83-$96.** 1050 N Norma St 93555. On US 395 business route, just w. Int corridors. **Pets:** Other species. $100 deposit/room. Service with restrictions, crate. [SAVE] 🛜 🕭ᴹ 🖨 🖵 🍴 ⇻

∞ ▼▼▼ Quality Inn M
(760) 375-9731. **$80-$150.** 507 S China Lake Blvd 93555. On US 395 business route; south end of town. Ext corridors. **Pets:** Small. $35 daily fee/pet. Designated rooms, service with restrictions, supervision.
[SAVE] 🛜 ✕ 🖨 🖵 ⇻

RIO DELL

∞ ▼ Humboldt Gables Motel M
(707) 764-5609. **$60-$135.** 40 W Davis St 95562. US 101 exit Wildwood Ave, 0.5 mi w. Ext corridors. **Pets:** Small, dogs only. $20 daily fee/room. Supervision. [SAVE] 🛜 ✕ 🕭ᴹ 🖨 🖵 🍴

RIPON

∞ ▼▼▼ La Quinta Inn & Suites Manteca - Ripon H
(209) 599-8999. **$83-$150.** 1524 Colony Rd 95366. SR 99 exit Jack Tone Rd, just e. Int corridors. **Pets:** Service with restrictions, supervision.
[SAVE] 🛜 🕭ᴹ 🖨 🖵 ⇻

RIVERSIDE

▼▼ Comfort Inn University M
(951) 683-6000. **$79-$99.** 1590 University Ave 92507. I-215 and SR 60 exit 32 (University Ave), 0.5 mi w. Ext corridors. **Pets:** Small. $15 daily fee/pet. Designated rooms, service with restrictions, supervision.
🛜 🖨 🖵 ⇻

▼▼▼ Hampton Inn & Suites Riverside/Corona East H
(951) 352-5020. **$79-$119.** 4250 Riverwalk Pkwy 92505. SR 91 exit 54 (Pierce St/Riverwalk Pkwy) eastbound, 0.4 mi n; exit 55A (Magnolia Ave) westbound, just w, then 0.5 mi n on Pierce St/Riverwalk Pkwy. Int corridors. **Pets:** Large. $35 one-time fee/room. Service with restrictions, crate.
🛜 🕭ᴹ 🖨 🖵 ⇻

∞ ▼▼▼ Rodeway Inn Riverside M
(951) 359-0770. **Call for rates.** 10518 Magnolia Ave 92505. SR 91 exit 56 (Tyler St), 0.5 mi n, then 0.3 mi w. Ext corridors. **Pets:** Small. $100 deposit/room, $20 daily fee/pet. Designated rooms, service with restrictions, supervision. [SAVE] 🛜 🖨 🖵 ⇻

ROCKLIN

▼▼ Heritage Inn Express, Rocklin H
(916) 632-3366. **$65-$75.** 4480 Rocklin Rd 95677. I-80 exit Rocklin Rd, just w, then just s. Int corridors. **Pets:** Accepted.
🛜 🕭ᴹ 🖨 🖵 ⇻

▼▼ Howard Johnson Hotel H
(916) 624-4500. **$59-$119.** 4420 Rocklin Rd 95677. I-80 exit Rocklin Rd, just w, then just s. Int corridors. **Pets:** Accepted.
🛜 🕭ᴹ 🖨 🖵 ⇻

▼▼ Staybridge Suites H
(916) 781-7500. **$99-$159.** 6664 Lonetree Blvd 95765. SR 65 exit Blue Oaks Blvd, just e, just n to Redwood Dr, then just w;.behind Blue Oaks Town Center (directly behind Petco). Int corridors. **Pets:** Medium. $35 one-time fee/pet. Service with restrictions, crate.
🛜 ✕ 🕭ᴹ 🖨 🖵 ⇻ ✕

ROSEVILLE

∞ ▼▼▼ BEST WESTERN PLUS Roseville Inn H
(916) 782-4434. **Call for rates.** 220 Harding Blvd 95678. I-80 exit 103 westbound; exit 103B eastbound, just w, then just n. Ext corridors.
Pets: Accepted. [SAVE] 🛜 🕭ᴹ 🖨 🖵 ⇻

▼▼ Extended StayAmerica-Sacramento-Roseville H
(916) 781-9001. **$84-$99.** 1000 Lead Hill Blvd 95678. I-80 Douglas Blvd w exit 103B (eastbound), just w, then 0.6 mi n on Harding Blvd, just e; exit 103 Douglas Blvd/Sunrise Ave (westbound), just w, then 0.6 mi n on Harding Blvd, just e. Int corridors. **Pets:** $25 daily fee/pet. Designated rooms, service with restrictions. 🛜 🖨 🖵

▼▼▼ Homewood Suites by Hilton H ☘
(916) 783-7455. **$109-$179.** 401 Creekside Ridge Ct 95678. I-80 exit SR 65, 1 mi w to Galleria Blvd, 0.5 mi s to Antelope Creek Rd, then just e. Int corridors. **Pets:** Small, other species. $75 one-time fee/room. Service with restrictions, supervision. 🛜 🕭ᴹ 🖨 🖵 ⇻

▼▼▼ Larkspur Landing Roseville H
(916) 773-1717. **$89-$219.** 1931 Taylor Rd 95661. I-80 exit 105A (Atlantic St/Eureka Rd), just e on Eureka Rd, then 0.4 mi n. Int corridors.
Pets: Accepted. 🛜 🕭ᴹ 🖨 🖵

∞ ▼▼ Orchid Suites Roseville H
(916) 784-2222. **$80-$199.** 130 N Sunrise Ave 95661. I-80 exit Douglas Blvd, just e, then 0.3 mi n. Ext/int corridors. **Pets:** Medium, other species. $20 daily fee/pet. Designated rooms, service with restrictions, supervision.
[SAVE] 🛜 🕭ᴹ 🖨 🖵 ⇻ ✕

▼▼ Residence Inn by Marriott H
(916) 772-5500. **$109-$149.** 1930 Taylor Rd 95661. I-80 exit 105A (Atlantic St/Eureka Rd), just n. Int corridors. **Pets:** Medium, other species. $100 one-time fee/room. Service with restrictions, crate.
🛜 ✕ 🕭ᴹ 🖨 🖵 ⇻ ✕

▼▼▼ TownePlace Suites by Marriott Roseville H
(916) 782-2232. **$99-$169.** 10569 Fairway Dr 95678. SR 65 exit Blue Oaks Blvd, just e. Int corridors. **Pets:** Large. $100 one-time fee/room. Service with restrictions. 🛜 ✕ 🕭ᴹ 🖨 🖵 ⇻ ✕

SACRAMENTO

∞ ▼▼▼ BEST WESTERN John Jay Inn H
(916) 689-4425. **$70-$130, 3 day notice.** 15 Massie Ct 95823. SR 99 exit Stockton Blvd/Mack Rd northbound, 0.8 mi n, then just w; exit Mack Rd E southbound, just e, just n on Stockton Blvd, then just w. Int corridors. **Pets:** Accepted. [SAVE] 🛜 🕭ᴹ 🖨 🖵 ⇻ ✕

∞ ▼▼▼ BEST WESTERN Sandman Motel H
(916) 443-6515. **$69-$100.** 236 Jibboom St 95811. I-5 exit Richards Blvd, just w. Ext corridors. **Pets:** Accepted.
[SAVE] 🛜 🕭ᴹ 🖨 🖵 🍴 ⇻

▼▼▼ The Citizen, a Joie de Vivre hotel H
(916) 447-2700. **$139-$299.** 926 J St 95814. I-5 exit J St (Old Sacramento), 0.6 mi e; jct 10th St. Int corridors. **Pets:** Large, other species. $200 deposit/room. Service with restrictions, crate.
[ECO] 🛜 ✕ 🕭ᴹ 🖨 🖵 🍴

∞ ▼▼▼ Days Inn-Sacramento Downtown H
(916) 443-4811. **$55-$109.** 228 Jibboom St 95814. I-5 exit Richards Blvd, just w. Int corridors. **Pets:** Medium, dogs only. $10 daily fee/pet. Service with restrictions, supervision. [SAVE] 🛜 🕭ᴹ 🖨 🖵 ⇻

∞ ▼▼▼ DoubleTree by Hilton Hotel Sacramento H
(916) 929-8855. **$89-$229.** 2001 Point West Way 95815. Business Rt I-80 exit Arden Way, just e. Int corridors. **Pets:** Accepted.
[ECO] [SAVE] 🛜 🕭ᴹ 🖨 🖵 🍴 ⇻

Econo Lodge M
(916) 443-6631. **$49-$99.** 711 16th St 95814. Business Rt I-80 exit SR 160, 3.5 mi sw to N 12th St, 0.5 mi s to H St, just se, then just n; I-5 exit J St (Old Sacramento), 1 mi e, then just n. Ext corridors. **Pets:** Accepted.

Extended StayAmerica-Sacramento-Arden Way H
(916) 921-9942. **$76-$91.** 2100 Harvard St 95815. I-80 business route exit Arden Way, just w. Ext corridors. **Pets:** $25 daily fee/pet. Designated rooms, service with restrictions.

Hilton Sacramento Arden West H
(916) 922-4700. **$89-$239.** 2200 Harvard St 95815. Business Rt I-80 exit Arden Way, just w, then just n. Int corridors. **Pets:** Accepted.

Holiday Inn Express Sacramento Convention Center H
(916) 444-4436. **$89-$199.** 728 16th St 95814. Jct H and 16th sts. Int corridors. **Pets:** Medium, other species. $50 one-time fee/room. Service with restrictions, crate.

Hyatt Regency Sacramento H ✿
(916) 443-1234. **$99-$369.** 1209 L St 95814. 1/2 blk from state capitol; jct 12th and L sts. Int corridors. **Pets:** Medium, dogs only. $50 daily fee/room. Designated rooms, service with restrictions, supervision.

La Quinta Inn Sacramento North H
(916) 348-0900. **$71-$133.** 4604 Madison Ave 95841. I-80 exit Madison Ave, 0.3 mi e. Ext corridors. **Pets:** Service with restrictions, supervision.

Larkspur Landing Sacramento H
(916) 646-1212. **$109-$189, 7 day notice.** 555 Howe Ave 95825. US 50 exit Howe Ave, 1.5 mi n. Int corridors. **Pets:** Accepted.

Lions Gate Hotel & Conference Center H
(916) 643-6222. **$99-$109.** 3410 Westover St 95652. I-80 exit Watt Ave, 1.3 mi n to Palm St, just w, then just s on Arnold Ave. Ext/int corridors. **Pets:** Small. $25 daily fee/pet. Service with restrictions, supervision.

Quality Inn & Suites H ✿
(916) 922-9833. **Call for rates.** 1413 Howe Ave 95825. US 50 exit Howe Ave, 2.5 mi n; I-80 business route exit Howe Ave, 2 mi s; just n of jct Hurley and Howe aves. Int corridors. **Pets:** Other species. $25 one-time fee/room. Service with restrictions, crate.

Quality Inn Natomas H
(916) 927-7117. **$55-$90.** 3796 Northgate Blvd 95834. I-80 exit Northgate Blvd, just s. Ext corridors. **Pets:** Medium. $25 deposit/pet. Designated rooms, service with restrictions, supervision.

Red Lion Hotel Woodlake Conference Center Sacramento H
(916) 922-2020. **$89-$209.** 500 Leisure Ln 95815. Business Rt I-80 exit Cal Expo/Exposition Blvd, 0.4 mi w on Exposition Blvd; SR 160 exit 47B (Exposition Blvd) eastbound, just sw; SR 160 exit 47A (Leisure Ln/Canterbury Rd) westbound, just e. Ext corridors. **Pets:** Large, other species. Service with restrictions, supervision.

Residence Inn by Marriott-Sacramento Airport Natomas H
(916) 649-1300. **$189-$199.** 2410 W El Camino Ave 95833. I-5 exit 521B (W El Camino Ave) northbound only, just w, then just s on Gateway Oaks Dr; I-80 exit W El Camino Ave, 1.5 mi e, then just s on Gateway Oaks Dr. Ext corridors. **Pets:** Large. $75 one-time fee/room. Service with restrictions, supervision.

Residence Inn by Marriott- Sacramento Downtown at Capitol Park H
(916) 443-0500. **$118-$313.** 1121 15th St 95814. Jct 15th and L sts; just e of state capitol. Int corridors. **Pets:** Medium. $100 one-time fee/pet. Service with restrictions, supervision.

Sheraton Grand Sacramento Hotel H
(916) 447-1700. **$119-$359.** 1230 J St 95814. I-5 exit J St (Old Sacramento), 1 mi e; jct 12th St. Int corridors. **Pets:** Accepted.

Staybridge Suites Sacramento Airport/Natomas H
(916) 575-7907. **$99-$159.** 140 Promenade Cir 95834. I-80 exit Truxel Rd, just nw, n on Gateway Park Blvd, e on N Freeway Blvd, then just s. Int corridors. **Pets:** Medium. $75 one-time fee/pet. Service with restrictions, supervision.

TownePlace Suites by Marriott Sacramento Cal Expo H ✿
(916) 920-5400. **$79-$159.** 1784 Tribute Rd 95815. Business Rt I-80 exit Cal Expo westbound; exit Exposition Blvd eastbound, just w, then just s. Int corridors. **Pets:** Medium. $100 one-time fee/pet. Service with restrictions, crate.

Vagabond Executive Inn Old Town H
(916) 446-1481. **$79-$150.** 909 3rd St 95814. I-5 exit J St (Old Sacramento); 8 blks w of state capitol; jct J and 3rd sts. Ext corridors. **Pets:** Medium. $10 daily fee/room. Supervision.

SALIDA

La Quinta Inn & Suites Modesto Salida H
(209) 579-8723. **$89-$161.** 4909 Sisk Rd 95368. SR 99 exit SR 219, just e. Int corridors. **Pets:** Service with restrictions, supervision.

SALINAS

BEST WESTERN PLUS Salinas Valley Inn & Suites H
(831) 751-6411. **$89-$299.** 187 Kern St 93905. US 101 exit Market St, just e. Int corridors. **Pets:** Medium, dogs only. $200 deposit/pet, $20 daily fee/pet. Designated rooms, service with restrictions, supervision.

Residence Inn by Marriott-Salinas H ✿
(831) 775-0410. **$119-$349.** 17215 El Rancho Way 93907. US 101 exit Laurel Dr, just w. Int corridors. **Pets:** Medium, other species. $100 one-time fee/room. Designated rooms, service with restrictions.

SAN ANDREAS

The Robins Nest BB ✿
(209) 754-1076. **$100-$175, 7 day notice.** 247 W St. Charles St 95249. SR 49; north end of town. Int corridors. **Pets:** Other species. Designated rooms, service with restrictions.

SAN BERNARDINO

BEST WESTERN Hospitality Lane M
(909) 381-1681. **$100-$150.** 294 E Hospitality Ln 92408. I-10 exit 73 (Waterman Ave) westbound; exit 73B (Waterman Ave) eastbound, just nw. Ext corridors. **Pets:** Medium. $50 deposit/pet, $10 daily fee/pet. Designated rooms, service with restrictions, supervision.

Hilton-San Bernardino H
(909) 889-0133. **$89-$169.** 285 E Hospitality Ln 92408. I-10 exit 73 (Waterman Ave) westbound; exit 73B (Waterman Ave) eastbound, just n, then just w. Int corridors. **Pets:** Accepted.

WWW Residence Inn by Marriott San Bernardino H
(909) 382-4564. **$149-$249.** 1040 E Harriman Pl 92408. I-10 exit 74 (Tippecanoe Ave) eastbound; exit 74 (Anderson St/Tippecanoe Ave) westbound, just n, then just w. Int corridors. **Pets:** Medium. $100 one-time fee/room. Service with restrictions, crate.
📶 ❌ 🔳 🛗 🅿 🚳

SAN CLEMENTE

AAA WWW BEST WESTERN PLUS Casablanca Inn H
(949) 361-1644. **$90-$170.** 1601 N El Camino Real 92672. I-5 exit 76 (Avenida Pico), 0.8 mi sw, then just s. Ext/int corridors. **Pets:** $20 daily fee/room. Designated rooms, service with restrictions, supervision.
SAVE 📶 ❌ 🛗 🅿 🚳

AAA WWW Casa Tropicana A Boutique Beach Front Inn BB ☙
(949) 492-1234. **$225-$775, 10 day notice.** 610 Avenida Victoria 92672. I-5 exit 75 (Avenida Palizada) southbound, just w, just s on El Camino Real, then 1 mi sw on Avenida Del Mar; exit Avenida Presidio northbound, just w, just n on El Camino Real, then 1 mi sw on Avenida Del Mar. Ext corridors. **Pets:** Small, dogs only. $25 daily fee/pet. Designated rooms, service with restrictions, supervision. SAVE 📶 ❌ 🛗 ⏹

WWW Holiday Inn-San Clemente Resort H
(949) 361-3000. **$119-$250.** 111 S Avenida de Estrella 92672. I-5 exit 75 (Avenida Palizada) southbound, just w, then just s; exit Avenida Presidio northbound, just w, then just n. Int corridors. **Pets:** Accepted.
📶 ❌ 🛗 🔳 🅿 🚳

SAN DIEGO METROPOLITAN AREA

CHULA VISTA

AAA WWW Holiday Inn Express-San Diego South H
(619) 426-2500. **Call for rates.** 632 E St 91910. I-5 exit 8B (E St), just e. Int corridors. **Pets:** Small, dogs only. $35 one-time fee/room. Designated rooms, service with restrictions, supervision.
SAVE 📶 ❌ 🛗 🔳 🅿 🚳

WWW La Quinta Inn San Diego Chula Vista M
(619) 691-1211. **$95-$177.** 150 Bonita Rd 91910. I-805 exit 7C (E St/Bonita Rd), just w. Ext/int corridors. **Pets:** Service with restrictions, supervision. 📶 🔳 🅿 🚳

CORONADO

WW Crown City Inn M ☙
(619) 435-3116. **$100-$300.** 520 Orange Ave 92118. I-5 exit 14A (Coronado Bridge), 2.4 mi nw, then just sw. Ext corridors. **Pets:** Other species. $8 daily fee/pet. Designated rooms, service with restrictions, supervision.
📶 🛗 🔳 🅿 🍴 🚳

AAA WWWW Loews Coronado Bay H
(619) 424-4000. **Call for rates.** 4000 Loews Coronado Bay Rd 92118. I-5 exit 14A (Coronado Bridge), 2.4 mi nw to Orange Ave, 1 mi sw to Silver Strand Blvd, 4.5 mi s to Coronado Cays, then just e. Ext/int corridors. **Pets:** Accepted. SAVE 📶 ❌ 🔳 🅿 🍴 🚳 🚳

DEL MAR

WWWW Hilton San Diego Del Mar H ☙
(858) 792-5200. **$119-$349.** 15575 Jimmy Durante Blvd 92014. I-5 exit 36 (Via de la Valle), just w, then just s. Int corridors. **Pets:** Large. $50 one-time fee/pet. Designated rooms, service with restrictions, supervision.
📶 ❌ 🛗 🔳 🅿 🍴 🚳

AAA WWW Hotel Indigo Del Mar M ☙
(858) 755-1501. **$129-$309, 3 day notice.** 710 Camino Del Mar 92014. I-5 exit 34 (Del Mar Heights Rd), 1 mi w, then just n. Ext corridors. **Pets:** Other species. $75 one-time fee/room. Service with restrictions, supervision. SAVE 📶 ❌ 🛗 🔳 🅿 🍴 🚳 🚳

AAA WWWW L'Auberge Del Mar H ☙
(858) 259-1515. **$295-$720, 3 day notice.** 1540 Camino Del Mar 92014. I-5 exit 34 (Del Mar Heights Rd), 1 mi w, then 1 mi n. Int corridors. **Pets:** Very small, dogs only. $100 one-time fee/pet. Service with restrictions, supervision.
ECO 🔌 SAVE 📶 ❌ 🛗 🔳 🍴 🚳 🚳

EL CAJON

AAA WWW BEST WESTERN Courtesy Inn M
(619) 440-7378. **$59-$109.** 1355 E Main St 92021. I-8 exit 19 (2nd St), 0.5 mi s, then just e. Ext corridors. **Pets:** Other species. $20 daily fee/pet. Service with restrictions, supervision. SAVE 📶 ❌ 🔳 🅿 🚳

LA JOLLA

WWW Empress Hotel of La Jolla H
(858) 454-3001. **$139-$369.** 7766 Fay Ave 92037. I-5 exit 28 (La Jolla Village Dr) southbound, 0.7 mi w to Torrey Pines Rd, 2.5 mi sw to Prospect St, 0.8 mi sw, then just s; exit 26A (La Jolla Pkwy) northbound, 1.5 mi n to Torrey Pines Rd, 1 mi sw to Prospect St, 0.8 mi sw, then just s. Int corridors. **Pets:** Small, dogs only. $75 one-time fee/pet. Designated rooms, service with restrictions, supervision. 📶 ❌ 🛗 🔳 🍴

AAA WWWW Holiday Inn Express La Jolla M
(858) 454-7101. **$109-$289.** 6705 La Jolla Blvd 92037. I-5 exit 28 (La Jolla Village Dr) southbound, 0.7 mi w to Torrey Pines Rd, 3 mi sw to Girard Ave, just s to Pearl St, 0.4 mi w, then 0.6 mi s; exit 26A (La Jolla Pkwy) northbound, 1.5 mi n to Torrey Pines Rd, 1.5 mi sw to Girard Ave, just s to Pearl St, 0.4 mi w, then 0.6 mi s. Ext corridors. **Pets:** Accepted. SAVE 📶 ❌ 🛗 🔳 🚳

WWWW Hotel La Jolla H
(858) 459-0261. **Call for rates.** 7955 La Jolla Shores Dr 92037. I-5 exit 28 (La Jolla Village Dr) southbound, 0.7 mi w to Torrey Pines Rd, 1.7 mi sw, then just n; exit 26A (La Jolla Pkwy) northbound, 1.5 mi n to Torrey Pines Rd, just w, then just n. Ext corridors. **Pets:** Accepted.
📶 ❌ 🛗 🔳 🍴 🚳

AAA WWW WWW Hyatt Regency La Jolla H
(858) 552-1234. **$99-$316, 3 day notice.** 3777 La Jolla Village Dr 92122. I-5 exit 28 (La Jolla Village Dr), just e. Int corridors. **Pets:** Accepted. ECO 🔌 SAVE 📶 ❌ 🛗 🔳 🍴 🚳 🚳

AAA WWWW La Valencia Hotel H
(858) 454-0771. **$279-$795, 3 day notice.** 1132 Prospect St 92037. I-5 exit 26A (La Jolla Pkwy) northbound, 1.5 mi n to Torrey Pines Rd, 1 mi sw to Prospect St, then 0.6 mi sw; exit 28 (La Jolla Village Dr) southbound, 0.7 mi w to Torrey Pines Rd, 2.5 mi sw to Prospect St, then 0.6 mi sw. Ext/int corridors. **Pets:** Accepted.
SAVE 📶 ❌ 🛗 🔳 🍴 🚳 🚳

WWW Residence Inn by Marriott San Diego La Jolla H ☙
(858) 587-1770. **$149-$269.** 8901 Gilman Dr 92037. I-5 exit 27 (Gilman Dr), 1.3 mi nw. Ext corridors. **Pets:** Other species. $100 one-time fee/room. Designated rooms, service with restrictions, supervision.
ECO 📶 ❌ 🛗 🔳 🅿 🚳 🚳

WWW San Diego Marriott La Jolla H
(858) 587-1414. **$129-$349.** 4240 La Jolla Village Dr 92037. I-5 exit 28 (La Jolla Village Dr), 0.8 mi e. Int corridors. **Pets:** Accepted.
📶 ❌ 🛗 🔳 🍴 🚳

WWW Scripps Inn M
(858) 454-3391. **$185-$475, 7 day notice.** 555 Coast Blvd S 92037. I-5 exit 28 (La Jolla Village Dr) southbound, 0.7 mi w to Torrey Pines Rd, 2.5 mi sw to Prospect St, 1 mi sw to Cuvier St, just w, then just s; exit 26A (La Jolla Pkwy) northbound, 1.5 mi n to Torrey Pines Rd, 1 mi sw to Prospect St, 1 mi sw to Cuvier St, just w, then just s. Ext corridors. **Pets:** Small, dogs only. $50 one-time fee/room. Designated rooms, service with restrictions, supervision. 📶 ❌ 🔳 🅿 🅰

Sheraton La Jolla Hotel 🏨 ❀

(858) 453-5500. **$149-$350.** 3299 Holiday Ct 92037. I-5 exit 28 (La Jolla Village Dr), just w to Villa La Jolla Dr, just s, then just e. Ext/int corridors. **Pets:** Large, dogs only. $40 one-time fee/room. Designated rooms, service with restrictions, supervision.

ECO SAVE 📶 ✖ ♿ 📠 💻 🍴 🌊

NATIONAL CITY

BEST WESTERN PLUS Marina Gateway Hotel 🏨

(619) 259-2800. **$110-$170.** 800 Bay Marina Dr 91950. I-5 exit 10 (Bay Marina Dr), just w. Int corridors. **Pets:** Small, other species. $20 deposit/room, $20 daily fee/room. Designated rooms, service with restrictions, supervision. SAVE 📶 ✖ ♿ 📠 💻 🍴 🌊

Clarion Hotel 🏨

(619) 474-2800. **$89-$129.** 700 National City Blvd 91950. I-5 exit 11B (8th St) southbound, just e; exit 11B (Plaza Blvd) northbound, just e, then just n. Ext corridors. **Pets:** $50 one-time fee/room.

SAVE 📶 ♿ 📠 💻 🍴 🌊

POWAY

BEST WESTERN PLUS Poway/San Diego Hotel 🅼

(858) 748-6320. **$72-$149.** 13845 Poway Rd 92064. I-15 exit 18 (Poway Rd), 4.5 mi e. Ext corridors. **Pets:** Accepted.

ECO SAVE 📶 📠 💻 🌊

RANCHO BERNARDO

DoubleTree by Hilton Golf Resort San Diego 🏨 ❀

(858) 672-9100. **$89-$199.** 14455 Penasquitos Dr 92129. I-15 exit 21 (Carmel Mountain Rd), just w. Ext corridors. **Pets:** Medium. $30 daily fee/pet. Service with restrictions, crate.

ECO SAVE 📶 ✖ ♿ 📠 💻 🍴 🌊 ✖

Radisson Hotel San Diego-Rancho Bernardo 🏨

(858) 451-6600. **$149-$219.** 11520 W Bernardo Ct 92127. I-15 exit 24 (Rancho Bernardo Rd), just w, then 0.5 mi s on W Bernardo Dr, then just w. Ext corridors. **Pets:** Accepted. 📶 ✖ 📠 💻 🍴 🌊

Rancho Bernardo Inn 🏨

(858) 675-8500. **Call for rates.** 17550 Bernardo Oaks Dr 92128. I-15 exit 24 (Rancho Bernardo Rd), 1 mi e, then 1 mi n. Ext/int corridors. **Pets:** Medium. $100 one-time fee/room. Service with restrictions.

SAVE 📶 ✖ ♿ 📠 💻 🍴 🌊 ✖

Residence Inn San Diego Rancho Bernardo/Carmel Mountain Ranch 🏨 ❀

(858) 673-1900. **$139-$269.** 11002 Rancho Carmel Dr 92128. I-15 exit 21 (Carmel Mountain Rd), just e, just s, then just w on Windcrest Ln. Ext/int corridors. **Pets:** Large, other species. $100 one-time fee/room. Service with restrictions. SAVE 📶 ✖ ♿ 📠 💻 🌊 ✖

Staybridge Suites San Diego-Rancho Bernardo 🏨

(858) 487-0900. **$119-$159, 3 day notice.** 11855 Ave of Industry 92128. I-15 exit 21 (Carmel Mountain Rd), 1 mi ne to second Rancho Carmel Dr, just w to Innovation Dr, just n, then just e. Int corridors. **Pets:** Accepted.

📶 ♿ 📠 💻 🌊 ✖

RANCHO SANTA FE

The Inn at Rancho Santa Fe 🏨

(858) 756-1131. **$290-$1500, 3 day notice.** 5951 Linea del Cielo 92067. I-5 exit 37 (Lomas Santa Fe Dr), 4 mi e on CR S-8. Ext/int corridors. **Pets:** Accepted. 📶 ✖ 📠 💻 🍴 🌊 ✖

Morgan Run Resort & Club 🏨

(858) 756-2471. **$129-$299.** 5690 Cancha de Golf 92091. I-5 exit 36 (Via de la Valle), 3 mi e. Int corridors. **Pets:** Medium. $25 daily fee/room. Designated rooms, service with restrictions, supervision.

📶 ✖ 📠 💻 🍴 🌊 ✖

SAN DIEGO

Andaz San Diego 🏨 ❀

(619) 849-1234. **$153-$450, 3 day notice.** 600 F St 92101. I-5 exit 16B (6th Ave) northbound, 1 mi s, then just e; exit 17 (Front St) southbound, 0.9 mi s to Broadway, 0.5 mi e to 8th Ave, just s, then just w. Int corridors. **Pets:** Medium. $40 daily fee/room. Service with restrictions.

SAVE 📶 ✖ 💻 🍴 🌊

BEST WESTERN Lamplighter Inn & Suites at SDSU 🅼

(619) 582-3088. **$95-$130.** 6474 El Cajon Blvd 92115. I-8 exit 11 (70th St/Lake Murray Blvd), 0.4 mi s on 70th St, then 0.8 mi w. Ext corridors. **Pets:** Accepted. SAVE 📶 📠 💻 🌊

BEST WESTERN Mission Bay 🅼

(619) 275-5700. **$79-$279.** 2575 Clairemont Dr 92117. I-5 exit 22 (Clairemont Dr/Mission Bay Dr), just e. Ext corridors. **Pets:** Medium. $15 daily fee/room. Service with restrictions, supervision.

SAVE 📶 📠 💻 🌊

BEST WESTERN PLUS Hacienda Hotel Old Town 🏨

(619) 298-4707. **$179-$249.** 4041 Harney St 92110. I-5 exit 19 (Old Town Ave), just e, 0.3 mi n on San Diego Ave, then just e. Ext corridors. **Pets:** Large, other species. $50 deposit/room. Designated rooms, service with restrictions, crate. SAVE 📶 ✖ ♿ 📠 💻 🌊

BEST WESTERN PLUS San Diego/Miramar Hotel 🅼

(858) 578-6600. **$75-$149.** 9310 Kearny Mesa Rd 92126. I-15 exit 14 (Miramar Rd/Pomerado Rd), just w, then just s. Ext corridors. **Pets:** Small, dogs only. $25 daily fee/room. Designated rooms, service with restrictions, supervision. ECO SAVE 📶 📠 💻 🌊

The Bristol 🏨 ❀

(619) 232-6141. **$139-$359.** 1055 First Ave 92101. I-5 exit 17 (Front St) southbound, 0.5 mi s, just e on C St, then just s; exit 15B (B St) northbound, 1 mi w to 1st Ave, then just s. Int corridors. **Pets:** Other species. Service with restrictions. ECO SAVE 📶 ✖ 💻 🍴

Comfort Suites Mission Valley SeaWorld Area 🏨

(619) 881-4000. **$89-$249.** 631 Camino del Rio S 92108. I-8 exit 5 (Mission Center Rd), just sw. Ext/int corridors. **Pets:** Very small, dogs only. $50 one-time fee/room. Service with restrictions, supervision.

ECO SAVE 📶 ✖ ♿ 📠 💻 🌊

Country Inn & Suites By Carlson San Diego North 🏨 ❀

(858) 558-1818. **$99-$249.** 5975 Lusk Blvd 92121. I-805 exit 27 (Mira Mesa Blvd), 1 mi e, then just n. Int corridors. **Pets:** Dogs only. $75 one-time fee/room. Designated rooms, service with restrictions, supervision.

ECO 📶 ✖ ♿ 📠 💻 🍴 🌊

Crowne Plaza San Diego 🏨

(619) 297-1101. **$149-$189.** 2270 Hotel Cir N 92108. I-8 exit 3 (Taylor St), just n, then just e. Ext corridors. **Pets:** Large. $75 one-time fee/pet. Service with restrictions, supervision.

ECO 📶 ✖ ♿ 📠 💻 🍴 🌊 ✖

DoubleTree by Hilton Hotel San Diego - Del Mar 🏨

(858) 481-5900. **$99-$249.** 11915 El Camino Real 92130. I-5 exit 33 (Carmel Valley Rd), 0.3 mi n, then just n. Int corridors. **Pets:** Accepted.

ECO SAVE 📶 📠 💻 🍴 🌊

Embassy Suites Hotel San Diego Bay-Downtown 🏨

(619) 239-2400. **$149-$299.** 601 Pacific Hwy 92101. I-5 exit 17 (Front St) southbound, 1.2 mi s to Market St, just w; exit 16B (6th Ave) northbound, just s to Market St, then 1.4 mi w. Int corridors.

Pets: Accepted. 📶 ♿ 📠 💻 🍴 🌊

(AAA) ▼▼▼▼ The Grand Del Mar ⊞ ❀
(858) 314-2000. **$395-$495, 7 day notice.** 5300 Grand Del Mar Ct 92130. I-5 exit 33 (Carmel Valley Rd), 1.5 mi e on SR 56, 0.5 mi s on Carmel Country Rd, 0.5 mi e on Grand Del Mar Way, then just se. Int corridors. **Pets:** Small, dogs only. $100 one-time fee/room. Designated rooms, service with restrictions, supervision.
[ECO] [⊟] [SAVE] [⊚] [✕] [⊟] [⊡] [❙❙] [⇌] [✕]

▼▼▼▼ Hampton Inn-Del Mar ⊞
(858) 792-5557. **Call for rates.** 11920 El Camino Real 92130. I-5 exit 33 (Carmel Valley Rd), just ne. Int corridors. **Pets:** Medium, other species. $50 one-time fee/room. Service with restrictions, supervision.
[⊚] [✕] [⊟] [⊡] [⇌]

▼▼▼▼ Handlery Hotel & Resort ⊞ ❀
(619) 298-0511. **$99-$289.** 950 Hotel Cir N 92108. I-8 exit 4A (Hotel Cir), north side. Ext/int corridors. **Pets:** Very small, dogs only. $25 deposit/ room. Designated rooms, service with restrictions, crate.
[ECO] [⊚] [✕] [⊟] [⊡] [❙❙] [⇌]

(AAA) ▼▼▼◇ Hilton San Diego Airport/Harbor Island ⊞
(619) 291-6700. **$129-$229.** 1960 Harbor Island Dr 92101. I-5 exit 184 (Laurel St) southbound, 1.5 mi w; exit 17 (Hawthorn St) northbound, 0.5 mi w to Harbor Dr, 1.5 mi nw. Int corridors. **Pets:** Accepted.
[ECO] [SAVE] [⊚] [&M] [⊟] [⊡] [❙❙] [⇌]

(AAA) ▼▼▼◇ Hilton San Diego Bayfront ⊞ ❀
(619) 564-3333. **$179-$499.** One Park Blvd 92101. I-5 exit 17 (Front St) southbound, 1.5 mi s, just w to Harbor Dr, then just s; exit 16B (6th Ave) northbound, 1.3 mi s, just w on Market, just s on Front St, just w to Harbor Dr, then just s. Int corridors. **Pets:** Large. $75 one-time fee/room. Service with restrictions.
[ECO] [SAVE] [⊚] [✕] [&M] [⊟] [⊡] [❙❙] [⇌] [✕]

▼▼▼▼ Hilton San Diego Gaslamp Quarter ⊞
(619) 231-4040. **Call for rates.** 401 K St 92101. I-5 exit 7B (J St) northbound, 0.8 mi w to 4th Ave, then just s; exit 17 (Front St) southbound, 0.5 mi e to 4th Ave, then 1 mi s; in Historic Gaslamp Quarter. Int corridors. **Pets:** Accepted.
[⊚] [✕] [&M] [⊟] [⊡] [❙❙] [⇌]

▼▼▼▼ Hilton San Diego Mission Valley ⊞
(619) 543-9000. **$119-$249.** 901 Camino del Rio S 92108. I-8 exit 5 (Mission Center Rd), just s, then just w. Int corridors. **Pets:** Accepted.
[ECO] [⊚] [✕] [&M] [⊟] [⊡] [❙❙] [⇌]

▼▼▼▼ Holiday Inn on the Bay ⊞ ❀
(619) 232-3861. **$129-$249.** 1355 N Harbor Dr 92101. I-5 exit 17 (Hawthorn St) northbound, 0.4 mi w, then 0.4 mi s; exit 17 (Front St) southbound, 0.5 mi s to Ash St, then just w. Int corridors. **Pets:** $25 daily fee/ pet. Service with restrictions, supervision.
[ECO] [⊚] [✕] [⊟] [⊡] [❙❙] [⇌]

▼▼▼▼ Hotel Indigo San Diego Gaslamp Quarter ⊞ ❀
(619) 727-4000. **$129-$399, 3 day notice.** 509 9th Ave 92101. I-5 exit 17 (Front St) southbound, 0.3 mi s, 0.5 mi e on A St, 0.5 mi s on 6th Ave, then just e on Island Ave; exit 16B (6th Ave) northbound, 0.5 mi s, then just e on Island Ave. Int corridors. **Pets:** Service with restrictions, crate. [ECO] [⊚] [✕] [&M] [⊟] [⊡] [❙❙]

(AAA) ▼▼▼◇ Howard Johnson San Diego SeaWorld Area Ⓜ
(619) 224-8266. **$75-$277.** 3330 Rosecrans St 92110. I-5 exit 20 (Rosecrans St) southbound, 0.8 mi s; exit 18A (Pacific Hwy) northbound, 1.5 mi n, just nw on Barnett Ave, 0.5 mi n on Midway Dr, then just w. Ext corridors. **Pets:** Accepted. [ECO] [SAVE] [⊚] [✕] [⊟] [⊡] [❙❙] [⇌]

(AAA) ▼▼▼◇ Hyatt house San Diego/Sorrento Mesa ⊞
(858) 597-0500. **$114-$229.** 10044 Pacific Mesa Blvd 92121. I-805 exit 27 (Mira Mesa Blvd), 1.5 mi e, just n on Pacific Heights, then just w. Int corridors. **Pets:** Medium. $150 one-time fee/pet. Service with restrictions, supervision. [SAVE] [⊚] [✕] [&M] [⊟] [⊡] [❙❙] [⇌]

(AAA) ▼▼▼◇ Hyatt Regency Mission Bay Spa and Marina ⊞ ❀
(619) 224-1234. **$117-$414.** 1441 Quivira Rd 92109. I-8 exit 1 (Ingraham St/Mission Bay Dr), 0.7 mi n, just w on Mission Bay Dr, then just sw. Ext/int corridors. **Pets:** Medium, dogs only. $50 daily fee/pet. Service with restrictions, supervision. [ECO] [SAVE] [⊚] [⊟] [⊡] [❙❙] [⇌] [✕]

(AAA) ▼▼▼◇ Kona Kai Resort Spa & Marina ⊞
(619) 221-8000. **$119-$369.** 1551 Shelter Island Dr 92106. I-5 exit 20 (Rosecrans St) southbound, 3 mi sw, then 1.5 mi sw; exit 17 (Hawthorn St) northbound, 3 mi nw on Harbor Dr to Scott Rd, then 1.5 mi sw. Ext/ int corridors. **Pets:** Accepted. [SAVE] [⊚] [&M] [⊟] [⊡] [❙❙] [⇌] [✕]

▼▼▼▼ La Quinta Inn & Suites San Diego/Mission Beach ⊞
(858) 483-9800. **$87-$299.** 4610 De Soto St 92109. I-5 exit 23A (Grand Ave/Garnet Ave) northbound, 1 mi n on Mission Bay Dr, then just e on Damon Ave; exit 23B (Balboa Ave/Garnet Ave) southbound, just s, then just e on Damon Ave. Int corridors. **Pets:** Service with restrictions, supervision. [⊚] [✕] [&M] [⊟] [⊡] [⇌]

▼▼▼▼ La Quinta Inn & Suites San Diego Mission Valley Ⓜ
(619) 295-6886. **$83-$298.** 641 Camino Del Rio S 92108. I-8 exit 5 (Mission Center Rd), just s, then just w. Ext corridors. **Pets:** Service with restrictions, supervision. [⊚] [✕] [&M] [⊟] [⊡] [⇌]

▼▼▼▼ La Quinta Inn San Diego Old Town/Airport Ⓜ
(619) 291-9100. **$107-$299.** 2380 Moore St 92110. I-5 exit 19 (Old Town Ave), just n via Frontage Rd; on east side of freeway. Ext/int corridors. **Pets:** Service with restrictions, supervision.
[ECO] [⊚] [✕] [&M] [⊟] [⊡] [⇌]

(AAA) ▼▼▼▼ Manchester Grand Hyatt San Diego ⊞ ❀
(619) 232-1234. **$99-$414, 7 day notice.** 1 Market Pl 92101. I-5 exit 17 (Front St), 1.3 mi s, then just w. Int corridors. **Pets:** Medium. $30 daily fee/pet. Designated rooms, service with restrictions, supervision.
[SAVE] [⊚] [&M] [⊟] [⊡] [❙❙] [⇌] [✕]

(AAA) ▼▼▼◇ Marina Inn & Suites Ⓜ
(619) 232-7551. **$49-$289.** 1943 Pacific Hwy 92101. I-5 exit 17 (Front St) southbound, just s to Cedar St, 0.3 mi n; exit 17 (Hawthorn St) northbound, 0.4 mi w, then just s. Ext corridors. **Pets:** Medium. $20 daily fee/pet. Service with restrictions, crate. [SAVE] [⊚] [⊟] [⊡]

▼▼ ▼ Old Town Inn Ⓜ
(619) 260-8024. **Call for rates.** 4444 Pacific Hwy 92110. I-5 exit 21 (SeaWorld Dr/Tecolote St), just sw, then 1 mi se. Ext corridors. **Pets:** Accepted. [⊚] [⊟] [⊡] [⇌]

▼▼▼▼ Omni San Diego Hotel ⊞ ❀
(619) 231-6664. **Call for rates.** 675 L St 92101. I-5 exit 17 (Front St) southbound, 0.3 mi s, 0.3 mi e on A St, 0.6 mi s on 6th Ave, then just e; exit 16B (6th Ave) northbound, just s on 6th Ave, then just e; connected via skybridge to Petco Park. Int corridors. **Pets:** Small. $50 one-time fee/ room. Service with restrictions, crate.
[⊚] [✕] [&M] [⊟] [⊡] [❙❙] [⇌] [✕]

(AAA) ▼▼▼◇ Pacific Inn Hotel & Suites Ⓜ
(619) 232-6391. **$49-$289.** 1655 Pacific Hwy 92101. I-5 exit 17 (Front St) southbound, just s to Cedar St, 0.5 mi w, then just n; exit 17 (Hawthorn St) northbound, 0.6 mi w, then just s. Ext corridors. **Pets:** Medium, other species. $20 daily fee/pet. Service with restrictions, crate.
[SAVE] [⊚] [⊟] [⊡] [⇌]

(AAA) ▼▼▼ Pacific Shores Inn Ⓜ
(858) 483-6300. **$109-$269, 3 day notice.** 4802 Mission Blvd 92109. I-5 exit 23A (Garnet Ave), via Mission Bay Dr to Garnet Ave, 2.2 mi w, then 0.3 mi n. Ext corridors. **Pets:** Medium, dogs only. $35 one-time fee/room. Service with restrictions, crate. [SAVE] [⊚] [✕] [⊟] [⊡] [⇌]

Paradise Point

(858) 274-4630. **$150-$450, 7 day notice.** 1404 Vacation Rd 92109. I-5 exit 21 (SeaWorld Dr/Tecolote Rd), 2.4 mi sw via Ingraham St, then just w. Ext corridors. **Pets:** Small, other species. $150 deposit/room, $100 one-time fee/room. Service with restrictions.

Point Loma Inn & Suites

(619) 222-4704. **$39-$129.** 2933 Fenelon St 92106. I-8 exit Nimitz Blvd, 2 mi s, then 0.4 mi w on Rosecrans Ave. Ext corridors. **Pets:** Medium. $20 daily fee/pet. Service with restrictions, crate.

Porto Vista Hotel

(619) 544-0164. **$99-$499.** 1835 Columbia St 92101. I-5 exit 17 (Front St) southbound, just w on Cedar St, then just n on State St; exit 17 (Hawthorn St) northbound, just e, then just s. Ext/int corridors. **Pets:** Accepted.

Quality Inn I-15 Miramar

(858) 578-4350. **$50-$89.** 9350 Kearny Mesa Rd 92126. I-15 exit 14 (Miramar Rd/Pomerado), just w, then just s. Int corridors. **Pets:** Accepted.

Red Roof Inn-Pacific Beach/SeaWorld Area, San Diego

(858) 483-4222. **$59-$299.** 4545 Mission Bay Dr 92109. I-5 exit 23A (Grand Ave/Garnet Ave) northbound, 0.5 mi n; exit 23B (Garnet Ave/Balboa Ave) southbound, 0.3 mi s. Ext corridors. **Pets:** Large, other species. Service with restrictions, supervision.

Residence Inn by Marriott-San Diego Central

(858) 278-2100. **$115-$299.** 5400 Kearny Mesa Rd 92111. SR 163 exit 8 (Clairemont Mesa Blvd) just w, then just n. Ext corridors. **Pets:** Large, other species. $75 one-time fee/room. Service with restrictions, supervision.

Residence Inn by Marriott San Diego Downtown

(619) 338-8200. **$119-$779.** 1747 Pacific Hwy 92101. I-5 exit 17 (Front St) southbound, just s to Cedar St, 0.3 mi w, then just n; exit 17 (Hawthorn St) northbound, 0.4 mi w, then just s. Int corridors. **Pets:** Small. $100 one-time fee/room. Service with restrictions.

Residence Inn by Marriott San Diego Downtown Gaslamp Quarter

(619) 487-1200. **$149-$650.** 356 6th Ave 92101. I-5 exit 17 (Front St/Civic Center) southbound, 0.3 mi s, 0.3 mi e on A St, then 0.6 mi s; exit 16B (6th Ave) northbound, 1 mi s. Int corridors. **Pets:** Other species. $100 one-time fee/pet. Service with restrictions.

Residence Inn by Marriott San Diego/Mission Valley/SeaWorld Area

(619) 881-3600. **$139-$229.** 1865 Hotel Cir S 92108. I-8 exit 4A (Hotel Cir), south side. Int corridors. **Pets:** Other species. $100 one-time fee/pet. Designated rooms.

Residence Inn by Marriott San Diego Rancho Bernardo/Scripps Poway

(858) 635-5724. **$113-$239.** 12011 Scripps Highlands Dr 92131. I-805 exit 17 (Mercy Rd/Scripps Poway Pkwy), just e, then just n. Int corridors. **Pets:** Large, other species. $75 one-time fee/room. Service with restrictions, supervision.

Residence Inn by Marriott San Diego-Sorrento Mesa

(858) 552-9100. **$149-$289.** 5995 Pacific Mesa Ct 92121. I-805 exit 27 (Mira Mesa Blvd), 1.5 mi e, just n on Pacific Heights, then just se. Int corridors. **Pets:** Accepted.

San Diego Marriott Del Mar

(858) 523-1700. **$149-$289.** 11966 El Camino Real 92130. I-5 exit 33 (Carmel Valley Rd), just ne. Int corridors. **Pets:** Medium. $75 one-time fee/room. Service with restrictions, supervision.

Sheraton Mission Valley, San Diego Hotel

(619) 260-0111. **$99-$299.** 1433 Camino del Rio S 92108. I-8 exit 5 (Mission Center Rd), south side. Int corridors. **Pets:** $50 one-time fee/room. Designated rooms, service with restrictions.

Sheraton San Diego Hotel & Marina

(619) 291-2900. **$119-$469, 3 day notice.** 1380 Harbor Island Dr 92101. I-5 exit 17 (Hawthorn St) northbound, just e to Harbor Dr, 1.5 mi w, then just s; exit 18A (Kettner/Hancock) southbound, just s to Laurel St, just w to Harbor Dr, 1.5 mi w, then just s. Ext/int corridors. **Pets:** Small, dogs only. Designated rooms, service with restrictions, supervision.

Sheraton Suites San Diego at Symphony Hall

(619) 696-9800. **$139-$399.** 701 A St 92101. I-5 exit 16 (10th Ave) southbound, just s to B St, just w, then just n on 7th St; exit 16B (6th Ave) northbound, just s, then just e. Int corridors. **Pets:** Accepted.

The Sofia Hotel

(619) 234-9200. **$149-$229.** 150 W Broadway 92101. I-5 exit 17 (Front St) southbound, 0.5 mi s, just w on Broadway; exit 15B (B St) northbound, 1 mi w to 3rd Ave, just s to Broadway, then just w. Int corridors. **Pets:** Other species. $25 daily fee/pet. Designated rooms, service with restrictions, supervision.

Sommerset Suites Hotel

(619) 692-5200. **$119-$329.** 606 Washington St 92103. SR 163 exit 2B (Washington St), just w. Ext/int corridors. **Pets:** Other species. $75 one-time fee/pet. Designated rooms, service with restrictions, supervision.

Staybridge Suites-Sorrento Mesa

(858) 453-5343. **$169-$269.** 6639 Mira Mesa Blvd 92121. I-805 exit 27 (Mira Mesa Blvd), 2.3 mi e. Int corridors. **Pets:** $15 daily fee/room. Service with restrictions.

The US Grant, A Luxury Collection Hotel

(619) 232-3121. **$179-$569, 3 day notice.** 326 Broadway 92101. I-5 exit 17 (Front St) southbound, 0.9 mi s to Broadway, then just e; exit 16B (6th Ave) northbound, 0.6 mi s, then just w. Int corridors. **Pets:** Medium. $150 one-time fee/room. Service with restrictions, supervision.

Vagabond Inn SeaWorld

(619) 297-1691. **$49-$289.** 625 Hotel Cir S 92108. I-8 exit 4A (Hotel Cir), south side. Ext corridors. **Pets:** Medium. $20 daily fee/pet. Service with restrictions, crate.

The Westin Gaslamp Quarter

(619) 239-2200. **$169-$449, 3 day notice.** 910 Broadway Cir 92101. I-5 exit 17 (Front St) southbound, 0.9 mi s to Broadway, just e, then just s; exit 16B (6th Ave) northbound, 0.6 mi s, just w, then just s. Int corridors. **Pets:** Accepted.

The Westin San Diego

(619) 239-4500. **$159-$459.** 400 W Broadway 92101. I-5 exit 17 (Front St) southbound, 0.9 mi s, then just w; exit 16B (6th Ave) northbound, 0.6 mi s, then just w. Int corridors. **Pets:** Medium, dogs only. Designated rooms, service with restrictions, supervision.

W San Diego H
(619) 398-3100. **$179-$499, 3 day notice.** 421 W B St 92101. I-5 exit 17 (Front St) southbound, 0.6 mi s, then just w; exit 16B (6th St) northbound, just s, then just w. Int corridors. **Pets:** Accepted.

SAVE 🛜 ✕ 🛄 🖥 🍴 🏊

SANTEE

BEST WESTERN Santee Lodge M
(619) 449-2626. **$69-$169.** 10726 Woodside Ave 92071. SR 52 exit 14 (Mission Gorge Rd), 2 mi e. Ext corridors. **Pets:** Medium. $10 daily fee/pet. Designated rooms, no service, supervision.

SAVE 🛜 ᴹ 🛄 🖥 🏊

END METROPOLITAN AREA

SAN FRANCISCO METROPOLITAN AREA

BELMONT

Hyatt house Belmont/Redwood Shores H
(650) 591-8600. **$119-$219.** 400 Concourse Dr 94002. US 101 exit 412 (Ralston Ave/Belmont), just e, then 0.3 mi n on Island Pkwy. Ext corridors. **Pets:** Accepted. SAVE 🛜 ✕ ᴹ 🛄 🖥 🏊 ✕

BURLINGAME

Crowne Plaza H
(650) 342-9200. **$129-$229.** 1177 Airport Blvd 94010. US 101 exit Broadway-Burlingame or Old Bayshore Hwy, just e. Int corridors. **Pets:** Accepted. 🛜 ✕ 🛄 🖥 🍴 🏊

DoubleTree by Hilton Hotel San Francisco Airport H
(650) 344-5500. **$129-$309.** 835 Airport Blvd 94010. US 101 exit Broadway-Burlingame or Anza Blvd, just e. Int corridors. **Pets:** Accepted.

ECO 🛜 ᴹ 🛄 🖥 🍴

Embassy Suites San Francisco Airport - Waterfront H ❖
(650) 342-4600. **$150-$350.** 150 Anza Blvd 94010. US 101 exit Broadway-Burlingame, just e. Int corridors. **Pets:** $50 deposit/pet. Service with restrictions, supervision. ECO 🛜 ᴹ 🛄 🖥 🍴 🏊 ✕

Hilton San Francisco Airport Bayfront H ❖
(650) 340-8500. **Call for rates.** 600 Airport Blvd 94010. US 101 exit Broadway-Burlingame or Anza Blvd, 0.3 mi e. Int corridors. **Pets:** Large. $50 one-time fee/pet. Designated rooms, service with restrictions, supervision. SAVE 🛜 ᴹ 🛄 🖥 🍴 🏊

Hyatt Regency San Francisco Airport H ❖
(650) 347-1234. **$81-$360.** 1333 Bayshore Hwy 94010. US 101 exit Broadway-Burlingame, just e. Int corridors. **Pets:** Medium, dogs only. $50 one-time fee/room. Designated rooms, service with restrictions, supervision. ECO SAVE 🛜 ᴹ 🛄 🖥 🍴 🏊 ✕

Red Roof Inn San Francisco Airport M
(650) 342-7772. **$60-$140.** 777 Airport Blvd 94010. US 101 exit Broadway-Burlingame or E Anza Blvd; just s of airport. Ext corridors. **Pets:** Large, other species. Service with restrictions, supervision.

SAVE 🛜 ᴹ 🛄 🍴 🏊

San Francisco Airport Marriott Waterfront H
(650) 692-9100. **$169-$329.** 1800 Old Bayshore Hwy 94010. US 101 exit Millbrae Ave, just e. Int corridors. **Pets:** Other species. $75 one-time fee/room. ECO 🛜 ✕ ᴹ 🛄 🖥 🍴 🏊 ✕

CORTE MADERA

Marin Suites Hotel H ❖
(415) 924-3608. **$109-$280.** 45 Tamal Vista Blvd 94925. US 101 exit Lucky Dr southbound, just w on Fifer Ave, 0.4 mi s; exit Tamalpais Rd/Paradise Dr northbound, 0.5 mi n on Madera Blvd (which becomes Tamal Vista Blvd). Ext corridors. **Pets:** Other species. $20 daily fee/pet. Designated rooms, service with restrictions, supervision.

SAVE 🛜 ✕ ᴹ 🛄 🖥 🏊 ✕ 🅰

HALF MOON BAY

Coastside Inn Half Moon Bay H
(650) 726-3400. **$89-$239.** 230 S Cabrillo Hwy 94019. On SR 1, just s of SR 92. Ext corridors. **Pets:** $20 deposit/pet. Designated rooms, service with restrictions, supervision. ECO SAVE 🛜 ✕ ᴹ 🛄 🖥

Comfort Inn Half Moon Bay H
(650) 712-1999. **$100-$230.** 2930 Cabrillo Hwy N 94019. On SR 1, 2 mi n of jct SR 92 and 1. Ext corridors. **Pets:** $20 daily fee/pet. Designated rooms, supervision. SAVE 🛜 ✕ ᴹ 🛄 🖥

Half Moon Bay Lodge H ❖
(650) 726-9000. **$149-$239.** 2400 Cabrillo Hwy S 94019. 2.5 mi s of jct SR 92 and 1, just w. Ext corridors. **Pets:** $75 one-time fee/room. Designated rooms, service with restrictions, supervision.

SAVE 🛜 ✕ ᴹ 🛄 🖥 🏊 ✕ 🅰

Harbor View Inn M
(650) 726-2329. **$79-$249.** 51 Ave Alhambra 94018. SR 1 exit Capistrano Ave, just e; 4 mi n of jct SR 92. Ext corridors. **Pets:** Small, dogs only. $20 one-time fee/pet. Designated rooms, service with restrictions, supervision. SAVE 🛜 ✕ ᴹ 🛄 🖥 🅰

Landis Shores Oceanfront Inn BB ❖
(650) 726-6642. **$225-$345, 7 day notice.** 211 Mirada Rd 94019. 3 mi n of jct SR 1 and 92 to Medio Ave, just w, then just n. Int corridors. **Pets:** Medium, dogs only. $30 daily fee/pet. Designated rooms, service with restrictions, supervision. 🛜 ✕ ᴹ 🛄 ✕ 🅰

The Ritz-Carlton, Half Moon Bay H ❖
(650) 712-7000. **$355-$4050.** 1 Miramontes Point Rd 94019. 2.5 mi s of jct SR 1 (Cabrillo Hwy S) and 92, 0.8 mi w. Ext/int corridors. **Pets:** Medium, dogs only. $125 one-time fee/room. Designated rooms, supervision. SAVE 🛜 ✕ ᴹ 🛄 🖥 🍴 🏊 ✕

MILLBRAE

The Westin San Francisco Airport H
(650) 692-3500. **$129-$409.** 1 Old Bayshore Hwy 94030. Just e of US 101 exit Millbrae Ave. Int corridors. **Pets:** Accepted.

ECO ♿ SAVE 🛜 ✕ ᴹ 🖥 🍴 🏊 ✕

MILL VALLEY

▽▽▽▽ **Acqua Hotel** 🄷
(415) 380-0400. **Call for rates.** 555 Redwood Hwy 94941. US 101 exit Seminary Dr. Ext/int corridors. **Pets:** Medium, dogs only. $35 one-time fee/room, $15 daily fee/room. Designated rooms, service with restrictions, crate. 🛜 ⊠ 🕭M 🄷

▽▽▽▽ **Tam Woods Hotel** 🄷
(415) 332-5700. **$139-$229.** 160 Shoreline Hwy 94941. US 101 exit Stinson Beach southbound, just nw; exit Mill Valley/SR 1/Stinson Beach northbound, 0.4 mi nw. Int corridors. **Pets:** Accepted.
ECO 🛜 ⊠ 🕭M 🄷 🖵 ⇌ ⊠

MOSS BEACH

▽▽▽▽ **Seal Cove Inn** 🄱🄱 ❀
(650) 728-4114. **$245-$360, 7 day notice.** 221 Cypress Ave 94038. 6.5 mi n of jct SR 1 and 92 to Cypress Ave, then just w. Int corridors. **Pets:** Dogs only. $65 one-time fee/room. Designated rooms, service with restrictions, crate. 🛜 ⊠ 🄷 🖵 🄰🄲

PACIFICA

AAA ▽▽▽▽ **BEST WESTERN PLUS Lighthouse Hotel** 🄷 ❀
(650) 355-6300. **$139-$209.** 105 Rockaway Beach Ave 94044. SR 1 exit Rockaway Beach Ave, just w. Int corridors. **Pets:** Medium, dogs only. $75 one-time fee/room. Designated rooms, service with restrictions, supervision. SAVE 🛜 ⊠ 🕭M 🄷 🖵 ⇌ 🄰🄲

SAN BRUNO

AAA ▽▽▽ **Staybridge Suites** 🄷
(650) 588-0770. **$129-$309.** 1350 Huntington Ave 94066. I-380 exit El Camino Real N, e on Sneath Ln, then just n. Ext corridors. **Pets:** Other species. $15 daily fee/room. SAVE 🛜 🕭M 🄷 🖵 ⇌ ⊠

SAN FRANCISCO

AAA ▽▽▽▽ **Argonaut Hotel** 🄷
(415) 563-0800. **$209-$719.** 495 Jefferson St 94109. Fisherman's Wharf; adjacent to The Cannery. Int corridors. **Pets:** Accepted.
ECO SAVE 🛜 ⊠ 🕭M 🄷 🖵 🍴

AAA ▽▽▽▽ **Beresford Arms Hotel & Suites** 🄷
(415) 673-2600. **$89-$299.** 701 Post St 94109. 3 blks w of Union Square; at Jones St. Int corridors. **Pets:** Other species. $25 one-time fee/pet. Designated rooms, service with restrictions, supervision.
SAVE 🛜 🕭M 🄷 🖵 🄰🄲

AAA ▽▽▽ **Beresford Hotel** 🄷
(415) 673-9900. **$79-$169.** 635 Sutter St 94102. 1 blk nw of Union Square at Mason St. Int corridors. **Pets:** Other species. $25 one-time fee/pet. Designated rooms, service with restrictions, supervision.
SAVE 🛜 🍴 🄰🄲

AAA ▽▽▽▽ **BEST WESTERN PLUS Americania** 🄷
(415) 626-0200. **$119-$349.** 121 7th St 94103. Just s of Market St; between Minna and Natoma sts. Ext corridors. **Pets:** Accepted.
SAVE 🛜 ⊠ 🕭M 🄷 🖵 🍴 ⇌ 🄰🄲

AAA ▽▽▽▽ **BEST WESTERN PLUS Tuscan Inn at Fisherman's Wharf** 🄷 ❀
(415) 561-1100. **$189-$389.** 425 Northpoint St 94133. Just s of Fisherman's Wharf at Mason St. Int corridors. **Pets:** Other species. Service with restrictions, supervision. ECO SAVE 🛜 🕭M 🖵 🍴

AAA ▽▽▽▽ **BEST WESTERN The Hotel California** 🄷
(415) 441-2700. **Call for rates.** 580 Geary St 94102. 0.3 mi w of Union Square at Jones St. Int corridors. **Pets:** Accepted.
SAVE 🛜 ⊠ 🕭M 🄷 🖵 🍴 🄰🄲

AAA ▽▽▽▽ **The Fairmont San Francisco** 🄷 ❀
(415) 772-5000. **$199-$999.** 950 Mason St (atop Nob Hill) 94108. Atop Nob Hill at California St. Int corridors. **Pets:** Small, other species. $75 one-time fee/room. Service with restrictions, supervision.
ECO SAVE 🛜 🕭M 🍴

▽▽▽ ▽▽▽ **Four Seasons Hotel San Francisco** 🄷 ❀
(415) 633-3000. **$395-$795, 3 day notice.** 757 Market St 94103. Between 3rd and 4th sts. Int corridors. **Pets:** Small, other species. $50 one-time fee/room. Service with restrictions, crate.
🛜 🕭M 🄷 🖵 🍴 ⇌

▽▽▽ ▽▽▽ **Galleria Park Hotel, a Joie de Vivre hotel** 🄷
(415) 781-3060. **Call for rates.** 191 Sutter St 94104. 2 blks ne of Union Square; between Kearny and Trinity sts. Int corridors. **Pets:** Accepted.
ECO 🛜 ⊠ 🕭M 🖵 🍴 ⊠

AAA ▽▽▽ **The Good Hotel** 🄷
(415) 621-7001. **$99-$289.** 112 7th St 94103. Just s of Market St; at Mission St. Int corridors. **Pets:** Accepted.
SAVE 🛜 ⊠ 🄷 🖵 🍴

AAA ▽▽▽ ▽▽▽ **Grand Hyatt San Francisco** 🄷
(415) 398-1234. **$153-$423.** 345 Stockton St 94108. On Union Square at Sutter St. Int corridors. **Pets:** Accepted.
ECO SAVE 🛜 🕭M 🄷 🖵 🍴

AAA ▽▽▽ ▽▽▽ **The Handlery Union Square Hotel** 🄷
(415) 781-7800. **$189-$499.** 351 Geary St 94102. Between Powell and Mason sts; just sw of Union Square. Ext/int corridors. **Pets:** Accepted.
ECO SAVE 🛜 ⊠ 🕭M 🄷 🖵 🍴 ⇌

AAA ▽▽▽▽ **Harbor Court Hotel** 🄷 ❀
(415) 882-1300. **$209-$359.** 165 Steuart St 94105. On Embarcadero; between Howard and Mission sts. Int corridors. **Pets:** Other species. Designated rooms, service with restrictions, supervision.
ECO SAVE 🛜 ⊠ 🕭M 🍴

AAA ▽▽▽ ▽▽▽ **Hilton San Francisco Financial District** 🄷
(415) 433-6600. **$189-$339.** 750 Kearny St 94108. Between Clay and Washington sts. Int corridors. **Pets:** Accepted.
⊟ SAVE 🛜 ⊠ 🕭M 🄷 🖵 🍴

▽▽▽ ▽▽▽ **Hilton San Francisco Union Square** 🄷
(415) 771-1400. **$109-$299.** 333 O'Farrell St 94102. Just w of Mason and O'Farrell sts. Int corridors. **Pets:** Accepted.
ECO 🛜 🕭M 🄷 🖵 🍴 ⇌ ⊠

AAA ▽▽▽ ▽▽▽ **Holiday Inn Civic Center** 🄷
(415) 626-6103. **$99-$339.** 50 8th St 94103. Between Market and Mission sts. Int corridors. **Pets:** Small. $75 one-time fee/room. Service with restrictions, supervision. ECO SAVE 🛜 🕭M 🄷 🖵 🍴 ⇌

AAA ▽▽▽ ▽▽▽ **Holiday Inn Fisherman's Wharf** 🄷
(415) 771-9000. **$125-$365.** 1300 Columbus Ave 94133. Jct North Point St. Int corridors. **Pets:** Accepted.
ECO SAVE ⊠ 🄷 🖵 🍴 ⇌

AAA ▽▽▽ ▽▽▽ **Holiday Inn Golden Gateway** 🄷
(415) 441-4000. **Call for rates.** 1500 Van Ness Ave 94109. US 101 (Van Ness Ave) at Pine St. Int corridors. **Pets:** Accepted.
SAVE 🛜 ⊠ 🕭M 🄷 🖵 🍴 ⇌

AAA ▽▽▽ ▽▽▽ **Hotel Abri** 🄷 ❀
(415) 392-8800. **$229-$389.** 127 Ellis St 94102. Just w of Union Square at Mason St. Int corridors. **Pets:** Medium. $75 one-time fee/room. Designated rooms, service with restrictions, crate.
ECO SAVE ⊠ 🕭M 🄷 🖵

▽▽▽ ▽▽▽ **Hotel Carlton, a Joie de Vivre hotel** 🄷
(415) 673-0242. **$109-$499.** 1075 Sutter St 94109. 0.5 mi w of Union Square; between Hyde and Larkin sts. Int corridors. **Pets:** Accepted.
ECO 🛜 ⊠ 🕭M 🄷 🖵 🍴 🄰🄲

▽▽ ▽▽ **Hotel Cartwright Union Square** 🄷
(415) 421-2865. **Call for rates.** 524 Sutter St 94102. Union Square at Powell St. Int corridors. **Pets:** Accepted.
ECO 🛜 ⊠ 🕭M 🄷 🖵 🄰🄲

Hotel Del Sol, a Joie de Vivre hotel M ❀
(415) 921-5520. **$129-$269.** 3100 Webster St 94123. Just s of Lombard St at Greenwich St. Ext corridors. **Pets:** Supervision.

Hotel Diva H ❀
(415) 885-0200. **$199-$369.** 440 Geary St 94102. Between Taylor and Mason sts; on Theater Row. Int corridors. **Pets:** Small, dogs only. $25 deposit/pet, $25 one-time fee/pet. Designated rooms, service with restrictions, supervision.

Hotel Kabuki, a Joie de Vivre hotel H
(415) 922-3200. **Call for rates.** 1625 Post St 94115. Jct Laguna St; in Japan Center. Int corridors. **Pets:** Accepted.

Hotel Mark Twain H ❀
(415) 673-2332. **$109-$399.** 345 Taylor St 94102. Just w of Union Square. Int corridors. **Pets:** Medium, dogs only. $50 one-time fee/room. Designated rooms, service with restrictions, crate.

Hotel Monaco H
(415) 292-0100. **$189-$459.** 501 Geary St 94102. Just w of Union Square at Taylor St. Int corridors. **Pets:** Accepted.

Hotel Nikko San Francisco H
(415) 394-1111. **$169-$399.** 222 Mason St 94102. At O'Farrell St. Int corridors. **Pets:** Accepted.

Hotel Palomar H
(415) 348-1111. **Call for rates.** 12 4th St 94103. At Market St. Int corridors. **Pets:** Accepted.

Hotel Triton H
(415) 394-0500. **$149-$489.** 342 Grant Ave 94108. Near Union Square at Bush St. Int corridors. **Pets:** Accepted.

Hotel Union Square H ❀
(415) 397-3000. **Call for rates.** 114 Powell St 94102. At Ellis St; just n of cable car turnaround. Int corridors. **Pets:** Large. $25 one-time fee/room. Service with restrictions, supervision.

Hotel Vitale, a Joie de Vivre hotel H
(415) 278-3700. **$499-$3500.** 8 Mission St 94105. At The Embarcadero and Mission St. Int corridors. **Pets:** Accepted.

Hyatt Regency San Francisco H ❀
(415) 788-1234. **$126-$423.** 5 Embarcadero Center 94111. Foot of California and Market sts; in Financial District. Int corridors. **Pets:** Medium, dogs only. $75 daily fee/room. Service with restrictions, crate.

InterContinental Mark Hopkins San Francisco H ❀
(415) 392-3434. **$159-$489.** One Nob Hill 94108. Corner of California and Mason sts. Int corridors. **Pets:** Small. $50 daily fee/pet. Service with restrictions, supervision.

InterContinental San Francisco H ❀
(415) 616-6500. **$159-$489.** 888 Howard St 94103. Between 4th and 5th sts; in SoMa District. Int corridors. **Pets:** Medium. $50 daily fee/pet. Designated rooms, service with restrictions, supervision.

JW Marriott San Francisco H
(415) 771-8600. **$219-$489.** 500 Post St 94102. Just w of Union Square at Mason St. Int corridors. **Pets:** Accepted.

Kensington Park Hotel H
(415) 788-6400. **$199-$399.** 450 Post St 94102. Just w of Union Square. Int corridors. **Pets:** Accepted.

Laurel Inn, a Joie de Vivre hotel H ❀
(415) 567-8467. **$159-$329.** 444 Presidio Ave 94115. 1 mi w of US 101 (Van Ness Ave); 1 mi e of Park Presidio Blvd (SR 1) at California St. Int corridors. **Pets:** $50 deposit/pet. Designated rooms, service with restrictions, supervision.

Le Meridien San Francisco H
(415) 296-2900. **$179-$699.** 333 Battery St 94111. Just s of Clay and Battery sts; in Financial District. Int corridors. **Pets:** Accepted.

Marina Motel M ❀
(415) 921-9406. **Call for rates.** 2576 Lombard St 94123. Between Broderick and Divisadero sts. Ext/int corridors. **Pets:** Dogs only. $10 daily fee/pet. Designated rooms, service with restrictions, crate.

Omni San Francisco Hotel H
(415) 677-9494. **$189-$699.** 500 California St 94104. At Montgomery St; in Financial District. Int corridors. **Pets:** Accepted.

Palace Hotel H
(415) 512-1111. **$179-$619.** 2 New Montgomery St 94105. Just e of Union Square; at Market St. Int corridors. **Pets:** Accepted.

Parc 55 Wyndham San Francisco Union Square H
(415) 392-8000. **$159-$400, 3 day notice.** 55 Cyril Magnin St 94102. Corner of Cyril Magnin and Eddy sts; just sw of Union Square. Int corridors. **Pets:** Accepted.

The Powell Hotel H ❀
(415) 398-3200. **Call for rates.** 28 Cyril Magnin St 94102. At Powell St cable car turnaround. Int corridors. **Pets:** Small. $150 deposit/room. Service with restrictions, crate.

The Prescott Hotel H
(415) 563-0303. **Call for rates.** 545 Post St 94102. Just w of Union Square. Int corridors. **Pets:** Accepted.

Radisson Hotel Fisherman's Wharf H
(415) 392-6700. **$139-$559.** 250 Beach St 94133. At Powell St. Int corridors. **Pets:** Large. $75 one-time fee/room. Service with restrictions, supervision.

The Ritz-Carlton, San Francisco H
(415) 296-7465. **Call for rates.** 600 Stockton St 94108. Just n of Union Square at California St. Int corridors. **Pets:** Accepted.

St. Regis Hotel San Francisco H ❀
(415) 284-4000. **$329-$649.** 125 3rd St 94103. At Mission St. Int corridors. **Pets:** Medium, dogs only. $150 one-time fee/room. Designated rooms, service with restrictions, supervision.

San Francisco Marriott Fisherman's Wharf H ❀
(415) 775-7555. **$169-$589.** 1250 Columbus Ave 94133. Just s of Fisherman's Wharf at Bay St. Int corridors. **Pets:** Other species. $100 daily fee/room. Service with restrictions, supervision.

Serrano Hotel H
(415) 885-2500. **Call for rates.** 405 Taylor St 94102. Just w of Union Square at O'Farrell St. Int corridors. **Pets:** Accepted.

Sheraton Fisherman's Wharf H ❀
(415) 362-5500. **$139-$479.** 2500 Mason St 94133. Just se of Fisherman's Wharf at Beach St. Int corridors. **Pets:** Large, dogs only. Designated rooms, supervision.
ECO SAVE 🛰 ✕ &M 🛎 💻 ▯▯ ➹

Sir Francis Drake Hotel H
(415) 392-7755. **$129-$509.** 450 Powell St 94102. Just n of Union Square at Sutter St. Int corridors. **Pets:** Accepted.
ECO SAVE 🛰 ✕ &M ▯▯

The Stanford Court, A Renaissance Hotel H ❀
(415) 989-3500. **$179-$399.** 905 California St 94108. Atop Nob Hill; corner of California and Powell sts. Int corridors. **Pets:** Small, dogs only. $25 one-time fee/room. Service with restrictions, supervision.
ECO SAVE 🛰 ✕ &M 🛎 💻 ▯▯

Taj Campton Place San Francisco H
(415) 781-5555. **Call for rates.** 340 Stockton St 94108. Just n of Union Square; jct Sutter St. Int corridors. **Pets:** Accepted.
ECO 🛰 ✕ &M 💻 ▯▯

Travelodge at the Presidio M
(415) 931-8581. **$129-$259.** 2755 Lombard St 94123. Between Lyon and Baker sts. Ext corridors. **Pets:** Medium. $20 daily fee/pet. Supervision.
🛰 ✕ 🛎 💻

Travelodge By The Bay M ❀
(415) 673-0691. **$69-$209.** 1450 Lombard St 94123. On US 101 (Lombard St); between Van Ness Ave and Franklin St. Ext/int corridors. **Pets:** Dogs only. $20 daily fee/pet. Designated rooms, service with restrictions, crate. SAVE 🛰 ✕ &M 💻

The Westin St. Francis San Francisco on Union Square H
(415) 397-7000. **$199-$629, 3 day notice.** 335 Powell St 94102. On Union Square. Int corridors. **Pets:** Accepted.
SAVE 🛰 ✕ &M 🛎 💻 ▯▯ ✕

Westin San Francisco Market Street H ❀
(415) 974-6400. **$159-$899, 3 day notice.** 50 3rd St 94103. Just n of Moscone Convention Center; between Jessie and Stevenson sts. Int corridors. **Pets:** Medium, other species. Service with restrictions, supervision.
SAVE 🛰 ✕ &M 💻 ▯▯

The Wharf Inn M
(415) 673-7411. **$119-$225.** 2601 Mason St 94133. At Beach St; adjacent to Fisherman's Wharf and San Francisco Bay. Ext corridors. **Pets:** Small, dogs only. $15 daily fee/pet. Designated rooms, service with restrictions, supervision. SAVE 🛰 ✕ &M A̶C

W San Francisco H ❀
(415) 777-5300. **$249-$669.** 181 3rd St 94103. At Howard St. Int corridors. **Pets:** Medium. $100 one-time fee/room. Designated rooms, service with restrictions. ECO SAVE 🛰 ✕ &M 🛎 ▯▯ ➹ ✕

SAN MATEO

Residence Inn by Marriott H
(650) 574-4700. **$229-$269.** 2000 Winward Way 94404. US 101 exit 414B (SR 92/E Hayward/Fashion Island) to Mariners Island exit, then just e. Ext corridors. **Pets:** Accepted. 🛰 ✕ &M 🛎 💻 ➹ ✕

SAN RAFAEL

Extended StayAmerica-SanRafael-Francisco Blvd E H
(415) 451-1887. **$119-$154.** 1775 Francisco Blvd E 94901. US 101 exit 451 (I-580/Richmond Br/Oakland) northbound; exit 451B (I-580/Richmond/Oakland) southbound, just e on Bellam Blvd, then 1 mi s. Int corridors. **Pets:** $25 daily fee/pet. Designated rooms, service with restrictions.
🛰 &M 🛎 💻 ➹

Gerstle Park Inn BB
(415) 721-7611. **$189-$275, 3 day notice.** 34 Grove St 94901. US 101 exit Central San Rafael, 0.5 mi w on 4th St, 0.5 mi s on D St, then just w on San Rafael Ave. Ext/int corridors. **Pets:** Dogs only. $10 daily fee/pet. Designated rooms, service with restrictions, supervision. 🛰 ✕ &M

SOUTH SAN FRANCISCO

Embassy Suites San Francisco Airport-South San Francisco H ❀
(650) 589-3400. **$140-$350.** 250 Gateway Blvd 94080. US 101 exit 425A (Grand Ave), just e. Int corridors. **Pets:** Medium. $50 one-time fee/room. Designated rooms, service with restrictions, crate.
ECO 🛰 &M 🛎 💻 ▯▯ ➹

Larkspur Landing South San Francisco H
(650) 827-1515. **$109-$309.** 690 Gateway Blvd 94080. US 101 exit 425A (Grand Ave), 0.4 mi e, then 0.4 mi n. Int corridors. **Pets:** Accepted.
ECO 🛰 ✕ &M 🛎 💻

Residence Inn by Marriott at Oyster Point H
(650) 837-9000. **$159-$285.** 1350 Veterans Blvd 94080. US 101 exit 425B (Oyster Point Blvd), just ne. Int corridors. **Pets:** Other species. $100 one-time fee/room. Service with restrictions, supervision.
ECO 🛰 ✕ &M 🛎 💻 ▯▯ ➹ ✕

TIBURON

The Lodge at Tiburon H ❀
(415) 435-3133. **$149-$469, 3 day notice.** 1651 Tiburon Blvd 94920. US 101 exit Tiburon-Belvedere, 4 mi e; in village; 1 blk from bay. Ext corridors. **Pets:** Medium, other species. $75 one-time fee/room. Service with restrictions. ECO 🛰 ✕ &M 🛎 💻 ▯▯ ➹

END METROPOLITAN AREA

SANGER

Wonder Valley Ranch Resort R▲
(559) 787-2551. **$149-$278.** 6450 Elwood Rd 93657. SR 180, 7.8 mi n on Piedra Rd, 5.4 mi e. Ext corridors. **Pets:** Small, dogs only. $25 daily fee/room. Designated rooms, supervision.
🛰 ✕ &M 🛎 💻 ✕

SAN JOSE

DoubleTree by Hilton Hotel San Jose H
(408) 453-4000. **$199-$459.** 2050 Gateway Pl 95110. 0.3 mi e of Norman Y. Mineta San Jose International Airport via Airport Blvd; w of US 101 exit N 1st St; US 101 exit Brokaw Rd northbound. Int corridors. **Pets:** Large. $50 one-time fee/room. Service with restrictions, crate.
ECO SAVE 🛰 ✕ &M 🛎 💻 ▯▯ ➹

Extended Stay America/San Jose Downtown H
(408) 573-0648. **$89-$104.** 1560 N 1st St 95112. 1 mi e of Norman Y. Mineta San Jose International Airport; US 101 exit N 1st St, then s. Int corridors. **Pets:** $25 daily fee/pet. Designated rooms, service with restrictions.
🛰 &M 🛎 💻

Fairfield Inn & Suites by Marriott H
(408) 453-3133. **$145-$160.** 1755 N 1st St 95112. US 101 exit N 1st St, just w. Int corridors. **Pets:** Accepted.
SAVE 🛰 ✕ &M 🛎 💻 ➹

The Fairmont San Jose H ❀
(408) 998-1900. **$129-$429, 3 day notice.** 170 S Market St 95113. At Fairmont Plaza. Int corridors. **Pets:** Large, dogs only. $75 one-time fee/room. Supervision. ECO SAVE 🛰 ✕ &M 💻 ▯▯ ➹ ✕

Four Points by Sheraton San Jose Silicon Valley H

(408) 972-7800. **$89-$204.** 399 Silicon Valley Blvd 95138. US 101 exit Bernal Rd, just e. Int corridors. **Pets:** Accepted.

Hilton San Jose H

(408) 287-2100. **$99-$319.** 300 Almaden Blvd 95110. SR 87 exit Santa Clara St E, 0.4 mi s; at W San Carlos St. Int corridors. **Pets:** Accepted.

Homewood Suites by Hilton H ❖

(408) 428-9900. **Call for rates.** 10 W Trimble Rd 95131. US 101 exit Trimble Rd, 1.3 mi e; 2 mi ne of Norman Y. Mineta San Jose International Airport. Ext/int corridors. **Pets:** Dogs only. Service with restrictions.

Hotel De Anza H

(408) 286-1000. **$129-$399.** 233 W Santa Clara St 95113. SR 87 exit Santa Clara St, just e. Int corridors. **Pets:** Small. $50 one-time fee/room. Designated rooms, service with restrictions, crate.

Hyatt Place San Jose/Downtown H

(408) 998-0400. **$109-$285.** 282 Almaden Blvd 95113. I-280 exit Almaden-Vine, 6 blks n. Int corridors. **Pets:** Accepted.

La Quinta Inn San Jose Airport H

(408) 435-8800. **$77-$210, 7 day notice.** 2585 Seaboard Ave 95131. US 101 exit Trimble Rd E; 1 mi ne of Norman Y. Mineta San Jose International Airport. Int corridors. **Pets:** Service with restrictions, supervision.

Residence Inn by Marriott H

(408) 226-7676. **$94-$169.** 6111 San Ignacio Ave 95119. US 101 exit Bernal Rd w, then just n. Int corridors. **Pets:** Large. $100 one-time fee/room. Service with restrictions, supervision.

San Jose Airport Garden Hotel H

(408) 793-3300. **$89-$209.** 1740 N 1st St 95112. W of US 101 exit N 1st St; 0.5 mi e of Norman Y. Mineta San Jose International Airport via Airport Pkwy. Int corridors. **Pets:** Accepted.

San Jose Marriott H ❖

(408) 280-1300. **$129-$319.** 301 S Market St 95113. SR 87 exit Santa Clara St E, s on Almaden Blvd, then just e on San Carlos St. Int corridors. **Pets:** Medium. $75 one-time fee/room. Designated rooms, service with restrictions, supervision.

Staybridge Suites San Jose H

(408) 436-1600. **Call for rates.** 1602 Crane Ct 95112. US 101 exit 1st St/Brokaw Rd, 0.4 mi e to Bering Dr, then 0.5 mi s. Ext corridors. **Pets:** Accepted.

TownePlace Suites by Marriott San Jose/Cupertino H

(408) 984-5903. **$129-$249.** 440 Saratoga Ave 95129. I-280 exit Saratoga Ave, just n. Int corridors. **Pets:** Accepted.

SAN JUAN CAPISTRANO

BEST WESTERN Capistrano Inn M

(949) 493-5661. **$114-$149.** 27174 Ortega Hwy 92675. I-5 exit 82 (SR 74/Ortega Hwy), just e. Ext corridors. **Pets:** Medium. $25 one-time fee/room.

Residence Inn by Marriott San Juan Capistrano H ❖

(949) 443-3600. **$169-$339.** 33711 Camino Capistrano 92675. I-5 exit Camino Capistrano, just w, then 1.3 mi s. Int corridors. **Pets:** Other species. $100 one-time fee/room. Service with restrictions.

SAN LUIS OBISPO

BEST WESTERN PLUS Royal Oak Hotel M ❖

(805) 544-4410. **$99-$319.** 214 Madonna Rd 93405. US 101 exit 201 (Madonna Rd), just s. Ext/int corridors. **Pets:** Large. $15 daily fee/pet. Service with restrictions, supervision.

Embassy Suites Hotel H

(805) 549-0800. **$119-$389.** 333 Madonna Rd 93405. US 101 exit 201 (Madonna Rd), 0.5 mi sw. Int corridors. **Pets:** Accepted.

Heritage Inn Bed & Breakfast BB ❖

(805) 544-7440. **$85-$185, 7 day notice.** 978 Olive St 93405. US 101 exit 203B (SR 1/Morro Bay) northbound, just w on Santa Rosa St, then just s; exit 203A (Santa Rosa St) southbound, just ne. Int corridors. **Pets:** Medium, other species. $35 one-time fee/pet. Designated rooms, service with restrictions, supervision.

Holiday Inn Express H

(805) 544-8600. **$139-$259.** 1800 Monterey St 93401. US 101 exit 204 (Monterey St), just w. Int corridors. **Pets:** Accepted.

Petit Soleil Bed & Breakfast BB ❖

(805) 549-0321. **$159-$309, 3 day notice.** 1473 Monterey St 93401. US 101 exit 204 (Monterey St), 0.3 mi sw. Ext corridors. **Pets:** Other species. $25 one-time fee/room. Service with restrictions, supervision.

Ramada Inn Olive Tree M

(805) 544-2800. **$59-$229.** 1000 Olive St 93405. US 101 exit 203B (Morro Bay) northbound, just w on Santa Rosa St, then just s; exit 203A (Santa Rosa St) southbound, just ne. Int corridors. **Pets:** Small, dogs only. $50 deposit/room, $10 daily fee/pet. Designated rooms, service with restrictions, supervision.

Sands Inn & Suites M

(805) 544-0500. **Call for rates.** 1930 Monterey St 93401. US 101 exit 204 (Monterey St), just sw. Ext corridors. **Pets:** $25 one-time fee/room. Designated rooms, service with restrictions, crate.

Super 8 M

(805) 544-6888. **$69-$279.** 1951 Monterey St 93401. US 101 exit 204 (Monterey St), just e. Ext corridors. **Pets:** Medium, dogs only. $10 daily fee/pet. Service with restrictions, supervision.

SAN MARCOS

Residence Inn by Marriott San Diego North/San Marcos H

(760) 591-9828. **$129-$189.** 1245 Los Vallecitos Blvd 92069. SR 78 exit Las Posas Rd, just ne. Int corridors. **Pets:** Medium. $100 one-time fee/room. Service with restrictions, supervision.

SAN RAMON

Extended StayAmerica-San Ramon-Bishop Ranch-West H

(925) 277-0833. **$94-$109.** 18000 San Ramon Valley Blvd 94583. I-680 exit Bollinger Canyon Rd E, just n. Ext corridors. **Pets:** $25 daily fee/pet. Designated rooms, service with restrictions.

◆◆◆◆ **Residence Inn by Marriott** 🏨 ❀

(925) 277-9292. **$123-$224.** 1071 Market Pl 94583. I-680 exit Bollinger Canyon Rd E, 0.5 mi e. Ext corridors. **Pets:** Large, other species. $100 one-time fee/room. Service with restrictions, supervision.

◆◆◆◆ **San Ramon Marriott at Bishop Ranch** 🏨

(925) 867-9200. **$109-$299.** 2600 Bishop Dr 94583. I-680 exit Bollinger Canyon Rd E, n on Sunset, then just w. Int corridors. **Pets:** Medium, other species. $100 one-time fee/room. Service with restrictions.

SAN SIMEON

🔺🔺🔺 ◆◆◆◆ **BEST WESTERN PLUS Cavalier Oceanfront Resort** 🏨 ❀

(805) 927-4688. **$109-$319, 3 day notice.** 9415 Hearst Dr 93452. Just w of SR 1. Ext corridors. **Pets:** Supervision.

🔺🔺🔺 ◆◆◆ **Courtesy Inn** 🅼

(805) 927-4691. **$69-$109, 7 day notice.** 9450 Castillo Dr 93452. Just e of SR 1. Ext corridors. **Pets:** Dogs only. $25 daily fee/pet. Designated rooms, service with restrictions, supervision.

◆◆◆◆ **The Morgan San Simeon** 🏨 ❀

(805) 927-3878. **$79-$225.** 9135 Hearst Dr 93452. Just w of SR 1. Int corridors. **Pets:** Dogs only. $25 daily fee/room. No service, supervision.

◆◆◆ **Sands by the Sea** 🅼 ❀

(805) 927-3243. **$69-$129, 3 day notice.** 9355 Hearst Dr 93452. Just w of SR 1. Ext corridors. **Pets:** Supervision.

🔺🔺🔺 ◆◆◆ **San Simeon Lodge** 🏨 ❀

(805) 927-4601. **$50-$240, 3 day notice.** 9520 Castillo Dr 93452. On SR 1. Ext corridors. **Pets:** Small, dogs only. $15 daily fee/pet. Designated rooms, service with restrictions, supervision.

🔺🔺🔺 ◆◆◆ **Silver Surf Motel** 🅼

(805) 927-4661. **$59-$199.** 9390 Castillo Dr 93452. Just e of SR 1. Ext corridors. **Pets:** Small. $15 daily fee/pet. Designated rooms, service with restrictions, supervision.

SANTA ANA

◆◆◆◆ **La Quinta Inn & Suites Orange County-Santa Ana** 🅼

(714) 540-1111. **$83-$166.** 2721 Hotel Terrace Dr 92705. SR 55 exit 8 (Dyer Rd) northbound; exit 8B (Dyer Rd W) southbound, just w, then just s. Ext corridors. **Pets:** Service with restrictions, supervision.

SANTA BARBARA

🔺🔺🔺 ◆◆◆ **BEST WESTERN Beachside Inn** 🅼

(805) 965-6556. **$120-$400.** 336 W Cabrillo Blvd 93101. US 101 exit 96 (Garden St) northbound, just w; exit 97 (Castillo St/Harbor) southbound, 0.3 mi w to Cabrillo Blvd, then 0.5 mi n; corner of Cabrillo Blvd and Castillo St. Ext corridors. **Pets:** Other species. $20 one-time fee/room. Designated rooms, supervision.

◆◆◆ **Blue Sands Motel** 🅼

(805) 965-1624. **$95-$285, 3 day notice.** 421 S Milpas St 93103. US 101 exit 96A (Milpas St), 0.3 mi s. Ext corridors. **Pets:** Dogs only. $10 daily fee/pet. Service with restrictions.

◆◆◆ **Extended StayAmerica Santa Barbara-Calle Real** 🏨

(805) 692-1882. **$125-$135.** 4870 Calle Real 93111. US 101 exit Turnpike Rd, just e, then just n. Int corridors. **Pets:** $25 daily fee/pet. Designated rooms, service with restrictions.

🪐 ◆◆◆ ◆◆◆ **The Fess Parker, A DoubleTree by Hilton Resort** 🏨 ❀

(805) 564-4333. **$229-$609.** 633 E Cabrillo Blvd 93103. US 101 exit 96A (Milpas St), just s, then just w. Ext/int corridors. **Pets:** Large, other species. $25 daily fee/room. Designated rooms, supervision.

🪐 ◆◆◆ **Four Seasons Biltmore Santa Barbara** 🏨

(805) 969-2261. **$395-$795, 3 day notice.** 1260 Channel Dr 93108. US 101 exit 94A (Olive Mill Rd), 0.3 mi s; in Montecito. Ext corridors. **Pets:** Accepted.

🪐 ◆◆◆◆ **Hyatt Santa Barbara** 🏨

(805) 882-1234. **$90-$495, 3 day notice.** 1111 E Cabrillo Blvd 93103. US 101 exit 96A (Milpas St), 0.3 mi s, then just e. Int corridors. **Pets:** Accepted.

◆◆◆ **Marina Beach Motel** 🅼

(805) 963-9311. **$120-$295.** 21 Bath St 93101. US 101 exit 96B (Garden St), 0.3 mi w to Cabrillo Blvd, 0.4 mi n to Bath St, then just e. Ext corridors. **Pets:** Small. $15 daily fee/pet. Designated rooms, service with restrictions, supervision.

◆◆◆ **Pacifica Suites** 🏨

(805) 683-6722. **$179-$459.** 5490 Hollister Ave 93111. US 101 exit 104A (Patterson Ave), 0.5 mi w, then 0.5 mi n. Ext/int corridors. **Pets:** Medium, dogs only. $25 daily fee/pet. Designated rooms, service with restrictions, supervision.

◆◆◆◆ **The Parkside Inn** 🅼

(805) 963-0744. **$79-$249, 3 day notice.** 424 Por La Mar 93103. I-101 exit 96A (Milpas St), 0.3 mi s, just e on Cabrillo Blvd, then just n. Int corridors. **Pets:** Accepted.

◆◆◆ **The Secret Garden Inn & Cottages** 🅱🅱

(805) 687-2300. **Call for rates.** 1908 Bath St 93101. US 101 exit 98B (Arrellaga St) northbound, just e, then just n; exit 99 (Mission St) southbound, just e, then just s. Ext/int corridors. **Pets:** Accepted.

SANTA CLARA

🪐 ◆◆◆◆ **Avatar Hotel Great America** 🏨

(408) 235-8900. **$79-$249.** 4200 Great America Pkwy 95054. 0.5 mi e off US 101 exit Great America Pkwy; 0.8 mi s of California's Great America theme park. Ext corridors. **Pets:** Accepted.

🪐 ◆◆◆◆ **Biltmore Hotel & Suites/Silicon Valley** 🏨 ❀

(408) 988-8411. **$129-$299.** 2151 Laurelwood Rd 95054. US 101 exit Montague Expwy, just e; 1 mi s of Great America Pkwy. Ext/int corridors. **Pets:** Small. $50 one-time fee/room. Designated rooms, service with restrictions, supervision.

◆◆◆ **Candlewood Suites-Silicon Valley/San Jose** 🏨

(408) 241-9305. **$119-$159.** 481 El Camino Real 95050. I-880 exit The Alameda, 1.5 mi w. Int corridors. **Pets:** Accepted.

🪐 ◆◆◆◆ **Hilton Santa Clara Hotel** 🏨

(408) 330-0001. **$95-$389.** 4949 Great America Pkwy 95054. US 101 exit Great America Pkwy, 0.5 mi n. Int corridors. **Pets:** Accepted.

🪐 ◆◆◆◆ **Hyatt Regency Santa Clara** 🏨

(408) 200-1234. **$72-$288.** 5101 Great America Pkwy 95054. US 101 exit Great America Pkwy, 0.8 mi e. Int corridors. **Pets:** Accepted.

🪐 ◆◆◆ **Quality Inn & Suites Silicon Valley** 🅼

(408) 241-3010. **$94-$105.** 2930 El Camino Real 95051. SR 82, 0.5 mi w of San Tomas Expwy; US 101 exit S Bowers Ave. Ext corridors. **Pets:** Accepted.

WWW Santa Clara Marriott Hotel H
(408) 988-1500. $99-$319. 2700 Mission College Blvd 95054. 0.5 mi e off US 101 exit Great America Pkwy; 0.8 mi s of California's Great America theme park. Int corridors. Pets: Accepted.
ECO 🛜 ✕ 🕭ᴹ 🔋 💻 🍴 🏊 ✕

SANTA CRUZ

WWW WWW Chaminade Resort & Spa H
(831) 475-5600. $199-$439, 3 day notice. 1 Chaminade Ln 95065. 1.5 mi e of SR 1 and 17; SR 1 exit Soquel Ave, just w to Paul Sweet Rd, then 0.5 mi n. Int corridors. Pets: Accepted.
SAVE 🛜 ✕ 🕭ᴹ 🔋 💻 🍴 🏊 ✕

WWW WWW Edgewater Beach Inn & Suites M ❀
(831) 423-0440. $129-$319, 3 day notice. 525 Second St 95060. Across from beach and Boardwalk. Ext corridors. Pets: Large, other species. $35 one-time fee/pet. Designated rooms, service with restrictions, supervision. SAVE 🛜 ✕ 🔋 💻 🏊 ✕

WWW WWW Hilton Santa Cruz/Scotts Valley H ❀
(831) 440-1000. $99-$399. 6001 La Madrona Dr 95060. SR 17 exit Mt Hermon Rd. Int corridors. Pets: Large, dogs only. $50 one-time fee/room. Designated rooms, service with restrictions, supervision.
SAVE 🛜 ✕ 🕭ᴹ 🔋 💻 🍴 🏊

WWW WWW The Inn at Pasatiempo H ❀
(831) 423-5000. $75-$305. 555 Hwy 17 95060. 0.8 mi n of jct SR 1 and 17; SR 17 exit Pasatiempo Dr. Ext corridors. Pets: Small, dogs only. $25 daily fee/room. Designated rooms, service with restrictions, crate.
SAVE 🛜 ✕ 🕭ᴹ 🔋 💻 🍴 🏊 ✕

WWW WWW Ocean Pacific Lodge H ❀
(831) 457-1234. $69-$399. 301 Pacific Ave 95060. SR 1 and 17 exit w via Ocean St, 1 mi w to Broadway, turn right, left on Front St to Pacific Ave, then just right. Ext corridors. Pets: $30 daily fee/pet. Designated rooms, service with restrictions, supervision.
SAVE 🛜 ✕ 🕭ᴹ 🔋 💻 🏊

WWW West Cliff Inn BB ❀
(831) 457-2200. $195-$410, 7 day notice. 174 W Cliff Dr 95060. Just n of boardwalk and adjacent to Fisherman's Wharf. Int corridors. Pets: Medium, dogs only. $40 one-time fee/room. Designated rooms, service with restrictions, crate. 🛜 ✕ 🕭ᴹ 🔋 💻

SANTA MARIA

WWW BEST WESTERN PLUS Big
America M ❀
(805) 922-5200. $107-$223. 1725 N Broadway 93454. US 101 exit 173 (SR 135/S Broadway), 0.5 mi s. Ext corridors. Pets: Other species. Service with restrictions, supervision. SAVE 🛜 ✕ 🔋 💻 🏊

WWW Candlewood Suites H
(805) 928-4155. $79-$149. 2079 N Roemer Ct 93454. US 101 exit 173 (SR 135/S Broadway), 0.8 mi sw, then just s. Int corridors.
Pets: Accepted. 🛜 ✕ 🔋 💻

WWW Historic Santa Maria Inn H ❀
(805) 928-7777. $121-$283. 801 S Broadway 93454. US 101 exit 171 (Main St), 1 mi w, then 0.5 mi s. Int corridors. Pets: Medium, other species. $50 one-time fee/room. Designated rooms, service with restrictions, supervision. 🛜 🔋 💻 🍴 🏊 ✕

WWW WWW Holiday Inn & Suites H ❀
(805) 928-6000. $114-$194, 3 day notice. 2100 N Broadway 93454. US 101 exit 173 (SR 135/S Broadway), just s. Int corridors. Pets: Small. $25 one-time fee/pet, $25 daily fee/pet. Designated rooms, service with restrictions, supervision. SAVE 🛜 🕭ᴹ 🔋 💻 🍴 🏊

WWW WWW Quality Inn & Suites M
(805) 922-5891. $97-$102. 210 S Nicholson Ave 93454. US 101 exit 171 (Main St), just e, then just s. Int corridors. Pets: Small, dogs only. $25 one-time fee/pet. Service with restrictions, supervision.
SAVE 🛜 🔋 💻 🏊

WWW WWW Radisson Hotel Santa Maria H
(805) 928-8000. $107-$161. 3455 Skyway Dr 93455. US 101 exit 169 (Betteravia Rd), 2.3 mi w, then 1.8 mi s. Ext/int corridors. Pets: $50 one-time fee/room. Designated rooms, service with restrictions, supervision.
SAVE 🛜 ✕ 🔋 💻 🍴 🏊 ✕

SANTA NELLA

WWW WWW BEST WESTERN Andersen's Inn H
(209) 826-5534. Call for rates. 12367 Hwy 33 S 95322. I-5 exit 407 (SR 33), just e. Ext corridors. Pets: Dogs only. $20 one-time fee/room. Designated rooms, service with restrictions, supervision.
SAVE 🛜 🕭ᴹ 🔋 💻 🏊

WWW WWW Holiday Inn Express H
(209) 826-8282. $79-$99. 28976 Plaza Dr 95322. I-5 exit 407 (SR 33), just e. Ext corridors. Pets: Medium. $12 one-time fee/pet. Designated rooms, service with restrictions, supervision.
SAVE 🛜 🕭ᴹ 🔋 💻 🏊

SANTA PAULA

WWW Glen Tavern Inn H
(805) 933-5550. $79-$99. 134 N Mill St 93060. SR 126 exit 12 (10th St) northbound, 0.5 mi w, just s on Santa Barbara St, then just e. Int corridors. Pets: Accepted. 🛜 ✕ 🔋 💻 🍴 🏊

SCOTTS VALLEY

WWW WWW BEST WESTERN PLUS Inn Scotts
Valley H
(831) 438-6666. $89-$199. 6020 Scotts Valley Dr 95066. SR 17 exit Granite Creek, just w. Ext corridors. Pets: Accepted.
SAVE 🛜 ✕ 🕭ᴹ 🔋 💻 🏊

SELMA

WWW WWW Holiday Inn-Swan Court H ❀
(559) 891-8000. $82-$104. 2950 Pea Soup Anderson Blvd 93662. SR 99 exit Floral Ave, just w. Int corridors. Pets: Dogs only. $50 one-time fee/pet. Designated rooms, service with restrictions, supervision.
SAVE 🛜 ✕ 🕭ᴹ 🔋 💻 🍴 🏊

WWW Super 8 Selma/Fresno Area H
(559) 896-2800. $65-$125. 3142 S Highland Ave 93662. SR 99 exit Floral Ave, just e. Int corridors. Pets: Small, dogs only. $10 daily fee/pet. Designated rooms, service with restrictions, supervision.
SAVE 🛜 🔋 💻 🏊

SIERRA CITY

WWW WWW Herrington's Sierra Pines Resort M
(530) 862-1151. $79-$140, 10 day notice. 104 Main St 96125. 0.5 mi w of center on SR 49; 12 mi n of Downieville. Ext corridors.
Pets: Accepted. SAVE 🛜 ✕ 💻 🍴 ✕ ✕ ✕

SIMI VALLEY

WWW Extended StayAmerica-Los Angeles-Simi Valley H
(805) 584-8880. $89-$139. 2498 Stearns St 93063. SR 118 exit 28 (Stearns St), just s. Int corridors. Pets: $25 daily fee/pet. Designated rooms, service with restrictions. 🛜 🔋 💻

SOLVANG

WWW WWW Hadsten House Inn M
(805) 688-3210. $109-$399, 7 day notice. 1450 Mission Dr 93463. On SR 246. Ext corridors. Pets: Accepted.
SAVE 🛜 ✕ 🕭ᴹ 🔋 💻 🍴 🏊

WWW Meadowlark Inn M ❀
(805) 688-4631. $135-$285, 7 day notice. 2644 Mission Dr 93463. SR 246, 1.6 mi e. Ext corridors. Pets: Dogs only. $100 deposit/pet, $25 daily fee/pet. Designated rooms, service with restrictions, supervision.
🛜 ✕ 🔋 💻 🏊

Royal Copenhagen Inn M
(805) 688-5561. **$85-$275, 3 day notice.** 1579 Mission Dr 93463. On SR 246; center of town. Ext corridors. **Pets:** Other species. $15 daily fee/pet. Designated rooms, service with restrictions, supervision.

Viking Motel M
(805) 688-1337. **$59-$180, 3 day notice.** 1506 Mission Dr 93463. On SR 246. Ext corridors. **Pets:** Medium. $15 daily fee/pet. Designated rooms, service with restrictions, supervision.

Wine Valley Inn & Cottages H
(805) 688-2111. **$149-$369.** 1564 Copenhagen Dr 93463. SR 246, just s on 5th St. Ext/int corridors. **Pets:** Other species. $50 one-time fee/pet. Service with restrictions, supervision.

SONORA

Aladdin Motor Inn H
(209) 533-4971. **$81-$145.** 14260 Mono Way (Hwy 108) 95370. On SR 108, 3.5 mi e. Ext/int corridors. **Pets:** Medium, other species. $15 one-time fee/room. Designated rooms, service with restrictions, supervision.

Barretta Gardens Inn BB
(209) 532-6039. **$149-$250, 14 day notice.** 700 S Barretta St 95370. Downtown. Int corridors. **Pets:** Dogs only. Designated rooms, service with restrictions, supervision.

BEST WESTERN PLUS Sonora Oaks Hotel & Conference Center H
(209) 533-4400. **$99-$149.** 19551 Hess Ave 95370. 3.5 mi e on SR 108. Ext/int corridors. **Pets:** Medium, dogs only. $20 daily fee/room. Designated rooms, service with restrictions, supervision.

Inns of California-Sonora H
(209) 532-3633. **$70-$130.** 350 S Washington St 95370. 3 blks e of jct SR 49 and 108; downtown. Ext corridors. **Pets:** $100 deposit/room, $25 one-time fee/room. Designated rooms, service with restrictions, supervision.

Union Hill Inn BB
(209) 533-1494. **$150-$195, 3 day notice.** 21645 Parrotts Ferry Rd 95370. Jct SR 49 and Parrotts Ferry Rd; 3 mi n of downtown. Ext corridors. **Pets:** Large, other species.

STOCKTON

BEST WESTERN PLUS Heritage Inn H
(209) 474-3301. **$70-$130.** 111 E March Ln 95207. I-5 exit March Ln, 2.5 mi e; corner of El Dorado St. Int corridors. **Pets:** Medium. $20 daily fee/pet. Designated rooms, service with restrictions, supervision.

La Quinta Inn Stockton H
(209) 952-7800. **$59-$122.** 2710 W March Ln 95219. I-5 exit March Ln, just w. Ext corridors. **Pets:** Service with restrictions, supervision.

Residence Inn by Marriott H
(209) 472-9800. **$107-$149.** 3240 W March Ln 95219. I-5 exit March Ln, 0.5 mi w. Int corridors. **Pets:** $100 one-time fee/room. Service with restrictions, supervision.

University Plaza Waterfront Hotel H
(209) 944-1140. **$99-$149.** 110 W Fremont St 95202. SR 4 exit Downtown Stockton, 0.5 mi n on El Dorado St, then just w. Int corridors. **Pets:** Medium. $20 daily fee/room. Designated rooms, service with restrictions, crate.

SUISUN CITY

Hampton Inn & Suites Suisun City Waterfront H
(707) 429-0900. **$109-$159.** 2 Harbor Center Dr 94585. I-80 exit SR 12, 2.6 mi e to Suisun City exit, then just s. Int corridors. **Pets:** Medium, dogs only. Designated rooms, service with restrictions, crate.

SUN CITY

Motel 6 Menifee #4599 M
(951) 679-1133. **$57-$90.** 27955 Encanto Dr 92586. I-215 exit 12 (McCall Blvd), just e, then just s. Ext corridors. **Pets:** Other species. Service with restrictions, supervision.

SUNNYVALE

Larkspur Landing Sunnyvale H
(408) 733-1212. **$99-$199.** 748 N Mathilda Ave 94085. US 101 exit Mathilda Ave, just s. Int corridors. **Pets:** Accepted.

Maple Tree Inn H
(408) 720-9700. **$109-$169.** 711 E El Camino Real 94087. US 101 exit 394 (Lawrence Expwy), 2.9 mi w to El Camino Real exit, then 1.8 mi n. Int corridors. **Pets:** Medium. $20 daily fee/pet. Designated rooms, service with restrictions, crate.

Quality Inn Santa Clara Convention Center H
(408) 744-1100. **$79-$189.** 1280 Persian Dr 94089. US 101 exit Lawrence Expwy N, 1 mi n to Persian Dr, then 0.3 mi w. Int corridors. **Pets:** Accepted.

Residence Inn by Marriott Silicon Valley I H
(408) 720-1000. **$169-$289.** 750 Lakeway Dr 94085. US 101 exit Lawrence Expwy S, e on Oakmead Pkwy. Ext corridors. **Pets:** Accepted.

Residence Inn by Marriott Sunnyvale Silicon Valley II H
(408) 720-8893. **$129-$239.** 1080 Stewart Dr 94086. US 101 exit Lawrence Expwy S, n on Duane Ave, just w. Ext corridors. **Pets:** Accepted.

Sheraton Sunnyvale H
(408) 745-6000. **$89-$329.** 1100 N Mathilda Ave 94089. US 101 exit Mathilda Ave. Int corridors. **Pets:** Accepted.

Staybridge Suites H
(408) 745-1515. **$140-$269.** 900 Hamlin Ct 94089. SR 237 exit Mathilda Ave S, w on Ross Dr. Ext corridors. **Pets:** Large. $150 one-time fee/room. Service with restrictions.

TownePlace Suites by Marriott Sunnyvale/Mountain View H
(408) 733-4200. **$129-$249.** 606 S Bernardo Ave 94087. SR 85 exit SR 82, 0.5 mi s. Int corridors. **Pets:** $75 one-time fee/room. Service with restrictions, crate.

Wild Palms Hotel H
(408) 738-0500. **$99-$209.** 910 E Fremont Ave 94087. US 101 exit Lawrence Expwy S, 1.5 mi s, 0.9 mi n on E El Camino Real, just w on S Wolfe Rd, then just s. Ext/int corridors. **Pets:** Accepted.

SUSANVILLE

BEST WESTERN PLUS Trailside Inn M
(530) 257-4123. **$80-$85.** 2785 Main St 96130. 0.7 mi se of jct SR 36 (Main St) and 139. Ext corridors. **Pets:** Dogs only. $15 daily fee/pet. Designated rooms, service with restrictions, supervision.

River Inn Motel M
(530) 257-6051. **$60-$90.** 1710 Main St 96130. Jct SR 36 and 139, just e on SR 36. Ext corridors. **Pets:** Other species. $11 daily fee/room. Designated rooms, service with restrictions, supervision.

The Roseberry House Bed & Breakfast BB
(530) 257-5675. **$110-$135.** 609 North St 96130. Jct SR 36 and 139, 0.7 mi nw to N Lassen St, then just ne. Int corridors. **Pets:** Other species. $10 daily fee/pet. No service, crate.

Super 8 M
(530) 257-2782. **$72-$82.** 2975 Johnstonville Rd 96130. Jct SR 36 and 139, 1 mi se on SR 139. Ext corridors. **Pets:** Other species. $10 daily fee/room. Service with restrictions, crate.

TEHACHAPI

BEST WESTERN Mountain Inn M
(661) 822-5591. **Call for rates.** 418 W Tehachapi Blvd 93561. SR 58 exit 148 (SR 202), 1 mi s, then e. Ext corridors. **Pets:** Other species. Designated rooms, service with restrictions, crate.

Holiday Inn Express & Suites H
(661) 822-9837. **$99-$129.** 901 Capital Hills Pkwy 93561. SR 58 exit 149 (Mill St), just n. Int corridors. **Pets:** Medium, other species. $25 one-time fee/room. Designated rooms, service with restrictions, supervision.

La Quinta Inn Tehachapi M
(661) 823-8000. **$71-$155.** 500 E Steuber Rd 93561. SR 58 exit 151 (Monolith St/Tehachapi Blvd), just s. Int corridors. **Pets:** Service with restrictions, supervision.

TEMECULA

Embassy Suites H
(951) 676-5656. **Call for rates.** 29345 Rancho California Rd 92591. I-15 exit 59 (Rancho California Rd), just e. Int corridors. **Pets:** Accepted.

La Quinta Inn & Suites Temecula H
(951) 296-1003. **$83-$221.** 27330 Jefferson Ave 92590. I-15 exit 61 (SR 79 N/Winchester Rd), just w, then just n; east side of Rancho Temecula Plaza. Int corridors. **Pets:** Service with restrictions, supervision.

Ponte Vineyard Inn H ❧
(951) 587-6688. **$219-$349, 3 day notice.** 35001 Rancho California Rd 92591. I-15 exit 59 (Rancho California Rd), 6.5 mi e. Ext/int corridors. **Pets:** Medium. $50 one-time fee/room. Designated rooms, service with restrictions, supervision.

Quality Inn Temecula Wine Country M
(951) 296-3788. **$54-$89.** 27338 Jefferson Ave 92590. I-15 exit 61 (SR 79 N/Winchester Rd), just w, then just n; east side of Rancho Temecula Plaza. Ext corridors. **Pets:** Medium. $20 daily fee/room. Designated rooms, supervision.

Temecula Creek Inn H
(951) 694-1000. **$119-$249, 3 day notice.** 44501 Rainbow Canyon Rd 92592. I-15 exit 58 (SR 79 S), 1 mi e to Pechanga Pkwy, then 0.5 mi s. Ext corridors. **Pets:** Medium, dogs only. $50 one-time fee/room. Service with restrictions, crate.

THOUSAND OAKS

La Quinta Inn & Suites Thousand Oaks Newbury Park M
(805) 499-5910. **$83-$166.** 1320 Newbury Rd 91320. US 101 exit 46 (Ventu Park Rd), just se. Ext corridors. **Pets:** Service with restrictions, supervision.

Motel 6 #1360 Thousand Oaks M
(805) 499-0711. **$55-$65.** 1516 Newbury Rd 91320. US 101 exit 46 (Ventu Park Rd), just w, then just n. Ext corridors. **Pets:** Other species. Service with restrictions, supervision.

Palm Garden Hotel H ❧
(805) 716-4200. **$89-$295.** 495 N Ventu Park Rd 91320. US 101 exit 46 (Ventu Park Rd), just n. Ext corridors. **Pets:** Other species. $50 one-time fee/pet. Designated rooms, service with restrictions, crate.

Premier Inn M
(805) 499-0755. **Call for rates.** 2434 W Hillcrest Dr 91320. US 101 exit 47B (Borchard Rd), just e, then just n. Ext corridors. **Pets:** Accepted.

TownePlace Suites by Marriott H ❧
(805) 499-3111. **$90-$155.** 1712 Newbury Rd 91320. US 101 exit 46 (Ventu Park Rd), just w, then just n. Int corridors. **Pets:** Other species. $100 one-time fee/room. Service with restrictions.

THREE RIVERS

Americas Best Value Inn - Lazy J Ranch M
(559) 561-4449. **$135, 3 day notice.** 39625 Sierra Dr 93271. SR 198, 3 mi sw of town center. Ext corridors. **Pets:** Other species. $10 one-time fee/pet. Service with restrictions, supervision.

Buckeye Tree Lodge M ❧
(559) 561-5900. **$73-$156, 7 day notice.** 46000 Sierra Dr 93271. SR 198, north end of town, 0.5 mi from national forest gate. Ext corridors. **Pets:** Large, other species. $10 daily fee/pet. Service with restrictions, crate.

Comfort Inn & Suites M
(559) 561-9000. **$60-$219.** 40820 Sierra Dr 93271. SR 198, 1.5 mi sw of town center. Ext/int corridors. **Pets:** Small, other species. $35 one-time fee/pet. Designated rooms, service with restrictions, crate.

Gateway Lodge M
(559) 561-4133. **$79-$179, 3 day notice.** 45978 Sierra Dr 93271. SR 198, 6 mi ne of town center; 0.5 mi sw of entrance to Sequoia National Park. Ext corridors. **Pets:** Medium. $10 daily fee/pet. Service with restrictions, crate.

Sequoia River Dance Bed & Breakfast BB
(559) 561-4411. **$105-$145, 14 day notice.** 40534 Cherokee Oaks Dr 93271. SR 198, 2 mi sw of town center, 0.3 mi e. Int corridors. **Pets:** Other species. $20 one-time fee/room. Service with restrictions, supervision.

Sequoia Village Inn M ❧
(559) 561-3652. **$73-$305, 7 day notice.** 45971 Sierra Dr 93271. SR 198, 6 mi ne of town center; 0.5 mi sw of entrance to Sequoia National Park. Ext corridors. **Pets:** Large, other species. $10 daily fee/pet. Service with restrictions, crate.

TRACY

BEST WESTERN Luxury Inn H
(209) 832-0271. **$70-$80.** 811 W Clover Rd 95376. I-205 exit Central Tracy/Tracy Blvd, just s, then just w. Int corridors. **Pets:** Medium. $10 daily fee/pet. Designated rooms, service with restrictions, crate.

TRINIDAD

Emerald Forest of Trinidad CA
(707) 677-3554. **Call for rates.** 753 Patrick's Point Dr 95570. US 101 exit Trinidad, just w on Main St, then 0.7 mi n. Ext corridors. **Pets:** Small, other species. $10 one-time fee/room. Designated rooms, service with restrictions.

▼▼▼ Lost Whale Bed & Breakfast Inn BB
(707) 677-3425. **$199-$315, 7 day notice.** 3452 Patrick's Point Dr 95570. US 101 exit Patrick's Point Dr, 1.1 mi w. Int corridors.
Pets: Accepted. 🔊 ✕ 🐾 🐾 🐾

AAA ▼▼▼ Trinidad Inn M
(707) 677-3349. **$110-$200.** 1170 Patrick's Point Dr 95570. US 101 exit Trinidad, just w on Main St, then 1.3 mi n. Ext corridors. **Pets:** Dogs only. $10 one-time fee/pet. Designated rooms, supervision.
SAVE 🔊 ✕ 🖥 📺 🐾

TULARE

AAA ▼▼▼ BEST WESTERN PLUS Town & Country Lodge M
(559) 688-7537. **$80-$200.** 1051 N Blackstone St 93274. SR 99 exit 88 (Prosperity Ave/Blackstone St), just w. Int corridors. **Pets:** $20 daily fee/pet. Service with restrictions, supervision. SAVE 🔊 🖥 📺 🐾

AAA ▼▼▼▼ Charter Inn & Suites H 🐾
(559) 685-9500. **$89-$199.** 1016 E Prosperity Ave 93274. SR 99 exit 88 (Prosperity Ave/Blackstone St), just e. Int corridors. **Pets:** Small. $100 deposit/room, $10 daily fee/pet. Service with restrictions, crate.
SAVE 🔊 🐾 🖥 📺 🐾

▼▼▼ La Quinta Inn & Suites Tulare H
(559) 685-8900. **$80-$138.** 1500 Cherry Ct 93274. SR 99 exit 88 (Prosperity Ave/Blackstone St), just w. Int corridors. **Pets:** Service with restrictions, supervision. 🔊 ✕ 🖥 📺 🐾

AAA ▼▼▼ Quality Inn M
(559) 686-3432. **$60-$140.** 1010 E Prosperity Ave 93274. SR 99 exit 88 (Prosperity Ave/Blackstone St), just e. Int corridors. **Pets:** Small, dogs only. $15 daily fee/pet. Service with restrictions, supervision.
SAVE 🔊 🖥 📺 🐾 ✕

TURLOCK

AAA ▼▼▼ BEST WESTERN PLUS Orchard Inn H
(209) 667-2827. **$79-$84, 3 day notice.** 5025 N Golden State Blvd 95382. SR 99 exit Taylor Rd, just e. Ext corridors. **Pets:** Other species. $20 one-time fee/room. Service with restrictions.
SAVE 🔊 🐾 🖥 📺 🐾

AAA ▼▼▼ Candlewood Suites H
(209) 250-1501. **$89-$249.** 1000 Powers Ct 95380. SR 99 exit Monte Vista Ave, just w. Int corridors. **Pets:** Medium, other species. $75 one-time fee/pet. Service with restrictions, supervision.
SAVE 🔊 ✕ 🐾 🖥 📺

AAA ▼▼▼ Comfort Suites H
(209) 667-7777. **$79-$149.** 191 N Tully Rd 95380. SR 99 exit West Main St E, just n. Int corridors. **Pets:** $20 daily fee/pet. Service with restrictions, supervision. SAVE 🔊 ✕ 🐾 🖥 📺 🐾

TWAIN HARTE

AAA ▼▼▼▼ McCaffrey House Bed & Breakfast Inn BB
(209) 586-0757. **$149-$199, 8 day notice.** 23251 Hwy 108 95383. On SR 108, 0.5 mi e; just beyond 4000' elevation marker. Int corridors.
Pets: Other species. $25 daily fee/pet. Designated rooms, service with restrictions, supervision. SAVE 🔊 ✕

TWENTYNINE PALMS

▼▼▼ Roughley Manor BB
(760) 367-3238. **$135-$160, 3 day notice.** 74744 Joe Davis Rd 92277. SR 62, 0.7 mi n on Utah Tr, 0.4 mi e on Joe Davis Rd, then just n. Ext/int corridors. **Pets:** Dogs only. Designated rooms, no service, crate.
🔊 ✕ 🖥 📺 🐾 🐾

VACAVILLE

AAA ▼▼▼ BEST WESTERN Heritage Inn M
(707) 448-8453. **$60-$85.** 1420 E Monte Vista Ave 95688. I-80 exit Monte Vista Ave, just nw. Ext corridors. **Pets:** $20 one-time fee/room. Service with restrictions, crate. SAVE 🔊 🐾 🖥 📺 🐾

▼▼▼ Extended StayAmerica-Sacramento-Vacaville H
(707) 469-1371. **$74-$89.** 799 Orange Dr 95687. I-80 exit Leisure Town Rd, just s; just e of I-505 interchange. Int corridors. **Pets:** $25 daily fee/pet. Designated rooms, service with restrictions. 🔊 🐾 🖥 📺

AAA ▼▼▼ Hampton Inn & Suites Vacaville/Napa Valley Area H 🐾
(707) 469-6200. **$99-$129.** 800 Mason St 95688. I-80 exit Davis St eastbound, just n, then ne on Porter Way; exit Mason St westbound, just w; jct Porter Way. Int corridors. **Pets:** Other species.
SAVE 🔊 ✕ 🐾 🖥 📺 🐾 ✕

▼▼▼ Quality Inn & Suites Vacaville M
(707) 446-8888. **$55-$109.** 1050 Orange Dr 95687. I-80 exit Leisure Town Rd, just s, then just e. Ext corridors. **Pets:** $99 daily fee/room. Designated rooms, service with restrictions. 🔊 🐾 🖥 📺 🐾

▼▼▼▼ Residence Inn by Marriott H
(707) 469-0300. **$109-$179.** 360 Orange Dr 95687. I-80 exit Orange Dr eastbound, 0.5 mi ne; exit Monte Vista Ave westbound to freeway overpass to E Nut Tree Pkwy, then just ne. Int corridors. **Pets:** Other species. $100 one-time fee/room. Service with restrictions, crate.
🔊 ✕ 🐾 🖥 📺 🐾 ✕

VALLEJO

AAA ▼▼▼▼ BEST WESTERN PLUS Inn & Suites at Discovery Kingdom H
(707) 554-9655. **Call for rates.** 1596 Fairgrounds Dr 94589. I-80 exit SR 37 N (Marine World Pkwy), 0.3 mi w. Int corridors. **Pets:** $35 one-time fee/pet. Designated rooms, service with restrictions, crate.
SAVE 🔊 ✕ 🐾 🖥 📺 🐾

▼▼▼▼ Courtyard by Marriott H
(707) 644-1200. **$79-$299.** 1000 Fairgrounds Dr 94589. I-80 exit SR 37 (Marine World Pkwy), 0.3 mi n. Int corridors. **Pets:** Large, dogs only. $75 one-time fee/room. Service with restrictions, supervision.
🔊 ✕ 🐾 🖥 📺 🍴 🐾

VALLEY CENTER

AAA ▼▼▼ ▼▼▼ Harrah's Rincon Casino & Resort H 🐾
(760) 751-3100. **$60-$750, 3 day notice.** 777 Harrah's Rincon Way 92082. I-15 exit 46 (SR 76/Pala/Oceanside), 17 mi n, then 1 mi s on CR 6. Int corridors. **Pets:** Medium, dogs only. $200 deposit/room, $40 daily fee/room. Designated rooms, service with restrictions, supervision.
🍴 SAVE 🔊 🐾 🖥 📺 🍴 🐾 ✕

VENTURA

▼▼▼▼ Crowne Plaza Ventura Beach Resort H
(805) 648-2100. **$139-$199.** 450 E Harbor Blvd 93001. US 101 exit 70A (California St) northbound, just s; exit 71 (Main St) southbound, 0.5 mi e to California St, then just s. Int corridors. **Pets:** Dogs only. $75 one-time fee/room. Designated rooms, service with restrictions, supervision.
🔊 ✕ 🖥 📺 🍴 🐾

AAA ▼▼▼ Four Points by Sheraton Ventura Harbor Resort H
(805) 658-1212. **$115-$350.** 1050 Schooner Dr 93001. US 101 exit 68 (Seaward Ave), just w, then 1.5 mi s on Harbor Blvd; at Ventura Harbor. Ext/int corridors. **Pets:** Large. $75 one-time fee/room. Designated rooms, service with restrictions, supervision.
SAVE 🔊 ✕ 🖥 📺 🍴 🐾 ✕

▼▼▼▼ Holiday Inn Express Ventura Harbor 🄷
(805) 856-9533. **$99-$225.** 1080 Navigator Dr 93001. US 101 exit 68 (Seaward Ave), just w, then 1.5 mi s; at Ventura Harbor. Ext/int corridors. **Pets:** Other species. $75 one-time fee/room. Service with restrictions, supervision. 📶 ⊠ ♿ 🛏 💻 🍽 ➳

▼▼▼▼ Marriott Ventura Beach Hotel 🄷
(805) 643-6000. **$119-$239.** 2055 E Harbor Blvd 93001. US 101 exit 68 (Seaward Ave), just w, then 0.5 mi n. Int corridors. **Pets:** Accepted.
🄴🄲🄾 📶 ⊠ ♿ 🛏 💻 🍽 ➳ ⊠

▼▼ Vagabond Inn Ventura 🄼
(805) 648-5371. **$69-$249.** 756 E Thompson Blvd 93001. US 101 exit 70A (California St) northbound, just n, then just e; exit 70A (Ventura Ave) southbound, 0.6 mi e. Ext corridors. **Pets:** Other species. $10 daily fee/pet. Service with restrictions, supervision. 📶 🛏 💻 ➳

VICTORVILLE
▼▼▼ Hawthorn Suites 🄷 ❀
(760) 949-4700. **$99-$199.** 11750 Dunia Rd 92392. I-15 exit 147 (Bear Valley Rd), just w, 0.3 mi s on Amargosa Rd, then just w. Int corridors. **Pets:** Other species. $10 daily fee/pet. Service with restrictions, crate.
📶 ♿ 🛏 💻 ➳ ⊠

VISALIA
▼▼▼ Ben Maddox House 🄱🄱
(559) 739-0721. **Call for rates.** 601 N Encina St 93291. SR 198 exit 107A (Central Visalia/SR 63 N), 0.4 mi n to Murray St, just w, then just n. Ext/int corridors. **Pets:** Accepted. 📶 ⊠ 🛏 💻 ➳ ⊠

⊛ ▼▼▼ Comfort Inn & Suites 🄷
(559) 651-3700. **$74-$89.** 9300 W Airport Dr 93277. SR 198 exit 102 (Plaza Dr), just s, then just w. Int corridors. **Pets:** Medium, other species. $25 one-time fee/room. Service with restrictions, supervision.
🅂🄰🅅🄴 📶 🛏 💻 ➳ ⊠

▼▼▼ Holiday Inn Hotel & Conference Center 🄷
(559) 651-5000. **$89-$139.** 9000 W Airport Dr 93277. SR 198 exit 102 (Plaza Dr), just s. Int corridors. **Pets:** Accepted.
📶 ⊠ ♿ 🛏 💻 🍽 ➳

⊛ ▼▼▼ Lamp Liter Inn 🄼
(559) 732-4511. **$79-$169.** 3300 W Mineral King Ave 93291. SR 198 exit 105B (SR 63 S/Mooney Blvd) westbound, 0.5 mi w; exit eastbound, just n, then 0.5 mi w. Ext corridors. **Pets:** Small. $25 daily fee/room. Service with restrictions, supervision. 🅂🄰🅅🄴 📶 ⊠ 🛏 💻 🍽 ➳

▼▼▼ La Quinta Inn & Suites Visalia/Sequoia Gateway 🄷
(559) 739-9800. **$95-$172.** 5438 W Cypress Ave 93277. SR 198 exit 104 (Akers St), just s, then just w. Int corridors. **Pets:** Service with restrictions, supervision. 📶 ⊠ 🛏 💻 ➳

⊛ ▼▼▼ Marriott Visalia at the Convention Center 🄷
(559) 636-1111. **$84-$159.** 300 S Court St 93291. SR 198 exit 107A (Central Visalia/SR 63 N), just ne. Int corridors. **Pets:** Other species. $75 one-time fee/room. Service with restrictions.
🅂🄰🅅🄴 📶 ⊠ 🛏 💻 🍽 ➳

VISTA
⊛ ▼▼▼ Hyatt Place San Diego-Vista/Carlsbad 🄷
(760) 814-8879. **$119-$229.** 2645 S Melrose Dr 92081. SR 78 exit 6 (Vista Village Dr), just s, just w on Hacienda, then 4 mi se. Int corridors. **Pets:** Accepted. 🅂🄰🅅🄴 📶 ⊠ ♿ 🛏 💻 🍽 ➳

WALNUT CREEK
▼▼▼ Holiday Inn Express Walnut Creek 🄷
(925) 932-3332. **$89-$199.** 2730 N Main St 94597. I-680 exit N Main St, just n. Int corridors. **Pets:** Small, dogs only. $20 daily fee/pet. Designated rooms, service with restrictions, supervision.
📶 ⊠ ♿ 🛏 💻 ➳

▼▼▼ Walnut Creek Marriott 🄷 ❀
(925) 934-2000. **$132-$256.** 2355 N Main St 94596. I-680 exit N Main St, 0.3 mi e, then s at Parkside Dr. Int corridors. **Pets:** Other species. $35 daily fee/pet. Designated rooms, service with restrictions, supervision.
🄴🄲🄾 📶 ⊠ ♿ 🛏 💻 🍽 ➳

WATSONVILLE
⊛ ▼▼▼ BEST WESTERN PLUS Rose Garden Inn 🄷
(831) 724-3367. **$100-$300.** 740 Freedom Blvd 95076. On SR 152 at the jct of Main St. Ext corridors. **Pets:** Large, dogs only. $20 daily fee/room. Designated rooms, service with restrictions, crate.
🅂🄰🅅🄴 📶 ⊠ ♿ 🛏 💻 ➳

⊛ ▼▼▼ Comfort Inn 🄷
(831) 728-2300. **$89-$159.** 112 Airport Blvd 95019. SR 1 exit Airport Blvd, 1 mi e. Int corridors. **Pets:** Medium, other species. $15 daily fee/pet. Service with restrictions, supervision. 🅂🄰🅅🄴 📶 ⊠ ♿ 🛏 💻

WEAVERVILLE
⊛ ▼▼▼ 49er Gold Country Inn 🄼
(530) 623-4937. **$60-$120, 3 day notice.** 880 Main St (Hwy 299) 96093. Jct SR 3 and 299, just se on SR 299 (Main St). Ext corridors. **Pets:** Accepted. 🅂🄰🅅🄴 📶 ⊠ 🛏 💻 ➳

▼▼▼ Weaverville Victorian Inn 🄼
(530) 623-4432. **$79-$169.** 2051 Main St 96093. Jct SR 3 and 299, 1.5 mi se on SR 299. Ext corridors. **Pets:** Accepted. 📶 🛏 💻 ➳

WESTLAKE VILLAGE
⊛ ▼▼▼▼ Four Seasons Hotel Westlake Village 🄷 ❀
(818) 575-3000. **$235-$1050.** Two Dole Dr 91362. US 101 exit 39 (Lindero Canyon Rd), just e, then just n on Via Colinas. Int corridors. **Pets:** Very small. $50 one-time fee/room. Service with restrictions, supervision. 🄴🄲🄾 🅂🄰🅅🄴 📶 ⊠ ♿ 🛏 💻 🍽 ➳ ⊠

⊛ ▼▼▼ Hyatt Westlake Plaza Hotel 🄷 ❀
(805) 557-1234. **$90-$279.** 880 S Westlake Blvd 91361. US 101 exit 40 (Westlake Blvd), just s. Int corridors. **Pets:** Medium, dogs only. $50 daily fee/room. Service with restrictions, crate.
🄴🄲🄾 🅂🄰🅅🄴 📶 ⊠ ♿ 🛏 💻 🍽 ➳ ⊠

▼▼▼ Residence Inn by Marriott 🄷
(818) 707-4411. **$118-$182.** 30950 Russell Ranch Rd 91362. US 101 exit 39 (Lindero Canyon Rd), just e, then just s. Int corridors. **Pets:** Medium. $100 one-time fee/room. Service with restrictions, crate.
📶 ⊠ 🛏 💻 ➳ ⊠

WESTLEY
▼▼▼ Days Inn Westley 🄼
(209) 894-5500. **$54-$89.** 7144 McCracken Rd 95387. I-5 exit Westley, just e. Ext corridors. **Pets:** Medium. $10 daily fee/pet. Service with restrictions, supervision. 📶 🛏 💻 ➳

▼▼▼ Holiday Inn Express 🄷 ❀
(209) 894-8940. **Call for rates.** 4525 Howard Rd 95387. I-5 exit Westley, just e. Int corridors. **Pets:** Other species. $20 one-time fee/room. Designated rooms, supervision. 📶 🛏 💻 ➳

WESTMORLAND
▼▼▼ Americas Best Value Inn 🄼
(760) 351-7100. **Call for rates.** 351 W Main St 92281. On SR 86/78. Int corridors. **Pets:** Medium, other species. $20 daily fee/pet. Service with restrictions, crate. 📶 🛏 💻 ➳

WEST SACRAMENTO

▼▼ Extended StayAmerica-Sacramento-West
Sacramento �H

(916) 371-1270. **$84-$99.** 795 Stillwater Rd 95605. I-80 exit Reed Ave, just n, just w, then just s. Int corridors. **Pets:** $25 daily fee/pet. Designated rooms, service with restrictions. 🛰 🔌 🖳

🐾 ▼ Rodeway Inn Capitol 🅼

(916) 371-6983. **$50-$70.** 817 W Capitol Ave 95691. Business Rt I-80 (Capital City Frwy) exit Jefferson Blvd westbound, 0.3 mi n, then just e; exit Jefferson Blvd eastbound, just s (make U-turn), 0.3 mi n on Jefferson Blvd, then just e. Ext corridors. **Pets:** Small, dogs only. $10 daily fee/pet. Service with restrictions, supervision. ⟨SAVE⟩ 🛰 🔌 🖳

WILLIAMS

🐾 ▼▼▼ Granzella's Inn 🅷

(530) 473-3310. **$89-$139.** 391 6th St 95987. I-5 exit 577 (Williams), 0.5 mi w, then just n. Int corridors. **Pets:** Other species. $10 daily fee/room. Service with restrictions, supervision.

⟨SAVE⟩ 🛰 🔌M 🔌 🖳 🍴 🐾

🐾 ▼▼ Quality Inn 🅼

(530) 473-2381. **$65-$125.** 400 C St 95987. I-5 exit 577 (Williams), just w on E St (SR 20 business route), just n on 4th St (at 76 gas station), then just e. Ext corridors. **Pets:** Other species. $15 daily fee/pet. Service with restrictions, supervision. ⟨SAVE⟩ 🛰 🔌M 🔌 🖳 🐾

🐾 ▼▼ Ramada 🅷

(530) 473-5120. **$79-$84.** 374 Ruggeri Way 95987. I-5 exit 577 (Williams), just e. Int corridors. **Pets:** $10 daily fee/pet. Designated rooms, service with restrictions, supervision. ⟨SAVE⟩ 🛰 ✖ 🔌M 🔌 🖳

🐾 ▼▼ Traveler's Inn 🅼

(530) 473-5387. **$38-$60.** 215 N 7th St 95987. I-5 exit 577 (Williams), just w on E St (SR 20 business route), then 0.3 mi n. Ext corridors. **Pets:** Medium, dogs only. $15 daily fee/pet. Designated rooms, service with restrictions, crate. ⟨SAVE⟩ 🛰 ✖ 🔌M 🔌 🐾

WILLOW CREEK

▼ Bigfoot Motel 🅼

(530) 629-2142. **$70-$140.** 39039 Hwy 299 95573. On SR 299; just e of SR 96; center. Ext corridors. **Pets:** Accepted. 🛰 🔌

WILLOWS

🐾 ▼▼◆ Baymont Inn & Suites Willows 🅷

(530) 934-9700. **$70-$190.** 199 N Humboldt Ave 95988. I-5 exit 603 (SR 162/Willows/Oroville), just e, then s. Int corridors. **Pets:** $10 one-time fee/room. Designated rooms, service with restrictions, supervision. ⟨SAVE⟩ 🛰 🔌 🖳 🐾

🐾 ▼▼◆ Days Inn 🅼

(530) 934-4444. **$55-$195.** 475 N Humboldt Ave 95988. I-5 exit 603 (SR 162/Willows/Oroville), just e, then just n. Ext corridors. **Pets:** $10 daily fee/pet. Designated rooms, no service, supervision. ⟨SAVE⟩ 🛰 🔌M 🔌 🖳 🐾

🐾 ▼▼ Economy Inn 🅼

(530) 934-4224. **$60-$90, 3 day notice.** 435 N Tehama St 95988. I-5 exit 603 (SR 162/Willows/Oroville), 1 mi e, then just n. Ext corridors. **Pets:** Small. $5 daily fee/pet. Designated rooms, service with restrictions, supervision. ⟨SAVE⟩ 🛰 🔌 🖳

🐾 ▼▼◆ Holiday Inn Express Willows 🅷

(530) 934-8900. **$119-$139.** 545 N Humboldt Ave 95988. I-5 exit 603 (SR 162/Willows/Oroville), just e, then just n. Int corridors. **Pets:** Other species. $20 one-time fee/room. Designated rooms, service with restrictions, supervision. ⟨SAVE⟩ 🛰 🔌M 🔌 🖳 🐾

🐾 ▼ Motel 6 #4273 🅼

(530) 934-7026. **$49-$99.** 452 N Humboldt Ave 95988. I-5 exit 603 (SR 162/Willows/Oroville), just e, then just n. Ext corridors. **Pets:** Other species. Service with restrictions, supervision. ⟨SAVE⟩ 🛰 🔌 🐾

WINE COUNTRY AREA

ALBION

▼▼ Fensalden Inn 🅱🅱

(707) 937-4042. **$149-$253, 7 day notice.** 33810 Navarro Ridge Rd 95410. 1.5 mi s on SR 1, 0.5 mi e. Ext/int corridors. **Pets:** Dogs only. $25 one-time fee/room. Designated rooms, service with restrictions, supervision. 🛰 ✖ 🔌 🖳 🥇 🚷 🅉

AMERICAN CANYON

▼▼▼ Holiday Inn Express & Suites - Napa Valley American
Canyon 🅷

(707) 552-8100. **$119-$259.** 5001 Main St 94503. Off SR 29. Int corridors. **Pets:** Accepted. 🛰 ✖ 🔌M 🔌 🖳 🐾

CALISTOGA

🐾 ▼▼ Brannan Cottage Inn 🅱🅱 🐾

(707) 942-4200. **$160-$285, 7 day notice.** 109 Wapoo Ave 94515. At Lincoln Ave. Ext corridors. **Pets:** Other species. $100 deposit/room, $25 daily fee/room. Designated rooms, service with restrictions, crate.

⟨SAVE⟩ 🛰 ✖ 🔌 🅉

CLEARLAKE

▼▼ Clear Lake Cottages and Marina 🅲🅰 🐾

(707) 995-5253. **$119-$209, 14 day notice.** 13885 Lakeshore Dr 95422. SR 53 exit Lakeshore Dr, 2.1 mi w. Ext corridors. **Pets:** $20 daily fee/pet. Designated rooms, service with restrictions, supervision.

🛰 ✖ 🔌 🖳 🐾 🅉

CLOVERDALE

▼▼▼ Auberge on the Vineyard 🅱🅱

(707) 894-5956. **$135-$325, 7 day notice.** 29955 River Rd 95425. US 101 exit Citrus Fair Dr, just e, 0.5 mi n on Asti Rd, then 0.8 mi on Crocker Rd. Int corridors. **Pets:** Accepted. 🛰 ✖ 🔌 🖳 🅉

🐾 ▼▼◆ Old Crocker Inn 🅱🅱

(707) 894-4000. **$165-$275, 8 day notice.** 1126 Old Crocker Inn Rd 95425. US 101 exit Citrus Fair Dr, just e, 0.5 mi n on Asti Rd, 0.8 mi e on Crocker Rd, 3.8 mi s on River Rd, 1.1 mi e on Asti Ridge Rd, then just n. Ext corridors. **Pets:** Dogs only. $25 one-time fee/room. Designated rooms, supervision. ⟨SAVE⟩ 🛰 ✖ 🔌 🐾 🅉

FORT BRAGG

🐾 ▼▼◆ Beachcomber Motel 🅼 🐾

(707) 964-2402. **$119-$269, 3 day notice.** 1111 N Main St 95437. 1 mi n on SR 1. Ext corridors. **Pets:** Other species. $20 daily fee/pet. Supervision. ⟨SAVE⟩ 🛰 ✖ 🔌 🖳 🥇

🐾 ▼▼ Beach House Inn 🅼

(707) 961-1700. **$69-$250.** 100 Pudding Creek Rd 95437. 0.7 mi n on SR 1. Int corridors. **Pets:** Large, other species. $16 daily fee/pet. Designated rooms, service with restrictions, supervision.

⟨SAVE⟩ 🛰 ✖ 🔌 🖳 🥇

▼▼ Coast Inn and Spa 🅼 🐾

(707) 964-2852. **$80-$390, 3 day notice.** 18661 N Hwy 1 95437. 0.3 mi s of SR 20. Ext corridors. **Pets:** Dogs only. $25 daily fee/pet. Designated rooms, service with restrictions, supervision. 🛰 ✖ 🔌 🖳 🥇

🐾 ▼▼◆ Emerald Dolphin Inn & Mini Golf 🅷 🐾

(707) 964-6699. **$65-$185, 7 day notice.** 1211 S Main St 95437. On SR 1; at Harbor View Dr. Ext corridors. **Pets:** Dogs only. $10 daily fee/room. Designated rooms, service with restrictions, supervision.

⟨SAVE⟩ 🛰 🔌M 🔌 🖳 ✖ 🥇

△△△ ▽▽▽▽ **Holiday Inn Express** **H**
(707) 964-1100. **$119-$199.** 250 Hwy 20 95437. On SR 20, just e of jct SR 1. Ext/int corridors. **Pets:** $100 deposit/room, $20 daily fee/pet. Designated rooms, supervision. [SAVE] 🛜 ⓜ 📶 🖥 🏊

△△△ ▽▽▽ **Seabird Lodge** **M**
(707) 964-4731. **$75-$150.** 191 South St 95437. 0.8 mi n of Noyo River Bridge; 1 blk e off SR 1. Ext corridors. **Pets:** Other species. $10 daily fee/room. Service with restrictions, supervision.
[SAVE] 🛜 📶 🖥 🏊 ⓚ

▽▽▽ **Shoreline Cottages** **CA** 🐾
(707) 964-2977. **$95-$160, 3 day notice.** 18725 N Hwy 1 95437. On SR 1, 0.3 mi s of SR 20. Ext corridors. **Pets:** Dogs only. $10 daily fee/room. Designated rooms, supervision. 🛜 ❌ 📶 🖥 ⓚ 🅩

▽▽▽ **Super 8** **M** 🐾
(707) 964-4003. **$82-$199.** 888 S Main St 95437. 0.5 mi s on SR 1; north end of Noyo River Bridge. Ext corridors. **Pets:** Dogs only. $10 one-time fee/pet. Designated rooms, service with restrictions, supervision.
🛜 ⓜ 📶 🖥

△△△ ▽▽▽ **Surf Motel & Gardens** **M** 🐾
(707) 964-5361. **$59-$275, 3 day notice.** 1220 S Main St 95437. At Oceanview Dr. Ext corridors. **Pets:** Dogs only. $15 daily fee/pet. Designated rooms, service with restrictions, supervision.
[SAVE] 🛜 📶 🖥 ⓚ

▽▽▽▽ **Weller House Inn** **BB**
(707) 964-4415. **Call for rates.** 524 Stewart St 95437. Just w of SR 1 via Pine St, just n. Int corridors. **Pets:** Accepted.
🛜 ❌ 📶 ⓚ 🅩

GUALALA

△△△ ▽▽▽ **Gualala Country Inn** **M**
(707) 884-4343. **$77-$190, 3 day notice.** 47975 Center St 95445. South end of town; just n of Old State Hwy. Ext/int corridors. **Pets:** Other species. $10 one-time fee/pet. Service with restrictions, supervision.
[SAVE] 🛜 ❌ 📶 🖥 ⓚ

▽▽▽▽ **North Coast Country Inn** **BB**
(707) 884-4537. **$195-$225, 3 day notice.** 34591 S Hwy 1 95445. On SR 1, 4.5 mi n. Ext corridors. **Pets:** Dogs only. $25 one-time fee/pet. Designated rooms, service with restrictions, supervision.
🛜 ❌ 📶 🖥 ⓚ 🅦 🅩

△△△ ▽▽▽ **Surf Motel** **M** 🐾
(707) 884-3571. **$89-$209, 3 day notice.** 39170 S SR 1 95445. Center. Ext/int corridors. **Pets:** Other species. $15 daily fee/pet. Service with restrictions, supervision. [SAVE] 🛜 ❌ 📶 🖥 ⓚ

GUERNEVILLE

▽▽▽ **Cottages on River Road** **CA** 🐾
(707) 869-3848. **$80-$250, 3 day notice.** 14880 River Rd 95446. 1.6 mi ne of jct SR 116. Ext corridors. **Pets:** Dogs only. $25 daily fee/pet. Supervision. 🛜 📶 🖥 🏊 ⓚ 🅩

△△△ ▽▽▽ **Ferngrove Cottages** **CA**
(707) 869-8105. **$89-$269, 3 day notice.** 16650 Hwy 116 95446. Just w of downtown. Ext corridors. **Pets:** Other species. $25 daily fee/pet. Service with restrictions, supervision.
[SAVE] 🛜 ❌ 📶 🖥 🏊 ⓚ 🅩

▽▽▽ **West Sonoma Inn & Spa** **M** 🐾
(707) 869-2470. **$109-$299, 14 day notice.** 14100 Brookside Ln 95446. Just n of SR 116; on west end of downtown. Ext corridors. **Pets:** Small, dogs only. $25 one-time fee/pet. Designated rooms, service with restrictions, supervision. 🛜 ❌ 📶 🖥 ⓚ

HEALDSBURG

▽▽▽ **Americas Best Value Inn & Suites** **M**
(707) 433-5548. **Call for rates.** 74 Healdsburg Ave 95448. US 101 exit Central Healdsburg, just se. Ext corridors. **Pets:** Accepted.
🛜 ❌ ⓜ 📶 🖥 🏊

▽▽▽ **Bella Villa Messina** **BB**
(707) 433-6655. **$220-$390, 7 day notice.** 316 Burgundy Rd 95448. US 101 exit Dry Creek Rd, just e to Grove St, 0.5 mi n to Chiquita Rd, then 0.5 mi w. Int corridors. **Pets:** Accepted. 🛜 ❌ ⓜ

△△△ ▽▽▽ **BEST WESTERN PLUS Dry Creek Inn** **H**
(707) 433-0300. **$99-$299.** 198 Dry Creek Rd 95448. US 101 exit Dry Creek Rd, just se. Ext corridors. **Pets:** $30 daily fee/room. Designated rooms, service with restrictions, supervision.
[SAVE] 🛜 ⓜ 📶 🖥 🏊 ❌

▽▽▽ **Healdsburg Inn on the Plaza** **H**
(707) 433-6991. **$310-$425, 7 day notice.** 112 Matheson St 95448. On the Plaza; downtown. Int corridors. **Pets:** Large, dogs only. $65 one-time fee/room. Designated rooms, service with restrictions, supervision.
🛜 ❌

JENNER

▽▽▽ **Jenner Inn & Cottages** **CI**
(707) 865-2377. **$118-$348, 10 day notice.** 10400 Hwy 1 95450. On SR 1, 1 mi n of SR 116. Ext corridors. **Pets:** Dogs only. $35 one-time fee/pet. Designated rooms, service with restrictions.
🛜 ❌ ⓜ 📶 🖥 🍴 ❌ ⓚ

KENWOOD

▽▽▽ **Birmingham Bed & Breakfast** **BB**
(707) 833-6996. **Call for rates.** 8790 Hwy 12 95452. SR 12, just n of town. Int corridors. **Pets:** Accepted. 🛜 ❌ 🅩

LEGGETT

△△△ ▽▽▽ **Redwoods River Resort** **CA**
(707) 925-6249. **$75-$175, 7 day notice.** 75000 Hwy 101 95585. 6.5 mi n of jct SR 1. Ext corridors. **Pets:** Accepted.
[SAVE] 🛜 ❌ 📶 🖥 🏊 ❌ ⓚ 🅩

LITTLE RIVER

▽▽▽ **The Inn at Schoolhouse Creek** **CI**
(707) 937-5525. **Call for rates.** 7051 N SR 1 95456. SR 1, 0.8 mi s of Van Damme State Park entrance. Ext corridors. **Pets:** Accepted.
🛜 ❌ 📶 🖥 🍴 ❌ ⓚ

▽▽▽ **Little River Inn** **CI** 🐾
(707) 937-5942. **$130-$365, 5 day notice.** 7901 N SR 1 95456. On SR 1, just s of Van Damme State Park entrance. Ext/int corridors. **Pets:** Other species. $25 daily fee/pet. Designated rooms, service with restrictions, supervision. 🛜 ❌ 📶 🖥 🍴 ❌ ⓚ

△△△ ▽▽▽▽ **Stevenswood Spa Resort** **CI** 🐾
(707) 937-2810. **$159-$399, 99 day notice.** 8211 N Hwy 1 95456. On SR 1, 0.4 mi n of Van Damme State Park entrance. Int corridors. **Pets:** Dogs only. $50 one-time fee/pet. Service with restrictions.
[SAVE] 🛜 ❌ 📶 🍴 ❌ ⓚ

MENDOCINO

▽▽▽▽ **Agate Cove Inn** **CA** 🐾
(707) 937-0551. **$189-$349, 14 day notice.** 11201 N Lansing St 95460. Just w on Little Lake Rd from jct SR 1, then 0.6 mi n. Ext corridors. **Pets:** $25 daily fee/pet. Designated rooms, service with restrictions, crate. 🛜 ❌ 📶 🖥 ⓚ 🅩

△△△ ▽▽▽ **Blackberry Inn** **M** 🐾
(707) 937-5281. **$100-$225, 7 day notice.** 44951 Larkin Rd 95460. 0.5 mi n on SR 1, then just e. Ext corridors. **Pets:** $15 daily fee/pet. Designated rooms, supervision. [SAVE] 🛜 ❌ 📶 🖥 ⓚ

△△△ ▽▽▽▽ **Hill House Inn** **H**
(707) 937-0554. **$203-$309.** 10701 Pallette Dr 95460. Just w on Little Lake St from jct SR 1, then just n on Lansing St. Ext corridors.
Pets: Accepted. [SAVE] 🛜 ❌ 📶 🖥 ⓚ

▽▽▽ **Mendocino Hotel & Garden Suites** **H**
(707) 937-0511. **Call for rates.** 45080 Main St 95460. 0.4 mi w on Main St from jct SR 1. Ext/int corridors. **Pets:** Accepted.
🛜 ❌ 🖥 🍴 ⓚ

(AAA) ▼▼▼ ▼▼▼ **Mendocino Seaside Cottage** [CA]
(707) 485-0239. **$187-$299, 7 day notice.** 10940 Lansing St 95460. Just w on Little Lake Rd from jct SR 1, 0.3 mi n. Ext/int corridors. **Pets:** Accepted. [SAVE] 🛜 ✕ 📦 💻 🐾

▼▼ ▼▼ **Nicholson House Inn** [BB]
(707) 937-0934. **$99-$239, 3 day notice.** 951 Ukiah St 95460. Just e of Lansing St; center. Ext/int corridors. **Pets:** $35 one-time fee/room. Service with restrictions, supervision. 🛜 ✕ 📦 💻 🐾

(AAA) ▼▼ ▼▼ **Stanford Inn by the Sea Eco-Lodge** [CI] 🐾
(707) 937-5615. **$199-$460, 7 day notice.** 44850 Comptche-Ukiah Rd 95460. SR 1 exit Comptche-Ukiah Rd, just e. Ext corridors. **Pets:** Other species. $45 one-time fee/pet. Supervision.
[SAVE] 🛜 ✕ 📦 💻 🍴 🏊 ✕ 🐾

MIDDLETOWN

▼▼ ▼▼ **Backyard Garden Oasis Bed and Breakfast Inn** [BB]
(707) 987-0505. **$139-$159, 5 day notice.** 24019 Hilderbrand Dr 95461. 3.9 mi s on SR 29, just e. Ext/int corridors. **Pets:** Accepted.
🛜 ✕ 📦 💻

MONTE RIO

▼▼ ▼▼ **Rio Villa Beach Resort** [M]
(707) 865-1143. **$100-$300, 7 day notice.** 20292 Hwy 116 95462. Center. Ext corridors. **Pets:** $25 daily fee/room. Designated rooms, service with restrictions, supervision. 🛜 ✕ 📦 💻

NAPA

▼▼ ▼▼ **Blackbird Inn** [BB]
(707) 226-2450. **$195-$310, 7 day notice.** 1755 1st St 94559. SR 29 exit 1st St, 0.5 mi e to Jefferson St, then just n. Int corridors. **Pets:** Accepted. 🛜 ✕ 🐾

▼▼ ▼▼ **The Chablis Inn** [M]
(707) 257-1944. **$79-$179, 3 day notice.** 3360 Solano Ave 94558. Just w off SR 29 via Redwood Rd, then just s. Ext corridors. **Pets:** Accepted.
🛜 ✕ 📦 💻 🏊

▼▼ ▼▼ **Embassy Suites Napa Valley** [H]
(707) 253-9540. **$179-$399.** 1075 California Blvd 94559. SR 29 exit 1st St E. Ext/int corridors. **Pets:** Accepted.
[ECO] 🛜 🐾 📦 💻 🍴 🏊 ✕

(AAA) ▼▼ ▼▼ **The Inn on First** [BB] 🐾
(707) 253-1331. **$199-$425, 30 day notice.** 1938 1st St 94559. SR 29 exit 1st St, just e via Clay St. Ext/int corridors. **Pets:** Dogs only. $50 one-time fee/room. Designated rooms, service with restrictions, crate.
[ECO] [SAVE] 🛜 ✕ 🐾 📦 💻 🐾

(AAA) ▼▼ ▼▼ **The Meritage Resort and Spa** [H]
(707) 251-1900. **Call for rates.** 875 Bordeaux Way 94558. 0.5 mi n of jct SR 29 and 121; SR 121 N, follow Downtown Napa/Lake Berryessa, w on Napa Valley Corporate Way, then just s. Int corridors. **Pets:** Accepted.
[SAVE] 🛜 ✕ 🐾 📦 💻 🍴 🏊 ✕

(AAA) ▼▼ ▼▼ **The Napa Inn** [BB]
(707) 257-1444. **$149-$295, 10 day notice.** 1137 Warren St 94559. SR 29 exit 1st St, 0.5 mi e, then 0.3 mi n. Int corridors. **Pets:** $30 daily fee/room. Designated rooms, service with restrictions, supervision.
[SAVE] 🛜 ✕ 📦 💻

▼▼ ▼▼ **Napa River Inn** [H] 🐾
(707) 251-8500. **$209-$599.** 500 Main St 94559. Downtown. Int corridors. **Pets:** $25 daily fee/pet. Designated rooms, service with restrictions, supervision. 🛜 ✕ 🐾 📦 💻

(AAA) ▼▼ ▼▼ **Quality Inn Napa Winery Inn** [H] 🐾
(707) 257-7220. **$149-$399, 3 day notice.** 1998 Trower Ave 94558. SR 29 exit E Trower Ave. Int corridors. **Pets:** Medium, other species. $50 one-time fee/room. Designated rooms.
[SAVE] 🛜 ✕ 🐾 📦 💻

(AAA) ▼▼ ▼▼ **The Westin Verasa, Napa** [H]
(707) 257-1800. **$159-$699, 3 day notice.** 1314 McKinstry St 94559. Jct Soscol Ave. Int corridors. **Pets:** Accepted.
[ECO] [SAVE] 🛜 ✕ 🐾 📦 💻 🍴 🏊 ✕

NICE

▼▼ ▼▼ **Featherbed Railroad Co.** [BB] 🐾
(707) 274-8378. **$99-$220, 3 day notice.** 2870 Lakeshore Blvd 95464. 0.5 mi s of SR 20. Ext corridors. **Pets:** Medium, dogs only. $30 one-time fee/room. Designated rooms, crate. 🛜 ✕ 📦 💻 🐾 ✕ 🐾

OCCIDENTAL

▼▼ ▼▼ **Inn at Occidental** [BB] 🐾
(707) 874-1047. **$199-$379, 10 day notice.** 3657 Church St 95465. Town center. Ext/int corridors. **Pets:** Medium, dogs only. $40 daily fee/room. Designated rooms, service with restrictions, supervision.
🛜 ✕ 🐾 🐾

▼▼ ▼▼ **Occidental Hotel** [M]
(707) 874-3623. **$95-$180, 3 day notice.** 3610 Bohemian Hwy 95465. In the village. Ext corridors. **Pets:** Small, dogs only. $20 daily fee/pet. Designated rooms, supervision. 🛜 ✕ 🐾 📦 💻 🏊

PETALUMA

(AAA) ▼▼ ▼▼ **BEST WESTERN Petaluma Inn** [H]
(707) 763-0994. **$80-$190.** 200 S McDowell Blvd 94954. US 101 exit Washington St, just e. Ext corridors. **Pets:** Accepted.
[SAVE] 🛜 🐾 📦 💻 🏊

(AAA) ▼▼ ▼▼ **Quality Inn-Petaluma** [H]
(707) 664-1155. **$69-$289.** 5100 Montero Way 94954. US 101 exit Old Redwood Hwy-Penngrove northbound; exit Petaluma Blvd N-Penngrove southbound (east side), just n on N McDowell Blvd, then just e. Ext/int corridors. **Pets:** $15 daily fee/room. Service with restrictions, supervision.
[SAVE] 🛜 🐾 📦 💻 🏊 ✕

(AAA) ▼▼ ▼▼ **Sheraton Sonoma County-Petaluma** [H] 🐾
(707) 283-2888. **$119-$339, 3 day notice.** 745 Baywood Dr 94954. US 101 exit SR 116 (Lakeville Hwy), just se. Int corridors. **Pets:** Large. Designated rooms, service with restrictions, supervision.
[SAVE] 🛜 ✕ 🐾 📦 💻 🍴 🏊

POINT ARENA

▼▼ ▼▼ **Wharf Master's Inn** [H]
(707) 882-3171. **$105-$395, 3 day notice.** 785 Port Rd 95468. 1 mi w on Iversen Ave from jct SR 1; at wharf. Ext corridors. **Pets:** Small, dogs only. $25 daily fee/pet. Designated rooms, supervision.
🛜 ✕ 🐾 📦 🐾

ROHNERT PARK

(AAA) ▼▼ ▼▼ **BEST WESTERN Inn** [M] 🐾
(707) 584-7435. **$95-$104.** 6500 Redwood Dr 94928. US 101 exit Rohnert Park Expwy, just w. Ext corridors. **Pets:** Medium. $20 daily fee/room. Designated rooms, service with restrictions, supervision.
[SAVE] 🛜 🐾 📦 💻 🏊

▼▼ ▼▼ **DoubleTree by Hilton Sonoma Wine Country** [H]
(707) 584-5466. **$129-$349.** One Doubletree Dr 94928. US 101 exit Golf Course Dr; 3 mi s of Santa Rosa. Int corridors. **Pets:** Medium, dogs only. $50 one-time fee/room. Designated rooms, supervision.
[ECO] 🛜 🐾 📦 💻 🍴 🏊 ✕

▼▼ ▼▼ **Rodeway Inn** [M]
(707) 584-1600. **Call for rates.** 6288 Redwood Dr 94928. US 101 exit W Rohnert Park Expwy, just n. Ext corridors. **Pets:** Accepted.
🛜 🐾 📦 💻 🏊

RUTHERFORD

▼▼ ▼▼ **Rancho Caymus** [H]
(707) 963-1777. **$149-$499, 3 day notice.** 1140 Rutherford Rd 94573. Just e of SR 29 and 128; 4 mi s of St. Helena. Ext corridors.
Pets: Accepted. 🛜 ✕ 🐾 📦 💻

ST. HELENA

El Bonita Motel M

(707) 963-3216. **$80-$300, 3 day notice.** 195 Main St 94574. 1 mi s of center on SR 29; at El Bonita Ave and Main St (SR 29). Ext corridors. **Pets:** Medium, other species. $20 daily fee/pet. Service with restrictions.

Harvest Inn H ❀

(707) 963-9463. **$229-$899, 14 day notice.** One Main St 94574. 1.5 mi s of center on SR 29 (Main St). Ext corridors. **Pets:** Medium, dogs only. $100 one-time fee/room. Designated rooms, service with restrictions, supervision.

SANTA ROSA

Americas Best Value Inn M

(707) 523-3480. **$70-$179.** 1800 Santa Rosa Ave 95407. US 101 exit Baker Ave northbound; exit Corby Ave southbound. Ext corridors. **Pets:** Accepted.

BEST WESTERN PLUS Garden Inn H ❀

(707) 546-4031. **$99-$224.** 1500 Santa Rosa Ave 95404. US 101 exit Baker Ave northbound, just n; exit Corby Ave southbound. Ext corridors. **Pets:** Dogs only. $15 daily fee/pet. Designated rooms, service with restrictions, supervision.

BEST WESTERN PLUS Wine Country Inn & Suites H ❀

(707) 545-9000. **$119-$169.** 870 Hopper Ave 95403. US 101 exit Mendocino Ave/Old Redwood Hwy northbound, just w; exit Hopper Ave southbound. Ext corridors. **Pets:** Dogs only. $20 one-time fee/room. Designated rooms, service with restrictions, supervision.

Extended StayAmerica-Santa Rosa-North H

(707) 541-0959. **$89-$104.** 100 Fountain Grove Pkwy 95403. US 101 exit Mendocino Ave/Old Redwood Hwy northbound, 0.3 mi e; exit Hopper Ave southbound, 0.6 mi e. Int corridors. **Pets:** $25 daily fee/pet. Designated rooms, service with restrictions.

Extended StayAmerica-Santa Rosa-South H

(707) 546-4808. **$79-$94.** 2600 Corby Ave 95407. US 101 exit Hearn Ave/Yolanda Ave northbound; exit Hearn Ave southbound. Ext corridors. **Pets:** $25 daily fee/pet. Designated rooms, service with restrictions.

Flamingo Conference Resort and Spa H

(707) 545-8530. **$109-$299.** 2777 4th St 95405. Off SR 12; at Farmers Ln. Int corridors. **Pets:** Medium. $50 one-time fee/room. Designated rooms, service with restrictions, supervision.

Fountaingrove Inn, Hotel & Conference Center H ❀

(707) 578-6101. **$99-$299.** 101 Fountaingrove Pkwy 95403. 2.5 mi n on US 101 exit Mendocino Ave/Old Redwood Hwy, just e. Int corridors. **Pets:** Medium, dogs only. $25 daily fee/room. Designated rooms, service with restrictions, supervision.

Hillside Inn Motel M

(707) 546-9353. **$84-$99, 3 day notice.** 2901 4th St 95409. US 101, 2.5 mi e on SR 12; at Farmers Ln and 4th St. Ext corridors. **Pets:** Very small. Service with restrictions, supervision.

Hilton Sonoma Wine Country H

(707) 523-7555. **$109-$349.** 3555 Round Barn Blvd 95403. US 101 exit Mendocino Ave/Old Redwood Hwy; just ne at top of hill. Int corridors. **Pets:** Accepted.

Hyatt Vineyard Creek Hotel and Spa in Sonoma County H ❀

(707) 284-1234. **$90-$540.** 170 Railroad St 95401. US 101 exit downtown Santa Rosa, just w; jct 3rd St. Int corridors. **Pets:** Dogs only. $30 one-time fee/room. Designated rooms, service with restrictions, crate.

Quality Inn & Suites Santa Rosa H

(707) 521-2100. **$80-$300.** 3000 Santa Rosa Ave 95407. US 101 exit Todd Rd, 1.2 mi n. Int corridors. **Pets:** Medium. $50 deposit/pet, $15 daily fee/pet. Service with restrictions, supervision.

Sandman Inn H

(707) 544-8570. **$89-$125.** 3421 Cleveland Ave 95403. US 101 exit W Mendocino Ave/Old Redwood Hwy. Ext corridors. **Pets:** Medium. $25 one-time fee/pet. Designated rooms, service with restrictions, supervision.

Santa Rosa Downtown Travelodge M

(707) 544-4141. **$100-$179.** 635 Healdsburg Ave 95401. US 101 exit College Ave, 0.3 mi e, then just s; at Mendocino Ave. Ext corridors. **Pets:** Accepted.

Travelodge M

(707) 542-3472. **$70-$170.** 1815 Santa Rosa Ave 95407. US 101 exit Baker Ave northbound; exit Corby Ave southbound. Ext corridors. **Pets:** Dogs only. $15 daily fee/pet. Service with restrictions, supervision.

Vagabond Inn Santa Rosa H

(707) 542-5544. **$59-$119.** 2632 Cleveland Ave 95403. US 101 exit Steele Ln, 1 mi n. Int corridors. **Pets:** Other species. $15 daily fee/room. Service with restrictions.

SONOMA

BEST WESTERN PLUS Sonoma Valley Inn & Krug Event Center H

(707) 938-9200. **$109-$295, 3 day notice.** 550 2nd St W 95476. 1 blk w of town plaza. Ext corridors. **Pets:** Accepted.

The Fairmont Sonoma Mission Inn & Spa H ❀

(707) 938-9000. **$199-$649, 5 day notice.** 100 Boyes Blvd 95476. 2.5 mi n on SR 12. Ext/int corridors. **Pets:** $25 daily fee/pet. Designated rooms, service with restrictions, supervision.

Inn at Sonoma BB

(707) 939-1340. **$225-$325, 7 day notice.** 630 Broadway 95476. On SR 12, just s of Sonoma Plaza. Int corridors. **Pets:** Accepted.

The Lodge at Sonoma, A Renaissance Resort & Spa H ❀

(707) 935-6600. **$209-$599, 3 day notice.** 1325 Broadway 95476. On SR 12, 1 mi s of Sonoma Plaza. Ext/int corridors. **Pets:** Small, dogs only. $75 one-time fee/room. Designated rooms, service with restrictions, supervision.

Sonoma Creek Inn M

(707) 939-9463. **$89-$199, 7 day notice.** 239 Boyes Blvd 95476. SR 12, 0.5 mi w. Ext corridors. **Pets:** Large, dogs only. $25 one-time fee/pet. Designated rooms, service with restrictions, supervision.

UKIAH

AAA ◆◆◆◆ **BEST WESTERN PLUS Orchard Inn** H

(707) 462-1514. **$99-$170.** 555 S Orchard Ave 95482. US 101 exit Gobbi St, 0.5 mi w. Int corridors. **Pets:** Medium. $20 daily fee/pet. Service with restrictions, supervision.

◆◆◆◆ **Comfort Inn & Suites** H

(707) 462-3442. **$89-$149.** 1220 Airport Park Blvd 95482. US 101 exit Talmage Rd, just w, then just s. Int corridors. **Pets:** $20 daily fee/pet. Designated rooms, service with restrictions, supervision.

AAA ◆◆◆ **Days Inn** M

(707) 462-7584. **$52-$109.** 950 N State St 95482. US 101 exit N State St, 0.5 mi s. Ext corridors. **Pets:** Medium. $10 daily fee/pet. Designated rooms, no service, supervision.

AAA ◆◆◆ **Quality Inn** M

(707) 462-2906. **$75-$95.** 1050 S State St 95482. US 101 exit Talmage Rd, 0.4 mi w, then just n. Ext corridors. **Pets:** Dogs only. $10 daily fee/pet. Service with restrictions, supervision.

AAA ◆◆◆ **Super 8 Ukiah** M ❖

(707) 468-8181. **$59-$89.** 693 S Orchard Ave 95482. US 101 exit Gobbi St W, just nw. Ext corridors. **Pets:** Other species. $10 daily fee/pet. Designated rooms, service with restrictions, supervision.

AAA ◆◆◆ **Travelodge Ukiah** H

(707) 462-5745. **$70-$90.** 1720 N State St 95482. US 101 exit N State St. Ext corridors. **Pets:** $20 daily fee/pet. Designated rooms, service with restrictions, supervision.

UPPER LAKE

AAA ◆◆◆ **Super 8** M

(707) 275-0888. **$70-$229, 3 day notice.** 450 E Hwy 20 95485. Jct SR 29, 0.5 mi e. Ext corridors. **Pets:** Dogs only. $10 daily fee/pet. Service with restrictions, crate.

WILLITS

AAA ◆◆◆◆ **Baechtel Creek Inn & Spa, an Ascend Collection hotel** H ❖

(707) 459-9063. **$109-$189.** 101 Gregory Ln 95490. US 101, just w. Ext corridors. **Pets:** Small, dogs only. $20 daily fee/pet. Designated rooms, service with restrictions, supervision.

AAA ◆◆◆ **Old West Inn** M

(707) 459-4201. **$55-$95.** 1221 S Main St 95490. US 101, 0.5 mi s of jct SR 20. Ext corridors. **Pets:** Small, dogs only. $10 daily fee/pet. Designated rooms, service with restrictions, supervision.

YOUNTVILLE

◆◆◆ **Lavender** BB

(707) 944-1388. **$235-$350, 7 day notice.** 2020 Webber Ave 94599. SR 29 exit Yountville, just w of Yount St at Webber Ave and Jefferson St; center. Ext/int corridors. **Pets:** Accepted.

AAA ◆◆◆◆ **Vintage Inn** H ❖

(707) 944-1112. **$225-$700, 7 day notice.** 6541 Washington St 94599. SR 29 exit Yountville; at Humboldt and Washington sts; center. Ext corridors. **Pets:** Other species. $40 one-time fee/room. Designated rooms, service with restrictions, crate.

END AREA

WOODLAND

AAA ◆◆◆ **Days Inn** H

(530) 666-3800. **$55.** 1524 E Main St 95776. I-5 exit 537 (Main St) northbound; exit SR 113 (Davis) southbound, just w; behind McDonalds. Int corridors. **Pets:** Medium, dogs only. $10 daily fee/pet. Designated rooms, service with restrictions, supervision.

AAA ◆◆◆◆ **Holiday Inn Express Hotel & Suites** H

(530) 662-7750. **$109-$179.** 2070 Freeway Dr 95776. I-5 exit 536 (CR 102), just n, just e on E Main St, then just s. Int corridors. **Pets:** Small. $20 daily fee/pet. Designated rooms, service with restrictions, supervision.

AAA ◆◆◆ **Valley Oaks Inn** M

(530) 666-5511. **Call for rates.** 600 N East St 95776. I-5 exit 538 (Yuba City/East St), northbound just s; southbound just n. Ext corridors. **Pets:** Medium. $15 daily fee/pet. Designated rooms, service with restrictions, supervision.

YERMO

◆◆◆ **Oak Tree Inn** M

(760) 254-1148. **$55-$65.** 35450 Yermo Rd 92398. I-15 exit 191 (Ghost Town Rd), just se. Int corridors. **Pets:** $10 daily fee/pet. Service with restrictions, crate.

YOSEMITE NATIONAL PARK AREA

YOSEMITE NATIONAL PARK

◆◆◆ **The Redwoods In Yosemite** VH

(209) 375-6666. **Call for rates.** 8038 Chilnualna Falls Rd 95389. 6 mi inside southern entrance via SR 41 and Chilnualna Falls Rd. Ext corridors. **Pets:** Other species. $25 daily fee/pet.

END AREA

YREKA

AAA ◆◆◆ **Baymont Inn & Suites** H

(530) 841-1300. **$59-$90.** 148 Moonlit Oaks Ave 96097. I-5 exit 773, just w. Int corridors. **Pets:** Service with restrictions, supervision.

AAA ◆◆◆◆ **BEST WESTERN Miner's Inn and Convention Center** M

(530) 842-4355. **$106-$124.** 122 E Miner St 96097. I-5 exit 776, just w to N Main St, then just s; exit 775, just w to N Main St, then just n; center. Ext corridors. **Pets:** Other species. $10 daily fee/pet. Designated rooms, supervision.

Comfort Inn H
(530) 842-1612. **$70-$150.** 1804-B Fort Jones Rd 96097. I-5 exit 773, just w. Int corridors. **Pets:** Accepted. ⟨SAVE⟩ 🛜 🛗 🖵 🏊

Econo Lodge Inn & Suites M
(530) 842-4404. **$46-$130.** 526 S Main St 96097. I-5 exit 775, just w to Main St, then just s. Ext corridors. **Pets:** Medium. $100 deposit/room, $10 daily fee/pet. Designated rooms, service with restrictions, supervision. ⟨SAVE⟩ 🛜 🛗 🖵 🏊

Rodeway Inn M
(530) 842-4412. **$46-$70.** 1235 S Main St 96097. I-5 exit 775 southbound, just w to Main St, then 0.9 mi s; exit 773 northbound, just w to Main St, then 1.1 mi n. Ext corridors. **Pets:** $5 daily fee/pet. Service with restrictions, supervision. ⟨SAVE⟩ 🛜 🛗 🖵 🏊

Super 8 M
(530) 842-5781. **$55-$75.** 136 Montague Rd 96097. I-5 exit 776, just w. Ext corridors. **Pets:** $10 daily fee/pet. Designated rooms, service with restrictions, supervision. ⟨SAVE⟩ 🛜 🛗 🖵 🏊

YUBA CITY

BEST WESTERN Yuba City Inn M
(530) 674-1650. **$80-$120.** 894 W Onstott Rd 95991. Just s of jct SR 99 and 20. Ext corridors. **Pets:** Medium. $10 daily fee/pet. Designated rooms, service with restrictions, crate. ⟨SAVE⟩ 🛜 ⌧ 🔥 🛗 🖵 🏊

The Harkey House BB
(530) 674-1942. **$120-$235, 7 day notice.** 212 C St 95991. At C and 2nd sts; downtown. Int corridors. **Pets:** Accepted. 🛜 🛗 🖵 🏊 ⊘

COLORADO

CITY INDEX

ALAMOSA

BEST WESTERN Alamosa Inn M 🐾
(719) 589-2567. **$63-$149.** 2005 W Main St 81101. On US 160, 1 mi w of center. Ext corridors. **Pets:** Medium, dogs only. $10 daily fee/pet. Designated rooms, service with restrictions, supervision. ⟨SAVE⟩ 🛜 ⌧ 🛗 🖵 🏊

Comfort Inn of Alamosa H
(719) 587-9000. **$80-$135.** 6301 Rd 107 S 81101. On US 160, 2.3 mi w of center. Int corridors. **Pets:** Medium, dogs only. $20 daily fee/pet. Designated rooms, service with restrictions, supervision. ⟨SAVE⟩ 🛜 ⌧ 🛗 🖵 🏊

Holiday Inn Express H
(719) 589-4026. **Call for rates.** 3418 Mariposa St 81101. On US 160, 2 mi w of center. Int corridors. **Pets:** Medium. $35 daily fee/room. Designated rooms, service with restrictions, supervision. 🛜 🛗 🖵 🏊 ⌧

ASPEN

Aspen Meadows Resort, A Dolce Resort H
(970) 925-4240. **$125-$800, 30 day notice.** 845 Meadows Rd 81611. 0.3 mi n of SR 82 via N 7th Ave, just w. Ext/int corridors. **Pets:** Accepted. ⟨SAVE⟩ 🛜 ⌧ 🛗 🖵 ⑪ 🏊 ⌧ 🐾

Aspen Mountain Lodge H
(970) 925-7650. **Call for rates.** 311 W Main St 81611. 0.4 mi w on SR 82; between S 2nd and S 3rd sts. Int corridors. **Pets:** Accepted. 🛜 ⌧ 🛗 🖵 🏊 ⌧

Chateau Aspen Condominiums CO
(970) 925-8717. **$150-$425, 30 day notice.** 630 E Cooper Ave 81611. Jct E Cooper Ave and S Spring St; downtown. Ext corridors. **Pets:** Accepted. 🛜 ⌧ 🛗 🖵 ⌧ 🐾

Hotel Jerome, An Auberge Resort H 🐾
(970) 920-1000. **$320-$1850, 30 day notice.** 330 E Main St 81611. Jct E Main and N Mill sts; downtown. Int corridors. **Pets:** $100 one-time fee/room. Service with restrictions. ⟨SAVE⟩ 🛜 ⌧ 🖵 ⑪ 🏊 ⌧

Hotel Lenado H 🐾
(970) 925-6246. **$175-$565, 30 day notice.** 200 S Aspen St 81611. 0.3 mi w on SR 82, just s to jct S Aspen and E Hopkins sts. Int corridors. **Pets:** Other species. Service with restrictions. 🛜 ⌧ 🛗 🖵 ⌧

The Limelight Hotel H
(970) 925-3025. **$115-$2520, 30 day notice.** 355 S Monarch St 81611. Just s of SR 82; at S Monarch and E Cooper sts; downtown. Int corridors. **Pets:** Dogs only. $25 daily fee/pet. Designated rooms, service with restrictions, crate. ⟨SAVE⟩ 🛜 ⌧ 🛗 🖵 ⑪ 🏊

The Little Nell 🅷 ❀
(970) 920-4600. **$280-$1250, 30 day notice.** 675 E Durant Ave 81611. Jct E Durant Ave and S Spring St; downtown; beside gondola at base of Aspen Mountain. Int corridors. **Pets:** Large, dogs only. $125 one-time fee/pet, $25 daily fee/pet. Crate.

Mountain House Lodge 🅼
(970) 920-2550. **$99-$299, 30 day notice.** 905 E Hopkins St 81611. 0.3 mi e on SR 82, just e. Int corridors. **Pets:** Accepted.

The Residence Hotel 🅷
(970) 920-6532. **Call for rates.** 305 S Galena St 81611. Jct S Galena St and E Hyman Ave; downtown. Int corridors. **Pets:** Accepted.

The St. Regis Aspen Resort 🅷 ❀
(970) 920-3300. **$199-$2099, 60 day notice.** 315 E Dean St 81611. Jct S Monarch and E Dean sts; downtown. Int corridors. **Pets:** Dogs only. $25 one-time fee/room, $25 daily fee/room. Designated rooms, service with restrictions.

Sky Hotel - A Kimpton Hotel 🅷 ❀
(970) 925-6760. **$200-$869, 30 day notice.** 709 E Durant Ave 81611. Corner of S Spring St and E Durant Ave; downtown; at base of Aspen Mountain. Ext/int corridors. **Pets:** Other species. Service with restrictions, supervision.

AVON

Comfort Inn Vail/Beaver Creek 🅷
(970) 949-5511. **$99-$249.** 161 W Beaver Creek Blvd 81620. I-70 exit 167, just s on Avon Rd, then just w. Int corridors. **Pets:** Medium. $25 one-time fee/pet. Service with restrictions, supervision.

Westin Riverfront Resort & Spa, Avon 🅷 ❀
(970) 790-6000. **$179-$889, 30 day notice.** 126 Riverfront Ln 81620. I-70 exit 167, 0.6 mi s on Avon Rd, then just w. Int corridors. **Pets:** Dogs only. Designated rooms, service with restrictions, supervision.

BAYFIELD

Wilderness Trails Ranch 🆁🅰
(970) 247-0722. **$199-$2495, 120 day notice.** 23486 CR 501 81122. 35 mi e of Durango to CR 501, then 18.5 mi ne. Ext corridors.
Pets: Accepted.

BEAVER CREEK

Park Hyatt Beaver Creek Resort & Spa 🅷 ❀
(970) 949-1234. **$109-$859, 3 day notice.** 136 E Thomas Pl 81620. I-70 exit 167, 3 mi s on Avon and Village rds, 0.4 mi e on Offerson Rd, then just s. Int corridors. **Pets:** Medium, dogs only. $50 one-time fee/room. Service with restrictions, crate.

The Ritz-Carlton, Bachelor Gulch 🅷
(970) 748-6200. **Call for rates.** 0130 Daybreak Ridge 81620. I-70 exit 167, just s through the Beaver Creek Village gatehouse to Prater Rd, then just w; follow signs to Bachelor Gulch Village. Int corridors.
Pets: Accepted.

BOULDER

BEST WESTERN PLUS Boulder Inn 🅷
(303) 449-3800. **$110-$200.** 770 28th St 80303. US 36 (28th St) at Baseline Rd. Int corridors. **Pets:** Small, other species. $50 deposit/room. Designated rooms, supervision.

Boulder Outlook Hotel & Suites 🅷
(303) 443-3322. **$79-$159.** 800 28th St 80303. US 36 (28th St) exit Baseline Rd via Frontage Rd. Ext/int corridors. **Pets:** Accepted.

Boulder University Inn 🅼
(303) 417-1700. **$79-$179.** 1632 Broadway 80302. US 36 (28th St) exit Baseline Rd, 0.3 mi s, then 3 mi nw. Ext corridors. **Pets:** Medium, other species. $100 deposit/room, $15 daily fee/pet. Designated rooms, service with restrictions, supervision.

Foot of The Mountain Motel 🅼
(303) 442-5688. **$90.** 200 Arapahoe Ave 80302. 1.8 mi w of US 36 (28th St). Ext corridors. **Pets:** Other species. $50 deposit/room, $5 daily fee/pet. Designated rooms, supervision.

Holiday Inn Express 🅷
(303) 442-6600. **$99-$199.** 4777 N Broadway 80304. 3 mi n of Pearl Street Pedestrian Mall; jct US 36 (28th St), 0.3 mi s. Int corridors. **Pets:** Other species. $25 daily fee/room. Service with restrictions, supervision.

Homewood Suites by Hilton 🅷
(303) 499-9922. **$99-$329.** 4950 Baseline Rd 80303. 1.2 mi e of US 36 (28th St); jct SR 157 (Foothills Pkwy), just w; entry off Baseline Rd. Ext/int corridors. **Pets:** Accepted.

Quality Inn & Suites Boulder Creek 🅷 ❀
(303) 449-7550. **$120-$167.** 2020 Arapahoe Ave 80302. US 36 (28th St), 0.5 mi w. Ext/int corridors. **Pets:** Large. $100 deposit/room, $15 daily fee/room. Designated rooms, service with restrictions, supervision.

Residence Inn by Marriott 🅷 ❀
(303) 449-5545. **$161-$259.** 3030 Center Green Dr 80301. 0.5 mi e of US 36 (28th St), e on Valmont Rd; from Foothills Pkwy, just w on Valmont Rd. Ext corridors. **Pets:** Other species. $75 one-time fee/room.

BRECKENRIDGE

Beaver Run Resort & Conference Center 🅷 ❀
(970) 453-6000. **$120-$650, 3 day notice.** 620 Village Rd 80424. 0.4 mi sw of SR 9 and Village Rd; at base of Peak 9. Int corridors. **Pets:** Medium, dogs only. $40 daily fee/pet. Designated rooms, service with restrictions, supervision.

DoubleTree by Hilton Breckenridge 🅷
(970) 547-5550. **$149-$399.** 550 Village Rd 80424. Jct Main St, just w on S Park Ave, then just sw. Int corridors. **Pets:** Accepted.

The Lodge & Spa at Breckenridge 🅷
(970) 453-9300. **$89-$340.** 112 Overlook Rd 80424. 0.3 m s of Main St and Ski Hill Rd to Boreas Pass Rd then 2.2 mi w (uphill) to Overlook Rd. Ext/int corridors. **Pets:** Dogs only. $20 daily fee/room. Service with restrictions.

BROOMFIELD

Aloft Broomfield Denver 🅷 ❀
(303) 635-2000. **$89-$199.** 8300 Arista Pl 80021. US 36 (Boulder Tpke) exit US 287/CR 121, 0.6 mi s, then 0.4 mi w on Uptown Ave. Int corridors. **Pets:** Medium, dogs only. Designated rooms, service with restrictions, crate.

Hyatt house Boulder/Broomfield 🅷
(720) 890-4811. **$99-$249.** 13351 W Midway Blvd 80020. US 36 (Boulder Tpke) exit Storagetek Dr/Interlocken Loop, 0.3 mi n, then just e on Via Varra Rd. Int corridors. **Pets:** Medium. $150 one-time fee/room. Service with restrictions, crate.

AAA ▼▼ ▼▼ Omni Interlocken Resort H
(303) 438-6600. **$119-$389.** 500 Interlocken Blvd 80021. US 36 (Boulder Tpke) exit Interlocken Loop, 0.4 mi s, then 0.4 mi e. Int corridors. **Pets:** Accepted. ▣ 🛜 ⊠ 🔥M 🖪 🖵 🍴 ⊛ ⊠

AAA ▼▼▼ TownePlace Suites by Marriott Boulder/Broomfield H
(303) 466-2200. **$79-$249.** 480 Flatiron Blvd 80021. US 36 (Boulder Tpke) exit Interlocken Loop, 0.4 mi s, just w on Interlocken Blvd, then just s. Int corridors. **Pets:** Other species. $100 one-time fee/room. Service with restrictions, crate. ▣ 🛜 ⊠ 🔥M 🖪 🖵 ⊛

BURLINGTON

AAA ▼▼▼ BEST WESTERN PLUS Carousel Inn & Suites H
(719) 346-7777. **$120-$140.** 605 S Lincoln St 80807. I-70 exit 437, just s. Int corridors. **Pets:** $50 deposit/room, $20 daily fee/pet. Designated rooms, service with restrictions, supervision.
▣ 🛜 ⊠ 🔥M 🖪 🖵 🍴 ⊛

AAA ▼ Chaparral Motor Inn M
(719) 346-5361. **$49-$65.** 405 S Lincoln St 80807. I-70 exit 437, just n on US 385. Ext corridors. **Pets:** $7 daily fee/pet. Designated rooms, service with restrictions, supervision. ▣ 🛜 🖪 🖵 ⊛

▼▼ Comfort Inn Burlington H
(719) 346-7676. **$89-$129.** 282 S Lincoln St 80807. I-70 exit 437, just n on US 385. Int corridors. **Pets:** Large. $50 deposit/room, $15 daily fee/room. Designated rooms, service with restrictions, supervision.
🛜 ⊠ 🖪 🖵 ⊛

CAÑON CITY

▼▼ Americas Best Value Inn M
(719) 275-3377. **$59-$143.** 1925 Fremont Dr 81212. From 9th St, 0.8 mi e on US 50. Int/int corridors. **Pets:** Large, dogs only. $10 daily fee/pet. Designated rooms, service with restrictions, supervision.
🛜 🖪 🖵 ⊛ ⊠

AAA ▼▼ BEST WESTERN Canon City H
(719) 275-2400. **$80-$149.** 110 Latigo Ln 81212. From 9th St, 3 mi e on US 50, then just n. Int corridors. **Pets:** Other species. $15 daily fee/pet. Designated rooms, no service, supervision.
▣ 🛜 ⊠ 🖪 🖵 ⊛

▼▼ Hampton Inn H
(719) 269-1112. **Call for rates.** 102 McCormick Pkwy 81212. From 9th St, 2.7 mi e on US 50. Int corridors. **Pets:** Accepted.
🛜 ⊠ 🖵 ⊛ ⊠

CARBONDALE

▼▼▼ Comfort Inn & Suites H
(970) 963-8880. **$84-$149.** 920 Cowen Dr 81623. Jct SR 82 and 133, just sw. Int corridors. **Pets:** Large. $15 daily fee/pet. Designated rooms, supervision. 🛜 ⊠ 🖪 🖵 ⊛ ⊠

CASTLE ROCK

AAA ▼▼▼ BEST WESTERN Inn & Suites of Castle Rock H ❀
(303) 814-8800. **$99-$189.** 595 Genoa Way 80109. I-25 exit 184 (Meadows Pkwy), just w to Castleton Way, just s, then e. Int corridors. **Pets:** Large. $20 daily fee/room. Designated rooms, service with restrictions, supervision. ▣ 🛜 ⊠ 🖪 🖵 ⊛

▼▼▼ Hampton Inn H
(303) 660-9800. **Call for rates.** 4830 Castleton Way 80104. I-25 exit 184 (Meadows Pkwy), sw to N Castleton Rd, just s, then e. Int corridors. **Pets:** Accepted. 🛜 🔥M 🖪 🖵 ⊛

CLIFTON

AAA ▼▼▼ BEST WESTERN Grande River Inn & Suites H ❀
(970) 434-3400. **$119-$149.** 3228 I-70 Business Loop 81520. I-70 exit 37, 0.8 mi s. Ext corridors. **Pets:** Small. $10 daily fee/pet. Designated rooms, service with restrictions, supervision. ▣ 🛜 🖪 🖵 ⊛

COLORADO SPRINGS METROPOLITAN AREA

CHIPITA PARK

▼▼▼▼ Chipita Lodge B & B BB ❀
(719) 684-8454. **$125-$190, 7 day notice.** 9090 Chipita Park Rd 80809. Jct US 24, just s on Fountain Blvd (Pine Peak Hwy), then 1.5 mi w; right at fork. Ext/int corridors. **Pets:** Dogs only. $25 one-time fee/pet. Designated rooms, crate. 🛜 ⊠ 🎾 🎬 🇿

COLORADO SPRINGS

▼▼ The Academy Hotel Colorado Springs H
(719) 598-5770. **$79-$139.** 8110 N Academy Blvd 80920. I-25 exit 150, just s. Int corridors. **Pets:** Medium. $10 daily fee/pet. Designated rooms, service with restrictions, supervision.
🛜 ⊠ 🔥M 🖪 🖵 🍴 ⊛ ⊠

AAA ▼▼▼ Antlers Hilton Colorado Springs H
(719) 473-5600. **Call for rates.** 4 S Cascade Ave 80903. I-25 exit 142 (Bijou St), just e, then just s; downtown. Int corridors. **Pets:** Accepted.
▣ 🛜 🔥M 🖪 🖵 🍴 ⊛ ⊠

AAA ▼▼▼ BEST WESTERN Executive Inn & Suites H
(719) 576-2371. **$68-$85.** 1440 Harrison Rd 80905. I-25 exit 138, just w; on northwest corner of interchange; entrance through restaurant. Int corridors. **Pets:** $10 daily fee/room. Service with restrictions, crate.
▣ 🛜 🔥M 🖪 🖵 ⊛

AAA ▼▼▼▼ The Broadmoor H ❀
(719) 634-7711. **$325-$7800, 7 day notice.** 1 Lake Ave 80906. I-25 exit 138, 3 mi w on Circle Dr (which becomes Lake Ave). Ext/int corridors. **Pets:** $50 daily fee/pet. Designated rooms, service with restrictions.
▣ 🛜 ⊠ 🔥M 🖪 🖵 🍴 ⊛ ⊠

AAA ▼▼▼ Cheyenne Mountain Resort H ❀
(719) 538-4000. **$99-$399, 7 day notice.** 3225 Broadmoor Valley Rd 80906. I-25 exit 138, 1.4 mi w to SR 115, 0.5 mi s, just w on Cheyenne Mountain Blvd, then just s. Ext/int corridors. **Pets:** Medium, dogs only. $35 one-time fee/room. Service with restrictions.
▣ 🛜 ⊠ 🔥M 🖪 🖵 🍴 ⊛ ⊠

AAA ▼▼▼ Comfort Inn H
(719) 380-9000. **$90-$160.** 2115 Aerotech Dr 80916. I-25 exit 139, 4.2 mi e on US 24 Bypass, 0.4 mi s on Powers Blvd, just w on Astrozon Blvd, then just n. Int corridors. **Pets:** Dogs only. $10 daily fee/pet. Designated rooms, service with restrictions, supervision. ▣ 🛜 🖪 🖵 ⊛

AAA ▼▼ Comfort Inn South H ❀
(719) 579-6900. **$69-$109.** 1410 Harrison Rd 80905. I-25 exit 138, just w to Rand Rd, then ne. Int corridors. **Pets:** Other species. $35 one-time fee/pet. Designated rooms, service with restrictions, supervision.
▣ 🛜 🖪 🖵 ⊛

▼▼▼ Crowne Plaza Colorado Springs H
(719) 576-5900. **$79-$189.** 2886 S Circle Dr 80906. I-25 exit 138, just e. Int corridors. **Pets:** Accepted. 🛜 ⊠ 🖪 🖵 🍴 ⊛ ⊠

▼▼ Drury Inn-Pikes Peak H
(719) 598-2500. **$65-$139.** 8155 N Academy Blvd 80920. I-25 exit 150, just s, then e. Int corridors. **Pets:** Service with restrictions, supervision.
🛜 🖪 🖵 ⊛

Fairfield Inn & Suites by Marriott Colorado Springs North Air Force Academy H
(719) 488-4644. **$89-$143.** 15275 W Struthers Rd 80921. I-25 exit 158, just e on Baptist Rd, then just s. Int corridors. **Pets:** Medium. $50 one-time fee/room. Service with restrictions, crate.

Fairfield Inn & Suites by Marriott Colorado Springs/South H
(719) 576-1717. **$104-$161.** 2725 Geyser Dr 80906. I-25 exit 138, just w to E Cheyenne Mountain Blvd, then just s. Int corridors. **Pets:** Medium. $75 one-time fee/room. Service with restrictions, supervision.

Hampton Inn & Suites Colorado Springs Air Force Academy/I-25 North @ Interquest H
(719) 598-6911. **$84-$149.** 1307 Republic Dr 80921. I-25 exit 153, 0.5 mi e, then just s. Int corridors. **Pets:** $50 one-time fee/room. Designated rooms, service with restrictions, supervision.

Homewood Suites by Hilton Colorado Springs-North H
(719) 265-6600. **$89-$169.** 9130 Explorer Dr 80920. I-25 exit 151 (Briargate Pkwy), 0.8 mi e; across from Focus on the Family. Int corridors. **Pets:** Large, other species. $25 one-time fee/pet. Service with restrictions.

Hyatt house Colorado Springs H
(719) 268-9990. **$89-$219.** 5805 Delmonico Dr 80919. I-25 exit 148 (Rockrimmon Blvd), just nw, then ne; entry around the bank. Int corridors. **Pets:** Medium. $150 one-time fee/room. Service with restrictions, crate.

Radisson Hotel Colorado Springs Airport H
(719) 597-7000. **$119-$185.** 1645 N Newport Rd 80916. I-25 exit 139, 4.5 mi e on US 24 Bypass. Int corridors. **Pets:** Medium, other species. $100 deposit/room, $25 one-time fee/pet. Designated rooms, service with restrictions, crate.

Residence Inn by Marriott Air Force Academy H
(719) 388-9300. **$99-$349.** 9805 Federal Dr 80921. I-25 exit 153, just e, then s. Int corridors. **Pets:** $75 one-time fee/room. Service with restrictions.

Residence Inn by Marriott Colorado Springs Central H
(719) 574-0370. **$139-$209.** 3880 N Academy Blvd 80917. I-25 exit 146 (Garden of the Gods Rd), 4.5 mi e, then 0.3 mi s. Ext corridors. **Pets:** Large, other species. $75 one-time fee/room. Service with restrictions, crate.

Residence Inn by Marriott-Colorado Springs South H
(719) 576-0101. **$113-$161.** 2765 Geyser Dr 80906. I-25 exit 138, just w to E Cheyenne Mountain Blvd, then just s. Int corridors. **Pets:** Medium. $75 one-time fee/room. Service with restrictions, supervision.

TownePlace Suites by Marriott Colorado Springs South H
(719) 638-0800. **$99-$179.** 1530 N Newport Rd 80916. I-25 exit 139, 5 mi e on US 24 Bypass, then just n. Int corridors. **Pets:** Accepted.

Travelodge H
(719) 632-4600. **$55-$100.** 2625 Ore Mill Rd 80904. I-25 exit 141, 2.3 mi nw on US 24; entry via 26th St. Int corridors. **Pets:** Other species. $15 one-time fee/pet. Service with restrictions, crate.

MANITOU SPRINGS

El Colorado Lodge CA
(719) 685-5485. **$56-$175, 14 day notice.** 23 Manitou Ave 80829. I-25 exit 141, 4 mi w on US 24, then just ne on US 24 business route. Ext corridors. **Pets:** Dogs only. $10 daily fee/room. Designated rooms, service with restrictions, crate.

Park Row Lodge M
(719) 685-5216. **Call for rates.** 54 Manitou Ave 80829. I-25 exit 141, 4 mi w on US 24, then just ne on US 24 business route. Ext corridors. **Pets:** Accepted.

Silver Saddle Motel M
(719) 685-5611. **Call for rates.** 215 Manitou Ave 80829. I-25 exit 141, 4 mi w on US 24, then just sw on US 24 business route. Ext corridors. **Pets:** Accepted.

END METROPOLITAN AREA

CORTEZ

Baymont Inn & Suites H
(970) 565-3400. **$80-$125.** 2321 E Main St 81321. 1.3 mi e of center on US 160. Ext/int corridors. **Pets:** Other species. $10 one-time fee/room. Designated rooms, service with restrictions.

BEST WESTERN Turquoise Inn & Suites M
(970) 565-3778. **$79-$129, 14 day notice.** 535 E Main St 81321. 0.6 mi e of center on US 160. Ext corridors. **Pets:** Small. $20 one-time fee/room. Designated rooms, service with restrictions, crate.

CRAIG

BEST WESTERN PLUS Deer Park Inn & Suites H
(970) 824-9282. **$109-$199.** 262 Commerce St 81625. 0.3 mi s of jct US 40 and SR 13. Int corridors. **Pets:** Large, other species. $100 deposit/room, $10 one-time fee/room. Designated rooms, service with restrictions, supervision.

Candlewood Suites H
(970) 824-8400. **$89-$169.** 92 Commerce St 81625. 0.4 mi s of jct US 40 and SR 13. Int corridors. **Pets:** Accepted.

CRESTED BUTTE

Elevation Hotel & Spa H
(970) 251-3000. **$169-$375, 3 day notice.** 500 Gothic Rd 81225. 5.9 mi n of Elk Ave. Int corridors. **Pets:** Dogs only. $30 daily fee/pet.

Elk Mountain Lodge BB
(970) 349-7533. **$119-$189, 14 day notice.** 129 Gothic Ave 81224. 0.3 mi w on Elk Ave to Second St, then just n. Int corridors. **Pets:** Accepted.

The Grand Lodge H
(970) 349-8000. **$99-$269, 3 day notice.** 6 Emmons Loop 81225. 2.3 mi n of center. Int corridors. **Pets:** Other species. $30 daily fee/pet. Designated rooms, service with restrictions, crate.

WW Old Town Inn 🅷 ✿

(970) 349-6184. **$89-$149.** 708 Sixth St 81224. On SR 135, just s of Elk Ave. Int corridors. **Pets:** Other species. $10 daily fee/room. Designated rooms, service with restrictions. 📶

WWW WestWall Lodge 🆑

(970) 349-1280. **$250-$2329, 30 day notice.** 14 Hunter Hill Rd 81225. 2.2 mi n, then just e; at Mt. Crested Butte. Int corridors. **Pets:** Accepted.
📶 ❎ 🛏 💻 ➿ ❌ ⚿

DELTA

WW Comfort Inn 🅷

(970) 874-1000. **$65-$120.** 180 Gunnison River Dr 81416. Just n of jct US 50 and SR 92. Int corridors. **Pets:** Accepted. 📶 🛏 💻

WWW Days Inn Sundance Ⓜ

(970) 874-9781. **$77-$150.** 903 Main St 81416. 0.5 mi s on US 50. Ext corridors. **Pets:** $10 daily fee/pet. Service with restrictions, crate.
🆂🅰🆅🅴 📶 🛏 💻 🍽 ➿

DENVER METROPOLITAN AREA

AURORA

WWW Aloft Denver International Airport 🅷

(303) 371-9500. **$79-$245.** 16470 E 40th Cir 80011. I-70 exit 283 (Chambers Rd), just n, 0.7 mi e, then just s. Int corridors.
Pets: Accepted. 🆂🅰🆅🅴 📶 ❎ 🛏 💻 🍽 ➿

WWW BEST WESTERN PLUS Gateway Inn & Suites 🅷

(720) 748-4800. **$70-$130.** 800 S Abilene St 80012. I-225 exit 7 (Mississippi Ave), just e, then 0.3 mi n. Int corridors. **Pets:** Medium. $15 daily fee/room. Service with restrictions, crate.
🆂🅰🆅🅴 📶 🍽 🛏 💻 ➿ ❎

WWW Holiday Inn Express & Suites Denver-Aurora 🅷

(303) 369-8400. **Call for rates.** 1500 S Abilene St 80012. I-225 exit 7 (Mississippi Ave), just e, then 0.5 mi s. Int corridors. **Pets:** Accepted.
📶 ❎ 🍽 🛏 💻 ➿

WWW Residence Inn by Marriott 🅷

(303) 459-8000. **$89-$198.** 16490 E 40th Cir 80011. I-70 exit 283 (Chambers Rd), just n, 0.5 mi e, then just s. Int corridors.
Pets: Accepted. 📶 ❎ 🍽 🛏 💻 ➿ ❌

WW Sleep Inn Denver International Airport 🅷

(303) 373-1616. **$50-$125.** 15900 E 40th Ave 80011. I-70 exit 283 (Chambers Rd); from airport, Pena Blvd S to 40th Ave W. Int corridors. **Pets:** Accepted. 📶 🍽 🛏 💻 ➿

BRIGHTON

WW BEST WESTERN Brighton Inn 🅷

(303) 637-7710. **$105-$125.** 15151 Brighton Rd 80601. US 85, 1 mi s of jct SR 7, just w. Int corridors. **Pets:** Medium, dogs only. $20 daily fee/pet. Designated rooms, service with restrictions, supervision.
🆂🅰🆅🅴 📶 🍽 🛏 💻 ➿

CENTENNIAL

WWW Drury Inn & Suites-Denver Near the Tech Center 🅷

(303) 694-3400. **$90-$169.** 9445 E Dry Creek Rd 80112. I-25 exit 196 (Dry Creek Rd), just w; on northwest corner. Int corridors. **Pets:** Service with restrictions, supervision. 📶 🛏 💻 ➿

WWW Embassy Suites Denver Tech Center 🅷

(303) 792-0433. **$99-$189.** 10250 E Costilla Ave 80112. I-25 exit 197 (Arapahoe Rd), 1 mi e, 0.3 mi s on Havana St, then w. Int corridors. **Pets:** Large, dogs only. $50 one-time fee/pet. Service with restrictions, supervision. 🆂🅰🆅🅴 📶 🍽 🛏 💻 🍽 ➿

WW Hawthorn Suites by Wyndham Denver Tech Center 🅷

(303) 792-5393. **$64-$130.** 6780 S Galena St 80112. I-25 exit 197 (Arapahoe Rd), 0.7 mi e, then just s. Int corridors. **Pets:** Accepted.
📶 🛏 💻

WWW Staybridge Suites Denver Tech Center 🅷

(303) 858-9990. **$89-$109, 3 day notice.** 7150 S Clinton St 80112. I-25 exit 197 (Arapahoe Rd), just e to Clinton St, 0.5 mi s, then just e. Int corridors. **Pets:** Accepted. 📶 ❎ 🍽 🛏 💻 ➿

WW TownePlace Suites by Marriott Denver Tech Center 🅷

(720) 875-1113. **$79-$229.** 7877 S Chester St 80112. I-25 exit 196 (Dry Creek Rd), just w to Chester St, then 0.3 mi s. Int corridors.
Pets: Accepted. 📶 ❎ 🍽 🛏 💻 ➿

DENVER

WWW BEST WESTERN PLUS Denver Hotel 🅷

(303) 388-6161. **$105-$140.** 3737 Quebec St 80207. I-70 exit 278, just s. Int corridors. **Pets:** Accepted. 🆂🅰🆅🅴 📶 ❎ 🛏 💻 ➿

WWW The Brown Palace Hotel and Spa, Autograph Collection 🅷

(303) 297-3111. **$189-$489.** 321 17th St 80202. From Broadway and Tremont Pl, just sw. Int corridors. **Pets:** Accepted.
🆂🅰🆅🅴 📶 ❎ 🛏 💻 🍽 ❌

WWW Comfort Inn Central 🅷

(303) 297-1717. **$99-$109.** 401 E 58th Ave 80216. I-25 exit 215, just e, then n on Logan St; connected to Denver Merchandise Mart. Int corridors. **Pets:** Other species. $10 one-time fee/pet. Designated rooms, service with restrictions, crate. 🆂🅰🆅🅴 📶 ❎ 🍽 🛏 💻 ➿

WWW Comfort Inn Downtown Denver 🅷

(303) 296-0400. **$99-$299.** 401 17th St 80202. From Broadway and Tremont Pl, just sw. Int corridors. **Pets:** Accepted.
🆂🅰🆅🅴 📶 ❎ 🛏 💻

WWW Courtyard by Marriott Denver Stapleton 🅷

(303) 333-3303. **$84-$149.** 7415 E 41st Ave 80216. I-70 exit 278, s on Quebec St, exit Smith Rd, then e to Frontage Rd; I-270 exit 4. Int corridors. **Pets:** Large. $75 one-time fee/room. Designated rooms, service with restrictions, supervision. 🅴🅲🅾 🆂🅰🆅🅴 📶 ❎ 🛏 💻 🍽 ➿

WWW Crowne Plaza Denver International Airport 🅷

(303) 371-9494. **$99-$199.** 15500 E 40th Ave 80239. I-70 exit 283 (Chambers Rd), just n, then just e. Int corridors. **Pets:** $30 one-time fee/room. Service with restrictions, crate.
📶 ❎ 🍽 🛏 💻 🍽 ➿

WWW the Curtis - a DoubleTree by Hilton Hotel 🅷 ✿

(303) 571-0300. **$109-$319.** 1405 Curtis St 80202. I-25 exit 212 (Speer Blvd S), s to Lawrence St, just ne, just se on 14th St, then just n. Int corridors. **Pets:** Other species. $25 daily fee/room. Designated rooms, service with restrictions, crate. 🆂🅰🆅🅴 📶 ❎ 🍽 🛏 💻 🍽

WWW DoubleTree by Hilton Denver-Stapleton North 🅷

(303) 321-6666. **$72-$160.** 4040 Quebec St 80216. I-70 exit 278, s on Quebec St to Smith Rd exit, then e to Frontage Rd. Int corridors. **Pets:** Other species. $15 one-time fee/room. Service with restrictions, crate. 📶 🛏 💻 🍽 ➿

WWW DoubleTree by Hilton Hotel Denver 🅷

(303) 321-3333. **$79-$224.** 3203 Quebec St 80207. I-70 exit 278, 0.5 mi s; I-270 exit 4. Int corridors. **Pets:** Accepted.
📶 ❎ 🛏 💻 ➿ ❌

▼▼▼ Drury Inn-Denver East 🅷
(303) 373-1983. **$90-$144.** 4380 Peoria St 80239. I-70 exit 281 eastbound; exit 282 westbound, just n. Int corridors. **Pets:** Service with restrictions, supervision. 🛜 🛏 🖥 ⊠

🆃 ▼▼▼ Embassy Suites Denver-Aurora 🅷
(303) 375-0400. **$119-$199.** 4444 N Havana St 80239. I-70 exit 280, just n. Int corridors. **Pets:** Accepted.
💾 🛜 ✕ 🔧M 🛏 🖥 🍴 ⊠ ⊠

▼▼▼▼ Four Seasons Hotel Denver 🅷 🐾
(303) 389-3000. **$295-$640, 3 day notice.** 1111 14th St 80202. Between Lawrence and Arapahoe sts. Int corridors. **Pets:** Small, dogs only. Service with restrictions, supervision.
🛜 ✕ 🖥 🍴 ⊠ ⊠

🆃 ▼▼▼ ▼▼▼ Grand Hyatt Denver 🅷 🐾
(303) 295-1234. **$89-$399.** 1750 Welton St 80202. Between 17th and 18th sts. Int corridors. **Pets:** Medium, dogs only. $25 one-time fee/room. Service with restrictions, supervision.
🅴🅲🅾 💾 🛜 ✕ 🔧M 🛏 🖥 🍴 ⊠ ⊠

▼▼▼▼ Hampton Inn & Suites Denver Tech Center 🅷
(303) 804-9900. **$99-$189.** 5001 S Ulster St 80237. I-25 exit 199, e to Ulster St, then just n. Int corridors. **Pets:** Other species. $25 one-time fee/pet. Designated rooms, service with restrictions, crate.
🛜 ✕ 🔧M 🛏 🖥 ⊠

▼▼▼▼ Hampton Inn DIA 🅷
(303) 371-0200. **$119-$189.** 6290 Tower Rd 80249. I-70 exit 286 (Tower Rd), 3.5 mi n. Int corridors. **Pets:** Accepted. 🛜 🔧M 🖥 ⊠

🆃 ▼▼▼ Holiday Inn Denver East - Stapleton 🅷
(303) 321-3500. **Call for rates.** 3333 Quebec St 80207. I-70 exit 278, 0.3 mi s; I-270 exit 4. Int corridors. **Pets:** Small, dogs only. $40 one-time fee/pet. Designated rooms, service with restrictions, supervision.
💾 🛜 ✕ 🔧M 🛏 🖥 🍴 ⊠ ⊠

🆃 ▼▼▼ Hotel Monaco Denver 🅷
(303) 296-1717. **$159-$399.** 1717 Champa St 80202. Between 17th and 18th sts. Int corridors. **Pets:** Accepted.
🅴🅲🅾 💾 🛜 ✕ 🔧M 🛏 🍴 ⊠

🆃 ▼▼▼ Hotel Teatro 🅷 🐾
(303) 228-1100. **$159-$1500.** 1100 14th St 80202. Between Lawrence and Arapahoe sts. Int corridors. **Pets:** Dogs only.
💾 🛜 ✕ 🛏 🖥 🍴 ⊠

🆃 ▼▼▼ Hyatt house Denver Airport 🅷
(303) 628-7777. **$89-$169.** 18741 E 71st Ave 80249. I-70 exit 286 (Tower Rd), 4.6 mi n, then just e; from Pena Blvd exit 5 (Tower Rd/SR 32), just s. Int corridors. **Pets:** Medium. $150 one-time fee/room. Designated rooms, service with restrictions, crate.
💾 🛜 ✕ 🛏 🖥 ⊠

🆃 ▼▼▼ ▼▼▼ Hyatt Regency Denver Tech Center 🅷 🐾
(303) 779-1234. **$69-$289.** 7800 E Tufts Ave 80237. I-225 exit 2 (Tamarac St), just s to Tufts Ave; I-25 exit 199 (Belleview Ave), e to S Ulster St, then 0.5 mi n. Int corridors. **Pets:** Medium, dogs only. $25 one-time fee/room. Designated rooms, service with restrictions.
💾 🛜 🔧M 🛏 🖥 🍴 ⊠ ⊠

🆃 ▼▼▼ The Inn at Cherry Creek 🅷
(303) 350-4440. **Call for rates.** 233 Clayton St 80206. Between 2nd and 3rd aves; in Cherry Creek Village. Int corridors. **Pets:** Accepted.
💾 🛜 ✕ 🛏 🖥

🆃 ▼▼▼ ▼▼▼ JW Marriott Denver At Cherry Creek 🅷 🐾
(303) 316-2700. **$209-$449.** 150 Clayton Ln 80206. I-25 exit 205 (University Blvd), 2.4 mi n to 1st Ave, just e, then just n. Int corridors. **Pets:** Service with restrictions, supervision. 💾 🛜 ✕ 🔧M 🖥 🍴 ⊠

▼▼▼ La Quinta Inn & Suites Denver Airport DIA 🅷
(303) 371-0888. **$78-$184.** 6801 Tower Rd 80249. I-70 exit 286 (Tower Rd), 4.2 mi n; 0.8 mi s of Pena Blvd. Int corridors. **Pets:** Service with restrictions, supervision. 🛜 🔧M 🛏 🖥 ⊠

▼▼▼ La Quinta Inn & Suites Denver Gateway Park 🅷
(303) 373-2525. **$95-$166.** 4460 Peoria St 80239. I-70 exit 281, just n. Int corridors. **Pets:** Service with restrictions, supervision.
🛜 ✕ 🛏 🖥 ⊠

▼▼▼ La Quinta Inn Denver Cherry Creek 🅷
(303) 758-8886. **$59-$155.** 1975 S Colorado Blvd 80222. I-25 exit 204, just s. Ext corridors. **Pets:** Service with restrictions, supervision.
🛜 🛏 🖥 ⊠

🆃 ▼▼▼ The Oxford Hotel 🅷 🐾
(303) 628-5400. **$180-$380.** 1600 17th St 80202. Corner of 17th and Wazee sts. Int corridors. **Pets:** Other species. Service with restrictions.
💾 🛜 ✕ 🛏 🖥 🍴 ⊠

🆃 ▼▼▼ Quality Inn & Suites-DIA 🅷
(303) 371-1044. **$65-$140.** 6890 Tower Rd 80249. I-70 exit 286 (Tower Rd), 4.2 mi n; 0.8 mi s of Pena Blvd. Int corridors. **Pets:** Medium. $25 one-time fee/pet. Designated rooms, service with restrictions, supervision.
💾 🛜 ✕ 🔧M 🛏 🖥 ⊠

▼▼ Quality Inn Denver East 🅷
(303) 371-5640. **Call for rates.** 3975 Peoria Way 80239. I-70 exit 281 eastbound; exit 282 westbound, just s. Ext corridors. **Pets:** Accepted.
🛜 🛏 🖥 ⊠

🆃 ▼▼▼ Renaissance Denver Hotel 🅷
(303) 399-7500. **$99-$289.** 3801 Quebec St 80207. I-70 exit 278, just s via Smith Rd exit. Int corridors. **Pets:** Dogs only. $75 one-time fee/room. Designated rooms, service with restrictions, crate.
💾 🛜 ✕ 🛏 🖥 🍴 ⊠

🆃 ▼▼▼ Residence Inn by Marriott Denver City Center 🅷
(303) 296-3444. **$119-$359.** 1725 Champa St 80202. Between 17th and 18th sts. Int corridors. **Pets:** Other species. $75 one-time fee/pet. Designated rooms, service with restrictions. 💾 🛜 ✕ 🛏 🖥

▼▼▼ Residence Inn by Marriott Denver Downtown 🅷
(303) 458-5318. **$160-$180.** 2777 Zuni St 80211. I-25 exit 212B (Speer Blvd) southbound; exit 212A (Speer Blvd S) northbound, just w, then just n. Ext corridors. **Pets:** Accepted. 🛜 ✕ 🛏 🖥 ⊠

🆃 ▼▼▼ The Ritz-Carlton, Denver 🅷
(303) 312-3800. **$239-$379.** 1881 Curtis St 80202. Between 18th and 19th sts. Int corridors. **Pets:** Accepted.
💾 🛜 ✕ 🔧M 🛏 🖥 🍴 ⊠ ⊠

🆃 ▼▼▼ Sheraton Denver Downtown Hotel 🅷
(303) 893-3333. **$119-$369.** 1550 Court Pl 80202. Between 15th and 16th sts. Int corridors. **Pets:** Accepted.
💾 🛜 ✕ 🛏 🖥 🍴 ⊠

▼▼▼ Staybridge Suites 🅷
(303) 574-0888. **$79-$179.** 6951 Tower Rd 80249. Just s of jct Pena Blvd. Int corridors. **Pets:** Accepted. 🛜 ✕ 🔧M 🛏 🖥

🆃 ▼▼▼ Timbers Hotel 🅷
(303) 373-1444. **Call for rates.** 4411 Peoria St 80239. I-70 exit 281, just n. Int corridors. **Pets:** Accepted. 💾 🛜 ✕ 🔧M 🛏 🖥 🍴

▼▼ TownePlace Suites by Marriott-Denver Southeast 🅷 🐾
(303) 759-9393. **$79-$229.** 3699 S Monaco Pkwy 80237. I-25 exit 201, just e to Monaco Pkwy, then s. Int corridors. **Pets:** Other species. $100 one-time fee/room. Service with restrictions, crate.
🛜 ✕ 🛏 🖥 ⊠

TownePlace Suites by Marriott DIA @ Gateway Park Ⓗ ☆

(303) 373-4243. **$79-$109.** 4100 N Kittredge St 80239. I-70 exit 283 (Chambers Rd), just n to 40th Ave, 0.3 mi e, then just n. Int corridors. **Pets:** Medium. $100 one-time fee/pet. Service with restrictions, supervision. (SAVE) 🛜 ✕ ▣ 🛏 🖃 ⌲

TownePlace Suites by Marriott Downtown Denver Ⓗ ☆

(303) 722-2322. **$69-$319.** 685 Speer Blvd 80204. I-25 exit 209A (6th Ave), 1.4 mi w, then just n on Acoma St. Int corridors. **Pets:** $100 one-time fee/room. Service with restrictions, supervision.

(SAVE) 🛜 ✕ ⒧Ⓜ 🛏 🖃 ⌲

Warwick Denver Hotel Ⓗ 🐾

(303) 861-2000. **$109-$499.** 1776 Grant St 80203. Between 17th and 18th aves. Int corridors. **Pets:** Dogs only. $50 one-time fee/room. Designated rooms, service with restrictions, crate.

(SAVE) 🛜 ✕ 🛏 🖃 🍴 ⌲

The Westin Denver Downtown Ⓗ ☆

(303) 572-9100. **$169-$389.** 1672 Lawrence St 80202. Between 16th and 17th sts. Int corridors. **Pets:** Small, dogs only. Service with restrictions, supervision. (SAVE) 🛜 ✕ ⒧Ⓜ 🛏 🖃 🍴 ⌲ ✕⌲

ENGLEWOOD

Homewood Suites by Hilton - DTC/Inverness Ⓗ ☆

(303) 706-0102. **$79-$199.** 199 Inverness Dr W 80112. I-25 exit 195 (County Line Rd), 0.3 mi ne to traffic light, then just n. Int corridors. **Pets:** Medium. $100 one-time fee/room. Designated rooms, service with restrictions, crate. 🛜 🛏 🖃 ⌲ ✕⌲

Residence Inn by Marriott Denver South / Park Meadows Ⓗ

(720) 895-0200. **$67-$177.** 8322 S Valley Hwy 80112. I-25 exit 195 (County Line Rd), just e to S Valley Hwy, then just s. Int corridors. **Pets:** Accepted. 🛜 ✕ ⒧Ⓜ 🛏 🖃 ⌲ ✕⌲

GLENDALE

Loews Denver Hotel Ⓗ

(303) 782-9300. **$89-$279.** 4150 E Mississippi Ave 80246. I-25 exit 204, 0.8 mi n on Colorado Blvd, then just e. Int corridors. **Pets:** Accepted.

🛜 ✕ ⒧Ⓜ 🛏 🖃 🍴

GOLDEN

The Golden Hotel, an Ascend Collection hotel Ⓗ 🐾

(303) 279-0100. **$139-$199.** 800 11th St 80401. At 11th St and Washington Ave; downtown. Int corridors. **Pets:** Medium, dogs only. $100 deposit/room, $20 daily fee/pet. Designated rooms, service with restrictions, supervision. 🛜 ✕ 🛏 🖃 🍴

Residence Inn by Marriott Denver West/Golden Ⓗ

(303) 271-0909. **$85-$269.** 14600 W 6th Ave, Frontage Rd 80401. US 6 exit Indiana Ave, just s to frontage road, then just e. Int corridors. **Pets:** Accepted. 🛜 ✕ ⒧Ⓜ 🛏 🖃 ⌲ ✕⌲

Table Mountain Inn Ⓗ 🐾

(303) 277-9898. **$141-$290.** 1310 Washington Ave 80401. US 6 exit 19th St, 0.5 mi n to Washington Ave, 0.5 mi w; downtown, just s of arch. Int corridors. **Pets:** Other species. $10 daily fee/room. Designated rooms, service with restrictions. (SAVE) 🛜 ✕ 🛏 🖃 🍴

GREENWOOD VILLAGE

Hampton Inn Denver Southeast Ⓗ

(303) 792-9999. **$69-$149.** 9231 E Arapahoe Rd 80112. I-25 exit 197 (Arapahoe Rd), just e. Int corridors. **Pets:** Accepted.

🛜 ✕ ⒧Ⓜ 🛏 🖃 ⌲

Hyatt house Denver Tech Center Ⓗ

(303) 706-1945. **$89-$229.** 9280 E Costilla Ave 80112. I-25 exit 197 (Arapahoe Rd), e to Clinton St, then just s. Int corridors. **Pets:** Medium. $200 one-time fee/room. Designated rooms, service with restrictions, crate. (SAVE) 🛜 ✕ ⒧Ⓜ 🛏 🖃 ⌲

La Quinta Inn & Suites Denver Tech Center Ⓗ

(303) 649-9969. **$59-$166.** 7077 S Clinton St 80112. I-25 exit 197 (Arapahoe Rd), e to Clinton St, then 0.5 mi s. Int corridors. **Pets:** Service with restrictions, supervision. 🛜 ⒧Ⓜ 🛏 🖃 ⌲

Residence Inn by Marriott-Denver Tech Center Ⓗ

(303) 740-7177. **$72-$189.** 6565 S Yosemite St 80111. I-25 exit 197 (Arapahoe Rd), just w, then n. Ext corridors. **Pets:** Other species. $75 one-time fee/room. Service with restrictions. 🛜 ✕ 🛏 🖃 ⌲

HIGHLANDS RANCH

Comfort Suites-Denver South Ⓗ ☆

(303) 770-5400. **$65-$195.** 7060 E County Line Rd 80126. SR 470 exit Quebec St, just n to County Line Rd, just w, then just s; at Quebec Highlands Center. Int corridors. **Pets:** Medium. $15 daily fee/pet. Designated rooms, service with restrictions, supervision.

(SAVE) 🛜 ✕ ⒧Ⓜ 🛏 🖃

Residence Inn by Marriott Denver Highlands Ranch Ⓗ

(303) 683-5500. **$90-$162.** 93 W Centennial Blvd 80126. SR 470 exit Broadway, just s, then w. Int corridors. **Pets:** Medium. $100 one-time fee/pet. Service with restrictions, supervision.

🛜 ✕ ⒧Ⓜ 🛏 🖃 ⌲ ✕⌲

LAKEWOOD

AmericInn Hotel & Suites/Denver West- Federal Center Ⓗ

(303) 231-9929. **Call for rates.** 11909 W 6th Ave 80401. US 6 exit Simms St/Union Blvd, westbound turn right at traffic light, but do not use right turn lane, follow signs to frontage road. Int corridors. **Pets:** Accepted.

(SAVE) 🛜 ✕ 🛏 🖃 ⌲ ✕⌲

BEST WESTERN Denver Southwest Ⓗ 🐾

(303) 989-5500. **$89-$149.** 3440 S Vance St 80227. Just ne of jct US 285 (Hampden Ave) and S Wadsworth Blvd, e on Girton Dr, then just s. Int corridors. **Pets:** Large, other species. Designated rooms, service with restrictions, crate. (SAVE) 🛜 ✕ 🛏 🖃

Holiday Inn Denver Lakewood Ⓗ

(303) 980-9200. **$89-$129.** 7390 W Hampden Ave 80227. US 285 (W Hampden Ave) exit S Wadsworth Blvd, just e on Jefferson Ave, then n on Vance St. Int corridors. **Pets:** Small. $50 one-time fee/room. Crate. (SAVE) 🛜 🛏 🖃 🍴 ⌲ ✕⌲

Lakewood Comfort Suites Ⓗ

(303) 988-8600. **$69-$189.** 7260 W Jefferson Ave 80235. Just se of US 285 (W Hampden Ave) and S Wadsworth Blvd, then e. Int corridors. **Pets:** Small, dogs only. $15 daily fee/pet. Designated rooms, service with restrictions, supervision. 🛜 ✕ 🛏 🖃 ⌲

Residence Inn by Marriott Denver SW/Lakewood Ⓗ

(303) 985-7676. **$86-$154.** 7050 W Hampden Ave 80227. Just se of jct US 285 (W Hampden Ave) and Wadsworth Blvd, e on Jefferson Ave, then n on frontage road. Int corridors. **Pets:** Other species. $50 one-time fee/pet. Service with restrictions, crate.

🛜 ✕ ⒧Ⓜ 🛏 🖃 ⌲ ✕⌲

Sheraton-Denver West Hotel Ⓗ

(303) 987-2000. **$89-$409.** 360 Union Blvd 80228. US 6 exit Simms St/Union Blvd, just s on Union Blvd. Int corridors. **Pets:** Accepted.

(SAVE) 🛜 ✕ 🛏 🖃 🍴 ⌲ ✕⌲

▽▽ ▽▽ TownePlace Suites by Marriott-Denver West/Federal Center **H**

(303) 232-7790. **$69-$199.** 800 Tabor St 80401. US 6 exit Simms St/Union Blvd, just n to 8th St, then w. Int corridors. **Pets:** Accepted.

📶 ✕ 🛎 🍴 💻 🏊

LITTLETON

▽▽▽▽ Holiday Inn Express Hotel & Suites **H** ✣

(720) 981-1000. **$89-$169.** 12683 W Indore Pl 80127. I-70 to SR 470 and Ken Caryl Ave; I-25 to SR 470 and Ken Caryl Ave, to Shaffer Ave, just n, then w. Int corridors. **Pets:** Medium, dogs only. $100 deposit/room, $15 daily fee/pet. Designated rooms, service with restrictions, supervision.

📶 ✕ 🛎 🍴 💻 🏊

④④④ ▽▽▽▽ Homewood Suites by Hilton-Denver Littleton **H** ✣

(720) 981-4763. **$89-$309.** 7630 Shaffer Pkwy 80127. SR 470 exit Ken Caryl Ave, just e, then just s. Int corridors. **Pets:** $50 one-time fee/room. Service with restrictions, supervision.

SAVE 📶 🍴 🛎 💻 🏊 ✕

▽▽ ▽▽ TownePlace Suites by Marriott-Littleton Denver Southwest **H**

(303) 972-0555. **$79-$229.** 10902 W Toller Dr 80127. SR 470 exit Kipling Pkwy, just s, then 0.4 mi w on Ute St. Int corridors. **Pets:** Other species. $100 one-time fee/room, $25 daily fee/room. Service with restrictions.

📶 ✕ 🛎 💻 🏊

LONE TREE

④④④ ▽▽▽▽ Element Denver Park Meadows **H** ✣

(303) 790-2100. **$89-$199.** 9985 Park Meadows Dr 80124. Jct Yosemite St, 0.4 mi e. Int corridors. **Pets:** Other species. Service with restrictions, supervision.

ECO ♿ SAVE 📶 ✕ 🛎 💻 🏊

▽▽▽▽ Staybridge Suites Denver South-Lone Tree **H**

(303) 649-1010. **$79-$189.** 7820 Park Meadows Dr 80124. I-25 exit 195 (County Line Rd), w to Acres Green Dr, s to E Park Meadows Dr, then just w; SR 470 exit Quebec St, just s, then just e. Int corridors.
Pets: Accepted. 📶 🛎 🍴 💻 🏊

THORNTON

④④④ ▽▽▽▽ Holiday Inn Express Hotel & Suites - Denver North/Thornton **H**

(303) 452-0800. **$99-$179.** 12030 Grant St 80241. Int corridors.
Pets: Small. $150 deposit/room, $25 daily fee/pet. Designated rooms, supervision. SAVE 📶 🍴 🛎 💻 🏊

④④④ ▽▽ ▽▽ Sleep Inn North Denver **H**

(303) 280-9818. **Call for rates.** 12101 Grant St 80241. I-25 exit 223, e to Grant St, then n. Int corridors. **Pets:** Accepted.

SAVE 📶 🍴 🛎 💻 🏊

WESTMINSTER

④④④ ▽▽ ▽▽ Comfort Inn Northwest **H**

(303) 428-3333. **$69-$130.** 8500 Turnpike Dr 80031. US 36 (Boulder Tpke) exit Sheridan Ave, just s, left on Turnpike Dr at 87th Ave, then 0.4 mi. Int corridors. **Pets:** Accepted. SAVE 📶 ✕ 🍴 🛎 💻 🏊

④④④ ▽▽ ▽▽ Comfort Suites Denver North **H**

(303) 429-5500. **$69-$124.** 12085 Delaware St 80234. I-25 exit 223, just w. Int corridors. **Pets:** Accepted. SAVE 📶 ✕ 🛎 💻 🏊

▽▽▽▽ DoubleTree by Hilton Hotel Denver - Westminster **H** ✣

(303) 427-4000. **Call for rates.** 8773 Yates Dr 80031. US 36 (Boulder Tpke) exit Sheridan Ave, n to 92nd Ave, e to Yates Dr, then 0.5 mi s. Int corridors. **Pets:** Other species. $25 one-time fee/room. Service with restrictions, crate. 📶 🛎 💻 🍴 🏊

▽▽▽▽ Residence Inn by Marriott **H**

(303) 427-9500. **$99-$299.** 5010 W 88th Pl 80031. US 36 (Boulder Tpke) exit Sheridan Ave, n to 92nd Ave, e to Yates Dr, then s. Int corridors.
Pets: Accepted. 📶 ✕ 🍴 🛎 💻 🏊 ✕

④④④ ▽▽▽▽ The Westin Westminster **H** ✣

(303) 410-5000. **$99-$329, 3 day notice.** 10600 Westminster Blvd 80020. US 36 (Boulder Tpke) exit 104th Ave, just n. Int corridors.
Pets: Medium, dogs only. Designated rooms, service with restrictions, supervision. SAVE 📶 ✕ 🍴 🛎 💻 🍴 🏊 ✕

END METROPOLITAN AREA

DILLON

④④④ ▽▽ ▽▽ BEST WESTERN Ptarmigan Lodge **M**

(970) 468-2341. **$76-$190.** 652 Lake Dillon Dr 80435. I-70 exit 205, 1.3 mi s on US 6 to Lake Dillon Dr stop light, then 0.3 mi s; opposite Lake Dillon. Ext/int corridors. **Pets:** $50 deposit/pet, $10 daily fee/pet. Designated rooms, service with restrictions, supervision.

SAVE 📶 ✕ 🛎 💻 ✕ 🎿

▽▽ Super 8 Dillon **M**

(970) 468-8888. **$50-$145.** 808 Little Beaver Tr 80435. I-70 exit 205, 0.3 mi s, then just e. Int corridors. **Pets:** Accepted. 📶 🛎 💻

DURANGO

▽▽▽▽ Apple Orchard Inn **BB**

(970) 247-0751. **$90-$250, 21 day notice.** 7758 CR 203 81301. 8.5 mi n on US 550, just w at Trimble Ln, then 1.3 mi n. Ext/int corridors.
Pets: Dogs only. $20 daily fee/pet. Designated rooms, service with restrictions, supervision. 📶 ✕ 🛎 💻 🎿

④④④ ▽▽ ▽▽ BEST WESTERN Durango Inn & Suites **M**

(970) 247-3251. **$79-$189.** 21382 US Hwy 160 W 81303. On US 160, 1 mi w. Ext corridors. **Pets:** Accepted. SAVE 📶 🛎 💻 🍴 🏊

▽▽ Caboose Motel **M**

(970) 247-1191. **$58-$190.** 3363 Main Ave 81301. 2.5 mi n on US 550. Ext corridors. **Pets:** Medium, dogs only. $10 daily fee/pet. Designated rooms, service with restrictions, supervision. 📶 ✕ 🛎 💻 🎿

▽▽▽▽ DoubleTree by Hilton Hotel Durango **H**

(970) 259-6580. **$119-$249.** 501 Camino Del Rio 81301. Jct US 160 and 550. Int corridors. **Pets:** Accepted. ECO 📶 🛎 💻 🍴 🏊 ✕

④④④ ▽▽ ▽▽ Durango Downtown Inn **M**

(970) 247-5393. **$109-$189.** 800 Camino Del Rio 81301. On US 550, just n of jct US 160. Ext corridors. **Pets:** Other species. $10 daily fee/pet. Designated rooms, service with restrictions, crate.

SAVE 📶 🛎 💻 🍴 🏊 ✕

▽▽▽▽ Leland House Bed & Breakfast Suites **BB** ✣

(970) 385-1920. **$129-$399, 14 day notice.** 721 E 2nd Ave 81301. Just e of Main Ave via 7th St, then just n. Ext/int corridors. **Pets:** $20 daily fee/pet. Designated rooms, supervision. 📶 ✕ 🛎 💻

▽▽ ▽▽ Quality Inn **M**

(970) 259-5373. **$69-$159.** 2930 N Main Ave 81301. 2 mi n on US 550. Ext corridors. **Pets:** Accepted. 📶 🛎 💻 🏊

▽▽ ▽▽ Residence Inn by Marriott **H**

(970) 259-6200. **$130-$256.** 21691 Hwy 160 W 81301. On US 160, just w. Int corridors. **Pets:** Accepted. 📶 ✕ 🍴 🛎 💻 🏊 ✕

▽▽▽▽ The Rochester Hotel **BB** ✣

(970) 385-1920. **$129-$399, 14 day notice.** 726 E 2nd Ave 81301. Just e of Main Ave via 7th St, then just n. **Pets:** $20 daily fee/pet. Designated rooms, supervision. 📶 ✕ 🛎

▼▼▼ Siesta Motel **M**

(970) 247-0741. **$58-$145.** 3475 N Main Ave 81301. 2.6 mi n on US 550. Ext corridors. **Pets:** Small, dogs only. $25 daily fee/pet. Designated rooms, service with restrictions, supervision. 🛜 ✕ 🗋 💻 📶

AAA ▼▼▼ Strater Hotel **H** ❀

(970) 247-4431. **$99-$289.** 699 Main Ave 81301. Corner of 7th St and Main Ave; historic downtown. Int corridors. **Pets:** Small, dogs only. $50 deposit/pet. Designated rooms, service with restrictions, crate. ECO SAVE 🛜 ✕ 🍴

ESTES PARK

AAA ▼▼▼ Castle Mountain Lodge LLC **CA**

(970) 586-3664. **$75-$575, 30 day notice.** 1520 Fall River Rd 80517. 1 mi w on US 34. Ext corridors. **Pets:** Dogs only. $15 daily fee/pet. Designated rooms, service with restrictions, supervision.
SAVE 🛜 ✕ 🗋 💻 🐾 �K 📶

▼▼ Hotel Estes **M**

(970) 586-3382. **$69-$179, 3 day notice.** 1240 Big Thompson Ave 80517. 0.8 mi e of jct US 34 and 36. Ext corridors. **Pets:** Accepted. 🛜 ✕ 🗋 💻 🐾 ✕

▼▼ Mountain Shadows Resort **CA**

(970) 577-0397. **Call for rates.** 871 Riverside Dr 80517. Jct Elkhorn and Moraine aves, 1.4 mi sw to Lake Marys Rd, 0.3 mi s, then just e. Ext corridors. **Pets:** Accepted. 🛜 ✕ 🗋 💻 📶

▼▼ Murphy's River Lodge **H**

(970) 480-5081. **$99-$209.** 481 W Elkhorn Ave 80517. 0.4 mi w of jct Elkhorn and Moraine aves; west end of downtown. Ext corridors. **Pets:** $20 daily fee/pet. Designated rooms, service with restrictions, crate. 🛜 ✕ 🗋 💻 🐾 📶

AAA ▼▼▼ Rocky Mountain Park Inn **H** ❀

(970) 586-2332. **$80-$220.** 101 S Saint Vrain Ave 80517. 0.4 mi se on US 36 to SR 7, then just s. Int corridors. **Pets:** Other species. $15 daily fee/room. Designated rooms, service with restrictions, supervision. SAVE 🛜 ✕ 🗋 💻 🍴 🐾

▼▼▼ Silver Moon Inn **M**

(970) 586-6006. **$80-$300.** 175 Spruce Dr 80517. Just w of jct Elkhorn and Moraine aves; west end of downtown. Ext/int corridors.
Pets: Accepted. 🛜 ✕ 🗋 💻 🐾 ✕

EVERGREEN

▼▼▼ Comfort Suites at Evergreen Parkway **H** ❀

(303) 526-2000. **$109-$179.** 29300 US Hwy 40 80439. I-70 exit 252 (Evergreen Pkwy) westbound; exit 251 eastbound; on west side of El Rancho Restaurant. Int corridors. **Pets:** $10 daily fee/pet. Designated rooms, service with restrictions, supervision.
🛜 ✕ 🗋 💻 🐾 ✕

FIRESTONE

AAA ▼▼▼ Comfort Suites **H**

(720) 864-2970. **$99-$199.** 11292 Business Park Cir 80504. I-25 exit 240, just e on Firestone Blvd, just n on Frontage Rd, then just e. Int corridors. **Pets:** Accepted. SAVE 🛜 ✕ 🗋 💻 🐾

FORT COLLINS

AAA ▼▼◆ BEST WESTERN Kiva Inn **H** ❀

(970) 484-2444. **$80-$190.** 1638 E Mulberry St 80524. I-25 exit 269B, 1.5 mi w on SR 14. Ext/int corridors. **Pets:** Medium. $10 daily fee/pet. Designated rooms, service with restrictions, supervision.
SAVE 🛜 💻 ✕

AAA ▼▼▼ BEST WESTERN University Inn **M**

(970) 484-1984. **Call for rates.** 914 S College Ave 80524. I-25 exit 268, 4 mi w to College Ave, then just n on US 287. Ext/int corridors.
Pets: Other species. $15 daily fee/pet. Designated rooms, service with restrictions. SAVE 🛜 ✕ 🗋 💻 🐾

▼▼▼ Comfort Suites Fort Collins **H** ❀

(970) 206-4597. **$79-$199.** 1415 Oakridge Dr 80525. I-25 exit 265 (Harmony Rd), 3.3 mi w to McMurry Ave, just s, then w. Int corridors.
Pets: Medium. $15 daily fee/room. Service with restrictions, crate.
🛜 ✕ 🗋 💻 🐾

▼▼▼ Courtyard by Marriott **H**

(970) 282-1700. **$99-$159.** 1200 Oakridge Dr 80525. I-25 exit 265 (Harmony Rd), 3.3 mi w; entry via Lemay Ave. Int corridors. **Pets:** Other species. $50 one-time fee/room. Service with restrictions, crate.
ECO 🛜 ✕ 🗋 💻 🍴 🐾

▼▼▼ Fort Collins Marriott **H**

(970) 226-5200. **$139-$219.** 350 E Horsetooth Rd 80525. Jct College Ave and Horsetooth Rd, just e, then just n on John F Kennedy Pkwy. Int corridors. **Pets:** Other species. $30 daily fee/room. Designated rooms, service with restrictions, supervision.
ECO 🛜 ✕ 🗋 💻 🍴 🐾

▼▼▼ Hilton Ft Collins **H**

(970) 482-2626. **$99-$189.** 425 W Prospect Rd 80526. I-25 exit 268, 4.3 mi w. Int corridors. **Pets:** Accepted. 🛜 🗋 💻 🍴 🐾 ✕

▼▼▼ Holiday Inn Express & Suites **H**

(970) 225-2200. **Call for rates.** 1426 Oakridge Dr 80525. I-25 exit 265 (Harmony Rd), 3 mi w, just s on McMurry Ave, then just w. Int corridors.
Pets: Dogs only. $30 one-time fee/pet. Service with restrictions, supervision. 🛜 ✕ 🗋 💻

AAA ▼▼▼ Homewood Suites by Hilton Fort Collins **H**

(970) 225-2400. **$99-$159.** 1521 Oakridge Dr 80525. I-25 exit 265 (Harmony Rd), 3 mi w, just s on McMurry Ave, then just w. Int corridors.
Pets: Medium. $75 one-time fee/pet. Designated rooms, service with restrictions, supervision. SAVE 🛜 🗋 💻 ✕

▼▼▼ Residence Inn by Marriott Fort Collins **H** ❀

(970) 223-5700. **$129-$219.** 1127 Oakridge Dr 80525. I-25 exit 265 (Harmony Rd), 3.3 mi w to Lemay Ave, then s to Oakridge Dr. Int corridors.
Pets: $25 daily fee/room. Service with restrictions.
ECO 🛜 ✕ 🗋 💻 🐾 ✕

▼▼ Super 8 **H**

(970) 493-7701. **$55-$135.** 409 Centro Way 80524. I-25 exit 269B, just w. Int corridors. **Pets:** Large, other species. $10 daily fee/pet. Service with restrictions, supervision. 🛜 🗋 💻 ✕

FORT MORGAN

AAA ▼▼ Central Motel **M**

(970) 867-2401. **$52-$69.** 201 W Platte Ave 80701. I-76 exit 80, 0.6 mi s, then w on US 34. Ext corridors. **Pets:** $10 one-time fee/room. Service with restrictions. SAVE 🛜 🗋 💻

▼▼▼ Clarion Inn Fort Morgan **H**

(970) 867-8200. **$109-$119.** 14378 Hwy 34 80701. I-76 exit 75, 0.3 mi s. Int corridors. **Pets:** Small, other species. $15 daily fee/pet. Designated rooms, service with restrictions. 🛜 ✕ 🗋 💻 🍴 🐾

▼▼ Fort Morgan Super 8 **H**

(970) 867-9443. **$72-$74.** 1220 N Main St 80701. I-76 exit 80, just s, then just e. Int corridors. **Pets:** Accepted. 🛜 🗋 💻

▼▼ Rodeway Inn **M**

(970) 867-9481. **$65-$119.** 1409 Barlow Rd 80701. I-76 exit 82 (Barlow Rd), just n. Ext/int corridors. **Pets:** Accepted. 🛜 🗋 💻 🍴

FRISCO

AAA ▼▼▼ BEST WESTERN Lake Dillon Lodge **H**

(970) 668-5094. **Call for rates.** 1202 N Summit Blvd 80443. I-70 exit 203, just sw. Int corridors. **Pets:** $15 daily fee/room. Designated rooms, service with restrictions, supervision.
SAVE 🛜 ✕ 🗋 💻 🐾 ✕

▼▼▼▼ **Holiday Inn** 🅷
(970) 668-5000. **Call for rates.** 1129 N Summit Blvd 80443. I-70 exit
203, just s, then just e. Int corridors. **Pets:** Accepted.

▼▼ **Hotel Frisco** 🅷 🐾
(970) 668-5009. **$89-$319, 14 day notice.** 308 Main St 80443. I-70 exit
201, 0.7 mi e. Int corridors. **Pets:** Dogs only. $15 daily fee/pet. Service
with restrictions, crate.

Ⓐ ▼▼▼ **New Summit Inn** 🅷
(970) 668-3220. **$49-$159, 15 day notice.** 1205 N Summit Blvd 80443.
I-70 exit 203, just s to Dam Rd, then just e. Int corridors. **Pets:** Dogs
only. $10 daily fee/pet. Designated rooms, service with restrictions, super-
vision.

FRUITA

▼▼ **Balanced Rock Motel** Ⓜ
(970) 858-7333. **Call for rates.** 126 S Coulson St 81521. I-70 exit 19,
just n to Aspen Ave, then just w. Ext corridors. **Pets:** Accepted.

▼▼ **Comfort Inn** 🅷
(970) 858-1333. **$69-$139.** 400 Jurassic Ave 81521. I-70 exit 19, 0.3 mi
s; just e of Dinosaur Journey Museum. Int corridors. **Pets:** Other species.
Designated rooms, service with restrictions, supervision.

Ⓐ ▼▼▼ **La Quinta Inn & Suites Fruita** 🅷
(970) 858-8850. **$83-$210.** 570 Raptor Rd 81521. I-70 exit 19, 0.3 mi s.
Int corridors. **Pets:** Service with restrictions, supervision.

Ⓐ ▼▼▼ **Super 8** 🅷
(970) 858-0808. **$60-$119.** 399 Jurassic Ave 81521. I-70 exit 19, 0.3 mi
s; just e of Dinosaur Journey Museum. Int corridors. **Pets:** Large. $10
daily fee/pet. Designated rooms, service with restrictions, supervision.

GATEWAY

Ⓐ ▼▼▼▼ **Gateway Canyons Resort** 🅷 🐾
(970) 931-2458. **$249-$1699, 3 day notice.** 43200 Hwy 141 81522. On
SR 141, 43 mi w of US 50; 49 mi n of CR 90. Ext/int corridors.
Pets: Dogs only. $30 daily fee/pet. Designated rooms, service with restric-
tions, supervision.

GLENWOOD SPRINGS

Ⓐ ▼▼▼ **BEST WESTERN Antlers Motel** Ⓜ
(970) 945-8535. **$80-$180.** 171 W 6th St 81601. I-70 exit 116, just n,
then just w. Ext corridors. **Pets:** Small, dogs only. $35 one-time fee/pet.
Designated rooms, service with restrictions, supervision.

▼▼▼ **Caravan Inn** Ⓜ
(970) 945-7451. **$59-$159.** 1826 Grand Ave (SR 82) 81601. I-70 exit
116, 0.9 mi s. Ext corridors. **Pets:** $100 deposit/pet, $10 daily fee/pet.
Designated rooms, service with restrictions, crate.

Ⓐ ▼▼▼ **Hotel Colorado** 🅷 🐾
(970) 945-6511. **$99-$129.** 526 Pine St 81601. I-70 exit 116, just ne. Int
corridors. **Pets:** Medium, dogs only. $25 daily fee/pet. Service with restric-
tions, supervision.

▼▼▼▼ **The Hotel Denver** 🅷
(970) 945-6565. **$124-$339.** 402 7th St 81601. I-70 exit 116; across from
historic train station; in town center. Int corridors. **Pets:** Designated rooms,
service with restrictions, supervision.

▼▼▼ **Hotel Glenwood Springs** 🅷
(970) 928-8188. **$99-$235.** 52000 Two Rivers Plaza Rd 81601. I-70 exit
116, 0.3 mi w on US 6 and 24. Int corridors. **Pets:** Dogs only. $15 daily
fee/room. Designated rooms, service with restrictions.

▼▼▼ **Quality Inn & Suites** 🅷
(970) 945-5995. **$69-$179.** 2650 Gilstrap Ct 81601. I-70 exit 114, just s,
then just w. Int corridors. **Pets:** Other species. $25 deposit/room, $10
daily fee/room. Designated rooms, service with restrictions, supervision.

▼▼▼ **Residence Inn by Marriott** 🅷
(970) 928-0900. **$98-$159.** 125 Wulfsohn Rd 81601. I-70 exit 114, 2nd
exit at roundabout, 1.5 mi e on Midland Ave, then just s. Int corridors.
Pets: Accepted.

GRAND JUNCTION

Ⓐ ▼▼▼ **Americas Best Value Inn** Ⓜ
(970) 245-1410. **$62-$120.** 754 Horizon Dr 81506. I-70 exit 31, just n.
Ext corridors. **Pets:** Medium, other species. $10 daily fee/room. Service
with restrictions, supervision.

Ⓐ ▼▼▼ **BEST WESTERN Sandman Motel** Ⓜ
(970) 243-4150. **$63-$89.** 708 Horizon Dr 81506. I-70 exit 31, 0.3 mi s.
Ext corridors. **Pets:** $25 one-time fee/room. Designated rooms, service
with restrictions, supervision.

▼▼▼ **Candlewood Suites** 🅷
(970) 255-8093. **Call for rates.** 654 Market St 81506. I-70 exit 28 (24
Rd), 1.3 mi s to F Rd, just e, then just n. Int corridors. **Pets:** Accepted.

Ⓐ ▼▼▼ **Clarion Inn** 🅷
(970) 243-6790. **$79-$109.** 755 Horizon Dr 81506. I-70 exit 31, just n.
Ext/int corridors. **Pets:** Other species. Designated rooms, supervision.

Ⓐ ▼▼▼ **Econo Lodge** 🅷
(970) 257-1140. **Call for rates.** 751 Horizon Dr 81506. I-70 exit 31, just
n. Int corridors. **Pets:** Other species. Designated rooms, supervision.

▼▼▼ **Fairfield Inn & Suites by Marriott Grand
Junction** 🅷 🐾
(970) 242-2525. **$99-$219.** 225 Main St 81501. At 2nd and Main sts. Int
corridors. **Pets:** $25 daily fee/room. Designated rooms, service with
restrictions, crate.

▼▼▼ **La Quinta Inn & Suites Grand Junction** 🅷
(970) 241-2929. **$90-$184.** 2761 Crossroads Blvd 81506. I-70 exit 31,
0.3 mi n, then 0.3 mi w. Int corridors. **Pets:** Service with restrictions,
supervision.

Ⓐ ▼▼▼ **Quality Inn of Grand Junction** 🅷
(970) 245-7200. **$65-$99.** 733 Horizon Dr 81506. I-70 exit 31, just s. Int
corridors. **Pets:** $10 daily fee/room. Designated rooms, service with
restrictions, supervision.

▼▼▼ **Residence Inn by Marriott** 🅷 🐾
(970) 263-4004. **$90-$170.** 767 Horizon Dr 81506. I-70 exit 31, 0.3 mi n.
Int corridors. **Pets:** Large, other species. $25 one-time fee/room. Service
with restrictions, crate.

▼▼▼▼ **SpringHill Suites by Marriott - Downtown** 🅷
(970) 424-5777. **$110-$240.** 236 Main St 81501. 3rd and Main sts. Int
corridors. **Pets:** $25 daily fee/pet. Designated rooms, service with restric-
tions, crate.

GRAND LAKE

Ⓐ ▼▼▼ **Spirit Lake Lodge** Ⓜ
(970) 627-3344. **$55-$200, 7 day notice.** 829 Grand Ave 80447. 0.3 mi
e to Grand Ave, then 0.4 mi e. Ext corridors. **Pets:** Other species. $15
daily fee/pet. Designated rooms, no service, supervision.

GREELEY

Comfort Inn-Greeley 🏨 🐾

(970) 330-6380. **$104-$139.** 2467 W 29th St 80631. US 34 Bypass exit 23rd Ave, just sw. Int corridors. **Pets:** Other species. $15 daily fee/pet. Service with restrictions, crate.

Country Inn & Suites By Carlson 🏨 🐾

(970) 330-3404. **$95-$180, 3 day notice.** 2501 W 29th St 80631. US 34 Bypass exit 23rd Ave, just s, then w. Int corridors. **Pets:** Other species. $40 one-time fee/room. Service with restrictions, crate.

GUNNISON

Alpine Inn 🏨

(970) 641-2804. **$56-$180.** 1011 W Rio Grande Rd 81230. 0.5 mi w of center, then 0.5 mi s; at US 50 and Rio Grande Ave. Int corridors. **Pets:** Small, dogs only. $10 daily fee/pet. Designated rooms, service with restrictions, supervision.

Rodeway Inn 🅼

(970) 641-0500. **Call for rates.** 37760 W Hwy 50 81230. 0.5 mi w of center, then 2 mi sw. Ext corridors. **Pets:** Medium, dogs only. $10 daily fee/pet. Designated rooms, service with restrictions, supervision.

The Seasons Inn 🅼

(970) 641-0700. **$48-$95.** 412 E Tomichi Ave 81230. 0.3 mi e of center on US 50. Ext corridors. **Pets:** Accepted.

Super 8 🏨

(970) 641-3068. **$63-$119.** 411 E Tomichi Ave 81230. On US 50, 0.3 mi e of center. Int corridors. **Pets:** Accepted.

HOT SULPHUR SPRINGS

Canyon Motel 🅼

(970) 725-3395. **$59-$139.** 221 Byers Ave 80451. On US 40, center. Ext corridors. **Pets:** Other species. $10 one-time fee/room. Service with restrictions, supervision.

IGNACIO

Sky Ute Casino Resort 🏨

(970) 563-7777. **$100-$300.** 14324 Hwy 172 N 81137. Jct US 172 and CR 517. Int corridors. **Pets:** Accepted.

JULESBURG

Budget Host Platte Valley Inn 🏨

(970) 474-3336. **Call for rates.** 15225 Hwy 385 80737. I-76 exit 180, just n. Ext corridors. **Pets:** Accepted.

KEYSTONE

The Inn at Keystone 🏨 🐾

(970) 496-4825. **$119-$249, 21 day notice.** 23044 Hwy 6 80435. I-70 exit 205, 6.5 mi e. Int corridors. **Pets:** Dogs only. $25 daily fee/room. Designated rooms, service with restrictions.

KREMMLING

Allington Inn & Suites 🏨

(970) 724-9800. **$97-$117.** 215 W Central Ave 80459. 0.5 mi w of jct US 40 and SR 9, then just n. Int corridors. **Pets:** Other species. $10 daily fee/pet. Designated rooms, service with restrictions, supervision.

LA JUNTA

Holiday Inn Express 🏨

(719) 384-2900. **$99-$119.** 27994 US Hwy 50 Frontage Rd 81050. On US 50 Frontage Rd, 0.8 mi w. Int corridors. **Pets:** $20 daily fee/room. Designated rooms, service with restrictions, supervision.

Stagecoach Motel 🅼

(719) 384-5476. **$55-$70.** 905 W 3rd St 81050. Jct US 50 and 350. Ext corridors. **Pets:** Accepted.

LAKE GEORGE

M Lazy C Ranch & Mule Creek Outfitters 🆁🅰

(719) 748-3302. **Call for rates.** 801 CR 453 80827. 5 mi w on US 24, then 1 mi n on dirt road. Ext corridors. **Pets:** Accepted.

LAMAR

Blue Spruce Motel 🅼

(719) 336-7454. **$60-$90, 3 day notice.** 1801 S Main St 81052. 1.3 mi s on US 287 and 385. Ext corridors. **Pets:** Medium, other species. $25 daily fee/pet. Designated rooms, service with restrictions, crate.

Holiday Inn Express & Suites 🏨

(719) 931-4010. **Call for rates.** 1304 N Main St 81052. 0.8 mi n on US 50 and 287. Int corridors. **Pets:** Accepted.

LEADVILLE

Alps Motel 🅼

(719) 486-1223. **$60-$85, 5 day notice.** 207 Elm St 80461. Just s of center on US 24. Ext corridors. **Pets:** Other species. $18 daily fee/pet. Supervision.

LIMON

Safari Inn 🅼

(719) 775-2363. **$45-$130, 3 day notice.** 637 Main St 80828. I-70 exit 361, 0.8 mi w. Ext corridors. **Pets:** Other species. $10 daily fee/pet. Designated rooms, service with restrictions, supervision.

LONGMONT

BEST WESTERN PLUS Plaza Hotel 🏨 🐾

(303) 776-2000. **$100-$170.** 1900 Ken Pratt Blvd 80501. Jct US 287, 1.3 mi sw on Ken Pratt Blvd (SR 119). Int corridors. **Pets:** Other species. $50 deposit/room. Designated rooms, service with restrictions, crate.

Holiday Inn Express & Suites 🏨

(303) 684-0404. **$119-$169.** 1355 Dry Creek Dr 80503. Jct Main St and Ken Pratt Blvd (SR 119), 2.2 mi w, just n, then just ne. Int corridors. **Pets:** Other species. $30 one-time fee/room. Service with restrictions, supervision.

Residence Inn by Marriott Boulder/Longmont 🏨

(303) 702-9933. **$129-$225.** 1450 Dry Creek Dr 80503. Jct Main St and Ken Pratt Blvd (SR 119), 2.2 mi w, just n, then just ne; jct Hoover Rd and SR 119. Int corridors. **Pets:** Other species. $75 one-time fee/room. Service with restrictions, supervision.

Super 8 Twin Peaks, Longmont 🏨

(303) 772-8106. **$63-$109.** 2446 N Main St 80501. I-25 exit 243, 6.4 mi w on SR 66. Int corridors. **Pets:** Small. $10 daily fee/pet. Designated rooms, service with restrictions, supervision.

LOUISVILLE

BEST WESTERN PLUS Louisville Inn & Suites 🏨

(303) 327-1215. **Call for rates.** 960 W Dillon Rd 80027. US 36 (Boulder Tpke) exit Superior (SR 170), just n on McCaslin Blvd to Dillon Rd, then just e. Int corridors. **Pets:** Accepted.

◆◆◆◆ **Residence Inn by Marriott-Boulder/Louisville** H
(303) 665-2661. **$139-$199.** 845 Coal Creek Cir 80027. US 36 (Boulder Tpke) exit Superior (SR 170), n on McCaslin Blvd to Dillon Rd, then 0.6 mi e. Int corridors. **Pets:** Other species. $100 one-time fee/room. Service with restrictions.

LOVELAND

◆◆◆ ◆◆◆◆ **BEST WESTERN PLUS Crossroads Inn & Conference Center** H
(970) 667-7810. **$59-$179.** 5542 E US Hwy 34 80537. I-25 exit 257B, just w. Ext/int corridors. **Pets:** Medium, other species. $18 daily fee/room. Designated rooms, service with restrictions, supervision.
SAVE ◆◆◆◆◆◆◆◆

◆◆◆◆ **Candlewood Suites** H
(970) 667-5444. **Call for rates.** 6046 E Crossroads Blvd 80538. I-25 exit 259, just e. Int corridors. **Pets:** Accepted. ◆◆◆◆◆

◆◆◆◆ **Embassy Suites Loveland** H
(970) 593-6200. **$159-$209.** 4705 Clydesdale Pkwy 80538. I-25 exit 259, just e, then just n. Int corridors. **Pets:** $25 one-time fee/room. Designated rooms, service with restrictions, crate.
◆◆◆◆◆◆◆

◆◆◆◆ **La Quinta Inn & Suites Loveland** H
(970) 622-8600. **$84-$183.** 1450 Cascade Ave 80538. I-25 exit 257B, 7.3 mi w. Int corridors. **Pets:** Service with restrictions, supervision.
◆◆◆◆◆

◆◆◆◆ **Residence Inn by Marriott Loveland** H ◆
(970) 622-7000. **$109-$209.** 5450 McWhinney Blvd 80538. I-25 exit 257B, 0.5 mi w to outlet mall entry, just n, then just e. Int corridors. **Pets:** Other species. $75 one-time fee/room. Service with restrictions.
◆◆◆◆◆◆

MANCOS

◆◆◆ ◆◆◆ **Mesa Verde Motel** M ◆
(970) 533-7741. **$55-$108, 3 day notice.** 191 W Railroad Ave 81328. On US 160 at SR 184; 7 mi e of Mesa Verde National Park entrance. Ext corridors. **Pets:** Other species. $5 daily fee/pet. Designated rooms, service with restrictions. SAVE ◆◆◆◆

MESA VERDE NATIONAL PARK

◆◆◆ ◆◆◆ **Far View Lodge** M
(970) 529-4422. **$110-$153, 3 day notice.** 1 Navajo Hill, MM 15 81330. 14 mi from park gate. Ext corridors. **Pets:** Accepted.
SAVE ◆◆◆◆◆◆

MONTE VISTA

◆◆◆ ◆◆◆ **BEST WESTERN Movie Manor** H
(719) 852-5921. **$85-$160.** 2830 W Hwy 160 81144. 2 mi w of center on US 160. Ext corridors. **Pets:** Accepted. SAVE ◆◆◆◆

MONTROSE

◆◆◆ ◆◆◆ **BEST WESTERN Red Arrow** M ◆
(970) 249-9641. **$69-$139.** 1702 E Main St 81401. 1 mi e on US 50. Ext/int corridors. **Pets:** Other species. $10 daily fee/pet. Designated rooms, service with restrictions, supervision.
SAVE ◆◆◆◆◆

◆◆◆ **Days Inn** M
(970) 249-4507. **$55-$140.** 1417 E Main St 81401. 0.8 mi e on US 50. Ext corridors. **Pets:** Other species. $10 daily fee/pet. Designated rooms, service with restrictions, supervision. ◆◆◆◆

◆◆◆◆ **Hampton Inn** H
(970) 252-3300. **$119-$139.** 1980 N Townsend Ave 81401. 1.5 mi n on US 550. Int corridors. **Pets:** Accepted. ◆◆◆◆◆

◆◆ **Quality Inn & Suites** H
(970) 249-1011. **$70-$109.** 2751 Commercial Way 81401. 2 mi s on US 550, then just w on O'Delle Rd. Int corridors. **Pets:** Large. $10 daily fee/pet. Designated rooms, service with restrictions.
◆◆◆◆◆

◆◆ **Super 8** H
(970) 240-8200. **$55-$100.** 1705 E Main St 81401. 1 mi e on US 50. Int corridors. **Pets:** $5 daily fee/pet. Designated rooms, service with restrictions, supervision. ◆◆◆

◆ **Western Motel** M
(970) 249-3481. **$52-$165.** 1200 E Main St 81401. 0.8 mi e on US 50. Ext corridors. **Pets:** Small, dogs only. $25 deposit/pet, $5 one-time fee/pet. Designated rooms, supervision. ◆◆◆

NEDERLAND

◆◆◆ ◆◆◆ **BEST WESTERN Lodge at Nederland** H
(303) 258-9463. **$146-$166, 3 day notice.** 55 Lakeview Dr 80466. SR 119; across from Visitor's Center. Int corridors. **Pets:** Accepted.
SAVE ◆◆◆◆

NEW CASTLE

◆◆◆ ◆◆◆ **Econo Lodge Inn & Suites** H ◆
(970) 984-2363. **Call for rates.** 781 Burning Mountain Ave 81647. I-70 exit 105, just n, then w. Int corridors. **Pets:** Other species. $10 daily fee/pet. Service with restrictions, supervision. SAVE ◆◆◆◆

OURAY

◆◆ **Comfort Inn** M
(970) 325-7203. **$69-$149.** 191 5th Ave 81427. Just w of US 550 (Main St) via 5th Ave. Ext corridors. **Pets:** Dogs only. $15 daily fee/pet. Designated rooms, service with restrictions, supervision. ◆◆◆

◆ **Matterhorn Motel** M
(970) 325-4938. **Call for rates.** 201 6th Ave 81427. Just w of US 550 (Main St), at 6th Ave and 2nd St. Ext corridors. **Pets:** Accepted.
◆◆◆◆◆◆

◆◆◆ ◆◆◆ **Ouray Riverside Inn & Cabins** M
(970) 325-4061. **$62-$212, 3 day notice.** 1804 N Main St 81427. 1 mi n of center on US 550 (Main St). Ext corridors. **Pets:** $5 daily fee/pet. Designated rooms, service with restrictions, supervision.
SAVE ◆◆◆◆◆

◆◆◆ ◆◆◆ **Ouray Victorian Inn** M ◆
(970) 325-7222. **$77-$199.** 50 3rd Ave 81427. Just w of US 550 (Main St) to 3rd Ave. Ext corridors. **Pets:** Dogs only. $10 daily fee/pet. Designated rooms, service with restrictions, supervision.
SAVE ◆◆◆◆

◆◆◆ ◆◆◆ **River's Edge Motel** M
(970) 325-4621. **$64-$150.** 110 7th Ave 81427. Just w of US 550 (Main St) via 7th Ave. Ext corridors. **Pets:** Accepted. SAVE ◆◆◆◆

◆◆◆ ◆◆◆◆ **Twin Peaks Lodge & Hot Springs** M ◆
(970) 325-4427. **$111-$500.** 125 3rd Ave 81427. Just s on US 550 (Main St), then just w. Ext corridors. **Pets:** Medium, dogs only. $20 deposit/pet. Designated rooms, service with restrictions, supervision.
SAVE ◆◆◆◆◆◆

PAGOSA SPRINGS

◆ **Alpine Inn of Pagosa Springs** M
(970) 731-4005. **Call for rates.** 8 Solomon Dr 81147. 2.5 mi w of downtown to Piedra Rd, then just n. Ext/int corridors. **Pets:** Accepted.
◆◆◆◆

◆◆◆ **Fireside Inn Cabins** CA ◆
(970) 264-9204. **$105-$199, 30 day notice.** 1600 E Hwy 160 81147. On US 160, 1.3 mi e of downtown. Ext corridors. **Pets:** Dogs only. $10 one-time fee/pet. No service, crate. ◆◆◆◆◆

▼▼ ▼▼ High Country Lodge & Cabins M ✿
(970) 264-4181. **$89-$210.** 3821 E Hwy 160 81147. On US 160, 3 mi e; downtown. Ext corridors. **Pets:** Dogs only. $10 daily fee/pet. Service with restrictions, crate. 🛜 📶 🛏 💻 ⊠

▼▼ ▼▼ Pagosa Springs Inn & Suites H
(970) 731-3400. **$65-$189.** 519 Village Dr 81147. On US 160, 3.8 mi w of downtown. **Pets:** Medium. $10 daily fee/pet. Designated rooms, service with restrictions, supervision. 🛜 🛏 💻 🏊

PALISADE

▲▲▲ ▼▼▼▼ Wine Country Inn H
(970) 464-5777. **$105-$275.** 777 Grande River Dr 81526. I-70 exit 42, 0.3 mi w. Int corridors. **Pets:** Medium, dogs only. $50 deposit/room, $35 one-time fee/room. Designated rooms, service with restrictions, crate. 🆂🅰🆅🅴 🛜 ⊠ 🛢 🛏 💻 🍴 🏊

PARACHUTE

▼▼▼▼ Candlewood Suites H ✿
(970) 285-9880. **Call for rates.** 233 Grand Valley Way 81635. I-70 exit 75, just se. Int corridors. **Pets:** Other species. $25 one-time fee/room. Service with restrictions, crate. 🛜 ⊠ 🛏 💻 🏊

▼▼▼▼ Holiday Inn Express & Suites H
(970) 285-2330. **Call for rates.** 221 Grand Valley Way 81635. I-70 exit 25, just se. Int corridors. **Pets:** Small, other species. $25 one-time fee/room. Service with restrictions, crate. 🛜 🛏 💻 🏊 ⊠

PARKER

▼▼▼▼ Holiday Inn H
(303) 248-2147. **Call for rates.** 19308 Cottonwood Dr 80138. E470 toll road exit 5 (Parker Rd/SR 83) eastbound, straight at light, follow signs to Cottonwood Dr; exit westbound, just s to Crown Crest Blvd, follow signs to Cottonwood Dr. Int corridors. **Pets:** Accepted.
🛜 ⊠ 🛏 💻 🍴 🏊

PUEBLO

▲▲▲ ▼▼▼▼ BEST WESTERN Eagleridge Inn & Suites H ✿
(719) 543-4644. **$99-$119.** 4727 N Elizabeth St 81008. I-25 exit 102, just w, then just n. Int corridors. **Pets:** Large. $20 daily fee/room. Designated rooms, service with restrictions, supervision.
🆂🅰🆅🅴 🛜 ⊠ 🛏 💻 🏊 ⊠

▲▲▲ ▼▼▼▼ Courtyard by Marriott Pueblo H ✿
(719) 542-3200. **$99-$189.** 110 W 1st St 81003. I-25 exit 98B, just w. Int corridors. **Pets:** Other species. $75 one-time fee/room, $10 daily fee/room. Designated rooms, service with restrictions, supervision.
🆂🅰🆅🅴 🛜 ⊠ 🛏 💻 🍴 🏊 ⊠

▼▼▼▼ Holiday Inn Express & Suites H
(719) 542-8888. **$105-$160.** 4530 Dillon Dr 81008. I-25 exit 102, just e, then just s. Int corridors. **Pets:** $25 one-time fee/pet. Service with restrictions, supervision. 🛜 ⊠ 🛏 💻 🏊

▼▼ ▼▼ La Quinta Inn & Suites Pueblo H
(719) 542-3500. **$78-$159.** 4801 N Elizabeth St 81008. I-25 exit 102, just w, then 0.3 mi n. Int corridors. **Pets:** Service with restrictions, supervision.
🛜 🛏 💻 🏊 ⊠

▼▼ ▼▼ Microtel Inn & Suites by Wyndham Pueblo H
(719) 242-2020. **$55-$105.** 3343 Gateway Dr 81004. I-25 exit 94, just w, then just s. Int corridors. **Pets:** Accepted. 🛜 🛏 💻

RIDGWAY

▼▼ ▼▼ Ridgway Lodge & Suites H
(970) 626-5444. **$79-$104.** 373 Palomino Tr 81432. Just e of jct US 550 and SR 62, then just s. Int corridors. **Pets:** Large, dogs only. $15 daily fee/pet. Designated rooms, service with restrictions, supervision.
🛜 ⊠ 🛏 💻 🏊 ⊠

RIFLE

▼▼▼▼ Comfort Inn & Suites H
(970) 625-9912. **$79-$89.** 301 S 7th St 81650. I-70 exit 90, just s, then just w. Int corridors. **Pets:** Accepted. 🛜 ⊠ 🛏 💻 🏊 ⊠

▲▲▲ ▼▼▼▼ Hampton Inn & Suites H ✿
(970) 625-1500. **$89-$129.** 499 Airport Rd 81650. I-70 exit 90, just s, then just e. Int corridors. **Pets:** Service with restrictions, supervision.
🆂🅰🆅🅴 🛜 ⊠ 🛏 💻 🏊

▼▼▼▼ La Quinta Inn & Suites Rifle H
(970) 625-2676. **$83-$144.** 600 Wapiti Ct 81650. I-70 exit 90, just s, then just e. Int corridors. **Pets:** Service with restrictions, supervision.
🛜 ⊠ 🛏 💻 🏊

▲▲▲ ▼▼▼▼ Rusty Cannon Motel M
(970) 625-4004. **Call for rates.** 701 Taughenbaugh Blvd 81650. I-70 exit 90, just s of roundabout. Ext corridors. **Pets:** Dogs only. $10 one-time fee/pet. Service with restrictions, supervision. 🆂🅰🆅🅴 🛜 🛏 💻 🏊

SALIDA

▼▼▼▼ Chalets at Tudor Rose 🆅🅷 ✿
(719) 539-2002. **$185-$265, 30 day notice.** 6720 CR 104 81201. East end of US 50, just s on CR 104, then 0.5 mi up the hill. Ext corridors. **Pets:** Dogs only. $10 daily fee/pet. No service, crate.
🛜 ⊠ 🛢 🛏 💻 ⊠

▼▼▼▼ Hampton Inn & Suites H
(719) 539-0800. **Call for rates.** 785 E US 50 81201. On US 50, 0.6 mi e of G St. Int corridors. **Pets:** Dogs only. $30 one-time fee/pet. Service with restrictions. 🛜 ⊠ 🛏 💻 🏊

▲▲▲ ▼▼▼▼ Woodland Motel M ✿
(719) 539-4980. **$48-$136.** 903 W 1st St 81201. 0.5 mi nw on 1st St (SR 291); nw of historic downtown. Ext corridors. **Pets:** Other species.
🆂🅰🆅🅴 🛜 ⊠ 🛏 💻 🏊

SILVERTON

▲▲▲ ▼▼▼▼ Inn of the Rockies at the Historic Alma House 🅱🅱
(970) 387-5336. **$99-$149, 7 day notice.** 220 E 10th St 81433. Just se of 10th and Main sts. Int corridors. **Pets:** Medium, dogs only. $20 daily fee/pet. Service with restrictions, crate. 🆂🅰🆅🅴 🛜 ⊠ 🅰🅲 ☎

▼▼ ▼▼ Villa Dallavalle Bed & Breakfast 🅱🅱
(970) 387-5555. **$109-$125, 3 day notice.** 1257 Blair St 81433. Corner of 13th and Blair sts. Int corridors. **Pets:** Dogs only. $20 one-time fee/room. Designated rooms, supervision. 🛜 ⊠ 🅰🅲

▼▼▼▼ The Wyman Hotel & Inn 🅱🅱
(970) 387-5372. **$95-$240, 3 day notice.** 1371 Greene St 81433. Corner of 14th and Main sts. Int corridors. **Pets:** Accepted.
🛜 ⊠ 🛏 💻 🅰🅲

SNOWMASS VILLAGE

▼▼ ▼▼ Snowmass Mountain Chalet H
(970) 923-3900. **$79-$375, 45 day notice.** 115 Daly Ln 81615. 4 mi sw of SR 82 via Brush Creek and Lower Village rds; Lot 5. Ext/int corridors. **Pets:** Accepted. 🛜 ⊠ 🛢 🛏 💻 🏊 ⊠ 🅰🅲

SOUTH FORK

▼▼ ▼▼ Ute Bluff Lodge & Cabins M
(719) 873-5595. **Call for rates.** 27680 W Hwy 160 81154. 2.7 mi e of jct US 160 and SR 149. Ext corridors. **Pets:** $5 daily fee/pet. Designated rooms, service with restrictions, supervision. 🛜 🛏 💻 🅰🅲

STEAMBOAT SPRINGS

⌬ ▽▽ ▽▽ Fairfield Inn & Suites by Marriott ⊞
(970) 870-9000. **$85-$180.** 3200 S Lincoln Ave 80477. On US 40 (Lincoln Ave), 3.1 mi s of downtown; near Steamboat Ski Resort. Int corridors. **Pets:** $20 daily fee/pet. Designated rooms, service with restrictions, supervision. SAVE 🛜 ✕ 🖥 🛏 🍽 🛋

▽▽▽▽ Hampton Inn & Suites ⊞
(970) 871-8900. **$98-$179.** 725 S Lincoln Ave 80487. 1.1 mi e of center on US 40 (Lincoln Ave). Int corridors. **Pets:** Accepted.
🛜 🌆 🛏 🖥 🛋

▽▽▽▽ Holiday Inn Steamboat Springs ⊞ ❀
(970) 879-2250. **$109-$159, 3 day notice.** 3190 S Lincoln Ave 80487. On US 40, 3 mi s of downtown. Int corridors. **Pets:** Other species. $20 daily fee/room. Designated rooms, service with restrictions, supervision. 🛜 ✕ 🌆 🛏 🖥 🍽 🛋 🖾

▽▽ ▽▽ La Quinta Inn Steamboat Springs ⊞
(970) 871-1219. **$87-$221.** 3155 Ingles Ln 80487. On US 40 (Lincoln Ave), 3 mi s of downtown; near Steamboat Ski Resort. Int corridors. **Pets:** Service with restrictions, supervision. 🛜 ✕ 🛏 🖥 🛋

▽▽ ▽▽ Nordic Lodge ⓜ
(970) 879-0531. **Call for rates.** 1036 Lincoln Ave 80477. On US 40 (Lincoln Ave), just w of 10th St; downtown. Ext corridors. **Pets:** Accepted.
🛜 ✕ 🛏 🛋

▽▽ ▽▽ Rabbit Ears Motel ⓜ
(970) 879-1150. **$89-$189, 3 day notice.** 201 Lincoln Ave 80477. On US 40 (Lincoln Ave), just se of 3rd St; downtown. Ext corridors. **Pets:** $20 one-time fee/room. Service with restrictions, supervision.
🛜 ✕ 🛏 🛋

⌬ ▽▽▽▽ Sheraton Steamboat Resort ⊞
(970) 879-2220. **$149-$579, 30 day notice.** 2200 Village Inn Ct 80487. 2.3 mi s from center on US 40 (Lincoln Ave) to Mt. Werner Rd exit, 0.8 mi e, 0.3 mi ne on Mt. Werner Cir, just ne at Ski Time Sq, then just s. Int corridors. **Pets:** Accepted. SAVE 🛜 ✕ 🛏 🖥 🍽 🛋 🖾

▽▽▽▽ Steamboat Hotel ⊞
(970) 879-5230. **$59-$115.** 3195 S Lincoln Ave 80487. On US 40 (Lincoln Ave), 3 mi s of downtown. Int corridors. **Pets:** Accepted.
🛜 ✕ 🛏 🖥 🛋

STERLING

⌬ ▽▽▽▽ BEST WESTERN Sundowner ⓜ ❀
(970) 522-6265. **$89-$189.** 125 Overland Trail St 80751. I-76 exit 125, just w. Ext/int corridors. **Pets:** $20 daily fee/room. Designated rooms, service with restrictions, supervision. SAVE 🛜 ✕ 🛏 🖥 🛋

STRATTON

▽▽ ▽▽ Rodeway Inn Golden Prairie ⊞
(719) 348-5311. **$89-$120.** 700 Colorado Ave 80836. I-70 exit 419, just n. Ext corridors. **Pets:** Accepted. 🛜 🛏 🖥 🛋

TELLURIDE

▽▽▽▽ ▽▽▽▽ Fairmont Heritage Place, Franz Klammer Lodge ⓒⓞ ❀
(970) 728-3318. **$250-$2200, 45 day notice.** 567 Mountain Village Blvd 81435. 2.3 mi e; in Mountain Village. Int corridors. **Pets:** Dogs only. $20 daily fee/room. Designated rooms, service with restrictions.
ⒺⒸⓄ 🛜 ✕ 🛏 🖥 🛋 🖾 🖾

⌬ ▽▽▽▽ Hotel Columbia ⊞ ❀
(970) 728-0660. **$175-$1625, 30 day notice.** 301 W San Juan Ave 81435. At Aspen St and San Juan Ave; opposite gondola. Int corridors. **Pets:** Dogs only. $25 daily fee/pet. Designated rooms, service with restrictions. SAVE 🛜 ✕ 🖥 🍽

▽▽▽▽ ▽▽▽▽ Hotel Madeline Telluride ⊞ ❀
(970) 369-0880. **$150-$395, 30 day notice.** 568 Mountain Village Blvd 81435. 2.2 mi e; in Mountain Village. Int corridors. **Pets:** Dogs only. $25 daily fee/pet. Designated rooms, service with restrictions, supervision.
SAVE 🛜 ✕ 🛏 🖥 🍽 🛋 🖾

▽▽▽▽ The Hotel Telluride ⊞ ❀
(970) 369-1188. **$179-$279, 30 day notice.** 199 N Cornet St 81435. Just s of roundabout, then just e. Int corridors. **Pets:** Other species. $50 one-time fee/room. Service with restrictions, supervision.
🛜 ✕ 🌆 🛏 🖥 🍽 🖾

▽▽▽▽ Ice House Lodge & Condominiums ⊞
(970) 728-6300. **Call for rates.** 310 S Fir St 81435. Just s of SR 145 (Colorado Ave); end of Fir St. Int corridors. **Pets:** Other species. $20 daily fee/pet. Service with restrictions. 🛜 ✕ 🛏 🖥 🛋 🖾 🖾

▽▽▽▽ The Peaks, A Grand Heritage Resort & Spa ⊞
(970) 728-6800. **$119-$399, 30 day notice.** 136 Country Club Dr 81435. 2.5 mi e; in Mountain Village. Int corridors. **Pets:** Large, dogs only. $75 one-time fee/room. Designated rooms, service with restrictions.
🛜 ✕ 🛏 🖥 🍽 🛋 🖾 🖾

TRINIDAD

⌬ ▽▽▽▽ BEST WESTERN Trinidad Inn ⓜ
(719) 846-2215. **$60-$120.** 900 W Adams St 81082. I-25 exit 13A northbound; exit 13B southbound, just e to Santa Fe Trail, then 0.3 mi s. Ext corridors. **Pets:** Large. $10 daily fee/pet. Designated rooms, service with restrictions, supervision. SAVE 🛜 🛏 🖥 🛋

▽▽▽▽ Holiday Inn Hotel & Suites ⊞
(719) 845-8400. **$89-$119.** 3130 Santa Fe Trail Dr 81082. I-25 exit 11 (Starkville), just e, then 1.2 mi n. Int corridors. **Pets:** Medium, other species. $20 one-time fee/pet. Designated rooms, service with restrictions, supervision. 🛜 ✕ 🌆 🛏 🖥 🍽 🛋

▽▽▽▽ La Quinta Inn & Suites Trinidad ⊞
(719) 845-0102. **$83-$177.** 2833 Toupal Dr 81082. I-25 exit 11 (Starkville), just w, then n. Int corridors. **Pets:** Service with restrictions, supervision. 🛜 🛏 🖥 🍽 🛋 🖾

▽▽▽▽ Super 8 ⊞
(719) 846-8280. **$55-$96.** 1924 Freedom Rd 81082. I-25 exit 15 (Kit Carson Trail), just e, then n. Int corridors. **Pets:** Accepted. 🛜 🛏 🖥

VAIL

⌬ ▽▽▽▽ ▽▽▽▽ The Arrabelle at Vail Square, A RockResort ⊞
(970) 754-7777. **Call for rates.** 675 Lionshead Pl 81657. I-70 exit 176, just s to roundabout, 1 mi w on Frontage Rd to W Lionshead Cir, continue just s past no outlet sign. Int corridors. **Pets:** Accepted.
SAVE 🛜 ✕ 🛏 🖥 🛋 🖾

▽▽▽▽ Evergreen Lodge at Vail ⊞
(970) 476-7810. **$99-$570, 30 day notice.** 250 S Frontage Rd W 81657. I-70 exit 176, just s, then just w. Int corridors. **Pets:** Other species. $25 daily fee/room. Designated rooms, service with restrictions, crate. 🛜 ✕ 🛏 🖥 🍽 🛋 🖾 🖾

▽▽▽▽ Four Seasons Resort Vail ⊞
(970) 477-8600. **Call for rates.** One Vail Rd 81657. I-70 exit 176, just s, then just w of roundabout. Int corridors. **Pets:** Accepted.
🛜 ✕ 🛏 🖥 🍽 🛋 🖾

▽▽▽▽ Holiday Inn Apex Vail ⊞
(970) 476-2739. **Call for rates.** 2211 N Frontage Rd 81657. I-70 exit 173, just n to roundabout, then 0.3 mi e. Int corridors. **Pets:** Medium, dogs only. $25 daily fee/room. Designated rooms, service with restrictions, supervision. 🛜 ✕ 🛏 🖥 🍽 🛋 🖾

▼▼▼▼ The Lodge at Vail, A RockResort & Spa ⬛
(970) 754-7800. **Call for rates.** 174 E Gore Creek Dr 81657. I-70 exit 176, 0.3 mi s on Vail Rd to Gore Creek Dr. Ext/int corridors.
Pets: Accepted. 🛜 ⊗ 🛏 💻 🍴 🏊 ⊗

🏅 ▼▼▼▼ The Sebastian Vail ⬛
(970) 477-8000. **$239-$5850, 31 day notice.** 16 Vail Rd 81657. I-70 exit 176, just s, take 2nd exit at roundabout, then just s. Int corridors.
Pets: Accepted. 🅂🅰🆅🅴 🛜 ⊗ 🅼 🛏 💻 🍴 🏊 ⊗

🏅 ▼▼▼▼ Sonnenalp Resort of Vail ⬛
(970) 476-5656. **$175-$3100, 30 day notice.** 20 Vail Rd 81657. I-70 exit 176, just s, take 2nd exit at the roundabout, then just s. Int corridors.
Pets: Medium, dogs only. $100 one-time fee/room. Designated rooms, supervision. 🅴🅲🅾 🅂🅰🆅🅴 🛜 🍴 🏊 ⊗

🏅 ▼▼▼▼ Vail Cascade Resort & Spa ⬛
(970) 476-7111. **$99-$659, 3 day notice.** 1300 Westhaven Dr 81657. I-70 exit 176, 1.3 mi w via S Frontage Rd; 1 mi e of exit 173. Int corridors. **Pets:** Accepted. 🅂🅰🆅🅴 🛜 ⊗ 🅼 🛏 💻 🍴 🏊 ⊗

WALSENBURG

🏅 ▼▼ BEST WESTERN Rambler Ⓜ
(719) 738-1121. **$80-$96, 3 day notice.** 457 US Hwy 85-87 81089. I-25 exit 52, just w. Ext/int corridors. **Pets:** Medium. $10 daily fee/pet. Designated rooms, service with restrictions, supervision.

🅂🅰🆅🅴 🛜 ⊗ 🛏 💻 🏊

WINTER PARK

🏅 ▼▼ BEST WESTERN Alpenglo Lodge ⬛ ❀
(970) 726-8088. **$82-$167.** 78665 US Hwy 40 80482. On US 40, 0.3 mi n of center. Int corridors. **Pets:** Other species. $10 daily fee/pet. Designated rooms, service with restrictions, supervision.

🅂🅰🆅🅴 🛜 ⊗ 🅼 🛏 💻 ⊗

WOODLAND PARK

▼▼▼ Bristlecone Lodge 🅲🅰
(719) 687-9518. **$89-$140, 14 day notice.** 510 N Hwy 67 80863. 0.5 mi n. Ext corridors. **Pets:** Accepted. 🛜 ⊗ 🛏 💻 🅺 🐾

▼▼ Woodland Country Lodge ⬛ ❀
(719) 687-6277. **$85-$145.** 723 US Hwy 24 W 80863. US 24, just w of jct SR 67. Int corridors. **Pets:** $10 daily fee/pet. Designated rooms, service with restrictions, supervision. 🛜 ⊗ 🅼 🛏 💻 🏊

YAMPA

▼▼ Oak Tree Inn Ⓜ
(970) 638-1000. **Call for rates.** 98 Moffat Ave 80483. 0.3 mi w of SR 131. Int corridors. **Pets:** Accepted. 🛜 ⊗ 🛏 💻 🍴

CONNECTICUT

CITY INDEX

BETHEL

▼▼ Microtel Inn & Suites by Wyndham Bethel ⬛
(203) 748-8318. **$74-$84.** 80 Benedict Rd 06801. I-84 exit 8, 1 mi e on US 6. Int corridors. **Pets:** $100 deposit/pet, $11 daily fee/pet. Supervision.

🛜 🅼 🛏 💻

BRANFORD

▼▼ Baymont Inn & Suites New Haven/Branford ⬛
(203) 488-4991. **$80-$180.** 3 Business Park Dr 06405. I-95 exit 56, just n. Int corridors. **Pets:** Medium. $50 deposit/room, $20 daily fee/pet. Service with restrictions, supervision. 🛜 🛏 💻 🏊

BRIDGEPORT

▼▼▼ Bridgeport Holiday Inn & Convention Center ⬛
(203) 334-1234. **$119-$159.** 1070 Main St 06604. SR 8 exit 2 northbound, 0.7 mi se; exit southbound, just s, then just e. Int corridors.
Pets: Accepted. 🛜 🅼 🛏 💻 🍴 🏊

BROOKFIELD

▼▼ Newbury Inn Ⓜ
(203) 775-0220. **$79-$119, 3 day notice.** 1030 Federal Rd 06804. Jct SR 25, 0.9 mi nw. Ext/int corridors. **Pets:** $100 deposit/pet, $11 daily fee/pet. Supervision. 🛜 🛏 💻

DANBURY

▼▼▼ Ethan Allen Hotel ⬛ ❀
(203) 744-1776. **Call for rates.** 21 Lake Ave Ext 06811. I-84 exit 4, 0.3 mi w on US 6 and 202. Int corridors. **Pets:** Small. $250 deposit/room, $25 daily fee/pet. Designated rooms, service with restrictions, supervision.

🛜 ⊗ 🛏 💻 🍴 🏊

▼▼▼ Holiday Inn ⬛
(203) 792-4000. **Call for rates.** 80 Newtown Rd 06810. I-84 exit 8 (Newtown Rd), 0.5 mi s on US 6 W. Int corridors. **Pets:** Accepted.
🛜 🛏 💻 🍴 🏊

🏅 ▼▼▼ La Quinta Inn & Suites ⬛
(203) 798-1200. **$107-$177.** 116 Newtown Rd 06810. I-84 exit 8 (Newtown Rd), just sw. Int corridors. **Pets:** Service with restrictions, supervision. 🅂🅰🆅🅴 🛜 🛏 💻 🍴 🏊

▼▼ Maron Hotel & Suites ⬛
(203) 791-2200. **$99-$199.** 42 Lake Ave Ext 06811. I-84 exit 4, 0.5 mi w on US 6 and 202. Int corridors. **Pets:** Medium. $25 daily fee/pet. Designated rooms, service with restrictions, supervision.

🛜 🅼 🛏 💻 🍴

▼▼▼ Residence Inn by Marriott Danbury ⬛ ❀
(203) 797-1256. **$109-$199.** 22 Segar St 06810. I-84 exit 4 eastbound, just n; exit westbound, just e on Lake Ave Ext, then just s. Int corridors.
Pets: Other species. $75 one-time fee/room. Designated rooms, service with restrictions. 🅴🅲🅾 🛜 ⊗ 🛏 💻 🏊

DAYVILLE

▼▼▼▼ Comfort Inn & Suites **H**
(860) 779-3200. **$134-$147.** 16 Tracy Rd 06241. I-395 exit 94, just w. Int corridors. **Pets:** Medium. $15 daily fee/pet. Designated rooms, service with restrictions, supervision. 🛜 ⓜ 🔌 💻 🛟

FAIRFIELD

🅐🅐🅐 ▼▼▼▼ BEST WESTERN PLUS Black Rock Inn **H** ❧
(203) 659-2200. **$99-$189.** 100 Kings Hwy Cutoff 06824. I-95 exit 24, just sw. Int corridors. **Pets:** Large, dogs only. $20 one-time fee/pet. Designated rooms, service with restrictions, supervision.
SAVE 🛜 ✖ ⓜ 🔌 💻

GREENWICH

▼▼▼▼ The Stanton House Inn **BB**
(203) 869-2110. **$159-$239, 7 day notice.** 76 Maple Ave 06830. Just n of US 1; center. Ext/int corridors. **Pets:** Accepted. 🛜 ✖ 🔌 🛟

HAMDEN

▼▼▼ Clarion Hotel & Suites Hamden-New Haven **M** ❧
(203) 288-3831. **$119-$229.** 2260 Whitney Ave 06518. Just n off SR 15 exit 61. Int corridors. **Pets:** Small. $50 deposit/room. Service with restrictions, supervision. 🛜 ✖ ⓜ 🔌 💻 🛟

HARTFORD METROPOLITAN AREA

AVON

▼▼▼▼ Avon Old Farms Hotel **H** ❧
(860) 677-1651. **$109-$259.** 279 Avon Mountain Rd 06001. Jct US 44 and SR 10. Ext/int corridors. **Pets:** Other species. $20 daily fee/room. Designated rooms, service with restrictions. 🛜 🔌 💻 🍴 🛟

▼▼▼▼ Residence Inn by Marriott Hartford-Avon **H**
(860) 678-1666. **$152-$233.** 55 Simsbury Rd (SR 202 & SR 10) 06001. Jct US 44, just n. Int corridors. **Pets:** Accepted.
🛜 ✖ ⓜ 🔌 💻 🛟 ✖

CROMWELL

▼▼▼ Super 8 **H**
(860) 632-8888. **$65-$160.** 1 Industrial Park Rd 06416. I-91 exit 21, just w on SR 372. Int corridors. **Pets:** Other species. $10 daily fee/pet. Designated rooms, service with restrictions, supervision.
ECO 🛜 ⓜ 🔌 💻

EAST HARTFORD

▼▼▼▼ The Hartford Plaza Hotel **H**
(860) 528-9703. **$90-$126.** 100 E River Dr 06108. I-84 exit 53 eastbound, just s; exit 54 westbound to exit 3 (Darlin St), just n. Int corridors. **Pets:** Accepted. 🛜 ✖ ⓜ 🔌 💻 🍴 🛟

ENFIELD

▼▼▼▼ Holiday Inn Hotel Enfield-Springfield **H**
(860) 741-2211. **Call for rates.** 1 Bright Meadow Blvd 06082. I-91 exit 49, just e on service road. Int corridors. **Pets:** Accepted.
🛜 ⓜ 🔌 💻 🍴 🛟 ✖

🅐🅐🅐 ▼ Red Roof Inn # 7105 **M**
(860) 741-2571. **$44-$112.** 5 Hazard Ave 06082. I-91 exit 47E. Ext corridors. **Pets:** Large, other species. Service with restrictions, supervision.
SAVE 🛜 ⓜ 🔌 💻

FARMINGTON

▼▼ Centennial Inn Hotel & Apartments **H**
(860) 677-4647. **Call for rates.** 5 Spring Ln 06032. US 6, 0.3 mi e of jct SR 177. Ext/int corridors. **Pets:** Accepted. 🛜 ⓜ 🔌 💻 🛟

▼▼ Extended Stay Deluxe Hartford-Farmington **H**
(860) 676-2790. **$105-$139.** 1 Batterson Park Rd 06032. I-84 exit 37, just ne. Int corridors. **Pets:** $25 daily fee/pet. Designated rooms, service with restrictions. 🛜 ⓜ 🔌 💻

▼▼▼▼ The Farmington Inn **H** ❧
(860) 269-3401. **$109-$179.** 827 Farmington Ave 06032. I-84 exit 39, 1.8 mi w on SR 4. Int corridors. **Pets:** Large, other species. $100 deposit/room, $20 daily fee/room. Designated rooms, service with restrictions, crate. 🛜 🔌 💻

▼▼▼▼ Homewood Suites by Hilton Hartford-Farmington **H**
(860) 321-0000. **$139-$169.** 2 Farm Glen Blvd 06032. I-84 exit 39, 0.6 mi e on SR 4. Int corridors. **Pets:** Accepted. 🛜 ⓜ 🔌 💻 🛟

GLASTONBURY

🅐🅐🅐 ▼▼▼▼ Homewood Suites by Hilton Hartford South/Glastonbury **H**
(860) 652-8111. **$129-$229.** 65 Glastonbury Blvd 06033. SR 3 exit Main St, just se. Int corridors. **Pets:** Accepted. SAVE 🛜 ⓜ 🔌 💻 🛟

HARTFORD

▼▼▼▼ The Hilton Hartford Hotel **H**
(860) 728-5151. **$139-$309.** 315 Trumbull St 06103. Downtown. Int corridors. **Pets:** Accepted. ECO 🛜 ⓜ 🔌 💻 🍴 🛟 ✖

▼▼▼▼ Holiday Inn Express Downtown Hartford **H**
(860) 246-9900. **Call for rates.** 440 Asylum St 06103. I-84 exit 48, just se to Spring St. Int corridors. **Pets:** Accepted. 🛜 🔌 💻

▼▼▼▼ Holiday Inn Express Hotel & Suites Hartford **H**
(860) 525-1000. **$99-$149.** 185 Brainard Rd 06114. I-91 exit 27, just e, then just s. Int corridors. **Pets:** Accepted. 🛜 🔌 💻 🛟

▼▼▼▼ Homewood Suites by Hilton Hartford Downtown **H**
(860) 524-0223. **$169-$299.** 338 Asylum St 06103. Between Ann and High sts; downtown. Int corridors. **Pets:** Accepted. 🛜 ⓜ 🔌 💻

▼▼▼▼ Ramada Plaza Hartford Downtown **H**
(860) 549-2400. **$129-$315.** 50 Morgan St 06120. I-91 exit 32B; I-84 exit 50 eastbound; exit 52 westbound. Int corridors. **Pets:** Accepted.
🛜 ⓜ 🔌 💻 🍴 🛟

▼▼▼▼ Residence Inn by Marriott Downtown Hartford **H**
(860) 524-5550. **$149-$299.** 942 Main St 06103. I-91 exit 29A northbound; exit 31 southbound. Int corridors. **Pets:** Medium. $100 one-time fee/pet. ECO 🛜 ✖ 🔌 💻

MANCHESTER

▼▼▼ Extended StayAmerica Hartford-Manchester **H**
(860) 643-5140. **$85-$119.** 340 Tolland Tpke 06040. I-84 exit 63, 0.3 mi se on SR 30, then just sw. Int corridors. **Pets:** $25 daily fee/pet. Designated rooms, service with restrictions. 🛜 ⓜ 🔌 💻

🅐🅐🅐 ▼▼▼▼ Residence Inn by Marriott Hartford/Manchester **H** ❧
(860) 432-4242. **$139-$229.** 201 Hale Rd 06042. I-84 exit 63, 0.5 mi nw, then 0.6 mi sw. Int corridors. **Pets:** Other species. $75 one-time fee/room. Designated rooms, service with restrictions, crate.
SAVE 🛜 ✖ ⓜ 🔌 💻 🛟 ✖

NEW BRITAIN

▼▼▼ La Quinta Inn & Suites New Britain/Hartford South **H**

(860) 348-1463. **$63-$133.** 65 Columbus Blvd 06051. SR 9 exit 26 northbound; exit 27 southbound, just nw. Int corridors. **Pets:** Service with restrictions, supervision.

ROCKY HILL

▼▼▼ Residence Inn by Marriott Hartford-Rocky Hill **H** 🐾

(860) 257-7500. **$123-$238.** 680 Cromwell Ave 06067. I-91 exit 23, 0.4 mi w on West St, then just n. Int corridors. **Pets:** Medium. $100 one-time fee/room. Service with restrictions.

SIMSBURY

▼▼▼ Simsbury Inn **H** 🐾

(860) 651-5700. **$169-$229.** 397 Hopmeadow St 06070. On US 202/SR 10, 0.4 mi n of jct SR 185. Int corridors. **Pets:** Medium. $20 daily fee/room. Service with restrictions, supervision.

SOUTHINGTON

▼▼▼ Residence Inn by Marriott Southington **H**

(860) 621-4440. **$149-$179.** 778 West St 06489. I-84 exit 31, just s. Int corridors. **Pets:** $100 one-time fee/room. Designated rooms, service with restrictions, crate.

WINDSOR

🔷 ▼▼▼ Hyatt house Hartford North/Windsor **H** 🐾

(860) 298-8000. **$99-$199.** 200 Corporate Dr 06095. I-91 exit 38 northbound; exit 38B southbound. Int corridors. **Pets:** Medium. $150 one-time fee/pet. Service with restrictions, crate.

▼▼▼ Residence Inn by Marriott Hartford-Windsor **H**

(860) 688-7474. **$122-$143.** 100 Dunfey Ln 06095. I-91 exit 37, just w on SR 305 to Dunfey Ln, then 0.3 mi n. Ext corridors. **Pets:** Accepted.

WINDSOR LOCKS

▼▼▼ Candlewood Suites **H**

(860) 623-2000. **$99-$149.** 149 Ella T Grasso Tpke 06096. I-91 exit 40, 2.5 mi w on SR 20, then 0.6 mi w on SR 75. Int corridors. **Pets:** Medium. $75 one-time fee/pet. Service with restrictions, crate.

▼▼ La Quinta Inn Hartford Bradley Airport **H**

(860) 623-3336. **$78-$144.** 64 Ella T Grasso Tpke 06096. I-91 exit 40, 2.5 mi w on SR 20, then just n on SR 75. Int corridors. **Pets:** Service with restrictions, supervision.

▼▼ Ramada Inn Bradley International Airport **H**

(860) 623-9494. **$89.** 5 Ella T Grasso Tpke 06096. I-91 exit 40, 2.5 mi w on SR 20, then just n on SR 75. Int corridors. **Pets:** Accepted.

🔷 ▼▼▼ Sheraton Hartford Hotel At Bradley Airport **H**

(860) 627-5311. **$99-$299.** 1 Bradley International Airport 06096. Jct SR 75, 0.6 mi w on Schoephoester Rd, 0.5 mi nw on Terminal Rd. Int corridors. **Pets:** Accepted.

END METROPOLITAN AREA

IVORYTON

▼▼▼ The Copper Beech Inn **CI**

(860) 767-0330. **$209-$400, 14 day notice.** 46 Main St 06442. SR 9 exit 3, 1.7 mi w. Int corridors. **Pets:** Medium, dogs only. $85 one-time fee/room. Designated rooms, service with restrictions, supervision.

LAKEVILLE

▼▼▼ Interlaken Inn Resort and Conference Center **H** 🐾

(860) 435-9878. **$199-$299, 7 day notice.** 74 Interlaken Rd 06039. On SR 112, 0.5 mi w of jct SR 41. Ext/int corridors. **Pets:** Dogs only. $25 daily fee/room. Designated rooms, service with restrictions, supervision.

LEDYARD

▼▼▼ Almost In Mystic/Mares Inn **BB**

(860) 572-7556. **$125-$225, 14 day notice.** 333 Colonel Ledyard Hwy 06339. I-95 exit 89, 1 mi ne to Gold Star Hwy, 0.6 mi w, then 0.7 mi n. Int corridors. **Pets:** Other species. $100 deposit/pet. Designated rooms, no service.

MASHANTUCKET

▼▼▼ Two Trees Inn at Foxwoods Resort Casino **H**

(860) 312-3000. **Call for rates.** 240 Indiantown Rd 06339. Jct SR 214 and 2. Int corridors. **Pets:** Accepted.

MERIDEN

▼▼ Extended StayAmerica Hartford-Meriden **H**

(203) 630-1927. **$85-$119.** 366 Bee St 06450. I-91 exit 17 northbound, just e on E Main St, then 0.7 mi n; exit 19 southbound, 0.5 mi w on Baldwin Ave, then 0.6 mi s. Int corridors. **Pets:** $25 daily fee/pet. Designated rooms, service with restrictions.

🔷 ▼▼▼ Four Points by Sheraton Meriden **H**

(203) 238-2380. **$80-$180.** 275 Research Pkwy 06450. I-91 exit 17 southbound; exit 16 northbound, 0.5 mi e, then 0.5 mi s. Int corridors. **Pets:** Accepted.

MILFORD

🔷 ▼▼▼ The Red Roof Inn Milford #197 **M**

(203) 877-6060. **$61-$120.** 10 Rowe Ave 06460. I-95 exit 35, just nw. Ext corridors. **Pets:** Large, other species. Service with restrictions, supervision.

▼▼▼ Residence Inn by Marriott Milford **H**

(203) 283-2100. **$139-$189.** 62 Rowe Ave 06460. I-95 exit 35, just nw. Int corridors. **Pets:** Medium. $100 one-time fee/room. Service with restrictions, crate.

MORRIS

🔷 ▼▼▼▼ Winvian **H** 🐾

(860) 567-9600. **$549-$2300, 60 day notice.** 155 Alain White Rd 06763. Jct SR 109, 1 mi n. Ext/int corridors. **Pets:** Dogs only. $75 one-time fee/pet. Designated rooms, service with restrictions, crate.

MYSTIC

◆◆◆◆ Comfort Inn Mystic 🄷
(860) 572-8531. **$79-$209.** 48 Whitehall Ave 06355. I-95 exit 90, just n on SR 27. Int corridors. **Pets:** Accepted.

◆◆◆◆ Hampton Inn & Suites/Mystic 🄷
(860) 536-2536. **$99-$279.** 6 Hendel Dr 06355. I-95 exit 90. Int corridors. **Pets:** Other species. Service with restrictions.

◆◆◆◆ Inn at Mystic 🄼
(860) 536-9604. **$115-$275.** 3 Williams Ave 06355. On US 1 at SR 27. Ext/int corridors. **Pets:** Other species. $25 deposit/room, $25 daily fee/pet. Designated rooms, service with restrictions, supervision.

◆◆◆◆ Residence Inn by Marriott 🄷
(860) 536-5150. **$129-$389.** 40 Whitehall Ave 06355. I-95 exit 90, just n on SR 27. Int corridors. **Pets:** Other species. $100 one-time fee/room. Designated rooms, service with restrictions, crate.

NAUGATUCK

◆◆◆◆ Comfort Inn Naugatuck 🄷
(203) 723-9356. **$95-$119.** 716 New Haven Rd 06770. Jct SR 63 and 8, 0.8 mi s. Int corridors. **Pets:** $50 daily fee/pet. Designated rooms, service with restrictions, supervision.

NEW HAVEN

◆◆◆◆ Omni New Haven Hotel at Yale 🄷
(203) 772-6664. **$129-$499.** 155 Temple St 06510. Between Chapel and Crown sts; downtown. Int corridors. **Pets:** Small, dogs only. $50 one-time fee/room. Designated rooms, service with restrictions, crate.

◆◆◆◆ Premiere Hotel & Suites 🄷
(203) 777-5337. **$149-$239.** 3 Long Wharf Dr 06511. I-95 exit 46, 0.6 mi nw. Ext corridors. **Pets:** $75 one-time fee/room.

NEW LONDON

◆◆◆◆ Clarion Inn New London 🄷
(860) 442-0631. **Call for rates.** 269 N Frontage Rd 06320. I-95 exit 82A northbound, 0.8 mi n, just w on Colman St, then 0.6 mi s; exit 83 southbound, 0.6 mi s. Int corridors. **Pets:** Large, dogs only. $10 daily fee/pet. Designated rooms, service with restrictions, supervision.

◆◆◆◆ Red Roof Inn #7145 🄼
(860) 444-0001. **$59-$120.** 707 Colman St 06320. I-95 exit 82A northbound, 0.4 mi n, then just n; exit 83 southbound, 0.6 mi s. Ext corridors. **Pets:** Large, other species. Service with restrictions, supervision.

NEW MILFORD

◆◆◆ The Homestead Inn 🄱🄱
(860) 354-4080. **$105-$250.** 5 Elm St 06776. Jct US 202, just w. Ext/int corridors. **Pets:** Other species. $10 daily fee/room. Designated rooms, service with restrictions, supervision.

NIANTIC

◆ Motel 6 - #1063 🄼
(860) 739-6991. **$45-$65.** 269 Flanders Rd 06357. I-95 exit 74, just s. Ext corridors. **Pets:** Other species. Service with restrictions, supervision.

NORTH STONINGTON

◆◆◆◆ The Inn at Lower Farm B & B 🄱🄱
(860) 535-9075. **$105-$185, 7 day notice.** 119 Mystic Rd 06359. I-95 exit 90, 1.5 mi n on SR 27, 1.4 mi e on SR 184, then 3.4 mi n on SR 201. Int corridors. **Pets:** Medium, dogs only. $10 daily fee/pet. Designated rooms, service with restrictions, supervision.

NORWALK

◆◆◆ Extended Stay America - Norwalk 🄷
(203) 847-6888. **$120-$199.** 400 Main Ave 06851. I-95 exit 15, 3.5 mi n on US 7, just e, then 1 mi s. Int corridors. **Pets:** $25 daily fee/pet. Designated rooms, service with restrictions.

◆◆◆◆ Four Points by Sheraton Norwalk 🄷
(203) 849-9828. **$89-$219.** 426 Main Ave 06851. I-95 exit 15, 3.5 mi n on US 7, just e, then 0.7 mi s. Int corridors. **Pets:** Accepted.

OLD GREENWICH

◆◆◆◆◆ Hyatt Regency Greenwich 🄷 ❀
(203) 637-1234. **$105-$299.** 1800 E Putnam Ave 06870. I-95 exit 5, 0.5 mi n on US 1. Int corridors. **Pets:** Medium, dogs only. $50 daily fee/pet. Designated rooms, service with restrictions, supervision.

OLD SAYBROOK

◆ Days Inn Old Saybrook 🄼
(860) 388-3453. **$59-$169.** 1430 Boston Post Rd 06475. I-95 exit 66, 0.3 mi s on SR 166, then 0.5 mi e on US 1 N. Ext corridors. **Pets:** Accepted.

◆ Liberty Inn 🄼
(860) 388-1777. **$58-$130.** 55 Spring Brook Rd 06475. I-95 exit 68 southbound; exit 67 northbound, 0.9 mi n on US 1, then w. Ext corridors. **Pets:** Medium, dogs only. $15 daily fee/pet. Crate.

◆◆◆◆ Saybrook Point Inn & Spa 🄷
(860) 395-2000. **$229-$899, 3 day notice.** 2 Bridge St 06475. On SR 154, 2.2 mi s of jct US 1; at Saybrook Point. Int corridors. **Pets:** Accepted.

PAWCATUCK

◆◆◆◆ La Quinta Inn & Suites 🄷
(860) 599-2400. **$95-$309.** 349 Liberty St 06379. I-95 exit 92, 1 mi s on SR 2. Int corridors. **Pets:** Service with restrictions, supervision.

PLAINFIELD

◆◆ Quality Inn 🄷
(860) 564-4021. **Call for rates.** 55 Lathrop Rd 06374. I-395 exit 87, just se. Int corridors. **Pets:** $10 deposit/pet. Designated rooms, service with restrictions.

RIVERTON

◆◆◆ Old Riverton Inn 🄲
(860) 379-8678. **$99-$225, 10 day notice.** 436 E River Rd (SR 20) 06065. Center. Int corridors. **Pets:** Accepted.

SHELTON

◆◆ Extended Stay America - Shelton - Fairfield County 🄷
(203) 926-6868. **$105-$199.** 945 Bridgeport Ave 06484. SR 8 exit 11, 0.5 mi w. Int corridors. **Pets:** $25 daily fee/pet. Designated rooms, service with restrictions.

◆◆◆ Hampton Inn Shelton 🄷
(203) 925-5900. **$139-$159.** 695 Bridgeport Ave 06484. SR 8 exit 12, 0.3 mi w, then just s. Int corridors. **Pets:** Accepted.

◆◆◆ Residence Inn by Marriott Shelton Fairfield County 🄷
(203) 926-9000. **$129-$179.** 1001 Bridgeport Ave 06484. SR 8 exit 11, 0.3 mi w. Ext corridors. **Pets:** Other species. $100 one-time fee/room. Service with restrictions, crate.

SOUTHBURY

 Cornucopia at Oldfield Bed and Breakfast BB
(203) 267-6772. **$160-$275, 14 day notice.** 782 Main St N 06488. I-84 exit 15, 1.5 mi n. Int corridors. **Pets:** Small, dogs only. $25 daily fee/pet. Supervision. ECO 🛜 ✕ 🔄 Ⓩ

🔷🔷🔷 **Crowne Plaza Southbury** H
(203) 598-7600. **$99-$229.** 1284 Strongtown Rd 06488. I-84 exit 16, just n on SR 188. Int corridors. **Pets:** Other species. $25 one-time fee/room. Designated rooms, service with restrictions, crate.
🛜 ᴦM 🔌 🖥 🍴 🔄 ✕

🔷🔷🔷 **Heritage Hotel** H
(203) 264-8200. **$99-$199.** 522 Heritage Rd 06488. I-84 exit 15, 0.4 mi n on SR 67, then 1 mi w. Int corridors. **Pets:** Accepted.
🛜 ✕ ᴦM 🔌 🖥 🍴 🔄 ✕

SOUTHPORT

🔷🔷🔷🔷 **Delamar Southport** H 🐾
(203) 259-2800. **$355.** 275 Old Post Rd 06890. I-95 exit 19, just e. Int corridors. **Pets:** Small, dogs only. $50 daily fee/pet. Service with restrictions, supervision. 🛜 ✕ 🖥 🍴 ✕

STAMFORD

 Amsterdam Hotel - Greenwich/Stamford H
(203) 327-4300. **$90-$120.** 19 Clarks Hill Ave 06902. I-95 exit 8 northbound, just n on Atlantic St, 0.6 mi ne on Tresser Blvd, then just s; exit southbound, just nw on Elm St, ne on Main St, then just s. Int corridors. **Pets:** $30 deposit/pet, $30 daily fee/pet. Designated rooms, service with restrictions, supervision. SAVE 🛜 ᴦM 🔌 🖥

🔷🔷🔷 **Hilton Stamford Hotel & Executive Meeting Center** H
(203) 967-2222. **$119-$269.** 1 First Stamford Pl 06902. I-95 exit 7 northbound, just s on Greenwich Ave, then just w; exit 6 southbound, just s on West Ave, 0.3 mi w on Baxter Ave, just n on Fairfield Ave, then just e. Int corridors. **Pets:** Accepted. SAVE 🛜 ✕ 🔌 🖥 🍴 🔄 ✕

🔷🔷 **La Quinta Inn & Suites Stamford-NYC Area** H
(203) 357-7100. **$83-$177.** 135 Harvard Ave 06902. I-95 exit 6 northbound, just s; exit southbound, just w on Grenhart Rd, then just s. Int corridors. **Pets:** Service with restrictions, supervision.
🛜 ᴦM 🔌 🖥 🍴 🔄

🔷🔷🔷 **Sheraton Stamford Hotel** H 🐾
(203) 358-8400. **$109-$329.** 700 E Main St 06901. I-95 exit 8 southbound, just n on Atlantic St; exit northbound, just n on Atlantic St, 0.3 mi e on Tresser Blvd, then just n on Elm St; downtown. Int corridors. **Pets:** Other species. Designated rooms, service with restrictions, crate.
SAVE 🛜 ✕ 🔌 🖥 🍴 🔄

🔷 🔷🔷🔷 **Stamford Marriott Hotel & Spa** H
(203) 357-9555. **$119-$289.** 243 Tresser Blvd 06901. I-95 exit 8, just n under viaduct, then n. Int corridors. **Pets:** $49 deposit/pet. Designated rooms, service with restrictions, supervision.
SAVE 🛜 ✕ ᴦM 🔌 🖥 🍴 🔄 ✕

STONINGTON

🔷 🔷🔷🔷 **Another Second Penny Inn** BB
(860) 535-1710. **$129-$199, 7 day notice.** 870 Pequot Tr 06378. I-95 exit 91, 0.8 mi s on SR 234. Int corridors. **Pets:** $25 one-time fee/pet. Designated rooms, service with restrictions, crate. SAVE 🛜 ✕ 🔌

STRATFORD

🔷🔷🔷 **Homewood Suites by Hilton** H
(203) 377-3322. **$179-$209.** 6905 Main St 06614. SR 15 exit 53, just n. Int corridors. **Pets:** Medium, other species. $15 daily fee/room. Service with restrictions, crate. 🛜 ᴦM 🔌 🖥 🔄

WALLINGFORD

🔷🔷🔷 **Homewood Suites by Hilton New Haven/Wallingford** H
(203) 284-2600. **$129-$199.** 90 Miles Dr 06492. I-91 exit 15, nw on SR 68, then just s. Int corridors. **Pets:** Accepted.
🛜 ᴦM 🔌 🖥 🔄 ✕

WATERFORD

🔷 **Rodeway Inn at Crossroad** M
(860) 442-7227. **Call for rates.** 211 Parkway N 06385. I-95 exit 81 northbound, just nw; exit southbound, 0.6 mi w. Ext corridors. **Pets:** Other species. $25 daily fee/pet. Service with restrictions. 🛜 🔌 🔄

WESTPORT

🔷 🔷🔷🔷 **The Westport Inn, an Ascend Collection hotel** H 🐾
(203) 259-5236. **Call for rates.** 1595 Post Rd E 06880. I-95 exit 18 northbound, n to US 1, then 1.5 mi e; exit 19 southbound, 1 mi w. Ext/int corridors. **Pets:** Medium, other species. $50 one-time fee/pet. Designated rooms, service with restrictions, crate.
SAVE 🛜 ✕ 🔌 🖥 🍴 🔄

WOODSTOCK

🔷🔷🔷 **Inn at Woodstock Hill** CI
(860) 928-0528. **$135-$250, 3 day notice.** 94 Plaine Hill Rd 06281. 0.8 mi n on SR 169. Int corridors. **Pets:** $25 daily fee/room. Designated rooms, service with restrictions, supervision.
ECO 🛜 ✕ 🔌 🖥 🍴

DELAWARE

BEAR

△△△ ▽▽ BEST WESTERN PLUS of Newark/Christiana Inn **H**

(302) 326-2500. **$110-$160.** 875 Pulaski Hwy 19701. I-95 exit 4, 3.3 mi se on SR 1 exit 160, then just e on US 40. Int corridors. **Pets:** Small, dogs only. $15 daily fee/pet. Designated rooms, service with restrictions, crate. 🛡️ 📶 ✕ ᴍ 🛏️ 💻 🏊

DEWEY BEACH

▽ Bellbuoy Motel **M**

(302) 227-6000. **$49-$375, 3 day notice.** 21 Van Dyke St 19971. SR 1; on ocean side. Ext corridors. **Pets:** Accepted. 📶 ✕ 🛏️ 🅿️

DOVER

△△△ ▽▽ Days Inn Dover **M**

(302) 674-8002. **$62-$650.** 272 N DuPont Hwy 19901. SR 1 exit 104, 2.8 mi s on US 13. Ext corridors. **Pets:** Medium, dogs only. $25 daily fee/room. Service with restrictions, crate. 🛡️ 📶 🛏️ 💻

▽▽▽ Hampton Inn-Dover **H**

(302) 736-3500. **$79-$300.** 1568 N DuPont Hwy 19901. SR 1 exit 104, 1 mi s. Int corridors. **Pets:** Accepted. 📶 ᴍ 🛏️ 💻 🏊

▽▽▽ Holiday Inn Express Hotel & Suites Dover **H** ✿

(302) 678-0600. **Call for rates.** 1780 N DuPont Hwy 19901. SR 1 exit 104, just s on US 13. Int corridors. **Pets:** Large, other species. $20 daily fee/pet. Service with restrictions, crate. 📶 ᴍ 🛏️ 💻 🏊

▽▽▽ MainStay Suites Dover **H**

(302) 678-8383. **Call for rates.** 201 Stover Blvd 19901. SR 1 exit 95 northbound, just n on Bay Rd; exit 95 southbound, 1.5 mi n on Bay Rd; 0.7 mi s of jct US 13. Int corridors. **Pets:** Accepted. 🅴🅲🅾 📶 ᴍ 🛏️ 💻 🏊

▽▽▽ Residence Inn by Marriott-Dover **H**

(302) 677-0777. **$125-$169.** 600 Jefferic Blvd 19901. SR 1 exit 104, 2.7 mi s on US 13. Int corridors. **Pets:** Accepted. 📶 ✕ ᴍ 🛏️ 💻 🏊 ✕

△△△ ▽▽▽ Sheraton Dover Hotel **H**

(302) 678-8500. **$99-$229.** 1570 N DuPont Hwy 19901. SR 1 exit 104, 1 mi s on US 13. Int corridors. **Pets:** Accepted. 🛡️ 📶 ✕ 🛏️ 💻 🍴 🏊

▽▽ Sleep Inn & Suites Dover **H** ✿

(302) 735-7770. **Call for rates.** 1784 N DuPont Hwy 19901. SR 1 exit 104, just s on US 13. Int corridors. **Pets:** Other species. $20 deposit/pet, $20 daily fee/pet. Service with restrictions, crate. 📶 ✕ ᴍ 🛏️ 💻

GEORGETOWN

▽▽ Comfort Inn & Suites-Georgetown **H**

(302) 854-9400. **Call for rates.** 20530 DuPont Blvd 19947. On US 113, 0.5 mi n of jct SR 404. Int corridors. **Pets:** Other species. $30 daily fee/pet. Designated rooms, service with restrictions, supervision. 📶 🛏️ 💻 🏊

HARRINGTON

▽▽ AmericInn Lodge & Suites of Harrington **H**

(302) 398-3900. **$89-$199.** 1259 Corn Crib Rd 19952. On US 13, 0.6 mi s of jct SR 14. Int corridors. **Pets:** Accepted. 📶 ✕ ᴍ 🛏️ 💻 🏊

LEWES

△△△ ▽▽▽ The Inn at Canal Square **H**

(302) 644-3377. **$105-$310, 7 day notice.** 122 Market St 19958. On the canal. Int corridors. **Pets:** Medium, other species. Designated rooms, service with restrictions, supervision. 🛡️ 📶 ✕ 🛏️ 💻 ✕

▽▽ Sleep Inn & Suites **H**

(302) 645-6464. **Call for rates.** 18451 Coastal Hwy 19958. On SR 1, 1.5 mi s. Int corridors. **Pets:** Accepted. 📶 🛏️ 💻 🏊

MILLSBORO

▽▽ Atlantic Inn-Millsboro **M**

(302) 934-6711. **$89-$179.** 28534 DuPont Blvd 19966. US 113, just s of SR 24. Ext corridors. **Pets:** Dogs only. $25 daily fee/pet. Designated rooms, service with restrictions. 📶 🛏️ 🏊

NEWARK

△△△ ▽▽▽ Courtyard by Marriott-Newark at the University of Delaware **H** ✿

(302) 737-0900. **$149-$359.** 400 David Hollowell Dr 19716. I-95 exit 1B southbound; exit 1 northbound, 3 mi on SR 896. Int corridors. **Pets:** Medium. $75 one-time fee/room. Designated rooms, service with restrictions, supervision. 🅴🅲🅾 🛡️ 📶 ✕ ᴍ 🛏️ 💻 🏊

▽▽▽ Hilton Wilmington/Christiana **H** ✿

(302) 454-1500. **$109-$329.** 100 Continental Dr 19713. I-95 exit 4B; 0.3 mi n on SR 7 exit 166, then 0.4 mi w on SR 58 (Churchmans Rd). Int corridors. **Pets:** $49 one-time fee/room. Designated rooms, service with restrictions, crate. 🅴🅲🅾 📶 🛏️ 💻 🍴 🏊

▽▽▽ Homestead Studio Suites Hotel-Newark/Christiana **H**

(302) 283-0800. **$94-$174.** 333 Continental Dr 19713. I-95 exit 4B; 0.3 mi n on SR 7 exit 166, then 0.4 mi w on SR 58 (Churchmans Rd). Int corridors. **Pets:** $25 daily fee/pet. Designated rooms, service with restrictions. 📶 ᴍ 🛏️ 💻

▽▽▽ Homewood Suites by Hilton Newark/Wilmington South **H**

(302) 453-9700. **$109-$179.** 640 S College Ave 19713. I-95 exit 1B southbound; exit 1 northbound, 0.8 mi n on SR 896. Int corridors. **Pets:** Accepted. 📶 ᴍ 🛏️ 💻 🏊

△△△ ▽▽ Ramada Newark/Wilmington **H**

(302) 738-3400. **$74-$199.** 260 Chapman Rd 19702. I-95 exit 3 southbound; exit 3A northbound, 0.3 mi e on SR 273 E, then just s. Int corridors. **Pets:** Small, other species. $25 deposit/pet, $25 daily fee/pet. Service with restrictions, supervision. 🛡️ 📶 🛏️ 💻 🍴 🏊

△△△ ▽▽ Red Roof Inn-Wilmington **M**

(302) 292-2870. **$59-$130.** 415 Stanton Christiana Rd 19713. I-95 exit 4B, 0.5 mi n on SR 7. Ext corridors. **Pets:** Large, other species. Service with restrictions, supervision. 🛡️ 📶 ✕ ᴍ 🛏️

▽▽▽ Residence Inn by Marriott Wilmington/Newark **H**

(302) 453-9200. **$129-$249.** 240 Chapman Rd 19702. I-95 exit 3 southbound; exit 3A northbound, 0.3 mi e on SR 273 E, then 0.5 mi s. Ext corridors. **Pets:** Accepted. 📶 ✕ 🛏️ 💻 🏊 ✕

▽▽▽ Staybridge Suites-Newark/Wilmington **H**

(302) 366-8097. **$119-$149.** 270 Chapman Rd 19702. I-95 exit 3 southbound; exit 3A northbound, 0.3 mi e on SR 273 E, then just s. Int corridors. **Pets:** Accepted. 📶 ✕ ᴍ 🛏️ 💻 🏊

▼▼ TownePlace Suites by
Marriott-Wilmington/Christiana/Newark 🄷
(302) 369-6212. **$129-$269.** 410 Eagle Run Rd 19702. I-95 exit 3 south-bound; exit 3A northbound, just e. Int corridors. **Pets:** Accepted.

🛜 ✕ ♿ 🛏 💻 🌊

NEW CASTLE
▼▼▼ Clarion Hotel-The Belle 🄷
(302) 428-1000. **Call for rates.** 1612 N DuPont Hwy 19720. Jct I-295, just n on SR 13. Int corridors. **Pets:** Medium, other species. $10 daily fee/room. Designated rooms, service with restrictions, supervision.

🌱 🛜 ♿ 🛏 💻 🍴 🌊

🅰🅰🅰 ▼▼▼▼ Sheraton Wilmington South New Castle 🄷
(302) 328-6200. **$99-$199.** 365 Airport Rd 19720. I-95 exit 5A (SR 141 S). Int corridors. **Pets:** Accepted.

SAVE 🛜 ✕ ♿ 🛏 💻 🍴 🌊

REHOBOTH BEACH
▼▼ AmericInn Lodge & Suites of Rehoboth Beach 🄷
(302) 226-0700. **$99-$299.** 36012 Airport Rd 19971. Just w of SR 1; just w on Miller Rd, then just s. Int corridors. **Pets:** Accepted.

🛜 ✕ ♿ 🛏 💻 🌊

▼▼ The Breakers Hotel & Suites 🄼
(302) 227-6688. **Call for rates.** 105 2nd St 19971. Just n of Rehoboth Ave. Ext corridors. **Pets:** Accepted. 🛜 ✕ 🛏 💻 🌊

▼▼ Sea-Esta IV 🄼
(302) 227-5882. **$38-$249, 3 day notice.** 20902 Coastal Hwy 19971. 1 mi s of jct SR 24. Ext corridors. **Pets:** Accepted.

🛜 ✕ 🛏 💻 🌊

SEAFORD
▼▼▼ Comfort Suites 🄷
(302) 628-5400. **Call for rates.** 23420 Sussex Hwy 19973. On US 13, just n of jct SR 20. Int corridors. **Pets:** Small, other species. $25 daily fee/pet. Designated rooms, service with restrictions.

🛜 ✕ ♿ 🛏 💻 🌊

WILMINGTON
🅰🅰🅰 ▼▼ BEST WESTERN PLUS Brandywine Valley Inn 🄷
(302) 656-9436. **Call for rates.** 1807 Concord Pike 19803. I-95 exit 8, 1 mi n on US 202. Ext corridors. **Pets:** Medium, other species. $25 one-time fee/room. Designated rooms, service with restrictions, supervision.

SAVE 🛜 🛏 💻 🌊

🅰🅰🅰 ▼▼▼▼ Hotel du Pont 🄷
(302) 594-3100. **$229-$899.** 1007 Market St 19801. I-95 exit 7, 0.5 mi se; at 11th St; downtown. Int corridors. **Pets:** Small, dogs only. $150 one-time fee/pet. Service with restrictions, crate.

SAVE 🛜 ✕ 🛏 💻 🍴 ✕

🅰🅰🅰 ▼▼▼▼ Sheraton Suites Wilmington 🄷 🐾
(302) 654-8300. **$119-$349.** 422 Delaware Ave 19801. I-95 exit 7 north-bound; exit 7A southbound, 0.3 mi e; downtown. Int corridors. **Pets:** Medium, dogs only. Designated rooms, service with restrictions, crate. SAVE 🛜 ✕ ♿ 🛏 💻 🍴 🌊

DISTRICT OF COLUMBIA

WASHINGTON, D.C. METROPOLITAN AREA

WASHINGTON, D.C.
▼▼▼ Avenue Suites 🄷
(202) 333-8060. **Call for rates.** 2500 Pennsylvania Ave NW 20037. Jct 25th St NW and Pennsylvania Ave. Int corridors. **Pets:** Accepted.

🛜 ✕ 🛏 💻

🅰🅰🅰 ▼▼▼ Capitol Hill Hotel 🄷 🐾
(202) 543-6000. **$129-$799.** 200 C St SE 20003. 2 blks from Capitol grounds; at 2nd and C sts SE. Int corridors. **Pets:** Small, other species. Designated rooms, service with restrictions, crate.

SAVE 🛜 ✕ 🛏 💻

▼▼▼ DoubleTree Suites by Hilton Hotel Washington DC 🄷
(202) 785-2000. **Call for rates.** 801 New Hampshire Ave NW 20037. Just sw at Washington Circle. Int corridors. **Pets:** Accepted.

🛜 ♿ 🛏 💻 🌊

🅰🅰🅰 ▼▼▼ The Dupont Circle Hotel 🄷
(202) 483-6000. **$169-$609.** 1500 New Hampshire Ave NW 20036. At Dupont Circle, Connecticut and Massachusetts aves NW. Int corridors. **Pets:** Accepted. SAVE 🛜 ✕ 💻 🍴

🅰🅰🅰 ▼▼▼ ▼▼▼ Fairmont Washington, D.C., Georgetown 🄷
(202) 429-2400. **$189-$950.** 2401 M St NW 20037. 24th and M sts NW. Int corridors. **Pets:** Accepted.

🌱 SAVE 🛜 ♿ 🛏 💻 🍴 🌊 ✕

🅰🅰🅰 ▼▼▼ Four Points by Sheraton Washington DC Downtown 🄷
(202) 289-7600. **$109-$519.** 1201 K St NW 20005. 12th and K sts NW. Int corridors. **Pets:** Other species. $125 deposit/room, $25 daily fee/room. Designated rooms, service with restrictions, crate.

🌱 SAVE 🛜 ✕ 🛏 💻 🍴 🌊

🅰🅰🅰 ▼▼▼▼▼ Four Seasons Hotel Washington, D.C. 🄷 🐾
(202) 342-0444. **$495-$2500, 30 day notice.** 2800 Pennsylvania Ave NW 20007. In Georgetown. Int corridors. **Pets:** Very small, other species. Service with restrictions, supervision.

SAVE 🛜 ♿ 🛏 💻 🌊 ✕

🅰🅰🅰 ▼▼▼ Hamilton Crowne Plaza Hotel Washington DC 🄷
(202) 682-0111. **$129-$379.** 1001 14th St NW 20005. 14th and K sts NW. Int corridors. **Pets:** Accepted. SAVE 🛜 ✕ ♿ 🛏 💻 🍴

🅰🅰🅰 ▼▼▼ The Hay-Adams 🄷
(202) 638-6600. **$399-$1050.** 800 16th St NW 20006. 16th and H sts NW; just n of the White House. Int corridors. **Pets:** Accepted.

🌱 SAVE 🛜 🛏 🍴

🅰🅰🅰 ▼▼▼ Hotel George-A Kimpton Hotel 🄷
(202) 347-4200. **$169-$499.** 15 E St NW 20001. On Capitol Hill, just n of Capitol grounds. Int corridors. **Pets:** Accepted.

🌱 SAVE 🛜 ✕ ♿ 🛏 💻 🍴

Hotel Helix-A Kimpton Hotel 🅷
(202) 462-9001. **$129-$409.** 1430 Rhode Island Ave NW 20005. Just e of Scott Circle. Int corridors. **Pets:** Accepted.

Hotel Madera-A Kimpton Hotel 🅷
(202) 296-7600. **$149-$449.** 1310 New Hampshire Ave NW 20036. Between 20th and N sts NW. Int corridors. **Pets:** Accepted.

Hotel Monaco Washington DC-A Kimpton Hotel 🅷 🐾
(202) 628-7177. **$189-$499.** 700 F St NW 20004. Between 7th and 8th sts NW. Int corridors. **Pets:** Dogs only. Service with restrictions, supervision.

Hotel Palomar Washington, DC-A Kimpton Hotel 🅷 🐾
(202) 448-1800. **$159-$399.** 2121 P St NW 20037. Between 21st and 22nd sts NW; just w of Dupont Circle. Int corridors. **Pets:** Other species. Service with restrictions, crate.

Hotel Rouge-A Kimpton Hotel 🅷 🐾
(202) 232-8000. **$139-$429.** 1315 16th St NW 20036. Just n of Scott Circle. Int corridors. **Pets:** Other species. Designated rooms.

L'Enfant Plaza Hotel 🅷 🐾
(202) 484-1000. **$99-$579.** 480 L'Enfant Plaza SW 20024. I-395 exit L'Enfant Plaza/12th St. Int corridors. **Pets:** Medium. $25 daily fee/pet. Designated rooms, service with restrictions, supervision.

The Liaison Capitol Hill, An Affinia Hotel 🅷
(202) 638-1616. **$139-$459.** 415 New Jersey Ave NW 20001. On Capitol Hill, just n of Capitol grounds. Int corridors. **Pets:** Accepted.

The Madison 🅷
(202) 862-1600. **$152-$489.** 1177 15th St NW 20005. 15th and M sts NW. Int corridors. **Pets:** Accepted.

Mandarin Oriental, Washington D.C. 🅷
(202) 554-8588. **$235-$695.** 1330 Maryland Ave SW 20024. Jct Independence Ave SW, just s on 12th St SW. Int corridors. **Pets:** Accepted.

The Mayflower Renaissance Hotel 🅷 🐾
(202) 347-3000. **$99-$479.** 1127 Connecticut Ave NW 20036. Just n of K St NW; in business district. Int corridors. **Pets:** Large, other species. $100 one-time fee/room. Service with restrictions, crate.

The Melrose Hotel, Washington DC 🅷
(202) 955-6400. **$129-$589.** 2430 Pennsylvania Ave NW 20037. Between 24th and 25th sts NW. Int corridors. **Pets:** Accepted.

The Normandy Hotel 🅷
(202) 483-1350. **$89-$429.** 2118 Wyoming Ave NW 20008. Just w of Connecticut Ave. Int corridors. **Pets:** Accepted.

Omni Shoreham Hotel 🅷
(202) 234-0700. **$149-$599.** 2500 Calvert St NW 20008. Just w of Connecticut Ave. Int corridors. **Pets:** Accepted.

Park Hyatt Washington D. C. 🅷 🐾
(202) 789-1234. **$179-$845, 3 day notice.** 1201 24th St NW 20037. 24th and M sts NW. Int corridors. **Pets:** $150 one-time fee/room. Service with restrictions, supervision.

The Quincy 🅷
(202) 223-4320. **$99-$539.** 1823 L St NW 20036. Between 18th and 19th sts NW. Int corridors. **Pets:** Accepted.

Residence Inn by Marriott Capitol 🅷
(202) 484-8280. **$141-$509.** 333 E St SW 20024. Between 3rd and 4th sts SW. Int corridors. **Pets:** Accepted.

Residence Inn by Marriott-Dupont Circle 🅷
(202) 466-6800. **$139-$389.** 2120 P St NW 20037. Between 21st and 22nd sts NW; just w of Dupont Circle. Int corridors. **Pets:** Accepted.

Residence Inn by Marriott-Washington DC-Vermont Ave 🅷 🐾
(202) 898-1100. **$79-$479.** 1199 Vermont Ave NW 20005. Jct 14th St and Vermont Ave NW, at Thomas Circle. Int corridors. **Pets:** Medium. $175 one-time fee/room. Service with restrictions, supervision.

The Ritz-Carlton Georgetown, Washington DC 🅷
(202) 912-4100. **Call for rates.** 3100 South St NW 20007. Just s of jct M St and Wisconsin Ave; in Georgetown. Int corridors. **Pets:** Accepted.

The Ritz-Carlton, Washington, D.C. 🅷 🐾
(202) 835-0500. **Call for rates.** 1150 22nd St NW 20037. At 22nd and M sts NW. Int corridors. **Pets:** Other species. Service with restrictions.

The River Inn 🅷
(202) 337-7600. **$169-$550.** 924 25th St NW 20037. Between K and I sts NW. Int corridors. **Pets:** Accepted.

The St. Regis Washington, D.C. 🅷 🐾
(202) 638-2626. **$285-$1200.** 923 16th St NW 20006. 16th and K sts; just n of the White House. Int corridors. **Pets:** Small, dogs only. $100 one-time fee/pet, $25 daily fee/pet. Service with restrictions, supervision.

Topaz Hotel-A Kimpton Hotel 🅷
(202) 393-3000. **$149-$449.** 1733 N St NW 20036. Just e of Connecticut Ave. Int corridors. **Pets:** Accepted.

The Washington Court Hotel 🅷
(202) 628-2100. **Call for rates.** 525 New Jersey Ave NW 20001. On Capitol Hill, 3 blks n of Capitol grounds. Int corridors. **Pets:** Accepted.

Washington Hilton 🅷
(202) 483-3000. **$119-$399.** 1919 Connecticut Ave NW 20009. Just n of Dupont Circle at T St NW. Int corridors. **Pets:** Accepted.

Washington Marriott Wardman Park 🅷
(202) 328-2000. **$89-$479.** 2660 Woodley Rd NW 20008. Just w of Connecticut Ave. Int corridors. **Pets:** Medium, other species. $50 one-time fee/room. Service with restrictions.

🏛 ▼▼▼ ▼▼▼ **The Westin Georgetown, Washington, D.C.** 🅷

(202) 429-0100. **$149-$649.** 2350 M St NW 20037. 24th and M sts NW. Int corridors. **Pets:** Accepted. 💰 📶 ✕ Ⓜ 🛗 🖥 🍴 🏊

🏛 ▼▼▼ ▼▼▼ **The Westin Washington DC City Center Hotel** 🅷 ❀

(202) 429-1700. **$120-$500.** 1400 M St NW 20005. Just w of Thomas Circle. Int corridors. **Pets:** Small, dogs only. $50 one-time fee/room. Service with restrictions, supervision. 💰 📶 ✕ 🛗 🖥 🍴

🏛 ▼▼▼ ▼▼▼ **The Willard InterContinental** 🅷

(202) 628-9100. **$229-$629.** 1401 Pennsylvania Ave NW 20004. Just e of the White House; jct 14th St NW. Int corridors. **Pets:** Accepted. 💰 📶 ✕ Ⓜ 🖥 🍴 🏊

🏛 ▼▼▼ ▼▼▼ **W Washington, D.C.** 🅷

(202) 661-2400. **$299-$499.** 515 15th St NW 20004. 15th St and Pennsylvania Ave NW. Int corridors. **Pets:** Accepted. 💰 📶 ✕ Ⓜ 🍴 🏊

END METROPOLITAN AREA

FLORIDA

CITY INDEX

ALFORD

▼▼▼ **La Maison de Lucy Bed & Breakfast & Event Center** 🅱🅱

(850) 579-0138. **$190-$290, 3 day notice.** 2388 Park Ave 32420. I-10 exit 130, 3.8 mi s on US 231, then 0.5 mi w on CR 276. Int corridors. **Pets:** Accepted. 📶 ✕ Ⓜ 🛗 🚶 ✕ 🐾

APALACHICOLA

▼▼▼▼ **Coombs House Inn** 🅱🅱

(850) 653-9199. **$119-$289, 7 day notice.** 80 Sixth St 32320. US 98 (Market St) and Ave E. Int corridors. **Pets:** Medium, other species. $25 daily fee/room. Designated rooms, service with restrictions. 📶 ✕ 🛗 🖥

🏛 ▼▼▼ ▼▼▼ **Gibson Inn** 🅲🅸

(850) 653-2191. **$115-$260, 14 day notice.** 51 Ave C 32329. US 98 at west end of bridge; downtown. Int corridors. **Pets:** Other species. $25 daily fee/pet. Designated rooms, service with restrictions, supervision. 💰 📶 ✕ 🍴

▼▼▼ **Water Street Hotel & Marina** 🅲🅾

(850) 653-3700. **$169-$275.** 329 Water St 32320. Jct Ave I. Ext corridors. **Pets:** Other species. $25 daily fee/pet. Service with restrictions, supervision. 📶 ✕ Ⓜ 🛗 🖥 🚶 ✕

ARCADIA

🏛 ▼▼ ▼▼ **Knights Inn-Arcadia** 🅼

(863) 494-4884. **$50-$60.** 504 S Brevard Ave 34266. 0.6 mi s of SR 70; on US 17. Ext corridors. **Pets:** Dogs only. $10 daily fee/room. Service with restrictions, supervision. 💰 📶 🛗 🖥 🏊

BOCA RATON

▼▼▼▼ **Boca Raton Bridge Hotel** 🅷

(561) 368-9500. **$89-$289.** 999 E Camino Real 33432. I-95 exit 44 (Palmetto Park Rd), 2.1 mi e to US 1 (Federal Hwy), 0.7 mi s to E Camino Real, then 0.8 mi e. Int corridors. **Pets:** Medium, dogs only. $100 one-time fee/room. Designated rooms, service with restrictions, supervision. 📶 ✕ 🛗 🖥 🍴 🚶 ✕

△△△ ▽▽▽▽ Boca Raton Resort & Club, A Waldorf Astoria Resort 🄷

(561) 447-3000. **Call for rates.** 501 E Camino Real 33432. I-95 exit 44 (Palmetto Park Rd), 1.9 mi e to US 1 (Federal Hwy), just s to Camino Real, then 0.5 mi e. Ext/int corridors. **Pets:** Accepted.

🄴🄲🄾 ⓢⒶⓥⒺ 🛜 ⌨ 🕭Ⓜ 🚪 🖥 ⍿ 🌊 ☒

△△△ ▽▽▽▽ Fairfield Inn & Suites by Marriott-Boca Raton 🄷

(561) 417-8585. **$79-$169.** 3400 Airport Rd 33431. I-95 exit 45 (SR 808/Glades Rd), just e to Airport Rd, then 1.1 mi n. Int corridors. **Pets:** Medium, other species. Designated rooms, service with restrictions, crate. 🄴🄲🄾 🛜 ☒ 🕭Ⓜ 🚪 🖥 🌊

△△△ ▽▽▽▽ Hilton Boca Raton Suites 🄷 ❀

(561) 483-3600. **$99-$239.** 7920 Glades Rd 33434. I-95 exit 45 (SR 808/Glades Rd), 3.4 mi w; Florida Tpke exit 75 (SR 808/Glades Rd), just e; in Arvida Parkway Center. Int corridors. **Pets:** Small. $50 one-time fee/room. Service with restrictions. 🄴🄲🄾 ⓢⒶⓥⒺ 🛜 🚪 🖥 🌊

△△△ ▽▽▽ Quality Inn-Boca Raton Ⓜ

(561) 395-7172. **$65-$199.** 2899 N Federal Hwy 33431. I-95 exit 48 (Yamato Rd), 1.2 mi e to US 1 (Federal Hwy), then 1.3 mi s. Ext corridors. **Pets:** Other species. $25 one-time fee/room. Service with restrictions. ⓢⒶⓥⒺ 🛜 🚪 🖥 🌊

△△△ ▽▽▽▽ Residence Inn by Marriott-Boca Raton 🄷 ❀

(561) 994-3222. **$89-$206.** 525 NW 77th St 33487. I-95 exit 50 (Congress Ave), merge onto NW 82nd St, just s on Congress Ave to NW 6th Ave, just e, then n; in Boca Commerce Center. Ext corridors. **Pets:** Large, other species. $85 one-time fee/room. Service with restrictions.

ⓢⒶⓥⒺ 🛜 ☒ 🚪 🖥 🌊 ☒

△△△ ▽▽▽▽ TownePlace Suites by Marriott-Boca Raton 🄷

(561) 994-7232. **$79-$249.** 5110 NW 8th Ave 33487. I-95 exit 48 (Yamato Rd), just w; in Arvida Park of Commerce. Int corridors. **Pets:** Accepted. 🄴🄲🄾 ⓢⒶⓥⒺ 🛜 ☒ 🕭Ⓜ 🚪 🖥 🌊

△△△ ▽▽▽▽ Wyndham Hotel-Boca Raton 🄷

(561) 368-5200. **$129-$325.** 1950 Glades Rd 33431. I-95 exit 45 (SR 808/Glades Rd), just w. Ext/int corridors. **Pets:** Accepted.

🄴🄲🄾 ⓢⒶⓥⒺ 🛜 ☒ 🕭Ⓜ 🚪 🖥 🌊

BONITA SPRINGS

△△△ ▽▽▽▽ Holiday Inn Express Hotel & Suites Bonita Springs 🄷 ❀

(239) 948-0699. **$59-$139.** 27891 Crown Lake Blvd 34135. I-75 exit 116, 3.4 mi w on Bonita Beach Rd SE (CR 865), then just n. Int corridors. **Pets:** Medium. $25 one-time fee/room. Designated rooms, service with restrictions, supervision. 🄴🄲🄾 ⓢⒶⓥⒺ 🛜 🕭Ⓜ 🚪 🖥 🌊

△△△ ▽▽▽▽ Hyatt Regency Coconut Point Resort & Spa 🄷

(239) 444-1234. **$126-$513, 3 day notice.** 5001 Coconut Rd 34134. I-75 exit 123, 1.9 mi w on Corkscrew Rd, 2.3 mi s on US 41 (Tamiami Tr), then 1.5 mi w. Int corridors. **Pets:** Accepted.

🄴🄲🄾 ⓢⒶⓥⒺ 🛜 🚪 🖥 ⍿ 🌊 ☒

BRADENTON

△△△ ▽▽▽ Quality Inn Bradenton Ⓜ

(941) 758-7199. **$60-$190.** 6727 14th St W 34207. On US 41, 2 mi s of jct SR 70. Ext corridors. **Pets:** Small, dogs only. $10 daily fee/pet. Designated rooms, service with restrictions, supervision.

ⓢⒶⓥⒺ 🛜 🚪 🖥 🌊

△△△ ▽▽▽ Super 8-Bradenton Ⓜ

(941) 756-6656. **$59-$139.** 6516 14th St W 34207. On US 41, 1.5 mi s of jct SR 70. Ext corridors. **Pets:** Small, dogs only. $10 daily fee/pet. Designated rooms, service with restrictions, supervision. ⓢⒶⓥⒺ 🚪 🌊

BRADENTON BEACH

▽▽▽▽ Tortuga Inn Beach Resort 🄲🄾

(941) 778-6611. **Call for rates.** 1325 Gulf Dr N 34217. On Sarasota Bay and Anna Maria Island; on SR 789, 0.3 mi n of jct SR 684 (Cortez Rd). Ext corridors. **Pets:** Accepted. 🛜 🚪 🖥 🌊

BROOKSVILLE

▽▽▽ Microtel Inn & Suites by Wyndham Brooksville 🄷

(352) 796-9025. **$60-$90.** 6298 Nature Coast Blvd 34602. I-75 exit 301, just w on US 98/SR 50, then just s. Int corridors. **Pets:** Other species. $25 one-time fee/room. Service with restrictions, supervision.

🛜 🕭Ⓜ 🚪 🖥 🌊

▽▽▽ Quality Inn & Suites Ⓜ

(352) 796-9481. **$69-$119.** 30307 Cortez Blvd 34602. I-75 exit 301, just w on US 98/SR 50. Ext corridors. **Pets:** Accepted.

🛜 🕭Ⓜ 🚪 🖥 🌊

CAPE CANAVERAL

▽▽▽ Residence Inn by Marriott Cape Canaveral/Cocoa Beach 🄷

(321) 323-1100. **$149-$209.** 8959 Astronaut Blvd 32920. On SR A1A, 0.3 mi s of jct SR 528. Int corridors. **Pets:** Medium, other species. $100 one-time fee/pet. Designated rooms, service with restrictions, crate.

🄴🄲🄾 🛜 ☒ 🚪 🖥 🌊 ☒

CAPE CORAL

▽▽▽ Hampton Inn & Suites Cape Coral 🄷

(239) 540-1050. **$119-$189.** 619 SE 47th Terr 33904. Just w of jct Coronado Pkwy. Int corridors. **Pets:** Other species. Service with restrictions, supervision. 🛜 🕭Ⓜ 🚪 🖥 🌊

▽▽▽ Holiday Inn Express Cape Coral 🄷

(239) 542-2121. **$89-$169.** 1538 Cape Coral Pkwy E 33904. Jct Del Prado Blvd. Int corridors. **Pets:** Small, other species. $20 daily fee/room. Designated rooms, service with restrictions, supervision.

🛜 ☒ 🕭Ⓜ 🚪 🖥 🌊

CEDAR KEY

△△△ ▽▽▽ Park Place Motel & Condominiums 🄲🄾

(352) 543-5737. **$65-$115.** 211 2nd St 32625. Just ne of jct SR 24; at A St. Ext corridors. **Pets:** Small, other species. $7 daily fee/pet. Service with restrictions, supervision. 🄴🄲🄾 ⓢⒶⓥⒺ 🛜 🚪 🖥

▽▽▽ Seahorse Landing Waterfront Condominiums 🄲🄾

(352) 543-5860. **$100-$175, 3 day notice.** 4050 G St 32625. Just sw of jct SR 24, on 6th St. Ext corridors. **Pets:** Medium, dogs only. $15 daily fee/room. Designated rooms, service with restrictions, crate.

🄴🄲🄾 🛜 🚪 🖥 🌊 ☒

CHIEFLAND

△△△ ▽▽ BEST WESTERN Suwannee Valley Inn Ⓜ ❀

(352) 493-0663. **$82-$97.** 1125 N Young Blvd 32626. On Alternate Rt US 27/19/98, just n of jct US 129. Ext corridors. **Pets:** Medium, other species. $20 daily fee/room. Designated rooms, service with restrictions, supervision. ⓢⒶⓥⒺ 🛜 🚪 🖥 🌊

▽▽▽ Days Inn Chiefland Ⓜ

(352) 493-9400. **$56-$80.** 809 NW 21st Ave 32626. Just e of US 19/98; 1 mi n of jct US 129. Ext corridors. **Pets:** Accepted.

🛜 🕭Ⓜ 🚪 🖥 🌊

COCOA

△△△ ▽▽▽ BEST WESTERN Cocoa Inn Ⓜ

(321) 632-1065. **$70-$200.** 4225 W King St 32926. I-95 exit 201 (SR 520), just e. Ext corridors. **Pets:** Small. $10 deposit/pet. Service with restrictions, supervision. ⓢⒶⓥⒺ 🛜 🚪 🖥 🌊

COCOA BEACH

BEST WESTERN Ocean Beach Hotel & Suites H

(321) 783-7621. **$89-$199.** 5600 N Atlantic Ave 32931. SR A1A (Atlantic Ave), 0.8 mi n of jct SR 520. Ext/int corridors. **Pets:** Accepted.

Days Inn Cocoa Beach M

(321) 784-2550. **$90-$170.** 5500 N Atlantic Ave 32931. On SR A1A (Atlantic Ave), 0.8 mi n of SR 520. Ext corridors. **Pets:** Medium, other species. $15 daily fee/pet. Designated rooms, service with restrictions, crate.

Four Points by Sheraton - Cocoa Beach H

(321) 783-8717. **$95-$145.** 4001 N Atlantic Ave 32931. SR A1A (Atlantic Ave), just s of SR 520. Int corridors. **Pets:** Medium, dogs only. Service with restrictions, supervision.

International Palms Resort and Conference Center H

(321) 783-2271. **$79-$259.** 1300 N Atlantic Ave 32931. SR A1A (Atlantic Ave), 1.8 mi s of jct SR 520. Ext corridors. **Pets:** Accepted.

La Quinta Inn Cocoa Beach H

(321) 783-2252. **$81-$183.** 1275 N Atlantic Ave 32931. SR A1A (Atlantic Ave), 1.7 mi s of SR 520. Ext corridors. **Pets:** Service with restrictions, supervision.

Surf Studio Beach Resort M

(321) 783-7100. **$110-$265, 7 day notice.** 1801 S Atlantic Ave 32931. SR A1A northbound, 5 mi s of jct SR 520 at Francis St; 1.3 mi n of Patrick AFB. Ext corridors. **Pets:** Other species. $20 daily fee/pet. Service with restrictions, supervision.

CRESCENT BEACH

Beacher's Lodge Oceanfront Suites H

(904) 471-8849. **$79-$225.** 6970 A1A S 32080. On SR A1A (Atlantic Ave), just s of SR 206. Ext corridors. **Pets:** Large, other species. $50 one-time fee/pet. Designated rooms, service with restrictions.

CRESTVIEW

Quality Inn H

(850) 683-1778. **Call for rates.** 151 Cracker Barrel Dr 32536. I-10 exit 56, just s. Int corridors. **Pets:** Small, other species. $15 daily fee/pet. Designated rooms, service with restrictions, supervision.

CRYSTAL RIVER

BEST WESTERN Crystal River Resort H

(352) 795-3171. **$120-$135.** 614 NW Hwy 19 34428. On US 19/98, 0.8 mi n of jct SR 44. Ext corridors. **Pets:** Large, other species. $5 daily fee/pet. Service with restrictions, supervision.

DAYTONA BEACH

Comfort Inn & Suites Oceanfront H

(386) 255-5491. **$90-$180.** 730 N Atlantic Ave 32118. On SR A1A (Atlantic Ave), 1.1 mi n of jct US 92. Ext/int corridors. **Pets:** Small. $20 one-time fee/pet. Service with restrictions, crate.

Extended Stay Deluxe Daytona Beach-International Speedway H

(386) 257-4311. **$70-$500.** 255 Bill France Blvd 32114. I-95 exit 261 (US 92), 2.1 mi e to Bill France Blvd, then just n. Int corridors. **Pets:** $25 daily fee/pet. Designated rooms, service with restrictions.

Hilton Daytona Beach Oceanfront Resort H

(386) 254-8200. **$99-$399.** 100 N Atlantic Ave 32118. I-95 exit 261 (US 92), 6.1 mi e to SR A1A (Atlantic Ave), then 0.5 mi n. Int corridors. **Pets:** Accepted.

Holiday Inn - Daytona Beach LPGA H

(386) 236-0200. **Call for rates.** 137 AutoMall Cir 32124. I-95 exit 265, just sw. Int corridors. **Pets:** Accepted.

Homewood Suites by Hilton - Daytona Beach Airport/Speedway H

(386) 258-2828. **$99-$159.** 165 Bill France Blvd 32114. I-95 exit 261 (US 92), 2.1 mi e to Bill France Blvd, then just n. Int corridors. **Pets:** Other species. $50 one-time fee/pet. Designated rooms, service with restrictions, crate.

La Quinta Inn - Daytona Beach International Speedway H

(386) 255-7412. **$59-$144.** 2725 W International Speedway Blvd 32114. I-95 exit 261 (US 92), just e. Int corridors. **Pets:** Service with restrictions, supervision.

Residence Inn by Marriott - Daytona Beach H

(386) 252-3949. **$109-$152.** 1725 Richard Petty Blvd 32114. I-95 exit 261 (US 92), 2.4 mi e to Midway Ave, just s to Richard Petty Blvd, then just e. Int corridors. **Pets:** Accepted.

DAYTONA BEACH SHORES

Atlantic Ocean Palm Inn M

(386) 761-8450. **$49-$199, 30 day notice.** 3247 S Atlantic Ave 32118. On SR A1A (Atlantic Ave), 5 mi s of jct US 92 (International Speedway Blvd). Ext corridors. **Pets:** Small. $15 daily fee/pet. Designated rooms, service with restrictions, supervision.

The Shores Resort & Spa H ☙

(386) 767-7350. **$119-$659, 3 day notice.** 2637 S Atlantic Ave 32118. On SR A1A (Atlantic Ave), 3.2 mi s of jct US 92 (International Speedway Blvd). Int corridors. **Pets:** Medium, other species. $250 deposit/room, $50 daily fee/room. Crate.

DE FUNIAK SPRINGS

BEST WESTERN Crossroads Inn H

(850) 892-5111. **$80-$100.** 2343 US Hwy 331 S 32435. I-10 exit 85, just s. Ext/int corridors. **Pets:** Medium, other species. $10 one-time fee/room. Service with restrictions, supervision.

DELAND

University Inn M

(386) 734-5711. **$79-$199.** 644 N Woodland Blvd 32720. US 17, 0.9 mi n of jct SR 44. Ext corridors. **Pets:** Medium. $10 daily fee/pet. Designated rooms, service with restrictions, supervision.

DELRAY BEACH

The Colony Hotel & Cabana Club H ☙

(561) 276-4123. **$99-$329, 3 day notice.** 525 E Atlantic Ave 33483. I-95 exit 52 (SR 806/Atlantic Ave), 1.4 mi e. Int corridors. **Pets:** Other species. $25 daily fee/pet.

Delray Beach Marriott H

(561) 274-3200. **$289-$379.** 10 N Ocean Blvd 33483. I-95 exit 52 (SR 806/Atlantic Ave), 1.8 mi e, then just n. Int corridors. **Pets:** Small, dogs only. $75 one-time fee/room. Designated rooms, service with restrictions, crate.

▼▼▼▼ Residence Inn by Marriott - Delray Beach �H ❀
(561) 276-7441. **$269-$349.** 1111 E Atlantic Ave 33483. I-95 exit 52 (SR 806/Atlantic Ave), 1.7 mi e. Int corridors. **Pets:** Other species. $100 one-time fee/room. Service with restrictions, crate.
ECO 🛜 ✕ 💪M 🛏 🖵 ➥

▼▼▼▼ Sundy House �H
(561) 272-5678. **$139-$349, 7 day notice.** 106 S Swinton Ave 33444. I-95 exit 52 (SR 806/Atlantic Ave), 1.1 mi e to Swinton Ave, then just s. Ext corridors. **Pets:** $250 one-time fee/pet. Designated rooms, service with restrictions. 🛜 ✕ 🛏 🖵 🍽 ➥

DELTONA
AAA ▼▼▼ Deltona Inn �H
(386) 860-3000. **Call for rates.** 481 Deltona Blvd 32725. I-4 exit 108, just ne. Ext corridors. **Pets:** Accepted. SAVE 🛜 🛏 🖵 🍽 ➥

DESTIN
AAA ▼▼▼▼ Residence Inn by Marriott Sandestin at Grand Boulevard �H ❀
(850) 650-7811. **$109-$399.** 300 Grand Blvd 32550. On US 98, jct Baytowne Ln. Int corridors. **Pets:** Medium, other species. $100 one-time fee/room. Service with restrictions, crate.
ECO SAVE 🛜 ✕ 💪M 🛏 🖵 ➥ ✕

AAA ▼▼▼▼ SummerPlace Inn �H ❀
(850) 650-8003. **$80-$250.** 14047 Emerald Coast Pkwy 32541. Jct SR 293 and US 98, 2.5 mi w. Int corridors. **Pets:** Other species. $26 one-time fee/pet. Designated rooms, service with restrictions, crate.
SAVE 🛜 ✕ 🛏 🖵 ➥

THE FLORIDA KEYS AREA

ISLAMORADA
▼▼▼▼ Islander Resort 🅜
(305) 664-2031. **$135-$245, 4 day notice.** 82100 Overseas Hwy 33036. US 1 at MM 82.1. Ext corridors. **Pets:** Large, other species. $75 one-time fee/pet. Designated rooms, service with restrictions, supervision.
🛜 🛏 🖵 🍽 ➥ ✕

▼▼▼ Pelican Cove Resort & Marina 🅒🅞
(305) 664-4435. **$99-$359, 5 day notice.** 84457 Old Overseas Hwy 33036. US 1 at MM 84.5, oceanside. Ext corridors. **Pets:** Small, other species. $80 one-time fee/room. Designated rooms, service with restrictions, crate. 🛜 ✕ 🛏 🖵 ➥ ✕

AAA ▼▼▼▼ Postcard Inn Beach Resort and Marina at Holiday Isle �H
(305) 664-2321. **$159-$359, 3 day notice.** 84001 Overseas Hwy 33036. US 1, MM 84.5. Ext corridors. **Pets:** Accepted.
SAVE 🛜 ✕ 🛏 🖵 ➥ ✕

AAA ▼▼▼▼ Sands of Islamorada 🅜 ❀
(305) 664-2791. **$120-$350, 3 day notice.** 80051 Overseas Hwy 33036. US 1 at MM 80. Ext corridors. **Pets:** $100 deposit/room. Service with restrictions, supervision. SAVE 🛜 ✕ 🛏 🖵 ➥ ✕

KEY LARGO
AAA ▼▼▼▼ Hilton Key Largo Resort �H
(305) 852-5553. **$129-$399.** 97000 S Overseas Hwy 33037. US 1 at MM 97; bayside. Ext corridors. **Pets:** Accepted.
SAVE 🛜 🛏 🖵 🍽 ➥ ✕

▼▼▼▼ Tarpon Flats Inn & Marina 🅜
(305) 453-1313. **$139-$220, 7 day notice.** 29 Shoreland Dr 33037. US 1 at MM 103.5, 0.3 mi e on Transylvania Ave, then s on Oceanview to Shoreland Dr. Ext corridors. **Pets:** Accepted.
🛜 ✕ 🛏 🖵 ➥ ✕

KEY WEST
AAA ▼▼▼ BEST WESTERN Key Ambassador Resort Inn 🅜 ❀
(305) 296-3500. **$149-$349.** 3755 S Roosevelt Blvd 33040. On SR A1A, 1 mi s of jct US 1. Ext corridors. **Pets:** Large, dogs only. $20 daily fee/room. Designated rooms, service with restrictions.
SAVE 🛜 ✕ 🛏 🖵 🍽 ➥

AAA ▼▼▼▼ Casa Marina, A Waldorf Astoria Resort �H
(305) 296-3535. **$199-$529.** 1500 Reynolds St 33040. 4 mi s on Flagler (CR 5A) from jct SR A1A. Ext/int corridors. **Pets:** Small, dogs only. $75 daily fee/pet. Service with restrictions, supervision.
ECO SAVE 🛜 ✕ 🛏 🖵 🍽 ➥ ✕

AAA ▼▼ Courtney's Place Historic Cottages & Inn 🅑🅑
(305) 294-3480. **$119-$389, 21 day notice.** 720 Whitmarsh Ln 33040. Just e of jct Petronia and Simonton sts; in Old Town. Ext corridors. **Pets:** Other species. $10 daily fee/pet. Service with restrictions.
SAVE 🛜 ✕ 🛏 🖵 ➥

AAA ▼▼▼ DoubleTree Resort by Hilton Hotel Grand Key-Key West �H
(305) 293-1818. **Call for rates.** 3990 S Roosevelt Blvd 33040. From US 1, 0.5 mi s on SR A1A. Int corridors. **Pets:** Medium. $75 one-time fee/room. Service with restrictions, supervision.
ECO SAVE 🛜 💪M 🛏 🖵 🍽 ➥ ✕

AAA ▼▼▼ ▼▼▼ Hyatt Key West Resort & Spa �H
(305) 809-1234. **$198-$536, 7 day notice.** 601 Front St 33040. Simonton and Front sts; just n of Mallory Square; in Old Town. Ext corridors. **Pets:** Accepted. ECO SAVE 🛜 🛏 🖵 🍽 ➥ ✕

AAA ▼▼▼ Ocean Breeze Inn 🅜
(305) 296-2829. **$129-$219, 14 day notice.** 625 South St 33040. Just n of Duval St. Ext corridors. **Pets:** Medium. $200 deposit/room, $25 daily fee/room. Designated rooms, service with restrictions, supervision.
ECO SAVE 🛜 ✕ 🛏 🖵 ➥ ✉

AAA ▼▼▼ Quality Inn - Key West 🅜 ❀
(305) 294-3773. **$134-$244, 3 day notice.** 3824 N Roosevelt Blvd 33040. On US 1; in New Town. Ext corridors. **Pets:** Large, other species. $75 one-time fee/room. Service with restrictions, supervision.
SAVE 🛜 💪M 🛏 🖵 ➥

AAA ▼▼▼ ▼▼ The Reach, A Waldorf Astoria Resort �H
(305) 296-5000. **$199-$529.** 1435 Simonton St 33040. Just s of jct Truman Ave and Simonton St. Ext corridors. **Pets:** Accepted.
ECO SAVE 🛜 ✕ 🛏 🖵 🍽 ➥ ✕

AAA ▼▼▼▼ Sheraton Suites-Key West �H
(305) 292-9800. **$149-$469, 3 day notice.** 2001 S Roosevelt Blvd 33040. Jct US 1 and SR A1A, 3 mi s. Ext/int corridors. **Pets:** Accepted.
ECO SAVE 🛜 ✕ 💪M 🛏 🖵 🍽 ➥ ✕

AAA ▼▼▼ ▼▼▼ The Westin Key West Resort & Marina �H ❀
(305) 294-4000. **$229-$599, 3 day notice.** 245 Front St 33040. Corner of Front and Greene sts; in Old Town. Ext/int corridors. **Pets:** Small, dogs only. Service with restrictions, supervision.
ECO SAVE 🛜 ✕ 💪M 🛏 🖵 🍽 ➥ ✕

▼▼▼ Wicker Guesthouse BB
(305) 296-4275. **Call for rates.** 913 Duval St 33040. Just n of Truman Ave/US 1. Ext corridors. **Pets:** Small, dogs only. $25 daily fee/room. Designated rooms, service with restrictions.
ECO 🛰 ✕ 🖬 🖵 ⇆ ⊠

MARATHON
▼ Royal Hawaiian Motel/Botel M
(305) 743-7500. **$99-$175, 30 day notice.** 12020 Overseas Hwy 33050. US 1 at MM 53; gulfside. Ext corridors. **Pets:** Small. $25 one-time fee/pet. Service with restrictions, supervision. 🛰 ✕ 🖬 🖵 ⇆ ⊠

END AREA

FORT LAUDERDALE METROPOLITAN AREA

CORAL SPRINGS
▼▼ La Quinta Inn & Suites-Coral Springs University Dr H
(954) 753-9000. **$69-$140.** 3701 N University Dr 33065. SR 869 (Sawgrass Expwy) exit 15 (University Dr/SR 817), 1.9 mi s. Int corridors. **Pets:** Service with restrictions, supervision. 🛰 ⌂M 🖬 🖵 ⇆

▼▼ La Quinta Inn & Suites-Ft. Lauderdale University Drive South H
(954) 344-2200. **$63-$133.** 3100 N University Dr 33065. SR 869 (Sawgrass Expwy) exit 15 (University Dr/SR 817), 2.4 mi s. Int corridors. **Pets:** Service with restrictions, supervision. 🛰 🖬 🖵 ⇆

DANIA BEACH
▼▼▼ Hilton Fort Lauderdale Airport Hotel H
(954) 920-3300. **$79-$199.** 1870 Griffin Rd 33004. I-95 exit 23 (Griffin Rd), just e. Ext/int corridors. **Pets:** Accepted. ECO 🛰 🖵 🍽 ⇆

AAA⁺ ▼▼▼ Hyatt house Fort Lauderdale Airport & Cruise Port H
(954) 922-0271. **$139-$399.** 90 SW 18th Ave 33004. I-95 exit 22 (Stirling Rd), just e to SW 18th Ave, then just n. Int corridors. **Pets:** Accepted.
SAVE 🛰 ✕ 🖬 🖵 ⇆

AAA⁺ ▼▼▼ Sheraton Fort Lauderdale Airport & Cruise Port Hotel H
(954) 920-3500. **$89-$329.** 1825 Griffin Rd 33004. I-95 exit 23 (Griffin Rd), just e. Int corridors. **Pets:** Accepted.
ECO SAVE 🛰 ✕ ⌂M 🖬 🖵 🍽 ⇆ ⊠

DEERFIELD BEACH
AAA⁺ ▼▼▼ Comfort Inn Oceanside H ☙
(954) 428-0650. **$75-$190, 3 day notice.** 50 S Ocean Dr (SR A1A) 33441. I-95 exit 42A (Hillsboro Blvd), 2.6 mi e; jct Hillsboro Blvd and SR A1A. Int corridors. **Pets:** Medium, other species. $25 daily fee/pet. Designated rooms, service with restrictions, crate.
SAVE 🛰 🖬 🖵 ⇆ ⊠

▼▼ Comfort Suites Deerfield Beach H
(954) 570-8887. **$49-$149.** 1040 E Newport Center Dr 33442. I-95 exit 41 (SW 10th St), just w; in Newport Center Complex. Ext corridors. **Pets:** Accepted. 🛰 ✕ 🖬 🖵 ⇆

AAA⁺ ▼▼▼ DoubleTree by Hilton Deerfield Beach-Boca Raton H
(954) 427-7700. **$89-$239.** 100 Fairway Rd 33441. I-95 exit 42A (Hillsboro Blvd E), just e to Fairway Dr. Int corridors. **Pets:** Medium. $75 one-time fee/room. Designated rooms, service with restrictions, supervision.
ECO SAVE 🛰 ✕ 🖬 🖵 🍽 ⇆

▼▼ Extended StayAmerica - Fort Lauderdale - Deerfield Beach H
(954) 428-5997. **$60-$140.** 1200 FAU Research Park Blvd 33441. I-95 exit 41 (SW 10th St), just e to FAU Research Park Rd, then just s. Int corridors. **Pets:** $25 daily fee/pet. Designated rooms, service with restrictions. 🛰 ⌂M 🖬 🖵

▼▼ La Quinta Inn & Suites-Ft. Lauderdale Deerfield Beach H
(954) 428-0661. **$59-$151.** 100 SW 12th Ave 33442. I-95 exit 42B (Hillsboro Blvd), just w to SW 12th Ave, then just s. Int corridors. **Pets:** Service with restrictions, supervision. 🛰 ⌂M 🖬 🖵 ⇆

▼▼ La Quinta Inn-Deerfield Beach I-95 at Hillsboro East H
(954) 421-1004. **$66-$144.** 351 W Hillsboro Blvd 33441. I-95 exit 42 (Hillsboro Blvd), 0.3 mi e. Ext/int corridors. **Pets:** Service with restrictions, supervision. 🛰 ⌂M 🖬 🖵 ⇆

▼▼▼ Wyndham Deerfield Beach Resort H ☙
(954) 428-2850. **$152-$260.** 2096 NE 2nd St 33441. I-95 exit 42 (Hillsboro Blvd), 2.6 mi e to SR A1A (Ocean Blvd), then just ne. Int corridors. **Pets:** Small. $35 daily fee/room. Designated rooms, service with restrictions, crate. 🛰 ✕ 🖬 🖵 🍽 ⇆ ⊠

FORT LAUDERDALE
▼▼▼ Bahia Mar Fort Lauderdale Beach, A DoubleTree by Hilton H
(954) 764-2233. **$99-$399.** 801 Seabreeze Blvd 33316. I-95 exit 29 (Sunrise Blvd), 4.1 mi e to SR A1A (Fort Lauderdale Beach Blvd), then 2 mi s. Int corridors. **Pets:** Accepted. ECO 🛰 🖬 🖵 🍽 ⇆ ⊠

AAA⁺ ▼▼▼ Candlewood Suites Fort Lauderdale Airport/Cruise Port H
(954) 522-8822. **$79-$269.** 1120 W State Road 84 33315. I-95 exit 25 (SR 84), 0.8 mi e. Int corridors. **Pets:** Accepted.
SAVE 🛰 ⌂M 🖬 🖵

▼▼▼ Embassy Suites Fort Lauderdale - 17th Street H
(954) 527-2700. **$119-$299.** 1100 SE 17th St 33316. I-95 exit 25 (SR 84), 2 mi e to US 1 (SE 6th Ave), 0.5 mi n to SE 17th St, then 0.3 mi e. Int corridors. **Pets:** Accepted. ECO 🛰 🖬 🖵 🍽 ⇆ ⊠

▼▼ Extended Stay Deluxe - Fort Lauderdale - Cypress Creek - NW 6th Way H
(954) 772-3155. **$60-$140.** 6001 NW 6th Way 33309. I-95 exit 33 (Cypress Creek Rd), 0.4 mi w, then just s. Int corridors. **Pets:** $25 daily fee/pet. Designated rooms, service with restrictions.
🛰 ✕ ⌂M 🖬 🖵 ⇆

▼▼▼ Hampton Inn Fort Lauderdale Airport North H
(954) 524-9900. **$89-$169.** 2301 SW 12th Ave 33315. I-95 exit 25 (SR 84), 0.7 mi e to SW 12th Ave, then just n. Int corridors. **Pets:** Accepted.
ECO 🛰 ✕ ⌂M 🖬 🖵

AAA⁺ ▼▼▼ Hilton Fort Lauderdale Marina H
(954) 463-4000. **$99-$349.** 1881 SE 17th St Cswy 33316. I-95 exit 25 (SR 84), 2 mi e to SE 6th Ave (US 1), 0.5 mi n SE 17th St, then 1 mi e. Ext/int corridors. **Pets:** Accepted. SAVE 🛰 🖬 🖵 🍽 ⇆ ⊠

▼▼▼ Holiday Inn Express & Suites-Ft Lauderdale Executive Airport 🅷 ✿
(954) 772-3032. **$109-$149.** 1500 W Commercial Blvd 33309. I-95 exit 32 (Commercial Blvd), 0.7 mi w. Int corridors. **Pets:** Small, dogs only. $25 daily fee/room. Designated rooms, service with restrictions.
🛰 🅷 💻 🏊

AAA▼ ▼▼▼▼ Il Lugano Suite Hotel 🅷
(954) 564-4400. **$109-$999, 3 day notice.** 3333 NE 32nd Ave 33308. 1.4 mi s of Commercial Blvd on N Ocean Dr (SR A1A), w on NE 34th St; on Intracoastal Waterway. Int corridors. **Pets:** Accepted.
SAVE 🛰 ✕ 🅛🅜 🅷 💻 🍴 🏊 ✕

▼▼▼ La Quinta Inn & Suites-Ft Lauderdale Cypress Creek/I-95 🅷
(954) 491-7666. **$59-$133.** 999 W Cypress Creek Rd 33309. I-95 exit 33 (Cypress Creek Rd), 0.7 mi w. Int corridors. **Pets:** Service with restrictions, supervision. 🛰 🅷 💻 🏊

▼▼▼▼ La Quinta Inn-Fort Lauderdale Northeast 🅷
(954) 491-2500. **$59-$129.** 5727 N Federal Hwy 33308. I-95 exit 32 (Commercial Blvd), 2.7 mi e to US1 (Federal Hwy), then 0.7 mi n. Ext/int corridors. **Pets:** Service with restrictions, supervision.
🛰 🅛🅜 🅷 💻 🏊

AAA▼ ▼▼▼▼▼ The Ritz-Carlton, Fort Lauderdale 🅷 ✿
(954) 465-2300. **$219-$2499, 7 day notice.** 1 N Fort Lauderdale Beach Blvd 33304. I-95 exit 29 (Sunrise Blvd), 4.1 mi e to SR A1A (Fort Lauderdale Beach Blvd), then 1.2 mi s. Int corridors. **Pets:** Small. $250 one-time fee/room. ECO SAVE 🛰 ✕ 🅛🅜 🅷 💻 🍴 🏊 ✕

AAA▼ ▼▼▼▼ Riverside Hotel, The International Hotel of Fort Lauderdale 🅷 ✿
(954) 467-0671. **$119-$359, 3 day notice.** 620 E Las Olas Blvd 33301. I-95 exit 27 (Broward Blvd), 2.4 mi e to US 1, just s to Las Olas Blvd, then just e; downtown. Int corridors. **Pets:** Medium. $75 one-time fee/pet. Service with restrictions, crate. SAVE 🛰 ✕ 🅷 💻 🍴 🏊 ✕

AAA▼ ▼▼▼▼ Sheraton Fort Lauderdale Beach Hotel 🅷
(954) 524-5551. **$109-$850, 3 day notice.** 1140 Seabreeze Blvd 33316. SR A1A, just s of Bahia Mar Marina. Ext/int corridors. **Pets:** Accepted.
SAVE 🛰 ✕ 🅛🅜 💻 🍴 🏊

AAA▼ ▼▼▼▼ Sheraton Suites Cypress Creek, Ft. Lauderdale 🅷 ✿
(954) 772-5400. **$99-$269.** 555 NW 62nd St 33309. I-95 exit 33 (Cypress Creek Rd), just w. Int corridors. **Pets:** Medium, other species. $25 daily fee/pet. Designated rooms, service with restrictions, crate.
ECO SAVE 🛰 ✕ 🅷 💻 🍴 🏊 ✕

AAA▼ ▼▼▼▼ TownePlace Suites by Marriott-Fort Lauderdale West 🅷
(954) 484-2214. **$79-$249.** 3100 Prospect Rd 33309. I-95 exit 33 (Cypress Creek Rd), just w to NW 31st St, then 0.5 mi s. Int corridors. **Pets:** Accepted. SAVE 🛰 ✕ 🅷 💻 🏊

AAA▼ ▼▼▼▼ The Westin Beach Resort & Spa, Fort Lauderdale 🅷
(954) 467-1111. **$169-$1100, 3 day notice.** 321 N Fort Lauderdale Beach Blvd (SR A1A) 33304. I-95 exit 29 (Sunrise Blvd), 4.2 mi e to SR A1A (Fort Lauderdale Beach Blvd), then 0.8 mi s. Int corridors. **Pets:** Accepted. ECO SAVE 🛰 ✕ 💻 🍴 🏊 ✕

AAA▼ ▼▼▼▼ The Westin Fort Lauderdale 🅷
(954) 772-1331. **$79-$499.** 400 Corporate Dr 33334. I-95 exit 33A (Cypress Creek Rd), just e; in Radice Corporate Park. Int corridors. **Pets:** Accepted. SAVE 🛰 ✕ 💻 🍴 🏊 ✕

AAA▼ ▼▼▼▼ W Fort Lauderdale 🅷
(954) 414-8200. **$199-$499, 3 day notice.** 401 N Fort Lauderdale Beach Blvd 33304. I-95 exit 29 (Sunrise Blvd), 4.2 mi e to SR A1A (Fort Lauderdale Beach Blvd), then 0.7 mi s. Int corridors. **Pets:** Accepted.
SAVE 🛰 ✕ 🅛🅜 🅷 💻 🍴 🏊 ✕

HILLSBORO BEACH

AAA▼ ▼▼▼ Seabonay Beach Resort 🅷
(954) 427-2525. **Call for rates.** 1159 Hillsboro Mile 33062. I-95 exit 42 (Hillsboro Blvd), 2.6 mi e to SR A1A (Ocean Blvd), then 1.4 mi s. Ext/int corridors. **Pets:** Accepted. SAVE 🛰 ✕ 🅷 💻 🏊

HOLLYWOOD

AAA▼ ▼▼▼ Comfort Inn-Ft. Lauderdale Airport/Cruise Port South 🅷
(954) 922-1600. **$59-$189.** 2520 Stirling Rd 33020. I-95 exit 22 (Stirling Rd), 0.4 mi e. Ext corridors. **Pets:** Small. $25 one-time fee/pet. Service with restrictions, supervision. SAVE 🛰 🅛🅜 🅷 💻 🏊

▼▼▼ Days Inn - Fort Lauderdale/Hollywood Airport South 🅷
(954) 923-7300. **$99-$169.** 2601 N 29th Ave 33020. I-95 exit 21 (Sheridan St), just w. Int corridors. **Pets:** Medium. $10 daily fee/pet. Designated rooms, service with restrictions, crate. ECO 🛰 🅷 💻 🏊

▼▼▼ La Quinta Inn & Suites-Ft. Lauderdale Airport 🅷
(954) 922-2295. **$90-$188.** 2620 N 26th Ave 33020. I-95 exit 21 (Sheridan St), just e to Oakwood Blvd (N 26th Ave), then just n. Int corridors. **Pets:** Service with restrictions, supervision. 🛰 🅷 💻 🏊

AAA▼ ▼▼▼ Quality Inn & Suites - Hollywood Blvd Ⓜ
(954) 981-1800. **$80-$190.** 4900 Hollywood Blvd 33021. I-95 exit 20 (Hollywood Blvd), 1.6 mi w; Florida Tpke exit 49, 1.3 mi e. Ext corridors. **Pets:** Accepted. SAVE 🛰 🅷 💻 🏊

AAA▼ ▼▼▼▼ Seminole Hard Rock Hotel & Casino Hollywood 🅷
(954) 327-7625. **Call for rates.** 1 Seminole Way 33314. I-95 exit 22 (Stirling Rd), 2.9 mi w, then just n on SR 7/US 441; Florida Tpke exit 53, 0.5 mi e, then 0.8 mi s. Int corridors. **Pets:** Accepted.
ECO SAVE 🛰 🅛🅜 💻 🍴 🏊 ✕

MIRAMAR

▼▼▼ Residence Inn by Marriott-Fort Lauderdale SW/Miramar 🅷
(954) 450-2717. **$79-$189.** 14700 Hotel Rd 33027. I-75 exit 7A (Miramar Pkwy), just e to SW 148th Ave, just n to Hotel Rd, then just e. Int corridors. **Pets:** Other species. $100 one-time fee/room. Designated rooms, service with restrictions, crate. ECO 🛰 ✕ 🅛🅜 🅷 💻 🏊

PLANTATION

▼▼▼ Extended StayAmerica Fort Lauderdale-Plantation 🅷
(954) 382-8888. **$60-$150.** 7755 SW 6th St 33324. I-595 exit 5 (SR 817/ University Dr), 1.2 mi w to University Dr, 1 mi n to SW 6th St, then just w. Int corridors. **Pets:** $25 daily fee/pet. Designated rooms, service with restrictions. 🛰 🅷 💻 🏊

AAA▼ ▼▼▼▼ Holiday Inn Express Hotel & Suites-Plantation 🅷
(954) 472-5600. **$99-$199.** 1701 N University Dr 33322. On SR 817 (University Dr), just s of jct SR 838 (Sunrise Blvd). Int corridors. **Pets:** Medium. $50 one-time fee/pet. Designated rooms, service with restrictions, crate. SAVE 🛰 🅷 💻 🏊

▼▼▼ La Quinta Inn & Suites-Ft. Lauderdale Plantation 🅷
(954) 476-6047. **$85-$165.** 8101 Peters Rd 33324. I-595 exit 5 (SR 817 N/University Dr), just n, then just w; in Crossroad Office Park. Int corridors. **Pets:** Service with restrictions, supervision.
🛰 🅛🅜 🅷 💻 🏊

▼▼▼ La Quinta Inn & Suites-Ft Lauderdale Plantation at SW 6th St 🅷
(954) 473-8257. **$66-$155.** 7901 SW 6th St 33324. I-595 exit 5 (SR 817/ University Dr), 1.2 mi w to University Dr, 1 mi n to SW 6th St, then 0.3 mi w; in Wellesley Corporate Plaza. Int corridors. **Pets:** Service with restrictions, supervision. 🛰 🅷 💻 🏊

▼▼▼▼ Residence Inn by Marriott-Fort Lauderdale Plantation [H] ❀

(954) 723-0300. **$79-$179.** 130 N University Dr 33324. I-95 exit 27 (Broward Blvd), 5.2 mi w to University Dr, then just n. Int corridors. **Pets:** Other species. $100 one-time fee/room. Designated rooms, service with restrictions. [ECO] 🛜 ⊠ 🕹M 🛏 🖳 🐾 ⊠

🐾🐾 ▼▼▼▼ Sheraton Suites-Plantation [H]

(954) 424-3300. **$109-$189.** 311 N University Dr 33324. I-595 exit 5 (SR 817/University Dr), 1.2 mi w to University Dr, then 1.8 mi n. Int corridors. **Pets:** Accepted. [ECO] [SAVE] 🛜 ⊠ 🕹M 🛏 🖳 🍴 🐾 ⊠

▼▼▼▼ Staybridge Suites Ft. Lauderdale-Plantation [H]

(954) 577-9696. **$109-$139, 3 day notice.** 410 N Pine Island Rd 33324. I-595 exit 4 (Pine Island Rd), 1.7 mi n. Int corridors. **Pets:** Accepted. 🛜 🕹M 🛏 🖳 🐾

POMPANO BEACH

▼▼▼ Extended Stay Deluxe-Cypress Creek Park North [H]

(954) 783-1050. **$60-$140.** 1401 W McNab Rd 33069. I-95 exit 33B (Cypress Creek Rd), just w to Andrews Ave, 0.7 mi n to McNab Rd, then just w. Int corridors. **Pets:** $25 daily fee/pet. Designated rooms, service with restrictions. 🛜 🛏 🖳 🐾

▼▼▼▼ Residence Inn by Marriott-Fort Lauderdale Pompano Beach/Oceanfront [H]

(954) 590-1000. **$159-$349.** 1350 N Ocean Blvd 33062. I-95 exit 36 (Atlantic Blvd/SR 814), 2.7 mi e to SR A1A/Ocean Blvd, then 1.3 mi n. Ext/int corridors. **Pets:** Accepted. 🛜 ⊠ 🕹M 🛏 🖳 🍴 🐾 ⊠

SUNRISE

🐾🐾 ▼▼▼▼ DoubleTree by Hilton Sunrise-Sawgrass Mills [H]

(954) 851-1020. **$99-$219.** 13400 W Sunrise Blvd 33323. Sawgrass Expwy (SR 869) exit 1 (Sunrise Blvd), 1 mi e. Int corridors. **Pets:** Medium. $50 one-time fee/pet. Service with restrictions, crate. [SAVE] 🛜 🕹M 🛏 🖳 🍴 🐾

▼▼▼ La Quinta Inn & Suites-Ft Lauderdale Sawgrass Mills Outlet Mall [H]

(954) 846-1200. **$78-$155.** 13651 NW 2nd St 33325. I-595 exit 1A (SR 84), 0.5 mi w to NW 136th Ave, 0.4 mi n to NW 2nd St, then just w. Int corridors. **Pets:** Service with restrictions, supervision. 🛜 🛏 🖳 🐾

▼▼▼ La Quinta Inn & Suites-Ft Lauderdale Sunrise [H]

(954) 845-9929. **$78-$155.** 13600 NW 2nd St 33325. I-595 exit 1A (SR 84), 0.5 mi w to NW 136th Ave, 0.4 mi n to NW 2nd St, then just w. Int corridors. **Pets:** Service with restrictions, supervision. 🛜 🛏 🖳 🐾

TAMARAC

▼▼▼ La Quinta Inn & Suites-Tamarac [H]

(954) 484-6909. **$59-$129.** 5070 N SR 7 33319. I-95 exit 32 (Commercial Blvd), 3.2 mi w to SR 7 (US 441), then just n; Florida Tpke exit 62, 0.5 mi e to SR 7 (US 441), then just n. Int corridors. **Pets:** Service with restrictions, supervision. 🛜 🛏 🖳 🐾

▼▼▼ La Quinta Inn Tamarac East [H]

(954) 485-7900. **$59-$129.** 3800 W Commercial Blvd 33309. I-95 exit 32 (Commercial Blvd), 3 mi w; Florida Tpke exit 62, 0.7 mi e. Int corridors. **Pets:** Service with restrictions, supervision. 🛜 🛏 🖳 🐾

WESTON

🐾🐾 ▼▼▼▼ Comfort Suites [H]

(954) 659-1555. **$100-$300.** 2201 N Commerce Pkwy 33326. I-75 exit 15 (Royal Palm Blvd), just w to Weston Rd, n to N Commerce Pkwy, then just e. Int corridors. **Pets:** Medium, other species. $10 daily fee/pet. Designated rooms, service with restrictions, crate. [SAVE] 🛜 ⊠ 🕹M 🛏 🖳 🐾

▼▼▼▼ Residence Inn by Marriott-Fort Lauderdale Weston [H]

(954) 659-8585. **$109-$309.** 2605 Weston Rd 33331. I-75 exit 15 (Royal Palm Blvd), 0.3 mi w to Weston Rd, then just s. Int corridors. **Pets:** Other species. $100 one-time fee/room. Service with restrictions, crate. 🛜 ⊠ 🕹M 🛏 🖳 🐾 ⊠

▼▼▼ TownePlace Suites by Marriott-Fort Lauderdale Weston [H]

(954) 659-2234. **$89-$299.** 1545 Three Village Rd 33326. I-75 exit 15 (Royal Palm Blvd), 1.1 mi e to Bonaventure Blvd, 0.4 mi n to Three Village Rd, then just w. Int corridors. **Pets:** Other species. $100 one-time fee/room. Designated rooms, service with restrictions, crate. 🛜 ⊠ 🕹M 🛏 🖳 🐾

END METROPOLITAN AREA

FORT MYERS

🐾🐾 ▼▼▼ BEST WESTERN Airport Inn [H] ❀

(239) 561-7000. **$90-$150.** 8955 Daniels Pkwy 33912. I-75 exit 131, 0.6 mi w on CR 879 (Daniels Pkwy). Int corridors. **Pets:** Medium, dogs only. $250 deposit/room, $20 daily fee/pet. Designated rooms, service with restrictions, supervision. [SAVE] 🛜 ⊠ 🛏 🖳 🐾 ⊠

▼▼▼ Days Inn Springs Resort [M]

(239) 267-7900. **$64-$109.** 18051 S Tamiami Tr 33908. On US 41; jct Constitution Blvd. Ext corridors. **Pets:** Accepted. 🛜 🛏 🖳 🍴 🐾

🐾🐾 ▼▼▼ GrandStay Hotel & Suites [H]

(239) 791-5000. **$69-$259.** 10150 Daniels Pkwy 33913. I-75 exit 131, just e on CR 879 (Daniels Pkwy). Int corridors. **Pets:** Small, dogs only. $15 daily fee/pet. Designated rooms, service with restrictions, supervision. [SAVE] 🛜 ⊠ 🕹M 🛏 🖳 🐾

▼▼▼ Holiday Inn Downtown Historic District [H]

(239) 332-3232. **$80-$160.** 2431 Cleveland Ave 33901. On US 41, just s of jct Edison Ave. Int corridors. **Pets:** Accepted. [ECO] 🛜 ⊠ 🕹M 🛏 🖳 🍴 🐾

🐾🐾 ▼▼▼▼ Homewood Suites by Hilton-Ft. Myers [H] ❀

(239) 275-6000. **$109-$189.** 5255 Big Pine Way 33907. Just e of jct US 41; just n of jct Daniels Pkwy; in Bell Tower Shops. Int corridors. **Pets:** Large. $75 one-time fee/room. Service with restrictions, crate. [ECO] [SAVE] 🛜 🕹M 🛏 🖳 🐾

▼▼▼ Homewood Suites by Hilton Fort Myers Airport/FGCU [H]

(239) 210-7300. **$94-$189.** 16450 Corporate Commerce Way 33913. I-75 exit 128, 0.6 mi e on CR 840 (Alico Rd), just n on Ben Hill Griffin Pkwy, then just w; in Gulfcoast Landings. Int corridors. **Pets:** Accepted. 🛜 🕹M 🛏 🖳 🐾

▼▼▼ Hotel Indigo-Ft. Myers-River District Downtown [H]

(239) 337-3446. **$129-$149.** 1520 Broadway Ave 33901. Between First and Main sts; downtown. Int corridors. **Pets:** Accepted. [ECO] 🛜 🕹M 🛏 🖳 🍴 🐾

🐾🐾 ▼▼▼ La Quinta Inn & Suites-Airport [H]

(239) 466-0012. **$81-$139.** 9521 Marketplace Rd 33912. I-75 exit 131, 0.4 mi w on CR 879 (Daniels Pkwy), then just n on Danport Blvd. Int corridors. **Pets:** Service with restrictions, supervision. [ECO] [SAVE] 🛜 ⊠ 🕹M 🛏 🖳 🐾

Residence Inn by Marriott Fort Myers 🅷
(239) 936-0110. **$109-$299.** 2960 Colonial Blvd 33966. I-75 exit 136, 3.5 mi w on SR 884 (Colonial Blvd). Int corridors. **Pets:** Accepted.
ECO 🛜 ✕ 🅜 📶 💻 🏊 ✕

Residence Inn by Marriott Ft. Myers-Sanibel 🅷
(239) 415-4150. **$95-$209.** 20371 Summerlin Rd 33908. On CR 869, just ne of jct McGregor Blvd. Int corridors. **Pets:** Medium. $100 one-time fee/room. Designated rooms, service with restrictions, crate.
SAVE 🛜 ✕ 🅜 📶 💻 🏊 ✕

Suburban Extended Stay Hotel 🅷
(239) 938-0100. **$50-$120.** 10150 Metro Pkwy 33912. I-75 exit 136, 3.4 mi w on SR 884 (Colonial Blvd); just s on SR 739. Int corridors. **Pets:** Medium, dogs only. $25 daily fee/pet. Designated rooms, service with restrictions, supervision. ECO 🅜 📶 💻 🏊

FORT MYERS BEACH

BEST WESTERN PLUS Beach Resort 🅷
(239) 463-6000. **$189-$349, 7 day notice.** 684 Estero Blvd 33931. 0.4 mi n of Matanzas Pass Bridge (SR 865). Ext corridors. **Pets:** Small, dogs only. $20 daily fee/pet. Service with restrictions, supervision.
SAVE 🛜 ✕ 🅜 📶 💻 🏊

Carousel Inn on the Beach 🅼
(239) 463-6131. **$89-$189, 7 day notice.** 6230 Estero Blvd 33931. On SR 599, 4 mi se of jct Matanzas Pass Bridge (SR 865). Ext corridors. **Pets:** Large, other species. $20 daily fee/room. Designated rooms, service with restrictions. SAVE 🛜 📶 💻 🏊

Hampton Inn & Suites Ft. Myers Beach-Sanibel Gateway 🅷
(239) 437-8888. **$69-$159.** 11281 Summerlin Square Rd 33931. Just e of jct San Carlos Blvd (SR 865). Int corridors. **Pets:** Medium. Service with restrictions, supervision. ECO SAVE 🛜 🅜 📶 💻 🏊

Lighthouse Resort Inn & Suites 🅷 🐾
(239) 463-9392. **$72-$325, 3 day notice.** 1051 5th St 33931. Jct Matanzas Pass Bridge (SR 865). Ext corridors. **Pets:** Small, other species. $25 daily fee/pet. Designated rooms, service with restrictions, supervision.
SAVE 🛜 📶 💻 🍽 🏊

Matanzas Inn 🅼
(239) 463-9258. **$79-$199, 30 day notice.** 414 Crescent St 33931. Just e of Matanzas Pass Bridge (SR 865), then just n. Ext corridors. **Pets:** Small. $35 one-time fee/room. Designated rooms, service with restrictions. SAVE 🛜 📶 💻 🏊 ✕

FORT PIERCE

Holiday Inn Express & Suites-Fort Pierce West 🅷
(772) 464-5000. **$89-$129.** 7151 Okeechobee Rd 34945. I-95 exit 129 (Okeechobee Rd), 0.7 mi w; Florida Tpke exit 152, just e. Int corridors. **Pets:** Accepted. 🛜 ✕ 🅜 📶 💻 🏊

Royal Inn Beach Hotel-South Hutchinson Island 🅼
(772) 672-8888. **$79-$179.** 222 Hernando St 34949. From US 1, 2.5 mi e on Seaway Dr (SR A1A) to Hernando St, then just s. Ext corridors. **Pets:** $25 deposit/room. SAVE 🛜 ✕ 📶

The Sandhurst Hotel & Suites 🅷 🐾
(772) 595-0711. **$79-$189.** 1230 Seaway Dr 34949. From US 1, 2 mi e on Seaway Dr (SR A1A). Int corridors. **Pets:** Other species. $50 one-time fee/room. Service with restrictions, supervision.
SAVE 🛜 ✕ 📶 💻 🏊 ✕

FORT WALTON BEACH

La Quinta Inn & Suites Fort Walton Beach 🅷
(850) 244-1500. **$89-$221.** 3 SW Miracle Strip Pkwy 32548. Jct SR 189 and US 98. Int corridors. **Pets:** Service with restrictions, supervision.
🛜 ✕ 📶 💻 🏊

GAINESVILLE

Baymont Inn & Suites Gainesville 🅷 🐾
(352) 332-8292. **$69-$89.** 6901 NW 4th Blvd 32607. I-75 exit 387, just w on SR 26 to 75th St, just s to NW 4th Blvd, then e. Ext/int corridors. **Pets:** Other species. $10 daily fee/pet. Designated rooms, service with restrictions, supervision. SAVE 🛜 ✕ 📶 💻 🏊

BEST WESTERN PLUS Gateway Grand 🅷 🐾
(352) 331-3336. **$112-$149.** 4200 NW 97th Blvd 32606. I-75 exit 390, just n of SR 222, then just w. Int corridors. **Pets:** Other species. $20 daily fee/room. Designated rooms, service with restrictions, supervision.
ECO SAVE 🛜 ✕ 🅜 📶 💻 🍽 🏊 ✕

Comfort Inn West 🅷
(352) 264-1771. **$79-$139.** 3440 SW 40th Blvd 32608. I-75 exit 384, just e, then just n. Int corridors. **Pets:** Other species. $15 daily fee/pet. Designated rooms, service with restrictions, crate. 🛜 🅜 📶 💻 🏊

Extended Stay America 🅷
(352) 375-0073. **$54-$189.** 3600 SW 42nd St 32608. I-75 exit 384, just e. Ext corridors. **Pets:** $25 daily fee/pet. Designated rooms, service with restrictions. 🛜 📶 💻

Hilton University of Florida Conference Center Gainesville 🅷
(352) 371-3600. **$130-$249.** 1714 SW 34th St 32607. I-75 exit 384, 0.9 mi e on SR 24, then 0.7 mi n on SR 121; in University of Florida. Int corridors. **Pets:** Accepted.
ECO SAVE 🛜 🅜 📶 💻 🍽 🏊 ✕

Holiday Inn Express 🅷
(352) 376-0004. **$101-$154.** 3905 SW 43rd St 32608. I-75 exit 384, just w. Int corridors. **Pets:** Medium, other species. $25 daily fee/pet. Designated rooms, service with restrictions, supervision.
SAVE 🛜 🅜 📶 💻 🏊

Homewood Suites 🅷
(352) 335-3133. **Call for rates.** 3333 SW 42nd St 32608. I-75 exit 384, just e. Int corridors. **Pets:** Accepted.
ECO 🛜 🅜 📶 💻 🏊 ✕

Quality Inn 🅷
(352) 378-2405. **$66-$80.** 3455 SW Williston Rd 32608. I-75 exit 382, just w. Int corridors. **Pets:** Medium, dogs only. $20 daily fee/pet. Designated rooms, no service, supervision. 🛜 📶 💻 🏊

Quality Inn - University 🅷
(352) 373-6500. **$69-$99.** 2435 SW 13th St 32608. I-75 exit 382, 2 mi ne on SR 331, then 1 mi n on US 441. Int corridors. **Pets:** Medium. $10 daily fee/pet. Service with restrictions, crate. SAVE 🛜 📶 💻 🏊

Red Roof Inn-Gainesville 🅷
(352) 336-3311. **$52-$199.** 3500 SW 42nd St 32608. I-75 exit 384, just e. Int corridors. **Pets:** Large, other species. Service with restrictions, supervision. SAVE 🛜 🅜 📶 🏊

Residence Inn by Marriott Gainesville I-75 🅷
(352) 264-0000. **$119-$139.** 3275 SW 40th Blvd 32608. I-75 exit 384, just e to SW 40th Blvd, then n. Int corridors. **Pets:** Other species. $75 one-time fee/room. Service with restrictions.
ECO SAVE 🛜 ✕ 📶 💻 🏊

SpringHill Suites by Marriott Gainesville 🅷
(352) 376-8873. **$99-$149.** 4155 SW 40th Blvd 32608. I-75 exit 384, just e, then just s. Int corridors. **Pets:** Accepted.
ECO SAVE 🛜 ✕ 📶 💻 🏊

AAA ▼▼▼ Sweetwater Branch Inn Bed & Breakfast **BB** ❖

(352) 373-6760. **$109-$239.** 625 E University Ave 32601. 1.3 mi e of the University on SR 26; 7.3 mi e of I-75 exit 387. Int corridors. **Pets:** Other species. $100 deposit/room. Designated rooms, service with restrictions, crate. SAVE 🛰 ✕ 🛡 💻

HERNANDO

▼▼ Quality Inn Conference Center **M**

(352) 527-0015. **$69.** 350 E Norvell Bryant Hwy 34442. On CR 486 at Citrus Hills Blvd, 3.6 mi w of US 41. Int corridors. **Pets:** Small, other species. $20 daily fee/pet. Designated rooms, service with restrictions, crate. 🛰 &M 🛡 💻 🏊

JACKSONVILLE METROPOLITAN AREA

ATLANTIC BEACH

AAA ▼▼▼▼ One Ocean Resort & Spa **H**

(904) 249-7402. **$169-$450, 3 day notice.** One Ocean Blvd 32233. Jct SR A1A, just e on Atlantic Blvd. Int corridors. **Pets:** Accepted.

ECO SAVE 🛰 ✕ &M 🛡 🍴 🏊 🏊

BALDWIN

AAA ▼▼▼ BEST WESTERN Baldwin Inn **M**

(904) 266-9759. **$70.** 1088 US 301 S 32234. I-10 exit 343, just s. Ext corridors. **Pets:** Other species. $10 daily fee/pet. Designated rooms, no service, supervision. SAVE 🛰 🛡 💻 🏊

FERNANDINA BEACH

▼▼▼▼ Comfort Suites Amelia Island **H**

(904) 261-0193. **$85-$130.** 2801 Atlantic Ave 32034. In Fernandina Beach; SR A1A (Atlantic Ave), 1.5 mi e of downtown. Int corridors. **Pets:** Small, other species. $25 daily fee/pet. Designated rooms, service with restrictions, supervision. 🛰 ✕ &M 🛡 💻 🏊

AAA ▼▼▼ Days Inn & Suites **H**

(904) 277-2300. **$70-$400.** 2707 Sadler Rd 32034. In Fernandina Beach; 12.3 mi e on SR 200/A1A, 1.2 mi e. Ext corridors. **Pets:** Accepted.

SAVE 🛰 🛡 💻 🏊 🏊

AAA ▼▼▼▼ The Hoyt House **BB** ❖

(904) 277-4300. **$225-$300, 14 day notice.** 804 Atlantic Ave 32034. In Fernandina Beach; on Atlantic Ave/SR 200 at Centre and S 8th sts; in historic district. Int corridors. **Pets:** Medium, dogs only. $25 daily fee/pet. Designated rooms, crate. SAVE 🛰 ✕ 🏊 🏊

AAA ▼▼▼▼ Omni Amelia Island Plantation Resort **H** ❖

(904) 261-6161. **$189-$499, 7 day notice.** 6800 First Coast Hwy 32034. In Fernandina Beach; SR A1A (Atlantic Ave), 6.5 mi s of the bridge. Ext corridors. **Pets:** Medium. $50 one-time fee/room. Designated rooms, service with restrictions. ECO SAVE 🛰 ✕ 🛡 💻 🍴 🏊 🏊

AAA ▼▼▼▼ Residence Inn by Marriott-Amelia Island **H** ❖

(904) 277-2440. **$129-$299.** 2301 Sadler Rd 32034. In Fernandina Beach; on east side of island, just w of jct SR A1A (Atlantic Ave)and Sadler Rd. Int corridors. **Pets:** Medium, other species. $65 one-time fee/pet. Service with restrictions.

ECO SAVE 🛰 ✕ &M 🛡 💻 🏊 🏊

JACKSONVILLE

AAA ▼▼▼▼ Aloft Jacksonville Tapestry Park **H**

(904) 998-4448. **$89-$299.** 4812 Deer Lake Dr W 32246. I-95 exit 340, 4.5 mi n to Southside Blvd, then e. Int corridors. **Pets:** Accepted.

SAVE 🛰 ✕ &M 🛡 💻 🏊

▼▼ Baymont Inn & Suites Jacksonville/At Butler Blvd **H**

(904) 296-0968. **Call for rates.** 7030 Bonneval Rd 32216. I-95 exit 344 (SR 202), just w. Int corridors. **Pets:** Accepted. 🛰 🛡 💻 🏊

AAA ▼▼▼ BEST WESTERN Hotel - JTB/Southpoint **H** ❖

(904) 281-0900. **$78-$179.** 4660 Salisbury Rd 32256. I-95 exit 344 (Butler Blvd/SR 202), just e to Salisbury Rd, then just s. Int corridors. **Pets:** Small. $10 daily fee/pet. Designated rooms, service with restrictions. SAVE 🛰 🛡 💻 🏊 🏊

AAA ▼▼▼ BEST WESTERN Jacksonville Airport **H**

(904) 741-4980. **$69-$89.** 1170 Airport Entrance Rd 32218. I-95 exit 363B, just w, then just s on Duval Rd. Ext corridors. **Pets:** Medium. $20 daily fee/pet. Designated rooms, service with restrictions, supervision. SAVE 🛰 &M 🛡 💻 🏊

▼▼▼ Candlewood Suites **H**

(904) 296-7785. **$62-$90.** 4990 Belfort Rd 32256. I-95 exit 344, ne to Belfort Rd, then just s. Int corridors. **Pets:** Large. $75 one-time fee/pet. Designated rooms, service with restrictions, crate. 🛰 &M 🛡 💻

▼▼▼ Courtyard by Marriott Jacksonville Airport Northeast **H**

(904) 741-1122. **$79-$159.** 14668 Duval Rd 32218. I-95 exit 363B, just w on Airport Rd, then just s. Int corridors. **Pets:** Accepted.

🛰 ✕ &M 🛡 💻 🍴 🏊

AAA ▼▼▼▼ Crowne Plaza Jacksonville Airport/I-95N **H**

(904) 741-4404. **$89-$179.** 14670 Duval Rd 32218. I-95 exit 363, just w. Int corridors. **Pets:** Accepted. SAVE 🛰 &M 🛡 💻 🍴 🏊

▼▼▼▼ Embassy Suites Jacksonville - Baymeadows **H**

(904) 731-3555. **$99-$199.** 9300 Baymeadows Rd 32256. I-95 exit 341 (Baymeadows Rd/SR 152), 0.5 mi e. Int corridors. **Pets:** Medium, other species. $50 one-time fee/room. Service with restrictions, crate.

ECO 🛰 🛡 💻 🍴 🏊

▼▼▼ Extended StayAmerica-Jacksonville-Butler Blvd **H**

(904) 296-0181. **$50-$70.** 6961 Lenoir Ave 32216. I-95 exit 344 (SR 202), just sw, then 0.3 mi n. Int corridors. **Pets:** $25 daily fee/pet. Designated rooms, service with restrictions. 🛰 🛡 💻

▼▼▼ Extended Stay Deluxe-Jacksonville-Butler Blvd **H**

(904) 332-6512. **$55-$80.** 4699 Lenoir Ave S 32216. I-95 exit 344 (SR 202), just sw, then just n. Int corridors. **Pets:** $25 daily fee/pet. Designated rooms, service with restrictions. 🛰 🛡 💻

▼▼▼ Extended Stay Deluxe (Jacksonville/Deerwood Park) **H**

(904) 620-9008. **$60-$90.** 8801 Perimeter Park Blvd 32216. I-95 exit 344 (SR 202), 2.5 mi e on J Turner Butler Blvd to Southside Blvd, then just n on west side of road. Int corridors. **Pets:** $25 daily fee/pet. Designated rooms, service with restrictions. 🛰 &M 🛡 💻 🏊

▼▼▼▼ Hampton Inn & Suites Deerwood Park **H** ❖

(904) 997-9100. **$79-$169.** 4415 Southside Blvd 32216. I-95 exit 344 (SR 202), 2.5 mi e on J Turner Butler Blvd, then 0.9 mi n on SR 115. Int corridors. **Pets:** Other species. Service with restrictions, supervision.

🛰 ✕ 🛡 💻 🏊

▼▼▼▼ Holiday Inn Express & Suites Jacksonville **H**

(904) 696-3333. **$82-$109, 3 day notice.** 10148 New Berlin Rd 32226. I-95 exit 362A southbound, 4.9 mi s on SR 9A to Heckscher Dr, then just w; exit 358A northbound, 5.8 mi ne on Heckscher Dr; 0.6 mi from Jaxport Cruise Terminal. Int corridors. **Pets:** Small. $30 one-time fee/room. Designated rooms, service with restrictions, supervision. 🛰 🛡 💻 🏊

▼▼▼▼ Holiday Inn Express & Suites Jacksonville-East **H**

(904) 997-9190. **Call for rates.** 53 Jefferson Rd 32225. Jct SR 9A and Atlantic Blvd, just ne. Int corridors. **Pets:** Medium. $30 one-time fee/room. Service with restrictions. 🛰 ✕ 🛡 💻 🏊

▼▼▼ **Holiday Inn Express Hotel & Suites** 🅷
(904) 652-2782. **$89-$109.** 537 Chaffee Point Blvd 32221. I-10 exit 351 (Chaffee Rd), just se. Int corridors. **Pets:** Other species. $33 one-time fee/room. Designated rooms, service with restrictions, crate.
🛜 ⊠ 🅼 🛏 💻 🐾

▼▼▼ **Holiday Inn Express Hotel & Suites - South** 🅷
(904) 332-9500. **$74-$104.** 4675 Salisbury Rd 32256. I-95 exit 344 (Butler Blvd/SR 202), just e to Salisbury Rd, then just s. Int corridors. **Pets:** Large. $25 one-time fee/pet. Service with restrictions, crate.
🛜 ⊠ 🅼 🛏 💻 🐾

▼▼▼ **Homewood Suites by Hilton - Jacksonville** 🅷
(904) 733-9299. **$72-$145.** 8737 Baymeadows Rd 32256. I-95 exit 341 (Baymeadows Rd/SR 152), 0.3 mi w. Ext/int corridors. **Pets:** $75 one-time fee/pet. Service with restrictions. 🛜 🛏 💻 🐾 ⊠

▼▼▼ **Homewood Suites by Hilton Jacksonville South/Town Center** 🅷
(904) 641-7988. **$80-$269.** 10434 Midtown Pkwy 32246. I-95 exit 344 (SR 202), 3.5 mi e on J Turner Butler Blvd to Gate Pkwy, 0.3 mi n to Town Center Pkwy, 0.5 mi e to Midtown Pkwy, then 0.3 mi s. Int corridors. **Pets:** Accepted. 🛜 🛏 💻 🐾 ⊠

▼▼▼ **Hotel Indigo Jacksonville-Deerwood Park** 🅷 ❀
(904) 996-7199. **$75-$175.** 9840 Tapestry Park Cir 32246. I-95 exit 340, 4.5 mi n to Southside Blvd, then e. Int corridors. **Pets:** Large. $25 one-time fee/room. Service with restrictions, crate.
🛜 ⊠ 🛏 💻 🍽 🐾

𝔸𝔸𝔸 ▼▼▼ **Hyatt Regency Jacksonville Riverfront** 🅷
(904) 588-1234. **$81-$360, 3 day notice.** 225 Coast Line Dr E 32202. Downtown; just e of The Landing. Int corridors. **Pets:** Accepted.
🄴🄲🄾 🅂🄰🅅🄴 🛜 🛏 💻 🍽 🐾 ⊠

▼▼ **La Quinta Inn & Suites - Jacksonville Mandarin/San Jose** 🅷
(904) 268-9999. **$66-$122.** 3199 Hartley Rd 32257. I-295 exit 5A northbound; exit 5 southbound at SR 13, just n and then e. Int corridors. **Pets:** Service with restrictions, supervision. 🛜 🛏 💻 🐾

𝔸𝔸𝔸 ▼▼▼▼ **Omni Jacksonville Hotel** 🅷
(904) 355-6664. **$139-$349, 5 day notice.** 245 Water St 32202. Corner of Pearl and Water sts; on north side of St. Johns River; downtown; adjacent to The Landing. Int corridors. **Pets:** Accepted.
🄴🄲🄾 🅂🄰🅅🄴 🛜 🛏 💻 🍽 🐾

▼▼ **Ramada Conference Center - Jacksonville** 🅷 ❀
(904) 268-8080. **$69-$139.** 3130 Hartley Rd 32257. I-295 exit 5A northbound; exit 5 southbound, then just n on SR 13. Ext corridors. **Pets:** Designated rooms, service with restrictions, supervision.
🛜 ⊠ 🛏 💻 🍽 🐾

▼▼▼ **Residence Inn by Marriott Butler Blvd** 🅷
(904) 996-8900. **$99-$149.** 10551 Deerwood Park Blvd 32256. I-95 exit 344 (SR 202/Butler Blvd), 3.3 mi e to Gate Parkway exit, then just s to Deerwood Park Blvd, then just w. Int corridors. **Pets:** Accepted.
🛜 ⊠ 🅼 🛏 💻 🐾 ⊠

𝔸𝔸𝔸 ▼▼▼ **Residence Inn by Marriott Jacksonville Baymeadows** 🅷
(904) 733-8088. **$84-$109.** 8365 Dix Ellis Tr 32256. I-95 exit 341 (Baymeadows Rd/SR 152), just w to Freedom Commerce Pkwy, then just s. Ext corridors. **Pets:** Accepted. 🅂🄰🅅🄴 🛜 ⊠ 🛏 💻 🐾 ⊠

𝔸𝔸𝔸 ▼▼▼ **Sheraton Jacksonville Hotel** 🅷 ❀
(904) 564-4772. **$99-$399.** 10605 Deerwood Park Blvd 32256. I-95 exit 344 (SR 202/Butler Blvd), 3.3 mi e to Gate Parkway exit, just s to Deerwood Park Blvd, then just w. Int corridors. **Pets:** Medium. Designated rooms, service with restrictions, supervision.
🅂🄰🅅🄴 🛜 ⊠ 🅼 💻 🍽 🐾

JACKSONVILLE BEACH

𝔸𝔸𝔸 ▼▼▼ **Holiday Inn Express Jacksonville Beach-Mayo Clinic** 🅷
(904) 435-3000. **$119-$179.** 1101 Beach Blvd 32250. 0.7 mi w of 3rd St/SR A1A. Int corridors. **Pets:** Medium. $25 daily fee/pet. Designated rooms, service with restrictions, supervision.
🄴🄲🄾 🅂🄰🅅🄴 🛜 ⊠ 🅼 🛏 💻 🐾 ⊠

𝔸𝔸𝔸 ▼▼▼ **Quality Suites Oceanfront - Mayo Clinic** 🅷
(904) 435-3535. **$150-$250.** 11 1st St N 32250. Just n of Beach Blvd (US 90). Int corridors. **Pets:** Medium. $35 daily fee/room. Designated rooms, service with restrictions, supervision.
🄴🄲🄾 🅂🄰🅅🄴 🛜 ⊠ 🅼 🛏 💻 🐾 ⊠

NEPTUNE BEACH

𝔸𝔸𝔸 ▼▼◆ **Days Inn Neptune Beach-Mayo Clinic** 🅷
(904) 249-2777. **$60-$150.** 1401 Atlantic Blvd 32266. SR 9A exit SR 10, 6.9 mi e. Int corridors. **Pets:** Other species. $15 daily fee/pet. Designated rooms, service with restrictions, supervision. 🅂🄰🅅🄴 🛜 🛏 💻 🐾

YULEE

𝔸𝔸𝔸 ▼▼▼ **BEST WESTERN PLUS First Coast Inn & Suites** 🅷
(904) 225-0182. **Call for rates.** 462577 SR 200 32097. I-95 exit 373, just e on SR 200/A1A. Int corridors. **Pets:** Medium, dogs only. $20 daily fee/room. Designated rooms, service with restrictions, supervision.
🅂🄰🅅🄴 🛜 ⊠ 🅼 🛏 💻 🐾

▼▼ **Comfort Inn** 🅷
(904) 225-2600. **$70-$110.** 76043 Sidney Pl 32097. I-95 exit 373, just e on SR 200/A1A. Int corridors. **Pets:** Accepted. 🛜 🛏 💻 🐾

END METROPOLITAN AREA

JUNO BEACH

▼▼▼ **Holiday Inn Express-Juno Beach** 🅷
(561) 622-4366. **$99-$239.** 13950 US Hwy 1 33408. I-95 exit 83 (Donald Ross Rd), 4.5 mi e; jct US 1 and Donald Ross Rd. Ext/int corridors. **Pets:** Small. $25 daily fee/pet. Service with restrictions, supervision.
🛜 ⊠ 🛏 💻 🐾

JUPITER

▼▼▼ **Fairfield Inn & Suites by Marriott-Jupiter/West Palm Beach** 🅷
(561) 748-5252. **$79-$169.** 6748 W Indiantown Rd 33458. I-95 exit 87A (Indiantown Rd), 0.8 mi e. Int corridors. **Pets:** Accepted.
🄴🄲🄾 🛜 ⊠ 🛏 💻 🐾

LAKE CITY

𝔸𝔸𝔸 ▼▼▼ **BEST WESTERN Lake City Inn** 🅷
(386) 752-3801. **$72-$82.** 3598 W Hwy 90 32055. I-75 exit 427, just w. Ext corridors. **Pets:** Medium, other species. $15 daily fee/room. Designated rooms, service with restrictions, supervision.
🅂🄰🅅🄴 🛜 🛏 💻 🐾 ⊠

𝔸𝔸𝔸 ▼▼▼ **Days Inn I-10** 🅷
(386) 758-4224. **$55-$80.** 3430 N Hwy 441 32055. I-10 exit 303, just s. Ext corridors. **Pets:** Other species. $10 daily fee/pet. Service with restrictions, crate. 🅂🄰🅅🄴 🛜 🛏 💻 🐾

𝔸𝔸𝔸 ▼▼▼ **Driftwood Inn** 🄼
(386) 755-3545. **$42-$70.** 2764 W Hwy 90 32055. I-75 exit 427, 0.7 mi e. Ext corridors. **Pets:** Medium, dogs only. $10 daily fee/pet. Designated rooms, service with restrictions, supervision. 🅂🄰🅅🄴 🛜 🛏

▼▼▼▼ Holiday Inn Hotel & Suites ⚑

(386) 754-1411. **Call for rates.** 213 SW Commerce Dr 32025. I-75 exit 427, just e. Int corridors. **Pets:** Accepted.

🌱 📶 ✕ 📠 💻 🍴 ⌫ ✕

▼▼ Red Roof Inn ⚑

(386) 752-6693. **$59-$99.** 414 SW Florida Gateway Dr 32024. I-75 exit 427, just w, then 0.4 mi s. Ext corridors. **Pets:** Large, other species. Service with restrictions, supervision. 📶 📠 ⌫

▼▼ Rodeway Inn 🅼

(386) 755-5203. **Call for rates.** 205 SW Commerce Dr 32025. I-75 exit 427, just e. Ext corridors. **Pets:** Accepted. 📶 📠 💻

LAKELAND

▼▼ Baymont Inn & Suites Lakeland ⚑

(863) 858-9070. **Call for rates.** 4375 Lakeland Park Dr 33809. I-4 exit 33, 0.6 mi s on SR 33, just nw on N Socrum Loop Rd, then just w. Int corridors. **Pets:** Accepted. 📶 ♿ 📠 💻 ⌫

▼▼▼▼ Crestwood Suites Extended Stay Hotel Lakeland ⚑

(863) 904-2050. **Call for rates.** 4360 Lakeland Park Dr 33809. I-4 exit 33, 0.6 mi se on SR 33; 0.4 mi n on Socrum Loop, just s. Int corridors. **Pets:** Accepted. 📶 ♿ 📠 💻 ⌫

▼▼▼▼ Residence Inn by Marriott Lakeland ⚑

(863) 680-2323. **$99-$279.** 3701 Harden Blvd 33803. SR 570 (Polk Pkwy) exit 5, just n. Int corridors. **Pets:** Accepted.

📶 ✕ 📠 💻 ⌫ ✕

LAKE WORTH

▲▲▲ **▼▼▼▼▼▼** Sabal Palm House B & B Inn 🅱🅱

(561) 582-1090. **$99-$249, 14 day notice.** 109 N Golfview Rd 33460. Just n of SR 802; west side of Intracoastal Bridge. Ext/int corridors. **Pets:** Small. $15 daily fee/pet. Designated rooms, service with restrictions.

🆂 📶 ✕ 📠 💻

LANTANA

▲▲▲ **▼▼** Super 8 Lantana 🅼

(561) 585-3970. **$59-$99.** 1255 Hypoluxo Rd 33462. I-95 exit 60 (Hypoluxo Rd), just e. Ext corridors. **Pets:** Accepted. 🆂 📶 📠 💻 ⌫

LECANTO

▼▼▼▼ Holiday Inn Express Hotel & Suites ⚑

(352) 341-3515. **$80-$140.** 903 E Gulf to Lake Hwy 34461. On SR 44, 4.2 mi e. Int corridors. **Pets:** Accepted.

🌱 📶 ✕ ♿ 📠 💻 ⌫

LIVE OAK

▲▲▲ **▼▼** Econo Lodge ⚑

(386) 362-7459. **$70-$80.** 6811 N US 129 & I-10 32060. I-10 exit 283, just s. Ext corridors. **Pets:** Accepted. 🆂 📶 📠 💻 ⌫

▲▲▲ **▼▼** Quality Inn ⚑

(386) 362-6000. **$70-$90.** 6819 US 129 N 32060. I-10 exit 283, 0.3 mi s. Ext corridors. **Pets:** Accepted. 🆂 📶 📠 💻 ⌫

LYNN HAVEN

▼▼▼▼ Wingate by Wyndham Lynn Haven ⚑

(850) 248-8080. **$95-$155.** 2610 Lynn Haven Pkwy 32444. On SR 77, 1.8 mi n of jct SR 368. Int corridors. **Pets:** Small, dogs only. $60 one-time fee/room. Service with restrictions, supervision.

📶 ✕ ♿ 📠 💻 ⌫ ✕

MACCLENNY

▲▲▲ **▼▼** Econo Lodge 🅼

(904) 259-3000. **$50-$90.** 151 Woodlawn Rd 32063. I-10 exit 335, just s of jct SR 121. Ext corridors. **Pets:** Accepted. 🆂 📶 📠 💻 ⌫

MANALAPAN

▲▲▲ **▼▼▼▼▼** The Ritz-Carlton, Palm Beach ⚑ 🐾

(561) 533-6000. **$199-$749, 14 day notice.** 100 S Ocean Blvd 33462. I-95 exit 61 (Lantana Rd), 1.1 mi e to US 1 (Dixie Hwy), just s to Ocean Ave, then 0.8 mi e. Int corridors. **Pets:** Small. $175 one-time fee/room. Designated rooms, service with restrictions, crate.

🌱 🆂 📶 ✕ 💻 🍴 ⌫ ✕

MARIANNA

▼▼▼▼ Microtel Inn & Suites by Wyndham Marianna ⚑ 🐾

(850) 526-5005. **$80-$110.** 4959 White Tail Dr 32448. I-10 exit 142, just n. Int corridors. **Pets:** Small, dogs only. $25 daily fee/pet. Designated rooms, service with restrictions, supervision. 📶 ♿ 📠 💻 ⌫

MELBOURNE

▼▼▼▼ Candlewood Suites Hotel ⚑

(321) 821-9009. **$79-$99.** 2930 Pineda Plaza Way 32940. I-95 exit 191 (CR 509/Wickham Rd), 4.5 mi e, then just n. Int corridors.

Pets: Accepted. 📶 📠 💻

▲▲▲ **▼▼▼▼** DoubleTree Guest Suites - Melbourne Beach Oceanfront ⚑

(321) 723-4222. **$119-$179.** 1665 N SR A1A 32903. On SR A1A, 1.5 mi n of jct US 192. Ext corridors. **Pets:** Accepted.

🌱 🆂 📶 ✕ 📠 💻 🍴 ⌫ ✕

▼▼ Extended Stay Deluxe Melbourne-Airport ⚑

(321) 733-6050. **$70-$120.** 1701 Evans Rd 32904. I-95 exit 180 (US 192/New Haven Ave), 3.2 mi e to Evans Rd, then 0.4 mi n. Int corridors. **Pets:** $25 daily fee/pet. Designated rooms, service with restrictions.

📶 📠 💻 ⌫

▲▲▲ **▼▼▼▼** Hilton Melbourne Beach Oceanfront ⚑

(321) 777-5000. **$109-$179.** 3003 N SR A1A 32903. 3 mi n of jct US 192. Int corridors. **Pets:** Medium. $50 one-time fee/pet. Designated rooms, service with restrictions, crate.

🌱 🆂 📶 📠 💻 🍴 ⌫ ✕

▼▼▼▼ Hilton Melbourne Rialto Place ⚑ 🐾

(321) 768-0200. **$89-$199.** 200 Rialto Pl 32901. I-95 exit 180 (US 192/New Haven Ave), 4.8 mi e to Airport Blvd, then 0.8 mi n to Rialto Pl. Int corridors. **Pets:** Large. $50 one-time fee/room. Service with restrictions.

📶 ♿ 📠 💻 🍴 ⌫ ✕

▼▼ La Quinta Inn & Suites - Melbourne ⚑

(321) 242-9400. **$83-$155.** 7200 George T Edwards Dr 32940. I-95 exit 191 (CR 509/Wickham Rd), just w. Int corridors. **Pets:** Service with restrictions, supervision. 📶 📠 💻 ⌫

▲▲▲ **▼▼▼▼** Residence Inn by Marriott Melbourne ⚑

(321) 723-5740. **$109-$239.** 1430 S Babcock St 32901. I-95 exit 180 (US 192/New Haven Ave), 5.1 mi e to Babcock St, then 0.5 mi n. Int corridors. **Pets:** Large, other species. $100 one-time fee/room. Service with restrictions, supervision. 🆂 📶 ✕ ♿ 📠 💻 ⌫ ✕

MIAMI-MIAMI BEACH METROPOLITAN AREA

AVENTURA

Residence Inn by Marriott-Aventura Mall 🄷
(786) 528-1001. **$134-$404.** 19900 W Country Club Dr 33180. I-95 exit 16 (Ives Dairy Rd), 1.1 mi e to US 1 (Biscayne Blvd), 0.5 mi s to 199th St, 0.5 mi e to W Country Club Dr, then just s. Int corridors. **Pets:** Medium. $100 one-time fee/pet. Service with restrictions, supervision. ECO SAVE 🛜 ⊠ ᴸᴹ 🖥 🖵 ⊇⊷ ⊠

Turnberry Isle Miami 🄷 ❀
(305) 932-6200. **$159-$3900, 3 day notice.** 19999 W Country Club Dr 33180. I-95 exit 16 (Ives Dairy Rd), 1.1 mi e to US 1 (Biscayne Blvd), just s to 199th St (Aventura Blvd), 0.5 mi e to Country Club Dr, then just s. Ext/int corridors. **Pets:** Small. $100 one-time fee/pet, $25 daily fee/pet. Designated rooms, service with restrictions, crate.
ECO SAVE 🛜 ⊠ ᴸᴹ 🖥 🖵 ¶¶ ⊇⊷ ⊠

BAL HARBOUR

ONE Bal Harbour Resort & Spa 🄷 ❀
(305) 455-5400. **$300-$1000, 3 day notice.** 10295 Collins Ave 33154. On SR A1A (Collins Ave); at Haulover Cswy. Int corridors. **Pets:** Small, dogs only. $150 one-time fee/pet. Designated rooms, service with restrictions, supervision. SAVE 🛜 ⊠ 🖥 🖵 ¶¶ ⊇⊷ ⊠

St. Regis Bal Harbour 🄷
(305) 993-3300. **$409-$1500, 3 day notice.** 9703 Collins Ave 33154. Just n of jct SR A1A (Collins Ave) and 922 (96th St). Int corridors.
Pets: Accepted. SAVE 🛜 ⊠ ᴸᴹ 🖥 ¶¶ 🖵 ⊇⊷ ⊠

COCONUT GROVE

Mayfair Hotel & Spa 🄷
(305) 441-0000. **$119-$409.** 3000 Florida Ave 33133. At Florida Ave and Virginia St; center. Ext/int corridors. **Pets:** Accepted.
SAVE 🛜 ⊠ 🖵 ¶¶ ⊇⊷

Residence Inn by Marriott Miami Coconut Grove 🄷 ❀
(305) 285-9303. **$99-$299.** 2835 Tigertail Ave 33133. S Bayshore Dr, w on SW 27th Ave (Cornelia Dr), then s. Ext corridors. **Pets:** Large, other species. $100 one-time fee/room. Service with restrictions.
SAVE 🛜 ⊠ 🖥 🖵 ⊇⊷

CORAL GABLES

The Biltmore Hotel Coral Gables 🄷
(305) 445-1926. **$195-$440.** 1200 Anastasia Ave 33134. From US 1, 1.4 mi w on Bird Rd (SW 40th St) to Granada Blvd, 0.5 mi n to Anastasia Ave, then just w. Int corridors. **Pets:** Accepted.
ECO 🛜 🖥 ¶¶ ⊇⊷ ⊠

Extended StayAmerica-Miami-Coral Gables 🄷
(305) 443-7444. **$60-$160.** 3640 Coral Way/SW 22nd St 33145. Just e of Douglas Rd. Int corridors. **Pets:** $25 daily fee/pet. Designated rooms, service with restrictions. 🛜 ᴸᴹ 🖥 🖵

Hyatt Regency Coral Gables 🄷
(305) 441-1234. **$117-$378.** 50 Alhambra Plaza 33134. At Alhambra Plaza and Douglas Rd; downtown. Int corridors. **Pets:** Accepted.
ECO SAVE 🛜 ᴸᴹ 🖵 ¶¶ ⊇⊷ ⊠

The Westin Colonnade Coral Gables 🄷
(305) 441-2600. **$109-$559.** 180 Aragon Ave 33134. At Aragon Ave and Ponce de Leon Blvd; downtown. Int corridors. **Pets:** Accepted.
ECO SAVE 🛜 ⊠ 🖥 🖵 ¶¶ ⊇⊷ ⊠

FLORIDA CITY

Travelodge-Florida City 🅼
(305) 248-9777. **$60-$200.** 409 SE 1st Ave 33034. On US 1, just s of Florida Tpke terminus. Ext corridors. **Pets:** $15 daily fee/pet. Service with restrictions, supervision. SAVE 🛜 ᴸᴹ 🖥 🖵 ⊇⊷

KEY BISCAYNE

The Ritz-Carlton Key Biscayne, Miami 🄷
(305) 365-4500. **Call for rates.** 455 Grand Bay Dr 33149. Jct Crandon Blvd, just e. Int corridors. **Pets:** Accepted.
ECO SAVE 🛜 ⊠ ᴸᴹ 🖥 🖵 ¶¶ ⊇⊷ ⊠

MIAMI

Candlewood Suites-Miami Airport West 🄷
(305) 591-9099. **$109-$189.** 8855 NW 27th St 33172. Florida Tpke exit 29 (NW 41st St), 3.2 mi e to NW 87th Ave, 0.7 mi s to NW 27th St, then just w. Int corridors. **Pets:** Accepted. 🛜 ᴸᴹ 🖥 🖵 ⊇⊷

DoubleTree by Hilton Hotel-Miami Airport & Convention Center 🄷
(305) 261-3800. **$99-$269.** 711 NW 72nd Ave 33126. SR 836 (Dolphin Expwy) exit NW 57th Ave/Red Rd, 0.6 mi s to NW 7th St, 1.5 mi w to NW 72nd Ave/Milam Dairy Rd, then just n. Int corridors. **Pets:** Accepted.
SAVE 🛜 🖵 ¶¶ ⊇⊷ ⊠

Epic Hotel 🄷
(305) 424-5226. **$269-$799, 3 day notice.** 270 Biscayne Boulevard Way 33131. Just e of US 1 (SE 2nd Ave). Int corridors. **Pets:** Accepted.
ECO SAVE 🛜 ⊠ ᴸᴹ ¶¶ ⊇⊷ ⊠

Extended Stay Deluxe-Miami-Airport-Doral 🄷
(305) 716-9005. **$55-$150.** 7750 NW 25th St 33122. SR 826 (Dolphin Expwy) exit NW 25th St, just w. Int corridors. **Pets:** $25 daily fee/pet. Designated rooms, service with restrictions. 🛜 ᴸᴹ 🖥 🖵 ⊇⊷

Four Seasons Hotel Miami 🄷 ❀
(305) 358-3535. **$255-$595, 3 day notice.** 1435 Brickell Ave 33131. Jct 14th Terr on US 1. Int corridors. **Pets:** Very small. Service with restrictions, supervision.
ECO ⊟ SAVE 🛜 ⊠ ᴸᴹ 🖥 🖵 ¶¶ ⊇⊷ ⊠

Hilton Miami Downtown 🄷
(305) 374-0000. **$109-$429.** 1601 Biscayne Blvd 33132. On US 1 (Biscayne Blvd), just n of NE 15th St. Int corridors. **Pets:** Accepted.
ECO SAVE 🛜 ⊠ ᴸᴹ 🖥 🖵 ⊇⊷

Hotel Indigo Miami-Dadeland 🄷
(305) 595-6000. **$109-$199.** 7600 N Kendall Dr 33156. SR 826 (Palmetto Expwy) exit SW 88th St (N Kendall Dr), just w. Int corridors.
Pets: Accepted. SAVE 🛜 ⊠ ᴸᴹ 🖥 🖵 ¶¶ ⊇⊷

Hotel Urbano at Brickell 🄷
(305) 854-2070. **$129-$399.** 2500 Brickell Ave 33129. Jct SE 25th Rd and Brickell Ave. Int corridors. **Pets:** Accepted.
SAVE 🛜 ⊠ ᴸᴹ 🖥 🖵 ¶¶ ⊇⊷

Hyatt house Miami Airport 🄷
(305) 269-1922. **$94-$399.** 5710 Blue Lagoon Dr 33126. SR 836 (Dolphin Expwy) exit NW 57th Ave/Red Rd, just s. Int corridors.
Pets: Accepted. SAVE 🛜 ⊠ ᴸᴹ 🖥 🖵 ⊇⊷

Hyatt Miami at The Blue 🄷
(305) 597-8600. **$99-$306.** 5300 NW 87th Ave 33178. SR 826 (Palmetto Expwy) exit NW 58th St, 0.9 mi w to NW 87th Ave, then 0.4 mi s. Ext corridors. **Pets:** Accepted. SAVE 🛜 ⊠ 🖥 🖵 ¶¶ ⊇⊷ ⊠

▼▼▼ La Quinta Inn & Suites-Miami Airport West 🅷
(305) 436-0830. **$78-$232.** 8730 NW 27th St 33172. Florida Tpke exit 29 (NW 41st St), 3.2 mi e to NW 87th Ave, 0.7 mi s to NW 27th St, then just w. Int corridors. **Pets:** Service with restrictions, supervision.
🛜 Ꮺᴹ 🛀

▼▼▼ La Quinta Inn Miami Airport North 🅷
(305) 599-9902. **$71-$144.** 7401 NW 36th St 33166. SR 826 (Palmetto Expwy) exit NW 36th St, just e. Ext/int corridors. **Pets:** Service with restrictions, supervision. 🛜 🛢 🖵 🛀

Ⓐ▲ ▼▼▼▼▼▼ Mandarin Oriental, Miami 🅷 ❀
(305) 913-8288. **$269-$699.** 500 Brickell Key Dr 33131. US 1 (Brickell Ave), just e on SE 8th St (Brickell Key Dr). Int corridors. **Pets:** Medium. $100 deposit/pet, $100 one-time fee/pet. Supervision.
ECO SAVE 🛜 ✕ Ꮺᴹ 🍴 🛀 ✕

Ⓐ▲ ▼▼▼▼ Residence Inn by Marriott Miami Airport 🅷
(305) 642-8570. **$127-$212.** 1201 NW LeJeune Rd 33126. SR 836 (Dolphin Expwy) exit LeJeune Rd (NW 42nd Ave), just s. Int corridors. **Pets:** Small, other species. $100 one-time fee/room. Service with restrictions, supervision. SAVE 🛜 ✕ Ꮺᴹ 🛢 🖵

▼▼▼▼ Residence Inn by Marriott-Miami Airport West/Doral Area 🅷
(305) 591-2211. **$139-$189.** 1212 NW 82nd Ave 33126. SR 826 (Palmetto Expwy) exit NW 25th St, 0.5 mi w to NW 82nd Ave, then 1 mi s. Ext corridors. **Pets:** $100 one-time fee/room. Service with restrictions, supervision. 🛜 ✕ 🛢 🖵 🛀 ✕

Ⓐ▲ ▼▼▼▼ Sheraton Miami Airport Hotel & Executive Meeting Center 🅷 ❀
(305) 871-3800. **$169-$399, 3 day notice.** 3900 NW 21st St 33142. SR 112 to LeJeune Rd (NW 42nd Ave), 0.3 mi e. Int corridors. **Pets:** Large, other species. ECO SAVE 🛜 ✕ 🛢 🖵 🍴 🛀

▼▼▼▼ Sofitel Miami 🅷 ❀
(305) 264-4888. **Call for rates.** 5800 Blue Lagoon Dr 33126. SR 836 (Dolphin Expwy) exit Red Rd/SR 959, just s to Blue Lagoon Dr, then just w. Int corridors. **Pets:** Medium. Designated rooms, service with restrictions. ECO 🛜 🖵 🍴 🛀 ✕

▼▼▼▼ Staybridge Suites Miami-Doral Area 🅷
(305) 500-9100. **$129-$149, 3 day notice.** 3265 NW 87th Ave 33172. Florida Tpke exit 29 (NW 41st St), 3.2 mi e to NW 87th Ave, then 0.3 mi s. Int corridors. **Pets:** Accepted. 🛜 🛢 🖵 🛀

Ⓐ▲ ▼▼▼▼ TownePlace Suites by Marriott-Miami Airport West/Doral Area 🅷
(305) 718-4144. **$101-$144.** 10505 NW 36th St 33178. Florida Tpke exit 29 (NW 41st St), 1.2 mi e to 107th Ave, then just s. Int corridors. **Pets:** Other species. $100 one-time fee/room. Service with restrictions. SAVE 🛜 ✕ 🛢 🛀

MIAMI BEACH

▼▼▼▼ The Betsy-South Beach 🅷
(305) 531-6100. **$329-$699, 3 day notice.** 1440 Ocean Dr 33139. Between 14th and 15th sts. Int corridors. **Pets:** Accepted.
🛜 ✕ 🖵 🍴 🛀

Ⓐ▲ ▼▼▼▼▼▼ Eden Roc Renaissance Miami Beach 🅷
(305) 531-0000. **$186-$459, 3 day notice.** 4525 Collins Ave 33140. SR A1A (Collins Ave), just n of 41st St. Int corridors. **Pets:** Accepted.
SAVE 🛜 ✕ 🛢 🖵 🍴 🛀 ✕

Ⓐ▲ ▼▼▼▼ Fontainebleau Miami Beach 🅷
(305) 538-2000. **Call for rates.** 4441 Collins Ave 33140. SR A1A (Collins Ave); just n of Arthur Godfrey Rd. Int corridors. **Pets:** Accepted.
ECO 🎫 SAVE 🛜 ✕ 🛢 🖵 🍴 🛀 ✕

▼▼▼▼ Grand Beach Hotel 🅷
(305) 538-8666. **$149-$539.** 4835 Collins Ave 33140. Between 48th and 49th sts. Int corridors. **Pets:** Accepted. 🛜 🛢 🖵 🍴 🛀

Ⓐ▲ ▼▼▼ ▼▼▼ Hilton Bentley Miami/South Beach 🅷
(305) 938-4600. **Call for rates.** 101 Ocean Dr 33139. Just e of SR A1A (Collins Ave); corner of Ocean Dr and 1st St. Int corridors.
Pets: Accepted. SAVE 🛜 ✕ Ꮺᴹ 🛢 🖵 🍴 🛀 ✕

Ⓐ▲ ▼▼▼▼ Loews Miami Beach Hotel 🅷
(305) 604-1601. **$199-$599, 3 day notice.** 1601 Collins Ave 33139. SR A1A, jct Collins and 16th aves. Int corridors. **Pets:** Accepted.
SAVE 🛜 ✕ Ꮺᴹ 🖵 🍴 🛀 ✕

Ⓐ▲ ▼▼▼▼ Marriott South Beach 🅷
(305) 536-7700. **$219-$459, 3 day notice.** 161 Ocean Dr 33139. Just e of SR A1A (Collins Ave); just s of 2nd St. Int corridors. **Pets:** Accepted.
SAVE 🛜 ✕ 🛢 🖵 🍴 🛀 ✕

▼▼▼▼ The National Hotel 🅷
(305) 532-2311. **Call for rates.** 1677 Collins Ave 33139. On SR A1A (Collins Ave) and 16th St. Int corridors. **Pets:** Accepted.
🛜 ✕ 🍴 🛀 ✕

▼▼▼▼ The Ritz-Carlton, South Beach 🅷
(786) 276-4000. **Call for rates.** 1 Lincoln Rd 33139. Jct SR A1A (Collins Ave). Int corridors. **Pets:** Very small, dogs only. $250 one-time fee/room. Designated rooms, service with restrictions, supervision.
ECO 🛜 Ꮺᴹ 🖵 🍴 🛀 ✕

▼▼▼▼ The Setai, Miami Beach 🅷
(305) 520-6000. **$550-$1400, 14 day notice.** 2001 Collins Ave 33139. On SR A1A (Collins Ave); at 20th St. Int corridors. **Pets:** Accepted.
ECO SAVE 🛜 ✕ Ꮺᴹ 🛢 🖵 🍴 🛀 ✕

Ⓐ▲ ▼▼▼▼ W South Beach 🅷
(305) 938-3000. **$369-$1409, 3 day notice.** 2201 Collins Ave 33139. Jct SR A1A (Collins Ave) and 22nd St. Int corridors. **Pets:** Accepted.
SAVE 🛜 ✕ Ꮺᴹ 🛢 🖵 🍴 🛀 ✕

MIAMI LAKES

▼▼▼ Hotel Indigo Miami Lakes 🅷
(305) 556-0100. **$99-$169.** 7601 Miami Lakes Dr 33014. From SR 826 (Palmetto Expwy) exit NW 154 St, just e. Int corridors. **Pets:** Accepted.
🛜 ✕ Ꮺᴹ 🖵 🍴 🛀

▼▼▼ La Quinta Inn & Suites-Miami Lakes 🅷
(305) 821-8274. **$90-$166.** 7925 NW 154th St 33016. Jct SR 826 (Palmetto Expwy) exit NW 154th St, just w. Int corridors. **Pets:** Service with restrictions, supervision. 🛜 🛢 🖵 🛀

Ⓐ▲ ▼▼▼ TownePlace Suites by Marriott-Miami Lakes Miramar Area 🅷
(305) 512-9191. **$93-$127.** 8079 NW 154th St 33016. SR 826 (Palmetto Expwy) exit NW 154th St, 0.4 mi w. Int corridors. **Pets:** Accepted.
SAVE 🛜 ✕ Ꮺᴹ 🛢 🖵 🛀

MIAMI SPRINGS

▼▼▼ La Quinta Inn & Suites-Miami Airport East 🅷
(305) 871-1777. **$78-$221.** 3501 NW LeJeune Rd 33142. LeJeune Rd (NW 42nd Ave), just s of SR 112. Int corridors. **Pets:** Service with restrictions, supervision. 🛜 🛢 🖵 🛀

Red Roof Inn-Miami Airport ⊞
(305) 871-4221. **$89-$269.** 3401 NW LeJeune Rd (NW 42nd Ave)
33142. On LeJeune Rd (NW 42nd Ave), just s of SR 112. Int corridors.
Pets: Large, other species. Service with restrictions, supervision.
[SAVE] 🛜 🛈 🖵 🏊

SUNNY ISLES BEACH

Acqualina Resort & Spa on the
Beach ⊞ 🐾
(305) 918-8000. **$475-$3250, 30 day notice.** 17875 Collins Ave 33160.
I-95 exit 16 (Ives Dairy Rd), 1.2 mi e to US 1 (Biscayne Blvd), 0.6 mi s
to William Lehman Cswy, 1.6 mi e to SR A1A (Collins Ave), then 0.8 mi
s. Int corridors. **Pets:** Small. $100 one-time fee/room. Service with restric-
tions, supervision. [SAVE] 🛜 ✕ ⫶M 🛈 🖵 ⎟⎟ 🏊 ✕

END METROPOLITAN AREA

MIDWAY

BEST WESTERN PLUS Panhandle Capital Inn
& Suites ⊞
(850) 514-2222. **$84-$119.** 85 River Park Dr 32343. I-10 exit 192, just s.
Int corridors. **Pets:** Large, other species. $10 one-time fee/room. Service
with restrictions. [SAVE] 🛜 🛈 🖵 🏊

MILTON

Comfort Inn ⊞ 🐾
(850) 623-1511. **$75-$110.** 8936 Hwy 87 S 32583. I-10 exit 31, just s. Int
corridors. **Pets:** Small. $20 daily fee/room. Designated rooms, service with
restrictions, supervision. [SAVE] 🛜 ⫶M 🛈 🖵 🏊

Red Roof Inn & Suites ⊞
(850) 995-6100. **$70-$104.** 2672 Avalon Blvd 32583. I-10 exit 22, just s.
Int corridors. **Pets:** Large, other species. Service with restrictions, supervision. [SAVE] 🛜 ⫶M 🛈 🖵 🏊

MONTICELLO

Days Inn Ⓜ
(850) 997-5988. **$60-$190.** 44 Woodworth Dr 32336. I-10 exit 225, just s
on US 19. Ext corridors. **Pets:** Accepted. 🛜 🛈 🖵 🏊

NAPLES

Hawthorn Suites By Wyndham of
Naples ⊞ 🐾
(239) 593-1300. **$159-$300.** 3557 Pine Ridge Rd 34109. I-75 exit 107,
0.5 mi w on Pine Ridge Rd (CR 896). Int corridors. **Pets:** Medium. $125
one-time fee/room. Designated rooms, service with restrictions, crate.
[ECO] [SAVE] 🛜 ✕ 🛈 🖵 🏊 ✕

Hilton Naples ⊞
(239) 430-4900. **$109-$339.** 5111 Tamiami Tr N 34103. On US 41
(Tamiami Tr), just s of jct Pine Ridge Rd (CR 896). Int corridors.
Pets: Accepted. [ECO] [SAVE] 🛜 ✕ ⫶M 🛈 🖵 ⎟⎟ 🏊 ✕

La Quinta Inn & Suites-Naples Downtown Ⓜ
(239) 793-4646. **$79-$189.** 1555 5th Ave S 34102. Just w of jct SR 84
(Davis Blvd) and US 41 (Tamiami Tr). Int corridors. **Pets:** Service with
restrictions, supervision. 🛜 🛈 🖵 🏊

Naples Bay Resort ⊞
(239) 530-1199. **$149-$799, 7 day notice.** 1500 5th Ave S 34102. On
US 41 (Tamiami Tr), just e of jct Goodlette-Frank Rd. Ext/int corridors.
Pets: Accepted. [SAVE] 🛜 ✕ 🛈 🖵 ⎟⎟ 🏊 ✕

Ramada Naples Ⓜ
(239) 263-3434. **$99-$199.** 1100 Tamiami Tr N 34102. US 41 (Tamiami
Tr), jct 13th Ave N. Ext corridors. **Pets:** Medium. $25 daily fee/room. Des-
ignated rooms, service with restrictions, supervision.
[ECO] [SAVE] 🛜 🛈 🖵 ⎟⎟ 🏊

Residence Inn by Marriott, Naples ⊞
(239) 659-1300. **$109-$299.** 4075 Tamiami Tr N 34103. I-75 exit 107, 3.8
mi w on Pine Ridge Rd (CR 896), then 1 mi s on US 41 (Tamiami Tr).
Int corridors. **Pets:** Accepted. 🛜 ✕ ⫶M 🛈 🖵 🏊 ✕

The Ritz-Carlton Golf Resort, Naples ⊞
(239) 593-2000. **$179-$579, 3 day notice.** 2600 Tiburon Dr 34109. I-75
exit 111, 1.6 mi w on Immokalee Rd, 1.3 mi s on CR 31 (Airport-Pulling
Rd), then just e. Int corridors. **Pets:** Accepted.
[ECO] [SAVE] 🛜 ✕ ⫶M 🛈 🖵 ⎟⎟ 🏊 ✕

Staybridge Suites by Holiday Inn ⊞
(239) 643-8002. **$99-$199.** 4805 Tamiami Tr N 34103. I-75 exit 107, 3.8
mi w on Pine Ridge Rd(CR 896), then 0.9 mi s on US 41 (Tamiami Tr).
Int corridors. **Pets:** Accepted. 🛜 ⫶M 🛈 🖵 🏊

NEW SMYRNA BEACH

Longboard Inn ⒷⒷ
(386) 428-3499. **$115-$160, 14 day notice.** 312 Washington St 32168.
Just e of US 1 (Dixie Frwy); 0.3 mi w of jct N Riverside Dr. Ext corridors.
Pets: Accepted. [SAVE] 🛜 ✕ 🛈

Night Swan Intracoastal Bed & Breakfast ⒷⒷ
(386) 423-4940. **$110-$225, 3 day notice.** 512 S Riverside Dr 32168.
I-95 exit 249 (SR 44), 4 mi e to Live Oak St, just s to Andrews St, just e
to S Riverside Dr, then just s; on west side of Intracoastal Waterway.
Ext/int corridors. **Pets:** Medium, other species. Designated rooms, service
with restrictions, crate. [ECO] 🛜 ✕ 🛈 🖵

NORTH FORT MYERS

BEST WESTERN Ft. Myers Waterfront ⊞
(239) 997-5511. **$90-$150.** 13021 N Cleveland Ave 33903. On US 41,
0.6 mi s of SR 78A (Pondella Rd), jct N Bay Dr; at base of Caloosa-
hatchee Bridge. Ext corridors. **Pets:** Large, dogs only. $35 one-time fee/
room. Designated rooms, service with restrictions, supervision.
[SAVE] 🛜 ✕ ⫶M 🛈 🖵 ⎟⎟ 🏊 ✕

OCALA

Hilton Ocala ⊞ 🐾
(352) 854-1400. **$109-$199.** 3600 SW 36th Ave 34474. I-75 exit 350, 0.3
mi e on SR 200, just s. Int corridors. **Pets:** $49 one-time fee/room. Desig-
nated rooms, service with restrictions, crate.
[ECO] [SAVE] 🛜 ⫶M 🛈 🖵 ⎟⎟ 🏊 ✕

Holiday Inn Express Midtown Medical ⊞
(352) 629-7300. **$79-$119.** 1212 S Pine Ave 34474. 0.8 mi s on US 27,
301 and 441; just s of SR 200. Int corridors. **Pets:** Small. $25 one-time
fee/pet. Designated rooms, service with restrictions, supervision.
[SAVE] 🛜 ✕ ⫶M 🛈 🖵 🏊

La Quinta Inn & Suites Ocala ⊞
(352) 861-1137. **$71-$166.** 3530 SW 36th Ave 34474. I-75 exit 350, just
e on SR 200. Int corridors. **Pets:** Service with restrictions, supervision.
🛜 ⫶M 🛈 🖵 🏊

Red Roof Inn & Suites ⊞
(352) 732-4590. **$59-$150.** 120 NW 40th Ave 34482. I-75 exit 352, just w
on SR 40. Int corridors. **Pets:** Large, other species. Service with restrictions, supervision. [SAVE] 🛜 🛈 🖵 🏊

Residence Inn by Marriott Ocala ⊞ 🐾
(352) 547-1600. **$119-$239.** 3610 SW 38th Ave 34474. I-75 exit 350, just
w on SR 200, then n. Int corridors. **Pets:** Large, other species. $75
deposit/room. Service with restrictions.
[ECO] [SAVE] 🛜 ✕ 🛈 🖵 🏊 ✕

▼▼▼▼ Sleep Inn & Suites 🏠

(352) 347-8383. **$69-$89.** 13600 SW 17th Ct 34473. I-75 exit 341, just e. Int corridors. **Pets:** Accepted. 🌱 🛜 ⊠ 🔋 💻 🐾

ORANGE CITY

▼▼▼ Alling House Bed and Breakfast 🅱🅱

(386) 775-7648. **$105-$155, 7 day notice.** 215 E French Ave 32763. I-4 exit 114, 3 mi nw on SR 472, 2.3 mi s on US 17-92, then just e. Ext/int corridors. **Pets:** Other species. $20 one-time fee/room. Designated rooms, crate. 🛜 ⊠ 🔋 💻 🎵

▼▼ Days Inn Ⓜ

(386) 775-4522. **$60-$200.** 2501 N Volusia Ave 32763. I-4 exit 114, 2.8 mi w on SR 472, then 0.3 mi s on US 17-92. Ext corridors. **Pets:** Accepted. 🛜 🔋 💻 🐾

▼▼ Quality Inn Ⓜ

(386) 775-7444. **Call for rates.** 445 S Volusia Ave 32763. I-4 exit 114, 2.8 mi w on SR 472, then 2 mi s on US 17-92. Ext corridors. **Pets:** Accepted. 🛜 ⊠ 🔋 💻 🐾

ORLANDO METROPOLITAN AREA

ALTAMONTE SPRINGS

▼▼ Days Inn & Suites 🏠

(407) 788-1411. **$50-$75.** 150 S Westmonte Dr 32714. I-4 exit 92, 0.3 mi w on SR 436, then just s. Ext corridors. **Pets:** Medium. $20 daily fee/pet. Designated rooms, service with restrictions, supervision.
🛜 🔋 💻 🐾

🤿 ▼▼▼ Embassy Suites Orlando North 🏠

(407) 834-2400. **$109-$209.** 225 Shorecrest Dr 32701. I-4 exit 92, 0.3 mi e on SR 436, then just n on Cranes Roost Blvd. Int corridors. **Pets:** Medium. $50 one-time fee/pet. Designated rooms, service with restrictions, crate. 🌱 SAVE 🛜 🔋 💻 🍴 🐾 ⊠

▼▼▼ Hawthorn Suites by Wyndham Orlando Altamonte Springs 🏠

(407) 767-5757. **Call for rates.** 644 Raymond Ave 32701. I-4 exit 92, just w to Douglas Ave, 0.8 mi n to Central Pkwy, then just e. Int corridors. **Pets:** Accepted. 🛜 🔋 💻 🐾

▼▼▼▼ Hilton Orlando/Altamonte Springs 🏠

(407) 830-1985. **$109-$139.** 350 S Northlake Blvd 32701. I-4 exit 92, just e on SR 436, then 0.5 mi s. Int corridors. **Pets:** Accepted.
🌱 🛜 🔋 💻 🍴 🐾 ⊠

▼▼▼▼ Residence Inn by Marriott Orlando Altamonte Springs/Maitland 🏠

(407) 788-7991. **$89-$149.** 270 Douglas Ave 32714. I-4 exit 92, just w on SR 436, then just n. Ext corridors. **Pets:** Accepted.
🛜 ⊠ 🔋 💻 🐾 ⊠

CELEBRATION

🤿 ▼▼▼ Bohemian Hotel Celebration, Autograph Collection 🏠 ❀

(407) 566-6000. **$152-$279, 3 day notice.** 700 Bloom St 34747. SR 417 exit 2 (Celebration Ave), 0.9 mi sw to Campus St, then just s; downtown. Int corridors. **Pets:** Small, dogs only. $150 one-time fee/room. Designated rooms, service with restrictions, crate.
SAVE 🛜 ⊠ 🔋 💻 🍴 🐾 ⊠

CHAMPIONSGATE

🤿 ▼▼ ▼▼ Omni Orlando Resort at ChampionsGate 🏠 ❀

(407) 390-6664. **Call for rates.** 1500 Masters Blvd 33896. I-4 exit 58, 0.5 mi w on ChampionsGate Blvd (CR 532) to Masters Blvd, then just n. Int corridors. **Pets:** Small. $50 one-time fee/room. Designated rooms, service with restrictions, crate. 🌱 SAVE 🛜 🔋 💻 🍴 🐾 ⊠

CLERMONT

🤿 ▼▼ ▼▼ Days Inn Clermont Theme Park West 🏠

(863) 424-6099. **$40-$60.** 9240 US Hwy 192 34711. On US 192; 0.8 mi e of jct US 27. Ext corridors. **Pets:** Accepted. SAVE 🛜 🔋 💻 🐾

▼▼▼ Fairfield Inn & Suites by Marriott Clermont 🏠 ❀

(352) 394-6585. **$99-$159.** 1750 Hunt Trace Blvd 34711. Jct SR 50 and US 27, 0.5 mi e on SR 50, just n on Citrus Tower Blvd. Int corridors. **Pets:** Large, other species. $75 one-time fee/room. Designated rooms, service with restrictions, supervision. 🌱 🛜 ⊠ 🔋 💻 🐾

🤿 ▼▼▼ Holiday Inn Express-Clermont 🏠

(352) 243-7878. **Call for rates.** 1810 S US 27 34711. Just s of jct SR 50. Int corridors. **Pets:** Medium, other species. $50 one-time fee/room. Designated rooms, service with restrictions, crate.

SAVE 🛜 🔋 💻 🐾

FERN PARK

▼▼▼ Days Inn North Orlando 🏠

(407) 339-3333. **$60-$90.** 8245 S Hwy 17-92 32730. Jct SR 436 and US 17-92, 1.3 mi s on US 17-92. Ext corridors. **Pets:** Medium. $25 daily fee/pet. Designated rooms, service with restrictions, supervision.
🛜 ⊠ 🔋 💻 🐾

KISSIMMEE

🤿 ▼▼▼ Celebration Suites 🏠

(407) 396-7900. **$59-$139, 3 day notice.** 5820 W Irlo Bronson Memorial Hwy 34746. I-4 exit 64 (US 192), 2.2 mi e. Ext corridors. **Pets:** Accepted.
SAVE 🛜 ⊠ 🔋 💻 🐾 ⊠

🤿 ▼▼ ▼▼ Champions World Resort 🏠

(407) 396-4500. **$42-$99.** 8660 W Irlo Bronson Memorial Hwy 34747. I-4 exit 64 (US 192), 6.7 mi w. Ext corridors. **Pets:** Accepted.
SAVE 🛜 ⊠ 🔋 💻 🍴 🐾 ⊠

🤿 ▼▼ ▼▼ The Palms Hotel & Villas 🏠 ❀

(407) 396-2229. **$79-$199.** 3100 Parkway Blvd 34747. I-4 exit 64 (US 192), 1.2 mi e to Parkway Blvd, then 0.4 mi n. Ext/int corridors. **Pets:** Medium, dogs only. $100 one-time fee/room. Designated rooms, service with restrictions, crate. SAVE 🛜 ⊠ 🔋 💻 🐾 ⊠

🤿 ▼▼ ▼▼ Ramada Gateway Hotel 🏠

(407) 396-4400. **$49-$104.** 7470 W Irlo Bronson Memorial Hwy 34747. I-4 exit 64 (US 192), 3.4 mi w. Ext/int corridors. **Pets:** Medium, other species. $50 one-time fee/room. Designated rooms, service with restrictions, crate. SAVE 🛜 ⊠ 🔋 💻 🍴 🐾 ⊠

🤿 ▼▼ ▼▼ Seralago Hotel & Suites - Main Gate East 🏠

(407) 396-4488. **$45-$89.** 5678 W Irlo Bronson Memorial Hwy 34746. I-4 exit 64 (US 192), 2.5 mi e. Ext corridors. **Pets:** Medium, dogs only. $40 one-time fee/room. Designated rooms, service with restrictions.
SAVE 🛜 ⊠ 🔋 💻 🍴 🐾 ⊠

LADY LAKE

🤿 ▼▼ ▼▼ Comfort Suites in the Villages 🏠

(352) 259-6578. **$71-$109.** 1202 Avenida Central N 32159. Just n on US 441. Int corridors. **Pets:** Medium. $35 one-time fee/pet. Designated rooms, service with restrictions, crate. SAVE 🛜 🔋 💻 🐾

▼▼▼ Hampton Inn & Suites - The Villages 🏠

(352) 259-8246. **$94-$135.** 11727 NE 63rd Dr 32162. I-75 exit 329 (SR 44/Wildwood), e to Wildwood, n on US 301 to Oxford, then e on CR 466. Int corridors. **Pets:** Accepted. 🛜 ⊠ 🔋 💻 🐾

▼▼ ▼▼ Microtel Inn & Suites by Wyndham Lady Lake/The Villages 🏠

(352) 259-0184. **$65-$140.** 850 US 27/441 32159. 1 mi s of downtown. Int corridors. **Pets:** Medium. $25 one-time fee/pet. Designated rooms, service with restrictions, supervision. 🛜 ⊠ 🔋 💻 🐾

TownePlace Suites by Marriott The Villages H
(352) 753-8686. **$99-$195.** 1141 Alonzo Ave 32159. US 441/27 to Main St. Int corridors. **Pets:** Large, other species. $100 one-time fee/room. Service with restrictions, crate. [icons]

LAKE BUENA VISTA

Clarion Inn Lake Buena Vista H ❖
(407) 996-7300. **$59-$109.** 8442 Palm Pkwy 32836. I-4 exit 68, 0.6 mi n on SR 535, then 0.5 mi e. Ext corridors. **Pets:** Medium. $50 deposit/pet, $10 daily fee/pet. Designated rooms, no service, crate. [icons]

Holiday Inn Express Lake Buena Vista H
(407) 239-8400. **$79-$179, 3 day notice.** 8686 Palm Pkwy 32836. I-4 exit 68, 0.5 mi n on SR 535, then 0.3 mi e. Int corridors. **Pets:** Accepted. [icons]

Holiday Inn Resort Lake Buena Vista H
(407) 239-4500. **$89-$179, 3 day notice.** 13351 SR 535 32821. I-4 exit 68, 0.3 mi se. Ext/int corridors. **Pets:** Medium, other species. $14 daily fee/pet. Designated rooms, no service. [icons]

Hyatt Regency Grand Cypress H ❖
(407) 239-1234. **$90-$270, 3 day notice.** 1 Grand Cypress Blvd 32836. I-4 exit 68, just w on SR 535; near entrance to Walt Disney World Village. Int corridors. **Pets:** Medium, dogs only. $100 one-time fee/room, $50 daily fee/room. Designated rooms, service with restrictions. [icons]

Residence Inn by Marriott Orlando Lake Buena Vista H ❖
(407) 465-0075. **$79-$350, 3 day notice.** 11450 Marbella Palms Ct 32836. I-4 exit 68, 0.4 mi n on SR 535, then 0.5 mi e on Palm Pkwy. Int corridors. **Pets:** Medium. $100 deposit/room. Service with restrictions, crate. [icons]

Sheraton Lake Buena Vista Resort H ❖
(407) 239-0444. **$99-$229.** 12205 Apopka-Vineland Rd 32836. I-4 exit 68, 0.5 mi n on SR 535. Ext/int corridors. **Pets:** Large, dogs only. Designated rooms, service with restrictions, supervision. [icons]

LAKE MARY

Candlewood Suites Lake Mary-Heathrow H
(407) 585-3000. **Call for rates.** 1130 Greenwood Blvd 32746. I-4 exit 98, just e to Lake Emma Rd, then 0.5 mi s. Int corridors. **Pets:** Accepted. [icons]

Extended StayAmerica/Lake Mary/Sanford H
(407) 833-0011. **$49-$125.** 1036 Greenwood Blvd 32746. I-4 exit 98, just e to Lake Emma Rd, then 0.5 mi. Int corridors. **Pets:** $25 daily fee/pet. Designated rooms, service with restrictions. [icons]

Homestead Studio Suites - Lake Mary/Sanford H
(407) 829-2332. **$54-$139.** 1040 Greenwood Blvd 32746. I-4 exit 98, 0.5 mi s on Lake Emma Rd; in Commerce Park. Int corridors. **Pets:** $25 daily fee/pet. Designated rooms, service with restrictions. [icons]

La Quinta Inn & Suites Orlando (Lake Mary) H
(407) 805-9901. **$59-$129.** 1060 Greenwood Blvd 32746. I-4 exit 98, just e to Lake Emma Rd, then 0.5 mi s. Int corridors. **Pets:** Service with restrictions, supervision. [icons]

Residence Inn by Marriott Lake Mary H
(407) 995-3400. **$134-$224.** 825 Heathrow Park Lane Pkwy 32746. I-4 exit 101A, just w, then just s on International Pkwy. Int corridors. **Pets:** Medium, other species. $100 one-time fee/room. Service with restrictions. [icons]

The Westin Lake Mary Orlando North H ❖
(407) 531-3555. **$129-$299.** 2974 International Pkwy 32746. I-4 exit 101C, just w. Int corridors. **Pets:** Small, dogs only. Designated rooms, service with restrictions, supervision. [icons]

LEESBURG

BEST WESTERN PLUS Chain of Lakes Inn & Suites H
(352) 460-0118. **$75-$99.** 1321 N 14th St 34748. Florida Tpke exit 285 (US 27), 15.9 mi n; jct US 27 and 441. Int corridors. **Pets:** Small, dogs only. $20 daily fee/room. Designated rooms, service with restrictions, supervision. [icons]

MAITLAND

Extended Stay Deluxe-Orlando-Maitland-Pembrook Dr H
(407) 475-1675. **$55-$129.** 1776 Pembrook Dr 32810. I-4 exit 90B, 0.5 mi w. Int corridors. **Pets:** $25 daily fee/pet. Designated rooms, service with restrictions. [icons]

Homewood Suites by Hilton Orlando North H
(407) 875-8777. **$119-$179.** 290 Southhall Ln 32751. I-4 exit 90, just w, then just s on Lake Destiny. Int corridors. **Pets:** Medium. $75 one-time fee/room. Service with restrictions. [icons]

Sheraton Orlando North H ❖
(407) 660-9000. **$99-$269.** 600 N Lake Destiny Dr 32751. I-4 exit 90B, just w. Int corridors. **Pets:** Medium, dogs only. Designated rooms, service with restrictions, crate. [icons]

MOUNT DORA

Heron Cay Lakeview Bed & Breakfast BB ❖
(352) 383-4050. **$125-$295.** 495 Old US Hwy 441 32757. On CR 441 (Old US 441), 0.3 mi w. Int corridors. **Pets:** Other species. $25 daily fee/room. Designated rooms, service with restrictions, supervision. [icons]

OCOEE

Red Roof Inn Orlando West H
(407) 347-0140. **$55-$83.** 11241 W Colonial Dr 34761. I-4 exit 84, 10 mi w on SR 50; Florida Tpke exit 267, 0.6 mi e. Int corridors. **Pets:** Large, other species. Service with restrictions, supervision. [icons]

ORLANDO

BEST WESTERN Inn & Suites-East Orlando H ❖
(407) 282-3900. **$79-$119.** 8750 E Colonial Dr 32817. SR 417 exit 34. Ext corridors. **Pets:** Large, other species. $20 daily fee/pet. Designated rooms, service with restrictions, supervision. [icons]

BEST WESTERN Orlando West H
(407) 841-8600. **$69-$159.** 2014 W Colonial Dr 32804. I-4 exit 84, 1.5 mi w on SR 50 (Colonial Dr); 0.4 mi e of SR 423. Int corridors. **Pets:** Small. $50 deposit/room, $5 daily fee/pet. Designated rooms, service with restrictions, supervision. [icons]

BEST WESTERN PLUS Orlando Gateway Hotel H ❖
(407) 351-5009. **$100-$170.** 7299 Universal Blvd 32819. I-4 exit 75A, just e of International Dr. Int corridors. **Pets:** Medium. $20 daily fee/room. Service with restrictions. [icons]

Comfort Suites Downtown [H]
(407) 228-4007. **$115-$145.** 2416 N Orange Ave 32804. I-4 exit 85, just e on Princeton, then just n. Int corridors. **Pets:** Small. $15 daily fee/pet. Designated rooms, service with restrictions, supervision.

Country Inn & Suites By Carlson-Orlando International Airport [H]
(407) 856-8896. **$79-$129.** 5440 Forbes Pl 32812. SR 528 (Beachline Expwy) exit 11, 0.6 mi n on SR 436, then just w. Int corridors. **Pets:** Medium. $75 one-time fee/room. Service with restrictions, crate.

Days Inn Airport/Florida Mall [M]
(407) 855-0308. **$58-$90.** 9301 S Orange Blossom Tr 32837. SR 528 (Beachline Expwy) exit 4, just s on US 17-92/441. Ext corridors. **Pets:** Small. $15 daily fee/pet. Designated rooms, service with restrictions, crate.

DoubleTree by Hilton Orlando at SeaWorld [H]
(407) 352-1100. **Call for rates.** 10100 International Dr 32821. I-4 exit 72, 0.5 mi e on SR 528 (Beachline Expwy) exit 1 (International Dr), just e. Ext/int corridors. **Pets:** Accepted.

Extended StayAmerica-Orlando Universal Studios [H]
(407) 351-1788. **$55-$179.** 5620 Major Blvd 32819. I-4 exit 75B, just n, then just e. Int corridors. **Pets:** $25 daily fee/pet. Designated rooms, service with restrictions.

Extended Stay Deluxe Orlando Convention Center/Pointe Orlando [H]
(407) 903-1500. **$60-$189.** 8750 Universal Blvd 32819. I-4 exit 74A, 0.5 mi e on SR 482 (Sand Lake Rd), then 0.7 mi s. Int corridors. **Pets:** $25 daily fee/pet. Designated rooms, service with restrictions.

Extended Stay Deluxe Orlando-Universal Studios [H]
(407) 370-4428. **$60-$189.** 5610 Vineland Rd 32819. I-4 exit 75B, just n, then e. Int corridors. **Pets:** $25 daily fee/pet. Designated rooms, service with restrictions.

The Florida Hotel and Conference Center [H] ❧
(407) 859-1500. **$89-$239, 3 day notice.** 1500 Sand Lake Rd 32809. Just s of jct Sand Lake Rd and S Orange Blossom Tr; south end of Florida Mall. Int corridors. **Pets:** Small. $75 one-time fee/room. Service with restrictions, crate.

Floridays Resort Orlando [CO] ❧
(407) 238-7700. **$150-$450, 3 day notice.** 12562 International Dr 32821. I-4 exit 72, 0.5 mi e on SR 528 (Beachline Expwy) exit 1 (International Dr), then 3 mi s. Ext corridors. **Pets:** Small. $200 one-time fee/room. Service with restrictions, crate.

The Grand Bohemian Hotel Autograph Collection [H]
(407) 313-9000. **$169-$279.** 325 S Orange Ave 32801. I-4 exit 82B, just e on South St, jct Jackson St. Int corridors. **Pets:** Accepted.

Hard Rock Hotel® at Universal Orlando [H] ❧
(407) 503-2000. **$254-$569, 5 day notice.** 5800 Universal Blvd 32819. I-4 exit 74B; exit 75A eastbound, 1 mi n. Int corridors. **Pets:** Other species. $25 one-time fee/room. Designated rooms, service with restrictions, crate.

Holiday Inn Resort Orlando-The Castle [H]
(407) 345-1511. **Call for rates.** 8629 International Dr 32819. I-4 exit 74A, 1 mi se, just e of International Dr; 0.5 mi s of SR 482 (Sand Lake Rd). Int corridors. **Pets:** Medium, dogs only. $75 one-time fee/room. Designated rooms, service with restrictions, crate.

International Palms Resort and Conference Center - Orlando [H]
(407) 351-3500. **$59-$139.** 6515 International Dr 32819. I-4 exit 74A, just e on SR 482 (Sand Lake Rd), then 0.5 mi n. Ext/int corridors.
Pets: Accepted.

La Quinta Inn & Suites Orlando (Convention Center) [H]
(407) 345-1365. **$66-$140.** 8504 Universal Blvd 32819. I-4 exit 74A, 0.5 mi e on SR 482 (Sand Lake Rd), then 0.5 mi s at jct Via Mercado W. Int corridors. **Pets:** Service with restrictions, supervision.

La Quinta Inn & Suites Orlando South [H]
(407) 240-0500. **$59-$118.** 2051 Consulate Dr 32837. SR 528 (Beachline Expwy) exit 4, just se; Florida Tpke exit 254, s on US 441, then right. Int corridors. **Pets:** Service with restrictions, supervision.

La Quinta Inn & Suites Orlando (U.C.F.) [H]
(407) 737-6075. **$71-$188.** 11805 Research Pkwy 32826. Just se of jct SR 434 (Alafaya Tr). Int corridors. **Pets:** Service with restrictions, supervision.

La Quinta Inn Orlando International Drive North [H]
(407) 351-4100. **$63-$148.** 5825 International Dr 32819. I-4 exit 75A, just w. Int corridors. **Pets:** Service with restrictions, supervision.

Loews Portofino Bay Hotel at Universal Orlando® [H] ❧
(407) 503-1000. **$289-$619, 5 day notice.** 5601 Universal Blvd 32819. I-4 exit 74B westbound; exit 75A eastbound, 1 mi n. Int corridors. **Pets:** $25 one-time fee/room. Designated rooms, service with restrictions, crate.

Loews Royal Pacific Resort at Universal Orlando® [H] ❧
(407) 503-3000. **$234-$499, 5 day notice.** 6300 Hollywood Way 32819. I-4 exit 74B westbound; exit 75A eastbound, just n on Universal Blvd, just w. Int corridors. **Pets:** Accepted.

Motel 6 Orlando-International Drive #1079 [H]
(407) 351-6500. **$45-$55.** 5909 American Way 32819. I-4 exit 75A, just w of SR 435 (Kirkman Rd), then just n. Int corridors. **Pets:** Other species. Service with restrictions, supervision.

Quality Inn International [H] ❧
(407) 996-1600. **$55-$99.** 7600 International Dr 32819. I-4 exit 74A, just e on SR 482 (Sand Lake Rd), then just n. Ext corridors. **Pets:** Medium. $10 daily fee/pet. Service with restrictions, crate.

Red Roof Inn Orlando/Convention Center [H]
(407) 352-1507. **$50-$126.** 9922 Hawaiian Ct 32819. I-4 exit 72, 0.9 mi e on SR 528 (Beachline Expwy) to exit 1 (International Dr), then just n. Ext corridors. **Pets:** Large, other species. Service with restrictions, supervision.

Residence Inn by Marriott Orlando Convention Center [H]
(407) 226-0288. **$94-$229.** 8800 Universal Blvd 32819. I-4 exit 74A, 0.5 mi e on SR 482 (Sand Lake Rd), then 0.8 mi s. Int corridors.
Pets: Accepted.

Residence Inn by Marriott/Orlando East UCF H
(407) 513-9000. **$98-$143.** 11651 University Blvd 32817. 2.2 mi e of SR 417 on University Blvd; just w of SR 434 (Álafaya Tr). Int corridors. **Pets:** Medium. $100 one-time fee/room. Service with restrictions, crate.

Residence Inn by Marriott Orlando International Airport H ❀
(407) 856-2444. **$119-$169.** 7024 Augusta National Dr 32822. SR 528 (Beach Line Expwy) exit 11, 1 mi n; 1 mi e of Orlando International Airport. Int corridors. **Pets:** Medium. $75 one-time fee/room. Service with restrictions, crate. SAVE

Residence Inn by Marriott-Orlando International Dr H
(407) 345-0117. **$79-$152.** 7975 Canada Ave 32819. I-4 exit 74A, just e on SR 482 (Sand Lake Rd). Ext corridors. **Pets:** Other species. $75 one-time fee/room. Service with restrictions.
SAVE

Residence Inn by Marriott SeaWorld International Center H
(407) 313-3600. **$93-$209.** 11000 Westwood Blvd 32821. I-4 exit 72. Int corridors. **Pets:** Other species. $75 one-time fee/room. Service with restrictions. SAVE

Rosen Inn H
(407) 996-4444. **$60-$150.** 6327 International Dr 32819. I-4 exit 74A, just e on SR 482 (Sand Lake Rd), then 0.7 mi n. Ext/int corridors. **Pets:** Medium. $10 daily fee/pet. Designated rooms, service with restrictions, crate. SAVE

Rosen Inn at Pointe Orlando H
(407) 996-8585. **$59-$129.** 9000 International Dr 32819. I-4 exit 74A, just e on SR 482 (Sand Lake Rd), then 1 mi s, jct Samoan Ct. Ext corridors. **Pets:** Accepted. SAVE

Sheraton Orlando Downtown Hotel H
(407) 843-6664. **$89-$296.** 400 W Livingston St 32801. I-4 exit 84 (SR 50/Colonial Dr) westbound; exit 83A (Robinson St) eastbound, just w; jct Livingston and Hughey sts. Int corridors. **Pets:** Accepted.
ECO SAVE

Sheraton Suites Orlando Airport H
(407) 240-5555. **$89-$279.** 7550 Augusta National Dr 32822. 2 mi n of airport terminal via SR 436 and TG Lee Blvd. Int corridors.
Pets: Accepted. ECO SAVE

Staybridge Suites Orlando Airport H
(407) 438-2121. **$99-$139, 3 day notice.** 7450 Augusta National Dr 32822. SR 528 (Beachline Expwy) exit 11, 0.5 mi n on SR 436, just e, then just s. Int corridors. **Pets:** Accepted.
ECO

TownePlace Suites by Marriott Orlando East/UCF H
(407) 243-6100. **$99-$129.** 11801 High Tech Ave 32817. 2.2 mi e of SR 417 on University Blvd; 1.2 mi w of jct SR 434 (Alafaya Tr), just n on Quadrangle Blvd. Int corridors. **Pets:** Accepted.

Ventura Cove-Ventura Country Club-Ventura Resort Rentals VH
(407) 273-8770. **$79-$500, 15 day notice.** 3763 Ventura Club 32822. 0.6 mi e of SR 436 (Semoran Blvd). Ext corridors. **Pets:** Small, other species. $100 deposit/pet, $100 one-time fee/pet. Designated rooms, service with restrictions, crate.

Villas Of Grand Cypress Golf Resort H
(407) 239-4700. **$175-$2000, 3 day notice.** 1 N Jacaranda St 32836. I-4 exit 68, 2.3 mi nw on SR 535. Ext corridors. **Pets:** Small, other species. $150 one-time fee/pet. Service with restrictions, supervision.
ECO SAVE

Westgate Palace CO
(407) 996-6000. **Call for rates.** 6145 Carrier Dr 32819. I-4 exit 74A, just e on SR 482 (Sand Lake Rd), 0.6 mi n on International Dr, then just e. Int corridors. **Pets:** Accepted.
SAVE

Wyndham Grand Orlando Resort, Bonnet Creek H
(407) 390-2300. **$105-$399.** 14651 Chelonia Pkwy 32821. I-4 exit 65 (W Osceola Pkwy), on Victory Way, e on Buena Vista Dr, then s. Int corridors. **Pets:** Accepted. SAVE

Wyndham Orlando Resort H
(407) 351-2420. **$89-$199, 3 day notice.** 8001 International Dr 32819. I-4 exit 74A, just e on SR 482 (Sand Lake Rd). Ext/int corridors. **Pets:** Large. $50 one-time fee/room. Service with restrictions, supervision.
SAVE

ST. CLOUD

Budget Inn of St Cloud M
(407) 892-2858. **$35-$90, 3 day notice.** 602 13th St 34769. On US 192, 0.5 mi e of The Water Tower, 2 mi w of jct CR 15. Ext corridors. **Pets:** Small, dogs only. $10 daily fee/pet. SAVE

SANFORD

Holiday Inn Express-Sanford/Lake Mary H
(407) 320-0845. **$70-$109.** 3401 S Orlando Dr 32773. I-4 exit 98, e on Lake Mary Blvd, then 0.5 mi n on US 17-92. Int corridors.
Pets: Accepted.

TAVARES

BEST WESTERN Lake County Inn & Suites H
(352) 253-2378. **$89-$189.** 1380 E Burleigh Blvd 32778-4305. On US 441 N. Int corridors. **Pets:** Accepted. ECO SAVE

WINTER PARK

BEST WESTERN Mt. Vernon Inn H ❀
(407) 647-1166. **$99-$169.** 110 S Orlando Ave 32789. I-4 exit 87 (Fairbanks Ave), 1 mi e, then 0.3 mi n on US 17-92. Ext/int corridors. **Pets:** Dogs only. $15 daily fee/pet. Designated rooms, service with restrictions, supervision. SAVE

END METROPOLITAN AREA

ORMOND BEACH

▼▼ ▼▼ Baymont Inn & Suites Ormond Beach 🏨
(386) 672-3675. **Call for rates.** 175 Interchange Blvd 32174. I-95 exit 268 (SR 40/Granada Blvd), just w to Interchange Blvd, then just s. Int corridors. **Pets:** Accepted. 🛜 🍴 💻 🏊

▼▼▼▼ Hampton Inn Daytona/Ormond Beach 🏨
(386) 677-9999. **$89-$139.** 155 Interchange Blvd 32174. I-95 exit 268 (SR 40/Granada Blvd), just w to Interchange Blvd, then just s. Int corridors. **Pets:** Small, other species. $25 daily fee/pet. Service with restrictions, supervision. 🛜 ✖ 🔥M 🍴 💻 🏊

▲▲▲◢ ▼▼▼▼ Howard Johnson Ormond Beach at Destination Daytona 🏨
(386) 944-1500. **$89-$350, 3 day notice.** 1635 N US Hwy 1 32174. I-95 exit 273 (US 1), just nw. Int corridors. **Pets:** Other species. $25 daily fee/room. Service with restrictions, supervision. 🆂🅰🆅🅴 🍴 💻 🏊

▼▼◢▼ Lotus Boutique Inn & Suites 🏨
(386) 310-7966. **Call for rates.** 505 S Atlantic Ave 32176. I-95 exit 268 (SR 40/Granada Blvd), 5.6 mi e to SR A1A (Atlantic Ave), then 1 mi s. Ext corridors. **Pets:** Accepted. 🛜 ✖ 🍴 💻 🏊

PALATKA

▼▼ ▼▼ Quality Inn & Suites Riverfront 🏨
(386) 328-3481. **$70-$110.** 201 N First St 32177. On US 17; at foot of St. Johns River Bridge. Ext corridors. **Pets:** Accepted.
🛜 🍴 💻 🏊

▼▼ ▼▼ Sleep Inn & Suites 🏨 🐾
(386) 325-8889. **$67-$89.** 3805 Reid St 32177. 2 mi n on SR 100, jct SR 19. Int corridors. **Pets:** Small. $20 daily fee/pet. Service with restrictions, supervision. 🛜 🍴 💻 🏊

PALM BAY

▼▼▼▼ Holiday Inn Express Hotel & Suites-Palm Bay 🏨
(321) 220-2003. **$89-$159.** 1206 SE Malabar Rd 32907. I-95 exit 173 (SR 514/Malabar Rd), just e. Int corridors. **Pets:** Small. $15 daily fee/pet. Designated rooms, service with restrictions, supervision.
🛜 🔥M 🍴 💻 🏊

▼▼ ▼▼ Quality Inn 🏨
(321) 725-2952. **Call for rates.** 890 Palm Bay Rd NE 32905. I-95 exit 176 (Palm Bay Rd NE), 0.5 mi e. Int corridors. **Pets:** Very small, dogs only. $15 daily fee/room. Designated rooms, service with restrictions, crate. 🛜 🔥M 🍴 💻 🏊

PALM BEACH

▲▲▲◢ ▼▼▼▼ The Brazilian Court Hotel & Beach Club 🏨
(561) 655-7740. **$249-$2999, 14 day notice.** 301 Australian Ave 33480. From Royal Palm Way, just s on Cocoanut Row to Australian Ave, then just e; corner of Hibiscus and Australian aves. Int corridors.
Pets: Accepted. 🆂🅰🆅🅴 🛜 ✖ 🍴 🍽 🏊 ✖

▲▲▲◢ ▼▼▼▼ The Chesterfield Hotel Palm Beach 🏨 🐾
(561) 659-5800. **$179-$929, 3 day notice.** 363 Cocoanut Row 33480. Jct Australian Ave and Cocoanut Row; 2 blks n of Worth Ave. Int corridors. **Pets:** Small. $75 deposit/pet, $75 one-time fee/pet. Supervision.
🆂🅰🆅🅴 🛜 🍴 🍽 🏊 ✖

▲▲▲◢ ▼▼▼▼▼ Four Seasons Resort Palm Beach 🏨
(561) 582-2800. **$249-$4950, 14 day notice.** 2800 S Ocean Blvd 33480. On SR A1A, 0.4 mi n of SR 802 (Lake Ave). Int corridors.
Pets: Accepted. 🆔🆒🅾 🆂🅰🆅🅴 🛜 ✖ 🔥M 💻 🍴 🏊 ✖

▲▲▲◢ ▼▼▼▼ The Omphoy Ocean Resort 🏨 🐾
(561) 540-6440. **$149-$1099, 14 day notice.** 2842 S Ocean Blvd 33480. On SR A1A (S Ocean Blvd), 0.4 mi n of SR 802 (Lake Ave). Int corridors. **Pets:** Medium, other species. $100 one-time fee/pet. Service with restrictions, crate. 🆂🅰🆅🅴 🛜 ✖ 🍴 🏊 ✖

PALM BEACH GARDENS

▲▲▲◢ ▼▼▼▼ DoubleTree by Hilton Hotel & Executive Meeting Center-Palm Beach Gardens 🏨
(561) 622-2260. **$79-$99.** 4431 PGA Blvd 33410. I-95 exit 79B (PGA Blvd), just w. Int corridors. **Pets:** Accepted.
🆔🆒🅾 🆂🅰🆅🅴 🛜 🔥M 🍴 💻 🍽 🏊

▲▲▲◢ ▼▼▼▼ Homewood Suites by Hilton-Palm Beach Gardens 🏨 🐾
(561) 622-7799. **$129-$249.** 4700 Donald Ross Rd 33418. I-95 exit 83 (Donald Ross Rd), 1.1 mi e; in Donald Ross Village Plaza. Int corridors. **Pets:** Medium, other species. $150 deposit/room, $75 one-time fee/room. Designated rooms, service with restrictions, crate.
🆂🅰🆅🅴 🛜 🔥M 🍴 💻 🏊 ✖

▲▲▲◢ ▼▼▼▼▼ PGA National Resort & Spa 🏨 🐾
(561) 627-2000. **$179-$599, 3 day notice.** 400 Ave of the Champions 33418. I-95 exit 79B (PGA Blvd), 2 mi w; Florida Tpke exit 109, just w. Int corridors. **Pets:** Medium. $150 one-time fee/pet. Designated rooms, crate. 🆔🆒🅾 🆂🅰🆅🅴 🛜 ✖ 🍴 🍽 🏊 ✖

PALM BEACH SHORES

▼▼▼ SeaSpray Inn Beach Resort 🏨
(561) 844-0233. **$90-$180, 14 day notice.** 123 S Ocean Ave 33404. On Singer Island; 0.5 mi s of SR A1A. Int corridors. **Pets:** Accepted.
🛜 🍴 💻 🍽 🏊

PALM COAST

▲▲▲◢ ▼▼▼▼ BEST WESTERN Palm Coast Ⓜ
(386) 446-4457. **$60-$90.** 5 Kingswood Dr 32137. I-95 exit 289 (Palm Coast Pkwy), just e to Kingswood Dr, then just s; in Kingswood Center. Ext corridors. **Pets:** Medium, other species. $20 daily fee/room. Service with restrictions. 🆂🅰🆅🅴 🛜 🍴 💻 🏊

▲▲▲◢ ▼▼▼▼ Days Inn Palm Coast 🏨
(386) 627-7734. **$69-$149.** 120 Garden St N 32137. I-95 exit 289 (Palm Coast Pkwy), just w to Boulder Rock Dr, just n to Garden St, then just e. Int corridors. **Pets:** $15 one-time fee/pet. Designated rooms, service with restrictions, crate. 🆂🅰🆅🅴 🛜 🔥M 🍴 💻 🏊

▼▼▼▼ Fairfield Inn & Suites by Marriott Palm Coast I-95 🏨
(386) 445-3450. **$75-$85.** 400 Old Kings Rd N 32137. I-95 exit 289 (Palm Coast Pkwy), just e Kingswood Dr, then 0.3 mi s. Int corridors.
Pets: Accepted. 🆔🆒🅾 🛜 ✖ 🔥M 🍴 💻 🏊

▲▲▲◢ ▼▼▼▼ Holiday Inn Express Hotel & Suites 🏨
(386) 439-3939. **$89-$109.** 200 Flagler Plaza Dr 32137. I-95 exit 284 (SR 100), just e. Int corridors. **Pets:** Accepted.
🆂🅰🆅🅴 🛜 🔥M 🍴 💻 🏊

▼▼ ▼▼ Microtel Inn & Suites by Wyndham 🏨
(386) 445-8976. **$55-$180.** 16 Kingswood Dr 32137. I-95 exit 289 (Palm Coast Pkwy), just e to Kingswood Dr, then just sw. Int corridors.
Pets: Accepted. 🛜 🔥M 🍴 💻 🏊

▲▲▲◢ ▼▼▼▼ Palm Coast Villas Ⓜ
(386) 445-3525. **$69-$89, 3 day notice.** 5454 N Oceanshore Blvd 32137. I-95 exit 289 (Palm Coast Pkwy), 3 mi ne to Camino Del Mar, just nw to Oceanshore Blvd, then 1.8 mi n. Ext corridors. **Pets:** Accepted.
🆂🅰🆅🅴 🛜 ✖ 🍴 💻 🏊

PANAMA CITY

▼▼ ▼▼ La Quinta Inn & Suites 🏨
(850) 914-0022. **$66-$151.** 1030 E 23rd St 32405. On SR 368 (23rd St), jct US 231. Int corridors. **Pets:** Service with restrictions, supervision.
🛜 🔥M 🍴 💻 🏊

▼▼ ▼▼ Red Roof Inn-Panama City 🏨
(850) 215-2727. **$59-$129.** 217 N Hwy 231 32401. On US 231, just ne of jct US 98. Int corridors. **Pets:** Large, other species. Service with restrictions, supervision. 🛜 🍴 💻 🏊

▼▼ Super 8-Panama City M
(850) 784-1988. **$59-$106.** 207 Hwy 231 N 32405. On US 231, just ne of jct US 98. Ext/int corridors. **Pets:** Medium, dogs only. $15 daily fee/pet. Designated rooms, service with restrictions, crate. 🛜 📶 💻 🏊

▼▼▼ TownePlace Suites by Marriott Panama City H
(850) 747-0609. **$116-$129.** 903 E 23rd Pl 32405. Just e of jct SR 77 on SR 368 (23rd St), then n on Palo Alto Ave. Int corridors. **Pets:** $100 one-time fee/room. Service with restrictions, crate.
🛜 ✕ 💪 📶 💻 🏊

PENSACOLA
▼▼▼ MainStay Suites H
(850) 479-1000. **$89-$169.** 7230 Plantation Rd 32504. I-10 exit 13, just s, then 0.3 mi w. Ext corridors. **Pets:** Medium. $25 daily fee/room. Designated rooms, service with restrictions, supervision.
🛜 ✕ 💪 📶 💻 🏊 ✕

▲▲▲ ▼▼ Red Roof Inn Pensacola M
(850) 476-7960. **$49-$99.** 7340 Plantation Rd 32504. I-10 exit 13, just s. Ext corridors. **Pets:** Large, other species. Service with restrictions, supervision. 📥 🛜 📶

▼▼ Red Roof Inn Pensacola West H
(850) 941-0908. **$55-$90.** 2591 Wilde Lake Blvd 32526. I-10 exit 7, just s. Int corridors. **Pets:** Large, other species. Service with restrictions, supervision. 🛜 💪 📶 💻 🏊

▼▼ TownePlace Suites by Marriott Pensacola H
(850) 484-7022. **$116-$129.** 481 Creighton Rd 32504. I-10 exit 13, 0.3 mi s, then just w. Int corridors. **Pets:** Large, other species. $100 one-time fee/room. Service with restrictions, crate. 🌿 🛜 ✕ 📶 💻 🏊

PORT CHARLOTTE
▼▼▼ Country Inn & Suites By Carlson H
(941) 235-1035. **$70-$200.** 24244 Corporate Ct 33954. I-75 exit 170, just w on CR 769 (Kings Hwy). Int corridors. **Pets:** Large, other species. $10 daily fee/pet. Service with restrictions, supervision.
🛜 💪 📶 💻 🏊

▲▲▲ ▼▼ Days Inn of Port Charlotte H 🐾
(941) 627-8900. **$74-$159.** 1941 Tamiami Tr 33948. On US 41, 2.3 mi s of jct Toledo Blade Blvd (CR 779). Ext corridors. **Pets:** Medium. $10 daily fee/pet. Designated rooms, service with restrictions, supervision.
📥 🛜 📶 💻 🍴 🏊

▲▲▲ ▼▼▼ La Quinta Inn & Suites Port Charlotte H
(941) 979-4200. **$78-$151.** 812 Kings Hwy 33980. I-75 exit 170, just w on CR 769 (Kings Hwy), then just s on Veterans Blvd. Int corridors. **Pets:** Service with restrictions, supervision.
📥 🛜 ✕ 💪 📶 🏊

PORT ORANGE
▼▼▼ La Quinta Inn & Suites - Port Orange H
(386) 756-3440. **$107-$210.** 1791 Dunlawton Ave 32129. I-95 exit 256, just e. Int corridors. **Pets:** Service with restrictions, supervision.
🛜 ✕ 💪 📶 💻 🏊

PORT ST. LUCIE
▼▼▼ Holiday Inn-Port St Lucie H
(772) 337-2200. **$80-$170.** 10120 S Federal Hwy 34952. On US 1, 0.6 mi n of jct SR 716 (Port St Lucie Blvd). Int corridors. **Pets:** $50 one-time fee/room. Designated rooms, service with restrictions, crate.
🌿 🛜 📶 💻 🍴 🏊 ✕

▼▼▼ Homewood Suites by Hilton Port St. Lucie-Tradition H
(772) 345-5300. **$119-$189.** 10301 SW Innovation Way 34987. I-95 exit 118 (Gatlin Blvd), 0.5 mi w to Village Pkwy, then just s. Int corridors. **Pets:** Accepted. 🛜 💪 📶 💻 🏊

▼▼ MainStay Suites at PGA Village H
(772) 460-8882. **$50-$190.** 8501 Champions Way 34986. I-95 exit 121 (St. Lucie West Blvd), just w. Int corridors. **Pets:** Medium, dogs only. $75 one-time fee/pet. Designated rooms, service with restrictions, supervision.
🛜 📶 💻 🏊

▲▲▲ ▼▼▼ Residence Inn by Marriott Port St. Lucie H
(772) 344-7814. **$95-$139.** 1920 SW Fountainview Blvd 34986. I-95 exit 121 (St Lucie West Blvd), just e to Paramount Dr, just s to SW Fountainview Blvd, then just sw. Int corridors. **Pets:** $100 one-time fee/room. Service with restrictions, crate. 📥 🛜 ✕ 💪 📶 💻 🏊 ✕

PUNTA GORDA
▲▲▲ ▼▼▼ Four Points by Sheraton Punta Gorda Harborside H ❀
(941) 637-6770. **$99-$209.** 33 Tamiami Tr 33950. On US 41; at Peace River Bridge. Int corridors. **Pets:** Medium, other species. $25 one-time fee/room. Designated rooms, service with restrictions, crate.
📥 🛜 ✕ 💪 📶 💻 🍴 🏊 ✕

▼▼▼ Wyvern Hotel H
(941) 639-7700. **Call for rates.** 101 E Retta Esplanade 33950. Jct US 41 northbound; just e of jct US 41 southbound. Int corridors.
Pets: Accepted. 🛜 ✕ 📶 💻 🍴 🏊

QUINCY
▼▼▼ Allison House Inn BB
(850) 875-2511. **$85-$175, 21 day notice.** 215 N Madison St 32351. Just n of town center; in historic district. Int corridors. **Pets:** Small, dogs only. Designated rooms, service with restrictions, crate. 🛜 ✕

RIVER RANCH
▼▼ Westgate River Ranch Resort M
(863) 692-1321. **Call for rates.** 3200 River Ranch Rd 33867. Florida Tpke exit 193 (SR 60), 22 mi w to River Ranch Blvd, then 2.7 mi s. Ext corridors. **Pets:** Accepted. 🛜 ✕ 📶 💻 🍴 🏊 ✕

▲▲▲ ▼▼▼ Westgate River Ranch Resort Cabins CA
(863) 692-1321. **Call for rates.** 3200 River Ranch Blvd 33867. Florida Tpke exit 193 (SR 60), 22 mi w to River Ranch Blvd, then 2.7 mi s. Ext corridors. **Pets:** Accepted. 📥 🛜 ✕ 📶 💻 🍴 🏊 ✕

ST. AUGUSTINE
▼▼▼ Bayfront Marin House Bed & Breakfast Inn BB
(904) 824-4301. **$149-$309, 7 day notice.** 142 Avenida Menendez 32084. 1 blk s of Bridge of Lions. Ext corridors. **Pets:** Medium, dogs only. $30 daily fee/pet. Designated rooms, service with restrictions. 🛜 ✕

▲▲▲ ▼ BEST WESTERN Bayfront Inn M
(904) 824-4482. **$89-$189.** 16 Avenida Menendez 32084. I-95 exit 318 (SR 16), 5.5 mi e to San Marco Ave, then 1.7 mi s; in historic district. Ext corridors. **Pets:** Accepted. 📥 🛜 ✕ 📶 💻 🏊

▲▲▲ ▼▼▼ BEST WESTERN I-95 St. Augustine M
(904) 829-1999. **$60-$200.** 2445 SR 16 32092. I-95 exit 318, just w. Ext corridors. **Pets:** Accepted. 📥 🛜 💻 🏊

▲▲▲ ▼▼▼ Casablanca Inn on the Bay BB
(904) 829-0928. **Call for rates.** 24 Avenida Menendez 32084. I-95 exit 318 (SR 16), 5.5 mi e to San Marco Ave, then 1.8 mi s; in historic district. Ext/int corridors. **Pets:** Accepted. 📥 🛜 ✕ 📶 💻

▼▼▼ Casa De Solana Bed & Breakfast Inn BB
(904) 824-3555. **$129-$259, 14 day notice.** 21 Aviles St 32084. Aviles St at Cadiz St; in historic district. Int corridors. **Pets:** $35 daily fee/pet. Designated rooms, service with restrictions. 🛜 ✕ 📶 ✉

Casa Monica Hotel, Autograph Collection 🅗 ❀

(904) 827-1888. **$169-$299, 3 day notice.** 95 Cordova St 32084. Downtown; across from Lightner Museum and Flagler College. Int corridors. **Pets:** Medium, dogs only. $150 one-time fee/pet. Designated rooms, service with restrictions, supervision.

Comfort Suites World Golf Village Resort 🅗

(904) 940-9500. **$69-$129.** 475 Commerce Lake Dr 32095. I-95 exit 323 (International Golf Pkwy), just e to Center Place Way, then just s. Int corridors. **Pets:** Other species. Service with restrictions, supervision.

The Cozy Inn Ⓜ

(904) 824-2449. **$69-$209, 30 day notice.** 202 San Marco Ave 32084. I-95 exit 318 (SR 16), 5.5 mi e to San Marco Ave, the 0.4 mi s. Ext corridors. **Pets:** Dogs only. $50 one-time fee/pet. Service with restrictions.

La Quinta Inn & Suites - St. Augustine 🅗

(904) 209-2580. **$75-$199.** 250 Outlet Mall Blvd 32084. I-95 exit 318 (SR 16), just e to Prime Outlet Blvd, then just n. Int corridors. **Pets:** Service with restrictions, supervision.

Peace and Plenty Inn 🄱🄱

(904) 829-8209. **$89-$189, 7 day notice.** 87 Cedar St 32084. From King St, just s on Granada St, then just w. Int corridors. **Pets:** $35 one-time fee/pet. Designated rooms, service with restrictions, supervision.

Quality Inn Ⓜ

(904) 823-8636. **$60-$160.** 2310 SR 16 32084. I-95 exit 318 (SR 16), just e. Ext corridors. **Pets:** $15 daily fee/pet. Designated rooms, service with restrictions, supervision.

ST. AUGUSTINE BEACH

Holiday Isle Oceanfront Resort 🅗 ❀

(904) 471-2555. **$89-$189.** 860 A1A Beach Blvd 32080. On Business Rt SR A1A, 1.8 mi s of jct SR 312 and A1A. Int corridors. **Pets:** Other species. $20 daily fee/pet. Designated rooms, service with restrictions, supervision.

House of Sea and Sun 🄱🄱 ❀

(904) 461-1716. **$169-$229, 7 day notice.** 2 B St 32080. Jct SR 312 and A1A, 1.9 mi s to B St, then just e. Ext/int corridors. **Pets:** Other species. Service with restrictions.

ST. PETERSBURG-CLEARWATER AND BEACHES AREA

CLEARWATER

Holiday Inn Express Clearwater East-Icot Center 🅗 ❀

(727) 536-7275. **$69-$189.** 13625 Icot Blvd 33760. 0.5 mi e of jct US 19; just n of Ulmerton Rd (SR 688); in Icot Center Business Park. Int corridors. **Pets:** Medium. $49 one-time fee/room. Service with restrictions, supervision.

Homestead Studio Suites Hotel-St Petersburg-Clearwater Ⓜ

(727) 572-4800. **$52-$115.** 2311 Ulmerton Rd 33762. I-275 exit 31 southbound, 1.3 mi w on SR 688 (Ulmerton Rd); exit 30 northbound, 1.4 mi w on SR 686, then 0.6 mi e on SR 688 (Ulmerton Rd). Ext corridors. **Pets:** $25 daily fee/pet. Designated rooms, service with restrictions.

Howard Johnson Inn & Suites Ⓜ

(727) 796-0135. **$59-$175.** 27988 US Hwy 19 N 33761. On US 19, 0.6 mi n of jct SR 580. Ext corridors. **Pets:** Medium. $50 deposit/room, $10 daily fee/pet. Designated rooms, service with restrictions, supervision.

La Quinta Inn Tampa Bay Clearwater Airport 🅗

(727) 572-7222. **$83-$155.** 3301 Ulmerton Rd 33762. I-275 exit 31 southbound, 1.7 mi w on SR 688 (Ulmerton Rd); exit 30 northbound, 1.4 mi w on SR 686, then just w on SR 688 (Ulmerton Rd); in The Centres Office Park. Int corridors. **Pets:** Service with restrictions, supervision.

Residence Inn by Marriott Clearwater Downtown 🅗

(727) 562-5400. **$109-$209.** 940 Court St 33756. On SR 60, jct S Prospect Ave. Int corridors. **Pets:** Other species. $100 one-time fee/room. Designated rooms, service with restrictions.

Residence Inn by Marriott St. Petersburg/Clearwater 🅗 ❀

(727) 573-4444. **$89-$229.** 5050 Ulmerton Rd 33760. I-275 exit 31 southbound, 3.1 mi w on SR 688 (Ulmerton Rd); exit 30 northbound, 1.4 mi w on SR 686, then 1.7 mi w on SR 688 (Ulmerton Rd). Ext corridors. **Pets:** $100 one-time fee/room. Service with restrictions, crate.

Super 8 Clearwater/St. Petersburg Airport/ Tampa Bay 🅗

(727) 572-8881. **$45-$170.** 13260 34th St N 33762. I-275 exit 31 southbound, 1.8 mi w on SR 688 (Ulmerton Rd), then just s; exit 30 northbound, 1.4 mi w on SR 686, just w on SR 688 (Ulmerton Rd), just s. Int corridors. **Pets:** Accepted.

TownePlace Suites by Marriott St. Petersburg/Clearwater 🅗

(727) 299-9229. **$129-$199.** 13200 49th St N 33762. I-275 exit 31 southbound, 3.4 mi w on SR 688 (Ulmerton Rd); exit 30 northbound, 1.4 mi w on SR 686, 3 mi w on SR 688 (Ulmerton Rd), then just s; in Turtle Creek. Int corridors. **Pets:** Accepted.

CLEARWATER BEACH

Chart House Suites on Clearwater Bay 🅗

(727) 449-8007. **$89-$199.** 850 Bayway Blvd 33767. 1.3 mi s of jct roundabout via Gulf View Blvd. Ext/int corridors. **Pets:** Other species. $30 one-time fee/pet. Designated rooms, service with restrictions.

INDIAN SHORES

Sea Club Resort Condominiums 🄲🄾

(727) 596-2046. **$80-$165, 45 day notice.** 19725 Gulf Blvd 33785. On SR 699, 1.1 mi n of jct CR 694. Ext corridors. **Pets:** Accepted.

LARGO

Hampton Inn & Suites 🅗

(727) 585-3333. **$105-$189.** 100 E Bay Dr 33770. On SR 686 (W Bay/E Bay drs), 3.4 mi w of jct US 19; jct Alternate Rt US 19 (Seminole Blvd). Int corridors. **Pets:** Medium. Service with restrictions, supervision.

Holiday Inn Express & Suites Largo Central Park 🅗

(727) 581-3900. **$105-$169.** 210 Seminole Blvd 33770. On Alternate Rt US 19, just s of jct SR 686 (W Bay/E Bay drs). Int corridors. **Pets:** Medium. $35 one-time fee/pet. Designated rooms, service with restrictions, crate.

OLDSMAR

Residence Inn by Marriott Tampa/Oldsmar 🅷

(813) 818-9400. **$125-$199.** 4012 Tampa Rd 34677. On SR 580; jct St. Pete Dr. Int corridors. **Pets:** Large, other species. $25 daily fee/room. Service with restrictions. 🅔🅒🅞 ⬛ 🛜 ❌ ♿ ⬛ ⬛ ⬛ ⬛ ❌

PORT RICHEY

Homewood Suites by Hilton Tampa/Port Richey 🅷

(727) 819-1000. **$109-$179.** 11115 US 19 N 34668. On US 19, 0.9 mi s of SR 52 at jct Hammock/Ranch Rd. Int corridors. **Pets:** Medium. $75 one-time fee/room. Designated rooms, service with restrictions, supervision. 🛜 ♿ ⬛ ⬛ ⬛ ❌

ST. PETE BEACH

Alden Suites A Beachfront Resort 🅷 ✿

(727) 360-7081. **$129-$349.** 5900 Gulf Blvd 33706. On SR 699, 1.7 mi n of Pinellas Bayway. Ext corridors. **Pets:** Medium, dogs only. $25 one-time fee/pet. Designated rooms, service with restrictions, crate.
⬛ 🛜 ❌ ⬛ ⬛ ⬛ ❌

Bay Palms Waterfront Resort 🅼 ✿

(727) 360-7642. **$59-$229, 14 day notice.** 4237 Gulf Blvd 33706. On SR 699, 0.6 mi n of Pinellas Bayway. Ext corridors. **Pets:** Medium, other species. $50 deposit/pet, $25 daily fee/pet. Designated rooms, service with restrictions, crate. 🅔🅒🅞 ⬛ 🛜 ❌ ⬛ ⬛ ⬛ ❌

Bayview Plaza Waterfront Resort 🅼 ✿

(727) 367-2791. **$59-$229, 14 day notice.** 4321 Gulf Blvd 33706. On SR 699, 0.6 mi n of Pinellas Bayway. Ext/int corridors. **Pets:** Medium, other species. $50 deposit/pet, $25 daily fee/pet. Designated rooms, service with restrictions, crate. 🅔🅒🅞 ⬛ 🛜 ❌ ⬛ ⬛ ⬛ ❌

Island's End Resort 🅒🅐 ✿

(727) 360-5023. **$163-$390.** 1 Pass-A-Grille Way 33706. 2 mi s of Pinellas Bayway; in historic Pass-A-Grille. Ext corridors. **Pets:** Dogs only. $100 deposit/room, $20 daily fee/pet. Service with restrictions.
⬛ 🛜 ❌ ⬛ ⬛

Loews Don CeSar Hotel 🅷 ✿

(727) 360-1881. **$179-$799, 3 day notice.** 3400 Gulf Blvd 33706. On SR 699, jct Pinellas Bayway. Int corridors. **Pets:** Other species. $25 one-time fee/room. Designated rooms, service with restrictions, crate.
🅔🅒🅞 🅒 ⬛ 🛜 ❌ ♿ ⬛ ⬛ ⬛ ⬛ ❌

TradeWinds Island Grand Beach Resort 🅷 ✿

(727) 367-6461. **$188-$543.** 5500 Gulf Blvd 33706. On SR 699, 1 mi n of Pinellas Bayway. Ext/int corridors. **Pets:** Large, other species. $100 deposit/room, $30 daily fee/room. Designated rooms, service with restrictions. 🅔🅒🅞 ⬛ 🛜 ❌ ⬛ ⬛ ⬛ ⬛ ❌

ST. PETERSBURG

Hotel Indigo-Downtown St Petersburg 🅷

(727) 822-4814. **$129-$229.** 234 3rd Ave N 33701. Jct 2nd St N. Int corridors. **Pets:** Accepted. 🛜 ❌ ♿ ⬛ ⬛ ⬛ ⬛ ⬛ ❌

La Quinta Inn & Suites St. Petersburg Northeast 🅷

(727) 525-1800. **$99-$188.** 6638 4th St N 33702. I-275 exit 26, 1.7 mi e on 54th Ave N (CR 202), then 0.8 mi n. Int corridors. **Pets:** Service with restrictions, supervision. 🛜 ♿ ⬛ ⬛ ⬛

Magnuson Hotel Marina Cove 🅼 ✿

(727) 867-1151. **$80-$180.** 6800 Sunshine Skyway Ln S 33711. I-275 exit 16, just e on Pinellas Point Dr S, then just s. Ext/int corridors. **Pets:** Medium. $20 daily fee/pet. Designated rooms, service with restrictions, crate. ⬛ 🛜 ♿ ⬛ ⬛ ⬛ ⬛ ❌

TREASURE ISLAND

Residence Inn by Marriott St. Petersburg Treasure Island 🅷 ✿

(727) 367-2761. **$149-$399, 3 day notice.** 11908 Gulf Blvd 33706. On SR 699, 0.7 mi n of jct Treasure Island Cswy. Ext/int corridors. **Pets:** Medium. $100 one-time fee/room. Designated rooms, service with restrictions, supervision. ⬛ 🛜 ❌ ♿ ⬛ ⬛ ⬛

END AREA

SANIBEL

Sanibel Moorings Condominium Resort 🅒🅞

(239) 472-4119. **30 day notice.** 845 E Gulf Dr 33957. Just ne of jct Lindgren Blvd. Ext corridors. **Pets:** Medium. $15 daily fee/pet. Designated rooms, no service, supervision.
🛜 ❌ ⬛ ⬛ ⬛ ❌

SARASOTA

Hampton Inn & Suites Sarasota Bradenton Airport 🅷

(941) 355-8140. **$109-$159.** 975 University Pkwy 34234. Just e of jct US 41 (N Tamiami Tr). Int corridors. **Pets:** Accepted.
🅒 🛜 ❌ ♿ ⬛ ⬛ ⬛

Holiday Inn Express & Suites Sarasota East I-75 🅷

(941) 925-0631. **$89-$189.** 5730 Gantt Rd 34233. I-75 exit 205, 0.3 mi w on SR 72 (Clark Rd), then just n on Hospitality Way. Int corridors. **Pets:** Small, dogs only. $25 daily fee/pet. Designated rooms, service with restrictions, supervision. 🅔🅒🅞 ⬛ 🛜 ❌ ♿ ⬛ ⬛ ⬛

Holiday Inn Lido Beach 🅷

(941) 388-5555. **$159-$399.** 233 Ben Franklin Dr 34236. On Lido Key at Lido Beach; 0.4 mi s of St. Armands Circle. Int corridors. **Pets:** Medium, dogs only. $75 one-time fee/room. Designated rooms, service with restrictions, crate. 🅔🅒🅞 ⬛ 🛜 ❌ ⬛ ⬛ ⬛

Holiday Inn Sarasota Bradenton Airport 🅷 ✿

(941) 355-9000. **$99-$199.** 8009 Fifteenth St E 34243. 1.2 mi nw on W University Pkwy from jct University Pkwy (CR 610). Int corridors. **Pets:** $75 one-time fee/room. Service with restrictions, crate.
⬛ 🛜 ❌ ♿ ⬛ ⬛ ⬛ ⬛ ❌

Homewood Suites by Hilton Sarasota 🅷

(941) 365-7300. **$109-$199.** 3470 Fruitville Rd 34237. I-75 exit 210, 3.2 mi w on SR 780 (Fruitville Rd). Int corridors. **Pets:** Accepted.
🅔🅒🅞 🛜 ♿ ⬛ ⬛ ⬛ ❌

Hotel Indigo Sarasota 🅷

(941) 487-3800. **$134-$264.** 1223 Boulevard of the Arts 34236. Jct US 41 (N Tamiami Tr). Int corridors. **Pets:** Accepted.
🛜 ❌ ♿ ⬛ ⬛ ⬛ ⬛

Hyatt Regency Sarasota 🅷 ✿

(941) 953-1234. **$90-$333, 3 day notice.** 1000 Boulevard of the Arts 34236. Just w of jct US 41 (Tamiami Tr). Int corridors. **Pets:** Medium. $40 daily fee/room. Designated rooms, service with restrictions, crate.
🅔🅒🅞 ⬛ 🛜 ❌ ⬛ ⬛ ⬛ ⬛ ❌

The Inn at Sarasota 🅷 ✿

(941) 921-7750. **$84-$139.** 5778 Clark Rd 34233. I-75 exit 205, just w on SR 72 (Clark Rd). Int corridors. **Pets:** Other species. $25 deposit/room, $10 daily fee/pet. Designated rooms, service with restrictions.
🅔🅒🅞 🛜 ♿ ⬛ ⬛ ⬛

AAA ▼▼▼ **Lido Beach Resort** H

(941) 388-2161. **$169-$299.** 700 Ben Franklin Dr 34236. On Lido Key at Lido Beach; 0.8 mi s of St. Armands Circle. Ext/int corridors. **Pets:** Small, dogs only. $100 one-time fee/pet. Designated rooms, service with restrictions, crate. ECO SAVE 🛜 ✕ ⚙M 🛏 💻 ¶¶ 🏊

AAA ▼▼▼ **Residence Inn by Marriott Sarasota-Bradenton** H

(941) 358-1468. **$134-$209.** 1040 University Pkwy 34234. Just e of jct US 41 (Tamiami Tr). Int corridors. **Pets:** Other species. $75 one-time fee/room. Service with restrictions, crate.

ECO 🛜 ✕ ⚙M 🛏 💻 🏊 ✕

AAA ▼▼▼▼ **The Ritz-Carlton, Sarasota** H

(941) 309-2000. **$209-$699, 3 day notice.** 1111 Ritz-Carlton Dr 34236. On US 41, jct John Ringling Blvd. Int corridors. **Pets:** Small, other species. $125 deposit/room. Designated rooms, service with restrictions, crate. ECO SAVE 🛜 ✕ ⚙M 🛏 💻 ¶¶ 🏊 ✕

SEBASTIAN

AAA ▼▼▼ **BEST WESTERN PLUS Sebastian Hotel & Suites** H

(772) 388-9300. **$89-$130.** 1655 US Hwy 1 32958. I-95 exit 156 (Fellsmere Rd/CR 512), 6.5 mi e to US 1, then 1.2 mi n. Int corridors. **Pets:** Accepted. SAVE 🛜 ✕ 🛏 💻 🏊

SEBRING

AAA ▼▼▼ **Inn On The Lakes** H ❀

(863) 471-9400. **$89-$219.** 3101 Golfview Rd 33875. On US 27, 4.9 mi n of jct SR 98. Ext/int corridors. **Pets:** Other species. $40 one-time fee/room. Designated rooms, service with restrictions.

SAVE 🛜 🛏 💻 ¶¶ 🏊

AAA ▼▼▼ **La Quinta Inn & Suites-Sebring** H

(863) 386-1000. **$90-$162.** 4115 US Hwy 27 S 33870. On US 27, just n of Sebring Pkwy. Int corridors. **Pets:** Service with restrictions, supervision.

🛜 ✕ ⚙M 🛏 💻 🏊

AAA ▼▼▼ **Residence Inn by Marriott - Sebring** H

(863) 314-9100. **$107-$418.** 3221 Tubbs Rd 33875. On US 27, 4.5 mi n of jct SR 98; south side of Lake Jackson. Int corridors. **Pets:** Accepted.

SAVE 🛜 ✕ 🛏 💻 🏊 ✕

SILVER SPRINGS

▼▼▼ **Holiday Inn Express Hotel & Suites** H

(352) 304-6111. **$70-$120.** 5360 E Silver Springs Blvd 34488. On SR 40, just e of jct NE 25th St. Int corridors. **Pets:** Small, other species. $15 daily fee/pet. Service with restrictions, supervision.

ECO 🛜 ✕ 🛏 💻 🏊

STARKE

AAA ▼▼▼ **BEST WESTERN Starke** H

(904) 964-6744. **$72-$77.** 1290 N Temple Ave 32091. 1 mi n on US 301 from jct SR 100 (Reid St). Ext corridors. **Pets:** Medium. $10 daily fee/pet. Service with restrictions, supervision. SAVE 🛜 🛏 💻 🏊

▼▼ **Hometown Inn** M

(904) 964-7357. **Call for rates.** 880 N Temple Ave 32091. 0.7 mi n on US 301 from jct SR 100. Ext corridors. **Pets:** Accepted. 🛜 🛏 🏊

STUART

AAA ▼▼▼ **BEST WESTERN PLUS Downtown Stuart** M ❀

(772) 287-6200. **$69-$120.** 1209 S Federal Hwy 34994. On US 1, 0.5 mi s of jct SR 76. Ext corridors. **Pets:** Large. $15 daily fee/room. Designated rooms, service with restrictions, supervision. SAVE 🛜 🛏 💻 🏊

▼▼▼ **Courtyard by Marriott-Stuart** H

(772) 781-3344. **$94-$142.** 7615 SW Lost River Rd 34997. I-95 exit 101 (SR 76), 0.7 mi e to SW Lost River Rd, then just nw. Int corridors. **Pets:** Accepted. 🛜 ✕ ⚙M 🛏 💻 🏊

▼▼▼ **Hampton Inn & Suites Stuart-North, FL** H

(772) 692-6922. **$99-$169.** 1150 NW Federal Hwy 34994. On US 1 (Federal Hwy), 2.1 mi nw of SR 76 (SW Kanner Hwy). Int corridors. **Pets:** Accepted. 🛜 ⚙M 🛏 💻 🏊

▼▼ **Monterey Inn & Marina** M ❀

(772) 283-3500. **$65-$129.** 300 SW Monterey Rd 34994. Jct SR 76 (S Kanner Hwy) and CR 714 (SW Monterey Rd), just w; base of east side of Palm City Bridge. Ext corridors. **Pets:** Large, other species. $20 daily fee/pet. Designated rooms, service with restrictions, crate. 🛜 🛏 💻

▼▼▼ **Pirate's Cove Resort & Marina** H

(772) 287-2500. **Call for rates.** 4307 SE Bayview St 34997. From US 1, 0.4 mi ne on SE Indian St to SE Dixie Hwy, 2 mi se to SE Bayview St, then 0.3 mi e. Ext corridors. **Pets:** Accepted.

🛜 🛏 💻 ¶¶ 🏊 ✕

TALLAHASSEE

AAA ▼▼▼ **Aloft Tallahassee Downtown** H ❀

(850) 513-0313. **$109-$249.** 200 N Monroe St 32301. 0.4 mi n of Capitol. Int corridors. **Pets:** Medium, dogs only. Service with restrictions.

SAVE 🛜 ✕ 🛏 💻 🏊

AAA ▼▼▼ **BEST WESTERN Pride Inn & Suites** M

(850) 656-6312. **$69-$299.** 2016 Apalachee Pkwy 32301. 1 mi se of US 27. Ext corridors. **Pets:** $10 daily fee/pet. No service, crate.

SAVE 🛜 🛏 💻 🏊

AAA ▼▼▼ **BEST WESTERN Seminole Inn** M

(850) 656-2938. **$60-$190.** 6737 Mahan Dr 32308. I-10 exit 209A, just w on US 90. Ext corridors. **Pets:** Medium. $10 daily fee/pet. Service with restrictions, supervision. SAVE 🛜 🛏 💻 🏊

AAA ▼▼▼ **Econo Lodge** M

(850) 385-6155. **$60.** 2681 N Monroe St 32303. I-10 exit 199, 0.5 mi s. Ext corridors. **Pets:** Accepted. SAVE 🛜 🛏 💻

▼▼▼ **Holiday Inn Capitol Center** H

(850) 877-3171. **$79-$150, 3 day notice.** 1355 Apalachee Pkwy 32301. 1.3 mi se on US 27. Int corridors. **Pets:** Accepted.

🛜 🛏 💻 ¶¶ 🏊

▼▼▼ **Homewood Suites by Hilton** H

(850) 402-9400. **Call for rates.** 2987 Apalachee Pkwy 32301. US 27, 3.5 mi s. Int corridors. **Pets:** Accepted. ECO 🛜 🛏 💻 🏊 ✕

▼▼ **La Quinta Inn Tallahassee (North)** H

(850) 385-7172. **$59-$199.** 2905 N Monroe St 32303. I-10 exit 199, just s on US 27. Ext corridors. **Pets:** Service with restrictions, supervision.

🛜 🛏 💻 🏊

▼▼ **La Quinta Inn Tallahassee (South)** H

(850) 878-5099. **$59-$199.** 2850 Apalachee Pkwy 32301. 3 mi se on US 27. Ext corridors. **Pets:** Service with restrictions, supervision.

🛜 ⚙M 🛏 💻 🏊

▼▼▼ **Residence Inn by Marriott Tallahassee North I-10 Capital Circle by Marriott** H

(850) 422-0093. **$109-$139.** 1880 Raymond Diehl Rd 32308. I-10 exit 203, just s. Int corridors. **Pets:** Accepted.

ECO 🛜 ✕ ⚙M 🛏 💻 🏊 ✕

AAA ▼▼▼▼ **Residence Inn by Marriott Tallahassee Universities at the Capitol** H ❀

(850) 329-9080. **$109-$229.** 600 W Gaines St 32304. 0.5 mi w of S Monroe St; downtown. Int corridors. **Pets:** Other species. $100 one-time fee/room. Service with restrictions, crate.

ECO SAVE 🛜 ✕ ⚙M 🛏 💻 🏊

▼▼▼ **Staybridge Suites Tallahassee** H

(850) 219-7000. **Call for rates.** 1600 Summit Lake Dr 32317. I-10 exit 209B, just n. Int corridors. **Pets:** Accepted.

ECO 🛜 ✕ 🛏 💻 🏊

▼▼ ▼▼ **StudioPLUS-Tallahassee-Killearn** ⊞
(850) 383-1700. **$60-$190.** 1950 Raymond Diehl Rd 32308. I-10 exit 203, 2.4 mi s, then just n. Int corridors. **Pets:** $25 daily fee/pet. Designated rooms, service with restrictions. 🤚 🕭M 🔂 🔲 🌊

▼▼ ▼▼ **TownePlace Suites by Marriott Tallahassee North/ Capital Circle** ⊞
(850) 219-0122. **$89-$109.** 1876 Capital Cir NE 32308. 3.3 mi e on US 90, 1 mi n on US 319. Int corridors. **Pets:** Accepted.
ECO 🤚 ✕ 🕭M 🔂 🔲 🌊

TAMPA METROPOLITAN AREA

BRANDON
▼▼▼▼ **La Quinta Inn & Suites Tampa Brandon Regency Park** ⊞
(813) 643-0574. **$78-$144.** 310 Grand Regency Blvd 33510. I-75 exit 257, just e on SR 60, then 0.5 mi n; in Regency Corporate Office Park. Int corridors. **Pets:** Service with restrictions, supervision.
🤚 🕭M 🔂 🔲 🌊

LUTZ
ⒶⒶ▷ ▼▼▼▼ **Residence Inn by Marriott Tampa Suncoast Parkway at NorthPointe Village** ⊞
(813) 792-8400. **$129-$199.** 2101 NorthPointe Pkwy 33558. Suncoast Pkwy exit 19, just w on SR 54, then just ne; in NorthPointe at Suncoast Crossings. Int corridors. **Pets:** Large, other species. $100 one-time fee/room. Service with restrictions, crate.
ECO SAVE 🤚 ✕ 🕭M 🔂 🔲 🌊

PLANT CITY
▼▼ ▼▼ **Comfort Inn of Plant City** ⊞
(813) 707-6000. **$59-$139.** 2003 S Frontage Rd 33566. I-4 exit 22, just s on Park Rd. Int corridors. **Pets:** Accepted. 🤚 🕭M 🔂 🔲 🌊

RUSKIN
▼▼▼▼ **Southern Comfort Bed & Breakfast** ⒷⒷ
(813) 645-6361. **Call for rates.** 2409 Ravine Dr W 33570. Jct US 41, 1.1 mi sw on 1st St, just w on 24th Ave SW, then just s. Ext/int corridors. **Pets:** Accepted. 🤚 ✕ 🔂 🔲 🌊 ✕ 🄯

SEFFNER
ⒶⒶ▷ ▼▼▼▼ **Country Inn & Suites By Carlson Tampa East/Seffner** ⊞
(813) 675-8600. **$89-$199.** 11551 Discovery Ln 33584. I-4 exit 10, just n on CR 579. Int corridors. **Pets:** Other species. $16 daily fee/pet. Designated rooms, service with restrictions.
SAVE 🤚 ✕ 🕭M 🔂 🔲 🌊

ⒶⒶ▷ ▼▼▼▼ **Hampton Inn & Suites Tampa East** ⊞
(813) 630-4321. **$89-$149.** 11740 Tampa Gateway Blvd 33584. I-4 exit 10, just n of CR 579, just e. Int corridors. **Pets:** Small. Designated rooms, service with restrictions. SAVE 🤚 🕭M 🔂 🔲 🌊

TAMPA
ⒶⒶ▷ ▼▼ ▼▼ **BEST WESTERN Hotel Brandon** Ⓜ
(813) 621-5555. **$69-$299.** 9331 Adamo Dr 33619. I-75 exit 257, 1.2 mi w on SR 60. Ext corridors. **Pets:** Large. $35 deposit/room. Designated rooms, service with restrictions, crate. SAVE 🤚 🔂 🔲 🍴 🌊

▼▼ ▼▼ **Extended StayAmerica** ⊞
(813) 886-5253. **$65-$115.** 4811 Memorial Hwy 33634. Veteran's Expwy exit 3, just sw on CR 576. Int corridors. **Pets:** $25 daily fee/pet. Designated rooms, service with restrictions. 🤚 🕭M 🔂 🔲 🌊

▼▼ ▼▼ **Extended StayAmerica-Tampa-Airport-N West Shore Blvd** ⊞
(813) 637-8990. **$65-$115.** 1805 N Westshore Blvd 33607. I-275 exit 40A southbound, 0.5 mi nw; exit 39A northbound, 1 mi e on SR 60 (Kennedy Blvd), then 1.3 mi nw. Int corridors. **Pets:** $25 daily fee/pet. Designated rooms, service with restrictions. 🤚 🕭M 🔂 🔲 🌊

ⒶⒶ▷ ▼▼▼▼ ▼▼▼▼ **Grand Hyatt Tampa Bay** ⊞
(813) 874-1234. **$90-$360.** 2900 Bayport Dr 33607. On SR 60 (Kennedy Blvd), east end of Courtney Campbell Cswy. Ext/int corridors.
Pets: Accepted. ECO SAVE 🤚 🕭M 🔂 🔲 🍴 🌊 ✕

▼▼▼▼ **Hampton Inn Tampa- Veterans Expwy/Airport North** ⊞ 🐾
(813) 901-5900. **$99-$169.** 5628 W Waters Ave 33634. Veteran's Expwy (SR 589) exit 6A, just e on CR 584. Int corridors. **Pets:** Large, other species. $20 one-time fee/pet. Designated rooms, service with restrictions, supervision. 🤚 🕭M 🔂 🔲 🌊

ⒶⒶⒶ▷ ▼▼▼▼ **Holiday Inn Express Hotel & Suites** ⊞
(813) 910-7171. **$90-$150.** 8310 Galbraith Rd 33647. I-75 exit 270, 0.3 mi n on CR 581 (Bruce B Downs Blvd), just w on Highwoods Preserve Pkwy, then just n; in Highwoods Preserve. Int corridors. **Pets:** Accepted.
ECO SAVE 🤚 🕭M 🔂 🔲 🌊

▼▼▼▼ **Homewood Suites by Hilton Tampa Airport/Westshore** ⊞
(813) 282-1950. **$149-$229.** 5325 Avion Park Dr 33607. I-275 exit 40A southbound, 0.7 mi n on Westshore Blvd; exit 39A northbound, 1 mi e on Kennedy Blvd (SR 60), 1.2 mi n on Westshore Blvd, just w on Spruce St, then just s on O'Brien St; in Avion Park Westshore. Int corridors.
Pets: Accepted. ECO 🤚 🕭M 🔂 🔲 🌊

▼▼▼▼ **Homewood Suites by Hilton Tampa/Brandon** ⊞
(813) 685-7099. **$139-$179.** 10240 Palm River Rd 33619. I-75 exit 257, 0.4 mi w on SR 60 (Kennedy Blvd), just s on S Falkenburg Rd, then 0.3 mi e. Int corridors. **Pets:** Medium. $100 one-time fee/room. Service with restrictions, crate. ECO 🤚 🕭M 🔂 🔲 🌊 ✕

▼▼ ▼▼ **La Quinta Inn & Suites Tampa Bay Fairgrounds** ⊞
(813) 626-0885. **$59-$144.** 4811 US 301 N 33610. I-4 exit 7 westbound; exit 7A eastbound, just se. Int corridors. **Pets:** Service with restrictions, supervision. 🤚 🕭M 🔂 🔲 🌊

▼▼ ▼▼ **La Quinta Inn & Suites Tampa Brandon West** ⊞
(813) 684-4007. **$59-$126.** 602 S Falkenburg Rd 33619. I-75 exit 257, just w on SR 60 (Kennedy Blvd), then just n. Int corridors. **Pets:** Service with restrictions, supervision. 🤚 🔂 🔲 🌊

▼▼ ▼▼ **La Quinta Inn & Suites USF (near Busch Gardens)** ⊞
(813) 910-7500. **$71-$155.** 3701 E Fowler Ave 33612. I-275 exit 51, 2.2 mi e on SR 582 (Fowler Ave). Int corridors. **Pets:** Service with restrictions, supervision. 🤚 🕭M 🔂 🔲 🌊

▼▼▼▼ **La Quinta Inn Tampa South** ⊞
(813) 835-6262. **$87-$166.** 4620 W Gandy Blvd 33611. Just e of jct S Westshore Blvd. Int corridors. **Pets:** Service with restrictions, supervision. 🤚 ✕ 🕭M 🔂 🔲 🌊

▼▼▼▼ **MainStay Suites By Choice** Ⓜ
(813) 622-8557. **Call for rates.** 10007 Princess Palm Ave 33619. I-75 exit 260 southbound; exit 260B northbound, 0.5 mi w on SR 574 (Dr. Martin Luther King Jr Blvd), just s on Falkenburg Rd, then just w; in Sabal Corporate Park. Int corridors. **Pets:** Accepted.
🤚 ✕ 🔂 🔲 🌊

ⒶⒶ▷ ▼▼ ▼▼ **Red Roof Inn-Fairgrounds** Ⓜ
(813) 623-5245. **$40-$199.** 5001 N US 301 33610. I-4 exit 7 westbound; exit 7A eastbound, just se. Ext corridors. **Pets:** Large, other species. Service with restrictions, supervision. SAVE 🤚 🔂

▼▼▼▼ **Residence Inn by Marriott Tampa Downtown** ⊞
(813) 221-4224. **$139-$209.** 101 E Tyler St 33602. I-275 exit 44, 0.5 mi se on W Ashley Dr/Tampa St; exit 45A southbound, 1.5 mi se on W Ashley Dr. Int corridors. **Pets:** $100 one-time fee/room. Service with restrictions. 🤚 ✕ 🕭M 🔂 🔲 🌊 ✕

▼▼▼▼ **Residence Inn by Marriott Tampa North I-75 Fletcher** H
(813) 972-4400. **$107-$179.** 13420 N Telecom Pkwy 33637. I-75 exit 266, 1.1 mi w on Fletcher Ave (CR 582A), then just s; in Telecom Tampa Park. Int corridors. **Pets:** Accepted.

▼▼▼ **Residence Inn by Marriott Tampa Sabal Park/Brandon** H ❖
(813) 627-8855. **$109-$169.** 9719 Princess Palm Ave 33619. I-75 exit 260 southbound; exit 260B northbound, just w on SR 574 (Dr. Martin Luther King Jr Blvd), just s on Falkenburg Rd, then 0.4 mi w; in Sabal Corporate Center. Int corridors. **Pets:** Other species. $100 one-time fee/room. Service with restrictions.

▼▼▼ **Residence Inn by Marriott Tampa Westshore/Airport** H
(813) 877-7988. **$109-$269.** 4312 W Boy Scout Blvd 33607. I-275 exit 40B, 0.8 mi n on Lois Ave. Int corridors. **Pets:** Accepted.

(AAA) ▼▼▼▼ **Seminole Hard Rock Hotel & Casino Tampa** H
(813) 627-7625. **$189-$449.** 5223 N Orient Rd 33610. I-4 exit 6, just w. Int corridors. **Pets:** Accepted.

(AAA) ▼▼▼▼ **Sheraton Suites Tampa Airport Westshore** H ❖
(813) 873-8675. **$99-$405.** 4400 W Cypress St 33607. I-275 exit 40A southbound; exit 39A northbound, just nw on Westshore Blvd (CR 587), then just e. Int corridors. **Pets:** Large, dogs only. Service with restrictions, supervision.

(AAA) ▼▼▼▼ **Sheraton Tampa Riverwalk** H ❖
(813) 223-2222. **$99-$339.** 200 N Ashley Dr 33602. I-275 exit 44, 0.8 mi s. Int corridors. **Pets:** Service with restrictions.

▼▼▼▼ **Staybridge Suites-Tampa East** H
(813) 227-4000. **$89-$269, 3 day notice.** 3624 N Falkenburg Rd 33619. I-75 exit 260 southbound; exit 260B northbound, just w on SR 574 (Dr. Martin Luther King Jr Blvd), then just s. Int corridors. **Pets:** Accepted.

▼▼▼▼ **Tahitian Inn Hotel Cafe Spa** H
(813) 877-6721. **$89-$209.** 601 S Dale Mabry Hwy 33609. I-275 exit 41A, 1.1 mi s at jct W Dale Ave. Ext/int corridors. **Pets:** Medium. $35 one-time fee/pet. Designated rooms, service with restrictions, crate.

▼▼▼ **TownePlace Suites by Marriott Tampa North/I-75 Fletcher** H
(813) 975-9777. **$99-$269.** 6800 Woodstork Rd 33637. I-75 exit 266, 1.1 mi w on Fletcher Ave (CR 582A), then just s on N Telecom Dr; in Telecom Tampa Park. Int corridors. **Pets:** Accepted.

▼▼▼▼ **TownePlace Suites by Marriott Tampa Westshore/Airport** H
(813) 282-1081. **$109-$169.** 5302 Avion Park Dr 33607. I-275 exit 40A southbound, 0.7 mi n on Westshore Blvd; exit 39A northbound, 1 mi e on SR 60 (Kennedy Blvd), 1.2 mi n on Westshore Blvd, just w on Spruce St, then just s on O'Brien St; in Avion Park Westshore. Int corridors. **Pets:** Accepted.

(AAA) ▼▼▼ ▼▼▼ **The Westin Tampa Bay** H ❖
(813) 281-0000. **$109-$469.** 7627 Courtney Campbell Cswy 33607. On SR 60, at east end of Courtney Campbell Cswy. Int corridors. **Pets:** Medium, dogs only. Service with restrictions, supervision.

(AAA) ▼▼▼▼ **The Westin Tampa Harbour Island** H
(813) 229-5000. **$109-$439, 3 day notice.** 725 S Harbour Island Blvd 33602. I-275 exit 44, 2.4 mi e on W Ashley Dr/Tampa St, on Harbour Island; exit 45A southbound, 3.9 mi e. Int corridors. **Pets:** Accepted.

(AAA) ▼▼▼▼ **Wyndham Tampa Westshore** H
(813) 289-8200. **$149-$250.** 700 N Westshore Blvd 33609. I-275 exit 40A southbound, just nw on CR 587; exit 39A northbound, 1 mi e on Kennedy Blvd, then 0.9 mi nw on CR 587, jct W Cypress St. Int corridors. **Pets:** Medium. $30 one-time fee/room. Designated rooms, service with restrictions, supervision.

TEMPLE TERRACE
▼▼ ▼▼ **Extended StayAmerica-Tampa North-USF Attractions** H
(813) 989-2264. **$60-$130.** 12242 Morris Bridge Rd 33637. I-75 exit 266, just w on Fletcher Ave (CR 582A). Int corridors. **Pets:** $25 daily fee/pet. Designated rooms, service with restrictions.

WESLEY CHAPEL
(AAA) ▼▼ ▼▼ **Holiday Inn Express** H
(813) 907-1379. **$69-$99.** 27615 SR 54 W 33543. I-75 exit 279, just w. Int corridors. **Pets:** Accepted.

ZEPHYRHILLS
▼▼ ▼▼ **Microtel Inn & Suites by Wyndham Zephyrhills** H
(813) 783-2211. **$55-$110.** 7839 Gall Blvd 33541. On US 301; 0.9 mi n of jct Daugherty Rd. Int corridors. **Pets:** Accepted.

END METROPOLITAN AREA

TITUSVILLE
(AAA) ▼▼ ▼▼ **BEST WESTERN Space Shuttle Inn** H ❖
(321) 269-9100. **$60-$129.** 3455 Cheney Hwy 32780. I-95 exit 215 (SR 50), just e. Ext corridors. **Pets:** Other species. $10 daily fee/room. Service with restrictions.

(AAA) ▼▼ ▼▼ **Days Inn Titusville Kennedy Space Center** M
(321) 269-4480. **$59-$89.** 3755 Cheney Hwy 32780. I-95 exit 215 (SR 50), just w. Ext corridors. **Pets:** Accepted.

(AAA) ▼▼▼ **Fairfield Inn & Suites by Marriott - Titusville Kennedy Space Center** H
(321) 385-1818. **$89-$159.** 4735 Helen Hauser Blvd 32780. I-95 exit 215 (SR 50), just w. Int corridors. **Pets:** Small, dogs only. $50 one-time fee/room. Designated rooms, service with restrictions, crate.

▼▼▼▼ **Hampton Inn - Titusville I-95/Kennedy Space Center** H
(321) 383-9191. **$99-$139.** 4760 Helen Hauser Blvd 32780. I-95 exit 215 (SR 50), just w. Int corridors. **Pets:** Medium, other species. $25 one-time fee/pet. Designated rooms, service with restrictions, crate.

▼▼▼▼ Holiday Inn Titusville - Kennedy Space Center ⛶

(321) 383-0200. **Call for rates.** 4715 Helen Hauser Blvd 32780. I-95 exit 215 (SR 50), just w to Helen Hauser Blvd, then just n. Int corridors. **Pets:** Medium. $50 one-time fee/room. Service with restrictions, supervision. 🤖 🖴 🅼 🔒 🖳 🍽 🏊

VENICE

▼▼▼▼ Holiday Inn Express Hotel & Suites ⛶ 🐾

(941) 584-6800. **$89-$145.** 380 Commercial Ct 34292. I-75 exit 193, just w on Jacaranda Blvd (CR 765), then just n. Int corridors. **Pets:** Other species. $30 one-time fee/room. Service with restrictions, crate.

🤖 🅼 🔒 🏊

▼▼▼▼ Horse and Chaise Inn A Bed & Breakfast 🅱🅱

(941) 488-2702. **$115-$189, 14 day notice.** 317 Ponce de Leon 34285. Just s of jct Venice Ave on Nassau St, just sw; downtown. Ext/int corridors. **Pets:** Small. Designated rooms. 🤖 🔒 🐾

VERO BEACH

🔷🔷 ▼▼▼▼ The Caribbean Court Boutique Hotel ⛶

(772) 231-7211. **$99-$299.** 1601 S Ocean Dr 32963. US 1, 4.3 mi n on Indian River Blvd (CR 603), 1.3 mi e on 17th St (SR 656) to Ocean Dr, then just s; jct Ocean Dr and Jasmine Ln. Ext corridors. **Pets:** Accepted.

[SAVE] 🤖 🅧 🔒 🖳 🍽 🏊

🔷🔷 ▼▼▼ ▼▼▼ Costa d' Este Beach Resort ⛶ 🐾

(772) 562-9919. **$159-$459, 7 day notice.** 3244 Ocean Dr 32963. I-95 exit 147 (SR 60), 8.7 mi e to Indian River Blvd, 1 mi n to Merril P Barber Bridge/SR 60, 1.7 mi e to Ocean Dr, then just s. Int corridors. **Pets:** Dogs only. Supervision. [SAVE] 🤖 🅧 🅼 🔒 🍽 🏊 🅧

▼▼▼ Country Inn & Suites By Carlson, Vero Beach I-95 ⛶

(772) 257-0252. **$69-$199.** 9330 19th Ln 32966. I-95 exit 147 (20th St/SR 60), just w. Int corridors. **Pets:** Accepted.

🤖 🅧 🔒 🖳 🏊

🔷🔷 ▼▼▼ Holiday Inn Hotel & Suites Vero Beach-Oceanside ⛶

(772) 231-2300. **$119-$269.** 3384 Ocean Dr 32963. E of SR A1A; at end of SR 60. Ext corridors. **Pets:** Medium. $50 one-time fee/room. Designated rooms, service with restrictions, crate.

[ECO] [SAVE] 🤖 🅧 🔒 🖳 🍽 🏊

🔷🔷 ▼▼▼ ▼▼▼ Vero Beach Hotel & Spa ⛶ 🐾

(772) 231-5666. **$149-$999.** 3500 Ocean Dr 32963. On Ocean Dr, just n of SR 60. Ext/int corridors. **Pets:** Other species. Designated rooms, service with restrictions. [ECO] [SAVE] 🤖 🅧 🅼 🔒 🍽 🏊 🅧

WEEKI WACHEE

🔷🔷 ▼▼▼ BEST WESTERN Nature Coast 🅼

(352) 596-9000. **$69-$99.** 9373 Cortez Blvd 34613. On SR 50, just e of jct US 19. Ext corridors. **Pets:** $20 daily fee/pet. Designated rooms, service with restrictions, supervision. [SAVE] 🤖 🔒 🖳 🏊

WEST MELBOURNE

🔷🔷 ▼▼▼▼ Fairfield Inn & Suites by Marriott - Melbourne ⛶

(321) 722-2220. **$89-$159.** 4355 W New Haven Ave 32904. I-95 exit 180 (US 192/New Haven Ave), just e. Int corridors. **Pets:** Small, dogs only. $50 one-time fee/room. Designated rooms, service with restrictions, supervision. [SAVE] 🤖 🅧 🅼 🔒 🖳 🏊

WEST PALM BEACH

🔷🔷 ▼▼▼ BEST WESTERN Palm Beach Lakes Inn ⛶

(561) 683-8810. **$89-$129.** 1800 Palm Beach Lakes Blvd 33401. I-95 exit 71 (Palm Beach Lakes Blvd), just e. Ext/int corridors. **Pets:** Small. $100 deposit/room, $15 daily fee/pet. Designated rooms, service with restrictions, crate. [ECO] [SAVE] 🤖 🔒 🖳 🏊

🔷🔷 ▼▼▼ Casa Grandview West Palm Beach 🅲🅰

(561) 655-8932. **$175-$400, 30 day notice.** 1410 Georgia Ave 33401. I-95 exit 70 (Okeechobee Blvd), 1 mi e to Parker Ave, 0.5 mi s to Park Pl, just e to Georgia Ave, then just n. Ext/int corridors. **Pets:** Accepted.

[SAVE] 🤖 🅧 🔒 🖳 🏊 🅧 🐾

▼▼▼ Days Inn-Airport North 🅼

(561) 689-0450. **$63-$110.** 2300 45th St 33407. I-95 exit 74 (45th St), just e. Ext corridors. **Pets:** Accepted. 🤖 🔒 🖳 🍽 🏊 🅧

▼▼▼ La Quinta Inn-West Palm Beach City Place 🅼

(561) 697-3388. **$59-$144.** 5981 Okeechobee Blvd 33417. I-95 exit 70B (Okeechobee Blvd), 3.6 mi w; Florida Tpke exit 99 (Okeechobee Blvd), just e. Ext corridors. **Pets:** Service with restrictions, supervision.

🤖 🔒 🖳 🏊

▼▼▼ Residence Inn by Marriott-West Palm Beach ⛶

(561) 687-4747. **$89-$189.** 2461 Metrocentre Blvd E 33407. I-95 exit 74 (45th St), just w to Metrocentre Blvd, then just se; in Metrocentre Corporate Park. Int corridors. **Pets:** Medium. $75 one-time fee/room. Service with restrictions, crate. 🤖 🅧 🅼 🔒 🖳 🏊 🅧

🔷🔷 ▼▼▼ Stay Inn West Palm Beach Airport Hotel 🅼

(561) 471-8700. **$80-$180.** 1505 Belvedere Rd 33406. I-95 exit 69A (Belvedere Rd), just w. Ext corridors. **Pets:** Medium. $100 deposit/room, $20 daily fee/pet. Service with restrictions, supervision.

[SAVE] 🤖 🔒 🖳 🏊

WILDWOOD

▼▼▼ Sleep Inn & Suites Wildwood- The Villages ⛶

(352) 748-0507. **$69-$89.** 1224 S Main St 34785. Florida Tpke exit 304, just n on US 301. Int corridors. **Pets:** Medium. $25 one-time fee/room. Designated rooms, service with restrictions, crate.

[ECO] 🤖 🅧 🅼 🔒 🖳 🏊

GEORGIA

ADAIRSVILLE

🌼 ▼▼ Quality Inn Ⓜ
(770) 773-2886. **$66-$90.** 107 Princeton Blvd 30103. I-75 exit 306, just w. Ext corridors. **Pets:** Medium. $15 daily fee/pet. Service with restrictions, supervision. ⬛ 🛜 ⬛ ⬛ ⬛ ⬛

▼▼ Ramada Limited Ⓜ
(770) 769-9726. **$65-$110.** 500 Georgia North Cir 30103. I-75 exit 306, 0.3 mi w. Ext corridors. **Pets:** Accepted. 🛜 ⬛ ⬛ ⬛ ⬛

ADEL

▼▼ Days Inn Ⓗ
(229) 896-4574. **$50-$90.** 1204 W 4th St 31620. I-75 exit 39, just w. Ext corridors. **Pets:** Accepted. 🛜 ⬛ ⬛ ⬛ ⬛

▼▼▼ Hampton Inn Ⓗ
(229) 896-3099. **$75-$115.** 1500 W 4th St 31620. I-75 exit 39, just w. Int corridors. **Pets:** Accepted. 🛜 ⬛ ⬛ ⬛ ⬛

ALBANY

▼▼ Baymont Inn & Suites Albany Ⓗ
(229) 435-3737. **Call for rates.** 2720 Dawson Rd 31707. 0.5 mi se of jct US 82 and SR 520. Ext corridors. **Pets:** Accepted. 🛜 ⬛ ⬛ ⬛

🌼 ▼▼▼ BEST WESTERN Albany Mall Inn & Suites Ⓗ
(229) 446-2001. **$65-$75.** 2729 Pointe North Blvd 31721. Just se of jct Dawson Rd and US 82 W. Int corridors. **Pets:** Accepted.
⬛ 🛜 ⬛ ⬛ ⬛ ⬛

▼▼ Merry Acres Inn Ⓜ
(229) 435-7721. **$100-$140.** 1500 Dawson Rd 31707. 3.3 mi w. Ext corridors. **Pets:** Accepted. 🛜 ❌ ⬛ ⬛ ⬛

▼▼▼ Wingate by Wyndham Ⓗ
(229) 883-9800. **$117-$123.** 2735 Dawson Rd 31707. Jct US 82 and SR 520, 0.4 mi se. Int corridors. **Pets:** Accepted. 🛜 ⬛ ⬛ ⬛ ⬛

ALMA

▼▼ Days Inn Ⓜ
(912) 632-7000. **$54-$75.** 930 S Pierce St 31510. Jct SR 32/US 1, 0.4 mi s on US 1. Ext corridors. **Pets:** Accepted. 🛜 ⬛ ⬛ ⬛

AMERICUS

▼▼ Quality Inn Ⓗ
(229) 924-4431. **$65-$100.** 1205 S Martin Luther King Jr Blvd 31719. On US 19 S, 1 mi w of downtown. Ext corridors. **Pets:** $15 daily fee/pet. Designated rooms, service with restrictions, crate.
🛜 ⬛ ⬛ ⬛ ⬛

ASHBURN

🌼 ▼▼▼ BEST WESTERN Ashburn Inn Ⓗ
(229) 567-0080. **$65-$75.** 820 Shoney's Dr 31714. I-75 exit 82, just w. Ext corridors. **Pets:** Medium, dogs only. $10 daily fee/pet. Designated rooms, service with restrictions, supervision. ⬛ 🛜 ⬛ ⬛ ⬛

🌼 ▼▼ Days Inn Ⓗ
(229) 567-3346. **$52.** 823 E Washington Ave 31714. I-75 exit 82, just w on SR 112. Ext corridors. **Pets:** Medium, dogs only. $10 daily fee/pet. Designated rooms, service with restrictions, supervision.
⬛ 🛜 ⬛ ⬛ ⬛

▼▼ Super 8 Ⓗ
(229) 567-4688. **$51.** 749 E Washington Ave 31714. I-75 exit 82, just w. Ext corridors. **Pets:** Medium, other species. $5 daily fee/pet. Crate.
🛜 ⬛ ⬛

ATHENS

🌼 ▼▼▼ BEST WESTERN Athens Ⓜ
(706) 546-7311. **$65-$260.** 170 N Milledge Ave 30601. Jct US 78 business route (Broad St), 0.5 mi w on SR 15. Ext corridors. **Pets:** Medium. $10 daily fee/pet. Designated rooms, service with restrictions, crate.
⬛ 🛜 ⬛ ⬛ ⬛

▼▼▼ Candlewood Suites Ⓗ
(706) 548-9663. **Call for rates.** 156 Classic Rd 30622. Jct SR 8/10 Loop and US 29/78, 1.1 mi w on US 29/78 to Classic Rd, then just s. Int corridors. **Pets:** Accepted. 🛜 ⬛ ⬛ ⬛

▼▼▼ Comfort Inn & Suites Ⓗ
(706) 227-9700. **$79-$210.** 3980 Atlanta Hwy 30622. SR 10 Loop exit 18 (Atlanta Hwy), 0.7 mi w. Int corridors. **Pets:** Accepted.
🛜 ⬛ ⬛ ⬛

🌼 ▼▼▼ Comfort Suites Downtown Athens Ⓗ
(706) 995-4000. **$70-$139.** 255 North Ave 30601. SR 10 Loop exit 11B (Dougherty St/North Ave); 1 mi n of downtown. Int corridors. **Pets:** Medium. $25 daily fee/pet. Designated rooms, service with restrictions, supervision. ⬛ 🛜 ❌ ⬛ ⬛ ⬛

WWW Foundry Park Inn & Spa M ✿
(706) 549-7020. **$94-$135.** 295 E Dougherty St 30601. Jct Thomas and Dougherty sts; downtown. Ext/int corridors. **Pets:** Small, dogs only. $25 deposit/pet. Crate. 🛜 🖬 🖳 🍴 ➿

WWW Holiday Inn H
(706) 549-4433. **$99-$109.** 197 E Broad St 30603. On US 78 business route (Broad St); jct N Hull St; center. Int corridors. **Pets:** Accepted.
🛜 🖬 🖳 🍴 ➿

AAA WWW Hotel Indigo H ✿
(706) 546-0430. **$139-$209.** 500 College Ave 30601. Just n of center. Int corridors. **Pets:** Medium, other species. $75 one-time fee/room. Designated rooms, service with restrictions, crate.
ECO SAVE 🛜 ✕ ⅗M 🖬 🖳 🍴

AAA WWW Microtel Inn by Wyndham Athens H
(706) 548-5676. **$50-$175.** 1050 Ultimate Dr 30605. Jct US 78 business route (Broad St) and SR 10 Loop, 1.4 mi e. Int corridors. **Pets:** Medium, dogs only. $25 one-time fee/room. Service with restrictions, crate.
SAVE 🛜 ⅗M 🖬 🖳

WW Sleep Inn & Suites H
(706) 850-1261. **$69-$189.** 109 Florence Dr 30622. Jct SR 8/10 Loop and US 29/78, 1.2 mi w on US 29/78 to Florence Rd, then just s. Int corridors. **Pets:** Small. $15 daily fee/pet. Service with restrictions, supervision. 🛜 ⅗M 🖬 🖳 ➿

ATLANTA METROPOLITAN AREA

ACWORTH

AAA WWW BEST WESTERN Acworth Inn M
(770) 974-0116. **$60-$100.** 5155 Cowan Rd 30101. I-75 exit 277, just w. Ext corridors. **Pets:** Medium, other species. $10 daily fee/pet. Service with restrictions, supervision. SAVE 🛜 🖬 🖳 ➿

WW Days Inn Acworth M
(770) 975-9000. **$55-$120, 3 day notice.** 164 N Point Way 30102. I-75 exit 277, just e. Ext corridors. **Pets:** Accepted. 🛜 🖬 🖳

WWW La Quinta Inn Acworth H
(770) 975-9920. **$90-$156.** 184 N Point Way 30102. I-75 exit 277, just e. Ext/int corridors. **Pets:** Service with restrictions, supervision.
🛜 ⅗M 🖬 🖳 ➿

WWW Super 8 M
(770) 966-9700. **$55-$60.** 4970 Cowan Rd 30101. I-75 exit 277, just w. Ext corridors. **Pets:** Medium. $10 daily fee/pet. Service with restrictions, supervision. 🛜 🖬 🖳 ➿

ALPHARETTA

WWW Embassy Suites Hotel Alpharetta H
(678) 566-8800. **$119-$189.** 5955 North Point Pkwy 30022. SR 400 exit 9, just e to North Point Pkwy, then just n. Int corridors. **Pets:** Accepted.
🛜 ⅗M 🖬 🖳 ➿

WWW Holiday Inn Express Alpharetta H
(770) 552-0006. **Call for rates.** 2950 Mansell Rd 30022. SR 400 exit 8, 0.7 mi e. Int corridors. **Pets:** Accepted. 🛜 ⅗M 🖬 🖳 ➿

WWW Homewood Suites H
(770) 998-1622. **$62-$129.** 10775 Davis Dr 30009. SR 400 exit 8; northwest corner. Int corridors. **Pets:** Accepted. 🛜 ⅗M 🖬 🖳 ➿

WWW La Quinta Inn & Suites Atlanta Alpharetta H
(770) 754-7800. **$59-$144.** 1350 North Point Dr 30022. SR 400 exit 9, 0.5 mi e. Int corridors. **Pets:** Service with restrictions, supervision.
🛜 ⅗M 🖬 🖳 ➿

AAA WWWW Residence Inn by Marriott Atlanta Alpharetta North Point Mall H ✿
(770) 587-1151. **$59-$159.** 1325 North Point Dr 30022. SR 400 exit 9, just e to North Point Dr, then just s. Int corridors. **Pets:** Other species. $100 one-time fee/room. Service with restrictions, crate.
SAVE 🛜 ✕ ⅗M 🖬 🖳 ➿ ✕

AAA WWWW Residence Inn by Marriott Atlanta Alpharetta/Windward H
(770) 664-0664. **$69-$179.** 5465 Windward Pkwy W 30004. SR 400 exit 11, 0.4 mi w. Ext/int corridors. **Pets:** Large, other species. $100 one-time fee/room. Service with restrictions. SAVE 🛜 ✕ ⅗M 🖬 🖳 ➿

WWWW Staybridge Suites H
(770) 569-7200. **$74-$162.** 3980 North Point Pkwy 30005. SR 400 exit 10, 0.5 mi e. Int corridors. **Pets:** Accepted.
🛜 ✕ ⅗M 🖬 🖳 ➿ ✕

WWWW TownePlace Suites by Marriott Alpharetta H ✿
(770) 664-1300. **$66-$118.** 7925 Westside Pkwy 30009. SR 400 exit 9, 0.3 mi w. Int corridors. **Pets:** Other species. $75 one-time fee/room. Service with restrictions, supervision. 🛜 ✕ ⅗M 🖬 🖳 ➿

WWWW Wingate by Wyndham Alpharetta H ✿
(770) 649-0955. **$51-$119.** 1005 Kingswood Pl 30004. SR 400 exit 8, 0.7 mi w. Int corridors. **Pets:** Medium, other species. $25 one-time fee/room. Service with restrictions, crate. 🛜 ✕ ⅗M 🖬 🖳

ATLANTA

WWWW Artmore Hotel H
(404) 876-6100. **Call for rates.** 1302 W Peachtree St 30309. I-75/85 exit 250 (14th St), just e, then just n on W Peachtree St to 16th St. Int corridors. **Pets:** Accepted. 🛜 ✕ 🖬 🖳 🍴

WWWW Atlanta Perimeter Hotel & Suites H
(770) 396-6800. **Call for rates.** 111 Perimeter Center W 30346. I-285 exit 29 (Ashford-Dunwoody Rd), 0.5 mi n. Int corridors. **Pets:** Accepted.
🛜 ✕ ⅗M 🖬 🖳 🍴 ➿ ✕

AAA WWWW BEST WESTERN PLUS Inn at the Peachtrees M
(404) 577-6970. **$109-$299.** 330 W Peachtree St 30308. I-75/85 exit 248C northbound, 0.4 mi w to Peachtree St, then 0.3 mi n; exit 249C southbound, just s to Peachtree Pl, then just e. Ext/int corridors. **Pets:** Large, dogs only. $25 daily fee/pet. Service with restrictions, crate.
SAVE 🛜 ✕ ⅗M 🖬 🖳

WWWW Beverly Hills Inn BB
(404) 233-8520. **$129-$249, 3 day notice.** 65 Sheridan Dr NE 30305. Jct Piedmont and Peachtree rds, 1.1 mi s on Peachtree Rd to Sheridan Dr, then just e. Int corridors. **Pets:** Accepted. 🛜 ✕ 🖬

WWWW Courtyard by Marriott-Atlanta Vinings H
(770) 432-5555. **$80-$189.** 2857 Paces Ferry Rd 30339. I-285 exit 18, 0.6 mi e. Int corridors. **Pets:** Accepted.
🛜 ✕ ⅗M 🖬 🖳 🍴 ➿

AAA WWWW Embassy Suites Atlanta-Galleria H
(770) 984-9300. **$99-$189.** 2815 Akers Mill Rd 30339. I-75 exit 258, just w. Int corridors. **Pets:** Accepted. SAVE 🛜 ⅗M 🖬 🖳 🍴 ➿

WWWW Extended StayAmerica Atlanta-Clairmont H
(404) 679-4333. **$61-$105.** 3115 Clairmont Rd 30329. I-85 exit 91, 0.6 mi w. Int corridors. **Pets:** $25 daily fee/pet. Designated rooms, service with restrictions. 🛜 ⅗M 🖬 🖳

Extended StayAmerica Atlanta-Perimeter H
(770) 396-5600. **$52-$75.** 905 S Crestline Pkwy 30328. I-285 exit 28 westbound, 0.7 mi n; exit 26 eastbound, 0.5 mi n to Hammond Dr, 0.5 mi e, then 0.3 mi n. Int corridors. **Pets:** $25 daily fee/pet. Designated rooms, service with restrictions. 🛰 ⓜ 🖥 💻

Extended Stay Deluxe Atlanta-Lenox H
(404) 237-9100. **$68-$100.** 3967 Peachtree Rd 30319. I-85 exit 89, 2.8 mi w. Int corridors. **Pets:** $25 daily fee/pet. Designated rooms, service with restrictions. 🛰 ⓜ 🖥 💻 🏊

Extended Stay Deluxe (Atlanta/Marietta/Powers Ferry Rd) H
(770) 933-8010. **$63-$83.** 2010 Powers Ferry Rd 30339. I-75 exit 260 (Windy Hill Rd), 0.5 mi e, then just s. Int corridors. **Pets:** $25 daily fee/pet. Designated rooms, service with restrictions.
🛰 ⓜ 🖥 💻 🏊

Extended Stay Deluxe (Atlanta/Marietta/Windy Hill/Int N Pkwy) H
(770) 226-0242. **$52-$91.** 2225 Interstate North Pkwy 30339. I-75 exit 260, just e to Interstate North Pkwy, then just s. Int corridors. **Pets:** $25 daily fee/pet. Designated rooms, service with restrictions.
🛰 ⓜ 🖥 💻 🏊

Extended Stay Deluxe Atlanta-Perimeter H
(770) 379-0111. **$61-$81.** 6330 Peachtree-Dunwoody Rd NE 30328. I-285 exit 28 westbound, 0.7 mi n; exit 26 eastbound, 0.5 mi n to Hammond Dr, 0.5 mi e, then 0.3 mi n. Int corridors. **Pets:** $25 daily fee/pet. Designated rooms, service with restrictions. 🛰 ⓜ 🖥 💻 🏊

Extended Stay Deluxe Atlanta-Vinings H
(770) 436-1511. **$65-$109.** 2474 Cumberland Pkwy SE 30339. I-285 exit 18, just e. Int corridors. **Pets:** $25 daily fee/pet. Designated rooms, service with restrictions. 🛰 ⓜ 🖥 💻 🏊

Four Seasons Hotel Atlanta H ❀
(404) 881-9898. **$249-$4000.** 75 14th St NE 30309. I-75/85 exit 250 (14th St), 0.4 mi n. Int corridors. **Pets:** Service with restrictions, crate.
SAVE 🛰 ⓜ 🍴 🏊 ⊠

The Georgian Terrace Hotel H
(404) 897-1991. **$126-$349.** 659 Peachtree St 30308. I-75/85 exit 249D, 0.5 mi e to Peachtree St, then just n. Int corridors. **Pets:** Medium. $75 one-time fee/pet. Designated rooms, service with restrictions, supervision.
SAVE 🛰 ⊠ 🖥 💻 🍴 🏊

Glenn Hotel, Autograph Collection H
(404) 521-2250. **$119-$289, 3 day notice.** 110 Marietta St NW 30303. I-75/85 exit 248C northbound, 0.8 mi w, then just s; exit 249A southbound, just s to Baker St, just w, then just s. Int corridors.
Pets: Accepted. SAVE 🛰 ⊠ ⓜ 💻 🍴

Grand Hyatt Atlanta H
(404) 237-1234. **$126-$369.** 3300 Peachtree Rd NE 30305. Corner of Peachtree and Piedmont rds. Int corridors. **Pets:** Accepted.
ECO SAVE 🛰 ⓜ 🖥 💻 🍴 🏊 ⊠

Hawthorn Suites by Wyndham Atlanta Northwest H
(770) 952-9595. **$69-$139.** 1500 Parkwood Cir 30339. I-75 exit 260 (Windy Hill Rd), 0.5 mi e, then 0.3 mi s on Powers Ferry Rd. Ext corridors. **Pets:** Accepted. 🛰 🖥 💻 ⊠

Hilton Atlanta H
(404) 659-2000. **$119-$299.** 255 Courtland St NE 30303. I-75/85 exit 249A southbound; exit 248C northbound, just w to Piedmont Ave, just n to Baker St, then just w. Int corridors. **Pets:** Accepted.
ECO 🛰 ⓜ 💻 🍴 🏊 ⊠

Hilton Suites Atlanta Perimeter H
(770) 668-0808. **$89-$179.** 6120 Peachtree-Dunwoody Rd 30328. I-285 exit 28 westbound, 0.4 mi n; exit 26 eastbound, 0.5 mi n to Hammond Dr, 0.5 mi e to Peachtree-Dunwoody Rd, then just n. Int corridors.
Pets: Accepted. 🛰 ⓜ 🖥 💻 🍴 🏊

Holiday Inn Atlanta Perimeter H
(770) 457-6363. **$79-$129.** 4386 Chamblee-Dunwoody Rd 30341. I-285 exit 30 eastbound, just s; exit westbound, follow access road 1.3 mi to Chamblee-Dunwoody Rd, then just s. Int corridors. **Pets:** Other species. $75 deposit/room. Service with restrictions, supervision.
SAVE 🛰 ⊠ ⓜ 🖥 💻 🍴 🏊

Homestead Studio Suites Atlanta/Perimeter H
(770) 522-0025. **$51-$86.** 1050 Hammond Dr 30328. I-285 exit 26 eastbound, 0.5 mi n to Hammond Dr, then 0.5 mi e; exit 28 westbound, just n to Hammond Dr, then just w. Ext corridors. **Pets:** $25 daily fee/pet. Designated rooms, service with restrictions. 🛰 ⓜ 🖥 💻 🏊

Homewood Suites-Atlanta Buckhead H
(404) 365-0001. **$119-$189.** 3566 Piedmont Rd 30305. SR 400 exit 2, just s to Piedmont Rd, then 1 mi w. Int corridors. **Pets:** Accepted.
🛰 ⓜ 🖥 💻 🏊

Homewood Suites-Cumberland H
(770) 988-9449. **$99-$189.** 3200 Cobb Pkwy SW 30339. I-285 exit 19 eastbound; exit 20 westbound, 0.7 mi se on US 41 (Cobb Pkwy). Ext/int corridors. **Pets:** Accepted. 🛰 ⓜ 🖥 💻 🏊 ⊠

Hotel Indigo Atlanta Midtown H ❀
(404) 874-9200. **$99-$229.** 683 Peachtree St NE 30308. I-75/85 exit 249D, 0.5 mi e to Peachtree St, then just n. Int corridors. **Pets:** Other species. $25 one-time fee/room. Designated rooms, service with restrictions. 🛰 ⓜ 🖥 💻 🍴

InterContinental Buckhead Atlanta H
(404) 946-9000. **$159-$349.** 3315 Peachtree Rd NE 30326. Jct Piedmont and Peachtree rds NE, just e. Int corridors. **Pets:** Accepted.
SAVE 🛰 ⓜ 💻 🍴 🏊

La Quinta Inn & Suites Atlanta (Paces Ferry/Vinings) H
(770) 801-9002. **$66-$155.** 2415 Paces Ferry Rd SE 30339. I-285 exit 18, just w. Int corridors. **Pets:** Service with restrictions, supervision.
🛰 ⓜ 🖥 💻 🏊

La Quinta Inn & Suites Atlanta (Perimeter/Medical Center) H
(770) 350-6177. **$63-$151.** 6260 Peachtree-Dunwoody Rd 30328. I-285 exit 28 westbound, 0.7 mi n; exit 26 eastbound, 0.5 mi n to Hammond Dr, 0.7 mi e, then 0.5 mi n. Int corridors. **Pets:** Service with restrictions, supervision. 🛰 ⓜ 🖥 💻 🏊

La Quinta Inn Atlanta Lenox Buckhead H
(404) 321-0999. **$71-$133.** 2535 Chantilly Dr NE 30324. I-85 exit 88 southbound; exit 86 northbound, 2 mi on Buford Hwy to Lenox Rd, then just e under highway. Int corridors. **Pets:** Service with restrictions, supervision. 🛰 🖥 💻

Loews Hotel Atlanta H
(404) 745-5000. **$189-$349.** 1075 Peachtree St NE 30309. I-75/85 exit 251 (10th St), 0.5 mi e to Peachtree St NE, then just n. Int corridors.
Pets: Accepted. 🛰 ⊠ ⓜ 🖥 💻 🍴 ⊠

Mandarin Oriental, Atlanta H
(404) 995-7500. **$295-$495.** 3376 Peachtree Rd NE 30326. Jct Peachtree and Lenox rds, just s. Int corridors. **Pets:** Accepted.
🛰 ⊠ ⓜ 💻 🍴 🏊 ⊠ 🅦

Melia Hotel Atlanta H
(404) 877-9000. **$89-$189.** 590 W Peachtree St NW 30308. I-75/85 exit 249D southbound; exit 249C northbound, just e. Int corridors.
Pets: Medium, dogs only. $100 one-time fee/room. Service with restrictions, supervision. 🛰 ⊠ ⓜ 🖥 💻 🍴

Microtel Inn & Suites by Wyndham Atlanta/Buckhead Area H
(404) 325-4446. **$65-$80.** 1840 Corporate Blvd 30329. I-85 exit 89, just w to Buford Hwy, 0.3 mi n to Corporate Blvd, then just e. Int corridors.
Pets: Medium. $25 one-time fee/room. Service with restrictions, supervision. 🛰 ⓜ 🖥 💻

Omni Hotel at CNN Center H
(404) 659-0000. **$159-$359.** 100 CNN Center 30303. I-75/85 exit 248C northbound, 0.8 mi w; exit 249C southbound to International Blvd, then 0.5 mi w. Int corridors. **Pets:** Small. $50 one-time fee/room. Service with restrictions, supervision. [SAVE] [icons]

Red Roof Inn Atlanta-Buckhead M
(404) 321-1653. **$49-$84.** 1960 N Druid Hills Rd 30329. I-85 exit 89, just w. Ext corridors. **Pets:** Large, other species. Service with restrictions, supervision. [SAVE] [icons]

Renaissance Atlanta Midtown H
(678) 412-2400. **$129-$399.** 866 W Peachtree St NW 30308. I-75/85 exit 249D, just e to W Peachtree St NW, then 0.6 mi n. Int corridors.
Pets: Accepted. [ECO] [SAVE] [icons]

Residence Inn by Marriott-Atlanta/Buckhead H
(404) 239-0677. **$109-$219.** 2960 Piedmont Rd NE 30305. Jct Piedmont and Pharr rds, just s. Ext corridors. **Pets:** Accepted.

Residence Inn by Marriott Atlanta Buckhead/ Lenox Park H
(404) 467-1660. **$89-$219.** 2220 Lake Blvd 30319. I-85 exit 89, 1.6 mi w on N Druid Hills (which becomes E Roxboro Rd), then just n on Lenox Park Blvd. Int corridors. **Pets:** Large. $100 one-time fee/room. Service with restrictions. [SAVE] [icons]

Residence Inn by Marriott Atlanta - Downtown H
(404) 522-0950. **$109-$179.** 134 Peachtree St NW 30303. I-75/85 exit 248C northbound, 0.4 mi w, then just s; exit 249A southbound to International Blvd, just w, then just s. Int corridors. **Pets:** Medium. $100 one-time fee/room. Service with restrictions. [icons]

Residence Inn by Marriott Atlanta Midtown at 17th Street H
(404) 745-1000. **$99-$249.** 1365 Peachtree St 30309. I-75/85 exit 250 (14th St), 0.5 mi e to Peachtree St, then 0.3 mi n. Int corridors.
Pets: Accepted. [icons]

Residence Inn by Marriott Atlanta - Midtown / Historic H
(404) 872-8885. **$119-$169.** 1041 W Peachtree St 30309. I-75/85 exit 250 (10th St), just e to W Peachtree St, then just n; corner of 11th St. Int corridors. **Pets:** $100 one-time fee/room. Service with restrictions.
[icons]

Residence Inn by Marriott Atlanta - Perimeter Center H
(404) 252-5066. **$89-$159.** 6096 Barfield Rd 30328. I-285 exit 26 eastbound, 0.5 mi n on Glenridge to Hammond Dr, then 0.3 mi e to Barfield Rd; exit 28 westbound (Peachtree-Dunwoody Rd), 0.5 mi n to Hammond Dr, then just w. Ext corridors. **Pets:** Accepted.
[SAVE] [icons]

Residence Inn by Marriott Atlanta Perimeter/Dunwoody H
(770) 455-4446. **$89-$149.** 1901 Savoy Dr 30341. I-285 exit 30, just e. Ext corridors. **Pets:** Accepted. [SAVE] [icons]

The Ritz-Carlton, Buckhead H
(404) 237-2700. **$229-$499.** 3434 Peachtree Rd NE 30326. I-85 exit 86, 1.8 mi n on Lenox Rd. Int corridors. **Pets:** Accepted.
[SAVE] [icons]

St. Regis Atlanta Hotel & Residences H 🐾
(404) 563-7900. **$350-$650.** 88 W Paces Ferry Rd 30305. Jct Peachtree and W Paces Ferry rds, just w. Int corridors. **Pets:** Small. $100 one-time fee/room, $25 daily fee/pet. Service with restrictions, supervision.
[SAVE] [icons]

Sheraton Atlanta Hotel H
(404) 659-6500. **$119-$399, 3 day notice.** 165 Courtland St NE 30303. I-75/85 exit 249A southbound; exit 248C northbound, just w. Int corridors. **Pets:** Medium, dogs only. $65 deposit/room, $35 one-time fee/room. Service with restrictions, supervision. [SAVE] [icons]

Sheraton Suites Galleria H 🐾
(770) 955-3900. **$89-$279.** 2844 Cobb Pkwy SE 30339. I-285 exit 20 westbound; exit 19 eastbound, just s on US 41 (Cobb Pkwy). Int corridors. **Pets:** Medium. $25 one-time fee/room. Designated rooms, service with restrictions. [SAVE] [icons]

Sonesta ES Suites Atlanta H
(404) 250-0110. **Call for rates.** 760 Mt Vernon Hwy NE 30328. I-285 exit 25, 0.8 mi n on Roswell Rd, then 1 mi e. Ext/int corridors.
Pets: Accepted. [SAVE] [icons]

Staybridge Suites-Atlanta/Buckhead H
(404) 842-0800. **$99-$250.** 540 Pharr Rd 30305. Jct Pharr and Piedmont rds, just w. Int corridors. **Pets:** Medium, other species. $75 one-time fee/room. Service with restrictions, supervision. [icons]

Staybridge Suites Atlanta Perimeter H
(678) 320-0111. **$129-$159.** 4601 Ridgeview Rd 30338. I-285 exit 29 (Ashford-Dunwoody Rd), 0.5 mi n, 0.5 mi w on Perimeter Center W to Crowne Pointe Dr, then just n. Int corridors. **Pets:** Accepted.
[icons]

Stonehurst Place Bed & Breakfast BB 🐾
(404) 881-0722. **$159-$449, 3 day notice.** 923 Piedmont Ave NE 30309. I-75 exit 251 (10th St), 0.6 mi e to Juniper St, just s to 8th St, just e to Piedmont Ave, then just n. Int corridors. **Pets:** Medium, dogs only. $50 one-time fee/room. Designated rooms, service with restrictions, crate.
[icons]

TownePlace Suites by Marriott Atlanta Buckhead H
(404) 949-4820. **$109-$199.** 820 Sidney Marcus Blvd 30324. I-85 exit 86 northbound, 1.9 mi n to Sidney Marcus Blvd, then just w; exit 88 southbound, just w to Sidney Marcus Blvd, then just w. Int corridors.
Pets: Small. $100 one-time fee/room. [icons]

TWELVE Centennial Park H
(404) 418-1212. **$149-$409.** 400 W Peachtree St NW 30308. I-75/85 exit 248C, 0.4 mi s to W Peachtree Pl, just e to W Peachtree St, then just n. Int corridors. **Pets:** Small. Service with restrictions, supervision.
[icons]

University Inn at Emory M 🐾
(404) 634-7327. **$80-$175.** 1767 N Decatur Rd 30307. Adjacent to Emory University. Ext corridors. **Pets:** Other species. $25 daily fee/room. Service with restrictions. [SAVE] [icons]

W Atlanta Buckhead H
(678) 500-3100. **$169-$539.** 3377 Peachtree Rd NE 30326. Jct Piedmont and Peachtree rds, 0.3 mi e. Int corridors. **Pets:** Accepted.
[SAVE] [icons]

W Atlanta Downtown H 🐾
(404) 582-5800. **$159-$459.** 45 Ivan Allen Jr Blvd 30308. I-75/85 exit 249C, just s. Int corridors. **Pets:** Small, other species. $100 one-time fee/room, $25 daily fee/pet. Service with restrictions.
[SAVE] [icons]

W Atlanta Midtown H
(404) 892-6000. **$129-$539.** 188 14th St NE 30361. I-75/85 exit 250 (14th St), 0.5 mi e. Int corridors. **Pets:** Accepted.
[SAVE] [icons]

The Westin Atlanta North H
(770) 395-3900. **$119-$369.** 7 Concourse Pkwy 30328. I-285 exit 28 westbound; exit 26 eastbound, 0.5 mi n to Hammond Dr, then 0.4 mi e. Int corridors. **Pets:** Accepted. [SAVE] [icons]

AAA ♦♦♦ ♦♦♦ The Westin Buckhead Atlanta H
(404) 365-0065. **$129-$479.** 3391 Peachtree Rd NE 30326. Adjacent to Lenox Square Mall. Int corridors. **Pets:** Accepted.
SAVE 📶 ✕ &M 💻 🍴 ➤ ✕

AAA ♦♦♦ ♦♦♦ The Westin Peachtree Plaza H
(404) 659-1400. **$120-$400.** 210 Peachtree St 30303. I-75/85 exit 248C northbound, 0.4 mi w; exit 249C southbound, 0.5 mi s. Int corridors.
Pets: Accepted. ECO SAVE 📶 ✕ 💻 🍴 ➤

♦♦♦ ♦♦♦ Wyndham Atlanta Perimeter H
(770) 955-1700. **$65-$159.** 6345 Powers Ferry Rd NW 30339. I-285 exit 22, just s. Int corridors. **Pets:** Medium, dogs only. $75 deposit/pet. Service with restrictions, supervision. 📶 ✕ &M 🔋 💻 🍴 ➤

AUSTELL
♦♦ ♦♦ Super 8 Austell/Six Flags M
(770) 944-2110. **$60-$70.** 7377 Six Flags Dr 30168. I-20 exit 46 eastbound; exit 46B westbound, just n. Ext/int corridors. **Pets:** Other species. $10 daily fee/pet. Service with restrictions, supervision.
📶 🔋 💻 ➤

COLLEGE PARK
♦♦♦ ♦♦♦ Embassy Suites Hotel at Atlanta Airport H
(404) 767-1988. **$89-$169.** 4700 Southport Rd 30337. I-85 exit 71, 0.3 mi w on Riverdale Rd. Int corridors. **Pets:** Accepted.
📶 &M 🔋 💻 🍴 ➤ ✕

♦♦♦ Holiday Inn Express-Atlanta Airport H
(404) 761-6500. **$79-$139.** 4601 Best Rd 30337. I-85 exit 71; northwest corner. Int corridors. **Pets:** Accepted. 📶 ✕ &M 🔋 💻 ➤

♦♦♦ ♦♦♦ La Quinta Inn & Suites Atlanta Airport H
(770) 996-0000. **$71-$166.** 4820 Massachusetts Blvd 30337. I-85 exit 71, just e to Airport Rd, then just s. Int corridors. **Pets:** Service with restrictions, supervision. 📶 🔋 💻 ➤

♦♦ ♦♦ Microtel Inn by Wyndham Atlanta Airport H
(770) 994-3003. **$47-$69.** 4839 Massachusetts Blvd 30337. I-85 exit 71, just e to Airport Rd, then just s; I-285 exit 60 (Riverdale Rd N), 1 mi to Sullivan Rd, then just s. Int corridors. **Pets:** Accepted. 📶 &M 🔋

AAA ♦♦♦ ♦♦♦ Sheraton Gateway Hotel, Atlanta Airport H
(770) 997-1100. **$79-$279.** 1900 Sullivan Rd 30337. I-85 exit 71, just e to Airport Rd, then just s. Int corridors. **Pets:** Accepted.
SAVE 📶 ✕ &M 🔋 💻 🍴 ➤

AAA ♦♦♦ ♦♦♦ The Westin Hotel-Atlanta Airport H 🐾
(404) 762-7676. **$99-$369.** 4736 Best Rd 30337. I-85 exit 71, just w, se on access road to Best Rd, then just s. Int corridors. **Pets:** Medium, dogs only. $100 one-time fee/room. Service with restrictions, crate.
SAVE 📶 ✕ &M 🔋 💻 🍴 ➤ ✕

DECATUR
♦♦ ♦♦ America's Best Inn & Suites M
(404) 286-2500. **$60.** 4095 Covington Hwy 30032. I-285 exit 43, just w. Ext corridors. **Pets:** Accepted. 📶 &M 🔋 ➤

♦♦ ♦♦ Courtyard by Marriott Atlanta Decatur Downtown/Emory H
(404) 371-0204. **$99-$219.** 130 Clairemont Ave 30030. Downtown. Int corridors. **Pets:** Accepted. 📶 ✕ &M 🔋 💻 🍴 ➤

DORAVILLE
AAA ♦♦♦ ♦♦♦ Comfort Inn & Conference Center Northeast H
(770) 455-3700. **$65-$83.** 2001 Clearview Ave 30340. I-285 exit 32; southeast corner. Int corridors. **Pets:** Other species. $25 one-time fee/room. Service with restrictions, crate. SAVE 📶 &M 🔋 💻 ➤

DOUGLASVILLE
♦♦ ♦♦ Days Inn M
(770) 949-1499. **$55-$65.** 5489 Westmoreland Plaza 30134. I-20 exit 37, just n. Ext corridors. **Pets:** Medium, other species. $20 deposit/pet, $20 daily fee/pet. Service with restrictions. 📶 🔋 💻 ➤

♦♦♦ ♦♦♦ Econo Lodge Inn & Suites H
(770) 489-4863. **$60-$75.** 8304 Cherokee Blvd 30134. I-20 exit 37, just n to Cherokee Blvd, then just e. Int corridors. **Pets:** Medium. $15 daily fee/pet. Designated rooms, service with restrictions, supervision.
📶 &M 🔋 💻 ➤

♦♦♦ ♦♦♦ La Quinta Inn & Suites Atlanta Douglasville H
(770) 577-3838. **$71-$155.** 1000 Linnenkohl Dr 30134. I-20 exit 34, just n. Int corridors. **Pets:** Service with restrictions, supervision.
📶 &M 🔋 💻 ➤

DULUTH
♦♦♦ Candlewood Suites-Atlanta H
(678) 380-0414. **$65-$95.** 3665 Shackleford Rd 30096. I-85 exit 104, just e, then just s. Int corridors. **Pets:** Accepted. 📶 &M 🔋 💻

♦♦♦ ♦♦♦ Extended Stay Deluxe Atlanta-Gwinnett Place H
(770) 623-6800. **$60-$84.** 3390 Venture Pkwy NW 30096. I-85 exit 104, just w to Venture Pkwy, then just n. Int corridors. **Pets:** $25 daily fee/pet. Designated rooms, service with restrictions. 📶 &M 🔋 💻 ➤

♦♦♦ ♦♦♦ Holiday Inn Express H
(770) 935-7171. **$74-$94.** 3670 Shackleford Rd 30096. I-85 exit 104, just e to Shackleford Rd, then just s. Int corridors. **Pets:** Other species. $50 one-time fee/pet. Designated rooms, service with restrictions, supervision.
📶 &M 🔋 💻 ➤

♦♦♦ ♦♦♦ Holiday Inn-Gwinnett Center H
(770) 476-2022. **$79-$159.** 6310 Sugarloaf Pkwy 30097. I-85 exit 108, just w. Int corridors. **Pets:** Accepted. 📶 &M 🔋 💻 🍴 ➤

AAA ♦♦♦ ♦♦♦ La Quinta Inn Atlanta Duluth H
(678) 957-0500. **$71-$161.** 2370 Stephen Center Dr 30096. I-85 exit 107 southbound, just w; exit 105 northbound, to Boggs Rd, 0.5 mi w to Satellite Blvd, then 0.5 mi n. Int corridors. **Pets:** Service with restrictions, supervision. SAVE 📶 ✕ &M 🔋 💻 ➤

♦♦ ♦♦ Quality Inn - Gwinnett Mall M
(770) 623-9300. **$50-$120.** 3500 Venture Pkwy 30096. I-85 exit 104, just w to Venture Pkwy, then just n. Ext/int corridors. **Pets:** Accepted.
📶 &M 🔋 💻 ➤

♦♦♦ ♦♦♦ Residence Inn by Marriott Atlanta Gwinnett Place H
(770) 921-2202. **$89-$169.** 1760 Pineland Rd 30096. I-85 exit 104, just e to Shackleford Rd, just s to Pineland Rd, then just e. Int corridors. **Pets:** Small. $100 one-time fee/pet. Service with restrictions, supervision.
📶 ✕ &M 🔋 💻 ➤ ✕

EAST POINT
♦♦ ♦♦ Comfort Inn & Suites Atlanta Airport Camp Creek H
(404) 762-5566. **$63-$76.** 3601 N Desert Dr 30344. I-285 exit 2, just e. Int corridors. **Pets:** Small. $50 one-time fee/pet. Designated rooms, service with restrictions, supervision. 📶 &M 🔋 💻 ➤

♦♦♦ ♦♦♦ Crowne Plaza Atlanta Airport H
(404) 768-6660. **$89-$189.** 1325 Virginia Ave 30344. I-85 exit 73 southbound; exit 73B northbound, just w. Int corridors. **Pets:** Accepted.
📶 ✕ &M 🔋 💻 🍴 ➤

♦♦♦ ♦♦♦ Drury Inn & Suites-Atlanta Airport H
(404) 761-4900. **$99-$179.** 1270 Virginia Ave 30344. I-85 exit 73 southbound; exit 73A northbound, just e. Int corridors. **Pets:** Service with restrictions, supervision. 📶 &M 🔋 💻 ➤

▼▼ Motel 6 Atlanta Airport North #4589 **H**
(404) 209-1800. **$55-$99.** 1200 Virginia Ave 30344. I-85 exit 73 southbound; exit 73A northbound, just e. Int corridors. **Pets:** Other species.
Service with restrictions, supervision.

FAIRBURN
▼▼▼ Country Inn & Suites By Carlson **H**
(678) 782-4900. **$89-$109.** 7815 Senoia Rd 30213. I-85 exit 61, just e.
Int corridors. **Pets:** Small. $30 daily fee/pet. Designated rooms, service
with restrictions, supervision.

▼▼▼ Sleep Inn & Suites **H**
(678) 782-4700. **$72-$109.** 1005 Oakley Industrial Blvd 30213. I-85 exit
61, just e. Int corridors. **Pets:** Accepted.

FOREST PARK
▼▼ Econo Lodge **M**
(404) 363-6429. **Call for rates.** 5060 Frontage Rd 30297. I-75 exit 237,
just e to Frontage Rd, then just s. Ext corridors. **Pets:** Accepted.

▼▼ Super 8 **M**
(404) 363-8811. **$45-$100.** 410 Old Dixie Way 30297. I-75 exit 235, just
e. Ext corridors. **Pets:** Accepted.

HAPEVILLE
AAA ▼▼▼ Hilton Atlanta Airport **H**
(404) 767-9000. **$89-$199.** 1031 Virginia Ave 30354. I-85 exit 73 southbound; exit 73A northbound, just e. Int corridors. **Pets:** Accepted.

AAA ▼▼▼ Residence Inn by Marriott Atlanta Airport
North/Virginia Avenue **H**
(404) 761-0511. **$74-$179.** 3401 International Blvd 30354. I-85 exit 73
southbound; exit 73A northbound, 0.5 mi e to International Blvd, then just
n. Ext/int corridors. **Pets:** Accepted.

KENNESAW
AAA ▼▼▼ BEST WESTERN Kennesaw Inn **M** ❀
(770) 424-7666. **$72.** 3375 Busbee Dr 30144. I-75 exit 271, just e. Ext
corridors. **Pets:** Other species. $10 daily fee/pet. Service with restrictions,
crate.

▼▼ Days Inn **M**
(770) 419-1576. **$50-$85.** 760 Cobb Place Blvd 30144. I-75 exit 269, just
w. Ext corridors. **Pets:** Medium. $15 daily fee/pet. Service with restrictions,
crate.

▼▼ Embassy Suites Atlanta-Kennesaw Town
Center **H**
(770) 420-2505. **$109-$169.** 620 Chastain Rd 30144. I-75 exit 271, 0.4
mi w. Int corridors. **Pets:** Small. $75 one-time fee/room. Designated
rooms, service with restrictions, supervision.

▼▼ Extended StayAmerica Atlanta Kennesaw **H**
(770) 422-1403. **$52-$95.** 3000 George Busbee Pkwy 30144. I-75 exit
269, just e to George Busbee Pkwy, then 0.8 mi n. Int corridors.
Pets: $25 daily fee/pet. Designated rooms, service with restrictions.

▼▼ Green Roof Inn & Suites **M**
(770) 529-3370. **$45-$55.** 3027 Cobb Pkwy NW 30152. I-75 exit 271, 2.5
mi w, then 2.2 mi n on US 41. Ext corridors. **Pets:** Accepted.

▼▼▼ La Quinta Inn Kennesaw **H**
(770) 426-0045. **$84-$133.** 2625 George Busbee Pkwy 30144. I-75 exit
269, just e to George Busbee Pkwy, then just n. Int corridors. **Pets:** Service with restrictions, supervision.

▼▼ Magnuson Hotel Kennesaw **M**
(770) 590-0519. **$49-$89.** 1460 George Busbee Pkwy 30144. I-75 exit
273, just e. Ext corridors. **Pets:** Medium, other species. $15 daily fee/pet.
Designated rooms, service with restrictions, supervision.

▼▼ Quality Inn **M**
(770) 419-1530. **$55-$90.** 750 Cobb Place Blvd 30144. I-75 exit 269, just
w. Ext corridors. **Pets:** Medium. $15 daily fee/pet. Service with restrictions,
crate.

AAA ▼▼ Red Roof Inn-Town Center Mall **M**
(770) 429-0323. **$44-$69.** 520 Roberts Ct NW 30144. I-75 exit 269, just
e. Ext corridors. **Pets:** Large, other species. Service with restrictions,
supervision.

AAA ▼▼▼ Residence Inn by Marriott Atlanta Kennesaw/
Town Center **H** ❀
(770) 218-1018. **$99-$199.** 3443 Busbee Dr 30144. I-75 exit 271, just e.
Int corridors. **Pets:** Small. $100 one-time fee/room. Designated rooms,
service with restrictions, supervision.

▼▼ StudioPLUS Atlanta-Kennesaw **H**
(770) 425-6101. **$45-$87.** 3316 Busbee Dr 30144. I-75 exit 271, just e to
Busbee Dr, then just s. Int corridors. **Pets:** $25 daily fee/pet. Designated
rooms, service with restrictions.

LAWRENCEVILLE
AAA ▼▼ Days Inn **M**
(770) 995-7782. **$58-$63.** 731 Duluth Hwy 30046. Jct SR 316, just e on
SR 120. Ext corridors. **Pets:** Medium. $20 deposit/pet, $20 one-time fee/
pet. Service with restrictions, crate.

▼▼ Extended StayAmerica Atlanta-Lawrenceville **H**
(770) 962-5660. **$50-$75.** 474 W Pike St 30045. SR 316 exit SR 120,
0.8 mi s. Ext corridors. **Pets:** $25 daily fee/pet. Designated rooms, service
with restrictions.

▼▼ Magnuson Hotel Lawrenceville **H**
(770) 513-0028. **$50-$65.** 571 Buford Dr 30045. Jct SR 316 and 20/124,
0.5 mi s. Int corridors. **Pets:** Accepted.

LITHONIA
AAA ▼▼▼ Red Roof Inn **H**
(770) 322-1400. **$69-$90.** 5400 Fairington Rd 30038. I-20 exit 71, just s
to Fairington Rd, then just ne. Int corridors. **Pets:** Large, other species.
Service with restrictions, supervision.

MARIETTA
▼▼▼ Clarion Hotel Atlanta-Marietta **H**
(770) 428-4400. **$65-$115.** 1775 Parkway Pl NW 30067. I-75 exit 263,
just w. Int corridors. **Pets:** Other species. $25 daily fee/pet. Designated
rooms, service with restrictions, crate.

▼▼▼ Drury Inn & Suites-Atlanta Northwest **H**
(770) 612-0900. **$94-$159.** 1170 Powers Ferry Pl 30067. I-75 exit 261,
just e. Int corridors. **Pets:** Service with restrictions, supervision.

▼▼ Extended StayAmerica Atlanta-Marietta Windy
Hill **H**
(770) 690-9477. **$45-$65.** 1967 Leland Dr 30067. I-75 exit 260, just e to
Leland Dr, then just n. Int corridors. **Pets:** $25 daily fee/pet. Designated
rooms, service with restrictions.

AAA ▼▼▼ Hilton Atlanta/Marietta Hotel & Conference
Center **H** ❀
(770) 427-2500. **$89-$179.** 500 Powder Springs St 30064. I-75 exit 263,
3.5 mi w to Powder Springs St, then just w. Int corridors. **Pets:** Large,
other species. $75 one-time fee/room. Service with restrictions.

▼▼ Homestead Studio Suites Hotel-Atlanta-Marietta-Powers Ferry Rd H

(770) 303-0043. **$45-$86.** 2239 Powers Ferry Rd 30067. I-285 exit 22, just n. Int corridors. **Pets:** $25 daily fee/pet. Designated rooms, service with restrictions. 📶 &M 🛏️ 💻

▼▼ Hometown Inn Atlanta-Marietta-Canton Rd M

(770) 499-9550. **Call for rates.** 1051 Canton Rd 30066. I-75 exit 267A northbound, 1.8 mi w. Ext corridors. **Pets:** Accepted. 📶 🛏️ 💻

AAA ▼▼▼ Hyatt Regency Suites Atlanta NW H ❀

(770) 956-1234. **$72-$243, 3 day notice.** 2999 Windy Hill Rd 30067. I-75 exit 260, 0.5 mi e at Powers Ferry Rd. Int corridors. **Pets:** Small, dogs only. $50 one-time fee/pet. Designated rooms, service with restrictions, supervision. SAVE 📶 &M 🛏️ 💻 🍴 🏊

▼▼ La Quinta Inn M

(770) 951-0026. **$59-$111.** 2170 Delk Rd 30067. I-75 exit 261, 0.3 mi w. Ext/int corridors. **Pets:** Service with restrictions, supervision. 📶 🛏️ 💻 🏊

MORROW

AAA ▼▼ BEST WESTERN Southlake Inn M

(770) 961-6300. **$59-$99.** 6437 Jonesboro Rd 30260. I-75 exit 233, just e. Ext corridors. **Pets:** Medium, other species. $10 daily fee/pet. Designated rooms, service with restrictions, crate. SAVE 📶 🛏️ 💻 🏊

▼▼▼ Drury Inn & Suites-Atlanta South H

(770) 960-0500. **$104-$164.** 6520 S Lee St 30260. I-75 exit 233, just e. Int corridors. **Pets:** Service with restrictions, supervision. 📶 &M 💻 🏊

▼▼ Extended StayAmerica-Atlanta-Morrow H

(770) 472-0727. **$55-$85.** 2265 Mt. Zion Pkwy 30260. I-75 exit 231, just w, then just s. Int corridors. **Pets:** $25 daily fee/pet. Designated rooms, service with restrictions. 📶 🛏️ 💻

▼▼ Quality Inn & Suites M

(770) 960-1957. **$54-$99.** 6597 Jonesboro Rd 30260. I-75 exit 233, just w. Ext corridors. **Pets:** Other species. $10 deposit/pet. Designated rooms, service with restrictions, crate. 📶 &M 🛏️ 💻 🏊

AAA ▼▼▼ Red Roof Inn-South M

(770) 968-1483. **$45-$69.** 1348 Southlake Plaza Dr 30260. I-75 exit 233, just e to Southlake Plaza Dr, then just n. Ext corridors. **Pets:** Large, other species. Service with restrictions, supervision. SAVE 📶 &M 🛏️

AAA ▼▼ Sleep Inn H

(770) 472-9800. **$54-$99.** 2185 Mt. Zion Pkwy 30260. I-75 exit 231, just w to Mt. Zion Pkwy, then just s. Int corridors. **Pets:** Medium. $10 daily fee/pet. Designated rooms, service with restrictions, supervision. SAVE 📶 &M 🛏️ 💻 🏊

NORCROSS

▼▼▼▼ Comfort Inn & Suites H

(770) 263-8883. **$70-$100.** 5200 Peachtree Industrial Blvd 30071. I-285 exit 31B, 5.5 mi n; I-85 exit 99, 4 mi w to Peachtree Industrial Blvd, then 1.5 mi n. Int corridors. **Pets:** Accepted. 📶 &M 🛏️ 💻 🏊

▼▼ Crossland Economy Studios-Jimmy Carter Blvd M

(770) 446-9245. **$40-$75.** 6295 Jimmy Carter Blvd 30071. I-85 exit 99, 1.5 mi w. Ext corridors. **Pets:** $25 daily fee/pet. Designated rooms, service with restrictions. 📶 &M 🛏️ 💻

▼▼ Days Inn & Suites H

(770) 416-9021. **$43-$90.** 5385 Peachtree Industrial Blvd 30092. I-285 exit 31B, 5.5 mi n; I-85 exit 99, 4 mi w to Peachtree Industrial Blvd, then 1.5 mi n. Int corridors. **Pets:** Accepted. 📶 &M 🛏️ 💻 🏊

▼▼▼▼ Drury Inn & Suites-Atlanta Northeast H

(770) 729-0060. **$79-$159.** 5655 Jimmy Carter Blvd 30071. I-85 exit 99, just w. Int corridors. **Pets:** Service with restrictions, supervision. 📶 &M 🛏️ 💻 🏊

▼▼▼▼ Hilton Atlanta Northeast H ❀

(770) 447-4747. **$79-$149.** 5993 Peachtree Industrial Blvd 30092. I-285 exit 31B, 4.5 mi ne. Int corridors. **Pets:** Other species. $25 one-time fee/ pet. Service with restrictions, crate. 📶 &M 🛏️ 💻 🍴 🏊

▼▼▼ Homestead Studio Suites Hotel-Atlanta/Peachtree Corners M

(770) 449-9966. **$49-$69.** 7049 Jimmy Carter Blvd 30092. I-85 exit 99, 4 mi n; I-285 exit 31B, 4 mi n. Ext corridors. **Pets:** $25 daily fee/pet. Designated rooms, service with restrictions. 📶 &M 💻

▼▼▼▼ Homewood Suites by Hilton H

(770) 448-4663. **$109-$139.** 450 Technology Pkwy 30092. I-85 exit 99, 4 mi w to Peachtree Industrial Blvd, 0.4 mi n, w on Holcomb Bridge Rd, then 2 blks n on Peachtree Pkwy; I-285 exit 31B, 5 mi n on SR 141. Ext/int corridors. **Pets:** Accepted. 📶 &M 🛏️ 💻 🏊 ❌

▼▼▼▼ La Quinta Inn Norcross H

(770) 368-9400. **$59-$133.** 5945 Oakbrook Pkwy 30093. I-85 exit 99, 0.5 mi e to Live Oak Pkwy, then 0.8 mi w. Int corridors. **Pets:** Service with restrictions, supervision. 📶 🛏️ 💻 🏊

▼▼▼▼ TownePlace Suites by Marriott Atlanta Norcross/ Peachtree Corners H

(770) 447-8446. **$60-$94.** 6640 Bay Cir 30071. I-285 exit 31B, 3 mi n on Peachtree Industrial Blvd to Jones Mill Rd. Int corridors. **Pets:** Medium, other species. $75 one-time fee/room. Service with restrictions, crate. ECO 📶 ❌ &M 🛏️ 💻 🏊

SMYRNA

▼▼▼ Baymont Inn & Suites H

(404) 794-1600. **$71-$79.** 5130 S Cobb Dr 30082. I-285 exit 15, 0.3 mi w. Int corridors. **Pets:** Accepted. 📶 &M 🛏️ 💻 🏊 ❌

▼▼▼ Cobb Galleria Inn H

(770) 435-4990. **$69-$169.** 2855 Spring Hill Pkwy 30080. I-285 exit 20 westbound; exit 19 eastbound, just n on US 41 (Cobb Pkwy), then just w on Spring Rd. Int corridors. **Pets:** Medium, dogs only. 📶 &M 🛏️ 💻 🏊

▼▼▼ Homestead Studio Suites Hotel-Atlanta/Cumberland Mall M

(770) 432-4000. **$48-$89.** 3103 Sports Ave 30080. I-285 exit 20 westbound; exit 19 eastbound, just n to Spring Rd, then 0.3 mi w. Ext corridors. **Pets:** $25 daily fee/pet. Designated rooms, service with restrictions. 📶 &M 🛏️ 💻

AAA ▼▼▼ Red Roof Inn-North M

(770) 952-6966. **$36-$69.** 2200 Corporate Plaza 30080. I-75 exit 260, just w to Corporate Plaza, then just s. Ext corridors. **Pets:** Large, other species. Service with restrictions, supervision. SAVE 📶 &M 🛏️

AAA ▼▼▼▼ Residence Inn by Marriott-Atlanta Cumberland H

(770) 433-8877. **$75-$199.** 2771 Cumberland Blvd 30080. I-285 exit 20 westbound; exit 19 eastbound, just n to Spring Rd, 0.3 mi w to Cumberland Blvd, then just n. Ext corridors. **Pets:** Accepted. SAVE 📶 ❌ &M 🛏️ 💻 🏊 ❌

SNELLVILLE

▼▼▼ Crestwood Suites H

(770) 982-5250. **$55-$72.** 1784 Presidential Cir 30078. Jct Ronald Reagan Pkwy and SR 124, just w. Int corridors. **Pets:** Small. $15 daily fee/ pet. Designated rooms, service with restrictions, supervision. 📶 🛏️ 💻

AAA ▼▼▼ La Quinta Inn & Suites Snellville - Stone Mountain H

(770) 736-4723. **$93-$162.** 2971 Main St W 30078. Jct US 78 and SR 124, 0.9 mi w. Int corridors. **Pets:** Service with restrictions, supervision. SAVE 📶 ❌ &M 🛏️ 💻 🏊

STONE MOUNTAIN

△△△ ▼▼ **BEST WESTERN Stone Mountain** Ⓜ
(770) 465-1022. **$80-$130.** 1595 E Park Place Blvd 30087. US 78 exit 9, just n. Ext corridors. **Pets:** Small, dogs only. $25 daily fee/pet. Designated rooms, service with restrictions, supervision. ⓢ ⊚ 🔓 🖥 🏊

SUWANEE

△△△ ▼▼ **Comfort Inn** Ⓜ
(770) 945-1608. **$80-$110.** 2945 Lawrenceville Suwanee Rd 30024. I-85 exit 111, just e. Ext corridors. **Pets:** Other species. $25 one-time fee/pet. Crate. ⓢ ⊚ 🔓 🖥 🏊

TUCKER

△△△ ▼▼▼▼ **DoubleTree by Hilton Hotel Atlanta - Northlake** Ⓗ
(770) 938-1026. **$79-$119.** 4156 Lavista Rd 30084. I-285 exit 37, just w. Int corridors. **Pets:** Accepted. ⓢ ⊚ 🔓 🖥 🍴 🏊

△△△ ▼▼ **Econo Lodge** Ⓜ
(770) 939-8440. **$50-$60.** 1820 Mountain Industrial Blvd 30084. US 78 exit 4, just n. Int corridors. **Pets:** Medium. $10 daily fee/pet. Designated rooms, service with restrictions, supervision. ⓢ ⊚ 🔓 🖥

△△△ ▼▼ **Masters Inn Tucker** Ⓜ
(770) 938-3552. **$42-$75.** 1435 Montreal Rd 30084. I-285 exit 38, just w. Ext corridors. **Pets:** Small. $10 daily fee/pet. Service with restrictions, crate. ⓢ ⊚ 🔓 🏊

△△△ ▼▼ **Quality Inn Atlanta/Northlake** Ⓜ
(770) 491-7444. **$67-$80.** 2155 Ranchwood Dr 30345. I-285 exit 37, 0.4 mi w, then just n. Ext/int corridors. **Pets:** Small. $15 daily fee/pet. Designated rooms, service with restrictions, crate.
ⓢ ⊚ 🔓 🖥 🏊

▼▼ ▼▼ TownePlace Suites by Marriott Atlanta Northlake Ⓗ
(770) 938-0408. **$69-$139.** 3300 Northlake Pkwy 30345. I-285 exit 36 southbound, just w; exit 37 northbound, just w to Parklake Dr, 0.5 mi n, then just w. Int corridors. **Pets:** Accepted.
🌱 ⊚ ✕ 🔓 🖥 🏊

UNION CITY

▼▼ ▼▼ Magnuson Hotel Atlanta South Ⓜ
(770) 306-6067. **$50-$125.** 6840 Shannon Pkwy S 30291. I-85 exit 64, 0.3 mi w to Shannon Pkwy, then just s. Ext corridors. **Pets:** Medium, dogs only. $10 daily fee/pet. Service with restrictions, crate. ⊚ 🔓 🖥 🏊

AUGUSTA

△△△ ▼▼▼▼ **Augusta Marriott At The Convention Center** Ⓗ
(706) 722-8900. **$151-$179.** 2 10th St 30901. I-20 exit 200 (River Watch Pkwy), 5.4 mi se, then just n; downtown. Int corridors. **Pets:** Accepted.
ⓢ ⊚ ✕ 🔓 🖥 🍴 🏊 ✕

▼▼▼▼ Candlewood Suites Augusta Ⓗ
(706) 733-3300. **$70-$86.** 1080 Claussen Rd 30907. I-20 exit 200 (River Watch Pkwy), just nw, then just sw. Int corridors. **Pets:** Medium. $25 daily fee/pet. Service with restrictions, supervision. ⊚ 🔓 🖥

△△△ ▼▼ **Clarion Suites** Ⓜ
(706) 868-1800. **$95-$159.** 3038 Washington Rd 30907. I-20 exit 199 (Washington Rd), just w. Ext corridors. **Pets:** Small, dogs only. $25 one-time fee/pet. Service with restrictions, crate.
ⓢ ⊚ 🔓 🖥 🍴 🏊

▼▼▼▼ DoubleTree by Hilton Hotel Augusta Ⓗ
(706) 855-8100. **Call for rates.** 2651 Perimeter Pkwy 30909. I-520 exit 1C (Wheeler Rd), just w to Perimeter Pkwy, then just n. Int corridors.
Pets: Accepted. ⊚ ✕ 🔓 🖥 🍴 🏊 ✕

△△△ ▼▼ **Holiday Inn Gordon Highway at Bobby Jones** Ⓜ
(706) 737-2300. **$75-$89, 3 day notice.** 2155 Gordon Hwy 30909. I-520 exit 3A (US 78), just w. Ext corridors. **Pets:** Accepted.
ⓢ ⊚ ✕ 🔓 🖥 🍴 🏊

▼▼▼▼ Jameson Suites Ⓗ
(706) 733-4656. **Call for rates.** 1062 Clausen Rd 30907. I-20 exit 200 (River Watch Pkwy), just nw, then just sw. Int corridors. **Pets:** $15 daily fee/pet. Designated rooms, service with restrictions, crate.
⊚ 🔓 🖥 🏊

▼▼ ▼▼ La Quinta Inn Augusta Ⓜ
(706) 733-2660. **$59-$115.** 3020 Washington Rd 30907. I-20 exit 199 (Washington Rd), just w. Ext/int corridors. **Pets:** Service with restrictions, supervision. ⊚ 🔓 🔓 🖥 🏊

▼▼▼▼ The Partridge Inn Ⓗ
(706) 737-8888. **Call for rates.** 2110 Walton Way 30904. 1.3 mi w off 15th St. Int corridors. **Pets:** Accepted. ⊚ 🔓 🖥 🍴 🏊

△△△ ▼▼▼▼ **Sheraton Augusta Hotel** Ⓗ 🐾
(706) 396-1000. **$99-$179.** 1069 Stevens Creek Rd 30907. I-20 exit 199 (Washington Rd), just w, then just ne. Int corridors. **Pets:** Medium. $50 one-time fee/room. Designated rooms, service with restrictions, supervision. ⓢ ⊚ ✕ 🔓 🖥 🍴 🏊

BAINBRIDGE

▼▼ ▼▼ Quality Inn Ⓗ
(229) 243-7000. **Call for rates.** 1403 Tallahassee Hwy 39819. Just s of US 84 Bypass on US 27. Ext corridors. **Pets:** Accepted.
⊚ 🔓 🖥 🏊

BLUE RIDGE

△△△ ▼▼▼▼ **The Blue Ridge Lodge by Comfort Inn & Suites** Ⓗ 🐾
(706) 946-3333. **$79-$129.** 83 Blue Ridge Overlook 30513. Just off SR 515 and US 76; behind Arby's. Int corridors. **Pets:** Other species. $50 one-time fee/room. Service with restrictions, supervision.
ⓢ ⊚ ✕ 🔓 🖥

▼▼ ▼▼ Days Inn Ⓜ
(706) 632-2100. **$55-$100.** 4970 Appalachian Hwy 30513. On SR 515 and US 76. Ext corridors. **Pets:** Accepted. ⊚ 🔓 🖥 🏊

▼▼ ▼▼ Douglas Inn & Suites Ⓜ
(706) 258-3600. **Call for rates.** 1192 Windy Ridge Rd 30513. Just off SR 515 and US 76; behind Wendy's. Ext corridors. **Pets:** Accepted.
⊚ 🔓 🖥 🏊

BRASELTON

△△△ ▼▼ **BEST WESTERN Braselton Inn** Ⓜ
(706) 654-3081. **$79-$169.** 303 Zion Church Rd 30517. I-85 exit 129, just e, then 0.3 mi n. Ext corridors. **Pets:** Accepted.
ⓢ ⊚ 🔓 🖥 🏊

BREMEN

▼▼ ▼▼ Days Inn Ⓜ
(770) 537-4646. **$56, 3 day notice.** 35 Price Creek Rd 30110. I-20 exit 11, just n. Ext corridors. **Pets:** $10 daily fee/pet. Service with restrictions, crate. ⊚ 🔓 🖥 🏊

BRUNSWICK

Super 8 H
(912) 264-8800. **$50-$60.** 5280 New Jesup Hwy 31523. I-95 exit 36B (New Jesup Hwy/US 25), just nw. Int corridors. **Pets:** $10 daily fee/pet. Service with restrictions, supervision. SAVE

BYRON

BEST WESTERN Inn & Suites M ❀
(478) 956-3056. **$59-$69.** 101 Dunbar Rd 31008. I-75 exit 149 (SR 49), just ne. Ext corridors. **Pets:** Large. $10 daily fee/pet. Designated rooms, service with restrictions, crate. SAVE

Econo Lodge M 🐾
(478) 956-2800. **$50-$60.** 12003 Watson Blvd 31008. I-75 exit 146, just nw. Ext corridors. **Pets:** Medium, other species. $10 daily fee/pet. Designated rooms, service with restrictions. SAVE

Super 8 H
(478) 956-3311. **$54-$55.** 305 Hwy 49 N 31008. I-75 exit 149 (SR 49), just ne. Ext corridors. **Pets:** Small, other species. $10 daily fee/pet. Service with restrictions, supervision. SAVE

CAIRO

BEST WESTERN Executive Inn H
(229) 377-8000. **$70-$90.** 2800 Hwy 84 E 39828. 2 mi e. Ext corridors. **Pets:** Small, other species. $10 daily fee/pet. Designated rooms, service with restrictions, supervision. SAVE

CALHOUN

Baymont Inn & Suites M
(706) 629-8133. **Call for rates.** 189 Jameson St 30701. I-75 exit 312, just w. Ext corridors. **Pets:** Small, other species. $15 daily fee/room. Designated rooms, service with restrictions, supervision.

Country Inn & Suites By Carlson H
(706) 625-6500. **$80-$179, 3 day notice.** 1033 Fairmount Hwy 30701. I-75 exit 312, just e. Int corridors. **Pets:** Medium, other species. Service with restrictions, supervision.

Days Inn M
(706) 629-9501. **$60-$80.** 915 Hwy 53 E SE 30701. I-75 exit 312, just e. Ext corridors. **Pets:** Small, dogs only. $10 daily fee/pet. No service, supervision.

La Quinta Inn H
(706) 629-2559. **$71-$139.** 150 Cracker Barrel Rd 30701. I-75 exit 312, just e. Int corridors. **Pets:** Service with restrictions, supervision.
SAVE

Motel 6 - #4485 M
(706) 629-8271. **$44-$69.** 742 Hwy 53 SE 30701. I-75 exit 312, just w. Ext corridors. **Pets:** Other species. Service with restrictions, supervision.

Ramada Calhoun M
(706) 629-9207. **$68-$90.** 1204 Red Bud Rd NE 30701. I-75 exit 315, just w. Ext corridors. **Pets:** Small. $10 daily fee/pet. Designated rooms, service with restrictions, supervision.

CANTON

Econo Lodge Inn & Suites H
(770) 345-1994. **$70-$104.** 138 Keith Dr 30114. I-575 exit 20, just e. Int corridors. **Pets:** Accepted.

Microtel Inn & Suites by Wyndham Canton H
(770) 345-8700. **$74-$84.** 114 River Pointe Pkwy 30114. I-575 exit 20, just e. Int corridors. **Pets:** Accepted.

CARROLLTON

Quality Inn M
(770) 834-2600. **Call for rates.** 700 S Park St 30117. On US 27, just s of downtown. Ext corridors. **Pets:** Accepted.

CARTERSVILLE

BEST WESTERN Garden Inn & Suites M
(770) 386-1569. **$75-$100.** 5663 Hwy 20 NE 30121. I-75 exit 290, 0.3 mi e. Ext corridors. **Pets:** Small. $10 daily fee/pet. Designated rooms, service with restrictions, supervision. SAVE

Cartersville North Inn & Suites H
(770) 386-9259. **$60-$74.** 11 Kent Dr 30121. I-75 exit 296, just e. Int corridors. **Pets:** Medium. $10 daily fee/room. Designated rooms, service with restrictions, crate.

Country Inn & Suites By Carlson H
(770) 386-5888. **$80-$169, 3 day notice.** 43 SR 20 Spur 30121. I-75 exit 290, 0.3 mi se. Int corridors. **Pets:** Medium. $5 one-time fee/room. Service with restrictions, crate.

Holiday Inn H
(770) 386-0830. **Call for rates.** 2336 Hwy 411 30120. I-75 exit 293, just w. Int corridors. **Pets:** Other species. $25 one-time fee/room. Service with restrictions, supervision.

Knights Inn M
(770) 386-7263. **$48-$55.** 420 E Church St 30121. I-75 exit 288, 1.5 mi w. Ext corridors. **Pets:** Medium, dogs only. $10 daily fee/pet. Designated rooms, service with restrictions, crate. SAVE

Motel 6 - #4046 M
(770) 386-1449. **$43-$47.** 5657 Hwy 20 NE 30121. I-75 exit 290, 0.3 mi e. Ext corridors. **Pets:** Other species. Service with restrictions, supervision.

Red Roof Inn M
(770) 387-1800. **$49-$79.** 28 SR 20 Spur 30121. I-75 exit 290, 0.3 mi se. Ext corridors. **Pets:** Large, other species. Service with restrictions, supervision.

Super 8 H
(770) 382-8881. **$60.** 41 SR 20 Spur SE 30121. I-75 exit 290, 0.3 mi e. Int corridors. **Pets:** Other species. $5 daily fee/pet. Service with restrictions, supervision.

CEDARTOWN

Country Hearth Inn H
(770) 749-9951. **Call for rates.** 925 N Main St 30125. 1.5 mi n on US 27. Int corridors. **Pets:** Accepted.

CHATSWORTH

Key West Inn M
(706) 517-1155. **Call for rates.** 501 GI Maddox Pkwy 30705. Jct US 76/411. Ext corridors. **Pets:** Accepted.

CLAYTON

Americas Best Value Inn H
(706) 782-4702. **Call for rates.** 698 Hwy 441 S 30525. 0.8 mi s. Int corridors. **Pets:** Very small, dogs only. $10 daily fee/room. Designated rooms, service with restrictions, supervision.

Days Inn M
(706) 782-4258. **$60-$115.** 54 Hwy 441 30525. Center. Ext corridors. **Pets:** Very small, dogs only. $10 daily fee/pet. Designated rooms, service with restrictions, supervision.

Historic Old Clayton Inn H
(706) 782-7722. **$69-$119, 7 day notice.** 60 S Main St 30525. 1 blk s of US 76; 2 blks w of US 441; downtown. Int corridors. **Pets:** Accepted.

Regal Inn M

(706) 782-4269. **$40-$95.** 707 Hwy 441 S 30525. 0.8 mi s. Ext corridors. **Pets:** Small, dogs only. $10 daily fee/pet. Designated rooms, service with restrictions, supervision. 🛰 📶 🐾 💻

COLQUITT

Tarrer Inn CI

(229) 758-2888. **$99-$149, 7 day notice.** 155 S Cuthbert St 39837. Corner of SR 91 and 27; center of town square. Int corridors. **Pets:** Accepted. 🛰 ✕ 🐾 💻 🍴

COLUMBUS

Extended StayAmerica-Columbus-Bradley Park H

(706) 653-9938. **$65-$85.** 1721 Rollins Way 31904. I-185 exit 10 (US 80 and SR 22), 1.5 mi w on US 80 exit 3A, just s to Whittlesey Rd, 0.3 mi e to Rollins Way, then just n. Int corridors. **Pets:** $25 daily fee/pet. Designated rooms, service with restrictions. 🛰 📶 💻

Holiday Inn Express & Suites H

(706) 507-7080. **Call for rates.** 3901 Victory Dr 31903. I-185 exit 1B, 1 mi w. Int corridors. **Pets:** Accepted. 🛰 🐾 📶 💻 ⤳

Holiday Inn North H ✿

(706) 324-0231. **$59-$149.** 2800 Manchester Expwy 31904. I-185 exit 7 (Manchester Expwy), just w. Int corridors. **Pets:** $25 one-time fee/pet. Service with restrictions, supervision.

SAVE 🛰 ✕ 📶 💻 🍴 ⤳

La Quinta Inn Columbus Midtown M

(706) 568-1740. **$59-$118.** 3201 Macon Rd, Suite 200 31906. I-185 exit 6, just w. Ext/int corridors. **Pets:** Service with restrictions, supervision.

🛰 💻 ⤳

La Quinta Inn Columbus State University H

(706) 323-4344. **$63-$144.** 2919 Warm Springs Rd 31909. I-185 exit 7 southbound; exit 7A northbound, just e. Int corridors. **Pets:** Service with restrictions, supervision. 🛰 🐾 📶 💻 ⤳

Microtel Inn & Suites by Wyndham Columbus/Near Fort Benning H

(706) 685-2305. **$70-$110.** 3930 St. Mary's Rd 31907. I-185 exit 3, just e. Int corridors. **Pets:** Accepted. 🛰 📶 💻 ⤳

Microtel Inn & Suites by Wyndham Columbus North H

(706) 653-7004. **$65-$90.** 1728 Fountain Ct 31904. I-185 exit 12, just w. Int corridors. **Pets:** Accepted. 🛰 🐾 📶 💻

Rothschild-Pound House Inn BB

(706) 322-4075. **Call for rates.** 201 7th St 31901. Jct US 27 (Veterans Pkwy/7th St), just w; downtown. Ext/int corridors. **Pets:** Accepted.

🛰 ✕ 📶 💻 🎁

Staybridge Suites H

(706) 507-7700. **Call for rates.** 1678 Whittlesey Rd 31904. I-185 exit 8, just w on Whitesville Rd, then just s. Int corridors. **Pets:** Large, other species. $75 one-time fee/room. Service with restrictions, crate.

SAVE 🛰 📶 💻 ⤳

COMMERCE

BEST WESTERN Commerce Inn H

(706) 335-3640. **$60-$169.** 157 Eisenhower Dr 30529. I-85 exit 149, just ne. Int corridors. **Pets:** Medium. $10 daily fee/pet. Designated rooms, service with restrictions, supervision. SAVE 🛰 🐾 📶 💻 ⤳

Comfort Suites Commerce H

(706) 336-0000. **$90-$200.** 30490 Hwy 441 S 30529. I-85 exit 149, just w. Int corridors. **Pets:** Accepted. 🛰 ✕ 🐾 📶 💻 ⤳

Quality Inn M

(706) 335-9001. **$46-$96.** 165 Eisenhower Dr 30529. I-85 exit 149, just w. Ext corridors. **Pets:** Other species. $15 daily fee/pet. Service with restrictions, crate. 🛰 💻 ⤳

CONYERS

Comfort Inn H

(770) 760-0300. **$66-$70.** 1363 Klondike Rd 30094. I-20 exit 80, just s. Int corridors. **Pets:** Accepted. SAVE 🛰 🐾 📶 💻 ⤳

Country Inn & Suites By Carlson H

(770) 785-2400. **$87-$120, 3 day notice.** 1312 Old Covington Hwy SE 30012. I-20 exit 82, just n. Int corridors. **Pets:** Medium. $45 one-time fee/pet. Designated rooms, service with restrictions, supervision.

🛰 🐾 📶 💻 ⤳

Hampton Inn H ✿

(770) 483-8838. **$77-$109.** 1340 Dogwood Dr SE 30013. I-20 exit 82, just n, then just e. Int corridors. **Pets:** Other species. Designated rooms, supervision. 🛰 🐾 📶 💻 ⤳

La Quinta Inn & Suites Atlanta (Conyers) H

(770) 918-0092. **$78-$140.** 1184 Dogwood Dr 30012. I-20 exit 82, just n, then just w. Int corridors. **Pets:** Service with restrictions, supervision.

🛰 🐾 📶 💻 ⤳

Motel 6 Conyers #4747 M

(770) 483-3220. **Call for rates.** 1351 Dogwood Dr SW 30012. I-20 exit 80, just n, then 0.4 mi w. Ext corridors. **Pets:** Other species. Service with restrictions, supervision. SAVE 🛰 🐾 📶 💻 ⤳

Quality Inn M

(770) 760-1230. **Call for rates.** 1164 Dogwood Dr 30012. I-20 exit 82, just n, then just w. Ext corridors. **Pets:** Accepted. 🛰 📶 💻 ⤳

CORDELE

BEST WESTERN Colonial Inn H ✿

(229) 273-5420. **$63-$70.** 1706 E 16th Ave (US 280) 31015. I-75 exit 101 (US 280), just w. Ext/int corridors. **Pets:** Large, other species. $10 daily fee/pet. Designated rooms, service with restrictions, supervision.

SAVE 🛰 📶 💻 ⤳

Hampton Inn H

(229) 273-0737. **$82-$119.** 1603 16th Ave E (US 280) 31015. I-75 exit 101 (US 280), just w. Ext corridors. **Pets:** Medium. $10 one-time fee/room. Designated rooms, service with restrictions. 🛰 📶 💻 ⤳

Lake Blackshear Resort & Golf Club H

(229) 276-1004. **$59-$199, 7 day notice.** 2459-H US 280 W 31015. I-75 exit 101 (US 280), 10 mi w. Ext/int corridors. **Pets:** Designated rooms, service with restrictions.

ECO SAVE 🛰 🐾 📶 💻 🍴 ⤳ ✕

Quality Inn Cordele H

(229) 273-2371. **$56-$129.** 1601 E 16th Ave (US 280) 31015. I-75 exit 101 (US 280), just w. Ext corridors. **Pets:** Medium. $15 daily fee/pet. Designated rooms, service with restrictions, supervision.

SAVE 🛰 📶 💻 ⤳

Ramada Cordele H

(229) 273-5000. **$59-$89.** 2016 E 16th Ave (US 280) 31015. I-75 exit 101 (US 280), just e. Ext corridors. **Pets:** Accepted.

SAVE 🛰 📶 💻 ⤳

CORNELIA

Super 8 H

(706) 778-9573. **$50-$85.** 2965 J Warren Rd 30531. Jct SR 365 and US 441 business route, just w. Int corridors. **Pets:** Medium, dogs only. $25 one-time fee/pet, $25 daily fee/pet. Service with restrictions, crate.

🛰 🐾 📶 💻 ⤳

COVINGTON

Baymont Inn & Suites M

(770) 787-4900. **$64-$134.** 10111 Alcovy Rd 30014. I-20 exit 92, just n. Ext corridors. **Pets:** Small, dogs only. $15 daily fee/pet. No service, supervision. SAVE 🛰 🐾 📶 💻 ⤳

DAHLONEGA

◆◆◆◆ Super 8 **M**

(706) 864-4343. **$55-$149, 3 day notice.** 20 Mountain Dr 30533. 0.5 mi s on US 19 and SR 60. Ext corridors. **Pets:** Accepted.

DALTON

◆◆◆ ◆◆◆◆ Baymont Inn & Suites Dalton **M**

(706) 226-5022. **$70.** 2106 Chattanooga Rd 30720. I-75 exit 336, just w. Ext corridors. **Pets:** Accepted. [SAVE]

◆◆◆◆ Comfort Inn & Suites **H**

(706) 259-2583. **$85-$120.** 905 Westbridge Rd 30720. I-75 exit 333, just w to Westbridge Rd, then just s. Int corridors. **Pets:** Medium. $15 daily fee/pet. Designated rooms, service with restrictions, supervision.

◆◆◆◆ Holiday Inn & Suites Dalton **H**

(706) 529-6000. **Call for rates.** 879 College Dr 30720. I-75 exit 333, just w. Int corridors. **Pets:** Accepted.

◆◆◆ Howard Johnson Dalton **M**

(706) 281-1880. **Call for rates.** 790 College Dr 30720. I-75 exit 333, just w, then 0.3 mi n. Ext corridors. **Pets:** Accepted.

◆◆◆◆ La Quinta Inn & Suites Dalton **H**

(706) 272-9099. **$90-$166.** 715 College Dr 30720. I-75 exit 333, just w to Holiday Dr, then 0.5 mi n. Int corridors. **Pets:** Service with restrictions, supervision.

◆◆◆ Quality Inn **M**

(706) 278-0500. **$60-$95.** 875 College Dr 30720. I-75 exit 333, just w. Ext corridors. **Pets:** Other species. $10 daily fee/pet. Service with restrictions, crate.

DARIEN

◆◆◆ ◆◆◆◆ Comfort Inn **H**

(912) 437-4200. **$60-$70.** 12924 GA Hwy 251 Rd 31305. I-95 exit 49 (SR 251), just nw. Int corridors. **Pets:** Medium. $15 daily fee/pet. Designated rooms, service with restrictions, supervision.

[SAVE]

DAWSONVILLE

◆◆◆ ◆◆◆◆ BEST WESTERN Dawson Village Inn **H**

(706) 216-4410. **$69-$99, 7 day notice.** 76 N Georgia Ave 30534. Jct SR 400/53, 0.5 mi s. Int corridors. **Pets:** Dogs only. $20 daily fee/pet. Service with restrictions, supervision. [SAVE]

◆◆◆◆ Comfort Inn **H**

(706) 216-1900. **$59-$90.** 127 Beartooth Pkwy 30534. Jct SR 400/53, 0.5 mi s. Int corridors. **Pets:** Large, other species. $15 daily fee/pet. Designated rooms, service with restrictions, crate.

◆◆◆ Super 8 **H**

(706) 216-6801. **$50-$136, 3 day notice.** 205 N 400 Center Ln 30534. Jct SR 400/53, just n. Int corridors. **Pets:** Accepted.

DILLARD

◆◆◆ ◆◆◆◆ Dillard House **M**

(706) 746-5348. **$69-$179, 3 day notice.** 768 Franklin St 30537. US 441, just e via Old Dillard Rd. Ext corridors. **Pets:** Dogs only. $15 daily fee/pet. Designated rooms, service with restrictions, supervision.

[SAVE]

◆◆◆ ◆◆◆◆ Mountain Valley Inn **M**

(706) 746-5373. **$35-$110.** 13 Royalty Ln 30537. Just n of town center. Ext corridors. **Pets:** Small, dogs only. $10 daily fee/pet. Designated rooms, service with restrictions, supervision. [SAVE]

DOUGLAS

◆◆◆ Jameson Inn **H**

(912) 384-9432. **Call for rates.** 1628 S Peterson Ave 31535. Jct US 221/441/SR 31 and SR 206/353, just s. Ext corridors. **Pets:** Medium. $15 daily fee/pet. Designated rooms, service with restrictions, supervision.

DUBLIN

◆◆◆ Baymont Inn & Suites Dublin **H**

(478) 275-3008. **Call for rates.** 100 PM Watson Dr 31021. I-16 exit 51 (US 441), just n. Ext corridors. **Pets:** Accepted.

◆◆◆ ◆◆◆◆ La Quinta Inn & Suites Dublin **H**

(478) 272-3110. **$93-$166.** 101 Travel Center Blvd 31021. I-16 exit 51 (US 441), just s. Int corridors. **Pets:** Service with restrictions, supervision.

◆◆◆ Quality Inn & Suites **H**

(478) 274-8000. **$65-$80.** 2110 Hwy 441 S 31021. I-16 exit 51 (US 441), 0.6 mi n. Ext corridors. **Pets:** Accepted.

EAST ELLIJAY

◆◆◆ ◆◆◆◆ Stratford Motor Inn **M**

(706) 276-1080. **$60-$100.** 79 Maddox Cir 30540. Jct Maddox Cir and SR 515. Ext corridors. **Pets:** Accepted. [SAVE]

EATONTON

◆◆◆◆ The Lodge on Lake Oconee **H**

(706) 485-7785. **$109-$169.** 930 Lake Oconee Pkwy 31024. I-20 exit 130 (SR 44), 10.6 mi s. Int corridors. **Pets:** Accepted.

FITZGERALD

◆◆◆ Western Motel **H**

(229) 424-9500. **$45-$55.** 111 Bull Run Rd 31750. Just n of US 319/107, on US 129. Ext corridors. **Pets:** Accepted.

FORSYTH

◆◆◆ ◆◆◆◆ Comfort Inn **H**

(478) 994-3400. **$65-$85.** 333 Harold G Clark Pkwy 31029. I-75 exit 185 (SR 18), just w. Ext corridors. **Pets:** Medium, other species. $15 daily fee/pet. Designated rooms, service with restrictions, crate.

[SAVE]

◆◆◆ ◆◆◆◆ Econo Lodge **M**

(478) 994-5603. **Call for rates.** 320 Cabiness Rd 31029. I-75 exit 187, just e. Int corridors. **Pets:** Medium. $6 daily fee/pet. Designated rooms, service with restrictions, supervision. [SAVE]

◆◆◆ ◆◆◆◆ Hilltop Garden Inn, a Magnuson Hotel **M**

(478) 994-9260. **$60-$80.** 951 Hwy 42 N 31029. I-75 exit 188, just e; on Frontage Rd. Ext corridors. **Pets:** Accepted. [SAVE]

◆◆◆◆ Holiday Inn Express **H**

(478) 994-9697. **$78-$119.** 520 Holiday Cir 31029. I-75 exit 186 (Juliette Rd), just w, then just s on Aaron St. Int corridors. **Pets:** Medium, other species. $15 one-time fee/room. Designated rooms, service with restrictions, supervision.

◆◆◆ Ramada Conference Center Forsyth **M**

(478) 994-5691. **Call for rates.** 480 Holiday Cir 31029. I-75 exit 186 (Juliette Rd), just w, then just s on Aaron St. Ext corridors. **Pets:** Medium. $10 one-time fee/pet. Designated rooms, service with restrictions, supervision.

◆◆◆ ◆◆◆◆ Super 8 **M**

(478) 994-5101. **$57-$112.** 436 Tift College Dr 31029. I-75 exit 186 (Juliette Rd), just w. Ext/int corridors. **Pets:** Medium. $15 daily fee/pet. Designated rooms, service with restrictions, supervision.

[SAVE]

FORT OGLETHORPE

AAA ▼▼ ▼▼ **BEST WESTERN Battlefield Inn** **M**

(706) 866-0222. **$65-$90.** 2120 Lafayette Rd 30742. Jct US 27 and SR 2, just n. Ext corridors. **Pets:** Small. $15 daily fee/pet. Service with restrictions, supervision. [SAVE] 🛜 🛅 📺 🏊

GAINESVILLE

AAA ▼▼ ▼▼ **GuestHouse Inn & Suites** **M**

(770) 535-8100. **$54-$99.** 520 Queen City Pkwy SW 30501. I-985 exit 20, 1.8 mi nw on SR 60/Queen City Pkwy. Ext corridors. **Pets:** Other species. $15 daily fee/pet. Designated rooms, service with restrictions, crate. [SAVE] 🛜 🛅 📺 🏊

GOLDEN ISLES AREA

JEKYLL ISLAND

AAA ▼▼▼▼ **Hampton Inn & Suites Jekyll Island** **H**

(912) 635-3733. **$139-$239.** 200 S Beachview Dr 31527. Jct Ben Fortson Pkwy (SR 520/Beachview Dr), 2 mi s. Int corridors. **Pets:** Small. $10 deposit/pet. Designated rooms, service with restrictions, supervision.
[SAVE] 🛜 ✖ 🛗M 🛅 📺 🏊 ✖

AAA ▼▼▼▼ **Villas by the Sea** **CO** ❀

(912) 635-2521. **$139-$400, 7 day notice.** 1175 N Beachview Dr 31527. Jct Ben Fortson Pkwy (SR 520/Beachview Dr), 4 mi n. Ext corridors. **Pets:** Medium, dogs only. $75 one-time fee/room. Designated rooms, service with restrictions, crate.
[SAVE] 🛜 🛗M 🛅 📺 🍴 🏊 ✖

ST. SIMONS ISLAND

AAA ▼▼▼▼▼ **The Lodge at Sea Island** **H** ❀

(912) 634-3992. **Call for rates.** 100 Retreat Ave 31522. FJ Torras Cswy, 1.6 mi se on Kings Way, just s. Int corridors. **Pets:** Small, other species. $175 one-time fee/room. Service with restrictions, crate.
[SAVE] 🛜 ✖ 🍴 ✖

▼▼▼▼ **Sea Palms Inn** **H** ❀

(912) 634-0660. **$109-$149, 14 day notice.** 411 Longview Plaza 31522. Jct Frederica and Demere rds, 0.4 mi n on Frederica Rd. Ext corridors. **Pets:** Dogs only. $50 one-time fee/room. Designated rooms, service with restrictions, crate. 🛜 🛅 📺 🏊 ✖

END AREA

GREENSBORO

▼▼▼▼▼ **The Ritz-Carlton Lodge, Reynolds Plantation** **H** ❀

(706) 467-0600. **$249-$499.** One Lake Oconee Tr 30642. I-20 exit 130, 7.2 mi sw on SR 44 (Old Eatonton Rd), 1.5 mi e on Linger Longer Rd, then 2 mi ne. Ext/int corridors. **Pets:** Dogs only. $150 one-time fee/room. Designated rooms, service with restrictions.
🛜 ✖ 🛗M 🛅 📺 🍴 🏊 ✖

GROVETOWN

▼▼▼▼ **Hawthorn Suites by Wyndham Augusta** **H**

(706) 228-1990. **$85-$499.** 4049 Jimmie Dyess Pkwy 30909. I-20 exit 194 (SR 383), 0.5 mi s. Int corridors. **Pets:** $75 one-time fee/room. Service with restrictions, crate. 🛜 🛗M 🛅 📺 🏊

▼▼▼▼ **Super 8-Augusta** **H**

(706) 396-1600. **$65-$275.** 456 Park West Dr 30813. I-20 exit 194 (SR 383), just s, then w. Int corridors. **Pets:** Accepted. 🛜 🛅 📺 🏊

HARTWELL

AAA ▼▼ ▼▼ **BEST WESTERN Lake Hartwell Inn & Suites** **H**

(706) 376-4700. **$79-$149.** 1357 E Franklin St 30643. I-85 exit 177, 2 mi on US 29 E. Int corridors. **Pets:** Other species. $20 one-time fee/room. Service with restrictions, crate. [SAVE] 🛜 ✖ 🛅 📺 🏊

HELEN

▼▼ ▼▼ **The Helendorf River Inn & Conference Center** **M**

(706) 878-2271. **$44-$169, 10 day notice.** 33 Munich Strasse 30545. SR 17 and 75; center. Ext corridors. **Pets:** Other species. $20 daily fee/pet. Designated rooms, service with restrictions, supervision.
🛜 🛅 📺 🏊

▼▼ ▼▼ **Kountry Peddler Tanglewood Resort Cabins** **CA**

(706) 878-3286. **$79-$179, 14 day notice.** 3387 Hwy 356 30571. 1 mi n on SR 75, then 3 mi ne. Ext corridors. **Pets:** Accepted. 🛜 🛅 📺

AAA ▼▼ ▼▼ **Quality Inn** **M**

(706) 878-2268. **$55-$130.** 15 Yonah St 30545. Just w of Mack St. Ext corridors. **Pets:** Small. $20 daily fee/pet. Service with restrictions.
[SAVE] 🛜 🛅 📺 🏊

AAA ▼▼ ▼▼ **Riverbend Motel & Cabins** **M**

(706) 878-2155. **$49-$289, 3 day notice.** 134 River St 30545. Just w off Main St. Ext corridors. **Pets:** Small. $20 daily fee/pet. Service with restrictions. [SAVE] 🛜 🛅 📺

HIAWASSEE

▼▼ ▼▼ **Enota B & B, Cabins & Conference Lodge** **CA**

(706) 896-9966. **Call for rates.** 1000 Hwy 180 30546. E on US 76 to SR 75/17, 6 mi s to SR 180, then 2.5 mi w. Ext corridors. **Pets:** Other species. $15 daily fee/pet. No service, supervision.
🛜 ✖ 🛅 📺 ✖ ✖

HINESVILLE

▼▼▼▼ **La Quinta Inn & Suites Hinesville/Ft Stewart** **H**

(912) 369-3000. **$89-$155.** 1740 E Oglethorpe Hwy 31313. Jct US 84 and SR 38C, 0.8 mi ne. Int corridors. **Pets:** Service with restrictions, supervision. 🛜 ✖ 🛗M 🛅 📺 🏊

HIRAM

▼▼▼▼ **Country Inn & Suites By Carlson** **H**

(770) 222-0456. **$85-$140.** 70 Enterprise Path 30134. Jct SR 92/6 and US 278, 0.3 mi w. Int corridors. **Pets:** Small. $15 daily fee/pet. Service with restrictions, crate. 🛜 🛅 📺 🏊

HOGANSVILLE

▼▼ ▼▼ **Woodstream Inn** **M**

(706) 637-9395. **$50-$120.** 1888 E Main St 30230. I-85 exit 28, just w. Ext corridors. **Pets:** Very small, dogs only. $10 daily fee/pet. Designated rooms, service with restrictions, supervision. 🛜 🛅 📺 🏊

JASPER

▼▼ ▼▼ **Microtel Inn & Suites by Wyndham Jasper** **H**

(706) 299-5500. **$60-$90.** 171 H Mullins Ct 30143. Jct SR 515/53, 0.9 mi n. Int corridors. **Pets:** Accepted. 🛜 🛗M 🛅 📺

▼▼ ▼▼ **Super 8** **M**

(706) 253-3297. **$63-$93.** 100 Whitfield Dr 30143. Jct SR 515/53; in Lawsons Crossing. Ext corridors. **Pets:** Accepted.
🛜 🛗M 🛅 📺 🏊

KINGSLAND

▼▼ Baymont Inn & Suites Kingsland 🄷
(912) 729-9600. **Call for rates.** 105 May Creek Blvd 31548. I-95 exit 3 (SR 40), just w, then s at Boone Ave. Ext corridors. **Pets:** Accepted.
🛜 🕎 🛗 📺 🌊

▼▼ Country Inn & Suites By Carlson 🄷
(912) 576-1616. **$95.** 135 The Lakes Blvd 31548. I-95 exit 3 (SR 40), just se. Int corridors. **Pets:** Accepted. 🛜 🕎 🛗 📺 🌊

AAA ▼▼▼ La Quinta Inn Kingsland Kings Bay 🄷
(912) 882-8010. **$83-$155.** 104 May Creek Dr 31548. I-95 exit 3 (SR 40), just sw. Int corridors. **Pets:** Service with restrictions, supervision.
SAVE 🛜 ✕ 🕎 🛗 📺 🌊

AAA ▼▼▼ Microtel Inn & Suites by Wyndham Kingsland 🄷
(912) 729-1555. **$43-$70.** 1325 E King Ave 31548. I-95 exit 3 (SR 40), just ne. Int corridors. **Pets:** Other species. $10 daily fee/pet. Designated rooms, service with restrictions, supervision. SAVE 🛜 🛗 📺 🌊

▼▼ Sleep Inn & Suites 🄷
(912) 673-7116. **$45-$89.** 1321 Hospitality Ave 31548. I-95 exit 3 (SR 40), just e. Int corridors. **Pets:** Accepted. 🛜 🕎 🛗 📺 🌊

LA FAYETTE

▼▼ Days Inn Ⓜ
(706) 639-9362. **$60-$65.** 2209 N Main St 30728. 2.5 mi n on US 27. Ext corridors. **Pets:** Medium. $10 daily fee/pet. Service with restrictions, crate. 🛜 🛗 📺 🌊

▼▼ Key West Inn Ⓜ
(706) 638-8200. **$49-$89.** 2221 N Main St 30728. 2.5 mi n on US 27. Ext corridors. **Pets:** Small. $15 daily fee/pet. Service with restrictions, crate. 🛜 🕎 🛗 🌊

LAGRANGE

▼▼ Baymont Inn & Suites 🄷 ❀
(706) 885-9002. **$69-$85.** 107 Hoffman Dr 30240. I-85 exit 18 (Lafayette Pkwy), just w. Int corridors. **Pets:** Medium. $10 daily fee/pet. Service with restrictions, supervision. 🛜 🛗 📺 🌊 ✕

AAA ▼▼▼ BEST WESTERN PLUS Lafayette Garden Inn & Conference Center Ⓜ ❀
(706) 884-6175. **$70-$75.** 1513 Lafayette Pkwy 30241. I-85 exit 18 (Lafayette Pkwy), just w. Ext corridors. **Pets:** Medium, other species. $15 daily fee/pet. Designated rooms, no service, supervision.
SAVE 🛜 🛗 📺 🍴 🌊

AAA ▼▼▼ Days Inn-LaGrange/Callaway Gardens Ⓜ
(706) 882-8881. **$55-$150.** 2606 Whitesville Rd 30240. I-85 exit 13, just e. Ext corridors. **Pets:** Other species. $15 daily fee/pet. Designated rooms, no service, supervision. SAVE 🛜 🛗 📺 🌊

▼▼ Quality Inn Ⓜ
(706) 882-8700. **Call for rates.** 110 Jameson Dr 30240. I-85 exit 18 (Lafayette Pkwy), 0.3 mi w. Ext corridors. **Pets:** Accepted.
🛜 🕎 🛗 📺 🌊

▼▼ Red Roof Inn LaGrange Ⓜ
(706) 882-9540. **$59-$99.** 1601 Lafayette Pkwy 30241. I-85 exit 18 (Lafayette Pkwy), just e. Ext corridors. **Pets:** Large, other species. Service with restrictions, supervision. 🛜 🛗 📺 🌊

LAKE PARK

AAA ▼▼ Days Inn 🄷
(229) 559-0229. **$59-$89.** 4913 Timber Dr 31636. I-75 exit 5, just nw. Ext corridors. **Pets:** Accepted. SAVE 🛜 ✕ 🛗 📺 🌊

LAVONIA

▼▼▼ Holiday Inn Express & Suites 🄷
(706) 356-2100. **Call for rates.** 110 Owens Dr 30553. I-85 exit 173, just w. Int corridors. **Pets:** Small. $31 one-time fee/room. Designated rooms, service with restrictions, supervision. 🛜 🕎 🛗 📺 🌊

LOCUST GROVE

AAA ▼▼▼ La Quinta Inn & Suites Locust Grove 🄷
(678) 583-8088. **$71-$155.** 4832 Bill Gardner Pkwy 30248. I-75 exit 212, just e. Int corridors. **Pets:** Service with restrictions, supervision.
SAVE 🛜 ✕ 🕎 🛗 📺 🌊

AAA ▼▼▼ Red Roof Inn 🄷
(678) 583-0004. **$59-$89.** 4840 Bill Gardner Pkwy 30248. I-75 exit 212, just e. Int corridors. **Pets:** Large, other species. Service with restrictions, supervision. SAVE 🛜 🕎 🛗 📺

AAA ▼▼▼ Super 8 Ⓜ
(770) 957-2936. **$54-$96, 3 day notice.** 4605 Bill Gardner Pkwy 30248. I-75 exit 212, just w. Ext corridors. **Pets:** Small, dogs only. $10 daily fee/pet. Designated rooms, service with restrictions, supervision.
SAVE 🛜 🛗 📺

MACON

AAA ▼▼ BEST WESTERN Inn & Suites of Macon Ⓜ ❀
(478) 781-5300. **$70-$80.** 4681 Chambers Rd 31206. I-475 exit 3 (Eisenhower Pkwy/US 80), just ne, then just se. Ext corridors. **Pets:** Large. $10 daily fee/pet. Service with restrictions. SAVE 🛜 🛗 📺 🌊

▼▼▼ Candlewood Suites 🄷
(478) 254-3530. **$81-$99.** 3957 River Place Dr 31210. I-75 exit 169 (Arkwright Rd), just e, then just s. Int corridors. **Pets:** Other species. $75 one-time fee/room. Service with restrictions. 🛜 🕎 🛗 📺 🌊

▼▼▼ La Quinta Inn & Suites Macon 🄷
(478) 475-0206. **$63-$129.** 3944 River Place Dr 31210. I-75 exit 169 (Arkwright Rd), just n, then e. Int corridors. **Pets:** Service with restrictions, supervision. 🛜 🕎 🛗 📺 🌊

▼▼▼ La Quinta Inn & Suites Macon West 🄷
(478) 788-6226. **$78-$188.** 4615 Chambers Rd 31206. I-475 exit 3 (Eisenhower Pkwy/US 80), just e, then 0.5 mi s. Int corridors. **Pets:** Service with restrictions, supervision. 🛜 ✕ 🛗 📺 🌊

AAA ▼▼▼ Rodeway Inn Ⓜ
(478) 781-4343. **$45-$50.** 4999 Eisenhower Pkwy 31206. I-475 exit 3 (Eisenhower Pkwy/US 80), just ne. Ext corridors. **Pets:** Medium. $10 daily fee/pet. Designated rooms, service with restrictions, crate.
SAVE 🛜 🛗 📺 🌊

MCDONOUGH

▼▼▼ Baymont Inn & Suites McDonough Ⓜ
(770) 954-9110. **$59-$99.** 80 Hwy 81 W 30253. I-75 exit 218, just nw. Ext corridors. **Pets:** Accepted. 🛜 🛗 📺 🌊

AAA ▼▼▼ Country Inn & Suites By Carlson 🄷
(770) 957-0082. **$89-$190.** 115 E Greenwood Rd 30253. I-75 exit 216, just w. Int corridors. **Pets:** Small, other species. $25 daily fee/pet. Designated rooms, service with restrictions, crate.
SAVE 🛜 🕎 🛗 📺 🌊

AAA ▼▼ Econo Lodge Ⓜ
(770) 957-2651. **$40-$100.** 1279 Hwy 20 W 30253. I-75 exit 218, just w. Ext corridors. **Pets:** Small. $10 daily fee/pet. Designated rooms, service with restrictions, supervision. SAVE 🛜 🛗 📺

AAA ▼▼▼ Quality Inn & Suites Conference Center Ⓜ
(770) 957-5291. **$64-$124.** 930 Hwy 155 S 30253. I-75 exit 216, just w. Ext corridors. **Pets:** Medium. $10 daily fee/room. Service with restrictions, crate. SAVE 🛜 🕎 🛗 📺 🌊

AAA **WWW** Sleep Inn **H**
(770) 898-0804. **$60-$74.** 945 Hwy 155 S 30253. I-75 exit 216, just w. Int corridors. **Pets:** Medium. $10 daily fee/pet. Service with restrictions.
[SAVE] [icons]

MILLEDGEVILLE
WWW Antebellum Inn **BB**
(478) 453-3993. **$119-$199, 3 day notice.** 200 N Columbia St 31061. Just s of Business Rt US 441 (Columbia St); between SR 22 and 49; downtown. Int corridors. **Pets:** Small. $25 daily fee/pet. Designated rooms, service with restrictions, supervision. [icons]

WW Super 8 Milledgeville **M**
(478) 453-9491. **$50-$75.** 2474 N Columbia St 31061. US 441, 2.6 mi n of downtown. Ext corridors. **Pets:** Medium, other species. $10 daily fee/pet. Designated rooms, service with restrictions, supervision.
[icons]

MOULTRIE
WW Econo Lodge **H**
(229) 890-8652. **$65-$79.** 1300 Veterans Pkwy 31788. Northern jct US 319 and 319 business route, just e. Int corridors. **Pets:** Accepted.
[icons]

NEWNAN
AAA **WWW** BEST WESTERN Shenandoah Inn **M**
(770) 304-9700. **$69-$75.** 620 Hwy 34 E 30265. I-85 exit 47, just w. Ext corridors. **Pets:** Medium. $10 daily fee/pet. Service with restrictions, supervision. [SAVE] [icons]

WW Howard Johnson Inn **M**
(770) 683-1499. **$50-$59.** 1310 Hwy 29 S 30263. I-85 exit 41, just w. Ext corridors. **Pets:** Small. $10 daily fee/pet. Designated rooms, service with restrictions, supervision. [icons]

WWW La Quinta Inn & Suites Atlanta South - Newnan **H**
(770) 502-8430. **$66-$134.** 600 Bullsboro Dr 30265. I-85 exit 47, 0.3 mi w. Int corridors. **Pets:** Service with restrictions, supervision.
[icons]

OAKWOOD
WW Jameson Inn **M**
(770) 533-9400. **Call for rates.** 3530 Thurman Tanner Pkwy 30566. I-985 exit 16, 0.4 mi w. Ext corridors. **Pets:** Very small, dogs only. $15 daily fee/pet. Designated rooms, service with restrictions, supervision.
[icons]

PEACHTREE CITY
AAA **WWW** BEST WESTERN Inn & Suites **M**
(770) 632-9700. **$70-$100.** 976 Crosstown Dr 30269. Jct SR 74 and 54, 2.1 mi s on SR 74. Ext corridors. **Pets:** Medium. $20 daily fee/pet. Designated rooms, service with restrictions, crate.
[SAVE] [icons]

WWWW Wyndham Peachtree Hotel & Conference Center **H**
(770) 487-2000. **$76-$161.** 2443 Hwy 54 W 30269. Jct SR 74 and 54, 1 mi e. Int corridors. **Pets:** Accepted. [icons]

PERRY
AAA **WWW** Econo Lodge **M**
(478) 987-2142. **$50-$100.** 102 Valley Dr 31069. I-75 exit 136, just w, then just s. Int corridors. **Pets:** Accepted. [SAVE] [icons]

WW Microtel Inn & Suites by Wyndham Perry **H**
(478) 987-4004. **$45-$89.** 110 Fairview Dr 31069. I-75 exit 134, just nw. Int corridors. **Pets:** Accepted. [icons]

WW Ramada Inn **H**
(478) 987-3313. **$65-$89.** 200 Valley Dr 31069. I-75 exit 136 (Sam Nunn Blvd), just w, then s. Ext corridors. **Pets:** Accepted.
[icons]

PINE MOUNTAIN
AAA **WWWW** Mountain Creek Inn at Callaway Gardens **M**
(706) 663-2281. **$109-$159, 7 day notice.** 17800 Hwy 27 31822. Jct SR 354, 1.5 mi s on US 27/SR 1; in Callaway Gardens. Ext corridors. **Pets:** Small, other species. $95 one-time fee/room. Designated rooms, service with restrictions, crate. [SAVE] [icons]

WW White Columns Motel **M**
(706) 663-2312. **$59-$80, 3 day notice.** 524 S Main Ave 31822. Jct SR 354, just n on US 27/SR 1. Ext corridors. **Pets:** Accepted. [icons]

POOLER
WW Bradbury Suites **H**
(912) 330-0330. **$62-$199.** 155 Bourne Ave 31322. I-95 exit 102 (US 80), just e. Int corridors. **Pets:** Accepted.
[icons]

AAA **WWWW** Holiday Inn Hotel & Suites - Savannah/Pooler **H**
(912) 330-5100. **$109-$119.** 103 San Dr 31322. I-95 exit 102 (US 80), just w. Int corridors. **Pets:** Accepted.
[SAVE] [icons]

WWWW La Quinta Inn & Suites Savannah Airport - Pooler **H**
(912) 748-3771. **$101-$177.** 414 Gray St 31322. I-95 exit 102 (US 80), just w. Int corridors. **Pets:** Service with restrictions, supervision.
[icons]

WW Quality Inn **H**
(912) 748-0017. **Call for rates.** 125 Bourne Ave 31322. I-95 exit 102 (US 80), just e. Int corridors. **Pets:** Accepted. [icons]

PORT WENTWORTH
WWW Comfort Suites Savannah North **H**
(912) 965-1445. **$79-$109.** 115 Travelers Way 31407. I-95 exit 109 (SR 21), just n. Int corridors. **Pets:** Small. $20 daily fee/pet. Designated rooms, service with restrictions, supervision.
[icons]

AAA **WWW** Hampton Inn Savannah North **H** ❀
(912) 966-2000. **$99-$139.** 7050 Hwy 21 31407. I-95 exit 109 (SR 21), just s. Int corridors. **Pets:** Other species. Designated rooms, service with restrictions. [SAVE] [icons]

WWW Wingate by Wyndham **H**
(912) 964-0840. **$80-$139.** 115 O' Leary Rd 31407. I-95 exit 109 (SR 21), just s, then just n. Int corridors. **Pets:** Accepted.
[icons]

RICHMOND HILL
AAA **WWWW** BEST WESTERN PLUS Richmond Hill Inn **H** ❀
(912) 756-7070. **$64-$129.** 4564 Hwy 17 31324. I-95 exit 87 (Ocean Hwy/US 17), just w. Int corridors. **Pets:** Other species. $20 daily fee/pet. Designated rooms, service with restrictions, supervision.
[SAVE] [icons]

AAA **WWW** Econo Lodge-Richmond Hill **M**
(912) 756-3312. **$50-$60.** 4701 US 17 31324. I-95 exit 87 (Ocean Hwy/US 17), 0.4 mi sw. Ext corridors. **Pets:** Very small. $20 daily fee/pet. Designated rooms, supervision. [SAVE] [icons]

Holiday Inn Express ⊞
(912) 756-6668. **$79-$99.** 4601 Hwy 17 31324. I-95 exit 87 (Ocean Hwy/US 17), 0.4 mi sw. Int corridors. **Pets:** Other species. $35 daily fee/pet. Designated rooms, service with restrictions, crate.
🅂🄰🅅🄴 🛜 ⊠ 🛏 💻 🐾 ⊠

RINGGOLD

 Hometown Inn ⊞ ❀
(706) 937-7070. **$60-$99.** 22 Gateway Business Park Dr 30736. I-75 exit 350, just e. Int corridors. **Pets:** Medium, other species. $10 daily fee/pet. Designated rooms, service with restrictions, supervision.
🅂🄰🅅🄴 🛜 ♿M 🛏 💻 🐾

ROCKMART

▼▼ Western Inn Ⓜ
(770) 684-9955. **Call for rates.** 105 GTM Pkwy 30165. Jct US 278 and SR 101, just n. Ext corridors. **Pets:** Accepted. 🛜 ♿M 🛏 💻

ROME

▼▼▼ La Quinta Inn & Suites ⊞
(706) 291-1034. **$84-$156.** 15 Chateau Dr SE 30161. 2 mi e on US 411. Int corridors. **Pets:** Service with restrictions, supervision.
🛜 ⊠ 🛏 💻 🐾

▼▼ Quality Inn ⊞
(706) 291-7797. **Call for rates.** 40 Grace Dr 30161. On US 411, 2.2 mi e. Int corridors. **Pets:** Accepted. 🛜 ♿M 🛏 💻 🐾

SANDERSVILLE

▼▼ Days Inn Sandersville Ⓜ
(478) 553-0393. **$69-$99.** 128 Commerce St 31082. On SR 15, jct SR 24/88, just s. Ext corridors. **Pets:** Accepted. 🛜 ♿M 🛏 💻 🐾

SAVANNAH

▼▼▼ Baymont Inn & Suites ⊞
(912) 925-9494. **$70-$150.** 393 Canebrake Rd 31419. I-95 exit 94 (SR 204/Abercorn St), just se. Int corridors. **Pets:** Medium. $20 daily fee/pet. Designated rooms, service with restrictions, supervision.
🛜 ⊠ ♿M 🛏 💻 🐾

🄰🄰🄰 ▼▼▼ BEST WESTERN PLUS Savannah Historic District Ⓜ
(912) 233-1011. **$99-$229.** 412 W Bay St 31401. Jct Montgomery St. Ext corridors. **Pets:** Large, dogs only. $50 deposit/pet, $20 daily fee/room. Supervision. 🅂🄰🅅🄴 🛜 ⊠ 🛏 💻 🐾

🄰🄰🄰 ▼▼▼▼ Bohemian Hotel Savannah Riverfront, Autograph Collection ⊞ ❀
(912) 721-3800. **$199-$409, 3 day notice.** 102 W Bay St 31401. Between Bull and Whitaker sts. Int corridors. **Pets:** Dogs only. $150 one-time fee/pet. Designated rooms, service with restrictions.
🅂🄰🅅🄴 🛜 ⊠ ♿M 💻 🍽

▼▼▼ Candlewood Suites ⊞
(912) 966-9644. **$59-$129.** 50 Stephen S Green Dr 31408. I-95 exit 104, just e, then s. Int corridors. **Pets:** Accepted. 🛜 ♿M 🛏 💻 🐾

▼▼▼ Catherine Ward House Inn ⒷⒷ
(912) 234-8564. **$159-$259, 3 day notice.** 118 E Waldburg St 31401. Between Drayton and Abercorn sts. Ext/int corridors. **Pets:** Dogs only. $35 one-time fee/room. Designated rooms, service with restrictions.
🛜 ⊠ 🛏 🅕

🄰🄰🄰 ▼▼▼▼ Comfort Suites Historic District ⊞ ❀
(912) 629-2001. **$99-$239.** 630 W Bay St 31401. Between Fahm and W Boundary sts; on west side of historic district. Int corridors. **Pets:** Small. $50 one-time fee/pet. Designated rooms, crate.
🅂🄰🅅🄴 🛜 ⊠ ♿M 🛏 💻 🐾

🄰🄰🄰 ▼▼▼ East Bay Inn ⒸⒾ
(912) 238-1225. **$189-$325, 7 day notice.** 225 E Bay St 31401. Between Abercorn and Lincoln sts. Int corridors. **Pets:** Accepted.
🅂🄰🅅🄴 🛜 ⊠ 🍽

▼▼ Extended StayAmerica Savannah-Midtown ⊞
(912) 692-0076. **$60-$110.** 5511 Abercorn St 31405. Jct SR 21 and 204 (Abercorn St), just s. Int corridors. **Pets:** $25 daily fee/pet. Designated rooms, service with restrictions. 🛜 🛏 💻

🄰🄰🄰 ▼▼▼ Foley House Inn ⒷⒷ ❀
(912) 232-6622. **$199-$399, 3 day notice.** 14 W Hull St 31401. Between Bull and Whitaker sts; on Chippewa Square. Ext/int corridors. **Pets:** Other species. $50 one-time fee/pet. Designated rooms, service with restrictions. 🅂🄰🅅🄴 🛜 ⊠

▼▼▼ The Forsyth Park Inn ⒷⒷ
(912) 233-6800. **$175-$295, 14 day notice.** 102 W Hall St 31401. Between Whitaker and Howard sts; across from Forsyth Park. Int corridors. **Pets:** Accepted. 🛜 ⊠ 🛏

🄰🄰🄰 ▼▼▼▼ Hamilton-Turner Inn ⒷⒷ
(912) 233-1833. **$189-$389, 10 day notice.** 330 Abercorn St 31401. Between E Charlton and E Harris sts; overlooking Lafayette Square. Ext/int corridors. **Pets:** Small, other species. $50 one-time fee/room. Designated rooms, service with restrictions, supervision. 🅂🄰🅅🄴 🛜 ⊠

▼▼▼ Homewood Suites by Hilton ⊞
(912) 353-8500. **$129-$399.** 5820 White Bluff Rd 31405. Jct SR 21 and 204 (Abercorn St), 0.5 mi s. Ext/int corridors. **Pets:** Medium. $75 one-time fee/room. Service with restrictions, crate. 🛜 🛏 💻 🐾 ⊠

▼▼▼ La Quinta Inn & Suites ⊞
(912) 927-7660. **$63-$144.** 8484 Abercorn St 31406. 2.4 mi s of jct SR 21 and 204 (Abercorn St). Int corridors. **Pets:** Service with restrictions, supervision. 🛜 ⊠ 💻 🐾

🄰🄰🄰 ▼▼▼▼ Mansion on Forsyth Park Hotel and Spa, Autograph Collection ⊞
(912) 238-5158. **$159-$379.** 700 Drayton St 31401. Between E Hall and E Gwinnett sts; on Forsyth Park. Int corridors. **Pets:** Medium, dogs only. $150 one-time fee/pet. Service with restrictions, crate.
🄴🄲🄾 🅂🄰🅅🄴 🛜 ⊠ 🛏 💻 🍽 🐾

▼▼▼ The Mulberry-A Holiday Inn Hotel ⊞
(912) 238-1200. **Call for rates.** 601 E Bay St 31401. Between Broad and Houston sts; east side of historic district. Ext/int corridors. **Pets:** Accepted. 🛜 ♿M 🛏 💻 🍽 🐾

🄰🄰🄰 ▼▼▼ Olde Harbour Inn ⒷⒷ
(912) 234-4100. **$159-$300, 7 day notice.** 508 E Factors Walk 31401. Lincoln St ramp off E Bay St. Ext corridors. **Pets:** Accepted.
🅂🄰🅅🄴 🛜 ⊠ 🛏 💻

🄰🄰🄰 ▼▼ Quality Inn Heart of Savannah Ⓜ
(912) 236-6321. **$89-$199.** 300 W Bay St 31401. Between N Montgomery and N Jefferson sts. Ext corridors. **Pets:** Small. $25 one-time fee/pet. Designated rooms, service with restrictions, supervision.
🅂🄰🅅🄴 🛜 ⊠ 🛏 💻

▼▼▼ Quality Inn Midtown Ⓜ
(912) 352-7100. **$75-$100.** 7100 Abercorn St 31406. Jct SR 21, 1.2 mi s on SR 204 (Abercorn St). Ext corridors. **Pets:** Accepted.
🛜 🛏 💻 🐾

▼▼▼ Residence Inn by Marriott Savannah Midtown ⊞
(912) 356-3266. **$109-$289.** 5710 White Bluff Rd 31405. Jct SR 21, 0.5 mi s. Int corridors. **Pets:** Small, other species. $100 one-time fee/room. Designated rooms, service with restrictions, crate.
🛜 ⊠ 🛏 💻 🐾 ⊠

ⓐⓐⓐ ◈◈◈ **Staybridge Suites Savannah Historic**
District 🏠 🐾

(912) 721-9000. **$99-$139.** 301 E Bay St 31401. Corner of Lincoln St. Int corridors. **Pets:** Large, other species. $75 one-time fee/room. Designated rooms, service with restrictions. 🆂🅰🆅🅴 📶 ♿ 🛏 💻

◈◈ **Super 8 Gateway** 🏠

(912) 925-6996. **$60-$95.** 387 Canebrake Rd 31419. I-95 exit 94 (SR 204/Abercorn St), just e, then s. Int corridors. **Pets:** Small. $10 daily fee/pet. Designated rooms, service with restrictions, supervision. 📶 ⓧ ♿ 🛏 💻

◈◈ **TownePlace Suites by Marriott Savannah**
Airport 🏠

(912) 629-7775. **$79-$139.** 4 Jay R Turner Dr 31408. I-95 exit 104, just e. Int corridors. **Pets:** Other species. $35 daily fee/room. Service with restrictions, crate. 📶 ⓧ ♿ 🛏 💻

◈◈ **TownePlace Suites by Marriott Savannah**
Midtown 🏠

(912) 920-9080. **$99-$249.** 11309 Abercorn St 31419. Jct SR 21 and 204 (Abercorn St), 4.6 mi s. Int corridors. **Pets:** Accepted. 📶 ⓧ 🛏 💻 ⤳

ⓐⓐⓐ ◈◈◈◈ **The Westin Savannah Harbor Golf Resort**
and Spa 🏠

(912) 201-2000. **$179-$449, 3 day notice.** 1 Resort Dr 31421. On Hutchinson Island; 1 mi se of first exit after Eugene Talmadge Memorial Bridge and US 17. Int corridors. **Pets:** Accepted. 🅴🅲🅾 🆂🅰🆅🅴 📶 ⓧ ♿ 🛏 💻 🍴 ⤳ ⓧ

◈◈ **Wingate by Wyndham Savannah Airport** 🏠 🐾

(912) 544-1180. **$89-$209.** 50 Sylvester C Formey Dr 31408. I-95 exit 104, 0.4 mi e. Int corridors. **Pets:** Medium, other species. $25 one-time fee/pet. Designated rooms, service with restrictions, supervision. 📶 ⓧ ♿ 🛏 💻 ⤳

STATESBORO

ⓐⓐⓐ ◈◈ **BEST WESTERN University Inn** Ⓜ

(912) 681-7900. **$59-$89.** 1 Jameson Ave 30458. Jct US 25/301 and SR 67, 0.9 mi s on US 25/301. Ext corridors. **Pets:** Accepted. 🆂🅰🆅🅴 📶 🛏 💻 ⤳

STOCKBRIDGE

ⓐⓐⓐ ◈◈◈ **La Quinta Inn & Suites Atlanta**
Stockbridge 🏠

(770) 506-9991. **$90-$155.** 3581 Cameron Pkwy 30281. I-75 exit 228, just e on SR 138, then just n; I-675 exit 1, just w on SR 138, then just n. Int corridors. **Pets:** Service with restrictions, supervision. 🆂🅰🆅🅴 📶 ♿ 🛏 💻 ⤳ ⓧ

◈◈ **Microtel Inn & Suites by Wyndham Stockbridge/Atlanta**
South/At Eagles Landing 🏠

(678) 782-6100. **$70-$110, 3 day notice.** 195 Country Club Dr 30281. I-75 exit 224, just e, then just s. Int corridors. **Pets:** Small. $10 daily fee/pet. Designated rooms, no service, crate. 📶 ♿ 🛏 💻 ⤳

◈◈ **Sleep Inn & Suites** 🏠

(770) 474-3870. **$70-$74.** 7423 Davidson Cir W 30281. I-675 exit 1, just e, then just s; I-75 exit 228, 1 mi e, then just s. Int corridors. **Pets:** $10 daily fee/pet. Designated rooms, service with restrictions, supervision. 📶 ⓧ ♿ 🛏 💻 ⤳

SWAINSBORO

ⓐⓐⓐ ◈◈◈ **BEST WESTERN Bradford Inn** 🏠

(478) 237-2400. **$65.** 688 S Main St 30401. I-16 exit 90 (US 1), 12.4 mi n. Ext corridors. **Pets:** Accepted. 🆂🅰🆅🅴 📶 🛏 💻 ⤳

THOMASTON

◈◈ **Quality Inn** Ⓜ

(706) 648-2232. **Call for rates.** 1010 Hwy 19 N 30286. Jct SR 74, 2.3 mi n. Ext corridors. **Pets:** Accepted. 📶 ♿ 🛏 💻 ⤳

THOMASVILLE

ⓐⓐⓐ ◈◈◈ **Quality Inn & Suites Conference Center** Ⓜ

(229) 225-2134. **$60-$75.** 15138 US Hwy 19 S 31757. 0.3 mi s of US 319. Ext corridors. **Pets:** Medium. $10 deposit/pet. Service with restrictions, supervision. 🆂🅰🆅🅴 📶 ♿ 🛏 💻 🍴 ⤳

THOMSON

ⓐⓐⓐ ◈◈◈ **BEST WESTERN White Columns Inn** Ⓜ

(706) 595-8000. **$85-$95.** 1890 Washington Rd 30824. I-20 exit 172 (US 78), just s. Ext corridors. **Pets:** $10 daily fee/pet. Designated rooms, service with restrictions, crate. 🆂🅰🆅🅴 📶 🛏 💻 ⤳

TIFTON

◈◈◈ **Country Inn & Suites By Carlson** 🏠

(229) 382-8100. **$70-$109.** 310 S Virginia Ave W 31794. I-75 exit 62, just e on US 82 and 319. Int corridors. **Pets:** Small. $25 daily fee/pet. Service with restrictions, supervision. 📶 ⓧ 🛏 💻 ⤳

◈◈ **Days Inn & Suites** 🏠

(229) 382-8505. **$57-$160.** 1199 Hwy 82 W 31793. I-75 exit 62, just w. Int corridors. **Pets:** Accepted. 📶 🛏 💻

VALDOSTA

ⓐⓐⓐ ◈◈◈ **BEST WESTERN PLUS Valdosta Hotel &**
Suites 🏠 🐾

(229) 241-9221. **$79-$109.** 4025 Northlake Dr 31602. I-75 exit 22, just e on N Valdosta Rd, then just n. Int corridors. **Pets:** Other species. $20 deposit/room. Designated rooms, service with restrictions. 🆂🅰🆅🅴 📶 ⓧ ♿ 🛏 💻 ⤳

ⓐⓐⓐ ◈◈◈ **Clarion Inn Conference Center** 🏠

(229) 242-1212. **$75-$100.** 2101 W Hill Ave 31602. I-75 exit 16, just w. Ext/int corridors. **Pets:** Medium. $25 daily fee/room. Service with restrictions, crate. 🆂🅰🆅🅴 📶 🛏 💻 🍴 ⤳ ⓧ

ⓐⓐⓐ ◈◈ **Econo Lodge** 🏠

(229) 671-1511. **$49-$89.** 3022 James Cir 31602. I-75 exit 18, just w. Int corridors. **Pets:** Accepted. 🆂🅰🆅🅴 📶 ♿ 🛏 💻 ⤳

◈◈ **Howard Johnson Valdosta** 🏠

(229) 244-4460. **$50-$60.** 4598 N Valdosta Rd 31602. I-75 exit 22, just w. Ext corridors. **Pets:** Medium. $10 daily fee/pet. Service with restrictions, supervision. 📶 🛏 💻 ⤳

ⓐⓐⓐ ◈◈◈ **La Quinta Inn & Suites Valdosta / Moody**
AFB 🏠

(229) 247-7755. **$77-$177.** 1800 Clubhouse Dr 31601. I-75 exit 18, 0.3 mi e, then just s off SR 94. Int corridors. **Pets:** Service with restrictions, supervision. 🆂🅰🆅🅴 📶 ⓧ 🛏 💻 ⤳ ⓧ

◈◈ **Quality Inn South** 🏠

(229) 244-4520. **$50-$70.** 1902 W Hill Ave 31601. I-75 exit 16, just e on US 84. Ext corridors. **Pets:** Medium, other species. $8 daily fee/pet. Service with restrictions, crate. 📶 🛏 💻 ⤳

VILLA RICA

◈◈ **Days Inn** 🏠

(770) 459-8888. **$63-$80.** 195 Hwy 61 Connector 30180. I-20 exit 24, just n. Int corridors. **Pets:** $10 daily fee/pet. Designated rooms, service with restrictions, supervision. 📶 ♿ 🛏 💻 ⤳

◈◈ **Super 8** Ⓜ

(770) 459-8000. **$55-$69, 3 day notice.** 128 Hwy 61 Connector 30180. I-20 exit 24, just n. Ext corridors. **Pets:** Accepted. 📶 🛏 💻 ⤳

WARNER ROBINS

◈◈ **Baymont Inn & Suites Warner Robins** 🏠

(478) 953-5522. **Call for rates.** 2731 Watson Blvd 31093. I-75 exit 146 (SR 247C), 4.1 mi e. Ext corridors. **Pets:** Medium. $15 daily fee/room. Service with restrictions, crate. 📶 🛏 💻 ⤳

AAA ▼▼▼ BEST WESTERN Peach Inn H
(478) 953-3800. **$56-$67.** 2739 Watson Blvd 31093. I-75 exit 146 (SR 247C), 4.1 mi e. Ext corridors. **Pets:** Other species. $10 daily fee/pet. Designated rooms, service with restrictions.

▼▼ Comfort Inn & Suites H
(478) 922-7555. **$79-$89.** 95 Georgia Hwy 247 S 31088. Jct SR 247C and US 129/SR 247, 1.6 mi s on US 129/SR 247. Ext/int corridors. **Pets:** Medium. $15 daily fee/room. Service with restrictions, crate.

WAYCROSS
▼▼ Baymont Inn & Suites Waycross M
(912) 283-3800. **Call for rates.** 950 City Blvd 31501. Between US 1 and 82; east of city. Ext corridors. **Pets:** Accepted.

▼▼▼ Comfort Suites H
(912) 548-0555. **$74-$89.** 1922 Memorial Dr 31501. Between US 1 and 82. Int corridors. **Pets:** Small. $20 one-time fee/pet. Designated rooms, service with restrictions, supervision.

▼▼▼ Holiday Inn Express & Suites H
(912) 548-0720. **$77-$99.** 1761 Memorial Dr 31501. Between US 1 and 82. Int corridors. **Pets:** Accepted.

WAYNESBORO
▼▼ Quality Inn M
(706) 437-0500. **Call for rates.** 1436 N Liberty St 30830. 0.9 mi n of downtown center on US 25. Ext corridors. **Pets:** Accepted.

WINDER
AAA ▼▼▼ BEST WESTERN Winder Hotel H
(770) 868-5303. **Call for rates.** 177 W Athens St 30680. Jct Broad St, 0.8 mi n; downtown. Int corridors. **Pets:** Accepted.

▼▼ Jameson Inn M
(770) 867-1880. **Call for rates.** 9 Stafford St 30680. Jct SR 81, 11, 53 and 8; center. Ext corridors. **Pets:** Accepted.

WOODSTOCK
▼▼▼ Comfort Suites H
(770) 517-9650. **$70-$119.** 340 Parkway 575 30188. I-575 exit 7, just e to Parkway 575, then just n. Int corridors. **Pets:** Accepted.

YOUNG HARRIS
▼▼▼ Brasstown Valley Resort H
(706) 379-9900. **$129-$269, 7 day notice.** 6321 US Hwy 76 30582. US 76 and US 76/SR 515. Int corridors. **Pets:** Medium, other species. $75 one-time fee/pet. Designated rooms.

HAWAII

HONOLULU METROPOLITAN AREA

HONOLULU
AAA ▼▼▼ Airport Honolulu Hotel H ❀
(808) 836-0661. **$115-$169, 3 day notice.** 3401 N Nimitz Hwy 96819. Jct Rodgers Blvd. Int corridors. **Pets:** Medium, other species. $25 daily fee/pet. Designated rooms, service with restrictions, crate.

▼▼▼ Aqua Lotus Honolulu H ❀
(808) 922-1700. **$199-$349, 3 day notice.** 2885 Kalakaua Ave 96815. East end of Kapiolani Park. Ext corridors. **Pets:** Small, dogs only. $100 deposit/room, $25 daily fee/pet. Service with restrictions, supervision.

▼▼ Aqua Waikiki Wave Hotel H
(808) 922-1262. **$127-$400, 3 day notice.** 2299 Kuhio Ave 96815. Just s of Seaside Ave. Int corridors. **Pets:** Accepted.

AAA ▼▼ BEST WESTERN The Plaza Hotel H ❀
(808) 836-3636. **$169-$189.** 3253 N Nimitz Hwy 96819. Just e of jct Paiea St. Ext/int corridors. **Pets:** Medium, other species. $25 daily fee/pet. Designated rooms, service with restrictions, crate.

▼▼▼ Hotel Renew H
(808) 687-7700. **$143-$399, 3 day notice.** 129 Paoakalani Ave 96815. Between Kalakaua Ave and Lemon Rd. Int corridors. **Pets:** Accepted.

AAA ▼▼▼▼ Hyatt Regency Waikiki Beach Resort & Spa H
(808) 923-1234. **$135-$432, 3 day notice.** 2424 Kalakaua Ave 96815. Between Kaiulani Ave and Uluniu St; entrance on Uluniu St. Int corridors. **Pets:** Accepted.

AAA ▼▼▼▼ The Kahala Hotel & Resort H ❀
(808) 739-8888. **$525-$10000, 3 day notice.** 5000 Kahala Ave 96816. E of Diamond Head at end of Kahala Ave. Int corridors. **Pets:** Medium, dogs only. $150 one-time fee/pet. Supervision.

▼▼▼▼ The Modern Honolulu H ❀
(808) 943-5800. **$359-$899, 3 day notice.** 1775 Ala Moana Blvd 96815. Jct Hobron Ln. Int corridors. **Pets:** Small. $50 daily fee/pet. Designated rooms, crate.

▼▼▼▼ Trump International Hotel Waikiki Beach Walk H
(808) 683-7777. **$379-$629, 3 day notice.** 223 Saratoga Rd 96815. Just sw on Kalakaua Ave via Saratoga Rd. Int corridors. **Pets:** Accepted.

KAHUKU
▼▼▼ Turtle Bay Resort H ❀
(808) 293-6000. **$249-$1399, 7 day notice.** 57-091 Kamehameha Hwy 96731. 3 mi nw off SR 83. Ext/int corridors. **Pets:** Small, dogs only. $150 deposit/room. Designated rooms, service with restrictions, supervision.

END METROPOLITAN AREA

KĀ'ANAPALI

Hyatt Regency Maui Resort & Spa 🅗 ❀

(808) 661-1234. **$234-$405, 3 day notice.** 200 Nohea Kai Dr 96761. Off SR 30, via Kaanapali Pkwy; in Kaanapali Beach resort area. Ext/int corridors. **Pets:** Small, dogs only. $50 daily fee/room. Designated rooms, service with restrictions.

KAUPULEHU

Four Seasons Resort Hualalai at Historic Ka'upulehu 🅗 ❀

(808) 325-8000. **$635-$1295, 21 day notice.** 72-100 Ka'upulehu Dr 96740. Off SR 19, 6 mi n of Kona International Airport, 1.3 mi sw. Ext corridors. **Pets:** Very small. Service with restrictions, supervision.

KOHALA COAST

The Fairmont Orchid, Hawaii 🅗 ❀

(808) 885-2000. **$449-$3900, 14 day notice.** 1 N Kaniku Dr 96743. On SR 19, 19 mi n of Kona International Airport, 2 mi w; in Mauna Lani resort area. Int corridors. **Pets:** Small. $25 daily fee/pet. Designated rooms, supervision.

Kings Land by Hilton Grand Vacations Club 🆒

(808) 881-3000. **$224-$589.** 69-699 Waikoloa Beach Dr 96738. Off SR 19, 17 mi n of Kona International Airport, 2 mi w; in Waikoloa Beach resort area. Ext corridors. **Pets:** Accepted.

LĀNA'I CITY

Four Seasons Resort Lana'i at Manele Bay 🅗

(808) 565-2000. **$399-$5399, 21 day notice.** 1 Manele Bay Rd 96763. From airport, 4 mi e on Kaumalapau Hwy to Lana'i City, 7 mi s on SR 440. Ext corridors. **Pets:** Accepted.

Four Seasons Resort Lana'i, The Lodge at Koele 🅗

(808) 565-4000. **$335-$1530, 21 day notice.** One Keomoku Hwy 96763. From airport, 4 mi e on Kaumalapau Hwy to Lana'i City, 2 mi n on SR 440, follow signs. Int corridors. **Pets:** Accepted.

WAILEA

Four Seasons Resort Maui at Wailea 🅗

(808) 874-8000. **$445-$1995, 21 day notice.** 3900 Wailea Alanui Dr 96753. From end of SR 31, 0.5 mi s. Int corridors. **Pets:** Accepted.

IDAHO

CITY INDEX

AHSAHKA

The High Country Inn - Orofino 🅱🅱

(208) 476-7570. **$89-$129, 7 day notice.** 70 High Country Ln 83520. 0.5 mi w to Dworshak Visitors Center Rd, 2 mi n, then just w, follow signs. Ext/int corridors. **Pets:** Medium, dogs only. $25 one-time fee/room. Crate.

ATHOL

Log Spirit Bed & Breakfast 🅱🅱

(208) 683-4722. **$140-$200, 14 day notice.** 31328 N Tiara Ln 83801. US 95, just e on SR 54 to Howard Rd, 1.8 mi n, then 0.5 mi e. Int corridors. **Pets:** Medium, dogs only. $25 daily fee/pet. Supervision.

BLACKFOOT

BEST WESTERN Blackfoot Inn 🅗 ❀

(208) 785-4144. **Call for rates.** 750 Jensen Grove Dr 83221. I-15 exit 93, 0.3 mi e to Parkway Dr, then 0.4 mi n. Int corridors. **Pets:** Large, dogs only. Service with restrictions, supervision.

BOISE

BEST WESTERN Airport Inn 🅼

(208) 384-5000. **$70-$100.** 2660 Airport Way 83705. I-84 exit 53 (Vista Ave), just s, then just e. Ext corridors. **Pets:** Dogs only. $10 deposit/pet, $10 daily fee/pet. Designated rooms, no service, supervision.

BEST WESTERN PLUS Northwest Lodge 🅗 ❀

(208) 287-2300. **Call for rates.** 6989 Federal Way 83716. I-84 exit 57 (Gowen Rd/Idaho City), just e, then just s. Int corridors. **Pets:** Medium, dogs only. $20 daily fee/room. Designated rooms, service with restrictions, supervision.

BEST WESTERN PLUS Vista Inn at the Airport 🅗

(208) 336-8100. **Call for rates.** 2645 Airport Way 83705. I-84 exit 53 (Vista Ave), just s. Ext/int corridors. **Pets:** Medium, dogs only. $20 daily fee/room. Designated rooms, service with restrictions, crate.

▼▼▼▼ Candlewood Suites - Boise Towne Square 🅷

(208) 322-4300. **$74-$109.** 700 N Cole Rd 83704. I-184 exit 1B westbound, just n; exit 1A eastbound, just e, then 0.5 mi n. Int corridors. **Pets:** Accepted.

AAA ▼▼▼ Fairfield Inn by Marriott - Airport 🅷

(208) 331-5656. **$79-$159.** 3300 S Shoshone St 83705. I-84 exit 53 (Vista Ave), just n to Elder St, then just w. Int corridors. **Pets:** Other species. $20 daily fee/pet. Service with restrictions, supervision.

▼▼▼▼ Hampton Inn Boise - Airport 🅷

(208) 331-5600. **$99-$149.** 3270 S Shoshone St 83705. I-84 exit 53 (Vista Ave), just n to Elder St, then just w. Int corridors. **Pets:** Small. Designated rooms, service with restrictions, supervision.

▼▼ Holiday Inn Express - Airport 🅷

(208) 388-0800. **Call for rates.** 2613 S Vista Ave 83705. I-84 exit 53 (Vista Ave), 0.6 mi n. Int corridors. **Pets:** Accepted.

AAA ▼▼▼ Inn America - Airport 🅷

(208) 389-9800. **$49-$69.** 2275 Airport Way 83705. I-84 exit 53 (Vista Ave), 0.3 mi se. Int corridors. **Pets:** Dogs only. $20 daily fee/room. Designated rooms, service with restrictions, supervision.

▼▼ Modern Hotel & Bar 🅷

(208) 424-8244. **Call for rates.** 1314 W Grove St 83702. At 14th and W Grove sts; downtown. Ext/int corridors. **Pets:** Accepted.

AAA ▼▼▼▼ Oxford Suites - Boise/Spectrum 🅷 🐾

(208) 322-8000. **$89-$169.** 1426 S Entertainment Ave 83709. I-84 exit 50A, just s to Spectrum Way, just w, then just n. Int corridors. **Pets:** Medium. Service with restrictions, crate.

▼▼▼ Red Lion Hotel Boise Downtowner 🅷

(208) 344-7691. **$69-$249.** 1800 Fairview Ave 83702. I-184 exit 3 (Fairview Ave), 1 mi n. Int corridors. **Pets:** Other species. $15 one-time fee/room. Service with restrictions, crate.

AAA ▼▼▼▼ Residence Inn by Marriott Boise West 🅷

(208) 385-9000. **$94-$129.** 7303 W Denton St 83704. I-84 exit 50A westbound; exit 50B eastbound, 2 mi n on Cole Rd, then just w. Int corridors. **Pets:** Accepted.

AAA ▼▼▼▼ Residence Inn by Marriott - Downtown 🅷

(208) 344-1200. **$99-$199.** 1401 S Lusk Ave 83706. I-84 exit 53 (Vista Ave), 2.4 mi n, just w on Ann Morrison Park Dr, then just s on Lois Ave. Ext corridors. **Pets:** Other species. $75 one-time fee/room. Service with restrictions, crate.

▼▼ The Riverside Hotel 🅷 🐾

(208) 343-1871. **$89-$159.** 2900 W Chinden Blvd 83714. I-84 exit 49 (Franklin Rd/City Center), 2.7 mi ne on I-184 exit 3 (Fairview Ave), just n, then just w. Int corridors. **Pets:** Large, other species. $35 one-time fee/room. Service with restrictions, supervision.

▼▼▼▼ Safari Inn Downtown 🅷

(208) 344-6556. **$69-$99.** 1070 Grove St 83702. Corner of 11th and Grove sts. Int corridors. **Pets:** $10 one-time fee/room. Designated rooms, service with restrictions, supervision.

▼▼ Shilo Inn Suites - Boise Airport 🅷

(208) 343-7662. **$59-$130.** 4111 Broadway Ave 83705. I-84 exit 54 (Broadway Ave), just sw. Int corridors. **Pets:** Dogs only. $25 one-time fee/room. Designated rooms, service with restrictions, supervision.

▼▼▼▼ SpringHill Suites by Marriott - Boise 🅷

(208) 939-8266. **$99-$139.** 6325 N Cloverdale Rd 83713. I-84 exit 46 (Eagle Rd), 4.3 mi n to Chinden Blvd, 0.9 mi e, then just s; in Boise Research Center. Int corridors. **Pets:** Accepted.

▼▼▼▼ SpringHill Suites by Marriott - Boise/ParkCenter 🅷

(208) 342-1044. **$89-$169.** 424 E ParkCenter Blvd 83706. I-84 exit 54 (Broadway Ave), 2.3 mi n to Beacon St, 0.3 mi e, then 0.7 mi se. Int corridors. **Pets:** Accepted.

AAA ▼▼▼▼ TownePlace Suites by Marriott - Downtown 🅷

(208) 429-8881. **$89-$179.** 1455 S Capitol Blvd 83706. I-84 exit 53 (Vista Ave), 2.4 mi n. Int corridors. **Pets:** Other species. $50 one-time fee/room. Service with restrictions, supervision.

BONNERS FERRY

AAA ▼▼▼ BEST WESTERN PLUS Kootenai River Inn Casino & Spa 🅷

(208) 267-8511. **$104-$150.** 7169 Plaza St 83805. On US 95; city center. Int corridors. **Pets:** Other species. $20 daily fee/pet. Service with restrictions, supervision.

▼▼▼▼ Northside School Bed & Breakfast 🅱🅱

(208) 267-1826. **$80-$140.** 6497 Comanche St 83805. US 95, w on Chinook St, just n on Bingham St, then just e. Int corridors. **Pets:** Small, dogs only. $10 one-time fee/room. Designated rooms, service with restrictions, supervision.

BURLEY

AAA ▼▼▼▼ BEST WESTERN PLUS Burley Inn & Convention Center 🅷

(208) 678-3501. **$75-$100.** 800 N Overland Ave 83318. I-84 exit 208, just s. Ext/int corridors. **Pets:** Medium. $10 daily fee/pet. Designated rooms, service with restrictions, supervision.

AAA ▼▼▼ Super 8 Burley 🅷

(208) 678-7000. **$75-$129.** 336 S 600 W 83318. I-84 exit 208, just n. Int corridors. **Pets:** Accepted.

CALDWELL

AAA ▼▼▼ BEST WESTERN PLUS Caldwell Inn & Suites 🅷

(208) 454-7225. **$71-$99.** 908 Specht Ave 83605. I-84 exit 29, just s. Int corridors. **Pets:** Accepted.

▼▼ La Quinta Inn Caldwell 🅷

(208) 454-2222. **$59-$144.** 901 Specht Ave 83605. I-84 exit 29, just s. Int corridors. **Pets:** Service with restrictions, supervision.

COEUR D'ALENE

AAA ▼▼▼ BEST WESTERN PLUS Coeur d'Alene Inn 🅷 🐾

(208) 765-3200. **Call for rates.** W 506 Appleway Ave 83814. I-90 exit 12, just nw. Int corridors. **Pets:** Large, dogs only. $20 daily fee/room. Service with restrictions, crate.

▼▼ ▼▼ The Coeur d'Alene Resort 🅷

(208) 765-4000. **$129-$549, 3 day notice.** 115 S 2nd St 83814. I-90 exit 11 (Northwest Blvd), 2 mi s. Ext/int corridors. **Pets:** Medium. $75 daily fee/room. Service with restrictions.

▼▼ **Comfort Inn Coeur d'Alene** H
(208) 664-1649. **Call for rates.** 2303 N 4th St 83814. I-90 exit 13 (4th St), just n. Int corridors. **Pets:** Other species. $30 one-time fee/pet. Designated rooms, service with restrictions, crate. 🛰 ✕ 🛏 💻 🚬

▼▼ **Days Inn-Coeur d'Alene** H
(208) 667-8668. **$70-$200.** 2200 Northwest Blvd 83814. I-90 exit 11 (Northwest Blvd), just se. Int corridors. **Pets:** Accepted.
🛰 ✕ 🚹 🛏 💻

▼▼▼ **Holiday Inn Express Hotel & Suites Coeur d'Alene** H
(208) 667-3100. **Call for rates.** 2300 W Seltice Way 83814. I-90 exit 11 (Northwest Blvd), just s. Int corridors. **Pets:** Dogs only. $15 one-time fee/room. Designated rooms, service with restrictions, supervision.
🛰 ✕ 🛏 💻 🚬

▼▼ **La Quinta Inn & Suites Coeur d'Alene East** H
(208) 667-6777. **$90-$243.** 2209 E Sherman Ave 83814. I-90 exit 15 (Sherman Ave), just s. Int corridors. **Pets:** Service with restrictions, supervision. 🛰 🚹 🛏 💻 🚬

▼▼ **La Quinta Inn Coeur d'Alene Appleway** H
(208) 765-5500. **$71-$210.** 280 W Appleway Ave 83814. I-90 exit 12, just ne. Int corridors. **Pets:** Service with restrictions, supervision.
🛰 ✕ 🚹 🛏 💻 🚬 ✕

▼▼▼ **The Roosevelt Inn and Spa** BB
(208) 765-5200. **$99-$339, 14 day notice.** 105 E Wallace Ave 83814. I-90 exit 13 (4th St), 2 mi s, then just w; downtown. Int corridors. **Pets:** Other species. $25 one-time fee/room. Designated rooms, supervision. 🛰 ✕ ✕ 🎬 🎵

▼▼ **Shilo Inn Suites - Coeur d'Alene** H
(208) 664-2300. **$60-$140.** 702 W Appleway Ave 83814. I-90 exit 12, just n, then just w. Int corridors. **Pets:** Dogs only. $25 one-time fee/room. Designated rooms, service with restrictions, supervision.
🛰 ✕ 🚹 🛏 💻 🚬 ✕

GRANGEVILLE
▼ **Down Towner Inn** M
(208) 983-1110. **$55-$70.** 113 E North St 83530. Jct US 95 and SR 13, 0.5 mi e to Hall St, then just n. Ext corridors. **Pets:** Accepted.
🛰 ✕ 🛏

◈◈◈ ▼▼▼ **Gateway Inn - Grangeville** M
(208) 983-2500. **$55-$99.** 700 W Main St 83530. Jct US 95 and SR 13. Ext corridors. **Pets:** $10 daily fee/room. Designated rooms, service with restrictions, supervision. 💾 🛰 ✕ 🚹 💻

HAGERMAN
◈◈◈ ▼ **Hagerman Valley Inn** M
(208) 837-6196. **$65-$108.** 661 Frog's Landing 83332. South end of town on US 30. Ext corridors. **Pets:** $10 one-time fee/room. Designated rooms, service with restrictions, supervision. 💾 🛰 ✕ 🚹 💻 🍴

HAILEY
▼▼ **Airport Inn** M
(208) 788-2477. **$80-$150, 3 day notice.** 820 S 4th Ave 83333. 1 mi s of center to 4th Ave via Main St (SR 75); south end of town. Ext corridors. **Pets:** Accepted. 🛰 🚹 💻

▼▼▼ **AmericInn Lodge & Suites-Hailey/Sun Valley** H
(208) 788-7950. **Call for rates.** 51 Cobblestone Ln 83333. 0.5 mi n of center. Int corridors. **Pets:** Dogs only. $25 one-time fee/room. Designated rooms, service with restrictions, supervision.
🛰 ✕ 🚹 💻 🚬 ✕

▼▼▼ **Wood River Inn** H
(208) 578-0600. **$89-$159.** 603 N Main St 83333. 0.3 mi n of center. Int corridors. **Pets:** Large. $25 one-time fee/room. Designated rooms, supervision. 🛰 ✕ 🚹 💻 🚬 ✕

HAYDEN
▼▼▼ **Holiday Inn Express Hotel & Suites** H 🐾
(208) 772-7900. **$90-$399.** 151 W Orchard Ave 83835. I-90 exit 12, 3.5 mi n. Int corridors. **Pets:** Other species. $10 daily fee/pet. Service with restrictions, supervision. 🛰 ✕ 🚹 🛏 💻 ✕

IDAHO FALLS
◈◈◈ ▼▼▼ **BEST WESTERN PLUS CottonTree Inn** H
(208) 523-6000. **$79-$169.** 900 Lindsay Blvd 83402. I-15 exit 119, just e. Int corridors. **Pets:** Large, other species. $15 daily fee/pet. Service with restrictions, crate. ECO 💾 🛰 🚹 💻 🚬

◈◈◈ ▼▼▼ **BEST WESTERN PLUS Driftwood Inn** M
(208) 523-2242. **$79-$149.** 575 River Pkwy 83402. I-15 exit 118 (Broadway), 0.5 mi e, then 0.3 mi n. Ext corridors. **Pets:** Other species. $10 daily fee/room. Service with restrictions, supervision.
💾 🛰 ✕ 🚹 💻 🚬 ✕

▼▼ **Candlewood Suites** H
(208) 525-9800. **$79-$150.** 665 Pancheri Dr 83402. I-15 exit 118 (Broadway), 1 mi e (cross bridge), 0.5 mi s on S Capital Ave. Int corridors. **Pets:** Accepted. 🛰 🚹 💻

▼▼ **Hotel on the Falls** H
(208) 523-8000. **Call for rates.** 475 River Pkwy 83402. I-15 exit 118 (Broadway), 0.5 mi e, then just n. Ext/int corridors. **Pets:** Medium. $15 daily fee/pet. Designated rooms, service with restrictions, supervision.
🛰 🚹 💻 🍴 🚬 ✕

◈◈◈ ▼▼▼ **Le Ritz Hotel & Suites** H 🐾
(208) 528-0880. **$78-$128.** 720 Lindsay Blvd 83402. I-15 exit 118 (Broadway), 0.5 mi e, then just n. Int corridors. **Pets:** $15 daily fee/room. Designated rooms, service with restrictions, crate.
💾 🛰 🚹 💻 🚬

JACKSON HOLE AREA (NEARBY WYOMING)

DRIGGS
▼▼ **Teton Valley Cabins** M
(208) 354-8153. **$69-$99, 7 day notice.** 388 Ski Hill Rd 83422. 0.8 mi e on Little Ave from SR 33 E. Ext corridors. **Pets:** Dogs only. $10 daily fee/room. Designated rooms, service with restrictions, supervision.
🛰 ✕ 🚹 💻 ✕ 🐾

END AREA

JEROME

 BEST WESTERN PLUS Sawtooth Inn & Suites 🅷 🐾

(208) 324-9200. **$69-$109.** 2653 S Lincoln Ave 83338. I-84 exit 168, just n. Int corridors. **Pets:** Other species. $100 deposit/room. Designated rooms, service with restrictions. 🆂🆅 📶 ⊠ 🔌 💻 ⇢ 🚫

Comfort Inn & Suites 🅷

(208) 644-1200. **Call for rates.** 379 Crossroads Point Blvd 83338. I-84 exit 173, 0.3 mi n. Int corridors. **Pets:** Medium. $10 daily fee/pet. Designated rooms, service with restrictions, supervision.

📶 ⊠ 🔌 💻 🏊

Days Inn Twin Falls/Jerome 🅷 🐾

(208) 324-6400. **$69-$106.** 1200 Centennial Spur 83338. I-84 exit 173, just n on US 93. Int corridors. **Pets:** Medium, other species. $15 daily fee/pet. Designated rooms, service with restrictions, supervision.

📶 🔌 💻

KAMIAH

Clearwater 12 Motel 🅼

(208) 935-2671. **Call for rates.** 108 E 3rd St (Hwy 12) 83536. On US 12, just e of center. Ext corridors. **Pets:** Accepted. 📶 🔌 💻

KELLOGG

GuestHouse Inn & Suites 🅷

(208) 783-1234. **$79-$259.** 601 Bunker Ave 83837. I-90 exit 49, 0.5 mi se. Int corridors. **Pets:** Other species. $10 daily fee/pet. Service with restrictions, crate. 📶 🔌 💻 ⇢ 🚫

Morning Star Lodge 🅒🅞

(208) 783-0202. **$101-$400.** 602 Bunker Ave 83837. I-90 exit 49, 0.5 mi se. Int corridors. **Pets:** Accepted. ⊠ 🔌 💻 🍴 🚫

Silverhorn Motor Inn 🅷 🐾

(208) 783-1151. **$69-$120.** 699 W Cameron Ave 83837. I-90 exit 49, just ne. Int corridors. **Pets:** Other species. Supervision. 📶 🔌 🍴

KETCHUM

 BEST WESTERN Tyrolean Lodge 🅷

(208) 726-5336. **Call for rates.** 260 Cottonwood St 83340. Just s of center to Rivers St, w to 2nd Ave, s to Cottonwood St, then just w. Int corridors. **Pets:** Accepted. 🆂🆅 📶 ⊠ 🔌 💻 ⇢ 🚫

Tamarack Lodge 🅼

(208) 726-3344. **$101-$179.** 291 Walnut Ave N 83340. 0.3 mi e on Sun Valley Rd. Ext/int corridors. **Pets:** Large. $25 one-time fee/room. Supervision. 📶 ⊠ 🔌 💻 🏊

KOOSKIA

River Dance Lodge Resort 🅒🅐

(208) 926-4300. **Call for rates.** 7743 Hwy 12 83539. On US 12, 16 mi e of Kooskia at MM 89. Ext corridors. **Pets:** Accepted.

📶 🔌 💻 🍴 🚫 🅚 🅦 🅩

LEWISTON

Holiday Inn Express 🅷

(208) 750-1600. **Call for rates.** 2425 Nez Perce Dr 83501. 1.2 mi s on US 12 from jct US 95, 1.2 mi s on 21st St, then just e. Int corridors. **Pets:** Other species. $10 daily fee/room. Service with restrictions, supervision. 🆂🆅 📶 ⊠ 🅜 🔌 💻 🏊

Inn America 🅼

(208) 746-4600. **Call for rates.** 702 21st St 83501. 1.2 mi s on US 12 from jct US 95, just s. Int corridors. **Pets:** Accepted.

📶 🅜 🔌 💻 🏊

MCCALL

Americas Best Value Inn & Suites 🅷 🐾

(208) 634-6300. **$69-$129.** 415 N 3rd St 83638. 0.4 mi s of center on SR 55. Int corridors. **Pets:** $10 daily fee/pet. Service with restrictions, crate. 📶 ⊠ 🔌 💻 🏊

BEST WESTERN PLUS McCall Lodge & Suites 🅷 🐾

(208) 634-2230. **$100-$180.** 211 S 3rd St 83638. 1 mi s of center on SR 55. Int corridors. **Pets:** Large, dogs only. $20 daily fee/room. Designated rooms, service with restrictions, supervision.

🆂🆅 📶 ⊠ 🅜 🔌 💻 🏊 🚫

Shore Lodge 🅷

(208) 634-2244. **Call for rates.** 501 W Lake St 83638. 1 mi w of center on SR 55. Int corridors. **Pets:** Accepted.

🆂🆅 📶 ⊠ 🔌 💻 🍴 🏊 🚫

Super 8 🅷 🐾

(208) 634-4637. **$69-$139.** 303 S 3rd St 83638. 1.1 mi s of center on SR 55. Int corridors. **Pets:** Other species. $10 one-time fee/room. Designated rooms, service with restrictions, supervision. 📶 🔌 💻

MERIDIAN

BEST WESTERN PLUS Rama Inn 🅷

(208) 887-7888. **$65-$90.** 1019 S Progress Ave 83642. I-84 exit 44 (Meridian/Kuna), just ne. Int corridors. **Pets:** Accepted.

🆂🆅 📶 ⊠ 🔌 💻 🏊

Candlewood Suites - Meridian/West Boise 🅷 🐾

(208) 888-5121. **$80-$100.** 1855 S Silverstone Way 83642. I-84 exit 46 (Eagle Rd), 0.6 mi s, just e on Overland Rd, then just s. Int corridors. **Pets:** Medium. $13 daily fee/room. Service with restrictions, crate.

📶 🅜 🔌 💻 🚫

Country Inn & Suites By Carlson-Boise West 🅷

(208) 639-3300. **Call for rates.** 3355 E Pine Ave 83642. I-84 exit 46 (Eagle Rd), 0.7 mi n, then just e. Int corridors. **Pets:** $35 one-time fee/ pet. Service with restrictions, supervision.

🆂🆅 📶 ⊠ 🔌 💻 ⇢ 🚫

Holiday Inn Express & Suites Boise West - Meridian 🅷

(208) 288-2060. **$95-$143.** 2610 E Freeway Dr 83642. I-84 exit 46 (Eagle Rd), just n, then 0.3 mi w. Int corridors. **Pets:** Dogs only. $200 deposit/room, $30 daily fee/pet. Designated rooms, service with restrictions, crate. 🆂🆅 📶 ⊠ 🔌 💻 ⇢ 🚫

TownePlace Suites by Marriott - Meridian/West Boise 🅷 🐾

(208) 884-8550. **$89-$139.** 1415 S Eagle Rd 83642. I-84 exit 46 (Eagle Rd), just sw. Int corridors. **Pets:** Large. $50 one-time fee/room. Service with restrictions, crate. 🆂🆅 📶 ⊠ 🔌 💻 🏊

MONTPELIER

Clover Creek Inn & Suites 🅼

(208) 847-1782. **$75-$125.** 243 N 4th St 83254. On US 30, just n of jct US 89. Ext corridors. **Pets:** Dogs only. $10 one-time fee/pet. Designated rooms, service with restrictions, supervision. 🆂🆅 📶 🔌 💻

MOSCOW

BEST WESTERN PLUS University Inn 🅷 🐾

(208) 882-0550. **$100-$200.** 1516 Pullman Rd 83843. Jct US 95, 1 mi w on SR 8. Int corridors. **Pets:** Medium. $20 daily fee/room. Designated rooms, service with restrictions, crate.

🆂🆅 📶 ⊠ 🅜 🔌 💻 🍴 ⇢ 🚫

La Quinta Inn & Suites Moscow Pullman
(208) 882-5365. **$90-$243.** 185 Warbonnet Dr 83843. 1.6 mi w on SR 8 from jct US 95, just n. Int corridors. **Pets:** Service with restrictions, supervision.

Super 8
(208) 883-1503. **$66-$196.** 175 Peterson Dr 83843. Jct US 95, 0.8 mi w on SR 8, just n. Int corridors. **Pets:** Accepted.

MOUNTAIN HOME

BEST WESTERN Foothills Inn
(208) 587-8477. **$94-$134.** 1080 Hwy 20 83647. I-84 exit 95, just n. Ext corridors. **Pets:** Large, dogs only. $15 daily fee/room. Designated rooms, service with restrictions, supervision.

Mountain Home Inn
(208) 587-9743. **$84-$99.** 1180 Hwy 20 83647. I-84 exit 95, just n. Int corridors. **Pets:** Small. $10 daily fee/room. Service with restrictions, supervision.

NAMPA

Sleep Inn
(208) 463-6300. **Call for rates.** 1315 Industrial Rd 83687. I-84 exit 36 (Franklin Blvd), just s. Int corridors. **Pets:** Accepted.

OROFINO

BEST WESTERN PLUS Lodge at River's Edge
(208) 476-9999. **$91-$116.** 615 Main St 83544. From US 12, 0.3 mi e to Main St, then 0.3 mi s. Int corridors. **Pets:** Small, dogs only. $20 daily fee/pet. Designated rooms, service with restrictions, supervision.

Helgeson Hotel
(208) 476-5729. **$56-$77.** 125 Johnson Ave 83544. US 12, 0.3 mi e. Int corridors. **Pets:** Medium, dogs only. $20 daily fee/pet. Designated rooms, service with restrictions, supervision.

Konkolville Motel
(208) 476-5584. **Call for rates.** 2600 Michigan Ave 83544. US 12, 3 mi e. Ext corridors. **Pets:** Accepted.

POCATELLO

BEST WESTERN PLUS CottonTree Inn
(208) 237-7650. **$100.** 1415 Bench Rd 83201. I-15 exit 71, just e. Int corridors. **Pets:** Other species. Service with restrictions, supervision.

Clarion Inn
(208) 237-1400. **$89-$119.** 1399 Bench Rd 83201. I-15 exit 71, just e. Ext/int corridors. **Pets:** Accepted.

Red Lion Hotel
(208) 233-2200. **Call for rates.** 1555 Pocatello Creek Rd 83201. I-15 exit 71, just e. Int corridors. **Pets:** Other species. $15 one-time fee/room. Service with restrictions, crate.

Super 8
(208) 234-0888. **$60-$100.** 1330 Bench Rd 83201. I-15 exit 71, just e. Int corridors. **Pets:** Other species. $15 one-time fee/room. Designated rooms, service with restrictions, supervision.

Thunderbird Motel
(208) 232-6330. **$46-$59.** 1415 S 5th Ave 83201. I-15 exit 67 (5th Ave), 1.3 mi n; just s of Idaho State University. Ext corridors. **Pets:** Other species. $5 daily fee/pet. Service with restrictions, supervision.

TownePlace Suites by Marriott
(208) 478-7000. **$114-$199.** 2376 Via Caporatti Dr 83201. I-15 exit 69 (Clark St), 0.3 mi e. Int corridors. **Pets:** Large, other species. $50 one-time fee/room. Service with restrictions, crate.

PONDERAY

GuestHouse Lodge-Sandpoint
(208) 263-2210. **$45-$153.** 476841 Hwy 95 N 83852. 0.7 mi n on US 95 from jct SR 200. Int corridors. **Pets:** Dogs only. $10 daily fee/pet. Designated rooms, service with restrictions, crate.

Holiday Inn Express & Suites
(208) 255-4500. **Call for rates.** 477326 Hwy 95 N 83852. 0.7 mi n on US 95 from jct SR 200. Int corridors. **Pets:** Small. $10 daily fee/room. Designated rooms, service with restrictions, supervision.

Howard Johnson Sandpoint/Ponderay
(208) 263-5383. **$56-$141.** 477255 Hwy 95 N 83852. 1.2 mi n on US 95 from jct SR 200. Int corridors. **Pets:** Accepted.

POST FALLS

Red Lion Templin's Hotel on the River - Post Falls
(208) 773-1611. **$139-$229.** 414 E First Ave 83854. I-90 exit 5 eastbound, just s to First Ave; exit 6 westbound, 0.7 mi w on Seltice Way to Spokane St, 0.5 mi s, then just e. Int corridors. **Pets:** Other species. $15 one-time fee/room. Service with restrictions, crate.

Sleep Inn
(208) 777-9394. **Call for rates.** 157 S Pleasant View Rd 83854. I-90 exit 2, just s. Int corridors. **Pets:** Medium, dogs only. $15 one-time fee/room. Service with restrictions, supervision.

PRIEST RIVER

Eagle's Nest Motel
(208) 448-2000. **$59-$125, 3 day notice.** 5722 Hwy 2 83856. US 2, 0.5 mi w. Ext corridors. **Pets:** Accepted.

REXBURG

AmericInn Lodge & Suites of Rexburg
(208) 356-5333. **$89-$210.** 1098 Golden Beauty Dr 83440. US 20 exit 332 (S Rexburg). Int corridors. **Pets:** Accepted.

Quality Inn
(208) 359-1311. **$74-$139.** 885 W Main St 83440. US 20 exit 333 (Salmon), just e. Int corridors. **Pets:** Medium. Service with restrictions, supervision.

RIGBY

Blue Heron Inn
(208) 745-9922. **$109-$199, 7 day notice.** 706 N Yellowstone Hwy 83442. US 20 exit 325, just e. Ext/int corridors. **Pets:** Accepted.

RIGGINS

BEST WESTERN PLUS Salmon Rapids Lodge
(208) 628-2743. **$90-$127.** 1010 S Main St 83549. 0.3 mi s of center. Int corridors. **Pets:** Dogs only. $15 deposit/pet, $15 daily fee/pet. Designated rooms, service with restrictions, supervision.

▼▼ ▼▼ Pinehurst Resort Cabins & RV
(208) 628-3323. **$65-$95.** 5604 Hwy 95 83654. MM 182 on US 95; 13 mi s of center. Ext corridors. **Pets:** Accepted.

SAGLE

▼▼ ▼▼ Bottle Bay Resort & Marina 🅲🅰
(208) 265-0951. **Call for rates.** 115 Resort Rd 83860. 8.3 mi e on Bottle Bay Rd from US 95. Ext corridors. **Pets:** Accepted.

(AAA) ▼▼▼ The Lodge at Sandpoint 🅷
(208) 263-2211. **$99-$459, 14 day notice.** 41 Lakeshore Dr 83860. 1 mi s of Sandpoint on US 95; just s of Long Bridge. Int corridors. **Pets:** Dogs only. $20 daily fee/pet. Designated rooms, service with restrictions, supervision.

ST. ANTHONY

▼▼ ▼▼ GuestHouse International Henry's Fork Inn 🅷 🐾
(208) 624-3711. **$60-$98.** 115 S Bridge St 83445. US 20 exit 346, just e. Ext corridors. **Pets:** Other species. $10 daily fee/pet. Designated rooms, service with restrictions, supervision.

SALMON

▼▼ ▼▼ Stagecoach Inn Ⓜ
(208) 756-2919. **Call for rates.** 201 Riverfront Dr (US 93 N) 83467. Just n on US 93 from jct SR 28. Int corridors. **Pets:** Accepted.

SANDPOINT

(AAA) ▼▼▼ BEST WESTERN PLUS Edgewater Resort 🅷
(208) 263-3194. **$149-$299.** 56 Bridge St 83864. Just e of US 95; downtown. Int corridors. **Pets:** Accepted.

▼▼▼ La Quinta Inn Sandpoint 🅷
(208) 263-9581. **$71-$243.** 415 Cedar St 83864. Jct US 2 and 95; downtown. Ext/int corridors. **Pets:** Service with restrictions, supervision.

▼▼ ▼▼ Quality Inn Sandpoint 🅷
(208) 263-2111. **$79-$159.** 807 N 5th Ave 83864. US 2 and 95, just s of jct SR 200. Int corridors. **Pets:** Other species. $10 daily fee/pet. Service with restrictions, supervision.

STANLEY

(AAA) ▼▼ Jerrys Country Store, Cabins & Motel Ⓜ
(208) 774-3566. **$80-$140, 7 day notice.** 55 Lower Stanley (US Hwy 75) 83278. 1 mi n of jct US 75 and SR 21. Ext corridors. **Pets:** $10 daily fee/pet. Service with restrictions, supervision.

TWIN FALLS

(AAA) ▼▼▼ BEST WESTERN PLUS Twin Falls Hotel 🅷 🐾
(208) 736-8000. **Call for rates.** 1377 Blue Lakes Blvd N 83301. I-84 exit 173, 4 mi s on US 93. Int corridors. **Pets:** $20 daily fee/room. Designated rooms, service with restrictions, supervision.

▼▼▼ La Quinta Inn & Suites 🅷
(208) 736-9600. **$96-$177.** 539 Pole Line Rd 83301. I-84 exit 173, 3 mi s to Pole Line Rd, then 0.3 mi w. Int corridors. **Pets:** Service with restrictions, supervision.

▼▼ ▼▼ Quality Inn & Suites 🅷
(208) 734-7494. **$79-$139.** 1910 Fillmore St N 83301. I-84 exit 173, 3.1 mi s to Fillmore St, then 0.5 mi sw. Int corridors. **Pets:** $20 daily fee/pet. Service with restrictions, supervision.

(AAA) ▼▼▼ Red Lion Hotel Canyon Springs 🅷
(208) 734-5000. **$79-$129.** 1357 Blue Lakes Blvd N 83301. I-84 exit 173, 4 mi s on US 93. Int corridors. **Pets:** Other species. $15 one-time fee/room. Service with restrictions, crate.

▼▼ ▼▼ Shilo Inn Suites Hotel - Twin Falls 🅷
(208) 733-7545. **$77-$170.** 1586 Blue Lakes Blvd N 83301. I-84 exit 173, 3.7 mi s on US 93. Int corridors. **Pets:** Dogs only. $25 one-time fee/room. Designated rooms, service with restrictions, supervision.

▼▼ ▼▼ Super 8 Twin Falls Ⓜ
(208) 734-5801. **$62-$115.** 1260 Blue Lakes Blvd N 83301. I-84 exit 173, 4 mi s, then just s of College Rd. Int corridors. **Pets:** Medium, other species. $10 daily fee/pet. Service with restrictions, supervision.

WALLACE

(AAA) ▼▼▼ The Wallace Inn 🅷
(208) 752-1252. **$72-$175.** 100 Front St 83873. I-90 exit 61 (Business Rt 90), just se. Int corridors. **Pets:** Other species. $20 daily fee/room. Service with restrictions, supervision.

WHITE BIRD

▼▼ ▼▼ Hells Canyon Jet Boat Trips & Lodging Ⓜ
(208) 839-2255. **$70-$80, 7 day notice.** 3252 Waterfront Dr 83554. Take the White Bird exit off US 95, then 1 mi s of center. Ext corridors. **Pets:** $15 daily fee/pet. Service with restrictions, crate.

WORLEY

▼▼▼ Coeur d'Alene Casino Resort Hotel 🅷
(208) 769-2600. **Call for rates.** 27068 S Hwy 95 83876. On US 95, 3 mi n. Int corridors. **Pets:** Accepted.

ILLINOIS

ALTON

▲▲▲ ▼▼▼▼ BEST WESTERN PLUS Parkway Hotel 🅷
(618) 433-9900. **$86-$140.** 1900 Homer M Adams Pkwy 62002. On SR 111, 1.8 mi e of jct US 67. Int corridors. **Pets:** Large. $10 daily fee/pet. Service with restrictions, crate. SAVE 🛜 ✕ 🅼 🛗 💻 🏊

▼▼ Comfort Inn 🅷
(618) 465-9999. **$90-$110.** 11 Crossroads Ct 62002. Off SR 3, jct SR 140. Int corridors. **Pets:** Accepted. 🛜 🅼 🛗 💻 🏊

ANNAWAN

▲▲▲ ▼▼▼▼ BEST WESTERN Annawan Inn 🅷
(309) 935-6565. **Call for rates.** 315 N Canal St 61234. I-80 exit 33, just s. Int corridors. **Pets:** $25 daily fee/pet. Designated rooms, service with restrictions, supervision. SAVE 🛜 🅼 🛗 💻 🏊

ARCOLA

▼▼ Comfort Inn 🅷
(217) 268-4000. **Call for rates.** 610 E Springfield Rd 61910. I-57 exit 203 (SR 133), just w. Int corridors. **Pets:** Medium. $10 daily fee/pet. Crate. 🛜 🛗 💻 🏊

BLOOMINGTON

▲▲▲ ▼▼ Baymont Inn & Suites 🅷
(309) 662-2800. **$74-$95.** 604 1/2 IAA Dr 61701. I-55 exit 167 southbound, follow I-55 business route (Veterans Pkwy), 2.8 mi s to jct SR 9, just e, then just n via service road; exit 157B (Veterans Pkwy) northbound, 4 mi n to SR 9. Int corridors. **Pets:** Large, other species. $10 daily fee/pet. Service with restrictions, crate. SAVE 🛜 🛗 💻 🏊

▼▼▼ The Chateau Hotel and Conference Center 🅷
(309) 662-2020. **$79-$119.** 1601 Jumer Dr 61704. I-55 exit 167, follow I-55 business route (Veterans Pkwy), just e; 1.3 mi n of jct SR 9; 1 mi s of jct I-55. Int corridors. **Pets:** Accepted. 🛜 🛗 💻 🏊 ✕

▼▼ Country Inn & Suites By Carlson Bloomington/Normal West 🅷 🐾
(309) 828-7177. **$79-$129.** 923 Maple Hill Rd 61704. I-55/74 exit 160 (SR 9), 0.3 mi w to Wylie Dr, just n, then just e. Int corridors. **Pets:** $25 daily fee/room. Service with restrictions, crate.
🛜 ✕ 🅼 🛗 💻 🏊

▼▼▼ Doubletree Hotel & Conference Center-Bloomington 🅷
(309) 664-6446. **$98-$179.** 10 Brickyard Dr 61701. I-55 business route (Veterans Pkwy), just n of US 150. Int corridors. **Pets:** Accepted.
🛜 🛗 💻 🍴 🏊 ✕

▼▼▼ Eastland Suites Hotel & Conference Center 🅷
(309) 662-0000. **Call for rates.** 1801 Eastland Dr 61704. Jct I-55 business route (Veterans Pkwy) and SR 9, just s to Eastland Dr, then just e. Ext/int corridors. **Pets:** Accepted. 🛜 🛗 💻 🏊

▼▼▼ Holiday Inn Express Bloomington West 🅷
(309) 820-9990. **$104-$129, 3 day notice.** 1031 Wylie Dr 61705. I-55/74 exit 160 (SR 9), just w, then just n. Int corridors. **Pets:** Medium. $50 deposit/pet, $15 daily fee/pet. Service with restrictions, crate.
🛜 ✕ 🛗 💻 🏊

▼▼▼ Holiday Inn Hotel & Suites 🅷 🐾
(309) 662-4700. **$89-$179.** 3202 E Empire St 61704. Jct I-55 business route (Veterans Pkwy) and SR 9, 2.3 mi e on SR 9. Int corridors. **Pets:** Dogs only. $20 daily fee/room. Designated rooms, service with restrictions, supervision. 🛜 ✕ 🅼 🛗 💻 🍴 🏊 ✕

▼▼▼ La Quinta Inn Bloomington - Normal 🅷
(309) 828-6000. **$60-$145.** 505 Brock Dr 61701. I-55/74 exit 160 (SR 9), just e. Int corridors. **Pets:** Service with restrictions, supervision.
🛜 🛗 💻

▼▼▼ Ramada Limited and Suites Bloomington 🅷
(309) 828-0900. **$60-$129.** 919 Maple Hill Rd 61705. I-55/74 exit 160 (SR 9), 0.3 mi w to Wylie Dr, just n, then just e. Int corridors. **Pets:** Accepted. 🛜 🛗 💻 🏊

CARBONDALE

▼▼▼ Hampton Inn 🅷
(618) 549-6900. **$99-$129.** 2175 Reed Station Pkwy 62901. I-57 exit 54B, 11.7 mi w on SR 13. Int corridors. **Pets:** Medium. $25 one-time fee/room. Service with restrictions, crate. 🛜 🅼 💻 🏊 ✕

▼▼▼ Holiday Inn Hotel and Conference Center 🅷
(618) 549-2600. **$129-$179.** 2300 Reed Station Pkwy 62901. I-57 exit 54B, 12 mi w on SR 13. Int corridors. **Pets:** Accepted.
🛜 🅼 🛗 💻 🍴 🏊 ✕

▼ Super 8 ⊞
(618) 457-8822. **$45-$79.** 1180 E Main St 62901. I-57 exit 54B, 13.9 mi w on SR 13. Int corridors. **Pets:** $10 daily fee/pet. Service with restrictions, supervision. ⊛ ⊠ 🛏 💻

CHAMPAIGN

▼▼ Baymont Inn & Suites ⊞
(217) 356-8900. **$74-$190.** 302 W Anthony Dr 61822. I-74 exit 182 (Neil St), just nw. Int corridors. **Pets:** Medium, other species. $15 daily fee/pet. Designated rooms, service with restrictions, crate. ⊛ 🛏 💻

▼▼▼ Drury Inn & Suites-Champaign ⊞
(217) 398-0030. **$105-$224.** 905 W Anthony Dr 61821. I-74 exit 181 (Prospect Ave), just n. Int corridors. **Pets:** Service with restrictions, supervision. ⊛ 🔥M 🛏 💻 🏊 ⊠

▼▼ Extended StayAmerica-Champaign-Urbana ⊞
(217) 351-8899. **$59-$84.** 610 W Marketview Dr 61822. I-74 exit 181 (Prospect Ave), just n, then just e. Int corridors. **Pets:** $25 daily fee/pet. Designated rooms, service with restrictions. ⊛ 🛏 💻

◈◈ ▼▼▼ Hawthorn Suites by Wyndham ⊞
(217) 398-3400. **$95-$310.** 101 Trade Centre Dr 61820. I-74 exit 182 (Neil St), 2.7 mi s. Int corridors. **Pets:** $25 deposit/room. Service with restrictions, crate. SAVE ⊛ ⊠ 🔥M 🛏 💻 🏊

▼▼ La Quinta Inn Champaign ⊞
(217) 356-4000. **$71-$191.** 1900 Center Dr 61820. I-74 exit 182 (Neil St), just n. Int corridors. **Pets:** Service with restrictions, supervision. ⊛ 🔥M 🛏 💻 🏊

▼▼ Quality Inn & Suites ⊞
(217) 352-4055. **$59-$160.** 305 Marketview Dr 61821. I-74 exit 182 (Neil St), just n to Marketview Dr, then just w. Int corridors. **Pets:** Accepted. ⊛ 🛏 💻 🏊

CHESTER

◈◈ ▼▼▼ BEST WESTERN Reid's Inn ⊞
(618) 826-3034. **$80-$120.** 2150 State St 62233. SR 150, 1 mi e of SR 3. Int corridors. **Pets:** Small. $5 daily fee/pet. Designated rooms, service with restrictions, crate. SAVE ⊛ 🔥M 🛏 💻 🏊

CHICAGO METROPOLITAN AREA

ALSIP

▼▼ Baymont Inn & Suites Chicago/Alsip ⊞
(708) 597-3900. **$84-$180.** 12801 S Cicero Ave 60803. I-294 exit SR 50 (Cicero Ave S). Int corridors. **Pets:** Accepted. ⊛ 🛏 💻

ARLINGTON HEIGHTS

▼▼▼ DoubleTree by Hilton Hotel Chicago - Arlington Heights ⊞
(847) 364-7600. **$89-$259.** 75 W Algonquin Rd 60005. I-90 exit Arlington Heights Rd, just n to Algonquin Rd, then just w. Int corridors. **Pets:** Accepted. ⊛ 🔥M 🛏 💻 🍽 🏊 ⊠

▼▼ Holiday Inn Express ⊞
(847) 593-9400. **Call for rates.** 2120 S Arlington Heights Rd 60005. I-90 exit Arlington Heights Rd, 0.6 mi n. Int corridors. **Pets:** Accepted. ⊛ 🔥M 🛏 💻

▼▼ Jameson Suites Chicago-Arlington Heights ⊞
(847) 956-1400. **Call for rates.** 2111 S Arlington Heights Rd 60005. I-90 exit Arlington Heights Rd, 0.6 mi n. Int corridors. **Pets:** Medium, other species. $15 daily fee/pet. Service with restrictions, crate. ⊛ 🛏 💻 ⊠

▼▼ La Quinta Inn Chicago Arlington Heights ⊞
(847) 253-8777. **$59-$133.** 1415 W Dundee Rd 60004. SR 53 exit Dundee Rd, just e. Int corridors. **Pets:** Service with restrictions, supervision. ⊛ 🛏 💻 🏊

▼ Red Roof Inn #102 Ⓜ
(847) 228-6650. **$45-$90.** 22 W Algonquin Rd 60005. I-90 exit Arlington Heights Rd, 0.5 mi n, then just w. Ext corridors. **Pets:** Large, other species. Service with restrictions, supervision. ⊛ 🛏

AURORA

▼▼▼ Staybridge Suites Aurora/Naperville ⊞
(630) 978-2222. **Call for rates.** 4320 Meridian Pkwy 60504. I-88 exit SR 59, 2 mi s to Meridian Pkwy, then just w. Int corridors. **Pets:** Accepted. ⊛ 🔥M 🛏 💻 🏊 ⊠

BANNOCKBURN

▼▼▼ La Quinta Inn & Suites Chicago North Shore ⊞
(847) 317-7300. **$66-$177.** 2000 S Lakeside Dr 60015. I-94 exit Half Day Rd (SR 22), just e to Lakeside Dr, then just s. Int corridors. **Pets:** Service with restrictions, supervision. ⊛ 🔥M 🛏 💻 🏊 ⊠

BEDFORD PARK

▼▼ Extended StayAmerica Chicago-Midway ⊞
(708) 496-8211. **$70-$120.** 7524 State Rd 60638. Jct SR 50, just w. Int corridors. **Pets:** $25 daily fee/pet. Designated rooms, service with restrictions. ⊛ 🔥M

▼▼▼ Residence Inn by Marriott Chicago Midway Airport ⊞ ❀
(708) 458-7790. **$159-$219.** 6638 S Cicero Ave 60638. Jct 65th St. Int corridors. **Pets:** Large, other species. $100 one-time fee/room. Service with restrictions. ⊛ ⊠ 🔥M 🛏 💻 🏊 ⊠

BLOOMINGDALE

▼▼▼ Courtyard by Marriott Chicago Bloomingdale ⊞
(630) 529-9200. **$139-$189.** 275 Knollwood Dr 60108. I-355 exit Army Trail Rd, 4 mi w, then just n. Int corridors. **Pets:** Accepted. ⊛ ⊠ 🔥M 🛏 💻 🍽 🏊

◈◈ ▼▼▼ Hilton Chicago Indian Lakes Resort ⊞
(630) 529-0200. **$99-$199.** 250 W Schick Rd 60108. I-355 exit Lake St (US 20), 2.5 mi w, just s on Bloomingdale Rd, then 0.6 mi w. Int corridors. **Pets:** Large. $50 one-time fee/room. Service with restrictions, crate. SAVE ⊛ 🍽 🏊 🏊

▼▼▼ Residence Inn by Marriott ⊞
(630) 893-9200. **$109-$499.** 295 Knollwood Dr 60108. I-355 exit Army Trail Rd, 4 mi w, then just n. Int corridors. **Pets:** Accepted. ⊛ ⊠ 🔥M 🛏 💻 🏊 ⊠

BOLINGBROOK

◈◈ ▼▼▼ Aloft Bolingbrook ⊞ ❀
(630) 410-6367. **$99-$199.** 500 Janes Ave 60440. I-355 exit Boughton Rd, just sw. Int corridors. **Pets:** Designated rooms, service with restrictions, supervision. SAVE ⊛ ⊠ 🔥M 🛏 💻 🏊

▼▼ La Quinta Inn & Suites Bolingbrook ⊞
(630) 226-0000. **$83-$199.** 225 W South Frontage Rd 60440. I-55 exit 267, 0.5 mi sw. Int corridors. **Pets:** Service with restrictions, supervision. ⊛ 🛏 💻 🏊

◈◈ ▼▼ Quality Inn ⊞ ❀
(630) 378-5300. **$89-$119, 7 day notice.** 175 W Remington Blvd 60440. I-55 exit 267, just n on SR 53. Int corridors. **Pets:** Small, dogs only. $25 one-time fee/pet. Service with restrictions, supervision. SAVE ⊛ 🔥M 🛏 💻 🏊

BRIDGEVIEW

▼▼ **Days Inn Bridgeview** ⊞
(708) 430-1818. **$74-$104.** 9625 S 76th Ave 60455. I-294 exit 95th St, just sw. Int corridors. **Pets:** Medium, other species. $25 one-time fee/room. Service with restrictions, crate. 🛰 🗏 🗏

BUFFALO GROVE

▼▼ **Extended StayAmerica-Chicago-Buffalo Grove-Deerfield** ⊞
(847) 215-0641. **$55-$105.** 1525 Busch Pkwy 60089. I-94 exit W Lake Cook Rd, 2 mi w to Milwaukee Ave (US 45/SR 21), then 1.3 mi n. Int corridors. **Pets:** $25 daily fee/pet. Designated rooms, service with restrictions. 🛰 🗏 🗏

BURR RIDGE

▼▼ ▼▼ **Extended StayAmerica Chicago-Burr Ridge** ⊞
(630) 323-6630. **$55-$100.** 15 W 122nd S Frontage Rd 60527. I-55 exit 276A (County Line Rd), just sw. Int corridors. **Pets:** $25 daily fee/pet. Designated rooms, service with restrictions. 🛰 🗏 🗏

CHICAGO

◉ ▼▼▼▼ **Allegro Chicago, A Kimpton Hotel** ⊞
(312) 236-0123. **$129-$409.** 171 W Randolph St 60601. Jct La Salle St; in theater district. Int corridors. **Pets:** Accepted.
ECO SAVE 🛰 ✕ 🗏 🍴

▼▼▼▼ **Amalfi Hotel Chicago** ⊞
(312) 395-9000. **$139-$649.** 20 W Kinzie St 60654. Between State and Dearborn sts. Int corridors. **Pets:** Accepted.
🛰 ✕ 🗏 🗏 🗏 🍴 🌐

▼▼▼▼ **Avenue Crowne Plaza Chicago Downtown Magnificent Mile** ⊞
(312) 787-2900. **$109-$379.** 160 E Huron St 60611. Just e of N Michigan Ave. Int corridors. **Pets:** Accepted. 🛰 ✕ 🗏 🗏 🍴 🌐

◉ ▼▼▼▼ **The Blackstone, A Renaissance Hotel** ⊞
(312) 447-0955. **$169-$319.** 636 S Michigan Ave 60605. Jct Congress Pkwy, just s. Int corridors. **Pets:** Accepted.
SAVE 🛰 ✕ 🗏 🗏 🍴

◉ ▼▼ ▼▼ **Carlton Inn Midway** Ⓜ 🐾
(773) 582-0900. **$89-$189.** 4944 S Archer Ave 60632. I-55 exit 287 (Pulaski Rd), 1.8 mi s to Archer Ave, then just e. Ext corridors. **Pets:** Medium. $50 deposit/room, $10 daily fee/pet. Designated rooms, service with restrictions, supervision. SAVE 🛰 🗏 🗏

◉ ▼▼▼▼ **Conrad Chicago** ⊞
(312) 645-1500. **$149-$495.** 521 N Rush St 60611. Jct Grand Ave. Int corridors. **Pets:** Accepted. SAVE 🛰 ✕ 🗏 🗏 🍴

◉ ▼▼▼▼ **Crowne Plaza Chicago Metro** ⊞
(312) 829-5000. **$149-$229.** 733 W Madison St 60661. I-90/94 exit 51D (Madison St); jct Halsted St. Int corridors. **Pets:** Accepted.
SAVE 🛰 🗏 🍴

▼▼▼▼ **The Drake Hotel, Chicago** ⊞
(312) 787-2200. **$119-$495.** 140 E Walton Pl 60611. Jct N Michigan Ave and Lake Shore Dr. Int corridors. **Pets:** Accepted.
🛰 ✕ 🗏 🗏 🍴 🌐

◉ ▼▼▼▼ **Fairmont Chicago, Millennium Park** ⊞
(312) 565-8000. **Call for rates.** 200 N Columbus Dr 60601. Jct Michigan Ave and Wacker Dr, just e. Int corridors. **Pets:** Accepted.
ECO SAVE 🛰 ✕ 🗏 🗏 🍴

▼▼▼▼▼ **Four Seasons Hotel Chicago** ⊞ 🐾
(312) 280-8800. **Call for rates.** 120 E Delaware Pl 60611. Jct Michigan Ave; just nw of John Hancock Building. Int corridors. **Pets:** Very small. Designated rooms, service with restrictions, supervision.
ECO 🛰 🗏 🗏 🗏 🍴 🌐

◉ ▼▼▼▼ **Hard Rock Hotel Chicago** ⊞
(312) 345-1000. **Call for rates.** 230 N Michigan Ave 60601. Between Lake St and Wacker Dr. Int corridors. **Pets:** Accepted.
SAVE 🛰 ✕ 🗏 🗏 🍴 🌐

◉ ▼▼▼▼ **Hilton Chicago** ⊞ 🐾
(312) 922-4400. **$119-$495.** 720 S Michigan Ave 60605. I-290 (Congress Pkwy) exit Michigan Ave, just s. Int corridors. **Pets:** Large, other species. $50 one-time fee/pet. Designated rooms, service with restrictions.
ECO SAVE 🛰 ✕ 🗏 🍴 🌐 🌐

◉ ▼▼▼▼ **Hilton Chicago O'Hare Airport** ⊞
(773) 686-8000. **$119-$495.** O'Hare Int'l Airport 60666. Opposite and connected to terminal buildings at Chicago O'Hare International Airport, accessed via I-190. Int corridors. **Pets:** Accepted.
SAVE 🛰 🗏 🍴 🌐 🌐

◉ ▼▼▼▼ **Hilton Suites Chicago/Magnificent Mile** ⊞
(312) 664-1100. **$189-$399.** 198 E Delaware Pl 60611. Just e of Michigan Ave. Int corridors. **Pets:** Accepted.
SAVE 🛰 🗏 🗏 🗏 🍴 🌐 🌐

◉ ▼▼▼▼ **Holiday Inn & Suites Downtown Chicago** ⊞
(312) 957-9100. **$129-$349.** 506 W Harrison St 60607. I-290 exit Canal St, just s. Int corridors. **Pets:** Accepted. SAVE 🛰 🗏 🗏 🍴 🌐

◉ ▼▼▼▼ **Holiday Inn Chicago O'Hare** ⊞
(773) 693-5800. **$79-$309.** 5615 N Cumberland Ave 60631. I-90 exit 79B (N Cumberland Ave), just s. Int corridors. **Pets:** Medium, other species. $50 one-time fee/pet. Service with restrictions, supervision.
SAVE 🛰 🗏 🗏 🍴 🌐

◉ ▼▼▼▼ **Hotel Burnham Chicago** ⊞ 🐾
(312) 782-1111. **$139-$509.** One W Washington St 60602. Jct State St. Int corridors. **Pets:** Other species. Designated rooms, service with restrictions, crate. ECO SAVE 🛰 ✕ 🗏 🍴

▼▼▼▼ **Hotel Indigo Chicago Downtown Gold Coast** ⊞ 🐾
(312) 787-4980. **$139-$399.** 1244 N Dearborn Pkwy 60610. Just n of Division St. Int corridors. **Pets:** Large, other species. $75 one-time fee/room. Service with restrictions, crate. 🛰 🗏 🍴

◉ ▼▼▼▼ **Hotel Monaco Chicago** ⊞
(312) 960-8500. **$199-$509.** 225 N Wabash Ave 60601. Jct Wacker Dr. Int corridors. **Pets:** Accepted. ECO SAVE 🛰 ✕ 🗏 🍴 🌐

▼▼▼▼ **Hotel Palomar Chicago** ⊞ 🐾
(312) 755-9703. **$129-$799.** 505 N State St 60654. Between Grand and Illinois sts. Int corridors. **Pets:** Other species. Designated rooms.
🛰 ✕ 🗏 🍴 🌐 🌐

▼▼▼▼ **InterContinental Chicago Magnificent Mile** ⊞
(312) 944-4100. **Call for rates.** 505 N Michigan Ave 60611. Just n of Chicago River; between E Grand Ave and E Illinois St. Int corridors. **Pets:** Accepted. ECO 🛰 🗏 🗏 🌐 🌐

▼▼▼▼ **The James Chicago** ⊞
(312) 337-1000. **Call for rates.** 55 E Ontario St 60611. Just w of N Michigan Ave. Int corridors. **Pets:** Accepted. 🛰 🗏 🗏 🍴 🌐

▼▼▼▼ **La Quinta Inn & Suites Chicago Downtown** ⊞
(312) 558-1020. **$119-$364.** 1 S Franklin St 60606. Jct Madison Ave. Int corridors. **Pets:** Service with restrictions, supervision.
🛰 🗏 🗏 🗏 🍴 🌐 🌐

◉ ▼▼▼▼ **MileNorth, A Chicago Hotel** ⊞ 🐾
(312) 787-6000. **$169-$499.** 166 E Superior St 60611. Just e of Michigan Ave. Int corridors. **Pets:** Small, dogs only. $75 one-time fee/pet. Designated rooms, service with restrictions, supervision.
SAVE 🛰 ✕ 🗏 🗏

Omni Chicago Hotel H
(312) 944-6664. **$199-$479.** 676 N Michigan Ave 60611. Jct Huron St.
Int corridors. **Pets:** Accepted.

Palmer House - A Hilton Hotel H
(312) 726-7500. **$119-$495.** 17 E Monroe St 60603. Between State St
and Wabash Ave. Int corridors. **Pets:** Accepted.

Park Hyatt Chicago H
(312) 335-1234. **$265-$845, 3 day notice.** 800 N Michigan Ave 60611.
Jct Chicago Ave at Water Tower Square. Int corridors. **Pets:** Accepted.

The Peninsula Chicago H
(312) 337-2888. **$450-$1425.** 108 E Superior St 60611. Jct Michigan
Ave. Int corridors. **Pets:** Accepted.

Radisson Blu Aqua Hotel H
(312) 565-5258. **$199-$459.** 221 N Columbus Dr 60601. Jct E Water St,
just s of the Chicago River. Int corridors. **Pets:** Accepted.

Renaissance Chicago Downtown H
(312) 372-7200. **$189-$479.** 1 W Wacker Dr 60601. Jct State St. Int
corridors. **Pets:** Accepted.

**Residence Inn by Marriott Chicago Downtown/
Magnificent Mile** H
(312) 943-9800. **$139-$459.** 201 E Walton Pl 60611. Just e of Michigan
Ave at Mies van der Rohe Way. Int corridors. **Pets:** Accepted.

**Residence Inn by Marriott Chicago Downtown River
North** H
(312) 494-9301. **$99-$399.** 410 N Dearborn St 60654. Between W Kinzie
and W Hubbard sts. Int corridors. **Pets:** Accepted.

**The Ritz-Carlton Chicago (A Four Seasons
Hotel)** H
(312) 266-1000. **Call for rates.** 160 E Pearson St 60611. Jct N Michigan
Ave. Int corridors. **Pets:** Accepted.

Sheraton Chicago Hotel & Towers H
(312) 464-1000. **$109-$659.** 301 E North Water St 60611. Columbus Dr
at Chicago River; just e of Michigan Ave. Int corridors. **Pets:** Accepted.

Sofitel Chicago Water Tower H
(312) 324-4000. **Call for rates.** 20 E Chestnut St 60611. Jct Wabash
Ave and Chestnut St, 1/2 blk w of Rush St. Int corridors. **Pets:** Accepted.

**Trump International Hotel &
Tower** H ❀
(312) 588-8000. **$395-$2000.** 401 N Wabash Ave 60611. Between Hubbard and Kinzie sts; just s of Kinzie St. Int corridors. **Pets:** Small, dogs
only. Service with restrictions, supervision.

Waldorf Astoria Chicago H ❀
(312) 646-1300. **Call for rates.** 11 E Walton St 60611. Between State
and Rush sts. Int corridors. **Pets:** Medium. Service with restrictions.

W Chicago-City Center H ❀
(312) 332-1200. **$169-$629.** 172 W Adams St 60603. Between La Salle
and Wells sts. Int corridors. **Pets:** Small. $100 one-time fee/room, $25
daily fee/room. Service with restrictions, crate.

W Chicago Lakeshore H
(312) 943-9200. **$159-$739.** 644 N Lake Shore Dr 60611. Jct Ontario St.
Int corridors. **Pets:** Accepted.

The Westin Chicago River North H
(312) 744-1900. **$129-$799.** 320 N Dearborn St 60654. Just n of Chicago River; between Dearborn and Clark sts. Int corridors.
Pets: Accepted.

**The Westin Michigan Avenue
Chicago** H
(312) 943-7200. **$199-$689.** 909 N Michigan Ave 60611. Across from
John Hancock Center. Int corridors. **Pets:** Accepted.

Wyndham Blake Chicago H
(312) 986-1234. **$79-$209.** 500 S Dearborn St 60605. Jct I-290 (Congress Pkwy). Int corridors. **Pets:** Accepted.

CRYSTAL LAKE

Comfort Inn by Choice Hotels H
(815) 444-0040. **$79-$109.** 595 Tracy Tr 60014. Jct US 14 and SR 31,
0.4 mi w, just n on Pingree Rd, then just n. Int corridors. **Pets:** Accepted.

Country Inn & Suites By Carlson H
(815) 477-3500. **$114-$159.** 600 Tracy Tr 60014. Jct US 14 and SR 31,
0.4 mi w, then just n on Pingree Rd. Int corridors. **Pets:** $25 daily fee/
room. Designated rooms, service with restrictions, crate.

Holiday Inn Chicago-Crystal Lake H
(815) 477-7000. **$89-$139.** 800 S SR 31 60014. At Three Oaks Rd, 0.3
mi s of jct US 14. Int corridors. **Pets:** Small. $25 daily fee/pet. Designated
rooms, service with restrictions, crate.

Super 8 H
(815) 788-8888. **$69-$99.** 577 Crystal Point Dr 60014. On US 14, 1 mi w
of jct SR 31. Int corridors. **Pets:** Accepted.

DARIEN

Extended StayAmerica Chicago-Darien H
(630) 985-4708. **$55-$100.** 2345 Sokol Ct 60561. I-55 exit 271A, 0.5 mi
s to Westgate Rd, then 0.5 mi ne via frontage road. Int corridors.
Pets: $25 daily fee/pet. Designated rooms, service with restrictions.

DEERFIELD

Chicago Marriott Suites Deerfield H
(847) 405-9666. **$79-$279.** 2 Parkway North 60015. I-94 exit Deerfield
Rd northbound, just w; exit Lake Cook Rd southbound, 0.3 mi e to Saunders Rd, then 0.5 mi n. Int corridors. **Pets:** Accepted.

Red Roof Inn #188 M
(847) 205-1755. **$54-$99.** 340 S Waukegan Rd 60015. I-94 exit SR 43
(Waukegan Rd). Ext corridors. **Pets:** Large, other species. Service with
restrictions, supervision.

Residence Inn by Marriott Chicago/Deerfield H
(847) 940-4644. **$99-$229.** 530 Lake Cook Rd 60015. I-94 exit Lake
Cook Rd, 1.8 mi e, then 3 blks n on Corporate 500 Dr access road. Ext
corridors. **Pets:** Accepted.

DES PLAINES

Comfort Inn O'Hare 🅷
(847) 635-1300. **$129-$190.** 2175 E Touhy Ave 60018. I-294 exit Touhy Ave westbound, just w; exit Golf Rd (SR 58) eastbound, 0.3 mi w to River Rd, then 5.5 mi s. Int corridors. **Pets:** Small. $20 daily fee/pet. Designated rooms, no service, supervision.

Extended StayAmerica-Chicago O'Hare 🅷
(847) 294-9693. **$55-$110.** 1201 E Touhy Ave 60018. SR 72 (Higgins Rd), 0.6 mi, w of US 12/45 (Mannheim Rd). Int corridors. **Pets:** $25 daily fee/pet. Designated rooms, service with restrictions.

Extended Stay Deluxe Chicago O'Hare 🅷
(847) 768-0395. **$60-$120.** 1207 E Touhy Ave 60018. SR 72 (Higgins Rd), 0.6 mi w of US 12/45 (Mannheim Rd). Int corridors. **Pets:** $25 daily fee/pet. Designated rooms, service with restrictions.

DOWNERS GROVE

Holiday Inn Express 🅷
(630) 810-9500. **Call for rates.** 3031 Finley Rd 60515. I-355 exit Butterfield Rd (SR 56), just e. Int corridors. **Pets:** Medium, dogs only. $10 daily fee/pet. Designated rooms, service with restrictions, supervision.

Red Roof Inn #087 Ⓜ
(630) 963-4205. **$59-$109.** 1113 Butterfield Rd 60515. I-355 exit Butterfield Rd (SR 56), on frontage road; I-88 exit Highland Ave N, just w. Ext corridors. **Pets:** Large, other species. Service with restrictions, supervision.

ELGIN

Quality Inn-Elgin 🅷
(847) 608-7300. **$69-$99.** 500 Tollgate Rd 60123. I-90 exit SR 31 N, just n. Int corridors. **Pets:** Accepted.

ELK GROVE VILLAGE

Baymont Inn & Suites O'Hare 🅷
(847) 803-9400. **$64-$109.** 2881 Touhy Ave 60007. Jct SR 72 (Higgins Rd) and 83 (Busse Rd), 1.5 mi e on SR 72 (Higgins Rd). Int corridors. **Pets:** Other species. $25 one-time fee/room. Designated rooms, service with restrictions, supervision.

Days Inn Schaumburg/Elk Grove 🅷
(847) 895-2085. **$54-$130.** 1000 W Devon Ave 60007. I-290 exit Thorndale Ave, 0.5 mi w to Rohlwing Rd, 0.3 mi n to Devon Ave, then 0.3 mi e. Int corridors. **Pets:** Accepted.

La Quinta Inn Chicago O'Hare Airport 🅷
(847) 439-6767. **$81-$144.** 1900 E Oakton St 60007. Jct SR 72 (Higgins Rd) and 83 (Busse Rd). Int corridors. **Pets:** Service with restrictions, supervision.

Sheraton Suites Chicago Elk Grove 🅷
(847) 290-1600. **$99-$189.** 121 Northwest Point Blvd 60007. I-90 exit Arlington Heights Rd, just s; in Northwest Point Corporate Park. Int corridors. **Pets:** Accepted.

Super 8 O'Hare 🅷
(847) 827-3133. **$63-$145.** 2951 Touhy Ave 60007. Jct SR 72 (Higgins Rd) and 83 (Busse Rd); 1.5 mi e on SR 72 (Higgins Rd). Int corridors. **Pets:** Medium. $20 deposit/pet, $20 daily fee/pet. Designated rooms, service with restrictions, supervision.

ELMHURST

Extended StayAmerica Chicago-Elmhurst-O'Hare 🅷
(630) 530-4353. **$50-$100.** 550 W Grand Ave 60126. Jct US 20 (Lake St), 0.4 mi ne; adjacent to I-290 overpass. Int corridors. **Pets:** $25 daily fee/pet. Designated rooms, service with restrictions.

EVANSTON

Hilton Orrington/Evanston 🅷 🌼
(847) 866-8700. **$139-$239.** 1710 Orrington Ave 60201. Jct Church St. Int corridors. **Pets:** Medium, other species. $50 one-time fee/room. Designated rooms, service with restrictions, crate.

GLEN ELLYN

Crowne Plaza Glen Ellyn-Lombard 🅷
(630) 629-6000. **$74-$139.** 1250 Roosevelt Rd 60137. I-355 exit Roosevelt Rd, 0.8 mi e on SR 38. Int corridors. **Pets:** Medium. Designated rooms, service with restrictions, crate.

GLENVIEW

Staybridge Suites 🅷
(847) 657-0002. **$89-$149.** 2600 Lehigh Ave 60026. I-294 exit Willow Rd, 2.4 mi e. Int corridors. **Pets:** Medium, other species. $50 one-time fee/pet, $10 daily fee/pet. Service with restrictions, crate.

Wyndham Glenview Suites 🅷
(847) 803-9800. **$98-$250.** 1400 N Milwaukee Ave 60025. I-294 exit Willow Rd, 0.3 mi w to Sanders Rd, 1.3 mi s to Milwaukee Ave (SR 21), then 1 mi s. Int corridors. **Pets:** Accepted.

GRAYSLAKE

Comfort Suites by Choice Hotels 🅷
(847) 223-5050. **$89-$159.** 1775 E Belvidere Rd 60030. Just w of jct US 45. Int corridors. **Pets:** Medium. $35 one-time fee/pet. Designated rooms, service with restrictions, supervision.

GURNEE

BEST WESTERN Gurnee Hotel & Suites 🅷
(847) 782-0890. **$75-$175.** 5430 Grand Ave 60031. I-94 exit Grand Ave (SR 132 E), 0.5 mi e. Int corridors. **Pets:** Accepted.

Comfort Inn by Choice Hotels 🅷
(847) 855-8866. **$69-$120.** 6080 Gurnee Mills Cir E 60031. I-94 exit Grand Ave (SR 132 W), just nw. Int corridors. **Pets:** Medium, other species. $30 daily fee/pet. Designated rooms, service with restrictions, supervision.

Country Inn & Suites By Carlson 🅷
(847) 625-9700. **Call for rates.** 5420 Grand Ave 60031. I-94 exit Grand Ave (SR 132 E), 0.5 mi e. Int corridors. **Pets:** Medium, dogs only. $50 one-time fee/room.

Holiday Inn Gurnee Convention Center 🅷
(847) 336-6300. **Call for rates.** 6161 W Grand Ave 60031. I-94 exit Grand Ave (SR 132 W), 0.3 mi w. Int corridors. **Pets:** Accepted.

La Quinta Inn & Suites Chicago Gurnee 🅷
(847) 662-7600. **$63-$173.** 5688 Northridge Dr 60031. I-94 exit Grand Ave (SR 132 E), just e via service road. Int corridors. **Pets:** Service with restrictions, supervision.

HANOVER PARK

Extended StayAmerica-Chicago-Hanover Park 🅷
(630) 893-4823. **$55-$100.** 1075 Lake St 60133. On US 20; between Gary Ave and Elgin-O'Hare Expwy. Int corridors. **Pets:** $25 daily fee/pet. Designated rooms, service with restrictions.

HILLSIDE

BEST WESTERN PLUS Chicago Hillside Hotel 🅷
(708) 544-9300. **$90-$140.** 4400 Frontage Rd 60162. I-290 exit 14B eastbound to US 12/45 (Mannheim Rd), just nw via frontage road; exit 17 westbound to US 12/45 (Mannheim Rd), just nw via frontage road. Int corridors. **Pets:** $50 one-time fee/room. Service with restrictions, supervision.

HOFFMAN ESTATES

▼▼▼ **La Quinta Inn Chicago Hoffman Estates** 🅗
(847) 882-3312. **$59-$144.** 2280 Barrington Rd 60169. I-90 exit Barrington Rd westbound, 0.3 mi s; exit SR 59 eastbound, 0.5 mi n to SR 72 (Higgins Rd), 2 mi e to Barrington Rd, then just n. Int corridors. **Pets:** Service with restrictions, supervision. 🛜 💻 🏊

▼ **Red Roof Inn #199** Ⓜ
(847) 885-7877. **$44-$90.** 2500 Hassell Rd 60169. I-90 exit Barrington Rd westbound, 0.3 mi s; exit SR 59 eastbound, 0.5 mi n to SR 72 (Higgins Rd), 2 mi e to Barrington Rd, then just n. Ext corridors. **Pets:** Large, other species. Service with restrictions, supervision. 🛜 🛗

ITASCA

▼▼ **Extended StayAmerica-Chicago-Itasca** 🅗
(630) 250-1111. **$50-$100.** 1181 Rohlwing Rd 60143. I-290 exit Thorndale Ave, 0.5 mi w. Int corridors. **Pets:** $25 daily fee/pet. Designated rooms, service with restrictions. 🛜 ♿ 🛗 💻

🅐🅐🅐 ▼▼ ▼▼ **The Westin Chicago Northwest** 🅗 ❀
(630) 773-4000. **$99-$349, 3 day notice.** 400 Park Blvd 60143. I-290 exit Thorndale Ave, just e. Int corridors. **Pets:** Medium. Service with restrictions, crate. 🆂🅰🆅🅴 🛜 ✖ 🛗 💻 🍴 🏊 ❎

JOLIET

▼▼ **Comfort Inn by Choice Hotels Joliet North** 🅗
(815) 436-5141. **Call for rates.** 3235 Norman Ave 60435. I-55 exit 257, just e. Int corridors. **Pets:** Accepted. 🛜 🛗 💻 🏊

▼▼ **Comfort Inn by Choice Hotels-South** 🅗
(815) 744-1770. **Call for rates.** 135 S Larkin Ave 60436. I-80 exit 130B, 0.5 mi n. Int corridors. **Pets:** Accepted. 🛜 🛗 💻 🏊

▼▼ **Fairfield Inn by Marriott Joliet South** 🅗
(815) 741-3499. **$99-$259.** 1501 Riverboat Center Dr 60436. I-80 exit 127, just n. Int corridors. **Pets:** Accepted. 🛜 ✖ 🛗 💻 🏊

🅐🅐🅐 ▼▼ **Red Roof Inn #071** Ⓜ
(815) 741-2304. **$49-$131.** 1750 McDonough St 60436. I-80 exit 130B, just off Larkin Ave. Ext corridors. **Pets:** Large, other species. Service with restrictions, supervision. 🆂🅰🆅🅴 🛜 🛗

🅐🅐🅐 ▼▼▼ **TownePlace Suites by Marriott Joliet** 🅗 ❀
(815) 741-2400. **$107-$180.** 1515 Riverboat Center Dr 60431. I-80 exit 127, just n. Int corridors. **Pets:** Medium, other species. $50 one-time fee/room, $10 daily fee/room. Service with restrictions, crate.
🆂🅰🆅🅴 🛜 ✖ ♿ 🛗 💻 🏊 ❎

LAKE ZURICH

▼▼▼ **Holiday Inn Express & Suites Lake Zurich-Barrington** 🅗
(847) 726-7500. **Call for rates.** 197 S Rand Rd 60047. On US 12, 0.3 mi nw of SR 22. Int corridors. **Pets:** Accepted.
🛜 ✖ ♿ 🛗 💻 🏊 ❎

LANSING

▼▼ **Extended StayAmerica-Chicago-Lansing** 🅗
(708) 895-6402. **$55-$110.** 2520 173rd St 60438. I-80/94 exit 161 (Torrence Ave), just n to 173rd St, then just e. Int corridors. **Pets:** $25 daily fee/pet. Designated rooms, service with restrictions. 🛜 ♿ 🛗 💻

LIBERTYVILLE

▼▼ **Candlewood Suites Chicago-Libertyville** 🅗
(847) 247-9900. **$80-$120.** 1100 N US 45 60048. I-94 exit SR 137 (Buckley Rd), 5.6 mi w to US 45, then 1.4 mi s. Int corridors. **Pets:** Accepted. 🛜 ✖ ♿ 🛗 💻

▼▼▼ **Holiday Inn Express & Suites** 🅗
(847) 549-7878. **Call for rates.** 77 Buckley Rd 60048. I-94 exit SR 137 (Buckley Rd), 2.3 mi w. Int corridors. **Pets:** Other species. $50 one-time fee/room. Service with restrictions, crate. 🛜 🛗 💻 🏊

LINCOLNSHIRE

▼▼▼ **Homewood Suites by Hilton Chicago-Lincolnshire** 🅗
(847) 945-9300. **$109-$189.** 10 Westminster Way 60069. I-94 exit Half Day Rd, just w. Int corridors. **Pets:** Small. $75 one-time fee/pet. Designated rooms, service with restrictions, crate. 🛜 🛗 💻 🏊

▼▼▼ **Staybridge Suites Lincolnshire** 🅗
(847) 821-0002. **Call for rates.** 100 Barclay Blvd 60069. I-94 exit Half Day Rd, 2.2 mi w to Barclay Blvd, then just s; just w of jct US 45 and SR 21; in Lincolnshire Corporate Center. Int corridors. **Pets:** Medium. $13 one-time fee/pet. Service with restrictions, supervision.
🛜 ✖ ♿ 🛗 💻 🏊

LISLE

▼▼ **Extended StayAmerica-Chicago-Lisle** 🅗
(630) 434-7710. **$45-$95.** 445 Warrenville Rd 60532. I-355 exit Ogden Ave, just nw. Int corridors. **Pets:** $25 daily fee/pet. Designated rooms, service with restrictions. 🛜 🛗 💻

🅐🅐🅐 ▼▼▼ **Hyatt Lisle** 🅗
(630) 852-1234. **$49-$219.** 1400 Corporetum Dr 60532. I-88 exit SR 53 westbound, 0.3 mi s; exit Naperville Rd eastbound to Warrenville Rd, 2 mi e to jct SR 53. Int corridors. **Pets:** Medium. $75 one-time fee/room. Service with restrictions, supervision. 🆂🅰🆅🅴 🛜 💻 🍴 🏊 ❎

LOMBARD

🅐🅐🅐 ▼▼▼ **Embassy Suites Hotel Chicago-Lombard/Oak Brook** 🅗
(630) 969-7500. **$99-$159.** 707 E Butterfield Rd 60148. I-88 exit Highland Ave, just n to Butterfield Rd (SR 56), then 0.5 mi e. Int corridors. **Pets:** Other species. $50 one-time fee/pet. Designated rooms, service with restrictions, crate. 🆂🅰🆅🅴 🛜 ♿ 🛗 💻 🍴 🏊 ❎

▼▼ **Extended Stay Deluxe-Chicago-Lombard-Oak Brook** 🅗
(630) 424-1000. **$65-$105.** 260 E 22nd St 60148. I-88 exit Highland Ave, 0.8 mi n to 22nd St, then just e. Int corridors. **Pets:** $25 daily fee/pet. Designated rooms, service with restrictions. 🛜 ♿ 🛗 💻 ❎

▼▼ **Homestead Studio Suites Hotel-Chicago/Lombard-Oak Brook** 🅗
(630) 928-0202. **$45-$100.** 2701 Technology Dr 60148. I-88 exit Highland Ave, just n, 0.6 mi e on Butterfield Rd (SR 56), then just s. Int corridors. **Pets:** $25 daily fee/pet. Designated rooms, service with restrictions.
🛜 ♿ 🛗 💻

🅐🅐🅐 ▼▼▼ **Residence Inn by Marriott Chicago-Lombard** 🅗
(630) 629-7800. **$69-$189.** 2001 S Highland Ave 60148. I-88 exit Highland Ave, 0.8 mi n. Ext corridors. **Pets:** $75 one-time fee/room. Service with restrictions, crate. 🆂🅰🆅🅴 🛜 ✖ 🛗 💻 🏊 ❎

🅐🅐🅐 ▼▼▼ **TownePlace Suites by Marriott Chicago Lombard** 🅗
(630) 932-4400. **$99-$199.** 455 E 22nd St 60148. I-88 exit Highland Ave, 0.8 mi n, then 0.3 mi e. Int corridors. **Pets:** Accepted.
🆂🅰🆅🅴 🛜 ✖ ♿ 🛗 💻 🏊

🅐🅐🅐 ▼▼▼ **The Westin Lombard Yorktown Center** 🅗 ❀
(630) 719-8000. **$199-$309.** 70 Yorktown Center 60148. I-88 exit Highland Ave, just n to Butterfield Rd (SR 56), then just e; in The Shops on Butterfield. Int corridors. **Pets:** Medium, dogs only. Service with restrictions, supervision. 🄴🄲🄾 🆂🅰🆅🅴 🛜 ✖ ♿ 🛗 💻 🍴 🏊 ❎

MATTESON

▼▼ **La Quinta Inn Chicago Matteson** 🅗
(708) 503-0999. **$71-$144.** 5210 Southwick Dr 60443. I-57 exit 340A, 0.3 mi e on US 30, then 0.3 mi s on Cicero Ave (SR 50). Int corridors. **Pets:** Service with restrictions, supervision. 🛜 🛗 💻

METTAWA

 Residence Inn by Marriott Chicago Lake Forest-Mettawa �H

(847) 615-2701. **$89-$289.** 26325 N Riverwoods Blvd 60045. I-94 exit SR 60 (Townline Rd), just nw. Int corridors. **Pets:** Accepted.

MONEE

Red Roof Inn #748 �H

(708) 534-0022. **$49-$89.** 25640 S Friendship Dr 60449. I-57 exit 335, just se. Int corridors. **Pets:** Large, other species. Service with restrictions, supervision.

MORTON GROVE

BEST WESTERN Morton Grove Inn 🅼

(847) 965-6400. **$64-$159.** 9424 Waukegan Rd 60053. SR 43, just s of Golf Rd (SR 58). Ext corridors. **Pets:** Accepted.

MUNDELEIN

DoubleTree by Hilton Libertyville - Mundelein �H ❀

(847) 949-5100. **$89-$229.** 510 E Illinois (Rt 83) 60060. Jct US 45. Int corridors. **Pets:** Other species. $50 daily fee/room. Designated rooms, service with restrictions, crate.

NAPERVILLE

Baymont Inn & Suites Naperville �H

(630) 357-0022. **$56-$79.** 1585 Naperville/Wheaton Rd 60563. I-88 exit Naperville Rd, 0.5 mi s. Int corridors. **Pets:** Accepted.

BEST WESTERN Naperville Inn �H ❀

(630) 505-0200. **$80-$150.** 1617 N Naperville Wheaton Rd 60563. I-88 exit Naperville Rd, just e on Diehl Rd to Naperville Rd, then just s. Ext/int corridors. **Pets:** Medium, dogs only. $10 daily fee/pet. Designated rooms, service with restrictions, supervision.

Country Inn & Suites By Carlson �H ❀

(630) 505-3353. **$79-$179.** 1837 Centre Point Cir 60563. I-88 exit Naperville Rd, 0.3 mi s to Diehl Rd, 0.7 mi w, then just n. Int corridors. **Pets:** Other species. $100 one-time fee/room. Service with restrictions, crate.

Homestead Studio Suites Hotel-Chicago-Naperville �H

(630) 577-0200. **$50-$100.** 1827 Centre Point Cir 60563. I-88 exit Naperville Rd, just s to Diehl Rd, 0.8 mi w, then just n. Int corridors. **Pets:** $25 daily fee/pet. Designated rooms, service with restrictions.

Hotel Arista at CityGate Centre �H

(630) 579-4100. **Call for rates.** 2139 CityGate Ln 60563. I-88 exit SR 59, just n. Int corridors. **Pets:** Accepted.

Red Roof Inn #195 🅼

(630) 369-2500. **$55-$90.** 1698 W Diehl Rd 60563. I-88 exit SR 59, just s. Ext corridors. **Pets:** Large, other species. Service with restrictions, supervision.

Sleep Inn by Choice Hotels �H

(630) 778-5900. **$80-$90.** 1831 W Diehl Rd 60563. I-88 exit SR 59, just sw. Int corridors. **Pets:** Medium. $30 one-time fee/pet. Designated rooms, service with restrictions, supervision.

TownePlace Suites by Marriott Naperville �H

(630) 548-0881. **$140-$170.** 1843 W Diehl Rd 60563. I-88 exit SR 59, just s to Diehl Rd, then just w. Int corridors. **Pets:** Large, other species. $100 one-time fee/room. Service with restrictions, crate.

NORTHBROOK

Hilton Chicago/Northbrook �H ❀

(847) 480-7500. **$99-$109.** 2855 N Milwaukee Ave 60062. On SR 21, s of jct US 45 and Willow Rd. Int corridors. **Pets:** Large, other species. $50 one-time fee/pet. Designated rooms.

Renaissance Chicago North Shore �H

(847) 498-6500. **$89-$399.** 933 Skokie Blvd 60062. I-94 exit Dundee Rd W northbound; exit SR 43 (Waukegan Rd) southbound, 0.5 mi s to SR 68, then 1.5 mi e. Int corridors. **Pets:** $75 one-time fee/room. Designated rooms, service with restrictions, supervision.

Sheraton Chicago Northbrook Hotel �H

(847) 480-1900. **$109-$339, 3 day notice.** 1110 Willow Rd 60062. 2 mi w of jct I-94; 3.2 mi e of jct I-294. Int corridors. **Pets:** Accepted.

OAK BROOK

Residence Inn by Marriott Chicago/Oak Brook �H

(630) 571-1200. **$89-$399.** 790 Jorie Blvd 60523. I-88 exit Midwest Rd eastbound, just n to 22nd St (Cermak Rd), 1.7 mi e to Jorie Blvd, then just sw; exit 22nd St (Cermak Rd) westbound, 0.4 mi e to Jorie Blvd. Int corridors. **Pets:** Other species. $100 one-time fee/room. Service with restrictions.

OAKBROOK TERRACE

Holiday Inn Chicago-Oak Brook �H

(630) 833-3600. **$79-$209.** 17 W 350 22nd St 60181. I-88 exit Midwest Rd eastbound, 0.4 mi n to 22nd St (Cermak Rd), then just e; exit 22nd St (Cermak Rd) westbound, then 0.9 mi w. Int corridors. **Pets:** Medium. $50 one-time fee/pet. Service with restrictions, supervision.

La Quinta Inn Chicago Oakbrook Terrace �H

(630) 495-4600. **$75-$162.** 1 S 666 Midwest Rd 60181. I-88 exit Midwest Rd eastbound, 0.4 mi n, then just n of 22nd St (Cermak Rd); exit 22nd St (Cermak Rd) westbound, 1.1 mi w to Midwest Rd, then just n. Int corridors. **Pets:** Service with restrictions, supervision.

Staybridge Suites Chicago-Oakbrook Terrace �H

(630) 953-9393. **Call for rates.** 200 Royce Blvd 60181. I-88 exit Midwest Rd eastbound to 22nd St (Cermak Rd), 0.4 mi w to Butterfield Rd (SR 56), just n, then just n on Renaissance Blvd; exit 22nd St (Cermak Rd) westbound, 2.5 mi w on 22nd St to SR 56, just n, then just n on Renaissance Blvd. Int corridors. **Pets:** Accepted.

PALATINE

Holiday Inn Express Palatine/Arlington Heights �H

(847) 934-4900. **$72-$108.** 1550 E Dundee Rd 60074. SR 53 exit Dundee Rd (SR 68), just w. Int corridors. **Pets:** Accepted.

PROSPECT HEIGHTS

Comfort Inn & Suites Conference Center �H

(847) 419-3600. **$129-$169.** 600 N Milwaukee Ave 60070. Jct SR 21 and US 45. Int corridors. **Pets:** Accepted.

Super 8-Prospect Heights �H

(847) 459-0545. **$54-$69.** 540 N Milwaukee Ave 60070. Jct SR 21 and US 45. Int corridors. **Pets:** Medium. $25 daily fee/room. Service with restrictions.

RICHMOND

Super 8 Richmond/Geneva Lakes �H

(815) 678-4711. **$65-$165.** 11200 N US Hwy 12 60071. 0.5 mi n of jct SR 173. Int corridors. **Pets:** Medium, dogs only. $20 daily fee/pet. Designated rooms, service with restrictions, supervision.

ROMEOVILLE

▼▼ Country Inn & Suites By Carlson, Romeoville (Chicago) H
(630) 378-1052. **$100-$170.** 1265 Lakeview Dr 60446. I-55 exit 263, just n. Int corridors. **Pets:** Accepted. 📶 🛗 🖵 🏊

▼▼ Extended StayAmerica Chicago-Romeoville H
(630) 226-8966. **$60-$106.** 1225 Lakeview Dr 60446. I-55 exit 263, just n. Int corridors. **Pets:** $25 daily fee/pet. Designated rooms, service with restrictions. 📶 🛗 🖵

ROSEMONT

◈◈ ▼▼▼ Aloft Chicago O'Hare H
(847) 671-4444. **$99-$309, 3 day notice.** 9700 Balmoral Ave 60018. I-190 exit 1B, just s. Int corridors. **Pets:** Accepted.
[SAVE] 📶 ✕ 📶 🛗 🖵 🏊

◈◈ ▼▼▼ Crowne Plaza Chicago O'Hare Hotel & Conference Center H
(847) 671-6350. **$79-$199.** 5440 N River Rd 60018. I-190 exit 1B (River Rd), just s. Int corridors. **Pets:** Accepted.
[SAVE] 📶 📶 🛗 🖵 🍴 🏊

◈◈ ▼▼▼ ▼▼▼ DoubleTree by Hilton Chicago O'Hare Airport-Rosemont H
(847) 292-9100. **$89-$299.** 5460 N River Rd 60018. I-190 exit 1B (River Rd), just s. Int corridors. **Pets:** Accepted.
[SAVE] 📶 📶 🖵 🍴 🏊 ✕

◈◈ ▼▼▼ ▼▼▼ Embassy Suites Hotel O'Hare Rosemont H
(847) 678-4000. **$99-$309.** 5500 N River Rd 60018. I-190 exit 1B (River Rd), just s. Int corridors. **Pets:** Accepted. [SAVE] 📶 🛗 🖵 🍴 🏊

◈◈ ▼▼▼ ▼▼▼ Hilton Rosemont Chicago O'Hare H
(847) 678-4488. **$119-$495.** 5550 N River Rd 60018. I-190 exit 1B (River Rd), just s. Int corridors. **Pets:** Accepted. [SAVE] 📶 📶 🖵 🍴 🏊

◈◈ ▼▼▼ ▼▼▼ InterContinental Chicago O'Hare H
(847) 544-5300. **Call for rates.** 5300 N River Rd 60018. I-190 exit 1B (River Rd), 0.4 mi s. Int corridors. **Pets:** Accepted.
[SAVE] 📶 ✕ 📶 🖵 🍴

▼▼◈ Residence Inn by Marriott Chicago-O'Hare H
(847) 375-9000. **$109-$169.** 7101 Chestnut St 60018. Jct US 12, 45 and Touhy Ave. Int corridors. **Pets:** Accepted. 📶 ✕ 🛗 🖵 🏊 ✕

◈◈ ▼▼▼ Sheraton Chicago O'Hare H 🐾
(847) 699-6300. **$99-$399, 3 day notice.** 6501 N Mannheim Rd 60018. On US 12 and 45, at SR 72 (Higgins Rd). Int corridors. **Pets:** Large. $75 deposit/room. Crate. [SAVE] 📶 ✕ 🛗 🖵 🍴

◈◈ ▼▼▼ ▼▼▼ The Westin O'Hare H
(847) 698-6000. **$99-$329.** 6100 N River Rd 60018. I-190 exit 1B (River Rd), just n. Int corridors. **Pets:** Accepted.
[SAVE] 📶 ✕ 📶 🖵 🍴 🏊 ✕

ST. CHARLES

◈◈ ▼▼ BEST WESTERN Inn of St. Charles H
(630) 584-4550. **$80-$110.** 1635 E Main St 60174. On SR 64, 0.5 mi e of SR 25. Ext/int corridors. **Pets:** Medium, dogs only. $10 daily fee/pet. Designated rooms, service with restrictions, supervision.
[SAVE] 📶 🛗 🖵 🏊

▼▼▼ Country Inn & Suites By Carlson H
(630) 587-6564. **$79-$149.** 155 38th Ave 60174. On SR 64, 3.1 mi w of SR 59. Int corridors. **Pets:** Accepted. 📶 📶 🛗 🖵 🏊 ✕

▼▼▼ Courtyard by Marriott Chicago-St Charles H
(630) 377-6370. **$119-$149.** 700 Courtyard Dr 60174. Jct SR 59 and 64, 3.4 mi w on SR 64, just n on Kirk Rd, then just w on Foxfield. Int corridors. **Pets:** Accepted. [ECO] 📶 ✕ 📶 🛗 🖵 🍴 🏊

▼▼ Holiday Inn Express H 🐾
(630) 584-5300. **$89-$139.** 1600 E Main St 60174. On SR 64, 0.5 mi e of SR 25. Int corridors. **Pets:** Medium. $50 one-time fee/pet. Designated rooms, service with restrictions, crate. 📶 🛗 🖵 🏊

SCHAUMBURG

▼▼ Extended StayAmerica Chicago-Schaumburg Convention Center H
(847) 882-7011. **$48-$95.** 2000 N Roselle Rd 60195. I-90 exit Roselle Rd, just sw. Int corridors. **Pets:** $25 daily fee/pet. Designated rooms, service with restrictions. 📶 🛗 🖵

▼▼▼ Extended StayAmerica-Chicago-Woodfield H
(847) 517-7255. **$55-$105.** 1200 American Ln 60173. I-290 exit SR 72 (Higgins Rd), 0.5 mi w to Meacham Rd, 0.5 mi n to American Ln, then just w. Int corridors. **Pets:** $25 daily fee/pet. Designated rooms, service with restrictions. 📶 🛗 🖵

▼▼▼ Hawthorn Suites by Wyndham Chicago-Schaumburg H 🐾
(847) 517-7644. **$80-$150.** 1200 E Bank Dr 60173. I-290 exit SR 72 (Higgins Rd), 0.8 mi w to National Pkwy, then just n. Int corridors. **Pets:** Other species. $15 daily fee/pet. Service with restrictions.
📶 🛗 🖵

▼▼▼ Homestead Studio Suites Chicago-Schaumburg H
(847) 882-6900. **$50-$100.** 51 E State Pkwy 60173. I-90 exit Roselle Rd, 0.8 mi s, then just e. Int corridors. **Pets:** $25 daily fee/pet. Designated rooms, service with restrictions. 📶 📶 🛗 🖵

▼▼▼ Homewood Suites by Hilton-Schaumburg H
(847) 605-0400. **Call for rates.** 815 E American Ln 60173. I-290 exit SR 72 (Higgins Rd), 1.5 mi w, then 0.4 mi n on Plum Grove Rd. Ext/int corridors. **Pets:** Accepted. 📶 📶 🛗 🖵 🏊 ✕

◈◈ ▼▼▼ Hyatt house Chicago/Schaumburg H
(847) 706-9007. **$89-$159.** 1251 E American Ln 60173. I-290 exit SR 72 (Higgins Rd), 0.5 mi w to Meacham Rd, 0.5 mi n to American Ln, then just w. Int corridors. **Pets:** Medium. $25 daily fee/pet. Service with restrictions, crate. [SAVE] 📶 ✕ 📶 🛗 🖵 🏊 ✕

▼▼ La Quinta Inn (Schaumburg) H
(847) 517-8484. **$59-$144.** 1730 E Higgins Rd 60173. I-290 exit SR 72 (Higgins Rd), just w. Int corridors. **Pets:** Service with restrictions, supervision. 📶 🛗 🖵 🏊

▼▼▼ Residence Inn by Marriott-Chicago/Schaumburg H
(847) 517-9200. **$129-$499.** 1610 McConnor Pkwy 60173. I-290 exit 1A (Woodfield Rd/Golf Rd) northbound, follow signs just n to Golf Rd, just w to McConnor Pkwy, then 0.8 mi n; exit 1B (Woodfield Rd/Golf Rd) southbound. Int corridors. **Pets:** Medium. $100 one-time fee/room. Service with restrictions. 📶 ✕ 📶 🛗 🖵 🏊 ✕

◈◈ ▼▼▼ Sonesta ES Suites H
(847) 619-6677. **Call for rates.** 901 E Woodfield Office Ct 60173. I-290 exit SR 72 (Higgins Rd), 1.5 mi w, then 0.3 mi n on Plum Grove Rd. Ext/int corridors. **Pets:** Accepted. [SAVE] 📶 🛗 🖵 🏊 ✕

▼▼ Stay Inn Chicago-Schaumburg H
(847) 619-1000. **$69-$199, 7 day notice.** 1300 E Higgins Rd 60173. I-290 exit SR 72 (Higgins Rd), 0.5 mi w. Int corridors. **Pets:** Medium. $75 one-time fee/room. Designated rooms, service with restrictions, crate.
📶 📶 🖵

SCHILLER PARK

▼▼▼ Comfort Suites O'Hare Airport H
(847) 233-9000. **$79-$129.** 4200 N River Rd 60176. Jct SR 19 (Irving Park Rd) and Des Plaines St/River Rd, just n. Int corridors. **Pets:** Other species. $50 one-time fee/pet. Service with restrictions, crate.
📶 ✕ 📶 🛗 🖵 🍴

Four Points by Sheraton Chicago O'Hare Airport H

(847) 671-6000. **$79-$250.** 10249 W Irving Park Rd 60176. Jct US 12, 45 and SR 19 (Irving Park Rd). Int corridors. **Pets:** Medium, other species. $100 deposit/room. Designated rooms, service with restrictions, crate. [SAVE]

Hampton Inn Chicago O'Hare Airport H ❀

(847) 671-1700. **$89-$179.** 3939 N Mannheim Rd 60176. Jct US 12 and 45, 0.5 mi s of SR 19 (Irving Park Rd). Int corridors. **Pets:** Small, dogs only. $50 one-time fee/pet. Designated rooms, service with restrictions, supervision.

SKOKIE

Comfort Inn Northshore-Skokie H

(847) 679-4200. **$99-$139.** 9333 Skokie Blvd 60077. I-94 exit 35 (Old Orchard Rd), 0.4 mi e to Skokie Blvd (US 41), then 0.3 mi s. Int corridors. **Pets:** Other species. $15 daily fee/room. Designated rooms, service with restrictions.

Extended StayAmerica-Chicago-Skokie H

(847) 663-9031. **$60-$115.** 5211 Old Orchard Rd 60077. I-94 exit 35 (Old Orchard Rd). Int corridors. **Pets:** $25 daily fee/pet. Designated rooms, service with restrictions.

Holiday Inn Chicago North Shore H

(847) 679-8900. **$79-$169.** 5300 W Touhy Ave 60077. I-94 exit 39A, 0.5 mi w. Int corridors. **Pets:** Accepted. [SAVE]

TINLEY PARK

La Quinta Inn & Suites Chicago-Tinley Park H

(708) 633-1200. **$83-$184.** 7255 W 183rd St 60477. I-80 exit 148B, 0.5 mi n to 183rd St, then just w to North Creek Business Center. Int corridors. **Pets:** Service with restrictions, supervision.

VERNON HILLS

Extended StayAmerica-Chicago-Vernon Hills-Lake Forest H

(847) 821-7101. **$55-$105.** 215 N Milwaukee Ave 60061. I-94 exit SR 60 (Townline Rd), 2.1 mi w to SR 21 (Milwaukee Ave), then 0.3 mi s; in The Marketplace At Vernon Hills. Int corridors. **Pets:** $25 daily fee/pet. Designated rooms, service with restrictions.

Holiday Inn Express/Vernon Hills H

(847) 367-8031. **$79-$159.** 975 Lakeview Pkwy 60061. Jct SR 21 (Milwaukee Ave), 0.7 mi w on SR 60 (Townline Rd) to Lakeview Pkwy, then just n. Int corridors. **Pets:** Accepted.

Homestead Studio Suites Hotel-Chicago/Vernon Hills-Lincolnshire H

(847) 955-1111. **$55-$110.** 675 Woodlands Pkwy 60061. I-94 exit SR 60 (Townline Rd), 2.1 mi w to SR 21 (Milwaukee Ave), 1.9 mi s to Woodlands Pkwy, then just w. Int corridors. **Pets:** $25 daily fee/pet. Designated rooms, service with restrictions.

Hotel Indigo Chicago/Vernon Hills H

(847) 918-1400. **$89-$199.** 450 N Milwaukee Ave 60061. I-94 exit SR 60 (Townline Rd), 2.1 mi w to SR 21 (Milwaukee Ave), then 0.3 mi s. Int corridors. **Pets:** Medium. $75 one-time fee/pet. Designated rooms, service with restrictions, crate.

WARRENVILLE

Hyatt house Chicago/Naperville/Warrenville H

(630) 836-2960. **$89-$259.** 27554 Maecliff Dr 60555. I-88 exit Winfield Rd, just n to Ferry Rd, then just e. Int corridors. **Pets:** Medium. $150 one-time fee/pet. Service with restrictions.

Residence Inn by Marriott Chicago Naperville/Warrenville H

(630) 393-3444. **$79-$199.** 28500 Bella Vista Pkwy 60555. I-88 exit Winfield Rd, just n to Ferry Rd, then just e. Int corridors. **Pets:** Accepted.

WAUKEGAN

Candlewood Suites Chicago/Waukegan H

(847) 578-5250. **$85-$125.** 1151 S Waukegan Rd 60085. I-94 exit SR 137 (Buckley Rd), 0.5 mi e to SR 43 (Waukegan Rd), then 1.9 mi n. Int corridors. **Pets:** Accepted.

Residence Inn by Marriott Chicago-Waukegan/Gurnee H 🐾

(847) 689-9240. **$89-$179.** 1440 S White Oak Dr 60085. I-94 exit SR 137 (Buckley Rd), 0.5 mi e to SR 43 (Waukegan Rd), 1.5 mi n to Lakeside Dr, then just e. Int corridors. **Pets:** Other species. $100 one-time fee/room. Service with restrictions.

WEST DUNDEE

TownePlace Suites by Marriott Chicago West Dundee/Elgin H ❀

(847) 608-6320. **$89-$169.** 2185 Marriott Dr 60118. I-90 exit SR 31, 0.4 mi n to Marriott Dr, then just e. Int corridors. **Pets:** Other species. Service with restrictions, crate.

WESTMONT

ClubHouse Inn & Suites H

(630) 920-2200. **Call for rates.** 630 Pasquinelli Dr 60559. Just off US 34 (Ogden Ave), 0.3 mi nw of jct SR 83. Int corridors. **Pets:** Other species. $10 daily fee/pet. Designated rooms, service with restrictions, supervision.

Homestead Studio Suites - Chicago - Westmont - Oak Brook H

(630) 323-9292. **$50-$100.** 855 Pasquinelli Dr 60559. SR 83 exit US 34 (Ogden Ave), just w to Pasquinelli Dr, then 0.5 mi n. Int corridors. **Pets:** $25 daily fee/pet. Designated rooms, service with restrictions.

WHEELING

The Westin Chicago North Shore H

(847) 777-6500. **$89-$389.** 601 N Milwaukee Ave 60090. Jct Lake Cook Rd, just s. Int corridors. **Pets:** Accepted.

WILLOWBROOK

La Quinta Inn Chicago-Willowbrook H

(630) 654-0077. **$83-$155.** 855 79th St 60527. I-55 exit 274, just n. Int corridors. **Pets:** Service with restrictions, supervision.

Red Roof Inn #0167 M

(630) 323-8811. **$45-$86.** 7535 Kingery Hwy Route 83 60527. I-55 exit 274, 0.5 mi n on SR 83. Ext corridors. **Pets:** Large, other species. Service with restrictions, supervision. [SAVE]

WOODSTOCK

BEST WESTERN Woodstock Inn H

(815) 337-0065. **$85-$95.** 990 Lake Ave 60098. On SR 47, 0.5 mi n of jct US 14. Int corridors. **Pets:** Medium, dogs only. $50 deposit/pet, $20 daily fee/pet. Designated rooms, supervision.

Super 8 H

(815) 337-8808. **$65.** 1220 Davis Rd 60098. On SR 47, s of jct US 14. Int corridors. **Pets:** Accepted.

END METROPOLITAN AREA

COLLINSVILLE

DoubleTree by Hilton Hotel Collinsville - St. Louis H

(618) 345-2800. **Call for rates.** 1000 Eastport Plaza Dr 62234. I-55/70 exit 11 (SR 157), just nw. Int corridors. **Pets:** Accepted.

[SAVE] 🛜 ✕ 🛏 🖨 🍴 ⊰

Drury Inn-St. Louis/Collinsville H

(618) 345-7700. **$100-$174.** 602 N Bluff Rd 62234. I-55/70 exit 11 (SR 157), just n. Int corridors. **Pets:** Service with restrictions, supervision.

🛜 🅜 🛏 🖨 ⊰

Super 8-Collinsville H

(618) 345-8008. **$59-$90.** 2 Gateway Dr 62234. I-55/70 exit 11 (SR 157), just n. Int corridors. **Pets:** Other species. $15 one-time fee/room. Supervision. 🛜 🛏 🖨

COLUMBIA

Hampton Inn H

(618) 281-9000. **$89-$119.** 165 Admiral Trost Dr 62236. I-255 exit 6 (SR 3), 2.4 mi s, then just e. Int corridors. **Pets:** Other species. $100 deposit/room. Service with restrictions, supervision.

🛜 ✕ 🅜 🛏 🖨 ⊰

DANVILLE

BEST WESTERN Regency Inn H

(217) 446-2111. **$69-$139.** 360 Eastgate Dr 61834. I-74 exit 220 (Lynch Dr), just n. Ext/int corridors. **Pets:** Accepted. [SAVE] 🛜 🛏 🖨 ⊰

Sleep Inn & Suites H

(217) 442-6600. **$69-$99.** 361 Lynch Dr 61834. I-74 exit 220 (Lynch Dr), just n. Int corridors. **Pets:** $15 daily fee/pet. Service with restrictions, supervision. 🛜 ✕ 🛏 🖨 ⊰

Super 8 H

(217) 443-4499. **$50.** 377 Lynch Dr 61834. I-74 exit 220 (Lynch Dr), just n. Int corridors. **Pets:** Accepted. 🛜 🛏 🖨

DECATUR

Decatur Conference Center & Hotel H

(217) 422-8800. **$99-$109, 3 day notice.** 4191 W Hwy 36 62522. I-72 exit 133A (US 36), 1 mi e. Int corridors. **Pets:** Accepted.

🛜 🅜 🛏 🖨 🍴 ⊰ ✕

Sleep Inn H

(217) 872-7700. **$70-$100.** 3920 E Hospitality Ln 62521. I-72 exit 144 (SR 48), just s to Brush College Rd, then just e. Int corridors. **Pets:** Small. $10 daily fee/pet. Designated rooms, service with restrictions, crate. 🛜 🛏 🖨 ⊰

DEKALB

BEST WESTERN DeKalb Inn & Suites H

(815) 758-8661. **$89-$149.** 1212 W Lincoln Hwy 60115. I-88 exit Annie Glidden Rd, 2 mi n to W Lincoln Hwy (SR 38), then just w. Ext/int corridors. **Pets:** Accepted. [SAVE] 🛜 🛏 🖨 ⊰

DIXON

Comfort Inn by Choice Hotels H

(815) 284-0500. **$75-$120.** 136 Plaza Dr 61021. I-88 exit SR 26, just n, then just e. Int corridors. **Pets:** $15 daily fee/pet. Service with restrictions, crate. [SAVE] 🛜 🛏 🖨 ⊰ ✕

EAST MOLINE

Comfort Inn & Suites H

(309) 792-4660. **$85-$105.** 2209 John Deere Expwy 61244. I-74 exit 4B (John Deere Rd), 5 mi e; I-80 exit 4A, 6 mi w on SR 5. Int corridors. **Pets:** Accepted. 🛜 ✕ 🅜 🛏 🖨 ⊰

Super 8-East Moline H

(309) 796-1999. **$60-$99.** 2201 John Deere Rd 61244. I-74 exit 4B (John Deere Rd), 5.5 mi e on SR 5. Int corridors. **Pets:** Accepted.

🛜 🛏 🖨

EAST PEORIA

Stoney Creek Inn & Conference Center H

(309) 694-1300. **Call for rates.** 101 Mariners Way 61611. I-74 exit 95 (Main St) westbound; exit 95A eastbound, just n. Int corridors. **Pets:** Accepted. 🛜 ✕ 🅜 🛏 🖨 ⊰ ✕

Super 8 H

(309) 698-8889. **$59-$80.** 725 Taylor St 61611. I-74 exit 96, just e. Int corridors. **Pets:** Accepted. 🛜 🛏 🖨

EFFINGHAM

BEST WESTERN Raintree Inn H

(217) 342-4121. **$65-$70.** 1811 W Fayette Ave 62401. I-57/70 exit 159, just n. Ext/int corridors. **Pets:** Accepted. [SAVE] 🛜 🛏 🖨 🍴 ⊰

Fairfield Inn & Suites by Marriott H

(217) 540-5454. **$109-$159.** 1111 N Henrietta St 62401. I-57/70 exit 160 (SR 32/33), just se. Int corridors. **Pets:** $20 one-time fee/pet. Service with restrictions, supervision. 🛜 ✕ 🅜 🛏 🖨 ⊰

Quality Inn H

(217) 347-5050. **$71-$80.** 1304 W Evergreen Ave 62401. I-57/70 exit 160 (SR 32/33), just e, then just n. Int corridors. **Pets:** Other species. $10 deposit/pet, $10 daily fee/pet. Designated rooms, service with restrictions, supervision. 🛜 🅜 🛏 🖨 ⊰

Super 8-Effingham M

(217) 342-6888. **$56-$105.** 1400 Thelma Keller Ave 62401. I-57/70 exit 160 (SR 32/33), 0.5 mi n. Int corridors. **Pets:** Other species. Service with restrictions, crate. 🛜 🛏 🖨

FAIRFIELD

Briarwood Inn Fairfield H

(618) 842-3667. **$82-$110.** 116 N Market Ave 62837. West end of town. Int corridors. **Pets:** Small, dogs only. $10 daily fee/pet. Service with restrictions, crate. 🛜 🅜 🛏 🖨 ⊰

FAIRVIEW HEIGHTS

Americas Best Value Inn H

(618) 624-3636. **$50-$90.** 305 Salem Pl 62208. I-64 exit 12 (SR 159), just n. Int corridors. **Pets:** Medium. $10 daily fee/pet. Designated rooms, service with restrictions, supervision. [SAVE] 🛜 🛏 🖨 ⊰

Comfort Suites H

(618) 394-0202. **$89-$139.** 137 Ludwig Dr 62208. I-64 exit 12 (SR 159), just n to Ludwig Dr, then 0.4 mi w. Int corridors. **Pets:** Medium. $10 daily fee/pet. Service with restrictions. 🛜 ✕ 🅜 🛏 🖨 ⊰

Drury Inn & Suites-Fairview Heights H

(618) 398-8530. **$100-$179.** 12 Ludwig Dr 62208. I-64 exit 12 (SR 159), just n. Int corridors. **Pets:** Service with restrictions, supervision.

🛜 🛏 🖨 ⊰ ✕

Fairfield Inn by Marriott H

(618) 398-7124. **$89-$299.** 140 Ludwig Dr 62208. I-64 exit 12 (SR 159), 1 mi nw. Int corridors. **Pets:** Accepted. 🛜 ✕ 🅜 🛏 🖨 ⊰

FLORA

BEST WESTERN Lorson Inn H

(618) 662-3054. **$72-$80.** 201 Hagen Dr 62839. Jct US 45 and 50. Int corridors. **Pets:** $8 daily fee/pet. Designated rooms, service with restrictions, supervision. [SAVE] 🛜 🅜 🛏 🖨

FORSYTH

▼▼▼ **Hampton Inn Decatur-Forsyth** H

(217) 877-5577. **$99-$279.** 1429 Hickory Point Dr 62535. I-72 exit 141B (US 51), 0.5 mi n. Int corridors. **Pets:** Medium, other species. Designated rooms, service with restrictions. 🛰 ✕ ⓜ 🔋 💻 ⌇ ✕

▼▼ **Quality Inn Forsyth** H

(217) 875-1166. **$79-$100.** 134 Barnett Ave 62535. I-72 exit 141B (US 51), 0.5 mi n. Int corridors. **Pets:** $10 one-time fee/room. Service with restrictions, supervision. 🛰 🔋 💻 ⌇

FREEPORT

▼▼ **Baymont Inn & Suites-Freeport** H

(815) 599-8510. **$89-$119.** 1060 Rt 26 61032. Jct US 20 Bypass and SR 26, just s. Int corridors. **Pets:** Other species. $35 one-time fee/room. Service with restrictions, supervision. 🛰 🔋 💻 ⌇

GALENA

𝔸𝔸𝔸 ▼▼ **BEST WESTERN Designer Inn & Suites** H

(815) 777-2577. **$89-$249.** 9923 US Rt 20 W 61036. On US 20, 1 mi e. Ext/int corridors. **Pets:** Small, dogs only. $15 daily fee/pet. Designated rooms, service with restrictions. SAVE 🛰 🔋 💻 ⌇

𝔸𝔸𝔸 ▼▼▼ **Eagle Ridge Resort & Spa** H 🐾

(815) 777-5000. **$139-$319, 7 day notice.** 444 Eagle Ridge Dr 61036. US 20, 6 mi e to E Glen Hollow Rd, 4.5 mi n. Ext/int corridors. **Pets:** Medium, dogs only. $75 one-time fee/pet. Designated rooms, service with restrictions, crate. SAVE 🛰 🔋 💻 🍽 ⌇ ✕

▼▼ **Stoney Creek Inn** H 🐾

(815) 777-2223. **Call for rates.** 940 Galena Square Dr 61036. On US 20, 1.8 mi w. Int corridors. **Pets:** Medium, other species. $25 daily fee/pet. Designated rooms, service with restrictions, supervision. 🛰 ✕ 🔋 💻 ⌇ ✕

GALESBURG

𝔸𝔸𝔸 ▼▼▼ **BEST WESTERN PLUS Prairie Inn** H

(309) 343-7151. **$100-$120.** 300 S Soangetaha Rd 61401. I-74 exit 48 (Main St), just e, then just s. Int corridors. **Pets:** Medium. $20 daily fee/room. Designated rooms, service with restrictions, crate. SAVE 🛰 🔋 💻 🍽 ⌇

▼▼ **Comfort Inn by Choice Hotels** H

(309) 344-5445. **Call for rates.** 907 W Carl Sandburg Dr 61401. US 34 exit US 150 E. Int corridors. **Pets:** Accepted. 🛰 ⓜ 🔋 💻

▼▼▼ **Holiday Inn Express** H 🐾

(309) 343-7100. **$89-$149.** 2285 Washington St 61401. I-74 exit 48A (US 150), just w to Michigan Ave, just s to Washington St, then just e. Int corridors. **Pets:** Other species. $25 one-time fee/room. Service with restrictions, supervision. 🛰 ⓜ 🔋 💻 ⌇ ✕

GILMAN

𝔸𝔸𝔸 ▼▼ **Super 8** H

(815) 265-7000. **$56-$66.** 1301 S Crescent St 60938. I-57 exit 283, 0.3 mi e. Int corridors. **Pets:** Large. $10 daily fee/pet. Service with restrictions, supervision. SAVE 🛰 🔋 💻

GRAYVILLE

▼▼ **Super 8** H

(618) 375-7288. **$55-$105.** 2060 CR 2450 N 62844. I-64 exit 130 (SR 1), just n. Int corridors. **Pets:** Medium, other species. $15 one-time fee/room. Service with restrictions, crate. 🛰 ⓜ 🔋 💻

GREENVILLE

𝔸𝔸𝔸 ▼▼▼ **Econo Lodge Inn & Suites** M

(618) 664-3030. **$53-$160.** 1731 S SR 127 62246. I-70 exit 45, just n. Ext/int corridors. **Pets:** $10 daily fee/pet. Designated rooms, service with restrictions, supervision. SAVE 🛰 🔋 💻 ⌇

▼▼ **Super 8-Greenville** H

(618) 664-0800. **$50-$68.** 1700 SR 127 S 62246. I-70 exit 45, just n. Int corridors. **Pets:** Accepted. 🛰 🔋 💻

JACKSONVILLE

𝔸𝔸𝔸 ▼ **Starlite Motel** M

(217) 245-7184. **$40-$85.** 1910 W Morton Ave 62650. I-72 exit 64, 2.3 mi n on SR 267 (Main St) to SR 104 (Morton Ave), then 1.8 mi w. Ext corridors. **Pets:** Small. $5 daily fee/pet. Service with restrictions, crate. SAVE 🛰 🔋 💻

▼▼ **Super 8** H

(217) 479-0303. **$50-$100.** 1003 W Morton Ave 62650. I-72 exit 64, 2.3 mi n on SR 267 (Main St) to SR 104 (Morton Ave), then 0.8 mi w. Int corridors. **Pets:** Other species. $10 daily fee/pet. Designated rooms, crate. 🛰 🔋 💻

KEWANEE

▼▼ **AmericInn Lodge & Suites of Kewanee** H

(309) 856-7200. **$100-$160.** 925 S Tenney St 61443. On SR 78, 1.9 mi s of jct US 34. Int corridors. **Pets:** Accepted. 🛰 ⓜ 🔋 💻 ⌇

LEROY

▼▼▼ **Holiday Inn Express** H

(309) 962-4439. **$89-$129.** 705 S Persimmons Ct 61752. I-74 exit 149, just ne. Int corridors. **Pets:** Large. $25 one-time fee/room. Designated rooms, service with restrictions, supervision. 🛰 ⓜ 🔋 💻 ⌇

▼▼ **Red Roof Inn Le Roy** M

(309) 962-4700. **$71-$111.** 1 Demma Dr 61752. I-74 exit 149, just sw. Int corridors. **Pets:** Large, other species. Service with restrictions, supervision. 🛰 🔋 💻

LINCOLN

𝔸𝔸𝔸 ▼▼▼ **BEST WESTERN PLUS Lincoln Inn** H

(217) 732-9641. **$78-$85.** 1750 5th St 62656. I-55 exit 126 (US 121), 1.6 mi e to Lincoln Pkwy, then 0.5 mi s. Int corridors. **Pets:** Medium. $15 daily fee/pet. Service with restrictions, supervision. SAVE 🛰 🔋 💻 ⌇

▼▼▼ **Hampton Inn - Lincoln** H

(217) 732-6729. **$80-$90.** 1019 N Heitman Dr 62656. I-55 exit 126 (US 121), just e. Int corridors. **Pets:** Accepted. 🛰 ⓜ 🔋 💻 ⌇

▼▼ **Holiday Inn Express** H 🐾

(217) 735-5800. **$60-$129, 3 day notice.** 130 Olson Dr 62656. I-55 exit 126 (US 121), just e. Int corridors. **Pets:** Medium. Service with restrictions, supervision. 🛰 🔋 💻 ⌇

LITCHFIELD

▼▼▼ **Hampton Inn** H

(217) 324-4441. **$76-$98.** 11 Thunderbird Cir 62056. I-55 exit 52 (SR 16), on Corvette Dr, then just e. Int corridors. **Pets:** Large. $50 deposit/room. Service with restrictions, crate. 🛰 ⓜ 🔋 💻 ⌇

▼▼ **Holiday Inn Express** H

(217) 324-4556. **$99-$159.** 1405 W Hudson Dr 62056. I-55 exit 52 (SR 16), just e to Ohren Ln, just s to W Hudson Dr, then just w. Int corridors. **Pets:** Other species. Service with restrictions, supervision. 🛰 🔋 💻 ⌇

𝔸𝔸𝔸 ▼▼▼ **Quality Inn & Suites Litchfield** H

(217) 324-9260. **$65-$74.** 1010 E Columbian Blvd N 62056. I-55 exit 52 (SR 16), just e to Ohren Ln, just s to W Hudson Dr, then just w. Int corridors. **Pets:** Small. $10 daily fee/pet. Service with restrictions, supervision. SAVE 🛰 🔋 💻 ⌇

LOVES PARK

AAA **▼▼▼▼** Holiday Inn Express Hotel & Suites Rockford North **H**

(815) 654-4100. **Call for rates.** 7552 Park Pl 61111. I-39/90 exit E Riverside Blvd, just nw. Int corridors. **Pets:** Medium, other species. $25 daily fee/room. Designated rooms, service with restrictions, supervision.

SAVE 🛜 🕹M 🛄 🖵 🏊 ⊠

▼▼ Quality Inn & Suites Rockford/Loves Park **H**

(815) 282-9300. **Call for rates.** 4313 N Bell School Rd 61111. I-39/90 exit E Riverside Blvd, just nw. Int corridors. **Pets:** Accepted.

🛜 🕹M 🛄 🖵 🏊

MACOMB

▼▼ Super 8 **H**

(309) 836-8888. **$55-$135.** 313 University Dr 61455. 1.1 mi n on US 67 to University Dr, 0.5 mi w. Int corridors. **Pets:** Accepted. 🛜 🛄 🖵

MANTENO

AAA **▼▼▼▼** Country Inn & Suites By Carlson **H**

(815) 468-2600. **$79-$199.** 380 S Cypress St 60950. I-57 exit 322, just se via frontage road. Int corridors. **Pets:** Medium, other species. $15 daily fee/pet. Designated rooms, service with restrictions, supervision.

SAVE 🛜 ⊠ 🕹M 🛄 🖵 🏊

MARION

▼▼▼ Country Inn & Suites By Carlson **H**

(618) 997-2444. **$86.** 1306 Halfway Rd 62959. Int corridors. **Pets:** Other species. $15 one-time fee/pet. Service with restrictions, supervision.

🛜 ⊠ 🛄 🖵 🏊 ⊠

▼▼ Drury Inn-Marion **H**

(618) 997-9600. **$105-$174.** 2706 W DeYoung St 62959. I-57 exit 54B (SR 13), 0.5 mi w. Int corridors. **Pets:** Service with restrictions, supervision. 🛜 🕹M 🛄 🖵 🏊

▼ Super 8 **H**

(618) 993-5577. **$61-$83.** 2601 W Vernell Rd 62959. I-57 exit 54B (SR 13), just w. Int corridors. **Pets:** Accepted. 🛜 🛄 🖵

MASCOUTAH

▼▼▼▼ La Quinta Inn & Suites O'Fallon / Mascoutah **H**

(618) 808-0280. **$83-$139.** 9730 Hayden Dr 62258. I-64 exit 23, just n. Int corridors. **Pets:** Service with restrictions, supervision.

🛜 ⊠ 🕹M 🛄 🖵 🏊

MATTOON

▼▼ Baymont Inn & Suites **H**

(217) 234-2420. **$75-$105.** 206 McFall Rd 61938. I-57 exit 190B, just w. Int corridors. **Pets:** Accepted. 🛜 🛄 🖵 🏊

▼▼▼▼ Holiday Inn Express Hotel & Suites **H**

(217) 235-2060. **$90-$139.** 121 Swords Dr 61938. I-57 exit 190B, just w. Int corridors. **Pets:** $10 daily fee/pet. Designated rooms, service with restrictions, supervision. 🛜 ⊠ 🕹M 🛄 🖵 🏊 ⊠

▼▼ Super 8 **M**

(217) 235-8888. **$51-$80.** 205 McFall Rd 61938. I-57 exit 190B, just w. Int corridors. **Pets:** Small, other species. $10 one-time fee/pet. Designated rooms, service with restrictions, supervision. 🛜 🛄 🖵

METROPOLIS

AAA **▼▼▼▼** Harrah's Metropolis Casino & Hotel **H**

(618) 524-2628. **$70-$770.** 100 E Front St 62960. I-24 exit 37 (US 45), 3.5 mi w, then just s on Ferry St; between Metropolis and Ferry sts. Int corridors. **Pets:** Accepted. SAVE 🛜 🕹M 🛄 🖵 🍴

MONMOUTH

▼▼▼ AmericInn Lodge & Suites of Monmouth **H**

(309) 734-9958. **Call for rates.** 1 AmericInn Way 61462. Jct US 34 and N Main St, just s; 18 mi w of jct I-74 and US 34. Int corridors. **Pets:** Medium, other species. $75 one-time fee/room. Service with restrictions, crate. 🛜 ⊠ 🕹M 🛄 🖵 🏊

MONTICELLO

AAA **▼▼▼** BEST WESTERN Monticello Gateway Inn **H** 🐾

(217) 762-9436. **Call for rates.** 805 Iron Horse Pl 61856. I-72 exit 166, just s. Ext/int corridors. **Pets:** Large. $10 daily fee/pet. Service with restrictions, supervision. SAVE 🛜 ⊠ 🛄 🖵 🏊

MORRIS

▼▼▼ Comfort Inn by Choice Hotels **H**

(815) 942-1433. **Call for rates.** 70 Gore Rd W 60450. I-80 exit 112 (SR 47), 0.3 mi nw. Int corridors. **Pets:** Accepted. 🛜 🛄 🖵 🏊

▼▼▼ Holiday Inn Express & Suites **H**

(815) 941-8700. **$93-$150, 3 day notice.** 222 Gore Rd 60450. I-80 exit 112 (SR 47), just nw. Int corridors. **Pets:** Accepted.

🛜 🕹M 🛄 🖵 🏊

MORTON

AAA **▼▼▼** Baymont Inn & Suites **H**

(309) 266-8888. **$75-$105.** 210 E Ashland St 61550. I-74 exit 102, 0.4 mi ne. Int corridors. **Pets:** $10 daily fee/pet. Designated rooms, service with restrictions, supervision. SAVE 🛜 🛄 🖵 🏊

AAA **▼▼▼▼** BEST WESTERN Ashland House & Conference Center **H**

(309) 263-5116. **$85-$100.** 201 E Ashland St 61550. I-74 exit 102, 0.3 mi ne. Int corridors. **Pets:** Medium, dogs only. $15 daily fee/room. Designated rooms, service with restrictions, supervision.

SAVE 🛜 🛄 🖵 🍴 🏊

▼▼▼ Quality Inn by Choice Hotels **H**

(309) 266-8310. **$65-$89.** 115 E Ashland Ave 61550. I-74 exit 102B, just w. Ext/int corridors. **Pets:** Accepted. 🛜 🛄 🖵

MOUNT VERNON

▼▼▼ Comfort Suites **H** 🐾

(618) 244-2700. **Call for rates.** 404 S 44th St 62864. I-57/64 exit 95 (SR 15), just e. Int corridors. **Pets:** Dogs only. $25 daily fee/room. Designated rooms, service with restrictions, crate.

🛜 ⊠ 🕹M 🛄 🖵 🏊

▼▼ Drury Inn-Mount Vernon **H**

(618) 244-4550. **$95-$139.** 145 N 44th St 62864. I-57/64 exit 95 (SR 15), just e, then just n; entry through restaurant parking lot. Int corridors. **Pets:** Service with restrictions, supervision. 🛜 🛄 🖵 🏊

▼▼▼ Holiday Inn **H**

(618) 244-7100. **$90-$115.** 222 Potomac Blvd 62864. I-57/64 exit 95 (SR 15), just w to Potomac Blvd, then just n. Int corridors. **Pets:** Accepted.

🛜 🕹M 🛄 🖵 🍴 🏊 ⊠

▼ Thrifty Inn-Mt. Vernon **H**

(618) 244-7750. **$50-$104.** 100 N 44th St 62864. I-57/64 exit 95 (SR 15), just e. Ext corridors. **Pets:** Service with restrictions, supervision.

🛜 🛄 🖵

NASHVILLE

AAA **▼▼▼** BEST WESTERN U.S. Inn **H**

(618) 478-5341. **$70-$85.** 11640 SR 127 62263. I-64 exit 50 (SR 127), 0.3 mi s. Int corridors. **Pets:** Small. $10 daily fee/pet. Designated rooms, service with restrictions, supervision. SAVE 🛜 🕹M 🛄 🖵 🏊

NORMAL

▼▼ ▼▼ Comfort Suites by Choice Hotels Bloomington/Normal

(309) 452-8588. **$80-$130.** 310 B Greenbriar Dr 61761. I-55 exit 167, follow I-55 business route (Veterans Pkwy), 1.3 mi s; jct Fort Jesse Rd. Int corridors. **Pets:** Other species. $20 daily fee/room. Service with restrictions, crate. 🛰 ✖ 🕊 🛏 💻 🏊

O'FALLON

▼▼ ▼▼ Candlewood Suites

(618) 622-9555. **Call for rates.** 1332 Park Plaza Dr 62269. I-64 exit 14 (US 50), just s on Lincoln Hwy, 0.5 mi w on Hartman Ln, then just n on 2nd entrance to Park Plaza Dr. Int corridors. **Pets:** Accepted.
🛰 🕊 🛏 💻

▼▼▼▼ Drury Inn & Suites-O'Fallon 🄷

(618) 624-2211. **$105-$199.** 1118 Central Park Dr 62269. I-64 exit 16, just s. Int corridors. **Pets:** Service with restrictions, supervision.
🛰 🕊 🛏 💻

▼▼ ▼▼ Extended StayAmerica-St. Louis-O'Fallon 🄷

(618) 624-1757. **$59-$84.** 154 Regency Park Dr 62269. I-64 exit 14 (US 50), just w to Regency Park Dr, then 0.4 mi s. Int corridors. **Pets:** $25 daily fee/pet. Designated rooms, service with restrictions.
🛰 🕊 🛏 💻

▼▼ ▼▼ Suburban Extended Stay Hotel 🄷

(618) 589-3696. **Call for rates.** 148 Regency Park Dr 62269. I-64 exit 14 (US 50), 0.5 mi e. Int corridors. **Pets:** Accepted. 🛰 🛏 💻 🏊

OGLESBY

🄰🄰🄰 ▼▼ ▼▼ BEST WESTERN Oglesby Inn 🄷

(815) 883-3535. **$79-$129.** 900 Holiday St 61348. I-39 exit 54, just e. Int corridors. **Pets:** Accepted. 🆂🄰🆅🄴 🛰 🛏 💻 🏊

▼▼ ▼▼ Days Inn Oglesby/Starved Rock 🄷

(815) 883-9600. **$85-$120.** 120 N Lewis Ave 61348. I-39 exit 54, just e. Int corridors. **Pets:** Other species. $15 one-time fee/pet. Service with restrictions, supervision. 🛰 ✖ 🕊 🛏 💻 🏊

OSWEGO

▼▼ ▼▼ AmericInn Lodge & Suites of Oswego 🄷

(630) 554-9090. **Call for rates.** 1050 Douglas Rd 60543. Between US 30 and 34. Int corridors. **Pets:** Accepted. 🛰 🕊 🛏 💻 🏊 ✖

OTTAWA

▼▼▼▼▼ Fairfield Inn & Suites by Marriott Ottawa/Starved Rock Area 🄷 🐾

(815) 431-8955. **$104-$129.** 3000 Fairfield Ln 61350. I-80 exit 90 (SR 23), just s to Etna Rd, then just e. Int corridors. **Pets:** Small. $35 one-time fee/room. Service with restrictions, crate.
🛰 ✖ 🕊 🛏 💻 🏊

▼▼ ▼▼ Hampton Inn-Starved Rock Area 🄷

(815) 434-6040. **Call for rates.** 4115 Holiday Ln 61350. I-80 exit 90 (SR 23), just n. Int corridors. **Pets:** Accepted. 🛰 🕊 🛏 💻 🏊

▼▼ ▼▼ Holiday Inn Express 🄷

(815) 433-0029. **$89-$132, 3 day notice.** 120 W Stevenson Rd 61350. I-80 exit 90 (SR 23), just n. Int corridors. **Pets:** Other species. Service with restrictions, supervision. 🛰 🛏 💻 🏊

PEORIA

▼▼ ▼▼ Candlewood Suites Peoria at Grand Prairie 🄷

(309) 691-1690. **$109-$124.** 5300 W Landens Way 61615. SR 6 exit 2 (US 150/War Memorial Dr), follow US 150 NW to Summershade Cir, then just w. Int corridors. **Pets:** Accepted. 🛰 🕊 🛏 💻 🏊

▼▼ ▼▼ Comfort Suites by Choice Hotels 🄷

(309) 688-3800. **Call for rates.** 1812 W War Memorial Dr 61614. I-74 exit 89 (US 150/War Memorial Dr), just e, then just s. Int corridors.
Pets: Accepted. 🛰 ✖ 🛏 💻 🏊

▼▼ ▼▼ Country Inn & Suites By Carlson Peoria-North 🄷 🐾

(309) 589-0044. **$129-$149.** 5309 W Landens Way 61615. SR 6 exit 2 (US 150/War Memorial Dr), just n. Int corridors. **Pets:** $75 one-time fee/pet. Service with restrictions, supervision.
🛰 ✖ 🕊 🛏 💻 🏊 ✖

🄰🄰🄰 ▼▼▼▼ Four Points by Sheraton Peoria Downtown 🄷

(309) 674-2500. **$159-$199.** 500 Hamilton Blvd 61602. I-74 exit 93 (Washington/Adams), just sw. Int corridors. **Pets:** Accepted.
🆂🄰🆅🄴 🛰 ✖ 🛏 💻 🍴 💻 ✖

🄰🄰🄰 ▼▼▼▼ Quality Inn & Suites 🄷

(309) 685-2556. **Call for rates.** 4112 N Brandywine Dr 61614. I-74 exit 89 (US 150/War Memorial Dr), just e. Int corridors. **Pets:** Other species. $15 daily fee/pet. Service with restrictions. 🆂🄰🆅🄴 🛰 🛏 💻 🏊

▼▼ ▼▼ Residence Inn by Marriott 🄷 🐾

(309) 681-9000. **$129-$279.** 2000 W War Memorial Dr 61614. I-74 exit 89 (US 150/War Memorial Dr), just w; entrance through Northwoods Mall. Int corridors. **Pets:** Other species. $100 one-time fee/room. Service with restrictions. 🛰 ✖ 🛏 💻 🏊 ✖

▼▼ ▼▼ Super 8 🄷

(309) 688-8074. **$59-$93.** 1816 W War Memorial Dr 61614. I-74 exit 89 (US 150/War Memorial Dr), just e. Int corridors. **Pets:** Other species. $50 deposit/room. Service with restrictions, crate. 🛰 🛏 💻

▼▼ ▼▼ Wingate by Wyndham Peoria 🄷 🐾

(309) 589-0033. **$109-$189.** 7708 N Rt 91 61615. SR 6 exit 2 (US 150/War Memorial Dr), just w, then 0.3 mi n. Int corridors. **Pets:** Other species. $75 one-time fee/room. Service with restrictions, crate.
🛰 ✖ 🕊 🛏 💻 🏊 ✖

PERU

▼▼ ▼▼ La Quinta Inn & Suites Peru 🄷

(815) 224-9000. **$82-$167.** 4389 Venture Dr 61354. I-80 exit 75 (SR 251), 0.4 mi s to 38th St, just w to Venture Dr, then 0.4 mi nw. Int corridors. **Pets:** Service with restrictions, supervision. 🛰 🛏 💻 🏊

PONTIAC

🄰🄰🄰 ▼▼ ▼▼ BEST WESTERN Pontiac Inn 🄷

(815) 842-2777. **$95-$110, 3 day notice.** 1821 W Reynolds St 61764. I-55 exit 197 (SR 116), just e. Int corridors. **Pets:** Accepted.
🆂🄰🆅🄴 🛰 ✖ 🛏 💻 🏊

QUAD CITIES AREA

MOLINE

▼▼ Comfort Inn by Choice Hotels H
(309) 762-7000. **$85-$119.** 2600 52nd Ave 61265. I-280/74 exit 18A eastbound; exit 5B westbound, just s on US 6 and 150, then 0.5 mi nw on 27th St. Int corridors. **Pets:** $15 daily fee/pet. Service with restrictions, supervision. 📶 🍴 💻 🏊

▼▼ Days Inn & Suites H
(309) 762-8300. **$55-$80.** 6910 27th St 61265. I-280/74 exit 18A eastbound; exit 5B westbound, just s on US 6 and 150, then just nw. Int corridors. **Pets:** Accepted. 📶 🍴 💻

▼▼ Fairfield Inn by Marriott H
(309) 762-9083. **$100-$160.** 2705 48th Ave 61265. I-280/74 exit 5B westbound; exit 18A eastbound, just s on US 6 to traffic light, then 1 mi nw on 27th St. Int corridors. **Pets:** Accepted. 📶 ✖ 🅼 🍴 💻 🏊

▼▼ La Quinta Inn Moline Airport H
(309) 762-9008. **$71-$144.** 5450 27th St 61265. I-280/74 exit 18A eastbound; exit 5B westbound, just s on US 6 and 150 to traffic light, then just nw. Int corridors. **Pets:** Service with restrictions, supervision. 📶 🅼 🍴 💻 🏊

▼▼▼ Stoney Creek Inn & Conference Center H ✿
(309) 743-0101. **Call for rates.** 101 18th St 61265. Jct 18th St and 2nd Ave; along Mississippi River. Int corridors. **Pets:** Medium. $25 daily fee/pet. Designated rooms, service with restrictions, crate. 📶 ✖ 🅼 🍴 💻 🏊 ✖

▼▼ Super 8 H
(309) 797-5580. **$49-$79.** 2501 52nd Ave 61265. I-280/74 exit 18A eastbound; exit 5B westbound, just s on US 6 and 150, then 1 mi nw on 27th St. Int corridors. **Pets:** Small, other species. $25 daily fee/pet. Designated rooms, service with restrictions, crate. 📶 🍴 💻

END AREA

QUINCY

▼▼ Comfort Inn by Choice Hotels H
(217) 228-2700. **Call for rates.** 4122 Broadway St 62305. I-172 exit 14 (SR 104), 1.3 mi w. Int corridors. **Pets:** Accepted. 📶 🍴 💻 🏊

▼▼ Microtel Inn & Suites by Wyndham Quincy H
(217) 222-5620. **$69-$109.** 200 S 3rd St 62301. Jct US 24 and SR 57, just sw. Int corridors. **Pets:** $15 daily fee/pet. Service with restrictions. 📶 🍴 💻 🏊

▼▼ Quincy Inn & Suites H
(217) 228-8808. **$51-$71.** 224 N 36th St 62301. I-172 exit 14 (SR 104), 1.8 mi w, then just s. Int corridors. **Pets:** Accepted. 📶 🅼 🍴 💻

▼▼ Stoney Creek Inn H ✿
(217) 223-2255. **Call for rates.** 3809 Broadway St 62305. I-172 exit 14 (SR 104), 1 mi w. Int corridors. **Pets:** Medium, dogs only. $25 daily fee/pet. Service with restrictions, crate. 📶 ✖ 🍴 💻 🏊 ✖

RANTOUL

ꊒ ▼▼ Magnuson Hotel Heritage Inn M
(217) 892-9292. **$58-$63.** 420 S Murray Rd 61866. I-57 exit 250 (US 136), 0.5 mi e, then just s. Ext corridors. **Pets:** Medium. $8 daily fee/pet. No service, supervision. SAVE 📶 🍴 💻 🏊

▼▼ Super 8 H
(217) 893-8888. **$60-$90.** 207 S Murray Rd 61866. I-57 exit 250 (US 136), just e. Int corridors. **Pets:** Small, dogs only. $10 daily fee/pet. Designated rooms, service with restrictions, supervision. 📶 🍴 💻

RAYMOND

ꊒ ▼▼ Magnuson Grand Hotel & Conference Center H
(217) 324-2100. **$80-$120.** 19067 W Frontage Rd 62560. I-55 exit 60 (SR 108), just w. Int corridors. **Pets:** Medium, other species. $15 daily fee/pet. Designated rooms, service with restrictions, supervision. SAVE 📶 ✖ 🍴 💻 🍴 🏊 ✖

ROBINSON

ꊒ ▼▼▼ BEST WESTERN Robinson Inn H
(618) 544-8448. **Call for rates.** 1500 W Main St 62454. 1.2 mi w on SR 33. Int corridors. **Pets:** Other species. $5 daily fee/room. Service with restrictions. SAVE 📶 🍴 💻

ROCHELLE

ꊒ ▼▼▼ Comfort Inn & Suites by Choice Hotels H
(815) 562-5551. **$79-$125.** 1133 N 7th St 61068. I-39 exit 99 (SR 38), 2.5 mi w; jct SR 38 and 251; downtown. Int corridors. **Pets:** Other species. $15 daily fee/pet. Service with restrictions, supervision. SAVE 📶 🍴 💻 🍴 🏊 ✖

ꊒ ▼▼▼ Holiday Inn Express H
(815) 562-9994. **$119-$139.** 1240 Dement Rd 61068. I-39 exit 99 (SR 38), just nw. Int corridors. **Pets:** Small. $25 one-time fee/pet. Designated rooms, service with restrictions, supervision. SAVE 📶 🅼 🍴 💻 🏊

ROCKFORD

ꊒ ▼▼▼ Baymont Inn & Suites Rockford H
(815) 229-8200. **$75-$140.** 662 N Lyford Rd 61107. I-90 exit US 20 business route, just e, then just n. Int corridors. **Pets:** Other species. $10 daily fee/pet. Designated rooms, service with restrictions, supervision. SAVE 📶 🍴 💻 🏊

ꊒ ▼▼▼ BEST WESTERN Clock Tower Resort H
(815) 398-6000. **$89-$129.** 7801 E State St 61108. I-90 exit US 20 business route, just e. Int corridors. **Pets:** Accepted. SAVE 📶 ✖ 🍴 💻 🍴 🏊 ✖

▼▼ Candlewood Suites H ✿
(815) 229-9300. **$99-$129.** 7555 Walton St 61108. I-90 exit US 20 business route, 0.3 mi e to Bell School Rd, just s to Walton St, then just e. Int corridors. **Pets:** Large, other species. $75 deposit/pet. Designated rooms, service with restrictions, crate. 📶 🅼 🍴 💻

▼▼ Comfort Inn by Choice Hotels H
(815) 398-7061. **$89-$104.** 7392 Argus Dr 61107. I-90 exit US 20 business route, just w to Bell School Rd, then just n. Int corridors. **Pets:** Accepted. 📶 🍴 💻 🏊

▼▼ Days Inn Rockford H
(815) 332-4915. **$60-$100.** 220 S Lyford Rd 61108. I-90 exit US 20 business route, just e, then just s. Int corridors. **Pets:** Accepted. 📶 🍴 💻

▼▼ Extended StayAmerica-Rockford East H
(815) 226-8969. **$45-$85.** 653 Clark Dr 61107. I-90 exit US 20 business route, just w. Int corridors. **Pets:** $25 daily fee/pet. Designated rooms, service with restrictions. 📶 🅼 🍴 💻

▼▼▼▼ Holiday Inn 🅷
(815) 398-2200. **$99-$159.** 7550 E State St 61108. I-90 exit US 20 business route, 0.3 mi w to Bell School Rd. Int corridors. **Pets:** Accepted.
🛜 ᴍ 🅗 🅟 ❌ 🍽 ➹ ⊠

Ⓐ ▼▼▼ Red Roof Inn #7035 Ⓜ
(815) 398-9750. **$49-$90.** 7434 E State St 61108. I-90 exit US 20 business route, just w. Ext corridors. **Pets:** Large, other species. Service with restrictions, supervision. 🆂🅰🆅🅴 🛜 🅗

▼▼▼▼ Residence Inn by Marriott 🅷 ❀
(815) 227-0013. **$140-$230.** 7542 Colosseum Dr 61107. I-90 exit US 20 business route, 0.3 mi w to Bell School Rd, then just n. Int corridors. **Pets:** Other species. $112 one-time fee/room. Designated rooms, service with restrictions, crate. 🛜 ❌ 🅗 🅟 ➹ ⊠

▼▼▼ Sleep Inn-Rockford 🅷
(815) 398-8900. **Call for rates.** 725 Clark Dr 61107. I-90 exit US 20 business route, just w to Bell School Rd, just n to Clark Dr, then 0.4 mi ne. Int corridors. **Pets:** $15 daily fee/pet. Service with restrictions, supervision. 🛜 🅗 🅟

▼▼▼▼ Staybridge Suites 🅷
(815) 397-0200. **$139-$249, 3 day notice.** 633 N Bell School Rd 61107. I-90 exit US 20 business route, 0.3 mi w to Bell School Rd, then just n. Int corridors. **Pets:** Accepted. 🛜 ᴍ 🅗 🅟 ➹ ⊠

▼▼▼ StudioPLUS Deluxe Studios Rockford-East 🅷
(815) 397-8316. **$58-$90.** 747 N Bell School Rd 61107. I-90 exit US 20 business route, just w to Bell School Rd, then 0.3 mi n. Int corridors. **Pets:** $25 daily fee/pet. Designated rooms, service with restrictions. 🛜 🅗 🅟

SALEM
▼ Super 8 🅷
(618) 548-5882. **$64-$79.** 118 Woods Ln 62881. I-57 exit 116 (US 50), just w. Ext/int corridors. **Pets:** Service with restrictions, supervision. 🛜 ᴍ 🅗 🅟

SAVOY
Ⓐ ▼▼▼ BEST WESTERN Paradise Inn 🅷 ❀
(217) 356-1824. **$91-$100.** 709 N Dunlap Ave 61874. I-57 exit 229, 2.5 mi e to US 45, then 2.5 mi n. Ext corridors. **Pets:** Small. $10 daily fee/pet. Designated rooms, service with restrictions, crate.
🆂🅰🆅🅴 🛜 🅗 🅟 ➹

SOUTH BELOIT
Ⓐ ▼▼▼▼ BEST WESTERN Legacy Inn & Suites
Beloit/South Beloit 🅷 ❀
(815) 389-4211. **$84-$139.** 5910 Technology Dr 61080. I-90/39 exit 1, just sw. Int corridors. **Pets:** Other species. $15 one-time fee/room. Service with restrictions, crate. 🆂🅰🆅🅴 🛜 ❌ ᴍ 🅗 🅟 ➹ ⊠

SOUTH JACKSONVILLE
▼▼▼▼ Comfort Inn by Choice Hotels-South
Jacksonville 🅷
(217) 245-8372. **Call for rates.** 200 Comfort Dr 62650. I-72 exit 64, just n. Int corridors. **Pets:** Medium. $15 daily fee/pet. Service with restrictions, supervision. 🛜 ᴍ 🅗 🅟 ➹

▼▼▼▼ Holiday Inn Express & Suites Jacksonville 🅷
(217) 245-6500. **Call for rates.** 2501 Holliday Ln 62650. I-72 exit 64, just n. Int corridors. **Pets:** Accepted. 🛜 ❌ ᴍ 🅟 ➹

SPRINGFIELD
▼▼▼ Baymont Inn & Suites Springfield 🅷
(217) 529-6655. **$65-$160.** 5871 S 6th St 62703. I-55 exit 90 (Toronto Rd), just e to 6th St, then just n. Int corridors. **Pets:** Medium. $10 daily fee/pet. Designated rooms, service with restrictions, supervision.
🛜 ❌ ᴍ 🅗 🅟 ➹

Ⓐ ▼▼▼ BEST WESTERN Clearlake Plaza 🅷
(217) 525-7420. **$89-$135.** 3440 E Clearlake Ave 62702. I-55 exit 98B, just w. Int corridors. **Pets:** Medium, other species. $20 daily fee/pet. Service with restrictions, crate. 🆂🅰🆅🅴 🛜 ᴍ 🅗 🅟 ➹

▼▼▼ Candlewood Suites 🅷
(217) 522-5100. **$75-$119.** 2501 Sunrise Dr 62703. I-55 exit 94 (Stevenson Dr), just w to Dirksen Pkwy, then 0.4 mi n. Int corridors. **Pets:** $75 one-time fee/pet. Designated rooms, service with restrictions, crate.
🛜 ❌ ᴍ 🅗 🅟

▼▼▼ Drury Inn & Suites-Springfield 🅷
(217) 529-3900. **$100-$169.** 3180 S Dirksen Pkwy 62703. I-55 exit 94 (Stevenson Dr), just w to Dirksen Pkwy, then just n. Int corridors. **Pets:** Service with restrictions, supervision.
🛜 ᴍ 🅗 🅟 ➹ ⊠

▼▼▼ Fairfield Inn by Marriott 🅷
(217) 793-9277. **$99-$169.** 3446 Freedom Dr 62704. I-72 exit 93 (Veterans Pkwy), 0.7 mi n to Lindbergh Blvd, just w to Freedom Dr, then just s. Int corridors. **Pets:** Accepted. 🛜 ❌ 🅗 🅟 ➹

▼▼▼ Holiday Inn Express Hotel & Suites 🅷
(217) 529-7771. **Call for rates.** 3050 S Dirksen Pkwy 62703. I-55 exit 94 (Stevenson Dr), just w to S Dirksen Pkwy, then 0.4 mi n. Int corridors. **Pets:** Medium. $40 one-time fee/room. Service with restrictions, crate.
🛜 ᴍ 🅗 🅟

Ⓐ ▼▼▼ Mansion View Inn & Suites 🅷
(217) 544-7411. **Call for rates.** 529 S 4th St 62701. I-55 exit 92 (6th St), 3.9 mi n to Edwards St, then just w, follow signs. Ext/int corridors. **Pets:** Accepted. 🆂🅰🆅🅴 🛜 ❌ 🅗 🅟

▼▼▼ Microtel Inn & Suites by Wyndham Springfield 🅷
(217) 753-2636. **$74-$99.** 2636 Sunrise Dr 62703. I-55 exit 94 (Stevenson Dr), just w to Dirksen Pkwy, then 0.4 mi n. Int corridors. **Pets:** Medium, dogs only. $5 daily fee/pet. Service with restrictions, crate.
🛜 ❌ ᴍ 🅗 🅟

▼▼▼ Quality Inn & Suites Springfield 🅷
(217) 787-2250. **$80-$120.** 3442 Freedom Dr 62704. I-72 exit 93 (Veterans Pkwy), 0.7 mi n to Lindbergh Blvd, just w to Freedom Dr, then just s. Int corridors. **Pets:** Accepted. 🛜 🅗 🅟 ➹

▼▼▼ Sleep Inn by Choice Hotels 🅷
(217) 787-6200. **$79-$130.** 3470 Freedom Dr 62704. I-72 exit 93 (Veterans Pkwy), 0.7 mi n to Lindbergh Blvd, just w to Freedom Dr, then just s. Int corridors. **Pets:** $25 one-time fee/room. Service with restrictions, crate.
🛜 🅗 🅟

▼▼▼ Staybridge Suites Springfield South 🅷 ❀
(217) 793-6700. **$99-$199.** 4231 Schooner Dr 62711. I-72 exit 93 (Veterans Pkwy), 0.4 mi se. Int corridors. **Pets:** Dogs only. $50 one-time fee/room. Service with restrictions, supervision.
🛜 ᴍ 🅗 🅟 ➹ ⊠

STAUNTON
▼▼▼ Staunton Super 8 🅷
(618) 635-5353. **$50-$70.** 1527 Herman Rd 62088. I-55 exit 41, 0.5 mi w. Int corridors. **Pets:** Medium. $10 one-time fee/room. Service with restrictions, supervision. 🛜 🅗 🅟

STOCKTON
▼▼▼ Country Inn & Suites By Carlson 🅷
(815) 947-6060. **$92-$142.** 200 Dillon Ave 61085. On US 20, just e of SR 78. Int corridors. **Pets:** $20 daily fee/pet. Designated rooms, service with restrictions, supervision. 🛜 ᴍ 🅗 🅟 ➹

STREATOR
▼▼▼ Budget Inn & Suites Ⓜ
(815) 672-0080. **$71-$99.** 1705 N Bloomington St 61364. Jct SR 18 and 23, 1.5 mi n. Int corridors. **Pets:** Other species. $15 daily fee/pet. Designated rooms, service with restrictions, supervision.
🛜 ᴍ 🅗 🅟 ➹

SYCAMORE

◆ **Motel 6 Sycamore #4628** 🄷

(815) 899-6500. **Call for rates.** 1860 Dekalb Ave 60178. On SR 23, 0.9 mi s of Peace Rd. Int corridors. **Pets:** Other species. Service with restrictions, supervision. 🛜 Ⓜ 📳

TROY

🅰🅰🅰 ◆◆ **Super 8** 🄷

(618) 667-8888. **$57-$100, 3 day notice.** 910 Edwardsville Rd 62294. I-55/70 exit 18, just w. Int corridors. **Pets:** Accepted.

SAVE 🛜 📳 💻 🏊

TUSCOLA

◆◆ **Baymont Inn & Suites** 🄷

(217) 253-3500. **$76-$109.** 1006 Southline Rd 61953. I-57 exit 212 (US 36), 0.3 mi w. Int corridors. **Pets:** Small, dogs only. $10 daily fee/pet. Service with restrictions, supervision. 🛜 Ⓜ 📳 💻 🏊

◆◆◆ **Holiday Inn Express** 🄷

(217) 253-6363. **$94-$125, 3 day notice.** 1201 Tuscola Blvd 61953. I-57 exit 212 (US 36), 0.3 mi w to Progress Blvd, just s to Tuscola Blvd, then 0.4 mi se. Int corridors. **Pets:** Large, other species. Service with restrictions. 🛜 📳 💻 🏊

URBANA

◆◆◆ **Comfort Suites by Choice Hotels Urbana/Champaign** 🄷

(217) 328-3500. **$99-$129.** 2001 N Lincoln Ave 61801. I-74 exit 183 (Lincoln Ave), 0.5 mi s. Int corridors. **Pets:** Other species. $20 one-time fee/room. Designated rooms, service with restrictions, crate.

🛜 ❌ Ⓜ 📳 💻 🏊

🅰🅰🅰 ◆◆◆ **Ramada-Urbana/Champaign** 🄷

(217) 328-4400. **$78-$99.** 902 W Killarney St 61801. I-74 exit 183 (Lincoln Ave), just s to Killarney St, then just w. Int corridors. **Pets:** Large. $20 daily fee/pet. Designated rooms, service with restrictions.

SAVE 🛜 📳 💻 🏊

◆◆◆ **Sleep Inn by Choice Hotels** 🄷

(217) 367-6000. **Call for rates.** 1908 N Lincoln Ave 61801. I-74 exit 183 (Lincoln Ave), 0.5 mi s. Int corridors. **Pets:** Small. $10 daily fee/pet. Service with restrictions, supervision. SAVE 🛜 📳 💻 🏊

VANDALIA

◆◆◆ **Holiday Inn Express Hotel & Suites** 🄷

(618) 283-0010. **Call for rates.** 21 Mattes Ave 62471. I-70 exit 61, just s. Int corridors. **Pets:** Accepted. 🛜 ❌ Ⓜ 📳 💻 🏊

🅰🅰🅰 ◆◆◆ **Jay's Inn** Ⓜ

(618) 283-1200. **$56-$65.** 720 Gochenour St 62471. I-70 exit 63 (US 51), just s. Ext corridors. **Pets:** Other species. Service with restrictions. SAVE 🛜 📳 💻

◆◆ **Ramada Vandalia** 🄷

(618) 283-1400. **$60-$81.** 2707 Veterans Ave 62471. I-70 exit 61, just s. Int corridors. **Pets:** Medium. $10 daily fee/pet. Designated rooms, service with restrictions, supervision. 🛜 📳 💻 🏊

WASHINGTON

◆◆ **Super 8** 🄷

(309) 444-8881. **$51-$63.** 1884 Washington Rd 61571. On Business Rt US 24, 1.5 mi w. Int corridors. **Pets:** Medium. $50 deposit/pet, $8 daily fee/pet. Designated rooms, service with restrictions. 🛜 📳 💻

WATSEKA

🅰🅰🅰 ◆◆ **Super 8** 🄷

(815) 432-6000. **$58-$87.** 710 W Walnut St 60970. On US 24; center of downtown. Int corridors. **Pets:** Small, dogs only. $6 daily fee/pet. Designated rooms, service with restrictions, supervision. SAVE 🛜 📳 💻

WENONA

◆◆ **Super 8** Ⓜ

(815) 853-4371. **$50-$68.** 5 Cavalry Dr 61377. I-39 exit 35, just e. Int corridors. **Pets:** Large. $5 daily fee/pet. Designated rooms, service with restrictions, supervision. 🛜 📳 💻

INDIANA

ANGOLA

▽▽ ▽▽ Ramada Angola Hotel H

(260) 665-9471. **$89-$150.** 3855 N SR 127 & I-69 exit 354 46703. I-69 exit 354, just e, then 0.4 mi s. Int corridors. **Pets:** Other species. $25 daily fee/room. Service with restrictions, crate. 🛜 🛏 🖥 🏊 ⊠

AUBURN

🔷 ▽▽ ▽▽ Quality Inn H

(260) 925-6363. **Call for rates.** 225 Touring Dr 46706. I-69 exit 329 (SR 8), just e, then just s. Int corridors. **Pets:** Other species. $20 one-time fee/pet. Designated rooms, service with restrictions, crate.
〔SAVE〕 🛜 🛏 🖥 🏊

▽▽ ▽▽ Super 8-Auburn H

(260) 927-8800. **$64-$169.** 503 Ley Dr 46706. I-69 exit 329 (SR 8), just e, then just s. Int corridors. **Pets:** Accepted. 🛜 🛏 🖥

BEDFORD

🔷 ▽▽ ▽▽ Bedford Comfort Inn H

(812) 279-8111. **$89-$109.** 911 Constitution Ave 47421. Jct SR 37 and 58, just s on SR 37. Int corridors. **Pets:** Small. $25 one-time fee/pet. Service with restrictions, supervision. 〔SAVE〕 🛜 🔥 🛏 🖥 🏊

▽▽ ▽▽ Bedford Super 8 H

(812) 275-8881. **$65-$175.** 501 Bell Back Rd 47421. Jct SR 37 and 58, just e on SR 58. Int corridors. **Pets:** $10 daily fee/pet. No service, supervision. 🛜 🛏 🖥 🏊 ⊠

🔷 ▽▽ ▽▽ Holiday Inn Express & Suites H

(812) 279-1206. **$112-$128.** 2800 Express Ln 47421. On US 50/SR 37, 1.4 mi s of jct SR 450. Int corridors. **Pets:** Medium, dogs only. $15 daily fee/pet. Designated rooms, service with restrictions, supervision.
〔SAVE〕 🛜 ⊠ 🛏 🖥 🏊

BERNE

▽▽ ▽▽ Black Bear Inn & Suites H

(260) 589-8955. **Call for rates.** 1335 US 27 N 46711. On US 27, 1 mi n. Int corridors. **Pets:** Accepted. 🛜 🛏 🖥 🏊

BLOOMINGTON

▽▽ 🔷 ▽▽ Comfort Inn Bloomington H

(812) 650-0010. **$99-$299.** 1700 N Kinser Pike 47404. On SR 45 and 46 Bypass, 1 mi e of jct SR 37. Int corridors. **Pets:** Small, other species. $25 one-time fee/room. Designated rooms, service with restrictions.
🛜 ⊠ 🛏 🖥 🏊

▽▽ ▽▽ ▽▽ Fairfield Inn by Marriott H 🐾

(812) 331-1122. **$89-$429.** 120 Fairfield Dr 47404. Just e from SR 37 at 3rd St. Int corridors. **Pets:** Medium. $75 one-time fee/room. Service with restrictions, supervision. 🛜 ⊠ 🔥 🛏 🖥 🏊 ⊠

▽▽ ▽▽ ▽▽ Hampton Inn H 🐾

(812) 334-2100. **$109-$189.** 2100 N Walnut St 47404. 1 mi e of jct SR 37 on SR 45 and 46 Bypass, then just s on College Ave/Walnut St. Int corridors. **Pets:** Large. $40 one-time fee/pet. Service with restrictions, crate. 🛜 🛏 🖥 🏊

▽▽ ▽▽ ▽▽ Holiday Inn Bloomington H

(812) 334-3252. **$89-$169, 3 day notice.** 1710 N Kinser Pike 47404. On SR 45 and 46 Bypass, 1 mi e of jct SR 37. Int corridors. **Pets:** Small. $25 one-time fee/room. Designated rooms, service with restrictions, crate.
🛜 ⊠ 🔥 🛏 🖥 🍴 🏊

▽▽ ▽▽ ▽▽ TownePlace Suites by Marriott H 🐾

(812) 334-1234. **$99-$399.** 105 S Franklin Rd 47404. Just e from SR 37 at 3rd St, then 0.3 mi n. Int corridors. **Pets:** Other species. $75 one-time fee/room. Service with restrictions, crate. 🛜 ⊠ 🛏 🖥 🏊

BLUFFTON

▽▽ ▽▽ Bluffton Inn & Suites H

(260) 824-5553. **$64-$89.** 100 Charles Deam Ct 46714. Jct SR 1 and 124 (E Division Rd), just n. Int corridors. **Pets:** Accepted. 🛜 🛏 🖥

BREMEN

▽▽ ▽▽ ▽▽ Scottish Bed and Breakfast BB

(574) 220-6672. **$109-$149, 14 day notice.** 2180 Miami Tr 46506. Jct SR 331, 2 mi w on SR 106, just s. Int corridors. **Pets:** Small, dogs only. $25 one-time fee/room. Designated rooms, crate.
🛜 ⊠ 🛏 🏊 🗎

CENTERVILLE

▽▽ ▽▽ ▽▽ Historic Lantz House Inn BB

(765) 855-2936. **$111-$139, 14 day notice.** 214 W Main St 47330. I-70 exit 145, 3 mi s to US 40 (W Main St), then just w. Int corridors. **Pets:** Medium, other species. $12 daily fee/pet. Designated rooms, service with restrictions, crate. 🛜 ⊠ 🗒 🗎

CHESTERTON

▽▽ ▽▽ ▽▽ Gray Goose Inn BB 🐾

(219) 926-5781. **$110-$195, 10 day notice.** 350 Indian Boundary Rd 46304. I-94 exit 26A, 0.6 mi s, then just w. Int corridors. **Pets:** $25 one-time fee/pet. Service with restrictions, supervision. 🛜 ⊠

CINCINNATI METROPOLITAN AREA (NEARBY OHIO)

BATESVILLE

Hampton Inn Batesville H
(812) 934-6262. **$98-$135.** 1030 SR 229 N 47006. I-74 exit 149, just n. Int corridors. **Pets:** Medium. Service with restrictions, crate.

LAWRENCEBURG

Comfort Inn & Suites H
(812) 539-3600. **$70-$110.** 1610 Flossie Dr 47025. I-275 exit 16, 0.3 mi e. Int corridors. **Pets:** Accepted.

Modern Inn & Suites H
(812) 539-4770. **Call for rates.** 1000 E Eads Pkwy 47025. I-275 exit 16, 0.5 mi w on US 50. Int corridors. **Pets:** $20 daily fee/pet. Service with restrictions.

END METROPOLITAN AREA

CLARKSVILLE

BEST WESTERN Green Tree Inn M ✿
(812) 288-9281. **$86-$265, 30 day notice.** 1425 Broadway St 47129. I-65 exit 4, just w. Ext corridors. **Pets:** Dogs only. $15 one-time fee/room. Service with restrictions, crate.

Candlewood Suites Louisville North H
(812) 284-6113. **$79-$119.** 1419 Bales Ln 47129. I-65 exit 4, just w. Int corridors. **Pets:** Accepted.

CLOVERDALE

Super 8 Cloverdale/Greencastle H
(765) 795-7373. **$57-$204.** 1020 N Main St 46120. I-70 exit 41, just s on US 231. Int corridors. **Pets:** Medium, dogs only. $10 daily fee/room. Service with restrictions, supervision.

COLUMBIA CITY

Quality Inn H
(260) 248-4551. **$70-$90.** 701 W Connexion Way 46725. 1 mi w of SR 9, just off US 30. Int corridors. **Pets:** Very small. $15 one-time fee/room. Designated rooms, service with restrictions, supervision.

COLUMBUS

Hotel Indigo H ✿
(812) 375-9100. **$99-$229.** 400 Brown St 47201. Jct 4th St. Int corridors. **Pets:** Large. $35 one-time fee/room. Service with restrictions.

La Quinta Inn & Suites H
(812) 379-4657. **$75-$166.** 101 Carrie Ln 47201. I-65 exit 68, just w on SR 46. Int corridors. **Pets:** Service with restrictions, supervision.

Residence Inn by Marriott H ✿
(812) 342-2400. **$109-$179.** 4525 W SR 46 47201. I-65 exit 68, 0.8 mi w. Int corridors. **Pets:** Other species. $100 one-time fee/pet. Service with restrictions, supervision.

CORYDON

Comfort Inn Corydon H
(812) 738-3900. **$70-$100.** 115 Skypark Dr 47112. I-64 exit 105, just n. Int corridors. **Pets:** Other species. $10 daily fee/pet. Designated rooms, service with restrictions, supervision.

Holiday Inn Express H
(812) 738-1623. **$94-$119.** 249 Federal Dr 47112. I-64 exit 105, 0.6 mi s, then just w. Int corridors. **Pets:** Other species. $25 one-time fee/pet. Service with restrictions, supervision.

CRAWFORDSVILLE

Comfort Inn H
(765) 361-0665. **$69-$110.** 2991 N Gandhi Dr 47933. I-74 exit 34, just s on US 231. Int corridors. **Pets:** $15 daily fee/pet. Service with restrictions, supervision.

Hampton Inn & Suites H
(765) 362-8884. **$109-$149.** 2895 Gandhi Dr 47933. I-74 exit 34, just s on US 231. Int corridors. **Pets:** $25 daily fee/pet. Designated rooms, service with restrictions, supervision.

Holiday Inn Express Hotel & Suites H
(765) 323-4575. **$99-$107.** 2506 N Lafayette Rd 47933. I-74 exit 34, 0.3 mi s on US 231. Int corridors. **Pets:** Accepted.

Quality Inn Crawfordsville H
(765) 362-8700. **$70-$84.** 2500 N Lafayette Rd 47933. I-74 exit 34, 0.3 mi s on US 231. Ext corridors. **Pets:** Small. $15 one-time fee/pet. Service with restrictions, supervision.

DALE

BEST WESTERN PLUS Lincoln Land Inn H
(812) 937-7000. **Call for rates.** 1339 N Washington St 47523. I-64 exit 57A, just s. Int corridors. **Pets:** $100 deposit/room, $10 daily fee/pet. Designated rooms, service with restrictions, supervision.

DECATUR

Baymont Inn & Suites H
(260) 728-4600. **$79-$89.** 1201 S 13th St 46733. On US 27 and 33, 1 mi s of jct US 224. Int corridors. **Pets:** Accepted.

ELKHART

Baymont Inn & Suites Elkhart H
(574) 264-7222. **Call for rates.** 3010 Brittany Ct 46514. I-80/90 exit 92, 0.3 mi s on SR 19. Int corridors. **Pets:** Accepted.

Candlewood Suites H
(574) 262-8600. **Call for rates.** 300 Northpointe Blvd 46514. I-80/90 exit 92, just n on SR 19, then just w. Int corridors. **Pets:** Medium, other species. $25 daily fee/room. Designated rooms, service with restrictions.

Staybridge Suites Elkhart North H ✿
(574) 970-8488. **$109-$139, 7 day notice.** 3252 Cassopolis St 46514. I-80/90 exit 92, just n on SR 19. Int corridors. **Pets:** $25 one-time fee/room. Designated rooms, no service, supervision.

EVANSVILLE

▼▼▼▼ Baymont Inn & Suites Evansville East 🅷
(812) 477-2677. **$74-$120.** 8005 E Division St 47715. I-164 exit 7B (SR 66/Lloyd Expwy), 0.5 mi w to Cross Pointe Blvd, just n to Division St, then 0.5 mi e. Int corridors. **Pets:** Small. $10 daily fee/room. Service with restrictions, crate. 🛜 ⓜ 🛏 📺 🏊

🅰🅰🅰 ▼▼ BEST WESTERN PLUS Gateway Inn & Suites 🅷 🐾
(812) 868-8000. **$70-$180.** 324 Rusher Creek Rd 47725. I-64 exit 25A (US 41), 0.5 mi s, then just w. Int corridors. **Pets:** Medium, other species. $20 one-time fee/room. Service with restrictions, crate.
🆂🅰🆅🅴 🛜 ⓜ 🛏 📺 🏊

🅰🅰🅰 ▼▼▼ Casino Aztar Hotel 🅷
(812) 433-4000. **$99-$299.** 421 NW Riverside Dr 47708. SR 62 (Lloyd Expwy), just s on Fulton. Int corridors. **Pets:** Accepted.
🆂🅰🆅🅴 🛜 ⓜ 🛏 📺 🍽

▼▼ Comfort Inn East 🅷
(812) 476-3600. **$79-$94.** 8331 E Walnut St 47715. I-164 exit 7B (SR 66/Lloyd Expwy), to Eagle Crest Blvd, 0.3 mi se to Fuquay St, just s to Walnut St, then 0.4 mi e. Int corridors. **Pets:** Accepted.
🛜 ✖ ⓜ 🛏 📺 🏊 ✖

▼▼ Comfort Inn North 🅷
(812) 867-1600. **Call for rates.** 19622 Elpers Rd 47725. I-64 exit 25A (US 41), 0.5 mi s, then just w. Int corridors. **Pets:** Accepted.
🛜 🛏 📺 🏊

▼▼▼▼ Drury Inn & Suites-Evansville East 🅷
(812) 471-3400. **$95-$179.** 100 Cross Pointe Blvd 47715. I-164 exit 7B (SR 66/Lloyd Expwy), 0.5 mi w. Int corridors. **Pets:** Service with restrictions, supervision. 🛜 ⓜ 🛏 📺 🏊 ✖

▼▼▼▼ Drury Inn & Suites-Evansville North 🅷
(812) 423-5818. **$75-$159.** 3901 US 41 N 47711. US 41, 2.5 mi n of jct SR 62 and 66 (Lloyd Expwy), 3.3 mi sw of Evansville Regional Airport entrance. Int corridors. **Pets:** Service with restrictions, supervision.
🛜 🛏 📺 🏊

▼▼▼ Holiday Inn Express 🅷 🐾
(812) 867-1100. **$69-$99.** 19600 Elpers Rd 47725. I-64 exit 25A (US 41), 0.6 mi s. Int corridors. **Pets:** Small. $25 one-time fee/room. Service with restrictions, supervision. 🛜 ✖ ⓜ 🛏 📺 🏊

▼▼▼ Holiday Inn Express - Evansville West 🅷 🐾
(812) 421-9773. **$120-$200.** 5737 Pearl Dr 47712. Jct US 41 and SR 62, 5.7 mi w on SR 62, then just s on Boehne Camp Rd. Int corridors. **Pets:** Small. $15 one-time fee/pet. Service with restrictions, supervision.
🛜 ⓜ 🛏 📺 🏊

▼▼ HomeLife Studios & Suites 🅜
(812) 475-1700. **$59-$119.** 100 S Green River Rd 47715. I-164 exit 7B (SR 66/Lloyd Expwy), to Green River Rd, then just s. Ext corridors. **Pets:** Medium. $50 daily fee/room. Service with restrictions, crate. 🛜 🛏 📺 🏊

▼▼▼▼ Howard Johnson Evansville East 🅷
(812) 476-9626. **$78-$139.** 1101 N Green River Rd 47715. I-164 exit 9 (SR 62 E/Morgan Ave), 1.5 mi w on SR 62, then just s. Int corridors. **Pets:** Medium, other species. $15 daily fee/pet. Service with restrictions, crate. 🛜 ⓜ 🛏 📺 🏊

▼▼▼▼ La Quinta Inn & Suites Evansville 🅷
(812) 471-3414. **$77-$151.** 8015 E Division St 47715. I-164 exit 7B (SR 66/Lloyd Expwy), 0.5 mi w to Cross Pointe Blvd, just n, then 0.5 mi e. Int corridors. **Pets:** Service with restrictions, supervision.
🛜 🛏 📺 🏊

▼▼▼▼ Residence Inn by Marriott Evansville East 🅷
(812) 471-7191. **$99-$169.** 8283 E Walnut St 47715. I-164 exit 7B (SR 66/Lloyd Expwy), 0.5 mi w to Eagle Crest Blvd, 0.3 mi se to Fuquay St, then 0.3 mi e. Int corridors. **Pets:** Medium, other species. $100 one-time fee/room. Service with restrictions, supervision.
🛜 ✖ ⓜ 🛏 📺 🏊 ✖

▼▼ StudioPLUS Evansville East 🅷
(812) 479-0103. **$50-$85.** 301 Eagle Crest Dr 47715. I-164 exit 7B (SR 66/Lloyd Expwy), 0.5 mi w to Eagle Crest Blvd, 0.5 mi s, then just e. Int corridors. **Pets:** $25 daily fee/pet. Designated rooms, service with restrictions. 🛜 🛏 📺

FORT WAYNE

▼▼ Baymont Inn Fort Wayne 🅷
(260) 489-2220. **$58-$75.** 1005 W Washington Center Rd 46825. I-69 exit 311B, just n on SR 3, then 0.4 mi e. Int corridors. **Pets:** Other species. $25 one-time fee/pet. Service with restrictions, supervision.
🛜 🛏 📺

🅰🅰🅰 ▼▼▼▼ BEST WESTERN Luxbury Inn Fort Wayne 🅷 🐾
(260) 436-0242. **$80-$110.** 5501 Coventry Ln 46804. I-69 exit 302, just w. Int corridors. **Pets:** Medium. $20 daily fee/room. Designated rooms, service with restrictions, supervision. 🆂🅰🆅🅴 🛜 🛏 📺 🏊

▼▼▼ Candlewood Suites 🅷
(260) 484-1400. **$89-$119.** 5250 Distribution Dr 46825. I-69 exit 311A, just e. Int corridors. **Pets:** Other species. $12 daily fee/pet. Supervision.
🛜 ⓜ 🛏 📺 🏊

▼▼ Don Hall's Guesthouse 🅷
(260) 489-2524. **$89-$99, 3 day notice.** 1313 W Washington Center Rd 46825. I-69 exit 311B, just n on SR 3, then 0.3 mi e. Ext/int corridors. **Pets:** $10 daily fee/pet. Designated rooms, service with restrictions, crate.
🛜 🛏 📺 🍽 🏊 ✖

▼▼ Extended StayAmerica-Fort Wayne-South 🅷
(260) 432-1916. **$50-$90.** 8309 W Jefferson Blvd 46804. I-69 exit 302, 0.4 mi e on US 24, then 0.6 mi s. Int corridors. **Pets:** $25 daily fee/pet. Designated rooms, service with restrictions. 🛜 🛏 📺

🅰🅰🅰 ▼▼▼▼ Hilton Fort Wayne at Grand Wayne Convention Center 🅷 🐾
(260) 420-1100. **$99-$189.** 1020 S Calhoun St 46802. Jct Jefferson Blvd; center. Int corridors. **Pets:** $50 one-time fee/room. Service with restrictions, crate. 🆂🅰🆅🅴 🛜 ⓜ 🛏 📺 🍽 🏊

🅰🅰🅰 ▼▼▼▼ Holiday Inn at IPFW & The Coliseum 🅷
(260) 482-3800. **Call for rates.** 4111 Paul Shaffer Dr 46825. I-69 exit 311A, 1.2 mi s on Lima Rd, then 1.5 mi e. Int corridors. **Pets:** $25 one-time fee/room. Service with restrictions, supervision.
🆂🅰🆅🅴 🛜 ✖ ⓜ 🛏 📺 🍽 🏊 ✖

🅰🅰🅰 ▼▼▼ Quality Inn 🅷
(260) 489-5554. **$75-$100.** 1734 W Washington Center Rd 46818. I-69 exit 311B, just n on SR 3. Int corridors. **Pets:** Medium. $15 daily fee/pet. Service with restrictions, crate. 🆂🅰🆅🅴 🛜 🛏 📺 🏊

▼▼▼▼ Residence Inn by Marriott Southwest 🅷
(260) 432-8000. **$89-$149.** 7811 W Jefferson Blvd 46804. I-69 exit 302, 0.5 mi e. Int corridors. **Pets:** Accepted. 🛜 ✖ 🛏 📺 🏊 ✖

▼▼▼ Staybridge Suites 🅷
(260) 432-2427. **Call for rates.** 5925 Ellison Rd 46804. I-69 exit 302, just w. Int corridors. **Pets:** Accepted. 🛜 ⓜ 🛏 📺 🏊 ✖

▼▼▼ Stay Inn Suites 🅷
(260) 484-4700. **$109-$129.** 4919 Lima Rd 46808. I-69 exit 311A, 0.4 mi s on US 27. Ext corridors. **Pets:** Other species. $100 one-time fee/room. Service with restrictions, crate. 🛜 ✖ 🛏 📺 🏊 ✖

▼▼▼ TownePlace Suites by Marriott Fort Wayne North 🅷
(260) 483-1160. **$94-$124.** 3949 Ice Way 46805. I-69 exit 311A, 1.2 mi se on Lima Rd. Int corridors. **Pets:** Medium, other species. $100 one-time fee/room. 🛜 ✖ ⓜ 🛏 📺 🏊

FRENCH LICK

▼▼▼ Comfort Suites **H**

(812) 936-5300. **$105-$135.** 9530 W SR 56 47432. Jct SR 145, 1.2 mi sw. Int corridors. **Pets:** Accepted. 🤚 ⊠ 🔥 🛢 🖥 🏊

△△△ ▼▼▼▼ French Lick Resort **H**

(812) 936-9300. **$139-$299.** 8670 W SR 56 47432. Jct SR 145. Int corridors. **Pets:** Accepted. 🆂🅰🆅🅴 🤚 ⊠ 🔥 🛢 🖥 🍴 🏊 ⊠

GAS CITY

△△△ ▼▼▼ BEST WESTERN PLUS Gas City **H**

(765) 998-2331. **$85-$125.** 4936 Kaybee Dr 46933. I-69 exit 259, just e. Int corridors. **Pets:** Large. $20 one-time fee/pet. Designated rooms, service with restrictions, supervision. 🆂🅰🆅🅴 🤚 🔥 🛢 🖥 🏊

GOSHEN

△△△ ▼▼▼ BEST WESTERN Inn **M**

(574) 533-0408. **$89-$99.** 900 Lincolnway E 46526. 1 mi se on US 33. Ext corridors. **Pets:** Service with restrictions, crate. 🆂🅰🆅🅴 🤚 🛢 🖥

GREENSBURG

▼▼▼ Hampton Inn & Suites **H** ❖

(812) 663-5000. **$79-$109.** 2075 N Michigan Ave 47240. I-74 exit 132, just se. Int corridors. **Pets:** Medium. Service with restrictions.
🤚 🔥 🛢 🖥 🏊

▼▼▼ Holiday Inn Express **H**

(812) 663-5500. **$89-$119.** 915 Ann Blvd 47240. I-74 exit 134A, 1.4 mi s on SR 3. Int corridors. **Pets:** Other species. $15 daily fee/pet. Service with restrictions, crate. 🤚 🔥 🛢 🖥 🏊

HAMMOND

△△△ ▼▼▼ BEST WESTERN Northwest Indiana Inn **H**

(219) 844-2140. **Call for rates.** 3830 179th St 46323. I-80/94 exit 5, 0.6 mi s on Cline Ave (SR 912), then 0.6 mi n on frontage road (179th St). Int corridors. **Pets:** Accepted. 🆂🅰🆅🅴 🤚 🛢 🖥 🍴 🏊

▼▼▼▼ Residence Inn by Marriott Chicago Southeast **H** ❖

(219) 844-8440. **$116-$179.** 7740 Corinne Dr 46323. I-80/94 exit 3 (Kennedy Ave S), just s. Int corridors. **Pets:** Small, other species. $100 one-time fee/room. Service with restrictions, crate.
🤚 ⊠ 🔥 🛢 🖥 🏊 ⊠

HOWE

▼▼▼ Holiday Inn Express-Howe/Sturgis **H**

(260) 562-3660. **Call for rates.** 45 W 750 N 46746. I-80/90 exit 121 (US 66). Int corridors. **Pets:** Medium. $40 one-time fee/room. Designated rooms, service with restrictions, crate. 🤚 ⊠ 🔥 🛢 🖥 🏊

HUNTINGTON

▼▼ Super 8 **H**

(260) 358-8888. **$65-$70.** 2801 Guilford St 46750. US 24, just n. Int corridors. **Pets:** $10 daily fee/pet. Designated rooms, no service, supervision. 🤚 🛢 🖥 🏊

INDIANAPOLIS METROPOLITAN AREA

BROWNSBURG

▼▼▼ Holiday Inn Express Brownsburg **H**

(317) 852-5353. **Call for rates.** 31 Maplehurst Dr 46112. I-74 exit 66, just n on SR 267. Int corridors. **Pets:** Accepted.
🤚 ⊠ 🛢 🖥 🏊

CARMEL

▼▼▼ Comfort Inn **H**

(317) 816-1616. **Call for rates.** 10201 N Meridian St 46290. I-465 exit 31, 0.3 mi n on US 31. Int corridors. **Pets:** Accepted.
🤚 🔥 🛢 🖥 🏊 ⊠

▼▼▼ Residence Inn by Marriott Indianapolis/Carmel **H**

(317) 846-2000. **$89-$199.** 11895 N Meridian St 46032. I-465 exit 31, 2 mi n on US 31, just e on 116th St, then just n on N Pennsylvania St. Int corridors. **Pets:** Accepted. 🤚 ⊠ 🔥 🛢 🖥 🏊 ⊠

▼▼▼ Staybridge Suites Indianapolis-Carmel **H**

(317) 582-1500. **$89-$199.** 10675 N Pennsylvania St 46280. I-465 exit 31, 0.7 mi n to 106th St, just e, then just n. Int corridors. **Pets:** Large. $150 one-time fee/room. Service with restrictions, crate.
🤚 ⊠ 🔥 🛢 🖥 🏊

EDINBURGH

△△△ ▼▼▼ BEST WESTERN Horizon Inn **H**

(812) 526-9883. **$90-$100.** 11780 N US 31 46124. I-65 exit 76B, just n. Int corridors. **Pets:** Medium, other species. $10 daily fee/pet. Designated rooms, service with restrictions, crate. 🆂🅰🆅🅴 🤚 🛢 🖥 🏊

FISHERS

△△△ ▼▼▼ Comfort Suites **H**

(317) 578-1200. **$82-$129.** 9760 Crosspoint Blvd 46256. I-69 exit 203, just w on 96th St, then just n. Int corridors. **Pets:** Large. $25 daily fee/pet. Designated rooms, service with restrictions, crate.
🆂🅰🆅🅴 🤚 ⊠ 🛢 🖥 🏊

▼▼▼ Holiday Inn Express-Fishers **H**

(317) 578-2000. **$79-$159.** 9790 North by Northeast Blvd 46038. I-69 exit 203, just ne. Int corridors. **Pets:** Accepted. 🤚 🔥 🛢 🖥 🏊

▼▼▼ Residence Inn by Marriott Indianapolis/Fishers **H**

(317) 842-1111. **$89-$199.** 9765 Crosspoint Blvd 46256. I-69 exit 203, just nw. Int corridors. **Pets:** Accepted.
🤚 ⊠ 🔥 🛢 🖥 🏊 ⊠

▼▼▼ Staybridge Suites Indianapolis-Fishers **H** ❖

(317) 577-9500. **$89-$149.** 9780 Crosspoint Blvd 46256. I-69 exit 203, just nw. Int corridors. **Pets:** Medium, other species. $75 one-time fee/room. Service with restrictions, crate. 🤚 🔥 🛢 🖥 🏊 ⊠

GREENFIELD

△△△ ▼▼▼ Comfort Inn-Greenfield/Indianapolis **H**

(317) 467-9999. **$82-$170.** 178 E Martindale Dr 46140. I-70 exit 104, 0.4 mi s on State St. Int corridors. **Pets:** Accepted.
🆂🅰🆅🅴 🤚 🛢 🖥 🏊

▼▼ Quality Inn Greenfield **H** ❖

(317) 462-7112. **$79-$134.** 2270 N State St 46140. I-70 exit 104, just s. Int corridors. **Pets:** Other species. $10 daily fee/room. Service with restrictions, supervision. 🤚 🛢 🖥 🏊

GREENWOOD

▼▼▼ Candlewood Suites Indy-South **H**

(317) 882-4300. **$89-$109.** 1190 N Graham Rd 46143. I-65 exit 101, just e. Int corridors. **Pets:** Large, other species. $125 one-time fee/pet. Service with restrictions, crate. 🤚 🔥 🛢 🖥

△△△ ▼▼ Red Roof Inn **M**

(317) 887-1515. **$59-$199.** 110 Sheek Rd 46143. I-65 exit 99, just w. Ext corridors. **Pets:** Large, other species. Service with restrictions, supervision. 🆂🅰🆅🅴 🤚 🛢 🖥 🏊

INDIANAPOLIS

▼▼ Baymont Inn & Suites **H**
(317) 322-2000. **$95-$159, 3 day notice.** 1540 Brookville Crossing Way 46239. I-465 exit 47, 0.3 mi e. Int corridors. **Pets:** Other species. $25 one-time fee/room. Designated rooms, service with restrictions, crate.

▼▼▼ Baymont Inn & Suites Indianapolis South **H**
(317) 784-7006. **$85-$105.** 4402 E Creekview Dr 46237. I-65 exit 103, just w. Int corridors. **Pets:** Medium. $16 daily fee/pet. Service with restrictions, supervision.

AAA ▼▼▼▼ BEST WESTERN Airport Suites **H**
(317) 246-1505. **Call for rates.** 55 S High School Rd 46241. I-465 exit 13B, just w. Int corridors. **Pets:** Accepted.

AAA ▼▼ BEST WESTERN Country Suites **H**
(317) 879-1700. **$85-$99.** 3871 W 92nd St 46268. I-465 exit 27, just s on Michigan Rd. Int corridors. **Pets:** Medium. $25 one-time fee/room. Designated rooms, service with restrictions, supervision.

AAA ▼▼▼▼ BEST WESTERN Crossroads **H**
(317) 353-6966. **$79-$129.** 7610 Old Trails Rd 46219. I-465 exit 46, just sw. Int corridors. **Pets:** $25 one-time fee/room. Service with restrictions, supervision.

▼▼ Candlewood Suites Indianapolis NE **H**
(317) 595-9292. **$89-$129.** 8111 Bash St 46250. I-69 exit 201, just w. Int corridors. **Pets:** Large, other species. $75 one-time fee/room. Service with restrictions.

▼▼▼ Candlewood Suites Indianapolis NW **H**
(317) 298-8000. **Call for rates.** 7455 Woodland Dr 46278. I-465 exit 21 (73rd St), just n. Int corridors. **Pets:** Accepted.

▼▼ Comfort Inn-East **H**
(317) 359-9999. **$79-$92.** 2295 N Shadeland Ave 46219. I-70 exit 89, 0.5 mi w of jct I-465. Int corridors. **Pets:** Accepted.

▼▼▼ Conrad Indianapolis **H** 🐾
(317) 713-5000. **$169-$399.** 50 W Washington St 46204. Jct Illinois St. Int corridors. **Pets:** Medium, dogs only. $100 deposit/room, $150 one-time fee/room. Service with restrictions, crate.

▼▼▼ Drury Inn & Suites Indianapolis Northeast **H**
(317) 849-8900. **$110-$224.** 8180 N Shadeland Ave 46250. I-69 exit 201, just e. Int corridors. **Pets:** Service with restrictions, supervision.

▼▼▼ Drury Inn-Indianapolis **H**
(317) 876-9777. **$90-$174.** 9320 N Michigan Rd 46268. I-465 exit 27, just s. Int corridors. **Pets:** Service with restrictions, supervision.

▼▼ Extended StayAmerica Indianapolis - North - Carmel **H**
(317) 843-1181. **$47-$100.** 9750 Lakeshore Dr 46280. I-465 exit 33, 0.4 mi n on Keystone Dr, 0.6 mi e on 96th St, then just n on Bauer Dr. Int corridors. **Pets:** $25 daily fee/pet. Designated rooms, service with restrictions.

AAA ▼▼▼▼ Hilton Indianapolis Hotel & Suites **H**
(317) 972-0600. **$99-$259.** 120 W Market St 46204. Jct Illinois St. Int corridors. **Pets:** Accepted.

AAA ▼▼▼▼ The Historic Canterbury Hotel **H**
(317) 634-3000. **$139-$399.** 123 S Illinois St 46225. Between Georgia and Maryland sts. Int corridors. **Pets:** Accepted.

▼▼▼ Holiday Inn Express South **H**
(317) 783-5151. **$92-$144.** 5151 S East St 46227. I-465 exit 2B, 0.3 mi s. Int corridors. **Pets:** Other species. $50 one-time fee/pet. Service with restrictions.

▼▼ Homestead Studio Suites Hotel-Indianapolis/Northwest **H**
(317) 334-7829. **$50-$100.** 8520 Northwest Blvd 46278. I-465 exit 23, just e. Int corridors. **Pets:** $25 daily fee/pet. Designated rooms, service with restrictions.

AAA ▼▼▼▼ Indianapolis Marriott East **H**
(317) 352-1231. **$101-$212.** 7202 E 21st St 46219. I-70 exit 89, 0.3 mi se; 0.5 mi w of jct I-465. Int corridors. **Pets:** Accepted.

▼▼▼▼ Jameson Inn Indy West **H**
(317) 299-6165. **$85-$105.** 3850 Eagle View Dr 46254. I-465 exit 17, just w on 38th St, then just n. Int corridors. **Pets:** Dogs only. $15 daily fee/pet. Service with restrictions, crate.

▼▼ La Quinta Inn Indianapolis Airport Executive Drive **H**
(317) 244-8100. **$59-$144.** 2650 Executive Dr 46241. I-465 exit 11 southbound; exit 11B northbound, 0.3 mi e. Int corridors. **Pets:** Service with restrictions, supervision.

▼▼ La Quinta Inn Indianapolis Airport Lynhurst **H**
(317) 247-4281. **$59-$133.** 5316 W Southern Ave 46241. I-465 exit 11A, 0.5 mi e on Sam Jones Expwy to Lynhurst Dr. Int corridors. **Pets:** Service with restrictions, supervision.

▼▼ La Quinta Inn Indianapolis East **H**
(317) 359-1021. **$59-$144.** 7304 E 21st St 46219. I-70 exit 89, just s, then just e; 0.5 mi w of jct I-465. Int corridors. **Pets:** Service with restrictions, supervision.

AAA ▼▼▼▼ Omni Severin Hotel **H**
(317) 634-6664. **Call for rates.** 40 W Jackson Pl 46225. Corner of Illinois and Georgia sts. Int corridors. **Pets:** Accepted.

▼▼▼ Quality Inn **H**
(317) 849-8555. **Call for rates.** 8380 Kelly Ln 46250. I-465 exit 35 (Allisonville Rd), just s. Int corridors. **Pets:** Accepted.

▼▼ Radisson Hotel Indianapolis Airport **H**
(317) 244-3361. **Call for rates.** 2500 S High School Rd 46241. I-465 exit 11 southbound; exit 11B northbound, just w. Int corridors. **Pets:** Accepted.

▼▼▼ Ramada Limited **M**
(317) 297-1848. **$65-$175, 3 day notice.** 3851 Shore Dr 46254. I-465 exit 17, just w on 38th St, then just n. Ext corridors. **Pets:** Other species. $15 daily fee/pet. Service with restrictions, crate.

▼▼▼ Residence Inn by Marriott Indianapolis Airport **H**
(317) 244-1500. **$190-$300.** 5224 W Southern Ave 46241. I-465 exit 11A, 0.5 mi e on Sam Jones Expwy exit Lynhurst Dr. Int corridors. **Pets:** Accepted.

▼▼▼ Residence Inn by Marriott Indianapolis Downtown on the Canal **H**
(317) 822-0840. **$149-$289.** 350 W New York St 46202. Jct Senate Ave. Int corridors. **Pets:** Accepted.

▼▼▼ Residence Inn by Marriott Northwest-Indianapolis **H**
(317) 275-6000. **$119-$159.** 6220 Digital Way 46278. I-465 exit 21, just w. Int corridors. **Pets:** Other species. $100 one-time fee/room. Designated rooms, service with restrictions, crate.

Sheraton Hotel City Centre H ❤
(317) 635-2000. **$99-$209, 3 day notice.** 31 W Ohio St 46204. Jct Meridian St; just n of Monument Cir. Int corridors. **Pets:** Medium, dogs only. Designated rooms, service with restrictions, supervision.
SAVE 🛜 ✕ ♿M ⊞ 🛢 ▣ 🍴 ⊅

Sheraton Indianapolis at Keystone Crossing H ❤
(317) 846-2700. **$119-$399.** 8787 Keystone Crossing 46240. I-465 exit 33, 0.5 mi s on SR 431, just e on 86th St, then just n. Int corridors. **Pets:** Medium, dogs only. Service with restrictions, supervision.
ECO SAVE 🛜 ✕ ♿M ▣ 🛢 🍴 ⊅

Sleep Inn Airport H
(317) 247-4100. **$54-$94.** 5845 Rockville Rd 46224. I-465 exit 13A, just e. Int corridors. **Pets:** Accepted. SAVE 🛜 🛢 ▣

Staybridge Suites City Centre H
(317) 536-7500. **Call for rates.** 535 S West St 46225. Just s of South St. Int corridors. **Pets:** Accepted. 🛜 ✕ ♿M 🛢 ▣ ⊅

Suburban Extended Stay Hotel H
(317) 598-1914. **$59-$89.** 8055 Bash St 46250. I-69 exit 201, just w. Int corridors. **Pets:** Large, other species. $25 daily fee/pet. Service with restrictions. 🛜 ♿M 🛢 ▣

TownePlace Suites by Marriott Keystone H
(317) 255-3700. **$89-$199.** 8468 Union Chapel Rd 46240. I-465 exit 33, 0.5 mi s on SR 431, just e on 86th St, then just s. Int corridors. **Pets:** Accepted. 🛜 ✕ 🛢 ▣ ⊅

TownePlace Suites by Marriott Park 100 H
(317) 290-8900. **$79-$179.** 5802 W 71st St 46278. I-465 exit 21, 0.3 mi e. Int corridors. **Pets:** Large. $100 one-time fee/room. Designated rooms, service with restrictions, crate. 🛜 ✕ 🛢 ▣ ⊅

The Westin Indianapolis H
(317) 262-8100. **$109-$525.** 50 S Capitol Ave 46204. Jct Washington and Maryland sts. Int corridors. **Pets:** Accepted.
SAVE 🛜 ✕ ♿M ▣ 🍴 ⊅ ✕

Wingate Inn-Airport H
(317) 243-8310. **$99-$200.** 5797 Rockville Rd 46224. I-465 exit 13A, just e. Int corridors. **Pets:** Other species. $25 one-time fee/room. Service with restrictions, crate. 🛜 ✕ ♿M 🛢 ▣ ⊅

Wyndham Indianapolis West H
(317) 248-2481. **$89-$319.** 2544 Executive Dr 46241. I-465 exit 11A southbound; exit 11B northbound, just e on Sam Jones Expwy to Executive Dr. Int corridors. **Pets:** Medium, dogs only. $50 one-time fee/room. Service with restrictions, supervision.
SAVE 🛜 ✕ ♿M 🛢 🛢 ▣ 🍴 ⊅

LEBANON

Holiday Inn Express H
(765) 483-4100. **$99-$129.** 335 N Mt Zion Rd 46052. I-65 exit 140, just w. Int corridors. **Pets:** Medium. $15 daily fee/pet. Designated rooms, no service, supervision. 🛜 ♿M 🛢 ▣ ⊅

MARTINSVILLE

BEST WESTERN Martinsville Inn H
(765) 342-1842. **$70-$149.** 50 Bill's Blvd 46151. SR 37 to Ohio St, just w. Int corridors. **Pets:** Accepted. SAVE 🛜 ♿M 🛢 ▣

NOBLESVILLE

Quality Inn & Suites H ❤
(317) 770-6772. **$70-$90.** 16025 Prosperity Dr 46060. I-69 exit 205, 4 mi n on SR 37. Int corridors. **Pets:** Large, other species. $20 daily fee/pet. Designated rooms, service with restrictions, crate.
🛜 ✕ 🛢 ▣ ⊅

Super 8 Noblesville H ❤
(317) 776-7088. **$59-$174.** 17070 Dragonfly Dr 46060. Jct SR 37 and 38, 0.5 mi s on SR 37. Int corridors. **Pets:** Other species. $10 daily fee/pet. Crate. SAVE 🛜 🛢 ▣ ⊅

PLAINFIELD

Holiday Inn Express-Indianapolis Airport H ❤
(317) 839-9000. **$109-$169.** 6296 Cambridge Way 46168. I-70 exit 66, 0.4 mi n on SR 267, just e on Hadley Rd, then just s. Int corridors. **Pets:** Other species. $25 one-time fee/room. Service with restrictions, supervision. 🛜 ✕ ♿M 🛢 ▣ ⊅

La Quinta Inn & Suites Indianapolis Airport-Plainfield H
(317) 279-2650. **$89-$166.** 2251 Manchester Dr 46168. I-70 exit 66, 0.4 mi n on SR 267, just e on Perry Rd. Int corridors. **Pets:** Service with restrictions, supervision. SAVE 🛜 ✕ ♿M 🛢 ▣ ⊅

Staybridge Suites Indianapolis Airport H
(317) 839-2700. **$109-$199.** 6295 Cambridge Way 46168. I-70 exit 66, 0.4 mi n on SR 267, just e on Hadley Rd, then just s. Int corridors. **Pets:** Accepted. 🛜 ✕ ♿M 🛢 ▣ ⊅

END METROPOLITAN AREA

JASPER

Days Inn Jasper H
(812) 482-6000. **$74-$114.** 272 Brucke Strasse 47546. Jct SR 164, just w. Ext/int corridors. **Pets:** Small. $15 daily fee/pet. Designated rooms, service with restrictions, supervision. 🛜 ✕ 🛢 ▣ 🍴 ⊅

JEFFERSONVILLE

Comfort Suites Louisville North H
(812) 282-2100. **$79-$99.** 360 Eastern Blvd 47130. I-65 exit 2 (Eastern Blvd), just e. Int corridors. **Pets:** Accepted. 🛜 ✕ ♿M 🛢 ▣

Sheraton Louisville Riverside Hotel H ❤
(812) 284-6711. **$109-$349.** 700 W Riverside Dr 47130. I-65 exit 0, just w. Int corridors. **Pets:** Large, other species. Service with restrictions.
SAVE 🛜 ✕ 🛢 ▣ 🍴 ⊅

TownePlace Suites by Marriott H
(812) 280-8200. **$89-$132.** 703 N Shore Dr 47130. I-65 exit 0, just w. Int corridors. **Pets:** Accepted. 🛜 ✕ 🛢 ▣ ⊅

KENDALLVILLE

BEST WESTERN Kendallville Inn H ❤
(260) 347-5263. **$73-$109.** 621 Professional Way 46755. 1 mi e on US 6. Int corridors. **Pets:** Other species. $15 one-time fee/room. Service with restrictions, supervision. SAVE 🛜 🛢 ▣ ⊅ ✕

Holiday Inn Express Kendallville H
(260) 343-0000. **$75-$125.** 1917 Dowling St 46755. I-69 exit 134, 9.3 mi e on US 6. Int corridors. **Pets:** Accepted.
SAVE 🛜 ♿M 🛢 ▣ ⊅ ✕

KOKOMO

▼▼ ▼▼ Comfort Inn by Choice Hotels H

(765) 452-5050. **$69-$110.** 522 Essex Dr 46901. Jct US 35, 0.3 mi n on US 31. Int corridors. **Pets:** Accepted. 🛜 📶 💻 🏊

▼▼ ▼▼ Fairfield Inn by Marriott H

(765) 453-8822. **$89-$129.** 1717 E Lincoln Rd 46902. US 31, 2 mi s of jct US 35. Int corridors. **Pets:** Accepted. 🛜 ❌ 🔧 📶 💻 🏊

▼▼▼▼ Hampton Inn & Suites H

(765) 455-2900. **$109-$129.** 2920 S Reed Rd (US Hwy 31) 46902. US 31, 2 mi s of jct US 35. Int corridors. **Pets:** Dogs only. Designated rooms, service with restrictions, supervision. 🛜 🔧 📶 💻 🏊 ❌

LAFAYETTE

◆◆◆ ▼▼▼▼ Baymont Inn & Suites H

(765) 449-4808. **$69-$300.** 201 Frontage Rd 47905. I-65 exit 172, just e on SR 26, then just n. Int corridors. **Pets:** Medium, dogs only. $10 daily fee/pet. Designated rooms, service with restrictions, supervision.

SAVE 🛜 ❌ 📶 💻

◆◆◆ ▼▼▼▼ BEST WESTERN Lafayette Executive Plaza & Conference Center H ❋

(765) 447-0575. **$120-$160.** 4343 South St 47905. I-65 exit 172, just w. Int corridors. **Pets:** Medium. $20 daily fee/room. Designated rooms, supervision. SAVE 🛜 ❌ 🔧 📶 💻 🍽 🏊 ❌

▼▼▼▼ Candlewood Suites H

(765) 807-5735. **$95-$226, 7 day notice.** 240 Meijer Dr 47905. I-65 exit 172, just e on SR 26. Int corridors. **Pets:** $100 one-time fee/pet. Service with restrictions, crate. 🛜 ❌ 🔧 📶 💻 🏊

▼▼▼▼ Comfort Inn H

(765) 447-3434. **$79-$100.** 4701 Meijer Ct 47905. I-65 exit 172, just e on SR 26. Int corridors. **Pets:** Small, other species. $15 one-time fee/pet. Designated rooms, service with restrictions, supervision.

🛜 📶 💻 🏊

▼▼ ▼▼ Days Inn & Suites H ❋

(765) 446-8558. **$60-$139.** 151 Frontage Rd 47905. I-65 exit 172, just e. Int corridors. **Pets:** Small. $10 daily fee/pet. Service with restrictions, crate. 🛜 📶 💻

▼▼▼▼ Homewood Suites by Hilton H

(765) 449-9700. **$149-$159.** 3939 SR 26 E 47905. I-65 exit 172, 0.8 mi w. Ext/int corridors. **Pets:** Large, other species. $50 one-time fee/pet. Service with restrictions, supervision. 🛜 📶 💻 🏊 ❌

▼▼ ▼▼ Motel 6 #4291 M

(765) 447-7566. **$50-$119.** 139 Frontage Rd 47905. I-65 exit 172. Ext corridors. **Pets:** Other species. Service with restrictions, supervision. 🛜 📶

▼▼ ▼▼ Quality Inn & Suites H

(765) 447-9460. **Call for rates.** 4221 SR 26 E 47905. I-65 exit 172, 0.3 mi w. Int corridors. **Pets:** Accepted. 🛜 📶 💻 🏊 ❌

▼▼ ▼▼ Red Roof Inn-Lafayette #7062 M

(765) 448-4671. **$60-$199.** 4201 SR 26 E 47905. I-65 exit 172, 0.3 mi w. Ext corridors. **Pets:** Large, other species. Service with restrictions, supervision. 🛜 📶

◆◆◆ ▼▼▼▼ TownePlace Suites by Marriott H

(765) 446-8668. **$89-$229.** 163 Frontage Rd 47905. I-65 exit 172, just e. Int corridors. **Pets:** Other species. $75 one-time fee/room. Service with restrictions. SAVE 🛜 ❌ 📶 💻 🏊 ❌

LA PORTE

◆◆◆ ▼▼▼▼ BEST WESTERN PLUS LaPorte Hotel & Conference Center H

(219) 362-4585. **$109-$119, 3 day notice.** 444 Pine Lake Ave 46350. 1.5 mi n on US 35. Int corridors. **Pets:** $25 one-time fee/room. Designated rooms, service with restrictions, supervision.

SAVE 🛜 📶 💻 🍽 🏊 ❌

▼▼ ▼▼ Holiday Inn Express-LaPorte @Pine Lake H ❋

(219) 326-7900. **Call for rates.** 100 Eastshore Ct 46350. I-80/90 exit 49, 2.5 mi s on SR 39/US 35. Int corridors. **Pets:** Other species. $35 one-time fee/pet. Service with restrictions, crate. 🛜 ❌ 📶 💻 🏊

MERRILLVILLE

▼▼ ▼▼ Candlewood Suites H ❋

(219) 791-9100. **$99-$109.** 8339 Ohio St 46410. I-65 exit 253, 0.3 mi e, just s on Mississippi St, 0.4 mi w on 83rd Ave, then just s. Int corridors. **Pets:** Small, dogs only. $75 one-time fee/pet. Service with restrictions, supervision. 🛜 📶 💻

▼▼ ▼▼ Extended StayAmerica-Merrillville-US Rte 30 H

(219) 769-4740. **$60-$100.** 1355 E 83rd Ave 46410. I-65 exit 253, 0.3 mi e on US 30, just s on Mississippi St, then 0.4 mi w. Int corridors. **Pets:** $25 daily fee/pet. Designated rooms, service with restrictions. 🛜 📶 💻

▼▼▼▼ Residence Inn by Marriott Merrillville H

(219) 791-9000. **$123-$189.** 8018 Delaware Pl 46410. I-65 exit 253, just nw. Int corridors. **Pets:** Accepted. 🛜 ❌ 🔧 📶 💻 🏊 ❌

MISHAWAKA

▼▼▼▼ Country Inn & Suites By Carlson H

(574) 271-1700. **Call for rates.** 120 W University Dr 46545. I-80/90 exit 83, just n on SR 331 to SR 23, 0.6 mi sw on SR 23, then just s on Main St. Int corridors. **Pets:** Accepted. 🛜 🔧 📶 💻 🏊

▼▼▼▼ Holiday Inn Express Mishawaka H

(574) 277-2520. **Call for rates.** 420 W University Dr 46545. I-80/90 exit 83, just n on SR 331 to 23, 1.6 mi sw to Main St, just s to University Dr, then just w. Int corridors. **Pets:** $35 one-time fee/pet. Designated rooms, service with restrictions. 🛜 🔧 📶 💻 🏊

▼▼▼▼ Residence Inn by Marriott South Bend/Mishawaka H

(574) 271-9283. **$90-$360.** 231 Park Pl 46545. I-80/90 exit 83, just n on SR 331 to SR 23, 1.6 mi sw, then 1.3 mi s on Main St. Int corridors. **Pets:** Other species. $100 one-time fee/room. Service with restrictions. 🛜 ❌ 🔧 📶 💻 🏊 ❌

MOUNT VERNON

▼▼ ▼▼ Four Seasons Motel M

(812) 838-4821. **$77-$104.** 70 Hwy 62 W 47620. 1.8 mi w. Ext corridors. **Pets:** Medium, other species. $25 one-time fee/pet. Service with restrictions, supervision. 🛜 📶 💻 🏊

MUNCIE

▼▼ ▼▼ Super 8 H

(765) 286-4333. **$48-$94, 3 day notice.** 3601 W Fox Ridge Ln 47304. I-69 exit 241, 6.3 mi e on SR 332. Int corridors. **Pets:** Small, dogs only. $10 one-time fee/pet. Service with restrictions, supervision. 🛜 ❌ 📶

NORTH VERNON

▼▼ ▼▼ Comfort Inn H

(812) 352-9999. **Call for rates.** 150 FDR Dr 47265. Jct US 50, 0.6 mi n on SR 7. Int corridors. **Pets:** Accepted. 🛜 📶 💻 🏊

PERU

BEST WESTERN Circus City Inn ♿ 🐾
(765) 473-8800. **Call for rates.** 2642 Business Rt US 31 S 46970. Just e of jct US 31. Int corridors. **Pets:** Large, other species. $10 daily fee/pet. Supervision. [SAVE] 🛜 🅿 📺

PORTAGE

Comfort Inn ♿
(219) 763-7177. **Call for rates.** 2300 Willowcreek Rd 46368. I-80/90 exit 23; I-94 exit 19, 1.5 mi s on CR 249. Int corridors. **Pets:** Small, dogs only. $20 one-time fee/pet. Service with restrictions, supervision.
🛜 🅿 📺

PRINCETON

Fairfield Inn by Marriott ♿ 🐾
(812) 385-4300. **$79-$139.** 2828 Dixon St 47670. Jct US 41 and SR 64, 0.3 mi w. Int corridors. **Pets:** Medium, other species. $30 one-time fee/room. Service with restrictions, crate. 🛜 ✖ 🅿 📺 ≋

REMINGTON

Super 8-Remington ♿
(219) 261-2883. **$73-$140.** 4278 W US 24 47977. I-65 exit 201, 0.5 mi w. Int corridors. **Pets:** Accepted. 🛜 🅿 📺

RICHMOND

BEST WESTERN Classic Inn ♿
(765) 939-9500. **Call for rates.** 533 W Eaton Pike 47374. I-70 exit 156A, just s. Int corridors. **Pets:** Large. $10 daily fee/pet. Service with restrictions, supervision. [SAVE] 🛜 🅿 📺 ≋

Days Inn 🅼
(765) 966-4900. **$56-$81.** 5775 National Rd E 47374. I-70 exit 156A, just s. Ext corridors. **Pets:** $10 daily fee/pet. Service with restrictions, crate.
🛜 🅿 📺

Knights Inn 🅼
(765) 966-1505. **$50-$55.** 3020 E Main St 47374. I-70 exit 156A, 2 mi w. Ext corridors. **Pets:** Small. $8 daily fee/pet. Service with restrictions, supervision. [SAVE] 🛜 🅿 📺

Quality Inn Richmond Conference Center ♿
(765) 966-7511. **$72-$125.** 5501 National Rd E 47374. I-70 exit 156A, 0.3 mi w. Int corridors. **Pets:** $20 one-time fee/room. Service with restrictions, crate. 🛜 🅿 📺 ≋ ✖

RUSHVILLE

Comfort Inn ♿
(765) 932-2999. **Call for rates.** 320 Conrad Harcourt Way 46173. Just e of SR 3. Int corridors. **Pets:** Accepted. 🛜 🅿 📺

SCOTTSBURG

Hampton Inn & Suites ♿
(812) 752-1999. **Call for rates.** 1535 W McClain Ave 47170. I-65 exit 29, just w. Int corridors. **Pets:** Accepted. 🛜 ✖ 🅿 📺 ≋

SELLERSBURG

Home Lodge ♿
(812) 246-6332. **$59-$64.** 363 Triangle Dr 47172. I-65 exit 9, just e. Int corridors. **Pets:** Accepted. 🛜 🅿 📺

Ramada ♿
(812) 246-3131. **$74-$550.** 360 Triangle Dr 47172. I-65 exit 9, just e. Int corridors. **Pets:** Accepted. 🛜 ✖ 🅿 📺 ≋

SOUTH BEND

Comfort Suites University Area ♿ 🐾
(574) 272-1500. **$69-$99.** 52939 SR 933 N 46637. I-80/90 exit 77, just e to Business Rt US 31/SR 933, then 1 mi n. Int corridors. **Pets:** Medium. $20 one-time fee/pet. Designated rooms, service with restrictions, supervision. 🛜 ✖ 🅿 📺

Oliver Inn Bed & Breakfast 🅱🅱
(574) 232-4545. **$140-$339, 14 day notice.** 630 W Washington St 46601. 0.3 mi w of SR 933 and Business Rt US 31. Int corridors. **Pets:** Other species. $10 daily fee/pet. Designated rooms, service with restrictions, supervision. 🛜 ✖ 🅿 📺

Sleep Inn ♿
(574) 232-3200. **$75-$110.** 4134 Lincolnway W 46628. I-80/90 exit 72, 1.5 mi s on US 31 to South Bend Regional Airport exit, then 2 mi e. Int corridors. **Pets:** Medium. $10 daily fee/pet. Designated rooms, service with restrictions, crate. [SAVE] 🛜 ✖ 🅿 📺 ≋

Staybridge Suites South Bend-University Area ♿
(574) 968-7440. **Call for rates.** 52860 SR 933 N 46637. I-80/90 exit 77, 1 mi n. Int corridors. **Pets:** Large, other species. $150 one-time fee/room. Designated rooms, service with restrictions, crate.
🛜 🅼 🅿 📺 ≋

Suburban Extended Stay Hotel ♿
(574) 968-4737. **$59-$79.** 52825 SR 933 N 46637. I-80/90 exit 77, 1 mi n. Int corridors. **Pets:** Accepted. 🛜 🅼 🅿 📺 ≋

Waterford Estates Lodge ♿
(574) 272-5220. **$109-$119.** 52890 SR 933 N 46637. I-80/90 exit 77, 1 mi n. Int corridors. **Pets:** $30 one-time fee/pet. Designated rooms, service with restrictions, supervision. 🛜 ✖ 🅼 🅿 📺 🍴 ≋

TAYLORSVILLE

Red Roof Inn 🅼
(812) 526-9747. **$69-$100.** 10330 US 31 47280. I-65 exit 76A, just s. Ext corridors. **Pets:** Large, other species. Service with restrictions, supervision.
🛜 ✖ 🅿 📺 ≋

TELL CITY

Holiday Inn Express ♿
(812) 547-0800. **$88-$120.** 310 Orchard Hill Dr 47586. Just off SR 66, 1.7 mi se of jct SR 37. Int corridors. **Pets:** Accepted.
🛜 🅼 🅿 📺

Ramada Limited ♿
(812) 547-3234. **$79-$119.** 235 Orchard Hill Dr 47586. Just off SR 66, 1.7 mi se of jct SR 37. Int corridors. **Pets:** Other species. $15 deposit/room. Service with restrictions, supervision. 🛜 🅿 📺 ≋

TERRE HAUTE

Candlewood Suites ♿
(812) 234-3400. **$89-$99.** 721 Wabash Ave 47807. I-70 exit 7 (US 41/150), 2.2 mi n, 0.4 mi e, then just s. Int corridors. **Pets:** Other species. $25 one-time fee/pet. Service with restrictions, crate.
🛜 ✖ 🅼 🅿 📺

Drury Inn-Terre Haute ♿
(812) 238-1206. **$105-$179.** 3040 Hwy 41 S 47802. I-70 exit 7 (US 41/150), just n. Int corridors. **Pets:** Service with restrictions, supervision.
🛜 🅼 🅿 📺 ≋ ✖

Holiday Inn ♿ 🐾
(812) 232-6081. **$99-$119.** 3300 US 41 S 47802. I-70 exit 7 (US 41/150), just s. Int corridors. **Pets:** Large. $25 one-time fee/room. Service with restrictions, supervision. 🛜 🅿 📺 🍴 ≋ ✖

Holiday Inn Express & Suites 🅷
(812) 234-3200. **Call for rates.** 2645 S Joe Fox St 47803. I-70 exit 11, just n. Int corridors. **Pets:** Other species. $75 one-time fee/room. Service with restrictions.

Pear Tree Inn by Drury-Terre Haute 🅷
(812) 234-4268. **$65-$134.** 3050 US 41 S 47802. I-70 exit 7 (US 41/150), just n. Int corridors. **Pets:** Service with restrictions, supervision.

VALPARAISO

Courtyard by Marriott Valparaiso 🅷
(219) 465-1700. **$89-$124.** 2301 E Morthland Dr 46383. US 30, just w of jct SR 49. Int corridors. **Pets:** Accepted.

The Inn at Aberdeen 🅱🅱
(219) 465-3753. **$106-$201.** 3158 S SR 2 46385. Jct US 30, 2.7 mi w, just n. Int corridors. **Pets:** $25 daily fee/pet. Designated rooms, service with restrictions, supervision.

VINCENNES

TownePlace Suites by Marriott Vincennes 🅷
(812) 255-1500. **$113-$125.** 1320 Willow St 47591. Jct US 41 Bypass and Willow Rd, 1 mi nw. Int corridors. **Pets:** Accepted.

WARSAW

Holiday Inn Express Hotel & Suites-Warsaw 🅷
(574) 268-1600. **Call for rates.** 3825 Lake City Hwy 46580. Jct US 30 and SR 15, 4 mi e on US 30. Int corridors. **Pets:** Medium, other species. $15 daily fee/pet. Service with restrictions, supervision.

Wyndham Garden of Warsaw 🅷
(574) 269-2323. **$94-$129.** 2519 E Center St 46580. 2.8 mi e of SR 15 on US 30, just s. Int corridors. **Pets:** Large, other species. $50 one-time fee/room. Crate.

WASHINGTON

Baymont Inn & Suites Washington 🅷
(812) 254-7000. **$85-$135.** 7 Cumberland Dr 47501. Just ne of jct US 50 and SR 257. Int corridors. **Pets:** Accepted.

Holiday Inn Express 🅷
(812) 254-6666. **Call for rates.** 1808 E National Hwy 47501. On US 50 business route, 0.4 mi e of SR 257. Int corridors. **Pets:** Accepted.

WEST BADEN SPRINGS

West Baden Springs Hotel 🅷
(812) 936-1902. **$180-$325.** 8538 W Baden Ave 47469. On SR 56. Int corridors. **Pets:** Accepted.

WEST LAFAYETTE

Four Points by Sheraton West Lafayette 🅷
(765) 463-5511. **$134-$175.** 1600 Cumberland Ave 47906. I-65 exit 175, 1.5 mi sw on Schuyler Ave, then 3.8 mi nw on US 52. Int corridors. **Pets:** Small, dogs only. Service with restrictions, supervision.

IOWA

CITY INDEX

ALBIA

Indian Hills Inn 🅷
(641) 932-7181. **$68-$149.** 100 Hwy 34 E 52531. Just e of jct US 34 and SR 5. Ext/int corridors. **Pets:** Accepted.

ALGONA

AmericInn Lodge & Suites of Algona 🅷
(515) 295-3333. **$91-$156.** 600 Hwy 18 W 50511. Just w of jct US 169/18. Int corridors. **Pets:** Accepted.

ALTOONA

Settle Inn & Suites-Altoona 🅷
(515) 967-7888. **Call for rates.** 2101 Adventureland Dr 50009. I-80 exit 142A, just se. Int corridors. **Pets:** Small, dogs only. $15 daily fee/room. Designated rooms, service with restrictions, supervision.

AMES

AmericInn of Ames 🅷
(515) 233-1005. **Call for rates.** 2507 SE 16th St 50010. exit 111B, US 30 exit 150, just ne. Int corridors. **Pets:** Accepted.

AAA ◆◆◆ BEST WESTERN PLUS University Park Inn & Suites H
(515) 296-2500. **$99-$169.** 2500 University Blvd 50010. US 30 exit 146, then just s. Int corridors. **Pets:** Large. $10 one-time fee/room. Service with restrictions, supervision. SAVE 🛜 🔲 💻 🏊

◆◆ Comfort Inn-Ames H
(515) 232-0689. **Call for rates.** 1605 S Dayton Pl 50010. US 30 exit 150, then just ne. Int corridors. **Pets:** Accepted. 🛜 🔲 💻 🏊

◆◆ Country Inn & Suites By Carlson H
(515) 233-3935. **$99-$189.** 2605 SE 16th St 50010. US 30 exit 150, then just ne. Int corridors. **Pets:** Accepted. 🛜 ✕ ♿ 🔲 💻 🏊

◆◆ Econo Lodge H
(515) 233-6060. **Call for rates.** 2600 SE 16th St 50010. US 30 exit 150, then just ne. Int corridors. **Pets:** Accepted. 🛜 🔲 💻 🏊

◆◆◆ Gateway Hotel & Conference Center H
(515) 292-8600. **Call for rates.** 2100 Green Hills Dr 50014. US 30 exit 146, then just sw. Int corridors. **Pets:** Accepted.
🛜 ✕ ♿ 🔲 💻 🍴 🏊 ✕

AAA ◆◆◆ GrandStay Residential Suites Hotel H
(515) 232-8363. **$90-$210.** 1606 S Kellogg Ave 50010. US 30 exit 148, then just n. Int corridors. **Pets:** Other species. $250 deposit/pet, $10 daily fee/pet. Designated rooms, service with restrictions, supervision.
SAVE 🛜 ✕ ♿ 🔲 💻 🏊

◆◆◆ Holiday Inn Ames Conference Center at ISU H
(515) 268-8808. **$89-$189.** 2609 University Blvd 50010. US 30 exit 146, then just s. Int corridors. **Pets:** Small. $25 daily fee/pet. Service with restrictions, supervision. 🛜 ♿ 🔲 💻 🍴 🏊

◆◆ Microtel Inn & Suites by Wyndham Ames H
(515) 233-4444. **$60-$124.** 2216 SE 16th St 50010. US 30 exit 150, then just ne. Int corridors. **Pets:** Other species. $10 daily fee/pet. Designated rooms, service with restrictions, crate. 🛜 ♿ 🔲 💻 🏊

◆◆◆ Quality Inn & Suites Starlite Village Conference Center H ❀
(515) 232-9260. **$89-$139.** 2601 E 13th St 50010. I-35 exit 113 (13th St), 0.5 mi w. Int corridors. **Pets:** Medium. $20 daily fee/room. Service with restrictions, crate. 🛜 ♿ 🔲 💻 🍴 🏊

ANAMOSA
◆◆◆ AmericInn Lodge & Suites H
(319) 462-4119. **$90-$165.** 101 Harley Ave 52205. US 151 exit 54, 1 mi n. Int corridors. **Pets:** Accepted. 🛜 ✕ ♿ 🔲 💻 🏊

◆◆ Super 8-Anamosa H
(319) 462-3888. **$60-$120.** 100 Grant Wood Dr 52205. US 151 exit 54, just e on SR 64. Int corridors. **Pets:** Accepted. 🛜 🔲 💻

ANKENY
AAA ◆◆◆ Comfort Inn H
(515) 963-1100. **$89-$170.** 2602 SE Creekview Dr 50021. I-35 exit 90, just ne. Int corridors. **Pets:** Very small. $25 daily fee/pet. Designated rooms, no service, supervision. SAVE 🛜 🔲 💻 🏊

ARNOLDS PARK
◆◆ Bridges Bay Resort CO
(712) 332-2202. **Call for rates.** 630 Linden Dr 51331. Just e of US 71. Int corridors. **Pets:** Accepted. 🛜 ✕ 🔲 💻 🍴 🏊 ✕

◆◆ Fillenwarth Beach M
(712) 332-5646. **$114-$1680, 60 day notice.** 87 Lake Shore Dr 51331. Just w of US 71. Ext corridors. **Pets:** Accepted.
🛜 ✕ 🔲 💻 🏊 ✕

ATLANTIC
◆◆ Americas Best Value Inn H
(712) 243-4067. **$60-$90.** 64968 Boston Rd 50022. I-80 exit 60 (US 71), 0.3 mi s. Int corridors. **Pets:** Other species. Service with restrictions, supervision. 🛜 🔲 💻 🏊

◆◆ Super 8 H
(712) 243-4723. **$75-$85.** 1902 E 7th St 50022. I-80 exit 60 (US 71), 6 mi s, then 2 mi w; east side of town. Int corridors. **Pets:** Medium, other species. $5 one-time fee/room. Service with restrictions, supervision.
🛜 ✕ ♿ 🔲 💻 🏊

BURLINGTON
AAA ◆◆◆ Comfort Suites Hotel & Conference Center H
(319) 753-1300. **$90-$121.** 1780 Stonegate Center Dr 52601. On US 61, 2 mi s of US 34. Int corridors. **Pets:** Large, other species. $15 daily fee/pet. Designated rooms, service with restrictions, supervision.
SAVE 🛜 ✕ ♿ 🔲 💻 🍴 🏊 ✕

AAA ◆◆◆ Quality Inn H
(319) 753-0000. **Call for rates.** 3051 Kirkwood St 52601. Jct US 61 and 34, just n. Int corridors. **Pets:** Medium. $10 daily fee/pet. Service with restrictions, supervision. SAVE 🛜 🔲 💻 🏊

◆◆ Super 8 H
(319) 752-9806. **$70.** 3001 Kirkwood St 52601. Jct US 61 and 34, just n. Int corridors. **Pets:** Accepted. 🛜 🔲 💻

CARTER LAKE
AAA ◆◆◆ Holiday Inn Express & Suites-Omaha Airport H
(402) 505-4900. **Call for rates.** 2510 Abbott Plaza 51510. I-480 W exit 4 to 10th St, 2 mi n, follow Eppley Airfield signs. Int corridors.
Pets: Accepted. SAVE 🛜 ✕ ♿ 🔲 💻 🏊

AAA ◆◆◆ La Quinta Inn & Suites Omaha Airport - Carter Lake H
(712) 347-6595. **$95-$320.** 1201 Ave H 51510. I-480 W exit 4 to 10th St, 2 mi n, follow Eppley Airfield signs. Int corridors. **Pets:** Service with restrictions, supervision. SAVE 🛜 ♿ 🔲 💻 🏊

◆◆ Super 8 H ❀
(712) 347-5588. **$61-$100.** 3000 Airport Dr 51510. I-480 W exit 4 to 10th St, 2.3 mi n, follow Eppley Airfield signs. Int corridors. **Pets:** Other species. $10 one-time fee/pet. Service with restrictions, crate.
🛜 ✕ 🔲 💻 🏊

CEDAR FALLS
◆◆ AmericInn Lodge & Suites of Cedar Falls H
(319) 277-6166. **$79-$99.** 5818 Nordic Dr 50613. US 20 exit 225, 1.4 mi n on SR 58. Int corridors. **Pets:** Small. $15 daily fee/pet. Service with restrictions, crate. 🛜 🔲 💻 🏊

◆◆ Comfort Suites H ❀
(319) 273-9999. **$84-$140.** 7402 Nordic Dr 50613. US 20 exit 225, just nw. Int corridors. **Pets:** Medium, dogs only. $10 daily fee/pet. Designated rooms, service with restrictions, crate. 🛜 ✕ ♿ 🔲 💻 🏊

AAA ◆◆◆ Days Inn H
(319) 266-1222. **$53-$75.** 5924 University Ave. 0.7 mi e of jct SR 58. Int corridors. **Pets:** Medium, other species. Service with restrictions, crate.
SAVE 🛜 🔲 💻

◆◆◆ Suburban Extended Stay Hotel H
(319) 268-2222. **$79-$170.** 300 Viking Rd 50613. Jct US 20 and SR 58 exit 225, 1.4 mi n on SR 58, then just w. Int corridors. **Pets:** Medium, dogs only. $75 one-time fee/pet. Service with restrictions, supervision.
🛜 ✕ ♿ 🔲 💻 🏊

CEDAR RAPIDS

▼▼▼ AmericInn Lodge & Suites of Cedar Rapids 🅷
(319) 632-1800. **$90-$196.** 8910 6th St SW 52404. I-380 exit 13, just nw. Int corridors. **Pets:** $25 daily fee/pet. Designated rooms, service with restrictions, supervision. 🛰 📶 🔌 🖥 🏊 ✕

AAA ▼▼ Baymont Inn & Suites 🅷
(319) 378-8000. **$75-$110.** 1220 Park Pl NE 52402. I-380 exit 24A (SR 100/Collins Rd), 0.9 mi e, then just n. Int corridors. **Pets:** Small. $10 daily fee/pet. Designated rooms, service with restrictions, crate.
SAVE 🛰 ✕ 📶 🔌 🖥 🏊

AAA ▼▼▼ BEST WESTERN Cooper's Mill Hotel 🅷
(319) 366-5323. **$100-$160.** 100 F Ave NW 52405. I-380 exit 19C northbound, at south end of exit make immediate U-turn under I-380; exit 20A southbound, cross river, then just n on 1st St NW. Int corridors. **Pets:** Medium, other species. $10 daily fee/pet. Service with restrictions.
SAVE 🛰 🔌 🖥 🍽 🏊 ✕

AAA ▼▼▼ BEST WESTERN PLUS Longbranch Hotel & Convention Center 🅷
(319) 377-6386. **$120-$160.** 90 Twixt Town Rd NE 52402. I-380 exit 24A (SR 100/Collins Rd), 2.5 mi e, then just n. Int corridors. **Pets:** Medium, other species. $10 daily fee/pet. Designated rooms, service with restrictions. SAVE 🛰 🔌 🖥 🍽 🏊 ✕

▼▼ Clarion Hotel & Convention Center 🅷
(319) 366-8671. **$84-$175.** 525 33rd Ave SW 52404. I-380 exit 17 (33rd Ave SW), just w. Int corridors. **Pets:** Small. $100 deposit/pet, $15 daily fee/pet. Designated rooms, service with restrictions, supervision.
🛰 🔌 🖥 🍽 🏊 ✕

▼▼ Collins Inn & Suites 🅷
(319) 378-8888. **$76-$126.** 2025 Werner Ave NE 52402. I-380 exit 24A (SR 100/Collins Rd), just se. Int corridors. **Pets:** Accepted.
🛰 🔌 🖥 🏊

▼▼ Comfort Inn by Choice Hotels North 🅷
(319) 393-8247. **$80-$100.** 5055 Rockwell Dr NE 52402. I-380 exit 24A (SR 100/Collins Rd), 1 mi e. Int corridors. **Pets:** Small. $15 daily fee/pet. Designated rooms, service with restrictions, crate. 🛰 🔌 🖥

AAA ▼▼ Country Inn & Suites By Carlson, Cedar Rapids Airport 🅷
(319) 363-3789. **$99-$199.** 9100 Atlantic Dr SW 52405. I-380 exit 13, just w. Int corridors. **Pets:** Medium. $20 one-time fee/pet, $10 daily fee/pet. Designated rooms, service with restrictions, supervision.
SAVE 🛰 📶 🔌 🖥 🏊

▼▼ Hometown Inn & Suites 🅷
(319) 362-9012. **$60-$130.** 3315 Southgate Ct SW 52404. I-380 exit 17 (33rd Ave SW), just sw. Int corridors. **Pets:** Accepted.
🛰 🔌 🖥 🏊

▼▼ Homewood Suites 🅷
(319) 378-1140. **$99-$199.** 1140 Park Pl NE 52402. I-380 exit 24A (SR 100/Collins Rd) to Collins Rd, n on Council St, then just e. Int corridors. **Pets:** Accepted. 🛰 📶 🔌 🖥 🏊

▼▼ Howard Johnson Ⓜ
(319) 366-2475. **$54-$79.** 616 33rd Ave SW 52404. I-380 exit 17 (33rd Ave SW), 0.3 mi w. Int corridors. **Pets:** Accepted. 🛰 🔌 🖥

▼▼▼ MainStay Suites 🅷
(319) 363-7829. **$79-$169.** 5145 Rockwell Dr NE 52402. I-380 exit 24A (SR 100/Collins Rd), 1 mi e, then just n. Int corridors. **Pets:** Medium. $25 daily fee/room. Designated rooms, service with restrictions, supervision.
🛰 📶 🔌 🖥 🏊

▼▼ Quality Inn South by Choice Hotels 🅷
(319) 363-7934. **$69-$110.** 390 33rd Ave SW 52404. I-380 exit 17 (33rd Ave SW), just w. Int corridors. **Pets:** Accepted. 🛰 🔌 🖥

▼▼ Red Roof Inn Cedar Rapids 🅷
(319) 364-2000. **$54-$89.** 3243 S Ridge Dr SW 52404. I-380 exit 17 (33rd Ave SW), just nw. Ext/int corridors. **Pets:** Large, other species. Service with restrictions, supervision. 🛰 📶 🔌 🖥 🏊

▼▼▼ Residence Inn by Marriott 🅷
(319) 395-0111. **$119-$219.** 1900 Dodge Rd NE 52402. I-380 exit 24A (SR 100/Collins Rd), just e. Int corridors. **Pets:** Accepted.
🛰 ✕ 📶 🔌 🖥 🏊 ✕

▼▼ Super 8 🅷
(319) 362-6002. **$56-$100, 3 day notice.** 720 33rd Ave SW 52404. I-380 exit 17 (33rd Ave SW), 0.4 mi w. Int corridors. **Pets:** Medium, other species. $10 daily fee/room. Service with restrictions, supervision.
🛰 🔌 🖥

CHARLES CITY

▼▼▼ Sleep Inn & Suites 🅷
(641) 257-6700. **$85-$100.** 1416 S Grand Ave 50616. US 218/18 exit 218, 0.7 mi n on US 218 business route; south side of town. Int corridors. **Pets:** Accepted. 🛰 📶 🔌 🖥 🏊

▼▼ Super 8 - Charles City 🅷
(641) 228-2888. **$62-$90.** 1411 S Grand Ave 50616. US 218/18 exit 218, 0.8 mi n on US 218 business route; south side of town. Int corridors. **Pets:** Very small. $10 daily fee/pet. Service with restrictions, supervision.
🛰 📶 🔌 🖥

CHEROKEE

AAA ▼▼ BEST WESTERN La Grande Hacienda 🅷
(712) 225-5701. **$90-$100.** 1401 N 2nd St 51012. Just s of jct SR 3 and US 59 (N 2nd St). Int corridors. **Pets:** Other species. $50 deposit/room. Service with restrictions, supervision.
SAVE 🛰 ✕ 📶 🖥 🍽 🏊

CLARINDA

▼▼ Clarinda Super 8 🅷
(712) 542-6333. **$65-$72.** 1203 S 12th St 51632. Jct US 71 and SR 2, just e. Int corridors. **Pets:** Accepted. 🛰 📶 🔌 🖥 🏊

CLEAR LAKE

▼▼ AmericInn Lodge & Suites of Clear Lake 🅷
(641) 357-8954. **$91-$111.** 1406 N 25th St 50428. I-35 exit 194 (US 18), just nw. Int corridors. **Pets:** Designated rooms, service with restrictions, supervision. 🛰 🔌 🖥

AAA ▼▼ BEST WESTERN Holiday Lodge 🅷 🐾
(641) 357-5253. **$89-$109.** 2023 7th Ave N 50428. I-35 exit 194 (US 18), 0.3 mi w. Ext/int corridors. **Pets:** $10 daily fee/room. Service with restrictions, supervision. SAVE 🛰 📶 🔌 🖥 🍽 🏊 ✕

▼▼ Budget Inn Ⓜ
(641) 357-8700. **Call for rates.** 1306 N 25th St 50428. I-35 exit 194 (US 18), just nw. Int corridors. **Pets:** Accepted. 🛰 🔌 🖥

▼▼ Lake Country Inn Ⓜ
(641) 357-2184. **$55-$75.** 518 US 18 50428. I-35 exit 194 (US 18), 1.9 mi w. Ext corridors. **Pets:** Other species. $5 daily fee/pet. Designated rooms, service with restrictions, supervision. 🛰 🔌

▼▼ Microtel Inn by Wyndham Clear Lake 🅷
(641) 357-0966. **$65-$103.** 1305 N 25th St 50428. I-35 exit 194 (US 18), just nw. Int corridors. **Pets:** Designated rooms, service with restrictions, supervision. 🛰 📶 🔌 🖥

CLINTON

AAA ▼▼▼ Country Inn & Suites By Carlson 🅷
(563) 244-9922. **$89-$149.** 2224 Lincoln Way 52732. On US 30, just e of jct US 30 and 67. Int corridors. **Pets:** $10 daily fee/pet. Service with restrictions, supervision. SAVE 🛰 📶 🔌 🖥 🏊

▼▼▼ Oak Tree Inn 🏨
(563) 243-1000. **Call for rates.** 2300 Valley West Ct 52732. Just n of jct US 30 and 67; west side of town. Int corridors. **Pets:** Accepted.
🛰 ⊠ 🔊 🛏 🖵 ➤

CLIVE

🄰🄰🄰 ▼▼▼ BEST WESTERN PLUS Des Moines West Inn & Suites 🏨
(515) 221-2345. **$85-$115.** 1450 NW 118th St 50325. I-80/35 exit 124 (University Ave), just nw. Int corridors. **Pets:** Dogs only. $15 daily fee/pet. Supervision. SAVE 🛰 ⊠ 🔊 🛏 🖵 ➤

▼▼▼ Chase Suite Hotel 🏨
(515) 223-7700. **$109-$159.** 11428 Forest Ave 50325. I-80/35 exit 124 (University Ave), just ne. Ext corridors. **Pets:** Accepted.
🛰 ⊠ 🔊 🛏 🖵 ➤

🄰🄰🄰 ▼▼▼ Country Inn & Suites By Carlson, Des Moines-West 🏨
(515) 223-9254. **$89-$159.** 1350 NW 118th St 50325. I-80/35 exit 124 (University Ave), just nw. Int corridors. **Pets:** Medium, dogs only. $25 one-time fee/room. Designated rooms, service with restrictions, crate.
SAVE 🛰 ⊠ 🔊 🛏 🖵 ➤

▼▼ La Quinta Inn & Suites Des Moines West Clive 🏨
(515) 221-9200. **$71-$144.** 1390 NW 118th St 50325. I-80/35 exit 124 (University Ave). Int corridors. **Pets:** Service with restrictions, supervision.
🛰 🔊 🛏 🖵 ➤

▼▼ Super 8 🏨
(515) 226-0414. **$64-$99.** 11414 Forest Ave 50325. I-80/35 exit 124 (University Ave), just e. Int corridors. **Pets:** Small. $10 one-time fee/room. Designated rooms, service with restrictions, supervision.
🛰 🛏 🖵 ⊠

COLFAX

🄰🄰🄰 ▼▼▼ Microtel Inn & Suites by Wyndham Colfax/Newton 🏨
(515) 674-0600. **$60-$149.** 11000 Federal Ave 50054. I-80 exit 155 (SR 117). Int corridors. **Pets:** Other species. $10 daily fee/room. Supervision.
SAVE 🛰 🔊 🛏 🖵

CORALVILLE

▼▼ AmericInn of Coralville 🏨
(319) 625-2400. **$80-$200, 3 day notice.** 2597 Holiday Rd 52241. I-80 exit 240, just n. Int corridors. **Pets:** Small. $20 daily fee/pet. Designated rooms, supervision. 🛰 🔊 🛏 🖵 ➤

🄰🄰🄰 ▼▼▼ Baymont Inn & Suites 🏨
(319) 337-9797. **$80-$190.** 200 6th St 52241. I-80 exit 242, just s on 1st Ave, then just w. Int corridors. **Pets:** Other species. $10 daily fee/pet. Designated rooms, service with restrictions. SAVE 🛰 🛏 🖵 ➤

🄰🄰🄰 ▼▼▼ BEST WESTERN Cantebury Inn & Suites 🏨
(319) 351-0400. **Call for rates.** 704 1st Ave 52241. I-80 exit 242, just s. Int corridors. **Pets:** Small, dogs only. $20 daily fee/room. Designated rooms, service with restrictions, crate. SAVE 🛰 🛏 🖵 🍽 ➤

▼▼ Comfort Inn by Choice Hotels 🏨
(319) 351-8144. **$79-$109.** 209 W 9th St 52241. I-80 exit 242, just s. Int corridors. **Pets:** Accepted. 🛰 🔊 🛏 🖵 ➤

▼▼▼ Country Inn & Suites By Carlson 🏨
(319) 545-8464. **$89-$239, 3 day notice.** 2571 Heartland Pl 52241. I-80 exit 240, just n. Int corridors. **Pets:** Large, other species. $30 one-time fee/room. Designated rooms, service with restrictions.
🛰 🔊 🛏 🖵 ➤

▼▼▼ Holiday Inn 🏨
(319) 351-5049. **$89-$180.** 1220 1st Ave 52241. I-80 exit 242, just n. Int corridors. **Pets:** Large, other species. $20 one-time fee/room. Designated rooms, service with restrictions, supervision.
🛰 🔊 🛏 🖵 🍽 ➤

▼▼▼ Fairfield Inn by Marriott 🏨
(319) 337-8382. **$94-$250.** 214 W 9th St 52241. I-80 exit 242, just s. Int corridors. **Pets:** Accepted. 🛰 ⊠ 🔊 🛏 🖵 ➤

▼▼▼ Residence Inn by Marriott 🏨
(319) 338-6000. **$122-$299.** 2681 James St 52241. I-80 exit 240, just s. Int corridors. **Pets:** Medium, other species. $100 one-time fee/room. Service with restrictions, crate. 🛰 ⊠ 🔊 🛏 🖵 ➤ ⊠

🄰🄰🄰 ▼▼ Super 8 🏨
(319) 337-8388. **$70-$149.** 611 1st Ave 52241. I-80 exit 242, 0.4 mi s. Int corridors. **Pets:** Other species. $10 one-time fee/room. Service with restrictions. SAVE 🛰 🔊 🛏 🖵

COUNCIL BLUFFS

🄰🄰🄰 ▼▼ BEST WESTERN Crossroads of the Bluffs 🏨
(712) 322-3150. **Call for rates.** 2216 27th Ave 51501. I-29/80 exit 1B (24th St), just ne. Int corridors. **Pets:** Accepted.
SAVE 🛰 🛏 🖵 ➤

🄰🄰🄰 ▼▼▼ Comfort Suites 🏨
(712) 323-9760. **Call for rates.** 1801 S 35th St 51503. I-29 exit 52, just e. Int corridors. **Pets:** Small. $20 daily fee/room. Service with restrictions, supervision. SAVE 🛰 ⊠ 🔊 🛏 🖵 ➤

▼▼ Days Inn 🏨
(712) 366-9699. **$50-$106.** 3208 S 7th St 51501. I-29/80 exit 3 (US 92), just sw. Int corridors. **Pets:** Accepted. 🛰 🛏 🖵

▼▼ Days Inn 🏨
(712) 323-2200. **$55-$110.** 3619 9th Ave 51501. I-29 exit 53A (9th Ave). Int corridors. **Pets:** Accepted. 🛰 🛏 🖵

▼▼▼ Harrah's Casino & Hotel 🏨
(712) 329-6000. **Call for rates.** 1 Harrahs Blvd 51501. I-29 exit 53A (9th Ave), just w. Int corridors. **Pets:** Accepted. 🛰 🔊 🛏 🖵 🍽

▼▼ Microtel Inn & Suites by Wyndham Council Bluffs 🏨
(712) 256-2900. **$75-$200.** 2141 S 35th St 51501. I-29/80 exit 1B (24th St), 0.4 mi n, then 0.8 mi w on 23rd Ave. Int corridors. **Pets:** Other species. $25 daily fee/room. Service with restrictions, crate.
🛰 ⊠ 🔊 🛏 🖵 ➤

▼▼ Super 8 🏨
(712) 322-2888. **$65-$97.** 2712 S 24th St 51501. I-29/80 exit 1B (24th St), just nw. Int corridors. **Pets:** Accepted. 🛰 🖵

🄰🄰🄰 ▼▼▼ Western Inn 🏨
(712) 322-4499. **$59-$145.** 1842 Madison Ave 51503. I-80 exit 5 (Madison Ave), just s. Int corridors. **Pets:** Small. $10 one-time fee/pet. Service with restrictions. SAVE 🛰 ⊠ ➤

CRESCO

🄰🄰🄰 ▼ Cresco Motel Ⓜ
(563) 547-2240. **$53-$81.** 620 2nd Ave SE (Hwy 9) 52136. East side of town. Ext corridors. **Pets:** Dogs only. Designated rooms, supervision.
SAVE 🛰 🔊 🛏 🖵

CRESTON

◆◆ ◆◆ Super 8-Creston 🅗
(641) 782-6541. **$65-$80.** 804 W Taylor St 50801. On US 34; jct US 34 and SR 25. Int corridors. **Pets:** Accepted. 🛜 🍴 🖵

DECORAH

◆◆ ◆◆ Quality Inn & Suites 🅗
(563) 382-2269. **$85-$155.** 705 Commerce Dr 52101. Jct US 52, 1.5 mi e on SR 9. Int corridors. **Pets:** Accepted. 🛜 ✕ 🍴 🖵 🏊

DENISON

◆◆ ◆◆ Denison Super 8 🅗
(712) 263-5081. **$52-$62.** 502 Boyer Valley Rd 51442. Jct US 30/59 and SR 141, 0.3 mi sw. Int corridors. **Pets:** $10 daily fee/pet. Designated rooms, no service, crate. 🛜 🍴 🖵

DES MOINES

◆◆ ◆◆ Comfort Inn 🅗
(515) 266-6800. **Call for rates.** 4950 NE 14th St 50313. I-80 exit 136 (US 69), just n. Int corridors. **Pets:** Small. $10 daily fee/pet. Service with restrictions, supervision. 🛜 🅖M 🍴 🖵 🏊

🅐🅐🅐 ◆◆◆◆ Des Moines Marriott Downtown 🅗
(515) 245-5500. **$116-$289.** 700 Grand Ave 50309. Downtown. Int corridors. **Pets:** Very small. $75 one-time fee/pet. Service with restrictions, supervision. 🆂🅰🆅🅴 🛜 ✕ 🅖M 🍴 🖵 🍴 🏊

🅐🅐🅐 ◆◆ ◆◆ Econo Lodge 🅗
(515) 278-8858. **$54-$70.** 4755 Merle Hay Rd 50322. I-80/35 exit 131 (Merle Hay Rd), just s. Int corridors. **Pets:** $10 daily fee/room. Service with restrictions, supervision. 🆂🅰🆅🅴 🛜 🍴 🖵

◆◆◆◆ Holiday Inn Airport & Conference Center 🅗
(515) 287-2400. **$135-$205.** 6111 Fleur Dr 50321. SR 5 exit 97, 1 mi n; opposite the airport. Int corridors. **Pets:** Other species. $25 one-time fee/room. Designated rooms, service with restrictions, crate.
🛜 ✕ 🅖M 🍴 🖵 🍴 🏊 ✕

🅐🅐🅐 ◆◆◆◆ Magnuson Hotel Des Moines Airport 🅗
(515) 287-6464. **Call for rates.** 1810 Army Post Rd 50315. SR 5 exit 97, 1 mi n, then just e; just e of airport. Int corridors. **Pets:** Accepted.
🆂🅰🆅🅴 🛜 ✕ 🅖M 🍴 🖵 🍴 🏊

◆◆ ◆◆ Quality Inn & Suites 🅗
(515) 287-3434. **$69-$150.** 5231 Fleur Dr 50321. Opposite the airport. Int corridors. **Pets:** Small, dogs only. $10 daily fee/pet. Service with restrictions, supervision. 🛜 🅖M 🍴 🖵 🏊

DE WITT

◆◆ ◆◆ De Witt Super 8 🅗
(563) 659-8888. **$55-$95.** 918 Westwood Dr 52742. On US 30, just e of jct US 30 and 61. Int corridors. **Pets:** Accepted. 🛜 🅖M 🍴 🖵

DUBUQUE

🅐🅐🅐 ◆◆◆◆ BEST WESTERN PLUS Dubuque Hotel &
Conference Center 🅗 🐾
(563) 557-8000. **$90-$150.** 3100 Dodge St 52003. US 20, 2.3 mi w of jct US 52/61/151 and Mississippi Bridge. Int corridors. **Pets:** Large, other species. $15 daily fee/room. Designated rooms, service with restrictions, supervision. 🆂🅰🆅🅴 🛜 🅖M 🍴 🖵 🍴 🏊 ✕

◆◆ ◆◆ Comfort Inn by Choice Hotels 🅗
(563) 556-3006. **$55-$120.** 4055 McDonald Dr 52002. US 20, 3.8 mi w of jct US 52/61/151 and Mississippi Bridge. Int corridors. **Pets:** Accepted.
🛜 🍴 🖵 🏊

🅐🅐🅐 ◆◆ ◆◆ Days Inn 🅗
(563) 583-3297. **$50-$90.** 1111 Dodge St 52003. US 20, 0.8 mi w of jct US 52/61/151 and Mississippi Bridge exit Hill/Bryant sts. Ext corridors. **Pets:** Small. $10 one-time fee/pet. Designated rooms, service with restrictions, supervision. 🆂🅰🆅🅴 🛜 🍴 🖵 🏊

🅐🅐🅐 ◆◆◆◆ Holiday Inn Dubuque/Galena 🅗
(563) 556-2000. **$79-$135.** 450 Main St 52001. At Main and 4th sts; downtown. Int corridors. **Pets:** Other species. $25 one-time fee/room. Service with restrictions. 🆂🅰🆅🅴 🛜 🅖M 🍴 🖵 🍴 🏊 ✕

◆◆◆◆ MainStay Suites 🅗
(563) 557-7829. **$79-$171.** 1275 Associates Dr 52002. Just n of jct US 20 and NW Arterial Rd; west side of town. Int corridors. **Pets:** Small, other species. $100 deposit/room, $20 daily fee/room. Service with restrictions, supervision. 🛜 🅖M 🍴 🖵

DYERSVILLE

◆◆ ◆◆ Comfort Inn 🅗
(563) 875-7700. **$85-$114.** 527 16th Ave SE 52040. US 20 exit 294 (SR 136), just nw. Int corridors. **Pets:** Medium. $20 daily fee/room. Designated rooms, service with restrictions, supervision. 🛜 🍴 🖵 🏊

◆◆ ◆◆ Super 8 🅗
(563) 875-8885. **$55-$82.** 925 15th Ave SE 52040. US 20 exit 294 (SR 136), just n. Int corridors. **Pets:** Small. $15 daily fee/pet. Designated rooms, service with restrictions, supervision. 🛜 🍴 🖵

EMMETSBURG

◆◆ ◆◆ Super 8 🅗
(712) 852-2667. **$54-$67.** 3501 Main St 50536. Jct US 18 and SR 4, 0.8 mi w. Int corridors. **Pets:** Large, other species. $10 daily fee/pet. Designated rooms, service with restrictions, supervision. 🛜 ✕ 🍴 🖵

ESTHERVILLE

◆◆◆◆ Sleep Inn & Suites 🅗
(712) 362-5522. **Call for rates.** 2008 Central Ave 51334. Jct SR 4 and 9, 1 mi e. Int corridors. **Pets:** Other species. $20 one-time fee/room. Service with restrictions, supervision. 🛜 🍴 🖵

◆◆ ◆◆ Super 8 🅗
(712) 362-2400. **$53-$66.** 1919 Central Ave 51334. Jct SR 4 and 9, 1 mi e. Int corridors. **Pets:** Small, dogs only. $6 daily fee/pet. Designated rooms, service with restrictions, supervision. 🛜 🍴 🖵

EVANSDALE

◆◆ ◆◆ Days Inn 🅗
(319) 235-1111. **$79-$120.** 450 Evansdale Dr 50707. I-380/US 20 exit 68, just n. Int corridors. **Pets:** Accepted. 🛜 🅖M 🍴 🖵 🏊

FAIRFIELD

🅐🅐🅐 ◆◆◆◆ AmericInn Hotel & Suites Fairfield 🅗
(641) 451-6600. **$90-$180.** 2104 S Main St 52556. US 34 exit 212, just sw. Int corridors. **Pets:** Accepted. 🆂🅰🆅🅴 🛜 🅖M 🖵 🏊

🅐🅐🅐 ◆◆◆◆ BEST WESTERN Fairfield Inn 🅗
(641) 472-2200. **Call for rates.** 2200 W Burlington Ave 52556. On US 34, 1 mi w of jct SR 1. Int corridors. **Pets:** $20 one-time fee/pet. Service with restrictions, supervision. 🆂🅰🆅🅴 🛜 🍴 🖵 🍴 🏊

🅐🅐🅐 ◆◆◆◆ Super 8 🅗
(641) 469-2000. **$65-$100.** 3001 W Burlington Ave 52556. On US 34, 1.5 mi w of jct SR 1. Int corridors. **Pets:** Accepted.
🆂🅰🆅🅴 🛜 🍴 🖵 🏊

FORT DODGE

◆◆ ◆◆ AmericInn Lodge & Suites of Fort Dodge 🅗
(515) 576-2100. **$120-$225.** 100 W Kenyon Rd 50501. 3 mi n of jct US 20 and 169. Int corridors. **Pets:** Medium. $10 daily fee/room. Designated rooms, service with restrictions, supervision. 🛜 🅖M 🍴 🖵 🏊

◆◆ ◆◆ Comfort Inn 🅗
(515) 573-5000. **$99-$150.** 2938 5th Ave S 50501. US 20 exit 124 (Coalville), 3.5 mi n on CR P59, then 1.3 mi w on 5th Ave and Business Rt US 20. Int corridors. **Pets:** Accepted. 🛜 🅖M 🍴 🖵 🏊

▼▼▼ Days Inn 🄷

(515) 576-8000. **$62-$125, 7 day notice.** 3040 5th Ave S 50501. US 20 exit 124 (Coalville), 3.5 mi n on CR P59, then 1.2 mi w on Business Rt US 20. Int corridors. **Pets:** Medium, other species. $10 daily fee/pet. Service with restrictions, supervision. 🛜 🈁 🄷 💻

FORT MADISON

▼▼▼ Comfort Inn & Suites 🄷

(319) 372-6800. **Call for rates.** 6169 Reve Ct 52627. Just e of jct US 61 and SR 2, on US 61. Int corridors. **Pets:** Accepted.

🛜 🈁 💻 ≋

▼▼ Super 8-Ft Madison 🄷

(319) 372-8500. **$65-$70.** 5107 Ave O 52627. 1 mi e of jct US 61 and SR 2. Int corridors. **Pets:** Accepted. 🛜 🈁 💻

GRINNELL

◆◆◆ ▼▼▼▼ BEST WESTERN PLUS Pioneer Inn & Suites 🄷

(641) 236-6116. **Call for rates.** 2210 West St S 50112. I-80 exit 182, just n. Int corridors. **Pets:** Medium, other species. $20 daily fee/pet. Service with restrictions, supervision. 🆂🅰🆅🅴 🛜 🈁 🄷 💻 ≋

▼▼▼ Comfort Inn & Suites 🄷

(641) 236-5236. **$85-$105.** 1630 West St S 50112. I-80 exit 182, 0.7 mi n. Int corridors. **Pets:** Accepted. 🛜 ✖ 🈁 🄷 💻 ≋

▼▼ Country Inn & Suites By Carlson 🄷

(641) 236-9600. **$72-$179.** 1710 West St S 50112. I-80 exit 182, 0.7 mi n. Int corridors. **Pets:** Small. $15 daily fee/room. Designated rooms, service with restrictions, supervision. 🛜 ✖ 🈁 🄷 💻 ≋

GRUNDY CENTER

▼▼▼ AmericInn Motel & Suites of Grundy Center 🄷

(319) 824-5272. **$79-$114.** 2101 Commerce Dr 50638. SR 175, 1.2 mi w of jct SR 14 and 175; west side of town. Int corridors. **Pets:** Small. $25 one-time fee/room. Designated rooms, service with restrictions, crate.

🛜 🈁 🄷 💻 ≋ ✖

HAMPTON

◆◆◆ ▼▼▼ AmericInn Lodge & Suites of Hampton 🄷

(641) 456-5559. **$81-$146.** 702 Central Ave W 50441. On SR 3 (Central Ave W), 0.7 mi w of jct US 65 and SR 3. Int corridors. **Pets:** Other species. $15 daily fee/pet. Designated rooms, service with restrictions, supervision. 🆂🅰🆅🅴 🛜 🈁 🄷 💻 ≋ ✖

IDA GROVE

▼▼▼ Super 8 🄷

(712) 364-3988. **$57-$66.** 90 E Hwy 175 51445. Just n of SR 175/US 59. Int corridors. **Pets:** Accepted. 🛜 🈁 🄷 💻

INDEPENDENCE

▼▼▼ Super 8 🄷

(319) 334-7041. **$60-$112.** 2000 1st St W 50644. US 20 exit 252, 1.4 mi n. Int corridors. **Pets:** Small. $15 daily fee/pet. Service with restrictions, crate. 🛜 🈁 🄷 💻

IOWA CITY

◆◆◆ ▼▼▼ Alexis Park Inn & Suites 🄷

(319) 337-6800. **Call for rates.** 1165 S Riverside Dr 52246. I-80 exit 239 (US 218), 5 mi s, 2 mi e on US 6, then just s. Ext/int corridors. **Pets:** Medium. $15 daily fee/pet. Designated rooms, service with restrictions, supervision. 🆂🅰🆅🅴 🛜 🈁 💻

◆◆◆ ▼▼▼▼ hotelVetro conference center 🄷

(319) 337-4961. **$139-$399.** 201 S Linn St 52240. I-80 exit 244, s on Dubuque St, e on Washington St, then just s. Int corridors. **Pets:** Accepted. 🆂🅰🆅🅴 🛜 ✖ 🈁 🄷 💻 ≋

▼▼▼▼ Sheraton Iowa City Hotel 🄷

(319) 337-4058. **$119-$369.** 210 S Dubuque St 52240. Jct Dubuque and Burlington sts (SR 1); downtown. Int corridors. **Pets:** Accepted.

🆂🅰🆅🅴 🛜 ✖ 🈁 💻 🍽 ≋

IOWA FALLS

▼▼▼ Iowa Falls Super 8 🄷

(641) 648-4618. **$64-$99.** 839 S Oak St 50126. Jct US 65 and Washington Ave, 1 mi s; US 20 exit 168, 3.8 mi n. Int corridors. **Pets:** Other species. $15 one-time fee/pet. Service with restrictions, crate.

🛜 🈁 🄷 💻

KEOKUK

▼▼▼ Holiday Inn Express 🄷

(319) 524-8000. **Call for rates.** 325 Main St 52632. Jct 4th and Main sts; downtown. Int corridors. **Pets:** Accepted.

🛜 🈁 🄷 💻 ≋ ✖

▼▼▼ Super 8-Keokuk 🄷

(319) 524-3888. **$69-$81.** 3511 Main St 52632. On Business Rt US 61/218, 2 mi n of jct US 136. Int corridors. **Pets:** Accepted.

🛜 🈁 💻

LE CLAIRE

▼▼▼ Comfort Inn & Suites-Riverview 🄷 🐾

(563) 289-4747. **$85-$145.** 902 Mississippi View Ct 52753. I-80 exit 306 (US 67), 0.5 mi n to Eagle Ridge Rd, then just sw. Int corridors. **Pets:** Medium. $10 daily fee/pet. Service with restrictions, crate.

🛜 🈁 🄷 💻

▼▼▼▼ Holiday Inn Express 🄷

(563) 289-9978. **$110-$199.** 1201 Canal Shore Dr SW 52753. I-80 exit 306 (US 67), just n. Int corridors. **Pets:** Medium. $25 one-time fee/room. Service with restrictions, supervision. 🛜 ✖ 🈁 🄷 💻 ≋

▼▼▼ Super 8 of Le Claire 🄷 🐾

(563) 289-5888. **$73-$129.** 1552 Welcome Center Dr 52753. I-80 exit 306 (US 67), 0.5 mi n to Eagle Ridge Rd, then just sw to Mississippi View Ct. Int corridors. **Pets:** Medium. $10 daily fee/pet. Service with restrictions, crate. 🛜 ✖ 🈁 🄷 💻

LE MARS

◆◆◆ ▼▼▼ Baymont Inn & Suites 🄷

(712) 548-4910. **$84-$125.** 1314 12th St SW 51031. US 75 exit 116, 1.7 mi ne. Int corridors. **Pets:** $10 one-time fee/room. Service with restrictions, crate. 🆂🅰🆅🅴 🛜 🈁 🄷 💻 ≋ ✖

MANCHESTER

▼▼▼ Super 8 🄷

(563) 927-2533. **$58-$73.** 1020 W Main St 52057. Jct US 20 and SR 13 exit 275, 1.3 mi n, then 0.3 mi e. Int corridors. **Pets:** Other species. $10 deposit/room, $10 daily fee/room. Designated rooms, crate.

🛜 🈁 🄷 💻

MARQUETTE

▼▼ The Frontier Motel 🄼

(563) 873-3497. **$50-$110.** 101 S 1st St 52158. Just s of jct US 18 and SR 76; between Mississippi River Bridge and casino. Ext corridors. **Pets:** Accepted. 🛜 🈁 🄷 💻 ≋

MARSHALLTOWN

◆◆◆ ▼▼▼▼ BEST WESTERN Regency Inn 🄷

(641) 752-6321. **$75-$175.** 3303 S Center St 50158. Jct US 30 and SR 14. Int corridors. **Pets:** Medium. $50 deposit/room, $10 daily fee/room. Designated rooms, service with restrictions, supervision.

🆂🅰🆅🅴 🛜 🈁 🄷 💻 🍽 ≋

▼▼▼ Comfort Inn 🄷

(641) 752-6000. **$64-$125.** 2613 S Center St 50158. 0.5 mi n of jct US 30 and SR 14. Int corridors. **Pets:** Accepted. 🛜 🈁 🄷 💻 ≋

◆◆ Super 8 H

(641) 753-3333. **$65-$99.** 3315 S Center St 50158. Just n of jct US 30 and SR 14. Int corridors. **Pets:** Accepted. 🛜 🛗 💻

MASON CITY

◭ ◆◆ Clarion Inn H

(641) 423-1640. **$89-$149.** 2101 4th St SW (Hwy 122) 50401. I-35 exit 194 (SR 122), 6 mi e. Ext/int corridors. **Pets:** $25 one-time fee/room. Service with restrictions. 🅂🄰🅅🄴 🛜 🛗 💻 🍴 ➶ ⊠

◆◆ Days Inn Mason City H

(641) 424-0210. **$60-$120.** 2301 4th St SW 50401. I-35 exit 194 (SR 122), 6 mi e. Int corridors. **Pets:** Accepted. 🛜 🛗 💻

◆◆ Mason City Super 8 H

(641) 423-8855. **$65-$100.** 3010 4th St SW 50401. I-35 exit 194 (SR 122), 5.3 mi e. Int corridors. **Pets:** Other species. $10 daily fee/pet. Service with restrictions, supervision. 🛜 🛗 🛗 💻 ➶

MISSOURI VALLEY

◭ ◆◆ Oak Tree Inn H

(712) 642-3000. **$68-$76.** 128 S Willow Rd 51555. I-29 exit 75, 0.4 mi ne. Int corridors. **Pets:** $8 daily fee/pet. Service with restrictions, supervision. 🅂🄰🅅🄴 🛜 ⊠ 🛗 🛗 💻

MORAVIA

◭ ◆◆◆ Honey Creek Resort State Park on Rathbun Lake H

(641) 724-9100. **$99-$189, 14 day notice.** 12633 Resort Dr 52571. Jct SR 5 and CR J18, 5.4 mi w on CR J18, 1.3 mi s. Int corridors. **Pets:** Small, dogs only. $25 daily fee/room. Designated rooms, service with restrictions, crate. 🄴🄲🄾 🅂🄰🅅🄴 🛜 ⊠ 🛗 💻 🍴 ➶ ⊠

MOUNT PLEASANT

◭ ◆◆◆ BEST WESTERN Mt. Pleasant Inn H

(319) 385-2102. **$69-$199.** 810 N Grand Ave 52641. US 218 exit 45, 0.6 mi s. Int corridors. **Pets:** Accepted. 🅂🄰🅅🄴 🛜 ⊠ 🛗 💻 ➶ ⊠

◆◆◆ Comfort Inn & Suites H

(319) 385-0571. **Call for rates.** 1200 E Baker St 52641. US 218 exit 45, 0.6 mi s. Int corridors. **Pets:** Accepted. 🛜 ⊠ 🛗 💻

◆◆ Super 8 H ❀

(319) 385-8888. **$56-$108.** 1000 N Grand Ave 52641. US 218 exit 45, 0.6 mi s. Int corridors. **Pets:** Other species. $10 daily fee/pet. Service with restrictions, supervision. 🛜 🛗 💻

MOUNT VERNON

◆◆◆ Sleep Inn & Suites H

(319) 895-0055. **$80-$100.** 310 Virgil Ave 52314. Jct US 30 and SR 1, just se. Int corridors. **Pets:** Small, dogs only. $13 daily fee/pet. Service with restrictions, supervision. 🛜 🛗 🛗 💻 ➶

MUSCATINE

◆◆ AmericInn Lodge & Suites of Muscatine H

(563) 263-0880. **Call for rates.** 3115 Hwy 61 N 52761. Jct US 61 and SR 38, just n. Int corridors. **Pets:** Accepted. 🛜 🛗 🛗 💻 ➶

◭ ◆◆◆ Musatine Clarion Hotel H

(563) 264-5550. **$70-$100.** 2915 N Hwy 61 52761. Jct US 61 and SR 38, just n. Int corridors. **Pets:** Medium. $50 deposit/room, $10 daily fee/pet. Designated rooms, service with restrictions, crate. 🅂🄰🅅🄴 🛜 ⊠ 🛗 💻 ➶ ⊠

◆◆ Super 8 Muscatine H

(563) 263-9100. **$55-$80.** 2900 N Hwy 61 52761. Jct US 61 and SR 38. Int corridors. **Pets:** Accepted. 🛜 🛗 💻

NEW HAMPTON

◆◆ Southgate Inn M

(641) 394-4145. **$47-$70.** 2199 S Linn Ave 50659. US 63 exit 201, 0.9 mi ne on US 63 business route. Ext corridors. **Pets:** Dogs only. $15 daily fee/room. Designated rooms, service with restrictions, crate. 🛜 🛗 🛗 💻

◆◆ Super 8-New Hampton H

(641) 394-3838. **$64-$112.** 825 S Linn Ave 50659. US 63 exit 201, 1.5 mi ne on US 63 business route. Int corridors. **Pets:** Dogs only. $15 daily fee/room. Designated rooms, service with restrictions, crate. 🛜 ⊠ 🛗 🛗 💻 ➶ ⊠

NEWTON

◭ ◆◆◆ AmericInn of Newton H

(641) 791-1160. **$105-$180.** 4401 S 22nd Ave E 50208. I-80 exit 168, just sw. Int corridors. **Pets:** Medium. $15 daily fee/pet. Designated rooms, service with restrictions, supervision. 🅂🄰🅅🄴 🛜 🛗 🛗 💻 ➶

◆◆◆ Holiday Inn Express H

(641) 792-3333. **Call for rates.** 208 W 4th St N 50208. Downtown. Int corridors. **Pets:** Accepted. 🛜 🛗 🛗 💻 ➶

NORTH LIBERTY

◆◆◆ Sleep Inn & Suites H

(319) 665-2700. **$79-$100.** 485 Madison Ave N 52317. I-380 exit 4. Int corridors. **Pets:** Small, dogs only. $13 one-time fee/room. Service with restrictions, supervision. 🛜 🛗 🛗 💻 ➶

NORTHWOOD

◆◆◆ Country Inn & Suites By Carlson H

(641) 323-7000. **$130, 14 day notice.** 711 Diamond Jo Ln 50459. I-35 exit 214, just nw. Int corridors. **Pets:** Small. $25 one-time fee/room. Designated rooms, service with restrictions, supervision. 🛜 🛗 🛗 💻 ➶

◭ ◆◆◆ Holiday Inn Express & Suites H

(641) 323-7500. **$89-$109.** 4712 Wheelerwood Rd 50459. I-35 exit 214, just nw. Int corridors. **Pets:** Large. $25 one-time fee/room. Designated rooms, service with restrictions, crate. 🅂🄰🅅🄴 🛜 ⊠ 🛗 🛗 💻 ➶

OELWEIN

◆◆ Super 8-Oelwein M

(319) 283-2888. **$70-$90.** 210 10th St SE 50662. Jct SR 3 and 150, 1 mi s on SR 150; south end of downtown. Int corridors. **Pets:** Other species. $10 daily fee/pet. Service with restrictions, supervision. 🛜 🛗 💻

OKOBOJI

◆◆ AmericInn Lodge & Suites of Okoboji H

(712) 332-9000. **$89-$289, 7 day notice.** 1005 Brooks Park Dr 51355. Jct US 71 and SR 9, 2.5 mi s on US 71. Int corridors. **Pets:** Medium, dogs only. $200 deposit/room, $25 one-time fee/pet. Designated rooms, service with restrictions, supervision. 🛜 ⊠ 🛗 🛗 💻 ➶

◆◆◆ Arrowwood Resort & Conference Center H

(712) 332-2161. **Call for rates.** 1405 US 71 S 51355. Jct US 71 and SR 9, 3 mi s. Ext/int corridors. **Pets:** Medium. Service with restrictions, crate. 🛜 🛗 🛗 💻 🍴 ➶ ⊠

OSCEOLA

◭ ◆◆◆ Americas Best Value Inn M

(641) 342-2123. **$68-$76.** 1520 Jeffreys Dr 50213. I-35 exit 33 (Osceola/US 34), just e. Int corridors. **Pets:** Accepted. 🅂🄰🅅🄴 🛜 💻

◆◆ AmericInn Lodge & Suites of Osceola H

(641) 342-9400. **$90-$160.** 111 Ariel Cir 50213. I-35 exit 33 (Osceola/US 34), just w. Int corridors. **Pets:** Small, dogs only. $50 deposit/room, $25 one-time fee/room. Designated rooms, service with restrictions, supervision. 🛜 ⊠ 🛗 🛗 💻 ➶

▼▼ Days Inn 🔡
(641) 342-6666. **$65-$110.** 710 Warren Ave 50213. I-35 exit 33
(Osceola/US 34), just e. Int corridors. **Pets:** Accepted.
🛰 🛏 💻 🐾

OSKALOOSA
▼▼▼ Comfort Inn 🔡
(641) 676-6000. **$99-$150.** 2401 A Ave W 52577. SR 163 exit 57 (SR
92), just e. Int corridors. **Pets:** Accepted. 🛰 🛏 💻 🐾

▼▼ Super 8-Oskaloosa 🔡
(641) 673-8481. **$55-$90.** 306 S 17th St 52577. Just s of SR 92 and 23.
Int corridors. **Pets:** Accepted. 🛰 ♿ 🛏 💻

OTTUMWA
▼▼ AmericInn of Ottumwa 🔡
(641) 684-8222. **$74-$125.** 222 W 2nd St 52501. Just se of US 63 and
4th St W; downtown. Int corridors. **Pets:** Accepted.
🛰 ♿ 🛏 💻 🐾

▼▼♦ Quality Inn & Suites 🔡
(641) 682-8526. **$69-$99.** 125 W Joseph Ave 52501. Jct US 34, 2 mi n
on US 63. Int corridors. **Pets:** Large, other species. $15 daily fee/pet.
Designated rooms, service with restrictions, supervision.
🛰 ❌ 🛏 💻 🐾

PELLA
🅰🅰🅰 ▼▼▼ Super 8 🔡
(641) 628-8181. **$70-$115.** 105 E Oskaloosa St 50219. SR 163 exit 42,
1 mi n, then 0.5 mi e. Int corridors. **Pets:** Other species. $10 daily fee/
pet. Designated rooms, service with restrictions, crate.
[SAVE] 🛰 ♿ 🛏 💻

PEOSTA
▼▼ ▼▼ Quality Inn & Suites 🔡
(563) 557-8878. **Call for rates.** 100 Peosta St 52068. I-20 exit 308, just
n. Int corridors. **Pets:** Accepted. 🛰 ❌ ♿ 🛏 💻 🐾

PERCIVAL
▼▼ Americas Best Value Inn & Suites - Percival/Nebraska
City 🔡
(712) 382-2100. **$78-$86.** 2113 Sapp Bros Dr 51648. I-29 exit 10 (SR 2),
just w. Int corridors. **Pets:** Small, dogs only. $20 one-time fee/pet. Service
with restrictions, supervision. 🛰 ❌ 🛏 💻

▼▼ Super 8 - Percival/Nebraska City 🔡
(712) 382-2828. **$60-$110.** 2103 249th St 51648. I-29 exit 10 (SR 2), just
w. Int corridors. **Pets:** Dogs only. $10 one-time fee/pet. Service with
restrictions, supervision. 🛰 ❌ ♿ 🛏 💻

PLEASANT HILL
▼▼ Sleep Inn & Suites 🔡 🐾
(515) 299-9922. **$95-$115.** 5850 Morning Star Ct 50327. US 65 exit 79
(SR 163/E University Ave), just e. Int corridors. **Pets:** Other species. $15
daily fee/pet. Service with restrictions, crate. 🛰 ♿ 🛏 💻 🐾

QUAD CITIES AREA

BETTENDORF
🅰🅰🅰 ▼▼ Econo Lodge Inn & Suites 🔡
(563) 355-6336. **$80-$110.** 815 Golden Valley Dr 52722. I-74 exit 2, just
e, then just n on Utica Ridge Rd. Int corridors. **Pets:** Medium, dogs only.
$10 daily fee/pet. Designated rooms, service with restrictions, supervision.
[SAVE] 🛰 🛏 💻 🐾

▼▼▼ Isle Casino Hotel Bettendorf 🔡
(563) 441-7000. **Call for rates.** 1777 Isle Pkwy 52722. I-74 exit 4 (US
67/State St), just e on State St, then just s, follow signs. Int corridors.
Pets: Accepted. 🛰 ♿ 🛏 💻 🍴 🐾 ❌

▼▼▼▼ The Lodge Hotel & Conference Center 🔡
(563) 359-7141. **$109-$127.** 900 Spruce Hills Dr 52722. I-74 exit 2, just
e. Int corridors. **Pets:** Very small, dogs only. $10 daily fee/room. Desig-
nated rooms, service with restrictions, crate.
🛰 🛏 💻 🍴 🐾 ❌

▼▼▼ Ramada Bettendorf/Davenport 🔡
(563) 355-7575. **$70-$140.** 3020 Utica Ridge Rd 52722. I-74 exit 2, just
e. Int corridors. **Pets:** Accepted. 🛰 ♿ 🛏 💻 🐾

DAVENPORT
🅰🅰🅰 ▼▼▼▼ BEST WESTERN PLUS SteepleGate Inn 🔡
(563) 386-6900. **$110-$150.** 100 W 76th St 52806. I-80 exit 295A (US
61), 0.5 mi s to 65th St and west frontage road entrance, then just nw.
Int corridors. **Pets:** Medium. $10 daily fee/pet. Designated rooms, service
with restrictions, supervision. [SAVE] 🛰 ♿ 🛏 💻 🍴 🐾

🅰🅰🅰 ▼▼▼▼ Clarion Hotel & Conference Center 🔡
(563) 391-1230. **$69-$119.** 5202 Brady St 52806. I-80 exit 295A (US 61),
1.6 mi s. Int corridors. **Pets:** Other species. $10 daily fee/room. Service
with restrictions, supervision. [SAVE] 🛰 ♿ 🛏 💻 🍴 🐾 ❌

🅰🅰🅰 ▼▼▼▼ Comfort Inn & Suites-Davenport 🔡
(563) 324-8300. **$74-$135.** 8300 Northwest Blvd 52806. I-80 exit 292
(Northwest Blvd), just n. Int corridors. **Pets:** Dogs only. $10 daily fee/pet.
Designated rooms, service with restrictions, supervision.
[SAVE] 🛰 ❌ ♿ 🛏 💻 🐾

▼▼ Country Inn & Suites By Carlson 🔡
(563) 388-6444. **$99-$179.** 140 E 55th St 52806. I-80 exit 295A (US 61),
1.4 mi s. Int corridors. **Pets:** Medium. $25 one-time fee/room. Service
with restrictions, crate. 🛰 ♿ 🛏 💻 🐾

🅰🅰🅰 ▼▼ Crossings by GrandStay Inn & Suites 🔡
(563) 386-5000. **$80-$190, 7 day notice.** 301 Jason Way Ct 52806.
I-80 exit 295A (US 61), just s to 65th St, then 0.4 mi ne on frontage road.
Int corridors. **Pets:** Accepted. [SAVE] 🛰 ♿ 🛏 🐾

▼▼ Days Inn Davenport 🔡
(563) 391-8222. **$55-$70.** 7222 Northwest Blvd 52806. I-80 exit 292
(Northwest Blvd), 0.3 mi s. Ext corridors. **Pets:** Accepted.
🛰 ♿ 🛏 💻

▼▼ Fairfield Inn by Marriott 🔡
(563) 355-2264. **$89-$199.** 3206 E Kimberly Rd 52807. I-74 exit 2, just
w. Int corridors. **Pets:** Accepted. 🛰 ❌ ♿ 🛏 💻 🐾

🅰🅰🅰 ▼▼ ▼▼ Hotel Blackhawk 🔡 🐾
(563) 322-5000. **$134-$699.** 200 E 3rd St 52801. Between Brady St (US
61 N) and Pershing Ave; downtown. Int corridors. **Pets:** $50 daily fee/pet.
Designated rooms, service with restrictions, supervision.
[SAVE] 🛰 ❌ ♿ 🛏 💻 🍴 🐾 ❌

▼▼▼▼ Residence Inn by Marriott 🔡
(563) 391-8877. **$109-$499.** 120 E 55th St 52806. I-80 exit 295A (US
61), 1.4 mi s. Int corridors. **Pets:** Accepted.
🛰 ❌ ♿ 🛏 💻 🐾 ❌

▼▼▼ Staybridge Suites ⊞

(563) 359-7829. **$110-$160.** 4729 Progress Dr 52807. I-74 exit 1 (53rd St), 0.5 mi e, then 0.4 mi s on CR 216 (Utica Ridge Rd). Int corridors. **Pets:** Large, other species. $10 daily fee/pet. Service with restrictions, crate. 🛜 ⊠ 🅜 🔲 🖵 ⤳

▼▼ Super 8 ⊞

(563) 388-9810. **$55-$100.** 410 E 65th St 52807. I-80 exit 295A (US 61), 0.5 mi s, then just e. Int corridors. **Pets:** $10 deposit/pet. Service with restrictions, supervision. 🛜 🔲 🖵

END AREA

RIVERSIDE

▼▼▼ Riverside Casino & Golf Resort ⊞

(319) 648-1234. **$70-$250.** 3184 Hwy 22 52327. I-218 exit 80, 1.5 mi ne. Int corridors. **Pets:** Accepted. 🛜 🅜 🔲 🖵 🍴 ⤳ ⊠

ROCK RAPIDS

◆◆◆▽ ▼ Four Seasons Motel 🅜

(712) 472-2565. **$60-$85.** 810 1st Ave 51246. Jct US 75, just w on SR 9. Ext/int corridors. **Pets:** Small, dogs only. Service with restrictions, crate. (SAVE) 🛜 🔲 🖵

SHELDON

▼▼▼ Holiday Inn Express & Suites ⊞

(712) 324-3000. **Call for rates.** 201 34th Ave 51201. SR 60 exit 34, just sw. Int corridors. **Pets:** Accepted. 🛜 ⊠ 🅜 🔲 🖵 ⤳

▼▼ Super 8 🅜

(712) 324-8400. **$66-$83.** 210 N 2nd Ave 51201. SR 60 exit 34, 2 mi w on US 18, then just n on Business Rt SR 60. Int corridors. **Pets:** Accepted. 🛜 🅜 🔲 🖵 ⤳

SIGOURNEY

▼▼ Belva Deer Inn ⊞

(641) 622-3200. **$74-$99.** 21638 Hwy 92 52591. Jct SR 149 and 92, 1.1 mi e. Int corridors. **Pets:** Accepted. 🛜 ⊠ 🅜 🔲 🖵

SIOUX CENTER

▼▼ Econo Lodge 🅜

(712) 722-4000. **$75-$87.** 86 9th St Cir NE 51250. On US 75, 1 mi n of jct SR 840; north side of town. Ext/int corridors. **Pets:** $10 daily fee/pet. Designated rooms, service with restrictions, crate. 🛜 ⊠ 🅜 🔲 🖵

SIOUX CITY

▼▼ AmericInn Lodge & Suites of Sioux City ⊞

(712) 255-1800. **$70-$170.** 4230 S Lewis Blvd 51106. I-29 exit 143, just e. Int corridors. **Pets:** Other species. $10 daily fee/room. Designated rooms, service with restrictions, supervision. 🛜 🅜 🔲 🖵 ⤳

▼▼ Comfort Inn by Choice Hotels ⊞

(712) 274-1300. **$59-$120.** 4202 S Lakeport St 51106. I-29 exit 144A, 1 mi e on US 20, then just s. Int corridors. **Pets:** $15 daily fee/room. Service with restrictions, supervision. 🛜 🔲 🖵 ⤳

▼▼ Fairfield Inn by Marriott ⊞

(712) 276-5600. **$99-$299.** 4716 Southern Hills Dr 51106. I-29 exit 144A, 1 mi e on US 20, then just s. Int corridors. **Pets:** Other species. $15 daily fee/room. Service with restrictions, supervision. 🛜 ⊠ 🔲 🖵 ⤳

▼▼▼ Hilton Garden Inn-Sioux City Riverfront ⊞

(712) 255-4200. **Call for rates.** 1132 Larsen Park Rd 51103. I-29 exit 149, just sw. Int corridors. **Pets:** Accepted. 🛜 ⊠ 🅜 🔲 🖵 🍴 ⤳

▼▼ Quality Inn & Suites ⊞

(712) 274-1400. **Call for rates.** 4230 S Lakeport St 51106. I-29 exit 144A, 1 mi e on US 20, then just s. Int corridors. **Pets:** Accepted. 🛜 🅜 🔲 🖵

▼▼▼ Stoney Creek Inn ⊞

(712) 234-1100. **$89-$275.** 300 3rd St 51101. I-29 exit 147B (Tyson Event Center), 0.3 mi w on US 20 (Gordon Dr), then just n. Int corridors. **Pets:** Accepted. 🛜 ⊠ 🅜 🔲 🖵 ⤳ ⊠

▼▼ Super 8 ⊞

(712) 274-1520. **$50-$55.** 4307 Stone Ave 51106. I-29 exit 144A northbound; US 75 exit 4B, 1.5 mi w on Gordon Dr; exit 147B southbound to Gordon Dr, 3 mi e. Int corridors. **Pets:** $10 daily fee/pet. Service with restrictions, crate. 🛜 🔲 🖵

SLOAN

▼▼ WinnaVegas Inn ⊞

(712) 428-4280. **Call for rates.** 1862 Hwy 141 51055. I-29 exit 127, just e. Int corridors. **Pets:** $5 daily fee/pet. No service, supervision. 🛜 ⊠ 🅜 🔲 🖵

SPENCER

▼▼ AmericInn of Spencer ⊞

(712) 262-7525. **$89-$169, 3 day notice.** 1005 13th St SW 51301. On US 71, 1 mi w of southern jct US 18 and 71. Int corridors. **Pets:** Medium, other species. $10 daily fee/pet. Designated rooms, supervision. 🛜 ⊠ 🅜 🔲 🖵

SPIRIT LAKE

▼▼ Spirit Lake Super 8 ⊞

(712) 336-4901. **$62-$135.** 2203 Circle Dr W 51360. Jct US 71 and SR 9. Int corridors. **Pets:** Accepted. 🛜 🅜 🔲 🖵

STORM LAKE

◆◆◆▽ ▼▼▼ King's Pointe Waterpark Resort ⊞

(712) 213-4500. **$99-$399, 3 day notice.** 1520 E Lakeshore Dr 50588. Just n, jct Business Rt US 71 and SR 7. Int corridors. **Pets:** Accepted. (SAVE) 🛜 ⊠ 🅜 🔲 🖵 🍴 ⤳ ⊠

STORY CITY

▼▼ Comfort Inn ⊞

(515) 733-6363. **$89-$120.** 425 Timberland Dr 50248. I-35 exit 124, just sw. Int corridors. **Pets:** Other species. $13 one-time fee/room. Service with restrictions, supervision. 🛜 🅜 🔲 🖵 ⤳

▼▼ Super 8 ⊞

(515) 733-5281. **$61-$97.** 515 Factory Outlet Dr 50248. I-35 exit 124, just sw. Int corridors. **Pets:** Large. $10 daily fee/room. Designated rooms, service with restrictions, supervision. 🛜 🔲 🖵

STUART

▼▼ AmericInn Lodge & Suites of Stuart ⊞

(515) 523-9000. **Call for rates.** 420 SW 8th St 50250. I-80 exit 93, just w. Int corridors. **Pets:** Accepted. 🛜 ⊠ 🅜 🔲 🖵 ⤳ ⊠

▼▼ Super 8 ⊞

(515) 523-2888. **$56-$83.** 203 SE 7th St 50250. I-80 exit 93, just ne. Int corridors. **Pets:** Accepted. 🛜 🅜 🔲 🖵

TOLEDO

▼▼ Designer Inn & Suites ⊞

(641) 484-5678. **$50-$199.** 403 Hwy 30 W 52342. Jct US 63 and 30, just nw. Int corridors. **Pets:** $7 daily fee/pet. Designated rooms, service with restrictions. 🛜 🔲 🖵 ⤳

▼▼ Super 8-Toledo 🅷

(641) 484-5888. **$70-$84.** 207 Hwy 30 W 52342. Jct US 63 and 30, just nw. Ext/int corridors. **Pets:** Accepted. 🛜 ⓜ 🛢 🖥

URBANA

▼▼ Urbana Inn & Suites 🅷

(319) 443-8888. **$59-$71.** 5369 Hutton Dr 52345. I-380 exit 43, just s on east access road. Int corridors. **Pets:** Small. $15 one-time fee/room. Service with restrictions, supervision. 🛜 ✕ ⓜ 🛢 🖥 ➿

URBANDALE

▼▼ Extended StayAmerica Des Moines-Urbandale 🅷

(515) 276-1929. **$59-$74.** 3940 114th St 50322. I-35/80 exit 126 (Douglas Ave), just e to 114th St, then 0.4 mi nw. Int corridors. **Pets:** $25 daily fee/pet. Designated rooms, service with restrictions. 🛜 ⓜ 🛢 🖥

📖 ▼▼▼▼ Holiday Inn Hotel & Suites Northwest 🅷

(515) 278-4755. **$89-$149.** 4800 Merle Hay Rd 50322. I-35/80 exit 131 (Merle Hay Rd), just s. Int corridors. **Pets:** Accepted.
SAVE 🛜 ✕ ⓜ 🛢 🖥 🍴 ➿ ✕

▼▼ Microtel Inn & Suites by Wyndham Urbandale/Des Moines 🅷

(515) 727-5424. **$59-$100.** 8711 Plum Dr 50322. I-35/80 exit 129 (86th St). Int corridors. **Pets:** Other species. $10 daily fee/pet. Service with restrictions, crate. 🛜 ⓜ 🛢 🖥

▼▼▼▼ Ramada Tropics Resort/Conference Center Des Moines 🅷

(515) 278-0271. **$99-$300.** 5000 Merle Hay Rd 50322. I-35/80 exit 131 (Merle Hay Rd), just s. Ext/int corridors. **Pets:** Accepted.
🛜 ✕ 🛢 🖥 🍴 ➿ ✕

▼▼ Sleep Inn 🅷

(515) 270-2424. **$79-$129.** 11211 Hickman Rd 50322. I-35/80 exit 125 (Hickman Rd), just ne. Int corridors. **Pets:** Medium, other species. $25 one-time fee/room. Supervision. 🛜 ⓜ 🛢 🖥

▼▼▼ TownePlace Suites by Marriott Des Moines/Urbandale 🅷

(515) 727-4066. **$89-$199.** 8800 Northpark Dr 50131. I-35/80 exit 129 (86th St), just nw. Int corridors. **Pets:** Accepted.
🛜 ✕ 🛢 🖥 ➿

VINTON

▼▼ Cobblestone Inn & Suites 🅷

(319) 472-2220. **Call for rates.** 1202 W 11th St 52349. Jct US 218, just sw. Int corridors. **Pets:** Accepted. 🛜 ✕ ⓜ 🛢 🖥

WALCOTT

📖 ▼▼ Davenport/Walcott Comfort Inn 🅷

(563) 284-9000. **$89-$110.** 501 W Walker St 52773. I-80 exit 284, just nw. Int corridors. **Pets:** Small. $20 daily fee/pet. Service with restrictions, supervision. SAVE 🛜 ⓜ 🖥 ➿

WALNUT

▼▼ Super 8 🅷

(712) 784-2221. **$55-$80.** 2109 Antique City Dr 51577. I-80 exit 46, just n. Int corridors. **Pets:** Designated rooms, service with restrictions, supervision. 🛜 ⓜ 🛢 🖥 ➿

WATERLOO

▼▼ Comfort Inn by Choice Hotels 🅷

(319) 234-7411. **Call for rates.** 1945 LaPorte Rd 50702. I-380 exit 72 (E San Marnan Dr). Int corridors. **Pets:** Accepted. 🛜 🛢 🖥 ➿

▼▼ Days Inn & Suites 🅷

(319) 235-4461. **$79-$145.** 1809 LaPorte Rd 50702. I-380 exit 72 (E San Marnan Dr), just nw. Int corridors. **Pets:** Accepted. 🛜 🛢 🖥 ➿

▼▼ Fairfield Inn by Marriott 🅷

(319) 234-5452. **$99-$120.** 2011 LaPorte Rd 50702. I-380 exit 72 (E San Marnan Dr), just w. Int corridors. **Pets:** Accepted.
🛜 ✕ ⓜ 🛢 🖥 ➿

▼▼ Howard Johnson 🅷

(319) 232-7467. **$79-$129.** 3052 Marnie Ave 50701. 1 mi n of jct US 20 and 63 exit 227. Int corridors. **Pets:** Dogs only. $10 daily fee/pet. Designated rooms, service with restrictions, supervision. 🛜 🛢 🖥 ➿

▼▼ Motel 6 - Crossroads Mall-Waterloo-Cedar Falls # 4746 🅷

(319) 233-9191. **$62-$119.** 2141 LaPorte Rd 50702. I-380 exit 72 (E San Marnan Dr), just sw. Int corridors. **Pets:** Other species. Service with restrictions, supervision. 🛜 ⓜ 🛢 🖥 ➿

▼▼ Ramada Hotel & Convention Center 🅷

(319) 233-7560. **$50-$100.** 205 W 4th St 50701. At 4th and Commercial sts; downtown. Int corridors. **Pets:** Accepted.
🛜 ✕ ⓜ 🛢 🖥 🍴 ➿ ✕

▼▼ Super 8 🅷

(319) 233-1800. **$60-$99.** 1825 LaPorte Rd 50702. I-380 exit 72 (E San Marnan Dr), just nw. Int corridors. **Pets:** Accepted. 🛜 🛢 🖥

WAUKON

▼▼ Stoney Creek Inn 🅷 🐾

(563) 568-2220. **$69-$142.** 407 Rossville Rd 52172. Jct SR 9 and 76, 1.7 mi n. Int corridors. **Pets:** Medium, dogs only. $25 daily fee/room. Designated rooms, service with restrictions, crate. 🛜 ⓜ 🛢 🖥

WAVERLY

▼▼ Comfort Inn 🅷

(319) 352-0399. **$99-$170.** 404 29th Ave SW 50677. US 218 exit 198, 0.7 mi n. Int corridors. **Pets:** Medium, dogs only. $10 daily fee/pet. Designated rooms, service with restrictions, supervision.
🛜 ⓜ 🛢 🖥 ➿ ✕

▼▼ Super 8 Waverly 🅷

(319) 352-0888. **$66-$130.** 301 13th Ave SW 50677. US 218 exit 198, 1.4 mi n. Int corridors. **Pets:** Accepted. 🛜 ⓜ 🛢 🖥

WEBSTER CITY

▼▼▼ AmericInn Motel & Suites of Webster City 🅷

(515) 832-3999. **$75-$125.** 411 Closz Dr 50595. Just s of jct US 20 and SR 17. Int corridors. **Pets:** Other species. $25 one-time fee/room. Designated rooms, service with restrictions, crate. 🛜 ⓜ 🛢 🖥 ➿

WEST BURLINGTON

▼▼ AmericInn Lodge & Suites of Burlington 🅷

(319) 758-9000. **$70-$150.** 628 S Gear Ave 52655. US 34 exit 260 (Gear Ave), just ne. Int corridors. **Pets:** Accepted. 🛜 🛢 🖥 ➿

WEST DES MOINES

▼▼▼ Candlewood Suites-West Des Moines 🅷

(515) 221-0001. **Call for rates.** 7625 Office Plaza Dr N 50266. I-80 exit 121 (Jordan Creek Pkwy), just sw. Int corridors. **Pets:** Medium. $15 daily fee/pet. Designated rooms, service with restrictions, crate.
🛜 ⓜ 🛢 🖥

▼▼▼ Drury Inn & Suites 🅷

(515) 457-9500. **$115-$204.** 5505 Mills Civic Pkwy 50266. I-35 exit 70 (Mills Civic Pkwy), just w. Int corridors. **Pets:** Service with restrictions, supervision. 🛜 ✕ ⓜ 🛢 🖥 ➿

▼▼▼ Residence Inn by Marriott-Des Moines West 🅷

(515) 267-0338. **$109-$499.** 160 S Jordan Creek Pkwy 50266. I-35 exit 70 (Mills Civic Pkwy), 1.2 mi w to 68th St, then just nw. Int corridors. **Pets:** Other species. $100 one-time fee/room. Service with restrictions.

🛜 ✕ ⓜ 🛢 🖥 ➿ ✕

AAA **WWWW** Sheraton West Des Moines 🅷 ❀

(515) 223-1800. **$59-$200, 3 day notice.** 1800 50th St 50266. I-35/80 exit 124 (University Ave), just e. Int corridors. **Pets:** Medium, other species. $50 one-time fee/room. Service with restrictions, crate.

🆂🅰🆅🅴 📶 ✖ ♿ 🈯 💻 🍴 ⤳

WWWW Staybridge Suites 🅷 ❀

(515) 223-0000. **Call for rates.** 6905 Lake Dr 50266. I-80 exit 121 (Jordan Creek Pkwy), just ne. Int corridors. **Pets:** $35 one-time fee/room. Service with restrictions, supervision. 📶 ♿ 🈯 💻 ⤳ ✖

WWWW West Des Moines Marriott 🅷

(515) 267-1500. **$119-$269.** 1250 Jordan Creek Pkwy 50266. I-80 exit 121 (Jordan Creek Pkwy), just sw. Int corridors. **Pets:** Accepted.

📶 ✖ ♿ 🈯 💻 🍴 ⤳

WILLIAMS

AAA **WWWW** BEST WESTERN Norseman Inn 🅼

(515) 854-2281. **Call for rates.** 3086 220th St 50271. I-35 exit 144, just e. Int corridors. **Pets:** Medium, dogs only. $10 daily fee/pet. Designated rooms, service with restrictions, supervision. 🆂🅰🆅🅴 📶 🈯 💻

WILLIAMSBURG

AAA **WWWW** BEST WESTERN Cozy House & Suites 🅷 ❀

(319) 668-9777. **$90-$150.** 1708 N Highland St 52361. I-80 exit 220, 0.8 mi n. Int corridors. **Pets:** $20 daily fee/pet. Designated rooms, service with restrictions, supervision. 🆂🅰🆅🅴 📶 🈯 💻

AAA **WWWW** Crest Country Inn 🅼 ❀

(319) 668-1522. **$70-$90.** 340 W Evans St 52361. I-80 exit 220, just nw. Ext corridors. **Pets:** $7 daily fee/pet. Designated rooms, service with restrictions, supervision. 🆂🅰🆅🅴 📶 🈯

WWWW Heritage Inn Hotel & Suites Amana Colonies 🅷

(319) 668-2700. **$77-$160.** 2185 U Ave 52361. I-80 exit 225 (US 151), just n. Int corridors. **Pets:** Medium, dogs only. $15 daily fee/pet. Designated rooms, no service, supervision. 📶 ✖ 🈯 💻 ⤳

KANSAS

CITY INDEX

ABILENE

WWWW Holiday Inn Express Hotel & Suites 🅷

(785) 263-4049. **Call for rates.** 110 E Lafayette Ave 67410. I-70 exit 275, just n. Int corridors. **Pets:** $20 daily fee/pet. Service with restrictions.

📶 ♿ 🈯 💻 ⤳ ✖

ANDOVER

AAA **WWWW** Days Inn Andover 🅼

(316) 733-8881. **$54-$67.** 222 W US Hwy 54 67002. 2.2 mi e of jct SR 96. Ext corridors. **Pets:** Medium, dogs only. $10 daily fee/pet. Service with restrictions, crate. 🆂🅰🆅🅴 📶 🈯 💻 ⤳

WWWW Holiday Inn Express & Suites 🅷

(316) 733-8833. **$90-$119.** 600 S Allen St 67002. 2.2 mi e of jct SR 96 and US 54, then just s. Int corridors. **Pets:** Other species. $10 one-time fee/pet. Service with restrictions, crate. 📶 ✖ ♿ 🈯 💻 ⤳

BELOIT

WWWW Super 8 🅷

(785) 738-4300. **$56-$125, 3 day notice.** 3018 W Hwy 24 67420. Just e of jct SR 14. Ext/int corridors. **Pets:** Accepted.

📶 ✖ ♿ 🈯 💻

BURLINGTON

WWWW Country Haven Inn 🅷

(620) 364-8260. **$67-$75.** 207 Cross St 66839. Just e of US 75; 1 mi n of center. Int corridors. **Pets:** Very small, dogs only. $56 deposit/pet. Designated rooms, service with restrictions, supervision.

📶 ✖ ♿ 🈯

CLAY CENTER

WWWW Cedar Court Motel 🅼

(785) 632-2148. **$57-$85.** 905 Crawford St 67432. On US 24, just e of jct SR 15. Ext corridors. **Pets:** Accepted. 📶 ♿ 🈯 💻 ⤳

COFFEYVILLE

AAA **WWWW** BEST WESTERN Bricktown Lodge 🅷

(620) 251-3700. **$86-$92.** 605 Northeast St 67337. 1 mi e of center. Int corridors. **Pets:** Dogs only. $20 daily fee/pet. Service with restrictions, supervision. 🆂🅰🆅🅴 📶 ✖ 🈯 💻 ⤳

COLBY

WWWW Comfort Inn 🅷 ❀

(785) 462-3833. **$79-$109.** 2225 S Range Ave 67701. I-70 exit 53 (SR 25), just s. Int corridors. **Pets:** Other species. $10 daily fee/pet. Designated rooms, service with restrictions, supervision.

📶 🈯 💻 🍴 ⤳

AAA **WWWW** Days Inn 🅷

(785) 462-8691. **$73-$90.** 1925 S Range Ave 67701. I-70 exit 53 (SR 25), 0.3 mi n. Int corridors. **Pets:** Small, dogs only. $10 daily fee/pet. Designated rooms, service with restrictions, supervision.

🆂🅰🆅🅴 📶 🈯 💻 ⤳

AAA **WWWW** Holiday Inn Express Hotel & Suites 🅷

(785) 462-8787. **$115-$145.** 645 W Willow St 67701. I-70 exit 53 (SR 25), just ne. Int corridors. **Pets:** Other species. $25 one-time fee/room. Designated rooms, service with restrictions, supervision.

🆂🅰🆅🅴 📶 ✖ ♿ 🈯 💻 ⤳

AAA **WWW** **Knights Inn** **M**
(785) 462-3943. **$50-$75.** 2320 S Range Ave 67701. I-70 exit 53 (SR 25), just s. Ext corridors. **Pets:** Accepted. [SAVE] 🛰 🛏 💻 🏊

WWW **Sleep Inn & Suites** **H**
(785) 460-0310. **$86-$105.** 2075 Sewell Ave 67701. I-70 exit 53 (SR 25), just ne. Int corridors. **Pets:** Medium, other species. $15 daily fee/pet. Designated rooms, service with restrictions, supervision.
🛰 ✖ 🛏 💻 🏊

AAA **WWW** **Super 8** **H**
(785) 462-8248. **$65-$80.** 1040 Zelfer Ave 67701. I-70 exit 53 (SR 25), 0.3 mi n, then just w. Int corridors. **Pets:** Medium, other species. $10 one-time fee/pet. Service with restrictions, supervision.
[SAVE] 🛰 🛏 💻

COTTONWOOD FALLS

AAA **WWW** **Grand Central Hotel** **CI**
(620) 273-6763. **$160-$190.** 215 Broadway 66845. US 177, just w on Main St, then just s; center of downtown. Int corridors. **Pets:** Designated rooms, service with restrictions, supervision. [SAVE] 🛰 ✖ 💻 🍽

DERBY

WWW **Hampton Inn Derby** **H**
(316) 425-7900. **$129-$169.** 1701 Cambridge St 67037. Just sw of jct Rock Rd. Int corridors. **Pets:** Small. Designated rooms, supervision.
🛰 ✖ 🐾M 🛏 💻 🏊

DODGE CITY

AAA **WWW** **BEST WESTERN PLUS Country Inn & Suites** **H**
(620) 225-7378. **$130.** 506 N 14th Ave 67801. Just n of jct US 50 business route. Ext/int corridors. **Pets:** Medium, dogs only. $20 daily fee/pet. Designated rooms, service with restrictions, supervision.
[SAVE] 🛰 ✖ 🐾M 🛏 💻 🏊

WWW **Holiday Inn Express** **H**
(620) 227-5000. **$111-$123.** 2320 W Wyatt Earp Blvd 67801. 1.4 mi w on US 50 business route. Int corridors. **Pets:** Medium. $25 one-time fee/pet. Service with restrictions, crate. 🛰 🛏 💻 🏊

WWW **La Quinta Inn & Suites Dodge City** **H**
(620) 225-7373. **$114-$188.** 2400 W Wyatt Earp Blvd 67801. 1.4 mi w on US 50 business route. Int corridors. **Pets:** Service with restrictions, supervision. 🛰 🐾M 💻 🏊

WWW **Super 8** **H**
(620) 225-3924. **$75-$116.** 1708 W Wyatt Earp Blvd 67801. 1.2 mi w on US 50 business route. Int corridors. **Pets:** Accepted. 🛰 🛏 💻 🏊

EL DORADO

AAA **WWW** **BEST WESTERN Red Coach Inn** **H**
(316) 321-6900. **$68-$80.** 2525 W Central Ave 67042. I-35 exit 71, 0.5 mi e. Ext corridors. **Pets:** Very small, dogs only. $15 daily fee/pet. Designated rooms, service with restrictions, supervision.
[SAVE] 🛰 🛏 💻

WWW **Super 8-El Dorado** **M**
(316) 321-4888. **$69-$74.** 2530 W Central Ave 67042. I-35 exit 71, 0.5 mi e. Int corridors. **Pets:** Other species. $15 daily fee/pet. Service with restrictions, crate. 🛰 🛏 💻

ELLIS

WWW **Days Inn** **H**
(785) 726-2511. **$70-$95.** 205 N Washington St 67637. I-70 exit 145, just s. Int corridors. **Pets:** $5 daily fee/room. Designated rooms, service with restrictions, supervision. 🛰 ✖ 🐾M 🛏 💻 🏊

EMPORIA

AAA **WWW** **BEST WESTERN Hospitality House** **H**
(620) 342-7587. **$70-$110.** 3021 W US Hwy 50 66801. I-35 exit 127A, just s to US 50, follow roundabout directions, then 0.5 mi e. Ext/int corridors. **Pets:** Other species. $10 one-time fee/room. Designated rooms, no service, crate. [SAVE] 🛰 ✖ 🛏 💻 🍽 🏊

WWW **Candlewood Suites** **H**
(620) 343-7756. **$82-$150.** 2602 Candlewood Dr 66801. I-35 exit 128 (Industrial St), just n, then just e. Int corridors. **Pets:** Medium. $50 daily fee/pet. Service with restrictions, crate. 🛰 ✖ 🛏 💻

AAA **WWW** **Comfort Inn** **H**
(620) 342-9700. **Call for rates.** 2836 W 18th Ave 66801. I-35 exit 128 (Industrial St), just nw. Int corridors. **Pets:** Other species. $15 one-time fee/room. Service with restrictions, supervision.
[SAVE] 🛰 ✖ 🛏 💻 🏊

AAA **WWW** **Super 8** **M**
(620) 342-7567. **$55-$95.** 2913 W US Hwy 50 66801. I-35 exit 127A, just s to US 50, follow roundabout directions, then 0.7 mi e. Int corridors. **Pets:** Small. $10 daily fee/pet. Service with restrictions, supervision.
[SAVE] 🛰 🛏 💻

FORT SCOTT

WWW **Lyons' Twin Mansions B & B Hotel and Spa** **BB**
(620) 223-3644. **Call for rates.** 742 S National Ave 66701. Jct US 69 and 54 E, 0.3 mi w on Wall St, then 0.6 mi s. Int corridors.
Pets: Accepted. 🛰 ✖ 🛏 💻 🍽

GARDEN CITY

WWW **AmericInn Lodge & Suites of Garden City** **H** ❀
(620) 272-9860. **$89-$165.** 3020 E Kansas Ave 67846. Jct US 50, 83 and SR 156. Int corridors. **Pets:** Other species. $20 one-time fee/room. Designated rooms, service with restrictions.
🛰 ✖ 🛏 💻 🏊 ✖

AAA **WWW** **Clarion Inn & Conference Center** **H**
(620) 275-7471. **$119-$140.** 1911 E Kansas Ave 67846. 0.5 mi w of US 50 and 83 Bypass, on SR 156. Int corridors. **Pets:** Medium. $45 one-time fee/room. Service with restrictions, crate.
[SAVE] 🛰 ✖ 🛏 💻 🍽 ✖

WWW **Comfort Inn** **H** 🐾
(620) 275-5800. **$100-$135.** 2608 E Kansas Ave 67846. Jct US 50, 83 and SR 156. Int corridors. **Pets:** Medium. $15 daily fee/room. Service with restrictions, supervision. 🛰 ✖ 🛏 💻 🏊 ✖

WWW **Holiday Inn Express Hotel & Suites** **H**
(620) 275-5900. **Call for rates.** 2502 E Kansas Ave 67846. Jct US 50, 83 and SR 156. Int corridors. **Pets:** Accepted. 🛰 ✖ 🛏 💻 🏊

WWW **Magnuson Hotel Red Baron** **H**
(620) 275-4164. **$79-$119, 5 day notice.** 2205 E Fulton St 67846. 2.3 mi e on US 50 business route, at US 83 Bypass. Ext corridors. **Pets:** Very small. $10 daily fee/pet. Service with restrictions, supervision.
🛰 🛏 💻 🏊

GOODLAND

AAA **WWW** **Comfort Inn** **H**
(785) 899-7181. **Call for rates.** 2519 Enterprise Rd 67735. I-70 exit 17 (SR 27), just n. Int corridors. **Pets:** Accepted.
[SAVE] 🛰 ✖ 🐾M 🛏 💻 🏊

AAA **WWW** **Holiday Inn Express Hotel & Suites** **H**
(785) 890-9060. **$109-$129.** 2631 Enterprise Rd 67735. I-70 exit 17 (SR 27), just s. Int corridors. **Pets:** Small, other species. $25 one-time fee/room. Designated rooms, service with restrictions, supervision.
[SAVE] 🛰 ✖ 🐾M 🛏 💻 🏊

▼▼ Super 8 **H**
(785) 890-7566. **$55-$90.** 2520 Commerce Rd 67735. I-70 exit 17 (SR 27), just n. Ext corridors. **Pets:** Accepted. 🤖 🗐 💻

GREAT BEND
△△△ ▼▼ BEST WESTERN Angus Inn **H**
(620) 792-3541. **$81-$92.** 2920 10th St 67530. 0.8 mi w on US 56 and SR 96/156. Ext/int corridors. **Pets:** Other species. $5 daily fee/pet. Designated rooms, service with restrictions, crate.
[SAVE] 🤖 🗐 💻 🍽 🌊 ⊠

GREENSBURG
△△△ ▼▼▼ BEST WESTERN PLUS Night Watchman Inn & Suites **H** 🐾
(620) 723-2244. **$99-$109.** 515 W Kansas Ave 67054. US 54, just e of US 183 and 54. Int corridors. **Pets:** $25 deposit/pet. Service with restrictions, crate. [SAVE] 🤖 ⊠ 🗐 💻 🌊

HAYS
▼▼ Americas Best Value Inn Vagabond **M**
(785) 625-2511. **$65-$149, 7 day notice.** 2524 Vine St 67601. I-70 exit 159 (US 183), 1 mi s. Ext corridors. **Pets:** Large, other species. $5 daily fee/pet. Designated rooms, service with restrictions, supervision.
🤖 🗐 💻 🌊

▼▼▼▼ Fairfield Inn by Marriott Hays **H**
(785) 625-3344. **$84-$93.** 377 Mopar Dr 67601. I-70 exit 159 (US 183), just n to 43rd St, then just w. Int corridors. **Pets:** Accepted.
🤖 ⊠ 🔼M 🗐 💻 🌊

▼▼▼▼ Hampton Inn **H**
(785) 621-4444. **$99-$149.** 4002 General Hays Rd 67601. I-70 exit 159 (US 183), just n, then e. Int corridors. **Pets:** Accepted.
🤖 🔼M 🗐 💻 🌊

HERINGTON
▼▼ Herington Inn & Suites **H**
(785) 258-3300. **$72-$92.** 565 Hwy 77 67449. US 77, just w. Int corridors. **Pets:** Accepted. ⊠ 🔼M 🗐 💻

HESSTON
▼▼ AmericInn Lodge & Suites of Hesston **H**
(620) 327-2053. **Call for rates.** 2 Leonard Ct 67062. I-135 exit 40, just e. Int corridors. **Pets:** Small, other species. $30 one-time fee/pet. Designated rooms, service with restrictions, crate. 🤖 🗐 💻 🌊 ⊠

HILLSBORO
▼▼ Country Haven Inn **H**
(620) 947-2929. **$78-$84.** 804 Western Heights Cir 67063. On US 56; center. Int corridors. **Pets:** $50 deposit/room, $28 one-time fee/room. Service with restrictions, supervision. 🤖 ⊠ 🗐

HUTCHINSON
▼▼ Comfort Inn **H**
(620) 663-7822. **$59-$160.** 1621 Super Plaza 67501. Just w of jct SR 61 and N 17th Ave. Int corridors. **Pets:** Medium, other species. $15 one-time fee/pet. Designated rooms, service with restrictions, supervision.
🤖 🗐 💻 🌊

▼▼▼▼ Holiday Inn Express Hotel & Suites **H**
(620) 669-5200. **$105-$165.** 1601 Super Plaza 67501. Just w of jct SR 61 and N 17th Ave. Int corridors. **Pets:** Accepted.
🤖 🔼M 🗐 💻 🌊

INDEPENDENCE
▼▼ Appletree Inn **H**
(620) 331-5500. **Call for rates.** 201 N 8th St 67301. At 8th and Laurel sts. Ext/int corridors. **Pets:** Accepted. 🤖 🗐 💻 🌊

IOLA
△△△ ▼▼ Americas Best Value Inn Iola **M**
(620) 365-5161. **Call for rates.** 1315 N State St 66749. Jct US 54 and 169, 1.5 mi w on US 54, then 0.8 mi n. Ext corridors. **Pets:** Accepted.
[SAVE] 🤖 🔼M 🗐 💻 🍽 🌊

JUNCTION CITY
△△△ ▼▼ BEST WESTERN J.C. Inn **H**
(785) 210-1212. **$84-$129.** 604 E Chestnut St 66441. I-70 exit 298, just w. Int corridors. **Pets:** Accepted. [SAVE] 🤖 🔼M 🗐 💻 🌊

▼▼▼▼ Candlewood Suites **H**
(785) 238-1454. **$86-$115.** 100 S Hammons Dr 66441. I-70 exit 298, just w. Int corridors. **Pets:** Accepted. 🤖 🔼M 🗐 💻 ⊠

▼▼▼▼ Courtyard by Marriott Junction City **H**
(785) 210-1500. **$89-$129.** 310 Hammons Dr 66441. I-70 exit 298, just w. Int corridors. **Pets:** Accepted. 🤖 ⊠ 🔼M 🗐 💻 🌊

▼▼▼▼ Holiday Inn Express **H**
(785) 762-4200. **$109-$150.** 120 N East St 66441. I-70 exit 298, just nw. Int corridors. **Pets:** Small. $50 deposit/pet, $5 daily fee/pet. Designated rooms, service with restrictions, supervision. 🤖 🔼M 🗐 💻 🌊

KANSAS CITY METROPOLITAN AREA

BONNER SPRINGS
▼▼▼▼ Holiday Inn Express **H**
(913) 721-5300. **$99-$159.** 13031 Ridge Dr 66012. I-70 exit 224. Int corridors. **Pets:** Other species. $20 one-time fee/room. Service with restrictions, supervision. 🤖 🔼M 🗐 💻 🌊

GARDNER
▼▼ Super 8 **H**
(913) 856-8887. **$64-$110.** 2001 E Santa Fe 66030. I-35 exit 210. Int corridors. **Pets:** Other species. $10 daily fee/pet. Service with restrictions, supervision. 🤖 🔼M 🗐 💻 🌊

KANSAS CITY
△△△ ▼▼ BEST WESTERN Kansas City Inn **H**
(913) 677-3060. **$90-$100.** 501 Southwest Blvd 66103. I-35 exit 234 (7th St), 0.4 mi s to Southwest Blvd, then just w. Int corridors. **Pets:** Accepted.
[SAVE] 🤖 🗐 💻 🌊

▼▼▼▼ Candlewood Suites **H**
(913) 788-9929. **Call for rates.** 10920 Parallel Pkwy 66109. I-435 exit 14B, just w. Int corridors. **Pets:** Large. $10 daily fee/pet. Service with restrictions, crate. 🤖 🔼M 🗐 💻

LEAWOOD
△△△ ▼▼▼▼ Aloft Leawood-Overland Park **H**
(913) 345-9430. **$89-$229.** 11620 Ash St 66211. I-435 exit 77B (Nall Ave), 1.1 mi s, then just e; in Town Center shopping area. Int corridors. **Pets:** Accepted. [SAVE] 🤖 ⊠ 🔼M 🗐 💻 🌊

LENEXA
▼▼ La Quinta Inn Kansas City Lenexa **H**
(913) 492-5500. **$59-$118.** 9461 Lenexa Dr 66215. I-35 exit 224 (95th St), just ne; entrance left on Monrovia Rd off 95th St. Int corridors. **Pets:** Service with restrictions, supervision. 🤖 ⊠ 🗐 💻 🌊

MERRIAM

▼▼ Drury Inn-Merriam/Shawnee Mission Parkway 🅷
(913) 236-9200. **$80-$159.** 9009 W Shawnee Mission Pkwy 66202. I-35 exit 228B (Shawnee Mission Pkwy), just se. Int corridors. **Pets:** Service with restrictions, supervision. 🤖 ᴹ 🔲 🔳 ➷

OLATHE

AAA ▼▼▼ BEST WESTERN PLUS Olathe Hotel & Suites 🅷
(913) 440-9762. **$99-$179.** 1580 S Hamilton Cir 66061. I-35 exit 215 (151st St), just nw. Int corridors. **Pets:** Medium. $10 daily fee/pet. Service with restrictions, supervision. SAVE 🤖 🔲 🔳 ➷

▼▼ Candlewood Suites Olathe 🅷
(913) 768-8888. **$85-$99.** 15490 S Rogers Rd 66062. I-35 exit 215 (151st St), just sw. Int corridors. **Pets:** Medium. $75 one-time fee/room. Service with restrictions, crate. 🤖 ᴹ 🔲 🔳

▼▼ Days Inn Olathe Medical Center 🅷
(913) 390-9500. **$58-$142.** 20662 W 151st St 66061. I-35 exit 215 (151st St), 0.4 mi sw, follow signs. Int corridors. **Pets:** Accepted.
🤖 ᴹ 🔲 🔳 ➷

▼▼▼ Holiday Inn at Olathe Medical Center 🅷
(913) 829-4000. **Call for rates.** 101 W 151st St 66061. I-35 exit 215 (151st St). Int corridors. **Pets:** Accepted.
🤖 ✖ 🔲 🔳 🍴 ➷ ✖

AAA ▼▼▼ La Quinta Inn & Suites Olathe 🅷
(913) 254-0111. **$82-$194.** 20570 W 151st St 66061. I-35 exit 215 (151st St), just w. Int corridors. **Pets:** Service with restrictions, supervision.
SAVE 🤖 ✖ 🔲 🔳 ➷

AAA ▼▼▼ Residence Inn by Marriott 🅷
(913) 829-6700. **$99-$179.** 12215 S Strang Line Rd 66062. I-35 exit 220 (119th St), just e to Strang Line Rd, then 0.8 mi s. Int corridors. **Pets:** $75 one-time fee/room. Service with restrictions, crate.
SAVE 🤖 ✖ ᴹ 🔲 🔳 ➷ ✖

OVERLAND PARK

▼▼▼ Candlewood Suites 🅷
(913) 469-5557. **Call for rates.** 11001 Oakmont St 66210. I-435 exit 82 (Quivira Rd), 0.5 mi s, 0.3 mi w on College Blvd, then just n. Int corridors. **Pets:** Accepted. 🤖 ✖ ᴹ 🔲 🔳

▼▼▼▼ Chase Suite Hotels - Overland Park 🅷
(913) 491-3333. **$79-$139.** 6300 W 110th St 66211. I-435 exit 79 (Metcalf Ave/US 169), 0.3 mi s on US 169, 0.5 mi e on College Blvd to Lamar Ave, then just n. Ext corridors. **Pets:** Medium, other species. $10 daily fee/room. Service with restrictions, crate. 🤖 ✖ 🔲 🔳 ➷

▼▼▼ Clarion Hotel 🅷
(913) 383-2550. **Call for rates.** 7000 W 108th St 66211. I-435 exit 79 (Metcalf Ave/US 169), just ne. Int corridors. **Pets:** Accepted.
🤖 ✖ ᴹ 🔲 🔳 🍴 ➷

AAA ▼▼▼ Comfort Inn & Suites 🅷
(913) 648-7858. **$74-$94.** 7200 W 107th St 66212. I-435 exit 79 (Metcalf Ave/US 169), just nw. Int corridors. **Pets:** Medium. $25 one-time fee/pet. Designated rooms, service with restrictions, supervision.
SAVE 🤖 ✖ ᴹ 🔲 🔳 ➷

▼▼ Days Inn Overland Park-Convention Center 🅼
(913) 341-0100. **$50-$90.** 6800 W 108th St 66211. I-435 exit 79 (Metcalf Ave/US 169), just ne. Ext corridors. **Pets:** Accepted. 🤖 ✖ ᴹ 🔲

▼▼ Drury Inn & Suites-Overland Park 🅷
(913) 345-1500. **$85-$214.** 10963 Metcalf Ave 66210. I-435 exit 79 (Metcalf Ave/US 169), just se. Int corridors. **Pets:** Service with restrictions, supervision. 🤖 ✖ ᴹ 🔲 🔳 ➷ ✖

▼▼ Econo Lodge Inn & Suites 🅷
(913) 262-9600. **Call for rates.** 7508 Shawnee Mission Pkwy 66202. I-35 exit 228B, 0.5 mi e. Ext corridors. **Pets:** Accepted.
🤖 ✖ 🔲 🔳 ➷

▼▼ La Quinta Inn & Suites Overland Park 🅷
(913) 648-5555. **$59-$199.** 10610 Marty St 66212. I-435 exit 79 (Metcalf Ave/US 169), just nw. Int corridors. **Pets:** Service with restrictions, supervision. 🤖 ✖ 🔲 🔳 ➷

▼▼ Pear Tree Inn by Drury-Overland Park 🅷
(913) 451-0200. **$70-$139.** 10951 Metcalf Ave 66210. I-435 exit 79 (Metcalf Ave/US 169), just se. Int corridors. **Pets:** Service with restrictions, supervision. 🤖 ✖ ᴹ 🔲 🔳 ➷

▼▼ Residence Inn by Marriott 🅷
(913) 491-4444. **$79-$129.** 12010 Blue Valley Pkwy 66213. I-435 exit 79 (Metcalf Ave/US 169), 1.3 mi s. Int corridors. **Pets:** Accepted.
🤖 ✖ ᴹ 🔲 🔳 ➷ ✖

AAA ▼▼▼ Sheraton Overland Park Hotel at the Convention Center 🅷
(913) 234-2100. **$99-$369.** 6100 College Blvd 66211. I-435 exit 79 (Metcalf Ave/US 169), just s to College Blvd, then 0.6 mi e. Int corridors. **Pets:** Accepted. ECO SAVE 🤖 ✖ ᴹ 🔲 🍴 ➷

END METROPOLITAN AREA

LANSING

▼▼ Econo Lodge 🅷
(913) 727-2777. **Call for rates.** 504 N Main 66043. I-70 exit 224 (Leavenworth), 10 mi n on US 73 and SR 7. Int corridors. **Pets:** Accepted.
🤖 🔲 🔳

LAWRENCE

AAA ▼▼▼ Baymont Inn & Suites 🅷
(785) 838-4242. **$70-$160.** 740 Iowa St 66044. I-70 exit 202, 1 mi s on US 59. Int corridors. **Pets:** Medium. $15 daily fee/pet. Designated rooms, service with restrictions, supervision. SAVE 🤖 ᴹ 🔲 🔳 ➷

AAA ▼▼▼ BEST WESTERN Lawrence 🅷
(785) 843-9100. **$69-$130.** 2309 Iowa St 66046. On US 59; jct SR 10. Ext/int corridors. **Pets:** Accepted. SAVE 🤖 ᴹ 🔲 🔳 ➷

▼▼ Comfort Inn & Suites 🅷
(785) 330-7241. **Call for rates.** 151 McDonald Dr 66044. I-70 exit 202, 0.5 mi s on US 59. Int corridors. **Pets:** Medium, other species. $10 daily fee/pet. Service with restrictions, supervision. 🤖 ✖ 🔲 🔳 ➷

AAA ▼▼▼ Holiday Inn Express Hotel & Suites 🅷
(785) 749-7555. **$104-$149.** 3411 SW Iowa St 66046. I-70 exit 197 (SR 10), 8.4 mi e to US 59, then just n. Int corridors. **Pets:** Accepted.
SAVE 🤖 ✖ ᴹ 🔲 🔳 ➷ ✖

▼▼ Holiday Inn Hotel & Convention Center 🅷
(785) 841-7077. **$99-$199.** 200 McDonald Dr 66044. I-70 exit 202, 0.5 mi s on US 59. Int corridors. **Pets:** Other species. $25 one-time fee/room. Service with restrictions, supervision.
🤖 ✖ 🔲 🔳 🍴 ➷ ✖

▼▼ Super 8 🅷
(785) 842-5721. **$55-$110.** 515 McDonald Dr 66049. I-70 exit 202, 0.8 mi s, then just w. Int corridors. **Pets:** Accepted. 🤖 🔲 🔳

LIBERAL

Americas Best Value Inn M
(620) 624-6203. **$54-$64.** 564 E Pancake Blvd 67901. 0.8 mi w of jct US 54 and 83. Ext corridors. **Pets:** $10 daily fee/pet. Service with restrictions, supervision. [SAVE]

LYONS

Celebration Centre Inn & Suites H
(620) 680-6022. **$65-$100.** 1108 E Hwy 56 67554. 2 mi e of jct SR 14 and US 56. Int corridors. **Pets:** $20 one-time fee/room. Designated rooms, service with restrictions, crate.

MAIZE

Holiday Inn Express & Suites Wichita Northwest Airport Area H
(316) 260-4070. **$99-$159.** 10750 Hampton Lakes 67101. Jct Maize Rd, just w. Int corridors. **Pets:** Small. $25 one-time fee/pet. Service with restrictions, supervision. [SAVE]

MANHATTAN

Holiday Inn at the Campus H
(785) 539-7531. **$99-$199.** 1641 Anderson Ave 66502. 1 mi n of SR 18 (Ft. Riley Blvd). Int corridors. **Pets:** Other species. $25 one-time fee/room. Service with restrictions, supervision.

Parkwood Inn & Suites H
(785) 320-5440. **$81-$190.** 505 S 17th St 66502. 1.5 mi w of jct SR 177 and 18 (Ft. Riley Blvd), just n. Int corridors. **Pets:** Large. $10 daily fee/pet. [SAVE]

MARYSVILLE

Heritage Inn Express H
(785) 562-5588. **$56-$95.** 1155 Pony Express Hwy 66508. 2 mi e on US 36 (Pony Express Hwy). Int corridors. **Pets:** Accepted.

Marysville Surf Motel M
(785) 562-2354. **Call for rates.** 2105 Center St 66508. 1 mi e on US 36 (Pony Express Hwy). Ext/int corridors. **Pets:** Accepted.

Oak Tree Inn H
(785) 562-1234. **$69-$79.** 1127 Pony Express Hwy 66508. 1.6 mi e on US 36 (Pony Express Hwy). Int corridors. **Pets:** Other species. Service with restrictions, crate. [SAVE]

MCPHERSON

BEST WESTERN Holiday Manor H 🐾
(620) 241-5343. **$75-$100.** 2211 E Kansas Ave 67460. I-135 exit 60, just w. Ext/int corridors. **Pets:** Medium, other species. $10 daily fee/pet. Supervision. [SAVE]

NEWTON

BEST WESTERN Red Coach Inn H
(316) 283-9120. **$85-$110.** 1301 E 1st St 67114. I-135 exit 31, just w; exit southbound, just w at 2nd roundabout. Ext/int corridors. **Pets:** Medium, dogs only. $15 daily fee/pet. Designated rooms, service with restrictions, supervision. [SAVE]

Comfort Inn & Suites H
(316) 804-4866. **Call for rates.** 1205 E 1st St 67114. I-135 exit 31 northbound, just w; exit southbound, just w at second roundabout. Int corridors. **Pets:** $10 daily fee/pet. Service with restrictions, supervision. [SAVE]

OAKLEY

Sleep Inn & Suites of Oakley H
(785) 671-1111. **Call for rates.** 3596 E Hwy 40 67748. I-70 exit 76, just w. Int corridors. **Pets:** Small. $10 daily fee/pet. Designated rooms, service with restrictions, supervision. [SAVE]

OTTAWA

BEST WESTERN Ottawa Inn H
(785) 242-2224. **$81-$90.** 212 E 23rd St 66067. I-35 exit 183 (US 59). Ext/int corridors. **Pets:** Medium. $20 daily fee/pet. Service with restrictions, supervision. [SAVE]

PAOLA

Paola Inn & Suites H
(913) 294-3700. **$107-$111.** 1600 E Hedge Lane Ct 66071. US 169 exit 127 (Baptiste Dr), just w. Int corridors. **Pets:** Other species. $10 daily fee/pet. Designated rooms, service with restrictions, crate.

PARK CITY

BEST WESTERN Wichita North Hotel & Suites H
(316) 832-9387. **$80-$100.** 915 E 53rd St N 67219. I-135 exit 13, just w. Ext/int corridors. **Pets:** Large, other species. $10 daily fee/room. Service with restrictions, supervision. [SAVE]

Quality Inn & Suites H
(316) 927-3900. **$64-$85.** 792 Beaumont St 67219. I-135 exit 14, just sw. Int corridors. **Pets:** Medium, dogs only. $10 daily fee/pet. Service with restrictions, supervision. [SAVE]

Super 8-Wichita North/Park City M
(316) 744-2071. **$55-$65.** 6075 N Air Cap Dr 67219. I-135 exit 14, just sw. Int corridors. **Pets:** Accepted.

PARSONS

BEST WESTERN Parsons Inn H
(620) 423-0303. **Call for rates.** 101 E Main St 67357. 1.5 mi e. Int corridors. **Pets:** Small. $20 daily fee/pet. Service with restrictions, supervision. [SAVE]

Sleep Inn & Suites H
(620) 421-6126. **Call for rates.** 1807 Harding Dr 67357. Just sw of jct US 59 and 400. Int corridors. **Pets:** Small. $25 one-time fee/pet. Service with restrictions, supervision. [SAVE]

PHILLIPSBURG

Cottonwood Inn M
(785) 543-2125. **$80-$199, 7 day notice.** 1200 State St 67661. 1 mi e on US 36/183. Ext corridors. **Pets:** Designated rooms, service with restrictions, supervision.

PITTSBURG

Lamplighter Inn & Suites H
(620) 231-8700. **$79-$129.** 4020 Parkview Dr 66762. 2.3 mi n on US 69 from jct SR 126. Ext/int corridors. **Pets:** Small, dogs only. $10 daily fee/pet. Designated rooms, service with restrictions, supervision. [SAVE]

PRATT

Comfort Suites H
(620) 672-9999. **Call for rates.** 704 Allison Ln 67124. Jct US 54 and SR 61, just n. Int corridors. **Pets:** Medium. $25 one-time fee/pet. Service with restrictions, supervision. [SAVE]

Evergreen Inn & RV Park M
(620) 672-6431. **$59-$100.** 20001 W US Hwy 54 67124. 3 mi w. Ext corridors. **Pets:** Other species. $5 daily fee/pet. Supervision.

SALINA

AmericInn Hotel & Suites Salina H
(785) 826-1711. **Call for rates.** 1820 W Crawford St 67401. I-135 exit 92, just e. Int corridors. **Pets:** Accepted.

▼▼▼ **Candlewood Suites** H
(785) 823-6939. **$69-$109.** 2650 Planet Ave 67401. I-135 exit 89 (Schilling Rd), just e to S 9th St, 0.5 mi n to Belmont Blvd, then just w. Int corridors. **Pets:** Large, other species. $20 one-time fee/room. Service with restrictions, crate. 🛰 ✕ 🕹M 🛏 💻

▼▼ **Days Inn** H
(785) 823-9791. **$70-$75.** 407 W Diamond Dr 67401. I-70 exit 252, just n. Int corridors. **Pets:** Accepted. 🛰 ✕ 🛏 💻 🏊

▼▼▼ **La Quinta Inn & Suites** H
(785) 827-9000. **$95-$177.** 201 E Diamond Dr 67401. I-70 exit 252, just ne. Int corridors. **Pets:** Service with restrictions, supervision.
🛰 ✕ 🕹M 🛏 💻 🏊

▼▼ **Rodeway Inn Salina** M
(785) 827-0356. **Call for rates.** 1846 N 9th St 67401. I-70 exit 252, just s. Ext corridors. **Pets:** Accepted. 🛰 ✕ 🕹M 💻 🏊

▼▼◆ **Sleep Inn & Suites** H ❀
(785) 404-6777. **$84-$105.** 3932 S 9th St 67401. I-135 exit 88, just e, then just s. Int corridors. **Pets:** Other species. Service with restrictions, supervision. 🛰 ✕ 🛏 💻 🏊

◆◆◆ ▼▼ **Super 8 I-70** H
(785) 823-8808. **$72-$82.** 120 E Diamond Dr 67401. I-70 exit 252, just ne. Int corridors. **Pets:** Accepted. SAVE 🛰 ✕ 🛏 💻 🏊

SHARON SPRINGS
▼▼ **Oak Tree Inn** H
(785) 852-4664. **Call for rates.** 801 N Hwy 27 67758. Jct US 40 and SR 27. Ext/int corridors. **Pets:** Accepted. 🛰 ✕ 🕹M 🛏 💻

TOPEKA
▼▼ **AmericInn of Topeka** H
(785) 273-5365. **Call for rates.** 1518 SW Wanamaker Rd 66604. I-470 exit 1 (Wanamaker Rd). Int corridors. **Pets:** Accepted.
🛰 🛏 💻 🏊

◆◆◆ ▼◆ **BEST WESTERN Topeka Inn & Suites** H
(785) 228-2223. **Call for rates.** 700 SW Fairlawn Rd 66606. I-70 exit 357A, just ne. Int corridors. **Pets:** Large, other species. $10 one-time fee/pet. Designated rooms, service with restrictions, supervision.
SAVE 🛰 ✕ 🛏 💻 🏊

◆◆◆ ▼▼▼ **Capitol Plaza Hotel** H
(785) 431-7200. **$79-$149.** 1717 SW Topeka Blvd 66612. I-70 exit 362B (SE 8th Ave), 1.6 mi s; I-470 exit 177 (Topeka Blvd), 2.9 mi n. Int corridors. **Pets:** Accepted. SAVE 🛰 ✕ 🕹M 🛏 🛏 🍴 🏊 ✕

▼▼▼▼ **ClubHouse Inn & Suites** H ❀
(785) 273-8888. **Call for rates.** 924 SW Henderson 66615. I-70 exit 356 (Wanamaker Rd), just sw. Int corridors. **Pets:** Other species. $10 daily fee/pet. Service with restrictions, crate. 🛰 🛏 💻 🏊

◆◆ ▼▼ **Ramada Convention Center Downtown Topeka** H ❀
(785) 234-5400. **$99-$129.** 420 SE 6th Ave 66607. I-70 exit 362B, just e. Int corridors. **Pets:** Large, other species. $40 one-time fee/room. Designated rooms, service with restrictions, crate.
🛰 ✕ 🕹M 🛏 💻 🍴 🏊 ✕

▼▼ **Sleep Inn & Suites** H
(785) 228-2500. **$69-$149.** 1024 SW Wanamaker Rd 66604. I-70 exit 356 (Wanamaker Rd), just s. Int corridors. **Pets:** Other species. $10 daily fee/pet. Service with restrictions, supervision. 🛰 🕹M 🛏 💻 🏊

◆◆◆ ▼▼◆ **Super 8 at Forbes Landing** H ❀
(785) 862-2222. **$70-$135.** 5922 SW Topeka Blvd 66619. I-470 exit 6, 2.2 mi s. Int corridors. **Pets:** Dogs only. $20 one-time fee/room. Crate.
SAVE 🛰 🕹M 🛏 💻 🏊

ULYSSES
▼▼ **Single Tree Inn** H
(620) 356-1500. **$73-$77.** 2033 W Oklahoma Ave 67880. 1.5 mi w on US 160. Int corridors. **Pets:** Dogs only. $10 daily fee/pet. Designated rooms, service with restrictions, supervision. 🛰 ✕ 🛏 💻

UNIONTOWN
▼ **Wyatt Earp Inn & Hotel** M
(620) 756-4990. **Call for rates.** 100 5th St 66779. On SR 3; west side of town. Int corridors. **Pets:** Accepted. 🛰 ✕ 🛏 💻

WAKEENEY
◆◆◆ ▼▼◆ **BEST WESTERN PLUS Wakeeney Inn & Suites** H ❀
(785) 743-2700. **$95-$100.** 525 S 1st St 67672. I-70 exit 127, just n. Int corridors. **Pets:** Other species. $10 daily fee/pet. Designated rooms, service with restrictions, supervision. SAVE 🛰 ✕ 🕹M 🛏 💻 🏊

◆◆◆ ▼▼▼ **Super 8** H
(785) 743-6442. **$68-$88.** 709 S 13th St 67672. I-70 exit 128, just n. Int corridors. **Pets:** Other species. $10 daily fee/pet. Service with restrictions, supervision. SAVE 🛰 🛏 💻

WICHITA
◆◆◆ ▼▼▼ **BEST WESTERN Airport Inn & Conference Center** H ❀
(316) 942-5600. **$120-$135.** 6815 W Kellogg St 67209. I-235 exit 7, 0.6 mi w on US 54 (S Frontage Rd). Int corridors. **Pets:** Small. Service with restrictions, crate. SAVE 🛰 ✕ 🛏 💻 🍴 🏊 ✕

◆◆◆ ▼▼▼ **BEST WESTERN Governors Inn & Suites** H
(316) 522-0775. **$79-$150.** 4742 S Emporia St 67216. I-135 exit 1A/B (47th St S), just sw. Int corridors. **Pets:** Very small, dogs only. $20 deposit/room. Service with restrictions, supervision.
SAVE 🛰 🛏 💻 🏊

▼▼▼ **Candlewood Suites** H
(316) 942-0400. **$79-$129.** 570 S Julia St 67209. I-235 exit 7, 0.3 mi w to Dugan St, just n to Taft St, just e, then just s. Int corridors. **Pets:** Other species. $15 daily fee/room. Service with restrictions, supervision.
🛰 🛏 💻

▼▼▼ **Candlewood Suites-Wichita Northeast** H
(316) 634-6070. **$69-$119.** 3141 N Webb Rd 67226. SR 96 exit Webb Rd, just nw. Int corridors. **Pets:** Small, dogs only. $15 daily fee/pet. Service with restrictions, crate. 🛰 🕹M 🛏 💻

▼▼ **Comfort Inn by Choice Hotels** H
(316) 686-2844. **$85-$99.** 9525 E Corporate Hills Dr 67207. I-35 exit 50, just ne. Int corridors. **Pets:** Accepted. 🛰 🛏 💻 🏊

▼▼ **Cresthill Suites Hotel** H
(316) 689-8000. **$140.** 12111 E Central Ave 67206. 1.7 mi e of jct Webb Rd. Int corridors. **Pets:** Medium, other species. $50 one-time fee/room. Designated rooms, service with restrictions, crate. 🛰 🛏 💻 🏊

▼▼▼ **Drury Plaza Hotel Broadview-Wichita** H
(316) 262-5000. **$95-$339.** 400 W Douglas Ave 67202. Jct Waco St; downtown. Int corridors. **Pets:** Service with restrictions, supervision.
🛰 ✕ 🛏 💻 🍴 🏊 ✕

▼▼▼ **Hampton Inn by Hilton** H
(316) 686-3576. **$109-$139.** 9449 E Corporate Hills Dr 67207. I-35 exit 50, just ne. Int corridors. **Pets:** Accepted. 🛰 🕹M 🛏 💻 🏊

▼▼▼ **Homewood Suites by Hilton at The Waterfront** H ❀
(316) 260-8844. **$129-$309.** 1550 N Waterfront Pkwy 67206. Just e of jct 13th St and Webb Rd, then just n. Int corridors. **Pets:** Other species. $100 deposit/room, $50 one-time fee/room. Designated rooms, service with restrictions, crate. 🛰 🕹M 🛏 💻 🏊 ✕

▼▼▼▼ **La Quinta Inn & Suites Wichita Airport** 🅷
(316) 943-2181. **$66-$155.** 5500 W Kellogg Dr 67209. I-235 exit 7, just nw. Int corridors. **Pets:** Service with restrictions, supervision.
🛜 ☒ 🛗 💻 🍴 🐾

▼▼▼▼ **Residence Inn by Marriott at Plazzio** 🅷
(316) 682-7300. **$89-$229.** 1212 N Greenwich Rd 67206. SR 96 exit 13th St, 0.5 mi sw. Int corridors. **Pets:** $75 one-time fee/room. Service with restrictions. 🛜 ☒ 🅼 🛗 💻 🐾 ☒

▼▼▼▼ **Staybridge Suites** 🅷
(316) 927-3888. **$99-$169.** 2250 N Greenwich Rd 67226. Just e of jct 21st St and Greenwich Rd. Int corridors. **Pets:** Medium. $75 one-time fee/pet. Service with restrictions, crate. 🛜 🅼 🛗 💻 🐾

▼▼ **TownePlace Suites by Marriott** 🅷
(316) 631-3773. **$94-$199.** 9444 E 29th St N 67226. SR 96 exit Webb Rd, just sw. Int corridors. **Pets:** Accepted. 🛜 ☒ 🅼 🛗 💻

▼▼▼▼ **Wesley Inn** 🅷
(316) 858-3343. **$91.** 3343 E Central Ave 67208. Just e of jct Hillside St. Int corridors. **Pets:** Small. $25 one-time fee/room. Service with restrictions, crate. 🛜 ☒ 🛗 💻

WINFIELD
▼▼▼▼ **Comfort Inn** 🅷
(620) 221-7529. **Call for rates.** 3800 S Pike Rd 67156. On US 77, 1 mi s. Ext/int corridors. **Pets:** $10 daily fee/pet. Service with restrictions.
🛜 🛗 💻 🐾

KENTUCKY

ASHLAND
ⒶⒶⒶ ▼▼▼▼ **BEST WESTERN River Cities** 🅷
(606) 326-0357. **$97-$111.** 31 Russell Plaza Dr 41101. I-64 exit 185, 6 mi nw on US 60, then 3 mi n on US 23. Int corridors. **Pets:** Small, dogs only. $10 daily fee/pet. Designated rooms, service with restrictions.
ⓢⒶⓥⒺ 🛜 🅼 🛗 💻 🐾

▼▼ **Quality Inn** 🅷
(606) 325-8989. **$68-$75.** 4708 Winchester Ave 41101. I-64 exit 191, 4.8 mi n on US 23. Ext corridors. **Pets:** Medium. $15 daily fee/pet. Service with restrictions, supervision. 🛜 🅼 🛗 💻 🐾

BARDSTOWN
ⒶⒶⒶ ▼▼▼ **BEST WESTERN General Nelson** 🅷 🐾
(502) 348-3977. **$63-$140.** 411 W Stephen Foster Ave 40004. 0.5 mi w on US 62. Ext corridors. **Pets:** Medium, dogs only. $15 one-time fee/room. Service with restrictions, crate. ⓢⒶⓥⒺ 🛜 ☒ 🛗 💻 🐾

▼▼▼▼ **Hampton Inn** 🅷
(502) 349-0100. **$104-$129.** 985 Chambers Blvd 40004. Just s of US 245. Int corridors. **Pets:** Accepted. 🛜 ☒ 🅼 🛗 💻 🐾

BENTON
▼▼ **Comfort Inn & Suites** 🅷
(270) 527-5300. **$110.** 173 Carroll Rd 42025. Just ne of jct US 68/641. Int corridors. **Pets:** Other species. $10 daily fee/pet. Service with restrictions, crate. 🛜 🅼 🛗 💻 🐾

BEREA
ⒶⒶⒶ ▼▼▼▼ **Boone Tavern Hotel & Restaurant of Berea College** 🅷
(859) 985-3700. **$99-$165.** 100 Main St 40404. I-75 exit 76, 1.5 mi ne on SR 21. Int corridors. **Pets:** Medium. $50 one-time fee/room. Service with restrictions, crate. ⒺⒸⓄ ⓢⒶⓥⒺ 🛜 ☒ 🅼 🛗 💻 🍴

▼▼ **Comfort Inn & Suites** 🅷
(859) 985-5500. **$69-$130.** 219 Paint Lick Rd 40403. I-75 exit 76, just w. Int corridors. **Pets:** Medium, other species. $20 one-time fee/room. Service with restrictions, supervision. 🛜 🅼 🛗 💻 🐾

BOWLING GREEN
ⒶⒶⒶ ▼▼▼▼ **Baymont Bowling Green** 🅷
(270) 782-3800. **Call for rates.** 166 Cumberland Trace Rd 42103. I-65 exit 22 (Scottsville Rd), just e. Int corridors. **Pets:** Medium, other species. $10 daily fee/pet. Service with restrictions, supervision.
ⓢⒶⓥⒺ 🛜 🅼 🛗 💻 🐾 ☒

ⒶⒶⒶ ▼▼▼▼ **Candlewood Suites** 🅷 🐾
(270) 843-5505. **$99-$159.** 540 Wall St 42103. I-65 exit 22 (Scottsville Rd), just n. Int corridors. **Pets:** Medium, other species. $100 one-time fee/room. Service with restrictions, crate. ⓢⒶⓥⒺ 🛜 🅼 🛗 💻 🐾

ⒶⒶⒶ ▼▼ **Country Hearth Inn** 🅷
(270) 783-4443. **$45-$90.** 395 Corvette Dr 42101. I-65 exit 28, just w. Int corridors. **Pets:** Medium. $5 daily fee/pet. No service, supervision.
ⓢⒶⓥⒺ 🛜 🛗

▼▼▼▼ **Country Inn & Suites By Carlson** 🅷
(270) 781-7200. **$79-$199.** 535 Wall St 42104. I-65 exit 22 (Scottsville Rd), just w. Int corridors. **Pets:** Other species. $15 daily fee/pet. Service with restrictions, crate. 🛜 ☒ 🅼 🛗 💻 🐾

▼▼▼▼ **Drury Inn-Bowling Green** 🅷
(270) 842-7100. **$105-$174.** 3250 Scottsville Rd 42104. I-65 exit 22 (Scottsville Rd), just w. Int corridors. **Pets:** Service with restrictions, supervision. 🛜 🅼 🛗 💻 🐾

▼▼▼▼ **Hampton Inn** 🅷
(270) 842-4100. **$99-$149.** 233 Three Springs Rd 42104. I-65 exit 22 (Scottsville Rd), 0.3 mi w. Int corridors. **Pets:** Accepted.
🛜 🅼 🛗 💻 🐾

▼▼▼ Holiday Inn University Plaza 🄷

(270) 745-0088. **$99-$179.** 1021 Wilkinson Trace 42103. I-65 exit 22 (Scottsville Rd), 2.5 mi w, then just n. Int corridors. **Pets:** Medium. $50 one-time fee/room. Designated rooms, service with restrictions, crate.

🛜 🈁 🔌 💻 🍽 ➿

▼▼▼ La Quinta Inn & Suites 🄷

(270) 783-0083. **$75-$155.** 1953 Mel Browning St 42104. I-65 exit 22 (Scottsville Rd), just e. Int corridors. **Pets:** Service with restrictions, supervision. 🛜 ❌ 🔌 💻 ➿

AAA▷ ▼▼▼ News Inn of Bowling Green 🄼

(270) 781-3460. **Call for rates.** 3160 Scottsville Rd 42104. I-65 exit 22 (Scottsville Rd), just w. Ext corridors. **Pets:** Medium. $7 daily fee/pet. Service with restrictions, supervision. [SAVE] 🛜 🔌 💻 ➿

▼▼ Red Roof Inn 🄷

(270) 781-6550. **$50-$150.** 3140 Scottsville Rd 42104. I-65 exit 22 (Scottsville Rd), 0.3 mi w. Ext corridors. **Pets:** Large, other species. Service with restrictions, supervision. 🛜 🔌

BUCKHORN LAKE STATE RESORT PARK

▼▼ Buckhorn Lake State Resort Park 🄷

(606) 398-7510. **Call for rates.** 4441 Hwy 1833 41721. 5 mi off SR 28 via SR 1833. Ext corridors. **Pets:** Accepted. 🛜 💻 🍽 ➿ ❌

BURKESVILLE

▼▼ Dale Hollow Lake State Resort Park 🄷

(270) 433-7431. **Call for rates.** 5970 State Park Rd 42717. Jct SR 90, 4.5 mi sw on SR 449, 6 mi s on SR 1206. Ext corridors. **Pets:** Other species. $25 daily fee/pet. Designated rooms, service with restrictions, crate. 🛜 ❌ 🔌ᴹ 🔌 💻 🍽 ➿ ❌

CADIZ

▼▼▼ Lake Barkley State Resort Park 🄷

(270) 924-1131. **Call for rates.** 3500 State Park Rd 42211. I-24 exit 65, 9.1 mi sw on US 68 and SR 80 to SR 1489, 3.3 mi nw to State Park Rd, then n, follow signs. Ext corridors. **Pets:** $27 one-time fee/room. Designated rooms, service with restrictions, supervision.

🛜 ❌ 🔌 💻 🍽 ➿ ❌

CALVERT CITY

▼▼ Super 8 Calvert City/KY Lake Area 🄷

(270) 395-5566. **$54-$184.** 86 Campbell Dr 42029. I-24 exit 27 (US 62), just e. Int corridors. **Pets:** Small, dogs only. $10 one-time fee/pet. Designated rooms, service with restrictions, supervision.

🛜 🔌ᴹ 🔌 💻 ➿

CARROLLTON

AAA▷ ▼▼▼ BEST WESTERN Executive Inn 🄷

(502) 732-8444. **$80.** 10 Slumber Ln 41008. I-71 exit 44, just nw. Int corridors. **Pets:** Accepted. [SAVE] 🛜 🔌ᴹ 🔌 💻 ➿

▼▼▼ General Butler State Resort Park 🄷

(502) 732-4384. **Call for rates.** 1608 Hwy 227 41008. I-71 exit 44, 2 mi n. Ext/int corridors. **Pets:** $25 one-time fee/room. Designated rooms. 🛜 🔌ᴹ 🔌 💻 🍽 ➿ ❌

▼▼▼ Super 8 Carrollton 🄷

(502) 732-0252. **$60-$199.** 130 Slumber Ln 41008. I-71 exit 44, just nw. Int corridors. **Pets:** Accepted. 🛜 🔌 💻

CATLETTSBURG

▼▼▼ Ramada Limited Hotel 🄷

(606) 739-5700. **$98-$99.** 6000 Crider Dr 41129. I-64 exit 191, 0.5 mi n on US 23. Int corridors. **Pets:** Other species. $15 daily fee/pet. Designated rooms, service with restrictions, supervision. 🛜 🔌 💻 ➿

CAVE CITY

AAA▷ ▼▼▼ Super 8 🄼

(270) 773-2500. **$61-$90.** 799 Mammoth Cave St 42127. I-65 exit 53, just ne. Ext corridors. **Pets:** Medium. $10 daily fee/pet. Service with restrictions, crate. [SAVE] 🛜 🔌ᴹ 🔌 💻 ➿

COLUMBIA

AAA▷ ▼▼▼ BEST WESTERN Columbia Inn 🄼

(270) 384-9744. **$80-$110.** 710 Bomar Heights 42728. Cumberland Pkwy exit 49, just n on SR 55, then just w. Ext corridors. **Pets:** Other species. $20 one-time fee/pet. Designated rooms, service with restrictions, supervision. [SAVE] 🛜 🔌 💻 ➿

CORBIN

AAA▷ ▼▼▼ BEST WESTERN Corbin Inn 🄼

(606) 528-2100. **$90-$111.** 2630 Cumberland Falls Hwy 40701. I-75 exit 25, just w. Ext corridors. **Pets:** $15 deposit/pet, $15 daily fee/pet. Designated rooms, service with restrictions, supervision.

[SAVE] 🛜 🔌 💻 ➿

COVINGTON

AAA▷ ▼▼▼▼ Embassy Suites Cincinnati RiverCenter 🄷

(859) 261-8400. **$139-$209.** 10 E RiverCenter Blvd 41011. I-71/75 exit 192, 0.8 mi e on 5th St, then 0.3 mi n on Madison Ave. Int corridors.
Pets: Accepted. [SAVE] 🛜 🔌ᴹ 🔌 💻 🍽 ➿ ❌

CUMBERLAND FALLS STATE RESORT PARK

▼▼▼ Cumberland Falls State Resort Park 🄷

(606) 528-4121. **Call for rates.** 7351 Hwy 90 40701. Jct SR 25 W, 8 mi w. Ext/int corridors. **Pets:** Accepted.

🛜 ❌ 🔌ᴹ 🔌 💻 🍽 ➿ ❌

DANVILLE

AAA▷ ▼▼▼ BEST WESTERN Danville Inn 🄷

(859) 236-5525. **Call for rates.** 210 Brenda Ave 40422. Just e on US 127 Bypass and 150. Int corridors. **Pets:** Accepted.

[SAVE] 🛜 🔌ᴹ 🔌 💻 ➿

AAA▷ ▼▼▼ Comfort Suites 🄷

(859) 936-9300. **Call for rates.** 864 Ben Ali Dr 40422. Jct US 127 Bypass, just w on US 150 (Perryville Rd). Int corridors. **Pets:** Accepted.

[SAVE] 🛜 ❌ 🔌ᴹ 🔌 💻 ➿

▼▼▼ Quality Inn 🄷

(859) 236-8600. **$68-$99.** 96 Daniel Dr 40422. Jct US 127, just e on US 150. Int corridors. **Pets:** Large. $10 daily fee/pet. Service with restrictions, supervision. 🛜 🔌ᴹ 🔌 💻 ➿

DAWSON SPRINGS

▼▼▼ Pennyrile Forest State Resort Park 🄷

(270) 797-3421. **Call for rates.** 20781 Pennyrile Lodge Rd 42408. Western Kentucky Pkwy exit 24, 9.5 mi se on SR 109, then 1.8 mi w on SR 398. Ext corridors. **Pets:** Accepted.

🛜 ❌ 🔌ᴹ 🔌 💻 🍽 ➿ ❌

DRY RIDGE

▼▼▼ Comfort Inn 🄷

(859) 824-7121. **$79-$190.** 1050 Fashion Ridge Rd 41035. I-75 exit 159, just nw. Int corridors. **Pets:** $10 daily fee/pet. Service with restrictions, supervision. 🛜 ❌ 🔌 💻

▼▼▼ Hampton Inn 🄷

(859) 823-7111. **Call for rates.** 1200 Cull Rd 41035. I-75 exit 159, just nw. Int corridors. **Pets:** Medium. $25 one-time fee/pet. Service with restrictions, supervision. 🛜 🔌 💻 ➿

EDDYVILLE

▼▼ Holiday Hills Resort Townhouses **CO**
(270) 388-7236. **$80-$210, 30 day notice.** 1 Holiday Hills Rd 42038. I-24 exit 45, 2 mi s. Ext corridors. **Pets:** $20 daily fee/pet. Designated rooms, crate. 🛰 🔌 🖥 ⤴ ⊠ ☒

ELIZABETHTOWN

▼▼ Baymont Inn & Suites **H**
(270) 769-9616. **$65-$119.** 209 Commerce Dr 42701. I-65 exit 94, just nw. Int corridors. **Pets:** Accepted. 🛰 🔌M 🔌 🖥 ⤴ ⊠

◆◆◆ ▼▼ BEST WESTERN Atrium Gardens **H**
(270) 769-3030. **$90-$140.** 1043 Executive Dr 42701. I-65 exit 94, just nw. Int corridors. **Pets:** Other species. $20 one-time fee/room, $5 daily fee/room. Designated rooms, service with restrictions, crate.
SAVE 🛰 🔌 🖥 ⤴

▼▼ Comfort Inn **H**
(270) 765-4166. **Call for rates.** 2009 N Mulberry St 42701. I-65 exit 94, just sw. Int corridors. **Pets:** Medium, other species. $10 daily fee/pet. Designated rooms, service with restrictions, supervision.
🛰 🔌M 🔌 🖥 ⤴

▼▼▼ Holiday Inn Express **H**
(270) 769-1334. **$99-$129.** 107 Buffalo Creek Dr 42701. I-65 exit 94, just w. Int corridors. **Pets:** Medium. $50 daily fee/room. Designated rooms, service with restrictions, crate. 🛰 ⊠ 🔌M 🔌 🖥 ⤴

▼▼ Howard Johnson Inn **H**
(270) 769-2344. **$69.** 1058 N Mulberry St 42701. I-65 exit 94, just nw. Ext corridors. **Pets:** Service with restrictions. 🛰 🔌 🖥 ⤴

◆◆◆ ▼▼▼ La Quinta Inn & Suites Elizabethtown **H**
(270) 765-4747. **$84-$156.** 210 Commerce Dr 42701. I-65 exit 94, just nw. Int corridors. **Pets:** Service with restrictions, supervision.
SAVE 🛰 ⊠ 🔌M 🔌 🖥 ⤴ ⊠

ERLANGER

▼▼▼ Residence Inn by Marriott, Cincinnati Airport **H** ❄
(859) 282-7400. **$139-$180.** 2811 Circleport Dr 41018. I-275 exit 2, just s. Int corridors. **Pets:** $100 one-time fee/room. Designated rooms, service with restrictions, supervision. 🛰 ⊠ 🔌M 🔌 🖥 ⤴ ⊠

FALLS OF ROUGH

▼▼ Rough River Dam State Resort Park **H**
(270) 257-2311. **Call for rates.** 450 Lodge Rd 40119. On SR 79, at Rough River Dam. Ext corridors. **Pets:** $25 one-time fee/room. Designated rooms, service with restrictions, supervision.
🛰 ⊠ 🔌 🖥 🍴 ⤴ ⊠

FLORENCE

▼▼▼ Ashley Quarters Hotel **H** ❄
(859) 525-9997. **$100-$175.** 4880 Houston Rd 41042. I-71/75 exit 182, 0.6 mi w on Turfway and Houston rds. Int corridors. **Pets:** Other species. $75 one-time fee/room. Service with restrictions, crate.
🛰 🔌 🖥 ⤴

◆◆◆ ▼▼▼ BEST WESTERN Inn Florence **H**
(859) 525-0090. **$80-$250.** 7821 Commerce Dr 41042. I-71/75 exit 181, just ne. Int corridors. **Pets:** Medium. $15 daily fee/pet. Designated rooms, service with restrictions, crate. SAVE 🛰 🔌M 🔌 🖥 ⤴

◆◆◆ ▼▼ Comfort Inn Greater Cincinnati Airport on Turfway Rd **M**
(859) 647-2700. **$80-$99.** 7454 Turfway Rd 41042. I-71/75 exit 182, 0.8 mi sw. Int corridors. **Pets:** Small. $10 daily fee/pet. Service with restrictions, crate. SAVE 🛰 🔌 🖥

◆◆◆ ▼▼▼ Hilton Cincinnati Airport **H**
(859) 371-4400. **$90-$180.** 7373 Turfway Rd 41042. I-71/75 exit 182, 0.4 mi sw. Int corridors. **Pets:** Accepted.
SAVE 🛰 🔌M 🔌 🖥 🍴 ⤴

▼▼▼ Homewood Suites **H**
(859) 283-2111. **$109-$189.** 1090 Vandercar Way 41042. I-71/75 exit 182, just w. Int corridors. **Pets:** Accepted. 🛰 🔌 🖥 ⤴ ⊠

▼▼▼ La Quinta Inn & Suites Cincinnati Airport Florence **H**
(859) 282-8212. **$89-$177.** 350 Meijer Dr 41042. I-71/75 exit 182, 0.4 mi sw. Int corridors. **Pets:** Service with restrictions, supervision.
🛰 ⊠ 🔌M 🔌 🖥 ⤴

▼▼ Microtel Inn & Suites by Wyndham Florence/Cincinnati Airport **H**
(859) 746-8100. **$70-$301.** 7490 Woodspoint Dr 41042. I-71/75 exit 181, just w. Int corridors. **Pets:** Accepted. 🛰 🔌M 🔌 🖥

FRANKFORT

◆◆◆ ▼▼▼ BEST WESTERN Parkside Inn **H** ❄
(502) 695-6111. **$85-$109.** 80 Chenault Rd 40601. I-64 exit 58, just e. Ext/int corridors. **Pets:** Large, other species. $20 daily fee/pet. Designated rooms, service with restrictions, crate. SAVE 🛰 ⊠ 🔌 🖥 ⤴

▼▼▼ Capital Plaza Hotel **H**
(502) 227-5100. **Call for rates.** 405 Wilkinson Blvd 40601. Adjacent to Frankfort Convention Center. Int corridors. **Pets:** Medium, other species. $25 one-time fee/pet. Designated rooms, service with restrictions, supervision. 🛰 🔌M 🔌 🖥 🍴 ⤴

FRANKLIN

▼▼▼ Holiday Inn Express & Suites-Franklin **H**
(270) 586-7626. **$85-$129.** 85 Neha Dr 42134. I-65 exit 2, just n. Int corridors. **Pets:** Large. $25 daily fee/pet. Designated rooms, service with restrictions, supervision. 🛰 ⊠ 🔌M 🔌 🖥 ⤴

GEORGETOWN

◆◆◆ ▼▼▼ BEST WESTERN PLUS Georgetown Corporate Center Hotel **H**
(502) 868-0055. **Call for rates.** 132 Darby Dr 40324. I-75 exit 126, just nw. Int corridors. **Pets:** Accepted. SAVE 🛰 🔌M 🔌 🖥 ⤴ ⊠

▼▼▼ Country Inn & Suites By Carlson **H**
(502) 868-6800. **Call for rates.** 131 Darby Dr 40324. I-75 exit 126, just nw. Int corridors. **Pets:** Small, dogs only. $25 daily fee/pet. Service with restrictions, supervision. 🛰 ⊠ 🔌M 🔌 🖥 ⤴

GILBERTSVILLE

▼▼▼ Kentucky Dam Village State Resort Park **H**
(270) 362-4271. **Call for rates.** 166 Upper Village Dr 42044. I-24 exit 27, 2 mi w on US 62, follow signs. Ext/int corridors. **Pets:** Accepted.
🛰 🔌 🖥 🍴 ⤴ ⊠

GLASGOW

▼▼ Comfort Inn **M**
(270) 651-9099. **$75-$110.** 210 Cavalry Dr 42141. Cumberland Pkwy exit 11, just n. Ext corridors. **Pets:** Accepted. 🛰 🔌 🖥 ⤴

GRAND RIVERS

▼▼ Americas Best Value Inn **M**
(270) 928-2700. **Call for rates.** 720 Complex Dr 42045. I-24 exit 31 (SR 453), just s. Ext/int corridors. **Pets:** Accepted. 🛰 🔌 🖥 ⤴

◆◆◆ ▼▼▼ Green Turtle Bay Resort **CO**
(270) 362-8364. **$125-$500, 7 day notice.** 263 Green Turtle Bay Dr 42045. I-24 exit 31 (SR 453), 3 mi s to Grand Rivers business district, just e to JH O'Bryan Ave, just n to Barkley Dr, then 0.7 mi w. Ext corridors. **Pets:** $45 one-time fee/pet. Designated rooms, no service, supervision. SAVE 🛰 ⊠ 🔌 🖥 🍴 ⤴ ⊠

◆◆ **Patti's Inn and Suites** 🅷

(270) 928-2740. **$65-$70.** 1017 Dover Rd 42045. I-24 exit 31 (SR 453), just n. Int corridors. **Pets:** Small. $15 one-time fee/room. Designated rooms, service with restrictions, supervision.
🛜 ✕ ♿ 🛏 💻 ⌲

GRAYSON

◆◆ **Quality Inn-Grayson, KY** 🅼

(606) 474-7854. **Call for rates.** 205 SR 1947 41143. I-64 exit 172, just n. Ext corridors. **Pets:** Accepted. 🛜 ♿ 🛏 💻 ⌲

♦♦♦ ◆◆◆ **Super 8** 🅷

(606) 474-8811. **$50-$90.** 125 Super 8 Ln 41143. I-64 exit 172, just s. Int corridors. **Pets:** Small. $10 daily fee/pet. Designated rooms, service with restrictions, supervision. 🆂🅰🆅🅴 🛜 ♿ 🛏 💻

GREENUP

◆◆ **Greenbo Lake State Resort Park** 🅷

(606) 473-7324. **Call for rates.** 965 Lodge Rd 41144. I-64 exit 172, 15 mi ne on SR 1. Ext corridors. **Pets:** Accepted.
🛜 ✕ 🛏 💻 🍽 ⌲ ✕

HARDIN

◆◆ **Kenlake State Resort Park** 🅷

(270) 474-2211. **Call for rates.** 542 Kenlake Rd 42048. Just se of jct US 68 and SR 80. Int corridors. **Pets:** Accepted.
🛜 ✕ ♿ 🛏 💻 🍽 ⌲ ✕

HARLAN

◆◆ **Comfort Inn** 🅷

(606) 573-3385. **Call for rates.** 2608 S Hwy 421 40831. On US 421, 2.8 mi s. Int corridors. **Pets:** Small. $10 daily fee/pet. Crate.
🛜 🛏 💻 ⌲

HARRODSBURG

◆◆ **Country Hearth Inn** 🅷

(859) 734-2400. **$65-$130.** 105 Commercial Dr 40330. Jct US 68, 1 mi n on US 127, just e. Int corridors. **Pets:** Small. $20 one-time fee/pet. Service with restrictions, supervision. 🛜 🛏 💻

◆◆ **Shaker Village of Pleasant Hill** 🅲

(859) 734-5411. **$95-$250.** 3501 Lexington Rd 40330. On US 68, 7 mi ne; jct SR 33. Ext/int corridors. **Pets:** Medium, other species. $20 daily fee/pet. Designated rooms, service with restrictions, supervision.
🛜 ✕ 🛏 💻 🍽

HEBRON

♦♦♦ ◆◆◆◆ **DoubleTree by Hilton Hotel Cincinnati Airport** 🅷

(859) 371-6166. **Call for rates.** 2826 Terminal Dr 41048. I-71/75 exit 185 (I-275), 4 mi w to exit 4B (SR 212), then 1.3 mi w. Int corridors. **Pets:** Accepted. 🆂🅰🆅🅴 🛜 ✕ ♿ 🛏 💻 🍽 ⌲

HENDERSON

◆◆◆ **Ramada Inn** 🅷

(270) 826-6600. **$72-$160.** 2044 US 41 N 42420. On US 41, 1 mi n. Int corridors. **Pets:** $20 daily fee/pet. Designated rooms, service with restrictions. 🛜 🛏 💻 🍽 ⌲

HOPKINSVILLE

♦♦♦ ◆◆ **BEST WESTERN Hopkinsville** 🅷

(270) 886-9000. **Call for rates.** 4101 Ft Campbell Blvd 42240. Pennyrile Pkwy exit 7, just s. Int corridors. **Pets:** Small, dogs only. $20 daily fee/room. Designated rooms, supervision. 🆂🅰🆅🅴 🛜 🛏 💻 ⌲

♦♦♦ ◆◆◆◆ **Holiday Inn** 🅷

(270) 886-4413. **$89-$149.** 2910 Ft Campbell Blvd 42240. Pennyrile Pkwy exit 7, 0.6 mi n on US 41A. Int corridors. **Pets:** Accepted.
🆂🅰🆅🅴 🛜 🛏 💻 🍽 ⌲ ✕

JAMESTOWN

◆◆ **Lake Cumberland State Resort Park** 🅷

(270) 343-3111. **Call for rates.** 5465 State Park Rd 42629. Jct SR 55, 2.5 mi s on US 127, 4 mi e. Ext/int corridors. **Pets:** Accepted.
🛜 ✕ ♿ 🛏 💻 🍽 ⌲ ✕

KUTTAWA

◆◆ **Days Inn** 🅼

(270) 388-4060. **$65-$115.** 139 Days Inn Dr 42055. I-24 exit 40 (US 62), just s. Ext corridors. **Pets:** Accepted. 🛜 ♿ 🛏 💻 ⌲

◆◆ **Relax Inn** 🅼

(270) 388-2285. **$55-$90.** 224 New Circle Dr 42055. I-24 exit 40 (US 62), just e. Ext corridors. **Pets:** Small, dogs only. $10 deposit/pet. Designated rooms, service with restrictions, supervision. 🛜 🛏 💻

LEBANON

◆◆◆ **Hampton Inn Lebanon** 🅷

(270) 699-4000. **$85-$125.** 1125 Loretto Rd 40033. Jct SR 49 and 84. Int corridors. **Pets:** Medium. $45 one-time fee/room. Service with restrictions, crate. 🛜 ♿ 🛏 💻 ⌲

LEITCHFIELD

◆◆ **Hatfield Inn** 🅷

(270) 259-0464. **$83-$135.** 769 White St 42754. Western Kentucky Pkwy exit 107, just nw. Int corridors. **Pets:** Medium. $20 deposit/pet, $20 daily fee/pet. Service with restrictions, crate. 🛜 🛏 💻

LEWISPORT

◆◆ **Quality Inn** 🅼

(270) 295-3234. **Call for rates.** 9040 US Hwy 60 W 42351. On US 60. Int corridors. **Pets:** Accepted. 🛜 🛏 💻 ⌲

LEXINGTON

♦♦♦ ◆◆ **BEST WESTERN Lexington Conference Center Hotel** 🅷

(859) 263-5241. **$90-$100.** 5532 Athens-Boonesboro Rd 40509. I-75 exit 104, just e. Int corridors. **Pets:** Large, other species. $20 daily fee/pet. Service with restrictions, crate. 🆂🅰🆅🅴 🛜 🛏 💻 ⌲ ✕

◆◆◆ **Candlewood Suites** 🅷

(859) 967-1940. **$60-$150.** 603 Adcolor Dr 40511. Jct SR 4 (New Circle Rd) and Newtown Pike, just s. Int corridors. **Pets:** Dogs only. $75 daily fee/pet. Service with restrictions, supervision. 🛜 ♿ 🛏 💻 ⌲

♦♦♦ ◆◆◆ **Clarion Hotel** 🅷

(859) 233-0512. **$89-$129.** 1950 Newtown Pike 40511. I-75/64 exit 115, just s on SR 922. Ext/int corridors. **Pets:** Other species. $35 one-time fee/room. Service with restrictions, supervision.
🆂🅰🆅🅴 🛜 ♿ 🛏 💻 🍽 ⌲ ✕

◆◆◆ **Comfort Suites by Choice Hotels** 🅷

(859) 296-4446. **Call for rates.** 3060 Fieldstone Way 40513. Jct New Circle and Harrodsburg rds, just sw. Int corridors. **Pets:** $40 one-time fee/pet. 🛜 ✕ ♿ 🛏 💻 ⌲ ✕

◆◆◆ **Crowne Plaza Lexington-The Campbell House** 🅷

(859) 255-4281. **$79-$159.** 1375 S Broadway 40504. I-75/64 exit 113, 4.8 mi sw on US 68 (Broadway). Int corridors. **Pets:** Accepted.
🛜 ♿ 🛏 💻 🍽 ⌲

◆◆◆ **Days Inn-South** 🅼

(859) 263-3100. **$55-$68.** 5575 Athens-Boonesboro Rd 40509. I-75 exit 104, just e. Ext corridors. **Pets:** Accepted. 🛜 🛏 💻

◆◆◆ **DoubleTree Suites by Hilton Hotel Lexington** 🅷

(859) 268-0060. **Call for rates.** 2601 Richmond Rd 40509. SR 4 (New Circle Rd) exit 15, just s on US 25/421. Int corridors. **Pets:** Medium, other species. $75 one-time fee/room. Service with restrictions, crate.
🛜 ♿ 🛏 💻 🍽 ⌲

Fairfield Inn & Suites by Marriott-Lexington North H 🌸

(859) 977-5870. **$89-$99.** 2100 Hackney Pl 40511. I-75/64 exit 115, just n, then 0.3 mi e on Stanton Way. Int corridors. **Pets:** Other species. $75 one-time fee/room. Designated rooms, service with restrictions, crate.

Four Points by Sheraton Hotel H

(859) 259-1311. **$69-$169, 3 day notice.** 1938 Stanton Way 40511. I-75/64 exit 115, just n on SR 922, then just e. Int corridors. **Pets:** Large. $25 daily fee/room. Service with restrictions, crate.

Hampton Inn I-75 H

(859) 299-2613. **Call for rates.** 2251 Elkhorn Rd 40505. I-75 exit 110, 0.4 mi nw. Int corridors. **Pets:** Service with restrictions, supervision.

Hilton Suites of Lexington Green H

(859) 271-4000. **$199-$229.** 245 Lexington Green Cir 40503. SR 4 (New Circle Rd) exit 19, just s on US 27 (Nicholasville Rd), then just w. Int corridors. **Pets:** Medium, dogs only. $50 daily fee/room. Designated rooms, service with restrictions.

Holiday Inn Express Hotel & Suites-Lexington H

(859) 389-6800. **$89-$199.** 1000 Export St 40504. I-75/64 exit 113, 4.5 mi s, then just e. Int corridors. **Pets:** Accepted.

Howard Johnson Regency H

(859) 293-2202. **$48-$96.** 2241 Elkhorn Rd 40505. I-75 exit 110, just w on US 60 (Winchester Rd), then just n. Ext/int corridors. **Pets:** Accepted.

La Quinta Inn H

(859) 231-7551. **$71-$140.** 1920 Stanton Way 40511. I-75/64 exit 115, just se off SR 922. Int corridors. **Pets:** Service with restrictions, supervision.

La Quinta Inn & Suites Lexington South/Hamburg H

(859) 543-1877. **$66-$173.** 100 Canebrake Dr 40509. I-75 exit 104, just e. Int corridors. **Pets:** Service with restrictions, supervision.

Lyndon House Bed & Breakfast BB 🌸

(859) 420-2683. **$169-$289.** 507 N Broadway 40508. I-75/64 exit 113, 2.5 mi w on US 27, then just n. Int corridors. **Pets:** $35 one-time fee/room. Designated rooms.

Marriott Griffin Gate Resort & Spa H

(859) 231-5100. **$189-$299.** 1800 Newtown Pike 40511. I-75/64 exit 115, 0.5 mi s on SR 922. Int corridors. **Pets:** Accepted.

Red Roof Inn-North H

(859) 293-2626. **$45-$99.** 1980 Haggard Ct 40505. I-75/64 exit 113, 0.3 mi nw. Ext corridors. **Pets:** Large, other species. Service with restrictions, supervision.

Red Roof Inn South H

(859) 277-9400. **$50-$99.** 2651 Wilhite Dr 40503. Jct US 27 and SR 4 (New Circle Rd). Ext corridors. **Pets:** Large, other species. Service with restrictions, supervision.

Residence Inn by Marriott H

(859) 296-0460. **$140-$240.** 3110 Wall St 40513. Jct New Circle and Harrodsburg rds. Int corridors. **Pets:** Accepted.

Residence Inn by Marriott Lexington North H

(859) 231-6191. **$99-$199.** 1080 Newtown Pike 40511. I-75/64 exit 115, 1 mi s on SR 922. Ext corridors. **Pets:** Other species. $75 one-time fee/room. Service with restrictions, supervision.

Residence Inn by Marriott Lexington South/Hamburg Place H

(859) 263-9979. **$99-$229.** 2688 Pink Pigeon Pkwy 40509. I-75 exit 108, just se. Int corridors. **Pets:** Accepted.

Sleep Inn Lexington H

(859) 543-8400. **$81-$99.** 1920 Plaudit Pl 40509. I-75 exit 108, just sw. Int corridors. **Pets:** Accepted.

LONDON

Country Inn & Suites By Carlson H

(606) 878-9900. **$69-$109.** 2035 W Hwy 192 40741. I-75 exit 38, just e. Int corridors. **Pets:** $25 one-time fee/room. Service with restrictions, supervision.

Red Roof Inn H

(606) 862-8844. **$59-$114.** 110 Melcon Ln 40741. I-75 exit 41, southwest corner. Int corridors. **Pets:** Large, other species. Service with restrictions, supervision.

LOUISA

Super 8-Louisa H

(606) 638-7888. **$63-$109.** 191 Falls Creek Dr 41230. Jct US 23 and SR 3. Int corridors. **Pets:** Accepted.

LOUISVILLE METROPOLITAN AREA

BROOKS

Baymont Inn H

(502) 957-6900. **$60-$300.** 149 Willabrook Dr 40109. I-65 exit 121, just nw. Int corridors. **Pets:** Accepted.

HURSTBOURNE

Drury Inn & Suites-Louisville H

(502) 326-4170. **$100-$179.** 9501 Blairwood Rd 40222. I-64 exit 15, just n. Int corridors. **Pets:** Service with restrictions, supervision.

Red Roof Inn Louisville - East #034 H

(502) 426-7621. **$49-$199.** 9330 Blairwood Rd 40222. I-64 exit 15, 0.3 mi nw of Hurstbourne Pkwy. Ext corridors. **Pets:** Large, other species. Service with restrictions, supervision.

JEFFERSONTOWN

BEST WESTERN Louisville East H

(502) 499-0000. **Call for rates.** 9802 Bunsen Way 40299. I-64 exit 15, just s. Int corridors. **Pets:** Accepted.

Holiday Inn Louisville East Hurstbourne H

(502) 426-2600. **Call for rates.** 1325 S Hurstbourne Pkwy 40222. I-64 exit 15, just n. Ext/int corridors. **Pets:** Dogs only. $39 one-time fee/room. Service with restrictions, supervision.

La Quinta Inn & Suites Louisville Expo East H

(502) 267-8889. **$87-$166.** 1501 Alliant Ave 40299. I-64 exit 17, just e. Int corridors. **Pets:** Service with restrictions, supervision.

▼▼ **Microtel Inn by Wyndham Louisville East** 🏨
(502) 266-6590. **$53-$200.** 1221 Kentucky Mills Dr 40299. I-64 exit 17, just s. Int corridors. **Pets:** Medium, dogs only. $20 one-time fee/pet. Designated rooms, service with restrictions, supervision. 🛜 🅼

▼▼ **Quality Inn** 🏨
(502) 267-8100. **Call for rates.** 1301 Kentucky Mills Dr 40299. I-64 exit 17, just s. Ext/int corridors. **Pets:** Accepted. 🛜 🅼 🛏 🖥 🏊

LA GRANGE
▼▼▼ **Holiday Inn Express** 🏨
(502) 222-5678. **Call for rates.** 1001 Paige Pl 40031. I-71 exit 22, just se. Int corridors. **Pets:** Accepted. 🛜 🅼 🛏 🖥 🏊

LOUISVILLE
▼▼▼ **21c Museum Hotel** 🏨
(502) 217-6300. **Call for rates.** 700 W Main St 40202. Jct 7th and Main sts. Int corridors. **Pets:** Accepted. 🛜 🗙 🅼 🖥 🍴 🗙

▼▼▼ **Aleksander House Bed and Breakfast** 🅱🅱 🐾
(502) 637-4985. **Call for rates.** 1213 S 1st St 40203. I-65 exit 135 (St Catherine St), just s. Int corridors. **Pets:** $50 one-time fee/room. Designated rooms, service with restrictions, crate. 🛜 🗙 🛏 🖥

🔼 ▼▼ **BEST WESTERN PLUS Airport East/Expo Center** 🏨
(502) 456-4411. **$84.** 1921 Bishop Ln 40218. I-264 exit 15B westbound, 0.3 mi s; exit 15 eastbound. Int corridors. **Pets:** Other species. $25 one-time fee/room. Service with restrictions, crate.
🆂🅰🆅🅴 🛜 🅼 🛏 🖥 🍴 🏊

▼▼ **Candlewood Suites Louisville Airport** 🏨
(502) 357-3577. **Call for rates.** 1367 Gardiner Ln 40213. I-264 exit 14, just s, then just e. Int corridors. **Pets:** Accepted. 🛜 🛏 🖥 🗙

▼▼ **Crowne Plaza Louisville** 🏨
(502) 367-2251. **$99-$159.** 830 Phillips Ln 40209. I-264 exit 11 (Fairgrounds/Expo Center Main Gate). Int corridors. **Pets:** Other species. $250 one-time fee/room. Service with restrictions, crate.
🛜 🗙 🅼 🛏 🖥 🍴 🏊

▼▼ **Homewood Suites** 🏨
(502) 429-9070. **$169-$189.** 9401 Hurstbourne Trace 40222. I-64 exit 15, 2.5 mi n. Int corridors. **Pets:** Other species. $100 one-time fee/room. Service with restrictions, crate. 🛜 🅼 🛏 🖥 🏊 🗙

🔼 ▼▼▼ **La Quinta Inn & Suites Louisville Airport Expo** 🏨
(502) 368-0007. **$87-$239.** 4125 Preston Hwy 40213. I-65 exit 130, 1 mi n. Int corridors. **Pets:** Service with restrictions, supervision.
🆂🅰🆅🅴 🛜 🗙 🅼 🛏 🖥 🏊

▼▼ **Ramada Limited Airport & Fair/Expo Center** 🏨
(502) 637-6336. **$70-$460.** 2912 Crittenden Dr 40209. I-264 exit 11 (Fairgrounds/Expo Center Main Gate), 0.6 mi n. Int corridors. **Pets:** $25 one-time fee/pet. Designated rooms, service with restrictions, crate.
🛜 🗙 🛏 🖥 🏊

🔼 ▼▼ **Red Roof Inn-Airport-Fairgrounds** 🏨
(502) 968-0151. **$59-$265.** 4704 Preston Hwy 40213. I-65 exit 130, northeast corner. Ext corridors. **Pets:** Large, other species. Service with restrictions, supervision. 🆂🅰🆅🅴 🛜 🛏

🔼 ▼▼ **Red Roof Inn-Southeast-Fairgrounds** 🏨
(502) 456-2993. **$55-$250.** 3322 Red Roof Inn Pl 40218. I-264 exit 15B westbound, 0.3 mi s; exit 15 eastbound. Ext corridors. **Pets:** Large, other species. Service with restrictions, supervision. 🆂🅰🆅🅴 🛜 🛏 🖥

▼▼ **Residence Inn by Marriott-Louisville Airport** 🏨 🐾
(502) 363-8800. **$99-$199.** 700 Phillips Ln 40209. I-264 exit 11 (Fairgrounds/Expo Center Main Gate), 0.4 mi w. Int corridors. **Pets:** Other species. $100 one-time fee/room. Service with restrictions, crate.
🛜 🗙 🅼 🛏 🖥 🏊 🗙

▼▼ **Residence Inn by Marriott Louisville Downtown** 🏨
(502) 589-8998. **$99-$139.** 333 E Market St 40202. Corner of Preston and E Market sts. Int corridors. **Pets:** Accepted.
🛜 🗙 🅼 🛏 🖥 🏊 🗙

▼▼ **Residence Inn by Marriott Louisville East** 🏨
(502) 425-1821. **$99-$199.** 120 N Hurstbourne Pkwy 40222. I-64 exit 15, 1.8 mi n. Ext corridors. **Pets:** $100 one-time fee/room. Service with restrictions. 🛜 🗙 🛏 🖥 🏊 🗙

▼▼ **Residence Inn by Marriott-Louisville NE** 🏨
(502) 412-1311. **$97-$139.** 3500 Springhurst Commons Dr 40241. I-265 exit 32, 0.5 mi w on Westport Rd, then just n. Int corridors. **Pets:** Accepted. 🛜 🗙 🅼 🛏 🖥 🏊 🗙

▼▼ **Rodeway Inn** Ⓜ
(502) 361-5008. **$95-$325.** 571 Phillips Ln 40209. I-264 exit 11 (Fairgrounds/Expo Center Main Gate), 0.5 mi w. Ext corridors. **Pets:** Medium. $35 one-time fee/pet. Designated rooms, service with restrictions, supervision. 🛜 🅼 🖥

🔼 ▼▼ ▼▼ **The Seelbach Hilton Louisville** 🏨 🐾
(502) 585-3200. **Call for rates.** 500 4th St 40202. I-65 exit 136C (Muhammad Ali Blvd), 0.3 mi w, then just s. Int corridors. **Pets:** $50 one-time fee/room. Designated rooms, service with restrictions, crate.
🆂🅰🆅🅴 🛜 🗙 🅼 🛏 🖥 🍴 🗙

▼▼ **Sleep Inn Fairgrounds** 🏨
(502) 368-9597. **$69-$149, 3 day notice.** 3330 Preston Hwy 40213. I-264 exit 11 (Fairgrounds/Expo Center Main Gate), 0.5 mi e on Phillips Ln, then just n. Int corridors. **Pets:** Accepted.
🛜 🗙 🅼 🛏 🖥

▼▼▼ **Staybridge Suites Louisville East** 🏨
(502) 244-9511. **Call for rates.** 11711 Gateworth Way 40299. I-64 exit 17, just n. Int corridors. **Pets:** Accepted. 🛜 🅼 🛏 🖥 🏊

▼▼ **Super 8** 🏨
(502) 635-0799. **$60-$160.** 101 Central Ave 40209. I-65 exit 132, just s. Int corridors. **Pets:** Accepted. 🛜 🅼 🛏 🖥

SHEPHERDSVILLE
🔼 ▼▼▼ **BEST WESTERN PLUS South** 🏨
(502) 543-7097. **$78-$89.** 211 S Lakeview Dr 40165. I-65 exit 117 (SR 44 W), just se. Int corridors. **Pets:** Large. $20 one-time fee/pet. Service with restrictions, crate. 🆂🅰🆅🅴 🛜 🛏 🖥

▼▼▼ **Comfort Inn Pirates Bay Indoor Water Park Louisville South** 🏨 🐾
(502) 955-5566. **$69-$179.** 191 Brenton Way 40165. I-65 exit 121, just ne. Int corridors. **Pets:** Medium, other species. $25 one-time fee/pet. Service with restrictions. 🛜 🗙 🛏 🖥 🏊 🗙

▼▼▼ **Fairfield Inn by Marriott Louisville South** 🏨
(502) 955-5533. **$99-$109.** 362 Brenton Way 40165. I-65 exit 121, just ne. Int corridors. **Pets:** Accepted. 🛜 🗙 🅼 🛏 🖥 🏊 🗙

▼▼▼ **Sleep Inn & Suites - Louisville South** 🏨
(502) 921-1001. **Call for rates.** 130 Spring Pointe Dr 40165. I-65 exit 117 (SR 44 W), just e. Int corridors. **Pets:** Accepted.
🛜 🅼 🛏 🖥 🏊

◆◆ Super 8 H
(502) 543-8870. **$59-$190.** 275 Keystone Crossroads 40165. I-65 exit 117 (SR 44 W), just w. Int corridors. **Pets:** Medium, dogs only. $10 daily fee/pet. Service with restrictions, supervision.

SHIVELY
◆◆◆◆ Holiday Inn Southwest Fair Expo H
(502) 448-2020. **Call for rates.** 4110 Dixie Hwy 40216. I-264 exit 8B, just n on US 31 W and 60. Int corridors. **Pets:** $25 daily fee/pet.

END METROPOLITAN AREA

LUCAS
◆◆ Barren River Lake State Resort Park H
(270) 646-2151. **Call for rates.** 1149 State Park Rd 42156. Cumberland Pkwy exit 11, 10 mi s on US 31 E. Ext corridors. **Pets:** Other species. $25 one-time fee/room. Designated rooms, service with restrictions.

MADISONVILLE
AAA ◆◆◆◆ BEST WESTERN PLUS Madisonville Inn H
(270) 821-2121. **$90-$110.** 1891 Lantaff Blvd 42431. Pennyrile Pkwy exit 44. Int corridors. **Pets:** Medium. $10 daily fee/pet. Service with restrictions.

MAYSVILLE
◆◆ Super 8 H
(606) 759-8888. **$61-$71.** 550 Tucker Dr 41056. Just e of US 68. Int corridors. **Pets:** Accepted.

MOREHEAD
AAA ◆◆◆ Comfort Inn & Suites H
(606) 780-7378. **$69-$130.** 2650 Kentucky 801 N 40351. I-64 exit 133, just s. Int corridors. **Pets:** Other species. $10 daily fee/pet. Service with restrictions, crate.

◆◆◆◆ Holiday Inn Express of Morehead H
(606) 784-5796. **$89-$129.** 110 Toms Dr 40351. I-64 exit 137 (SR 32), just sw. Int corridors. **Pets:** Small, other species. $15 daily fee/pet. Designated rooms, service with restrictions, supervision.

MORTONS GAP
AAA ◆◆ Executive Pennyrile Inn M
(270) 258-5201. **Call for rates.** 1562 Mortons Gap Rd 42440. Pennyrile Pkwy exit 37 (US 41). Ext corridors. **Pets:** Dogs only. $8 daily fee/pet. Service with restrictions.

MOUNT OLIVET
◆◆◆ Blue Licks Battlefield State Resort Park H
(859) 289-5507. **Call for rates.** 10299 Maysville Rd 41064. I-75/64 exit 113, 45 mi n on US 68. Ext corridors. **Pets:** Accepted.

MOUNT VERNON
◆◆◆ Days Inn-Renfro Valley H
(606) 256-3300. **$60-$106.** 1630 Richmond St 40456. I-75 exit 62, just w. Ext corridors. **Pets:** Small. $20 one-time fee/pet. Service with restrictions, supervision.

MURRAY
AAA ◆◆◆ BEST WESTERN University Inn H
(270) 753-5353. **$75-$125.** 1503 N 12th St 42071. 1.9 mi n on US 641. Ext corridors. **Pets:** Very small, dogs only. $20 daily fee/room. Designated rooms, service with restrictions, supervision.

OAK GROVE
AAA ◆◆◆ Quality Inn @ Ft. Campbell H
(270) 439-3311. **$69-$120.** 201 Auburn St 42262. I-24 exit 86, just se. Ext corridors. **Pets:** $20 daily fee/pet. Service with restrictions, supervision.

OLIVE HILL
◆◆◆ Carter Caves State Resort Park H
(606) 286-4411. **Call for rates.** 344 Caveland Dr 41164. I-64 exit 161, just n. Ext corridors. **Pets:** Other species. $27 one-time fee/room. Designated rooms, service with restrictions, supervision.

OWENSBORO
◆◆ Super 8-Owensboro H
(270) 685-3388. **$70-$80.** 1027 Goetz Rd 42301. US 60 Bypass exit 4 at US 431. Int corridors. **Pets:** $20 daily fee/pet. Service with restrictions.

PADUCAH
◆◆◆◆ Candlewood Suites H
(270) 442-3969. **Call for rates.** 3940 Coleman Crossing Cir 42001. I-24 exit 4 (US 60), just ne. Int corridors. **Pets:** Large. $25 one-time fee/room. Service with restrictions, supervision.

◆◆ Days Inn H
(270) 442-7500. **$50-$66.** 3901 Hinkleville Rd 42001. I-24 exit 4 (US 60), just e. Ext corridors. **Pets:** Small, dogs only. $10 one-time fee/room. Designated rooms, service with restrictions, supervision.

◆◆◆ Drury Inn H
(270) 443-3313. **$105-$174.** 3975 Hinkleville Rd 42001. I-24 exit 4 (US 60), just e. Int corridors. **Pets:** Service with restrictions, supervision.

◆◆◆◆ Drury Suites H
(270) 441-0024. **$100-$184.** 2930 James Sanders Blvd 42001. I-24 exit 4 (US 60), just w. Int corridors. **Pets:** Service with restrictions, supervision.

◆◆◆◆ Holiday Inn Express H
(270) 442-8874. **$99-$139.** 3994 Hinkleville Rd 42001. I-24 exit 4 (US 60), just se. Int corridors. **Pets:** Other species. $10 daily fee/room. Service with restrictions, supervision.

◆◆ Pear Tree Inn by Drury H
(270) 444-7200. **$75-$119.** 5006 Hinkleville Rd 42001. I-24 exit 4 (US 60), just w. Int corridors. **Pets:** Service with restrictions, supervision.

◆◆◆◆ Residence Inn by Marriott H ❀
(270) 444-3966. **$104-$169.** 3900 Coleman Crossing Cir 42001. I-24 exit 4 (US 60), just ne. Int corridors. **Pets:** Medium, other species. $50 one-time fee/room. Designated rooms, service with restrictions.

PINEVILLE

▼▼ Pine Mountain State Resort Park H

(606) 337-3066. **Call for rates.** 1050 State Park Rd 40977. Jct US 25 E and SR 190, 5.5 mi w. Ext corridors. **Pets:** $25 one-time fee/pet. Designated rooms, service with restrictions, crate.

🛜 📶 💻 🍽 ⊃ ⊠

PRESTONSBURG

▼▼▼ Heritage House Hotel H

(606) 886-0001. **Call for rates.** 1887 N US 23 41653. On US 23, 2 mi s. Ext corridors. **Pets:** Accepted. 🛜 📶 📶 💻 ⊃ ⊠

▼▼ Jenny Wiley State Resort Park H

(606) 889-1790. **Call for rates.** 75 Theatre Ct 41653. 3.5 mi s on US 23 and 460, 3 mi e on SR 3; SR 80, 4 mi n on SR 302. Ext corridors. **Pets:** Accepted. 🛜 📶 📶 💻 🍽 ⊃ ⊠

RADCLIFF

▼▼ Super 8 Radcliff/Fort Knox M

(270) 352-1888. **$85.** 395 Redmar Blvd 40160. Jct US 31 W and SR 1646 (Bullion Blvd), 1.5 mi s. Int corridors. **Pets:** Accepted.

🛜 📶 💻

RICHMOND

▼▼▼ Holiday Inn Express Hotel & Suites H

(859) 624-4055. **$89-$129, 3 day notice.** 1990 Colby Taylor Dr 40745. I-75 exit 87, just w. Int corridors. **Pets:** Other species. $25 daily fee/pet. Designated rooms, service with restrictions, supervision.

🛜 📶 📶 💻

▼▼ Quality Inn H

(859) 623-0063. **$85-$105.** 1007 Colby Taylor Dr 40475. I-75 exit 87, just w. Int corridors. **Pets:** Accepted. 🛜 📶 📶 💻 ⊃

AAA ▼▼ Super 8 H

(859) 624-1550. **$45-$70.** 107 N Keeneland Dr 40475. I-75 exit 90 or 90B, just n on US 25/421, then just nw. Int corridors. **Pets:** Small, dogs only. $10 daily fee/pet. Designated rooms, service with restrictions, supervision. SAVE 🛜 📶 💻

RUSSELLVILLE

▼▼ Econo Lodge H

(270) 726-2488. **$70-$100.** 1450 Bowling Green Rd 42276. 1.4 mi e on SR 80 and US 68. Ext corridors. **Pets:** Accepted. 🛜 📶 💻 ⊃

SHELBYVILLE

AAA ▼▼▼ BEST WESTERN Shelbyville Lodge H ✿

(502) 633-4400. **$83-$200.** 115 Isaac Shelby Dr 40065. I-64 exit 32, 0.5 mi n on SR 55. Int corridors. **Pets:** Dogs only. $20 daily fee/pet. Service with restrictions, supervision. SAVE 🛜 📶 💻 ⊃

AAA ▼▼ Country Hearth Inn H

(502) 633-5771. **$55-$145.** 100 Howard Dr 40065. I-64 exit 32, 0.5 mi n on SR 55. Int corridors. **Pets:** Medium, dogs only. $10 daily fee/pet. Service with restrictions, supervision. SAVE 🛜 📶 💻

Ramada H

▼▼▼ Ramada H

(502) 633-9933. **$84-$349, 3 day notice.** 251 Breighton Cir 40065. I-64 exit 32, just s. Int corridors. **Pets:** Large. $25 one-time fee/room. Designated rooms, service with restrictions, supervision.

🛜 ⊠ 📶 📶 💻 ⊃

SLADE

▼▼▼ Natural Bridge State Resort Park H

(606) 663-2214. **Call for rates.** 2135 Natural Bridge Rd 40376. Mountain Pkwy exit 33, 2 mi s on SR 11. Ext/int corridors. **Pets:** Accepted.

🛜 ⊠ 📶 📶 💻 🍽 ⊃ ⊠

SMITHS GROVE

▼▼ Bryce Inn M

(270) 563-5141. **$59-$75.** 592 S Main St 42171. I-65 exit 38, 0.3 mi w. Ext corridors. **Pets:** Medium, dogs only. $10 one-time fee/pet. Designated rooms, service with restrictions, crate. 🛜 📶 💻 ⊃

SOMERSET

▼▼▼ Quality Inn & Suites H

(606) 678-2023. **$65-$99.** 240 N Hwy 27 42503. Jct SR 80, just n; at traffic light 2. Int corridors. **Pets:** Accepted. 🛜 📶 📶 💻 ⊃

SPARTA

▼▼▼ Ramada at the Kentucky Speedway H

(859) 567-7223. **$79-$525, 3 day notice.** 525 Dale Dr 41086. I-71 exit 57, just w. Int corridors. **Pets:** Medium. $25 one-time fee/room. Designated rooms, service with restrictions, crate. 🛜 📶 📶 💻 ⊃

VERSAILLES

▼▼▼ 1823 Historic Rose Hill Inn BB

(859) 873-5957. **Call for rates.** 233 Rose Hill Ave 40383. Just s on SR 33 (S Main St), then just w. Ext/int corridors. **Pets:** Accepted.

🛜 ⊠ 📶 💻

WEST LIBERTY

▼▼ Days Inn H

(606) 743-4206. **$70-$160.** 1613 W Main St 41472. Jct SR 519 and 460, just w. Int corridors. **Pets:** Accepted. 🛜 📶 📶 💻

WILLIAMSBURG

AAA ▼▼▼ Cumberland Inn H

(606) 539-4100. **$80-$100.** 649 S 10th St 40769. I-75 exit 11, just e on SR 92, then just n on SR 2386. Int corridors. **Pets:** $15 daily fee/pet. Designated rooms, service with restrictions, supervision.

SAVE 🛜 ⊠ 📶 📶 💻 🍽 ⊃

WINCHESTER

AAA ▼▼▼ BEST WESTERN Country Squire M

(859) 744-7210. **$69-$149, 7 day notice.** 1307 W Lexington Ave 40391. I-64 exit 94 (US 60), 0.9 mi se. Ext corridors. **Pets:** Very small. $50 deposit/room, $20 daily fee/pet. Designated rooms, service with restrictions, supervision. SAVE 🛜 📶 💻 ⊃

LOUISIANA

ALEXANDRIA

BEST WESTERN of Alexandria Inn & Suites & Conference Center H ❀

(318) 445-5530. **$78-$99.** 2720 N MacArthur Dr 71303. I-49 exit 86 (MacArthur Dr), 1.3 mi sw. Ext/int corridors. **Pets:** $10 one-time fee/pet. Designated rooms, service with restrictions, supervision.

SAVE 🛜 🛏 🖵 🌊

La Quinta Inn & Suites Alexandria Airport H

(318) 442-3700. **$102-$173.** 6116 W Calhoun Dr 71303. I-49 exit 90 (Air Base Rd), just w. Int corridors. **Pets:** Service with restrictions, supervision.

🛜 🔊ᴹ 🛏 🖵 🌊

Ramada H

(318) 448-1611. **$59-$80.** 742 MacArthur Dr 71303. 0.4 mi s of jct SR 28 and US 71/165 (MacArthur Dr). Ext corridors. **Pets:** Accepted.

🛜 🛏 🖵 🌊

BATON ROUGE

BEST WESTERN Chateau Louisianne Suite Hotel H

(225) 927-6700. **$80-$150.** 710 N Lobdell Blvd 70806. 4.6 mi e on Florida Blvd, then 0.3 mi n. Int corridors. **Pets:** $20 daily fee/pet. Service with restrictions, crate. SAVE 🛜 🛏 🖵 🌊 ⊠

BEST WESTERN PLUS Richmond Inn & Suites - Baton Rouge H ❀

(225) 924-6500. **$99-$149.** 2683 Energy Dr 70808. I-10 exit 158 (College Dr), just ne. Int corridors. **Pets:** Other species. $20 daily fee/room. Service with restrictions, crate. SAVE 🛜 ⊠ 🛏 🖵 🌊 ⊠

Chase Suites by Woodfin H

(225) 927-6400. **Call for rates.** 5522 Corporate Blvd 70808. I-10 exit 158 (College Dr), just n, then just e. Ext corridors. **Pets:** Accepted.

🛜 ⊠ 🛏 🖵 🌊 ⊠

Courtyard by Marriott Baton Rouge Acadian Center H

(225) 924-6400. **$100-$239.** 2421 S Acadian Thruway 70808. I-10 exit 157B, just s. Int corridors. **Pets:** Other species. $75 one-time fee/room. Service with restrictions. ECO SAVE 🛜 ⊠ 🔊ᴹ 🛏 🖵 🍴 🌊

Crowne Plaza Executive Center H

(225) 925-2244. **$109-$189.** 4728 Constitution Ave 70808. I-10 exit 158 (College Dr), just s, then just e. Int corridors. **Pets:** Accepted.

SAVE 🛜 🔊ᴹ 🛏 🖵 🍴 🌊

Drury Inn & Suites Baton Rouge H

(225) 766-2022. **$99-$229.** 7939 Essen Park Ave 70809. I-10 exit 160 (Essen Ln), just s. Int corridors. **Pets:** Service with restrictions, supervision. 🛜 🔊ᴹ 🛏 🖵 🌊

Hilton Baton Rouge Capitol Center H

(225) 344-5866. **$159-$249.** 201 Lafayette St 70801. I-110 exit 1C (Florida Blvd), 0.5 mi w to Lafayette St, then just s. Int corridors. **Pets:** Accepted. SAVE 🛜 ⊠ 🛏 🖵 🍴 🌊

Holiday Inn-College @ I-10 H

(225) 448-2030. **$99-$119.** 4848 Constitution Ave 70808. I-10 exit 158 (College Dr), just s, then just e. Int corridors. **Pets:** Medium, other species. $30 one-time fee/pet. Designated rooms, service with restrictions, crate. SAVE 🛜 🛏 🖵 🍴 🌊

Holiday Inn-South Baton Rouge H

(225) 924-7021. **$99-$119.** 9940 Airline Hwy 70816. I-12 exit 2B, just n on US 61. Ext/int corridors. **Pets:** Accepted. 🛜 🛏 🖵 🍴 🌊

Hotel Indigo Baton Rouge Downtown Riverfront H ❀

(225) 343-1515. **$189-$249.** 200 Convention St 70801. Corner of Lafayette St; downtown. Int corridors. **Pets:** Medium. $50 one-time fee/pet. Designated rooms, service with restrictions.

SAVE 🛜 ⊠ 🔊ᴹ 🛏 🖵 🍴 ⊠

La Quinta Inn Baton Rouge-Siegen Lane H

(225) 291-6600. **$66-$173.** 10555 Reiger Rd 70809. I-10 exit 163 (Siegen Ln), just n, then just e. Int corridors. **Pets:** Service with restrictions, supervision. 🛜 🛏 🖵 🌊

La Quinta Inn Baton Rouge University Area M

(225) 924-9600. **$59-$210.** 2333 S Acadian Thruway 70808. I-10 exit 157B, just n. Ext corridors. **Pets:** Service with restrictions, supervision.

🛜 🛏 🖵 🌊

Microtel Inn & Suites by Wyndham Baton Rouge Airport H ❀

(225) 356-9191. **$60-$109.** 3444 Harding Blvd 70807. I-110 exit 6, just e. Int corridors. **Pets:** Small, other species. $35 daily fee/pet. Service with restrictions, supervision. 🛜 ⊠ 🔊ᴹ 🛏 🖵 🌊

Radisson Hotel Baton Rouge H

(225) 236-4000. **$129-$409, 3 day notice.** 2445 S Acadian Thruway 70808. I-10 exit 157B, just n. Int corridors. **Pets:** Other species. $25 daily fee/pet. Service with restrictions, supervision.

SAVE 🛜 ⊠ 🛏 🖵 🍴 ⊠

Residence Inn by Marriott-Baton Rouge-Siegen Lane H

(225) 293-8700. **$159-$189.** 10333 N Mall Dr 70809. I-10 exit 163, just s on Siegen Ln; in Siegen Marketplace. Int corridors. **Pets:** Medium, other species. $109 one-time fee/room. Service with restrictions.

🛜 ⊠ 🔊ᴹ 🛏 🖵 🌊 ⊠

Residence Inn by Marriott Baton Rouge-Towne Center at Cedar Lodge H ❀

(225) 925-9100. **$99-$169.** 7061 Commerce Cir 70810. I-10 exit 158 (College Dr), just n to Corporate Blvd, then 1.8 mi e. Int corridors. **Pets:** Large, other species. $75 one-time fee/room. Service with restrictions, crate. SAVE 🛜 ⊠ 🔊ᴹ 🛏 🖵 🌊 ⊠

TownePlace Suites by Marriott Baton Rouge South H

(225) 819-2112. **$99-$149.** 8735 Summa Ave 70809. I-10 exit 162 (Bluebonnet Blvd), just s to Picardy Ave, just w to Summa Ave, then 0.5 mi nw. Int corridors. **Pets:** Accepted. 🛜 ⊠ 🔊ᴹ 🛏 🖵 🌊

BOSSIER CITY

▼▼▼ **Hampton Inn** 🏨
(318) 752-1112. **$89-$129.** 1005 Gould Dr 71111. I-20 exit 21 (Old Minden Rd), just n, then 0.5 mi e. Int corridors. **Pets:** Small. Service with restrictions, supervision. 🛜 🔥M 🛏 💻 ➿

▼▼▼ **Microtel Inn & Suites by Wyndham Bossier City** 🏨
(318) 742-7882. **$60-$100.** 2713 Village Ln 71112. I-20 exit 22 (Airline Dr), just s, then just w. Int corridors. **Pets:** Medium. $25 one-time fee/pet. Service with restrictions, supervision. 🛜 🔥M 🛏 💻

▼▼ **Quality Inn & Suites** 🏨
(318) 742-7890. **$69-$99.** 2717 Village Ln 71112. I-20 exit 22 (Airline Dr), just s, then just w. Int corridors. **Pets:** Accepted.
🛜 🔥M 🛏 💻

BREAUX BRIDGE

▼▼ **Holiday Inn Express of Breaux Bridge** 🏨
(337) 667-8913. **$95-$120.** 2942 H Grand Point Hwy 70517. I-10 exit 115, just n. Int corridors. **Pets:** Accepted. 🛜 🔥M 🛏 💻 ➿

BROUSSARD

▼▼▼ **La Quinta Inn & Suites Broussard - Lafayette Area** 🏨
(337) 330-8081. **$95-$199.** 104 Sweetland Dr 70518. US 90, just w on Albertson Pkwy, then just n. Int corridors. **Pets:** Service with restrictions, supervision. 🛜 ✖ 🔥M 🛏 💻 ➿

DELHI

AAA **▼▼▼** **BEST WESTERN Delhi Inn** Ⓜ
(318) 878-5126. **$75-$95.** 135 Snider Rd 71232. I-20 exit 153, just s. Ext corridors. **Pets:** Accepted. 🆂🅰🆅🅴 🛜 🛏 💻 ➿

FRANKLIN

AAA **▼▼▼** **Comfort Inn & Suites** 🏨
(337) 828-1134. **Call for rates.** 1819 Main St 70538. US 90, 1.7 mi n on SR 3211, just e. Int corridors. **Pets:** Accepted.
🆂🅰🆅🅴 🛜 🔥M 🛏 💻 ➿

HAMMOND

AAA **▼▼▼** **Historic Michabelle Inn** Ⓒ
(985) 419-0550. **$75-$125, 5 day notice.** 1106 S Holly St 70403. I-12 exit 40 (US 51), 0.8 mi n, just e on Old Covington Hwy, then n, follow signs. Ext/int corridors. **Pets:** Medium. Designated rooms, service with restrictions, supervision. 🆂🅰🆅🅴 🛜 ✖ 🛏 💻 🍽 ➿ ✖

▼▼▼ **La Quinta Inn & Suites Hammond** 🏨
(985) 345-4742. **$99-$177.** 42126 Veterans Ave 70403. I-12 exit 40 (US 51), just s. Int corridors. **Pets:** Service with restrictions, supervision.
🛜 ✖ 🔥M 🛏 💻 ➿

AAA **▼▼** **Lexington Inn** 🏨
(985) 345-0003. **$75-$80.** 46053 N Puma Dr 70401. I-55 exit 32 (Wardline/University), just e. Ext corridors. **Pets:** Other species. $25 daily fee/room. Service with restrictions, supervision. 🆂🅰🆅🅴 🛜 🛏 💻 ➿

▼▼▼ **Quality Inn & Conference Center** 🏨
(985) 345-0556. **$70-$110.** 2000 S Morrison Blvd 70403. I-55 exit 28 (US 51), 0.5 mi nw. Ext/int corridors. **Pets:** Other species. $25 one-time fee/room. Service with restrictions, supervision. 🛜 🛏 💻 ➿

HOUMA

▼▼▼ **La Quinta Inn & Suites Houma** 🏨
(985) 879-1646. **$72-$199.** 189 Synergy Center Blvd 70364. US 90 exit 202, 3.4 mi s on Main St to Martin Luther King Jr Blvd, then just w. Int corridors. **Pets:** Service with restrictions, supervision.
🛜 ✖ 🔥M 🛏 💻 ➿ ✖

IOWA

▼▼▼ **La Quinta Inn & Suites Iowa** 🏨
(337) 582-2261. **$95-$185.** 204 W Frontage Rd 70647. I-10 exit 43, just n. Int corridors. **Pets:** Service with restrictions, supervision.
🛜 ✖ 🛏 💻 ➿

KINDER

AAA **▼▼▼** **BEST WESTERN Inn At Coushatta** 🏨
(337) 738-4800. **$109.** 12102 US Hwy 165 N 70648. 5 mi n of jct US 190/165. Int corridors. **Pets:** Small, other species. $25 deposit/pet. Service with restrictions, supervision. 🆂🅰🆅🅴 🛜 🔥M 🛏 💻 ➿

LAFAYETTE

▼▼▼ **Baymont Inn & Suites Lafayette Airport** 🏨
(337) 291-2916. **$69-$89, 30 day notice.** 2200 NE Evangeline Thruway 70501. I-10 exit 103A, just s. Int corridors. **Pets:** Small. $15 daily fee/room. Service with restrictions, supervision. 🛜 🛏 💻 ➿

AAA **▼▼▼** **BEST WESTERN Lafayette Inn** 🏨
(337) 769-2900. **$67-$110.** 2207 NW Evangeline Thruway 70501. I-10 exit 103A, just s. Int corridors. **Pets:** Medium. $15 daily fee/pet. Designated rooms, service with restrictions, supervision.
🆂🅰🆅🅴 🛜 🛏 💻 ➿

▼▼▼ **Candlewood Suites** 🏨
(337) 984-6900. **$85-$105.** 2105 Kaliste Saloom Rd 70508. I-10 exit 103A, 3.9 mi s, then 3.6 mi w. Int corridors. **Pets:** Accepted.
🛜 ✖ 🔥M 🛏 💻

AAA **▼▼▼▼** **Carriage House Hotel** 🏨
(337) 769-8400. **$199-$299.** 603 Silverstone Rd 70508. I-10 exit 103A, 3 mi s to Pinhook Rd, 2.1 mi sw to Kaliste Saloom Rd, 2 mi sw to Camelia Blvd, 0.4 mi nw to Silverstone Rd, then just w. Int corridors.
Pets: Accepted. 🆂🅰🆅🅴 🛜 ✖ 🛏 💻 🍽 ➿ ✖

▼▼▼▼ **Drury Inn & Suites-Lafayette** 🏨
(337) 262-0202. **$94-$164.** 120 Alcide Dominique 70506. I-10 exit 101 (SR 182), just s on University Ave, then just w. Int corridors. **Pets:** Service with restrictions, supervision. 🛜 🔥M 🛏 💻 ➿

▼▼▼▼ **Fairfield Inn & Suites by Marriott I-10** 🏨
(337) 235-9898. **$79-$139.** 2225 NW Evangeline Thruway 70501. I-10 exit 103A, just sw. Int corridors. **Pets:** Accepted.
🛜 ✖ 🔥M 🛏 💻 ➿

AAA **▼▼▼▼** **Hilton Lafayette** 🏨
(337) 235-6111. **$89-$259.** 1521 W Pinhook Rd 70503. I-10 exit 103A, 3.5 mi s, then 1.3 mi w. Int corridors. **Pets:** Medium. $50 one-time fee/room. Designated rooms, service with restrictions, crate.
🆂🅰🆅🅴 🛜 🛏 💻 🍽 ➿

▼▼▼▼ **Holiday Inn Lafayette US 167 Conference Center** 🏨
(337) 233-6815. **Call for rates.** 2032 NE Evangeline Thruway 70501. I-10 exit 103A, 0.5 mi s. Ext/int corridors. **Pets:** Accepted.
🛜 🛏 💻 🍽 ➿ ✖

▼▼▼ **La Quinta Inn & Suites Lafayette Oil Center** 🏨
(337) 291-1088. **$102-$173.** 1015 W Pinhook Rd 70503. I-10 exit 103A, 2.9 mi s on Evangeline Thruway, then 1 mi w. Int corridors. **Pets:** Service with restrictions, supervision. 🛜 ✖ 🛏 💻 ➿

▼▼▼ **La Quinta Inn Lafayette North** Ⓜ
(337) 233-5610. **$59-$115.** 2100 NE Evangeline Thruway 70501. I-10 exit 103A, 0.3 mi s on US 167. Ext corridors. **Pets:** Service with restrictions, supervision. 🛜 🛏 💻 ➿

▼▼▼ **Pear Tree Inn By Drury** 🏨
(337) 289-9907. **$84-$134.** 126 Alcide Dominique 70506. I-10 exit 101, just s on University Ave, then just w. Int corridors. **Pets:** Service with restrictions, supervision. 🛜 🔥M 💻 ➿

Residence Inn by Marriott, Lafayette Airport ⚅

(337) 232-3341. **$116-$179.** 128 James Comeaux Rd 70508. I-10 exit 103A, 3.9 mi s to Kaliste Saloom Rd, then 1 mi w. Int corridors. **Pets:** Large, other species. $100 one-time fee/room. Service with restrictions, crate. 🛜 ✖ 🔥M 🛏 ▣ 🐾 ✖

Staybridge Suites Lafayette Airport ⚅

(337) 267-4666. **$89-$219.** 129 E Kaliste Saloom Rd 70508. I-10 exit 103A, 3.9 mi s on US 90 to Kaliste Saloom Rd, then 0.7 mi w. Int corridors. **Pets:** Other species. $15 daily fee/pet. Designated rooms, service with restrictions, crate. 🛜 ✖ 🔥M 🛏 ▣ 🐾 ✖

LAKE CHARLES
Comfort Suites ⚅

(337) 436-6400. **$99-$104.** 1016 N Martin Luther King Hwy 70601. I-10 exit 33, 0.3 mi n on US 171 (Martin Luther King Hwy). Int corridors. **Pets:** Other species. $25 one-time fee/room. Designated rooms, service with restrictions, crate. 🛜 ✖ 🔥M 🛏 ▣ 🐾

La Quinta Inn & Suites-Prien ⚅

(337) 478-9889. **$131-$210.** 1201 W Prien Lake Rd 70601. I-210 exit 4 (Nelson Rd), just n, then 0.5 mi e. Int corridors. **Pets:** Service with restrictions, supervision. SAVE 🛜 ✖ 🛏 ▣ 🐾

Super 8-Lake Charles ⚅

(337) 477-1606. **$70-$150, 3 day notice.** 1350 E Prien Lake Rd 70601. I-210 exit 6B (Enterprise Blvd), 0.3 mi e, then just n. Int corridors. **Pets:** Accepted. 🛜 🛏 ▣ 🐾

MANY
Cypress Bend Resort Golf, Spa & Conference Center ⚅

(318) 590-1500. **$129-$189, 7 day notice.** 2000 Cypress Bend Pkwy 71449. 13 mi w on SR 6, 3 mi s on SR 191, 3 mi w on Cypress Bend Dr, then 1.5 mi w. Int corridors. **Pets:** Dogs only. $75 one-time fee/room. Designated rooms, service with restrictions, supervision.

SAVE 🛜 ✖ 🔥M 🛏 ▣ 🍴 🐾 ✖

MINDEN
BEST WESTERN Minden Inn ⚅

(318) 377-1001. **$85-$95.** 1411 Sibley Rd 71055. I-20 exit 47, just n. Ext corridors. **Pets:** Small. $15 daily fee/pet. Service with restrictions, supervision. SAVE 🛜 🛏 ▣ 🐾

MONROE
Residence Inn by Marriott ⚅

(318) 387-0210. **$139-$175.** 4960 Millhaven Rd 71203. I-20 exit 120, just n of Pecanland Mall. Int corridors. **Pets:** Other species. $75 one-time fee/room. Service with restrictions, supervision.

SAVE 🛜 ✖ 🔥M 🛏 ▣ 🐾 ✖

TownePlace Suites by Marriott ⚅

(318) 387-7277. **$115-$125.** 4919 Pecanland Mall Dr 71203. I-20 exit 120. Int corridors. **Pets:** Medium. $75 one-time fee/room. Service with restrictions, crate. SAVE 🛜 ✖ 🔥M 🛏 ▣ 🐾

MORGAN CITY
Holiday Inn-Morgan City ⚅

(985) 385-2200. **$110-$169.** 520 Roderick St 70380. 1.5 mi s of jct US 90 and SR 70. Ext corridors. **Pets:** Medium. $50 one-time fee/room. Service with restrictions, supervision. 🛜 🔥M 🛏 ▣ 🍴 🐾

La Quinta Inn & Suites Morgan City ⚅

(985) 300-0200. **$78-$150.** 2018 Allison St 70380. US 90 exit Dr Martin Luther King Jr Blvd, just s. Int corridors. **Pets:** Service with restrictions, supervision. 🛜 ✖ 🔥M 🛏 ▣ 🐾

NATCHITOCHES
BEST WESTERN Natchitoches Inn ⚅

(318) 352-6655. **$113-$120.** 5131 University Pkwy 71457. I-49 exit 138, just e. Int corridors. **Pets:** Accepted. SAVE 🛜 🛏 ▣ 🐾

NEW IBERIA
La Quinta Inn & Suites ⚅

(337) 321-6000. **$89-$161.** 611A Queen City Dr 70560. US 90 exit SR 14, just e. Int corridors. **Pets:** Service with restrictions, supervision. SAVE 🛜 ✖ 🛏 ▣ 🐾

Le Rosier Country Inn 🆑

(337) 367-5306. **Call for rates.** 314 E Main St 70560. US 90, 3 mi e on SR 14, just w on SR 182. Ext corridors. **Pets:** Accepted. 🛜 ✖ 🛏 ▣ 🖉

Super 8 of New Iberia ⚅

(337) 364-3030. **$85-$90.** 2714 Hwy 14 70560. 0.3 mi e of jct US 90. Ext/int corridors. **Pets:** Small, dogs only. $25 deposit/room. Designated rooms, service with restrictions, crate. 🛜 🛏 ▣ 🍴 🐾

NEW ORLEANS METROPOLITAN AREA

COVINGTON
BEST WESTERN Northpark Inn ⚅ ❀

(985) 892-2681. **$75-$149.** 625 N Hwy 190 70433. I-12 exit 63B, just n. Ext corridors. **Pets:** Large, other species. $20 daily fee/room. Designated rooms, service with restrictions, crate. SAVE 🛜 🛏 ▣ 🐾

Residence Inn New Orleans Covington/North Shore ⚅ ❀

(985) 246-7222. **$99-$189.** 101 Park Pl Blvd 70433. I-12 exit 63B, 0.5 mi n, then just w. Int corridors. **Pets:** Medium. $75 one-time fee/pet. Service with restrictions, crate. SAVE 🛜 ✖ 🛏 ▣ 🐾 ✖

Staybridge Suites Covington-Northpark ⚅

(985) 892-0003. **$119-$139.** 140 Holiday Blvd 70433. I-12 exit 63B, just n, then just w. Int corridors. **Pets:** Accepted. 🛜 🛏 ▣ 🐾 ✖

Super 8 Covington Ⓜ

(985) 892-4470. **$94.** 120 Holiday Blvd 70433. I-12 exit 63B, just nw. Ext corridors. **Pets:** Small, dogs only. $20 one-time fee/pet. Service with restrictions, supervision. SAVE 🛜 🛏 ▣ 🐾

GRETNA
La Quinta Inn New Orleans West Bank / Gretna ⚅

(504) 368-5600. **$74-$144.** 50 Terry Pkwy 70056. US 90 business route exit 9A (Terry Pkwy) southbound; US 90 (Westbank Expwy) exit 9 (Terry Pkwy/General DeGaulle) northbound. Ext corridors. **Pets:** Service with restrictions, supervision. 🛜 🛏 ▣ 🐾

KENNER
Days Inn New Orleans Airport ⚅

(504) 464-1644. **$69-$410.** 1021 Airline Dr 70062. US 61, 0.6 mi w from jct SR 49. Ext corridors. **Pets:** Accepted. 🛜 🛏 ▣ 🍴 🐾

DoubleTree by Hilton Hotel New Orleans Airport ⚅

(504) 467-3111. **$99-$209.** 2150 Veterans Blvd 70062. I-10 exit 223A (Williams Blvd), just s, then just e. Int corridors. **Pets:** Accepted. 🛜 ✖ 🛏 ▣ 🍴 🐾

Hilton New Orleans Airport ⚅ ❀

(504) 469-5000. **$99-$189.** 901 Airline Dr 70062. I-10 exit 223A (Williams Blvd), 2 mi s, then 0.8 mi w. Int corridors. **Pets:** Large, other species. $50 one-time fee/room. Designated rooms, service with restrictions, crate. SAVE 🛜 🛏 ▣ 🍴 🐾

▼▼▼ La Quinta Inn New Orleans (Airport) H
(504) 466-1401. $71-$144. 2610 Williams Blvd 70062. I-10 exit 223A (Williams Blvd), 0.3 mi s. Int corridors. Pets: Service with restrictions, supervision. 🛜 ⬛M 🛏 💻 🍴 ➤

LA PLACE

AAA ▼▼▼ BEST WESTERN La Place Inn M
(985) 651-4000. $100. 4289 Main St 70068. I-10 exit 209, just s. Ext corridors. Pets: Accepted. SAVE 🛜 🛏 💻 ➤

METAIRIE

▼▼▼ La Quinta Inn New Orleans Causeway M
(504) 835-8511. $71-$133. 3100 S I-10 Service Rd E 70001. I-10 exit 228 (Causeway Blvd), just s. Ext corridors. Pets: Service with restrictions, supervision. 🛜 ⬛M 🛏 💻 ➤

AAA ▼▼▼ Sheraton Metairie New Orleans H
(504) 837-6707. $99-$159. 4 Galleria Blvd 70001. I-10 exit 228 (Causeway Blvd), just s to 36th St, just e, then just n. Int corridors.
Pets: Accepted. SAVE 🛜 ✖ ⬛M 💻 🍴 ➤

NEW ORLEANS

AAA ▼▼▼ BEST WESTERN PLUS St. Charles Inn H
(504) 899-8888. $119-$289. 3636 St. Charles Ave 70115. US 90 business route exit St. Charles Ave, 1.8 mi s. Int corridors. Pets: $20 daily fee/room. Service with restrictions. SAVE 🛜 ✖ 🛏 💻

AAA ▼▼▼ BEST WESTERN PLUS St. Christopher Hotel H
(504) 648-0444. $99-$299. 114 Magazine St 70130. Between Canal and Common sts. Int corridors. Pets: Small. $50 deposit/room, $20 daily fee/room. Designated rooms, service with restrictions, supervision.
SAVE 🛜 🛏 💻

AAA ▼▼▼ The Bienville House Hotel H 🐾
(504) 529-2345. $79-$369, 3 day notice. 320 Decatur St 70130. Between Conti and Bienville sts. Ext/int corridors. Pets: Medium. $100 one-time fee/pet, $25 daily fee/pet. Designated rooms, service with restrictions, crate. SAVE 🛜 ✖ 🛏 🍴 ➤

▼▼▼ Clarion Inn & Suites H
(504) 299-9900. $90-$200, 3 day notice. 1300 Canal St 70112. Jct Saratoga St. Int corridors. Pets: Accepted. 🛜 ✖ 🛏 💻

▼▼▼ DoubleTree by Hilton Hotel New Orleans H
(504) 581-1300. $119-$269. 300 Canal St 70130. Corner of Canal and Tchoupitoulas sts. Int corridors. Pets: Accepted.
🛜 ✖ 🛏 💻 🍴 ➤

▼▼▼ Drury Inn & Suites-New Orleans H
(504) 529-7800. $119-$269. 820 Poydras St 70112. Between Baronne and Carondelet sts. Int corridors. Pets: Service with restrictions, supervision. 🛜 ⬛M 🛏 💻 ➤

AAA ▼▼▼ ▼▼▼ Hilton New Orleans St. Charles Avenue H
(504) 524-8890. Call for rates. 333 St. Charles Ave 70130. Jct Perdido St. Int corridors. Pets: Accepted. SAVE 🛜 ⬛M 🛏 💻 🍴 ➤

▼▼▼ The Hotel Modern New Orleans H
(504) 962-0900. Call for rates. 2 Lee Cir 70130. Just e of US 90 business route exit St. Charles Ave; on southeast block of circle. Int corridors.
Pets: Accepted. 🛜 💻 🍴

AAA ▼▼▼ ▼▼▼ Hotel Monteleone H 🐾
(504) 523-3341. $169-$399, 3 day notice. 214 Royal St 70130. Between Iberville and Bienville sts. Int corridors. Pets: $100 one-time fee/room, $25 daily fee/room. Designated rooms, service with restrictions, crate. ECO SAVE 🛜 ✖ 🛏 💻 🍴 ➤

AAA ▼▼▼ ▼▼▼ InterContinental New Orleans H
(504) 525-5566. $109-$699. 444 St. Charles Ave 70130. Between Perdido and Poydras sts. Int corridors. Pets: Accepted.
SAVE 🛜 ⬛M 🛏 💻 🍴 ➤

▼▼▼ La Quinta Inn & Suites New Orleans French Quarter H
(504) 598-9977. $83-$276. 301 Camp St 70130. Corner of Gravier and Camp sts. Int corridors. Pets: Service with restrictions, supervision.
🛜 ⬛M 🛏 💻 ➤

AAA ▼▼▼ ▼▼▼ Loews New Orleans Hotel H 🐾
(504) 595-3300. $149-$750. 300 Poydras St 70130. Corner of S Peters St. Int corridors. Pets: Other species. $25 one-time fee/room. Designated rooms, service with restrictions, supervision.
SAVE 🛜 ✖ 💻 🍴 ➤ ✖

AAA ▼▼▼ ▼▼▼ Maison Dupuy Hotel H
(504) 586-8000. $89-$289, 3 day notice. 1001 Toulouse St 70112. Between Burgundy and Rampart sts. Int corridors. Pets: Small, dogs only. $50 one-time fee/pet. Service with restrictions, crate.
SAVE 🛜 ✖ 🛏 💻 🍴 ✖

AAA ▼▼▼ Omni Royal Crescent Hotel H
(504) 527-0006. $99-$289, 3 day notice. 535 Gravier St 70130. 0.3 mi w of Canal St. Int corridors. Pets: Small. $50 one-time fee/pet. Service with restrictions, supervision. SAVE 🛜 ✖ 🛏 💻 🍴 ✖

AAA ▼▼▼ Omni Royal Orleans Hotel H
(504) 529-5333. $139-$399, 3 day notice. 621 St. Louis St 70140. At Royal and St. Louis sts. Int corridors. Pets: Small, other species. $50 one-time fee/room. Designated rooms, service with restrictions, crate.
SAVE 🛜 ✖ 🛏 💻 🍴 ➤

AAA ▼▼▼ Quality Inn & Suites Maison St. Charles H
(504) 522-0187. Call for rates. 1319 St. Charles Ave 70130. Just s of US 90 business route (Pontchartrain Expwy). Ext corridors.
Pets: Medium. $50 one-time fee/room. Designated rooms, service with restrictions, crate. SAVE 🛜 ✖ 🛏 💻 ➤

AAA ▼▼▼ Residence Inn by Marriott Downtown New Orleans H
(504) 522-1300. $104-$239, 3 day notice. 345 St. Joseph St 70130. At Tchoupitoulas St. Int corridors. Pets: Accepted.
SAVE 🛜 ✖ ⬛M 🛏 💻 ➤

AAA ▼▼▼ ▼▼▼ The Ritz-Carlton, New Orleans H
(504) 524-1331. $199-$499, 3 day notice. 921 Canal St 70112. Between Dauphine and Burgundy sts. Int corridors. Pets: Accepted.
SAVE 🛜 ✖ ⬛M 💻 🍴 ✖

AAA ▼▼▼ ▼▼▼ The Roosevelt New Orleans, A Waldorf Astoria Hotel H
(504) 648-1200. $179-$499. 123 Baronne St 70112. Just s of Canal St. Int corridors. Pets: Small. $175 one-time fee/room. Designated rooms, service with restrictions, crate. SAVE 🛜 ✖ ⬛M 🛏 🍴 ➤ ✖

AAA ▼▼▼ ▼▼▼ Royal Sonesta Hotel New Orleans H
(504) 586-0300. $179-$499, 3 day notice. 300 Bourbon St 70130. Garage entrance on Conti or Bienville sts. Int corridors. Pets: Accepted.
SAVE 🛜 ⬛M 🛏 🍴 ➤

AAA ▼▼▼ Sheraton New Orleans Hotel H
(504) 525-2500. $89-$389, 3 day notice. 500 Canal St 70130. Between Camp and Magazine sts. Int corridors. Pets: Accepted.
SAVE 🛜 ✖ ⬛M 💻 🍴 ➤ ✖

AAA ▼▼▼ Staybridge Suites Hotel H
(504) 571-1818. $89-$199. 501 Tchoupitoulas St 70130. Corner of Poydras St. Int corridors. Pets: Large, other species. $30 deposit/room, $10 daily fee/room. Designated rooms, service with restrictions, crate.
SAVE 🛜 ⬛M 🛏 💻 ➤

(AAA) ▼▼ ▼▼ **Westin New Orleans Canal Place** H ❀

(504) 566-7006. **$99-$329, 3 day notice.** 100 Iberville St 70130. At Canal Place, near Mississippi River. Int corridors. **Pets:** Medium, dogs only. Service with restrictions, supervision.

SAVE 🛜 ✕ 🍴 💻 🍴 ➰

(AAA) ▼▼▼ **W French Quarter** H

(504) 581-1200. **$139-$429, 3 day notice.** 316 Chartres St 70130. Between Conti and Bienville sts. Int corridors. **Pets:** Accepted.

SAVE 🛜 ✕ 💻 ➰

(AAA) ▼▼ ▼▼ **Windsor Court Hotel** H ❀

(504) 523-6000. **$190-$685, 3 day notice.** 300 Gravier St 70130. Between Magazine and Tchoupitoulas sts. Int corridors. **Pets:** Medium. $150 one-time fee/room. Service with restrictions, supervision.

SAVE 🛜 ✕ 💻 🍴 ➰ ✕

(AAA) ▼▼ ▼▼ **W New Orleans** H

(504) 525-9444. **$109-$339, 3 day notice.** 333 Poydras St 70130. Jct Poydras and S Peters sts; close to Riverfront area/convention center. Int corridors. **Pets:** Accepted. SAVE 🛜 ✕ 🗄 🍴 ➰

SLIDELL

▼▼ ▼▼ **La Quinta Inn New Orleans/Slidell** H

(985) 643-9770. **$63-$129.** 794 E I-10 Service Rd 70461. I-10 exit 266 (Gause Blvd), just se. Ext corridors. **Pets:** Service with restrictions, supervision. 🛜 🍴 💻 ➰

END METROPOLITAN AREA

OPELOUSAS

▼▼▼ **Evangeline Downs Hotel, an Ascend Collection hotel** H

(337) 407-2121. **$89-$125.** 2235 Creswell Ln Lot B 70570. I-49 exit 18, 0.6 mi e on SR 31, then 0.7 mi n on entry driveway. Int corridors. **Pets:** Small. $25 daily fee/pet. Service with restrictions, supervision.

🛜 🗄 🍴 💻 🍴 ➰

RUSTON

▼▼▼ **Days Inn** H

(318) 251-2360. **$70-$150.** 1801 N Service Rd E 71270. I-20 exit 86, just ne. Ext corridors. **Pets:** Small. $20 daily fee/room. Service with restrictions, supervision. 🛜 🍴 💻 ➰

ST. FRANCISVILLE

▼▼ ▼▼ **Lake Rosemound Inn Bed & Breakfast** BB

(225) 635-3176. **$80-$135, 4 day notice.** 10473 Lindsey Ln 70775. 13 mi n on SR 61, then 3 mi w using Rosemound Loop, Sligo Rd, Lake Rosemound Rd and Lindsey Ln, follow signs. Ext/int corridors. **Pets:** Dogs only. No service. 🛜 ✕ ✕

SCOTT

▼▼ ▼▼ **Howard Johnson Inn Lafayette West** H

(337) 593-0849. **$55-$65.** 103 Harold Gauthe Dr 70583. I-10 exit 97, just s. Int corridors. **Pets:** Medium, other species. $10 daily fee/pet. Service with restrictions, crate. 🛜 🍴 💻 ➰

SHREVEPORT

▼▼ ▼▼ **Candlewood Suites** H

(318) 635-8062. **$69-$109.** 5020 Hollywood Ave 71109. I-20 exit 13, 0.4 mi s, then just e. Int corridors. **Pets:** Small. $25 one-time fee/pet. Service with restrictions, supervision. 🛜 ✕ 🗄 🍴 💻 ➰

(AAA) ▼▼ ▼▼ **Eldorado Resort Casino Shreveport** H

(318) 220-0711. **$92-$212.** 451 Clyde Fant Pkwy 71101. I-20 exit 19A (Spring St), 0.8 mi n to Crockett St, just e, then just n. Int corridors. **Pets:** Accepted. SAVE 🛜 🍴 💻 🍴

(AAA) ▼▼ ▼▼ **Holiday Inn Shreveport Airport West** H

(318) 688-3000. **Call for rates.** 5555 Financial Plaza 71129. I-20 exit 10 (Pines Rd), 1 mi e on frontage road. Int corridors. **Pets:** Accepted.

SAVE 🛜 ✕ 💻 🍴 ➰ ✕

▼▼ ▼▼ **Homewood Suites - Shreveport** H

(318) 549-2000. **$111-$129.** 5485 Financial Plaza 71129. I-20 exit 10 (Pines Rd), just s, then 1.2 mi e. Int corridors. **Pets:** Large, other species. $20 daily fee/room. Service with restrictions, supervision.

🛜 🍴 💻 ➰ ✕

▼▼ ▼▼ **La Quinta Inn & Suites Shreveport Airport** H

(318) 671-1100. **$87-$166.** 6700 Financial Cir 71129. I-20 exit 10 (Pines Rd), just s, then 0.5 mi e. Int corridors. **Pets:** Service with restrictions, supervision. 🛜 🗄 🍴 💻 ➰

(AAA) ▼▼ ▼▼ **Residence Inn by Marriott Shreveport - Airport** H

(318) 635-8000. **$95-$107.** 4910 W Monkhouse Dr 71109. I-20 exit 13, just nw. Int corridors. **Pets:** Accepted.

SAVE 🛜 ✕ 🗄 🍴 💻 ➰ ✕

VILLE PLATTE

(AAA) ▼▼ ▼▼ **BEST WESTERN Ville Platte** H

(337) 360-9961. **$91.** 1919 E Main St (Hwy 167) 70586. I-49 exit 23, 14 mi nw. Int corridors. **Pets:** Small, dogs only. $10 daily fee/pet. Designated rooms, service with restrictions, crate. SAVE 🛜 🍴 💻 ➰

WALKER

▼▼ ▼▼ **La Quinta Inn & Suites Walker** H

(225) 667-1966. **$111-$175.** 13450 Vera McGowan 70785. I-12 exit 15, just n. Int corridors. **Pets:** Service with restrictions, supervision.

🛜 ✕ 🍴 💻 ➰

WEST MONROE

▼▼ ▼▼ **Quality Inn & Suites-West Monroe** H

(318) 387-2711. **$77-$120.** 503 Constitution Dr 71292. I-20 exit 114 (Thomas Rd), just s to Constitution Dr, then 0.6 mi w. Int corridors. **Pets:** Medium. $25 one-time fee/room. Designated rooms, crate.

🛜 🗄 🍴 💻 ➰

WINNFIELD

(AAA) ▼▼ ▼▼ **BEST WESTERN of Winnfield** M

(318) 628-3993. **$66-$87.** 700 W Court St 71483. Jct US 84 and 167, just e. Ext corridors. **Pets:** Other species. $10 daily fee/room. Service with restrictions. SAVE 🛜 🍴 💻 🍴 ➰

ZACHARY

(AAA) ▼▼ ▼▼ **BEST WESTERN Zachary Inn** H ❀

(225) 658-2550. **$91.** 4030 Hwy 19 70791. Just s of jct SR 64. Int corridors. **Pets:** Medium, other species. $20 daily fee/room. Service with restrictions, crate. SAVE 🛜 🍴 💻 ➰

MAINE

AUBURN

▼▼ Fireside Inn & Suites 🅷 🐾

(207) 777-1777. **$80-$120.** 1777 Washington St 04210. I-95 exit 75, 0.5 mi s on US 202, SR 4 and 100. Ext/int corridors. **Pets:** $20 daily fee/pet. Designated rooms, service with restrictions, supervision.

▼▼▼▼ Residence Inn by Marriott Auburn 🅷

(207) 777-3400. **$119-$309.** 670 Turner St 04210. I-95 exit 80 southbound; exit 75 northbound; from SR 100, just w. Int corridors.
Pets: Accepted. 🛰 ⨉ 🕭M 🔌 💻 🛳 ⨉

▼ Sleepy Time Motel 🅼

(207) 783-1435. **$89-$99.** 46 Danville Corner Rd 04210. I-95 exit 75, 0.5 mi ne on US 202, then just e. Ext corridors. **Pets:** Small. $10 daily fee/pet. Designated rooms, service with restrictions, supervision.

🛰 ⨉ 🔌 💻

AUGUSTA

⟨AAA⟩ ▼▼▼ BEST WESTERN PLUS Civic Center Inn 🅷 🐾

(207) 622-4751. **$89-$189.** 110 Community Dr 04330. I-95 exit 112A northbound; exit 112 southbound, just s on SR 8, 11 and 27. Int corridors. **Pets:** Large, other species. $10 daily fee/room. Service with restrictions, supervision. 💲AVE 🛰 🕭M 🔌 💻 🍴 🛳

▼▼▼ Comfort Inn 🅷 🐾

(207) 623-1000. **$89-$149, 3 day notice.** 281 Civic Center Dr 04330. I-95 exit 112B northbound; exit 112 southbound. Int corridors. **Pets:** Large, other species. $10 one-time fee/room. Designated rooms, service with restrictions, crate. 🛰 🔌 💻 🛳

▼▼▼ Senator Inn & Spa 🅷 🐾

(207) 622-5804. **$80-$229.** 284 Western Ave 04330. I-95 exit 109 northbound; exit 109A southbound, on US 202, SR 11 and 100. Ext/int corridors. **Pets:** Other species. $12 daily fee/room. Service with restrictions.

🄴🄲🄾 🛰 ⨉ 🔌 💻 🍴 🛳 ⨉

BANGOR

⟨AAA⟩ ▼▼▼▼ BEST WESTERN White House 🅷 🐾

(207) 862-3737. **$112-$290.** 155 Littlefield Ave 04401. I-95 exit 180 (Coldbrook Rd), 5.5 mi s of downtown. Ext/int corridors. **Pets:** Large, other species. $10 daily fee/pet. Designated rooms, service with restrictions, supervision. 💲AVE 🛰 🔌 💻 🛳 ⨉

▼▼ Econo Lodge Inn & Suites 🅼

(207) 945-0111. **$75-$175.** 327 Odlin Rd 04401. I-95 exit 182B, just e on US 2 and SR 100. Int corridors. **Pets:** Other species. $10 deposit/room. Service with restrictions, supervision. 🛰 🕭M 🔌 💻 🛳

⟨AAA⟩ ▼▼▼▼ Fairfield Inn by Marriott Bangor 🅷

(207) 990-0001. **$129-$199.** 300 Odlin Rd 04401. I-95 exit 182B, just e on US 2 and SR 100. Int corridors. **Pets:** Other species. $20 daily fee/room. Service with restrictions, crate.

🄴🄲🄾 💲AVE 🛰 ⨉ 🕭M 🔌 💻 🛳

▼▼ Fireside Inn & Suites 🅷 🐾

(207) 942-1234. **$89-$189, 7 day notice.** 570 Main St 04401. I-395 exit 3B. Int corridors. **Pets:** Other species. $10 daily fee/pet. Service with restrictions, supervision. 🄴🄲🄾 🛰 🔌 💻 🍴

⟨AAA⟩ ▼▼▼▼ Four Points by Sheraton Bangor 🅷 🐾

(207) 947-6721. **$125-$199.** 308 Godfrey Blvd 04401. At Bangor International Airport. Int corridors. **Pets:** Large. $20 one-time fee/room. Service with restrictions, supervision. 💲AVE 🛰 ⨉ 🕭M 🔌 💻 🍴 🛳

▼▼▼ Holiday Inn-Bangor 🅷

(207) 947-0101. **Call for rates.** 404 Odlin Rd 04401. I-95 exit 182B; jct Odlin Rd and I-395. Int corridors. **Pets:** Accepted.

🛰 ⨉ 🕭M 🔌 💻 🍴 🛳 ⨉

⟨AAA⟩ ▼▼▼ Howard Johnson Inn 🅷

(207) 942-5251. **$55-$122.** 336 Odlin Rd 04401. I-95 exit 182B; jct Odlin Rd and I-395. Int corridors. **Pets:** Dogs only. $10 daily fee/pet. Designated rooms, service with restrictions, supervision.

💲AVE 🛰 🔌 💻 🍴 🛳

▼▼ Quality Inn Bangor 🅷

(207) 942-7899. **$69-$139.** 750 Hogan Rd 04401. I-95 exit 187 (Hogan Rd), 0.5 mi nw. Int corridors. **Pets:** $10 one-time fee/room. Service with restrictions, supervision. 🛰 ⨉ 🔌 💻

▼▼ Ramada 🅷

(207) 947-6961. **$89-$129.** 357 Odlin Rd 04401. I-95 exit 182B; jct Odlin Rd and I-395. Int corridors. **Pets:** Accepted. 🛰 🔌 💻 🍴 🛳

▼▼ Riverside Inn 🅷

(207) 973-4100. **$99-$159, 7 day notice.** 495 State St 04401. Adjacent to Eastern Maine Medical Center. Int corridors. **Pets:** Medium. $100 deposit/pet, $5 daily fee/pet. Designated rooms, service with restrictions, supervision. 🛰 ⨉ 🔌 💻

BAR HARBOR

⟨AAA⟩ ▼▼▼▼ Atlantic Eyrie Lodge 🅷

(207) 288-9786. **$85-$249, 7 day notice.** 6 Norman Rd 04609. 1 mi w on SR 3 to Highbrook Rd. Ext corridors. **Pets:** Large. $35 one-time fee/room. Designated rooms, service with restrictions, supervision.

💲AVE 🛰 ⨉ 🕭M 🔌 💻 🛳

⟨AAA⟩ ▼▼▼▼ Atlantic Oceanside Hotel & Conference Center 🅷 🐾

(207) 288-5801. **$119-$399, 7 day notice.** 119 Eden St 04609. 1.8 mi w on SR 3. Ext/int corridors. **Pets:** Dogs only. $35 daily fee/pet. Designated rooms, service with restrictions, supervision.

🄴🄲🄾 💲AVE 🛰 ⨉ 🔌 💻 🛳 ⨉

⟨AAA⟩ ▼▼▼ A Wonder View Inn 🅷 🐾

(207) 288-3358. **$99-$269, 3 day notice.** 50 Eden St 04609. 0.5 mi w on SR 3. Ext corridors. **Pets:** $20 daily fee/pet. Designated rooms, service with restrictions, supervision. 💲AVE 🛰 ⨉ 🔌 💻 🍴 🛳

◆◆◆ ▽▽▽ Balance Rock Inn 1903 [BB]
(207) 288-2610. **$155-$635, 14 day notice.** 21 Albert Meadow 04609. Just s of Main St; center. Ext/int corridors. **Pets:** Other species. $40 daily fee/pet. Designated rooms, service with restrictions, crate.
[SAVE] 📶 ✕ 🛏 🖵 🏊

◆◆◆ ▽▽▽▽ Bar Harbor Regency Holiday Inn [H]
(207) 288-9723. **Call for rates.** 123 Eden St 04609. 1 mi w on SR 3. Int corridors. **Pets:** Accepted. [SAVE] 📶 ✕ 🛏 🖵 🍴 🏊 ✕

▽▽ ▽▽ Hutchins Mountain View Cottages [CA] ❀
(207) 288-4833. **$74-$98, 14 day notice.** 286 State Rt 3 04609. On SR 3, 4 mi w. Ext corridors. **Pets:** Other species. Service with restrictions.
[ECO] 📶 🛏 🖵 🏊 🐾 ✕

◆◆◆ ▽▽▽▽ West Street Hotel [H]
(207) 288-0825. **$139-$1200, 3 day notice.** 50 West St 04609. Jct Main St. Int corridors. **Pets:** Accepted.
[SAVE] 📶 ✕ �òM 🛏 🖵 🍴 🏊

BATH

◆◆◆ ▽▽▽▽ Holiday Inn Bath/Brunswick [H]
(207) 443-9741. **$79-$199.** 139 Richardson St 04530. 0.3 mi s on US 1. Int corridors. **Pets:** Other species. $25 one-time fee/pet. Designated rooms, service with restrictions, supervision.
[ECO] [SAVE] 📶 ✕ �òM 🛏 🖵 🍴 🏊

BELFAST

◆◆◆ ▽▽▽ Belfast Harbor Inn [H]
(207) 338-2740. **$64-$169.** 91 Searsport Ave (Rt 1) 04915. On US 1, 1.2 mi n from jct SR 3. Ext/int corridors. **Pets:** Dogs only. $10 daily fee/pet. Designated rooms, service with restrictions, supervision.
[SAVE] 📶 🛏 🏊

▽▽▽▽ Fireside Inn & Suites, Ocean's Edge [H] ❀
(207) 338-2090. **$85-$329.** 159 Searsport Ave 04915. On US 1, 2 mi n from jct SR 3. Int corridors. **Pets:** $20 daily fee/room. Designated rooms, service with restrictions, supervision.
[ECO] 📶 �òM 🛏 🖵 🍴 🏊 ✕

▽▽ Gull Motel [M]
(207) 338-4030. **$59-$159, 3 day notice.** 196 Searsport Ave 04915. On US 1, 3 mi n from jct SR 3. Ext corridors. **Pets:** Medium, dogs only. $20 daily fee/pet. Designated rooms, service with restrictions, supervision.
📶 🛏

◆◆◆ ▽▽ ▽▽ Yankee Clipper Motel [M]
(207) 338-2353. **$69-$139.** 50 Searsport Ave 04915. On US 1, 1 mi n from jct SR 3. Ext corridors. **Pets:** Dogs only. $10 daily fee/pet. Designated rooms, service with restrictions, supervision.
[SAVE] 📶 ✕ 🛏 🖵

BETHEL

▽▽ ▽▽ The Inn At the Rostay [M]
(207) 824-3111. **$68-$140, 14 day notice.** 186 Mayville Rd (US 2) 04217. On US 2, 2 mi e. Ext corridors. **Pets:** Other species. $20 daily fee/pet. Designated rooms, service with restrictions, supervision.
📶 ✕ 🛏 🏊

BOOTHBAY HARBOR

▽▽ ▽▽ Beach Cove Waterfront Inn [M] ❀
(207) 633-0353. **Call for rates.** 48 Lakeview Rd 04538. Off SR 27. Ext corridors. **Pets:** Medium, dogs only. $20 one-time fee/pet. Designated rooms, service with restrictions, supervision. 📶 ✕ 🛏 🖵 🏊

▽▽ ▽▽ Boothbay Harbor Inn [H] ❀
(207) 633-6302. **$99-$249, 3 day notice.** 31 Atlantic Ave 04538. 0.3 mi e of SR 27; on east side of Boothbay Harbor. Ext/int corridors. **Pets:** Other species. $20 daily fee/room. Designated rooms, service with restrictions, supervision. 📶 ✕ 🛏 🖵 🍴

▽▽ ▽▽ Cap'n Fish's Waterfront Inn [H]
(207) 633-6605. **$75-$175, 7 day notice.** 65 Atlantic Ave 04538. 0.3 mi se of SR 27; on east side of Boothbay Harbor. Ext corridors.
Pets: Accepted. 📶 🛏 🖵

◆◆◆ ▽▽▽ Flagship Inn [M] ❀
(207) 633-5094. **$74-$144, 3 day notice.** 200 Townsend Ave 04538. On SR 27, just n of jct SR 96. Ext corridors. **Pets:** $10 daily fee/pet. Designated rooms, service with restrictions. [ECO] [SAVE] 📶 🛏 🏊

◆◆◆ ▽▽▽ Tugboat Inn [H] ❀
(207) 633-4434. **$85-$265, 3 day notice.** 80 Commercial St 04538. Center. Ext corridors. **Pets:** $20 daily fee/pet. Designated rooms, service with restrictions, supervision. [SAVE] 📶 ✕ 🛏 🖵 🍴

BRUNSWICK

◆◆◆ ▽▽▽▽ The Inn at Brunswick Station [H] ❀
(207) 837-6565. **$129-$229.** 4 Noble St 04011. Center. Int corridors. **Pets:** $50 one-time fee/room. Designated rooms, service with restrictions, supervision. [SAVE] 📶 ✕ �òM 🖵 🍴

BRYANT POND

▽▽ Mollyockett Motel & Swim Spa [M]
(207) 674-2345. **$70-$99.** 1132 S Main St 04219. 1.3 mi n on SR 26 from jct SR 219. Ext/int corridors. **Pets:** Dogs only. Service with restrictions, supervision. 📶 ✕ 🛏 🖵 🍴 🏊 ✕

BUCKSPORT

▽▽ Bucksport Motor Inn [M]
(207) 469-3111. **$69-$109.** 70 US Route 1 04416. Center. Ext corridors. **Pets:** Dogs only. $20 one-time fee/room. Designated rooms, service with restrictions, supervision. 📶 ✕ 🛏 🖵

CAMDEN

◆◆◆ ▽▽▽▽ Camden Riverhouse Hotel [H] ❀
(207) 236-0500. **$109-$250, 14 day notice.** 11 Tannery Ln 04843. Center; just e of Washington St. Int corridors. **Pets:** Dogs only. $15 daily fee/room. Designated rooms, service with restrictions, supervision.
[ECO] [SAVE] 📶 ✕ 🛏 🖵 🏊 ✕

◆◆◆ ▽▽▽▽ Grand Harbor Inn [H] ❀
(207) 230-7177. **$159-$549.** 14 Bay View Landing 04843. Center; just e of Main St. Int corridors. **Pets:** Dogs only. $35 daily fee/pet. Designated rooms, service with restrictions, supervision. [SAVE] 📶 ✕ 🛏 🖵

◆◆◆ ▽▽▽▽ Hartstone Inn & Hideaway [CI] ❀
(207) 236-4259. **$105-$295, 14 day notice.** 41 Elm St 04843. US 1, just s of Washington St; center. Ext/int corridors. **Pets:** Small, dogs only. $20 one-time fee/room. Designated rooms, supervision.
[SAVE] 📶 ✕ 🛏 🖵 🍴

◆◆◆ ▽▽▽▽ Lord Camden Inn [H] ❀
(207) 236-4325. **$99-$349.** 24 Main St 04843. Just n of Washington St; center. Int corridors. **Pets:** Dogs only. $25 daily fee/pet. Designated rooms, service with restrictions, crate. [ECO] [SAVE] 📶 ✕ 🛏 🖵

CAPE ELIZABETH

◆◆◆ ▽▽ ▽▽ Inn by the Sea [H]
(207) 799-3134. **$199-$1799, 14 day notice.** 40 Bowery Beach Rd (SR 77) 04107. On SR 77, 7 mi s. Ext/int corridors. **Pets:** Accepted.
[ECO] [SAVE] 📶 ✕ �òM 🛏 🖵 🍴 🏊 ✕

CARIBOU

◆◆◆ ▽▽▽▽ Caribou Inn & Convention Center [H]
(207) 498-3733. **$98-$146.** 19 Main St 04736. 3 mi s on US 1. Int corridors. **Pets:** Other species. $35 one-time fee/room. Designated rooms, service with restrictions, supervision.
[SAVE] 📶 🛏 🖵 🍴 🏊 ✕

◈◈ Crown Park Inn **H**

(207) 493-3311. **Call for rates.** 30 Access Hwy 04736. On SR 89, 0.4 mi e of jct US 1. Int corridors. **Pets:** Accepted.

CASCO

◈◈ Alyssas Motel on Thomas Pond **M**

(207) 655-2223. **$75-$169, 30 day notice.** 11 Roosevelt Tr 04015. On US 302 at the Casco/Raymond line. Ext corridors. **Pets:** Accepted.

CASTINE

◈◈◈ Pentagoet Inn **CI**

(207) 326-8616. **Call for rates.** 26 Main St 04421. Center. Int corridors. **Pets:** Accepted.

EAGLE LAKE

◈◈◈ Overlook Motel & Lakeside Cabins **M**

(207) 444-4535. **$78.** 3232 Aroostook Rd 04739. On SR 11; center. Ext/int corridors. **Pets:** $10 daily fee/pet. Service with restrictions, supervision.

EASTPORT

◈◈ The Motel East **M** ❖

(207) 853-4747. **$75-$150.** 23A Water St 04631. Center. Ext corridors. **Pets:** Other species. $20 one-time fee/room. Designated rooms, service with restrictions, supervision.

EDGECOMB

AAA ◈◈◈ Sheepscot Harbour Village & Resort **H**

(207) 882-6343. **$119-$369, 14 day notice.** 306 Eddy Rd 04556. 1 mi w on US 1; on east side of Davies Bridge; 1 mi e of Wiscasset. Ext/int corridors. **Pets:** Accepted.

ELLSWORTH

AAA ◈ Acadia Birches Knights Inn **M**

(207) 667-3621. **$95-$145.** 19 Thorsen Rd 04605. US 1, 1.5 mi n of SR 3. Ext corridors. **Pets:** Dogs only. $25 one-time fee/pet. Designated rooms, service with restrictions, supervision.

AAA ◈◈ Comfort Inn **H** ❖

(207) 667-1345. **$109-$159.** 130 High St 04605. Center on US 1 and SR 3. Int corridors. **Pets:** $25 daily fee/pet. Designated rooms, supervision.

AAA ◈◈ Ellsworth Ramada **H**

(207) 667-9341. **$119-$189.** 215 High St 04605. Jct US 1, 1A and SR 3. Int corridors. **Pets:** Dogs only. $20 daily fee/pet. Designated rooms, service with restrictions, supervision.

AAA ◈◈ Sunset Motel **CA**

(207) 667-8390. **$65-$78.** 210 Twin Hill Rd 04605. 6 mi s on US 1 and SR 3. Ext corridors. **Pets:** Medium. $10 daily fee/pet. Service with restrictions, supervision.

AAA ◈◈◈ Twilite Motel **M**

(207) 667-8165. **$54-$126.** 147 Bucksport Rd 04605. Jct US 1A, 1.5 mi w on US 1 and SR 3. Ext corridors. **Pets:** Small, dogs only. $10 daily fee/room. Designated rooms, service with restrictions, supervision.

FALMOUTH

AAA ◈ Falmouth Inn **M**

(207) 781-2120. **$69-$156.** 209 US 1 04105. I-295 exit 10, just e on Buckman Rd, then just s. Ext corridors. **Pets:** Dogs only. $10 daily fee/pet. Designated rooms, service with restrictions, supervision.

FREEPORT

AAA ◈◈◈◈ BEST WESTERN PLUS Freeport Inn **H** ❖

(207) 865-3106. **$90-$220.** 31 US 1 04032. I-295 exit 17, 1 mi n. Ext/int corridors. **Pets:** Other species. $20 one-time fee/room. Designated rooms, service with restrictions.

◈◈◈ Captain Briggs House B & B **BB**

(207) 865-1868. **$105-$235, 5 day notice.** 8 Maple Ave 04032. Just n of downtown, then just w. Int corridors. **Pets:** Dogs only. $15 one-time fee/room.

AAA ◈◈ Econo Lodge **M** ❖

(207) 865-3777. **$75-$160.** 537 US Rt 1 04032. I-295 exit 20, 0.3 mi s. Ext corridors. **Pets:** Large, other species. $10 daily fee/room. Designated rooms, service with restrictions.

AAA ◈◈◈ Harraseeket Inn **CI** ❖

(207) 865-9377. **$135-$305, 3 day notice.** 162 Main St 04032. I-295 exit 22, 0.5 mi e. Int corridors. **Pets:** Other species. $25 daily fee/pet. Designated rooms, service with restrictions.

GREENVILLE

◈◈ Chalet Moosehead Lakefront Motel **M**

(207) 695-2950. **$79-$165, 7 day notice.** 12 N Birch St 04442. 1.5 mi w on SR 15. Ext corridors. **Pets:** Dogs only. $20 deposit/pet. Designated rooms, service with restrictions, supervision.

AAA ◈◈ Kineo View Motor Lodge **M**

(207) 695-4470. **$79-$199.** 50 Overlook Dr 04441. 2.5 mi s on SR 15; gravel access road from highway. Ext corridors. **Pets:** $10 daily fee/room. Designated rooms, service with restrictions, supervision.

AAA ◈◈◈◈ The Lodge at Moosehead Lake **CI**

(207) 695-4400. **$250-$695, 21 day notice.** 368 Lily Bay Rd 04441. 2.5 mi n. Int corridors. **Pets:** Accepted.

HANCOCK

◈◈◈ Le Domaine Inn **CI**

(207) 422-3395. **Call for rates.** 1513 US Rt 1 04640. On US 1, 9 mi e of Ellsworth; center. Ext corridors. **Pets:** Accepted.

JACKMAN

◈◈ Bishop's Country Inn Motel **M**

(207) 668-3231. **$65-$100.** 461 Main St 04945. On US 201; center. Ext corridors. **Pets:** $10 daily fee/pet. Service with restrictions, crate.

KENNEBUNK

AAA ◈◈ Turnpike Motel **M**

(207) 985-4404. **Call for rates.** 77 Old Alewive Rd 04043. I-95 exit 25, just e on SR 35, then just n. Ext/int corridors. **Pets:** Very small, other species. $10 daily fee/pet. Designated rooms, supervision.

KENNEBUNKPORT

◈◈◈ The Captain Jefferds Inn **BB**

(207) 967-2311. **$149-$399, 14 day notice.** 5 Pearl St 04046. From Dock Square, 0.3 mi s on Ocean Ave, then just ne; corner of Pearl and Pleasant sts. Ext/int corridors. **Pets:** Accepted.

AAA ◈◈◈ The Colony Hotel **H** ❖

(207) 967-3331. **$134-$294, 7 day notice.** 140 Ocean Ave 04046. From Dock Square, 1 mi s. Int corridors. **Pets:** Other species. $30 daily fee/pet. Service with restrictions.

Lodge At Turbat's Creek M

(207) 967-8700. **$69-$179, 14 day notice.** 7 Turbats Creek Rd 04046. From Dock Square, 0.5 mi se on Maine St, 0.6 mi ne on Wildes District Rd, then just se. Ext corridors. **Pets:** $25 daily fee/room. Designated rooms, service with restrictions, supervision. 🛰️ ❌ 🆓 🛏️ 🔄

The Yachtsman Lodge & Marina M

(207) 967-2511. **$129-$399, 30 day notice.** 57 Ocean Ave 04046. From Dock Square, just s. Ext corridors. **Pets:** Accepted.
🛰️ ❌ 🆓 🛏️ 🔄

KITTERY

The Coachman Inn M

(207) 439-4434. **$69-$209.** 380 US Rt 1 03904. I-95 exit 2, 1 mi n. Ext/ int corridors. **Pets:** $10 daily fee/pet. Designated rooms, service with restrictions, supervision. 🆓 🛰️ ❌ 🆓 🛏️ 🔄

LINCOLNVILLE

Victorian By The Sea BB

(207) 236-3785. **$149-$269, 10 day notice.** 33 Seaview Dr 04849. On US 1, 1.2 mi s of jct SR 173. Int corridors. **Pets:** Small. $15 daily fee/pet. Designated rooms, service with restrictions, supervision.
🛰️ ❌ 🔤 🔤 🔄

LUBEC

The Eastland Motel M 🐾

(207) 733-5501. **$70-$85.** 385 County Rd 04652. Jct US 1 and SR 189, 8.4 mi e on SR 189. Ext/int corridors. **Pets:** $10 daily fee/room. Designated rooms, supervision. 🛰️ ❌ 🆓 🛏️ 🔄

MACHIAS

The Bluebird Motel M

(207) 255-3332. **$75-$85, 7 day notice.** 231 Dublin St 04654. On US 1, 1 mi s. Ext corridors. **Pets:** Accepted. 🆓 🛰️ 🆓 🛏️

Machias Motor Inn M

(207) 255-4861. **$84-$124.** 103 Main St 04654. 0.5 mi e on US 1. Ext corridors. **Pets:** Dogs only. $10 daily fee/pet. Service with restrictions, supervision. 🆓 🛰️ 🛏️ 🔄

MILFORD

Milford Motel On The River M

(207) 827-3200. **$72-$135, 3 day notice.** 174 Main Rd 04461. 0.5 mi n on US 2. Ext/int corridors. **Pets:** Medium, dogs only. Designated rooms, service with restrictions, supervision. 🆓 🛰️ 🛏️ 🔄

MILLINOCKET

Baxter Park Inn H

(207) 723-9777. **$79-$119.** 935 Central St 04462. 0.8 mi e on SR 11 and 157. Int corridors. **Pets:** Medium, dogs only. $10 daily fee/pet. Service with restrictions, supervision. 🛰️ 🛏️ 🔄

NAPLES

Augustus Bove House BB

(207) 693-6365. **$125-$250, 45 day notice.** 11 Sebago Rd 04055. Corner of US 302 and SR 114. Int corridors. **Pets:** Large, dogs only. $10 daily fee/pet. Designated rooms, service with restrictions, supervision.
🛰️ ❌ 🛏️ 🔄

NEWCASTLE

Newcastle Inn BB

(207) 563-5685. **$155-$275, 14 day notice.** 60 River Rd 04553. Jct US 1 and River Rd, 0.5 mi nw. Ext/int corridors. **Pets:** Accepted.
🛰️ ❌ 🔤

NORTHPORT

Point Lookout Resort & Conference Center CA

(207) 789-2000. **$129-$449, 3 day notice.** 67 Atlantic Hwy 04849. 4 mi s on US 1; at Lincolnville town line. Ext corridors. **Pets:** $15 daily fee/pet. Designated rooms, service with restrictions, crate.
🌿 🆓 🛰️ ❌ 🛏️ 🖥️ 🍴 ❌

OGUNQUIT

Studio East Motor Inn M

(207) 646-7297. **Call for rates.** 267 Main St 03907. On US 1; center. Ext corridors. **Pets:** Accepted. 🛰️ ❌ 🛏️

OLD ORCHARD BEACH

Sea View Inn H

(207) 934-4180. **Call for rates.** 65 W Grand Ave (SR 9) 04064. 0.5 mi w on SR 9 (W Grand Ave). Ext corridors. **Pets:** Dogs only. $10 daily fee/pet. Supervision. 🆓 🛰️ ❌ 🛏️ 🖥️ 🔄

ORONO

Black Bear Inn Conference Center & Suites H

(207) 866-7120. **$99-$189, 7 day notice.** 4 Godfrey Dr 04473. I-95 exit 193 (Stillwater Ave). Int corridors. **Pets:** $10 deposit/pet. Designated rooms, service with restrictions, supervision.
🛰️ ❌ 🆓 🛏️ 🖥️ 🍴

University Inn Academic Suites H

(207) 866-4921. **$86-$149.** 5 College Ave 04473. I-95 exit 191, 1.6 mi n on US 2; 8 mi n of Bangor. Int corridors. **Pets:** Designated rooms, service with restrictions, supervision. 🛰️ ❌ 🛏️ 🖥️ 🔄

POLAND SPRING

Wolf Cove Inn BB 🐾

(207) 998-4976. **$129-$169, 14 day notice.** 5 Jordan Shore Dr 04274. Just w of SR 11. Int corridors. **Pets:** Dogs only. $25 one-time fee/room. Service with restrictions, supervision. 🛰️ ❌ 🔤

PORTLAND

Clarion Portland H

(207) 774-5611. **$79-$239.** 1230 Congress St 04102. I-295 exit 5, just w on SR 22. Int corridors. **Pets:** Accepted.
🛰️ ❌ 🆓 🛏️ 🖥️ 🍴 🔄

Embassy Suites Hotel H

(207) 775-2200. **$109-$289.** 1050 Westbrook St 04102. At Portland International Jetport. Int corridors. **Pets:** Medium. $50 one-time fee/pet. Designated rooms, service with restrictions.
🆓 🛰️ 🆓 🛏️ 🖥️ 🍴 🔄 ❌

Fireside Inn & Suites H 🐾

(207) 774-5601. **$110-$240.** 81 Riverside St 04103. I-95 exit 48. Int corridors. **Pets:** Other species. $10 daily fee/pet. Designated rooms, service with restrictions, supervision. 🛰️ 🆓 🛏️ 🖥️ 🍴 🔄 ❌

Hilton Garden Inn Portland Airport H

(207) 828-1117. **$129-$309.** 145 Jetport Blvd 04102. At Portland International Jetport. Int corridors. **Pets:** Medium, dogs only. $50 one-time fee/ pet. Designated rooms, service with restrictions, supervision.
🆓 🛰️ 🆓 🛏️ 🖥️ 🍴 🔄

Hilton Garden Inn Portland Downtown Waterfront H

(207) 780-0780. **$159-$339.** 65 Commercial St 04101. In the Old Port; across from Casco Bay ferry terminal. Int corridors. **Pets:** Accepted.
🛰️ ❌ 🆓 🛏️ 🖥️ 🍴 🔄

▼▼▼ La Quinta Inn & Suites Portland 🅷
(207) 871-0611. **$87-$254.** 340 Park Ave 04102. I-295 exit 5A southbound; exit 5 northbound, e on SR 22. Int corridors. **Pets:** Service with restrictions, supervision.

⨁ ▼▼▼ ▼▼▼ Portland Harbor Hotel 🅷
(207) 775-9090. **$189-$399.** 468 Fore St 04101. In the Old Port. Int corridors. **Pets:** Accepted. (SAVE) 🛜 ✕ &M 🛏 💻 🍴

▼▼▼ Residence Inn by Marriott Portland
Downtown/Waterfront 🅷
(207) 761-1660. **$139-$559.** 145 Fore St 04101. In the Old Port; across from Casco Bay ferry terminal. Int corridors. **Pets:** Accepted.
🛜 ✕ &M 🛏 💻 🛝

PRESQUE ISLE

▼ Budget Traveler Inn & Suites 🅼
(207) 769-0111. **Call for rates.** 71 Main St 04769. 1.3 mi s on US 1. Int corridors. **Pets:** Accepted. 🛜 🛏

⨁ ▼▼▼ Presque Isle Inn & Convention Center 🅷
(207) 764-3321. **$88-$150.** 116 Main St 04769. 1 mi s on US 1. Int corridors. **Pets:** Other species. $25 one-time fee/room. Designated rooms, service with restrictions, supervision. (SAVE) 🛜 🛏 💻 🍴 🛝

RANGELEY

⨁ ▼▼▼ Rangeley Saddleback Inn 🅷 ✿
(207) 864-3434. **$85-$250, 3 day notice.** 2303 Main St 04970. On SR 4, just s of village. Ext corridors. **Pets:** Other species. $10 daily fee/room. Designated rooms, service with restrictions.
(SAVE) 🛜 ✕ &M 🛏 💻 🍴 🛝

ROCKLAND

⨁ ▼▼ Navigator Motor Inn 🅷
(207) 594-2131. **$79-$169.** 520 Main St 04841. On US 1; between Talbot and Summer sts. Int corridors. **Pets:** Dogs only. $10 daily fee/pet. Designated rooms, service with restrictions, crate. (SAVE) 🛜 ✕ 🛏 🍴

▼▼ Trade Winds Motor Inn 🅷
(207) 596-6661. **$74-$234.** 2 Park Dr 04841. On US 1; center. Ext/int corridors. **Pets:** Dogs only. $10 daily fee/pet. Designated rooms, service with restrictions, crate. (SAVE) 🛜 ✕ 🛏 💻 🍴 🛝 🐾

ROCKPORT

⨁ ▼▼▼ The Country Inn At
Camden/Rockport 🅷 ✿
(207) 236-2725. **$109-$239.** 8 Country Inn Way 04856. Jct SR 90, 0.9 mi n on US 1. Ext/int corridors. **Pets:** Other species. $10 daily fee/pet. Designated rooms, supervision. (SAVE) 🛜 ✕ 🛏 💻 🛝 🐾

⨁ ▼▼▼ Glen Cove Inn & Suites 🅼 ✿
(207) 594-4062. **$69-$299, 3 day notice.** 866 Commercial St 04856. Jct SR 90, 3 mi s on US 1. Ext corridors. **Pets:** Large, dogs only. $10 daily fee/pet. Designated rooms, service with restrictions, supervision.
(SAVE) 🛜 ✕ 🛏 🛝

⨁ ▼▼▼▼ Samoset Resort 🅷
(207) 594-2511. **$159-$1599, 3 day notice.** 220 Warrenton St 04856. 3.5 mi s on US 1, then 0.5 mi e on Waldo Rd. Int corridors. **Pets:** Small. $30 one-time fee/pet. Designated rooms, service with restrictions, crate.
(ECO) (SAVE) 🛜 ✕ &M 🛏 💻 🍴 🛝 🐾

SACO

⨁ ▼▼▼▼ Hampton Inn 🅷
(207) 282-7222. **$99-$259.** 48 Industrial Park Rd 04072. I-95 exit 36 (I-195) to exit 1 (Industrial Park Rd), just ne. Int corridors. **Pets:** Other species. Designated rooms, service with restrictions, supervision.
(SAVE) 🛜 ✕ &M 🛏 💻 🛝

⨁ ▼▼▼ ▼▼▼ Ramada Saco Old Orchard Beach
Area 🅷 ✿
(207) 286-9600. **$80-$230.** 352 North St (SR 112) 04072. I-95 exit 36 (I-195) to exit 1 (Industrial Park Rd), 0.6 mi sw to SR 112, then 0.4 mi nw. Int corridors. **Pets:** Other species. $25 one-time fee/room. Designated rooms, service with restrictions, supervision.
(SAVE) 🛜 ✕ &M 🛏 💻 🛝

⨁ ▼ Saco Motel 🅼
(207) 284-6952. **$50-$90, 3 day notice.** 473 Main St 04072. I-95 exit 36 (I-195) to exit 2A (US 1), just sw. Ext corridors. **Pets:** Small, dogs only. $5 daily fee/pet. Designated rooms, service with restrictions, supervision. (SAVE) 🛜 ✕ 🛏 🛝

▼▼ Wagon Wheel Motel 🅼
(207) 283-3258. **Call for rates.** 726 Portland Rd (US 1) 04072. I-95 exit 36 (I-195), 1.5 mi se to US 1, then 0.7 mi ne. Ext corridors.
Pets: Accepted. 🛜 ✕ 🛏 💻 🛝 🐾

SANFORD

▼▼ Super 8 🅷
(207) 324-8823. **$52-$113.** 1892 Main St (Rt 109) 04073. I-95 exit 19, 7 mi nw. Int corridors. **Pets:** Accepted. 🛜 🛏 💻

SCARBOROUGH

⨁ ▼▼▼ Homewood Suites Portland 🅷 ✿
(207) 775-2700. **Call for rates.** 200 Southborough Dr 04074. I-95 exit 45, just s. Int corridors. **Pets:** Other species. $75 one-time fee/room. Designated rooms. (SAVE) 🛜 &M 🛏 💻 🍴 🛝 🐾

▼ Pride Motel & Cottages 🅲🅰
(207) 883-4816. **$65-$225, 7 day notice.** 677 US Rt 1 04074. I-95 exit 36, 0.5 mi e to US 1, then 4.5 mi n. Ext corridors. **Pets:** Accepted.
(ECO) 🛜 ✕ 🛏 💻 🛝 🐾

▼▼▼ Residence Inn by Marriott 🅷
(207) 883-0400. **$139-$329.** 800 Roundwood Dr 04074. I-95 exit 42, 1.5 mi n on Payne Rd. Int corridors. **Pets:** Accepted.
🛜 ✕ &M 🛏 💻 🛝 🐾

▼▼▼ TownePlace Suites by Marriott 🅷
(207) 883-6800. **$99-$259.** 700 Roundwood Dr 04074. I-95 exit 42, 1.5 mi n on Payne Rd. Int corridors. **Pets:** Other species. $75 one-time fee/room. Service with restrictions. 🛜 ✕ &M 🛏 💻 🛝

SKOWHEGAN

⨁ ▼▼▼ Belmont Motel 🅼
(207) 474-8315. **$85-$125.** 273 Madison Ave 04976. 1 mi n on US 201. Ext corridors. **Pets:** Accepted. (SAVE) 🛜 ✕ &M 🛏 💻 🛝

⨁ ▼▼ Breezy Acres Motel 🅼
(207) 474-2703. **$65-$78.** 315 Waterville Rd 04976. 1.5 mi s on US 201. Ext corridors. **Pets:** Accepted. (SAVE) 🛜 ✕ 🛏 💻 🛝 🐾

SOUTHPORT

⨁ ▼▼▼ Ocean Gate Resort 🅷
(207) 633-3321. **$104-$384, 7 day notice.** 70 Ocean Gate Rd 04576. SR 27, 2.5 mi s of Boothbay Harbor, 0.5 mi s of bridge to Southport Island. Ext corridors. **Pets:** Accepted.
(SAVE) 🛜 ✕ 🛏 💻 🛝 🐾

SOUTH PORTLAND

⨁ ▼▼▼ BEST WESTERN Merry Manor Inn 🅷 ✿
(207) 774-6151. **$99-$209.** 700 Main St 04106. I-95 exit 45, 1.3 mi e to US 1. Ext/int corridors. **Pets:** $20 daily fee/pet. Service with restrictions, crate. (SAVE) 🛜 ✕ &M 🛏 💻 🍴 🛝 🐾

◇◇ ▽▽▽ Comfort Inn 🅷 ❀
(207) 775-0409. **$74-$189.** 90 Maine Mall Rd 04106. I-95 exit 45, 1 mi n. Int corridors. **Pets:** Other species. $10 daily fee/pet. Service with restrictions, supervision. ⓔⓒⓞ (Ṡᴬᵛᴱ) 🛰 ✕ &ᴹ 🔋 💻

◇◇ ▽▽▽ Days Inn Portland-South Portland 🅷
(207) 772-3450. **$45-$350.** 461 Maine Mall Rd 04106. I-95 exit 45. Int corridors. **Pets:** Accepted. (Ṡᴬᵛᴱ) 🛰 🔋 💻 ⤳

◇◇ ▽▽▽▽ DoubleTree by Hilton 🅷
(207) 775-6161. **$109-$349.** 363 Maine Mall Rd 04106. I-95 exit 45. Int corridors. **Pets:** Medium. Designated rooms, service with restrictions, supervision. (Ṡᴬᵛᴱ) 🛰 &ᴹ 🔋 💻 ⑪ ⤳

▽▽▽▽ Hampton Inn Portland Airport 🅷
(207) 773-4400. **$99-$269.** 171 Philbrook Ave 04106. I-95 exit 45, just ne. Int corridors. **Pets:** Accepted. 🛰 ✕ &ᴹ 🔋 💻 ⤳ ✕

◇◇ ▽▽▽▽ Holiday Inn Express & Suites 🅷
(207) 775-3900. **Call for rates.** 303 Sable Oaks Dr 04106. I-95 exit 45, just n on Maine Mall Rd, then just w on Running Hill Rd. Int corridors. **Pets:** Accepted. ⓔⓒⓞ (Ṡᴬᵛᴱ) 🛰 ✕ 🔋 💻 ⤳

▽▽▽ Howard Johnson Hotel 🅷
(207) 775-5343. **$70-$180.** 675 Main St 04106. I-95 exit 45, 1.3 mi e to US 1. Int corridors. **Pets:** Medium. $10 daily fee/pet. Designated rooms, service with restrictions, supervision. 🛰 🔋 💻 ⤳

◇◇ ▽▽▽▽ Portland Marriott at Sable Oaks 🅷
(207) 871-8000. **$129-$329.** 200 Sable Oaks Dr 04106. I-95 exit 45, just n on Maine Mall Rd, then just w on Running Hill Rd. Int corridors. **Pets:** Accepted. ⓔⓒⓞ (Ṡᴬᵛᴱ) 🛰 ✕ &ᴹ 🔋 💻 ⑪ ⤳ ✕

SPRUCE HEAD
▽▽ ▽▽ The Craignair Inn & Restaurant 🅲🅸
(207) 594-7644. **$100-$200, 14 day notice.** 5 Third St 04859. 2.5 mi w on SR 73, 1.5 mi s on Clark Island Rd; 10 mi s of Rockland. Ext/int corridors. **Pets:** Accepted. ⓔⓒⓞ 🛰 ✕ ⑪

STANDISH
▽▽ ▽▽ Sebago Lake Lodge and Cottages 🅱🅱
(207) 892-2698. **$62-$275, 30 day notice.** 661 White's Bridge Rd 04084. 1 mi w on US 302. Ext/int corridors. **Pets:** $15 daily fee/pet. Designated rooms, no service, supervision.
🛰 ✕ 🔋 💻 ✕ 🎤 🏷

WATERVILLE
◇◇ ▽▽▽▽ BEST WESTERN PLUS Waterville 🅷 ❀
(207) 873-0111. **$99-$249.** 375 Main St 04901. I-95 exit 130 (Main St), on SR 104. Int corridors. **Pets:** Other species. Service with restrictions.
ⓔⓒⓞ (Ṡᴬᵛᴱ) 🛰 🔋 💻 ⑪ ⤳

▽▽ ▽▽ Comfort Inn & Suites 🅷
(207) 873-2777. **Call for rates.** 332 Main St 04901. I-95 exit 130 (Main St), 0.4 mi e on SR 104. Int corridors. **Pets:** Accepted.
🛰 🔋 💻 ⤳

▽▽ ▽▽ Fireside Inn & Suites 🅷 ❀
(207) 873-3335. **$89-$249.** 356 Main St 04901. I-95 exit 130 (Main St). Int corridors. **Pets:** $20 one-time fee/room. Designated rooms, service with restrictions, supervision. ⓔⓒⓞ 🛰 ✕ 🔋 💻 ⑪ ⤳ ✕

WELLS
▽▽▽ Wells-Moody Motel 🅼
(207) 646-5601. **$49-$149, 10 day notice.** 119 Post Rd (US 1) 04054. I-95 exit 19, jct SR 109 and US 1, 3.4 mi s. Ext corridors. **Pets:** Accepted. 🛰 ✕ 🔋 💻 ⤳

WESTBROOK
◇◇ ▽▽▽ Super 8 🅷
(207) 854-1881. **$58-$130.** 208 Larrabee Rd 04092. I-95 exit 48. Int corridors. **Pets:** Other species. $25 one-time fee/room. Designated rooms, service with restrictions, supervision. (Ṡᴬᵛᴱ) 🛰 🔋 💻 ⤳

WEST FORKS
◇◇ ▽▽▽ Inn by the River 🅲🅸
(207) 663-2181. **$89-$129, 30 day notice.** 2777 US Rt 201 04985. Center. Int corridors. **Pets:** Designated rooms, supervision.
(Ṡᴬᵛᴱ) 🛰 ✕ 💻 ⑪ ✕ 🎤 🏷

WESTPORT
▽▽▽▽ The Squire Tarbox Inn 🅲🅸
(207) 882-7693. **$115-$199, 14 day notice.** 1181 Main Rd 04578. Jct US 1 and SR 144; in Wiscasset; 8.5 mi s on SR 144, follow signs. Ext/int corridors. **Pets:** Accepted. 🛰 ✕ ⑪ ✕ 🎤 🏷

WILTON
▽▽▽▽ Farmington/Wilton Comfort Inn & Suites 🅷 🐾
(207) 645-5155. **$99-$140.** 1026 US Rt 2 04294. On US 2, just w of jct SR 133. Int corridors. **Pets:** Small, other species. $35 one-time fee/room. Designated rooms, service with restrictions, crate.
🛰 ✕ &ᴹ 🔋 💻 ⤳

YARMOUTH
◇◇ ▽▽▽ Down-East Village Motel 🅼
(207) 846-5161. **$89-$129.** 705 US Rt 1 04096. I-295 exit 15 northbound; exit 17 southbound. Ext corridors. **Pets:** Other species. $8 daily fee/pet. Service with restrictions, crate. (Ṡᴬᵛᴱ) 🛰 ✕ 🔋 💻 ⤳

YORK HARBOR
▽▽▽▽ Inn at Harmon Park 🅱🅱
(207) 363-2031. **$99-$139, 7 day notice.** 415 York St 03911. I-95 exit 7, 0.3 mi s on US 1, then 1.5 mi n; to York Village. Int corridors. **Pets:** Designated rooms, service with restrictions, supervision.
🛰 ✕ 🏷

▽▽▽▽ York Harbor Inn 🅲🅸
(207) 363-5119. **$109-$349, 14 day notice.** 480 York St 03911. On US 1A; center. Ext/int corridors. **Pets:** Accepted. ⓔⓒⓞ 🛰 ✕ ⑪

MARYLAND

BALTIMORE METROPOLITAN AREA

ABERDEEN

Clarion Aberdeen H
(410) 273-6300. **$89-$129.** 980 Hospitality Way 21001. I-95 exit 85, just e on SR 22. Int corridors. **Pets:** Accepted.

La Quinta Inn Aberdeen H
(410) 272-6000. **$71-$166.** 793 W Bel Air Ave 21001. I-95 exit 85, just e. Int corridors. **Pets:** Service with restrictions, supervision.

Residence Inn by Marriott Aberdeen at Ripken Stadium H
(410) 272-0444. **$99-$229.** 830 Long Dr 21001. I-95 exit 85, 0.5 mi w on SR 22, then 0.5 mi n. Int corridors. **Pets:** Accepted.

Super 8 Aberdeen M
(410) 272-5420. **$59-$150.** 1008 Beards Hill Rd 21001. I-95 exit 85, just e on SR 22. Int corridors. **Pets:** Accepted.

ANNAPOLIS

BEST WESTERN Annapolis M
(410) 224-2800. **$79-$169.** 2520 Riva Rd 21401. 2.3 mi sw on US 50 and 301 exit 22, just e. Ext/int corridors. **Pets:** $15 daily fee/room. Designated rooms, service with restrictions, supervision.

Country Inn & Suites By Carlson H
(410) 571-6700. **$85-$259.** 2600 Housley Rd 21401. US 50 and 301 exit 23 eastbound; exit 23B westbound, 1 mi w on SR 450. Int corridors. **Pets:** Other species. $75 one-time fee/room. Designated rooms, service with restrictions.

DoubleTree by Hilton Hotel Annapolis H
(410) 224-3150. **$99-$239.** 210 Holiday Ct 21401. 2.3 mi sw on US 50 and 301 exit 22 to Riva Rd, 0.3 mi n. Int corridors. **Pets:** Accepted.

Hampton Inn & Suites-Annapolis H
(410) 571-0200. **$99-$299.** 124 Womack Dr 21401. 2.3 mi sw on US 50 and 301 exit 22, just s, then just e on Admiral Cochrane Dr, just n on Spruill Rd, then just w. Int corridors. **Pets:** Large, other species. Service with restrictions, crate.

Homestead Studio Suites Hotel-Annapolis-Admiral Cochrane Dr H
(410) 571-6600. **$109-$309.** 120 Admiral Cochrane Dr 21401. 2.3 mi sw on US 50 and 301 exit 22, just s, then just e. Int corridors. **Pets:** $25 daily fee/pet. Designated rooms, service with restrictions.

Loews Annapolis Hotel H
(410) 263-7777. **$149-$339.** 126 West St 21401. US 50 and 301 exit 24 eastbound; exit 24A westbound, 1.4 mi s on SR 70, just sw on Calvert St, then just w. Int corridors. **Pets:** Accepted.

Quality Inn M
(410) 974-4440. **$80-$140.** 1542 Whitehall Rd 21409. 1 mi w of Chesapeake Bay Bridge, off US 50 and 301 exit 30 eastbound; exit 32 westbound. Int corridors. **Pets:** Accepted.

Sheraton Annapolis Hotel H
(410) 266-3131. **$109-$249.** 173 Jennifer Rd 21401. North side of US 50 and 301 exit 23B westbound; exit 23 eastbound. Int corridors. **Pets:** Medium, dogs only. $50 one-time fee/pet. Designated rooms, service with restrictions, crate.

The Westin Annapolis H
(410) 972-4300. **$159-$429.** 100 Westgate Cir 21401. US 50 and 301 exit 24 eastbound; exit 24A westbound, 0.7 mi s on SR 70, then 0.8 mi e on SR 435; 0.5 mi n of Church Circle. Int corridors. **Pets:** Medium, dogs only. Designated rooms, service with restrictions, supervision.

BALTIMORE

Admiral Fell Inn H
(410) 522-7377. **$169-$249.** 888 S Broadway St 21231. Corner of Broadway and Thames sts; facing the waterfront. Int corridors. **Pets:** Accepted.

Brookshire Suites H
(410) 625-1300. **$144-$162, 3 day notice.** 120 E Lombard St 21202. Corner of Calvert and Lombard sts. Int corridors. **Pets:** Accepted.

Celie's Waterfront Inn BB
(410) 522-2323. **Call for rates.** 1714 Thames St 21231. In historic Fells Point area. Int corridors. **Pets:** Accepted.

Days Inn Inner Harbor Baltimore H
(410) 576-1000. **$149-$219.** 100 Hopkins Pl 21201. Opposite First Mariner Arena; 1 blk from Baltimore Convention Center. Int corridors. **Pets:** Accepted.

Four Seasons Hotel Baltimore H
(410) 576-5800. **$359-$579.** 200 International Dr 21202. In Harbor East section of the Inner Harbor. Int corridors. **Pets:** Accepted.

▼▼▼▼ **Hilton Baltimore** 🅗
(443) 573-8700. **$159-$359.** 401 W Pratt St 21201. I-95 exit 53, just w of Camden Yards. Int corridors. **Pets:** Accepted.
🛜 ❌ 🔌ᴹ 🛏 🖥 🍽 ⇌ ⌧

▼▼▼ **Holiday Inn Express Baltimore/Downtown** 🅗
(410) 400-8045. **$99-$179.** 221 N Gay St 21202. Jct N Gay St and Fallsway. Int corridors. **Pets:** Small, other species. $50 one-time fee/pet. Service with restrictions, crate. 🛜 ❌ 🔌ᴹ 🛏 🖥

🅐🅐🅐 ▼▼▼▼ **Holiday Inn-Inner Harbor** 🅗
(410) 685-3500. **$119-$329.** 301 W Lombard St 21201. Just w of Camden Yards. Int corridors. **Pets:** Accepted.
🆂🅰🆅🅴 🛜 ❌ 🛏 🖥 🍽 ⇌ ⌧

▼▼▼▼ **Home2 Suites by Hilton-Downtown Baltimore** 🅗
(410) 576-1200. **$129-$179.** 8 E Pleasant St 21202. Just s of US 40 E, off Charles St. Int corridors. **Pets:** Accepted. 🛜 🛏 🖥

▼▼▼ **Homewood Suites by Hilton Baltimore Inner Harbor** 🅗
(410) 234-0999. **$189-$289.** 625 S President St 21202. In Harbor East section of Inner Harbor. Int corridors. **Pets:** Medium. $150 one-time fee/pet. Service with restrictions, supervision. 🛜 🔌ᴹ 🛏 🖥

▼ ▼▼ **Hotel Brexton** 🅗
(443) 478-2100. **$129-$199.** 868 Park Ave 21201. Between Tyson and Brexton sts; 1 blk e of Martin Luther King Jr Blvd. Int corridors.
Pets: Small. $50 daily fee/pet. Designated rooms, service with restrictions.
🛜 ❌ 🛏 🖥

🅐🅐🅐 ▼▼▼ ▼▼▼ **Hotel Monaco Baltimore** 🅗
(443) 692-6170. **$139-$299.** 2 N Charles St 21201. Jct Baltimore and N Charles sts. Int corridors. **Pets:** Accepted.
🅴🅲🅾 🆂🅰🆅🅴 🛜 ❌ 🛏 🖥 🍽

▼▼▼▼ **Inn at The Colonnade Baltimore - A DoubleTree by Hilton Hotel** 🅗
(410) 235-5400. **$143-$299.** 4 W University Pkwy 21218. I-83 exit 9A, 0.5 mi on Cold Springs Ln to Roland Ave/University Pkwy, then 1 mi s. Int corridors. **Pets:** Accepted. 🅴🅲🅾 🛜 ❌ 🛏 🖥 🍽

▼▼▼ **Pier 5 Hotel** 🅗
(410) 539-2000. **$199-$299.** 711 Eastern Ave 21202. On the Inner Harbor, at Pier 5. Int corridors. **Pets:** Accepted. 🛜 ❌ 🛏 🖥 🍽

▼▼▼ **Radisson Hotel at Cross Keys** 🅗 🐾
(410) 532-6900. **$119-$189.** 100 Village Sq 21210. I-83 exit 10A (Northern Pkwy), just e, then 0.4 mi s on Falls Rd; in Village of Cross Keys. Int corridors. **Pets:** Medium, other species. $25 one-time fee/pet. Service with restrictions, crate. 🛜 ❌ 🔌ᴹ 🛏 🖥 ⇌ ⌧

🅐🅐🅐 ▼▼▼▼ **Radisson Plaza Lord Baltimore** 🅗 🐾
(410) 539-8400. **$109-$209.** 20 W Baltimore St 21201. At Baltimore and Hanover sts. Int corridors. **Pets:** Medium. $25 one-time fee/room, $10 daily fee/room. Designated rooms, service with restrictions, supervision.
🅴🅲🅾 🆂🅰🆅🅴 🛜 ❌ 🛏 🖥 🍽

▼▼▼ **Residence Inn by Marriott-Baltimore Downtown/Inner Harbor** 🅗
(410) 962-1220. **Call for rates.** 17 Light St 21202. Jct Redwood and Light sts. Int corridors. **Pets:** Large. $100 one-time fee/room. Service with restrictions, crate. 🛜 ❌ 🔌ᴹ 🛏 🖥 🍽

🅐🅐🅐 ▼▼▼ ▼▼▼ **Royal Sonesta Harbor Court** 🅗 🐾
(410) 234-0550. **$159-$479.** 550 Light St 21202. Facing Inner Harbor. Int corridors. **Pets:** Medium. $150 one-time fee/pet. Service with restrictions, supervision. 🆂🅰🆅🅴 🛜 ❌ 🔌ᴹ 🛏 🖥 🍽 ⇌ ⌧

🅐🅐🅐 ▼▼▼ **Sheraton Baltimore City Center Hotel** 🅗
(410) 752-1100. **$100-$389.** 101 W Fayette St 21201. Between Charles and Liberty sts. Int corridors. **Pets:** Accepted.
🆂🅰🆅🅴 🛜 ❌ 🛏 🖥 🍽 ⇌

🅐🅐🅐 ▼▼▼ **Sheraton Inner Harbor Hotel** 🅗
(410) 962-8300. **$99-$509, 3 day notice.** 300 S Charles St 21201. At Conway St; 1 blk from the Inner Harbor. Int corridors. **Pets:** Accepted.
🆂🅰🆅🅴 🛜 ❌ 🛏 🖥 🍽 ⇌ ⌧

🅐🅐🅐 ▼▼▼ **Sleep Inn & Suites Downtown/Inner Harbor** 🅗 🐾
(410) 779-6166. **$99-$179.** 301 Fallsway 21202. Between E Lexington and Gay sts. Int corridors. **Pets:** Medium, other species. $35 daily fee/room. Designated rooms, service with restrictions.
🆂🅰🆅🅴 🛜 ❌ 🔌ᴹ 🛏 🖥

🅐🅐🅐 ▼▼▼ **Wyndham Baltimore Peabody Court** 🅗 🐾
(410) 727-7101. **$99-$209.** 612 Cathedral St 21201. Cathedral St and Mt. Vernon Square. Int corridors. **Pets:** Small, dogs only. $50 daily fee/pet. Service with restrictions, crate. 🆂🅰🆅🅴 🛜 ❌ 🛏 🖥 🍽

BELCAMP
▼▼▼ **Candlewood Suites Aberdeen** 🅗 🐾
(410) 914-3060. **$119-$129.** 4216 Philadelphia Rd 21015. I-95 exit 80 (SR 543), just s to SR 7 (Philadelphia Rd N), then just w. Int corridors. **Pets:** Large, other species. $10 daily fee/pet. Designated rooms, service with restrictions, crate. 🛜 🔌ᴹ 🛏 🖥

▼▼▼ **Extended StayAmerica-Baltimore-Bel Air-Aberdeen** 🅗
(410) 273-0194. **$79-$199.** 1361 James Way 21015. I-95 exit 80 (SR 543), just ne. Int corridors. **Pets:** $25 daily fee/pet. Designated rooms, service with restrictions. 🛜 🔌ᴹ 🛏 🖥

▼▼▼ **Homewood Suites by Hilton Aberdeen/Bel Air** 🅗
(410) 297-8585. **$109-$159.** 4170 Philadelphia Rd 21015. I-95 exit 80 (SR 543), just s to SR 7 (Philadelphia Rd N), then just w. Int corridors. **Pets:** Medium. $100 one-time fee/room. Service with restrictions, crate.
🛜 🔌ᴹ 🛏 🖥 ⇌ ⌧

COLUMBIA
▼▼▼ **Homewood Suites by Hilton Columbia** 🅗
(410) 872-9200. **$99-$209.** 8320 Benson Dr 21045. I-95 exit 41B, 0.5 mi w on SR 175 (Little Patuxent Pkwy), just nw on SR 108, then just w on Lark Brown Rd. Int corridors. **Pets:** Other species. $15 daily fee/room. Service with restrictions, crate. 🛜 🔌ᴹ 🛏 🖥 ⇌ ⌧

🅐🅐🅐 ▼▼▼ ▼▼▼ **Sheraton Columbia Town Center Hotel** 🅗
(410) 730-3900. **$119-$299.** 10207 Wincopin Cir 21044. 1.2 mi w on SR 175 (Little Patuxent Pkwy) from jct US 29, then just s; center. Int corridors. **Pets:** Medium. Designated rooms, service with restrictions, crate.
🅴🅲🅾 🆂🅰🆅🅴 🛜 ❌ 🛏 🖥 🍽 ⌧

🅐🅐🅐 ▼▼▼ ▼▼▼ **Sonesta ES Suites Columbia** 🅗
(410) 964-9494. **$89-$159.** 8844 Columbia 100 Pkwy 21045. I-95 exit 43B, 4 mi w on SR 100 exit 1B, then just e. Int corridors.
Pets: Accepted. 🆂🅰🆅🅴 🛜 🔌ᴹ 🛏 🖥 ⇌ ⌧

EDGEWOOD
🅐🅐🅐 ▼▼▼ **BEST WESTERN Invitation Inn** 🅜
(410) 679-9700. **$84-$104.** 1709 Edgewood Rd 21040. I-95 exit 77A, just e on SR 24. Ext corridors. **Pets:** Medium. $15 daily fee/room. Service with restrictions, crate. 🆂🅰🆅🅴 🛜 🛏 🖥 ⇌

▼▼▼ **La Quinta Inn & Suites** 🅗
(410) 676-6969. **$95-$188.** 2112B Emmorton Park Rd 21040. I-95 exit 77A, just e on SR 24. Int corridors. **Pets:** Service with restrictions, supervision. 🛜 ❌ 🔌ᴹ 🛏 🖥

ELLICOTT CITY
▼▼▼ **Residence Inn by Marriott Columbia** 🅗 🐾
(410) 997-7200. **$95-$199.** 4950 Beaver Run Way 21043. I-95 exit 43B, 4 mi w on SR 100 exit 1B (Executive Park Dr). Int corridors. **Pets:** Other species. $150 one-time fee/room. Service with restrictions.
🅴🅲🅾 🛜 ❌ 🔌ᴹ 🛏 🖥 ⇌ ⌧

◇◇◇◇ Turf Valley H

(410) 465-1500. **Call for rates.** 2700 Turf Valley Rd 21042. I-70 exit 82 eastbound, 1.5 mi e on US 40 exit 83 westbound, 0.6 mi s on Marriottsville Rd, then 0.8 mi e on US 40. Int corridors. **Pets:** Accepted.

ECO SAVE 🛜 ✕ 🛏 🖥 🍽 🏊 🐾

GLEN BURNIE

◇◇ Days Inn-Baltimore South/Glen Burnie M

(410) 761-8300. **$75-$114.** 6600 Ritchie Hwy 21061. I-695 exit 3B eastbound; exit 2 westbound, 0.5 mi s on SR 2. Ext corridors. **Pets:** Medium. $21 daily fee/pet. Designated rooms, service with restrictions, supervision.

SAVE 🛜 🛏 🖥

◇◇◇ Extended StayAmerica Baltimore-Glen Burnie H

(410) 761-2708. **$99-$289.** 104 Chesapeake Centre Ct 21061. I-695 exit 3B, 0.9 mi s on SR 2, just e on E Ordnance Rd, then just s. Int corridors. **Pets:** $25 daily fee/pet. Designated rooms, service with restrictions.

🛜 ♿M 🛏 🖥

◇◇◇ La Quinta Inn & Suites Baltimore South Glen Burnie H

(410) 636-4300. **$83-$188.** 6323 Ritchie Hwy 21061. I-695 exit 3A eastbound; exit 2 westbound, jct SR 2. Int corridors. **Pets:** Service with restrictions, supervision. SAVE 🛜 ♿M 🛏 🖥 🏊

HANOVER

◇◇◇◇ Aloft Arundel Mills H

(443) 577-0077. **$99-$250.** 7520 Teague Rd 21076. I-95 exit 43A, 3.6 mi e on SR 100 exit 10A (Arundel Mills Blvd), then 0.4 mi s to SR 713. Int corridors. **Pets:** Accepted. ECO SAVE 🛜 ✕ ♿M 🛏 🖥 🏊

◇◇◇◇ Element Arundel Mills H 🐾

(443) 577-0050. **$99-$250.** 7522 Teague Rd 21076. I-95 exit 43A, 3.6 mi e on SR 100 exit 10A (Arundel Mills Blvd), then 0.4 mi s to SR 713. Int corridors. **Pets:** Large, dogs only. Service with restrictions, crate.

ECO ♿ SAVE 🛜 ✕ ♿M 🛏 🖥 🏊

◇◇◇◇ Homewood Suites by Hilton Baltimore/Arundel Mills H 🐾

(410) 878-7201. **$129-$279.** 7491-B New Ridge Rd 21076. SR 100 exit 10B, 0.3 mi n on SR 713. Int corridors. **Pets:** Large. $75 one-time fee/room. Service with restrictions, crate. 🛜 ♿M 🛏 🖥 🏊 🐾

◇◇◇ Red Roof Inn Baltimore-Washington BW Parkway M

(410) 712-4070. **$60-$130.** 7306 Parkway Dr S 21076. I-95 exit 43A, 2 mi e on SR 100 exit 8 (Coca Cola Dr), then 0.5 mi se. Ext corridors. **Pets:** Large, other species. Service with restrictions, supervision.

SAVE 🛜 ✕ ♿M 🛏

◇◇◇◇ Residence Inn by Marriott-Arundel Mills/BWI H 🐾

(410) 799-7332. **$141-$284.** 7035 Arundel Mills Cir 21076. I-95 exit 43A, 3.6 mi e on SR 100 exit 10A (Arundel Mills Blvd). Int corridors. **Pets:** Medium, other species. $100 one-time fee/room. Designated rooms, service with restrictions, crate. 🛜 ✕ ♿M 🛏 🖥 🐾 🐾

◇◇◇ TownePlace Suites by Marriott Arundel Mills/BWI H

(410) 379-9000. **$119-$219.** 7021 Arundel Mills Cir 21076. I-95 exit 43A, 3.6 mi e on SR 100 exit 10A (Arundel Mills Blvd). Int corridors. **Pets:** Small, other species. $100 one-time fee/room. Service with restrictions. 🛜 ✕ ♿M 🛏 🖥 🏊 🐾

HAVRE DE GRACE

◇◇ Super 8 Havre de Grace M

(410) 939-1880. **$59-$150.** 929 Pulaski Hwy 21078. I-95 exit 89, 2.5 mi e on SR 155, then 0.3 mi w on US 40. Int corridors. **Pets:** Accepted.

🛜 🛏 🖥

HUNT VALLEY

◇◇◇ Residence Inn by Marriott Baltimore Hunt Valley H 🐾

(410) 527-2333. **$149-$299.** 45 Schilling Rd 21031. I-83 exit 20A (Shawan Rd), just e on Shawan Rd, just s on McCormick Rd, then just e. Int corridors. **Pets:** Other species. $75 one-time fee/room. Designated rooms, service with restrictions. 🛜 ✕ ♿M 🛏 🖥 🐾 🐾

JESSUP

◇◇◇ Extended StayAmerica-Columbia-Laurel-Ft. Meade H

(301) 725-3877. **$99-$289.** 8550 Washington Blvd 20794. I-95 exit 38A, 1.4 mi e on SR 32, then 0.5 mi n on US 1. Int corridors. **Pets:** $25 daily fee/pet. Designated rooms, service with restrictions. 🛜 🛏 🖥

◇◇◇ Holiday Inn Columbia H

(410) 799-7500. **$89-$189.** 7900 Washington Blvd 20794. I-95 exit 41A; jct US 1 and SR 175. Int corridors. **Pets:** Accepted.

🛜 🛏 🖥 🍽 🏊

◇◇◇ La Quinta Inn & Suites Columbia Jessup H

(410) 799-1500. **$78-$188.** 7300 Crestmount Rd 20794. I-95 exit 41A, just s of jct US 1 and SR 175. Int corridors. **Pets:** Service with restrictions, supervision. 🛜 ♿M 🛏 🖥

◇◇◇ Red Roof Inn-Columbia/Fort Meade M

(410) 796-0380. **$60-$130.** 8000 Washington Blvd 20794. I-95 exit 41A, 0.3 mi s of jct US 1 and SR 175. Ext corridors. **Pets:** Large, other species. Service with restrictions, supervision. SAVE 🛜 ♿M 🛏 🖥

LINTHICUM HEIGHTS

◇◇◇ Aloft Baltimore Washington Intl Airport H 🐾

(410) 691-6969. **$149-$299.** 1741 W Nursery Rd 21090. I-695 exit 7A, 1 mi s on SR 295, then 1.2 mi e. Int corridors. **Pets:** Medium, dogs only. Designated rooms, supervision. SAVE 🛜 ✕ ♿M 🛏 🖥 🏊

◇◇◇ Candlewood Suites-BWI H

(410) 850-9214. **$89-$159.** 1247 Winterson Rd 21090. I-695 exit 7A, 1 mi s on SR 295, 1.3 mi e on W Nursery Rd, then 0.3 mi w. Int corridors. **Pets:** Large. $150 daily fee/room. Service with restrictions, supervision.

🛜 🛏 🖥

◇◇◇ DoubleTree by Hilton Baltimore - BWI Airport H

(410) 859-8400. **$89-$209.** 890 Elkridge Landing Rd 21090. I-695 exit 7A, 1 mi s on SR 295, 1.3 mi e on W Nursery Rd, then 0.5 mi w. Int corridors. **Pets:** Accepted. 🛜 ♿M 🛏 🖥 🍽 🏊 ✕

◇◇◇◇ Four Points by Sheraton BWI Airport H 🐾

(410) 859-3300. **$90-$190, 7 day notice.** 1001 Scott Dr 21240. I-195 exit 1A, 0.5 mi n on SR 170, then just e. Int corridors. **Pets:** $25 daily fee/pet. Designated rooms, service with restrictions, crate.

SAVE 🛜 ✕ ♿M 🛏 🖥 🍽 🐾

◇◇◇ Hampton Inn BWI Airport H

(410) 850-0600. **$79-$179.** 829 Elkridge Landing Rd 21090. I-695 exit 7A, 1 mi s on SR 295, 1.3 mi e on W Nursery Rd, then just w. Int corridors. **Pets:** $50 one-time fee/pet. Designated rooms, service with restrictions, crate. 🛜 ✕ ♿M 🛏 🖥

◇◇◇ Holiday Inn BWI H 🐾

(410) 691-1000. **$70-$180.** 815 Elkridge Landing Rd 21090. I-695 exit 7A, 1 mi s on SR 295, then 1.3 mi e on W Nursery Rd. Int corridors. **Pets:** $30 deposit/pet. Designated rooms, service with restrictions, supervision. 🛜 ✕ ♿M 🛏 🖥

◇◇◇ La Quinta Inn & Suites BWI Airport H

(410) 859-2333. **$71-$188.** 1734 W Nursery Rd 21090. I-695 exit 7A, 1 mi s on SR 295, then 1.3 mi e on W Nursery Rd. Int corridors. **Pets:** Service with restrictions, supervision. 🛜 🛏 🖥 🏊

ⓐⓐⓐ ▽▽ ▽▽ Red Roof Inn-BWI Airport Ⓜ
(410) 850-7600. **$60-$130.** 827 Elkridge Landing Rd 21090. I-695 exit 7A, 1 mi s on SR 295, 1.3 mi e on W Nursery Rd, then just w. Ext corridors. **Pets:** Large, other species. Service with restrictions, supervision.
〔SAVE〕 ⓢ 🛏 📺 📶

ⓐⓐⓐ ▽▽ ▽▽ Residence Inn by Marriott-BWI Airport Ⓗ
(410) 691-0255. **$89-$199.** 1160 Winterson Rd 21090. I-695 exit 7A, 1 mi s on SR 295, 0.7 mi e on W Nursery Rd, then just n. Int corridors. **Pets:** Other species. $100 one-time fee/room. Service with restrictions.
ⒺⒸⓄ 〔SAVE〕 ⓢ ✕ ⓖⓂ 🛏 📺 ↝ ⌧

ⓐⓐⓐ ▽▽ ▽▽ Sheraton Baltimore Washington Airport Hotel Ⓗ
(443) 577-2100. **$99-$300.** 1100 Old Elkridge Landing Rd 21090. I-695 exit 7A, 1 mi s on SR 295, 1.3 mi e on W Nursery Rd, then 0.4 mi w on Winterson Rd. Int corridors. **Pets:** Accepted.
〔SAVE〕 ⓢ ✕ ⓖⓂ 🛏 📺 🍴 ↝ ⌧

▽▽ ▽▽ Sleep Inn & Suites BWI Airport Ⓗ
(410) 789-7223. **$79-$129.** 6055 Belle Grove Rd 21225. I-695 exit 6A eastbound; exit 5 westbound, 0.3 mi n to jct SR 170/648. Int corridors. **Pets:** Accepted. ⓢ ⓖⓂ 🛏 📺

▽▽ ▽▽ ▽▽ Staybridge Suites BWI Ⓗ
(410) 850-5666. **$119-$359.** 1301 Winterson Rd 21090. I-695 exit 7A, 1 mi s on SR 295, 1.3 mi e on Nursery Rd, then 0.4 mi w. Int corridors. **Pets:** Accepted. ⓢ ⓖⓂ 🛏 📺 ↝

ⓐⓐⓐ ▽▽ ▽▽ ▽▽ TownePlace Suites by Marriott Baltimore/BWI Airport Ⓗ ☙
(410) 694-0060. **$129-$159.** 1171 Winterson Rd 21090. I-695 exit 7A, 1 mi s on SR 295, 0.7 mi e on W Nursery Rd, then just n. Int corridors. **Pets:** Other species. $100 one-time fee/room. Crate.
ⒺⒸⓄ 〔SAVE〕 ⓢ ✕ ⓖⓂ 🛏 📺 ↝

ⓐⓐⓐ ▽▽ ▽▽ ▽▽ The Westin-Baltimore Washington Airport Ⓗ
(443) 577-2300. **$119-$350.** 1110 Old Elkridge Landing Rd 21090. I-695 exit 7A, 1 mi s on SR 295, 1.3 mi e on W Nursery Rd, then 0.4 mi w on Winterson Rd. Int corridors. **Pets:** Accepted.
〔SAVE〕 ⓢ ✕ ⓖⓂ 🛏 📺 🍴 ↝ ⌧

ROSEDALE
▽▽ ▽▽ La Quinta Inn & Suites Baltimore North Ⓗ
(410) 574-8100. **$90-$166.** 4 Philadelphia Ct 21237. I-695 exit 34, just n. Int corridors. **Pets:** Service with restrictions, supervision.
ⓢ 🛏 📺 ↝

SYKESVILLE
▽▽ ▽▽ ▽▽ Inn at Norwood ⒷⒷ
(410) 549-7868. **$135-$225, 7 day notice.** 7514 Norwood Ave 21784. I-70 exit 80 (SR 32), 3.6 mi n, 0.6 mi w on West Friendship Rd (which becomes Main St), then just s on Church St. Int corridors. **Pets:** Dogs only. $20 daily fee/pet. Designated rooms, service with restrictions.
ⓢ ✕ 🛏 📺 ⌧

TIMONIUM
ⓐⓐⓐ ▽▽ ▽▽ Red Roof Inn-Timonium Ⓜ
(410) 666-0380. **$65-$110.** 111 W Timonium Rd 21093. I-83 exit 16A northbound; exit 16 southbound, just e. Ext corridors. **Pets:** Large, other species. Service with restrictions, supervision.
〔SAVE〕 ⓢ ✕ ⓖⓂ 🛏 📺

TOWSON
ⓐⓐⓐ ▽▽ ▽▽ ▽▽ Sheraton Baltimore North Hotel Ⓗ
(410) 321-7400. **$99-$259.** 903 Dulaney Valley Rd 21204. I-695 exit 27A (Dulaney Valley Rd), 0.3 mi s. Int corridors. **Pets:** Accepted.
〔SAVE〕 ⓢ ✕ 🛏 📺 🍴 ↝ ⌧

WESTMINSTER
ⓐⓐⓐ ▽▽ ▽▽ BEST WESTERN Westminster Catering and Conference Center Ⓗ ☙
(410) 857-1900. **$100-$132.** 451 WMC Dr 21158. 1.7 mi w on SR 140 from jct SR 27. Int corridors. **Pets:** Medium, dogs only. $10 daily fee/pet. Service with restrictions. 〔SAVE〕 ⓢ ✕ 🛏 📺 ↝

▽▽ The Boston Inn Ⓜ
(410) 848-9095. **$47-$75.** 533 Baltimore Blvd 21157. 0.9 mi se on SR 97/140 from jct SR 27. Ext corridors. **Pets:** Dogs only. Service with restrictions, crate. ⓢ 🛏 📺 ↝

WHITE MARSH
▽▽ ▽▽ Residence Inn by Marriott Baltimore/White Marsh Ⓗ
(410) 933-9554. **$149-$169.** 4980 Mercantile Rd 21236. I-95 exit 67B, 0.5 mi w on SR 43 (White Marsh Blvd), just s to Mercantile Rd, then just e. Int corridors. **Pets:** Other species. $75 one-time fee/room. Designated rooms, service with restrictions, crate.
ⓢ ✕ ⓖⓂ 🛏 📺 ↝ ⌧

END METROPOLITAN AREA

CALIFORNIA
▽▽ ▽▽ La Quinta Inn & Suites Lexington Park - Patuxent Ⓗ
(301) 862-4100. **$95-$177.** 22769 Three Notch Rd 20619. 3.2 mi n on SR 235. Int corridors. **Pets:** Service with restrictions, supervision.
ⓢ ✕ 🛏 📺 ↝

CAMBRIDGE
▽▽ ▽▽ ▽▽ Comfort Inn & Suites Cambridge Ⓗ
(410) 901-0150. **$110-$150.** 2936 Ocean Gateway 21613. On US 50, 0.8 mi e of jct SR 16. Int corridors. **Pets:** Accepted.
ⓢ ✕ ⓖⓂ 🛏 📺 ↝

ⓐⓐⓐ ▽▽ ▽▽ ▽▽ Hyatt Regency Chesapeake Bay Golf Resort, Spa and Marina Ⓗ ☙
(410) 901-1234. **$139-$419, 3 day notice.** 100 Heron Blvd 21613. US 50 E, 1.2 mi e of Frederick C Malkus Jr Bridge. Int corridors. **Pets:** Large, dogs only. $50 daily fee/pet. Designated rooms, service with restrictions. ⒺⒸⓄ 〔SAVE〕 ⓢ ⓖⓂ 🛏 📺 🍴 ↝ ⌧

CHESTERTOWN
▽▽ ▽▽ ▽▽ Holiday Inn Express Hotel & Suites Chestertown Ⓗ
(410) 778-0778. **Call for rates.** 150 Scheeler Rd 21620. 0.4 mi ne of jct SR 213 and 291. Int corridors. **Pets:** Accepted.
ⓢ ✕ ⓖⓂ 🛏 📺 ↝

CUMBERLAND
▽▽ ▽▽ ▽▽ Holiday Inn Ⓗ
(301) 724-8800. **$89-$129.** 100 S George St 21502. I-68 exit 43C, just n; downtown. Int corridors. **Pets:** Accepted. ⓢ 🛏 📺 🍴 ↝

EASTON
▽▽ ▽▽ Comfort Inn Easton Ⓜ
(410) 820-8333. **$65-$129, 3 day notice.** 8523 Ocean Gateway 21601. US 50, 0.7 mi n of jct SR 331. Ext corridors. **Pets:** Accepted.
ⓢ 🛏 📺 ↝

▲▲▲ ▼▼▼▼ Inn at 202 Dover [CI]
(410) 819-8007. **$279-$500, 7 day notice.** 202 E Dover St 21601. 0.7 mi w on SR 331 from jct US 50. Int corridors. **Pets:** Medium, dogs only. $50 one-time fee/room. Designated rooms, service with restrictions, crate.
[SAVE] 🛜 ⊠ ⑪

▼▼▼ Tidewater Inn [H]
(410) 822-1300. **Call for rates.** 101 E Dover St 21601. On SR 231, 0.8 mi w of US 50; center. Int corridors. **Pets:** Accepted.
🛜 ⊠ 🔋 💷 ⑪

ELKTON

▼▼▼▼ Elk Forge Inn & Spa [BB]
(410) 392-9007. **Call for rates.** 807 Elk Mills Rd 21921. I-95 exit 109B, 1 mi w on SR 279 to Fletchwood Rd (SR 277), then 2 mi s. Ext/int corridors. **Pets:** Accepted. 🛜 ⊠ 🔋 ⊠

EMMITSBURG

▼▼▼ Sleep Inn & Suites in Emmitsburg [H]
(301) 447-0044. **Call for rates.** 501 Silo Hill Pkwy 21727. US 15 exit SR 140, just w, then just n. Int corridors. **Pets:** Accepted.
🛜 ⊠ 🔋 💷 ⊋

FREDERICK

▲▲▲ ▼▼▼ Comfort Inn Frederick [H]
(301) 668-7272. **$99-$139.** 7300 Executive Way 21704. I-270 exit 31B, 0.9 mi sw on SR 85. Int corridors. **Pets:** Medium. $10 daily fee/pet. Designated rooms, service with restrictions, supervision.
[SAVE] 🛜 🔋M 💷

▲▲▲ ▼▼▼ Days Inn [M]
(301) 694-6600. **$79-$99, 3 day notice.** 5646 Buckeystown Pike 21704. I-270 exit 31A, 0.5 mi e on SR 85; I-70 exit 54, 0.5 mi w. Ext corridors. **Pets:** Small. $20 daily fee/pet. Designated rooms, service with restrictions, crate. [SAVE] 🛜 🔋 💷 ⊋

▼▼▼ Extended StayAmerica-Frederick-Westview Dr [M]
(301) 668-0808. **$89-$279.** 5240 Westview Dr 21703. I-270 exit 31B, 0.5 mi sw on SR 85, then 0.4 mi n. Int corridors. **Pets:** $25 daily fee/pet. Designated rooms, service with restrictions. 🛜 🔋M 🔋 💷

▲▲▲ ▼▼▼▼ Hampton Inn Frederick [H] ✿
(301) 698-2500. **$109-$179.** 5311 Buckeystown Pike (SR 85) 21704. I-270 exit 31B, 0.6 mi w. Int corridors. **Pets:** Medium. Service with restrictions, supervision. [SAVE] 🛜 🔋 💷 ⑪ ⊋

▼▼▼▼ Holiday Inn & Conference Center [H]
(301) 694-7500. **$109-$189.** 5400 Holiday Dr 21703. I-270 exit 31A, just se of SR 85. Int corridors. **Pets:** Accepted.
🛜 🔋 💷 ⑪ ⊋ ⊠

▼▼▼ Holiday Inn Express-FSK Mall [H]
(301) 695-2881. **$99-$179.** 5579 Spectrum Dr 21703. I-270 exit 31A, just e on SR 85. Int corridors. **Pets:** Accepted. 🛜 🔋 💷

▲▲▲ ▼▼▼ MainStay Suites Frederick [H]
(301) 668-4600. **$90-$130.** 7310 Executive Way 21704. I-270 exit 31B, 0.7 mi sw on SR 85. Int corridors. **Pets:** Medium. $10 daily fee/pet. Designated rooms, service with restrictions, supervision.
[SAVE] 🛜 🔋 💷 ⊋

▼▼▼▼ Residence Inn by Marriott Frederick [H]
(301) 360-0010. **$189-$219.** 5230 Westview Dr 21703. I-270 exit 31B, 0.5 mi sw on SR 85, then 0.3 mi n on Crestwood Blvd. Int corridors.
Pets: Accepted. 🛜 ⊠ 🔋M 🔋 💷 ⊋ ⊠

▲▲▲ ▼▼▼ Travelodge Frederick [H]
(301) 663-0500. **$58-$95.** 20 Monocacy Blvd 21704. I-70 exit 54, just n. Int corridors. **Pets:** Medium, dogs only. $25 deposit/room. Designated rooms, service with restrictions, supervision. [SAVE] 🛜 🔋 💷

FROSTBURG

▲▲▲ ▼▼▼ Days Inn & Suites [M]
(301) 689-2050. **$80-$125.** 11100 New Georges Creek Rd 21532. I-68 exit 34, 1 mi n on SR 36. Int corridors. **Pets:** $20 daily fee/pet. Service with restrictions, supervision. [SAVE] 🛜 🔋 💷 ⊠

GRASONVILLE

▲▲▲ ▼▼▼ BEST WESTERN Kent Narrows Inn [M] ✿
(410) 827-6767. **$79-$229.** 3101 Main St 21638. US 50 and 301 exit 42; at Kent Narrows Bridge. Ext corridors. **Pets:** Medium. $10 daily fee/pet. Service with restrictions, crate. [SAVE] 🛜 🔋 💷 ⊋

HAGERSTOWN

▼▼▼ Days Inn Hagerstown [M]
(301) 733-2700. **$60-$70.** 1101 Dual Hwy 21740. I-70 exit 32B, 2.2 mi w on US 40. Int corridors. **Pets:** Small, other species. $12 daily fee/pet. Designated rooms, service with restrictions, supervision. 🛜 🔋 💷

▼▼▼ Halfway Hagerstown Super 8 [M]
(301) 582-1992. **$59-$150.** 16805 Blake Rd 21740. I-81 exit 5B, just w. Int corridors. **Pets:** Medium, dogs only. $15 deposit/pet, $10 daily fee/pet. Designated rooms, service with restrictions, supervision. 🛜 🔋 💷

▲▲▲ ▼▼▼ Holiday Inn Express Hotel & Suites [H] ✿
(301) 745-5644. **Call for rates.** 241 Railway Ln 21740. I-81 exit 5A, just e. Int corridors. **Pets:** Other species. $25 one-time fee/room. Designated rooms, service with restrictions, supervision.
[SAVE] 🛜 🔋M 🔋 💷 ⊋ ⊠

▲▲▲ ▼▼▼ Sleep Inn & Suites [H]
(301) 766-9449. **$85-$100.** 18216 Col Henry K Douglas Dr 21740. I-70 exit 29, just s. Int corridors. **Pets:** Other species. $10 daily fee/pet. Designated rooms, supervision. [SAVE] 🛜 🔋 💷

INDIAN HEAD

▲▲▲ ▼▼▼ Super 8 Indian Head [M]
(301) 753-8100. **$59-$150.** 4694 Indian Head Hwy 20640. SR 210, 0.6 mi s of jct SR 225. Int corridors. **Pets:** Medium, dogs only. $10 daily fee/pet. Service with restrictions, supervision. [SAVE] 🛜 🔋M 🔋 💷

LA VALE

▲▲▲ ▼▼▼▼ BEST WESTERN PLUS Braddock Motor Inn [H]
(301) 729-3300. **$70-$75, 7 day notice.** 1268 National Hwy 21502. On US 40, jct SR 53, adjacent to I-68 exit 39W/40E. Int corridors.
Pets: Accepted. [SAVE] 🛜 🔋 💷 ⑪ ⊋ ⊠

LEXINGTON PARK

▼▼▼▼ Home2 Suites by Hilton Lexington Park/Pax River NAS [H]
(301) 866-1416. **$89-$239.** 46058 Valley Dr 20653. On SR 235, 0.9 mi n of jct SR 246. Int corridors. **Pets:** Large, other species. $75 one-time fee/pet. Designated rooms, service with restrictions, crate.
[ECO] 🛜 ⊠ 🔋M 🔋 💷 ⊋

▼▼▼▼ TownePlace Suites by Marriott Patuxent River Naval Air Station [H] ✿
(301) 863-1111. **$129-$199.** 22520 Three Notch Rd 20653. From Gate 1 at Patuxent River Naval Air Station, 1 mi n on SR 235. Int corridors. **Pets:** Other species. $100 one-time fee/room. Service with restrictions.
🛜 ⊠ 🔋M 🔋 💷 ⊋

MCHENRY

▼▼▼▼ Wisp Resort Hotel & Conference Center [H]
(301) 387-5581. **$79-$369, 7 day notice.** 290 Marsh Hill Rd 21541. 1 mi s on US 219 from jct SR 42, just w on Sang Run Rd, then 0.3 mi s. Int corridors. **Pets:** Accepted. 🛜 ⊠ 🔋 💷 ⑪ ⊋ ⊠

NORTH EAST

BEST WESTERN North East Inn 🅷
(410) 287-5450. **Call for rates.** 39 Elwoods Rd 21901. I-95 exit 100 southbound; exit 100B northbound, 0.5 mi n on SR 272, then just w on Joseph Biggs Hwy to Old Bayview Rd. Int corridors. **Pets:** Large, other species. $10 daily fee/pet. Service with restrictions.

Comfort Inn & Suites North East 🅷
(410) 287-7100. **$89-$130.** 1 Center Dr 21901. I-95 exit 100 southbound; exit 100A northbound, just s on SR 272. Int corridors. **Pets:** Small, dogs only. $15 daily fee/pet. Designated rooms, service with restrictions, supervision.

OCEAN CITY

Clarion Resort Fontainebleau Hotel 🅷
(410) 524-3535. **$79-$389, 3 day notice.** 10100 Coastal Hwy 21842. At 101st St. Int corridors. **Pets:** Other species. $35 daily fee/pet. Designated rooms, service with restrictions.

Coastal Palms Inn & Suites 🅼
(410) 250-4000. **$49-$299, 3 day notice.** 12000 Coastal Hwy 21842. At 120th St. Ext corridors. **Pets:** Accepted.

Comfort Suites Ocean City 🅷 ❀
(410) 213-7171. **Call for rates.** 12718 Ocean Gateway 21842. US 50; 0.7 mi w of Ocean City Bridge. Int corridors. **Pets:** Medium. $35 daily fee/pet. Designated rooms, service with restrictions, crate.

PERRYVILLE

Days Inn Perryville 🅼
(410) 642-2866. **$69-$84.** 61 Heather Ln 21903. I-95 exit 93, just e. Ext corridors. **Pets:** Accepted.

ROCK HALL

Inn at Huntingfield Creek 🅱🅱
(410) 639-7779. **$179-$325, 14 day notice.** 4928 Eastern Neck Rd 21661. 1.8 mi s on SR 445 from jct SR 20. Ext/int corridors. **Pets:** Dogs only. $30 daily fee/pet. Designated rooms.

Mariners Motel 🅼
(410) 639-2291. **$75-$95.** 5681 S Hawthorne Ave 21661. 0.3 mi e of SR 20. Ext corridors. **Pets:** Other species. $10 one-time fee/room. Service with restrictions, crate.

ST. MICHAELS

BEST WESTERN St. Michaels Motor Inn 🅼
(410) 745-3333. **$109-$189.** 1228 S Talbot St 21663. 1 mi e on SR 33. Ext/int corridors. **Pets:** Accepted.

St. Michaels Harbour Inn, Marina & Spa 🅷
(410) 745-9001. **$129-$525, 3 day notice.** 101 N Harbor Rd 21663. 0.3 mi e on SR 33, just n on Seymour Ave, then just w on Meadow St. Int corridors. **Pets:** Medium, dogs only. $100 one-time fee/pet. Designated rooms, service with restrictions, supervision.

SALISBURY

BEST WESTERN Salisbury Plaza 🅼 ❀
(410) 546-1300. **$59-$130.** 1735 N Salisbury Blvd 21801. US 13 business route, 0.5 mi s of US 50 Bypass. Ext corridors. **Pets:** Other species. Service with restrictions, crate.

Holiday Inn Salisbury Downtown 🅷
(410) 546-4400. **Call for rates.** 300 S Salisbury Blvd 21801. US 13 business route, 0.4 mi s of jct US 50 business route; downtown. Int corridors. **Pets:** Medium. $25 daily fee/pet. Designated rooms, service with restrictions, crate.

Residence Inn by Marriott Salisbury 🅷 ❀
(410) 543-0033. **$113-$189.** 140 Centre Rd 21801. Just off US 13 business route at US 50. Int corridors. **Pets:** Other species. $100 one-time fee/room. Service with restrictions.

SNOW HILL

River House Inn 🅱🅱
(410) 632-2722. **$99-$325, 7 day notice.** 201 E Market St 21863. 1 mi w on SR 394 from jct SR 113. Ext/int corridors. **Pets:** Dogs only. $10 daily fee/pet. Designated rooms, service with restrictions, crate.

THURMONT

Cozy Country Inn 🅼
(301) 271-4301. **Call for rates.** 103 Frederick Rd 21788. US 15, just e to SR 806, 0.4 mi n. Ext corridors. **Pets:** Large, dogs only. $25 one-time fee/room. Designated rooms, service with restrictions.

Super 8-Thurmont 🅼
(301) 271-7888. **$59-$150.** 300 Tippin Dr 21788. US 15, just w on SR 806. Int corridors. **Pets:** Medium. $10 daily fee/pet. Service with restrictions, supervision.

TILGHMAN ISLAND

Knapp's Narrows Marina & Inn 🅼
(410) 886-2720. **$80-$170, 7 day notice.** 6176 Tilghman Island Rd 21671. On SR 33, east side of the bridge. Ext corridors. **Pets:** Other species. $25 daily fee/pet. Designated rooms, service with restrictions, supervision.

WALDORF

La Quinta Inn Waldorf 🅷
(301) 645-0022. **$72-$155.** 11770 Business Park Dr 20601. 1 mi n on US 301 from jct SR 228. Int corridors. **Pets:** Service with restrictions, supervision.

Residence Inn by Marriott Waldorf 🅷
(301) 632-2111. **$154-$199.** 3020 Technology Pl 20601. SR 228, just w of jct US 301. Int corridors. **Pets:** Other species. $100 one-time fee/room. Service with restrictions, supervision.

WASHINGTON, D.C. METROPOLITAN AREA

BELTSVILLE

Comfort Inn Capital Beltway/I-95 North 🅷
(301) 572-7100. **$89-$149.** 4050 Powder Mill Rd 20705. I-95 exit 29B, just w on SR 212. Int corridors. **Pets:** Other species. $25 one-time fee/room. Service with restrictions, crate.

Sheraton Washington North Hotel 🅷 ❀
(301) 937-4422. **$89-$199.** 4095 Powder Mill Rd 20705. I-95 exit 29B, just w on SR 212; 2 mi n of I-495. Int corridors. **Pets:** Medium, dogs only. $25 daily fee/pet. Designated rooms, service with restrictions, crate.

BETHESDA

Hyatt Regency Bethesda H
(301) 657-1234. **$89-$315.** One Bethesda Metro Center 20814. I-495 exit 34, 2.5 mi s on SR 355; jct Wisconsin Ave and Old Georgetown Rd. Int corridors. **Pets:** Accepted.

Residence Inn by Marriott-Bethesda Downtown H
(301) 718-0200. **$101-$299.** 7335 Wisconsin Ave 20814. I-495 exit 34, 2.5 mi s on SR 355; entrance on Waverly St. Int corridors.
Pets: Accepted.

BOWIE

Comfort Inn Conference Center-Bowie H
(301) 464-0089. **$85-$132.** 4500 NW Crain Hwy 20716. US 50 exit 13A, jct US 50/301 and SR 3. Int corridors. **Pets:** Medium, other species. $15 daily fee/pet. Designated rooms, service with restrictions, crate.

CAMP SPRINGS

Country Inn & Suites By Carlson Andrews Air Force Base/DC Area H
(240) 492-1070. **$99-$200.** 4950 Mercedes Blvd 20746. I-95/495 exit 7B, just e to Auth Rd, then just n. Int corridors. **Pets:** Medium. $50 daily fee/pet. Designated rooms, service with restrictions, supervision.

CHEVERLY

Howard Johnson Washington, DC North/BW Pkwy H
(301) 779-7700. **$89-$319.** 5811 Annapolis Rd 20784. Jct Baltimore-Washington Pkwy and SR 450. Int corridors. **Pets:** Accepted.

CLINTON

TownePlace Suites by Marriott Clinton/Andrews AFB H
(301) 856-2266. **$169-$289.** 7800 Ferry Ave 20735. I-95/495 exit 7A, 2.9 mi s on SR 5 exit Coventry Way E, follow signs to Andrews AFB, then 0.5 mi ne on Old Alexandria Ferry Rd. Int corridors. **Pets:** Medium, other species. $400 deposit/room, $100 one-time fee/room. Designated rooms, service with restrictions, supervision.

COLLEGE PARK

Clarion Inn & Fundome H
(301) 474-2800. **$75-$149.** 8601 Baltimore Ave 20740. I-95/495 exit 25 northbound; exit 25B southbound, 1.5 mi s on US 1. Ext/int corridors. **Pets:** Medium. $20 daily fee/pet. Designated rooms, service with restrictions, supervision.

Comfort Inn & Suites College Park H
(301) 441-8110. **$109-$159.** 9020 Baltimore Ave 20740. I-95/495 exit 25 northbound; exit 25B southbound, 1.3 mi s on US 1. Int corridors. **Pets:** Medium, other species. $25 daily fee/pet. Service with restrictions, supervision.

Super 8-College Park M
(301) 474-0894. **$59-$150.** 9150 Baltimore Ave 20740. I-95/495 exit 25 northbound; exit 25B southbound, 0.9 mi s on US 1. Int corridors. **Pets:** Small. $11 daily fee/pet. Designated rooms, service with restrictions, supervision.

GAITHERSBURG

Comfort Inn Shady Grove H
(301) 330-0023. **$79-$159.** 16216 Frederick Rd 20877. I-270 exit 8, 1 mi e on Shady Grove Rd at SR 355. Int corridors. **Pets:** Other species. $15 daily fee/pet. Service with restrictions.

Extended Stay America-Washington DC-Rockville H
(301) 987-9100. **$109-$299.** 2621 Research Blvd 20850. I-270 exit 8, just w, then just n. Int corridors. **Pets:** $25 daily fee/pet. Designated rooms, service with restrictions.

Hilton Washington DC North/Gaithersburg H
(301) 977-8900. **$129-$149.** 620 Perry Pkwy 20877. I-270 exit 11, then e. Int corridors. **Pets:** Medium, other species. $50 deposit/pet. Designated rooms, service with restrictions, supervision.

Holiday Inn-Gaithersburg H
(301) 948-8900. **Call for rates.** 2 Montgomery Village Ave 20879. I-270 exit 11, 0.3 mi e. Int corridors. **Pets:** Accepted.

Hyatt house Gaithersburg H
(301) 527-6000. **$89-$229.** 200 Skidmore Blvd 20877. I-370 exit SR 355, just n to Westland Rd. Ext corridors. **Pets:** Accepted.

Residence Inn by Marriott-Gaithersburg H
(301) 590-3003. **$94-$170.** 9721 Washingtonian Blvd 20878. I-270 exit 9B (I-370/Sam Eig Hwy), just w to Fields Rd, 0.8 mi se, then just ne. Int corridors. **Pets:** $100 one-time fee/room. Service with restrictions.

TownePlace Suites by Marriott-Gaithersburg H
(301) 590-2300. **$79-$249.** 212 Perry Pkwy 20877. I-270 exit 10 northbound, just e; exit 11 southbound, just e on SR 124 to SR 355, 0.3 mi s, then 0.5 mi sw. Int corridors. **Pets:** Accepted.

GREENBELT

Residence Inn by Marriott-Greenbelt H
(301) 982-1600. **$98-$224.** 6320 Golden Triangle Dr 20770. I-95/495 exit 23, 0.5 mi sw of jct SR 201; off SR 193 (Greenbelt Rd), just n on Walker Dr. Int corridors. **Pets:** Accepted.

LAUREL

Holiday Inn Express & Suites Laurel Lakes H
(301) 206-2600. **Call for rates.** 14402 Laurel Pl 20707. On US 1, 0.9 mi s of jct SR 198. Int corridors. **Pets:** Accepted.

Holiday Inn Laurel-West H
(301) 776-5300. **$89-$149.** 15101 Sweitzer Ln 20707. I-95 exit 33B, just w on SR 198. Ext/int corridors. **Pets:** Accepted.

NATIONAL HARBOR

Aloft Washington National Harbor H
(301) 749-9000. **$119-$299.** 156 Waterfront St 20745. I-95/495 exit 2A, 0.5 mi e. Int corridors. **Pets:** Accepted.

Residence Inn by Marriott National Harbor H
(301) 749-4755. **$149-$259.** 192 Waterfront St 20745. I-95/495 exit 2A, 0.5 mi e. Int corridors. **Pets:** Other species. $200 one-time fee/room. Designated rooms, service with restrictions.

The Westin Washington National Harbor H
(301) 567-3999. **$199-$309.** 171 Waterfront St 20745. I-95/495 exit 2A, 0.5 mi e. Int corridors. **Pets:** Small, dogs only. $25 deposit/room. Designated rooms, service with restrictions, crate.

ROCKVILLE

BEST WESTERN PLUS Rockville Hotel & Suites H
(301) 424-4940. **Call for rates.** 1251 W Montgomery Ave 20850. I-270 exit 6B, just w on SR 28. Int corridors. **Pets:** Medium. $20 deposit/pet, $20 daily fee/pet. Crate.

▼▼▼ Hilton Rockville Hotel & Executive Meeting
Center **H** ❀
(301) 468-1100. **$89-$309.** 1750 Rockville Pike 20852. SR 355, 2 mi s of jct SR 28. Int corridors. **Pets:** Large. $50 one-time fee/room. Designated rooms, service with restrictions.
📶 ✕ 🔥M 🛏 🖥 🍽 ⤴ 🚫

𝄢 ▼▼▼ Red Roof Inn-Rockville **M**
(301) 987-0965. **$69-$145.** 16001 Shady Grove Rd 20850. I-270 exit 8 (Shady Grove Rd), 0.5 mi e. Ext corridors. **Pets:** Large, other species. Service with restrictions, supervision. SAVE 📶 🔥M 🛏

𝄢 ▼▼▼ Sheraton Rockville **H**
(240) 912-8200. **$89-$400.** 920 King Farm Blvd 20850. I-270 exit 8 (Shady Grove Rd), 0.3 mi e to Choke Cherry Rd, just s to Piccard Dr, then just sw; 1 mi w of SR 355 via Redland Blvd. Int corridors.
Pets: Accepted. SAVE 📶 ✕ 🔥M 🛏 🖥 🍽 ⤴ 🚫

𝄢 ▼▼▼ Sleep Inn-Rockville **H**
(301) 948-8000. **$59-$139.** 2 Research Ct 20850. I-270 exit 8 (Shady Grove Rd), just sw. Int corridors. **Pets:** Medium. $15 daily fee/pet. Service with restrictions, crate. SAVE 📶 🔥M 🛏 🖥

SILVER SPRING
▼▼▼ Residence Inn by Marriott Silver Spring **H**
(301) 572-2322. **$93-$299.** 12000 Plum Orchard Dr 20904. I-95 exit 29B, 1.2 mi w on SR 212, then 1 mi n on Cherry Hill Rd. Int corridors.
Pets: Medium, other species. $125 one-time fee/room. Service with restrictions, crate. ECO 📶 ✕ 🔥M 🛏 🖥 ⤴ 🚫

𝄢 ▼▼▼ Sheraton Silver Spring **H**
(301) 589-0800. **$99-$229.** 8777 Georgia Ave 20910. I-495 exit 31B, 1 mi s. Int corridors. **Pets:** Accepted.
SAVE 📶 ✕ 🔥M 🛏 🖥 🍽 ⤴ 🚫

UPPER MARLBORO
𝄢 ▼▼▼ Executive Inn & Suites **M**
(301) 627-3969. **$70-$120.** 2901 Crain Hwy 20774. On US 301, 2.5 mi n of jct SR 4; 7 mi s of jct US 50. Ext corridors. **Pets:** Medium. $5 daily fee/pet. Service with restrictions, supervision. SAVE 📶 🔥M 🛏 🖥

END METROPOLITAN AREA

WILLIAMSPORT
𝄢 ▼▼▼ Red Roof Inn **M**
(301) 582-3500. **$49-$99.** 310 E Potomac St 21795. I-81 exit 2, 0.3 mi sw on US 11. Ext corridors. **Pets:** Large, other species. Service with restrictions, supervision. SAVE 📶 🛏

MASSACHUSETTS

CITY INDEX

AMHERST
▼ University Lodge **M**
(413) 256-8111. **Call for rates.** 345 N Pleasant St 01002. 0.6 mi n. Ext corridors. **Pets:** Accepted. 📶 ✕ 🛏 🖥

AUBURN
▼▼ Comfort Inn **H**
(508) 832-8300. **Call for rates.** 426 Southbridge St 01501. I-90 exit 10, 1 mi n on SR 12; I-290 exit 9 to SR 12. Int corridors. **Pets:** Accepted.
📶 🔥M 🛏 🖥

▼▼ La Quinta Inn Auburn Worcester **H**
(508) 832-7000. **$95-$162.** 446 Southbridge St 01501. I-90 exit 10, 1.2 mi n on SR 12. Int corridors. **Pets:** Service with restrictions, supervision.
📶 🛏 🖥

BARRE
▼▼▼ Jenkins Inn **CI**
(978) 355-6444. **$185-$260, 7 day notice.** 7 West St 01005. On SR 122 and 32. Int corridors. **Pets:** Dogs only. $10 daily fee/pet. Supervision.
📶 ✕ 🛏 🖥 🍽

BOSTON METROPOLITAN AREA

ANDOVER

Homewood Suites by Hilton Boston/Andover 🏨
(978) 475-6000. **$109-$139.** 4 Riverside Dr 01810. I-93 exit 45, 0.5 mi e.
Int corridors. **Pets:** Accepted.

La Quinta Inn & Suites Andover 🏨
(978) 685-6200. **$87-$166.** 131 River Rd 01810. I-93 exit 45, just w;
I-495 exit 40B, 2 mi n. Int corridors. **Pets:** Service with restrictions, supervision.

Residence Inn by Marriott Boston-Andover 🏨
(978) 683-0382. **$109-$209.** 500 Minuteman Rd 01810. I-93 exit 45, 0.3
mi w, then 0.5 mi n. Int corridors. **Pets:** Accepted.

Sonesta ES Suites 🏨
(978) 686-2000. **$135-$162.** 4 Tech Dr 01810. I-93 exit 45, just sw to
Shattuck Rd. Int corridors. **Pets:** Accepted.

Wyndham Boston/Andover Hotel 🏨 🐾
(978) 975-3600. **$109-$219.** 123 Old River Rd 01810. I-93 exit 45, just e
on River Rd. Int corridors. **Pets:** Medium. $50 one-time fee/room. Service
with restrictions, supervision.

BEDFORD

Homewood Suites by Hilton 🏨
(978) 670-7111. **$129-$139.** 35 Middlesex Tpke 01730. I-95 exit 32B, 2.5
mi n. Int corridors. **Pets:** Accepted.

BOSTON

Ames Hotel 🏨
(617) 979-8100. **$200-$700.** 1 Court St 02108. Across from Old State
House. Int corridors. **Pets:** Small. $100 one-time fee/room. Service with
restrictions.

BEST WESTERN PLUS Roundhouse Suites 🏨
(617) 989-1000. **Call for rates.** 891 Massachusetts Ave 02118. I-93 exit
18, just sw; just n of Newmarket Square. Int corridors. **Pets:** Medium. $20
daily fee/pet. Designated rooms, service with restrictions, crate.

Boston Harbor Hotel 🏨 🐾
(617) 439-7000. **Call for rates.** 70 Rowes Wharf 02110. At Rowes
Wharf. Int corridors. **Pets:** Other species. $100 one-time fee/room. Service with restrictions, supervision.

The Boston Park Plaza Hotel & Towers 🏨
(617) 426-2000. **Call for rates.** 100 Columbus Ave 02116. At Park Plaza
and Arlington St, just s of Boston Common and Public Gardens. Int corridors. **Pets:** Accepted.

Bulfinch Hotel 🏨
(617) 624-0202. **Call for rates.** 107 Merrimac St 02114. At Lancaster St.
Int corridors. **Pets:** Medium, other species. $30 deposit/room. Designated
rooms, service with restrictions.

The Colonnade Hotel Boston 🏨
(617) 424-7000. **Call for rates.** 120 Huntington Ave 02116. Just s of
Copley Square. Int corridors. **Pets:** Accepted.

Comfort Inn Boston 🏨
(617) 287-9200. **Call for rates.** 900 William T Morrissey Blvd 02122.
I-93 exit 13 northbound, 0.5 mi sw; exit 12 southbound, follow signs. Int
corridors. **Pets:** Designated rooms, service with restrictions, supervision.

Copley Square Hotel 🏨 🐾
(617) 536-9000. **$159-$599.** 47 Huntington Ave 02116. I-90 exit 22, just
n. Int corridors. **Pets:** Large, dogs only. $60 one-time fee/pet. Service with
restrictions, supervision.

DoubleTree Suites by Hilton Boston 🏨
(617) 783-0090. **$139-$399.** 400 Soldiers Field Rd 02134. I-90 exit 20
westbound; exit 18 eastbound. Int corridors. **Pets:** Accepted.

The Eliot Hotel 🏨 🐾
(617) 267-1607. **$285-$545.** 370 Commonwealth Ave 02215. Corner of
Massachusetts Ave. Int corridors. **Pets:** Service with restrictions, crate.

Fairmont Battery Wharf 🏨 🐾
(617) 994-9000. **$209-$2200.** Three Battery Wharf 02109. At Battery
Wharf; east of North End. Int corridors. **Pets:** Small, other species. $25
daily fee/pet. Service with restrictions, supervision.

The Fairmont Copley Plaza Boston 🏨 🐾
(617) 267-5300. **$299-$579.** 138 St. James Ave 02116. At Copley
Square. Int corridors. **Pets:** Medium. $25 daily fee/pet. Service with
restrictions, supervision.

Fifteen Beacon 🏨 🐾
(617) 670-1500. **$325-$1600.** 15 Beacon St 02108. Center. Int corridors.
Pets: Dogs only. Designated rooms, service with restrictions, supervision.

Four Seasons Hotel Boston 🏨
(617) 338-4400. **$395-$995.** 200 Boylston St 02116. Between Arlington
and Charles sts. Int corridors. **Pets:** Accepted.

Hilton Boston Financial District 🏨
(617) 556-0006. **$189-$299.** 89 Broad St 02110. Corner of Broad and
Franklin sts. Int corridors. **Pets:** Accepted.

Hilton Boston Logan Airport 🏨 🐾
(617) 568-6700. **$159-$409.** 1 Hotel Dr 02128. At Boston Logan International Airport. Int corridors. **Pets:** Large, other species. $25 one-time fee/
room. Designated rooms, service with restrictions, supervision.

Hotel Commonwealth 🏨
(617) 933-5000. **$179-$569.** 500 Commonwealth Ave 02215. On SR 2;
at Beacon St and Brookline Ave. Int corridors. **Pets:** Accepted.

Hyatt Regency Boston 🏨 🐾
(617) 912-1234. **$159-$599.** 1 Avenue De Lafayette 02111. Just e of
Boston Common at Lafayette Pl. Int corridors. **Pets:** Large. $50 one-time
fee/room. Service with restrictions, crate.

InterContinental Boston 🏨
(617) 747-1000. **Call for rates.** 510 Atlantic Ave 02210. I-93 exit 23
southbound; exit 20 northbound; at Pearl St. Int corridors. **Pets:** Accepted.

The Langham, Boston 🏨
(617) 451-1900. **$205-$575.** 250 Franklin St 02110. On Post Office
Square; center. Int corridors. **Pets:** Medium, dogs only. $100 one-time
fee/pet. Designated rooms, service with restrictions, supervision.

▼▼ ▼▼ The Lenox Hotel 🏨 🐾
(617) 536-5300. **$195-$495.** 61 Exeter St 02116. I-90 exit 22, just n at Boylston St. Int corridors. **Pets:** Medium, dogs only. $125 one-time fee/room. Supervision. 🄴🄲🄾 🔌 📶 ✕ 🍴

◈ ▼▼ ▼▼ The Liberty, A Luxury Collection Hotel 🏨
(617) 224-4000. **$299-$699.** 215 Charles St 02114. I-93 exit 26 (Storrow Dr). Int corridors. **Pets:** Accepted. [SAVE] 📶 ✕ ♿M 🍴

◈ ▼◈▼◈▼ Mandarin Oriental, Boston 🏨 🐾
(617) 535-8888. **$345-$995.** 776 Boylston St 02199. At Prudential Center. Int corridors. **Pets:** Medium, dogs only. Designated rooms, service with restrictions, supervision. [SAVE] 📶 ✕ ♿M 🍴

◈ ▼▼ ▼▼ The Midtown Hotel 🏨 🐾
(617) 262-1000. **$99-$309.** 220 Huntington Ave 02115. 3 blks sw of Copley Pl; just n of Symphony Hall and Massachusetts Ave. Int corridors. **Pets:** Other species. $30 one-time fee/pet. Service with restrictions, crate. [SAVE] 📶 ✕ 🍴 ≈

◈ ▼▼ ▼▼ Nine Zero Hotel 🏨
(617) 772-5800. **$209-$539.** 90 Tremont St 02108. Just ne of Boston Common; motor entrance on Bosworth. Int corridors. **Pets:** Accepted. 🄴🄲🄾 [SAVE] 📶 ✕ ♿M

◈ ▼▼ ▼▼ Omni Parker House 🏨
(617) 227-8600. **Call for rates.** 60 School St 02108. Corner of Tremont St; northeast corner of Boston Common. Int corridors. **Pets:** Medium. $51 one-time fee/room. Service with restrictions, supervision.
[SAVE] 📶 ✕ 💻 🍴

◈ ▼▼ ▼▼ Onyx Hotel 🏨
(617) 557-9955. **$159-$499.** 155 Portland St 02114. Corner of Merrimac and Traverse sts, just n; 3 blks s of TD Bank North Garden. Int corridors. **Pets:** Accepted. 🄴🄲🄾 [SAVE] 📶 ✕ 🍴 ✕

▼▼ ▼▼ Ramada Boston 🏨
(617) 287-9100. **$99-$259.** 800 William T Morrissey Blvd 02122. I-93 exit 13 northbound, 0.5 mi sw; exit 12 southbound, follow signs. Int corridors. **Pets:** Designated rooms, service with restrictions, supervision.
📶 ✕ 💻 ≈

◈ ▼▼ ▼▼ Residence Inn by Marriott Boston Harbor on Tudor Wharf 🏨 🐾
(617) 242-9000. **$179-$499.** 34-44 Charles River Ave 02129. Just se of SR 99 at Charlestown Bridge. Int corridors. **Pets:** Medium. $100 one-time fee/room. Service with restrictions.
[SAVE] 📶 ✕ ♿M 💻 🍴 ≈

◈ ▼◈▼◈▼ Revere Hotel/Boston Common 🏨 🐾
(617) 482-1800. **$179-$699.** 200 Stuart St 02116. At Park Square and Charles St; in Back Bay. Int corridors. **Pets:** Other species. Service with restrictions. [SAVE] 📶 ✕ 💻 🍴 ≈

◈ ▼◈▼◈▼ The Ritz-Carlton, Boston Common 🏨 🐾
(617) 574-7100. **$395-$725.** 10 Avery St 02111. At Washington and Avery sts; 1 blk e of Boston Common. Int corridors. **Pets:** Medium. $150 one-time fee/room. Service with restrictions, supervision.
[SAVE] 📶 ✕ ♿M 🍴 ≈ ✕

◈ ▼▼ ▼▼ Seaport Hotel & Seaport World Trade Center 🏨 🐾
(617) 385-4000. **$149-$499.** 1 Seaport Ln 02210. At Seaport World Trade Center. Int corridors. **Pets:** Medium, dogs only. Designated rooms, service with restrictions, supervision.
🄴🄲🄾 🔌 [SAVE] 📶 ✕ ♿M 💻 🍴 ≈ ✕

◈ ▼▼ ▼▼ Sheraton Boston 🏨 🐾
(617) 236-2000. **$159-$549.** 39 Dalton St 02199. I-90 exit 22. Int corridors. **Pets:** Medium, dogs only. Service with restrictions, supervision.
🄴🄲🄾 [SAVE] 📶 ✕ ♿M 💻 🍴 ≈

▼▼ ▼▼ Taj Boston 🏨 🐾
(617) 536-5700. **$249-$5000.** 15 Arlington St 02117. At Arlington and Newbury sts; overlooks the Public Gardens. Int corridors. **Pets:** Large. Service with restrictions, supervision. 🄴🄲🄾 📶 ✕ 🍴 ✕

◈ ▼▼ ▼▼ W Boston Hotel & Residences 🏨 🐾
(617) 261-8700. **$259-$679.** 100 Stuart St 02116. At Tremont St. Int corridors. **Pets:** Medium. $50 one-time fee/room. Service with restrictions.
[SAVE] 📶 ✕ ♿M 🍴

◈ ▼▼ ▼▼ Westin Boston Waterfront 🏨
(617) 532-4600. **$199-$579.** 425 Summer St 02210. I-93 exit 23, 1 mi se on Purchase St to Summer St. Int corridors. **Pets:** Accepted.
[SAVE] 📶 ✕ ♿M 💻 🍴 ≈

◈ ▼▼ ▼▼ The Westin Copley Place Boston 🏨
(617) 262-9600. **$279-$639.** 10 Huntington Ave 02116. I-90 exit 22; at Copley Square. Int corridors. **Pets:** Accepted.
🄴🄲🄾 [SAVE] 📶 ✕ 💻 🍴 ≈ ✕

BOXBOROUGH

▼▼ ▼▼ Holiday Inn Boxborough 🏨 🐾
(978) 263-8701. **Call for rates.** 242 Adams Pl 01719. I-495 exit 28, just e on SR 111. Int corridors. **Pets:** $25 one-time fee/room. Service with restrictions, crate. 📶 ✕ 💻 🍴 ≈

BRAINTREE

▼▼ Candlewood Suites Boston - Braintree 🏨
(781) 849-7450. **$100-$115.** 235 Wood Rd 02184. I-93 exit 6, just n on SR 37, then 0.5 mi w. Int corridors. **Pets:** Large, other species. $15 daily fee/room. 📶 💻

◈ ▼▼ ▼▼ Hampton Inn Braintree 🏨
(781) 380-3300. **$129-$249.** 215 Wood Rd 02184. I-93 exit 6, just n on SR 37, then 0.5 mi w. Int corridors. **Pets:** Accepted.
[SAVE] 📶 ♿M 💻 ≈

BROOKLINE

▼▼ ▼▼ Holiday Inn Boston-Brookline 🏨
(617) 277-1200. **$189-$309.** 1200 Beacon St 02446. 1 mi sw of Kenmore Square, on SR 2. Int corridors. **Pets:** Accepted.
📶 ✕ ♿M 💻 🍴 ≈

BURLINGTON

▼▼ ▼▼ Candlewood Suites Boston-Burlington 🏨
(781) 229-4300. **$89-$129.** 130 Middlesex Tpke 01803. I-95 exit 32B, just n. Int corridors. **Pets:** Accepted. 📶 ♿M 💻

◈ ▼▼ ▼▼ Hyatt house Boston/Burlington 🏨
(781) 270-0800. **$99-$239.** 2 Van de Graaff Dr 01803. I-95 exit 33A, just s on US 3, then 0.5 mi w on Wayside Rd. Int corridors. **Pets:** Medium. $150 one-time fee/room. Service with restrictions, crate.
[SAVE] 📶 ✕ ♿M 💻 ≈ ✕

◈ ▼▼ ▼▼ Sonesta ES Suites 🏨
(781) 221-2233. **Call for rates.** 11 Old Concord Rd 01803. I-95 exit 32B, just s on Middlesex Tpke. Int corridors. **Pets:** Accepted.
[SAVE] 📶 ♿M 💻 ≈

CAMBRIDGE

◈ ▼▼ ▼▼ BEST WESTERN PLUS Hotel Tria 🏨 🐾
(617) 491-8000. **$159-$369.** 220 Alewife Brook Pkwy 02138. Jct SR 2, 16 and US 3; I-90 (Massachusetts Tpke) exit Cambridge/Allston to SR 2 W (Fresh Pond Pkwy). Int corridors. **Pets:** Medium. $20 daily fee/room. Designated rooms, service with restrictions, supervision.
[SAVE] 📶 ♿M 💻 🍴

◈ ▼▼ ▼▼ The Charles Hotel, Harvard Square 🏨
(617) 864-1200. **Call for rates.** One Bennett St 02138. Just s of Harvard Square; at Eliot St. Int corridors. **Pets:** Accepted.
🔌 [SAVE] 📶 ✕ ♿M 🍴 ≈ ✕

ⓐⓐⓐ ▼▼▼▼ **Hotel Marlowe** Ⓗ ❀
(617) 868-8000. **$159-$569.** 25 Edwin H Land Blvd 02141. Just sw of jct SR 28. Int corridors. **Pets:** Other species.
ⒺⒸⓄ ⓈⒶⓋⒺ 🛜 ✕ 🔥ᴹ ▮▮ 🍽 🚫

ⓐⓐⓐ ▼▼▼▼ **Hyatt Regency Cambridge** Ⓗ
(617) 492-1234. **$129-$459.** 575 Memorial Dr 02139. On US 3 and SR 2. Int corridors. **Pets:** Accepted.
ⓈⒶⓋⒺ 🛜 🔥ᴹ 🖥 🖥 🍽 🚣 ✕

ⓐⓐⓐ ▼▼▼▼ **Le Meridien Cambridge** Ⓗ ❀
(617) 577-0200. **$139-$499, 3 day notice.** 20 Sidney St 02139. On SR 2A, 1 mi n of river. Int corridors. **Pets:** Dogs only. $150 deposit/room. Service with restrictions, supervision. ⓈⒶⓋⒺ 🛜 ✕ 🔥ᴹ 🖥 🍽

▼▼▼▼ **Residence Inn by Marriott Boston Cambridge Center** Ⓗ ❀
(617) 349-0700. **$99-$499.** 6 Cambridge Center 02142. Corner of Ames St and Broadway. Int corridors. **Pets:** Other species. $150 one-time fee/room. Service with restrictions. 🛜 ✕ 🔥ᴹ 🖥 🖥 🚣

ⓐⓐⓐ ▼▼▼▼ **Sheraton Commander Hotel** Ⓗ ❀
(617) 547-4800. **$119-$800.** 16 Garden St 02138. Just n of Harvard Square. Int corridors. **Pets:** Medium, dogs only. Service with restrictions, supervision. ⓈⒶⓋⒺ 🛜 ✕ 🖥 🍽

CHELSEA
▼▼▼▼ **Residence Inn by Marriott Boston Logan Airport/Chelsea** Ⓗ
(617) 889-9990. **Call for rates.** 200 Maple St 02150. 0.3 mi se of SR 16. Int corridors. **Pets:** Large, other species. $100 one-time fee/room. Designated rooms, service with restrictions, crate.
🛜 ✕ 🔥ᴹ 🖥 🖥 🚣

CONCORD
ⓐⓐⓐ ▼▼▼▼ **BEST WESTERN PLUS at Historic Concord** Ⓗ
(978) 369-6100. **$159-$199.** 740 Elm St 01742. 1.8 mi w, just off SR 2 and 2A. Int corridors. **Pets:** $15 daily fee/room. Designated rooms, service with restrictions, supervision. ⓈⒶⓋⒺ 🛜 ✕ 🖥 🖥 🚣

▼▼▼▼ **The Hawthorne Inn** ⒷⒷ
(978) 369-5610. **$159-$359, 14 day notice.** 462 Lexington Rd 01742. 0.8 mi e of town square. Int corridors. **Pets:** Small. $200 deposit/room, $25 one-time fee/pet. Designated rooms, supervision. 🛜 ✕ Ⓦ

DANVERS
ⓐⓐⓐ ▼▼▼▼ **Comfort Inn North Shore** Ⓗ
(978) 777-1700. **$85-$150.** 50 Dayton St 01923. Just w of US 1, 0.8 mi n of jct SR 114 exit Center St northbound; w under US 1 exit Dayton St southbound. Int corridors. **Pets:** Medium. $25 one-time fee/room, $10 daily fee/room. Service with restrictions, supervision.
ⓈⒶⓋⒺ 🛜 🔥ᴹ 🖥 🖥 🚣

ⓐⓐⓐ ▼▼▼▼ **DoubleTree by Hilton Boston North Shore** Ⓗ
(978) 777-2500. **$99-$229.** 50 Ferncroft Rd 01923. I-95 exit 50, follow signs for US 1 S to Ferncroft Village. Int corridors. **Pets:** Accepted.
ⓈⒶⓋⒺ 🛜 ✕ 🔥ᴹ 🖥 🖥 🍽 🚣 🚫

▼▼▼▼ **Residence Inn by Marriott Boston-North Shore/Danvers** Ⓗ
(978) 777-7171. **$109-$189.** 51 Newbury St 01923. US 1 N, just s of jct SR 114. Ext corridors. **Pets:** Accepted. 🛜 ✕ 🖥 🖥 🚣

▼▼▼▼ **TownePlace Suites by Marriott Boston-North Shore/Danvers** Ⓗ
(978) 777-6222. **$109-$179.** 238 Andover St 01923. SR 114 eastbound, enter just w of US 1 (no westbound entrance); US 1 southbound, enter through shopping center; southwest corner of jct US 1 and SR 114. Int corridors. **Pets:** Accepted. ⒺⒸⓄ 🛜 ✕ 🔥ᴹ 🖥 🖥 🚣

DEDHAM
ⓐⓐⓐ ▼▼▼▼ **Hilton Boston/Dedham** Ⓗ
(781) 329-7900. **$89-$289.** 25 Allied Dr 02026. I-95 exit 14, just e. Int corridors. **Pets:** Accepted. ⓈⒶⓋⒺ 🛜 🖥 🖥 🍽 🚣 🚫

▼▼▼▼ **Residence Inn by Marriott** Ⓗ
(781) 407-0999. **$109-$209.** 259 Elm St 02026. I-95 exit 15A, just n, then 0.4 mi e. Int corridors. **Pets:** Medium. $100 one-time fee/room. Service with restrictions. 🛜 ✕ 🖥 🖥 🚣 🚫

FOXBORO
▼▼▼▼ **Residence Inn by Marriott Foxborough** Ⓗ ❀
(508) 698-2800. **$119-$269.** 250 Foxborough Blvd 02035. I-95 exit 7A, 0.6 mi s on SR 140, 0.7 mi e, then just n. Int corridors. **Pets:** Other species. $100 one-time fee/room. Designated rooms, service with restrictions, crate. 🛜 ✕ 🔥ᴹ 🖥 🖥 🚣 🚫

FRAMINGHAM
ⓐⓐⓐ ▼▼▼ **BEST WESTERN Framingham** Ⓗ ❀
(508) 872-8811. **Call for rates.** 130 Worcester Rd 01702. I-90 exit 13, 0.5 mi s to SR 9; 1 mi w of Speen St; just w of Shopper's World Mall. Int corridors. **Pets:** Medium. Designated rooms, service with restrictions, supervision. ⓈⒶⓋⒺ 🛜 🖥 🖥 🍽 🚣

ⓐⓐⓐ ▼▼▼ **Red Roof Inn #068** Ⓜ
(508) 872-4499. **$71-$149.** 650 Cochituate Rd 01701. I-90 exit 13, follow SR 30 E. Ext corridors. **Pets:** Large, other species. Service with restrictions, supervision. ⓈⒶⓋⒺ 🛜 🖥

ⓐⓐⓐ ▼▼▼▼ **Residence Inn by Marriott Boston/Framingham** Ⓗ
(508) 370-0001. **$129-$259.** 400 Staples Dr 01702. SR 9 W to Crossing Blvd, then s. Int corridors. **Pets:** Medium, other species. $100 one-time fee/room. Service with restrictions, crate.
ⓈⒶⓋⒺ 🛜 ✕ 🔥ᴹ 🖥 🖥 🚣

ⓐⓐⓐ ▼▼▼▼ **Sheraton Framingham Hotel & Conference Center** Ⓗ ❀
(508) 879-7200. **$95-$285.** 1657 Worcester Rd 01701. I-90 exit 12, follow signs to SR 9 W. Int corridors. **Pets:** Small, dogs only. Designated rooms, service with restrictions, supervision.
ⓈⒶⓋⒺ 🛜 ✕ 🖥 🖥 🍽 🚣

FRANKLIN
ⓐⓐⓐ ▼▼▼▼ **Hawthorn Suites by Wyndham Franklin** Ⓗ
(508) 553-3500. **$149-$179.** 835 Upper Union St 02038. I-495 exit 16, just s, then 0.3 mi e. Int corridors. **Pets:** $50 one-time fee/room. Service with restrictions, crate. ⓈⒶⓋⒺ 🛜 ✕ 🔥ᴹ 🖥 🖥 🚣 🚫

▼▼▼▼ **Residence Inn by Marriott-Franklin** Ⓗ
(508) 541-8188. **$129-$199.** 4 Forge Pkwy 02038. I-495 exit 17, 0.7 mi nw off SR 140 N. Int corridors. **Pets:** Accepted.
🛜 ✕ 🔥ᴹ 🖥 🖥 🚣 🚫

GLOUCESTER
ⓐⓐⓐ ▼▼ **Cape Ann Motor Inn** Ⓜ ❀
(978) 281-2900. **$85-$185, 7 day notice.** 33 Rockport Rd 01930. 2 mi n of terminus of SR 128 on SR 127A. Ext corridors. **Pets:** Service with restrictions, supervision. ⓈⒶⓋⒺ 🛜 ✕ 🖥 Ⓐ

HAVERHILL
ⓐⓐⓐ ▼▼▼▼ **BEST WESTERN PLUS Merrimack Valley** Ⓗ
(978) 373-1511. **$100-$250.** 401 Lowell Ave 01832. I-495 exit 49 (SR 110). Int corridors. **Pets:** Large, other species. $20 daily fee/pet. Supervision. ⓈⒶⓋⒺ 🛜 ✕ 🖥 🖥 🚣

LAWRENCE
ⓐⓐⓐ ▼▼▼ **Holiday Inn Express** Ⓗ
(978) 975-4050. **$79-$129.** 224 Winthrop Ave 01843. I-495 exit 42A, just s on SR 114. Int corridors. **Pets:** Accepted. ⓈⒶⓋⒺ 🛜 ✕ 🔥ᴹ 🖥

LEXINGTON

Aloft Lexington �H ❀
(781) 761-1700. **$99-$349.** 727 Marrett Rd - A 02421. I-95 exit 30B, just w. Int corridors. **Pets:** Other species. Designated rooms, service with restrictions, crate.

Element Lexington �H 🐾
(781) 761-1750. **$109-$369.** 727 Marrett Rd - B 02421. I-95 exit 30B. Int corridors. **Pets:** Other species. Designated rooms, service with restrictions, crate.

MARLBOROUGH

BEST WESTERN Royal Plaza Hotel & Trade Center �H
(508) 460-0700. **Call for rates.** 181 Boston Post Rd W 01752. I-495 exit 24B, 1 mi w on US 20. Int corridors. **Pets:** Medium. $20 daily fee/room. Designated rooms, service with restrictions, supervision.

Courtyard by Marriott Boston Marlborough �H
(508) 480-0015. **$109-$209.** 75 Felton St 01752. I-495 exit 24B, just w; just off US 20. Int corridors. **Pets:** Accepted.

Embassy Suites Hotel-Boston Marlborough �H
(508) 485-5900. **$129-$199.** 123 Boston Post Rd W 01752. I-495 exit 24B, 0.5 mi w; just off US 20. Int corridors. **Pets:** Accepted.

Residence Inn by Marriott Boston Marlborough �H
(508) 481-1500. **$149-$209.** 112 Donald Lynch Blvd 01752. I-290 exit 25B, 3 mi ne. Int corridors. **Pets:** Accepted.

MEDFORD

Hyatt Place Boston/Medford �H
(781) 395-8500. **$109-$329.** 116 Riverside Ave NE 02155. I-93 exit 32, just sw to SR 60 and River St. Int corridors. **Pets:** Medium, dogs only. $150 one-time fee/room. Service with restrictions, crate.

NATICK

The Verve, Crowne Plaza �H 🐾
(508) 653-8800. **$129-$279, 7 day notice.** 1360 Worcester St 01760. I-90 exit 12, 5 mi e; SR 9, 4 mi e of Framingham Center. Int corridors. **Pets:** Other species. $50 one-time fee/room. Designated rooms, service with restrictions, crate.

NEEDHAM

Sheraton Needham Hotel �H 🐾
(781) 444-1110. **$99-$349.** 100 Cabot St 02494. I-95 exit 19A, just e. Int corridors. **Pets:** Large. Designated rooms, service with restrictions, supervision.

NEWBURYPORT

Garrison Inn �H
(978) 499-8500. **$190-$370, 7 day notice.** 11 Brown Square 01950. I-95 exit 57, 2.6 mi e on SR 1A, just n on Green St, just w on Pleasant St, then just s. Int corridors. **Pets:** $30 daily fee/pet. Service with restrictions, crate.

NEWTON

Hotel Indigo Boston-Newton Riverside �H
(617) 969-5300. **$109-$259, 3 day notice.** 399 Grove St 02462. I-95 exit 22, just e. Int corridors. **Pets:** Dogs only. $50 one-time fee/pet. Designated rooms, service with restrictions, crate.

NORWOOD

Hampton Inn Boston - Norwood �H
(781) 769-7000. **$109-$199.** 434 Providence Hwy 02062. I-95 exit 9 northbound, 5.9 mi ne on US 1; exit 11B southbound, 1.3 mi nw on Neponset St, then 0.4 mi n on US 1. Int corridors. **Pets:** Accepted.

Residence Inn by Marriott Boston-Norwood-Canton �H ❀
(781) 278-9595. **$109-$199.** 275 Norwood Park S 02062. I-95 exit 9 northbound, 3.7 mi n on US 1; exit 11B southbound, 0.5 mi nw on Neponset St, 0.6 mi w on Dean St, then 0.8 mi s on US 1. Int corridors. **Pets:** Other species. $100 one-time fee/room. Service with restrictions, crate.

PEABODY

Homewood Suites by Hilton �H
(978) 536-5050. **$139-$189.** 57 Newbury St 01960. On US 1 northbound. Int corridors. **Pets:** Accepted.

REVERE

Comfort Inn & Suites Boston Airport �H
(781) 485-3600. **$89-$249.** 85 American Legion Hwy 02151. Jct SR 1A and 60; 3 mi n of Boston Logan International Airport. Int corridors. **Pets:** Accepted.

Hampton Inn Boston Logan Airport �H
(781) 286-5665. **$139-$299.** 230 Lee Burbank Hwy 02151. On SR 1A, 0.6 mi s of terminus SR 60, 1.9 mi n of Boston Logan International Airport. Int corridors. **Pets:** Accepted.

ROCKPORT

Rockport Inn & Suites Ⓜ 🐾
(978) 546-3300. **$109-$259, 3 day notice.** 183 Main St 01966. On SR 127. Ext corridors. **Pets:** Other species. $30 daily fee/room. Service with restrictions.

ROWLEY

Country Garden Inn & Spa 🅱🅱
(978) 948-7773. **$99-$339, 10 day notice.** 101 Main St 01969. On SR 1A. Ext corridors. **Pets:** Dogs only. $30 daily fee/pet. Designated rooms, crate.

SALEM

Hawthorne Hotel �H 🐾
(978) 744-4080. **$114-$320, 3 day notice.** 18 Washington Square W 01970. On SR 1A. Int corridors. **Pets:** Other species. $15 daily fee/pet. Designated rooms, service with restrictions.

The Salem Inn 🅱🅱
(978) 741-0680. **$129-$370, 7 day notice.** 7 Summer St 01970. On SR 114 at Essex St; SR 128 exit 25A, 3 mi e. Int corridors. **Pets:** Other species. $15 daily fee/pet. Designated rooms, service with restrictions.

SAUGUS

Red Roof Inn -Boston Logan #305 �H
(781) 941-1400. **$89-$189.** 920 Broadway 01906. I-95 exit 44 northbound, 3.2 mi s on US 1 exit Main St/Saugus; southbound to U-turn. Int corridors. **Pets:** Large, other species. Service with restrictions, supervision.

SOMERVILLE

La Quinta Inn & Suites Boston Somerville �H
(617) 625-5300. **$99-$243.** 23 Cummings St 02143. I-93 exit 29 northbound, just ne on SR 28, then just s on Middlesex Ave; exit 31 southbound 1 mi e on SR 16, then 0.5 mi s on SR 28 to Middlesex Ave. Int corridors. **Pets:** Service with restrictions, supervision.

TEWKSBURY

◆◆ Extended StayAmerica Boston-Tewksbury 🅷
(978) 863-9888. **$90-$139.** 1910 Andover St 01876. I-93 exit 43B, just w; I-495 exit 39, just e. Int corridors. **Pets:** $25 daily fee/pet. Designated rooms, service with restrictions. 🛜 📶 💻

Ⓐ ◆◆◆ Holiday Inn Tewksbury-Andover 🅷
(978) 640-9000. **$99-$199.** 4 Highwood Dr 01876. I-495 exit 39, just w on SR 133. Int corridors. **Pets:** Accepted.
SAVE 🛜 ✖ 📶 💻 🍴 🛬 ✖

◆◆◆ Residence Inn by Marriott
Boston-Tewksbury-Andover 🅷
(978) 640-1003. **$129-$219.** 1775 Andover St 01876. I-495 exit 39, 0.3 mi w on SR 133. Ext corridors. **Pets:** Accepted.
🛜 ✖ 📶 📶 💻 🛬 ✖

◆◆◆ TownePlace Suites by Marriott Boston
Tewksbury 🅷
(978) 863-9800. **$99-$184.** 20 International Pl 01876. I-495 exit 39, 0.3 mi nw. Int corridors. **Pets:** Other species. $75 one-time fee/pet. Service with restrictions. ECO 🛜 ✖ 📶 📶 📶 💻 🛬

WAKEFIELD

ⒶⒶ ◆◆◆ Sheraton Colonial Hotel Boston North &
Conference Center 🅷
(781) 245-9300. **$105-$255.** 1 Audubon Rd 01880. I-95 exit 42, just n. Int corridors. **Pets:** Accepted. SAVE 🛜 ✖ 📶 💻 🍴 🛬 ✖

WALTHAM

◆◆◆ Courtyard by Marriott Boston-Waltham 🅷
(781) 419-0900. **$89-$239.** 387 Winter St 02451. I-95 exit 27B northbound; exit 27A southbound; on northeast corner. Int corridors. **Pets:** Other species. $50 one-time fee/room. Service with restrictions, crate. 🛜 ✖ 📶 💻 🍴 🛬

◆◆◆ Holiday Inn Express Boston/Waltham 🅷
(781) 890-2800. **$89-$229.** 385 Winter St 02451. I-95 exit 27B northbound; exit 27A southbound, just ne. Int corridors. **Pets:** Other species. $50 one-time fee/room. Service with restrictions, crate.
🛜 ✖ 📶 📶 💻

ⒶⒶ ◆◆◆◆ The Westin Waltham-Boston 🅷
(781) 290-5600. **$109-$349.** 70 3rd Ave 02451. I-95 exit 27A, just se. Int corridors. **Pets:** Accepted.
ECO SAVE 🛜 ✖ 📶 💻 🍴 🛬 ✖

WESTFORD

◆◆◆ Residence Inn by Marriott Boston
Westford 🅷 🐾
(978) 392-1407. **$139-$199.** 7 Lan Dr 01886. I-495 exit 32, just s, then 0.5 w on SR 110. Int corridors. **Pets:** $100 one-time fee/room. Service with restrictions, supervision. 🛜 ✖ 📶 📶 💻 🛬 ✖

WOBURN

ⒶⒶ ◆◆◆ BEST WESTERN PLUS New Englander 🅷
(781) 935-8160. **$89-$189.** 1 Rainin Rd 01801. I-93 exit 36, just e. Int corridors. **Pets:** Medium, dogs only. $50 deposit/room, $20 daily fee/room. Designated rooms, service with restrictions, supervision.
SAVE 🛜 ✖ 📶 📶 💻 🛬

◆◆ Extended Stay Deluxe Boston-Woburn 🅷
(781) 938-3737. **$110-$199.** 831 Main St 01801. I-95 exit 35, just n on SR 38. Int corridors. **Pets:** $25 daily fee/pet. Designated rooms, service with restrictions. 🛜 📶 📶 💻 🛬

◆◆◆ Hilton Boston/Woburn 🅷
(781) 932-0999. **$90-$260.** 2 Forbes Rd 01801. I-95 exit 36, 0.5 mi s via Washington St, then just e at Lukoil; jct Cedar St. Int corridors. **Pets:** Accepted. 🛜 📶 💻 🍴

ⒶⒶ ◆◆◆ Red Roof Inn Woburn #238 🅷
(781) 935-7110. **$79-$180.** 19 Commerce Way 01801. I-95 exit 36, just n, then just w on Mishawum Rd. Int corridors. **Pets:** Large, other species. Service with restrictions, supervision. SAVE 🛜 📶 📶 💻 🛬

ⒶⒶ ◆◆◆ Residence Inn by
Marriott-Boston/Woburn 🅷 🐾
(781) 376-4000. **$109-$289.** 300 Presidential Way 01801. I-93 exit 37C, just nw. Int corridors. **Pets:** Other species. $100 one-time fee/room. Service with restrictions, crate. SAVE 🛜 ✖ 📶 📶 💻 🛬 ✖

END METROPOLITAN AREA

BROCKTON

◆◆◆ Residence Inn by Marriott Boston Brockton 🅷
(508) 583-3600. **$134-$161.** 124 Liberty St 02301. I-93 exit 7B, just w, just s on Pearl St, then 0.3 mi se to Mill St connector. Int corridors. **Pets:** Other species. $100 one-time fee/room. Service with restrictions, crate. 🛜 ✖ 📶 📶 💻 🛬 ✖

CAPE COD AREA

BUZZARDS BAY

ⒶⒶ ◆ Bay Motor Inn Ⓜ
(508) 759-3989. **$72-$159, 7 day notice.** 223 Main St 02532. SR 25 exit 3, 0.5 mi w of Bourne rotary. Ext corridors. **Pets:** $15 daily fee/room. Designated rooms, service with restrictions, supervision.
SAVE 🛜 ✖ 📶 💻 🛬

EAST FALMOUTH

◆◆ Capewind Waterfront Motel Ⓜ
(508) 548-3400. **$109-$289, 30 day notice.** 34 Maravista Ext 02536. 2.2 mi e to SR 28, just s, follow signs. Ext corridors. **Pets:** Accepted.
🛜 ✖ 📶 💻 🛬 ✖

EASTHAM

◆ Ocean Park Inn Ⓜ 🐾
(508) 255-1132. **Call for rates.** 3900 State Hwy 02642. On US 6; 1 mi n of National Seashore Visitor's Center. Ext corridors. **Pets:** Dogs only. $25 daily fee/room. Designated rooms, service with restrictions, supervision.
🛜 ✖ 📶 💻

FALMOUTH

ⒶⒶ ◆◆ Seaside Inn Ⓜ
(508) 540-4120. **$59-$345, 14 day notice.** 263 Grand Ave 02540. Jct SR 28, 1.3 mi s from Falmouth Heights Rd. Ext/int corridors. **Pets:** Medium. $15 daily fee/pet. Designated rooms, service with restrictions, supervision. SAVE 🛜 ✖ 📶 💻

HYANNIS

Cape Cod Harbor House Inn **M**
(508) 771-1880. **Call for rates.** 119 Ocean St 02601. Opposite ferry docks. Ext corridors. **Pets:** Accepted. 🛜 ⊠ 🛏 💻

Comfort Inn Cape Cod **H**
(508) 771-4804. **Call for rates.** 1470 Iyannough Rd 02601. US 6 exit 6, 1.3 mi se on SR 132. Ext/int corridors. **Pets:** Accepted.
🛜 ⊠ 🛏 💻 ⇶ 🗙

ORLEANS

Orleans Inn **CI**
(508) 255-2222. **$250-$450.** 21 SR 6A 02653. On SR 28 and 6A exit rotary, just w. Int corridors. **Pets:** Dogs only. Service with restrictions.
🛜 ⊠ 🛏 🍴

Skaket Beach Motel **M**
(508) 255-1020. **$65-$175, 10 day notice.** 203 Cranberry Hwy (Rt 6A) 02653. US 6 exit 12, just e. Ext corridors. **Pets:** Dogs only. $12 daily fee/pet. Designated rooms, service with restrictions, supervision.
(SAVE) 🛜 🛏 💻 ⇶

PROVINCETOWN

Bayshore & Chandler **CO**
(508) 487-9133. **$105-$325, 30 day notice.** 493 Commercial St 02657. 0.8 mi e of Town Hall. Ext corridors. **Pets:** $20 daily fee/pet. Service with restrictions. 🛜 ⊠ 🛏 💻

Crowne Pointe Historic Inn & Spa **CI** ❀
(508) 487-6767. **$109-$659, 21 day notice.** 82 Bradford St 02657. On SR 6A, just w of Town Hall. Ext/int corridors. **Pets:** Large, dogs only. $30 daily fee/pet. Designated rooms, service with restrictions, supervision.
(SAVE) 🛜 ⊠ 🛏 💻 🍴 ⇶ 🗙

White Wind Inn **BB**
(508) 487-1526. **$85-$300, 14 day notice.** 174 Commercial St 02657. Just w of Town Hall. Int corridors. **Pets:** Accepted. 🛜 ⊠ 🛏

SOUTH YARMOUTH

Ambassador Inn & Suites **H**
(508) 394-4000. **$60-$250.** 1314 Main St 02664. On SR 28, just w of Bass River Bridge. Int corridors. **Pets:** $20 daily fee/pet. Designated rooms, service with restrictions, supervision.
(SAVE) 🛜 🛏 💻 ⇶ 🗙

Red Jacket Beach Resort **H**
(508) 398-6941. **Call for rates.** 1 S Shore Dr 02664. 2 mi s off SR 28. Ext/int corridors. **Pets:** Accepted. (SAVE) 🛜 ⊠ 🛏 🍴 ⇶ 🗙

Red Jacket Blue Rock Resort **M**
(508) 398-6962. **$89-$219, 10 day notice.** 39 Todd Rd 02664. SR 28, 1 mi ne via N Main St and High Bank Rd, then 0.5 mi nw on Country Club Dr, follow signs. Ext corridors. **Pets:** Accepted.
(SAVE) 🛜 ⊠ 🛏 🍴 ⇶ 🗙

Red Jacket Blue Water Resort on the Ocean **H** ❀
(508) 398-2288. **$100-$395, 30 day notice.** 291 S Shore Dr 02664. 1 mi s off SR 28. Ext/int corridors. **Pets:** Medium, other species. $40 daily fee/pet. Designated rooms, service with restrictions, supervision.
(SAVE) 🛜 ⊠ 🛏 🍴 ⇶

WEST DENNIS

Inn at Swan River **M**
(508) 394-5415. **Call for rates.** 829 Main St 02670. On SR 28, just w of SR 134. Ext corridors. **Pets:** Other species. $35 one-time fee/pet. Designated rooms, no service, crate. 🛜 ⊠ 🛏 💻 ⇶

WEST YARMOUTH

The Yarmouth Resort **M** ❀
(508) 775-5155. **$59-$199.** 343 Main St 02673. On SR 28, 2 mi e of jct SR 132. Ext/int corridors. **Pets:** Medium, dogs only. $15 daily fee/pet. Designated rooms, service with restrictions, supervision.
🛜 🛏 💻 ⇶ 🗙

END AREA

EAST WAREHAM

Atlantic Motel **M**
(508) 295-0210. **$80-$200, 10 day notice.** 7 Depot St 02538. Jct SR 25 exit 1; between eastbound and westbound lanes of US 6/SR 28. Ext corridors. **Pets:** Medium, dogs only. $25 daily fee/pet. Designated rooms, service with restrictions, supervision. (SAVE) 🛜 🛏 💻 ⇶

FAIRHAVEN

Seaport Inn Conference Center & Marina **H** ❀
(508) 997-1281. **$99-$159.** 110 Middle St 02719. I-195 exit 15, 1 mi s, then just off US 6. Int corridors. **Pets:** Other species. $25 one-time fee/room. Designated rooms, service with restrictions, supervision.
🛜 🛏 💻 🍴

FALL RIVER

Comfort Inn & Suites **H**
(508) 672-0011. **$75-$139.** 360 Airport Rd 02720. SR 79 and 24 exit 8; at Fall River Airport. Int corridors. **Pets:** Medium, other species. $15 daily fee/pet. Designated rooms, service with restrictions, crate.
🛜 ⊠ 🛏 💻 ⇶

FITCHBURG

Holiday Inn Fitchburg Waterpark **H**
(978) 342-7100. **Call for rates.** 150 Royal Plaza Dr 01420. SR 2 exit 28, just s on SR 31. Int corridors. **Pets:** Accepted.
🛜 ⊠ 🔼M 💻 🍴 ⇶

GARDNER

Colonial Hotel **H**
(978) 630-2500. **$99-$149.** 625 Betty Spring Rd 01440. SR 2 exit 24 eastbound; exit 24B westbound, 0.9 mi n on SR 140, then 0.5 mi w. Int corridors. **Pets:** Small, other species. $25 one-time fee/pet. Designated rooms, service with restrictions, supervision.
🛜 🛏 💻 🍴 ⇶ 🗙

GREENFIELD

The Brandt House B&B **BB**
(413) 774-3329. **$105-$359, 30 day notice.** 29 Highland Ave 01301. I-91 exit 26, 1.8 mi e on SR 2A, then se on Crescent St. Int corridors. **Pets:** Accepted. 🛜 ⊠

HADLEY

Comfort Inn **H**
(413) 584-9816. **$89-$165.** 237 Russell St 01035. I-91 exit 19 northbound; exit 20 southbound, 3 mi e on SR 9. Int corridors. **Pets:** $25 daily fee/pet. Designated rooms, service with restrictions, supervision.
(SAVE) 🛜 🛏 💻 ⇶

Howard Johnson Inn Hadley **H**
(413) 586-0114. **$69-$270.** 401 Russell St 01035. I-91 exit 19 northbound, 4.3 mi e on SR 9; exit 24 southbound, 10 mi s on SR 116, then just w on SR 9. Int corridors. **Pets:** Other species. $20 daily fee/room. Designated rooms, service with restrictions. 🛜 🔼M 🛏 💻 ⇶

HOLLAND

▼▼▼ The Inn at Restful Paws BB ❖

(413) 245-7792. **$174, 14 day notice.** 70 Allen Hill Rd 01521. SR 20, 2.1 mi s on E Brimfield Rd, 0.4 mi on Alexander Rd, then 0.7 mi n. Int corridors. **Pets:** No service, supervision. 🐾 ✕ 💻 �W 🅩

HOLYOKE

▼▼▼ Homewood Suites by Hilton Holyoke-Springfield North H ❖

(413) 532-3100. **$114-$309.** 375 Whitney Ave 01040. I-91 exit 15, just w on Lower Westfield Rd, then 0.4 mi s. Int corridors. **Pets:** Other species. $75 one-time fee/room. Service with restrictions, crate.

🐾 ♿ 📦 💻 ➿ ✕

LENOX

▼▼▼ ▼▼▼ Wheatleigh CI

(413) 637-0610. **$715-$2100.** 11 Hawthorne Rd 01240. 1.8 mi s on SR 183, 1 mi e. Int corridors. **Pets:** Accepted. 🐾 ✕ 🍴 ➿ ✕

MANSFIELD

▼▼▼ Holiday Inn Mansfield H

(508) 339-2200. **$99-$179.** 31 Hampshire St 02048. I-95 exit 7A, 0.5 mi s on SR 140, then 1 mi w on Forbes Rd; I-495 exit 12, 2 mi n on SR 140, then w on Forbes Rd. Int corridors. **Pets:** Small. $15 daily fee/pet. Service with restrictions, supervision.

🐾 ♿ 📦 💻 🍴 ➿ ✕

AAA ▼▼▼ Red Roof Inn - Mansfield/Foxboro H

(508) 339-2323. **$50-$150.** 60 Forbes Blvd 02048. I-95 exit 7A, 1.3 mi n; I-495 exit 12, just off SR 140. Int corridors. **Pets:** Large, other species. Service with restrictions, supervision. SAVE 🐾 📦 ➿

MARTHA'S VINEYARD AREA

EDGARTOWN

▼▼▼ Hob Knob Inn BB

(508) 627-9510. **$150-$675, 30 day notice.** 128 Main St 02539. Corner of Tilton Way; center. Int corridors. **Pets:** Small. $150 one-time fee/room. Designated rooms, service with restrictions. 🐾 ✕ 📦 ✕

▼▼▼ Vineyard Square Hotel & Suites CI

(508) 627-4711. **$95-$945, 14 day notice.** 38 N Water St 02539. Just n from Main St. Int corridors. **Pets:** Dogs only. Designated rooms, service with restrictions, crate. 🐾 ✕ 📦 💻 🍴

VINEYARD HAVEN

▼▼▼ The Doctor's House Bed & Breakfast BB

(508) 696-0859. **$175-$350, 21 day notice.** 60 Mt. Aldworth Rd 02568. 0.4 mi sw to road to Edgartown, 1 blk e. Int corridors. **Pets:** Dogs only. $25 daily fee/pet. Supervision. 🐾 ✕ ✕ 🅩

▼▼▼ Mansion House Inn, Health Club & Spa H

(508) 693-2200. **$99-$509, 14 day notice.** 9 Main St 02568. West of ferry dock; corner of Beach Rd. Int corridors. **Pets:** $50 one-time fee/pet. Designated rooms, service with restrictions, supervision.

🐾 ✕ 📦 💻 🍴 ➿ ✕

END AREA

MILFORD

▼▼▼ Holiday Inn Express H

(508) 634-1054. **$99-$159.** 50 Fortune Blvd 01757. I-495 exit 20, just sw on SR 85, then just se. Int corridors. **Pets:** Accepted.

🐾 ♿ 📦 💻 ➿

NORTHAMPTON

▼▼ ▼ Clarion Hotel & Conference Center H

(413) 586-1211. **$110-$170.** 1 Atwood Dr 01060. I-91 exit 18, just s on US 5. Int corridors. **Pets:** Large. $20 daily fee/room. Designated rooms, service with restrictions. 🐾 ✕ ♿ 📦 💻 🍴 ➿ ✕

NORTH DARTMOUTH

AAA ▼▼▼ Residence Inn by Marriott New Bedford/Dartmouth H

(508) 984-5858. **$139-$199.** 181 Faunce Corner Rd 02747. I-195 exit 12A westbound; exit 12 eastbound, just s. Int corridors. **Pets:** Other species. $100 one-time fee/room. Service with restrictions, supervision.

SAVE 🐾 ✕ ♿ 📦 💻 ➿ ✕

NORTON

▼▼ ▼ Extended StayAmerica-Foxboro-Norton H

(508) 285-7800. **$100-$149.** 280 S Washington St 02766. I-495 exit 9, 0.3 mi se on Bay St, then 0.5 mi nw via Industrial Park Rd. Int corridors. **Pets:** $25 daily fee/pet. Designated rooms, service with restrictions.

🐾 ♿ 📦 💻

PITTSFIELD

▼▼▼ Crowne Plaza Hotel-Berkshires H

(413) 499-2000. **$99-$349, 3 day notice.** 1 West St 01201. Center. Int corridors. **Pets:** Small. $50 one-time fee/room. Designated rooms, service with restrictions, supervision. 🐾 ♿ 📦 💻 🍴 ➿ ✕

PLYMOUTH

▼▼▼ Hampton Inn & Suites - Plymouth Kingston H

(508) 747-5000. **$109-$199.** 10 Plaza Way 02360. SR 3 exit 7. Int corridors. **Pets:** Accepted. 🐾 ♿ 📦 💻 ➿

RAYNHAM

AAA ▼▼▼ Quality Inn of Raynham-Taunton M

(508) 824-8647. **$84-$139.** 164 New State Hwy 02767. SR 24 exit 13B, 0.8 mi w on US 44. Ext/int corridors. **Pets:** Medium. $10 daily fee/pet. Designated rooms, service with restrictions, supervision.

SAVE 🐾 📦 💻 ➿

REHOBOTH

▼▼▼ Five Bridge Inn Bed & Breakfast BB

(508) 252-3190. **Call for rates.** 152 Pine St 02769. 1.6 mi n of US 44; 3.3 mi w of jct SR 118; US 44, n on Blanding Rd, e on Broad St, n on Salisbury St, then w. Int corridors. **Pets:** Accepted.

🐾 ✕ 📦 💻 ➿ ✕ 🅩

RICHMOND

◆◆◆ The Inn at Richmond ⅢⅢ
(413) 698-2566. **Call for rates.** 802 State Rd (SR 41) 01254. 2.5 mi s of jct US 20. Ext/int corridors. **Pets:** Accepted. 🛰 ✕ ▯ ▣ ✕

SEEKONK

◆◆◆ Clarion Providence-Seekonk ⅡⅡ ✿
(508) 336-7300. **$99-$269.** 940 Fall River Ave 02771. I-195 exit 1, just s. Int corridors. **Pets:** Small, dogs only. $75 one-time fee/room. Designated rooms, service with restrictions, supervision.
🛰 ▯ ▣ ⅢⅢ ⅞ ✕

◆◆◆ Motel 6 - #1289 Ⅲ
(508) 336-7800. **$55-$65.** 821 Fall River Ave 02771. I-195 exit 1, just n on SR 114A. Int corridors. **Pets:** Other species. Service with restrictions, supervision. 🛰 ⅏Ⅿ

SOMERSET

◆◆◆ ◆◆◆ Quality Inn-Fall River/Somerset ⅡⅡ ✿
(508) 678-4545. **$75-$205.** 1878 Wilbur Ave 02725. Jct SR 103 and I-195 exit 4 eastbound; exit 4A westbound. Int corridors. **Pets:** $50 deposit/room. Designated rooms, service with restrictions, supervision.
🛡 🛰 ▯ ▣ ⅞ ✕

SOUTHBOROUGH

◆◆◆ ◆◆◆ Red Roof Inn # 7075 Ⅲ
(508) 481-3904. **$49-$89.** 367 Turnpike Rd 01772. I-495 exit 23A, just e on SR 9. Ext corridors. **Pets:** Large, other species. Service with restrictions, supervision. 🛡 🛰 ✕ ▯

SPRINGFIELD

◆◆◆ ◆◆◆ Sheraton Springfield Monarch Place Hotel Ⅲ
(413) 781-1010. **$109-$239.** 1 Boland Way 01144. I-91 exit 6 northbound; exit 7 southbound, just n; downtown. Int corridors. **Pets:** Accepted.
🛡 🛰 ✕ ⅏Ⅿ ▯ ▣ ⅢⅢ ⅞ ✕

STURBRIDGE

◆◆◆ ◆◆◆ Comfort Inn & Suites Colonial Ⅲ
(508) 347-3306. **Call for rates.** 215 Charlton Rd 01566. I-90 exit 9, 0.5 mi e; I-84 exit 3A. Ext/int corridors. **Pets:** Accepted.
🛡 🛰 ✕ ⅏Ⅿ ▯ ▣ ⅞

◆◆◆ Publick House Historic Inn & Country Lodge ⅠⅠ
(508) 347-3313. **Call for rates.** 277 Main St 01566. I-84 exit 3B, 0.5 mi s of jct US 20. Ext/int corridors. **Pets:** Accepted.
🛰 ▯ ▣ ⅢⅢ ⅞

◆◆◆ ◆◆◆ Sturbridge Host Hotel & Conference Center on Cedar Lake Ⅲ
(508) 347-7393. **$115-$199.** 366 Main St 01566. I-90 exit 9, just w on US 20; I-84 exit 3B. Int corridors. **Pets:** $25 daily fee/room. Designated rooms, service with restrictions, supervision.
🛡 🛰 ▯ ▣ ⅢⅢ ⅞ ✕

◆◆◆ Super 8 Sturbridge Ⅲ
(508) 347-9000. **$69-$250.** 358 Main St 01566. I-84 exit 3B; on US 20. Ext corridors. **Pets:** Medium, other species. $30 daily fee/pet. Service with restrictions, crate. 🛰 ▯ ▣ ⅞

WESTBOROUGH

◆◆◆ Extended Stay Deluxe-Boston-Westborough Ⅲ
(508) 616-9213. **$90-$129.** 180 E Main St 01581. I-495 exit 23B, 1.4 mi w, then just sw on SR 30. Int corridors. **Pets:** $25 daily fee/pet. Designated rooms, service with restrictions. 🛰 ⅏Ⅿ ▯ ▣

◆◆◆ Residence Inn by Marriott Boston/Westborough Ⅲ
(508) 366-7700. **$109-$189.** 25 Connector Rd 01581. I-495 exit 23B, just w on SR 9 exit Computer and Research drs, then 0.3 mi s. Ext/int corridors. **Pets:** Accepted. 🜨 🛰 ✕ ⅏Ⅿ ▯ ▣ ⅞ ✕

WESTMINSTER

◆◆◆ ◆◆◆ Wachusett Village Inn & Conference Center Ⅲ
(978) 874-2000. **$89-$159.** 9 Village Inn Rd 01473. SR 2 exit 27 westbound, 0.3 mi e; exit 26 eastbound. Ext/int corridors. **Pets:** Medium. $50 one-time fee/pet. Designated rooms, service with restrictions, supervision.
🛡 🛰 ✕ ▯ ▣ ⅢⅢ ⅞ ✕

WESTPORT

◆◆◆ Hampton Inn-Fall River-Westport Ⅲ
(508) 675-8500. **$99-$219.** 53 Old Bedford Rd 02790. I-195 exit 9 eastbound; exit 10 westbound, just s to US 6, then 1.3 mi w. Int corridors. **Pets:** Medium. $35 daily fee/room. Designated rooms, service with restrictions, supervision. 🛰 ▯ ▣ ⅞ ✕

WEST SPRINGFIELD

◆◆◆ Candlewood Suites Ⅲ
(413) 739-1122. **Call for rates.** 572 Riverdale St 01089. I-91 exit 13B, 1.3 mi s. Int corridors. **Pets:** $25 daily fee/pet. Service with restrictions, crate. 🛰 ⅏Ⅿ ▯ ▣ ⅞

◆◆◆ Hampton Inn Ⅲ
(413) 732-1300. **$139-$179.** 1011 Riverdale St (US 5) 01089. I-91 exit 13B, 0.3 mi s. Int corridors. **Pets:** Accepted.
🛰 ✕ ⅏Ⅿ ▯ ▣ ⅞

◆◆◆ Residence Inn by Marriott West Springfield Ⅲ
(413) 732-9543. **$129-$319.** 64 Border Way 01089. I-91 exit 13A, on US 5. Int corridors. **Pets:** $75 one-time fee/pet. Service with restrictions, crate. 🛰 ✕ ⅏Ⅿ ▯ ▣ ⅞ ✕

WILLIAMSTOWN

◆◆◆ ◆◆◆ Cozy Corner Motel Ⅲ
(413) 458-8006. **$50-$135, 4 day notice.** 284 Sand Springs Rd (Rt 7) 01267. On US 7, 1.5 mi n of jct SR 2. Ext corridors. **Pets:** Medium. $25 daily fee/pet. Service with restrictions, crate. 🛡 🛰 ✕ ▯ ▣

◆◆◆ Maple Terrace Motel Ⅲ
(413) 458-9677. **$68-$185, 10 day notice.** 555 Main St 01267. On SR 2, 1 mi e of jct US 7. Ext corridors. **Pets:** Dogs only. $17 one-time fee/pet. Designated rooms, service with restrictions, supervision.
🛰 ✕ ▯ ▣ ⅞

◆◆◆ ◆◆ The Villager Motel Ⅲ
(413) 458-4046. **Call for rates.** 953 Simonds Rd 01267. On US 7, 1.7 mi n of jct SR 2. Ext corridors. **Pets:** Accepted.
🛡 🛰 ✕ ▯ ▣

WORCESTER

◆◆◆ ◆◆◆ Beechwood Hotel Ⅲ
(508) 754-5789. **$159-$390.** 363 Plantation St 01605. I-290 exit 22 westbound, 0.5 mi w on Lincoln St, then 1.5 mi s; exit 21 eastbound, 1.3 mi s. Int corridors. **Pets:** Medium. $60 daily fee/pet. Service with restrictions, crate. 🛡 🛰 ✕ ⅏Ⅿ ▯ ▣ ⅢⅢ ✕

◆◆◆ Residence Inn by Marriott Worcester Ⅲ
(508) 753-6300. **$139-$229.** 503 Plantation St 01605. I-290 exit 21, 0.5 mi sw. Int corridors. **Pets:** Accepted. 🛰 ✕ ⅏Ⅿ ▯ ▣ ⅞

MICHIGAN

ACME

▼▼▼ Sleep Inn & Suites H

(231) 938-7000. $50-$130. 5520 US 31 N 49610. Jct US 31 and SR 72, 0.5 mi sw. Int corridors. Pets: Accepted. 🛜 ✕ 🔥M 🔒 📺 🏊

ADRIAN

▼▼▼ Carlton Lodge H

(517) 263-7000. $91-$101. 1629 W Maumee St 49221. Jct US 223 and SR 52, 3 mi w on US 223. Int corridors. Pets: Accepted.
🛜 ✕ 🔒 📺 🍴 🏊

▼▼▼ Holiday Inn Express H

(517) 265-5700. Call for rates. 1077 W US 223 49221. Jct US 223 and SR 52, just w. Int corridors. Pets: Accepted. 🛜 ✕ 🔒 📺 🏊

▼▼ Super 8 H

(517) 265-8888. $80-$276. 1091 W US 223 49221. Jct US 223 and SR 52, just w. Int corridors. Pets: Other species. $25 one-time fee/room. Service with restrictions, supervision. 🛜 ✕ 🔒 📺

ALMA

🅰️ ▼▼▼ Triangle Motel M

(989) 463-2296. $60-$65. 131 W Lincoln Rd 48801. US 127 exit 123 (Lincoln Rd) northbound; exit 124 (State Rd) southbound, just w on US 127 business route. Ext corridors. Pets: Small, dogs only. Designated rooms, service with restrictions, supervision. SAVE 🛜 ✕ 🔒

ALPENA

🅰️ ▼▼▼ BEST WESTERN of Alpena H

(989) 356-9087. $79-$92. 1285 Hwy M-32 W 49707. 2.3 mi w of jct US 23. Ext/int corridors. Pets: Dogs only. $5 daily fee/pet. Service with restrictions, supervision. SAVE 🛜 ✕ 🔒 📺 🏊 ✕

◆◆ Days Inn H ❀

(989) 356-6118. $82-$122. 1496 Hwy M-32 W 49707. 2.5 mi w of jct US 23. Int corridors. Pets: Dogs only. $10 daily fee/room. Designated rooms, service with restrictions, supervision. 🛜 ✕ 🔒 📺 🏊 ✕

▼▼ Holiday Inn H

(989) 356-2151. $109-$159. 1000 Hwy 23 N 49707. On US 23, 1 mi n. Int corridors. Pets: Other species. Designated rooms, service with restrictions, supervision. 🛜 ✕ 🔒 📺 🍴 🏊 ✕

ANN ARBOR

▼▼▼ Candlewood Suites H

(734) 663-2818. Call for rates. 701 Waymarket Way 48103. I-94 exit 175 (Ann Arbor/Saline Rd), just e on Eisenhower Rd. Int corridors. Pets: Accepted. 🛜 ✕ 🔥M 🔒 📺

▼▼▼ Extended Stay Deluxe Detroit-Ann Arbor H

(734) 997-7623. $77-$112. 3265 Boardwalk St 48108. I-94 exit 177 (State St), just n, then just e on Victors Way. Int corridors. Pets: $25 daily fee/pet. Designated rooms, service with restrictions. 🛜 ✕ 🔒 📺

▼▼▼ Hampton Inn-North H

(734) 996-4444. $109-$319. 2300 Green Rd 48105. US 23 exit 41 (Plymouth Rd), just nw. Int corridors. Pets: Accepted.
🛜 ✕ 🔥M 🔒 📺 🍴 🏊

▼▼▼ Hawthorn Suites H

(734) 327-0011. $109-$299. 3535 Green Ct 48105. US 23 exit 41 (Plymouth Rd), just sw. Int corridors. Pets: Accepted.
🛜 ✕ 🔥M 🔒 📺 🏊 ✕

🅰️ ▼▼▼ Holiday Inn Near the University of Michigan H

(734) 769-9800. $159-$229. 3600 Plymouth Rd 48105. US 23 exit 41 (Plymouth Rd), just sw. Int corridors. Pets: $22 daily fee/room. Designated rooms, service with restrictions, crate.
SAVE 🛜 ✕ 🔒 📺 🍴 🏊 ✕

🅰️ ▼▼ Red Roof Inn #10045 M

(734) 996-5800. $60-$190. 3621 Plymouth Rd 48105. US 23 exit 41 (Plymouth Rd), just nw. Ext corridors. Pets: Large, other species. Service with restrictions, supervision. SAVE 🛜 ✕ 🔥M 🔒 📺

▼▼▼▼ Residence Inn by Marriott H ❀

(734) 996-5666. $151-$180. 800 Victors Way 48108. I-94 exit 177 (State St), just ne. Ext/int corridors. Pets: $25 daily fee/room. Service with restrictions, crate. 🛜 ✕ 🔥M 🔒 📺 🏊 ✕

🅰️ ▼▼▼▼ Sheraton Ann Arbor Hotel H ❀

(734) 996-0600. $99-$359, 3 day notice. 3200 Boardwalk St 48108. I-94 exit 177 (State St), just ne. Int corridors. Pets: Medium, dogs only. Service with restrictions, supervision.
SAVE 🛜 ✕ 🔒 📺 🍴 🏊 ✕

▼▼▼ TownePlace Suites by Marriott Ann Arbor
   South 🏨 🐾

(734) 327-5900. **$89-$299.** 1301 Briarwood Circle Dr 48108. I-94 exit 177, just n on State St, then 0.6 mi w. Int corridors. **Pets:** Other species. $100 one-time fee/room. Service with restrictions.

BAD AXE

▼▼ Econo Lodge Inn & Suites 🏨 🐾

(989) 269-3200. **$60-$80.** 898 N Van Dyke Rd 48413. 0.4 mi s of jct SR 142 and 53 (Van Dyke Rd). Int corridors. **Pets:** Medium. $10 daily fee/pet. Designated rooms, service with restrictions, supervision.

BATTLE CREEK

▼▼ Baymont Inn & Suites-Battle Creek 🏨

(269) 979-5400. **$99-$239.** 4725 Beckley Rd 49015. I-94 exit 97 (Capital Ave), just sw. Int corridors. **Pets:** Accepted.

BAY CITY

▼▼ Fairfield Inn by Marriott 🏨

(989) 667-7050. **$109-$149.** 4015 E Wilder Rd 48706. 1 mi e of SR 13. Int corridors. **Pets:** Very small. $50 one-time fee/room. Designated rooms, service with restrictions, crate.

▼▼▼ Holiday Inn Express & Suites 🏨

(989) 667-3800. **$99-$149.** 3959 Traxler Ct 48706. I-75 exit 164 (SR 13/Wilder Rd), 0.3 mi e. Int corridors. **Pets:** Medium. $25 one-time fee/pet. Designated rooms, service with restrictions, supervision.

BEAR LAKE

AAA ▼ Bella Vista Inn Ⓜ

(231) 864-3000. **$55-$106, 7 day notice.** 12273 West St 49614. On US 31; center. Ext corridors. **Pets:** Medium, dogs only. $15 daily fee/pet. Designated rooms, service with restrictions, supervision.

BELLAIRE

▼▼▼ Shanty Creek Resorts Lakeview Hotel 🏨

(231) 533-8621. **$144-$255, 5 day notice.** 5780 Shanty Creek Rd 49615. Jct SR 88, 4 mi nw to Summit Village. Int corridors. **Pets:** Medium, other species. $20 daily fee/pet. Designated rooms, service with restrictions, supervision.

BEULAH

AAA ▼▼▼ BEST WESTERN Scenic Hill
   Resort 🏨 🐾

(231) 882-7754. **$150-$190.** 1400 US Hwy 31 49617. On US 31, 0.8 mi e. Int corridors. **Pets:** Large, dogs only. $50 deposit/room, $20 daily fee/pet. Designated rooms, service with restrictions, supervision.

BIG RAPIDS

▼▼ Big Rapids Quality Inn & Suites Ⓜ

(231) 592-5150. **Call for rates.** 1705 S State St 49307. US 131 exit 139, 1.7 mi e on SR 20, then 0.8 mi s. Ext/int corridors. **Pets:** $10 daily fee/pet. Designated rooms, service with restrictions, supervision.

▼▼ Holiday Inn Hotel & Conference Center 🏨

(231) 796-4400. **Call for rates.** 1005 Perry Ave 49307. US 131 exit 139, 1.3 mi e on SR 20. Int corridors. **Pets:** Other species. $20 daily fee/pet. Service with restrictions, supervision.

BIRCH RUN

▼▼ Americas Best Value Inn & Suites 🏨

(989) 624-4440. **$50-$140.** 9235 E Birch Run Rd 48415. I-75 exit 136 (Birch Run Rd), just e. Int corridors. **Pets:** Small. Designated rooms, service with restrictions, supervision.

AAA ▼▼ BEST WESTERN of Birch
   Run/Frankenmuth

(989) 624-9395. **$70-$150.** 9087 Birch Run Rd 48415. I-75 exit 136 (Birch Run Rd), just e. Ext/int corridors. **Pets:** Other species. $20 one-time fee/room. Designated rooms, service with restrictions, supervision.

▼▼▼ Holiday Inn Express 🏨

(989) 624-9300. **$95-$149.** 12150 Dixie Hwy 48415. I-75 exit 136 (Birch Run Rd), just e. Int corridors. **Pets:** Medium, dogs only. $35 one-time fee/pet. Designated rooms, service with restrictions, supervision.

BRIDGEPORT

▼▼ Baymont Inn & Suites-Frankenmuth/Bridgeport 🏨

(989) 777-3000. **$89-$159.** 6460 Dixie Hwy 48722. I-75 exit 144A. Int corridors. **Pets:** Dogs only. $25 one-time fee/pet. Service with restrictions, supervision.

BRIGHTON

AAA ▼▼▼ Courtyard by Marriott 🏨

(810) 225-9200. **$89-$149.** 7799 Conference Center Dr 48114. I-96 exit 145 (Grand River Ave S), just ne. Int corridors. **Pets:** Accepted.

BROOKLYN

▼▼ Super 8-Brooklyn 🏨

(517) 592-0888. **$76-$111.** 419 S Main/M-50 49230. Jct SR 50 (Main St) and 124; downtown. Int corridors. **Pets:** Other species. $5 daily fee/pet. Service with restrictions, supervision.

BYRON CENTER

▼▼▼ Comfort Suites-Grand Rapids South 🏨

(616) 301-2255. **$89-$120.** 7644 Caterpillar Ct SW 49548. US 131 exit 75. Int corridors. **Pets:** Service with restrictions, crate.

CADILLAC

AAA ▼▼ McGuire's Resort 🏨

(231) 775-9947. **$79-$119.** 7880 Mackinaw Tr 49601. US 131 exit 177, 0.7 mi n, then 0.5 mi w. Int corridors. **Pets:** Other species. $20 daily fee/room. Designated rooms, service with restrictions.

CALUMET

▼▼ AmericInn Lodge & Suites of Calumet 🏨 🐾

(906) 337-6463. **$95-$146.** 56925 S 6th St 49913. On US 41; just w of Visitors Center. Int corridors. **Pets:** Dogs only. $20 one-time fee/room. Designated rooms, service with restrictions, supervision.

CASCADE

▼▼ Baymont Inn-Grand Rapids Airport 🏨

(616) 956-3300. **$59-$129.** 2873 Kraft Ave SE 49512. I-96 exit 43B, just e. Int corridors. **Pets:** Other species. $10 one-time fee/pet. Service with restrictions, crate.

AAA ▼▼▼ BEST WESTERN Hospitality Hotel &
   Suites 🏨 🐾

(616) 949-8400. **$69-$120.** 5500 28th St SE 49512. I-96 exit 43B, just e on SR 11. Int corridors. **Pets:** Large, other species. $10 daily fee/room. Service with restrictions, supervision.

♥♥ ♥♥ Clarion Inn & Suites Grand Rapids Airport H
(616) 956-9304. **$74-$129.** 4981 28th St SE 49512. I-96 exit 43A, 0.5 mi w on SR 11. Int corridors. **Pets:** Accepted. 🛰 ✕ 🔌 💻 🏊

♥♥♦♥♥ Crowne Plaza Grand Rapids H
(616) 957-1770. **$82-$159.** 5700 28th St SE 49546. I-96 exit 43B, 0.3 mi e on SR 11. Int corridors. **Pets:** Accepted.
🛰 ✕ 🔌 🔌 💻 🍴 🏊 ✕

♥♥ ♥♥ Holiday Inn Express Suites Airport H
(616) 940-8100. **$94-$129.** 5401 28th St Ct SE 49546. I-96 exit 43B, just e on SR 11. Int corridors. **Pets:** Other species. $10 daily fee/room. Designated rooms, service with restrictions, crate.
🛰 ✕ 🔌 🔌 💻 🏊 ✕

♠♠♠ ♥♥ Red Roof Inn #7011 M
(616) 942-0800. **$52-$80.** 5131 28th St SE 49512. I-96 exit 43A, 0.3 mi w on SR 11. Ext corridors. **Pets:** Large, other species. Service with restrictions, supervision. SAVE 🛰 ✕ 🔌 💻

♥♥ ♥♥ Super 8-Grand Rapids Airport H
(616) 957-3000. **$59-$64.** 4855 28th St SE 49512. I-96 exit 43A, 0.5 mi w on SR 11. Int corridors. **Pets:** Accepted. 🛰 ✕ 🔌 💻

CHARLEVOIX

♥♥ ♥♥ AmericInn Lodge & Suites of Charlevoix H
(231) 237-0988. **Call for rates.** 11800 US 31 N 49720. On US 31, 2.4 mi n. Int corridors. **Pets:** Accepted. 🛰 ✕ 🔌 🔌 💻 🏊

CHEBOYGAN

♠♠♠ ♥♥♥ BEST WESTERN River Terrace H
(231) 627-5688. **$79-$209.** 847 S Main St 49721. 1 mi s on SR 27. Ext/ int corridors. **Pets:** Medium, dogs only. $10 daily fee/pet. Designated rooms, service with restrictions, supervision.
SAVE 🛰 ✕ 🔌 💻 🏊 ✕

♥♥ Birch Haus Motel M
(231) 627-5862. **$40-$85.** 1301 Mackinaw Ave 49721. On US 23, 0.8 mi nw. Ext corridors. **Pets:** Small, dogs only. $5 daily fee/pet. Designated rooms, service with restrictions, supervision. 🛰 ✕ 🔌

♥♥ ♥♥ Continental Inn M
(231) 627-7164. **$39-$99.** 613 N Main St 49721. Jct US 23 and SR 27. Ext corridors. **Pets:** Dogs only. $10 daily fee/room. Service with restrictions, crate. 🛰 ✕ 🔌 🏊

CHELSEA

♥♦ ♦♥ Chelsea Comfort Inn & Village Conference Center H
(734) 433-8000. **$91-$110.** 1645 Commerce Park Dr 48118. I-94 exit 159 (SR 52/Main St), just n. Int corridors. **Pets:** Other species. $20 daily fee/ room. Service with restrictions, supervision.
🛰 ✕ 🔌 🔌 💻 🏊 ✕

♥♥♥♥ Holiday Inn Express H
(734) 433-1600. **Call for rates.** 1540 Commerce Park Dr 48118. I-94 exit 159 (SR 52/Main St), 0.3 mi n. Int corridors. **Pets:** Accepted.
🛰 ✕ 🔌 🔌 💻 🏊

CHESANING

♠♠♠ ♥♥ Colonial Motel M
(989) 845-3292. **$60-$130, 3 day notice.** 9475 E M-57 48616. On SR 57, 0.5 mi e. Ext corridors. **Pets:** $10 daily fee/pet. Supervision.
SAVE 🛰 ✕ 🔌 💻

CLARE

♥♥ ♥♥ Days Inn of Clare H
(989) 386-1111. **$80-$140.** 10318 S Clare Ave 48617. On Business Rt US 10 and 127; just w of jct US 127 and Old US 27. Int corridors. **Pets:** Other species. $10 daily fee/room. Designated rooms, service with restrictions, supervision. 🛰 ✕ 🔌 💻 🏊

COMSTOCK PARK

♥♥♦♥♥ Comfort Suites Grand Rapids North H
(616) 785-7899. **$100-$145.** 350 Dodge St 49321. US 131 exit 91. Int corridors. **Pets:** Accepted. 🛰 ✕ 🔌 🔌 💻 🏊

COPPER HARBOR

♥♥ Lake Fanny Hooe Resort M
(906) 289-4451. **$100-$135, 7 day notice.** 505 2nd St 49918. Just s on Manganese Rd. Ext corridors. **Pets:** Accepted.
🛰 ✕ 🔌 💻 ✕ 🎿 📠

DETROIT METROPOLITAN AREA

ALLEN PARK

♠♠♠ ♥♥♥ BEST WESTERN Greenfield Inn H 🐾
(313) 271-1600. **Call for rates.** 3000 Enterprise Dr 48101. I-94 exit 206 (Oakwood Blvd), just s, then just w. Int corridors. **Pets:** $10 daily fee/ room. Service with restrictions, supervision.
SAVE 🛰 ✕ 🔌 💻 🍴 🏊 ✕

AUBURN HILLS

♥♥ Extended Stay Deluxe-Detroit Auburn Hills-Featherstone H
(248) 335-5200. **$75-$100.** 2100 Featherstone Rd 48326. I-75 exit 79 (University Dr), just w to Opdyke Rd, s to Featherstone Rd, then just e. Int corridors. **Pets:** $25 daily fee/pet. Designated rooms, service with restrictions. 🛰 ✕ 🔌 🔌 💻 🏊

♥♥ ♥♥ Hawthorn Suites by Wyndham Detroit Auburn Hills H
(248) 373-3342. **$68-$145.** 1650 N Opdyke Rd 48326. I-75 exit 79 (University Dr), just w, then 0.4 mi n. Int corridors. **Pets:** Medium. $15 daily fee/pet. Service with restrictions, supervision. 🛰 ✕ 🔌 💻

♠♠♠ ♥♥♥ Hilton Suites Auburn Hills H
(248) 334-2222. **$107-$205.** 2300 Featherstone Rd 48326. I-75 exit 79 (University Dr), just w, 0.5 mi s on Opdyke Rd, then just e. Int corridors. **Pets:** Dogs only. $75 one-time fee/room. Designated rooms, service with restrictions, supervision. SAVE 🛰 ✕ 🔌 💻 🍴 🏊 ✕

♥♥ ♥♥ Homestead Studio Suites Hotel-Detroit/Auburn Hills H
(248) 340-8888. **$72-$95.** 3315 University Dr 48326. I-75 exit 79 (University Dr), 0.9 mi e. Int corridors. **Pets:** $25 daily fee/pet. Designated rooms, service with restrictions. 🛰 ✕ 🔌 💻

♠♠♠ ♥♥♥ Sonesta ES Suites H
(248) 322-4600. **$110-$149.** 2050 Featherstone Rd 48326. I-75 exit 79 (University Dr), just w, 0.5 mi s on Opdyke Rd, then just e. Int corridors. **Pets:** Large. $15 one-time fee/room, $10 daily fee/room. Service with restrictions. SAVE 🛰 ✕ 🔌 💻 🏊

BELLEVILLE

♥♥♦♥♥ Holiday Inn Express Hotel & Suites H
(734) 857-6200. **Call for rates.** 46194 N I-94 Service Dr 48111. I-94 exit 190 (Belleville Rd), just n, then just w. Int corridors. **Pets:** Medium, dogs only. $50 one-time fee/pet. Service with restrictions.
🛰 ✕ 🔌 🔌 💻 🏊 ✕

♥♥ ♥♥ Red Roof Inn Metro Airport #7183 M
(734) 697-2244. **$49-$79.** 45501 N I-94 Service Dr 48111. I-94 exit 190 (Belleville Rd), just n. Ext corridors. **Pets:** Large, other species. Service with restrictions, supervision. 🛰 ✕ 🔌

BIRMINGHAM

The Townsend Hotel [H] ❖
(248) 642-7900. **$320-$440.** 100 Townsend St 48009. Center. Int corridors. **Pets:** Dogs only. $150 one-time fee/room, $5 daily fee/room. Service with restrictions, crate. [ECO] [SAVE] 🛜 ✕ [&M] [📶] [🍴] ✕

CANTON

La Quinta Inn Detroit Canton [H]
(734) 981-1808. **$63-$129.** 41211 Ford Rd 48187. I-275 exit 25 (Ford Rd), just w to jct Haggerty Rd. Int corridors. **Pets:** Service with restrictions, supervision. 🛜 ✕ [📶]

Super 8-Canton [H]
(734) 722-8880. **$50-$90.** 3933 Lotz Rd 48188. I-275 exit 22 (Michigan Ave), just e on US 12, then just s. Int corridors. **Pets:** Medium. $10 daily fee/pet. Designated rooms, service with restrictions, crate. 🛜 ✕ [📶]

DEARBORN

Adoba Hotel Dearborn/Detroit [H] ❖
(313) 593-1234. **$109-$399.** 600 Town Center Dr 48126. Jct SR 39 (Southfield Frwy), 0.3 mi w on Michigan Ave, 0.3 mi n on Evergreen Rd, then e on Fairlane Rd. Int corridors. **Pets:** Small, dogs only. $35 daily fee/pet. Designated rooms, service with restrictions, supervision. [ECO] [SAVE] 🛜 ✕ [&M] [📶] [🍴] ✕

Extended StayAmerica Detroit Dearborn [H]
(313) 336-0021. **$85-$112.** 260 Towne Center Dr 48126. SR 39 (Southfield Frwy); between Ford Rd and Michigan Ave exits; just w of jct Service and Hubbard drs. Int corridors. **Pets:** $25 daily fee/pet. Designated rooms, service with restrictions. 🛜 ✕ [&M] [📶]

The Henry, Autograph Collection [H]
(313) 441-2000. **$149-$339.** 300 Town Center Dr 48126. SR 39 (Southfield Frwy); between Ford Rd and Michigan Ave exits, on Service Dr. Int corridors. **Pets:** Medium. $75 one-time fee/room. Service with restrictions. [SAVE] 🛜 ✕ [&M] [📶] [🍴] ✕

Red Roof Inn-Dearborn #7182 [M]
(313) 278-9732. **$61-$96.** 24130 Michigan Ave 48124. Jct US 24 (Telegraph Rd) and 12 (Michigan Ave). Ext corridors. **Pets:** Large, other species. Service with restrictions, supervision. [SAVE] 🛜 ✕ [📶]

TownePlace Suites by Marriott [H]
(313) 271-0200. **$121-$161.** 6141 Mercury Dr 48126. SR 39 (Southfield Frwy) exit 7 (Ford Rd), just e, then 0.8 mi n. Int corridors. **Pets:** Small. $100 one-time fee/room. Service with restrictions. 🛜 ✕ [📶]

DETROIT

DoubleTree Suites by Hilton Detroit Downtown-Fort Shelby [H]
(313) 963-5600. **$129-$209.** 525 W Lafayette Blvd 48226. Jct First Ave. Int corridors. **Pets:** Accepted. 🛜 ✕ [📶] [🍴]

Holiday Inn Express & Suites [H]
(313) 887-7000. **Call for rates.** 1020 Washington Blvd 48226. Corner of Washington Blvd and Michigan Ave. Int corridors. **Pets:** Accepted. 🛜 ✕ [&M] [📶] [🍴] ✕

MotorCity Casino Hotel [H]
(313) 237-7711. **$179-$599.** 2901 Grand River Ave 48201. I-75 exit 50 (Grand River Ave), just n. Int corridors. **Pets:** Small, dogs only. $125 one-time fee/room. Service with restrictions, supervision. [SAVE] 🛜 ✕ [📶] [🍴] ✕

The Westin Book Cadillac Detroit [H] ❖
(313) 442-1600. **$179-$459.** 1114 Washington Blvd 48226. Corner of Washington Blvd and Michigan Ave. **Pets:** Medium, dogs only. Service with restrictions, supervision. [SAVE] 🛜 ✕ [&M] [📶] [🍴] ✕

FARMINGTON HILLS

Extended StayAmerica Detroit-Farmington Hills [H]
(248) 473-4000. **$60-$82.** 27775 Stansbury Blvd 48334. I-696 exit 5 (Orchard Lake Rd), just n, just e on 12 Mile Rd, then just s. Int corridors. **Pets:** $25 daily fee/pet. Designated rooms, service with restrictions. 🛜 ✕ [&M] [📶]

Hawthorn Suites by Wyndham Detroit Farmington Hills [H]
(248) 324-0540. **$73-$150.** 37555 Hills Tech Dr 48331. I-696 exit I-96 E/I-275 S/SR 5, just s to SR 5 N, 2 mi n to 12 Mile Rd, 1.3 mi e, then 0.3 mi s on Halsted Rd. Int corridors. **Pets:** Accepted. 🛜 ✕ [&M] [📶]

Holiday Inn & Suites [H]
(248) 477-7800. **$99-$160.** 37529 Grand River Ave 48335. I-275 exit 165 (SR 5/Grand River Ave), 1 mi e. Int corridors. **Pets:** Small, dogs only. $50 daily fee/pet. Designated rooms, service with restrictions, supervision. [SAVE] 🛜 ✕ [&M] [📶] [🍴] ✕

Red Roof Inn-Farmington Hills #7038 [M]
(248) 478-8640. **$45-$99.** 24300 Sinacola Ct 48335. I-96/275 and SR 5 exit 165 (Grand River Ave), just w. Ext corridors. **Pets:** Large, other species. Service with restrictions, supervision. [SAVE] 🛜 ✕ [&M] [📶]

LAKE ORION

Palace Inn [H]
(248) 391-2755. **$89-$109.** 2755 N Lapeer Rd 48360. I-75 exit 81 (Lapeer Rd), 3.3 mi n. Ext/int corridors. **Pets:** Accepted. 🛜 ✕ [📶] ✕

LIVONIA

Comfort Inn Livonia [H]
(734) 458-7111. **$79-$100.** 29235 Buckingham Dr 48154. I-96 exit 176 (Middlebelt Rd), just n. Int corridors. **Pets:** Medium, dogs only. $50 deposit/room. Service with restrictions, supervision. [SAVE] 🛜 ✕ [📶]

Embassy Suites Hotel [H]
(734) 462-6000. **$109-$209.** 19525 Victor Pkwy 48152. I-275 exit 169 (7 Mile Rd), just e, then 0.5 mi n. Int corridors. **Pets:** Accepted. 🛜 ✕ [📶]

Livonia Marriott [H]
(734) 462-3100. **$94-$155.** 17100 Laurel Park Dr N 48152. I-275 exit 170 (6 Mile Rd), just w. Int corridors. **Pets:** Accepted. [ECO] 🛜 ✕ [📶] [🍴] ✕

Residence Inn by Marriott Detroit-Livonia [H]
(734) 462-4201. **$99-$149.** 17250 Fox Dr 48152. I-275 exit 170 (6 Mile Rd), just w. Int corridors. **Pets:** Accepted. 🛜 ✕ [📶] ✕

TownePlace Suites by Marriott [H] ❖
(734) 542-7400. **$71-$170.** 17450 Fox Dr 48152. I-275 exit 170 (6 Mile Rd), just nw. Int corridors. **Pets:** Other species. $100 one-time fee/room. Designated rooms. 🛜 ✕ [&M] [📶] ✕

MADISON HEIGHTS

Motel 6 Madison Heights #1109 [M]
(248) 583-0500. **$45-$55.** 32700 Barrington Rd 48071. I-75 exit 65A (14 Mile Rd), just e. Ext corridors. **Pets:** Other species. Service with restrictions, supervision. 🛜 ✕ [&M]

Red Roof Inn #7084 [M]
(248) 583-4700. **$39-$85.** 32511 Concord Dr 48071. I-75 exit 65A (14 Mile Rd), just e, then just s. Ext corridors. **Pets:** Large, other species. Service with restrictions, supervision. [SAVE] 🛜 ✕ [&M] [📶]

▼▼▼ Residence Inn by Marriott-Detroit Troy/Madison Heights **H**

(248) 583-4322. **$99-$209.** 32650 Stephenson Hwy 48071. I-75 exit 65B (14 Mile Rd), just w, then just s. Ext corridors. **Pets:** Accepted.
🛜 ✕ 🛗 📺 ⊷ ⊠

MOUNT CLEMENS

▼▼▼ Concorde Inn of Clinton Township **H**

(586) 493-7300. **Call for rates.** 44315 Gratiot Ave 48036. I-94 exit 240B (SR 59), 0.3 mi w, then 0.3 mi s. Int corridors. **Pets:** Accepted.
🛜 ✕ 🖥 🛗 📺 ⊷ ⊠

NOVI

▼▼▼ Extended StayAmerica-Detroit-Novi **H**

(248) 305-9955. **$80-$105.** 21555 Haggerty Rd 48375. I-275 exit 167 (8 Mile Rd), just w, then 0.5 mi n. Int corridors. **Pets:** $25 daily fee/pet. Designated rooms, service with restrictions. 🛜 ✕ 🖥 🛗 📺

▼▼▼ Residence Inn by Marriott-Detroit/Novi **H**

(248) 735-7400. **$107-$159.** 27477 Cabaret Dr 48377. I-96 exit 162 (Novi Rd), just n to 12 Mile Rd, then just w. Int corridors. **Pets:** Other species. $100 one-time fee/room. Service with restrictions.
🛜 ✕ 🛗 📺 ⊷ ⊠

ⒶⒶⒶ◿ ▼▼▼ Sheraton-Detroit-Novi **H**

(248) 349-4000. **$87-$229.** 21111 Haggerty Rd 48375. I-275 exit 167 (8 Mile Rd), just w to Haggerty Rd, then just n. Int corridors.
Pets: Accepted. 🌿 SAVE 🛜 ✕ 🛗 🖥 📺 ⫙ ⊷

▼▼▼ Staybridge Suites **H**

(248) 349-4600. **$119-$149, 3 day notice.** 27000 Providence 48374. I-96 exit 160 (Beck Rd), just s to Grand River Ave, then 0.6 mi w. Int corridors. **Pets:** Large. $75 one-time fee/pet. Designated rooms, service with restrictions, crate. 🛜 ✕ 🛗 🖥 📺 ⊷ ⊠

▼▼▼ TownePlace Suites by Marriott **H**

(248) 305-5533. **$71-$123.** 42600 11 Mile Rd 48375. I-96 exit 162 (Novi Rd), just s, 0.5 mi e on Crescent Dr, then just s on Town Center Dr. Int corridors. **Pets:** Small, dogs only. $75 one-time fee/room. Designated rooms, crate. 🌿 ✕ 🛗 🖥 📺 ⊷

PLYMOUTH

ⒶⒶⒶ◿ ▼▼▼ Red Roof Inn-Plymouth #016 **M**

(734) 459-3300. **$45-$110.** 39700 Ann Arbor Rd 48170. I-275 exit 28 (Ann Arbor Rd), just e. Ext corridors. **Pets:** Large, other species. Service with restrictions, supervision. SAVE 🛜 ✕ 🖥 📺

PONTIAC

▼▼▼ Residence Inn by Marriott Detroit Pontiac/Auburn Hills **H**

(248) 858-8664. **$90-$155.** 3333 Centerpoint Pkwy 48341. I-75 exit 75 (Square Lake Rd), w via Opdyke Rd. Int corridors. **Pets:** $100 one-time fee/room. Service with restrictions. 🛜 ✕ 🖥 📺 ⊷ ⊠

ROCHESTER HILLS

ⒶⒶⒶ◿ ▼▼▼ Red Roof Inn #7191 **M**

(248) 853-6400. **$45-$99.** 2580 Crooks Rd 48309. Jct Hall Rd (SR 59). Ext corridors. **Pets:** Large, other species. Service with restrictions, supervision. SAVE 🛜 ✕ 🖥 📺

ROMULUS

▼▼▼ Baymont Inn & Suites Detroit-Airport **H**

(734) 722-6000. **$59-$89.** 9000 Wickham Rd 48174. I-94 exit 198 (Merriman Rd), just n, then just w. Int corridors. **Pets:** Accepted.
🛜 ✕ 🖥 📺

▼▼▼ Days Inn and Suites **H**

(734) 946-4300. **$65-$120.** 9501 Middlebelt Rd 48174. I-94 exit 199 (Middlebelt Rd), 0.4 mi n. Int corridors. **Pets:** Small, dogs only. $25 one-time fee/pet. Designated rooms, service with restrictions, supervision.
🛜 ✕ 🖥 📺 ⫙

▼▼▼ Extended StayAmerica Detroit-Metro Airport **H**

(734) 722-7780. **$65-$88.** 30325 Flynn Dr 48174. I-94 exit 198 (Merriman Rd), just n, then 0.4 mi e. Int corridors. **Pets:** $25 daily fee/pet. Designated rooms, service with restrictions. 🛜 ✕ 🖥 📺

▼▼▼ La Quinta Inn Detroit Airport Romulus **H**

(734) 641-9006. **$83-$155.** 7680 Merriman Rd 48174. I-94 exit 198 (Merriman Rd), just n. Int corridors. **Pets:** Service with restrictions, supervision. 🛜 ✕ 🖥 📺

▼▼▼ Red Roof Inn **H**

(734) 595-7400. **$39-$60.** 9095 Wickham Rd 48174. I-94 exit 198 (Merriman Rd), just n, then just w. Int corridors. **Pets:** Large, other species. Service with restrictions, supervision. 🛜 ✕ 🖥 📺

ⒶⒶⒶ◿ ▼▼▼ ▼▼▼ The Westin Detroit Metropolitan Airport **H**

(734) 942-6500. **$99-$379.** 2501 Worldgateway Pl 48242. I-94 exit 198 (Merriman Rd); at McNamara Terminal. Int corridors. **Pets:** Accepted.
SAVE 🛜 ✕ 🛗 🖥 📺 ⫙ ⊷

ROSEVILLE

ⒶⒶⒶ◿ ▼▼▼▼ BEST WESTERN PLUS Georgian Inn **M**

(586) 294-0400. **Call for rates.** 31327 Gratiot Ave 48066. I-94 exit 232 (Little Mack Ave), just s, 0.5 mi n on 13 Mile Rd, then just n. Ext corridors. **Pets:** Dogs only. $8 daily fee/pet. Service with restrictions, supervision. SAVE 🛜 ✕ 🖥 📺 ⫙ ⊷

ⒶⒶⒶ◿ ▼▼▼ Red Roof Inn #10012 **M**

(586) 296-0310. **$45-$89.** 31800 Little Mack Ave 48066. I-94 exit 232 (Little Mack Ave), just n. Ext corridors. **Pets:** Large, other species. Service with restrictions, supervision. SAVE 🛜 ✕ 🛗 🖥 📺

SOUTHFIELD

▼▼▼ Candlewood Suites **H**

(248) 945-0010. **$90-$120.** 1 Corporate Dr 48076. SR 10 (Northwestern Hwy) exit Lahser Rd, just e. Int corridors. **Pets:** Large. $15 daily fee/pet. Service with restrictions, crate. 🛜 ✕ 🛗 🖥 📺

▼▼▼▼ Hampton Inn-Southfield **H**

(248) 356-5500. **$69-$89.** 27500 Northwestern Service Dr 48034. I-696 exit 9 (Telegraph Rd), just n to 11 Mile Rd, then 0.5 mi e. Int corridors. **Pets:** Accepted. 🛜 ✕ 🖥 📺 ⊷

▼▼▼ Red Roof Inn-Southfield #7133 **M**

(248) 353-7200. **$49-$111.** 27660 Northwestern Hwy 48034. I-696 exit 9 (Telegraph Rd), just nw. Ext corridors. **Pets:** Large, other species. Service with restrictions, supervision. 🛜 ✕ 🛗 🖥 📺

ⒶⒶⒶ◿ ▼▼▼ ▼▼▼ The Westin Southfield Detroit **H**

(248) 827-4000. **$99-$309.** 1500 Town Center 48075. SR 10 (Northwestern Hwy) exit 10 (10 Mile Rd/Evergreen Rd), 0.3 mi n. Int corridors. **Pets:** Accepted. SAVE 🛜 ✕ 🛗 🖥 📺 ⫙ ⊷ ⊠

SOUTHGATE

▼▼ La Quinta Inn Detroit Southgate **H**

(734) 374-3000. **$59-$122.** 12888 Reeck Rd 48195. I-75 exit 37 (Northline Rd), just w. Int corridors. **Pets:** Service with restrictions, supervision.
🛜 ✕ 🖥 📺

STERLING HEIGHTS

▼▼▼ TownePlace Suites by Marriott **H**

(586) 566-0900. **$70-$120.** 14800 Lakeside Cir 48313. 1 mi e of jct SR 53 (Van Dyke Ave) and 59 (Hall Rd). Int corridors. **Pets:** Medium, other species. $100 one-time fee/room. Service with restrictions, crate.
🛜 ✕ 🛗 🖥 📺 ⊷

TAYLOR

ⒶⒶⒶ◿ ▼▼▼ Red Roof Inn-Taylor #7189 **M**

(734) 374-1150. **$44-$89.** 21230 Eureka Rd 48180. I-75 exit 36 (Eureka Rd), just w. Ext corridors. **Pets:** Large, other species. Service with restrictions, supervision. SAVE 🛜 ✕ 🖥 📺

TROY

▼▼▼▼ Drury Inn & Suites-Troy 🅷

(248) 528-3330. **$90-$229.** 575 W Big Beaver Rd 48084. I-75 exit 69 (Big Beaver Rd), just e. Int corridors. **Pets:** Service with restrictions, supervision. 🛜 ☒ 🖧ᴹ 🛏 💻 �ⅱ 🌊

▼▼ ▼▼ Hawthorn Suites by Wyndham Troy 🅷

(248) 689-6856. **$99-$129.** 2600 Livernois Rd 48083. I-75 exit 69 (Big Beaver Rd), 0.5 mi e to Livernois Rd, then 0.5 mi s. Ext corridors. **Pets:** Dogs only. $25 daily fee/pet. Service with restrictions, supervision. 🛜 ☒ 🛏 💻 🌊 ☒

▼▼▼▼ The MET Hotel Troy Detroit 🅷

(248) 879-2100. **Call for rates.** 5500 Crooks Rd 48098. I-75 exit 72 (Crooks Rd), just n. Int corridors. **Pets:** Medium. Designated rooms, supervision. 🛜 ☒ 🖧ᴹ 🛏 💻 🌊

▼▼ ▼▼ Quality Inn Detroit-Troy 🅷

(248) 689-7500. **$72-$89.** 2537 Rochester Ct 48083. I-75 exit 67 (Rochester Rd), 0.3 mi sw, then just w. Int corridors. **Pets:** Accepted. ECO 🛜 ☒ 🛏 💻 ⅱ 🌊

⋘⋙ ▼▼▼▼ Red Roof Inn-Troy #7021 Ⓜ

(248) 689-4391. **$40-$99.** 2350 Rochester Ct 48083. I-75 exit 67 (Rochester Rd), 0.3 mi sw. Ext corridors. **Pets:** Large, other species. Service with restrictions, supervision. SAVE 🛜 ☒ 🖧ᴹ 🛏 💻

UTICA

⋘⋙ ▼▼▼▼ Comfort Inn 🅷

(586) 739-7111. **$79-$100.** 11401 Hall Rd 48317. Jct Van Dyke Ave (SR 53). Int corridors. **Pets:** Medium, dogs only. Service with restrictions, supervision. SAVE 🛜 ☒ 🛏 💻

▼▼▼▼ La Quinta Inn & Suites Detroit Utica 🅷

(586) 731-4700. **$78-$144.** 45311 Park Ave 48315. Jct Van Dyke Ave (SR 53) and Hall Rd (SR 59), just n. Int corridors. **Pets:** Service with restrictions, supervision. 🛜 ☒ 🛏 💻 🌊

▼▼▼▼ Staybridge Suites-Utica 🅷

(586) 323-0101. **$119-$129.** 46155 Utica Park Blvd 48315. Jct Van Dyke Ave (SR 53) and Hall Rd (SR 59), just n. Int corridors. **Pets:** Large. $75 deposit/room. Designated rooms, service with restrictions, crate. 🛜 ☒ 🖧ᴹ 🛏 💻 🌊

WARREN

▼▼ ▼▼ Candlewood Suites-Detroit Warren 🅷 🐾

(586) 978-1261. **$89-$99.** 7010 Convention Blvd 48092. I-696 exit 23 (Van Dyke Ave), 2.8 mi n. Int corridors. **Pets:** Other species. $15 daily fee/room. Service with restrictions. 🛜 ☒ 🖧ᴹ 🛏 💻

▼▼ ▼▼ Extended Stay Deluxe Detroit-Warren 🅷

(586) 558-5554. **$68-$78.** 30125 N Civic Center Blvd 48093. I-696 exit 23 (Van Dyke Ave), 1.5 mi n, then just e. Int corridors. **Pets:** $25 daily fee/pet. Designated rooms, service with restrictions. 🛜 ☒ 🖧ᴹ 🛏 💻

▼▼▼▼ Hawthorn Suites 🅷

(586) 558-7870. **$79-$119, 3 day notice.** 30180 N Civic Center Blvd 48093. I-696 exit 23 (Van Dyke Ave), 1.8 mi n. Ext/int corridors. **Pets:** Other species. $75 one-time fee/pet. Designated rooms, service with restrictions, crate. 🛜 ☒ 🖧ᴹ 🛏 💻 🌊

▼▼ ▼▼ La Quinta Inn Detroit Warren Tech Center 🅷

(586) 574-0550. **$59-$118.** 30900 Van Dyke Ave 48093. I-696 exit 23 (Van Dyke Ave), 1.8 mi n on SR 53. Int corridors. **Pets:** Service with restrictions, supervision. 🛜 ☒ 🖧ᴹ 🛏 💻

⋘⋙ ▼▼ ▼▼ Red Roof Inn-Warren #070 Ⓜ

(586) 573-4300. **$54-$74.** 26300 Dequindre Rd 48091. I-696 exit 20 (Dequindre Rd), just ne. Ext corridors. **Pets:** Large, other species. Service with restrictions, supervision. SAVE 🛜 ☒ 🖧ᴹ 🛏 💻

⋘⋙ ▼▼▼▼ TownePlace Suites by Marriott-Warren 🅷

(586) 264-8800. **$89-$199.** 7601 Chicago Rd 48092. I-696 exit 23 (Van Dyke Ave), 2 mi n. Int corridors. **Pets:** Small, other species. $100 one-time fee/pet. Designated rooms, service with restrictions, supervision. SAVE 🛜 ☒ 🖧ᴹ 🛏 💻 🌊

WATERFORD

▼▼▼▼ Comfort Inn 🅷

(248) 666-8555. **Call for rates.** 7076 Highland Rd 48327. Jct SR 59 (Highland Rd) and Airport Rd, 1 mi w. Int corridors. **Pets:** Accepted. 🛜 ☒ 🛏 💻 🌊 ☒

WOODHAVEN

⋘⋙ ▼▼ ▼▼ BEST WESTERN Woodhaven Inn 🅷

(734) 676-8000. **$72-$79.** 21700 West Rd 48183. I-75 exit 32 (West Rd), just w. Int corridors. **Pets:** Medium. $20 daily fee/room. Designated rooms, service with restrictions, supervision. SAVE 🛜 ☒ 🛏 💻 ⅱ 🌊 ☒

END METROPOLITAN AREA

DEWITT

⋘⋙ ▼▼ ▼▼ Sleep Inn 🅷

(517) 669-8823. **$69-$189.** 1101 Commerce Park Dr 48820. I-69 exit 87 (Old US 27), 0.8 mi n. Int corridors. **Pets:** Small, dogs only. $25 daily fee/pet. Service with restrictions, supervision. SAVE 🛜 ☒ 🛏 💻 🌊

DOUGLAS

▼▼ ▼▼ AmericInn Lodge & Suites of Douglas 🅷

(269) 857-8581. **$79-$249.** 2905 Blue Star Hwy 49406. I-196 exit 36, 0.3 mi n. Int corridors. **Pets:** Accepted. 🛜 ☒ 🖧ᴹ 🛏 💻 🌊

⋘⋙ ▼▼▼▼ The Kirby House 🅱🅱

(269) 857-2904. **Call for rates.** 294 W Center St 49406. Center. Int corridors. **Pets:** Accepted. SAVE 🛜 ☒ 🌊 🄕

EAST LANSING

▼▼▼▼ Gatehouse Suites East Lansing 🅷

(517) 332-7711. **Call for rates.** 1600 E Grand River Ave 48823. US 127 exit 78, 2.6 mi se on SR 43. Ext corridors. **Pets:** Accepted. 🛜 ☒ 🛏 💻 🌊

▼▼▼▼ Hampton Inn East Lansing 🅷

(517) 324-2072. **$139-$199.** 2500 Coolidge Rd 48823. US 127 exit 79 (Lake Lansing Rd), just e. Int corridors. **Pets:** Accepted. 🛜 ☒ 🖧ᴹ 🛏 💻 🌊 ☒

EAST TAWAS

⋘⋙ ▼▼▼▼ Tawas Bay Beach Resort 🅷

(989) 362-8600. **$70-$189, 3 day notice.** 300 E Bay St 48730. On US 23 W. Int corridors. **Pets:** Accepted. SAVE 🛜 ☒ 🛏 💻 ⅱ 🌊 ☒

ESCANABA

▼ Bay View Motel M

(906) 786-2843. **Call for rates.** 7110 US Hwy 2 & 41 & M-35 49837. 4.5 mi n on US 2/41 and SR 35. Ext/int corridors. **Pets:** Accepted.

🛰 ✕ 🛏 💻 ✕

⚠ ▼ Econo Lodge H

(906) 789-1066. **$65-$95.** 921 N Lincoln Rd 49829. 0.5 mi n on US 2/41 and SR 35. Int corridors. **Pets:** Small. $10 daily fee/pet. Designated rooms, service with restrictions, supervision.

SAVE 🛰 ✕ 🛏 💻 ✕

FENTON

▼▼▼ Holiday Inn Express & Suites H

(810) 714-7171. **$99-$129.** 17800 Silver Pkwy 48430. US 23 exit 78 (Owen Rd), just w, then 0.4 mi n. Int corridors. **Pets:** Small. Designated rooms, service with restrictions, supervision.

🛰 ✕ 🔊 🛏 💻 ⤵

FLINT

⚠ ▼▼▼ Americas Best Value Inn & Suites H

(810) 233-9000. **$69-$139.** 6075 Hill 23 Dr 48507. US 23 exit 90 (Hill Rd), just w. Int corridors. **Pets:** $25 one-time fee/pet. Service with restrictions, crate. SAVE 🛰 ✕ 🔊 🛏 💻 ⤵ ✕

▼ Baymont Inn & Suites-Flint/Flushing H

(810) 732-2300. **$49-$129.** 4160 Pier North Blvd 48504. I-75 exit 122 (Pierson Rd), just w. Int corridors. **Pets:** Other species. $25 one-time fee/room. Designated rooms, service with restrictions, supervision.

🛰 ✕ 🛏 💻 ⤵

▼▼▼ Courtyard by Marriott H 🐾

(810) 232-3500. **$99-$149.** 5205 Gateway Center 48507. US 23 exit 90 (Hill Rd), just e to Gateway Center, then just n. Int corridors. **Pets:** Medium. $75 one-time fee/room. Service with restrictions, supervision. 🛰 ✕ 🔊 🛏 💻 🍴 ⤵

▼▼▼ Holiday Inn Express Flint Campus Area H

(810) 238-7744. **$95-$149.** 1150 Robert T Longway Blvd 48503. I-475 exit 8A (Robert T Longway Blvd), just w. Int corridors. **Pets:** $25 one-time fee/pet. Service with restrictions, crate. 🛰 ✕ 🔊 🛏 💻

▼▼▼ Residence Inn by Marriott H

(810) 424-7000. **$89-$145.** 2202 W Hill Rd 48507. US 23 exit 90 (Hill Rd), just e. Int corridors. **Pets:** Accepted.

🛰 ✕ 🔊 🛏 💻 ⤵ ✕

FRANKENMUTH

▼ ▼ Drury Inn & Suites H

(989) 652-2800. **$120-$209.** 260 S Main St 48734. On SR 83; downtown. Int corridors. **Pets:** Service with restrictions, supervision.

🛰 ✕ 🔊 🛏 💻 ⤵

⚠ ▼ Frankenmuth Motel M

(989) 652-6171. **$49-$99.** 1218 Weiss St 48734. Just e of SR 83. Ext corridors. **Pets:** Other species. $10 one-time fee/room. Designated rooms, service with restrictions. SAVE 🛰 ✕ 🛏

GAYLORD

▼ Alpine Lodge H

(989) 732-2431. **$69-$119, 14 day notice.** 833 W Main St 49735. I-75 exit 282, 0.3 mi e on SR 32. Ext/int corridors. **Pets:** Medium, dogs only. Designated rooms, service with restrictions, supervision.

🛰 ✕ 🛏 💻 🍴 ⤵ ✕

⚠ ▼ Downtown Motel M

(989) 732-5010. **Call for rates.** 208 S Otsego Ave 49735. I-75 exit 282, 0.5 mi e, then 0.3 mi s on I-75 business loop. Ext corridors. **Pets:** Dogs only. $10 deposit/pet. Service with restrictions, supervision.

SAVE 🛰 ✕ 🛏 💻

GRAND BLANC

▼▼ ▼▼ Comfort Inn H

(810) 694-0000. **$69-$129.** 9040 Holly Rd 48439. I-75 exit 108 (Holly Rd), just e. Int corridors. **Pets:** Small. $50 one-time fee/room. Designated rooms, service with restrictions, crate. 🛰 ✕ 🔊 🛏 💻 ⤵

GRAND HAVEN

▼▼ Days Inn Grand Haven H

(616) 842-1999. **$76-$180.** 1500 S Beacon Blvd 49417. 1.5 mi s on US 31. Int corridors. **Pets:** $150 deposit/room, $10 daily fee/pet. Service with restrictions, supervision. 🛰 ✕ 🛏 💻 ⤵ ✕

GRAND RAPIDS

⚠ ▼▼▼ Holiday Inn Grand Rapids Downtown H

(616) 235-7611. **$133-$199.** 310 Pearl St NW 49504. US 131 exit 85B (Pearl St), just e. Int corridors. **Pets:** Other species. $25 daily fee/room. Designated rooms, service with restrictions, crate.

ECO SAVE 🛰 ✕ 🔊 🛏 💻 🍴 ⤵ ✕

▼▼▼ Homewood Suites by Hilton H 🐾

(616) 285-7100. **$99-$209.** 3920 Stahl Dr SE 49546. I-96 exit 43A (28th St SW), 1.5 mi w to E Paris Ave, then just n. Int corridors. **Pets:** Other species. Service with restrictions, crate. 🛰 ✕ 🔊 🛏 💻 ⤵

GRANDVILLE

⚠ ▼▼ Days Inn & Suites H

(616) 531-5263. **$70-$75.** 3825 28th St SW 49418. I-196 exit 70/70A, 0.3 mi e. Int corridors. **Pets:** Small, dogs only. $50 deposit/room, $10 daily fee/pet. Designated rooms, service with restrictions, supervision.

SAVE 🛰 ✕ 🛏 💻

▼▼ Grandville Inn H 🐾

(616) 532-3222. **$79-$89.** 3425 Fairlanes Ave 49418. I-196 exit 69A, 0.3 mi e to Fairlanes Ave, then just s. Int corridors. **Pets:** Medium. $20 daily fee/room. Designated rooms, service with restrictions, supervision.

🛰 ✕ 🛏 💻 ⤵ ✕

▼▼▼ Residence Inn by Marriott Grand Rapids West H

(616) 538-1100. **$89-$179.** 3451 Rivertown Point Ct SW 49418. I-196 exit 67, 1.7 mi e. Int corridors. **Pets:** Other species. $75 one-time fee/room. Service with restrictions, crate.

ECO 🛰 ✕ 🔊 🛏 💻 ⤵ ✕

GRAYLING

▼▼ ▼▼ Ramada Hotel & Conference Center H

(989) 348-7611. **$65-$120.** 2650 S Business Loop 49738. I-75 business loop, 0.8 mi s. Ext/int corridors. **Pets:** $35 daily fee/pet. Service with restrictions. 🛰 ✕ 🔊 🛏 💻 🍴 ⤵ ✕

▼▼ Super 8 H 🐾

(989) 348-8888. **$69-$112.** 5828 Nelson A Miles Pkwy 49738. I-75 exit 251, just w. Int corridors. **Pets:** Other species. $8 daily fee/pet. Service with restrictions, crate. 🛰 ✕ 🛏 💻 ⤵ ✕

GREENVILLE

▼▼ ▼▼ AmericInn Lodge & Suites of Greenville H

(616) 754-4500. **$95-$105.** 2525 W Washington St 48838. US 131 exit 101 (SR 57), 13 mi e. Int corridors. **Pets:** Other species. $15 daily fee/room. Designated rooms, service with restrictions, crate.

🛰 ✕ 🔊 🛏 💻 ⤵ ✕

HANCOCK

▼▼ ▼▼ Magnuson Hotel Copper Crown H

(906) 482-6111. **$66-$70.** 235 Hancock St 49930. On US 41 S; downtown. Ext/int corridors. **Pets:** Other species. $10 daily fee/room. Designated rooms, service with restrictions, supervision.

🛰 ✕ 🛏 💻 ⤵

HARRISON

AAA **WV** Lakeside Motel & Cottages **M**

(989) 539-0706. **$62-$99.** 515 E Park St, Business US 127 48625. US 127 exit US 127 business route/SR 61, 2.2 mi w. Ext corridors. **Pets:** Other species. Service with restrictions, supervision.

HARTLAND

AAA **WV WV** BEST WESTERN of Hartland **M**

(810) 632-7177. **$99-$150.** 10087 M-59 48353. On SR 59; US 23 exit 67. Ext corridors. **Pets:** Small, dogs only. $50 deposit/pet. Service with restrictions, supervision.

HILLMAN

WV WV Thunder Bay Golf Resort **M**

(989) 742-4502. **$69-$89, 14 day notice.** 27800 Hwy M-32 E 49746. On SR 32, just e. Ext corridors. **Pets:** Accepted.

HOLLAND

WV WV WV Residence Inn by Marriott **H**

(616) 393-6900. **$129-$199.** 631 Southpoint Ridge Rd 49423. I-196 exit 49, 0.7 mi n on SR 40. Int corridors. **Pets:** $75 one-time fee/room. Service with restrictions, crate.

HOUGHTON

WV WV WV Country Inn & Suites By Carlson **H** ✿

(906) 487-6700. **Call for rates.** 919 Razorback Dr 49931. 1.3 mi w on SR 26. Int corridors. **Pets:** Other species. $10 daily fee/room. Designated rooms, service with restrictions, supervision.

WV WV Magnuson Hotel-Franklin Square Inn **H**

(906) 487-1700. **$80-$110.** 820 Shelden Ave 49931. On US 41; downtown. Int corridors. **Pets:** Other species. $20 daily fee/room. Designated rooms, service with restrictions, supervision.

HOUGHTON LAKE

WV WV Super 8 **H**

(989) 422-3119. **$60-$120.** 9580 W Lake City Rd 48629. Jct US 127 and SR 55. Int corridors. **Pets:** Medium, other species. $10 deposit/pet. Service with restrictions, supervision.

HOWELL

WV WV Baymont Inn & Suites-Howell **H**

(517) 546-0712. **$69-$139.** 4120 Lambert Dr 48855. I-96 exit 133 (US 59/Grand River Ave), just n, then 0.5 mi e. Int corridors. **Pets:** Medium, dogs only. $50 deposit/pet. $10 daily fee/pet. Designated rooms, service with restrictions, crate.

AAA **WV WV** BEST WESTERN Howell **M**

(517) 548-2900. **$89-$145.** 1500 Pinckney Rd 48843. I-96 exit 137 (Pinckney Rd), just s on CR D19. Ext corridors. **Pets:** Small, dogs only. $20 daily fee/pet. Designated rooms, service with restrictions, supervision.

WV WV WV Holiday Inn Express & Suites **H**

(517) 548-0100. **$99-$139.** 1397 N Burkhart Rd 48855. I-96 exit 133 (US 59/Grand River Ave), just n, then 0.5 mi e. Int corridors. **Pets:** Small. $25 one-time fee/pet. Service with restrictions, crate.

IMLAY CITY

WV WV Super 8-Imlay City **H**

(810) 724-8700. **$58-$90.** 6951 Newark Rd 48444. I-69 exit 168 (SR 53/Van Dyke Rd), just n, then just e. Int corridors. **Pets:** $10 one-time fee/room. Service with restrictions, supervision.

IRON MOUNTAIN

AAA **WV WV** Comfort Inn by Choice Hotels **H**

(906) 774-5505. **$84-$109.** 1565 N Stephenson Ave 49801. On US 2, 1.3 mi nw. Int corridors. **Pets:** Medium, dogs only. $15 daily fee/pet. Designated rooms, service with restrictions, crate.

WV WV WV Country Inn & Suites By Carlson **H**

(906) 774-1900. **$86-$160.** 2005 S Stephenson Ave 49801. Jct SR 141, 0.8 mi w on US 2. Int corridors. **Pets:** Dogs only. $20 daily fee/room. Designated rooms, service with restrictions, supervision.

IRON RIVER

WV WV AmericInn Lodge & Suites of Iron River **H**

(906) 265-9100. **$99-$136.** 40 E Adams St 49935. On US 2; downtown. Int corridors. **Pets:** Dogs only. $10 daily fee/pet. Designated rooms, service with restrictions, supervision.

IRONWOOD

WV Americas Best Value Inn **H**

(906) 932-3395. **Call for rates.** 160 E Cloverland Dr 49938. Jct US 2 and 2 business route. Int corridors. **Pets:** $10 daily fee/pet. Designated rooms, service with restrictions, supervision.

WV WV AmericInn of Ironwood **H**

(906) 932-7200. **Call for rates.** 1117 E Cloverland Dr 49938. 0.8 mi e on US 2. Int corridors. **Pets:** Accepted.

ISHPEMING

AAA **WV WV** BEST WESTERN Country Inn **H**

(906) 485-6345. **$93-$114.** 850 US 41 W 49849. US 41, just n of town. Int corridors. **Pets:** Medium. Designated rooms, service with restrictions, supervision.

JACKSON

WV WV Baymont Inn-Jackson **H**

(517) 789-6000. **$89-$209.** 2035 Bondsteel Dr 49202. I-94 exit 138 (US 127), just nw. Int corridors. **Pets:** Medium. $10 daily fee/pet. Service with restrictions, crate.

WV WV Hampton Inn by Hilton **H**

(517) 789-5151. **$109-$149.** 2225 Shirley Dr 49202. I-94 exit 138 (US 127), just n to Springport Rd, then just e. Int corridors. **Pets:** Medium. Designated rooms, service with restrictions, supervision.

KALAMAZOO

WV WV AmericInn Hotel & Suites **H**

(269) 344-7774. **$89-$119.** 1550 E Kilgore Rd 49001. I-94 exit 78 (Portage Rd), just n, then just w. Int corridors. **Pets:** Accepted.

WV WV Baymont Inn & Suites **H**

(269) 372-7999. **$79-$199.** 2203 S 11th St 49009. US 131 exit 36B (Stadium Dr), just w. Int corridors. **Pets:** $10 daily fee/room. Service with restrictions, crate.

AAA **WV WV** BEST WESTERN Hospitality Inn **H**

(269) 381-1900. **Call for rates.** 3640 E Cork St 49001. I-94 exit 80 (Sprinkle Rd), just nw. Int corridors. **Pets:** Other species. $15 daily fee/pet. Service with restrictions, supervision.

AAA **WV WV WV** BEST WESTERN PLUS Kalamazoo Suites **H**

(269) 350-5522. **$90-$170.** 2575 S 11th St 49009. US 131 exit 36B (Stadium Dr), just w. Int corridors. **Pets:** Large. $25 one-time fee/room. Service with restrictions, crate.

▼▼▼▼ Candlewood Suites 🇭

(269) 270-3203. **$89-$109.** 3443 Retail Place Dr 49048. I-94 exit 80 (Sprinkle Rd), just s. Int corridors. **Pets:** Other species. $25 daily fee/room. Service with restrictions, crate. 🛜 ⊗ &M 🔋 💻

ⓐⓐⓐ ▼▼▼▼ Four Points by Sheraton Kalamazoo 🇭

(269) 385-3922. **$89-$229.** 3600 E Cork Street Ct 49001. I-94 exit 80 (Sprinkle Rd), 0.3 mi n, then 0.4 mi w. Int corridors. **Pets:** Medium, dogs only. $25 one-time fee/pet. Service with restrictions, crate.
SAVE 🛜 ⊗ 🔋 💻 🍴 🏊

▼▼▼▼ Holiday Inn-West 🇭

(269) 375-6000. **Call for rates.** 2747 S 11th St 49009. US 131 exit 36B (Stadium Dr), just w. Int corridors. **Pets:** Accepted.
ECO 🛜 ⊗ &M 🔋 💻 🍴 🏊 ⊗

ⓐⓐⓐ ▼▼▼ Quality Inn 🇭

(269) 381-7000. **Call for rates.** 3820 S Sprinkle Rd 49001. I-94 exit 80 (Sprinkle Rd), 0.3 mi s. Int corridors. **Pets:** Medium. $15 one-time fee/pet. Service with restrictions, supervision. SAVE 🛜 ⊗ 🔋 💻 🏊

ⓐⓐⓐ ▼▼▼ Red Roof Inn-West #7025 🇭

(269) 375-7400. **$49-$110.** 5425 W Michigan Ave 49009. US 131 exit 36B (Stadium Dr), just nw. Ext corridors. **Pets:** Large, other species. Service with restrictions, supervision. SAVE 🛜 ⊗ &M 🔋 💻

▼▼▼▼ Residence Inn by Marriott 🇭

(269) 349-0855. **$129-$159.** 1500 E Kilgore Rd 49001. I-94 exit 78 (Portage Rd), just n, then just w. Int corridors. **Pets:** Accepted.
ECO 🛜 ⊗ &M 🔋 💻 🏊 ⊗

▼▼▼▼ Staybridge Suites-Kalamazoo 🇭

(269) 372-8000. **$119-$159.** 2001 Seneca Ln 49008. US 131 exit 36A (Stadium Dr), 0.3 mi e. Int corridors. **Pets:** Medium. $25 daily fee/room. Service with restrictions, crate. 🛜 ⊗ &M 🔋 💻 🏊

▼▼▼▼ TownePlace Suites by Marriott Kalamazoo 🇭

(269) 353-1500. **$129-$179.** 5683 S 9th St 49009. I-94 exit 72 (9th St), just s. Int corridors. **Pets:** Medium, dogs only. $25 daily fee/room. Designated rooms, service with restrictions, crate.
🛜 ⊗ &M 🔋 💻 🏊

KALKASKA

▼▼▼ All Seasons Resort 🇭

(231) 258-0000. **Call for rates.** 760 S Cedar St 49646. On US 131 and SR 72, 0.8 mi e. Int corridors. **Pets:** Accepted. 🛜 ⊗ 🔋 🏊 ⊗

KENTWOOD

▼▼▼ Comfort Inn Airport 🇭

(616) 957-2080. **$70-$160.** 4155 28th St SE 49512. I-96 exit 43A, 1.5 mi w on SR 11. Int corridors. **Pets:** Other species. $95 daily fee/pet. Designated rooms, supervision. 🛜 ⊗ 🔋 💻

▼▼▼ Extended StayAmerica Grand Rapids-Kentwood 🇭

(616) 977-6750. **$45-$80.** 3747 29th St SE 49512. I-96 exit 43A, 2 mi w on SR 11, then just s. Int corridors. **Pets:** $25 daily fee/pet. Designated rooms, service with restrictions. 🛜 ⊗ 🔋 💻

▼▼▼ Hawthorn Suites by Wyndham Grand Rapids 🇭

(616) 957-8111. **$99-$119.** 2701 E Beltline Ave 49546. Jct 28th St (SR 11) and E Beltline Ave (SR 37). Ext corridors. **Pets:** Accepted.
🛜 ⊗ 🔋 💻 🏊 ⊗

▼▼▼ Sleep Inn & Suites 🇭

(616) 975-9000. **$69-$119.** 4284 29th St 49512. I-96 exit 43A, 1 mi w on SR 11, then just s on Acquest Ave. Int corridors. **Pets:** Accepted.
🛜 ⊗ &M 🔋 💻 🏊

▼▼▼▼ Staybridge Suites 🇭

(616) 464-3200. **Call for rates.** 3000 Lake Eastbrook Blvd SE 49512. I-96 exit 43A, 2 mi w on SR 11, then just s. Int corridors. **Pets:** Small. $15 daily fee/room. Service with restrictions.
🛜 ⊗ &M 🔋 💻 🏊

LANSING

ⓐⓐⓐ ▼▼▼▼ BEST WESTERN PLUS Lansing 🇭

(517) 694-8123. **Call for rates.** 6820 S Cedar St 48911. I-96 exit 104. Int corridors. **Pets:** Other species. $50 one-time fee/room. Designated rooms, service with restrictions, supervision.
SAVE 🛜 ⊗ &M 🔋 💻 🍴 🏊 ⊗

ⓐⓐⓐ ▼▼▼▼ Candlewood Suites 🇭

(517) 351-8181. **$59-$189.** 3545 Forest Rd 48910. I-496 exit 11 (Jolly Rd), 0.3 mi e to Collins Rd, 0.7 mi n, then just w. Int corridors. **Pets:** $75 one-time fee/room. Service with restrictions, crate.
SAVE 🛜 ⊗ &M 🔋 💻 🍴 ⊗

ⓐⓐⓐ ▼▼▼▼ Courtyard by Marriott 🇭 ❀

(517) 482-0500. **$89-$149.** 2710 Lake Lansing Rd 48912. US 127 exit 79 (Lake Lansing Rd), just w. Int corridors. **Pets:** Medium, dogs only. $75 one-time fee/room. Service with restrictions, crate.
SAVE 🛜 ⊗ &M 🔋 💻 🍴 ⊗

▼▼▼▼ Hampton Inn of Lansing 🇭

(517) 627-8381. **$75-$115.** 525 N Canal Rd 48917. I-96 exit 93B (SR 43/Saginaw Hwy), just e. Int corridors. **Pets:** Medium, dogs only. $50 deposit/pet. Designated rooms, service with restrictions, supervision.
🛜 ⊗ 🔋 💻 🏊 ⊗

ⓐⓐⓐ ▼▼▼▼ Lexington Lansing Hotel 🇭

(517) 323-7100. **$119-$300.** 925 S Creyts Rd 48917. I-496 exit 1 (Creyts Rd), just n. Int corridors. **Pets:** Accepted.
SAVE 🛜 ⊗ 🔋 💻 🍴 🏊 ⊗

ⓐⓐⓐ ▼▼▼▼ Quality Suites Hotel 🇭 ❀

(517) 886-0600. **$99-$129.** 901 Delta Commerce Dr 48917. I-96 exit 93B (SR 43/Saginaw Hwy), 0.3 mi e to Bennigan's, then just n. Int corridors. **Pets:** Other species. $25 one-time fee/room. Service with restrictions.
ECO SAVE 🛜 ⊗ 🔋 💻 ⊗

ⓐⓐⓐ ▼▼▼ Red Roof Inn-West #7020 🇭

(517) 321-7246. **$47-$68.** 7412 W Saginaw Hwy 48917. I-96 exit 93B (SR 43/Saginaw Hwy), just e. Ext corridors. **Pets:** Large, other species. Service with restrictions, supervision. SAVE 🛜 ⊗ 🔋 💻

▼▼▼▼ Residence Inn by Marriott West 🇭

(517) 886-5030. **$130-$220.** 922 Delta Commerce Dr 48917. I-96 exit 93B (SR 43/Saginaw Hwy), 0.4 mi e; behind Bennigan's. Int corridors. **Pets:** Accepted. 🛜 ⊗ &M 🔋 💻 🏊 ⊗

LUDINGTON

ⓐⓐⓐ ▼▼▼ BEST WESTERN Splash Park Inn 🇭

(231) 843-2140. **Call for rates.** 5005 W US 10 49431. US 31 exit 170B, 1 mi w. Int corridors. **Pets:** Accepted.
SAVE 🛜 ⊗ 🔋 💻 🏊 ⊗

▼▼▼ Holiday Inn Express 🇭 ❀

(231) 845-7004. **$89-$249, 3 day notice.** 5323 W US 10 49431. US 31 exit 170B, 1.3 mi w. Int corridors. **Pets:** Dogs only. $10 daily fee/pet. Service with restrictions, supervision. ECO 🛜 ⊗ 🔋 💻 🏊 ⊗

MACKINAW CITY

ⓐⓐⓐ ▼▼▼▼ Americas Best Value Inn Mackinaw City Ⓜ

(231) 436-5544. **$49-$209.** 112 Old US 31 49701. I-75 exit 337 northbound, just ne; exit 338 southbound, 0.7 mi se. Ext corridors. **Pets:** Accepted. SAVE 🛜 ⊗ 🔋 💻 🏊

▼▼▼▼ Baymont Inn & Suites-Mackinaw City 🇭

(231) 436-7737. **$59-$265.** 109 S Nicolet St 49701. I-75 exit 338 southbound, just n. Int corridors. **Pets:** Large, dogs only. $15 daily fee/room. Designated rooms, supervision. 🛜 ⊗ 🔋 💻 🏊

▼▼▼ The Beach House 🄲🄰

(231) 436-5353. **Call for rates.** 11490 W US 23 49701. 1.3 mi s. Ext corridors. **Pets:** Accepted. 🛜 ⊗ 🔋 💻 🏊 ⊗ ⊘

Days Inn & Suites "Bridgeview Lodge" Ⓜ ❀
(231) 436-8961. **$59-$300.** 206 N Nicolet St 49701. I-75 exit 339; at bridge. Ext/int corridors. **Pets:** Medium, dogs only. Designated rooms, service with restrictions, supervision. 🛰 ✕ 🗎 💻 ➴

Days Inn Lakeview Ⓜ
(231) 436-5557. **$39-$299, 3 day notice.** 825 S Huron Ave 49701. I-75 exit 337 northbound, 0.5 mi n to US 23, then 0.3 mi e; exit 338 southbound, 0.8 mi se on US 23. Ext corridors. **Pets:** Dogs only. $20 daily fee/pet. Service with restrictions, supervision.
SAVE 🛰 ✕ 🗎 💻 ➴ ✕

Econo Lodge Bayview Ⓜ
(231) 436-5777. **$39-$299, 3 day notice.** 712 S Huron Ave 49701. I-75 exit 337 northbound, 0.5 mi n to US 23, 0.3 mi e, then just n; exit 338 southbound, 0.8 mi se on US 23, then just n. Ext corridors. **Pets:** Dogs only. $20 daily fee/pet. Service with restrictions, supervision.
SAVE 🛰 ✕ 🗎 💻 ➴ ✕

Fairview Beachfront Inn Ⓜ
(231) 436-8831. **$38-$198, 3 day notice.** 907 S Huron St 49701. 0.8 mi se on US 23. Ext corridors. **Pets:** Dogs only. $20 daily fee/pet. Service with restrictions, supervision. SAVE 🛰 ✕ 🗎 💻 ➴

Holiday Inn Express at the Bridge Ⓗ ❀
(231) 436-7100. **$49-$249.** 364 Louvigny St 49701. I-75 exit 339. Int corridors. **Pets:** Medium, dogs only. Designated rooms, service with restrictions, supervision. 🛰 ✕ ♿M 🗎 💻 ➴ ✕

Lamplighter Motel Ⓜ
(231) 436-5350. **Call for rates.** 303 Jamet St 49701. I-75 exit 339, just n of town. Ext corridors. **Pets:** Medium, other species. $5 daily fee/pet. Service with restrictions, supervision. 🛰 ✕ 🗎 💻

Mackinaw City Stay Inn Ⓜ
(231) 436-5026. **Call for rates.** 412 N Nicolet St 49701. I-75 exit 339, just ne. Ext corridors. **Pets:** Accepted. 🛰 ✕ 🗎 💻

Quality Inn & Suites Beachfront Ⓜ
(231) 436-5051. **$39-$249, 3 day notice.** 917 S Huron Ave 49701. 1 mi se on US 23. Ext corridors. **Pets:** Dogs only. $20 daily fee/pet. Service with restrictions, supervision. SAVE 🛰 ✕ 🗎 💻 ➴

Super 8 Beachfront Ⓜ
(231) 436-7111. **$49-$299, 3 day notice.** 519 S Huron Ave 49701. I-75 exit 337 northbound, 0.5 mi n to US 23, 0.3 mi e, then just n; exit 338 southbound, 0.8 mi se on US 23, then just n. Ext corridors. **Pets:** Dogs only. $20 daily fee/pet. Service with restrictions, supervision.
SAVE 🛰 ✕ 🗎 💻 ➴

Super 8 Bridgeview Ⓗ
(231) 436-5252. **$49-$299, 3 day notice.** 601 N Huron Ave 49701. I-75 exit 339 northbound, just n, then just e. Ext/int corridors. **Pets:** Dogs only. $20 daily fee/pet. Service with restrictions, supervision.
SAVE 🛰 ✕ 🗎 💻 ➴

Thunderbird Inn Mackinaw City Ⓜ
(231) 436-5433. **$49-$169.** 146 Old US 31 49701. I-75 exit 337 northbound, just ne; exit 338 southbound, 0.7 mi se. Ext corridors. **Pets:** Accepted. SAVE 🛰 ✕ 🗎 💻 ➴

MANISTIQUE

Comfort Inn by Choice Hotels Ⓗ
(906) 341-6981. **$90-$180.** 617 E Lakeshore Dr 49854. 0.5 mi e on US 2. Int corridors. **Pets:** $25 one-time fee/room. Service with restrictions, supervision. 🛰 ✕ 🗎 💻

Econo Lodge Lakeshore Ⓜ
(906) 341-6014. **$60-$120.** 1101 E Lakeshore Dr 49854. 1.5 mi e on US 2. Ext/int corridors. **Pets:** Accepted. 🛰 ✕ 🗎 💻

Peninsula Pointe Hotel Ⓗ
(906) 341-3777. **$79-$129.** 955 E Lakeshore Dr 49854. 1.4 mi e on US 2. Int corridors. **Pets:** Accepted. 🛰 ✕ 🗎 💻

MARQUETTE

Birchmont Motel Ⓜ
(906) 228-7538. **$60-$80.** 2090 US 41 S 49855. On US 41, 1.8 mi n of jct SR 28; 4.3 mi s of downtown. Ext corridors. **Pets:** Accepted.
SAVE 🛰 ✕ 🗎 💻

Days Inn Ⓗ 🐾
(906) 225-1393. **$89-$119, 3 day notice.** 2403 US 41 W 49855. On US 41 and SR 28, 2.3 mi w. Int corridors. **Pets:** Dogs only. $15 daily fee/room. Designated rooms, service with restrictions, supervision.
🛰 ✕ 🗎 💻 ➴ ✕

Econo Lodge Lakeside Ⓜ
(906) 225-1305. **$55-$149.** 2050 US 41 S 49855. On US 41, 2 mi n of SR 28; 4.1 mi s of downtown. Ext/int corridors. **Pets:** Other species. $10 daily fee/pet. Service with restrictions. 🛰 ✕ 🗎 💻

Holiday Inn Ⓗ
(906) 225-1351. **$129-$199.** 1951 US 41 W 49855. On US 41 and SR 28, 1.8 mi w. Int corridors. **Pets:** Dogs only. $25 deposit/room. Designated rooms, service with restrictions.
🛰 ✕ ♿M 🗎 💻 ¶1 ➴ ✕

Ramada Marquette Ⓗ
(906) 228-6000. **$99-$139.** 412 W Washington St 49855. 0.5 mi w on US 42 business route. Int corridors. **Pets:** Large. $25 one-time fee/pet. Service with restrictions, crate. 🛰 ✕ 🗎 💻 ¶1 ➴ ✕

Super 8 Ⓗ
(906) 228-8100. **$59-$95.** 1275 US 41 W 49855. On US 41 and SR 28, 1 mi w. Int corridors. **Pets:** Dogs only. $20 one-time fee/room. Designated rooms, service with restrictions, supervision. 🛰 ✕ 🗎 💻 ➴

MARSHALL

Arbor Inn of Historic Marshall Ⓜ
(269) 781-7772. **$45-$69.** 15435 W Michigan Ave 49068. I-69 exit 36 (Michigan Ave), just w. Ext corridors. **Pets:** Medium. $5 daily fee/pet. Service with restrictions, supervision. SAVE 🛰 ✕ ➴

Comfort Inn Ⓗ
(269) 789-7890. **$79-$180.** 204 Winston Dr 49068. I-69 exit 36 (Michigan Ave), just se. Int corridors. **Pets:** $35 one-time fee/pet. Designated rooms, service with restrictions, crate. 🛰 ✕ ♿M 🗎 💻 ➴ ✕

Hampton Inn Marshall Ⓗ
(269) 789-0131. **Call for rates.** 325 Sam Hill Dr 49068. I-94 exit 110 (SR 227), just s. Int corridors. **Pets:** Accepted.
🛰 ✕ ♿M 🗎 💻 ➴

Holiday Inn Express-Marshall Ⓗ
(269) 789-9301. **Call for rates.** 329 Sam Hill Dr 49068. I-94 exit 110 (SR 227), just s. Int corridors. **Pets:** $35 daily fee/pet. Designated rooms, service with restrictions, supervision. 🛰 ✕ ♿M 🗎 💻 ➴

MENOMINEE

AmericInn of Menominee Ⓗ
(906) 863-8699. **$94-$139.** 2330 10th St 49858. 0.8 mi n on US 41. Int corridors. **Pets:** Small. $30 daily fee/room. Designated rooms, supervision.
🛰 ✕ 🗎 💻 ➴ ✕

Econo Lodge On The Bay Ⓗ
(906) 863-4431. **Call for rates.** 2516 10th St 49858. 1 mi n on US 41. Int corridors. **Pets:** $20 daily fee/pet. Designated rooms, supervision.
🛰 ✕ 🗎 💻 ✕

MIDLAND

BEST WESTERN Valley Plaza Inn Ⓗ
(989) 496-2700. **Call for rates.** 5221 Bay City Rd 48642. US 10 exit Midland/Bay City Rd. Int corridors. **Pets:** Accepted.
SAVE 🛰 ✕ 🗎 💻 ¶1 ➴ ✕

▼▼ ▼▼ **Fairview Inn & Suites** 🄷
(989) 631-0070. **$89-$125.** 2200 W Wackerly St 48640. Jct US 10 and Eastman Ave. Int corridors. **Pets:** Accepted. 🛜 ☒ 🛌 📖 ➿

▼▼▼ **Residence Inn by Marriott** 🄷
(989) 837-9990. **$146-$249.** 850 Joe Mann Blvd 48642. US 10 exit Eastman Ave, 1 mi e. Int corridors. **Pets:** Accepted.
🛜 ☒ ㊑ 🛌 📖 ➿ ☒

▼▼ ▼▼ **Sleep Inn of Midland** 🄷
(989) 837-1010. **$79-$110.** 2100 W Wackerly St 48640. Jct US 10 and Eastman Ave. Int corridors. **Pets:** Accepted. 🛜 ☒ 🛌 📖 ➿

MOUNT PLEASANT
▼▼ ▼▼ **Comfort Inn & Suites Hotel and Conference Center** 🄷
(989) 772-4000. **$99-$129.** 2424 S Mission St 48858. 2 mi s on US 127 business route. Int corridors. **Pets:** $20 one-time fee/room. Crate.
🛜 ☒ 🛌 📖 ➿ ☒

▼▼ ▼▼ **Fairfield Inn & Suites by Marriott** 🄷 🐾
(989) 775-5000. **$99-$129.** 2525 S University Park Dr 48858. 2.5 mi s on US 127 business route. Int corridors. **Pets:** Other species. $20 daily fee/room. No service, supervision. 🛜 ☒ 🛌 📖 ➿

▼▼ ▼▼ **Super 8** 🄷
(989) 773-8888. **$70-$249.** 2323 S Mission St 48858. 1.8 mi s on US 127 business route. Int corridors. **Pets:** Accepted.
🛜 ☒ ㊑ 🛌 📖

MUNISING
▼▼ **Alger Falls Motel** Ⓜ
(906) 387-3536. **$45-$175.** E9427 Hwy M-28 49862. 2 mi e on SR 28 and 94. Ext corridors. **Pets:** Small, dogs only. $5 one-time fee/pet. Designated rooms, service with restrictions, supervision. 🛜 ☒ 🛌

▼▼ ▼▼ **AmericInn Lodge & Suites of Munising** 🄷
(906) 387-2000. **$70-$170.** E9926 Hwy M-28 49854. On SR 28, 2.7 mi e. Int corridors. **Pets:** Small. $10 daily fee/pet. Designated rooms, service with restrictions, supervision. 🛜 ☒ ㊑ 🛌 📖 ➿ ☒

▼▼ ▼▼ **Holiday Inn Express Lakeview** 🄷 🐾
(906) 387-4800. **Call for rates.** E8890 M-28 49862. On SR 28, 2 mi w of town. Int corridors. **Pets:** $10 daily fee/room. Designated rooms, service with restrictions. 🛜 ☒ ㊑ 🛌 📖 ➿ ☒

🔺 ▼ **Terrace Motel** Ⓜ
(906) 387-2735. **$50-$75.** 420 Prospect St 49862. 0.5 mi e, just off SR 28. Ext corridors. **Pets:** $10 daily fee/room. Designated rooms, service with restrictions, crate. [SAVE] 🛜 ☒ ☒ 🅰 ⓩ

NEWBERRY
▼▼ ▼▼ **Comfort Inn Tahquamenon Falls** 🄷
(906) 293-3218. **Call for rates.** 13954 Hwy M-28 49868. Jct SR 28 and 123. Int corridors. **Pets:** Accepted. 🛜 ☒ 🛌 📖 ☒

NEW BUFFALO
▼▼▼▼ **Fairfield Inn & Suites by Marriott** 🄷
(269) 586-2222. **$99-$329.** 11400 Holiday Dr 49117. I-94 exit 1 (La Porte Rd). Int corridors. **Pets:** Accepted. 🛜 ☒ ㊑ 🛌 📖 ➿

▼▼▼▼ **Holiday Inn Express Hotel & Suites** 🄷
(269) 469-1400. **$130-$310.** 11500 Holiday Dr 49117. I-94 exit 1 (La Porte Rd), just w. Int corridors. **Pets:** Accepted.
🛜 ☒ ㊑ 🛌 📖 ➿

NILES
▼▼ **Comfort Inn & Suites** 🄷
(269) 684-3900. **Call for rates.** 1265 S 11th St (M-51) 49120. Jct US 12, 0.8 mi n on SR 51. Int corridors. **Pets:** Large. $25 daily fee/pet. Designated rooms, service with restrictions, supervision.
🛜 ☒ 🛌 📖 ➿

NORWAY
▼▼ **Norway Inn Lodge & Suites** 🄷
(906) 563-7500. **$81-$88.** W6002 US Hwy 2 49870. 0.7 mi w. Int corridors. **Pets:** Accepted. 🛜 ☒ 🛌 📖 ➿ ☒

OKEMOS
▼▼ **Comfort Inn-E Lansing/Okemos** 🄷
(517) 347-6690. **$95-$140.** 2187 University Park Dr 48864. I-96 exit 110 (Okemos Rd), just n, then just e. Int corridors. **Pets:** Accepted.
🛜 ☒ ㊑ 🛌 📖

▼▼▼ **Holiday Inn Express & Suites** 🄷
(517) 349-8700. **Call for rates.** 2209 University Park Dr 48864. I-96 exit 110 (Okemos Rd), just n, then just e. Int corridors. **Pets:** Large, dogs only. $25 one-time fee/pet. Service with restrictions, crate.
🛜 ☒ ㊑ 🛌 📖 ➿ ☒

▼▼▼ **Staybridge Suites-Lansing/Okemos** 🄷
(517) 347-3044. **Call for rates.** 3553 Meridian Crossing Dr 48864. I-96 exit 110 (Okemos Rd), just n. Int corridors. **Pets:** Medium. $75 one-time fee/room. Service with restrictions, supervision.
🛜 ☒ ㊑ 🛌 📖 ➿

PAW PAW
▼▼ **Comfort Inn & Suites** 🄷
(269) 655-0303. **$65-$150.** 153 Ampey Rd 49079. I-94 exit 60 (SR 40), just nw. Int corridors. **Pets:** Accepted. 🛜 ☒ ㊑ 🛌 📖 ➿

PETOSKEY
🔺 ▼▼ **Days Inn Petoskey** Ⓜ
(231) 348-3900. **$59-$142.** 1420 US 131 49770. 1.3 mi s on US 131. Ext corridors. **Pets:** Other species. $12 daily fee/pet. Designated rooms, service with restrictions, supervision. [SAVE] 🛜 ☒ 🛌 📖 🍴

▼▼▼ **Holiday Inn Express Hotel & Suites** 🄷
(231) 487-0991. **$79-$299.** 1751 US 131 S 49770. I-75 exit 282, w on SR 32 to US 131 N. Int corridors. **Pets:** Accepted.
🛜 ☒ 🛌 📖 ☒

PLAINWELL
🔺 ▼▼▼ **Comfort Inn** 🄷
(269) 685-9891. **$90-$130.** 622 Allegan St 49080. US 131 exit 49A, just e. Int corridors. **Pets:** Medium. $15 daily fee/pet. Designated rooms, service with restrictions, supervision. [SAVE] 🛜 ☒ 🛌 📖 ➿

PORT HURON
🔺 ▼▼ **Baymont Inn & Suites** 🄷
(810) 364-8000. **$65-$149.** 1611 Range Rd 48074. I-94 exit 269 (Range Rd), just w. Int corridors. **Pets:** Medium. $15 daily fee/pet. Designated rooms, service with restrictions, crate. [SAVE] 🛜 ☒ 🛌 📖 ➿

▼▼▼ **Comfort Inn** 🄷
(810) 982-5500. **$90-$170.** 1700 Yeager St 48060. I-94 exit 274 (Water St), just s, then just w. Int corridors. **Pets:** Dogs only. $20 daily fee/pet. Designated rooms, service with restrictions, supervision.
🛜 ☒ 🛌 📖 ➿

PORTLAND
🔺 ▼▼ **American Heritage Inn** 🄷
(517) 647-2200. **$69-$149.** 1681 E Grand River Ave 48875. I-96 exit 77, just n. Int corridors. **Pets:** Small, dogs only. $25 daily fee/pet. Service with restrictions, supervision. [SAVE] 🛜 ☒ ㊑ 🛌 📖 ➿

SAGINAW

◆◆ Comfort Suites by Choice Hotels **H**
(989) 797-8000. **$84-$145.** 5180 Fashion Square Blvd 48603. I-675 exit 6, 0.6 mi w on Tittabawassee Rd. Int corridors. **Pets:** Medium, other species. $50 one-time fee/room. Service with restrictions, crate.

◆◆◆ Country Inn & Suites By Carlson Saginaw **H**
(989) 792-7666. **Call for rates.** 2222 Tittabawassee Rd 48604. I-675 exit 6, just w. Int corridors. **Pets:** Other species. $25 daily fee/pet. Designated rooms, service with restrictions, supervision.

◆◆◆ Residence Inn by Marriott **H**
(989) 799-9000. **$159-$174.** 5230 Fashion Square Blvd 48604. I-675 exit 6, 0.8 mi w, then just n. Int corridors. **Pets:** Accepted.

ST. IGNACE

◆◆◆ ◆◆ Budget Host Inn & Suites **H**
(906) 643-9666. **$70-$156.** 700 N State St 49781. 1.8 mi n of bridge tollgate on I-75 business route. Ext/int corridors. **Pets:** Other species. $10 one-time fee/room. Service with restrictions, supervision.

ST. JOSEPH

◆◆ Silver Beach Hotel **H**
(269) 983-7341. **Call for rates.** 100 Main St 49085. I-94 exit 23, 6 mi nw on Business Rt I-94. Int corridors. **Pets:** Accepted.

SANDUSKY

◆◆ DeMott's West Park Inn **H**
(810) 648-4300. **Call for rates.** 440 W Sanilac Rd 48471. 0.7 mi w on SR 46. Ext/int corridors. **Pets:** Small. Service with restrictions, crate.

SAULT STE. MARIE

◆◆ Americas Best Value Inn **H**
(906) 632-8882. **Call for rates.** 3826 I-75 Business Loop 49783. I-75 exit 392, 0.5 mi ne. Int corridors. **Pets:** Accepted.

◆◆◆ ◆ Budget Host Crestview Inn **M**
(906) 635-5213. **$59-$99.** 1200 Ashmun St 49783. I-75 exit 392, 2.8 mi ne on I-75 business loop. Ext corridors. **Pets:** Other species. $5 one-time fee/pet. Designated rooms, service with restrictions, supervision.

◆◆◆ ◆◆ Days Inn **H**
(906) 635-5200. **$75-$119.** 3651 I-75 Business Spur 49783. I-75 exit 392, 0.8 mi ne on I-75 business loop. Int corridors. **Pets:** Medium. $5 daily fee/room. Designated rooms, service with restrictions, crate.

◆◆◆ ◆◆ Park Inn by Radisson Sault Sainte Marie, MI **H**
(906) 632-6000. **$65-$90.** 3525 I-75 Business Spur 49783. I-75 exit 392, 0.7 mi ne. Int corridors. **Pets:** Dogs only. $10 daily fee/room. Designated rooms, service with restrictions, supervision.

◆◆◆ ◆◆◆ Ramada Plaza Ojibway Hotel **H**
(906) 632-4100. **$99-$159.** 240 Portage St W 49783. Just w of jct Ashmun St; downtown. Int corridors. **Pets:** $25 one-time fee/pet. Crate.

SILVER CITY

◆◆◆ AmericInn Lodge & Suites **H**
(906) 885-5311. **$100-$170.** 120 Lincoln Ave 49953. SR 107, 0.3 mi w of SR 64. Int corridors. **Pets:** Accepted.

SOUTH HAVEN

◆◆◆ ◆◆◆ Comfort Suites **H**
(269) 639-2014. **$79-$209.** 1755 Phoenix St 49090. I-196 exit 20, 0.5 mi e. Int corridors. **Pets:** Small. $25 deposit/pet. Service with restrictions, supervision.

SPRING LAKE

◆◆◆ Grand Haven Waterfront Holiday Inn **H** ❀
(616) 846-1000. **Call for rates.** 940 W Savidge St 49456. On SR 104, just e of US 31. Int corridors. **Pets:** Medium, dogs only. $25 daily fee/pet. Designated rooms, service with restrictions, supervision.

STEVENSVILLE

◆◆ Candlewood Suites **H** ❀
(269) 428-4400. **Call for rates.** 2567 W Marquette Woods Rd 49127. I-94 exit 23 (Red Arrow Hwy). Int corridors. **Pets:** Medium. $75 one-time fee/pet. Designated rooms, service with restrictions, supervision.

◆◆◆ Hampton Inn of St. Joseph I-94 **H**
(269) 429-2700. **$99-$199.** 5050 Red Arrow Hwy 49127. I-94 exit 23 (Red Arrow Hwy), just se. Int corridors. **Pets:** Large, other species. Service with restrictions, crate.

SUTTONS BAY

◆ Red Lion Motor Lodge **M**
(231) 271-6694. **$59-$195.** 4290 S West Bayshore Dr 49682. 5 mi s on SR 22. Ext corridors. **Pets:** Other species. $15 one-time fee/room. Service with restrictions, crate.

TAWAS CITY

◆◆◆ ◆◆ Bay Inn Tawas **H**
(989) 362-0088. **$63-$135, 3 day notice.** 1020 W Lake St 48763. 1.5 mi s on US 23. Int corridors. **Pets:** Small, other species. $150 deposit/room. Service with restrictions, supervision.

THOMPSONVILLE

◆◆◆ ◆◆◆ Crystal Mountain **H** ❀
(231) 378-2000. **$139-$389, 14 day notice.** 12500 Crystal Mountain Dr 49683. On SR 115, 2 mi w. Ext/int corridors. **Pets:** Other species. $50 one-time fee/pet. Designated rooms, service with restrictions.

THREE RIVERS

◆◆ Super 8 **H**
(269) 279-8888. **$69-$125.** 689 Super 8 Way 49093. Jct US 131 and SR 60 (W Broadway St), 0.3 mi s on US 131. Int corridors. **Pets:** Very small, dogs only. $50 deposit/pet, $11 daily fee/pet. Designated rooms, service with restrictions, supervision.

TRAVERSE CITY

◆◆ Baymont Inn & Suites-Traverse City **H**
(231) 933-4454. **$70-$200.** 2326 US 31 S 49684. 3.5 mi s on SR 37. Int corridors. **Pets:** $10 daily fee/pet. Designated rooms, service with restrictions, supervision.

◆◆◆ ◆◆ BEST WESTERN Four Seasons **H**
(231) 946-8424. **$59-$349.** 305 Munson Ave 49686. 2 mi e on US 31. Int corridors. **Pets:** Other species. $15 daily fee/room. Service with restrictions, supervision.

◆◆ Days Inn & Suites **H**
(231) 941-0208. **$67-$210.** 420 Munson Ave 49686. 2 mi e on US 31. Int corridors. **Pets:** Other species. $15 daily fee/room. Designated rooms, service with restrictions, supervision.

Holiday Inn, West Bay H ❀
(231) 947-3700. **$100-$305, 3 day notice.** 615 E Front St 49686. 0.5 mi e on US 31. Int corridors. **Pets:** Other species. $150 deposit/room, $15 daily fee/pet. Service with restrictions, supervision.
📶 ⊗ 🛗M 🛄 🖵 🍴 🏊 ⊠

Park Place Hotel H
(231) 946-5000. **Call for rates.** 300 E State St 49684. Corner of E State and Park sts; downtown. Int corridors. **Pets:** Accepted.
ECO 📶 ⊗ 🛄 🖵 🍴 🏊 ⊠

AAA **Quality Inn** H
(231) 929-4423. **$50-$200.** 1492 US 31 N 49686. On US 31, 3.3 mi e. Ext/int corridors. **Pets:** Large, other species. $10 daily fee/room. Designated rooms, service with restrictions, supervision.
SAVE 📶 ⊗ 🛄 🖵 🏊

Traverse Victorian Inn H
(231) 947-5525. **$60-$150.** 461 Munson Ave 49686. 2.4 mi e on US 31. Int corridors. **Pets:** Accepted. 📶 ⊗ 🛄 🖵 🏊

WALKER

Baymont Inn & Suites-Grand Rapids North H
(616) 735-9595. **$79-$149.** 2151 Holton Ct NW 49544. I-96 exit 28 (Walker Ave), just s. Int corridors. **Pets:** Accepted.
📶 ⊗ 🛄 🖵 🏊

Hampton Inn-Grand Rapids North H
(616) 647-1000. **$119-$199.** 500 Center Dr NW 49544. I-96 exit 30, just n on Alpine Rd, then 0.3 mi e. Int corridors. **Pets:** Designated rooms, service with restrictions. 📶 ⊗ 🛗M 🛄 🖵 🏊 ⊠

Quality Inn Grand Rapids North H
(616) 791-8500. **$69-$110.** 2171 Holton Ct 49544. I-96 exit 28 (Walker Ave), just s. Int corridors. **Pets:** Small. $10 daily fee/pet. Designated rooms, service with restrictions, supervision. 📶 ⊗ 🛄 🖵 🏊

SpringHill Suites by Marriott H
(616) 785-1600. **$119-$199.** 450 Center Dr 49544. I-96 exit 30, just n on Alpine Rd, then 0.3 mi e. Int corridors. **Pets:** Accepted.
📶 ⊗ 🛗M 🛄 🖵 🏊

WATERSMEET

Dancing Eagles Resort Lac Vieux Desert Casino H
(906) 358-4949. **$45-$90.** N5384 US Hwy 45 49969. 1.8 mi n of US 2. Int corridors. **Pets:** Accepted. 📶 ⊗ 🛄 🖵 🍴 🏊 ⊠

WHITEHALL

Comfort Inn H
(231) 893-4833. **Call for rates.** 2822 N Durham Rd 49461. US 31 exit 128, just e. Int corridors. **Pets:** Very small, other species. $30 one-time fee/pet. Designated rooms, service with restrictions, crate.
📶 ⊗ 🛄 🖵 🏊

WHITMORE LAKE

AAA **BEST WESTERN of Whitmore Lake** M
(734) 449-2058. **$79-$159.** 9897 Main St 48189. US 23 exit 53, just e. Ext corridors. **Pets:** Other species. $20 daily fee/pet. Designated rooms, service with restrictions, supervision. SAVE 📶 ⊗ 🛄 🖵 🏊

MINNESOTA

CITY INDEX

AITKIN

Ripple River Motel & RV Park M
(218) 927-3734. **$57-$97.** 701 Minnesota Ave S 56431. US 169, 0.8 mi s of jct SR 210. Ext corridors. **Pets:** Dogs only. $10 daily fee/pet. Designated rooms, service with restrictions, crate. 📶 🛄

ALBERT LEA

AmericInn Lodge & Suites of Albert Lea H
(507) 373-4324. **Call for rates.** 811 E Plaza St 56007. I-90 exit 157 (CR 22), just se. Int corridors. **Pets:** Accepted. 📶 🛄 🖵 🏊 ⊠

AAA **BEST WESTERN PLUS Albert Lea** H ❀
I-90/I-35
(507) 373-4000. **$90-$130.** 821 Plaza St 56007. I-90 exit 157 (CR 22), just se. Int corridors. **Pets:** Medium. $20 daily fee/room. Designated rooms, service with restrictions, supervision.
SAVE 📶 ⊗ 🛗M 🛄 🖵 🏊

Comfort Inn H
(507) 377-1100. **Call for rates.** 810 Happy Trails Ln 56007. I-35 exit 11, just se. Int corridors. **Pets:** Medium. $25 one-time fee/pet. Service with restrictions, supervision. 📶 🛗M 🛄 🖵 🏊 ⊠

◆◆◆◆ Country Inn & Suites By Carlson H
(507) 373-5513. **Call for rates.** 2214 E Main St 56007. I-35 exit 12 southbound; exit 11 northbound, 1 mi w. Int corridors. **Pets:** $20 one-time fee/room. Designated rooms, service with restrictions, supervision.
🛜 🛗 🛏 🖥 🏊

ALEXANDRIA

◆◆◆◆ AmericInn Lodge & Suites of Alexandria H
(320) 763-6808. **Call for rates.** 4520 Hwy 29 S 56308. I-94 exit 103, 0.3 mi n. Int corridors. **Pets:** Accepted. 🛜 ✖ 🛗 🛏 🖥 🏊

◆◆◆ BEST WESTERN Alexandria Inn H
(320) 762-5161. **$86-$120.** 508 Twin Blvd 56308. I-94 exit 103, just n, then just e on 50th St. Int corridors. **Pets:** Large. $10 daily fee/pet. Designated rooms, service with restrictions, supervision.
[SAVE] 🛜 🛏 🖥 🏊 ✖

◆◆ Country Inn & Suites By Carlson H
(320) 763-9900. **$79-$139, 21 day notice.** 5304 Hwy 29 S 56308. I-94 exit 103, just sw. Int corridors. **Pets:** $10 one-time fee/pet. Designated rooms, service with restrictions, supervision.
🛜 🛗 🛏 🖥 🏊 ✖

◆◆◆◆ Holiday Inn Alexandria H
(320) 763-6577. **$140-$180.** 5637 Hwy 29 S 56308. I-94 exit 103, just s. Int corridors. **Pets:** Other species. Designated rooms, service with restrictions, crate. 🛜 🛗 🛏 🖥 🍽 🏊 ✖

◆◆ Super 8 H
(320) 763-6552. **$64-$100, 3 day notice.** 4620 Hwy 29 S 56308. I-94 exit 103, 0.3 mi nw. Int corridors. **Pets:** Medium, dogs only. $11 one-time fee/pet. Designated rooms, service with restrictions, supervision.
🛜 🛏 🖥

AUSTIN

◆◆ Days Inn H
(507) 433-8600. **$73.** 700 16th Ave NW 55912. I-90 exit 178A (4th St NW), just nw. Int corridors. **Pets:** Accepted. 🛜 🛏 🖥

◆◆◆◆ Holiday Inn & Austin Conference Center H
(507) 433-1000. **$119-$149.** 1701 4th St NW 55912. I-90 exit 178A (4th St NW), just nw. Int corridors. **Pets:** Accepted.
🛜 ✖ 🛗 🛏 🖥 🍽 🏊

BABBITT

◆◆◆◆ Timber Bay Lodge & Houseboats CA
(218) 827-3682. **$165-$798, 60 day notice.** 8347 Timber Bay Rd 55706. 2.8 mi e of jct CR 21 via CR 70 and 623. Ext corridors. **Pets:** Dogs only. $15 daily fee/pet. Service with restrictions, crate.
🛜 ✖ 🛏 🖥 ✖ ⊠

BAUDETTE

◆◆ AmericInn Lodge & Suites of Baudette H
(218) 634-3200. **Call for rates.** 1179 Main St W 56623. 0.5 mi w on SR 11. Int corridors. **Pets:** Accepted. 🛜 🛗 🛏 🖥 🏊 ✖

BAXTER

◆◆◆ Country Inn & Suites By Carlson H 🐾
(218) 828-2161. **$89-$179.** 15058 Dellwood Dr N 56425. Jct SR 371 and 210, 1 mi n on SR 371. Int corridors. **Pets:** Medium. $30 one-time fee/room. Designated rooms, service with restrictions, supervision.
🛜 🛗 🛏 🖥 🏊

◆◆◆ Holiday Inn Express, Three Bear Waterpark H
(218) 824-3232. **$104-$189.** 15739 Audubon Way 56425. Just se of jct SR 371 and CR 77. Int corridors. **Pets:** Dogs only. $40 daily fee/pet. Designated rooms, service with restrictions, supervision.
🛜 ✖ 🛗 🛏 🖥 ✖

◆◆◆ Super 8 M 🐾
(218) 828-4288. **$75-$152.** 14341 Edgewood Dr 56425. 0.5 mi n of jct SR 371 on SR 210. Int corridors. **Pets:** Dogs only. Service with restrictions, supervision. [SAVE] 🛜 🛏 🖥

BEMIDJI

◆◆◆ ◆◆◆ AmericInn Lodge & Suites of Bemidji H 🐾
(218) 751-3000. **$80-$160.** 1200 Paul Bunyan Dr NW 56601. 0.5 mi e of northwest jct US 2, 71 and SR 197. Int corridors. **Pets:** $15 daily fee/room. Designated rooms, service with restrictions, supervision.
[SAVE] 🛜 ✖ 🛏 🖥 🏊 ✖

◆◆◆ ◆◆◆ BEST WESTERN Bemidji Inn H
(218) 751-0390. **$94-$114.** 2420 Paul Bunyan Dr 56601. Jct US 71 N and SR 197. Int corridors. **Pets:** Large, other species. $15 daily fee/room. Designated rooms, service with restrictions, supervision.
[SAVE] 🛜 ✖ 🛏 🖥 🏊 ✖

◆◆◆ ◆◆◆ Ruttger's Birchmont Lodge CA
(218) 444-3463. **$76-$390, 30 day notice.** 7598 Bemidji Rd NE 56601. Jct SR 197, 3.6 mi n on CR 21 (Bemidji Ave N). Ext/int corridors. **Pets:** Other species. $15 daily fee/pet. Designated rooms, service with restrictions, crate. [SAVE] 🛜 ✖ 🛏 🖥 🍽 🏊 ✖

CALEDONIA

◆◆◆ Fairbridge Inn & Suites Caledonia H
(507) 725-8000. **Call for rates.** 508 N Kruckow Ave 55921. Jct SR 44 and 76, just sw. Int corridors. **Pets:** Accepted. 🛜 🛏 🖥

CANBY

◆◆◆ Canby Inn & Suites M
(507) 223-6868. **$90-$175.** 127 1st St W 56220. Just w of US 75; center. Int corridors. **Pets:** Other species. $20 one-time fee/room. Service with restrictions, crate. 🛜 ✖ 🛗 🛏 🖥 🏊

CANNON FALLS

◆◆◆ ◆◆◆ BEST WESTERN Saratoga Inn H
(507) 263-7272. **$60-$120.** 31591 64th Ave 55009. Jct SR 19, 1 mi sw on US 52. Int corridors. **Pets:** Accepted. [SAVE] 🛜 🛏 🖥 🏊

CLOQUET

◆◆◆ AmericInn Lodge & Suites of Cloquet H
(218) 879-1231. **Call for rates.** 111 Big Lake Rd 55720. I-35 exit 237 (SR 33), 2 mi nw. Int corridors. **Pets:** Accepted.
🛜 🛏 🖥 🏊 ✖

◆◆◆ Super 8 H
(218) 879-1250. **$70-$125.** 121 Big Lake Rd 55720. I-35 exit 237 (SR 33), 2 mi nw. Int corridors. **Pets:** Accepted. 🛜 🛗 🛏 🖥

COOK

◆◆◆ Ludlow's Island Resort CA
(218) 666-5407. **$200-$600, 90 day notice.** 8166 Ludlow Dr 55723. US 53, 3.5 mi ne on CR 24, 5.1 mi e on CR 78 and 540. Ext corridors. **Pets:** Other species. $30 daily fee/pet. Designated rooms, crate.
🛜 🛏 🖥 ✖

CROSSLAKE

◆◆◆◆ Pine Peaks Lodge and Suites H
(218) 692-7829. **$80-$170, 3 day notice.** 14047 Swann Dr 56442. Jct CR 66 and Swann Dr. Int corridors. **Pets:** Small, dogs only. $25 one-time fee/room. Designated rooms, service with restrictions, supervision.
🛜 ✖ 🛏 🖥 ✖

DEER RIVER

◆◆◆ ◆◆◆ White Oak Inn & Suites H
(218) 246-9400. **$67-$160.** 201 4th Ave NW 56636. On US 2. Int corridors. **Pets:** $15 daily fee/pet. Designated rooms, service with restrictions, supervision. [SAVE] 🛜 🛏 🖥 🏊 ✖

DEERWOOD

AAA **▼▼▼** **Country Inn of Deerwood** **H** ❖
(218) 534-3101. **$79-$139.** 23885 Front St 56444. On SR 6 and 210, e of jct CR 12. Int corridors. **Pets:** Other species. $10 daily fee/pet. Service with restrictions, supervision. SAVE 🛜 🖫M 🛏 🖵 🌊

DETROIT LAKES

◈◈ **AmericInn Lodge & Suites of Detroit Lakes** **H**
(218) 847-8795. **$80-$190.** 777 Hwy 10 E 56501. 1.4 mi se. Int corridors. **Pets:** Other species. $10 daily fee/room. Service with restrictions.
🛜 🖫M 🛏 🖵 🌊 ✖

AAA **▼◈◈** **BEST WESTERN PLUS Holland House** **H**
(218) 847-4483. **Call for rates.** 615 Hwy 10 E 56501. 1.3 mi se. Ext/int corridors. **Pets:** Accepted. SAVE 🛜 ✖ 🖫M 🛏 🖵 🌊

▼◈◈ **Holiday Inn on the Lake** **H**
(218) 847-2121. **$79-$119.** 1155 US 10 E 56501. 2 mi se. Int corridors. **Pets:** Other species. $20 one-time fee/room. Designated rooms.
🛜 ✖ 🖫M 🛏 🖵 🍴 🌊 ✖

DULUTH

AAA **▼◈◈** **AmericInn Hotel & Suites of Duluth South** **H**
(218) 624-1026. **$84-$210.** 185 US 2 55810. Jct I-35 and US 2, 0.8 mi n. Int corridors. **Pets:** $25 one-time fee/room. Service with restrictions, supervision. SAVE 🛜 ✖ 🛏 🖵 🍴 🌊

AAA **▼◈◈** **BEST WESTERN Downtown Motel** **M**
(218) 727-6851. **$75-$175.** 131 W 2nd St 55802. 2nd St at 2nd Ave W; center. Ext/int corridors. **Pets:** Accepted. SAVE 🛜 🛏 🖵

AAA **▼◈◈** **Country Inn & Suites By Carlson North** **H** ❖
(218) 740-4500. **$119-$229.** 4257 Haines Rd 55811. Just n of US 53. Int corridors. **Pets:** Other species. $30 one-time fee/room. Designated rooms, service with restrictions, supervision. 🛜 ✖ 🛏 🖵 🌊 ✖

AAA **▼◈◈** **Country Inn & Suites By Carlson South** **H**
(218) 628-0668. **$79-$350.** 9330 W Skyline Pkwy 55810. I-35 exit 249 (Boundary Ave), just se. Int corridors. **Pets:** Small, dogs only. $20 one-time fee/pet. Designated rooms, service with restrictions, supervision.
SAVE 🛜 ✖ 🛏 🖵 🌊 ✖

▼◈◈ **Days Inn-Duluth** **H**
(218) 727-3110. **$85-$220.** 909 Cottonwood Ave 55811. SR 194, just n of jct US 53. Int corridors. **Pets:** Other species. $5 daily fee/room. Service with restrictions, supervision. 🛜 🛏 🖵

AAA **▼◈◈** **Econo Lodge Airport** **H**
(218) 722-5522. **$70-$139.** 4197 Haines Rd 55811. Just s of US 53. Int corridors. **Pets:** Medium, other species. $10 one-time fee/room. Service with restrictions, supervision. SAVE 🛜 🛏 🖵 ✖

AAA **▼◈◈** **Edgewater Resort & Waterpark** **H** ❖
(218) 728-3601. **Call for rates.** 2400 London Rd 55812. I-35 exit 258 (21st Ave E), just nw. Ext/int corridors. **Pets:** $20 daily fee/room. Service with restrictions, supervision. SAVE 🛜 ✖ 🛏 🖵 🍴 🌊 ✖

AAA **▼◈◈** **Fitger's Inn** **H**
(218) 722-8826. **$129-$369.** 600 E Superior St 55802. I-35 exit 256B (Lake Ave), just ne. Int corridors. **Pets:** Large, other species. Designated rooms, service with restrictions, supervision.
SAVE 🛜 ✖ 🛏 🖵 🍴 ✖

▼◈◈ **Radisson Hotel Duluth-Harborview** **H**
(218) 727-8981. **$89-$259.** 505 W Superior St 55802. At 5th Ave W; center. Int corridors. **Pets:** $25 daily fee/room. Designated rooms, service with restrictions. 🛜 🛏 🖵 🍴 🌊 ✖

▼◈◈ **Residence Inn by Marriott** **H** ❖
(218) 279-2885. **$129-$239.** 517 W Central Entrance 55811. Just e on SR 194 from jct US 53. Int corridors. **Pets:** Medium. $75 one-time fee/room. Service with restrictions, supervision.
🛜 ✖ 🖫M 🛏 🖵

AAA **▼◈◈** **Sheraton Duluth Hotel** **H** ❖
(218) 733-5660. **$99-$299.** 301 E Superior St 55802. I-35 exit 256B (Lake Ave), just nw. Int corridors. **Pets:** Dogs only. Service with restrictions, supervision. SAVE 🛜 ✖ 🖫M 🛏 🖵 🍴 🌊

AAA **▼◈◈** **The Suites Hotel at Waterfront Plaza** **H**
(218) 727-4663. **$89-$549.** 325 Lake Ave S 55802. In Canal Park area. Int corridors. **Pets:** $15 daily fee/pet. Designated rooms, service with restrictions, supervision. SAVE 🛜 🖫M 🛏 🖵 🍴 🌊 ✖

◈ **Voyageur Lakewalk Inn** **M**
(218) 722-3911. **Call for rates.** 333 E Superior St 55802. I-35 exit 256 (Superior St), just n; jct 4th Ave E and Superior St. Ext corridors. **Pets:** Dogs only. $15 one-time fee/room. Designated rooms, service with restrictions, supervision. 🛜 🛏 🖵

ELY

AAA **▼◈◈** **Grand Ely Lodge Resort and Conference Center** **H** ❖
(218) 365-6565. **$109-$290, 14 day notice.** 400 N Pioneer Rd 55731. SR 169 to Central Ave, just n to Pioneer Rd, then 1 mi n. Ext/int corridors. **Pets:** $15 daily fee/pet. Designated rooms, service with restrictions, crate. SAVE 🛜 🛏 🖵 🍴 🌊 ✖

AAA **▼◈◈** **Motel Ely-Budget Host** **M**
(218) 365-3237. **$50-$130, 3 day notice.** 1047 E Sheridan St 55731. SR 1 and 169. Ext corridors. **Pets:** Dogs only. $15 one-time fee/pet. Service with restrictions, crate. SAVE 🛜 🛏 🖵

EVELETH

▼◈ **Super 8** **H**
(218) 744-1661. **$80-$160.** 1080 Industrial Park Dr 55734. On US 53, 0.5 mi n of jct SR 37. Int corridors. **Pets:** Accepted.
🛜 🖫M 🛏 🖵 🌊 ✖

FAIRMONT

▼◈ **Comfort Inn** **H** ❖
(507) 238-5444. **Call for rates.** 2225 N State St 56031. I-90 exit 102 (SR 15), just s. Int corridors. **Pets:** Other species. $25 one-time fee/room. Service with restrictions, supervision. 🛜 🛏 🖵 🌊

AAA **▼◈◈** **Hampton Inn Fairmont** **H** ❖
(507) 235-2626. **Call for rates.** 100 Hampton Dr 56031. I-90 exit 102 (SR 15), just sw. Int corridors. **Pets:** Other species. $25 one-time fee/room. Service with restrictions, supervision.
SAVE 🛜 ✖ 🖫M 🛏 🖵

▼◈◈ **Holiday Inn** **H** ❖
(507) 238-4771. **$124-$149.** 1201 Torgerson Dr 56031. I-90 exit 102 (SR 15), just s. Int corridors. **Pets:** Medium. $25 one-time fee/pet. Service with restrictions, supervision. 🛜 🖫M 🛏 🖵 🍴 🌊 ✖

▼◈ **Super 8** **H** ❖
(507) 238-9444. **$75-$110.** 1200 Torgerson Dr 56031. I-90 exit 102 (SR 15), just s. Int corridors. **Pets:** Medium. $25 one-time fee/pet. Service with restrictions, supervision. 🛜 🛏

FARIBAULT

▼◈ **AmericInn Motel & Suites of Faribault** **H**
(507) 334-9464. **$80-$95.** 1801 Lavender Dr 55021. I-35 exit 59 (SR 21), 0.3 mi e. Int corridors. **Pets:** $25 one-time fee/room. Service with restrictions, crate. 🛜 ✖ 🛏 🖵 🌊 ✖

▼◈ **Days Inn & Suites** **H**
(507) 334-6835. **$67-$130.** 1920 Cardinal Ln 55021. I-35 exit 59 (SR 21), just ne. Int corridors. **Pets:** Accepted. 🛜 🖫M 🛏 🖵 🌊

FERGUS FALLS

▼▼ AmericInn Lodge & Suites of Fergus Falls 🚫 ❀
(218) 739-3900. **$84-$155.** 526 Western Ave N 56537. I-94 exit 54 (SR 210), just se. Int corridors. **Pets:** Other species. $50 deposit/room, $10 one-time fee/room. Designated rooms, service with restrictions, supervision. 🛜 💪ᴹ 🔌 💻 🏊 ⬜

FINLAYSON

▼ Americas Best Value Inn 🚫
(320) 245-5284. **Call for rates.** 60671 State Hwy 23 55735. I-35 exit 195 (SR 23), just ne. Int corridors. **Pets:** Accepted. 🛜 🔌

FOSSTON

▼▼ Super 8 🚫
(218) 435-1088. **$58-$98.** 108 S Amber Ave 56542. US 2, 0.5 mi e. Int corridors. **Pets:** Dogs only. $5 one-time fee/pet. Designated rooms, supervision. 🛜 ⬜ 🔌 💻

GARRISON

▼▼ Garrison Inn & Suites 🚫
(320) 692-4050. **Call for rates.** 9243 Hwy 169 56540. SR 169, just s of jct SR 18. Int corridors. **Pets:** Accepted. 🛜 🔌 💻 🏊

GRAND MARAIS

ⒶⒶⒶ ▼▼▼ BEST WESTERN PLUS Superior Inn & Suites 🚫 ❀
(218) 387-2240. **$90-$226, 3 day notice.** 104 1st Ave E 55604. SR 61, just ne of center. Int corridors. **Pets:** Medium, other species. $15 daily fee/pet. Designated rooms, service with restrictions, supervision.
[SAVE] 🛜 ⬜ 🔌 💻

▼▼▼ Gunflint Lodge ⓋⒽ ❀
(218) 388-2294. **$99-$399, 31 day notice.** 143 S Gunflint Lake 55604. 43 mi nw on CR 12 (Gunflint Tr) from jct SR 61; 0.8 mi e on CR 50. Ext corridors. **Pets:** Other species. $20 daily fee/pet. Service with restrictions, crate. 🛜 ⬜ 💪ᴹ 🔌 💻 🍴 ⬜ 🐾 ☎

▼▼▼ Nor'Wester Lodge and Outfitter ⒸⒶ
(218) 388-2252. **$119-$289, 60 day notice.** 7778 Gunflint Tr 55604. 30 mi nw on CR 12 (Gunflint Tr) from jct SR 61. Ext corridors. **Pets:** $15 daily fee/pet. Designated rooms, no service, supervision.
🛜 ⬜ 🔌 💻 ⬜ 🐾 ⓦ ☎

▼ Outpost Motel Ⓜ
(218) 387-1833. **$49-$89.** 2935 SR 61 E 55604. SR 61, 9 mi ne. Ext corridors. **Pets:** Other species. $10 daily fee/pet. Service with restrictions, supervision. 🛜 ⬜ 🔌 💻 ⬜ 🐾

▼ Wedgewood Motel Ⓜ
(218) 387-2944. **$59-$89, 3 day notice.** 1663 E Hwy 61 55604. SR 61, 2.5 mi ne. Ext corridors. **Pets:** Dogs only. $10 one-time fee/pet. Designated rooms, service with restrictions, supervision.
[SAVE] 🛜 ⬜ 🔌 🐾 ☎

GRAND RAPIDS

ⒶⒶⒶ ▼▼▼ Country Inn & Suites By Carlson 🚫 ❀
(218) 327-4960. **$89-$99.** 2601 S Hwy 169 55744. US 2, 2 mi s. Int corridors. **Pets:** Small, dogs only. Supervision.
[SAVE] 🛜 💪ᴹ 🔌 💻 🏊

ⒶⒶⒶ ▼▼▼ Sawmill Inn 🚫
(218) 326-8501. **$69-$109.** 2301 S Hwy 169 55744. US 2, 2 mi s. Ext/int corridors. **Pets:** Other species. Service with restrictions, supervision.
[SAVE] 🛜 🔌 💻 🍴 🏊 ⬜

GRANITE FALLS

▼▼ Granite Falls Super Motel Ⓜ
(320) 564-4075. **$59-$129.** 845 W SR 212 56241. Jct SR 23, 0.5 mi w. Int corridors. **Pets:** Small. $10 daily fee/pet. Designated rooms, service with restrictions, crate. 🛜 💪ᴹ 🔌 🏊

HUTCHINSON

▼▼ AmericInn of Hutchinson 🚫 ❀
(320) 587-5515. **$79-$140.** 1115 Hwy 7 E 55350. 1 mi e of jct SR 15. Int corridors. **Pets:** Dogs only. $15 daily fee/room. Designated rooms, service with restrictions, supervision. 🛜 💪ᴹ 🔌 💻 🏊 ⬜

ⒶⒶⒶ ▼▼ BEST WESTERN Victorian Inn 🚫
(320) 587-6030. **$73-$95.** 1000 Hwy 7 W 55350. SR 15, 1 mi w. Int corridors. **Pets:** $10 one-time fee/room. Service with restrictions, supervision. [SAVE] 🛜 🔌 💻 🍴 🏊

INTERNATIONAL FALLS

▼▼ AmericInn of International Falls 🚫
(218) 283-8000. **Call for rates.** 1500 US 71 W 56649. 1.5 mi w on US 71 and SR 11 W. Int corridors. **Pets:** Accepted.
🛜 🔌 💻 🍴 🏊 ⬜

ⒶⒶⒶ ▼▼ Hilltop Motel Ⓜ
(218) 283-2505. **$59-$89.** 2002 2nd Ave W 56649. US 53, 1 mi s of jct US 53 and SR 11. Ext corridors. **Pets:** Small, dogs only. $5 daily fee/pet. Service with restrictions, supervision. [SAVE] 🛜 ⬜

JACKSON

ⒶⒶⒶ ▼▼▼ AmericInn Lodge & Suites of Jackson 🚫
(507) 847-2444. **$95-$180.** 110 Belmont Ln 56143. I-90 exit 73 (US 71), just sw. Int corridors. **Pets:** Dogs only. $10 daily fee/pet. Designated rooms, service with restrictions, supervision.
[SAVE] 🛜 💪ᴹ 🔌 💻 🏊

KASSON

▼▼ AmericInn Motel & Suites of Kasson 🚫
(507) 634-3444. **$79-$159.** 301 8th St SE 55944. Just se of jct US 14 and SR 57. Int corridors. **Pets:** Accepted. 🛜 💪ᴹ 🔌 💻 🏊

LE CENTER

▼▼ Guardian Inn Motel Ⓜ
(507) 357-2239. **Call for rates.** 550 Commerce Dr 56057. 1 mi e on SR 99. Ext/int corridors. **Pets:** Accepted. 🛜 ⬜ 🔌 💻

LITCHFIELD

▼▼ Knights Inn Ⓜ
(320) 693-2496. **$55-$80.** 1017 E Frontage Rd 55355. On US 12. Int corridors. **Pets:** Small. $10 daily fee/pet. Service with restrictions, supervision. 🛜 🔌 🏊

LONG PRAIRIE

ⒶⒶⒶ ▼▼ Budget Host Inn Ⓜ
(320) 732-6118. **$66-$89, 3 day notice.** 417 Lake St 56347. On US 71 and SR 27, just s of jct SR 287. Ext corridors. **Pets:** $5 daily fee/room. Designated rooms, service with restrictions, supervision.
[SAVE] 🛜 🔌 💻

LUTSEN

▼▼ Solbakken Resort Ⓜ
(218) 663-7566. **$59-$89, 14 day notice.** 4874 W SR 61 55612. SR 61, 1.3 mi n of jct CR 4 (Caribou Tr). Ext corridors. **Pets:** Other species. $10 daily fee/pet. Designated rooms, no service, supervision.
⬜ 🔌 💻 ⬜ 🐾

MAHNOMEN

▼▼ Shooting Star Casino Hotel & Events Center 🚫
(218) 935-2701. **Call for rates.** 777 Casino Rd 56557. 1 mi s on SR 59. Int corridors. **Pets:** Accepted. 🛜 💪ᴹ 💻 🍴 🏊 ⬜

MANHATTAN BEACH

▼▼▼ Manhattan Beach Lodge ⒸⒾ
(218) 692-3381. **Call for rates.** 39051 CR 66 56442. On CR 66. Int corridors. **Pets:** Accepted. 🛜 ⬜ 🔌 💻 🍴 ⬜

MANKATO

BEST WESTERN PLUS Hotel & Restaurant 🏠 🐾
(507) 625-9333. **$79-$145.** 1111 Range St 56003. 0.6 mi s of jct US 169 and 14. Int corridors. **Pets:** $10 daily fee/room. Designated rooms, service with restrictions, supervision. (SAVE) 🛜 🛏 🖥 🍴 ➔ 🗙

Comfort Inn by Choice Hotels 🏠
(507) 388-5107. **Call for rates.** 131 Apache Pl 56001. Just s of US 14 and SR 22 S. Int corridors. **Pets:** Accepted. 🛜 🛏 🖥 ➔

Days Inn 🏠 🐾
(507) 387-3332. **$55-$87.** 1285 Range St 56001. 0.3 mi s of jct US 169 and 14. Int corridors. **Pets:** $10 daily fee/pet. No service, supervision. 🛜 🛏 🖥 ➔

GrandStay Residential Suites Hotel 🏠
(507) 388-8688. **Call for rates.** 1000 Raintree Rd 56001. 0.4 mi se of jct US 14 and CR 3. Int corridors. **Pets:** Medium. $10 daily fee/pet. Designated rooms, service with restrictions, crate. (SAVE) 🛜 🛏 🖥 ➔ 🗙

Microtel Inn & Suites by Wyndham Mankato 🏠 🐾
(507) 388-2818. **$72-$92.** 200 St. Andrews Dr 56001. US 14 exit CR 3, 0.4 mi n. Int corridors. **Pets:** Other species. $15 one-time fee/room. Service with restrictions, crate. 🛜 🛏 🖥

Super 8 🏠
(507) 387-0600. **$55-$86, 3 day notice.** 51578 US Hwy 169 N 56001. Jct US 169 and 14, just n. Int corridors. **Pets:** Accepted. 🛜 🛏 🖥

MARSHALL

AmericInn Lodge & Suites of Marshall 🏠
(507) 537-9424. **$92-$112.** 1406 E Lyon St 56258. Just se on US 59 from jct SR 23. Int corridors. **Pets:** Dogs only. $15 daily fee/pet. Designated rooms, service with restrictions, supervision.
🛜 🗙 🛏 🖥 ➔

Comfort Inn 🏠 🐾
(507) 532-3070. **$80-$100.** 1511 E College Dr 56258. SR 19, w of jct SR 23. Int corridors. **Pets:** Large. $10 daily fee/pet. Service with restrictions, crate. 🛜 🗙 🔊 🛏 🖥 ➔

Ramada Marshall 🏠
(507) 532-3221. **$99-$117.** 1500 E College Dr 56258. SR 19, just w of jct SR 23. Int corridors. **Pets:** Accepted.
🛜 🗙 🛏 🖥 🍴 ➔ 🗙

Super 8 🅼
(507) 537-1461. **$63-$78.** 1106 E Main St 56258. 0.3 mi se on US 59 from jct SR 23. Int corridors. **Pets:** Accepted. 🛜 🛏 🖥

MCGREGOR

Country Meadows Inn & Suites 🏠
(218) 768-7378. **$69-$129.** 403 Meadows Dr 55760. Jct SR 65 and 210. Int corridors. **Pets:** Accepted. 🛜 🛏 🖥 ➔

MINNEAPOLIS-ST. PAUL METROPOLITAN AREA

ANNANDALE

Annandale Lodge & Suites 🏠
(320) 274-3006. **$70-$139.** 620 Elm St E 55302. On SR 55. Int corridors. **Pets:** Other species. Designated rooms, service with restrictions, supervision. 🛜 🔊 🛏 🖥 ➔

BECKER

Crossings by GrandStay Inn & Suites of Becker 🏠
(763) 262-7700. **$69-$100.** 14435 Bank St 55308. Just e on US 10. Int corridors. **Pets:** $10 daily fee/pet. Designated rooms, service with restrictions, supervision. (SAVE) 🛜 🛏 🖥 ➔ 🗙

BLAINE

Comfort Suites 🏠
(763) 792-0750. **$89-$159.** 10580 Baltimore St NE 55449. 1.5 mi n of jct SR 65 and US 10 to 107th Ave NE, just e to Baltimore St NE, then just s. Int corridors. **Pets:** Accepted. 🛜 🗙 🔊 🛏 🖥 ➔ 🗙

Super 8 🏠
(763) 786-8888. **$80-$190.** 9410 Baltimore St NE 55449. Just n of jct US 10 and SR 65 to 93rd Ln, just e to Baltimore St NE, then just n. Int corridors. **Pets:** Accepted. 🛜 🔊 🛏 🖥 ➔

BLOOMINGTON

DoubleTree by Hilton Bloomington - Minneapolis South 🏠
(952) 835-7800. **$99-$219.** 7800 Normandale Blvd 55439. Just nw of jct I-494 and SR 100, access via SR 100 and Industrial Blvd. Int corridors. **Pets:** Accepted. 🛜 🗙 🛏 🖥 🍴 ➔ 🗙

Extended StayAmerica Minneapolis-Bloomington 🏠
(952) 884-1400. **$69-$84.** 7956 Lyndale Ave S 55420. I-494 exit 4B (Lyndale Ave), just sw. Int corridors. **Pets:** $25 daily fee/pet. Designated rooms, service with restrictions. 🛜 🛏 🖥

Hilton Minneapolis/Bloomington 🏠
(952) 893-9500. **$89-$239.** 3900 American Blvd W 55437. I-494 exit 6B (France Ave), just sw. Int corridors. **Pets:** Medium, dogs only. $50 one-time fee/room. Service with restrictions, supervision.
(SAVE) 🛜 🛏 🖥 🍴 ➔

Hilton Minneapolis/St. Paul Airport Mall of America 🏠
(952) 854-2100. **$89-$239.** 3800 American Blvd E 55425. I-494 exit 1B (34th Ave), just se. Int corridors. **Pets:** Accepted.
(SAVE) 🛜 🔊 🛏 🖥 🍴 ➔

La Quinta Inn & Suites Minneapolis Bloomington NW 🏠
(952) 830-1300. **$71-$155.** 5151 American Blvd W 55437. I-494 exit 6B (France Ave), just se of SR 100, 1 mi w on frontage road. Int corridors. **Pets:** Service with restrictions, supervision.
🛜 🔊 🛏 🖥 🍴 ➔ 🗙

La Quinta Inn Minneapolis Airport Bloomington 🏠
(952) 881-7311. **$66-$129.** 7815 Nicollet Ave S 55420. I-494 exit 4A (Nicollet Ave), just s. Int corridors. **Pets:** Service with restrictions, supervision. 🛏 🖥

Le Bourget Aero Suites, an Ascend Collection hotel 🏠 🐾
(952) 893-9999. **$89-$149.** 7770 Johnson Ave 55435. I-494 exit 6B (France Ave), 0.5 mi nw on frontage road (78th St). Int corridors. **Pets:** Other species. $10 daily fee/pet. Service with restrictions, supervision. (SAVE) 🛜 🔊 🛏 🖥 🍴 ➔

Park Plaza Hotel Bloomington 🏠
(952) 831-3131. **$99-$129.** 4460 W 78th Street Cir 55435. I-494 exit 6B (France Ave), 0.5 mi nw. Int corridors. **Pets:** Accepted.
(ECO) 🛜 🛏 🖥 🍴 ➔ 🗙

Ramada Mall of America - Airport H
(952) 854-3411. $105-$240. 2300 E American Blvd 55425. I-494 exit 2A (24th Ave), just s. Int corridors. Pets: Accepted.

Residence Inn by Marriott H
(952) 876-0900. $89-$209. 7850 Bloomington Ave S 55425. I-494 exit 3 (Portland Ave/12th Ave), on south frontage road; behind Courtyard by Marriott Minneapolis/Bloomington. Int corridors. Pets: Accepted.

Sofitel Minneapolis H ✿
(952) 835-1900. $115-$305. 5601 W 78th St 55439. Just nw of jct I-494 and SR 100, access via SR 100 and Industrial Blvd. Int corridors. Pets: Other species. Designated rooms, service with restrictions.

Staybridge Suites H ✿
(952) 831-7900. $89-$269. 5150 American Blvd 55437. I-494 exit 6B (France Ave), just se of SR 100, then 1 mi w on frontage road. Int corridors. Pets: Medium. $75 one-time fee/room. Service with restrictions, crate.

Super 8 H
(952) 888-8800. $69-$94. 7800 S 2nd Ave 55420. I-494 exit 4A (Nicollet Ave), just se. Int corridors. Pets: $10 daily fee/pet. Service with restrictions, supervision.

BROOKLYN CENTER

Comfort Inn by Choice Hotels H
(763) 560-7464. $74-$105. 1600 James Cir N 55430. I-94/694 exit 34 (Shingle Creek Pkwy), just ne. Int corridors. Pets: Other species. $15 one-time fee/pet.

Country Inn & Suites By Carlson H
(763) 561-0900. $81-$159. 2550 Freeway Blvd 55430. I-94/694 exit 34 (Shingle Creek Pkwy), just nw. Int corridors. Pets: Accepted.

Extended StayAmerica-Minneapolis-Brooklyn Center H
(763) 549-5571. $59-$79. 2701 Freeway Blvd 55430. I-94/694 exit 34 (Shingle Creek Pkwy), 0.5 mi nw. Int corridors. Pets: $25 daily fee/pet. Designated rooms, service with restrictions.

BROOKLYN PARK

La Quinta Inn & Suites Brooklyn Park H
(763) 971-8000. $59-$144. 7011 Northland Cir 55428. I-94/694 exit 30 (Boone Ave), just ne. Int corridors. Pets: Service with restrictions, supervision.

BURNSVILLE

BEST WESTERN PREMIER Nicollet Inn H
(952) 435-2100. Call for rates. 14201 Nicollet Ave 55337. Just n of jct I-35W and CR 42. Int corridors. Pets: Accepted.

CHANHASSEN

AmericInn of Chanhassen H
(952) 934-3888. $119-$195, 7 day notice. 570 Pond Promenade 55317. Just se of jct SR 5 and 101 S. Int corridors. Pets: Medium. $130 deposit/pet, $30 one-time fee/pet. Designated rooms, service with restrictions, crate.

COON RAPIDS

Quality Inn Northtown H
(763) 785-4746. Call for rates. 9052 University Ave NW 55448. US 10 exit Foley Blvd, 0.6 mi. Int corridors. Pets: Medium, other species. $10 daily fee/pet. Service with restrictions, supervision.

EAGAN

BEST WESTERN PLUS Dakota Ridge H
(651) 452-0100. $89-$169. 3450 Washington Dr 55122. I-35E exit 97B (Yankee Doodle Rd), just sw. Int corridors. Pets: Large. $20 daily fee/room. Designated rooms, service with restrictions, crate.

Days Inn H
(651) 681-1770. $76-$105. 4510 Erin Dr 55122. Just ne of jct SR 77 and Cliff Rd. Int corridors. Pets: Other species. $100 deposit/pet, $5 daily fee/pet. Designated rooms, service with restrictions, supervision.

Extended StayAmerica Minneapolis-Airport-Eagan H
(651) 681-9991. $69-$79. 3384 Norwest Ct 55121. I-35E exit 97, just nw. Int corridors. Pets: $25 daily fee/pet. Designated rooms, service with restrictions.

Homestead Studio Suites Hotel-Minneapolis-Airport-Eagan H
(651) 905-1778. $69-$79. 3015 Denmark Ave 55121. I-35E exit 98 (Lone Oak Rd), just se. Int corridors. Pets: $25 daily fee/pet. Designated rooms, service with restrictions.

Microtel Inn & Suites by Wyndham Eagan/St Paul H
(651) 405-0988. $55-$110, 3 day notice. 3000 Denmark Ave 55121. I-35E exit 98 (Lone Oak Rd), just se. Int corridors. Pets: Medium. $15 daily fee/room. Service with restrictions, supervision.

Residence Inn by Marriott Minneapolis-St. Paul Airport/Eagan H
(651) 688-0363. $89-$149. 3040 Eagandale Pl 55121. I-35E exit 98 (Lone Oak Rd), just sw. Ext corridors. Pets: Other species. $50 one-time fee/room. Service with restrictions.

Staybridge Suites H
(651) 994-7810. $89-$179. 4675 Rahncliff Rd 55122. I-35E exit 93 (Cliff Rd), just w, then just s. Int corridors. Pets: Accepted.

TownePlace Suites by Marriott Minneapolis St. Paul Airport/Eagan H
(651) 994-4600. $89-$119. 3615 Crestridge Dr 55122. I-35E exit 97A (Pilot Knob Rd), just se. Int corridors. Pets: Other species. $75 one-time fee/room. Designated rooms, service with restrictions, crate.

EDEN PRAIRIE

BEST WESTERN Eden Prairie Inn H
(952) 829-0888. $89-$120. 11500 W 78th St 55344. I-494 exit 11A (Prairie Center Dr), just sw. Int corridors. Pets: Dogs only. $10 daily fee/pet. Service with restrictions, supervision.

Extended StayAmerica Minneapolis-Eden Prairie H
(952) 941-1113. $69-$79. 7550 Office Ridge Cir 55344. I-494 exit 12, just se. Int corridors. Pets: $25 daily fee/pet. Designated rooms, service with restrictions.

Homestead Studio Suites Hotel-Minneapolis-Eden Prairie H
(952) 942-6818. $69-$79. 11905 Technology Dr 55344. Just sw of jct I-494 and US 212 (Flying Cloud Dr). Int corridors. Pets: $25 daily fee/pet. Designated rooms, service with restrictions.

Residence Inn by Marriott-Minneapolis SW H
(952) 829-0033. $80-$179. 7780 Flying Cloud Dr 55344. I-494 exit 11A (Prairie Center Dr); on US 169 S and 212 (Flying Cloud Dr). Int corridors. Pets: Accepted.

EDINA

Residence Inn by Marriott Minneapolis-Edina [H]
(952) 893-9300. **$99-$241.** 3400 Edinborough Way 55435. I-494 exit 6B (France Ave), 0.3 mi n to Minnesota Dr, then just e. Int corridors.
Pets: Accepted.

The Westin Edina Galleria [H] ☘
(952) 567-5000. **$119-$439.** 3201 Galleria 55435. I-494 exit 6B (France Ave), 1.5 mi n, then just e; at the Galleria. Int corridors. **Pets:** Medium. Service with restrictions, supervision.

FOREST LAKE

AmericInn Motel of Forest Lake [H]
(651) 464-1930. **Call for rates.** 1291 W Broadway Ave 55025. I-35 exit 131 (CR 2), just ne. Int corridors. **Pets:** Accepted.

HASTINGS

AmericInn Lodge & Suites of Hastings [H]
(651) **Call for rates.** 2400 Vermillion St 55033. 1.5 mi s on US 61. Int corridors. **Pets:** Accepted.

LAKE ELMO

Holiday Inn & Suites St. Paul NE-Lake Elmo [H]
(651) 714-8068. **Call for rates.** 8511 Hudson Blvd 55042. I-94 exit 250 (Inwood Ave/Radio Dr), just ne. Int corridors. **Pets:** Accepted.

MAPLE GROVE

Extended StayAmerica Minneapolis-Maple Grove [H]
(763) 694-9747. **$69-$84.** 12970 63rd Ave N 55369. I-494 exit 26 (Bass Lake Rd), just ne. Int corridors. **Pets:** $25 daily fee/pet. Designated rooms, service with restrictions.

Staybridge Suites Minneapolis-Maple Grove [H]
(763) 494-8856. **Call for rates.** 7821 Elm Creek Blvd 55369. Just ne of jct I-94/494/694. Int corridors. **Pets:** Accepted.

MAPLEWOOD

Emerald Inn [H]
(651) 777-8131. **$54-$80.** 2025 County Rd D E 55109. I-694 exit 50 (White Bear Ave), just se. Int corridors. **Pets:** Accepted.

MINNEAPOLIS

Aloft Minneapolis [H] ☘
(612) 455-8400. **$99-$299.** 900 Washington Ave S 55415. Jct 9th Ave. Int corridors. **Pets:** Dogs only.

BEST WESTERN PLUS The Normandy Inn & Suites [H]
(612) 370-1400. **$89-$209.** 405 S 8th St 55404. Corner of S 8th St and S 4th Ave. Int corridors. **Pets:** Large, dogs only. $10 daily fee/room. Designated rooms, service with restrictions, crate.

Days Hotel on University [H]
(612) 623-3999. **$69-$209.** 2407 University Ave SE 55414. I-35W exit University Ave, 1 mi se. Int corridors. **Pets:** $20 one-time fee/room. Designated rooms, service with restrictions, supervision.

The Grand Hotel Minneapolis-A Kimpton Hotel [H]
(612) 288-8888. **Call for rates.** 615 2nd Ave S 55402. Corner of 2nd Ave S and S 7th St. Int corridors. **Pets:** Accepted.

Graves 601 Hotel, Wyndham Grand Collection [H]
(612) 677-1100. **$149-$375.** 601 1st Ave N 55403. Between 6th and 7th sts. Int corridors. **Pets:** Accepted.

Hilton Minneapolis [H]
(612) 376-1000. **$99-$339.** 1001 Marquette Ave S 55403. Between S 10th and S 11th sts. Int corridors. **Pets:** Accepted.

Hotel Ivy [H]
(612) 746-4600. **$499, 3 day notice.** 201 S 11th St 55403. 2nd Ave and 11th St. Int corridors. **Pets:** Accepted.

The Marquette Hotel [H] ☘
(612) 333-4545. **$95-$349.** 710 Marquette Ave 55402. Jct Marquette Ave and S 7th St. Int corridors. **Pets:** Medium, dogs only. $50 one-time fee/pet. Designated rooms, service with restrictions, crate.

Minneapolis Marriott City Center [H]
(612) 349-4000. **$109-$319.** 30 S 7th St 55402. Between Hennepin and Nicollet aves; in City Center Shopping Complex. Int corridors.
Pets: Accepted.

Radisson Plaza Hotel Minneapolis [H]
(612) 339-4900. **$99-$429.** 35 S 7th St 55402. Between Nicollet and Hennepin aves. Int corridors. **Pets:** Medium, other species. $75 one-time fee/room. Service with restrictions, supervision.

Ramada Plaza Minneapolis [H] ☘
(612) 331-1900. **$110-$175.** 1330 Industrial Blvd NE 55413. I-35W exit 22, 3 mi n of downtown. Int corridors. **Pets:** Medium. $150 deposit/room, $10 daily fee/pet. Service with restrictions, crate.

The Residence Inn by Marriott at The Depot [H]
(612) 340-1300. **$129-$289.** 425 S 2nd St 55401. Jct S 2nd St and 5th Ave S. Int corridors. **Pets:** Accepted.

Residence Inn by Marriott Minneapolis Downtown City Center [H]
(612) 677-1000. **$99-$399.** 45 S 8th St 55402. At 8th St and LaSalle Ave. Int corridors. **Pets:** Accepted.

Sheraton Minneapolis Midtown Hotel [H] ☘
(612) 821-7600. **$109-$349.** 2901 Chicago Ave S 55407. At Lake St. Int corridors. **Pets:** Medium, dogs only. Service with restrictions, supervision.

The Westin Minneapolis [H]
(612) 333-4006. **$129-$679.** 88 S 6th St 55402. At Marquette Ave. Int corridors. **Pets:** Medium. Service with restrictions, supervision.

W Minneapolis - The Foshay [H] ☘
(612) 215-3700. **$109-$799.** 821 Marquette Ave 55402. Between 9th and 8th sts. Int corridors. **Pets:** Medium, other species. $100 one-time fee/room. Service with restrictions.

MINNETONKA

Minneapolis Marriott-Southwest [H]
(952) 935-5500. **$69-$229.** 5801 Opus Pkwy 55343. Just nw of jct US 169 and SR 62, exit Bren Rd. Int corridors. **Pets:** $25 daily fee/room. Service with restrictions, crate.

Sheraton Minneapolis West Hotel H ✿
(952) 593-0000. **$89-$199.** 12201 Ridgedale Dr 55305. I-394 exit 1C (Ridgedale Dr), 0.3 mi s. Int corridors. **Pets:** Large, dogs only. Service with restrictions, supervision. SAVE 📶 ✕ 🛏 🖥 🍴 ➰

MONTICELLO

BEST WESTERN Chelsea Inn & Suites H ✿
(763) 271-8880. **$90-$140.** 89 Chelsea Rd 55362. I-94 exit 193, 0.3 mi se. Int corridors. **Pets:** Other species. $10 daily fee/room. Designated rooms, service with restrictions, supervision.
SAVE 📶 ✕ 🛏 🖥 ➰ ✕

Days Inn H
(763) 295-1111. **$50-$80.** 200 E Oakwood Dr 55362. I-94 exit 193, 0.3 mi se. Int corridors. **Pets:** Accepted. SAVE 📶 🛏 🖥

Super 8 H
(763) 295-5900. **$70-$100.** 1114 Cedar St 55362. I-94 exit 193, 0.3 mi se. Int corridors. **Pets:** $10 daily fee/room. Designated rooms, service with restrictions, crate. SAVE 📶 🛏 🖥 ➰

NEW BRIGHTON

Homewood Suites New Brighton H
(651) 631-8002. **$99-$189.** 1815 Old Hwy 8 NW 55112. I-35W exit 28A (CR 96). Int corridors. **Pets:** Medium, other species. $150 one-time fee/pet. Service with restrictions, crate. 📶 🛏 🖥 ➰ ✕

NORTH BRANCH

AmericInn Lodge & Suites of North Branch H
(651) 674-8627. **$79-$180.** 38675 14th Ave 55056. I-35 exit 147 (SR 95), just e, just s on Oakview Ave, then w on Oak St. Int corridors. **Pets:** Other species. $30 one-time fee/room. Service with restrictions, supervision. 📶 🛏 🖥 ➰ ✕

OAKDALE

AmericInn Lodge & Suites of Oakdale H
(651) 730-5700. **$79-$169.** 6630 Hudson Blvd N 55128. I-94 exit 247 (Century Ave), 0.7 mi n on Frontage Rd (Hudson Blvd). Int corridors. **Pets:** Large, dogs only. $20 daily fee/room. Designated rooms, service with restrictions, crate. 📶 🛏 🖥 ➰ ✕

BEST WESTERN Regency Plaza Hotel H ✿
(651) 578-8466. **Call for rates.** 970 Helena Ave N 55128. I-694 exit 57, just e, then just s. Int corridors. **Pets:** Large, dogs only. $20 daily fee/room. Designated rooms, service with restrictions, crate.
SAVE 📶 🛏 🖥

OAK PARK HEIGHTS

AmericInn Lodge & Suites of Oak Park Heights H
(651) 275-0980. **Call for rates.** 13025 60th St N 55082. SR 36 at Stillwater Blvd, just se. Int corridors. **Pets:** Other species. $15 daily fee/room. Service with restrictions, crate. 📶 ✕ 🛏 🖥 ➰ ✕

PLYMOUTH

BEST WESTERN PLUS Kelly Inn H
(763) 553-1600. **$99-$119.** 2705 N Annapolis Ln 55441. I-494 exit 22 (SR 55), just e. Int corridors. **Pets:** Designated rooms, service with restrictions, supervision. SAVE 📶 🛏 🖥 🍴 ➰ ✕

Comfort Inn H
(763) 559-1222. **$74-$120.** 3000 Harbor Ln 55447. I-494 exit 22 (SR 55), 0.3 mi nw. Int corridors. **Pets:** $10 daily fee/pet. Designated rooms, service with restrictions, supervision. SAVE 📶 🛏 🖥 🍴 ➰ ✕

Crowne Plaza Minneapolis West H ✿
(763) 559-6600. **$79-$259.** 3131 Campus Dr 55441. I-494 exit 22 (SR 55), just e to CR 61 (Northwest Blvd), then 0.8 mi nw. Int corridors. **Pets:** Service with restrictions. 📶 🖥 🍴 ➰ ✕

Days Inn Minneapolis/West H
(763) 559-2400. **$60-$93.** 2955 Empire Ln 55447. I-494 exit 22 (SR 55), just w. Int corridors. **Pets:** Other species. $10 daily fee/room. Service with restrictions, crate. SAVE 📶 🛏 🖥

Red Roof Inn M
(763) 553-1751. **$50-$89.** 2600 Annapolis Cir N 55441. I-494 exit 22 (SR 55), just se. Ext corridors. **Pets:** Large, other species. Service with restrictions, supervision. SAVE 📶 🛏

Residence Inn by Marriott H
(763) 577-1600. **$79-$229.** 2750 Annapolis Cir N 55441. I-494 exit 22 (SR 55), just e to CR 61, just nw. Int corridors. **Pets:** Accepted.
📶 ✕ 🛏 🖥 ➰

RICHFIELD

Candlewood Suites H
(612) 869-7704. **$105-$150.** 351 W 77th St 55423. I-494 exit 4B (Lyndale Ave), just ne. Int corridors. **Pets:** Accepted. 📶 🛏 🖥

Four Points by Sheraton Minneapolis Airport H ✿
(612) 861-1000. **$99-$209, 7 day notice.** 7745 Lyndale Ave S 55423. I-494 exit 4B (Lyndale Ave), just ne. Int corridors. **Pets:** Medium, dogs only. Designated rooms, service with restrictions.
SAVE 📶 ✕ 🛏 🖥 🍴 ➰

ROGERS

AmericInn Lodge & Suites of Rogers H
(763) 428-4346. **$79-$149.** 21800 Industrial Blvd 55374. I-94 exit 207 (SR 101), just sw. Int corridors. **Pets:** Medium. $10 daily fee/pet. Designated rooms, service with restrictions, supervision.
SAVE 📶 🛏 🖥 ➰

Hampton Inn & Suites H
(763) 425-0044. **$89-$149.** 13550 Commerce Blvd 55374. I-94 exit 207 (SR 101), 0.4 mi ne. Int corridors. **Pets:** Medium.
SAVE 📶 ✕ 🛏 🖥 ➰ ✕

ROSEVILLE

Days Inn St. Paul NW/Roseville H
(651) 636-6730. **$69-$199.** 2550 Cleveland Ave N 55113. I-35W exit 24 (CR C), 0.3 mi se. Int corridors. **Pets:** Accepted. SAVE 📶 🛏 🖥

Residence Inn by Marriott H
(651) 636-0680. **$79-$189.** 2985 Centre Pointe Dr 55113. I-35W exit 25A (CR D), just se. Int corridors. **Pets:** Accepted.
📶 ✕ 🛏 🖥 ➰ ✕

ST. LOUIS PARK

DoubleTree by Hilton Hotel Minneapolis - Park Place H ✿
(952) 542-8600. **$89-$219.** 1500 Park Place Blvd 55416. I-394 exit 5 (Park Place Blvd), just sw. Int corridors. **Pets:** Medium. $25 one-time fee/room. Service with restrictions, supervision. 📶 🛏 🖥 🍴 ➰

Homewood Suites St. Louis Park/Minneapolis West H
(952) 544-0495. **$99-$219.** 5305 Wayzata Blvd 55416. I-394 exit 5 (Park Place Blvd), just se. Int corridors. **Pets:** Other species. $150 one-time fee/room. Service with restrictions. 📶 🛏 🖥 ➰

TownePlace Suites by Marriott Minneapolis West St. Louis Park H
(952) 847-6900. **$89-$199.** 1400 Zarthan Ave S 55416. I-394 exit 5 (Park Place Blvd), 0.3 mi w on 16th, then just n. Int corridors. **Pets:** Accepted.
📶 ✕ 🛏 🖥 ➰

ST. PAUL

(AAA) ♦♦♦ BEST WESTERN Bandana Square **H**
(651) 647-1637. **$99-$199, 15 day notice.** 1010 Bandana Blvd W
55108. I-94 exit 239B (Lexington Pkwy), 1.3 mi n, then 0.3 mi w on
Energy Park Dr. Int corridors. **Pets:** Dogs only. $10 daily fee/room. Ser-
vice with restrictions, crate. [SAVE] 🛜 🗇 🖥 🖵 🏊 ⊠

(AAA) ♦♦♦♦ BEST WESTERN PLUS Kelly Inn **H**
(651) 227-8711. **$99-$249.** 161 St. Anthony Ave 55103. Jct I-35E and 94.
Int corridors. **Pets:** Medium. Service with restrictions, crate.
[SAVE] 🛜 🗇 🖵 🍽 🏊 ⊠

♦♦♦ Super 8 **H**
(651) 771-5566. **$64-$109.** 1739 Old Hudson Rd 55106. I-94 exit 245
(White Bear Ave), just nw. Int corridors. **Pets:** Accepted. 🛜 🗇 🖵

SHAKOPEE

♦♦♦ Americas Best Value Inn & Suites **H**
(952) 445-3644. **$89-$139.** 1244 Canterbury Rd 55379. Just nw of US
169. Int corridors. **Pets:** Medium. $10 daily fee/room. Service with restric-
tions, supervision. 🛜 🗇 🖵 🍽 🏊

♦♦♦♦ Country Inn & Suites By Carlson **H**
(952) 445-0200. **Call for rates.** 1204 Ramsey St 55379. Just ne of US
169. Int corridors. **Pets:** Accepted. 🛜 🗇 🖥 🖵 🏊

♦♦♦ Sandalwood Studios & Suites **H**
(952) 277-0100. **$39-$109.** 3910 12th Ave E 55379. Just nw of US 169.
Int corridors. **Pets:** Medium. $10 daily fee/room. Designated rooms, ser-
vice with restrictions, supervision. 🛜 🗇

SOUTH ST. PAUL

♦♦♦ Clarion South Saint Paul Hotel & Conference
Center **H**
(651) 455-3600. **$71-$120.** 701 Concord St S 55075. I-494 exit 64B (SR
56/Concord St), 0.3 mi n. Int corridors. **Pets:** Accepted.
🛜 🗇 🖥 🖵 🍽 🏊

STILLWATER

(AAA) ♦♦♦ Americas Best Value Inn **H**
(651) 430-1300. **$50-$120.** 1750 Frontage Rd W 55082. SR 36 at Washington Ave, just ne. Int corridors. **Pets:** Small, other species. $10 daily
fee/pet. Designated rooms, service with restrictions, supervision.
[SAVE] 🛜 🗇 🖥 🖵 🏊

♦♦♦ Super 8 **H**
(651) 430-3990. **$49-$112.** 2190 W Frontage Rd 55082. SR 36 at Washington Ave. Int corridors. **Pets:** Accepted. 🛜 🗇 🖵

WACONIA

♦♦♦ AmericInn Lodge & Suites of Waconia **H** 🐾
(952) 442-8787. **$90-$120.** 550 Cherry Dr 55387. Just nw of jct SR 5. Int
corridors. **Pets:** Small, dogs only. $10 daily fee/pet. Designated rooms,
service with restrictions, crate. 🛜 ⊠ 🗇 🖥 🖵 🏊 ⊠

♦♦♦ Waconia Inn & Suites **M**
(952) 442-5147. **Call for rates.** 301 E Frontage Rd 55387. On SR 5; jct
CR 10. Int corridors. **Pets:** $10 deposit/pet. Designated rooms, service
with restrictions, crate. 🛜 🖵

WHITE BEAR LAKE

♦♦♦ AmericInn Lodge & Suites of White Bear Lake **H**
(651) 429-7131. **$89-$149.** 4675 White Bear Pkwy 55110. I-35E exit 117,
just ne of jct SR 96. Int corridors. **Pets:** Medium, dogs only. $15 one-time
fee/pet. Designated rooms, service with restrictions, supervision.
🛜 ⊠ 🗇 🖥 🖵 🏊 ⊠

(AAA) ♦♦♦ BEST WESTERN PLUS White Bear Country
Inn **H**
(651) 429-5393. **$89-$169.** 4940 N Hwy 61 55110. Jct SR 96, 1 mi n. Int
corridors. **Pets:** Medium, other species. $10 daily fee/pet. Service with
restrictions, supervision. [SAVE] 🛜 🗇 🖥 🖵 🍽 🏊 ⊠

WOODBURY

♦♦♦ Extended StayAmerica-Minneapolis-Woodbury **H**
(651) 501-1085. **$69-$79.** 10020 Hudson Rd 55125. I-94 exit 251, just
se. Int corridors. **Pets:** $25 daily fee/pet. Designated rooms, service with
restrictions. 🛜 🗇 🖵

♦♦♦ Holiday Inn Express Hotel & Suites **H**
(651) 702-0200. **$89-$129.** 9840 Norma Ln 55125. I-94 exit 251, just sw.
Int corridors. **Pets:** Large. $10 daily fee/pet. Designated rooms, supervi-
sion. 🛜 ⊠ 🗇 🖵 🏊

(AAA) ♦♦♦ Red Roof Inn #7063 **M**
(651) 738-7160. **$49-$85.** 1806 Wooddale Dr 55125. I-494 exit 59 (Valley
Creek Rd), just se. Ext corridors. **Pets:** Large, other species. Service with
restrictions, supervision. [SAVE] 🛜

(AAA) ♦♦♦ Sheraton St. Paul Woodbury Hotel **H**
(651) 209-3280. **$109-$309.** 676 Bielenberg Dr 55125. I-494 exit 59C
(Tamarack Rd), just ne. Int corridors. **Pets:** Accepted.
[SAVE] 🛜 ⊠ 🗇 🖥 🖵 🍽 🏊

END METROPOLITAN AREA

MONTEVIDEO

(AAA) ♦♦♦ Crossings by GrandStay Inn & Suites **H**
(320) 269-8000. **$89-$152.** 1805 E SR 7 56265. On SR 7; east of downtown. Int corridors. **Pets:** Large, other species. $200 deposit/room, $10
daily fee/pet. Designated rooms, service with restrictions, supervision.
[SAVE] 🛜 🗇 🖥 🏊

MOORHEAD

♦♦♦ Travelodge & Suites **H**
(218) 233-5333. **$80-$140.** 3027 S Frontage Rd 56560. Just s of US 10
E; east of downtown. Int corridors. **Pets:** Medium. Designated rooms,
service with restrictions, supervision. 🛜 🗇 🖥 🖵 🏊

MOOSE LAKE

♦♦♦ AmericInn Lodge & Suites of Moose Lake **H**
(218) 485-8885. **$70-$170.** 400 Park Place Dr 55767. I-35 exit 214 (SR
73), just sw. Int corridors. **Pets:** Medium. $50 deposit/room, $15 daily
fee/room. Designated rooms, service with restrictions, crate.
🛜 ⊠ 🗇 🖵 🏊

MOUNTAIN IRON

♦♦♦ AmericInn Lodge & Suites of Virginia **H**
(218) 741-7839. **$108-$167.** 5480 Mountain Iron Dr 55792. Us SR 53, just s
of jct US 169. Int corridors. **Pets:** Medium, dogs only. $15 one-time fee/
pet. Designated rooms, service with restrictions, supervision.
🛜 🗇 🖥 🏊 ⊠

♦♦♦ Holiday Inn Express & Suites **H**
(218) 741-7411. **$119-$169.** 8570 Rock Ridge Dr 55768. On US 169,
just w of jct US 53. Int corridors. **Pets:** Medium, dogs only. $20 daily
fee/pet. Service with restrictions, supervision. 🛜 🗇 🖵 🏊

NEW ULM

♦♦♦ Holiday Inn **H**
(507) 359-2941. **$95-$139.** 2101 S Broadway 56073. SR 15/68, 1.8 mi
se. Int corridors. **Pets:** Accepted. 🛜 🗇 🖥 🖵 🍽 🏊 ⊠

◆◆ **Microtel Inn & Suites by Wyndham New Ulm** Ⓗ

(507) 354-9800. **$65-$105.** 424 20th St S 56073. Just e of jct SR 15/68 and CR 37. Int corridors. **Pets:** Medium. $10 daily fee/room. Designated rooms, service with restrictions, supervision.

⟦SAVE⟧ 🛜 🖶 📟 ⟦≈⟧

NISSWA

◆◆ **Nisswa Motel** Ⓜ

(218) 963-7611. **$59-$109, 5 day notice.** 5370 Merrill Ave 56468. Just sw of Main St; center. Ext corridors. **Pets:** Accepted.

⟦SAVE⟧ 🛜 🖶 📟

ORR

◆◆ **North Country Inn** Ⓗ

(218) 757-3778. **Call for rates.** 4483 Hwy 53 55771. 0.3 mi s. Int corridors. **Pets:** Accepted. 🛜 ⟦✗⟧ 🖶

OTTERTAIL

◆◆◆◆ **Thumper Pond Resort** Ⓗ

(218) 367-2000. **$93-$161, 3 day notice.** 300 Thumper Lodge Rd 56571. Jct SR 108 and 78. Int corridors. **Pets:** Accepted.

⟦SAVE⟧ 🛜 ⟦✗⟧ 🖶 📟 ⟦🍴⟧ ⟦≈⟧

OWATONNA

◆◆ **AmericInn of Owatonna** Ⓗ

(507) 455-1142. **Call for rates.** 245 Florence Ave 55060. I-35 exit 41 (Bridge St), 0.3 mi ne. Int corridors. **Pets:** Accepted.

🛜 🖶 📟 ⟦≈⟧ ⟦✗⟧

◆◆◆◆ **Comfort Inn** Ⓗ 🐾

(507) 444-0818. **$85-$140.** 2345 43rd St NW 55060. I-35 exit 45 (Clinton Falls), just sw. Int corridors. **Pets:** Other species. $10 deposit/pet. Service with restrictions, supervision. 🛜 ⟦&M⟧ 🖶 📟 ⟦≈⟧

◆◆◆ **Holiday Inn Hotel & Suites** Ⓗ

(507) 446-8900. **Call for rates.** 2365 43rd St NW 55060. I-35 exit 45 (Clinton Falls), just sw. Int corridors. **Pets:** Accepted.

🛜 ⟦✗⟧ 🖶 📟 ⟦🍴⟧ ⟦≈⟧ ⟦✗⟧

◆◆ **Microtel Inn & Suites by Wyndham Owatonna** Ⓗ

(507) 446-0228. **$60-$90.** 150 St. John Dr NW 55060. I-35 exit 41 (Bridge St), just nw. Int corridors. **Pets:** Large, other species. $15 one-time fee/pet. Service with restrictions, supervision. 🛜 ⟦&M⟧ 🖶 📟

PARKERS PRAIRIE

◆◆◆ ◆◆ **Crossings by GrandStay Inn & Suites of Parkers Prairie** Ⓗ 🐾

(218) 338-3380. **$81-$119.** 211 W Main St 56361. Just w of jct SR 29 and 235 (Main St). Int corridors. **Pets:** Large, dogs only. $150 deposit/pet, $25 daily fee/pet. Designated rooms, service with restrictions, supervision.

⟦SAVE⟧ 🛜 ⟦&M⟧ 🖶 📟

PARK RAPIDS

◆◆ **C'mon Inn** Ⓗ

(218) 732-1471. **$90-$174.** 1009 1st St E 56470. SR 34, 0.8 mi e of jct US 71. Int corridors. **Pets:** Dogs only. Service with restrictions, crate.

🛜 🖶 📟 ⟦≈⟧

PAYNESVILLE

◆◆ **Paynesville Inn & Suites** Ⓗ

(320) 243-4146. **$85-$99.** 700 W Hwy 23 56362. Jct SR 55, 0.3 mi s. Int corridors. **Pets:** $25 deposit/room, $10 daily fee/pet. Designated rooms, service with restrictions, supervision. 🛜 🖶 📟 ⟦≈⟧

PEQUOT LAKES

◆◆ **AmericInn Lodge & Suites of Pequot Lakes** Ⓗ

(218) 568-8400. **Call for rates.** 32912 Paul Bunyan Trail Dr (SR 371/CR 16) 56472. SR 371, 2 mi n of downtown. Int corridors. **Pets:** Dogs only. $15 daily fee/pet. Designated rooms, service with restrictions, supervision.

🛜 ⟦✗⟧ 🖶 📟 ⟦≈⟧ ⟦✗⟧

PERHAM

◆◆ **Super 8** Ⓗ

(218) 346-7888. **$65-$90.** 106 Jake St SE 56573. SR 78, just nw of jct US 10. Int corridors. **Pets:** Accepted. 🛜 🖶 📟

PINE RIVER

◆◆ **Rodeway Inn** Ⓜ

(218) 587-4499. **Call for rates.** 2684 SR 371 SW 56474. 1 mi s. Ext corridors. **Pets:** Medium. $10 daily fee/pet. Designated rooms, service with restrictions, supervision. 🛜 🖶 📟 ⟦✗⟧

RED WING

◆◆ **Days Inn** Ⓜ

(651) 388-3568. **$56-$94.** 955 E 7th St 55066. US 61/63, 1.7 mi se. Ext corridors. **Pets:** Accepted. 🛜 🖶 📟 ⟦≈⟧

ROCHESTER

◆◆ **AmericInn Hotel & Suites Rochester Airport** Ⓗ

(507) 536-7000. **$80-$150.** 7320 Airport View Dr SW 55902. On US 63 (Broadway), airport exit. Int corridors. **Pets:** Other species. $25 one-time fee/pet. Service with restrictions, supervision.

🛜 ⟦✗⟧ ⟦&M⟧ 🖶 📟 ⟦≈⟧

◆◆◆ **Aspen Suites** Ⓗ

(507) 289-6600. **Call for rates.** 1211 2nd St SW 55902. US 52/14 exit 55B (2nd St SW), just e. Int corridors. **Pets:** Accepted.

🛜 ⟦✗⟧ ⟦&M⟧ 🖶 📟 ⟦≈⟧

◆◆◆ ◆◆◆ **BEST WESTERN PLUS Soldiers Field Tower & Suites** Ⓗ

(507) 288-2677. **$120-$135.** 401 6th St SW 55902. 4th Ave SW at 6th St; just s of Mayo Clinic. Ext/int corridors. **Pets:** Large. $10 daily fee/pet. Designated rooms, service with restrictions, crate.

⟦SAVE⟧ 🛜 🖶 📟 ⟦🍴⟧ ⟦≈⟧ ⟦✗⟧

◆◆◆ **Clarion Inn** Ⓗ

(507) 288-1844. **$74-$100.** 1630 S Broadway 55904. 0.5 mi s of jct US 14 and 63 (Broadway). Ext/int corridors. **Pets:** Accepted.

🛜 🖶 📟 ⟦🍴⟧ ⟦≈⟧ ⟦✗⟧

◆◆◆ **Comfort Inn** Ⓗ

(507) 289-3344. **$80-$95.** 5708 Bandel Rd NW 55901. US 52 exit 55th St, just n on E Frontage Rd. Int corridors. **Pets:** Accepted.

🛜 ⟦✗⟧ ⟦&M⟧ 🖶 📟 ⟦≈⟧ ⟦✗⟧

◆◆◆ **Extended StayAmerica-Rochester North** Ⓗ

(507) 289-7444. **$59-$79.** 2814 43rd St NW 55901. Just nw from jct US 52. Int corridors. **Pets:** $25 daily fee/pet. Designated rooms, service with restrictions. 🛜 🖶 📟

◆◆◆ **Extended StayAmerica-Rochester-South** Ⓗ

(507) 536-7444. **$59-$79.** 55 Wood Lake Dr SE 55904. US 63 (Broadway) exit 49th St S, 0.7 mi ne. Int corridors. **Pets:** $25 daily fee/pet. Designated rooms, service with restrictions. 🛜 🖶 📟

◆◆◆ ◆◆◆ **GuestHouse International Inn & Suites** Ⓗ

(507) 288-9090. **$70.** 435 16th Ave NW 55901. Just se of jct US 14 and 52; exit Civic Center Dr. Int corridors. **Pets:** $15 one-time fee/room. Designated rooms, no service, supervision.

⟦SAVE⟧ 🛜 ⟦✗⟧ ⟦&M⟧ 🖶 📟 ⟦🍴⟧ ⟦≈⟧ ⟦✗⟧

▼▼▼ Holiday Inn Rochester Downtown H
(507) 252-8200. **Call for rates.** 220 S Broadway 55904. On US 63 (Broadway); downtown. Int corridors. **Pets:** Accepted.
🛜 ✕ ⌖M 🔌 💻 🍽 🏊 ✕

▲▲▲ ▼▼▼ ▼▼▼ International Hotel H
(507) 328-8000. **Call for rates.** 20 SW 2nd Ave 55902. Opposite Mayo Clinic and Methodist Hospital; 11th Floor of The Kahler Grand Hotel. Int corridors. **Pets:** Accepted. SAVE 🛜 ✕ 🔌 💻 🍽 🏊 ✕

▲▲▲ ▼▼▼ The Kahler Grand Hotel H
(507) 280-6200. **Call for rates.** 20 SW 2nd Ave 55902. Opposite Mayo Clinic and Methodist Hospital. Int corridors. **Pets:** Accepted.
SAVE 🛜 ✕ 🔌 💻 🍽 🏊 ✕

▲▲▲ ◆◆◆ Kahler Inn & Suites H
(507) 285-9200. **$119-$159.** 9 NW 3rd Ave 55901. Just n of Mayo Clinic. Int corridors. **Pets:** Accepted. SAVE 🛜 ✕ 🔌 💻 🍽 🏊 ✕

▼▼▼ ◆◆◆ Marriott Hotel H
(507) 280-6000. **$259-$289.** 101 1st Ave SW 55902. Just e of Mayo Clinic. Int corridors. **Pets:** Accepted. 🛜 ✕ 🔌 💻 🍽 🏊

▼▼▼ ◆◆◆ Microtel Inn & Suites by Wyndham Rochester H
(507) 286-8780. **$60-$130.** 4210 Hwy 52 N 55901. US 52 exit 58 (41st St NW), just w. Int corridors. **Pets:** Accepted. 🛜 ⌖M 🔌 💻

▲▲▲ ▼▼▼ ◆◆◆ Quality Inn & Suites H
(507) 282-8091. **$70-$200.** 1620 1st Ave SE 55904. On US 63 (Broadway) from jct US 14, 0.5 mi s, just e on 16th St, then just s. Ext/int corridors. **Pets:** $15 daily fee/pet. Service with restrictions, crate.
SAVE 🛜 ✕ 🔌 💻

▼▼▼ ▼▼▼ Residence Inn by Marriott H
(507) 292-1400. **$199-$369.** 441 W Center St 55902. Just n of Mayo Clinic; downtown. Int corridors. **Pets:** Accepted.
🛜 ✕ ⌖M 🔌 💻

▼▼▼ ▼▼▼ TownePlace Suites by Marriott H
(507) 281-1200. **$99-$199.** 2829 NW 43rd St 55901. US 52 exit 41st St NW, just w, just n on W Frontage Rd, then just w. Int corridors. **Pets:** $100 one-time fee/room. Service with restrictions, crate.
🛜 ✕ ⌖M 🔌 💻 🏊 ✕

ROSEAU

▲▲▲ ▼▼▼ ▼▼▼ AmericInn Lodge & Suites of Roseau H
(218) 463-1045. **$71-$141.** 1110 3rd St NW 56751. 1 mi w on SR 11. Int corridors. **Pets:** Other species. $25 one-time fee/room. Designated rooms, service with restrictions. SAVE 🛜 ✕ ⌖M 🔌 💻 🏊 ✕

▼▼▼ ▼▼▼ North Country Inn H
(218) 463-9444. **$72-$120.** 902 3rd St NW 56751. 0.8 mi w on SR 11. Int corridors. **Pets:** $7 daily fee/pet. Designated rooms, service with restrictions, supervision. 🛜 ✕ 🔌 💻 🏊

ST. CLOUD

▲▲▲ ▼▼▼ ▼▼▼ AmericInn Lodge & Suites of St. Cloud H
(320) 253-6337. **Call for rates.** 4385 Clearwater Rd 56301. I-94 exit 171 (CR 75), just ne. Int corridors. **Pets:** Accepted.
SAVE 🛜 ⌖M 🔌 💻 🏊

▲▲▲ ▼▼▼▼ BEST WESTERN PLUS Kelly Inn H
(320) 253-0606. **$95-$140.** 100 4th Ave S 56301. SR 23 at 4th Ave S; center. Int corridors. **Pets:** Designated rooms, service with restrictions, supervision. SAVE 🛜 ⌖M 🔌 💻 🍽 🏊 ✕

▲▲▲ ▼▼▼▼ Country Inn & Suites By Carlson-St. Cloud West H
(320) 259-8999. **Call for rates.** 235 S Park Ave 56301. Jct SR 15 and 23 W, just w. Int corridors. **Pets:** Small, dogs only. $15 one-time fee/pet. Designated rooms, service with restrictions, supervision.
SAVE 🛜 ⌖M 🔌 💻 🏊

▲▲▲ ▼▼▼▼ GrandStay Residential Suites Hotel H
(320) 251-5400. **$77-$170.** 213 6th Ave S 56301. SR 23 at 6th Ave S; center. Int corridors. **Pets:** Large. $10 daily fee/pet. Service with restrictions, crate. SAVE 🛜 🔌 💻 🏊 ✕

▼▼▼▼ Holiday Inn Hotel & Suites H
(320) 253-9000. **$95-$125.** 75 S 37th Ave 56301. Jct SR 15 and 23. Int corridors. **Pets:** Other species. Service with restrictions.
🛜 🔌 💻 🏊 ✕

▲▲▲ ▼▼▼▼ Le St-Germain Suite Hotel H
(320) 654-1661. **$89-$139.** 404 W St. Germain St 56301. Just n of SR 23; center. Int corridors. **Pets:** Accepted.
SAVE 🛜 ✕ ⌖M 🔌 💻 🏊 ✕

ST. JAMES

▼▼▼ Super 8 St. James M 🐾
(507) 375-4708. **$60-$100.** 1210 Heckman Ct 56081. SR 60 exit 30/730th Ave, just n, then just e. Int corridors. **Pets:** Other species. $10 daily fee/pet. Designated rooms, service with restrictions, crate.
🛜 🔌 💻

SAUK CENTRE

▼▼▼ ▼▼▼ AmericInn Lodge & Suites of Sauk Centre H
(320) 352-2800. **$79-$149.** 1230 Timberlane Dr 56378. I-94 exit 127, just ne. Int corridors. **Pets:** Medium, dogs only. $10 daily fee/pet. Designated rooms, service with restrictions, supervision. 🛜 🔌 💻 🏊 ✕

▼▼▼ ▼▼▼ GuestHouse International Hotel H
(320) 351-7256. **$72-$86.** 322 12th St S 56378. I-94 exit 127, just ne. Int corridors. **Pets:** Medium, dogs only. $10 one-time fee/pet. Designated rooms, service with restrictions, supervision. 🛜 🔌 💻 🍽 🏊

SILVER BAY

▲▲▲ ▼▼▼▼ AmericInn Lodge & Suites of Silver Bay H
(218) 226-4300. **$105-$165.** 150 Mensing Dr 55614. On SR 61, 0.5 mi ne of jct SR 61 and Outer Dr. Int corridors. **Pets:** Dogs only. $20 one-time fee/pet. Designated rooms, service with restrictions, crate.
SAVE 🛜 ✕ ⌖M 🔌 💻 🏊 ✕

▲▲▲ ▼▼▼ Mariner Motel M
(218) 226-4488. **$55-$75, 3 day notice.** 46 Outer Dr 55614. Just w off SR 61; at traffic signal. Ext corridors. **Pets:** Dogs only. $10 daily fee/pet. Service with restrictions, supervision. SAVE 🛜 🔌 💻 🐾

SLEEPY EYE

▼▼▼ Inn of Seven Gables H
(507) 794-5390. **Call for rates.** 1100 E Main St 56085. US 14, 0.8 mi e of jct CR 4 and US 14. Int corridors. **Pets:** Accepted.
🛜 🔌 💻 🏊

SPICER

▼▼▼ Northern Inn Hotel & Suites H
(320) 796-2091. **$60-$160.** 154 Lake Ave S 56288. Just e of jct SR 23 and CR 10. Int corridors. **Pets:** Other species. $10 daily fee/pet. Designated rooms, service with restrictions, crate. 🛜 🔌 💻 🏊

SPRINGFIELD

▼▼▼ Microtel Inn & Suites by Wyndham Springfield H
(507) 723-8200. **$62-$79.** 502 E Rock St 56087. On US 14. Int corridors. **Pets:** Designated rooms, service with restrictions, supervision.
🛜 ✕ ⌖M 🔌 💻 🏊

SPRING VALLEY

▼▼▼ Spring Valley Inn & Suites H
(507) 346-7788. **$65-$69.** 745 N Broadway 55975. Just w on US 63. Int corridors. **Pets:** Accepted. 🛜 ✕ ⌖M 🔌 💻

STEWARTVILLE

▼▼ Relax Inn M

(507) 533-4747. **Call for rates.** 1700 2nd Ave NW 55976. I-90 exit 209A, 1 mi s on US 63. Int corridors. **Pets:** Accepted.

TOFTE

▼▼ AmericInn Lodge & Suites of Tofte H

(218) 663-7899. **$70-$150.** 7231 W SR 61 55615. On SR 61. Int corridors. **Pets:** $15 daily fee/room. Designated rooms, service with restrictions, crate.

▼▼▼ Bluefin Bay on Lake Superior CO

(218) 663-7296. **Call for rates.** 7198 W Hwy 61 55615. SR 61. Ext corridors. **Pets:** Dogs only. $20 daily fee/room. Designated rooms, service with restrictions, crate.

▼▼▼▼ Surfside on Lake Superior CO

(218) 663-6870. **Call for rates.** 10 Surfside (Hwy 61) Dr 55615. On SR 61. Ext corridors. **Pets:** Dogs only. $20 daily fee/room. Designated rooms, service with restrictions, crate.

TWO HARBORS

▼▼ AmericInn Lodge & Suites of Two Harbors H

(218) 834-3000. **$109-$264.** 1088 SR 61 N 55616. On SR 61, 0.7 mi s. Int corridors. **Pets:** Medium, dogs only. $15 daily fee/room. Designated rooms, service with restrictions, crate.

▼▼▼ Superior Shores Resort CO

(218) 834-5671. **$59-$479, 14 day notice.** 1521 Superior Shores Dr 55616. On SR 61, 1.5 mi n of center. Ext/int corridors. **Pets:** Dogs only. $15 daily fee/room. Designated rooms, service with restrictions, supervision.

VIRGINIA

▼ Lakeshor Motor Inn M

(218) 741-3360. **$55-$104.** 404 6th Ave N 55792. Just n of Chestnut St; center. Ext corridors. **Pets:** Dogs only. $5 daily fee/room. Designated rooms, supervision.

▼ Pine View Inn M

(218) 741-8918. **$59-$109.** 903 N 17th St 55792. Jct US 53 and 169, 0.5 mi n on US 53, 0.7 mi e on 9th St N, then 0.5 mi n on 9th Ave W. Ext/int corridors. **Pets:** Accepted.

WABASHA

▼▼ AmericInn Lodge & Suites of Wabasha H

(651) 565-5366. **$77-$180.** 150 Commerce Dr 55981. Just ne of jct US 61 and SR 60. Int corridors. **Pets:** Other species. $15 daily fee/room. Designated rooms, service with restrictions, crate.

WALKER

▼▼▼ Country Inn Walker H

(218) 547-1400. **$76-$225.** 442 Walker Bay Blvd 56484. 1 mi s on SR 371. Int corridors. **Pets:** Medium. $30 one-time fee/room. Service with restrictions, crate.

WARROAD

▼▼ America's Best Inn Warroad H

(218) 386-3807. **$65-$129.** 406 Main Ave NE 56763. 0.5 mi w on SR 11. Int corridors. **Pets:** Accepted.

▼▼ The Patch Motel H

(218) 386-2723. **Call for rates.** 801 State St N 56763. 0.6 mi w on SR 11. Int corridors. **Pets:** Accepted.

WILLMAR

▼▼ AmericInn Motel of Willmar H

(320) 231-1962. **$83-$93.** 2404 E US 12 56201. 2 mi e. Int corridors. **Pets:** Accepted.

▼▼ Comfort Inn H

(320) 231-2601. **$89-$150.** 2200 E US 12 56201. 1.8 mi e. Int corridors. **Pets:** $10 daily fee/pet. Service with restrictions, supervision.

▼▼ Days Inn-Willmar H

(320) 231-1275. **$70-$82.** 225 28th St SE 56201. 2.3 mi e on US 12. Int corridors. **Pets:** Other species. $10 daily fee/pet. Service with restrictions, supervision.

▼▼▼ Holiday Inn & Willmar Conference Center H

(320) 235-6060. **$99-$150.** 2100 US 12 E 56201. 1.8 mi e. Int corridors. **Pets:** Other species. $10 daily fee/pet. Service with restrictions, supervision.

WINDOM

▼▼ Guardian Inn Motel M

(507) 831-1809. **$60-$100.** 1955 1st Ave 56101. Just ne on SR 60 from jct US 71. Ext/int corridors. **Pets:** $15 one-time fee/room. Designated rooms, service with restrictions, crate.

WINONA

▼▼ Express Suites Riverport Inn H

(507) 452-0606. **Call for rates.** 900 Bruski Dr 55987. Jct US 14/61 and SR 43, just ne. Int corridors. **Pets:** Accepted.

▼▼▼ Holiday Inn Express & Suites H

(507) 474-1700. **Call for rates.** 1128 Homer Rd 55987. Jct SR 43, just sw. Int corridors. **Pets:** Accepted.

▼▼▼ The Plaza Hotel & Suites H

(507) 453-0303. **$109-$205.** 1025 Hwy 61 E 55987. Jct SR 43, just sw. Int corridors. **Pets:** Other species. $25 daily fee/room. Designated rooms, supervision.

WORTHINGTON

▼▼▼ AmericInn Lodge & Suites of Worthington H

(507) 376-4500. **$130-$155.** 1475 Darling Dr 56187. I-90 exit 43 (US 59), just se. Int corridors. **Pets:** Other species. $10 one-time fee/room. Supervision.

MISSISSIPPI

ABERDEEN

 Americas Best Value Inn & Suites Ⓜ

(662) 369-4343. **$75-$80.** 801 E Commerce St 39730. On US 45, just n of jct SR 25 and Tenn-Tom Bridge. Ext corridors. **Pets:** Accepted.
🛜 🗄 💻 ⊇

AMORY

▼▼ **Briarwood Inn** Ⓜ

(662) 256-2120. **Call for rates.** 915 Hwy 278 E 38821. Jct SR 25 (Main St), 0.6 mi e. Ext corridors. **Pets:** Small, dogs only. $10 daily fee/pet. Service with restrictions, supervision. 🛜 🗄 💻 ⊇

BILOXI

𝔸𝔸𝔸 ▼▼ **Edgewater Inn** Ⓗ

(228) 388-1100. **$99-$495, 3 day notice.** 1936 Beach Blvd 39531. I-110 exit 1B, 3.4 mi w on US 90. Ext corridors. **Pets:** Large, other species. $75 deposit/pet. Designated rooms. SAVE 🛜 🗄 💻 ⊇

𝔸𝔸𝔸 ▼▼▼▼ **Hard Rock Hotel & Casino Biloxi** Ⓗ

(228) 374-7625. **$109-$499.** 777 Beach Blvd 39530. I-110 exit 1A (US 90), just e. Int corridors. **Pets:** Small. $75 one-time fee/room. Service with restrictions, supervision. SAVE 🛜 &M 🗄 💻 🍴 ⊇ ⊠

▼▼▼ **La Quinta Inn & Suites** Ⓗ

(228) 392-5978. **$79-$179.** 957 Cedar Lake Rd 39532. I-10 exit 44, just s. Int corridors. **Pets:** Service with restrictions, supervision.
🛜 ⊠ &M 🗄 💻 ⊇

CANTON

𝔸𝔸𝔸 ▼▼▼▼ **BEST WESTERN Canton Inn** Ⓗ

(601) 859-8600. **$70-$100.** 137 Soldier Colony Rd 39046. I-55 exit 119, just se. Int corridors. **Pets:** Large, other species. $10 daily fee/pet. Service with restrictions, supervision. SAVE 🛜 🗄 💻 ⊇

▼▼▼ **Brentwood Inn & Suites** Ⓗ

(601) 859-7575. **Call for rates.** 145 Soldier Colony Rd 39046. I-55 exit 119, just se. Int corridors. **Pets:** Accepted. 🛜 🗄 💻 ⊇

CLARKSDALE

▼▼ **Comfort Inn of Clarksdale** Ⓗ

(662) 627-5122. **$85-$120.** 818 S State St 38614. 1.2 mi s of jct US 49 and SR 161. Int corridors. **Pets:** Accepted. 🛜 🗄 💻 ⊇

CLEVELAND

▼▼▼ **Holiday Inn Express** Ⓗ

(662) 843-9300. **$109-$114.** 808 N Davis Ave 38732. 1 mi n of jct US 61 and SR 8. Int corridors. **Pets:** Accepted. 🛜 &M 🗄 💻 ⊇

CLINTON

𝔸𝔸𝔸 ▼▼ **BEST WESTERN Ridgeland Inn** Ⓗ

(601) 926-4323. **$75-$85.** 102 Clinton Loop Dr 39056. I-20 exit 36, just s, then just w on Clinton Center Dr. Int corridors. **Pets:** Accepted.
SAVE 🛜 🗄 💻 ⊇

COLUMBIA

▼▼ **Comfort Inn** Ⓗ

(601) 731-9955. **$75-$85.** 820 Hwy 98 Bypass 39429. Just e of jct US 98 Bypass and SR 13. Int corridors. **Pets:** Accepted.
🛜 🗄 💻 ⊇

COLUMBUS

▼▼ **Quality Inn** Ⓗ

(662) 329-2422. **$72-$80.** 1210 US Hwy 45 N 39705. Jct US 82 Bypass and 45 N. Ext corridors. **Pets:** Accepted. 🛜 🗄 💻

CORINTH

▼▼ **Quality Inn** Ⓜ

(662) 287-4421. **Call for rates.** 2101 Hwy 72 W 38834. Jct US 72 and 45, just e. Ext corridors. **Pets:** Accepted. 🛜 🗄 💻 ⊇

D'IBERVILLE

▼▼▼ **Suburban Extended Stay Hotel** Ⓗ

(228) 396-5780. **$49-$99.** 10221 Rodriguez St 39540. I-110 exit 2, just sw. Ext corridors. **Pets:** Accepted. 🛜 🗄 💻

▼▼▼ **Wingate by Wyndham** Ⓗ

(228) 396-0036. **$99-$179.** 12009 Indian River Rd 39540. I-10 exit 46B, just ne. Int corridors. **Pets:** Dogs only. $50 one-time fee/pet. Designated rooms, service with restrictions, supervision. 🛜 ⊠ 🗄 💻 ⊇

FLOWOOD

𝔸𝔸𝔸 ▼▼ **Sleep Inn-Flowood** Ⓗ

(601) 936-0007. **$52-$85.** 4351 Lakeland Dr 39232. I-55 exit 98B northbound, 4 mi e to jct Airport Rd. Int corridors. **Pets:** Medium. $10 daily fee/room. Service with restrictions, crate. SAVE 🛜 &M 🗄 💻 ⊇

GRENADA

▼▼▼ **Comfort Inn & Suites** Ⓗ

(662) 227-8444. **$86-$130.** 255 SW Frontage Rd 38901. I-55 exit 206, just sw. Int corridors. **Pets:** Medium. $25 one-time fee/room. Service with restrictions, supervision. 🛜 🗄 💻 ⊇

GULFPORT

𝔸𝔸𝔸 ▼▼▼▼ **BEST WESTERN PLUS Seaway Inn** Ⓗ 🐾

(228) 864-0050. **$70-$130.** 9475 Hwy 49 39503. I-10 exit 34A, just sw. Ext corridors. **Pets:** Other species. $15 daily fee/pet. Designated rooms, service with restrictions, crate. SAVE 🛜 🗄 💻 ⊇

𝔸𝔸𝔸 ▼▼▼ **Clarion Inn Gulfport/Airport** Ⓗ

(228) 868-3300. **$79-$199.** 9445 Hwy 49 39503. I-10 exit 34A, just sw. Ext corridors. **Pets:** Small. $25 one-time fee/room. Service with restrictions, supervision. SAVE 🛜 🗄 💻 ⊇

▼▼ **Quality Inn Gulfport** Ⓗ

(228) 864-7222. **$60-$130.** 9435 Hwy 49 39503. I-10 exit 34A, 0.6 mi s. Ext corridors. **Pets:** Accepted. 🛜 🗄 💻

▼▼ ▼▼ **Ramada Inn Hotel & Convention Center** 🄷
(228) 868-8200. **$60-$120.** 9415 Hwy 49 39503. I-10 exit 34A, 0.6 mi s. Ext corridors. **Pets:** Accepted. 🛜 🛗 💻 🍴 ≋

▼▼ ▼▼ **Residence Inn by Marriott Gulfport-Biloxi Airport** 🄷
(228) 867-1722. **$129-$169.** 14100 Airport Rd 39503. I-10 exit 34A, 0.8 mi s on US 49, then 1.2 mi e. Int corridors. **Pets:** Accepted.
🛜 ✕ 🛗 🛗 💻 ≋ 🗙

HATTIESBURG

▼▼ ▼▼ **Candlewood Suites** 🄷
(601) 264-9666. **Call for rates.** 9 Gateway Dr 39402. I-59 exit 67B, just nw to Classic Dr, then just sw. Int corridors. **Pets:** Large, other species. $75 one-time fee/room. Service with restrictions, supervision.
🛜 🛗 🛗 💻

▼▼ ▼▼ **Comfort Inn University** 🄷
(601) 264-1881. **Call for rates.** 6541 Hwy 49 39401. I-59 exit 67A, just s. Ext/int corridors. **Pets:** Accepted. 🛜 🛗 💻 ≋

▼▼ ▼▼ **Hampton Inn of Hattiesburg** 🄷
(601) 264-8080. **$99-$109.** 4301 Hardy St 39402. I-59 exit 65, just nw. Ext/int corridors. **Pets:** Medium. $30 one-time fee/room. Designated rooms, service with restrictions, supervision. 🛜 🛗 💻 ≋

🄰🄰🄰 ▼▼ ▼▼ **La Quinta Inn** 🄷
(601) 268-2850. **$66-$144.** 6563 Hwy 49 N 39401. I-59 exit 67A, just se. Int corridors. **Pets:** Service with restrictions, supervision.
SAVE 🛜 🛗 💻 ≋

▼▼ ▼▼ **Residence Inn by Marriott Hattiesburg** 🄷
(601) 264-9202. **$142-$199.** 116 Grand Dr 39401. I-59 exit 65, jct N 40th St, then just w. Int corridors. **Pets:** Accepted.
🛜 ✕ 🛗 🛗 💻 ≋ 🗙

HOLLY SPRINGS

▼▼ ▼▼ **Econo Lodge** 🄷
(662) 252-5444. **Call for rates.** 100 Brooks Rd 38635. US 78 exit 30, just sw. Int corridors. **Pets:** Accepted. 🛜 🛗 💻 ≋

HORN LAKE

🄰🄰🄰 ▼▼ ▼▼ **BEST WESTERN PLUS Goodman Inn & Suites** 🄷
(662) 510-6999. **$100-$120.** 6910 Windchase Dr 38637. I-55 exit 289, just w, then just s. Int corridors. **Pets:** Accepted.
SAVE 🛜 ✕ 🛗 🛗 💻 ≋

▼▼ ▼▼ **Comfort Inn** 🄷
(662) 349-3493. **$89-$104.** 801 Desoto Cove 38637. I-55 exit 289, just w, then just n. Int corridors. **Pets:** Accepted. 🛜 🛗 🛗 💻 ≋

▼▼ ▼▼ **Drury Inn & Suites-Memphis South** 🄷
(662) 349-6622. **$109-$189.** 735 Goodman Rd W 38637. I-55 exit 289, just w, then just s. Int corridors. **Pets:** Service with restrictions, supervision. 🛜 🛗 🛗 💻 ≋

▼▼ ▼▼ **La Quinta Inn & Suites Horn Lake** 🄷
(662) 510-6500. **$78-$178.** 721 Southwest Dr 38637. I-55 exit 289, just sw. Int corridors. **Pets:** Service with restrictions, supervision.
🛜 ✕ 🛗 🛗 💻 ≋

JACKSON

🄰🄰🄰 ▼▼ ▼▼ **Hilton Jackson** 🄷 🐾
(601) 957-2800. **$99-$209.** 1001 E County Line Rd 39211. I-55 exit 103 (County Line Rd), just e. Int corridors. **Pets:** Medium. $75 one-time fee/room. Designated rooms, no service, supervision.
SAVE 🛜 🛗 💻 🍴 ≋

▼▼ ▼▼ **Howard Johnson Jackson North Ridgeland** 🄷
(601) 206-8923. **Call for rates.** 585 E Beasley Rd 39206. I-55 exit 102, just w. Int corridors. **Pets:** Accepted. 🛜 🛗 🛗 💻 ≋

▼▼ ▼▼ **La Quinta Inn Jackson (North)** 🄷
(601) 957-1741. **$59-$107.** 616 Briarwood Dr 39211. I-55 exit 102A northbound, just ne on Frontage Rd. Ext corridors. **Pets:** Service with restrictions, supervision. 🛜 🛗 🛗 💻 ≋

KOSCIUSKO

🄰🄰🄰 ▼▼ ▼▼ **Americas Best Value Inn** 🄼
(662) 289-6252. **$57-$65.** 1052 Veterans Memorial Dr 39090. Just sw of jct SR 35 and Natchez Trace Pkwy. Ext corridors. **Pets:** Accepted.
SAVE 🛜 🛗 💻 ≋

LUCEDALE

▼▼ ▼▼ **Holiday Inn Express & Suites** 🄷
(601) 947-2099. **Call for rates.** 1287 Beaver Dam Rd 39452. Jct US 98 and SR 63, 1.5 mi se. Int corridors. **Pets:** Accepted. 🛜 🛗 💻 ≋

MCCOMB

▼▼ ▼▼ **Ramada** 🄷
(601) 684-8655. **$90.** 2001 Veteran's Blvd 39648. I-55 exit 18, just w. Int corridors. **Pets:** Accepted. 🛜 🛗 🛗 💻 ≋

MERIDIAN

▼▼ ▼▼ **Baymont Inn & Suites Meridian** 🄷
(601) 483-3315. **Call for rates.** 524 Bonita Lakes Dr 39301. I-20/59 exit 154 southbound; exit 154A northbound, just s. Ext corridors. **Pets:** Accepted. 🛜 🛗 🛗 💻 ≋

🄰🄰🄰 ▼▼ ▼▼ **BEST WESTERN of Meridian** 🄷
(601) 693-3210. **$61-$64.** 2219 S Frontage Rd 39301. I-20/59 exit 153, just sw. Ext/int corridors. **Pets:** Small, dogs only. $10 daily fee/pet. Service with restrictions, crate. SAVE 🛜 🛗 💻 ≋

▼▼ ▼▼ **Drury Inn & Suites** 🄷
(601) 483-5570. **$114-$199.** 112 Hwy 11 & 80 N 39301. I-20/59 exit 154, jct US 11/80 N. Int corridors. **Pets:** Service with restrictions, supervision.
🛜 🛗 🛗 💻 ≋

▼▼ ▼▼ **La Quinta Inn & Suites - Meridian** 🄷
(601) 693-2300. **$59-$144.** 1400 Roebuck Dr 39301. I-20/59 exit 153, just s. Int corridors. **Pets:** Service with restrictions, supervision.
🛜 🛗 💻 ≋

▼▼ ▼▼ **Microtel Inn & Suites by Wyndham Meridian** 🄷
(601) 553-8100. **$59-$70.** 518 Bonita Lakes Dr 39301. I-20/59 exit 154 westbound, 0.4 mi s to Bonita Lakes Dr, then just sw; exit 154A eastbound, just s. Int corridors. **Pets:** Accepted. 🛜 🛗 🛗 💻

🄰🄰🄰 ▼▼ ▼▼ **Super 8** 🄼
(601) 482-8088. **$67-$74.** 124 Hwy 11 & 80 E 39301. I-20/59 exit 154 westbound; exit 154B eastbound, on northeast frontage road. Ext corridors. **Pets:** Accepted. SAVE 🛜 🛗 💻

MOSS POINT

🄰🄰🄰 ▼▼ ▼▼ **BEST WESTERN Flagship Inn** 🄷
(228) 475-5000. **$80-$90.** 4830 Amoco Dr 39563. I-10 exit 69, just s. Ext corridors. **Pets:** Small. $20 one-time fee/room. Designated rooms, supervision. SAVE 🛜 🛗 💻 ≋

▼▼ ▼▼ **Quality Inn** 🄷
(228) 475-2477. **$59-$79.** 6800 Hwy 63 N 39563. I-10 exit 69, just s. Ext corridors. **Pets:** Small, other species. $15 daily fee/pet. Designated rooms, service with restrictions, crate. 🛜 🛗 💻 ≋

NATCHEZ

▼▼ ▼▼ **Hampton Inn & Suites** 🄷
(601) 446-6770. **$104-$129.** 627 S Canal St 39120. US 84/65 exit just before Mississippi River. Int corridors. **Pets:** Small. $30 daily fee/pet. Designated rooms, service with restrictions, crate. 🛜 🛗 🛗 💻 ≋

OCEAN SPRINGS
▼▼▼ Ramada Limited **H**
(228) 872-2323. **$50-$130, 3 day notice.** 8011 Tucker Rd 39532. I-10 exit 50, just n. Ext corridors. **Pets:** Other species. $15 daily fee/pet. Designated rooms, service with restrictions, crate. 🛜 📶 🖨 💻 🏊

OLIVE BRANCH
▼▼▼ Candlewood Suites **H**
(662) 890-7491. **Call for rates.** 7448 Craft Goodman Rd 38654. US 78 exit 1 westbound, 0.5 mi se; exit 2 (SR 302) eastbound, 1.4 mi ne. Int corridors. **Pets:** Large, other species. $10 daily fee/pet. Designated rooms, supervision. 🛜 ♿ 🖨 💻

▼▼ Magnolia Inn & Suites **H**
(662) 895-4545. **$55-$100.** 6935 W Hamilton Cir 38654. US 78 exit 2 (SR 302), 0.5 mi w. Int corridors. **Pets:** Medium, dogs only. $20 daily fee/pet. Service with restrictions, supervision. 🛜 🖨 💻 🏊

〰 ▼▼▼ Whispering Woods Hotel and Conference Center **H**
(662) 895-2941. **$109, 3 day notice.** 11200 E Goodman Rd 38654. US 78 exit 2 (SR 302), 3.6 mi e. Int corridors. **Pets:** Accepted.
SAVE 🛜 ✕ 🖨 💻 🍴 🏊

PASCAGOULA
▼▼ Super 8 **M**
(228) 762-9414. **$90-$120, 3 day notice.** 4919 Denny Ave 39581. I-10 exit 69, 3.5 mi s on SR 63, then just w on US 90. Int corridors. **Pets:** Small. $50 deposit/room, $15 one-time fee/pet. Designated rooms, service with restrictions, supervision. 🛜 ♿ 🖨 💻 🏊

PEARL
▼▼▼ Baymont Inn & Suites Pearl **H**
(601) 932-6030. **Call for rates.** 434 Riverwind Dr 39208. I-20 exit 48, just nw. Int corridors. **Pets:** Small. $15 daily fee/pet. Service with restrictions, supervision. 🛜 ♿ 🖨 💻 🏊

▼▼▼ Candlewood Suites **H**
(601) 936-3442. **$85-$95.** 632 S Pearson Rd 39208. I-20 exit 48, just s. Int corridors. **Pets:** Other species. $25 one-time fee/room.
🛜 ♿ 🖨 💻

▼▼ La Quinta Inn & Suites Jackson Airport **H**
(601) 664-0065. **$78-$161.** 501 S Pearson Rd 39208. I-20 exit 48, just s. Int corridors. **Pets:** Service with restrictions, supervision.
🛜 🖨 💻 🏊

▼▼ Ramada Jackson Airport **H**
(601) 933-1122. **$54-$80.** 341 Airport Rd 39208. I-20 exit 52, just nw. Int corridors. **Pets:** Medium. $25 one-time fee/room. Service with restrictions, crate. 🛜 🖨 💻

PHILADELPHIA
▼▼▼ Golden Moon Hotel & Casino **H**
(601) 650-1234. **$69-$199.** 13541 Hwy 16 W 39350. Jct SR 15, 2 mi w. Int corridors. **Pets:** Accepted. 🛜 ♿ 🖨 💻 🍴 🏊 ✕

▼▼ Silver Star Hotel & Casino **H**
(601) 650-1234. **Call for rates.** 13540 Hwy 16 W 39350. Jct SR 15, 2 mi w. Int corridors. **Pets:** Accepted. 🛜 ♿ 🖨 💻 🍴 🏊 ✕

PICAYUNE
▼▼ Days Inn **H**
(601) 799-1339. **$70-$400.** 450 S Lofton Ave 39466. I-59 exit 4, just nw. Ext corridors. **Pets:** Accepted. 🛜 🖨 💻 🏊

RIDGELAND
▼▼▼ Drury Inn & Suites Ridgeland-Jackson **H**
(601) 956-6100. **$99-$174.** 610 E County Line Rd 39157. I-55 exit 103 (County Line Rd), just w. Int corridors. **Pets:** Service with restrictions, supervision. 🛜 ♿ 🖨 💻 🏊 ✕

▼▼▼ Homewood Suites by Hilton **H**
(601) 899-8611. **Call for rates.** 853 Centre St 39157. I-55 exit 103 (County Line Rd), just e to Ridgewood Rd, 0.4 mi ne, then just e. Int corridors. **Pets:** Accepted. 🛜 ♿ 🖨 💻 🏊

▼▼▼ Residence Inn by Marriott Jackson Ridgeland **H**
(601) 206-7755. **$149-$169.** 855 Centre St 39157. I-55 exit 103 (County Line Rd), just e to Ridgewood Rd, then just e. Int corridors. **Pets:** Accepted. 🛜 ✕ ♿ 🖨 💻 🏊 ✕

RIPLEY
〰 ▼▼▼ BEST WESTERN Ripley **M**
(662) 837-0002. **$91.** 922 City Ave S 38663. Jct US 4 and 15, 0.5 mi s. Ext corridors. **Pets:** Accepted. SAVE 🛜 🖨 💻 🏊

SOUTHAVEN
▼▼▼ Magnolia Inn & Suites **H**
(662) 280-5555. **$50-$95.** 5069 Pepper Chase Dr 38671. I-55 exit 287, just w. Int corridors. **Pets:** Medium, dogs only. $20 one-time fee/pet. Designated rooms, service with restrictions, supervision. 🛜 🖨

▼▼▼ Residence Inn by Marriott Memphis Southaven **H**
(662) 996-1500. **$104-$144.** 7165 Sleepy Hollow Dr 38671. I-55 exit 289, just e to Southcrest Pkwy, just n, then just w. Int corridors. **Pets:** Medium. $100 one-time fee/room. Service with restrictions, crate.
🛜 ✕ ♿ 🖨 💻 🏊

STARKVILLE
▼▼▼ Comfort Suites Starkville **H**
(662) 324-9595. **$109-$159.** 801 Russell St 39759. 0.5 mi w of jct US 82 and SR 12. Int corridors. **Pets:** Accepted. 🛜 ✕ 🖨 💻 🏊

▼▼▼ Hampton Inn **H**
(662) 324-1333. **$104-$129.** 700 Hwy 12 E 39759. 1.1 mi sw of jct SR 182. Int corridors. **Pets:** Medium, other species. Service with restrictions, supervision. 🛜 ✕ ♿ 🖨 💻 🏊

TUNICA
▼▼ Key West Inn Tunica **M**
(662) 363-0021. **$40-$150.** 11635 Hwy 61 N 38664. US 61, 0.3 mi n of SR 304. Ext corridors. **Pets:** Small, dogs only. $10 daily fee/pet. Designated rooms, service with restrictions, supervision. 🛜 🖨 💻

TUPELO
▼▼ America's Best Inn **M**
(662) 842-4403. **$55-$100, 3 day notice.** 897 Harmony Ln 38804. US 45 exit Barnes Crossing, 0.5 mi sw, then just e. Ext corridors. **Pets:** Accepted. 🛜 ♿ 🖨 💻

〰 ▼▼▼ Days Inn **M**
(662) 842-0088. **$75-$85.** 1015 N Gloster St 38804. On SR 145, just n of McCullough Blvd. Ext corridors. **Pets:** Accepted.
SAVE 🛜 ♿ 🖨 💻

〰 ▼▼▼ La Quinta Inn & Suites **M**
(662) 847-8000. **$90-$195.** 1013 N Gloster St 38804. On SR 145, just n of McCullough Blvd. Int corridors. **Pets:** Service with restrictions, supervision. SAVE 🛜 ✕ ♿ 🖨 💻 🏊

▼▼ Quality Inn Tupelo **H**
(662) 842-5100. **$72-$76.** 1190 N Gloster St 38804. Jct McCullough Blvd and SR 145, 1.3 mi s to McCullough Blvd, w to N Gloster St, then 0.3 mi n. Ext corridors. **Pets:** Accepted. 🛜 🖨 💻

▼▼ Super 8 **M**
(662) 842-0448. **$65-$75.** 3898 McCullough Blvd 38801. US 78 exit 81, just sw. Ext corridors. **Pets:** Medium, dogs only. $10 deposit/pet. Service with restrictions. 🛜 🖨 💻 🏊

VICKSBURG

▼▼ ◆◆ Baymont Inn & Suites Vicksburg **H**
(601) 619-7799. **Call for rates.** 3975 S Frontage Rd 39180. I-20 exit 4A, on southeast frontage road. Ext corridors. **Pets:** Accepted.
🛜 ♿ 🛏 💻 🏊

◭◭◭ ▼▼▼ BEST WESTERN Vicksburg **H**
(601) 636-5800. **$77-$110.** 2445 N Frontage Rd 39180. I-20 exit 3, just w on NW Frontage Rd. Ext corridors. **Pets:** Large. $15 daily fee/room. Service with restrictions, crate. 〔SAVE〕🛜 🛏 💻 🏊

◭◭◭ ▼▼▼ Cedar Grove Mansion Inn & Restaurant **CI**
(601) 636-1000. **$100-$215, 3 day notice.** 2200 Oak St 39180. I-20 exit 1A, 2.3 mi n on Washington St, then w on Klein St; to gated entrance. Ext/int corridors. **Pets:** Medium, dogs only. $50 one-time fee/room. Designated rooms, service with restrictions, supervision.
〔SAVE〕🛜 ❌ 🛏 💻 🍴 🏊

▼▼▼ Corners Mansion Inn, a Bed & Breakfast **BB**
(601) 636-7421. **$125-$210, 3 day notice.** 601 Klein St 39180. I-20 exit 1A, 2.3 mi n on Washington St, then just w. Ext/int corridors. **Pets:** $25 daily fee/pet. Designated rooms. 🛜 ❌ 🛏 💻

▼▼▼ La Quinta Inn & Suites **H**
(601) 802-0525. **$95-$172.** 4160 S Frontage Rd 39180. I-20 exit 4A eastbound; exit 5B westbound, just s. Int corridors. **Pets:** Service with restrictions, supervision. 🛜 ❌ 🛏 💻 🏊

▼ Motel 6 #4189 **H**
(601) 638-5077. **$60-$80.** 4127 I-20 Frontage Rd 39183. I-20 exit 4B (Clay St), just ne. Int corridors. **Pets:** Other species. Service with restrictions, supervision. 🛜 🛏 🏊

▼▼ Travel Inn **M**
(601) 630-0100. **$45-$100.** 1675 N Frontage Rd 39180. I-20 exit 1C, on northeast frontage road. Ext corridors. **Pets:** Accepted. 🛜 🛏

WINONA

◭◭◭ ▼▼▼ Holiday Inn Express Inn & Suites Winona North Mississippi **H**
(662) 283-9992. **$89-$99.** 413 SE Frontage Rd 38967. I-55 exit 185, just e, then just s. Int corridors. **Pets:** Other species. $25 one-time fee/room. Service with restrictions. 〔SAVE〕🛜 ♿ 🛏 💻 🏊

MISSOURI

CITY INDEX

ARNOLD

▼▼▼ Drury Inn & Suites Arnold **H**
(636) 287-3111. **$95-$179.** 3800 SR 141 63010. I-55 exit 191 (SR 141), 0.3 mi e. Int corridors. **Pets:** Service with restrictions, supervision.
🛜 ♿ 🛏 💻 🏊

▼▼ Pear Tree Inn Arnold **H**
(636) 296-9600. **$70-$134.** 1201 Drury Ln 63010. I-55 exit 191 (SR 141), 0.3 mi e. Int corridors. **Pets:** Service with restrictions, supervision.
🛜 🛏 💻 🏊

AVA

▼▼ Ava Super 8 **H**
(417) 683-1343. **$65-$75.** 1711 S Jefferson St 65608. 1.8 mi s of jct SR 5, 14 and 76. Int corridors. **Pets:** Accepted. 🛜 ♿ 🛏 💻

BOONVILLE

◭◭◭ ▼ ◆◆ Boonville Comfort Inn **H**
(660) 882-5317. **$69-$99.** 2427 Mid America Industrial Dr 65233. I-70 exit 101, just sw. Int corridors. **Pets:** Small. $10 daily fee/pet. Designated rooms, service with restrictions, supervision. 〔SAVE〕🛜 🛏 💻 🏊

BRANSON METROPOLITAN AREA

BRANSON

◭◭◭ ▼▼▼▼ Baymont Inn & Suites **H**
(417) 334-1985. **$67-$117.** 1000 W Main St 65616. Just sw of jct US 65 and SR 76 (Country Blvd). Int corridors. **Pets:** Small, dogs only. $25 one-time fee/pet. Service with restrictions, crate.
〔SAVE〕🛜 ❌ 🛏 💻 🏊

◭◭◭ ▼▼◆◆ BEST WESTERN PLUS Landing View Inn & Suites **H**
(417) 334-6464. **$89-$199.** 403 W Main (Hwy 76) 65616. 0.3 mi e of jct SR 76 (Country Blvd) and US 65. Ext corridors. **Pets:** Medium, dogs only. $10 daily fee/pet. Designated rooms, service with restrictions, supervision.
〔SAVE〕🛜 🛏 💻 🏊

◭◭◭ ▼▼▼ ▼▼▼ Chateau on the Lake Resort & Spa **H**
(417) 334-1161. **$139-$359, 3 day notice.** 415 N State Hwy 265 65616. Just n of jct SR 165. Int corridors. **Pets:** Small, dogs only. $30 one-time fee/room. Designated rooms, service with restrictions, crate.
〔SAVE〕🛜 ❌ ♿ 🛏 💻 🍴 🏊 ❌

◭◭◭ ▼▼▼ Econo Lodge **M**
(417) 336-4849. **Call for rates.** 230 S Wildwood Dr 65616. Just s of jct SR 76 (Country Blvd). Ext corridors. **Pets:** Accepted.
〔SAVE〕🛜 ♿ 🛏 💻 🏊

AAA ▼▼▼ Fall Creek Inn & Suites H
(417) 348-1683. **$49-$99.** 995 Hwy 165 65616. Jct SR 76 (Country Blvd), 1.5 mi s on SR 165. Ext corridors. **Pets:** Dogs only. $50 deposit/room, $15 daily fee/pet. Designated rooms, service with restrictions.
[SAVE] 🛜 🖥 🏊

▼▼▼ Grand Crowne Resorts CO
(417) 332-8536. **Call for rates.** 405 SR 165 Dr 65616. 0.7 mi s of jct SR 76 (Country Blvd). Ext corridors. **Pets:** Medium, dogs only. $75 deposit/pet. Designated rooms, service with restrictions, crate.
🛜 ♿ 🖥 🏊 ✕

AAA ▼▼▼ Hampton Inn Branson Hills H
(417) 243-7800. **$99-$189.** 200 Payne Stewart Dr 65616. 1.5 mi nw of jct US 65 and Branson Hills Pkwy. Int corridors. **Pets:** Accepted.
[SAVE] 🛜 ♿ 🖥 🏊

▼▼▼ Hilton Promenade at Branson Landing H 🐾
(417) 336-5500. **$89-$199.** 3 Branson Landing 65616. Jct Main St, just e; in Branson Landing Shopping District. Int corridors. **Pets:** Large. $50 one-time fee/room. Service with restrictions, supervision.
🛜 ♿ 🖥 🍽 🏊

AAA ▼▼▼ HomeStay Inn Branson H
(417) 336-2666. **$59-$89.** 3221 Shepherd of the Hills Expwy 65616. 0.3 mi e of jct SR 76 (Country Blvd). Ext corridors. **Pets:** Accepted.
[SAVE] 🛜 🖥 🏊

AAA ▼▼▼ Hotel Grand Victorian H
(417) 336-2935. **$70-$130.** 2325 W Hwy 76 (Country Blvd) 65616. 2.3 mi w of jct US 65. Ext/int corridors. **Pets:** Accepted.
[SAVE] 🛜 🖥 🏊 ✕

▼▼ La Quinta Inn Branson Music City Centre H
(417) 336-1600. **$59-$155.** 1835 W Hwy 76 65616. 1.6 mi w of jct US 65. Ext/int corridors. **Pets:** Service with restrictions, supervision.
🛜 ✕ 🖥 🏊

▼▼ Lazy Valley Resort M
(417) 334-2397. **Call for rates.** 285 River Ln 65616. 2.5 mi s of jct SR 76 (Country Blvd); on Fall Creek Rd to River Valley Rd. Ext corridors. **Pets:** Accepted. ♿ 🖥 🏊 ✕ ✎

AAA ▼▼▼ Lodge at the Falls H
(417) 336-3255. **$59-$79.** 3245 Falls Pkwy 65616. 0.9 mi s of jct SR 165 and SR 76 (Country Blvd). Ext corridors. **Pets:** Small. $10 daily fee/pet. Designated rooms, service with restrictions. [SAVE] 🛜 🖥 🏊

▼▼ Plantation Inn H
(417) 336-3300. **$43-$60.** 3470 Keeter St 65616. Just sw of jct SR 76 (Country Blvd). Ext corridors. **Pets:** Accepted. 🛜 ♿ 🖥 🏊

▼▼ Quality Inn & Suites on the Strip H
(417) 334-1194. **$59-$129.** 2834 W Hwy 76 65616. 2.5 mi w of jct US 65. Ext corridors. **Pets:** Other species. $10 daily fee/pet. Service with restrictions. 🛜 🖥 🏊

AAA ▼▼▼ Radisson Hotel Branson H
(417) 335-5767. **$89-$239, 3 day notice.** 120 S Wildwood Dr 65616. Just s of jct SR 76 (Country Blvd). Int corridors. **Pets:** Medium. Designated rooms, service with restrictions, supervision.
[SAVE] 🛜 ✕ ♿ 🖥 🍽 🏊 ✕

▼▼ Ramada Resort & Conference Center H
(417) 334-1000. **$49-$79.** 1700 Hwy 76 W 65616. 1.5 mi w of jct US 65. Ext corridors. **Pets:** Other species. $15 one-time fee/room. Service with restrictions. 🛜 🖥 🍽 🏊 ✕

▼▼▼ Residence Inn by Marriott H
(417) 336-4077. **$99-$200.** 280 Wildwood Dr S 65616. Just s of jct Green Mountain Dr. Int corridors. **Pets:** Other species. $100 one-time fee/room. Service with restrictions, crate.
🛜 ✕ ♿ 🖥 🏊 ✕

AAA ▼▼▼ The Village At Indian Point CO
(417) 338-8800. **$130-$305, 31 day notice.** 24 Village Tr 65616. 2.5 mi s of jct SR 76 (Country Blvd) on Indian Point Rd. Ext corridors. **Pets:** Medium, dogs only. $15 daily fee/room. Designated rooms, no service, crate. [SAVE] 🛜 ✕ 🖥 🏊 ✕

HOLLISTER

AAA ▼▼▼ Westgate Branson Lakes at Emerald Pointe CO
(417) 334-4944. **$79-$259, 3 day notice.** 750 Emerald Pointe Dr 65672. Jct US 65 and SR 265, 1 mi w to Hill Haven Rd, then 2 mi s. Ext corridors. **Pets:** Accepted. [SAVE] 🛜 ✕ ♿ 🖥 🏊 ✕

END METROPOLITAN AREA

BROOKFIELD

AAA ▼▼▼ BEST WESTERN Brookfield H
(660) 258-4900. **$99-$119.** 28622 Hwy 11 64628. US 36 exit Business Rt 36, just se. Int corridors. **Pets:** Medium, dogs only. $10 daily fee/pet. Designated rooms, service with restrictions, crate.
[SAVE] 🛜 ♿ 🖥 🏊

CAMERON

AAA ▼▼▼ BEST WESTERN Acorn Inn M
(816) 632-2187. **$77-$85.** 2210 E US 36 64429. I-35 exit 54, 0.3 mi e. Ext corridors. **Pets:** Accepted. [SAVE] 🛜 🖥 🏊

▼▼ Days Inn H
(816) 632-6666. **$60-$67.** 601 E Bryan Rd 64429. I-35 exit 54, 0.5 mi w on US 36. Int corridors. **Pets:** Accepted. 🛜 🖥 🏊

▼▼ Super 8 H
(816) 632-8888. **$57-$150.** 1710 N Walnut St 64429. I-35 exit 54, 0.5 mi w on US 36. Int corridors. **Pets:** Small. $10 daily fee/pet. Designated rooms, service with restrictions, supervision. 🛜 🖥 🏊

CANTON

▼▼ Comfort Inn Canton H
(573) 288-8800. **$70-$104, 3 day notice.** 1701 Oak St 63435. US 61 exit US 61 business route/CR P, just e. Int corridors. **Pets:** Accepted.
🛜 🖥 🏊 ✕

CAPE GIRARDEAU

▼▼ Auburn Place Hotel & Suites H
(573) 651-4486. **$79-$139.** 3265 William St 63701. I-55 exit 96 (William St), just e. Ext/int corridors. **Pets:** Accepted.
🛜 ♿ 🖥 🏊 ✕

▼▼▼ Drury Lodge-Cape Girardeau H
(573) 334-7151. **$85-$144.** 104 S Vantage Dr 63701. I-55 exit 96 (William St), just e. Ext/int corridors. **Pets:** Service with restrictions, supervision. 🛜 🖥 🏊

▼▼▼ Drury Suites-Cape Girardeau H
(573) 339-9500. **$100-$154.** 3303 Campster Dr 63701. I-55 exit 96 (William St), just w. Int corridors. **Pets:** Service with restrictions, supervision.
🛜 ♿ 🖥 🏊 ✕

▼▼ **Hampton Inn-Cape Girardeau** 🅗
(573) 651-3000. **$98-$104.** 103 Cape W Pkwy 63701. I-55 exit 96 (William St), 0.3 mi sw. Int corridors. **Pets:** Accepted.
📶 ❌ 🅑ᴹ 🈁 🖥️

▼ **Pear Tree Inn by Drury-Cape Girardeau** 🅗
(573) 334-3000. **$65-$124.** 3248 William St 63701. I-55 exit 96 (William St), just e. Int corridors. **Pets:** Service with restrictions, supervision.
📶 🈁 ➦

CARTHAGE

🅐🅐🅐 ▼▼▼ **BEST WESTERN Precious Moments Hotel** 🅗
(417) 359-5900. **$80-$90.** 2701 Hazel St 64836. Just e of jct US 71 and SR HH. Int corridors. **Pets:** Medium, dogs only. $10 daily fee/room. Service with restrictions, crate. 🆂🅰🆅🅴 📶 ❌ 🈁 🖥️ 🏊

▼▼ **Econo Lodge** 🅗
(417) 358-3900. **Call for rates.** 1441 W Central Ave 64836. Just ne of jct US 71 and SR 96. Ext/int corridors. **Pets:** Accepted. 📶 🈁 ➦

▼▼ **Super 8** 🅗
(417) 359-9000. **$60-$90.** 416 W Fir Rd 64836. Just e of jct US 71 and SR HH. Int corridors. **Pets:** Accepted. 📶 🈁 🖥️

CHILLICOTHE

▼ **Chillicothe Super 8** 🅗
(660) 646-7888. **$57-$75.** 580 Business Hwy 36 E 64601. Jct US 36 and 65 (Washington St), 0.8 mi e. Int corridors. **Pets:** Other species. $10 daily fee/pet. Designated rooms, service with restrictions, supervision.
📶 🈁 🖥️

▼▼ **Econo Lodge Inn & Suites Chillicothe** 🅗
(660) 646-0572. **Call for rates.** 1020 S Washington St 64601. Jct US 36 and 65 (Washington St), just nw. Ext/int corridors. **Pets:** Accepted.
📶 ❌ 🅑ᴹ 🈁 🖥️ 🏊

COLUMBIA

▼▼ **Candlewood Suites** 🅗
(573) 817-0525. **Call for rates.** 3100 Wingate Ct 65201. I-70 exit 128A (US 63), just s, just e on I-70 Dr SE, then just s on Keene St. Int corridors. **Pets:** Accepted. 📶 🅑ᴹ 🈁 🖥️

▼▼▼ **Drury Inn-Columbia** 🅗
(573) 445-1800. **$115-$189.** 1000 Knipp St 65203. I-70 exit 124 (Stadium Blvd), just s. Int corridors. **Pets:** Service with restrictions, supervision.
📶 🈁 🖥️ ➦

▼▼ **Extended StayAmerica-Columbia-Stadium Blvd** 🅗
(573) 445-6800. **$59-$84.** 2000 Business Loop 70 W 65203. I-70 exit 124 (Stadium Blvd), just ne. Int corridors. **Pets:** $25 daily fee/pet. Designated rooms, service with restrictions. 📶 🈁 🖥️

🅐🅐🅐 ▼▼▼ **Holiday Inn Executive Center** 🅗
(573) 445-8531. **$119-$139.** 2200 I-70 Dr SW 65203. I-70 exit 124 (Stadium Blvd), just w. Int corridors. **Pets:** $30 one-time fee/room. Designated rooms, service with restrictions, supervision.
🆂🅰🆅🅴 📶 🅑ᴹ 🈁 🖥️ 🍴 ➦ ❌

▼▼ **Quality Inn** 🅗
(573) 449-2491. **$59-$129.** 1612 N Providence Rd 65202. I-70 exit 126 (Providence Rd), just n. Ext/int corridors. **Pets:** Medium. $15 daily fee/pet. Designated rooms, service with restrictions, supervision.
📶 🅑ᴹ 🈁 🖥️ ➦ ❌

▼▼ **Ramada** 🅗
(573) 443-4141. **$60-$140.** 901 Conley Rd 65201. I-70 exit 128A (US 63), just sw. Int corridors. **Pets:** $15 one-time fee/pet. Service with restrictions, supervision. 📶 🅑ᴹ 🈁 🖥️ ➦

▼▼▼ **Residence Inn by Marriott** 🅗
(573) 442-5601. **Call for rates.** 1100 Woodland Springs Ct 65202. I-70 exit 128A (US 63), just n, then 0.4 mi e. Int corridors. **Pets:** Accepted.
🆂🅰🆅🅴 📶 ❌ 🅑ᴹ 🈁 🖥️ ➦ ❌

▼▼▼ **Stoney Creek Inn & Conference Center** 🅗 🐾
(573) 442-6400. **$78-$300, 3 day notice.** 2601 S Providence Rd 65203. I-70 exit 126 (Providence Rd), 3 mi s; on west outer road. Int corridors. **Pets:** $25 daily fee/room. Designated rooms, service with restrictions, crate. 📶 ❌ 🈁 🖥️ ➦ ❌

▼ **Super 8 Columbia Clark Lane** 🅜
(573) 474-8488. **$59-$130.** 3216 Clark Ln 65202. I-70 exit 128A (US 63); northeast corner. Int corridors. **Pets:** Medium, other species. $15 daily fee/pet. Service with restrictions, supervision. 📶 🈁 🖥️

CUBA

🅐🅐🅐 ▼▼▼ **BEST WESTERN Cuba Inn** 🅜
(573) 885-7707. **$80-$100.** 246 Hwy P 65453. I-44 exit 208 (SR 19), just n, then just e. Ext corridors. **Pets:** Medium. $10 daily fee/pet. Designated rooms, service with restrictions, supervision. 🆂🅰🆅🅴 📶 🈁 🖥️ ➦

▼ **Super 8** 🅗
(573) 885-2087. **$60-$72.** 28 Hwy P 65453. I-44 exit 208 (SR 19), just n, then just w. Ext/int corridors. **Pets:** $15 one-time fee/pet. Designated rooms, service with restrictions, supervision. 📶 🈁 🖥️

FESTUS

▼▼ **Drury Inn-Festus** 🅗
(636) 933-2400. **$90-$149.** 1001 Veterans Blvd 63028. I-55 exit 175, just e. Int corridors. **Pets:** Service with restrictions, supervision.
📶 🈁 🖥️ ➦

FULTON

▼▼▼ **Loganberry Inn Bed & Breakfast** 🅑🅑 🐾
(573) 642-9229. **$99-$199, 14 day notice.** 310 W 7th St 65251. Jct US 54 exit CR F, 1 mi e, just n to Westminster Ave, then just e. Int corridors. **Pets:** Dogs only. $15 one-time fee/room. Designated rooms, service with restrictions, crate. 📶 ❌ 🈁 🖥️ 🆉

HANNIBAL

🅐🅐🅐 ▼▼▼ **Quality Inn & Suites** 🅗
(573) 221-4001. **$80-$120.** 120 Lindsey Dr 63401. 2 mi w on US 36 exit Shinn Ln to south service road, then 0.6 mi e. Int corridors. **Pets:** Medium. $10 daily fee/pet. Designated rooms, service with restrictions, supervision. 🆂🅰🆅🅴 📶 🈁 🖥️ ➦ ❌

▼ **Super 8** 🅜
(573) 221-5863. **$56-$110.** 120 Huckleberry Heights Dr 63401. Jct US 36, 1.5 mi s on US 61. Int corridors. **Pets:** Small, other species. $15 daily fee/pet. Designated rooms, service with restrictions, supervision.
📶 🈁 🖥️ ➦

HARRISONVILLE

🅐🅐🅐 ▼▼▼ **Comfort Inn & Suites** 🅗
(816) 884-4124. **$70-$85.** 2304 S Commercial St 64701. US 71 exit Commercial St, just e. Int corridors. **Pets:** Very small, dogs only. $10 daily fee/pet. Designated rooms, service with restrictions, supervision.
🆂🅰🆅🅴 📶 🅑ᴹ 🈁 🖥️ ➦

HAYTI

▼▼ **Drury Inn & Suites Hayti/Caruthersville** 🅗
(573) 359-2702. **$85-$149.** 1317 Hwy 84 63851. I-55 exit 19 (US 412/SR 84), just w. Int corridors. **Pets:** Service with restrictions, supervision.
📶 🈁 🖥️ ➦

JACKSON

🅐🅐🅐 ▼▼▼ **Comfort Suites** 🅗
(573) 204-0014. **$75-$140.** 2904 Old Orchard Rd 63755. I-55 exit 99, 0.5 mi e, then just n. Int corridors. **Pets:** Dogs only. $20 daily fee/pet. Designated rooms, service with restrictions, crate.
🆂🅰🆅🅴 📶 ❌ 🅑ᴹ 🈁 🖥️ ➦

▼▼▼▼ **Drury Inn & Suites-Jackson, MO** 🅷
(573) 243-9200. **$80-$164.** 225 Drury Ln 63755. I-55 exit 105 (SR 61), 0.3 mi w. Int corridors. **Pets:** Service with restrictions, supervision.
📶 🕭ᴹ 🛅 🖳 🏊

JANE
▼▼ ▼▼ **Booneslick Lodge** 🅷
(417) 226-1888. **$55-$76.** 21140 US Hwy 71 64856. Just s on US 71. Int corridors. **Pets:** Small. $10 daily fee/pet. Service with restrictions, supervision. 📶 🛅 🖳 🏊

JEFFERSON CITY
▼▼▼ **Capitol Plaza Hotel & Convention Center** 🅷
(573) 635-1234. **Call for rates.** 415 W McCarty St 65101. On US 50 and 63 S, just e of jct US 54. Int corridors. **Pets:** Medium, dogs only. $20 one-time fee/room. Service with restrictions, crate.
📶 ⊗ 🕭ᴹ 🛅 🖳 🍽 🏊

▼▼ ▼▼ **Super 8 Jefferson City** 🅷
(573) 636-5456. **$51-$75.** 1710 Jefferson St 65110. US 54 exit Ellis Blvd, 0.3 mi nw on frontage road. Int corridors. **Pets:** Accepted. 📶 🛅 🖳

JOPLIN
𝒜𝒜𝒜 ▼▼▼ **BEST WESTERN Oasis Inn & Suites** 🅷
(417) 781-6776. **$79-$149.** 3508 S Range Line Rd 64804. I-44 exit 8B, just nw. Ext corridors. **Pets:** Other species. $10 daily fee/pet. Service with restrictions, supervision. 🆂🅰🆅🅴 📶 🛅 🖳 🏊

𝒜𝒜𝒜 ▼▼▼▼ **Candlewood Suites** 🅷 🐾
(417) 623-9595. **$89-$139.** 3512 S Range Line Rd 64804. I-44 exit 8B, just nw. Int corridors. **Pets:** Other species. $75 one-time fee/pet. Crate.
🆂🅰🆅🅴 📶 🕭ᴹ 🛅 🖳

▼▼▼▼ **Drury Inn & Suites-Joplin** 🅷
(417) 781-8000. **$110-$189.** 3601 S Range Line Rd 64804. I-44 exit 8B, just ne. Int corridors. **Pets:** Service with restrictions, supervision.
📶 🕭ᴹ 🛅 🖳 🏊

▼▼▼ **Holiday Inn and Convention Center Joplin** 🅷
(417) 782-1000. **$109-$149.** 3615 S Range Line Rd 64804. I-44 exit 8B, just ne. Int corridors. **Pets:** Accepted. 📶 🛅 🖳 🍽 🏊

▼▼▼ **La Quinta Inn Joplin** 🅷
(417) 781-0500. **$83-$166.** 3320 S Range Line Rd 64804. I-44 exit 8B, just n. Int corridors. **Pets:** Service with restrictions, supervision.
📶 🛅 🖳 🍽 🏊

▼▼▼▼ **Residence Inn by Marriott-Joplin** 🅷 🐾
(417) 782-0908. **$99-$169.** 3128 E Hammons Blvd 64804. I-44 exit 8B, just ne. Int corridors. **Pets:** Large, other species. $75 one-time fee/room. Service with restrictions, crate. 📶 ⊗ 🕭ᴹ 🛅 🖳 🏊 ⊗

𝒜𝒜𝒜 ▼▼▼ **Sleep Inn** 🅷
(417) 782-1212. **Call for rates.** 4100 Hwy 43 S 64803. I-44 exit 4, just s. Int corridors. **Pets:** Large, other species. $15 one-time fee/room. Service with restrictions, supervision. 🆂🅰🆅🅴 📶 🖳

▼▼▼▼ **TownePlace Suites by Marriott Joplin** 🅷
(417) 659-8111. **$49-$109.** 4026 Arizona Ave 64804. I-44 exit 8A, just sw. Int corridors. **Pets:** Other species. $75 one-time fee/room. Service with restrictions. 📶 ⊗ 🕭ᴹ 🛅 🖳 🏊

KANSAS CITY METROPOLITAN AREA

BLUE SPRINGS
▼▼▼▼ **Hampton Inn Blue Springs** 🅷
(816) 220-3844. **$79-$99.** 900 NW South Outer Rd 64015. I-70 exit 20, just s on SR 7, then just w. Int corridors. **Pets:** Service with restrictions, supervision. 📶 🛅 🖳 🏊

INDEPENDENCE
𝒜𝒜𝒜 ▼▼▼ **BEST WESTERN Truman Inn** 🅷 🐾
(816) 254-0100. **$60-$100.** 4048 S Lynn Court Dr 64055. I-70 exit 12, just n on Noland Rd, then just w. Ext corridors. **Pets:** Medium, other species. $10 daily fee/pet. Service with restrictions, supervision.
🆂🅰🆅🅴 📶 🛅 🖳 🏊

▼▼▼▼ **Drury Inn & Suites Kansas City - Independence** 🅷
(816) 795-9393. **$105-$184.** 20300 E 42nd St S 64015. I-70 exit 17 (Little Blue Pkwy), just s. Int corridors. **Pets:** Service with restrictions, supervision. 📶 ⊗ 🕭ᴹ 🛅 🖳 🏊

▼▼◆▼ **Fairfield Inn by Marriott** 🅷
(816) 795-1616. **$89-$179.** 18700 E 37th Terr S 64057. I-70 exit 15B (SR 291 N), just e on 39th St, then just n on Arrowhead Ave. Int corridors. **Pets:** Accepted. 📶 ⊗ 🛅 🖳 🏊

𝒜𝒜𝒜 ▼▼▼▼ **Holiday Inn Express & Suites - Independence/ Kansas City** 🅷 🐾
(816) 795-8889. **Call for rates.** 19901 E Valley View Pkwy 64057. I-70 exit 17 (Little Blue Pkwy), just s, then just w. Int corridors. **Pets:** $25 one-time fee/pet. Designated rooms, service with restrictions, crate.
🆂🅰🆅🅴 📶 ⊗ 🕭ᴹ 🛅 🖳 🏊

𝒜𝒜𝒜 ▼▼ ▼▼ **Quality Inn & Suites-East** 🅷
(816) 373-8856. **$65-$160.** 4200 S Noland Rd 64055. I-70 exit 12, just s. Int corridors. **Pets:** Medium, other species. $10 daily fee/pet. Service with restrictions, supervision. 🆂🅰🆅🅴 📶 🛅 🖳 🏊

▼▼ ▼▼ **Super 8 Independence** 🅷
(816) 833-1888. **$55-$125.** 4032 S Lynn Court Dr 64055. I-70 exit 12, just n on Noland Rd, then just w. Int corridors. **Pets:** Medium, other species. $10 daily fee/pet. Service with restrictions, supervision.
📶 🛅 🖳 🏊

KANSAS CITY
𝒜𝒜𝒜 ▼▼▼ **BEST WESTERN Country Inn-North** Ⓜ
(816) 459-7222. **$55-$190.** 2633 NE 43rd St 64117. I-35 exit 8C (Antioch Rd), just s on SR 1, then just e. Ext corridors. **Pets:** Medium, other species. $10 daily fee/pet. Designated rooms, service with restrictions, crate.
🆂🅰🆅🅴 📶 🛅 🖳 🏊

𝒜𝒜𝒜 ▼▼▼ **BEST WESTERN PLUS Seville Plaza Hotel** 🅷
(816) 561-9600. **Call for rates.** 4309 Main St 64111. Jct 43rd St, just s. Int corridors. **Pets:** Large, dogs only. $10 daily fee/pet. Designated rooms, service with restrictions. 🆂🅰🆅🅴 📶 ⊗ 🕭ᴹ 🛅 🖳

▼▼▼▼ **Candlewood Suites Kansas City Airport** 🅷 🐾
(816) 886-9700. **$86-$96.** 11110 NW Ambassador Dr 64153. I-29 exit 12, just se. Int corridors. **Pets:** Medium, other species. $20 daily fee/pet. Designated rooms, service with restrictions, supervision. 📶 🕭ᴹ 🛅 🖳

▼▼▼▼ **Candlewood Suites Kansas City Northeast** 🅷
(816) 886-9311. **$79-$149.** 4450 N Randolph Rd 64117. I-435 exit 54, just s. Int corridors. **Pets:** Accepted. 📶 🛅 🖳 🏊

▼▼▼▼ **Chase Suite Hotel** 🅷
(816) 891-9009. **$99-$159.** 9900 NW Prairie View Rd 64153. I-29 exit 10, just w, then just n. Ext corridors. **Pets:** $150 deposit/room, $10 daily fee/pet. Designated rooms, service with restrictions, crate.
📶 ⊗ 🛅 🖳 🏊 ⊗

▼▼▼ Clarion Hotel 🅷
(816) 464-2423. **$89-$129.** 11828 NW Plaza Cir 64153. I-29 exit 13, just e on CR D, just s on Ambassador Dr, then just w. Int corridors.
Pets: Accepted. 🛜 ᴴ 🗐 💻 🍴 ᔕ

▼▼▼ Comfort Inn-Kansas City Airport 🅷 🐾
(816) 569-2500. **$70-$120.** 11100 NW Ambassador Dr 64153. I-29 exit 12, just se. Int corridors. **Pets:** Medium, other species. $20 daily fee/pet. Designated rooms, service with restrictions, supervision.
🛜 ✕ 🗐 💻 ᔕ

▼▼▼ Drury Inn & Suites-Kansas City Airport 🅷
(816) 880-9700. **$90-$199.** 7900 NW Tiffany Springs Pkwy 64153. I-29 exit 10, just w. Int corridors. **Pets:** Service with restrictions, supervision.
🛜 ᴴ 🗐 💻 ᔕ

▼▼▼ Drury Inn & Suites-Kansas City Stadium 🅷
(816) 923-3000. **$100-$184.** 3830 Blue Ridge Cutoff 64133. I-70 exit 9 (Blue Ridge Cutoff), just nw. Int corridors. **Pets:** Service with restrictions, supervision. 🛜 ᴴ 🗐 💻 ᔕ

▼▼▼ Embassy Suites Kansas City-International Airport 🅷
(816) 891-7788. **$109-$239.** 7640 NW Tiffany Springs Pkwy 64153. I-29 exit 10, just e. Int corridors. **Pets:** Accepted.
🛜 ᴴ 🗐 💻 🍴 ᔕ

▼▼▼ Fairfield Inn & Suites by Marriott Kansas City North Near Worlds of Fun 🅷
(816) 452-6212. **$109-$159.** 4231 N Corrington Ave 64117. I-435 exit 54 northbound, just w on Parvin Rd; exit southbound, 1 mi s on service road, just w on Parvin Rd, then just n. Int corridors. **Pets:** Accepted.
🛜 ✕ ᴴ 🗐 💻 ᔕ

AAA ▼▼▼ Hilton Kansas City Airport 🅷
(816) 891-8900. **$89-$189.** 8801 NW 112th St 64153. I-29 exit 12, just se. Int corridors. **Pets:** Medium, dogs only. $75 one-time fee/room. Designated rooms, supervision. SAVE 🛜 ᴴ 🗐 💻 🍴 ᔕ ✕

AAA ▼▼▼ Holiday Inn Country Club Plaza 🅷
(816) 753-7400. **$89-$149.** 1 E 45th St 64111. Jct Main St; in Country Club Plaza. Int corridors. **Pets:** Other species. $50 deposit/pet, $25 daily fee/pet. Designated rooms, service with restrictions, supervision.
SAVE 🛜 ✕ ᴴ 🗐 💻 ᔕ

AAA ▼▼▼ Holiday Inn Kansas City Northeast 🅷
(816) 455-1060. **$79-$129.** 7333 NE Parvin Rd 64117. I-435 exit 54, just w. Int corridors. **Pets:** $25 one-time fee/room. Service with restrictions, crate. SAVE 🛜 ᴴ 🗐 💻 🍴 ᔕ ✕

▼▼▼ Holiday Inn Kansas City SE - Water Park 🅷
(816) 737-0200. **$119-$149.** 9103 E 39th St 64133. I-70 exit 8B eastbound; 9 westbound, just ne. Int corridors. **Pets:** Accepted.
🛜 ✕ 🗐 💻 🍴 ᔕ ✕

AAA ▼▼▼ Holiday Inn KCI Airport & Expo Center 🅷 🐾
(816) 801-8400. **$109-$149.** 11728 NW Ambassador Dr 64153. I-29 exit 13, just e on CR D, then just s. Int corridors. **Pets:** Small, other species. $35 one-time fee/room. Designated rooms, service with restrictions, supervision. SAVE 🛜 ✕ ᴴ 🗐 💻 🍴 ᔕ

▼▼ Homestead Studio Suites-Kansas City/Country Club Plaza 🅷
(816) 531-2212. **$81-$114.** 4535 Main St 64111. Jct 45th St, just s; just ne of Country Club Plaza. Int corridors. **Pets:** $25 daily fee/pet. Designated rooms, service with restrictions. 🛜 ᴴ 🗐 💻

▼▼▼ Homewood Suites by Hilton 🅷
(816) 880-9880. **$99-$219.** 7312 NW Polo Dr 64153. I-29 exit 10, just e. Int corridors. **Pets:** Large, other species. $75 one-time fee/room. Service with restrictions. 🛜 🗐 💻 ᔕ ✕

AAA ▼▼▼ Hotel Phillips 🅷 🐾
(816) 221-7000. **$109-$249.** 106 W 12th St 64105. Jct Wyandotte St, just e. Int corridors. **Pets:** Large, other species. $50 one-time fee/pet. Designated rooms, service with restrictions, crate.
SAVE 🛜 ✕ 💻 🍴

AAA ▼▼▼▼ The InterContinental Kansas City at the Plaza 🅷
(816) 756-1500. **$149-$309.** 401 Ward Pkwy 64112. Jct Wornall Rd; in Country Club Plaza. Int corridors. **Pets:** Accepted.
SAVE 🛜 ✕ 💻 🍴 ᔕ ✕

▼▼▼ The Q Hotel + Spa 🅷
(816) 931-0001. **$109-$139.** 560 Westport Rd 64111. Jct Main St, 0.4 mi w; in Westport Plaza area. Int corridors. **Pets:** Medium. $50 one-time fee/room. Designated rooms. ECO 🛜 ✕ 🗐 💻

▼▼▼ Residence Inn by Marriott Downtown/Union Hill 🅷
(816) 561-3000. **$109-$219.** 2975 Main St 64108. Jct 31st St, just n. Ext corridors. **Pets:** Accepted. ECO 🛜 ✕ 🗐 💻 ᔕ

▼▼▼ Residence Inn by Marriott, Kansas City Airport 🅷
(816) 741-2300. **$89-$209.** 10300 N Ambassador Dr 64153. I-29 exit 10, 1.5 mi ne. Int corridors. **Pets:** Medium, other species. $100 one-time fee/room. Designated rooms, service with restrictions.
🛜 ✕ ᴴ 🗐 💻 ✕

▼▼▼ Residence Inn by Marriott Kansas City Country Club Plaza 🅷
(816) 753-0033. **$129-$189.** 4601 Broadway Blvd 64112. Jct J.C. Nichols Pkwy, just w on 46th Terr; in Country Club Plaza. Int corridors. **Pets:** Medium. $100 one-time fee/room. Service with restrictions, supervision. 🛜 ✕ 🗐 💻 ᔕ ✕

AAA ▼▼▼ The Sheraton Kansas City Hotel at Crown Center 🅷
(816) 841-1000. **$99-$399.** 2345 McGee St 64108. In Crown Center area. Int corridors. **Pets:** Accepted.
ECO SAVE 🛜 ✕ ᴴ 🗐 💻 🍴 ᔕ ✕

AAA ▼▼▼ Sheraton Suites Country Club Plaza 🅷
(816) 931-4400. **$149-$329.** 770 W 47th St 64112. Jct Summit St; in Country Club Plaza. Int corridors. **Pets:** Accepted.
SAVE 🛜 ✕ ᴴ 🗐 💻 ᔕ

▼▼ Sleep Inn-KCI 🅷
(816) 891-0111. **$54-$100.** 7611 NW 97th Terr 64153. I-29 exit 10, just sw. Int corridors. **Pets:** Large. $20 one-time fee/room. Designated rooms, service with restrictions, supervision. 🛜 ᴴ 🗐 💻 ᔕ

AAA ▼▼▼▼ The Westin Kansas City at Crown Center 🅷
(816) 474-4400. **$99-$359.** 1 E Pershing Rd 64108. 0.5 mi s. Int corridors. **Pets:** Accepted. SAVE 🛜 ✕ ᴴ 🗐 💻 🍴 ᔕ ✕

KEARNEY

AAA ▼▼▼ Kearney Super 8 🅷
(816) 628-6800. **$49-$108.** 210 Platte Clay Way 64060. I-35 exit 26, just e on SR 92, then just n. Int corridors. **Pets:** Medium. $10 daily fee/pet. Designated rooms, service with restrictions, crate.
SAVE 🛜 🗐 ᔕ

▼▼ Quality Inn 🅷
(816) 628-5000. **Call for rates.** 601 Centerville Ave 64060. I-35 exit 26, just w. Int corridors. **Pets:** Medium, dogs only. $10 daily fee/pet. Service with restrictions, supervision. 🛜 🗐 💻 ᔕ

NORTH KANSAS CITY

▼▼▼ Harrah's North Kansas City Casino and Hotel 🅷
(816) 472-7777. **Call for rates.** One Riverboat Dr 64116. I-29/35 exit 6A, 1.4 mi e on SR 210, then just s on Chouteau Thrwy. Int corridors.
Pets: Accepted. 🛜 ᴴ 🗐 💻 🍴

▼▼▼ La Quinta Inn Kansas City North **H**

(816) 221-1200. **$59-$129.** 2214 Taney Rd 64116. I-29/35 exit 6A, just e on SR 210, then just n. Int corridors. **Pets:** Service with restrictions, supervision. 🛜 📶 🖥️

OAK GROVE (JACKSON COUNTY)

▼ Econo Lodge **M**

(816) 690-3681. **Call for rates.** 410 SE 1st St 64075. I-70 exit 28, just s on Broadway St, just e on SE 4th St, then just n. Ext corridors. **Pets:** Small. $10 daily fee/pet. Service with restrictions, supervision. 🛜 📶 🖥️

PLATTE CITY

◉◉◉ **▼▼▼** BEST WESTERN Airport Inn & Suites/KCI North **H** 🐾

(816) 858-0200. **Call for rates.** 2512 NW Prairie View Rd 64079. I-29 exit 18, just e, then just s. Int corridors. **Pets:** Large, other species. $25 one-time fee/pet. Designated rooms, service with restrictions, supervision. ⟨SAVE⟩ 🛜 ♿M 📶 🖥️ 🏊

END METROPOLITAN AREA

KIRKSVILLE

▼ Super 8-Kirksville **M**

(660) 665-8826. **$69-$89.** 1101 Country Club Dr 63501. On US 63 and SR 6. Int corridors. **Pets:** Other species. $10 daily fee/pet. Designated rooms, service with restrictions, crate. 🛜 📶 🖥️

LAKE OZARK

▼▼▼ The Resort at Port Arrowhead **H**

(573) 365-2334. **$80-$140, 3 day notice.** 3080 Bagnell Dam Blvd 65049. 2.6 mi s of Bagnell Dam. Ext/int corridors. **Pets:** Accepted. 🛜 ♿M 📶 🖥️ 🍴 🏊 ⊗

LAMAR

▼ ▼ Super 8-Lamar **H**

(417) 682-6888. **$60-$83.** 45 SE 1st Ln 64759. Jct US 71 and 160. Ext/int corridors. **Pets:** Accepted. 🛜 📶 🖥️ 🏊

LEBANON

◉◉◉ **▼▼▼** BEST WESTERN Wyota Inn **H**

(417) 532-6171. **$77-$101.** 1221 Mill Creek Rd 65536. I-44 exit 130, just nw. Ext corridors. **Pets:** Accepted. ⟨SAVE⟩ 🛜 📶 🖥️ 🏊

LICKING

▼ Scenic Rivers Inn **M**

(573) 674-4809. **$60-$70.** 209 S Hwy 63 65542. On US 63. Ext corridors. **Pets:** Medium. $10 daily fee/pet. Designated rooms, service with restrictions, supervision. 🛜 📶 🖥️ 🏊

LINN

▼ Settle Inn & Suites **H**

(573) 897-9903. **$79-$119.** 1639 US Hwy 50 E 65051. 1 mi e of jct US 50 and SR 89. Int corridors. **Pets:** Medium, dogs only. $15 daily fee/pet. Designated rooms, service with restrictions, supervision. 🛜 📶 🖥️ 🏊

MACON

▼ Super 8 **H**

(660) 385-5788. **$79-$84.** 203 E Briggs Dr 63552. Jct US 36 and 63. Int corridors. **Pets:** Other species. $25 one-time fee/room. Service with restrictions, crate. 🛜 ⊗ 📶 🖥️

MARSHFIELD

▼▼ Holiday Inn Express **H**

(417) 859-6000. **$95-$105.** 1301 Banning St 65706. I-44 exit 100 (SR 38); on southeast corner. Int corridors. **Pets:** Accepted. 🛜 ♿M 📶 🖥️ 🏊

MARYVILLE

▼▼ Super 8 **H**

(660) 582-8088. **$52-$60.** 222 E Summit Dr 64468. On Business Rt US 71; just n of US 71 Bypass. Int corridors. **Pets:** Other species. $10 deposit/room. Service with restrictions, supervision. 🛜 ⊗ 📶 🖥️

MINER

▼▼▼ Drury Inn & Suites-Sikeston **H**

(573) 472-2299. **$105-$174.** 2608 E Malone Ave 63801. I-55 exit 67, just nw. Int corridors. **Pets:** Service with restrictions, supervision. 🛜 📶 🖥️ 🏊

▼▼ Pear Tree Inn by Drury **H**

(573) 471-4100. **$80-$149.** 2602 E Malone Ave 63801. I-55 exit 67, just nw. Int corridors. **Pets:** Service with restrictions, supervision. 🛜 ♿M 📶 🖥️ 🏊

OSAGE BEACH

▼▼ Dogwood Hills Golf Resort **H**

(573) 348-1735. **$53-$115.** 1252 State Hwy KK 65065. US 54 exit SR KK; 0.5 mi n. Ext corridors. **Pets:** Accepted. 🛜 📶 🖥️ 🍴 🏊

PACIFIC

◉◉◉ **▼▼▼** Quality Inn Near Six Flags **H**

(636) 257-8400. **$69-$109.** 1400 W Osage St 63069. I-44 exit 257, just se. Ext/int corridors. **Pets:** Medium. $10 daily fee/pet. Designated rooms, service with restrictions, supervision. ⟨SAVE⟩ 🛜 📶 🖥️ 🏊

PERRYVILLE

▼▼ Days Inn **M**

(573) 547-1091. **$60-$105.** 1500 Liberty St 63775. I-55 exit 129 (SR 51). Int corridors. **Pets:** Small, dogs only. $10 daily fee/pet. Designated rooms, service with restrictions, supervision. 🛜 📶 🏊

POPLAR BLUFF

▼▼ Drury Inn-Poplar Bluff **H**

(573) 686-2451. **$95-$134.** 2220 N Westwood Blvd 63901. 1.4 mi se of jct US 60 and 67. Int corridors. **Pets:** Service with restrictions, supervision. 🛜 📶 🖥️ 🏊 ⊗

▼▼ Super 8 **H**

(573) 785-0176. **$65-$70.** 2831 N Westwood Blvd 63901. 0.7 mi se of jct US 60 and 67. Int corridors. **Pets:** Medium. $50 one-time fee/room. Designated rooms, service with restrictions, supervision. 🛜 📶 🖥️

POTOSI

▼ Potosi Super 8 **H**

(573) 438-8888. **$60-$64.** 820 E High St 63664. Jct SR 8 and 21. Ext/int corridors. **Pets:** $10 one-time fee/pet. Designated rooms, service with restrictions, supervision. 🛜 📶 🖥️

REPUBLIC

▼▼ AmericInn Lodge & Suites of Republic **H** 🐾

(417) 732-5335. **$85-$140.** 950 N Austin Ln 65738. I-44 exit 67, 4.4 mi s to SR 174, then 0.7 mi e. Int corridors. **Pets:** Medium. $10 daily fee/pet. Designated rooms, service with restrictions, supervision. 🛜 📶 🖥️ 🏊

ROLLA

▼▼ ▼▼ Baymont Inn & Suites 🏨
(573) 364-7000. **$85-$119.** 1801 Martin Springs Dr 65401. I-44 exit 184, just sw. Int corridors. **Pets:** Accepted. 🛜 ⓜ 🛏 💻 ⤷

◈◈◈⁄ ▼▼▼ BEST WESTERN Coachlight Ⓜ
(573) 341-2511. **$70-$90.** 1403 Martin Springs Dr 65401. Jct I-44 and Business Rt 44 S exit 184. Ext corridors. **Pets:** Other species. $20 daily fee/pet. Designated rooms, service with restrictions, crate.
🆂🅰🆅🅴 🛜 🛏 💻 ⤷

▼▼ ▼▼ Drury Inn-Rolla 🏨
(573) 364-4000. **$90-$129.** 2006 N Bishop Ave 65401. I-44 exit 186 (US 63), just ne. Int corridors. **Pets:** Service with restrictions, supervision.
🛜 🛏 💻 ⤷

◈◈◈⁄ ▼▼ ▼▼ Super 8 Rolla 🏨 🐾
(573) 426-6688. **$74-$89.** 1641 Martin Springs Dr 65401. I-44 exit 184, just sw. Int corridors. **Pets:** Other species. $25 one-time fee/pet. Service with restrictions. 🆂🅰🆅🅴 🛜 ⓜ 🛏 💻 ⤷

ST. CLAIR

▼▼ ▼▼ Budget Lodging Ⓜ
(636) 629-1000. **$69-$79.** 866 S Outer Rd 63077. I-44 exit 240, just w. Ext corridors. **Pets:** Dogs only. $10 daily fee/pet. Designated rooms, service with restrictions, supervision. 🛜 🛏 💻 ⤷

ST. JOSEPH

▼▼▼ Drury Inn & Suites-St. Joseph 🏨
(816) 364-4700. **$105-$164.** 4213 Frederick Blvd 64506. I-29 exit 47, just e. Int corridors. **Pets:** Service with restrictions, supervision.
🛜 ⓜ 🛏 💻 ⤷ 🗙

▼▼ ▼▼ ▼ St. Joseph Holiday Inn-Riverfront 🏨
(816) 279-8000. **Call for rates.** 102 S Third St 64501. I-229 exit Edmond St northbound; exit Felix St southbound; downtown. Int corridors.
Pets: Accepted. 🛜 ⓜ 🛏 💻 🍴 ⤷ 🗙

ST. LOUIS METROPOLITAN AREA

BRIDGETON

◈◈◈⁄ ▼▼▼▼ Crowne Plaza St. Louis Airport 🏨
(314) 291-6700. **$89-$169.** 11228 Lone Eagle Dr 63044. I-70 exit 235A (Lindbergh Blvd/US 67), just s, then just w. Int corridors. **Pets:** Medium, other species. $50 deposit/room. Designated rooms, service with restrictions, crate. 🆂🅰🆅🅴 🛜 ⓜ 🛏 💻 🍴 ⤷

CHESTERFIELD

▼▼▼▼ Drury Plaza Hotel-Chesterfield 🏨
(636) 532-3300. **$110-$314.** 355 Chesterfield Center E 63017. I-64/US 40 exit 19B (Clarkson Rd/Olive Blvd); jct I-64/US 40 and Clarkson Rd; southwest corner. Int corridors. **Pets:** Service with restrictions, supervision.
🛜 ⓜ 🛏 💻 🍴 ⤷

▼▼▼▼ Hampton Inn-Chesterfield 🏨
(636) 537-2500. **$104-$124.** 16201 Swingley Ridge Rd 63017. I-64/US 40 exit 19B (Clarkson Rd/Olive Blvd). Int corridors. **Pets:** Accepted.
🛜 🛏 💻 ⤷ 🗙

▼▼ ▼▼ Homewood Suites by Hilton 🏨
(636) 530-0305. **$89-$139.** 840 Chesterfield Pkwy W 63017. I-64/US 40 exit 20 (Chesterfield Pkwy), 0.6 mi n. Int corridors. **Pets:** Other species. $25 daily fee/room. Service with restrictions. 🛜 🛏 💻 ⤷

CLAYTON

◈◈◈⁄ ▼▼▼ Crowne Plaza St. Louis-Clayton 🏨 🐾
(314) 726-5400. **$99-$199.** 7750 Carondelet Ave 63105. I-64 exit 32B (Hanley Rd), 1.3 mi n, then just w. Int corridors. **Pets:** Dogs only. $25 deposit/pet. Designated rooms, service with restrictions, crate.
🆂🅰🆅🅴 🛜 🛏 💻 🍴 ⤷

◈◈◈⁄ ▼▼ ▼▼ The Ritz-Carlton, St. Louis 🏨
(314) 863-6300. **$199-$499.** 100 Carondelet Plaza 63105. I-64 exit 32B (Hanley Rd), 1.2 mi n, then just w. Int corridors. **Pets:** Accepted.
🆂🅰🆅🅴 🛜 🗙 💻 🍴 ⤷ 🗙

◈◈◈⁄ ▼▼ ▼▼ Sheraton Clayton Plaza Hotel 🏨
(314) 863-0400. **$89-$309, 3 day notice.** 7730 Bonhomme Ave 63105. I-64 exit 31 (Brentwood Blvd), 1.3 mi n, then 0.7 mi e. Int corridors.
Pets: Accepted. 🆂🅰🆅🅴 🛜 🗙 🛏 💻 🍴 ⤷

CREVE COEUR

▼▼▼ Drury Inn & Suites-Creve Coeur 🏨
(314) 989-1100. **$85-$189.** 11980 Olive Blvd 63141. I-270 exit 14 (Olive Blvd), just e. Int corridors. **Pets:** Service with restrictions, supervision.
🛜 🗙 ⓜ 🛏 💻 ⤷

EARTH CITY

▼▼ ▼▼ Candlewood Suites St. Louis 🏨
(314) 770-2744. **$70-$100.** 3250 Rider Tr S 63045. I-70 exit 231B (Earth City Expwy N), just n, then just e. Int corridors. **Pets:** Accepted.
🛜 🛏 💻

▼▼ ▼▼ Residence Inn by Marriott St. Louis Airport/Earth City 🏨
(314) 209-0995. **$85-$130.** 3290 Rider Tr S 63045. I-70 exit 231B (Earth City Expwy N), just n, then just e. Int corridors. **Pets:** Accepted.
🛜 🗙 ⓜ 🛏 💻 ⤷ 🗙

EDMUNDSON

▼▼▼ Drury Inn-St. Louis Airport 🏨
(314) 423-7700. **$90-$194.** 10490 Natural Bridge Rd 63134. I-70 exit 236 (Lambert Airport), just s, then just n. Int corridors. **Pets:** Service with restrictions, supervision. 🛜 ⓜ 🛏 💻 ⤷

◈◈◈⁄ ▼▼▼▼ Marriott-St. Louis Airport 🏨
(314) 423-9700. **$79-$209.** 10700 Pear Tree Ln 63134. I-70 exit 236 (Lambert Airport), just s. Int corridors. **Pets:** Accepted.
🆂🅰🆅🅴 🛜 🗙 🛏 💻 🍴 ⤷

EUREKA

▼▼▼ Holiday Inn at Six Flags 🏨
(636) 938-6661. **$99-$159, 3 day notice.** 4901 Six Flags Rd 63025. I-44 exit 261 (Allenton Rd). Ext/int corridors. **Pets:** $25 daily fee/room. Service with restrictions, crate. 🛜 🛏 💻 🍴 ⤷ 🗙

FENTON

▼▼▼ Drury Inn & Suites-Fenton 🏨
(636) 343-7822. **$90-$174.** 1088 S Highway Dr 63026. I-44 exit 274 (Bowles Ave), just se. Int corridors. **Pets:** Service with restrictions, supervision. 🛜 🛏 💻 ⤷

▼▼ ▼▼ Pear Tree Inn by Drury-Fenton 🏨
(636) 343-8820. **$65-$134.** 1100 S Highway Dr 63026. I-44 exit 274 (Bowles Ave), just s. Int corridors. **Pets:** Service with restrictions, supervision. 🛜 🛏 💻 ⤷

▼▼ ▼▼ TownePlace Suites by Marriott 🏨
(636) 305-7000. **$89-$139.** 1662 Fenton Business Park Ct 63026. I-44 exit 275 westbound; exit 274 eastbound to S Highway Dr, just s. Int corridors. **Pets:** Other species. $50 one-time fee/room. Designated rooms, service with restrictions, crate. 🛜 🗙 ⓜ 🛏 💻 ⤷

FORISTELL

AAA ▼▼▼ **Quality Inn** H
(636) 673-2900. **$65-$95.** 12 Hwy W 63348. I-70 exit 203 (CR W), just n. Int corridors. **Pets:** Large. $15 daily fee/room. Service with restrictions, supervision. (SAVE) 🛰 🖥 🖵

KIRKWOOD

AAA ▼▼▼ **BEST WESTERN Kirkwood Inn** H 🐾
(314) 821-3950. **$90-$140.** 1200 S Kirkwood Rd 63122. I-44 exit 277B (Lindbergh Blvd), just n. Int corridors. **Pets:** Large, other species. $10 daily fee/pet. Designated rooms, service with restrictions, crate.
(SAVE) 🛰 ✕ 🖥 🖵 ⍟ ⌕

MARYLAND HEIGHTS

AAA ▼▼▼ **DoubleTree by Hilton Hotel St. Louis-Westport** H
(314) 434-0100. **$85-$179.** 1973 Craigshire Rd 63146. I-270 exit 16A (Page Ave), just e to Lackland Rd, then 0.4 mi sw on Lackland and Craigshire rds. Int corridors. **Pets:** Accepted.
(ECO) (SAVE) 🛰 🖥 🖵 ⍟ ⌕ ✕

▼▼▼ **Drury Inn & Suites-St. Louis-Westport** H
(314) 576-9966. **$95-$179.** 12220 Dorsett Rd 63043. I-270 exit 17 (Dorsett Rd), just e. Int corridors. **Pets:** Service with restrictions, supervision. 🛰 🖥 🖵 ⍟

AAA ▼▼▼▼ **Hollywood Casino & Hotel** H
(314) 770-8100. **$89-$499.** 777 Casino Center Dr 63043. I-70 exit 231A (Earth City Expwy S), 1 mi s, then 1.2 mi nw. Int corridors.
Pets: Accepted. (SAVE) 🛰 ⌕ 🖥 🖵 ⍟

▼▼▼▼ **Residence Inn by Marriott-Westport** H
(314) 469-0060. **$99-$209.** 1881 Craigshire Rd 63146. I-270 exit 16A (Page Ave), 0.8 mi e to Lackland Rd exit, just w, just s on Craig Rd, then just w. Ext corridors. **Pets:** Accepted. 🛰 ✕ 🖥 🖵 ⍟ ✕

▼▼▼▼ **Sheraton Westport Lakeside Chalet** H
(314) 878-1500. **$89-$179.** 191 Westport Plaza Dr 63146. I-270 exit 16A (Page Ave), 0.8 mi e to Lackland Rd exit, just w, then 0.4 mi n. Int corridors. **Pets:** Accepted. (SAVE) 🛰 ✕ ⌕ 🖥 🖵 ⍟ ⌕ ✕

AAA ▼▼▼▼ **Sheraton Westport Plaza Tower** H
(314) 878-1500. **$89-$199.** 900 Westport Plaza 63146. I-270 exit 16A (Page Ave), 0.8 mi e; exit Lackland Rd, just w, then just n. Int corridors. **Pets:** Accepted. (SAVE) 🛰 ✕ ⌕ 🖥 🖵 ⍟ ⌕

AAA ▼▼▼▼ **Sonesta ES Suites** H
(314) 878-1555. **Call for rates.** 1855 Craigshire Rd 63146. I-270 exit 16A (Page Ave), 0.8 mi e to Lackland Rd exit, 1 mi w, 0.4 mi s on Craig Rd, then just e. Ext/int corridors. **Pets:** Large, other species. $15 daily fee/room. Service with restrictions. (SAVE) 🛰 🖥 🖵 ⍟ ✕

MEHLVILLE

AAA ▼▼▼ **BEST WESTERN St. Louis Inn** H
(314) 416-7639. **$70-$110.** 6224 Heimos Industrial Park Dr 63129. I-55 exit 193, just e on Meramec Bottom Rd, then just n. Int corridors. **Pets:** Small, other species. $10 daily fee/pet. Designated rooms, no service, supervision. (SAVE) 🛰 🖥 🖵 ⍟

▼▼▼▼ **Holiday Inn St. Louis-South I-55** H
(314) 894-0700. **$109-$179.** 4234 Butler Hill Rd 63129. I-55 exit 195 (Butler Hill Rd), just e, then just s. Ext/int corridors. **Pets:** Medium, other species. $15 daily fee/room. Service with restrictions, crate.
🛰 🖥 🖵 ⍟ ⌕ ✕

O'FALLON

AAA ▼▼▼▼ **Hilton Garden Inn St. Louis/O'Fallon** H
(636) 625-2700. **$89-$219.** 2310 Technology Dr 63368. US 40/61 exit 6 (Wing Haven Blvd/CR DD), just ne; I-70 exit 216 (Bryan Rd), 4.2 mi s. Int corridors. **Pets:** Accepted. (SAVE) 🛰 ✕ ⌕ 🖥 🖵 ⍟ ⌕

▼▼▼▼ **Staybridge Suites O'Fallon** H
(636) 300-0999. **$99-$159.** 1155 Technology Dr 63368. US 40/61 exit 9 (CR K), just nw. Int corridors. **Pets:** Large. $50 one-time fee/room. Service with restrictions, crate. 🛰 ⌕ 🖥 🖵 ⍟

RICHMOND HEIGHTS

▼▼▼ **Residence Inn by Marriott-St. Louis Galleria** H
(314) 862-1900. **$119-$199.** 8011 Galleria Pkwy 63117. I-170 exit 1C (Brentwood Blvd) northbound; exit 1D southbound, just s, just e on Galleria Pkwy, then just s. Ext corridors. **Pets:** Accepted.
(ECO) 🛰 ✕ ⌕ 🖥 🖵 ⍟ ✕

ST. ANN

▼▼▼ **Hampton Inn-St. Louis Airport** H
(314) 429-2000. **$89-$189.** 10820 Pear Tree Ln 63074. I-70 exit 236 (Airport Dr), just sw. Int corridors. **Pets:** Accepted. 🛰 🖥 🖵 ⍟

▼▼ **Pear Tree Inn by Drury-St. Louis Airport** H
(314) 427-3400. **$75-$140.** 10810 Pear Tree Ln 63074. I-70 exit 236 (Airport Dr), just sw. Int corridors. **Pets:** Service with restrictions, supervision. 🛰 🖥 🖵 ⍟

ST. CHARLES

▼▼▼ **Comfort Suites-St. Charles** H
(636) 949-0694. **Call for rates.** 1400 S 5th St 63301. I-70 exit 229 (5th St), just ne. Int corridors. **Pets:** Accepted. 🛰 ✕ ⌕ 🖥 🖵 ⍟

▼▼▼ **TownePlace Suites by Marriott** H
(636) 949-6800. **$89-$99.** 1800 Zumbehl Rd 63303. I-70 exit 227 (Zumbehl Rd), 0.6 mi s, then just se. Int corridors. **Pets:** Accepted.
🛰 ✕ 🖥 🖵 ⍟

ST. LOUIS

AAA ▼▼▼▼ **The Cheshire** H
(314) 647-7300. **$131-$316.** 6300 Clayton Rd 63117. I-64/US 40 exit 34A (Clayton Rd/Skinker Blvd), 0.4 mi w. Int corridors. **Pets:** Accepted.
(SAVE) 🛰 ✕ 🖥 🖵 ⍟ ⌕

AAA ▼▼▼▼ **Crowne Plaza St. Louis Downtown** H
(314) 621-8200. **$79-$189.** 200 N 4th St 63102. I-70 exit 250B (Stadium/Memorial Dr), just w; at 4th and Pine sts. Int corridors. **Pets:** Accepted.
(SAVE) 🛰 🖥 🖵 ⍟ ⌕

▼▼▼ **Drury Inn & Suites Near Forest Park** H
(314) 646-0770. **$125-$239.** 2111 Sulphur Ave 63139. I-44 exit 286, just s. Int corridors. **Pets:** Service with restrictions, supervision.
🛰 ⌕ 🖥 🖵 ⍟ ⌕

▼▼▼ **Drury Inn & Suites-St. Louis-Convention Center** H
(314) 231-8100. **$100-$219.** 711 N Broadway 63102. I-70 exit 250B (Stadium/Memorial Dr), at convention center. Int corridors. **Pets:** Service with restrictions, supervision. 🛰 🖥 🖵 ⍟ ⌕

▼▼▼ **Drury Inn-St. Louis/Union Station** H
(314) 231-3900. **$120-$204.** 201 S 20th St 63103. Just e of Jefferson Ave; between Market St and Clark Ave. Int corridors. **Pets:** Service with restrictions, supervision. 🛰 🖥 🖵 ⍟ ⌕

▼▼▼ **Drury Plaza Hotel-St. Louis at the Arch** H
(314) 231-3003. **$105-$309.** 2 S 4th St 63102. I-70 exit 250B (Stadium/Memorial Dr), just w on Pine St to Broadway, just s to Walnut St, just e to 4th St, then just n. Int corridors. **Pets:** Service with restrictions, supervision. 🛰 ⌕ 🖥 🖵 ⍟ ⌕

AAA ▼▼▼▼ **Four Seasons Hotel St. Louis** H 🐾
(314) 881-5800. **$235-$495.** 999 N 2nd St 63102. I-70 exit 250A, just s, 1.1 mi e, then just s. Int corridors. **Pets:** Medium, other species. Service with restrictions, crate. (SAVE) 🛰 ⌕ 🖵 ⍟ ⌕ ✕

Hilton St. Louis at the Ballpark H ❀
(314) 421-1776. **$94-$294.** 1 S Broadway 63102. Between Walnut and Market sts. Int corridors. **Pets:** Medium, other species. $75 one-time fee/room. Service with restrictions, supervision.

Hilton-St. Louis Downtown H ❀
(314) 436-0002. **$98-$224.** 400 Olive St 63102. I-70 exit 249C/251C (6th St) to N Broadway to Olive St. Int corridors. **Pets:** Large, other species. $50 one-time fee/room. Service with restrictions, crate.

Holiday Inn Forest Park H
(314) 645-0700. **$99-$159.** 5915 Wilson Ave 63110. I-44 exit 286, just n. Int corridors. **Pets:** Accepted.

Hotel Ignacio H
(314) 977-4400. **Call for rates.** 3411 Olive St 63103. Jct Compton Ave and Olive St, 0.3 mi w. Int corridors. **Pets:** Large, dogs only. $75 one-time fee/room. Designated rooms, service with restrictions, crate.

Hyatt Regency St. Louis at The Arch H
(314) 655-1234. **$71-$342.** 315 Chestnut St 63102. I-70 exit 250B (Stadium/Memorial Dr); at 4th and Chestnut sts. Int corridors. **Pets:** Accepted.

Moonrise Hotel H ❀
(314) 721-1111. **$119-$279.** 6177 Delmar Blvd 63112. I-64 exit 38A, 2.4 mi on Forest Park Pkwy, 0.4 mi n on Skinker Blvd, then just e; in The Loop. Int corridors. **Pets:** $50 one-time fee/pet. Designated rooms, service with restrictions.

Omni Majestic Hotel H ❀
(314) 436-2355. **$159-$279.** 1019 Pine St 63101. Jct N Broadway, just w; at 10th St. Int corridors. **Pets:** Small. $50 one-time fee/room. Service with restrictions.

The Parkway Hotel H
(314) 256-7777. **$118-$269.** 4550 Forest Park Ave 63108. I-64 exit 36A (Kingshighway Blvd), 0.6 mi n, then just e. Int corridors. **Pets:** Medium. $20 daily fee/pet. Designated rooms, service with restrictions, crate.

Pear Tree Inn Union Station H
(314) 241-3200. **$90-$174.** 2211 Market St 63103. I-64/US 40 exit 39, just n on Jefferson Ave, then just e. Int corridors. **Pets:** Service with restrictions, supervision.

Residence Inn by Marriott St. Louis Downtown H
(314) 289-7500. **$139-$179.** 525 S Jefferson Ave 63103. I-64/US 40 exit 38C westbound; exit 38A (Jefferson Ave) eastbound, just s. Int corridors. **Pets:** Other species. $75 one-time fee/room. Service with restrictions.

St. Louis Union Station Hotel A DoubleTree by Hilton Hotel H
(314) 621-5262. **$99-$304.** 1820 Market St 63103. I-64 exit 38C eastbound; exit 39A westbound, just n on N Jefferson Ave, then 0.5 mi e on Market St. Int corridors. **Pets:** Accepted.

The Westin St. Louis H
(314) 621-2000. **$132-$409.** 811 Spruce St 63102. I-64 exit 39C eastbound, just n on 11th St, then just e; exit 40A westbound, just n, just e on Clark Ave, just s on 8th St, then just w. Int corridors. **Pets:** Accepted.

ST. PETERS
Drury Inn St. Peters H
(636) 397-9700. **$100-$184.** 170 Mid Rivers Mall Cir 63376. I-70 exit 222 (Mid Rivers Mall Dr), just se. Int corridors. **Pets:** Service with restrictions, supervision.

VALLEY PARK
Drury Inn & Suites-St. Louis Southwest H
(636) 861-8300. **$100-$164.** 5 Lambert Drury Pl 63088. I-44 exit 272 (SR 141), just sw. Int corridors. **Pets:** Service with restrictions, supervision.

Hampton Inn-St. Louis Southwest near Six Flags H
(636) 529-9020. **Call for rates.** 9 Lambert Drury Pl 63088. I-44 exit 272 (SR 141), just sw. Int corridors. **Pets:** Service with restrictions, crate.

WELDON SPRING
Wingate by Wyndham Weldon Spring H
(636) 329-8503. **$89-$119.** 32 Research Park Cir 63304. I-64/40 exit 11 (Research Park Cir), just se. Int corridors. **Pets:** Small. $10 daily fee/pet. Service with restrictions, crate.

WOODSON TERRACE
Hilton St. Louis Airport H
(314) 426-5500. **$85-$289.** 10330 Natural Bridge Rd 63134. I-70 exit 236 (Lambert Airport), 0.5 mi se. Int corridors. **Pets:** Accepted.

END METROPOLITAN AREA

ST. ROBERT
Americas Best Value Inn H
(573) 451-3100. **$71-$105.** 110 Carmel Valley Way 65584. I-44 exit 161, just nw. Int corridors. **Pets:** Other species. $10 daily fee/pet. Service with restrictions, crate.

Baymont Inn & Suites Ft. Leonard Wood-St. Robert H
(573) 336-5050. **$85-$143.** 139 Carmel Valley Way 65584. I-44 exit 161, just nw. Int corridors. **Pets:** Small. $50 deposit/room, $10 daily fee/pet. Designated rooms, service with restrictions, supervision.

BEST WESTERN Montis Inn H
(573) 336-4299. **$75.** 14086 Hwy Z 65584. I-44 exit 163, just s. Ext corridors. **Pets:** Small, dogs only. $10 daily fee/pet. Designated rooms, service with restrictions, supervision.

Days Inn H
(573) 336-5556. **$65-$70.** 14125 Hwy Z 65584. I-44 exit 163, just sw. Ext corridors. **Pets:** Accepted.

MainStay Suites H
(573) 451-2700. **$105-$180.** 227 St. Robert Blvd 65584. I-44 exit 159, 0.8 mi nw. Ext/int corridors. **Pets:** Other species. $15 daily fee/room. Service with restrictions, crate.

STE. GENEVIEVE
Microtel Inn & Suites by Wyndham Sainte Genevieve H
(573) 883-8884. **$70-$130.** 21958 Hwy 32 63670. I-55 exit 150 (SR 32), 3.9 mi e. Int corridors. **Pets:** $10 daily fee/pet. Service with restrictions.

SEDALIA

BEST WESTERN State Fair Inn H
(660) 826-6100. **Call for rates.** 3120 S Limit Ave 65301. Jct US 50, 1.5 mi s on US 65. Ext/int corridors. **Pets:** Other species. Designated rooms.

Hotel Bothwell, an Ascend Collection hotel H
(660) 826-5588. **$75-$160.** 103 E 4th St 65301. Corner of 4th and S Ohio sts; downtown. Int corridors. **Pets:** Accepted.

SEYMOUR

Americas Best Value Inn H
(417) 935-9888. **$73.** 1000 E Clinton Rd 65746. Just s of jct US 60. Int corridors. **Pets:** Medium. $15 daily fee/pet. Designated rooms, service with restrictions, supervision.

SIKESTON

Comfort Inn & Suites H
(573) 472-0197. **$87-$170.** 109 Matthews Ln 63801. I-55 exit 67, just sw. Int corridors. **Pets:** Dogs only. $15 daily fee/pet. Designated rooms, service with restrictions, supervision.

SPRINGFIELD

Baymont Inn & Suites H
(417) 889-8188. **$80-$110.** 3776 S Glenstone Ave 65804. On US 60 (James River Expwy). Int corridors. **Pets:** Large. $10 daily fee/pet. Designated rooms, service with restrictions, crate.

BEST WESTERN Coach House Inn H ✿
(417) 862-0701. **$79-$139.** 2535 N Glenstone Ave 65803. I-44 exit 80, just s. Ext corridors. **Pets:** $10 daily fee/pet. Service with restrictions, crate.

BEST WESTERN PLUS Springfield Airport Inn H
(417) 799-2200. **$70-$85.** 4445 W Chestnut Expwy 65802. I-44 exit 72, 0.8 mi s. Int corridors. **Pets:** Medium, other species. $10 daily fee/pet. Service with restrictions, supervision.

BEST WESTERN Route 66 Rail Haven M
(417) 866-1963. **$69-$129.** 203 S Glenstone Ave 65802. I-44 exit 80, 3 mi s. Ext corridors. **Pets:** Large, other species. $10 daily fee/pet. Designated rooms, service with restrictions, supervision.

Candlewood Suites South H
(417) 881-8500. **$89-$139.** 1035 E Republic Rd 65807. US 60 (James River Expwy) exit National Ave, just s. Int corridors. **Pets:** Accepted.

Candlewood Suites Springfield I-44 H
(417) 866-4242. **$89-$139.** 1920 E Kerr St 65803. I-44 exit 80A, just e to Evergreen St. Int corridors. **Pets:** Accepted.

Courtyard by Marriott Airport H ✿
(417) 869-6700. **$89-$149.** 3527 W Kearney St 65803. I-44 exit 75 (US 160 W Bypass), just se to SR 744, then just w. Int corridors. **Pets:** Other species. $75 one-time fee/room. Service with restrictions.

DoubleTree by Hilton Hotel Springfield H ✿
(417) 831-3131. **$89-$139.** 2431 N Glenstone Ave 65803. I-44 exit 80A, just s. Int corridors. **Pets:** Large, other species. $25 one-time fee/room. Service with restrictions, supervision.

Drury Inn & Suites-Springfield H
(417) 863-8400. **$95-$199.** 2715 N Glenstone Ave 65803. I-44 exit 80A, just s. Int corridors. **Pets:** Service with restrictions, supervision.

Greenstay Hotel & Suites H
(417) 863-1440. **$89-$129.** 222 N Ingram Mill Rd 65802. US 65 exit Chestnut Expwy, just sw. Ext/int corridors. **Pets:** Medium. $10 daily fee/pet. Service with restrictions, crate.

Hilton Garden Inn Springfield H
(417) 875-8800. **$89-$169.** 4155 S Nature Center Way 65804. US 60 (James River Expwy) exit Glenstone Ave (US 65 business route), just s. Int corridors. **Pets:** Accepted.

La Quinta Inn & Suites Springfield Airport Plaza H
(417) 447-4466. **$78-$162.** 2445 N Airport Plaza Ave 65803. I-44 exit 75, just se. Int corridors. **Pets:** Service with restrictions, supervision.

La Quinta Inn Springfield South H
(417) 890-6060. **$69-$142.** 2535 S Campbell Ave 65807. Jct Battlefield Rd and Campbell Ave, 0.5 mi n. Int corridors. **Pets:** Service with restrictions, supervision.

Quality Inn & Suites H ✿
(417) 888-0898. **$60-$100.** 3930 S Overland Ave 65807. US 60 (James River Expwy) exit Kansas Expwy, just n to Chesterfield Blvd, then just w. Int corridors. **Pets:** Medium, dogs only. $10 one-time fee/pet. Service with restrictions, crate.

Quality Inn & Suites North H
(417) 869-0001. **$65-$80.** 2745 N Glenstone Ave 65803. I-44 exit 80, just sw. Ext/int corridors. **Pets:** $25 daily fee/pet. Service with restrictions, supervision.

Sleep Inn of Springfield H
(417) 886-2464. **$75-$100.** 233 El Camino Alto 65810. US 60 (James River Expwy) exit Campbell Ave, just se. Int corridors. **Pets:** Medium. $20 one-time fee/room. Designated rooms, service with restrictions, supervision.

University Plaza Hotel and Convention Center H ✿
(417) 864-7333. **Call for rates.** 333 John Q Hammons Pkwy 65806. 0.5 mi e on St. Louis St. Int corridors. **Pets:** $25 one-time fee/room. Service with restrictions.

SULLIVAN

Baymont Inn & Suites H
(573) 860-3333. **$82-$115.** 275 N Service Rd W 63080. I-44 exit 225. Int corridors. **Pets:** $8 one-time fee/pet. Service with restrictions, supervision.

Comfort Inn H
(573) 468-7800. **Call for rates.** 736 S Service Rd W 63080. I-44 exit 225, just sw. Int corridors. **Pets:** Medium. $15 daily fee/room. Designated rooms, service with restrictions, supervision.

TRENTON

Country Home Inn H
(660) 359-2988. **$66-$79.** 1845A E 28th St 64683. US 65, 1 mi n of jct SR 6 and US 65. Int corridors. **Pets:** $10 one-time fee/room. Service with restrictions, supervision.

UNION

Super 8 H
(636) 583-8808. **$80-$97.** 1015 E Main St 63084. I-44 exit 247 (US 50), 4.7 mi w; just w of jct SR 47. Int corridors. **Pets:** Small, dogs only. $10 daily fee/pet. Service with restrictions, supervision.

WASHINGTON

Brick Inn Bed & Breakfast BB
(636) 390-3264. **$109-$159, 7 day notice.** 516 W 3rd St 63090. Jct SR 47 and 3rd St, 1 mi nw. Int corridors. **Pets:** Accepted.

▼▼ Sleep Inn & Suites **H**
(636) 390-8877. **Call for rates.** 2621 E 5th St 63090. I-44 exit 251, 8.5
mi w on SR 100. Int corridors. **Pets:** Medium. $25 daily fee/pet. Service
with restrictions. 🛜 ⊠ 🛏 🖵 🏊

▼▼ Super 8 Washington **H**
(636) 390-0088. **$79-$85.** 2081 Eckelkamp Ct 63090. I-44 exit 251, 10
mi w on SR 100; just s of SR 100 and 47. Int corridors. **Pets:** Small,
dogs only. $10 daily fee/pet. Designated rooms, service with restrictions,
supervision. 🛜 🛏 🖵

WEST PLAINS

◢◣◥ **▼▼** BEST WESTERN Grand Villa **H**
(417) 257-2711. **$85-$100.** 220 Jan Howard Expwy 65775. 0.5 mi nw of
jct US 63 and 160. Int corridors. **Pets:** Accepted.
SAVE 🛜 🛏 🖵 🏊

WILLOW SPRINGS

▼▼ Comfort Inn of Willow Springs **H**
(417) 469-0410. **Call for rates.** 1204 E Main St 65793. Just n of US
60/63. Int corridors. **Pets:** Accepted. 🛜 🛏 🖵

MONTANA

CITY INDEX

ALBERTON

▼▼ The Ghost Rails Inn B & B **BB**
(406) 722-4990. **Call for rates.** 702 Railroad Ave 59820. Downtown. Int
corridors. **Pets:** Accepted. 🛜 ⊠ 🖋 🍽

BELGRADE

◈◈◈◈ Gallatin River Lodge **CI**
(406) 388-0148. **$170-$400, 7 day notice.** 9105 Thorpe Rd 59718. I-90
exit 298, 2.7 mi s on SR 85, 1 mi w on Valley Center Rd (gravel), then
0.5 mi s, follow signs. Ext/int corridors. **Pets:** Accepted.
🛜 ⊠ 🛏 🍴 🍽

▼▼ La Quinta Inn & Suites Belgrade / Bozeman **H**
(406) 388-2222. **$65-$188.** 6445 Jackrabbit Ln 59714. I-90 exit 298, just
s on SR 85. Int corridors. **Pets:** Service with restrictions, supervision.
🛜 🛏 🖵 🏊 🍽

◢◣◥ **▼▼** Quality Inn **H** 🐾
(406) 388-0800. **$69-$149.** 6261 Jackrabbit Ln 59714. I-90 exit 298, just
s on SR 85. Int corridors. **Pets:** Other species. $5 one-time fee/pet.
Supervision. SAVE 🛜 ⊠ 🛗 🛏 🖵

◢◣◥ **▼▼** Super 8-Belgrade/Bozeman Airport **H**
(406) 388-1493. **$70-$130.** 6450 Jackrabbit Ln 59714. I-90 exit 298, just
s on SR 85. Int corridors. **Pets:** Large. $5 daily fee/pet. Designated
rooms, service with restrictions, supervision. SAVE 🛜 🛏 🖵 🏊

BIGFORK

◢◣◥ **▼◈▼** Mountain Lake Lodge **H** 🐾
(406) 837-3800. **$205-$285, 7 day notice.** 14735 Sylvan Dr 59911. On
SR 35, 5 mi s. Ext corridors. **Pets:** $15 daily fee/pet. Designated rooms,
service with restrictions, supervision.
SAVE 🛜 🛗 🛏 🖵 🍴 🏊 🍽

◢◣◥ **▼▼** Timbers Motel **M**
(406) 837-6200. **$60-$160, 7 day notice.** 8540 Hwy 35 59911. Just n
on SR 35 from jct SR 209. Ext corridors. **Pets:** Accepted.
SAVE 🛜 🛏 🖵 🏊

BIG SKY

▼▼ Buck's T-4 Lodge **H**
(406) 995-4111. **$99-$159.** 46625 Gallatin Rd 59716. US 191, 1 mi s of
Big Sky entrance. Ext/int corridors. **Pets:** Accepted.
🛜 ⊠ 🛏 🖵 🍴 🍽

▼▼▼ Rainbow Ranch Lodge **H** 🐾
(406) 995-4132. **$295-$450, 14 day notice.** 42950 Gallatin Rd 59730. 5
mi s on US 191. Ext corridors. **Pets:** $40 one-time fee/pet. Designated
rooms, service with restrictions, supervision.
🛜 ⊠ 🛏 🖵 🍴 🍽 🚫

BIG TIMBER

◈▼▼ Big Timber Super 8 **H** 🐾
(406) 932-8888. **$80-$115.** 20A Big Timber Loop Rd 59011. I-90 exit 367.
Int corridors. **Pets:** Medium, other species. $10 daily fee/pet. Designated
rooms, service with restrictions, supervision. 🛜 🛗 🛏 🖵

▼ River Valley Inn **H**
(406) 932-4943. **Call for rates.** 600 W 2nd St 59011. I-90 exit 367, just
n, then 0.6 mi e. Int corridors. **Pets:** Medium, other species. $10 one-time
fee/room. Service with restrictions, supervision. 🛜 🛏

BILLINGS

◢◣◥ **▼◈▼** BEST WESTERN PLUS Clocktower
Inn **H** 🐾
(406) 259-5511. **Call for rates.** 2511 1st Ave N 59101. On I-90 business
loop; downtown. Ext/int corridors. **Pets:** Large, other species. $20 daily
fee/pet. Service with restrictions, supervision.
SAVE 🛜 ⊠ 🛏 🖵 🍴 🏊

◢◣◥ **▼◈▼** BEST WESTERN PLUS Kelly Inn &
Suites **H** 🐾
(406) 256-9400. **$110-$160.** 4915 Southgate Dr 59101. I-90 exit 447, just
w. Ext/int corridors. **Pets:** Designated rooms, service with restrictions,
supervision. SAVE 🛜 ⊠ 🛗 🛏 🖵 🏊

◢◣◥ **▼▼** Billings Inn by Riversage **H**
(406) 252-6800. **$75-$85.** 880 N 29th St 59101. I-90 exit 450, 2 mi n on
27th St, then just w on 9th Ave. Int corridors. **Pets:** Other species. $7
daily fee/pet. Designated rooms, service with restrictions, crate.
SAVE 🛜 ⊠ 🛏 🖵

◢◣◥ **▼▼** Billings Super 8 **H**
(406) 248-8842. **$79-$125.** 5400 Southgate Dr 59102. I-90 exit 447, just
n on S Billings Blvd, 0.8 mi w on King Ave, then just s on Parkway Ln.
Int corridors. **Pets:** Small, dogs only. $10 one-time fee/pet. Designated
rooms, service with restrictions, supervision. SAVE 🛜 🛗 🛏 🖵

Cherry Tree Inn H
(406) 252-5603. **$68.** 823 N Broadway 59101. I-90 exit 450, 2 mi n on 27th St, then just w on 9th Ave. Int corridors. **Pets:** Other species. Designated rooms, service with restrictions, crate. SAVE 🛰 ☒ 🖥 🖵 🖃

Comfort Inn by Choice Hotels H
(406) 652-5200. **Call for rates.** 2030 Overland Ave 59102. I-90 exit 446, 0.5 mi n, then just s. Int corridors. **Pets:** Other species. $20 daily fee/pet. Designated rooms, service with restrictions, supervision.
🛰 🖎 🖥 🖵 🖃

Days Inn H
(406) 252-4007. **$73-$119.** 843 Parkway Ln 59101. I-90 exit 447, just n on S Billings Blvd, 0.8 mi w on King Ave, then just s. Int corridors. **Pets:** Dogs only. $8 daily fee/pet. Service with restrictions, supervision.
🛰 ☒ 🖥 🖵

Econo Lodge H
(406) 252-2700. **$70-$190.** 5425 Midland Rd 59101. I-90 exit 446, just se. Ext/int corridors. **Pets:** Large, other species. Supervision.
🛰 🖥 🖵 🖃

Extended StayAmerica-Billings-West End H
(406) 245-3980. **$85-$119.** 4950 Southgate Dr 59101. I-90 exit 447, just w. Int corridors. **Pets:** $25 daily fee/pet. Designated rooms, service with restrictions. 🛰 🖎 🖥 🖵

Hilltop Inn by Riversage H
(406) 245-5000. **$75-$85.** 1116 N 28th St 59101. I-90 exit 450, 2 mi n on 27th St, just w on 11th Ave, then just n. Int corridors. **Pets:** Other species. $7 daily fee/pet. Designated rooms, service with restrictions, crate.
SAVE 🛰 ☒ 🖎 🖥 🖵

Holiday Inn Grand Montana Billings H
(406) 248-7701. **$119-$149.** 5500 Midland Rd 59101. I-90 exit 446. Int corridors. **Pets:** Other species. $50 one-time fee/room. Service with restrictions, supervision. SAVE 🛰 🖎 🖥 🖵 🍴 🖃 ☒

Kelly Inn H
(406) 248-9800. **Call for rates.** 5610 S Frontage Rd 59101. I-90 exit 446, just s. Ext/int corridors. **Pets:** Accepted.
🛰 ☒ 🖎 🖥 🖵 🖃

Motel 6 #1150 Billings North H
(406) 248-7551. **$61-$81.** 5353 Midland Rd 59102. I-90 exit 446, just se. Int corridors. **Pets:** Other species. Service with restrictions, supervision.
🛰 🖎 🖥 🖃

Motel 6 #178 Billings South M
(406) 252-0093. **$55-$75.** 5400 Midland Rd 59101. I-90 exit 446, just se. Ext corridors. **Pets:** Other species. Service with restrictions, supervision.
🛰 🖎

Quality Inn Homestead H
(406) 652-1320. **$85-$160.** 2036 Overland Ave 59102. I-90 exit 446, 0.5 mi n, then just s. Int corridors. **Pets:** Accepted. 🛰 🖥 🖵 🖃 ☒

Residence Inn by Marriott H
(406) 656-3900. **$129-$189.** 956 S 25th St W 59102. I-90 exit 446, 1.5 mi w, just s on S 24th St, then just s; behind Home Depot. Int corridors. **Pets:** Large, other species. $75 one-time fee/room. Service with restrictions. SAVE 🛰 ☒ 🖎 🖥 🖵 🖃 ☒

Western Executive Inn H
(406) 294-8888. **$80-$210.** 3121 King Ave W 59102. I-90 exit 446, 2.5 mi w. Int corridors. **Pets:** Small. $10 daily fee/pet. Service with restrictions, supervision. SAVE 🛰 🖎 🖥 🖵

Westwood's Rimview Inn M
(406) 248-2622. **Call for rates.** 1025 N 27th St 59101. I-90 exit 450, 2 mi n. Ext/int corridors. **Pets:** Small, dogs only. $10 daily fee/pet. Designated rooms, service with restrictions, supervision. SAVE 🛰 🖥 🖵

BOZEMAN

BEST WESTERN PLUS GranTree Inn H 🐾
(406) 587-5261. **Call for rates.** 1325 N 7th Ave 59715. I-90 exit 306, just s. Int corridors. **Pets:** Other species. Supervision.
SAVE 🛰 ☒ 🖥 🖵 🍴 🖃

Bozeman Days Inn & Suites H
(406) 587-5251. **$60-$130.** 1321 N 7th Ave 59715. I-90 exit 306, just s. Int corridors. **Pets:** Accepted. 🛰 🖥 🖵 🖃 ☒

Bozeman Inn M
(406) 587-3176. **$60-$100.** 1235 N 7th Ave 59715. I-90 exit 306, just s. Ext corridors. **Pets:** Other species. $5 daily fee/pet. Service with restrictions, supervision. SAVE 🛰 🖥 🖵 🖃

Bozeman's Western Heritage Inn H
(406) 586-8534. **$78-$158.** 1200 E Main St 59715. I-90 exit 309, 0.5 mi w. Int corridors. **Pets:** Accepted. 🛰 ☒ 🖥 🖵

Comfort Inn of Bozeman H
(406) 587-2322. **$69-$115.** 1370 N 7th Ave 59715. I-90 exit 306, just s. Int corridors. **Pets:** Accepted. 🛰 ☒ 🖥 🖵 🖃

Holiday Inn Bozeman H
(406) 587-4561. **$79-$159.** 5 E Baxter Ln 59715. I-90 exit 306, just s. Int corridors. **Pets:** Large, other species. Service with restrictions, supervision.
🛰 🖥 🖵 🍴 🖃

Holiday Inn Express & Suites H
(406) 582-4995. **$109-$169.** 2305 Catron St 59718. I-90 exit 305, just s on CR 41 (19th St), then just w on E Valley Center Rd. Int corridors.
Pets: Accepted. ECO 🛰 ☒ 🖎 🖥 🖵 🖃

La Quinta Inn & Suites H
(406) 585-9300. **$87-$199.** 620 Nikles Dr 59715. I-90 exit 306, just ne. Int corridors. **Pets:** Service with restrictions, supervision.
🛰 ☒ 🖎 🖥 🖵 🖃

Microtel Inn & Suites by Wyndham Bozeman H
(406) 586-3797. **$60-$140.** 612 Nikles Dr 59715. I-90 exit 306, just ne. Int corridors. **Pets:** Accepted. 🛰 ☒ 🖥 🖵 🖃

MountainView Lodge & Suites H
(406) 522-8686. **$89-$179.** 1121 Reeves Rd W 59718. I-90 exit 305, just n. Int corridors. **Pets:** Dogs only. $10 daily fee/pet. Designated rooms, service with restrictions, supervision. 🖎 🖥 🖵 🖃 ☒

Rainbow Motel M
(406) 587-4201. **$65-$85.** 510 N 7th Ave 59715. I-90 exit 306, 0.8 mi s. Ext corridors. **Pets:** Medium, dogs only. $7 daily fee/pet. Designated rooms, service with restrictions, supervision. SAVE 🛰 🖥 🖵 🖃

Ramada Limited H
(406) 585-2626. **$40-$129, 3 day notice.** 2020 Wheat Dr 59715. I-90 exit 306, just n, then just w. Ext/int corridors. **Pets:** Accepted.
SAVE 🛰 ☒ 🖥 🖵 🖃 ☒

Rodeway Inn H
(406) 585-7888. **Call for rates.** 817 Wheat Dr 59718. I-90 exit 306, just n. Int corridors. **Pets:** Accepted. 🛰 ☒ 🖎 🖥 🖵 🖃

Royal "7" Budget Inn M
(406) 587-3103. **$48-$69.** 310 N 7th Ave 59715. I-90 exit 306, 0.8 mi s. Ext corridors. **Pets:** $3 daily fee/pet. Designated rooms, service with restrictions, supervision. SAVE 🛰 ☒ 🖥 🖵

Super 8 H 🐾
(406) 586-1521. **$59-$119.** 800 Wheat Dr 59715. I-90 exit 306, just n, then just w. Int corridors. **Pets:** Dogs only. $8 daily fee/pet. Designated rooms, service with restrictions, supervision. 🛰 🖥 🖵

YOUR FURRY FRIEND WILL FEEL RIGHT AT HOME

With over 1,600 pet-friendly hotels,* we're sure to have the perfect hotel for you. Best Western® recognizes the ever-growing need for pet-friendly accommodations, so we strive to offer our guests and their pets a comfortable stay at all of our pet-friendly hotels. For more information call 1.866.430.9022.

Preferred Hotels

bestwestern.com/aaapet
bestwestern.com/caapet

WATCH "Traveling With Your Dog" with Cesar Millan

MORE CHOICES. MORE REWARDS. MORE LOCATIONS.

You travel for many reasons, which is why we now have BEST WESTERN®, BEST WESTERN PLUS® and BEST WESTERN PREMIER®. Our hotel offerings provide you with everything you need for a quick overnight stay or a vacation with more time to relax. You can rest assured, there's a Best Western hotel that's right for your trip.

Join our FREE rewards program, AAA/CAA Preferred℠ Best Western Rewards® and start earning free nights, gas cards, and savings of 10% or more at participating hotels. For more information call 1.866.430.9022.

Show Your Card & Save®

Preferred Hotels

bestwestern.com/aaa | bestwestern.com/caa

AAA PetBook® Photo Contest Entries

Each year, the winning entry in AAA's PetBook Photo Contest, sponsored by Best Western®appears on a cover of *Traveling With Your Pet: The AAA PetBook®* and also receives other great prizes. You have already met the contest winners, but here are more great entries that we just had to make room for!

Check out AAA.com/PetBook for pictures, contest rules and an entry form for next year's contest. And keep traveling with your pet!

Shorty on Route 66, Rainbow Bridge, Kansas
Owner: Rebecca A. Murray from Belgrade, Mont.

Maddi in Shell Canyon, Shell, Wyoming
Owner: Mar Sension from Altoona, Pa.

Blitzen Rainier in Salem, Oregon
Owner: Beverly L. Peterson from Salem, Ore.

Rigel Orion at Gold Beach, Oregon
Owner: Cynthia Franke from Vancouver, Wash.

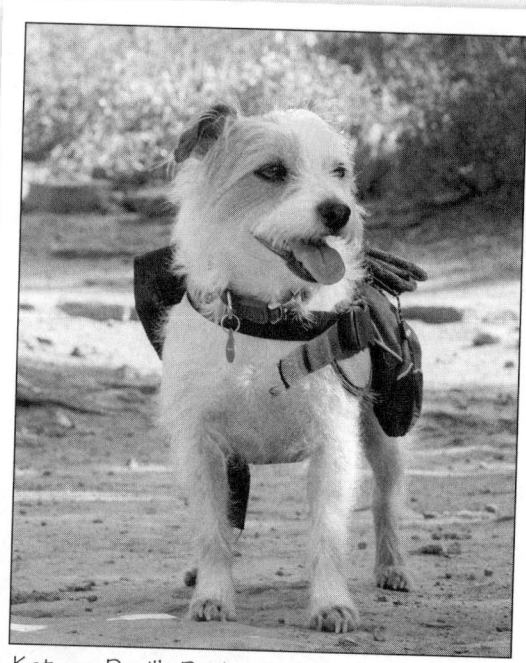

Katy on Devil's Bridge Trail, Sedona, Arizona
Owner: Christopher Meyer from
Santa Monica, Calif.

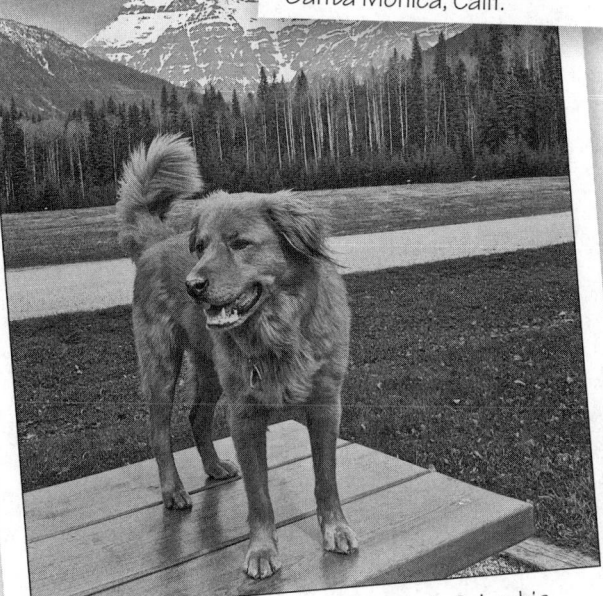

Sasha at Canadian Route 16, British Columbia
Owner: Michelle Kirkhoff from Big Bear City, Calif.

Bagel in Nags Head, North Carolina
Owner: Geneve Bergeron from Washington, D.C.

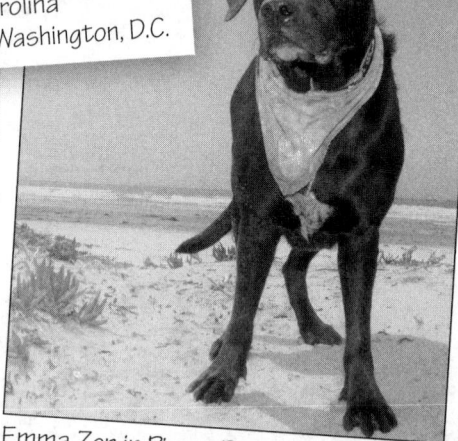

Emma Zen in Pismo Beach, California
Owner: Debra Jo Chiapuzio from
Anaheim, Calif.

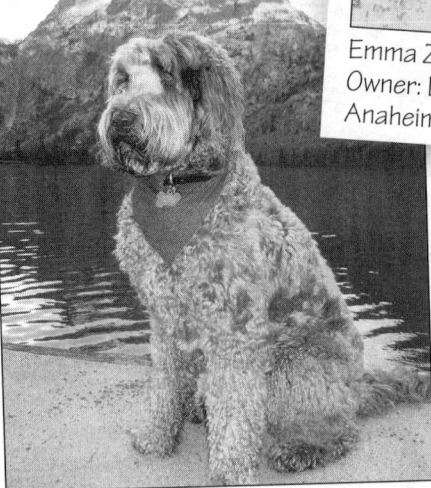

Monroe visiting Silver Lake, California
Owner: Susan Gribbons from Newhall, Calif.

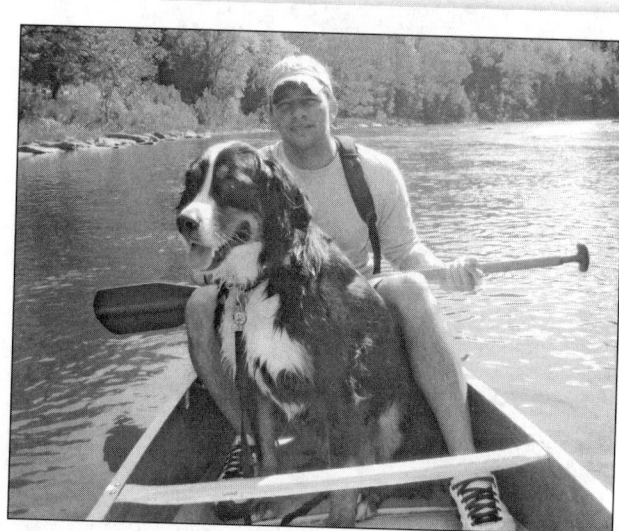

Moose in Cook Forest State Park, Pennsylvania
Owner: Rhonda Johnson from Pittsfield, Pa.

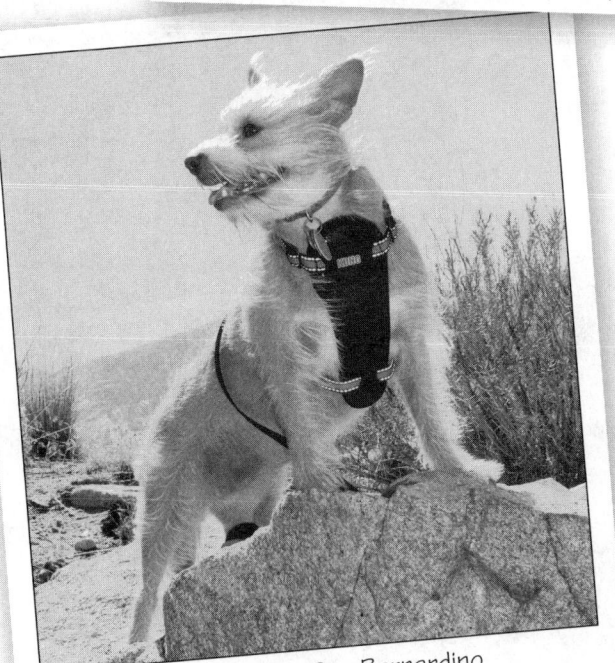

Lexie at Mormon Rocks, San Bernardino
National Forest, California
Owner: Lisa Gonzalez from Fontana, Calif.

Stewart at Walnut Creek Park, Austin, Texas
Owner: Janel Poon from San Marino, Calif.

Quincy at Touisset Point, Mount Hope Bay,
Massachusetts & Rhode Island border
Owner: Jacque Gorman from Portsmouth, R.I.

Ziggy in Carmel, California
Owner: Susan Heberer from Poway, Calif.

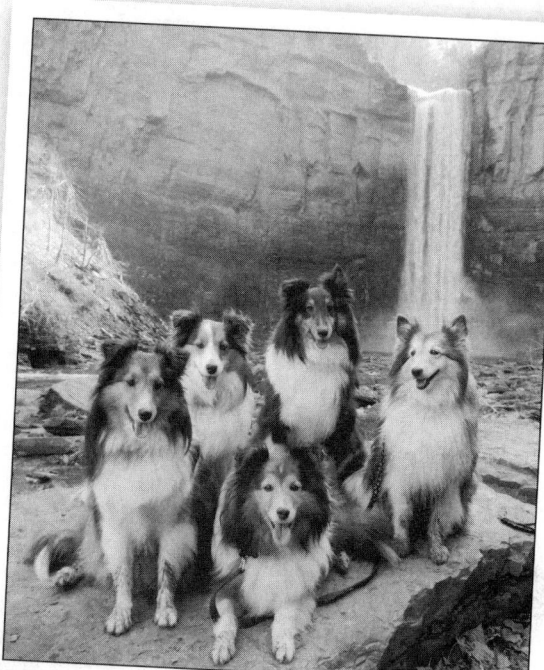

Heather, Abby, Heidi, Bailey & Greta at Taughannock Falls State Park, New York
Owner: Amy K. Litwiler from Horseheads, N.Y.

Bella enjoying Narragansett Bay, Rhode Island
Owner: Jennifer Priestley from Warwick, R.I.

Benson at Salt Creek Beach, Laguna Niguel, California
Owners: Donna, Dean & Nicky Lofgren from Torrance, Calif.

Minie Me visiting West Branch State Park, Ravenna, Ohio
Owner: Louis Jordan from Rootstown, Ohio

Buddy enjoying Carefree, Arizona
Owner: Robert Brown from Clinton, Wash.

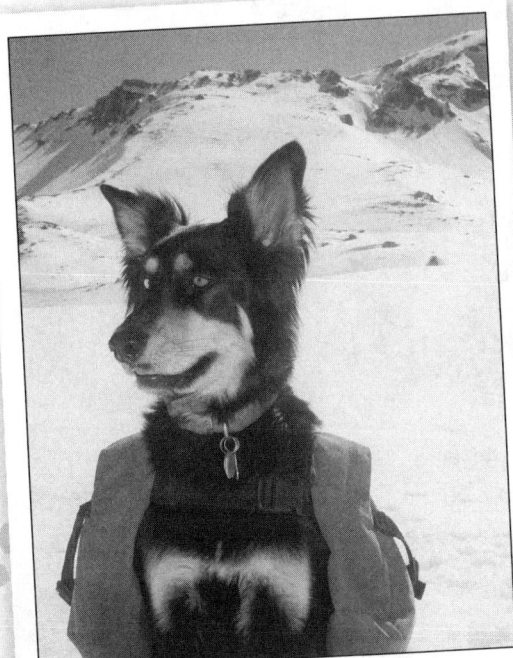

Natalena in Central Sierras, California
Owner: Michael Dong from San Diego, Calif.

Hannah visiting Balboa Park, San Diego, California
Owner: Rachel Peters from Lemon Grove, Calif.

Mochi & Sumiko visiting Mammoth Lakes, California
Owner: Rose Sato from Gardena, Calif.

Penny vacationing in Boca Grande, Florida
Owner: Alane Palmer from Pittsburgh, Pa.

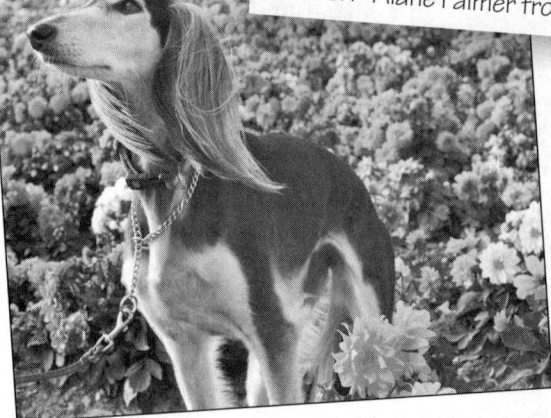

Zoe in Lompoc, California
Owner: Ken Bornstein from Los Angeles, Calif.

Rusty in Ruidoso, New Mexico
Owner: Erica Asmus-Otero from Rio Rancho, N.M.

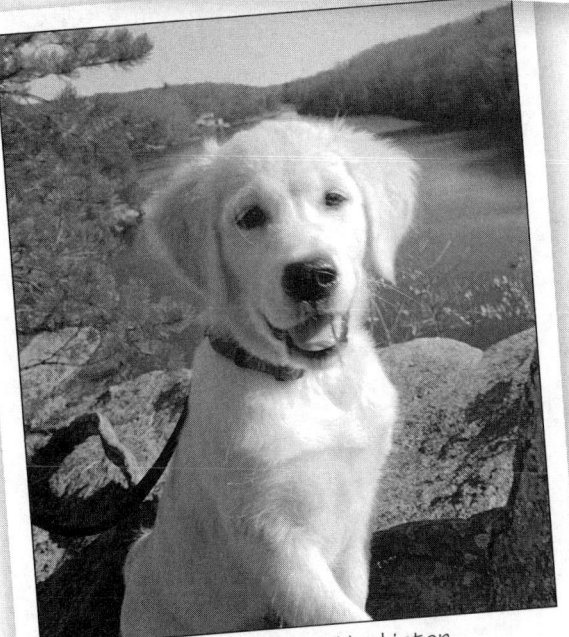

Reece enjoying Long Pond, Hopkinton,
Rhode Island
Owner: Kristen Longo from Ashaway, R.I.

Nika visiting Glacier National Park, Montana
Owner: Susanna Sovek from Pittsburgh, Pa.

Finnega & Fiona in Branford, Connecticut
Owner: Holly Haringa, Branford, Conn.

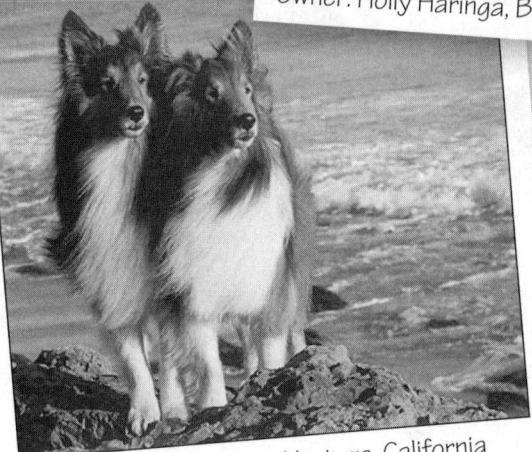

Boomer & Remington in Ventura, California
Owner: Karen Velguth from Bakersfield, Calif.

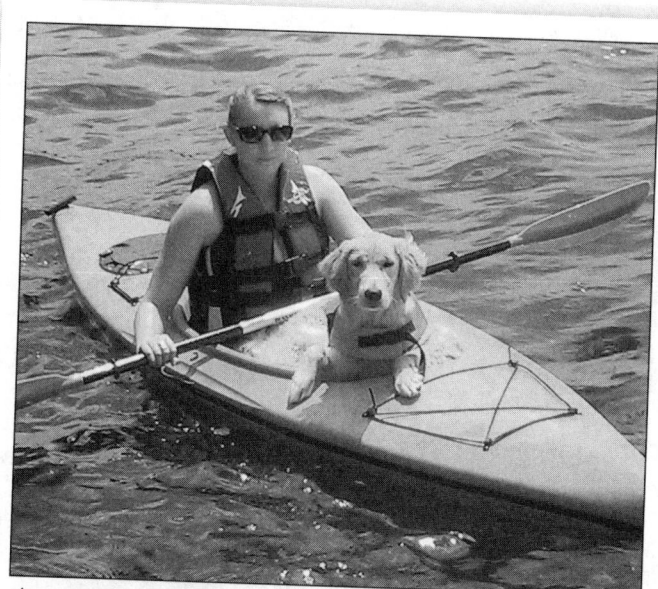

Annabelle in Meredith, New Hampshire
Owner: Esther Dussault from Hollis, N.H.

Chara & Ella in Bushkill Falls, Pennsylvania
Owners: Arthur & Linda Everly from Blackstone, Mass.

Ruger & Grizwald at Matanuska River,
Matanuska-Susitna Valley, Alaska
Owner: Lisa Stratton from Palmer, Alaska

Mitzi at Lake Tahoe, California
Owner: Walter T. Farrell from Palm Springs, Calif.

Bumble vacationing on St. George Island, Florida
Owner: Lisa Wingerter from Evansville, Ind.

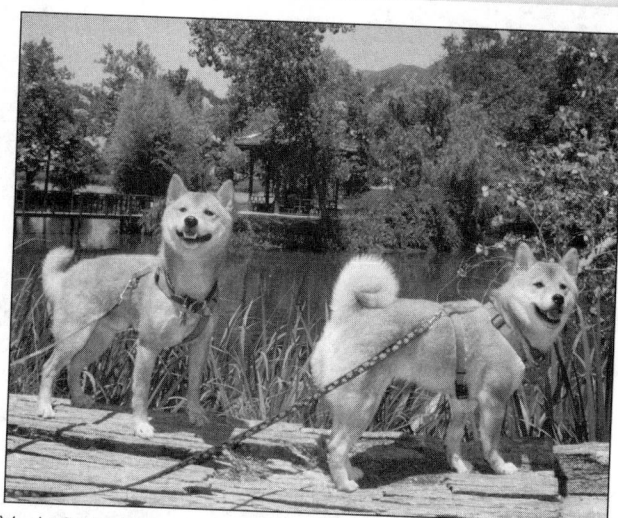

Yoshi & Sachi at the Chateau Montelena Winery, Calistoga, California
Owners: Bill & Jean Mumbleau from Rancho Cucamonga, Calif.

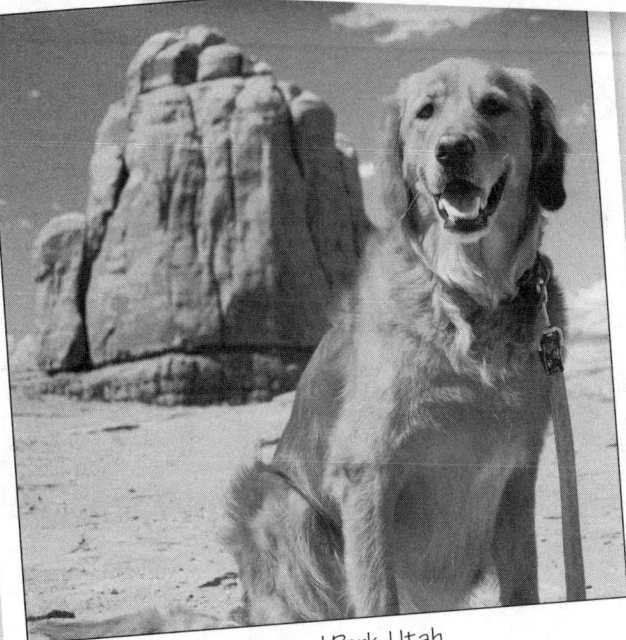

Maggie at Arches National Park, Utah
Owner: Puja Buch from Claremont, Calif.

A few more tail-wagging travelers

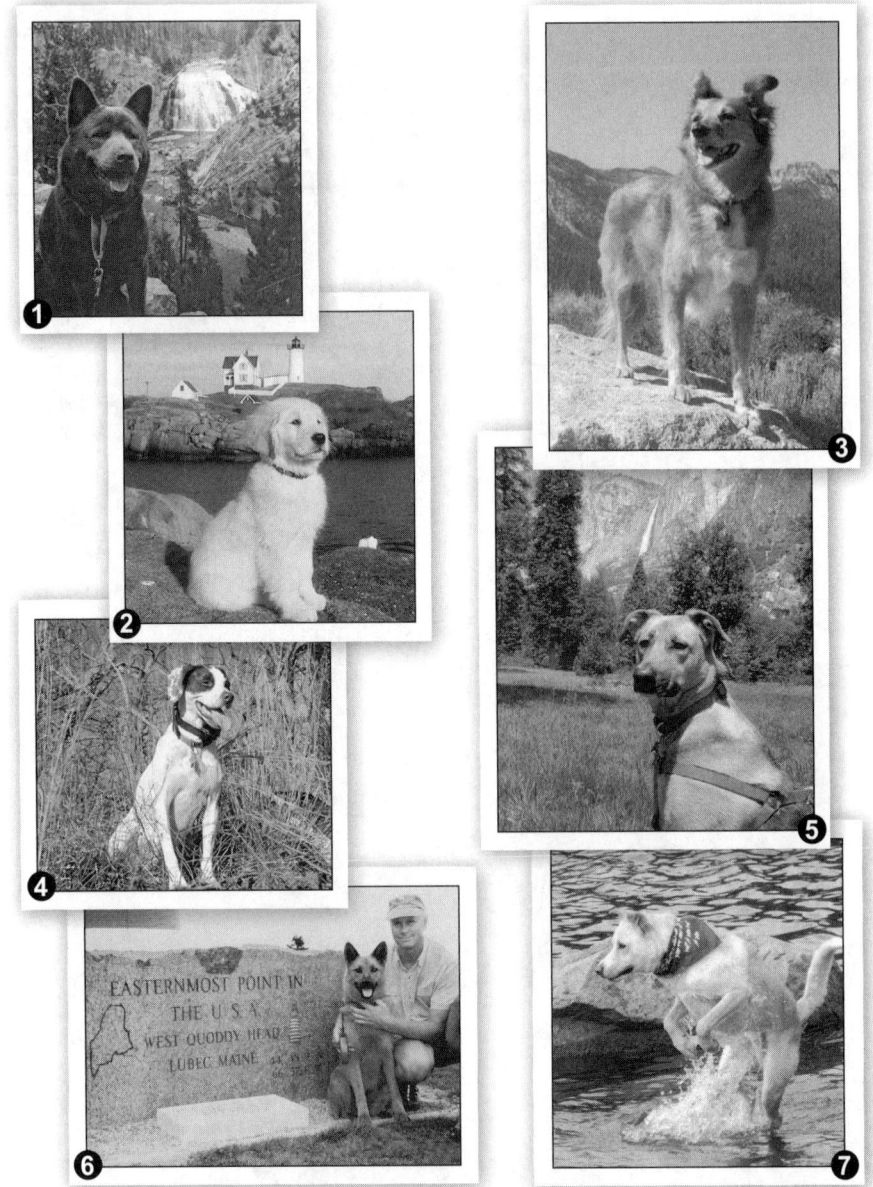

1) Sherpa at Yellowstone National Park, Montana, Owner: William Celentano from Glendale, Calif. 2) McGee at the Nubble Lighthouse, York, Maine, Owners: Renee Savage & Louise Paradis from Rochester, N.H. 3) Roxy at Mammoth Lakes, California, Owner: Toni Gavello from Orange, Calif. 4) Cookie at Delaware Water Gap National Recreation Area, Pennsylvania, Owner: Kelly L. Althouse from Milford, Pa. 5) Mia in Yosemite Valley, California, Owner: Tom Doyle from Livermore, Calif. 6) Lia in Lubec, Maine, Owner: Barry Oberpriller from Leverett, Mass. 7) Dillon visiting Head's Pond Trail, Hooksett, New Hampshire, Owner: Barbara Lupien from Manchester, N.H.

BROWNING

Western Motel LLC M
(406) 338-7572. **$88-$174, 4 day notice.** 121 Central Ave E 59417. On US 2; center. Ext corridors. **Pets:** Accepted. [SAVE] 🔋 ⊠ 📶

BUTTE

BEST WESTERN PLUS Butte Plaza Inn H
(406) 494-3500. **$115-$155.** 2900 Harrison Ave 59701. I-90/15 exit 127 (Harrison Ave). Int corridors. **Pets:** Other species. Designated rooms, service with restrictions, supervision.
[SAVE] 🔋 ⊠ 📶 📶 🍴 🏊 ⊠

Comfort Inn of Butte H 🐾
(406) 494-8850. **$110-$170.** 2777 Harrison Ave 59701. I-90/15 exit 127 (Harrison Ave), just s. Int corridors. **Pets:** Other species. $20 daily fee/pet. Supervision. [ECO] [SAVE] 🔋 📶 📶 🏊 ⊠

Finlen Hotel H
(406) 723-5461. **$62-$100.** 100 E Broadway 59701. Jct Wyoming St; in Historic Uptown. Ext/int corridors. **Pets:** Accepted. 🔋 ⊠ 📶

La Quinta Inn & Suites H
(406) 494-6999. **$89-$188.** 1 Holiday Park Dr 59701. I-90/15 exit 127 (Harrison Ave), just n to Cornell St, then just e, follow signs. Int corridors. **Pets:** Service with restrictions, supervision. 🔋 ⊠ 📶 📶 📶

Quality Inn & Suites Butte H
(406) 494-7800. **$85-$149.** 2100 Cornell Ave 59701. I-90/15 exit 127B (Harrison Ave), just n, then just e. Int corridors. **Pets:** Accepted.
[SAVE] 🔋 📶 📶 🍴 🏊 ⊠

Rocker Inn M
(406) 723-5464. **$46-$61.** 122001 W Brown's Gulch Rd 59701. I-90/15 exit 122 (Rocker Rd). Int corridors. **Pets:** Medium. $10 daily fee/room. Designated rooms, service with restrictions, supervision. [SAVE] 🔋 📶

Super 8 of Butte H
(406) 494-6000. **$79-$119.** 2929 Harrison Ave 59701. I-90/15 exit 127 (Harrison Ave), just s. Int corridors. **Pets:** Large. $15 one-time fee/pet. Designated rooms, service with restrictions, supervision.
[SAVE] 🔋 ⊠ 📶 📶

CHINOOK

Chinook Motor Inn M
(406) 357-2248. **$69-$79.** 100 Indiana St 59523. On US 2. Int corridors. **Pets:** $10 daily fee/pet. Service with restrictions, supervision.
[SAVE] 🔋 ⊠ 📶 🍴

COLUMBUS

Super 8 of Columbus H
(406) 322-4101. **$73-$116.** 602 8th Ave N 59019. I-90 exit 408, just s on SR 78. Int corridors. **Pets:** Accepted. [SAVE] 🔋 📶 📶 📶

CONRAD

Super 8 H
(406) 278-7676. **$81-$110.** 215 N Main St 59425. I-15 exit 339, just w. Int corridors. **Pets:** Other species. $10 daily fee/pet. Service with restrictions, crate. 🔋 📶 📶

COOKE CITY

Elk Horn Lodge M
(406) 838-2332. **$99-$125, 7 day notice.** 103 Main St 59020. Center. Ext corridors. **Pets:** Accepted. 🔋 📶 📶 📶 ⊠

DARBY

Rye Creek Lodge CA
(406) 821-3366. **$200-$500, 60 day notice.** 458 Rye Creek Rd 59829. US 93, 4.5 mi s, 1.5 mi e. Ext corridors. **Pets:** Other species. $25 one-time fee/room. Designated rooms, no service, crate.
🔋 ⊠ 📶 📶 ⊠

DEER LODGE

Travelodge M
(406) 846-2370. **$78-$90.** 1150 N Main St 59722. I-90 exit 184, 0.3 mi s. Int corridors. **Pets:** Other species. $10 one-time fee/room. Service with restrictions, supervision. [SAVE] 🔋 ⊠ 📶 📶 📶

Western Big Sky Inn M
(406) 846-2590. **$50-$85.** 210 N Main St 59722. I-90 exit 184, 1 mi w. Ext corridors. **Pets:** Accepted. 🔋 ⊠ 📶 📶 📶

DILLON

BEST WESTERN Paradise Inn H
(406) 683-4214. **$80-$150.** 650 N Montana St 59725. I-15 exit 63, 0.3 mi s on SR 41. Ext corridors. **Pets:** Accepted.
[SAVE] 🔋 ⊠ 📶 📶 🍴

Comfort Inn of Dillon H
(406) 683-6831. **$110-$145.** 450 N Interchange 59725. I-15 exit 63. Int corridors. **Pets:** Accepted. [SAVE] 🔋 📶 📶 🏊

GuestHouse International Inn & Suites H
(406) 683-3636. **$69-$199.** 580 Sinclair St 59725. I-15 exit 63. Int corridors. **Pets:** Accepted. 🔋 ⊠ 📶 📶 📶 🏊

EAST GLACIER PARK

Dancing Bears Inn LLC M
(406) 226-4402. **$88-$174, 4 day notice.** 40 Montana Ave 59434. Just off US 2, follow signs; center. Ext/int corridors. **Pets:** Small, other species. $10 daily fee/pet. Designated rooms, supervision. [SAVE] 🔋 ⊠ 📶

EMIGRANT

Paradise Gateway Bed & Breakfast & Guest Cabin BB
(406) 333-4063. **$85-$400, 14 day notice.** 2644 Hwy 89 S 59027. I-90 exit 333 (US 89), 4.5 mi s of town; between MM 26 and 27, 0.3 mi e on gravel road. Ext/int corridors. **Pets:** $50 one-time fee/pet. Designated rooms, crate. [SAVE] 🔋 ⊠ 📶 📶

FORSYTH

Magnuson Hotels Sundowner Inn M
(406) 346-2115. **$95-$130.** 1018 Front St 59327. I-94 exit 95, 0.5 mi nw on north frontage road. Ext corridors. **Pets:** Dogs only. $10 daily fee/pet. Service with restrictions, supervision. [SAVE] 🔋 📶 📶

Rails Inn Motel H
(406) 346-2242. **$65-$83, 3 day notice.** 290 Front St 59327. I-94 exit 93, just n, then 0.5 mi e on frontage road. Int corridors. **Pets:** $6 daily fee/pet. Service with restrictions, supervision. [SAVE] 🔋 📶 📶

Restwel Motel M
(406) 346-2771. **$67-$80.** 810 Front St 59327. I-94 exit 95, 0.8 mi nw on north frontage road. Ext corridors. **Pets:** Accepted. [SAVE] 🔋 📶

Westwind Motor Inn M
(406) 346-2038. **$65-$83, 3 day notice.** 225 Westwind Ln 59327. I-94 exit 93, 0.3 mi n. Int corridors. **Pets:** $6 daily fee/pet. Service with restrictions, supervision. [SAVE] 🔋 ⊠ 📶 📶

GARDINER

BEST WESTERN PLUS By Mammoth Hot Springs M 🐾
(406) 848-7311. **$85-$215, 3 day notice.** 905 Scott St W 59030. 0.5 mi n. Ext/int corridors. **Pets:** Other species. $20 daily fee/room. Designated rooms, service with restrictions, crate.
[SAVE] 🔋 ⊠ 📶 📶 🍴 🏊 ⊠

Yellowstone River Motel M
(406) 848-7303. **$62-$112.** 14 E Park St 59030. Just e of US 89. Ext corridors. **Pets:** Accepted. [SAVE] 🔋 ⊠ 📶 📶 📶

▼▼ Yellowstone Super 8-Gardiner H
(406) 848-7401. **$50-$150.** Hwy 89 S 59030. On US 89. Int corridors.
Pets: Other species. $10 daily fee/pet. Designated rooms, supervision.

GLASGOW

▼▼ Cottonwood Inn H
(406) 228-8213. **$85-$110.** 45 1st Ave NE 59230. 0.5 mi e on US 2. Int
corridors. **Pets:** $5 daily fee/room. Designated rooms, service with restrictions, supervision.

GREAT FALLS

▲▲▲ ▼▼▼▼ BEST WESTERN PLUS Heritage Inn H
(406) 761-1900. **$110-$140.** 1700 Fox Farm Rd 59404. I-15 exit 278, 0.8
mi e on 10th Ave S, US 87/89 and SR 3/200. **Pets:** $15
one-time fee/room. Designated rooms, service with restrictions, supervision.

▼▼ Comfort Inn by Choice Hotels H
(406) 454-2727. **$79-$135.** 1120 9th St S 59405. I-15 exit 278, 3 mi e on
10th Ave S, US 87/89 and SR 3/200, just s. Int corridors.
Pets: Other species. $20 daily fee/room. Designated rooms, service with
restrictions.

▼▼ Days Inn of Great Falls H
(406) 727-6565. **$74-$99.** 101 14th Ave NW 59404. I-15 exit 280 (Central
Ave), 1.3 mi e on Central Ave/Business Rt I-15, 0.8 mi n on 3rd St NW,
then just w. Int corridors. **Pets:** Dogs only. $5 daily fee/room. Designated
rooms, service with restrictions, supervision.

**▼▼ Extended StayAmerica-Great Falls-Missouri
River** H
(406) 761-7524. **$62-$100.** 800 River Dr S 59405. I-15 exit 278, 1.7 mi e
on 10th Ave S, then 0.7 mi n. Int corridors. **Pets:** $25 daily fee/pet. Designated rooms, service with restrictions.

▲▲▲ ▼▼▼ The Great Falls Inn by Riversage H
(406) 453-6000. **$75-$85.** 1400 28th St S 59405. I-15 exit 278, 5.3 mi e
on 10th Ave S, 0.3 mi s on 26th St S, then just e on 15th Ave S. Int
corridors. **Pets:** Other species. $7 daily fee/pet. Designated rooms, service with restrictions, supervision.

▼▼▼▼ Hampton Inn H
(406) 453-2675. **$129-$159.** 2301 14th St SW 59404. I-15 exit 278, just
sw. Int corridors. **Pets:** Medium, dogs only. $20 daily fee/room. Service
with restrictions, supervision.

▲▲▲ ▼▼▼▼ Holiday Inn H
(406) 727-7200. **Call for rates.** 400 10th Ave S 59405. I-15 exit 278, 2
mi e on 10th Ave S, then just s. Int corridors. **Pets:** Other species. $20
one-time fee/room. Designated rooms, supervision.

▼▼▼▼ La Quinta Inn & Suites Great Falls H
(406) 761-2600. **$83-$177.** 600 River Dr S 59405. I-15 exit 278, 1.7 mi e
on 10th Ave S, then 0.8 mi n. Int corridors. **Pets:** Service with restrictions,
supervision.

▲▲▲ ▼ Motel 6 #4238 M
(406) 453-1602. **$67-$95.** 2 Treasure State Dr 59404. I-15 exit 278, 0.8
mi e on 10th Ave S and US 87/89 and SR 3/200. Int corridors.
Pets: Other species. Service with restrictions, supervision.

▼ O'Haire Motor Inn M
(406) 454-2141. **Call for rates.** 17 7th St S 59403. Center of downtown.
Ext/int corridors. **Pets:** Accepted.

▲▲▲ ▼▼ Quality Inn H
(406) 761-3410. **$69-$130.** 220 Central Ave 59401. Downtown. Ext/int
corridors. **Pets:** Small, dogs only. $10 daily fee/pet. Service with restrictions, supervision.

▼▼▼ Staybridge Suites H
(406) 761-4903. **$99-$199.** 201 3rd St NW (US 87) 59404. I-15 exit 280
(Central Ave), 1.2 mi w, then just n. Int corridors. **Pets:** Accepted.

▲▲▲ ▼▼▼ TownHouse Inn of Great Falls M
(406) 761-4600. **Call for rates.** 1411 10th Ave S 59405. I-15 exit 278,
2.6 mi e on 10th Ave S and US 87/89 and SR 3/200. Int corridors.
Pets: Accepted.

HAMILTON

▼▼ Bitterroot River Inn & Conference Center H
(406) 375-2525. **$69-$139.** 139 Bitterroot Plaza Dr 59840. US 93, 1 mi
n, then just w. Ext/int corridors. **Pets:** Large. Designated rooms, service
with restrictions, supervision.

▼▼ Magnuson Hotel Hamilton Black Bear Inn M
(406) 363-2142. **$87-$105.** 409 S 1st St (US 93) 59840. On US 93, s of
City Center, jct Madison. Ext corridors. **Pets:** Other species. $10 daily
fee/pet. Service with restrictions, supervision.

▲▲▲ ▼▼▼ Town House Inns H ❀
(406) 363-6600. **$65-$100.** 1113 N 1st St 59840. On US 93, n of City
Center. Int corridors. **Pets:** Other species. $10 daily fee/pet. Service with
restrictions, supervision.

HARDIN

▼ Rodeway Inn H
(406) 665-1870. **Call for rates.** 1324 N Crawford Ave 59034. I-90 exit
495, just s on SR 47. Ext corridors. **Pets:** Other species. $10 daily fee/
pet. Designated rooms, service with restrictions, supervision.

▼ Western Motel M
(406) 665-2296. **$65-$110.** 830 W 3rd St 59034. I-90 exit 495 eastbound,
1.3 mi s on SR 47 and CR 313, then just e; exit 497 westbound, 0.3 mi
w on I-90 business loop, continue on 3rd St for 0.7 mi. Ext corridors.
Pets: $5 daily fee/pet. Service with restrictions, supervision.

HARLOWTON

▼ Countryside Inn M
(406) 632-4119. **$54-$67.** 309 3rd St NE 59036. US 12 E. Ext corridors.
Pets: Accepted.

HAVRE

▼▼ TownHouse Inn of Havre H
(406) 265-6711. **Call for rates.** 601 1st St W 59501. Just w of town
center on US 2. Int corridors. **Pets:** Accepted.

HELENA

▼▼▼ Barrister Bed & Breakfast BB ❀
(406) 443-7330. **$130-$145, 4 day notice.** 416 N Ewing St 59601. I-15
exit 192 (Prospect Ave), 1.5 mi sw via Prospect and Montana aves to 9th
Ave, 0.8 mi w, then just s. Int corridors. **Pets:** Dogs only.

**▲▲▲ ▼▼▼ BEST WESTERN PREMIER Helena Great
Northern Hotel** H ❀
(406) 457-5500. **$167.** 835 Great Northern Blvd 59601. I-15 exit 193
(Cedar St), 2 mi w, just w on Lyndale Ave, then just s on Getchell St;
downtown. Int corridors. **Pets:** Small, dogs only. $15 daily fee/pet. Designated rooms, service with restrictions, supervision.

▼▼ Days Inn Helena H
(406) 442-3280. **$80-$115.** 2001 Prospect Ave 59601. I-15 exit 192
(Prospect Ave), just w. Int corridors. **Pets:** Accepted.

▲▲▲ ▼▼▼ Helena Super 8 H
(406) 443-2450. **$65-$95.** 2200 11th Ave 59601. I-15 exit 192 (Prospect
Ave) northbound; exit west business district southbound on US 12. Int
corridors. **Pets:** Accepted.

▼▼▼▼ **Holiday Inn Conference Center Downtown** H
(406) 443-2200. **$119-$159, 3 day notice.** 22 N Last Chance Gulch 59601. Jct Park and Broadway aves. Int corridors. **Pets:** Medium. $10 daily fee/pet. Designated rooms, service with restrictions, supervision.
🛜 ⊠ 📧 💻 🍴 ➤

▲▲▲ ▼▼▼ **Jorgenson's Inn & Suites** H
(406) 442-1770. **$70-$129.** 1714 11th Ave 59601. I-15 exit 192 (Prospect Ave), just w of I-15 and US 287/12. Ext/int corridors. **Pets:** Other species. $20 one-time fee/room. Service with restrictions, crate.
SAVE 🛜 📧 💻 🍴 ➤

▼▼▼ **La Quinta Inn & Suites Helena** H
(406) 449-4000. **$89-$166.** 701 Washington St 59601. I-15 exit 192 (Prospect Ave), just w. Int corridors. **Pets:** Service with restrictions, supervision. 🛜 ⊠ 🅜 📧 💻

▼▼▼▼ **Red Lion Colonial Hotel** H
(406) 443-2100. **Call for rates.** 2301 Colonial Dr 59601. I-15 exit 192 (Prospect Ave) southbound; exit 192B northbound. Int corridors. **Pets:** Other species. $15 one-time fee/room. Service with restrictions, crate. 🛜 ⊠ 📧 💻 🍴 ➤ ⊠

▼▼▼ **Residence Inn by Marriott** H
(406) 443-8010. **$119-$179.** 2500 E Custer Ave 59602. I-15 exit 194 (Custer Ave), just e. Int corridors. **Pets:** $100 one-time fee/room. Service with restrictions, crate. 🛜 ⊠ 🅜 📧 ➤

▼▼▼▼ **Wingate by Wyndham** H 🐾
(406) 449-3000. **$130.** 2007 N Oakes St 59601. I-15 exit 193 (Cedar St), just sw. Int corridors. **Pets:** $10 daily fee/pet. Designated rooms, service with restrictions, supervision. 🛜 🅜 📧 💻 ➤

HUNGRY HORSE

▲▲▲ ▼▼▼ **Mini Golden Inns Motel** M
(406) 387-4313. **$86-$160, 30 day notice.** 8955 US 2 E 59919. East end of town. Ext corridors. **Pets:** Accepted. SAVE 🛜 🅜 📧 💻

KALISPELL

▲▲▲ ▼▼ **Aero Inn** H 🐾
(406) 755-3798. **$49-$104.** 1830 US 93 S 59901. 1.3 mi s on US 93 from jct US 2. Int corridors. **Pets:** Other species. $20 deposit/room. Designated rooms, service with restrictions, supervision. SAVE 🛜 📧 ➤

▼▼ **Americas Best Value Inn** H
(406) 756-3222. **$60-$135.** 1550 Hwy 93 N 59901. 1.3 mi n on US 93 from jct US 2. Int corridors. **Pets:** Small, dogs only. $10 daily fee/room. Designated rooms, service with restrictions, supervision. 🛜 ⊠ 📧

▲▲▲ ▼▼▼ **Comfort Inn** H
(406) 755-6700. **$70-$250.** 1330 Hwy 2 W 59901. 1 mi w on US 2 from jct US 93. Int corridors. **Pets:** Medium. $20 one-time fee/pet. Designated rooms, service with restrictions, supervision.
SAVE 🛜 ⊠ 📧 💻 ➤

▼▼▼▼ **Holiday Inn Express & Suites** H
(406) 755-7405. **$99-$249.** 275 Treeline Rd 59901. 3 mi n on US 93 from jct US 2, just w. Int corridors. **Pets:** Dogs only. $35 one-time fee/room. Service with restrictions, supervision.
🛜 ⊠ 🅜 📧 💻 ➤

▼▼ **Kalispell/Glacier Int'l Airport area Super 8** H
(406) 755-1888. **$53-$122.** 1341 1st Ave E 59901. 1.2 mi s on US 93 from jct US 2. Int corridors. **Pets:** Other species. $10 one-time fee/pet. Designated rooms, service with restrictions, supervision.
🛜 ⊠ 🅜 📧 💻

▼▼▼ **Kalispell Grand Hotel** H 🐾
(406) 755-8100. **$80-$150.** 100 Main St 59901. On US 93; jct 1st St; downtown. Int corridors. **Pets:** Other species. Service with restrictions, crate. 🛜 ⊠

▼▼▼▼ **La Quinta Inn & Suites Kalispell** H
(406) 257-5255. **$65-$260.** 255 Montclair Dr 59901. Jct US 93 and 2, 1 mi e. Int corridors. **Pets:** Service with restrictions, supervision.
🛜 ⊠ 🅜 📧 💻 ➤

▼▼▼▼ **Red Lion Hotel Kalispell** H
(406) 751-5050. **Call for rates.** 20 N Main St 59901. Just s on US 93 from jct US 2; connected to Kalispell Center Mall. Int corridors. **Pets:** Other species. $15 one-time fee/room. Service with restrictions, crate. 🛜 ⊠ 🅜 📧 💻 ➤ ⊠

LAUREL

▲▲▲ ▼▼▼ **BEST WESTERN Yellowstone Crossing** H
(406) 628-6888. **$89-$99.** 205 SE 4th St 59044. I-90 exit 434, just n, then just e. Int corridors. **Pets:** $15 deposit/pet. Designated rooms, service with restrictions, supervision. SAVE 🛜 🅜 📧 💻 ➤

LEWISTOWN

▼▼ **B & B Motel** M
(406) 535-5496. **Call for rates.** 520 E Main St 59457. Downtown. Ext corridors. **Pets:** Dogs only. $10 one-time fee/pet. Designated rooms, supervision. 🛜 📧 💻

▼▼ **Lewistown Super 8** H
(406) 538-2581. **$80-$100.** 102 Wendell Ave 59457. West side of town, on US 87; near airport. Int corridors. **Pets:** Accepted.
🛜 ⊠ 📧 💻

LIBBY

▼▼ **Sandman Motel** M
(406) 293-8831. **$55-$85, 7 day notice.** 31901 US 2 59923. Just w on US 2 from jct SR 37. Ext corridors. **Pets:** Accepted. 🛜 📧

LIVINGSTON

▲▲▲ ▼▼▼ **BEST WESTERN Yellowstone Inn** H
(406) 222-6110. **$86-$154.** 1515 W Park St 59047. I-90 exit 333, just n. Int corridors. **Pets:** Other species. $10 daily fee/pet. Designated rooms, service with restrictions, supervision. SAVE 🛜 📧 💻 🍴 ➤

▼▼ **Livingston Rodeway Inn** M
(406) 222-6320. **$60-$130.** 102 Rogers Ln 59047. I-90 exit 333, just n on US 89, then just w. Ext/int corridors. **Pets:** $10 daily fee/pet. Designated rooms, service with restrictions, supervision. 🛜 📧 💻 🍴 ➤

LOLO

▼▼ **Days Inn** H
(406) 273-2121. **$80-$120, 3 day notice.** 11225 US 93 S 59847. North edge of town. Ext/int corridors. **Pets:** Dogs only. $10 daily fee/pet. Service with restrictions, supervision. 🛜 ⊠ 🅜 📧 💻

MALTA

▲▲▲ ▼▼ **Maltana Motel** M
(406) 654-2610. **$70-$80.** 138 S 1st Ave W 59538. Just s of US 2 via US 191, then just w; downtown. Ext corridors. **Pets:** Accepted.
SAVE 🛜 ⊠ 📧 💻

MILES CITY

▲▲▲ ▼▼▼ **BEST WESTERN War Bonnet Inn** M 🐾
(406) 234-4560. **$90-$200.** 1015 S Haynes Ave 59301. I-94 exit 138 (Broadus), 0.3 mi n. Ext corridors. **Pets:** Large. $20 daily fee/room. Designated rooms, service with restrictions, crate.
SAVE 🛜 ⊠ 📧 💻 ➤ ⊠

▲▲▲ ▼▼▼ **GuestHouse International Inn & Suites** H 🐾
(406) 232-3661. **$90-$120.** 3111 Steel St 59301. I-94 exit 138 (Broadus), just s. Int corridors. **Pets:** $15 daily fee/pet. Designated rooms, service with restrictions, supervision. SAVE 🛜 ⊠ 🅜 📧 💻 ➤

MISSOULA

BEST WESTERN PLUS Grant Creek Inn H ❀
(406) 543-0700. **$109-$209.** 5280 Grant Creek Rd 59808. I-90 exit 101 (Reserve St), just n. Int corridors. **Pets:** $10 daily fee/pet. Designated rooms, service with restrictions, supervision.

Broadway Inn Conference Center H ❀
(406) 532-3300. **$70-$100.** 1609 W Broadway 59808. I-90 exit 104 (Orange St), 0.5 mi s, then 1 mi w. Int corridors. **Pets:** Dogs only. $10 daily fee/pet. Designated rooms, supervision.

Campus Inn M
(406) 549-5134. **$70-$150.** 744 E Broadway 59802. I-90 exit 105 (Van Buren St), just s to Broadway, then just w. Ext/int corridors. **Pets:** Other species. $6 daily fee/pet. Service with restrictions.

Days Inn/Missoula Airport H ❀
(406) 721-9776. **$60-$95.** 8600 Truck Stop Rd 59808. I-90 exit 96, just n. Int corridors. **Pets:** Other species. $10 daily fee/pet. Designated rooms, service with restrictions, supervision.

Days Inn University H
(406) 543-7221. **$79-$100.** 201 E Main St 59802. I-90 exit 104 (Orange St), 0.5 mi s to Broadway, 0.5 mi e to Washington St, just s to Main St, then just w. Ext corridors. **Pets:** Accepted.

DoubleTree by Hilton Hotel Missoula - Edgewater H
(406) 728-3100. **$109-$199.** 100 Madison St 59802. I-90 exit 105 (Van Buren St), just s, then just w on Front St. Int corridors. **Pets:** Other species. $30 one-time fee/room. Designated rooms, service with restrictions, supervision.

Econo Lodge H
(406) 542-7550. **$60-$110.** 4953 N Reserve St 59808. I-90 exit 101 (Reserve St), just s. Int corridors. **Pets:** Medium. $10 daily fee/pet. Designated rooms, service with restrictions, supervision.

Family Inn M
(406) 543-7371. **Call for rates.** 1031 E Broadway 59802. I-90 exit 105 (Van Buren St), just s, then just e. Ext corridors. **Pets:** $10 daily fee/room.

GuestHouse Inn & Suites - Missoula H
(406) 251-2665. **$69-$109.** 3803 Brooks St 59804. I-90 exit 101 (Reserve St), 5 mi s to Brooks St, then just w. Int corridors. **Pets:** Accepted.

Hampton Inn H ❀
(406) 549-1800. **$109-$149.** 4805 N Reserve St 59808. I-90 exit 101 (Reserve St), just s. Int corridors. **Pets:** Large, other species. $10 one-time fee/room. Service with restrictions, supervision.

Holiday Inn Missoula-Downtown at the Park H ❀
(406) 721-8550. **Call for rates.** 200 S Pattee St 59802. I-90 exit 104 (Orange St), 0.5 mi s to Broadway, just e to Pattee St, then just s. Int corridors. **Pets:** Other species. $20 one-time fee/room. Designated rooms, service with restrictions, supervision.

La Quinta Inn Missoula H
(406) 549-9000. **$83-$205.** 5059 N Reserve St 59808. I-90 exit 101 (Reserve St), just s. Int corridors. **Pets:** Service with restrictions, supervision.

Quality Inn & Suites H
(406) 542-0888. **$79-$129.** 4545 N Reserve St 59808. I-90 exit 101 (Reserve St), 0.5 mi s. Int corridors. **Pets:** Accepted.

Red Lion Inn M
(406) 728-3300. **Call for rates.** 700 W Broadway 59802. I-90 exit 104 (Orange St), just s, then just w. Ext corridors. **Pets:** Other species. $15 one-time fee/room. Service with restrictions, crate.

Ruby's Inn & Convention Center H
(406) 721-0990. **$79-$125, 7 day notice.** 4825 N Reserve St 59808. I-90 exit 101 (Reserve St), just s. Ext/int corridors. **Pets:** Accepted.

Sleep Inn by Choice Hotels H ❀
(406) 543-5883. **$85-$119.** 3425 Dore Ln 59801. I-90 exit 101 (Reserve St), 5 mi s, then just e on Brooks St. Int corridors. **Pets:** Other species. $20 one-time fee/room. Designated rooms, service with restrictions, supervision.

Staybridge Suites H
(406) 830-3900. **$99-$169.** 120 Expressway Blvd 59808. I-90 exit 101 (Reserve St), just s. Int corridors. **Pets:** Medium. $50 one-time fee/room. Designated rooms, service with restrictions, supervision.

Super 8-Brooks St H
(406) 251-2255. **$57-$94.** 3901 Brooks St 59804. I-90 exit 101 (Reserve St), 5 mi s to Brooks St, then just w. Int corridors. **Pets:** Accepted.

Thunderbird Motel M
(406) 543-7251. **Call for rates.** 1009 E Broadway 59802. I-90 exit 105 (Van Buren St), just s to Broadway, then just e. Ext/int corridors. **Pets:** Medium, dogs only. $10 one-time fee/pet. Designated rooms, service with restrictions, supervision.

MONTANA CITY

Elkhorn Mountain Inn H
(406) 442-6625. **$70-$90.** 1 Jackson Creek Rd 59634. I-15 exit 187 (Montana City), just w. Int corridors. **Pets:** Other species. $10 daily fee/pet. Designated rooms, service with restrictions, supervision.

POLSON

BEST WESTERN PLUS KwaTaqNuk Resort H ❀
(406) 883-3636. **$80-$161.** 49708 US Hwy 93 E 59860. Just s of downtown. Int corridors. **Pets:** Medium. $20 daily fee/room. Designated rooms, service with restrictions, supervision.

RED LODGE

Comfort Inn of Red Lodge H
(406) 446-4469. **Call for rates.** 612 N Broadway 59068. Jct US 212 and SR 78, north entrance. Int corridors. **Pets:** Other species. $10 daily fee/room. Designated rooms, service with restrictions, supervision.

Lu Pine Inn H
(406) 446-1321. **$69-$149.** 702 S Hauser Ave 59068. 0.4 mi s, just w of US 212. Int corridors. **Pets:** Designated rooms, service with restrictions, supervision.

Yodeler Motel M
(406) 446-1435. **$60-$140.** 601 S Broadway Ave 59068. Just s on US 212. Ext corridors. **Pets:** Accepted.

RONAN

Starlite Motel M
(406) 676-7000. **Call for rates.** 18 Main St SW 59864. Just w of jct US 93 and Main St. Ext corridors. **Pets:** Accepted.

ST. IGNATIUS

💎 Sunset Motel Ⓜ

(406) 745-3900. **$60-$80.** 333 Mountain View 59865. Just s of downtown, exit US 93. Ext corridors. **Pets:** Dogs only. $5 daily fee/pet. Supervision. 🛜 ⊠ 🔲

ST. REGIS

🛆 💎 Little River Motel Ⓜ

(406) 649-2713. **$45-$80.** 424 Little River Ln 59866. I-90 exit 33, just n to flashing light, just w, then just sw. Ext corridors. **Pets:** Medium. $10 daily fee/pet. Designated rooms, service with restrictions, supervision.
[SAVE] 🛜 🔲 🔳 Ⓧ 🔲

🛆 💎💎 Super 8-St. Regis 🄷

(406) 649-2422. **$60-$100.** 9 Old Hwy 10 E 59866. I-90 exit 33, just n. Ext/int corridors. **Pets:** Accepted. [SAVE] 🛜 🔲 🔳

SHELBY

🛆 💎💎 Comfort Inn of Shelby 🄷

(406) 434-2212. **$110-$170.** 455 McKinley Ave 59474. I-15 exit 363, just e, then just s. Int corridors. **Pets:** Accepted. [SAVE] 🛜 🔲 🔳 ⊠

🛆 💎 O'Haire Manor Motel Ⓜ

(406) 434-5555. **Call for rates.** 204 2nd St S 59474. Just s of Main St via Maple St. Ext/int corridors. **Pets:** Accepted. [SAVE] 🛜 🔲

SIDNEY

💎💎 Holiday Inn Express & Suites 🄷

(406) 433-3200. **Call for rates.** 251 W Holly St 59270. Just nw of jct SR 16 and 200. Int corridors. **Pets:** Accepted. 🛜 ⊠ 🔲 🔳 🛥

🛆 💎💎 Richland Motor Inn Ⓜ

(406) 433-6400. **$116-$125.** 1200 S Central Ave 59270. 1.5 mi n of jct SR 16 and 200. Int corridors. **Pets:** Other species. $10 daily fee/pet. Service with restrictions, crate. [SAVE] 🛜 🔲 🔳

THREE FORKS

🛆 💎 Broken Spur Motel Ⓜ

(406) 285-3237. **$60-$120.** 124 W Elm (Hwy 2) 59752. I-90 exit 278 westbound, 1.3 mi sw; exit 274 eastbound, 1 mi s on SR 287 to jct SR 2, then 3 mi se. Ext corridors. **Pets:** Other species. $5 one-time fee/pet. Designated rooms, service with restrictions, supervision. [SAVE] 🛜 🔲

💎 Fort Three Forks Motel & RV Park Ⓜ

(406) 285-3233. **$48-$109.** 10776 Hwy 287 59752. I-90 exit 274, just n. Ext corridors. **Pets:** $10 one-time fee/pet. Designated rooms, service with restrictions, supervision. 🛜 🔲 🔳

WEST YELLOWSTONE

🛆 💎💎 BEST WESTERN Cross Winds Motor Inn Ⓜ

(406) 646-9557. **Call for rates.** 201 Firehole Ave 59758. Just w of US 191 and 287, on US 20 at Dunraven St and Firehole Ave. Ext corridors. **Pets:** $20 one-time fee/room. Designated rooms, service with restrictions, supervision. [SAVE] 🛜 ⊠ 🔲 🔳 🛥

🛆 💎💎💎 BEST WESTERN Desert Inn 🄷 🐾

(406) 646-7376. **$79-$205.** 133 Canyon St 59758. US 191 at US 20; corner of Canyon St and Firehole Ave. Int corridors. **Pets:** Large, dogs only. Designated rooms, service with restrictions, supervision.
[SAVE] 🛜 ⊠ 🔲 🔳 🛥

🛆 💎💎 BEST WESTERN Weston Inn Ⓜ

(406) 646-7373. **$190-$210.** 108 Gibbon Ave 59758. US 191; jct Canyon St. Ext/int corridors. **Pets:** Accepted. [SAVE] 🛜 ⊠ 🔲 🔳 🛥

🛆 💎💎💎 Brandin' Iron Inn Ⓜ

(406) 646-9411. **$79-$159, 3 day notice.** 201 Canyon St 59758. Just w; just n of park entrance. Ext corridors. **Pets:** Other species. $15 one-time fee/room. Designated rooms, service with restrictions, supervision.
[SAVE] 🛜 ⊠ Ⓧ 🔲 🔳

🛆 💎 City Center Motel Ⓜ

(406) 646-7337. **$69-$119, 3 day notice.** 214 Madison Ave 59758. W of US 191 at Madison Ave and Dunraven St; just nw of park entrance. Ext corridors. **Pets:** Other species. $15 one-time fee/room. Designated rooms, service with restrictions, supervision. [SAVE] 🛜 ⊠ 🔲 Ⓩ

💎💎💎 ClubHouse Inn 🄷

(406) 646-4892. **$100-$260.** 105 S Electric St 59758. Just sw of jct US 191, 187 and 20; just w of park entrance. Int corridors. **Pets:** Large, other species. Designated rooms, service with restrictions, supervision.
🛜 ⊠ Ⓧ 🔲 🔳 🛥

💎💎💎 Comfort Inn 🄷

(406) 646-4212. **Call for rates.** 638 Madison Ave 59758. US 191, 0.6 mi w; US 20, just e, then 0.4 mi s on Iris St. Int corridors. **Pets:** Large, other species. Designated rooms, service with restrictions, supervision.
🛜 ⊠ 🔲 🔳 🛥

🛆 💎💎 Gray Wolf Inn & Suites 🄷

(406) 646-0000. **$69-$279, 3 day notice.** 250 S Canyon St 59758. Just w of park entrance. Int corridors. **Pets:** Dogs only. Designated rooms, service with restrictions, supervision.
[SAVE] 🛜 ⊠ Ⓧ 🔲 🔳 🛥

🛆 💎💎💎 Holiday Inn West Yellowstone 🄷

(406) 646-7365. **$119-$299, 3 day notice.** 315 Yellowstone Ave 59758. Just w of park entrance. Int corridors. **Pets:** Other species. $50 one-time fee/room. Designated rooms, service with restrictions, supervision.
[SAVE] 🛜 ⊠ Ⓧ 🔲 🔳 🍽 🛥 ⊠

💎💎 Kelly Inn 🄷 🐾

(406) 646-4544. **Call for rates.** 104 S Canyon Ave 59758. S of jct US 191, 287 and 20; just w of park entrance. Ext/int corridors. **Pets:** Designated rooms, service with restrictions, supervision.
🛜 ⊠ 🔲 🔳 🛥

🛆 💎💎💎 Stage Coach Inn 🄷

(406) 646-7381. **$69-$239.** 209 Madison Ave 59758. Corner of Dunraven St and Madison Ave, just w of park entrance. Int corridors. **Pets:** $25 daily fee/room. Crate. [SAVE] 🛜 ⊠ 🔲 🔳 ⊠

🛆 💎💎💎 Three Bear Lodge 🄷

(406) 646-7353. **$69-$229.** 217 Yellowstone Ave 59758. Just w of park entrance. Ext/int corridors. **Pets:** $25 daily fee/pet. Designated rooms, service with restrictions, crate. [SAVE] 🛜 ⊠ 🔲 🔳 🍽 🛥 ⊠

💎💎 Yellowstone Lodge 🄷

(406) 646-0020. **$69-$209.** 251 S Electric St 59758. Just w of park entrance. Int corridors. **Pets:** Medium, other species. Designated rooms, service with restrictions, supervision. 🛜 ⊠ 🔲 🔳 🛥

WHITEFISH

💎💎 Bay Point on the Lake 🄒🄾

(406) 862-2331. **$133-$164, 30 day notice.** 300 Bay Point Dr 59937. Jct US 93 and SR 487, 0.6 mi n on SR 487 to Skyles Pl, 0.3 mi w to Dakota Ave, 0.3 mi n, then just w. Ext corridors. **Pets:** Dogs only. $35 one-time fee/room. Designated rooms, no service, crate.
🛜 🔲 🔳 🛥 ⊠

🛆 💎💎💎 BEST WESTERN Rocky Mountain Lodge 🄷

(406) 862-2569. **$102-$176.** 6510 Hwy 93 S 59937. 1.3 mi s on US 93 from jct SR 487. Ext/int corridors. **Pets:** Accepted.
[SAVE] 🛜 ⊠ Ⓧ 🔲 🔳 🛥

🛆 💎💎💎 Grouse Mountain Lodge 🄷

(406) 862-3000. **$109-$399, 14 day notice.** 2 Fairway Dr 59937. 1 mi w on US 93 from jct SR 487. Int corridors. **Pets:** $25 one-time fee/room. Service with restrictions, supervision.
[SAVE] 🛜 ⊠ 🔲 🔳 🍽 🛥 ⊠

Kristianna Mountain Homes CO
(406) 862-2860. **$220-$440, 90 day notice.** 331 Karrow Ave 59937. Jct US 93 and SR 487, 2.4 mi n on SR 487, at flashing light go 5.2 mi on Big Mountain Rd, just n on Gelande St, then just w on Kristianna Close. Ext/int corridors. **Pets:** Accepted.

North Forty Resort CA
(406) 862-7740. **$119-$269, 14 day notice.** 3765 Hwy 40 W 59912. 2.5 mi e on SR 40 from jct US 93. Ext corridors. **Pets:** Other species. $10 daily fee/pet. Designated rooms, service with restrictions, crate.

Pine Lodge H
(406) 862-7600. **$79-$170.** 920 Spokane Ave 59937. 1 mi s on US 93 from jct SR 487. Int corridors. **Pets:** Other species. Service with restrictions, supervision.

WHITE SULPHUR SPRINGS

All Seasons Inn & Suites H
(406) 547-8888. **$77-$165.** 808 3rd Ave SW 59645. On US 89/12, south end of town. Int corridors. **Pets:** Dogs only. $10 one-time fee/pet. Service with restrictions, supervision.

NEBRASKA

BELLEVUE

BEST WESTERN White House Inn H
(402) 293-1600. **$90-$140.** 305 Fort Crook Rd N 68005. US 75, 1.8 mi n of jct SR 370 and Fort Crook Rd N. Int corridors. **Pets:** Accepted.

Candlewood Suites-Bellevue H
(402) 932-8144. **$89-$120.** 10902 S 15th St 68123. Jct US 75 and Cornhusker Rd, just e on Cornhusker Rd, then 0.3 mi s. Int corridors. **Pets:** Medium. $100 one-time fee/pet. Service with restrictions, crate.

Hampton Inn H
(402) 292-1607. **$129-$219.** 3404 Samson Way 68123. US 75, 1 mi n on SR 370, just w on Golden Blvd, then 0.3 mi n. Int corridors. **Pets:** Medium. $50 one-time fee/room. Designated rooms, service with restrictions, crate.

Microtel Inn & Suites by Wyndham Bellevue H
(402) 292-0191. **$65-$170.** 3008 Samson Way 68123. US 75, 1 mi w on SR 370, n on Golden Blvd, then just w. Int corridors. **Pets:** Other species. $25 one-time fee/room. Service with restrictions, supervision.

Settle Inn & Suites H
(402) 292-1155. **$69-$200.** 2105 Pratt Ave 68123. US 75 exit Cornhusker Rd, just w. Int corridors. **Pets:** Dogs only. $15 daily fee/room. Designated rooms, service with restrictions, crate.

BROKEN BOW

The Arrow Hotel H
(308) 872-6662. **$80-$166.** 509 S 9th Ave 68822. On SR 2/92; downtown. Int corridors. **Pets:** Other species. $10 daily fee/pet. Service with restrictions, supervision.

CHADRON

BEST WESTERN West Hills Inn H
(308) 432-3305. **$74-$102.** 1100 W 10th St 69337. Just s of jct US 385 and 20. Ext/int corridors. **Pets:** $20 daily fee/pet. Designated rooms, service with restrictions, crate.

Grand Westerner Motel M
(308) 432-5595. **Call for rates.** 1050 W Hwy 20 69337. On US 20, 0.8 mi w; just e of jct US 385. Ext corridors. **Pets:** Dogs only. $5 deposit/pet. Service with restrictions, supervision.

Westerner Motel M
(308) 432-5577. **Call for rates.** 300 Oak St 69337. On US 20; 0.5 mi e of jct US 385 and SR 87. Ext corridors. **Pets:** Accepted.

COLUMBUS

Sleep Inn & Suites Hotel H
(402) 562-5200. **$79-$139.** 303 23rd St 68601. On US 30, 2 mi e of jct US 30 and 81; east side of town. Int corridors. **Pets:** Medium. $25 daily fee/pet. Designated rooms, service with restrictions, crate.

COZAD

Rodeway Inn H
(308) 784-4900. **$55-$68.** 809 S Meridian Ave 69130. I-80 exit 222, just n. Int corridors. **Pets:** Other species. Service with restrictions, supervision.

FREMONT

Oak Tree Inn H
(402) 721-3700. **Call for rates.** 2700 N Diers Pkwy 68025. US 30, just n. Int corridors. **Pets:** Accepted.

GERING

Monument Inn & Suites H
(308) 436-1950. **$70-$80.** 1130 M St 69341. 1 mi e of SR 71, just w of M (SR 92) and 10th sts. Int corridors. **Pets:** Medium, dogs only. $15 one-time fee/room. Service with restrictions, crate.

GOTHENBURG

Comfort Suites H
(308) 537-7378. **Call for rates.** 315 Platte River Dr 69138. I-80 exit 211 (SR 47), just n, then just w. Int corridors. **Pets:** Accepted.

GRAND ISLAND

Quality Inn and Conference Center H
(308) 384-7770. **$79-$130.** 7838 S US Hwy 281 68803. I-80 exit 312 (US 281), just s. Int corridors. **Pets:** Medium. $15 daily fee/pet. Designated rooms, service with restrictions, supervision.

Rodeway Inn H
(308) 384-1333. **$55-$100.** 3205 S Locust St 68801. I-80 exit 314, 4 mi n. Int corridors. **Pets:** Medium. $100 deposit/pet. Service with restrictions, supervision.

♦♦♦ ▼▼▼ Super 8 H
(308) 384-4380. **$54-$67.** 2603 S Locust St 68801. I-80 exit 314, 4.7 mi n. Int corridors. **Pets:** Cats only. $10 daily fee/room. Service with restrictions, supervision. 〔SAVE〕 📶 🅼 🖥 💻 🏊

KEARNEY

♦♦♦ ▼▼▼ AmericInn Lodge & Suites of Kearney H
(308) 234-7800. **$89-$159.** 215 W Talmadge Rd 68845. I-80 exit 272 (SR 44), just n. Int corridors. **Pets:** Medium, dogs only. $10 daily fee/room. Designated rooms, service with restrictions, crate.
〔SAVE〕 📶 ✖ 🅼 🖥 💻 🏊

♦♦♦ ▼▼▼ BEST WESTERN Inn of Kearney H
(308) 237-5185. **$80.** 1010 3rd Ave 68845. I-80 exit 272 (SR 44), 1 mi n, then just w. Ext/int corridors. **Pets:** Accepted.
〔SAVE〕 📶 ✖ 🅼 🖥 💻 🍴 🏊 ✖

▼▼ Econo Lodge H
(308) 237-2671. **Call for rates.** 709 2nd Ave 68847. I-80 exit 272 (SR 44), 1 mi n. Int corridors. **Pets:** Large, other species. $15 one-time fee/room. Service with restrictions, supervision. 📶 ✖ 🅼 🖥 💻

▼▼ Microtel Inn & Suites by Wyndham Kearney H
(308) 698-3003. **$60-$80.** 104 Talmadge Rd 68847. I-80 exit 272 (SR 44), just se. Int corridors. **Pets:** $5 daily fee/pet. Service with restrictions, supervision. 📶 ✖ 🅼 🖥 💻

▼▼ Quality Inn by Choice Hotels H
(308) 237-0838. **Call for rates.** 121 3rd Ave 68845. I-80 exit 272 (SR 44), 0.3 mi n. Int corridors. **Pets:** Medium. $15 daily fee/pet. Designated rooms, service with restrictions, supervision.
📶 ✖ 🅼 🖥 💻 🏊

♦♦♦ ▼▼▼ Ramada Kearney Hotel H
(308) 237-3141. **$80-$200.** 301 2nd Ave 68847. I-80 exit 272 (SR 44), 0.7 mi n. Int corridors. **Pets:** Accepted.
〔SAVE〕 📶 🅼 🖥 💻 🍴 🏊 ✖

▼▼ Rodeway Inn & Suites H
(308) 698-2810. **Call for rates.** 411 2nd Ave 68847. I-80 exit 272 (SR 44), 0.8 mi n. Int corridors. **Pets:** Large, other species. $15 daily fee/room. Service with restrictions, supervision. 📶 ✖ 🅼 🖥 💻

LEXINGTON

▼▼ Days Inn H
(308) 324-6440. **$70-$105.** 2506 Plum Creek Pkwy 68850. I-80 exit 237 (US 283), 0.6 mi n. Int corridors. **Pets:** Dogs only. $10 daily fee/pet. Designated rooms, no service, supervision. 📶 🅼 🖥 💻

▼▼▼ Holiday Inn Express Suites H
(308) 324-9900. **$120-$175.** 2605 Plum Creek Pkwy 68850. I-80 exit 237 (US 283), 0.5 mi n. Int corridors. **Pets:** Other species. $15 daily fee/room. Designated rooms, service with restrictions, supervision.
📶 ✖ 🅼 🖥 💻 🏊

▼▼▼ Lexington Comfort Inn H
(308) 324-3747. **$85-$112.** 2810 Plum Creek Pkwy 68850. I-80 exit 237 (US 283), 0.3 mi n. Ext/int corridors. **Pets:** Medium. $15 deposit/pet. Designated rooms, service with restrictions, supervision.
📶 🅼 🖥 💻 🏊

LINCOLN

♦♦♦ ▼▼▼ AmericInn Lodge & Suites of Lincoln North H
(402) 435-1600. **Call for rates.** 6555 N 27th St 68521. I-80 exit 403 (27th St), 0.3 mi s, just w on Whitehead Dr, then just s. Int corridors.
Pets: Accepted. 〔SAVE〕 📶 🅼 🖥 💻 🏊

▼▼▼ AmericInn Lodge & Suites of Lincoln South H
(402) 420-0027. **Call for rates.** 8701 Amber Hill Ct 68526. 5.8 mi se on SR 2 (Nebraska Hwy), just w at 87th St. Int corridors. **Pets:** Accepted.
📶 ✖ 🅼 🖥 💻 🏊

♦♦♦ ▼▼▼ BEST WESTERN Crown Inn H
(402) 438-4700. **Call for rates.** 6501 N 28th St 68504. I-80 exit 403 (27th St), just s to Wildcat Dr, then 0.3 mi s. Int corridors. **Pets:** Medium, dogs only. $100 deposit/room, $15 daily fee/pet. Designated rooms, service with restrictions, supervision. 〔SAVE〕 📶 ✖ 🅼 🖥 💻 🏊

▼▼▼ Comfort Suites H
(402) 476-8080. **$79-$130, 3 day notice.** 4231 Industrial Ave 68504. I-80 exit 403 (27th St), 2.3 mi s. Int corridors. **Pets:** $10 daily fee/pet. Service with restrictions, supervision. 📶 ✖ 🅼 🖥 💻 🏊

♦♦♦ ▼▼▼ Comfort Suites East H
(402) 325-8800. **Call for rates.** 331 N Cotner Blvd 68505. From I-180 (9th St), 3.3 mi e on US 34 (O St), then 0.3 mi n. Int corridors. **Pets:** $25 one-time fee/pet. Service with restrictions.
〔SAVE〕 📶 ✖ 🅼 🖥 💻 🏊

♦♦♦ ▼▼▼▼ Country Inn & Suites By Carlson North H
(402) 476-5353. **$89-$250.** 5353 N 27th St 68521. I-80 exit 403 (27th St), 1.5 mi s. Int corridors. **Pets:** Other species. $20 daily fee/room. Designated rooms, service with restrictions, crate.
〔SAVE〕 📶 🅼 🖥 💻 🍴 🏊 ✖

♦♦♦ ▼▼▼ Countryside Suites H
(402) 742-7575. **Call for rates.** 6750 Wildcat Dr 68504. I-80 exit 403 (27th St), just s, then e. Int corridors. **Pets:** Medium, other species. $10 daily fee/room. Service with restrictions, supervision.
〔SAVE〕 📶 ✖ 🅼 🖥 💻 🏊

▼▼▼ Holiday Inn Express & Suites H
(402) 464-0588. **Call for rates.** 1101 W Commerce Way 68521. I-80 exit 399, just n, then just e. Int corridors. **Pets:** Other species. $25 one-time fee/pet. Crate. 📶 ✖ 🅼 🖥 💻 🏊

♦♦♦ ▼▼▼ La Quinta Inn Lincoln H
(402) 476-2222. **$71-$188.** 4433 N 27th St 68521. I-80 exit 403 (27th St), 2.3 mi s. Int corridors. **Pets:** Service with restrictions, supervision.
〔SAVE〕 📶 ✖ 🅼 🖥 💻 🏊

♦♦♦ ▼▼▼ Microtel Inn & Suites by Wyndham Lincoln H
(402) 476-2591. **$50-$170.** 2505 Fairfield St 68521. I-80 exit 403 (27th St), 2.7 mi s, then just w. Int corridors. **Pets:** Accepted.
〔SAVE〕 📶 🅼 🖥 💻 🏊

▼▼ New Victorian Suites H ♣
(402) 464-4400. **$69-$149.** 225 N 50th St 68504. 2.5 mi e on US 6 and 34; just ne of jct O St; entrance off 48th St. Int corridors. **Pets:** Medium, dogs only. $15 daily fee/pet. Designated rooms, supervision.
📶 🅼 🖥 💻

▼▼▼ Residence Inn by Marriott - Lincoln South H
(402) 423-1555. **$119-$169.** 5865 Boboli Ln 68516. 1 mi s of SR 2 (Nebraska Hwy) via 56th St, then just e on Pine Lake Rd (Southeast Lincoln). Int corridors. **Pets:** $25 daily fee/room. Service with restrictions, crate. 📶 ✖ 🅼 🖥 💻 🏊 ✖

▼▼▼ Staybridge Suites Lincoln-I-80 H
(402) 438-7829. **$99-$200.** 2701 Fletcher Ave 68504. I-80 exit 403 (27th St), 0.4 mi s, then just e. Int corridors. **Pets:** Other species. $20 one-time fee/room. Service with restrictions, crate. 📶 🅼 🖥 💻 🏊 ✖

▼▼ Super 8-Lincoln/West "O" Street H
(402) 476-8887. **$53-$129.** 2635 West O St 68528. I-80 exit 396 eastbound, 0.5 mi w; exit 397 westbound, 0.5 mi w. Int corridors. **Pets:** Other species. $11 daily fee/pet. Service with restrictions, supervision.
📶 🅼 🖥 💻

MORRILL

▼▼ Oak Tree Inn M
(308) 247-2111. **$62-$70.** 707 E Webster St 69358. 0.4 mi e of center on US 26. Ext/int corridors. **Pets:** $5 one-time fee/room. Service with restrictions. 📶 ✖ 🖥 💻 🍴

NORTH PLATTE

Americas Best Value Travelers Inn M
(308) 534-4020. **$40-$70.** 602 E 4th St 69101. I-80 exit 177 (US 83), 1.5 mi n, then 0.3 mi e. Ext corridors. **Pets:** Other species. Designated rooms, service with restrictions, supervision. (SAVE)

Comfort Inn H
(308) 532-6144. **$89-$119.** 2901 S Jeffers St 69101. I-80 exit 177 (US 83), just s. Int corridors. **Pets:** Medium. $15 daily fee/pet. Service with restrictions, supervision.

Holiday Inn Express Hotel & Suites H
(308) 532-9500. **$119-$229.** 300 Holiday Frontage Rd 69101. I-80 exit 177 (US 83), just s. Int corridors. **Pets:** Accepted.

La Quinta Inn & Suites North Platte H
(308) 534-0700. **$89-$184.** 2600 Eagles Wings Pl 69101. I-80 exit 179, just n, then just w. Int corridors. **Pets:** Service with restrictions, supervision. (SAVE)

Oak Tree Inn H
(308) 535-9900. **Call for rates.** 451 Halligan Dr 69101. I-80 exit 177 (US 83), 0.3 mi n, then 0.3 mi e on service road. Int corridors.
Pets: Accepted.

OGALLALA

BEST WESTERN Stagecoach Inn H
(308) 284-3656. **$80-$100.** 201 Stagecoach Tr 69153. I-80 exit 126 (US 26/SR 61), just n, then e on frontage road. Ext corridors. **Pets:** Accepted.
(SAVE)

Days Inn M
(308) 284-6365. **$69-$86.** 601 Stagecoach Tr 69153. I-80 exit 126 (US 26/SR 61), just n, then e on frontage road. Int corridors. **Pets:** Other species. $10 daily fee/room. Designated rooms, service with restrictions, supervision. (SAVE)

OMAHA

BEST WESTERN PLUS Kelly Inn H 🐾
(402) 339-7400. **$79-$249.** 4706 S 108th St 68137. I-80 exit 445 (L St E), 0.3 mi e, then just s. Int corridors. **Pets:** Other species. Service with restrictions, crate. (SAVE)

BEST WESTERN Settle Inn H
(402) 431-1246. **$80-$169.** 650 N 109th Ct 68154. I-680 exit 3 (Dodge St W), 0.7 mi w to 108th St and Old Mill Rd, then just w on Mill Valley Rd. Int corridors. **Pets:** Large, dogs only. $15 daily fee/room. Designated rooms, service with restrictions, supervision.
(SAVE)

Comfort Inn at the Zoo H
(402) 342-8000. **$89-$150.** 2920 S 13th Ct 68108. I-80 exit 454 (13th St) westbound; exit 454 (13th St N) eastbound, just w. Int corridors.
Pets: Other species. $20 one-time fee/room. Service with restrictions, crate. (SAVE)

Comfort Inn-Southwest H
(402) 593-2380. **$99-$179.** 10728 L St 68127. I-80 exit 445 (L St E), just n on 108th St, then e. Int corridors. **Pets:** $10 daily fee/pet. Designated rooms, service with restrictions, crate. (SAVE)

Countryside Suites M
(402) 884-2644. **$55-$75.** 9477 S 142nd St 68138. I-80 exit 440, just ne. Ext corridors. **Pets:** Other species. $10 daily fee/pet. Service with restrictions. (SAVE)

DoubleTree by Hilton Hotel Omaha Downtown H
(402) 346-7600. **$95-$379.** 1616 Dodge St 68102. Downtown. Int corridors. **Pets:** Accepted.

DoubleTree Suites by Hilton Hotel Omaha H
(402) 397-5141. **$85-$180.** 7270 Cedar St 68124. I-80 exit 449 (72nd St), 1.3 mi n. Int corridors. **Pets:** Accepted.
(SAVE)

Element Omaha Midtown Crossing H
(402) 614-8080. **$99-$229.** 3253 Dodge St 68131. I-480 exit 2B westbound; exit 2A northbound, just w. Int corridors. **Pets:** Accepted.
(SAVE)

Hawthorn Suites by Wyndham Omaha H
(402) 758-2848. **$79-$149.** 360 S 108th Ave 68154. I-680 exit 3 (Dodge St W), 0.7 mi to 108th Ave, then 0.8 mi s. Int corridors. **Pets:** $50 one-time fee/pet. Designated rooms, service with restrictions, crate.

Hilton Omaha H 🐾
(402) 998-3400. **$99-$349.** 1001 Cass St 68102. Jct Cass and 10th sts; downtown. Int corridors. **Pets:** Large, dogs only. $50 one-time fee/room. Service with restrictions, crate.
(SAVE)

Holiday Inn Express Hotel & Suites-West H 🐾
(402) 333-5566. **$105-$179.** 17677 Wright St 68130. I-80 exit 445 (L St W), 5.5 mi w, then just s. Int corridors. **Pets:** Other species. $25 one-time fee/room. Service with restrictions, supervision.

Hotel Deco XV H
(402) 991-4981. **Call for rates.** 1504 Harney St 68102. Jct Harney and 15th sts; downtown. Int corridors. **Pets:** Accepted.
(SAVE)

La Quinta Inn Omaha Southwest H
(402) 592-5200. **$59-$129.** 10760 M St 68127. I-80 exit 445 (L St E), 0.3 mi e, s on 108th St, then just e. Int corridors. **Pets:** Service with restrictions, supervision.

Magnolia Hotel H
(402) 341-2500. **Call for rates.** 1615 Howard St 68102. Jct 16th St. Int corridors. **Pets:** $50 one-time fee/pet. Service with restrictions, crate.
(SAVE)

Relax Inn Motel & Suites M
(402) 731-7300. **$50-$60.** 4578 S 60th St 68117. I-80 exit 450 (60th St), 0.8 mi s. Ext corridors. **Pets:** Very small, dogs only. $20 deposit/pet, $10 daily fee/pet. Service with restrictions, supervision.
(SAVE)

Residence Inn by Marriott Omaha-Central H
(402) 553-8898. **$89-$239.** 6990 Dodge St 68132. I-680 exit 3 (Dodge St E), 3 mi e. Int corridors. **Pets:** Medium, other species. $100 one-time fee/room. Service with restrictions.

Satellite Motel M
(402) 733-7373. **$45-$55.** 6006 L St 68117. I-80 exit 450 (60th St), 0.8 mi s; just n of US 275 and SR 92. Ext/int corridors. **Pets:** Very small, dogs only. $20 deposit/pet, $10 daily fee/pet. Service with restrictions, supervision. (SAVE)

Sheraton Omaha Hotel H 🐾
(402) 496-0850. **$99-$329.** 655 N 108th Ave 68154. I-680 exit 3 (Dodge Rd W), 0.7 mi to 108th St to 108th Ave and N Old Mill Rd exits, then just n. Int corridors. **Pets:** Medium. $50 one-time fee/room. Service with restrictions, crate. (SAVE)

Sleep Inn & Suites H
(402) 342-2525. **$60-$129.** 2525 Abbott Dr 68110. I-480 E exit 14th St (Cuming St), 2 mi n, follow signs. Int corridors. **Pets:** $10 daily fee/pet. Service with restrictions, crate. (SAVE)

▼▼▼▼ Staybridge Suites Omaha 🅗
(402) 933-8901. **Call for rates.** 7825 Davenport St 68114. I-680 exit 3 (Dodge St E), 2.2 mi e, then just n. Int corridors. **Pets:** Accepted.
🛜 ⊠ 🛏 🖵 ⌇

▼▼▼▼ TownePlace Suites by Marriott Omaha West 🅗
(402) 590-2800. **$104-$346.** 10865 W Dodge Rd 68154. I-680 exit 3 (Dodge St), 0.7 mi to 108th St to 108th Ave and N Old Mill Rd exits, then just s. Int corridors. **Pets:** Accepted. 🛜 ⊠ 🆓 🛏 🖵 ⌇

◈◈ ▼▼ University Plaza Downtown Motel 6 🅗
(402) 345-2222. **$54-$69.** 330 N 30th St 68131. I-480 exit 2B westbound; exit 2A northbound, just w on Dodge St, then just n on 30th St. Int corridors. **Pets:** Designated rooms, service with restrictions, crate.
SAVE 🛜 🆓 🛏 🖵

SCOTTSBLUFF

▼▼ Comfort Inn 🅗
(308) 632-7510. **$90-$109.** 1902 21st Ave 69361. 1.8 mi e on US 26, just n. Ext/int corridors. **Pets:** Accepted. 🛜 🆓 🛏 🖵 ⌇ ⊠

◈◈ ▼▼ Scottsbluff Super 8 🅗 🐾
(308) 635-1600. **$65.** 2202 Delta Dr 69361. 1.8 mi e on US 26. Int corridors. **Pets:** $10 one-time fee/pet. Designated rooms, service with restrictions, supervision. 🛜 🆓 🛏 🖵 ⌇

SIDNEY

◈◈◈ ▼▼▼ BEST WESTERN PLUS Sidney Lodge 🅗
(308) 254-0100. **$89-$199.** 645 Cabela Dr 69162. I-80 exit 59, just nw. Int corridors. **Pets:** Other species. $20 daily fee/room. Designated rooms, service with restrictions, supervision.
SAVE 🛜 ⊠ 🆓 🛏 🖵 ⌇ ⊠

◈◈◈ ▼▼▼ Days Inn 🅗
(308) 254-2121. **$85-$140.** 3042 Silverberg Dr 69162. I-80 exit 59, just n. Int corridors. **Pets:** Medium. $10 daily fee/pet. Designated rooms, service with restrictions, crate. SAVE 🛜 ⊠ 🆓 🛏 🖵 ⌇

▼▼▼▼ Holiday Inn & Conference Center 🅗
(308) 254-2000. **$99-$179.** 664 Chase Blvd 69162. I-80 exit 59, just s. Int corridors. **Pets:** $20 one-time fee/room. Service with restrictions, supervision. 🛜 🆓 🛏 🖵 🍴 ⌇

▼▼ Sidney Comfort Inn 🅗
(308) 254-5011. **$85-$119.** 730 E Jennifer Ln 69162. I-80 exit 59, just n. Int corridors. **Pets:** Accepted. 🛜 🆓 🛏 🖵 ⌇

SOUTH SIOUX CITY

▼▼▼▼ Marina Inn Conference Center 🅗
(402) 494-4000. **Call for rates.** 385 E 4th St 68776. I-29 exit 149 southbound; exit 148 northbound, e at traffic light by Nebraska side of bridge; on banks of Missouri River. Int corridors. **Pets:** Accepted.
🛜 ⊠ 🆓 🛏 🖵 🍴 ⌇

VALENTINE

▼▼ Dunes Lodge & Suites Ⓜ 🐾
(402) 376-3131. **$54-$179.** 340 E Hwys 20 & 83 69201. Jct US 20/83, 0.3 mi e. Ext corridors. **Pets:** Medium. $10 daily fee/pet. Designated rooms, service with restrictions, supervision. 🛜 🛏 🖵

▼▼ Trade Winds Motel Ⓜ
(402) 376-1600. **$66-$105.** 1009 E Hwy 20 69201. Jct US 20/83, 1 mi se. Ext corridors. **Pets:** $10 daily fee/pet. Designated rooms, service with restrictions, supervision. 🛜 🛏 🖵

YORK

◈◈◈ ▼▼▼ Americas Best Value Inn-Palmer Inn Ⓜ 🐾
(402) 362-5585. **$45-$95.** 2426 S Lincoln Ave 68467. I-80 exit 353 (US 81), 1 mi n. Ext corridors. **Pets:** Other species. $10 daily fee/pet. Designated rooms, service with restrictions, supervision.
SAVE 🛜 🆓 🛏 🖵 ⌇

◈◈◈ ▼▼▼ Comfort Inn 🅗
(402) 362-6555. **Call for rates.** 3815 S Lincoln Ave 68467. I-80 exit 353 (US 81), just n. Ext/int corridors. **Pets:** Other species. $20 one-time fee/pet. Designated rooms, service with restrictions, supervision.
SAVE 🛜 🆓 🛏 🖵 ⌇

◈◈◈ ▼▼▼ Holiday Inn 🅗
(402) 362-6661. **$79-$150.** 4619 S Lincoln Ave 68467. I-80 exit 353 (US 81), just s. Int corridors. **Pets:** Other species. $25 deposit/room, $25 one-time fee/pet. Designated rooms.
SAVE 🛜 ⊠ 🆓 🛏 🖵 🍴 ⌇

NEVADA

CITY INDEX

BEATTY

▼▼ Death Valley Inn & RV Park 🅗
(775) 553-9400. **$70-$125.** 651 Hwy 95 S 89003. Just s. Ext corridors. **Pets:** Accepted. 🛜 ⊠ 🛏 🖵 ⌇

◈◈◈ ▼▼▼ Stagecoach Hotel Casino Ⓜ
(775) 553-2419. **$66-$76.** 900 E Hwy 95 N 89003. North end of town; west side of US 95. Ext/int corridors. **Pets:** Medium, other species. $10 deposit/room, $5 one-time fee/room. Designated rooms, service with restrictions. SAVE 🛜 🆓 🛏 🖵 🍴 ⌇

CARSON CITY

▼▼▼ Holiday Inn Express & Suites 🅗
(775) 283-4055. **$100-$179.** 4055 N Carson St 89701. US 395 exit 43, 0.7 mi se. Int corridors. **Pets:** Medium, other species. $20 one-time fee/pet. Designated rooms, service with restrictions, supervision.
🛜 🆓 🛏 🖵 ⌇ ⊠

ELKO

◈◈◈ ▼▼▼ Americas Best Value Gold Country Inn & Casino Ⓜ
(775) 738-8421. **$79-$159, 14 day notice.** 2050 Idaho St 89801. I-80 exit 303, just s. Ext corridors. **Pets:** Other species. $15 one-time fee/room. Designated rooms, service with restrictions, crate.
SAVE 🛜 🛏 🖵 🍴 ⌇

◈◈◈ ▼▼▼ BEST WESTERN Elko Inn 🅗 🐾
(775) 738-8787. **$140-$170.** 1930 Idaho St 89801. I-80 exit 303, 0.3 mi sw. Int corridors. **Pets:** Medium, other species. $15 daily fee/pet. Designated rooms, service with restrictions, supervision.
SAVE 🛜 🛏 🖵 ⌇

▼▼ Oak Tree Inn 🅗
(775) 777-2222. **$89-$109.** 95 Spruce Rd 89801. I-80 exit 301, just n. Int corridors. **Pets:** Accepted. 🛜 ⊠ 🛏 🖵 ⊠

Red Lion Hotel & Casino H
(775) 738-2111. **$89-$289.** 2065 Idaho St 89801. I-80 exit 303, just s. Int corridors. **Pets:** Other species. $15 one-time fee/room. Service with restrictions, crate. ⎯

Shilo Inn Suites - Elko H
(775) 738-5522. **$110-$185.** 2401 Mountain City Hwy 89801. I-80 exit 301, just n. Int corridors. **Pets:** Dogs only. $25 one-time fee/room. Designated rooms, service with restrictions, supervision.

Thunderbird Motel M
(775) 738-7115. **$79-$89.** 345 Idaho St 89801. Just sw of 4th and Idaho sts. Ext corridors. **Pets:** Accepted.

TownePlace Suites by Marriott H
(775) 738-9900. **$104-$199.** 2625 E Jennings Way 89801. I-80 exit 303, 0.3 mi nw. Int corridors. **Pets:** Other species. $100 one-time fee/room.

ELY

BEST WESTERN Park Vue Motel M
(775) 289-4497. **$70-$90.** 930 Aultman St 89301. 0.8 mi w of jct US 50 and 93. Ext corridors. **Pets:** Accepted.

Four Sevens Motel M
(775) 289-4747. **$35-$48, 7 day notice.** 500 High St 89301. Just n of 5th St; downtown. Ext corridors. **Pets:** Other species. $10 daily fee/pet. Service with restrictions, supervision.

Historic Hotel Nevada & Gambling Hall H
(775) 289-6665. **$45-$55, 7 day notice.** 501 Aultman St 89301. 1.1 mi w of jct US 50 and 93. Int corridors. **Pets:** Other species. $10 daily fee/pet. Service with restrictions, supervision.

La Quinta Inn & Suites-Ely H
(775) 289-8833. **$77-$172.** 1591 Great Basin Blvd 89301. 0.4 mi s of jct US 6, 50 and 93. Int corridors. **Pets:** Service with restrictions, supervision.

Prospector Hotel Gambling Hall H
(775) 289-8900. **$79.** 1501 E Aultman St 89301. 0.8 mi e of jct US 50 and 93. Int corridors. **Pets:** Medium. $10 daily fee/pet. Designated rooms, service with restrictions, supervision.

EUREKA

BEST WESTERN PLUS Eureka Inn H
(775) 237-5247. **$100-$106.** 251 N Main St 89316. On east side of Main St; center. Int corridors. **Pets:** Large. $15 daily fee/pet. Designated rooms, service with restrictions, supervision.

FALLON

BEST WESTERN Fallon Inn and Suites H
(775) 423-6005. **$90-$110.** 1035 W Williams Ave 89406. 0.4 mi w of jct US 50 and 95. Ext corridors. **Pets:** Medium. $15 daily fee/pet. Designated rooms, service with restrictions, supervision.

Econo Lodge M
(775) 423-2194. **$50-$99.** 70 E Williams Ave 89406. Just e of jct US 50 and 95. Ext corridors. **Pets:** Accepted.

Holiday Inn Express H
(775) 428-2588. **$119-$139.** 55 Commercial Way 89406. At Williams Ave, 0.8 mi w of US 95. Int corridors. **Pets:** Other species. $25 one-time fee/room. Service with restrictions, supervision.

Motel 6 #4140 M
(775) 423-2277. **$48-$89.** 1705 S Taylor St 89406. 0.8 mi s of jct US 50. Ext corridors. **Pets:** Other species. Service with restrictions, supervision.

Super 8 H
(775) 423-6031. **$60-$75.** 855 W Williams Ave 89406. 0.4 mi w of jct US 50 and 95. Ext/int corridors. **Pets:** Accepted.

FERNLEY

BEST WESTERN Fernley Inn M 🐾
(775) 575-6776. **$80-$105.** 1405 E Newlands Dr 89408. I-80 exit 48 (Craig Rd), just s. Ext corridors. **Pets:** Other species. $10 one-time fee/pet. Designated rooms, service with restrictions, crate.

GARDNERVILLE

BEST WESTERN Topaz Lake Inn H
(775) 266-4661. **Call for rates.** 3410 Sandy Bowers Ave 89410. US 395 S at Topaz Lake, 20 mi s. Ext/int corridors. **Pets:** Medium, dogs only. $12 daily fee/pet. Designated rooms, service with restrictions, supervision.

Topaz Lodge Super 8 H
(775) 266-3338. **$59-$99, 3 day notice.** 1979 US 395 S 89410. US 395 S at Topaz Lake, 20 mi s. Ext corridors. **Pets:** Dogs only. $12 daily fee/pet. Designated rooms, service with restrictions.

Westerner Motel M
(775) 782-3602. **$45-$89.** 1353 US Hwy S 395 89410. On US 395, south end of town. Ext corridors. **Pets:** Dogs only. Designated rooms, service with restrictions, crate.

HAWTHORNE

America's Best Inn & Suites M
(775) 945-2660. **$100-$120.** 1402 E 5th St 89415. US 95, 0.5 mi e. Ext corridors. **Pets:** Other species. $10 daily fee/room. Designated rooms, service with restrictions, crate.

JACKPOT

Horseshu Hotel & Casino H
(775) 755-2321. **$55-$89.** 1385 Hwy 93 89825. On US 93; center. Int corridors. **Pets:** Accepted.

LAKE TAHOE AREA

INCLINE VILLAGE

(A) ▼▼▼ ▼▼▼ **Hyatt Regency Lake Tahoe Resort, Spa and Casino** H

(775) 832-1234. **$108-$450, 3 day notice.** 111 Country Club Dr at Lakeshore 89450. 0.4 mi w of SR 28, toward lake via Country Club Dr; 2 mi s of Mt. Rose Hwy. Int corridors. **Pets:** Accepted.

ECO SAVE 🛜 ⊠ ♿ 📶 💻 ⛽ 🍴 ≈ 🐾

ZEPHYR COVE

▼▼ ▼▼ **Zephyr Cove Resort** CA

(775) 589-4907. **Call for rates.** 760 Hwy 50 89449. 4 mi n of Stateline, NV. Ext/int corridors. **Pets:** Accepted. 🛜 ⊠ 📶 💻 🍴 🐾

END AREA

LAS VEGAS METROPOLITAN AREA

BOULDER CITY

▼▼ **Quality Inn** H

(702) 293-6444. **Call for rates.** 110 Ville Dr 89005. Jct US 93. Ext corridors. **Pets:** Accepted. 🛜 📶 💻 ≈

HENDERSON

(A) ▼▼▼ ▼▼▼ **BEST WESTERN PLUS Henderson Hotel** H

(702) 564-9200. **$69-$149.** 1553 N Boulder Hwy 89011. Jct Sunset Rd, 0.5 mi s. Int corridors. **Pets:** Other species. $20 daily fee/pet. Service with restrictions, supervision. SAVE 🛜 ♿ 📶 💻 🍴 ≈

(A) ▼▼ ▼▼ **Fiesta-Henderson** H

(702) 558-7000. **$30-$299.** 777 W Lake Mead Pkwy 89015. I-515 exit 61A southbound; exit 61 northbound (Lake Mead Pkwy), just e. Int corridors. **Pets:** Medium, dogs only. $50 one-time fee/room. Designated rooms, service with restrictions, supervision.

SAVE 🛜 ♿ 📶 🍴 ≈

▼▼▼ **Hampton Inn & Suites** H

(702) 992-9292. **$79-$89.** 421 Astaire Dr 89014. I-215 exit 3A (Stephanie St) eastbound, 1.8 mi n, just e on Warm Springs Rd, then just n; exit 3 (Stephanie St) westbound. Int corridors. **Pets:** Medium, other species. Designated rooms, service with restrictions, supervision.

🛜 ♿ 📶 💻 ≈

▼▼ ▼▼ **Hawthorn Inn & Suites** H

(702) 568-7800. **$66-$222.** 910 S Boulder Hwy 89015. Jct Lake Mead Pkwy, 1.4 mi s. Int corridors. **Pets:** Accepted. 🛜 📶 💻 ≈

(A) ▼▼▼ ▼▼▼ **Ravella A Dolce Hotel & Resort** H

(702) 567-4700. **$119-$1200.** 1610 Lake Las Vegas Pkwy 89011. I-515 exit 61A southbound; exit 61 northbound (Lake Mead Pkwy), 6.3 mi ne, then n, follow signs. Int corridors. **Pets:** Medium. $50 one-time fee/room. Designated rooms, service with restrictions.

SAVE 🛜 ⊠ ♿ 💻 🍴 ≈ 🐾

▼▼▼ ▼▼▼ **Residence Inn by Marriott-Green Valley** H

(702) 434-2700. **$94-$169.** 2190 Olympic Ave 89014. I-215 exit 5 (Green Valley Pkwy), 3 mi n at Sunset Rd. Int corridors. **Pets:** Accepted.

ECO 🛜 ⊠ ♿ 💻 ≈ 🐾

(A) ▼▼▼ ▼▼▼ **Sunset Station Hotel & Casino** H

(702) 547-7777. **$30-$299.** 1301 W Sunset Rd 89014. I-515 exit 64A (Sunset Rd), just w. Int corridors. **Pets:** Accepted.

SAVE 🛜 ♿ 📶 💻 🍴 ≈

▼▼▼ ▼▼▼ **TownePlace Suites by Marriott Las Vegas Henderson** H

(702) 896-2900. **$89-$149.** 1471 Paseo Verde Pkwy 89012. I-215 exit 3A (Stephanie St) eastbound; exit 3 westbound, just s. Int corridors. **Pets:** Accepted. 🛜 ⊠ 📶 💻 ≈ 🐾

(A) ▼▼▼ ▼▼▼ **The Westin Lake Las Vegas Resort & Spa** H

(702) 567-6000. **$109-$699, 3 day notice.** 101 Montelago Blvd 89011. I-515 exit 61A southbound; exit 61 northbound (Lake Mead Pkwy), 6.3 mi ne, then n, follow signs. Int corridors. **Pets:** Accepted.

SAVE 🛜 ⊠ ♿ 📶 💻 🍴 ≈ 🐾

LAS VEGAS

(A) ▼▼ ▼▼ **Alexis Park All Suite Resort** H

(702) 796-3300. **$59-$289.** 375 E Harmon Ave 89169. Jct Las Vegas Blvd, just e. Ext corridors. **Pets:** Large, dogs only. $50 one-time fee/room. Designated rooms, service with restrictions, supervision.

SAVE 🛜 ♿ 📶 💻 🍴 ≈ 🐾

(A) ▼▼ ▼▼ **Ambassador Strip Inn Travelodge** M

(702) 736-3600. **$49-$299.** 5075 S Koval Ln 89119. I-15 exit 37 (Tropicana Ave), 0.5 mi e. Ext corridors. **Pets:** Medium, other species. $10 daily fee/pet. Service with restrictions, crate. SAVE 🛜 📶 💻 ≈

▼▼▼ ▼▼▼ **Artisan Hotel** H

(702) 214-4000. **Call for rates.** 1501 W Sahara Ave 89102. I-15 exit 40 (Sahara Ave), just s. Int corridors. **Pets:** Accepted.

🛜 ⊠ 📶 🍴 ≈

▼▼ ▼▼ **Bally's Las Vegas** H

(702) 967-4111. **Call for rates.** 3645 Las Vegas Blvd S 89109. I-15 exit 38 (Flamingo Rd), just e to the Strip. Int corridors. **Pets:** Accepted.

🛜 ♿ 📶 💻 🍴 ≈ 🐾

▼▼ ▼▼ **Baymont Inn & Suites Las Vegas South Strip** H

(702) 273-2500. **$90-$191.** 55 E Robindale Rd 89123. I-15 exit 33 (Blue Diamond Rd), just e, then just n. Int corridors. **Pets:** Accepted.

🛜 ⊠ 📶 💻 ≈

(A) ▼▼ ▼▼ **BEST WESTERN Main Street Inn** M

(702) 382-3455. **$49-$179.** 1000 N Main St 89101. I-15 exit 43E northbound; exit 44E southbound. Ext corridors. **Pets:** Other species. $15 daily fee/room. Service with restrictions, supervision.

SAVE 🛜 📶 💻 🍴 ≈

(A) ▼▼ ▼ **BEST WESTERN Mardi Gras Hotel & Casino** H

(702) 731-2020. **$49-$199.** 3500 Paradise Rd 89169. 0.5 mi s of convention center. Ext corridors. **Pets:** Accepted.

SAVE 🛜 📶 💻 🍴 ≈

(A) ▼▼▼ ▼▼▼ **BEST WESTERN PLUS Las Vegas West** H

(702) 256-3766. **$79-$129.** 8669 W Sahara Ave 89117. Jct Durango Dr. Int corridors. **Pets:** Large. $20 daily fee/room. Designated rooms, service with restrictions, crate. SAVE 🛜 📶 💻 ≈

Caesars Palace H
(702) 731-7110. **$109-$929, 3 day notice.** 3570 Las Vegas Blvd S 89109. I-15 exit 38 (Flamingo Rd), just e at the Strip. Int corridors. **Pets:** Accepted. ⟨SAVE⟩ 📶 🖥️ 🛏️ 💻 🍴 🏊 🗙

Candlewood Suites H
(702) 836-3660. **$69-$129.** 4034 S Paradise Rd 89169. I-15 exit 38 (Flamingo Rd) to Paradise Rd, just ne. Int corridors. **Pets:** Large. $15 daily fee/pet. Service with restrictions, crate. 📶 🖥️ 🛏️ 💻 🏊

City Center Motel M
(702) 382-4766. **Call for rates.** 700 E Fremont St 89101. Jct 7th and Fremont sts. Ext corridors. **Pets:** Accepted. 📶 🛏️ 💻 🏊

The Cosmopolitan of Las Vegas H
(702) 698-7000. **$160-$600, 3 day notice.** 3708 Las Vegas Blvd S 89109. Between Flamingo Rd and Tropicana Ave; on the Strip. Int corridors. **Pets:** Accepted. ⟨SAVE⟩ 📶 🗙 🖥️ 🛏️ 🍴 🏊 🗙

Element by Westin Las Vegas Summerlin H
(702) 589-2000. **$109-$329, 14 day notice.** 10555 Discovery Dr 89135. I-215 exit 23 (Town Center), just n. Int corridors. **Pets:** Dogs only. $50 one-time fee/room. Designated rooms, service with restrictions, supervision. 🔌 ⟨SAVE⟩ 📶 🗙 🖥️ 🛏️ 💻 🏊

Embassy Suites Convention Center H
(702) 893-8000. **$109-$229.** 3600 Paradise Rd 89169. 0.5 mi s of convention center. Int corridors. **Pets:** Accepted. 📶 🖥️ 🛏️ 💻 🍴 🏊

Flamingo Las Vegas H
(702) 733-3111. **Call for rates.** 3555 Las Vegas Blvd S 89109. I-15 exit 38 (Flamingo Rd), just n on the Strip. Int corridors. **Pets:** Accepted. 📶 🖥️ 🛏️ 💻 🍴 🏊 🗙

Four Seasons Hotel Las Vegas H ✿
(702) 632-5000. **$229-$5000.** 3960 Las Vegas Blvd S 89119. I-15 exit 37 (Tropicana Ave), just s on the Strip. Int corridors. **Pets:** Small, other species. $50 one-time fee/pet. Designated rooms, service with restrictions, supervision. ⟨SAVE⟩ 📶 🗙 🖥️ 🛏️ 💻 🍴 🏊 🗙

Harrah's-Las Vegas H ✿
(702) 369-5000. **$40-$499, 3 day notice.** 3475 Las Vegas Blvd S 89109. I-15 exit 38 (Flamingo Rd), just n on the Strip. Int corridors. **Pets:** Medium, dogs only. $100 deposit/room, $50 daily fee/room. Designated rooms, service with restrictions, crate. 📶 🖥️ 🛏️ 💻 🍴 🏊

Homestead Studio Suites Hotel-Las Vegas/Midtown H
(702) 369-1414. **$50-$105.** 3045 S Maryland Pkwy 89109. I-15 exit 40 (Sahara Ave E), then 0.6 mi s. Int corridors. **Pets:** $25 daily fee/pet. Designated rooms, service with restrictions. 📶 🖥️ 🛏️ 💻

Homewood Suites by Hilton Las Vegas Airport H
(702) 407-0075. **Call for rates.** 230 Hidden Well Rd 89119. Jct E Sunset and Bermuda rds; 1 mi s, 0.5 mi w. Int corridors. **Pets:** Medium, other species. $100 one-time fee/room. 📶 🛏️ 💻 🏊 🗙

La Quinta Inn & Suites Airport South H
(702) 492-8900. **$95-$188.** 6560 Surrey St 89119. Jct Eastern Ave, just w. Int corridors. **Pets:** Service with restrictions, supervision. 📶 🗙 🖥️ 🛏️ 💻 🏊

La Quinta Inn & Suites Las Vegas Redrock/Summerlin M
(702) 243-0356. **$95-$177.** 9570 W Sahara Ave 89117. Jct Fort Apache Rd, just w. Int corridors. **Pets:** Service with restrictions, supervision. 📶 🗙 🖥️ 🛏️ 💻 🏊

La Quinta Inn Las Vegas Nellis H
(702) 632-0229. **$71-$144.** 4288 N Nellis Blvd 89115. I-15 exit 48 (Craig Rd), e to N Las Vegas Blvd. Int corridors. **Pets:** Service with restrictions, supervision. ⟨SAVE⟩ 📶 🖥️ 🛏️ 💻 🏊

Paris Las Vegas H
(702) 946-7000. **Call for rates.** 3655 Las Vegas Blvd S 89109. I-15 exit 38 (Flamingo Rd), e to the Strip, then just s. Int corridors. **Pets:** Accepted. 📶 🖥️ 🛏️ 💻 🍴 🏊 🗙

Planet Hollywood Resort & Casino H
(702) 785-5555. **Call for rates.** 3667 Las Vegas Blvd S 89109. I-15 exit 38 (Flamingo Rd), just e to the Strip, then just s. Int corridors. **Pets:** Accepted. 📶 🖥️ 🛏️ 💻 🍴 🏊 🗙

Platinum Hotel & Spa H
(702) 365-5000. **Call for rates.** 211 E Flamingo Rd 89169. I-15 exit 38 (Flamingo Rd), 1.2 mi e. Int corridors. **Pets:** Accepted. 📶 🗙 🖥️ 🛏️ 💻 🍴 🏊 🗙

Residence Inn by Marriott-Hughes Center H
(702) 650-0040. **$107-$199.** 370 Hughes Center Dr 89169. Jct Flamingo and Paradise rds, just n. Int corridors. **Pets:** Other species. $100 one-time fee/room. Service with restrictions. 🔌 📶 🗙 🖥️ 🛏️ 💻 🏊 🗙

Residence Inn by Marriott Las Vegas Convention Center H ❀
(702) 796-9300. **$98-$209.** 3225 Paradise Rd 89169. Opposite convention center. Ext corridors. **Pets:** Other species. $100 one-time fee/room. Designated rooms, service with restrictions. 🔌 📶 🗙 🖥️ 🛏️ 💻 🏊 🗙

Residence Inn by Marriott Las Vegas South H
(702) 795-7378. **$107-$169.** 5875 Dean Martin Rd 89118. I-15 exit 36 (Russell Rd), just sw. Int corridors. **Pets:** Accepted. 📶 🗙 🖥️ 🛏️ 💻 🏊 🗙

Rio All Suite Hotel & Casino H
(702) 777-7777. **$49-$399, 3 day notice.** 3700 W Flamingo Rd 89103. I-15 exit 38 (Flamingo Rd), 0.3 mi w. Int corridors. **Pets:** Accepted. 📶 🖥️ 🛏️ 💻 🍴 🏊 🗙

Staybridge Suites Las Vegas South H
(702) 259-2663. **$119-$169.** 5735 Dean Martin Dr 89118. I-15 exit 36 (Russell Rd), just w. Int corridors. **Pets:** Accepted. 📶 🗙 🖥️ 🛏️ 💻 🏊

Super 8 M
(702) 794-0888. **$39-$199.** 4250 Koval Ln 89109. Jct Flamingo Rd and Koval Ln, just s. Int corridors. **Pets:** Other species. $15 one-time fee/pet. Service with restrictions, supervision. ⟨SAVE⟩ 📶 🛏️ 💻 🏊

THEhotel at Mandalay Bay H
(702) 632-7777. **$105-$2000.** 3950 Las Vegas Blvd S 89119. I-15 exit 36 (Russell Rd), e to the Strip, then just n. Int corridors. **Pets:** Accepted. ⟨SAVE⟩ 📶 🗙 🖥️ 🛏️ 💻 🍴 🏊 🗙

Trump International Hotel Las Vegas H
(702) 982-0000. **$129-$499, 3 day notice.** 2000 Fashion Show Dr 89109. Jct Las Vegas Blvd, just w. Int corridors. **Pets:** Accepted. 📶 🗙 🛏️ 💻 🍴 🏊

Westgate Flamingo Bay CO
(702) 252-6000. **$79-$209, 3 day notice.** 5625 W Flamingo Rd 89103. Jct Jones Blvd, just e. Ext corridors. **Pets:** Large, other species. $80 one-time fee/room. Service with restrictions. ⟨SAVE⟩ 📶 🗙 🖥️ 💻 🏊 🗙

The Westin Las Vegas Hotel, Casino and Spa H
(702) 836-5900. **$100-$500.** 160 E Flamingo Rd 89109. I-15 exit 38 (Flamingo Rd), 1.1 mi e. Int corridors. **Pets:** Accepted. ⟨SAVE⟩ 📶 🗙 🖥️ 🛏️ 💻 🍴 🏊 🗙

LAUGHLIN

▼▼▼ Harrah's Casino Hotel **H** ❀

(702) 298-4600. **Call for rates.** 2900 S Casino Dr 89029. 5 mi s of Davis Dam. Int corridors. **Pets:** Medium, dogs only. $150 deposit/pet, $45 daily fee/room. Designated rooms, service with restrictions, supervision.

🛜 🏋 🕳 💻 🍽 🏊 ⊗

MESQUITE

✦ **▼▼▼** BEST WESTERN Mesquite Inn **M**

(702) 346-7444. **$79-$125.** 390 N Sandhill Blvd 89027. I-15 exit 122. Ext corridors. **Pets:** Small. $20 daily fee/room. Designated rooms, service with restrictions, supervision. (SAVE) 🛜 🕳 💻 🏊

▼▼▼ Holiday Inn Express **H**

(702) 346-2200. **$59-$149.** 1030 W Pioneer Blvd 89027. I-15 exit 120, just w. Int corridors. **Pets:** Large, other species. $20 daily fee/room. Designated rooms, service with restrictions, crate.

🛜 ⊗ 🕳 💻 🏊 ⊗

▼▼▼ Virgin River Hotel Casino Bingo **M**

(702) 346-7777. **Call for rates.** 100 Pioneer Blvd 89027. I-15 exit 122, just w. Ext corridors. **Pets:** Accepted. 🛜 🏋 🕳 🍽 🏊

NORTH LAS VEGAS

✦ **▼▼▼** **▼▼▼** Aliante Casino + Hotel **H**

(702) 692-7777. **$35-$500.** 7300 Aliante Pkwy 89084. I-215 exit 43 (Aliante Pkwy), just n. Int corridors. **Pets:** Accepted.

(SAVE) 🛜 🏋 🕳 💻 🍽 🏊 ⊗

✦ **▼▼▼** BEST WESTERN PLUS North Las Vegas Inn & Suites **H**

(702) 649-3000. **Call for rates.** 4540 Donovan Way 89081. I-15 exit 48 (Craig Rd), just w to Donovan Way. Int corridors. **Pets:** Accepted.

(SAVE) 🛜 🕳 💻 🏊

OVERTON

▼▼ North Shore Inn at Lake Mead **H**

(702) 397-6000. **$85-$125.** 520 N Moapa Valley Blvd 89040. I-15 exit 93, 10 mi ne on SR 169. Int corridors. **Pets:** Large. $10 daily fee/room. Designated rooms, service with restrictions, supervision.

🛜 ⊗ 🕳 💻 🏊

PAHRUMP

✦ **▼▼▼** BEST WESTERN Pahrump Station **M** ❀

(775) 727-5100. **$80-$110.** 1101 S Hwy 160 89048. Downtown. Ext/int corridors. **Pets:** Dogs only. $10 daily fee/pet. Designated rooms, service with restrictions, supervision. (SAVE) 🛜 🏋 🕳 💻 🍽 🏊

END METROPOLITAN AREA

MINDEN

▼▼▼▼ Holiday Inn Express & Suites Minden **H**

(775) 782-7500. **$109-$209.** 1659 SR 88 89423. Jct US 395 N. Int corridors. **Pets:** Other species. $20 one-time fee/pet. Designated rooms, service with restrictions, supervision. 🛜 ⊗ 🕳 💻 🏊

▼▼▼ Quality Inn & Suites **M**

(775) 782-7766. **Call for rates.** 1795 Ironwood Dr 89423. Just w of jct US 395. Ext corridors. **Pets:** Accepted. 🛜 ⊗ 🏋 🕳 💻 🏊

RENO

✦ **▼▼▼** BEST WESTERN PLUS Airport Plaza Hotel **H** ❀

(775) 348-6370. **$67-$169.** 1981 Terminal Way 89502. US 395 exit 65A southbound (E Plumb Ln/Villanova Dr), just e on E Plumb Ln; exit 65 northbound, just e on E Plumb Ln. Int corridors. **Pets:** Other species. $100 deposit/room. Designated rooms, service with restrictions, supervision. (SAVE) 🛜 🏋 🕳 💻 🍽 🏊 ⊗

▼▼ Extended StayAmerica-Reno-South Meadows **H**

(775) 852-5611. **$69-$84.** 9795 Gateway Dr 89521. US 395 exit 60 (S Meadows Pkwy), just e, then n. Int corridors. **Pets:** $25 daily fee/pet. Designated rooms, service with restrictions. 🛜 🕳 💻

▼▼▼▼ Grand Sierra Resort & Casino **H**

(775) 789-2000. **Call for rates.** 2500 E 2nd St 89595. 0.5 mi s of jct I-80 and US 395; US 395 exit 66 (Mill St). Int corridors. **Pets:** Accepted.

🛜 🏋 🕳 💻 🍽 🏊 ⊗

✦ **▼▼▼▼** Harrah's **H** ❀

(775) 786-3232. **$33-$350.** 219 N Center St 89501. I-80 exit 13 (Virginia St), 0.6 mi s; jct 2nd st; downtown. Int corridors. **Pets:** Medium, dogs only. $100 deposit/room, $30 daily fee/room. Designated rooms, service with restrictions, crate. (SAVE) 🛜 🏋 🕳 💻 🍽 🏊 ⊗

▼▼▼▼ Holiday Inn Express & Suites Reno Airport **H**

(775) 229-7070. **$99-$139.** 2375 Market St 89502. US 395 exit 66, just n. Int corridors. **Pets:** Medium. $10 deposit/room, $20 daily fee/pet. Designated rooms, service with restrictions, supervision.

🛜 ⊗ 🏋 🕳 💻 🏊

✦ **▼▼▼** Homewood Suites by Hilton Reno **H**

(775) 853-7100. **$109-$169.** 5450 Kietzke Ln 89511. US 395 exit 62 (Neil Rd), just sw. Int corridors. **Pets:** Medium. $75 one-time fee/room. Service with restrictions. (SAVE) 🛜 🕳 💻 🏊 ⊗

▼▼ La Quinta Inn Reno **M**

(775) 348-6100. **$59-$129.** 4001 Market St 89502. US 395 exit 65A southbound (E Plumb Ln/Villanova Dr), just w on Villanova Dr; exit 65 northbound, just n, then just w on Villanova Dr. Ext corridors. **Pets:** Service with restrictions, supervision. 🛜 🏋 🕳 💻 🏊

✦ **▼▼▼** Ramada Reno Hotel & Casino **H** ❀

(775) 786-5151. **$55-$140.** 1000 E 6th St 89512. I-80 exit 14 (Wells Ave), just s, then just e. Int corridors. **Pets:** Medium, other species. $10 daily fee/room. Designated rooms, service with restrictions, supervision.

(SAVE) 🛜 🏋 🕳 💻 🍽 🏊

▼▼▼ Residence Inn by Marriott **H**

(775) 853-8800. **$107-$199.** 9845 Gateway Dr 89521. US 395 exit 60 (S Meadows Pkwy), just e. Int corridors. **Pets:** Accepted.

(ECO) 🛜 ⊗ 🏋 🕳 💻 🏊 ⊗

▼▼ Sands Regency Casino Hotel **H**

(775) 348-2200. **Call for rates.** 345 N Arlington Ave 89501. At 3rd St. Int corridors. **Pets:** Medium, dogs only. $15 daily fee/pet. Designated rooms, service with restrictions, crate. 🛜 🕳 🍽 🏊 ⊗

✦ **▼▼▼** Siena Hotel Spa Casino **H**

(775) 327-4362. **$59-$329.** 1 S Lake St 89501. I-80 exit 13 (Virginia St), 0.8 mi s; at Mill St. Int corridors. **Pets:** Accepted.

(SAVE) 🛜 🏋 🕳 💻 🍽 🏊

▼▼ Staybridge Suites Reno **H**

(775) 657-8999. **$89-$189.** 10559 Professional Cir 89511. US 395 exit 59 (Damonte Ranch Pkwy), just e, just n on Double R Blvd, then just w. Int corridors. **Pets:** Accepted. 🛜 ⊗ 🏋 🕳 💻 🏊

SPARKS

✦ **▼▼▼** Holiday Inn-Reno/Sparks **H** ❀

(775) 358-6900. **$89-$149, 3 day notice.** 55 E Nugget Ave 89431. I-80 exit 19 (McCarran Blvd), just se. Int corridors. **Pets:** Large. $50 deposit/room, $20 daily fee/pet. Designated rooms, service with restrictions, supervision. (SAVE) 🛜 🏋 🕳 💻 🍽 🏊 ⊗

△△△ **▽▽▽** John Ascuaga's Nugget Hotel Tower 🄷

(775) 356-3300. **$49-$179.** 1100 Nugget Ave 89431. I-80 exit 17 (Nugget Ave) eastbound; exit 18 (Pyramid Way) westbound. Int corridors. **Pets:** Medium. $50 deposit/pet, $20 daily fee/pet. Designated rooms, service with restrictions, supervision.

[SAVE] 🛜 🄻🄼 🛏 💻 🍴 ⇌ ✕

△△△ **▽▽▽** Super 8-Sparks/Reno 🄷

(775) 358-8884. **$80-$160.** 1900 E Greg St 89431. I-80 exit 20, 0.6 mi s, then just e. Int corridors. **Pets:** Large, other species. $10 daily fee/pet. Service with restrictions. [SAVE] 🛜 🛏 💻 ⇌

TONOPAH

△△△ **▽▽▽** BEST WESTERN Hi-Desert Inn 🄷 🐾

(775) 482-3511. **$104-$125.** 320 Main St 89049. On US 6 and 95. Int corridors. **Pets:** Dogs only. Designated rooms, service with restrictions, supervision. [ECO] [SAVE] 🛜 🄻🄼 🛏 💻 ⇌

△△△ **▽▽▽** Tonopah Station 🄼

(775) 482-9777. **$60-$70.** 1137 S Main St 89049. On US 6 and 95. Int corridors. **Pets:** Accepted. [SAVE] 🛜 ✕ 🄻🄼 🛏 💻 🍴

VIRGINIA CITY

△△△ **▽▽▽** Silverland Inn and Suites 🄷 🐾

(775) 847-4484. **$89-$169, 3 day notice.** 100 North E St 89440. Center. Int corridors. **Pets:** Other species. $20 daily fee/pet. Service with restrictions, supervision. [SAVE] 🛜 🛏 💻 ⇌

WINNEMUCCA

△△△ **▽▽▽** BEST WESTERN PLUS Gold Country Inn 🄷 🐾

(775) 623-6999. **$129-$135.** 921 W Winnemucca Blvd 89445. 0.6 mi sw of center. Int corridors. **Pets:** Other species. $10 daily fee/room. Designated rooms, service with restrictions, supervision.

[SAVE] 🛜 🛏 💻 ⇌

▽▽▽ Holiday Inn Express 🄷

(775) 625-3100. **$129-$224.** 1987 W Winnemucca Blvd 89445. I-80 exit 176, just s. Int corridors. **Pets:** Other species. $20 daily fee/pet. Designated rooms, service with restrictions, supervision.

🛜 ✕ 🄻🄼 🛏 💻 🍴 ⇌

△△△ **▽▽▽** Town House Motel 🄼

(775) 623-3620. **$84-$92.** 375 Monroe St 89445. 0.4 mi sw of center. Monroe St, then just se. Ext corridors. **Pets:** Small, dogs only. $10 one-time fee/pet. Service with restrictions, supervision.

[SAVE] 🛜 ✕ 🛏 💻 ⇌

△△△ **▽▽▽** Winnemucca Holiday Motel 🄼

(775) 623-3684. **$79-$149.** 670 W Winnemucca Blvd 89445. 0.4 mi sw of center. Ext corridors. **Pets:** Other species. $75 deposit/pet. Designated rooms, service with restrictions, supervision. [SAVE] 🛜 🛏 💻 ⇌

△△△ **▽▽▽** The Winnemucca Inn 🄷

(775) 623-2565. **$99-$149.** 741 W Winnemucca Blvd 89445. I-80 exit 176, 1.1 mi nw. Ext/int corridors. **Pets:** Accepted.

[SAVE] 🛜 🛏 💻 🍴 ⇌

NEW HAMPSHIRE

CITY INDEX

ASHLAND

▽▽▽ Glynn House Inn 🄱🄱

(603) 968-3775. **Call for rates.** 59 Highland St 03217. I-93 exit 24 (SR 25 and US 3), 0.8 mi e to flag pole in center of town (Highland St), then 0.3 mi nw. Ext/int corridors. **Pets:** Accepted. [ECO] 🛜 ✕ ✍

△△△ **▽▽▽** Lakes Region Comfort Inn 🄷

(603) 968-7668. **Call for rates.** 53 West St 03217. I-93 exit 24 (SR 25 and US 3), just e. Int corridors. **Pets:** $20 daily fee/pet. Designated rooms, supervision. [SAVE] 🛜 🛏 💻 ⇌

BARTLETT

△△△ **▽▽▽** The Bartlett Inn 🄱🄱

(603) 374-2353. **$109-$248, 14 day notice.** 1477 US Rt 302 03812. On US 302, 7 mi w of jct SR 16. Ext/int corridors. **Pets:** Dogs only. $15 one-time fee/pet. Designated rooms, service with restrictions, supervision.

[SAVE] 🛜 ✕ 🛏 💻 ⇌ ✕ ✍

▽▽▽ The Villager Motel 🄼

(603) 374-2742. **Call for rates.** 1126 US 302 03812. 1 mi e on US 302; 1.3 mi w of Attitash Mountain. Ext corridors. **Pets:** Accepted.

🛜 ✕ 🛏 💻 ⇌ ✕

BRETTON WOODS

▽▽▽ Omni Bretton Arms Inn 🄲🄸

(603) 278-3000. **$129-$479, 7 day notice.** 173 Mount Washington Hotel Rd (US 302) 03575. Center. Int corridors. **Pets:** Accepted.

🛜 ✕ 🛏 🍴 ✕

CAMPTON

▽▽▽ Days Inn Campton/Plymouth 🄷

(603) 536-3520. **$75-$189.** 1513 Daniel Webster Hwy 03223. I-93 exit 27, just e, then just n. Int corridors. **Pets:** $20 daily fee/pet. Designated rooms, service with restrictions, supervision. 🛜 🛏 💻 ⇌ ✕

CHESTERFIELD

▽▽▽ Chesterfield Inn 🄲🄸

(603) 256-3211. **$149-$345, 5 day notice.** 20 Cross Rd 03466. I-91 exit 3, 2 mi e on SR 9. Ext/int corridors. **Pets:** Large, other species. Designated rooms, service with restrictions, crate.

[ECO] 🛜 ✕ 🛏 💻 🍴

COLEBROOK

△△△ **▽▽▽** Northern Comfort Motel 🄼

(603) 237-4440. **$79-$89, 3 day notice.** 1 Trooper Scott Phillips Hwy 03576. 1.5 mi s on US 3. Ext corridors. **Pets:** Accepted.

[SAVE] 🛜 ✕ 🛏 ⇌ ✕

CONCORD

BEST WESTERN Concord Inn & Suites [H]
(603) 228-4300. **$89-$249.** 97 Hall St 03301. I-93 exit 13, just n on Main St, then 0.5 mi w. Int corridors. **Pets:** $15 daily fee/pet. Designated rooms, service with restrictions, supervision. [SAVE]

Concord Comfort Inn [H]
(603) 226-4100. **$59-$179.** 71 Hall St 03301. I-93 exit 13, just n on Main St, then 0.3 mi w. Int corridors. **Pets:** Accepted.

Residence Inn by Marriott Concord [H]
(603) 226-0012. **$99-$179.** 91 Hall St 03301. I-93 exit 13, just n on Main St, then 0.5 mi w. Int corridors. **Pets:** Accepted.

DOVER

Comfort Inn & Suites [H]
(603) 750-7507. **$89-$200.** 10 Hotel Dr 03820. SR 16 exit 9, 0.4 mi ne. Int corridors. **Pets:** Accepted.

Days Inn [M]
(603) 742-0400. **$89-$179.** 481 Central Ave 03820. Spaulding Tpke exit 7, 2 mi n on SR 108; downtown. Ext/int corridors. **Pets:** Other species. $50 deposit/room, $10 daily fee/pet. Service with restrictions, supervision.

Homewood Suites Dover [H]
(603) 516-0929. **$129-$229.** 21 Members Way 03820. SR 16 exit 9, 0.4 mi w. Int corridors. **Pets:** Accepted.

DURHAM

Holiday Inn Express Durham-UNH [H]
(603) 868-1234. **$99-$189.** 2 Main St 03824. On SR 108; center. Int corridors. **Pets:** Large. $50 one-time fee/room. Designated rooms, service with restrictions, supervision.

Three Chimneys Inn [CI]
(603) 868-7800. **$139-$239, 7 day notice.** 17 Newmarket Rd 03824. On SR 108; center. Ext/int corridors. **Pets:** Dogs only. $25 one-time fee/room. Designated rooms, service with restrictions, crate.
[SAVE]

EXETER

Hampton Inn & Suites [H]
(603) 658-5555. **$109-$179.** 59 Portsmouth Ave 03833. I-101 exit 11. Int corridors. **Pets:** Large. Designated rooms, service with restrictions, supervision. [SAVE]

FRANCONIA

BEST WESTERN White Mountain Inn [H] ❖
(603) 823-7422. **$90-$210, 3 day notice.** 87 Wallace Hill Rd 03580. I-93 exit 38, just e. Int corridors. **Pets:** Large, other species. $20 daily fee/room. Designated rooms, service with restrictions, crate.
[SAVE]

Gale River Motel [M]
(603) 823-5655. **$60-$220, 7 day notice.** 1 Main St 03580. I-93 exit 38, 0.8 mi n on SR 18. Ext corridors. **Pets:** Dogs only. $10 daily fee/pet. Designated rooms, service with restrictions, supervision.

Lovetts Inn by Lafayette Brook [CI]
(603) 823-7761. **$155-$255, 7 day notice.** 1474 Profile Rd 03580. I-93 exit 38, just w on Wallace Hill Rd, then 2.1 mi s on SR 18. Ext/int corridors. **Pets:** Accepted.

GILFORD

Fireside Resort Inn & Suites [H] ❖
(603) 293-7526. **$90-$270.** 17 Harris Shore Rd 03249. Jct SR 11 and 11B, 2.5 mi e of jct US 3 N. Int corridors. **Pets:** Medium. $20 deposit/pet. Designated rooms, service with restrictions, supervision.

TownePlace Suites by Marriott Gilford [H] ❖
(603) 524-5533. **$119-$329.** 14 Sawmill Rd 03249. Just e of jct SR 3 and 11A. Int corridors. **Pets:** Large, other species. $100 one-time fee/room. Service with restrictions, supervision.

GLEN

Will's Inn [M]
(603) 383-6757. **$49-$235, 10 day notice.** 440 US 302 03838. On US 302, 2 mi w of jct SR 16. Ext corridors. **Pets:** Accepted.
[SAVE]

GORHAM

Moose Brook Motel [M]
(603) 466-5400. **$59-$89, 7 day notice.** 65 Lancaster Rd 03581. Jct SR 16, 0.5 mi w on US 2. Ext corridors. **Pets:** $10 one-time fee/pet. Service with restrictions, crate.

Royalty Inn [H]
(603) 466-3312. **$69-$169.** 130 Main St 03581. On US 2 and SR 16; center. Ext/int corridors. **Pets:** Other species. $5 daily fee/pet. Designated rooms, service with restrictions.

Top Notch Inn [M]
(603) 466-5496. **$69-$149.** 265 Main St 03581. On US 2 and SR 16; center. Ext/int corridors. **Pets:** Medium, dogs only. Designated rooms, service with restrictions, supervision. [SAVE]

Town & Country Inn & Resort [H]
(603) 466-3315. **$68-$148.** 20 SR 2 03581. 0.5 mi e of jct SR 16. Ext/int corridors. **Pets:** Accepted.

HAMPTON

Lamie's Inn and The Old Salt [CI] ❖
(603) 926-0330. **$99-$180, 3 day notice.** 490 Lafayette Rd 03842. Jct SR 27 on US 1. Int corridors. **Pets:** Medium, other species. $10 daily fee/pet. Designated rooms, supervision. [SAVE]

Seascape Inn [M]
(603) 926-1750. **$79-$175, 7 day notice.** 955 Ocean Blvd 03842. On SR 1A. Ext corridors. **Pets:** Other species. $10 one-time fee/room. Designated rooms, service with restrictions, crate. [SAVE]

HANCOCK

The Hancock Inn [CI]
(603) 525-3318. **Call for rates.** 33 Main St 03449. Jct SR 123 and 137; center. Int corridors. **Pets:** Accepted.

HANOVER

Six South Street Hotel Hanover [H] ❖
(603) 643-0600. **$259-$389.** 6 South St 03755. I-89 exit 18, n on SR 120 to Lebanon St, left on Sanborn Rd (which becomes South St). Int corridors. **Pets:** $25 daily fee/room. Designated rooms, service with restrictions, supervision. [SAVE]

HARTS LOCATION

Notchland Inn [CI]
(603) 374-6131. **Call for rates.** 2 Morey Rd 03812. On US 302, 6.4 mi w of town. Ext/int corridors. **Pets:** Other species. $15 daily fee/pet. Designated rooms, service with restrictions, crate.

HEBRON

▼▼▼▼ Coppertoppe Inn & Retreat Center BB ❖
(603) 744-3636. **$139-$279, 14 day notice.** 8 Range Rd 03241. I-93 exit 23, 6 mi w on SR 104, 8.7 mi n on SR 3A, then 0.6 mi w on N Shore Rd. Int corridors. **Pets:** Other species. $15 daily fee/pet.
ECO 🛰 ✕ 🛡 🖵 🖵 ✕ ✆

HENNIKER

▼▼ Henniker Motel M
(603) 428-3536. **$90-$139, 14 day notice.** 61 Craney Pond Rd 03242. I-89 exit 5, 6.5 mi w on US 202 and SR 9 to jct SR 114, 3 mi s to Flanders Rd, then 0.5 mi w, follow signs; adjacent to Pat's Peak. Ext/int corridors. **Pets:** Accepted. 🛰 ✕ 🛡 🖵 🖵 ≈

JACKSON

▼▼▼ Christmas Farm Inn & Spa CI ❖
(603) 383-4313. **Call for rates.** 3 Blitzen Way (Rt 16B) 03846. Jct SR 16, 0.6 mi e on SR 16A (through Jackson Covered Bridge), then 0.4 mi. Ext/int corridors. **Pets:** $25 daily fee/room. Designated rooms, service with restrictions, crate. 🛰 ✕ 🛡 🖵 🖵 🍴 ≈ ✕

▼▼▼▼ The Eagle Mountain House & Golf Club H
(603) 383-9111. **$79-$229, 3 day notice.** 179 Carter Notch Rd 03846. Jct SR 16B, from village center follow SR 16B across the Jackson Covered Bridge to immediate right turn, 0.7 mi n. Int corridors. **Pets:** Medium. $35 daily fee/pet. Designated rooms, service with restrictions, supervision. ECO 🛰 ✕ 🛡 🖵 🍴 ≈ ✕

▼▼ The Lodge at Jackson Village H
(603) 383-0999. **$119-$249, 14 day notice.** 153 Rt 16 03846. Jct SR 16 and 16A at Jackson Covered Bridge, 0.5 mi n. Int corridors. **Pets:** Accepted. ECO 🛰 ✕ 🛡M 🛡 🖵 ≈ ✕

◊◊◊ ▼▼▼▼ Nordic Village Resort CO
(603) 383-9101. **$89-$869, 7 day notice.** Rt 16 03846. 1 mi n of jct US 302. Ext/int corridors. **Pets:** $25 daily fee/pet. Designated rooms, service with restrictions, supervision. SAVE 🛰 ✕ 🛡 🖵 ≈ ✕

▼▼▼ Snowflake Inn BB ❖
(603) 383-8259. **$169-$375, 14 day notice.** 95 Main St (SR 16A) 03846. On SR 16A; center. Int corridors. **Pets:** Dogs only. $30 daily fee/pet. Designated rooms, service with restrictions. 🛰 ✕ ≈

JEFFERSON

◊◊◊ ▼▼▼ Jefferson Inn BB
(603) 586-7998. **Call for rates.** 6 Renaissance Ln 03583. US 2, 0.5 mi e of SR 116. Int corridors. **Pets:** Accepted.
SAVE 🛰 ✕ 🛡 ✕ ✆

KEENE

◊◊◊ ▼▼▼▼ BEST WESTERN PLUS Sovereign Hotel H ❖
(603) 357-3038. **$89-$299.** 401 Winchester St 03431. SR 10, just s of jct SR 12 and 101. Int corridors. **Pets:** Other species. $20 daily fee/room. Designated rooms, service with restrictions, supervision.
SAVE 🛰 🛡 🖵 🍴 ≈

▼▼▼▼ Courtyard by Marriott Keene Downtown H
(603) 354-7900. **$109-$259.** 75 Railroad St 03431. Just off Main St; downtown. Int corridors. **Pets:** Accepted.
ECO 🛰 ✕ 🛡 🖵 🍴 ≈

◊◊◊ ▼▼▼ Days Inn of Keene H
(603) 352-9780. **$75-$260.** 3 Ash Brook Rd 03431. Jct SR 9 and 12, just w. Int corridors. **Pets:** $20 one-time fee/room. Service with restrictions, supervision. SAVE 🛰 🛡 🖵 ≈

▼▼▼▼ Holiday Inn Express H
(603) 352-7616. **$89-$199.** 175 Key Rd 03431. SR 101, just n, via Winchester St, then 0.3 mi w. Int corridors. **Pets:** Accepted.
🛰 ✕ 🛡M 🛡 🖵 ≈

▼▼▼▼ The Lane Hotel, an Ascend Collection hotel H
(603) 357-7070. **$129-$229.** 30 Main St 03431. Between Church and Roxbury sts; downtown. Int corridors. **Pets:** Accepted.
🛰 ✕ 🛡M 🛡 🖵

LANCASTER

◊◊◊ ▼▼▼ The Cabot Inn & Suites H
(603) 788-3346. **$79-$159.** 200 Portland St 03584. On US 2, 1.5 mi e of jct US 3. Int corridors. **Pets:** Dogs only. $15 daily fee/pet. Designated rooms, supervision. SAVE 🛰 ✕ 🛡 🖵 🍴 ≈ ✕

◊◊◊ ▼▼▼ Coos Motor Inn H
(603) 788-3079. **$49-$110.** 209 Main St 03584. On US 2 and 3; center. Int corridors. **Pets:** Accepted. SAVE 🛰 ✕ 🛡 🖵

LEBANON

◊◊◊ ▼▼▼▼ Residence Inn by Marriott Hanover Lebanon H
(603) 643-4511. **$139-$259.** 32 Centerra Pkwy 03766. I-89 exit 18, 2.5 mi n on SR 120. Int corridors. **Pets:** Other species. $100 one-time fee/room. Designated rooms. SAVE 🛰 ✕ 🛡M 🛡 🖵 ≈ ✕

LINCOLN

◊◊◊ ▼▼▼ Comfort Inn & Suites H
(603) 745-6700. **$99-$249, 3 day notice.** 21 Railroad St 03251. I-93 exit 32 (SR 112), just e; at Hobo Railroad. Int corridors. **Pets:** $15 daily fee/pet. Designated rooms, service with restrictions.
SAVE 🛰 ✕ 🛡M 🛡 🖵 ✕

◊◊◊ ▼▼▼ Econo Lodge Inn & Suites M
(603) 745-3661. **$60-$250.** 381 US Rt 3 03251. I-93 exit 33 (US 3), 0.3 mi ne. Ext/int corridors. **Pets:** Medium, dogs only. $15 daily fee/pet. Designated rooms, service with restrictions, crate.
SAVE 🛰 ✕ 🛡 ≈ ✕

◊◊◊ ▼▼ Parker's Motel M
(603) 745-8341. **$59-$99, 3 day notice.** 750 US Rt 3 03251. I-93 exit 33 (US 3), 2 mi ne. Ext corridors. **Pets:** $10 daily fee/pet. Designated rooms, service with restrictions, supervision.
SAVE 🛰 🛡 🖵 ≈ ✕

◊◊◊ ▼▼ Woodward's Resort M
(603) 745-8141. **Call for rates.** 527 US 3 03251. I-93 exit 33 (US 3), 1.4 mi ne. Ext/int corridors. **Pets:** Medium. Designated rooms, supervision. SAVE 🛰 🛡 🖵 🍴 ≈ ✕

LITTLETON

▼▼▼ The Beal House Inn CI
(603) 444-2661. **Call for rates.** 2 W Main St 03561. I-93 exit 42, 0.8 mi e on US 302 and SR 10. Int corridors. **Pets:** Small. $30 daily fee/room. Designated rooms, supervision. 🛰 ✕ 🛡 🖵 🍴 ✆

◊◊◊ ▼▼▼ Eastgate Motor Inn M
(603) 444-3971. **$69-$135.** 335 Cottage St 03561. I-93 exit 41, just e. Ext/int corridors. **Pets:** Dogs only. $10 daily fee/pet. Service with restrictions, supervision. SAVE 🛰 🛡 🖵

▼▼ Thayers Inn H
(603) 444-6469. **Call for rates.** 111 Main St 03561. I-93 exit 42, 1.3 mi e on US 302 and SR 10; center. Int corridors. **Pets:** Accepted.
🛰 ✕ 🛡 🖵 🍴

LOUDON

◊◊◊ ▼▼▼ Red Roof Inn Loudon #586 H
(603) 225-8399. **$80-$216.** 2 Staniels Rd 03307. I-393 exit 3, 1.5 mi n. Int corridors. **Pets:** Large, other species. Service with restrictions, supervision. SAVE 🛰 ✕ 🛡M 🛡 ≈

MANCHESTER

(AAA) ▼▼▼▼ BEST WESTERN PLUS Executive Court Inn & Conference Center H ❀

(603) 627-2525. **$107-$117.** 13500 S Willow St 03103. I-293 exit 1, 0.5 mi s on SR 28, then 1 mi e. Int corridors. **Pets:** Medium, other species. $10 daily fee/pet. Designated rooms, service with restrictions, crate.

[SAVE] 📶 🔲 💻 🍴 ≈ ✕

(AAA) ▼▼▼ Comfort Inn H

(603) 668-2600. **$79-$119.** 298 Queen City Ave 03102. I-293 exit 4, just w. Int corridors. **Pets:** Accepted. [SAVE] 📶 🔲 💻 ≈

(AAA) ▼▼▼ Four Points by Sheraton H

(603) 668-6110. **$89-$195, 3 day notice.** 55 John E Devine Dr 03103. I-293 exit 1, just nw on SR 28. Int corridors. **Pets:** Dogs only. $75 one-time fee/room. Service with restrictions, crate.

[SAVE] 📶 ✕ 🔲💻 🔲 💻 🍴 ≈

▼▼▼▼ Holiday Inn Express Hotel & Suites - Manchester Airport H

(603) 669-6800. **Call for rates.** 1298 S Porter St 03103. I-293 exit 1. Int corridors. **Pets:** Accepted. 📶 ✕ 🔲💻 🔲 💻 ≈

▼▼▼▼ Homewood Suites by Hilton H

(603) 668-2200. **$103-$189.** 1000 Perimeter Rd 03103. I-293 exit 2, follow signs to Manchester-Boston Regional Airport. Int corridors. **Pets:** Accepted. 📶 🔲💻 🔲 💻 ≈ ✕

▼▼▼▼ La Quinta Inn & Suites Manchester H

(603) 669-5400. **$68-$287.** 21 Front St 03102. I-293 exit 6, just se. Int corridors. **Pets:** Service with restrictions, supervision.

📶 ✕ 🔲💻 🔲 💻 ≈

(AAA) ▼▼▼▼ Radisson Hotel Manchester Downtown H

(603) 625-1000. **$119-$209.** 700 Elm St 03101. Jct Granite St; downtown. Int corridors. **Pets:** Accepted.

[ECO] [SAVE] 📶 ✕ 🔲💻 🔲 💻 🍴 ≈ ✕

▼▼ TownePlace Suites by Marriott Manchester-Boston Regional Airport H

(603) 641-2288. **$89-$179.** 686 Huse Rd 03103. I-293 exit 1, 0.5 mi se on SR 28. Int corridors. **Pets:** Accepted. 📶 ✕ 🔲💻 🔲 💻 ≈

MEREDITH

▼▼▼▼ Church Landing at Mill Falls H ❀

(603) 279-7006. **$239-$509, 3 day notice.** 281 Daniel Webster Hwy 03253. Jct US 3 and SR 104, 0.6 mi n. Ext/int corridors. **Pets:** $25 daily fee/pet. Designated rooms, service with restrictions, supervision.

📶 ✕ 🔲💻 🔲 💻 🍴 ≈ ✕

▼▼▼▼ The Inn at Mill Falls H

(603) 279-7006. **$109-$289, 3 day notice.** 312 Daniel Webster Hwy 03253. Jct US 3 and SR 25; center. Int corridors. **Pets:** Accepted.

[ECO] 📶 ✕ 🔲💻 🔲 💻 ≈

MERRIMACK

(AAA) ▼▼▼ Residence Inn by Marriott Nashua-Merrimack H

(603) 424-8100. **$94-$179.** 246 Daniel Webster Hwy 03054. Everett Tpke exit 11, just e, then 0.6 mi s on US 3. Ext/int corridors. **Pets:** Large, other species. $100 one-time fee/room.

[ECO] [SAVE] 📶 ✕ 🔲💻 🔲 💻 ≈ ✕

NASHUA

(AAA) ▼▼ BEST WESTERN Granite Inn M

(603) 883-7700. **$80-$231.** 10 St. Laurent St 03060. US 3 (Everett Tpke) exit 7E, just e. Int corridors. **Pets:** Other species. $25 one-time fee/room. Designated rooms, service with restrictions. [SAVE] 📶 🔲💻 🔲 💻 ≈

▼▼▼▼ Hampton Inn Nashua H

(603) 883-5333. **$89-$169.** 407 Amherst St 03063. US 3 (Everett Tpke) exit 8. Int corridors. **Pets:** Accepted.

[ECO] 📶 ✕ 🔲💻 🔲 💻 ≈

▼▼▼▼ Holiday Inn & Suites Nashua H

(603) 888-1551. **Call for rates.** 9 Northeastern Blvd 03062. US 3 (Everett Tpke) exit 4, just w, then 0.3 mi n. Int corridors. **Pets:** Accepted.

📶 🔲💻 🔲 💻 🍴 ≈

◆ Motel 6 #2019 M

(603) 888-1893. **$53-$59.** 77 Spitbrook Rd 03060. US 3 (Everett Tpke) exit 1, just e. Ext corridors. **Pets:** Other species. Service with restrictions, supervision. 📶 🔲💻

(AAA) ▼▼▼▼ Radisson Hotel Nashua H

(603) 888-9970. **$89-$219.** 11 Tara Blvd 03062. US 3 (Everett Tpke) exit 1, just w. Int corridors. **Pets:** Medium. Service with restrictions, supervision. [ECO] [SAVE] 📶 ✕ 🔲💻 🔲 💻 🍴 ≈ ✕

NEWBURY

(AAA) ▼▼ BEST WESTERN Sunapee Lake Lodge H ❀

(603) 763-2010. **Call for rates.** 1403 SR 103 03255. Jct SR 103B, just e. Int corridors. **Pets:** $10 one-time fee/pet. Designated rooms, service with restrictions, crate. [SAVE] 📶 ✕ 🔲💻 🔲 💻 ≈ ✕

NEW CASTLE

(AAA) ▼▼▼▼ Wentworth By The Sea Marriott Hotel & Spa H

(603) 422-7322. **$199-$469, 3 day notice.** 588 Wentworth Rd 03854. On SR 1B, 2 mi e of SR 1A. Ext/int corridors. **Pets:** Accepted.

[SAVE] 📶 ✕ 🔲 💻 🍴 ≈ ✕

NEW LONDON

▼▼ Fairway Motel at Lake Sunapee Country Club M

(603) 526-0202. **$69-$109, 14 day notice.** 344 Andover Rd 03257. I-89 exit 11, 3 mi e on SR 11. Ext corridors. **Pets:** Small. $25 daily fee/room. Designated rooms, service with restrictions, supervision.

📶 ✕ 🔲💻 ≈

(AAA) ▼▼▼▼ New London Inn CI

(603) 526-2791. **$144-$259, 3 day notice.** 353 Main St 03257. Center. Int corridors. **Pets:** Dogs only. Designated rooms, crate.

[SAVE] 📶 ✕ 🍴

NORTH CONWAY

▼▼▼▼ North Conway Hampton Inn & Suites H ❀

(603) 356-7736. **$85-$225.** 1788 White Mountain Hwy 03860. Jct US 302/SR 16, 1 mi n. Int corridors. **Pets:** Medium. Service with restrictions, supervision. [ECO] 📶 ✕ 🔲💻 🔲 💻 ✕

(AAA) ▼▼ North Conway Mountain Inn M

(603) 356-2803. **$79-$199.** 2114 White Mountain Hwy 03860. 1 mi s on US 302/SR 16. Ext corridors. **Pets:** $20 daily fee/pet. Designated rooms, service with restrictions, crate. [SAVE] 📶 ✕ 🔲💻 🔲 💻

(AAA) ▼▼▼▼ Red Jacket Mountain View Resort and Indoor Water Park H ❀

(603) 356-5411. **$109-$339.** 2251 White Mountain Hwy 03860. 1 mi s on US 302/SR 16. Ext/int corridors. **Pets:** Medium. $35 daily fee/pet. Designated rooms, no service, supervision.

[ECO] [SAVE] 📶 ✕ 🔲💻 🔲 💻 🍴 ≈ ✕

(AAA) ▼▼▼▼ Residence Inn by Marriott, North Conway H

(603) 356-3024. **$94-$236.** 1801 White Mountain Hwy 03860. Jct US 302/SR 16, 1 mi n. Int corridors. **Pets:** Accepted.

[SAVE] 📶 ✕ 🔲💻 🔲 💻 ≈ ✕

▽ White Trellis Motel **M**
(603) 356-2492. **$59-$269, 3 day notice.** 3245 White Mountain Hwy 03860. 0.8 mi n on US 302/SR 16; village center. Ext corridors.
Pets: Accepted. 🛜 📶

NORTH WOODSTOCK
▽ Autumn Breeze Motor Lodge **M**
(603) 745-8549. **Call for rates.** 183 Main St 03262. I-93 exit 32, 0.5 mi w on SR 112, then just n on US 3. Ext corridors. **Pets:** Small, dogs only. $10 daily fee/pet. Designated rooms, service with restrictions, supervision.
🛜 ✕ 📶 💷

PITTSBURG
▽ The Glen **CA**
(603) 538-6500. **Call for rates.** 118 Glen Rd 03592. 9 mi n on US 3, from jct SR 145 to Varney Rd, then 0.3 mi s to Glen Rd, follow signs. Ext/int corridors. **Pets:** Accepted.
✕ 📶 💷 🍴 ✕ ✕ ✕ ✕

PORTSMOUTH
◈ **▽▽▽▽** Anchorage Inn & Suites **H**
(603) 431-8111. **$89-$349.** 417 Woodbury Ave 03801. Jct US 1 and I-95; at Portsmouth Traffic Circle. Int corridors. **Pets:** Medium. $20 daily fee/pet. Designated rooms, service with restrictions, supervision.
SAVE 🛜 📶 💷 ✕

▽▽▽▽ Hampton Inn-Portsmouth **H**
(603) 431-6111. **Call for rates.** 99 Durgin Ln 03801. I-95 exit 7, 1 mi w via Market St and Woodbury Ave to Durgin Ln, then 0.3 mi s. Int corridors. **Pets:** Medium, other species. $50 one-time fee/room. Service with restrictions, supervision. 🛜 ✕ 📶 📶 💷 ✕

▽▽▽ Homewood Suites by Hilton **H**
(603) 427-5400. **$129-$399.** 100 Portsmouth Blvd 03801. I-95 exit 7, 0.5 mi w, then 0.3 mi n. Int corridors. **Pets:** Accepted.
🛜 📶 📶 💷 ✕

▽▽▽ Residence Inn by Marriott **H**
(603) 436-8880. **$139-$339.** 1 International Dr 03801. SR 4/16 exit 1, just s. Int corridors. **Pets:** Other species. $75 one-time fee/room. Service with restrictions. ECO 🛜 ✕ 📶 📶 💷 ✕

▽▽▽ Residence Inn by Marriott Downtown/
Waterfront **H**
(603) 422-9200. **$129-$489.** 100 Deer St 03801. Downtown. Int corridors.
Pets: Accepted. 🛜 ✕ 📶 📶 💷 ✕

◈ **▽▽▽▽** Sheraton Portsmouth Harborside Hotel &
Conference Center **H**
(603) 431-2300. **$139-$649.** 250 Market St 03801. Downtown. Int corridors. **Pets:** Accepted.
ECO SAVE 🛜 ✕ 📶 📶 💷 🍴 ✕ ✕

ROCHESTER
◈ **▽** Anchorage Inn **M**
(603) 332-3350. **$89-$159.** 13 Wadleigh Rd 03867. Jct Spaulding Tpke and SR 125 exit 12. Ext corridors. **Pets:** Medium. $20 daily fee/pet. Designated rooms, service with restrictions, supervision. SAVE 🛜 📶 ✕

▽▽▽ The Governor's Inn **CI**
(603) 332-0107. **Call for rates.** 78 Wakefield St 03867. On SR 125 and 108, just n of monument; center. Int corridors. **Pets:** Accepted.
🛜 ✕ 📶 💷 🍴

▽▽▽ Holiday Inn Express Hotel & Suites Rochester **H**
(603) 994-1175. **$79-$159.** 77 Farmington Rd 03867. I-16 exit 15, 1 mi w on SR 11. Int corridors. **Pets:** Small. $50 one-time fee/room. Service with restrictions, supervision. 🛜 📶 📶 💷 ✕

SALEM
▽▽ La Quinta Inn & Suites Salem **H**
(603) 893-4722. **$75-$188.** 8 Keewaydin Dr 03079. I-93 exit 2, just sw. Int corridors. **Pets:** Service with restrictions, supervision.
🛜 📶 📶 💷 ✕

◈◈ **▽▽** Red Roof Inn #151 **M**
(603) 898-6422. **$50-$110.** 15 Red Roof Ln 03079. I-93 exit 2, just se. Ext corridors. **Pets:** Large, other species. Service with restrictions, supervision. SAVE 🛜 📶 📶 💷

SEABROOK
◈◈ **▽▽** Hampshire Inn **M**
(603) 474-5700. **Call for rates.** 20 Spur Rd 03874. I-95 exit 1 on SR 107. Int corridors. **Pets:** Accepted. SAVE 🛜 ✕ 📶 💷 ✕

SUGAR HILL
▽▽▽ The Hilltop Inn **BB** 🐾
(603) 823-5695. **$120-$195, 8 day notice.** 9 Norton Ln 03586. I-93 exit 38, 0.5 mi n on SR 18, then 2.8 mi w on SR 117. Int corridors.
Pets: Dogs only. $10 daily fee/room. 🛜 ✕ 📶 ✕ ✕ ✕

▽▽▽▽ Sunset Hill House-A Grand Inn **CI**
(603) 823-5522. **$149-$499, 14 day notice.** 231 Sunset Hill Rd 03586. I-93 exit 38, 0.5 mi n on SR 18, 2.2 mi w on SR 117, then 0.5 mi s. Int corridors. **Pets:** Accepted. ECO 🛜 ✕ 📶 🍴 ✕ ✕

SUNAPEE
▽▽ Dexter's Inn **CI** 🐾
(603) 763-5571. **$110-$185, 7 day notice.** 258 Stagecoach Rd 03782. Jct SR 103B and 11, 0.4 mi e on SR 11, then 1.8 mi s on Winn Hill Rd. Ext/int corridors. **Pets:** Other species. $10 daily fee/pet. Designated rooms, service with restrictions. 🛜 ✕ 📶 💷 🍴 ✕ ✕

THORNTON
▽ Shamrock Motel **M**
(603) 726-3534. **$63-$85, 7 day notice.** 2913 US 3 03285. I-93 exit 29, 2.3 mi n. Ext corridors. **Pets:** Other species. $5 one-time fee/room. Designated rooms, no service, crate.
ECO 🛜 ✕ 📶 💷 ✕ ✕ ✕

TILTON
▽▽▽ Black Swan Inn **BB**
(603) 628-4524. **$99-$159, 10 day notice.** 354 W Main St 03276. I-93 exit 20 southbound, 1.5 mi w on SR 3 and 11. Int corridors.
Pets: Accepted. 🛜 ✕ 📶 💷 ✕

TROY
▽▽ The Inn at East Hill Farm **CI**
(603) 242-6495. **$248-$292, 21 day notice.** 460 Monadnock St 03465. Jct SR 12 and Monadnock St, 2 mi e. Ext/int corridors. **Pets:** Accepted.
ECO ✕ 📶 🍴 ✕ ✕ ✕

WATERVILLE VALLEY
◈◈ **▽▽▽** BEST WESTERN Silver Fox Inn **H**
(603) 236-3699. **Call for rates.** 70 Packards Rd 03215. I-93 exit 28, 11 mi e on SR 49, then just n. Int corridors. **Pets:** Accepted.
SAVE 🛜 ✕ 💷

WEST LEBANON
▽▽ A Fireside Inn and Suites **H** 🐾
(603) 298-5900. **$120-$200.** 25 Airport Rd 03784. I-89 exit 20 (SR 12A), just s. Int corridors. **Pets:** Dogs only. $20 daily fee/pet. Designated rooms, supervision. 🛜 ✕ 📶 💷 🍴 ✕

👐 ☜☜ Baymont Inn 🅼
(603) 298-8888. **$90-$250.** 45 Airport Rd 03784. I-89 exit 20 (SR 12A), just s, then just e. Int corridors. **Pets:** Accepted.
[SAVE] 🛜 🔊 🍴 🖵 🏊

WOODSVILLE
👐 ☜ All Seasons Motel 🅼
(603) 747-2157. **$60-$125, 3 day notice.** 36 Smith St 03785. I-91 exit 17, 4.1 mi e on US 302, then just s. Ext corridors. **Pets:** $5 daily fee/pet. Designated rooms, service with restrictions, supervision.
[SAVE] 🛜 🍴 🖵 🏊

👐 ☜☜ Nootka Lodge 🅼
(603) 747-2418. **$75-$235, 3 day notice.** 4982 Dartmouth College Hwy 03785. I-91 exit 17, 4.5 mi e on US 302. Ext corridors. **Pets:** $5 daily fee/pet. Designated rooms, service with restrictions, supervision.
[SAVE] 🛜 🍴 🏊 ✖

NEW JERSEY

CITY INDEX

ATLANTIC CITY METROPOLITAN AREA

ABSECON
☜☜ Quality Inn & Suites Atlantic City Marina District 🅷 🐾
(609) 652-3300. **Call for rates.** 328 E White Horse Pike (US 30) 08205. Garden State Pkwy exit 40 southbound; exit northbound, U-turn through Atlantic City Service Plaza, s to exit 40, then just e. Ext corridors. **Pets:** Medium, other species. $20 daily fee/pet. Service with restrictions, crate. 🛜 🍴 🖵 🏊

ATLANTIC CITY
👐 ☜☜☜ Sheraton Atlantic City Convention Center Hotel 🅷 🐾
(609) 344-3535. **$99-$499, 3 day notice.** 2 Convention Blvd 08401. Garden State Pkwy exit 38 to Atlantic City Expwy to Arctic Ave, just e to Michigan Ave, then just n. Int corridors. **Pets:** Large, dogs only. Supervision. [SAVE] 🛜 ✖ 🍴 🖵 🍴 🏊

GALLOWAY
👐 ☜☜☜ Stockton Seaview Hotel & Golf Club-A Dolce Resort 🅷
(609) 652-1800. **$99-$379.** 401 S New York Rd 08205. US 9, 2.5 mi ne of White Horse Pike (US 30). Int corridors. **Pets:** Medium, dogs only. $50 one-time fee/pet. Designated rooms, service with restrictions, crate.
[SAVE] 🛜 ✖ 🍴 🖵 🍴 🏊 ✖

SOMERS POINT
☜☜☜ Residence Inn by Marriott Atlantic City Somers Point 🅷
(609) 927-6400. **$89-$349.** 900 Mays Landing Rd 08244. Garden State Pkwy exit 30 southbound; exit 29 northbound, 1 mi e. Ext corridors.
Pets: Accepted. 🛜 ✖ 🍴 🖵 🏊 ✖

END METROPOLITAN AREA

BASKING RIDGE
☜☜☜ Hotel Indigo 🅷 🐾
(908) 580-1300. **$99-$199.** 80 Allen Rd 07920. I-78 exit 33, 0.3 mi n on CR 525, then 0.3 mi w. Int corridors. **Pets:** Medium, other species. $75 one-time fee/room. Designated rooms, service with restrictions, crate.
🛜 ✖ 🍴 🖵 🍴

BAY HEAD
☜☜ Grenville Hotel 🅷
(732) 892-3100. **$89-$359, 14 day notice.** 345 Main Ave (SR 35) 08742. SR 35 S; at Bridge Ave. Int corridors. **Pets:** Accepted.
🛜 ✖ 🍴 🍴 🎫

BRIDGEWATER
👐 ☜☜ Days Inn Conference Center 🅷
(908) 526-9500. **$70-$105.** 1260 US 22 E 08807. I-287 exit 17 to US 202/206 S, just s, exit US 22, then 2 mi e; exit 14B northbound, 1 mi w on US 22, U-turn at Adamsville Rd, then 1 mi e. Int corridors.
Pets: Accepted. [SAVE] 🛜 🍴 🖵 🏊

👐 ☜☜☜ Hyatt house Bridgewater 🅷
(908) 725-0800. **$99-$239.** 530 US 22 E 08807. I-287 exit 14B northbound; exit 17 southbound to US 22 W, then 0.8 mi. Ext corridors. **Pets:** Large. $150 one-time fee/room. Service with restrictions, crate.
[SAVE] 🛜 ✖ 🔊 🍴 🖵 🏊 ✖

CAPE MAY

▼▼▼ Madison Avenue Beach Club Motel M
(609) 884-8266. **$80-$220, 7 day notice.** 605 Madison Ave 08204. Jct Columbia Ave. Ext corridors. **Pets:** Accepted. 🤶 ✖ 📶 ◨ 🏊

◈◈◈ ▼▼◈ Marquis de Lafayette Hotel H
(609) 884-3500. **$116-$545, 10 day notice.** 501 Beach Ave 08204. Between Decatur and Ocean sts. Ext/int corridors. **Pets:** Other species. $100 deposit/room, $25 daily fee/pet. Designated rooms, service with restrictions. SAVE 🤶 ✖ 🏳M ◨ 📶 ◨ 🍴 🏊

◈◈◈ ▼▼◈ Palace Hotel of Cape May H ❀
(609) 898-8100. **$89-$329, 7 day notice.** 1101 Beach Ave 08204. Jct Beach and Philadelphia aves. Int corridors. **Pets:** Medium. $25 deposit/pet. Designated rooms, service with restrictions, crate.
SAVE 🤶 ✖ 🏳M ◨ 📶

CAPE MAY COURT HOUSE

▼▼▼ The Doctors Inn BB
(609) 463-9330. **$100-$350, 14 day notice.** 2 N Main St 08210. At Main (US 9) and Mechanic sts; just s of Garden State Pkwy. Int corridors. **Pets:** Small. $25 daily fee/pet. Designated rooms, supervision.
🤶 ✖ ◨ ☒

CLINTON

▼▼▼ Holiday Inn-Clinton H
(908) 735-5111. **$99-$129.** 111 Rt 173 08809. I-78 exit 15, just nw. Int corridors. **Pets:** $50 daily fee/pet. Service with restrictions, supervision.
🤶 ◨ 📶 🍴 🏊

COOKSTOWN

▼▼▼ Quality Inn McGuire AFB H
(609) 723-6500. **$126-$155.** 21 Wrightstown/Cookstown Rd 08511. From main entrance to McGuire Air Force Base, 0.3 mi n. Int corridors. **Pets:** $100 deposit/room, $35 one-time fee/room. Designated rooms, service with restrictions, supervision. 🤶 🏳M ◨ 📶 🏊

CRANBURY

▼▼▼ Courtyard by Marriott Cranbury/South Brunswick H
(609) 655-9950. **$99-$229.** 420 Forsgate Dr 08512. New Jersey Tpke exit 8A to SR 32 W toward town, just w. Int corridors. **Pets:** Accepted.
🤶 ✖ 🏳M ◨ 📶 🍴 🏊

◈◈◈ ▼▼◈ Residence Inn by Marriott/Cranbury-South Brunswick H ❀
(609) 395-9447. **$99-$150.** 2662 US 130 08512. New Jersey Tpke exit 8A to SR 32 W toward town, 2 mi w on S River Rd. Int corridors. **Pets:** $100 one-time fee/room. Designated rooms, service with restrictions, crate. SAVE 🤶 ✖ 🏳M ◨ 📶 🏊 🏊

▼▼▼ Staybridge Suites/Cranbury H
(609) 409-7181. **$79-$249.** 1272 S River Rd 08512. New Jersey Tpke exit 8A to SR 32 W toward town, 2 mi w. Int corridors. **Pets:** Accepted.
🤶 ✖ ◨ 📶 🏊

DOVER

▼▼▼ Homewood Suites by Hilton Dover-Rockaway H
(973) 989-8899. **$149-$169.** 2 Commerce Center Dr 07801. 1.2 mi n on Mt Hope Ave, just w on Mt Pleasant Ave. Int corridors. **Pets:** Accepted.
🤶 🏳M ◨ 📶 🏊

EAST BRUNSWICK

◈◈◈ ▼▼ ▼ BEST WESTERN East Brunswick Inn H
(732) 238-4900. **$85-$160.** 764 SR 18 N 08816. Between Rue Ln and Racetrack Rd; New Jersey Tpke exit 9 (SR 18 N), 4 mi s. Ext/int corridors. **Pets:** Accepted. SAVE 🤶 🏳M ◨ 📶

▼ Motel 6 East Brunswick #1083 M
(732) 390-4545. **$55-$69.** 244 SR 18 N 08816. New Jersey Tpke exit 9 (SR 18), 1 mi s, U-turn at Edgeboro Rd, then just e. Ext/int corridors. **Pets:** Other species. Service with restrictions, supervision. 🤶 🏳M ◨

▼▼ Studio 6 East Brunswick #6020 H
(732) 238-3330. **$73-$83.** 246 Rt 18 at Edgeboro Rd 08816. New Jersey Tpke exit 9 (SR 18), 1 mi s, U-turn at Edgeboro Rd, then just e. Int corridors. **Pets:** Other species. $10 daily fee/room. Service with restrictions, supervision. 🤶 ✖ ◨ 📶

EAST RUTHERFORD

▼▼▼ Residence Inn by Marriott East Rutherford Meadowlands H
(201) 939-0020. **$161-$251.** 10 Murray Hill Pkwy 07073. New Jersey Tpke exit 16W (from western spur) to SR 3 W to SR 17 N, 1.5 mi n to Paterson Plank Rd (SR 120), then just e. Int corridors. **Pets:** Accepted.
🤶 ✖ 🏳M ◨ 📶 🏊 ☒

◈◈◈ ▼▼◈ Sheraton Meadowlands Hotel & Conference Center H
(201) 896-0500. **$104-$850, 3 day notice.** 2 Meadowlands Plaza 07073. New Jersey Tpke exit 16W (from western spur), sports complex right after toll to Sheraton Plaza Dr. Int corridors. **Pets:** Accepted.
SAVE 🤶 ✖ 🏳M ◨ 📶 🍴 🏊 ☒

EAST WINDSOR

◈◈◈ ▼▼▼ Quality Inn East Windsor H
(609) 448-7399. **$80-$200.** 351 Franklin St 08520. New Jersey Tpke exit 8, just w. Ext/int corridors. **Pets:** Medium. $20 daily fee/pet. Designated rooms, service with restrictions, crate. SAVE 🤶 🏳M ◨ 📶

EATONTOWN

◈◈◈ ▼▼▼ Staybridge Suites Hotel Eatontown-Tinton Falls H
(732) 380-9300. **$99-$209.** 4 Industrial Way E 07724. Garden State Pkwy exit 105, 0.7 mi e on SR 36, then 1 mi s on SR 35. Int corridors. **Pets:** Medium. $75 one-time fee/pet. Service with restrictions, crate.
SAVE 🤶 🏳M ◨ 📶 🏊

EDISON

▼ Red Roof Inn #7194 M
(732) 248-9300. **$59-$99.** 860 New Durham Rd 08817. I-287 exit 2A northbound, 0.3 mi w via Bridge St, then left; exit 3 southbound, just w. Ext corridors. **Pets:** Large, other species. Service with restrictions, supervision. 🤶 🏳M ◨

◈◈◈ ▼▼▼ Sheraton Edison Hotel Raritan Center H ❀
(732) 225-8300. **$99-$289.** 125 Raritan Center Pkwy 08837. New Jersey Tpke exit 10, 0.5 mi se on CR 514, keep right after tolls. Int corridors. **Pets:** Medium, dogs only. $150 deposit/room. Designated rooms, service with restrictions, supervision.
SAVE 🤶 ✖ 🏳M ◨ 📶 🍴 🏊 ☒

ELIZABETH

▼▼▼ Residence Inn by Marriott Newark Elizabeth/Liberty International Airport H
(908) 352-4300. **$127-$309.** 83 Glimcher Realty Way 07201. New Jersey Tpke exit 13A, 1 mi se on Jersey Garden Blvd, just n on Kapkowski Rd, then just w. Int corridors. **Pets:** Medium. $100 one-time fee/room. Service with restrictions, supervision. 🤶 ✖ 🏳M ◨ 📶 🏊

EWING

◈◈◈ ▼▼▼ Element Ewing Princeton H ❀
(609) 671-0050. **$149-$329, 7 day notice.** 1000 Sam Weinroth Rd E 08628. I-95 exit 3A, n on Sam Weinroth Rd, then just e. Int corridors. **Pets:** Medium, other species. Service with restrictions.
⬛ SAVE 🤶 ✖ 🏳M ◨ 📶 🏊 ☒

FAIRFIELD

▼▼▼ La Quinta Inn & Suites Fairfield H
(973) 575-1742. **$83-$173.** 38 Two Bridges Rd 07004. I-80 exit 52 westbound; exit 47B (Caldwells) eastbound, 7 mi e on US 46 exit Passaic Ave. Int corridors. **Pets:** Service with restrictions, supervision.
🤶 ◨ 📶 🏊

FORT LEE

BEST WESTERN Fort Lee M
(201) 461-7000. **$129-$189.** 2300 Rt 4 W 07024. 0.5 mi w of George Washington Bridge (SR 4 W). Int corridors. **Pets:** Accepted.

HAZLET

Holiday Inn/Hazlet H
(732) 888-2000. **$89-$189.** 2870 SR 35 07730. Garden State Pkwy exit 117 to SR 35 S, 2.5 mi s. Int corridors. **Pets:** Accepted.

HOBOKEN

W Hoboken H
(201) 253-2400. **$329-$929.** 225 River St 07030. Between 1st and 2nd sts. Int corridors. **Pets:** Accepted.

JERSEY CITY

The Westin Jersey City Newport H
(201) 626-2900. **$169-$599.** 479 Washington Blvd 07310. At 6th St. Int corridors. **Pets:** Accepted.

LAWRENCEVILLE

Red Roof Inn-Princeton #10111 M
(609) 896-3388. **$58-$89.** 3203 Brunswick Pike (US 1) 08648. I-295 exit 67A, just n. Ext corridors. **Pets:** Large, other species. Service with restrictions, supervision.

LEDGEWOOD

Quality Inn H
(973) 347-5100. **Call for rates.** 1691 US 46 W 07852. I-80 exit 27, 2 mi e via US 206 N and 183 N. Int corridors. **Pets:** Accepted.

LONG BRANCH

Ocean Place Resort & Spa H
(732) 571-4000. **$125-$629, 7 day notice.** 1 Ocean Blvd 07740. Jct SR 71, 3 mi e on SR 36, then 0.5 mi s. Int corridors. **Pets:** Medium, other species. $150 one-time fee/room. Designated rooms, service with restrictions, crate.

MAHWAH

Homewood Suites by Hilton H
(201) 760-9994. **$119-$179.** 375 Corporate Dr 07430. I-287 exit 66, 1.7 mi on SR 17 S to MacArthur Blvd, then 0.4 mi w. Int corridors. **Pets:** Other species. $150 one-time fee/room. Service with restrictions, supervision.

Sheraton Mahwah Hotel H
(201) 529-1660. **$109-$249.** 1 International Blvd (Rt 17) 07495. I-287 exit 66; at SR 17 N. Int corridors. **Pets:** Accepted.

MIDDLETOWN

Comfort Inn Middletown-Red Bank H
(732) 671-3400. **$105-$275.** 750 State Rt 35 S 07748. Garden State Pkwy exit 114, 2 mi e on Red Hill Rd, 1 mi s on Kings Hwy to SR 35, then 0.3 mi s. Int corridors. **Pets:** Medium. $30 daily fee/room. Service with restrictions, supervision.

MONMOUTH JUNCTION

Red Roof Inn/Princeton North #198 M
(732) 821-8800. **$60-$133.** 208 New Rd 08852. On US 1 S. Ext corridors. **Pets:** Large, other species. Service with restrictions, supervision.

Residence Inn by Marriott Princeton-South Brunswick H
(732) 329-9600. **$80-$269.** 4225 US 1 S 08543. 0.5 mi s of Raymond Rd. Int corridors. **Pets:** Accepted.

MORRIS PLAINS

Candlewood Suites Parsippany-Morris Plains H
(973) 984-9960. **$110-$130.** 100 Candlewood Dr 07950. I-287 exit 39 northbound; exit 39B southbound, 2 mi w on SR 10. Int corridors. **Pets:** Accepted.

MORRISTOWN

Hyatt house Morristown H
(973) 971-0008. **$99-$289.** 194 Park Ave 07960. SR 24 exit 2A (Morristown), stay in far left lane. Int corridors. **Pets:** Medium. $150 one-time fee/pet. Service with restrictions, supervision.

The Westin Governor Morris H
(973) 539-7300. **$119-$459.** 2 Whippany Rd 07960. I-287 exit 36 southbound, left lane to light, left to stop sign, then 1 mi e; exit 36A northbound to Morris Ave, 0.8 mi e, follow signs. Int corridors. **Pets:** Accepted.

MOUNT OLIVE

Residence Inn by Marriott Mt. Olive at The International Trade Center H
(973) 691-1720. **$110-$171.** 271 Continental Dr 07828. I-80 exit 25, just n, follow signs for International Trade Center. Int corridors. **Pets:** Accepted.

NEPTUNE

Residence Inn by Marriott Neptune at Gateway Centre H
(732) 643-9350. **$89-$219.** 230 Jumping Brook Rd 07753. Garden State Pkwy exit 100B, 0.5 mi e on SR 33, then 0.5 mi n. Int corridors. **Pets:** Accepted.

NEWARK

Fairfield Inn & Suites by Marriott Newark Liberty International Airport H
(973) 242-2600. **$99-$199.** 618-50 Rt 1 & 9 S 07114. US 1 and 9 N to Frontage Rd, U-turn to US 1 and 9 S (local lane), past hotel to Courtyard by Marriott entrance. Int corridors. **Pets:** Accepted.

Hilton Newark Penn Station H
(973) 622-5000. **$159-$289.** Gateway Center - 1048 Raymond Blvd 07102. New Jersey Tpke exit 15E, 3 mi w via Raymond Blvd. Int corridors. **Pets:** Large. $150 one-time fee/pet. Service with restrictions, crate.

SpringHill Suites by Marriott Newark Liberty International Airport H
(973) 624-5300. **$79-$199.** 652 Rt 1 & 9 S 07114. I-95 exit 14, 1 mi sw via US 1 and 9 S. Int corridors. **Pets:** Accepted.

NORTH BRUNSWICK

Brunswick Hotel H
(732) 297-7400. **$89-$149.** 2880 US 1 N 08902. Between Finnegan and Black Horse Ins. Int corridors. **Pets:** Accepted.

PARAMUS

La Quinta Inn H
(201) 265-4200. **$95-$173.** 393 Rt 17 S 07652. Garden State Pkwy exit 163 northbound to SR 17 N, 0.6 mi to Midland Ave, then U-turn to SR 17 S; exit 165 southbound to Richwood Ave, 1 mi s. Int corridors. **Pets:** Service with restrictions, supervision.

PARSIPPANY

WWWW Embassy Suites Parsippany H
(973) 334-1440. **Call for rates.** 909 Parsippany Blvd 07054. I-80 exit 42 to US 202 N; just ne of jct US 202 and 46 W. Int corridors.
Pets: Accepted. 🛜 🛏 💻 🍴 🏊

AAA WWWW Hyatt house Parsippany-East H
(973) 428-8875. **$94-$309.** 299 Smith Rd 07054. I-287 exit 41A northbound; exit 42 southbound to US 46 E, 0.5 mi s. Int corridors.
Pets: Accepted. 🚰 🛜 ✖ 🛏 💻 🏊 ✖

AAA WWWW Red Roof Inn #7072 M
(973) 334-3737. **$55-$99.** 855 US Hwy 46 E 07054. I-80 exit 47 westbound; exit 45 eastbound, 0.5 mi e. Ext corridors. **Pets:** Large, other species. Service with restrictions, supervision. 🚰 🛜 🛏 💻

WWWW Residence Inn by Marriott Parsippany H
(973) 984-3313. **$99-$199.** 3 Gatehall Dr 07054. I-287 exit 39 northbound; exit 39B southbound, 2 mi w on SR 10. Ext/int corridors.
Pets: $100 one-time fee/room. Service with restrictions.
🛜 ✖ 🛏 💻 🏊 ✖

AAA WWWW Sheraton Parsippany Hotel H
(973) 515-2000. **$75-$369.** 199 Smith Rd 07054. I-287 exit 41A northbound; exit 42 to US 46 E, 0.4 mi s. **Pets:** Accepted.
🌱 🚰 🛜 ✖ 🚰 🛏 💻 🍴 🏊 ✖

AAA WWWW Sonesta ES Suites Parsippany H 🐾
(973) 334-2907. **$89-$179.** 61 Interpace Pkwy 07054. I-80 exit 42, 0.3 mi s on Cherry Hill Rd, then just w. Int corridors. **Pets:** Medium. $15 daily fee/pet. Designated rooms, service with restrictions, supervision.
🚰 🛜 ✖ 🚰 🛏 💻 🏊

PHILADELPHIA METROPOLITAN AREA (NEARBY PENNSYLVANIA)

BORDENTOWN

AAA WWWW BEST WESTERN Bordentown Inn M 🐾
(609) 298-8000. **$80-$120.** 1068 US Hwy 206 S 08505. New Jersey Tpke exit 7, 0.8 mi n. Ext corridors. **Pets:** Large. $20 daily fee/pet. Designated rooms, service with restrictions. 🚰 🛜 🛏 💻 🏊 ✖

AAA WWW Days Inn-Bordentown M
(609) 298-6100. **$69-$110.** 1073 US Hwy 206 N 08505. New Jersey Tpke exit 7, 0.8 mi n. Ext corridors. **Pets:** Accepted.
🚰 🛜 🛏 💻 🍴 🏊

BRIDGEPORT

WWW Hampton Inn-Bridgeport H 🐾
(856) 467-6200. **$129-$159.** 2 Pureland Dr 08085. I-295 exit 10, just se. Int corridors. **Pets:** $75 deposit/room. Designated rooms, service with restrictions, supervision. 🛜 ✖ 🚰 🛏 💻 🏊

CARNEYS POINT

WWWW Comfort Inn & Suites H
(856) 299-8282. **$80-$129.** 634 Sodders Rd 08069. I-295 exit 2B, just e on Pennsville-Auburn Rd, then 0.3 mi s. Int corridors. **Pets:** Accepted.
🛜 🚰 🛏 💻

AAA WWWW Holiday Inn Express Hotel & Suites H
(856) 351-9222. **$110-$140.** 506 S Pennsville-Auburn Rd 08069. I-295 exit 2B, just e. Int corridors. **Pets:** Other species. $10 daily fee/pet. Service with restrictions, supervision. 🚰 🛜 🛏 💻

CHERRY HILL

WWW Extended StayAmerica-Philadelphia/Cherry Hill H
(856) 616-1200. **$82-$149.** 1653 E SR 70 (Marlton Pike) 08034. I-295 exit 34A, just e. Int corridors. **Pets:** $25 daily fee/pet. Designated rooms, service with restrictions. 🛜 🛏 💻

AAA WWWW Holiday Inn Philadelphia-Cherry Hill H
(856) 663-5300. **$99-$169.** 2175 W Marlton Pike 08002. I-295 exit 34B, 2.5 mi w. Int corridors. **Pets:** Medium, dogs only. $75 deposit/room. Designated rooms, service with restrictions, supervision.
🚰 🛜 ✖ 🚰 🛏 💻 🍴 🏊

DEPTFORD

WWW Residence Inn by Marriott Deptford H
(856) 686-9188. **$159-$189.** 1154 Hurffville Rd 08096. SR 42 exit Deptford, Runnemede, Woodbury to CR 544, just e to CR 415. Int corridors. **Pets:** Medium, other species. $75 one-time fee/room. Service with restrictions, supervision. 🛜 ✖ 🛏 💻 🏊 ✖

HADDONFIELD

WWWW Haddonfield Inn BB 🐾
(856) 428-2195. **$139-$299, 7 day notice.** 44 W End Ave 08033. I-295 exit 28, 0.7 mi n on SR 168, 2.6 mi e on Kings Hwy, then just n. Int corridors. **Pets:** Dogs only. $25 daily fee/pet. Designated rooms, service with restrictions, supervision. 🛜 ✖ 🚰 🛏

MOUNT LAUREL

AAA WWWW Aloft Mount Laurel H
(856) 234-1880. **$99-$399.** 558 Fellowship Rd 08054. I-295 exit 36A, just se on SR 73 to Fellowship Rd, then just n. Int corridors. **Pets:** Accepted.
🚰 🛜 ✖ 🚰 🛏 💻 🏊

WWW Candlewood Suites H
(856) 642-7567. **$75-$100.** 4000 Crawford Pl 08054. New Jersey Tpke exit 4, 1 mi s on SR 73 S. Int corridors. **Pets:** Accepted. 🛜 🛏 💻

WWW Extended Stay Deluxe-Philadelphia-Mt. Laurel H
(856) 608-9820. **$105-$149.** 500 Diemer Dr 08054. New Jersey Tpke exit 4, 1 mi se on SR 73, just n on Crawford Pl, then just e. Int corridors. **Pets:** $25 daily fee/pet. Designated rooms, service with restrictions.
🛜 🛏 💻

AAA WWWW Hyatt house Mt. Laurel H
(856) 222-1313. **$99-$249.** 3000 Crawford Pl 08054. I-295 exit 36A, 1.5 mi s on SR 73. Ext corridors. **Pets:** Accepted.
🚰 🛜 ✖ 🚰 🛏 💻 🏊

WWWW Philadelphia/Mount Laurel Homewood Suites by Hilton H
(856) 222-9001. **$99-$169.** 1422 Nixon Dr 08054. I-295 exit 36B, follow ramp to end, then just n. Int corridors. **Pets:** Accepted.
🛜 🚰 🛏 💻 🏊 ✖

WWWW Red Roof Inn #7066 M
(856) 234-5589. **$70-$85.** 603 Fellowship Rd 08054. I-295 exit 36A, just se on SR 73 to Fellowship Rd, then just s. Ext corridors. **Pets:** Large, other species. Service with restrictions, supervision. 🚰 🛜 🛏 💻

WWWW Residence Inn by Marriott Mount Laurel at Bishop's Gate H
(856) 234-1025. **$119-$269.** 1001 Sunburst Ln 08054. I-295 exit 40A, just e. Int corridors. **Pets:** Accepted.
🛜 ✖ 🚰 🛏 💻 🏊 ✖

AAA WWWW Staybridge Suites H
(856) 722-1900. **$99-$199.** 4115 Church Rd 08054. New Jersey Tpke exit 4, 0.5 mi s on SR 73, then 0.5 mi w. Int corridors. **Pets:** Accepted.
🚰 🛜 ✖ 🛏 💻 🏊 ✖

Wyndham Philadelphia-Mount Laurel H
(856) 234-7000. **$108-$150.** 1111 SR 73 08054. New Jersey Tpke exit 4; I-295 exit 36A, 0.5 mi se. Int corridors. **Pets:** $100 deposit/room, $50 one-time fee/room. Service with restrictions, crate.
[ECO] [SAVE] 🤶 ✕ (&M) 🍴 💻 🍴 🏊

WESTAMPTON
BEST WESTERN Burlington Inn H
(609) 261-3800. **$115-$129, 3 day notice.** 2020 Burlington Mt Holly Rd 08060. New Jersey Tpke exit 5, just n. Int corridors. **Pets:** Accepted.
[SAVE] 🤶 🍴 💻 🏊

END METROPOLITAN AREA

PISCATAWAY
Embassy Suites Hotel Piscataway-Somerset H
(732) 980-0500. **$99-$159.** 121 Centennial Ave 08854. I-287 exit 9 (Highland Park), just s to Centennial Ave. Int corridors. **Pets:** Accepted.
🤶 🍴 💻 🍴 🏊

Extended StayAmerica Piscataway-Rutgers University H
(732) 235-1000. **$105-$169.** 410 S Randolphville Rd 08854. I-287 exit 7, 0.4 mi s. Int corridors. **Pets:** $25 daily fee/pet. Designated rooms, service with restrictions. 🤶 🍴 💻 🏊

Motel 6 Piscataway #1084 H
(732) 981-9200. **$61-$71.** 1012 Stelton Rd 08854. I-287 exit 5, just e. Ext/int corridors. **Pets:** Other species. Service with restrictions, supervision. 🤶

POMPTON PLAINS
BEST WESTERN PLUS Regency House Hotel H
(973) 696-0900. **Call for rates.** 140 SR 23 N 07444. 6 mi n of jct I-80, US 46 and SR 23. Int corridors. **Pets:** $20 daily fee/pet. Designated rooms, service with restrictions, crate. [SAVE] 🤶 🍴 💻 🍴 🏊

PRINCETON
Chauncey Hotel and Conference Center H
(609) 921-3600. **$139-$319.** 660 Rosedale Rd 08541. 0.5 mi w on Stockton Rd, 0.5 mi n on Elm Rd, 1.8 mi w on Rosedale Rd; enter through the ETS campus. Int corridors. **Pets:** Accepted.
🤶 ✕ (&M) 🍴 💻 🍴 🏊 ✕

Clarion Hotel The Palmer Inn H
(609) 452-2500. **Call for rates.** 3499 US 1 S 08540. 2 mi s of jct CR 526 and 571. Ext/int corridors. **Pets:** Accepted.
[SAVE] 🤶 🍴 💻 🍴 🏊

Hampton Inn Princeton H
(609) 951-0066. **$109-$239.** 4385 US 1 S 08540. Just past Ridge Rd. Int corridors. **Pets:** Accepted. 🤶 ✕ (&M) 🍴 💻 🏊

Holiday Inn Princeton H
(609) 520-1200. **$89-$149.** 100 Independence Way 08540. I-295 exit 67A (SR 1) northbound; exit 67 (SR 1) southbound, 7 mi n. Int corridors.
Pets: Accepted. 🤶 🍴 💻 🍴 🏊 ✕

Nassau Inn H ❀
(609) 921-7500. **$159-$209.** 10 Palmer Square E 08542. Center. Int corridors. **Pets:** Large. $75 one-time fee/room. Designated rooms, service with restrictions, crate. [SAVE] 🤶 🍴 💻 🍴

Residence Inn by Marriott-Princeton at Carnegie Center H
(609) 799-0550. **$139-$229.** 3563 US 1 S 08540. 1.5 mi s of jct CR 527 and 571. Int corridors. **Pets:** Accepted.
🤶 ✕ (&M) 🍴 💻 🏊 ✕

Sonesta ES Suites Princeton H
(609) 951-0009. **Call for rates.** 4375 US 1 S 08543. Just past Ridge Rd. Ext corridors. **Pets:** Accepted. [SAVE] 🤶 🍴 💻 🏊 ✕

Westin Princeton at Forrestal Village H ❀
(609) 452-7900. **$119-$359.** 201 Village Blvd 08540. On US 1 southbound, 1.5 mi n of CR 571. Int corridors. **Pets:** Medium. Service with restrictions, supervision. [SAVE] 🤶 ✕ (&M) 🍴 💻 🍴 🏊 ✕

RAHWAY
Hotel Indigo Rahway H
(732) 340-0076. **Call for rates.** 1 Carriage City Plaza 07065. Across from train station; center. Int corridors. **Pets:** Small. $75 one-time fee/room. Service with restrictions, crate. 🤶 ✕ 🍴 💻

RAMSEY
BEST WESTERN The Inn at Ramsey H ❀
(201) 327-6700. **$84-$119.** 1315 Rt 17 S 07446. Jct I-287 and SR 17 S, 3 mi s. Int corridors. **Pets:** Dogs only. $50 deposit/room, $20 daily fee/room. Designated rooms, service with restrictions, supervision.
[SAVE] 🤶 (&M) 🍴 💻

RUTHERFORD
Extended StayAmerica-Meadowlands-Rutherford H
(201) 635-0266. **$115-$199.** 750 Edwin L Ward Sr Memorial Hwy 07070. I-95 exit 16W, 1.5 mi w on SR 3 to SR 17 N service road exit, then 0.5 mi e. Int corridors. **Pets:** $25 daily fee/pet. Designated rooms, service with restrictions. 🤶 🍴 💻

SECAUCUS
Embassy Suites-Secaucus-Meadowlands H
(201) 864-7300. **Call for rates.** 455 Plaza Dr 07094. New Jersey Tpke eastern spur exit 16E northbound; exit 17 southbound, just e on SR 3 to Harmon Meadow Blvd. Int corridors. **Pets:** Accepted.
🤶 🍴 💻 🍴 🏊

La Quinta Inn & Suites Secaucus Meadowlands H
(201) 863-8700. **$131-$232.** 350 Lighting Way 07094. Between eastern and western spurs of New Jersey Tpke exits 16E, 17 or 16W via SR 3 W and Harmon Meadow Blvd; in Mill Creek Mall. Int corridors. **Pets:** Service with restrictions, supervision. 🤶 🍴 💻 🏊

SOMERSET
Candlewood Suites H
(732) 748-1400. **Call for rates.** 41 Worlds Fair Dr 08873. I-287 exit 10 (CR 527), left on ramp (CR 527 S/Easton Ave), 0.3 mi, then 0.5 mi w. Int corridors. **Pets:** Accepted. 🤶 🍴 💻

Holiday Inn-Somerset H
(732) 356-1700. **Call for rates.** 195 Davidson Ave 08873. I-287 exit 10 (CR 527), just n (direction Bound Brook), then 0.5 mi sw. Int corridors. **Pets:** Other species. $50 one-time fee/pet. Designated rooms, service with restrictions, supervision. [SAVE] 🤶 (&M) 🍴 💻 🍴 🏊

▼▼▼▼ Homewood Suites by Hilton-Somerset 🅷

(732) 868-9155. $99-$289. 101 Pierce St 08873. I-287 exit 10 (CR 527), left on ramp (CR 527 S/Easton Ave), 0.3 mi, 0.7 mi w on Worlds Fair Dr, then just s. Int corridors. **Pets:** Accepted. 🛜 ♿ 🍴 📺 🏊 ⊠

▼▼▼▼ La Quinta Inn & Suites Somerset 🅷

(732) 560-9880. $75-$172. 60 Cottontail Ln 08873. I-287 exit 12, just sw via Weston Canal Rd (Cottontail Ln signage). Int corridors. **Pets:** Service with restrictions, supervision. 🛜 📺 🍴 🏊

▼▼▼▼ Residence Inn by Marriott-Somerset 🅷

(732) 627-0881. $105-$214. 37 Worlds Fair Dr 08873. I-287 exit 10 (CR 527), 0.3 mi left on ramp (CR 527 S/Easton Ave), then 0.5 mi w. Int corridors. **Pets:** Accepted. 🛜 ⊠ ♿ 🍴 📺 🏊 ⊠

♿ ▼▼▼▼ Sonesta ES Suites Somerset 🅷

(732) 356-8000. $99-$129. 260 Davidson Ave 08873. I-287 exit 10 (CR 527), just n (direction Bound Brook) to Davidson Ave, then 0.8 mi sw. Ext corridors. **Pets:** Medium, dogs only. $15 one-time fee/pet, $10 daily fee/pet. Service with restrictions. SAVE 🛜 🍴 📺 🏊 ⊠

SOUTH PLAINFIELD

♿ ▼▼▼ BEST WESTERN The Garden Executive Hotel 🅷

(908) 561-4488. $84-$94. 101 New World Way 07080. I-287 exit 5, just s. Int corridors. **Pets:** Small. $50 deposit/room. Designated rooms, service with restrictions, supervision. SAVE 🛜 🍴 📺 🍴

STOCKTON

▼▼▼▼ Woolverton Inn 🅱🅱 🐾

(609) 397-0802. $150-$435, 10 day notice. 6 Woolverton Rd 08559. Jct CR 523 N and SR 29 N, just n to Woolverton Rd, then just w. Int corridors. **Pets:** Dogs only. Designated rooms. 🛜 ⊠ 🍴 📺 🎦

TINTON FALLS

♿ ▼ Red Roof Inn #211 🅼

(732) 389-4646. $79-$145. 11 Centre Plaza 07724. Garden State Pkwy exit 105, just right at 1st light after toll. Ext corridors. **Pets:** Large, other species. Service with restrictions, supervision.

SAVE 🛜 ⊠ ♿ 🍴 📺

▼▼▼▼ Residence Inn by Marriott Tinton Falls 🅷

(732) 389-8100. $139-$219. 90 Park Rd 07724. Garden State Pkwy exit 105, 1st jughandle after toll, immediate left before Courtyard by Marriott, just n, then e. Ext corridors. **Pets:** Accepted.

🛜 ⊠ 🍴 📺 🏊 ⊠

TOMS RIVER

♿ ▼▼▼ Howard Johnson Hotel-Toms River 🅷

(732) 244-1000. $79-$299. 955 Hooper Ave 08753. Garden State Pkwy exit 82, 1 mi e on SR 37. Int corridors. **Pets:** Accepted.

SAVE 🛜 ⊠ 🍴 📺 🍴 🏊

VERNON

♿ ▼▼▼ Appalachian Motel 🅼

(973) 764-6070. $55-$125, 3 day notice. 367 Rt 94 N 07462. 1 mi n. Ext corridors. **Pets:** Small. $20 daily fee/pet. Designated rooms, service with restrictions, supervision. SAVE 🛜 🍴

WANTAGE

▼ High Point Country Inn 🅼

(973) 702-1860. $79-$89. 1328 SR 23 N 07461. 1 mi n of Colesville Village Center. Ext corridors. **Pets:** Other species. $5 daily fee/pet. Service with restrictions. 🛜 ⊠ 🍴 📞

WAYNE

▼▼▼▼ La Quinta Inns & Suites 🅷

(973) 696-8050. $71-$144. 1850 SR 23 07470. I-80 exit 53 (Butler-Verona) westbound to SR 23 N, 3 mi to Ratzer Rd (service road), then just n; exit 54 eastbound to Minnisink Rd, U-turn for US 80 W exit 53. Int corridors. **Pets:** Service with restrictions, supervision.

🛜 ♿ 🍴 📺 🏊

▼▼▼▼ Residence Inn by Marriott Wayne 🅷

(973) 872-7100. $129-$174. 30 Nevins Rd 07470. Jct CR 640 (Riverview Dr) and 681 (Valley Rd), 3.5 mi n, just w on Barbour Pond Dr, then just n. Int corridors. **Pets:** Accepted. 🛜 ⊠ ♿ 🍴 📺 🏊

WEEHAWKEN

♿ ▼▼▼▼ Sheraton Lincoln Harbor Hotel 🅷

(201) 617-5600. $149-$1325. 500 Harbor Blvd 07086. I-495 E toward Lincoln Tunnel exit Weehawken/Hoboken, bear right at bottom of hill, then 0.4 mi e to Lincoln Harbor Complex; on 19th St. Int corridors.

Pets: Accepted. SAVE 🛜 ⊠ 🍴 📺 🍴 🏊

WEST ORANGE

▼▼▼▼ Residence Inn by Marriott-West Orange 🅷

(973) 669-4700. $200-$220. 107 Prospect Ave 07052. I-280 exit 8B, 1 mi n on CR 577 (Prospect Ave). Int corridors. **Pets:** Accepted.

🛜 ⊠ 🍴 📺 🏊

♿ ▼▼▼▼ The Wilshire Grand Hotel 🅷 🐾

(973) 731-7007. $199-$389, 3 day notice. 350 Pleasant Valley Way 07052. I-280 exit 8B, just n to Eagle Rock Ave, 0.9 mi w, then just n. Int corridors. **Pets:** Medium. $30 daily fee/pet. Designated rooms, service with restrictions, supervision. SAVE 🛜 ⊠ 🍴 📺 🍴 ⊠

WHIPPANY

♿ ▼▼▼▼ Hyatt house Parsippany/Whippany 🅷

(973) 605-1001. $89-$269. 1 Ridgedale Ave N 07981. I-287 exit 39, just nw. Int corridors. **Pets:** Large. $150 one-time fee/room. Service with restrictions, crate. SAVE 🛜 ⊠ ♿ 🍴 📺 🏊

WOODBRIDGE

▼▼ Extended StayAmerica Woodbridge-Edison 🅷

(732) 442-8333. $95-$139. 1 Hoover Way 07095. New Jersey Tpke exit 11, 1.4 mi to US 9 N, then just w on King Georges Post Rd. Int corridors. **Pets:** $25 daily fee/pet. Designated rooms, service with restrictions.

🛜 ♿ 🍴 📺

WOODCLIFF LAKE

▼▼▼▼ Hilton Woodcliff Lake 🅷

(201) 391-3600. $99-$299. 200 Tice Blvd 07677. Garden State Pkwy exit 171 northbound, left on Glen Rd from exit ramp, right on Chestnut Ridge Rd, 0.5 mi to Tice Blvd, then just left. Int corridors. **Pets:** Medium. $75 one-time fee/room. Designated rooms, service with restrictions, supervision. 🛜 ♿ 🍴 📺 🍴 🏊 ⊠

NEW MEXICO

ALAMOGORDO

BEST WESTERN Desert Aire Inn M 🐾

(575) 437-2110. **$83-$90.** 1021 S White Sands Blvd 88310. 1.6 mi s of jct US 82/70 and 54. Ext corridors. **Pets:** Dogs only. $10 daily fee/pet. Designated rooms, service with restrictions, supervision.

[SAVE] 🛜 [&M] 🍴 📟 ☎

Super 8-Alamogordo H

(575) 434-4205. **$60-$70.** 3204 N White Sands Blvd 88310. Just s of jct US 54/70 and 82. Int corridors. **Pets:** Other species. $10 one-time fee/pet. Service with restrictions, crate. [SAVE] 🛜 🍴 📟

ALBUQUERQUE

Albuquerque Sheraton Uptown Hotel H

(505) 881-0000. **$99-$229.** 2600 Louisiana Blvd NE 87110. I-40 exit 162, 0.8 mi n. Int corridors. **Pets:** Accepted.

[SAVE] 🛜 ☒ [&M] 🍴 📟 [�“] ☎

Baymont Inn & Suites H

(505) 344-1555. **$80-$89.** 5101 Ellison St NE 87109. I-25 exit 231 (San Antonio Dr), just w. Ext corridors. **Pets:** Other species. Service with restrictions, supervision. 🛜 [&M] 🍴 📟 ☎

BEST WESTERN Airport Albuquerque InnSuites Hotel H

(505) 242-7022. **$69-$169.** 2400 Yale Blvd SE 87106. I-25 exit 222 (Gibson Blvd) northbound; exit 222A southbound, 1 mi e, then just s. Int corridors. **Pets:** Large, other species. $20 one-time fee/room. Designated rooms, service with restrictions, supervision. [SAVE] 🛜 🍴 📟 ☎

BEST WESTERN PLUS Rio Grande Inn H 🐾

(505) 843-9500. **$89-$129.** 1015 Rio Grande Blvd NW 87104. I-40 exit 157A (Rio Grande Blvd), just s. Int corridors. **Pets:** Medium, dogs only. $20 one-time fee/pet. Designated rooms, service with restrictions, supervision. [SAVE] 🛜 ☒ 🍴 📟 [�“] ☎

Bottger Mansion Bed and Breakfast BB

(505) 243-3639. **$115-$179, 14 day notice.** 110 San Felipe St NW 87104. I-40 exit 157A (Rio Grande Blvd), 1.5 mi s, then just e; off Central Ave. Int corridors. **Pets:** Accepted. 🛜 ☒

Candlewood Suites H

(505) 888-3424. **Call for rates.** 3025 Menaul Blvd NE 87107. I-40 exit 160, just n to Menaul Blvd, then 0.5 mi w. Int corridors. **Pets:** Large, other species. $10 daily fee/pet. Service with restrictions, crate.

[&M] 🍴 📟

ClubHouse Inn & Suites H

(505) 345-0010. **$79-$129.** 1315 Menaul Blvd NE 87107. I-25 exit 227A southbound, 1.5 mi s to Menaul Blvd, then just w; exit 225 northbound, 1.8 mi, then just w. Int corridors. **Pets:** $15 daily fee/pet. Service with restrictions, crate. 🛜 ☒ [&M] 🍴 📟

Comfort Inn & Suites by Choice Hotels H

(505) 822-1090. **$65-$75.** 5811 Signal Ave NE 87113. I-25 exit 233, just e via Alameda Blvd. Int corridors. **Pets:** Accepted.

🛜 [&M] 🍴 📟 ☎

Country Inn & Suites By Carlson Albuquerque Airport H 🐾

(505) 246-9600. **$54-$153.** 2601 Mulberry St SE 87106. I-25 exit 222 (Gibson Blvd), just e. Int corridors. **Pets:** Medium, other species. $25 one-time fee/pet. Designated rooms, service with restrictions, supervision.

🛜 ☒ 🍴 📟 ☎

Crowne Plaza Albuquerque H

(505) 884-2500. **$89-$159.** 1901 University Blvd NE 87102. I-40 exit 160, just n to Menaul Blvd, then 1.1 mi w. Int corridors. **Pets:** Other species. $75 daily fee/room. Designated rooms, service with restrictions, supervision. [SAVE] 🛜 ☒ [&M] 🍴 📟 [�“] ☎

Drury Inn & Suites-Albuquerque H

(505) 341-3600. **$119-$189.** 4310 The 25 Way NE 87109. I-25 exit Jefferson St NE; northwest quadrant of exchange. Int corridors. **Pets:** Service with restrictions, supervision. 🛜 [&M] 🍴 📟 ☎

Econo Lodge Downtown/University M

(505) 243-1321. **$39-$109.** 817 Central Ave NE 87102. I-25 exit 224A northbound; exit 224B southbound, just w. Ext corridors. **Pets:** Medium. $10 deposit/pet, $10 daily fee/pet. Service with restrictions, supervision.

[SAVE] 🛜 🍴 📟

Econo Lodge East H

(505) 292-7600. **Call for rates.** 13211 Central Ave NE 87123. I-40 exit 167 (Central Ave), just w. Ext corridors. **Pets:** Other species. $7 daily fee/pet. Service with restrictions, supervision. [SAVE] 🛜 🍴

Econo Lodge Midtown H

(505) 880-0080. **$45-$60.** 2412 Carlisle Blvd NE 87110. I-40 exit 160, just n. Int corridors. **Pets:** Medium, other species. $15 daily fee/pet. Service with restrictions, supervision. [SAVE] 🛜 🍴

Fairfield Inn by Marriott Albuquerque-University Area H

(505) 889-4000. **$89-$199.** 1760 Menaul Blvd NE 87102. I-40 exit 160, just n to Menaul Blvd, then 1 mi w. Int corridors. **Pets:** Accepted.

🛜 ☒ [&M] 🍴 📟 ☎ ☒

Hotel Andaluz H 🐾

(505) 242-9090. **$139-$329.** 125 2nd St NW 87102. I-25 exit 224A northbound; exit 224B southbound, jct Copper Ave and 2nd St; downtown. Int corridors. **Pets:** $50 one-time fee/pet. Designated rooms, service with restrictions, supervision. [SAVE] 🛜 ☒ [�“]

The Hotel Blue H

(505) 924-2400. **$69-$139.** 717 Central Ave NW 87102. 8th St and Central Ave. Ext corridors. **Pets:** Accepted. 🛜 🍴 📟 ☎

Hotel Parq Central H 🐾

(505) 242-0040. **$140-$420.** 806 Central Ave SE 87102. I-25 exit 224A northbound, just south, just w. Int corridors. **Pets:** Medium. $75 one-time fee/pet. Designated rooms, service with restrictions, supervision. [SAVE] 🛜 ☒ [&M] 🍴 [❚❚] ☒

Hyatt Regency Albuquerque H 🐾

(505) 842-1234. **$81-$217.** 330 Tijeras Ave NW 87102. I-25 exit 224B, 0.5 mi w. Int corridors. **Pets:** Medium. $75 one-time fee/pet. Supervision. [ECO] [SAVE] 🛜 [&M] 🍴 [❚❚] ☎ ☒

▼▼ La Quinta Inn Albuquerque Airport 🅗
(505) 243-5500. **$59-$129.** 2116 Yale Blvd SE 87106. I-25 exit 222 (Gibson Blvd) northbound; exit 222A southbound, 1 mi e. Ext corridors. **Pets:** Service with restrictions, supervision. 🛜 🛁 🛏 🖵 ⇌

▼▼ La Quinta Inn Albuquerque Northeast Ⓜ
(505) 821-9000. **$59-$122.** 5241 San Antonio Dr NE 87109. I-25 exit 231 (San Antonio Dr), just e. Ext corridors. **Pets:** Service with restrictions, supervision. 🛜 🛁 🛏 🖵

▼▼ La Quinta Inn & Suites Albuquerque Journal Ctr NW 🅗
(505) 345-7500. **$59-$129.** 7439 Pan American Frwy NE 87109. I-25 exit 231 (San Antonio Dr), just w. Int corridors. **Pets:** Service with restrictions, supervision. 🛜 🛏 🖵 ⇌

▼▼ La Quinta Inn & Suites Albuquerque Midtown 🅗
(505) 761-5600. **$89-$172.** 2011 Menaul Blvd 87107. Jct University and Menaul blvds, just e. Int corridors. **Pets:** Service with restrictions, supervision. 🛜 🛁 🛏 🖵 ⇌

▼▼ La Quinta Inn & Suites Albuquerque West 🅗
(505) 839-1744. **$59-$140.** 6101 Iliff Rd NW 87121. I-40 exit 155, just sw. Int corridors. **Pets:** Service with restrictions, supervision. 🛜 🛁 🛏 🖵 ⇌

🆀 ▼▼ Mauger Bed & Breakfast Inn 🅱🅱 🐾
(505) 242-8755. **$99-$204, 10 day notice.** 701 Roma Ave NW 87102. I-25 exit 225, 1 mi w, then just s on 7th Ave. Int corridors. **Pets:** Dogs only. $20 one-time fee/room. Designated rooms, service with restrictions. 🆂🅰🆅🅴 🛜 ✕ 🛏 🖵

▼▼ MCM Elegante Hotel 🅗 🐾
(505) 884-2511. **$69-$149.** 2020 Menaul Blvd NE 87107. I-40 exit 160, 0.3 mi n to Menaul Blvd, then 1 mi w. Int corridors. **Pets:** $25 one-time fee/room. Designated rooms, service with restrictions, crate. 🛜 ✕ 🛁 🛏 🖵 🍴 ⇌

▼▼ Nativo Lodge 🅗
(505) 798-4300. **$69-$159.** 6000 Pan American Frwy NE 87109. I-25 exit 230, just e. Int corridors. **Pets:** Accepted. 🛜 ✕ 🛏 🖵 🍴 ⇌ ✕

▼▼ Residence Inn by Marriott Albuquerque Airport 🅗
(505) 242-2844. **$118-$219.** 2301 International Dr SE 87106. I-25 exit 222 (Gibson Blvd) northbound; exit 222A southbound, 1 mi e of jct Yale Blvd SE, then just n. Int corridors. **Pets:** Accepted. 🛜 ✕ 🛁 🛏 ⇌ ✕

🆀 ▼▼ Residence Inn by Marriott North 🅗
(505) 761-0200. **$139-$209.** 4331 The Lane at 25 NE 87109. I-25 exit 229 (Jefferson St), just w, just n to The Lane at 25 NE, then just e. Int corridors. **Pets:** Accepted. 🆂🅰🆅🅴 🛜 ✕ 🛁 🛏 🖵 ⇌

🆀 ▼▼ Sheraton Albuquerque Airport Hotel 🅗
(505) 843-7000. **$89-$219.** 2910 Yale Blvd SE 87106. I-25 exit 222 northbound; exit 222A southbound, 1 mi e on Gibson Blvd, then 0.5 mi s. Int corridors. **Pets:** Accepted. 🆂🅰🆅🅴 🛜 ✕ 🛁 🛏 🖵 🍴 ⇌

▼▼ Staybridge Suites Albuquerque Airport 🅗 🐾
(505) 338-3900. **$80-$120.** 1350 Sunport Pl SE 87106. I-25 exit 221, 0.3 mi e to University Blvd exit, then just n to Woodward Rd. Int corridors. **Pets:** Large, other species. $25 one-time fee/room. Service with restrictions, crate. 🛜 ✕ 🛁 🛏 🖵 ⇌ ✕

▼▼ Staybridge Suites Albuquerque North 🅗 🐾
(505) 266-7829. **$89-$359, 7 day notice.** 5817 Signal Ave NE 87113. I-25 exit 233 (Alameda Blvd), just e; jct Alameda Blvd and Signal Ave. Int corridors. **Pets:** Large, other species. $10 daily fee/room. Designated rooms, service with restrictions, supervision. 🛜 ✕ 🛁 🛏 🖵 ⇌ ✕

▼▼ Suburban Extended Stay Hotels Ⓜ
(505) 883-8888. **$40-$70.** 2401 Wellesley Dr NE 87107. I-40 exit 160, just n to Menaul Blvd, just w, then just s. Ext corridors. **Pets:** Small. $15 daily fee/pet. Designated rooms, service with restrictions, crate. 🛜 🖵

▼▼ TownePlace Suites by Marriott 🅗
(505) 232-5800. **$69-$139.** 2400 Centre Ave SE 87106. I-25 exit 222 (Gibson Blvd) northbound; exit 222A southbound, 1 mi e to Yale Blvd, at northeast jct of Gibson and Yale blvds, then just e. Int corridors. **Pets:** Accepted. 🛜 ✕ 🛁 🛏 🖵 ⇌

ALGODONES

▼▼ Hacienda Vargas Bed and Breakfast Inn 🅱🅱
(505) 867-9115. **Call for rates.** 1431 SR 313 (El Camino Real) 87001. I-25 exit 248, 0.3 mi w, then 0.3 mi s. Int corridors. **Pets:** Other species. $15 one-time fee/room. Crate. ✕ 🆆 🇿

ARROYO SECO

▼▼ Adobe and Stars B & B 🅱🅱
(575) 776-2776. **Call for rates.** 584 State Hwy 150 87571. 1.1 mi ne of Arroyo Seco village, at Valdez Rd. Ext/int corridors. **Pets:** Accepted. 🛜 ✕ 🛁 🅺 🇿

▼▼ Cottonwood Inn Bed & Breakfast 🅱🅱
(575) 776-5826. **Call for rates.** 2 SR 230 87514. On SR 150 at SR 230. Ext/int corridors. **Pets:** Accepted. 🛜 ✕ 🛁 🖵 ✕ 🅺 🇿

ARTESIA

🆀 ▼▼ Artesia Inn Ⓜ
(575) 746-9801. **$75-$110.** 1820 S 1st St 88210. 1.5 mi s on US 285. Ext corridors. **Pets:** $15 one-time fee/room. Service with restrictions, supervision. 🆂🅰🆅🅴 🛜 🛁 🛏 🖵 ⇌

🆀 ▼▼ BEST WESTERN Pecos Inn 🅗
(575) 748-3324. **$110-$150.** 2209 W Main St 88210. 1.5 mi w on US 82. Int corridors. **Pets:** Accepted. 🆂🅰🆅🅴 🛜 🛁 🛏 🖵 🍴 ⇌ ✕

BERNALILLO

▼▼ Days Inn Bernalillo 🅗
(505) 771-7000. **$65-$140.** 107 N Camino del Pueblo 87004. I-25 exit 242, just w. Int corridors. **Pets:** Small. $30 deposit/pet. Service with restrictions, supervision. 🛜 ✕ 🛁 🖵 ⇌

🆀 ▼▼ Hyatt Regency Tamaya Resort and Spa 🅗 🐾
(505) 867-1234. **$108-$279, 7 day notice.** 1300 Tuyuna Tr 87004. I-25 exit 242, 1 mi w on US 550 to Tamaya Blvd, then 1 mi n, follow signs. Int corridors. **Pets:** Medium, dogs only. $65 one-time fee/room. Service with restrictions. 🅴🅲🅾 🆂🅰🆅🅴 🛜 🛁 🛏 🖵 🍴 ⇌ ✕

BLOOMFIELD

▼▼ Super 8 Ⓜ
(505) 632-8886. **$56-$74, 3 day notice.** 525 W Broadway Blvd 87413. Jct of US 64 and 550. Int corridors. **Pets:** Medium. $15 one-time fee/pet. Designated rooms, supervision. 🛜 🖵

CARLSBAD

🆀 ▼▼ BEST WESTERN Stevens Inn 🅗
(575) 887-2851. **$101-$199.** 1829 S Canal St 88220. 1 mi s on US 62, 180 and 285. Ext corridors. **Pets:** $20 daily fee/pet. Service with restrictions, supervision. 🆂🅰🆅🅴 🛜 🛁 🛏 🖵 🍴 ⇌

CHIMAYÓ

▼▼ Casa Escondida Bed & Breakfast 🅱🅱
(505) 351-4805. **$109-$169, 14 day notice.** 64 CR 100 87522. Jct SR 76 and 98, just w on SR 76, then 0.5 mi ne, follow signs; 7.5 mi e of Espanola on SR 76. Ext/int corridors. **Pets:** Accepted. 🛜 ✕ 🛁 🖵 🆆 🇿

CIMARRON

 Cimarron Inn & RV Park Ⓜ ☀
(575) 376-2268. **$49-$75.** 212 10th St 87714. On US 64. Ext corridors. **Pets:** Large, other species. $10 one-time fee/room. Service with restrictions, crate. 🆂🆅Ⓔ 🛜 ☒ 🛄 🖵

CLAYTON

BEST WESTERN Kokopelli Lodge 🄷 ☀
(575) 374-2589. **$110-$140.** 702 S 1st St 88415. US 87, 0.5 mi se of jct US 56 and 64. Ext corridors. **Pets:** Large. $10 daily fee/pet. Service with restrictions, supervision. 🆂🆅Ⓔ 🛜 ☒ 🛄 🖵 ⌦

Days Inn & Suites 🄷
(575) 374-0133. **$99-$157.** 1120 S 1st St 88415. US 87, 1 mi s of jct US 56 and 64. Int corridors. **Pets:** Medium. $10 daily fee/pet. Designated rooms, service with restrictions, supervision.
🆂🆅Ⓔ 🛜 ☒ 🛄 🖵 ⌦

CLOUDCROFT

The Lodge Resort 🄷
(575) 682-2566. **$115-$335, 14 day notice.** 601 Corona Pl 88317. US 82, 0.3 mi s on Curlew Pl/Corona Pl. Int corridors. **Pets:** $25 one-time fee/room. Designated rooms, service with restrictions, supervision.
🆂🆅Ⓔ 🛜 ☒ 🛄 🖵 🍴 ⌦ ☒

CLOVIS

BEST WESTERN Clovis Inn & Suites 🄷
(575) 762-5600. **$73-$81.** 2912 Mabry Dr 88101. 1.8 mi e on US 60/70/84. Ext corridors. **Pets:** Accepted. 🆂🆅Ⓔ 🛜 🛄 🖵 ⌦

Comfort Inn & Suites 🄷
(575) 762-4536. **$85-$104.** 201 Schepps Blvd 88101. Jct US 60/70/84 and Schepps Blvd, just n. Int corridors. **Pets:** Accepted.
🛜 🛄 🖵 ⌦

Econo Lodge Ⓜ
(575) 763-3439. **$49-$89.** 1400 E Mabry Dr 88101. 0.5 mi e on US 60/70/84. Ext corridors. **Pets:** Accepted. 🛜 🛄 🖵 ⌦

La Quinta Inn & Suites Clovis 🄷
(575) 763-8777. **$89-$172.** 4521 N Prince St 88101. Jct US 60/84 and Prince St, 3 mi n. Int corridors. **Pets:** Service with restrictions, supervision. 🛜 ☒ 🛄 🖵 ⌦

DEMING

BEST WESTERN Mimbres Valley Inn 🄷 ☀
(575) 546-4544. **$69-$149.** 1500 W Pine St 88030. I-10 exit 81, just e. Ext corridors. **Pets:** Medium, other species. $15 daily fee/pet. Designated rooms, service with restrictions, supervision. 🆂🆅Ⓔ 🛜 🛄 🖵 ⌦

Days Inn Ⓜ ☀
(575) 546-8813. **$57-$62.** 1601 E Pine St 88030. I-10 exit 85 westbound, 2 mi w on business loop; exit 81 eastbound, 1 mi e on business loop. Ext corridors. **Pets:** Small. $7 daily fee/pet. Service with restrictions, supervision. 🆂🆅Ⓔ 🛜 🛄 🖵 ⌦

Grand Motor Inn 🄷
(575) 546-2632. **$48-$65.** 1721 E Pine St 88030. I-10 exit 85 westbound, 2 mi w on business loop; exit 82 eastbound, 1 mi e on business loop. Ext/int corridors. **Pets:** Medium, other species. $5 daily fee/pet. Designated rooms, service with restrictions, supervision.
🆂🆅Ⓔ 🛜 🛄 🍴 ⌦

Hampton Inn 🄷
(575) 546-2022. **$89-$99.** 3751 E Cedar St 88030. I-10 exit 85, just s to Cedar St, just w. Int corridors. **Pets:** Small, other species. Designated rooms, service with restrictions, supervision.
🛜 ☒ 🆎 🛄 🖵 ⌦

La Quinta Inn & Suites Deming 🄷
(575) 546-0600. **$71-$166.** 4300 E Pine St 88030. I-10 exit 85, just w. Int corridors. **Pets:** Service with restrictions, supervision.
🆂🆅Ⓔ 🛜 ☒ 🆎 🛄 🖵 ⌦

DULCE

Wild Horse Casino & Hotel 🄷
(575) 759-3663. **Call for rates.** 13603 US Hwy 64 87528. Center. Int corridors. **Pets:** Accepted. 🆂🆅Ⓔ 🛜 🛄 🖵 🍴

ELEPHANT BUTTE

Elephant Butte Inn & Spa 🄷 ☀
(575) 744-5431. **$80-$140.** 401 Hwy 195 87935. I-25 exit 83, 4 mi e. Ext corridors. **Pets:** $20 one-time fee/pet. Designated rooms, service with restrictions, supervision. 🆂🆅Ⓔ 🛜 ☒ 🆎 🛄 🖵 🍴 ⌦

ESPAÑOLA

Comfort Inn 🄷
(505) 753-2419. **Call for rates.** 604-B S Riverside Dr 87532. US 84 and 285, just s of jct SR 68. Int corridors. **Pets:** Accepted.
🛜 🛄 🖵 ⌦

Inn at the Delta 🄱🄱
(505) 753-9466. **Call for rates.** 243 Paseo de Onate 87532. US 84 and 285, 1 mi n of jct SR 68; 0.3 mi n of jct SR 30. Ext corridors.
Pets: Accepted. 🛜 ☒ 🛄 🖵

FARMINGTON

Comfort Inn 🄷
(505) 325-2626. **$79-$119.** 555 Scott Ave 87401. 1 mi e on SR 516 (Main St), just s. Int corridors. **Pets:** Accepted.
🆂🆅Ⓔ 🛜 ☒ 🛄 🖵 ⌦

Holiday Inn Express 🄷 ☀
(505) 325-2545. **$99-$169.** 2110 Bloomfield Blvd 87401. 1.6 mi e on US 64 (Bloomfield Blvd), just past jct Broadway; on Frontage Rd. Int corridors. **Pets:** Large, other species. $25 one-time fee/room. Service with restrictions, crate. 🛜 ☒ 🛄 🖵 ⌦

La Quinta Inn Farmington 🄷
(505) 327-4706. **$66-$151.** 675 Scott Ave 87401. 1 mi e on SR 516 (Main St), just s. Ext/int corridors. **Pets:** Service with restrictions, supervision. 🛜 🛄 🖵 ⌦

Red Lion Hotel Farmington 🄷
(505) 327-5221. **$69-$129.** 700 Scott Ave 87401. 1 mi e on SR 516 (Main St), just s. Int corridors. **Pets:** Other species. $15 one-time fee/room. Service with restrictions, crate. 🛜 🛄 🖵 🍴 ⌦ ☒

TownePlace Suites by Marriott 🄷
(505) 327-2442. **$85-$170.** 4200 Sierra Vista Dr 87402. 5 mi e on SR 516 (E Main St), just s. Int corridors. **Pets:** Medium. $100 one-time fee/room. Designated rooms, service with restrictions, crate.
🛜 ☒ 🛄 🖵 🍴 ⌦

GALLUP

Americas Best Value Inn & Suites Ⓜ
(505) 722-0757. **$63-$99.** 2003 Hwy 66 W 87301. I-40 exit 20, 1 mi w. Ext/int corridors. **Pets:** Other species. $10 daily fee/room. Service with restrictions, crate. 🆂🆅Ⓔ 🛜 🛄 🖵

Comfort Suites 🄷
(505) 863-3445. **$109-$129.** 3940 E Hwy 66 87301. I-40 exit 26, just e. Int corridors. **Pets:** Small, other species. $15 daily fee/pet. Service with restrictions, supervision. 🆂🆅Ⓔ 🛜 ☒ 🛄 🖵 ⌦

La Quinta Inn & Suites Gallup 🄷
(505) 722-2233. **$89-$177.** 3880 E Hwy 66 87301. I-40 exit 26, just e. Int corridors. **Pets:** Service with restrictions, supervision.
🛜 ☒ 🛄 🖵 ⌦ ☒

ⓐⓐ 🔷🔷 Quality Inn & Suites Ⓜ
(505) 726-1000. **$100-$150.** 1500 W Maloney Ave 87301. I-40 exit 20, just n on Muñoz Dr, then just w. Ext/int corridors. **Pets:** Large. $15 one-time fee/pet. Service with restrictions, supervision.
[SAVE] 🛜 🖥 🖵 🏊

🔷🔷 Red Lion Hotel Gallup Ⓗ
(505) 722-2221. **$39-$189.** 3009 W US 66 87301. I-40 exit 16, 1 mi e. Int corridors. **Pets:** Other species. $15 one-time fee/room. Service with restrictions, crate. 🛜 🖥 🖵 🍴 🏊

ⓐⓐ 🔷🔷 Red Roof Inn Ⓜ
(505) 722-7765. **$44-$59.** 3304 W Hwy 66 87301. I-40 exit 16, just se. Ext corridors. **Pets:** Large, other species. Service with restrictions, supervision. [SAVE] 🛜 🖥 🖵 🏊

GRANTS
🔷🔷 Comfort Inn Ⓗ
(505) 287-8700. **Call for rates.** 1551 E Santa Fe Ave 87020. I-40 exit 85, 0.3 mi n. Int corridors. **Pets:** Other species. $10 one-time fee/room. Service with restrictions, supervision. 🛜 🖥 🖵 🏊

ⓐⓐ 🔷🔷 Quality Inn & Suites Ⓗ
(505) 285-4676. **$90-$110.** 1496 E Santa Fe Ave 87020. I-40 exit 85, 0.3 mi n. Int corridors. **Pets:** Small, other species. $20 daily fee/pet. Designated rooms, service with restrictions, crate.
[SAVE] 🛜 ✕ 🖥 🖵 🏊

🔷🔷🔷 Red Lion Hotel Grants Ⓗ
(505) 287-7901. **$114-$183.** 1501 E Santa Fe Ave 87020. I-40 exit 85, just w. Int corridors. **Pets:** Other species. $15 one-time fee/room. Service with restrictions, crate. 🛜 🖥 🖵 🍴 🏊 ✕

HOBBS
ⓐⓐ 🔷🔷 BEST WESTERN Executive Inn Ⓗ
(575) 397-7171. **$90-$150.** 309 N Marland Blvd 88240. US 62, 180 and Snyder St. Ext corridors. **Pets:** Accepted. [SAVE] 🛜 🖥 🖵 🏊

🔷🔷 Days Inn Ⓜ
(575) 397-6541. **$80-$110.** 211 N Marland Blvd 88240. 2 mi e on US 62 and 180. Ext corridors. **Pets:** Small. $10 daily fee/pet. Designated rooms, service with restrictions, supervision. 🛜 🖥 🖵 🏊

🔷🔷 Econo Lodge Ⓗ
(575) 397-3591. **Call for rates.** 619 N Marland Blvd 88240. 2.5 mi e on US 62 and 180. Ext corridors. **Pets:** Accepted. 🛜 🖥 🖵 🏊

🔷🔷🔷 La Quinta Inn & Suites Hobbs Ⓗ
(575) 397-8777. **$114-$183.** 3312 N Lovington Hwy 88240. SR 18 N (Lovington Hwy), just s of jct Joe Harvey Blvd. Int corridors. **Pets:** Service with restrictions, supervision. 🛜 ✕ 🖥 🖵 🏊

ⓐⓐ 🔷🔷 Sleep Inn & Suites Ⓗ
(575) 393-3355. **$129-$189.** 4630 Lovington Hwy 88240. Jct SR 18 N (Lovington Hwy) and W Millen Dr, 0.8 mi s. Int corridors. **Pets:** Small. $10 daily fee/pet. Service with restrictions, crate.
[SAVE] 🛜 ✕ 🖥 🖵 🏊

LAS CRUCES
ⓐⓐ 🔷🔷🔷 BEST WESTERN Mission Inn Ⓗ 🐾
(575) 524-8591. **$80-$85.** 1765 S Main St 88005. I-10 exit 142 (University Ave), 1 mi n. Ext corridors. **Pets:** Other species. $10 daily fee/pet. Designated rooms, service with restrictions, supervision.
[SAVE] 🛜 🖥 🖵 🏊

🔷🔷🔷 Comfort Inn & Suites de Mesilla Ⓗ
(575) 527-1050. **Call for rates.** 1300 Avenida de Mesilla 88005. I-10 exit 140, just s. Int corridors. **Pets:** Accepted. 🛜 🖥 🖵 🏊

🔷🔷 Comfort Suites by Choice Hotels Ⓗ
(575) 522-1300. **$82-$109.** 2101 S Triviz Dr 88001. I-25 exit 1 (University Ave), just w, then just n. Int corridors. **Pets:** Medium. $25 one-time fee/room. Service with restrictions, supervision.
🛜 ✕ 🖥 🖵 🏊

🔷🔷🔷 Days Inn Las Cruces Ⓗ
(575) 526-8311. **$60-$200.** 755 Avenida de Mesilla 88005. I-10 exit 140, just e. Ext corridors. **Pets:** Other species. $13 daily fee/pet. Service with restrictions. 🛜 🖥 🖵 🏊

🔷🔷🔷 Drury Inn & Suites Las Cruces Ⓗ
(575) 523-4100. **$100-$159.** 1631 Hickory Loop 88005. I-10 exit 140, just e. Int corridors. **Pets:** Service with restrictions, supervision.
🛜 🖥 🖵 🏊

🔷🔷🔷 Holiday Inn Express & Suites Ⓗ
(575) 522-0700. **$104-$129.** 2142 Telshor Ct 88011. I-25 exit 6 (US 70), just s. Int corridors. **Pets:** Medium, dogs only. $10 daily fee/pet. Designated rooms, service with restrictions, supervision.
🛜 ✕ 🖥 🖵 🏊

ⓐⓐⓐ 🔷🔷🔷 Hotel Encanto de Las Cruces Ⓗ 🐾
(575) 522-4300. **$109-$179.** 705 S Telshor Blvd 88011. I-25 exit 3 (Lohman Ave), just e, then just s. Int corridors. **Pets:** Large, other species. $25 daily fee/pet. Designated rooms, service with restrictions, supervision.
[SAVE] 🛜 ✕ 🖥 🖵 🍴 🏊

🔷🔷 La Quinta Inn & Suites Las Cruces Organ Mountain Ⓗ
(575) 523-0100. **$63-$140.** 1500 Hickory Dr 88005. I-10 exit 140, just se of jct I-25 and Avenida de Mesilla. Int corridors. **Pets:** Service with restrictions, supervision. 🛜 🖥 🖵 🏊

🔷🔷 La Quinta Inn Las Cruces Mesilla Valley Ⓗ
(575) 524-0331. **$63-$151.** 790 Avenida de Mesilla 88005. I-10 exit 140, just e. Int corridors. **Pets:** Service with restrictions, supervision.
🛜 🖥 🖵 🏊

🔷🔷 Lundeen's Inn of the Arts ⒷⒷ
(575) 526-3326. **$79-$125, 3 day notice.** 618 S Alameda Blvd 88005. Jct Lohman Ave, just s; center. Int corridors. **Pets:** Accepted.
🛜 ✕ 🖥 🖵

🔷🔷 Quality Inn & Suites Ⓗ
(575) 524-4663. **Call for rates.** 2200 S Valley Dr 88007. I-10 exit 142 (University Ave), 2 blks w. Ext corridors. **Pets:** Accepted.
🛜 🖥 🖵 🏊

🔷🔷🔷 Ramada Palms de Las Cruces Ⓗ
(575) 526-4411. **$89-$109.** 201 E University Ave 88005. I-10 exit 142 (University Ave), just n. Int corridors. **Pets:** Accepted.
🛜 ✕ 🖥 🖵 🍴 🏊

🔷🔷🔷 Staybridge Suites Ⓗ
(575) 521-7999. **$84-$209, 3 day notice.** 2651 Northrise Dr 88011. I-25 exit 6 (US 70), just e. Int corridors. **Pets:** Accepted.
🛜 ✕ 🖥 🖵 🏊 ✕

🔷🔷🔷 TownePlace Suites by Marriott Las Cruces Ⓗ 🐾
(575) 532-6500. **$109-$159.** 2143 Telshor Ct 88011. I-25 exit 6 (US 70), just s. Int corridors. **Pets:** Other species. $75 one-time fee/room. Service with restrictions, supervision. 🛜 ✕ 🖥 🖵 🏊

LAS VEGAS
ⓐⓐ 🔷🔷🔷 BEST WESTERN PLUS Montezuma Inn & Suites Ⓗ
(505) 426-8000. **$72-$120.** 2020 N Grand Ave 87701. I-25 exit 347, just sw. Int corridors. **Pets:** Accepted.
[SAVE] 🛜 ✕ 🖥 🖵 🏊 ✕

◇◇ ▼▼▼ Comfort Inn H
(505) 425-1100. **$65-$90.** 2500 N Grand Ave 87701. I-25 exit 347, just sw; US 85/25 business route. Int corridors. **Pets:** Medium, other species. $15 daily fee/room. Designated rooms.

▼▼▼▼ Holiday Inn Express Hotel & Suites H
(505) 426-8182. **$95-$125.** 816 S Grand Ave 87701. I-25 exit 343, just n. Int corridors. **Pets:** Accepted.

◇◇ ▼▼▼ Plaza Hotel H
(505) 425-3591. **$99-$108.** 230 Plaza St 87701. I-25 exit 343W, just w, follow signs to Old Town Plaza. Int corridors. **Pets:** $10 daily fee/pet. Service with restrictions.

LORDSBURG
◇◇ ▼▼▼ Comfort Inn & Suites H
(575) 542-3355. **$70-$120.** 400 W Wabash St 88045. I-10 exit 22, just n, then w. Int corridors. **Pets:** Medium. $10 daily fee/pet. Service with restrictions, supervision.

▼▼▼▼ Hampton Inn H
(575) 542-8900. **$89-$109.** 412 W Wabash St 88045. I-10 exit 22, just w. Int corridors. **Pets:** Medium, other species. Service with restrictions, supervision.

LOS ALAMOS
▼▼▼▼ Holiday Inn Express & Suites H
(505) 661-2646. **$114-$199.** 60 Entrada Dr 87544. Jct Airport Basin Dr and SR 502. Int corridors. **Pets:** Accepted.

LOS LUNAS
◇◇ ▼▼ Western Skies Inn & Suites H
(505) 865-0001. **$65-$95.** 2258 Sun Ranch Village Loop 87031. I-25 exit 203, just w. Int corridors. **Pets:** Other species. $10 daily fee/pet. Service with restrictions, supervision.

MORIARTY
◇◇ ▼▼▼ Americas Best Value Inn H
(505) 832-4457. **$52-$85.** 1316 Route 66 W 87035. I-40 exit 194, 0.5 mi se on US 66 and I-40 business loop. Int corridors. **Pets:** Other species. $7 daily fee/pet. Designated rooms, service with restrictions, supervision.

◇◇ ▼▼▼▼ BEST WESTERN Moriarty Heritage Inn H ❀
(505) 832-5000. **$90-$120.** 111 Anaya Blvd 87035. I-40 exit 194, 0.4 mi e. Int corridors. **Pets:** Medium, other species. $15 one-time fee/room. Designated rooms, service with restrictions, supervision.

▼▼ Comfort Inn H 🐾
(505) 832-6666. **$79-$109.** 119 Route 66 E 87035. I-40 exit 196, just s, then just e. Int corridors. **Pets:** Other species. $10 one-time fee/room. Service with restrictions.

◇◇ ▼▼▼ Super 8 H
(505) 832-6730. **$62-$85.** 1611 W Old Route 66 87035. I-40 exit 194, 0.5 mi e on Central Ave. Int corridors. **Pets:** Other species. $10 daily fee/pet. Designated rooms, service with restrictions, supervision.

OJO CALIENTE
▼▼▼▼ Rancho de San Juan Country Inn & Restaurant CI
(505) 753-6818. **$525-$1050, 30 day notice.** RR 34020, US Hwy 285 87549. 3 mi nw of jct US 285 and 84, just n of MM 340. Ext corridors. **Pets:** Accepted.

PINOS ALTOS
▼▼▼ Bear Creek Motel & Cabins CA
(575) 388-4501. **$109-$189.** 88 Main St 88053. 1 mi n of town on SR 15. Ext corridors. **Pets:** Accepted.

RATON
◇◇ ▼▼▼▼ BEST WESTERN PLUS Raton Hotel H
(575) 445-8501. **$110-$150.** 473 Clayton Rd 87740. I-25 exit 451, just w. Ext/int corridors. **Pets:** Medium, dogs only. $20 deposit/room. Designated rooms, service with restrictions, supervision.

◇◇ ▼▼▼▼ Budget Host Raton M
(575) 445-3655. **$59-$87.** 136 Canyon Dr 87740. I-25 exit 454, 0.8 mi s on I-25 business loop. Ext corridors. **Pets:** Medium. $5 daily fee/pet. Service with restrictions, supervision.

◇◇ ▼▼▼▼ Holiday Inn Express Hotel & Suites H
(575) 445-1500. **Call for rates.** 101 Card Ave 87740. I-25 exit 450, just w. Int corridors. **Pets:** Dogs only. $10 daily fee/pet. Designated rooms, service with restrictions, supervision.

▼▼ Microtel Inn & Suites by Wyndham Raton H
(575) 445-9100. **$65-$80.** 1640 Cedar St 87740. I-25 exit 451, just w. Int corridors. **Pets:** Accepted.

▼▼ Raton Pass Inn M
(575) 445-3641. **$48-$64.** 308 Canyon Dr 87740. I-25 exit 454, 0.8 mi s. Ext corridors. **Pets:** Dogs only. $2 daily fee/pet. Service with restrictions, supervision.

RED RIVER
◇◇ ▼▼▼ BEST WESTERN Rivers Edge H
(575) 754-1766. **$80-$200, 7 day notice.** 301 W River St 87558. 1 blk s of W Main St (SR 38); center. Ext corridors. **Pets:** Accepted.

RIO RANCHO
▼▼▼ Extended StayAmerica Albuquerque-Rio Rancho M
(505) 792-1338. **$64-$99.** 2608 The American Rd NW 87124. Corner of SR 528 and Cottonwood Dr, just n, then just w. Int corridors. **Pets:** $25 daily fee/pet. Designated rooms, service with restrictions.

◇◇ ▼▼▼ Inn at Rio Rancho Hotel and Conference Center H
(505) 892-1700. **$59-$119.** 1465 Rio Rancho Dr SE 87124. I-25 exit 233 (Alameda Blvd), 6.5 mi w; I-40 exit 155, 10 mi n on Coors Rd/Coors Bypass to SR 528, then 1 mi n. Ext corridors. **Pets:** $25 daily fee/room. Designated rooms, service with restrictions.

▼▼ Rio Rancho Super 8 H
(505) 896-8888. **$47-$60.** 4100 Barbara Loop SE 87124. I-25 exit 233 (Alameda Blvd), 0.5 mi w, 3.8 mi nw on SR 528, then just e. Int corridors. **Pets:** Medium. $10 one-time fee/pet. Service with restrictions, crate.

ROSWELL
◇◇ ▼▼▼ BEST WESTERN El Rancho Palacio H
(575) 622-2721. **$70-$110.** 2205 N Main St 88201. 1.8 mi n on US 70 and 285. Ext corridors. **Pets:** Large. Service with restrictions, crate.

◇◇ ▼▼▼ BEST WESTERN PLUS Sally Port Inn & Suites H
(575) 622-6430. **$109-$149.** 2000 N Main St 88201. 1.5 mi n on US 70 and 285. Int corridors. **Pets:** Accepted.

Candlewood Suites Roswell [H] 🐾
(575) 623-4300. **$109-$159.** 4 Military Heights Dr 88201. Jct US 70 and 285, just n of US 385. Int corridors. **Pets:** Large. $15 daily fee/pet. Service with restrictions, crate. [SAVE] [icons]

Comfort Inn [H]
(575) 623-4567. **$89-$109.** 3595 N Main St 88201. 3 mi n on US 70 and 285. Int corridors. **Pets:** Medium. Service with restrictions, supervision. [SAVE] [icons]

Days Inn [H]
(575) 623-4021. **$76.** 1310 N Main St 88201. 0.8 mi n on US 70 and 285. Ext corridors. **Pets:** Large. Service with restrictions, crate. [SAVE] [icons]

Holiday Inn Express [H]
(575) 627-9900. **$110-$139.** 2300 N Main St 88201. 1.8 mi n on US 70 and 285. Int corridors. **Pets:** Medium, other species. $10 daily fee/pet. Service with restrictions, supervision. [SAVE] [icons]

La Quinta Inn & Suites Roswell [H]
(575) 622-8000. **$95-$188.** 200 E 19th St 88201. Jct N Main and 19th sts, 2 blks e. Int corridors. **Pets:** Service with restrictions, supervision. [SAVE] [icons]

RUIDOSO

The Lodge at Sierra Blanca [H]
(575) 258-5500. **$109-$199.** 107 Sierra Blanca Dr 88345. Jct Sudderth Dr. Int corridors. **Pets:** Accepted. [icons]

Whispering Pine Cabins [CA]
(575) 257-4311. **$99-$450, 14 day notice.** 422 Main Rd 88345. 0.9 mi w of jct SR 48 and Sudderth Dr. Ext corridors. **Pets:** Other species. $15 one-time fee/pet. No service, crate. [icons]

RUIDOSO DOWNS

BEST WESTERN Pine Springs Inn [H]
(575) 378-8100. **Call for rates.** 111 Pine Springs Dr 88346. Just e of jct US 70 and SR 48. Ext corridors. **Pets:** Accepted. [SAVE] [icons]

La Quinta Inn & Suites [H]
(575) 378-3333. **$95-$265.** 26147 US Hwy 70 E 88346. Just e of jct US 70 and SR 48. Int corridors. **Pets:** Service with restrictions, supervision. [icons]

SANTA FE

BEST WESTERN PLUS Inn of Santa Fe [H] 🐾
(505) 438-3822. **$70-$150.** 3650 Cerrillos Rd 87507. I-25 exit 278, 2.8 mi n. Int corridors. **Pets:** Service with restrictions, supervision. [SAVE] [icons]

Bishop's Lodge Ranch Resort & Spa [H] 🐾
(505) 983-6377. **$125-$1299, 3 day notice.** 1297 N Bishop's Lodge Rd 87501. 3.5 mi n of jct Paseo de Peralta. Ext/int corridors. **Pets:** Other species. $20 daily fee/pet. Designated rooms, supervision. [SAVE] [icons]

Eldorado Hotel & Spa [H]
(505) 988-4455. **$139-$419, 3 day notice.** 309 W San Francisco St 87501. Just w of The Plaza; at Sandoval St. Int corridors.
Pets: Accepted. [SAVE] [icons]

El Paradero Bed & Breakfast [BB]
(505) 988-1177. **$100-$200, 14 day notice.** 220 W Manhattan Ave 87501. 0.3 mi s on Cerrillos Rd, 1/2 blk e. Ext/int corridors. **Pets:** Dogs only. $20 deposit/pet, $20 daily fee/pet. Designated rooms, service with restrictions, supervision. [SAVE] [icons]

Four Seasons Resort Rancho Encantado Santa Fe [H] 🐾
(505) 946-5700. **$275-$675, 14 day notice.** 198 SR 592 87506. US 285/84 N exit 172 (CR 73/Tesuque), 0.5 mi se to SR 592, then 2 mi ne. Ext corridors. **Pets:** Other species. $100 deposit/room. Service with restrictions, supervision. [SAVE] [icons]

Hacienda Nicholas [BB] 🐾
(505) 986-1431. **$110-$260, 14 day notice.** 320 E Marcy St 87501. Just e of jct Paseo de Peralta; 4 blks e of historic plaza. Ext/int corridors. **Pets:** Other species. $25 one-time fee/pet. Service with restrictions, crate. [icons]

Hampton Inn Santa Fe [H]
(505) 474-3900. **$89-$159.** 3625 Cerrillos Rd 87505. I-25 exit 278, 2.5 mi n. Int corridors. **Pets:** Medium, other species. Designated rooms, service with restrictions, supervision. [SAVE] [icons]

Hilton Santa Fe Buffalo Thunder [H] 🐾
(505) 455-5555. **$149-$249.** 20 Buffalo Thunder Tr 87506. North on US 285 exit Buffalo Thunder Rd, just e. Int corridors. **Pets:** Large. $50 one-time fee/room. Designated rooms, service with restrictions, supervision. [SAVE] [icons]

Hilton Santa Fe Historic Plaza [H]
(505) 988-2811. **$142-$284.** 100 Sandoval St 87501. Just sw of The Plaza; between San Francisco and W Alameda sts. Ext/int corridors. **Pets:** Accepted. [SAVE] [icons]

Holiday Inn Express-Santa Fe [H]
(505) 474-7570. **$79-$119.** 3450 Cerrillos Rd 87507. I-25 exit 278, 3 mi n. Int corridors. **Pets:** Small, other species. $15 daily fee/pet. Designated rooms, service with restrictions, supervision. [icons]

Homewood Suites By Hilton-Santa Fe North [H]
(505) 455-9100. **$129-$249.** 10 Buffalo Thunder Tr 87506. US 84/285 exit 177, just e. Ext/int corridors. **Pets:** Small, dogs only. $75 one-time fee/room. Service with restrictions, crate. [SAVE] [icons]

Hotel Chimayó de Santa Fe [H]
(505) 988-4900. **Call for rates.** 125 Washington Ave 87501. Just ne of The Plaza; center. Ext/int corridors. **Pets:** Accepted. [icons]

Hotel Santa Fe, The Hacienda & Spa [H] 🐾
(505) 982-1200. **$119-$600, 3 day notice.** 1501 Paseo de Peralta 87501. At Cerrillos Rd, 0.6 mi s of The Plaza. Int corridors. **Pets:** Dogs only. $20 daily fee/pet. Service with restrictions, supervision. [SAVE] [icons]

The Inn & Spa at Loretto [H]
(505) 988-5531. **$189-$599, 3 day notice.** 211 Old Santa Fe Tr 87501. Just s of The Plaza. Int corridors. **Pets:** Accepted. [SAVE] [icons]

Inn at Santa Fe [H] 🐾
(505) 474-9500. **$89-$249.** 8376 Cerrillos Rd 87507. I-25 exit 278, 0.3 mi n. Int corridors. **Pets:** Other species. $25 one-time fee/pet. Designated rooms, service with restrictions, supervision. [icons]

The Inn of The Five Graces [CI] 🐾
(505) 992-0957. **$425-$2500, 3 day notice.** 150 E DeVargas St 87501. Jct Old Pecos Trail. Ext/int corridors. **Pets:** Medium, dogs only. $75 daily fee/pet. Designated rooms, service with restrictions, crate. [icons]

◆◆◇ Inn On The Alameda 🅗 ✿

(505) 984-2121. **$135-$400, 3 day notice.** 303 E Alameda St 87501. Just e of The Plaza; jct Paseo de Peralta. Ext/int corridors. **Pets:** Small, other species. $30 daily fee/pet. Designated rooms, service with restrictions. 〔SAVE〕 🛜 ✕ 🛢 🖵 ⊠

◇◇ Inn on the Paseo 🅱🅱

(505) 984-8200. **$79-$259.** 630 Paseo de Peralta 87501. I-25 exit 282, 2 mi e; jct St. Francis Dr. Ext/int corridors. **Pets:** $20 daily fee/room. Service with restrictions, supervision. 🛜 ✕

◇◇◇ La Fonda On the Plaza 🅗 ✿

(505) 982-5511. **$229-$829.** 100 E San Francisco St 87501. On The Plaza. Int corridors. **Pets:** Medium, dogs only. $25 daily fee/room. Service with restrictions. 🛜 ✕ ♿ 🛢 🖵 ❚¶ ⊷ ⊠

◆◆◇ ◇◇◇ La Posada de Santa Fe Resort & Spa 🅗

(505) 986-0000. **$169-$659, 3 day notice.** 330 E Palace Ave 87501. Jct Paseo de Peralta and E Palace Ave. Ext corridors. **Pets:** Accepted. 〔SAVE〕 🛜 ✕ 🖵 ❚¶ ⊷ ⊠

◇◇◇ La Quinta Inn Santa Fe 🅗

(505) 471-1142. **$59-$188.** 4298 Cerrillos Rd 87507. I-25 exit 278, 1.8 mi n. Ext/int corridors. **Pets:** Service with restrictions, supervision. 🛜 🛢 🖵 ⊷

◆◆◇ ◇◇◇ Las Palomas 🅗 ✿

(505) 982-5560. **$99-$600.** 460 W San Francisco St 87501. Just w of jct Guadalupe St. Ext corridors. **Pets:** Dogs only. $20 daily fee/pet. Service with restrictions, supervision. 〔SAVE〕 🛜 ✕ 🛢 🖵

◇◇◇ The Lodge at Santa Fe 🅗

(505) 992-5800. **Call for rates.** 750 N St. Francis Dr 87501. Jct of Cerrillos Rd and St. Francis Dr (US 84/285), 1.1 mi nw to Alamo Dr, just w, then just n. Ext/int corridors. **Pets:** Accepted. 🛜 ✕ 🛢 🖵 ❚¶

◇ Motel 6-150 🅜

(505) 473-1380. **$45-$75.** 3007 Cerrillos Rd 87507. I-25 exit 278, 3.8 mi n. Ext corridors. **Pets:** Other species. Service with restrictions, supervision. 🛜 🛢 ⊷

◆◆◇ ◇◇◇ The Old Santa Fe Inn 🅜 ✿

(505) 995-0800. **$99-$390, 3 day notice.** 320 Galisteo St 87501. Just sw of The Plaza; center. Ext/int corridors. **Pets:** $20 daily fee/pet. Designated rooms, service with restrictions, supervision. 〔SAVE〕 🛜 ✕ 🛢 🖵

◆◆◇ ◇◇◇ Pecos Trail Inn 🅜

(505) 982-1943. **$89-$155.** 2239 Old Pecos Tr 87505. I-25 exit 284, 0.8 mi n on CR 466 (Old Pecos Tr). Ext corridors. **Pets:** Accepted. 〔SAVE〕 🛜 ✕ 🛢 🖵 ❚¶ ⊷

◇◇◇ ◇◇◇ Rosewood Inn of the Anasazi 🅗

(505) 988-3030. **Call for rates.** 113 Washington Ave 87501. Just ne of The Plaza. Int corridors. **Pets:** Accepted. 🛜 ✕ 🖵 ❚¶

◆◆◇ ◇◇◇ Santa Fe Motel & Inn 🅜

(505) 982-1039. **$79-$199, 3 day notice.** 510 Cerrillos Rd 87501. 4 blks sw of The Plaza. Ext corridors. **Pets:** Accepted. 〔SAVE〕 🛜 🛢 🖵

◆◆◇ ◇◇◇ Santa Fe Sage Inn 🅗 ✿

(505) 982-5952. **$45-$140.** 725 Cerrillos Rd 87505. 0.4 mi ne of St. Francis Dr (US 84). Ext corridors. **Pets:** $15 daily fee/pet. Designated rooms, service with restrictions, supervision. 〔SAVE〕 🛜 🛢 🖵 ⊷

◇ The Santa Fe Suites 🅜

(505) 989-3600. **Call for rates.** 3007 S St. Francis Dr 87505. 0.8 mi n on S St. Francis Dr, just e on Zia Rd via access drive. Ext corridors. **Pets:** Accepted. 🛜 ♿ 🛢 🖵

SANTA ROSA

◆◆◇ ◇◇◇ BEST WESTERN Adobe Inn 🅗

(575) 472-3446. **$55-$109.** 2255 Historic Route 66 88435. I-40 exit 275. Ext corridors. **Pets:** Medium. $10 one-time fee/room. Service with restrictions, supervision. 〔SAVE〕 🛜 🛢 🖵 ⊷

◆◆◇ ◇◇◇ BEST WESTERN Santa Rosa Inn 🅜

(575) 472-5877. **$70-$120.** 2491 Historic Route 66 88435. I-40 exit 277, 0.5 mi w. Ext corridors. **Pets:** Medium. $10 daily fee/pet. Designated rooms, service with restrictions, supervision. 〔SAVE〕 🛜 🛢 🖵 ⊷

◇◇◇ Holiday Inn Express 🅗 ✿

(575) 472-5411. **$80-$199, 3 day notice.** 2516 Historic Route 66 88435. I-40 exit 277, 0.4 mi w. Int corridors. **Pets:** Other species. $25 one-time fee/room. Designated rooms, service with restrictions, supervision. 🛜 ♿ 🛢 🖵 ⊷ ⊠

◇◇◇ La Quinta Inn Santa Rosa 🅗

(575) 472-4800. **$93-$166.** 2277 Historic Route 66 88435. I-40 exit 275, just e. Int corridors. **Pets:** Service with restrictions, supervision. 🛜 🛢 🖵 ⊷

◇◇ Quality Inn 🅗

(575) 472-5570. **$71-$81.** 2533 E Historic Route 66 88435. I-40 exit 277, 0.3 mi w. Ext corridors. **Pets:** $10 one-time fee/pet. Designated rooms, service with restrictions, supervision. 🛜 🛢 🖵 ⊷

◇◇◇ Super 8-Santa Rosa 🅜

(575) 472-5388. **$65-$80.** 2075 Historic Route 66 88435. I-40 exit 275, just w. Int corridors. **Pets:** Medium, other species. $10 daily fee/pet. Designated rooms, service with restrictions, supervision. 🛜 ♿ 🛢 🖵

SILVER CITY

◆◆◇ ◇◇◇ Comfort Inn 🅗

(575) 534-1883. **$75-$250.** 1060 E Hwy 180 88061. Just e of jct SR 15. Int corridors. **Pets:** $20 deposit/pet, $7 daily fee/pet. Service with restrictions, supervision. 〔SAVE〕 🛜 ✕ 🛢 🖵 ⊷

◆◆◇ ◇◇◇ Econo Lodge Silver City 🅗

(575) 534-1111. **$79-$159.** 1120 Hwy 180 E 88061. 1.5 mi ne on US 180 and SR 90. Int corridors. **Pets:** Other species. $7 one-time fee/pet. Designated rooms, service with restrictions, crate. 〔SAVE〕 🛜 ♿ 🛢 🖵 ⊷

◆◆◇ ◇◇◇ Holiday Inn Express 🅗

(575) 538-2525. **$113-$124.** 1103 Superior St 88061. 3 mi ne on US 180 and SR 90. Int corridors. **Pets:** Other species. Designated rooms, service with restrictions, supervision. 〔SAVE〕 🛜 ✕ 🛢 🖵

SOCORRO

◆◆◇ ◇◇◇ BEST WESTERN Socorro Hotel & Suites 🅗

(575) 838-0556. **$105.** 1100 California Ave NE 87801. I-25 exit 150, just s. Ext/int corridors. **Pets:** Large. $10 daily fee/pet. Designated rooms, service with restrictions, supervision. 〔SAVE〕 🛜 ✕ ♿ 🛢 🖵 ⊷ ⊠

◇◇◇ Comfort Inn & Suites 🅗

(575) 838-4400. **$90-$105.** 1259 Frontage Rd NW 87801. I-25 exit 150, just nw. Int corridors. **Pets:** Accepted. 🛜 ♿ 🛢 🖵 ⊷

◇◇◇ Econo Lodge 🅜

(575) 835-1500. **$65-$150.** 713 N California St NW 87801. I-25 exit 150, 1 mi s. Ext corridors. **Pets:** Medium, dogs only. $10 one-time fee/pet. Designated rooms, service with restrictions, supervision. 🛜 🛢 🖵 ⊷ ⊠

TAOS

◬ ▽▽▽ American Artists Gallery House Bed & Breakfast BB

(575) 758-4446. **$109-$225, 14 day notice.** 132 Frontier Ln 87571. 1 mi s of jct US 64 and Taos Plaza, 0.3 mi e. Ext/int corridors. **Pets:** Dogs only. $25 daily fee/room. Designated rooms, service with restrictions, supervision. SAVE 🛜 ⊠ 🛏 🖵

◬ ▽▽▽▽ An Inn On The Rio BB

(575) 758-7199. **$125-$225, 14 day notice.** 910 Kit Carson Rd 87571. US 64, 1.5 mi e of jct SR 68 and Taos Plaza. Ext corridors.
Pets: Accepted. SAVE 🛜 ⊠ 🖵 🌊 ⊠ 🐾

◬ ▽▽▽ ▽▽▽ El Monte Sagrado, Autograph Collection H ❀

(575) 758-3502. **$169-$309, 3 day notice.** 317 Kit Carson Rd 87571. 0.5 mi e of jct US 64 and SR 68. Ext corridors. **Pets:** Dogs only. $75 one-time fee/room. Designated rooms, service with restrictions, crate.
SAVE 🛜 ⊠ 🖵 🍽 🌊 ⊠

◬ ▽▽▽ ▽▽▽ Inn on La Loma Plaza BB

(575) 758-1717. **$150-$450, 15 day notice.** 315 Ranchitos Rd 87571. 0.3 mi sw, just w of Taos Plaza; in La Loma Plaza Historic District. Ext/int corridors. **Pets:** Medium, dogs only. $25 daily fee/pet. Designated rooms, service with restrictions, supervision. SAVE 🛜 🛏 🖵 ⊠

◬ ▽▽▽ La Posada de Taos BB

(575) 758-8164. **$149-$250, 5 day notice.** 309 Juanita Ln 87571. From Taos Plaza, just w on Don Fernando St, just s on Manzanares St, then just w. Ext/int corridors. **Pets:** Medium, dogs only. $50 one-time fee/room. Service with restrictions, crate. SAVE 🛜 ⊠ 🖵 🎇

▽▽▽ Sagebrush Inn H

(575) 758-2254. **$79-$219.** 1508 Paseo del Pueblo Sur 87571. SR 68, 3 mi sw of jct US 64 and Taos Plaza. Ext corridors. **Pets:** Other species. $7 daily fee/pet. Designated rooms, service with restrictions, supervision.
🛜 🛏 🖵 🍽 🌊

◬ ▽▽▽ San Geronimo Lodge BB

(575) 751-3776. **Call for rates.** 1101 Witt Rd 87571. 1.3 mi e of jct SR 68 and Taos Plaza on US 64, 0.6 mi s. Ext/int corridors. **Pets:** Accepted.
SAVE 🛜 ⊠ 🛏 🖵 🌊 🐾

TRUTH OR CONSEQUENCES

▽▽▽ Comfort Inn & Suites H

(575) 894-1660. **$85-$109.** 2205 N Date St 87901. I-25 exit 79, just e. Int corridors. **Pets:** Large. Designated rooms, supervision.
🛜 ♿ 🛏 🖵 🌊

▽▽▽ Holiday Inn Express & Suites H

(575) 894-3900. **Call for rates.** 2201 FG Amin St 87901. I-25 exit 79, just e. Int corridors. **Pets:** Accepted. 🛜 ⊠ ♿ 🛏 🖵 🌊

▽▽▽ Sierra Grande Lodge & Spa H

(575) 894-6976. **$99-$395.** 501 McAdoo St 87901. Just w of Foch St; center. Ext/int corridors. **Pets:** Small, other species. $25 daily fee/pet. Designated rooms, service with restrictions, supervision. 🛜 ⊠

TUCUMCARI

◬ ▽▽▽ BEST WESTERN Discovery Inn H

(575) 461-4884. **Call for rates.** 200 E Estrella Ave 88401. I-40 exit 332, just n. Ext corridors. **Pets:** Accepted. SAVE 🛜 🛏 🖵 🌊

▽▽ Days Inn H

(575) 461-3158. **$60-$102.** 2623 S 1st St 88401. I-40 exit 332, just n. Ext/int corridors. **Pets:** Accepted. 🛜 🛏 🖵

◬ ▽▽▽ La Quinta Inn & Suites Tucumcari H

(575) 461-2233. **$100-$176.** 2516 S Adams St 88401. I-40 exit 332, just n. Int corridors. **Pets:** Service with restrictions, supervision.
SAVE 🛜 🛏 🖵 🌊

NEW YORK

CITY INDEX

ALBANY

BEST WESTERN Sovereign H
(518) 489-2981. $90-$120. 1228 Western Ave 12203. I-90 exit 1S, 1 mi e on US 20 (Western Ave). Int corridors. Pets: Accepted.

CrestHill Suites H
(518) 454-0007. $99-$209. 1415 Washington Ave 12206. I-90 exit 2 westbound, just s on Fuller Rd, then just e; exit eastbound, just e. Int corridors. Pets: Accepted.

Days Inn-Albany/Sunny H
(518) 489-4423. $74-$119. 1230 Western Ave 12203. I-90 exit 1S, 0.7 mi e on US 20 (Western Ave). Int corridors. Pets: Large, dogs only. $30 one-time fee/room. Service with restrictions, supervision.

Extended StayAmerica Albany-Capital H
(518) 446-0680. $85-$119. 1395 Washington Ave 12206. I-90 exit 2 westbound, just s on Fuller Rd, then 0.5 mi e; exit eastbound, just e. Int corridors. Pets: $25 daily fee/pet. Designated rooms, service with restrictions.

TownePlace Suites by Marriott Albany Downtown/ Medical Center H
(518) 860-1500. $113-$161. 22 Holland Ave 12209. I-90 exit 5 (Everett Rd), 2.6 mi on SR 5, then just e. Int corridors. Pets: Medium, other species. $100 one-time fee/room. Designated rooms, service with restrictions, crate.

TownePlace Suites by Marriott Albany SUNY H
(518) 435-1900. $89-$299. 1379 Washington Ave 12206. I-90 exit 2 westbound, just s on Fuller Rd, then 0.6 mi e; exit eastbound, just e. Int corridors. Pets: Medium. $75 one-time fee/room. Service with restrictions, supervision.

ALEXANDRIA BAY

The Ship Motel M
(315) 482-4503. $75-$135. 6 Market St 13607. Center. Ext corridors. Pets: Accepted.

ALLEGANY

Microtel Inn & Suites by Wyndham Olean/Allegany H
(716) 373-5333. $90-$121. 3234 NYS Rt 417 14760. I-86 exit 25 westbound; exit 24 eastbound, 2.1 mi e on SR 417 (State St). Int corridors. Pets: Other species. $15 daily fee/room. Service with restrictions, crate.

AMSTERDAM

Super 8 H
(518) 843-5888. $69-$100. 5502 Rt 30 S 12010. I-90 exit 27 (SR 30), just sw. Int corridors. Pets: Accepted.

APALACHIN

Quality Inn H
(607) 625-4441. Call for rates. 7666 SR 434 13732. SR 17 exit 66, just e. Int corridors. Pets: Other species. $10 daily fee/pet. Service with restrictions, supervision.

AUBURN

Days Inn Auburn/Finger Lakes Region H
(315) 252-7567. $60-$150. 37 William St 13021. Just s on SR 34, just w. Ext/int corridors. Pets: Accepted.

Holiday Inn-Auburn/Finger Lakes H
(315) 253-4531. $89-$169. 75 North St 13021. On SR 34, just n of US 20/SR 5. Int corridors. Pets: Small. Designated rooms, service with restrictions, crate.

Inn at the Finger Lakes H
(315) 253-5000. $99-$189, 3 day notice. 12 Seminary Ave 13021. Jct SR 34/38, just e on US 20/SR 5; center. Int corridors. Pets: Other species. $15 one-time fee/pet. Service with restrictions, supervision.

AVERILL PARK

La Perla at the Gregory House Country Inn & Restaurant CI
(518) 674-3774. $115-$160, 7 day notice. 3016 SR 43 12018. Center. Int corridors. Pets: Small, dogs only. Service with restrictions, supervision.

BALDWINSVILLE

Microtel Inn & Suites by Wyndham Baldwinsville/Syracuse H
(315) 635-9556. **$70-$125.** 131 Downer St 13027. SR 690 exit SR 31 W, 0.4 mi e. Int corridors. **Pets:** Large, other species. $10 daily fee/pet. Service with restrictions, crate. ⊡ ⊡ ⊡ ⊡

The Red Mill Inn H
(315) 635-4871. **$92-$299.** 4 Syracuse St 13027. Just w of jct SR 31 on SR 48; center. Int corridors. **Pets:** Medium. $50 one-time fee/room. Designated rooms, service with restrictions, supervision. ⊡ ⊡ ⊡

BATAVIA

Budget Inn M
(585) 343-7921. **$49-$129.** 301 Oak St 14020. I-90 exit 48, just n. Int corridors. **Pets:** Medium, dogs only. $7 daily fee/pet. Designated rooms, no service, supervision. ⊡ ⊡ ⊡

Clarion Hotel Palm Island Indoor Water Park H
(585) 344-2100. **$89-$139.** 8250 Park Rd 14020. I-90 exit 48, just w. Int corridors. **Pets:** $20 one-time fee/room. Service with restrictions, supervision. ⊡ ⊡ ⊡ ⊡

Comfort Inn H
(585) 344-9999. **Call for rates.** 4371 Federal Dr 14020. I-90 exit 48, just n on SR 98. Int corridors. **Pets:** Accepted.
⊡ ⊡ ⊡ ⊡ ⊡ ⊡

Quality Inn & Suites H
(585) 344-7000. **Call for rates.** 8200 Park Rd 14020. I-90 exit 48, just w. Int corridors. **Pets:** $10 daily fee/pet. Designated rooms, service with restrictions, supervision. ⊡ ⊡ ⊡ ⊡ ⊡ ⊡

Super 8 H
(585) 345-0800. **$70-$165.** 202 Oak St 14020. I-90 exit 48, just s. Int corridors. **Pets:** Accepted. ⊡ ⊡ ⊡ ⊡ ⊡

BATH

Bath Super 8 H
(607) 776-2187. **$50-$150, 3 day notice.** 333 W Morris St 14810. I-86 exit 38, just n. Int corridors. **Pets:** $10 daily fee/pet. Designated rooms, service with restrictions, supervision. ⊡ ⊡ ⊡

Microtel Inn & Suites by Wyndham Bath H
(607) 776-5333. **$70-$115.** 370 W Morris St 14810. I-86 exit 38, just n. Int corridors. **Pets:** Accepted. ⊡ ⊡ ⊡ ⊡

BELLEROSE

Comfort Inn Bellerose H
(718) 343-4400. **Call for rates.** 249-05 Jericho Tpke 11426. Cross Island Pkwy exit 27 northbound; exit 27E southbound. Int corridors. **Pets:** Small. $25 daily fee/pet. Service with restrictions, crate. ⊡ ⊡ ⊡ ⊡

BINGHAMTON

Comfort Inn of Binghamton H
(607) 724-3297. **Call for rates.** 1000 Upper Front St 13905. I-81 exit 5, 1 mi n on US 11 (Front St). Int corridors. **Pets:** $5 daily fee/room. Designated rooms, service with restrictions, supervision.
⊡ ⊡ ⊡ ⊡ ⊡ ⊡

Grand Royale Hotel H
(607) 722-0000. **$79-$94.** 79 Collier St 13901. Just n of jct Hawley St; downtown. Int corridors. **Pets:** Small. $25 daily fee/pet. Service with restrictions. ⊡ ⊡ ⊡

Holiday Inn Arena H
(607) 722-1212. **$129-$159.** 2-8 Hawley St 13901. Downtown. Int corridors. **Pets:** $30 one-time fee/room. Designated rooms, service with restrictions. ⊡ ⊡ ⊡ ⊡ ⊡ ⊡

BOHEMIA

La Quinta Inn & Suites Islip Macarthur Airport H
(631) 881-7700. **$114-$210.** 10 Aero Rd 11716. I-495 exit 57, 5.1 mi se on SR 454, just s on Johnson Ave, then just e. Int corridors. **Pets:** Service with restrictions, supervision. ⊡ ⊡ ⊡ ⊡

BRIGHTON

La Quinta Inn & Suites Rochester South H
(585) 272-7800. **$101-$221.** 717 E Henrietta Rd 14623. I-390 exit 16B (Henrietta Rd) southbound; exit 16 northbound, just w. Int corridors. **Pets:** Service with restrictions, supervision. ⊡ ⊡ ⊡ ⊡ ⊡ ⊡

Towpath Motel M
(585) 271-2147. **$65-$110.** 2323 Monroe Ave (US 31) 14618. I-590 exit 2 northbound; exit 2A southbound, just w. Ext corridors. **Pets:** Small. $10 daily fee/pet. Designated rooms, service with restrictions, supervision. ⊡ ⊡ ⊡

BROCKPORT

Dollinger's Inn and Suites H
(585) 395-1000. **$100-$150.** 4908 Lake Rd S 14420. Just s of jct SR 31, on SR 19 S. Int corridors. **Pets:** Other species. $25 one-time fee/room. Service with restrictions, supervision. ⊡ ⊡ ⊡ ⊡ ⊡

BUFFALO METROPOLITAN AREA

AMHERST

Candlewood Suites H
(716) 688-2100. **$129-$189.** 20 Flint Rd 14226. I-290 exit 5B, just n on SR 263 (Millersport Hwy). Int corridors. **Pets:** $25 one-time fee/pet. Service with restrictions, supervision. ⊡ ⊡ ⊡ ⊡ ⊡

Comfort Inn University H ❀
(716) 688-0811. **$74-$159.** 1 Flint Rd 14226. I-290 exit 5B, just n on SR 263 (Millersport Hwy), then just w. Int corridors. **Pets:** $20 daily fee/room. Designated rooms, service with restrictions, crate.
⊡ ⊡ ⊡ ⊡ ⊡

DoubleTree by Hilton Buffalo-Amherst H
(716) 689-4414. **$140-$180.** 10 Flint Rd 14226. I-290 exit 5B, just n on SR 263 (Millersport Hwy). Int corridors. **Pets:** $50 one-time fee/room. Designated rooms, service with restrictions, supervision.
⊡ ⊡ ⊡ ⊡ ⊡ ⊡ ⊡ ⊡

Homewood Suites Buffalo/Amherst H
(716) 833-2277. **Call for rates.** 1138 Millersport Hwy 14226. I-290 exit 5A, just w. Int corridors. **Pets:** Accepted. ⊡ ⊡ ⊡ ⊡ ⊡ ⊡

Red Roof Inn #7104 M
(716) 689-7474. **$44-$129.** 42 Flint Rd 14226. I-290 exit 5B, just n on SR 263 (Millersport Hwy). Ext corridors. **Pets:** Large, other species. Service with restrictions, supervision. ⊡ ⊡ ⊡ ⊡

BLASDELL

Econo Lodge South M
(716) 825-7530. **$56-$106.** 4344 Milestrip Rd 14219. I-90 exit 56, just e on SR 179. Ext corridors. **Pets:** Small. $10 daily fee/room. Designated rooms, service with restrictions, supervision. ⊡ ⊡ ⊡ ⊡

BOWMANSVILLE

La Quinta Inn Buffalo Airport H
(716) 633-1011. **$71-$210.** 6619 Transit Rd 14026. I-90 exit 49, just n. Int corridors. **Pets:** Service with restrictions, supervision.
⊡ ⊡ ⊡ ⊡

▽▽ Red Roof Inn-Buffalo Airport #7137 **M**
(716) 633-1100. **$60-$130.** 146 Maple Dr 14026. Just e of SR 78; just n of entrance to I-90 (New York State Thruway) exit 49. Ext corridors. **Pets:** Large, other species. Service with restrictions, supervision.
(SAVE) 🛈 🖥

BUFFALO

 ▽▽ BEST WESTERN On The Avenue **H** ❀
(716) 886-8333. **$109-$159.** 510 Delaware Ave 14202. Between Virginia and Allen sts; downtown. Int corridors. **Pets:** Medium, dogs only. Designated rooms, service with restrictions, supervision.
(SAVE) 🛈 &M 🖥 🖥

▽▽▽ Hyatt Regency Buffalo/Hotel and Conference Center **H**
(716) 856-1234. **$89-$249.** 2 Fountain Plaza 14202. On Pearl St at W Huron St; downtown. Int corridors. **Pets:** Accepted.
(SAVE) 🛈 🖥 🖥 ⓘⓘ ☞

CHEEKTOWAGA

 ▽▽▽ Comfort Inn-Cheektowaga **H**
(716) 896-2800. **Call for rates.** 475 Dingens St 14206. Just n of I-90 exit 53 (I-190); I-190 exit 1 (S Ogden St), just w. Int corridors. **Pets:** Medium, dogs only. $10 daily fee/pet. Service with restrictions, supervision. (SAVE) 🛈 &M 🖥 🖥 ☞

▽▽▽ Comfort Suites-Buffalo Airport **H**
(716) 633-6000. **$109-$200.** 901 Dick Rd 14225. SR 33 exit Dick Rd, just sw. Int corridors. **Pets:** Medium, dogs only. $15 daily fee/pet. Service with restrictions, supervision. 🛈 ⓧ &M 🖥 🖥 ☞

▽▽▽ Holiday Inn-Buffalo Airport **H**
(716) 634-6969. **$119-$169.** 4600 Genesee St 14225. I-90 exit 51, 1 mi e on SR 33. Int corridors. **Pets:** Small. $50 one-time fee/room. Service with restrictions, supervision. 🛈 ⓧ 🖥 🖥 ⓘⓘ ☞ ⓧ

▽▽▽ Holiday Inn Express Hotel & Suites-Buffalo Airport **H**
(716) 631-8700. **$129-$169.** 131 Buell Ave 14225. I-90 exit 51, just e on Genesee St (SR 33), then just s. Int corridors. **Pets:** Small. $40 one-time fee/room. Service with restrictions, supervision.
🛈 ⓧ &M 🖥 🖥 ☞ ⓧ

▽▽▽ Homewood Suites by Hilton **H**
(716) 685-0700. **$149-$309.** 760 Dick Rd 14225. SR 33 exit Dick Rd, 0.3 mi sw. Int corridors. **Pets:** Other species. $100 one-time fee/room. Service with restrictions, supervision. 🛈 🖥 🖥 ☞

▽▽ Oak Tree Inn **H**
(716) 681-2600. **$99-$150.** 3475 Union Rd 14225. I-90 exit 52, 0.3 mi e on Walden Ave, just n on SR 277 (Union Rd). Int corridors.
Pets: Accepted. 🛈 &M 🖥 🖥

▽▽▽ Residence Inn by Marriott Buffalo-Cheektowaga **H**
(716) 892-5410. **$139-$199.** 107 Anderson Rd 14225. I-90 exit 52 westbound, stay to left off exit ramp. Int corridors. **Pets:** $100 one-time fee/room. Service with restrictions, crate.
🛈 ⓧ &M 🖥 🖥 ☞ ⓧ

CLARENCE

 ▽▽▽ Asa Ransom House **CI**
(716) 759-2315. **$135-$198, 7 day notice.** 10529 Main St 14031. Jct SR 78 (Transit Rd), 5.3 mi e on SR 5 (Main St). Int corridors. **Pets:** Dogs only. $100 deposit/room. Designated rooms, service with restrictions, crate. (ECO) (SAVE) 🛈 ⓧ &M 🖥 ⓘⓘ

▽▽▽ Staybridge Suites-Buffalo Airport **H**
(716) 810-7829. **$169-$219.** 8005 Sheridan Dr 14221. I-90 exit 49, 3 mi n on SR 78 (Transit Rd); jct SR 324; next to Eastern Hills Mall. Int corridors. **Pets:** Medium. $75 one-time fee/room. Service with restrictions.
🛈 &M 🖥 🖥 ☞ ⓧ

HAMBURG

 ▽▽ Comfort Inn & Suites **H**
(716) 648-2922. **Call for rates.** 3615 Commerce Pl 14075. I-90 exit 57, just w. Int corridors. **Pets:** Accepted. (SAVE) 🛈 &M 🖥 🖥 ☞

▽▽▽ Quality Inn Hamburg **H**
(716) 649-0500. **$69-$229.** 5440 Camp Rd 14075. I-90 exit 57, 0.3 mi se on SR 75. Int corridors. **Pets:** Accepted. (SAVE) 🛈 🖥 🖥 ⓘⓘ ☞

▽▽▽ Red Roof Inn #055 **M**
(716) 648-7222. **$50-$120.** 5370 Camp Rd 14075. I-90 exit 57, just se on SR 75. Ext corridors. **Pets:** Large, other species. Service with restrictions, supervision. (SAVE) 🛈 🖥

▽▽▽ Super 8 Hamburg **H**
(716) 649-0505. **$60-$120.** 5442 Camp Rd 14075. I-90 exit 57, 0.3 mi se on SR 75. Int corridors. **Pets:** $10 daily fee/pet. Service with restrictions, supervision. (SAVE) 🛈 🖥 🖥

KENMORE

▽ Super 8-Buffalo/Niagara Falls **H**
(716) 876-4020. **$45-$115.** 1288 Sheridan Dr 14217. I-190 exit 15, 1.5 mi e on SR 324 (Sheridan Dr). Int corridors. **Pets:** Medium. Service with restrictions, supervision. 🛈 🖥 🖥

SPRINGVILLE

▽▽ Microtel Inn & Suites by Wyndham Springville **H**
(716) 592-3141. **$70-$100.** 270 S Cascade Dr 14141. Just s off SR 39 E. Int corridors. **Pets:** Accepted. 🛈 ⓧ 🖥 🖥

TONAWANDA

▽▽ Econo Lodge **M**
(716) 694-6696. **Call for rates.** 2000 Niagara Falls Blvd 14150. I-290 exit 3 (Niagara Falls Blvd), 0.5 mi n on US 62. Ext/int corridors. **Pets:** Accepted. 🛈

WEST SENECA

▽▽▽ Staybridge Suites Buffalo-South **H** ❀
(716) 939-3100. **$139-$429.** 164 Slade Ave 14224. I-90 exit 55 (Ridge Rd E), just n. Int corridors. **Pets:** Medium. $75 one-time fee/room. Service with restrictions, supervision. 🛈 &M 🖥 🖥 ☞ ⓧ

WILLIAMSVILLE

▽▽▽ Residence Inn by Marriott Buffalo/Amherst **H**
(716) 632-6622. **$149-$259.** 100 Maple Rd 14221. I-290 exit 5B, just n on Millersport Hwy exit Maple Rd, then just e. Ext corridors.
Pets: Accepted. 🛈 ⓧ &M 🖥 🖥 ☞ ⓧ

▽▽ Super 8 Buffalo/Williamsville Airport **H**
(716) 634-1500. **$60-$110.** 7200 Transit Rd 14221. I-90 exit 49 (SR 78), 1.2 mi n. Int corridors. **Pets:** Small. $10 one-time fee/pet. Service with restrictions, supervision. 🛈 🖥 🖥

END METROPOLITAN AREA

CALCIUM

◆◆ ◆◆ Microtel Inn by Wyndham Calcium/Near Fort Drum **H**

(315) 629-5000. **$82-$118.** 8000 Virginia Smith Dr 13616. Jct SR 342 and US 11, just s. Int corridors. **Pets:** Other species. $15 daily fee/room. Service with restrictions, supervision. 🛜 📵 📺

CANANDAIGUA

◆◆◆ ◆◆◆ The Inn On The Lake **H**

(585) 394-7800. **$117-$205.** 770 S Main St 14424. I-90 exit 44 (SR 332), just s of jct US 20 and SR 5. Int corridors. **Pets:** Dogs only. $25 daily fee/pet. Designated rooms, service with restrictions, crate.

SAVE 🛜 ✕ 📵 📺 🍴 🏊 ✕

◆◆◆ ◆◆◆◆ Morgan-Samuels Inn/BB & Spa **BB**

(585) 394-9232. **Call for rates.** 2920 Smith Rd 14424. I-90 exit 43, 4.1 mi s on SR 21, just e on SR 488 to East Ave/Smith Rd, then 2 mi s. Ext/int corridors. **Pets:** Accepted. SAVE 🛜 ✕ 📵 ✕ 🅿

◆◆ ◆◆ Super 8 **H**

(585) 396-7224. **$68-$105.** 4450 Eastern Blvd 14424. Jct SR 332, 5 and US 20, 0.5 mi e. Int corridors. **Pets:** Other species. $10 daily fee/room. Designated rooms, service with restrictions, supervision. 🛜 📵 📺

CAZENOVIA

◆◆◆◆ Brae Loch Inn **CI**

(315) 655-3431. **Call for rates.** 5 Albany St 13035. On US 20. Int corridors. **Pets:** Accepted. 🛜 ✕ 📺 🍴

CHESTER

◆◆◆ ◆◆◆ Holiday Inn Express Hotel & Suites Chester/Monroe/Goshen **H**

(845) 469-3000. **Call for rates.** 2 Bryle Pl 10918. SR 17 exit 126, just n on SR 94, then just w on SR 17M (Brookside Ave). Int corridors. **Pets:** Accepted. SAVE 🛜 📵 📵 📺 🏊

CICERO

◆◆◆ ◆◆ Budget Inn **M**

(315) 458-3510. **$55-$145, 7 day notice.** 901 South Bay Rd 13039. I-481 exit 10, just n. Ext corridors. **Pets:** Small, dogs only. $10 daily fee/pet. Designated rooms, service with restrictions, supervision.

SAVE 🛜 📵 📺

◆◆◆ ◆◆◆ Comfort Suites Syracuse-Cicero **H**

(315) 752-0150. **$90-$229.** 5875 Carmenica Dr 13039. I-80 exit 31, just e. Int corridors. **Pets:** Medium. $25 one-time fee/room. Designated rooms, service with restrictions, supervision.

SAVE 🛜 ✕ 📵 📵 📺 🏊

CLAY

◆◆◆◆ Hampton Inn-Syracuse/Clay **H**

(315) 622-3443. **$129-$239.** 3948 SR 31 13090. SR 481 exit 12, just w. Int corridors. **Pets:** Accepted. 🛜 📵 📵 📺 🏊 ✕

CLAYTON

◆◆ Fair Wind Lodge **M**

(315) 686-5251. **$50-$85, 3 day notice.** 38201 NYS Rt 12E 13624. 2.3 mi sw. Ext corridors. **Pets:** Accepted. 🛜 ✕ 📵 📺 🏊 🅿

CLINTON

◆◆◆◆ Amidst the Hedges **BB**

(315) 723-2035. **$95-$225, 20 day notice.** 180 Sanford Ave 13323. SR 412 (College St), 0.3 mi n on Elm St. Int corridors. **Pets:** Small, dogs only. Designated rooms, no service, supervision. 🛜 ✕ 📵 📺

COBLESKILL

◆◆◆ ◆◆◆◆ BEST WESTERN PLUS Inn of Cobleskill **H**

(518) 234-4321. **$129-$169.** 121 Burgin Dr 12043. I-88 exit 21 eastbound on SR 7, 0.8 mi e of jct SR 10; exit 22 westbound, 2.9 mi w on SR 7. Int corridors. **Pets:** Other species. $15 one-time fee/room. Designated rooms, service with restrictions, supervision.

SAVE 🛜 ✕ 📵 📵 📺 🍴 🏊

◆◆ ◆◆ Super 8 **H**

(518) 234-4888. **$85-$140.** 955 E Main St 12043. I-88 exit 22 westbound, 2.4 mi w on SR 7; exit 21 eastbound, 3.1 mi e on SR 7. Int corridors. **Pets:** Dogs only. $10 daily fee/pet. Service with restrictions, supervision. 🛜 📵 📵 📺

COLONIE

◆◆◆ ◆◆◆ BEST WESTERN Albany Airport Inn **H** 🐾

(518) 458-1000. **Call for rates.** 200 Wolf Rd 12205. I-87 exit 4, just se to Wolf Rd, then just sw. Int corridors. **Pets:** $20 daily fee/pet. Designated rooms, service with restrictions, supervision.

SAVE 🛜 📵 📵 📺 🍴 🏊

◆◆◆ ◆◆◆ Cocca's Inn & Suites, Wolf Rd **M**

(518) 459-2240. **$59-$149.** 2 Wolf Rd 12205. I-87 exit 2E, just e. Ext/int corridors. **Pets:** Accepted. SAVE 🛜 📵 📺

◆◆◆◆ Holiday Inn Albany on Wolf Road **H**

(518) 458-7250. **$99-$199.** 205 Wolf Rd 12205. I-87 exit 4, 0.3 mi se. Int corridors. **Pets:** Large, other species. $35 daily fee/room. Service with restrictions, supervision. 🛜 📵 📵 📺 🍴 🏊 ✕

◆◆◆ ◆◆ Red Roof Inn #7112 **M**

(518) 459-1971. **$49-$130.** 188 Wolf Rd 12205. I-87 exit 4, just se to Wolf Rd, then just sw. Ext corridors. **Pets:** Large, other species. Service with restrictions, supervision. SAVE 🛜 📵 📵 📺

◆◆◆ ◆◆◆ Travelodge Inn & Suites, Albany Airport **H**

(518) 459-5670. **$65-$100.** 42 Wolf Rd 12205. I-87 exit 2E, just e, then just n. Int corridors. **Pets:** Small. $10 daily fee/pet. Service with restrictions, supervision. SAVE 🛜 📵 📺

CORNING

◆◆◆ ◆◆◆ Radisson Hotel Corning **H**

(607) 962-5000. **$109-$399.** 125 Denison Pkwy E 14830. Downtown. Int corridors. **Pets:** Other species. $75 one-time fee/pet. Designated rooms, supervision. 🌿 🛜 📵 📵 📺 🍴 🏊 ✕

◆◆◆ ◆◆◆ Staybridge Suites **H**

(607) 936-7800. **$150-$189.** 201 Townley Ave 14830. I-86/SR 17 exit 46, just s. Int corridors. **Pets:** Accepted. 🛜 ✕ 📵 📵 📺 🏊 ✕

CUBA

◆◆◆ Cuba Econo Lodge **M**

(585) 968-1992. **$59-$150.** 1 N Branch Rd 14727. I-86 exit 28, just n to N Branch Rd, then e. Int corridors. **Pets:** Medium. $10 daily fee/pet. Service with restrictions, supervision. 🛜 📵

DEWITT

◆◆◆ ◆◆◆ Econo Lodge **M**

(315) 446-3300. **$78-$175.** 3400 Erie Blvd E 13214. I-481 exit 3, 1.2 mi w on SR 5; I-690 exit 17S (Bridge St), just e on Erie Blvd (SR 5). Ext corridors. **Pets:** Small. $15 daily fee/pet. Designated rooms, service with restrictions, supervision. SAVE 🛜 📵

DUNKIRK

◆◆◆ ◆◆◆◆ BEST WESTERN PLUS Dunkirk & Fredonia Inn **H**

(716) 366-7100. **$90-$200.** 3912 Vineyard Dr 14048. I-90 exit 59, just w. Int corridors. **Pets:** Medium, other species. $10 daily fee/pet. Service with restrictions, supervision. SAVE 🛜 ✕ 📵 📵 📺 🏊

Comfort Inn H

(716) 672-4450. **Call for rates.** 3925 Vineyard Dr 14048. I-90 exit 59, just se on SR 75 (Camp Rd), then just w. Int corridors. **Pets:** Medium, other species. $10 daily fee/pet. Service with restrictions, supervision.

SAVE 📶

EAST GREENBUSH

Residence Inn by Marriott Albany East Greenbush/ Tech Valley H

(518) 720-3600. **$93-$170.** 3 Tech Valley Dr 12061. I-90 exit 9, just e. Int corridors. **Pets:** Other species. $75 one-time fee/room. Service with restrictions. 📶 ✕ ♿ 🍴 💻 🏊 ✕

EAST SYRACUSE

BEST WESTERN PLUS Carrier Circle Syracuse H 🐾

(315) 437-2761. **$89-$189.** 6555 Old Collamer Rd S 13057. I-90 exit 35 (Carrier Cir) to SR 298 E, just n. Int corridors. **Pets:** Large. $20 daily fee/room. Service with restrictions, supervision.

SAVE 📶 🍴 💻 🍴 🏊 ✕

Candlewood Suites Syracuse H 🐾

(315) 432-1684. **$99-$129.** 6550 Baptist Way 13057. I-90 exit 35 (Carrier Cir) to SR 298 E to Old Collamer Rd, just n. Int corridors. **Pets:** $25 one-time fee/pet. Service with restrictions, crate.

SAVE 📶 ♿ 🍴 💻

CrestHill Suites H

(315) 432-5595. **$109-$249.** 6410 New Venture Gear Dr 13057. I-90 exit 35 (Carrier Cir) to SR 298 E, 0.7 mi s, then just e. Int corridors. **Pets:** $50 one-time fee/pet. Designated rooms, service with restrictions, supervision. 📶 🍴 💻 🍴

Quality Inn Syracuse H

(315) 432-9333. **$59-$139.** 6611 Old Collamer Rd S 13057. I-90 exit 35 (Carrier Cir) to SR 298 E, just n. Ext/int corridors. **Pets:** Large. $15 daily fee/room. Designated rooms, service with restrictions, crate.

📶 ♿ 🍴 💻

Residence Inn by Marriott Syracuse H

(315) 432-4488. **$159-$359.** 6420 Yorktown Cir 13057. I-90 exit 35 (Carrier Cir), SR 298 E to Old Collamer Rd, then just n. Ext/int corridors. **Pets:** Accepted. 📶 ✕ ♿ 🍴 💻 🏊 ✕

ELLICOTTVILLE

The Jefferson Inn of Ellicottville BB

(716) 699-5869. **$89-$269, 30 day notice.** 3 Jefferson St 14731. Just n of jct US 219 and SR 242. Ext/int corridors. **Pets:** Other species. $15 daily fee/pet. Designated rooms, service with restrictions.

SAVE 📶 ✕ 🍴 💻

Sugar Pine Lodge BB

(716) 699-4855. **Call for rates.** 6158 Jefferson St (Rt 219 S) 14731. Jct US 219 and SR 242, 0.5 mi s on US 219. Ext/int corridors. **Pets:** Accepted. 📶 ✕ 🍴 💻 🏊

ELMIRA

Coachman Motor Lodge M

(607) 733-5526. **$90-$120.** 908 Pennsylvania Ave 14904. I-86/SR 17 exit 56, 0.7 mi w on SR 352 (Church St), 0.5 mi s on Madison Ave (which becomes Pennsylvania Ave), then 1.4 mi s. Ext corridors. **Pets:** Small. $15 daily fee/pet. Service with restrictions, supervision.

SAVE 📶 🍴 💻

Holiday Inn-Elmira Riverview H

(607) 734-4211. **$109-$300.** 760 E Water St 14901. I-86/SR 17 exit 56, 0.5 mi s. Int corridors. **Pets:** $25 one-time fee/room. Designated rooms, service with restrictions, supervision. 📶 🍴 💻 🍴 🏊

EVANS MILLS

Candlewood Suites Watertown/Fort Drum H

(315) 629-6990. **Call for rates.** 26513 Herrick Dr 13637. Jct US 11, just n. Int corridors. **Pets:** Accepted. 📶 ✕ ♿ 🍴 💻

FARMINGTON

Budget Inn M

(585) 924-5020. **$49-$109, 3 day notice.** 6001 Rt 96 14425. I-90 exit 44, 1 mi s on SR 332, then just e. Ext corridors. **Pets:** Small, dogs only. $15 daily fee/pet. Service with restrictions, supervision.

SAVE 📶 💻

FAYETTEVILLE

Craftsman Inn and Conference Center H

(315) 637-8000. **$109-$189, 7 day notice.** 7300 E Genesee St (SR 5) 13066. Across from Fayetteville Towne Center. Int corridors.

Pets: Accepted. SAVE 📶 ✕ ♿ 🍴 💻 🍴

FISHKILL

Extended StayAmerica-Fishkill-Poughkeepsie H

(845) 896-0592. **$110-$199.** 55 W Merritt Blvd 12524. I-84 exit 13, just n. Int corridors. **Pets:** $25 daily fee/pet. Designated rooms, service with restrictions. 📶 ♿ 🍴 💻

Homestead Studio Suites-Fishkill-Poughkeepsie H

(845) 897-2400. **$95-$199.** 25 Merritt Blvd 12524. I-84 exit 13, just n. Int corridors. **Pets:** $25 daily fee/pet. Designated rooms, service with restrictions. 📶 🍴 💻 ✕

Residence Inn by Marriott Fishkill H

(845) 896-5210. **$108-$269.** 14 Schuyler Blvd 12524. I-84 exit 13, just n. Ext corridors. **Pets:** Other species. $100 one-time fee/room. Service with restrictions, crate. SAVE 📶 ✕ ♿ 🍴 💻 🏊 ✕

FLORAL PARK

Quality Inn Floral Park H

(718) 343-9600. **Call for rates.** 256-15 Jericho Tpke 11001. At Keene Ave. Int corridors. **Pets:** Accepted. 📶 ✕ 💻

GARDEN CITY

La Quinta Inn & Suites Garden City H

(516) 705-9000. **$167-$232.** 821 Stewart Ave 11530. Meadowbrook Pkwy exit 3, 0.5 mi w. Int corridors. **Pets:** Service with restrictions, supervision. 📶 ♿ 🍴 💻

GATES

Holiday Inn-Rochester Airport H

(585) 328-6000. **$129-$169.** 911 Brooks Ave 14624. I-390 exit 18A (SR 204), just e. Int corridors. **Pets:** Small. $50 deposit/room. Designated rooms, service with restrictions, supervision.

📶 🍴 💻 🍴 🏊 ✕

Quality Inn-Rochester H

(585) 464-8800. **$89-$129.** 1273 Chili Ave 14624. I-390 exit 19, just w on SR 33. Int corridors. **Pets:** Large. $50 deposit/room. Service with restrictions, crate. 📶 🍴 💻 🍴 🏊

GENESEO

Quality Inn Geneseo H

(585) 243-0500. **$99-$189.** 4242 Lakeville Rd 14454. I-390 exit 8, 3.4 mi w on SR 20A. Int corridors. **Pets:** Accepted. 📶 ✕ 🍴 💻 🏊

GENEVA

Cobtree Vacation Rentals Resort VH 🐾

(315) 789-1144. **$125-$585, 90 day notice.** 440-458 Armstrong Rd 14456. 3 mi n on SR 14. Ext corridors. **Pets:** Other species. $8 daily fee/pet. No service. SAVE 📶 ✕ 🍴 💻 ✕

Microtel Inn & Suites by Wyndham Geneva H

(315) 789-7890. **$59-$125.** 550 Hamilton St 14456. Jct SR 14, 2 mi w on US 20/SR 5. Int corridors. **Pets:** Accepted. 📶 ✕ ♿ 🍴 💻

GLENS FALLS

Queensbury Hotel ⊞

(518) 792-1121. **$89-$209.** 88 Ridge St 12801. Corner of Maple St. Int corridors. **Pets:** Large, other species. $100 deposit/room, $25 daily fee/room. Designated rooms, service with restrictions, crate.

SAVE 🛜 ✕ 🛢 🖃 🍴 ➴ ✕

GREAT NECK

▼▼▼ The Andrew Hotel ⊞

(516) 482-2900. **$199-$309.** 75 N Station Plaza 11021. Jct SR 25A, 0.8 mi n on Middle Neck Rd, just e. Int corridors. **Pets:** Medium. $150 one-time fee/pet. Service with restrictions, crate. 🛜 ✕ 🛢 🖃

▼▼▼ Inn at Great Neck ⊞

(516) 773-2000. **$205-$285.** 30 Cutter Mill Rd 11021. Jct SR 25A, 0.8 mi n on Middle Neck Rd, just w. Int corridors. **Pets:** Medium, dogs only. $50 one-time fee/room. Service with restrictions, crate.

🛜 ⓜ 🛢 🖃 🍴 ✕

GREECE

▼▼ Comfort Inn West ⊞

(585) 621-5700. **$79-$159.** 1501 W Ridge Rd 14615. Jct I-390 and SR 104 (Ridge Rd), 0.5 mi e. Int corridors. **Pets:** Other species. $15 daily fee/room. Service with restrictions, supervision. 🛜 🛢 🖃

▼▼▼ Hampton Inn-Rochester North ⊞

(585) 663-6070. **$119-$179.** 500 Center Place Dr 14615. I-390 exit 24A, just e on SR 104 (Ridge Rd), then just n on Buckman Rd. Int corridors. **Pets:** Accepted. 🛜 ✕ ⓜ 🛢 🖃 ➴ ✕

▼▼▼ Residence Inn by Marriott Rochester West/Greece ⊞

(585) 865-2090. **$134-$289.** 500 Paddy Creek Cir 14615. I-390 exit 24A, just e on SR 104 (Ridge Rd), just s on Hoover Dr, then just w. Int corridors. **Pets:** Accepted. 🛜 ✕ 🛢 🖃 ➴ ✕

HANCOCK

▼▼ Smith's Colonial Motel Ⓜ

(607) 637-2989. **Call for rates.** 23085 State Hwy 97 13783. SR 17 exit 87, 2.7 mi s. Ext corridors. **Pets:** Accepted. 🛢 🖃

HAUPPAUGE

Hyatt Regency Long Island at Wind Watch Golf Club, New York ⊞

(631) 784-1234. **$89-$299.** 1717 Motor Pkwy (SR 67) 11788. I-495 exit 57, just n to Long Island Motor Pkwy (SR 67), then 1.3 mi ne. Int corridors. **Pets:** Accepted. ECO SAVE 🛜 ⓜ 🛢 🖃 🍴 ➴ ✕

▼▼▼ Residence Inn by Marriott Long Island-Hauppauge/Islandia ⊞

(631) 724-4188. **$149-$189.** 850 Veterans Memorial Hwy 11788. I-495 exit 57, 1.2 mi nw. Int corridors. **Pets:** Accepted.

🛜 ✕ ⓜ 🛢 🖃 ➴

▼▼▼ Sheraton Long Island Hotel ⊞

(631) 231-1100. **$109-$229.** 110 Vanderbilt Motor Pkwy 11788. I-495 exit 53 (Wicks Rd), just n, then 0.3 mi e. Int corridors. **Pets:** Large, dogs only. $50 one-time fee/pet. Service with restrictions, crate.

SAVE 🛜 ✕ ⓜ 🛢 🖃 🍴 ➴

HENRIETTA

▼▼▼ Homewood Suites by Hilton-Rochester ⊞

(585) 334-9150. **$139-$209.** 2095 Hylan Dr 14623. I-390 exit 13, just e. Int corridors. **Pets:** Large, other species. $75 one-time fee/room. Service with restrictions, crate. 🛜 ⓜ 🛢 🖃 ➴ ✕

▼ Microtel Inn by Wyndham Henrietta/Rochester ⊞

(585) 334-3400. **$60-$119.** 905 Lehigh Station Rd 14467. I-390 exit 12 northbound; exit 12A southbound, just w on SR 253. Int corridors. **Pets:** $15 deposit/pet. Designated rooms, service with restrictions, supervision. 🛜 🛢

▼▼▼ Radisson Rochester Airport ⊞

(585) 475-1910. **$109-$229, 3 day notice.** 175 Jefferson Rd 14623. I-390 exit 14A southbound; exit 14 northbound, 3 mi w on SR 252 (Jefferson Rd). Int corridors. **Pets:** $25 one-time fee/room. Designated rooms, service with restrictions, crate. 🛜 ⓜ 🛢 🖃 🍴 ➴

▼▼ Red Roof Inn-Henrietta #7042 Ⓜ

(585) 359-1100. **$49-$119.** 4820 W Henrietta Rd 14467. I-390 exit 12 northbound; exit 12A southbound, 0.5 mi w on SR 253, then just s on SR 15 (Henrietta Rd). Ext corridors. **Pets:** Large, other species. Service with restrictions, supervision. SAVE 🛜 🛢 🖃

▼▼▼ Residence Inn by Marriott Rochester ⊞ 🐾

(585) 272-8850. **$166-$183.** 1300 Jefferson Rd 14623. I-390 exit 14A southbound, 0.5 mi e on SR 252 (Jefferson Rd); exit 14 northbound, just n on SR 15A, then 0.5 mi e on SR 252 (Jefferson Rd). Ext/int corridors. **Pets:** $100 one-time fee/room. Designated rooms, service with restrictions, crate.

🛜 ✕ 🛢 🖃 ➴ ✕

▼▼▼ R I T Inn & Conference Center ⊞

(585) 359-1800. **$109-$189.** 5257 W Henrietta Rd 14586. I-390 exit 12 northbound; exit 12A southbound, 0.5 mi w on SR 253, then 0.7 mi s. Int corridors. **Pets:** Other species. $50 one-time fee/pet. Designated rooms, service with restrictions, supervision.

ECO 🛜 ✕ 🛢 🖃 🍴 ➴ ✕

HERKIMER

▼▼▼ Herkimer Motel & Suites Ⓜ

(315) 866-0490. **$78-$150.** 100 Marginal Rd 13350. I-90 exit 30, just n on SR 28. Ext/int corridors. **Pets:** Other species. $10 daily fee/pet. Designated rooms, service with restrictions, supervision.

SAVE 🛜 🛢 🖃 ➴

HIGHLAND

▼▼ Super 8 Ⓜ

(845) 691-6888. **$5-$140.** 3423 Rt 9W 12528. Just s of jct SR 299 and US 9W. Int corridors. **Pets:** Accepted. 🛜 ⓜ 🛢 🖃

HOGANSBURG

▼▼▼ Comfort Inn & Suites Hogansburg ⊞

(518) 358-1000. **$130-$260.** 865 State Route 37 13655. Jct SR 95, 0.3 mi w. Int corridors. **Pets:** Medium, other species. $10 daily fee/pet. Service with restrictions, supervision. SAVE 🛜 ✕ 🛢 🖃 ➴

HORSEHEADS

▼▼▼ Candlewood Suites ⊞

(607) 873-7676. **$79-$299.** 198 Colonial Dr 14845. I-86/SR 17 exit 51A eastbound, just e; exit 51B westbound. Int corridors. **Pets:** $75 one-time fee/room. Service with restrictions, supervision. 🛜 ✕ 🛢 🖃

▼▼▼ Country Inn & Suites By Carlson, Big Flats ⊞

(607) 739-9205. **$109-$259.** 105 E Mall Rd 14845. I-86/SR 17 exit 51A eastbound; exit 51B westbound, then just e on Colonial Dr. Int corridors. **Pets:** Accepted. 🛜 🛢 🖃 ➴ ✕

INLET

▼ Marina Motel Ⓜ 🐾

(315) 357-3883. **$79-$189, 14 day notice.** 6 S Shore Rd 13360. Center. Ext corridors. **Pets:** $50 deposit/pet, $15 daily fee/pet. Designated rooms, crate. SAVE 🛜 ✕ 🛢

IRONDEQUOIT

▼▼▼ Holiday Inn Express ⊞

(585) 342-0430. **$139-$179.** 2200 Goodman St N 14609. SR 104 exit Goodman St, just n. Int corridors. **Pets:** Medium, other species. $25 one-time fee/room. Designated rooms, service with restrictions, supervision.

🛜 ⓜ 🛢 🖃 ➴

ITHACA

BEST WESTERN University Inn M ❄
(607) 272-6100. **$160-$209.** 1020 Ellis Hollow Rd 14850. SR 79 E, 1 mi ne on Pine Tree Rd, just n; in East Hill Plaza. Int corridors. **Pets:** Medium, other species. $30 daily fee/room. Service with restrictions, supervision. SAVE 📶 🌐 🛅 🖥 🏊

Comfort Inn H ❄
(607) 272-0100. **$90-$120.** 356 Elmira Rd 14850. Jct SR 96, 89 and 79, 1.5 mi sw on SR 13. Int corridors. **Pets:** $25 one-time fee/pet. Designated rooms, service with restrictions, crate.
SAVE 📶 ✕ 🛅 🖥

Country Inn & Suites By Carlson H ❄
(607) 256-1100. **$99-$359.** 1100 Danby Rd (SR 96B) 14850. 0.5 mi past entrance to Ithaca College and jct SR 96B. Int corridors. **Pets:** Other species. $25 daily fee/pet. Designated rooms, service with restrictions, supervision. SAVE 📶 ✕ 🛅 🖥 🏊

Hampton Inn H
(607) 277-5500. **$119-$299.** 337 Elmira Rd 14850. On SR 13. Int corridors. **Pets:** Dogs only. Service with restrictions, supervision.
SAVE 📶 🛅 🖥 🏊

La Tourelle Resort and Spa CI ❄
(607) 273-2734. **$154-$700, 3 day notice.** 1150 Danby Rd 14850. 2.7 mi s on SR 96B. Int corridors. **Pets:** Other species. Designated rooms, service with restrictions, crate. ECO 📶 ✕ 🛅 🖥 🍴 🏊

Rodeway Inn & Suites M
(607) 272-5252. **Call for rates.** 654 Elmira Rd 14850. On SR 13 S. Ext/int corridors. **Pets:** Medium. $15 daily fee/pet. Service with restrictions, supervision. SAVE 📶 🛅 🖥

JAMESTOWN

BEST WESTERN PLUS Downtown Jamestown H ❄
(716) 484-8400. **$119-$159.** 200 W 3rd St 14701. I-86/SR 17 exit 12, 2 mi s on SR 60 (Washington St). Int corridors. **Pets:** Medium. $15 daily fee/room. Designated rooms, service with restrictions.
SAVE 📶 ✕ 🛅 🖥 🏊

Comfort Inn H ❄
(716) 664-5920. **$99-$160.** 2800 N Main St 14701. I-86/SR 17 exit 12, just s on SR 60 (Main St). Int corridors. **Pets:** Other species. $25 one-time fee/pet. Service with restrictions, supervision. 📶 🛅 🖥

JOHNSON CITY

BEST WESTERN PLUS of Johnson City H
(607) 729-9194. **$99-$139.** 569 Harry L Dr 13790. SR 17 exit 70N, 0.3 mi n. Int corridors. **Pets:** Large. $10 daily fee/room. Designated rooms, service with restrictions, crate. SAVE 📶 🛅 🖥

La Quinta Inn Binghamton - Johnson City H
(607) 770-9333. **$95-$166.** 581 Harry L Dr 13790. SR 17 exit 70N, 0.3 mi n. Int corridors. **Pets:** Service with restrictions, supervision.
SAVE 📶 🛅 🖥

Red Roof Inn-Binghamton #7203 M
(607) 729-8940. **$65-$175.** 590 Fairview St 13790. SR 17 exit 70N, 0.3 mi n, then just n on Reynolds Rd. Ext corridors. **Pets:** Large, other species. Service with restrictions, supervision. SAVE 📶 🛅 🖥

JOHNSTOWN

Holiday Inn H
(518) 762-4686. **$109-$159.** 308 N Comrie Ave 12095. Jct SR 30A and 29 E, 1.3 mi n. Int corridors. **Pets:** Accepted.
📶 ♿ 🛅 🖥 🍴 🏊

Super 8 H
(518) 736-1800. **$70-$100.** 301 N Comrie Ave 12095. Jct SR 30A and 29 E, 1.2 mi n. Int corridors. **Pets:** Medium. $15 daily fee/pet. Service with restrictions, supervision. SAVE 📶 🛅 🖥

KINGSTON

Holiday Inn H
(845) 338-0400. **$139-$209, 3 day notice.** 503 Washington Ave 12401. I-87 exit 19, just e of traffic circle. Int corridors. **Pets:** $25 daily fee/room. Service with restrictions, supervision.
SAVE 📶 ✕ 🛅 🖥 🍴 🏊 🏊

LAKE GEORGE

Green Haven Resort M
(518) 668-2489. **$64-$139, 10 day notice.** 3136 Lake Shore Dr 12845. I-87 exit 22, 0.8 mi n on SR 9N. Ext corridors. **Pets:** Dogs only. $20 one-time fee/pet. Service with restrictions, supervision.
📶 ✕ 🛅 🖥 🏊 🏊

Lake George Inn M
(518) 668-2673. **$48-$175, 10 day notice.** 444 Canada St 12845. I-87 exit 22, 0.3 mi s on US 9. Ext corridors. **Pets:** Other species. $15 daily fee/pet. Designated rooms, service with restrictions, supervision.
📶 ✕ 🛅 🖥 🏊

Lake Haven Motel M
(518) 668-2260. **$49-$132, 10 day notice.** 442 Canada St 12845. I-87 exit 22, 0.4 mi s on US 9. Ext corridors. **Pets:** Medium, dogs only. $15 daily fee/pet. Designated rooms, service with restrictions, crate.
SAVE 📶 ✕ 🛅 🖥 🏊

Roaring Brook Ranch & Tennis Resort H
(518) 668-5767. **$170-$246, 10 day notice.** 2206 Rt 9N S 12845. I-87 exit 21, 1 mi s. Ext/int corridors. **Pets:** $10 daily fee/pet. Service with restrictions, crate. 📶 🛅 🍴 🏊 🏊

Travelodge of Lake George M
(518) 668-5421. **$59-$169.** 2011 US 9 12845. I-87 exit 21, just s. Ext/int corridors. **Pets:** Other species. $20 daily fee/pet. Designated rooms, service with restrictions, crate. 📶 🛅 🏊

LAKE PLACID

Art Devlin's Olympic Motor Inn, Inc. M
(518) 523-3700. **$76-$498, 14 day notice.** 2764 Main St 12946. 0.5 mi e on SR 86. Ext corridors. **Pets:** Dogs only. $4 daily fee/pet. Service with restrictions, crate. SAVE 📶 ✕ 🛅 🖥

Comfort Inn on Lake Placid H
(518) 523-9555. **$90-$250.** 2125 Saranac Ave 12946. 0.5 mi w on SR 86. Ext/int corridors. **Pets:** Large, other species. $15 daily fee/pet. Service with restrictions, supervision. SAVE 📶 ✕ 🛅 🖥 🍴 🏊

Crowne Plaza Resort & Golf Club Lake Placid H
(518) 523-2556. **$119-$259, 7 day notice.** 101 Olympic Dr 12946. Downtown. Ext/int corridors. **Pets:** Dogs only. $10 daily fee/pet. Designated rooms, service with restrictions, supervision.
SAVE 📶 ✕ ♿ 🛅 🖥 🍴 🏊 🏊

Golden Arrow Lakeside Resort H
(518) 523-3353. **Call for rates.** 2559 Main St 12946. On SR 86; center. Int corridors. **Pets:** Accepted. ECO 📶 ✕ 🛅 🖥 🍴 🏊 🏊

High Peaks Resort H
(518) 523-4411. **$129-$349, 7 day notice.** 2384 Saranac Ave 12946. 0.3 mi w on SR 86. Int corridors. **Pets:** Accepted.
SAVE 📶 ✕ ♿ 🛅 🖥 🍴 🏊 🏊

The Lakeview H
(518) 523-4411. **$79-$229, 7 day notice.** 1 Mirror Lake Dr 12946. 0.3 mi w on SR 86. Int corridors. **Pets:** Medium, dogs only. $100 deposit/room. Designated rooms, service with restrictions, supervision.
📶 ✕ ♿ 🛅 🖥 🏊

LANSING

▼▼▼ Homewood Suites by Hilton H ❀
(607) 266-0000. **$119-$359.** 36 Cinema Dr 14850. SR 13 exit Triphammer Rd, just e, then just n on Sheraton Dr (which becomes Cinema Dr). Int corridors. **Pets:** Other species. $100 one-time fee/room. Service with restrictions, crate. 🛰 🔌 🛗 🛏 💻 ➦ ⊠

▼▼▼ Ithaca Courtyard by Marriott H
(607) 330-1000. **$43-$229.** 29 Thornwood Dr 14850. Jct SR 13 N and Warren Rd, just w to Brown Rd, then just e. Int corridors. **Pets:** Accepted. 🛰 ⊠ 🔌 🛗 💻 ➦

▼▼ Ramada Inn Ithaca H
(607) 257-3100. **$120-$325.** 2310 N Triphammer Rd 14850. SR 13 exit Triphammer Rd, just w; adjoins Triphammer Mall. Int corridors. **Pets:** $20 one-time fee/room. Designated rooms, service with restrictions, supervision. 🛰 ⊠ 🛗 💻 🍴 ➦ ⊠

LATHAM

◭ ▼▼▼ The Century House, A Clarion Hotel & Conference Center H
(518) 785-0931. **$90-$160.** 997 New Loudon Rd 12110. I-87 exit 7 (SR 7), just e, then 0.5 mi n on US 9. Int corridors. **Pets:** Other species. $20 daily fee/pet. Designated rooms, service with restrictions, supervision. SAVE 🛰 ⊠ 🛗 💻 🍴 ➦

◭ ▼▼▼ Days Inn Airport & Conference Center H
(518) 783-1900. **$64-$120.** 20 Airport Park Blvd 12110. I-87 exit 4, 2.2 mi nw on Albany Shaker Rd. Int corridors. **Pets:** Other species. $25 deposit/room, $25 daily fee/room. Designated rooms, service with restrictions, supervision. SAVE 🛰 🛗 💻

▼▼▼ Hotel Indigo H
(518) 869-9100. **Call for rates.** 254 Old Wolf Rd 12110. I-87 exit 4, just w on Albany Shaker Rd. Int corridors. **Pets:** Accepted. 🛰 ⊠ 🔌 🛗 💻 🍴

◭ ▼▼▼ La Quinta Inn & Suites Latham Albany Airport H
(518) 640-2200. **$101-$216.** 833 New Loudon Rd 12110. I-87 exit 7 (SR 7), just s on US 9 to Latham Cir, then just n on US 9. **Pets:** Service with restrictions, supervision. SAVE 🛰 ⊠ 🔌 🛗 💻 ➦

◭ ▼▼▼ Microtel Inn by Wyndham Albany Airport H
(518) 782-9161. **$65-$120.** 7 Rensselaer Ave 12110. I-87 exit 6, just w. Int corridors. **Pets:** Medium. $10 daily fee/pet. Designated rooms, service with restrictions, supervision. SAVE 🛰 🔌 🛗

▼▼▼ Residence Inn by Marriott Albany Airport H
(518) 783-0600. **$119-$229.** 1 Residence Inn Dr 12110. I-87 exit 6, 2 mi w on SR 7. Ext corridors. **Pets:** Accepted. 🛰 ⊠ 🛗 💻 ➦ ⊠

LITTLE FALLS

◭ ▼▼▼ Knights Inn of Little Falls H
(315) 823-4954. **$80-$85, 3 day notice.** 20 Albany St 13365. On SR 5 and 167. Int corridors. **Pets:** Other species. $10 one-time fee/pet. Designated rooms, service with restrictions, crate. SAVE 🛰 🛗 💻 🍴

LIVERPOOL

◭ ▼▼▼ BEST WESTERN PLUS Liverpool Grace Inn & Suites H
(315) 701-4400. **$80-$200.** 136 Transistor Pkwy 13088. I-90 exit 37 (Electronics Pkwy), just n. Int corridors. **Pets:** Medium. $25 one-time fee/pet. Service with restrictions, supervision. SAVE 🛰 ⊠ 🔌 🛗 💻 ➦

▼▼▼ Homewood Suites H ❀
(315) 451-3800. **$129-$239.** 275 Elwood Davis Rd 13088. I-81 exit 25 (7th North St), 1 mi w; I-90 exit 36. Int corridors. **Pets:** Other species. $100 one-time fee/room. Designated rooms, service with restrictions, crate. 🛰 🔌 🛗 💻 ➦ ⊠

◭ ▼▼▼ Knights Inn M
(315) 453-6330. **$59-$169.** 430 Electronics Pkwy 13088. I-90 exit 37 (Electronics Pkwy), just w; I-81 exit 25 (7th North St), 1.3 mi nw, then just w. Ext corridors. **Pets:** Medium. $25 daily fee/pet. Designated rooms, no service, supervision. SAVE 🛰 🛗

◭ ▼▼▼ Super 8 Route 57 H
(315) 451-8550. **$69-$129, 3 day notice.** 7360 Oswego Rd 13090. I-90 exit 38, 1 mi n on CR 57. Int corridors. **Pets:** Medium, dogs only. $15 daily fee/pet. Designated rooms, service with restrictions, supervision. SAVE 🛰 🛗 💻

MALONE

◭ ▼▼▼ Four Seasons Motel M
(518) 483-3490. **$55-$99, 3 day notice.** 206 W Main St 12953. 1 mi w on US 11. Ext corridors. **Pets:** Accepted. SAVE 🛰 🛗 ➦

▼▼▼ Super 8 at Jons H
(518) 483-8123. **$80-$99.** 42 Finney Blvd 12953. On SR 30, just s of jct US 11. Int corridors. **Pets:** Accepted. 🛰 ⊠ 🔌 🛗 💻 🍴

MALTA

◭ ▼▼▼ Hyatt Place Saratoga/Malta H
(518) 885-1109. **$119-$369.** 20 State Farm Pl 12020. I-87 exit 12, just w. Int corridors. **Pets:** Medium, dogs only. $150 one-time fee/pet. Designated rooms, service with restrictions, crate. ECO SAVE 🛰 ⊠ 🔌 🛗 💻 ➦

MANCHESTER

◭ ▼▼ Scottish Inns M
(585) 289-3811. **$49-$139.** 4078 Rt 96 14504. I-90 exit 43, just s, then just w. Ext/int corridors. **Pets:** Accepted. SAVE 🛰 🛗

MARGARETVILLE

▼▼▼ Hanah Mountain Resort and Country Club H
(845) 586-4849. **Call for rates.** 576 W Hubbell Hill Rd 12455. 2.5 mi n on SR 30. Ext corridors. **Pets:** Accepted. 🛰 ⊠ 🛗 💻 🍴 ➦ ⊠

MASSENA

▼▼ Econo Lodge-Meadow View Motel H
(315) 764-0246. **Call for rates.** 15054 State Hwy 37 13662. On SR 37, 2.7 mi sw. Int corridors. **Pets:** Medium. $10 daily fee/pet. Designated rooms, service with restrictions, crate. 🛰 🛗 💻

MCGRAW

◭ ▼▼▼ Cortland Days Inn H
(607) 753-7594. **$54-$159.** 3775 US Rt 11 13101. I-81 exit 10 (McGraw/Cortland), just n. Int corridors. **Pets:** Accepted. SAVE 🛰 🛗 💻

MELVILLE

▼▼ Extended StayAmerica-Long Island-Melville H
(631) 777-3999. **$120-$299.** 100 Spagnoli Rd 11747. I-495 exit 49S eastbound, 0.5 mi e on south service road, then 1.1 mi s on SR 110; exit westbound, 1.5 mi s on SR 110. Int corridors. **Pets:** $25 daily fee/pet. Designated rooms, service with restrictions. 🛰 🔌 🛗 💻

MIDDLETOWN

▼▼▼ Microtel Inn & Suites by Wyndham Middletown H ❀
(845) 692-0098. **$99-$139.** 19 Crystal Run Crossing 10941. SR 17 exit 122, just nw. Int corridors. **Pets:** Small, other species. $20 daily fee/pet. Service with restrictions, supervision. 🛰 ⊠ 🔌 🛗

▼▼▼ Middletown Hampton Inn H
(845) 344-3400. **$129-$169.** 20 Crystal Run Crossing 10941. SR 17 exit 122, just ne. Int corridors. **Pets:** Other species. Service with restrictions, crate. 🛰 🔌 🛗 💻

MOUNT MORRIS

▼▼▼▼ Country Inn & Suites By Carlson 🅗 ❀

(585) 658-4080. **$120-$220.** 130 N Main St 14510. On SR 36; center. Int corridors. **Pets:** Dogs only. $25 daily fee/room. Designated rooms, service with restrictions, crate. 📶 ☒ 🛏 🖭 ≈

NEWARK

▼▼ ▼▼ Quality Inn Finger Lakes Region 🅗

(315) 331-9500. **Call for rates.** 125 N Main St 14513. Jct SR 31, just n on SR 88. Int corridors. **Pets:** Small, dogs only. $25 deposit/pet. Service with restrictions. 📶 ☒ 🛏 🖭 ¶¶ ≈

NEWBURGH

▼▼ ▼▼ Super 8 🅜

(845) 564-5700. **$55-$145.** 1287 Rt 300 12550. I-87 exit 17, just w; I-84 exit 6, 2 mi e. Int corridors. **Pets:** Large. $25 deposit/pet, $25 daily fee/pet. Designated rooms, service with restrictions, supervision. 📶 🛏 🖭

NEW HARTFORD

▼▼▼▼ Holiday Inn Utica 🅗

(315) 797-2131. **$89-$189.** 1777 Burrstone Rd 13413. I-90 (New York State Thruway) exit 31, 4.5 mi w on SR 5 W and 12 S exit Burrstone Rd, then 1 mi nw. Int corridors. **Pets:** Accepted. 🄴🄲🄾 📶 🛄 🛏 🖭 ¶¶ ≈

NEW YORK CITY METROPOLITAN AREA

ARMONK

▼▼▼▼ La Quinta Inn & Suites Armonk 🅗

(914) 273-9090. **$102-$188.** 94 Business Park Dr 10504. I-684 exit 3S northbound; exit 3 southbound, 0.3 mi s on SR 22. Int corridors. **Pets:** Service with restrictions, supervision.

📶 ☒ 🛄 🛏 🖭 ¶¶

BROOKLYN

🄰🄰🄰 ▼▼▼▼ Aloft New York Brooklyn 🅗

(718) 256-3833. **$129-$599, 3 day notice.** 216 Duffield St 11201. Between Willoughby St and Fulton Mall. Int corridors. **Pets:** Accepted.

🅂🄰� 📶 ☒ 🛄 🛏 🖭 ¶¶ ≈

▼▼▼▼ Fairfield Inn & Suites by Marriott New
    York-Brooklyn 🅗

(718) 522-4000. **$219-$239.** 181 3rd Ave 11217. In Park Slope; jct Butler St. Int corridors. **Pets:** Accepted. 📶 ☒ 🛏 🖭

▼▼▼▼ Holiday Inn Express Brooklyn 🅗

(718) 797-1133. **$129-$399.** 625 Union St 11215. Between 3rd and 4th aves. Int corridors. **Pets:** Accepted. 📶 🛏 🖭

▼▼▼▼ Holiday Inn Express Brooklyn Downtown 🅗

(718) 855-9600. **Call for rates.** 279 Butler St 11217. In Park Slope; between 3rd Ave and Nevins St. Int corridors. **Pets:** Accepted.

📶 🛏 🖭

🄰🄰🄰 ▼▼▼▼ Hotel Indigo Brooklyn 🅗

(718) 254-7800. **$199-$699.** 229 Duffield St 11201. Between Willoughby St and Fulton Mall. Int corridors. **Pets:** Small. $75 one-time fee/pet.

🅂🄰� 📶 ☒ 🛏 🖭

▼▼▼▼ King & Grove Williamsburg 🅗

(718) 218-7500. **Call for rates.** 160 N 12th St 11211. In Williamsburg; between Bedford Ave and Berry St. Int corridors. **Pets:** Accepted.

📶 ☒ 🛏 ¶¶ ≈

🄰🄰🄰 ▼▼▼▼ Nu Hotel Brooklyn 🅗

(718) 852-8585. **$119-$349.** 85 Smith St 11201. Between Atlantic and State sts. Int corridors. **Pets:** Accepted. 🅂🄰� 📶 ☒

🄰🄰🄰 ▼▼▼▼ Sheraton Brooklyn New York Hotel 🅗

(718) 855-1900. **$149-$649, 3 day notice.** 228 Duffield St 11201. Between Willoughby St and Fulton Mall. Int corridors. **Pets:** Accepted.

🅂🄰� 📶 ☒ 🛏 🖭 ¶¶ ≈

CORONA

▼▼▼▼ Holiday Inn LaGuardia Airport Hotel 🅗

(718) 651-2100. **Call for rates.** 37-10 114th St 11368. In Flushing; Grand Central Pkwy W exit 9W (Northern Blvd W), s on 114th St, then just s; exit 8 (111th St) eastbound, e at stop sign, e at 1st light, then just s on Astoria Blvd (which becomes 114th St). Int corridors.
Pets: Accepted. 📶 ☒ ♿ 🛏 🖭 ¶¶ ≈

CROTON-ON-HUDSON

▼▼▼▼ Alexander Hamilton House 🄱🄱

(914) 271-6737. **$142-$299, 14 day notice.** 49 Van Wyck St 10520. US 9 exit SR 129, just e on Municipal Place, just n on Riverside Ave, just e on Grand St, then just n on Hamilton Ave. Int corridors. **Pets:** Accepted.

📶 ☒ 🛏 ≈ 🄴

ELMSFORD

▼▼ ▼▼ Extended StayAmerica-White Plains-Elmsford 🅗

(914) 347-8073. **$130-$249.** 118 Tarrytown Rd 10523. I-87 exit 8, just w. Int corridors. **Pets:** $25 daily fee/pet. Designated rooms, service with restrictions. 📶 ♿ 🛏 🖭

FLUSHING

▼▼ ▼▼ Extended StayAmerica-NY City-LaGuardia
    Airport 🅗

(718) 357-3661. **$145-$349.** 18-30 Whitestone Expwy 11357. In Flushing; I-678 (Van Wyck Expwy) exit 15, just w; in Whitestone. Int corridors. **Pets:** $25 daily fee/pet. Designated rooms, service with restrictions.

📶 🛏 🖭

🄰🄰🄰 ▼▼▼▼ Sheraton LaGuardia East Hotel 🅗

(718) 460-6666. **$169-$389.** 135-20 39th Ave 11354. In Flushing; Grand Central Pkwy to Northern Blvd, 1 mi e to Main St, 0.3 mi s to 39th Ave, then just w. Int corridors. **Pets:** Accepted. 🅂🄰� 📶 ☒ 🛏 🖭 ¶¶

JAMAICA

▼▼▼▼ DoubleTree by Hilton Hotel JFK Airport 🅗

(718) 322-2300. **Call for rates.** 135-30 140th St 11436. In Jamaica; I-678 (Van Wyck Expwy) exit 2 (Rockaway Blvd), just e to 140th St, then s. Int corridors. **Pets:** Accepted. 📶 🛏 🖭 ¶¶

🄰🄰🄰 ▼▼▼▼ Sheraton JFK Airport Hotel 🅗

(718) 322-7190. **$269-$349, 3 day notice.** 132-26 S Conduit Ave 11430. In Jamaica; between S Conduit and 149th aves; off Nassau Expwy. Int corridors. **Pets:** Accepted. 🅂🄰� 📶 ☒ 🛏 🖭 ¶¶

MOUNT KISCO

🄰🄰🄰 ▼▼▼▼ Holiday Inn 🅗

(914) 241-2600. **$159-$205.** 1 Holiday Inn Dr 10549. Saw Mill River Pkwy exit 37, just e. Int corridors. **Pets:** Other species. $49 one-time fee/room. Service with restrictions, supervision.

🅂🄰� 📶 ☒ ♿ 🛏 🖭 ¶¶ ≈

NANUET

▼▼▼▼ Candlewood Suites 🅗

(845) 371-4445. **Call for rates.** 20 Overlook Blvd 10954. I-287/87 (New York State Thruway) exit 14 (SR 59 W) to New Clarkstown Rd. Int corridors. **Pets:** Accepted. 📶 🛏 🖭

▼▼▼▼ Comfort Inn & Suites 🅗

(845) 623-6000. **$119-$169.** 425 E Rt 59 10954. Palisades Interstate Pkwy exit 8W, just w. Int corridors. **Pets:** Accepted.

📶 🛏 🖭 ¶¶ ≈

Days Inn Nanuet Ⓜ
(845) 623-4567. **$85-$140.** 367 W Rt 59 10954. I-287/87 (New York State Thruway) exit 14 (SR 59) northbound, just e; exit southbound, just w. Ext/int corridors. **Pets:** Medium. $20 daily fee/pet. Service with restrictions, supervision.

NEW YORK

70 Park Avenue Hotel Ⓗ
(212) 973-2400. **$199-$899.** 70 Park Ave 10016. At 38th St. Int corridors. **Pets:** Accepted.

Ace Hotel - New York Ⓗ
(212) 679-2222. **Call for rates.** 20 W 29th St 10001. Between Broadway and 5th Ave. Int corridors. **Pets:** Accepted.

Affinia 50 Ⓗ
(212) 751-5710. **Call for rates.** 155 E 50th St 10022. Between 3rd and Lexington aves. Int corridors. **Pets:** Accepted.

Affinia Dumont Ⓗ 🐾
(212) 481-7600. **$189-$699.** 150 E 34th St 10016. Between Lexington and 3rd aves. Int corridors. **Pets:** Large, other species. $25 one-time fee/pet. Service with restrictions.

Affinia Gardens Ⓗ
(212) 355-1230. **Call for rates.** 215 E 64th St 10021. Between 2nd and 3rd aves. Int corridors. **Pets:** Accepted.

Affinia Manhattan Ⓗ
(212) 563-1800. **$199-$519.** 371 7th Ave 10001. At 31st St. Int corridors. **Pets:** Accepted.

Affinia Shelburne Ⓗ
(212) 689-5200. **$189-$699.** 303 Lexington Ave 10016. Between 37th and 38th sts. Int corridors. **Pets:** Accepted.

The Alex Ⓗ
(212) 867-5100. **$450-$3700, 3 day notice.** 205 E 45th St 10017. At 3rd Ave. Int corridors. **Pets:** Accepted.

Algonquin Hotel Autograph Collection Ⓗ 🐾
(212) 840-6800. **$219-$669.** 59 W 44th St 10036. Between 5th and 6th (Ave of the Americas) aves. Int corridors. **Pets:** Large, other species. $100 deposit/room. Service with restrictions, supervision.

Aloft Harlem Hotel Ⓗ 🐾
(212) 749-4000. **$189-$429.** 2296 Frederick Douglass Blvd 10027. At W 124th St. Int corridors. **Pets:** Other species. Service with restrictions, supervision.

Andaz 5th Avenue Ⓗ
(212) 601-1234. **$225-$775.** 485 5th Ave 10017. At 41st St. Int corridors. **Pets:** Accepted.

Andaz Wall Street Ⓗ
(212) 590-1234. **$170-$695.** 75 Wall St 10005. Between Pearl and Water sts. Int corridors. **Pets:** Accepted.

The Benjamin Hotel Ⓗ 🐾
(212) 715-2500. **$249-$799.** 125 E 50th St 10022. Between Lexington and 3rd aves. Int corridors. **Pets:** Other species. Designated rooms, service with restrictions, crate.

BEST WESTERN PLUS Seaport Inn Downtown Ⓗ
(212) 766-6600. **Call for rates.** 33 Peck Slip on Front St 10038. North end of South St Seaport. Int corridors. **Pets:** Accepted.

The Bowery Hotel Ⓗ
(212) 505-9100. **Call for rates.** 335 Bowery 10003. Between E 2nd and 3rd sts. Int corridors. **Pets:** Accepted.

Candlewood Suites Times Square Ⓗ
(212) 967-2254. **$149-$499.** 339 39th St 10018. Between 8th and 9th aves. Int corridors. **Pets:** Accepted.

The Carlton Hotel Ⓗ
(212) 532-4100. **$269-$619.** 88 Madison Ave 10016. Between 28th and 29th sts. Int corridors. **Pets:** Accepted.

The Carlyle, A Rosewood Hotel Ⓗ
(212) 744-1600. **$495-$900.** 35 E 76th St 10021. At Madison Ave. Int corridors. **Pets:** Accepted.

Chambers Hotel Ⓗ
(212) 974-5656. **Call for rates.** 15 W 56th St 10019. Between 5th and 6th (Ave of the Americas) aves. Int corridors. **Pets:** Accepted.

The Chatwal, A Luxury Collection Hotel Ⓗ
(212) 764-6200. **$495-$795.** 130 W 44th St 10036. Between 6th (Ave of the Americas) and 7th aves. Int corridors. **Pets:** Accepted.

Comfort Inn Manhattan Bridge Ⓗ
(212) 925-1212. **$119-$319.** 61-63 Chrystie St 10002. At Hester and Canal sts. Int corridors. **Pets:** Accepted.

Comfort Inn Times Square South Ⓗ
(212) 268-3040. **$119-$389.** 305 W 39th St 10018. At 8th Ave. Int corridors. **Pets:** Small. $10 daily fee/pet. Service with restrictions.

Conrad New York Ⓗ 🐾
(212) 945-0100. **Call for rates.** 102 North End Ave 10282. In Battery Park City; between Vesey and Murray sts. Int corridors. **Pets:** Medium. Service with restrictions, supervision.

The Court - A St Giles Premier Hotel Ⓗ
(212) 685-1100. **$149-$899.** 130 E 39th St 10016. Between Park and Lexington aves. Int corridors. **Pets:** Accepted.

Courtyard by Marriott/Manhattan-Times Square South Ⓗ
(212) 391-0088. **$179-$499.** 114 W 40th St 10018. Between Broadway and 6th Ave (Ave of the Americas). Int corridors. **Pets:** Accepted.

Crowne Plaza Times Square Manhattan Ⓗ
(212) 977-4000. **Call for rates.** 1605 Broadway 10019. Between 48th and 49th sts. Int corridors. **Pets:** Accepted.

DoubleTree by Hilton Metropolitan Hotel-New York City Ⓗ 🐾
(212) 752-7000. **$139-$599.** 569 Lexington Ave 10022. At E 51st St. Int corridors. **Pets:** Large. $100 one-time fee/pet. Designated rooms, service with restrictions, crate.

DoubleTree by Hilton New York City-Chelsea Ⓗ
(212) 564-0994. **$159-$999.** 128 W 29th St 10001. Between 6th (Ave of the Americas) and 7th aves. Int corridors. **Pets:** Accepted.

DoubleTree by Hilton Times Square South Ⓗ
(212) 542-8990. **$179-$399.** 341 W 36th St 10018. Between 8th and 9th aves. Int corridors. **Pets:** Accepted.

AAA ▼▼▼ DoubleTree Suites by Hilton New York City - Times Square H
(212) 719-1600. **$169-$599.** 1568 Broadway 10036. Jct 47th St and 7th Ave. Int corridors. **Pets:** Medium, other species. $60 deposit/room. Service with restrictions. [SAVE] 📶 ✕ 🏋M 🍴 📺 🍴

▼▼▼ ▼▼▼ Dream Downtown H
(212) 229-2559. **$150-$700.** 355 W 16th St 10011. Between 8th and 9th aves. Int corridors. **Pets:** Accepted. 📶 🏋M 🍴 🏊

AAA ▼▼▼ Duane Street Hotel H
(212) 964-4600. **$199-$599.** 130 Duane St 10013. Between Church St and W Broadway. Int corridors. **Pets:** Accepted. [SAVE] 📶 ✕ 🍴

▼▼ ▼▼ Eastgate Tower Hotel H
(212) 687-8000. **Call for rates.** 222 E 39th St 10016. Between 2nd and 3rd aves. Int corridors. **Pets:** Accepted. 📶 🏋M 🍴 📺

AAA ▼▼▼ Element by Westin Times Square West H
(212) 643-0770. **$159-$699, 3 day notice.** 311 W 39th St 10018. Between 8th and 9th aves. Int corridors. **Pets:** Accepted. [SAVE] 📶 ✕ 🍴 📺

AAA ▼▼▼ Eventi-A Kimpton Hotel H 🐾
(212) 564-4567. **$299-$599.** 851 6th Ave (Ave of the Americas) 10001. At 30th St. Int corridors. **Pets:** Other species. [SAVE] 📶 ✕ 🏋M 🍴 📺 🍴 🗷

▼▼◆▼ Four Seasons Hotel New York H 🐾
(212) 758-5700. **$595-$1650.** 57 E 57th St 10022. Between Park and Madison aves. Int corridors. **Pets:** Small, dogs only. Service with restrictions, supervision. 📶 ✕ 🏋M 🍴 🍴 🗷

AAA ▼▼▼ The Franklin Hotel H
(212) 369-1000. **Call for rates.** 164 E 87th St 10128. Between 3rd and Lexington aves. Int corridors. **Pets:** Service with restrictions, crate. [SAVE] 📶 🍴

▼▼◆▼ Gansevoort Meatpacking NYC H
(212) 660-6700. **Call for rates.** 18 9th Ave 10014. At 13th St. Int corridors. **Pets:** Accepted. 📶 🏋M 🍴 📺 🍴 🏊 🗷

▼▼ Gracie Inn Hotel/B & B BB
(212) 628-1700. **$149-$399, 3 day notice.** 502 E 81st St 10028. Between York and East End aves. Int corridors. **Pets:** Accepted. 📶 ✕ 🍴 📺

AAA ▼▼▼ Hampton Inn-Manhattan/Chelsea H
(212) 414-1000. **$249-$419.** 108 W 24th St 10011. Between 6th (Ave of the Americas) and 7th aves. Int corridors. **Pets:** Accepted. [SAVE] 📶 🍴 📺

AAA ▼▼▼ Hampton Inn Manhattan/Madison Square Garden Area H
(212) 947-9700. **$249-$419.** 116 W 31st St 10001. Between 6th (Ave of the Americas) and 7th aves. Int corridors. **Pets:** Accepted. [SAVE] 📶 ✕ 🏋M 🍴 📺

AAA ▼▼▼ Hampton Inn-Manhattan/Seaport/Financial District H
(212) 571-4400. **$149-$499.** 320 Pearl St 10038. Between Peck Slip and Dover St. Int corridors. **Pets:** Accepted. [SAVE] 📶 ✕ 🏋M 🍴 📺

AAA ▼▼▼ Hampton Inn Manhattan/Times Square South H
(212) 967-2344. **$249-$419.** 337 W 39th St 10018. Between 8th and 9th aves. Int corridors. **Pets:** Accepted. [SAVE] 📶 ✕ 🍴 📺

▼▼▼ Hampton Inn/New York-35th Street/Empire State Bldg H
(212) 564-3688. **$149-$499.** 59 W 35th St 10001. Between 5th and 6th (Ave of the Americas) aves. Int corridors. **Pets:** Accepted. 📶 ✕ 🍴 📺

▼▼▼ Hilton Club New York H
(646) 459-6500. **$369-$899.** 1335 Ave of the Americas, 37th Floor 10019. At W 54th St; between 6th (Ave of the Americas) and 7th aves. Int corridors. **Pets:** Accepted. 📶 ✕ 🏋M 🍴 🍴 🗷

▼▼▼ Hilton New York H
(212) 586-7000. **$249-$599.** 1335 Ave of the Americas 10019. Between 53rd and 54th sts. Int corridors. **Pets:** Accepted. 📶 ✕ 🏋M 🍴 🍴 🗷

AAA ▼◆▼ Hilton Times Square H 🐾
(212) 840-8222. **$169-$699.** 234 W 42nd St 10036. Between 7th and 8th aves. Int corridors. **Pets:** Large, other species. $75 one-time fee/room. Service with restrictions, crate. [SAVE] 📶 🏋M 🍴 📺 🍴

▼▼◆▼ Holiday Inn Express Fifth Ave H
(212) 302-9088. **$159-$499.** 15 W 45th St 10036. At 5th Ave. Int corridors. **Pets:** Accepted. 📶 🏋M 🍴 📺

▼▼◆▼ Holiday Inn Express NYC/Madison Square Garden H
(212) 695-7200. **Call for rates.** 232 W 29th St 10001. Between 7th and 8th aves. Int corridors. **Pets:** Accepted. [SAVE] 📶 ✕ 🏋M 🍴 📺

▼▼▼ Holiday Inn NYC/Manhattan 6th Avenue H
(212) 430-8500. **Call for rates.** 125 W 26th St 10001. Between 6th (Ave of the Americas) and 7th aves. Int corridors. **Pets:** Accepted. 📶 🍴 📺

AAA ▼◆▼ Hotel 373 Fifth Avenue H
(212) 213-3388. **Call for rates.** 373 Fifth Ave 10016. Jct 35th St. Int corridors. **Pets:** Accepted. [SAVE] 📶 ✕ 📺

▼▼▼ Hotel Indigo New York City-Chelsea H
(212) 973-9000. **Call for rates.** 127 W 28th St 10001. Between 6th (Ave of the Americas) and 7th aves. Int corridors. **Pets:** Accepted. 📶 ✕ 🏋M 📺 🍴

AAA ▼▼▼ Hotel Mela H
(212) 710-7000. **Call for rates.** 120 W 44th St 10036. Between Broadway and 6th Ave (Ave of the Americas). Int corridors. **Pets:** Accepted. [SAVE] 📶 ✕ 🏋M 🍴 📺 🍴

▼▼ ▼▼▼ Hotel Plaza Athenee H 🐾
(212) 734-9100. **Call for rates.** 37 E 64th St 10065. Between Madison and Park aves. Int corridors. **Pets:** Small. $100 one-time fee/pet. Service with restrictions, crate. 📶 🏋M 🍴 📺 🍴 🗷

AAA ▼▼▼ Hotel Wales H
(212) 876-6000. **$195-$695.** 1295 Madison Ave 10128. Between 92nd and 93rd sts E. Int corridors. **Pets:** Accepted. [SAVE] 📶 ✕ 🍴 🍴

AAA ▼▼ ▼▼ Ink 48 New York City, A Kimpton Hotel H
(212) 757-0088. **Call for rates.** 653 11th Ave 10036. Between 47th and 48th sts. Int corridors. **Pets:** Accepted. [SAVE] 📶 ✕ 📺 🍴

AAA ▼▼▼ InterContinental New York Barclay H
(212) 755-5900. **Call for rates.** 111 E 48th St 10017. Between Park and Lexington aves. Int corridors. **Pets:** Accepted. [SAVE] 📶 ✕ 🍴 📺 🍴 🗷

AAA ▼▼▼ ▼▼▼ InterContinental New York Times Square [H]

(212) 803-4500. **Call for rates.** 300 W 44th St 10036. Between 8th and 9th aves. Int corridors. **Pets:** Medium, other species. $250 one-time fee/room. Service with restrictions, crate.

[SAVE] [📶] [✕] [👤M] [📠] [💻] [🍴]

AAA ▼▼▼ ▼▼▼ The James Hotel New York Soho [H]

(212) 465-2000. **Call for rates.** 27 Grand St 10013. Between 6th Ave (Ave of the Americas) and Thompson St. Int corridors. **Pets:** Accepted.

[SAVE] [📶] [✕] [📠] [💻] [🍴] [🏊]

▼▼▼ ▼▼▼ JW Marriott Essex House New York [H]

(212) 247-0300. **Call for rates.** 160 Central Park S 10019. Between 6th (Ave of the Americas) and 7th aves. Int corridors. **Pets:** Accepted.

[📶] [✕] [👤M] [📠] [💻] [🍴]

AAA ▼▼▼ ▼▼▼ Le Parker Meridien New York [H] ❀

(212) 245-5000. **$309-$1169.** 119 W 56th St 10019. Between 6th (Ave of the Americas) and 7th aves. Int corridors. **Pets:** Other species. $50 daily fee/room. Service with restrictions, crate.

[SAVE] [📶] [✕] [📠] [💻] [🍴] [🏊] [✕]

▼▼▼ ▼▼▼ The London NYC [H]

(212) 307-5000. **Call for rates.** 151 W 54th St 10019. Between 6th (Ave of the Americas) and 7th aves. Int corridors. **Pets:** Accepted.

[📶] [👤M] [📠] [🍴] [✕]

▼▼▼ ▼▼▼ The Lowell Hotel [H] ❀

(212) 838-1400. **$700-$900, 3 day notice.** 28 E 63rd St 10021. Between Park and Madison aves. Int corridors. **Pets:** Other species. $200 one-time fee/room. Service with restrictions.

[📶] [✕] [📠] [💻] [🍴] [✕]

AAA ▼▼▼ Mandarin Oriental, New York [H]

(212) 805-8800. **$695-$955.** 80 Columbus Cir at 60th St 10023. At 60th St. Int corridors. **Pets:** Accepted. [SAVE] [📶] [💻] [🍴] [🏊]

AAA ▼▼▼ The Mansfield [H]

(212) 277-8700. **Call for rates.** 12 W 44th St 10036. Between 5th and 6th (Ave of the Americas) aves. Int corridors. **Pets:** Accepted.

[SAVE] [📶] [🍴]

▼▼▼ Millennium Broadway Hotel-Times Square-New York [H]

(212) 768-4400. **$179-$599.** 145 W 44th St 10036. Between 6th Ave (Ave of the Americas) and Broadway; in Times Square. Int corridors. **Pets:** Accepted. [📶] [👤M] [💻] [🍴]

AAA ▼▼▼ ▼▼▼ Mondrian SoHo [H]

(212) 389-1000. **$299-$549.** 9 Crosby St 10013. Just s of Grand St. Int corridors. **Pets:** Accepted. [SAVE] [📶] [✕] [💻] [🍴]

AAA ▼▼▼ ▼▼▼ The Muse Hotel [H]

(212) 485-2400. **Call for rates.** 130 W 46th St 10036. Between 6th (Ave of the Americas) and 7th aves. Int corridors. **Pets:** Accepted.

[ECO] [SAVE] [📶] [✕] [📠] [💻] [🍴] [✕]

▼▼▼ ▼▼▼ New York Marriott Marquis [H]

(212) 398-1900. **$179-$799.** 1535 Broadway 10036. Between 45th and 46th sts; motor entrance on 46th St. Int corridors. **Pets:** Accepted.

[📶] [✕] [📠] [💻] [🍴]

▼▼▼ ▼▼▼ The New York Palace [H] ❀

(212) 888-7000. **$249-$950.** 455 Madison Ave 10022. Between 50th and 51st sts. Int corridors. **Pets:** Small, dogs only. Service with restrictions, supervision. [📶] [✕] [👤M] [📠] [💻] [🍴] [✕]

AAA ▼▼▼ ▼▼▼ Novotel New York Times Square [H]

(212) 315-0100. **Call for rates.** 226 W 52nd St 10019. At Broadway. Int corridors. **Pets:** Accepted. [SAVE] [📶] [👤M] [📠] [🍴]

AAA ▼▼▼ ▼▼▼ Omni Berkshire Place [H] ❀

(212) 753-5800. **$269-$699.** 21 E 52nd St 10022. Between Madison and 5th aves. Int corridors. **Pets:** Small. $50 one-time fee/room. Crate.

[SAVE] [📶] [✕] [👤M] [📠] [🍴] [✕]

AAA ▼▼▼ On The Ave Hotel [H]

(212) 362-1100. **$129-$699.** 2178 Broadway 10024. At 77th St. Int corridors. **Pets:** Accepted. [SAVE] [📶] [✕] [💻] [🍴]

AAA ▼▼▼▼ The Paramount Hotel New York [H]

(212) 764-5500. **Call for rates.** 235 W 46th St 10036. Between Broadway and 8th Ave. Int corridors. **Pets:** Small. $125 one-time fee/pet. Supervision. [SAVE] [📶] [✕] [🍴]

AAA ▼▼▼▼ The Peninsula New York [H]

(212) 956-2888. **$595-$1045.** 700 5th Ave 10019. At 55th St. Int corridors. **Pets:** Accepted. [SAVE] [📶] [📠] [💻] [🍴] [🏊] [✕]

AAA ▼▼▼▼ The Pierre New York-A Taj Hotel [H]

(212) 838-8000. **$795-$1045.** 2 E 61st St 10065. At 5th Ave. Int corridors. **Pets:** Accepted. [ECO] [SAVE] [📶] [👤M] [📠] [💻] [🍴] [✕]

AAA ▼▼▼ ▼▼▼ The Plaza Hotel [H]

(212) 759-3000. **Call for rates.** 5th Ave at Central Park S 10019. Corner of 5th Ave and Central Park S. Int corridors. **Pets:** Accepted.

[SAVE] [📶] [✕] [👤M] [📠] [💻] [🍴] [✕]

AAA ▼▼▼ ▼▼▼ Radisson Martinique on Broadway [H]

(212) 736-3800. **$235-$525.** 49 W 32nd St 10001. Between Broadway and 5th Ave. Int corridors. **Pets:** Small, dogs only. $100 deposit/pet, $25 daily fee/pet. Service with restrictions, supervision.

[SAVE] [📶] [👤M] [📠] [💻] [🍴] [✕]

▼▼▼ ▼▼▼ Renaissance New York Hotel 57 [H]

(212) 753-8841. **$229-$599.** 130 E 57th St 10022. At Lexington Ave. Int corridors. **Pets:** Accepted. [📶] [✕] [📠] [💻] [🍴]

AAA ▼▼▼ ▼▼▼ Renaissance New York Hotel Times Square [H]

(212) 765-7676. **$249-$899.** 2 Times Square, 7th Ave at W 48th St 10036. At Broadway and 7th Ave; motor access from 7th Ave, s of W 48th St. Int corridors. **Pets:** Accepted. [SAVE] [📶] [✕] [💻] [🍴]

AAA ▼▼▼ ▼▼▼ The Ritz-Carlton New York, Battery Park [H]

(212) 344-0800. **$495-$845, 3 day notice.** Two West St 10004. Jct Battery Pl. Int corridors. **Pets:** Accepted.

[SAVE] [📶] [✕] [👤M] [📠] [💻] [🍴]

AAA ▼▼▼▼ The Ritz-Carlton New York, Central Park [H] ❀

(212) 308-9100. **Call for rates.** 50 Central Park S 10019. Jct 59th St (Central Park S) and 6th Ave (Ave of the Americas). Int corridors. **Pets:** Large, other species. $125 one-time fee/room. Service with restrictions, crate. [SAVE] [📶] [✕] [👤M] [📠] [💻] [🍴] [✕]

AAA ▼▼▼ ▼▼▼ Royalton Hotel [H]

(212) 869-4400. **Call for rates.** 44 W 44th St 10036. Between 5th and 6th (Ave of the Americas) aves. Int corridors. **Pets:** Accepted.

[SAVE] [📶] [✕] [🍴] [✕]

▼▼▼ ▼▼▼ St Giles Hotel The Tuscany [H]

(212) 686-1600. **Call for rates.** 120 E 39th St 10016. Between Park and Lexington aves. Int corridors. **Pets:** Accepted. [📶] [✕] [📠] [💻] [🍴]

▼▼▼ ▼▼▼ The St. Regis New York [H]

(212) 753-4500. **Call for rates.** 2 E 55th St 10022. Between Madison and 5th aves. Int corridors. **Pets:** Accepted.

[📶] [👤M] [📠] [💻] [🍴] [✕]

▼▼▼ ▼▼▼ The Setai Fifth Avenue 🅷 ❀
(212) 695-4005. **$595-$895.** 400 Fifth Ave 10018. Between 36th and 37th sts. Int corridors. **Pets:** Very small, dogs only. Designated rooms, service with restrictions, supervision. 📶 ✕ 🏋M 🔌 💻 ¶¶

ⒶⒶ ▼▼▼ ▼▼▼ Sheraton New York Times Square Hotel 🅷 ❀
(212) 581-1000. **$199-$699.** 811 7th Ave 10019. At 52nd St. Int corridors. **Pets:** Medium, dogs only. Service with restrictions.
SAVE 📶 ✕ 🏋M 🔌 💻 ¶¶

ⒶⒶ ▼▼▼ ▼▼▼ Sheraton Tribeca New York Hotel 🅷
(212) 966-3400. **$129-$599.** 370 Canal St 10013. Just e of Broadway. Int corridors. **Pets:** Accepted. SAVE 📶 ✕ 🏋M 🔌 💻 ¶¶

ⒶⒶ ▼▼▼ ▼▼▼ The Shoreham Hotel 🅷
(212) 247-6700. **Call for rates.** 33 W 55th St 10019. Between 5th and 6th (Ave of the Americas) aves. Int corridors. **Pets:** Accepted.
SAVE 📶 ¶¶

▼▼▼ ▼▼▼ Skyline Hotel 🅷 ❀
(212) 586-3400. **$139-$650.** 725 10th Ave 10019. At 49th and 50th sts. Int corridors. **Pets:** Large. $200 deposit/pet. Service with restrictions, crate. 📶 ✕ 🔌 ¶¶ ⚓

ⒶⒶ ▼▼▼ ▼▼▼ Sofitel New York 🅷
(212) 354-8844. **$255-$895.** 45 W 44th St 10036. Between 5th and 6th (Ave of the Americas) aves. Int corridors. **Pets:** Accepted.
ECO SAVE ✕ 🔌 💻 ¶¶ ⚓

ⒶⒶ ▼▼▼ ▼▼▼ Staybridge Suites Times Square 🅷 ❀
(212) 757-9000. **$199-$499.** 340 W 40th St 10018. Between 8th and 9th aves. Int corridors. **Pets:** Other species. $150 one-time fee/room. Service with restrictions, crate. SAVE 📶 ✕ 🔌 💻

ⒶⒶ ▼▼▼ ▼▼▼ The Surrey 🅷 ❀
(212) 288-3700. **$625-$795.** 20 E 76th St 10021. Jct E 76th St and Madison Ave. Int corridors. **Pets:** Medium. $100 deposit/pet. Service with restrictions, crate. SAVE 📶 ✕ 🏋M 🔌 💻 ¶¶

ⒶⒶ ▼▼▼▼▼▼ Trump International Hotel & Tower 🅷 ❀
(212) 299-1000. **Call for rates.** 1 Central Park W 10023. Jct Central Park S; at Columbus Cir. Int corridors. **Pets:** Small, dogs only. $260 one-time fee/room. SAVE 📶 ✕ 🔌 💻 ¶¶ ⚓ ✕

ⒶⒶ ▼▼▼ ▼▼▼ TRYP Times Square South 🅷 ❀
(212) 600-2440. **$159-$459.** 345 W 35th St 10001. Between 8th and 9th aves. Int corridors. **Pets:** Small. $30 daily fee/room. Service with restrictions. SAVE 📶 ✕ 🔌 💻 ¶¶

ⒶⒶ ▼▼▼ ▼▼▼ The Waldorf=Astoria 🅷
(212) 355-3000. **Call for rates.** 301 Park Ave 10022. Between E 49th and 50th sts. Int corridors. **Pets:** Accepted.
SAVE 📶 🏋M 🔌 💻 ¶¶

ⒶⒶ ▼▼▼ ▼▼▼ The Westin New York at Times Square 🅷
(212) 201-2700. **$229-$899.** 270 W 43rd St 10036. Corner of 8th Ave. Int corridors. **Pets:** Accepted.
ECO SAVE 📶 ✕ 🏋M 🔌 💻 ¶¶ ✕

ⒶⒶ ▼▼▼ ▼▼▼ The Westin New York Grand Central 🅷
(212) 490-8900. **$199-$699.** 212 E 42nd St 10017. Between 2nd and 3rd aves. Int corridors. **Pets:** Accepted. SAVE 📶 ✕ 🔌 💻 ¶¶

ⒶⒶ ▼▼▼ ▼▼▼ W New York 🅷
(212) 755-1200. **$229-$849.** 541 Lexington Ave 10022. At 49th St. Int corridors. **Pets:** Accepted. SAVE 📶 ✕ 🏋M 🔌 💻 ¶¶

ⒶⒶ ▼▼▼ ▼▼▼ W New York Downtown 🅷
(646) 826-8600. **$249-$789.** 123 Washington St 10006. At Albany St. Int corridors. **Pets:** Accepted. SAVE 📶 ✕ 🏋M 🔌 💻 ¶¶

ⒶⒶ ▼▼▼ ▼▼▼ W New York Times Square 🅷
(212) 930-7400. **$269-$899.** 1567 Broadway at 47th St 10036. Corner of 47th St. Int corridors. **Pets:** Accepted. SAVE 📶 🏋M 🔌 💻 ¶¶

ⒶⒶ ▼▼▼ ▼▼▼ W New York-Union Square 🅷
(212) 253-9119. **$299-$999.** 201 Park Ave S 10003. At 17th St. Int corridors. **Pets:** Accepted. SAVE 📶 ✕ 🏋M 🔌 💻 ¶¶ ✕

RYE BROOK

ⒶⒶ ▼▼▼ ▼▼▼ Hilton Westchester 🅷
(914) 939-6300. **Call for rates.** 699 Westchester Ave 10573. I-287 (Cross Westchester Expwy) exit 10 eastbound, 0.6 mi ne on SR 120A; exit westbound, 0.3 mi n on Webb Ave, then 0.4 mi ne on SR 120A. Int corridors. **Pets:** Accepted.
SAVE 📶 ✕ 🏋M 🔌 💻 ¶¶ ⚓ ✕

STATEN ISLAND

ⒶⒶ ▼▼▼ ▼▼▼ Hilton Garden Inn Staten Island 🅷
(718) 477-2400. **Call for rates.** 1100 South Ave 10314. I-278 exit 6 (South Ave) westbound, just s; exit 5 eastbound to SR 440 S to South Ave exit, just s, 1 mi n to Lois Ln, then just w. Int corridors.
Pets: Accepted. SAVE 📶 🔌 💻 ¶¶ ⚓ ✕

SUFFERN

ⒶⒶ ▼▼▼ ▼▼▼ Crowne Plaza Hotel and Conference Center 🅷 ❀
(845) 357-4800. **$129-$189.** 3 Executive Blvd 10901. I-87 (New York State Thruway) exit 14B, just n. Int corridors. **Pets:** Medium, dogs only. $50 deposit/room. Designated rooms, service with restrictions, crate.
SAVE 📶 ✕ 🔌 💻 ¶¶

TARRYTOWN

ⒶⒶ ▼▼▼ ▼▼▼ Sheraton Tarrytown Hotel 🅷 ❀
(914) 332-7900. **$89-$299.** 600 White Plains Rd 10591. I-87 exit 9 northbound, 0.8 mi e on SR 119; exit southbound, just n on US 9, then 1 mi e on SR 119. Int corridors. **Pets:** Dogs only. $50 one-time fee/room. Designated rooms, service with restrictions, supervision.
SAVE 📶 ✕ 🏋M 🔌 💻 ¶¶ ⚓

▼▼▼ ▼▼▼ Westchester Marriott Hotel 🅷
(914) 631-2200. **$139-$309.** 670 White Plains Rd 10591. I-87 (New York State Thruway) exit 9 northbound, 0.8 mi e on SR 119; exit southbound, just n on US 9, then 1 mi e on SR 119. Int corridors. **Pets:** Accepted.
ECO 📶 ✕ 🔌 💻 ¶¶ ⚓ ✕

WHITE PLAINS

ⒶⒶ ▼▼▼ ▼▼▼ Hyatt house White Plains 🅷
(914) 251-9700. **$129-$289.** 101 Corporate Park Dr 10604. I-287 (Cross Westchester Expwy) exit 9A eastbound, 0.6 mi e on Westchester Ave, then 0.3 mi n; exit 9N-S westbound, 0.9 mi w on Westchester Ave. Int corridors. **Pets:** Medium. $150 one-time fee/room. Service with restrictions, supervision. SAVE 📶 ✕ 🏋M 🔌 💻 ⚓ ✕

▼▼▼ ▼▼▼ Residence Inn by Marriott White Plains 🅷
(914) 761-7700. **$161-$249.** 5 Barker Ave 10601. I-287 exit 6 westbound, w on service road to SR 22 (Broadway), 0.8 mi s to Barker Ave, then 0.5 mi w; exit eastbound, s on Broadway. Int corridors. **Pets:** Accepted.
📶 ✕ 🔌 💻 ¶¶

The Ritz-Carlton, Westchester **H**
(914) 946-5500. **Call for rates.** 3 Renaissance Square 10601. Jct SR 22, just w on Main St, then just n. Int corridors. **Pets:** Accepted.

YONKERS

Hampton Inn & Suites **H** ❀
(914) 377-1144. **$139-$259.** 160 Corporate Blvd 10701. Sawmill Pkwy exit 9, 0.8 mi w. Int corridors. **Pets:** Dogs only. $250 deposit/pet. Service with restrictions.

END METROPOLITAN AREA

NIAGARA FALLS METROPOLITAN AREA

LOCKPORT

BEST WESTERN PLUS Lockport **H**
(716) 434-6151. **$95-$150.** 515 S Transit St 14094. 1 mi s on SR 78. Int corridors. **Pets:** Accepted.

Comfort Inn **H**
(716) 434-4411. **$70-$160.** 551 S Transit St 14094. 1 mi s on SR 78. Int corridors. **Pets:** Medium. $10 daily fee/pet. Service with restrictions, supervision.

NEWFANE

Lake Ontario Motel **M**
(716) 778-5004. **$69-$105, 5 day notice.** 3330 Lockport-Olcott Rd 14108. 2.5 mi n of jct SR 104 on SR 78. Int corridors. **Pets:** Other species. $5 daily fee/pet. Service with restrictions, supervision.

NIAGARA FALLS

Four Points by Sheraton Niagara Falls **H**
(716) 299-0344. **$65-$300.** 7001 Buffalo Ave 14304. I-190 exit 21 (Robert Moses Pkwy), just e. Int corridors. **Pets:** Small, dogs only. $40 one-time fee/pet. Service with restrictions, supervision.

Holiday Inn Express Niagara Falls **H**
(716) 298-4500. **$89-$499.** 10111 Niagara Falls Blvd 14304. I-190 exit 22, 2.1 mi e on US 62. Int corridors. **Pets:** $50 daily fee/pet. Designated rooms, no service, supervision.

Motel 6 **H**
(716) 297-9902. **$45-$250.** 9100 Niagara Falls Blvd 14304. I-190 exit 22, 1.8 mi e. Int corridors. **Pets:** Other species. Service with restrictions, supervision.

Quality Hotel & Suites "At the Falls" **H**
(716) 282-1212. **$59-$199.** 240 First St 14303. I-190 exit 21 (Robert Moses Pkwy) eastbound to City Traffic exit, just w; downtown. Int corridors. **Pets:** Large. $30 one-time fee/pet. Service with restrictions, supervision.

Sheraton At The Falls **H** ❀
(716) 285-3361. **$119-$299.** 300 3rd St 14303. I-190 exit 21 (Robert Moses Pkwy) to City Traffic exit, just w on Rainbow Blvd, then just n. Int corridors. **Pets:** Small, dogs only. Designated rooms, service with restrictions, supervision.

END METROPOLITAN AREA

NORTH SYRACUSE

BEST WESTERN Syracuse Airport Inn **H**
(315) 455-7362. **$100-$180.** 900 Col. Eileen Collins Blvd 13212. I-81 exit 27 (Syracuse Hancock International Airport). Int corridors. **Pets:** $25 one-time fee/pet. Supervision.

Candlewood Suites Syracuse Airport **H**
(315) 454-8999. **Call for rates.** 5414 South Bay Rd 13212. I-90 exit 36; I-81 exit 26 (Mattydale Rd), follow South Bay Rd signs, just n. Int corridors. **Pets:** Other species. $10 daily fee/pet. Service with restrictions, crate.

Comfort Inn & Suites/Syracuse Airport **H** ❀
(315) 457-4000. **$85-$179.** 6701 Buckley Rd 13212. I-81 exit 25 (7th North St), just w. Int corridors. **Pets:** Medium. $25 one-time fee/pet. Service with restrictions, supervision.

NORWICH

Super 8 of Norwich **H**
(607) 336-8880. **$55-$101.** 6067 State Hwy 12 13815. On SR 12, 0.9 mi n. Int corridors. **Pets:** Large. $11 daily fee/pet. Designated rooms, supervision.

OGDENSBURG

Quality Inn Gran-View **M**
(315) 393-4550. **$101-$275.** 6765 SR 37 13669. On SR 37, 3 mi sw. Ext/int corridors. **Pets:** Other species. $10 daily fee/pet. Designated rooms, service with restrictions, crate.

Windjammer Lodge **M**
(315) 393-6300. **$80-$175.** 5843 SR 37 13669. On SR 37, 5 mi sw. Ext corridors. **Pets:** Other species. $10 daily fee/pet. Service with restrictions, crate.

OLD FORGE

Adirondack Lodge Old Forge **M**
(315) 369-6836. **$59-$299, 7 day notice.** 2752 SR 28 13420. 0.3 mi s. Ext/int corridors. **Pets:** Dogs only. $25 one-time fee/pet. Designated rooms, service with restrictions, crate.

ONEIDA

Super 8-Oneida **H**
(315) 363-5168. **$60-$120.** 215 Genesee St 13421. I-90 exit 33, 4 mi s on SR 365 to SR 5, then 0.5 mi w. Int corridors. **Pets:** Accepted.

ONEONTA

(AAA) ▼▼▼ Holiday Inn Oneonta/Cooperstown Area [H]
(607) 433-2250. **$89-$199.** 5206 State Hwy 23 13820. I-88 exit 15 (SR 23 and 28), 1.5 mi e. Int corridors. **Pets:** Accepted.
[SAVE] 📶 ✕ 🚹M 🛏 🖥 ¶¶ 🏊 ✕

OSWEGO

▼▼ Quality Inn & Suites - Riverfront [H]
(315) 343-1600. **$109-$184.** 70 E 1st St 13126. Just n on SR 481. Int corridors. **Pets:** Small. $10 daily fee/pet. Designated rooms, service with restrictions, supervision. 📶 ✕ 🛏 🖥 ¶¶

PAINTED POST

(AAA) ▼▼ Americas Best Value Inn Lodge on the Green [M] 🐾
(607) 962-2456. **$76-$160.** 196 S Hamilton St 14870. I-86/SR 17 exit 44B; US 15 exit 3, 1 mi n, then just w on Canada Rd. Ext corridors. **Pets:** Dogs only. $10 one-time fee/room. Service with restrictions, crate.
[SAVE] 📶 🛏 🖥 🏊

▼▼ Econo Lodge [H]
(607) 962-4444. **$89-$129.** 200 Robert Dann Dr 14870. I-86/SR 17 exit 44A westbound; exit 44B eastbound; US 15 N exit 3 (Gang Mills), just n on Hamilton St, then just w. Int corridors. **Pets:** Accepted.
📶 🚹M 🛏 🖥

PEMBROKE

▼▼ Darien Lakes Econo Lodge [H] 🐾
(585) 599-4681. **$70-$180.** 8493 Alleghany Rd 14036. I-90 exit 48A, just s. Int corridors. **Pets:** Other species. Designated rooms, service with restrictions, supervision. 📶 🅲 🖥

PENN YAN

(AAA) ▼▼▼ BEST WESTERN PLUS Vineyard Inn & Suites [H] 🐾
(315) 536-8473. **$108-$153.** 142 Lake St 14527. I-90 exit 43, just e on SR 54, then just s; corner of SR 54 and 14A. Int corridors. **Pets:** Medium, dogs only. $20 daily fee/pet. Service with restrictions, supervision. [SAVE] 📶 ✕ 🛏 🖥 🏊

PINE VALLEY

(AAA) ▼▼▼ Rodeway Inn Marshall Manor [M]
(607) 739-3891. **$89-$180, 7 day notice.** 3527 Watkins Rd 14845. I-86 exit 52B, 5 mi n on SR 14. Ext corridors. **Pets:** Large. $20 daily fee/room. Designated rooms, service with restrictions, supervision.
[SAVE] 📶 🛏 🖥 🏊

PLAINVIEW

▼▼▼ Homewood Suites Long Island Melville [H]
(516) 293-4663. **$209-$249.** 1585 Round Swamp Rd 11803. I-495 exit 48, just s. Int corridors. **Pets:** Accepted. 📶 🚹M 🛏 🖥 🏊 ✕

▼▼▼ Residence Inn by Marriott Plainview Long Island [H]
(516) 433-6200. **$229-$269.** 9 Gerhard Rd 11803. I-495 exit 44, 1.6 mi s on SR 135 exit 10, then just e on Old Country Rd. Int corridors.
Pets: Accepted. 📶 ✕ 🚹M 🛏 🖥 ¶¶ 🏊 ✕

PLATTSBURGH

(AAA) ▼▼▼ BEST WESTERN PLUS The Inn at Smithfield [H]
(518) 561-7750. **$95-$125.** 446 Rt 3 12901. I-87 exit 37, just e. Int corridors. **Pets:** Large, other species. $10 daily fee/room. Service with restrictions, crate. [SAVE] 📶 ✕ 🚹M 🛏 🖥 ¶¶ 🏊

▼▼▼ Comfort Inn & Suites Plattsburgh New York [H]
(518) 562-2730. **$89-$149.** 411 Rt 3 12901. I-87 exit 37, 0.5 mi e. Int corridors. **Pets:** Service with restrictions, supervision.
📶 ✕ 🚹M 🛏 🖥 ¶¶ 🏊 ✕

▼▼▼ La Quinta Inn & Suites Plattsburgh [H]
(518) 562-4000. **$83-$173.** 16 Plaza Blvd 12901. I-87 exit 37, just w. Int corridors. **Pets:** Service with restrictions, supervision.
📶 🚹M 🛏 🖥 🏊

▼▼▼ Microtel Inn & Suites by Wyndham Plattsburgh [H]
(518) 324-3800. **$69-$154.** 554 SR 3 12901. I-87 exit 37, just w. Int corridors. **Pets:** Medium. $10 daily fee/room. Service with restrictions, supervision. 📶 🚹M 🛏 🖥

POUGHKEEPSIE

(AAA) ▼▼▼ BEST WESTERN PLUS The Inn & Suites at the Falls [H]
(845) 462-5770. **Call for rates.** 50 Red Oaks Mill Rd (CR 44) 12603. Jct SR 376 and CR 113, just se. Int corridors. **Pets:** Medium, dogs only. $100 deposit/room, $25 daily fee/room. Designated rooms, service with restrictions, supervision. [SAVE] 📶 ✕ 🛏 🖥

(AAA) ▼▼▼ Days Inn [M]
(845) 454-1010. **$100-$239.** 536 Haight Ave 12603. 2 mi e of Mid-Hudson Bridge on US 44 and SR 55. Ext/int corridors. **Pets:** Dogs only. $30 one-time fee/pet. Designated rooms, service with restrictions, crate.
[SAVE] 📶 🛏 🖥 🏊

QUEENSBURY

▼▼▼ Quality Inn of Glens Falls [H]
(518) 793-3800. **Call for rates.** 547 Aviation Rd 12804. I-87 exit 19, just e. Int corridors. **Pets:** Accepted. 📶 ✕ 🚹M 🛏 🖥 🏊

RHINEBECK

▼▼▼ Beekman Arms & Delamater Inn and Conference Center [CI]
(845) 876-7077. **$120-$300, 14 day notice.** 6387 Mill St (Rt 9) 12572. Jct US 9 and SR 308; center of village. Ext/int corridors. **Pets:** Other species. $15 daily fee/pet. Designated rooms, service with restrictions.
📶 🛏 🖥 ¶¶

RIVERHEAD

▼▼▼ Holiday Inn Express East End [H]
(631) 548-1000. **Call for rates.** 1707 Old Country Rd (SR 58) 11901. I-495 exit 73, 0.5 mi e. Int corridors. **Pets:** Accepted.
📶 🚹M 🛏 🖥 🏊

▼▼▼ Hotel Indigo East End [H]
(631) 369-2200. **$149-$399, 3 day notice.** 1830 SR 25 11901. I-495 exit 72 (SR 25 E). Int corridors. **Pets:** $50 one-time fee/room. Service with restrictions, crate. 📶 ✕ 🛏 🖥 ¶¶ 🏊

ROCHESTER

▼▼▼ La Quinta Inn Rochester North [H]
(585) 254-1000. **$71-$173.** 1956 Lyell Ave 14606. I-390 exit 21 (SR 31), just e. Int corridors. **Pets:** Service with restrictions, supervision.
📶 🛏 🖥

▼▼▼ Radisson Hotel Rochester Riverside [H]
(585) 546-6400. **$99-$299.** 120 E Main St 14604. Downtown. Int corridors. **Pets:** Medium. $50 one-time fee/room. Service with restrictions, crate. 📶 🚹M 🛏 🖥 ¶¶

(AAA) ▼▼▼ Rochester Plaza Hotel & Conference Center [H]
(585) 546-3450. **$99-$269, 7 day notice.** 70 State St 14614. Jct Main St; downtown. Int corridors. **Pets:** Accepted.
[SAVE] 📶 🛏 🖥 ¶¶ 🏊

ROCKVILLE CENTRE

(AAA) ▼▼▼ BEST WESTERN Mill River Manor [H] 🐾
(516) 678-1300. **$129-$199.** 173 Sunrise Hwy 11570. On SR 27; between N Village and N Centre aves. Ext corridors. **Pets:** $15 daily fee/room. Designated rooms, service with restrictions, supervision.
[SAVE] 📶 🚹M 🛏 🖥 ¶¶ 🏊

ROME

▼▼ Econo Lodge M
(315) 337-9400. **Call for rates.** 145 E Whitesboro St 13440. Just s of jct SR 26 (Turin Rd) and 46. Ext corridors. **Pets:** Accepted. 🛜 🍴 💻

◈◈◈ ▼▼ Inn at the Beeches M
(315) 336-1775. **$95-$295.** 7900 Turin Rd 13440. Jct SR 46, 2 mi n on SR 26 (Turin Rd). Ext corridors. **Pets:** Other species. $10 daily fee/pet. Designated rooms, service with restrictions, crate.
SAVE 🍴 💻 ▥ ⤵

ROSCOE

◈◈◈ ▼ Roscoe Motel M
(607) 498-5220. **$70-$85, 7 day notice.** 2054 Old Rt 17 12776. SR 17 exit 94, 0.5 mi n on SR 206, then just w. Ext corridors. **Pets:** $10 daily fee/pet. Service with restrictions, supervision. SAVE 🛜 ✕ 🍴 💻

SACKETS HARBOR

▼▼▼ Ontario Place Hotel H
(315) 646-8000. **Call for rates.** 103 General Smith Dr 13685. Corner of W Main St; center. Int corridors. **Pets:** Accepted. 🛜 ✕ 🍴 💻

SALAMANCA

▼▼▼ Holiday Inn Express Hotel & Suites H
(716) 945-7600. **$140-$190.** 779 Broad St 14779. I-86 exit 20, just n. Int corridors. **Pets:** Large, other species. $50 deposit/room, $25 one-time fee/room. Designated rooms, service with restrictions, supervision.
🛜 ♿ 🍴 💻 ⤵

SARANAC LAKE

▼ Adirondack Motel M
(518) 891-2116. **$79-$265.** 248 Lake Flower Ave 12983. 0.5 mi e on SR 86. Ext corridors. **Pets:** Dogs only. $15 daily fee/pet. Designated rooms, service with restrictions, supervision. 🛜 ✕ 🍴 💻 ⤵

◈◈◈ ▼▼▼ BEST WESTERN Mountain Lake Inn H
(518) 891-1970. **Call for rates.** 487 Lake Flower Ave 12983. 1.1 mi e on SR 86. Int corridors. **Pets:** Other species. $20 one-time fee/room. Designated rooms, service with restrictions, supervision.
SAVE 🛜 ✕ ♿ 🍴 💻 ▥ ⤵

▼ Lake Flower Inn M
(518) 891-2310. **$78-$148, 14 day notice.** 234 Lake Flower Ave 12983. 0.5 mi e on SR 86. Ext corridors. **Pets:** Accepted.
🛜 ✕ 🍴 ⤵ ☒

▼ Lake Side Motel M
(518) 891-4333. **Call for rates.** 256 Lake Flower Ave 12983. 0.6 mi e on SR 86. Ext corridors. **Pets:** Dogs only. $10 daily fee/pet. Designated rooms, service with restrictions, supervision. 🛜 ✕ 🍴 ⤵ ☒

SARATOGA SPRINGS

▼▼▼▼ Adelphi Hotel H
(518) 587-4688. **Call for rates.** 365 Broadway 12866. Downtown. Int corridors. **Pets:** Accepted. 🛜 ✕ ⤵

◈◈◈ ▼▼▼▼ BEST WESTERN PLUS Park Inn H
(518) 584-2350. **$89-$389, 3 day notice.** 3291 S Broadway 12866. I-87 exit 13N, 1.1 mi n on US 9. Int corridors. **Pets:** $25 daily fee/pet. Designated rooms, service with restrictions, supervision.
SAVE 🛜 ✕ ♿ 🍴 💻 ⤵

◈◈◈ ▼▼▼▼ Comfort Inn & Suites H
(518) 587-6244. **$99-$305.** 17 Old Gick Rd 12866. I-87 exit 15, just e, then just n. Int corridors. **Pets:** Dogs only. $20 daily fee/pet. Designated rooms, service with restrictions, crate.
SAVE 🛜 ✕ ♿ 🍴 💻 ⤵

▼▼▼ Holiday Inn H
(518) 584-4550. **Call for rates.** 232 Broadway 12866. On US 9, jct SR 50. Int corridors. **Pets:** Other species. Service with restrictions.
🛜 ✕ 🍴 💻 ▥ ⤵

▼▼▼ Residence Inn by Marriott-Saratoga Springs H ☙
(518) 584-9600. **$149-$469.** 295 Excelsior Ave 12866. I-87 exit 15, just n, just s, then just e. Int corridors. **Pets:** Other species. $75 one-time fee/room. Service with restrictions, crate.
🛜 ✕ ♿ 🍴 💻 ⤵ ☒

▼▼▼ Roosevelt Inn & Suites H
(518) 584-0980. **$99-$495, 14 day notice.** 2961 S Broadway 12866. I-87 exit 13N, just n. Ext/int corridors. **Pets:** Accepted.
🛜 ♿ 🍴 💻 ▥ ⤵ ☒

◈◈◈ ▼▼▼ Saratoga Downtowner Motel M
(518) 584-6160. **$79-$249, 7 day notice.** 413 Broadway 12866. On US 9; corner of Division St. Ext/int corridors. **Pets:** Dogs only. $25 one-time fee/pet. Service with restrictions, crate. SAVE 🛜 ✕ 🍴 ⤵

▼▼▼▼ The Saratoga Hilton H
(518) 584-4000. **$119-$459.** 534 Broadway 12866. I-87 exit 15, on SR 50. Int corridors. **Pets:** Accepted. 🛜 ♿ 🍴 💻 ▥ ⤵

▼▼▼▼ Union Gables Bed & Breakfast BB
(518) 584-1558. **$125-$450.** 55 Union Ave 12866. I-87 exit 14, 1.5 mi w. Int corridors. **Pets:** $25 one-time fee/pet. Designated rooms, service with restrictions. 🛜 ✕ 🍴 ☑

SAUGERTIES

◈◈◈ ▼▼▼ Comfort Inn H ☙
(845) 246-1565. **Call for rates.** 2790 SR 32 12477. I-87 exit 20, just n. Int corridors. **Pets:** $10 daily fee/pet. Service with restrictions, supervision.
SAVE 🛜 🍴 💻

SENECA FALLS

◈◈◈ ▼▼▼ Microtel Inn & Suites by Wyndham Seneca Falls H
(315) 539-8438. **$60-$130.** 1966 Rt 5 & 20 13148. I-90 (New York State Thruway) exit 41, 4 mi s on SR 414, then just e. Int corridors. **Pets:** Other species. $15 daily fee/room. Service with restrictions, supervision. SAVE 🛜 ♿ 🍴 💻

SKANEATELES

◈◈◈ ▼▼▼ Finger Lakes Lodging M
(315) 217-0222. **$79-$310, 7 day notice.** 834 W Genesee St 13152. On US 20, just w. Ext/int corridors. **Pets:** Dogs only. $40 one-time fee/pet. Designated rooms, no service, supervision. SAVE 🛜 ✕ 🍴

▼▼▼ Skaneateles Suites M
(315) 685-7568. **$99-$175.** 4114 W Genesee St 13152. On US 20, 2 mi w. Ext corridors. **Pets:** Other species. $35 one-time fee/pet. Service with restrictions, crate. 🛜 ✕ 🍴 💻

SOLVAY

▼▼ Clarion Inn & Suites H
(315) 457-8700. **$69-$169.** 100 Farrell Rd 13209. I-690 exit 4 (John Glenn Blvd) eastbound, just n to Farrell Rd; exit 3 (Farrell Rd) westbound. Int corridors. **Pets:** Medium. $25 one-time fee/pet. Service with restrictions, crate. 🛜 🍴 💻 ▥ ⤵

SOUTHAMPTON

◈◈◈ ▼▼▼ Southampton Inn H
(631) 283-6500. **$159-$525, 30 day notice.** 91 Hill St 11968. 0.3 mi n from corner of Main St and Jobs Ln. Ext corridors. **Pets:** Accepted.
SAVE 🛜 ✕ ♿ 🍴 ⤵ ☒

SYLVAN BEACH

▼ Cinderella's Cafe & Suites M
(315) 762-4280. **$59-$199, 15 day notice.** 1208 N Main St 13157. On SR 13; center. Ext corridors. **Pets:** $100 deposit/pet. Service with restrictions, crate. 🛜 ✕ 🍴 💻 ▥

SYRACUSE

▼▼ ▼▼ Comfort Inn-Carrier Circle 🏨 ❖
(315) 437-0222. **$79-$169.** 6491 Thompson Rd S 13206. I-90 exit 35 (Carrier Cir), just s. Ext/int corridors. **Pets:** Medium. $15 daily fee/room. Designated rooms, service with restrictions, crate. 📶 🛅 🖥

▼▼▼▼ Crowne Plaza Hotel Syracuse 🏨
(315) 479-7000. **$129-$269.** 701 E Genesee St 13210. Jct Almond St; downtown. Int corridors. **Pets:** Medium, other species. $50 one-time fee/room. 📶 ☒ 🔊M 🛅 🖥 🍴

▼▼▼▼ Genesee Grande Hotel 🏨
(315) 476-4212. **$169-$529.** 1060 E Genesee St 13210. I-81 exit 18, 0.7 mi e on SR 92 (Genesee St). Int corridors. **Pets:** Accepted.
📶 ☒ 🛅 🖥 🍴

AAA ▼▼ ▼▼ Red Roof Inn #7157 Ⓜ
(315) 437-3309. **$50-$160.** 6614 N Thompson Rd 13206. I-90 exit 35 (Carrier Cir), just n. Ext corridors. **Pets:** Large, other species. Service with restrictions, supervision. 📶 📶 🛅 🖥

AAA ▼▼▼▼ Sheraton Syracuse University Hotel & Conference Center 🏨 ❖
(315) 475-3000. **$145-$355.** 801 University Ave 13210. I-81 exit 18. Int corridors. **Pets:** Large, dogs only. Supervision.
ⒺⒸⓄ 📶 📶 ☒ 🛅 🖥 🍴 🏊

TICONDEROGA

▼▼ ▼▼ Super 8-Ticonderoga 🏨
(518) 585-2617. **$70-$85.** 1144 Wicker St 12883. Jct SR 9N and 74/22. Int corridors. **Pets:** Accepted. 📶 ☒ 🛅 🖥

TROY

AAA ▼▼▼▼ BEST WESTERN PLUS Franklin Square Inn 🏨 ❖
(518) 274-8800. **$130-$200.** One 4th St 12180. I-787 exit 8, just e on 23rd to Federal, just e to 4th St, then just s; downtown. Int corridors. **Pets:** Medium, other species. $25 one-time fee/room. Service with restrictions, supervision. 📶 📶 ☒ 🔊M 🛅 🖥

TULLY

AAA ▼▼ ▼▼ BEST WESTERN Tully Inn 🏨
(315) 696-6061. **$75-$200.** 5779 SR 80 13159. I-81 exit 14, just e. Int corridors. **Pets:** Medium, dogs only. $10 daily fee/pet. Designated rooms, no service, supervision. 📶 📶 🖥

UTICA

▼▼▼▼ Hotel Utica, an Ascend Collection hotel 🏨
(315) 724-7829. **$109-$189.** 102 Lafayette St 13502. I-90 (New York State Thruway) exit 31, 1.1 mi s on Genesee St; center. Int corridors. **Pets:** Small. $25 daily fee/pet. Designated rooms, service with restrictions, supervision. 📶 🛅 🖥 🍴

AAA ▼▼▼▼ Red Roof Inn #7180 Ⓜ
(315) 724-7128. **$52-$170.** 20 Weaver St 13502. I-90 (New York State Thruway) exit 31. Ext corridors. **Pets:** Large, other species. Service with restrictions, supervision. 📶 📶 🛅 🖥

▼▼▼▼ Rosemont Inn Bed & Breakfast Ⓑ
(315) 797-9033. **Call for rates.** 1423 Genesee St 13501. I-90 (New York State Thruway) exit 31, 2.5 mi s. Int corridors. **Pets:** Accepted.
📶 ☒ ☎

VERONA

▼▼▼▼ La Quinta Inn & Suites Verona 🏨
(315) 231-5080. **$167-$287.** 5394 Willow Pl 13478. I-90 exit 33, just s on SR 365, then 0.5 mi n. Int corridors. **Pets:** Service with restrictions, supervision. 📶 🔊M 🛅 🖥 🏊

VICTOR

AAA ▼▼ ▼▼ BEST WESTERN PLUS Victor Inn & Suites 🏨
(585) 924-3933. **$90-$130.** 7449 SR 96 14564. I-90 (New York State Thruway) exit 45, 0.5 mi s. Int corridors. **Pets:** Small, dogs only. $35 daily fee/pet. Designated rooms, service with restrictions, supervision.
Ⓢ🄰🅅🄴 📶 🔊M 🛅 🖥 🏊

AAA ▼▼ ▼▼ Hampton Inn & Suites-Rochester/Victor 🏨 ❖
(585) 924-4400. **$134-$199.** 7637 Pittsford-Victor Rd/St Rt 96 14564. I-90 (New York State Thruway) exit 45, just n. Int corridors. **Pets:** Designated rooms, service with restrictions, supervision.
Ⓢ🄰🅅🄴 📶 ☒ 🛅 🖥 🏊

▼▼▼▼ Microtel Inn by Wyndham Victor/Rochester 🏨
(585) 924-9240. **$55-$119.** 7498 Main St Fishers 14564. I-90 (New York State Thruway) exit 45, just s on SR 96, then just e. Int corridors. **Pets:** Accepted. 📶 ☒ 🛅 🖥

WARRENSBURG

▼▼▼▼ Super 8 Ⓜ ❖
(518) 623-2811. **$60-$95.** 3619 SR 9 12845. I-87 exit 23, just w. Int corridors. **Pets:** Other species. $15 one-time fee/room. Service with restrictions, crate. 📶 🛅 🖥

WATERLOO

AAA ▼▼▼▼ Holiday Inn Waterloo-Seneca Falls 🏨
(315) 539-5011. **$89-$199.** 2468 SR 414 13165. I-90 (New York State Thruway) exit 41, 4 mi s; just n of jct SR 414/5 and US 20. Int corridors. **Pets:** Medium. $15 daily fee/room. Designated rooms, service with restrictions, crate. Ⓢ🄰🅅🄴 📶 🔊M 🛅 🖥 🍴 🏊 ☒

WATERTOWN

AAA ▼▼▼▼ BEST WESTERN Carriage House Inn 🏨 ❖
(315) 782-8000. **Call for rates.** 300 Washington St 13601. Center. Int corridors. **Pets:** Other species. $15 daily fee/pet. Designated rooms, service with restrictions, crate. ⒺⒸⓄ Ⓢ🄰🅅🄴 📶 🛅 🖥 🍴 🏊

▼▼▼▼ Comfort Inn & Suites 🏨
(315) 782-2700. **$119-$149.** 110 Commerce Park Dr 13601. I-81 exit 45, 0.4 mi e on Arsenal St, then just n. Int corridors. **Pets:** Other species. $25 one-time fee/pet. Service with restrictions, crate. 📶 🛅 🖥 🏊

WATKINS GLEN

AAA ▼▼ ▼▼ Anchor Inn and Marina Ⓜ
(607) 535-4159. **$69-$189, 15 day notice.** 3425 Salt Point Rd 14891. Just n on SR 14, 0.8 mi n. Ext corridors. **Pets:** Medium, dogs only. $25 deposit/pet. Service with restrictions, supervision.
Ⓢ🄰🅅🄴 📶 ☒ 🛅 ☒

AAA ▼▼ ▼▼ Chieftain Motel Ⓜ
(607) 535-4759. **$69-$189, 15 day notice.** 3815 SR 14 14891. 3 mi n of town; on west side of SR 14. Ext corridors. **Pets:** Medium, other species. $25 deposit/pet. Service with restrictions, supervision.
Ⓢ🄰🅅🄴 📶 🛅 🖥

WELLSVILLE

▼▼ ▼▼ Microtel Inn & Suites by Wyndham Wellsville 🏨
(585) 593-3449. **$70-$100.** 30 W Dyke St 14895. Just n off SR 19 and 417. Int corridors. **Pets:** Accepted. 📶 🛅 🖥

WESTBURY

▼▼▼▼ Viana Hotel & Spa 🏨
(516) 338-7777. **Call for rates.** 3998 Brush Hollow Rd 11590. Northern Pkwy exit 34, just ne. Int corridors. **Pets:** Accepted.
📶 ☒ 🛅 🖥 🍴 🏊 ☒

WEST COXSACKIE

◆◆ ▼▼▼ BEST WESTERN New Baltimore Inn ⊞
(518) 731-8100. **$90-$150.** 12600 Rt 9W 12192. I-87 (New York State Thruway) exit 21B, 0.5 mi s. Int corridors. **Pets:** Medium. $20 daily fee/room. Service with restrictions, supervision.

SAVE 📶 ⊠ 🛏 🖵 ⤳ ⊠

WILMINGTON

▼▼▼ Hungry Trout Resort Ⓜ
(518) 946-2217. **$79-$269, 7 day notice.** 5239 Rt 86 12997. On SR 86, 2 mi w. Ext corridors. **Pets:** Accepted.

📶 ⊠ 🛏 🖵 🍽 ⤳ ⊠

▼▼◆ Ledge Rock at Whiteface Ⓜ
(518) 946-2379. **$79-$179, 10 day notice.** 5078 NYS Rt 86 12997. On SR 86, 3 mi w. Ext corridors. **Pets:** $25 one-time fee/pet, $5 daily fee/pet. Designated rooms, service with restrictions, crate.

📶 ⊠ 🛏 🖵 ⤳

◆◆ ▼▼▼ Willkommen Hof Bed & Breakfast ⅭⅭ ✿
(518) 946-7669. **$79-$259, 14 day notice.** 5367 SR 86 12997. On SR 86, 1.5 mi sw of jct CR 431. Int corridors. **Pets:** Large, other species. $10 daily fee/pet. Designated rooms, crate.

SAVE 📶 ⊠ 🛏 🖵 ⊠ 🗲

WOODBURY

◆◆ ▼▼▼ BEST WESTERN Woodbury Inn Ⓜ
(516) 921-6900. **$89-$189.** 7940 Jericho Tpke (SR 25) 11797. Jct SR 25 and 135, 0.9 mi e. Ext/int corridors. **Pets:** Accepted.

SAVE 📶 ⊠ 🛏 🖵 🍽 ⤳

◆◆ ▼▼▼ Executive Inn at Woodbury Ⓜ
(516) 921-8500. **$99-$209.** 8030 Jericho Tpke (SR 25) 11797. Jct SR 25 and 135, 1 mi e. Ext corridors. **Pets:** Accepted.

SAVE 📶 🛏 🖵 ⤳

NORTH CAROLINA

CITY INDEX

ABERDEEN

◆◆ ▼▼▼ Hampton Inn & Suites ⊞
(910) 693-4330. **$89-$119.** 200 Columbus Dr 28315. Jct US 1, just n on US 15/501, then just s. Int corridors. **Pets:** Service with restrictions, crate.

SAVE 📶 🛏 🖵 ⤳

▼ Motel 6-1234 Ⓜ
(910) 944-5633. **$45-$55.** 1408 Sandhills Blvd 28315. Jct US 15/501 N, just s on US 1. Ext corridors. **Pets:** Other species. Service with restrictions, supervision. 📶 🛏 🖵 ⤳

ALBEMARLE

▼▼ Quality Inn Ⓜ
(704) 983-6990. **Call for rates.** 735 NC 24/27 Bypass E 28001. Jct US 52 S, 1.4 mi e. Ext corridors. **Pets:** Medium. $25 daily fee/pet. Designated rooms, service with restrictions, supervision. 📶 🛏 🖵 ⤳

APEX

▼▼▼ Candlewood Suites-Apex/Raleigh ⊞
(919) 387-8595. **$79-$109.** 1005 Marco Dr 27502. US 1 exit 95, just w on SR 55. Int corridors. **Pets:** Medium, other species. $75 one-time fee/room. Service with restrictions, supervision. 📶 ♿ 🛏 🖵

ARCHDALE

◆◆ ▼▼▼ Comfort Inn Archdale-High Point ⊞
(336) 434-4797. **$65-$80.** 10123 N Main St 27263. I-85 exit 111, just n on US 311 business route, then just sw on Balfour Dr. Int corridors. **Pets:** Small. $25 one-time fee/pet. Service with restrictions, crate.

SAVE 📶 ♿ 🛏 🖵 ⤳

▼▼ Days Inn High Point/Archdale Ⓜ
(336) 434-5151. **$50-$200.** 10002 S Main St 27263. I-85 exit 111, just s on US 311 business route. Ext/int corridors. **Pets:** Accepted.

📶 🛏 ⤳

▼▼▼ Hampton Inn-High Point ⊞
(336) 434-5200. **$99-$129.** 10066 N Main St 27263. I-85 exit 111, just n on US 311 business route. Int corridors. **Pets:** Accepted.

📶 🛏 🖵 ⤳

▼▼▼ Holiday Inn Express Hotel & Suites ⊞
(336) 861-3310. **$95-$99.** 10050 N Main St 27263. I-85 exit 111, just n on US 311 business route. Int corridors. **Pets:** Medium, other species. $50 one-time fee/room. Designated rooms, service with restrictions.

📶 ♿ 🛏 🖵 ⤳

▼▼ Quality Inn-High Point **H**

(336) 861-3000. **Call for rates.** 1202 Liberty Rd 27263. I-85 exit 113A, just s on SR 62. Int corridors. **Pets:** $10 daily fee/room. Service with restrictions. 🛜 🅗 ▦ 🖵 🏊

ARDEN

▼▼ Quality Inn & Suites Biltmore South **H**

(828) 684-6688. **$70-$140.** 1 Skyland Inn Dr 28704. I-26 exit 37, just e. Int corridors. **Pets:** Other species. $25 one-time fee/room. Designated rooms, service with restrictions. 🛜 🅼 ▦ 🖵 🏊

ASHEBORO

𝄢 ▼▼▼ Comfort Inn **H**

(336) 626-4414. **$75-$89.** 825 W Dixie Dr 27205. Jct US 220, just e on US 64. Int corridors. **Pets:** Small. $15 daily fee/pet. Designated rooms, service with restrictions. **SAVE** 🛜 ▦ 🖵 🏊

▼▼▼ Holiday Inn Express Hotel & Suites **H**

(336) 636-5222. **Call for rates.** 1113 E Dixie Dr 27203. Jct SR 42, 0.5 mi w on US 64. Int corridors. **Pets:** Medium. $35 one-time fee/pet. Designated rooms, service with restrictions, crate.
🛜 ✕ 🅼 ▦ 🖵 🏊

𝄢 ▼▼▼ Quality Inn **H** 🐾

(336) 626-3680. **Call for rates.** 242 Lakecrest Rd 27203. US 64, just nw on SR 42. Ext corridors. **Pets:** Medium, other species. $15 daily fee/pet. Service with restrictions, crate. **SAVE** 🛜 ▦ 🖵 🏊

ASHEVILLE

𝄢 ▼▼▼ 1889 WhiteGate Inn & Cottage **BB** 🐾

(828) 253-2553. **$169-$379, 14 day notice.** 173 E Chestnut St 28801. I-240 exit 5B (Charlotte St), just n, then just w; in historic district. Ext/int corridors. **Pets:** Dogs only. $50 one-time fee/room. Designated rooms, service with restrictions, crate. **SAVE** 🛜 ▦ 🖵

𝄢 ▼▼▼ 1900 Inn on Montford **BB** 🐾

(828) 254-9569. **$145-$625, 14 day notice.** 296 Montford Ave 28801. I-240 exit 4C (Montford Ave/Haywood St), 0.7 mi n; in historic district. Ext/int corridors. **Pets:** Other species. Designated rooms, service with restrictions. **SAVE** 🛜 🖵 🅩

𝄢 ▼▼▼ Abbington Green Bed & Breakfast Inn **BB**

(828) 251-2454. **$150-$450, 30 day notice.** 46 Cumberland Cir 28801. I-240 exit 4C (Montford Ave/Haywood St), just n on Montford Ave, just e on W Chestnut St, just n on Cumberland Ave, then just ne; in historic district. Ext/int corridors. **Pets:** Accepted. **SAVE** 🛜 ✕ ▦ 🖵 🅩

𝄢 ▼▼▼ Applewood Manor Inn Bed & Breakfast **BB**

(828) 254-2244. **$160-$250, 7 day notice.** 62 Cumberland Cir 28801. I-240 exit 4C (Montford Ave/Haywood St), just n on Montford Ave, just e on W Chestnut St, just n on Cumberland Ave, then just ne; in historic district. Ext/int corridors. **Pets:** Dogs only. $10 daily fee/pet. Designated rooms, crate. **SAVE** 🛜 ✕ ▦ 🖵 🅩

𝄢 ▼▼ BEST WESTERN of Asheville Biltmore East **M** 🐾

(828) 298-5562. **$59-$299.** 501 Tunnel Rd 28805. I-240 exit 7, 0.5 mi e on US 70 (Tunnel Rd). Ext corridors. **Pets:** Medium, dogs only. $10 daily fee/pet. No service, supervision. **SAVE** 🛜 ▦ 🖵 🏊

𝄢 ▼▼▼ Biltmore Village Inn **BB**

(828) 274-8707. **$199-$335, 21 day notice.** 119 Dodge St 28803. I-40 exit 50/50B (US 25 N), 0.5 mi n, just e on Lula St, just n on Reed St, just e on Warren Ave, then just s. Ext/int corridors. **Pets:** Accepted.
SAVE 🛜 ✕ ▦ 🖵

𝄢 ▼▼▼ Cedar Crest Inn **BB** 🐾

(828) 252-1389. **$129-$300, 30 day notice.** 674 Biltmore Ave 28803. I-40 exit 50, 1.1 mi n. Ext/int corridors. **Pets:** Other species. $50 fee/room. Designated rooms, no service. **SAVE** 🛜 ✕ 🅼 ▦ 🖵

▼▼ Comfort Inn-West **H**

(828) 665-6500. **$59-$169.** 15 Crowell St 28806. I-40 exit 44, just n on US 19 and 23, just w on Old Haywood Rd, then just s. Int corridors. **Pets:** Medium. $15 daily fee/pet. Service with restrictions, supervision.
🛜 🅼 ▦ 🖵

𝄢 ▼▼▼ Comfort Suites Biltmore **H** 🐾

(828) 665-4000. **$60-$100.** 890 Brevard Rd 28806. I-26 exit 33, 0.3 mi w. Int corridors. **Pets:** Other species. $25 daily fee/room. Designated rooms, service with restrictions, crate.
SAVE 🛜 ✕ 🅼 ▦ 🖵 🏊

𝄢 ▼▼▼ Crowne Plaza Tennis & Golf Resort **H** 🐾

(828) 254-3211. **$90-$300.** 1 Resort Dr 28806. I-240 exit 3B (Resort Dr), just w. Int corridors. **Pets:** Medium. $25 daily fee/room. Designated rooms, service with restrictions, supervision.
SAVE 🛜 ✕ 🅼 ▦ 🖵 🍴 🏊 ✕

𝄢 ▼▼▼ Days Inn-Asheville Mall **M**

(828) 252-4000. **$59-$159.** 201 Tunnel Rd 28805. I-240 exit 6, 0.5 mi e, on south side of road. Ext corridors. **Pets:** Large. $20 one-time fee/pet, $10 daily fee/pet. Designated rooms, service with restrictions.
SAVE 🛜 ▦ 🖵 🏊

𝄢 ▼▼▼ Days Inn-Biltmore East **H** 🐾

(828) 298-4000. **$65-$150.** 1435 Tunnel Rd 28805. I-40 exit 55, just n. Int corridors. **Pets:** Small, dogs only. $10 daily fee/pet. Service with restrictions, crate. **SAVE** 🛜 🅼 ▦ 🖵 🏊

▼▼ Extended StayAmerica Asheville-Tunnel Rd **H**

(828) 253-3483. **Call for rates.** 6 Kenilworth Knoll 28805. I-240 exit 6, 0.7 mi e on US 70 (Tunnel Rd), then just n. Int corridors. **Pets:** $25 daily fee/pet. Designated rooms, service with restrictions. 🛜 🅼 ▦ 🖵

𝄢 ▼▼▼ Four Points by Sheraton Asheville Downtown **H** 🐾

(828) 253-1851. **$89-$309.** 22 Woodfin St 28801. I-240 exit 5A (Merrimon Ave), just s, then just w. Int corridors. **Pets:** $50 one-time fee/room. Designated rooms, service with restrictions.
SAVE 🛜 ✕ 🅼 ▦ 🖵 🍴 🏊

𝄢 ▼▼▼ Grand Bohemian Hotel Asheville, Autograph Collection **H** 🐾

(828) 505-2949. **$169-$499, 3 day notice.** 11 Boston Way 28803. I-40 exit 50/50B, 0.8 mi n on US 25, follow signs for Biltmore Estate Historic Biltmore Village. Int corridors. **Pets:** Dogs only. $100 one-time fee/room. Designated rooms, service with restrictions, supervision.
SAVE 🛜 ✕ 🅼 ▦ 🖵 🍴

𝄢 ▼▼ ▼▼ The Grove Park Inn **H**

(828) 252-2711. **$179-$300, 3 day notice.** 290 Macon Ave 28804. I-240 exit 5B (Charlotte St), 2 mi n on Macon Ave via Charlotte St, follow signs. Int corridors. **Pets:** Accepted. **SAVE** 🛜 🅼 ▦ 🖵 🍴 🏊 ✕

𝄢 ▼▼◆ ▼▼◆ Haywood Park Hotel & Promenade **H** 🐾

(828) 252-2522. **$159-$479, 3 day notice.** One Battery Park Ave 28801. I-240 exit 4C (Montford Ave/Haywood St), just s, 0.6 mi se on Haywood St, then just w. Int corridors. **Pets:** Medium, dogs only. $50 one-time fee/pet. Designated rooms, service with restrictions.
SAVE 🛜 ✕ ▦ 🖵

𝄢 ▼▼◆ ▼▼◆ Hilton Asheville Biltmore Park **H** 🐾

(828) 209-2700. **$139-$269.** 43 Town Square Blvd 28803. I-26 exit 37, just e (Long Shoals Rd), then w; in Biltmore Town Square. Int corridors. **Pets:** Large. $50 one-time fee/room. Designated rooms, service with restrictions. 🌿 🅴 **SAVE** 🛜 🅼 ▦ 🖵 🍴 🏊 ✕

▼▼▼ Holiday Inn-Biltmore East at the Blue Ridge Parkway **H** 🐾

(828) 298-5611. **$79-$199.** 1450 Tunnel Rd 28805. I-40 exit 55, just n. Int corridors. **Pets:** Other species. $25 daily fee/room. Designated rooms, service with restrictions. 🛜 🅼 ▦ 🖵 🍴 🏊

▼▼▼▼ Hotel Indigo 🄷 🐾
(828) 239-0239. **$149-$369.** 151 Haywood St 28801. I-240 exit 4C (Montford Ave/Haywood St), just s, then just w. Int corridors. **Pets:** Large. $50 one-time fee/room. Designated rooms, service with restrictions, supervision. 🛜 ✕ ㋔Ⓜ 🛗 🖵 🍴

▲▲▲▷ ▼▼▼ Ramada 🄷
(828) 298-9141. **$75-$124, 3 day notice.** 800 Fairview Rd 28803. I-240 exit 8; jct I-40 and US 74. Int corridors. **Pets:** Medium. $15 deposit/pet. Designated rooms, service with restrictions, supervision.
(SAVE) 🛜 🛗 🖵 ⤳ ✕

▲▲▲▷ ▼▼▼ Red Roof Inn-West 🄼
(828) 667-9803. **$47-$159.** 16 Crowell Rd 28806. I-40 exit 44, just n on US 19 and 23, just w on Old Haywood Rd, then just s. Ext corridors. **Pets:** Large, other species. Service with restrictions, supervision.
(SAVE) 🛜 ㋔Ⓜ 🛗

▲▲▲▷ ▼▼▼▼ Renaissance Asheville Hotel 🄷
(828) 252-8211. **$107-$233.** 31 Woodfin St 28801. I-240 exit 5A (Merrimon Ave). Int corridors. **Pets:** Medium, dogs only. $75 one-time fee/pet. Designated rooms, service with restrictions.
(SAVE) 🛜 ✕ ㋔Ⓜ 🛗 🖵 🍴 ⤳

▼▼ ▼▼ Rodeway Inn & Suites Biltmore Square 🄷
(828) 670-8800. **$49-$179.** 9 Wedgefield Dr 28806. I-26 exit 33, just nw. Int corridors. **Pets:** Medium, other species. $15 daily fee/pet.
🛜 ㋔Ⓜ 🛗 🖵

▼▼ Rodeway Inn Asheville 🄼
(828) 667-8706. **$49-$149.** 8 Crowell Rd 28806. I-40 exit 44, just n on US 19 and 23. Int corridors. **Pets:** Accepted. 🛜 🛗 🖵

▼▼ ▼▼ Sleep Inn Biltmore 🄷 🐾
(828) 277-1800. **$69-$169.** 117 Hendersonville Rd 28803. I-40 exit 50 eastbound; exit 50B westbound, just n on US 25. Int corridors. **Pets:** Other species. $75 one-time fee/room. Designated rooms, service with restrictions, crate. 🛜 ㋔Ⓜ 🛗 🖵

BANNER ELK

▼▼▼▼ The Banner Elk Inn B&B and Cottages 🄱🄱
(828) 898-6223. **$95-$250, 30 day notice.** 407 Main St E 28604. Jct SR 184 and 194, just n on SR 194; center. Int corridors. **Pets:** Dogs only. Designated rooms, service with restrictions, crate. 🛜 ✕ 🛗 🖵

▲▲▲▷ ▼▼▼▼ BEST WESTERN PLUS Mountain Lodge at Banner Elk 🄷
(828) 898-4571. **$70-$170.** 1615 Tynecastle Hwy 28604. Jct SR 194, 1.3 mi s on SR 184. Ext corridors. **Pets:** Other species. $10 daily fee/room. Designated rooms, service with restrictions.
(SAVE) 🛜 ✕ ㋔Ⓜ 🛗 🖵 🍴 ⤳

▲▲▲▷ ▼▼▼▼ Lodges At Eagle's Nest by Ashemore Luxury Rentals 🅅🄷 🐾
(828) 963-7310. **$425-$1075.** 3054 Eagle's Nest Tr 28604. 3.7 mi w on SR 194. Int corridors. **Pets:** Dogs only. $100 one-time fee/pet. Crate.
(SAVE) 🛜 ✕ 🛗 🖵 ✕

BLACK MOUNTAIN

▲▲▲▷ ▼▼▼ Comfort Inn 🄼
(828) 669-9950. **$70-$150.** 585 NC Hwy 9 28711. I-40 exit 64, just s. Ext corridors. **Pets:** $20 daily fee/pet. Designated rooms, service with restrictions, crate. (SAVE) 🛜 ㋔Ⓜ 🛗 🖵 ⤳

BLOWING ROCK

▼▼ ▼▼ Alpine Village Inn 🄼 🐾
(828) 295-7206. **$70-$190, 7 day notice.** 297 Sunset Dr 28605. Jct US 321, just w. Ext corridors. **Pets:** Dogs only. $75 one-time fee/room. Service with restrictions, supervision. 🛜 ✕ 🛗 🖵

▲▲▲▷ ▼▼ Hillwinds Inn 🄼
(828) 295-7660. **$69-$299, 3 day notice.** 315 Sunset Dr 28605. Jct US 321, just w. Ext/int corridors. **Pets:** Other species. $25 daily fee/pet. Designated rooms, service with restrictions. (SAVE) 🛜 ✕ 🛗 🖵

▼▼ ▼▼ Homestead Inn 🄼 🐾
(828) 295-9559. **$49-$99, 4 day notice.** 153 Morris St 28605. Jct US 321 business route (Main St), just e. Ext corridors. **Pets:** Other species. $10 daily fee/pet. Designated rooms, service with restrictions.
🛜 ✕ ㋔Ⓜ 🛗 🖵

▼▼▼▼ The Village Inn 🄼
(828) 295-3380. **Call for rates.** 7876 Valley Blvd 28605. Jct Sunset Dr, just s on US 321. Ext corridors. **Pets:** Accepted.
🛜 ✕ ㋔Ⓜ 🛗 🖵

BOONE

▼▼▼▼ La Quinta Inn & Suites Boone 🄷
(828) 262-1234. **$72-$288.** 165 Hwy 105 N Ext 28607. US 421, just s on SR 105. Int corridors. **Pets:** Service with restrictions, supervision.
🛜 ✕ ㋔Ⓜ 🛗 🖵 ⤳

BREVARD

▼▼▼ Hampton Inn-Brevard 🄷
(828) 883-4800. **$79-$159.** 275 Forest Gate Dr 28768. Jct US 64, just e on SR 280, then just n. Int corridors. **Pets:** Accepted.
🛜 ㋔Ⓜ 🛗 🖵 ⤳

▲▲▲▷ ▼▼▼▼ Holiday Inn Express 🄷
(828) 862-8900. **Call for rates.** 2228 Asheville Hwy 28712. Jct SR 280, just w on US 64. Int corridors. **Pets:** Other species. $25 daily fee/room. Designated rooms, service with restrictions, crate.
(SAVE) 🛜 ✕ ㋔Ⓜ 🛗 🖵 ⤳

▲▲▲▷ ▼▼▼ The Inn at Brevard 🄱🄱 🐾
(828) 884-2105. **$115-$235, 14 day notice.** 315 E Main St 28712. Jct US 64 (Broad St), just e; center. Ext/int corridors. **Pets:** Dogs only. $25 deposit/pet. Designated rooms. (SAVE) 🛜 ✕ 🖵 ⊘

BRYSON CITY

▼▼ ▼▼ Settlers Mountain 🅅🄷
(828) 488-8622. **$90-$250, 30 day notice.** 340 E Alarka Rd 28713. US 74 exit 64, 1.5 mi s on Alarka Rd, then 0.4 mi e. Ext corridors. **Pets:** Dogs only. $50 one-time fee/room. Crate. 🛜 ✕ 🛗 🖵

BURLINGTON

▲▲▲▷ ▼▼▼ Quality Inn 🄷 🐾
(336) 229-5203. **Call for rates.** 2444 Maple Ave 27215. I-40/85 exit 145, just n on SR 49. Int corridors. **Pets:** Other species. $25 one-time fee/pet. Designated rooms. (SAVE) 🛜 ㋔Ⓜ 🛗 🖵 ⤳

CANDLER

▲▲▲▷ ▼▼▼ Days Inn Asheville West #6116 🄼
(828) 667-9321. **$45-$110.** 2551 Smokey Park Hwy 28715. I-40 exit 37, just s, then w. Ext corridors. **Pets:** $10 daily fee/room. Designated rooms, service with restrictions, supervision. (SAVE) 🛜 🛗 🖵 ⤳

CANTON

▼▼ ▼▼ Comfort Inn 🄷
(828) 648-4881. **Call for rates.** 737 Champion Dr 28716. I-40 exit 31, just s. Int corridors. **Pets:** Accepted. 🛜 🛗 🖵 ⤳

▼▼ ▼▼ Days Inn 🄼
(828) 648-0300. **$75-$119.** 1963 Champion Dr 28716. I-40 exit 31, just n. Ext corridors. **Pets:** Accepted. 🛜 🛗 🖵 ⤳

CARY

BEST WESTERN PLUS Cary-NC State 🅷
(919) 481-1200. **$74-$95.** 1722 Walnut St 27511. I-40 exit 293A, just s on US 1 exit 101A, then just e. Ext/int corridors. **Pets:** Accepted.
[SAVE] 📶 🛏 💻 🏊

Comfort Suites Hotel 🅷
(919) 852-4318. **$99-$124.** 350 Ashville Ave 27518. US 1 exit 98A, 0.8 mi e on Tryon Rd, then just n. Int corridors. **Pets:** Medium, other species. $50 one-time fee/pet. Designated rooms, service with restrictions, supervision. 📶 ✖ 🅼 🛏 💻 🏊 ✖

Extended StayAmerica Cary-Regency Parkway North 🅷
(919) 468-5828. **$58-$83.** 1500 Regency Pkwy 27518. US 1 exit 98A, 0.5 mi e on Tryon Rd, then just s. Int corridors. **Pets:** $25 daily fee/pet. Designated rooms, service with restrictions. 📶 🛏 💻

Extended StayAmerica Cary-Regency Parkway South 🅷
(919) 460-1161. **$65-$90.** 3100 Regency Pkwy 27511. US 1 exit 98A, 0.5 mi e on Tryon Rd, then just s. Int corridors. **Pets:** $25 daily fee/pet. Designated rooms, service with restrictions. 📶 🛏 💻

Hampton Inn & Suites 🅷
(919) 233-1798. **$79-$139.** 111 Hampton Woods Ln 27607. I-40 exit 290, just w on SR 54, then just s. Int corridors. **Pets:** Accepted.
📶 ✖ 🅼 🛏 💻 🏊

Hawthorn Suites by Wyndham Raleigh 🅷
(919) 468-4222. **$79-$120.** 1020 Buck Jones Rd 27606. I-40 exit 293A, just s on US 1 exit 101B, 0.5 mi nw; in Buck Jones Village. Int corridors. **Pets:** Other species. $15 daily fee/room. Service with restrictions.
📶 🛏 💻

La Quinta Inn & Suites Raleigh (Cary) 🅷
(919) 851-2850. **$66-$151.** 191 Crescent Commons Dr 27511. US 1 exit 98A, 0.5 mi e on Tryon Rd, then just n. Int corridors. **Pets:** Service with restrictions, supervision. 📶 🅼 🛏 💻 🏊

Residence Inn by Marriott Raleigh Cary 🅷
(919) 467-4080. **$85-$139.** 2900 Regency Pkwy 27518. US 1 exit 98A, 0.5 mi e on Tryon Rd, then just s. Int corridors. **Pets:** $100 one-time fee/room. Service with restrictions, crate.
[ECO] 📶 ✖ 🅼 🛏 💻 🏊 ✖

StudioPLUS-Raleigh-Cary-Harrison Ave 🅷
(919) 677-9910. **$70-$95.** 600 Weston Pkwy 27513. I-40 exit 287, 0.5 mi s on Harrison Ave, then just w. Int corridors. **Pets:** $25 daily fee/pet. Designated rooms, service with restrictions. 📶 🛏 💻 🏊

TownePlace Suites by Marriott-Raleigh/Cary/ Weston Parkway 🅷
(919) 678-0005. **$79-$139.** 120 Sage Commons Way 27513. I-40 exit 287, 0.5 mi s on Harrison Ave, 2.3 w on Weston Pkwy, then just n. Int corridors. **Pets:** Medium. $100 one-time fee/room. No service, supervision. [SAVE] 📶 ✖ 🅼 🛏 💻 🏊

The Umstead Hotel & Spa 🅷 🐾
(919) 447-4000. **$239-$619.** 100 Woodland Pond Dr 27513. I-40 exit 287, just s on Harrison Ave, just e on SAS Campus Dr, then just n. Int corridors. **Pets:** Dogs only. $200 one-time fee/room. Service with restrictions, crate. ▣ [SAVE] 📶 ✖ 🅼 💻 🍴 🏊 ✖

CASHIERS

High Hampton Inn & Country Club 🅷 🐾
(828) 743-2411. **$271-$380, 21 day notice.** 1525 Hwy 107 S 28717. Jct US 64, 1.5 mi s. Ext/int corridors. **Pets:** Large. $50 one-time fee/pet. Designated rooms, service with restrictions.
[SAVE] 📶 ✖ 🛏 💻 🍴 ✖ 🎾 🎾 🎿

CHAPEL HILL

Aloft - Chapel Hill 🅷 🐾
(919) 932-7772. **$99-$279.** 1001 S Hamilton Rd 27517. I-40 exit 273/ 273A, 2.6 mi w on SR 54, then just s. Int corridors. **Pets:** Medium, dogs only. Designated rooms, service with restrictions, supervision.
[SAVE] 📶 ✖ 🅼 🛏 💻 🏊

Chapel Hill University Inn Ⓜ
(919) 929-2171. **$75-$115.** 1301 N Fordham Blvd 27514. I-40 exit 270, 2 mi s on US 15/501. Ext corridors. **Pets:** Accepted.
[SAVE] 📶 🛏 💻 🍴 🏊

Residence Inn by Marriott-Chapel Hill 🅷
(919) 933-4848. **$139-$199.** 101 Erwin Rd 27514. I-40 exit 270, 1.2 mi s on US 15/501, then just w. Int corridors. **Pets:** Medium. $100 one-time fee/room. Designated rooms, service with restrictions.
[SAVE] 📶 ✖ 🅼 🛏 💻 🏊 ✖

Sheraton Chapel Hill 🅷
(919) 968-4900. **$99-$350.** 1 Europa Dr 27517. I-40 exit 270, 1 mi s, then just e. Int corridors. **Pets:** Accepted.
[SAVE] 📶 ✖ 🛏 💻 🍴 🏊

The Siena Hotel 🅷
(919) 929-4000. **$119-$350.** 1505 E Franklin St 27514. I-40 exit 270, 2 mi s on US 15/501, then 0.5 mi w. Int corridors. **Pets:** Medium, dogs only. $75 one-time fee/room. Designated rooms, service with restrictions.
[SAVE] 📶 ✖ 🅼 🛏 💻 🍴

CHARLOTTE METROPOLITAN AREA

CHARLOTTE

Aloft Charlotte-Ballantyne 🅷 🐾
(704) 247-2222. **$99-$299.** 13139 Ballantyne Corporate Pl 28277. I-485 exit 61 or 61B, 0.5 mi s on US 521 (Johnston Rd), just e on Ballantyne Commons Pkwy, then just n. Int corridors. **Pets:** Other species. $100 one-time fee/room. Designated rooms, service with restrictions, supervision. [ECO] [SAVE] 📶 ✖ 🅼 🛏 💻 🏊

Aloft Charlotte Uptown @ the EpiCentre 🅷 🐾
(704) 333-1999. **$109-$699.** 210 E Trade St 28202. I-77 exit 10 or 10B, 0.9 mi e, then just n; jct College St. Int corridors. **Pets:** Medium, dogs only. Designated rooms, service with restrictions, supervision.
[SAVE] 📶 ✖ 🅼 🛏 💻 🏊

Candlewood Suites-Charlotte University 🅷
(704) 598-9863. **$60-$130.** 8812 University East Dr 28213. I-85 exit 45A (W. T. Harris Blvd), 2.5 mi e on SR 24, then just s; in University East Business Park. Int corridors. **Pets:** Other species. $75 one-time fee/room. Service with restrictions, crate. 📶 ✖ 🛏 💻

Comfort Suites-Airport 🅷
(704) 971-4400. **$79-$139.** 3425 Mulberry Church Rd 28208. I-85 exit 33, just e, then just n. Int corridors. **Pets:** Other species. $25 one-time fee/room. Service with restrictions, crate.
[SAVE] 📶 ✖ 🅼 🛏 💻 🏊

Comfort Suites-University 🅷
(704) 547-0049. **$95-$149.** 7735 University City Blvd 28213. I-85 exit 45A (W. T. Harris Blvd), 2 mi e on SR 24, then 0.5 mi s on SR 49. Int corridors. **Pets:** $25 one-time fee/pet. Designated rooms, service with restrictions, supervision. 📶 ✖ 🅼 🛏 💻 🏊

Country Inn & Suites By Carlson-Charlotte University 🅷
(704) 549-8770. **Call for rates.** 131 E McCullough Dr 28262. I-85 exit 45A (W. T. Harris Blvd), 0.5 mi e on SR 24, 0.4 mi s on US 29 (N Tryon St), then just e. Int corridors. **Pets:** Accepted.
📶 ✖ 🅼 🛏 💻 🏊

DoubleTree Suites by Hilton Hotel Charlotte-SouthPark ❖
(704) 364-2400. **$99-$219.** 6300 Morrison Blvd 28211. I-77 exit 5 (Tyvola Rd), 3.3 mi e on Tyvola/Fairview rds, just n on Barclay Downs, then just e. Int corridors. **Pets:** Large, other species. $50 daily fee/room. Service with restrictions, crate. [SAVE] 🛰 🛠 🍴 ☕ 🐾

Drury Inn & Suites-Charlotte North
(704) 593-0700. **$99-$204.** 415 W W. T. Harris Blvd 28262. I-85 exit 45A (W. T. Harris Blvd), just e on SR 24. Int corridors. **Pets:** Service with restrictions, supervision. 🛰 🛠 🍴 ☕ 🏊

Drury Inn & Suites-Charlotte Northlake
(704) 599-8882. **$94-$204.** 6920 Northlake Mall Dr 28216. I-77 exit 18 (W. T. Harris Blvd), just w on SR 24. Int corridors. **Pets:** Service with restrictions, supervision. 🛰 🛠 🍴 ☕ 🏊

Extended StayAmerica-Charlotte/Airport
(704) 676-0083. **$65-$90.** 710 Yorkmont Rd 28217. I-77 exit 6B northbound, just w, just s on S Tryon St, then just w; exit southbound, just s on S Tryon St, then just w. Ext corridors. **Pets:** $25 daily fee/pet. Designated rooms, service with restrictions. 🛰 🍴 ☕

Extended StayAmerica-Charlotte-Pineville-Park Rd
(704) 341-0929. **$75-$100.** 10930 Park Rd 28226. I-485 exit 64A, just n on SR 51, then just e; behind Terraces at Park Place Shopping Center. Int corridors. **Pets:** $25 daily fee/pet. Designated rooms, service with restrictions. 🛰 🛠 🍴 ☕

Extended StayAmerica-Charlotte-Pineville-Pineville Matthews Rd
(704) 542-9521. **$95-$120.** 8405 Pineville-Matthews Rd 28226. I-485 exit 64A, 0.7 mi n on SR 51. Int corridors. **Pets:** $25 daily fee/pet. Designated rooms, service with restrictions. 🛰 🍴 ☕ 🏊

Extended StayAmerica-Charlotte-Tyvola Rd-Executive Park
(704) 527-1960. **$63-$88.** 5830 Westpark Dr 28217. I-77 exit 5 (Tyvola Rd), just e, then 0.4 mi s. Int corridors. **Pets:** $25 daily fee/pet. Designated rooms, service with restrictions. 🛰 🍴 ☕ 🏊

Extended StayAmerica-Charlotte-University Place
(704) 510-1636. **$65-$90.** 8211 University Executive Park Dr 28262. I-85 exit 45A (W. T. Harris Blvd), 0.5 mi e on SR 24, then 0.5 mi s on US 29 (N Tryon St). Int corridors. **Pets:** $25 daily fee/pet. Designated rooms, service with restrictions. 🛰 🍴 ☕

Hawthorn Suites by Wyndham Charlotte-Coliseum
(704) 529-7500. **$69-$199.** 5840 Westpark Dr 28217. I-77 exit 5 (Tyvola Rd), just e, then 0.5 mi s. Int corridors. **Pets:** Accepted. 🛰 🛠 🍴 ☕

Holiday Inn Airport
(704) 394-4301. **Call for rates.** 2707 Little Rock Rd 28214. I-85 exit 32, just e. Int corridors. **Pets:** Accepted. 🛰 🍴 ☕ 🍴 🏊

Holiday Inn at University Executive Park
(704) 547-0999. **Call for rates.** 8520 University Executive Park Dr 28262. I-85 exit 45A (W. T. Harris Blvd), just e on SR 24, then just s. Int corridors. **Pets:** Accepted. 🛰 🛠 🍴 ☕ 🍴 🏊

Homewood Suites by Hilton Airport
(704) 357-0500. **$99-$199.** 2770 Yorkmont Rd 28208. I-77 exit 6B, 2 mi nw on Billy Graham Pkwy exit Coliseum/Tyvola Rd, just se on Tyvola Rd, then just w. Int corridors. **Pets:** Accepted. 🛰 🛠 🍴 ☕ 🏊

Homewood Suites by Hilton-University Research Park
(704) 549-8800. **$99-$199.** 8340 N Tryon St 28262. I-85 exit 45A (W. T. Harris Blvd), 0.5 mi e on SR 24, then just s on US 29. Ext/int corridors. **Pets:** Accepted. 🛰 🛠 🍴 ☕ 🏊 🐾

Hyatt house Charlotte Airport
(704) 525-2600. **$89-$239.** 4920 S Tryon St 28217. I-77 exit 6B northbound, just w, then just s; exit southbound, just s. Int corridors. **Pets:** Medium. $150 one-time fee/room. Designated rooms, service with restrictions, crate. [SAVE] 🛰 🐾 🛠 🍴 ☕ 🐾

La Quinta Inn & Suites Charlotte Airport North
(704) 392-1600. **$63-$133.** 3127 Sloan Dr 28208. I-85 exit 33, just w, then just s. Int corridors. **Pets:** Service with restrictions, supervision. 🛰 🛠 🍴 ☕

La Quinta Inn & Suites Charlotte Airport South
(704) 523-5599. **$71-$144.** 4900 S Tryon St 28217. I-77 exit 6B northbound, just w, then just s; exit southbound, just s. Int corridors. **Pets:** Service with restrictions, supervision. 🛰 🛠 🍴 ☕ 🏊

MainStay Suites
(704) 521-3232. **$70-$120.** 7926 Forest Pine Dr 28273. I-77 exit 3 southbound; exit 2 northbound, just e, then just s. Int corridors. **Pets:** Accepted. 🛰 🐾 🍴 ☕ 🏊

Microtel Inn & Suites by Wyndham Charlotte/Northlake
(704) 227-3377. **$59-$140.** 6309 Banner Elk Dr 28216. I-77 exit 16B, just w on Sunset Rd, then just s. Int corridors. **Pets:** Small. $20 one-time fee/pet. Service with restrictions, supervision. [SAVE] 🛰 🐾 🍴 ☕ 🏊

Morehead Inn 🄱🄱
(704) 376-3357. **$144-$199.** 1122 E Morehead St 28204. I-277 exit Kenilworth Ave, 0.9 mi s, then just w; corner of Berkeley Ave. Ext/int corridors. **Pets:** Accepted. 🛰 🐾 ☕

Omni Charlotte Hotel
(704) 377-0400. **$129-$425.** 132 E Trade St 28202. I-77 exit 10 or 10B, 0.8 mi e; jct Tryon St. Int corridors. **Pets:** Accepted.
[SAVE] 🛰 🐾 🍴 ☕ 🍴 🏊 🐾

Quality Inn & Suites Airport
(704) 393-5306. **$59-$69.** 3100 Queen City Dr 28208. I-85 exit 33, just w, then just n. Ext/int corridors. **Pets:** Large, other species. $20 one-time fee/pet. Service with restrictions, supervision. 🛰 🛠 🍴 ☕ 🏊

Quality Inn-Executive Park
(704) 525-0747. **$70-$190.** 440 Griffith Rd 28217. I-77 exit 5 (Tyvola Rd), just e, just s on Westpark Dr, then just e. Int corridors. **Pets:** Other species. $35 one-time fee/room. Designated rooms, service with restrictions. [SAVE] 🛰 🍴 ☕ 🏊

Renaissance Charlotte Uptown Hotel
(704) 372-7550. **$129-$209.** 201 S McDowell St 28204. I-277 exit 2A, just w on 4th St, then just s. Int corridors. **Pets:** Accepted. [SAVE] 🛰 🐾 🍴 ☕ 🍴 🏊

Residence Inn by Marriott Charlotte South at I-77/Tyvola Rd
(704) 527-8110. **$79-$149.** 5816 Westpark Dr 28217. I-77 exit 5 (Tyvola Rd), just e, then 0.4 mi s. Ext/int corridors. **Pets:** Accepted. 🛰 🐾 🛠 🍴 ☕ 🏊 🐾

Residence Inn by Marriott Charlotte SouthPark
(704) 554-7001. **$169-$185.** 6030 Piedmont Row Dr S 28210. I-77 exit 5 (Tyvola Rd), 3.2 mi e on Tyvola/Fairview rds, then just s. Int corridors. **Pets:** Accepted. 🛰 🐾 🛠 🍴 ☕ 🏊 🐾

Residence Inn by Marriott-Charlotte University Research Park
(704) 547-1122. **$125-$135.** 8503 N Tryon St 28262. I-85 exit 45A (W. T. Harris Blvd), 0.5 mi e on SR 24, then just s on US 29 (N Tryon St). Ext corridors. **Pets:** Accepted. 🛰 🐾 🛠 🍴 ☕ 🏊 🐾

AAA ▼▼▼▼ Residence Inn by Marriott-Charlotte Uptown H ❀

(704) 340-4000. **$109-$229.** 404 S Mint St 28202. I-77 exit 10 or 10B, 0.6 mi e on Trade St, then just s. Int corridors. **Pets:** Large, other species. $100 one-time fee/room. Designated rooms, service with restrictions.

ECO **SAVE** 🛜 ⊠ 🔥 🔒 💻 🍴

▼▼▼▼ Residence Inn by Marriott-Piper Glen H

(704) 319-3900. **$109-$189.** 5115 Piper Station Dr 28277. I-485 exit 59, just s on Rea Rd, then just e. Int corridors. **Pets:** Accepted.

🛜 ⊠ 🔥 🔒 💻 🌊 ⊠

AAA ▼▼▼ Sheraton Charlotte Airport Hotel H

(704) 392-1200. **$99-$269.** 3315 Scott Futrell Dr 28208. I-85 exit 33, just e, then just s. Int corridors. **Pets:** Accepted.

SAVE 🛜 ⊠ 🔒 💻 🍴 🌊

AAA ▼▼▼ Sleep Inn H ❀

(704) 549-4544. **$69-$89.** 8525 N Tryon St 28262. I-85 exit 45A (W. T. Harris Blvd), 0.5 mi e on SR 24, just s on US 29 (N Tryon St). Int corridors. **Pets:** Medium, other species. $25 one-time fee/room. Designated rooms, service with restrictions, crate. **SAVE** 🛜 🔥 🔒 💻 🌊

▼▼▼ Sleep Inn-Billy Graham Parkway H

(704) 525-5005. **$70-$150.** 701 Yorkmont Rd 28217. I-77 exit 6B northbound, just w, just s on S Tryon St; exit southbound, just s on S Tryon St, then just w. Int corridors. **Pets:** Small. $20 daily fee/pet. Designated rooms, service with restrictions, crate.

🛜 🔥 🔒 💻 🌊

AAA ▼▼▼ Sleep Inn Northlake H

(704) 399-7778. **$60-$130.** 6300 Banner Elk Dr 28216. I-77 exit 16B, just w on Sunset Rd, then just s. Int corridors. **Pets:** Small. $15 one-time fee/pet. Designated rooms, service with restrictions, supervision.

SAVE 🛜 ⊠ 🔒 💻 🌊

AAA ▼▼▼▼ Sonesta ES Suites Charlotte H ❀

(704) 527-6767. **Call for rates.** 7925 Forest Pine Dr 28273. I-77 exit 3 southbound; exit 2 northbound, just e, then just s. Int corridors. **Pets:** Medium, other species. $100 one-time fee/room. Service with restrictions, crate. **SAVE** 🛜 🔥 🔒 💻 🌊

▼▼▼▼ Staybridge Suites Charlotte-Ballantyne H

(704) 248-5000. **Call for rates.** 15735 John J Delaney Dr 28277. I-485 exit 61 or 61B, just s, then just w. Int corridors. **Pets:** Accepted.

🛜 ⊠ 🔥 🔒 💻 🌊 ⊠

▼▼▼▼ TownePlace Suites by Marriott Charlotte Arrowood H

(704) 227-2000. **$79-$199.** 7805 Forest Point Blvd 28217. I-77 exit 3 southbound; exit 2 northbound, just e. Int corridors. **Pets:** $75 one-time fee/room. Designated rooms, service with restrictions, supervision.

🛜 ⊠ 🔥 🔒 💻 🌊

AAA ▼▼▼ TownePlace Suites by Marriott-University H

(704) 548-0388. **$89-$139.** 8710 Research Dr 28262. I-85 exit 45B (W. T. Harris Blvd), just w on SR 24, then just n. Int corridors. **Pets:** Accepted. **SAVE** 🛜 ⊠ 🔥 🔒 💻 🌊

AAA ▼▼▼▼ The Westin Charlotte H

(704) 375-2600. **$199-$529.** 601 S College St 28202. I-277 exit College St, just n; jct E Stonewall St. Int corridors. **Pets:** Accepted.

SAVE 🛜 ⊠ 🔥 🔒 💻 🍴 🌊 ⊠

CONCORD

▼ Americas Best Value Inn M

(704) 788-8550. **$53-$145.** 2451 Kannapolis Hwy 28025. I-85 exit 58, just s on US 29, then just w. Ext corridors. **Pets:** Small, dogs only. $20 one-time fee/room. Designated rooms, service with restrictions, supervision. 🛜 🔒 💻

AAA ▼▼▼▼ Comfort Suites-Concord Mills H

(704) 979-3800. **$90-$250.** 7800 Gateway Ln NW 28027. I-85 exit 49, just e, just n on Weddington Rd, then just w. Int corridors. **Pets:** Accepted. **SAVE** 🛜 ⊠ 🔥 🔒 💻 🌊

▼▼▼▼ Embassy Suites Charlotte-Concord Golf Resort & Spa H ❀

(704) 455-8200. **$109-$299.** 5400 John Q Hammons Dr 28027. I-85 exit 49, just e, then just n. Int corridors. **Pets:** Medium, dogs only. $65 one-time fee/room. Supervision. 🛜 🔥 🔒 💻 🍴 🌊 ⊠

▼▼▼▼ Hampton Inn H

(704) 793-9700. **$89-$139.** 612 Dickens Pl NE 28025. I-85 exit 60, just e, then just s. Int corridors. **Pets:** Small, other species. Designated rooms, service with restrictions, crate. 🛜 🔥 🔒 💻 🌊

▼▼▼▼ Residence Inn by Marriott Charlotte Concord H

(704) 454-7862. **$99-$189.** 7601 Scott Padgett Pkwy 28027. I-85 exit 49, 1 mi e, then just n. Int corridors. **Pets:** Medium. $75 one-time fee/room. Service with restrictions, crate. 🛜 ⊠ 🔥 🔒 💻 🌊 ⊠

AAA ▼▼▼ Sleep Inn-Concord H ❀

(704) 788-2150. **$67-$84.** 1120 Copperfield Blvd 28025. I-85 exit 60, just e. Int corridors. **Pets:** Medium. $25 one-time fee/pet, $5 daily fee/pet. Designated rooms, service with restrictions, crate.

SAVE 🛜 ⊠ 🔥 🔒 💻 🌊

▼▼▼▼ Wingate by Wyndham H

(704) 979-1300. **$99-$399, 3 day notice.** 7841 Gateway Ln NW 28027. I-85 exit 49, just e, just n on Weddington Rd, then just w. Int corridors. **Pets:** Medium. $50 one-time fee/pet. Designated rooms, service with restrictions, crate. 🛜 ⊠ 🔥 🔒 💻 🌊

CORNELIUS

AAA ▼▼▼ Clarion Inn-Lake Norman H

(704) 896-0660. **$69-$129.** 19608 Liverpool Pkwy 28031. I-77 exit 28, just w, then s. Int corridors. **Pets:** Accepted. **SAVE** 🛜 🔒 💻 🌊

AAA ▼▼▼▼ Comfort Inn & Suites H

(704) 896-7622. **$85-$99.** 19521 Liverpool Pkwy 28031. I-77 exit 28, just w, then s. Int corridors. **Pets:** Medium. $25 daily fee/pet. Designated rooms, supervision. **SAVE** 🛜 🔒 💻 🌊

▼▼▼ Econo Lodge Inn & Suites M

(704) 892-3500. **$69-$180.** 20740 Torrence Chapel Rd 28031. I-77 exit 28, just w, then just n. Ext corridors. **Pets:** $15 daily fee/pet. Designated rooms, service with restrictions, supervision. 🛜 🔒 💻 🌊

HUNTERSVILLE

AAA ▼▼▼ BEST WESTERN PLUS Huntersville Inn & Suites H

(704) 875-7880. **$88-$130.** 13830 Statesville Rd 28078. I-77 exit 23, just e, then s on US 21. Int corridors. **Pets:** Other species. $20 daily fee/room. Designated rooms, service with restrictions, supervision.

SAVE 🛜 🔒 💻 🌊

▼▼▼ Candlewood Suites H ❀

(704) 895-3434. **Call for rates.** 16530 Northcross Dr 28078. I-77 exit 25, just w on SR 73, then just s. Int corridors. **Pets:** Large, other species. $150 one-time fee/room. Designated rooms, service with restrictions.

🛜 🔒 💻

▼▼▼▼ Hampton Inn & Suites-Huntersville H

(704) 947-5510. **$99-$144.** 10305 Wilmington St 28078. I-77 exit 23, just e, then just n on US 21. Int corridors. **Pets:** Small. Designated rooms, service with restrictions, crate. 🛜 🔥 🔒 💻 🌊

▼▼▼▼ Residence Inn by Marriott-Lake Norman H

(704) 584-0000. **$109-$189.** 16830 Kenton Dr 28078. I-77 exit 25, 1 mi w on SR 73, then just n. Int corridors. **Pets:** Large. $100 one-time fee/room. Service with restrictions, crate.

🛜 ⊠ 🔥 🔒 💻 🌊 ⊠

MATTHEWS

AAA ◆◆◆ **Country Inn & Suites By Carlson-Matthews** H

(704) 846-8000. **$80-$129.** 2001 Mount Harmony Church Rd 28104. I-485 exit 51B, 0.5 mi e on US 74, just n on Independence Commerce Dr, then just w. Int corridors. **Pets:** Other species. $15 daily fee/room. Service with restrictions, crate. [SAVE] 📶 (&M) 🍴 🖥 🏊

◆◆ **Hampton Inn-Matthews** H ✿

(704) 841-1155. **$129-$159.** 9615 Independence Point Pkwy 28105. I-485 exit 51A, 2 mi w on US 74, then just s. Int corridors. **Pets:** Medium. Service with restrictions, supervision. 📶 (&M) 🍴 🖥 🏊

END METROPOLITAN AREA

CHEROKEE

◆◆ **Great Smokies Inn by Magnuson Hotels** M

(828) 497-2020. **$49-$139.** 1636 Acquoni Rd 28719. Jct US 19, 1.7 mi n. Ext corridors. **Pets:** Small, dogs only. $25 daily fee/pet. Designated rooms, service with restrictions, supervision. 📶 🍴 🖥 🍴 🏊

◆◆ **Microtel Inn & Suites by Wyndham Cherokee** H

(828) 497-7800. **$65-$150.** 674 Casino Tr 28719. Jct US 441, just n on US 441 business route. Int corridors. **Pets:** Accepted. 📶 (&M) 🍴 🖥 🏊

◆ **Pioneer Motel** M

(828) 497-2435. **$48-$80, 3 day notice.** 122 Tsalagi Rd 28719. Jct US 441, just s on US 19. Ext corridors. **Pets:** Accepted. (&M) 🍴 🖥 🏊 ✖

CHOCOWINITY

◆◆ **Super 8** M

(252) 946-8001. **$63-$75.** 3635 US Hwy 17 S 27817. On US 17 business route. Ext corridors. **Pets:** Accepted. 📶 🍴 🖥 🏊

CLEMMONS

◆◆ **Super 8 Clemmons** H

(336) 778-0931. **$65-$90.** 6204 Ramada Dr 27012. I-40 exit 184, just s, then just e. Int corridors. **Pets:** Medium. $10 daily fee/pet. Service with restrictions, supervision. 📶 (&M) 🍴 🖥

COLUMBUS

AAA ◆◆ **Days Inn** M

(828) 894-3303. **$75-$126.** 626 W Mills St 28722. I-26 exit 67, just w on SR 108. Ext corridors. **Pets:** Accepted. [SAVE] 📶 🍴 🖥 🏊

CONOVER

◆◆◆ **La Quinta Inn & Suites Hickory/Conover** H

(828) 465-1100. **$93-$155.** 1607 Fairgrove Church Rd 28613. I-40 exit 128, just s. Int corridors. **Pets:** Service with restrictions, supervision. 📶 ✖ (&M) 🍴 🖥 🍴 🏊

DILLSBORO

◆◆ **Mountain Brook Cottages** CA ✿

(828) 586-4329. **$100-$160, 30 day notice.** 208 Mountain Brook Rd 28779. Jct US 74 exit 81A, 9 mi s on US 23/441, then just w. Ext corridors. **Pets:** Medium. $50 one-time fee/room. Designated rooms, no service, supervision. 📶 🍴 🖥 ✖ W 🔔

DUNN

◆◆ **Baymont Inn & Suites Dunn** M

(910) 891-5758. **Call for rates.** 901 Jackson Rd 28334. I-95 exit 73, just w, then just s. Ext corridors. **Pets:** Accepted. 📶 (&M) 🍴 🖥 🏊

◆◆ **Comfort Inn** H

(910) 891-2511. **Call for rates.** 131 Bud Hawkins Rd 28334. I-95 exit 72 (Pope Rd), just e, then just s. Int corridors. **Pets:** Accepted. 📶 (&M) 🍴 🖥 🏊

DURHAM

◆◆ **Candlewood Suites** H

(919) 484-9922. **Call for rates.** 1818 E NC Hwy 54 27713. I-40 exit 278, just s, then just w. Int corridors. **Pets:** Accepted. 📶 (&M) 🍴 🖥

◆◆◆ **Comfort Inn Medical Park** H

(919) 471-6100. **Call for rates.** 1816 Hillandale Rd 27705. I-85 exit 174, just w. Int corridors. **Pets:** Medium. $49 deposit/pet. Designated rooms, service with restrictions, crate. 📶 🍴 🖥 🏊

◆◆ **DoubleTree by Hilton-Raleigh-Durham Airport at Research Triangle Park** H

(919) 941-6000. **$79-$279.** 4810 Page Creek Ln 27703. I-40 exit 282, just s on Page Rd, then just w on Creekstone Dr. Int corridors. **Pets:** Accepted. 📶 ✖ (&M) 🍴 🖥 🍴 🏊

◆◆ **Durham Skyland Inn, A Magnuson Hotel** M

(919) 237-3131. **Call for rates.** 5400 US 70 W 27705. I-85 exit 170, just e on US 70, then just n. Ext corridors. **Pets:** Accepted. 📶 🍴 🖥

◆◆ **Extended Stay Deluxe-Durham-RTP-Miami Blvd North** H

(919) 941-2878. **$75-$100.** 4610 S Miami Blvd 27703. I-40 exit 281, just n. Int corridors. **Pets:** $25 daily fee/pet. Designated rooms, service with restrictions. 📶 🍴 🖥 🏊

◆◆ **Extended Stay Deluxe-Durham-RTP-Miami-South** H

(919) 998-0400. **$75-$100.** 4919 S Miami Blvd 27703. I-40 exit 281, just s. Int corridors. **Pets:** $25 daily fee/pet. Designated rooms, service with restrictions. 📶 (&M) 🍴 🖥 🏊

AAA ◆◆◆ **Four Points by Sheraton-Durham at Southpoint** H

(919) 806-8200. **$105-$275.** 7807 Leonardo Dr 27713. I-40 exit 274, just s on SR 751. Int corridors. **Pets:** Dogs only. $50 one-time fee/pet. Designated rooms, service with restrictions, crate. [SAVE] 📶 ✖ 🍴 🖥 🍴 🏊

AAA ◆◆◆ **Hilton Durham near Duke University** H ✿

(919) 564-2900. **$99-$209.** 3800 Hillsborough Rd 27705. I-85 exit 173, just e on Cole Mill Rd, then 0.5 mi w on US 70 business route. Int corridors. **Pets:** Large, dogs only. $50 one-time fee/pet. Designated rooms, service with restrictions, crate. [SAVE] 📶 🍴 🖥 🍴 🏊

◆◆◆ **Holiday Inn Express** H

(919) 313-3244. **$89-$119.** 2516 Guess Rd 27705. I-85 exit 175, just e. Int corridors. **Pets:** Medium, dogs only. $50 one-time fee/pet. Designated rooms, service with restrictions, supervision. 📶 🍴 🖥 🏊

◆◆◆ **Holiday Inn Express Hotel & Suites-RTP** H

(919) 474-9800. **$85-$134.** 4912 S Miami Blvd 27703. I-40 exit 281, just s. Int corridors. **Pets:** Medium. $50 one-time fee/room. Designated rooms, service with restrictions, crate. 📶 (&M) 🍴 🖥

◆◆ **Homestead Studio Suites Hotel-Durham/University** M

(919) 402-1700. **$63-$88.** 1920 Ivy Creek Blvd 27707. I-40 exit 270, 2 mi n on US 15/501 exit 105B, just e on Martin Luther King Jr Pkwy, then just s; in University Place. Ext corridors. **Pets:** $25 daily fee/pet. Designated rooms, service with restrictions. 📶 🍴 🖥

◆◆ **Hotel Indigo** �H
(919) 474-3000. **$89-$179, 3 day notice.** 151 Tatum Dr 27703. I-40 exit 281, just s on Miami Blvd, then just e. Int corridors. **Pets:** Accepted.
📶 ❌ ᴹ 🛏 💻 🍽 ≋

◆◆ **La Quinta Inn & Suites Raleigh (Durham-Chapel Hill)** �H
(919) 401-9660. **$63-$144.** 4414 Durham Chapel Hill Blvd 27707. I-40 exit 270, 1.7 mi n on US 15/501. Int corridors. **Pets:** Service with restrictions, supervision. 📶 ᴹ 🛏 💻 ≋

◆◆◆ **La Quinta Inn & Suites Raleigh (Research Triangle Park)** �H
(919) 484-1422. **$71-$144.** 1910 W Westpark Dr 27713. I-40 exit 278, just n on SR 55, then just e. Int corridors. **Pets:** Service with restrictions, supervision. 📶 ᴹ 🛏 💻 ≋

◆◆ **Quality Inn & Suites** �H
(919) 382-3388. **$75-$90.** 3710 Hillsborough Rd 27705. I-85 exit 173, just e on Cole Mill Rd, then just w on US 70 business route. Ext/int corridors. **Pets:** Accepted. 📶 🛏 💻 ≋

AAA ◆◆ **Residence Inn by Marriott Durham/Research Triangle Park** �H
(919) 361-1266. **$90-$189.** 201 Residence Inn Blvd 27713. I-40 exit 278, just s on SR 55, then just w. Ext/int corridors. **Pets:** Medium, other species. $75 one-time fee/room. Service with restrictions.
SAVE 📶 ❌ ᴹ 🛏 💻 ≋ ❌

◆◆◆ **Staybridge Suites of Durham** �H
(919) 401-9800. **$89-$139.** 3704 Mt. Moriah Rd 27707. I-40 exit 270, just n on US 15/501, then just e. Int corridors. **Pets:** Accepted.
📶 ᴹ 🛏 💻 ≋

AAA ◆◆ ◆◆ **Washington Duke Inn & Golf Club** �H
(919) 490-0999. **$349-$379.** 3001 Cameron Blvd 27705. US 15/501 Bypass exit 107, 0.8 mi s on SR 751. Int corridors. **Pets:** Medium, dogs only. $50 one-time fee/room. Designated rooms, service with restrictions, supervision. SAVE 📶 ❌ 🛏 💻 🍽 ≋ ❌

EDEN
◆◆ **Baymont Inn & Suites Eden** M
(336) 627-0472. **Call for rates.** 716 Linden Dr 27288. Jct SR 700/770, 1.4 mi s on SR 87/14, then just e. Ext corridors. **Pets:** Accepted.
📶 ᴹ 🛏

AAA ◆◆ **Econo Lodge** M
(336) 627-5131. **$60-$80.** 110 E Arbor Ln 27288. Jct SR 700/770, 1.4 mi s on SR 87/14, then just e. Ext corridors. **Pets:** Medium. $10 daily fee/pet. Designated rooms, service with restrictions, supervision.
SAVE 📶 🛏

FAYETTEVILLE
AAA ◆◆ **Ambassador Inn** M
(910) 485-8135. **$63-$70.** 2035 Eastern Blvd 28306. Jct SR 87, 1.2 mi s on I-95 business route/US 301; jct Owen Dr. Ext corridors. **Pets:** Other species. $15 daily fee/room. Service with restrictions, crate.
SAVE 📶 🛏 💻 ≋

◆◆◆ **Comfort Inn near Fort Bragg** �H
(910) 867-1777. **$85-$110.** 1922 Skibo Rd 28314. All American Frwy exit US 401 Bypass, 0.8 mi s. Int corridors. **Pets:** Medium, other species. $49 one-time fee/pet. Designated rooms, service with restrictions, supervision.
📶 🛏 💻 ≋

AAA ◆◆ **Country Hearth Inn & Suites** M
(910) 438-0748. **$60-$90.** 1902 Cedar Creek Rd 28312. I-95 exit 49, just w. Ext corridors. **Pets:** $10 daily fee/pet. Service with restrictions, supervision. SAVE 📶 ᴹ 🛏 💻 ≋

AAA ◆◆ **Econo Lodge I-95** M
(910) 433-2100. **$59-$85.** 1952 Cedar Creek Rd 28312. I-95 exit 49, just w. Ext corridors. **Pets:** Medium, other species. $10 daily fee/pet. Service with restrictions, supervision. SAVE 📶 🛏 ≋

◆◆ **Extended StayAmerica Fayetteville-Owen Dr.** M
(910) 485-2747. **$78-$105.** 408 Owen Dr 28304. Jct All American Frwy. Ext corridors. **Pets:** $25 daily fee/pet. Designated rooms, service with restrictions. 📶 🛏 💻

◆◆◆ **Extended Stay Deluxe Fayetteville-Cross Creek Mall** �H
(910) 868-5662. **$94-$120.** 4105 Sycamore Dairy Rd 28303. All American Frwy exit Morganton Rd, just e, then just n. Int corridors. **Pets:** $25 daily fee/pet. Designated rooms, service with restrictions. 📶 🛏 💻 ≋

◆◆◆ **Holiday Inn Fayetteville-Bordeaux** �H 🐾
(910) 323-0111. **$79-$129.** 1707 Owen Dr 28304. Jct I-95 business route/US 301 S, 2.3 mi w. Ext/int corridors. **Pets:** Medium. $50 one-time fee/room. Service with restrictions, crate. 📶 ❌ 🛏 💻 🍽 ≋

◆◆◆ **Holiday Inn I-95** �H
(910) 323-1600. **$79-$129, 7 day notice.** 1944 Cedar Creek Rd 28312. I-95 exit 49, just w. Ext/int corridors. **Pets:** Medium, other species. $35 one-time fee/room. Designated rooms, service with restrictions, supervision. 📶 ❌ 🛏 💻 🍽 ≋

◆◆◆ **Home2 Suites by Hilton** �H
(910) 223-1170. **$109-$132.** 4035 Sycamore Dairy Rd 28303. US 401 Bypass, just e on McPherson Church Rd, then just s. Int corridors. **Pets:** Accepted. 📶 ᴹ 🛏 💻 ≋

◆◆ **Innkeeper-Cross Creek** M
(910) 867-7659. **Call for rates.** 1720 Skibo Rd 28303. All American Frwy exit US 401 Bypass, just s; enter thru Cross Creek Plaza entrance. Ext/int corridors. **Pets:** Accepted. 📶 🛏 💻 ≋

AAA ◆◆ **Residence Inn by Marriott Fayetteville Cross Creek** �H
(910) 868-9005. **$143-$188.** 1468 Skibo Rd 28303. Jct SR 24/87, just s on US 401 Bypass. Int corridors. **Pets:** Other species. $100 one-time fee/room. Service with restrictions.
SAVE 📶 ❌ ᴹ 🛏 💻 ≋ ❌

AAA ◆◆ **TownePlace Suites by Marriott Fayetteville Cross Creek** �H
(910) 764-1100. **$107-$125.** 1464 Skibo Rd 28303. Jct SR 24/87, just s on US 401 Bypass. Int corridors. **Pets:** Accepted.
SAVE 📶 ❌ 🛏 💻 ≋ ❌

FEARRINGTON VILLAGE
AAA ◆◆◆◆ **The Fearrington House Inn** CI
(919) 542-2121. **$299-$635.** 2000 Fearrington Village Center 27312. US 64 exit 383, 6 mi n on US 15/501. Ext/int corridors. **Pets:** Accepted.
SAVE 📶 ❌ ᴹ 🍽 ≋ ❌

FLAT ROCK
◆◆ **Highland Lake Inn** �H
(828) 693-6812. **$79-$309, 7 day notice.** 86 Lily Pad Ln 28731. I-26 exit 53, 1.1 mi w on Upward Rd, 0.5 mi w on N Highland Lake Rd, then just s on Highland Lake Dr. Ext/int corridors. **Pets:** Accepted.
📶 ❌ 🛏 💻 🍽 ≋

◆◆ **Mountain Inn & Suites** �H
(828) 692-7772. **$69-$139.** 755 Upward Rd 28731. I-26 exit 53, just e. Int corridors. **Pets:** Other species. $25 one-time fee/room.
📶 ᴹ 🛏 💻

◆◆ **Mountain Lodge** �H
(828) 693-9910. **Call for rates.** 755 Upward Rd 28731. I-26 exit 53, just e. Int corridors. **Pets:** Accepted. 📶 ❌ ᴹ 🛏 💻 ≋

FLETCHER
◆◆ **Comfort Inn Asheville Airport** �H
(828) 687-9199. **Call for rates.** 15 Rockwood Rd 28732. I-26 exit 40, just e on SR 280, then just s. Int corridors. **Pets:** Large. $20 daily fee/room. Service with restrictions, supervision. 📶 🛏 💻 ≋

FOREST CITY

▼▼ Baymont Inn & Suites Forest City Ⓜ
(828) 287-8788. **Call for rates.** 164 Jameson Inn Dr 28043. US 74 Bypass exit 181, 1.8 mi nw on US 74A. Ext corridors. **Pets:** Accepted.
🛰 📶 🛏 🖥 🏊

▼▼ Quality Inn Ⓜ
(828) 248-3400. **Call for rates.** 205 Commercial Dr 28043. US 74 Bypass exit 181, 1.8 mi nw on US 74A. Ext corridors. **Pets:** Accepted.
🛰 🛏 🖥 🏊

FRANKLIN

▼▼ Comfort Inn Ⓗ
(828) 369-9200. **Call for rates.** 313 Cunningham Rd 28734. Jct US 441 Bypass, just e on Hyatt Rd, then just n. Int corridors. **Pets:** Accepted.
🛰 📶 🛏 🖥 🏊

▼▼ Microtel Inn by Wyndham Franklin Ⓗ
(828) 349-9000. **$70-$100.** 81 Allman Dr 28734. Jct US 441 Bypass, 0.4 mi s on US 441/23. Int corridors. **Pets:** Accepted. 🛰 📶 🛏 🖥

FUQUAY-VARINA

▼▼ Comfort Inn Ⓗ
(919) 557-9000. **$90-$180.** 7616 Purfoy Rd 27526. Jct SR 55, 1 mi n on US 401/SR 55, then just e. Int corridors. **Pets:** Medium, other species. $10 daily fee/pet. Designated rooms, service with restrictions, supervision.
🛰 🛏 🖥 🏊

GARNER

▼▼ Super 8 Ⓜ
(919) 661-1991. **$59-$79.** 101 Leone Ct 27529. I-40 exit 312, just e on SR 42, then just s. Ext corridors. **Pets:** Medium. $5 daily fee/pet. Service with restrictions, supervision. 🛰 🛏 🖥 🏊

GASTONIA

ⒶⒶⒶ ▼▼▼▼ BEST WESTERN PLUS Executive Inn Ⓗ
(704) 868-2000. **$70-$90.** 360 Best Western Ct 28054. I-85 exit 20, just n on SR 279, then just e. Ext/int corridors. **Pets:** Accepted.
SAVE 🛰 🛏 🖥 🏊

ⒶⒶⒶ ▼▼▼ Days Inn Ⓜ
(704) 864-9981. **$50-$225.** 1700 N Chester St 28052. I-85 exit 17, just s on US 321. Ext/int corridors. **Pets:** Other species. $10 daily fee/pet. Service with restrictions, supervision. SAVE 🛰 🛏 🖥 🍴 🏊

▼▼▼▼ Hampton Inn Ⓗ
(704) 866-9090. **$89-$129.** 1859 Remount Rd 28054. I-85 exit 20, just n on SR 279, then just e. Int corridors. **Pets:** Accepted.
🛰 📶 🛏 🖥

GOLDSBORO

ⒶⒶⒶ ▼▼▼ Days Inn Goldsboro Ⓜ
(919) 735-7911. **$59-$79.** 801 US 70 E Bypass 27534. US 70 E Bypass exit Wayne Memorial Dr eastbound, just n, just w on 11th St, then 0.5 mi sw on Lincoln Mercury Dr; exit westbound, straight on 11th St, then 0.5 mi sw on Lincoln Mercury Dr. Ext corridors. **Pets:** Small, dogs only. $10 daily fee/pet. Designated rooms, service with restrictions, supervision.
SAVE 🛰 🛏 🖥 🏊

▼▼▼▼ Hampton Inn Ⓗ
(919) 778-1800. **$99-$129.** 905 N Spence Ave 27534. US 70 E Bypass exit Spence Ave, just s. Int corridors. **Pets:** Accepted.
🛰 🛏 🖥 🏊

▼▼▼▼ Holiday Inn Express Goldsboro Ⓗ
(919) 751-1999. **Call for rates.** 909 N Spence Ave 27534. US 70 E Bypass exit Spence Ave, just s. Int corridors. **Pets:** Medium. $20 deposit/pet. Service with restrictions, supervision. 🛰 🛏 🖥 🏊

GREENSBORO

ⒶⒶⒶ ▼▼▼▼ BEST WESTERN PLUS Windsor Suites Ⓗ
(336) 294-9100. **$89-$149.** 2006 Veasley St 27407. I-40 exit 217, just s on High Point Rd, then just w. Int corridors. **Pets:** Large. $20 daily fee/pet. Designated rooms, service with restrictions, supervision.
SAVE 🛰 ✖ 🛏 🖥 🏊

▼▼▼ Comfort Inn Greensboro Ⓗ
(336) 297-1055. **$74-$169.** 1103 Lanada Rd 27407. I-40 exit 214 or 214A, just sw on Wendover Ave, then just e on Stanley Rd. Int corridors. **Pets:** Accepted. 🛰 🛏 🖥 🏊

▼▼▼ Comfort Suites Airport Ⓗ
(336) 882-6666. **$90-$140.** 7619 Thorndike Rd 27409. I-40 exit 210 (SR 68), just s, then just w. Int corridors. **Pets:** Other species. $20 daily fee/pet. Designated rooms, service with restrictions, crate.
🛰 ✖ 📶 🛏 🖥 🏊

▼▼▼ Drury Inn & Suites-Greensboro Ⓗ
(336) 856-9696. **$94-$174.** 3220 High Point Rd 27407. I-40 exit 217, just s. Int corridors. **Pets:** Service with restrictions, supervision.
🛰 🛏 🖥

▼▼ Extended Stay Deluxe-Greensboro-Airport Ⓗ
(336) 454-0080. **$70-$85.** 7617 Thorndike Rd 27409. I-40 exit 210 (SR 68), just s, then just w. Int corridors. **Pets:** $25 daily fee/pet. Designated rooms, service with restrictions. 🛰 🛏 🖥 🏊

▼▼▼ Fairfield Inn by Marriott Greensboro/Airport Ⓗ
(336) 841-0140. **$85-$139.** 7615 Thorndike Rd 27409. I-40 exit 210 (SR 68), just s, then just w. Int corridors. **Pets:** Medium. $50 one-time fee/room. Designated rooms, service with restrictions, crate.
🛰 ✖ 📶 🛏 🖥 🏊

▼▼ Hawthorn Suites by Wyndham Greensboro Ⓗ
(336) 454-0078. **Call for rates.** 7623 Thorndike Rd 27409. I-40 exit 210 (SR 68), just s, then just w. Int corridors. **Pets:** Accepted.
🛰 📶 🛏 🖥

▼▼▼ Holiday Inn Express & Suites-Airport Ⓗ
(336) 882-0004. **Call for rates.** 645 S Regional Rd 27409. I-40 exit 210 (SR 68), just s, then just e. Int corridors. **Pets:** Medium. $50 deposit/room, $50 one-time fee/room. Designated rooms, service with restrictions, crate. 🛰 🛏 🖥 🏊

▼▼▼ Holiday Inn Express-I-40 at Wendover Ⓗ
(336) 854-0090. **$89-$99.** 4305 Big Tree Way 27409. I-40 exit 214 or 214B, just ne on Wendover Ave, then just w. Int corridors. **Pets:** Medium, other species. $50 one-time fee/pet. Designated rooms, service with restrictions, crate. 🛰 📶 🛏 🖥 🏊

▼▼▼ The Inn at Greensboro Airport Ⓗ 🐾
(336) 668-0421. **$69-$189.** 6426 Burnt Poplar Rd 27409. I-40 exit 211, just n on Gallimore Dairy Rd, then just w. Int corridors. **Pets:** Medium. $10 daily fee/pet. Designated rooms, service with restrictions, supervision.
🛰 ✖ 🛏 🖥 🍴 🏊

▼▼▼ Quality Inn & Suites-Airpark East Ⓗ
(336) 668-3638. **$69-$75, 3 day notice.** 7067 Albert Pick Rd 27409. I-40 exit 210 (SR 68) westbound, just s, then just e; exit eastbound, just e. Int corridors. **Pets:** Accepted. 🛰 🛏 🖥 🏊

▼▼ Red Roof Inn Airport Ⓜ
(336) 271-2636. **$34-$79.** 615 Regional Rd S 27409. I-40 exit 210 (SR 68), just s, then just e. Ext corridors. **Pets:** Large, other species. Service with restrictions, supervision. 🛰 📶 🛏 🖥

▼▼▼ Residence Inn by Marriott-Greensboro Airport Ⓗ
(336) 632-4666. **$109-$159.** 7616 Thorndike Rd 27409. I-40 exit 210 (SR 68), just s, then just w. Int corridors. **Pets:** Medium. $100 one-time fee/room. Service with restrictions, crate.
🛰 ✖ 📶 🛏 🖥 🏊 ✖

▼▼ Sleep Inn-Airport H

(336) 931-1272. **$59-$89.** 7 Sharps Airpark Ct 27409. I-40 exit 210 (SR 68) westbound, follow Regional Rd sign, then just n; exit 210 eastbound, straight on Albert Pick Rd, then just n on Regional Rd. Int corridors. **Pets:** Small, other species. $20 daily fee/pet. Designated rooms, service with restrictions, supervision. ▨ ▨ ▨ ▨ ▨

GREENVILLE

▼▼▼ Candlewood Suites H

(252) 317-3000. **$46-$103.** 1055 Waterford Commons Dr 27834. Just e of US 264; jct Stantonsburg and B's Barbeque rds; just w of Pitt County Memorial Hospital. Int corridors. **Pets:** Large. $75 one-time fee/pet. Service with restrictions, crate. ▨ ▨ ▨ ▨

▼▼ City Hotel & Bistro H

(252) 355-8300. **$79-$159.** 203 W Greenville Blvd 27834. Jct SR 11/903, 1 mi e on US 264A. Int corridors. **Pets:** Accepted.
▨ ▨ ▨ ▨ ▨

▼▼ Econo Lodge M

(252) 752-7382. **Call for rates.** 920 Crosswinds St 27834. Jct US 264 alternate route, just s on US 13/SR 11, then just w. Ext corridors. **Pets:** Accepted. ▨ ▨ ▨ ▨ ▨

▼▼ Hilton Greenville H ❁

(252) 355-5000. **Call for rates.** 207 SW Greenville Blvd 27834. Jct SR 11/903, 1 mi e on US 264 alternate route. Int corridors. **Pets:** Medium. $75 one-time fee/room. Designated rooms, service with restrictions.
▨ ▨ ▨ ▨ ▨

▼▼ Home-Towne Suites H

(252) 752-3411. **$59-$130.** 2111 W Arlington Blvd 27834. Jct US 13/SR 11, 0.4 mi w on Stantonsburg Rd, then just s. Int corridors. **Pets:** Medium. $25 daily fee/room. Service with restrictions, supervision.
▨ ▨ ▨

HAVELOCK

▼▼▼ Holiday Inn Express & Suites H

(252) 447-9000. **Call for rates.** 103 Branchside Dr 28532. Jct SR 101, 1 mi w on US 70. Int corridors. **Pets:** $35 one-time fee/pet. Designated rooms, service with restrictions, supervision.
▨ ▨ ▨ ▨ ▨ ▨

HENDERSON

▼▼ Budget Host Inn M

(252) 492-2013. **$49-$69.** 1727 N Garnett St 27536. I-85 exit 215, just e, then just w on US 158. Ext corridors. **Pets:** Small. $15 daily fee/pet. Designated rooms, service with restrictions, crate. ▨ ▨ ▨

▼▼ Lamplight Inn B&B BB ❁

(252) 438-6311. **$90-$120, 7 day notice.** 1680 Flemingtown Rd 27537. I-85 exit 220, 1.5 mi nw. Int corridors. **Pets:** Small, dogs only. Designated rooms, service with restrictions, crate. ▨ ▨

▲▲▲ ▼▼ Sleep Inn H

(252) 433-9449. **$65-$80.** 18 Market St 27537. I-85 exit 212, just w on Ruin Creek Rd, then just se on Zeb Robinson Rd. Int corridors. **Pets:** Small. $15 daily fee/pet. Designated rooms, service with restrictions, supervision. ▨ ▨ ▨ ▨

HENDERSONVILLE

▼▼ 1898 Waverly Inn BB

(828) 693-9193. **$189-$305, 7 day notice.** 783 N Main St 28792. I-26 exit 49B, 2 mi w on US 64, then just n. Int corridors. **Pets:** Designated rooms, no service, crate. ▨ ▨ ▨ ▨

▲▲▲ ▼▼▼ BEST WESTERN Hendersonville Inn M

(828) 692-0521. **$55-$110.** 105 Sugarloaf Rd 28792. I-26 exit 49A, just e on US 64. Ext corridors. **Pets:** Large, other species. $10 daily fee/pet. Service with restrictions, crate. ▨ ▨ ▨ ▨ ▨ ▨ ▨

▲▲▲ ▼▼▼ Comfort Inn M ❁

(828) 693-8800. **Call for rates.** 206 Mitchelle Dr 28792. I-26 exit 49B, just w on US 64, just s on Orr Camp Dr, then just e. Ext corridors. **Pets:** $10 daily fee/pet. Designated rooms, service with restrictions.
▨ ▨ ▨ ▨ ▨

▼▼▼ Inn on Church CI ❁

(828) 696-2001. **$149-$275, 7 day notice.** 201 3rd Ave W 28739. I-26 exit 49B, 2 mi w on US 64, just s on Main St, then just w. Int corridors. **Pets:** Small. $40 daily fee/room. Designated rooms, supervision.
▨ ▨ ▨

▲▲▲ ▼▼▼ Ramada H

(828) 697-0006. **$55-$140.** 150 Sugarloaf Rd 28792. I-26 exit 49A, just e on US 64, then just s. Int corridors. **Pets:** Small. $15 daily fee/pet. Service with restrictions, supervision. ▨ ▨ ▨ ▨ ▨

HICKORY

▼▼▼ Baymont Inn & Suites Hickory M

(828) 304-0410. **Call for rates.** 1120 13th Ave Dr SE 28602. I-40 exit 125, just s, then 0.4 mi w. Ext corridors. **Pets:** Accepted.
▨ ▨ ▨ ▨ ▨

▲▲▲ ▼▼▼ BEST WESTERN Hickory H ❁

(828) 323-1150. **$80-$95.** 1520 13th Ave Dr SE 28602. I-40 exit 125, just s on Lenoir Rhyne Blvd, then just e. Ext/int corridors. **Pets:** Large, other species. $20 one-time fee/pet. Service with restrictions.
▨ ▨ ▨ ▨ ▨

▼▼▼ Crowne Plaza H

(828) 323-1000. **$89-$119.** 1385 Lenoir Rhyne Blvd SE 28602. I-40 exit 125, just s. Ext/int corridors. **Pets:** Accepted. ▨ ▨ ▨ ▨ ▨

▼▼ Gateway Hotel & Conference Center H

(828) 328-5101. **$64-$149.** 909 US 70 SW 28602. I-40 exit 123, just n on US 321 exit 44, then just e. Ext/int corridors. **Pets:** Medium, other species. Designated rooms, service with restrictions, crate.
▨ ▨ ▨ ▨ ▨

▲▲▲ ▼▼▼ Red Roof Inn Hickory M

(828) 323-1500. **$47-$79.** 1184 Lenoir Rhyne Blvd 28602. I-40 exit 125, just n. Ext corridors. **Pets:** Large, other species. Service with restrictions, supervision. ▨ ▨ ▨ ▨

HIGHLANDS

▼▼ Mountain High Lodge M

(828) 526-2790. **$49-$189, 7 day notice.** 200 Main St 28741. Just w on US 64; downtown. Ext corridors. **Pets:** Other species. Designated rooms. ▨ ▨ ▨

HILLSBOROUGH

▲▲▲ ▼▼▼ Holiday Inn Express H

(919) 644-7997. **$100-$129.** 202 Cardinal Dr 27278. I-85 exit 164, just se, then just s; I-40 exit 261, 1.2 mi n, then just w. Int corridors. **Pets:** Medium. $25 daily fee/pet. Designated rooms, service with restrictions, supervision. ▨ ▨ ▨ ▨ ▨ ▨

JACKSONVILLE

▼▼▼ Baymont Inn & Suites Jacksonville H

(910) 347-6500. **$89-$155, 3 day notice.** 474 Western Blvd 28546. Jct US 17, just n. Ext corridors. **Pets:** Medium, other species. $50 deposit/room, $10 daily fee/pet. Service with restrictions. ▨ ▨ ▨ ▨

▼▼▼ Candlewood Suites H ❁

(910) 333-0494. **$92-$129.** 119 Penny Ln 28546. Jct Western Blvd, just n on US 17, then just w. Int corridors. **Pets:** Other species. $30 daily fee/room. Service with restrictions, crate. ▨ ▨ ▨ ▨ ▨

▼▼ Extended StayAmerica Jacksonville Camp Lejeune H

(910) 347-7684. **$79-$110.** 20 McDaniel Dr 28546. Jct Western Blvd, just n on US 17, then just w. Int corridors. **Pets:** $25 daily fee/pet. Designated rooms, service with restrictions. ▨ ▨ ▨ ▨

▼▼▼▼ TownePlace Suites by Marriott
　　Jacksonville 🅷 ❀
(910) 478-9795. **$115-$150.** 400 Northwest Dr 28546. Jct US 17, 2 mi w on Western Blvd, then just s. Int corridors. **Pets:** $100 one-time fee/room. Service with restrictions, supervision. 📶 ⊠ ᕇM 🛏 💻 ⇶

JONESVILLE

🔺🔺🔺 ▼▼▼▼ BEST WESTERN Yadkin Valley Inn &
　　Suites 🅷
(336) 835-6000. **$90-$140.** 1713 NC Hwy 67 28642. I-77 exit 82, just e. Int corridors. **Pets:** Small. $15 daily fee/pet. Designated rooms, service with restrictions, supervision. SAVE 📶 ᕇM 🛏 💻 ⇶

🔺🔺🔺 ▼▼▼ Comfort Inn 🅼 ❀
(336) 835-9400. **$80-$100.** 1633 Winston Rd 28642. I-77 exit 82, just w on SR 67. Ext corridors. **Pets:** Medium, other species. $15 one-time fee/room. Service with restrictions, crate. SAVE 📶 ᕇM 🛏 💻 ⇶

▼▼▼ Days Inn Jonesville-Elkin 🅼
(336) 526-6777. **$73-$120.** 1540 NC Hwy 67 28642. I-77 exit 82, just w. Ext corridors. **Pets:** Other species. $12 daily fee/pet. Designated rooms, service with restrictions, crate. 📶 🛏 💻 ⇶

KENLY

▼▼▼ Quality Inn 🅼
(919) 284-1000. **$55-$100.** 405 S Church St 27542. I-95 exit 107, just e. Ext corridors. **Pets:** Accepted. 📶 🛏 💻 ⇶

LAKE TOXAWAY

▼▼▼ Cabins at Seven Foxes 🅲🅰 ❀
(828) 877-6333. **$170-$285, 30 day notice.** Seven Foxes Ln 28747. Jct US 64, 1.4 mi n on SR 281, 1.4 mi w on Slick Fisher Rd, then just s. Ext corridors. **Pets:** Dogs only. $75 one-time fee/pet. ⊠ 🛏 💻

LAURINBURG

▼▼▼ Quality Inn 🅼
(910) 277-0080. **Call for rates.** 14 Jameson Inn Ct 28352. Jct US 74 Bypass exit 183, just n on US 15/401 Bypass, then just e. Ext corridors. **Pets:** Other species. $15 daily fee/pet. Service with restrictions, crate. 📶 🛏 💻 ⇶

LELAND

🔺🔺🔺 ▼▼▼▼ BEST WESTERN PLUS Westgate Inn &
　　Suites 🅷
(910) 371-2858. **$89-$129.** 1120 Towne Lake Dr 28451. Jct US 74/76, 2 mi s on US 17. Int corridors. **Pets:** $20 daily fee/room. Designated rooms, service with restrictions, supervision.
SAVE 📶 ⊠ ᕇM 🛏 💻 ⇶

▼▼▼ Comfort Suites-Magnolia Greens 🅷 ❀
(910) 383-3300. **$79-$179.** 1020 Grandiflora Dr 28451. Jct US 74/76, 2 mi s on US 17, just w. Int corridors. **Pets:** Medium. $40 one-time fee/pet. Designated rooms, service with restrictions, crate.
📶 ⊠ ᕇM 🛏 💻 ⇶

LENOIR

▼▼▼ Days Inn 🅼
(828) 754-0731. **$66-$76.** 206 Blowing Rock Blvd 28645. Jct US 64/SR 18, just n on US 321. Ext corridors. **Pets:** Accepted. 📶 🛏 💻

LEXINGTON

▼▼▼ Days Inn 🅷
(336) 357-2333. **$80-$99.** 1620 Cotton Grove Rd 27292. I-85 exit 91, just s on SR 8, then just ne. Ext/int corridors. **Pets:** $10 daily fee/pet. Designated rooms, service with restrictions, supervision.
📶 ᕇM 🛏 💻 ⇶

▼▼▼ Quality Inn 🅷
(336) 243-2929. **Call for rates.** 101 Plaza Pkwy 27292. I-85 exit 91, just n on SR 8, then 0.4 mi ne. Int corridors. **Pets:** Accepted.
📶 ᕇM 🛏 💻 ⇶

LILLINGTON

▼▼▼ Microtel Inn & Suites by Wyndham Lillington 🅷
(910) 893-2626. **$70-$90.** 300 E Cornelius Harnett Blvd 27546. Jct US 401/SR 210, just ne on US 421/SR 27. Int corridors. **Pets:** $15 deposit/pet. Designated rooms, no service, supervision.
📶 ᕇM 🛏 💻 ⇶

LUMBERTON

🔺🔺🔺 ▼▼▼▼ BEST WESTERN Lumberton 🅼
(910) 618-9799. **$90-$150.** 201 Jackson Ct 28358. I-95 exit 22, just e, then just s. Ext corridors. **Pets:** Medium. $10 daily fee/pet. Service with restrictions, supervision. SAVE 📶 🛏 💻 ⇶

MAGGIE VALLEY

🔺🔺🔺 ▼▼▼ Comfort Inn 🅷
(828) 926-9106. **Call for rates.** 3282 Soco Rd 28751. Jct US 276, 3.3 mi w on US 19. Int corridors. **Pets:** Accepted.
SAVE 📶 ⊠ 🛏 💻 ⇶

▼▼▼ Microtel Inn & Suites by Wyndham Maggie
　　Valley 🅷
(828) 926-8554. **$55-$170.** 3777 Soco Rd 28751. Jct US 276, 4 mi w on US 19. Int corridors. **Pets:** Small. $10 daily fee/pet. Designated rooms, service with restrictions, supervision. 📶 ᕇM 🛏 💻 ⇶

MARION

▼▼▼ Comfort Inn 🅷
(828) 652-4888. **Call for rates.** 178 Hwy 70 W 28752. I-40 exit 85, 5 mi n; jct US 221 N Bypass and 70. Int corridors. **Pets:** Accepted.
📶 ᕇM 🛏 💻 ⇶

MILLS RIVER

▼▼▼ Barkwells 🅲🅰 ❀
(828) 891-8288. **$198-$330, 30 day notice.** 234-333 Barkwells Ln 28759. I-26 exit 40, 0.8 mi n on US 25 (Boylston Hwy), 2.4 mi w on Old Fanning Bridge Rd, then 0.3 mi s, follow signs to gated entrance. Ext corridors. **Pets:** Dogs only. $100 deposit/room, $25 one-time fee/pet. No service. 📶 ⊠ 🛏 💻 ⊠

MOCKSVILLE

▼▼▼ Quality Inn 🅼
(336) 751-7310. **$59-$79.** 1500 Yadkinville Rd 27028. I-40 exit 170, just s on US 601. Ext corridors. **Pets:** Medium. $15 deposit/room. Service with restrictions, supervision. 📶 🛏 💻 ⇶

MONROE

▼▼▼ Super 8 🅼
(704) 289-1555. **$71-$91.** 608-E W Roosevelt Blvd 28110. Jct US 601, 1 mi e on US 74. Ext corridors. **Pets:** Accepted. 📶 ᕇM 🛏 💻 ⇶

MOORESVILLE

▼▼▼▼ Holiday Inn Express Hotel & Suites 🅷
(704) 662-6900. **$99-$109.** 130 Norman Station Blvd 28117. I-77 exit 36, just e on SR 150, then just s. Int corridors. **Pets:** Medium, other species. $25 one-time fee/room. Designated rooms, service with restrictions.
📶 ᕇM 🛏 💻 ⇶

▼▼▼ TownePlace Suites by Marriott Charlotte
　　Mooresville 🅷
(704) 659-8600. **$89-$139.** 139 Gateway Blvd 28117. I-77 exit 33, just ne on US 21, then just w. Int corridors. **Pets:** Accepted.
📶 ⊠ ᕇM 🛏 💻 ⇶

MOREHEAD CITY

▼▼▼ Holiday Inn Express Hotel & Suites H 🐾

(252) 247-5001. **$89-$179.** 5063 Executive Dr 28557. Jct US 70 and SR 24. Int corridors. **Pets:** Large. $35 one-time fee/room. Designated rooms, service with restrictions, crate. 🛜 ✖ 📶 💻 🏊

MORGANTON

△△△ ▼▼▼ Comfort Inn & Suites H

(828) 430-4000. **Call for rates.** 1273 Burkemont Ave 28655. I-40 exit 103, just s. Int corridors. **Pets:** Accepted. 🆂🅰🆅🅴 🛜 ♿ 📶 💻 🏊

▼▼▼ Quality Inn H

(828) 437-0171. **$79-$85.** 2400 S Sterling St 28655. I-40 exit 105 (SR 18), just s. Ext corridors. **Pets:** Medium, other species. $25 one-time fee/room. Service with restrictions. 🛜 ♿ 📶 💻 🍽 🏊

▼▼ Sleep Inn H

(828) 433-9000. **$75-$100.** 2400A S Sterling St 28655. I-40 exit 105 (SR 18), just s. Int corridors. **Pets:** Accepted. 🛜 ♿ 📶 💻

MORRISVILLE

▼▼▼▼ Holiday Inn Express H

(919) 653-2260. **$119-$139, 3 day notice.** 1014 Airport Blvd 27560. I-40 exit 284 or 284A, just s. Int corridors. **Pets:** Accepted.
🛜 ♿ 📶 💻 🏊

▼▼▼ Holiday Inn-Raleigh-Durham Airport H

(919) 465-1910. **$91-$117.** 930 Airport Blvd 27560. I-40 exit 284 or 284A, 0.5 mi s. Int corridors. **Pets:** Small. $50 one-time fee/pet. Service with restrictions, supervision. 🛜 ♿ 📶 💻 🍽 🏊

▼▼▼ La Quinta Inn & Suites Raleigh Durham Airport South H

(919) 481-3600. **$63-$140.** 1001 Aerial Center Pkwy 27560. I-40 exit 284 or 284A, just s, then just e; in Aerial Center Park. Int corridors. **Pets:** Service with restrictions, supervision. 🛜 ♿ 📶 💻 🏊

▼▼▼ La Quinta Inn & Suites (Raleigh-Durham Int'l Airport) H

(919) 461-1771. **$63-$166.** 1001 Hospitality Ct 27560. I-40 exit 284 or 284A, just s, just e on Aerial Center Pkwy, then just ne; in Aerial Center Park. Int corridors. **Pets:** Service with restrictions, supervision.
🛜 ♿ 📶 💻 🏊

▼▼▼▼ Residence Inn by Marriott Raleigh-Durham Airport H

(919) 467-8689. **$71-$139.** 2020 Hospitality Ct 27560. I-40 exit 284 or 284A, just s on Airport Blvd, just e on Aerial Center Pkwy, then just ne. Int corridors. **Pets:** Other species. $100 one-time fee/room. Designated rooms, service with restrictions, crate.
🌱 🛜 ✖ ♿ 📶 💻 🏊 ✖

▼▼▼▼ Staybridge Suites Raleigh Durham Airport H

(919) 468-0180. **$80-$180.** 1012 Airport Blvd 27560. I-40 exit 284 or 284A, just s; enter between Hampton Inn-RDU and Holiday Inn Express. Int corridors. **Pets:** Large, other species. $50 one-time fee/pet. Service with restrictions, crate. 🛜 ♿ 📶 💻

MOUNT AIRY

▼▼▼ Holiday Inn Express & Suites H

(336) 719-1731. **Call for rates.** 1320 EMS Dr 27030. Jct US 52, 0.5 mi s on US 601, then just w. Int corridors. **Pets:** Medium. $25 daily fee/pet. Designated rooms, service with restrictions, supervision.
🛜 ✖ ♿ 📶 💻

▼▼▼ Quality Inn M

(336) 789-2000. **$69-$130.** 2136 Rockford St 27030. Jct US 52, 0.6 mi s on US 601. Ext corridors. **Pets:** Medium. $25 one-time fee/room. Designated rooms, service with restrictions, supervision. 🛜 📶 💻 🏊

MURPHY

△△△ ▼▼▼ BEST WESTERN of Murphy M 🐾

(828) 837-3060. **$69-$109.** 1522 Andrews Rd 28906. US 74, 19 and 129 exit Andrews Rd. Ext corridors. **Pets:** Large, other species. $15 daily fee/room. Designated rooms, service with restrictions.
🆂🅰🆅🅴 🛜 ♿ 📶 💻 🏊

▼▼ Days Inn M

(828) 837-8030. **$59-$99.** 754 Hwy 64 W 28906. US 64 W/19 S/74 W and 129 S. Ext corridors. **Pets:** Accepted. 🛜 📶 💻 🏊

NEW BERN

△△△ ▼▼▼ Bridge Pointe Hotel & Marina H 🐾

(252) 636-3637. **$80-$135.** 101 Howell Rd 28562. US 70 Bypass exit 417, just w on US 70 business route, then just s. Int corridors. **Pets:** Large, other species. $250 deposit/room, $25 daily fee/pet. Designated rooms, no service, crate. 🆂🅰🆅🅴 🛜 📶 💻 🏊

▼▼▼▼ DoubleTree by Hilton New Bern Riverfront H 🐾

(252) 638-3585. **$119-$149.** 100 Middle St 28560. On waterfront; downtown. Int corridors. **Pets:** Medium. $50 one-time fee/room. Designated rooms, service with restrictions, supervision.
🛜 ♿ 📶 💻 🍽 🏊

OCEAN ISLE BEACH

△△△ ▼▼▼ The Islander Inn H

(910) 575-7000. **Call for rates.** 57 W First St 28469. Jct SR 904, just s. Int corridors. **Pets:** Accepted. 🆂🅰🆅🅴 🛜 ✖ 📶 💻 🏊

△△△ ▼▼▼ The Winds Resort Beach Club H

(910) 579-6275. **$71-$363, 30 day notice.** 310 E First St 28469. SR 904, 1.6 mi n. Ext/int corridors. **Pets:** Medium. $25 daily fee/pet. Designated rooms, service with restrictions, crate.
🆂🅰🆅🅴 🛜 ✖ 📶 💻 🏊 ✖

OLD FORT

▼▼▼ Inn On Mill Creek BB 🐾

(828) 668-1115. **$149-$199, 14 day notice.** 3895 Mill Creek Rd 28762. I-40 exit 66, just n, 0.9 mi e on Ridgecrest Rd, 0.9 mi n on Yates Ave, then 1.5 mi n. Ext/int corridors. **Pets:** Other species. $10 daily fee/pet. Designated rooms, service with restrictions. 🛜 ✖ ✖ 📧

ORIENTAL

▼▼ Oriental Marina & Inn CO

(252) 249-1818. **$99-$234.** 103 Wall St 28571. Jct SR 55 (Broad St), just ne on Hodges St. Ext corridors. **Pets:** Other species. $50 one-time fee/room. Service with restrictions, supervision.
🛜 ✖ 📶 💻 🍽 🏊

OUTER BANKS AREA

BUXTON

▼▼ Lighthouse View Oceanfront Lodging M
(252) 995-5680. **$64-$169, 7 day notice.** 46677 Hwy 12 27920. On SR 12; 0.5 mi n of Cape Hatteras Lighthouse. Ext corridors. **Pets:** $10 daily fee/pet. Designated rooms, no service. 📶 🛇 🖥 🐾

KILL DEVIL HILLS

▼▼▼ Comfort Inn North Oceanfront ⊞ ✿
(252) 441-6333. **$59-$279.** 1601 S Virginia Dare Tr 27948. SR 12, at MM 9.5. Int corridors. **Pets:** Other species. $25 daily fee/room. Designated rooms, service with restrictions, supervision.
📶 🛇 🖥 🍴 🐾 ⊠

▼▼▼▼ First Flight Retreat Condominiums ⓒⓄ
(252) 489-4747. **$145-$399.** 815 S Virginia Dare Tr 27948. SR 12, at MM 8.5. Int corridors. **Pets:** Dogs only. $125 one-time fee/pet. Designated rooms, no service, crate. 📶 ⊠ 🛇 🖥 🐾 ⊠

▼▼ John Yancey Oceanfront Inn M
(252) 441-7141. **$50-$190, 3 day notice.** 2009 S Virginia Dare Tr 27948. SR 12, at MM 10.3. Ext/int corridors. **Pets:** Other species. $20 daily fee/pet. Designated rooms, service with restrictions, supervision.
📶 🛇 🖥 🐾

◈ ▼▼▼▼ Ramada Plaza Nags Head Beach ⊞ ✿
(252) 441-2151. **$69-$299, 3 day notice.** 1701 S Virginia Dare Tr 27948. SR 12, at MM 9.5. Int corridors. **Pets:** $25 daily fee/room. Designated rooms, service with restrictions, supervision.
[SAVE] 📶 ⊠ 🛇 🖥 🍴 🐾

◈ ▼▼ Travelodge-Nags Head Beach ⊞
(252) 441-0411. **$50-$210, 3 day notice.** 804 N Virginia Dare Tr 27948. SR 12, at MM 8.1. Ext/int corridors. **Pets:** Other species. Designated rooms, service with restrictions. [SAVE] 📶 🖥 🛇 🖥 🐾

NAGS HEAD

▼▼▼ Comfort Inn Oceanfront South ⊞
(252) 441-6315. **$59-$279.** 8031 Old Oregon Inlet Rd 27959. SR 12, at MM 17. Int corridors. **Pets:** Accepted. 📶 🛇 🐾

▼ Dolphin Oceanfront Motel M
(252) 441-7488. **$49-$399, 30 day notice.** 8017 S Old Oregon Inlet Rd 27959. Jct SR 12, just s, at MM 16.5. Ext corridors. **Pets:** Other species. $10 daily fee/pet. Service with restrictions. 📶 🛇 🖥 🐾 🐾

OCRACOKE

◈ ▼▼ The Anchorage Inn M ✿
(252) 928-1101. **$99-$250, 7 day notice.** 205 Irvin Garrish Hwy (SR 12) 27960. From Cedar Island Ferry, just n. Ext corridors. **Pets:** Large, other species. $25 daily fee/room. Designated rooms, service with restrictions, supervision. [SAVE] 📶 🛇 🖥 🐾 ⊠

END AREA

OXFORD

◈ ▼▼▼▼ Comfort Inn & Suites ⊞
(919) 692-1000. **$60-$90.** 1000 Linden Ave 27565. I-85 exit 204, just e. Int corridors. **Pets:** $15 one-time fee/pet. Service with restrictions, supervision. [SAVE] 📶 🛇 🖥 🐾

PEMBROKE

▼▼▼ Holiday Inn Express ⊞
(910) 521-1311. **Call for rates.** 605 Redmond Rd 28372. Jct SR 710, just se on SR 711, then just s. Int corridors. **Pets:** Large, other species. $10 daily fee/pet. Designated rooms, service with restrictions, crate.
📶 ⌖ 🛇 🖥 🐾

PINEHURST

◈ ▼▼▼▼ Homewood Suites by Hilton-Olmstead Village near Pinehurst ⊞
(910) 255-0300. **$119-$199.** 250 Central Park Ave 28374. Jct SR 5 and 211, just n; in Olmstead Village. Int corridors. **Pets:** Accepted.
[SAVE] 📶 ⌖ 🛇 🖥 🐾

PLYMOUTH

▼▼▼▼ Holiday Inn Express ⊞
(252) 793-4700. **$84-$89.** 840 US Hwy 64 W 27962. Jct SR 32 S, 1 mi w. Ext/int corridors. **Pets:** $25 one-time fee/room. Designated rooms, service with restrictions, supervision. 📶 ⊠ ⌖ 🛇 🖥 🐾

RALEIGH

◈ ▼▼ Americas Best Value Inn-Crabtree ⊞
(919) 277-8485. **$55-$65.** 3921 Arrow Dr 27612. I-440 exit 7 or 7B, just w on US 70, just s on Blue Ridge Rd, then 0.4 mi e on Summit Park Ln. Ext/int corridors. **Pets:** Dogs only. Crate. [SAVE] 📶 🛇

◈ ▼▼▼ BEST WESTERN PLUS Raleigh North ⊞
(919) 872-5000. **Call for rates.** 2715 Capital Blvd 27604. I-440 exit 11 or 11B, just n on US 1. Int corridors. **Pets:** Accepted.
[SAVE] 📶 🛇 🖥 🐾

▼▼ Candlewood Suites-Crabtree ⊞
(919) 789-4840. **Call for rates.** 4433 Lead Mine Rd 27612. I-440 exit 7 or 7B, just w, then just n. Int corridors. **Pets:** Accepted.
📶 ⌖ 🛇 🖥

▼▼▼ Comfort Inn & Suites Crabtree ⊞
(919) 782-1112. **$59-$85.** 6209 Glenwood Ave 27612. I-440 exit 7 or 7B, 2.5 mi w on US 70. Int corridors. **Pets:** Small, other species. $25 daily fee/room. Designated rooms, service with restrictions, crate.
📶 ⌖ 🛇 🖥 🐾

▼▼ Comfort Suites ⊞
(919) 876-2211. **$79-$119.** 4400 Capital Blvd 27604. I-440 exit 11 and 11B, 2.5 mi n on US 1. Int corridors. **Pets:** Other species. $25 one-time fee/room, $10 daily fee/room. Designated rooms, service with restrictions, crate. 📶 ⊠ ⌖ 🛇 🖥 🐾

▼▼ Days Inn M
(919) 878-9310. **$55-$70.** 3201 Wake Forest Rd 27609. I-440 exit 10 (Wake Forest Rd), just n, then just w. Ext corridors. **Pets:** $20 daily fee/room. Designated rooms, service with restrictions, crate.
📶 🛇 🖥 🐾

▼▼ Extended StayAmerica-Raleigh-North Raleigh ⊞
(919) 829-7271. **$62-$90.** 911 Wake Towne Dr 27609. I-440 exit 10 (Wake Forest Rd), just s, then w. Int corridors. **Pets:** $25 daily fee/pet. Designated rooms, service with restrictions. 📶 🛇 🖥

Fairfield Inn & Suites by Marriott Raleigh Crabtree Valley H

(919) 881-9800. **$79-$154.** 2201 Summit Park Ln 27612. I-440 exit 7 or 7B, just w on US 70, just s on Blue Ridge Rd, then just e. Int corridors. **Pets:** Large. $75 one-time fee/room. Designated rooms, service with restrictions, supervision. [SAVE] 🛜 ✕ 🅼 🛏 🖵 🏊

Hilton North Raleigh Midtown H

(919) 872-2323. **$99-$229.** 3415 Wake Forest Rd 27609. I-440 exit 10 (Wake Forest Rd), 0.4 mi n. Int corridors. **Pets:** Accepted.
🛜 🅼 🛏 🖵 🍽 🏊

Holiday Inn Crabtree Valley H

(919) 782-8600. **Call for rates.** 4100 Glenwood Ave 27612. I-440 exit 7 or 7B, just w on US 70. Int corridors. **Pets:** Large, other species. $25 daily fee/room. Service with restrictions, supervision.
[SAVE] 🛜 🅼 🛏 🖵 🍽 🏊 ✕

Holiday Inn Express & Suites near NC State/Southwest H

(919) 854-0001. **$89-$129.** 3741 Thistledown Dr 27606. I-40 exit 295, just n on Gorman St, then just e. Int corridors. **Pets:** Medium, dogs only. $25 daily fee/pet. Designated rooms, service with restrictions, supervision.
🛜 ✕ 🅼 🛏 🖵 🏊

Holiday Inn Express Hotel & Suites H

(919) 570-5550. **$89-$109.** 11400 Common Oaks Dr 27614. Jct SR 98, 1.2 mi s on US 1, then just w. Int corridors. **Pets:** Small. $25 daily fee/room. Designated rooms, service with restrictions, crate.
🛜 🅼 🛏 🖵 🏊

Holiday Inn Raleigh-North H

(919) 872-3500. **$79-$129.** 2805 Highwoods Blvd 27604. I-440 exit 11 or 11B, just n on US 1, then just w. Int corridors. **Pets:** Accepted.
[SAVE] 🛜 🅼 🛏 🖵 🍽 🏊 ✕

Homestead Studio Suites Hotel-Raleigh/Crabtree Valley H

(919) 510-8551. **$62-$87.** 4810 Bluestone Dr 27612. I-440 exit 7 or 7B, 1.6 mi w on US 70, then just s. Ext corridors. **Pets:** $25 daily fee/pet. Designated rooms, service with restrictions. 🛜 🛏 🖵

Homestead Studio Suites Hotel-Raleigh/Northeast H

(919) 807-9970. **$65-$90.** 2601 Appliance Ct 27604. I-440 exit 11 or 11B, just n on US 1, then 0.5 mi e. Int corridors. **Pets:** $25 daily fee/pet. Designated rooms, service with restrictions. 🛜 🛏 🖵 🏊

Homestead Studio Suites Hotel-Raleigh/North Raleigh M

(919) 981-7353. **$57-$85.** 3531 Wake Forest Rd 27609. I-440 exit 10 (Wake Forest Rd), 0.5 mi n. Ext corridors. **Pets:** $25 daily fee/pet. Designated rooms, service with restrictions. 🛜 🅼 🛏 🖵

La Quinta Inn & Suites Raleigh (Crabtree) H

(919) 785-0071. **$66-$172.** 2211 Summit Park Ln 27612. I-440 exit 7 or 7B, just w on US 70, just s on Blue Ridge Rd, then just e. Int corridors. **Pets:** Service with restrictions, supervision. 🛜 🅼 🛏 🖵 🏊

Ramada-Blue Ridge H

(919) 832-4100. **$79-$132.** 1520 Blue Ridge Rd 27607. I-40 exit 289, 2 mi e on Wade Ave exit Blue Ridge Rd, then just s; I-440 exit 4 or 4B, just w on Wade Ave exit Blue Ridge Rd, then just s. Int corridors. **Pets:** Large. $25 one-time fee/room. Designated rooms, service with restrictions, crate. 🛜 ✕ 🅼 🛏 🖵 🍽 🏊

Red Roof Inn-Convention Center H

(919) 833-6005. **$49-$79.** 1813 S Saunders St 27603. I-40 exit 298B, just n. Int corridors. **Pets:** Large, other species. Service with restrictions, supervision. [SAVE] 🛜 🅼 🛏

Residence Inn by Marriott Raleigh Crabtree Valley H

(919) 279-3000. **$98-$188.** 2200 Summit Park Ln 27612. I-440 exit 7 or 7B, just w on US 70, just s on Blue Ridge Rd, then just e. Int corridors. **Pets:** Medium. $100 one-time fee/pet. Service with restrictions, supervision. [SAVE] 🛜 ✕ 🅼 🛏 🖵 🏊 ✕

Residence Inn by Marriott-Raleigh Midtown H

(919) 878-6100. **$89-$159.** 1000 Navaho Dr 27609. I-440 exit 10 (Wake Forest Rd), just n, then w. Ext corridors. **Pets:** Large. $100 one-time fee/room. Service with restrictions, crate.
[SAVE] 🛜 ✕ 🅼 🛏 🖵 🏊 ✕

REIDSVILLE

Days Inn of Reidsville M

(336) 342-2800. **$64-$179.** 2205 Barnes St 27320. US 29 exit 150 (Barnes St), just e. Ext corridors. **Pets:** Very small. $15 daily fee/pet. Service with restrictions, supervision. [SAVE] 🛜 🛏 🖵

Quality Inn M

(336) 634-1275. **Call for rates.** 2203 Barnes St 27320. US 29 exit 150 (Barnes St), just e. Ext corridors. **Pets:** Small. $15 daily fee/pet. Service with restrictions, supervision. [SAVE] 🛜 🅼 🛏 🖵 🏊

RESEARCH TRIANGLE PARK

Radisson Hotel in Research Triangle Park H

(919) 549-8631. **Call for rates.** 150 Park Dr 27709. I-40 exit 280, just s, then just w. Int corridors. **Pets:** Accepted.
[ECO] 🛜 ✕ 🛏 🖵 🍽 🏊 ✕

ROANOKE RAPIDS

Baymont Inn & Suites Roanoke Rapids M

(252) 533-0022. **Call for rates.** 101 S Old Farm Rd 27870. I-95 exit 173, 0.5 mi w on US 158, then just e. Ext corridors. **Pets:** Accepted.
🛜 🛏 🖵 🏊

Quality Inn M

(252) 537-9927. **Call for rates.** 1914 Julian R Allsbrook Hwy 27870. I-95 exit 173, just w. Ext corridors. **Pets:** Medium, other species. $15 one-time fee/room. Designated rooms, service with restrictions, supervision. 🛜 🛏 🖵 🏊

Super 8 Roanoke Rapids M

(252) 537-1011. **Call for rates.** 6785 NC 46 Hwy 27831. I-95 exit 176, just w. Ext corridors. **Pets:** Medium, other species. Service with restrictions. 🛜 🛏 🖵 🍽 🏊

ROBBINSVILLE

Microtel Inn & Suites by Wyndham Robbinsville H

(828) 479-6772. **$65-$85.** 111 Rodney Orr Bypass (US 129) 28771. Center of downtown. Int corridors. **Pets:** Accepted. 🛜 ✕ 🛏 🖵

ROCKY MOUNT

BEST WESTERN Inn I-95/Goldrock M 🐾

(252) 985-1450. **$60-$110.** 7095 NC 4 27809. I-95 exit 145, just e. Ext corridors. **Pets:** Medium. $20 one-time fee/room. Designated rooms, supervision. [SAVE] 🛜 🛏 🖵

Candlewood Suites H 🐾

(252) 467-2550. **Call for rates.** 688 English Rd 27804. I-95 exit 138, 1 mi e on US 64 exit 466, just n on Winstead Ave, then just w. Int corridors. **Pets:** Medium, other species. $25 one-time fee/room. Service with restrictions, crate. 🛜 🅼 🛏 🖵

Comfort Inn H

(252) 937-7765. **$80-$120.** 200 Gateway Blvd 27804. I-95 exit 138, 1 mi e on US 64 exit 466, just s on Winstead Ave, just e on Curtis Ellis Dr, then just ne. Int corridors. **Pets:** Accepted. [SAVE] 🛜 🛏 🖵

Country Inn & Suites By Carlson ◨ ✿
(252) 442-0500. **$79-$169, 14 day notice.** 672 English Rd 27804. I-95 exit 138, 1 mi e on US 64 exit 466, just n on Winstead Ave, then just w. Int corridors. **Pets:** Other species. $15 one-time fee/room. Designated rooms, service with restrictions, crate.

Residence Inn by Marriott Rocky Mount ◨ ✿
(252) 451-5600. **$99-$199.** 230 Gateway Blvd 27804. I-95 exit 138, 1 mi e on US 64 exit 466, just s on Winstead Ave, just e on Curtis Ellis Dr, then just ne. Int corridors. **Pets:** Other species. $40 one-time fee/room. Designated rooms, service with restrictions.

Rocky Mount Inn M
(252) 442-8101. **$50-$99.** 1921 N Wesleyan Blvd 27804. US 64 exit 468A, 2.2 mi n on US 301 Bypass. Ext corridors. **Pets:** Accepted.

ROXBORO
Hampton Inn ◨
(336) 599-8800. **Call for rates.** 920 Durham Rd 27573. Jct US 158, n on US 501. Int corridors. **Pets:** Accepted.

Innkeeper M
(336) 599-3800. **Call for rates.** 906 Durham Rd 27573. Jct US 158, n on US 501. Ext/int corridors. **Pets:** Medium. $50 one-time fee/room. Designated rooms, service with restrictions, supervision.

SALISBURY
Hampton Inn ◨
(704) 637-8000. **$129-$199.** 1001 Klumac Rd 28144. I-85 exit 75, just n on US 601, then just sw. Int corridors. **Pets:** Designated rooms, service with restrictions, supervision.

Holiday Inn Hotel & Conference Center ◨
(704) 637-3100. **$89-$129.** 530 Jake Alexander Blvd S 28147. I-85 exit 75, 0.5 mi n on US 601. Ext/int corridors. **Pets:** Small. $25 one-time fee/pet. Service with restrictions, supervision.

SALUDA
The Oaks Bed & Breakfast BB ✿
(828) 749-2000. **$139-$199, 14 day notice.** 339 Greenville St 28773. I-26 exit 59, 1.1 mi sw, 0.5 mi w on US 176, then cross railway tracks. Ext/int corridors. **Pets:** Other species. $50 one-time fee/room. Designated rooms, service with restrictions, supervision.

SANFORD
Hampton Inn ◨
(919) 775-2000. **$85-$119.** 1904 S Horner Blvd 27330. Jct US 1 exit 69A, 3.2 mi s on US 421 and SR 87. Int corridors. **Pets:** Accepted.

Holiday Inn Express Hotel & Suites ◨ ✿
(919) 776-6600. **Call for rates.** 2110 Dalrymple St 27330. Jct US 1 exit 69A, 3.5 mi s on US 421 and SR 87, then just w. Int corridors. **Pets:** Medium, other species. $35 one-time fee/pet. Designated rooms, service with restrictions, crate.

Jameson Inn M
(919) 708-7400. **Call for rates.** 2614 S Horner Blvd 27330. Jct US 1 exit 69A, 4.1 mi s on US 421 and SR 87. Ext corridors. **Pets:** Accepted.

SCOTLAND NECK
Scotland Neck Inn M
(252) 826-5141. **$60-$90, 3 day notice.** 308 S Main St 27874. Jct SR 125 S, just s on US 258. Int corridors. **Pets:** $10 daily fee/pet. Designated rooms, service with restrictions, supervision.

SELMA
Days Inn ◨
(919) 965-4000. **$65-$80.** 115 US 70A 27576. I-95 exit 97, just e, then just n. Int corridors. **Pets:** Medium, other species. $15 one-time fee/pet. Service with restrictions, crate.

Quality Inn M
(919) 965-5200. **Call for rates.** 1705 Industrial Park Dr 27576. I-95 exit 97, just w, then just s. Ext corridors. **Pets:** $15 daily fee/room. Service with restrictions, supervision.

SHALLOTTE
Days Inn Shallotte ◨
(910) 754-3300. **$55-$150.** 3670 Express Dr 28470. Jct SR 130, 0.9 mi n on US 17, just w on N Mulberry Dr, then just s. Int corridors. **Pets:** Accepted.

SMITHFIELD
Baymont Inn & Suites Smithfield M
(919) 989-5901. **Call for rates.** 125 S Equity Dr 27577. I-95 exit 95, just w on US 70 business route, just n on Industrial Park Blvd, then just w. Ext corridors. **Pets:** Accepted.

Super 8 ◨ ✿
(919) 989-8988. **$67-$89.** 735 Industrial Park Dr 27577. I-95 exit 95, just w on US 70 business route, then just n. Int corridors. **Pets:** Medium. $15 daily fee/room. Designated rooms, service with restrictions, supervision.

SOUTHERN PINES
BEST WESTERN Pinehurst Inn ◨
(910) 692-0640. **$80-$110.** 1675 US Hwy 1 S 28387. Jct US 15/501, 0.5 mi n on US 1. Ext corridors. **Pets:** Accepted.

Econo Lodge Inn & Suites ◨
(910) 692-2063. **$65-$99.** 408 W Morganton Rd 28387. US 1 exit Morganton Rd, just w. Int corridors. **Pets:** Medium, other species. $20 daily fee/pet. Service with restrictions, supervision.

Residence Inn by Marriott-Pinehurst/Southern Pines ◨
(910) 693-3400. **$98-$179.** 105 Brucewood Rd 28387. Jct US 1, 1.2 mi n on US 15/501, then just e. Int corridors. **Pets:** $125 one-time fee/room. Service with restrictions.

SOUTHPORT
Comfort Suites ◨
(910) 454-7444. **$89-$134.** 4963 Southport Supply Rd (SR 211) 28461. Jct SR 87, 1.8 mi n. Int corridors. **Pets:** Accepted.

SPRUCE PINE
Richmond Inn BB
(828) 765-6993. **Call for rates.** 51 Pine Ave 28777. Jct US 19E, just n on SR 226 business route (Highland Ave), just e on Oak St, just n on Walnut Ave, just w on Balsam Ave, then just ne. Int corridors. **Pets:** Accepted.

STATESVILLE
BEST WESTERN Statesville Inn M ✿
(704) 881-0111. **$77-$110.** 1121 Morland Dr 28677. I-77 exit 49A, just e on US 70. Ext corridors. **Pets:** Small. $20 daily fee/pet. Designated rooms, service with restrictions, supervision.

Comfort Inn & Suites ◨
(704) 873-2044. **Call for rates.** 1214 Greenland Dr 28677. I-77 exit 49A, just e on US 70, then just s. Int corridors. **Pets:** Small, other species. $15 one-time fee/room. Designated rooms, service with restrictions, supervision.

Courtyard by Marriott Statesville Mooresville/ Lake Norman 🅷 ❀

(704) 768-2400. **$99-$154.** 1530 Cinema Dr 28625. I-77 exit 49B, just e on Salisbury Rd, 0.6 mi n on Folger Dr, then just e. Int corridors.
Pets: Medium, other species. $50 one-time fee/room. Designated rooms, service with restrictions, crate. (SAVE) 📶 ⊠ 🅺M 🛗 🖵 ¶ ⚤

Quality Inn & Suites 🅼

(704) 878-2721. **Call for rates.** 715 Sullivan Rd 28677. I-40 exit 151, just s on US 21. Ext corridors. **Pets:** Accepted. 📶 🛗 🖵 ⚤

Red Roof Inn 🅼

(704) 878-2051. **$44-$79.** 1508 E Broad St 28625. I-77 exit 50, just e, then just s on Middleton St. Ext corridors. **Pets:** Large, other species. Service with restrictions, supervision. (SAVE) 📶 🅺M 🛗 🖵

SYLVA
Holiday Inn Express 🅷

(828) 631-1111. **$99-$149.** 26 Rufus Robinson Rd 28779. US 23/74 exit 81B, just n. Int corridors. **Pets:** Large. $25 daily fee/pet. Service with restrictions, crate. 📶 🅺M 🛗 🖵 ⚤

THOMASVILLE
Comfort Inn-Thomasville 🅷

(336) 472-6600. **$59-$79.** 895 Lake Rd 27360. I-85 exit 102, just w, then just s. Int corridors. **Pets:** Medium, dogs only. $15 daily fee/pet. Designated rooms, no service, supervision. (SAVE) 📶 🛗 🖵 ⚤

Microtel Inn & Suites by Wyndham Thomasville/High Point/Lexington 🅷

(336) 474-4515. **$55-$130.** 959 Lake Rd 27360. I-85 exit 102, just w, then just s. Int corridors. **Pets:** Small, dogs only. $20 daily fee/room. Designated rooms, service with restrictions, supervision. 📶 🅺M 🛗 🖵 ⚤

WAKE FOREST
Candlewood Suites 🅷

(919) 554-6901. **$104-$114.** 12050 Retail Dr 27587. Jct US 1, just w on SR 98 (Durham Rd), then just s. Int corridors. **Pets:** Accepted.
📶 🅺M 🛗 🖵

Hampton Inn 🅷

(919) 554-0222. **$89-$129.** 12318 Wake Union Church Rd 27587. Jct SR 98, 0.5 mi n on US 1, then 0.5 mi w. Int corridors. **Pets:** Accepted.
📶 🅺M 🛗 🖵 ⚤

WAYNESVILLE
Rodeway Inn 🅼

(828) 452-9009. **$80-$110.** 232 Phillips Rd 28786. US 23/74 exit 102 (US 276), just sw. Ext corridors. **Pets:** Accepted.
📶 🅺M 🛗 🖵 ⚤

Super 8 🅼

(828) 454-9667. **$50-$120.** 79 Liner Cove Rd 28786. I-40 exit 27, to US 23/74, 3 mi; exit 104 (Liner Cove Rd). Ext corridors. **Pets:** Medium, dogs only. $15 daily fee/pet. No service, supervision. 📶 🅺M 🛗 🖵 ⚤

The Waynesville Inn Golf Resort & Spa 🅷

(828) 456-3551. **$79-$169.** 176 Country Club Dr 28786. US 23 S/74 W exit 100, 0.6 mi s on Hazelwood Ave, then 0.3 mi e on Virginia Ave. Ext/int corridors. **Pets:** Accepted. (SAVE) 📶 🅺M 🛗 🖵 ¶ ⚤

The Yellow House on Plott Creek Road 🅱🅱

(828) 452-0991. **$165-$265, 15 day notice.** 89 Oakview Dr 28786. US 23/74 exit 100 eastbound, 1.3 mi nw on Plott Creek Rd; exit 100 westbound, just se, just w on Sulphur Springs Rd, then 1.4 mi nw on Plott Creek Rd. Ext/int corridors. **Pets:** Other species. Designated rooms, service with restrictions. 📶 ⊠ 🛗 🖵

WEST JEFFERSON
Nation's Inn 🅼

(336) 246-2080. **$81-$91.** 107 Beaver Creek School Rd 28694. Jct US 221, just n on SR 194, then just w. Ext corridors. **Pets:** Accepted.
📶 🅺M 🛗 🖵 ⚤

WHITEVILLE
Econo Lodge 🅼

(910) 642-2378. **Call for rates.** 503 N J K Powell Blvd 28472. Jct US 74/76, 1 mi s on US 701 Bypass. Ext corridors. **Pets:** Accepted.
📶 🛗 🖵 ⚤

WILKESBORO
Holiday Inn Express 🅷

(336) 838-1800. **$70-$100.** 1700 Winkler St 28697. Jct SR 16 N, 2 mi nw on US 421/SR 16. Int corridors. **Pets:** Medium. $30 daily fee/pet. Designated rooms, service with restrictions, crate.
(SAVE) 📶 🅺M 🛗 🖵 ⚤

WILLIAMSTON
The Inn at Moratoc 🅷

(252) 792-3184. **Call for rates.** 101 East Blvd 27892. US 64 exit 514, 1.5 mi n on US 17 business route. Ext/int corridors. **Pets:** Accepted.
📶 🛗 🖵 ¶ ⚤

WILMINGTON
Baymont Inn 🅼

(910) 392-6767. **$63-$103, 3 day notice.** 306 S College Rd 28403. Jct US 17 business route, just s on SR 132. Ext/int corridors. **Pets:** $10 deposit/pet. Designated rooms, service with restrictions, supervision.
📶 🛗 🖵 ⚤

BEST WESTERN PLUS Coastline Inn 🅷 ❀

(910) 763-2800. **$99-$189.** 503 Nutt St 28401. Jct Market St, just w on Front St, just s on Red Cross St, then just w. Ext corridors. **Pets:** Large, dogs only. $20 daily fee/room. Designated rooms, service with restrictions, supervision. (SAVE) 📶 ⊠ 🛗 🖵

BEST WESTERN PLUS University Inn 🅷

(910) 799-4292. **$70-$149.** 5345 Market St 28405. Jct SR 132, just s on US 17 business route. Int corridors. **Pets:** Small, dogs only. $50 one-time fee/room. Service with restrictions, crate. (SAVE) 📶 🛗 🖵 ⚤

Comfort Inn University 🅷

(910) 791-4841. **Call for rates.** 151 S College Rd 28403. Jct US 17 business route, just s on SR 132. Int corridors. **Pets:** Accepted.
📶 🛗 🖵 ⚤

Days Inn 🅼

(910) 799-6300. **$51-$100.** 5040 Market St 28405. Jct SR 132, 0.6 mi s on US 17 business route. Ext corridors. **Pets:** Other species. $15 daily fee/room. Service with restrictions, crate. 📶 🛗 🖵 ¶ ⚤

Jameson Inn 🅷

(910) 452-5660. **Call for rates.** 5102 Dunlea Ct 28405. Jct SR 132, 0.5 mi s on US 17 business route, just w on New Centre Dr. Int corridors.
Pets: Accepted. 📶 🛗 🖵 ⚤

MainStay Suites 🅷

(910) 392-1741. **$69-$129.** 5229 Market St 28405. Jct SR 132, just s on US 17 business route. Int corridors. **Pets:** Accepted. 📶 🅺M 🛗 🖵

Quality Inn 🅼

(910) 791-8850. **Call for rates.** 4926 Market St 28405. Jct SR 132, 0.9 mi s on US 17 business route. Ext corridors. **Pets:** Medium, other species. $25 one-time fee/pet, $5 daily fee/pet. Designated rooms, service with restrictions, supervision. 📶 🛗 🖵 ⚤

Residence Inn by Marriott Wilmington Landfall 🅷

(910) 256-0098. **$109-$209.** 1200 Culbreth Dr 28405. Jct US 17 business route, 2.4 mi e on US 74, 0.4 mi n on Military Cutoff Rd, then just e. Int corridors. **Pets:** Medium. $100 one-time fee/room. Designated rooms, service with restrictions.

Staybridge Suites Wilmington East 🅷

(910) 202-8500. **$89-$199.** 5010 New Centre Dr 28403. Jct SR 132, 0.5 mi s on US 17 business route, then just e. Int corridors. **Pets:** Large, dogs only. $150 one-time fee/pet. Service with restrictions, supervision.

 TownePlace Suites by Marriott Wilmington/ Wrightsville Beach 🅷 🐾

(910) 332-3326. **$79-$189.** 305 Eastwood Rd 28403. Jct US 17 business route, just e on US 74. Int corridors. **Pets:** Medium, other species. $75 one-time fee/room. Designated rooms, service with restrictions, crate.

WILSON

 Days Inn Ⓜ

(252) 291-2323. **$70-$95.** 1801 S Tarboro St 27893. US 264 exit 40, 3.3 mi e on SR 42. Ext corridors. **Pets:** Medium. $15 daily fee/pet. Service with restrictions, supervision.

WINDSOR

The Inn at Grays Landing 🅲🅸

(252) 794-2255. **$70-$140.** 401 S King St 27983. US 17, just w on SR 308. Int corridors. **Pets:** Medium. $25 one-time fee/pet. Designated rooms, service with restrictions.

WINSTON-SALEM

Augustus T Zevely Inn 🅱🅱

(336) 748-9299. **$95-$240, 14 day notice.** 803 S Main St 27101. I-40 business route exit 5D eastbound, 0.5 mi s on Liberty St to Old Salem Rd, just e on Academy St, then just s; exit 5C westbound, just n on Cherry St, just e on 2nd St, 1 mi s on Liberty St to Old Salem Rd, just e on Academy St, then just s. Ext/int corridors. **Pets:** Accepted.

Embassy Suites-Winston-Salem 🅷 🐾

(336) 724-2300. **Call for rates.** 460 N Cherry St 27101. I-40 business route exit 5C (Cherry St), just n. Int corridors. **Pets:** Large, other species. $75 one-time fee/room. Designated rooms, no service, crate.

Extended StayAmerica Winston-Salem-Hanes Mall Blvd Ⓜ

(336) 768-0075. **$55-$80.** 1995 Hampton Inn Ct 27103. I-40 exit 189 (Stratford Rd), just s, just e on Hanes Mall Blvd, then just n. Ext corridors. **Pets:** $25 daily fee/pet. Designated rooms, service with restrictions.

Fairfield Inn & Suites by Marriott Winston-Salem Hanes Mall 🅷

(336) 714-3000. **$84-$109.** 1680 Westbrook Plaza Dr 27103. I-40 exit 189 (Stratford Rd), 0.5 mi n, just w, then just s. Int corridors. **Pets:** Accepted.

 The Hawthorne Inn & Conference Center 🅷

(336) 777-3000. **$80-$165.** 420 High St 27101. I-40 business route exit 5C (Cherry St) eastbound, just e; exit westbound, just w on 1st St, then just s on Marshall St. Int corridors. **Pets:** Medium. $15 daily fee/pet. Designated rooms, service with restrictions, crate.

Innkeeper Ⓜ

(336) 721-0062. **Call for rates.** 2115 Peters Creek Pkwy 27127. I-40 exit 192 (Peters Creek Pkwy), just ne on SR 150. Ext/int corridors. **Pets:** Medium, other species. $25 daily fee/room. Designated rooms, service with restrictions, crate.

La Quinta Inns & Suites Winston-Salem 🅷

(336) 765-8777. **$63-$166.** 2020 Griffith Rd 27103. I-40 exit 189 (Stratford Rd), just s, just e on Hanes Mall Blvd, then just s. Int corridors. **Pets:** Service with restrictions, supervision.

Quality Inn & Suites-Hanes Mall 🅷

(336) 765-6670. **$55-$170.** 2008 S Hawthorne Rd 27103. I-40 business route exit 2A, 0.5 mi s on Silas Creek Pkwy, then just e. Ext corridors. **Pets:** Medium. $25 one-time fee/pet. Designated rooms, service with restrictions, crate.

Quality Inn-Coliseum 🅷

(336) 767-8240. **$60-$110.** 531 Akron Dr 27105. US 52 exit 112, just e. Int corridors. **Pets:** Medium. $20 daily fee/pet. Service with restrictions, crate.

Residence Inn by Marriott Winston-Salem 🅷

(336) 759-0777. **$119-$149.** 7835 North Point Blvd 27106. US 52 exit 115B, 2 mi s on University Pkwy, then just e. Ext corridors. **Pets:** Accepted.

Sleep Inn-Hanes Mall 🅷

(336) 774-8020. **Call for rates.** 1985 Hampton Inn Ct 27103. I-40 exit 189 (Stratford Rd), just s, just e on Hanes Mall Blvd, then just n. Int corridors. **Pets:** Medium. $25 daily fee/pet. Designated rooms, service with restrictions, crate.

Sundance Plaza Hotel, Spa & Wellness Center 🅷

(336) 723-2911. **$90-$160.** 3050 University Pkwy 27105. I-40 business route exit 5C (Cherry St), 3 mi n. Int corridors. **Pets:** Accepted.

Wingate by Wyndham 🅷

(336) 714-2800. **$89-$129.** 125 S Main St 27101. I-40 business route exit 5D, just n. Int corridors. **Pets:** Other species. $50 one-time fee/room. Service with restrictions, supervision.

NORTH DAKOTA

BEULAH

▼▼ AmericInn Lodge & Suites of Beulah H
(701) 873-2220. **$113-$186.** 2100 2nd Ave NW 58523. Jct SR 49/200, 1.2 mi s. Int corridors. **Pets:** Accepted. 🛜 ⊠ &M 🛢 🖵 �

BISMARCK

 ▼▼◆ Americas Best Value Inn & Suites M
(701) 223-8060. **$74-$117.** 1505 Interchange Ave 58501. I-94 exit 159 (US 83), just se. Int corridors. **Pets:** Other species. $10 daily fee/pet. Designated rooms, service with restrictions, supervision.
SAVE 🛜 ⊠ &M 🛢 🖵

◆◆ ▼◆▼◆ BEST WESTERN PLUS Ramkota Hotel H ❀
(701) 258-7700. **$109-$139.** 800 S 3rd St 58504. Just s of jct I-94 business loop (Bismarck Expwy) and S 3rd St. Int corridors. **Pets:** $10 daily fee/room. Designated rooms, service with restrictions, supervision.
SAVE 🛜 ⊠ &M 🛢 🖵 🍽 ⊸ ⊠

▼◆▼ Candlewood Suites H
(701) 751-8900. **$130-$150.** 4400 Skyline Crossings 58503. I-94 exit 159 (US 83), 1.7 mi n, then just e. Int corridors. **Pets:** Accepted.
🛜 &M 🛢 🖵 ⊸

▼◆▼ Comfort Inn H
(701) 223-1911. **$80-$145.** 1030 Interstate Ave 58503. I-94 exit 159 (US 83), 0.3 mi nw. Int corridors. **Pets:** Accepted.
🛜 &M 🛢 🖵 ⊸ ⊠

▼◆▼ Days Inn-Bismarck H
(701) 223-9151. **$80-$170.** 1300 E Capitol Ave 58501. I-94 exit 159 (US 83), just s. Int corridors. **Pets:** Accepted.
🛜 ⊠ &M 🛢 🖵 ⊸ ⊠

▼◆▼ Kelly Inn M
(701) 223-8001. **$109-$149.** 1800 N 12th St 58501. I-94 exit 159 (US 83), 0.3 mi s. Int corridors. **Pets:** Accepted.
🛜 ⊠ &M 🛢 🖵 🍽 ⊸ ⊠

▼◆▼◆ La Quinta Inn & Suites Bismarck H
(701) 751-3313. **$113-$205.** 2240 N 12th St 58501. I-94 exit 159 (US 83), just s. Int corridors. **Pets:** Service with restrictions, supervision.
🛜 ⊠ &M 🛢 🖵 ⊸ ⊠

▼◆▼◆ Radisson Hotel Bismarck H
(701) 255-6000. **$124-$139.** 605 E Broadway Ave 58501. Jct 6th St; center. Int corridors. **Pets:** Large, other species. $20 one-time fee/room. Designated rooms, service with restrictions, supervision.
🛜 ⊠ &M 🛢 🖵 🍽 ⊸ ⊠

◆◆ ▼◆ ▼◆ Ramada Bismarck Hotel H ❀
(701) 258-7000. **Call for rates.** 1400 E Interchange Ave 58501. I-94 exit 159 (US 83), just s. Int corridors. **Pets:** $10 daily fee/room. Designated rooms, service with restrictions, supervision.
SAVE 🛜 ⊠ &M 🛢 🖵 🍽 ⊠

◆◆◆ ▼◆▼◆ Ramada Limited Bismarck H
(701) 221-3030. **$134-$249.** 3808 E Divide Ave 58501. I-94 exit 161, just s on E Bismarck Expwy. Int corridors. **Pets:** Large, other species. $10 daily fee/room. Designated rooms, crate. SAVE 🛜 &M 🛢 🖵 ⊸

▼◆▼◆ Residence Inn by Marriott Bismarck H
(701) 258-6088. **$119-$299.** 3421 N 14th St 58503. I-94 exit 159 (US 83), just n. Int corridors. **Pets:** Accepted. 🛜 ⊠ &M 🛢 🖵

◆◆◆ ▼◆▼◆ Super 8 M
(701) 255-1314. **$55-$150, 3 day notice.** 1124 E Capitol Ave 58501. I-94 exit 159 (US 83), just s. Int corridors. **Pets:** Accepted.
SAVE 🛜 🛢 🖵

BOTTINEAU

▼◆▼ Super 8 of Bottineau H
(701) 228-2125. **$86.** 1007 11th St E 58318. 0.5 mi e on SR 5. Int corridors. **Pets:** Accepted. 🛜 &M 🛢 🖵

CARRINGTON

▼◆▼ Carrington Inn & Suites M
(701) 652-3982. **$65-$105.** 101 4th Ave S 58421. Jct US 52 and 281, 0.5 mi s on US 52; just s of jct SR 200. Int corridors. **Pets:** Small. $10 daily fee/pet. Designated rooms, service with restrictions, supervision.
🛜 🛢

▼◆▼ Chieftain Conference Center M
(701) 652-3131. **$71-$120.** 60 4th Ave S 58421. Jct US 52 and 281, 0.5 mi s on US 52; just s of jct SR 200. Ext/int corridors. **Pets:** Accepted.
🛜 &M 🛢 🖵 🍽

CASSELTON

▼◆▼ Days Inn & Governors Conference Center H
(701) 347-4524. **$65-$130.** 2050 Governors Dr 58012. I-94 exit 331, just n on SR 18. Int corridors. **Pets:** Dogs only. $10 daily fee/pet. Service with restrictions, supervision. 🛜 &M 🛢 🖵 🍽 ⊸ ⊠

DICKINSON

◆◆◆ ▼◆▼ Comfort Inn H
(701) 264-7300. **Call for rates.** 493 Elks Dr 58601. I-94 exit 61 (SR 22), just n, then w. Int corridors. **Pets:** $10 daily fee/pet. Service with restrictions, supervision. SAVE 🛜 ⊠ &M 🛢 🖵 ⊸ ⊠

▼◆▼◆ Holiday Inn Express Hotel & Suites H
(701) 456-8000. **$159-$175.** 103 14th St W 58601. I-94 exit 61 (SR 22), just n, then just e. Int corridors. **Pets:** Medium, dogs only. $50 one-time fee/room. Service with restrictions, supervision.
🛜 ⊠ &M 🛢 🖵 ⊸ ⊠

▼◆▼◆ La Quinta Inn & Suites H
(701) 456-2500. **$131-$276.** 552 12th St W 58601. I-94 exit 61 (SR 22), just s, then just w. Int corridors. **Pets:** Service with restrictions, supervision. 🛜 ⊠ &M 🛢 🖵 ⊸

▼◆▼◆ Microtel Inn & Suites by Wyndham Dickinson H
(701) 456-2000. **$130-$190.** 1597 6th Ave W 58601. I-94 exit 61 (SR 22), just n, then w. Int corridors. **Pets:** Accepted.
🛜 ⊠ &M 🛢 🖵 ⊸

◆◆◆ ▼◆▼◆ Quality Inn & Suites-Dickinson H
(701) 225-9510. **$109-$189.** 71 Museum Dr 58601. I-94 exit 61 (SR 22), just s, then just e. Int corridors. **Pets:** Medium, other species. $10 daily fee/pet. Designated rooms, service with restrictions, supervision.
SAVE 🛜 &M 🛢 🖵 ⊠

FARGO

◆◆◆ ▼◆▼ AmericInn Lodge & Suites of Fargo H
(701) 234-9946. **$78-$142.** 1423 35th St SW 58103. I-29 exit 64 (13th Ave S), just e, just s on 34th St SW, then just w. Int corridors.
Pets: Accepted. SAVE 🛜 ⊠ &M 🛢 🖵 ⊸ ⊠

AAA ▼▼ ◆ **BEST WESTERN Fargo Doublewood Inn** 🅷 ☙

(701) 235-3333. **$95-$115.** 3333 13th Ave S 58103. I-29 exit 64 (13th Ave S), 0.3 mi e. Int corridors. **Pets:** Medium. $15 one-time fee/pet. Designated rooms, service with restrictions, supervision.

SAVE 🛜 ✕ &M 🔒 🖵 🖳 ⑪ ⇲ ✕

AAA ▼▼◆▼ **BEST WESTERN PLUS Kelly Inn & Suites** 🅷 ☙

(701) 282-2143. **$99-$160.** 1767 44th St S 58103. I-94 exit 348 (45th St SW), just n, then just e on 18th Ave. Ext/int corridors. **Pets:** Medium. Service with restrictions, supervision.

SAVE 🛜 ✕ &M 🔒 🖵 🖳 ⇲ ✕

▼▼◆▼ **Candlewood Suites** 🅷

(701) 235-8200. **Call for rates.** 1831 NDSU Research Park Dr 58102. I-29 exit 67 (19th Ave), 1.6 mi e. Int corridors. **Pets:** Large, other species. $25 one-time fee/room. Service with restrictions, crate.

🛜 &M 🔒 🖵

AAA ▼▼◆▼ **Country Inn & Suites By Carlson** 🅷

(701) 234-0565. **Call for rates.** 3316 13th Ave S 58103. I-29 exit 64 (13th Ave S), 0.3 mi e. Int corridors. **Pets:** $10 daily fee/pet. Designated rooms, service with restrictions, supervision.

SAVE 🛜 ✕ &M 🔒 🖵 🖳 ⇲ ✕

▼▼◆ **Days Inn Fargo** 🅷

(701) 235-5566. **$80-$180.** 3431 14th Ave SW 58103. I-29 exit 64 (13th Ave SW), just e, just s on 34th St SW, then just w. Int corridors. **Pets:** Other species. $15 daily fee/room. Service with restrictions.

🛜 &M 🔒 🖵 ⇲

▼▼◆ **Econo Lodge** 🅼

(701) 232-3412. **$69-$139.** 1401 35th St SW 58103. I-29 exit 64 (13th Ave S), just e, just s on 34th St SW, then just w. Int corridors. **Pets:** $10 daily fee/room. Service with restrictions, crate. 🛜 ✕ &M 🔒 🖵

▼▼◆ **Econo Lodge West** 🅷

(701) 282-9596. **Call for rates.** 3825 9th Ave SW 58103. I-29 exit 64 (13th Ave S), just n on west frontage road (38th St SW), then just w. Int corridors. **Pets:** Accepted. 🛜 ✕ 🔒 🖵 ⇲

AAA ▼▼◆▼ **Fargo Inn & Suites** 🅷

(701) 282-6300. **$65-$85.** 1025 38th St SW 58103. I-29 exit 64 (13th Ave S), just n on west frontage road (38th St SW). Int corridors. **Pets:** Medium. $25 deposit/room, $5 daily fee/pet. Service with restrictions, supervision. SAVE 🛜 🔒 🖵

AAA ▼▼◆▼ **Holiday Inn of Fargo** 🅷

(701) 282-2700. **$129-$179.** 3803 13th Ave S 58103. I-29 exit 64 (13th Ave S), just nw. Int corridors. **Pets:** Large, other species. $30 daily fee/pet. Service with restrictions, supervision.

SAVE 🛜 ✕ &M 🔒 🖵 ⑪ ⇲ ✕

▼▼◆ **Kelly Inn** 🅷

(701) 281-9700. **$84-$150, 3 day notice.** 3800 Main Ave (US 10) 58103. I-29 exit 65, just sw on US 10. Ext/int corridors. **Pets:** Medium. Service with restrictions, supervision.

🛜 &M 🔒 🖵 ⑪ ⇲ ✕

▼▼◆ **Kelly Inn 13th Avenue** 🅷

(701) 277-8821. **$88-$134, 5 day notice.** 4207 13th Ave SW 58103. I-29 exit 64 (13th Ave S), 0.4 mi w. Ext/int corridors. **Pets:** Medium. Service with restrictions, supervision. 🛜 ✕ &M 🔒 🖵 ⇲

▼▼◆▼ **La Quinta Inn & Suites Fargo** 🅷

(701) 499-2000. **$107-$177.** 2355 46th St S 58104. I-94 exit 348 (45th St SW), just s, then just w. Int corridors. **Pets:** Service with restrictions, supervision. 🛜 ✕ &M 🔒 🖵 ⇲

▼▼◆ **MainStay Suites** 🅷

(701) 277-4627. **$80-$173.** 1901 44th St SW 58103. I-94 exit 348 (45th St SW), just n, then just e. Int corridors. **Pets:** $25 one-time fee/room. Crate. 🛜 &M 🔒 🖵 ⇲

▼▼◆ **Quality Inn** 🅷

(701) 280-9666. **Call for rates.** 1407 35th St SW 58103. I-29 exit 64 (13th Ave S), just e, just s on 34th St SW, then just w. Int corridors. **Pets:** $15 one-time fee/pet. Service with restrictions, supervision.

🛜 🔒 🖵 ⇲

▼▼◆ **Quality Suites** 🅷

(701) 237-5911. **Call for rates.** 1415 35th St SW 58103. I-29 exit 64 (13th Ave S), just e, just s on 34th St SW, then just w. Int corridors. **Pets:** Accepted. 🛜 ✕ &M 🔒 🖵 ⇲

AAA ▼▼◆ **Sleep Inn** 🅷

(701) 281-8240. **$59-$117.** 1921 44th St SW 58103. I-94 exit 348 (45th St SW), just n, just e on 19th Ave S, then just s. Int corridors. **Pets:** Accepted. SAVE 🛜 🔒 🖵 ⇲

AAA ▼▼◆▼ **Staybridge Suites** 🅷

(701) 281-4900. **$89-$199.** 4300 20th Ave S 58103. I-94 exit 348 (45th St SW), just n, just e on 19th Ave, just s on 44th St S, then just e. Int corridors. **Pets:** Large, other species. $50 one-time fee/room. Designated rooms, service with restrictions, crate.

SAVE 🛜 &M 🔒 🖵 ⇲ ✕

▼▼◆ **Super 8 Fargo/I-29/West Acres Mall** 🅷

(701) 232-9202. **$60-$131.** 3518 Interstate Blvd 58103. I-29 exit 64 (13th Ave S), just n on east frontage road via 35th St. Int corridors. **Pets:** Accepted. 🛜 &M 🔒 🖵 ⇲

GRAND FORKS

AAA ▼◆ **Americas Best Value Inn of Grand Forks** 🅼 🐾

(701) 775-0555. **$50-$100.** 1000 N 42nd St 58203. I-29 exit 141, just e on US 2 (Gateway Dr), then just s. Int corridors. **Pets:** Other species. $10 daily fee/pet. Designated rooms, service with restrictions, supervision.

SAVE 🛜 ✕ 🔒

AAA ▼▼◆ **Days Inn - Columbia Mall** 🅷

(701) 775-0060. **$75-$120.** 3101 S 34th St 58201. I-29 exit 138, 0.4 mi e on 32nd Ave S, then just n. Int corridors. **Pets:** Small. $10 daily fee/pet. Designated rooms, service with restrictions, supervision.

SAVE 🛜 🔒 🖵 ⇲

AAA ▼▼◆ **GuestHouse International Town House** 🅷

(701) 746-5411. **$73-$130.** 710 1st Ave N 58203. I-29 exit 140, 2.8 mi e on DeMers Ave, then just n; downtown. Int corridors. **Pets:** Other species. $15 one-time fee/room. Designated rooms, service with restrictions, supervision. SAVE 🛜 🔒 🖵 ⑪ ⇲ ✕

AAA ▼▼◆ **Howard Johnson Grand Forks** 🅷 ☙

(701) 772-7131. **$69-$139.** 1210 N 43rd St 58203. I-29 exit 141, just e on US 2 (Gateway Dr), then just s. Ext/int corridors. **Pets:** $15 daily fee/room. Crate. SAVE 🛜 🔒 🖵 ⑪ ⇲ ✕

▼▼◆ **Ramada Inn** 🅷

(701) 775-3951. **$64-$104.** 1205 N 43rd St 58203. I-29 exit 141, just e on US 2 (Gateway Dr), then just s. Int corridors. **Pets:** $10 daily fee/pet. Designated rooms, service with restrictions, supervision.

🛜 🔒 🖵 ⑪ ⇲ ✕

JAMESTOWN

▼▼◆ **Quality Inn & Suites** 🅷

(701) 252-3611. **Call for rates.** 507 25th St SW 58401. I-94 exit 258 (US 281), just se. Int corridors. **Pets:** Other species. $10 daily fee/room. Designated rooms, service with restrictions.

🛜 🔒 🖵 ⑪ ⇲ ✕

AAA ▼▼◆ **Super 8** 🅷

(701) 252-4715. **$55-$90.** 2623 Hwy 281 S 58401. I-94 exit 258 (US 281), just s. Int corridors. **Pets:** Accepted. SAVE 🛜 🔒 🖵

MANDAN

 BEST WESTERN PLUS Seven Seas Hotel & Waterpark ⊞

(701) 663-7401. **$112-$132.** 2611 Old Red Tr 58554. I-94 exit 152, just n on Sunset Dr, then just w. Int corridors. **Pets:** Accepted.

[SAVE] 🛜 ✕ ᴴᴹ 🔋 💻 ⍚ 🏊 ✕

MINOT

 BEST WESTERN Kelly Inn Ⓜ ❀

(701) 852-4300. **$119-$150.** 1510 26th Ave SW 58701. US 2 and 52 Bypass, at 16th St SW. Ext/int corridors. **Pets:** Service with restrictions, crate. [SAVE] 🛜 ✕ ᴴᴹ 🔋 💻 🏊 ✕

▽▽▽ Candlewood Suites ⊞ ❀

(701) 858-7700. **Call for rates.** 900 37th Ave SW 58701. US 83, 0.6 mi s of US 2 and 52 Bypass, then just w. Int corridors. **Pets:** Medium. $75 one-time fee/room. Service with restrictions, crate.

🛜 ✕ ᴴᴹ 🔋 💻

 Comfort Inn ⊞

(701) 852-2201. **$125-$200.** 1515 22nd Ave SW 58701. US 2 and 52 Bypass, at 16th St SW. Int corridors. **Pets:** Medium. $10 daily fee/room. Designated rooms, service with restrictions, supervision.

[SAVE] 🛜 ✕ ᴴᴹ 🔋 💻 🏊

▽▽ Days Inn Minot Ⓜ

(701) 852-3646. **$120-$186.** 2100 4th St SW 58701. Jct US 2 and 52 Bypass, just n. Int corridors. **Pets:** Accepted. 🛜 🔋 💻 🏊

▽▽▽ Holiday Inn Riverside Minot ⊞

(701) 852-2504. **Call for rates.** 2200 Burdick Expwy E 58702. 1.3 mi e on US 2 business route (Burdick Expwy E). Int corridors. **Pets:** Accepted.

🛜 ᴴᴹ 🔋 💻 ⍚ 🏊 ✕

▽▽▽ Sleep Inn & Suites ⊞

(701) 837-3100. **Call for rates.** 2400 10th St SW 58701. US 2 and 52 Bypass, 0.4 mi s on 16th St SW, then 0.4 mi e. Int corridors. **Pets:** Very small, dogs only. Service with restrictions, supervision.

🛜 ✕ ᴴᴹ 🔋 💻 🏊 ✕

VALLEY CITY

 AmericInn Lodge & Suites of Valley City ⊞

(701) 845-5551. **$85-$140.** 280 Winter Show Rd SE 58072. I-94 exit 292, just ne. Int corridors. **Pets:** Dogs only. $10 daily fee/pet. Designated rooms, service with restrictions, crate.

🛜 ✕ ᴴᴹ 🔋 💻 🏊 ✕

WAHPETON

▽▽ Baymont Inn & Suites ⊞

(701) 642-5000. **$75-$155.** 1800 Two Ten Dr 58075. 1 mi n on SR 210 Bypass. Int corridors. **Pets:** Accepted. 🛜 ᴴᴹ 🔋 💻 🏊 ✕

▽▽ Rodeway Inn ⊞

(701) 642-1115. **Call for rates.** 209 13th St S 58075. SR 13, 0.3 mi e of jct SR 210 Bypass. Int corridors. **Pets:** Accepted. 🛜 🔋 💻 🏊

WATFORD CITY

 Roosevelt Inn & Suites ⊞

(701) 842-3686. **$115.** 600 2nd Ave SW 58854. US 85, 0.3 mi w. Int corridors. **Pets:** Medium. $10 daily fee/pet. Designated rooms, service with restrictions, crate. [SAVE] 🛜 ✕ 🔋 💻 🏊

WILLISTON

▽▽▽ Candlewood Suites ⊞

(701) 572-3716. **$140-$250.** 3716 6th Ave W 58801. 1.3 mi n on US 2 and 85 Bypass, just w. Int corridors. **Pets:** Medium. $5 daily fee/room. Service with restrictions, supervision. 🛜 ✕ ᴴᴹ 🔋 💻

 El Rancho Motor Hotel ⊞

(701) 572-6321. **$126-$136.** 1623 2nd Ave W 58801. 1 mi n on US 2 and 85 N Bypass. Ext/int corridors. **Pets:** Accepted.

[SAVE] 🛜 ᴴᴹ 🔋 💻 ⍚

▽▽▽ HomStay Suites ⊞

(701) 577-3701. **$195-$310, 7 day notice.** 3701 4th Ave W 58801. 1.3 mi n on US 2 and 85 Bypass, just w. Int corridors. **Pets:** Large. $5 daily fee/pet. Service with restrictions, crate. 🛜 ✕ 🔋 💻 ⍚

 Marquis Plaza & Suites ⊞

(701) 774-3250. **$125-$147.** 1525 9th Ave NW 58801. US 2 and 85 Bypass, 4 mi e of jct US 85 Bypass. Int corridors. **Pets:** Small. $15 daily fee/pet. Designated rooms, service with restrictions, supervision.

[SAVE] 🛜 ✕ ᴴᴹ 🔋 💻 🏊 ✕

▽▽▽ Microtel Inn & Suites by Wyndham Williston ⊞

(701) 577-4900. **$130-$180, 3 day notice.** 3820 4th Ave W 58801. 1.3 mi n on US 2 and 85 Bypass, just w. Int corridors. **Pets:** Accepted.

🛜 ✕ ᴴᴹ 🔋 💻 🏊

 Missouri Flats Inn Ⓜ

(701) 572-4242. **$108-$115.** 213 35th St W 58801. 1.3 mi n on US 2 and 85 Bypass. Int corridors. **Pets:** Small. $15 daily fee/pet. Designated rooms, service with restrictions, supervision.

[SAVE] 🛜 ✕ ᴴᴹ 🔋 💻

OHIO

CITY INDEX

AKRON

Red Roof Inn-Akron South #0207 M
(330) 644-7748. **$54-$119.** 2939 S Arlington Rd 44312. I-77 exit 120, just n. Ext corridors. **Pets:** Large, other species. Service with restrictions, supervision. [SAVE]

ALLIANCE

Holiday Inn Express Hotel & Suites H
(330) 821-6700. **$99-$199.** 2341 W State St 44601. 2 mi w on US 62. Int corridors. **Pets:** Accepted.

Super 8 M
(330) 821-5688. **$58-$92.** 2330 W State St 44601. 2 mi w on US 62. Ext corridors. **Pets:** $5 daily fee/pet. Service with restrictions, crate. [SAVE]

AMHERST

Days Inn M
(440) 985-1428. **$65-$126.** 934 N Leavitt Rd 44001. I-80/90 exit 140, 2.7 mi n on SR 58. Ext/int corridors. **Pets:** Medium. $10 daily fee/pet. Designated rooms, service with restrictions, supervision.

ASHTABULA

Cedars Motel M
(440) 992-5406. **$50-$140.** 2015 W Prospect Rd 44004. Jct SR 11, 3 mi w on US 20. Ext corridors. **Pets:** Other species. $10 daily fee/pet. Service with restrictions, supervision.

ATHENS

The Ohio University Inn & Conference Center H
(740) 593-6661. **Call for rates.** 331 Richland Ave 45701. 1 mi w on US 33 and 50. Int corridors. **Pets:** Accepted.

AUSTINTOWN

Austintown Super 8 M
(330) 793-7788. **$60-$75.** 5280 76 Dr 44515. I-80 exit 223, just s on SR 46. Int corridors. **Pets:** $10 daily fee/pet. Designated rooms, service with restrictions, supervision. [SAVE]

BEST WESTERN Meander Inn H
(330) 544-2378. **Call for rates.** 870 N Canfield-Niles Rd 44515. I-80 exit 223, 0.3 mi s on SR 46. Int corridors. **Pets:** Large, other species. $10 daily fee/pet. Service with restrictions, supervision.
[SAVE]

Comfort Inn M
(330) 792-9740. **Call for rates.** 5425 Clarkins Dr 44515. I-80 exit 223B, just n. Ext corridors. **Pets:** Other species. $15 daily fee/room. Service with restrictions.

Sleep Inn H
(330) 544-5555. **$64-$89.** 5555 Interstate Blvd 44515. I-80 exit 223, just s on SR 46. Int corridors. **Pets:** Medium. $10 daily fee/room. Service with restrictions, crate. [SAVE]

BEAVERCREEK

Residence Inn by Marriott Beavercreek H
(937) 427-3914. **$110-$160.** 2779 Fairfield Commons Blvd 45431. I-675 exit 17, just s on N Fairfield Rd, just w on Pentagon Rd, then just s. Int corridors. **Pets:** Accepted.

BLUFFTON

Comfort Inn H
(419) 358-6000. **$81-$91.** 117 Commerce Ln 45817. I-75 exit 142, just w on SR 103. Int corridors. **Pets:** Medium, other species. $25 one-time fee/pet. Service with restrictions, supervision.

BOARDMAN

Americas Best Value Inn & Suites M
(330) 549-0157. **$49-$121.** 9988 Market St 44452. 0.5 mi n on SR 7. Int corridors. **Pets:** Medium. $10 daily fee/pet. Service with restrictions, supervision.

BOWLING GREEN

Holiday Inn Express H
(419) 353-5500. **Call for rates.** 2150 E Wooster St 43402. I-75 exit 181, just e. Int corridors. **Pets:** Accepted.

BROOKVILLE

 Holiday Inn Express Hotel & Suites Dayton West (Brookville) **H**
(937) 833-9998. **Call for rates.** 95 N Parkview Dr 45309. I-70 exit 21, just s. Int corridors. **Pets:** Other species. $25 one-time fee/pet. Designated rooms, no service, supervision. [SAVE] 🛜 [&M] 🛗 🖵 🏊

BRUNSWICK

Quality Inn **H**
(330) 273-1112. **$69-$100.** 1435 S Carpenter Rd 44212. I-71 exit 226, 0.3 mi w on SR 303, then just s. Int corridors. **Pets:** Accepted.
🛜 🛗 🖵 🏊

BRYAN

 Colonial Manor Motel **M**
(419) 636-3123. **$67-$97.** 924 E High St 43506. US 127, 0.8 mi e on SR 2/34. Ext corridors. **Pets:** Other species. $10 one-time fee/room. Designated rooms, service with restrictions, supervision.
[SAVE] 🛜 🛗 🖵 🍽

Plaza Motel **M**
(419) 636-3159. **$69-$93.** 1604 S Main St 43506. 1.3 mi s on US 127 and SR 15. Ext corridors. **Pets:** Designated rooms, service with restrictions, supervision. [SAVE] 🛜 🛗 🖵

BUCYRUS

Hideaway Country Inn **C** 🐾
(419) 562-3013. **$119-$375, 14 day notice.** 1601 SR 4 44820. 4.5 mi s. Ext/int corridors. **Pets:** Small, dogs only. $50 daily fee/pet. Designated rooms, service with restrictions, supervision. 🛜 ✕ 🛗 🖵 🍽

CAMBRIDGE

Baymont Inn & Suites **M**
(740) 439-1505. **$80-$130.** 61595 Southgate Pkwy 43725. I-70 exit 178, just s on SR 209. Int corridors. **Pets:** Accepted.
🛜 [&M] 🛗 🖵 🏊

Budget Inn **M**
(740) 432-2304. **$50-$60.** 6405 Glenn Hwy 43725. I-70 exit 176, just e on US 40. Ext/int corridors. **Pets:** Accepted. 🛜 🛗 🖵

 Comfort Inn **H**
(740) 435-3200. **$110-$130.** 2327 Southgate Pkwy 43725. I-70 exit 178, just n on SR 209. Int corridors. **Pets:** $25 daily fee/pet. Service with restrictions, crate. [SAVE] 🛜 🛗 🖵 🏊

Days Inn-Cambridge **M**
(740) 432-5691. **$70-$100, 3 day notice.** 2328 Southgate Pkwy 43725. I-70 exit 178, just n on SR 209. Int corridors. **Pets:** Small. $10 daily fee/pet. Service with restrictions, crate. 🛜 🛗 🖵 🏊

CANTON

 Comfort Inn-Hall of Fame **H**
(330) 492-1331. **$99-$149.** 5345 Broadmoor Cir NW 44709. I-77 exit 109, 0.5 mi e on Everhard Rd. Int corridors. **Pets:** Small. $25 daily fee/pet. Designated rooms, service with restrictions, crate.
[SAVE] 🛜 🛗 🖵 🏊

La Quinta Inn & Suites Canton **H**
(330) 492-0151. **$101-$172.** 5335 Broadmoor Cir NW 44709. I-77 exit 109, 0.5 mi e on Everhard Rd. Int corridors. **Pets:** Service with restrictions, supervision. 🛜 [&M] 🛗 🖵 🏊

Red Roof Inn #7019 **M**
(330) 499-1970. **$55-$99.** 5353 Inn Circle Ct NW 44720. I-77 exit 109, just w on Everhard Rd. Ext corridors. **Pets:** Large, other species. Service with restrictions, supervision. [SAVE] 🛜 ✕ 🛗 🖵

Residence Inn by Marriott **H**
(330) 493-0004. **$200-$340.** 5280 Broadmoor Cir NW 44709. I-77 exit 109, 0.5 mi e on Everhard Rd. Int corridors. **Pets:** Accepted.
🛜 ✕ [&M] 🛗 🖵 🏊 ✕

CARROLLTON

Carrollton Days Inn **H**
(330) 627-9314. **$89-$149, 3 day notice.** 1111 Canton Rd 44615. On SR 43, 0.5 mi n of SR 39. Int corridors. **Pets:** Accepted.
🛜 🛗 🖵 🏊

CEDARVILLE

Hearthstone Inn & Suites **H**
(937) 766-3000. **$109-$169.** 10 S Main St 45314. I-70 exit 54, 11 mi s. Int corridors. **Pets:** Small, dogs only. $15 daily fee/pet. Service with restrictions, supervision. 🛜 ✕ 🛗 🖵

CHILLICOTHE

Christopher Inn & Suites **H**
(740) 774-6835. **$100-$160.** 30 N Plaza Blvd 45601. US 35 exit Bridge St, just n on US 23. Int corridors. **Pets:** Accepted.
🛜 🛗 🖵 🏊 ✕

CINCINNATI METROPOLITAN AREA

BATAVIA

Ameristay Inn & Suites **H**
(513) 735-4678. **$76-$139.** 2188 Winemiller Ln 45103. I-275 exit 63B (SR 32), 7.3 mi e. Int corridors. **Pets:** Small. $25 one-time fee/room. Service with restrictions, supervision. 🛜 🛗 🖵 🏊

Hampton Inn-Cincinnati Eastgate **H**
(513) 752-8584. **$99-$199.** 858 Eastgate North Dr 45245. I-275 exit 63B (SR 32), just e, just n on Gleneste Withamsville Rd, then just w. Int corridors. **Pets:** Medium. Service with restrictions, crate. 🛜 🛗 🖵 🏊

Holiday Inn & Suites Cincinnati Eastgate **H**
(513) 752-4400. **$119-$169.** 4501 Eastgate Blvd 45245. I-275 exit 63B (SR 32), 0.5 mi e to Eastgate Mall exit, then 0.5 mi n. Int corridors.
Pets: Accepted. 🛜 🛗 🖵 🍽 🏊 ✕

BLUE ASH

Embassy Suites Hotel-Cincinnati Northeast **H**
(513) 733-8900. **$99-$159.** 4554 Lake Forest Dr 45242. I-275 exit 47, 2.3 mi s; I-71 exit 15, 1 mi w on Pfeiffer Rd. **Pets:** Small, dogs only. $50 one-time fee/room. Designated rooms, service with restrictions, supervision. 🛜 🛗 🖵 🍽 🏊 ✕

Extended StayAmerica - Cincinnati - Blue Ash - Kenwood Road **H**
(513) 469-8900. **$50-$82.** 11145 Kenwood Rd 45242. I-71 exit 15, 0.5 mi w on Pfeiffer Rd, then 1.3 mi n. Int corridors. **Pets:** $25 daily fee/pet. Designated rooms, service with restrictions. 🛜 🛗 🖵

Extended StayAmerica - Cincinnati - Blue Ash - Reagan Highway **H**
(513) 793-6750. **$62-$79.** 4260 Hunt Rd 45242. I-71 exit 14, 1.3 mi w on Ronald Reagan Hwy exit Hunt Rd, then just e. Int corridors. **Pets:** $25 daily fee/pet. Designated rooms, service with restrictions.
🛜 🛗 🖵 🏊

Residence Inn by Marriott-Blue Ash **H** 🐾
(513) 530-5060. **$109-$199.** 11401 Reed-Hartman Hwy 45241. I-275 exit 47, 0.8 mi s. Ext/int corridors. **Pets:** Large, other species. $100 one-time fee/room. Service with restrictions. 🛜 ✕ [&M] 🛗 🖵 🏊 ✕

 TownePlace Suites by Marriott Blue Ash **H**
(513) 469-8222. **$79-$189.** 4650 Cornell Rd 45241. I-275 exit 47, 0.9 mi s on Reed-Hartman Hwy, then just w. Int corridors. **Pets:** Accepted.
[SAVE] 🛜 ✕ 🛗 🖵 🏊

CHERRY GROVE

BEST WESTERN Clermont 🅜

(513) 528-7702. **$90-$150.** 4004 Williams Dr 45255. I-275 exit 65, just w, then just s. Ext corridors. **Pets:** Medium. $20 one-time fee/room. Service with restrictions, supervision. [SAVE] 🛰 🔲 💻 🏊

CINCINNATI

Holiday Inn Express Cincinnati West 🅗

(513) 574-6000. **$104-$199.** 5505 Rybolt Rd 45248. I-74 exit 11, just s. Int corridors. **Pets:** Medium. $25 one-time fee/room. Designated rooms, service with restrictions, supervision. [SAVE] 🛰 🔲 🔲 💻 🏊

Hyatt Regency Cincinnati 🅗 ❀

(513) 579-1234. **$99-$329.** 151 W 5th St 45202. At Hyatt-Saks Fifth Avenue Center. Int corridors. **Pets:** Medium, dogs only. $35 daily fee/ room. Designated rooms, service with restrictions, crate.
[ECO] [SAVE] 🛰 🔲 🔲 💻 🍴 🏊

Millennium Hotel Cincinnati 🅗

(513) 352-2100. **$69-$349.** 150 W 5th St 45202. Between Elm and Race sts. Int corridors. **Pets:** Large, other species. $65 deposit/pet, $35 one-time fee/pet. Designated rooms, service with restrictions, supervision.
🛰 ⊠ 🔲 🏊

**Residence Inn by Marriott Cincinnati
Downtown** 🅗

(513) 651-1234. **$179-$299.** 506 E Fourth St 45202. Center. Int corridors. **Pets:** Accepted. 🛰 ⊠ 🔲 💻

The Westin Cincinnati 🅗 ❀

(513) 621-7700. **$99-$339.** 21 E 5th St 45202. Between Vine and Walnut sts. Int corridors. **Pets:** Medium, dogs only. Service with restrictions, supervision. [SAVE] 🛰 ⊠ 🔲 🔲 💻 🍴 🏊 ⊠

HARRISON

**BEST WESTERN PLUS Miami Whitewater
Inn** 🅗 ❀

(513) 367-9666. **$54-$79.** 391 Comfort Dr 45030. I-74 exit 1, just n on New Haven Rd, then just e on Biggs Blvd. Int corridors. **Pets:** Other species. $20 one-time fee/room. Crate. [SAVE] 🛰 🔲 🔲 💻

MASON

Kings Island Resort & Conference Center 🅗

(513) 398-0115. **$49-$189.** 5691 Kings Island Dr 45040. I-71 exit 25, just e on Kings Mills Rd, then just s. Ext/int corridors. **Pets:** Dogs only. $25 one-time fee/room. Service with restrictions, crate.
🛰 ⊠ 🔲 🔲 💻 🍴 🏊 ⊠

TownePlace Suites by Marriott 🅗

(513) 774-0610. **$69-$189.** 9369 Waterstone Blvd 45249. I-71 exit 19, just e on Mason-Montgomery Rd, then 0.9 mi n on Fields-Ertel and Union Cemetery rds. Int corridors. **Pets:** Accepted.
[ECO] [SAVE] 🛰 ⊠ 🔲 🔲 💻

MIDDLETOWN

Middletown Drury Inn & Suites 🅗

(513) 425-6650. **$95-$169.** 3320 Village Dr 45005. I-75 exit 32, just w on SR 122. Int corridors. **Pets:** Service with restrictions, supervision.
🛰 🔲 🔲 💻 🏊 ⊠

MILFORD

Homewood Suites by Hilton 🅗

(513) 248-4663. **$99-$149.** 600 Chamber Dr 45150. I-275 exit 59 southbound; exit 59A northbound, 0.5 mi w on Milford Pkwy, then 0.5 mi s. Int corridors. **Pets:** Accepted. 🛰 🔲 🔲 💻

MOUNT ORAB

BEST WESTERN PLUS Mt. Orab Inn 🅗

(937) 444-6666. **$77-$95.** 100 Leininger St 45154. Jct US 68 and SR 32, just n on US 68. Int corridors. **Pets:** Large. $15 daily fee/pet. Designated rooms, service with restrictions, supervision. [SAVE] 🛰 🔲 🔲 💻

SHARONVILLE

Drury Inn & Suites-Cincinnati North 🅗

(513) 771-5601. **$110-$214.** 2265 E Sharon Rd 45241. I-75 exit 15, just e. Int corridors. **Pets:** Service with restrictions, supervision.
🛰 🔲 🔲 💻 🏊 ⊠

Hawthorn Suites by Wyndham 🅗

(513) 354-1000. **$60-$150.** 11180 Dowlin Dr 45241. I-75 exit 15, just e on Sharon Rd, then just n. Int corridors. **Pets:** Dogs only. $15 daily fee/ pet. Service with restrictions, crate. 🛰 🔲 🔲 💻

Holiday Inn Cincinnati I-275 North 🅗

(513) 563-8330. **Call for rates.** 3855 Hauck Rd 45241. I-275 exit 46, just n. Int corridors. **Pets:** Other species. $35 one-time fee/room. Service with restrictions, crate. 🛰 🔲 🔲 💻 🍴 🏊 ⊠

**Homewood Suites by Hilton-Cincinnati
North** 🅗 ❀

(513) 772-8888. **$124-$169.** 2670 E Kemper Rd 45241. I-275 exit 44, jct Mosteller Rd. Int corridors. **Pets:** Other species. $150 one-time fee/room, $25 daily fee/room. Service with restrictions. 🛰 🔲 🔲 💻 🏊 ⊠

La Quinta Inn & Suites Cincinnati Sharonville 🅗

(513) 771-0300. **$71-$166.** 11029 Dowlin Dr 45241. I-75 exit 15, just e. Int corridors. **Pets:** Service with restrictions, supervision.
🛰 🔲 🔲 💻 🏊 ⊠

Residence Inn by Marriott 🅗

(513) 771-2525. **$99-$161.** 11689 Chester Rd 45246. I-75 exit 15, just w on Sharon Rd, then 1 mi n. Ext corridors. **Pets:** Accepted.
🛰 ⊠ 🔲 🔲 💻 🏊 ⊠

SPRINGDALE

La Quinta Inn Cincinnati North 🅗

(513) 671-2300. **$63-$133.** 12150 Springfield Pike 45246. I-275 exit 41, just n on SR 4. Int corridors. **Pets:** Service with restrictions, supervision.
🛰 🔲 💻

WEST CHESTER

**Residence Inn by Marriott Cincinnati North/West
Chester** 🅗

(513) 341-4040. **$159-$199.** 6240 Muhlhauser Rd 45069. I-75 exit 19, just w on Union Centre Blvd, then just n. Int corridors. **Pets:** Accepted.
🛰 ⊠ 🔲 🔲 💻 🏊 ⊠

Staybridge Suites Cincinnati North 🅗

(513) 874-1900. **$99-$250.** 8955 Lakota Dr W 45069. I-75 exit 19, just w on Union Centre Blvd, then 0.5 mi n. Int corridors. **Pets:** Accepted.
🛰 🔲 🔲 💻 🏊 ⊠

WILMINGTON

**Holiday Inn Wilmington & Roberts Conference
Centre** 🅗

(937) 283-3200. **Call for rates.** 123 Gano Rd 45177. I-71 exit 50, just w. Int corridors. **Pets:** Accepted. 🛰 ⊠ 🔲 🔲 💻 🍴 🏊

END METROPOLITAN AREA

CLEVELAND METROPOLITAN AREA

BEACHWOOD

▼▼▼ Embassy Suites H

(216) 765-8066. **$119-$209.** 3775 Park East Dr 44122. I-271 exit 29, just w on Chagrin Blvd. Int corridors. **Pets:** Accepted.

📶 🛗 🖥 🍴 ➰ ⊠

▼▼ Extended StayAmerica-Cleveland-Beachwood H

(216) 595-9551. **$79-$114.** 3820 Orange Pl 44122. I-271 exit 29, 0.3 mi e on Chagrin Blvd, then 0.4 mi s. Int corridors. **Pets:** $25 daily fee/pet. Designated rooms, service with restrictions. 📶 🛗 🖥

▼▼ Homestead Studio Suites Hotel-Cleveland/Beachwood H

(216) 896-5555. **$79-$114.** 3625 Orange Pl 44122. I-271 exit 29, just e on Chagrin Blvd, then just s. Int corridors. **Pets:** $25 daily fee/pet. Designated rooms, service with restrictions. 📶 🛗 🖥

▼▼▼ Homewood Suites by Hilton H

(216) 464-9600. **$107-$199.** 25725 Central Pkwy 44122. I-271 exit 29, just w on Chagrin Blvd, then just n on Enterprise Pkwy. Int corridors. **Pets:** Accepted. 📶 🛗 🖥 ➰

▼▼▼ Residence Inn by Marriott Cleveland-Beachwood H

(216) 831-3030. **$139-$299.** 3628 Park East Dr 44122. I-271 exit 29, just w on Chagrin Blvd. Int corridors. **Pets:** Accepted.

📶 ⊠ 🛗 🖥 🖥 ➰ ⊠

BROOKLYN

▼▼ Extended StayAmerica Cleveland-Brooklyn H

(216) 267-7799. **$69-$104.** 10300 Cascade Crossing 44144. I-480 exit 13, just s. Int corridors. **Pets:** $25 daily fee/pet. Designated rooms, service with restrictions. 📶 🛗 🖥

BROOK PARK

🌐 ▼▼ BEST WESTERN Airport Inn & Suites H

(216) 267-9364. **$69-$99.** 16501 Snow Rd 44142. I-71 exit 237, just e. Int corridors. **Pets:** Accepted. 🆂🅰🆅 📶 🛗 🖥 ➰

CLEVELAND

▼▼ Comfort Inn Downtown Cleveland H

(216) 861-0001. **$89-$199.** 1800 Euclid Ave 44115. Corner of Euclid Ave and E 18th St. Int corridors. **Pets:** Accepted. 📶 ⊠ 🖥 🖥

▼▼ La Quinta Inn Cleveland Airport North H

(216) 251-8500. **$66-$140.** 4222 W 150th St 44135. I-71 exit 240, just n. Int corridors. **Pets:** Service with restrictions, supervision.

📶 🛗 🖥 🖥

🌐 ▼▼▼ Radisson Hotel Cleveland-Gateway H

(216) 377-9000. **$109-$229.** 651 Huron Rd E 44115. North side of Progressive Field. Int corridors. **Pets:** Medium. $35 daily fee/pet. Service with restrictions, supervision. 🆂🅰🆅 📶 ⊠ 🖥 🖥

▼▼▼ Residence Inn by Marriott H

(216) 443-9043. **$129-$299.** 527 Prospect Ave E 44115. Between E 9th and Ontario sts. Int corridors. **Pets:** Accepted. 📶 ⊠ 🖥 🖥

🌐 ▼▼▼ ▼▼ The Ritz-Carlton, Cleveland H 🐾

(216) 623-1300. **$199-$399.** 1515 W 3rd St 44113. In Tower City Center (3rd St side). Int corridors. **Pets:** $75 one-time fee/room. Designated rooms, service with restrictions.

🆂🅰🆅 📶 ⊠ 🛗 🖥 🖥 🍴 ➰ ⊠

🌐 ▼▼▼▼ Sheraton Cleveland Airport Hotel H 🐾

(216) 267-1500. **$99-$219.** 5300 Riverside Dr 44135. I-71 exit 237, just s of I-480 on SR 237, follow signs. Int corridors. **Pets:** Large. $200 deposit/ room. Designated rooms, service with restrictions, crate.

🆂🅰🆅 📶 ⊠ 🛗 🖥 🍴 ➰

INDEPENDENCE

▼▼ La Quinta Inn Cleveland Independence H

(216) 447-1133. **$78-$140.** 6161 Quarry Ln 44131. I-77 exit 155 (Rockside Rd), just e, then just s. Int corridors. **Pets:** Service with restrictions, supervision. 📶 🛗 🖥

🌐 ▼▼ Red Roof Inn #0028 M

(216) 447-0030. **$49-$99.** 6020 Quarry Ln 44131. I-77 exit 155 (Rockside Rd), just e, then just s. Ext corridors. **Pets:** Large, other species. Service with restrictions, supervision. 🆂🅰🆅 📶 🛗

▼▼▼ Residence Inn by Marriott H

(216) 520-1450. **$89-$199.** 5101 W Creek Rd 44131. I-77 exit 155 (Rockside Rd), just w, then just n. Ext/int corridors. **Pets:** Accepted.

📶 ⊠ 🛗 🖥 🖥 ➰ ⊠

MAYFIELD HEIGHTS

▼▼ Comfort Inn - Mayfield Heights H

(440) 442-8400. **$79-$119.** 1421 Golden Gate Blvd 44124. I-271 exit 34, 0.3 mi w on US 322, then just n. Int corridors. **Pets:** Accepted.

📶 ⊠ 🖥 🖥

▼▼▼ Staybridge Suites Cleveland East H 🐾

(440) 442-9200. **$109-$169.** 6103 Landerhaven Dr 44124. I-271 exit 32, just e on Cedar Rd, 0.7 mi n on Lander Rd, then just e. Int corridors. **Pets:** Small. $75 one-time fee/room. Service with restrictions, crate.

📶 ⊠ 🛗 🖥 🖥 ➰

MEDINA

▼▼ Quality Inn & Suites H

(330) 723-4994. **Call for rates.** 2850 Medina Rd 44256. I-71 exit 218, just e. Int corridors. **Pets:** Accepted. 📶 🛗 🖥 ➰

▼▼ Red Roof Inn M

(330) 725-1395. **$49-$130.** 5021 Eastpointe Dr 44256. I-71 exit 218, just w. Ext corridors. **Pets:** Large, other species. Service with restrictions, supervision. 📶 🛗 ➰

MIDDLEBURG HEIGHTS

🌐 ▼▼ Comfort Inn-Cleveland Airport H

(440) 234-3131. **$72-$124, 3 day notice.** 17550 Rosbough Dr 44130. I-71 exit 235, 0.3 mi w to Engle Rd, then 0.3 mi n. Int corridors. **Pets:** Medium. $45 one-time fee/room. Service with restrictions, crate.

🆂🅰🆅 📶 🛗 🖥 🖥 ➰

🌐 ▼▼ Days Inn Cleveland Airport South M

(440) 243-2277. **$59-$69.** 7233 Engle Rd 44130. I-71 exit 235, just w. Ext corridors. **Pets:** $20 one-time fee/room. Designated rooms, service with restrictions, supervision. 🆂🅰🆅 📶 🖥 🖥 ➰

🌐 ▼▼ Red Roof Inn-Middleburg Heights #7060 H

(440) 243-2441. **$49-$99.** 17555 Bagley Rd 44130. I-71 exit 235, just w, then just s. Ext/int corridors. **Pets:** Large, other species. Service with restrictions, supervision. 🆂🅰🆅 📶 🛗

▼▼▼ Residence Inn by Marriott H

(440) 234-6688. **$89-$199.** 17525 Rosbough Dr 44130. I-71 exit 235, just w on Bagley Rd, then just n on Engle Rd. Ext/int corridors. **Pets:** Other species. $100 one-time fee/room. Designated rooms, service with restrictions, crate. 📶 ⊠ 🛗 🖥 ➰ ⊠

▼▼▼ **StudioPLUS-Cleveland-Middleburg Heights** 🅷
(440) 243-7024. **$69-$104.** 17552 Rosbough Dr 44130. I-71 exit 235, 0.3 mi w to Engle Rd, then 0.3 mi n. Int corridors. **Pets:** $25 daily fee/pet. Designated rooms, service with restrictions. 🛜 🔋 💻

▼▼ **TownePlace Suites by Marriott Cleveland Airport** 🅷 🐾
(440) 816-9300. **$79-$179.** 7325 S Engle Rd 44130. I-71 exit 235, just w on Bagley Rd, then just s. Int corridors. **Pets:** Other species. $75 one-time fee/room. Service with restrictions, crate.
🌿 🛜 ✖ 🔋 💻 ⇝

NORTH OLMSTED

▼▼ **Candlewood Suites Cleveland/North Olmsted** 🅷 🐾
(440) 716-0584. **Call for rates.** 24741 Country Club Blvd 44070. I-480 exit 6B westbound; exit 6 eastbound, just n on SR 252. Int corridors. **Pets:** Medium, other species. $15 daily fee/room. Service with restrictions.
🛜 🔋 💻

▼▼ **Homestead Studio Suites Hotel-Cleveland/Airport/North Olmsted** 🅷
(440) 777-8585. **$69-$104.** 24851 Country Club Blvd 44070. I-480 exit 6B westbound; exit 6 eastbound, just n on SR 252. Int corridors. **Pets:** $25 daily fee/pet. Designated rooms, service with restrictions.
🛜 🔋 💻

▼▼▼ **La Quinta Inn & Suites Cleveland Airport West** 🅷
(440) 734-4477. **$87-$188.** 25105 Country Club Blvd 44070. I-480 exit 6B westbound; exit 6 eastbound, just n on SR 252. Int corridors. **Pets:** Service with restrictions, supervision.
🛜 ✖ 🔋 💻 ⇝

▼▼ **StudioPLUS Cleveland-Airport-N Olmsted** 🅷
(440) 716-2412. **$69-$104.** 25801 Country Club Blvd 44070. I-480 6B westbound; exit 6 eastbound, just n on SR 252, then 0.3 mi w. Int corridors. **Pets:** $25 daily fee/pet. Designated rooms, service with restrictions.
🛜 🔋 💻 ⇝

RICHFIELD

▼▼ **Days Inn & Suites Richfield** 🅷
(330) 659-6151. **$79-$109.** 4742 Brecksville Rd 44286. I-80 exit 173, just s; I-77 exit 145, 0.5 mi n. Int corridors. **Pets:** Accepted.
🛜 🔋 💻 🍽 ⇝ ✖

SOLON

▼▼▼ **Hampton Inn** 🅷
(440) 542-0400. **$99-$149.** 6035 Enterprise Pkwy 44139. US 422 exit Harper Rd, 0.6 mi s, then 0.4 mi e. Int corridors. **Pets:** $50 one-time fee/room. Designated rooms, service with restrictions, crate.
🛜 ✖ 🔋 💻 ⇝

TWINSBURG

▼▼▼ **Comfort Suites-Twinsburg** 🅷
(330) 963-5909. **$120-$140.** 2715 Creekside Dr 44087. I-480 exit 37, just n. Int corridors. **Pets:** Dogs only. $25 one-time fee/room, $5 daily fee/room. Designated rooms, service with restrictions, supervision.
🛜 ✖ 🔋 💻 ⇝

WESTLAKE

▼▼▼ **Extended Stay Deluxe Cleveland-Westlake** 🅷
(440) 899-4160. **$79-$114.** 30360 Clemens Rd 44145. I-90 exit 156, just n. Int corridors. **Pets:** $25 daily fee/pet. Designated rooms, service with restrictions. 🛜 🔋 💻

▼▼▼ **Holiday Inn Cleveland Westlake** 🅷
(440) 871-6000. **$89-$149.** 1100 Crocker Rd 44145. I-90 exit 156, just n. Int corridors. **Pets:** $25 daily fee/room. Designated rooms, service with restrictions, supervision. 🛜 🔋 💻 🍽 ⇝ ✖

🆎 ▼▼▼ **Red Roof Inn-Westlake #7094** Ⓜ
(440) 892-7920. **$49-$99.** 29595 Clemens Rd 44145. I-90 exit 156, just n. Ext corridors. **Pets:** Large, other species. Service with restrictions, supervision. 🆂🆅 🛜 🔋 💻

▼▼▼ **Residence Inn by Marriott Cleveland/Westlake** 🅷
(440) 892-2254. **$89-$199.** 30100 Clemens Rd 44145. I-90 exit 156, just n. Ext corridors. **Pets:** Accepted. 🛜 ✖ 🔋 💻 ⇝ ✖

WILLOUGHBY

🆎 ▼▼▼ **Red Roof Inn-East #053** Ⓜ
(440) 946-9872. **$50-$90.** 4166 SR 306 44094. I-90 exit 193, just s. Ext corridors. **Pets:** Large, other species. Service with restrictions, supervision.
🆂🆅 🛜 🔋

END METROPOLITAN AREA

CLYDE

▼▼ **Red Roof Inn** 🅷
(419) 547-6660. **$74-$140.** 1363 W McPherson Hwy 43410. 1 mi w on SR 20. Int corridors. **Pets:** Large, other species. Service with restrictions, supervision. 🛜 🔋 💻 ⇝

COLUMBUS METROPOLITAN AREA

CIRCLEVILLE

▼▼▼ **Holiday Inn Express Hotel & Suites** 🅷
(740) 420-7711. **Call for rates.** 23911 US 23 S 43113. Jct US 22, 1.2 mi s. Int corridors. **Pets:** Accepted. 🛜 🔋 💻 ⇝

COLUMBUS

▼▼ **Baymont Inn & Suites Columbus at Rickenbacker** 🅷
(614) 491-4400. **$69-$119.** 2323 Rickenbacker Pkwy W 43217. I-270 exit 49, 3.6 mi s, then just w. Int corridors. **Pets:** Small. $25 deposit/pet, $20 one-time fee/pet. Designated rooms, service with restrictions, supervision.
🛜 🔋 💻 ⇝

🆎 ▼▼▼ **BEST WESTERN PLUS Columbus North** 🅷
(614) 888-8230. **$90-$120.** 888 E Dublin Granville Rd 43229. I-71 exit 117, 0.5 mi w on SR 161. Int corridors. **Pets:** Medium, other species. $25 deposit/room. Service with restrictions, crate.
🆂🆅 🛜 🔋 💻 🍽 ⇝ ✖

▼▼▼ **Candlewood Suites Polaris** 🅷 🐾
(614) 436-6600. **$90-$109.** 8515 Lyra Dr 43240. I-71 exit 121, 0.3 mi w on SR 750. Int corridors. **Pets:** Medium, other species. $15 daily fee/room. Service with restrictions. 🛜 🔋 💻 ⇝ ✖

▼▼ **Comfort Inn North Conference Center** 🅷
(614) 885-4084. **Call for rates.** 1213 E Dublin Granville Rd 43229. I-71 exit 117, just e. Int corridors. **Pets:** Accepted. 🛜 🔋 💻 ⇝

▼▼▼ Comfort Inn Polaris ⊞ ❖
(614) 791-9700. **$79-$89.** 8400 Lyra Dr 43240. I-71 exit 121, just w. Int corridors. **Pets:** Medium. $25 one-time fee/room. Service with restrictions, crate. 🛜 ⊠ 🕹 ⊟ 🖵 ⚓ ⊠

AAA ▼▼▼ Comfort Suites Fairgrounds Ⓜ
(614) 586-1001. **Call for rates.** 1690 Clara St 43211. I-71 exit 111, just w. Int corridors. **Pets:** Accepted. 🆂🅰🆅🅴 🛜 ⊠ ⊟ 🖵 ⚓

AAA ▼▼▼ DoubleTree by Hilton Hotel Columbus - Worthington ⊞
(614) 885-3334. **$89-$149.** 175 Hutchinson Ave 43235. I-270 exit 23, just n on US 23, just e on Dimension Dr, then just s on High Cross Blvd. Int corridors. **Pets:** Accepted. 🆂🅰🆅🅴 🛜 🕹 ⊟ 🖵 ⏍ ⚓

▼▼▼ DoubleTree Suites by Hilton Columbus Downtown ⊞
(614) 228-4600. **Call for rates.** 50 S Front St 43215. Corner of Front and State sts, just n. Int corridors. **Pets:** Accepted. 🛜 ⊟ 🖵 ⏍

▼▼▼ Drury Inn & Suites-Columbus Convention Center ⊞
(614) 221-7008. **$105-$204.** 88 E Nationwide Blvd 43215. 0.3 mi n on US 23. Int corridors. **Pets:** Service with restrictions, supervision.
🛜 🕹 ⊟ 🖵 ⚓ ⊠

▼▼▼ Extended StayAmerica-Columbus-Easton ⊞
(614) 428-6022. **$75-$100.** 4200 Stelzer Rd 43230. I-270 exit 32, just w on Morse Rd, then just n. Int corridors. **Pets:** $25 daily fee/pet. Designated rooms, service with restrictions. 🛜 ⊟ 🖵

▼▼ Extended StayAmerica-Columbus-North ⊞
(614) 431-0033. **$55-$77.** 6255 Zumstein Dr 43229. I-71 exit 117, just w on SR 161, then 0.5 mi n. Int corridors. **Pets:** $25 daily fee/pet. Designated rooms, service with restrictions. 🛜 ⊟ 🖵

▼▼ Extended Stay Deluxe Columbus/Polaris ⊞
(614) 431-5522. **$85-$105.** 8555 Lyra Dr 43240. I-71 exit 121, just w on Polaris Pkwy. Int corridors. **Pets:** $25 daily fee/pet. Designated rooms, service with restrictions. 🛜 🕹 ⊟ 🖵 ⚓

▼▼▼ German Village Guest House 🅱🅱 ❖
(614) 437-9712. **$175-$275.** 748 Jaeger St 43206. I-70 exit 100B, just s on S 3rd St, 0.4 mi e on E Sycamore St, then just s. Int corridors.
Pets: $35 daily fee/room. Designated rooms. 🛜 ⊠ ⊟ 🖵

▼▼ Hawthorn Suites by Wyndham ⊞
(614) 853-6199. **$89-$149.** 5505 Keim Cir 43228. I-70 exit 91B, just n on Renner Rd. Int corridors. **Pets:** Medium. $25 daily fee/room. Service with restrictions, supervision. 🛜 🕹 ⊟ 🖵 ⚓ ⊠

AAA ▼▼▼▼ Hilton Columbus at Easton ⊞
(614) 414-5000. **Call for rates.** 3900 Chagrin Dr 43219. I-270 exit 33, 0.5 mi w. Int corridors. **Pets:** Medium, dogs only. $75 one-time fee/room. Service with restrictions, supervision.
🆂🅰🆅🅴 🛜 ⊠ 🕹 ⊟ 🖵 ⏍ ⚓ ⊠

AAA ▼▼▼▼ Hilton Columbus/Polaris ⊞
(614) 885-1600. **$129-$239.** 8700 Lyra Dr 43240. I-71 exit 121, just w on Polaris Pkwy, then just n. Int corridors. **Pets:** Accepted.
🆂🅰🆅🅴 🛜 ⊠ 🕹 ⊟ 🖵 ⏍ ⚓ ⊠

AAA ▼▼▼ Holiday Inn Columbus Downtown Capitol Square ⊞
(614) 221-3281. **$99-$179.** 175 E Town St 43215. I-70 exit 100B, 0.3 mi n on 4th St. Int corridors. **Pets:** Accepted.
🆂🅰🆅🅴 🛜 ⊠ 🕹 ⊟ 🖵 ⏍ ⚓

▼▼▼ Holiday Inn Express & Suites Columbus Southeast ⊞
(614) 920-2400. **$99-$109.** 4041 Hamilton Square Blvd 43125. US 33 exit Hamilton Rd, just n. Int corridors. **Pets:** Small. $25 daily fee/pet. Designated rooms, service with restrictions, supervision. 🛜 ⊟ 🖵 ⚓

AAA ▼▼▼ Hyatt Regency Columbus ⊞
(614) 463-1234. **$89-$319.** 350 N High St 43215. 0.3 mi n on US 23. Int corridors. **Pets:** Accepted. 🄴🄲🄾 🆂🅰🆅🅴 🛜 ⊠ 🕹 ⊟ 🖵 ⏍ ⚓

▼▼▼ La Quinta Inns & Suites Columbus West ⊞
(614) 878-8844. **$77-$150.** 5510 Trabue Rd 43228. I-70 exit 91 eastbound; exit 91B westbound, just n on Renner Rd, then just e. Int corridors. **Pets:** Service with restrictions, supervision.
🛜 ⊠ ⊟ 🖵 ⚓

▼▼▼ Quality Inn & Suites North/Polaris ⊞
(614) 436-0556. **$54-$175.** 7500 Vantage Dr 43235. I-270 exit 23, 0.4 mi n on US 23, just e on Dimension Dr, then just s. Int corridors.
Pets: Accepted. 🛜 🕹 ⊟ 🖵

▼▼ Red Roof Inn and Suites ⊞
(614) 870-3700. **$59-$89.** 4530 W Broad St 43228. I-270 exit 7B southbound; exit 7 northbound, just w. Int corridors. **Pets:** Large, other species. Service with restrictions, supervision. 🛜 ⊟ 🖵 ⚓

AAA ▼▼▼ Red Roof Inn Columbus Downtown - Convention Center ⊞
(614) 224-6539. **$80-$180.** 111 E Nationwide Blvd 43215. Jct 3rd St. Int corridors. **Pets:** Large, other species. Service with restrictions, supervision.
🆂🅰🆅🅴 🛜 ⊠ 🕹 ⊟ 🖵

AAA ▼▼▼ Red Roof Inn-OSU #121 Ⓜ
(614) 267-9941. **$70-$219.** 441 Ackerman Rd 43202. SR 315 exit Ackerman Rd, 0.6 mi e. Ext corridors. **Pets:** Large, other species. Service with restrictions, supervision. 🆂🅰🆅🅴 🛜 🕹 ⊟ 🖵

▼▼▼ Residence Inn by Marriott ⊞
(614) 222-2610. **$129-$299.** 36 E Gay St 43215. Between High and S 3rd sts. Int corridors. **Pets:** Other species. $75 one-time fee/room. Service with restrictions. 🛜 ⊠ 🕹 ⊟ 🖵

AAA ▼▼▼▼ Residence Inn by Marriott ⊞
(614) 885-0799. **$79-$179.** 7300 Huntington Park Dr 43235. I-270 exit 23, 0.4 mi n on US 23, 0.3 mi e on E Campus View Blvd, then 0.5 mi s. Int corridors. **Pets:** Other species. $100 one-time fee/room. Service with restrictions, crate. 🆂🅰🆅🅴 🛜 ⊠ 🕹 ⊟ 🖵 ⚓ ⊠

▼▼▼▼ Residence Inn by Marriott Easton ⊞
(614) 414-1000. **$139-$269.** 3999 Easton Loop W 43219. I-270 exit 33, 1 mi w, then just n. Int corridors. **Pets:** Accepted.
🛜 ⊠ 🕹 ⊟ 🖵 ⚓ ⊠

AAA ▼▼▼ Sheraton Columbus at Capitol Square ⊞ ❖
(614) 365-4500. **$99-$499.** 75 E State St 43215. Corner of State and 3rd sts. Int corridors. **Pets:** Service with restrictions, supervision.
🄴🄲🄾 🆂🅰🆅🅴 🛜 ⊠ 🕹 ⊟ 🖵 ⏍ ⊠

AAA ▼▼▼ Sheraton Suites Columbus ⊞ ❖
(614) 436-0004. **$109-$189.** 201 Hutchinson Ave 43235. I-270 exit 23, 0.3 mi n on US 23, just e on Dimension Dr, then 0.4 mi se on Vantage Dr. Int corridors. **Pets:** Large. Designated rooms, service with restrictions, crate. 🆂🅰🆅🅴 🛜 ⊠ 🕹 🕹 ⊟ 🖵 ⏍ ⚓

AAA ▼▼▼ TownePlace Suites by Marriott ⊞
(614) 885-1557. **$69-$159.** 7272 Huntington Park Dr 43235. I-270 exit 23, 0.4 mi n, 0.3 mi e on E Campus View Blvd, then 0.3 mi s. Int corridors. **Pets:** Accepted. 🄴🄲🄾 🆂🅰🆅🅴 🛜 ⊠ ⊟ 🖵 ⚓

AAA ▼▼▼ Varsity Inn North Ⓜ
(614) 267-4646. **Call for rates.** 3246 Olentangy River Rd 43202. SR 315 exit N Broadway, 0.3 mi s. Ext corridors. **Pets:** Accepted.
🆂🅰🆅🅴 🛜 ⊟ 🖵 ⚓

AAA ▼▼▼ The Varsity Inn South Ⓜ
(614) 291-2983. **Call for rates.** 1445 Olentangy River Rd 43212. SR 315 exit King Ave southbound; exit Lane Ave northbound, 1 mi s. Ext corridors. **Pets:** Accepted. 🆂🅰🆅🅴 🛜 ⊟ 🖵 ⚓

▼▼▼ ▼▼▼ The Westin Columbus �H ❄️
(614) 228-3800. **$119-$239.** 310 S High St 43215. Corner of Main and High sts. Int corridors. **Pets:** Small. Service with restrictions, supervision.
[SAVE] 📶 ⊠ 🛏 🖥 🍴

DELAWARE

▲▲▲ ▼▼▼ BEST WESTERN PLUS Delaware Inn �H
(740) 363-3510. **$80-$150.** 1720 Columbus Pike 43015. I-270 exit 23, 11 mi n on US 23. Int corridors. **Pets:** Other species. $20 daily fee/room. Designated rooms, service with restrictions, crate.
[SAVE] 📶 ♿ 🛏 🖥 ≋ ⊠

DUBLIN

▼▼ ▼▼ Chase Suite Hotel �H
(614) 766-7762. **$99-$179.** 4130 Tuller Rd 43017. I-270 exit 20, 0.3 mi s on Sawmill Rd via Village Pkwy and Dublin Center Dr. Ext corridors.
Pets: Accepted. 📶 ⊠ 🛏 🖥

▼▼▼ Drury Inn & Suites-Columbus Northwest �H
(614) 798-8802. **$95-$164.** 6170 Parkcenter Cir 43017. I-270 exit 15 (Tuttle Crossing Blvd), 0.3 mi e, then just n on Blazer Pkwy. Int corridors.
Pets: Service with restrictions, supervision. 📶 ♿ 🛏 🖥 ≋

▼▼▼ Dublin Homewood Suites by Hilton �H
(614) 791-8675. **$89-$159.** 5300 Parkcenter Ave 43017. I-270 exit 15 (Tuttle Crossing Blvd), just e, just n on Blazer Pkwy, then just e. Int corridors. **Pets:** Accepted. 📶 ♿ 🛏 🖥 ≋ ⊠

▼▼ ▼▼ Extended StayAmerica-Columbus-Dublin �H
(614) 760-0053. **$60-$82.** 450 Metro Pl N 43017. I-270 exit 17A, just e on SR 161, just s on Frantz Rd, then just w. Int corridors. **Pets:** $25 daily fee/pet. Designated rooms, service with restrictions. 📶 🛏 🖥

▼▼ ▼▼ Extended Stay Deluxe (Columbus/Tuttle) �H
(614) 760-0245. **$75-$100.** 5530 Tuttle Crossing Blvd 43016. I-270 exit 15 (Tuttle Crossing Blvd), 0.3 mi w. Int corridors. **Pets:** $25 daily fee/pet. Designated rooms, service with restrictions. 📶 🛏 🖥

▼▼▼ Holiday Inn Express �H
(614) 793-5500. **Call for rates.** 5500 Tuttle Crossing Blvd 43016. I-270 exit 15 (Tuttle Crossing Blvd), just w. Int corridors. **Pets:** Accepted.
📶 ♿ 🛏 🖥 ≋ ⊠

▼▼ ▼▼ La Quinta Inn Columbus Dublin �H
(614) 792-8300. **$63-$133.** 6145 Parkcenter Cir 43017. I-270 exit 15 (Tuttle Crossing Blvd), just e, then just n on Blazer Pkwy. Int corridors.
Pets: Service with restrictions, supervision. 📶 ♿ 🛏 🖥

▲▲▲ ▼▼▼ Red Roof Inn-Dublin #127 🅼
(614) 764-3993. **$49-$110.** 5125 Post Rd 43017. I-270 exit 17A, just ne. Ext corridors. **Pets:** Large, other species. Service with restrictions, supervision. [SAVE] 📶 ♿

▲▲▲ ▼▼▼ Sonesta ES Suites Dublin �H
(614) 791-0403. **Call for rates.** 435 Metro Pl S 43017. I-270 exit 17A, 0.5 mi e on SR 161, 0.5 mi s on Frantz Rd, then just w. Ext/int corridors.
Pets: Accepted. [SAVE] 📶 ⊠ ♿ 🛏 🖥 ≋ ⊠

GAHANNA

▼▼ ▼▼ Candlewood Suites Columbus Airport �H ❄️
(614) 863-4033. **Call for rates.** 590 Taylor Rd 43230. I-270 exit 37, 0.4 mi e, 0.6 mi s on Morrison Rd, then just e. Int corridors. **Pets:** Large, other species. $15 daily fee/room. Service with restrictions.
📶 🛏 🖥

▼▼▼ TownePlace Suites by Marriott Columbus Airport �H
(614) 861-1400. **$89-$179.** 695 Taylor Rd 43230. I-270 exit 37, just e, 0.6 mi s on Morrison Rd, then just e. Int corridors. **Pets:** Accepted.
[ECO] 📶 ⊠ 🛏 🖥 ≋

GROVE CITY

▲▲▲ ▼▼ ▼▼ BEST WESTERN Executive Inn 🅼
(614) 875-7770. **$76-$93.** 4026 Jackpot Rd 43123. I-71 exit 100, just e. Ext corridors. **Pets:** Small, dogs only. $10 daily fee/pet. Designated rooms, service with restrictions, supervision. [SAVE] 📶 🛏 🖥 ≋

▼▼▼ Drury Inn & Suites-Columbus South �H
(614) 875-7000. **$105-$214.** 4109 Parkway Centre Dr 43123. I-71 exit 100, just e. Int corridors. **Pets:** Service with restrictions, supervision.
📶 ♿ 🛏 🖥 ≋

▼▼▼ La Quinta Inn Grove City �H
(614) 539-6200. **$83-$170.** 3962 Jackpot Rd 43123. I-71 exit 100, just e. Int corridors. **Pets:** Service with restrictions, supervision.
📶 ⊠ 🛏 🖥 ≋ ⊠

▼▼ ▼▼ Red Roof Inn Columbus/Grove City 🅼
(614) 871-9617. **$54-$79.** 4055 Jackpot Rd 43123. I-71 exit 100, just e. Ext corridors. **Pets:** Large, other species. Service with restrictions, supervision. 📶 🛏 🖥 ≋

HEBRON

▼▼ ▼▼ Red Roof Inn �H
(740) 467-7663. **$49-$170.** 10668 Lancaster Rd SW 43025. I-70 exit 126, just s. Int corridors. **Pets:** Large, other species. Service with restrictions, supervision. 📶 ♿ 🛏 🖥

HILLIARD

▼▼ ▼▼ Comfort Suites by Choice Hotels-Columbus �H
(614) 529-8118. **$79-$129.** 3831 Park Mill Run Dr 43026. I-270 exit 13A northbound; exit 13 southbound, 0.3 mi e on Fishinger Blvd. Int corridors.
Pets: Accepted. 📶 ⊠ ♿ 🛏 🖥 ≋

▼▼ ▼▼ Homewood Suites by Hilton-Columbus �H
(614) 529-4100. **$99-$169.** 3841 Park Mill Run Dr 43026. I-270 exit 13 southbound; exit 13A northbound, 0.4 mi e on Fishinger Blvd. Int corridors. **Pets:** $25 one-time fee/pet, $10 daily fee/pet. Service with restrictions, supervision. 📶 ♿ 🛏 🖥 ≋ ⊠

MARYSVILLE

▼▼ ▼▼ Comfort Inn �H
(937) 644-0400. **$84-$90.** 16420 Allenby Dr 43040. Jct US 33 and 36. Int corridors. **Pets:** Accepted. 📶 🛏 🖥 ≋

NEWARK

▼▼▼ Cherry Valley Lodge �H ❄️
(740) 788-1200. **$99-$179.** 2299 Cherry Valley Rd 43055. 4.6 mi w on SR 16, 0.3 mi s. Int corridors. **Pets:** Medium. $25 daily fee/pet. Service with restrictions, crate. 📶 ⊠ ♿ 🛏 🖥 🍴 ≋ ⊠

OBETZ

▼▼▼ Comfort Inn Obetz Rickenbacker �H ❄️
(614) 492-9000. **$79-$140.** 4870 Old Rathmell Ct 43207. I-270 exit 49, just e. Int corridors. **Pets:** Large. $20 daily fee/pet. Designated rooms, service with restrictions, crate. 📶 ⊠ ♿ 🛏 🖥 ≋

REYNOLDSBURG

▼▼▼ The Fairfield Inn & Suites by Marriott Columbus East �H
(614) 864-4555. **$99-$159.** 2826 Taylor Rd Ext 43068. I-70 exit 112B eastbound; exit 112 westbound, just n, then just e. Int corridors.
Pets: Medium. $75 one-time fee/room. Service with restrictions, supervision. 📶 ⊠ ♿ 🛏 🖥 ≋

SUNBURY

▼▼▼ Hampton Inn-Columbus/Delaware **H**
(740) 363-4700. **Call for rates.** 7329 SR 37 E 43074. I-71 exit 131, just nw. Int corridors. **Pets:** Large, other species. Service with restrictions, crate. 🛜 🔌M 🔌 💻 ⚊

WESTERVILLE

◄◄◄ ▼▼◊ Red Roof Inn Columbus
Northeast-Westerville **M**
(614) 890-1244. **$55-$85.** 909 S State St 43081. I-270 exit 29, 0.4 mi n on SR 3, just w on Heatherdown Dr, then just s. Ext corridors.
Pets: Large, other species. Service with restrictions, supervision.
🅂🄰🅅🄴 🛜 🔌 💻 ⚊

END METROPOLITAN AREA

CONNEAUT

◄◄◄ ▼▼▼ Days Inn of Conneaut **H**
(440) 593-6000. **$70-$129.** 600 Days Blvd 44030. I-90 exit 241, 0.3 mi n. Int corridors. **Pets:** Accepted. 🅂🄰🅅🄴 🛜 🔌 💻 🍽 ⚊

CUYAHOGA FALLS

◄◄◄ ▼▼◊ Sheraton Suites Akron-Cuyahoga
Falls **H** ❀
(330) 929-3000. **$129-$329.** 1989 Front St 44221. SR 8 exit Broad Blvd, just w. Int corridors. **Pets:** Other species. Service with restrictions, crate.
🅂🄰🅅🄴 🛜 ⊠ 🔌M 🔌 💻 🍽 ⚊ ⊠

DANVILLE

▼▼▼ The White Oak Inn **BB**
(740) 599-6107. **Call for rates.** 29683 Walhonding Rd (SR 715) 43014. 3 mi s on US 62, 1.3 mi se on US 36, then 2.7 mi e on SR 715. Ext/int corridors. **Pets:** Accepted. 🛜 ⊠ 🔌 💻 ⚊

DAYTON

◄◄◄ ▼▼▼ Crowne Plaza Dayton **H**
(937) 224-0800. **Call for rates.** 33 E 5th St 45402. 5th and Jefferson sts; downtown. Int corridors. **Pets:** Accepted.
🅂🄰🅅🄴 🛜 ⊠ 🔌M 🔌 💻 🍽 ⚊

▼▼▼ Dayton Marriott Hotel **H**
(937) 223-1000. **$109-$199.** 1414 S Patterson Blvd 45409. I-75 exit 51, 0.6 mi e on Edwin C Moses Blvd, just s on Stewart St, then just w. Int corridors. **Pets:** Accepted. 🛜 ⊠ 🔌M 🔌 💻 🍽 ⚊ ⊠

▼▼▼ Drury Inn & Suites-Dayton North **H**
(937) 454-5200. **$105-$249.** 6616 Miller Ln 45414. I-75 exit 59 (Wyse Rd/Benchwood Rd), just w on Benchwood Rd, then just n. Int corridors.
Pets: Service with restrictions, supervision. 🛜 🔌M 🔌 💻 ⚊

▼▼ Extended StayAmerica Dayton South **H**
(937) 439-2022. **$52-$110.** 7851 Lois Cir 45459. I-75 exit 44, just e on SR 725. Int corridors. **Pets:** $25 daily fee/pet. Designated rooms, service with restrictions. 🛜 🔌 💻 ⚊

▼▼ Fairfield Inn by Marriott Dayton North **H**
(937) 898-1120. **$69-$119.** 6960 Miller Ln 45414. I-75 exit 59 (Wyse Rd/Benchwood Rd), just w on Benchwood Rd, then 0.5 mi n. Ext/int corridors. **Pets:** $30 one-time fee/pet. Designated rooms, service with restrictions, crate. 🛜 ⊠ 🔌M 🔌 💻 ⚊

◄◄◄ ▼▼◊ Red Roof Inn Dayton North #10023 **M**
(937) 898-1054. **$45-$99.** 7370 Miller Ln 45414. I-75 exit 59 (Wyse Rd/Benchwood Rd), just w on Benchwood Rd, then 0.8 mi n. Ext corridors. **Pets:** Large, other species. Service with restrictions, supervision.
🅂🄰🅅🄴 🛜 🔌 💻

▼▼▼ Residence Inn by Marriott Dayton North **H**
(937) 890-2244. **$130-$170.** 7227 York Center Dr 45414. I-75 exit 59 (Wyse Rd/Benchwood Rd), just w on Benchwood Rd, 0.6 mi n on Miller Lane, then just w. Int corridors. **Pets:** Accepted.
🛜 ⊠ 🔌M 🔌 💻 ⚊

▼▼▼ TownePlace Suites by Marriott Dayton North **H**
(937) 898-5700. **$65-$95.** 3642 Maxton Rd 45414. I-75 exit 59 (Wyse Rd/Benchwood Rd), just w on Wyse Rd, 0.5 mi n on Miller Ln. Int corridors. **Pets:** Accepted. 🛜 ⊠ 🔌M 🔌 💻

DELPHOS

▼▼ Microtel Inn & Suites by Wyndham Delphos **H**
(567) 765-1500. **$69-$89.** 480 Moxie Ln 45833. US 30 exit 5th St, 0.5 mi s. Int corridors. **Pets:** Accepted. 🛜 ⊠ 🔌M 🔌 💻

ENGLEWOOD

◄◄◄ ▼▼▼ BEST WESTERN PLUS Dayton
Northwest **H**
(937) 832-2222. **Call for rates.** 20 Rockridge Rd 45322. I-70 exit 29, just n. Int corridors. **Pets:** Accepted. 🅂🄰🅅🄴 🛜 ⊠ 🔌 💻

▼▼▼ Comfort Inn & Suites-Dayton **H**
(937) 836-9400. **$69-$179.** 9305 N Main St 45415. I-70 exit 29, just s. Int corridors. **Pets:** Medium. $25 daily fee/pet. Designated rooms, service with restrictions, supervision. 🛜 🔌 💻 ⚊

▼▼ Holiday Inn Dayton Airport **H**
(937) 832-1234. **Call for rates.** 10 Rockridge Rd 45322. I-70 exit 29, just n. Int corridors. **Pets:** Accepted. 🛜 🔌 💻 🍽 ⚊

FAIRBORN

◄◄◄ ▼▼▼ Baymont Inn & Suites Wright-Patterson Air
Force Base **H**
(937) 754-9109. **$79-$129.** 730 E Xenia Dr 45324. I-675 exit 22, 0.6 mi w. Int corridors. **Pets:** Accepted. 🅂🄰🅅🄴 🛜 🔌 💻

▼▼▼ Holiday Inn Dayton/Fairborn/I-675 **H**
(937) 426-7800. **Call for rates.** 2800 Presidential Dr 45324. I-675 exit 17 (N Fairfield Rd), just w. Int corridors. **Pets:** Accepted.
🛜 🔌M 🔌 💻 🍽 ⚊

▼▼▼ Homewood Suites by Hilton-Fairborn/Dayton **H**
(937) 429-0600. **$109-$189.** 2750 Presidential Dr 45324. I-675 exit 17 (N Fairfield Rd), just w. Ext/int corridors. **Pets:** Accepted.
🛜 🔌 💻 ⚊ ⊠

◄◄◄ ▼▼▼ Ramada Limited & Suites-Fairborn Ohio **H**
(937) 490-2000. **$72-$99.** 2540 University Blvd 45324. I-675 exit 15 (Colonel Glenn Hwy), 2 mi e, then just s. Int corridors. **Pets:** Medium, other species. $25 one-time fee/room. Service with restrictions, crate.
🅂🄰🅅🄴 🛜 🔌 💻 ⚊

▼▼ StudioPLUS Dayton-Fairborn **H**
(937) 429-0140. **$45-$115.** 3131 Presidential Dr 45324. I-675 exit 15 (Colonel Glenn Hwy), 1.5 mi e, then just s. Int corridors. **Pets:** $25 daily fee/pet. Designated rooms, service with restrictions. 🛜 🔌 💻 ⚊

FAIRLAWN

▼▼ Extended StayAmerica Akron-Copley **H**
(330) 668-9818. **$64-$99.** 185 Montrose West Ave 44321. I-77 exit 137B, just w on SR 18, then 0.6 mi s. Int corridors. **Pets:** $25 daily fee/pet. Designated rooms, service with restrictions. 🛜 🔌 💻

▼▼ StayPlace Suites **H**

(330) 666-4811. **$109-$259.** 120 Montrose West Ave 44321. I-77 exit 137B, just w on SR 18, then 0.5 mi s. Ext corridors. **Pets:** Other species. $75 one-time fee/room. Service with restrictions.

▼▼ StudioPLUS-Akron-Copley **H**

(330) 666-3177. **$64-$99.** 170 Montrose West Ave 44321. I-77 exit 137B, 0.3 mi w on SR 18, then 0.5 mi s. Int corridors. **Pets:** $25 daily fee/pet. Designated rooms, service with restrictions. 🛜 🛗 💻 🏊

FINDLAY

▼▼▼ Country Inn & Suites By Carlson **H**

(419) 422-4200. **Call for rates.** 903 Interstate Dr 45840. I-75 exit 159, just w. Int corridors. **Pets:** Accepted. 🛜 🗺 🛗 💻 🏊 ✕

▼▼ Drury Inn & Suites **H**

(419) 422-9700. **$105-$164.** 820 Trenton Ave 45840. I-75 exit 159, just e. Int corridors. **Pets:** Service with restrictions, supervision.

▼▼ Extended Stay Deluxe Findlay-Tiffin Ave **H**

(419) 425-9696. **$83-$100.** 2355 Tiffin Ave 45840. 3 mi e on US 224. Int corridors. **Pets:** $25 daily fee/pet. Designated rooms, service with restrictions. 🛜 🛗 💻 🏊 ✕

▼▼ Holiday Inn Express Hotel & Suites **H**

(419) 420-1776. **Call for rates.** 941 Interstate Dr 45840. I-75 exit 159, just w. Int corridors. **Pets:** Medium. $25 daily fee/pet. Service with restrictions, supervision. 🛜 🗺 🛗 💻 🏊 ✕

▼▼ Quality Inn **M** 🐾

(419) 423-4303. **$69-$84.** 1020 Interstate Ct 45840. I-75 exit 159, just w. Ext corridors. **Pets:** Medium. $15 daily fee/pet. Service with restrictions, crate. 🛜 🛗 🏊

▼▼ TownePlace Suites by Marriott Findlay **H**

(419) 425-9545. **$79-$199.** 2501 Tiffin Ave 45840. 3 mi e on US 224. Int corridors. **Pets:** Accepted. 🛜 ✕ 🛗 💻 🏊

FOSTORIA

◈◈◈ ▼▼▼ BEST WESTERN Fostoria Inn & Suites **H**

(419) 436-3600. **Call for rates.** 1690 N County Line Rd 44830. SR 12, 2 mi n on SR 23. Int corridors. **Pets:** Medium. $10 daily fee/pet. Designated rooms, service with restrictions, crate.

[SAVE] 🛜 🗺 🛗 💻 🏊

FREDERICKTOWN

▼▼▼ Heartland Country Resort **CA**

(419) 768-9300. **$180-$240, 7 day notice.** 3020 Township Rd 190 43019. I-71 exit 151, 2 mi e on SR 95, 0.6 mi s on SR 314, then 1.3 mi e. Ext corridors. **Pets:** Dogs only. $15 daily fee/room. Crate.

✕ 🛗 💻 ✕

FREMONT

▼▼ Days Inn **H**

(419) 334-9551. **$77-$141.** 3701 SR 53 N 43420. I-80/90 exit 91, just n. Int corridors. **Pets:** Small, dogs only. $50 deposit/pet. Service with restrictions, supervision. 🛜 🛗 💻 🍴 🏊

GENEVA

◈◈◈ ▼ Motel 6 #4476 **H**

(440) 466-1168. **$50-$96.** 1715 SR 534 S 44041. I-90 exit 218, just n. Int corridors. **Pets:** Other species. Service with restrictions, supervision.

[SAVE] 🛜 🛗 🏊

GENEVA-ON-THE-LAKE

◈◈◈ ▼▼▼ The Lodge & Conference Center at Geneva-on-the-Lake **H** 🐾

(440) 466-7100. **$89-$299, 3 day notice.** 4888 N Broadway (SR 534) 44041. I-90 exit 218, 6.1 mi n on SR 534. Int corridors. **Pets:** Medium, other species. $50 one-time fee/room. Designated rooms, service with restrictions, supervision. [SAVE] 🛜 ✕ 🗺 🛗 💻 🍴 🏊 ✕

GREEN

▼▼ Super 8 **H**

(330) 899-9888. **$70-$170.** 1605 Corporate Woods Pkwy 44685. I-77 exit 118, just w. Int corridors. **Pets:** Accepted. 🛜 🛗 💻 🏊

GREENVILLE

▼▼ Greenville Inn **H**

(937) 548-3613. **Call for rates.** 851 Martin St 45331. Jct US 36 and 127, 0.3 mi w on SR 571. Int corridors. **Pets:** $10 daily fee/pet. Designated rooms, service with restrictions, supervision. 🛜 🛗 💻

HILLSBORO

▼▼ Days Inn Hillsboro **H**

(937) 393-0299. **$70-$100.** 103 Harry Sauner Rd 45133. 1.9 mi ne on US 62. Int corridors. **Pets:** Accepted. 🛜 🛗 💻 🏊

HOLIDAY CITY

▼▼▼ Holiday Inn Express Hotel & Suites Bryan/ Montpelier **H**

(419) 485-0008. **$93-$220.** 13399 SR 15 43543. I-80/90 exit 13, just s. Int corridors. **Pets:** Other species. $10 daily fee/pet. Service with restrictions, crate. 🛜 🛗 💻 🏊

HOLLAND

▼ Extended StayAmerica Toledo-Holland **H**

(419) 861-1133. **$55-$77.** 6155 W Trust Dr 43528. I-475 exit 8, 0.5 mi e to Holland-Sylvania Rd, then just n. Int corridors. **Pets:** $25 daily fee/pet. Designated rooms, service with restrictions. 🛜 🛗 💻

HUBER HEIGHTS

▼▼▼ Holiday Inn Express Hotel & Suites **H** 🐾

(937) 235-2000. **$129-$149.** 5612 Merily Way 45424. I-70 exit 36, just se on SR 202. Int corridors. **Pets:** Other species. $25 one-time fee/room. Service with restrictions, crate. 🛜 🗺 🛗 💻 🏊 ✕

HUDSON

◈◈◈ ▼▼▼ Baymont Inn & Suites Hudson/Boston Heights **H**

(330) 650-2040. **$65-$150.** 6731 Industrial Pkwy 44236. SR 8 exit 15 southbound; exit 14A northbound. Int corridors. **Pets:** Large. $10 daily fee/pet. Service with restrictions, crate.

[SAVE] 🛜 ✕ 🗺 🛗 💻 🏊

◈◈◈ ▼▼▼ Clarion Inn and Conference Center **H**

(330) 653-9191. **$89-$129.** 6625 Dean Memorial Pkwy 44236. SR 8 exit 15 (southbound); exit 14A (northbound). Int corridors. **Pets:** Medium. $10 daily fee/room. Service with restrictions, supervision.

[SAVE] 🛜 🗺 🛗 💻 🍴 🏊 ✕

HURON

◈◈◈ ▼▼▼ Comfort Inn **H**

(419) 433-8000. **Call for rates.** 132 N Main St 44839. 3 blks n on Williams St to South St, just e. Int corridors. **Pets:** Accepted. [SAVE] 🛜 🏊

▼▼▼ Motel 6 Huron **H**

(419) 433-7829. **$39-$169, 3 day notice.** 601 Rye Beach Rd 44839. SR 2 exit Rye Beach, 2.5 mi w on US 6. Int corridors. **Pets:** Other species. Service with restrictions, supervision.

AAA ◇◇◇◇ **Sawmill Creek Resort** H
(419) 433-3800. **$129-$219, 3 day notice.** 400 Sawmill Creek W 44839. SR 2 exit Rye Beach, 3 mi w on US 6. Int corridors. **Pets:** Medium, dogs only. $25 daily fee/room. Service with restrictions, crate.
[SAVE] 🛜 ✕ 🛏 💻 🍽 ⌚ ✕

JACKSON
◇◇ **Red Roof Inn** M
(740) 288-1200. **$69-$107.** 1000 Acy Ave 45640. US 35 exit McCarty Ln, just nw. Int corridors. **Pets:** Large, other species. Service with restrictions, supervision. 🛜 🛏

KENT
◇◇ **Days Inn-Akron Kent** M
(330) 677-9400. **$55-$140.** 4422 Edson Rd 44240. I-76 exit 33. Ext corridors. **Pets:** $10 daily fee/pet. Service with restrictions, crate.
🛜 🛏 💻 ⌚

KINSMAN
◇◇◇ **Dream Horse Guesthouse** BB
(330) 876-0428. **Call for rates.** 9532 SR 7 44428. 0.5 mi n on SR 7. Int corridors. **Pets:** Other species. $20 daily fee/pet. No service, supervision.
🛜 ✕ 🛏 💻 ✕

LIMA
◇◇◇ **Country Inn & Suites By Carlson** H
(419) 999-9992. **$89-$129.** 804 S Leonard Ave 45804. I-75 exit 125A southbound; exit 125 northbound, just w. Int corridors. **Pets:** Accepted.
🛜 🛏 💻 ⌚

◇◇◇ **Holiday Inn & Suites** H
(419) 879-4000. **$99-$150.** 803 S Leonard Ave 45804. I-75 exit 125A southbound; exit 125 northbound, just w. Int corridors. **Pets:** Accepted.
🛜 ✕ 🆖 🛏 💻 🍽 ⌚ ✕

AAA ◇◇◇ **Howard Johnson Lima** H
(419) 222-0004. **$70-$125.** 1920 Roschman Ave 45804. I-75 exit 125A southbound; exit 125 northbound. Int corridors. **Pets:** Other species. $25 daily fee/room. Service with restrictions, supervision.
[SAVE] 🛜 🆖 🛏 💻 ⌚ ✕

LOGAN
AAA ◇◇◇◇ **Holiday Inn Express Hocking Hills** H
(740) 385-7700. **$74-$169.** 12916 Grey St 43138. SR 664, just w to Lake Logan Rd, then just n. Int corridors. **Pets:** Small, dogs only. Designated rooms, service with restrictions, supervision.
[SAVE] 🛜 🆖 🛏 💻 ⌚

◇◇◇ **The Inn & Spa At Cedar Falls** CI ❖
(740) 385-7489. **$129-$339.** 21190 SR 374 43138. 9.5 mi s on SR 664, 1 mi e. Int corridors. **Pets:** Large, dogs only. $45 one-time fee/room. Designated rooms, service with restrictions, crate.
🛜 ✕ 🛏 💻 🍽 ✕ W ☎

MANSFIELD
AAA ◇◇◇ **BEST WESTERN Richland Inn-Mansfield** H ❖
(419) 756-6670. **$75-$185.** 180 E Hanley Rd 44903. I-71 exit 169, jct SR 13. Int corridors. **Pets:** Large. $15 daily fee/room. Service with restrictions, crate. [SAVE] 🛜 🛏 💻 ⌚

◇◇ **La Quinta Inn & Suites Mansfield** H
(419) 774-0005. **$71-$133.** 120 Stander Ave 44903. I-71 exit 169. Int corridors. **Pets:** Service with restrictions, supervision.
🛜 🆖 🛏 💻 ⌚

◇◇ **Super 8** H
(419) 756-8875. **$50-$119.** 2425 Interstate Cir 44903. I-71 exit 169. Int corridors. **Pets:** Accepted. 🛜 🛏 💻

MARIETTA
AAA ◇◇◇ **Comfort Inn Marietta** H
(740) 374-8190. **$77-$89.** 700 Pike St 45750. I-77 exit 1, just e. Int corridors. **Pets:** Small, dogs only. $10 daily fee/pet. Service with restrictions, supervision. [SAVE] 🛜 🆖 🛏 💻 🍽 ⌚

◇◇ **The Lafayette Hotel** H
(740) 373-5522. **$65-$195.** 101 Front St 45750. I-77 exit 1; downtown. Int corridors. **Pets:** Accepted. 🛜 🛏 💻

◇◇ **Magnuson Hotel By The River** M
(740) 374-7211. **$66-$99.** 279 Muskingum Dr 45750. I-77 exit 6, 3.5 mi sw on SR 821, then 1 mi s on SR 60. Ext corridors. **Pets:** Accepted.
🛜 🛏 💻 ✕

AAA ◇◇◇ **Super 8-Marietta** M
(740) 374-8888. **$60-$145.** 46 Acme St 45750. I-77 exit 1, just w. Int corridors. **Pets:** $10 daily fee/pet. Designated rooms, service with restrictions, supervision. [SAVE] 🛜 🛏 💻

MARION
◇◇ **Comfort Inn by Choice Hotels** H
(740) 389-5552. **Call for rates.** 256 Jamesway Dr 43302. Jct US 23 and SR 95, just w. Int corridors. **Pets:** Accepted. 🛜 🛏 💻 ⌚

MAUMEE
◇◇◇ **Homewood Suites by Hilton Toledo/Maumee** H
(419) 897-0980. **$84-$229.** 1410 Arrowhead Rd 43537. I-475 exit 6, just e. Int corridors. **Pets:** Accepted. 🛜 🆖 🛏 💻 ⌚ ✕

AAA ◇◇ **Red Roof Inn-Maumee #7046** M
(419) 893-0292. **$50-$85.** 1570 S Reynolds Rd 43537. I-80/90 exit 59, just s. Ext/int corridors. **Pets:** Large, other species. Service with restrictions, supervision. [SAVE] 🛜 🛏 💻

◇◇◇ **Residence Inn by Marriott Maumee** H
(419) 891-2233. **$149-$159.** 1370 Arrowhead Dr 43537. I-475 exit 6, just e. Int corridors. **Pets:** Accepted. 🛜 ✕ 🛏 💻 ⌚ ✕

◇◇ **StudioPLUS-Toledo-Maumee** H
(419) 891-1211. **$60-$90.** 542 W Dussel Dr 43537. I-475 exit 6, just e. Int corridors. **Pets:** $25 daily fee/pet. Designated rooms, service with restrictions. 🛜 🛏 💻 ⌚

MENTOR
AAA ◇◇◇◇ **BEST WESTERN PLUS Lawnfield Inn & Suites** H ❖
(440) 205-7378. **Call for rates.** 8434 Mentor Ave 44060. I-90 exit 195, 1.5 mi n to SR 20 (Mentor Ave), then just e. Int corridors. **Pets:** $20 daily fee/room. Designated rooms, service with restrictions, supervision.
[SAVE] 🛜 ✕ 🆖 🛏 💻 🍽 ⌚

◇◇ **Comfort Inn & Suites** H
(440) 951-7333. **Call for rates.** 7701 Reynolds Rd 44060. On SR 306, just s of SR 2. Int corridors. **Pets:** Accepted. 🛜 🛏 💻 ⌚ ✕

◇◇◇ **Residence Inn by Marriott** H
(440) 392-0800. **$99-$299.** 5660 Emerald Ct 44060. Jct SR 2 and Heisley Rd, just s. Int corridors. **Pets:** $75 one-time fee/room. Service with restrictions. 🛜 ✕ 🛏 💻 ⌚ ✕

◇◇ **Super 8** H
(440) 951-8558. **$60-$85.** 7325 Palisades Pkwy 44060. On SR 306, just s of SR 2. Int corridors. **Pets:** Accepted. 🛜 🛏 💻

MIAMISBURG

▼▼▼ **DoubleTree Suites by Hilton Hotel Dayton - Miamisburg** H

(937) 436-2400. **$99-$159.** 300 Prestige Pl 45342. I-75 exit 44, just e on SR 725, just s on Prestige Plaza Dr, then just se. Int corridors. **Pets:** Medium. $25 one-time fee/room, $20 daily fee/pet. Designated rooms, service with restrictions, supervision.
🛜 ⓜ 🛗 🖥 🍴 🏊 ✕

▼▼▼ **Homewood Suites by Hilton-Dayton South** H

(937) 432-0000. **Call for rates.** 3100 Contemporary Ln 45342. I-75 exit 44, just e on SR 725, just se on Prestige Plaza Dr, then just s. Int corridors. **Pets:** Accepted. 🛜 ⓜ 🛗 🖥 🏊

▼▼▼ **Quality Inn & Suites Dayton South** H

(937) 865-0077. **Call for rates.** 250 Byers Rd 45342. I-75 exit 44, just w on SR 725, then just n. Int corridors. **Pets:** Other species. $10 daily fee/pet. Designated rooms, service with restrictions. 🛜 🛗 🖥 🏊

🅰🅰🅰 ▼▼▼ **Red Roof Inn-South #10006** M

(937) 866-0705. **$45-$99.** 222 Byers Rd 45342. I-75 exit 44, just w on SR 725. Ext corridors. **Pets:** Large, other species. Service with restrictions, supervision. [SAVE] 🛜 🛗 🖥

▼▼▼ **Super 8 Miamisburg/South Dayton** H

(937) 866-5500. **$50-$85.** 155 Monarch Ln 45342. I-75 exit 44, 0.5 mi w on SR 725. Int corridors. **Pets:** Accepted. 🛜 🛗 🖥

MILAN

▼▼▼ **Motel 6 - 4016** H

(419) 499-8001. **$39-$169, 3 day notice.** 11406 US 250 Milan Rd 44846. I-80/90 exit 118, 1.5 mi n. Int corridors. **Pets:** Other species. Service with restrictions, supervision. [ECO] 🛜 🏊

▼▼ **Red Roof Inn** H

(419) 499-4347. **$49-$165.** 11303 Rte 250 Milan Rd 44846. I-80/90 exit 118, 0.5 mi n. Int corridors. **Pets:** Large, other species. Service with restrictions, supervision. 🛜 🛗 🖥 🏊 ✕

▼▼ **Super 8** H

(419) 499-4671. **$49-$179.** 11313 US 250 Milan Rd 44846. I-80/90 exit 118, 0.5 mi n. Ext/int corridors. **Pets:** Small, dogs only. Service with restrictions, supervision. 🛜 🖥 🍴 🏊

MILLERSBURG

▼▼ **Comfort Inn Millersburg** H

(330) 674-7400. **Call for rates.** 1102 Glen Dr 44654. SR 39, 0.5 mi s on S Clay. Int corridors. **Pets:** Dogs only. $20 daily fee/pet. Designated rooms, service with restrictions, supervision.
🛜 ✕ 🛗 🖥 🏊 ✕

▼▼ **Hotel Millersburg** H

(330) 674-1457. **$79-$199, 3 day notice.** 35 W Jackson St 44654. Just w of jct SR 83; downtown. Int corridors. **Pets:** Medium. $12 daily fee/room. Designated rooms, service with restrictions, supervision.
🛜 ✕ 🛗 🖥 🍴

MOUNT VERNON

▼▼ **Comfort Inn** H

(740) 392-6886. **$100-$120.** 150 Howard St 43050. Jct SR 13; s of downtown. Int corridors. **Pets:** Other species. $10 daily fee/pet. Service with restrictions, supervision. 🛜 🛗 🖥 🏊

▼▼▼ **Holiday Inn Express** H

(740) 392-1900. **$119-$190.** 11555 Upper Gilchrist Rd 43050. 2.6 mi e on US 36, then just s. Int corridors. **Pets:** Very small. Designated rooms, service with restrictions, crate. 🛜 ✕ ⓜ 🛗 🖥 🏊

NAPOLEON

🅰🅰🅰 ▼▼▼▼ **BEST WESTERN PLUS Napoleon Inn & Suites** H

(419) 599-0850. **Call for rates.** 1290 Independence Dr 43545. US 6 and 24, just se. **Pets:** Accepted. [SAVE] 🛜 🛗 🖥 🏊 ✕

▼▼▼ **Holiday Inn Express Hotel & Suites** H

(419) 592-5599. **$89-$99.** 590 Bonaparte Dr 43545. Jct US 6 and 24, just n on SR 108. Int corridors. **Pets:** Large. $50 one-time fee/pet. Designated rooms, service with restrictions, supervision.
🛜 ⓜ 🛗 🖥 🏊

NEWCOMERSTOWN

▼▼▼ **Hampton Inn** H 🐾

(740) 498-9800. **$89-$139.** 200 Morris Crossing 43832. I-77 exit 65, 0.8 mi w. Int corridors. **Pets:** Medium, other species. Service with restrictions, supervision. 🛜 ⓜ 🛗 🖥 🏊

NEW PHILADELPHIA

🅰🅰🅰 ▼▼▼ **BEST WESTERN Dutch Valley Inn** H 🐾

(330) 339-6500. **$100-$130.** 161 Bluebell Dr SW 44663. I-77 exit 81, 0.7 mi e. Int corridors. **Pets:** Large, other species. $10 daily fee/room. Designated rooms, service with restrictions, supervision.
[SAVE] 🛜 ⓜ 🛗 🖥 🏊

NEWTON FALLS

🅰🅰🅰 ▼ **Econo Lodge** M

(330) 872-0988. **Call for rates.** 4248 SR 5 44444. I-80 exit 209, just w. Ext corridors. **Pets:** Accepted. [SAVE] 🛜 🛗 🖥

NORTH LIMA

▼▼ **Super 8** M

(330) 549-9190. **$48-$73.** 10076 Market St 44452. I-76 exit 232, 0.5 mi n. Ext corridors. **Pets:** Medium, other species. $15 one-time fee/pet. Service with restrictions, supervision. 🛜 🛗 🖥

NORWALK

🅰🅰🅰 ▼▼▼ **All American Inn & Suites** H 🐾

(419) 663-1922. **$59-$259, 7 day notice.** 415 Milan Ave 44857. 4 mi n on US 250; 5 mi s of I-80/90 (Ohio Tpke). Int corridors. **Pets:** Medium. $25 one-time fee/pet. Service with restrictions, crate.
[SAVE] 🛜 🛗 🖥 🏊

🅰🅰🅰 ▼▼▼ **BEST WESTERN Norwalk** H 🐾

(419) 663-3501. **$80-$270, 7 day notice.** 351 Milan Ave 44857. 3.5 mi n on US 250; 5.5 mi s of I-80/90 (Ohio Tpke). Int corridors. **Pets:** Medium. $20 one-time fee/pet. Service with restrictions, crate.
[SAVE] 🛜 🛗 🖥 🏊

▼▼ **Econo Lodge** M

(419) 668-5656. **$43-$149.** 342 Milan Ave 44857. 3 mi n on US 250; 6 mi s of I-80/90 (Ohio Tpke). Ext corridors. **Pets:** Medium, dogs only. $10 daily fee/pet. Designated rooms, service with restrictions, supervision.
🛜 🛗 🏊

OBERLIN

▼▼ **Oberlin Inn** H

(440) 775-1111. **$109-$189.** 7 N Main St 44074. On SR 58; jct College and Main sts; center. Int corridors. **Pets:** Accepted. 🛜 🛗 🖥 🍴

OREGON

🅰🅰🅰 ▼▼▼ **Comfort Inn East** H

(419) 691-8911. **$76-$106.** 2930 Navarre Ave 43616. I-280 exit 7, 0.3 mi n on access road, then 0.6 mi e on SR 2 (Navarre Ave). Int corridors. **Pets:** Other species. $15 one-time fee/room. Service with restrictions, supervision. [SAVE] 🛜 🛗 🖥 🏊

🅰🅰🅰 ▼▼▼ **Sleep Inn & Suites** H

(419) 697-7800. **$85-$106.** 1761 Meijer Cir 43616. I-280 exit 6 (Curtice Rd), just w. Int corridors. **Pets:** $15 one-time fee/room. Designated rooms, service with restrictions, crate. [SAVE] 🛜 🛗 🖥 🏊

PAINESVILLE

▼▼▼ **Quail Hollow Resort** H

(440) 497-1100. **Call for rates.** 11080 Concord-Hambden Rd 44077. I-90 exit 200, 0.3 mi s on SR 44, then just e on Auburn Rd. Int corridors. **Pets:** Accepted. 🛜 ✕ ⓜ 🛗 🖥 🍴 🏊 ✕

PERRYSBURG

▼▼ ▼▼ Candlewood Suites 🅷

(419) 872-6161. **$109-$119.** 27350 Lake Vue Dr 43551. I-75 exit 193, just e. Int corridors. **Pets:** Accepted. 🛜 📶 🔳 🔲

▼▼ ▼▼ La Quinta Inn Toledo Perrysburg 🅷

(419) 872-0000. **$66-$129.** 1154 Professional Dr 43551. I-75 exit 193, just w. Int corridors. **Pets:** Service with restrictions, supervision.
🛜 🔳 🔲

PIQUA

▼▼ ▼▼ Comfort Inn, Piqua, at Miami Valley Centre Mall 🅷

(937) 778-8100. **$74-$139.** 987 E Ash St 45356. I-75 exit 82, just w. Int corridors. **Pets:** Medium, other species. $20 one-time fee/pet. Service with restrictions. 🛜 🔳 🔲 🏊

POLAND

▼▼▼▼ Residence Inn by Marriott-Youngstown 🅷

(330) 726-1747. **$190-$220.** 7396 Tiffany S 44514. I-680 exit 11, just w. Int corridors. **Pets:** Accepted. 🛜 ❌ 🔳 🔲 🏊 🐾

PORT CLINTON

🆀🆀🆀 ▼▼ Best Budget Inn & Suites 🅷

(419) 734-5633. **$44-$179, 3 day notice.** 1735 E Perry St 43452. 1.5 mi e on SR 163, w of jct SR 2. Ext/int corridors. **Pets:** Other species. $50 deposit/pet. Service with restrictions, supervision. SAVE 🔳 🏊

▼▼ ▼▼ Comfort Inn, Waterfront 🅷

(419) 732-2929. **Call for rates.** 1723 E Perry St 43452. 1.5 mi e on SR 163, w of jct SR 2. Ext corridors. **Pets:** Other species. $50 deposit/pet. Service with restrictions, supervision. 🛜 🔳 🔲

▼▼ ▼▼ Commodore Perry Inn & Business Center 🅷

(419) 732-2645. **$50-$190, 3 day notice.** 255 W Lakeshore Dr 43452. SR 2 exit 121A, 2.4 mi e on SR 163. Int corridors. **Pets:** Medium, other species. Service with restrictions, crate. 🛜 🔳 🔲 🍴 🏊

▼▼ ▼▼ Sleep Inn & Suites 🅷

(419) 732-7707. **Call for rates.** 947 SE Catawba Rd (SR 53) 43452. SR 2 exit 124, just n on SR 53. Int corridors. **Pets:** Accepted.
🛜 📶 🔳 🔲

▼▼ ▼▼ Super 8 🅷

(419) 734-4446. **$49-$179.** 1704 E Perry St 43452. 1.7 mi e on SR 163, w of jct SR 2. Int corridors. **Pets:** Small, dogs only. $50 deposit/pet. Service with restrictions, supervision. 🛜 🔲

🆀🆀🆀 ▼▼▼▼ Travelodge Port Clinton 🅼

(419) 734-0769. **$60-$200.** 1811 E Perry St 43452. SR 163, 1.8 mi e to jct SR 2, then w. Ext/int corridors. **Pets:** Medium. $50 deposit/pet. Service with restrictions, supervision. SAVE 🛜 🔳 🔲 🏊

PORTSMOUTH

▼▼ ▼▼ Comfort Inn 🅼

(740) 353-3232. **$79-$90.** 5100 Old Scioto Tr 45662. 3.8 mi n of downtown. Int corridors. **Pets:** Small. $25 one-time fee/pet. Service with restrictions, supervision. 🛜 📶 🔳 🔲 🏊

ST. CLAIRSVILLE

🆀🆀🆀 ▼▼ Americas Best Value Inn St. Clairsville/Wheeling 🅼

(740) 695-5038. **$69-$149.** 51260 National Rd 43950. I-70 exit 218, 0.5 mi ne on US 40. Ext corridors. **Pets:** Other species. $10 one-time fee/room. Service with restrictions, crate. SAVE 🛜 🔳 🔲 🏊

🆀🆀🆀 ▼▼▼▼ Red Roof Inn #7101 🅼

(740) 695-4057. **$59-$99.** 68301 Red Roof Ln 43950. I-70 exit 218, just n. Ext corridors. **Pets:** Large, other species. Service with restrictions, supervision. SAVE 🛜 🔳

SANDUSKY

🆀🆀🆀 ▼▼ ▼▼ Budget Host Inn 🅼

(419) 626-3610. **$39-$119.** 2027 Cleveland Rd 44870. US 6, just e of Cedar Point Cswy. Ext/int corridors. **Pets:** Small, dogs only. $50 deposit/pet. Service with restrictions. SAVE 🛜 🔳 🏊

▼▼ ▼▼ Knights Inn Sandusky 🅼

(419) 621-9000. **$45-$149.** 2405 Cleveland Rd 44870. US 6, 2 mi e of Cedar Point Cswy. Ext/int corridors. **Pets:** Medium, dogs only. $25 deposit/pet, $10 daily fee/pet. Designated rooms, service with restrictions, crate. 🛜 🔳 🔲 🏊

▼▼ ▼▼ La Quinta Inn Sandusky-Cedar Point 🅼

(419) 626-6766. **$59-$254.** 3304 Milan Rd 44870. US 250, 2 mi n of SR 2. Int corridors. **Pets:** Service with restrictions, supervision.
🛜 🔳 🔲 🏊

SEAMAN

▼▼ ▼▼ Comfort Inn 🅼

(937) 386-2511. **Call for rates.** 55 Stern Dr 45679. Jct SR 32 and 247. Int corridors. **Pets:** Accepted. 🛜 🔳 🔲

SEVILLE

▼▼▼▼ Hawthorn Suites by Wyndham 🅷

(330) 769-5025. **$99-$109, 3 day notice.** 5025 Park Ave W 44273. I-76/US 224 exit 2, just n. Int corridors. **Pets:** Accepted.
🛜 🔳 🔲 🏊

▼▼ ▼▼ Super 8-Seville 🅷

(330) 769-8880. **$60-$80.** 6116 Speedway Dr 44273. Jct US 224 and Lake Rd, just s. Int corridors. **Pets:** Accepted. 🛜 📶 🔳 🔲

SPRINGFIELD

🆀🆀🆀 ▼▼▼▼ Courtyard by Marriott Springfield Downtown 🅷

(937) 322-3600. **$99-$169.** 100 S Fountain Ave 45502. I-70 exit 54, 2 mi n on SR 72 (Limestone St), just w on Main St, then downtown. Int corridors. **Pets:** Other species. $75 one-time fee/room. Service with restrictions, crate. SAVE 🛜 ❌ 🔳 🔲 🍴 🏊

▼▼ ▼▼ Quality Inn and Conference Center 🅷

(937) 323-8631. **Call for rates.** 383 E Leffel Ln 45505. I-70 exit 54, just n, then e. Int corridors. **Pets:** Accepted. 🛜 🔳 🔲 🍴 🏊 ❌

🆀🆀🆀 ▼▼ ▼▼ Red Roof Inn 🅷

(937) 325-5356. **$59-$129.** 155 W Leffel Ln 45506. I-70 exit 54, just n, then w. Int corridors. **Pets:** Large, other species. Service with restrictions, supervision. SAVE 🛜 🔳 🔲 🏊

STRASBURG

🆀🆀🆀 ▼▼▼▼ Ramada Limited Dover/Strasburg 🅷

(330) 878-1400. **$69-$135.** 509 S Wooster Ave 44680. I-77 exit 87, 0.4 mi n on US 250 and SR 21. Int corridors. **Pets:** Medium. $15 daily fee/room. Service with restrictions, supervision.
SAVE 🛜 📶 🔳 🔲 🏊

STREETSBORO

▼▼ ▼▼ TownePlace Suites by Marriott 🅷 🐾

(330) 422-1855. **$109-$149.** 795 Mondial Pkwy 44241. I-80 exit 187, 0.8 mi s. Int corridors. **Pets:** Medium, other species. $75 one-time fee/room. Designated rooms, service with restrictions, crate.
🛜 ❌ 🔳 🔲 🏊

SWANTON

▼▼ ▼▼ Days Inn 🅷

(419) 865-2002. **$55-$69.** 10753 Airport Hwy 43558. I-80/90 exit 52, just s, then 0.5 mi e. Int corridors. **Pets:** $15 daily fee/pet. Service with restrictions, supervision. 🛜 🔳 🔲 🏊

TIFFIN

▼▼▼ Holiday Inn Express **H**

(419) 443-5100. **$69-$99.** 78 Shaffer Park Dr 44883. US 224, just n on Market St, then just w. Int corridors. **Pets:** Medium, other species. $20 daily fee/room. Designated rooms, service with restrictions, supervision.
🛜 📺 💻 🏊

TIPP CITY

Ⓐ ▼▼▼ La Quinta Inn & Suites Dayton North-Tipp City **H**

(937) 667-1574. **$77-$155.** 19 Weller Dr 45371. I-75 exit 68, just w. Int corridors. **Pets:** Service with restrictions, supervision.
SAVE 🛜 ♿M 📺 💻 🏊

TOLEDO

▼▼ Park Inn Hotel Toledo **H**

(419) 241-3000. **Call for rates.** 101 N Summit St 43604. Between Jefferson and Monroe sts; downtown. Int corridors. **Pets:** Accepted.
🛜 📺 💻 🍴 ⊠

TROY

▼▼▼ Holiday Inn Express Hotel & Suites **H**

(937) 332-1700. **Call for rates.** 60 Troy Town Dr 45373. I-75 exit 74, just w. Int corridors. **Pets:** Accepted. 🛜 ♿M 📺 💻 🏊 ⊠

▼▼▼ Residence Inn by Marriott **H**

(937) 440-9303. **$109-$159.** 87 Troy Town Dr 45373. I-75 exit 74, just w. Int corridors. **Pets:** Accepted. 🛜 ⊠ 📺 💻 🏊 ⊠

UHRICHSVILLE

Ⓐ ▼▼▼ BEST WESTERN Country Inn **M**

(740) 922-0774. **$75-$90.** 111 W McCauley Dr 44683. US 250 exit McCauley Dr. Ext corridors. **Pets:** $10 daily fee/pet. Designated rooms, service with restrictions, crate. SAVE 🛜 📺 💻

VAN WERT

▼▼▼ Comfort Inn **H**

(419) 232-6040. **$89-$100.** 840 N Washington St 45891. US 127, s of jct US 30 and 224. Int corridors. **Pets:** Small. $20 daily fee/pet. Designated rooms, service with restrictions, supervision. 🛜 📺 💻 🏊

VERMILION

▼▼▼ Holiday Inn Express **H**

(440) 967-8770. **$99-$179.** 2417 SR 60 44089. Jct SR 2 and 60. Int corridors. **Pets:** Medium, other species. $35 one-time fee/pet. Designated rooms, service with restrictions, supervision. 🛜 📺 💻 🏊

WAPAKONETA

Ⓐ ▼▼▼ BEST WESTERN Wapakoneta Inn **H**

(419) 738-2050. **$85-$95.** 1008 Lunar Dr 45895. I-75 exit 111, just w. Int corridors. **Pets:** Accepted. SAVE 🛜 ⊠ ♿M 📺 🏊

WARREN

▼▼▼ Fairfield Inn by Marriott-Warren/Niles **H**

(330) 544-5774. **$99-$180.** 1860 Niles-Cortland Rd 44484. Jct US 422 and SR 46, 1 mi n on SR 46. Int corridors. **Pets:** Accepted.
🛜 ⊠ ♿M 📺 💻 🏊

WASHINGTON COURT HOUSE

▼▼▼ Holiday Inn Express **H**

(740) 335-9310. **Call for rates.** 101 Courthouse Pkwy 43160. Jct US 35, 0.4 mi sw on US 62. Int corridors. **Pets:** Accepted.
🛜 ♿M 📺 💻 🏊

WAUSEON

Ⓐ ▼▼▼ BEST WESTERN Del Mar **H**

(419) 335-1565. **$75-$146.** 8319 SR 108 43567. I-80/90 exit 34, just s. Ext corridors. **Pets:** Medium. $20 daily fee/room. Service with restrictions, crate. SAVE 🛜 📺 💻 🏊

WOOSTER

Ⓐ ▼▼▼ Econo Lodge **M**

(330) 264-8883. **Call for rates.** 2137 E Lincoln Way 44691. US 30, 3 mi e. Ext corridors. **Pets:** Accepted. SAVE 🛜 📺 🏊

YOUNGSTOWN

▼▼ Days Inn & Suites **M**

(330) 759-9820. **$70-$95, 3 day notice.** 1615 E Liberty St 44420. I-80 exit 229, just s. Int corridors. **Pets:** Accepted. 🛜 📺 💻 🏊

ZANESVILLE

▼▼▼ Baymont Inn & Suites Zanesville **M**

(740) 454-9332. **$79-$109.** 230 Scenic Crest Dr 43701. I-70 exit 155, just s. Int corridors. **Pets:** Accepted. 🛜 📺 💻 🏊

Ⓐ ▼▼▼ BEST WESTERN B. R. Guest **H**

(740) 453-6300. **$79-$134.** 4929 East Pike 43701. I-70 exit 160, just s. Int corridors. **Pets:** Other species. $10 daily fee/pet. Service with restrictions, supervision. SAVE 🛜 ♿M 📺 💻 🏊

Ⓐ ▼▼▼ Comfort Inn **H**

(740) 454-4144. **$129-$200.** 500 Monroe St 43701. I-70 exit 155 westbound; exit 7th St eastbound, e on Elberon to light, just n on Underwood St. Int corridors. **Pets:** Large, other species. $20 daily fee/pet. Designated rooms, service with restrictions, supervision.
SAVE 🛜 ♿M 📺 💻 🏊

▼▼ Super 8-Zanesville **M**

(740) 455-3124. **$64-$119.** 2440 National Rd 43701. I-70 exit 152, just n. Int corridors. **Pets:** Accepted. 🛜 📺 💻

OKLAHOMA

ALTUS

◆◆◆ ▼▼◆ BEST WESTERN Altus H
(580) 482-9300. $69-$99. 2804 N Main St 73521. 2 mi n on US 283. Ext corridors. Pets: Medium, other species. Designated rooms, service with restrictions, supervision. [SAVE] 🛜 🛑 💻 ➰ ⊠

▼▼◆ Hampton Inn & Suites Altus H
(580) 482-1273. $99-$159. 3601 N Main St 73521. 2.2 mi n on US 283. Int corridors. Pets: Accepted. 🛜 ⊠ 🆓M 🛑 💻 ➰

ARDMORE

◆◆◆ ▼▼◆ BEST WESTERN Ardmore Inn H
(580) 223-7525. $80-$175. 136 Holiday Dr 73401. I-35 exit 31A, just e, then just n. Int corridors. Pets: Large, other species. $10 daily fee/room. Designated rooms, service with restrictions. [SAVE] 🛜 🛑 💻 ➰

▼▼ La Quinta Inn Ardmore North H
(580) 223-7976. $69-$148. 2432 Veterans Blvd 73401. I-35 exit 33, just e. Ext corridors. Pets: Service with restrictions, supervision.
🛜 🛑 💻 ➰

▼▼ Quality Hotel H
(580) 223-7130. $80-$90. 2705 W Broadway 73401. I-35 exit 31A, just e. Ext corridors. Pets: Small, other species. $10 daily fee/room. Designated rooms, service with restrictions, crate. 🛜 🛑 💻 🍴 ➰

ATOKA

◆◆◆ ▼▼◆ BEST WESTERN Atoka Inn H ❀
(580) 889-7381. $79-$89. 2101 S Mississippi Ave 74525. 1 mi s. Ext corridors. Pets: Other species. $10 one-time fee/room. Service with restrictions, supervision. [SAVE] 🛜 🛑 💻 ➰

◆◆◆ ▼▼◆ Comfort Inn & Suites H
(580) 889-8999. Call for rates. 1502 S Mississippi Ave 74525. Just s of center. Int corridors. Pets: Small, dogs only. $25 one-time fee/pet. Designated rooms, service with restrictions, supervision. [SAVE] 🛜 🛑 💻

BARTLESVILLE

▼▼ Candlewood Suites H ❀
(918) 766-0044. Call for rates. 3812 SE Washington Pl 74006. Just s of jct US 60. Int corridors. Pets: Large, other species. $50 one-time fee/pet. 🛜 ⊠ 🆓M 🛑 💻

▼▼ Microtel Inn & Suites by Wyndham Bartlesville H
(918) 333-2100. $69-$109. 2696 SE Washington Blvd 74006. 1.4 mi s of jct US 60. Int corridors. Pets: Accepted. 🛜 🆓M 🛑 💻

BIG CABIN

▼▼ Super 8-Big Cabin M
(918) 783-5888. $57-$76. 30954 S Hwy 69 74301. I-44 exit 283, just ne. Ext/int corridors. Pets: Accepted. 🛜 🛑 💻 ➰

BLACKWELL

◆◆◆ ▼▼◆ BEST WESTERN Blackwell Inn H ❀
(580) 363-1300. Call for rates. 4545 W White Ave 74631. I-35 exit 222, just ne. Int corridors. Pets: $10 daily fee/room. Designated rooms, service with restrictions. [SAVE] 🛜 🛑 💻 ➰

◆◆◆ ▼▼◆ Econo Lodge Blackwell H ❀
(580) 363-7000. $92-$200. 1201 N 44th St 74631. I-35 exit 222, just ne. Int corridors. Pets: $10 daily fee/room. Designated rooms, service with restrictions. [SAVE] 🛜 ⊠ 🛑 💻 ➰

BROKEN BOW

◆◆◆ ▼▼◆ BEST WESTERN Broken Bow Hotel & Suites H
(580) 584-7400. Call for rates. 1699 S Park Dr 74728. On US 70/259, 1 mi s of SR 3. Int corridors. Pets: Medium. $25 daily fee/pet. Service with restrictions, supervision. [SAVE] 🛜 🛑 💻 ➰

CHICKASHA

◆◆◆ ▼▼◆ BEST WESTERN Chickasha Inn H
(405) 224-4890. $89-$99. 2101 S 4th St 73018. I-44 exit 80, just nw. Ext/int corridors. Pets: Small. $40 one-time fee/pet. Designated rooms, service with restrictions, supervision.
[SAVE] 🛜 🛑 💻 🍴 ➰ ⊠

DURANT

▼▼ Comfort Inn & Suites H
(580) 924-8881. $69-$119. 2112 W Main St 74701. Just e of jct US 75/69 and 70. Int corridors. Pets: Accepted. 🛜 🛑 💻 ➰

ENID

▼▼ Baymont Inn & Suites-Enid H
(580) 234-6800. $80-$129. 3614 W Owen K Garriott Rd 73703. 2 mi w of jct US 81. Int corridors. Pets: Accepted. 🛜 🆓M 🛑 💻 ➰

◆◆◆ ▼▼◆ BEST WESTERN Inn H
(580) 242-7110. $128-$139. 2818 S Van Buren St 73703. 1.6 mi s of jct US 412. Ext corridors. Pets: Accepted. [SAVE] 🛜 🛑 💻 🍴 ➰

▼▼ Holiday Inn Express Hotel & Suites H
(580) 237-7722. $119-$134. 4702 W Owen K Garriott Rd 73703. 2.3 mi w of jct US 81. Int corridors. Pets: Accepted. 🛜 🛑 💻 ➰

GROVE

◆◆◆ ▼▼◆ BEST WESTERN TimberRidge Inn H
(918) 786-6900. Call for rates. 120 W 18th St 74344. Just w of jct US 59. Ext/int corridors. Pets: Medium, dogs only. $10 daily fee/pet. Designated rooms, service with restrictions, supervision.
[SAVE] 🛜 ⊠ 🛑 💻 ➰

GUYMON

◆◆◆ ▼▼◆ BEST WESTERN PLUS Guymon Hotel & Suites H
(580) 338-0800. Call for rates. 1102 NE 6th St (Hwy 54) 73942. Just s of jct US 64. Ext/int corridors. Pets: Large, other species. $15 daily fee/pet. Designated rooms, service with restrictions, crate.
[SAVE] 🛜 🆓M 🛑 💻 🍴 ➰ ⊠

▼▼◆ Comfort Inn & Suites H
(580) 338-0831. Call for rates. 501 Hwy 54 E 73942. Just s of jct US 64. Int corridors. Pets: Medium. $15 daily fee/pet. Service with restrictions, supervision. 🛜 🛑 💻 ➰

♦♦♦♦♦ Holiday Inn Express Hotel & Suites Guymon **H**
(580) 338-4208. **$99-$129.** 701 SE Hwy 3 73942. Jct US 54/412, just e.
Int corridors. **Pets:** Accepted. 🛜 ✕ 🕭M 🛏 🖼 🏊

HENRYETTA

♦♦ **♦♦♦♦♦** Green Country Inn **M**
(918) 652-9988. **$45-$58.** 2004 Old Hwy 75 W 74437. I-40 exit 237, just
ne. Ext corridors. **Pets:** Medium. $10 daily fee/pet. Designated rooms,
service with restrictions, supervision. 🆂🅰🆅🅴 🛜 🛏 🏊

IDABEL

♦♦ Comfort Suites **H**
(580) 286-9393. **$80-$130.** 400 SE Lincoln Rd 74745. Just s of jct US
70 and 259. Int corridors. **Pets:** Accepted. 🛜 ✕ 🛏 🖼 🏊

♦♦ Super 8 **H**
(580) 286-2888. **$60-$80.** 401 NE Lincoln Rd 74745. On US 259. Ext
corridors. **Pets:** Accepted. 🛜 🛏 🖼 🏊

LAWTON

♦♦ **♦♦♦♦♦** BEST WESTERN PLUS Lawton Hotel &
     Convention Center **H**
(580) 353-0200. **$94-$99.** 1125 E Gore Blvd 73501. I-44 exit 37, just e.
Ext/int corridors. **Pets:** Large. $25 one-time fee/pet. Service with restric-
tions. 🆂🅰🆅🅴 🛜 🛏 🖼 🍴 🏊

♦♦♦♦♦ Sleep Inn & Suites **H**
(580) 353-5555. **$79-$109.** 421 SE Interstate Dr 73501. I-44 exit 37, just
w, then just s. Int corridors. **Pets:** Small. $25 one-time fee/pet. Service
with restrictions. 🛜 ✕ 🕭M 🛏 🖼 🏊

LOCUST GROVE

♦♦ **♦♦♦♦♦** BEST WESTERN PLUS Locust Grove Inn &
     Suites **H**
(918) 479-8082. **$77-$250.** 106 Holiday Ln 74352. Just nw of jct US 412
and SR 82. Int corridors. **Pets:** Small. $25 one-time fee/pet. Designated
rooms, service with restrictions, crate. 🆂🅰🆅🅴 🛜 🛏 🖼 🏊

MCALESTER

♦♦ **♦♦♦♦♦** BEST WESTERN Inn of McAlester **H**
(918) 426-0115. **$85-$90.** 1215 George Nigh Expwy 74502. 3 mi s on
US 69. Ext corridors. **Pets:** Accepted. 🆂🅰🆅🅴 🛜 🛏 🖼 🏊

♦♦♦♦♦ Candlewood Suites **H**
(918) 426-4171. **Call for rates.** 425 S George Nigh Expwy 74501. 2 mi
e on US 69. Int corridors. **Pets:** Accepted. 🛜 ✕ 🕭M 🛏 🖼 🏊

♦♦♦♦♦ Comfort Suites **H**
(918) 302-0001. **$71-$199.** 650 S George Nigh Expwy 74501. 1.2 mi s
on US 69. Int corridors. **Pets:** Accepted. 🛜 ✕ 🛏 🖼 🏊

♦♦ **♦♦♦♦♦** Econo Lodge **M**
(918) 426-4420. **$49-$65.** 731 S George Nigh Expwy 74501. 1.5 mi s on
US 69. Ext corridors. **Pets:** Small. $30 one-time fee/pet. Service with
restrictions, supervision. 🆂🅰🆅🅴 🛜 🛏 🖼

♦♦♦♦♦ Happy Days Hotel **H**
(918) 429-0910. **$60-$75.** 1400 S George Nigh Expwy 74501. 3.3 mi s
on US 69. Int corridors. **Pets:** Service with restrictions, supervision.
🆂🅰🆅🅴 🛜 ✕ 🛏 🖼 🏊

♦♦ **♦♦♦♦♦** Oak Tree Inn **H**
(918) 420-5002. **Call for rates.** 2200 E South Ave 74501. Just e of jct
US 69. Int corridors. **Pets:** Accepted. 🆂🅰🆅🅴 🛜 ✕ 🕭M 🛏 🖼

MUSKOGEE

♦♦ Comfort Inn **H**
(918) 682-3724. **Call for rates.** 3133 Azalea Park Dr 74401. Just sw of
jct US 62 and 69. Int corridors. **Pets:** Medium, dogs only. $10 daily fee/
pet. Designated rooms, service with restrictions, supervision.
🛜 🛏 🖼 🏊

♦♦ **♦♦♦♦♦** Quality Inn & Suites **H** 🐾
(918) 687-9000. **$95-$161.** 3031 Military Blvd 74401. Just se of jct US
62 and 69. Int corridors. **Pets:** Small. $100 deposit/room, $25 one-time
fee/pet. Designated rooms, service with restrictions, supervision.
🆂🅰🆅🅴 🛜 ✕ 🛏 🖼 🍴 🏊

OKLAHOMA CITY METROPOLITAN AREA

EDMOND

♦♦ **♦♦♦♦♦** BEST WESTERN Edmond Inn & Suites **H**
(405) 216-0300. **Call for rates.** 2700 E 2nd St 73034. I-35 exit 141, 1.1
mi w. Int corridors. **Pets:** Accepted. 🆂🅰🆅🅴 🛜 ✕ 🛏 🖼 🏊

♦♦ Sleep Inn & Suites **H**
(405) 844-3000. **$74-$84.** 3608 S Broadway Extension 73013. John Kilpatrick Tpke, 1.5 mi n on US 77. Int corridors. **Pets:** $15 daily fee/room.
Designated rooms, service with restrictions, crate.
🛜 🕭M 🛏 🖼 🏊

EL RENO

♦♦ **♦♦♦♦♦** BEST WESTERN Hensley's **H**
(405) 262-6490. **Call for rates.** 2701 S Country Club Rd 73036. I-40 exit
123, just s. Ext corridors. **Pets:** Medium. $25 deposit/pet, $5 daily fee/pet.
Service with restrictions, supervision. 🆂🅰🆅🅴 🛜 🛏 🖼 🏊

♦♦ **♦♦♦♦♦** Motel 6 El Reno #4267 **H**
(405) 262-6060. **$78-$84.** 1506 Domino Dr 73036. I-40 exit 123, just ne.
Int corridors. **Pets:** Other species. Service with restrictions, supervision.
🆂🅰🆅🅴 🛜 🛏 🏊

GUTHRIE

♦♦♦♦♦ Holiday Inn Express **H**
(405) 293-6464. **$89-$139.** 2227 E Oklahoma Ave 73044. I-35 exit 157,
just s. Int corridors. **Pets:** Medium. $25 one-time fee/pet. Designated
rooms, service with restrictions, supervision. 🛜 🕭M 🛏 🖼 🏊

MIDWEST CITY

♦♦♦♦♦ Hawthorn Suites by Wyndham **H**
(405) 737-7777. **$95-$110, 3 day notice.** 5701 Tinker Diagonal 73110.
I-40 exit 156A (Sooner Rd), just n. Int corridors. **Pets:** Medium. $10 daily
fee/pet. Designated rooms, service with restrictions, crate.
🛜 🕭M 🛏 🖼 🏊

♦♦ **♦♦♦♦♦** Sheraton Midwest City Hotel at the Reed
     Conference Center **H**
(405) 455-1800. **$89-$139, 3 day notice.** 5750 Will Rogers Rd 73110.
I-40 exit 156A (Sooner Rd), just ne. Int corridors. **Pets:** Large, other species. Service with restrictions, crate. 🆂🅰🆅🅴 🛜 ✕ 🛏 🖼 🍴 🏊

MOORE

♦♦ **♦♦♦♦♦** BEST WESTERN PLUS Greentree Inn &
     Suites **H**
(405) 912-8882. **$80-$100.** 1811 N Moore Ave 73160. I-35 exit 118, just
n on west frontage road. Int corridors. **Pets:** Small, dogs only. $10 daily
fee/pet. Service with restrictions, supervision. 🆂🅰🆅🅴 🛜 🛏 🖼 🏊

NORMAN

♦♦ **♦♦♦♦♦** BEST WESTERN Norman Inn & Suites **H**
(405) 701-4011. **Call for rates.** 2841 S Classen Blvd 73071. Just n of jct
SR 9. Int corridors. **Pets:** Accepted. 🆂🅰🆅🅴 🛜 ✕ 🕭M 🛏 🖼 🏊

▼▼▼▼ Country Inn & Suites By Carlson

(405) 360-0240. **$74-$169, 3 day notice.** 960 Ed Noble Pkwy 73072. I-35 exit 108B (Lindsey St), just nw. Int corridors. **Pets:** Medium. $10 daily fee/room. Service with restrictions, supervision.

🛰 ✕ 🕭M 🛏 💻 ⚓

▲▲▲ ▼▼▼▼ Econo Lodge Ⓜ

(405) 364-5554. **$65-$105.** 100 SW 26th Dr 73069. I-35 exit 109 (Main St), just se. Ext corridors. **Pets:** Small. $5 daily fee/pet. Service with restrictions, supervision. (SAVE) 🛰 🛏 💻

▼▼▼▼ Embassy Suites Norman-Hotel & Conference Center Ⓗ ❀

(405) 364-8040. **Call for rates.** 2501 Conference Dr 73069. 0.7 mi n of jct 24th Ave NW and Robinson. Int corridors. **Pets:** Large. $50 one-time fee/room. Designated rooms, service with restrictions.

ⒺⒸⓄ 🛰 🕭M 🛏 💻 🍴 ⚓

▼▼▼▼ La Quinta Inn & Suites Oklahoma City Norman Ⓗ

(405) 579-4000. **$78-$140.** 930 Ed Noble Dr 73072. I-35 exit 108B (Lindsey St), just nw. Int corridors. **Pets:** Service with restrictions, supervision.

🛰 🕭M 🛏 💻 ⚓

OKLAHOMA CITY

▼ Americas Best Value Inn Bricktown Ⓜ

(405) 677-1000. **$50.** 3030 S Prospect 73129. I-35 exit 124B northbound; exit 125A southbound, just n on service road. Ext corridors. **Pets:** Other species. $10 daily fee/pet. Service with restrictions. 🛰 💻

▲▲▲ ▼▼▼ Baymont Inn & Suites Ⓗ

(405) 943-4400. **$67-$80.** 4240 W I-40 Service Rd 73108. I-40 exit 145 (Meridian Ave), just e on south frontage road. Ext/int corridors. **Pets:** Small, dogs only. $10 daily fee/pet. Designated rooms, service with restrictions, supervision. (SAVE) 🛰 🛏 💻 ⚓

▲▲▲ ▼▼▼▼ BEST WESTERN PLUS Broadway Inn & Suites Ⓗ ❀

(405) 848-1919. **$79, 7 day notice.** 6101 N Santa Fe 73118. I-44 exit 127, just e on 63rd St, then just s. Int corridors. **Pets:** Medium. $20 daily fee/room. Designated rooms, supervision. (SAVE) 🛰 🛏 💻 🍴 ⚓

▲▲▲ ▼▼▼▼ BEST WESTERN PLUS Memorial Inn & Suites Ⓗ

(405) 286-5199. **$86-$160.** 1301 W Memorial Rd 73114. John Kilpatrick Tpke exit Western Ave, just nw. Int corridors. **Pets:** Medium. $25 daily fee/pet. Service with restrictions, supervision.

(SAVE) 🛰 🕭M 🛏 💻 ⚓

▲▲▲ ▼▼▼▼ BEST WESTERN PLUS Saddleback Inn & Conference Center Ⓗ

(405) 947-7000. **$90-$160.** 4300 SW 3rd St 73108. I-40 exit 145 (Meridian Ave), just ne. Ext/int corridors. **Pets:** Small. $15 daily fee/room. Designated rooms, service with restrictions, crate.

(SAVE) 🛰 🕭M 🛏 💻 🍴 ⚓ ✕

▼▼▼▼ Candlewood Suites Hotel Ⓗ

(405) 680-8770. **$79-$99.** 4400 W River Park Dr 73108. I-40 exit 145 (Meridian Ave), 1.1 mi s. Int corridors. **Pets:** Large, other species. $15 daily fee/room. Service with restrictions. 🛰 🕭M 🛏 💻

▼▼▼▼ Colcord Hotel Ⓗ

(405) 601-4300. **$139-$179.** 15 N Robinson Ave 73102. Jct Sheridan and Robinson aves. Int corridors. **Pets:** Accepted.

ⒺⒸⓄ 🛰 ✕ 🛏 💻 🍴

▼▼▼ Comfort Inn North Ⓗ

(405) 478-7282. **Call for rates.** 4625 NE 120th St 73131. I-35 exit 137 (122nd St), just sw. Int corridors. **Pets:** Medium, dogs only. $20 daily fee/pet. Designated rooms, service with restrictions, crate.

🛰 🛏 💻 ⚓

▼▼▼▼ Country Inn & Suites By Carlson Ⓗ

(405) 286-3555. **$70-$119.** 13501 Memorial Park Dr 73120. Just sw of jct Memorial Rd and Memorial Park Ln. Int corridors. **Pets:** Small. $20 daily fee/pet. Service with restrictions, crate. 🛰 ✕ 🕭M 🛏 💻 ⚓

▼▼▼▼ Courtyard by Marriott-NW Ⓗ

(405) 848-0808. **$81-$132.** 1515 Northwest Expwy 73118. I-44 exit 125C westbound; exit 125B eastbound, just e. Int corridors. **Pets:** Small. $75 one-time fee/room. Designated rooms, service with restrictions, supervision. ⒺⒸⓄ 🛰 ✕ 🕭M 🛏 💻 ⚓

▲▲▲ ▼▼▼▼ Courtyard by Marriott Oklahoma City Downtown Ⓗ

(405) 232-2290. **$119-$299.** 2 W Reno Ave 73102. Gaylord and Reno aves. Int corridors. **Pets:** Accepted.

(SAVE) 🛰 ✕ 🕭M 🛏 💻 🍴 ⚓

▼▼▼▼ Econo Lodge Ⓗ

(405) 478-0400. **Call for rates.** 12001 N I-35 Service Rd 73131. I-35 exit 137 (122nd St), just sw. Ext corridors. **Pets:** Small, dogs only. $10 daily fee/pet. Designated rooms, service with restrictions, supervision.

🛰 🛏 💻

▲▲▲ ▼▼▼▼ Embassy Suites Ⓗ

(405) 682-6000. **$109-$179.** 1815 S Meridian Ave 73108. I-40 exit 145 (Meridian Ave), 1 mi s. Int corridors. **Pets:** Medium. $50 one-time fee/room. Designated rooms, service with restrictions, crate.

(SAVE) 🛰 🛏 💻 🍴 ⚓ ✕

▲▲▲ ▼▼▼▼ Four Points by Sheraton Oklahoma City Airport Ⓗ

(405) 681-3500. **$90-$189.** 6300 Terminal Dr 73159. I-40 exit 145 (Meridian Ave), 4 mi s. Int corridors. **Pets:** Accepted.

(SAVE) 🛰 ✕ 🛏 💻 🍴 ⚓

▼▼▼▼ La Quinta Inn & Suites OKC North - Quail Springs Ⓗ

(405) 755-7000. **$83-$188.** 3003 W Memorial Rd 73134. John Kilpatrick Tpke exit May Ave, just nw. Int corridors. **Pets:** Service with restrictions, supervision. 🛰 ✕ 🕭M 🛏 💻 ⚓ ✕

▼▼▼▼ La Quinta Inn & Suites Oklahoma City NW Expwy Ⓗ

(405) 773-5575. **$66-$137.** 4829 Northwest Expwy 73132. 1.9 mi w of jct SR 3 and 74. Int corridors. **Pets:** Service with restrictions, supervision.

🛰 🛏 💻 ⚓

▼▼▼ Quality Inn Ⓗ

(405) 632-6666. **$59-$75.** 7800 CA Henderson Blvd 73139. I-240 exit 2A, just s. Ext corridors. **Pets:** Small, dogs only. $20 daily fee/pet. Service with restrictions, supervision. 🛰 🛏 💻 ⚓

▼▼▼ Residence Inn by Marriott Ⓗ

(405) 601-1700. **$189-$259.** 400 E Reno Ave 73104. Just se of jct Joe Carter Ave; in Bricktown. Int corridors. **Pets:** Medium, other species. $100 one-time fee/room. Service with restrictions, crate.

🛰 ✕ 🕭M 🛏 💻 ⚓ ✕

▼▼▼ Residence Inn by Marriott Oklahoma City South-Crossroads Mall Ⓗ

(405) 634-9696. **$142-$170.** 1111 E I-240 Service Rd 73149. I-240 exit 4C eastbound, 0.4 mi nw; exit 5 westbound, 0.8 mi nw. Int corridors. **Pets:** Large. $75 one-time fee/room. Service with restrictions, crate.

🛰 ✕ 🛏 💻 ⚓ ✕

▲▲▲ ▼▼▼▼ Residence Inn by Marriott-Oklahoma City West Ⓗ

(405) 942-4500. **$89-$189.** 4361 W Reno Ave 73107. I-40 exit 145 (Meridian Ave), 0.3 mi n, then just e. Ext corridors. **Pets:** Accepted.

(SAVE) 🛰 ✕ 🛏 💻 ⚓

AAA ▼▼▼ ▼▼▼ **Sheraton Oklahoma City** H ❀
(405) 235-2780. **$149-$339.** 1 N Broadway Ave 73102. Jct Sheridan and Broadway aves. Int corridors. **Pets:** Medium, dogs only. Service with restrictions, supervision. SAVE 🛜 ✕ 🗄 ▦ 🍽 ⊷

AAA ▼▼▼ ▼▼▼ **Skirvin Hilton** H
(405) 272-3040. **$134-$296.** 1 Park Ave 73102. Corner of N Broadway and Park aves. Int corridors. **Pets:** Accepted.
SAVE 🛜 ✕ 🕭 🗄 ▦ 🍽 ⊷ ⊠

▼▼▼ **SpringHill Suites by Marriott** H
(405) 604-0200. **$70-$149.** 510 S MacArthur Blvd 73128. I-40 exit 144, just ne. Int corridors. **Pets:** Accepted. 🛜 ✕ 🕭 🗄 ▦ ⊷

▼▼▼ **Staybridge Suites** H
(405) 429-4400. **$79-$99, 5 day notice.** 4411 SW 15th St 73108. I-40 exit 145 (Meridian Ave), 1 mi se. Int corridors. **Pets:** Accepted.
🛜 🕭 🗄 ▦ ⊷ ⊠

▼▼▼ **Wyndham Garden Hotel Oklahoma City Airport** H
(405) 685-4000. **$89-$129.** 2101 S Meridian Ave 73108: I-40 exit 145 (Meridian Ave), 1.3 mi s. Int corridors. **Pets:** Small. $75 one-time fee/ room. Service with restrictions, crate. 🛜 🗄 ▦ 🍽 ⊷

SHAWNEE

AAA ▼▼▼ ▼▼▼ **La Quinta Inn & Suites Shawnee** H
(405) 275-7930. **$71-$162.** 5401 Enterprise Ct 74804. I-40 exit 186, just ne. Int corridors. **Pets:** Service with restrictions, supervision.
SAVE 🛜 🕭 🗄 ▦ ⊷

YUKON

AAA ▼▼▼▼ **BEST WESTERN PLUS Yukon** H
(405) 265-9200. **Call for rates.** 11440 W I-40 Service Rd 73099. I-40 exit 138, just sw. Ext/int corridors. **Pets:** Medium. $25 deposit/pet, $6 daily fee/pet. Service with restrictions, crate. SAVE 🛜 🗄 ▦ ⊷

▼▼▼ **Comfort Suites** H
(405) 577-6500. **$91-$101.** 11424 NW 4th St 73099. I-40 exit 138, just nw. Int corridors. **Pets:** Other species. $10 daily fee/pet. Designated rooms, service with restrictions, crate. 🛜 ✕ 🗄 ▦ ⊷

▼▼▼ **La Quinta Inn & Suites Oklahoma City - Yukon** H
(405) 494-7600. **$95-$166.** 11500 W I-40 73099. I-40 exit 138, just s. Int corridors. **Pets:** Service with restrictions, supervision.
🛜 🕭 🗄 ▦ ⊷

END METROPOLITAN AREA

OKMULGEE

AAA ▼▼▼ **BEST WESTERN PLUS Okmulgee** H
(918) 756-9200. **$84-$87.** 3499 N Wood Dr 74447. Just n of jct US 75 and SR 56. Int corridors. **Pets:** Small. $50 deposit/pet. Supervision.
SAVE 🛜 🗄 ▦ ⊷

PAULS VALLEY

▼▼▼ **Comfort Inn & Suites** H ❀
(405) 207-9730. **$104-$125.** 103 S Humphrey Blvd 73075. I-35 exit 72, just e. Int corridors. **Pets:** Small. $10 daily fee/room. Designated rooms, service with restrictions, supervision. 🛜 🕭 🗄 ▦ ⊷

AAA ▼▼▼ **Days Inn** H
(405) 238-7548. **$74-$76.** 2606 W Grant Ave 73075. I-35 exit 72, just e. Int corridors. **Pets:** Small. Supervision. SAVE 🛜 🗄 ▦

PERRY

AAA ▼▼▼ **Comfort Inn & Suites** H
(580) 336-3800. **$99-$110.** 3112 W Fir St 73077. I-35 exit 186, just w. Int corridors. **Pets:** Small. $20 daily fee/pet. Designated rooms, service with restrictions, supervision. SAVE 🛜 ✕ 🕭 🗄 ▦ ⊷

▼▼▼ **Holiday Inn Express** H
(580) 336-5050. **Call for rates.** 3002 W Fir St 73077. I-35 exit 186, just w. Int corridors. **Pets:** Accepted. 🛜 ✕ 🕭 🗄 ▦ ⊷

PONCA CITY

AAA ▼▼▼ **Comfort Inn & Suites** H ❀
(580) 765-2322. **$92.** 3101 N 14th St 74604. I-35 exit 214, 3 mi n on US 77. Int corridors. **Pets:** Small, dogs only. $10 daily fee/pet.
SAVE 🛜 🕭 🗄 ▦ ⊷

POTEAU

▼▼▼ **Holiday Inn Express & Suites-Poteau** H
(918) 649-0123. **Call for rates.** 201 Hillview Pkwy 74953. Just ne of jct US 59/271 and SR 112. Int corridors. **Pets:** Accepted.
🛜 ✕ 🕭 🗄 ▦ ⊷

PRYOR

▼▼▼ **Holiday Inn Express & Suites** H
(918) 476-5400. **$109-$159.** 271 Mid America Dr 74361. 5 mi s on US 69. Int corridors. **Pets:** Accepted. 🛜 🕭 🗄 ▦ ⊷

STILLWATER

AAA ▼▼▼ **BEST WESTERN PLUS Cimarron Hotel & Suites** H ❀
(405) 372-2878. **$99-$139.** 315 N Husband St 74074. Just w of jct Hall of Fame Blvd and Main St. Int corridors. **Pets:** Large, other species. $20 daily fee/room. Designated rooms, service with restrictions, crate.
SAVE 🛜 ✕ 🕭 🗄 ▦ ⊷

▼▼▼ **Residence Inn by Marriott** H
(405) 707-0588. **$99-$200.** 800 S Murphy St 74074. Just s of jct SR 51. Int corridors. **Pets:** Accepted. 🛜 ✕ 🕭 🗄 ▦ ⊷

STROUD

AAA ▼▼▼ **BEST WESTERN Stroud Motor Lodge** H
(918) 968-9515. **$73-$81.** 1200 N 8th Ave 74079. I-44 exit 179, just ne. Ext corridors. **Pets:** $10 daily fee/pet. Service with restrictions, crate.
SAVE 🛜 🗄 🍽 ⊷

THACKERVILLE

▼▼ **The Inn at WinStar** H
(580) 276-4487. **$109-$229.** Rt 1, Box 682 73459. I-35 exit 1, 1.2 mi n on E Service Rd. Int corridors. **Pets:** Accepted. 🛜 🗄 ▦ ⊷

TULSA METROPOLITAN AREA

BROKEN ARROW

▼▼▼ Clarion Hotel 🄷
(918) 258-7085. **$62-$89.** 2600 N Aspen Ave 74012. Just s of jct SR 51. Int corridors. **Pets:** Accepted. 🛜 🅿 🍴 💻 ➳

▼▼▼▼ Homewood Suites by Hilton Tulsa South 🄷
(918) 392-7700. **$99-$159.** 4900 W Madison Pl 74012. Just ne of jct 71st St and Garnett Ave. Int corridors. **Pets:** Accepted.
🛜 ♿ 🅿 💻 ➳ ⊠

▼▼▼ TownePlace Suites by Marriott 🄷
(918) 355-9600. **$85-$119.** 2251 N Stonewood Cir 74012. Just ne of jct SR 51 and Elm Pl. Int corridors. **Pets:** Accepted.
🛜 ⊠ ♿ 🅿 💻 ➳

CATOOSA

▼▼▼▼ Hampton Inn & Suites 🄷
(918) 739-3939. **$99-$129.** 100 McNabb Field Rd 74015. I-44 exit 240A, just ne. Int corridors. **Pets:** Medium. $25 one-time fee/pet, $10 daily fee/pet. Designated rooms, service with restrictions, crate.
🛜 ⊠ ♿ 🅿 💻 ➳

CLAREMORE

🄰🄰🄰 ▼ Claremore Motor Inn 🄼
(918) 342-4545. **Call for rates.** 1709 N Lynn Riggs Blvd 74017. 1.2 mi n on SR 66. Ext/int corridors. **Pets:** Accepted. 🆂🅰🆅🅴 🛜 🅿 💻

▼▼ Comfort Inn Claremore 🄷
(918) 343-3297. **$83-$95.** 1720 S Lynn Riggs Blvd 74017. 1.6 mi s on SR 66. Int corridors. **Pets:** Medium, other species. $15 daily fee/pet. Designated rooms, service with restrictions, crate. 🛜 🅿 💻 ➳

▼▼ Microtel Inn & Suites by Wyndham Claremore 🄷
(918) 343-2868. **$75-$95.** 10600 E Mallard Lake Rd 74017. 2.6 mi s on SR 66. **Pets:** Other species. $15 daily fee/pet. Supervision.
🛜 🅿 💻 ➳

🄰🄰🄰 ▼▼▼ Super 8 🄷
(918) 341-2323. **$65-$99.** 1100 E Will Rogers Blvd 74017. I-44 exit 255, just w. Ext/int corridors. **Pets:** Medium. $10 daily fee/pet. Designated rooms, service with restrictions, crate. 🆂🅰🆅🅴 🛜 🅿 💻

GLENPOOL

🄰🄰🄰 ▼▼▼ BEST WESTERN Glenpool/Tulsa 🄷
(918) 322-5201. **$73-$90.** 14831 S Casper St 74033. I-44 exit 224, 9.5 mi s on US 75. Ext corridors. **Pets:** Accepted. 🆂🅰🆅🅴 🛜 🅿 💻 ➳

OWASSO

🄰🄰🄰 ▼▼▼ BEST WESTERN Owasso Inn & Suites 🄷
(918) 272-2000. **$80.** 7653 N Owasso Expwy 74055. Just ne of jct US 169 and 76th St. Ext/int corridors. **Pets:** Accepted.
🆂🅰🆅🅴 🛜 ⊠ 🅿 💻 ➳

▼▼▼ Candlewood Suites 🄷 🐾
(918) 272-4334. **$76-$96.** 11699 E 96th St N 74055. 0.4 mi nw of jct US 169. Int corridors. **Pets:** Other species. $50 one-time fee/room. Service with restrictions, crate. 🛜 ⊠ ♿ 🅿 💻

▼▼▼▼ TownePlace Suites by Marriott Tulsa North/Owasso 🄷
(918) 376-4400. **$89-$98.** 9355 N Owasso Expwy 74055. Just se of jct US 169 and 96th St. Int corridors. **Pets:** Medium, dogs only. $100 one-time fee/pet. Designated rooms, service with restrictions, crate.
🛜 ⊠ ♿ 🅿 💻 ➳

TULSA

🄰🄰🄰 ▼▼▼ Aloft Tulsa 🄷 🐾
(918) 949-9000. **$89-$159.** 6716 S 104th E Ave 74133. Just nw of jct US 169 and 71st St. Int corridors. **Pets:** Medium, dogs only. Designated rooms, service with restrictions, supervision.
🆂🅰🆅🅴 🛜 ⊠ ♿ 🅿 💻 ➳ ⊠

🄰🄰🄰 ▼▼▼ Ambassador Hotel Tulsa 🄷
(918) 587-8200. **$209-$299.** 1324 S Main St 74119. Jct 14th and Main sts. Int corridors. **Pets:** Accepted. 🆂🅰🆅🅴 🛜 ⊠ 🅿 💻 🍴

▼▼ Baymont Inn & Suites Tulsa 🄷
(918) 488-8777. **$59-$69.** 4530 E Skelly Dr 74135. I-44 exit 229 (Yale Ave), just sw. Int corridors. **Pets:** Accepted. 🛜 🅿 💻 ➳

🄰🄰🄰 ▼▼▼ BEST WESTERN Airport 🄷 🐾
(918) 438-0780. **$70-$90.** 222 N Garnett Rd 74116. I-244 exit 14 (Garnett Rd), just s. Ext corridors. **Pets:** Other species. $20 one-time fee/room. Service with restrictions, crate. 🆂🅰🆅🅴 🛜 🅿 💻 ➳

▼▼▼ Candlewood Suites 🄷
(918) 294-9000. **$79-$99.** 10008 E 73rd St S 74133. Just sw of jct 71st St and 101st E Ave. Int corridors. **Pets:** Accepted. 🛜 ♿ 🅿 💻

▼▼▼ Clarion Inn Tulsa International Airport 🄷
(918) 835-9911. **$89-$119.** 2201 N 77th E Ave 74115. SR 11 exit airport terminal. Int corridors. **Pets:** Small. $25 one-time fee/pet. Designated rooms, service with restrictions, crate. 🛜 ⊠ 🅿 💻 🍴 ➳

▼▼▼ Comfort Suites East 🄷 🐾
(918) 628-0900. **$74-$94.** 1737 S 101st E Ave 74128. I-44 exit 233 eastbound; exit 233B westbound, follow signs. Int corridors. **Pets:** Large, other species. $10 daily fee/pet. Service with restrictions, supervision.
🛜 ⊠ 🅿 💻 ➳

▼▼▼ Crowne Plaza Tulsa-Southern Hills 🄷
(918) 492-5000. **Call for rates.** 7902 S Lewis Ave 74136. I-44 exit 227 (Lewis Ave), 3 mi s. Int corridors. **Pets:** Accepted.
🛜 🅿 💻 🍴 ➳

▼▼▼ DoubleTree by Hilton Hotel Tulsa Downtown 🄷
(918) 587-8000. **$89-$149.** 616 W 7th St 74127. Jct 7th St and Houston Ave. Int corridors. **Pets:** Other species. $50 one-time fee/room. Service with restrictions, crate. 🛜 ⊠ 🅿 💻 🍴 ➳

▼▼▼ DoubleTree by Hilton Hotel Tulsa-Warren Place 🄷
(918) 495-1000. **$79-$159.** 6110 S Yale Ave 74136. I-44 exit 229 (Yale Ave), 1.3 mi s. Int corridors. **Pets:** Accepted.
🛜 ⊠ ♿ 🅿 💻 🍴 ➳ ⊠

▼▼▼ Holiday Inn & Suites 🄷
(918) 994-5000. **$69-$149.** 10020 E 81st St 74133. Just w of jct US 169. Int corridors. **Pets:** Accepted. 🛜 ⊠ ♿ 🅿 💻 🍴 ➳

▼▼ Holiday Inn Express 🄷
(918) 459-5321. **Call for rates.** 9010 E 71st St 74133. US 169 exit 71st St, 1 mi w. Int corridors. **Pets:** Accepted. 🛜 ⊠ 🅿 💻 ➳

🄰🄰🄰 ▼▼▼ Holiday Inn Tulsa City Center 🄷
(918) 585-5898. **$84-$159.** 17 W 7th St 74119. Jct Boulder Ave. Int corridors. **Pets:** Medium. $35 one-time fee/room. Designated rooms, service with restrictions, supervision. 🆂🅰🆅🅴 🛜 ⊠ ♿ 🅿 💻 🍴 ➳

Hyatt Regency Tulsa H
(918) 582-9000. **$62-$270.** 100 E 2nd St 74103. Jct 2nd St and Boston Ave; downtown. Int corridors. **Pets:** Accepted.

La Quinta Inn & Suites Tulsa Airport/Expo Square H
(918) 949-3600. **$83-$166.** 23 N 67th E Ave 74115. I-244 exit 11 (Sheridan Ave), just se. Int corridors. **Pets:** Service with restrictions, supervision.

La Quinta Inn & Suites Tulsa Central H
(918) 665-2630. **$90-$155.** 6030 E Skelly Dr 74135. I-44 exit 230, just s. Int corridors. **Pets:** Service with restrictions, supervision.

Ramada H
(918) 828-9128. **$80-$120, 3 day notice.** 8175 E Skelly Dr 74129. I-44 exit 231 (31st St) eastbound; exit 232 (Memorial Dr) westbound, just ne. Int corridors. **Pets:** Service with restrictions, supervision.

Red Roof Inn M
(918) 622-6776. **$50-$149.** 4717 S Yale Ave 74135. I-44 exit 229 (Yale Ave), just s. Ext corridors. **Pets:** Large, other species. Service with restrictions, supervision.

Renaissance Tulsa Hotel & Convention Center H
(918) 307-2600. **$95-$199.** 6808 S 107th E Ave 74133. Just ne of jct US 169 and 71st St. Int corridors. **Pets:** Accepted.

Residence Inn by Marriott H
(918) 250-4850. **$109-$149.** 11025 E 73rd St 74133. Just se of jct US 169 and 71st St. Int corridors. **Pets:** Other species. $75 one-time fee/room. Designated rooms, service with restrictions.

Sleep Inn & Suites Tulsa Central H
(918) 663-2777. **$79-$90.** 8021 E 33rd St S 74145. I-44 exit 231 (31st St) eastbound; exit 232 (Memorial Dr) westbound, just sw. Int corridors. **Pets:** Accepted.

Staybridge Suites H 🐾
(918) 461-2100. **$99-$155.** 11111 E 73rd St 74133. Just se of jct US 169 and 71st St. Int corridors. **Pets:** Small, dogs only. $75 one-time fee/room. Designated rooms, service with restrictions, supervision.

Tulsa Square Hotel H
(918) 663-1000. **$62-$72.** 3209 S 79th E Ave 74145. I-44 exit 231 (31st St) eastbound; exit 232 (Memorial Dr) westbound, just sw. Int corridors. **Pets:** Medium, other species. $50 deposit/pet. Designated rooms, service with restrictions, supervision.

Wyndham Tulsa H
(918) 627-5000. **$90-$125.** 10918 E 41st St 74146. Just e of US 169. Int corridors. **Pets:** Small, dogs only. $75 one-time fee/room. Service with restrictions, crate.

WAGONER

The Canebrake H
(918) 485-1810. **Call for rates.** 33241 E 732 Rd 74467. 1.7 mi n of jct SR 51 and S 330th Rd. Ext corridors. **Pets:** Accepted.

End Metropolitan Area

WEATHERFORD

BEST WESTERN PLUS Mark Motor Hotel H
(580) 772-3325. **$90-$170.** 525 E Main St 73096. I-40 exit 82, 0.5 mi n. Ext corridors. **Pets:** Medium, dogs only. $20 daily fee/pet. Designated rooms, service with restrictions, supervision.

WOODWARD

Northwest Inn H
(580) 256-7600. **$99-$119.** Hwy 270 S & 1st St 73802. 1.4 mi s of jct US 183 and 270, SR 3 and 34. Ext/int corridors. **Pets:** Designated rooms, service with restrictions, crate.

OREGON

ALBANY

BEST WESTERN PLUS Prairie Inn 🄷
(541) 928-5050. **$80-$160.** 1100 Price Rd SE 97322. I-5 exit 233, just e on Santiam Hwy (US 20), then just n. Int corridors. **Pets:** Large. $20 one-time fee/pet. Designated rooms, service with restrictions, supervision.
[SAVE] 🛜 ⌖ 🍴 🛗 🌊

Comfort Suites - Linn County Fairgrounds and Expo 🄷
(541) 928-2053. **$79-$149.** 100 Opal Ct NE 97322. I-5 exit 234A southbound; exit 234 northbound, just se. Int corridors. **Pets:** Medium, dogs only. $15 daily fee/pet. Service with restrictions, supervision.
[SAVE] 🛜 ✖ ⌖ 🍴 🛗 🌊 ✖

Econo Lodge 🄼
(541) 926-0170. **$59-$70.** 1212 SE Price Rd 97322. I-5 exit 233, just e on Santiam Hwy (US 20), then just n. Ext corridors. **Pets:** Medium, dogs only. $10 daily fee/room. Service with restrictions, supervision.
[SAVE] 🛜 🍴

Holiday Inn Express Hotel & Suites 🄷
(541) 928-8820. **Call for rates.** 105 Opal Ct NE 97322. I-5 exit 234A southbound; exit 234 northbound, just se. Int corridors. **Pets:** Medium. $15 daily fee/room. Service with restrictions, supervision.
[SAVE] 🛜 ✖ ⌖ 🍴 🛗 🌊 ✖

La Quinta Inn Albany 🄷
(541) 928-0921. **$71-$155.** 251 Airport Rd SE 97322. I-5 exit 234B southbound; exit 234 northbound, just sw. Int corridors. **Pets:** Service with restrictions, supervision. 🛜 ✖ 🍴 🛗 🌊 ✖

Motel 6 - #4124 🄼
(541) 926-4233. **$55-$111.** 2735 E Pacific Blvd 97321. I-5 exit 234B southbound; exit 234 northbound, 0.5 mi w. Ext corridors. **Pets:** Other species. Service with restrictions, supervision. [SAVE] 🛜 🍴

Phoenix Inn Suites-Albany 🄷
(541) 926-5696. **Call for rates.** 3410 Spicer Rd SE 97322. I-5 exit 233, just se. Int corridors. **Pets:** Other species. $25 one-time fee/room. Designated rooms, service with restrictions, crate. [SAVE] 🛜 🍴 🛗 🌊

Super 8 - Albany 🄷
(541) 928-6322. **$55-$149.** 315 Airport Rd SE 97322. I-5 exit 234B southbound; exit 234 northbound, just sw. Ext corridors. **Pets:** Large, other species. $10 daily fee/pet. Service with restrictions, crate.
[SAVE] 🛜 🍴 🛗 🌊

ASHLAND

Ashland Chanticleer Inn 🄱🄱
(541) 482-1919. **$130-$199, 31 day notice.** 120 Gresham St 97520. Just se of downtown on SR 99 (E Main St), just s. Int corridors. **Pets:** Dogs only. $10 daily fee/pet. Designated rooms, service with restrictions, crate. 🛜 ✖ 🗎

Ashland Springs Hotel 🄷
(541) 488-1700. **$89-$269, 3 day notice.** 212 E Main St 97520. Corner of 1st St; center. Int corridors. **Pets:** Small, dogs only. $30 one-time fee/pet. Designated rooms, service with restrictions, crate.
🛜 ✖ 🍴 🍴

BEST WESTERN Bard's Inn 🄷 🐾
(541) 482-0049. **$100-$169.** 132 N Main St 97520. From Downtown Plaza, just nw on SR 99 (N Main St). Ext/int corridors. **Pets:** $15 daily fee/pet. Designated rooms, service with restrictions, supervision.
[SAVE] 🛜 ✖ 🍴 🛗 🌊

BEST WESTERN Windsor Inn 🄷 🐾
(541) 488-2330. **$99-$159.** 2520 Ashland St 97520. I-5 exit 14, just se on Ashland St (SR 66). Ext corridors. **Pets:** Medium. $15 daily fee/pet. Designated rooms, service with restrictions, supervision.
[SAVE] 🛜 ✖ 🍴 🛗 🌊

Callahan's Lodge 🄲🄸
(541) 482-1299. **$135-$260.** 7100 Old Hwy 99 S 97520. I-5 exit 6 (Mt. Ashland), just e; 8 mi s of town. Int corridors. **Pets:** $20 daily fee/pet. Designated rooms, service with restrictions, crate.
[SAVE] 🛜 ✖ 🍴 🛗 🍴 ✖

Cedarwood Inn 🄼
(541) 488-2000. **$59-$119, 3 day notice.** 1801 Siskiyou Blvd 97520. I-5 exit 11 northbound, 2.6 mi nw; exit 14 southbound, just w on Ashland St (SR 66), 0.6 mi s on Tolman Creek Rd, then 0.6 mi w. Ext corridors.
Pets: Accepted. [SAVE] 🛜 🍴 🛗 🌊

Flagship Inn of Ashland 🄼
(541) 482-2641. **$59-$119, 3 day notice.** 1193 Siskiyou Blvd 97520. I-5 exit 14, 1.3 mi w on Ashland St (SR 66), then just n. Ext corridors. **Pets:** Medium, dogs only. $10 deposit/pet, $10 daily fee/pet. Designated rooms, service with restrictions, crate. [SAVE] 🛜 ✖ 🍴 🛗 🌊

Holiday Inn Express Hotel & Suites 🄷
(541) 201-0202. **$116-$189.** 565 Clover Ln 97520. I-5 exit 14, just e on Ashland St (SR 66), then just s. Int corridors. **Pets:** Dogs only. $15 fee/pet. Designated rooms, service with restrictions, supervision.
[SAVE] 🛜 ✖ ⌖ 🍴 🛗 🌊

La Quinta Inn & Suites Ashland 🄷
(541) 482-6932. **$83-$188.** 434 S Valley View Rd 97520. I-5 exit 19, just sw. Int corridors. **Pets:** Service with restrictions, supervision.
🛜 ✖ 🍴 🛗 🌊 ✖

Plaza Inn & Suites At Ashland Creek 🄷 🐾
(541) 488-8900. **$89-$309.** 98 Central Ave 97520. From Downtown Plaza, just nw on SR 99 (N Main St), just n on Water St, then just w. Int corridors. **Pets:** Large. $25 daily fee/room. Designated rooms, service with restrictions, supervision. [SAVE] 🛜 ✖ 🍴 🛗

▼▼ Village Suites at Ashland Hills 🄷 ❖

(541) 482-8310. **$89-$159.** 2525 Ashland St 97520. I-5 exit 14, just ne on Ashland St (SR 66). Int corridors. **Pets:** Designated rooms, service with restrictions, supervision. 🛜 ⊠ 🛎 💻 ⊠

ASTORIA

⊕⊘ ▼ Astoria Dunes Motel 🄼

(503) 325-7111. **$75-$165.** 288 W Marine Dr 97103. Just e of Astoria Bridge on US 30. Ext corridors. **Pets:** Medium, dogs only. $10 daily fee/pet. Service with restrictions, supervision. SAVE 🛜 🛎 💻 ≋

▼▼▼ Astoria Holiday Inn Express Hotel & Suites 🄷 ❖

(503) 325-6222. **$119-$339.** 204 W Marine Dr 97103. On US 30; west side of town. Int corridors. **Pets:** Other species. $15 daily fee/pet. Designated rooms, service with restrictions, supervision.

🛜 ⊠ 🖫 🛎 💻 ≋ ⊠

⊕⊘ ▼▼ BEST WESTERN Lincoln Inn 🄷

(503) 325-2205. **$89-$399.** 555 Hamburg Ave 97103. On US 101/30; at east end of Young's Bay Bridge. Int corridors. **Pets:** Medium, dogs only. $15 daily fee/pet. Designated rooms, service with restrictions, supervision.

SAVE 🛜 ⊠ 🛎 💻 ≋ ⊠

▼▼ Clementine's Bed & Breakfast 🄱🄱 ❖

(503) 325-2005. **Call for rates.** 847 Exchange St 97103. At 8th and Exchange sts; in historic downtown. Int corridors. **Pets:** $20 one-time fee/pet. Designated rooms, no service, supervision.

🛜 ⊠ 🛎 💻 🗶 ⊠

⊕⊘ ▼▼▼ Comfort Suites Columbia River 🄷

(503) 325-2000. **$100-$310.** 3420 Leif Erickson Dr 97103. 2.5 mi e of Astoria Bridge on US 30. Int corridors. **Pets:** Other species. $10 daily fee/pet. Designated rooms, service with restrictions, crate.

SAVE 🛜 ⊠ 🛎 💻 ≋ ⊠

▼▼ Crest Motel 🄼

(503) 325-3141. **$68-$135.** 5366 Leif Erickson Dr 97103. 4 mi e of Astoria Bridge on US 30. Ext corridors. **Pets:** Supervision.

🛜 🛎 💻 🗶

BAKER CITY

⊕⊘ ▼▼ BEST WESTERN Sunridge Inn 🄷 ❖

(541) 523-6444. **$89-$109.** 1 Sunridge Ln 97814. I-84 exit 304, just w. Int corridors. **Pets:** Large, other species. $15 daily fee/room. Designated rooms, service with restrictions, crate.

SAVE 🛜 ⊠ 🛎 💻 🍴 ≋

▼▼▼ Geiser Grand Hotel 🄷 ❖

(541) 523-1889. **$99-$259, 3 day notice.** 1996 Main St 97814. I-84 exit 304, 0.9 mi w on Campbell St, then 0.3 mi s; downtown. Int corridors. **Pets:** Large, other species. $75 deposit/room, $15 daily fee/pet. Service with restrictions. 🛜 ⊠ 🍴

BANDON

▼▼ Bandon Beach Vacation Rentals 🅅🄷

(541) 347-4801. **$100-$200, 30 day notice.** 54515 Beach Loop Rd 97411. 1 mi s on US 101, 0.8 mi w on Seabird Rd, then 1 mi s; registration in house behind property. Ext corridors. **Pets:** Dogs only. $20 one-time fee/pet. Supervision. 🛜 ⊠ 🛎 💻 🗶

⊕⊘ ▼▼▼ Bandon Inn 🄼 ❖

(541) 347-4417. **$79-$155.** 355 US 101 97411. Center. Ext corridors. **Pets:** Small, dogs only. $15 daily fee/pet. Designated rooms, service with restrictions, supervision. SAVE 🛜 ⊠ 🛎 💻 🗶

⊕⊘ ▼▼▼ BEST WESTERN Inn at Face Rock 🄷

(541) 347-9441. **Call for rates.** 3225 Beach Loop Dr 97411. 1 mi s on US 101, 0.8 mi w on Seabird Rd, then just s. Ext corridors. **Pets:** Other species. $20 one-time fee/room. Service with restrictions, supervision.

SAVE 🛜 ⊠ 🛎 💻 🍴 ≋ ⊠ 🗶

BEND

⊕⊘ ▼▼ 💎 Bend Quality Inn 🄷

(541) 318-0848. **$79-$100.** 20600 Grandview Dr 97701. On US 97; north end of town. Int corridors. **Pets:** Medium, other species. $10 daily fee/pet. Designated rooms, service with restrictions, supervision.

SAVE 🛜 🖫 🛎 💻 ≋

▼▼ Bend Riverside Inn & Suites 🄷

(541) 389-2363. **$78-$159, 3 day notice.** 1565 NW Wall St 97701. US 97 exit 137 (Revere Ave), just s. Ext corridors. **Pets:** Medium. $10 daily fee/room. Designated rooms, no service, supervision.

🛜 ⊠ 🛎 💻 ≋

⊕⊘ ▼▼ Bend Three Sisters Inn & Suites 🄷

(541) 382-1515. **$85-$150.** 721 NE 3rd St 97701. Jct US 20 and Business Rt US 97 (NE 3rd St), just s. Ext corridors. **Pets:** Accepted.

SAVE 🛜 🛎 💻 ≋

▼▼▼ Holiday Inn Express Hotel & Suites 🄷

(541) 317-8500. **$99-$249.** 20615 Grandview Dr 97701. On US 97; north end of town. Int corridors. **Pets:** Accepted.

🛜 ⊠ 🛎 💻 ≋

▼▼ La Quinta Inn Bend 🄷

(541) 388-2227. **$89-$216.** 61200 SE 3rd St (Business Rt US 97) 97702. From south end of jct US 97 and Business Rt US 97 (NE 3rd St), 0.5 mi n. Int corridors. **Pets:** Service with restrictions, supervision.

🛜 ⊠ 🛎 💻 ≋

⊕⊘ ▼▼▼▼ The Oxford Hotel 🄷

(541) 382-8436. **$189-$445.** 10 NW Minnesota Ave 97701. Jct NW Minnesota Ave and NW Lava Rd; downtown. Int corridors. **Pets:** Accepted.

SAVE 🛜 ⊠ 🖫 🛎 💻 🍴 🗶

▼▼ Pine Ridge Inn Hotel & Suites 🄷

(541) 389-6137. **Call for rates.** 1200 SW Mt Bachelor Dr 97702. US 97 exit 138 (Downtown/Mt Bachelor Dr), 1.6 mi sw on Colorado Ave, just s on Century Dr, then just w. Int corridors. **Pets:** Accepted.

🛜 ⊠ 🖫 🛎 💻 ≋

⊕⊘ ▼▼▼▼ Red Lion Hotel Bend 🄷

(541) 382-7011. **$89-$199.** 1415 NE 3rd St 97701. Jct US 20 and Business Rt US 97 (NE 3rd St), just n. Ext corridors. **Pets:** Other species. $15 one-time fee/room. Service with restrictions, crate.

SAVE 🛜 ⊠ 🖫 🛎 💻 ≋

⊕⊘ ▼▼▼▼ The Riverhouse Hotel & Convention Center 🄷 ❖

(541) 389-3111. **$99-$219.** 3075 N US 97 Business 97701. US 97 exit 137 (Revere Ave) northbound, just n on NE Division St, then just n; exit 136 (Butler Market Rd) southbound, just w. Ext/int corridors. **Pets:** Supervision. SAVE 🛜 ⊠ 🛎 💻 🍴 ≋ ⊠

⊕⊘ ▼▼▼▼ Seventh Mountain Resort 🄲🄾 ❖

(541) 382-8711. **$99-$499, 7 day notice.** 18575 SW Century Dr 97702. US 97 exit 139 (Reed Market Rd), 1.6 mi sw, then 3.5 mi sw. Ext corridors. **Pets:** Other species. $50 one-time fee/room. Service with restrictions, crate. SAVE 🛜 ⊠ 🛎 💻 🍴 ≋ ⊠

▼▼ Shilo Inn Suites Hotel - Bend 🄷

(541) 389-9600. **$69-$220.** 3105 OB Riley Rd 97701. US 97 exit 137 (Revere Ave) northbound, just n on NE Division St, then n; exit 136 (Butler Market Rd) southbound, just w. Ext corridors. **Pets:** Dogs only. $25 one-time fee/room. Designated rooms, service with restrictions, supervision. 🛜 ⊠ 🛎 💻 🍴 ≋ ⊠

▼▼ TownePlace Suites by Marriott 🄷

(541) 382-5006. **$89-$189.** 755 SW 13th Pl 97702. US 97 exit 138 (Downtown/Mt Bachelor Dr), 1.6 mi sw on NW Colorado Ave. Int corridors. **Pets:** Small. $75 one-time fee/room. Designated rooms, service with restrictions, crate. 🛜 ⊠ 🛎 💻 ≋ ⊠

BROOKINGS

◇◇◇ ▽▽▽▽ BEST WESTERN PLUS Beachfront Inn 🄷
(541) 469-7779. **Call for rates.** 16008 Boat Basin Rd 97415. US 101 exit Benham Ln, 0.6 mi w; 1.2 mi s of Chetco River Bridge. Ext corridors. **Pets:** $10 daily fee/pet. Designated rooms, service with restrictions, supervision. SAVE 🛜 ❄M 🛢 🖵 ⇌ ✕

◇◇◇ ▽▽▽ Spindrift Motel 🅼
(541) 469-5345. **$69-$89.** 1215 Chetco Ave (US 101) 97415. On US 101; north end of town. Ext corridors. **Pets:** Very small, dogs only. $15 daily fee/pet. Designated rooms, supervision. SAVE 🛜 🛢 🖵 ✕

◇◇◇ ▽▽▽ Westward Inn 🅼
(541) 469-7471. **$55-$99, 3 day notice.** 1026 Chetco Ave (US 101) 97415. On US 101; just n of downtown. Ext corridors. **Pets:** Medium, dogs only. $12 daily fee/pet. Designated rooms, supervision.
SAVE 🛜 ✕ 🛢 🖵

◇◇◇ ▽▽▽ Wild Rivers Motorlodge 🅼 🐾
(541) 469-5361. **$59-$119.** 437 Chetco Ave (US 101) 97415. On US 101; just n of Chetco River Bridge. Ext corridors. **Pets:** $10 daily fee/pet. Designated rooms, service with restrictions, supervision.
SAVE 🛜 🛢 🖵

BURNS

◇◇◇ ▽▽▽ America's Best Inn 🅼
(541) 573-1700. **$60-$77.** 999 Oregon Ave (US 395/20) 97720. 1 mi w on US 395/20 from jct SR 78. Ext/int corridors. **Pets:** Medium, dogs only. $20 deposit/room, $5 daily fee/pet. Designated rooms, service with restrictions, supervision. SAVE 🛜 ✕ 🛢 🖵 ⇌

◇◇◇ ▽▽ Silver Spur Motel 🅼
(541) 573-2077. **$42-$56.** 789 N Broadway Ave 97720. US 395; corner of W "D" St. Ext corridors. **Pets:** Other species. $5 daily fee/room. Designated rooms, service with restrictions, supervision. SAVE 🛜 🛢 🖵

CANNON BEACH

▽▽ Cannon Beach Ecola Creek Lodge 🅼 🐾
(503) 436-2776. **$79-$239, 7 day notice.** 208 E 5th St 97110. US 101 exit Ecola State Park northbound, just w; north end of downtown. Ext corridors. **Pets:** Medium, other species. $20 daily fee/pet. Designated rooms, service with restrictions, supervision.
🛜 ✕ ❄M 🛢 🖵 ✕

▽▽▽▽ Inn at Cannon Beach 🄷 🐾
(503) 436-9085. **$99-$289, 7 day notice.** 3215 S Hemlock St 97110. US 101 exit Tolovana Park, just w on Warren Way, then just n. Ext corridors. **Pets:** $15 daily fee/pet. Designated rooms, service with restrictions, supervision. 🛜 ✕ 🛢 🖵 ✕

▽▽▽ The Ocean Lodge 🄷 🐾
(503) 436-2241. **$199-$399, 7 day notice.** 2864 S Pacific St 97110. US 101 exit Tolovana Park, just w on Warren Way, just n on S Hemlock St, just w on W Chisana St, then just n. Ext/int corridors. **Pets:** Other species. $15 daily fee/pet. Service with restrictions, supervision.
🛜 ✕ 🛢 🖵

◇◇◇ ▽▽▽▽ Surfsand Resort 🄷 🐾
(503) 436-2274. **$129-$469, 3 day notice.** 148 W Gower St 97110. US 101 exit Cannon Beach (2nd exit); downtown. Ext corridors. **Pets:** Other species. $15 daily fee/pet. Designated rooms, supervision.
SAVE 🛜 ✕ 🛢 🖵 ⏸ ✕

◇◇◇ ▽▽▽▽ Tolovana Inn 🄲🄾
(503) 436-2211. **$69-$474, 3 day notice.** 3400 S Hemlock St 97145. US 101 exit Tolovana Park, just w on Warren Way, then just s. Ext corridors. **Pets:** Other species. $15 daily fee/pet. Designated rooms, service with restrictions, supervision. SAVE 🛜 ✕ 🛢 🖵 ⇌ ✕ ✕

CANYONVILLE

◇◇◇ ▽▽▽▽ Holiday Inn Express & Suites Canyonville 🄷
(541) 839-4200. **$99-$189.** 200 Creekside Dr 97417. I-5 exit 99, just w. Int corridors. **Pets:** Small. $10 daily fee/pet. Designated rooms, service with restrictions, supervision. SAVE 🛜 ✕ 🛢 🖵 ⇌

CASCADE LOCKS

◇◇◇ ▽▽▽▽ BEST WESTERN PLUS Columbia River Inn 🄷
(541) 374-8777. **$100-$190.** 735 WaNaPa St (US 30) 97014. I-84 exit 44 eastbound, 0.4 mi ne; exit westbound, 1.4 mi nw. Int corridors. **Pets:** Medium. $10 daily fee/pet. Designated rooms, service with restrictions, supervision. SAVE 🛜 ✕ ❄M 🛢 🖵 ⇌

CENTRAL POINT

▽▽▽ Holiday Inn Express Hotel & Suites 🄷
(541) 423-1010. **$89-$149.** 285 Peninger St 97502. I-5 exit 33, just se. Int corridors. **Pets:** Other species. $25 daily fee/pet. Supervision.
🛜 ❄M 🛢 🖵 ⇌

▽▽▽ Super 8 Inn & Suites 🄷
(541) 664-5888. **$71-$89.** 4999 Biddle Rd 97502. I-5 exit 33, 0.5 mi e. Int corridors. **Pets:** Other species. $50 one-time fee/room. Service with restrictions, supervision. 🛜 ❄M 🛢 🖵 ⇌

CLATSKANIE

◇◇◇ ▽▽▽ Clatskanie River Inn 🄷
(503) 728-9000. **$89-$149.** 600 E Columbia River Hwy (US 30) 97016. On US 30, just e. Int corridors. **Pets:** Medium. $20 one-time fee/pet. Designated rooms, service with restrictions, supervision.
SAVE 🛜 🛢 🖵 ⇌

COOS BAY

◇◇◇ ▽▽▽ BEST WESTERN Holiday Motel 🄷
(541) 269-5111. **$100-$210.** 411 N Bayshore Dr 97420. On US 101; just n of downtown. Ext/int corridors. **Pets:** Dogs only. $15 daily fee/pet. Service with restrictions, supervision. SAVE 🛜 ✕ 🛢 🖵 ⇌

◇◇◇ ▽▽▽▽ Red Lion Hotel Coos Bay 🄷
(541) 267-4141. **$89-$156.** 1313 N Bayshore Dr 97420. On US 101; 0.5 mi n of downtown. Ext corridors. **Pets:** Other species. $15 one-time fee/room. Service with restrictions, crate.
SAVE 🛜 ✕ ❄M 🛢 🖵 🍴 ⇌

◇◇◇ ▽▽▽ Super 8 Coos Bay 🅼
(541) 808-0700. **$70-$160.** 1001 N Bayshore Dr 97420. On US 101; just n of downtown. Ext corridors. **Pets:** Other species. $15 daily fee/room. Service with restrictions, supervision. SAVE 🛜 ✕ 🛢 🖵

COQUILLE

▽▽ Myrtle Lane Motel 🅼
(541) 396-2102. **$55-$80.** 787 N Central Blvd 97423. SR 42, 0.4 mi n. Ext corridors. **Pets:** Accepted. 🛜 🛢 🖵 ✕

CORVALLIS

◇◇◇ ▽▽▽ BEST WESTERN Grand Manor Inn 🄷
(541) 758-8571. **$100-$200.** 925 NW Garfield Ave 97330. Jct SR 34 and US 20, 0.3 mi w on NW Harrison Blvd, 1 mi n on NW 9th St, then just w. Int corridors. **Pets:** Medium, dogs only. $10 daily fee/pet. Designated rooms, service with restrictions, supervision.
SAVE 🛜 ✕ ❄M 🛢 🖵 ⇌ ✕

◇◇◇ ▽▽▽ Days Inn 🄷
(541) 754-7474. **$65-$170.** 1113 NW 9th St 97330. Jct SR 34 and US 20, 0.3 mi w on NW Harrison Blvd, 0.5 mi n. Int corridors. **Pets:** Other species. $10 daily fee/pet. Designated rooms, service with restrictions, supervision. SAVE 🛜 ✕ 🛢 🖵 ⇌

Holiday Inn Express On The River H ❀

(541) 752-0800. **$89-$199.** 781 NE 2nd St 97330. Jct SR 34 and US 20, 0.4 mi n. Int corridors. **Pets:** Other species. $25 daily fee/room. Designated rooms, service with restrictions, crate.

SAVE 🛜 ✕ ⅃ᴹ 🛢 ▣ ⇝ ✕

Motel 6 - #4243 H

(541) 758-9125. **$65-$199.** 935 NW Garfield Ave 97330. Jct SR 34 and US 20, 0.3 mi w on NW Harrison Blvd, 1 mi n on NW 9th St, then just w. Int corridors. **Pets:** Other species. Service with restrictions, supervision.

🛜 🛢

Rodeway Inn Willamette River M

(541) 752-9601. **$50-$80.** 345 NW 2nd St 97330. Between NW Harrison Blvd and NW Van Buren St; downtown. Ext/int corridors. **Pets:** Dogs only. $10 daily fee/pet. Designated rooms, service with restrictions, supervision.

🛜 🛢

Super 8 H 🐾

(541) 758-8088. **$55-$151.** 407 NW 2nd St 97330. Jct SR 34 and US 20, just n; downtown. Int corridors. **Pets:** Medium. $10 daily fee/pet. Designated rooms, service with restrictions, supervision.

🛜 ⅃ᴹ 🛢 ▣ ⇝

COTTAGE GROVE

BEST WESTERN Cottage Grove Inn H

(541) 942-1000. **Call for rates.** 1601 Gateway Blvd 97424. I-5 exit 174, just sw. Int corridors. **Pets:** Medium, other species. $15 daily fee/pet. Designated rooms, service with restrictions, supervision.

SAVE 🛜 ✕ ⅃ᴹ 🛢 ▣ ⇝

Comfort Inn H

(541) 942-9747. **$75-$125.** 845 Gateway Blvd 97424. I-5 exit 174, just sw. Ext/int corridors. **Pets:** Medium. $10 daily fee/pet. Designated rooms, service with restrictions. SAVE 🛜 🛢 ▣ ⇝

CRESWELL

Comfort Inn & Suites H

(541) 895-4025. **$84-$124.** 247 Melton Rd 97426. I-5 exit 182, just ne. Int corridors. **Pets:** Other species. $20 one-time fee/room. Designated rooms, service with restrictions, supervision. 🛜 ✕ 🛢 ▣ ⇝

Super 8 Creswell Inn M

(541) 895-3341. **$69-$220.** 345 E Oregon Ave 97426. I-5 exit 182, just sw. Ext corridors. **Pets:** Large, other species. $15 one-time fee/pet. Designated rooms, service with restrictions, supervision.

SAVE 🛜 🛢 ▣ ⇝

DALLAS

BEST WESTERN Dallas Inn & Suites H

(503) 623-6000. **$84-$125.** 250 Orchard Dr 97338. SR 223, just n. Int corridors. **Pets:** Large, other species. $20 daily fee/pet. Designated rooms, service with restrictions, supervision. SAVE 🛜 ⅃ᴹ 🛢 ▣

DEPOE BAY

Crown Pacifiq Motel M

(541) 765-7773. **$59-$129.** 50 NE Bechill St 97341. Just n of downtown. Ext/int corridors. **Pets:** Small, dogs only. $10 daily fee/pet. Designated rooms, service with restrictions, supervision. SAVE 🛜 🛢 ▣ 🎜

Surfrider Resort H ❀

(541) 764-2311. **$69-$199, 3 day notice.** 3115 NW US 101 97341. 2 mi n of Depoe Bay. Ext corridors. **Pets:** Small, dogs only. $10 daily fee/pet. Designated rooms, service with restrictions, supervision.

SAVE 🛜 ✕ 🛢 ▣ 🍴 ⇝ ✕ 🎜

ENTERPRISE

BEST WESTERN Rama Inn & Suites H

(541) 426-2000. **Call for rates.** 1200 Highland Ave 97828. 0.5 mi w on SR 82. Int corridors. **Pets:** Accepted.

SAVE 🛜 ✕ 🛢 ▣ ⇝ ✕

Ponderosa Motel M

(541) 426-3186. **$56-$72.** 102 E Greenwood St 97828. Center. Ext corridors. **Pets:** Dogs only. $10 daily fee/pet. Designated rooms, service with restrictions, supervision. 🛜 🛢 ▣

The Wilderness Inn M

(541) 426-4535. **$51-$70.** 301 W North St 97828. Corner of NW 2nd St. Ext corridors. **Pets:** Dogs only. $10 daily fee/pet. Service with restrictions, supervision. 🛜 🛢 ▣

EUGENE

Americas Best Value Inn M

(541) 343-0730. **$49-$149.** 1140 W 6th Ave 97402. I-5 exit 194B, 3.5 mi w on I-105, then 0.3 mi w on SR 99 N (6th Ave). Ext corridors. **Pets:** Accepted. SAVE 🛜 🛢

BEST WESTERN Greentree Inn H ❀

(541) 485-2727. **Call for rates.** 1759 Franklin Blvd 97403. I-5 exit 194B southbound to I-105 exit University of Oregon, 0.9 mi e; exit 192 northbound, 1.2 mi w. Ext/int corridors. **Pets:** Large. $50 deposit/room, $20 daily fee/room. Designated rooms, service with restrictions, crate.

SAVE 🛜 🛢 ▣ ⇝

BEST WESTERN New Oregon H ❀

(541) 683-3669. **Call for rates.** 1655 Franklin Blvd 97403. I-5 exit 194B southbound to I-105 exit University of Oregon, 0.9 mi e; exit 192 northbound, 1.2 mi w. Ext/int corridors. **Pets:** Large. $50 deposit/room, $20 daily fee/room. Designated rooms, service with restrictions, crate.

SAVE 🛜 🛢 ▣ ⇝ ✕

Broadway Inn M

(541) 344-5233. **$55-$150, 3 day notice.** 476 E Broadway 97401. I-5 exit 194B southbound, 1.3 mi w on I-105 exit 2 (Coburg Rd), 1.5 mi s, follow University of Oregon signs; exit 192 northbound, 2.2 mi w. Ext corridors. **Pets:** Small, dogs only. $15 daily fee/pet. Designated rooms, service with restrictions, supervision. SAVE 🛜 ✕ 🛢 ⇝

Campus Inn & Suites M

(541) 343-3376. **$81-$168.** 390 E Broadway 97401. I-5 exit 194B southbound, 1.3 mi w on I-105 exit 2 (Coburg Rd), 1.5 mi s, follow University of Oregon signs; exit 192 northbound, 2.2 mi w. Ext corridors. **Pets:** Medium. $50 deposit/room, $10 one-time fee/room. Designated rooms, service with restrictions, supervision. SAVE 🛜 ✕ 🛢 ▣

Express Inn & Suites M

(541) 868-1520. **$59-$99, 3 day notice.** 990 W 6th Ave 97402. I-5 exit 194B, 3.5 mi w on I-105, then 0.3 mi w on SR 99 N (6th Ave). Ext corridors. **Pets:** Small, dogs only. $10 daily fee/pet. Designated rooms, service with restrictions, supervision. SAVE 🛜 ✕ 🛢

Hilton Eugene H 🐾

(541) 342-2000. **$109-$169.** 66 E 6th Ave 97401. At 6th Ave and Oak St; center. Int corridors. **Pets:** Medium. $50 one-time fee/room. Service with restrictions, crate. 🍴 🛜 ✕ 🛢 ▣ 🍴 ⇝ ✕

Inn at the 5th H

(541) 743-4099. **$199-$585.** 205 E 6th Ave 97401. Jct Pearl St; downtown. Int corridors. **Pets:** Other species. $50 one-time fee/room. Service with restrictions, supervision. SAVE 🛜 ✕ ⅃ᴹ 🛢 ▣ 🍴 ✕

La Quinta Inn & Suites Eugene H

(541) 344-8335. **$102-$243.** 155 Day Island Rd 97401. I-5 exit 194B, 1.3 mi w on I-105 exit 2 (Coburg Rd), straight through jct Coburg Rd to Southwood Ln, just w, then 0.5 mi se on Country Club Rd, follow signs for Autzen Stadium. Int corridors. **Pets:** Service with restrictions, supervision. 🛜 ✕ 🛢 ▣ ⇝

Motel 6 - #36 M

(541) 687-2395. **$49-$65.** 3690 Glenwood Dr 97403. I-5 exit 191, just sw. Ext corridors. **Pets:** Other species. Service with restrictions, supervision. ECO 🛜 🛢 ⇝

Red Lion Hotel Eugene H
(541) 342-5201. **$94-$150.** 205 Coburg Rd 97401. I-5 exit 194B, 1.3 mi w on I-105 to exit 2 (Coburg Rd), then just n. Ext corridors. **Pets:** Other species. $15 one-time fee/room. Service with restrictions, crate.

Residence Inn by Marriott Eugene Springfield H
(541) 342-7171. **$189-$299.** 25 Club Rd 97401. I-5 exit 194B, 1.3 mi w on I-105 exit 2 (Coburg Rd), straight through jct Coburg Rd to Southwood Ln, just w, then se on Country Club Rd, follow signs for Autzen Stadium. Int corridors. **Pets:** Other species. $75 one-time fee/pet.

Valley River Inn H
(541) 743-1000. **$109-$239.** 1000 Valley River Way 97401. I-5 exit 194B, 2.5 mi w on I-105 exit 1, follow signs for Valley River Center. Int corridors. **Pets:** Accepted.

FLORENCE
BEST WESTERN PLUS Pier Point Inn H ❀
(541) 997-7191. **$139-$260.** 85625 US 101 S 97439. Jct SR 126, 1.1 mi s. Ext corridors. **Pets:** $20 daily fee/room. Designated rooms, service with restrictions, supervision.

Le Chateau Inn M
(541) 997-3481. **$49-$89.** 1084 US 101 N 97439. Jct SR 126, just n. Ext corridors. **Pets:** $12 one-time fee/room. Designated rooms, service with restrictions, supervision.

Ocean Breeze Motel M
(541) 997-2642. **$59-$150.** 85165 US 101 S 97439. Jct SR 126, 2 mi s. Ext corridors. **Pets:** Accepted.

Old Town Inn M ❀
(541) 997-7131. **$75-$99.** 170 US 101 S 97439. Jct SR 126, 0.4 mi s. Ext corridors. **Pets:** Other species. $10 daily fee/pet. Designated rooms, service with restrictions, supervision.

Park Motel M ❀
(541) 997-2634. **$55-$150, 7 day notice.** 85034 US 101 S 97439. Jct SR 126, 2.2 mi s. Ext corridors. **Pets:** $10 daily fee/pet. Service with restrictions, supervision.

FOREST GROVE
BEST WESTERN University Inn & Suites H
(503) 992-8888. **$90-$160.** 3933 Pacific Ave 97116. East end of town on SR 8. Int corridors. **Pets:** Medium, dogs only. $15 daily fee/pet. Designated rooms, service with restrictions, supervision.

GEARHART
Gearhart By The Sea CO
(503) 738-8331. **$126-$300, 3 day notice.** 1157 N Marion Ave 97138. US 101 exit City Center, 1 mi w. Ext corridors. **Pets:** Other species. $11 daily fee/pet. Designated rooms, service with restrictions, supervision.

GLENEDEN BEACH
Salishan H ❀
(541) 764-2371. **$159-$329, 3 day notice.** 7760 US 101 N 97388. Just e of US 101; center. Ext corridors. **Pets:** Large, other species. $35 one-time fee/room. Supervision.

GOLD BEACH
Gold Beach Inn M
(541) 247-7091. **$55-$149.** 29346 Ellensburg Ave (US 101) 97444. On US 101; center. Ext corridors. **Pets:** Accepted.

Gold Beach Resort and Condominiums H
(541) 247-7066. **$80-$186.** 29232 Ellensburg Ave (US 101) 97444. On US 101; south end of town. Ext corridors. **Pets:** Medium, dogs only. $15 daily fee/pet. Designated rooms, service with restrictions, supervision.

Inn of the Beachcomber M
(541) 247-6691. **$68-$179.** 29266 Ellensburg Ave (US 101) 97444. On US 101; south end of town. Ext/int corridors. **Pets:** Other species. $15 daily fee/pet. Service with restrictions, supervision.

Jot's Resort M
(541) 247-6676. **$65-$230, 3 day notice.** 94360 Wedderburn Loop 97491. Just w of US 101; north end of bridge. Ext corridors. **Pets:** Other species. $15 daily fee/pet. Designated rooms, supervision.

Motel 6 - #4047 M
(541) 247-4533. **Call for rates.** 94433 Jerry's Flat Rd 97444. Just e of jct US 101; south end of town. Ext corridors. **Pets:** Other species. Service with restrictions, supervision.

GOVERNMENT CAMP
BEST WESTERN Mt. Hood Inn H
(503) 272-3205. **$109-$189.** 87450 E Government Camp Loop 97028. 0.5 mi w of center. Int corridors. **Pets:** Small, other species. $10 daily fee/pet. Designated rooms, service with restrictions, crate.

GRANTS PASS
Bestway Inn M
(541) 479-2952. **$55-$75.** 1253 NE 6th St 97526. I-5 exit 58, 0.9 mi s on SR 99. Ext corridors. **Pets:** Medium, dogs only. $10 daily fee/pet. Service with restrictions, supervision.

BEST WESTERN Grants Pass Inn H
(541) 476-1117. **$77-$132.** 111 NE Agness Ave 97526. I-5 exit 55, just nw. Ext corridors. **Pets:** Accepted.

BEST WESTERN Inn at the Rogue H 🐾
(541) 582-2200. **$99-$169.** 8959 Rogue River Hwy 97527. I-5 exit 48, just nw. Int corridors. **Pets:** Large, other species. $20 daily fee/room. Service with restrictions, supervision.

Holiday Inn Express Grants Pass H ❀
(541) 471-6144. **$119-$169.** 105 NE Agness Ave 97526. I-5 exit 55, just nw. Int corridors. **Pets:** Other species. $10 daily fee/pet. Service with restrictions, supervision.

Knights Inn Motel M
(541) 479-5595. **$65-$85.** 104 SE 7th St 97526. I-5 exit 58, 1.7 mi s on SR 99, just e on G St, then just n. Ext corridors. **Pets:** Medium, dogs only. $10 deposit/room, $10 daily fee/pet. Service with restrictions, supervision.

La Quinta Inn & Suites Grants Pass H
(541) 472-1808. **$71-$199.** 243 NE Morgan Ln 97526. I-5 exit 58, 0.4 mi s on SR 99, just e on Hillcrest Dr to SR 99 N, then just n. Int corridors. **Pets:** Service with restrictions, supervision.

Motel 6 - #253 M
(541) 474-1331. **$45-$65.** 1800 NE 7th St 97526. I-5 exit 58, 0.3 mi s on SR 99. Ext corridors. **Pets:** Other species. Service with restrictions, supervision.

Redwood Motel & Hyperion Suites H 🐾
(541) 476-0878. **$63-$210.** 815 NE 6th St 97526. I-5 exit 58, 1.2 mi s on SR 99. Ext corridors. **Pets:** Medium. Designated rooms, service with restrictions, supervision.

AAA VVV Riverside Inn H
(541) 476-6873. **$125-$149, 3 day notice.** 986 SW 6th St 97526. I-5 exit 58, 2.5 mi s on SR 99. Ext corridors. **Pets:** Other species. $25 daily fee/room. Designated rooms, service with restrictions, supervision.
SAVE 🛰 ✕ ⓜ 🔲 💻 💻

VVV Shilo Inn - Grants Pass H
(541) 479-8391. **$69-$140.** 1880 NW 6th St 97526. I-5 exit 58, 0.3 mi s on SR 99. Int corridors. **Pets:** Dogs only. $25 one-time fee/room. Designated rooms, service with restrictions, supervision.
🛰 ✕ ⓜ 🔲 💻 🏊

VVV Super 8 - Grants Pass H
(541) 474-0888. **$57-$102.** 1949 NE 7th St 97526. I-5 exit 58, 0.4 mi s on SR 99, just e on Hillcrest Dr to SR 99 N, then just n. Int corridors. **Pets:** Accepted. 🛰 ⓜ 🔲 💻 🏊

AAA VVV Sweet Breeze Inn M
(541) 471-4434. **$59-$159.** 1627 NE 6th St 97526. I-5 exit 58, 0.5 mi s on SR 99. Ext/int corridors. **Pets:** Medium. $5 daily fee/pet. Designated rooms, service with restrictions, supervision. SAVE 🛰 ✕ 🔲

AAA VVV Travelodge M 🐾
(541) 479-6611. **$59-$140.** 1950 NW Vine St 97526. I-5 exit 58, just s on SR 99. Ext corridors. **Pets:** Medium. $10 daily fee/pet. Designated rooms, service with restrictions, crate. SAVE 🛰 🔲 💻 🏊

HALSEY
VVV Pioneer Villa Travelodge M
(541) 369-2804. **$79-$89.** 33180 SR 228 97348. I-5 exit 216, just se. Ext corridors. **Pets:** $10 daily fee/pet. Service with restrictions.
🛰 🔲 💻 🍴 🏊

HERMISTON
VVV Comfort Inn & Suites H
(541) 564-5911. **Call for rates.** 77514 SR 207 97838. I-84 exit 182, just nw. Int corridors. **Pets:** Other species. $20 one-time fee/pet. Service with restrictions, supervision. 🛰 🔲 💻 🏊

VVV Oak Tree Inn H
(541) 567-2330. **$69-$84.** 1110 SE 4th St 97838. 0.4 mi s on US 395, then just w. Int corridors. **Pets:** Medium. $10 daily fee/pet. Service with restrictions, crate. 🛰 ✕ 🔲 💻

AAA VVV Oxford Suites Hermiston H 🐾
(541) 564-8000. **$119-$139.** 1050 N 1st St 97838. 0.5 mi n on US 395. Int corridors. **Pets:** Small, dogs only. $25 one-time fee/pet. Designated rooms, service with restrictions, supervision. SAVE 🛰 🔲 💻 🏊

HINES
AAA VVV BEST WESTERN Rory & Ryan Inns H
(541) 573-5050. **Call for rates.** 534 US 20 N 97738. On US 20 (Central Oregon Hwy). Int corridors. **Pets:** Accepted.
SAVE 🛰 ✕ 🔲 💻 🏊

VVV Rory & Ryan Inns H
(541) 573-3370. **$55-$125.** 504 US 20 N 97738. On US 20 (Central Oregon Hwy). Int corridors. **Pets:** Dogs only. $10 daily fee/pet. Service with restrictions, supervision. 🛰 ✕ 🔲 💻 🏊

HOOD RIVER
AAA VVVV BEST WESTERN PLUS Hood River Inn H 🐾
(541) 386-2200. **$180-$190.** 1108 E Marina Way 97031. I-84 exit 64, just ne. Int corridors. **Pets:** Dogs only. $12 daily fee/pet. Designated rooms, supervision. SAVE 🛰 ✕ 🔲 💻 🍴 🏊 🐾

AAA VVVV Columbia Gorge Hotel CI
(541) 386-5566. **$159-$299.** 4000 Westcliff Dr 97031. I-84 exit 62, just sw of overpass. Int corridors. **Pets:** Medium, other species. $20 daily fee/pet. Designated rooms, supervision. SAVE 🛰 ✕ 🔲 🍴

AAA VVV Sunset Motel M
(541) 386-6322. **$79-$129, 3 day notice.** 2300 Cascade Ave 97031. I-84 exit 62, 0.7 mi se. Ext corridors. **Pets:** Accepted.
SAVE 🛰 ✕ ⓜ 🔲 💻

AAA VVV Vagabond Lodge M 🐾
(541) 386-2992. **$65-$120.** 4070 Westcliff Dr 97031. I-84 exit 62, 0.3 mi nw. Ext corridors. **Pets:** Other species. $5 daily fee/pet. Designated rooms, service with restrictions. SAVE 🛰 🔲 💻

JACKSONVILLE
AAA VVVV Jacksonville Inn CI
(541) 899-1900. **$159-$465, 3 day notice.** 175 E California St 97530. On California St (SR 238); between 3rd and 4th sts; center. Ext/int corridors. **Pets:** $15 daily fee/room. Designated rooms, service with restrictions, supervision. SAVE 🛰 ✕ 🔲 💻 🍴

VVVV Jacksonville's Magnolia Inn BB 🐾
(541) 899-0255. **$104-$174, 7 day notice.** 245 N 5th St 97530. At 5th (SR 238) and D sts. Int corridors. **Pets:** Dogs only. $25 one-time fee/room. Designated rooms, supervision. 🛰 ✕ ⓜ

VVV The Wine Country Inn M 🐾
(541) 899-2050. **$125-$295, 3 day notice.** 830 N 5th St 97530. 0.5 mi ne of downtown. Ext corridors. **Pets:** $25 daily fee/room. Designated rooms, service with restrictions, supervision. 🛰 ✕ 🔲 💻 🛎

JOHN DAY
AAA VVV BEST WESTERN John Day Inn H
(541) 575-1700. **$85-$120.** 315 W Main St 97845. Just w of jct US 26 and 395. Ext corridors. **Pets:** $15 daily fee/room. Designated rooms, service with restrictions, supervision. SAVE 🛰 ✕ 🔲 💻 🏊 ✕

AAA VVV Dreamers Lodge M
(541) 575-0526. **$50-$100.** 144 N Canyon Blvd 97845. Just n of jct US 26 and 395. Ext corridors. **Pets:** Medium, dogs only. $5 daily fee/pet. Service with restrictions, supervision. SAVE 🛰 ✕ 🔲 💻

KEIZER
VVV Keizer Renaissance Inn H
(503) 390-4733. **Call for rates.** 5188 Wittenberg Ln N 97303. I-5 exit 260B southbound; exit 260 northbound, 1.5 mi w via Chemawa Rd and Lockhaven Dr, just s on River Rd, just e on Claggett St NE, then just s. Int corridors. **Pets:** Accepted. 🛰 ✕ ⓜ 🔲 💻 🍴 🏊

KLAMATH FALLS
AAA VVV Econo Lodge M
(541) 884-7735. **Call for rates.** 75 Main St 97601. US 97 exit City Center Dr, just e. Ext corridors. **Pets:** Accepted. SAVE 🛰 🔲 💻

AAA VVV Golden West Motel M 🐾
(541) 882-1758. **$42-$68.** 6402 S 6th St 97603. On S 6th St (SR 140); at eastern edge of town. Ext corridors. **Pets:** $10 one-time fee/room. Service with restrictions, supervision. SAVE 🛰 ✕ 🔲 💻

AAA VVVV The Lodge At Running Y Ranch - A Holiday Inn Resort H
(541) 850-5500. **$79-$159, 3 day notice.** 5500 Running Y Rd 97601. Jct US 97, 7.5 mi nw on SR 140. Int corridors. **Pets:** Large. Designated rooms, service with restrictions, crate. SAVE 🛰 ✕ ⓜ 🔲 💻 🍴 🏊 ✕

VVV Majestic Inn & Suites M
(541) 883-7771. **$35-$99.** 5543 S 6th St 97603. 1 mi e on 6th St (SR 140) from jct SR 140 E/39 S and SR 39 N/US 97 business route. Ext corridors. **Pets:** Accepted. 🛰 🔲

AAA VVVV Maverick Motel M
(541) 882-6688. **$39-$99.** 1220 Main St 97601. US 97 exit City Center Dr, 0.9 mi e on S Klamath Ave, just n on S 12th St, then just e. Ext corridors. **Pets:** $5 daily fee/pet. Designated rooms, service with restrictions, supervision. SAVE 🛰 🔲 💻

Microtel Inn & Suites by Wyndham Klamath Falls H

(541) 273-0206. **$79-$99.** 2716 Dakota Ct 97603. US 97 exit 277, 2.7 mi e to SR 140 exit 3, 1 mi n on Washburn Way, just e on Laverne Ave, then just s on Brooke Dr. Int corridors. **Pets:** Medium, dogs only. $35 one-time fee/room. Service with restrictions, supervision.

Motel 6 - #226 M

(541) 884-2110. **$45-$65.** 5136 S 6th St 97603. 0.5 mi e on 6th St (SR 140) from jct SR 140 E/39 S and SR 39 N/US 97 business route. Ext corridors. **Pets:** Other species. Service with restrictions, supervision.

Shilo Inn Suites Hotel-Klamath Falls H

(541) 885-7980. **$90-$190.** 2500 Almond St 97601. On US 97; 1.5 mi n of downtown. Int corridors. **Pets:** Dogs only. $25 one-time fee/room. Designated rooms, service with restrictions, supervision.

Super 8 H

(541) 884-8880. **$52-$79.** 3805 US 97 97601. On US 97; 2 mi n of downtown. Int corridors. **Pets:** Other species. $10 daily fee/room. Service with restrictions, supervision.

Vagabond Inn & Suites M

(541) 882-1200. **$59-$119.** 4061 S 6th St 97603. Just w on 6th St (SR 140) from jct SR 140 E/39 S and SR 39 N/US 97 business route. Ext corridors. **Pets:** Medium. $15 daily fee/pet. Designated rooms, service with restrictions, supervision.

LA GRANDE

Americas Best Value Sandman Inn H

(541) 963-3707. **$79-$129.** 2410 E R Ave 97850. I-84 exit 261, just s on Island Ave, just e on N Albany St, then just n. Int corridors. **Pets:** Dogs only. $15 one-time fee/room. Designated rooms, service with restrictions, supervision.

Royal Motor Inn M

(541) 963-4154. **$40-$69.** 1510 Adams Ave 97850. I-84 exit 265 (US 30) to La Grande exit; downtown. Ext corridors. **Pets:** Accepted.

LAKEVIEW

BEST WESTERN Skyline Motor Lodge M

(541) 947-2194. **$99-$149.** 414 N G St 97630. Jct US 395 and SR 140. Ext corridors. **Pets:** Accepted.

LA PINE

BEST WESTERN Newberry Station H

(541) 536-5130. **$80-$120.** 16515 Reed Rd 97739. Just off US 97; north end of town. Int corridors. **Pets:** Dogs only. $20 daily fee/room. Designated rooms, supervision.

LINCOLN CITY

Ashley Inn & Suites H

(541) 996-7500. **$69-$199.** 3430 NE US 101 97367. Just n of downtown. Int corridors. **Pets:** Other species. $100 deposit/room, $25 daily fee/pet. Designated rooms, service with restrictions, crate.

The Coho Oceanfront Lodge H

(541) 994-3684. **$99-$299.** 1635 NW Harbor Ave 97367. US 101 exit N 17th St, just w. Ext corridors. **Pets:** Small, dogs only. $20 daily fee/pet. Designated rooms, service with restrictions, supervision.

Comfort Inn & Suites H

(541) 994-8155. **$90-$300.** 136 NE US 101 97367. Just n of D River. Int corridors. **Pets:** Small, dogs only. $20 daily fee/pet. Designated rooms, service with restrictions, supervision.

Inn at Wecoma H

(541) 994-2984. **$64-$199.** 2945 NW US 101 97367. Just s of NW 30th St; n of downtown. Int corridors. **Pets:** Small, dogs only. $15 daily fee/pet. Designated rooms, service with restrictions, supervision.

Looking Glass Inn H

(541) 996-3996. **$79-$259, 3 day notice.** 861 SW 51st St 97367. US 101 exit 51st St; south end of town. Ext corridors. **Pets:** Dogs only. $10 daily fee/pet. Designated rooms, service with restrictions, crate.

Motel 6 - #4172 H

(541) 996-9900. **$46-$100.** 3517 NW US 101 97367. North end of downtown. Int corridors. **Pets:** Other species. Service with restrictions, supervision.

Palace Inn & Suites H

(541) 996-9466. **$69-$209.** 550 SE US 101 97367. Center. Int corridors. **Pets:** Small, dogs only. $25 one-time fee/pet. Designated rooms, service with restrictions, crate.

Shearwater Inn H

(541) 994-4121. **$89-$279, 3 day notice.** 120 NW Inlet Ave 97367. On US 101 at D River. Int corridors. **Pets:** Small, dogs only. $10 daily fee/pet. Designated rooms, service with restrictions, crate.

MADRAS

BEST WESTERN Madras Inn H

(541) 475-6141. **Call for rates.** 12 SW 4th St 97741. On US 97/26 S; at B and 4th sts; downtown. Ext corridors. **Pets:** Large. $20 daily fee/room. Designated rooms, service with restrictions, supervision.

Budget Inn M

(541) 475-3831. **Call for rates.** 133 NE 5th St 97741. On US 97/26 N; downtown. Ext corridors. **Pets:** Accepted.

Inn at Cross Keys Station H

(541) 475-5800. **$77-$185.** 66 NW Cedar St 97741. On US 26; north end of town. Int corridors. **Pets:** Medium, dogs only. $30 daily fee/pet. Designated rooms, service with restrictions, supervision.

Sonny's Motel M

(541) 475-7217. **$58-$135.** 1539 SW US 97 97741. South end of town. Ext corridors. **Pets:** Other species. $10 daily fee/room. Service with restrictions, supervision.

MCMINNVILLE

Americas Best Value Inn & Suites M

(503) 472-5187. **$75-$100.** 381 NE SR 99 W 97128. North end of SR 99 W. Ext corridors. **Pets:** Medium. $10 daily fee/pet. Designated rooms, service with restrictions, supervision.

Comfort Inn & Suites H

(503) 472-1700. **$87-$155.** 2520 SE Stratus Ave 97128. Jct SR 99 W; 2.3 mi ne on SR 18. Int corridors. **Pets:** Accepted.

GuestHouse Vineyard Inn H

(503) 472-4900. **$95-$131.** 2035 S SR 99 W 97128. Jct SR 99 W and 18. Int corridors. **Pets:** $10 daily fee/pet. Designated rooms, service with restrictions, crate.

Red Lion Inn & Suites McMinnville H

(503) 472-1500. **$95-$136.** 2535 NE Cumulus Ave 97128. Jct SR 99 W, 2.3 mi ne on SR 18. Int corridors. **Pets:** Other species. $15 one-time fee/room. Service with restrictions, crate.

MEDFORD

BEST WESTERN Horizon Inn 🏨 ✳️
(541) 779-5085. **$90-$140.** 1154 E Barnett Rd 97504. I-5 exit 27 (Barnett Rd), just ne. Ext corridors. **Pets:** Other species. $10 daily fee/pet. Designated rooms, supervision. SAVE 🛜 🍴 🍽️ 🏊

Candlewood Suites Medford Airport 🏨
(541) 772-2800. **$79-$99.** 3548 Heathrow Way 97504. I-5 exit 33, 1.5 mi se via E Pine St and Biddle Rd, just w on O'Hare Pkwy, then just n. Int corridors. **Pets:** Accepted. SAVE 🛜 🍴ᴹ 🍴 🍽️

Comfort Inn North Medford 🏨
(541) 772-9500. **$99-$149.** 2280 Biddle Rd 97504. I-5 exit 30 southbound, just ne on Crater Lake Hwy, follow signs to Biddle Rd/Airport, then just n; exit northbound, follow signs to Biddle Rd/Airport, then just ne. Int corridors. **Pets:** Small, dogs only. $150 deposit/room, $10 daily fee/pet. Designated rooms, service with restrictions.
SAVE 🛜 ✖️ 🍴 🍽️ 🏊

Comfort Inn South 🏨
(541) 772-8000. **$89-$149.** 60 E Stewart Ave 97501. I-5 exit 27 (City Center), just w on Garfield St, 0.4 mi n on S Pacific Hwy, then just e. Int corridors. **Pets:** Small. $150 deposit/room, $10 daily fee/pet. Designated rooms, service with restrictions. SAVE 🛜 🍴 🍽️ 🏊

Homewood Suites by Hilton 🏨
(541) 779-9800. **$99-$159.** 2010 Hospitality Way 97504. I-5 exit 27 (Barnett Rd), 0.4 mi e, just s on Ellendale Dr, then just w. Int corridors. **Pets:** Medium. $75 one-time fee/room. Service with restrictions, supervision. SAVE 🛜 🍴ᴹ 🍴 🍽️ 🏊 ✖️

Motel 6-Medford North - #739 Ⓜ️
(541) 779-0550. **$49-$65.** 2400 Biddle Rd 97504. I-5 exit 30 southbound, just ne on Crater Lake Hwy, follow signs to Biddle Rd/Airport, then just n; exit northbound, follow signs to Biddle Rd/Airport, then just n. Ext corridors. **Pets:** Other species. Service with restrictions, supervision.
🛜 🍴ᴹ 🍴 🏊

Motel 6-Medford South - #89 Ⓜ️
(541) 773-4290. **$45-$61.** 950 Alba Dr 97504. I-5 exit 27 (Barnett Rd), just w, then just n. Ext corridors. **Pets:** Other species. Service with restrictions, supervision. 🛜 🍴ᴹ 🍴 🏊

Quality Inn & Suites 🏨
(541) 779-0050. **$79-$90.** 1950 Biddle Rd 97504. I-5 exit 30 southbound, just ne on Crater Lake Hwy, follow signs to Biddle Rd/Airport, then just s; exit northbound, follow signs to Biddle Rd/Airport, then just s. Int corridors. **Pets:** Accepted. SAVE 🛜 ✖️ 🍴ᴹ 🍴 🍽️ 🏊 ✖️

Ramada Medford and Convention Center 🏨
(541) 779-3141. **$75-$109.** 2250 Biddle Rd 97504. I-5 exit 30 southbound, just ne on Crater Lake Hwy, follow signs, then just s; exit northbound, follow signs to Biddle Rd/Airport, then just s. Int corridors. **Pets:** Dogs only. $20 one-time fee/room. Designated rooms, service with restrictions, supervision. SAVE 🛜 🍴 🍽️ 🏊

Red Lion Hotel Medford 🏨
(541) 779-5811. **Call for rates.** 200 N Riverside Ave 97501. I-5 exit 27 (City Center), 0.4 mi w on Garfield St, then 1.7 mi n on S Pacific Hwy. Ext corridors. **Pets:** Other species. $15 one-time fee/room. Service with restrictions, crate. 🛜 ✖️ 🍴ᴹ 🍴 🍽️ 🍴

Rogue Regency Inn & Suites 🏨
(541) 770-1234. **$113-$125.** 2300 Biddle Rd 97504. I-5 exit 30 southbound, just ne on Crater Lake Hwy, follow signs, then just n; exit northbound, follow signs to Biddle Rd/Airport, then just n. Int corridors. **Pets:** Dogs only. Designated rooms, supervision.
🛜 🍴ᴹ 🍴 🍽️ 🍴 🏊 ✖️

Shilo Inn-Medford 🏨
(541) 770-5151. **$69-$140.** 2111 Biddle Rd 97504. I-5 exit 30 southbound, just ne on Crater Lake Hwy, follow signs to Biddle Rd/Airport, then just s; exit northbound, follow signs to Biddle Rd/Airport, then just s. Int corridors. **Pets:** Dogs only. $25 one-time fee/room. Designated rooms, service with restrictions, supervision. 🛜 ✖️ 🍴 🍽️

TownePlace Suites by Marriott 🏨
(541) 842-5757. **$129-$179.** 1395 Center Dr 97501. I-5 exit 27 (City Center), just w on Garfield St, then just n. Int corridors. **Pets:** $25 daily fee/room. Designated rooms, service with restrictions, supervision.
🛜 ✖️ 🍴ᴹ 🍴 🍽️ 🏊

MERLIN

Morrison's Rogue River Lodge 🅒🅐
(541) 476-3825. **$72-$420, 45 day notice.** 8500 Galice Rd 97532. I-5 exit 61, 12 mi w on Merlin-Galice Rd. Ext/int corridors. **Pets:** Medium, dogs only. $15 daily fee/room. Designated rooms, service with restrictions, crate. 🛜 ✖️ 🍴 🍽️ 🍴 🏊 ✖️

MYRTLE POINT

Myrtle Trees Motel Ⓜ️
(541) 572-5811. **$70-$81.** 1010 8th St (SR 42) 97458. On SR 42, 0.5 mi e. Ext corridors. **Pets:** Small, dogs only. $20 one-time fee/pet. Designated rooms, service with restrictions, supervision. SAVE 🛜 ✖️ 🍴 🍴

NEWBERG

The Allison Inn & Spa 🏨 ✳️
(503) 554-2525. **$330-$1100.** 2525 Allison Ln 97132. Jct Portland Rd (SR 99), 1 mi n on Springbrook Rd; n of center. Int corridors. **Pets:** Dogs only. $50 one-time fee/pet. Designated rooms, service with restrictions.
ⒺⒸⓄ 🛜 ✖️ 🍴 🍴 🏊 ✖️

BEST WESTERN Newberg Inn 🏨 🐾
(503) 537-3000. **$80-$171.** 2211 Portland Rd 97132. Ne of center. Int corridors. **Pets:** Large. $10 daily fee/pet. Designated rooms, service with restrictions, supervision. SAVE 🛜 🍴 🍽️ 🏊 ✖️

NEWPORT

BEST WESTERN PLUS Agate Beach Inn 🏨 ✳️
(541) 265-9411. **$89-$160.** 3019 N Coast Hwy (US 101) 97365. Jct US 20, 1.5 mi n on US 101. Int corridors. **Pets:** Large. $20 daily fee/room. Designated rooms, service with restrictions, supervision.
SAVE 🛜 ✖️ 🍴 🍽️ 🍴 🏊 ✖️ 🍴

Elizabeth Street Inn 🏨 ✳️
(541) 265-9400. **$169-$319.** 232 SW Elizabeth St 97365. Jct US 20, 0.5 mi s on US 101, just w on SW Falls St, then just n. Int corridors. **Pets:** Large, dogs only. $25 one-time fee/room. Designated rooms, service with restrictions, supervision. 🛜 ✖️ 🍴ᴹ 🍴 🍽️ 🏊 🍴

Hallmark Resort Oceanfront 🏨 🐾
(541) 265-2600. **$89-$294.** 744 SW Elizabeth St 97365. Jct US 20, 0.7 mi s on US 101, then just w on SW Bay St. Ext corridors. **Pets:** Other species. $20 daily fee/pet. Designated rooms, service with restrictions, supervision. 🛜 ✖️ 🍴ᴹ 🍴 🍽️ 🍴 🏊 ✖️ 🍴

The Landing at Newport 🅒🅞 🐾
(541) 574-6777. **$99-$388.** 890 SE Bay Blvd 97365. Jct US 101, 0.5 mi e on US 20, then 0.3 mi s on John Moore Rd. Ext corridors. **Pets:** $75 deposit/room, $25 one-time fee/room, $10 daily fee/room. Designated rooms, service with restrictions, supervision.
SAVE 🛜 ✖️ 🍴 🍽️ 🍴

La Quinta Inn & Suites Newport 🏨
(541) 867-7727. **$83-$199.** 45 SE 32nd St 97365. US 101, just s of Yaquina Bay Bridge. Int corridors. **Pets:** Service with restrictions, supervision. 🛜 ✖️ 🍴ᴹ 🍴 🍽️ 🏊

Newport Belle Riverboat Bed & Breakfast 🅱🅱 🐾
(541) 867-6290. **$150-$165, 7 day notice.** 2126 SE Marine Science Dr, Dock H, South Beach Marina 97365. South end of Yaquina Bay Bridge, follow signs to Marine Science Center, blvd just w; moored at dock H. Ext corridors. **Pets:** Small, dogs only. $25 one-time fee/pet. Designated rooms, service with restrictions, crate.
🛜 ✖️ 🍴 🍽️ 🍴 🍴 ✖️

▼▼ ▼▼ **Shilo Inn Suites Oceanfront Hotel - Newport** 🏨
(541) 265-7701. **$95-$260.** 536 SW Elizabeth St 97365. Jct US 20, 0.5
mi s on US 101, then just w on SW Falls St. Ext/int corridors.
Pets: Dogs only. $25 one-time fee/room. Designated rooms, service with
restrictions, supervision. 🛜 ✕ 🛏 🖵 🍽 ➳ ⚷

▼▼ **Waves of Newport Motel and Vacation Rentals** 🏨
(541) 265-4661. **$68-$129, 3 day notice.** 820 NW Coast St 97365. Jct
US 20, 0.5 mi n on US 101, just w on NW 11th St, then just s on Spring
St. Ext corridors. **Pets:** Accepted. 🛜 🛏 🖵 ➳ ⚷

◆◆ ▼▼ **The Whaler Motel** Ⓜ
(541) 265-9261. **$96-$176.** 155 SW Elizabeth St 97365. Jct US 20, just s
on US 101, then 0.4 mi w on SW 2nd St. Ext corridors. **Pets:** Dogs only.
$10 daily fee/pet. Designated rooms, service with restrictions, supervision.
(SAVE) 🛜 ✕ ⚴M 🛏 🖵 ➳ ⚷

NORTH BEND
▼◆▼ **The Mill Casino & Hotel** 🏨 ☙
(541) 756-8800. **$104-$144.** 3201 Tremont Ave (US 101) 97459. 0.7 mi
n of Coos Bay on US 101; on bayfront. Int corridors. **Pets:** Dogs only.
$25 one-time fee/pet. Designated rooms, service with restrictions, supervi-
sion. 🛜 ⚴M 🛏 🖵 🍽 ➳ ✕

▼▼ **Quality Inn & Suites at Coos Bay** 🏨
(541) 756-3191. **$89-$189.** 1503 Virginia Ave 97459. 0.5 mi w of US
101. Ext/int corridors. **Pets:** Small, dogs only. $15 daily fee/pet. Service
with restrictions, supervision. 🛜 ✕ ⚴M 🛏 🖵

OAKLAND
▼▼ **Motel 6 - Rice Hill** 🏨
(541) 849-3335. **Call for rates.** 621 John Long Rd 97462. I-5 exit 148,
just e. Ext corridors. **Pets:** Other species. Service with restrictions, supervision. 🎟 🛜 🛏 ➳

OAKRIDGE
◆◆ ▼▼▼ **BEST WESTERN Oakridge Inn** 🏨 ☙
(541) 782-2212. **$106-$126.** 47433 SR 58 97463. West end of downtown. Ext corridors. **Pets:** $15 daily fee/pet. Designated rooms, service
with restrictions, supervision. (SAVE) 🛜 🛏 🖵 ➳

◆◆ ▼ **Cascade Motel** Ⓜ
(541) 782-2489. **$63-$80.** 47487 SR 58 97463. Center. Ext corridors.
Pets: Small, dogs only. $10 one-time fee/room. Designated rooms, ser-
vice with restrictions, crate. (SAVE) 🛜 🛏

ONTARIO
◆◆ ▼▼ **Clarion Inn** 🏨
(541) 889-8621. **$89-$124.** 1249 Tapadera Ave 97914. I-84 exit 376B,
just nw. Int corridors. **Pets:** Other species. $10 one-time fee/room. Desig-
nated rooms, service with restrictions, crate.
(SAVE) 🛜 🛏 🖵 🍽 ➳

◆◆ ▼ **Rodeway Inn** Ⓜ
(541) 889-9188. **$69-$74.** 615 E Idaho Ave 97914. I-84 exit 376A, just
sw. Ext corridors. **Pets:** Accepted. (SAVE) 🛏 🖵 ➳

◆◆ ▼▼◆ **Sleep Inn** 🏨
(541) 881-0007. **$59-$129.** 1221 SE 1st Ave 97914. I-84 exit 376B, just
ne. Int corridors. **Pets:** Dogs only. $10 daily fee/pet. Designated rooms,
service with restrictions, supervision. (SAVE) 🛜 ⚴M 🛏 🖵 ➳

PACIFIC CITY
◆◆ ▼▼◆ **Inn at Cape Kiwanda** 🏨 ☙
(503) 965-7001. **$129-$299.** 33105 Cape Kiwanda Dr 97135. Just w on
Pacific Ave, 1 mi n. Ext corridors. **Pets:** Dogs only. $20 daily fee/pet.
Designated rooms, service with restrictions, crate.
(SAVE) 🛜 ✕ ⚴M 🛏 🖵 🍽 ⚷

◆◆ ▼▼ **Pacific City Inn Inc** Ⓜ
(503) 965-6464. **$99, 3 day notice.** 35280 Brooten Rd 97135. Center.
Ext corridors. **Pets:** Accepted. (SAVE) 🛜 ✕ 🛏 🖵 🍽 ⚷

PENDLETON
◆◆ ▼▼ **Americas Best Value Inn** Ⓜ
(541) 276-1400. **$79-$99.** 201 SW Court Ave 97801. I-84 exit 210 (SR
11), 0.7 mi ne on SE 3rd Dr, then 0.6 mi w. Ext corridors. **Pets:** Other
species. $15 one-time fee/room. Designated rooms, supervision.
(SAVE) 🛜 ✕ 🛏 🖵

◆◆ ▼▼▼▼ **BEST WESTERN PLUS Pendleton Inn** 🏨
(541) 276-2135. **$109-$119.** 400 SE Nye Ave 97801. I-84 exit 210 (SR
11), just se. Int corridors. **Pets:** Small. $10 one-time fee/pet. Supervision.
(SAVE) 🛜 ✕ ⚴M 🛏 🖵 ➳

◆◆ ▼▼▼▼ **Holiday Inn Express** 🏨
(541) 966-6520. **$109-$139.** 600 SE Nye Ave 97801. I-84 exit 210 (SR
11), just se. Int corridors. **Pets:** Accepted.
(SAVE) 🛜 ✕ 🛏 🖵 ➳

▼ **Motel 6 - #349** Ⓜ
(541) 276-3160. **$45-$115.** 325 SE Nye Ave 97801. I-84 exit 210 (SR
11), just se. Ext corridors. **Pets:** Other species. Service with restrictions,
supervision. 🛜 🛏 ➳

◆◆ ▼▼▼ **Oxford Suites Pendleton** 🏨 ☙
(541) 276-6000. **$109-$139.** 2400 SW Court Pl 97801. I-84 exit 209, just
n on SW Emigrant Ave, just nw on SW 20th St, then just sw to SW
Court Pl. Int corridors. **Pets:** Medium, other species. $25 one-time fee/pet.
Designated rooms, service with restrictions, supervision.
(SAVE) 🛜 ⚴M 🛏 🖵 ➳

◆◆ ▼▼▼ **Red Lion Hotel Pendleton** 🏨
(541) 276-6111. **$109-$169.** 304 SE Nye Ave 97801. I-84 exit 210 (SR
11), just sw. Ext/int corridors. **Pets:** Other species. $15 one-time fee/room.
Service with restrictions, crate. (SAVE) 🛜 ✕ 🛏 🖵 🍽 ➳ ✕

◆◆ ▼▼ **Rodeway Inn** 🏨
(541) 276-6231. **$59-$70.** 310 SE Dorion Ave 97801. I-84 exit 210 (SR
11), 0.7 mi ne on SE 3rd St, 0.4 mi w on SE Court St, then just s on SE
3rd St. Ext corridors. **Pets:** Medium. $10 daily fee/pet. Service with
restrictions, supervision. (SAVE) 🛜 🛏 🖵 ➳

▼▼ ▼▼ **Rugged Country Lodge** 🏨
(541) 966-6800. **$72-$82.** 1807 SE Court Ave 97801. I-84 exit 210 (SR
11), 0.7 mi ne on SE 3rd Dr, then 0.4 mi e. Ext/int corridors. **Pets:** Other
species. $15 daily fee/pet. Designated rooms, service with restrictions.
🛜 ✕ 🛏 🖵

▼▼ ▼▼ **Super 8** 🏨
(541) 276-8881. **$70-$250.** 601 SE Nye Ave 97801. I-84 exit 210 (SR
11), just se. Int corridors. **Pets:** Medium, dogs only. $10 one-time fee/pet.
Designated rooms, service with restrictions, supervision.
🛜 🛏 🖵 ➳

◆◆ ▼▼ ▼▼ **Travelodge** Ⓜ ☙
(541) 276-7531. **$62-$90.** 411 SW Dorion Ave 97801. I-84 exit 209, 0.9
mi ne on SW Frazer Ave, then just nw on SW 4th St. Ext corridors.
Pets: Dogs only. $10 daily fee/pet. Designated rooms, service with restric-
tions. (SAVE) 🛜 ✕ 🛏 🖵

PORTLAND METROPOLITAN AREA

BEAVERTON

◆◆◆ Comfort Inn & Suites 🏨

(503) 643-9100. **$75-$97.** 13455 SW Tualatin Valley Hwy 97005. SR 217 exit 2A (Canyon Rd/SR 8), 1 mi w. Int corridors. **Pets:** Small, dogs only. $20 daily fee/pet. Service with restrictions, supervision.

◆◆◆ DoubleTree by Hilton Portland-Beaverton 🏨

(503) 614-8100. **$89-$269.** 15402 NW Cornell Rd 97006. US 26 exit 65, just ne. Int corridors. **Pets:** Accepted.

◆◆◆ Homewood Suites by Hilton 🏨 🐾

(503) 614-0900. **$99-$309.** 15525 NW Gateway Ct 97006. US 26 exit 65, just sw on NW Cornell Rd, just s on NW 158th Ave, just se on NW Waterhouse Ave, then just e. Int corridors. **Pets:** Small, dogs only. $15 daily fee/pet. Service with restrictions.

CLACKAMAS

◆◆◆ Comfort Suites 🏨

(503) 723-3450. **$75-$119.** 15929 SE McKinley Ave 97015. I-205 exit 12 northbound; exit 12B southbound, just w. Int corridors. **Pets:** Medium, other species. $10 daily fee/pet. Service with restrictions, supervision.

◆◆◆ Howard Johnson Clackamas 🏨 🐾

(503) 496-1000. **$70-$130.** 12855 SE 97th Ave 97015. I-205 exit 14, follow signs for Sunnyside Rd E, just e, then just s. Ext corridors. **Pets:** Other species. $10 daily fee/room. Designated rooms, service with restrictions, crate.

GLADSTONE

◆◆◆ Oxford Suites Gladstone 🏨 🐾

(503) 722-7777. **$89-$149.** 75 82nd Dr 97027. I-205 exit 11, 0.3 mi sw. Int corridors. **Pets:** Other species. $25 one-time fee/pet. Service with restrictions, supervision.

GRESHAM

◆◆◆ Days Inn & Suites 🏨

(503) 465-1515. **$55-$95.** 24124 SE Stark St 97030. I-84 exit 16, 1.5 mi s on NE 238th and NE 242nd drs, then just w. Int corridors. **Pets:** Dogs only. $10 daily fee/pet. Designated rooms, service with restrictions, supervision.

◆◆ Days Inn-Portland/Gresham 🏨

(503) 618-8400. **$55-$115.** 2261 NE 181st Ave 97230. I-84 exit 13, just sw. Int corridors. **Pets:** Medium. $15 daily fee/room. Designated rooms, service with restrictions, supervision.

◆◆ Extended StayAmerica Portland/Gresham 🏨

(503) 661-0226. **$70-$80.** 17777 NE Sacramento St 97230. I-84 exit 13, 0.3 mi s on NE 181st Ave, just w on NE San Rafael St, then just n on NE 178th Ave. Int corridors. **Pets:** $25 daily fee/pet. Designated rooms, service with restrictions.

◆◆◆ Holiday Inn Portland/Gresham 🏨

(503) 907-1777. **$89-$199.** 2752 NE Hogan Dr 97030. I-84 exit 16, 1.8 mi s on NE 238th, NE 242nd and NE Hogan drs. Int corridors. **Pets:** Small. $25 daily fee/pet. Designated rooms, service with restrictions, supervision.

◆◆◆ Howard Johnson Gresham 🏨

(503) 666-9545. **$60-$145.** 1572 NE Burnside Rd 97030. I-84 exit 16, 2.7 mi s on NE 238th, NE 242nd and NE Hogan drs, just w on Division St, then just se; I-205 exit 19, 5.5 mi e on Division St, then just se. Int corridors. **Pets:** $20 daily fee/pet. Designated rooms, service with restrictions, supervision.

◆◆◆ Super 8 🏨

(503) 661-5100. **$47-$70.** 121 NE 181st Ave 97230. I-84 exit 13, 1.3 mi s. Int corridors. **Pets:** Dogs only. $10 deposit/pet, $10 daily fee/pet. Designated rooms, service with restrictions, supervision.

HILLSBORO

◆◆ Extended StayAmerica-Portland-Beaverton 🏨

(503) 439-1515. **$85-$95.** 18665 NW Eider Ct 97006. US 26 exit 64, 0.7 mi s on NW 185th Ave, then just w. Int corridors. **Pets:** $25 daily fee/pet. Designated rooms, service with restrictions.

◆◆◆ Larkspur Landing Hillsboro/Portland 🏨

(503) 681-2121. **Call for rates.** 3133 NE Shute Rd 97124. US 26 exit 61, 1.1 mi s. Int corridors. **Pets:** Accepted.

◆◆◆ Residence Inn by Marriott-Portland West/Hillsboro 🏨

(503) 531-3200. **$109-$249.** 18855 NW Tanasbourne Dr 97124. US 26 exit 64, just s on NW 185th Ave, then just w. Ext/int corridors. **Pets:** Accepted.

◆◆◆ TownePlace Suites by Marriott-Portland Hillsboro 🏨

(503) 268-6000. **$89-$209.** 6550 NE Brighton St 97124. US 26 exit 62A westbound; exit 62 eastbound, 1 mi s on Cornelius Pass Rd, 0.7 mi w on NE Cornell Rd, just n on NW 229th Ave, then just w. Ext corridors. **Pets:** Accepted.

KING CITY

◆◆◆ BEST WESTERN PLUS Northwind Inn & Suites 🏨

(503) 431-2100. **$90-$150.** 16105 SW Pacific Hwy 97224. I-5 exit 292, just nw on SR 217 exit 6 (SR 99W), then 2.5 mi s. Int corridors. **Pets:** Accepted.

LAKE OSWEGO

◆◆◆ Crowne Plaza Hotel 🏨

(503) 624-8400. **$79-$239.** 14811 Kruse Oaks Dr 97035. I-5 exit 292B northbound; exit 292 southbound, just e on Kruse Way, then just s. Int corridors. **Pets:** Accepted.

◆◆ Lakeshore Inn 🏨

(503) 636-9679. **$89-$199, 3 day notice.** 210 N State St 97034. Jct N State St and Foothills Rd; downtown. Ext corridors. **Pets:** Accepted.

◆◆◆ Phoenix Inn Suites-Lake Oswego 🏨 🐾

(503) 624-7400. **Call for rates.** 14905 SW Bangy Rd 97035. I-5 292B northbound; exit 292 southbound, just s. Int corridors. **Pets:** Medium, dogs only. $20 daily fee/room. Designated rooms, service with restrictions, supervision.

◆◆◆ Residence Inn by Marriott-Portland South 🏨 🐾

(503) 684-2603. **$99-$199.** 15200 SW Bangy Rd 97035. I-5 exit 292B northbound; exit 292 southbound, just e, then 0.3 mi s. Ext corridors. **Pets:** Other species. $11 daily fee/room. Service with restrictions.

OREGON CITY

◆◆◆ BEST WESTERN PLUS Rivershore Hotel 🏨

(503) 655-7141. **$95-$115.** 1900 Clackamette Dr 97045. I-205 exit 9, just n. Int corridors. **Pets:** $5 daily fee/pet. Designated rooms, service with restrictions, supervision.

PORTLAND

Aloft Portland Airport at Cascade Station H

(503) 200-5678. **$119-$229.** 9920 NE Cascades Pkwy 97220. I-205 exit 24A northbound; exit 24 southbound, 0.5 mi w on Airport Way, 0.5 mi s on NE Mt Hood Ave, then just e. Int corridors. **Pets:** Accepted.

The Benson Hotel, a Coast Hotel H

(503) 228-2000. **$119-$359.** 309 SW Broadway 97205. At SW Broadway and Oak St. Int corridors. **Pets:** Accepted.

BEST WESTERN Inn at the Meadows H

(503) 286-9600. **$79-$139.** 1215 N Hayden Meadows Dr 97217. I-5 exit 306B, just e. Int corridors. **Pets:** Medium, other species. $20 daily fee/pet. Designated rooms, service with restrictions, supervision.

BEST WESTERN Pony Soldier Inn-Airport H

(503) 256-1504. **$107-$117.** 9901 NE Sandy Blvd 97220. I-205 exit 23A, just e. Int corridors. **Pets:** $10 daily fee/room. Designated rooms, service with restrictions, crate.

Candlewood Suites - Portland Airport H

(503) 255-4003. **$99-$199.** 11250 NE Holman St 97220. I-205 exit 24B northbound; exit 24 southbound, 0.4 mi e on Airport Way, then just sw. Int corridors. **Pets:** Accepted.

Courtyard by Marriott Portland City Center H

(503) 505-5000. **$107-$259.** 550 SW Oak St 97204. At SW Oak St and SW 6th Ave. Int corridors. **Pets:** Large. $50 one-time fee/room. Designated rooms, service with restrictions, supervision.

Days Inn-Portland H

(503) 289-1800. **$55-$99.** 9930 N Whitaker Rd 97217. I-5 exit 306B, just e. Int corridors. **Pets:** Other species. $15 one-time fee/room. Service with restrictions, supervision.

DoubleTree by Hilton Hotel Portland

(503) 281-6111. **$95-$225.** 1000 NE Multnomah St 97232. I-5 exit 302A, just e, just s on 9th Ave, then just e; I-84 exit Lloyd Center westbound. Int corridors. **Pets:** Accepted.

Embassy Suites at Portland Airport H

(503) 460-3000. **Call for rates.** 7900 NE 82nd Ave 97220. I-205 exit 24A northbound; exit 24 southbound, 1.3 mi w. Int corridors. **Pets:** $25 daily fee/pet. Designated rooms, service with restrictions, crate.

The Governor Hotel H

(503) 224-3400. **$139-$389.** 614 SW 11th Ave 97205. At 11th Ave and Alder St. Int corridors. **Pets:** Accepted.

The Heathman Hotel H

(503) 241-4100. **$219-$2500, 7 day notice.** 1001 SW Broadway 97205. At SW Broadway and Salmon St. Int corridors. **Pets:** $35 daily fee/pet. Service with restrictions, supervision.

Hilton Portland & Executive Tower H

(503) 226-1611. **$129-$229.** 921 SW 6th Ave 97204. I-405 exit 1B (6th Ave); at 6th Ave and Taylor St. Int corridors. **Pets:** Dogs only. $25 one-time fee/room. Service with restrictions, supervision.

Holiday Inn Portland Airport Hotel & Convention Center H

(503) 256-5000. **$80-$150.** 8439 NE Columbia Blvd 97220. I-205 exit 23B, 0.5 mi w. Int corridors. **Pets:** Other species. $20 daily fee/room. Designated rooms, service with restrictions, crate.

Hospitality Inn H

(503) 244-6684. **$79-$129.** 10155 SW Capitol Hwy 97219. I-5 exit 295 southbound, just e; exit 294 northbound, 1 mi n on SW Barbur Blvd, then just e. Int corridors. **Pets:** Medium, dogs only. $10 daily fee/pet. Designated rooms, service with restrictions, supervision.

Hotel deLuxe H

(503) 219-2094. **$129-$409.** 729 SW 15th Ave 97205. I-5 to I-405 exit Salmon St northbound, just n on 14th Ave, w on Morrison St, then s; exit Couch St/Burnside St southbound; at SW 15th Ave and Yamhill St. Int corridors. **Pets:** Accepted.

Hotel Fifty H

(503) 221-0711. **$129-$369.** 50 SW Morrison St 97204. At Morrison St and Naito Pkwy (formerly Front Ave). Int corridors. **Pets:** Accepted.

Hotel Lucia H

(503) 225-1717. **$139-$279.** 400 SW Broadway 97205. At SW Broadway and Stark St. Int corridors. **Pets:** $45 one-time fee/room. Designated rooms, service with restrictions, supervision.

Hotel Monaco Portland - A Kimpton Hotel H

(503) 222-0001. **$149-$409.** 506 SW Washington St 97204. At SW 5th Ave and SW Washington St. Int corridors. **Pets:** Accepted.

Hotel Vintage Plaza - A Kimpton Hotel H

(503) 228-1212. **$139-$259.** 422 SW Broadway 97205. At Broadway and Washington St. Int corridors. **Pets:** Accepted.

La Quinta Inn & Suites Portland Airport H

(503) 382-3820. **$71-$150.** 11207 NE Holman St 97220. I-205 exit 24B northbound; exit 24 southbound, 0.4 mi e on Airport Way, then just sw. Int corridors. **Pets:** Service with restrictions, supervision.

La Quinta Inn & Suites Portland NW-Downtown H

(503) 497-9044. **$77-$166.** 4319 NW Yeon Ave 97210. I-5 to I-405 exit 3 (US 30), 2.5 mi w. Int corridors. **Pets:** Service with restrictions, supervision.

The Mark Spencer Hotel H

(503) 224-3293. **$99-$249.** 409 SW 11th Ave 97205. At SW Stark St and SW 11th Ave. Int corridors. **Pets:** Other species. $20 daily fee/pet. Designated rooms, service with restrictions, supervision.

Motel 6 North Portland - #4198 H

(503) 247-3700. **$49-$80.** 1125 N Schmeer Rd 97217. I-5 exit 306B, 0.4 mi s on N Whitaker Rd, then just e. Int corridors. **Pets:** Other species. Service with restrictions, supervision.

The Nines H

(503) 222-9996. **$169-$599.** 525 SW Morrison St 97204. At SW Morrison St and SW 5th Ave. Int corridors. **Pets:** Accepted.

Oxford Suites Portland H ❀
(503) 283-3030. **$85-$179.** 12226 N Jantzen Dr 97217. I-5 exit 308, just e on Hayden Island Dr. Int corridors. **Pets:** Other species. $25 one-time fee/pet. Service with restrictions, crate.
[SAVE] 🛜 ✕ &M 🛏 💻 ⊒ 🛇

Park Lane Suites and Inn M
(503) 226-6288. **Call for rates.** 809 SW King Ave 97205. I-405 exit Couch St/Burnside St southbound, 0.5 mi w on Burnside St, then just s; exit Everett St northbound, 0.3 mi w on Glisan St, just s on NW 21st Ave, just w on Burnside St, then just s. Ext corridors. **Pets:** Accepted.
🛜 ✕ &M 🛏 💻

The Portlander Inn H
(503) 345-0300. **$80-$120.** 10350 N Vancouver Way 97217. I-5 exit 307, follow signs for Marine Dr E, just ne, then 0.7 mi se. Int corridors.
Pets: Accepted. 🛜 ✕ 🛏 💻 🍽 🛇

Quality Inn Downtown Convention Center H
(503) 233-7933. **$79-$118.** 431 NE Multnomah St 97232. I-5 exit 302A, just e on NE Weidler St, just s on NE Martin Luther King Jr Blvd, then just e. Int corridors. **Pets:** Medium, dogs only. $10 daily fee/pet. Designated rooms, service with restrictions, supervision.
🛜 ✕ 🛏 💻 ⊒

Ramada Portland Airport H
(503) 255-6511. **$79-$105.** 6221 NE 82nd Ave 97220. I-205 exit 23B (Killingsworth St), just w on Columbia Blvd, then just n on 80th Ave. Int corridors. **Pets:** Small, dogs only. $20 daily fee/pet. Designated rooms, service with restrictions, supervision.
[SAVE] 🛜 &M 🛏 💻 🍽 ⊒ 🛇

Ramada Portland South I-205 H
(503) 252-7400. **$79-$100.** 9707 SE Stark St 97216. I-205 exit 21A southbound; exit 20 northbound, just e on Washington St, just n on SE 99th Ave, then just w. Int corridors. **Pets:** Accepted.
🛜 ✕ &M 🛏 💻

Red Lion Hotel on the River Jantzen Beach-Portland H
(503) 283-4466. **$99-$189.** 909 N Hayden Island Dr 97217. I-5 exit 308, just ne. Int corridors. **Pets:** Other species. $15 one-time fee/room. Service with restrictions, crate. [ECO] 🛜 ✕ &M 🛏 💻 🍽 ⊒ 🛇

Red Lion Hotel Portland Airport H
(503) 255-6722. **$89-$109.** 7101 NE 82nd Ave 97220. I-205 exit 24A northbound; exit 24 southbound, 1.3 mi w on NE Airport Way, then 0.5 mi s. Ext/int corridors. **Pets:** Other species. $15 one-time fee/room. Service with restrictions. [SAVE] 🛜 ✕ 🛏 💻 🍽 ⊒

Red Lion Hotel Portland-Convention Center H
(503) 235-2100. **$129-$199.** 1021 NE Grand Ave 97232. I-5 exit 302A, just e on NE Weidler St, just s on NE Martin Luther King Jr Blvd, then just e. Int corridors. **Pets:** Other species. $15 one-time fee/room. Service with restrictions, crate. [SAVE] 🛜 ✕ 🛏 💻 🍽

Residence Inn by Marriott Portland Airport at Cascade Station H
(503) 284-1800. **$139-$259.** 9301 NE Cascades Pkwy 97220. I-205 exit 24A northbound; exit 24 southbound, 0.5 mi w on Airport Way, 0.5 mi s on NE Mt Hood Ave, then just w. Int corridors. **Pets:** Accepted.
🛜 ✕ &M 🛏 💻 ⊒ 🛇

Residence Inn by Marriott Portland Downtown at RiverPlace H
(503) 552-9500. **$129-$249.** 2115 SW River Pkwy 97201. At SW Moody Ave and SW River Pkwy; on Willamette River Waterfront. Int corridors.
Pets: Accepted. 🛜 ✕ 🛏 💻 ⊒ 🛇

Residence Inn by Marriott Portland Downtown/Lloyd Center H ❀
(503) 288-1400. **$99-$249.** 1710 NE Multnomah St 97232. I-5 exit 302A, 0.8 mi e on Weidler St, then just s on 15th Ave; I-84 exit 1 (Lloyd Center) westbound, just n on 13th St, then just e. Ext corridors. **Pets:** Other species. $75 one-time fee/room. Service with restrictions.
🛜 ✕ &M 🛏 💻 ⊒ 🛇

Residence Inn by Marriott-Portland North Harbour H
(503) 285-9888. **$119-$199.** 1250 N Anchor Way 97217. I-5 exit 307, follow signs to Marine Dr E, then just n. Int corridors. **Pets:** Accepted.
🛜 ✕ &M 🛏 💻 ⊒ 🛇

RiverPlace Hotel - A Kimpton Hotel H 🐾
(503) 228-3233. **$189-$550.** 1510 SW Harbor Way 97201. At Naito Pkwy (formerly Front Ave) and SW Harbor Way. Int corridors. **Pets:** Other species. Designated rooms, supervision. [SAVE] 🛜 ✕ &M 💻 🍽

Sheraton Portland Airport Hotel H ❀
(503) 281-2500. **$109-$309.** 8235 NE Airport Way 97220. I-205 exit 24A northbound; exit 24 southbound, 1.5 mi w. Int corridors. **Pets:** Medium. Designated rooms, service with restrictions, supervision.
[SAVE] 🛜 ✕ &M 💻 🍽 ⊒ 🛇

Shilo Inn-Portland/Rose Garden H
(503) 736-6300. **$79-$160.** 1506 NE 2nd Ave 97232. I-5 exit 302A, just e on NE Weidler St, then just s. Int corridors. **Pets:** Dogs only. $25 one-time fee/room. Designated rooms, service with restrictions, supervision.
🛜 ✕ 🛏 💻

Shilo Inn Suites Hotel-Portland Airport H
(503) 252-7500. **$89-$189.** 11707 NE Airport Way 97220. I-205 exit 24B northbound; exit 24 southbound, 0.5 mi e. Int corridors. **Pets:** Dogs only. $25 one-time fee/room. Designated rooms, service with restrictions, supervision. 🛜 ✕ &M 🛏 💻 🍽 ⊒ 🛇

Staybridge Suites Portland-Airport H
(503) 262-8888. **$109-$159.** 11936 NE Glenn Widing Dr 97220. I-205 exit 24B northbound; exit 24 southbound, 0.7 mi e, then just nw. Int corridors. **Pets:** Medium, dogs only. $75 one-time fee/pet. Service with restrictions, supervision. 🛜 ✕ &M 🛏 💻 ⊒ 🛇

University Place Hotel & Conference Center H
(503) 221-0140. **Call for rates.** 310 SW Lincoln St 97201. I-5 to I-405 exit 4th Ave, just n, then just e. Ext/int corridors. **Pets:** Dogs only. $15 daily fee/pet. Designated rooms, service with restrictions, supervision.
🛜 ✕ 🛏 💻 🍽 ⊒

The Westin Portland H
(503) 294-9000. **$159-$459.** 750 SW Alder St 97205. At Park Ave and SW Alder St. Int corridors. **Pets:** Accepted.
[SAVE] 🛜 ✕ &M 💻 🍽

TIGARD

Embassy Suites Hotel-Portland Washington Square H
(503) 644-4000. **$99-$209.** 9000 SW Washington Square Rd 97223. SR 217 exit 4 (Progress/Scholls Ferry Rd), just ne on SW Scholls Ferry Rd, just e on SW Hall Blvd, then just s. Int corridors. **Pets:** Medium, dogs only. $25 daily fee/room. Designated rooms, service with restrictions, supervision. [SAVE] 🛜 &M 🛏 💻 🍽 ⊒

Extended StayAmerica-Portland-Tigard H
(503) 670-0555. **$81-$91.** 13009 SW 68th Pkwy 97223. I-5 exit 293 (Haines St) southbound, 0.5 mi s on SW 68th Ave; exit 293 northbound, just w on Atlanta Ave, then 0.7 mi s; SR 217 exit 7 (72nd Ave), just ne, just e on Hampton St, then just s. Ext corridors. **Pets:** $25 daily fee/pet. Designated rooms, service with restrictions. 🛜 🛏 💻

Phoenix Inn Suites-Tigard H
(503) 624-9000. **Call for rates.** 9575 SW Locust St 97223. SR 217 exit 5 (Greenburg Rd), just ne on SW Greenburg Rd, then just e. Int corridors. **Pets:** Medium. $25 one-time fee/pet. Designated rooms, service with restrictions, crate. [SAVE] 🛜 &M 🛏 💻 ⊒ 🛇

TROUTDALE

Comfort Inn Columbia Gorge - Gateway H
(503) 492-2900. **Call for rates.** 1000 NW Graham Rd 97060. I-84 exit 17 eastbound, e on Frontage Rd, then just n; exit westbound, just n. Int corridors. **Pets:** Accepted. 🛜 🛏 💻

▼ Motel 6-Portland Troutdale - #407 **M**
(503) 665-2254. **$45-$55.** 1610 NW Frontage Rd 97060. I-84 exit 17 eastbound, just sw; exit westbound, just w on Frontage Rd, then just sw. Ext corridors. **Pets:** Other species. Service with restrictions, supervision.
🛰 ᴸᴹ 🛏 ➿

TUALATIN
◈ ▼▼▼ Comfort Inn & Suites **H**
(503) 612-9952. **$89-$199.** 7640 SW Warm Springs St 97062. I-5 exit 289, just w on Nyberg St, just s on Martinazzi Ave, then just e; just behind Fred Meyer. Int corridors. **Pets:** Small, dogs only. $20 one-time fee/pet. Designated rooms, supervision.
SAVE 🛰 ✕ ᴸᴹ 🛏 📁 ➿

WILSONVILLE
▼▼ GuestHouse Inn & Suites **H**
(503) 682-9000. **Call for rates.** 8855 SW Citizens Dr 97070. I-5 exit 283, just e on Wilsonville Rd, just n on Town Center Loop W, then just w. Int corridors. **Pets:** Accepted. 🛰 ᴸᴹ 🛏 📁 ➿

▼▼▼ Holiday Inn-Wilsonville **H** ❖
(503) 682-2211. **$69-$159.** 25425 SW 95th Ave 97070. I-5 exit 286, just w on Boones Ferry Rd, then just se. Int corridors. **Pets:** Other species. $15 daily fee/room. Designated rooms. 🛰 ✕ 🛏 📁 ❢ ➿

▼ La Quinta Inn Wilsonville **H**
(503) 682-3184. **$83-$172.** 8815 SW Sun Pl 97070. I-5 exit 286, just e on Elligsen Rd, just n on Parkway Ave, then just w. Int corridors.
Pets: Service with restrictions, supervision.
SAVE 🛰 ✕ ᴸᴹ 🛏 📁 ➿

◈ ▼▼▼ Quality Inn Wilsonville **H**
(503) 682-2288. **$69-$109.** 30800 SW Parkway Ave 97070. I-5 exit 283, just e on Wilsonville Rd, just s on Town Center Loop W, just w on Main St, then 0.4 mi s. Int corridors. **Pets:** Large. $10 daily fee/pet. Designated rooms, service with restrictions, supervision.
SAVE 🛰 ✕ 🛏 📁 ➿

◈ ▼▼▼ Super 8 - Wilsonville **H**
(503) 682-2088. **$57-$82.** 25438 SW Parkway Ave 97070. I-5 exit 286, just e on Elligsen Rd, then just n. Int corridors. **Pets:** Dogs only. $10 daily fee/pet. Designated rooms, service with restrictions, supervision.
SAVE 🛰 🛏 📁

END METROPOLITAN AREA

PORT ORFORD
▼ Castaway by the Sea **M**
(541) 332-4502. **Call for rates.** 545 W 5th St 97465. Jct US 101, 1 blk w on Harbor Dr, 1 blk n. Ext corridors. **Pets:** Accepted.
🛰 ✕ 🛏 📁 🎿

PRINEVILLE
◈ ▼▼ BEST WESTERN Prineville Inn **H**
(541) 447-8080. **$75-$108.** 1475 NE 3rd St 97754. 0.8 mi e on US 26. Int corridors. **Pets:** Medium, dogs only. $15 daily fee/room. Designated rooms, supervision. SAVE 🛰 ✕ ᴸᴹ 🛏 📁 ➿

▼ Econo Lodge **M**
(541) 447-6231. **$60-$90.** 123 NE 3rd St 97754. Downtown. Int corridors.
Pets: Medium, dogs only. $10 deposit/pet. No service, supervision.
🛰 🛏 📁

▼▼▼ Stafford Inn **H**
(541) 447-7100. **$82-$117.** 1773 NE 3rd St 97754. 1 mi e on US 26. Int corridors. **Pets:** $25 one-time fee/room. Service with restrictions, supervision. 🛰 ᴸᴹ 🛏 📁 ➿

PROSPECT
▼▼ Prospect Historic Hotel-Motel & Dinner House **M** ❖
(541) 560-3664. **$70-$205, 7 day notice.** 391 Mill Creek Dr 97536. Jct SR 62 (0.7 mi e of MM 43), 0.3 mi s on 1st St, then just w. Ext/int corridors. **Pets:** Other species. $15 one-time fee/pet. Designated rooms, service with restrictions, supervision. 🛰 ✕ 🛏 📁 ❢ ✕

REDMOND
▼▼▼ Comfort Suites-Redmond Airport **H**
(541) 504-8900. **$99-$250.** 2243 SW Yew Ave 97756. US 97 exit 124 (Yew Ave/Airport Way/Redmond Airport), just nw; 2 mi s of jct SR 126. Int corridors. **Pets:** Other species. $25 one-time fee/room. Service with restrictions, supervision. 🛰 ✕ 🛏 📁 ➿

◈ ▼▼▼ The Lodge At Eagle Crest - A Holiday Inn Resort **H**
(541) 923-2453. **$79-$179, 3 day notice.** 1522 Cline Falls Rd 97756. 4.5 mi w on SR 126, 1 mi s. Int corridors. **Pets:** Accepted.
SAVE 🛰 ✕ ᴸᴹ 🛏 📁 ❢ ➿ ✕

◈ ▼ Motel 6 Redmond - #4076 **H**
(541) 923-2100. **$60-$100.** 2247 S US 97 97756. 1.1 mi s on US 97 from jct SR 126, just w. Int corridors. **Pets:** Other species. Service with restrictions, supervision. ECO SAVE 🛰 ᴸᴹ 🛏

◈ ▼ Redmond Inn **M**
(541) 548-1091. **$45-$125.** 1545 S US 97 97756. Jct SR 126, 0.7 mi s. Ext corridors. **Pets:** Medium. $7 daily fee/pet. Designated rooms, service with restrictions, supervision. SAVE 🛰 🛏 📁 ➿

◈ ▼▼▼ Sleep Inn & Suites-Redmond **H** ❖
(541) 504-1500. **$94-$159.** 1847 NW US 97 97756. US 97 exit 119, 0.6 mi s on Business Rt US 97; 1 mi n of downtown. Int corridors.
Pets: Medium, other species. $10 daily fee/pet. Designated rooms, service with restrictions, supervision. SAVE 🛰 ✕ ᴸᴹ 🛏 📁 ➿

REEDSPORT
◈ ▼▼▼ BEST WESTERN PLUS Salbasgeon Inn & Suites of Reedsport **H**
(541) 271-4831. **$115-$286.** 1400 US 101 S 97467. Jct SR 38, 0.4 mi s. Ext corridors. **Pets:** Medium, dogs only. $20 daily fee/pet. Designated rooms, service with restrictions, supervision. SAVE 🛰 🛏 📁 ➿

▼▼ Salbasgeon Inn of the Umpqua **M** ❖
(541) 271-2025. **$85-$325.** 45209 SR 38 97467. Jct US 101, 7.5 mi n. Ext corridors. **Pets:** $10 daily fee/room. Designated rooms, service with restrictions, supervision. ✕ 🛏 📁 🎿

ROCKAWAY BEACH
◈ ▼▼ Silver Sands Oceanfront Motel **H**
(503) 355-2206. **$72-$166.** 215 S Pacific St 97136. US 101, just w on SW 2nd Ave. Ext corridors. **Pets:** Dogs only. $10 daily fee/pet. Designated rooms, service with restrictions, supervision.
SAVE 🛰 ✕ 🛏 📁 ➿ ✕ 🎿

◈ ▼▼▼ Tradewinds Motel **M** ❖
(503) 355-2112. **$65-$169, 7 day notice.** 523 N Pacific St 97136. US 101, just w on NW 6th Ave, just s. Ext corridors. **Pets:** Large, dogs only. $15 daily fee/pet. Designated rooms, service with restrictions, supervision.
SAVE 🛰 ✕ 🛏 📁 🎿

ROSEBURG

BEST WESTERN Garden Villa Inn M ❖
(541) 672-1601. **$80-$130.** 760 NW Garden Valley Blvd 97471. I-5 exit
125, just nw. Ext corridors. **Pets:** Other species. $15 deposit/pet, $30
one-time fee/pet. Service with restrictions.
SAVE 🛜 ✕ 🛏 💻 🌊

Econo Lodge & Suites H
(541) 464-8338. **$75-$90.** 2855 NW Edenbower Blvd 97471. I-5 exit 127,
just sw. Int corridors. **Pets:** $10 one-time fee/room. Service with restric-
tions, crate. 🛜 🅼 🛏 💻 🌊

Holiday Inn Express H
(541) 673-7517. **$77-$159.** 375 W Harvard Blvd 97470. I-5 exit 124, just
se. Ext/int corridors. **Pets:** $15 daily fee/room. Service with restrictions,
supervision. 🛜 ✕ 🅼 🛏 💻 🌊

Motel 6 - #4108 H
(541) 464-8000. **$49-$82.** 3100 NW Aviation Dr 97470. I-5 exit 127, just
se. Int corridors. **Pets:** Other species. Service with restrictions, supervision. 🛜 🅼 🛏

Quality Inn M
(541) 673-5561. **$75-$89.** 427 NW Garden Valley Blvd 97470. I-5 exit
125, just se. Ext corridors. **Pets:** Dogs only. $50 deposit/room, $10 daily
fee/room. Designated rooms, service with restrictions, crate.
SAVE 🛜 🛏 💻 🌊

Roseburg Travelodge M
(541) 672-4836. **$70-$100.** 315 W Harvard Ave 97470. I-5 exit 124, just
se. Ext corridors. **Pets:** Medium. $15 deposit/pet. Service with restrictions,
vice with restrictions, supervision. SAVE 🛜 🛏 💻 🌊

Shady Oaks Motel M
(541) 672-2608. **$45-$79.** 2954 Old Hwy 99 S 97471. I-5 exit 120, 0.5 mi
n. Ext corridors. **Pets:** Dogs only. $10 daily fee/pet. Designated rooms,
service with restrictions, supervision. SAVE 🛜 🛏

Super 8 H
(541) 672-8880. **$69-$95.** 3200 NW Aviation Dr 97470. I-5 exit 127, just
ne. Int corridors. **Pets:** Other species. $10 one-time fee/room. Service
with restrictions, supervision. 🛜 🅼 🛏 💻 🌊

Windmill Inn of Roseburg H
(541) 673-0901. **Call for rates.** 1450 NW Mulholland Dr 97470. I-5 exit
125, just ne. Int corridors. **Pets:** Accepted.
SAVE 🛜 ✕ 🛏 💻 🌊 ✕

ST. HELENS

BEST WESTERN Oak Meadows Inn H
(503) 397-3000. **$121-$131.** 585 S Columbia River Hwy (US 30) 97051.
South end of town. Int corridors. **Pets:** $10 one-time fee/pet. Service with
restrictions, supervision. SAVE 🛜 ✕ 🛏 💻 🌊

SALEM

BEST WESTERN Pacific Highway Inn H
(503) 390-3200. **$90-$108.** 4646 Portland Rd NE 97305. I-5 exit 258, 0.3
mi e. Ext corridors. **Pets:** Dogs only. $20 daily fee/room. Designated
rooms, service with restrictions, supervision. SAVE 🛜 🛏 💻 🌊

**BEST WESTERN PLUS Mill Creek
Inn** H ❖
(503) 585-3332. **$120-$175.** 3125 Ryan Dr SE 97301. I-5 exit 253, just
w on Mission St (SR 22), just n on Hawthorne Ave SE, then just w. Int
corridors. **Pets:** Large, dogs only. $20 daily fee/room. Service with restric-
tions, supervision. SAVE 🛜 ✕ 🛏 💻 🌊 ✕

Comfort Suites Airport H
(503) 585-9705. **$104-$169.** 630 Hawthorne Ave SE 97301. I-5 exit 253,
just w on Mission St (SR 22), 0.4 mi on Hawthorne Ave SE, then just
e. Int corridors. **Pets:** Medium. $10 daily fee/pet. Designated rooms, ser-
vice with restrictions, supervision. 🛜 ✕ 🅼 🛏 💻 🌊 ✕

Crossland Economy Studios - Salem - North M
(503) 363-7557. **$65-$75.** 3535 Fisher Rd NE 97305. I-5 exit 258, just e
on Portland Rd NE, 0.3 mi s on Ward Dr, then 0.8 mi s. Ext corridors.
Pets: $25 daily fee/pet. Designated rooms, service with restrictions.
🛜 🛏 💻

Days Inn Black Bear H
(503) 581-1559. **$55-$140.** 1600 Motor Ct NE 97301. I-5 exit 256, just e
on Market St NE, then just s. Ext corridors. **Pets:** Medium. $11 daily fee/
room. Designated rooms, service with restrictions, supervision.
SAVE 🛜 🛏 💻 🌊 ✕

DoubleTree by Hilton Salem - Oregon H
(503) 581-7004. **Call for rates.** 1590 Weston Ct NE 97301. I-5 exit 256,
just w on Market St, then just s. Int corridors. **Pets:** Accepted.
SAVE 🛜 🅼 🛏 💻 🌊

Howard Johnson Inn H
(503) 375-7710. **$55-$88.** 2250 Mission St SE 97302. I-5 exit 253, 1.4 mi
w. Int corridors. **Pets:** Small, dogs only. $15 daily fee/pet. Designated
rooms, service with restrictions, supervision.
SAVE 🛜 ✕ 🛏 💻 🌊

La Quinta Inn & Suites Salem H
(503) 391-7000. **$71-$177.** 890 Hawthorne Ave SE 97301. I-5 exit 253,
just w on Mission St (SR 22), then just n. Int corridors. **Pets:** Service with
restrictions, supervision. SAVE 🛜 ✕ 🅼 🛏 💻 🌊

Phoenix Inn Suites-South Salem H
(503) 588-9220. **Call for rates.** 4370 Commercial St SE 97302. I-5 exit
252, 1.5 mi w on Kuebler Rd, then 0.7 mi n. Int corridors. **Pets:** Other
species. $20 daily fee/room. Designated rooms, service with restrictions,
supervision. SAVE 🛜 🅼 🛏 💻 🌊 ✕

Red Lion Hotel Salem H
(503) 370-7888. **Call for rates.** 3301 Market St NE 97301. I-5 exit 256,
just w. Int corridors. **Pets:** Other species. $15 one-time fee/room. Service
with restrictions, crate. 🛜 ✕ 🅼 🛏 💻 🍴 🌊

Residence Inn by Marriott H
(503) 585-6500. **$153-$225.** 640 Hawthorne Ave SE 97301. I-5 exit 253,
just w on Mission St (SR 22), 0.4 mi n on Hawthorne Ave SE, then just
e. Int corridors. **Pets:** Other species. $100 one-time fee/room. Service
with restrictions. 🛜 ✕ 🅼 🛏 💻 🌊 ✕

Shilo Inn Suites-Salem H
(503) 581-4001. **$81-$140.** 3304 Market St NE 97301. I-5 exit 256, just
w. Int corridors. **Pets:** Dogs only. $25 one-time fee/room. Designated
rooms, service with restrictions, supervision.
🛜 ✕ 🛏 💻 🌊 ✕

Super 8 Salem H
(503) 370-8888. **$55-$109.** 1288 Hawthorne Ave NE 97301. I-5 exit 256,
just w on Market St, then just s. Int corridors. **Pets:** Accepted.
🛜 🛏 💻 🌊

Travelodge Salem Capital M
(503) 581-2466. **$49-$75.** 1555 State St 97301. I-5 exit 253, 1.8 mi w on
Mission St (SR 22), 0.4 mi n on 17th St SE, then just w. Ext corridors.
Pets: Medium. $10 daily fee/pet. Designated rooms, service with restric-
tions, supervision. SAVE 🛜 🛏 💻 🌊

SANDY

BEST WESTERN Sandy Inn H
(503) 668-7100. **$80-$125.** 37465 US 26 97055. West side of town. Int
corridors. **Pets:** Accepted. SAVE 🛜 ✕ 🅼 🛏 💻 🌊

SEASIDE

▲▲▲ ▼▼▼▼ BEST WESTERN Ocean View Resort 🅷 ❀

(503) 738-3334. **$59-$449, 3 day notice.** 414 N Prom 97138. US 101 exit 1st Ave, just w, just n on Necanicum Dr, then just w on 4th Ave. Ext/int corridors. **Pets:** Medium, dogs only. $20 daily fee/pet. Designated rooms, service with restrictions, supervision.

[SAVE] 🛜 ✕ 🅱 🖵 🍴 ⇴

▲▲▲ ▼▼▼▼ Comfort Inn & Suites by Seaside Convention Center/Boardwalk 🅷 ❀

(503) 738-3011. **$89-$400.** 545 Broadway St 97138. US 101, just w on Ave A; downtown. Int corridors. **Pets:** Medium, dogs only. $25 daily fee/pet. Designated rooms, service with restrictions, supervision.

[SAVE] 🛜 ✕ 🄼 🅱 🖵 ⇴

▲▲▲ ▼▼▼ Ebb-Tide Resort 🅷

(503) 738-8371. **$120-$220, 3 day notice.** 300 N Prom 97138. US 101 exit 1st Ave, 0.4 mi w, just n on Columbia St, then just w on 2nd Ave. Ext/int corridors. **Pets:** Small, other species. $20 one-time fee/pet. Designated rooms, service with restrictions, supervision.

[SAVE] 🛜 🅱 🖵 ⇴ ✕ 🄰

▼▼▼ GuestHouse Inn & Suites Seaside 🅷

(503) 738-8971. **$80-$199.** 2455 S Roosevelt Dr (US 101) 97138. Just s of downtown on US 101. Int corridors. **Pets:** Accepted.

🛜 ✕ 🄼 🅱 🖵

▲▲▲ ▼▼▼▼ Holiday Inn Express Hotel & Suites-Seaside Convention Center 🅷 ❀

(503) 717-8000. **$89-$399.** 34 N Holladay Dr 97138. US 101 exit Broadway St, just w, then just n. Int corridors. **Pets:** Medium, dogs only. $25 daily fee/pet. Designated rooms, service with restrictions, supervision.

[SAVE] 🛜 🄼 🅱 🖵 ⇴ ✕

▲▲▲ ▼▼▼ Inn at Seaside 🅷 ❀

(503) 738-9581. **$69-$249, 3 day notice.** 441 2nd Ave 97138. US 101 exit 1st Ave, then just w. Ext/int corridors. **Pets:** $15 deposit/pet. Service with restrictions. [SAVE] 🛜 ✕ 🅱 🖵 ⇴

▼▼▼ Inn At The Shore 🅜 ❀

(503) 738-3113. **$69-$249, 3 day notice.** 2275 S Prom 97138. US 101 exit Ave U, just w. Ext corridors. **Pets:** Other species. $20 one-time fee/pet. Designated rooms, service with restrictions, supervision.

🛜 ✕ 🅱 🖵 🄰

▲▲▲ ▼▼▼▼ Rivertide Suites 🅷 ❀

(503) 717-1100. **$99-$449, 3 day notice.** 102 N Holladay Dr 97138. US 101, just w on Broadway St, just n. Int corridors. **Pets:** Medium. $25 deposit/pet, $25 daily fee/pet. Service with restrictions, supervision.

[SAVE] 🛜 ✕ 🄼 🅱 🖵 ⇴

▲▲▲ ▼▼▼ Seashore Inn...on the Beach 🅷

(503) 738-6368. **$75-$249.** 60 N Prom 97138. US 101 exit 1st Ave, 0.4 mi w. Ext/int corridors. **Pets:** Small. $20 daily fee/pet. Designated rooms, service with restrictions, supervision.

[SAVE] 🛜 ✕ 🅱 🖵 ⇴ ✕ 🄰

▼▼▼ The Seaside Oceanfront Inn & Restaurant 🅷

(503) 738-6403. **$79-$299, 5 day notice.** 581 S Prom 97138. US 101 exit Ave G, 0.6 mi w, then just n. Int corridors. **Pets:** $25 daily fee/room. Designated rooms, service with restrictions, supervision.

🛜 ✕ 🖵 🍴

▼▼▼▼ Shilo Inn Suites Oceanfront Hotel-Seaside 🅷

(503) 738-9571. **$81-$410.** 30 N Prom 97138. US 101 exit Broadway St, 0.4 mi w. Ext corridors. **Pets:** Dogs only. $25 one-time fee/room. Designated rooms, service with restrictions, supervision.

🛜 ✕ 🅱 🖵 🍴 ⇴ ✕ 🄰

SISTERS

▲▲▲ ▼▼▼▼ BEST WESTERN Ponderosa Lodge 🅷 ❀

(541) 549-1234. **$100-$180.** 500 US 20 W 97759. Jct SR 242, just w on US 20; at Barclay Dr; west end of town. Ext corridors. **Pets:** $15 daily fee/room. Designated rooms, service with restrictions, supervision.

[SAVE] 🛜 ✕ 🅱 🖵 ⇴

▲▲▲ ▼▼▼▼ FivePine Lodge & Spa 🅒 ❀

(541) 549-5900. **$149-$317, 7 day notice.** 1021 Desperado Tr 97759. Jct SR 126 and US 20, just e on US 20; east end of town. Int corridors. **Pets:** $25 daily fee/room. Designated rooms, service with restrictions, supervision. [SAVE] 🛜 ✕ 🅱 🖵 ⇴ ✕

▲▲▲ ▼▼▼ Sisters Inn & Suites 🅜 ❀

(541) 549-7829. **$120-$166.** 605 N Arrow Leaf Tr 97759. Just w on US 20 from jct SR 242; west end of town. Ext corridors. **Pets:** $15 one-time fee/room. Designated rooms, service with restrictions, supervision.

[SAVE] 🛜 ✕ 🄼 🅱 🖵

SPRINGFIELD

▲▲▲ ▼▼▼ BEST WESTERN Grand Manor Inn 🅷

(541) 726-4769. **Call for rates.** 971 Kruse Way 97477. I-5 exit 195A, just se. Int corridors. **Pets:** Accepted.

[SAVE] 🛜 ✕ 🄼 🅱 🖵 ⇴

▼▼▼ Comfort Suites Eugene/Springfield 🅷

(541) 746-5359. **$109-$169.** 969 Kruse Way 97477. I-5 exit 195A, just se. Int corridors. **Pets:** Dogs only. $25 one-time fee/room. Designated rooms, supervision. 🛜 ✕ 🅱 🖵 ⇴

▼▼▼ Holiday Inn Eugene - Springfield 🅷

(541) 284-0707. **$119-$169.** 919 Kruse Way 97477. I-5 exit 195A, just se. Int corridors. **Pets:** Small, dogs only. $23 one-time fee/pet. Designated rooms, service with restrictions, supervision.

🛜 ✕ 🄼 🅱 🖵 🍴 ⇴

▼▼▼ Holiday Inn Express Hotel & Suites 🅷 ❀

(541) 746-8471. **$119-$159.** 3480 Hutton St 97477. I-5 exit 195A, just se. Int corridors. **Pets:** Other species. $20 daily fee/pet. Designated rooms, service with restrictions, supervision. 🛜 ✕ 🅱 🖵 ⇴

▼▼▼ Motel 6 - #418 🅜

(541) 741-1105. **$49-$65.** 3752 International Ct 97477. I-5 exit 195A, just e on Beltline Rd, just nw on Gateway St, then just n. Ext corridors. **Pets:** Other species. Service with restrictions, supervision.

[ECO] 🛜 🄼 🅱 ⇴

▼▼▼ Quality Inn & Suites 🅷 ❀

(541) 726-9266. **$89-$149.** 3550 Gateway St 97477. I-5 exit 195A, just e on Beltline Rd, then just nw. Int corridors. **Pets:** Other species. $5 daily fee/pet. Designated rooms, service with restrictions, supervision.

🛜 🄼 🅱 🖵 ⇴

▲▲▲ ▼▼▼ Super 8 🅷

(541) 746-1314. **$65-$203.** 3315 Gateway St 97477. I-5 exit 195A, just e on Beltline Rd, then just s. Int corridors. **Pets:** Medium, dogs only. $20 one-time fee/pet. Designated rooms, service with restrictions, supervision.

[SAVE] 🛜 🅱 🖵

▲▲▲ ▼▼▼ Village Inn 🅜

(541) 747-4546. **$64-$79.** 1875 Mohawk Blvd 97477. I-5 exit 194A, 2.5 mi e on SR 126 exit Mohawk Blvd, then just n. Ext corridors. **Pets:** $10 daily fee/pet. Service with restrictions, supervision.

[SAVE] 🛜 🅱 🖵 ⇴

SUNRIVER

Discover Sunriver Vacation Rentals VH
(541) 593-2482. **$99-$180, 60 day notice.** Sunriver Village Mall, Bldg 7 97707. US 97 exit 153 (S Century Dr), 2 mi w to Abbott Dr, then just n on Beaver Dr. Int corridors. **Pets:** Dogs only. $40 one-time fee/pet. Designated rooms, service with restrictions, supervision.

Sunriver Resort H
(541) 593-1000. **$139-$344, 21 day notice.** 17600 Center Dr 97707. US 97 exit 153 (S Century Dr), 1.5 mi w to Abbott Dr, then 0.6 mi w. Ext corridors. **Pets:** Other species. $75 one-time fee/room. Designated rooms, service with restrictions, supervision.

SUTHERLIN

BEST WESTERN PLUS Hartford Lodge H
(541) 459-1424. **$100-$130.** 150 Myrtle St 97479. I-5 exit 136, just ne. Ext corridors. **Pets:** Large, dogs only. $20 one-time fee/room. Designated rooms, service with restrictions, supervision.

GuestHouse Inn & Suites Sutherlin H
(541) 459-6800. **$59-$100.** 1400 Hospitality Way 97479. I-5 exit 136, just se. Int corridors. **Pets:** Medium, other species. $10 daily fee/room. Service with restrictions, supervision.

SWEET HOME

Sweet Home Inn M
(541) 367-5137. **$69-$155.** 805 Long St 97386. Just e of jct US 20 and SR 228; just s on 10th Ave, then just w. Ext corridors. **Pets:** Medium, dogs only. $15 daily fee/pet. Service with restrictions, supervision.

THE DALLES

Celilo Inn M
(541) 769-0001. **$119-$169.** 3550 E 2nd St 97058. I-84 exit 87, just s on US 197, just w on US 30, then 0.8 mi ne on SE Frontage Rd/E 2nd St. Ext corridors. **Pets:** Accepted.

Comfort Inn Columbia Gorge H
(541) 298-2800. **$110-$189.** 351 Lone Pine Dr 97058. I-84 exit 87, just nw. Int corridors. **Pets:** Accepted.

Cousins' Country Inn H
(541) 298-5161. **$89-$189.** 2114 W 6th St 97058. I-84 exit 83 eastbound, just nw; exit 84 westbound, just nw on W 2nd St, just sw on Webber St, then just n. Ext corridors. **Pets:** $10 daily fee/pet. Designated rooms, service with restrictions, crate.

Motel 6 - #4268 H
(541) 296-1191. **Call for rates.** 2500 W 6th St 97058. I-84 exit 83 eastbound, just nw; exit 84 westbound, just nw on W 2nd St, just sw on Webber St, then just n. Int corridors. **Pets:** Other species. Service with restrictions, supervision.

Shilo Inn Suites Hotel-The Dalles H
(541) 298-5502. **$80-$199.** 3223 Bret Clodfelter Way 97058. I-84 exit 87, just ne. Int corridors. **Pets:** Dogs only. $25 one-time fee/room. Designated rooms, service with restrictions, supervision.

Super 8 H
(541) 296-6888. **$70-$120.** 609 Cherry Heights Rd 97058. I-84 exit 84 eastbound, just se on W 2nd St, then just sw; exit 84 westbound, just nw on W 2nd St, just sw on Webber St, then just se on W 8th St. Int corridors. **Pets:** Large, other species. $10 daily fee/pet. Designated rooms, service with restrictions, supervision.

The Dalles Inn H
(541) 296-9107. **$84-$169.** 112 W 2nd St 97058. I-84 exit 84 eastbound, 0.6 mi se; exit 85 westbound, 0.8 mi nw; at Liberty and W 2nd sts; downtown. Ext/int corridors. **Pets:** Dogs only. $10 daily fee/pet. Designated rooms, service with restrictions, crate.

TILLAMOOK

Ashley Inn of Tillamook H
(503) 842-7599. **Call for rates.** 1722 N Makinster Rd 97141. 1 mi n on US 101. Int corridors. **Pets:** Accepted.

Mar-Clair Inn M
(503) 842-7571. **$86-$106.** 11 Main Ave 97141. US 101, just n of jct SR 6. Ext/int corridors. **Pets:** Very small, dogs only. $10 daily fee/pet. Service with restrictions, supervision.

Shilo Inn Suites Hotel-Tillamook H
(503) 842-7971. **$69-$209.** 2515 N Main Ave 97141. 1 mi n on US 101. Int corridors. **Pets:** Dogs only. $25 one-time fee/room. Designated rooms, service with restrictions, supervision.

WARRENTON

Shilo Inn Suites Hotel - Warrenton/Astoria H
(503) 861-2181. **$69-$209.** 1609 E Harbor Dr 97146. On US 26/101; near west end of Youngs Bay Bridge. Int corridors. **Pets:** Dogs only. $25 one-time fee/room. Designated rooms, service with restrictions, supervision.

WELCHES

The Resort at The Mountain H
(503) 622-3101. **$119-$379, 5 day notice.** 68010 E Fairway Ave 97067. 0.6 mi s of US 26 on E Welches Rd. Ext corridors. **Pets:** Accepted.

WHITE CITY

Brookside Inn & Suites H
(541) 826-0800. **$80-$144.** 2020 Leigh Way 97503. I-5 exit 30, 5.6 mi ne on Crater Lake Hwy (SR 62), then just w. Int corridors. **Pets:** Designated rooms, service with restrictions, supervision.

WOODBURN

BEST WESTERN Woodburn H
(503) 982-6515. **Call for rates.** 2887 Newberg Hwy 97071. I-5 exit 271, just ne. Int corridors. **Pets:** $10 deposit/pet. Designated rooms, service with restrictions, crate.

La Quinta Inn & Suites Woodburn H
(503) 982-1727. **$71-$166.** 120 Arney Rd NE 97071. I-5 exit 271, just nw. Int corridors. **Pets:** Service with restrictions, supervision.

Super 8 - Woodburn H
(503) 981-8881. **$55-$89.** 821 Evergreen Rd 97071. I-5 exit 271, just se. Int corridors. **Pets:** Small, dogs only. $10 daily fee/pet. Designated rooms, service with restrictions, supervision.

YACHATS

The Adobe Resort H
(541) 547-3141. **$75-$405.** 1555 US 101 97498. 0.5 mi n; just w of US 101. Int corridors. **Pets:** Other species. $10 daily fee/pet. Designated rooms, service with restrictions.

The Dublin House Ⓜ
(541) 547-3703. **$49-$135, 3 day notice.** 251 W 7th St 97498. US 101 at 7th St; downtown. Ext corridors. **Pets:** Accepted.

Ⓐ Ⓦ Ⓦ Ⓦ **Fireside Motel** Ⓜ 🐾
(541) 547-3636. **$60-$150.** 1881 US 101 N 97498. 0.6 mi n; just w of US 101. Ext corridors. **Pets:** $10 daily fee/pet. Service with restrictions, supervision. SAVE

PENNSYLVANIA

CITY INDEX

ABBOTTSTOWN

Ⓦ Ⓦ Ⓦ **The Altland House Inn and Suites** Ⓒⓘ
(717) 259-9535. **Call for rates.** 35 Fleet St 17301. Jct SR 194. Int corridors. **Pets:** Accepted.

ALLENTOWN

Ⓐⓐⓐ Ⓦ Ⓦ **Allentown Howard Johnson Inn & Suites** Ⓗ
(610) 439-4000. **$49-$199.** 3220 Hamilton Blvd 18103. I-78 exit 54 (Hamilton Blvd), 0.8 mi n. Int corridors. **Pets:** Accepted.
SAVE

Ⓦ Ⓦ Ⓦ **Comfort Inn Lehigh Valley-West** Ⓗ
(610) 391-0344. **$89-$129.** 7625 Imperial Way 18106. I-78 exit 49B (SR 100), just n. Int corridors. **Pets:** Medium, other species. $25 one-time fee/room. Service with restrictions, crate.

Ⓦ Ⓦ Ⓦ **Days Inn & Suites Allentown Bethlehem Airport** Ⓗ
(610) 266-1000. **$80-$150.** 3400 Airport Rd 18109. On SR 987 N (Airport Rd), 0.5 mi n of jct US 22. Int corridors. **Pets:** Accepted.

Ⓦ Ⓦ Ⓦ **Holiday Inn-Allentown Center City** Ⓗ
(610) 433-2221. **$89-$149.** 904 Hamilton St 18101. At 9th and Hamilton sts; downtown. Int corridors. **Pets:** Small, other species. $50 one-time fee/pet. Designated rooms, service with restrictions, supervision.

Ⓦ Ⓦ Ⓦ **Staybridge Suites Allentown Bethlehem Airport** Ⓗ
(610) 443-5000. **Call for rates.** 1787-A Airport Rd 18109. US 22 exit Airport Rd S, 0.3 mi s. Int corridors. **Pets:** Accepted.

ALTOONA

Ⓦ Ⓦ Ⓦ **Holiday Inn Express Altoona** Ⓗ
(814) 944-9661. **$99-$134.** 3306 Pleasant Valley Blvd 16602. I-99 exit 32, 0.5 mi n, then just n. Int corridors. **Pets:** Medium. $75 one-time fee/pet. Designated rooms, service with restrictions, crate.

Ⓦ **Motel 6 #1415** Ⓜ
(814) 946-7601. **$51-$61.** 1500 Sterling St 16602. I-99 exit 31 (Plank Rd), just w. Ext corridors. **Pets:** Other species. Service with restrictions, supervision.

Ⓦ Ⓦ **Super 8 Altoona** Ⓜ
(814) 942-5350. **$59-$200.** 3535 Fairway Dr 16602. I-99 exit 32, just w. Int corridors. **Pets:** Small. $15 daily fee/pet. Service with restrictions, supervision.

BARKEYVILLE

Ⓐⓐⓐ Ⓦ Ⓦ **Quality Inn-Barkeyville** Ⓜ
(814) 786-7901. **Call for rates.** 137 Gibb Rd 16038. I-80 exit 29, just n on SR 8. Ext corridors. **Pets:** Medium. $10 one-time fee/room. Designated rooms, service with restrictions, supervision. SAVE

BEDFORD

Ⓐⓐⓐ Ⓦ Ⓦ Ⓦ **Omni Bedford Springs Resort & Spa** Ⓗ 🐾
(814) 623-8100. **Call for rates.** 2138 Business Rt 220 15522. I-70/76 (Pennsylvania Tpke) exit 146, 3.9 mi s. Int corridors. **Pets:** Large, other species. $100 one-time fee/pet. Designated rooms, service with restrictions. SAVE

Quality Inn Bedford 🅷

(814) 623-5188. **$79-$155.** 4407 Business Rt 220 N 15522. I-70/76 (Pennsylvania Tpke) exit 146, just n. Ext/int corridors. **Pets:** Medium, other species. $15 one-time fee/room. Designated rooms, service with restrictions, crate.

Travelodge Bedford 🅷

(814) 623-9006. **$75-$89.** 4517 Business Rt 220 15522. I-70/76 (Pennsylvania Tpke) exit 146, 0.3 mi n. Ext/int corridors. **Pets:** Medium, $50 deposit/room, $15 daily fee/room. Service with restrictions, supervision.

BETHEL

Comfort Inn-Bethel/Midway 🅷

(717) 933-8888. **$69-$135.** 41 Diner Dr 19507. I-78 exit 16, just w. Int corridors. **Pets:** Other species. $10 daily fee/pet. Designated rooms, service with restrictions, supervision.

BETHLEHEM

BEST WESTERN PLUS Lehigh Valley Hotel & Conference Center 🅷

(610) 866-5800. **$79-$169.** 300 Gateway Dr 18017. US 22 exit Center St and SR 512. Ext/int corridors. **Pets:** Accepted.

Comfort Inn 🅷

(610) 865-6300. **Call for rates.** 3191 Highfield Dr 18020. US 22 exit SR 191, just s. Ext/int corridors. **Pets:** Accepted.

Comfort Suites University 🅷

(610) 882-9700. **$99-$179.** 120 W 3rd St 18015. SR 378 exit 3rd St; jct W 3rd and Brodhead sts; center. Int corridors. **Pets:** Small. $20 daily fee/pet. Designated rooms, service with restrictions, crate.

Extended StayAmerica-Allentown/Bethlehem 🅷

(610) 866-8480. **$73-$119.** 3050 Schoenersville Rd 18017. US 22 exit SR 378/Schoenersville Rd, follow signs for Schoenersville Rd, just n. Int corridors. **Pets:** $25 daily fee/pet. Designated rooms, service with restrictions.

Historic Hotel Bethlehem 🅷 🐾

(610) 625-5000. **$129-$219.** 437 Main St 18018. SR 378 S exit 3 (City Center), just n on 3rd Ave, 0.3 mi e on Union, then 0.3 mi s. Int corridors. **Pets:** $75 one-time fee/room. Designated rooms, service with restrictions, supervision.

Homewood Suites - Allentown/Bethlehem Airport 🅷

(610) 264-7500. **Call for rates.** 2031 Avenue C 18017. US 22 exit SR 378/Schoenersville Rd, follow signs for Schoenersville Rd, 0.7 mi n. Int corridors. **Pets:** $75 one-time fee/room. Service with restrictions, crate.

Residence Inn by Marriott Allentown Bethlehem/ Lehigh Valley Airport 🅷

(610) 317-2662. **$109-$199.** 2180 Motel Dr 18018. US 22 exit Airport Rd S, 0.8 mi se on Catasauqua Rd. Int corridors. **Pets:** Accepted.

BLOOMSBURG

 Econo Lodge at Bloomsburg 🅷 🐾

(570) 387-0490. **$70-$130.** 189 Columbia Mall Dr 17815. I-80 exit 232 (SR 42), just n. Int corridors. **Pets:** Medium, dogs only. $15 daily fee/pet. Service with restrictions, crate.

The Inn at Turkey Hill 🅒 🐾

(570) 387-1500. **$135-$245.** 991 Central Rd 17815. I-80 exit 236 eastbound; exit 236A westbound, just s. Ext/int corridors. **Pets:** Other species. $25 daily fee/room. Designated rooms, service with restrictions, supervision.

BLUE MOUNTAIN

Kenmar Motel 🅼

(717) 423-5915. **$65-$90.** 17788 Cumberland Hwy 17240. I-76 exit 201, just e on SR 997 N. Ext corridors. **Pets:** Small, dogs only. $10 one-time fee/pet. Designated rooms, supervision.

BRADFORD

BEST WESTERN PLUS Bradford Inn 🅷

(814) 362-4501. **$115-$130.** 100 Davis St S 16701. US 219 exit Forman St southbound, just w to Davis St, then 0.3 mi s; exit Elm St northbound, just w. Ext/int corridors. **Pets:** $10 daily fee/pet. Designated rooms, service with restrictions, crate.

Comfort Inn-Bradford 🅷

(814) 368-6772. **$90-$120.** 76 Elm St 16701. US 219 exit Forman St southbound, just w to Davis St, then 0.3 mi s; exit Elm St northbound, just w. Int corridors. **Pets:** Other species. $10 daily fee/pet. Service with restrictions, crate.

Glendorn 🅒

(814) 362-6511. **$430-$2050, 7 day notice.** 1000 Glendorn Dr 16701. US 219 exit Forman St, just s on Mechanic St, then 4.3 mi w on W Corydon St. Ext/int corridors. **Pets:** Accepted.

BREEZEWOOD

BEST WESTERN Plaza Inn 🅼

(814) 735-4352. **$80-$99.** 16407 Lincoln Hwy 15533. I-76 (Pennsylvania Tpke) exit 161, just w on US 30; I-70 exit 147. Ext corridors. **Pets:** $10 daily fee/pet. Service with restrictions, crate.

Wiltshire Motel 🅼

(814) 735-4361. **$44-$54.** 140 S Breezewood Rd 15533. I-76 (Pennsylvania Tpke) exit 161, just w on US 30; I-70 exit 147. Ext corridors. **Pets:** Medium, other species. Service with restrictions, supervision.

BROOKVILLE

Super 8 🅼

(814) 849-8840. **$55-$145.** 251 Allegheny Blvd 15825. I-80 exit 78, just n on SR 36. Int corridors. **Pets:** Large, other species. $10 daily fee/pet. Service with restrictions, supervision.

BURNHAM

Quality Inn & Suites of Lewistown 🅼

(717) 248-4961. **Call for rates.** 13015 Ferguson Valley Rd 17009. US 322 exit Burnham, just w. Ext corridors. **Pets:** Medium, other species. $25 one-time fee/pet. Designated rooms, service with restrictions, supervision.

CAMP HILL

Radisson Hotel Harrisburg 🅷

(717) 763-7117. **$95-$189.** 1150 Camp Hill Bypass 17011. Jct US 11, 15 and Erford Rd. Ext/int corridors. **Pets:** Accepted.

CARLISLE

Comfort Suites Hotel 🅷 🐾

(717) 960-1000. **$135-$161, 3 day notice.** 10 S Hanover St 17013. I-81 exit 47, 0.8 mi n on SR 34, just s of square; downtown. Int corridors. **Pets:** Medium, other species. $20 daily fee/pet. Designated rooms, service with restrictions.

Country Inn & Suites By Carlson 🅷 🐾

(717) 241-4900. **$90-$199.** 1529 Commerce Ave 17015. I-81 exit 44 (Plainfield Rd), s on SR 465 (Allen Rd), then left. Int corridors. **Pets:** Other species. $25 daily fee/pet. Designated rooms, service with restrictions, crate.

Days Inn Carlisle-South H ❀
(717) 258-4147. **$79-$145.** 101 Alexander Spring Rd 17015. I-81 exit 45, just sw. Int corridors. **Pets:** Other species. $15 daily fee/room. Designated rooms, service with restrictions, supervision.
SAVE 🛜 ✕ 🐾M 🛗 💷 🏊

Fairfield Inn & Suites by Marriott Carlisle H
(717) 243-2080. **$119-$139.** 1528 E Commerce Ave 17015. I-81 exit 44 (Plainfield Rd), just s, then just e. Int corridors. **Pets:** Other species. $75 deposit/room. 🛜 ✕ 🐾M 🛗 💷 🏊

Hampton Inn Carlisle H ❀
(717) 240-0200. **$139-$199.** 1164 Harrisburg Pike 17013. I-76 (Pennsylvania Tpke) exit 226, just n; I-81 exit 52 (US 11) southbound; exit 52B northbound, 0.8 mi s. Int corridors. **Pets:** Medium. Service with restrictions, crate. SAVE 🛜 ✕ 🐾M 🛗 💷 🏊

Pheasant Field Bed & Breakfast BB ❀
(717) 258-0717. **$135-$255, 7 day notice.** 150 Hickorytown Rd 17015. I-76 (Pennsylvania Tpke) exit 226, 0.4 mi n on US 11, 2.3 mi right on S Middlesex Rd, 0.4 mi left on Ridge Dr, then right. Ext/int corridors. **Pets:** Other species. $10 daily fee/room. Designated rooms, service with restrictions, supervision. SAVE 🛜 ✕ 🛗 ✕ ✉

Quality Inn Carlisle H
(717) 243-6000. **$69-$179.** 1255 Harrisburg Pike 17013. I-76 (Pennsylvania Tpke) exit 226, 0.8 mi n. Int corridors. **Pets:** Medium. $20 daily fee/pet. Designated rooms, service with restrictions, supervision.
SAVE 🛜 🛗 💷 🏊

Residence Inn by Marriott Harrisburg Carlisle H ❀
(717) 610-9050. **$134-$359.** 1 Hampton Ct 17013. I-76 (Pennsylvania Tpke) exit 226, just n; I-81 exit 52 (US 11) southbound; exit 52B northbound, 0.8 mi s. Int corridors. **Pets:** Medium. $100 daily fee/room. Service with restrictions, crate. SAVE 🛜 ✕ 🐾M 🛗 💷 🏊 ✕

Sleep Inn Carlisle H
(717) 249-8863. **Call for rates.** 5 E Garland Dr 17013. I-81 exit 47 northbound, just ne; exit 47A southbound. Int corridors. **Pets:** Accepted.
🛜 🐾M 🛗 💷 🏊

Super 8/Carlisle South M
(717) 245-9898. **$49-$150.** 100 Alexander Spring Rd 17015. I-81 exit 45, just se. Int corridors. **Pets:** Medium. $10 daily fee/pet. Service with restrictions, crate. SAVE 🛜 🐾M 🛗 💷

CHAMBERSBURG

Americas Best Value Inn Chambersburg M ❀
(717) 264-8005. **$49-$149.** 1110 Sheller Ave 17201. I-81 exit 14, just w on SR 316. Int corridors. **Pets:** Other species. $15 daily fee/pet. Designated rooms, service with restrictions, supervision. 🛜 🛗

BEST WESTERN Chambersburg H
(717) 262-4994. **$70-$250.** 211 Walker Rd 17201. I-81 exit 16, just w on US 30, then just n. Int corridors. **Pets:** Accepted.
SAVE 🛜 🛗 💷 🏊

Country Inn & Suites By Carlson H
(717) 261-0900. **$89-$189.** 399 Bedington Blvd 17201. I-81 exit 17 (Walker Rd), 0.6 mi s, then just w. Int corridors. **Pets:** Other species. $15 one-time fee/pet. Designated rooms, service with restrictions, supervision.
🛜 🐾M 🛗 💷 🏊

Days Inn H
(717) 263-1288. **$60-$169.** 30 Falling Spring Rd 17202. I-81 exit 16, just e on US 30. Int corridors. **Pets:** Accepted. 🛜 🛗 💷 🏊

La Quinta Inn & Suites Chambersburg H
(717) 446-0770. **$83-$183.** 199 Walker Rd 17201. I-81 exit 16, just w on US 30, then just n. Int corridors. **Pets:** Service with restrictions, supervision. 🛜 ✕ 🛗 💷 🏊

Red Carpet Inn M
(717) 267-2323. **$80.** 1175 Wayne Ave 17201. I-81 exit 14, just e on SR 316. Ext corridors. **Pets:** Accepted. 🛜 🛗

Sleep Inn & Suites H
(717) 263-0596. **$69-$109.** 1435 Doron Dr 17202. I-81 exit 20, just w. Int corridors. **Pets:** Medium. $15 daily fee/pet. Designated rooms, service with restrictions, crate. 🛜 🐾M 🛗 💷 🏊

Super 8 H
(717) 264-6288. **$49-$150.** 3648 Old Scotland Rd 17202. I-81 exit 20, just e, then just n on SR 696. Int corridors. **Pets:** Medium. $10 daily fee/pet. Service with restrictions, crate. SAVE 🛜 🛗 💷

CLARION

Comfort Inn-Clarion H
(814) 226-5230. **Call for rates.** 129 Dolby St 16214. I-80 exit 62, 0.6 mi n on SR 68. Int corridors. **Pets:** Other species. $10 one-time fee/pet. Service with restrictions, supervision. 🛜 🛗 💷 🏊

Holiday Inn Clarion H
(814) 226-8850. **$109-$149.** 45 Holiday Inn Rd 16214. I-80 exit 62, 0.5 mi n on SR 68. Int corridors. **Pets:** $10 daily fee/room. Service with restrictions, crate. 🛜 🛗 💷 🍽 🏊

CLEARFIELD

Budget Inn M
(814) 765-2639. **$36-$79.** 6321 Clearfield Woodland Hwy (US 322 E) 16830. I-80 exit 120, 1.5 mi sw on SR 879, then 1.2 mi e. Ext/int corridors. **Pets:** Medium. $16 daily fee/pet. Designated rooms, service with restrictions, supervision. SAVE 🛜 🛗

Super 8-Clearfield M
(814) 768-7580. **$68-$86.** 14597 Clearfield/Shawville Hwy (Rt 879) 16830. I-80 exit 120, just s. Int corridors. **Pets:** Accepted.
🛜 🐾M 🛗 💷

COUDERSPORT

Westgate Inn H
(814) 274-0400. **$82-$99.** 307 Rt 6 W 16915. On US 6, 1 mi w. Int corridors. **Pets:** Small, dogs only. $15 daily fee/pet. Designated rooms, service with restrictions, supervision. 🛜 🛗 💷

DANVILLE

BEST WESTERN PLUS Danville Inn H
(570) 275-5750. **$90-$140.** 79 Old Valley School Rd 17821. I-80 exit 224, just s. Int corridors. **Pets:** Other species. $15 one-time fee/room. Service with restrictions, supervision. SAVE 🛜 🛗 💷 🏊

Danville Super 8 M
(570) 275-4640. **$59-$200, 3 day notice.** 35 Sheraton Rd 17821. I-80 exit 224, just sw on SR 54. Ext corridors. **Pets:** Medium. $15 one-time fee/room. Designated rooms, service with restrictions.
SAVE 🛜 🛗 💷

Quality Inn & Suites Danville M
(570) 275-5100. **$79-$189, 3 day notice.** 15 Valley West Rd 17821. I-80 exit 224, just n on SR 54. Int corridors. **Pets:** Medium. $25 one-time fee/room. Designated rooms, service with restrictions.
SAVE 🛜 🛗 💷 🏊

DICKSON CITY

Days Inn Scranton H
(570) 383-9979. **$66-$174.** 1946 Scranton-Carbondale Hwy 18508. I-81 exit 191A, 2 mi e on US 6; I-476 (Pennsylvania Tpke NE Ext) exit 131 (Clarks Summit), 4.5 mi e on US 6. Int corridors. **Pets:** Other species. $10 daily fee/pet. Designated rooms, service with restrictions, crate.
🛜 🛗 💷 🍽 🏊 ✕

Residence Inn by Marriott-Scranton H
(570) 343-5121. **$109-$249.** 947 Viewmont Dr 18519. I-81 exit 190, just e, follow signs to Viewmont Dr. Int corridors. **Pets:** Other species. $100 one-time fee/room. Designated rooms, service with restrictions.
🛜 ✕ 🛗 💷 🏊 ✕

DU BOIS

(AAA) ▼▼◆ BEST WESTERN PLUS Inn & Conference Center H ❖

(814) 371-6200. **$109-$119.** 82 N Park Pl 15801. I-80 exit 97 eastbound, 2.5 mi e on DuBois Ave (US 219/SR 255), then just s; exit 101 westbound, 2.7 mi w on DuBois Ave (US 219/SR 255), then just s on US 219. Int corridors. **Pets:** $12 daily fee/pet. Service with restrictions.

SAVE 🛜 🔌 🖥 ✕

DUNMORE

(AAA) ▼▼◆▼ BEST WESTERN PLUS Scranton East Hotel & Convention Center H ❖

(570) 343-4771. **$100-$140.** 200 Tigue St 18512. I-84/380 exit 1 (Tigue St), 0.3 mi e of jct I-81. Int corridors. **Pets:** Other species. $15 daily fee/pet. Designated rooms, service with restrictions, supervision.

SAVE 🛜 🔌 🖥 🍴 🏊 ✕

(AAA) ▼▼◆ Quality Inn H

(570) 348-6101. **$69-$149.** 1226 Oneill Hwy 18512. I-81 exit 188 (Throop), just e at SR 347 N (Oneill Hwy). Int corridors. **Pets:** Medium, other species. $15 daily fee/pet. Service with restrictions, crate.

SAVE 🛜 🔌 🖥

(AAA) ▼▼◆ Sleep Inn & Suites H ❖

(570) 961-1116. **Call for rates.** 102 Monahan Ave 18512. I-81 exit 188 (Throop), just e at SR 347 N (O'Neill Hwy), then just s. Int corridors. **Pets:** Small. $15 daily fee/pet. Designated rooms, service with restrictions, crate. SAVE 🛜 🔌 🖥 🏊

EASTON

▼▼◆▼ Grand Eastonian Suites Hotel H

(610) 258-6350. **$109-$239.** 140 N Northampton St 18042. US 22 exit 4th St (SR 611), just e to 3rd St, just s to downtown square, then just e towards river. Int corridors. **Pets:** Medium. $25 daily fee/room. Designated rooms, service with restrictions, crate. 🛜 ✕ 🔌 🖥 🏊

▼▼◆▼ The Lafayette Inn BB ❖

(610) 253-4500. **$150-$250.** 525 W Monroe St 18042. US 22 exit 4th St (SR 611), just n on 3rd St, 0.3 mi ne on College Ave, then 0.3 mi n on Cattell St to jct Monroe St. Ext/int corridors. **Pets:** $20 daily fee/room. Designated rooms, service with restrictions, supervision.

🛜 ✕ 🔌 🖥

(AAA) ▼▼◆▼ TownePlace Suites by Marriott - Bethlehem/Easton H

(610) 829-2000. **$119-$209.** 3800 Easton Nazareth Hwy 18045. SR 33 exit CR 248 (Nazareth/Wilson), 0.6 mi w. Int corridors. **Pets:** Medium, other species. $100 one-time fee/room. Service with restrictions, crate.

SAVE 🛜 ✕ 🔌 🖥 🏊

EBENSBURG

▼▼◆ Comfort Inn H

(814) 472-6100. **Call for rates.** 111 Cook Rd 15931. Jct US 219, just e on US 22. Int corridors. **Pets:** Accepted. 🛜 ✕ 🔌 🖥 🏊

ERIE

▼▼◆▼ Fairfield Inn by Marriott Erie H ❖

(814) 868-0985. **$119-$199.** 2082 Interchange Rd 16506. I-79 exit 180, just e; in Pavilion Marketplace. Int corridors. **Pets:** Other species. $25 one-time fee/room. Service with restrictions.

🛜 ✕ 🔌 🖥 🏊

▼▼◆▼ Homewood Suites by Hilton H

(814) 866-8292. **$140-$300.** 2084 Interchange Rd 16565. I-79 exit 180, just e; in Pavilion Marketplace. Int corridors. **Pets:** Other species. $75 one-time fee/room. Service with restrictions.

🛜 🔌 🖥 🏊

(AAA) ▼▼◆▼ La Quinta Inn & Suites H

(814) 864-1812. **$71-$210.** 7820 Perry Hwy 16509. I-90 exit 27, just n. Int corridors. **Pets:** Service with restrictions, supervision.

SAVE 🛜 ✕ 🔌 🖥 🏊

(AAA) ▼▼◆▼ Microtel Inn by Wyndham Erie M

(814) 864-1010. **$59-$119.** 8100 Peach St 16509. I-90 exit 24, just s. Int corridors. **Pets:** $10 daily fee/pet. Service with restrictions, crate.

SAVE 🛜 🔌 🖥

(AAA) ▼▼◆▼ Red Roof Inn #7054 M

(814) 868-5246. **$60-$199.** 7865 Perry Hwy 16509. I-90 exit 27, just n on SR 97. Ext/int corridors. **Pets:** Large, other species. Service with restrictions, supervision. SAVE 🛜 ✕ 🔌 🖥

(AAA) ▼▼◆▼ Sheraton Erie Bayfront Hotel H ❖

(814) 454-2005. **$119-$459, 3 day notice.** 55 West Bay Dr 16507. I-90 exit 22B to Bayfront Connector; I-79 to Bayfront Pkwy. Int corridors. **Pets:** Medium, dogs only. $50 one-time fee/room. Service with restrictions, supervision. SAVE 🛜 ✕ 🔌 🖥 🍴 🏊 ✕

▼▼◆▼ TownePlace Suites by Marriott Erie H

(814) 866-7100. **$110-$200.** 2090 Interchange Rd 16565. I-79 exit 180, just e; in Pavilion Marketplace. Int corridors. **Pets:** Accepted.

🛜 ✕ 🔌 🖥 🏊

▼▼◆▼ Wingate by Wyndham H

(814) 860-3050. **$109-$199.** 8060 Old Oliver Rd 16509. I-90 exit 24, just s on Peach St, just w, just n, then just e. Int corridors. **Pets:** Accepted.

🛜 ✕ 🔌 🖥 🏊

FOGELSVILLE

▼▼◆▼ Glasbern CI

(610) 285-4723. **$150-$485, 7 day notice.** 2141 Packhouse Rd 18051. I-78 exit 49B (SR 100), 0.3 mi n to 1st traffic light, 0.3 mi w on Main St, 0.6 mi n on Church St, then 0.8 mi ne. Ext corridors. **Pets:** Other species. $25 daily fee/room. Designated rooms, service with restrictions.

🛜 🔌 🖥 🍴 🏊

▼▼◆▼ Holiday Inn Conference Center H

(610) 391-1000. **$109-$159.** 7736 Adrienne Dr 18031. I-78 exit 49A, 0.3 mi s on SR 100. Int corridors. **Pets:** Accepted.

🛜 ✕ 🔌 🖥 🍴 🏊

▼▼◆ Sleep Inn H

(610) 395-6603. **$70-$160.** 327 Star Rd 18106. I-78 exit 49A, 0.3 mi s on SR 100, e at 1st traffic light, then n on service road. Int corridors. **Pets:** $15 daily fee/pet. Designated rooms, service with restrictions, supervision. 🛜 🔌 🖥

▼▼◆▼ Staybridge Suites-Allentown West H

(610) 841-5100. **Call for rates.** 327 Star Rd 18106. I-78 exit 49A, 0.3 mi s on SR 100, e at traffic light, then n on service road. Int corridors. **Pets:** Accepted. 🛜 🔌 🖥 🏊 ✕

FRANKLIN

▼▼◆ Franklin Super 8 H

(814) 432-2101. **$55-$125.** 847 Allegheny Blvd 16323. 2 mi n on SR 8. Int corridors. **Pets:** Accepted. 🛜 🔌 🖥

GETTYSBURG

▼▼◆▼ 1863 Inn of Gettysburg H

(717) 334-6211. **$99-$325.** 516 Baltimore St 17325. Jct US 15 business route and SR 97. Ext/int corridors. **Pets:** Other species. $21 daily fee/room. Designated rooms, service with restrictions, supervision.

🛜 ✕ 🔌 🖥 🏊

(AAA) ▼▼◆ Americas Best Value Inn M

(717) 334-1188. **$58-$168.** 301 Steinwehr Ave 17325. 1 mi s on US 15 business route, just s of jct SR 134. Ext/int corridors. **Pets:** Designated rooms, service with restrictions, crate. SAVE 🛜 ✕ 🔌 🖥 🏊

▼▼◆ Battlefield Bed & Breakfast Inn BB

(717) 334-8804. **Call for rates.** 2264 Emmitsburg Rd 17325. 4 mi s on Steinwehr Ave and Baltimore Pike. Int corridors. **Pets:** Dogs only. Service with restrictions. 🛜 ✕ 🐾

▼▼ Comfort Inn-Gettysburg M ❖
(717) 337-2400. **$70-$140.** 871 York Rd 17325. 1 mi e on US 30. Int corridors. **Pets:** Other species. $20 daily fee/pet. Designated rooms, service with restrictions. 📶 ✕ 🍴 📷 📺 🏊

▼▼ Country Inn & Suites By Carlson H
(717) 337-9518. **$89-$189.** 1857 Gettysburg Village Dr 17325. US 15 exit SR 97, just e. Int corridors. **Pets:** Accepted. 📶 ✕ 🍴 📷 📺 🏊

▼▼ Gettysburg Travelodge M
(717) 334-9281. **$79-$179.** 613 Baltimore St 17325. On SR 97; at US 15 business route. Ext/int corridors. **Pets:** Medium, other species. $10 daily fee/room. Designated rooms, service with restrictions, supervision.
📶 ✕ 🍴 📷

▲▲ ▼▼ Super 8 M
(717) 337-1400. **$49-$199.** 869 York Rd 17325. 1 mi e on US 30. Int corridors. **Pets:** Other species. $10 daily fee/pet. Service with restrictions, supervision. 🆂 📶 📶 🍴 📷 🏊

▲▲ ▼▼▼ Wyndham Gettysburg H
(717) 339-0020. **$89-$219.** 95 Presidential Cir 17325. US 15 exit York St, just e on US 30. Int corridors. **Pets:** Medium, dogs only. $20 daily fee/pet. Service with restrictions, crate. 🆂 📶 ✕ 📶 🍴 📷 📺 🏊

GRANTVILLE
▼▼ Days Inn Grantville-Hershey M
(717) 469-0631. **$65-$110.** 252 Bow Creek Rd 17028. I-81 exit 80, 0.3 mi s. Ext corridors. **Pets:** Accepted. 📶 🍴 📷 📺

▲▲ ▼▼▼ Holiday Inn Harrisburg-Hershey Area, I-81 H
(717) 469-0661. **$99-$199.** 604 Station Rd 17028. I-81 exit 80. Int corridors. **Pets:** Medium. $25 one-time fee/room. Service with restrictions, crate. 🆂 📶 📶 🍴 📷 📺 🍴 🏊 ✕

GREENCASTLE
▲▲ ▼▼▼ Comfort Inn H
(717) 597-8164. **$70-$170.** 50 Pine Dr 17225. I-81 exit 3, just s on US 11. Int corridors. **Pets:** Large, other species. $20 daily fee/room. Designated rooms, service with restrictions, supervision.
🆂 📶 🍴 📷 📺 🍴 ✕

HAMBURG
▼▼ Microtel Inn & Suites by Wyndham Hamburg H
(610) 562-4234. **$74-$118.** 50 Industrial Dr 19526. I-78 exit 29B, 0.3 mi n on SR 61, then just e. Int corridors. **Pets:** Accepted.
📶 📶 🍴 📷 📺 🍴

HARRISBURG
▼▼▼▼ Candlewood Suites Harrisburg/Hershey H ❖
(717) 652-7800. **$110-$180.** 504 N Mountain Rd 17112. I-81 exit 72B, 0.4 mi n. Int corridors. **Pets:** Other species. $25 one-time fee/pet. Service with restrictions. 📶 🍴 📷 📺

▲▲ ▼▼▼ Comfort Inn Hershey/Harrisburg H
(717) 657-2200. **$79-$189.** 5680 Allentown Blvd 17112. I-81 exit 72, just s on N Mountain Rd, then just w on US 22. Int corridors. **Pets:** Other species. $25 daily fee/pet. Service with restrictions, crate.
🆂 📶 ✕ 📶 🍴 📷 📺 🏊

▼▼▼ Comfort Inn Riverfront H ❖
(717) 233-1611. **$80-$200.** 525 S Front St 17104. I-83 exit 43, 0.5 mi n. Int corridors. **Pets:** Small. $25 daily fee/room. Designated rooms, service with restrictions, supervision. 📶 ✕ 🍴 📷 📺 🏊

▲▲ ▼▼▼ Econo Lodge H
(717) 540-9100. **Call for rates.** 7930 Linglestown Rd 17112. I-81 exit 77. Int corridors. **Pets:** Accepted. 🆂 📶 🍴 📷 📺

▲▲ ▼▼▼ Hilton Harrisburg H
(717) 233-6000. **$129-$229.** One N 2nd St 17101. Jct Market St; downtown. Int corridors. **Pets:** Large. $75 one-time fee/room. Service with restrictions. 🆂 📶 📶 🍴 📷 📺 🍴 🏊 ✕

▲▲ ▼▼▼ Holiday Inn Express East H
(717) 561-8100. **Call for rates.** 4021 Union Deposit Rd 17109. I-83 exit 48, just w. Int corridors. **Pets:** Medium. $15 daily fee/room. Service with restrictions, crate. 🆂 📶 🍴 📷 📺

▲▲ ▼▼▼ Holiday Inn Harrisburg East-Airport H
(717) 939-7841. **$99-$169.** 4751 Lindle Rd 17111. I-283 exit 2, just e. Int corridors. **Pets:** Large, other species. $75 deposit/room, $25 one-time fee/room. Service with restrictions, crate.
🆂 📶 ✕ 📶 🍴 📷 📺 🍴 🏊 ✕

▲▲ ▼▼▼ Ramada Harrisburg H
(717) 652-7180. **$65-$175.** 300 N Mountain Rd 17112. I-81 exit 72 southbound; exit 72B northbound, just s. Int corridors. **Pets:** Other species. $25 daily fee/room. Service with restrictions, crate.
🆂 📶 🍴 📷 📺 🏊

▲▲ ▼▼▼ Red Roof Inn- Harrisburg/Hershey #7027 M
(717) 939-1331. **$50-$126.** 950 Eisenhower Blvd 17111. I-283 exit 2, just e. Ext/int corridors. **Pets:** Large, other species. Service with restrictions, supervision. 🆂 📶 🍴 📷

▲▲ ▼▼▼ Red Roof Inn-North #7037 M
(717) 657-1445. **$49-$126.** 400 Corporate Cir 17110. I-81 exit 69 (Progress Ave), just n. Ext/int corridors. **Pets:** Large, other species. Service with restrictions, supervision. 🆂 📶 🍴 📷

▼▼▼ Residence Inn by Marriott Harrisburg-Hershey H
(717) 561-1900. **$149-$269.** 4480 Lewis Rd 17111. US 322 exit Penhar Dr, just e. Ext/int corridors. **Pets:** $100 one-time fee/room. Designated rooms, service with restrictions, crate. 📶 ✕ 🍴 📷 📺 🏊 ✕

▲▲ ▼▼▼ Sheraton Harrisburg Hershey H
(717) 564-5511. **$125-$249, 3 day notice.** 4650 Lindle Rd 17111. I-283 exit 2, just e. Int corridors. **Pets:** Accepted.
🆂 📶 ✕ 📶 🍴 📷 📺 🍴 🏊 ✕

▲▲ ▼▼▼ Staybridge Suites Harrisburg H ❖
(717) 233-3304. **$130-$190.** 920 Wildwood Park Dr 17110. I-81 exit 67A/B, just w. Int corridors. **Pets:** Medium. $75 one-time fee/room. Service with restrictions, supervision. 🆂 📶 ✕ 🍴 📷 📺 🏊

▲▲ ▼▼▼ TownePlace Suites by Marriott Harrisburg Hershey H ❖
(717) 558-0200. **$125-$269.** 450 Friendship Rd 17111. I-83 exit 45, 0.7 mi on Paxton St, then 0.3 mi s. Int corridors. **Pets:** Medium, other species. $100 one-time fee/room. Service with restrictions, crate.
🆂 📶 ✕ 🍴 📷 📺 🏊 ✕

HAZLETON
▲▲ ▼▼ BEST WESTERN Genetti Inn & Suites H ❖
(570) 454-2494. **$89-$99.** 1341 N Church St 18202. I-80 exit 262, 6 mi s on SR 309. Ext/int corridors. **Pets:** $10 daily fee/pet. Service with restrictions, crate. 🆂 📶 🍴 📷 🏊

▼▼▼ Ramada Inn Hazleton H
(570) 455-2061. **$70-$100.** 1213 N Church St 18202. I-80 exit 262, 6 mi s on SR 309; I-81 exit 145, 0.5 mi s on SR 93, 1 mi e on Airport Rd, then 0.7 mi s. Ext/int corridors. **Pets:** Accepted.
📶 🍴 📷 📺 🍴 🏊

▼▼▼ Residence Inn by Marriott - Hazleton H
(570) 455-9555. **$149-$289.** 1 New St 18202. I-81 exit 143, just s on SR 924 S; at Humboldt Station, just e on Commerce Dr. Int corridors.
Pets: Accepted. 📶 ✕ 📶 🍴 📷 📺 🏊 ✕

HERSHEY

△△△ ▼▼▼ BEST WESTERN Inn Hershey M ❖
(717) 533-5665. **$99-$299.** US 422 & Sipe Ave 17033. Jct US 322, just e. Ext/int corridors. **Pets:** $75 deposit/room, $20 daily fee/room. Designated rooms, service with restrictions, crate.

[SAVE] 🛜 ⊠ 🛏 🖵 ⊷ ⊠

△△△ ▼▼▼ Days Inn Hershey H ❖
(717) 534-2162. **$110-$290.** 350 W Chocolate Ave 17033. On US 422; center. Int corridors. **Pets:** Large, dogs only. $15 daily fee/pet. Designated rooms, service with restrictions, crate.

[SAVE] 🛜 ⊠ (&M) 🛏 🖵 ⊷ ⊠

△△△ ▼▼▼▼ Hampton Inn & Suites Hershey H
(717) 533-8400. **$119-$319.** 749 E Chocolate Ave 17033. 0.9 mi e on US 422. Int corridors. **Pets:** Small, dogs only. Designated rooms, service with restrictions, crate. [SAVE] 🛜 ⊠ (&M) 🛏 🖵 ⊷ ⊠

▼▼ Hershey Econo Lodge M ❖
(717) 533-2515. **$59-$175.** 115 Lucy Ave 17036. Jct US 322, just e on US 422. Ext corridors. **Pets:** Dogs only. $15 daily fee/pet. Service with restrictions. 🛜 🛏 🖵

HUNTINGDON

△△△ ▼▼▼ Comfort Inn H
(814) 643-1600. **$62-$95.** 100 S 4th St 16652. I-99 exit 48, 8.8 mi on SR 453, then 9.8 mi on US 22 and S 4th St; just off US 22. Int corridors. **Pets:** Medium, other species. $50 deposit/pet, $15 daily fee/pet. Designated rooms, service with restrictions, supervision.

[SAVE] 🛜 (&M) 🛏 🖵 ⊷

▼▼ Huntingdon Motor Inn M 🐾
(814) 643-1133. **$51-$85, 3 day notice.** 6920 Motor Inn Dr 16652. On US 22 at SR 26. Ext corridors. **Pets:** $10 daily fee/pet. Service with restrictions, supervision. 🛜 🛏 🖵

INDIANA (INDIANA COUNTY)

▼▼▼ Holiday Inn H ❖
(724) 463-3561. **$109-$159.** 1395 Wayne Ave 15701. US 422 exit Wayne Ave, 1 mi n. Ext/int corridors. **Pets:** Medium. $10 one-time fee/room. Designated rooms, service with restrictions, crate.

🛜 (&M) 🛏 🖵 (¶) ⊷

JOHNSTOWN

▼▼▼ Comfort Inn & Suites H
(814) 266-3678. **$99-$115.** 455 Theatre Dr 15904. US 219 exit Elton (SR 756), just e. Int corridors. **Pets:** $15 daily fee/pet. Designated rooms, service with restrictions, crate. 🛜 ⊠ (&M) 🛏 🖵 ⊷

▼▼ Econo Lodge M
(814) 536-1114. **Call for rates.** 430 Napoleon Pl 15901. Jct SR 271 and 403; downtown. Int corridors. **Pets:** Medium, other species. $10 daily fee/room. Designated rooms, service with restrictions, supervision.

🛜 (&M) 🛏

▼▼▼ Holiday Inn Downtown H
(814) 535-7777. **Call for rates.** 250 Market St 15901. Corner of Market and Vine sts; downtown. Int corridors. **Pets:** Accepted.

🛜 ⊠ (&M) 🛏 🖵 (¶) ⊷ ⊠

▼▼ Holiday Inn Express Johnstown M
(814) 266-8789. **Call for rates.** 1440 Scalp Ave 15904. US 219 exit Windber (SR 56 E), just e. Int corridors. **Pets:** Other species. $25 daily fee/pet. Service with restrictions, supervision. 🛜 (&M) 🛏 🖵

▼▼ Sleep Inn H
(814) 262-9292. **$89-$99.** 453 Theatre Dr 15904. US 219 exit Elton (SR 756), just e. Int corridors. **Pets:** Large. $15 daily fee/pet. Designated rooms, service with restrictions, crate. 🛜 ⊠ (&M) 🛏 🖵

△△△ ▼▼▼ Super 8 Johnstown H
(814) 535-5600. **$59-$200.** 627 Solomon Run Rd 15904. US 219 exit Galleria Dr, just w. Int corridors. **Pets:** Accepted. [SAVE] 🛜 🛏 🖵

JONESTOWN

▼▼ Days Inn Lebanon/Lickdale H
(717) 865-4064. **$75-$149.** 3 Everest Ln 17038. I-81 exit 90. Int corridors. **Pets:** Accepted. 🛜 🛏 🖵

▼▼ Quality Inn Jonestown M
(717) 865-6600. **$60-$120.** 16 Marsanna Ln 17038. I-81 exit 90, just w. Int corridors. **Pets:** Accepted. 🛜 🛏 🖵 ⊷

KITTANNING

▼▼ Quality Inn Royle H
(724) 543-1159. **Call for rates.** 405 Butler Rd 16201. SR 28 exit US 422 W. Ext/int corridors. **Pets:** Accepted. 🛜 ⊠ 🛏 🖵

LAMAR

▼▼ Comfort Inn of Lamar H
(570) 726-4901. **$92-$149.** 31 Hospitality Ln 17751. I-80 exit 173, just n on SR 64. Int corridors. **Pets:** Other species. Designated rooms, service with restrictions, crate. 🛜 🛏 🖵 ⊷

LAUREL HIGHLANDS AREA

CHALK HILL

△△△ ▼▼▼ The Lodge at Chalk Hill M
(724) 438-8880. **$70-$150.** Rt 40 E 15421. I-40 exit 14B, just w. Ext corridors. **Pets:** Medium, dogs only. $20 daily fee/pet. Designated rooms, service with restrictions. [SAVE] 🛜 🛏 🖵 ⊠

FARMINGTON

▼▼▼ Historic Summit Inn H
(724) 438-8594. **$139-$299, 3 day notice.** 101 Skyline Dr 15437. On US 40; center. Int corridors. **Pets:** Accepted.

🛜 🛏 🖵 (¶) ⊷ ⊠

△△△ ▼▼▼▼ Nemacolin Woodlands Resort H ❖
(724) 329-8555. **$255-$909, 14 day notice.** 1001 Lafayette Dr 15437. 1 mi e on US 40. Ext/int corridors. **Pets:** Medium, dogs only. $150 one-time fee/room. Designated rooms, service with restrictions, supervision.

[SAVE] 🛜 🖵 (¶) ⊷ ⊠

GREENSBURG

▼▼▼ Ramada Hotel and Conference Greensburg H
(724) 836-6060. **$85-$140.** 100 Sheraton Dr 15601. I-76 (Pennsylvania Tpke) exit 75, 5.6 mi on US 119 N, 3 mi e on US 30, then just n. Int corridors. **Pets:** Other species. $25 one-time fee/room. Designated rooms, service with restrictions, crate. 🛜 ⊠ (&M) 🛏 🖵 (¶) ⊷

JONES MILLS

▼▼ Log Cabin Lodge & Suites M
(724) 593-8200. **Call for rates.** 288 Rt 711 15646. I-76 (Pennsylvania Tpke) exit 91, 2 mi on SR 31 E, then just s. Ext corridors. **Pets:** Accepted. 🛜 (&M) 🛏 🖵

NEW STANTON

▼▼ Super 8-New Stanton M
(724) 925-8915. **$69-$84.** 103 Bair Blvd 15672. I-76 exit 75, 0.5 mi se; I-70 exit 57B westbound; exit 57 eastbound. Int corridors. **Pets:** Accepted.

🛜 (&M) 🛏 🖵

SOMERSET

▽ **Budget Host Inn** Ⓜ
(814) 445-7988. **$45-$95, 3 day notice.** 799 N Center Ave 15501.
I-70/76 (Pennsylvania Tpke) exit 110, 0.3 mi s. Ext corridors. **Pets:** Very
small. $10 daily fee/pet. Designated rooms, no service, supervision.
🛜 📶

AAA ▽▽▽ **Comfort Inn** Ⓗ
(814) 445-9611. **$90-$130.** 202 Harmon St 15501. I-70/76 (Pennsylvania
Tpke) exit 110, just s. Int corridors. **Pets:** Small. $35 one-time fee/room.
Designated rooms, service with restrictions, supervision.
SAVE 🛜 🆓 📶 🛗 🏊

▽ **Dollar Inn** Ⓜ
(814) 445-2977. **$40-$95.** 1146 N Center Ave 15501. I-70/76 (Pennsylvania Tpke) exit 110, 0.3 mi s, then just n on SR 601/N Central Ave; at top
of hill. Ext corridors. **Pets:** Medium, dogs only. $7 daily fee/pet. Desig-
nated rooms, service with restrictions, crate. 🛜 📶

▽▽ **Glades Pike Inn** 🅱🅱
(814) 443-4978. **$75-$125, 3 day notice.** 2684 Glades Pike Rd 15501.
I-70/76 (Pennsylvania Tpke) exit 110, 6 mi w on SR 31; exit 91, 13 mi e
on SR 31. Int corridors. **Pets:** No service, crate. 🛜 ✖ ✖ ⓩ

UNIONTOWN

▽▽ **Uniontown Holiday Inn** Ⓗ
(724) 437-2816. **Call for rates.** 700 W Main St 15401. 1.8 mi w on US
40. Int corridors. **Pets:** Medium. $10 daily fee/pet. Designated rooms,
service with restrictions, supervision.
🛜 🆓 📶 🛗 🍽 🏊 ✖

END AREA

LEBANON (LEBANON COUNTY)

▽▽▽ **Berry Patch Bed and Breakfast** 🅱🅱 🐾
(717) 865-7219. **$125-$229, 14 day notice.** 115 Moore Rd 17046. I-81
exit 90, 2.8 mi s on SR 72, 1 mi e on New Bunker Hill St, 0.8 mi s on S
Lancaster St, just e, then follow signs. Ext/int corridors. **Pets:** Dogs only.
$25 one-time fee/pet. Designated rooms, service with restrictions, crate.
🛜 ✖ 📶

LINCOLN FALLS

▽▽▽ **Morgan Century Farm** 🅱🅱
(570) 924-4909. **$110-$149, 5 day notice.** 7043 Rt 154 18616. In village. Ext/int corridors. **Pets:** Medium. $15 one-time fee/pet. Designated
rooms, service with restrictions, supervision. 🛜 📶 🛗 ⓩ

LOCK HAVEN

AAA ▽▽▽ **BEST WESTERN Lock Haven** Ⓗ
(570) 748-3297. **$109-$189.** 101 E Walnut St 17745. US 220 exit 111
(SR 120 W), just w. Int corridors. **Pets:** $10 daily fee/pet. Service with
restrictions, supervision. SAVE 🛜 📶 🛗

MANSFIELD

AAA ▽▽▽ **Comfort Inn** Ⓗ
(570) 662-3000. **$99-$179.** 300 Gateway Dr 16933. Jct US 6 and 15. Int
corridors. **Pets:** Accepted. SAVE 🛜 📶 🛗 ✖

MARIENVILLE

▽ **The Forest Lodge & Campground** Ⓜ 🐾
(814) 927-8790. **$40-$85, 14 day notice.** 44078 Rt 66 16239. 6 mi n of
town. Ext/int corridors. **Pets:** Other species. $10 daily fee/pet. Designated
rooms, service with restrictions, supervision. 📶 🛗

MEADVILLE

▽▽ **Quality Inn Meadville** Ⓜ
(814) 333-8883. **$69-$99.** 17259 Conneaut Lake Rd 16335. I-79 exit
147B, just w on US 322. Ext/int corridors. **Pets:** Medium. $10 daily fee/
pet. Service with restrictions, crate. 🛜 📶 🛗

MECHANICSBURG

▽▽ **Comfort Inn Capital City** Ⓗ 🐾
(717) 766-3700. **$79-$139.** 1012 Wesley Dr 17055. I-76 (Pennsylvania
Tpke) exit 236, 1 mi n to Wesley Dr exit, then just w. Int corridors.
Pets: Other species. $25 daily fee/pet. Service with restrictions, crate.
🛜 🆓 📶 🛗 🏊

▽▽ **Comfort Inn West** Ⓗ 🐾
(717) 790-0924. **$79-$149.** 6325 Carlisle Pike 17050. Jct Carlisle Pike
and US 11, 1 mi w on US 11. Int corridors. **Pets:** Medium. $25 daily
fee/pet. Service with restrictions, supervision. 🛜 📶 🛗

▽▽ **Hampton Inn-Harrisburg West** Ⓗ
(717) 691-1300. **$110-$189.** 4950 Ritter Rd 17055. I-76 (Pennsylvania
Tpke) exit 236, 1 mi n to Rossmoyne Rd exit. Int corridors. **Pets:** Other
species. Designated rooms, service with restrictions, supervision.
🛜 🆓 📶 🛗 🏊

▽▽ **Homewood Suites by Hilton-Harrisburg West** Ⓗ
(717) 697-4900. **$149-$209.** 5001 Ritter Rd 17055. I-76 (Pennsylvania
Tpke) exit 236, 1 mi n to Rossmoyne Rd exit. Int corridors. **Pets:** $50
one-time fee/room. Designated rooms, service with restrictions, crate.
ECO 🛜 🆓 📶 🛗 🏊 ✖

▽▽ **Park Inn by Radisson Harrisburg West** Ⓗ
(717) 697-0321. **$99-$179.** 5401 Carlisle Pike 17050. Jct Carlisle Pike
and US 11, just w. Ext/int corridors. **Pets:** Medium. $25 one-time fee/
room. Service with restrictions, crate. 🛜 📶 🛗 🍽 🏊 ✖

MERCER

▽▽ **Comfort Inn Mercer** Ⓗ
(724) 748-3030. **$85-$92.** 835 Perry Hwy 16137. I-80 exit 15, just n on
US 19. Int corridors. **Pets:** Accepted. 🛜 📶 🛗 🏊 ✖

MIFFLINVILLE

▽▽ **Super 8 - Mifflinville** Ⓜ
(570) 759-6778. **$59-$150.** 450 W 3rd St 18631. I-80 exit 242 (SR 339),
just n. Ext corridors. **Pets:** $10 one-time fee/room. Service with restric-
tions, supervision. 🛜 📶 🛗

MILROY

AAA ▽▽▽ **BEST WESTERN Nittany Inn Milroy** Ⓗ
(717) 667-9595. **Call for rates.** 5 Commerce Dr 17063. US 322 exit
Milroy, just e. Int corridors. **Pets:** Accepted.
SAVE 🛜 ✖ 📶 🛗 🍽 🏊

MONTGOMERY

AAA ▽ **White Deer Motel** Ⓜ
(570) 547-1007. **$50-$120.** 6967 SR 15 17752. Jct SR 54, 1.4 mi s. Ext
corridors. **Pets:** Medium. Designated rooms, service with restrictions,
supervision. SAVE 🛜 ✖ 📶 🛗

MORGANTOWN

▽▽▽ **Holiday Inn** Ⓗ
(610) 286-3000. **$85-$145.** 6170 Morgantown Rd 19543. I-76 exit 298,
just s on SR 10. Int corridors. **Pets:** Medium. $25 daily fee/pet. Desig-
nated rooms, service with restrictions, supervision.
🛜 📶 🛗 🍽 🏊 ✖

NEW CASTLE

▼▼ Comfort Inn-New Castle [H]

(724) 658-7700. **$84-$114.** 1740 New Butler Rd (US Business 422) 16101. Jct SR 65, 1 mi e on US 422, then 1 mi w on US 422 business route. Int corridors. **Pets:** Small, dogs only. $20 deposit/pet, $6 daily fee/pet. Service with restrictions, supervision. 🛜 🛗 📺

NEW COLUMBIA

◈ ▼▼▼ Holiday Inn Express [H]

(570) 568-1100. **$109-$159.** 160 Commerce Park Dr 17856. I-80 exit 210A (US 15/New Columbia), just s. Int corridors. **Pets:** Small, other species. $20 daily fee/pet. Designated rooms, service with restrictions, crate. 🆂 🛜 ❌ 🔧 🛗 📺 ➰

◈ ▼▼ New Columbia Comfort Inn [H]

(570) 568-8000. **Call for rates.** 330 Commerce Park Dr 17856. I-80 exit 210A (US 15/New Columbia), just s. Int corridors. **Pets:** Other species. 🆂 🛜 ❌ 🔧 🛗 📺 🍴 ➰

NEW CUMBERLAND

◈ ▼▼▼ Clarion Hotel & Conference Center Harrisburg [H]

(717) 774-2721. **Call for rates.** 148 Sheraton Dr 17070. I-83 exit 40A, just se. Int corridors. **Pets:** Medium. $10 daily fee/room. Service with restrictions, crate. 🆂 🛜 🔧 🛗 📺 🍴 ➰

▼▼ Days Inn Harrisburg South [H]

(717) 774-4156. **$65-$120.** 353 Lewisberry Rd 17070. I-83 exit 39A, just ne. Int corridors. **Pets:** Accepted. 🛜 🔧 🛗 📺 ➰

PENNSYLVANIA DUTCH COUNTRY AREA

ADAMSTOWN

▼▼▼ Adamstown Inns & Cottages [BB]

(717) 484-0800. **$139-$270, 14 day notice.** 144 W Main St 19501. Center. Ext/int corridors. **Pets:** Dogs only. $50 one-time fee/pet. Designated rooms, no service, crate. 🛜 ❌ 🔧 🔲

AKRON

▼▼▼ Boxwood Inn [BB]

(717) 859-3466. **Call for rates.** 1320 Diamond St 17501. SR 272, 0.4 mi se on Main St to Diamond St, then 0.3 mi s. Ext/int corridors. **Pets:** Accepted. 🛜 ❌ 🔧 🛗 📺 🔲

BIRD-IN-HAND

▼▼ Amish Country Motel [M]

(717) 768-8396. **$79-$115.** 3013 Old Philadelphia Pike (Rt 340) 17505. On SR 340, 1 mi e. Ext corridors. **Pets:** Small, other species. $100 deposit/room, $50 one-time fee/pet. Designated rooms, service with restrictions, crate. 🛜 ❌ 🔧 ➰

DENVER

▼▼▼ Comfort Inn Lancaster County North [H]

(717) 336-7541. **$90-$130.** 1 Denver Rd 17517. I-76 (Pennsylvania Tpke) exit 286, 1 mi w to SR 272, then just s. Int corridors. **Pets:** Other species. $5 one-time fee/pet. Service with restrictions, supervision. 🛜 🛗ᴹ 🔧 🛗 📺 🍴 ➰

▼▼ Red Roof Inn [H]

(717) 336-4649. **$40-$160.** 2017 N Reading Rd 17517. I-76 (Pennsylvania Tpke) exit 286, 1 mi w to SR 272, then just s. Int corridors. **Pets:** Large, other species. Service with restrictions, supervision. 🛜 🔧 📺

ELIZABETHTOWN

◈ ▼▼ Holiday Inn Express Elizabethtown (Hershey Area) [H]

(717) 367-4000. **Call for rates.** 147 Merts Dr 17022. SR 283 exit Elizabethtown/Rheems. Int corridors. **Pets:** Large, other species. $25 daily fee/pet. Designated rooms, service with restrictions, crate. 🆂 🛜 🛗ᴹ 🔧 📺

GORDONVILLE

◈ ▼▼▼ Motel 6-Lancaster #4174 [M]

(717) 687-3880. **Call for rates.** 2959 Lincoln Hwy E 17529. On US 30 (Lincoln Hwy); center. Int corridors. **Pets:** Other species. Service with restrictions, supervision. 🆂 🛜 🛗ᴹ 🔧

LANCASTER

◈ ▼▼▼ BEST WESTERN PREMIER Eden Resort & Suites [H]

(717) 569-6444. **$140-$200.** 222 Eden Rd 17601. Jct US 30 (Lincoln Hwy) and SR 272 (Oregon Pike). Ext/int corridors. **Pets:** Large, other species. $15 daily fee/pet. Designated rooms, service with restrictions, crate. 🆂 🛜 ❌ 🛗ᴹ 🔧 📺 🍴 ➰ ❌

◈ ▼▼▼ Hawthorn Suites by Wyndham [H]

(717) 290-7100. **$89-$170.** 2045 Lincoln Hwy 17602. Jct US 30 (Lincoln Hwy E). Int corridors. **Pets:** Accepted. 🆂 🛜 ❌ 🔧 📺

◈ ▼▼ Lancaster Red Roof Inn [M]

(717) 299-9700. **$56-$139.** 2307 Lincoln Hwy E 17602. On US 30 (Lincoln Hwy), 5 mi e. Ext/int corridors. **Pets:** Large, other species. Service with restrictions, supervision. 🆂 🛜 ❌ 🛗ᴹ 🔧 📺 ➰

LITITZ

◈ ▼▼▼ Holiday Inn Express Suites [H]

(717) 625-2366. **$110-$175.** 101 Crosswinds Dr 17543. 1.4 mi s on SR 501 (Lititz Pike), then just w on Trolley Run Rd. Int corridors. **Pets:** Medium, other species. $25 one-time fee/pet. Service with restrictions, supervision. 🆂 🛜 🛗ᴹ 🔧 📺 ➰

MOUNTVILLE

◈ ▼▼ MainStay Suites [H]

(717) 285-2500. **$89-$169.** 314 Primrose Ln 17554. US 30 (Lincoln Hwy) exit Mountville, just n on Stoney Battery Rd, just w on Highland Dr, then just s. Int corridors. **Pets:** Medium. $10 daily fee/pet. Service with restrictions, crate. 🆂 🛜 🛗ᴹ 🔧 📺 ➰

RONKS

◈ ▼▼▼ La Quinta Inn & Suites [H]

(717) 392-8100. **$84-$221.** 25 Eastbrook Rd 17572. Jct US 30 (Lincoln Hwy), just n on SR 896. Int corridors. **Pets:** Service with restrictions, supervision. 🆂 🛜 ❌ 🛗ᴹ 🔧 📺 ➰

STRASBURG

▼▼ Carriage House Motor Inn [M]

(717) 687-7651. **$49-$109.** 144 E Main St 17579. 0.3 mi e on SR 896 and 741. Ext corridors. **Pets:** Accepted. 🛜 ❌ 🔧 📺

END AREA

PHILADELPHIA METROPOLITAN AREA

AUDUBON

Homewood Suites by Hilton 🅷 ❀
(610) 539-7300. **$99-$209.** 681 Shannondell Blvd 19403. I-422 exit Trooper Rd, 1.2 mi n. Int corridors. **Pets:** Other species. $75 one-time fee/pet. Designated rooms, service with restrictions, crate.
[SAVE] 🛜 Ⓜ 🛏 💻 🏊 ✕

BENSALEM

Extended StayAmerica-Philadelphia/Bensalem 🅷
(215) 633-6900. **$95-$139.** 3216 Tillman Dr 19020. I-95 exit 37 (SR 132), 2.5 mi w, then just s; I-276 (Pennsylvania Tpke) exit 351, 0.9 mi on US 1, 1.4 mi e, then just s. Int corridors. **Pets:** $25 daily fee/pet. Designated rooms, service with restrictions. 🛜 Ⓜ 🛏 💻

Holiday Inn-Philadelphia Northeast 🅷
(215) 638-1500. **$99-$139.** 3499 Street Rd 19020. I-276 (Pennsylvania Tpke) exit 351, just s on US 1, then 0.3 mi e on SR 132/Street Rd. Ext/int corridors. **Pets:** Medium. $25 one-time fee/pet. Designated rooms, service with restrictions, crate. [SAVE] 🛜 🛏 💻 🍴 🏊

Sleep Inn & Suites-Bensalem 🅷
(215) 244-2300. **Call for rates.** 3427 Street Rd 19020. I-276 (Pennsylvania Tpke) exit 351, just s on US 1, then 0.3 mi e on SR 132. Int corridors. **Pets:** Accepted. [SAVE] 🛜 Ⓜ 🛏 💻

BERWYN

Residence Inn by Marriott Philadelphia-Valley Forge 🅷
(610) 640-9494. **$99-$249.** 600 W Swedesford Rd 19312. US 202 exit Paoli/SR 252, 1 mi n. Ext corridors. **Pets:** Large, other species. $100 one-time fee/room. Service with restrictions, supervision.
[ECO] 🛜 ✕ Ⓜ 🛏 💻 🏊 ✕

CHADDS FORD

Brandywine River Hotel 🅷 ❀
(610) 388-1200. **Call for rates.** 1609 Baltimore Pike, Bldg 300 19317. Jct US 1 (Baltimore Pike) and SR 100, 2 mi w of US 202 (Wilmington Pike). Int corridors. **Pets:** $150 deposit/room, $45 daily fee/pet. Designated rooms, crate. 🛜 ✕ 🛏 💻

CHESTER

BEST WESTERN PLUS Philadelphia Airport South at Widener University 🅷
(610) 872-8100. **Call for rates.** 1450 Providence Ave (SR 320) 19013. I-95 exit 6, just e to SR 320, follow signs. Int corridors. **Pets:** Medium, other species. $20 one-time fee/room. Service with restrictions.
[SAVE] 🛜 ✕ 🛏 💻

CONSHOHOCKEN

Residence Inn by Marriott Philadelphia/Conshohocken 🅷
(610) 828-8800. **$109-$239.** 191 Washington St 19428. I-76 (Schuylkill Expwy) exit 332 (SR 23), 0.3 mi over Fayette Bridge to Elm St, then just se along river. Int corridors. **Pets:** Accepted.
🛜 ✕ Ⓜ 🛏 💻 🏊 ✕

EAST NORRITON

Hyatt house Philadelphia/Plymouth Meeting 🅷 ❀
(610) 313-9990. **$109-$239.** 501 E Germantown Pike 19401. I-476 exit 20, 2.5 mi w. Int corridors. **Pets:** Medium. $200 one-time fee/room. Service with restrictions, crate. [SAVE] 🛜 ✕ 🛏 💻 🏊

ERWINNA

Golden Pheasant Inn 🅲🅸
(610) 294-9595. **$175-$295, 21 day notice.** 763 River Rd 18920. SR 32, 0.5 mi n of jct Dark Hollow Rd. Int corridors. **Pets:** Accepted.
🛜 ✕ 🛏 💻 🍴 🇿

ESSINGTON

Red Roof Inn-Airport #7119 Ⓜ
(610) 521-5090. **$61-$109.** 49 Industrial Hwy 19029. I-95 exit 9A, 0.3 mi sw on SR 291. Ext corridors. **Pets:** Large, other species. Service with restrictions, supervision. [SAVE] 🛜 Ⓜ 🛏 💻

FORT WASHINGTON

BEST WESTERN Fort Washington Inn 🅷
(215) 542-7930. **$85-$95.** 285 Commerce Dr 19034. I-276 (Pennsylvania Tpke) exit 339 (SR 309 S), just w on Pennsylvania Ave, just n to Commerce Dr, then 0.3 mi e. Int corridors. **Pets:** Medium. $15 daily fee/pet. Designated rooms, service with restrictions, crate.
[SAVE] 🛜 🛏 💻 🏊

Hilton Garden Inn Philadelphia/Fort Washington 🅷
(215) 646-4637. **$109-$209.** 530 W Pennsylvania Ave 19034. I-276 (Pennsylvania Tpke) exit 339 (SR 309 S), just w. Int corridors.
Pets: Accepted. 🛜 Ⓜ 🛏 💻 🍴 🏊

Holiday Inn Fort Washington Hotel & Conference Center 🅷
(215) 643-3000. **$99-$169.** 432 W Pennsylvania Ave 19034. I-276 (Pennsylvania Tpke) exit 339, just w. Int corridors. **Pets:** Medium. $45 one-time fee/room. Service with restrictions. [SAVE] 🛜 Ⓜ 🛏 💻 🍴 🏊

GLEN MILLS

Sweetwater Farm Bed & Breakfast 🅱🅱
(610) 459-4711. **$150-$370, 14 day notice.** 50 Sweetwater Rd 19342. US 1, 2 mi w on Valley Rd, then 0.6 mi s. Int corridors. **Pets:** Accepted.
🛜 ✕ 🛏 💻 🏊 ✕

HORSHAM

Days Inn-Horsham/Philadelphia 🅷
(215) 674-2500. **$50-$130.** 245 Easton Rd 19044. I-276 (Pennsylvania Tpke) exit 343 (SR 611), 1 mi n. Int corridors. **Pets:** Other species. $10 daily fee/pet. Designated rooms, service with restrictions, crate.
[SAVE] 🛜 🛏 💻

Extended StayAmerica-Philadelphia/Horsham 🅷
(215) 784-9045. **$89-$134.** 114 Welsh Rd 19044. I-276 (Pennsylvania Tpke) exit 343 (SR 611), s toward Jenkintown, 0.6 mi w on Maryland Rd, 0.5 mi sw on Computer Ave, then just n. Int corridors. **Pets:** $25 daily fee/pet. Designated rooms, service with restrictions. 🛜 Ⓜ 🛏 💻

Residence Inn by Marriott-Willow Grove 🅷
(215) 443-7330. **$139-$290.** 3 Walnut Grove Dr 19044. I-276 (Pennsylvania Tpke) exit 343, 1 mi n on Easton Rd, then 1.3 mi w on Dresher Rd; in Pennsylvania Business Campus. Ext corridors. **Pets:** Accepted.
🛜 ✕ Ⓜ 🛏 💻 🏊 ✕

KING OF PRUSSIA

Hyatt house Philadelphia/King of Prussia 🅷
(610) 265-0300. **$109-$379.** 240 Mall Blvd 19406. I-76 (Pennsylvania Tpke) exit 326 (Valley Forge), 1 mi n of jct US 202 on Gulph Rd. Int corridors. **Pets:** Accepted. [SAVE] 🛜 ✕ Ⓜ 🛏 💻 🍴 🏊

◇◇◇ ▼▼▼▼ Sheraton Valley Forge 🅷 ❀
(484) 238-1800. **Call for rates.** 480 N Gulph Rd 19406. I-76 (Pennsylvania Tpke) exit 326, 0.5 mi w. Int corridors. **Pets:** Medium, dogs only. Designated rooms, supervision. [SAVE] 🛜 ✕ ⅙M 🯄 🖵 ⚊

KULPSVILLE

▼▼▼ Holiday Inn Lansdale 🅷
(215) 368-3800. **$99-$149.** 1750 Sumneytown Pike 19443. I-476 exit 31, just e. Int corridors. **Pets:** Other species. $20 daily fee/pet. Service with restrictions. 🛜 ⅙M 🯄 🖵 ⚊

LANGHORNE

◇◇◇ ▼▼▼▼ Residence Inn by Marriott Philadelphia Langhorne 🅷
(215) 946-6500. **$139-$309.** 15 E Cabot Blvd 19047. I-95 exit 46A (Oxford Valley Rd), just e off US 1 N; 0.5 mi n of Sesame Place. Int corridors. **Pets:** Accepted. [SAVE] 🛜 ✕ ⅙M 🯄 🖵 ⚊ ☒

◇◇◇ ▼▼▼▼ Sheraton Bucks County Hotel 🅷 ❀
(215) 547-4100. **$99-$259.** 400 Oxford Valley Rd 19047. I-95 exit 46A (Oxford Valley Rd), 0.8 mi e to exit off US 1 N; opposite Sesame Place. Int corridors. **Pets:** Medium, dogs only. Designated rooms, service with restrictions, crate. [SAVE] 🛜 ✕ ⅙M 🯄 🖵 ⚊ ☒

LIONVILLE

▼▼▼ Comfort Suites 🅷
(610) 594-4770. **$99-$149.** 700 W Uwchlan Ave 19341. I-76 (Pennsylvania Tpke) exit 312, 1 mi s on SR 100. Int corridors. **Pets:** Accepted.
🛜 ✕ ⅙M 🯄 🖵 ⚊

▼▼ Extended StayAmerica-Philadelphia/Exton 🅷
(610) 524-7185. **$104-$139.** 877 N Pottstown Pike (Rt 100) 19353. I-76 (Pennsylvania Tpke) exit 312, 1.8 mi s. Int corridors. **Pets:** $25 daily fee/pet. Designated rooms, service with restrictions. 🛜 🯄 🖵

▼▼▼ Hampton Inn Exton 🅷 ❀
(610) 363-5555. **$119-$179.** 4 N Pottstown Pike 19341. I-76 (Pennsylvania Tpke) exit 312, 0.5 mi s; jct SR 113 and 100. Int corridors. **Pets:** Large. Service with restrictions, crate. 🛜 ⅙M 🯄 🖵 ⚊

▼▼▼ Residence Inn by Marriott Philadelphia Great Valley/Exton 🅷
(610) 594-9705. **$169-$239.** 10 N Pottstown Pike 19341. I-76 (Pennsylvania Tpke) exit 312, 1 mi s on SR 100. **Pets:** Other species. $100 one-time fee/room. Service with restrictions.
🛜 ✕ 🯄 🖵 ⚊ ☒

▼▼▼▼ Wyndham Garden Exton Valley Forge 🅷
(610) 363-1100. **$99-$139.** 815 N Pottstown Pike 19341. I-76 (Pennsylvania Tpke) exit 312, 2 mi s on SR 100. Int corridors. **Pets:** Dogs only. $25 daily fee/pet. Designated rooms, service with restrictions, supervision. 🛜 ✕ 🯄 🖵 ⚊

MALVERN

▼▼▼▼ The Desmond Hotel and Conference Center Malvern 🅷
(610) 296-9800. **$169-$249.** 1 Liberty Blvd 19355. US 202 exit SR 29 N, 0.5 mi w. Int corridors. **Pets:** Accepted.
🛜 ✕ 🯄 🖵 ⚊ ☒

▼▼ Extended StayAmerica-Philadelphia/Malvern 🅷
(610) 240-0455. **$104-$139.** 300 Morehall Rd (SR 29) 19355. US 202 exit SR 29 N. Int corridors. **Pets:** $25 daily fee/pet. Designated rooms, service with restrictions. 🛜 ⅙M 🯄 🖵

▼▼▼ Homestead Studio Suites Hotel Philadelphia-Malvern 🅷
(610) 695-9200. **$99-$149.** 8 E Swedesford Rd 19355. Just w of US 202 and SR 29 N. Int corridors. **Pets:** $25 daily fee/pet. Designated rooms, service with restrictions. 🛜 🯄 🖵 ⚊

◇◇◇ ▼▼▼▼ Homewood Suites by Hilton 🅷
(610) 296-3500. **$109-$209.** 12 E Swedesford Rd 19355. US 202 exit SR 29, follow signs. Int corridors. **Pets:** $50 one-time fee/room. Service with restrictions, crate. 🛜 ⅙M 🯄 🖵

◇◇◇ ▼▼▼▼ Sheraton Great Valley Hotel 🅷 ❀
(610) 524-5500. **$99-$199.** 707 Lancaster Pike 19355. Jct US 202 and 30 E. Int corridors. **Pets:** Medium, dogs only. Service with restrictions, supervision. [SAVE] 🛜 ✕ ⅙M 🯄 🖵 ⚊

◇◇◇ ▼▼▼▼ Sonesta ES Suites Malvern 🅷
(610) 296-4343. **Call for rates.** 20 Morehall Rd 19355. Jct US 30 and SR 29, just nw. Ext/int corridors. **Pets:** Accepted.
[SAVE] 🛜 🯄 🖵 ⚊ ☒

MONTGOMERYVILLE

▼▼▼ Comfort Inn 🅷
(215) 361-3600. **Call for rates.** 678 Bethlehem Pike 18936. Jct SR 463 and US 202, 0.3 mi n on SR 309. Int corridors. **Pets:** Accepted.
🛜 🯄 🖵

▼▼▼ Residence Inn by Marriott Philadelphia/Montgomeryville 🅷
(267) 468-0111. **$129-$289.** 1110 Bethlehem Pike 19454. I-276 (Pennsylvania Tpke) exit 339, 6.5 mi n on SR 309. Int corridors. **Pets:** Accepted.
🛜 ✕ 🯄 🖵 ⚊ ☒

▼▼▼ Rodeway Inn 🅷
(215) 699-8800. **Call for rates.** 969 Bethlehem Pike 18936. I-276 (Pennsylvania Tpke) exit 339, 8 mi n on SR 309. Ext corridors. **Pets:** Medium. $25 daily fee/room. Designated rooms, service with restrictions, supervision. 🛜 ⅙M 🯄 🖵

MORRISVILLE

◇◇◇ ▼▼▼▼ Comfort Inn NJ State Capital Area 🅷 ❀
(215) 428-2600. **Call for rates.** 7 S Pennsylvania Ave 19067. US 1 exit Pennsylvania Ave, just n. Int corridors. **Pets:** Large, dogs only. $10 daily fee/room. Designated rooms, service with restrictions, supervision.
[SAVE] 🛜 ✕ ⅙M 🯄 🖵

NEW HOPE

▼▼▼▼ 1870 Wedgwood Inn of New Hope [BB]
(215) 862-2570. **$95-$295, 10 day notice.** 111 W Bridge St (SR 179) 18938. 0.5 mi w of SR 32; downtown. Int corridors. **Pets:** Accepted.
🛜 ✕ 🯄 🖵

PHILADELPHIA

◇◇◇ ▼▼▼▼ Aloft Philadelphia 🅷
(267) 298-1700. **$109-$309.** 4301 Island Ave 19153. Jct I-95 and SR 291 exit 13 northbound; exit 15 southbound. Int corridors. **Pets:** Accepted.
[SAVE] 🛜 ✕ ⅙M 🯄 🖵 ⚊

◇◇◇ ▼▼ BEST WESTERN Center City Hotel 🅷
(215) 568-8300. **$149-$169.** 501 N 22nd St 19130. I-95 exit 22, just n on Benjamin Franklin Pkwy. Int corridors. **Pets:** Medium, other species. $15 daily fee/room. Designated rooms, service with restrictions.
[SAVE] 🛜 ⅙M 🯄 🖵 ⚊

▼▼▼▼ Chestnut Hill Hotel 🅷
(215) 242-5905. **Call for rates.** 8229 Germantown Ave 19118. I-476 exit 19, 5.5 mi e. Int corridors. **Pets:** Medium, dogs only. $25 daily fee/pet. Service with restrictions, supervision. 🛜 ✕ 🯄 🯄

◇◇◇ ▼▼▼▼ Four Points by Sheraton Philadelphia Airport 🅷
(215) 492-0400. **$100-$260.** 4101 Island Ave 19153. Jct I-95 and SR 291 exit 13 northbound; exit 15 southbound. Int corridors. **Pets:** Accepted.
[SAVE] 🛜 ✕ 🯄 🖵 ⚊

Four Points by Sheraton Philadelphia Northeast H

(215) 671-9600. **$99-$199.** 9461 E Roosevelt Blvd 19114. I-276 (Pennsylvania Tpke) exit 351, 5 mi s on US 1. Int corridors. **Pets:** Medium. $100 one-time fee/room. Designated rooms, service with restrictions, crate.

Four Seasons Hotel Philadelphia H

(215) 963-1500. **$249-$599.** 1 Logan Square 19103. Corner of 18th St and Benjamin Franklin Pkwy. Int corridors. **Pets:** Accepted.

The Hilton Inn at Penn H

(215) 222-0200. **$169-$379.** 3600 Sansom St 19104. I-76 (Pennsylvania Tpke) exit 345 eastbound; exit 346A (Sansom St) westbound; between 36th and 37th sts. Int corridors. **Pets:** Accepted.

Hotel Monaco Philadelphia, A Kimpton Hotel H

(215) 925-2111. **Call for rates.** 433 Chestnut St 19106. Jct 5th and Chestnut sts. Int corridors. **Pets:** Other species. Supervision.

Hotel Palomar-Philadelphia H

(215) 563-5006. **Call for rates.** 117 S 17th St 19103. Corner of 17th and Samson sts. Int corridors. **Pets:** Accepted.

Hyatt at The Bellevue H

(215) 893-1234. **$119-$449, 3 day notice.** 200 S Broad St 19102. Between Walnut and Locust sts. Int corridors. **Pets:** Medium, dogs only. $30 daily fee/room. Service with restrictions, supervision.

Hyatt Regency Philadelphia At Penn's Landing H

(215) 928-1234. **$99-$499.** 201 S Columbus Blvd 19106. Jct S Columbus Blvd and Dock St. Int corridors. **Pets:** Medium, dogs only. $75 one-time fee/room. Designated rooms, service with restrictions, crate.

The Latham Hotel H

(215) 563-7474. **$129-$409.** 135 S 17th St 19103. Jct 17th and Walnut sts. Int corridors. **Pets:** Accepted.

Loews Philadelphia Hotel H

(215) 627-1200. **Call for rates.** 1200 Market St 19107. Corner of 12th and Market sts. Int corridors. **Pets:** Accepted.

Omni Hotel at Independence Park H

(215) 925-0000. **$139-$289.** 401 Chestnut St 19106. Jct 4th St. Int corridors. **Pets:** Accepted.

Philadelphia Airport Residence Inn by Marriott H

(215) 492-1611. **$99-$279.** 4630 Island Ave 19153. I-95 exit 13 northbound; exit 15 southbound, 0.5 mi e; just e of SR 291. Ext corridors. **Pets:** Large, other species. $100 one-time fee/room. Service with restrictions, crate.

Residence Inn by Marriott Philadelphia City Center H

(215) 557-0005. **$157-$425.** 1 E Penn Square 19107. Jct Market and Juniper sts. Int corridors. **Pets:** Accepted.

The Rittenhouse Hotel and Condominium Residences H

(215) 546-9000. **$349-$699, 3 day notice.** 210 W Rittenhouse Square 19103. Jct W Rittenhouse Square and Walnut St. Int corridors. **Pets:** $150 one-time fee/pet. Supervision.

The Ritz-Carlton Philadelphia H

(215) 523-8000. **Call for rates.** Ten Avenue of the Arts 19102. On Broad St; between Market and Chestnut sts. Int corridors. **Pets:** Accepted.

Sheraton Philadelphia Downtown Hotel H

(215) 448-2000. **$100-$360, 3 day notice.** 201 N 17th St 19103. Jct 17th and Race sts. Int corridors. **Pets:** Accepted.

Sheraton Philadelphia University City Hotel H

(215) 387-8000. **$189-$399, 3 day notice.** 3549 Chestnut St 19104. I-76 (Pennsylvania Tpke) exit 345, 0.5 mi w; jct 36th St. Int corridors. **Pets:** Medium, dogs only. Service with restrictions, supervision.

Sheraton Society Hill H

(215) 238-6000. **$169-$379.** One Dock St 19106. Just s of jct 2nd and Walnut sts. Int corridors. **Pets:** Large, dogs only. Service with restrictions, supervision.

Sheraton Suites Philadelphia Airport H

(215) 365-6600. **$109-$289.** 4101 Island Ave 19153. Jct I-95 and SR 291 exit 13 northbound; exit 15 southbound. Int corridors. **Pets:** Accepted.

Sofitel Philadelphia H

(215) 569-8300. **$175-$460.** 120 S 17th St 19103. Jct Sansom and 17th sts. Int corridors. **Pets:** Small. $300 deposit/room. Service with restrictions, crate.

The Westin Philadelphia H

(215) 563-1600. **$139-$599.** 99 S 17th St at Liberty Pl 19103. Between Market and Chestnut sts. Int corridors. **Pets:** Accepted.

POTTSTOWN

Comfort Inn & Suites H

(610) 326-5000. **$99-$159.** 99 Robinson St 19464. SR 100, 1 mi n of jct US 422. Int corridors. **Pets:** Medium, other species. $20 daily fee/pet. Designated rooms, service with restrictions, supervision.

Days Inn Pottstown H

(610) 327-3300. **$75-$115.** 1600 Industrial Hwy 19464. US 422 exit Armand Hammer Blvd. Int corridors. **Pets:** Other species. $100 deposit/pet. Service with restrictions, supervision.

QUAKERTOWN

Comfort Inn & Suites H

(215) 538-3000. **$80-$160.** 1905 John Fries Hwy (SR 663) 18951. I-476 (Pennsylvania Tpke) exit 44, just e. Ext corridors. **Pets:** Other species. $10 daily fee/room. Designated rooms, service with restrictions, crate.

Hampton Inn-Quakertown H

(215) 536-7779. **Call for rates.** 1915 John Fries Hwy (SR 663) 18951. I-476 (Pennsylvania Tpke) exit 44, just e. Int corridors. **Pets:** Medium. $10 daily fee/pet. Designated rooms, service with restrictions, crate.

ROYERSFORD

▼▼▼ Staybridge Suites Royersford/Valley Forge 🅷
(610) 792-9300. **$99-$179.** 88 Anchor Pkwy 19468. I-422 exit Royersford, just n. Int corridors. **Pets:** Large, other species. $75 one-time fee/room. Service with restrictions. 🛜 ⊠ &M 🗄 🖃 🛥

TREVOSE

▼▼ Comfort Inn Trevose Northeast Philadelphia 🅷
(215) 638-4554. **$100-$120.** 2779 Lincoln Hwy N 19053. I-276 (Pennsylvania Tpke) exit 351, 0.5 mi s. Int corridors. **Pets:** Accepted.
🛜 🗄 🖃 🛥

◯◯◯ ▼▼▼ Red Roof Inn #185 Ⓜ
(215) 244-9422. **$67-$89.** 3100 Lincoln Hwy 19053. I-276 (Pennsylvania Tpke) exit 351, 0.5 mi s on US 1 at US 132. Ext corridors. **Pets:** Large, other species. Service with restrictions, supervision.
[SAVE] 🛜 &M 🗄 🖃

UPPER BLACK EDDY

▼▼▼ The Bridgeton House on the Delaware 🅱🅱
(610) 982-5856. **$225-$579, 30 day notice.** 1525 River Rd 18972. On SR 32; center. Int corridors. **Pets:** Accepted. 🛜 ⊠ 🗄 🖃

END METROPOLITAN AREA

PINE GROVE

▼▼ Comfort Inn 🅷
(570) 345-8031. **$90-$145.** 433 Suedberg Rd 17963. I-81 exit 100, just e. Int corridors. **Pets:** Other species. $10 daily fee/room. Service with restrictions. 🛜 &M 🗄 🖃 🛥

▼▼▼ Hampton Inn Pine Grove 🅷 ❀
(570) 345-4505. **$89-$159.** 481 Suedberg Rd 17963. I-81 exit 100, just w. Int corridors. **Pets:** Other species. $25 daily fee/pet. Designated rooms, service with restrictions, supervision. 🛜 &M 🗄 🖃 🛥

PITTSBURGH METROPOLITAN AREA

BEAVER FALLS

▼▼▼ Holiday Inn 🅷
(724) 846-3700. **Call for rates.** 7195 Eastwood Rd 15010. I-76 (Pennsylvania Tpke) exit 13, just n. Int corridors. **Pets:** Accepted.
🛜 🗄 🖃 🍴 ⊠

BENTLEYVILLE

◯◯◯ ▼▼▼ BEST WESTERN Garden Inn 🅷
(724) 239-4321. **$109-$139.** 101 Gosai Dr 15314. I-70 exit 32B, just s. Int corridors. **Pets:** Medium, other species. $20 one-time fee/room. Designated rooms, service with restrictions, supervision.
[SAVE] 🛜 🗄 🖃

BETHEL PARK

▼▼▼ Crowne Plaza Pittsburgh South 🅷 🐾
(412) 833-5300. **$120-$199.** 164 Ft Couch Rd 15241. 1 mi n on US 19. Int corridors. **Pets:** $35 deposit/room. Designated rooms, service with restrictions, crate. 🛜 ⊠ &M 🗄 🖃 🍴 🛥

BUTLER

▼▼ Butler Days Inn Conference Center 🅷
(724) 287-6761. **$99-$109.** 139 Pittsburgh Rd 16001. 2 mi s. Int corridors. **Pets:** Accepted. 🛜 🗄 🖃 🍴 🛥

▼▼ Locust Brook Lodge 🅱🅱
(724) 283-8453. **$85-$150, 3 day notice.** 179 Eagle Mill Rd 16001. 5 mi w on US 422 to jct Eagle Mill Rd, then 0.8 mi s; I-79 exit 99, 10 mi e on US 422 to jct Eagle Mill Rd, then 0.8 mi s. Ext/int corridors. **Pets:** Other species. Designated rooms, no service, crate. 🛜 ⊠

▼▼▼ Super 8 Ⓜ
(724) 287-8888. **$67-$72.** 138 Pittsburgh Rd 16001. 2 mi s. Int corridors. **Pets:** Medium. $15 deposit/pet. Designated rooms, service with restrictions, supervision. 🛜 🗄 🖃

CORAOPOLIS

◯◯◯ ▼▼▼ Embassy Suites-Pittsburgh International Airport 🅷 🐾
(412) 269-9070. **$139-$279.** 550 Cherrington Pkwy 15108. Business I-376 Loop exit Thorn Run Rd. Int corridors. **Pets:** Medium. $75 one-time fee/room. Designated rooms, service with restrictions, crate.
[SAVE] 🛜 &M 🗄 🖃 🍴 🛥 ⊠

▼▼▼ Hampton Inn Pittsburgh Airport 🅷
(412) 264-0020. **$99-$169.** 8514 University Blvd 15108. Business I-376 Loop, 0.5 mi n. Int corridors. **Pets:** Accepted. 🛜 &M 🗄 🖃

◯◯◯ ▼▼▼ Holiday Inn-Pittsburgh Airport 🅷
(412) 262-3600. **Call for rates.** 8256 University Blvd 15108. Business I-376 Loop, 1 mi n. Int corridors. **Pets:** Large. $50 one-time fee/room. Designated rooms, service with restrictions, crate.
[SAVE] 🛜 ⊠ &M 🗄 🖃 🍴 🛥

◯◯◯ ▼▼▼ Hyatt Regency Pittsburgh International Airport 🅷
(724) 899-1234. **$89-$359.** 1111 Airport Blvd 15231. SR 60 exit 6 (Airport Blvd). Int corridors. **Pets:** Accepted.
[ECO] [SAVE] 🛜 🗄 🖃 🍴 🛥 ⊠

▼▼ La Quinta Inn Pittsburgh Airport 🅷
(412) 269-0400. **$90-$144.** 8507 University Blvd 15108. 1 mi n of Business I-376 Loop. Int corridors. **Pets:** Service with restrictions, supervision. 🛜 &M 🗄 🖃

▼▼ Pittsburgh Airport Super 8 Ⓜ
(412) 264-7888. **$65-$75.** 8991 University Blvd 15108. Business I-376 Loop, 1 mi n. Int corridors. **Pets:** Accepted. 🛜 &M 🗄 🖃

◯◯◯ ▼▼▼ Sheraton Pittsburgh Airport 🅷
(412) 262-2400. **$99-$299.** 1160 Thorn Run Rd 15108. Business I-376 Loop exit Thorn Run Rd. Int corridors. **Pets:** Accepted.
[SAVE] 🛜 ⊠ &M 🗄 🖃 🍴 🛥

CRANBERRY TOWNSHIP

▼▼▼ Holiday Inn Express 🅷
(724) 772-1000. **$99-$169.** 20003 Rt 19 16066. I-76 (Pennsylvania Tpke) exit 28, jct US 19 and I-76 (Pennsylvania Tpke); I-79 exit 76 northbound; exit 78 southbound, just s. Int corridors. **Pets:** $25 daily fee/room. Service with restrictions, supervision. 🛜 &M 🗄 🖃

◯◯◯ ▼▼ Red Roof Inn-Cranberry Township-Pittsburgh North #7079 Ⓜ
(724) 776-5670. **$70-$105.** 20009 Rt 19 16066. I-76 (Pennsylvania Tpke) exit 28; I-79 exit 76 northbound; exit 78 southbound. Ext corridors. **Pets:** Large, other species. Service with restrictions, supervision.
[SAVE] 🛜 🗄

▼▼▼ Residence Inn by Marriott Pittsburgh Cranberry Township 🅷
(724) 779-1000. **$151-$209.** 1308 Freedom Rd 16066. I-76 (Pennsylvania Tpke) exit 28, 0.5 mi n on US 19, then 0.3 mi w; I-79 exit 78 southbound, 0.5 mi w. Int corridors. **Pets:** Accepted.
🛜 ⊠ &M 🗄 🖃 🛥 ⊠

DELMONT

▼◆ Super 8 Ⓜ ❀

(724) 468-4888. **$59-$150.** 180 Sheffield Dr 15626. SR 66, just s of US 22. Int corridors. **Pets:** Other species. $10 daily fee/pet. Service with restrictions, supervision. 🛜 🔊 🛗 📺

GIBSONIA

▼▼ Quality Inn & Suites Pittsburgh-Gibsonia Ⓜ

(724) 444-8700. **$79-$199.** 5137 William Flynn Hwy 15044. I-76 (Pennsylvania Tpke) exit 39, just n. Ext corridors. **Pets:** Large, other species. $15 daily fee/pet. Service with restrictions, supervision. 🛜 🛗 📺

GREEN TREE

Ⓐ ▼▼ DoubleTree by Hilton Pittsburgh-Green Tree Ⓗ ❀

(412) 922-8400. **$129-$198.** 101 DoubleTree Dr 15205. I-376 exit 67, 1.1 mi nw via Mansfield Ave. Int corridors. **Pets:** $50 one-time fee/room. Designated rooms, service with restrictions, supervision.

SAVE 🛜 ☒ 🔊 🛗 📺 🍽 ⇨ ☒

▼▼ Hampton Inn Pittsburgh Green Tree Ⓗ

(412) 922-0100. **$109-$199.** 555 Trumbull Dr 15205. I-376 exit 4A northbound; exit 4B southbound; jct US 22 and 30, 1 mi nw via Mansfield Ave. Int corridors. **Pets:** Service with restrictions. 🛜 🛗 📺 ⇨

MARS

▼▼ Comfort Inn Cranberry Township Ⓗ

(724) 772-2700. **Call for rates.** 924 Sheraton Dr 16046. I-76 (Pennsylvania Tpke) exit 28; I-79 exit 76 (US 19 N) northbound; exit 78 southbound, 0.5 mi s on US 19. Int corridors. **Pets:** $20 one-time fee/pet. Designated rooms, service with restrictions, supervision. 🛜 🛗 📺

▼▼ Super 8-Cranberry Ⓗ

(724) 776-9700. **$90-$169.** 929 Sheraton Dr 16046. I-76 (Pennsylvania Tpke) exit 28; I-79 exit 76 (US 19 N) northbound; exit 78 southbound, 0.5 mi s on US 19. Int corridors. **Pets:** Accepted. 🛜 🛗 📺

MONACA

▼▼▼ Hampton Inn Beaver Valley/Pittsburgh Ⓗ

(724) 774-5580. **$129-$143.** 202 Fairview Dr 15061. SR 60 exit 12, just n. Int corridors. **Pets:** Medium, other species. Service with restrictions, crate. 🛜 🔊 🛗 📺 ⇨

▼▼▼ Holiday Inn Express Hotel & Suites-Center Township Ⓗ

(724) 728-5121. **Call for rates.** 105 Stone Quarry Rd 15061. SR 60 exit 12, just n. Int corridors. **Pets:** Accepted. 🛜 🔊 🛗 📺 ⇨

▼▼ The Inn Ⓗ

(724) 728-9270. **$79-$129.** 1525 Old Brodhead Rd 15061. SR 60 exit 12, 1 mi e. Int corridors. **Pets:** Accepted. 🛜 🛗 📺

MONROEVILLE

Ⓐ ▼▼▼ DoubleTree by Hilton Hotel Pittsburgh - Monroeville Convention Center Ⓗ

(412) 373-7300. **$119-$169.** 101 Mall Blvd 15146. I-76 (Pennsylvania Tpke) exit 57, 2 mi w on US 22. Int corridors. **Pets:** Small, other species. $50 one-time fee/room. Service with restrictions, crate.

SAVE 🛜 ☒ 📺 🍽 ⇨

▼▼ Extended StayAmerica-Pittsburgh-Monroeville Ⓗ

(412) 856-8400. **$89-$129.** 3851 Northern Pike 15146. I-76 (Pennsylvania Tpke) exit 57, 1.2 mi w on Business Rt US 22. Int corridors. **Pets:** $25 daily fee/pet. Designated rooms, service with restrictions. 🛜 🛗 📺

▼▼ Hampton Inn Monroeville/Pittsburgh Ⓗ

(412) 380-4000. **Call for rates.** 3000 Mosside Blvd 15146. I-76 (Pennsylvania Tpke) exit 57; I-376 exit 14A, 0.3 mi s on SR 48. Int corridors. **Pets:** Accepted. 🛜 ☒ 🔊 📺 ⇨

Ⓐ ▼▼▼ Holiday Inn Monroeville Ⓗ ❀

(412) 372-1022. **$95-$159.** 2750 Mosside Blvd 15146. I-76 (Pennsylvania Tpke) exit 57, 0.4 mi s on SR 48; I-376 exit 14A, 0.4 mi s on SR 48. Int corridors. **Pets:** Medium, other species. $35 one-time fee/room. Designated rooms, service with restrictions, crate.

SAVE 🛜 🔊 🛗 📺 🍽 ⇨

Ⓐ ▼▼▼ Red Roof Inn-Monroeville #7174 Ⓜ

(412) 856-4738. **$49-$109.** 2729 Mosside Blvd 15146. I-76 (Pennsylvania Tpke) exit 57; I-37 exit 14A, 0.8 mi s on SR 48. Ext corridors. **Pets:** Large, other species. Service with restrictions, supervision.

SAVE 🛜 🛗 📺

▼▼ Super 8 Pittsburgh/Monroeville Ⓜ

(724) 733-8008. **$59-$150.** 1807 Golden Mile Hwy (Rt 286) 15239. I-76 (Pennsylvania Tpke) exit 57; I-376 exit 14A, 2 mi e on US 22 E, then 2 mi e. Int corridors. **Pets:** Other species. $10 daily fee/pet. Designated rooms, service with restrictions, supervision. 🛜 🛗 📺

MOON RUN

▼▼ Extended Stay Deluxe Pittsburgh Airport Ⓗ

(412) 490-0979. **$94-$134.** 200 Chauvet Dr 15275. SR 60 exit 1 (Robinson Town Center Blvd), just s. Int corridors. **Pets:** $25 daily fee/pet. Designated rooms, service with restrictions. 🛜 🔊 🛗 📺

Ⓐ ▼▼▼ Four Points by Sheraton Pittsburgh Airport Ⓗ

(724) 695-0002. **$85-$215.** 1 Industry Ln 15275. SR 60 exit 2 (Montour Run Rd). Int corridors. **Pets:** Accepted.

SAVE 🛜 ☒ 🔊 🛗 📺 🍽 ⇨

▼▼▼ Holiday Inn Express & Suites Pittsburgh Airport Ⓗ

(412) 788-8400. **$89-$159.** 5311 Campbells Run Rd 15205. US 22 and 30 W exit SR 60 S (Crafton), just w. Int corridors. **Pets:** Accepted.

🛜 ☒ 🛗 📺 ⇨

▼▼▼ MainStay Suites Pittsburgh Airport Ⓗ

(412) 490-7343. **Call for rates.** 1000 Park Lane Dr 15275. SR 60 exit 2 (Montour Run Rd), just w on Cliff Mine Rd, then just s. Int corridors. **Pets:** Accepted. 🛜 🔊 🛗 📺 ☒

Ⓐ ▼▼▼ Pittsburgh Airport Marriott Ⓗ

(412) 788-8800. **$110-$246.** 777 Aten Rd 15108. SR 60 exit 2 (Montour Run Rd). Int corridors. **Pets:** Medium. $50 one-time fee/room. Service with restrictions, supervision. SAVE 🛜 ☒ 🛗 📺 🍽 ⇨

▼▼▼ Residence Inn by Marriott Pittsburgh Airport Coraopolis Ⓗ

(412) 787-3300. **$116-$128.** 1500 Park Lane Dr 15275. SR 60 exit 2 (Montour Run Rd), just w on Cliff Mine Dr to Summit Park Dr, just s to Park Lane Dr, then just e. Int corridors. **Pets:** Accepted.

🛜 ☒ 🔊 🛗 📺 ⇨ ☒

OAKDALE

Ⓐ ▼▼▼ Quality Inn Pittsburgh Airport Ⓗ

(412) 787-2600. **$90-$150.** 7011 Old Steubenville Pike 15071. US 22 and 30, jct SR 60; 4 mi w of jct I-279 and 79. Ext/int corridors. **Pets:** Medium, dogs only. $75 one-time fee/pet. Designated rooms, service with restrictions, supervision. SAVE 🛜 🛗 📺

PITTSBURGH

▼▼▼ DoubleTree by Hilton Hotel & Suites Pittsburgh Downtown Ⓗ

(412) 281-5800. **$159-$229.** One Bigelow Square 15219. Jct Bigelow Square and 6th St; just n of Grant St. Int corridors. **Pets:** Accepted.

ECO 🛜 ☒ 🛗 📺 🍽 ⇨ ☒

Fairmont Pittsburgh 🏠 ✿
(412) 773-8800. **$199-$569.** 510 Market St 15222. Between Market St and 5th Ave; in cultural district. Int corridors. **Pets:** Other species. $25 daily fee/room. Designated rooms, service with restrictions, supervision.
[ECO] [SAVE] 🛜 ✕ 🅼 📧 💻 🍴 ✕

Omni William Penn Hotel 🏠 ✿
(412) 281-7100. **$189-$379.** 530 William Penn Pl 15219. Jct 6th St and William Penn Pl. Int corridors. **Pets:** Small. $50 one-time fee/room. Service with restrictions, crate. [SAVE] 🛜 🅼 📧 💻 🍴 ✕

The Parador Inn [BB]
(412) 231-4800. **$150, 14 day notice.** 939 Western Ave 15233. At North Shore. Int corridors. **Pets:** Accepted. 🛜 ✕ 📧 💻

Residence Inn by Marriott Pittsburgh University/Medical Center 🏠 ✿
(412) 621-2200. **$179-$255.** 3896 Bigelow Blvd 15213. On SR 380. Int corridors. **Pets:** Other species. $100 one-time fee/room. Designated rooms, service with restrictions, crate.
[SAVE] 🛜 ✕ 📧 💻 ⇨ ✕

Residence Inn by Marriott-Wilkins 🏠
(412) 816-1300. **$98-$189.** 3455 William Penn Hwy 15235. I-76 exit 57, 3.5 mi n. Int corridors. **Pets:** Large, other species. $100 one-time fee/room. Service with restrictions, supervision. 🛜 ✕ 📧 💻 ⇨

Sheraton Station Square Hotel 🏠
(412) 261-2000. **$189-$389.** 300 W Station Square Dr 15219. I-376 exit Grant St, south end of Smithfield St Bridge; across river. Int corridors.
Pets: Accepted. [SAVE] 🛜 ✕ 📧 💻 🍴 ⇨ ✕

The Westin Convention Center Pittsburgh 🏠
(412) 281-3700. **$161-$500.** 1000 Penn Ave 15222. Jct 10th St; at Liberty Center. Int corridors. **Pets:** Accepted.
[SAVE] 🛜 ✕ 🅼 📧 💻 🍴 ⇨ ✕

Wyndham Grand Pittsburgh Downtown 🏠
(412) 391-4600. **$179-$329.** 600 Commonwealth Pl 15222. Jct I-279/376/SR 885; in Gateway Center. Int corridors. **Pets:** Accepted.
[SAVE] 🛜 ✕ 🅼 📧 💻 🍴

WASHINGTON

Ramada 🏠
(724) 225-9750. **$89-$115.** 1170 W Chestnut St 15301. I-70 exit 15, 0.5 mi e on US 40. Ext/int corridors. **Pets:** Small. $35 daily fee/room. Designated rooms, service with restrictions, supervision.
[SAVE] 🛜 🅼 📧 💻 🍴 ⇨

Red Roof Inn #10048 [M]
(724) 228-5750. **$69-$106.** 1399 W Chestnut St 15301. I-70 exit 15, just e on US 40. Ext/int corridors. **Pets:** Large, other species. Service with restrictions, supervision. [SAVE] 🛜 📧 💻

WEST MIFFLIN

Extended StayAmerica-Pittsburgh-West Mifflin 🏠
(412) 650-9096. **$94-$134.** 1303 Lebanon Church Rd 15122. 0.5 mi e of jct SR 51. Int corridors. **Pets:** $25 daily fee/pet. Designated rooms, service with restrictions. 🛜 🅼 📧 💻

Holiday Inn Express Hotel & Suites 🏠
(412) 469-1900. **Call for rates.** 3122 Lebanon Church Rd 15122. 1.5 mi e of jct SR 51. Int corridors. **Pets:** Other species. $10 daily fee/pet. Service with restrictions, supervision. 🛜 🅼 📧 💻

END METROPOLITAN AREA

POCONO MOUNTAINS AREA

BARTONSVILLE
Comfort Inn Bartonsville 🏠
(570) 476-1500. **$80-$150.** SR 611 18321. I-80 exit 302B, 0.4 mi n. Int corridors. **Pets:** Other species. Service with restrictions.
[SAVE] 🛜 📧 💻 🍴 ⇨ ✕

BLAKESLEE
BEST WESTERN Inn at Blakeslee-Pocono 🏠 ✿
(570) 646-6000. **$85-$175.** New Ventures Business Park, Rt 115 18610. I-80 exit 284, just n. Int corridors. **Pets:** $50 deposit/room. Service with restrictions, supervision. [SAVE] 🛜 ✕ 🅼 📧 💻 ⇨

EAST STROUDSBURG
Budget Inn & Suites 🏠 ✿
(570) 424-5451. **$67-$115.** 308 Greentree Dr 18301. I-80 exit 308, just se. Ext/int corridors. **Pets:** Other species. Designated rooms, service with restrictions, crate. [SAVE] 🛜 📧 💻 🍴

Super 8 East Stroudsburg [M]
(570) 424-7411. **$55-$110.** 340 Greentree Dr 18301. I-80 exit 308, just se. Int corridors. **Pets:** $10 daily fee/pet. Designated rooms, service with restrictions, supervision. 🛜 🅼 📧 💻

HAMLIN
Comfort Inn-Pocono Lakes Region 🏠
(570) 689-4148. **$89-$109.** 117 Twin Rocks Rd 18427. I-84 exit 17, just n on SR 191. Int corridors. **Pets:** $15 daily fee/pet. Designated rooms, service with restrictions, supervision. [SAVE] 🛜 📧 💻

MATAMORAS
BEST WESTERN Inn at Hunt's Landing 🏠 ✿
(570) 491-2400. **$99-$189.** 120 Rt 6 & 209 18336. I-84 exit 53. Int corridors. **Pets:** Medium. $20 daily fee/pet. Designated rooms, service with restrictions, crate. [SAVE] 🛜 📧 💻 🍴 ⇨

MILFORD
Hotel Fauchere 🏠
(570) 409-1212. **$179-$594, 14 day notice.** 401 Broad St 18337. In historic downtown. Int corridors. **Pets:** Accepted.
🛜 ✕ 📧 💻 🍴

Scottish Inns [M]
(570) 491-4414. **$50-$110, 3 day notice.** 274 Rt 6 & 209 18337. I-84 exit 53, 1 mi s. Ext corridors. **Pets:** Accepted. [SAVE] 🛜 📧 💻

STARLIGHT

◆◆◆ The Inn at Starlight Lake ⓒ
(570) 798-2519. **Call for rates.** 289 Starlight Lake Rd 18461. Off SR
370, 1 mi n, follow signs. Ext/int corridors. **Pets:** Accepted.
🛰 ⊠ 🍴 ⊠ 🎿 🎦 🐾

TANNERSVILLE

◆◆◆ ◆◆◆◆ The Chateau Resort & Conference
Center 🏢 🐾
(570) 629-5900. **$89-$324.** 475 Camelback Rd 18372. I-80 exit 299, 1 mi
w on Sullivan Tr, then 1.7 mi on Camelback Rd, follow signs to Camelback Ski area or Camelback Beach Water Park. Int corridors. **Pets:** Other
species. $75 deposit/room, $25 daily fee/pet. Designated rooms, service
with restrictions, crate. (SAVE) 🛰 🚪 🖵 🍴 🐾 ⊠

END AREA

SAYRE

◆◆◆ ◆◆◆◆ BEST WESTERN Grand Victorian
Inn 🏢 🐾
(570) 888-7711. **$140-$200.** 255 Spring St 18840. SR 17 exit 61, just s.
Int corridors. **Pets:** $10 daily fee/pet. Service with restrictions, crate.
(SAVE) 🛰 🚪 🖵 🍴 🐾 ⊠

SCRANTON

◆◆◆◆ Hilton Scranton & Conference Center 🏢
(570) 343-3000. **$139-$199.** 100 Adams Ave 18503. I-81 exit 185, just w
of jct Lackawanna Ave, Jefferson Ave and Spruce St; downtown. Int corridors. **Pets:** Accepted. 🌿 🛰 ♿ 🚪 🖵 🍴 🐾

◆◆◆◆ Radisson Lackawanna Station Hotel
Scranton 🏢 🐾
(570) 342-8300. **$119-$289.** 700 Lackawanna Ave 18503. I-81 exit 185,
jct Lackawanna Ave, Jefferson Ave and Spruce St; downtown. Int corridors. **Pets:** Medium, dogs only. $70 one-time fee/room. Service with
restrictions, crate. 🛰 ⊠ 🚪 🖵 🍴 ⊠

◆◆◆◆ TownePlace Suites by Marriott Scranton
Wilkes-Barre 🏢 🐾
(570) 207-6800. **$152-$179.** 26 Radcliffe Dr 18507. I-81 exit 182A southbound, just e to Montage Mountain Rd, just se to Glenmaura Blvd, just e
on National Blvd, then just n; exit 182 northbound. Int corridors.
Pets: $50 one-time fee/pet. Service with restrictions.
🛰 ⊠ ♿ 🚪 🖵 🐾

SELINSGROVE

◆◆ Comfort Inn 🏢
(570) 374-8880. **$89-$190.** 613 N Susquehanna Tr 17870. US 11 and
15, just n of US 522. Int corridors. **Pets:** Medium. $25 one-time fee/room.
Designated rooms, service with restrictions, supervision.
🛰 🚪 🖵 🍴 🐾

SHAMOKIN DAM

◆◆ Econo Lodge Inn & Suites 🏢
(570) 743-1111. **$69-$169.** 3249 N Susquehanna Tr 17876. US 11 and
15, just n of jct SR 61. Ext corridors. **Pets:** Small, other species. $15
daily fee/pet. Designated rooms, service with restrictions, supervision.
🛰 🚪 🖵 🍴 🐾

◆◆ Phillips Motel Ⓜ
(570) 743-3100. **$78-$159.** 2943 N Susquehanna Tr 17876. 3 mi n of
Selinsgrove. Ext corridors. **Pets:** Accepted. 🛰 🚪 🖵

SHILLINGTON

◆◆◆ ◆◆◆◆ BEST WESTERN PLUS Reading Inn &
Suites 🏢
(610) 777-7888. **$90-$190, 3 day notice.** 2299 Lancaster Pike 19607.
I-76 (Pennsylvania Tpke) exit 286, 9 mi n on US 222. Int corridors.
Pets: Medium. $50 deposit/room, $20 daily fee/room. Designated rooms,
service with restrictions, supervision. (SAVE) 🛰 🚪 🖵 🐾

SHIPPENSBURG

◆◆◆ ◆◆◆ BEST WESTERN Shippensburg Hotel 🏢
(717) 532-5200. **Call for rates.** 125 Walnut Bottom Rd 17257. I-81 exit
29, 0.5 mi w on SR 174. Int corridors. **Pets:** Medium. $10 daily fee/pet.
Service with restrictions, crate. (SAVE) 🛰 🚪 🖵 🐾 ⊠

STATE COLLEGE

◆◆◆ The Autoport Motel & Restaurant Ⓜ
(814) 237-7666. **$69-$119.** 1405 S Atherton St 16801. US 322 business
route, 1.4 mi e of jct SR 26. Ext/int corridors. **Pets:** Medium, dogs only.
$10 daily fee/pet. Designated rooms, service with restrictions, crate.
🛰 ⊠ 🚪 🖵 🍴 🏊

◆◆◆ Days Inn Penn State 🏢
(814) 238-8454. **$104-$600.** 240 S Pugh St 16801. Just e of SR 26
northbound; 0.4 mi n of jct US 322 business route; downtown. Int corridors. **Pets:** Accepted. 🛰 🚪 🖵 🍴 🐾

◆◆◆ ◆ Nittany Budget Motel Ⓜ
(814) 238-0015. **$49-$225, 30 day notice.** 2070 Cato Ave 16801. SR
26, 2.6 mi s of jct US 322 business route. Ext corridors. **Pets:** Dogs only.
$5 daily fee/pet. Service with restrictions, crate. (SAVE) 🛰 🚪

◆◆ Quality Inn Penn State Ⓜ
(814) 234-1600. **Call for rates.** 1274 N Atherton St 16803. US 322 business route, 1 mi w of jct SR 26. Int corridors. **Pets:** Accepted.
🛰 ⊠ ♿ 🚪 🖵

◆◆◆ Residence Inn by Marriott State College 🏢
(814) 235-6960. **$99-$189.** 1555 University Dr 16801. US 322 business
route, 1.5 mi e of jct SR 26. Int corridors. **Pets:** Accepted.
🛰 ⊠ 🚪 🖵 🐾 ⊠

◆◆◆ Super 8 State College 🏢
(814) 237-8005. **$59-$400.** 1663 S Atherton St 16801. US 322 business
route, 1.6 mi e of jct SR 26. Int corridors. **Pets:** $25 one-time fee/room.
Service with restrictions, supervision. 🛰 🚪 🖵

WARREN

◆◆◆ ◆◆◆◆ Holiday Inn of Warren 🏢
(814) 726-3000. **$119-$129.** 210 Ludlow St 16365. Jct US 6, just n on
Ludlow St (US 62 N). Int corridors. **Pets:** Designated rooms, service with
restrictions. (SAVE) 🛰 ♿ 🖵 🍴 🐾

◆◆ Warren Super 8 🏢
(814) 723-8881. **$74.** 204 Struthers St 16365. 1.5 mi w on US 6 exit
Ludlow St, w on Allegheny, then s. Ext/int corridors. **Pets:** Accepted.
🛰 ⊠ 🚪 🖵

WEST HAZLETON

◆◆◆ Candlewood Suites 🏢
(570) 459-1600. **Call for rates.** 9 Bowman's Mill Rd 18202. I-81 exit 145
southbound; exit SR 93 S northbound to Tom Hicken Rd. Int corridors.
Pets: Other species. $10 daily fee/pet. Service with restrictions, crate.
🛰 ♿ 🚪 🖵

WEST READING

▼▼▼ Candlewood Suites **H**
(610) 898-1910. **$109-$129.** 55 S 3rd Ave 19611. Jct Penn Ave. Int corridors. **Pets:** Accepted. 🛜 ⌨ 🛢 💻

WHITE HAVEN

▼▼ Comfort Inn-Pocono Mountain **H** ❀
(570) 443-8461. **Call for rates.** Rt 940 at I-80 & 476 18661. I-476 exit 95, just e; I-80 exit 277 (Lake Harmony). Int corridors. **Pets:** Medium, other species. $15 daily fee/pet. Designated rooms, service with restrictions, crate. 🛜 🛢 💻 ⇒ ⊠

WILKES-BARRE

Ⓐ ▼▼▼ BEST WESTERN Genetti Hotel & Conference Center **H** ❀
(570) 823-6152. **$85-$150.** 77 E Market St 18701. Jct Washington St; downtown. Int corridors. **Pets:** Medium, dogs only. $15 one-time fee/pet. Designated rooms, service with restrictions, supervision.
SAVE 🛜 🛢 💻 ⏏ ⇒

Ⓐ ▼▼ Days Inn **H**
(570) 826-0111. **$65-$231.** 760 Kidder St 18702. I-81 exit 170B, to exit 1 (SR 309 S business route), just w; I-76 (Pennsylvania Tpke) exit 105 to exit 1 (SR 115 N). Int corridors. **Pets:** Accepted. SAVE 🛜 🛢

Ⓐ ▼▼▼ Econo Lodge Arena **H** ❀
(570) 823-0600. **$60-$99.** 1075 Wilkes-Barre Township Blvd 18702. I-81 exit 165 southbound; exit 165B northbound, on SR 309 business route. Int corridors. **Pets:** Large, other species. $100 deposit/room, $10 daily fee/pet. Designated rooms, service with restrictions, supervision.
SAVE 🛜 🛢 💻

▼▼ Extended Stay Deluxe Wilkes-Barre Hwy 315 **H**
(570) 970-2500. **$100-$149.** 1067 Hwy 315 18702. I-81 exit 170B to exit 1 (SR 309 S business route), 0.3 mi n. Int corridors. **Pets:** $25 daily fee/pet. Designated rooms, service with restrictions. 🛜 ⌨ 🛢 💻

Ⓐ ▼▼▼ Host Inn All Suites Hotel **H**
(570) 270-4678. **$109-$199.** 860 Kidder St 18702. I-81 exit 170B to exit 1 (SR 309 S business route), 0.5 mi w. Int corridors. **Pets:** Other species. $20 daily fee/pet. Service with restrictions, crate.
SAVE 🛜 ⌨ 🛢 💻 ⇒

▼▼ Quality Inn & Suites **H** ❀
(570) 824-8901. **$89-$159.** 880 Kidder St 18702. I-81 exit 170B to exit 1 (SR 309 S business route) off expressway, 0.5 mi w. Ext corridors. **Pets:** $20 daily fee/pet. Designated rooms, service with restrictions, crate.
🛜 🛢 💻 ⏏

Ⓐ ▼▼▼ Red Roof Inn #7139 **M**
(570) 829-6422. **$49-$120.** 1035 Hwy 315 18702. I-81 exit 170B to exit 1 (SR 309 S business route) to SR 315, just n. Ext corridors. **Pets:** Large, other species. Service with restrictions, supervision. SAVE 🛜 🛢

▼▼▼ The Woodlands Inn, An Ascend Collection by Choice Hotels **H**
(570) 824-9831. **$139-$159.** 1073 Hwy 315 18702. I-81 exit 170B to exit 1 (SR 309 S business route), 0.3 mi n. Int corridors. **Pets:** Dogs only. $35 one-time fee/room. Designated rooms, service with restrictions, crate.
🛜 🛢 💻 ⏏ ⇒ ⊠

WILLIAMSPORT

Ⓐ ▼▼ BEST WESTERN Williamsport Inn **H**
(570) 326-1981. **$120-$220.** 1840 E 3rd St 17701. I-180 exit 25 (Faxon St), 0.5 mi e. Ext corridors. **Pets:** $15 daily fee/pet. Designated rooms, service with restrictions, crate. SAVE 🛜 ⌨ 🛢 💻 ⏏ ⇒

▼▼ Candlewood Suites **H**
(570) 601-9100. **Call for rates.** 1836 E 3rd St 17701. I-180 exit 25 (Faxon St), 0.5 mi e. Int corridors. **Pets:** Medium. $10 daily fee/pet. Designated rooms, service with restrictions, supervision.
🛜 ⌨ 🛢 💻 ⇒

Ⓐ ▼▼▼ Genetti Hotel & Suites **H**
(570) 326-6600. **$129-$229.** 200 W 4th St 17701. Jct William St; downtown. Ext/int corridors. **Pets:** Accepted. SAVE 🛜 🛢 💻 ⏏ ⇒

WYOMISSING

▼▼▼ Crowne Plaza Reading Hotel **H** ❀
(610) 376-3811. **$129-$189, 3 day notice.** 1741 W Papermill Rd 19610. US 422 exit Papermill Rd. Int corridors. **Pets:** Other species. $15 daily fee/room. Designated rooms, service with restrictions, crate.
🛜 ⌨ ⌨ 🛢 💻 ⏏ ⇒

▼▼ Econo Lodge Inn & Suites **H**
(610) 378-5105. **Call for rates.** 635 Spring St 19610. Just off US 422 to exit Papermill Rd. Int corridors. **Pets:** Accepted. 🛜 🛢 💻

▼▼▼ Homewood Suites-Reading/Wyomissing **H**
(610) 736-3100. **$129-$214.** 2801 Papermill Rd 19610. US 422 exit Papermill Rd, 1.8 mi nw; US 222 exit Spring Ridge Rd. Int corridors. **Pets:** Medium. $75 one-time fee/pet. Service with restrictions.
🛜 ⌨ 🛢 💻 ⇒

Ⓐ ▼▼▼ The Inn at Reading Hotel & Conference Center **H**
(610) 372-7811. **Call for rates.** 1040 N Park Rd 19610. US 222 exit on N Wyomissing Blvd, just n, then 0.3 mi e. Int corridors. **Pets:** Accepted.
SAVE 🛜 ⌨ 🛢 💻 ⏏ ⇒ ⊠

WYSOX

▼▼▼ Comfort Inn **H** ❀
(570) 265-5691. **Call for rates.** US 6 18854. Center. Int corridors. **Pets:** Large, other species. $25 one-time fee/pet. Service with restrictions, supervision. 🛜 ⌨ 🛢 💻 ⇒ ⊠

YORK

▼▼ Comfort Inn & Suites **H**
(717) 699-1919. **$89-$149.** 2250 N George St 17402. I-83 exit 22, just n. Int corridors. **Pets:** Other species. $50 one-time fee/pet. Service with restrictions, supervision. 🛜 ⌨ 🛢 💻

▼▼▼ Holiday Inn Express & Suites **H**
(717) 741-1000. **$95-$165.** 140 Leader Heights Rd 17403. I-83 exit 14, just w on SR 182. Int corridors. **Pets:** Dogs only. $50 one-time fee/room. Service with restrictions, crate. 🛜 ⌨ 🛢 💻

▼▼▼ Holiday Inn York - Route 74 and US 30 **H**
(717) 846-9500. **Call for rates.** 2000 Loucks Rd 17408. I-83 exit 21B, 2.5 mi w on US 30, then just n; exit 22 southbound, 0.5 mi s on SR 181, 2.2 mi w on US 30, then just n. Int corridors. **Pets:** Accepted.
🛜 🛢 💻 ⏏ ⇒ ⊠

▼▼ Red Roof Inn #315 **H**
(717) 843-8181. **$59-$114.** 125 Arsenal Rd 17404. I-83 exit 21B northbound, 0.3 mi w on US 30; exit 21 southbound, 0.5 mi s on SR 181 to US 30. Int corridors. **Pets:** Large, other species. Service with restrictions, supervision. 🛜 🛢 💻

Ⓐ ▼▼▼ The Yorktowne Hotel **H**
(717) 848-1111. **Call for rates.** 48 E Market St 17401. SR 462 eastbound and I-83 business route, just e of square, follow signs. Int corridors. **Pets:** Accepted. SAVE 🛜 🛢 💻 ⏏ ⊠

RHODE ISLAND

EAST PROVIDENCE

◆◆ **Extended StayAmerica Providence-East Providence** 🏨

(401) 272-1661. **$92-$199.** 1000 Warren Ave 02914. I-195 exit 8 eastbound, just e; exit 6 westbound, 1.1 mi e. Int corridors. **Pets:** $25 daily fee/pet. Designated rooms, service with restrictions.

MIDDLETOWN

◆◆◆ ◆◆ **The Ambassador Inn & Suites** Ⓜ

(401) 849-2718. **$49-$300.** 1359 W Main Rd 02842. On SR 114, just n of jct SR 214. Int corridors. **Pets:** Small, dogs only. $100 deposit/pet, $20 daily fee/pet. Designated rooms, service with restrictions, supervision.

[SAVE]

◆◆◆ ◆◆ **Howard Johnson Inn-Newport** 🏨 🐾

(401) 849-2000. **$54-$500.** 351 W Main Rd 02842. On SR 114, 0.3 mi s of jct SR 138. Int corridors. **Pets:** Other species. $10 daily fee/pet. Designated rooms, service with restrictions, supervision.

[SAVE]

◆◆◆ ◆◆◆ **Residence Inn by Marriott-Newport/Middletown** 🏨 🐾

(401) 845-2005. **$119-$369, 3 day notice.** 325 W Main Rd 02842. On SR 114, 0.3 mi s of jct SR 138. Int corridors. **Pets:** Other species. $76 one-time fee/room. Designated rooms, service with restrictions.

[SAVE]

NEWPORT

◆◆◆ ◆◆◆ **Beech Tree Inn** BB 🐾

(401) 847-9794. **$99-$359, 14 day notice.** 34 Rhode Island Ave 02840. Just e of SR 138; 0.8 mi s of jct SR 138. Int corridors. **Pets:** Other species. $25 one-time fee/pet. Designated rooms, no service.

[SAVE]

◆◆◆ ◆◆ **BEST WESTERN The Mainstay Inn** 🏨

(401) 849-9880. **$59-$250, 3 day notice.** 151 Admiral Kalbfus Rd 02840. SR 138; from Newport Bridge, 2nd exit. Int corridors. **Pets:** Accepted. [SAVE]

◆◆◆ **The Burbank Rose** BB

(401) 849-9457. **Call for rates.** 111 Memorial Blvd W 02840. Just e on SR 138A. Int corridors. **Pets:** Accepted.

◆◆◆ ◆◆◆ **Cliffside Inn** BB 🐾

(401) 847-1811. **$190-$509, 30 day notice.** 2 Seaview Ave 02840. Just s of Memorial Blvd via Cliff Ave. Ext/int corridors. **Pets:** Small, dogs only. $250 deposit/room, $50 one-time fee/pet. Designated rooms.

[SAVE]

◆◆◆ ◆◆◆ **Hyatt Regency Newport Hotel & Spa** 🏨 🐾

(401) 851-1234. **$109-$449, 3 day notice.** 1 Goat Island 02840. 0.8 mi w of America's Cup Ave, follow signs to Goat Island. Int corridors. **Pets:** $75 deposit/pet. Designated rooms, service with restrictions, crate.

[ECO] [SAVE]

◆◆◆ ◆◆ **Mill Street Inn** 🏨

(401) 849-9500. **$165-$525, 5 day notice.** 75 Mill St 02840. Just e of Thames St; between Spring and Corne sts; downtown. Int corridors. **Pets:** Accepted.

◆◆◆ **Pelham Court Hotel** ⒸⓄ

(401) 619-4950. **Call for rates.** 14 Pelham St 02840. Just n of Memorial Blvd (SR 138A) via Spring St, then just w. Int corridors. **Pets:** Designated rooms, service with restrictions, crate.

◆◆◆ ◆◆ **Vanderbilt Grace** 🏨

(401) 846-6200. **Call for rates.** 41 Mary St 02840. Just n of Thames St; downtown. Int corridors. **Pets:** Accepted.

[SAVE]

NORTH KINGSTOWN

◆◆ **Hamilton Village Inn** Ⓜ

(401) 295-0700. **$79-$139, 7 day notice.** 642 Boston Neck Rd 02852. SR 1A, 1.3 mi s of jct SR 102. Ext corridors. **Pets:** Other species. Designated rooms, service with restrictions, supervision.

◆◆◆ **TownePlace Suites by Marriott Providence/North Kingstown** 🏨

(401) 667-7500. **$119-$219.** 55 Gate Rd 02852. Jct SR 403, just n on US 1, then just e. Int corridors. **Pets:** Other species. $100 one-time fee/room. Service with restrictions, crate.

PAWTUCKET

◆◆◆ ◆◆ **Comfort Inn-Providence/Pawtucket** 🏨

(401) 723-6700. **$99-$129.** 2 George St 02860. I-95 exit 27, just e, then just n. Int corridors. **Pets:** Medium. $15 daily fee/pet. Service with restrictions, supervision. [SAVE]

PROVIDENCE

◆◆◆ ◆◆◆ **The Hotel Providence** 🏨

(401) 861-8000. **$149-$289.** 139 Mathewson St 02903. Corner of Westminster St. Int corridors. **Pets:** Accepted.

[ECO] [SAVE]

◆◆◆ ◆◆◆ **Marriott Providence Downtown** 🏨

(401) 272-2400. **$149-$329.** 1 Orms St 02904. I-95 exit 23 to state offices. Int corridors. **Pets:** Other species. $49 one-time fee/room. Supervision. [ECO] [SAVE]

◆◆◆ ◆◆◆ **Omni Providence Hotel** 🏨

(401) 598-8000. **$149-$509.** One W Exchange St 02903. I-95 exit 22A; downtown. Int corridors. **Pets:** Accepted.

[ECO] [SAVE]

◆◆◆ ◆◆◆ **Providence Biltmore Hotel** 🏨

(401) 421-0700. **Call for rates.** 11 Dorrance St 02903. Between Washington and Worcester sts. Int corridors. **Pets:** $75 one-time fee/pet. Designated rooms, service with restrictions, crate.

[ECO] [SAVE]

SMITHFIELD

◆◆◆ ◆◆ **All Seasons Inn & Suites** 🏨

(401) 232-2400. **$100-$300.** 355 George Washington Hwy 02917. I-295 exit 8B, 0.3 mi n on SR 7, then 0.6 mi e on SR 116. Int corridors. **Pets:** Medium, dogs only. $25 daily fee/pet. Designated rooms, service with restrictions, supervision. [SAVE]

Hampton Inn & Suites Providence/Smithfield H ✿
(401) 232-9200. **$119-$219.** 945 Douglas Pike 02917. I-295 exit 8B, 0.6 mi nw on SR 7. Int corridors. **Pets:** Other species. Service with restrictions. SAVE 📶 ✕ Ⓜ 🛏 🖥 🏊

WAKEFIELD

The Kings' Rose Inn BB
(401) 783-5222. **$110-$145, 14 day notice.** 1747 Mooresfield Rd (SR 138) 02879. I-95 exit 3A, 11 mi e on SR 138; 3.3 mi w of US 1. Int corridors. **Pets:** Accepted. 📶 ✕

WARWICK

BEST WESTERN Airport Inn H
(401) 737-7400. **$79-$159.** 2138 Post Rd 02886. I-95 exit 13, e to US 1, then just ne. Int corridors. **Pets:** Small. $25 daily fee/room. Designated rooms, service with restrictions, supervision. SAVE 📶 🛏 🖥

Comfort Inn-Airport H
(401) 732-0470. **$69-$159.** 1940 Post Rd 02886. I-95 exit 13, e to US 1, then 0.5 mi n. Int corridors. **Pets:** Accepted. 📶 🛏 🖥

Crowne Plaza Hotel at the Crossings H
(401) 732-6000. **$99-$179.** 801 Greenwich Ave 02886. I-95 exit 12A southbound; exit 12 northbound, 0.3 mi se on SR 5. Int corridors. **Pets:** Dogs only. $50 deposit/room. Service with restrictions, crate. ECO 📶 Ⓜ 🛏 🖥 🍴

Extended StayAmerica Providence-Airport-Warwick H
(401) 732-2547. **$80-$169.** 245 W Natick Rd 02886. I-295 exit 2 northbound, just sw; exit 3A southbound, 1.1 mi e on SR 37, 2 mi s on SR 2, then just sw. Int corridors. **Pets:** $25 daily fee/pet. Designated rooms, service with restrictions. 📶 Ⓜ 🛏 🖥

Hampton Inn & Suites Providence-Warwick Airport H
(401) 739-8888. **Call for rates.** 2100 Post Rd 02886. I-95 exit 13, e to US 1, then just n. Int corridors. **Pets:** Medium, other species. Service with restrictions, supervision. SAVE 📶 Ⓜ 🛏 🖥 🏊

Holiday Inn Express Hotel & Suites H ✿
(401) 736-5000. **$79-$229.** 901 Jefferson Blvd 02886. I-95 exit 13, 0.4 mi on Airport Connector Rd exit Jefferson Blvd. Int corridors. **Pets:** Medium, dogs only. $25 one-time fee/room. Designated rooms, service with restrictions, crate. ECO 📶 ✕ Ⓜ 🛏 🖥 🏊

Homestead Studio Suites Hotel-Providence/Airport/Warwick H
(401) 732-6667. **$85-$159.** 268 Metro Center Blvd 02886. I-95 exit 12A, 0.4 mi e on SR 113, 0.4 mi n on SR 5, then 0.4 mi e. Int corridors. **Pets:** $25 daily fee/pet. Designated rooms, service with restrictions. 📶 Ⓜ 🛏 🖥

Homewood Suites by Hilton H
(401) 738-0008. **$99-$189.** 33 International Way 02886. I-95 exit 13, 0.4 mi n on Jefferson Blvd, 0.5 mi nw on Kilvert St, then 0.4 mi sw on Metro Center Blvd. Int corridors. **Pets:** Large, other species. $75 one-time fee/room. Service with restrictions. 📶 Ⓜ 🛏 🖥 🏊 ✕

La Quinta Inn & Suites Warwick Providence Airport H
(401) 941-6600. **$75-$173.** 36 Jefferson Blvd 02888. I-95 exit 15, just se. Int corridors. **Pets:** Service with restrictions, supervision. 📶 🛏 🖥 🏊

Residence Inn by Marriott H
(401) 737-7100. **$89-$289.** 500 Kilvert St 02886. I-95 exit 13 to Jefferson Blvd, 0.4 mi n, then 0.6 mi w. Ext corridors. **Pets:** Other species. $100 one-time fee/room. Service with restrictions, supervision. 📶 ✕ Ⓜ 🛏 🖥 🏊 ✕

Sheraton Providence Airport Hotel H ✿
(401) 738-4000. **$89-$209.** 1850 Post Rd 02886. I-95 exit 13, 0.6 mi n on US 1. Int corridors. **Pets:** Medium, other species. $50 one-time fee/pet. Service with restrictions, supervision. SAVE 📶 ✕ Ⓜ 🛏 🖥 🍴 🏊

WATCH HILL

Ocean House H ✿
(401) 584-7000. **$260-$1500, 3 day notice.** 1 Bluff Ave 02891. Jct SR 1A, 0.4 mi sw via Westerly Rd. Int corridors. **Pets:** Small, dogs only. $150 one-time fee/pet. Designated rooms, service with restrictions, crate. SAVE 📶 ✕ Ⓜ 🛏 🖥 🍴 🏊 ✕

WESTERLY

Shelter Harbor Inn C
(401) 322-8883. **$106-$258, 7 day notice.** 10 Wagner Rd 02891. 4 mi ne of jct SR 78 on US 1. Ext/int corridors. **Pets:** Designated rooms, service with restrictions, supervision. 📶 ✕ 🍴 ✕

WEST GREENWICH

Residence Inn by Marriott Providence / Coventry H
(401) 828-1170. **$110-$200.** 755 Center of New England Blvd 02817. I-95 exit 7, just ne. Int corridors. **Pets:** $100 one-time fee/room. Service with restrictions, crate. 📶 ✕ Ⓜ 🛏 🖥 🏊 ✕

WEST WARWICK

Extended StayAmerica Providence-Airport-West Warwick H
(401) 885-3161. **$80-$199.** 1235 Division Rd 02893. I-95 exit 8A northbound, just s on SR 2, then just w; exit 8 southbound, just s on SR 2, then just w. Int corridors. **Pets:** $25 daily fee/pet. Designated rooms, service with restrictions. 📶 Ⓜ 🛏 🖥

WYOMING

Stagecoach House Inn BB
(401) 539-9600. **$100-$199.** 1136 Main St (SR 138) 02898. I-95 exit 3B northbound, 0.7 mi nw; exit southbound, 0.4 mi nw. Ext/int corridors. **Pets:** Large. $25 one-time fee/pet. Designated rooms, service with restrictions, supervision. SAVE 📶 ✕ 🛏 🖥

SOUTH CAROLINA

AIKEN

▼▼ Clarion Inn M

(803) 648-0999. **$70-$90.** 155 Colony Pkwy/Whiskey Rd 29803. Jct US 1/78 and SR 19 (Whiskey Rd), 1.8 mi s on SR 19 (Whiskey Rd). Ext corridors. **Pets:** Accepted. 🛜 🚭 💻 ⌁

▼▼ Quality Inn & Suites M

(803) 641-1100. **$60-$90.** 3608 Richland Ave W 29801. Jct US 1/78 and SR 19 (Whiskey Rd), 2.9 mi w on US 1/78. Ext corridors. **Pets:** Large. $15 deposit/pet, $15 daily fee/pet. Service with restrictions, supervision. 🛜 🚭 💻 ⌁

ANDERSON

▼▼ Baymont Inn & Suites Anderson/Clemson M

(864) 375-9800. **Call for rates.** 128 Interstate Blvd 29621. I-85 exit 19B, just n, then just se. Ext corridors. **Pets:** Accepted. 🛜 🚭M 🚭 💻 ⌁

▼◈▼ Country Inn & Suites By Carlson H ❀

(864) 622-2200. **Call for rates.** 116 Interstate Blvd 29621. I-85 exit 19B, just n, then just se. Int corridors. **Pets:** Medium, dogs only. $25 daily fee/pet. Designated rooms, service with restrictions, supervision. 🛜 🚭M 🚭 💻 ⌁

🌀 ▼▼ Days Inn M

(864) 375-0375. **$69-$175.** 1007 Smith Mill Rd 29625. I-85 exit 19A, just se. Ext corridors. **Pets:** Small, dogs only. $20 one-time fee/pet, $5 daily fee/pet. Service with restrictions, supervision. SAVE 🛜 🚭M 🚭 💻 ⌁

▼◈▼ Holiday Inn Express H

(864) 231-0231. **$94-$114.** 410 Alliance Pkwy 29621. I-85 exit 27, just s on SR 81. Int corridors. **Pets:** Medium. $25 one-time fee/room, $5 daily fee/pet. Designated rooms, service with restrictions, supervision. 🛜 🚫 🚭M 🚭 💻 ⌁

▼▼ Home-Towne Suites H

(864) 226-1112. **Call for rates.** 151 Civic Center Blvd 29625. I-85 exit 19A, 2.2 mi se on US 76, then 0.6 mi s. Int corridors. **Pets:** Accepted. 🛜 🚫 🚭 💻 ⌁

▼▼ La Quinta Inn Anderson M

(864) 225-3721. **$59-$151.** 3430 Clemson Blvd 29621. I-85 exit 19A, 2.9 mi se on US 76/SR 28 (Clemson Blvd); exit 21 southbound, 2.6 mi s on US 178. Ext corridors. **Pets:** Service with restrictions, supervision. 🛜 🚭 💻 ⌁

BEAUFORT

▼▼▼ City Loft Hotel H

(843) 379-5638. **Call for rates.** 311 Carteret St 29902. Jct Port Republic St. Ext corridors. **Pets:** Accepted. 🛜 🚫 🚭 💻

▼▼ Quality Inn at Town Center M

(843) 524-2144. **$65-$80.** 2001 Boundary St 29902. Jct SR 170/US 21, 1 mi e. Ext corridors. **Pets:** Medium, other species. $10 daily fee/pet. Designated rooms, service with restrictions, crate. 🛜 🚭 💻 ⌁

BENNETTSVILLE

🌀 ▼▼ BEST WESTERN Bennettsville Inn M

(843) 479-1700. **$79-$149.** 213 US Hwy 15 & 401 Bypass E 29512. 0.6 mi s of center, just ne on US 15/401/SR 9. Ext corridors. **Pets:** Medium. $25 daily fee/pet. Service with restrictions, crate. SAVE 🛜 🚭 💻 ⌁

BLUFFTON

🌀 ▼▼▼ Candlewood Suites H

(843) 705-9600. **$79-$129.** 5 Young Clyde Ct 29909. I-95 exit 8 (US 278), 7.2 mi e to Okatie Center Blvd S, then just s. Int corridors. **Pets:** Other species. $25 one-time fee/pet. Designated rooms, service with restrictions. SAVE 🛜 🚭M 🚭 💻 ⌁

🌀 ▼◈▼ Holiday Inn Express Hotel & Suites H ❀

(843) 757-2002. **$79-$129.** 35 Bluffton Rd 29910. Jct US 278 (William Hilton Pkwy)/SR 46 (Bluffton Rd), just se. Int corridors. **Pets:** Medium, dogs only. $50 one-time fee/room. Service with restrictions, crate. SAVE 🛜 🚫 🚭M 🚭 💻 ⌁

🌀 ▼◈▼▼ The Inn at Palmetto Bluff CA ❀

(843) 706-6500. **$425-$925, 7 day notice.** 476 Mount Pelia Rd 29910. Jct US 278/SR 170, 4.4 mi sw on SR 170, then 2.2 mi e on SR 46 (Bluffton Rd) to Palmetto Bluff Rd; check-in at gatehouse. Ext corridors. **Pets:** $25 daily fee/room. Service with restrictions. SAVE 🛜 🚫 🚭 💻 🍴 ⌁ 🚫

CHARLESTON METROPOLITAN AREA

CHARLESTON

🌀 ▼▼▼ BEST WESTERN Sweetgrass Inn M ❀

(843) 571-6100. **$60-$229.** 1540 Savannah Hwy 29407. US 17, 3.6 mi w of Ashley River Bridge; jct I-526 W terminus and US 17, 1.7 mi e. Ext corridors. **Pets:** Large, other species. $20 daily fee/room. Designated rooms, service with restrictions, crate. SAVE 🛜 🚭 💻 ⌁

🌀 ▼▼ Days Inn Historic District M

(843) 722-8411. **$109-$259.** 155 Meeting St 29401. Between Cumberland and S Market sts. Ext corridors. **Pets:** Medium. $40 deposit/pet, $15 daily fee/room. Designated rooms, service with restrictions, supervision. SAVE 🛜 🚭 💻 🍴 ⌁

▼▼▼ Hawthorn Suites H
(843) 225-4411. **$109-$279, 3 day notice.** 2455 Savannah Hwy 29414. Jct I-526/US 17/SR 7; 1.3 mi w on US 17. Int corridors. **Pets:** Accepted.

📶 ❌ 🅰ᴹ 🛏 📺 🏊

🅰🅰🅰 ▼▼▼ The Inn at Middleton Place CI ❀
(843) 556-0500. **$149-$749, 3 day notice.** 4290 Ashley River Rd 29414. I-526 exit 11B (Ashley River Rd/SR 61), 2.8 mi nw on Paul Cantrell Blvd/Glenn McConnell Pkwy to Bees Ferry Rd, 1.8 mi ne to Ashley River Rd/SR 61, then 9.2 mi nw, follow signs to historic plantations; adjacent to Middleton Place, National Historic Landmark. Ext corridors. **Pets:** Medium, other species. $50 one-time fee/room. Designated rooms, service with restrictions, crate. SAVE 📶 ❌ 🛏 📺 🍽 🏊 ❌

🅰🅰🅰 ▼▼▼ ▼▼▼ John Rutledge House Inn BB ❀
(843) 723-7999. **$219-$375, 3 day notice.** 116 Broad St 29401. Corner of King St. Int corridors. **Pets:** Large, dogs only. $25 daily fee/room. Designated rooms, service with restrictions. SAVE 📶 ❌ 🛏

🅰🅰🅰 ▼▼▼ Kings Courtyard Inn H ❀
(843) 723-7000. **$179-$290, 3 day notice.** 198 King St 29401. Between Market St and Horlbeck Alley. Ext/int corridors. **Pets:** Medium, dogs only. $25 daily fee/room. Designated rooms, service with restrictions.

SAVE 📶 ❌ 🛏

▼▼▼ La Quinta Inn & Suites Charleston Riverview H
(843) 556-5200. **$78-$206.** 11 Ashley Pointe Dr 29407. US 17, just over Ashley River Bridge to Albermarle Rd, then 0.4 mi s to Ashley Pointe Dr. Ext/int corridors. **Pets:** Service with restrictions, supervision.

📶 🛏 📺 🏊

▼▼▼ Residence Inn by Marriott Charleston Downtown/Riverview H ❀
(843) 571-7979. **$109-$289.** 90 Ripley Point Dr 29407. US 17, just over Ashley River Bridge to Albermarle Rd, then just s. Int corridors. **Pets:** Large, other species. $100 one-time fee/room. Service with restrictions. 📶 ❌ 🅰ᴹ 🛏 📺 🏊 ❌

🅰🅰🅰 ▼▼▼ Town & Country Inn & Suites H
(843) 571-1000. **$99-$249.** 2008 Savannah Hwy 29407. US 17, 3.5 mi nw of Ashley River Bridge; jct I-526 W to terminus and US 17, just se. Ext/int corridors. **Pets:** Large, other species. Designated rooms, service with restrictions. SAVE 📶 🛏 📺 🍽 🏊 ❌

🅰🅰🅰 ▼▼▼ Vendue Inn CI ❀
(843) 577-7970. **$199-$595, 3 day notice.** 19 Vendue Range 29401. Off E Bay St, 1 blk from Waterfront Park. Int corridors. **Pets:** $50 one-time fee/pet. Designated rooms, service with restrictions, supervision.

SAVE 📶 ❌ 🛏 🍽

FOLLY BEACH

🅰🅰🅰 ▼▼▼ Tides Folly Beach H ❀
(843) 588-6464. **$169-$399, 3 day notice.** 1 Center St 29439. Terminus of SR 171; center. Ext corridors. **Pets:** $85 one-time fee/room. Service with restrictions. SAVE 📶 ❌ 🛏 📺 🍽 🏊

KIAWAH ISLAND

▼▼▼ Kiawah Island Golf Resort - Courtside Villas CO
(843) 768-2121. **Call for rates.** 1401 Shipwatch Rd 29455. Just e of main gate to Kiawah Beach Dr, then just s; in West Beach Village area. Ext corridors. **Pets:** Dogs only. $25 daily fee/room. Designated rooms, service with restrictions. ❌ 🛏 📺 🏊 ❌

▼▼▼ Kiawah Island Golf Resort - Fairway Oaks Villas CO
(843) 768-2121. **Call for rates.** 1301 Kiawah Beach Dr 29455. Just e of main gate, then just s; in West Beach Village area. Ext corridors. **Pets:** Dogs only. $25 daily fee/room. Designated rooms, service with restrictions. 📶 ❌ 🛏 📺 🍽 ❌

▼▼▼ Kiawah Island Golf Resort - Mariners Watch Villas CO
(843) 768-2121. **Call for rates.** 4200 Sea Forest Dr 29455. 1.6 mi e of main gate, then just s; in East Beach Village area. Ext corridors. **Pets:** Dogs only. $25 daily fee/room. Designated rooms, service with restrictions. 📶 ❌ 🛏 📺 🍽 🏊 ❌

▼▼▼ Kiawah Island Golf Resort - Parkside Villas CO
(843) 768-2121. **Call for rates.** 4501 Park Lake Dr 29455. 2 mi e of main gate, then just s; in East Beach Village area. Ext corridors. **Pets:** Dogs only. $25 daily fee/room. Designated rooms, service with restrictions. 📶 ❌ 🛏 📺 🍽 🏊 ❌

▼▼▼ Kiawah Island Golf Resort - Seascape Villas CO
(843) 768-2121. **Call for rates.** 3510 Shipwatch Rd 29455. Just e of main gate, then just s; in West Beach Village area. Ext corridors. **Pets:** Dogs only. $25 daily fee/room. Designated rooms, service with restrictions. ❌ 🛏 📺 🏊 ❌

▼▼▼ Kiawah Island Golf Resort - Tennis Club Villas CO
(843) 768-2121. **Call for rates.** 4659 Tennis Club Ln 29455. 2.2 mi e of main gate, then just s; at Roy Barth Tennis Center. Ext corridors. **Pets:** Dogs only. $25 daily fee/room. Designated rooms, service with restrictions. 📶 ❌ 🛏 📺 🍽 🏊 ❌

▼▼▼ Kiawah Island Golf Resort - Turtle Cove Villas CO
(843) 768-2121. **Call for rates.** 5501 Green Dolphin Way 29455. 2.4 mi e of main gate, then just se; at Roy Barth Tennis Center. Ext corridors. **Pets:** Dogs only. $25 daily fee/room. Designated rooms, service with restrictions. 📶 ❌ 🛏 📺 🍽 🏊 ❌

▼▼▼ Kiawah Island Golf Resort - Turtle Point Villas CO
(843) 768-2121. **Call for rates.** 4901 Green Dolphin Way 29455. 2.4 mi e of main gate, then just se; at Roy Barth Tennis Center and Turtle Point Golf Club. Ext corridors. **Pets:** Dogs only. $25 daily fee/room. Designated rooms, service with restrictions. 📶 ❌ 🛏 📺 🍽 🏊 ❌

▼▼▼ Kiawah Island Golf Resort - Windswept Villas CO
(843) 768-2121. **Call for rates.** 4300 Sea Forest Dr 29455. 1.6 mi e of main gate, then just s; in East Beach Village area. Ext corridors. **Pets:** Dogs only. $25 daily fee/room. Designated rooms, service with restrictions. 📶 ❌ 🛏 📺 🍽 🏊 ❌

LADSON

🅰🅰🅰 ▼▼▼ BEST WESTERN PLUS Magnolia Inn and Suites H
(843) 553-8888. **$79-$129.** 747 Treeland Dr 29456. I-26 exit 203 (College Park Rd), just ne. Int corridors. **Pets:** Small. $20 daily fee/pet. Designated rooms, service with restrictions, supervision.

SAVE 📶 🅰ᴹ 🛏 📺 🏊

MOUNT PLEASANT

🅰🅰🅰 ▼▼▼ Days Inn Patriots Point M
(843) 881-1800. **$79-$179, 3 day notice.** 261 Johnnie Dodds Blvd 29464. Just e of base of Cooper River Bridge on US 17 (Johnnie Dodds Blvd). Ext corridors. **Pets:** Small, dogs only. $10 daily fee/pet. Designated rooms, service with restrictions, supervision. SAVE 📶 🛏 📺 🏊

▼▼ Extended StayAmerica-Charleston-Mount Pleasant H
(843) 884-4453. **Call for rates.** 304 Wingo Way 29464. Just e of Cooper River Bridge on US 17 (Johnnie Dodds Blvd), then just n. Int corridors. **Pets:** $25 daily fee/pet. Designated rooms, service with restrictions.

📶 🛏 📺

▼▼▼ Hampton Inn-Patriots Point H ❀
(843) 881-3300. **$89-$199.** 255 Sessions Way 29464. Just ne of base of Cooper River Bridge to McGrath-Darby Blvd, then just s. Int corridors. **Pets:** Medium, other species. Designated rooms, service with restrictions, supervision. 📶 🅰ᴹ 🛏 📺 🏊

▼▼▼ Holiday Inn Charleston/Mt. Pleasant H
(843) 884-6000. **Call for rates.** 250 Johnnie Dodds Blvd 29464. US 17 (Johnnie Dodds Blvd), just e of base of Cooper River Bridge. Int corridors. **Pets:** Accepted. 📶 🅰ᴹ 🛏 📺 🍽 🏊

▼▼▼ Homewood Suites by Hilton H
(843) 881-6950. **Call for rates.** 1998 Riviera Dr 29464. I-526 exit 32 (Georgetown/US 17 N), 1.4 mi ne on US 17 (Johnnie Dodds Blvd), 1 mi se on SR 517 (Isle of Palms Connector), then just sw. Int corridors. **Pets:** Other species. $75 one-time fee/room. Service with restrictions.

📶 🅰ᴹ 🛏 📺 🏊 ❌

Red Roof Inn M

(843) 884-1411. **$54-$135.** 301 Johnnie Dodds Blvd 29464. Just e of base of Cooper River Bridge on US 17 (Johnnie Dodds Blvd), then just s on McGrath-Darby Blvd. Ext corridors. **Pets:** Large, other species. Service with restrictions, supervision. [SAVE]

Residence Inn by Marriott Charleston Mt. Pleasant H

(843) 881-1599. **$116-$279.** 1116 Isle of Palms Connector 29464. I-526 exit 30 (Georgetown/US 17 N), 1.4 mi ne on US 17 (Johnnie Dodds Blvd) to SR 517 (Isle of Palms Connector), then just se. Int corridors. **Pets:** Accepted.

Sleep Inn Mt. Pleasant H

(843) 856-5000. **$59-$140.** 299 Wingo Way 29464. Just ne of base of Cooper River Bridge to McGrath Darby Blvd, then just n. Int corridors. **Pets:** Accepted.

NORTH CHARLESTON

Aloft Charleston Airport & Convention Center H

(843) 566-7300. **$99-$259.** 4875 Tanger Outlet Blvd 29418. I-26 exit 213A, follow signs to Tanger Outlet Mall. Int corridors. **Pets:** Accepted.

[SAVE]

Candlewood Suites H

(843) 797-3535. **$89-$99.** 2177 Northwoods Blvd 29406. I-26 exit 209 (Ashley Phosphate Rd), just e, then just n. Int corridors. **Pets:** Accepted.

Comfort Suites Charleston/N Charleston, SC H

(843) 725-5400. **$79-$159.** 2520 N Forest Dr 29420. I-26 exit 209 (Ashley Phosphate Rd), just w of Northside Dr. Int corridors. **Pets:** Accepted.

Hawthorn Suites by Wyndham - North Charleston H 🐾

(843) 572-5757. **$109-$172.** 7645 Northwoods Blvd 29406. I-26 exit 209 (Ashley Phosphate Rd), just e, then n. Ext corridors. **Pets:** Other species. $100 one-time fee/room. Service with restrictions.

Home2 Suites by Hilton Charleston Airport/ Convention Center H 🐾

(843) 744-4202. **$139-$179.** 3401 W Montague Ave 29418. I-26 exit 213A, 0.9 mi sw; I-526 exit 16, just e. Int corridors. **Pets:** Medium. $75 one-time fee/room. Designated rooms, service with restrictions.

Homestead Charleston-Airport-N Charleston H

(843) 740-3440. **Call for rates.** 5045 N Arco Ln 29418. I-26 exit 213 westbound; exit 213A eastbound; enter through Tanger Outlet access roads. Int corridors. **Pets:** $25 daily fee/pet. Designated rooms, service with restrictions.

La Quinta Inn Charleston North M

(843) 797-8181. **$59-$139.** 2499 La Quinta Ln 29420. I-26 exit 209 (Ashley Phosphate Rd), just w. Ext/int corridors. **Pets:** Service with restrictions, supervision.

Radisson Hotel Charleston Airport H

(843) 744-2501. **$69-$189.** 5991 Rivers Ave 29406. I-26 exit 211B (Aviation Ave), just ne. Int corridors. **Pets:** Accepted.

Red Roof Inn M

(843) 572-9100. **$44-$69.** 7480 Northwoods Blvd 29406. I-26 exit 209 (Ashley Phosphate Rd), just e, then just n. Ext corridors. **Pets:** Large, other species. Service with restrictions, supervision. [SAVE]

Residence Inn by Marriott Charleston Airport H

(843) 266-3434. **$129-$159.** 5035 International Blvd 29418. I-26 exit 213 westbound; exit 213A eastbound, just s; I-526 exit 16 (International Blvd), 0.7 mi e. Int corridors. **Pets:** Accepted.

Sheraton Charleston Airport Hotel H 🐾

(843) 747-1900. **$89-$159.** 4770 Goer Dr 29406. I-26 exit 213 westbound; exit 213B eastbound, just n. Int corridors. **Pets:** Medium, dogs only. $100 deposit/room. Designated rooms, service with restrictions, crate. [SAVE]

Sleep Inn Charleston North H

(843) 572-8400. **$54-$139.** 7435 Northside Dr 29420. I-26 exit 209 (Ashley Phosphate Rd), just w. Int corridors. **Pets:** Accepted.

Staybridge Suites North Charleston H

(843) 377-4600. **$129-$149.** 7329 Mazyck Rd 29406. I-26 exit 209A (Ashley Phosphate Rd), just sw, then just s. Int corridors. **Pets:** Accepted.

SUMMERVILLE

Country Inn & Suites By Carlson H

(843) 285-9000. **$99-$109.** 220 Holiday Dr 29483. I-26 exit 199A, just w on US 17 alternate route to Holiday Dr, then just n. Int corridors. **Pets:** Large, other species. $10 daily fee/room. Service with restrictions, supervision.

Holiday Inn Express-Charleston/Summerville H 🐾

(843) 875-3300. **$89-$149.** 120 Holiday Dr 29483. I-26 exit 199A, just w. Int corridors. **Pets:** Other species. Service with restrictions, supervision.

Sleep Inn H

(843) 851-9595. **$76-$100.** 115 Holiday Dr 29483. I-26 exit 199A, just w. Int corridors. **Pets:** Medium. $10 daily fee/pet. Service with restrictions, crate.

END METROPOLITAN AREA

CHARLOTTE METROPOLITAN AREA (NEARBY NORTH CAROLINA)

ROCK HILL

🐾 ▼▼▼ Baymont Inn & Suites 🅷
(803) 329-1330. **$75-$199.** 1106 N Anderson Rd 29730. I-77 exit 82B (US 21), 0.4 mi sw to US 21 Bypass, then just s. Int corridors. **Pets:** Medium. $10 daily fee/pet. Service with restrictions, supervision.
SAVE 🛜 🔒 💻 🏊

▼▼▼ Comfort Suites 🅷
(803) 326-3300. **$90-$120.** 1323 Old Springdale Rd 29732. I-77 exit 79, just se. Int corridors. **Pets:** Medium. $25 daily fee/pet. Designated rooms, service with restrictions, supervision. 🛜 ✖ 🔒 💻 🏊

▼▼ Howard Johnson Inn 🅼
(803) 329-7900. **$49-$169.** 911 Riverview Rd 29730. I-77 exit 82B (US 21), just sw, then just s. Ext corridors. **Pets:** Accepted. 🛜 🔒 💻

▼▼ Super 8 🅷
(803) 980-0400. **$49-$200.** 888 Riverview Rd 29730. I-77 exit 82B (US 21), just sw, then just s. Int corridors. **Pets:** Accepted.
🛜 🔒 🔒 💻

▼▼▼▼ TownePlace Suites by Marriott Rock Hill 🅷
(803) 327-0700. **$80-$119.** 2135 Tabor Dr 29730. I-77 exit 79, just e on Dave Lyle Blvd to Galleria Blvd, then just n. Int corridors. **Pets:** Accepted.
🛜 ✖ 🔒 🔒 💻 🏊

END METROPOLITAN AREA

CHERAW

▼▼▼ Quality Inn 🅼
(843) 537-5625. **Call for rates.** 885 Chesterfield Hwy 29520. Jct US 1/52/SR 9, 1.6 mi w on SR 9. Ext corridors. **Pets:** Accepted.
🛜 🔒 💻 🏊

CLEMSON

🐾 ▼▼▼ Comfort Inn-Clemson 🅷
(864) 653-3600. **$72-$108.** 1305 Tiger Blvd 29631. Jct SR 133 (College Ave) and US 76/123, 0.5 mi e. Int corridors. **Pets:** Accepted.
SAVE 🛜 🔒 💻 🏊

CLINTON

🐾 ▼▼▼ Quality Inn 🅼
(864) 833-5558. **$53-$69.** 105 Trade St 29325. I-26 exit 52, just n. Ext corridors. **Pets:** Medium. $10 daily fee/pet. Service with restrictions, supervision. SAVE 🛜 🔒 💻 🏊

COLUMBIA

▼▼▼ Affordable Suites Delux 🅷
(803) 779-7000. **Call for rates.** 150 Stoneridge Dr 29210. I-126 exit Greystone Blvd, just n, then just e. Ext corridors. **Pets:** Accepted.
🛜 ✖ 🔒 💻 🏊 ✖

🐾 ▼▼▼▼ Candlewood Suites Columbia-Fort Jackson 🅷 ❖
(803) 727-1299. **$99-$139.** 921 Atlas Rd 29209. I-77 exit 9A (Garners Ferry Rd), 0.9 mi se to Atlas Rd, then just sw. Int corridors. **Pets:** Large. $95 one-time fee/room. Service with restrictions, crate.
SAVE 🛜 🔒 🔒 💻 🏊

▼▼▼▼ Chesnut Cottage Bed & Breakfast 🅱🅱 ❖
(803) 256-1718. **$159-$229, 14 day notice.** 1718 Hampton St 29201. SR 12 (Taylor St), just s; between Henderson and Barnwell sts; downtown. Int corridors. **Pets:** Other species. 🛜 ✖ 🔒 🔒 📄

🐾 ▼▼▼ Comfort Inn Columbia 🅷
(803) 798-5101. **$80-$100.** 911 Bush River Rd 29210. I-26 exit 108A, just e. Int corridors. **Pets:** Medium. $15 daily fee/pet. Designated rooms, service with restrictions, crate. SAVE 🛜 🔒 💻 🏊

🐾 ▼▼▼▼ DoubleTree by Hilton Columbia 🅷
(803) 731-0300. **$109-$199.** 2100 Bush River Rd 29210. I-20 exit 63 (Bush River Rd), just e; I-26 exit 108 (Bush River Rd), 0.7 mi w. Int corridors. **Pets:** Large, other species. $40 one-time fee/room. Designated rooms, service with restrictions, crate. SAVE 🛜 🔒 💻 🍴 🏊

▼▼ Extended StayAmerica Columbia-Fort Jackson 🅼
(803) 782-2025. **Call for rates.** 5430 Forest Dr 29206. I-77 exit 12, just ne, then just s along service road; behind mall. Ext corridors. **Pets:** $25 daily fee/pet. Designated rooms, service with restrictions. 🛜 🔒 💻

🐾 ▼▼▼▼ Hilton Columbia Center 🅷 ❖
(803) 744-7800. **$149-$309.** 924 Senate St 29201. Jct US 1/SR 48, just s; downtown. Int corridors. **Pets:** Large. $50 one-time fee/room. Designated rooms, service with restrictions, supervision.
SAVE 🛜 ✖ 🔒 🔒 💻 🍴 🏊

▼▼ La Quinta Inn & Suites Columbia NE/Ft. Jackson Area 🅷
(803) 736-6400. **$59-$129.** 1538 Horseshoe Dr 29223. I-20 exit 74 (Two Notch Rd), just n; I-77 exit 17 (Two Notch Rd), 0.5 mi s. Int corridors. **Pets:** Service with restrictions, supervision. 🛜 🔒 💻 🏊

▼▼ La Quinta Inn-Maingate Ft. Jackson 🅷
(803) 783-5410. **$78-$137.** 7333 Garners Ferry Rd 29209. I-77 exit 9A (Garners Ferry Rd), just se. Int corridors. **Pets:** Service with restrictions, supervision. 🛜 🔒 💻 🏊

▼▼▼ Residence Inn by Marriott Columbia Northeast 🅷
(803) 788-8850. **$99-$159.** 2320 Legrand Rd 29223. I-77 exit 19 southbound, just ne on Farrow Rd to Rabon Rd, then just se; exit 18 northbound. Int corridors. **Pets:** Accepted. 🛜 ✖ 🔒 💻 🏊 ✖

🐾 ▼▼▼▼ Sheraton Columbia Downtown Hotel 🅷 ❖
(803) 988-1400. **$85-$319.** 1400 Main St 29201. Jct Washington St; center of downtown. Int corridors. **Pets:** Medium. $200 deposit/room. Designated rooms, no service, supervision. SAVE 🛜 ✖ 💻 🍴

▼▼▼ Staybridge Suites Columbia 🅷 ❖
(803) 451-5900. **$99-$199, 3 day notice.** 1913 Huger St 29201. I-126 exit 3B (US 21/Huger St), just s. Int corridors. **Pets:** Other species. $150 one-time fee/room. Designated rooms, no service, crate.
🛜 ✖ 🔒 💻 🏊

▼▼ Super 8 🅼
(803) 735-0008. **$52-$73.** 5719 Fairfield Rd 29203. I-20 exit 70, just s. Ext corridors. **Pets:** Accepted. 🛜 🔒 💻

▼▼▼ TownePlace Suites by Marriott Columbia Northwest/Harbison 🅷
(803) 781-9391. **$72-$129.** 350 Columbiana Dr 29212. I-26 exit 103 (Harbison Blvd), just sw to Columbiana Dr, then 0.7 mi nw. Int corridors. **Pets:** Accepted. 🛜 ✖ 🔒 🔒 💻 🏊

DUNCAN

▼▼ ▼▼ **Baymont Inn & Suites Duncan/Spartanburg** Ⓜ

(864) 433-8405. **Call for rates.** 1546 E Main St 29334. I-85 exit 63, 0.4 mi se on SR 290. Ext corridors. **Pets:** Medium, other species. $15 daily fee/room. Service with restrictions. 🛜 🛏 💻 🏊

𝔸𝔸𝔸 ▼▼▼▼ **Holiday Inn Express & Suites** Ⓗ

(864) 486-9191. **$85-$109.** 275 Frontage Rd 29334. I-85 exit 63, just nw on SR 290, just ne on S Main St, then just se. Int corridors.
Pets: Accepted. [SAVE] 🛜 ✕ 🔔M 🛏 💻 🏊

EASLEY

▼▼ ▼▼ **Baymont Inn & Suites Easley/Greenville** Ⓜ

(864) 306-9000. **Call for rates.** 211 Dayton School Rd 29642. Jct US 123/SR 93, 0.6 mi e on US 123; jct US 123/SR 153, 1.4 mi w. Ext corridors. **Pets:** Accepted. 🛜 🛏 💻 🏊

▼▼ ▼▼ **Quality Inn** Ⓜ

(864) 859-7520. **$62-$68.** 5539 Calhoun Memorial Hwy 29640. Jct US 123/SR 93, just e on US 123. Ext corridors. **Pets:** Medium, dogs only. $25 daily fee/pet. Designated rooms, service with restrictions, supervision. 🛜 🛏 💻 🏊

FLORENCE

𝔸𝔸𝔸 ▼▼ ▼▼ **Baymont Inn & Suites** Ⓜ

(843) 468-9994. **$69-$169, 3 day notice.** 1826 W Lucas St 29501. I-95 exit 164, just e on US 52. Ext corridors. **Pets:** Other species. $10 daily fee/pet. Designated rooms, service with restrictions, crate.
[SAVE] 🛜 🛏 🏊

𝔸𝔸𝔸 ▼▼ ▼▼ **Howard Johnson Express Inn &** **Suites** Ⓜ 🐾

(843) 664-9494. **$63-$176.** 3821 Bancroft Rd 29501. I-95 exit 157, just ne on US 76. Ext corridors. **Pets:** Medium. $10 one-time fee/pet. Service with restrictions, crate. [SAVE] 🛜 🛏 💻 🏊

▼▼ ▼▼ **Quality Inn & Suites** Ⓜ

(843) 664-2400. **$60-$199.** 150 Dunbarton Dr 29501. I-95 exit 160A, just e, then just n. Ext corridors. **Pets:** Medium. $20 one-time fee/room. Designated rooms, service with restrictions, supervision.
[SAVE] 🛜 🛏 💻 🏊

𝔸𝔸𝔸 ▼▼ ▼▼ **Ramada** Ⓜ

(843) 665-4555. **$80-$219.** 1819 W Lucas St 29501. I-95 exit 164, just se. Ext corridors. **Pets:** Other species. $15 one-time fee/room. Designated rooms, service with restrictions, crate.
[SAVE] 🛜 🔔M 🛏 💻 🍽 🏊

𝔸𝔸𝔸 ▼▼ ▼▼ **Red Roof Inn** Ⓜ

(843) 678-9000. **$39-$159.** 2690 David McLeod Blvd 29501. I-95 exit 160A, just e on service road. Ext corridors. **Pets:** Large, other species. Service with restrictions, supervision. [SAVE] 🛜 🔔M 🏊

▼▼ ▼▼ **Residence Inn by Marriott Florence** Ⓗ 🐾

(843) 468-2800. **$130-$143.** 2660 Hospitality Blvd 29501. I-95 exit 160A, just e, then s. Int corridors. **Pets:** Medium, other species. $100 one-time fee/room. Service with restrictions, supervision. 🛜 ✕ 🛏 💻 🏊

𝔸𝔸𝔸 ▼▼ ▼▼ **Super 8** Ⓜ

(843) 661-7267. **$60-$149.** 1832 1/2 W Lucas St 29501. I-95 exit 164, just se. Ext corridors. **Pets:** Medium, other species. $10 daily fee/pet. Service with restrictions. [SAVE] 🛜 🛏 💻 🏊

GAFFNEY

▼▼ ▼▼ **Baymont Inn & Suites Gaffney** Ⓜ

(864) 489-0240. **$75-$95.** 101 Stuard St 29341. I-85 exit 92, 0.5 mi se on SR 11/W Floyd Baker Blvd. Ext corridors. **Pets:** Accepted.
🛜 🛏 💻 🏊

𝔸𝔸𝔸 ▼▼ ▼▼ **Super 8** Ⓜ

(864) 489-1699. **$59-$79.** 100 Ellis Ferry Ave 29341. I-85 exit 92, 0.7 mi se on SR 11/W Floyd Baker Blvd. Ext corridors. **Pets:** Very small. $10 one-time fee/pet. Designated rooms, service with restrictions, supervision. [SAVE] 🛜 🛏 💻 🏊

THE GRAND STRAND AREA

CONWAY

▼▼ ▼▼ **Comfort Suites at the University** Ⓗ

(843) 347-9292. **$55-$170.** 2480 Hwy 501 E 29526. Jct US 501/501 business route, 1.6 mi se. Int corridors. **Pets:** Small, dogs only. $15 daily fee/room. Designated rooms, service with restrictions, supervision.
🛜 ✕ 🛏 💻 🏊

GEORGETOWN

▼▼ ▼▼ **Baymont Inn & Suites Georgetown/Near Georgetown** **Marina** Ⓜ

(843) 546-6090. **Call for rates.** 120 Church St 29440. Jct US 17/17 alternate route/701, 1.2 mi se on US 17; just w of ICW Bridge at Georgetown Landing. Ext corridors. **Pets:** Accepted. 🛜 🛏 💻 🏊

LITTLE RIVER

𝔸𝔸𝔸 ▼▼▼▼ **Holiday Inn Express Hotel and Suites-North** **Myrtle Beach** Ⓗ

(843) 281-9400. **Call for rates.** 722 Hwy 17 N 29566. Jct SR 9/US 17, 1 mi e; at Coquina Harbor. Int corridors. **Pets:** Medium. $25 daily fee/pet. Designated rooms, service with restrictions.
[SAVE] 🛜 🔔M 🛏 💻 🏊

MURRELLS INLET

▼▼▼▼ **Holiday Inn Express Hotel & Suites** Ⓗ 🐾

(843) 357-0100. **$69-$189.** 1303-A Tadlock Dr 29576. Jct US 17 Bypass and 17 S business route. Int corridors. **Pets:** Medium, other species. $50 one-time fee/room. Designated rooms, service with restrictions.
🛜 ✕ 🛏 💻 🏊

MYRTLE BEACH

𝔸𝔸𝔸 ▼▼▼▼ **BEST WESTERN PLUS Myrtle Beach** **Hotel** Ⓗ 🐾

(843) 213-1440. **$80-$210.** 9551 Hwy 17 N 29572. Jct SR 22, 1.4 mi sw on US 17. Int corridors. **Pets:** Large. $50 deposit/room, $20 daily fee/room. Designated rooms, service with restrictions.
[SAVE] 🛜 ✕ 🔔M 🛏 💻 🏊

𝔸𝔸𝔸 ▼▼▼▼ **Clarion Hotel** Ⓗ

(843) 236-1000. **$59-$130.** 101 Fantasy Harbour Blvd 29579. Jct US 17 Bypass, 0.7 mi n on US 501 exit River Oaks Rd/George Bishop Pkwy, just w on River Oaks Rd, then 0.7 mi s. Int corridors. **Pets:** Small, dogs only. $15 daily fee/room. Designated rooms, service with restrictions, supervision. [SAVE] 🛜 ✕ 🛏 💻 🍽 🏊 ✕

𝔸𝔸𝔸 ▼▼▼▼ **Compass Cove Oceanfront Resort** Ⓒ🅞 🐾

(843) 448-8373. **Call for rates.** 2311 S Ocean Blvd 29577. Jct 24th Ave S. Ext corridors. **Pets:** Medium. $25 daily fee/room. Designated rooms, service with restrictions, supervision.
[SAVE] 🛜 ✕ 🛏 💻 🍽 🏊 ✕

▼▼▼▼ **La Quinta Inn & Suites Myrtle Beach At 48th** **Avenue** Ⓗ

(843) 449-5231. **$59-$210.** 4709 N Kings Hwy 29577. Jct 48th Ave N and US 17 business route. Int corridors. **Pets:** Service with restrictions, supervision. 🛜 🛏 💻 🏊

◈◈◈◈ La Quinta Inn & Suites Myrtle Beach Broadway Area 🅷
(843) 916-8801. **$59-$254.** 1561 21st Ave N 29577. Jct US 17 Bypass, just se. Int corridors. **Pets:** Service with restrictions, supervision.
🛜 ⬟ 🛏 📺 ➴

ⒶⒶⒶ ◈◈◈ Ocean Park Resort 🅷 ❋
(843) 448-1915. **$49-$259.** 1905 S Ocean Blvd 29577. Jct 20th Ave S. Int corridors. **Pets:** Small, dogs only. $15 daily fee/pet. Service with restrictions, crate. SAVE 🛜 ❎ 🛏 📺 ➴ ⊠

ⒶⒶⒶ ◈◈◈◈ Patricia Grand Resort Hotel 🅷 ❋
(843) 448-8453. **$54-$237.** 2710 N Ocean Blvd 29577. Jct 27th Ave N. Ext corridors. **Pets:** Small, dogs only. $15 daily fee/pet. Designated rooms, service with restrictions, crate.
SAVE 🛜 ❎ 🛏 📺 ⫴ ➴ ⊠

ⒶⒶⒶ ◈◈◈◈ Red Roof Inn & Suites Myrtle Beach 🅷
(843) 626-4444. **$44-$225.** 2801 S Kings Hwy 29577. Between 27th Ave S and 29th Ave S on US 17 business route. Int corridors. **Pets:** Large, other species. Service with restrictions, supervision.
SAVE 🛜 🛏 📺 ➴

ⒶⒶⒶ ◈◈◈◈ Sonesta ES Suites Myrtle Beach 🅷 ❋
(843) 903-4000. **$65-$179.** 303 Fantasy Harbour Blvd 29579. Jct US 17 Bypass, 0.7 mi n on US 501 exit River Oaks Rd/George Bishop Pkwy, just w on River Oaks Rd, then 0.4 mi s. Int corridors. **Pets:** Large. $20 daily fee/room. Service with restrictions, crate.
SAVE 🛜 🛏 📺 ➴ ⊠

ⒶⒶ ◈◈◈ Springmaid Beach Resort & Conference Center 🅷
(843) 315-7100. **$49-$299.** 3200 S Ocean Blvd 29577. Jct 30th Ave S, 0.4 mi s. Ext corridors. **Pets:** Accepted.
SAVE 🛜 ❎ 🛏 📺 ⫴ ➴ ⊠

ⒶⒶⒶ ◈◈◈◈ Westgate Myrtle Beach Oceanfront Resort 🅷
(843) 448-4481. **$59-$299, 3 day notice.** 415 S Ocean Blvd 29577. Jct 6th Ave S, just ne. Int corridors. **Pets:** Large. $80 one-time fee/pet. Designated rooms, service with restrictions, supervision.
SAVE 🛜 ❎ 🛏 📺 ⫴ ➴ ⊠

SURFSIDE BEACH

ⒶⒶⒶ ◈◈◈◈ Holiday Inn Oceanfront at Surfside Beach 🅷 ❋
(843) 238-5601. **Call for rates.** 1601 N Ocean Blvd 29575. Jct 16th Ave N and N Ocean Blvd. Int corridors. **Pets:** Medium, other species. $100 one-time fee/room. Service with restrictions, crate.
SAVE 🛜 🛏 📺 ⫴ ➴ ⊠

END AREA

GREENVILLE

ⒶⒶⒶ ◈◈◈ BEST WESTERN Greenville Airport Inn Ⓜ ❋
(864) 297-5353. **$57-$89.** 5009 Pelham Rd 29615. I-85 exit 54 (Pelham Rd), just se. Ext corridors. **Pets:** Other species. $15 daily fee/pet. Designated rooms, service with restrictions, supervision.
SAVE 🛜 🛏 📺 ➴

ⒶⒶⒶ ◈◈◈ Clarion Inn & Suites Ⓜ
(864) 254-6383. **$62-$99.** 50 Orchard Park Dr 29615. I-385 exit 39 (Haywood Rd), just n, just e on Orchard Park Rd, then just s. Ext corridors. **Pets:** $20 one-time fee/room. Service with restrictions, crate.
SAVE 🛜 🛏 📺 ➴

◈◈◈◈ Drury Inn & Suites-Greenville 🅷
(864) 288-4401. **$94-$204.** 10 Carolina Point Pkwy 29607. I-85 exit 51A (Woodruff Rd), just se; I-385 exit 35 (Woodruff Rd), 0.6 mi nw. Int corridors. **Pets:** Service with restrictions, supervision. 🛜 🛏 📺 ➴

◈◈◈ Extended StayAmerica-Greenville Airport 🅷
(864) 213-9698. **Call for rates.** 3715 Pelham Rd 29615. I-85 exit 54 (Pelham Rd), 0.5 mi w. Int corridors. **Pets:** $25 daily fee/pet. Designated rooms, service with restrictions. 🛜 🛏 📺

◈◈◈ Hawthorn Suites 🅷
(864) 297-0099. **$79.** 48 McPrice Ct 29615. I-385 exit 39 (Haywood Rd), just n, just e on Orchard Park Rd, then just s. Ext corridors. **Pets:** Medium, other species. $15 one-time fee/room. Designated rooms, service with restrictions, supervision. 🛜 🛏 📺 ➴ ⊠

ⒶⒶⒶ ◈◈◈◈ Hilton Greenville 🅷 ❋
(864) 232-4747. **$99-$189.** 45 W Orchard Park Dr 29615. I-385 exit 39 (Haywood Rd), just n, then w. Int corridors. **Pets:** Large. $50 one-time fee/pet. Designated rooms, service with restrictions, supervision.
SAVE 🛜 ❎ ⬟ 🛏 📺 ⫴ ➴ ⊠

ⒶⒶⒶ ◈◈◈◈ Hyatt Regency Greenville 🅷
(864) 235-1234. **$72-$243.** 220 N Main St 29601. Just n of center. Int corridors. **Pets:** Accepted. ECO SAVE 🛜 🛏 📺 ⫴ ➴

◈◈◈ La Quinta Inn & Suites Greenville Haywood 🅷
(864) 233-8018. **$63-$144.** 65 W Orchard Park Dr 29615. I-385 exit 39 (Haywood Rd), just n, then w. Int corridors. **Pets:** Service with restrictions, supervision. 🛜 🛏 📺 ➴ ⊠

◈◈◈ La Quinta Inn Greenville (Woodruff Rd) Ⓜ
(864) 297-3500. **$59-$115.** 31 Old Country Rd 29607. I-85 exit 51A (Woodruff Rd), just nw on SR 146; I-385 exit 37, just sw on Roper Mountain Rd, then 0.9 mi se. Ext/int corridors. **Pets:** Service with restrictions, supervision. 🛜 🛏 📺 ➴

◈◈◈◈ The Phoenix Greenville's Inn Ⓜ
(864) 233-4651. **$79-$295.** 246 N Pleasantburg Dr 29607. I-385 exit 40B, 0.6 mi s on SR 291. Ext corridors. **Pets:** Accepted.
🛜 🛏 📺 ⫴ ➴

ⒶⒶⒶ ◈◈◈ Red Roof Inn Ⓜ
(864) 297-4458. **$41-$64.** 2801 Laurens Rd 29607. I-85 exit 48A, just se to Millennium Blvd, then just nw on Vision Ct. Ext corridors. **Pets:** Large, other species. Service with restrictions, supervision. SAVE 🛜 ⬟ 🛏

◈◈◈ Residence Inn by Marriott Greenville-Spartanburg Airport 🅷
(864) 627-0001. **$129-$142.** 120 Milestone Way 29615. I-85 exit 54 (Pelham Rd), 0.6 mi w to Milestone Way, then just n. Int corridors.
Pets: Accepted. 🛜 ❎ ⬟ 🛏 📺 ➴

◈◈◈ Sleep Inn at TD Convention Center 🅷
(864) 240-2006. **$49-$99.** 231 N Pleasantburg Dr 29607. I-385 exit 40B, 0.6 mi s on SR 291. Int corridors. **Pets:** $20 one-time fee/room. Service with restrictions, crate. 🛜 ⬟ 🛏 📺 ➴

◈◈◈ Staybridge Suites Greenville/Spartanburg 🅷
(864) 288-4448. **$84-$169.** 31 Market Point Dr 29607. I-85 exit 51A (Woodruff Rd), 0.5 mi se to Miller Rd, 0.5 mi s to S Oak Forest Dr, then just nw; I-385 exit 35 (Woodruff Rd), nw to Miller Rd, 0.5 mi s to S Oak Forest Dr, then just nw. Int corridors. **Pets:** Medium. $50 one-time fee/pet. Service with restrictions, supervision. 🛜 🛏 📺 ➴

WW StudioPLUS-Greenville-Haywood Mall H

(864) 288-4300. **Call for rates.** 530 Woods Lake Rd 29607. I-385 exit 39 (Haywood Rd), just s, then just w. Int corridors. **Pets:** $25 daily fee/pet. Designated rooms, service with restrictions. 🛜 📵 ⬛ 💻 🏊

WWW TownePlace Suites by Marriott Greenville Haywood Mall H

(864) 675-1670. **$89-$119.** 75 Mall Connector Rd 29607. I-385 exit 39 (Haywood Rd), just s to Woods Crossing Rd, just se to Mall Connector Rd, then just s. Int corridors. **Pets:** Accepted.
🛜 📵 ♿ ⬛ 💻 🏊

WWW The Westin Poinsett H

(864) 421-9700. **$99-$339.** 120 S Main St 29601. Just s of center. Int corridors. **Pets:** Accepted. ⬛ECO ⬛SAVE 🛜 📵 ⬛ 💻 🍴

GREENWOOD
WW Quality Inn M

(864) 229-5329. **$69-$79.** 719 Bypass Hwy 25 NE 29646. Jct US 25 Bypass NE/221, just se. Ext corridors. **Pets:** Medium, other species. $10 daily fee/pet. Service with restrictions, supervision. 🛜 ⬛ 💻 🏊

GREER
WWW Holiday Inn Express Hotel & Suites Greenville Airport H

(864) 213-9331. **Call for rates.** 2681 Dry Pocket Rd 29650. I-85 exit 54 (Pelham Rd), just w to The Parkway, just n to Parkway E, then just se. Int corridors. **Pets:** Accepted. 🛜 ⬛ 💻 🏊

WW MainStay Suites-Greenville H

(864) 987-5566. **$72-$99.** 2671 Dry Pocket Rd 29650. I-85 exit 54 (Pelham Rd), just w to The Parkway, just n to Parkway E, then just se. Int corridors. **Pets:** Large. $10 daily fee/pet. Service with restrictions.
🛜 ⬛ 💻 🏊

HARDEEVILLE
WWW Holiday Inn Express & Suites H ☀

(843) 784-2800. **$81-$139.** 145 Independence Blvd 29927. I-95 exit 8, just w. Int corridors. **Pets:** $25 one-time fee/room. Designated rooms, service with restrictions, crate. 🛜 ♿ ⬛ 💻 🏊

HILTON HEAD ISLAND
WWW Comfort Inn South Forest Beach H

(843) 842-6662. **$59-$159.** 2 Tanglewood Dr 29928. Sea Pines Cir, 1.1 mi se on Pope Ave, then just sw on Coligny Plaza. Int corridors. **Pets:** Medium, other species. $10 daily fee/room. Designated rooms, service with restrictions, supervision. SAVE 🛜 ⬛ 💻 🏊

WWWW OMNI Hilton Head Oceanfront Resort H ☀

(843) 842-8000. **$99-$359, 3 day notice.** 23 Ocean Ln 29928. Jct US 278 business route/Queens Folly Rd, 0.9 mi se to Ocean Ln, then just sw; in Palmetto Dunes Plantation. Ext/int corridors. **Pets:** Medium. $50 one-time fee/room. Designated rooms, service with restrictions, crate.
SAVE 🛜 📵 ♿ ⬛ 💻 🍴 🏊 ❌

WWW Park Lane Hotel & Suites H

(843) 686-5700. **Call for rates.** 12 Park Ln 29928. 10 mi of J Wilton Graves Bridge on US 278 business route. Int corridors. **Pets:** Large. $50 one-time fee/room. Service with restrictions, crate.
SAVE 🛜 ⬛ 💻 🏊 ❌

WWW Red Roof Inn-Hilton Head M

(843) 686-6808. **$39-$149, 3 day notice.** 5 Regency Pkwy 29928. 9 mi e of J Wilton Grave Bridge on US 278 business route; between Shipyard Plantation and Palmetto Dunes. Ext corridors. **Pets:** Large, other species. Service with restrictions, supervision. SAVE 🛜 ⬛ 🏊

WWWW Westin Hilton Head Island Resort & Spa H ☀

(843) 681-4000. **$99-$559, 5 day notice.** Two Grasslawn Ave 29928. 5.6 mi from J Wilton Graves Bridge on US 278 business route to Coggins Point Rd, then just e, follow signs. Int corridors. **Pets:** Small, dogs only. $150 one-time fee/pet. Designated rooms, service with restrictions, supervision. SAVE 🛜 ❌ ⬛ 💻 🍴 🏊 ❌

LANCASTER
WW Quality Inn M

(803) 283-1188. **$70-$90.** 114 Commerce Blvd 29720. Jct SR 9 Bypass and US 521, 1.3 mi w on SR 9 Bypass. Ext corridors. **Pets:** Accepted.
🛜 ♿ ⬛ 💻 🏊

LANDRUM
WWW The Red Horse Inn Cottages CA ☀

(864) 895-4968. **$210-$325, 30 day notice.** 45 Winstons Chase Ct 29356. Jct SR 14/414, 1.5 mi w on SR 414 to Campbell Rd, then 0.7 mi n. Ext corridors. **Pets:** $25 one-time fee/pet. Designated rooms, no service, supervision. 🛜 ❌ ⬛ 💻 ❌

MANNING
WWW Baymont Inn & Suites M ☀

(803) 473-5334. **$59-$109.** 2284 Raccoon Rd 29102. I-95 exit 119 (SR 261), just se, then s. Ext corridors. **Pets:** Medium. $20 one-time fee/pet. Supervision. SAVE 🛜 ⬛ 💻 🏊

WWW Days Inn of Manning M

(803) 473-4021. **$56-$90.** 2825 Paxville Hwy 29102. I-95 exit 119 (SR 261), just se. Ext corridors. **Pets:** Other species. $10 daily fee/pet. Service with restrictions. SAVE 🛜 ⬛ 💻 🏊

WW Ramada Inn M

(803) 473-5135. **$55-$70.** 2816 Paxville Hwy 29102. I-95 exit 119 (SR 261), just se. Ext corridors. **Pets:** Other species. $5 daily fee/pet. Service with restrictions, supervision. 🛜 ⬛ 💻 🏊

NEWBERRY
WWW Americas Best Value Inn M

(803) 276-5850. **$60-$75.** 11701 Hwy 34 29108. I-26 exit 74 (SR 34), just ne. Ext corridors. **Pets:** Medium, dogs only. $10 daily fee/pet. Service with restrictions, supervision. SAVE 🛜 ⬛ 💻

ORANGEBURG
WW Baymont Inn & Suites Orangeburg M

(803) 534-1611. **Call for rates.** 2350 Chestnut St NE 29115. I-26 exit 145A (US 601), 3.9 mi sw to jct US 601 and 21/178 Bypass, then 2 mi nw. Ext corridors. **Pets:** Accepted. 🛜 ⬛ 💻 🏊

WWW Country Inn & Suites By Carlson H

(803) 928-5300. **$105-$190.** 731 Citadel Rd 29118. I-26 exit 145B, just s. Int corridors. **Pets:** Other species. $10 one-time fee/room. Service with restrictions, supervision. 🛜 ♿ ⬛ 💻 🏊

RIDGELAND
WWW Quality Inn H

(843) 726-2121. **$60-$90.** Hwy 336 & I-95 29936. I-95 exit 21 (US 336), just nw. Ext/int corridors. **Pets:** Accepted. SAVE 🛜 ⬛ 💻 🏊

ST. GEORGE
WW Comfort Inn M

(843) 563-4180. **Call for rates.** 139 Motel Dr 29477. I-95 exit 77 (US 78), just e. Ext corridors. **Pets:** Medium. $10 daily fee/pet. Designated rooms, service with restrictions, supervision. 🛜 ⬛ 💻 🏊

△△△ ▽ Econo Lodge M
(843) 563-4195. **$50-$80.** 5971 W Jim Bilton Blvd 29477. I-95 exit 77 (US 78), just e. Ext corridors. **Pets:** Small. $5 daily fee/pet. Designated rooms, service with restrictions, supervision. 〔SAVE〕 🛜 🍴 💻 ⊃

▽▽ Quality Inn- St George M ☙
(843) 563-4581. **$60-$70.** 6014 W Jim Bilton Blvd 29477. I-95 exit 77 (US 78), just e. Ext corridors. **Pets:** Large. $10 daily fee/pet. Service with restrictions, supervision. 🛜 🔊M 🍴 💻 ⊃

SANTEE

△△△ ▽ Americas Best Value Inn M
(803) 854-3122. **Call for rates.** 9091 Old Hwy 6 29142. I-95 exit 98 (SR 6), 0.4 mi se. Ext corridors. **Pets:** Accepted. 〔SAVE〕 🛜 🍴 💻

△△△ ▽▽ Econo Lodge Santee M
(803) 854-3870. **$54-$58.** 9112 Old Hwy 6 29142. I-95 exit 98 (SR 6), 0.4 mi se. Ext corridors. **Pets:** $10 daily fee/pet. No service, crate.
〔SAVE〕 🛜 🍴 ⊃

▽▽▽ Holiday Inn Santee H
(803) 854-9800. **$89-$165.** 139 Bradford Blvd 29142. I-95 exit 98 (SR 6), just nw, then just sw. Int corridors. **Pets:** Small, other species. $20 daily fee/pet. Service with restrictions, supervision.
🛜 🔊M 🍴 🍽 ⊃

△△△ ▽▽ Quality Inn & Suites Santee M
(803) 854-2121. **Call for rates.** 8929 Old Number 6 Hwy 29142. I-95 exit 98 (SR 6), just nw. Ext corridors. **Pets:** Other species. $10 one-time fee/pet. Designated rooms, service with restrictions, crate.
〔SAVE〕 🛜 🍴 🍽 ⊃ ⊠

△△△ ▽▽ Super 8 M
(803) 854-3456. **$55-$75.** 9125 Old Hwy 6 29142. I-95 exit 98 (SR 6), 0.4 mi se. Ext corridors. **Pets:** Other species. $10 daily fee/pet. Service with restrictions. 〔SAVE〕 🛜 🍴 💻 ⊃

SENECA

▽▽▽ Quality Inn M
(864) 888-8300. **$75-$95.** 226 Hi-Tech Rd 29678. Jct SR 28 and US 76/123, 0.9 mi w on US 76/123, then just se. Ext corridors.
Pets: Accepted. 🛜 🔊M 🍴 💻 ⊃

SIMPSONVILLE

▽▽▽ Comfort Suites H
(864) 757-1552. **$84-$149.** 3971 Grandview Dr 29680. I-385 exit 26, just w, then just ne. Int corridors. **Pets:** Medium, other species. $50 deposit/room, $25 daily fee/room. Service with restrictions.
🛜 ⊠ 🔊M 🍴 💻 ⊃

▽▽ Days Inn M
(864) 963-7701. **$60-$86.** 45 Ray E Talley Ct 29680. I-385 exit 27, just s, then just e. Ext corridors. **Pets:** Accepted. 🛜 🍴 💻 ⊃

△△△ ▽▽ Quality Inn M ☙
(864) 963-2777. **$59-$79.** 3755 Grandview Dr 29680. I-385 exit 27, just s. Ext corridors. **Pets:** $10 one-time fee/pet. Service with restrictions, supervision. 〔SAVE〕 🛜 🍴 💻 ⊃

SPARTANBURG

△△△ ▽▽▽ Holiday Inn Express Hotel & Suites H ☙
(864) 699-7777. **Call for rates.** 895 Spartan Blvd 29301. I-26 exit 21B (US 29), just e to W Blackstock Rd, then 0.7 mi n. Int corridors.
Pets: Other species. $50 one-time fee/room. Designated rooms, service with restrictions, crate. 〔SAVE〕 🛜 🔊M 🍴 💻 ⊃

▽▽▽ Quality Inn & Suites H
(864) 542-0333. **$55-$82.** 160 Simuel Rd 29303. I-85 business route exit 4 (SR 56), just sw. Int corridors. **Pets:** Accepted.
🛜 ⊠ 🍴 💻 ⊃ ⊠

SUMMERTON

△△△ ▽▽▽ Days Inn of Summerton M
(803) 485-2865. **$70-$105.** 400 Bluff Blvd 29148. I-95 exit 108, just n. Ext corridors. **Pets:** Accepted. 〔SAVE〕 🛜 🍴 💻 ⊃

SUMTER

▽▽▽ Candlewood Suites H
(803) 469-4000. **Call for rates.** 2541 Broad St 29150. 1.1 mi w of jct US 76/378/521. Int corridors. **Pets:** Accepted. 🛜 ⊠ 🍴 💻 ⊃

△△△ ▽▽ Travelers Inn & Suites M
(803) 469-9210. **$55-$129.** 1210 Camden Rd 29151. Jct US 521/76. Ext corridors. **Pets:** Medium. $10 daily fee/pet. Service with restrictions, supervision. 〔SAVE〕 🛜 🍴 💻 ⊃

WALTERBORO

△△△ ▽▽▽ BEST WESTERN of Walterboro M ☙
(843) 538-3600. **$79-$109.** 1428 Sniders Hwy 29488. I-95 exit 53 (SR 63), just e. Ext corridors. **Pets:** Medium. $15 daily fee/pet. Designated rooms, service with restrictions, supervision. 〔SAVE〕 🛜 🍴 💻 ⊃

△△△ ▽▽ Microtel Inn & Suites by Wyndham Walterboro H
(843) 539-5656. **$56-$89.** 130 Cane Branch Rd 29488. I-95 exit 53 (SR 63), just w, then just s. Int corridors. **Pets:** Other species. $15 one-time fee/room. Service with restrictions, crate. 〔SAVE〕 🛜 🔊M 🍴 💻 ⊃

△△△ ▽▽ Rice Planters Inn M
(843) 538-8964. **$44.** 97 Ladson Ln 29488. I-95 exit 53 (SR 63), just e. Ext corridors. **Pets:** Other species. $5 daily fee/pet. Service with restrictions, crate. 〔SAVE〕 🛜 🍴 ⊃

△△△ ▽▽ Super 8 M
(843) 538-5383. **$62-$77.** 1972 Bells Hwy 29488. I-95 exit 57 (SR 64), just nw. Ext corridors. **Pets:** Small. $10 daily fee/pet. Designated rooms, service with restrictions, supervision. 〔SAVE〕 🛜 🍴 💻 ⊃

WEST COLUMBIA

▽▽ Days Inn & Suites Airport M
(803) 796-0044. **$69-$90.** 110 Branch Rd 29169. I-26 exit 113 (Airport Blvd), just sw. Ext corridors. **Pets:** Accepted. 🛜 🍴 💻 ⊃

▽▽ Quality Inn M
(803) 791-5160. **$70-$100.** 2516 Augusta Rd 29169. I-26 exit 111B (US 1 N), just e. Ext/int corridors. **Pets:** Small. $15 daily fee/pet. Designated rooms, service with restrictions, supervision. 🛜 🍴 💻 ⊃

WINNSBORO

▽▽ Days Inn M
(803) 635-1447. **$56-$63.** 1894 US Hwy 321 Bypass 29180. I-77 exit 34 (SR 34), 6.5 mi w; jct US 321/SR 34/213. Ext corridors. **Pets:** Small. $10 daily fee/pet. Designated rooms, service with restrictions, supervision.
🛜 🍴 💻 ⊃

YEMASSEE

△△△ ▽▽▽ BEST WESTERN Point South M ☙
(843) 726-8101. **$70-$90.** 3536 Point South Dr 29945. I-95 exit 33 (US 17), just ne. Ext corridors. **Pets:** Other species. $10 one-time fee/room. Designated rooms, service with restrictions, supervision.
〔SAVE〕 🛜 🍴 💻 ⊃

SOUTH DAKOTA

ABERDEEN

Aberdeen East Super 8 🅷
(605) 229-5005. **$70-$115.** 2405 6th Ave SE 57401. 1.8 mi e on US 12. Int corridors. **Pets:** Other species. $10 daily fee/pet. Designated rooms, service with restrictions, supervision.

Aberdeen North Super 8 🅼
(605) 226-2288. **$60-$120.** 1023 8th Ave NW 57401. 1.5 mi nw on US 281. Int corridors. **Pets:** Accepted.

AmericInn Lodge & Suites of Aberdeen 🅷
(605) 225-4565. **$100.** 301 Centennial St 57401. 2.2 mi e on US 12, just n. Int corridors. **Pets:** Accepted.

BEST WESTERN Ramkota Hotel 🅷 ❀
(605) 229-4040. **$90-$130.** 1400 8th Ave NW 57401. 1.5 mi nw on US 281. Ext/int corridors. **Pets:** Service with restrictions, crate.
[SAVE] icons

Holiday Inn Express Hotel & Suites 🅷
(605) 725-4000. **$119-$145.** 3310 7th Ave SE 57401. 2.1 mi e on US 12. Int corridors. **Pets:** Accepted.

ARLINGTON

Arlington Inn 🅼
(605) 983-4609. **$66-$98.** 402 S Hwy 81 57212. 1 mi s on US 81. Int corridors. **Pets:** Accepted.

BLACK HILLS AREA

BELLE FOURCHE

Ace Motel 🅼
(605) 892-2612. **$48-$88.** 109 6th Ave 57717. 0.5 mi n via US 85, just e; just s of US 212 Bypass. Ext corridors. **Pets:** Medium, dogs only. $10 daily fee/pet. Designated rooms, service with restrictions, supervision.

CUSTER CITY

Bavarian Inn Motel 🅼
(605) 673-2802. **$59-$139, 3 day notice.** 907 N 5th St 57730. 1 mi n on US 16 and 385. Ext/int corridors. **Pets:** $100 deposit/pet, $20 one-time fee/pet. Designated rooms, service with restrictions, supervision.

Creekside Lodge 🅷
(605) 255-4388. **Call for rates.** 13389 US Hwy 16A 57730. On Alternate Rt US 16, 14 mi e; in Custer State Park. Int corridors. **Pets:** Accepted.

Rock Crest Lodge and Cabins 🅲🅰
(605) 673-4323. **Call for rates.** 15 W Mt. Rushmore Rd 57730. US 16, 0.5 mi w. Ext/int corridors. **Pets:** Accepted.

Rocket Motel 🅼
(605) 673-4401. **$59-$99, 3 day notice.** 211 Mt. Rushmore Rd 57730. On US 16; center. Ext corridors. **Pets:** Medium, dogs only. $10 daily fee/pet. Service with restrictions, crate.

State Game Lodge 🅼
(605) 255-4541. **Call for rates.** 13389 US 16A 57730. On Alternate Rt US 16, 14 mi e; in Custer State Park. Ext/int corridors. **Pets:** Accepted.

Super 8 - Custer 🅷
(605) 673-2200. **$60-$220.** 535 W Mt. Rushmore Rd 57730. US 16, 0.8 mi w. Int corridors. **Pets:** $15 daily fee/pet. Designated rooms, no service, supervision.

DEADWOOD

Cadillac Jacks Gaming Resort, an Ascend Collection hotel 🅷
(605) 578-1500. **$39-$279.** 360 Main St 57732. 0.6 mi n on US 85. Int corridors. **Pets:** $25 daily fee/pet. Designated rooms, service with restrictions, crate.

Deadwood Gulch Gaming Resort 🅷
(605) 578-1294. **$59-$169.** 304 Cliff St 57732. 0.7 mi s on US 85 S. Ext/int corridors. **Pets:** Dogs only. $500 deposit/room, $20 one-time fee/pet. Designated rooms, service with restrictions.

First Gold Hotel & Gaming 🅷
(605) 578-9777. **$79-$299.** 270 Main St 57732. 0.7 mi n on US 85. Int corridors. **Pets:** Medium. $25 one-time fee/room. Designated rooms, service with restrictions, supervision.

Holiday Inn Express Hotel & Suites 🅷 ❀
(605) 578-3330. **Call for rates.** 22 Lee St 57732. Jct Main St; center. Int corridors. **Pets:** $25 one-time fee/room. Designated rooms, supervision.

The Lodge at Deadwood 🅷 ❀
(605) 584-4800. **$89-$540, 3 day notice.** 100 Pine Crest Ln 57732. Jct US 14, 1 mi n on US 85. Ext/int corridors. **Pets:** Dogs only. Service with restrictions, crate.

HILL CITY

BEST WESTERN PLUS Golden Spike Inn & Suites 🅷 ❀
(605) 574-2577. **$90-$239.** 601 E Main St 57745. Just n on US 16 and 385. Ext/int corridors. **Pets:** Medium, dogs only. $15 daily fee/pet. Designated rooms, service with restrictions, supervision.

🖤 ▼▼▼ Lantern Inn M
(605) 574-2582. **$64-$175.** 580 E Main St 57745. On US 16 and 385; north side of town. Ext corridors. **Pets:** Very small, dogs only. $10 daily fee/room. Designated rooms, service with restrictions, crate.
SAVE 🛰 ✕ 🎱 ➦

🖤 ▼▼▼ The Lodge at Palmer Gulch H 🐾
(605) 574-2525. **$50-$695, 10 day notice.** 12620 SR 244 57745. On SR 244, 5 mi w of Mt. Rushmore. Int corridors. **Pets:** Medium, dogs only. $20 daily fee/pet. Service with restrictions, supervision.
SAVE 🛰 ✕ 🔊 🎱 ➦ 🍴 ✕

HOT SPRINGS

🖤 ▼▼▼ BEST WESTERN Sundowner Inn H
(605) 745-7378. **$60-$180.** 737 S 6th St 57747. 0.5 mi se off US 18 and 385. Int corridors. **Pets:** Large. Designated rooms, service with restrictions. SAVE 🛰 🔊 🎱 🎱 ➦

🖤 ▼▼▼ Budget Host Hills Inn M
(605) 745-3130. **$49-$154.** 640 S 6th St 57747. 0.5 mi se off US 18 and 385. Ext corridors. **Pets:** Accepted. SAVE 🛰 🎱 🎱 ➦

🖤 ▼▼▼ Dollar Inn Hot Springs M
(605) 745-3182. **$50-$200.** 402 Battle Mountain Ave 57747. 1 mi n on US 385. Ext corridors. **Pets:** Accepted. SAVE 🛰 ✕ 🎱 🎱

🖤 ▼▼▼ Stay USA Hotel and Suites H
(605) 745-4411. **$56-$280.** 1401 Hwy 18 Bypass 57747. Jct US 18 and 385, 0.7 mi w on US 18 Bypass. Int corridors. **Pets:** Medium. $20 one-time fee/pet. Designated rooms, service with restrictions, crate.
SAVE 🛰 ✕ 🔊 🎱 🎱

▼▼▼ Super 8 - Hot Springs H
(605) 745-3888. **$49-$189.** 800 Mammoth St 57747. Jct US 18 and 385, 1 mi w on US 18 Bypass. Int corridors. **Pets:** Accepted.
🛰 🔊 🎱 🎱

KEYSTONE

🖤 ▼▼▼ Econo Lodge of Mt. Rushmore H
(605) 666-4417. **Call for rates.** 908 Madill St 57751. SR 40, 1 mi e of jct US 16A. Int corridors. **Pets:** Accepted. SAVE 🛰 🎱 🎱 ➦

🖤 ▼▼▼ Holy Smoke Resort CA
(605) 666-4616. **$60-$150, 3 day notice.** 24105 Hwy 16A 57751. On US 16A, 2 mi n. Ext corridors. **Pets:** Accepted.
SAVE 🛰 ✕ 🎱 🎱 🍴 🌀

🖤 ▼▼▼ Mt. Rushmore's Washington Inn H
(605) 666-5070. **$49-$99, 3 day notice.** 231 Winter St 57751. On US 16A; downtown. Ext/int corridors. **Pets:** Other species. Designated rooms, service with restrictions, crate. SAVE 🛰 🔊 🎱 🍴 ➦

🖤 ▼▼▼ Mt. Rushmore's White House Resort H
(605) 666-4917. **$49-$99, 3 day notice.** 115 Swanzey St 57751. Just e of jct US 16A and SR 40. Ext/int corridors. **Pets:** Other species. Designated rooms, service with restrictions, crate.
SAVE 🛰 ✕ 🔊 🎱 🍴 ➦

🖤 ▼▼▼ Powder House Lodge CA
(605) 666-4646. **$80-$300, 3 day notice.** 24125 Hwy 16A 57751. On US 16A, 1.5 mi n. Ext corridors. **Pets:** Accepted.
SAVE 🛰 ✕ 🔊 🎱 🎱 🍴 ➦

RAPID CITY

🖤 ▼▼▼▼ Adoba Eco Hotel Rapid City/Mt. Rushmore H
(605) 348-8300. **$79-$359.** 445 Mt. Rushmore Rd 57701. On I-90 business loop; jct Main St; center. Int corridors. **Pets:** Accepted.
SAVE 🛰 ✕ 🔊 🎱 🎱 🍴

▼▼▼ Americas Best Value Inn H
(605) 343-5434. **$59-$259, 7 day notice.** 620 Howard St 57701. I-90 exit 58 (Haines Ave), just nw. Int corridors. **Pets:** $10 daily fee/room. Service with restrictions, supervision. 🛰 🔊 🎱 🎱 ➦

🖤 ▼▼▼ AmericInn Lodge & Suites of Rapid City H
(605) 343-8424. **$39-$299, 3 day notice.** 1632 Rapp St 57701. I-90 exit 59 (LaCrosse St), just se. Int corridors. **Pets:** Accepted.
SAVE 🛰 ✕ 🔊 🎱 🎱 ➦ ✕

🖤 ▼▼▼ BEST WESTERN Ramkota Hotel & Conference Center H 🐾
(605) 343-8550. **$90-$230.** 2111 N LaCrosse St 57701. I-90 exit 59 (LaCrosse St), just n. Ext/int corridors. **Pets:** Large. Service with restrictions, supervision. SAVE 🛰 ✕ 🔊 🎱 🎱 🍴 ➦ ✕

🖤 ▼▼▼ BEST WESTERN Town 'N Country H 🐾
(605) 343-5383. **$50-$270.** 2505 Mt. Rushmore Rd 57701. 1.3 mi s on US 16. Ext corridors. **Pets:** Medium, dogs only. $20 daily fee/room. Service with restrictions, supervision. SAVE 🛰 ✕ 🔊 🎱 🎱 ➦

🖤 ▼▼▼ Big Sky Lodge M
(605) 348-3200. **$59-$159.** 4080 Tower Rd 57701. 3 mi s on US 16, 0.3 mi n on Skyline Dr, take service road off US 16. Ext corridors.
Pets: Dogs only. Designated rooms, service with restrictions, supervision.
SAVE 🛰 ✕ 🔊 🎱 🎱 🌀

🖤 ▼▼▼ Country Inn & Suites By Carlson H
(605) 394-0017. **Call for rates.** 2321 N LaCrosse St 57701. I-90 exit 59 (LaCrosse St), 0.3 mi n. Int corridors. **Pets:** Accepted.
SAVE 🛰 ✕ 🎱 🎱 ➦ ✕

🖤 ▼▼ Days Inn I-90 H
(605) 348-8410. **$55-$290.** 1570 N LaCrosse St 57701. I-90 exit 59 (LaCrosse St), just s. Int corridors. **Pets:** Small. $10 daily fee/pet. Designated rooms, service with restrictions, supervision.
SAVE 🛰 ✕ 🔊 🎱 🎱 ➦

🖤 ▼▼ Gold Star Motel M
(605) 341-7051. **$45-$150.** 801 E North St 57701. I-90 exit 60, 1.5 mi sw on I-90 business loop, 1.2 mi s, then just e, from exit 59 (LaCrosse St). Ext corridors. **Pets:** Dogs only. $5 daily fee/pet. Service with restrictions, supervision. SAVE 🛰 🔊 🎱

▼▼▼ Grand Gateway Hotel H
(605) 342-1300. **$59-$350.** 1721 N LaCrosse St 57701. I-90 exit 59 (LaCrosse St), just s. Int corridors. **Pets:** Small, dogs only. $20 daily fee/pet. Designated rooms, service with restrictions, supervision.
🛰 ✕ 🎱 🎱 🍴 ➦ ✕

🖤 ▼▼▼▼ GrandStay Residential Suites Hotel H
(605) 341-5100. **$89-$299.** 660 Disk Dr 57701. I-90 exit 58 (Haines Ave), just n, then just w. Int corridors. **Pets:** $100 deposit/room, $10 daily fee/pet. Service with restrictions, supervision.
SAVE 🛰 ✕ 🔊 🎱 🎱 ➦ ✕

▼▼▼ Holiday Inn Express H
(605) 341-9300. **Call for rates.** 750 Cathedral Dr 57701. 1.4 mi s on US 16, just e. Int corridors. **Pets:** Accepted. 🛰 🔊 🎱 🎱 ➦

▼▼▼ Holiday Inn Express Hotel & Suites I-90 H
(605) 355-9090. **$99-$199.** 645 E Disk Dr 57701. I-90 exit 59 (LaCrosse St), just ne. Int corridors. **Pets:** Large. $10 daily fee/room. Designated rooms, service with restrictions, crate. 🛰 🔊 🎱 🎱 ➦

▼▼▼ Holiday Inn-Rushmore Plaza H
(605) 348-4000. **$149-$209.** 505 N 5th St 57701. I-90 exit 58 (Haines Ave), 1.3 mi s. Int corridors. **Pets:** Accepted.
🛰 ✕ 🔊 🎱 🎱 🍴 ➦ ✕

**W W W W The Hotel Alex Johnson, an Ascend
Collection hotel** 🅷 ❖

(605) 342-1210. **$99-$159.** 523 6th St 57701. I-90 exit 57 (I-190 B.H.
Nat'l Forest/Mt. Rushmore), 1.8 mi s, just e on SR 44 (Omaha St), then
just s; jct St Joseph St. Int corridors. **Pets:** Other species. $25 daily fee/
pet. Designated rooms, service with restrictions, supervision.
SAVE 🛜 ✕ 🔌 🖥 🍴

W W W Howard Johnson Inn & Suites 🅷

(605) 737-4656. **$69-$375.** 950 North St 57701. I-90 exit 57 (I-190) exit
1C, then just e. Int corridors. **Pets:** Small, dogs only. $10 daily fee/room.
Service with restrictions, crate. SAVE 🛜 ✕ 🔌 🖥 ≋

W W W W La Quinta Inn & Suites Rapid City 🅷

(605) 718-7000. **$59-$364.** 1416 N Elk Vale Rd 57701. I-90 exit 61 (Elk
Vale Rd), just s, then just e. Int corridors. **Pets:** Service with restrictions,
supervision. SAVE 🛜 ✕ 🔌 🖥 🍴

W W Lazy U Motel Ⓜ

(605) 343-4242. **$42-$82.** 2215 Mt. Rushmore Rd 57701. 1 mi s on US
16. Ext corridors. **Pets:** Accepted. SAVE 🛜 🔌

**W W Microtel Inn & Suites by Wyndham Rapid
City** 🅷

(605) 348-2523. **$49-$239.** 1740 Rapp St 57701. I-90 exit 59 (LaCrosse
St), just se. Int corridors. **Pets:** Medium. $10 daily fee/room. Designated
rooms, service with restrictions, supervision.
SAVE 🛜 ✕ 🔌 🖥

W W W Rapid City Ramada 🅷 ❖

(605) 342-3322. **$40-$400.** 1902 N LaCrosse St 57701. I-90 exit 59
(LaCrosse St), just s. Ext/int corridors. **Pets:** Medium, other species. $10
daily fee/pet. Designated rooms, service with restrictions, supervision.
SAVE 🛜 ✕ 🔌 🖥 🍴 ≋

W W Sleep Inn & Suites 🅷

(605) 791-5678. **$59-$199.** 4031 Cheyenne Blvd 57703. I-90 exit 61 (Elk
Vale Rd), just s. Int corridors. **Pets:** Other species. $10 daily fee/pet. Ser-
vice with restrictions, supervision. 🛜 ✕ 🔌 🖥 ≋

W W W Super 8 LaCrosse St Ⓜ

(605) 348-8070. **$44-$199.** 2124 LaCrosse St 57701. I-90 exit 59
(LaCrosse St), just n. Int corridors. **Pets:** Medium, other species. $10
daily fee/pet. Service with restrictions, supervision.
SAVE 🛜 🔌 🖥

W W Super 8 Mt. Rushmore Rd Ⓜ

(605) 342-4911. **$43-$240.** 2520 Tower Rd 57701. 1.4 mi s on US 16,
then just e. Int corridors. **Pets:** Accepted. 🛜 🔌 🖥

W W Thrifty Motor Inn Ⓜ

(605) 342-0551. **Call for rates.** 1303 LaCrosse St 57701. I-90 exit 59
(LaCrosse St), 0.5 mi s. Ext corridors. **Pets:** Dogs only. $5 daily fee/pet.
Service with restrictions, supervision. SAVE 🛜 🔌 🖥

SPEARFISH

W W Bell's Motor Lodge Motel Ⓜ

(605) 642-3812. **$40-$88.** 230 N Main St 57783. 0.5 mi s of center. Ext
corridors. **Pets:** Very small, dogs only. $2 daily fee/pet. Designated rooms,
supervision. 🛜 🔌 🖥 ≋

W W W BEST WESTERN Black Hills Lodge 🅷

(605) 642-7795. **$64-$145.** 540 E Jackson Blvd 57783. I-90 exit 12, just
s. Ext/int corridors. **Pets:** Dogs only. $15 daily fee/room. Designated
rooms, service with restrictions, supervision.
SAVE 🛜 ✕ 🔌 🖥 ≋ ✕

W W Days Inn 🅷

(605) 642-7101. **$54-$271.** 240 Ryan Rd 57783. I-90 exit 10, 1.2 mi s.
Ext/int corridors. **Pets:** Accepted. 🛜 ✕ 🔌 🖥

**W W W W Holiday Inn Hotel & Convention
Center** 🅷 ❖

(605) 642-4683. **$99-$149.** 305 N 27th St 57783. I-90 exit 14 (Spearfish
Canyon), just n. Ext/int corridors. **Pets:** Other species. $100 deposit/room,
$25 one-time fee/pet. Designated rooms, service with restrictions, supervi-
sion. SAVE 🛜 🔌 🖥 🍴 ≋ ✕

W W Howard Johnson Inn 🅷 ❖

(605) 642-8105. **$57-$240.** 323 S 27th St 57783. I-90 exit 14 (Spearfish
Canyon), just s. Int corridors. **Pets:** Medium, other species. $10 daily
fee/room. Service with restrictions. 🛜 ✕ 🔌 🖥 ≋ ✕

W W Quality Inn 🅷

(605) 642-2337. **$65-$300.** 2725 1st Ave 57783. I-90 exit 14 (Spearfish
Canyon), just n. Int corridors. **Pets:** Medium. $20 daily fee/pet. Desig-
nated rooms, service with restrictions, supervision.
🛜 ✕ 🔌 🖥 ≋

W W W Spearfish Canyon Lodge 🅷 ❖

(605) 584-3435. **$89-$275, 5 day notice.** 10619 Roughlock Falls Rd
57754. I-90 exit 14 (Spearfish Canyon), 13 mi s. Int corridors. **Pets:** Other
species. $25 daily fee/pet. Service with restrictions, supervision.
SAVE 🛜 ✕ 🔌 🖥 🍴 ✕

W W Super 8-Spearfish 🅷

(605) 642-4721. **$55-$285.** 440 Heritage Dr 57783. I-90 exit 14
(Spearfish Canyon), just s, just e, then just s. Int corridors. **Pets:** Other
species. $10 daily fee/pet. Designated rooms, service with restrictions,
supervision. 🛜 🔌 🖥 ≋

STURGIS

W W W Holiday Inn Express & Suites - Sturgis 🅷

(605) 347-4140. **$99-$159.** 2721 Lazelle St 57785. I-90 exit 30 (US 14A),
just s. Int corridors. **Pets:** $20 one-time fee/room. Designated rooms,
service with restrictions, crate. 🛜 ✕ 🔌 🖥 ≋ ✕

END AREA

BRANDON

W W Comfort Inn 🅷

(605) 582-5777. **Call for rates.** 1105 N Splitrock Blvd 57005. I-90 exit
406, just s. Int corridors. **Pets:** Accepted. 🛜 🔌 🖥 ≋

W W W Holiday Inn Express & Suites 🅷 ❖

(605) 582-2901. **Call for rates.** 1103 N Splitrock Blvd 57005. I-90 exit
406, just s. Int corridors. **Pets:** $15 daily fee/pet. Service with restrictions,
crate. 🛜 ✕ 🔌 🖥 ≋ ✕

BROOKINGS

W W Brookings Super 8 🅷

(605) 692-6920. **$71-$119.** 3034 Lefevre Dr 57006. I-29 exit 132, just e.
Int corridors. **Pets:** Medium, other species. $10 daily fee/pet. Service with
restrictions, crate. 🛜 ✕ 🔌 🖥 ≋

W W W Holiday Inn Express Hotel & Suites 🅷

(605) 692-9060. **$115-$169.** 3020 Lefevre Dr 57006. I-29 exit 132, just
se. Int corridors. **Pets:** Small. $10 daily fee/room. Service with restrictions,
supervision. 🛜 ✕ 🔌 🖥 ≋ ✕

BUFFALO

▼▼ Tipperary Lodge M

(605) 375-3721. **$56.** 604 1st St W 57720. 0.5 mi n on US 85, turn at sign. Int corridors. **Pets:** Other species. Designated rooms, service with restrictions, supervision. 🛜 ✕ 🖁

CHAMBERLAIN

AAA ▼▼▼ BEST WESTERN Lee's Motor Inn M

(605) 734-5575. **$60-$100.** 220 W King Ave 57325. US 16 and I-90 business loop; downtown. Ext/int corridors. **Pets:** Accepted.

SAVE 🛜 ✕ 🖁M 🖁 🖵 ⟷ ✕

DE SMET

▼▼▼ De Smet Super Deluxe Inn & Suites H

(605) 854-9388. **$74-$96.** 288 Hwy 14 E 57231. US 14, just e. Int corridors. **Pets:** Accepted. 🛜 ✕ 🖁 🖵 ⟷

FAITH

AAA ▼▼▼ Prairie Vista Inn M

(605) 967-2343. **$78-$95.** 204 E 1st St 57626. On US 212; east end of town. Int corridors. **Pets:** Dogs only. $15 one-time fee/room. Designated rooms, service with restrictions, supervision. SAVE 🛜 🖁M 🖁 🖵

FAULKTON

▼▼ Faulkton Inn M

(605) 598-4567. **Call for rates.** 700 Main St 57438. On US 212; center. Int corridors. **Pets:** Accepted. 🛜 🖁 🖵

FORT PIERRE

▼▼▼ AmericInn Lodge & Suites of Fort Pierre H ❀

(605) 223-2358. **$106-$199.** 312 Island Dr 57532. Jct US 14 and SR 34, just w of Missouri River Bridge, then just s. Int corridors. **Pets:** Other species. $20 one-time fee/pet. Designated rooms, service with restrictions, supervision. 🛜 ✕ 🖁 🖵 ⟷

▼▼ Fort Pierre Motel M

(605) 223-3111. **$68-$88, 3 day notice.** 211 S 1st St 57532. On US 83, 1.2 mi s of jct US 14. Ext corridors. **Pets:** Accepted.

🛜 ✕ 🖁M 🖁 🖉

FREEMAN

▼▼ Freeman Country Inn M

(605) 925-4888. **$75-$116.** 1019 S Hwy 81 57029. On US 81, just s. Int corridors. **Pets:** Other species. $20 daily fee/pet. Designated rooms, service with restrictions, supervision. 🛜 ✕ 🖁M 🖁

HURON

AAA ▼▼▼ BEST WESTERN Of Huron H ❀

(605) 352-2000. **$81-$131.** 2000 Dakota Ave 57350. 1.3 mi s on SR 37. Ext/int corridors. **Pets:** Very small, dogs only. $10 daily fee/room. Service with restrictions, supervision. SAVE 🛜 🖁M 🖁 🖵 ✕

INTERIOR

AAA ▼ Badlands Budget Host Inn M

(605) 433-5335. **$59-$69.** 900 SD Hwy 377 57750. Jct SR 44 and 377, 2 mi s of Badlands National Park. Ext corridors. **Pets:** Accepted.

SAVE 🛜 🖵 ⟷ 🕅 🖉

KADOKA

AAA ▼ Budget Host Sundowner Motor Inn M

(605) 837-2296. **$54-$120.** 510 SD Hwy 73 57543. I-90 exit 150, just s. Ext corridors. **Pets:** Accepted. SAVE 🛜 🖁M 🖁 ⟷

MADISON

▼▼ AmericInn Lodge & Suites Madison H

(605) 256-3076. **Call for rates.** 504 10th St SE 57042. SR 34, 0.5 mi se; south side of town. Int corridors. **Pets:** Other species. $10 daily fee/room. Service with restrictions, supervision.

🛜 ✕ 🖁M 🖁 🖵 ⟷

MITCHELL

AAA ▼▼▼ Days Inn of Mitchell H

(605) 996-6208. **$74-$114.** 1506 S Burr St 57301. I-90 exit 332, just n. Int corridors. **Pets:** Dogs only. $10 daily fee/pet. Designated rooms, service with restrictions, supervision. SAVE 🛜 🖁M 🖁 🖵 ⟷ ✕

AAA ▼▼▼ Hampton Inn H

(605) 995-1575. **Call for rates.** 1920 Highland Way 57301. I-90 exit 332, just se. Int corridors. **Pets:** Dogs only. $20 one-time fee/room. Service with restrictions. SAVE 🛜 ✕ 🖁M 🖁 🖵 ⟷ ✕

AAA ▼▼▼ Kelly Inn & Suites H

(605) 995-0500. **$75-$130.** 1010 Cabela Dr 57301. I-90 exit 332, just sw. Ext/int corridors. **Pets:** Accepted. SAVE 🛜 ✕ 🖁M 🖁 🖵 ⟷

MOBRIDGE

▼▼ Wrangler Inn H

(605) 845-3641. **$69-$159.** 820 W Grand Crossing 57601. 0.5 mi w on US 12. Ext/int corridors. **Pets:** Accepted.

🛜 ✕ 🖁 🖵 🍴 ⟷ ✕

MURDO

AAA ▼▼▼ BEST WESTERN Graham's M

(605) 669-2441. **$60-$140.** 301 W 5th St 57559. On I-90 business loop, 0.5 mi w of jct US 83; I-90 exit 191 or 192. Ext corridors. **Pets:** Large, other species. $20 one-time fee/room. Designated rooms, service with restrictions, supervision. SAVE 🛜 ✕ 🖁M 🖁 🖵 ⟷

AAA ▼▼▼ Range Country H

(605) 669-2425. **$65-$159.** 302 W 5th St 57559. I-90 business loop, 0.5 mi w of jct US 83 exit 192 or 191. Ext/int corridors. **Pets:** $50 deposit/room. Supervision. SAVE 🛜 🖁M 🖁 🖵 ⟷

I1;2q

NORTH SIOUX CITY

▼▼▼ Hampton Inn H

(605) 232-9739. **$79-$139.** 101 S Sodrac Dr 57049. I-29 exit 2, just w. Int corridors. **Pets:** Small. Designated rooms, service with restrictions, crate. 🛜 🖁M 🖁 🖵 ⟷

OACOMA

AAA ▼▼▼ Oasis Inn H

(605) 734-6061. **Call for rates.** 1100 E Hwy 16 57365. I-90 exit 260, 0.4 mi e on US 16 and I-90 business loop. Ext/int corridors. **Pets:** Other species. Designated rooms, service with restrictions, supervision.

SAVE 🛜 ✕ 🖁M 🖁 🖵 ⟷

▼▼ Quality Inn H

(605) 734-5593. **Call for rates.** 100 W Hwy 16 57365. I-90 exit 260, just n. Int corridors. **Pets:** Accepted. 🛜 ✕ 🖁M 🖁 🖵 ⟷

PIERRE

AAA ▼▼▼▼ BEST WESTERN Ramkota Hotel H ❀

(605) 224-6877. **$90-$130.** 920 W Sioux Ave 57501. 1 mi w on US 14/83. Ext/int corridors. **Pets:** Other species. Service with restrictions, supervision. SAVE 🛜 ✕ 🖁M 🖁 🖵 🍴 ⟷ ✕

▼▼▼ **Governor's Inn** 🅷

(605) 224-4200. **$75-$140.** 700 W Sioux Ave 57501. 0.8 mi w on US 14/83 and SR 34. Ext/int corridors. **Pets:** Other species. $10 one-time fee/room. Service with restrictions, supervision.

🛜 ✕ ⓱ 🗄 💻 🏊

🔷 ▼▼▼ **River Lodge** Ⓜ 🐾

(605) 224-4140. **$59-$79.** 713 W Sioux Ave 57501. 0.8 mi w on US 14/83. Int corridors. **Pets:** $8 daily fee/pet. Service with restrictions, supervision. 🆂🅰🆅🅴 🛜 ⓱ 🗄 💻

▼▼ **Super 8** Ⓜ

(605) 224-1617. **$55-$145.** 320 W Sioux Ave 57501. 0.3 mi w on US 14/83 and SR 34. Int corridors. **Pets:** $10 one-time fee/pet.

🛜 🗄 💻

SIOUX FALLS

🔷 ▼▼▼ **BEST WESTERN Empire Towers** 🅷

(605) 361-3118. **$85-$170.** 4100 W Shirley Pl 57106. I-29 exit 77 (41st St), just ne. Int corridors. **Pets:** Small, other species. $15 daily fee/room. Designated rooms, service with restrictions, supervision.

🆂🅰🆅🅴 🛜 ✕ ⓱ 🗄 💻 🏊

🔷 ▼▼▼▼ **BEST WESTERN PLUS Ramkota Hotel** 🅷

(605) 336-0650. **$90-$170.** 3200 W Maple St 57107. I-29 exit 81 (Airport/ Russell St), just e. Ext/int corridors. **Pets:** Other species. Service with restrictions, supervision. 🆂🅰🆅🅴 🛜 ✕ ⓱ 🗄 💻 🍽 🏊 ✕

▼▼ **Brimark Inn** Ⓜ

(605) 332-2000. **Call for rates.** 3200 W Russell St 57107. I-29 exit 81 (Airport/Russell St), just e. Int corridors. **Pets:** Other species. $10 daily fee/pet. Service with restrictions, supervision. 🛜 🗄 💻 🏊

▼▼▼▼ **ClubHouse Hotel & Suites** 🅷 🐾

(605) 361-8700. **Call for rates.** 2320 S Louise Ave 57106. I-29 exit 78 (26th St), just e. Ext/int corridors. **Pets:** Service with restrictions, supervision. 🛜 ✕ ⓱ 🗄 💻 🍽 🏊 ✕

▼▼ **Comfort Inn by Choice Hotels South** Ⓜ

(605) 361-2822. **$70-$140.** 3216 S Carolyn Ave 57106. I-29 exit 77 (41st St), just e, then n. Int corridors. **Pets:** Medium. $10 daily fee/pet. Service with restrictions, supervision. 🛜 ⓱ 🗄 💻 🏊

▼▼▼▼ **Comfort Suites by Choice Hotels** 🅷

(605) 362-9711. **Call for rates.** 3208 S Carolyn Ave 57106. I-29 exit 77 (41st St), just e, then n. Int corridors. **Pets:** Medium. $10 daily fee/pet. Designated rooms, service with restrictions, supervision.

🛜 ✕ ⓱ 🗄 💻 🏊

🔷 ▼▼▼ **Days Inn Airport** Ⓜ 🐾

(605) 331-5959. **$72-$107.** 5001 N Cliff Ave 57104. I-90 exit 399 (Cliff Ave), just s. Int corridors. **Pets:** Other species. $10 daily fee/room. Service with restrictions, supervision. 🆂🅰🆅🅴 🛜 ⓱ 🗄 💻

🔷 ▼▼▼▼ **Holiday Inn Sioux Falls City Centre** 🅷

(605) 339-2000. **$109-$179.** 100 W 8th St 57104. Just w of Phillips Ave; downtown. Int corridors. **Pets:** Medium, dogs only. $25 one-time fee/room. Supervision. 🆂🅰🆅🅴 🛜 ✕ ⓱ 🗄 💻 🍽 🏊 ✕

▼▼▼▼ **Homewood Suites By Hilton** 🅷

(605) 338-8585. **$69-$239.** 3620 W Avera Dr 57108. I-229 exit 1C (Louise Ave), just s. Int corridors. **Pets:** Other species. $15 one-time fee/room, $5 daily fee/room. Service with restrictions, crate.

🛜 ⓱ 🗄 💻 🏊 ✕

▼▼ **Microtel Inn & Suites by Wyndham Sioux Falls** Ⓜ

(605) 361-7484. **$55-$80.** 2901 S Carolyn Ave 57106. I-29 exit 77 (41st St), just e, then n. Int corridors. **Pets:** Other species. $25 one-time fee/ room. Service with restrictions. 🛜 ⓱ 🗄 💻

▼▼▼▼ **Quality Inn & Suites** 🅷

(605) 336-1900. **Call for rates.** 5410 N Granite Ln 57107. I-29 exit 83 (SR 38), just e, then 0.3 mi n. Int corridors. **Pets:** Medium, other species. $10 daily fee/pet. Designated rooms, service with restrictions, supervision.

🛜 ✕ ⓱ 🗄 💻 🏊

▼▼ **Red Roof Inn** Ⓜ

(605) 361-1864. **$42-$82.** 3500 S Gateway Blvd 57106. I-29 exit 77 (41st St), just w. Int corridors. **Pets:** Large, other species. Service with restrictions, supervision. 🛜 ⓱ 🗄 💻

▼▼▼ **Residence Inn by Marriott** 🅷 🐾

(605) 361-2202. **$80-$300.** 4509 W Empire Pl 57106. I-29 exit 77 (41st St), 0.5 mi se. Int corridors. **Pets:** Other species. $75 one-time fee/room. Service with restrictions, supervision.

🛜 ✕ ⓱ 🗄 💻 🏊 ✕

🔷 ▼▼▼▼ **Sheraton Sioux Falls** 🅷 🐾

(605) 331-0100. **$79-$159.** 1211 N West Ave 57104. I-29 exit 81 (Airport/ Russell St), 1.3 mi e. Int corridors. **Pets:** Dogs only. Service with restrictions, supervision. 🆂🅰🆅🅴 🛜 ✕ ⓱ 🗄 💻 🍽 🏊 ✕

▼▼▼▼ **Staybridge Suites** 🅷 🐾

(605) 361-2298. **$139-$349.** 2505 S Carolyn Ave 57106. I-29 exit 78 (26th St), just se. Int corridors. **Pets:** Medium, other species. $50 daily fee/pet. Designated rooms, service with restrictions, supervision.

🛜 ⓱ 🗄 💻 🏊

▼▼▼ **Super 8-East** Ⓜ

(605) 338-8881. **$68-$92.** 2616 E 10th St 57103. I-229 exit 6, just e. Int corridors. **Pets:** Accepted. 🛜 ⓱ 🗄 💻 🏊

🔷 ▼▼▼ **Super 8/I-90/Airport East** Ⓜ

(605) 339-9212. **$70-$90, 3 day notice.** 4808 N Cliff Ave 57104. I-90 exit 399 (Cliff Ave), 0.3 mi s. Int corridors. **Pets:** Accepted. 🆂🅰🆅🅴 🛜 🗄 💻

▼▼▼ **TownePlace Suites by Marriott** 🅷

(605) 361-2626. **$109-$189.** 4545 W Homefield Dr 57106. I-29 exit 78 (26th St), just w. Int corridors. **Pets:** Medium. $75 one-time fee/room. Service with restrictions, crate. 🛜 ✕ ⓱ 🗄 💻 🏊 ✕

SUMMERSET
▼▼ **Ramada** 🅷

(605) 787-4844. **$62-$333.** 7900 Stagestop Rd 57718. I-90 exit 48, just s. Int corridors. **Pets:** Accepted. 🛜 ✕ ⓱ 🗄 💻 🏊

VERMILLION

🔷 ▼▼▼ **BEST WESTERN Vermillion Inn** 🅷 🐾

(605) 624-8333. **$90-$120, 3 day notice.** 701 W Cherry St 57069. I-29 exit 26 (SR 50), 7.5 mi w on Business Rt SR 50. Int corridors. **Pets:** $10 daily fee/pet. Designated rooms, service with restrictions, supervision.

🆂🅰🆅🅴 🛜 ✕ ⓱ 🗄 💻 🏊 ✕

▼▼ **Prairie Inn** 🅷

(605) 624-2824. **Call for rates.** 916 N Dakota St 57069. I-29 exit 26 (SR 50), 7 mi w, then 0.3 mi n. Int corridors. **Pets:** Accepted.

🛜 ✕ 🗄 💻 🍽

WALL

🔷 ▼▼▼ **BEST WESTERN Plains Motel** Ⓜ 🐾

(605) 279-2145. **$60-$176.** 712 Glenn St 57790. I-90 exit 110, just n. Ext corridors. **Pets:** Other species. $15 daily fee/pet. Service with restrictions, supervision. 🆂🅰🆅🅴 🛜 ⓱ 🗄 💻 🏊 ✕

🔷 ▼▼▼ **Econo Lodge** Ⓜ

(605) 279-2121. **$49-$109.** 804 Glenn St 57790. I-90 exit 110, just n. Int corridors. **Pets:** Other species. Designated rooms, service with restrictions, supervision. 🆂🅰🆅🅴 🛜 ⓱ 🗄 💻 🏊

◆◆◆ ▼ Sunshine Inn M
(605) 279-2178. **$53-$73.** 608 Main St 57790. Downtown. Ext corridors.
Pets: $5 one-time fee/room. Service with restrictions. SAVE 📶

WATERTOWN

◆◆◆ ▼▼▼▼ BEST WESTERN Ramkota Hotel H ☙
(605) 886-8011. **Call for rates.** 1901 9th Ave SW 57201. I-29 exit 177
(US 212), 4 mi w. Int corridors. **Pets:** Medium. Designated rooms, service
with restrictions, supervision.
SAVE 📶 ✕ ♿ 🛏 💻 🍴 ⊷ ✕

▼▼▼▼ Country Inn & Suites By Carlson H
(605) 886-8900. **$96-$140.** 3400 8th Ave SE 57201. I-29 exit 177 (US
212), just w. Int corridors. **Pets:** Accepted.
📶 ✕ ♿ 🛏 💻 ⊷

▼▼ Days Inn H
(605) 886-3500. **$70-$105.** 2900 9th Ave SE 57201. I-29 exit 177 (US
212), 0.5 mi w. Ext/int corridors. **Pets:** $15 one-time fee/room. Service
with restrictions, supervision. 📶 ♿ 🛏 💻 ⊷

▼▼ Econo Lodge M
(605) 882-2243. **$55-$75.** 920 14th St SE 57201. I-29 exit 177 (US 212),
1.5 mi w, then just s. Int corridors. **Pets:** Accepted. 📶 🛏 💻

▼▼▼ Holiday Inn Express Hotel & Suites H ☙
(605) 882-3636. **Call for rates.** 3901 9th Ave SE 57201. I-29 exit 177
(US 212), just e. Int corridors. **Pets:** Large, dogs only. $30 deposit/room.
Crate. 📶 ♿ 🛏 💻 ⊷ ✕

▼▼▼ Quality Inn & Suites H
(605) 886-3010. **$89-$139.** 800 35th St Cir 57201. I-29 exit 177 (US
212), just w. Ext/int corridors. **Pets:** Accepted. 📶 ♿ 🛏 💻 ⊷

▼ Super 8-Watertown M
(605) 882-1900. **$65-$75.** 503 14th Ave SE 57201. On US 81, 0.3 mi s
of jct US 212. Int corridors. **Pets:** $10 daily fee/pet. Designated rooms,
service with restrictions, supervision. 📶 ♿ 🛏 💻 ⊷

▼ Travel Host Motel M
(605) 886-6120. **Call for rates.** 1714 9th Ave SW 57201. I-29 exit 177
(US 212), 4 mi w. Int corridors. **Pets:** Accepted. 📶 🛏 💻

WINNER

▼▼▼ Holiday Inn Express Hotel & Suites Winner H
(605) 842-2255. **$100-$110.** 1360 E Hwy 44 57580. Just ne of jct US 18
and 183. Int corridors. **Pets:** Very small. $25 daily fee/pet. Service with
restrictions, supervision. 📶 ✕ ♿ 🛏 💻 ⊷

YANKTON

◆◆◆ ▼▼▼ BEST WESTERN Kelly Inn H ☙
(605) 665-2906. **$89-$109.** 1607 Hwy 50 E 57078. On US 50, 1.8 mi e.
Ext/int corridors. **Pets:** Other species. Service with restrictions, supervision. SAVE 📶 ✕ ♿ 🛏 💻 🍴 ⊷ ✕

◆◆◆ ▼▼▼ Days Inn M
(605) 665-8717. **$78.** 2410 Broadway St 57078. US 81, 1.7 mi n. Int
corridors. **Pets:** $10 one-time fee/pet. Service with restrictions.
SAVE 📶 ♿ 🛏 💻 ⊷

▼▼ Lewis & Clark Resort M
(605) 665-2680. **$70-$125, 30 day notice.** 43496 Shore Dr 57078. 4 mi
w on SR 52; in Lewis and Clark State Park, just w of marina. Ext corridors. **Pets:** Accepted. 📶 ✕ ♿ 🛏 💻 🍴 ⊷ ✕ 🚳

TENNESSEE

ALCOA

▼▼▼▼ Candlewood Suites Knoxville Airport/Alcoa 🄷
(865) 233-4411. **$74-$79.** 176 Cusick Rd 37701. US 129, just e. Int corridors. **Pets:** Medium, other species. $25 daily fee/room. Service with restrictions, crate. 🛜 🕭M 🛏 🖵 ⊇

▼▼▼▼ MainStay Suites 🄷
(865) 379-7799. **$80-$110.** 361 Fountain View Cir 37701. US 129, just n on SR 35, just se on Associates Blvd, then just w. Int corridors. **Pets:** Medium. $25 one-time fee/room. Designated rooms, service with restrictions, crate. 🛜 🕭M 🛏 🖵 ⊇ ⊠

▼▼▼ Quality Inn 🄷
(865) 984-6800. **$79-$99.** 206 Corporate Pl 37701. US 129, just s. Int corridors. **Pets:** Accepted. 🛜 🕭M 🛏 🖵 ⊇ ⊠

ATHENS

▼▼▼ Days Inn-Athens 🄼
(423) 745-5800. **$63-$73.** 2541 Decatur Pike 37303. I-75 exit 49, just e on SR 30. Ext corridors. **Pets:** Accepted. 🛜 🕭M 🛏 🖵 ⊇

BRENTWOOD

▼▼▼ Baymont Inn & Suites 🄷
(615) 376-4666. **$70-$129.** 111 Penn Warren Dr 37027. I-65 exit 74B, 1.5 mi w, then just s on West Park Dr. Int corridors. **Pets:** $15 daily fee/pet. Designated rooms, service with restrictions, crate.
🛜 🕭M 🛏 🖵 ⊇

▼▼▼ Candlewood Suites 🄷
(615) 309-0600. **$53-$90.** 5129 Virginia Way 37027. I-65 exit 74B, 0.5 mi w, 0.5 mi s on Franklin Rd (US 31), 1.2 mi w on Maryland Way, just s on Ward Cir, then just s. Int corridors. **Pets:** Accepted. ⊏🔳 🛜 🛏 🖵

▼▼▼ MainStay Suites-Brentwood 🄷
(615) 371-8477. **$90-$140.** 107 Brentwood Blvd 37027. I-65 exit 74B, 1 mi w. Int corridors. **Pets:** Accepted. 🛜 🕭M 🛏 🖵 ⊇

(AAA) ▼▼▼▼ Residence Inn by Marriott Nashville - Brentwood 🄷
(615) 371-0100. **$87-$219.** 206 Ward Cir 37027. I-65 exit 74B, 0.3 mi s on Franklin Rd (US 31 S), then 0.5 mi w on Maryland Way. Ext/int corridors. **Pets:** Accepted. 🆂🅰🆅🅴 🛜 ⊠ 🛏 🖵 ⊇ ⊠

▼▼▼ Sleep Inn 🄷
(615) 376-2122. **Call for rates.** 1611 Galleria Blvd 37027. I-65 exit 69, 0.4 mi w, then just n. Int corridors. **Pets:** Medium. $10 daily fee/pet. Designated rooms, service with restrictions, supervision.
🛜 🕭M 🛏 🖵 ⊇

BULLS GAP

(AAA) ▼▼▼ BEST WESTERN Executive Inn 🄷
(423) 235-9111. **$70-$190.** 50 Speedway Ln 37711. I-81 exit 23, just w. Int corridors. **Pets:** $15 daily fee/pet. Designated rooms, service with restrictions, crate. 🆂🅰🆅🅴 🛜 🕭M 🛏 🖵 ⊇

BUTLER

▼▼▼ Iron Mountain Inn B&B and Creekside Chalet 🄱🄱
(423) 768-2446. **$150-$400, 21 day notice.** 268 Moreland Dr 37640. 1.6 mi w on Pine Orchard Rd from SR 67 at Stout Store, follow signs; 13 mi w on SR 67 from US 421 in Mountain City, follow sign at Stout Store area; 15.1 mi from Shell station in Hampton to Pine Orchard Rd, 1.6 mi to Moreland Dr. Ext/int corridors. **Pets:** Dogs only. $50 one-time fee/pet. Designated rooms, no service, supervision. 🛜 🛏 🖵 ⊠

CHATTANOOGA

▼▼▼ America's Best Inn-Hamilton Mall Area 🄼
(423) 894-5454. **Call for rates.** 7717 Lee Hwy 37421. I-75 exit 7B northbound; exit 7 southbound, just w. Ext corridors. **Pets:** Accepted.
🛜 🛏 🖵 ⊇

▼▼▼ Baymont Inn & Suites-Chattanooga 🄷
(423) 821-1090. **$65-$102.** 3540 Cummings Hwy 37419. I-24 exit 174, 0.4 mi s. Int corridors. **Pets:** Other species. $10 daily fee/pet. Designated rooms, no service, supervision. 🛜 🛏 🖵 ⊇

(AAA) ▼▼▼ BEST WESTERN Heritage Inn 🄼 🐾
(423) 899-3311. **$60-$99.** 7641 Lee Hwy 37421. I-75 exit 7B northbound; exit 7 southbound, just w. Ext corridors. **Pets:** Small, dogs only. $10 daily fee/pet. Service with restrictions, crate. 🆂🅰🆅🅴 🛜 🕭M 🛏 🖷 🍴 ⊇

▼▼▼ Chattanooga Choo-Choo 🄷
(423) 266-5000. **$109-$229.** 1400 Market St 37402. I-24 exit 178 (Broad St) eastbound; exit Market St westbound, 0.5 mi n. Ext/int corridors. **Pets:** $25 one-time fee/room. Service with restrictions, supervision.
🄴🄲🄾 🆂🅰🆅🅴 🛜 ⊠ 🕭M 🛏 🖵 🍴 ⊇ ⊠

(AAA) ▼▼▼▼ The Chattanoogan 🄷
(423) 756-3400. **$139-$239.** 1201 Broad St 37402. I-24 exit 178 (Market St), follow signs to Broad St/US 11, then 0.6 mi n. Int corridors. **Pets:** Accepted.
🄴🄲🄾 ⊏🔳 🆂🅰🆅🅴 🛜 ⊠ 🕭M 🛏 🖵 🍴 ⊇ ⊠

(AAA) ▼▼▼ Country Inn & Suites By Carlson, Chattanooga I-24 West 🄷 🐾
(423) 825-6100. **$109-$199.** 3725 Modern Industries Blvd 37419. I-24 exit 174, just s. Int corridors. **Pets:** Small, dogs only. $25 one-time fee/pet. Designated rooms, service with restrictions, crate.
🆂🅰🆅🅴 🛜 🕭M 🛏 🖵 ⊇

(AAA) ▼▼▼ Days Inn-Lookout Mountain/Tiftonia M
(423) 821-6044. **$59-$84.** 3801 Cummings Hwy 37419. I-24 exit 174, just n. Ext corridors. **Pets:** $10 daily fee/pet. Designated rooms, service with restrictions, supervision. [SAVE] [icons]

▼▼ Extended StayAmerica-Chattanooga-Airport H
(423) 892-1315. **$50-$100.** 6240 Airpark Dr 37421. SR 153 exit 1 (Lee Hwy), 0.3 mi s to Vance Rd, then just w to cul de sac. Ext corridors. **Pets:** $25 daily fee/pet. Designated rooms, service with restrictions. [icons]

▼▼ GuestHouse International Inn M
(423) 510-0800. **Call for rates.** 2201 Park Dr 37421. I-75 exit 5 (Shallowford Rd), 0.5 mi w, then just s. Ext corridors. **Pets:** Accepted. [icons]

▼▼▼ Homewood Suites by Hilton H
(423) 510-8020. **$149-$259.** 2250 Center St 37421. I-75 exit 5 (Shallowford Rd), 0.5 mi w. Int corridors. **Pets:** Accepted. [icons]

(AAA) ▼▼▼ La Quinta Inn Chattanooga H
(423) 265-3151. **$71-$166.** 100 W 21st St 37408. I-24 exit 178, US 11 to Lookout Mountain, w to 20th St, w to Williams St, then w. Int corridors. **Pets:** Service with restrictions, supervision. [SAVE] [icons]

▼▼ La Quinta Inn Chattanooga/Hamilton Place M
(423) 855-0011. **$59-$122.** 7015 Shallowford Rd 37421. I-75 exit 5 (Shallowford Rd), just w. Ext corridors. **Pets:** Service with restrictions, supervision. [icons]

▼▼ MainStay Suites-Chattanooga H
(423) 485-9424. **$79-$129.** 7030 Amin Dr 37421. I-75 exit 5 (Shallowford Rd), just w, then s. Int corridors. **Pets:** Medium, dogs only. $15 daily fee/pet. Designated rooms, service with restrictions, crate. [icons]

▼ Motel 6 Downtown #4145 H
(423) 265-7300. **$36-$100.** 2440 Williams St 37408. I-24 exit 178 (Market St), just s. Int corridors. **Pets:** Other species. Service with restrictions, supervision. [icons]

(AAA) ▼▼▼ Quality Inn M
(423) 821-1499. **Call for rates.** 3109 Parker Ln 37419. I-24 exit 175, just s. Ext corridors. **Pets:** $15 daily fee/pet. Designated rooms, service with restrictions, supervision. [SAVE] [icons]

(AAA) ▼▼▼ Quality Suites M
(423) 892-1500. **$68-$82.** 7324 Shallowford Rd 37421. I-75 exit 5 (Shallowford Rd), just e. Ext corridors. **Pets:** Medium. $10 daily fee/pet. Service with restrictions, supervision. [SAVE] [icons]

(AAA) ▼▼▼ Ramada Limited-Lookout Mountain I-24 West M
(423) 821-7162. **$50-$100.** 30 Birmingham Hwy 37419. I-24 exit 174, just s. Ext/int corridors. **Pets:** Medium. $15 daily fee/pet. Designated rooms, service with restrictions, supervision. [SAVE] [icons]

(AAA) ▼▼▼ Red Roof Inn-Chattanooga M
(423) 899-0143. **$39-$89.** 7014 Shallowford Rd 37421. I-75 exit 5 (Shallowford Rd), just w. Ext corridors. **Pets:** Large, other species. Service with restrictions, supervision. [SAVE] [icons]

▼▼▼ Residence Inn by Marriott Chattanooga - Downtown H
(423) 266-0600. **$132-$199.** 215 Chestnut St 37402. US 27 N exit 1C (4th St), just n. Int corridors. **Pets:** Accepted. [icons]

▼▼▼ Residence Inn by Marriott Chattanooga near Hamilton Place H
(423) 468-7700. **$129-$289.** 2340 Center St 37421. I-75 exit 5 (Shallowford Rd), 0.5 mi w to Lee Hwy, then just n. Int corridors. **Pets:** $75 one-time fee/room. Service with restrictions. [icons]

(AAA) ▼▼▼ The Sheraton Read House Hotel Chattanooga H ❀
(423) 266-4121. **$129-$500.** 827 Broad St 37402. US 27 exit 1A, just e. Int corridors. **Pets:** Small, dogs only. $50 one-time fee/room. Service with restrictions, supervision. [SAVE] [icons]

▼▼▼ Staybridge Suites H
(423) 267-0900. **$129-$169.** 1300 Carter St 37402. US 27 N exit 1A (Dr Martin Luther King Blvd), just e to Carter St, then 0.3 mi s. Int corridors. **Pets:** Accepted. [icons]

▼▼▼ Staybridge Suites-Hamilton Place H
(423) 826-2700. **$129-$249.** 7015 Shallowford Rd 37421. I-75 exit 5 (Shallowford Rd), just w. Int corridors. **Pets:** Small. $75 one-time fee/room. Designated rooms, service with restrictions, supervision. [icons]

▼▼ Super 8 H
(423) 490-8560. **$55-$74.** 7024 McCutcheon Rd 37421. I-75 exit 5 (Shallowford Rd), just w, then 0.3 mi n on Shallowford Village Dr. Int corridors. **Pets:** Accepted. [icons]

CLARKSVILLE

▼▼▼ Candlewood Suites H
(931) 906-0900. **$114-$129.** 3050 Clay Lewis Rd 37040. I-24 exit 4, just s. Int corridors. **Pets:** Medium. $75 one-time fee/room. Service with restrictions, crate. [icons]

▼▼▼ MainStay Suites H
(931) 648-3400. **$99-$139.** 115 Fairbrook Pl 37043. I-24 exit 4, just sw. Int corridors. **Pets:** Small. $50 one-time fee/room. Designated rooms, service with restrictions, crate. [icons]

(AAA) ▼▼ Quality Inn-Exit 4 H
(931) 648-4848. **$77-$99.** 3095 Wilma Rudolph Blvd 37040. I-24 exit 4, just se. Ext corridors. **Pets:** Medium, other species. $25 daily fee/room. Service with restrictions, crate. [SAVE] [icons]

▼▼ Red Roof Inn H
(931) 905-1555. **$41-$79.** 197 Holiday Dr 37040. I-24 exit 4, just se. Ext corridors. **Pets:** Large, other species. Service with restrictions, supervision. [icons]

CLEVELAND

▼▼ Baymont Inn & Suites Cleveland H
(423) 614-5583. **Call for rates.** 360 Paul Huff Pkwy 37312. I-75 exit 27, 0.8 mi e. Ext corridors. **Pets:** Other species. $15 daily fee/room. Service with restrictions, crate. [icons]

▼▼ Colonial Inn M
(423) 472-6845. **$35-$45.** 1555 25th St 37311. I-75 exit 25, 0.3 mi e. Ext corridors. **Pets:** Very small, dogs only. $10 one-time fee/pet, $10 daily fee/pet. Service with restrictions, supervision. [icons]

(AAA) ▼▼▼ Douglas Inn & Suites H
(423) 559-5579. **$55-$115.** 2600 Westside Dr NW 37312. I-75 exit 25, just e, then just n. Ext/int corridors. **Pets:** Medium. $15 daily fee/pet. Designated rooms, service with restrictions, supervision. [SAVE] [icons]

▼▼ Mountain View Inn H
(423) 472-1500. **$62-$71.** 2400 Executive Park Dr 37312. I-75 exit 25, just w, then just n. Ext/int corridors. **Pets:** Accepted. [icons]

◆◆ **Quality Inn** 🅷

(423) 478-5265. **$60-$100.** 153 James Asbury Dr 37312. I-75 exit 27, just w, then just s. Ext/int corridors. **Pets:** Accepted. 🛜 📶 💻 ⇌

◆◆ **Super 8** Ⓜ

(423) 476-5555. **$60-$110.** 163 Bernham Dr 37312. I-75 exit 27, just w, then just s. Ext/int corridors. **Pets:** Accepted. 🛜 📶 💻 ⇌

CLINTON

◆◆ **Red Roof Inn & Suites** 🅷

(865) 457-9070. **$54-$99.** 141 Buffalo Rd 37716. I-75 exit 122, just w. Ext corridors. **Pets:** Large, other species. Service with restrictions, supervision. 🛜 ♿ 📶 💻 ⇌

COLUMBIA

◆◆ **Baymont Inn & Suites Columbia/Maury** 🅷

(931) 388-3326. **$90-$110.** 715 James M Campbell Blvd 38401. 0.9 mi w of jct SR 50 and US 31. Int corridors. **Pets:** Accepted.

🛜 📶 💻 ⇌

◆◆ **Super 8 Columbia** 🅷

(931) 380-1227. **$75.** 1554 Bear Creek Pike 38401. I-65 exit 46, just w. Ext corridors. **Pets:** Medium. $10 one-time fee/pet. Service with restrictions, supervision. 🛜 ♿ 📶 💻 ⇌

COOKEVILLE

◆◆ **Baymont Inn & Suites Cookeville** 🅷

(931) 525-6668. **$77-$94.** 1151 S Jefferson Ave 38506. I-40 exit 287, just s. Int corridors. **Pets:** Other species. $25 daily fee/pet. Service with restrictions. 🛜 ♿ 📶 💻 ⇌ ✕

◆◆◆ ◆◆ **BEST WESTERN Thunderbird Motel** 🅷

(931) 526-7115. **$54-$101.** 900 S Jefferson Ave 38501. I-40 exit 287, just n. Ext corridors. **Pets:** $20 daily fee/room. Designated rooms, service with restrictions, crate. SAVE 🛜 ♿ 📶 💻 🍽 ⇌

◆◆◆ ◆◆ **Clarion Inn** 🅷

(931) 526-7125. **$65-$110.** 970 S Jefferson Ave 38501. I-40 exit 287, just n. Ext/int corridors. **Pets:** Large, other species. $10 one-time fee/pet. Designated rooms, service with restrictions, supervision.
SAVE 🛜 ♿ 📶 💻 🍽 ⇌ ✕

◆◆◆ ◆◆ **Red Roof Inn Cookeville** Ⓜ

(931) 528-2020. **$50-$125.** 1292 S Walnut Ave 38501. I-40 exit 287. Ext corridors. **Pets:** Large, other species. Service with restrictions, supervision. SAVE 🛜 📶 💻 ⇌

CROSSVILLE

◆◆◆ ◆◆ **BEST WESTERN Leisure Inn** 🅷

(931) 484-1551. **$85-$95.** 4035 Hwy 127 N 38571. I-40 exit 317 (US 127), just n. Int corridors. **Pets:** Small. $15 daily fee/room. Designated rooms, supervision. SAVE 🛜 📶 💻 ⇌

◆◆◆ ◆◆ **La Quinta Inn-Crossville** 🅷

(931) 456-9338. **$84-$162.** 4038 Hwy 127 N 38571. I-40 exit 317 (US 127), just n. Int corridors. **Pets:** Service with restrictions, supervision. SAVE 🛜 ♿ 📶 💻 ⇌

DANDRIDGE

◆◆ **Jefferson Inn** 🅷

(865) 940-5042. **$60-$100.** 127 Sharon Dr 37725. I-40 exit 417, just s. Int corridors. **Pets:** Small, dogs only. $10 daily fee/pet. Designated rooms, service with restrictions, supervision. ♿ 📶 💻 ⇌

◆◆ **Super 8** 🅷

(865) 397-1200. **$50-$185.** 125 Sharon Dr 37725. I-40 exit 417, just s. Int corridors. **Pets:** $10 daily fee/pet. Supervision.
🛜 ♿ 📶 💻 ⇌

DAYTON

◆◆◆ ◆◆ **BEST WESTERN Dayton** Ⓜ

(423) 775-6560. **$76-$99.** 7835 Rhea County Hwy 37321. 1 mi n on US 27. Ext corridors. **Pets:** $10 daily fee/pet. Designated rooms, service with restrictions. SAVE 🛜 📶 💻 ⇌

DECHERD

◆◆ **Quality Inn** 🅷

(931) 962-0130. **$74-$94.** 1838 Decherd Blvd 37324. Jct Main St and SR 41A, just s. Ext corridors. **Pets:** Accepted. 🛜 📶 💻 ⇌

DICKSON

◆◆◆ ◆◆ **BEST WESTERN Executive Inn** 🅷 🐾

(615) 446-0541. **$69-$99.** 2338 Hwy 46 37055. I-40 exit 172, just n. Ext corridors. **Pets:** Dogs only. $10 daily fee/pet. Service with restrictions, supervision. SAVE 🛜 📶 💻 ⇌

◆◆◆ ◆◆ **Comfort Inn** 🅷

(615) 740-1000. **$55-$99.** 1085 E Christi Dr 37055. I-40 exit 172, just ne. Int corridors. **Pets:** Medium, other species. $30 daily fee/pet. Designated rooms, service with restrictions, supervision.
SAVE 🛜 ♿ 📶 💻 ⇌

◆◆ **Econo Lodge Inn & Suites** 🅷

(615) 441-5252. **Call for rates.** 1025 E Christi Dr 37055. I-40 exit 172, just ne. Int corridors. **Pets:** Small, dogs only. $10 daily fee/pet. Designated rooms, service with restrictions, supervision. 🛜 📶 💻 ⇌

◆◆◆ ◆◆ **Holiday Inn Express** 🅷

(615) 446-2781. **$90-$120.** 100 Barzani Blvd 37055. I-40 exit 172, just se. Int corridors. **Pets:** Small. $20 daily fee/pet. Service with restrictions, supervision. SAVE 🛜 ♿ 📶 💻 ⇌

◆◆◆ ◆◆ **Super 8** 🅷

(615) 446-1923. **$50-$60, 3 day notice.** 150 Suzanne Dr 37055. I-40 exit 172, just ne. Int corridors. **Pets:** Accepted. SAVE 🛜 📶 💻 ⇌

DYERSBURG

◆◆◆ ◆◆ **BEST WESTERN Dyersburg Inn** 🅷

(731) 285-8601. **$80-$100.** 770 Hwy 51 Bypass W 38024. I-155 exit 13, 0.5 mi s; jct US 51 Bypass and SR 78. Ext corridors. **Pets:** Accepted.
SAVE 🛜 📶 💻 🍽 ⇌

◆◆ **Days Inn** 🅷

(731) 287-0888. **$63-$71.** 2600 Lake Rd 38024. I-155 exit 13, just s. Int corridors. **Pets:** Very small, dogs only. $10 daily fee/pet. Designated rooms, service with restrictions, supervision. 🛜 ♿ 📶 💻

◆◆ **Executive Inn & Suites** 🅷

(731) 287-0044. **$45-$65.** 2331 Lake Rd 38024. I-155 exit 13, 0.5 mi s. Ext corridors. **Pets:** $10 daily fee/pet. Service with restrictions, supervision. 🛜 📶

◆◆◆ **Hampton Inn** 🅷

(731) 285-4778. **Call for rates.** 2750 Mall Loop Rd 38024. I-155 exit 13, just s. Int corridors. **Pets:** Medium, other species. Service with restrictions, supervision. 🛜 ♿ 📶 💻 ⇌

◆◆◆ **Holiday Inn Express & Suites** 🅷

(731) 286-1021. **$90-$99.** 822 Reelfoot Dr 38024. I-155 exit 13, just s. Int corridors. **Pets:** Very small. $10 daily fee/pet. Service with restrictions, supervision. 🛜 ♿ 📶 💻 ⇌

◆◆◆ **Sleep Inn & Suites** 🅷

(731) 287-0248. **$70-$85, 5 day notice.** 824 Reelfoot Dr 38024. I-155 exit 13, just s. Int corridors. **Pets:** Medium. $10 daily fee/pet. Designated rooms, service with restrictions, supervision.
🛜 ✕ ♿ 📶 💻 ⇌

FARRAGUT

(AAA) ▼▼▼ **Econo Lodge Knoxville** **M**
(865) 288-3641. **Call for rates.** 11717 Campbell Lakes Dr 37934. I-40/75 exit 373 (Campbell Station Rd), just s. Ext corridors. **Pets:** Medium. $10 daily fee/pet. Service with restrictions, crate.
[SAVE] 🛜 &M 🛏 🖵 ⇒

FAYETTEVILLE

(AAA) ▼▼▼ **BEST WESTERN Fayetteville Inn** **H**
(931) 433-0100. **$95-$100.** 3021 Thornton Taylor Pkwy 37334. 0.7 mi e of US 431, on US 64 and 231 Bypass. Ext corridors. **Pets:** Medium. $10 daily fee/pet. Service with restrictions, supervision.
[SAVE] 🛜 🛏 🖵 ⇒

FRANKLIN

(AAA) ▼▼▼▼ **Aloft Nashville-Cool Springs** **H**
(615) 435-8700. **$89-$209.** 7109 S Springs Dr 37067. I-65 exit 68B, just w, 0.3 mi n on Mallory Ln, then just e. Int corridors. **Pets:** Accepted.
[SAVE] 🛜 ✕ 🛏 🖵 ⇒

(AAA) ▼▼▼ **BEST WESTERN Franklin Inn** **H** ❧
(615) 790-0570. **$59-$89.** 1308 Murfreesboro Rd 37064. I-65 exit 65, just sw. Ext corridors. **Pets:** Medium. $10 one-time fee/room. Service with restrictions, supervision. [SAVE] 🛜 🛏 🖵 ⇒

▼▼ **Days Inn** **H**
(615) 790-1140. **$56-$85.** 3915 S Carothers Pkwy 37064. I-65 exit 65, just se. Ext corridors. **Pets:** Other species. $10 daily fee/pet. Service with restrictions, supervision. 🛜 🛏 🖵 ⇒

▼▼▼ **Embassy Suites Nashville South/Cool Springs** **H** ❧
(615) 515-5151. **$139-$239.** 820 Crescent Centre Dr 37067. I-65 exit 68A to Carothers Rd. Int corridors. **Pets:** Large. $50 one-time fee/room. Designated rooms, service with restrictions, supervision.
🛜 &M 🛏 🖵 ❙❙ ⇒ ✕

▼▼▼ **Holiday Inn Express Hotel & Suites** **H**
(615) 591-6660. **$116-$123, 3 day notice.** 4202 Franklin Commons Ct 37067. I-65 exit 65, just e. Int corridors. **Pets:** Accepted.
🛜 &M 🛏 🖵 ⇒

▼▼ **Homestead Studio Suites Hotel-Nashville/Franklin-Cool Springs** **H**
(615) 771-7600. **$50-$70.** 680 Bakers Bridge Ave 37067. I-65 exit 69 (Galleria Blvd), 0.3 mi e on Moores Ln to Carothers Pkwy, 0.5 mi s, then 0.3 mi w. Ext corridors. **Pets:** $25 daily fee/pet. Designated rooms, service with restrictions. 🛜 🛏 🖵

▼▼ **La Quinta Inn & Suites Nashville-Franklin** **H**
(615) 791-7700. **$59-$144.** 4207 Franklin Commons Ct 37067. I-65 exit 65, just e. Int corridors. **Pets:** Service with restrictions, supervision.
🛜 &M 🛏 🖵 ⇒

▼▼ **Residence Inn by Marriott Franklin Cool Springs** **H**
(615) 778-0002. **$109-$279.** 2009 Meridian Blvd 37067. I-65 exit 68A, just e on Cool Springs Blvd, then just n on Carothers Pkwy. Int corridors. **Pets:** Medium. $100 one-time fee/room. Designated rooms, service with restrictions, crate. 🛜 ✕ &M 🛏 🖵 ⇒ ✕

GALLATIN

▼▼ **Quality Inn** **M**
(615) 451-4494. **$79-$99.** 1001 Village Green Crossing 37066. 2 mi s on US 31. Ext corridors. **Pets:** Medium, other species. $15 daily fee/pet. Service with restrictions, supervision. 🛜 &M 🛏 🖵 ⇒

GATLINBURG

(AAA) ▼▼▼▼ **Cobbly Nob Rentals** **CA**
(865) 436-5298. **$100-$1999, 30 day notice.** 3722 E Parkway 37738. Jct US 441, 10.3 mi n on US 321. **Pets:** Small, dogs only. $15 daily fee/pet. Designated rooms, no service, supervision.
[SAVE] 🛜 ✕ 🛏 🖵 ⇒ ✕

(AAA) ▼▼▼▼ **Microtel Inn & Suites by Wyndham Gatlinburg** **H**
(865) 436-0107. **$40-$299, 3 day notice.** 211 Historic Nature Tr 37738. Just e of US 441 at traffic light 8. Int corridors. **Pets:** Accepted.
[SAVE] 🛜 &M 🛏 🖵

▼▼▼▼ **Outback Resort Rentals & Sales** **VH**
(865) 430-9385. **$120-$799, 30 day notice.** 902 Street of Dreams Way 37738. Jct US 441 on north end of town at Great Smoky Mountains Welcome Center, 1 mi sw on Wiley Oakley Dr, then 0.5 mi w on N Woodland Dr. Ext corridors. **Pets:** Medium, dogs only. $150 deposit/room. No service. ◈ ✕ 🛏 🖵 ⇒

▼▼ **Red.Roof Inn** **M**
(865) 436-7813. **$39-$199.** 309 Ownby St 37738. Traffic light 10 (Ski Mountain Rd), 0.4 mi n. Ext corridors. **Pets:** Large, other species. Service with restrictions, supervision. 🛜 🛏 🖵 ⇒

(AAA) ▼▼▼▼ **Westgate Smoky Mountain Resort & Spa** **CO**
(865) 430-4800. **Call for rates.** 915 Westgate Resort Rd 37738. Jct US 441, just e on Little Smoky Rd, then just s. Ext corridors. **Pets:** Accepted.
[SAVE] 🛜 ✕ 🛏 🖵 ❙❙ ⇒ ✕

GREENEVILLE

▼ **Andrew Johnson Inn** **M**
(423) 638-8124. **$42-$55, 7 day notice.** 2145 E Andrew Johnson Hwy 37745. US 11 E, 3.1 mi ne. Ext corridors. **Pets:** Very small. $10 daily fee/pet. Designated rooms, service with restrictions, supervision.
🛏 🖵 ⇒

▼▼ **Days Inn** **M**
(423) 639-2156. **$60-$200.** 935 E Andrew Johnson Hwy 37745. US 11 E, 2 mi ne. Ext corridors. **Pets:** Accepted. 🛜 🛏 🖵

▼▼▼ **Quality Inn** **H**
(423) 638-7511. **$74-$94.** 3160 E Andrew Johnson Hwy 37745. US 11 E Bypass, 3.6 mi ne. Int corridors. **Pets:** Accepted.
🛜 &M 🛏 🖵 ⇒

HARRIMAN

(AAA) ▼▼▼ **Days Inn Harriman** **M**
(865) 882-6200. **$60-$90.** 120 Childs Rd 37748. I-40 exit 347, just n on US 27. Ext corridors. **Pets:** Accepted. [SAVE] 🛜 &M 🛏 🖵

(AAA) ▼▼▼ **Quality Inn** **M**
(865) 882-5340. **$60-$100.** 1845A S Roane St 37748. I-40 exit 347, just s on US 27/SR 61. Ext corridors. **Pets:** $15 daily fee/pet. Crate.
[SAVE] 🛜 &M 🛏 🖵 ⇒

▼▼ **Rodeway Inn** **M**
(865) 882-5400. **Call for rates.** 1845B S Roane St 37748. I-40 exit 347, just s on US 27/SR 61. Int corridors. **Pets:** $15 daily fee/pet. Crate.
🛜 🛏 🖵

HURRICANE MILLS

(AAA) ▼▼▼ **BEST WESTERN of Hurricane Mills** **H**
(931) 296-4251. **$100-$140.** 15542 Hwy 13 S 37078. I-40 exit 143, just n. Ext corridors. **Pets:** Other species. $15 daily fee/pet. Designated rooms, service with restrictions, crate. [SAVE] 🛜 🛏 🖵 ⇒

JACKSON

(AAA) ▼▼▼ **BEST WESTERN Carriage House Inn & Suites** **H**
(731) 664-3030. **$74-$89.** 1936 Hwy 45 Bypass 38305. I-40 exit 80A, just s. Ext corridors. **Pets:** Accepted. [SAVE] 🛜 🛏 🖵 ⇒

▼▼▼ **Courtyard by Marriott** **H**
(731) 422-1818. **$149-$189.** 200 Campbell Oaks Dr 38305. I-40 exit 83, just sw. Int corridors. **Pets:** Accepted.
🛜 ✕ &M 🛏 🖵 ❙❙ ⇒

▼▼▼ **Hampton Inn & Suites** 🏨
(731) 427-6100. **$119-$169.** 150 Campbell Oaks Dr 38305. I-40 exit 83, just s. Int corridors. **Pets:** Accepted. 🛜 👤M 🛏 🖵 🏊

▼▼ **Howard Johnson Jackson** 🏨
(731) 660-8651. **$89-$109.** 1292 Vann Dr 38305. I-40 exit 80B, 0.6 mi w. Int corridors. **Pets:** Accepted. 🛜 🛏 🖵 🏊

▼▼ **Quality Inn** 🏨
(731) 668-1400. **$65-$79.** 535 Wiley Parker Rd 38305. I-40 exit 80A, just s, then e on Carriage House Dr. Ext/int corridors. **Pets:** Small. $15 one-time fee/pet. Service with restrictions, supervision. 🛜 🛏 🖵 🏊

▼▼▼ **Residence Inn by Marriott Jackson** 🏨
(731) 935-4100. **$129-$189.** 126 Old Medina Crossing 38305. I-40 exit 83, just ne. Int corridors. **Pets:** Other species. $75 one-time fee/room. Service with restrictions. 🛜 ❌ 🛏 🖵 🏊

JOHNSON CITY

AAA ▼▼▼ **BEST WESTERN PLUS Johnson City Hotel & Conference Center** 🏨
(423) 282-2161. **$60-$275.** 2406 N Roan St 37601. I-26 exit 20A westbound; exit 20 eastbound, just n. Ext/int corridors. **Pets:** Medium. $15 daily fee/pet. Designated rooms, service with restrictions, crate.
SAVE 🛜 👤M 🛏 🖵 🍴 🏊

AAA ▼▼▼ ▼▼▼ **Carnegie Hotel** 🏨
(423) 979-6400. **$122-$135.** 1216 W State of Franklin Rd 37604. I-26 exit 24, 2.2 mi se on US 321 S. Int corridors. **Pets:** Dogs only. $25 daily fee/pet. Designated rooms, service with restrictions, crate.
SAVE 🛜 🛏 🖵 🍴 🏊

▼▼ **Comfort Inn of Johnson City** 🏨
(423) 928-9600. **$69-$85.** 1900 S Roan St 37604. I-26 exit 24, just w on US 321. Ext corridors. **Pets:** Accepted. 🛜 🛏 🖵 🏊

▼▼▼ **Comfort Suites** 🏨
(423) 610-0010. **$88-$100.** 3118 Browns Mill Rd 37604. I-26 exit 19, just e, then just n. Int corridors. **Pets:** Medium, other species. $15 daily fee/pet. Designated rooms, service with restrictions, crate.
🛜 ❌ 👤M 🛏 🖵 🏊

▼▼▼ **DoubleTree by Hilton Hotel Johnson City** 🏨
(423) 929-2000. **$89-$199.** 211 Mockingbird Ln 37604. I-26 exit 20A westbound; exit 20 eastbound, just w on N Roan St. Int corridors.
Pets: Accepted. ECO 🛜 👤M 🛏 🖵 🍴 🏊

▼▼▼ **Holiday Inn-Johnson City** 🏨
(423) 282-4611. **$109-$119.** 101 W Springbrook Dr 37604. I-26 exit 20A westbound; exit 20 eastbound, just e on N Roan St, then just n. Int corridors. **Pets:** Small. $25 one-time fee/room. Service with restrictions, supervision. 🛜 👤M 🛏 🖵 🍴 🏊

▼▼ **Motel 6 Johnson City #4620** 🏨
(423) 282-3335. **Call for rates.** 207 E Mountcastle Dr 37601. I-26 exit 20B westbound; exit 20 eastbound, 0.5 mi w on N Roan St, then 0.3 mi s. Ext/int corridors. **Pets:** Other species. Service with restrictions, supervision. 🛜 👤M 🏊

▼▼ **Quality Inn** 🏨
(423) 282-0488. **$97-$117.** 119 Pinnacle Dr 37615. I-26 exit 17, just w on CR 354, then just s. Ext corridors. **Pets:** Accepted.
🛜 👤M 🛏 🖵 🏊

AAA ▼▼▼ **Red Roof Inn-Johnson City** Ⓜ
(423) 282-3040. **$50-$90.** 210 Broyles Dr 37601. I-26 exit 20A westbound; exit 20 eastbound, just w on N Roan St. Ext corridors.
Pets: Large, other species. Service with restrictions, supervision.
SAVE 🛜 👤M

▼▼ **Sleep Inn & Suites** 🏨
(423) 915-0081. **Call for rates.** 2020 Franklin Terrace Ct 37604. I-26 exit 19, just w, then just n, follow signs; entrance on Oakland Ave at light. Int corridors. **Pets:** Accepted. 🛜 👤M 🛏 🖵

JONESBOROUGH

AAA ▼▼▼ **AmericInn Lodge & Suites of Jonesborough** 🏨
(423) 753-3100. **$70-$100.** 376 E Jackson Blvd 37659. I-26 exit 17 (Boones Creek Rd); jct E Jackson Blvd (US 11 E). Int corridors.
Pets: Small, dogs only. $25 one-time fee/pet. Designated rooms, service with restrictions, supervision. SAVE 🛜 👤M 🛏 🖵 🏊

KIMBALL

AAA ▼▼▼ **Super 8 - Kimball** 🏨
(423) 837-7185. **$63-$97.** 395 Main St 37347. I-24 exit 152, 0.5 mi n. Ext corridors. **Pets:** Medium. $10 one-time fee/room. Designated rooms, service with restrictions, supervision. SAVE 🛜 🛏 🖵 🏊

KINGSPORT

▼▼▼ **Colonial Inn** Ⓜ
(423) 239-3400. **$50-$210.** 4234 Fort Henry Dr 37663. I-81 exit 59, 0.7 mi n on SR 36. Ext corridors. **Pets:** Accepted. 🛜 ❌ 👤M 🛏 🖵

▼▼▼ **La Quinta Inn & Suites Kingsport Tri-Cities Airport** 🏨
(423) 323-0500. **$71-$177.** 10150 Airport Pkwy 37663. I-81 exit 63, just e. Int corridors. **Pets:** Service with restrictions, supervision.
🛜 👤M 🛏 🖵 🏊

▼▼▼ **Quality Inn** 🏨
(423) 230-0534. **$81-$101.** 3004 Bay Meadow Pl 37664. I-26 exit 4, just n. Int corridors. **Pets:** Accepted. 🛜 👤M 🛏 🖵 🏊

▼▼ **Sleep Inn** 🏨
(423) 279-1811. **Call for rates.** 200 Hospitality Pl 37663. I-81 exit 63, just s. Int corridors. **Pets:** Accepted. 🛜 🛏 🖵

KINGSTON

▼▼ **Motel 6 #4403** Ⓜ
(865) 376-2069. **$43-$90.** 495 Gallaher Rd 37763. I-40 exit 356, just n. Ext corridors. **Pets:** Other species. Service with restrictions, supervision.
🛜 🛏

KINGSTON SPRINGS

AAA ▼▼▼ **BEST WESTERN Harpeth Inn** 🏨
(615) 952-3961. **$60-$100.** 116 Luyben Hills Rd 37082. I-40 exit 188, just n. Ext corridors. **Pets:** Large, other species. $10 daily fee/pet. Service with restrictions, supervision. SAVE 🛜 🛏 🖵 🏊

KNOXVILLE

AAA ▼▼▼ **BEST WESTERN Knoxville Suites** 🏨
(865) 687-9922. **$69-$150.** 5317 Pratt Rd 37912. I-75 exit 108 (Merchants Dr), just e, then n. Int corridors. **Pets:** Accepted.
SAVE 🛜 👤M 🛏 🖵 🏊

▼▼ **Candlewood Suites-Knoxville** 🏨
(865) 777-0400. **$89-$119.** 10206 Parkside Dr 37922. I-40/75 exit 374 (Lovell Rd), 0.5 mi s, then 1 mi e. Int corridors. **Pets:** Medium. $15 daily fee/room. Service with restrictions, crate. 🛜 👤M 🛏 🖵

▼▼ **The Clarion Inn** 🏨
(865) 687-8989. **$70-$90.** 5634 Merchants Center Blvd 37912. I-75 exit 108 (Merchants Dr), just w, then just n. Int corridors. **Pets:** Medium, other species. $20 deposit/pet, $20 daily fee/pet. Service with restrictions, supervision. 🛜 👤M 🛏 🖵 🏊

▼▼▼ **Crowne Plaza Knoxville** 🏨 🐾
(865) 522-2600. **$116-$140.** 401 W Summit Hill Dr 37902. Corner of Walnut St; downtown. Int corridors. **Pets:** Other species. $25 one-time fee/room. Service with restrictions. 🍽 🛜 👤M 🛏 🖵 🍴 🏊

AAA ▼▼▼ **Econo Lodge Inn & Suites - East Knoxville** **M**

(865) 932-1217. **$55-$125.** 7424 Strawberry Plains Pike 37924. I-40 exit 398 (Strawberry Plains Pike), just n. Ext corridors. **Pets:** Accepted.
SAVE 🛜 🛗 💻 ≈

▼▼▼ **Econo Lodge-North** **M**

(865) 687-5680. **$55-$75.** 5505 Merchants Center Blvd 37912. I-75 exit 108 (Merchants Dr), just w, then just n. Ext corridors. **Pets:** Small, dogs only. $10 daily fee/pet. Service with restrictions, supervision. 🛜 🛗

▼▼▼ **Extended StayAmerica Knoxville-Cedar Bluff** **M**

(865) 769-0822. **$60-$100.** 214 Langley Pl 37922. I-40/75 exit 378 (Cedar Bluff Rd), just s, then 1 mi w on N Peters Rd. Ext corridors. **Pets:** $25 daily fee/pet. Designated rooms, service with restrictions.
🛜 🛗 💻 ≈

▼▼▼ **Extended StayAmerica Knoxville-West Hills** **H**

(865) 694-4178. **$60-$120.** 1700 Winston Rd 37919. I-40/75 exit 380 (West Hills), just w on Kingston Pike, then just s. Int corridors. **Pets:** $25 daily fee/pet. Designated rooms, service with restrictions.
🛜 🛗 💻 ≈

▼▼▼ **Hilton Knoxville Downtown** **H**

(865) 523-2300. **$109-$169.** 501 W Church Ave 37902. Between Locust and Walnut sts; downtown. Int corridors. **Pets:** Accepted.
🛜 ⬇M 🛗 💻 🍴 ≈

▼▼▼ **Holiday Inn Cedar Bluff** **H** ☙

(865) 693-1011. **$99-$149.** 304 Cedar Bluff Rd 37923. I-40/75 exit 378 (Cedar Bluff Rd) eastbound; exit 378B westbound, just n to Executive Park Dr. Int corridors. **Pets:** Medium. $50 one-time fee/room. Designated rooms, service with restrictions, supervision.
🛜 ⬇M 🛗 💻 🍴 ≈ ⊠

▼▼▼ **Holiday Inn Express Knoxville-East** **H**

(865) 525-5100. **$99-$159.** 730 Rufus Graham Rd 37924. I-40 exit 398 (Strawberry Plains Pike), just n. Int corridors. **Pets:** Accepted.
🄴 🛜 ⬇M 🛗 💻 ≈

AAA ▼▼▼ **Holiday Inn World's Fair Park** **H**

(865) 522-2800. **$99-$199.** 525 Henley St 37902. Corner of Clinch Ave; downtown. Int corridors. **Pets:** Accepted.
ECO SAVE 🛜 ⬇M 🛗 💻 🍴 ≈

▼▼▼ **Homewood Suites by Hilton** **H**

(865) 777-0375. **Call for rates.** 10935 Turkey Dr 37922. I-40/75 exit 374 (Lovell Rd), just s to Parkside Dr, then 0.5 mi n on Snow Goose Dr. Int corridors. **Pets:** Accepted. 🛜 ⬇M 🛗 💻 ≈ ⊠

▼▼▼ **La Quinta Inn & Suites Knoxville Strawberry Plains** **H**

(865) 633-5100. **$83-$177.** 7210 Saddle Rack St 37914. I-40 exit 398 (Strawberry Plains Pike), just s, just e on Region Ln, then just se on Shumard Ave. Int corridors. **Pets:** Service with restrictions, supervision.
🛜 ⬇M 🛗 💻 ≈

▼▼▼ **La Quinta Inn Knoxville (West)** **M**

(865) 690-9777. **$59-$144.** 258 N Peters Rd 37923. I-40/75 exit 378 (Cedar Bluff Rd), just s, then just e. Ext corridors. **Pets:** Service with restrictions, supervision. 🛜 🛗 💻 ≈

▼▼▼ **MainStay Suites Knoxville** **H**

(865) 247-0222. **$99-$149.** 144 Merchant Dr 37912. I-75 exit 108 (Merchants Dr), just n. Int corridors. **Pets:** Accepted. $30 daily fee/pet. Designated rooms, service with restrictions, supervision. 🛜 ⬇M 🛗 💻

▼▼▼ **Quality Inn Merchants Dr** **M**

(865) 342-3701. **$70-$99.** 117 Cedar Ln 37912. I-75 exit 108 (Merchants Dr), just e. Ext corridors. **Pets:** Large. $10 daily fee/pet. Designated rooms, service with restrictions, crate. 🛜 ⬇M 🛗 💻 ≈

▼▼▼ **Red Roof Inn** **M**

(865) 688-1010. **$50-$99.** 5334 Central Ave Pike 37912. I-75 exit 108 (Merchants Dr), just e. Ext corridors. **Pets:** Large, other species. Service with restrictions, supervision. 🛜 💻 ≈

▼▼▼ **Red Roof Inn Knoxville Central-Papermill Road** **H**

(865) 584-3911. **$64-$175.** 1315 Kirby Rd 37909. I-40/75 exit 383 (Papermill Rd), 0.5 mi w. Int corridors. **Pets:** Large, other species. Service with restrictions, supervision. 🛜 ⬇M 🛗 💻 ≈

AAA ▼▼▼ **Red Roof Inn-Knoxville West** **M**

(865) 691-1664. **$50-$120.** 209 Advantage Pl 37922. I-40/75 exit 378 (Cedar Bluff Rd), just s to N Peters Rd, then w. Ext corridors. **Pets:** Large, other species. Service with restrictions, supervision.
SAVE 🛜 ⬇M ≈

▼▼▼ **Residence Inn by Marriott Knoxville Cedar Bluff** **H**

(865) 539-5339. **$124-$179.** 215 Langley Pl 37922. I-40 exit 378 (Cedar Bluff Rd), just s, then 1 mi w on N Peters Blvd. Int corridors. **Pets:** Other species. $100 one-time fee/room. Service with restrictions.
🛜 ⊠ 🛗 💻 ≈ ⊠

▼▼▼ **Value Inn & Suites Knoxville** **H**

(865) 246-3600. **$58-$94.** 814 Brakebill Rd 37914. I-40 exit 398 (Strawberry Plains Pike), just n, then w. Ext corridors. **Pets:** Accepted.
🛜 🛗 💻 ≈

LA VERGNE

▼▼ **Quality Inn & Suites** **H**

(615) 793-9999. **Call for rates.** 110 Enterprise Blvd 37086. I-24 exit 64, just e. Int corridors. **Pets:** Small. $15 daily fee/pet. Designated rooms, service with restrictions, supervision. 🛜 ⬇M 🛗 💻 ≈

LAWRENCEBURG

▼▼ **Americas Best Value Inn** **M**

(931) 762-4467. **Call for rates.** 1940 N Hwy 43 38464. Jct US 43 and 64, 1.6 mi n. Ext corridors. **Pets:** Very small. $15 daily fee/pet. Supervision. 🛜 ⬇M 🛗 💻 ≈

LEBANON

▼▼ **Days Inn - Lebanon** **M**

(615) 449-5781. **$40-$99.** 822 S Cumberland St 37087. I-40 exit 238, just n. Ext corridors. **Pets:** Very small. $12 daily fee/pet. Designated rooms, service with restrictions, supervision. 🛜 🛗 💻 ≈

▼▼ **Econo Lodge** **M**

(615) 444-1001. **$50-$90.** 829 S Cumberland St 37087. I-40 exit 238, just n. Ext corridors. **Pets:** Accepted. 🛜 🛗 💻 ≈

▼▼ **Quality Inn** **M** ☙

(615) 444-7020. **Call for rates.** 641 S Cumberland St 37087. I-40 exit 238, just n. Ext corridors. **Pets:** Small. $10 daily fee/pet. Service with restrictions, supervision. 🛜 ⬇M 🛗 💻 ≈

▼▼ **Sleep Inn & Suites-Lebanon/Nashville** **H**

(615) 449-7005. **$89-$109.** 150 S Eastgate Ct 37090. I-40 exit 232, just n. Int corridors. **Pets:** Medium. $25 daily fee/pet. Designated rooms, service with restrictions, supervision. 🛜 ⊠ ⬇M 🛗 💻 ≈

LENOIR CITY

▼▼ **Days Inn** **H**

(865) 986-2011. **$62-$69.** 1110 Hwy 321 N 37771. I-75 exit 81, just e. Ext corridors. **Pets:** Accepted. 🛜 🛗 💻 ≈

AAA ▼▼▼ **Econo Lodge** **H**

(865) 986-0295. **$52-$89.** 1211 Hwy 321 N 37771. I-75 exit 81, just w. Ext corridors. **Pets:** Accepted. SAVE 🛜 🛗 ≈

LOUDON

Americas Best Value Inn

(865) 458-5855. **$55-$69.** 15100 Hwy 72 37774. I-75 exit 72, just w. Ext corridors. **Pets:** Medium. $10 daily fee/pet. Service with restrictions, supervision.

MANCHESTER

Microtel Inn & Suites by Wyndham Manchester

(931) 723-7001. **$67-$250.** 201 Expressway Dr 37355. I-24 exit 114, 0.5 mi nw on SR 41, then just n. Int corridors. **Pets:** Other species. $25 one-time fee/room. Service with restrictions, supervision.

Sleep Inn & Suites

(931) 954-0580. **Call for rates.** 84 Relco Dr 37355. I-24 exit 114, just se. Int corridors. **Pets:** Accepted.

MARYVILLE

LuxBury Inn & Suites

(865) 983-9839. **$59-$129.** 805 Foothills Mall Dr 37801. Jct US 321 (Lamar Alexander Pkwy). Ext corridors. **Pets:** Accepted.

MCKENZIE

BEST WESTERN McKenzie

(731) 352-1083. **$73-$78.** 16180 N Highland Ave 38201. Jct US 79 and SR 22, just s. Ext corridors. **Pets:** Small. $10 daily fee/pet. Designated rooms, service with restrictions, supervision.

MCMINNVILLE

BEST WESTERN Tree City Inn

(931) 473-2159. **$82-$89.** 809 Sparta Hwy 37110. Jct US 70 S Bypass and Red Rd, 1 mi s, follow signs. Ext corridors. **Pets:** $10 daily fee/room. Service with restrictions, crate.

MEMPHIS METROPOLITAN AREA

ATOKA

Comfort Inn & Suites

(901) 837-7729. **Call for rates.** 10772 Hwy 51 S 38004. 0.5 mi n of jct SR 206. Int corridors. **Pets:** Accepted.

COLLIERVILLE

Hampton Inn Collierville

(901) 854-9400. **$109-$129.** 1280 W Poplar Ave 38017. 0.9 mi w of jct CR 175 on US 72. Int corridors. **Pets:** Accepted.

GERMANTOWN

Comfort Inn & Suites-Germantown

(901) 757-7800. **Call for rates.** 7787 Wolf River Blvd 38138. I-40 exit 16, 5 mi s on Germantown Pkwy to Wolf River Blvd, then just w. Int corridors. **Pets:** Other species. $25 one-time fee/room. Designated rooms, service with restrictions, supervision.

Homewood Suites by Hilton-Germantown

(901) 751-2500. **$99-$134.** 7855 Wolf River Blvd 38138. I-40 exit 16, 5.7 mi s on Germantown Pkwy, then just e. Int corridors. **Pets:** Large, other species. $50 one-time fee/room. Designated rooms, service with restrictions.

Residence Inn by Marriott Memphis/Germantown

(901) 752-0900. **$99-$179.** 9314 Poplar Pike 38138. I-240 exit 15 (Poplar Ave), 7 mi e. Int corridors. **Pets:** Accepted.

MEMPHIS

Baymont Inn & Suites Memphis East

(901) 377-2233. **$59-$79.** 6020 Shelby Oaks Dr 38134. I-40 exit 12, just n. Int corridors. **Pets:** Accepted.

BEST WESTERN Travelers Inn

(901) 363-8430. **$76-$86, 30 day notice.** 5024 Lamar Ave (US Hwy 78) 38118. I-240 exit 21 (US 78), 6 mi s. Ext corridors. **Pets:** Accepted.

Drury Inn & Suites-Memphis Northeast

(901) 373-8200. **$84-$169.** 1556 Sycamore View 38134. I-40 exit 12, just n. Int corridors. **Pets:** Service with restrictions, supervision.

Hilton Memphis

(901) 684-6664. **$109-$189.** 939 Ridge Lake Blvd 38120. I-240 exit 15 (Poplar Ave), just e, then n under overpass. Int corridors. **Pets:** Accepted.

Homewood Suites by Hilton-Poplar

(901) 763-0500. **$99-$139.** 5811 Poplar Ave 38119. I-240 exit 15 (Poplar Ave), just e. Ext/int corridors. **Pets:** Very small, dogs only. $50 one-time fee/pet. Designated rooms, service with restrictions, supervision.

Homewood Suites by Hilton-Southwind

(901) 758-5018. **$89-$119.** 3583 Hacks Cross Rd 38125. I-240 exit 16, 4 mi e on SR 385, then 1 mi n. Int corridors. **Pets:** Large, other species. $75 one-time fee/room. Supervision.

La Quinta Inn & Suites Memphis East-Sycamore View

(901) 381-0044. **$71-$151.** 6069 Macon Cove Rd 38134. I-40 exit 12, just s. Int corridors. **Pets:** Service with restrictions, supervision.

La Quinta Inn & Suites Memphis (Primacy Parkway)

(901) 374-0330. **$63-$155.** 1236 Primacy Pkwy 38119. I-240 exit 15 (Poplar Ave), 0.5 mi e, s on Ridgeway Rd, just w, then just s. Int corridors. **Pets:** Service with restrictions, supervision.

Madison Hotel

(901) 333-1200. **$187-$374, 3 day notice.** 79 Madison Ave 38103. Just w of jct Main St. Int corridors. **Pets:** Accepted.

Peabody Memphis

(901) 529-4000. **$199-$550, 3 day notice.** 149 Union Ave 38103. Just se of jct 2nd St. Int corridors. **Pets:** Medium. $75 one-time fee/room. Designated rooms, service with restrictions, crate.

Residence Inn by Marriott Memphis Downtown

(901) 578-3700. **$161-$171.** 110 Monroe Ave 38103. Just e of jct Main St. Int corridors. **Pets:** Accepted.

Residence Inn by Marriott Memphis East

(901) 685-9595. **$123-$164.** 6141 Poplar Pike 38119. I-240 exit 15 (Poplar Ave), 0.5 mi e. Int corridors. **Pets:** Small. $100 one-time fee/room. Designated rooms, service with restrictions, crate.

Sleep Inn

(901) 312-7777. **$58-$80.** 2855 Old Austin Peay Hwy 38128. I-40 exit 8A, 0.8 mi ne. Int corridors. **Pets:** Accepted.

▼▼▼▼ Staybridge Suites 🇭

(901) 682-1722. **Call for rates.** 1070 Ridge Lake Blvd 38120. I-240 exit 15 (Poplar Ave), just e, then n under overpass. Int corridors.
Pets: Accepted. 📶 ⊠ 🛆M 🔒 💻 ➿

♠ ▼▼▼▼ The Westin Memphis Beale Street 🇭

(901) 334-5900. **$199-$399.** 170 Lt. George W. Lee Ave 38103. Jct S 3rd St. Int corridors. **Pets:** Accepted. [SAVE] 📶 ⊠ 🛆M 💻 🍴

MILLINGTON

▼▼ ▼▼ Plantation Oaks Suites & Inn 🇭

(901) 872-8000. **$67.** 6656 Hwy 51 N 38053. 1.5 mi s of jct SR 385. Ext/int corridors. **Pets:** $40 one-time fee/room. Designated rooms, service with restrictions, crate. 📶 🔒 💻 ➿

END METROPOLITAN AREA

MONTEAGLE

♠ ▼▼ ▼▼ BEST WESTERN Smoke House Lodge 🇭

(931) 924-2091. **Call for rates.** 844 W Main St 37356. I-24 exit 134, just s. Ext corridors. **Pets:** Accepted.
🔌 [SAVE] 📶 🔒 💻 🍴 ➿ ⊠

▼▼ ▼▼ Edgeworth Inn 🇨

(931) 924-4000. **$165-$225, 14 day notice.** 19 Wilkins Ave 37356. I-24 exit 134, 0.4 mi e on US 41A, 2nd left through assembly gates, follow signs. Ext/int corridors. **Pets:** Medium. $25 one-time fee/pet. Designated rooms, service with restrictions, supervision.
📶 ⊠ 🔒 💻 🍴 ➿ 🇿

MORRISTOWN

♠ ▼▼▼▼ BEST WESTERN PLUS Morristown Conference Center Hotel 🇭 🌸

(423) 587-2400. **$120-$200.** 5435 S Davy Crockett Pkwy 37813. I-81 exit 8, just w. Int corridors. **Pets:** Medium. $20 daily fee/room. Service with restrictions, supervision. [SAVE] 📶 🛆M 🔒 💻 🍴 ➿

♠ ▼▼ ▼▼ Days Inn Ⓜ

(423) 587-2200. **$55-$205, 3 day notice.** 2512 E Andrew Johnson Hwy 37814. I-81 exit 8, 6 mi n on US 25 E to exit 2B (Greeneville-Morristown), then just w. Ext corridors. **Pets:** Medium. $10 daily fee/pet. Designated rooms, service with restrictions. [SAVE] 🛆M 🔒 💻 ➿

▼▼ Econo Lodge Ⓜ

(423) 586-8504. **$50-$60.** 5984 W Andrew Johnson Hwy 37814. 4.1 mi w on US 11 E. Int corridors. **Pets:** Accepted. 📶 🔒

▼▼ Super 8 Ⓜ

(423) 318-8888. **$50-$170.** 5400 S Davy Crockett Pkwy 37813. I-81 exit 8, just n. Int corridors. **Pets:** Medium. $9 daily fee/pet. Designated rooms, supervision. 📶 🛆M 🔒 💻

▼▼ Travelodge Ⓜ

(423) 581-8700. **$80-$129.** 3304 W Andrew Johnson Hwy 37814. 2.5 mi w on US 11 E. Ext corridors. **Pets:** Other species. $10 one-time fee/pet. Service with restrictions, crate. 📶 🛆M 🔒 💻 ➿

MOUNT JULIET

▼▼ ▼▼ Quality Inn & Suites 🇭

(615) 773-3600. **$70-$150.** 1000 Hershel Dr 37122. I-40 exit 226, just s. Int corridors. **Pets:** Small. $25 one-time fee/room. Service with restrictions, supervision. 📶 🔒 💻 ➿

MURFREESBORO

▼▼ ▼▼ Baymont Inn & Suites Ⓜ 🌸

(615) 896-1172. **$75-$160.** 2230 Armory Dr 37129. I-24 exit 78B, just n. Ext corridors. **Pets:** Large, other species. $25 daily fee/room. Designated rooms, service with restrictions, crate. 📶 🛆M 🔒 💻 ➿

♠ ▼▼▼▼ BEST WESTERN Chaffin Inn Ⓜ

(615) 895-3818. **$60-$130.** 168 Chaffin Pl 37129. I-24 exit 78B. Ext corridors. **Pets:** Accepted. [SAVE] 📶 🔒 💻 ➿

▼▼ ▼▼ Clarion Inn & Suites 🇭

(615) 896-2420. **$69-$129.** 2227 Old Fort Pkwy 37129. I-24 exit 78B, just s. Ext/int corridors. **Pets:** Accepted. 📶 🔒 💻 🍴 ➿ ⊠

▼▼▼▼ DoubleTree by Hilton Hotel Murfreesboro 🇭

(615) 895-5555. **$89-$169.** 1850 Old Fort Pkwy 37129. I-24 exit 78B, 0.6 mi n. Int corridors. **Pets:** Medium. $50 one-time fee/room. Service with restrictions, crate. 🄴🄲🄾 🔌 📶 🛆M 🔒 💻 🍴 ➿

♠ ▼▼ ▼▼ Econo Lodge Inn & Suites Ⓜ

(615) 890-2811. **Call for rates.** 110 N Thompson Ln 37129. I-24 exit 78B, just n. Ext corridors. **Pets:** $10 one-time fee/pet. Supervision. [SAVE] 📶 🔒 💻 ➿

▼▼▼▼ Hampton Inn & Suites 🇭

(615) 890-2424. **$109-$159.** 325 N Thompson Ln 37129. I-24 exit 78B, just n. Int corridors. **Pets:** Accepted. 📶 🛆M 🔒 💻 ➿

♠ ▼▼ ▼▼ Quality Inn Murfreesboro 🇭 🌸

(615) 890-1006. **$63-$95.** 2135 S Church St 37130. I-24 exit 81 westbound; exit 81B eastbound. Int corridors. **Pets:** $10 one-time fee/room. [SAVE] 📶 🔒 💻 ➿

NASHVILLE METROPOLITAN AREA

GOODLETTSVILLE

♠ ▼▼ ▼▼ BEST WESTERN Fairwinds Inn 🇭

(615) 851-1067. **$54-$100.** 100 Northcreek Blvd 37072. I-65 exit 97 (Long Hollow Pike), 0.5 mi e. Ext corridors. **Pets:** Medium. $15 daily fee/pet. Service with restrictions, supervision. [SAVE] 📶 🔒 💻 ➿

♠ ▼▼▼▼ Holiday Inn Express & Suites 🇭 🌸

(615) 851-1891. **Call for rates.** 120 S Cartwright Ct 37072. I-65 exit 97 (Long Hollow Pike), just w. Int corridors. **Pets:** Medium. $25 one-time fee/room. Designated rooms, service with restrictions, supervision. [SAVE] 📶 🛆M 🔒 💻 ➿

♠ ▼▼ ▼▼ Quality Inn 🇭

(615) 859-5400. **Call for rates.** 925 Conference Dr 37072. I-65 exit 97 (Long Hollow Pike), 0.6 mi e. Int corridors. **Pets:** Small. $10 deposit/pet, $10 daily fee/pet. Designated rooms, service with restrictions, supervision. [SAVE] 📶 🛆M 🔒 💻 ➿

HERMITAGE

♠ ▼▼ ▼▼ Super 8 🇭

(615) 871-4545. **$70-$110.** 1414 Princeton Pl 37076. I-40 exit 221 westbound; exit 221B eastbound, just n. Ext corridors. **Pets:** Small. $10 daily fee/pet. Service with restrictions. [SAVE] 📶 🔒 💻 ➿

NASHVILLE

▼▼▼ Aloft Nashville West End 🄷
(615) 329-4200. **$109-$299.** 1719 West End Ave 37203. I-40 exit 209B (Broadway), 0.4 mi w. Int corridors. **Pets:** Accepted.
🛜 ✕ 🔊 🔒 💻 🍴

▲▲▲ ▼▼▼ BEST WESTERN Airport Inn 🄷
(615) 889-9199. **$70-$90.** 701 Stewarts Ferry Pike 37214. I-40 exit 219 (Stewarts Ferry Pike), just s. Ext corridors. **Pets:** Accepted.
〔SAVE〕🛜 🔒 💻 🏊

▲▲▲ ▼▼▼ BEST WESTERN Music City Inn 🄼 🐾
(615) 641-7721. **$79-$149.** 13010 Old Hickory Blvd 37013. I-24 exit 62, just n. Ext corridors. **Pets:** Small. $15 daily fee/room. Designated rooms, service with restrictions, crate. 〔SAVE〕🛜 🔊 🔒 💻 🏊

▲▲▲ ▼▼▼ BEST WESTERN PLUS Music Row 🄷
(615) 242-1631. **$99-$299.** 1407 Division St 37203. I-40 exit 209B (Broadway), just w around circle, then just e. Int corridors. **Pets:** Small, other species. $10 daily fee/pet. 〔SAVE〕🛜 🔒 💻 🏊

▲▲▲ ▼▼▼ Comfort Inn 🄷
(615) 356-0888. **$70-$150.** 412 White Bridge Pl 37209. I-40 exit 204B, just s. Int corridors. **Pets:** Small. $10 daily fee/pet. Service with restrictions. 〔SAVE〕🛜 🔊 🔒 💻 🏊

▼▼▼ Comfort Inn Downtown 🄷
(615) 255-9977. **$80-$100.** 1501 Demonbreun St 37203. I-40 exit 209B (Broadway), just w. Ext corridors. **Pets:** Accepted.
🛜 🔊 🔒 💻 🏊

▲▲▲ ▼▼▼ Comfort Inn Opryland 🄷
(615) 889-0086. **Call for rates.** 2516 Music Valley Dr 37214. I-40 exit 215 (Briley Pkwy), 4 mi n; I-65 exit 90 to McGavock Pike exit, off Briley Pkwy. Int corridors. **Pets:** Small. $25 one-time fee/room. Designated rooms, service with restrictions, crate. 〔SAVE〕🛜 🔒 💻 🏊

▲▲▲ ▼▼▼ Days Inn 🄷
(615) 889-0090. **$65-$116.** 2460 Music Valley Dr 37214. I-40 exit 215B (Briley Pkwy), 4 mi n to exit 11 (McGavock Pike). Int corridors. **Pets:** Small. $10 one-time fee/pet. Designated rooms, service with restrictions, crate. 〔SAVE〕🛜 🔊 🔒 💻 🏊

▲▲▲ ▼▼▼ Days Inn North 🄼
(615) 228-3421. **$55-$105.** 3312 Dickerson Pike 37207. I-65 exit 90A (Dickerson Pike), just s. Ext corridors. **Pets:** $10 daily fee/pet. Designated rooms, service with restrictions, crate. 〔SAVE〕🛜 🔊 🔒 💻 🏊

▼▼▼▼ Drury Inn & Suites-Nashville Airport 🄷
(615) 902-0400. **$104-$179.** 555 Donelson Pike 37214. I-40 exit 216 (Donelson Pike), just n. Int corridors. **Pets:** Service with restrictions, supervision. 🛜 🔊 🔒 💻 🏊

▼▼▼ Extended StayAmerica-Nashville-Vanderbilt 🄷
(615) 383-7490. **$80-$200.** 3311 West End Ave 37203. I-440 exit 1A, just e. Int corridors. **Pets:** $25 daily fee/pet. Designated rooms, service with restrictions. 🛜 🔊 🔒 💻

▲▲▲ ▼▼▼▼ The Hermitage Hotel 🄷
(615) 244-3121. **$269-$389.** 231 6th Ave N 37219. Corner of Union St. Int corridors. **Pets:** Accepted. 〔SAVE〕🛜 ✕ 🔊 🔒 💻 🍴

▲▲▲ ▼▼▼▼ Holiday Inn Express-Airport/Opryland Area 🄷
(615) 883-1366. **$89-$139.** 1111 Airport Center Dr 37214. I-40 exit 216C (Donelson Pike N), 1 mi n, then 0.5 mi e. Int corridors. **Pets:** Accepted.
〔SAVE〕🛜 ✕ 🔊 🔒 💻 🏊

▼▼ ▼▼ Homestead Studio Suites Hotel-Nashville/Airport 🄼
(615) 316-9020. **$50-$70.** 727 McGavock Pike 37214. I-40 exit 215B (Briley Pkwy), 1 mi n to exit 7 (Elm Hill Pike), then just e. Ext corridors. **Pets:** $25 daily fee/pet. Designated rooms, service with restrictions.
🛜 🔊 🔒 💻

▼▼▼▼ Homewood Suites Nashville Downtown 🄷
(615) 742-5550. **$179-$239.** 706 Church St 37203. Jct 7th Ave N and Church St. Int corridors. **Pets:** Accepted. 🛜 🔊 🔒 💻 ✕

▲▲▲ ▼▼▼▼ Hotel Indigo-Nashville Downtown 🄷
(615) 891-6000. **Call for rates.** 301 Union St 37201. I-40 exit 209A (Church St), 0.8 mi e on Charlotte Ave, then just s. Int corridors. **Pets:** Other species. $75 one-time fee/room. Service with restrictions.
〔SAVE〕🛜 ✕ 🔊 🔒 💻 🍴

▲▲▲ ▼▼▼▼ Hotel Preston 🄷 🐾
(615) 361-5900. **$119-$249, 3 day notice.** 733 Briley Pkwy 37217. I-40 exit 215 (Briley Pkwy), just s. Int corridors. **Pets:** Medium, other species. $45 one-time fee/room. Designated rooms, service with restrictions, crate.
〔SAVE〕🛜 🔒 💻 🍴 🏊

▼▼ ▼▼▼ Hutton Hotel 🄷 🐾
(615) 340-9333. **$219-$349.** 1808 W End Ave 37203. I-40 W exit 209B (Broadway), 1 mi w. Int corridors. **Pets:** $50 one-time fee/pet. Designated rooms, service with restrictions, supervision.
ⒺⒸⓄ ⬅ 〔SAVE〕🛜 ✕ 🔊 🔒 💻 🍴 ✕

▼▼ ▼▼ La Quinta Inn & Suites Nashville-Airport 🄷
(615) 885-3100. **$59-$144.** 531 Donelson Pike 37214. I-40 exit 216C (Donelson Pike), 0.3 mi n. Int corridors. **Pets:** Service with restrictions, supervision. 🛜 🔒 💻 🏊

▲▲▲ ▼▼▼ Loews Vanderbilt Hotel Nashville 🄷 🐾
(615) 320-1700. **$199-$449.** 2100 West End Ave 37203. I-40 exit 209B (Broadway), 1.3 mi w. Int corridors. **Pets:** Small. $25 one-time fee/room. Designated rooms, service with restrictions, supervision.
ⒺⒸⓄ ⬅ 〔SAVE〕🛜 ✕ 🔊 🔒 💻 🍴 ✕

▲▲▲ ▼▼▼ Microtel Inn & Suites by Wyndham Nashville 🄷
(615) 662-0004. **$62-$90.** 100 Coley Davis Ct 37221. I-40 exit 196, just se. Int corridors. **Pets:** Medium. $25 daily fee/pet. Service with restrictions, supervision. 〔SAVE〕🛜 🔒 💻

▼▼▼ Red Roof Inn 🄷
(615) 226-3300. **Call for rates.** 2407 Brick Church Pike 37207. I-65 exit 87, just w. Int corridors. **Pets:** Large, other species. Service with restrictions, supervision. 🛜 🔒 💻 🏊

▲▲▲ ▼▼▼ Red Roof Inn Airport 🄼
(615) 872-0735. **$50-$100.** 510 Claridge Dr 37214. I-40 exit 216C (Donelson Pike), 0.3 mi n. Ext corridors. **Pets:** Large, other species. Service with restrictions, supervision. 〔SAVE〕🛜 🔒

▼▼▼ Residence Inn by Marriott Nashville Airport 🄷
(615) 889-8600. **$89-$199.** 2300 Elm Hill Pike 37214. I-40 exit 215B (Briley Pkwy), 1.5 mi n. Ext corridors. **Pets:** Other species. $100 one-time fee/pet. Service with restrictions, supervision.
ⒺⒸⓄ 🛜 ✕ 🔊 🔒 💻

▲▲▲ ▼▼▼ Sheraton Music City Hotel 🄷 🐾
(615) 885-2200. **$105-$299.** 777 McGavock Pike 37214. I-40 exit 215B (Briley Pkwy), 1 mi n to exit 7 (Elm Hill Pike), 0.5 mi e, then s. Int corridors. **Pets:** Medium, dogs only. $100 one-time fee/room. Service with restrictions, supervision. 〔SAVE〕🛜 ✕ 🔊 🔒 💻 🍴 🏊 ✕

⚫ ▼▼▼▼ Sheraton Nashville Downtown
Hotel 🅷 ❀

(615) 259-2000. **$109-$329.** 623 Union St 37219. I-40 exit 209, just s of State Capitol. Int corridors. **Pets:** Medium, dogs only. $100 deposit/room. Designated rooms, service with restrictions, crate.

⬛ SAVE 🛜 ✕ ♿M 🔌 💻 🍴 🏊 ✕

⚫ ▼▼▼ Super 8-West 🅼

(615) 356-6005. **$65-$125.** 6924 Charlotte Pike 37209. I-40 exit 201B, just n. Ext corridors. **Pets:** Medium. $10 daily fee/pet. Service with restrictions, supervision. SAVE 🛜 🔌 🏊

▼▼▼▼ TownePlace Suites by Marriott Nashville
Airport 🅷

(615) 232-3830. **$109-$219.** 2700 Elm Hill Pike 37214. I-40 exit 215 (Briley Pkwy N), 1 mi n to exit 7 (Elm Hill Pike), then just e. Int corridors. **Pets:** Medium. $100 one-time fee/room. Service with restrictions, crate.

🛜 ✕ ♿M 🔌 💻 🏊

END METROPOLITAN AREA

NEWPORT

⚫ ▼▼▼ BEST WESTERN Newport Inn 🅼 ❀

(423) 623-8713. **$50-$170, 7 day notice.** 1015 Cosby Hwy 37821. I-40 exit 435, just w. Ext corridors. **Pets:** Other species. $10 daily fee/pet. Service with restrictions, crate. SAVE 🛜 ♿M 🔌 💻 🏊

▼▼ Comfort Inn 🅷

(423) 623-5355. **$59-$79.** 1149 Smokey Mountain Ln 37821. I-40 exit 432B, just n. Int corridors. **Pets:** $10 daily fee/pet. Designated rooms, service with restrictions, supervision. 🛜 ♿M 🔌 💻 🏊

⚫ ▼ Motel 6-#4090 🅼

(423) 623-1850. **$42-$62.** 255 Heritage Blvd 37822. I-40 exit 435, just n. Int corridors. **Pets:** Other species. Service with restrictions, supervision. SAVE 🛜 ♿M 🏊

OAK RIDGE

▼▼▼ DoubleTree by Hilton Hotel Oak Ridge 🅷

(865) 481-2468. **$104-$139.** 215 S Illinois Ave 37830. 0.3 mi se of SR 95 on SR 62 (Oak Ridge Hwy). Int corridors. **Pets:** Accepted.

ECO 🛜 ♿M 🔌 💻 🍴 🏊

▼▼ Quality Inn 🅷

(865) 483-6809. **$84-$104.** 216 S Rutgers Ave 37830. Jct SR 95 and 62, 0.9 mi se on SR 62 (Oak Ridge Hwy) to Rutgers Ave, then 0.7 mi n. Int corridors. **Pets:** Accepted. 🛜 ♿M 🔌 💻 🏊

▼▼▼▼ Staybridge Suites 🅷

(865) 298-0050. **$129-$139.** 420 S Illinois Ave 37830. Jct Lafayette St and SR 62 (Oak Ridge Hwy). Int corridors. **Pets:** Accepted.

🛜 ✕ ♿M 🔌 💻 🏊

OOLTEWAH

▼▼ Super 8 🅼

(423) 238-5951. **$50-$70.** 8934 Lee Hwy 37363. I-75 exit 11, just w. Ext corridors. **Pets:** Accepted. 🛜 🔌 💻

PARIS

▼▼ Super 8 🅷

(731) 644-7008. **$58-$70.** 1309 E Wood St 38242. 1.6 mi ne of jct US 79 and 641. Ext/int corridors. **Pets:** Accepted. 🛜 🔌 💻 🏊

PICKWICK DAM

▼▼ Pickwick Landing State Resort Park Inn 🅷

(731) 689-3135. **$68.** 220 Playground Loop 38365. Jct US 57 and SR 128; in State Park. Ext/int corridors. **Pets:** Accepted.

🛜 ✕ 🔌 💻 🍴 🏊 ✕

PIGEON FORGE

▼▼▼ Bear Creek Crossing by Eden Crest Vacation
Rentals 🅲🅰

(865) 774-0059. **$100-$1000.** 652 Wears Valley Rd 37863. Jct US 441, 1 mi s on US 321 at traffic light 3. Ext corridors. **Pets:** Accepted.

🛜 ✕ 🔌 💻 🏊 ✕

▼▼▼ Black Bear Ridge by Eden Crest Vacation
Rentals 🅲🅰

(865) 774-0059. **$100-$1300.** 652 Wears Valley Rd 37863. Jct US 441, 1 mi s on US 321 at traffic light 3. Int corridors. **Pets:** Small, dogs only. $100 one-time fee/pet. No service, crate. 🛜 ✕ 🔌 💻

▼▼▼ Blackberry Ridge-Accommodations by Sunset
Cottage 🅲🅰

(865) 429-8478. **$135-$150.** 3630 S River Rd 37863. Jct US 441, just e on Dollywood Ln at traffic light 8, then just n. Ext corridors. **Pets:** Other species. $50 one-time fee/room. Designated rooms, no service, crate.

🛜 ✕ 🔌 💻 🏊

▼ Country Hearth Inn & Suites 🅼

(865) 429-3000. **$60-$100.** 117 Pinoak View Dr 37863. Jct US 441, just n of traffic light 1, then just e. Ext corridors. **Pets:** Small, dogs only. $10 daily fee/pet. Designated rooms, no service, supervision.

🛜 🔌 💻 🏊

▼▼▼ Hampton Inn & Suites 🅷 ❀

(865) 428-1600. **$79-$229.** 2025 Parkway 37863. On US 441, at traffic light 0. Int corridors. **Pets:** Medium. $25 daily fee/room. Designated rooms, service with restrictions, crate. 🛜 ♿M 🔌 💻 🏊

⚫ ▼ Motel 6 #4021 🅼

(865) 908-1244. **$29-$99.** 336 Henderson Chapel Rd 37863. Jct US 441, just w at traffic light 1. Int corridors. **Pets:** Other species. Service with restrictions, supervision. SAVE 🛜 ✕ ♿M 🏊

⚫ ▼▼▼▼ RiverStone Resort & Spa 🅲🅾 ❀

(865) 908-0660. **$110-$450, 7 day notice.** 212 Dollywood Ln 37863. Jct US 441, just e at traffic light 8. Ext corridors. **Pets:** Small, dogs only. $25 daily fee/pet. Designated rooms, service with restrictions, crate.

SAVE 🛜 ✕ 🔌 💻 🏊 ✕

▼▼▼ Smoky Cove by Eden Crest Vacation Rentals 🅲🅰

(865) 774-0059. **$100-$1000.** 652 Wears Valley Rd 37863. Jct US 441, 1 mi s on US 321 at traffic light 3. Ext corridors. **Pets:** Accepted.

🛜 ✕ 🔌 💻 🏊

⚫ ▼▼▼ Timbers Lodge 🅼 ❀

(865) 428-5216. **$65-$130, 3 day notice.** 134 Wears Valley Rd E 37863. Jct US 441, just e at traffic light 3. Ext corridors. **Pets:** Other species. $10 daily fee/pet. Designated rooms, service with restrictions, crate.

SAVE 🛜 🔌 💻 🏊

POWELL

▼▼ Super 8 of Powell 🅼

(865) 938-5501. **$60-$80.** 323 E Emory Rd 37849. I-75 exit 112. Ext corridors. **Pets:** Accepted. 🛜 🔌 💻 🏊

ROGERSVILLE

▼▼ Comfort Inn & Suites 🅷

(423) 272-8700. **$81-$249.** 128 James Richardson Ln 37857. US 11 W. Int corridors. **Pets:** Accepted. 🛜 ♿M 🔌 💻 🏊

▼▼ Quality Inn ⊞

(423) 272-1842. **$75-$85.** 7139 Hwy 11 W 37857. Jct SR 66 and US 11, 0.5 mi sw. Int corridors. **Pets:** Accepted. 🛜 🔊 🔋 💻 ➿

SELMER

▼▼ America's Best Inn ⊞

(731) 645-8880. **$55-$65.** 644 Mulberry Ave 38375. Jct SR 64 and 45, just s on SR 45. Ext corridors. **Pets:** Dogs only. $10 daily fee/pet. Designated rooms, supervision. 🛜 🔋 💻 ➿

SEVIERVILLE

▼◈▼ Baymont Inn & Suites ⊞

(865) 933-9448. **$65-$118.** 2863 Winfield Dunn Pkwy 37764. I-40 exit 407, 2.3 mi s on SR 66. Int corridors. **Pets:** Other species. $10 daily fee/pet. Designated rooms, service with restrictions. 🛜 ✖ 🔊 🔋 💻 ➿

◎ ▼◈ BEST WESTERN Greenbrier Inn Ⓜ

(865) 428-1000. **$45-$99.** 711 Parkway 37862. Jct US 411, 0.7 mi s on US 441. Ext corridors. **Pets:** Accepted. SAVE 🛜 🔋 💻 ➿

▼◈▼ La Quinta Inn & Suites Sevierville / Kodak ⊞

(865) 933-3339. **$72-$167.** 2428 Winfield Dunn Pkwy 37764. I-40 exit 407, 3.2 mi s on SR 66. Int corridors. **Pets:** Service with restrictions, supervision. 🛜 ✖ 🔊 🔋 💻 ➿

◎ ▼◈▼ Quality Inn & Suites River Suites Ⓜ

(865) 428-5519. **Call for rates.** 860 Winfield Dunn Pkwy 37876. Jct US 411, 1.3 mi n on SR 66. Ext corridors. **Pets:** Medium. $10 daily fee/pet. Designated rooms, service with restrictions, crate. SAVE 🛜 ✖ 🔋 💻 ➿

▼▼ Sleep Inn ⊞

(865) 429-0484. **Call for rates.** 1020 Parkway 37862. On US 441, 1.2 mi s of jct US 411. Int corridors. **Pets:** Medium. $12 daily fee/room. Designated rooms, service with restrictions, supervision. 🛜 🔊 🔋 💻 ➿

SHELBYVILLE

◎ ▼◈▼ BEST WESTERN PLUS Celebration Inn & Suites ⊞

(931) 684-2378. **$60-$200.** 724 Madison St 37160. Jct US 231 and 41. Ext corridors. **Pets:** Other species. $20 daily fee/room. Designated rooms, service with restrictions, supervision. SAVE 🛜 ✖ 🔋 💻 ➿

SMYRNA

▼◈▼ La Quinta Inn & Suites ⊞

(615) 220-8845. **$95-$177.** 2537 Highwood Blvd 37167. I-24 exit 66A, just w. Int corridors. **Pets:** Service with restrictions, supervision. 🎴 🛜 ✖ 🔊 🔋 💻 ➿

▼▼ Sleep Inn & Suites ⊞

(615) 220-2260. **$79-$109.** 2689 Highwood Blvd 37167. I-24 exit 66A, just w. Int corridors. **Pets:** Other species. $10 daily fee/room. Service with restrictions, crate. 🛜 ✖ 🔊 🔋 💻 ➿

SWEETWATER

◎◎◎ ▼◈▼ Econo Lodge West ⊞ 🐾

(423) 337-3353. **$65-$70.** 249 Hwy 68 37874. I-75 exit 60, just e. Ext/int corridors. **Pets:** Small. $10 daily fee/pet. Designated rooms, service with restrictions, crate. SAVE 🛜 ✖ 🔋 💻 ➿

▼▼ Magnuson Hotel ⊞

(423) 337-3541. **$54-$60.** 1421 Murray's Chapel Rd 37874. I-75 exit 60, just w. Ext/int corridors. **Pets:** Accepted. 🛜 🔋 💻 ➿

▼▼ Quality Inn & Suites ⊞

(423) 337-4900. **Call for rates.** 1116 Hwy 68 37874. I-75 exit 60, just w. Int corridors. **Pets:** Medium, dogs only. $25 daily fee/pet. Designated rooms, service with restrictions, crate. 🛜 🔊 🔋 💻 ➿

◎◎◎ ▼◈▼ Rodeway Inn Ⓜ

(423) 337-6646. **Call for rates.** 731 S Main St 37874. On US 11, jct SR 68. Ext/int corridors. **Pets:** $15 daily fee/pet. Service with restrictions, supervision. SAVE 🛜 🔋 💻 ➿

TOWNSEND

◎◎◎ ▼◈▼ BEST WESTERN Cades Cove Inn Ⓜ

(865) 448-9000. **Call for rates.** 7824 E Lamar Alexander Pkwy 37882. Jct SR 73, 0.7 mi s on US 321. Ext corridors. **Pets:** Other species. $20 daily fee/pet. Service with restrictions, supervision. SAVE 🛜 ✖ 🔊 🔋 💻 ➿

▼▼ Valley View Lodge Ⓜ

(865) 448-2237. **Call for rates.** 7726 E Lamar Alexander Pkwy 37882. Jct SR 73, 1.1 mi s on US 321. Ext corridors. **Pets:** Accepted. 🛜 🔊 🔋 💻 ➿ ✖

TULLAHOMA

▼▼ Baymont Inn & Suites Tullahoma ⊞

(931) 455-7891. **$75-$95.** 2113 N Jackson St 37388. 3 mi n on SR 41A (N Jackson St). Ext corridors. **Pets:** Accepted. 🛜 🔋 💻 ➿

WHITE HOUSE

▼▼▼ Holiday Inn Express ⊞

(615) 672-7200. **$89-$109.** 206 Knight Cir 37188. I-65 exit 108, just e. Int corridors. **Pets:** Other species. $25 one-time fee/room. Service with restrictions, supervision. 🛜 🔊 🔋 💻 ➿

WINCHESTER

◎◎◎ ▼▼ BEST WESTERN Inn Ⓜ

(931) 967-9444. **$80-$90.** 1602 Dinah Shore Blvd 37398. Jct US 41A and 41 Bypass, just w. Ext corridors. **Pets:** Medium, other species. $20 daily fee/room. Designated rooms. SAVE 🛜 🔊 🔋 💻 ➿

TEXAS

CITY INDEX

ABILENE

🏵 ▼▼▼ Americas Best Value Inn 🎁
(325) 673-5424. **$55-$60.** 1633 W Stamford St 79601. I-20 exit 285, 1 mi
e on S Frontage Rd. Ext corridors. **Pets:** Accepted. SAVE 🛜 📱 💻 ➿

🏵 ▼▼▼ BEST WESTERN Whitten South 🎁 🐾
(325) 695-1262. **Call for rates.** 3950 Ridgemont Dr 79606. US 83/84
exit Buffalo Gap Rd, just w. Ext corridors. **Pets:** Other
species. $10 daily fee/pet. Service with restrictions, crate.
SAVE 🛜 📱 💻 ➿

▼▼ La Quinta Inn Abilene 🎁
(325) 676-1676. **$59-$144.** 3501 W Lake Rd 79601. I-20 exit 286C, just
n. Ext corridors. **Pets:** Service with restrictions, supervision.
🛜 📱 💻 ➿

▼▼▼ MCM Elegante Suites 🎁
(325) 698-1234. **$129-$349.** 4250 Ridgemont Dr 79606. US 83/84 exit
Buffalo Gap Rd, 1 mi s of W Frontage Rd to Ridgemont Dr, then 0.5 mi
w. Ext/int corridors. **Pets:** Accepted. 🛜 📱 💻 🍴 ➿

▼▼ Quality Inn 🎁
(325) 676-0203. **$75-$99.** 1758 E I-20 79601. I-20 exit 288; on N Frontage Rd. Ext corridors. **Pets:** Accepted. 🛜 📱 💻 ➿

▼▼▼ Residence Inn by Marriott 🎁
(325) 677-8700. **$119-$189.** 1641 Musgrave Blvd 79601. I-20 exit 288;
on N Frontage Rd. Int corridors. **Pets:** Accepted.
🛜 ❌ 🅼 📱 💻 ➿ 🐾

🏵 ▼▼▼ Sleep Inn & Suites 🎁 🐾
(325) 437-1525. **$79-$169.** 3225 S Danville Dr 79605. US 83/84/277S
exit Buffalo Gap Rd; on E Frontage Rd. Int corridors. **Pets:** Medium,
other species. $35 one-time fee/room. Designated rooms, service with
restrictions, supervision. SAVE 🛜 🅼 📱 💻 ➿

🏵 ▼▼▼ Sleep Inn & Suites University 🎁
(325) 437-9601. **$80-$120.** 250 Killough Cove 79601. I-20 exit 286C, just
s. Int corridors. **Pets:** Medium. $25 daily fee/pet. Designated rooms, ser-
vice with restrictions, supervision. SAVE 🛜 ❌ 🅼 📱 💻 ➿

🏵 ▼▼ Super 8 🎁
(325) 701-4779. **$79-$99.** 4397 Sayles Blvd 79605. US 83/84 southbound exit Buffalo Gap Rd, just e to Industrial Blvd, 0.5 mi e to Sayles
Blvd, then just s; northbound exit Buffalo Gap Rd, just e. Int corridors.
Pets: Other species. $20 daily fee/pet. Designated rooms, service with
restrictions, supervision. SAVE 🛜 📱 💻 ➿

ALAMO

La Quinta Inn & Suites Alamo At East McAllen ⬛
(956) 783-6955. **$71-$162.** 909 E Frontage Rd 78516. US 83 exit Alamo Rd. Int corridors. **Pets:** Service with restrictions, supervision.

ALICE

La Quinta Inn & Suites Alice ⬛
(361) 661-1777. **$119-$232.** 2400 E Main St 78332. 0.8 mi e of downtown. Int corridors. **Pets:** Service with restrictions, supervision.

ALPINE

BEST WESTERN Alpine Classic Inn ⬛
(432) 837-1530. **Call for rates.** 2401 E Hwy 90 79830. Jct SR 118 and US 67/90, 1.5 mi e. Int corridors. **Pets:** Medium, other species. $50 one-time fee/room. Service with restrictions, crate.

The Holland Hotel ⬛ ✿
(432) 837-2800. **$85-$220.** 209 W Holland Ave 79830. On US 90 eastbound and 6th St; downtown. Int corridors. **Pets:** $30 one-time fee/pet. Service with restrictions, supervision.

Oak Tree Inn ⬛
(432) 837-5711. **Call for rates.** 2407 E Holland Ave (Hwy 90/67) 79830. US 90, 2 mi e. Int corridors. **Pets:** Accepted.

ALVARADO

La Quinta Inn & Suites Alvarado ⬛
(817) 783-8700. **$63-$118.** 1165 Hwy 67 W 76009. I-35W exit 26B, just e. Int corridors. **Pets:** Service with restrictions, supervision.

Super 8 ⬛
(817) 790-7378. **$59-$109.** 5445 S I-35W 76009. I-35W exit 27A (US 67), just e to 1st traffic light on US 67, then 0.4 mi n on access road. Int corridors. **Pets:** $10 daily fee/pet. Service with restrictions, crate.

ALVIN

Americas Best Value Inn & Suites Ⓜ
(281) 331-0335. **$56-$66.** 1588 S Hwy 35 Loop 77511. SR 35 Bypass, 0.5 mi sw of SR 6. Ext corridors. **Pets:** Medium. $15 daily fee/pet. Service with restrictions, supervision.

AMARILLO

Ambassador Hotel ⬛
(806) 358-6161. **$109-$139.** 3100 I-40 W 79102. I-40 exit 68 (Georgia St), just w on north frontage road. Int corridors. **Pets:** Accepted.

Baymont Inn & Suites ⬛ ✿
(806) 372-1425. **$65-$129.** 1700 I-40 E 79103. I-40 exit 71 (Ross-Osage), just e on south frontage road. Int corridors. **Pets:** Small. $15 one-time fee/pet. Service with restrictions, supervision.

Baymont Inn & Suites ⬛
(806) 356-6800. **$60-$110.** 3411 I-40 W 79109. I-40 exit 67, 0.3 mi e on south frontage road. Int corridors. **Pets:** Other species. $15 daily fee/pet. Designated rooms, service with restrictions, crate.

BEST WESTERN Medical Center Inn ⬛
(806) 358-7861. **$90-$130.** 1610 Coulter Dr 79106. I-40 exit 65 (Coulter Dr), 0.6 mi n. Ext/int corridors. **Pets:** Large. $20 one-time fee/pet. Designated rooms, service with restrictions, supervision.

BEST WESTERN Santa Fe ⬛
(806) 372-1885. **$80-$130.** 4600 I-40 E 79103. I-40 exit 73 (Eastern St) eastbound; exit Bolton St westbound, U-turn on south frontage road. Int corridors. **Pets:** Other species. $20 daily fee/room. Designated rooms, service with restrictions, supervision.

Big Texan Inn Ⓜ
(806) 372-5000. **$59-$90, 14 day notice.** 7701 I-40 E 79118. I-40 exit 75 (Lakeside Dr), 0.3 mi w on north frontage road. Ext corridors. **Pets:** Accepted.

Country Inn & Suites By Carlson, I-40 West ⬛
(806) 356-9977. **$79-$229.** 2000 Soncy Rd 79121. I-40 exit 64 (Soncy Rd), just n. Int corridors. **Pets:** Other species. $20 daily fee/pet. Service with restrictions, supervision.

Days Inn ⬛
(806) 359-9393. **$49-$120.** 2102 S Coulter Dr 79106. I-40 exit 65 (Coulter Dr), just n. Ext corridors. **Pets:** Medium. $25 daily fee/pet. Service with restrictions, supervision.

Days Inn East Amarillo ⬛
(806) 379-6255. **$69-$99.** 1701 I-40 E 79102. I-40 exit 71 (Ross-Osage), just w on north frontage road. Int corridors. **Pets:** Accepted.

Drury Inn & Suites-Amarillo ⬛
(806) 351-1111. **$110-$169.** 8540 W I-40 79121. I-40 exit 64 (Soncy Rd). Int corridors. **Pets:** Service with restrictions, supervision.

Holiday Inn Express & Suites ⬛
(806) 335-2500. **Call for rates.** 9401 I-40 E 79118. I-40 exit 76 (Airport Blvd), just w on north frontage road. Int corridors. **Pets:** Other species. $25 one-time fee/room. Service with restrictions, crate.

La Quinta Inn Amarillo East Airport Area ⬛
(806) 373-7486. **$63-$129.** 1708 I-40 E 79103. I-40 exit 71 (Ross-Osage), just e on south frontage road. Ext corridors. **Pets:** Service with restrictions, supervision.

Microtel Inn & Suites by Wyndham Amarillo ⬛
(806) 372-8373. **$70-$100.** 1501 S Ross St 79102. I-40 exit 71 (Ross-Osage), just n. Int corridors. **Pets:** Dogs only. $20 one-time fee/pet. Designated rooms, service with restrictions, supervision.

Residence Inn by Marriott ⬛
(806) 354-2978. **$99-$199.** 6700 I-40 W 79106. I-40 exit 66 (Bell St), 0.5 mi w on north frontage road. Int corridors. **Pets:** Other species. $50 one-time fee/pet. Service with restrictions, supervision.

ANGLETON

BEST WESTERN Angleton Inn ⬛
(979) 849-5822. **$75-$85.** 1809 N Velasco St 77515. Jct SR 35 and Business Rt SR 288, 1 mi n. Ext corridors. **Pets:** $20 one-time fee/pet. Service with restrictions, supervision.

La Quinta Inn & Suites Angelton ⬛
(979) 864-3383. **$89-$166.** 2400 W Mulberry 77515. Jct SR 35 and 288; on northwest corner. Int corridors. **Pets:** Service with restrictions, supervision.

ARLINGTON

BEST WESTERN Cooper Inn & Suites ⬛
(817) 784-9490. **$76.** 4024 Melear Dr 76015. I-20 exit 449B (Cooper St), just n, then just w. Ext corridors. **Pets:** Accepted.

▼▼▼ Comfort Suites Six Flags in Arlington 🏨
(817) 460-8700. **$90-$150.** 411 W Road To Six Flags St 76011. I-30 exit 27 (Cooper St) eastbound; exit 28 (Cooper St) westbound, just s, then just e. Int corridors. **Pets:** Accepted.
📶 ✕ 🐾M 🛗 🖥 ⊇ ⊠

▼▼▼ Hawthorn Suites by Wyndham 🏨
(817) 640-1188. **$89-$269.** 2401 Brookhollow Plaza Dr 76006. I-30 exit 30 (SR 360), just n to Lamar Blvd, just w to Brookhollow Plaza Dr, then just n. Ext corridors. **Pets:** Medium, dogs only. $51 one-time fee/pet. Service with restrictions, crate. 📶 🛗 🖥 ⊇ ⊠

▼▼▼ Homewood Suites by Hilton 🏨
(817) 633-1594. **$119-$179.** 2401 East Rd to Six Flags Dr 76011. I-30 exit 30 (SR 360), 0.5 mi s on southbound frontage road, then just w. Int corridors. **Pets:** Accepted. 📶 🐾M 🛗 🖥 ⊇

▼▼▼ La Quinta Inn & Suites Dallas/Arlington 6 Flags Dr 🏨
(817) 640-4142. **$107-$221.** 825 N Watson Rd 76011. SR 360 exit Six Flags Dr northbound; exit Ave H/Lamar Blvd southbound; on southbound frontage road. Int corridors. **Pets:** Service with restrictions, supervision.
📶 🛗 🖥 ⊇

🆀🆀 ▼▼▼ Microtel Inn by Wyndham Arlington/Dallas Area 🏨
(817) 557-8400. **$59-$79.** 1740 Oak Village Blvd 76017. I-20 exit 449B (Cooper St) westbound; exit 449A (Cooper St) eastbound, just s, then just w. Int corridors. **Pets:** Dogs only. $15 daily fee/pet. Service with restrictions, supervision. SAVE 📶 🛗 ⊇

🆀🆀 ▼▼▼ Sheraton Arlington Hotel 🏨 ✿
(817) 261-8200. **$119-$259.** 1500 Convention Center Dr 76011. I-30 exit 29 (Ballpark Way), 0.4 mi e on Copeland Rd to Convention Center Dr, then just s. Int corridors. **Pets:** Small. Service with restrictions, supervision. SAVE 📶 ✕ 🐾M 🛗 🖥 🍴 ⊇

▼▼▼ Studio 6-South Arlington #6036 🏨
(817) 465-8500. **$43-$63.** 1980 W Pleasant Ridge Rd 76015. I-20 exit 449 (Cooper St), 0.3 mi n, then just w. Ext corridors. **Pets:** Other species. $10 daily fee/room. Service with restrictions, supervision. 📶 🛗 🖥

▼▼▼ TownePlace Suites by Marriott Arlington Near Six Flags 🏨
(817) 861-8728. **$89-$134.** 1709 E Lamar Blvd 76006. 2 mi w of SR 360. Int corridors. **Pets:** Accepted. 📶 ✕ 🐾M 🛗 🖥 ⊇ ⊠

AUSTIN

🆀🆀 ▼▼▼ Aloft Austin at the Domain 🏨
(512) 491-0777. **$139-$299.** 11601 Domain Dr 78758. Loop 1 (Mo-Pac Expwy) exit Burnett Rd/Duval Rd, just e; in The Domain. Int corridors. **Pets:** Accepted. SAVE 📶 ✕ 🐾M 🛗 🖥 ⊇

🆀🆀 ▼▼▼ BEST WESTERN Atrium North 🏨
(512) 339-7311. **$99-$139.** 7928 Gessner Dr 78753. I-35 exit 240A, 0.4 mi w on US 183. Int corridors. **Pets:** Very small. $25 one-time fee/room. Service with restrictions. SAVE 📶 🛗 🖥 ⊇

🆀🆀 ▼▼▼ BEST WESTERN PLUS Austin Airport Inn & Suites 🏨
(512) 386-5455. **Call for rates.** 1805 Airport Commerce Dr 78741. Jct SR 71 (E Ben White Blvd) and Riverside Dr, just n; in Airport Commerce Park. Int corridors. **Pets:** Accepted. SAVE 📶 ✕ 🐾M 🛗 🖥 ⊇

🆀🆀 ▼▼▼ BEST WESTERN PLUS Austin City Hotel 🏨
(512) 444-0561. **Call for rates.** 2200 S I-35 78704. I-35 exit 232A (Oltorf Blvd); on west side access road. Ext/int corridors. **Pets:** $20 one-time fee/room. Service with restrictions, supervision.
SAVE 📶 🛗 🖥 🍴 ⊇

▼▼▼ Candlewood Suites Austin Northwest 🏨
(512) 338-1611. **$109-$139.** 9701 Stonelake Blvd 78759. Jct SR 360 (Capital of Texas Hwy) and Stonelake Blvd, just s. Int corridors. **Pets:** Accepted. 📶 🐾M 🛗 🖥

▼▼▼ Candlewood Suites-South 🏨
(512) 444-8882. **$79-$159.** 4320 S I-35 78745. I-35 exit 230 northbound; exit 230B (Ben White Blvd/SR 71) southbound; on southbound frontage road. Int corridors. **Pets:** Small. $15 daily fee/room. Designated rooms, service with restrictions, supervision. 📶 🐾M 🛗 🖥

▼ Crossland Studios Austin West 🏨
(512) 331-4747. **$34-$49.** 12621 Hymeadow Rd 78729. US 183 N exit Lake Creek Pkwy, just n, then just e. Ext corridors. **Pets:** $25 daily fee/pet. Designated rooms, service with restrictions. 📶 🛗 🖥

▼▼▼ DoubleTree Suites by Hilton Hotel Austin 🏨
(512) 478-7000. **$179-$229.** 303 W 15th St 78701. Just nw of state capitol building. Int corridors. **Pets:** Accepted. 📶 ✕ 🛗 🖥 🍴 ⊇

🆀🆀 ▼▼▼▼ The Driskill 🏨
(512) 474-5911. **$169-$649.** 604 Brazos St 78701. Jct 6th St. Int corridors. **Pets:** Accepted. ECO SAVE 📶 ✕ 🛗 🍴 ⊠

▼▼▼ Drury Inn & Suites-Austin North 🏨
(512) 467-9500. **$109-$174.** 6711 I-35 N 78752. I-35 exit 238A; on east frontage road. Int corridors. **Pets:** Service with restrictions, supervision.
📶 🛗 🖥 ⊇

▼▼ Econo Lodge 🏨
(512) 835-7070. **$60-$130.** 9102 Burnet Rd 78758. US 183 and Burnet Rd; on northeast corner. Ext corridors. **Pets:** Small. $50 deposit/pet, $25 one-time fee/pet. Designated rooms, no service, supervision.
📶 🛗 🖥

▼▼▼ Embassy Suites Austin Central 🏨
(512) 454-8004. **$129-$199.** 5901 I-35 N 78723. I-35 exit 238A; on east frontage road. Int corridors. **Pets:** Accepted. 📶 🛗 🖥 🍴 ⊇

▼▼ Extended StayAmerica Austin Arboretum 🏨
(512) 231-1520. **$69-$89, 3 day notice.** 10100 Capital of Texas Hwy 78759. Jct Loop 1 (Mo-Pac Expwy) and Capital of Texas Hwy (SR 360), just w. Int corridors. **Pets:** $25 daily fee/pet. Designated rooms, service with restrictions. 📶 🐾M 🛗 🖥

▼▼ Extended StayAmerica Austin Northwest Lakeline Mall 🏨
(512) 258-3365. **$54-$69.** 13858 US Hwy 183 N 78750. Jct US 183 and SR 620; on southwest corner. Int corridors. **Pets:** $25 daily fee/pet. Designated rooms, service with restrictions. 📶 🐾M 🛗 🖥

▼▼ Extended StayAmerica Austin Southwest 🏨
(512) 892-4272. **$65-$79.** 5100 US Hwy 290 W 78735. I-35 exit 230, US 290 W exit Brodie Ln, then 1 mi w. Int corridors. **Pets:** $25 daily fee/pet. Designated rooms, service with restrictions. 📶 🐾M 🛗 🖥

▼▼▼ Extended Stay Deluxe Austin-Arboretum-North 🏨
(512) 833-0898. **$69-$84.** 2700 Gracy Farms Ln 78758. 2 mi n of US 183 on Loop 1 (Mo-Pac Expwy) exit Burnet Rd. Int corridors. **Pets:** $25 daily fee/pet. Designated rooms, service with restrictions.
📶 🛗 🖥 ⊇

▼▼ Extended Stay Deluxe Austin Metro 🏨
(512) 452-0880. **$54-$69.** 6300 US Hwy 290 E 78723. Jct I-35 and US 290 E; on northeast corner. Int corridors. **Pets:** $25 daily fee/pet. Designated rooms, service with restrictions. 📶 🛗 🖥 ⊇

▼▼▼ Extended Stay Deluxe Austin-North Central 🏨
(512) 339-6005. **$54-$69.** 8221 N I-35 78753. I-35 exit 241; on east frontage road. Int corridors. **Pets:** $25 daily fee/pet. Designated rooms, service with restrictions. 📶 🛗 🖥 ⊇

▼▼▼ **Extended Stay Deluxe (Austin/Northwest/Research Park)** 🅷
(512) 219-6500. **$66-$79.** 12424 Research Blvd 78759. US 183 exit Oak Knoll Dr; on eastbound frontage road. Int corridors. **Pets:** $25 daily fee/pet. Designated rooms, service with restrictions.
🛰 🕹M 🛗 💻 ⌁

▼▼▼ **Fairfield Inn & Suites by Marriott Austin NW** 🅷
(512) 527-0734. **$79-$169.** 11201 N Mo-Pac Expwy 78759. US 183 N, 1.5 mi n on Loop 1 (Mo-Pac Expwy) exit Braker Ln; on east frontage road. Int corridors. **Pets:** Accepted. 🛰 ☒ 🕹M 🛗 💻 ⌁

🄬 ▼▼ ▼▼ **Four Seasons Hotel** 🅷 🐾
(512) 478-4500. **$449-$2900.** 98 San Jacinto Blvd 78701. Jct Congress Ave and Cesar Chavez St; 2 blks e on Lady Bird Lake. Int corridors. **Pets:** Very small. Designated rooms, service with restrictions, supervision.
🆂🅰🆅🅴 🛰 ☒ 🛗 💻 🍽 ⌁ ☒

▼▼▼ **Hampton Inn Northwest** 🅷
(512) 349-9898. **$129-$189.** 3908 W Braker Ln 78759. 1 mi n of US 183 on Loop 1 (Mo-Pac Expwy) exit W Braker Ln. Int corridors.
Pets: Accepted. 🛰 ☒ 🕹M 🛗 💻 ⌁

🄬 ▼▼ ▼▼ **Hilton Austin** 🅷
(512) 482-8000. **$160-$379.** 500 E 4th St 78701. Jct 4th and Neches sts. Int corridors. **Pets:** Accepted.
🆂🅰🆅🅴 🛰 🕹M 🛗 🍽 ⌁ ☒

🄬 ▼▼ ▼▼ **Hilton Austin Airport** 🅷
(512) 385-6767. **$79-$209.** 9515 Hotel Dr 78719. SR 71; service road exit at airport. Int corridors. **Pets:** Large, other species. $50 one-time fee/room. No service. 🄴🄲🄾 🆂🅰🆅🅴 🛰 ☒ 🕹M 🛗 💻 🍽 ⌁

▼▼▼ **Holiday Inn Express & Suites Austin Airport** 🅷
(512) 386-7600. **$90-$150.** 7601 E Ben White Blvd 78741. I-35 exit 230B (Ben White Blvd/SR 71), 3.2 mi e. Int corridors. **Pets:** Small, dogs only. $50 one-time fee/pet. Service with restrictions, crate.
🛰 ☒ 🕹M 🛗 💻 ⌁

▼▼▼ **Holiday Inn Express Hotel & Suites** 🅷
(512) 251-9110. **Call for rates.** 14620 N I-35 78728. I-35 exit 247; on west frontage road. Int corridors. **Pets:** Small. $50 one-time fee/room. Service with restrictions, crate. 🛰 ☒ 🕹M 🛗 💻

▼▼ **Homestead Studio Suites Hotel-Austin/Arboretum-South** 🅷
(512) 837-6677. **$49-$59.** 9100 Waterford Centre Blvd 78758. US 183 exit Burnet Rd; on westbound frontage road. Ext corridors. **Pets:** $25 daily fee/pet. Designated rooms, service with restrictions. 🛰 🛗 💻

▼▼▼ **Homestead Studio Suites Hotel-Austin/Downtown/Town Lake** 🅷
(512) 476-1818. **$74-$99.** 507 S 1st St 78704. I-35 exit 234B southbound; exit 234A northbound, 1.8 mi w on Cesar Chavez/E 1st sts, then 0.5 mi s. Int corridors. **Pets:** $25 daily fee/pet. Designated rooms, service with restrictions. 🛰 🛗 💻

🄬 ▼▼▼ **Homewood Suites-Austin South/Airport** 🅷
(512) 445-5050. **Call for rates.** 4143 Governor's Row 78744. I-35 exit 231 (Ben White Blvd/SR 71) southbound; exit 229 northbound; at Ben White Blvd. Int corridors. **Pets:** Accepted. 🆂🅰🆅🅴 🛰 🕹M 🛗 💻

▼▼▼ **Homewood Suites by Hilton Arboretum NW** 🅷
(512) 349-9966. **$149-$199.** 10925 Stonelake Blvd 78759. US 183 N to Loop 1 (Mo-Pac Expwy), 1.5 mi n to Braker Ln; on northwest corner. Int corridors. **Pets:** Accepted. 🛰 🕹M 🛗 💻 ⌁ ☒

▼▼▼ **Hotel Allandale** 🅷
(512) 452-9391. **$149-$209.** 7685 Northcross Dr 78757. Loop 1 (Mo-Pac Expwy) exit Anderson Rd, just e to Northcross Dr, then just s. Ext corridors. **Pets:** Accepted. 🛰 🛗 💻 ⌁

▼▼▼ **Hotel Saint Cecelia** 🅷
(512) 852-2400. **Call for rates.** 112 Academy Dr 78704. Jct S Congress Ave and Riverside Dr, 2 blks s. Ext corridors. **Pets:** Accepted.
🛰 ☒ 🛗 ⌁

🄬 ▼▼▼ **Hyatt house** 🅷
(512) 342-8080. **$99-$239.** 10001 N Capital of Texas Hwy 78759. US 183, N Capital of Texas Hwy (SR 360), just e. Int corridors.
Pets: Medium, dogs only. $150 one-time fee/pet. Service with restrictions, crate. 🆂🅰🆅🅴 🛰 ☒ 🛗 💻

🄬 ▼▼ ▼▼ **Hyatt Regency Austin** 🅷
(512) 477-1234. **$90-$399.** 208 Barton Springs Rd 78704. At south end of Congress Avenue Bridge; on south bank of Town Lake. Int corridors.
Pets: Accepted. 🄴🄲🄾 🆂🅰🆅🅴 🛰 🕹M 🛗 💻 🍽 ⌁ ☒

🄬 ▼▼ ▼▼ **Hyatt Regency Lost Pines Resort and Spa** 🅷 🐾
(512) 308-1234. **$117-$468, 3 day notice.** 575 Hyatt Lost Pines Rd 78612. SR 71, 13 mi e of Austin-Bergstrom International Airport; 9 mi w of Bastrop. Int corridors. **Pets:** Dogs only. $75 one-time fee/room. Designated rooms, service with restrictions, supervision.
🄴🄲🄾 🆂🅰🆅🅴 🛰 ☒ 🕹M 🛗 💻 🍽 ⌁ ☒

▼▼▼ **La Quinta Inn & Suites Austin Airport** 🅷
(512) 386-6800. **$95-$199.** 7625 E Ben White Blvd 78741. I-35 exit 230B (Ben White Blvd/SR 71), 8.8 mi e. Int corridors. **Pets:** Service with restrictions, supervision. 🛰 🕹M 🛗 💻 ⌁

🄬 ▼▼ ▼▼ **La Quinta Inn & Suites-Austin/Cedar Park-Lakeline** 🅷
(512) 568-3538. **$101-$299.** 10701 Lakeline Mall Dr 78717. Jct US 183 and Lakeline Dr, 0.5 mi e, then just s on Lake Creek Dr. Int corridors.
Pets: Service with restrictions, supervision.
🆂🅰🆅🅴 🛰 ☒ 🕹M 🛗 💻 ⌁

▼▼▼ **La Quinta Inn & Suites Austin Mopac North** 🅷
(512) 832-2121. **$83-$177.** 11901 N Mo-Pac Expwy 78759. US 183, 2 mi n on Loop 1 (Mo-Pac Expwy) exit Duval Rd. Int corridors. **Pets:** Service with restrictions, supervision. 🛰 🕹M 🛗 💻 ⌁

▼▼▼ **La Quinta Inn & Suites Austin Southwest at Mopac** 🅷
(512) 899-3000. **$119-$199.** 4424 S Loop 1 (Mo-Pac Expwy) 78735. Jct Loop 1 (Mo-Pac Expwy), US 290 and SR 71 E; on southbound frontage road. Int corridors. **Pets:** Service with restrictions, supervision.
🛰 🕹M 🛗 💻 ⌁

▼▼▼ **La Quinta Inn & Suites Round Rock South** 🅷
(512) 246-2800. **$75-$144.** 150 Parker Dr 78728. I-35 exit 250; on west frontage road. Int corridors. **Pets:** Service with restrictions, supervision.
🛰 🕹M 🛗 💻 ⌁

▼▼▼ **La Quinta Inn Austin Capitol** 🅷
(512) 476-1166. **$90-$299.** 300 E 11 St 78701. Just e of state capitol building. Ext/int corridors. **Pets:** Service with restrictions, supervision.
🛰 🛗 💻 ⌁

▼▼▼ **La Quinta Inn Austin Highland Mall** 🅷
(512) 459-4381. **$59-$166.** 5812 I-35 78751. I-35 exit 238A; on west frontage road. Ext corridors. **Pets:** Service with restrictions, supervision.
🛰 🛗 💻 ⌁

🄬 ▼▼▼ **La Quinta Inn Austin North** 🅷
(512) 467-1701. **$77-$299.** 7622 N I-35 & 183 78752. I-35 exit 240A; on west frontage road. Int corridors. **Pets:** Service with restrictions, supervision. 🆂🅰🆅🅴 🛰 🛗 💻 ⌁

▼▼▼ **La Quinta Inn Austin Oltorf** 🅷
(512) 447-6661. **$63-$188.** 1603 E Oltorf Blvd 78741. I-35 exit 232A (Oltorf Blvd), just s. Ext/int corridors. **Pets:** Service with restrictions, supervision. 🛰 🛗 💻 ⌁

▼▼ **La Quinta Inn Austin South/IH-35** 🄷
(512) 443-1774. **$59-$166.** 4200 I-35 S 78745. I-35 exit 231 southbound; exit 230 northbound, just s of jct US 290 and SR 71; on north frontage road. Ext corridors. **Pets:** Service with restrictions, supervision.

▲ ▼▼▼ **Mansion at Judges' Hill** 🄷 ❄
(512) 495-1800. **$139-$599, 3 day notice.** 1900 Rio Grande St 78705. Jct Rio Grande St and Martin Luther King Jr Blvd. Int corridors. **Pets:** Other species. $50 one-time fee/room. Service with restrictions, crate.

▲ ▼▼▼▼ **Omni Austin Hotel Downtown** 🄷 ❄
(512) 476-3700. **$169-$649.** 700 San Jacinto Blvd 78701. At 8th St and San Jacinto Blvd. Int corridors. **Pets:** Small. $50 one-time fee/room. Service with restrictions, crate.

▲ ▼▼▼▼ **Omni Austin Hotel Southpark** 🄷 ❄
(512) 448-2222. **$109-$799.** 4140 Governor's Row 78744. I-35 exit 230B (Ben White Blvd/SR 71) southbound; exit 230 northbound; on east frontage road. Int corridors. **Pets:** Small. $50 one-time fee/room. Service with restrictions, crate.

▲ ▼▼▼▼ **Renaissance Austin Hotel** 🄷
(512) 343-2626. **$169-$249.** 9721 Arboretum Blvd 78759. Jct US 183 and Capital of Texas Hwy (SR 360); southwest corner. Int corridors. **Pets:** Accepted.

▼▼▼ **Residence Inn by Marriott Austin Airport/South** 🄷
(512) 912-1100. **$117-$162.** 4537 S I-35 78744. I-35 exit 229 (Stassney Rd) southbound; exit 230 (Ben White Blvd/SR 71) northbound; on northbound frontage road. Int corridors. **Pets:** Accepted.

▼▼▼ **Residence Inn by Marriott Austin/Downtown/ Convention Center** 🄷
(512) 236-8008. **$239-$279.** 300 E 4th St 78701. Between Trinity St and San Jacinto Blvd. Int corridors. **Pets:** Medium. $100 one-time fee/room. Service with restrictions, crate.

▼▼▼ **Residence Inn by Marriott-Austin North/Parmer Lane** 🄷
(512) 977-0544. **$117-$180.** 12401 N Lamar Blvd 78753. I-35 exit 245, just w. Int corridors. **Pets:** Accepted.

▼▼▼ **Staybridge Suites Austin Airport** 🄷
(512) 389-9767. **$119-$159.** 1611 Airport Commerce Dr 78741. Jct SR 71 (E Ben White Blvd) and Riverside Dr, just n. Int corridors. **Pets:** Accepted.

▼▼▼ **Staybridge Suites Austin Arboretum** 🄷
(512) 349-0888. **$169-$199.** 10201 Stonelake Blvd 78759. Jct Capital of Texas Hwy (SR 360) and Stonelake Blvd, 1 blk n. Int corridors. **Pets:** Large, other species. $15 daily fee/room. Service with restrictions, crate.

▼▼▼ **Staybridge Suites Austin Northwest** 🄷
(512) 336-7829. **$93-$139.** 13087 Hwy 183 N, Lot 3 78750. US 183 N exit Anderson Mill Rd, just n of exit on east frontage road; s of Anderson Mill Rd. Int corridors. **Pets:** Accepted.

▼▼ **Studio 6-Northwest #6032** 🄼
(512) 258-3556. **$53-$63.** 11901 Pavilion Blvd 78759. US 183 exit Oak Knoll Dr westbound; exit Duval Rd/Balcones Woods Dr eastbound; on eastbound frontage road. Ext corridors. **Pets:** Other species. $10 daily fee/room. Service with restrictions, supervision.

▲ ▼▼▼ **Super 8 Austin North** 🄷
(512) 339-1300. **$60-$223.** 8128 N I-35 78753. I-35 exit 241; on west frontage road. Int corridors. **Pets:** Large, other species. $25 one-time fee/room. Service with restrictions.

▼▼ **Super 8 University Austin** 🄷
(512) 451-7001. **$70-$460.** 5526 I-35 N 78751. I-35 exit 238A southbound; exit 238B northbound; on southbound frontage road. Ext corridors. **Pets:** Accepted.

▲ ▼▼▼▼ **W Austin** 🄷 ❄
(512) 542-3600. **$239-$569.** 200 Lavaca St 78701. At Lavaca and 2nd sts. Int corridors. **Pets:** Medium. $100 one-time fee/room, $50 daily fee/pet. Service with restrictions.

▲ ▼▼▼▼ **Westin Austin at the Domain** 🄷 ❄
(512) 832-4197. **$139-$329.** 11301 Domain Dr 78758. Jct Braker and Burnet rds; on northwest corner; in The Domain. Int corridors. **Pets:** Medium. Designated rooms, service with restrictions, supervision.

▼▼▼ **Wyndham Garden Hotel** 🄷
(512) 448-2444. **$99-$200.** 3401 I-35 S 78741. I-35 exit 231 (Woodward St) southbound; exit 230 (Ben White Blvd/SR 71) northbound; on northbound frontage road. Ext/int corridors. **Pets:** $35 one-time fee/room. Designated rooms, service with restrictions.

BASTROP

▼▼▼ **Comfort Suites** 🄷
(512) 321-3377. **$80-$93.** 505 Agnes St 78602. SR 71 exit Hasler Blvd; on south frontage road. Int corridors. **Pets:** Medium. $25 one-time fee/pet. Designated rooms, service with restrictions, supervision.

▼▼ **Quality Inn** 🄷
(512) 321-3303. **$89-$300.** 106 Hasler Blvd 78602. Jct SR 71. Int corridors. **Pets:** Accepted.

BAY CITY

▼▼▼ **Comfort Suites** 🄷
(979) 245-9300. **$80-$170.** 5100 7th (7th St) 77414. SR 35 (7th St), 2.2 mi e. Int corridors. **Pets:** Accepted.

▼▼▼ **La Quinta Inn & Suites Bay City** 🄷
(979) 323-9095. **$95-$166.** 5300 7th St 77414. On SR 35 (7th St), 3 mi e of downtown. Int corridors. **Pets:** Service with restrictions, supervision.

BEAUMONT

▲ ▼▼▼ **BEST WESTERN Jefferson Inn** 🄷 ❄
(409) 842-0037. **$79-$109.** 1610 I-10 S 77707. I-10 exit 851 (College St); on westbound frontage road; 0.5 mi s of jct US 90. Ext corridors. **Pets:** Large. $10 one-time fee/pet. Service with restrictions, supervision.

▼▼▼ **Days Inn** 🄷 ❄
(409) 898-8150. **$59.** 2155 N 11th St 77703. I-10 exit 853B (11th St), just n. Ext corridors. **Pets:** Medium. $10 one-time fee/pet. Service with restrictions, crate.

▲ ▼▼▼ **Holiday Inn Express Inn & Suites** 🄷
(409) 892-3600. **$109-$129.** 7140 Eastex Frwy 77708. US 69 exit 105; on northbound service road. Int corridors. **Pets:** Accepted.

▲ ▼▼▼ **Holiday Inn Hotel & Suites Beaumont Plaza** 🄷
(409) 842-5995. **$109-$149.** 3950 I-10 S 77705. I-10 exit 848 (Walden Rd), just n. Int corridors. **Pets:** Accepted.

▼▼▼ **Homewood Suites by Hilton** 🄷
(409) 842-9990. **$99-$149.** 3745 IH-10 S 77705. I-10 exit 848 (Walden Rd); on eastbound frontage road. Int corridors. **Pets:** Service with restrictions, supervision.

MCM Elegante Hotel & Conference Center H

(409) 842-3600. **$65-$129.** 2355 I-10 S 77705. I-10 exit 850 (Washington Blvd); on eastbound frontage road. Int corridors. **Pets:** Accepted.

Ramada Beaumont H

(409) 842-4420. **$59-$74.** 3985 College St 77707. I-10 exit 851A (College St); on westbound frontage road. Int corridors. **Pets:** Accepted.

Red Roof Inn & Suites - Beaumont H

(409) 842-8200. **$79-$150.** 2310 S I-10 77707. I-10 exit 850 (Washington Blvd) westbound; exit 851 (College St) eastbound. Int corridors. **Pets:** Large, other species. Service with restrictions, supervision.

BEDFORD

La Quinta Inn & Suites DFW Airport West-Bedford H

(817) 545-8105. **$81-$155.** 1809 Hwy 121 S 76021. SR 183 exit Murphy Dr; on westbound frontage road. Int corridors. **Pets:** Service with restrictions, supervision.

BEEVILLE

BEST WESTERN Texan Inn H

(361) 358-9999. **Call for rates.** 2001 Hwy 59 78102. US 181 at US 59, just e. Ext/int corridors. **Pets:** Large, other species. $10 daily fee/pet. Service with restrictions, supervision.

BELTON

Budget Host Inn H

(254) 939-0744. **$49-$75, 3 day notice.** 1520 S I-35 76513. I-35 exit 292 southbound; exit 293A northbound; on east frontage road. Ext corridors. **Pets:** Dogs only. $7 daily fee/pet. Supervision.

La Quinta Inn & Suites Belton H

(254) 939-2772. **$89-$177.** 229 W Loop 121 76513. I-35 exit 292, just w. Int corridors. **Pets:** Service with restrictions, supervision.

BENBROOK

BEST WESTERN Winscott Inn & Suites H

(817) 249-0076. **$90-$100.** 590 Winscott Rd 76126. I-20 exit 429B, just n. Int corridors. **Pets:** Small. $10 daily fee/pet. Designated rooms, no service, supervision.

Comfort Suites H

(817) 249-8008. **$90-$110.** 8004 Winbrook Dr 76126. I-20 exit 429B, just n. Int corridors. **Pets:** Small. $15 daily fee/pet. Designated rooms, no service, supervision.

Motel 6 - #4051 H

(817) 249-8885. **$62-$74.** 8601 Benbrook Blvd (Hwy 377 S) 76126. I-20 exit 429A, 0.7 mi s. Int corridors. **Pets:** Other species. Service with restrictions, supervision.

BIG SPRING

Holiday Inn Express H

(432) 263-5400. **Call for rates.** 1109 N Aylesford St 79720. I-20 exit 177; on eastbound frontage road. Int corridors. **Pets:** Medium, other species. $30 one-time fee/room. Service with restrictions, crate.

La Quinta Inns & Suites Big Spring H

(432) 264-0222. **$113-$254.** 1102 I-20 W 79720. I-20 exit 177; on north frontage road. Int corridors. **Pets:** Service with restrictions, supervision.

BOERNE

Americas Best Value Inn M

(830) 249-9791. **$79-$103.** 35150 IH-10 W 78006. I-10 exit 540 (SR 46); westbound access road. Ext corridors. **Pets:** Medium. $25 one-time fee/pet. Service with restrictions, crate.

Comfort Inn & Suites H

(830) 249-6800. **$69-$139.** 35000 I-10 W 78006. I-10 exit 540 (SR 46), just e to Norris Ln, then just s. Int corridors. **Pets:** Small. $25 one-time fee/pet. Service with restrictions, supervision.

Fairfield Inn & Suites by Marriott San Antonio Boerne H

(830) 368-4167. **$89-$139.** 6 Cascade Caverns Rd 78006. I-10 exit 543 (Cascade Caverns Rd), just off westbound access road. Int corridors. **Pets:** $50 one-time fee/room. Service with restrictions, supervision.

La Quinta Inn & Suites Boerne H

(830) 249-1212. **$77-$177.** 36756 IH-10 W 78006. I-10 exit 539 (Johns Rd) westbound; exit 540 (Bandera Rd) eastbound, U-turn back; on westbound access road. Int corridors. **Pets:** Service with restrictions, supervision.

BORGER

BEST WESTERN PLUS Plus Borger Inn H

(806) 274-7050. **$80-$120.** 206 S Cedar St 79007. Jct SR 136 and 207, just n. Int corridors. **Pets:** Other species. $30 daily fee/pet. Designated rooms, service with restrictions, crate.

BOWIE

BEST WESTERN Bowie Inn & Suites H

(940) 872-9595. **$80-$90.** 900 W US Hwy 287 S 76230. Jct SR 59. Int corridors. **Pets:** Small. $15 one-time fee/pet. Service with restrictions, supervision.

Park's Inn M

(940) 872-1111. **$60-$70.** 708 W Wise St 76230. 0.5 mi n of jct SR 59; downtown. Ext corridors. **Pets:** Small. $10 daily fee/pet. Service with restrictions, supervision.

BRADY

BEST WESTERN Brady Inn H

(325) 597-3997. **$85-$90.** 2200 S Bridge St 76825. 1.1 mi s on US 87/377. Ext corridors. **Pets:** Small. $10 daily fee/pet. Designated rooms, service with restrictions, supervision.

Days Inn M

(325) 597-0789. **$65-$100.** 2108 S Bridge St 76825. 1 mi s on US 87/377 at US 190. Ext corridors. **Pets:** Accepted.

BRENHAM

BEST WESTERN PLUS Inn of Brenham H

(979) 251-7791. **$90-$150.** 1503 Hwy 290 E 77833. Jct SR 36 and US 290, 1.3 mi e. Ext corridors. **Pets:** Large. $20 daily fee/pet. Service with restrictions, crate.

Comfort Suites H

(979) 421-8100. **$80-$150.** 2350 S Day St 77833. US 290 exit SR 36 S, just n on Business Rt SR 36. Int corridors. **Pets:** Accepted.

BRIDGEPORT

Comfort Suites H

(940) 683-5777. **Call for rates.** 2302 10th St 76426. 0.6 mi e of jct US 380 and SR 114. Int corridors. **Pets:** Accepted.

BROWNFIELD

BEST WESTERN Caprock Inn H
(806) 637-9471. **$100-$115, 3 day notice.** 321 Lubbock Rd 79316. Jct US 385 and 82, 2 blks n. Ext corridors. **Pets:** Accepted.

BROWNSVILLE

Holiday Inn H
(956) 547-1500. **$77-$85.** 3777 N Expwy 78520. US 77 and 83 exit Ruben Torres Sr Blvd (FM 802); on southbound frontage road. Int corridors. **Pets:** Accepted.

Homewood Suites by Hilton H
(956) 574-6900. **$99-$139.** 3759 N 78520. US 77 and 83 exit Ruben Torres Sr Blvd (FM 802); on southbound frontage road. Int corridors. **Pets:** Very small, dogs only. $75 one-time fee/pet. Designated rooms, service with restrictions, crate.

La Quinta Inn & Suites Brownsville North H
(956) 350-2118. **$71-$178.** 5051 N Expwy US 77 78520. US 77 exit Alton Gloor Rd southbound; exit Stillman northbound U-turn; on southbound frontage road. Int corridors. **Pets:** Service with restrictions, supervision.

Residence Inn by Marriott Brownsville H
(956) 350-8100. **$89-$142.** 3975 N Expwy 83 78520. US 77 and 83 exit Ruben Torres Sr Blvd (FM 802). Int corridors. **Pets:** Accepted.

Staybridge Suites H
(956) 504-9500. **$99-$129.** 2900 Pablo Kisel Blvd 78526. US 77 and 83 exit Ruben Torres Sr Blvd (FM 802), 0.8 mi n on frontage road to Pablo Kisel Blvd, then 0.5 mi e. Int corridors. **Pets:** Medium. $75 one-time fee/room. Service with restrictions, crate.

BROWNWOOD

La Quinta Inn and Suites H
(325) 641-1731. **$102-$184.** 103 Market Place Blvd 76801. US 183, just e. Int corridors. **Pets:** Service with restrictions, supervision.

BRYAN

BEST WESTERN PREMIER, Old Town Center H
(979) 731-5300. **$115-$360.** 1920 Austins Colony Pkwy 77803. SR 6 exit Briarcrest Dr, just n on E Frontage Rd. Int corridors. **Pets:** Small. $20 daily fee/pet. Service with restrictions, supervision.

BUFFALO

Craigs Inn Buffalo H
(903) 322-5831. **Call for rates.** IH-45 & US 79 75831. I-45 exit 178, just n on NW Frontage Rd. Ext/int corridors. **Pets:** Accepted.

BURKBURNETT

Burkburnett Hampton Inn H
(940) 569-8109. **Call for rates.** 1008 Sheppard Rd 76354. I-44 exit 12, just e. Int corridors. **Pets:** $30 one-time fee/room. Service with restrictions, supervision.

BURLESON

BEST WESTERN PLUS Burleson Inn & Suites H
(817) 744-7747. **Call for rates.** 516 Memorial Plaza 76028. I-35W exit 36 northbound; exit 35 southbound; on northbound access road. Int corridors. **Pets:** Small. $15 deposit/pet. Designated rooms, service with restrictions, supervision.

Comfort Suites H
(817) 426-6666. **$70-$110.** 321 S Burleson Blvd 76028. I-35W exit 35 southbound, 2 mi s to crossover, U-turn; exit 36 northbound; on northbound access road. Int corridors. **Pets:** Large. $20 daily fee/pet. Designated rooms, service with restrictions, supervision.

La Quinta Inn & Suites H
(817) 447-6565. **$83-$162.** 225 E Alsbury Blvd 76028. I-35E exit 38 (E Alsbury Blvd), just e. Int corridors. **Pets:** Service with restrictions, supervision.

BURNET

BEST WESTERN Post Oak Inn M
(512) 756-4747. **$69-$105.** 908 Buchanan Dr 78611. Jct US 281 and FM 29, 1 mi w. Ext corridors. **Pets:** Small, other species. $15 daily fee/pet. Service with restrictions, crate.

Comfort Inn & Suites H
(512) 756-1789. **Call for rates.** 810 S Water St (US 281) 78611. Jct US 281 and FM 29, 0.5 mi s. Int corridors. **Pets:** Small. $10 one-time fee/pet. Service with restrictions, supervision.

Log Country Cove VH
(512) 756-9132. **$150-$3200, 60 day notice.** 617 Log Country Cove 78611. Jct FM 1431 and 2342, 2 mi n; Park Rd 4 and FM 2342, 3 mi s. Ext corridors. **Pets:** Accepted.

CAMERON

Budget Host Inn & Suites H
(254) 605-0610. **$89-$200.** 102 Lafferty Ave 76520. US 77/190, 0.5 mi s. Int corridors. **Pets:** Medium. $25 daily fee/pet. Designated rooms, service with restrictions, supervision.

CANTON

BEST WESTERN Canton Inn H
(903) 567-6591. **$79-$159, 3 day notice.** 2251 N Trade Days Blvd 75103. Jct I-20 and SR 19 exit 527. Ext corridors. **Pets:** Accepted.

Quality Inn & Suites H
(903) 567-0909. **Call for rates.** 2406 N Trade Days Blvd 75103. I-20 exit 527, just n. Ext corridors. **Pets:** Accepted.

Super 8 H
(903) 567-6567. **$59-$179.** 17350 I-20 75103. I-20 exit 527. Ext corridors. **Pets:** Accepted.

CANYON

BEST WESTERN Palo Duro Canyon Inn & Suites H
(806) 655-1818. **$84-$110.** 2801 4th Ave 79015. I-27 exit 106, 1 mi w. Int corridors. **Pets:** Small, dogs only. $15 daily fee/pet. Designated rooms, service with restrictions, supervision.

Holiday Inn Express Hotel & Suites H
(806) 655-4445. **$99-$149.** 2901 4th Ave 79015. I-27 exit 106, 2 mi w. Int corridors. **Pets:** Accepted.

CARTHAGE

Baymont Inn & Suites H
(903) 694-9075. **$100-$145, 3 day notice.** 2313 SE Loop 75633. Just n of jct E US 59 Loop and SR 699. Int corridors. **Pets:** Small. $25 one-time fee/pet. Designated rooms, service with restrictions, crate.

CEDAR PARK

▼▼▼▼ Candlewood Suites 🅷 🐾
(512) 986-4825. **$89-$159.** 1100 Cottonwood Creek Tr 78613. Jct US 183A and CR 1431, 1 mi e. Int corridors. **Pets:** Medium. $75 one-time fee/pet. Service with restrictions, crate. 📶 ✕ ⚙M 🅗 🖥 🍽

▼▼ Comfort Inn 🅷
(512) 259-1810. **$75-$120.** 300 E Whitestone Blvd 78613. Jct US 183 and CR 1431, just e. Int corridors. **Pets:** Large, other species. $10 daily fee/pet. Service with restrictions, supervision. 📶 ⚙M 🅗 🖥 🍽

▼▼▼▼ La Quinta Inn & Suites Austin - Cedar Park 🅷
(512) 528-9300. **$106-$184.** 1010 E Whitestone Blvd 78613. Jct US 183A and CR 1431; on southwest corner. Int corridors. **Pets:** Service with restrictions, supervision. 📶 ✕ ⚙M 🅗 🖥 🍽

CENTER

▼▼▼▼ Sleep Inn & Suites 🅷
(936) 590-9090. **$80-$110.** 181 Civic Center Dr 75935. On US 96, just w of jct SR 87. Int corridors. **Pets:** Small. $25 daily fee/pet. Service with restrictions, supervision. 📶 ⚙M 🅗 🖥 🍽

CHILDRESS

◈◈◈ ▼▼▼ BEST WESTERN Childress 🅷
(940) 937-6353. **$85.** 1801 Ave F NW (Hwy 287) 79201. On US 287, just s of jct US 62/83. Ext corridors. **Pets:** Accepted.
[SAVE] 📶 🅗 🖥 🍽

▼▼▼▼ Hampton Inn & Suites 🅷
(940) 937-3500. **$95-$119.** 400 Madison Ave 79201. Jct US 298/83/62, just w. Int corridors. **Pets:** Accepted. 📶 ✕ ⚙M 🅗 🖥 🍽

▼▼ Rodeway Inn 🅷
(940) 937-3695. **Call for rates.** 1612 Ave F NW 79201. On US 287, just s of jct US 62/83. Ext corridors. **Pets:** Accepted. 📶 🅗 🖥

◈◈◈ ▼▼▼ Super 8 Childress M
(940) 937-8825. **$60-$90.** 411 Ave F NE (Hwy 287 S) 79201. Jct US 83/287, 1.5 mi e. Ext corridors. **Pets:** Other species. $13 daily fee/pet. Service with restrictions, crate. [SAVE] 📶 🅗 🖥 🍽

CISCO

▼▼ Americas Best Value Inn M
(254) 442-3735. **Call for rates.** 1898 Hwy 206 W 76437. I-20 exit 330, just n. Ext corridors. **Pets:** Accepted. 📶 🅗 🖥 🍽

CLARENDON

◈◈◈ ▼▼▼▼ BEST WESTERN PLUS Red River Inn 🅷
(806) 874-0160. **$99-$119.** 902 W 2nd St 79226. Jct US 287 and SR 70. Int corridors. **Pets:** Medium, other species. $10 daily fee/pet. Designated rooms, service with restrictions, crate.
[SAVE] 📶 ✕ ⚙M 🅗 🖥 🍽

◈◈◈ ▼▼ Western Skies Motel M
(806) 874-3501. **$45-$99.** 800 W 2nd St 79226. 0.5 mi nw on US 287 and SR 70. Ext corridors. **Pets:** Accepted. [SAVE] 📶 🅗

CLAUDE

◈◈◈ ◈ L A Motel M
(806) 226-4981. **$35-$65, 5 day notice.** 300 E 1st St 79019. 0.3 mi s. Ext corridors. **Pets:** Medium. $5 one-time fee/pet, $5 daily fee/pet. Service with restrictions, supervision. [SAVE] 📶 🅗 🖥

CLEAR LAKE CITY

▼▼▼ Candlewood Suites-Houston-Clear Lake 🅷
(281) 461-3060. **Call for rates.** 2737 Bay Area Blvd 77058. I-45 exit 26 (Bay Area Blvd), 3.7 mi e. Int corridors. **Pets:** Large. $15 daily fee/pet. Service with restrictions. 📶 🅗 🖥

▼▼▼ Residence Inn by Marriott Houston Clear Lake 🅷
(281) 486-2424. **$116-$179.** 525 Bay Area Blvd 77058. I-45 exit 26 (Bay Area Blvd) southbound, 1.2 mi e. Ext/int corridors. **Pets:** Medium, other species. $100 one-time fee/room. Service with restrictions, crate. 📶 ✕ 🅗 🖥 🍽 ✕

CLEBURNE

▼▼▼ Budget Host Inn-Sagamar Inn M
(817) 556-3631. **$65-$80.** 2107 N Main St 76033. US 67 exit SR 174, just e. Ext corridors. **Pets:** Accepted. 📶 🅗 🖥

▼▼▼ Comfort Inn 🅷
(817) 641-4702. **$67-$118.** 2117 N Main St 76033. On SR 174, just s of jct US 67. Int corridors. **Pets:** Other species. $10 daily fee/pet. Service with restrictions. 📶 ⚙M 🅗 🖥 🍽

▼▼▼▼ Hampton Inn & Suites 🅷
(817) 641-7770. **$79-$89.** 1996 W Henderson St 76033. US 67, just e of US 67 S. Int corridors. **Pets:** Medium, other species. $25 one-time fee/room. Service with restrictions, crate. 📶 ⚙M 🅗 🖥 🍽

▼▼▼▼ La Quinta Inn & Suites Cleburne 🅷
(817) 641-4455. **$78-$151.** 107 E Kilpatrick Ave 76033. Just n of jct SR 171/174 and FM 4. Int corridors. **Pets:** Service with restrictions, supervision. 📶 ⚙M 🅗 🖥 🍽

CLUTE

◈◈◈ ▼▼▼▼ Baymont Inn & Suites Clute 🅷
(979) 388-0055. **$110-$125.** 900 Hwy 332 77531. Just w of jct Business Rt SR 288. Int corridors. **Pets:** Small, dogs only. $20 daily fee/pet. Service with restrictions, supervision. [SAVE] 📶 🅗 🖥 🍽

▼▼▼ La Quinta Inn Clute Lake Jackson M
(979) 265-7461. **$59-$122.** 1126 Hwy 332 W 77531. On SR 288/332, just w of jct Business Rt SR 288. Ext corridors. **Pets:** Service with restrictions, supervision. 📶 🅗 🖥 🍽

COLLEGE STATION

▼▼ Econo Lodge 🅷
(979) 260-9150. **$63-$180.** 901 University Dr E 77840. Jct SR 6, 1 mi e. Ext corridors. **Pets:** Accepted. 📶 ⚙M 🅗 🖥 🍽

▼▼▼▼ Hawthorn Suites 🅷
(979) 695-9500. **$109-$269.** 1010 University Dr E 77840. SR 6 exit University Dr, 0.5 mi w. Int corridors. **Pets:** Accepted.
📶 ⚙M 🅗 🖥 🍽

▼▼▼▼ Hilton College Station & Conference Center 🅷
(979) 693-7500. **$89-$249.** 801 University Dr E 77840. SR 6 exit University Dr, 1.1 mi w. Int corridors. **Pets:** Accepted.
📶 ✕ ⚙M 🅗 🖥 🍽 🍴 🍽

▼▼▼▼ Holiday Inn Express Hotel & Suites 🅷
(979) 846-8700. **$124-$134.** 1203 University Dr E 77840. SR 6 exit University Dr, 1 mi w. Int corridors. **Pets:** Accepted.
📶 ✕ ⚙M 🅗 🖥 🍽

◈◈◈ ▼▼▼▼ Homewood Suites-College Station 🅷
(979) 846-0400. **$179-$279.** 950 University Dr E 77840. Jct SR 6 and 60 (Texas Ave), 1.5 mi e. Int corridors. **Pets:** Accepted.
[SAVE] 📶 ⚙M 🅗 🖥 ✕

◈◈◈ ▼▼▼ Howard Johnson Express 🅷
(979) 693-6810. **$63-$500.** 3702 Hwy 6 S 77845. SR 6 exit Rock Prairie Rd southbound. Ext corridors. **Pets:** Medium, dogs only. $20 daily fee/pet. Designated rooms, service with restrictions, crate.
[SAVE] 📶 🅗 🖥 🍽

▼▼▼▼ La Quinta Inn College Station 🅷
(979) 696-7777. **$83-$177.** 607 Texas Ave 77840. Just s on jct SR 60 and 6 business route to Live Oak St, then just e. Ext corridors.
Pets: Service with restrictions, supervision. 📶 🅗 🖥 🍽

▼▼ ▼▼ Manor Inn College Station H
(979) 764-9540. **$55-$145, 14 day notice.** 2504 Texas Ave S 77840. 2.4 mi s of jct SR 60. Ext corridors. **Pets:** Large, other species. $40 one-time fee/pet. Designated rooms, service with restrictions, supervision.

(AAA) ▼▼▼ Residence Inn by Marriott College Station H
(979) 268-2200. **$134-$189.** 720 University Dr E 77840. Jct Texas Ave, 0.5 mi e. Int corridors. **Pets:** Other species. $100 one-time fee/room. Service with restrictions, crate. SAVE 🛰 ✕ &M 🛏 💻 �'re ✕

▼▼▼▼ TownePlace Suites by Marriott H
(979) 260-8500. **$142-$156.** 1300 University Dr E 77840. SR 6 exit University Dr, 1 mi w. Ext corridors. **Pets:** Accepted.
ECO 🛰 ✕ 🛏 💻 ➤

COLUMBUS
(AAA) ▼▼ Americas Best Value Inn H
(979) 732-6293. **$78-$150.** 2436 Hwy 71 S 78934. I-10 exit 696 (SR 71). Ext corridors. **Pets:** Small, dogs only. $20 daily fee/pet. Designated rooms, service with restrictions, supervision. SAVE 🛰 🛏 💻 ➤

▼▼▼▼ Comfort Inn & Suites H
(979) 732-3785. **$75-$89, 4 day notice.** 2535 Hwy 71 S 78934. I-10 exit 696 (SR 71), just s. Int corridors. **Pets:** $10 daily fee/pet. Service with restrictions, supervision. 🛰 ✕ &M 🛏 💻 ➤

(AAA) ▼▼▼▼ Holiday Inn Express Hotel & Suites H
(979) 733-9300. **$99-$123.** 4321 I-10 78934. I-10 exit 696 (SR 71), just w on westbound service road. Int corridors. **Pets:** Other species. $25 daily fee/pet. Service with restrictions, supervision.
SAVE 🛰 ✕ 🛏 💻 ➤

CORPUS CHRISTI
(AAA) ▼▼▼ BEST WESTERN Garden Inn M
(361) 241-6675. **$99-$150.** 11217 I-37 78410. I-37 exit 11B (Violet Rd); on southbound frontage road. Ext corridors. **Pets:** Medium. $15 daily fee/pet. Service with restrictions, supervision.
SAVE 🛰 &M 🛏 💻 ➤

▼▼ Budget Inn & Suites M
(361) 884-2485. **$60-$150.** 801 S Shoreline Blvd 78401. I-37 exit Shoreline Blvd; between Park and Fuman aves. Ext corridors. **Pets:** Small. $25 daily fee/pet. Designated rooms, supervision. 🛰 🛏 💻 ➤

(AAA) ▼▼▼ Econo Lodge Inn & Suites M
(361) 883-7400. **$55-$140.** 722 N Port Ave 78408. I-37 exit 1D (Port Ave); on southbound frontage road. Ext corridors. **Pets:** Small. $100 deposit/pet, $10 daily fee/pet. Service with restrictions, supervision.
SAVE 🛰 🛏 💻 ➤

▼▼▼▼ Holiday Inn-Emerald Beach H
(361) 883-5731. **Call for rates.** 1102 S Shoreline Blvd 78401. 1.5 mi s on bay from downtown marina. Ext/int corridors. **Pets:** Medium. $35 one-time fee/room. Service with restrictions, supervision.
🛰 &M 🛏 💻 🍴 ➤ ✕

▼▼▼▼ Homewood Suites by Hilton H
(361) 854-1331. **$99-$199.** 5201 Crosstown Expwy (SR 286) 78417. I-37 exit SR 358 E (Greenwood Dr), 0.6 mi e on eastbound access road. Int corridors. **Pets:** Accepted. 🛰 🛏 💻 ➤

▼▼▼▼ La Quinta Inn & Suites Corpus Christi Airport H
(361) 299-2600. **$99-$199.** 546 S Padre Island Dr 78405. SR 358 exit Old Brownsville Rd; on frontage road. Int corridors. **Pets:** Service with restrictions, supervision. 🛰 ✕ &M 🛏 💻 ➤

▼▼▼ La Quinta Inn Corpus Christi South H
(361) 991-5730. **$71-$177.** 6225 S Padre Island Dr 78412. SR 358 exit Airline Rd. Ext corridors. **Pets:** Service with restrictions, supervision.
🛰 🛏 💻 ➤

(AAA) ▼▼▼▼ Omni Corpus Christi Hotel-Bayfront Tower H ❀
(361) 887-1600. **$129-$209.** 900 N Shoreline Blvd 78401. Across from bay; downtown; in marina district. Int corridors. **Pets:** Small. $50 one-time fee/room. Service with restrictions, supervision.
SAVE 🛰 ✕ &M 🛏 💻 🍴 ➤ ✕

▼▼▼▼ Omni Corpus Christi Hotel-Marina Tower H
(361) 887-1600. **$129-$199.** 707 N Shoreline Blvd 78401. Just n across from bay. Int corridors. **Pets:** Accepted. 🛰 🛏 💻 🍴 ➤ ✕

▼▼▼ Plaza Inn Corpus Christi H ❀
(361) 289-8200. **$79-$179.** 2021 N Padre Island Dr 78408. I-37 exit SR 358, just se at Leopard St. Int corridors. **Pets:** $50 one-time fee/pet. Designated rooms, service with restrictions, crate. 🛰 🛏 💻 ➤

▼▼▼ Quality Inn & Suites Sandy Shores H
(361) 883-7456. **$70-$210, 3 day notice.** 3202 Surfside Blvd 78402. 1 mi n on US 181; at north end of Harbor Bridge exit Bridge St. Ext/int corridors. **Pets:** Small. $20 daily fee/pet. Service with restrictions, crate.
🛰 🛏 💻 ➤

(AAA) ▼▼▼ Surfside Condominiums CO
(361) 949-8128. **$140-$225, 3 day notice.** 15005 Windward Dr 78418. Park Rd 22 on N Padre Island Dr, jct Whitecap Blvd, 0.6 mi n to Windward Dr, then 0.8 mi w. Ext corridors. **Pets:** Medium. $20 daily fee/pet. Designated rooms, service with restrictions.
SAVE 🛰 ✕ 🛏 💻 ➤

CORSICANA
(AAA) ▼▼▼▼ BEST WESTERN PLUS Executive Inn H
(903) 872-0020. **$80-$200.** 2100 E Hwy 31 75109. I-45 exit 231, just e. Int corridors. **Pets:** $20 daily fee/pet. Service with restrictions.
SAVE 🛰 &M 🛏 💻 ➤

▼▼▼▼ La Quinta Inn & Suites Corsicana H
(903) 874-6292. **$71-$144.** 2020 Regal Dr 75110. I-45 exit 231, just e. Int corridors. **Pets:** Service with restrictions, supervision.
🛰 🛏 💻 ➤

COTULLA
(AAA) ▼▼▼▼ BEST WESTERN Cowboy Inn H
(830) 879-3100. **$176.** 145 W FM 468 78014. I-35 exit 57 (FM 468), just w. Ext/int corridors. **Pets:** Small. $10 daily fee/pet. Service with restrictions, supervision. SAVE 🛰 ✕ 🛏 💻 ➤

CRESSON
(AAA) ▼▼▼▼ BEST WESTERN Cresson Inn H
(817) 396-4480. **Call for rates.** 9120 E Hwy 377 76035. 0.4 mi s of jct US 377 and SR 171. Int corridors. **Pets:** Accepted.
SAVE 🛰 🛏 💻 ➤

DALHART
(AAA) ▼▼▼ BEST WESTERN Nursanickel Motel H
(806) 244-5637. **$79-$105.** 102 Scott Ave (Hwy 87 S) 79022. Just s of jct US 54 and 87. Ext corridors. **Pets:** Medium. $10 daily fee/pet. Service with restrictions, supervision. SAVE 🛰 🛏 💻 ➤

(AAA) ▼▼ Budget Inn M
(806) 244-4557. **$45-$60.** 415 Liberal St (Hwy 54) 79022. On US 54, just e of US 87 and 385. Ext corridors. **Pets:** Medium. $10 one-time fee/pet. Designated rooms, service with restrictions, supervision. SAVE 🛰 🛏

▼▼▼ Days Inn H
(806) 244-5246. **$110-$150.** 701 Liberal St (Hwy 54) 79022. On US 54, 0.5 mi e. Int corridors. **Pets:** Accepted. 🛰 🛏 💻 ➤

(AAA) ▼▼▼ Rodeway Inn M
(806) 249-8585. **$75-$85.** 918 Liberal St (Hwy 54 E) 79022. 0.5 mi e of jct US 54 and 87. Ext corridors. **Pets:** Small. $10 deposit/pet. Designated rooms. SAVE 🛰 🛏 💻

(AAA) ▼ Sands Motel M
(806) 244-4568. **$35-$85.** 301 Liberal St (Hwy 54) 79022. On US 54, just e of US 87 and 385. Ext corridors. **Pets:** Designated rooms, service with restrictions, supervision. [SAVE] [≈] [■]

(AAA) ▼▼▼ Super 8 M
(806) 249-8526. **$60-$75.** 403 Tanglewood Rd (Hwy 54 E) 79022. Jct US 87 and 54, 0.5 mi e. Int corridors. **Pets:** Small. $25 deposit/pet. Designated rooms, service with restrictions, supervision. [SAVE] [≈] [■] [■]

DALLAS METROPOLITAN AREA

ADDISON

(AAA) ▼▼▼▼ BEST WESTERN PLUS Addison Galleria Hotel H
(972) 701-0881. **$59-$89, 7 day notice.** 14975 Landmark Blvd 75254. Dallas North Tollway exit Beltline, just w, then just s. Int corridors. **Pets:** Accepted. [SAVE] [≈] [✕] [■] [■] [⇌]

(AAA) ▼▼▼▼ Comfort Suites by Choice Hotels H
(972) 503-6500. **$65-$95.** 4555 Belt Line Rd 75001. Just w of Addison Rd; behind Macaroni Grill. Int corridors. **Pets:** Accepted.
[SAVE] [≈] [✕] [■] [■] [⇌]

▼▼▼▼ Homewood Suites by Hilton H
(972) 788-1342. **$89-$159.** 4451 Belt Line Rd 75001. Just e of jct Belt Line and Midway rds. Ext/int corridors. **Pets:** Small, other species. $75 one-time fee/pet. Service with restrictions, supervision.
[≈] [&M] [■] [■] [⇌] [✕]

(AAA) ▼▼▼▼ Hyatt house Dallas/Addison H
(972) 661-3113. **$89-$179.** 4900 Edwin Lewis Dr 75001. Just n of jct Belt Line Rd and Quorum Dr to Edwin Lewis Dr, then just w. Ext corridors. **Pets:** Accepted. [SAVE] [≈] [✕] [&M] [■] [■] [✕]

▼▼▼▼ La Quinta Inn & Suites Dallas Addison Galleria H
(972) 404-0004. **$59-$133.** 14925 Landmark Blvd 75254. Jct Belt Line Rd and Landmark Blvd, just s. Int corridors. **Pets:** Service with restrictions, supervision. [≈] [&M] [■] [■] [⇌]

▼▼▼ Quality Inn & Suites H
(972) 991-8888. **$60-$250.** 4103 Belt Line Rd 75001. Between Midway Rd and Marsh Ln. Ext corridors. **Pets:** Accepted. [≈] [■] [■] [⇌]

▼▼▼▼ Residence Inn by Marriott-Addison H
(972) 866-9933. **$89-$194.** 14975 Quorum Dr 75254. Just s of jct Belt Line Rd and Quorum Dr. Int corridors. **Pets:** Large, other species. $150 one-time fee/room. Service with restrictions.
[≈] [✕] [■] [■] [⇌] [✕]

ALLEN

(AAA) ▼▼▼▼ La Quinta Inn & Suites Allen At The Village H
(214) 667-6772. **$93-$166.** 1220 N Central Expwy 75013. US 75 exit 36 (Exchange Pkwy), just e. Int corridors. **Pets:** Service with restrictions, supervision. [SAVE] [≈] [✕] [■] [■] [⇌]

▼▼▼ Pyramids Hotel H
(972) 396-9494. **$89-$149.** 407 Central Expwy S 75013. US 75 exit 33 (Bethany Dr), just n on frontage road. Int corridors. **Pets:** Other species. $30 one-time fee/room. Designated rooms, service with restrictions, supervision. [≈] [✕] [■] [■] [⇌] [✕]

CARROLLTON

▼▼ Rodeway Inn H
(972) 245-9900. **Call for rates.** 1832 N I-35 E 75006. I-35E exit 443C (Frontage Rd) northbound; exit 443B Belt Line Rd) southbound, U-turn, just 1 mi n. Int corridors. **Pets:** Accepted. [≈] [■]

CEDAR HILL

(AAA) ▼▼▼▼ La Quinta Inn & Suites H
(972) 291-0008. **$77-$177.** 1419 N Hwy 67 75104. US 67 exit Wintergreen Rd; on southbound frontage road. Int corridors. **Pets:** Service with restrictions, supervision. [SAVE] [≈] [✕] [&M] [■] [■] [⇌]

DALLAS

(AAA) ▼▼▼▼ The Adolphus H
(214) 742-8200. **$139-$309.** 1321 Commerce St 75202. Between Field and Akard sts. Int corridors. **Pets:** Medium. $50 one-time fee/pet. Service with restrictions, supervision. [SAVE] [≈] [✕] [&M] [■] [■] [⫶] [✕]

(AAA) ▼▼▼▼ Aloft Downtown Dallas H
(214) 761-0000. **$129-$329.** 1033 Young St 75202. Northeast corner of Griffin and Young sts. Int corridors. **Pets:** Accepted.
[⊟] [SAVE] [≈] [✕] [&M] [■] [■] [⇌]

▼▼▼▼ Baymont Inn & Suites Dallas Love Field H
(214) 350-5577. **$99-$129.** 2370 W Northwest Hwy 75220. I-35E exit 436 Northwest Hwy (Loop 12), 0.8 mi e. Int corridors. **Pets:** Accepted.
[≈] [■] [■] [⇌]

(AAA) ▼▼▼ BEST WESTERN Cityplace Inn H
(214) 827-6080. **$59-$149.** 4150 N Central Expwy 75204. US 75 exit 1B (Fitzhugh Ave) southbound; exit 2 (Fitzhugh Ave) northbound. Ext corridors. **Pets:** Small. $50 one-time fee/pet. Service with restrictions, supervision. [SAVE] [≈] [■] [■] [⫶] [⇌]

▼▼ Candlewood Suites-Dallas by the Galleria H
(972) 233-6888. **$70-$119.** 13939 Noel Rd 75240. Jct Dallas Pkwy and Spring Valley, just e to Noel Rd, then just s. Int corridors. **Pets:** Medium. $15 daily fee/pet. Designated rooms, service with restrictions, supervision.
[≈] [&M] [■] [■]

(AAA) ▼▼▼ Candlewood Suites Dallas Market Center H
(214) 631-3333. **$89-$119.** 7930 N Stemmons Frwy 75247. I-35 exit 433B (Mockingbird Ln); on northbound frontage road. Int corridors. **Pets:** Small. $75 one-time fee/pet. Designated rooms, service with restrictions, supervision. [SAVE] [≈] [■] [■] [⇌]

▼▼ Candlewood Suites Dallas North/Richardson H ❀
(972) 669-9606. **$99-$139.** 12525 Greenville Ave 75243. I-635 exit 18A (Greenville Ave), turn n, then just w on Amberton Pkwy. Int corridors. **Pets:** Medium. $15 daily fee/pet. Designated rooms, service with restrictions, crate. [≈] [&M] [■] [■]

(AAA) ▼▼▼ Comfort Inn & Suites Market Center H
(214) 461-2677. **$70-$130.** 7138 N Stemmons Frwy 75247. I-35E exit 433B (Mockingbird Ln) northbound; exit 432B (Commonwealth Dr) southbound, turn under freeway, 0.7 mi on north access road. Int corridors. **Pets:** Other species. $25 one-time fee/pet. Service with restrictions, supervision. [SAVE] [≈] [■] [■]

▼▼▼ Dallas Marriott Suites Medical/Market Center H
(214) 905-0050. **$87-$199.** 2493 N Stemmons Frwy 75207. I-35E exit 431 (Motor St); on southbound frontage road. Int corridors.
Pets: Accepted. [ECO] [≈] [✕] [&M] [■] [■] [⫶] [⇌]

(AAA) ▼▼▼▼ The Fairmont Dallas H ❀
(214) 720-2020. **$119-$799.** 1717 N Akard St 75201. Corner of Ross Ave and N Akard St. Int corridors. **Pets:** Other species. $25 daily fee/room. Service with restrictions, supervision.
[ECO] [SAVE] [≈] [&M] [■] [■] [⫶] [⇌] [✕]

▼▼▼ Hawthorn Suites by Wyndham Dallas Near the Galleria H
(972) 391-0000. **$85-$120.** 7880 Alpha Rd 75240. I-635 exit 19B (Coit Rd), 0.3 mi n, then just w. Int corridors. **Pets:** Large. $15 one-time fee/room, $10 daily fee/room. Designated rooms, service with restrictions, crate. [≈] [✕] [■] [■] [⇌]

Hilton Dallas Lincoln Centre ⛨
(972) 934-8400. **$129-$399.** 5410 LBJ Frwy 75240. Jct I-635 and North Dallas Tollway/Dallas Pkwy; I-635 exit 22D (Dallas Pkwy) eastbound; exit 22B (Dallas Pkwy/Inwood Rd) westbound, just e on frontage road. Int corridors. **Pets:** Large. $50 one-time fee/pet. Service with restrictions.

Hilton Dallas Park Cities ⛨
(214) 368-0400. **Call for rates.** 5954 Luther Ln 75225. North Dallas Tollway exit Northwest Hwy (Loop 12), just e to Douglas Ave, then just s. Int corridors. **Pets:** Accepted.

Holiday Inn Dallas Market Center ⛨
(214) 219-3333. **Call for rates.** 4500 Harry Hines Blvd 75219. I-35E exit 430B (Market Center Blvd), just e. Int corridors. **Pets:** Accepted.

Holiday Inn Dallas Park Cities ⛨
(214) 750-6060. **$99-$109.** 6070 N Central Expwy 75206. US 75 exit 3 (Mockingbird Ln); on northbound frontage road. Int corridors. **Pets:** Medium. $50 one-time fee/room. Service with restrictions, supervision.

Homewood Suites by Hilton - I-635 Greenville ⛨
(972) 437-6966. **$109-$209.** 9169 Markville Dr 75243. I-635 exit 18A (Greenville Ave S), just s, then just e. Int corridors. **Pets:** Accepted.

Homewood Suites Dallas Market Center ⛨
(214) 819-9700. **$109-$179.** 2747 N Stemmons Frwy 75207. I-35E exit 432A (Inwood Rd), just s. Int corridors. **Pets:** $75 one-time fee/room. Service with restrictions.

Hotel Indigo Dallas Downtown ⛨
(214) 741-7700. **$89-$149, 3 day notice.** 1933 Main St 75201. Main and Harwood sts; northwest corner. Int corridors. **Pets:** Large, other species. $75 one-time fee/pet. Service with restrictions, supervision.

Hotel Palomar ⛨ ❖
(214) 520-7969. **$169-$397.** 5300 E Mockingbird Ln 75206. US 75 exit 3 (Mockingbird Ln); on southeast corner. Int corridors. **Pets:** Other species. Service with restrictions.

Hotel St. Germain ⛨ ❖
(214) 871-2516. **$305-$700, 7 day notice.** 2516 Maple Ave 75201. I-35 exit 430A (Oak Lawn Ave), 0.5 mi e, then 1 mi s. Int corridors. **Pets:** Small, dogs only. $50 daily fee/pet. Designated rooms, service with restrictions, supervision.

Hotel ZaZa ⛨
(214) 468-8399. **$295-$415.** 2332 Leonard St 75201. Jct Maple Ave/ Routh St and McKinney Ave; southeast corner. Int corridors.
Pets: Accepted.

Hyatt house Dallas/Lincoln Park ⛨
(214) 696-1555. **$109-$219.** 8221 N Central Expwy 75225. US 75 exit 5A southbound; exit 4B northbound, just w on Caruth Haven to Lincoln Pl, then just n. Int corridors. **Pets:** Medium. $150 one-time fee/room. Service with restrictions, crate.

Hyatt house Dallas/Uptown ⛨ ❖
(214) 965-9990. **$109-$219.** 2914 Harry Hines Blvd 75201. I-35 exit 430A (Oak Lawn Ave), just n to Harry Hines Blvd, then 0.6 mi s. Int corridors. **Pets:** Medium. $200 one-time fee/room. Service with restrictions, crate.

La Quinta Inn & Suites Dallas North Central ⛨
(214) 361-8200. **$90-$173.** 10001 N Central Expwy 75231. US 75 exit 6 (Walnut Hill Ln/Meadow Rd) northbound, 0.5 mi n to Meadow Rd, then U-turn under highway; exit 7 (Royal St/Meadow Rd) southbound, 1 mi s on feeder. Int corridors. **Pets:** Service with restrictions, supervision.

The Luxe Stoneleigh Hotel and Spa ⛨ ❖
(214) 871-7111. **$219-$459.** 2927 Maple Ave 75201. I-35E exit 430A (Oak Lawn Ave), 0.5 mi e, then 1.2 mi s. Int corridors. **Pets:** $100 one-time fee/room. Designated rooms, service with restrictions, supervision.

Magnolia Hotel Dallas ⛨
(214) 915-6500. **$129-$259.** 1401 Commerce St 75201. Corner of Commerce and Akard sts. Int corridors. **Pets:** Medium. $50 one-time fee/room. Designated rooms, service with restrictions, supervision.

MCM Elegante Hotel & Suites ⛨
(214) 351-4477. **$89-$139, 7 day notice.** 2330 W Northwest Hwy 75220. I-35E exit 436, just e. Ext/int corridors. **Pets:** Medium. $50 one-time fee/room. Service with restrictions, crate.

Residence Inn by Marriott Dallas Central Expressway ⛨
(214) 750-8220. **$104-$132.** 10333 N Central Expwy 75231. US 75 exit 6 (Walnut Hill Ln/Meadow Rd) northbound, 0.5 mi n to Meadow Rd, U-turn under highway; exit 7 (Royal St/Meadow Rd) southbound, 1 mi s on access road. Ext/int corridors. **Pets:** Accepted.

Residence Inn by Marriott-Dallas Market Center ⛨
(214) 631-2472. **$85-$151.** 6950 N Stemmons Frwy 75247. I-35E exit 432B (Commonwealth Ln), 0.6 mi n on northbound frontage road. Ext/int corridors. **Pets:** Accepted.

Residence Inn by Marriott-Dallas Park Central ⛨ ❖
(972) 503-1333. **$85-$151.** 7642 LBJ Frwy 75251. I-635 exit 20 (Hillcrest Ave); on eastbound access road. Int corridors. **Pets:** Other species. $100 one-time fee/room. Service with restrictions.

The Ritz-Carlton, Dallas ⛨ ❖
(214) 922-0200. **Call for rates.** 2121 McKinney Ave 75201. SR 366 (Woodall Rodgers Frwy) exit Pearl St, just sw to Olive St, then just nw. Int corridors. **Pets:** Small, other species. $125 one-time fee/room. Service with restrictions.

Rosewood Crescent Hotel ⛨
(214) 871-3200. **Call for rates.** 400 Crescent Ct 75201. Corner of Crescent Ct and McKinney Ave; uptown. Int corridors. **Pets:** Accepted.

Rosewood Mansion on Turtle Creek ⛨
(214) 559-2100. **$695-$5000.** 2821 Turtle Creek Blvd 75219. 2 mi nw, entrance on Gillespie St, just e of jct Gillespie St and Oak Lawn Ave. Int corridors. **Pets:** Accepted.

Sheraton Dallas Hotel ⛨
(214) 922-8000. **$99-$369.** 400 N Olive St 75201. Live Oak and Olive sts, just w off Central Expwy. Int corridors. **Pets:** Accepted.

Staybridge Suites North Dallas ⛨
(972) 726-9990. **$109-$149.** 16060 N Dallas Pkwy 75248. North Dallas Tollway exit Keller Springs, just e to Knoll Tr, then just s. Int corridors.
Pets: Accepted.

Warwick Melrose Hotel Dallas ⛨ ❖
(214) 521-5151. **$149-$599.** 3015 Oak Lawn Ave 75219. I-35E exit 430 (Oak Lawn Ave), 0.8 mi n; entrance off Cedar Springs, just n. Int corridors. **Pets:** Medium, dogs only. $50 one-time fee/room. Designated rooms, service with restrictions, crate.

W Dallas Victory Hotel & Residences H

(214) 397-4100. **$199-$529, 3 day notice.** 2440 Victory Park Ln 75219. Southwest corner of Olive and N Houston sts; uptown Dallas; across from American Airlines Center. Int corridors. **Pets:** Accepted.
SAVE 🛜 ✕ ⊇

The Westin Dallas Park Central H

(972) 385-3000. **$349-$424.** 12720 Merit Dr 75251. I-635 exit 19C (Coit Rd) eastbound; exit 19B (US 75/Coit Rd) westbound; 0.3 mi w of jct US 75. Int corridors. **Pets:** Accepted. SAVE 🛜 ✕ 🍴 ⊇

The Westin Galleria, Dallas H

(972) 934-9494. **$119-$449.** 13340 Dallas Pkwy 75240. Just n of jct I-635 and N Dallas Pkwy. Int corridors. **Pets:** Accepted.
SAVE 🛜 ▸ ▣ ⊇

Wyndham Dallas Park Central H

(972) 233-7600. **$79-$149.** 7800 Alpha Rd 75240. I-635 exit 19C (Coit Rd) eastbound; exit 19B (Coit Rd) westbound, just n, then just w. Int corridors. **Pets:** Medium. $25 one-time fee/pet. Service with restrictions, supervision. SAVE 🛜 ▸ ▣ 🍴 ⊇

DENTON

Comfort Inn H

(940) 320-5150. **$75-$80.** 4050 Mesa Dr 76207. I-35 exit 469 (University Dr), just w, then just n. Int corridors. **Pets:** Accepted.
SAVE 🛜 ✕ ▸ ▣ ⊇

Days Inn Denton H

(940) 383-1471. **$46-$150.** 4211 I-35 N 76207. I-35 exit 469 (University Dr), just w, then just n. Int corridors. **Pets:** Small. $10 daily fee/pet. Designated rooms, service with restrictions, supervision. 🛜 ▸ ▣ ⊇

Homewood Suites by Hilton-Denton H

(940) 382-0420. **$88-$162.** 2907 Shoreline Dr 76210. I-35E exit 462 (State School Rd/Mayhill Rd), just w to Unicorn Lake, 0.4 mi n, then just w. Int corridors. **Pets:** Medium. $75 one-time fee/room. Designated rooms, service with restrictions, crate. 🛜 ▸ ▣ ⊇ ✕

La Quinta Inn & Suites Denton H

(940) 808-0444. **$88-$162.** 4465 N I-35 76207. I-35 exit 469 (University Dr), just w, n on Mesa Dr, w on Barcelona St, then around to hotel. Int corridors. **Pets:** Service with restrictions, supervision.
🛜 ✕ ▸ ▣ ⊇

Super 8-Denton H

(940) 380-8888. **$60-$146.** 620 S I-35 E 76205. I-35 exit 465A (Teasley Ln). Int corridors. **Pets:** $25 daily fee/pet. Service with restrictions, crate. 🛜 ▸ ▣ ⊇

DESOTO

TownePlace Suites by Marriott Dallas DeSoto H

(972) 780-9300. **$98-$108.** 2700 Travis St 75115. US 67 exit Cockrell Hill; on northbound service road. Int corridors. **Pets:** Other species. $100 one-time fee/room. Service with restrictions, crate.
🛜 ✕ 🅼 ▸ ▣ ⊇

FARMERS BRANCH

Fairfield Inn & Suites by Marriott Dallas North H

(972) 661-9800. **$87-$99.** 13900 Parkside Center Blvd 75244. I-635 exit 23 (Midway Rd), 0.9 mi n to Spring Valley Rd, just w, then just s. Int corridors. **Pets:** Other species. $75 one-time fee/room. Service with restrictions. 🛜 ✕ ▸ ▣ ⊇

Omni Dallas Hotel Park West H

(972) 869-4300. **$89-$209.** 1590 LBJ Frwy 75234. I-635 exit 29 (Luna Rd), just s. Int corridors. **Pets:** Accepted. 🛜 ✕ ▣ 🍴 ⊇ ✕

Sheraton Dallas Hotel by the Galleria H ✤

(972) 661-3600. **$79-$249.** 4801 LBJ Frwy 75244. I-635 exit 22D (Dallas Pkwy) eastbound; exit 22B (Dallas Pkwy) westbound; on westbound frontage road. Int corridors. **Pets:** $75 one-time fee/room. Service with restrictions, supervision. SAVE 🛜 ✕ 🅼 ▸ ▣ 🍴 ⊇

FORNEY

BEST WESTERN PLUS Christopher Inn & Suites H ✤

(972) 552-1412. **$100-$130.** 752 Pinson Rd 75126. US 80 exit FM 740 (Pinson Rd), just ne. Int corridors. **Pets:** Large. $10 daily fee/pet. Service with restrictions, supervision. SAVE 🛜 ✕ 🅼 ▸ ▣ ⊇

FRISCO

Aloft Frisco H ✤

(972) 668-6011. **$89-$289.** 3202 Parkwood Blvd 75034. N Dallas Tollway exit Warren Pkwy, 0.5 mi e to Parkwood Blvd, then just s. Int corridors. **Pets:** Dogs only. Designated rooms, service with restrictions, supervision. SAVE 🛜 ✕ 🅼 ▸ ▣ ⊇

Embassy Suites Dallas-Frisco Hotel, Convention Center & Spa H ✤

(972) 712-7200. **$120-$250.** 7600 John Q Hammons Dr 75034. SR 121 exit Parkwood, just n. Int corridors. **Pets:** Large. $75 one-time fee/room. Designated rooms, service with restrictions, crate.
⊟ SAVE 🛜 🅼 ▸ ▣ 🍴 ⊇ ✕

Sheraton Stonebriar Hotel H

(972) 668-8700. **$99-$349.** 5444 State Hwy 121 75034. SR 121 exit Legacy Dr; northwest corner. Int corridors. **Pets:** Accepted.
SAVE 🛜 ✕ 🅼 ▸ ▣ 🍴

The Westin Stonebriar H

(972) 668-8000. **$109-$389.** 1549 Legacy Dr 75034. 0.3 mi n of jct SR 121. Int corridors. **Pets:** Accepted.
SAVE 🛜 ✕ 🅼 ▸ ▣ 🍴 ⊇ ✕

GARLAND

BEST WESTERN Lakeview Inn H ✤

(972) 303-1601. **$65-$75.** 1635 E I-30 at Bass Pro Rd 75043. I-30 exit 62 (Bass Pro Rd) eastbound, s on Chaha Rd, over bridge to north frontage road. Ext corridors. **Pets:** Other species. $10 daily fee/pet. Designated rooms, service with restrictions, crate. SAVE 🛜 ▸ ▣ ⊇

GRAND PRAIRIE

Comfort Suites H

(214) 412-1022. **$94-$119.** 2504 I-20 W 75052. I-20 exit 454 (Great Southwest Pkwy), just n, then just e. Int corridors. **Pets:** Small. $25 one-time fee/pet. Service with restrictions, crate. 🛜 ✕ ▸ ▣ ⊇

La Quinta Inn & Suites South Grand Prairie H

(214) 412-3220. **$95-$188.** 2131 W I-20 75052. I-20 exit 454 (Great Southwest Pkwy); on eastbound frontage road. Int corridors. **Pets:** Service with restrictions, supervision. ⊟ 🛜 ✕ ▸ ▣ ⊇

Super 8 H

(972) 606-2800. **$60-$90.** 4020 Great Southwest Pkwy 75052. I-20 exit 454 (Great Southwest Pkwy), just s. Ext corridors. **Pets:** Dogs only. $15 daily fee/pet. Service with restrictions, supervision. 🛜 ▸ ▣ ⊇

GREENVILLE

BEST WESTERN PLUS Monica Royale Inn & Suites H

(903) 454-3700. **$110-$129.** 3001 Mustang Crossing 75402. I-30 exit 93. Int corridors. **Pets:** Medium. $100 deposit/room. Service with restrictions, crate. SAVE 🛜 ✕ 🅼 ▸ ▣ ⊇

Holiday Inn Express Hotel & Suites H

(903) 454-8680. **$99-$130.** 2901 Mustang Crossing 75402. I-30 exit 93A. Int corridors. **Pets:** Accepted. 🛜 🅼 ▸ ▣ ⊇

HUTCHINS

ⓐ ▼▼▼▼ La Quinta Inn & Suites 🄷
(214) 269-1015. **$83-$166.** 1000 Dowdy Ferry Rd 75141. I-45 exit 274, just e. Int corridors. **Pets:** Service with restrictions, supervision.

[SAVE] 🛜 🛢 💻 🏊

IRVING

ⓐ ▼▼▼▼ Aloft Las Colinas 🄷
(972) 717-6100. **$89-$289.** 122 E John Carpenter Frwy 75062. SR 114 exit O'Connor Rd, just s. Int corridors. **Pets:** Accepted.

[SAVE] 🛜 ✕ 🅼 🛢 💻 🏊

▼▼▼▼ Candlewood Suites Dallas/Las Colinas 🄷
(972) 714-9990. **$81-$109, 3 day notice.** 5300 Green Park Dr 75038. SR 114 exit Walnut Hill Ln, just s. Int corridors. **Pets:** Accepted.

🛜 🅼 🛢 💻 🏊

▼▼▼▼ Courtyard by Marriott-DFW Airport North 🄷
(972) 929-4004. **$69-$169.** 4949 Regent Blvd 75063. I-635 exit 34 (Freeport Pkwy), 0.5 mi s, then 0.5 mi w. Int corridors. **Pets:** Accepted.

🛜 ✕ 🅼 🛢 💻 🍴 🏊

ⓐ ▼▼▼▼ DoubleTree by Hilton Hotel DFW Airport-North 🄷
(972) 929-8181. **$99-$189.** 4441 Hwy 114 75063. N off SR 114 exit Esters Blvd. Int corridors. **Pets:** Accepted.

[SAVE] 🛜 ✕ 🛢 💻 🍴 🏊

ⓐ ▼▼▼▼ Element Dallas Fort Worth Airport North 🄷
(972) 929-9800. **$79-$229.** 3550 IH 635 75063. I-635 exit 33 (Belt Line Rd), just s. Int corridors. **Pets:** Accepted.

◧ [SAVE] 🛜 ✕ 🛢 💻 🏊

ⓐ ▼▼▼▼▼ Four Seasons Resort and Club 🄷
(972) 717-0700. **$265-$400.** 4150 N MacArthur Blvd 75038. SR 114 exit MacArthur Blvd, 1.5 mi s. Int corridors. **Pets:** Accepted.

[SAVE] 🛜 ✕ 🅼 🛢 💻 🍴 🏊 ✕

ⓐ ▼▼▼▼ Hyatt house Dallas/Las Colinas 🄷
(972) 831-0909. **$99-$179.** 5901 N MacArthur Blvd 75039. SR 114 exit MacArthur Blvd; northwest corner. Ext/int corridors. **Pets:** Accepted.

[SAVE] 🛜 ✕ 🅼 🛢 💻 🏊 ✕

▼▼▼▼ La Quinta Inn & Suites Dallas DFW Airport North 🄷
(972) 915-4022. **$71-$166.** 4850 W John Carpenter Frwy 75063. SR 114 exit Freeport Pkwy; on eastbound service road. Int corridors. **Pets:** Service with restrictions, supervision. 🛜 🅼 🛢 💻 🏊

▼▼▼ La Quinta Inn & Suites Dallas DFW Airport South/Irving 🄷
(972) 252-6546. **$59-$177.** 4105 W Airport Frwy 75062-5997. SR 183 exit Esters Rd westbound; exit North Beltline Rd eastbound; on westbound frontage road. Int corridors. **Pets:** Service with restrictions, supervision. 🛜 🛢 💻 🏊

▼▼▼ La Quinta Inn & Suites Dallas - Las Colinas 🄷
(972) 261-4900. **$71-$155.** 4225 N MacArthur Blvd 75038. Se off SR 114 exit MacArthur Blvd, 1.4 mi s. Int corridors. **Pets:** Service with restrictions, supervision. 🛜 ✕ 🛢 💻 🏊

▼ Motel 6 - #4725 DFW North 🄼
(972) 915-3993. **Call for rates.** 7800 Heathrow Dr 75063. SR 114 exit Freeport Pkwy, just se. Int corridors. **Pets:** Other species. Service with restrictions, supervision. 🛜 🏊

ⓐ ▼▼▼▼ NYLO Dallas/Las Colinas 🄷
(972) 373-8900. **$89-$499.** 1001 W Royal Ln 75039. SR 114 exit MacArthur, just n, then just w. Int corridors. **Pets:** Medium. $50 daily fee/pet. Designated rooms, service with restrictions, supervision.

[SAVE] 🛜 ✕ 💻 🍴 🏊

▼▼▼ ▼▼▼ Omni Mandalay Dallas at Las Colinas 🄷 🐾
(972) 556-0800. **Call for rates.** 221 E Las Colinas Blvd 75039. SR 114 exit O'Connor Rd, just n, then just e. Int corridors. **Pets:** Medium. $50 one-time fee/room. Service with restrictions, crate.

🛜 ✕ 🛢 💻 🍴 🏊 ✕

ⓐ ▼▼▼ Red Roof Inn/DFW Airport North 🄼
(972) 929-0020. **$49-$199.** 8150 Esters Blvd 75063. SR 114 exit Esters Blvd, just n. Ext corridors. **Pets:** Large, other species. Service with restrictions, supervision. [SAVE] 🛜 🛢

▼▼▼ ▼▼▼ Residence Inn by Marriott at Las Colinas 🄷 🐾
(972) 580-7773. **$89-$189.** 950 W Walnut Hill Ln 75038. SR 114 exit MacArthur Blvd, 0.5 mi s, then just e. Ext corridors. **Pets:** Other species. $150 one-time fee/room. Service with restrictions, crate.

[ECO] 🛜 ✕ 🅼 🛢 💻 🏊 ✕

▼▼▼ Residence Inn by Marriott-DFW North 🄷
(972) 871-1331. **$139-$209.** 8600 Esters Blvd 75063. SR 114 exit Esters Blvd, 0.9 mi n. Int corridors. **Pets:** $100 one-time fee/room. Service with restrictions. 🛜 ✕ 🅼 🛢 💻 🏊 ✕

ⓐ ▼▼▼▼ Sheraton DFW Airport Hotel 🄷 🐾
(972) 929-8400. **$99-$359.** 4440 W John Carpenter Frwy 75063. SR 114 exit Esters Blvd, just s. Int corridors. **Pets:** Medium. $35 one-time fee/room. Service with restrictions, supervision.

[SAVE] 🛜 ✕ 🛢 💻 🍴 🏊

▼▼▼ Staybridge Suites Dallas-Las Colinas 🄷
(972) 465-9400. **$89-$229.** 1201 Executive Cir 75038. SR 114 exit MacArthur Blvd, just s to W Walnut Hill Ln, then just w. Int corridors. **Pets:** Accepted. 🛜 🛢 💻 🏊

ⓐ ▼▼▼▼ The Westin Dallas Fort Worth Airport 🄷 🐾
(972) 929-4500. **$109-$349.** 4545 W John Carpenter Frwy 75063. SR 114 exit Esters Blvd, just n. Int corridors. **Pets:** Accepted.

[SAVE] 🛜 ✕ 🛢 💻 🍴 🏊

ⓐ ▼▼▼▼ Wyndham-Las Colinas 🄷
(972) 650-1600. **$79-$219.** 110 W John Carpenter Frwy 75039. Sw off SR 114 exit O'Connor Rd. Int corridors. **Pets:** Accepted.

[SAVE] 🛜 ✕ 🛢 💻 🍴 🏊

KAUFMAN

ⓐ ▼▼▼ BEST WESTERN La Hacienda Inn 🄼 🐾
(972) 962-6272. **$60-$120.** 200 E Hwy 175 75142. Just e of jct US 175 and SR 34. Ext corridors. **Pets:** Large. $15 daily fee/pet. Designated rooms, service with restrictions, supervision. [SAVE] 🛜 🛢 💻 🏊

LAKE DALLAS

ⓐ ▼▼▼▼ BEST WESTERN PLUS Lake Dallas Inn & Suites 🄷
(940) 497-1007. **$75-$95.** 305 Swisher Rd 75065. I-35E exit 458 (Swisher Rd), 0.6 mi on N Frontage Rd. Int corridors. **Pets:** Medium. $25 one-time fee/pet. Designated rooms, service with restrictions, supervision.

[SAVE] 🛜 ✕ 🛢 💻 🏊

LEWISVILLE

▼▼ Comfort Suites by Choice Hotels 🄷
(972) 315-6464. **$89-$109.** 755A Vista Ridge Mall Dr 75067. I-35E exit 448A (Round Grove Rd) southbound; 0.5 mi s of jct I-35 and Round Grove Rd on southbound service road to Vista Ridge Mall Dr, then just w; exit 447B northbound, just w on SR 121 Bypass. Int corridors. **Pets:** Other species. $25 one-time fee/room. Service with restrictions, crate. 🛜 ✕ 🛢 💻 🏊

▼▼▼ Country Inn & Suites By Carlson 🄷
(972) 315-6565. **Call for rates.** 755 E B E Vista Ridge Mall Dr 75067. I-35E exit 448A (Round Grove Rd) southbound, 0.5 mi s on service road to Vista Ridge Mall Dr, then just w; exit 447B northbound, just w on SR 121 Bypass. Int corridors. **Pets:** Accepted. 🛜 🛢 💻 🏊

◈◈ **Extended StayAmerica Dallas-Lewisville** H
(972) 315-7455. **$64-$119.** 1900 Lakepointe Dr 75057. I-35E exit 449 (Corporate Dr), just e to Lakepointe Dr, then just s. Int corridors. **Pets:** $25 daily fee/pet. Designated rooms, service with restrictions.
◈ 🛜 📶 📺 💻

◈ **Motel 6 - #1288** H
(972) 436-5008. **$45-$55.** 1705 Lakepointe Dr 75057. I-35E exit 449 (Corporate Dr), just n on service road. Int corridors. **Pets:** Other species. Service with restrictions, supervision. 🛜 📶 🏊

◈◈◈ **Residence Inn by Marriott Dallas/Lewisville** H
(972) 315-3777. **$99-$199.** 755 E Vista Ridge Mall Dr 75067. I-35E exit 448A (Round Grove Rd) southbound, 0.5 mi s on frontage road, then just w; exit 447B northbound, just w to Lake Vista, just n. Int corridors. **Pets:** Other species. $100 one-time fee/room. Service with restrictions, crate. 🛜 🍽 📶 📺 💻 🏊 ⊗

◈◈◈ **TownePlace Suites by Marriott Dallas Lewisville** H
(972) 459-1275. **$117-$135.** 731 E Vista Ridge Mall Dr 75067. I-35 exit 447B northbound, just e; exit 448A southbound 0.5 mi w to Lake Vista, then just n. Int corridors. **Pets:** Medium. $100 one-time fee/pet. Service with restrictions, supervision. 🛜 🍽 📶 📺 💻 🏊

MCKINNEY

AAA ◈◈◈ **La Quinta Inn & Suites** H
(972) 908-2370. **$77-$166.** 6501 Henneman Way 75070. SR 121 exit Stacy Rd, just n, then just w. Int corridors. **Pets:** Service with restrictions, supervision. SAVE 🛜 🍽 📶 📺 🏊

◈◈ **Quality Inn** H
(972) 542-9471. **$70-$100.** 1300 N Central Expwy 75070. US 75 exit 40B (Bob White Ave); on northbound frontage road. Ext corridors. **Pets:** Large, other species. $25 one-time fee/pet. Service with restrictions, supervision. 🛜 📶 📺 🏊

AAA ◈◈ **Super 8-McKinney** H
(972) 548-8880. **$60-$75.** 910 N Central Expwy 75070. US 75 exit 40A (Virginia St/Louisiana St), 0.5 mi n on northbound frontage road. Int corridors. **Pets:** Accepted. SAVE 🛜 📶 📺 🏊

MESQUITE

◈◈◈ **Comfort Inn** H
(972) 285-6300. **$65-$74.** 923 Windbell Cir 75149. I-635 exit 5, just e, then just s. Int corridors. **Pets:** Other species. $10 daily fee/pet. Service with restrictions, supervision. 🛜 📶 📺 💻 🏊

AAA ◈◈◈◈ **La Quinta Inn & Suites Dallas Mesquite** H
(972) 216-7460. **$83-$161.** 118 E Hwy 80 75149. US 80 E exit Belt Line Rd. Int corridors. **Pets:** Service with restrictions, supervision.
SAVE 🛜 📶 📶 📺 💻 🏊

MIDLOTHIAN

◈◈◈ **Americas Best Value Inn & Suites** H
(972) 775-1891. **$79-$110.** 220 N Hwy 67 76065. On US 67, just n of jct US 287. Ext corridors. **Pets:** Large, other species. $10 daily fee/pet. Designated rooms, service with restrictions, supervision. 🛜 📶 📺 💻 🏊

PLANO

AAA ◈◈◈ **Aloft Plano** H
(214) 474-2520. **$89-$289.** 6853 N Dallas Pkwy 75024. North Dallas Tollway exit Spring Creek Pkwy/Tennyson Pkwy, just s of Tennyson Pkwy; on frontage road. Int corridors. **Pets:** Accepted.
SAVE 🛜 🍽 📶 📶 📺 💻

AAA ◈◈◈ **BEST WESTERN Park Suites Hotel** H
(972) 578-2243. **$95-$110.** 640 Park Blvd E 75074. US 75 exit 29A northbound, just e; then 0.5 mi s on frontage road; exit 29 southbound, just e on 15th St, then 0.5 mi n on frontage road. Int corridors. **Pets:** Medium, dogs only. $20 daily fee/room. Designated rooms, service with restrictions. SAVE 🛜 🍽 📶 📶 📺 💻 🏊

◈◈ **Candlewood Suites-Plano** H
(972) 618-5446. **$69-$129.** 4701 Legacy Dr 75024. Jct SR 289 (Preston Rd) and Legacy Dr, just e. Int corridors. **Pets:** Accepted. 🛜 📶 💻

◈◈◈ **Homewood Suites by Hilton** H
(972) 758-8800. **$85-$159.** 4705 Old Shepard Pl 75093. Jct Plano Pkwy and SR 289 (Preston Rd), 0.4 mi n, then just e. Int corridors.
Pets: Accepted. 🛜 📶 📶 📺 💻 🏊 ⊗

◈◈◈ **La Quinta Inn & Suites Dallas Plano West** H
(972) 599-0700. **$66-$155.** 4800 W Plano Pkwy 75093. Just e of jct SR 289 (Preston Rd). Int corridors. **Pets:** Service with restrictions, supervision. 🛜 📶 📶 📺 💻 🏊

◈◈◈ **NYLO Plano at Legacy** H
(972) 624-6990. **$79-$495.** 8201 Preston Rd 75024. Just s of jct SR 121. Int corridors. **Pets:** Accepted. 🛜 🍽 📶 📺 💻 🍴 🏊

AAA ◈◈◈ **Southfork Hotel** H
(972) 578-8555. **$69-$99.** 1600 N Central Expwy 75074. US 75 exit 29A northbound; exit 29 southbound; on northbound frontage road. Int corridors. **Pets:** Accepted. SAVE 🛜 🍽 📶 📺 💻 🍴 🏊

AAA ◈◈◈ **Staybridge Suites Plano/Richardson** H
(972) 612-8180. **Call for rates.** 301 Silverglen Dr 75075. George Bush Toll Rd exit Coit Rd, n to Mapleshade Ln, just e, then just s. Int corridors. **Pets:** Medium. $75 one-time fee/pet. Service with restrictions, supervision. SAVE 🛜 🍽 📶 📶 📺 💻 🏊 ⊗

◈◈ **Super 8-Plano** H
(972) 423-8300. **$50-$65.** 1704 N Central Expwy 75074. US 75 exit 29A (Park Blvd) northbound, just e; exit 29 southbound, 0.5 mi s on frontage road, just e on 15th St, then just n on frontage road. Int corridors. **Pets:** Accepted. 🛜 📶 📶 📺 💻

◈◈ **TownePlace Suites by Marriott** H
(972) 943-8200. **$82-$132.** 5005 Whitestone Ln 75024. North Dallas Tollway exit Spring Creek Pkwy, 1.9 mi e, just n on SR 289 (Preston Rd) to Whitestone Ln, then just w. Int corridors. **Pets:** Accepted.
🛜 🍽 📶 📶 📺 💻 🏊

RICHARDSON

AAA ◈◈◈ **Hyatt house Dallas/Richardson** H
(972) 671-8080. **$89-$189.** 2301 N Central Expwy 75080. US 75 exit 26 (Campbell Rd), 0.5 mi w to Collins Blvd, then 0.6 mi n. Int corridors. **Pets:** Medium. $150 one-time fee/pet. Designated rooms, service with restrictions, crate. SAVE 🛜 🍽 📶 📶 📺 💻 🏊 ⊗

AAA ◈◈◈ **Hyatt Regency North Dallas/Richardson** H
(972) 619-1234. **$72-$225.** 701 E Campbell Rd 75081. US 75 exit 26 (Campbell Rd) southbound; exit northbound; on frontage road. Int corridors. **Pets:** Accepted. SAVE 🛜 📶 📶 📺 💻 🍴 🏊

AAA ◈◈◈◈ **Renaissance Dallas-Richardson Hotel** H
(972) 367-2000. **$79-$239.** 900 E Lookout Dr 75082. US 75 exit 27A (Gallatin Pkwy/Renner Rd) northbound; exit 26 (Gallatin Pkwy/Campbell Rd) southbound, just e. Int corridors. **Pets:** Accepted.
SAVE 🛜 🍽 📶 📺 💻 🍴 🏊 ⊗

◈◈◈ **Residence Inn by Marriott Richardson** H
(972) 669-5888. **$85-$179.** 1040 Waterwood Dr 75082. US 75 exit 26 (Campbell Rd), just e to Greenville Ave, 0.4 mi n to Glenville Rd, then just w. Int corridors. **Pets:** Accepted.
ECO 🛜 🍽 📶 📺 💻 🏊 ⊗

ROANOKE

◈◈ **Comfort Suites Near Alliance** H
(817) 490-1455. **$89-$149.** 801 Byron Nelson Blvd 76262. I-35 exit 70 (SR 114), 2 mi e. Int corridors. **Pets:** Medium. $10 daily fee/pet. Service with restrictions, crate. 🛜 🍽 📶 📶 📺 💻 🏊

AAA ▼▼◆ Speedway Sleep Inn & Suites **H**

(817) 491-3120. **$80-$110.** 13471 Raceway Dr 76262. I-35 exit 70 (SR 114), just e, then just s. Int corridors. **Pets:** Medium, other species. $30 deposit/room. Service with restrictions, supervision.

SAVE 🛜 ♿M 🍴 💻 🏊

ROCKWALL

AAA ▼▼▼ BEST WESTERN PLUS Rockwall Inn & Suites **H**

(972) 722-3265. **$75-$150.** 996 E I-30 75087. I-30 exit 68; on westbound frontage road. Int corridors. **Pets:** Medium. $10 daily fee/pet. Designated rooms, service with restrictions. SAVE 🛜 ♿M 🍴 💻 🏊

▼▼▼ La Quinta Inn & Suites Rockwall **H**

(972) 771-1685. **$76-$150.** 689 E I-30 75087. I-30 exit 67 (Ridge Rd) westbound; exit 67B (Horizon Rd) eastbound; on eastbound frontage road. Int corridors. **Pets:** Service with restrictions, supervision.

🛜 ♿M 🍴 💻 🏊

ROWLETT

▼▼▼ Comfort Suites Lake Ray Hubbard **H**

(972) 463-9595. **$79-$139.** 8701 E I-30 75088. I-30 exit 64 (Dalrock Rd). Int corridors. **Pets:** Medium. $10 daily fee/pet. Service with restrictions, supervision. 🛜 ✕ ♿M 🍴 💻 🏊

TERRELL

AAA ▼▼◆ BEST WESTERN Country Inn **H**

(972) 563-1521. **Call for rates.** 1604 Hwy 34 S 75160. I-20 exit 501 (SR 34), just n. Ext corridors. **Pets:** Accepted. SAVE 🛜 🍴 💻 🏊

THE COLONY

AAA ▼▼▼ Comfort Suites **H**

(972) 668-5555. **$80-$110.** 4796 Memorial Dr 75056. SR 121 exit Blair Oaks southbound; exit Main St northbound, just n to Memorial Dr, then just e. Int corridors. **Pets:** Small. $15 daily fee/pet. Designated rooms, service with restrictions, supervision.

SAVE 🛜 ✕ ♿M 🍴 💻 🏊

▼▼▼ Residence Inn by Marriott-Plano/Frisco/The Colony **H**

(214) 469-1155. **$89-$239.** 6600 Cascades Ct 75056. SR 121 exit Spring Creek Pkwy; on southwest frontage road. Int corridors. **Pets:** Accepted.

🔌 🛜 ✕ 🍴 💻 🏊 ✕

UNIVERSITY PARK

AAA ▼▼▼ The Lumen **H**

(214) 219-2400. **$199-$399.** 6101 Hillcrest Ave 75205. Just n of jct Mockingbird Ln and Hillcrest Ave. Int corridors. **Pets:** Accepted.

ECO 🔌 SAVE 🛜 ✕ 🍴 🍴 🏊

WYLIE

AAA ▼▼▼ BEST WESTERN PLUS Wylie Inn **H** 🌼

(972) 429-1771. **$76-$100.** 2011 Hwy 78 N 75098. 1.8 mi ne of SR 2514 (Ballard St); downtown. Int corridors. **Pets:** Other species. $20 one-time fee/pet. Service with restrictions, supervision.

SAVE 🛜 ♿M 🍴 💻 🏊

END METROPOLITAN AREA

DECATUR

AAA ▼▼▼ BEST WESTERN Decatur Inn **M**

(940) 627-5982. **$74-$79.** 1801 S Hwy 287 76234. 0.6 mi s of jct Business Rt US 380. Ext corridors. **Pets:** Small. $15 daily fee/pet. Service with restrictions, supervision. SAVE 🛜 🍴 💻 🏊

AAA ▼▼◆ Holiday Inn Express Hotel & Suites **H**

(940) 627-0776. **Call for rates.** 1051 N Hwy 287 76234. Just n of jct US 380 and 287. Int corridors. **Pets:** Small. $50 one-time fee/pet. Designated rooms, service with restrictions, crate. SAVE 🛜 🍴 💻 🏊

DEL RIO

AAA ▼▼▼ BEST WESTERN Inn of Del Rio **M**

(830) 775-7511. **$70.** 810 Veterans Blvd 78840. Between E 6th and E 7th sts. Ext corridors. **Pets:** Dogs only. $20 deposit/pet, $20 daily fee/pet. Service with restrictions, crate. SAVE 🛜 🍴 💻 🏊

▼▼ La Quinta Inn Del Rio **H**

(830) 775-7591. **$59-$122.** 2005 Veterans Blvd 78840. 1.8 mi nw on US 90, 277 and 377. Ext/int corridors. **Pets:** Service with restrictions, supervision. 🛜 🍴 💻 🏊

AAA ▼▼▼ Ramada **H**

(830) 775-1511. **$69-$119.** 2101 Veterans Blvd 78840. 1.8 mi nw on US 90, 277 and 377. Ext/int corridors. **Pets:** Other species. Designated rooms, service with restrictions. SAVE 🛜 🍴 💻 🍴 🏊 ✕

DENISON

AAA ▼▼▼ BEST WESTERN PLUS Texoma Hotel & Suites **H**

(903) 327-8883. **$95.** 810 N US Hwy 75 75020. US 75 exit 69 (Morton Rd); on northbound frontage road. Int corridors. **Pets:** Other species. $25 one-time fee/pet. Service with restrictions, supervision.

SAVE 🛜 ✕ ♿M 🍴 💻 🏊

DONNA

▼▼ Super 8 **M**

(956) 461-2226. **$52-$60.** 2005 E Expwy 83 78537. US 83 exit CR 493. Ext corridors. **Pets:** Accepted. 🛜 🍴 💻 🏊

▼▼ Victoria Palms Inn & Suites **H**

(956) 464-7801. **$50-$140.** 602 N Victoria Rd 78537. US 83 exit Victoria Rd. Ext corridors. **Pets:** Small, other species. $100 deposit/pet, $5 daily fee/pet. Designated rooms, service with restrictions, supervision.

🛜 ✕ 🍴 💻 🍴 🏊 ✕

DRIPPING SPRINGS

▼▼▼ Sleep Inn & Suites **H**

(512) 858-2400. **$109-$289.** 2720 E US Hwy 290 78620. 2.5 mi e on US 290. Int corridors. **Pets:** Accepted. 🛜 ✕ ♿M 🍴 💻 🏊

DUMAS

AAA ▼▼▼ BEST WESTERN Windsor Inn **H**

(806) 935-9644. **$79-$129.** 1701 S Dumas Ave 79029. US 287, 2 mi s of US 87 and SR 152. Ext corridors. **Pets:** Dogs only. $10 daily fee/pet. Service with restrictions, crate. SAVE 🛜 🍴 💻 🏊 ✕

AAA ▼▼▼ Days Inn & Suites **H**

(806) 935-2222. **$78-$130.** 1610 S Dumas Ave 79029. Just s on US 287. Int corridors. **Pets:** Dogs only. $25 daily fee/room. Service with restrictions, crate. SAVE 🛜 ♿M 🍴 💻 🏊 ✕

AAA ▼▼▼ Econo Lodge **H**

(806) 935-9098. **$60-$70.** 1719 S Dumas Ave 79029. US 287, 2 mi s of US 87 and SR 152. Int corridors. **Pets:** Medium, dogs only. $10 daily fee/pet. No service, supervision. SAVE 🛜 ✕ 🍴

▼▼▼ Quality Inn **H**

(806) 935-4000. **$79-$89.** 1525 S Dumas Ave 79029. US 287, 1.1 mi s of US 87 and SR 152. Int corridors. **Pets:** Other species. $30 daily fee/room. Service with restrictions, supervision. 🛜 🍴 💻 🏊

▼▼ Super 8 **M**
(806) 935-6222. **$79-$89.** 119 W 17th St 79029. US 287, 2 mi s of US 87 and SR 152. Ext corridors. **Pets:** Accepted. 📶 🛏 💻

EAGLE PASS
▼▼ La Quinta Inn Eagle Pass **M**
(830) 773-7000. **$107-$199.** 2525 E Main St 78852-4498. US 57 and Loop 431 (US 277). Ext corridors. **Pets:** Service with restrictions, supervision. 📶 🛏 💻 🏊

EASTLAND
▼▼▼ La Quinta Inn & Suites Eastland **H**
(254) 629-1414. **$89-$156.** 10150 IH-20 76448. I-10 exit 343; on north service road. Int corridors. **Pets:** Service with restrictions, supervision. 📶 ❌ ♿ 🛏 💻 🏊

▼▼ Super 8 & RV Park **M**
(254) 629-3336. **$50-$80.** 3900 I-20 E 76448. I-20 exit 343; on north service road. Ext corridors. **Pets:** Accepted. 📶 🛏 💻 🏊

EDINBURG
Ⓐ ▼▼▼ BEST WESTERN PLUS Edinburg Inn & Suites **H**
(956) 318-0442. **$79-$99.** 2708 S Bus Hwy 281 78539. US 281 exit Canton Ave, 1 mi w to Business Rt US 281. Ext corridors. **Pets:** Small. $15 daily fee/pet. Designated rooms, service with restrictions, supervision. 🆂🅰🆅🅴 📶 ♿ 🛏 💻 🏊

Ⓐ ▼▼▼ Comfort Inn Edinburg **H**
(956) 318-1117. **$59-$149.** 4001 S US Hwy 281 78539. US 281 exit Trenton Rd, just w, then just n. Int corridors. **Pets:** Small. $10 daily fee/pet. Service with restrictions, crate. 🆂🅰🆅🅴 📶 🛏 💻 🏊

EL PASO
Ⓐ ▼▼▼ BEST WESTERN Sunland Park Inn **M**
(915) 587-4900. **$79-$99.** 1045 Sunland Park Dr 79922. I-10 exit 13, just s. Ext corridors. **Pets:** $20 daily fee/pet. Service with restrictions, supervision. 🆂🅰🆅🅴 📶 🛏 💻 🏊

▼▼▼▼ Candlewood Suites **H**
(915) 755-9000. **$88-$147.** 4631 Cohen Ave 79924. US 54 exit 28 (Diana Dr) northbound, 1 mi n, then just e; exit southbound, 1 mi s, U-turn under freeway, 1 mi n, then just e. Int corridors. **Pets:** Accepted. 📶 ❌ ♿ 🛏 💻

▼▼▼▼ Chase Suites Hotel **H**
(915) 772-8000. **$129-$299.** 6791 Montana Ave 79925. I-10 exit 25 (Airway Blvd), 1 mi n, then just e. Ext corridors. **Pets:** Small. $250 deposit/pet, $10 daily fee/pet. Designated rooms, service with restrictions, supervision. 📶 ❌ 🛏 💻 🏊 ❌

▼▼ Comfort Suites by Choice Hotels **H**
(915) 587-5300. **$69-$94.** 949 Sunland Park Dr 79922. I-10 exit 13, just s. Int corridors. **Pets:** Accepted. 📶 ❌ 🛏 💻 🏊

▼▼▼▼ GuestHouse International Suites **H**
(915) 772-0395. **$69-$135.** 1940 Airway Blvd 79925. I-10 exit 25 (Airway Blvd), 1.2 mi n. Int corridors. **Pets:** Small. $75 deposit/pet, $10 daily fee/room. Service with restrictions, supervision. 📶 ❌ ♿ 🛏 💻 🏊

Ⓐ ▼▼▼ Holiday Inn El Paso Sunland Park **H**
(915) 833-2900. **$99-$149.** 900 Sunland Park Dr 79922. I-10 exit 13 (Sunland Park Dr), just s. Ext corridors. **Pets:** Other species. $50 one-time fee/room. Service with restrictions, crate. 🆂🅰🆅🅴 📶 🛏 💻 🍴 🏊

Ⓐ ▼▼▼ Holiday Inn Express El Paso-Central **H** ❀
(915) 544-3333. **$79-$139.** 409 E Missouri St 79901. I-10 exit 19B westbound (downtown); exit 19 eastbound, just e. Int corridors. **Pets:** $25 one-time fee/room. Service with restrictions, crate.
🆂🅰🆅🅴 📶 ❌ 🛏 💻 🏊

▼▼ La Quinta Inn & Suites El Paso East **H**
(915) 591-3300. **$63-$140.** 7944 Gateway Blvd E 79915. I-10 exit 28B. Int corridors. **Pets:** Service with restrictions, supervision.
📶 ♿ 🛏 💻 🏊

▼▼ La Quinta Inn El Paso Lomaland **H**
(915) 591-2244. **$59-$129.** 11033 Gateway Blvd W 79935. I-10 exit 29 eastbound; exit 30 westbound, 1 mi w. Ext corridors. **Pets:** Service with restrictions, supervision. 📶 ♿ 🛏 💻 🏊

▼▼ La Quinta Inn El Paso West **M**
(915) 833-2522. **$59-$129.** 7550 Remcon Cir 79912. I-10 exit 11 (Mesa St). Ext corridors. **Pets:** Service with restrictions, supervision.
📶 🛏 💻 🏊

▼▼ Microtel Inn & Suites by Wyndham El Paso Airport **H**
(915) 772-3650. **$50-$78.** 2001 Airway Blvd 79925. I-10 exit 25 (Airway Blvd), 1.3 mi n. Int corridors. **Pets:** Accepted. 📶 ♿ 🛏 💻

▼▼ Microtel Inn & Suites by Wyndham El Paso East **H**
(915) 858-1600. **$55-$62.** 12211 Gateway Blvd W 79936. I-10 exit 34 (Joe Battle Blvd); on westbound frontage road. Int corridors. **Pets:** Other species. $100 deposit/pet. Service with restrictions, crate.
📶 ♿ 🛏 💻 🏊

▼▼ Motel 6 El Paso-Airport-Fort Bliss - #4487 **M**
(915) 778-3311. **$49-$65.** 6363 Montana Ave 79925. I-10 exit 24 (Geronimo Dr) westbound; exit 24B (Geronimo Dr) eastbound, 0.5 mi n, then 0.5 mi e. Ext corridors. **Pets:** Other species. Service with restrictions, supervision. 🄴🄲🄾 📶 🛏 🏊

▼▼ Motel 6 El Paso West - #4583 **H**
(915) 584-4030. **$45-$65.** 7840 N Mesa St 79932. I-10 exit 11 (N Mesa St), just s. Ext corridors. **Pets:** Other species. Service with restrictions, supervision. 📶 🛏 🏊

▼▼ Residence Inn by Marriott El Paso **H**
(915) 771-0504. **$170-$199.** 6355 Gateway Blvd W 79925. I-10 exit 24B (Geronimo Dr) eastbound, n to Edgemere, then just e; exit 25 (Airway Blvd) westbound; on westbound frontage road. Int corridors. **Pets:** Other species. $100 one-time fee/room. Designated rooms, service with restrictions, supervision. 📶 ❌ 🛏 💻 🏊 ❌

▼▼ Sleep Inn by Choice Hotels **H**
(915) 585-7577. **$59-$84.** 953 Sunland Park Dr 79922. I-10 exit 13, just w. Int corridors. **Pets:** $20 one-time fee/room. Service with restrictions, supervision. 📶 🛏 🏊

▼▼ Staybridge Suites Airport **H**
(915) 775-1212. **$129-$169.** 6680 Gateway Blvd E 79915. I-10 exit 25 (Airway Blvd) eastbound, just e; exit westbound, 0.5 mi w to Airway Blvd, then just sw. Int corridors. **Pets:** Accepted.
📶 ❌ ♿ 🛏 💻 🏊

▼▼▼ Wingate by Wyndham **H** 🐾
(915) 772-4088. **$89-$157.** 6351 Gateway Blvd W 79925. I-10 exit 24B (Geronimo Dr) westbound; exit 25 (Airport Blvd) eastbound, U-turn, 0.5 mi. Int corridors. **Pets:** Small. $75 deposit/pet, $10 daily fee/pet. Service with restrictions, supervision. 📶 ❌ ♿ 🛏 💻 🏊

▼▼▼ Wyndham El Paso Airport **H**
(915) 778-4241. **$129-$199, 3 day notice.** 2027 Airway Blvd 79925. I-10 exit 25 (Airway Blvd), 1.3 mi n. Int corridors. **Pets:** Small. $30 one-time fee/room. Service with restrictions, crate.
📶 ❌ 🛏 💻 🍴 🏊 ❌

EULESS

La Quinta Inn & Suites DFW Airport West - Euless H
(817) 836-4000. **$71-$166.** 431 Airport Frwy 76040. SR 183 exit Ector Dr; on eastbound frontage road. Int corridors. **Pets:** Service with restrictions, supervision. [SAVE] 🛜 ✕ 🛏 🖥 ⊷

Microtel Inn & Suites by Wyndham Euless/DFW Airport H
(817) 545-1111. **$50-$80.** 901 W Airport Frwy 76040. SR 183 exit Industrial Blvd (FM 157); on eastbound frontage road. Int corridors. **Pets:** Medium, dogs only. $25 one-time fee/room. Service with restrictions, supervision. 🛜 ⛱M 🛏 🖥 ⊷

FALFURRIAS

Days Inn M
(361) 325-2515. **$60-$70.** 2116 Hwy 281 S 78355. 1.5 mi s of SR 285. Ext corridors. **Pets:** Accepted. 🛜 🛏 🖥

FOREST HILL

Comfort Inn H
(817) 551-5200. **$60-$80.** 3232 SE Loop 820 76140. I-20/SE Loop 820 exit 440A (Wichita St); on eastbound access road. Int corridors. **Pets:** Medium. $10 one-time fee/room. Service with restrictions, supervision. [SAVE] 🛜 🛏 🖥 ⊷

La Quinta Inn & Suites H
(817) 293-5800. **$90-$162.** 3346 Forest Hill Cir 76140. I-20 exit 440B (Forest Hill), just s, then just w. Int corridors. **Pets:** Service with restrictions, supervision. [SAVE] 🛜 ✕ 🛏 🖥 ⊷

FORT DAVIS

Historical Prude Guest Ranch R·A
(432) 426-3202. **$61-$180, 3 day notice.** 6 mi n Hwy 118 79734. 4.5 mi n of jct SR 118 and 17. Ext corridors. **Pets:** Medium. $10 daily fee/room. Designated rooms, no service, crate.
🛜 🛏 🖥 ⍾ ⊷ ✕ 🄿 ☎

FORT STOCKTON

Candlewood Suites H ❀
(432) 336-7700. **Call for rates.** 2469 I-10 W 79735. I-20 exit 257, just n; on north frontage road. Int corridors. **Pets:** Medium. $35 one-time fee/room. Designated rooms, service with restrictions, supervision.
🛜 🛏 🖥 ⊷

Days Inn H
(432) 336-7500. **$69-$109.** 1408 N US Hwy 285 79735. I-10 exit 257, just s. Ext corridors. **Pets:** Small. $15 daily fee/pet. Designated rooms, service with restrictions, supervision. [SAVE] 🛜 🛏 🖥 ⊷

La Quinta Inn Fort Stockton H
(432) 336-9781. **$71-$140.** 1537 N US Hwy 285 79735. I-10 exit 257. Ext corridors. **Pets:** Service with restrictions, supervision.
🛜 🛏 🖥 ⊷

Quality Inn H
(432) 336-5955. **$79-$109.** 1308 N US Hwy 285 79735. I-10 exit 257, just s. Ext corridors. **Pets:** $15 daily fee/room. Designated rooms, service with restrictions, crate. [SAVE] 🛜 🛏 🖥 ⊷

Sleep Inn & Suites H
(432) 336-8338. **$80-$120.** 3401 W Dickinson Blvd 79735. I-10 exit 256, just e. Int corridors. **Pets:** Medium, other species. $35 daily fee/pet. Designated rooms, service with restrictions, crate.
[SAVE] 🛜 ⛱M 🛏 🖥 ⊷

Super 8 H
(432) 336-8531. **$59-$109.** 3200 W Dickinson Blvd 79735. I-10 exit 256, just s. Int corridors. **Pets:** Accepted. [SAVE] 🛜 🛏 🖥 ⊷

FORT WORTH

The Ashton Hotel H ❀
(817) 332-0100. **$199-$799.** 610 Main St 76102. Jct 6th and Main sts; center. Int corridors. **Pets:** Medium, dogs only. Service with restrictions, crate. [SAVE] 🛜 ✕ 🖥 ¶

Candlewood Suites H
(817) 838-8229. **$89-$99.** 5201 Endicott Ave 76137. I-820 exit 17B (Beach St), just s, then w. Int corridors. **Pets:** Accepted. 🛜 🛏 🖥

Candlewood Suites DFW Airport South M
(817) 868-1900. **$79-$119.** 4200 Reggis Ct 76155. SR 360 exit Trinity Blvd, just e, then just n. Int corridors. **Pets:** Accepted.
[SAVE] 🛜 🛏 🖥

Fort Worth Hotel South H
(817) 293-3088. **Call for rates.** 100 Altamesa Blvd E 76134. I-35W exit 44. Int corridors. **Pets:** Accepted. 🛜 ✕ 🛏 🖥 ¶ ⊷

Historic Hilton Fort Worth H
(817) 870-2100. **$179-$249.** 815 Main St 76102. Northeast corner of Main and 8th sts; center. Int corridors. **Pets:** Medium. $50 one-time fee/pet. Designated rooms, service with restrictions, supervision.
🛜 ⛱M 🛏 🖥 ¶

Holiday Inn Express Hotel & Suites H ❀
(817) 744-7755. **Call for rates.** 3541 NW Loop 820 76106. I-820 exit 10A eastbound; exit 10B westbound. Int corridors. **Pets:** Small. $20 daily fee/pet. Service with restrictions, crate. 🛜 ⛱M 🛏 🖥 ⊷

Holiday Inn Express Hotel & Suites Fort Worth Downtown H
(817) 698-9595. **Call for rates.** 1111 W Lancaster Ave 76102. I-30 exit 13B (Henderson St), just n. Int corridors. **Pets:** Small. $150 deposit/room, $75 one-time fee/room. Designated rooms, service with restrictions, crate.
[SAVE] 🛜 ⛱M 🛏 🖥 ⊷

Holiday Inn Express Hotel & Suites-Fort Worth West H
(817) 560-4200. **Call for rates.** 2730 S Cherry Ln 76116. I-30 exit 7A (Cherry Ln), just s. Int corridors. **Pets:** Accepted. 🛜 🛏 🖥 ⊷

Homewood Suites by Hilton H
(817) 834-7400. **$69-$139.** 3701 Tanacross Dr 76137. I-820 exit 17B (Beach St), just s, then just w. Int corridors. **Pets:** Accepted.
🛜 ⛱M 🛏 🖥 ⊷

La Quinta Inn & Suites Fort Worth North H
(817) 222-2888. **$83-$155.** 4700 North Frwy 76137. I-35W exit 56A, just n. Int corridors. **Pets:** Service with restrictions, supervision.
🛜 🛏 🖥 ⊷

La Quinta Inn & Suites Fort Worth Southwest H
(817) 370-2700. **$102-$177.** 4900 Bryant Irvin Rd 76132. I-20 exit 431 (Bryant Irvin Rd), just s. Int corridors. **Pets:** Service with restrictions, supervision. 🛜 ⛱M 🛏 🖥 ⊷

La Quinta Inn & Suites Lake Worth H
(817) 237-9300. **$95-$199.** 5800 Quebec St 76135. I-820 exit 9 (Quebec St), just sw. Int corridors. **Pets:** Service with restrictions, supervision.
🛜 ✕ 🛏 🖥 ⊷

Omni Hotel H ❀
(817) 535-6664. **$169-$349.** 1300 Houston St 76102. Between 12th and 14th sts. Int corridors. **Pets:** Small. $50 one-time fee/pet. Service with restrictions, supervision. 🛜 ✕ 🖥 ¶ ⊷ ✕

Residence Inn by Marriott Fort Worth Alliance Airport H
(817) 750-7000. **$84-$251.** 13400 North Frwy 76177. I-35W exit 66. Int corridors. **Pets:** Accepted. 🛜 ✕ 🛏 🖥 ⊷ ✕

▼▼▼ **Residence Inn by Marriott Fort Worth Cultural District** ⊞

(817) 885-8250. **$132-$218.** 2500 Museum Way 76107. I-30 exit 13B (Henderson St), 0.4 mi n to 7th St, 0.8 mi w to Stayton St, then just s. Int corridors. **Pets:** Accepted. 🛰 ✕ ⊾ᴹ 🛏 🖵 🏊 ✕

▼▼▼ **Residence Inn by Marriott-Fossil Creek** ⊞

(817) 439-1300. **$98-$199.** 5801 Sandshell Dr 76137. I-35W exit 58 (Western Center Blvd) northbound to Sandshell Dr, 0.7 mi s; exit southbound, first road to right through strip center, just s to Sandshell Dr, then 0.7 mi s. Int corridors. **Pets:** Accepted.

ᴇᴄᴏ 🛰 ✕ ⊾ᴹ 🛏 🖵 🏊 ✕

▼▼▼ **Residence Inn by Marriott University** ⊞ 🐾

(817) 870-1011. **$137-$219.** 1701 S University Dr 76107. I-30 exit 12 (University Dr), 0.4 mi s. Ext corridors. **Pets:** Large, other species. $100 one-time fee/room. Service with restrictions, crate.

🛰 ✕ ⊾ᴹ 🛏 🖵 🏊 ✕

▼▼▼ **Staybridge Suites West Fort Worth** ⊞

(817) 935-6500. **$92-$179.** 229 Clifford Center Dr 76108. I-820 N exit 5A (Clifford Center Dr), just w. Int corridors. **Pets:** Accepted.

🛰 ✕ 🛏 🖵 🏊

▼▼ **TownePlace Suites by Marriott Fort Worth Southwest** ⊞

(817) 732-2224. **$89-$169.** 4200 International Plaza Dr 76109. I-20 exit 433 (Hulen St); on westbound frontage road. Int corridors.

Pets: Accepted. ᴇᴄᴏ 🛰 ✕ 🛏 🖵 🏊

🅰🅰🅰 ▼▼▼ **The Worthington Renaissance Fort Worth Hotel** ⊞

(817) 870-1000. **$180-$339.** 200 Main St 76102. Northwest corner of 2nd and Main sts. Int corridors. **Pets:** Large, other species. $200 deposit/room. Service with restrictions, crate.

ꜱᴀᴠᴇ 🛰 ✕ 🛏 🖵 🍴 🏊 ✕

FREDERICKSBURG

🅰🅰🅰 ▼▼▼ **BEST WESTERN PLUS Fredericksburg** ⊞ 🐾

(830) 992-2929. **$90-$190.** 314 E Highway St 78624. Jct US 87 and 290, 6 blks s. Int corridors. **Pets:** Large. $20 daily fee/room. Designated rooms, service with restrictions, supervision. ꜱᴀᴠᴇ 🛰 🛏 🖵 🏊

▼▼▼ **Days Inn Suites** ⊞

(830) 997-1086. **$60-$170.** 808 S Adams St 78624. 0.6 mi sw of jct US 290 and SR 16. Ext corridors. **Pets:** Accepted. 🛰 🛏 🖵 🏊

🅰🅰🅰 ▼▼ **Dietzel Motel** 🅼

(830) 997-3330. **$52-$99.** 1141 W US 290 78624. On US 290, 1 mi w; at US 87. Ext corridors. **Pets:** Other species. $10 daily fee/pet. Service with restrictions. ꜱᴀᴠᴇ 🛰 ✕ 🛏 🖵 🏊

🅰🅰🅰 ▼▼ **Fredericksburg Econo Lodge** 🅼

(830) 997-3437. **$60-$110.** 810 S Adams St 78624. Jct US 290 and SR 16 S, 1 mi s. Ext corridors. **Pets:** Other species. $15 daily fee/pet. Service with restrictions. ꜱᴀᴠᴇ 🛰 🛏 🖵 🏊

▼▼▼ **Fredericksburg Hill Country Hotel & Resort** ⊞

(830) 990-4200. **$60-$140.** 1220 N Hwy 87 78624. 1 mi w on US 290 at US 87. Int corridors. **Pets:** Small. $50 one-time fee/pet. Service with restrictions, crate. 🛰 ✕ ⊾ᴹ 🛏 🖵 🏊

🅰🅰🅰 ▼▼▼ **Fredericksburg Inn & Suites** ⊞

(830) 997-0202. **$79-$229.** 201 S Washington St 78624. US 290 and 87, 3 blks s. Ext corridors. **Pets:** Dogs only. $35 one-time fee/pet. Designated rooms, service with restrictions, crate. ꜱᴀᴠᴇ 🛰 ✕ 🛏 🖵 🏊

▼▼▼ **La Quinta Inn & Suites Fredericksburg** ⊞

(830) 990-2899. **$99-$243.** 1465 E Main St 78624. 1 mi e of downtown. Int corridors. **Pets:** Service with restrictions, supervision.

🛰 ✕ ⊾ᴹ 🛏 🖵 🏊

▼▼ **Quality Inn** ⊞

(830) 997-9811. **Call for rates.** 908 S Adams St 78624. 0.8 mi sw on SR 16; 0.8 mi sw of jct US 87 and 290. Ext corridors. **Pets:** Small. $20 daily fee/pet. Designated rooms, service with restrictions, supervision.

🛰 🛏 🖵 🏊

▼▼ **Sunday House Inn & Suites** ⊞

(830) 997-4484. **$99-$249.** 501 E Main St 78624. 0.4 mi e on US 290. Ext corridors. **Pets:** Small. $25 daily fee/pet. Designated rooms, service with restrictions, supervision. 🛰 🛏 🖵 🏊

🅰🅰🅰 ▼▼▼ **Sunset Inn Motel & Suites** 🅼

(830) 997-9581. **$55-$85.** 900 S Adams St 78624. 0.8 mi sw of jct US 290 and SR 16. Ext corridors. **Pets:** Small. Designated rooms, service with restrictions, supervision. ꜱᴀᴠᴇ 🛰 ✕ 🛏 🖵 🍴

GAINESVILLE

▼▼▼ **La Quinta Inn & Suites Gainesville** ⊞

(940) 665-5700. **$95-$177.** 4201 N I-35 76240. I-35 exit 501, just w on FM 1202, then just s on access road. Int corridors. **Pets:** Service with restrictions, supervision. 🛰 ⊾ᴹ 🛏 🖵 🏊

GALVESTON

▼▼▼ **La Quinta Inn & Suites Galveston Seawall West** ⊞

(409) 740-9100. **$59-$276.** 8710 Seawall Blvd 77554. Between 85th and 89th sts. Int corridors. **Pets:** Service with restrictions, supervision.

🛰 ✕ ⊾ᴹ 🛏 🖵 🏊

🅰🅰🅰 ▼▼▼ **The San Luis Resort Spa & Conference Center** ⊞

(409) 744-1500. **$119-$950, 3 day notice.** 5222 Seawall Blvd 77551. Just e of jct Seawall Blvd and 53rd St. Int corridors. **Pets:** Accepted.

ꜱᴀᴠᴇ 🛰 ✕ ⊾ᴹ 🛏 🖵 🍴 🏊 ✕

GATESVILLE

🅰🅰🅰 ▼▼▼ **BEST WESTERN Chateau Ville Motor Inn** ⊞

(254) 865-2281. **$72-$89.** 2501 E Main St 76528. Jct US 84 and SR 36, 0.5 mi w. Ext corridors. **Pets:** Service with restrictions, crate.

ꜱᴀᴠᴇ 🛰 🛏 🖵 🏊

GEORGETOWN

▼▼▼ **BEST WESTERN PLUS Georgetown Inn & Suites** ⊞

(512) 868-8555. **$90-$100.** 600 San Gabriel Village Blvd 78626. I-35 exit 261A, 0.5 mi n on east frontage road, then just e. Int corridors.

Pets: Accepted. 🛰 ✕ ⊾ᴹ 🛏 🖵 🏊

▼▼▼ **La Quinta Inn Georgetown** ⊞

(512) 869-2541. **$59-$320.** 333 I-35 N 78628. I-35 exit 264 northbound; exit 262 southbound; on west frontage road. Ext corridors. **Pets:** Service with restrictions, supervision. 🛰 🛏 🖵 🏊

GEORGE WEST

🅰🅰🅰 ▼▼▼ **BEST WESTERN George West Executive Inn** 🅼

(361) 449-3300. **$129-$139.** 208 N Nueces St 78022. Just n of US 59 on US 281. Ext corridors. **Pets:** $20 daily fee/room. Service with restrictions, crate. ꜱᴀᴠᴇ 🛰 🛏 🖵 🏊

GLEN ROSE

🅰🅰🅰 ▼▼▼ **BEST WESTERN Dinosaur Valley Inn & Suites** ⊞

(254) 897-4818. **$74-$112, 7 day notice.** 1311 NE Big Bend Tr 76043. On US 67. Int corridors. **Pets:** Medium. $25 one-time fee/pet. Service with restrictions, crate. ꜱᴀᴠᴇ 🛰 ✕ 🛏 🖵 🏊 ✕

GRANBURY

▼▼▼ Baymont Inn & Suites �H

(817) 579-9977. **$85-$110.** 1515 N Plaza Dr 76048. On US 377 Bypass, 2.2 mi of jct SR 144 and US 377. Int corridors. **Pets:** Accepted.
🛰 &M 🛏 🖵 ⊁

Ⓐ ▼▼▼ BEST WESTERN Granbury Inn & Suites �H ❀

(817) 573-4239. **$70-$90.** 1517 N Plaza Dr 76048. On US 377 Bypass; 2.2 mi n of jct SR 144 and US 377 Bypass. Int corridors. **Pets:** $25 one-time fee/room. Designated rooms, service with restrictions, crate.
SAVE 🛰 &M 🛏 🖵 ⊁

▼▼▼ Comfort Suites �H

(817) 579-5559. **$70-$125.** 903 Harbor Lakes Dr 76048. Jct SR 144 and US 377 Bypass, 1.9 mi n on US 377 Bypass. Int corridors. **Pets:** Medium, other species. Service with restrictions, supervision.
🛰 ✕ &M 🛏 🖵 ⊁

Ⓐ ▼▼▼ La Quinta Inns & Suites-Granbury �H

(817) 573-2007. **$71-$155.** 880 Harbor Lakes Dr 76048. Jct US 377 and SR 144. Int corridors. **Pets:** Service with restrictions, supervision.
SAVE 🛰 ✕ &M 🛏 🖵 ⊁

▼▼▼ Quality Inn & Suites �H ❀

(817) 573-4411. **$50-$90.** 800 Harbor Lakes Dr 76048. Jct SR 144 and US 377 Bypass, 1.9 mi n on US 377 Bypass. Int corridors. **Pets:** Medium. $10 daily fee/pet. Designated rooms, service with restrictions, supervision. 🛰 &M 🛏 🖵 ⊁

GRAPEVINE

Ⓐ ▼▼▼ Embassy Suites Outdoor World �H

(972) 724-2600. **$130-$290.** 2401 Bass Pro Dr 76051. SR 121 exit Bass Pro Dr, just w. Int corridors. **Pets:** Accepted.
SAVE 🛰 &M 🛏 🖵 ❝❞ ⊁ ✕

▼▼▼ Homewood Suites by Hilton �H

(972) 691-2427. **$125-$179.** 2214 Grapevine Mills Cir W 76051. SR 121 N exit Bass Pro Dr. Int corridors. **Pets:** Accepted.
🛰 &M 🛏 🖵 ⊁ ✕

Ⓐ ▼▼▼ Hyatt Regency DFW �H

(972) 453-1234. **$77-$288.** 2334 N International Pkwy 75261. In Dallas-Fort Worth International Airport Terminal C area. Int corridors.
Pets: Accepted. ECO SAVE 🛰 &M 🛏 🖵 ❝❞ ⊁

▼▼ Super 8-Grapevine �H ❀

(817) 329-7222. **$79-$129.** 250 E Hwy 114 76051. SR 114 exit Main St. Int corridors. **Pets:** Other species. $10 daily fee/pet. Designated rooms, service with restrictions, crate. 🛰 &M 🛏 🖵 ⊁

GROESBECK

Ⓐ ▼▼▼ BEST WESTERN Groesbeck Inn & Suites �H

(254) 729-0077. **Call for rates.** 1012 N Ellis St 76642. Jct SR 14 and 164, 1 mi n. Int corridors. **Pets:** Very small. $50 one-time fee/pet. Designated rooms, no service, supervision. SAVE 🛰 &M 🛏 🖵 ⊁

GROOM

Ⓐ ▼▼ Chalet Inn M

(806) 248-7524. **$39-$60.** I-40 FM 2300 79039. I-40 exit 113, just s. Ext corridors. **Pets:** Medium. $5 daily fee/pet. Designated rooms, service with restrictions, supervision. SAVE &M 🛏

HALLETTSVILLE

Ⓐ ▼▼▼ Chaparral Motel M

(361) 798-4385. **Call for rates.** 310 Hwy 77 S 77964. Jct US 77 S and Alternate US 90. Ext corridors. **Pets:** Very small. $10 daily fee/pet. Service with restrictions, supervision. SAVE 🛰 🛏 🖵 ⊁

Ⓐ ▼▼▼ Hotel Texas �H

(361) 798-5900. **$80-$130.** 1632 N Texana St 77964. Just s of CR 200. Int corridors. **Pets:** Accepted. SAVE 🛰 ✕ 🛏 🖵 ⊁

HARLINGEN

▼▼▼ La Quinta Inn Harlingen �H

(956) 428-6888. **$59-$144.** 1002 S Expwy 83 78552. US 83 and 77 exit M St. Ext corridors. **Pets:** Service with restrictions, supervision.
🛰 &M 🛏 🖵 ⊁

HEARNE

▼▼ Oak Tree Inn �H

(979) 279-5599. **$89-$120.** 1051 N Market St 77859. 0.6 mi n of jct US 79 and SR 6. Ext/int corridors. **Pets:** Accepted.
🛰 ✕ 🛏 🖵 ❝❞

HEBBRONVILLE

Ⓐ ▼▼▼ BEST WESTERN Hebbronville Inn �H

(361) 527-3600. **$92.** 37 E Hwy 359 78361. On CR 359, just e of SR 16. Int corridors. **Pets:** Large. $10 daily fee/pet. Designated rooms, service with restrictions, crate. SAVE 🛰 🛏 🖵 ⊁

HENDERSON

▼▼▼ Baymont Inn & Suites Henderson �H

(903) 657-7900. **$85-$119.** 410 Hwy 79 S 75654. Just n of jct US 259. Int corridors. **Pets:** Small. $50 deposit/pet, $10 daily fee/pet. Service with restrictions, supervision. 🛰 🛏 🖵 ⊁

Ⓐ ▼▼▼ BEST WESTERN Inn of Henderson �H

(903) 657-9561. **$80-$90.** 1500 Hwy 259 S 75654. 2 mi s on US 259, 0.7 mi s of jct US 79 and 259 S. Ext/int corridors. **Pets:** Accepted.
SAVE 🛰 🛏 🖵 ⊁

HEREFORD

Ⓐ ▼▼▼ BEST WESTERN Red Carpet Inn �H

(806) 364-0540. **$70-$80.** 830 W 1st St 79045. Just w of jct US 385 and 60. Ext corridors. **Pets:** Small. $5 daily fee/pet. Service with restrictions, supervision. SAVE 🛰 🛏 🖵 ⊁

Ⓐ ▼▼▼ Holiday Inn Express �H

(806) 364-3322. **$119-$145.** 1400 W 1st St 79045. Jct US 385 and 60, just w. Int corridors. **Pets:** Medium. $20 daily fee/pet. Service with restrictions, supervision. SAVE 🛰 &M 🛏 🖵 ⊁

HILLSBORO

▼▼ Econo Lodge Hillsboro �H

(254) 582-3333. **$55-$100.** 1515 Old Brandon Rd 76645. I-35 exit 368A northbound; exit 368B southbound, just w. Ext corridors. **Pets:** Medium, other species. $20 daily fee/pet. Designated rooms, service with restrictions. 🛰 &M 🛏 🖵 ⊁

Ⓐ ▼▼▼ La Quinta Inn & Suites Hillsboro I-35 �H

(254) 580-1300. **$77-$144.** 1513 Old Brandon Rd 76645. I-35 exit 368A northbound; exit 368B southbound, just w. Int corridors. **Pets:** Service with restrictions, supervision. SAVE 🛰 ✕ 🛏 🖵 ⊁

▼▼ Motel 6 - #4136 �H

(254) 580-9000. **Call for rates.** 1506 Hillview Dr 76645. I-35 exit 368 southbound; exit 368A northbound; on northbound side. Int corridors. **Pets:** Other species. Service with restrictions, supervision.
🛰 &M 🛏 🖵 ⊁

▼▼ Super 8 �H

(254) 580-0404. **$60-$152.** 1512 Hillview Dr 76645. I-35 exit 368A northbound; exit 368 southbound, just e. Int corridors. **Pets:** Accepted.
🛰 🛏 🖵 ⊁

HONDO

▲▲▲ **▼▼▼▼** BEST WESTERN Hondo Inn **H**
(830) 426-4466. **Call for rates.** 301 Hwy 90 E 78861. Just e of downtown. Int corridors. **Pets:** $25 daily fee/pet. Service with restrictions, supervision. [SAVE] 🛜 ✕ ᴸ🄼 🛏 🖳 ⊅

HORSESHOE BAY

▲▲▲ **▼▼▼▼** Marriott Horseshoe Bay Resort **H**
(830) 598-8600. **$134-$349, 3 day notice.** 200 Hi Cir N 78657. Jct US 281 and SR 2147, 6.6 mi w. Ext/int corridors. **Pets:** Accepted.
[SAVE] 🛜 ✕ ᴸ🄼 🛏 🖳 🍴 ⊅ ✕

HOUSTON METROPOLITAN AREA

BAYTOWN

▼▼▼▼ Baymont Inn & Suites by Wyndham **H**
(281) 839-1400. **$80-$160.** 7212 E Point Blvd 77521. I-10 exit 792 (Garth Rd), just n. Int corridors. **Pets:** Accepted. 🛜 🛏 🖳 ⊅

▼▼▼▼ Comfort Suites **H**
(281) 421-9764. **$100-$190.** 7209 Garth Rd 77521. I-10 exit 792 (Garth Rd), just n. Int corridors. **Pets:** Very small. $25 daily fee/pet. Designated rooms, service with restrictions, supervision.
🛜 ✕ ᴸ🄼 🛏 🖳 ⊅

▼▼▼ La Quinta Inn & Suites Baytown East **H**
(281) 421-5566. **$78-$137.** 5215 I-10 E 77521. I-10 exit 792 (Garth Rd), just ne. Int corridors. **Pets:** Service with restrictions, supervision.
🛜 ᴸ🄼 🛏 🖳 ⊅

BROOKSHIRE

▼▼▼▼ La Quinta Inn & Suites Brookshire **H**
(281) 375-8888. **$83-$166.** 721 FM 1489 77423. I-10 exit 731; on south frontage road. Int corridors. **Pets:** Service with restrictions, supervision.
🛜 ✕ ᴸ🄼 🛏 🖳 ⊅

CHANNELVIEW

▼▼▼ Days Inn & Suites of Channelview **M**
(281) 457-0140. **$55-$70.** 15765 I-10 E Frwy 77530. I-10 exit 783 (Sheldon Rd); on westbound frontage road. Ext corridors. **Pets:** Medium, dogs only. $10 daily fee/pet. Designated rooms, service with restrictions, supervision. 🛜 🛏 🖳

CLEVELAND

▼▼▼▼ La Quinta Inn & Suites **H**
(281) 806-3007. **$77-$155.** 1004 Hwy 59 S 77327. US 59 exit Washington Ave; on northbound frontage road. Int corridors. **Pets:** Service with restrictions, supervision. 🛜 ᴸ🄼 🛏 🖳 ⊅

▼▼ Super 8 **H**
(281) 432-8800. **$59-$102, 3 day notice.** 427 W Southline St 77327. US 59 exit SR 105, just e to W Southline St, then just s. Int corridors. **Pets:** Accepted. 🛜 🛏 🖳 ⊅

CONROE

▲▲▲ **▼▼▼** Baymont Inn & Suites-Conroe/Woodlands **H**
(936) 539-5100. **$70-$100.** 1506 Interstate 45 S 77304. I-45 exit 85 (Gladstell St) northbound; exit 84 (Frazier St) southbound. Int corridors. **Pets:** Medium, dogs only. $10 daily fee/pet. Service with restrictions, crate. [SAVE] 🛜 🛏 🖳 ⊅

▼▼▼▼ La Quinta Inn & Suites Conroe **H**
(936) 228-0790. **$90-$172.** 4006 Sprayberry Ln 77303. I-45 exit 91 (League Line Rd), just e. Int corridors. **Pets:** Service with restrictions, supervision. 🛜 ᴸ🄼 🛏 🖳 ⊅

DEER PARK

▲▲▲ **▼▼▼** BEST WESTERN Deer Park Inn & Suites **H**
(281) 476-1900. **$79-$99.** 1401 Center St 77536. SR 225 (La Porte Rd) exit Center St, 0.9 mi s. Ext corridors. **Pets:** Small, dogs only. $25 daily fee/pet. Service with restrictions, supervision.
[SAVE] 🛜 ᴸ🄼 🛏 🖳 ⊅

▼▼▼▼ La Quinta Inn & Suites Deer Park **H**
(281) 476-5300. **$99-$166.** 1400 East Blvd 77536. Jct SR 225 and East Blvd, 0.8 mi s. Int corridors. **Pets:** Service with restrictions, supervision.
🛜 ✕ ᴸ🄼 🛏 🖳 ⊅

HOUSTON

▲▲▲ **▼▼▼▼** Aloft Houston by the Galleria **H** ✿
(713) 622-7010. **$89-$399, 3 day notice.** 5415 Westheimer Rd 77056. I-610 exit 8C (Westheimer Rd) northbound; exit 9A (San Felipe Rd/Westheimer Rd) southbound, 0.8 mi w. Int corridors. **Pets:** Medium, dogs only. Service with restrictions, supervision.
[SAVE] 🛜 ✕ ᴸ🄼 🛏 🖳 ⊅

▲▲▲ **▼▼▼** BEST WESTERN Heritage Inn **H**
(713) 670-9100. **$80-$110.** 10521 E Frwy 77029. I-10 exit 776A (Mercury Dr) westbound; exit 776B (John Ralston Rd) eastbound; on westbound frontage road. Int corridors. **Pets:** Large. $20 daily fee/room. Designated rooms, service with restrictions, supervision.
[SAVE] 🛜 ✕ 🛏 🖳 ⊅

▲▲▲ **▼▼▼** BEST WESTERN PLUS Westchase Mini-Suites **H**
(713) 782-1515. **$89-$129.** 2950 W Sam Houston Pkwy S 77042. Just w of Sam Houston Pkwy (Beltway 8) and Westheimer Rd; on southbound frontage road. Int corridors. **Pets:** Accepted.
[SAVE] 🛜 ✕ ᴸ🄼 🛏 🖳 ⊅

▼▼ Candlewood Suites at CITYCENTRE - Energy Corridor **H**
(713) 464-2677. **$99-$120.** 10503 Town & Country Way 77024. I-10 exit 755 eastbound, 1.1 mi on frontage road to Town & Country Blvd, then 0.4 mi s; exit 756A westbound, U-turn under I-10, just e to Town & Country Blvd, then 0.4 mi s. Int corridors. **Pets:** Accepted. 🛜 ᴸ🄼 🛏 🖳 ⊅

▼▼ Candlewood Suites Houston by the Galleria **H**
(713) 839-9411. **$79-$109.** 4900 Loop Central Dr 77081. I-610 exit 7 (Furnace Rd) southbound; exit 7 (Westpark Dr) northbound; on northbound frontage road. Int corridors. **Pets:** Accepted. 🛜 🛏 🖳

▼▼ Candlewood Suites-Westchase **H** ✿
(713) 780-7881. **$89-$129.** 4033 W Sam Houston Pkwy S 77042. Sam Houston Pkwy (Beltway 8) exit Westpark Dr; southeast corner of Westpark Dr and Sam Houston Pkwy (Beltway 8); on northbound frontage road. Int corridors. **Pets:** Very small. $15 daily fee/pet. Service with restrictions, crate. 🛜 ᴸ🄼 🛏 🖳

▼▼▼ Candlewood Suites Willowbrook **H**
(832) 237-7300. **Call for rates.** 8719 FM 1960 W 77070. Corner of Mills Rd and FM 1960 W; just w of Tomball Pkwy. Int corridors.
Pets: Accepted. 🛜 ᴸ🄼 🛏 🖳 ⊅

▲▲▲ **▼▼▼▼** Comfort Suites Galleria **H**
(713) 787-0004. **$89-$139.** 6221 Richmond Ave 77057. US 59 exit Hillcroft St, 1 mi n to Richmond Ave, then 0.6 mi e. Int corridors.
Pets: Small. $50 one-time fee/room. Designated rooms, service with restrictions, supervision. [SAVE] 🛜 ✕ 🛏 🖳 ⊅

▼▼▼▼ Comfort Suites-Greenspoint/IAH West **H**
(281) 219-0400. **$80-$110.** 1350 N Sam Houston Pkwy E 77032. Sam Houston Pkwy (Beltway 8) exit Aldine Westfield Rd eastbound, 0.8 mi e on service road; exit Hardy Toll Rd westbound, U-turn, then 1 mi e on service road. Int corridors. **Pets:** Accepted. 🛜 ✕ 🛏 🖳 ⊅

▼▼ Crossland Economy Studios Houston-Northwest **H**
(713) 934-7600. **$44-$79.** 5959 Guhn Rd 77040. US 290 exit Fairbanks n Houston Rd, just e on eastbound frontage road, then just s. Ext corridors. **Pets:** $25 daily fee/pet. Designated rooms, service with restrictions.
🛜 ᴸ🄼 🛏 🖳

Crowne Plaza Houston Galleria Area H
(713) 680-2222. **Call for rates.** 7611 Katy Frwy 77024. I-10 exit 762 (Silber Rd); on eastbound frontage road. Int corridors. **Pets:** Small. $50 deposit/room, $50 one-time fee/room. Service with restrictions.
[SAVE] 🛜 ✕ 🏋 🛏 🖳 🍴 🏊

Crowne Plaza Northwest Hotel H
(713) 462-9977. **$59-$179.** 12801 Northwest Frwy 77040. Nw on US 290 exit Hollister Rd, 0.7 mi e on south service road. Ext/int corridors. **Pets:** Medium, other species. $25 one-time fee/room. Designated rooms, service with restrictions, crate. [SAVE] 🛜 ✕ 🛏 🖳 🍴 🏊

Crowne Plaza Suites Houston - Near Sugar Land H ❀
(713) 995-0123. **$79-$159, 3 day notice.** 9090 Southwest Frwy 77074. US 59 exit Beechnut St/Gessner Rd; on southbound frontage road. Int corridors. **Pets:** Small. $40 one-time fee/room. Designated rooms, service with restrictions, supervision. [SAVE] 🛜 ✕ 🏋 🛏 🖳 🍴 🏊

DoubleTree by Hilton Hotel Houston Downtown H
(713) 759-0202. **$99-$399.** 400 Dallas St 77002. At Dallas and Bagby sts. Int corridors. **Pets:** Accepted. 🛜 ✕ 🛏 🖳 🍴

DoubleTree by Hilton Houston Hobby Airport H
(713) 645-3000. **$109-$249.** 8181 Airport Blvd 77061. I-45 exit 36 (Airport Blvd/College Rd), 1.5 mi w. Int corridors. **Pets:** Accepted.
🛜 🛏 🖳 🍴 🏊

DoubleTree Suites by Hilton Hotel Houston by the Galleria H
(713) 961-9000. **$119-$459.** 5353 Westheimer Rd 77056. I-610 exit 8C (Westheimer Rd) northbound; exit 9A (San Felipe Rd/Westheimer Rd) southbound, 0.8 mi w. Int corridors. **Pets:** Accepted.
🛜 ✕ 🛏 🖳 🍴 🏊 🏋

Drury Inn & Suites-Houston Hobby H
(713) 941-4300. **$84-$164.** 7902 Mosley Rd 77061. I-45 exit 36 (Airport Blvd/College Rd) northbound, just w on Airport Blvd, then just n; exit southbound, follow frontage road to Mosley Rd. Int corridors. **Pets:** Service with restrictions, supervision. 🛜 🏋 🛏 🖳 🏊

Drury Inn & Suites-Houston Near the Galleria H
(713) 963-0700. **$94-$239.** 1615 W Loop S 77027. I-610 exit 9 (San Felipe Rd) northbound; exit 9A (San Felipe Rd/Westheimer Rd) southbound; on east service road. Int corridors. **Pets:** Service with restrictions, supervision. 🛜 🏋 🛏 🖳 🏊

Drury Inn & Suites-Houston West H
(281) 558-7007. **$84-$154.** 1000 N Hwy 6 77079. I-10 exit 751 (Addicks Rd/SR 6), just n on SR 6. Int corridors. **Pets:** Service with restrictions, supervision. 🛜 🏋 🛏 🖳 🏊

Element by Westin Houston Vintage Park H ❀
(281) 379-7300. **$79-$299.** 14555 Vintage Preserve Pkwy 77070. US 290 exit Louetta Rd, just e to Chasewood Park, then just s. Int corridors. **Pets:** Large. Designated rooms, service with restrictions.
[ECO] [◄] [SAVE] 🛜 ✕ 🛏 🖳 🏊

Embassy Suites Houston Downtown H
(713) 739-9100. **Call for rates.** 1515 Dallas St 77010. Between Crawford and La Branch sts. Int corridors. **Pets:** Accepted.
[◄] 🛜 ✕ 🏋 🛏 🖳 🍴 🏊 🏋

Extended Stay Deluxe Houston-Northwest H
(713) 895-0965. **$84-$149.** 5454 Hollister St 77040. US 290 exit Tidwell Rd/Hollister St, just s. Int corridors. **Pets:** $25 daily fee/pet. Designated rooms, service with restrictions. 🛜 🛏 🖳 🏊

Four Points by Sheraton Houston Hobby Airport H
(713) 948-0800. **$89-$209.** 8720 Gulf Frwy 77017. I-45 exit 38 (Monroe Rd); on south frontage road. Int corridors. **Pets:** Accepted.
[SAVE] 🛜 ✕ 🖳 🍴 🏊

Four Points by Sheraton Houston, Memorial City H
(281) 501-4600. **$99-$209.** 10655 Katy Frwy 77024. I-10 exit 756A westbound; exit 755 eastbound; southeast corner of I-10 and Sam Houston Pkwy (Beltway 8). Ext/int corridors. **Pets:** Accepted.
[SAVE] 🛜 ✕ 🛏 🖳 🍴 🏊

Four Seasons Hotel Houston H
(713) 650-1300. **$159-$435.** 1300 Lamar St 77010. Jct Lamar and Austin sts. Int corridors. **Pets:** Accepted.
[SAVE] 🛜 ✕ 🛏 🖳 🍴 🏊 🏋

Hilton Houston North H
(281) 875-2222. **$179-$189.** 12400 Greenspoint Dr 77060. I-45 exit 61 (Greens Rd), 0.5 mi e. Int corridors. **Pets:** Accepted.
🛜 🏋 🛏 🍴 🏊

Hilton Houston Post Oak H ❀
(713) 961-9300. **$109-$239.** 2001 Post Oak Blvd 77056. I-610 exit 8C (Westheimer Rd) northbound, just w; exit 9A (San Felipe Rd/Westheimer Rd) southbound; between San Felipe and Westheimer rds. Ext/int corridors. **Pets:** Medium. $75 one-time fee/room. Service with restrictions, supervision. [SAVE] 🛜 ✕ 🛏 🖳 🍴 🏊

Hilton Houston Westchase H
(713) 974-1000. **$99-$239.** 9999 Westheimer Rd 77042. Sam Houston Pkwy (Beltway 8) exit Westheimer Rd and Briar Forest Dr northbound; exit Westheimer Rd and Richmond Ave southbound, 0.5 mi e. Int corridors. **Pets:** Medium. $50 one-time fee/pet. Service with restrictions, supervision. 🛜 ✕ 🏋 🛏 🖳 🍴 🏊 🏋

Holiday Inn Express Hotel & Suites Memorial Area H
(713) 688-2800. **Call for rates.** 7625 Katy Frwy 77024. I-10 exit 762 (Silber Rd); on eastbound frontage road. Int corridors. **Pets:** Accepted.
[SAVE] 🛜 ✕ 🏋 🛏 🖳 🏊

Holiday Inn Express Northwest H
(832) 237-4300. **$85-$169.** 12915 FM 1960 W 77065. US 290 exit FM 1960, just e. Int corridors. **Pets:** Small, dogs only. $25 deposit/pet. Service with restrictions, supervision. [SAVE] 🛜 🏋 🛏 🖳 🏊

Holiday Inn Houston Hobby Airport H
(713) 946-8900. **$79-$189.** 8611 Airport Blvd 77061. I-45 exit 36 (Airport Blvd), 1.3 mi w. Int corridors. **Pets:** Small. $50 one-time fee/pet. Service with restrictions, supervision. [SAVE] 🛜 ✕ 🏋 🛏 🖳 🍴 🏊

Holiday Inn Houston Intercontinental Airport H
(281) 449-2311. **$79-$219.** 15222 John F Kennedy Blvd 77032. Jct N Sam Houston Pkwy (Beltway 8) E and John F Kennedy Blvd. Int corridors. **Pets:** Accepted. [SAVE] 🛜 ✕ 🛏 🖳 🍴 🏊 🏋

Holiday Inn Houston Reliant Park Area H
(713) 790-1900. **Call for rates.** 8111 Kirby Dr 77054. I-610 exit 1C, 0.9 mi n. Int corridors. **Pets:** Medium, dogs only. $75 one-time fee/room. Service with restrictions. [SAVE] 🛜 🛏 🖳 🍴 🏊

Holiday Inn Northwest Willowbrook H
(281) 970-4888. **$79-$129.** 18818 Tomball Pkwy 77070. SR 249 (Tomball Pkwy) exit Grant Rd/Schroeder Rd, just n on Prestonwood Forrest Dr. Int corridors. **Pets:** Accepted. 🛜 ✕ 🏋 🛏 🖳 🍴 🏊

Homestead Studio Suites Hotel-Houston/Galleria Area H
(713) 960-9660. **$89-$159.** 2300 W Loop S 77027. I-610 exit 9A (San Felipe Rd) southbound; exit 9 (San Felipe Rd) northbound; on southbound frontage road. Int corridors. **Pets:** $25 daily fee/pet. Designated rooms, service with restrictions. 🛜 🛏 🖳

Homewood Suites by Hilton Intercontinental Airport H

(281) 219-9100. **$79-$159.** 1340 N Sam Houston Pkwy E 77032. Sam Houston Pkwy (Beltway 8) exit Aldine Westfield Rd eastbound Rd, 0.8 mi e on frontage road; exit Hardy Toll Rd westbound, U-turn, then 1 mi e on frontage road. Int corridors. **Pets:** Accepted.

SAVE 🛜 ✉M 🖥 💻 🏊 ❌

Homewood Suites by Hilton Near the Galleria H

(713) 439-1305. **Call for rates.** 2950 Sage Rd 77056. I-610 exit 8C (Westheimer Rd), just w to Sage Rd, then just s. Int corridors. **Pets:** Accepted. 🛜 ✉M 🖥 💻 🏊 ❌

Homewood Suites by Hilton-Westchase H 🐾

(713) 334-2424. **$119-$299.** 2424 Rogerdale Rd 77042. Sam Houston Pkwy (Beltway 8) exit Westheimer Rd, just w to Rogerdale Rd, then just n. Int corridors. **Pets:** Other species. $75 one-time fee/room.

🛜 ✉M 🖥 💻 🏊 ❌

Homewood Suites by Hilton-Willowbrook H

(281) 955-5200. **$119-$219.** 7655 W FM 1960 77070. Just e of jct SR 249 and FM 1960. Int corridors. **Pets:** Accepted.

🛜 ✉M 🖥 💻 🏊 ❌

Hotel Derek H

(713) 961-3000. **Call for rates.** 2525 W Loop S 77027. I-610 exit 9A (San Felipe/Westheimer) southbound; exit 8C (Westheimer Rd) northbound. Int corridors. **Pets:** Accepted. 🛜 ❌ 🖥 💻 🍴 🏊

Hotel Indigo Houston at the Galleria H

(713) 621-8988. **$109-$229.** 5160 Hidalgo St 77056. I-610 exit 9A (San Felipe Rd/Westheimer Rd) southbound; exit 8C (Westheimer Rd) northbound, s to Post Oak, just e to Hidalgo St, then just s. Int corridors. **Pets:** Small. $75 one-time fee/room. Service with restrictions, supervision.

🛜 ❌ ✉M 🖥 💻 🍴

Hotel ZaZa Houston Museum District H

(713) 526-1991. **$239-$379.** 5701 Main St 77005. US 59 exit Main St northbound, 0.5 mi s; exit Fannin St southbound, 0.5 mi s to Ewing St, then just w. Int corridors. **Pets:** Accepted.

SAVE 🛜 ❌ ✉M 🖥 🍴 🏊 ❌

Houston Marriott at the Texas Medical Center H

(713) 796-0080. **$95-$289.** 6580 Fannin St 77030. I-610 exit 2 (Main St), 2.5 mi ne to Holcombe St, 0.3 mi e, then just n. Int corridors.

Pets: Accepted. 🛜 ❌ ✉M 🖥 💻 🏊

Houston Marriott South at Hobby Airport H

(713) 943-7979. **$89-$237.** 9100 Gulf Frwy 77017. I-45 exit 36 (Airport Blvd/College Rd) southbound; exit 38 (Monroe Rd) northbound, on southbound frontage road. Int corridors. **Pets:** Accepted.

🛜 ❌ 🖥 💻 🍴 🏊

Hyatt house Houston/Galleria H

(713) 629-9711. **$99-$279.** 3440 Sage Rd 77056. I-610 exit 9A (San Felipe Rd/Westheimer Rd) southbound; exit 8C (Westheimer Rd) northbound, just w to Sage Rd, then 0.8 mi s. Int corridors. **Pets:** Accepted.

SAVE 🛜 ❌ 🖥 💻 🏊 ❌

Hyatt house Houston-West/Energy Corridor H

(281) 646-9990. **$99-$239.** 15405 Katy Frwy (I-10) 77094. I-10 exit 751 (SR 6), just s to Grisby Rd, then just w. Int corridors. **Pets:** Medium. $150 one-time fee/room. Designated rooms, service with restrictions, supervision. SAVE 🛜 ❌ 🖥 💻 🏊

Hyatt North Houston H

(281) 445-9000. **$72-$225.** 425 N Sam Houston Pkwy E 77060. Sam Houston Pkwy (Beltway 8) exit Imperial Valley Dr westbound; exit Hardy Toll Rd eastbound; on westbound frontage road. Int corridors.

Pets: Accepted. SAVE 🛜 ❌ ✉M 💻 🍴 🏊

La Quinta Inn & Suites Energy Corridor H

(281) 668-1068. **$83-$188.** 2451 Shadow View Ln 77077. 2.5 mi w of Sam Houston Pkwy (Beltway 8) on Westheimer Rd, just n. Int corridors. **Pets:** Service with restrictions, supervision.

🛜 ❌ ✉M 🖥 💻 🏊

La Quinta Inn & Suites Houston Bush Intercontinental Airport South H

(281) 219-2000. **$71-$188.** 15510 John F Kennedy Blvd 77032. Sam Houston Pkwy (Beltway 8) exit John F Kennedy Blvd/Vickery Dr, just n. Int corridors. **Pets:** Service with restrictions, supervision.

🛜 ✉M 💻 🏊

La Quinta Inn & Suites Houston Channelview H

(281) 452-4402. **$89-$166.** 5520 E Sam Houston Pkwy N 77015. Sam Houston Pkwy exit Woodforest Blvd. Int corridors. **Pets:** Service with restrictions, supervision. SAVE 🛜 ❌ ✉M 🖥 💻 🏊

La Quinta Inn & Suites - Houston Clay Road H

(713) 939-1400. **$95-$210.** 4424 Westway Park Blvd 77041. Sam Houston Pkwy (Beltway 8) exit Clay Rd, just e. Int corridors. **Pets:** Service with restrictions, supervision. 🛜 ❌ ✉M 🖥 💻 🏊

La Quinta Inn & Suites Houston Galleria Area H

(713) 355-3440. **$71-$210.** 1625 W Loop S 77027. I-610 exit 9 (San Felipe Rd) northbound; exit 9A (San Felipe Rd/Westheimer Rd) southbound; on northbound service road. Int corridors. **Pets:** Service with restrictions, supervision. 🛜 ❌ 🖥 💻 🏊

La Quinta Inn & Suites Houston Hobby Airport H

(713) 490-1008. **$83-$177.** 8776 Airport Blvd 77061. I-45 exit 36 (Airport Blvd/College Rd), 1.3 mi w. Int corridors. **Pets:** Service with restrictions, supervision. 🛜 ❌ ✉M 🖥 💻 🏊

La Quinta Inn & Suites Houston I-45/1960 H

(281) 784-1112. **$90-$177.** 415 FM 1960 Rd E 77073. I-45 exit 66 (FM 1960), just e. Int corridors. **Pets:** Service with restrictions, supervision.

SAVE 🛜 🖥 💻 🏊

La Quinta Inn & Suites Houston - Normandy H

(713) 451-0009. **$77-$155.** 930 Normandy St 77015. I-10 exit 778B, just n. Int corridors. **Pets:** Service with restrictions, supervision.

🛜 ❌ 🖥 💻 🏊

La Quinta Inn & Suites Houston - Westchase H

(281) 495-7700. **$90-$188.** 10850 Harwin Dr 77072. Sam Houston Pkwy (Beltway 8) exit Bellaire Blvd/Harwin Dr northbound; exit Westpark Dr/Harwin Dr southbound. Int corridors. **Pets:** Service with restrictions, supervision. 🛜 ❌ 🖥 💻 🏊

La Quinta Inn & Suites Houston West Park 10 H

(281) 646-9200. **$63-$155.** 15225 Katy Frwy 77094. I-10 exit 748 (Barker Cypress Rd) eastbound, 2.6 mi on eastbound service road; exit 751 (SR 6) westbound, just s to Grisby Rd, then 0.5 mi w. Int corridors. **Pets:** Service with restrictions, supervision. 🛜 ❌ 🖥 💻 🏊

La Quinta Inn & Suites Willowbrook H

(281) 897-8868. **$83-$199.** 18828 State Hwy 249 (Tomball Pkwy) 77070. SR 249 exit Grant Rd/Schroeder Rd; on northbound frontage road. Int corridors. **Pets:** Service with restrictions, supervision.

🛜 ❌ ✉M 🖥 💻 🏊

La Quinta Inn Houston Cy-Fair M

(281) 469-4018. **$66-$144.** 13290 FM 1960 W 77065. Just w of jct US 290 and FM 1960. Ext/int corridors. **Pets:** Service with restrictions, supervision. 🛜 ✉M 🖥 💻 🏊

La Quinta Inn Houston Wilcrest M

(713) 932-0808. **$59-$122.** 11113 Katy Frwy 77079. I-10 exit 754 (Kirkwood Dr) westbound; exit 755 (Wilcrest Rd) eastbound; on eastbound service road. Ext corridors. **Pets:** Service with restrictions, supervision.

🛜 🖥 💻 🏊

Omni Houston Hotel H
(713) 871-8181. **$199-$499.** Four Riverway 77056. I-610 exit 10 (Woodway Dr), 0.3 mi w. Int corridors. **Pets:** Accepted.

Omni Houston Hotel Westside H ❖
(281) 558-8338. **$109-$379.** 13210 Katy Frwy 77079. I-10 exit 753A (Eldridge St), just n. Int corridors. **Pets:** Small. $50 one-time fee/room. Service with restrictions, supervision.

Quality Inn & Suites Houston West/Energy Corridor M
(281) 493-0444. **$72-$190.** 715 Hwy 6 S 77079. I-10 exit 751 (Addicks Rd/Howell Rd), 0.4 mi s. Ext corridors. **Pets:** Medium. $10 daily fee/pet. Designated rooms, service with restrictions, supervision.

Red Roof Houston IAH H
(832) 243-7650. **$59-$99.** 15675 John F Kennedy Blvd 77032. Sam Houston Pkwy (Beltway 8) exit John F Kennedy Blvd, just n. Int corridors. **Pets:** Large, other species. Service with restrictions, supervision.

Red Roof Inns H
(713) 785-9909. **$55-$75.** 2960 W Sam Houston Pkwy S 77042. Sam Houston Pkwy (Beltway 8) exit Westheimer Rd; on southbound frontage road. Ext/int corridors. **Pets:** Large, other species. Service with restrictions, supervision.

Residence Inn by Marriott Houston by the Galleria H
(713) 840-9757. **$103-$196.** 2500 McCue Rd 77056. I-610 exit 8C (Westheimer Rd) northbound; exit 9A (San Felipe Rd/Westheimer Rd) southbound, just w to McCue Rd, then just n. Ext/int corridors. **Pets:** Accepted.

Residence Inn by Marriott Houston Downtown/ Convention Center H
(832) 366-1000. **$95-$289.** 904 Dallas St 77002. At Main St. Int corridors. **Pets:** Accepted.

Residence Inn by Marriott-Medical Center/Reliant Park H
(713) 660-7993. **$109-$179.** 7710 S Main St 77030. I-610 exit 2 (S Main St/Buffalo Speedway), 1.5 mi n. Ext corridors. **Pets:** Accepted.

Residence Inn by Marriott-West University H
(713) 661-4660. **$79-$309.** 2939 Westpark Dr 77005. US 59 exit Kirby Dr, just s, then just w. Int corridors. **Pets:** Other species. $100 one-time fee/room. Designated rooms, service with restrictions, crate.

Residence Inn by Marriott Willowbrook H
(832) 237-2002. **$99-$289.** 7311 W Greens Rd 77064. SR 249 exit Greens Rd, just e. Int corridors. **Pets:** Other species. $100 one-time fee/room. Service with restrictions.

The St. Regis Houston H ❖
(713) 840-7600. **$199-$995.** 1919 Briar Oaks Ln 77027. I-610 exit 9A (San Felipe Rd/Westheimer Rd), 0.3 mi e. Int corridors. **Pets:** Medium, dogs only. $250 deposit/pet. Service with restrictions, supervision.

Sheraton Houston Brookhollow H ❖
(713) 688-0100. **$89-$249.** 3000 N Loop W 77092. I-610 exit 13C (TC Jester Blvd); on southbound frontage road. Int corridors. **Pets:** Medium. Service with restrictions, supervision.

Sheraton Houston West Hotel H
(281) 501-4200. **$109-$269.** 11191 Clay Rd 77041. Sam Houston Pkwy (Beltway 8) exit Clay Rd, just e. Int corridors. **Pets:** Accepted.

Sheraton North Houston Hotel H ❖
(281) 442-5100. **$99-$270.** 15700 John F Kennedy Blvd 77032. Sam Houston Pkwy (Beltway 8) exit John F Kennedy Blvd, just n. Int corridors. **Pets:** Small. Service with restrictions, supervision.

Sheraton Suites Houston Near The Galleria H
(713) 586-2444. **$99-$459.** 2400 W Loop S 77027. I-610 exit 9 (San Felipe Rd) northbound; exit 9A (San Felipe Rd/Westheimer Rd) southbound. Int corridors. **Pets:** Accepted.

Sonesta ES Suites Houston H
(713) 355-8888. **$99-$239.** 5190 Hidalgo St 77056. I-610 exit 9A (San Felipe Rd/Westheimer Rd) southbound; exit 8C (Westheimer Rd) northbound, 0.4 mi w to Sage Rd, then just s. Int corridors. **Pets:** Accepted.

Staybridge Suites Houston West Energy Corridor H
(281) 759-7829. **$119-$169.** 1225 Eldridge Pkwy 77077. I-10 exit 753A (Eldridge Pkwy), 1.8 mi s. Int corridors. **Pets:** Accepted.

TownePlace Suites by Marriott-Central H
(713) 690-4035. **$90-$259.** 12820 Northwest Frwy (US 290) 77040. US 290 exit Bingle Rd/43rd St eastbound; exit Bingle Rd/Pinemont Dr/43rd St westbound; on westbound feeder. Int corridors. **Pets:** Accepted.

TownePlace Suites by Marriott Houston I-10 West/Energy Corridor H
(281) 646-0058. **$99-$119.** 15155 Katy Frwy 77094. I-10 exit 751, just s on SR 6 to Grisby Rd, then w. Int corridors. **Pets:** Accepted.

The Westin Galleria, Houston H
(713) 960-8100. **$110-$331.** 5060 W Alabama St 77056. I-610 exit 8C (Westheimer Rd) northbound; exit 9A (San Felipe Rd/Westheimer Rd) southbound, 0.5 mi w on Westheimer Rd to Sage, just s, then just e. Int corridors. **Pets:** Accepted.

Westin Houston Memorial City H
(281) 501-4300. **$129-$329.** 945 Gessner Rd 77024. I-10 exit 757 (Gessner Rd), just s. Int corridors. **Pets:** Accepted.

Westin Oaks Houston at the Galleria H ❖
(713) 960-8100. **$110-$331.** 5011 Westheimer Rd 77056. I-610 exit 8C (Westheimer Rd) northbound; exit 9A (San Felipe Rd/Westheimer Rd) southbound. Int corridors. **Pets:** Medium, dogs only. Designated rooms, service with restrictions, crate.

Wingate by Wyndham Houston Bush Intercontinental Airport IAH H
(281) 372-1000. **$75-$159.** 1330 N Sam Houston Pkwy E 77032. Off Sam Houston Pkwy (Beltway 8) exit Aldine Westfield Rd eastbound, 0.8 mi e on service road; exit Hardy Toll Rd westbound, U-turn, then 1 mi e on service road. Int corridors. **Pets:** Accepted.

KATY

La Quinta Inn & Suites Katy H
(281) 392-9800. **$102-$177.** 22455 Katy Frwy (I-10) 77450. I-10 exit 745 (Mason Rd); on eastbound frontage road. Int corridors. **Pets:** Service with restrictions, supervision.

Residence Inn by Marriott Houston Katy Mills H
(281) 391-7501. **$134-$147.** 25401 Katy Mills Pkwy 77494. I-10 exit 740 (Pin Oak Rd) westbound; exit 741 (Pin Oak Rd) eastbound, just s; on south side of Kay Mills Mall. Int corridors. **Pets:** Accepted.

KINGWOOD

▼▼▼▼ Comfort Suites Kingwood-Humble 🅷 ❀
(281) 359-4448. **$81-$200.** 22223 Hwy 59 N 77339. US 59 exit Kingwood Dr northbound; exit McClellan southbound. Int corridors.
Pets: Other species. $25 daily fee/pet. Service with restrictions, supervision. 🛜 ✕ ⚿M 🛗 💻 ➳

◎◎◎ ▼▼▼▼ Holiday Inn Express Hotel &
Suites-Kingwood 🅷
(281) 359-2700. **$70-$159.** 22675 US 59 N 77339. US 59 exit Kingwood Dr; on southbound access road. Int corridors. **Pets:** Very small. $25 daily fee/pet. Designated rooms, service with restrictions, supervision.
[SAVE] 🛜 🛗 💻 ➳

MONTGOMERY

◎◎◎ ▼▼▼ BEST WESTERN Lake Conroe Inn 🅷
(936) 588-3030. **$80-$130.** 14643 Hwy 105 W 77356. Just w of McCaleb Rd. Ext corridors. **Pets:** Accepted. [SAVE] 🛜 🛗 💻 ➳

◎◎◎ ▼▼▼ ▼ La Torretta Lake Resort & Spa 🅷
(936) 448-4400. **$159-$499, 3 day notice.** 600 La Torretta Blvd 77356. SR 105, 2.5 mi n on Walden Rd to La Torretta Blvd. Ext/int corridors.
Pets: Accepted. [SAVE] 🛜 ✕ 🛗 💻 🍴 ➳ ✕

NASSAU BAY

▼▼▼▼ Hilton Houston NASA Clear Lake 🅷
(281) 333-9300. **$89-$169.** 3000 NASA Pkwy 77058. 2 mi e of NASA bypass road. Int corridors. **Pets:** Accepted.
🛜 ✕ 🛗 💻 🍴 ➳

ROSENBERG

▼▼▼ Americas Best Value Inn & Suites 🅷
(832) 595-6900. **$65-$85.** 28150 Southwest Frwy 77471. US 59 exit SR 36; on southbound frontage road. Ext corridors. **Pets:** Small. $15 daily fee/pet. Service with restrictions, supervision. 🛜 🛗 💻

▼▼▼▼ La Quinta Inn & Suites Rosenberg 🅷
(832) 595-6111. **$87-$155.** 28332 Southwest Frwy 77471. Jct US 59 and SR 36; on southbound frontage road. Int corridors. **Pets:** Service with restrictions, supervision. 🛜 ✕ 🛗 💻 ➳

SEABROOK

▼▼▼▼ Comfort Inn & Suites-NASA Clearlake 🅷
(281) 326-3301. **$89-$109.** 2901 NASA Pkwy 77586. 1 mi w of jct W SR 146. Int corridors. **Pets:** Accepted. 🛜 ✕ 🛗 💻 ➳

▼▼▼▼ Hampton Inn NASA/Johnson Space Center
Houston 🅷
(281) 532-9200. **$79-$179.** 3000 NASA Pkwy 77586. 1 mi w of jct SR 146. Int corridors. **Pets:** Accepted. 🛜 🛗 💻 ➳

▼▼▼▼ La Quinta Inn & Suites Houston NASA
Seabrook 🅷
(281) 326-7300. **$83-$177.** 3636 NASA Pkwy 77586. I-45 exit 25 (NASA Rd One), then 6 mi e; SR 146, 2 mi w. Int corridors. **Pets:** Service with restrictions, supervision. 🛜 ✕ 🛗 💻 ➳

SHENANDOAH

▼▼▼▼ TownePlace Suites by Marriott The Woodlands 🅷
(936) 273-7772. **$123-$180.** 107 Vision Park Blvd 77384. I-45 exit 79 (College Park/Needham Rd), 1 mi s; on southbound frontage road. Int corridors. **Pets:** Accepted. 🛜 ✕ ⚿M 🛗 💻 ➳

STAFFORD

▼▼▼ La Quinta Inn & Suites Houston
Stafford/Sugarland 🅷
(281) 240-2300. **$59-$144.** 12727 Southwest Frwy 77477. US 59 exit Corporate Dr southbound; exit Airport Blvd/Kirkwood Rd northbound; eastbound service road. Int corridors. **Pets:** Service with restrictions, supervision. 🛜 🛗 💻 ➳

◎◎◎ ▼▼▼▼ Residence Inn by Marriott Houston/Sugar
Land 🅷 ❀
(281) 277-0770. **$110-$240.** 12703 Southwest Frwy 77477. US 59 exit Corporate Dr southbound; exit Airport Blvd/Kirkwood Rd northbound; on northbound service road. Int corridors. **Pets:** Medium. $100 one-time fee/room. Service with restrictions. [SAVE] 🛜 ✕ 🛗 💻 ➳ ✕

▼▼▼▼ Staybridge Suites Stafford 🅷 🐾
(281) 302-6535. **$99-$159.** 11101 Fountain Lake Dr 77477. US 59 exit Kirkwood Rd, just nw. Int corridors. **Pets:** Medium, other species. $75 one-time fee/pet. Service with restrictions, supervision.
🛜 ✕ ⚿M 🛗 💻 ➳

SUGAR LAND

▼▼▼▼ Drury Inn & Suites-Houston/Sugar Land 🅷
(281) 277-9700. **$94-$179.** 13770 Southwest Frwy 77478. US 59 exit Dairy Ashford Rd/Sugar Creek Blvd; on north frontage road. Int corridors.
Pets: Service with restrictions, supervision. 🛜 🛗 💻 ➳

THE WOODLANDS

◎◎◎ ▼▼▼▼ BEST WESTERN PLUS The
Woodlands 🅷 🐾
(936) 271-2378. **$109.** 17081 I-45 S 77385. I-45 exit 79 (College Park/Needham Rd) northbound; northeast corner of SR 242; on northbound frontage. Int corridors. **Pets:** Large, other species. $20 daily fee/room. Service with restrictions, crate. [SAVE] 🛜 🛗 💻 ➳

▼▼▼▼ Drury Inn & Suites-Houston/The Woodlands 🅷
(281) 362-7222. **$104-$209.** 28099 I-45 N 77380. I-45 exit 77 (Research Forest Dr/Tamina Rd) southbound; on southbound frontage road. Int corridors. **Pets:** Service with restrictions, supervision.
🛜 ⚿M 🛗 💻 ➳

◎◎◎ ▼▼▼▼ Holiday Inn Express Hotel & Suites 🅷
(281) 681-8088. **$99-$149.** 24888 I-45 N 77386. I-45 exit 73 (Rayford Rd/Sawdust Rd); on northbound access road. Int corridors.
Pets: Accepted. [SAVE] 🛜 ✕ 🛗 💻 ➳ ✕

▼▼▼▼ La Quinta Inn & Suites - The Woodlands
South 🅷
(281) 681-9188. **$95-$199.** 24868 I-45 N 77386. I-45 exit 73 (Rayford Rd/Sawdust Rd); on northbound access road. Int corridors. **Pets:** Service with restrictions, supervision. 🛜 ✕ ⚿M 🛗 💻 ➳ ✕

▼▼▼▼ Residence Inn by Marriott Lake Front 🅷
(281) 292-3252. **$139-$199.** 1040 Lake Front Cir 77380. I-45 exit 79 (College Park Dr/Needham Rd) northbound; exit 77 (Research Forest Dr/Tamina Rd) southbound; just off southbound frontage road. Int corridors. **Pets:** Accepted. 🛜 ✕ 🛗 💻 ➳ ✕

WEBSTER

◎◎◎ ▼▼▼▼ Comfort Suites 🅷
(281) 554-5400. **$90-$150.** 16931 N Texas Ave 77598. I-45 exit 26 (Bay Area Blvd), 0.5 mi e to Texas Ave, then just s. Int corridors.
Pets: Medium. $10 daily fee/pet. Designated rooms, service with restrictions. [SAVE] 🛜 ✕ ⚿M 🛗 💻 ➳

▼▼ Extended Stay Deluxe Houston NASA-Bay Area
Blvd 🅷
(281) 338-7711. **$79-$124.** 720 W Bay Area Blvd 77598. I-45 exit 26 (Bay Area Blvd), just e. Int corridors. **Pets:** $25 daily fee/pet. Designated rooms, service with restrictions. 🛜 🛗 💻 ➳

▼▼▼▼ La Quinta Inn & Suites Clearlake/Webster 🅷
(281) 554-5290. **$90-$177.** 520 W Bay Area Blvd 77598. I-45 exit 26 (Bay Area Blvd), just e. Int corridors. **Pets:** Service with restrictions, supervision. 🛜 ✕ ⚿M 🛗 💻 ➳

▼▼▼▼ Staybridge Suites Houston/ Clear Lake 🅷
(281) 338-0900. **$99-$149.** 501 W Texas Ave 77598. I-45 exit 26 (Bay Area Blvd), right, then left at 3rd light. Int corridors. **Pets:** Medium. $150 one-time fee/pet. Service with restrictions, crate.
🛜 ✕ ⚿M 🛗 💻 ➳ ✕

🔷 ▼▼▼ Super 8-Houston-Webster-NASA M
(281) 333-5385. **$65-$150, 3 day notice.** 18103 Kingsrow Rd 77058.
I-45 exit 25 (NASA Rd 1), 1.5 mi e. Ext corridors. **Pets:** Other species.
$25 one-time fee/pet. Designated rooms, service with restrictions.
[SAVE] 🛜 🖥 💻 🏊

WINNIE
▼▼▼ Comfort Inn & Suites H
(409) 296-6200. **$89-$99.** 338 Spur 5 77665. I-10 exit 829, just s. Int
corridors. **Pets:** Accepted. 🛜 ✕ 🖥 💻 🏊

▼▼ Days Inn & Suites H
(409) 296-2866. **$69-$114.** 14932 FM 1663 77665. I-10 exit 829, just n.
Ext corridors. **Pets:** Medium. $20 daily fee/pet. Service with restrictions,
supervision. 🛜 🖥M 🖥 💻

▼▼ Winnie Inn & Suites H
(409) 296-2947. **$50-$90.** 205 Spur 5, Hwy 124 77665. I-10 exit 829, just
s. Ext corridors. **Pets:** Accepted. 🛜 🖥 💻 🏊

END METROPOLITAN AREA

HUNTSVILLE
🔷 ▼▼▼ BEST WESTERN PLUS Huntsville Inn & Suites H
(936) 295-9000. **Call for rates.** 201 W Hill Park Cir 77320. I-45 exit 116,
just w on US 190. Ext corridors. **Pets:** Medium. $20 daily fee/pet. Service
with restrictions, supervision. [SAVE] 🛜 🖥M 🖥 💻 🏊

INGLESIDE
🔷 ▼▼ BEST WESTERN Naval Station Inn M
(361) 776-2767. **$90-$130.** 2025 State Hwy 361 78362. Jct SR 1069, 1
mi e. Ext corridors. **Pets:** $15 daily fee/pet. Service with restrictions,
supervision. [SAVE] 🛜 🖥 💻 🏊

JACKSONVILLE
▼▼ Comfort Inn H
(903) 589-8500. **Call for rates.** 1848 S Jackson St 75766. On US 69, 2
mi s of jct US 69 and 79. Int corridors. **Pets:** Accepted.
🛜 🖥M 🖥 💻 🏊

▼▼▼ La Quinta Inn & Suites Jacksonville H
(903) 586-6504. **$80-$167.** 1902 S Jackson St 75766. On US 69, 2.1 mi
s of jct US 69 and 79. Int corridors. **Pets:** Service with restrictions, supervision. 🛜 🖥M 🖥 💻 🏊

JASPER
▼▼ Super 8 H
(409) 384-8600. **$65-$125.** 2100 N Wheeler St 75951. US 96, 1.8 mi n
of jct US 190. Ext corridors. **Pets:** Very small, dogs only. $25 one-time
fee/room. Supervision. 🛜 🖥 💻 🏊

JOHNSON CITY
🔷 ▼▼ BEST WESTERN Johnson City Inn H
(830) 868-4044. **$90-$130.** 107 S Hwy 290/281 78636. Jct US 281 and
290 N. Ext corridors. **Pets:** Accepted. [SAVE] 🖥 💻 🏊

JUNCTION
🔷 ▼▼▼ Motel 6 Junction - #4384 H
(325) 446-3572. **$65-$149.** 200 I-10 W 76849. I-10 exit 456; on N Frontage Rd. Ext corridors. **Pets:** Other species. Service with restrictions,
supervision. [SAVE] 🛜 🖥 💻 🏊

▼▼ Rodeway Inn H
(325) 446-4588. **$65-$70.** 2343 N Main St 76849. I-10 exit 456, just s on
US 377. Ext corridors. **Pets:** Accepted. 🛜 🖥 💻 🏊

KERRVILLE
🔷 ▼▼▼ BEST WESTERN Sunday House Inn H
(830) 896-1313. **$74-$99.** 2124 Sidney Baker St 78028. I-10 exit 508
(SR 16), just s. Ext corridors. **Pets:** Accepted.
[SAVE] 🛜 🖥 💻 🍴 🏊

🔷 ▼▼▼ Comfort Inn H
(830) 792-7700. **$79-$149.** 2001 Sidney Baker St 78028. I-10 exit 508
(SR 16), 0.4 mi s. Int corridors. **Pets:** Medium. $10 daily fee/pet. Desig-
nated rooms, service with restrictions, supervision.
[SAVE] 🛜 🖥 💻 🏊

▼▼ Days Inn of Kerrville M
(830) 896-1000. **$45-$109.** 2000 Sidney Baker St 78028. I-10 exit 508
(SR 16), 0.5 mi s. Ext/int corridors. **Pets:** Medium, other species. $10
daily fee/pet. Designated rooms, service with restrictions, supervision.
🛜 🖥 💻 🏊

▼▼ La Quinta Inn Kerrville H
(830) 896-9200. **$78-$188.** 1940 Sidney Baker St 78028. I-10 exit 508
(SR 16), 0.4 mi s. Int corridors. **Pets:** Service with restrictions, supervision. 🛜 🖥 💻 🏊

🔷 ▼▼▼ Y. O. Ranch Hotel & Conference Center H
(830) 257-4440. **$79-$129.** 2033 Sidney Baker St 78028. I-10 exit 508
(SR 16), 0.3 mi s. Ext/int corridors. **Pets:** Accepted.
[SAVE] 🛜 🖥 💻 🍴 🏊 ✕

KILGORE
🔷 ▼▼ BEST WESTERN Inn of Kilgore H
(903) 986-1195. **$80-$120.** 1411 N Hwy 259 75662. I-20 exit 589, 3.9 mi
s. Ext corridors. **Pets:** Dogs only. $50 deposit/room, $40 one-time fee/pet.
Service with restrictions, crate. [SAVE] 🛜 🖥 💻 🏊

KILLEEN
▼▼▼ Candlewood Suites - Ft. Hood/Killeen H
(254) 501-3990. **$99-$129.** 2300 Florence Rd 76542. US 90 exit Jasper
Rd, just s. Int corridors. **Pets:** Accepted. 🛜 🖥M 🖥 💻

🔷 ▼▼ Days Inn Killeen Mall H
(254) 554-2727. **$69.** 1602 E Central Texas Expwy 76541. US 190 exit
Trimmier Rd. Ext corridors. **Pets:** Large, other species. $25 one-time fee/
room. Service with restrictions. [SAVE] 🛜 🖥 💻

▼▼▼ Residence Inn by Marriott H
(254) 634-1020. **$134-$152.** 400 E Central Texas Expwy 76541. US 190
exit Fort Hood St/Jasper Rd (SR 195); on south frontage road. Int corridors. **Pets:** Accepted. 🛜 ✕ 🖥M 🖥 💻 🏊

▼▼▼ Shilo Inn Suites Hotel - Killeen H
(254) 699-0999. **$115-$225.** 3701 S WS Young Dr 76542. US 190 exit
WS Young Dr, 1 mi s. Int corridors. **Pets:** Dogs only. $25 one-time fee/
room. Designated rooms, service with restrictions, supervision.
🛜 🖥M 🖥 💻 🍴 🏊 ✕

▼▼▼ TownePlace Suites by Marriott H
(254) 554-8899. **$89-$119.** 2401 Florence Rd 76542. US 190 exit Trimmier Rd to Jasper Rd, on south access road, 1 blk e to Florence Rd,
then just s. Int corridors. **Pets:** Accepted. 🛜 ✕ 🖥M 🖥 💻 🏊

KINGSLAND

▼▼▼ Rio Vista Resort [CO]
(325) 388-6331. **$90-$950, 30 day notice.** 234 Rio Vista Dr 78639. Colorado River Bridge, 0.5 mi nw on FM 1431, 0.5 mi s on Reynolds St. Ext corridors. **Pets:** Accepted. 🛜 ✕ 🛗 💻 ⊇ ✕

KINGSVILLE

ⓐⓐⓐ ▼▼ Quality Inn 🅷
(361) 592-5251. **$50-$140.** 221 S Hwy 77 Bypass 78363. On US 77, just s of jct SR 141. Ext corridors. **Pets:** Small. $100 deposit/pet, $10 daily fee/pet. Service with restrictions, supervision. [SAVE] 🛜 🛗 💻 ⊇

▼▼ Super 8 🅼
(361) 592-6471. **$65-$70.** 105 S US Hwy 77 Bypass 78363. 0.8 mi e on US 77. Ext corridors. **Pets:** Accepted. 🛜 🛗 💻 ⊇

KYLE

▼▼▼ La Quinta Inn & Suites Kyle 🅷
(512) 295-5599. **$83-$166.** 18869 IH-35 N 78640. I-35 exit 217; on east frontage road. Int corridors. **Pets:** Service with restrictions, supervision. 🛜 ✕ 🅜 🛗 💻 ⊇

LA GRANGE

ⓐⓐⓐ ▼▼▼ BEST WESTERN PLUS La Grange Inn & Suites 🅷
(979) 968-6800. **$95-$145.** 600 E State Hwy 71 Bypass 78945. Jct US 77 and SR 71, just e on N Frontage Rd. Int corridors. **Pets:** Medium. $15 daily fee/pet. Supervision. [SAVE] 🛜 ✕ 🛗 💻 ⊇

LAJITAS

▼▼▼ Lajitas Golf Resort and Spa 🅷
(432) 424-5000. **Call for rates.** 1 Main St 79852. Center. Ext/int corridors. **Pets:** Accepted. 🛜 🛗 💻 🍴 ⊇ ✕

LAKE JACKSON

▼▼▼ Candlewood Suites-Lake Jackson-Clute 🅷
(979) 297-0011. **$89-$139.** 506 Hwy 332 77566. Jct SR 288/332 and Plantation Dr, just n. Int corridors. **Pets:** Medium, dogs only. $150 one-time fee/room. Service with restrictions, supervision. 🛜 🅜 🛗 💻 ⊇

ⓐⓐⓐ ▼▼▼ Cherotel Grand Mariner Hotel 🅷
(979) 297-1161. **$74-$94.** 925 Hwy 332 77566. On SR 288/332, just w of jct Business Rt SR 288. Int corridors. **Pets:** Accepted. [SAVE] 🛜 🛗 💻 🍴 ⊇

LAKEWAY

ⓐⓐⓐ ▼▼ ▼▼ Lakeway Resort & Spa 🅷 🐾
(512) 261-6600. **$119-$1300, 3 day notice.** 101 Lakeway Dr 78734. Jct FM 620 and Lakeway Blvd W, 1.5 mi to Lakeway Dr, then 2.1 mi n. Int corridors. **Pets:** Small, dogs only. $35 one-time fee/pet. Designated rooms, service with restrictions, crate. [SAVE] 🛜 ✕ 🅜 🛗 💻 🍴 ⊇ ✕

LAMESA

ⓐⓐⓐ ▼▼ Shiloh Inn 🅼
(806) 872-6721. **$69-$99, 3 day notice.** 1707 Lubbock Hwy 79331. Jct US 87 and 180, 1 mi n. Ext corridors. **Pets:** Small, dogs only. $20 daily fee/pet. Supervision. [SAVE] 🛜 🛗 💻 🍴 ⊇

LAMPASAS

ⓐⓐⓐ ▼▼ Inn at Lampasas 🅷
(512) 556-9292. **$99.** 1200 Central Texas Expwy 76550. 0.5 mi se of jct US 183 and 281. Int corridors. **Pets:** $15 one-time fee/room. Service with restrictions. [SAVE] 🛜 🅜 🛗 💻 ⊇

LAREDO

▼▼ Americas Best Value Inn 🅼
(956) 723-1510. **$60-$90.** 5240 San Bernardo Ave 78041. I-35 exit 3B (Mann Rd); on southbound frontage road. Ext corridors. **Pets:** Other species. $20 daily fee/pet. Designated rooms, service with restrictions, supervision. 🛜 🛗 ⊇

▼▼ Days Inn & Suites 🅷
(956) 724-8221. **$70-$100.** 7060 N San Bernardo Ave 78041. I-35 exit 4 (San Bernardo Ave), just s; on southbound access road. Ext/int corridors. **Pets:** Small. $10 deposit/pet, $10 daily fee/pet. Designated rooms, service with restrictions, supervision. 🛜 🛗 💻 🍴 ⊇

▼▼▼ La Posada Hotel & Suites 🅷
(956) 722-1701. **$109-$129.** 1000 Zaragoza St 78040. I-35 exit downtown; just e of International Bridge 1. Ext/int corridors. **Pets:** Accepted. 🛜 🛗 💻 🍴 ⊇

▼▼▼ La Quinta Inn & Suites Laredo Airport 🅷
(956) 724-7222. **$95-$188.** 7220 Bob Bullock Loop 78041. I-35 exit 8 (Bob Bullock Loop E), 5.8 mi e on Loop 20. Int corridors. **Pets:** Service with restrictions, supervision. 🛜 ✕ 🅜 🛗 💻 ⊇

▼▼▼ La Quinta Inn Laredo I-35 🅼
(956) 722-0511. **$75-$144.** 3610 Santa Ursula Ave 78041. I-35 exit 2 (Jefferson St). Ext corridors. **Pets:** Service with restrictions, supervision. 🛜 🛗 💻 ⊇

▼ Motel 6 South - #142 🅼
(956) 725-8187. **$55-$71.** 5310 San Bernardo Ave 78041. I-35 exit 3B (Mann Rd), just s. Ext corridors. **Pets:** Other species. Service with restrictions, supervision. 🛜 ⊇

▼▼▼ Residence Inn by Marriott Laredo 🅷
(956) 753-9700. **$104-$139.** 310 Lost Oaks Blvd 78041. I-35 exit 3B (Mann Rd), just n; on northbound access road. Int corridors. **Pets:** Accepted. 🛜 ✕ 🅜 🛗 💻 ⊇

▼▼▼ Staybridge Suites-Laredo 🅷
(956) 722-0444. **$109-$169, 3 day notice.** 7010 Bob Bullock Loop 78041. US 83 exit onto Loop 20 (Bob Bullock Loop); on west side. Int corridors. **Pets:** Accepted. 🛜 🛗 💻 ⊇

LEVELLAND

▼▼▼ Holiday Inn Express Hotel & Suites 🅷 🐾
(806) 894-8555. **Call for rates.** 703 E SR 114 79336. Jct US 385 and SR 114, 0.5 mi e. Int corridors. **Pets:** Other species. $25 one-time fee/pet. Designated rooms, service with restrictions, supervision. 🛜 🛗 💻 ⊇

LITTLEFIELD

ⓐⓐⓐ ▼▼▼ BEST WESTERN PLUS Littlefield Inn & Suites 🅷 🐾
(806) 385-3400. **$99-$129, 7 day notice.** 2600 Hall Ave 79339. Jct US 84 and 385, just s. Int corridors. **Pets:** $20 one-time fee/pet. Designated rooms, service with restrictions, supervision. [SAVE] 🛜 ✕ 🅜 🛗 💻 ⊇

LIVINGSTON

ⓐⓐⓐ ▼▼▼ BEST WESTERN PLUS Livingston Inn & Suites 🅷
(936) 327-8500. **$85-$95.** 335 Hwy 59 Loop S 77351. Just s of jct US 59 and 190; on southbound frontage road. Int corridors. **Pets:** Small. $100 deposit/room. Designated rooms, service with restrictions, crate. [SAVE] 🛜 🛗 💻 ⊇

LLANO

ⓐⓐⓐ ▼▼▼ BEST WESTERN Llano 🅷
(325) 247-4101. **$70-$100.** 901 W Young St 78643. 1 mi w on SR 71 and 29. Ext corridors. **Pets:** $10 daily fee/pet. Service with restrictions, supervision. [SAVE] 🛜 🛗 💻 ⊇

LONGVIEW

BEST WESTERN Regency Inn & Suites H
(903) 212-3333. **$80-$90, 7 day notice.** 707 N Access Rd 75602. I-20 exit 596 (Eastman Rd), just w. Int corridors. **Pets:** Small. $25 one-time fee/pet. Service with restrictions, crate.

La Quinta Inn & Suites Longview North H
(903) 663-6611. **$96-$167.** 908 E Hawkins Pkwy 75605. Just w of jct US 259 (Eastman Rd). Int corridors. **Pets:** Service with restrictions, supervision.

LUBBOCK

Americas Best Value Inn - Lubbock M
(806) 745-2515. **$50-$150.** 150 Slaton Rd 79404. I-27 exit 1B, just e on US 84. Ext corridors. **Pets:** Medium. $10 daily fee/pet. Designated rooms, no service, supervision.

Arbor Inn & Suites H
(806) 722-2726. **$89-$249.** 5310 Englewood Ave 79424. Loop 289 exit 50th St, just w. Int corridors. **Pets:** Dogs only. Service with restrictions, supervision.

Baymont Inn & Suites Lubbock H
(806) 792-5181. **$69-$198.** 3901 19th St 79410. Jct US 62/82 W and 19th St. Int corridors. **Pets:** Accepted.

BEST WESTERN PLUS Lubbock Windsor Inn H
(806) 762-8400. **$70-$200.** 5410 I-27 79404. 3.5 mi s on I-27 exit 1B southbound; U-turn at exit 1A (50th St) northbound. Int corridors. **Pets:** Large, other species. $20 daily fee/pet. Service with restrictions, supervision.

Extended StayAmerica Lubbock Southwest H
(806) 785-9881. **$72-$90.** 4802 S Loop 289 79414. S Loop 289 exit Slide Rd; on north frontage road. Int corridors. **Pets:** $25 daily fee/pet. Designated rooms, service with restrictions.

Hawthorn Suites H
(806) 792-3600. **$85-$519.** 4435 Marsha Sharp Frwy 79407. W Loop 289 exit US 62/82, 2.7 mi e. Int corridors. **Pets:** $125 one-time fee/room. Supervision.

Holiday Inn Park Plaza H
(806) 797-3241. **$79-$149.** 3201 S Loop 289 79423. Loop 289 S exit Indiana Ave; on south frontage road. Ext/int corridors. **Pets:** Medium, other species. $50 deposit/room. Designated rooms, service with restrictions, supervision.

La Quinta Inn & Suites Lubbock North H
(806) 749-1600. **$99-$184.** 5006 Auburn St 79416. Jct Loop 289 W and Quaker Ave, 1 mi s on west frontage road. Int corridors. **Pets:** Service with restrictions, supervision.

La Quinta Inn & Suites Lubbock West Medical Center H
(806) 792-0065. **$83-$155.** 4115 Marsha Sharp Frwy 79407. 3.3 mi sw; 2.5 mi ne of Loop 289 on US 62 and 82. Ext/int corridors. **Pets:** Service with restrictions, supervision.

La Quinta Inn Lubbock Civic Center H
(806) 763-9441. **$59-$155.** 601 Ave Q 79401. 0.8 mi nw on US 84. Ext corridors. **Pets:** Service with restrictions, supervision.

Lubbock Super 8 M
(806) 762-8726. **$45-$169.** 501 Ave Q 79401. 1 mi nw on US 84. Ext corridors. **Pets:** Other species. $10 daily fee/pet. Designated rooms, service with restrictions.

Radisson Hotel H
(806) 747-0171. **Call for rates.** 505 Ave Q 79401. I-27 exit 4, 0.9 mi w to US 84, then just s. Int corridors. **Pets:** Accepted.

Residence Inn by Marriott H
(806) 745-1963. **$99-$169.** 2551 S Loop 289 79423. Loop 289 exit University Ave; on south frontage road. Ext corridors. **Pets:** Other species. $150 one-time fee/pet. Service with restrictions, crate.

Sleep Inn & Suites H
(806) 368-6060. **$89-$109.** 5816 34th St 79407. Loop 289 W exit 34th St, just e. Int corridors. **Pets:** Designated rooms, service with restrictions, supervision.

Staybridge Suites H
(806) 765-8900. **Call for rates.** 2515 19th St 79410. Jct University Ave and 19th St; on southwest corner. Int corridors. **Pets:** Small, other species. $75 one-time fee/room. Service with restrictions, supervision.

TownePlace Suites by Marriott H
(806) 799-6226. **$74-$159.** 5310 W Loop 289 79424. W Loop 289 exit US 62/82 (Brownfield Rd), 0.5 mi s on west frontage road. Int corridors. **Pets:** Other species. $50 one-time fee/room. Service with restrictions.

LUFKIN

BEST WESTERN PLUS Crown Colony Inn & Suites H
(936) 634-3481. **$114.** 3211 S 1st St 75901. 2 mi s of jct US 59 and Loop 287. Int corridors. **Pets:** Small. $20 one-time fee/pet. Service with restrictions, crate.

La Quinta Inn Lufkin H
(936) 634-3351. **$87-$155.** 2119 S 1st St 75901. US 59 exit Carriage Way northbound, 0.3 mi s of jct S Loop 287 and US 59 business route. Ext corridors. **Pets:** Service with restrictions, supervision.

LUMBERTON

Econo Lodge M
(409) 751-5557. **Call for rates.** 131 N LHS Dr 77657. On US 69, 3 mi n of jct US 96. Int corridors. **Pets:** Accepted.

La Quinta Inn & Suites H
(409) 751-3999. **$89-$161.** 104 N LHS Dr 77657. On US 69, 3 mi n of jct US 96. Int corridors. **Pets:** Service with restrictions, supervision.

MADISONVILLE

BEST WESTERN Executive Inn & Suites H
(936) 349-1700. **$100-$110.** 3307 E Main St 77864. I-45 exit 142, just e. Int corridors. **Pets:** Accepted.

Woodbine Hotel and Restaurant CI
(936) 348-3333. **$85-$165, 7 day notice.** 209 N Madison St 77864. I-45 exit 142, 2.2 mi w to town square, then 2 blks n. Ext/int corridors. **Pets:** Medium, dogs only. $15 one-time fee/pet. Service with restrictions, supervision.

MANSFIELD

BEST WESTERN PLUS Mansfield Inn & Suites H
(817) 539-0707. **$84-$99.** 775 N Hwy 287 76063. US 287 exit Walnut Creek Rd; on southbound frontage road. Int corridors. **Pets:** Small, dogs only. $20 daily fee/pet. Service with restrictions, supervision.

Comfort Inn H
(817) 453-8848. **$60-$139.** 175 N Hwy 287 76063. US 287 S exit E Broad St. Int corridors. **Pets:** Medium, other species. $20 one-time fee/pet. Service with restrictions.

▼▼▼▼ Holiday Inn Express Hotel & Suites 🅗

(817) 453-8722. **Call for rates.** 201 Hwy 287 N 76063. US 287 exit Walnut Creek Rd, just s on frontage road. Int corridors. **Pets:** Very small. $20 daily fee/pet. Supervision. 🛜 ♿ 🛏 💻 🏊

▼▼▼▼ La Quinta Inn & Suites Mansfield 🅗

(817) 453-5040. **$93-$161.** 1503 Breckenridge Rd 76063. US 287 exit Walnut Creek Rd/Debbie Ln, 1.2 mi n to Debbie Ln, then just e to Breckenridge Rd. Int corridors. **Pets:** Service with restrictions, supervision. 🛜 ✕ ♿ 🛏 💻 🏊

MANVEL

◇◇◇ ▼▼▼ BEST WESTERN PLUS Manvel Inn & Suites 🅗

(281) 489-2266. **$82-$149.** 19301 Hwy 6 77578. 1.3 mi e of jct SR 288. Int corridors. **Pets:** $10 daily fee/pet. Service with restrictions, crate. 🆂🅰🆅🅴 🛜 ✕ 🛏 💻 🏊

MARBLE FALLS

◇◇◇ ▼▼▼ BEST WESTERN PLUS Marble Falls Inn 🅗

(830) 693-5122. **$59-$139.** 1403 US Hwy 281 78654. 0.4 mi n of jct SR 281 and FM 1431. Ext corridors. **Pets:** Medium. $10 daily fee/room. Designated rooms, service with restrictions, supervision. 🆂🅰🆅🅴 🛜 ♿ 🛏 💻 🏊

◇◇◇ ▼▼ Quality Inn-Marble Falls 🅗

(830) 693-7531. **$60-$160.** 1206 Hwy 281 N 78654. 0.3 mi n of jct US 281 and FM 1431. Ext corridors. **Pets:** Medium. $10 daily fee/pet. Service with restrictions, supervision. 🆂🅰🆅🅴 🛜 🛏 💻 🏊

MARFA

▼▼▼▼ Hotel Paisano 🅗

(432) 729-3669. **Call for rates.** 207 N Highland Ave 79843. Jct US 90 and SR 17, 3 blks n. Int corridors. **Pets:** Accepted. 🛜 ✕ 🛏 💻 🍴 🏊 🎬

MARLIN

◇◇◇ ▼▼▼ BEST WESTERN Marlin Inn & Suites 🅗

(254) 883-6000. **$72-$169, 7 day notice.** 100 FM 147 76661. Jct SR 6 and 7, 1 mi n. Int corridors. **Pets:** Small, dogs only. $25 one-time fee/room. Service with restrictions, supervision. 🆂🅰🆅🅴 🛜 ✕ 🛏 💻 🏊

MARSHALL

◇◇◇ ▼▼▼ BEST WESTERN Executive Inn 🅗

(903) 935-0707. **$69-$99.** 5201 E End Blvd S 75672. I-20 exit 617, 0.4 mi n on US 59. Ext corridors. **Pets:** Accepted. 🆂🅰🆅🅴 🛜 🛏 💻 🏊

▼▼ Motel 6 Marshall - #422 Ⓜ

(903) 935-4393. **$45-$55.** 300 I-20 E 75670. I-20 exit 617, just s, then just e. Ext corridors. **Pets:** Other species. Service with restrictions, supervision. 🛜 🛏 🏊

MCALLEN

▼▼▼ Drury Inn-McAllen 🅗

(956) 687-5100. **$84-$149.** 612 W Expwy 83 78501. US 83 exit 2nd St; on northwest frontage road. Int corridors. **Pets:** Service with restrictions, supervision. 🛜 🛏 💻 🏊

▼▼▼ Drury Suites-McAllen 🅗

(956) 682-3222. **$104-$224.** 228 W Expwy 83 78501. At US 83 and 6th St. Int corridors. **Pets:** Service with restrictions, supervision. 🛜 🛏 💻 🏊

▼▼ Motel 6 McAllen - #212 Ⓜ

(956) 687-3700. **$45-$59.** 700 W Expwy 83 78501. US 83 exit 2nd St; on northwest frontage road. Ext corridors. **Pets:** Other species. Service with restrictions, supervision. 🛜 🏊

▼▼▼ Pear Tree Inn by Drury 🅗

(956) 682-4900. **$69-$124.** 300 W Expwy 83 78501. US 83 exit 2nd St; on northwest frontage road. Int corridors. **Pets:** Service with restrictions, supervision. 🛜 🛏 💻 🏊

▼▼▼ Posada Ana Inn 🅗

(956) 631-6700. **$76-$99.** 620 W Expwy 83 78501. US 83 exit 2nd St; on northwest frontage road. Int corridors. **Pets:** Service with restrictions, supervision. 🛜 💻

▼▼▼ Residence Inn by Marriott 🅗

(956) 994-8626. **$84-$129.** 220 W Expwy 83 78501. US 83 exit 2nd St, just w, then just n on 2nd St. Int corridors. **Pets:** Medium. $75 one-time fee/room. Service with restrictions, crate. 🛜 ✕ 🛏 💻 🏊 ✕

▼▼▼ Staybridge Suites McAllen-Airport 🅗

(956) 213-7829. **$94-$190.** 620 Wichita Ave 78503. 0.4 mi s of US 83, just e of S 10th St. Int corridors. **Pets:** Accepted. 🛜 ✕ ♿ 🛏 💻 🏊

MEXIA

◇◇◇ ▼▼▼ BEST WESTERN Limestone Inn & Suites 🅗

(254) 562-0200. **$79-$89.** 1314 E Milam St 76667. Just e of SR 1365 on US 84; east side of town. Int corridors. **Pets:** Small. $10 daily fee/pet. Service with restrictions. 🆂🅰🆅🅴 🛜 🛏 💻 🏊

MIDLAND

◇◇◇ ▼▼ Baymont Inn & Suites Midland Airport 🅗

(432) 561-8000. **$110-$265.** 10000 Airport Rd 79706. I-20 exit 126, 0.8 mi n on I-20 business loop to W CR 117, then 0.4 mi e. Int corridors. **Pets:** Accepted. 🆂🅰🆅🅴 🛜 🛏 💻 🍴 🏊

◇◇◇ ▼▼▼ Grand Texan Hotel & Convention Center 🅗

(432) 697-3181. **Call for rates.** 4300 W Wall St 79703. I-20 exit 134 (Midkiff Rd), 1 mi n to I-20 business loop, then 0.7 mi w. Ext/int corridors. **Pets:** Accepted. 🆂🅰🆅🅴 🛜 🛏 💻 🏊 ✕

▼▼▼ La Quinta Inn & Suites Midland North 🅗

(432) 694-1200. **$239-$364.** 2606 N Loop 250 W 79707. Loop 250 W exit SR 158/191, 0.5 mi n on east frontage road. Int corridors. **Pets:** Service with restrictions, supervision. 🛜 ✕ ♿ 🛏 💻 🏊

▼▼▼ La Quinta Inn Midland 🅗

(432) 697-9900. **$107-$232.** 4130 W Wall St 79703. I-20 exit 131, 0.9 mi n on Loop 250 to exit 1A; 1.2 mi e on I-20 business route. Ext corridors. **Pets:** Service with restrictions, supervision. 🛜 🛏 💻 🏊

▼▼ Plaza Inn 🅗

(432) 686-8733. **Call for rates.** 4108 N Big Spring St 79705. I-20 exit 144, 6.1 mi on Loop 250 to SR 349 (Big Spring St), then just s on SR 349. Ext corridors. **Pets:** Accepted. 🛜 🛏 💻 🏊

▼▼▼ Residence Inn by Marriott Midland 🅗

(432) 689-3511. **$265-$275.** 5509 Deauville Blvd 79706. Loop 250 W exit SR 158/191; on south frontage road. Int corridors. **Pets:** Accepted. 🛜 ✕ ♿ 🛏 💻 🏊

MINERAL WELLS

◇◇◇ ▼▼▼▼ BEST WESTERN Club House Inn & Suites 🅗 🐾

(940) 325-2270. **$75.** 4410 Hwy 180 E 76067. Jct US 180 and SR 1195; in East Mineral Wells. Int corridors. **Pets:** Other species. $10 daily fee/pet. Service with restrictions, supervision. 🆂🅰🆅🅴 🛜 ♿ 🛏 💻 🏊

▼▼▼ Comfort Suites 🅗

(940) 327-0077. **$66-$79.** 105 Carl Kessler Blvd 76067. Jct US 281 and 180, 2.5 mi w. Int corridors. **Pets:** Medium, dogs only. $20 daily fee/pet. Service with restrictions, supervision. 🛜 ✕ ♿ 🛏 💻 🏊

MISSION

△△△ ▼▼▼▼ El Rocio Retreat **BB**
(956) 584-7432. **$75-$315, 3 day notice.** 2519 S Inspiration Rd 78572. Jct US 83 at Inspiration Rd, 2 mi s. Ext/int corridors. **Pets:** Other species. Service with restrictions, crate. (SAVE) 🛜 ❌ 💻

▼▼▼▼ La Quinta Inn & Suites **H**
(956) 581-7772. **$89-$155.** 805 Travis St 78572. US 83 exit Bryan Rd; on eastbound access road. Int corridors. **Pets:** Service with restrictions, supervision. 🛜 ❌ 💻 〰

MONAHANS

▼▼ Americas Best Value Colonial Inn **M**
(432) 943-4345. **$90-$300.** 702 W I-20 79756. I-20 exit 80, just s. Ext/int corridors. **Pets:** Accepted. 🛜 💻 📶

MOUNT PLEASANT

△△△ ▼▼▼ BEST WESTERN Mt. Pleasant Inn **M**
(903) 572-5051. **$72-$80.** 102 E Burton Rd 75455. I-30 exit 162, just e. Ext corridors. **Pets:** $10 daily fee/pet. Service with restrictions, supervision. (SAVE) 🛜 💻 📶

▼▼▼▼ La Quinta Inn & Suites Mt. Pleasant **H**
(903) 572-5514. **$84-$156.** 1620 Rotan Ave 75455. I-30 exit 160, just n. Int corridors. **Pets:** Service with restrictions, supervision.
🛜 ❌ 📶M 💻 〰

△△△ ▼▼▼ Quality Inn **H**
(903) 577-7553. **$62-$70.** 2515 W Ferguson Rd 75455. I-30 exit 160, just s. Ext corridors. **Pets:** Other species. $20 one-time fee/room. Service with restrictions, supervision. (SAVE) 🛜 💻 〰

▼▼▼ Super 8 **M**
(903) 572-9808. **$60-$130.** 204 Lakewood Dr 75455. I-30 exit 162 eastbound; exit 162A westbound, just n, then just w. Ext corridors.
Pets: Accepted. 🛜 💻 〰

MOUNT VERNON

△△△ ▼▼▼ Super 8 of Mount Vernon **H**
(903) 588-2882. **$60-$75.** 401 W I-30 75457. I-30 exit 147; on eastbound frontage road. Ext corridors. **Pets:** Small, dogs only. $10 daily fee/pet. Service with restrictions, supervision. (SAVE) 🛜 💻

NACOGDOCHES

△△△ ▼▼▼ BEST WESTERN Northpark Inn **H**
(936) 560-1906. **$70-$111.** 4809 NW Stallings Dr 75964. Jct US 59 N and Loop 224 exit Westward Dr. Ext corridors. **Pets:** Small, dogs only. $25 one-time fee/pet. Designated rooms, service with restrictions, supervision. (SAVE) 🛜 💻 〰

▼▼▼▼ Super 8 Nacogdoches **H**
(936) 560-2888. **$59-$169.** 3909 South St 75964. On US 59, just s of jct Loop 224. Int corridors. **Pets:** Dogs only. $20 daily fee/pet. Designated rooms, service with restrictions, supervision. 🛜 💻 〰

NAVASOTA

△△△ ▼▼▼ BEST WESTERN Inn of Navasota **H**
(936) 870-4100. **$80-$110, 3 day notice.** 8965 Hwy 6 N 77868. Jct SR 6 and 90; on southeast corner. Ext corridors. **Pets:** $20 one-time fee/pet. Service with restrictions, crate. (SAVE) 🛜 💻 〰

▼▼▼▼ Comfort Inn & Suites **H**
(936) 825-9464. **$90-$95.** 9345 State Hwy 6 Loop S 77868. SR 6 exit SR 105 and 90, 0.5 mi n on E Frontage Rd. Int corridors.
Pets: Accepted. 🛜 ❌ 💻 〰

NEW CANEY

△△△ ▼▼▼▼ BEST WESTERN PLUS New Caney Inn & Suites **H**
(281) 354-7222. **$80-$100.** 22033 N Hwy 59 77357. US 59 northbound exit Community Dr, just e; southbound exit FM 1314, make U-turn. Int corridors. **Pets:** Medium. $100 deposit/pet, $10 daily fee/pet. Designated rooms, service with restrictions, supervision.
(SAVE) 🛜 ❌ 📶M 💻 〰

△△△ ▼▼▼▼ La Quinta Inn & Suites-New Caney **H**
(281) 354-1904. **$83-$166.** 22025 US Hwy 59 77357. US 59 northbound exit Community Dr, just e; exit FM 1314 southbound, U-turn 1 mi n. Int corridors. **Pets:** Service with restrictions, supervision.
(SAVE) 🛜 ❌ 💻 〰

NORTH RICHLAND HILLS

△△△ ▼▼▼ BEST WESTERN NE Mall Inn & Suites **H**
(817) 656-8881. **$80-$140.** 8709 Airport Frwy 76180. SR 121/183 exit Precinct Line Rd eastbound; exit Bedford Euless Rd westbound; on westbound frontage road. Ext corridors. **Pets:** Medium. $20 daily fee/pet. Service with restrictions, crate. (SAVE) 🛜 💻 〰

ODESSA

△△△ ▼▼▼ BEST WESTERN Garden Oasis **H**
(432) 337-3006. **$99-$199.** 110 W I-20 79761. Jct I-20 and US 385 exit 116, just w. Ext/int corridors. **Pets:** Medium. Designated rooms, service with restrictions, supervision. (SAVE) 🛜 💻 〰 ❌

▼▼▼▼ Comfort Suites **H**
(432) 362-1500. **$149-$219.** 4801 E 50th St 79762. Jct JBS Pkwy and 42nd St, 0.5 mi n. Int corridors. **Pets:** Medium. $50 deposit/pet. Service with restrictions. 🛜 ❌ 📶M 💻 〰

▼▼▼▼ La Quinta Inn & Suites Odessa North **H**
(432) 288-9041. **$171-$364.** 4122 Faudree Rd 79765. Jct Loop 338 E and SR 191, 2 mi e. Int corridors. **Pets:** Service with restrictions, supervision. 🛜 ❌ 📶M 💻 〰

▼▼▼▼ La Quinta Inn Odessa **H**
(432) 333-2820. **$107-$243.** 5001 E Business Loop I-20 79761. I-20 exit 121, 0.8 mi n on Loop 338, then just w. Ext corridors. **Pets:** Service with restrictions, supervision. 🛜 💻 〰

▼▼▼ MCM Grande Hotel **H**
(432) 362-2311. **Call for rates.** 6201 E Business Loop I-20 79762. I-20 exit 121, 0.8 mi n on Loop 338, then 1 mi e. Ext/int corridors.
Pets: Accepted. 🛜 ❌ 💻 🍴 〰 ❌

▼▼ Motel 6 Odessa - #439 **M**
(432) 333-4025. **$91-$101.** 200 E I-20 Service Rd 79766. I-20 exit 116; on eastbound frontage road. Ext corridors. **Pets:** Other species. Service with restrictions, supervision. 🛜 〰

△△△ ▼▼▼ Quality Inn & Suites **H**
(432) 333-3931. **$119-$139.** 3001 E Business Loop I-20 79761. I-20 exit 121, 0.7 mi n on Loop 338, then 0.5 mi w. Ext/int corridors.
Pets: Accepted. (SAVE) 🛜 💻 〰 ❌

▼▼▼▼ TownePlace Suites by Marriott **H** 🐾
(432) 362-1077. **$132-$399.** 4412 Tanglewood Ln 79762. Jct JBS Pkwy and 42nd St, 2 blks w to Tanglewood Ln, then just n. Int corridors.
Pets: Medium, other species. $100 one-time fee/room. Service with restrictions. 🛜 ❌ 📶M 💻 〰

OLMITO

▼▼▼▼ La Quinta Inn Brownsville/Olmito **H**
(956) 350-8855. **$60-$156.** 8280 North Expwy 78575. US 77/83 exit SR 511, just e. Int corridors. **Pets:** Service with restrictions, supervision.
🛜 💻 〰

ORANGE

Holiday Inn Express & Suites Orange H
(409) 882-9222. **$89-$129.** 2655 I-10 E 77630. I-10 exit 877 eastbound; exit 876 westbound; on eastbound frontage road. Int corridors. **Pets:** Small. $10 daily fee/pet. Service with restrictions, supervision.
[SAVE] 🛜 🕹M 🛗 🖥 🏊

La Quinta Inn & Suites Orange H
(409) 883-0011. **$83-$166.** 2220 Hwy 62 S 77630. I-10 exit 873, just s. Int corridors. **Pets:** Service with restrictions, supervision.
🛜 ❌ 🛗 🖥 🏊

OZONA

Hillcrest Inn & Suites M
(325) 392-5515. **$60-$80.** 1204 Sheffield Rd/Loop 466 W 76943. I-10 exit 365, 2 blks n to Loop 466, then 1 mi w. Ext corridors. **Pets:** Medium. $15 daily fee/pet. Designated rooms, service with restrictions, supervision.
[SAVE] 🛜 🛗 🖥

PALESTINE

BEST WESTERN Palestine Inn H
(903) 723-4655. **$80-$150.** 1601 W Palestine Ave 75801. Jct US 287/SR 19, 0.7 mi sw on US 79. Ext corridors. **Pets:** Medium. $10 daily fee/pet. Designated rooms, service with restrictions, supervision.
[SAVE] 🛜 🛗 🖥 🏊

Express Inn & Suites M
(903) 729-3151. **$60.** 1100 E Palestine Ave 75801. Jct US 79 and Loop 256, 0.4 mi s on US 79. Ext corridors. **Pets:** Other species. $20 daily fee/room. Service with restrictions, supervision.
[SAVE] 🛜 🛗 🖥 🏊 ❌

La Quinta Inn & Suites Palestine H
(903) 731-1387. **$83-$155.** 3000 S Loop 256 75801. 1.8 mi e of jct US 79 and Loop 256. Int corridors. **Pets:** Service with restrictions, supervision.
🛜 🛗 🖥 🏊

PAMPA

AmericInn Lodge & Suites of Pampa H
(806) 665-4404. **$117-$135.** 1101 N Hobart St 79065. SR 70; jct Hobart and Somerville sts. Int corridors. **Pets:** $15 daily fee/room. Designated rooms, service with restrictions, crate.
[SAVE] 🛜 ❌ 🕹M 🛗 🖥 🏊 ❌

BEST WESTERN Northgate Inn H
(806) 665-0926. **$85-$130.** 2831 Perryton Pkwy 79065. SR 70, 3 mi n. Ext corridors. **Pets:** Accepted. [SAVE] 🛜 🛗 🖥 🏊

PARIS

Americas Best Value Inn Paris H
(903) 785-5566. **$59-$79.** 3755 NE Loop 286 75460. Jct US 82 and E Loop 286, just n. Ext corridors. **Pets:** Other species. $5 daily fee/pet. Designated rooms, service with restrictions. [SAVE] 🛜 🛗 🖥 🏊

PEARLAND

BEST WESTERN Pearland Inn H
(281) 997-2000. **$70-$130.** 1855 N Main St 77581. Jct Loop 8 S and SR 35, 1.5 mi s. Ext corridors. **Pets:** Other species. $20 daily fee/pet. Service with restrictions, supervision. [SAVE] 🛜 🛗 🖥 🏊

La Quinta Inn & Suites Pearland H
(281) 412-5454. **$87-$177.** 9002 Broadway St 77584. Jct SR 288 and 518, 1.6 mi e. Int corridors. **Pets:** Service with restrictions, supervision.
[SAVE] 🛜 ❌ 🕹M 🛗 🖥 🏊

PECOS

BEST WESTERN Swiss Clock Inn M 🐾
(432) 447-2215. **$125-$130.** 133 S Frontage Rd, I-20 79772. I-20 exit 40, just e. Ext corridors. **Pets:** Dogs only. $15 one-time fee/pet, $15 daily fee/pet. Designated rooms, service with restrictions, supervision.
[SAVE] 🛜 🛗 🖥 🍴 🏊

Knights Inn Laura Lodge Motel & Suites M
(432) 445-4924. **$70-$130.** 1000 E Business I-20 79772. I-20 exit 42, 1 mi nw to Business Rt I-20, then 0.5 mi e. Ext corridors. **Pets:** Small. $10 daily fee/pet. Designated rooms, service with restrictions, supervision.
[SAVE] 🛜 🛗 🖥

Oak Tree Inn H
(432) 445-1628. **Call for rates.** 22 N Frontage Rd 79772. I-20 exit 42, just w on north frontage road. Int corridors. **Pets:** Other species. Service with restrictions, supervision. 🛜 ❌ 🛗 🖥

PERRYTON

BEST WESTERN Perryton Inn H
(806) 434-2850. **Call for rates.** 3505 S Main St (US 83) 79070. US 83, 2.2 mi s. Int corridors. **Pets:** Other species. $15 daily fee/pet. Designated rooms, service with restrictions, crate.
[SAVE] 🛜 🕹M 🛗 🖥 🍴 🏊

PHARR

La Quinta Inn & Suites Pharr H
(956) 787-2900. **$83-$155.** 4603 N Cage Blvd 78577. US 281 northbound exit Nolana Loop, just w. Int corridors. **Pets:** Service with restrictions, supervision. 🛜 ❌ 🕹M 🛗 🖥 🏊

PLAINVIEW

BEST WESTERN Conestoga H
(806) 293-9454. **$79-$99.** 600 N I-27 79072. I-27 exit 49, just s of US 70; on eastbound access road. Ext corridors. **Pets:** Accepted.
[SAVE] 🛜 🛗 🖥 🏊

PORT ARANSAS

Beachgate CondoSuites & Motel CO
(361) 749-5900. **$40-$610, 30 day notice.** 2000 On the Beach Dr 78373. Between beach markers 8 and 9; street access on Anchor Rd off 11th St. Ext/int corridors. **Pets:** Accepted. 🛜 ❌ 🛗 🖥 🏊 ❌

BEST WESTERN Ocean Villa H
(361) 749-3010. **$69-$229.** 400 E Ave G 78373. Just se of S Alister St (SR 361). Ext corridors. **Pets:** Accepted. [SAVE] 🛜 🕹M 🛗 🖥 🏊

Plantation Suites & Conference Center M 🌿
(361) 749-3866. **$80-$200.** 1909 Hwy 361 78373. On SR 361, 0.4 mi s. Ext corridors. **Pets:** Medium. $50 one-time fee/room. Service with restrictions, crate. [SAVE] 🛜 ❌ 🛗 🖥 🏊

PORT LAVACA

BEST WESTERN Port Lavaca Inn H
(361) 553-6800. **$99-$139.** 2202 N Hwy 35 77979. Jct US 87 and SR 35, 2.5 mi e. Int corridors. **Pets:** Accepted. [SAVE] 🛜 🛗 🖥 🏊

La Quinta Inn & Suites Port Lavaca H
(361) 552-8800. **$107-$221.** 910 Hwy 35 N 77979. Jct US 87 and SR 35, 2 mi e. Int corridors. **Pets:** Service with restrictions, supervision.
[SAVE] 🛜 ❌ 🕹M 🛗 🖥 🏊

POST

BEST WESTERN Post Inn H
(806) 495-9933. **$87-$138.** 1011 N Broadway 79356. 1 mi n on US 84. Int corridors. **Pets:** Medium. $20 daily fee/pet. Designated rooms, service with restrictions, supervision. [SAVE] 🛜 🛗 🖥 🏊

RANCHO VIEJO

Rancho Viejo Resort & Country Club H
(956) 350-4000. **Call for rates.** 1 Rancho Viejo Dr 78575. US 77/83 exit Rancho Viejo. Ext corridors. **Pets:** Accepted.
🛜 🛗 🖥 🍴 🏊 ❌

RAYMONDVILLE

▼▼▼ **La Quinta Inn & Suites Raymondville** H
(956) 689-4000. **$90-$166.** 128 N Expwy 77 78580. US 77, jct FM 186; on southbound access road. Int corridors. **Pets:** Service with restrictions, supervision. 🛜 ⊠ ᴹ 🛄 ▦ ⇨

REFUGIO

🆑 ▼▼▼ **BEST WESTERN Refugio Inn** H
(361) 526-4600. **$119.** 1007 N Victoria St 78377. Just n of jct US 183 and 77. Int corridors. **Pets:** Accepted. ꜱᴀᴠᴇ 🛜 ⊠ 🛄 ▦ ⇨

RICHLAND HILLS

▼▼▼ **La Quinta Inn & Suites Fort Worth NE Mall** H
(817) 595-4442. **$90-$155.** 653 NE Loop 820 76118. I-820 exit 23, just s of Glenview Dr. Int corridors. **Pets:** Service with restrictions, supervision.
🛜 ⊠ ᴹ 🛄 ▦ ⇨

ROBSTOWN

▼▼▼ **Days Inn** M
(361) 387-8600. **$82-$143.** 650 Hwy 77 S 78380. Just n of jct CR 892 (Lincoln Ave) and US 77. Ext corridors. **Pets:** Small. $10 daily fee/pet. Service with restrictions, supervision. 🛜 🛄 ▦ ⇨

ROCKDALE

🆑 ▼▼▼ **BEST WESTERN Rockdale Inn** H
(512) 446-6163. **$72-$90.** 381 N US Hwy 77 76567. Jct US 77 and 79, just n. Ext corridors. **Pets:** Accepted. ꜱᴀᴠᴇ 🛜 🛄 ▦ ⇨

ROCKPORT

▼▼▼ **Days Inn** M
(361) 729-6379. **$65-$145.** 1212 Laurel St 78382. Jct Laurel St and Business Rt SR 35; center. Ext corridors. **Pets:** Small, dogs only. $15 daily fee/pet. Service with restrictions, supervision. 🛜 🛄 ▦ ⇨

ROUND ROCK

🆑 ▼▼▼ **BEST WESTERN Executive Inn** H
(512) 255-3222. **$76-$99.** 1851 N I-35 78664. I-35 exit 253 northbound; exit 253A (U-turn) southbound. Ext corridors. **Pets:** Other species. $5 daily fee/pet. Service with restrictions. ꜱᴀᴠᴇ 🛜 ᴹ 🛄 ▦ ⇨

▼▼▼ **Candlewood Suites** H
(512) 828-0899. **$89-$119.** 521 S I-35 78664. I-35 exit 252A, just n on northbound frontage road. Int corridors. **Pets:** Accepted. 🛜 🛄 ▦

▼▼ **Extended StayAmerica Austin-Round Rock-N** H
(512) 671-7872. **$54-$69.** 555 S I-35 City Centre Business Park 78664. I-35 exit 252A; on northbound frontage road. Int corridors. **Pets:** $25 daily fee/pet. Designated rooms, service with restrictions. 🛜 🛄 ▦

▼▼▼ **Hampton Inn Austin-Round Rock** H
(512) 248-9100. **$99-$169.** 110 Dell Way 78664. I-35 exit 251; on east frontage road. Int corridors. **Pets:** Accepted. 🛜 ᴹ 🛄 ▦ ⇨

▼▼▼ **Homewood Suites by Hilton** H
(512) 394-9200. **Call for rates.** 2201 S Mays St 78664. I-35 exit 251, just n on E Access Rd to Hesters Crossing, then just e. Int corridors. **Pets:** Medium, other species. $45 one-time fee/pet. Service with restrictions, crate. 🛜 ⊠ ᴹ 🛄 ▦ ⇨ ⊠

▼▼▼ **La Quinta Inn & Suites Austin Round Rock North** H
(512) 255-6666. **$71-$166.** 2004 I-35 N 78681. I-35 exit 254; on west frontage road. Int corridors. **Pets:** Service with restrictions, supervision.
🛜 🛄 ▦ ⇨

▼▼▼ **Residence Inn by Marriott Austin Round Rock** H
(512) 733-2400. **$108-$171.** 2505 S I-35 78664. I-35 exit 250 southbound; exit 251 northbound; on east frontage road. Int corridors.
Pets: Accepted. 🛜 ⊠ ᴹ 🛄 ▦ ⇨ ⊠

▼▼▼ **SpringHill Suites by Marriott** H
(512) 733-6700. **$109-$149.** 2960 Hoppe Tr 78681. I-35 exit 256 southbound; exit 254 northbound; on west frontage road. Int corridors.
Pets: Accepted. 🛜 ⊠ ᴹ 🛄 ▦ ⇨

▼▼▼ **Staybridge Suites Austin-Round Rock** H
(512) 733-0942. **Call for rates.** 520 I-35 S 78681. I-35 exit 252B northbound; exit 252AB southbound; on west frontage road. Int corridors.
Pets: Large. $25 daily fee/pet. Service with restrictions, crate.
🛜 ᴹ 🛄 ▦ ⇨

SALADO

▼▼▼ **Holiday Inn Express Salado** H
(254) 947-4004. **$100-$120.** 1991 N Stagecoach Rd 76571. I-35 exit 286. Int corridors. **Pets:** Accepted. 🛜 ⊠ ᴹ 🛄 ▦ ⇨

▼▼▼ **Stagecoach Inn** H
(254) 947-5111. **$69-$160.** 401 S Stagecoach Rd 76571. I-35 and US 81 exit 284 southbound; exit 283 northbound. Ext corridors. **Pets:** Accepted.
🛜 🛄 ▦ 🍴 ⇨ ⊠

SAN ANGELO

🆑 ▼▼ **BEST WESTERN San Angelo** H
(325) 223-1273. **$85-$125.** 3017 W Loop 306 76904. Loop 306 exit College Hills Blvd, just s. Ext corridors. **Pets:** Medium, dogs only. $15 daily fee/pet. Service with restrictions, supervision. ꜱᴀᴠᴇ 🛜 🛄 ▦ ⇨

▼▼ **Days Inn San Angelo** H
(325) 658-6594. **$50-$85.** 4613 S Jackson St 76903. Jct US 87 and Jackson St. Ext corridors. **Pets:** Medium, dogs only. $25 one-time fee/pet. Service with restrictions, supervision. 🛜 🛄 ▦ 🍴 ⇨

▼▼▼ **La Quinta Inn & Conference Center San Angelo** H
(325) 949-0515. **$78-$166.** 2307 Loop 306 76904. Loop 306 exit Knickerbocker Rd, just s. Ext corridors. **Pets:** Service with restrictions, supervision. 🛜 🛄 ▦ ⇨

▼▼ **Rodeway Inn** H
(325) 944-2578. **Call for rates.** 2502 Loop 306 76904. Loop 306 exit Knickerbocker Rd. Ext corridors. **Pets:** Small, dogs only. Service with restrictions, supervision. 🛜 🛄 ▦ ⇨

▼▼▼ **Staybridge Suites** H
(325) 653-1500. **$144-$162.** 1355 Knickerbocker Rd 76904. US 87 S, 1 mi w. Int corridors. **Pets:** Accepted. 🛜 🛄 ▦ ⇨

SAN ANTONIO METROPOLITAN AREA

FLORESVILLE

🆑 ▼▼▼ **BEST WESTERN Floresville Inn** M ✿
(830) 393-0443. **$135-$145.** 1720 S 10th St 78114. US 181, just s of downtown. Ext corridors. **Pets:** Dogs only. $15 daily fee/pet. Service with restrictions, crate. ꜱᴀᴠᴇ 🛜 🛄 ▦ ⇨

LIVE OAK

▼▼ **La Quinta Inn San Antonio I-35 North at Toepperwein** H
(210) 657-5500. **$59-$144.** 12822 I-35 N 78233. I-35 exit 170B (Toepperwein Rd); on northbound access road. Ext/int corridors. **Pets:** Service with restrictions, supervision. 🛜 🛄 ▦ ⇨

NEW BRAUNFELS

▼▼ ▼▼ **Executive Inn & Suites** M
(830) 625-3932. **$44-$179.** 808 Hwy 46 S 78130. I-35 exit 189, 0.4 mi e. Ext corridors. **Pets:** Small, dogs only. $25 daily fee/pet. Designated rooms, service with restrictions, crate. 📶 🛗 🍴 💻 🏊

▼▼▼▼ **La Quinta Inn & Suites New Braunfels** H
(830) 627-3333. **$77-$199.** 365 Hwy 46 S 78130. I-35 exit 189, just s. Int corridors. **Pets:** Service with restrictions, supervision.
📶 ❌ 🛗 🍴 💻 🏊

▼▼ ▼▼ **Quality Inn & Suites** H
(830) 643-9300. **$69-$189.** 1533 IH-35 N 78130. I-35 exit 190; on southbound access road. Int corridors. **Pets:** Accepted. 📶 🍴 💻 🏊

▼▼ ▼▼ **Ramada New Braunfels** H
(830) 625-8017. **$60-$160.** 1051 I-35 E 78130. I-35 exit 189; on southbound access road. Ext corridors. **Pets:** Small. $25 one-time fee/pet. Service with restrictions, crate. 📶 🛗 🍴 💻 🏊

▼▼ ▼▼ **Super 8-New Braunfels** M 🐾
(830) 629-1155. **$60-$180.** 510 Hwy 46 S 78130. I-35 exit 189, just e. Ext corridors. **Pets:** $25 daily fee/pet. Service with restrictions, crate. 📶 🍴 💻 🏊

🅰🅰🅰 ▼▼ ▼▼ **Wingate by Wyndham** H
(830) 515-4701. **$89-$425.** 245 FM 306 N 78130. I-35 exit 191 (FM 306), just w. Int corridors. **Pets:** Medium, other species. Service with restrictions, supervision. (SAVE) 📶 ❌ 🛗 🍴 💻 🏊

SAN ANTONIO

🅰🅰🅰 ▼▼ ▼▼ **Alamo Inn** M 🐾
(210) 227-2203. **$45-$120.** 2203 E Commerce St 78203. I-37 exit 141A, 1.2 mi e at Commerce St and New Braunfels Ave. Ext corridors. **Pets:** Small, other species. $15 daily fee/pet. Designated rooms, service with restrictions, crate. (SAVE) 📶 🍴 💻

🅰🅰🅰 ▼▼ ▼▼ **Aloft San Antonio Airport** H
(210) 541-8881. **$99-$289.** 838 NW Loop 410 78216. I-410 exit Blanco Rd, just s. Int corridors. **Pets:** Accepted. (SAVE) 📶 ❌ 🍴 💻 🏊

🅰🅰🅰 ▼▼ ▼▼ **Arbor House Suites Bed & Breakfast** BB
(210) 472-2005. **$129-$207, 14 day notice.** 109 Arciniega St 78205. Just s of E Nueva St; between S Presa and S St. Mary's sts; near La Villita Historic District. Ext/int corridors. **Pets:** Medium. Service with restrictions, crate. (SAVE) 📶 ❌ 🍴 💻 🏊

▼▼ ▼▼ **Baymont Inns & Suites** H
(210) 593-0338. **$45-$81.** 9542 I-10 W 78230. I-10 exit Wurzbach Rd, just e on eastbound access road. Ext corridors. **Pets:** Small. Service with restrictions, supervision. 📶 🍴 💻 🏊

🅰🅰🅰 ▼▼ ▼▼ **BEST WESTERN PLUS Posada Ana -Medical Center** H
(210) 691-9550. **$75-$109.** 9411 Wurzbach Rd 78240. I-10 exit 561 (Wurzbach Rd); on eastbound access road. Int corridors. **Pets:** Accepted. (SAVE) 📶 🛗 🍴 💻 🏊

🅰🅰🅰 ▼▼ ▼▼ **BEST WESTERN Posada Ana Inn-Airport** H
(210) 342-1400. **$75-$110.** 8600 Jones Maltsberger Rd 78216. Loop 410 exit 21A (Jones Maltsberger Rd), just s. Int corridors. **Pets:** Large, other species. $10 daily fee/pet. Designated rooms, service with restrictions, crate. (SAVE) 📶 🍴 💻 🏊

▼▼ ▼▼ **Candlewood Suites Hotel** H
(210) 615-0550. **$79-$99.** 9350 I-10 W 78230. I-10 W exit 561 (Wurzbach Rd), between Wurzbach Rd and Medical Dr; eastbound access road. Int corridors. **Pets:** Large. $15 daily fee/room. Service with restrictions, crate. 🛗 🍴 💻 🏊

▼▼ ▼▼ **Candlewood Suites San Antonio Downtown** H
(210) 226-7700. **Call for rates.** 1024 S Laredo St 78204. I-10/35 exit Laredo St; on access road. Int corridors. **Pets:** Accepted.
📶 ❌ 🍴 💻 🏊

▼▼ ▼▼ **Candlewood Suites San Antonio West SeaWorld Area** H
(210) 523-7666. **$89-$129.** 9502 Amelia Pass 78254. Loop 1604 at Braun Rd; on northbound access road. Int corridors. **Pets:** Large, other species. $15 daily fee/room. Service with restrictions, crate.
📶 🍴 💻 🏊

▼▼ ▼▼ **Candlewood Suites Stone Oak Area** H
(210) 545-2477. **$99-$259.** 21103 Encino Commons Blvd 78259. US 281 exit Evans Rd; on southbound access road. Int corridors. **Pets:** Accepted. 📶 ❌ 🍴 💻 🏊

▼▼ ▼▼ **Comfort Inn & Suites** H
(210) 733-8080. **$50-$150.** 6039 IH-10 W 78201. I-10 exit Vance Jackson Rd; on westbound access road. Int corridors. **Pets:** Accepted.
📶 ❌ 🍴 💻 🏊

🅰🅰🅰 ▼▼ ▼▼ **Comfort Inn & Suites Airport** H
(210) 249-2000. **$70-$160.** 8640 Crownhill Blvd 78209. I-410 exit Airport Blvd, just off I-410 eastbound access road; just e of Broadway Ave. Int corridors. **Pets:** Small. $25 one-time fee/pet. Service with restrictions, crate. (SAVE) 📶 🍴 💻 🏊

▼▼ ▼▼ **Comfort Inn-Fiesta** M
(210) 696-4766. **$69-$109.** 6755 N Loop 1604 W 78249. I-10 exit CR 1604 W, 0.5 mi w of La Cantera Blvd. Int corridors. **Pets:** Accepted.
📶 🛗 🍴 💻 🏊

🅰🅰🅰 ▼▼ ▼▼ **Crowne Plaza San Antonio Riverwalk** H
(210) 354-2800. **$79-$259.** 111 Pecan St E 78205. Corner of Pecan and Soledad sts. Int corridors. **Pets:** Accepted.
(SAVE) 📶 ❌ 🍴 💻 🍴 🏊 ❌

🅰🅰🅰 ▼▼ ▼▼ **Days Inn Lackland** H
(210) 675-9690. **$49-$200.** 6815 Hwy 90 W 78227. Loop 410 exit US 90, 0.8 mi e to Military Dr, 0.5 mi e on westbound access road. Ext corridors. **Pets:** Medium, other species. $25 one-time fee/room. Service with restrictions, crate. (SAVE) 📶 🍴 💻 🏊

▼▼ ▼▼ **Drury Inn & Suites Northeast** H
(210) 657-1107. **$104-$224.** 4900 Crestwind Dr 78239. I-35 exit 165 (Walzem Rd); on northbound access road. Int corridors. **Pets:** Service with restrictions, supervision. 📶 🛗 🍴 💻 🏊

▼▼ ▼▼ **Drury Inn & Suites-San Antonio Airport** H
(210) 308-8100. **$105-$199.** 95 NE Loop 410 78216. I-410 exit 21A (Jones Maltsberger Rd), 1.8 mi w of airport. Int corridors. **Pets:** Service with restrictions, supervision. 📶 🛗 🍴 💻 🏊

▼▼ ▼▼ **Drury Inn & Suites San Antonio-La Cantera** H
(210) 696-0800. **$94-$214.** 15806 IH-10 W 78249. I-10 exit Loop 1604; on eastbound access road. Int corridors. **Pets:** Service with restrictions, supervision. 📶 ❌ 🍴 💻 🏊

▼▼ ▼▼ **Drury Inn & Suites-San Antonio North** H
(210) 404-1600. **$94-$194.** 801 N Loop 1604 E 78232. Jct Loop 1604 and US 281, just w. Int corridors. **Pets:** Service with restrictions, supervision. 📶 🍴 💻 🏊

▼▼ ▼▼ **Drury Inn & Suites-San Antonio Northwest** H
(210) 561-2510. **$104-$289.** 9806 I-10 W 78230. I-10 exit 561 (Wurzbach Rd); on southeast corner. Int corridors. **Pets:** Service with restrictions, supervision. 📶 🍴 💻 🏊

▼▼ ▼▼ **Drury Inn & Suites-San Antonio Riverwalk** H
(210) 212-5200. **$139-$229.** 201 N St. Mary's St 78205. Just s of College St. Int corridors. **Pets:** Service with restrictions, supervision.
📶 🛗 🍴 💻 🍴 🏊

▼▼ ▼▼ **Drury Plaza Hotel-San Antonio Riverwalk** H
(210) 270-7799. **$139-$284.** 105 S St. Mary's St 78205. Jct Commerce, St. Mary's and Market sts. Int corridors. **Pets:** Service with restrictions, supervision. 📶 🛗 🍴 💻 🏊

▼▼▼ **Drury Plaza San Antonio North** H
(210) 494-2420. **$99-$204.** 823 N Loop 1604 E 78232. Jct Loop 1604 and US 281, just w. Int corridors. **Pets:** Service with restrictions, supervision. 🛜 ⓜ 🛏 💻 🏊

ⒶⒶⒶ ▼▼▼ **Econo Lodge Downtown South** H
(210) 927-4800. **$59-$149.** 606 Division Ave 78214. I-35 exit 152A (Division Ave); on northbound frontage road. Ext corridors. **Pets:** Small, other species. $100 deposit/room, $25 one-time fee/pet. Service with restrictions, supervision. 🅂🅰🆅🅴 🛜 🛏 💻 🏊

ⒶⒶⒶ ▼▼▼ **Econo Lodge Inn & Suites** M
(210) 229-9220. **$49-$229.** 2755 N Panam Expwy 78208. I-35 N exit 159B (Walters Ave); on southbound access road. Ext corridors. **Pets:** Accepted. 🅂🅰🆅🅴 🛜 🛏 💻 🏊

▼▼ ◈ **Econo Lodge Inn & Suites Fiesta Park** M ❖
(210) 690-5500. **$49-$129.** 13575 I-10 W 78249. I-10 exit 557 westbound; exit 558 eastbound; on westbound access road. Ext corridors. **Pets:** Small, dogs only. $10 daily fee/pet. Designated rooms, service with restrictions, supervision. 🛜 🛏 💻 🏊

ⒶⒶⒶ ▼▼▼ ▼▼▼ **Eilan Hotel Resort & Spa** H
(210) 598-2900. **Call for rates.** 17103 La Cantera Pkwy 78256. I-10 exit 554 (La Cantera Pkwy), just w in Eilan office/shopping complex. Int corridors. **Pets:** Accepted. 🅂🅰🆅🅴 🛜 ✕ 💻 🍴

ⒶⒶⒶ ▼▼▼▼ ▼▼▼ **Emily Morgan Hotel** H ❖
(210) 225-8486. **$149-$429.** 705 E Houston St 78205. Just n of Bonham St. Int corridors. **Pets:** Other species. $75 one-time fee/room. Service with restrictions, crate. 🅂🅰🆅🅴 🛜 ✕ ⓜ 💻 🍴 🏊

▼▼▼▼ **Extended Stay Deluxe-San Antonio-Colonnade** H
(210) 694-1229. **$64-$79.** 4331 Spectrum One 78230. I-10 exit 561 (Wurzbach Rd), just nw. Int corridors. **Pets:** $25 daily fee/pet. Designated rooms, service with restrictions. 🛜 🛏 💻 🏊

▼▼▼▼ **The Fairmount Hotel** H
(210) 224-8800. **Call for rates.** 401 S Alamo St 78205. Opposite convention center and Hemisfair Plaza. Ext/int corridors. **Pets:** Accepted.
🛜 ✕ 🛏 🍴 ✕

ⒶⒶⒶ ▼▼▼▼ ▼▼▼ **Grand Hyatt San Antonio** H ❖
(210) 224-1234. **$90-$324.** 600 E Market St 78205. I-37 exit 141A (Market St); between S Alamo St and I-37. Int corridors. **Pets:** Other species. $35 one-time fee/pet. Designated rooms, service with restrictions, crate.
🄴🄲🄾 🅂🅰🆅🅴 🛜 ⓜ 🛏 💻 🍴 🏊

▼▼▼▼ **Hawthorne Suites by Wyndham** H
(210) 561-9660. **$99-$199.** 4041 Bluemel Rd 78240. I-10 exit 561 (Wurzbach Rd), 0.3 mi w on eastbound access road; set back from interstate. Ext corridors. **Pets:** Small. $15 daily fee/pet. Designated rooms, service with restrictions, supervision. 🛜 ✕ 🛏 💻 🏊 ✕

▼▼▼▼ **Hilton Hill Country Hotel & Spa** H
(210) 509-9800. **$99-$159.** 9800 Westover Hills Blvd 78251. Between Loop 410 and 1604, just off CR 151. Int corridors. **Pets:** Accepted.
🛜 ✕ ⓜ 🛏 💻 🍴 🏊 ✕

ⒶⒶⒶ ▼▼▼▼ **The Historic Menger Hotel** H
(210) 223-4361. **$119-$299.** 204 Alamo Plaza 78205. Just s of the Alamo. Int corridors. **Pets:** Medium. $100 one-time fee/pet. Service with restrictions, crate. 🅂🅰🆅🅴 🛜 ✕ 🛏 🍴 🏊 ✕

▼▼▼▼ **Holiday Inn Express-San Antonio Airport** H
(210) 308-6700. **$99-$129.** 91 NE Loop 410 78216. Loop 410 exit 21A (Jones Maltsberger Rd) eastbound; exit 20B westbound; between San Pedro Ave and Jones Maltsberger Rd; on westbound access road. Int corridors. **Pets:** Medium, other species. Service with restrictions, crate.
🛜 ⓜ 🛏 💻 🏊

ⒶⒶⒶ ▼▼▼▼ **Holiday Inn Northwest-SeaWorld** H
(210) 520-2508. **$79-$219.** 10135 State Hwy 151 78251. I-410 exit SR 151, 3 mi n on northbound access road. Int corridors. **Pets:** Accepted.
🅂🅰🆅🅴 🛜 ✕ ⓜ 🛏 💻 🍴 🏊

ⒶⒶⒶ ▼▼▼▼ **Holiday Inn San Antonio International Airport** H
(210) 349-9900. **$79-$159.** 77 NE Loop 410 78216. I-410 exit 20B (McCullough St); on westbound access road. Int corridors.
Pets: Accepted. 🅂🅰🆅🅴 🛜 🛏 💻 🍴 🏊

▼▼▼▼ **Home2 Suites by Hilton San Antonio Downtown-Riverwalk** H
(210) 354-4366. **$129-$169.** 603 Navarro St 78205. Jct E Houston St. Int corridors. **Pets:** Accepted. 🛜 ✕ 🛏 💻 🏊

▼▼▼ **Homestead Studio Suites Hotel-San Antonio-Airport** M
(210) 491-9009. **$44-$59.** 1015 Central Pkwy S 78232. I-410 exit US 281 (San Pedro Ave), just n of Bitters Rd; on northbound access road. Ext corridors. **Pets:** $25 daily fee/pet. Designated rooms, service with restrictions. 🛜 🛏 💻 🏊

ⒶⒶⒶ ▼▼▼▼ **Hotel Contessa** H
(210) 229-9222. **Call for rates.** 306 W Market St 78205. At St. Mary's St. Int corridors. **Pets:** Accepted.
🅂🅰🆅🅴 🛜 ✕ 🛏 💻 🍴 🏊 ✕

▼▼▼▼ **Hotel Havana** CI
(210) 222-2008. **Call for rates.** 1015 Navarro St 78205. Just s of N St. Mary's St. Int corridors. **Pets:** Accepted. 🛜 ✕ 🛏 🍴

▼▼▼▼ **Hotel Indigo Riverwalk** H
(210) 527-1900. **$99-$139.** 830 N St. Mary's St 78205. Just n of Navarro St. Int corridors. **Pets:** Accepted. 🛜 ✕ 🛏 💻 🏊

ⒶⒶⒶ ▼▼▼▼▼ **Hyatt Regency Hill Country Resort and Spa** H
(210) 647-1234. **$117-$360, 3 day notice.** 9800 Hyatt Resort Dr 78251. Between Loop 410 and 1604, just off CR 151 exit Hyatt Resort Dr. Int corridors. **Pets:** Accepted.
🄴🄲🄾 🅂🅰🆅🅴 🛜 ⓜ 🛏 💻 🍴 🏊 ✕

ⒶⒶⒶ ▼▼▼▼ **Hyatt Regency San Antonio** H ❖
(210) 222-1234. **$90-$324.** 123 Losoya St 78205. Between College and Crockett sts. Int corridors. **Pets:** Medium, other species. $35 daily fee/pet. Service with restrictions, supervision.
🄴🄲🄾 🅂🅰🆅🅴 🛜 ✕ 💻 🍴 🏊

▼▼ ▼ **Inn on the Riverwalk** BB
(210) 225-6333. **Call for rates.** 129 Woodward Pl 78204. Just n of W Cesar E Chavez Blvd. Ext/int corridors. **Pets:** Accepted.
🛜 ✕ 🛏 💻

ⒶⒶⒶ ▼▼▼▼ **La Quinta Inn & Suites** H
(210) 447-8000. **$66-$188.** 11155 W Loop 1604 N 78023. On W Loop 1604 access road, just w of Bandera Rd. Int corridors. **Pets:** Service with restrictions, supervision. 🅂🅰🆅🅴 🛜 ✕ ⓜ 🛏 💻 🏊

▼▼▼▼ **La Quinta Inn & Suites Dominion** H
(210) 564-6700. **$77-$188.** 25042 IH-10 W 78257. I-10 exit 550 (Johns Rd), just e; on westbound access road. Int corridors. **Pets:** Service with restrictions, supervision. 🛜 ✕ 🛏 💻 🏊

▼▼▼▼ **La Quinta Inn & Suites-Fiesta Texas** H
(210) 696-0100. **$71-$188.** 5622 Utex Blvd 78249. I-10 exit Loop 1604, 0.7 mi e; on eastbound access road. Int corridors. **Pets:** Service with restrictions, supervision. 🛜 ✕ ⓜ 🛏 💻 🏊

▼▼▼▼ **La Quinta Inn & Suites San Antonio Airport** H
(210) 342-3738. **$83-$155.** 850 Halm Blvd 78216. I-410 exit US 281 S; southwest corner. Int corridors. **Pets:** Service with restrictions, supervision.
🛜 ⓜ 🛏 💻 🏊

▼▼▼▼ **La Quinta Inn & Suites San Antonio Convention Center** H
(210) 222-9181. **$119-$299.** 303 Blum St 78202. 0.5 mi ne. Ext/int corridors. **Pets:** Service with restrictions, supervision.
🛜 ⓜ 🛏 💻 🏊

▼▼▼▼ La Quinta Inn & Suites San Antonio Downtown 🅷

(210) 212-5400. **$83-$210.** 100 Cesar E Chavez Blvd 78204. I-35 exit 155B (Cesar E Chavez Blvd), 3 blks e of jct E Flores St. Int corridors. **Pets:** Service with restrictions, supervision. 🛜 🕭ᴹ 📧 📺 🏊

▼▼▼▼ La Quinta Inn & Suites San Antonio North Stone Oak 🅷

(210) 497-0506. **$95-$232.** 18502 Hardy Oak Blvd 78258. Jct Loop 1604 and US 281, just w. Int corridors. **Pets:** Service with restrictions, supervision. 🛜 ✖ 🕭ᴹ 📧 📺 🏊

🆂🆅🆅𝄜 ▼▼▼ La Quinta Inn San Antonio AlamoDome South 🅷

(210) 337-7171. **$102-$177.** 3180 Goliad Rd 78223. I-37 exit 135 (Brooks City Base/SE Military Dr), just w of interstate. Int corridors. **Pets:** Service with restrictions, supervision.

SAVE 🛜 ✖ 📧 📺 🏊

▼▼▼▼ La Quinta Inn San Antonio I-10 East 🅷

(210) 661-4545. **$78-$188.** 6075 IH-10 E Foster Rd 78219. I-10 exit 583 (Foster Rd); on westbound access road. Int corridors. **Pets:** Service with restrictions, supervision. 🛜 🕭ᴹ 📧 📺 🏊

▼▼ La Quinta Inn San Antonio I-35 North At Rittman Rd 🅷

(210) 653-6619. **$59-$144.** 6410 I-35 78218. I-35 exit 164A (Rittman Rd); on northbound access road. Ext corridors. **Pets:** Service with restrictions, supervision. 🛜 📧 📺 🏊

▼▼ La Quinta Inn San Antonio Lackland 🅷

(210) 674-3200. **$78-$144.** 6511 Military Dr W 78227. Sw of jct US 90 and Military Dr W. Ext corridors. **Pets:** Service with restrictions, supervision. 🛜 📧 📺 🏊

▼▼ La Quinta Inn San Antonio Market Square 🅷

(210) 271-0001. **$71-$188.** 900 Dolorosa St 78207. I-10/35 exit Cesar E Chavez Blvd, just n on Santa Rosa St, then just w on Nueva St. Ext corridors. **Pets:** Service with restrictions, supervision.

🛜 🕭ᴹ 📧 📺 🏊

▼▼ La Quinta Inn San Antonio SeaWorld/Ingram Park 🅷

(210) 680-8883. **$59-$206.** 7134 NW Loop 410 78238. I-410 exit 10 (Culebra Rd); on eastbound access road. Ext corridors. **Pets:** Service with restrictions, supervision. 🛜 📧 📺 🏊

▼▼ La Quinta Inn San Antonio South Park 🅷

(210) 922-2111. **$63-$144.** 7202 S Pan Am 78224. I-35 exit 150A (Military Dr) northbound; exit 150B southbound; se of jct I-35 and Military Dr SW. Ext corridors. **Pets:** Service with restrictions, supervision.

🛜 🕭ᴹ 📧 📺 🏊

▼▼ La Quinta Inn San Antonio Vance Jackson 🅼

(210) 734-7931. **$59-$133.** 5922 I-10 W 78201. I-10 exit 565B eastbound; exit 565C (Vance Jackson Rd) westbound; on eastbound access road. Ext corridors. **Pets:** Service with restrictions, supervision.

🛜 📧 📺 🏊

🆂🆅🆅𝄜 ▼▼▼▼ Marriott San Antonio Plaza 🅷

(210) 229-1000. **$109-$239.** 555 S Alamo St 78205. Opposite convention center and Hemisfair Plaza. Int corridors. **Pets:** Accepted.

SAVE 🛜 ✖ 🕭ᴹ 📧 📺 🍽 🏊 ✖

🆂🆅🆅𝄜 ▼▼▼ ▼▼▼ Mokara Hotel & Spa 🅷

(210) 396-5800. **$259-$459.** 212 W Crockett St 78205. Between St. Mary's and Navarro sts; on River Walk. Int corridors. **Pets:** Accepted.

SAVE 🛜 ✖ 🕭ᴹ 📺 🍽 🏊 ✖

▼▼▼ Motel 6 - #1122 🅼

(210) 225-1111. **$55-$139.** 211 N Pecos St 78207. I-10/35 exit 155B (Pecos St); on south access road. Ext corridors. **Pets:** Other species. Service with restrictions, supervision. 🛜 📧 🏊

▼▼ Motel 6 - #4341 🅷

(210) 447-9000. **Call for rates.** 126 Kenley Pl 78232. US 281 exit Brook Hollow Blvd, just n on northbound access road. Int corridors. **Pets:** Other species. Service with restrictions, supervision. 🛜 🕭ᴹ 📧 🏊

▼▼ Motel 6 - #651 🅼

(210) 673-9020. **$45-$85.** 2185 SW Loop 410 78227. I-410 exit 7 (Marbach Rd), 0.7 mi w; on westbound access road. Ext corridors. **Pets:** Other species. Service with restrictions, supervision. 🛜 📧 🏊

▼▼ Motel 6 East - #183 🅼

(210) 333-1850. **$41-$75.** 138 N WW White Rd 78219. I-10 exit 580 (WW White Rd), just off westbound access road. Ext corridors. **Pets:** Other species. Service with restrictions, supervision. 🛜 🏊

▼▼ Motel 6 Fort Sam Houston - #1350 🅼

(210) 661-8791. **$45-$65.** 5522 N Pan Am Expwy 78218. I-35/410 exit 164 (Rittman Rd), just s on northbound access road; just off Goldfield St. Ext corridors. **Pets:** Other species. Service with restrictions, supervision. 🛜 📺 🏊

▼▼▼ Motel 6 - Medical Center South - #4429 🅷

(210) 616-0030. **Call for rates.** 7500 Louis Pasteur Dr 78229. I-410 exit 14C (Babcock Rd), 1 mi nw, then 0.5 mi n. Int corridors. **Pets:** Other species. Service with restrictions, supervision. 🛜 ✖ 🕭ᴹ 🏊

🆂🆅🆅𝄜 ▼▼▼ ▼▼▼ Omni La Mansión del Rio 🅷 🐾

(210) 518-1000. **$169-$309.** 112 College St 78205. Just s on the River Walk. Ext/int corridors. **Pets:** Small, dogs only. $50 one-time fee/pet. Designated rooms, service with restrictions, crate.

SAVE 🛜 📧 📺 🍽 🏊

🆂🆅🆅𝄜 ▼▼▼ ▼▼▼ Omni San Antonio Hotel 🅷

(210) 691-8888. **$109-$219.** 9821 Colonnade Blvd 78230. I-10 exit Wurzbach Rd; on westbound access road. Int corridors. **Pets:** Accepted.

SAVE 🛜 📧 🍽 🏊 ✖

▼▼▼ Pear Tree Inn by Drury-San Antonio Northeast 🅷

(210) 654-1144. **$74-$149.** 8300 I-35 N 78239. I-35 exit 165 (Walzem Rd); northbound access road. Ext/int corridors. **Pets:** Service with restrictions, supervision. 🛜 📧 📺 🏊

▼▼ Pear Tree Inn San Antonio Airport 🅷

(210) 366-9300. **$75-$144.** 143 NE Loop 410 78216. I-410 W exit 21 (Jones Maltsberger Rd); between Airport Blvd and Jones Maltsberger Rd; on westbound access road. Int corridors. **Pets:** Service with restrictions, supervision. 🛜 📧 📺 🏊

▼▼ Quality Inn & Suites 🅷

(210) 226-4361. **$59-$129.** 3855 I-35 N 78219. I-35 exit 162 (Binz-Engleman Rd) southbound; exit 161 northbound, on southbound access road. Ext corridors. **Pets:** Accepted. 🛜 📧 📺 🍽 🏊

🆂🆅🆅𝄜 ▼▼▼ Quality Inn & Suites Northwoods 🅷

(210) 545-5400. **$90-$110.** 1505 Bexar Crossing 78232. US 281, Loop 1604 (Anderson Loop), 0.5 mi s on southbound access road. Int corridors. **Pets:** Small. $25 one-time fee/pet. Designated rooms, service with restrictions, supervision. **SAVE** 🛜 🕭ᴹ 📧 📺 🏊

🆂🆅🆅𝄜 ▼▼▼ Quality Inn Medical 🅷

(210) 684-8606. **$69-$119.** 4 Piano Pl 78228. I-410 exit Evers Rd westbound, U-turn; exit 14 (Callahan Rd/Babcock Rd) eastbound. Ext corridors. **Pets:** Small, dogs only. $25 daily fee/pet. Designated rooms, service with restrictions, supervision. **SAVE** 🛜 📧 📺 🏊

▼▼▼ Quality Inn Six Flags Area 🅷

(210) 561-9058. **$59-$199.** 11010 I-10 W 78230. I-10 exit 560 westbound; exit 559 (Huebner Rd) eastbound. Int corridors. **Pets:** Accepted. 🛜 📧 📺 🏊

🆂🆅🆅𝄜 ▼▼▼ Red Roof Inn 🅷

(210) 333-9430. **$55-$120.** 4403 I-10 E 78219. I-10 exit 580 (WW White Rd); on westbound access road. Ext corridors. **Pets:** Large, other species. Service with restrictions, supervision.

SAVE 🛜 📧 📺 🍽 🏊

AAA ▼▼▼ Red Roof Inn Lackland **H**
(210) 675-4120. **$60-$140.** 6861 Hwy 90 W 78227. Ne of jct US 90 and Military Dr W; access via Renwick St, off Military Dr, just n of jct US 90. Ext corridors. **Pets:** Large, other species. Service with restrictions, supervision. **SAVE** 🛜 ✕ 🛏

AAA ▼▼▼ Red Roof Inn-San Antonio Airport **H**
(210) 340-4055. **$50-$100.** 333 Wolfe Rd 78216. Just s of US 281 at Isom Rd; on southbound access road. Ext/int corridors. **Pets:** Large, other species. Service with restrictions, supervision. **SAVE** 🛜 🛏

AAA ▼▼▼ Red Roof Inn San Antonio (Downtown) **H**
(210) 229-9973. **$69-$199.** 1011 E Houston St 78205. I-37 exit 141 northbound; exit 141B southbound. Int corridors. **Pets:** Large, other species. Service with restrictions, supervision. **SAVE** 🛜 🛏 🖥 🏊

AAA ▼▼▼ Red Roof Inn San Antonio
(NW-SeaWorld) **H**
(210) 509-3434. **$49-$89.** 6880 NW Loop 410 78238. I-410 exit 11 (Alamo Downs Pkwy); on eastbound access road. Ext/int corridors. **Pets:** Large, other species. Service with restrictions, supervision.
SAVE 🛜 ♿ 🛏 🏊

▼▼▼ Residence Inn by Marriott Alamo Plaza **H**
(210) 212-5555. **$139-$189.** 425 Bonham St 78205. I-37/281 exit Commerce St, just w to Bowie St, then 4 blks n. Int corridors. **Pets:** Large. $100 one-time fee/room. Service with restrictions, crate.
🛜 ✕ 🛏 🖥 🏊

AAA ▼▼▼ Residence Inn by Marriott North San
Antonio **H**
(210) 490-1333. **$109-$149.** 1115 N SR 1604 E 78232. Loop 1604, just w of US 281; on westbound access road. Int corridors. **Pets:** Accepted.
SAVE 🛜 ✕ ♿ 🛏 🖥 🏊 ✕

▼▼▼ Residence Inn by Marriott San Antonio-Airport **H**
(210) 805-8118. **$99-$159.** 1014 NE Loop 410 78209. Loop 410 exit Broadway St, 0.4 mi e on eastbound access road. Ext corridors. **Pets:** Other species. $100 one-time fee/room. Service with restrictions, crate. **ECO** 🛜 ✕ 🛏 🖥 🏊 ✕

AAA ▼▼▼ Residence Inn by Marriott San Antonio
Downtown/Market Square **H**
(210) 231-6000. **$121-$161.** 628 S Santa Rosa Blvd 78204. I-10/35 exit Cesar E Chavez Blvd, 0.5 mi e. Int corridors. **Pets:** Accepted.
SAVE 🛜 ✕ 🛏 🖥 🏊 ✕

▼▼▼ Residence Inn by Marriott San Antonio Northwest at
The RIM **H**
(210) 561-0200. **$129-$149.** 5707 Rim Pass Dr 78257. I-10 exit 555 (La Cantera Pkwy); in Rim Shopping Complex; on westbound access road. Int corridors. **Pets:** Accepted. 🛜 ✕ ♿ 🛏 🖥 🏊 ✕

▼▼▼ Residence Inn by Marriott SeaWorld/Lackland
AFB **H**
(210) 509-3100. **$109-$189.** 2838 Cinema Ridge 78238. I-410 exit 10 (Ingram Rd); on eastbound access road. Int corridors. **Pets:** Accepted.
🛜 ✕ ♿ 🛏 🖥 🏊 ✕

▼ Rodeway Inn-Six Flags Fiesta **M**
(210) 698-3991. **$50-$99.** 19793 I-10 W 78257. I-10 exit 554 (Camp Bullis Rd), westbound exit 552 (Dominion) and U-turn onto eastbound access road. Ext corridors. **Pets:** Medium. $15 daily fee/pet. Service with restrictions, supervision. 🛜 🛏 🏊

AAA ▼▼▼ ▼▼▼ Sheraton Gunter **H** 🐾
(210) 227-3241. **$99-$329, 3 day notice.** 205 E Houston St 78205. Center. Int corridors. **Pets:** Medium, dogs only. Designated rooms, service with restrictions, supervision. **SAVE** 🛜 ✕ 🖥 🍴 🏊 ✕

▼▼▼ Staybridge Suites Downtown Convention
Center **H**
(210) 444-2700. **$109-$169.** 123 Hoefgen Blvd 78205. In historic downtown Sunset Station. Int corridors. **Pets:** Accepted. 🛜 🛏 🖥 🏊

▼▼▼ Staybridge Suites NW Near Six Flags Fietsa **H**
(210) 691-3443. **Call for rates.** 6919 N Loop 1604 W 78249. Loop 1604 exit La Cantera Pkwy; on westbound frontage road. Int corridors. **Pets:** Accepted. 🛜 ✕ 🛏 🖥 🏊

▼▼▼ Staybridge Suites San Antonio-Airport **H**
(210) 341-3220. **$119-$129.** 66 NE Loop 410 78216. I-410 exit 20B (McCullough St); on eastbound access road. Int corridors. **Pets:** Accepted. 🛜 ♿ 🛏 🖥 🏊

▼▼▼ Staybridge Suites San Antonio NW-Colonnade **H**
(210) 558-9009. **$149-$249.** 4320 Spectrum One 78230. I-10 exit 561 (Wurzbach Rd), 0.3 mi w; off westbound access road. Int corridors. **Pets:** Accepted. 🛜 🛏 🖥 🏊

▼▼▼ Staybridge Suites San Antonio-Stone Oak **H**
(210) 497-0100. **$99-$140.** 808 N Loop 1604 E 78232. On Loop 1604, 0.4 mi w of US 281. Int corridors. **Pets:** Large, other species. $150 one-time fee/room. Service with restrictions, crate.
🛜 ✕ ♿ 🛏 🖥 🏊

▼▼ Super 8 on Roland **H**
(210) 798-5500. **$60-$90.** 302 Roland Ave 78210. I-10 exit 577 (Roland Ave) eastbound. Ext corridors. **Pets:** Accepted. 🛜 🛏 🖥 🏊

▼▼ Super 8-Six Flags Fiesta **H**
(210) 696-6916. **$50-$90.** 5319 Casa Bella 78249. I-10 exit 557 westbound; exit 558 eastbound; on westbound access road. Int corridors. **Pets:** Accepted. 🛜 🛏 🖥 🏊

▼▼▼ TownePlace Suites by Marriott San Antonio
Downtown **H**
(210) 271-3444. **$109-$189.** 409 E Houston St 78205. 1 blk w of Broadway St. Int corridors. **Pets:** Accepted. 🛜 ✕ 🛏 🖥 🏊

▼▼▼ TownePlace Suites by Marriott San Antonio
Northwest **H**
(210) 694-5100. **$94-$149.** 5014 Prue Rd 78240. I-10 exit 560 westbound; exit 559 (Huebner Rd) eastbound, 1 blk sw to Fredericksburg Rd, then just n. Int corridors. **Pets:** Accepted. 🛜 ✕ ♿ 🛏 🖥 🏊

AAA ▼▼▼ ▼▼▼ The Westin Riverwalk **H** 🐾
(210) 224-6500. **$159-$539, 3 day notice.** 420 W Market St 78205. 2 blks w of Navarro St. Int corridors. **Pets:** Medium. $125 deposit/room. Service with restrictions, supervision.
SAVE 🛜 ✕ ♿ 🖥 🍴 🏊 ✕

SCHERTZ
▼▼▼ Fairfield Inn & Suites by Marriott **H**
(210) 658-1466. **$85-$132.** 5008 Corridor Loop Rd 78154. I-35 exit 175 (Natural Bridge Cavern Rd); just off northbound frontage road. Int corridors. **Pets:** Accepted. 🛜 ✕ 🛏 🖥 🏊

SEGUIN
▼▼▼ La Quinta Inn & Suites Seguin **H**
(830) 372-0567. **$95-$232.** 1501 Hwy 46 N 78155. I-10 exit 607 (SR 46). Int corridors. **Pets:** Service with restrictions, supervision.
🛜 ♿ 🛏 🏊

▼▼ Super 8 of Seguin **H**
(830) 379-6888. **$85-$200.** 1525 N Hwy 46 78155. I-10 exit 607 (SR 46); on eastbound frontage road. Int corridors. **Pets:** Small. $15 daily fee/pet. Designated rooms, service with restrictions, supervision. 🛜 🛏 🖥

SELMA

▼▼▼▼ Comfort Inn & Suites H
(210) 447-2305. **$79-$99.** 15771 IH 35 N 78154. I-35 exit 174A (Selma Shertz CR 1518); on southbound access road. Int corridors.
Pets: Accepted. 🛰 ⊗ 🛅 🖵 🌤

UNIVERSAL CITY

⚓ ▼▼▼▼ Hawthorn Suites by Wyndham H
(210) 655-9491. **$89-$149, 3 day notice.** 13101 E Loop 1604 N 78233. Loop 1604 at Pat Booker Rd; 0.8 mi e of I-35. Ext corridors.
Pets: Accepted. 💲 🛰 🛅 🖵 🌤

END METROPOLITAN AREA

SAN MARCOS

▼▼▼ Days Inn H
(512) 353-5050. **$55-$170.** 1005 I-35 N 78666. I-35 exit 205 northbound; exit 204B southbound, jct SR 80; on southbound frontage road. Ext corridors. **Pets:** Small, dogs only. $10 daily fee/pet. Designated rooms, service with restrictions, supervision. 🛰 🛅 🖵 🌤

⚓ ▼▼▼ Econo Lodge H
(512) 353-5300. **$45-$120.** 811 S Guadalupe St 78666. I-35 exit 204 northbound; exit 204A southbound; on west frontage road. Ext corridors. **Pets:** Medium. $15 one-time fee/room. Service with restrictions, supervision. 💲 🛰 🛅 🖵 🌤

▼▼▼▼ Embassy Suites-San Marcos Hotel, Spa and Conference Center H 🐾
(512) 392-6450. **$159-$244.** 1001 E McCarty Ln 78666. I-35 exit 201; on east frontage road. Int corridors. **Pets:** Medium. $50 one-time fee/room. Designated rooms, service with restrictions, supervision.
🛰 🔊 🛅 🖵 🍴 🌤 ⊗

▼▼▼▼ La Quinta Inn San Marcos H
(512) 392-8800. **$59-$177.** 1619 I-35 N 78666. I-35 exit 206 southbound, 0.5 mi s; on west frontage road; exit northbound, 1 mi n to turnaround to west frontage road, then 1.5 mi s. Ext/int corridors. **Pets:** Service with restrictions, supervision. 🛰 🔊 🛅 🖵 🌤

⚓ ▼▼▼ Ramada Limited H
(512) 395-8000. **$55-$900.** 1701 I-35 N 78666. I-35 exit 206 southbound, 0.4 mi s on west frontage road; exit northbound, 1 mi n to turnaround for west frontage road, then 1.4 mi s. Ext corridors. **Pets:** Small, dogs only. $20 daily fee/pet. Service with restrictions, crate.
💲 🛰 🛅 🖵 🌤

▼▼ Rodeway Inn H
(512) 353-8011. **Call for rates.** 1635 Aquarena Springs Dr 78666. I-35 exit 206, 0.5 mi s. Ext corridors. **Pets:** Accepted. 🛰 🛅 🖵 🌤

▼▼ Travelodge San Marcos H
(512) 396-5665. **$40-$250.** 1611 I-35 N 78666. I-35 exit 206; on southbound frontage road. Ext corridors. **Pets:** Medium. $10 daily fee/pet. Service with restrictions, supervision. 🛰 🛅 🖵 🌤

SCHULENBURG

⚓ ▼▼▼ BEST WESTERN PLUS Schulenburg Inn & Suites H
(979) 743-2030. **$79-$177, 3 day notice.** 101 Huser Blvd 78956. I-10 exit 674, just s. Int corridors. **Pets:** Medium, other species. $10 daily fee/pet. Service with restrictions, supervision.
💲 🛰 ⊗ 🔊 🛅 🌤

SEALY

⚓ ▼▼▼ Americas Best Value Inn of Sealy H
(979) 885-3707. **$70-$95, 3 day notice.** 2107 Hwy 36 S 77474. I-10 exit 720. Ext corridors. **Pets:** Very small, other species. $20 deposit/pet, $20 one-time fee/pet. Service with restrictions, supervision.
💲 🛰 🛅 🖵 🌤

▼▼ Super 8 H
(979) 885-2121. **$78-$108.** 267 Gebhardt Rd 77474. I-10 exit 720. Ext corridors. **Pets:** Small, other species. $10 daily fee/pet. Designated rooms, supervision. 🛰 🔊 🛅 🖵 🌤

SEMINOLE

⚓ ▼▼▼ Seminole Inn M
(432) 758-9881. **Call for rates.** 2200 Hobbs Hwy 79360. 1.5 mi w on US 62 and 180. Ext corridors. **Pets:** Accepted. 💲 🛰 🛅 🖵

SHAMROCK

⚓ ▼▼▼▼ BEST WESTERN PLUS Shamrock Inn & Suites H
(806) 256-1001. **$110.** 1802 N Main St 79079. I-40 exit 163, just n. Int corridors. **Pets:** Large, other species. $10 daily fee/pet. Designated rooms, service with restrictions, supervision.
💲 🛰 ⊗ 🔊 🛅 🖵 🌤

⚓ ▼ Western Motel M
(806) 256-3244. **$59-$129.** 104 E 12th St 79079. Business Rt I-40 and US 83. Ext corridors. **Pets:** Small. $15 daily fee/pet. Designated rooms, service with restrictions, supervision. 💲 🛰 🛅 🖵

SHERMAN

▼▼▼▼ Comfort Suites of Sherman H
(903) 893-0499. **$89-$114.** 2900 US Hwy 75 N 75090. US 75 exit 63, 0.3 mi s of jct US 82. Int corridors. **Pets:** Accepted.
🛰 ⊗ 🛅 🖵 🌤

▼▼▼▼ La Quinta Inn & Suites Sherman Denison H
(903) 870-1122. **$78-$151.** 2912 US 75 N 75090. US 75 exit 63; on southbound frontage road. Int corridors. **Pets:** Service with restrictions, supervision. 🛰 🛅 🖵 🌤

SINTON

⚓ ▼▼▼ BEST WESTERN Sinton M
(361) 364-2882. **$99-$110.** 8108 US Hwy 77 78387. 0.5 mi s of SR 188. Ext corridors. **Pets:** Accepted. 💲 🛰 🛅 🖵 🌤

SMITHVILLE

▼▼ Americas Best Value Inn & Suites M
(512) 237-2040. **$75-$99.** 1503 Dorothy Nichol Ln 78957. Jct SR 71 and Dorothy Nichol Ln. Ext corridors. **Pets:** Accepted. 🛰 🛅 🖵 🌤

SNYDER

⚓ ▼▼▼ Purple Sage Motel M
(325) 573-5491. **$55-$75.** 1501 E Coliseum Dr 79549. 1 mi w on US 180 from jct US 84. Ext corridors. **Pets:** Service with restrictions, supervision. 💲 🛰 🛅 🖵 🌤

SONORA

⚓ ▼▼▼ BEST WESTERN Sonora Inn H
(325) 387-9111. **Call for rates.** 270 Hwy 277 N 76950. I-10 exit 400, just s. Ext corridors. **Pets:** Medium, other species. $10 daily fee/pet. Designated rooms, service with restrictions, crate. 💲 🛰 🛅 🖵 🌤

⚓ ▼ Holiday Host Motel M
(325) 387-2532. **$45-$55.** 127 Loop 467 (Hwy 290) 76950. Loop 467 exit 404 westbound, 3 mi w; exit 399 eastbound, 3 mi e. Ext corridors. **Pets:** Very small. Designated rooms, no service, supervision.
💲 🛰 🛅 🖵 🌤

SOUTH PADRE ISLAND

The Inn at South Padre H
(956) 761-5658. **Call for rates.** 1709 Padre Blvd 78597. 0.9 mi n of Queen Isabella Cswy; corner of W Palm St. Int corridors. **Pets:** Accepted.

AAA Isla Grand Beach Resort H
(956) 761-6511. **$89-$625, 3 day notice.** 500 Padre Blvd 78597. 0.3 mi n of Queen Isabella Cswy. Ext/int corridors. **Pets:** Medium. $25 daily fee/room. Designated rooms, service with restrictions.

La Copa Inn Beach Hotel H
(956) 761-6000. **$50-$400, 3 day notice.** 350 Padre Blvd 78597. Just s of Queen Isabella Cswy. Int corridors. **Pets:** Accepted.

La Quinta Inn & Suites South Padre Beach H
(956) 772-7000. **$84-$299.** 7000 Padre Blvd 78597. 3 mi n of Queen Isabella Cswy. Int corridors. **Pets:** Service with restrictions, supervision.

Motel 6 South Padre Island - #1237 M
(956) 761-7911. **$35-$115.** 4013 Padre Blvd 78597. 2 mi n of Queen Isabella Cswy. Ext corridors. **Pets:** Other species. Service with restrictions, supervision.

Super 8 H
(956) 761-6300. **$35-$250.** 4205 Padre Blvd 78597. 2.7 mi n of Queen Isabella Cswy. Ext corridors. **Pets:** Very small, dogs only. $25 deposit/pet, $25 daily fee/pet. Designated rooms, service with restrictions, supervision.

Travelodge H
(956) 761-4744. **$50-$300.** 6200 Padre Blvd 78597. 3 mi n of Queen Isabella Cswy. Ext corridors. **Pets:** Other species. $10 daily fee/room. Service with restrictions, crate.

STANTON

Comfort Inn H
(432) 756-1100. **Call for rates.** 3414 W I-20 79782. I-20 exit 156 (SR 137); on south frontage road. Int corridors. **Pets:** Medium, other species. $150 deposit/room, $25 daily fee/pet. Designated rooms, service with restrictions, crate.

STEPHENVILLE

AAA Americas Best Value Inn - Cross Timbers H
(254) 968-2114. **$59-$64.** 1625 W South Loop (US 377) 76401. 1.8 mi sw on US 377 Bypass and 67. Ext corridors. **Pets:** Other species. $20 daily fee/room. Service with restrictions, supervision.

La Quinta Inn & Suites Stephenville H
(254) 918-2444. **$87-$177.** 105 Christy Plaza 76401. US 67/377 S, 5 mi s of jct US 281. Int corridors. **Pets:** Service with restrictions, supervision.

Stephenville Hampton Inn & Suites H
(254) 918-5400. **$100-$143.** 910 S Harbin Dr 76401. US 67/377 S, 3 mi s of jct US 281. Int corridors. **Pets:** Small. $25 daily fee/pet. No service, supervision.

SULPHUR SPRINGS

AAA BEST WESTERN Trail Dust Inn & Suites H
(903) 885-7515. **$75-$85.** 1521 Shannon Rd 75482. I-30 exit 127; on eastbound frontage road. **Pets:** Small. $10 one-time fee/pet, $10 daily fee/pet. Designated rooms, service with restrictions, supervision.

Comfort Suites H
(903) 438-0918. **$72-$80.** 1521 E Industrial Dr 75482. I-30 exit 127, just n. Int corridors. **Pets:** Other species. $5 daily fee/pet. Designated rooms, service with restrictions, supervision.

La Quinta Inn & Suites Sulphur Springs H
(903) 885-8181. **$90-$144.** 1344 Eaton Dr 75482. I-30 exit 125; on westbound frontage road. Int corridors. **Pets:** Service with restrictions, supervision.

SWEETWATER

AAA BEST WESTERN PLUS Sweetwater Inn & Suites H
(325) 236-6512. **Call for rates.** 300 NW Georgia Ave 79556. I-20 exit 244; jct US 70. Int corridors. **Pets:** Accepted.

AAA Ranch House Motel & Restaurant H
(325) 236-6341. **$65-$75.** 301 SW Georgia Ave 79556. I-20 exit 244, just w of jct SR 70; on south frontage road. Ext/int corridors. **Pets:** Small. $10 daily fee/room. Designated rooms, service with restrictions, supervision.

TEMPLE

AAA Baymont Inn & Suites Temple H
(254) 770-0300. **$65-$83, 3 day notice.** 1415 N General Bruce Dr 76504. I-35 exit 302. Int corridors. **Pets:** Small, dogs only. $15 daily fee/room. Service with restrictions, supervision.

La Quinta Inn & Suites Temple H
(254) 771-2980. **$66-$144.** 1604 W Barton Ave 76504. SR 53, just e; jct I-35 and US 81 exit 301. Ext/int corridors. **Pets:** Service with restrictions, supervision.

Residence Inn by Marriott H
(254) 773-8400. **$79-$159.** 4301 S General Bruce Dr 76502. I-35 exit 298; on east frontage road. Int corridors. **Pets:** Accepted.

TEXARKANA

AAA Candlewood Suites Texarkana H
(903) 334-7418. **$89-$99.** 2901 S Cowhorn Creek Loop 75503. I-30 exit 222 (Summerhill Rd); just w on frontage road to Cowhorn Creek Loop, then just s. Int corridors. **Pets:** Large. $50 daily fee/pet. Designated rooms, service with restrictions, crate.

Country Inn & Suites By Carlson Texarkana H
(903) 838-6955. **Call for rates.** 1918 University Ave 75503. I-30 exit 217, just s. Int corridors. **Pets:** Accepted.

Fairfield Inn & Suites by Marriott H
(903) 306-0473. **$100-$160.** 4209 Mall Dr 75501. I-30 exit 220B (Richmond Rd) westbound; on eastbound service road; exit 218 eastbound. Int corridors. **Pets:** Other species. $75 one-time fee/room. Designated rooms, service with restrictions, supervision.

AAA TownePlace Suites by Marriott H
(903) 334-8800. **$99-$165.** 5020 N Cowhorn Creek Loop 75503. I-30 exit 222 (Summerhill Rd), w on frontage road, then just n. Int corridors. **Pets:** Accepted.

THREE RIVERS

AAA BEST WESTERN Inn-Three Rivers M
(361) 786-2000. **$159-$199, 3 day notice.** 900 N Harborth Ave 78071. I-37 exit 72 (US 281), 1.8 mi s; jct US 281 and SR 72. Ext corridors. **Pets:** $25 daily fee/pet. Designated rooms, service with restrictions.

TULIA

◆◆ Executive Inn 🅜

(806) 995-3248. **Call for rates.** 1591 I-27 79088. I-27 exit 74; on W Frontage Rd. Ext corridors. **Pets:** Accepted. 🛜 🅼 ▯

TYLER

◆◆ Candlewood Suites 🅗

(903) 509-4131. **$81-$119.** 315 E Rieck Rd 75703. 1.1 mi s of jct Loop 323 and US 69 to Rieck Rd, just e. Int corridors. **Pets:** Large, other species. $150 one-time fee/room. Designated rooms, service with restrictions, crate. 🛜 ✕ 🅼 ▯ 💻

◆◆◆ Holiday Inn South Broadway 🅗

(903) 561-5800. **$99-$129.** 5701 S Broadway Ave 75703. 1.1 mi s of jct Loop 323 and US 69. Int corridors. **Pets:** Other species. $50 one-time fee/room. Service with restrictions, crate. 🛜 ▯ 💻 🍴 💦

◆◆◆◆ Residence Inn by Marriott 🅗

(903) 595-5188. **$89-$107.** 3303 Troup Hwy 75701. 0.3 mi n of jct E Loop 323 and SR 110. Ext corridors. **Pets:** Accepted.
🛜 ✕ ▯ 💻 💦 ✕

UVALDE

◆◆ Quality Inn of Uvalde 🅗

(830) 278-4511. **$89-$169.** 920 E Main St 78801. 0.5 mi e on US 90. Ext corridors. **Pets:** Accepted. 🛜 ▯ 💻 💦

VAN HORN

◉◉◉ ◆◆ Econo Lodge 🅗

(432) 283-2211. **$62-$86.** 1601 W Broadway St 79855. I-10 exit 138, 0.5 mi e on Business Rt I-10. Ext corridors. **Pets:** Medium. $25 daily fee/pet. Designated rooms, service with restrictions, supervision.
SAVE 🛜 ▯ 💻 💦

◉◉◉ ◆ Economy Inn 🅜

(432) 283-2754. **$32-$38.** 1500 W Broadway St 79855. I-10 exit 138, 0.5 mi e on US 80. Ext corridors. **Pets:** $5 daily fee/pet. No service, crate.
SAVE 🛜 ▯

◉◉◉ ◆◆◆ Hampton Inn 🅗

(432) 283-0088. **$99-$159.** 1921 SW Frontage Rd 79855. I-10 exit 138, just w on S Frontage Rd. Int corridors. **Pets:** Other species. Designated rooms, supervision. SAVE 🛜 ✕ 🅼 ▯ 💻 💦

◆◆◆◆ Hotel El Capitan 🅗

(432) 283-1220. **$89-$175.** 100 E Broadway 79855. I-10 exit 460, 1 mi w; downtown. Int corridors. **Pets:** $15 daily fee/pet. Service with restrictions, supervision. 🛜 ✕ ▯ 💻 🍴

VEGA

◉◉◉ ◆◆ BEST WESTERN Country Inn 🅜

(806) 267-2131. **$80-$90.** 1800 W Vega Blvd 79092. 0.5 mi w on US 40 business loop. Ext corridors. **Pets:** Medium. $10 daily fee/pet. Designated rooms, service with restrictions, supervision. SAVE 🛜 ▯ 💻 💦

◆◆ Days Inn Vega 🅗

(806) 267-0126. **$80.** 1005 S Main St 79092. I-40 exit 36. Int corridors. **Pets:** Accepted. 🛜 ▯ 💻

VERNON

◉◉◉ ◆◆ BEST WESTERN Village Inn 🅗

(940) 552-5417. **Call for rates.** 1615 US Hwy 287 E 76384. US 287 exit Main St, just w. Ext/int corridors. **Pets:** Accepted.
SAVE 🛜 ▯ 💻 🍴 💦

◆◆ GreenTree Inn 🅜

(940) 552-5421. **$45-$95.** 3029 Morton St 76384. US 287 exit Bentley St, just w. Ext corridors. **Pets:** Medium. $15 daily fee/pet. Designated rooms, service with restrictions, supervision. 🛜 ▯ 💻 💦

◆◆◆ Hampton Inn 🅗

(940) 552-2100. **$109-$129.** 4131 Western Trail Dr 76384. Jct US 287 and 70; on W Frontage Rd. Int corridors. **Pets:** Very small. Service with restrictions, supervision. 🛜 ✕ 🅼 ▯ 💻 💦

◆◆◆ Holiday Inn Express Hotel & Suites 🅗

(940) 552-0200. **$99-$108.** 700 Hillcrest Dr 76384. Jct US 287 and 70; on W Frontage Rd. Int corridors. **Pets:** Medium. $25 one-time fee/room. Service with restrictions, supervision. 🛜 ✕ 🅼 ▯ 💻 💦

VICTORIA

◉◉◉ ◆◆◆ BEST WESTERN PLUS Victoria Inn & Suites 🅗

(361) 485-2300. **$160-$300.** 8106 NE Zac Lenz Pkwy 77904. Jct Zac Lenz Pkwy and Invitational Dr. Int corridors. **Pets:** Large. $20 daily fee/pet. Service with restrictions, supervision. SAVE 🛜 ✕ ▯ 💻 💦

◆◆◆ La Quinta Inn Victoria 🅗

(361) 572-3585. **$111-$210.** 7603 N Navarro St (US 77 N) 77904. 4 mi n; at Loop 463. Ext corridors. **Pets:** Service with restrictions, supervision.
🛜 ✕ ▯ 💻 💦

◉◉◉ ◆◆ Lone Star Inn & Suites 🅗

(361) 579-0225. **$100-$170.** 1907 US 59 N 77905. US 59 exit Blooming-ton (US 185); on northeast corner. Ext corridors. **Pets:** Medium. $10 daily fee/pet. Service with restrictions, supervision. SAVE 🛜 ▯ 💻 💦

◆ Motel 6 Victoria - #4729 🅜

(361) 573-1273. **$60-$100.** 3716 Houston Hwy 77901. On Business Rt US 59. Ext corridors. **Pets:** Other species. Service with restrictions, supervision. 🛜 ▯ 💻

◆◆ Victory Inn 🅗

(361) 578-2030. **Call for rates.** 3112 E Houston Hwy (Business Rt 59) 77901. On Business Rt US 59, 2 mi ne. Ext corridors. **Pets:** Medium. $25 daily fee/pet. Service with restrictions, supervision.
🛜 ▯ 💻 💦

WACO

◉◉◉ ◆◆◆ Clarion Hotel 🅗

(254) 757-2000. **$70-$129.** 801 S 4th St 76706. I-35 exit 335A. Ext/int corridors. **Pets:** $50 one-time fee/room. Designated rooms, service with restrictions, crate. SAVE 🛜 ▯ 💻 🍴 💦

◆◆◆ Hilton-Waco 🅗 🌼

(254) 754-8484. **$109-$199.** 113 S University Parks Dr 76701. I-35 exit 335B, 0.5 mi w. Int corridors. **Pets:** Small, other species. $50 one-time fee/room. Designated rooms, service with restrictions, crate.
🛜 ▯ 💻 🍴 💦

◆◆ La Quinta Inn Waco University 🅗

(254) 752-9741. **$59-$144.** 1110 S 9th St 76706. I-35 exit 334 (17th St) southbound; exit 334A (18th St) northbound; on east frontage road. Ext corridors. **Pets:** Service with restrictions, supervision.
🛜 ▯ 💻 💦

◆◆◆ Magnuson Hotel Waco 🅗

(254) 752-1991. **$54-$150.** 1430 I-35 S 76706. I-35 exit 334 (17th St); on northbound frontage road. Ext corridors. **Pets:** Small, dogs only. $10 daily fee/pet. Designated rooms, service with restrictions, crate.
🛜 ▯ 💻 💦

◆◆◆ Residence Inn by Marriott 🅗

(254) 714-1386. **$140-$229.** 501 S University Parks Dr 76706. I-35 exit 335B, 0.3 mi w. Int corridors. **Pets:** Accepted.
🛜 ✕ ▯ 💻 💦 ✕

◆ Super 8-Waco 🅗

(254) 754-1023. **$49-$139.** 1320 S Jack Kultgen Frwy 76706. I-35 exit 334 (17th St), just n on east frontage road. Int corridors. **Pets:** Small, other species. $10 daily fee/pet. Designated rooms, service with restrictions, crate. 🛜 ▯ 💻

WASHINGTON

▼▼▼▼ The Inn at Dos Brisas 🔲

(979) 277-7750. **$560-$1382, 30 day notice.** 10000 Champion Dr 77880. US 290 exit Chapel Hill to FM 1155, 6.5 mi n. Ext corridors. **Pets:** Accepted. 📶 ✖ 🛄 🖵 🍴 🏊

WAXAHACHIE

▼▼ Super 8 🔢

(972) 938-9088. **$55-$125.** 400 N I-35 E 75165. I-35E exit 401B. Int corridors. **Pets:** Accepted. 📶 🛄 🖵 🏊

▼▼▼ Waxahachie Sleep Inn & Suites 🔢

(972) 938-1600. **Call for rates.** 1701 US Hwy 77 N 75165. US 287 exit US 77, just n. Int corridors. **Pets:** Small. $15 daily fee/pet. Service with restrictions, crate. 📶 🛄 🖵 🏊

WEATHERFORD

▼▼▼ Cutting Horse Inn & Suites 🔢 🐾

(817) 599-3300. **Call for rates.** 210 Alford Dr 76086. I-20 exit 408, just s on SR 171, then just w. Int corridors. **Pets:** Small, other species. $20 one-time fee/pet. Designated rooms, supervision.
📶 ✖ 🛄 🖵 🏊

▼▼▼ Hampton Inn 🔢

(817) 599-4800. **$90-$170.** 2524 S Main St 76087. I-20 exit 408. Int corridors. **Pets:** Small. $15 daily fee/pet. Designated rooms, service with restrictions, supervision. 📶 🛄 🖵 🏊

▼▼ Quality Inn & Suites 🔢

(817) 599-3700. **$85-$95.** 2500 S Main St 76087. I-20 exit 408, just s. Ext/int corridors. **Pets:** Designated rooms, supervision.
📶 🛄 🖵 🏊

▼▼ Weatherford Heritage Inn 🔢

(817) 594-7401. **$52-$55.** 1927 Santa Fe Dr 76086. I-20 exit 409 (Clear Lake Rd/FM 2552), 0.3 mi nw. Ext corridors. **Pets:** Small. $10 one-time fee/pet. Service with restrictions, supervision. 📶 🛄 🖵 🏊

WICHITA FALLS

🅰🅰🅰 ▼▼▼▼ BEST WESTERN PLUS University Inn & Suites 🔢

(940) 687-2025. **Call for rates.** 4540 Maplewood Ave 76308. Jct Southwest Pkwy (CR 369), just n. Int corridors. **Pets:** Other species. $15 daily fee/pet. Service with restrictions. 🆂🅰🆅🅴 📶 ✖ 🛄 🖵 🏊

▼▼▼▼ Holiday Inn 🔢

(940) 761-6000. **$79-$149, 3 day notice.** 100 Central Frwy 76306. I-287 exit 1C; on west side access road. Int corridors. **Pets:** Accepted.
📶 🛄 🖵 🍴 🏊

▼▼▼▼ La Quinta Inn Wichita Falls Airport Area 🔢

(940) 322-6971. **$59-$122.** 1128 Central Frwy N 76306. I-44 exit 2 (Maurine St), just w. Ext corridors. **Pets:** Service with restrictions, supervision.
📶 🛄 🖵 🏊

🅰🅰🅰 ▼▼▼▼ Lexington Suites of Wichita Falls 🔢

(940) 692-7900. **$90-$153.** 1917 Elmwood Ave N 76308. US 281 S exit Southwest Pkwy (CR 369), 2.3 mi w to Kemp Blvd, 2 blks n to Elmwood Ave, then just e. Int corridors. **Pets:** Accepted.
🆂🅰🆅🅴 📶 ✖ 🛄 🛄 🖵 🏊

🅰🅰🅰 ▼▼▼ Red Roof Inn 🔢

(940) 766-6881. **$60-$80.** 1032 Central Frwy 76306. I-44 exit 2, just w. Ext corridors. **Pets:** Large, other species. Service with restrictions, supervision. 🆂🅰🆅🅴 📶 🛄 🖵 🏊

WOODWAY

▼▼▼▼ La Quinta Inn & Suites 🔢

(254) 772-0200. **$107-$243.** 6003 Woodway Dr 76712. I-35 exit 330, 2.5 mi w on SR 6 to jct US 84, then just s on N Frontage Rd. Int corridors. **Pets:** Service with restrictions, supervision.
📶 ✖ 🛄 🛄 🖵 🏊

🅰🅰🅰 ▼▼▼ Super 8 Waco Mall 🔢

(254) 776-3194. **$70-$110.** 6624 Woodway Dr (Hwy 84 W) 76712. Jct US 84 and SR 6, just w. Ext corridors. **Pets:** Medium. $10 one-time fee/pet. Service with restrictions, supervision. 🆂🅰🆅🅴 📶 🛄 🖵 🏊

ZAPATA

🅰🅰🅰 ▼▼▼ BEST WESTERN Inn by the Lake 🔢

(956) 765-8403. **$95-$106.** 1896 S US Hwy 83 78076. On US 83, 0.5 mi se. Ext corridors. **Pets:** Other species. $10 daily fee/pet. Service with restrictions, crate. 🆂🅰🆅🅴 📶 🛄 🖵 🏊 ✖

UTAH

AMERICAN FORK

 Holiday Inn Express & Suites - American Fork/North Provo ▪

(801) 763-8500. **$89-$169, 3 day notice.** 712 S Utah Valley Dr 84003. I-15 exit 276, 0.3 mi n on S 500 E, just e on E 620 S, then 0.3 mi s. Int corridors. **Pets:** Dogs only. $15 daily fee/pet. Designated rooms.

BEAVER

BEST WESTERN Butch Cassidy Inn **M**

(435) 438-2438. **$59-$109.** 161 S Main St 84713. I-15 exit 112, 1.8 mi e. Ext corridors. **Pets:** Other species. $10 daily fee/pet. Supervision.

BEST WESTERN Paradise Inn ▪

(435) 438-2455. **Call for rates.** 314 W 1425 N 84713. I-15 exit 112, just e. Ext corridors. **Pets:** Accepted.

Quality Inn ▪

(435) 438-5426. **$65-$95.** 781 W 1800 S 84713. I-15 exit 109, just w. Int corridors. **Pets:** $10 daily fee/pet. Designated rooms, service with restrictions, supervision.

BLANDING

Super 8 **M**

(435) 678-3880. **$65-$130.** 755 S Main St 84511. On US 191. Int corridors. **Pets:** Medium. $10 daily fee/pet. Designated rooms, service with restrictions, supervision.

BLUFF

Kokopelli Inn **M**

(435) 672-2322. **$65-$75.** 160 E Main St 84512. On US 191 (Main St). Int corridors. **Pets:** $11 daily fee/pet. Designated rooms, service with restrictions, crate.

Recapture Lodge **M**

(435) 672-2281. **$85.** 220 E Main St 84512. On US 191 (Main St). Ext corridors. **Pets:** Other species. Designated rooms, service with restrictions, supervision.

BOULDER

Boulder Mountain Lodge ▪ ❀

(435) 335-7460. **$85-$210, 30 day notice.** 20 N Hwy 12 84716. Just s. Ext/int corridors. **Pets:** $15 daily fee/pet. Designated rooms, service with restrictions, supervision.

BRIAN HEAD

DoubleTree by Hilton Resort & Spa Brian Head ▪

(435) 677-9000. **Call for rates.** 314 Hunter Ridge Rd 84719. On SR 143. Int corridors. **Pets:** Accepted.

BRIGHAM CITY

Crystal Inn ▪

(435) 723-0440. **$84-$139.** 480 Westland Dr 84302. I-15 exit 362, 1 mi e to S 500 W, then just n. Int corridors. **Pets:** Accepted.

BRYCE CANYON CITY

 BEST WESTERN PLUS Ruby's Inn ▪

(435) 834-5341. **$59-$169.** 26 S Main St 84764. On SR 63, 1 mi s of SR 12. Ext/int corridors. **Pets:** Large, dogs only. $20 daily fee/pet. Service with restrictions, supervision.

Bryce View Lodge **M**

(435) 834-5180. **$60-$120.** 105 E Center St 84764. 1 mi s of SR 12. Ext corridors. **Pets:** Large, dogs only. $20 daily fee/pet. Service with restrictions, supervision.

CAINEVILLE

Rodeway Inn Capitol Reef **M** ❀

(435) 456-9900. **$68-$110.** 25 E SR 24 84775. West end of town. Ext corridors. **Pets:** Medium, dogs only. $15 daily fee/pet. Designated rooms, service with restrictions, supervision.

CEDAR CITY

Americas Best Value Inn **M**

(435) 867-4700. **$43-$95.** 333 N 1100 W 84720. I-15 exit 59, just e. Int corridors. **Pets:** Large, other species. $10 daily fee/room. Designated rooms, service with restrictions, crate.

Comfort Inn & Suites ▪

(435) 865-0003. **$75-$149.** 1288 S Main St 84720. I-15 exit 57, just e, then just n. Int corridors. **Pets:** Medium. $25 deposit/pet, $25 one-time fee/pet. Designated rooms, service with restrictions, supervision.

Crystal Inn Cedar City ▪

(435) 586-8888. **$69-$129.** 1575 W 200 N 84720. I-15 exit 59, just w. Ext/int corridors. **Pets:** Large, other species. $25 one-time fee/room. Designated rooms, service with restrictions, crate.

Days Inn **M**

(435) 867-8877. **$54-$150.** 1204 S Main St 84720. I-15 exit 57, 0.4 mi ne. Ext corridors. **Pets:** Medium. $12 daily fee/pet. Designated rooms, service with restrictions, supervision.

Holiday Inn Express Hotel & Suites ▪

(435) 865-7799. **Call for rates.** 1555 S Old Hwy 91 84720. I-15 exit 57, just e, then s. Int corridors. **Pets:** Other species. $15 daily fee/room. Designated rooms, service with restrictions, supervision.

▼▼ Motel 6 of Cedar City - 4041 **M**

(435) 586-9200. **Call for rates.** 1620 W 200 N 84720. I-15 exit 59, just w. Int corridors. **Pets:** Other species. Service with restrictions, supervision.
📶 ♿M ⬛

▼▼ Quality Inn **M**

(435) 586-2082. **$59-$129, 7 day notice.** 250 N 1100 W 84720. I-15 exit 59, just e. Ext corridors. **Pets:** Large, other species. $10 daily fee/room. Designated rooms, service with restrictions, crate.
📶 ✕ ⬛ 💻 ≈

▼▼ Super 8 Motel Cedar City **M**

(435) 586-8880. **$51-$120.** 145 N 1550 W 84720. I-15 exit 59, just w. Int corridors. **Pets:** Other species. $15 daily fee/pet. Designated rooms, service with restrictions, supervision. 📶 ♿M ⬛ 💻

COALVILLE

AAA ▼▼ BEST WESTERN Holiday Hills **H**

(435) 336-4444. **$80-$100.** 200 S 500 W 84017. I-80 exit 162, just w. Int corridors. **Pets:** Large, other species. $20 daily fee/room. Designated rooms, service with restrictions, crate. SAVE 📶 ⬛ 💻 ≈ ✕

DELTA

▼▼ Days Inn **M**

(435) 864-3882. **$70-$110.** 527 E Topaz Blvd 84624. Jct US 6 and 50. Ext corridors. **Pets:** Medium, other species. $15 one-time fee/room. Designated rooms, service with restrictions, supervision. 📶 ⬛ 💻 ≈

ESCALANTE

▼▼ Rainbow Country Bed & Breakfast **BB**

(435) 826-4567. **$79-$109, 3 day notice.** 585 E 300 S 84726. Just s of SR 12; east end of town. Int corridors. **Pets:** $10 daily fee/pet. Service with restrictions, supervision. 📶 ✕ W Z

FILLMORE

AAA ▼▼ BEST WESTERN Paradise Inn & Resort **M**

(435) 743-6895. **$80-$90.** 905 N Main St 84631. I-15 exit 167, just e. Ext corridors. **Pets:** Accepted. SAVE 📶 ⬛ 💻 ⎕⎕ ≈

▼▼ Comfort Inn & Suites **H** ❀

(435) 743-4334. **Call for rates.** 940 S Hwy 99 84631. I-15 exit 163, just e. Int corridors. **Pets:** Small. $10 daily fee/pet. Designated rooms, supervision. 📶 ✕ ⬛ 💻 ≈

GLENDALE

▼▼ Historic Smith Hotel Bed & Breakfast **BB** ❀

(435) 648-2156. **$48-$98.** 295 N Main St 84729. US 89; north end of town. Int corridors. **Pets:** Other species. Designated rooms, no service, crate. 📶 ✕ Z

GREEN RIVER

▼▼▼ Holiday Inn Express **H** ❀

(435) 564-4439. **Call for rates.** 1845 E Main St 84525. I-70 exit 164, 1.7 mi nw. Int corridors. **Pets:** $10 one-time fee/pet. Designated rooms, service with restrictions, supervision. 📶 ✕ ⬛ 💻 ≈

AAA ▼▼ Super 8 **M**

(435) 564-8888. **$59-$76.** 1248 E Main St 84525. I-70 exit 164, 1.3 mi n. Int corridors. **Pets:** $5 daily fee/pet. Service with restrictions, supervision. SAVE 📶 ⬛ 💻 ≈

HEBER CITY

AAA ▼▼ Swiss Alps Inn **M**

(435) 654-0722. **$70-$120.** 167 S Main St 84032. I-80 exit 146 (US 40), 15 mi s. Ext corridors. **Pets:** Large, other species. $10 daily fee/room. Designated rooms, service with restrictions, supervision.
SAVE 📶 ✕ ⬛ 💻 ⎕⎕ ≈ ✕

HUNTSVILLE

▼▼ ▼▼ Jackson Fork Inn **M**

(801) 745-0051. **$90-$160, 3 day notice.** 7345 E 900 S 84317. I-15 exit 344 (12th St), 12 mi e. Int corridors. **Pets:** $20 one-time fee/room. Designated rooms, service with restrictions, supervision. 📶 ✕ ⎕⎕ Z

KANAB

AAA ▼▼▼ BEST WESTERN Red Hills **M**

(435) 644-2675. **$69-$139.** 125 W Center St 84741. Center. Ext/int corridors. **Pets:** Large. $15 daily fee/room. Designated rooms, service with restrictions, supervision. SAVE 📶 ⬛ 💻 ≈

AAA ▼▼ Canyons Lodge **M**

(435) 644-3069. **$79-$149, 3 day notice.** 236 N 300 W 84741. On US 89. Ext corridors. **Pets:** Accepted. SAVE 📶 ✕ ⬛ ≈

▼▼ Comfort Inn Kanab **H**

(435) 644-8888. **Call for rates.** 815 E 300 S 84741. On US 89, just e. Int corridors. **Pets:** Accepted. 📶 ✕ ♿M ⬛ 💻 ≈

▼▼▼ Holiday Inn Express Hotel & Suites **H**

(435) 644-3100. **$99-$159.** 217 S 100 E 84741. On US 89; jct 200 S. Int corridors. **Pets:** Accepted. 📶 ✕ ⬛ 💻 ≈

▼ Parry Lodge **M**

(435) 644-2601. **$54-$120.** 89 E Center St 84741. On US 89; corner of 100 E; center. Ext/int corridors. **Pets:** Other species. $10 daily fee/pet. Designated rooms, service with restrictions, crate.
📶 ✕ ⬛ 💻 ⎕⎕ ≈

AAA ▼▼▼ Quail Park Lodge **M** ❀

(435) 215-1447. **$79-$169, 3 day notice.** 125 N 300 W (Hwy 89) 84741. On US 89. Ext corridors. **Pets:** Dogs only. Designated rooms, service with restrictions, crate. SAVE 📶 ✕ ⬛ ≈

▼▼ Shilo Inn Suites-Kanab **H**

(435) 644-2562. **$69-$209.** 296 W 100 N 84741. On US 89; n of downtown. Int corridors. **Pets:** Dogs only. $25 one-time fee/room. Designated rooms, service with restrictions, supervision. 📶 ✕ ⬛ 💻 ≈

▼▼▼ Victorian Inn **H**

(435) 644-8660. **$89-$199.** 190 N 300 W 84741. North end of town. Int corridors. **Pets:** Medium, other species. $20 daily fee/room. Designated rooms, service with restrictions, crate. 📶 ✕ ⬛ 💻

LAYTON

AAA ▼▼▼ Comfort Inn **H**

(801) 544-5577. **$69-$119.** 877 N 400 W 84041. I-15 exit 331, just e. Int corridors. **Pets:** Accepted. SAVE 📶 ⬛ 💻 ≈

▼▼▼ Hampton Inn **H** ❀

(801) 775-8800. **$99-$159.** 1700 Woodland Park Dr 84041. I-15 exit 332 (Antelope Dr), 0.3 mi e, then just s. Int corridors. **Pets:** Dogs only. Service with restrictions, supervision. 📶 ⬛ 💻 ≈

▼▼▼ Home2 Suites by Hilton **H**

(801) 820-9222. **Call for rates.** 803 W Heritage Park Blvd 84041. I-15 exit 331, 0.6 mi n to Heritage Blvd, then 0.4 mi w. Int corridors. **Pets:** Accepted. 📶 ⬛ 💻 ≈

▼▼ La Quinta Inn & Suites Salt Lake City Layton **H**

(801) 776-6700. **$71-$155.** 1965 N 1200 W 84041. I-15 exit 332 (Antelope Dr), just e. Int corridors. **Pets:** Service with restrictions, supervision. 📶 ⬛ 💻 ≈

▼▼ TownePlace Suites by Marriott **H**

(801) 779-2422. **$80-$134.** 1743 Woodland Park Dr 84041. I-15 exit 332 (Antelope Dr), 0.3 mi se. Int corridors. **Pets:** Other species. $75 one-time fee/room. Service with restrictions, crate. 📶 ✕ ⬛ 💻 ≈

LEHI

◇◇◇◇ ▽▼▽ BEST WESTERN PLUS Timpanogos Inn 🅷
(801) 768-1400. **Call for rates.** 195 S 850 E 84043. I-15 exit 279, just w, then just s. Int corridors. **Pets:** Accepted.
SAVE 🛜 ✕ 🍴 💻 🏊

LOGAN

◇◇◇◇ ▽▼▽ BEST WESTERN Baugh Motel 🅼
(435) 752-5220. **$85-$190.** 153 S Main St 84321. Just s of center. Ext corridors. **Pets:** $20 one-time fee/pet. Designated rooms, service with restrictions, supervision. SAVE 🛜 🍴 💻 🏊

◇◇◇◇ ▽▼▽ BEST WESTERN Weston Inn 🅷
(435) 752-5700. **$89-$129.** 250 N Main St 84321. 0.3 mi n of center. Ext corridors. **Pets:** Small. $15 daily fee/pet. Service with restrictions, supervision. ECO SAVE 🛜 ✕ 🍴 💻 🏊 ✕

▽▼▽ Crystal Inn 🅷
(435) 752-0707. **$73-$149.** 853 S Hwy 89 and 91 84321. 2 mi s of center. Int corridors. **Pets:** Accepted. 🛜 ✕ 🍴 💻 🏊

▽▼▽ Holiday Inn Express & Suites 🅷
(435) 752-3444. **Call for rates.** 2235 N Main St 84341. 2.8 mi n of center. Int corridors. **Pets:** Medium. $25 one-time fee/pet. Service with restrictions, supervision. 🛜 ✕ 🍴 💻 🏊

▽ Super 8 🅼
(435) 753-8883. **$57-$95.** 865 S Hwy 89/91 84321. 2 mi s of center. Int corridors. **Pets:** Other species. $10 daily fee/pet. Service with restrictions, supervision. 🛜 🍴 💻 🏊

MANTI

▽ Manti Country Village Motel 🅼
(435) 835-9300. **$69-$99.** 145 N Main St 84642. On US 89 (Main St), just n of center. Ext corridors. **Pets:** Medium, dogs only. $75 deposit/room. Designated rooms, service with restrictions, crate. 🛜 ✕ 🍴

MIDWAY

▽▼▽ Homestead Resort 🅷
(435) 654-1102. **Call for rates.** 700 N Homestead Dr 84049. I-80 exit 146 (US 40), 13 mi s to River Rd traffic light, 2.9 mi w to roundabout, 1.2 mi w, follow signs to Homestead Dr, then 0.4 mi s. Ext/int corridors. **Pets:** Accepted. 🛜 ✕ 🍴 💻 🍴 🏊 ✕

MOAB

◇◇◇◇ ▽▼▽ Big Horn Lodge 🅼
(435) 259-6171. **$50-$140.** 550 S Main St 84532. 0.5 mi s. Ext corridors. **Pets:** Other species. $5 daily fee/pet. Designated rooms, service with restrictions, supervision. SAVE 🛜 ✕ 🍴 💻 🍴

◇◇◇◇ ▽▼▽ Bowen Motel 🅼
(435) 259-7132. **$50-$134.** 169 N Main St 84532. Downtown. Ext corridors. **Pets:** Medium. $10 daily fee/room. Service with restrictions, supervision. SAVE 🛜 ✕ 🍴 💻 🏊

▽▼▽ Cali Cochitta Bed & Breakfast 🅱🅱
(435) 259-4961. **$90-$175, 15 day notice.** 110 S 200 E 84532. Corner of 100 S and 200 E. Ext/int corridors. **Pets:** Accepted.
🛜 ✕ 🍴 🛎

◇◇◇◇ ▽▼▽ The Gonzo Inn 🅷
(435) 259-2515. **$169-$349.** 100 W 200 S 84532. Just w of 200 S and S Main St. Ext/int corridors. **Pets:** $30 daily fee/room. No service, supervision. SAVE 🛜 ✕ 🍴 💻 🏊

◇◇◇◇ ▽▼▽ La Quinta Inn Moab 🅷
(435) 259-8700. **$59-$254.** 815 S Main St 84532. 0.8 mi s. Int corridors. **Pets:** Service with restrictions, supervision.
SAVE 🛜 ✕ 🍴 💻 🏊

▽▼▽ Moab Valley Inn 🅷
(435) 259-4419. **$69-$199.** 711 S Main St 84532. 0.7 mi s. Int corridors. **Pets:** Accepted. 🛜 ✕ 🍴 💻 🏊

▽ Motel 6 Moab #4119 🅼
(435) 259-6686. **$59-$199.** 1089 N Main St 84532. 1.5 mi n. Int corridors. **Pets:** Other species. Service with restrictions, supervision. 🛜 🏊

◇◇◇◇ ▽▼▽ Red Cliffs Lodge - Moab's Adventure Headquarters 🆁🅰
(435) 259-2002. **$99-$340, 30 day notice.** Milepost 14 Hwy 128 84532. 2.3 mi n to jct Hwy 191 and SR 128, then 14 mi e to MM 14. Ext corridors. **Pets:** Medium, dogs only. $20 daily fee/pet. Designated rooms, service with restrictions, supervision.
SAVE 🛜 ✕ 🍴 💻 🍴 🏊 ✕

◇◇◇◇ ▽▼▽ Red Stone Inn 🅼
(435) 259-3500. **$45-$125.** 535 S Main St 84532. 0.5 mi s. Int corridors. **Pets:** Medium. $5 daily fee/room. Designated rooms, service with restrictions, supervision. SAVE 🛜 ✕ 🍴 💻

◇◇◇◇ ▽▼▽ River Canyon Lodge, An Extended Stay Inn & Suites 🅼 🐾
(435) 259-8838. **$59-$290.** 71 W 200 N 84532. Just w of 200 N and Main St. Int corridors. **Pets:** Other species. $25 one-time fee/pet. Designated rooms, service with restrictions, supervision.
SAVE 🛜 ✕ 🍴 💻 🏊

◇◇◇◇ ▽▼ Silver Sage Inn 🅼
(435) 259-4420. **$45-$100.** 840 S Main St 84532. 0.9 mi s of the center. Int corridors. **Pets:** Medium. $10 daily fee/pet. Service with restrictions, supervision. SAVE 🛜 🍴 💻

▽▼▽ Sleep Inn 🅷
(435) 259-4655. **$69-$179.** 1051 S Main St 84532. 1.3 mi s. Int corridors. **Pets:** Other species. $50 deposit/room. Designated rooms, service with restrictions, supervision. 🛜 🍴 💻 🏊

◇◇◇◇ ▽▼▽ ▽▼▽ Sorrel River Ranch Resort & Spa 🅷 🐾
(435) 259-4642. **$429-$729, 45 day notice.** Hwy 128 at MM 17 84532. 17 mi e of jct US 191 and SR 128; at MM 17. Ext corridors. **Pets:** Medium, other species. $50 daily fee/pet. Service with restrictions, crate. SAVE 🛜 ✕ 🍴 💻 🍴 🏊 ✕

MONTICELLO

◇◇◇◇ ▽▼▽ Inn at the Canyons 🅼
(435) 587-2458. **$40-$150.** 533 N Main St 84535. On US 191; north end of town. Int corridors. **Pets:** Accepted. SAVE 🛜 ✕ 🆎 🍴 🏊

▽▼▽ Wayside Inn 🅼
(435) 587-2261. **$79-$100.** 197 E Central St 84535. On US 491, just e of US 191. Ext corridors. **Pets:** Accepted. 🛜 ✕ 🍴 💻 🏊

MONUMENT VALLEY

◇◇◇◇ ▽▼▽ Goulding's Lodge & Tours 🅷
(435) 727-3231. **$85-$218, 3 day notice.** 1000 Main St 84536. 2 mi w of US 163; 0.5 mi n of Arizona border. Ext corridors. **Pets:** $30 daily fee/room. Designated rooms, service with restrictions, crate.
SAVE 🛜 ✕ 🍴 💻 🍴 🏊

NEPHI

◇◇◇◇ ▽▼▽ BEST WESTERN Paradise Inn of Nephi 🅼
(435) 623-0624. **$80-$125.** 1025 S Main St 84648. I-15 exit 222, 0.5 mi n. Ext corridors. **Pets:** Other species. $10 daily fee/pet. Service with restrictions. SAVE 🛜 ✕ 🍴 💻 🏊

OGDEN

▼▼▼▼ Ben Lomond Suites Historic Hotel, an Ascend Collection H
(801) 627-1900. **$60-$139.** 2510 Washington Blvd 84401. I-15 exit 341 (31st St), 1 mi e, then 0.8 mi n; at 25th St and Washington Blvd. Int corridors. **Pets:** Other species. $50 one-time fee/room. Designated rooms, service with restrictions, supervision.

AAA ▼▼▼▼ BEST WESTERN PLUS High Country Inn H ❀
(801) 394-9474. **$79-$129.** 1335 W 12th St 84404. I-15 exit 344 (12th St), just e. Ext/int corridors. **Pets:** Medium. $10 daily fee/room. Crate.
SAVE ⦿ █ ▣ ⊞ ↝

▼▼▼▼ Comfort Suites H
(801) 621-2545. **$89-$139.** 2250 S 1200 W 84401. I-15 exit 343 (21st St), just se. Int corridors. **Pets:** Medium, other species. $25 one-time fee/room. Designated rooms, service with restrictions, supervision.
⦿ ✕ █ ▣ ⊞ ↝ ⊠

▼▼▼ Holiday Inn Express & Suites H
(801) 392-5000. **$99-$149.** 2245 S 1200 W 84401. I-15 exit 343 (21st St), 0.3 mi e. Int corridors. **Pets:** Medium, other species. $25 one-time fee/room. Designated rooms, service with restrictions, supervision.
⦿ ✕ █ ▣ ↝

▼▼▼ Marriott Ogden H
(801) 627-1190. **$99-$149.** 247 24th St 84401. I-15 exit 341 (31st St), 0.7 mi e, 1 mi n, then just e; exit 342 (24th St) 1.5 mi e. Int corridors. **Pets:** Other species. $50 one-time fee/room. Designated rooms, service with restrictions, supervision. ⦿ ✕ █ ▣ ⊞ ↝

AAA ▼▼▼ Sleep Inn H
(801) 731-6500. **$70-$100.** 1155 S 1700 W 84404. I-15 exit 344 (12th St), just w. Int corridors. **Pets:** Other species. $10 daily fee/pet. Designated rooms, service with restrictions, crate. SAVE ⦿ █ ▣

OREM

▼▼▼▼ Holiday Inn Express & Suites Orem - North Provo H
(801) 655-1515. **$99-$179.** 1290 W University Pkwy 84058. I-15 exit 269 (University Pkwy), 0.5 mi w. Int corridors. **Pets:** Accepted.
⦿ ✕ █ ▣ ↝ ⊠

▼▼▼▼ La Quinta Inn & Suites Orem University Parkway H
(801) 226-0440. **$66-$166.** 521 W University Pkwy 84058. I-15 exit 269, 0.4 mi e. Int corridors. **Pets:** Service with restrictions, supervision.
⦿ █ ▣ ↝

AAA ▼▼▼ La Quinta Inn Orem H
(801) 235-9555. **$65-$144.** 1100 W 780 N 84057. I-15 exit 272 (800 N), 0.3 mi e. Int corridors. **Pets:** Service with restrictions, supervision.
SAVE ⦿ █ ▣ ↝

▼▼▼▼ TownePlace Suites by Marriott Orem - North Provo H
(801) 225-4477. **$85-$159.** 873 N 1200 W 84057. I-15 exit 272 (800 N), just e. Int corridors. **Pets:** Accepted. ⦿ ✕ █ ▣ ↝ ⊠

PANGUITCH

AAA ▼ Color Country Motel M
(435) 676-2386. **Call for rates.** 526 N Main St 84759. 0.3 mi n of center. Ext corridors. **Pets:** Accepted. SAVE ⦿ █

▼▼ Harold's Place Cabins CA
(435) 676-2350. **$85-$95.** 3066 Hwy 12 84759. Jct US 89 and SR 12, 0.5 mi e. Ext corridors. **Pets:** Medium, dogs only. $20 deposit/pet. Designated rooms, service with restrictions. ⦿ ✕ ▣ ⊞ ⊘

▼▼▼ Harold's Place Inn M
(435) 676-2350. **$75-$95.** 3090 Hwy 12 84759. Jct US 89 and SR 12, 0.5 mi e. Int corridors. **Pets:** Medium, dogs only. Designated rooms, service with restrictions. ⦿ ✕ ⊞ ⊘

PARK CITY

AAA ▼▼▼▼ BEST WESTERN PLUS Landmark Inn & Pancake House H
(435) 649-7300. **Call for rates.** 6560 N Landmark Dr 84098. I-80 exit 145 (Kimball Jct), 0.3 mi s, then 0.3 mi nw. Int corridors. **Pets:** Large, other species. $10 daily fee/room. Designated rooms, service with restrictions, supervision. SAVE ⦿ ✕ █ ▣ ↝ ⊠

▼▼▼▼ Holiday Inn Express Hotel & Suites H
(435) 658-1600. **$89-$179.** 1501 W Ute Blvd 84098. I-80 exit 145 (Kimball Jct), just s to Ute Blvd, then 0.3 mi e. Int corridors. **Pets:** Accepted.
⦿ ✕ █ ▣ ↝ ⊠

▼▼▼▼ Montage Deer Valley H ❀
(435) 604-1300. **Call for rates.** 9100 Marsac Ave 84060. I-80 exit 145 (Kimball Jct), at roundabout, take Marsac Ave exit, 2 mi s to Guardsman Connection, then 2 mi sw on SR 224 (Park Ave). Int corridors. **Pets:** Small, dogs only. $100 one-time fee/room. Supervision.
⦿ ✕ █ ⊞ ↝ ⊠

AAA ▼▼▼▼ St. Regis Deer Valley H
(435) 940-5700. **$319-$3449.** 2300 Deer Valley Dr E 84060. I-80 exit 145 (Kimball Jct), 6 mi s to Deer Valley Dr, 1 mi se to roundabout, take 3rd exit (Deer Valley Dr), then 1.2 mi se. Int corridors. **Pets:** Accepted.
SAVE ⦿ ✕ █ ▣ ⊞ ↝ ⊠

▼▼▼▼ Washington School House H
(435) 649-3800. **Call for rates.** 543 Park Ave 84060. I-80 exit 145 (Kimball Jct), 6 mi se to Kearns Blvd and SR 224 (Park Ave), then 1.2 mi s. Int corridors. **Pets:** Accepted. ⦿ ✕ ↝

PAROWAN

▼▼ Days Inn Parowan M
(435) 477-3326. **$50-$124.** 625 W 200 S 84761. I-15 exit 75, 1.5 mi e. Ext corridors. **Pets:** Accepted. ⦿ █ ▣ ↝

PRICE

▼▼ Holiday Inn & Suites H
(435) 637-8880. **$89-$149.** 838 Westwood Blvd 84501. US 6 exit 240 (Business Loop), just e. Int corridors. **Pets:** Accepted.
⦿ █ ▣ ⊞ ↝

AAA ▼▼ Legacy Inn M
(435) 637-2424. **$59-$125.** 145 N Carbonville Rd 84501. US 6 exit 240 (Business Loop), 0.5 mi se, 0.3 mi e then just ne on N Carbonville Rd. Ext corridors. **Pets:** Other species. $25 daily fee/pet. Service with restrictions, crate. SAVE ⦿ █ ▣

PROVO

AAA ▼▼▼ BEST WESTERN PLUS CottonTree Inn H
(801) 373-7044. **Call for rates.** 2230 N University Pkwy 84604. I-15 exit 269 (University Pkwy), 3.2 mi e, then just n; in CottonTree Square. Int corridors. **Pets:** Accepted. SAVE ⦿ ✕ █ ▣ ↝

▼▼ Days Inn M
(801) 375-8600. **$55-$135.** 1675 N 200 W 84604. I-15 exit 269 (University Pkwy), 3.7 mi e, then just s on N Freedom Blvd; in Village Green Square. Ext corridors. **Pets:** Accepted. ⦿ █ ▣ ↝

▼▼ Econo Lodge M ❀
(801) 373-0099. **$54-$99.** 1625 W Center St 84601. I-15 exit 265 (Center St), just w. Ext corridors. **Pets:** Other species. $10 deposit/pet, $10 daily fee/pet. Designated rooms, service with restrictions, supervision.
⦿ █ ▣

▼▼▼▽ **La Quinta Inn Provo Town Center** 🅷
(801) 374-9750. **$78-$178.** 1460 S University Ave 84601. I-15 exit 263 (University Ave), 0.5 mi e. Int corridors. **Pets:** Service with restrictions, supervision. 🛜 ⊠ 🛏 🖵 ¶¶ ⊃

▼▼▽▽ **Residence Inn by Marriott** 🅷
(801) 374-1000. **$89-$309.** 252 W 2230 N 84604. I-15 exit 269 (University Pkwy), 3.2 mi e to W 2230 N, then 0.3 mi e. Int corridors.
Pets: Accepted. 🛜 ⊠ ♿M 🛏 🖵 ⊃ ⊠

▼▼ ▽ **Sleep Inn** 🅷
(801) 377-6597. **Call for rates.** 1505 S 40 E 84606. I-15 exit 263 (University Ave), just e. Int corridors. **Pets:** Medium. $10 daily fee/pet. Designated rooms, service with restrictions, crate. 🛜 ⊠ 🛏 🖵 ⊃

RICHFIELD

🆎 ▼▼▼ **BEST WESTERN Richfield Inn** 🅷
(435) 893-0100. **$79-$89, 7 day notice.** 1275 N Main St 84701. I-70 exit 40, just s. Int corridors. **Pets:** $15 deposit/pet. Designated rooms, no service, supervision. (SAVE) 🛜 ⊠ 🛏 🖵 ⊃

▼▼▼ **Holiday Inn Express & Suites** 🅷
(435) 896-8552. **$89-$199.** 20 W 1400 N 84701. I-70 exit 40, just s. Int corridors. **Pets:** Other species. $20 daily fee/pet. Designated rooms, service with restrictions, supervision. 🛜 ⊠ ♿M 🛏 🖵 ⊃ ⊠

▼▼▼ **Super 8** 🅼
(435) 896-9204. **$59-$78, 3 day notice.** 1377 N Main St 84701. I-70 exit 40, just s. Ext/int corridors. **Pets:** $15 deposit/pet, $15 daily fee/pet. Designated rooms, service with restrictions, supervision. 🛜 🛏 🖵

ROOSEVELT

▼▼ ▼ **Americas Best Value Inn** 🅼
(435) 722-4644. **$110-$150.** 2203 E Hwy 40 84066. 1 mi e of center. Ext corridors. **Pets:** Accepted. 🛜 🛏 🖵 ¶¶

ST. GEORGE

▼▼ ▼ **America's Best Inn & Suites** 🅼
(435) 652-3030. **Call for rates.** 245 N Red Cliffs Dr 84790. I-15 exit 8, just e. Ext corridors. **Pets:** Medium, dogs only. $20 daily fee/pet. Designated rooms, supervision. 🛜 🛏 🖵 ⊃

▼▼ ▼ **Americas Best Value Inn** 🅼
(435) 688-8383. **$49-$59.** 915 S Bluff St 84770. I-15 exit 6 (Bluff St), just w. Int corridors. **Pets:** $10 daily fee/pet. Designated rooms, service with restrictions. 🛜 ⊠ 🛏 🖵 ⊃

▼▼▼▼ **Comfort Inn** 🅷
(435) 628-8544. **Call for rates.** 138 E Riverside Dr 84790. I-15 exit 6 (Bluff St), just e. Int corridors. **Pets:** Other species. $10 daily fee/room. Designated rooms, service with restrictions, supervision.
🛜 ⊠ ♿M 🛏 🖵 ⊃

▼▼▼ **Crystal Inn St. George** 🅷 🌸
(435) 688-7477. **$69-$149.** 1450 S Hilton Dr 84770. I-15 exit 6 (Bluff St), just w. Int corridors. **Pets:** Other species. $25 one-time fee/room. Designated rooms, service with restrictions, supervision.
🛜 ⊠ 🛏 🖵 ⊃ ⊠

🆎 ▼▼ **Dixie Palm Motel** 🅼
(435) 673-3531. **$29-$89.** 185 E St. George Blvd 84770. I-15 exit 8, 0.9 mi w; downtown. Ext corridors. **Pets:** Dogs only. $17 daily fee/pet. Service with restrictions, supervision. (SAVE) 🛜 ⊠ 🛏 🖵

🆎 ▼▼▼ ▼▼▼ **The Green Valley Spa & Resort** 🅷
(435) 628-8060. **$129-$439.** 1871 W Canyon View Dr 84770. Jct Bluff and S Main sts, 4 mi sw via Hilton Dr to Dixie Dr, then just w to Canyon View Dr. Ext corridors. **Pets:** Other species. $500 deposit/pet, $5 daily fee/pet. Service with restrictions.
(SAVE) 🛜 ♿M 🛏 🖵 ¶¶ ⊃ ⊠

🆎 ▼▼▼ **Howard Johnson Inn** 🅼
(435) 628-8000. **$60-$125.** 1040 S Main St 84770. I-15 exit 6 (Bluff St), just w, then just e. Ext corridors. **Pets:** Other species. $15 daily fee/pet. Designated rooms, service with restrictions.
(SAVE) 🛜 ⊠ 🛏 🖵 ⊃

▼▼▼▼ **La Quinta Inn & Suites - St. George** 🅷
(435) 674-2664. **$83-$199.** 91 E 2680 S 84790. I-15 exit 4, just e on Brigham Rd. Int corridors. **Pets:** Service with restrictions, supervision.
🛜 ⊠ ♿M 🛏 🖵 ⊃

🆎 ▼▼▼ **Lexington Hotel** 🅷
(435) 628-4235. **$79-$159.** 850 S Bluff St 84770. I-15 exit 6 (Bluff St), just w. Ext/int corridors. **Pets:** Dogs only. $25 one-time fee/room. Designated rooms, service with restrictions, supervision.
(SAVE) 🛜 🛏 🖵 ¶¶ ⊃ ⊠

▼▼ ▼ **Quality Inn I-15 Red Cliffs** 🅷
(435) 673-3537. **$50-$150.** 912 W Red Cliffs Dr 84780. I-15 exit 10, just e. Ext/int corridors. **Pets:** $10 daily fee/room. Designated rooms, service with restrictions, supervision. 🛜 🛏 🖵 ⊃

▼▼ ▼ **Quality Inn St. George** 🅼
(435) 628-4481. **$59-$149.** 1165 S Bluff St 84770. I-15 exit 6 (Bluff St), just w. Ext corridors. **Pets:** Accepted. 🛜 🛏 🖵 ⊃

▼▼ ▼ **Ramada** 🅷
(435) 628-2828. **$89-$159.** 1440 E St. George Blvd 84790. I-15 exit 8, just e. Int corridors. **Pets:** Small. $15 daily fee/pet. Designated rooms, service with restrictions, supervision. 🛜 🛏 🖵 ⊃

▼▼ ▼ **St. George Inn & Suites** 🅷
(435) 673-6661. **$79-$119.** 1221 S Main St 84770. I-15 exit 6 (Bluff St), just w. Ext corridors. **Pets:** Other species. $15 daily fee/room. Designated rooms, service with restrictions, supervision. 🛜 🛏 🖵 ⊃ ⊠

▼▼▼▼ **Seven Wives Inn** 🅱🅱
(435) 628-3737. **$99-$195, 7 day notice.** 217 N 100 W 84770. I-15 exit 8, 2.1 mi w, then n. Ext/int corridors. **Pets:** $20 one-time fee/pet. Designated rooms, service with restrictions, crate. 🛜 ⊠ 🛏 ⊃

🆎 ▼▼▼▼ **TownePlace Suites by Marriott** 🅷
(435) 986-9955. **$109-$179.** 251 S 1470 E 84790. I-15 exit 8, just e. Int corridors. **Pets:** $100 one-time fee/room. Service with restrictions, supervision. (SAVE) 🛜 ⊠ ♿M 🛏 🖵 ⊃

SALINA

🆎 ▼▼▼ **Scenic Hills Super 8** 🅼
(435) 529-7483. **$60-$100.** 375 E 1620 S 84654. I-70 exit 56, just n. Ext corridors. **Pets:** Accepted. (SAVE) 🛜 🛏 🖵 ⊃

SALT LAKE CITY METROPOLITAN AREA

MIDVALE

ⒶⒶⒶ◇ ▼▼▼ BEST WESTERN PLUS Midvale Inn Ⓗ
(801) 566-4141. **$59-$129.** 280 W 7200 S 84047. I-15 exit 297 (7200 S),
just e. Int corridors. **Pets:** Accepted. (SAVE) 🛜 ✕ 📵 💻 🏊

▼▼ La Quinta Inn Salt Lake City Midvale Ⓗ
(801) 566-3291. **$59-$118.** 7231 S Catalpa St 84047. I-15 exit 297 (7200
S), just e, then just s. Int corridors. **Pets:** Service with restrictions, supervision. 🛜 📵 💻 🏊

ⒶⒶⒶ◇ ▼▼▼ Super 8 Ⓗ 🐾
(801) 255-5559. **$63-$120.** 7048 S 900 E 84047. I-15 exit 297 (7200 S),
2.4 mi e via 7200 S (Fort Union Blvd) to 900 E, then just n. Int corridors.
Pets: Dogs only. $100 deposit/room. Service with restrictions, supervision.
(SAVE) 🛜 ✕ 📵 💻

MURRAY

▼▼ Pavilion Inn Ⓗ
(801) 506-8000. **$80-$160.** 5335 S College Dr 84123. I-15 exit 300 (5300
S), 0.3 mi w. Int corridors. **Pets:** Accepted. 🛜 📵 🏊

NORTH SALT LAKE

ⒶⒶⒶ◇ ▼▼▼ BEST WESTERN PLUS CottonTree Inn Ⓗ
(801) 292-7666. **$115-$200.** 1030 N 400 E 84054. I-15 exit 315 (Woods
Cross), just e to Onion St, then just s. Int corridors. **Pets:** Dogs only.
Designated rooms, service with restrictions, supervision.
(SAVE) 🛜 📵 💻 🏊

SALT LAKE CITY

▼▼ Candlewood Suites - Airport East Ⓗ
(801) 359-7500. **$109-$129.** 2170 W N Temple 84116. 3 mi w of Temple
Square. Int corridors. **Pets:** Accepted. 🛜 📵 💻

▼▼ Comfort Inn Downtown Ⓗ
(801) 325-5300. **$89-$396.** 171 W 500 S 84101. Cross streets 100 W
and 500 S. Ext/int corridors. **Pets:** Accepted. 🛜 📵 💻

▼▼▼ Crystal Inn Downtown Ⓗ 🐾
(801) 328-4466. **$89-$199.** 230 W 500 S 84101. Cross streets 500 S
and 200 W. Int corridors. **Pets:** Other species. $25 one-time fee/room,
$10 daily fee/room. Designated rooms, service with restrictions, supervi-
sion. 🛜 📵 💻 🏊 ✕

**◈▼ Hawthorn Suites by Wyndham Salt Lake City-Fort
Union Ⓗ**
(801) 567-0111. **$60-$150.** 6990 Park Centre Dr 84121. I-15 exit 297
(7200 S), 2.4 mi e on 7200 S (Fort Union Blvd) to 1300 E, continue just
e to Park Centre Dr, then just s. Int corridors. **Pets:** Accepted.
🛜 📵 💻

ⒶⒶⒶ◇ ▼▼▼▼ Hilton Salt Lake City Airport Ⓗ 🐾
(801) 539-1515. **$82-$232.** 5151 Wiley Post Way 84116. I-80 exit 114
(Wright Brothers Dr), just n off ramp, then 0.4 mi w. Int corridors.
Pets: Large, other species. $50 one-time fee/room. Designated rooms,
service with restrictions, supervision.
(SAVE) 🛜 📵 💻 🍴 🏊 ✕

ⒶⒶⒶ◇ ▼▼▼▼ Hilton Salt Lake City Center Ⓗ
(801) 328-2000. **$109-$349.** 255 S West Temple 84101. Just s of cross
streets 200 S and S West Temple. Int corridors. **Pets:** Accepted.
(SAVE) 🛜 📵 💻 🍴 🏊

▼▼▼ Holiday Inn & Suites - Airport West Ⓗ
(801) 741-1800. **$75-$299.** 5001 W Wiley Post Way 84116. I-80 exit 114
(Wright Brothers Dr), just n off ramp, then 0.4 mi w. Int corridors.
Pets: Other species. $35 one-time fee/pet. Service with restrictions,
supervision. 🛜 📵 💻 🍴 🏊

▼▼▼ Holiday Inn Express - Airport East Ⓗ
(801) 741-1500. **$99-$130.** 200 N 2100 W 84116. 3 mi w of Temple
Square. Int corridors. **Pets:** Large. $20 daily fee/pet. Designated rooms,
service with restrictions, crate. 🛜 📵 💻 🏊

ⒶⒶⒶ◇ ▼▼▼▼ Hotel Monaco Ⓗ
(801) 595-0000. **Call for rates.** 15 W 200 S 84101. Cross streets 200 S
and Main St. Int corridors. **Pets:** Accepted.
(ECO) (SAVE) 🛜 ✕ 🍴 ✕

**ⒶⒶⒶ◇ ▼▼▼▼ Radisson Hotel Salt Lake City
Downtown Ⓗ**
(801) 531-7500. **$79-$299.** 215 W South Temple 84101. Cross streets
200 S and W South Temple. Int corridors. **Pets:** Accepted.
(ECO) (SAVE) 🛜 ✕ 📵 💻 🍴 🏊 ✕

ⒶⒶⒶ◇ ▼▼▼▼ Red Lion Hotel Salt Lake Downtown Ⓗ
(801) 521-7373. **$80-$170.** 161 W 600 S 84101. Cross streets S West
Temple and 600 S. Int corridors. **Pets:** Other species. $15 one-time fee/
room. Service with restrictions, crate.
(SAVE) 🛜 ✕ 📵 💻 🍴 🏊

▼▼▼ Residence Inn by Marriott - Airport West Ⓗ 🐾
(801) 532-4101. **$78-$155.** 4883 W Douglas Corrigan Way 84116. I-80
exit 114 (Wright Brothers Dr), just n off ramp. Int corridors. **Pets:** Other
species. $75 one-time fee/room. Service with restrictions.
🛜 ✕ 🗄 📵 💻 🏊 ✕

▼▼▼ Residence Inn by Marriott-City Center Ⓗ
(801) 355-3300. **$89-$209.** 285 W Broadway (300 S) 84101. Corner of
300 W and 300 S. Int corridors. **Pets:** Accepted.
🛜 ✕ 📵 💻 🏊

ⒶⒶⒶ◇ ▼▼▼▼ Sheraton Salt Lake City Hotel Ⓗ 🐾
(801) 401-2000. **$99-$359.** 150 W 500 S 84101. Cross streets 200 W
and 500 S. Int corridors. **Pets:** Other species. Service with restrictions.
(SAVE) 🛜 ✕ 📵 💻 🍴 🏊 ✕

SANDY

ⒶⒶⒶ◇ ▼▼▼▼ BEST WESTERN PLUS CottonTree Inn Ⓗ
(801) 523-8484. **$89-$134.** 10695 S Auto Mall Dr 84070. I-15 exit 293
(10600 S), 0.3 mi e, then just s. Int corridors. **Pets:** Accepted.
(SAVE) 🛜 ✕ 📵 💻 🏊

▼▼▼▼ Holiday Inn Express & Suites Ⓗ
(801) 495-1317. **$99-$139.** 10680 S Auto Mall Dr 84070. I-15 exit 293
(10600 S), 0.3 mi e, then just s. Int corridors. **Pets:** Other species. $10
daily fee/pet. Designated rooms, no service, supervision.
🛜 📵 💻 🏊

ⒶⒶⒶ◇ ▼▼▼▼ Hyatt house Salt Lake City/Sandy Ⓗ
(801) 304-5700. **$99-$339.** 9685 S Monroe St 84070. I-15 exit 295 (9000
S), 0.3 mi e to Frontage Rd, then 1 mi s. Int corridors. **Pets:** Accepted.
(SAVE) 🛜 ✕ 📵 💻 🏊

▼▼▼ Residence Inn by Marriott Ⓗ
(801) 561-5005. **$109-$279.** 270 W 10000 S 84070. I-15 exit 293 (10600
S), 0.4 mi e to State St, 0.7 mi n to 10000 S, then 0.3 mi w. Int corridors.
Pets: Accepted. 🛜 ✕ 📵 💻 🏊 ✕

WEST VALLEY CITY

▼▼ Baymont Inn & Suites Ⓗ
(801) 886-1300. **$73-$114.** 2229 W City Center Ct 84119. I-215 exit 18
(3500 S), just e, then just w. Int corridors. **Pets:** Medium. Service with
restrictions, crate. 🛜 📵 💻 🏊

▼▼ Country Inn & Suites By Carlson 🅷
(801) 908-0311. **$89-$129.** 3422 S Decker Lake Dr 84119. I-215 exit 18 (3500 S), just e, then just n. Int corridors. **Pets:** Large, other species. $10 daily fee/room. Designated rooms, service with restrictions.
📶 ✕ 🚹 💻 🏊

▼▼▼ Holiday Inn Express Waterpark West Valley 🅷
(801) 517-4000. **$90-$150.** 3036 S Decker Lake Dr 84119. I-215 exit 18A (3500 S), just e, 0.6 mi n, then just w. Int corridors. **Pets:** $15 daily fee/pet. Service with restrictions, supervision. 📶 🚹 💻 🏊 ✕

▼▼▼ Home2 Suites by Hilton® Salt Lake City / West Valley City 🅷
(801) 679-8222. **$99-$299.** 4028 Parkway Blvd 84120. I-15 exit 305A (West Valley/2100 S), 4.2 mi w on CR 201 exit 13 (Bangerter Hwy), 1.2 mi s to Parkway Blvd, then 0.3 mi w. Int corridors. **Pets:** Accepted.
📶 🚹 💻 🏊

▼▼ La Quinta Inn Salt Lake City West 🅷
(801) 954-9292. **$72-$166.** 3540 S 2200 W 84119. I-215 exit 18 (3500 S), just e, then just s. Int corridors. **Pets:** Service with restrictions, supervision. 📶 🚹 💻 🏊

▼▼▼ Staybridge Suites 🅷
(801) 746-8400. **$99-$169.** 3038 S Decker Lake Dr 84119. I-215 exit 18A (3500 S), just e, 0.6 mi n, then just w. Int corridors. **Pets:** Accepted.
📶 Ⓜ 🚹 💻 🏊 ✕

WOODS CROSS
▼▼▼ Hampton Inn - Salt Lake City North/Woods Cross 🅷
(801) 296-1211. **$89-$125.** 2393 S 800 W 84087. I-15 exit 315, just w, then just n. Int corridors. **Pets:** Other species. Supervision.
📶 ✕ 🚹 💻 🏊 ✕

END METROPOLITAN AREA

SPANISH FORK
🅰🅰🅰 ▼▼ Western Inn 🅷
(801) 798-9400. **$50-$80.** 632 Kirby Ln 84660. I-15 exit 257B, on US 6. Int corridors. **Pets:** Other species. $50 deposit/room, $6 daily fee/pet. Designated rooms, service with restrictions, supervision. SAVE 📶 ✕

SPRINGDALE
🅰🅰🅰 ▼▼▼ BEST WESTERN Zion Park Inn 🅷
(435) 772-3200. **$89-$179.** 1215 Zion Park Blvd 84767. 2 mi s of Zion National Park entrance. Int corridors. **Pets:** Small, dogs only. $25 one-time fee/room. Designated rooms, service with restrictions, crate.
SAVE 📶 🚹 💻 🏊 ✕

▼▼ Canyon Ranch Motel Ⓜ
(435) 772-3357. **Call for rates.** 668 Zion Park Blvd 84767. SR 9, just s of south gate to Zion National Park. Ext corridors. **Pets:** Accepted.
📶 ✕ 🚹 💻 🏊

SPRINGVILLE
🅰🅰🅰 ▼▼ BEST WESTERN Mountain View Inn 🅷 ✿
(801) 489-3641. **$76-$130.** 1455 N 1750 W 84663. I-15 exit 261, just e. Int corridors. **Pets:** $10 daily fee/pet. Designated rooms, service with restrictions, supervision. SAVE 📶 ✕ 🚹 💻 🏊

TOOELE
▼▼▼ Comfort Inn & Suites 🅷
(801) 250-3600. **Call for rates.** 8580 N SR 36 84074. I-80 exit 99, just s. Int corridors. **Pets:** Small, dogs only. $40 one-time fee/room. Designated rooms, supervision. 📶 ✕ 🚹 💻 🏊

▼▼▼ Holiday Inn Express & Suites 🅷
(435) 833-0500. **$89-$150.** 1531 N Main St 84074. I-80 exit 99, 11 mi s. Int corridors. **Pets:** Accepted. 📶 Ⓜ 🚹 💻 🏊

TORREY
🅰🅰🅰 ▼▼ BEST WESTERN Capitol Reef Resort Ⓜ
(435) 425-3761. **$110-$180.** 2600 E SR 24 84775. 2 mi e of jct SR 12 and 24. Ext corridors. **Pets:** Medium. Designated rooms, service with restrictions, supervision. SAVE 📶 🚹 💻 🍽 🏊 ✕

▼▼ Days Inn Torrey 🅷
(435) 425-3111. **$79-$114.** 825 E SR 24 84775. Jct SR 12 and 24. Int corridors. **Pets:** Accepted. 📶 ✕ 🚹 💻 🏊

▼▼ Howard Johnson 🅷
(435) 425-3866. **$79-$109.** 877 N SR 24 84775. 1.5 mi ne of jct SR 12 and 24. Ext corridors. **Pets:** $15 deposit/pet, $15 daily fee/pet. Designated rooms, service with restrictions, supervision. 📶 ✕ 🚹 💻 🍽

🅰🅰🅰 ▼▼ Red Sands Hotel 🅷
(435) 425-3688. **$79-$110.** 670 E SR 24 84775. 0.3 mi w of jct SR 12 and 24. Int corridors. **Pets:** Accepted. SAVE 📶 ✕ Ⓜ 🚹 🏊

🅰🅰🅰 ▼ Rim Rock Inn Ⓜ ✿
(435) 425-3398. **$54-$84.** 2523 E Hwy 24 84775. 2.5 mi ne of jct SR 12 and 24. Ext corridors. **Pets:** $10 one-time fee/pet. Designated rooms, supervision. SAVE 📶 ✕ 🍽

TREMONTON
▼▼▼ Hampton Inn 🅷
(435) 257-6000. **$89-$129.** 2145 W Main St 84337. I-84 exit 40, 0.4 mi e. Int corridors. **Pets:** Medium. Designated rooms, service with restrictions, supervision. 📶 ✕ 🚹 💻 🏊

WASHINGTON
▼▼▼ Holiday Inn Express & Suites 🅷
(435) 986-1313. **$89-$149, 3 day notice.** 2450 N Town Center Dr 84780. I-15 exit 16, just e. Int corridors. **Pets:** Accepted.
📶 ✕ 🚹 💻 🏊

VERMONT

ALBURG

▼▼▼ Ransom Bay Inn & Restaurant **BB**
(802) 796-3399. **$120-$135, 7 day notice.** 4 Center Bay Rd 05440. Jct SR 78, 0.5 mi s on US 2, then just e. Int corridors. **Pets:** Accepted.
🛰 ⊠ 📶 🐾 🏊

ARLINGTON

◈◈ ▼ Candlelight Motel **M**
(802) 375-6647. **$59-$115, 14 day notice.** 4893 SR 7A 05250. Historic SR 7A, 1 mi n. Ext corridors. **Pets:** Small, dogs only. $10 one-time fee/pet, $10 daily fee/pet. Designated rooms, service with restrictions, supervision. [SAVE] 🛰 🖥 🏊

BENNINGTON

◈◈ ▼▼ Bennington Motor Inn **M**
(802) 442-5479. **$65-$169, 3 day notice.** 143 W Main St 05201. Jct US 7, 0.4 mi w on SR 9. Ext corridors. **Pets:** Accepted. [SAVE] 🛰 🖥 🏊

◈◈ ▼ Harwood Hill Motel **M**
(802) 442-6278. **$67-$99, 3 day notice.** 864 Harwood Hill Rd (SR 7A) 05201. Jct SR 9, 1.2 mi n on US 7, then 1.7 mi n on Historic SR 7A. Ext corridors. **Pets:** Accepted. [SAVE] ⊠ 🖥 🏊

▼ Knotty Pine Motel **M**
(802) 442-5487. **$79-$99.** 130 Northside Dr (SR 7A) 05201. Jct SR 9, 1.2 mi n on US 7, then just n on Historic SR 7A. Ext corridors. **Pets:** Service with restrictions, supervision. 🛰 ⊠ 🖥 🏊 🐾

BRANDON

◈◈ ▼▼ Brandon Motor Lodge **M**
(802) 247-9594. **$69-$145.** 2095 Franklin St 05733. 2 mi s on US 7. Ext corridors. **Pets:** Large, other species. $10 one-time fee/room. Designated rooms, service with restrictions, supervision.
[ECO] [SAVE] 🛰 ⊠ 🖥 🏊 🐾

▼▼▼ The Lilac Inn **CI**
(802) 247-5463. **$145-$375, 30 day notice.** 53 Park St 05733. Just e on SR 73. Int corridors. **Pets:** Dogs only. $40 one-time fee/room. Service with restrictions, crate. [ECO] 🛰 ⊠ 📶 🏊

BRATTLEBORO

◈◈ ▼▼▼ Econo Lodge **M**
(802) 254-2360. **Call for rates.** 515 Canal St 05301. I-91 exit 1, 0.3 mi n on US 5. Ext/int corridors. **Pets:** Accepted. [SAVE] 🛰 🖥 🏊

BURLINGTON

◈◈ ▼▼▼ Hilton Burlington **H**
(802) 658-6500. **$99-$199.** 60 Battery St 05401. At Battery and College sts; just n of ferry terminal; center. Int corridors. **Pets:** Accepted.
[SAVE] 🛰 ⊠ 🐾ᴹ 🖥 🏊 📶 🐾

CAVENDISH

▼▼▼▼ The Pointe at Castle Hill Resort & Spa **H**
(802) 226-7688. **$79-$299, 14 day notice.** 2940 SR 103 05142. On SR 103, just n of jct SR 131. Int corridors. **Pets:** $40 daily fee/room. Designated rooms, service with restrictions, crate.
🛰 ⊠ 🖥 🏊 📶 🐾 🐾

COLCHESTER

▼▼ Days Inn Colchester **H**
(802) 655-0900. **$70-$150.** 124 College Pkwy 05446. I-89 exit 15 northbound, just e on SR 15; exit 16 southbound, 1.1 mi s on US 7, then 1 mi e on SR 15. Int corridors. **Pets:** Dogs only. $10 daily fee/pet. Designated rooms, service with restrictions, crate. 🛰 🐾ᴹ 🖥 🏊 🐾

▼▼ Hampton Inn & Event Center **H**
(802) 655-6177. **$129-$229.** 42 Lower Mountain View Dr 05446. I-89 exit 16, just n on US 7. Int corridors. **Pets:** Other species. Designated rooms, service with restrictions, supervision.
[ECO] 🛰 ⊠ 🐾ᴹ 🖥 🏊 🐾

▼▼ Motel 6 #1407 **H**
(802) 654-6860. **$59-$89.** 74 S Park Dr 05446. I-89 exit 16, just s on US 7. Int corridors. **Pets:** Other species. Service with restrictions, supervision.
🛰 🐾

◈◈ ▼▼▼ Quality Inn Colchester Burlington Area **H**
(802) 655-1400. **$109-$209.** 84 S Park Dr 05446. I-89 exit 16, just s on US 7. Ext/int corridors. **Pets:** Medium. $15 daily fee/pet. Designated rooms, service with restrictions. [SAVE] 🛰 🐾ᴹ 🖥 🏊 🐾

◈◈ ▼▼▼ Residence Inn by Marriott, Burlington-Colchester **H** 🐾
(802) 655-3100. **$159-$299.** 71 Rathe Rd 05446. I-89 exit 16, 0.6 mi n on US 2 W/7 N, then just w. Int corridors. **Pets:** Other species. $100 one-time fee/room. Service with restrictions, crate.
🛰 ⊠ 🐾ᴹ 🖥 🏊 🐾 🐾

ESSEX JUNCTION

◈◈ ▼▼▼ ▼▼▼ The Essex Resort & Spa **H** 🐾
(802) 878-1100. **$169-$349, 7 day notice.** 70 Essex Way 05452. SR 289 exit 10, 0.3 mi s. Int corridors. **Pets:** Other species. $25 daily fee/pet. Designated rooms, service with restrictions.
[ECO] [SAVE] 🛰 ⊠ 🐾ᴹ 🖥 🏊 📶 🐾 🐾

▼▼▼ Handy Suites-Essex **H**
(802) 872-5200. **$69-$249.** 27 Susie Wilson Rd 05452. I-89 exit 15 northbound, 2 mi e, then just n. Int corridors. **Pets:** Dogs only. $200 deposit/room. Designated rooms, service with restrictions.
🛰 🐾ᴹ 🖥 🏊 🐾

FLETCHER

▼▼▼▼ The Inn at Buck Hollow Farm **BB** 🐾
(802) 849-2400. **$100-$130, 14 day notice.** 2150 Buck Hollow Rd 05454. 6 mi n of jct SR 104 via Buck Hollow Rd. Int corridors. **Pets:** $20 daily fee/pet. Service with restrictions, supervision.
🛰 ⊠ 🐾 🐾 🏊

KILLINGTON

◆◇ ▼▼▼ The Cascades Lodge 🅷
(802) 422-3731. **$115-$299, 21 day notice.** 58 Old Mill Rd 05751. 3.6 mi s on Killington Rd from jct SR 100/US 4, then just e. Int corridors. **Pets:** Dogs only. $50 daily fee/pet. Designated rooms, service with restrictions, crate. ⓢⒶⓥⒺ 🛜 ❎ 🔋 🖵 🍴 🏊 ⊠

LONDONDERRY

▼ Snowdon Motel Ⓜ
(802) 824-6047. **$65-$125, 7 day notice.** 4071 VT Rt 11 05148. Jct SR 100, 2 mi e. Ext corridors. **Pets:** Dogs only. $10 daily fee/pet. Designated rooms, service with restrictions, crate. 🛜 ❎ 🔋 ⊠

LUDLOW

▼▼▼ Andrie Rose Inn ᴮᴮ 🐾
(802) 228-4846. **$110-$364, 20 day notice.** 13 Pleasant St 05149. Corner of Depot St; center. Int corridors. **Pets:** Other species. $25 one-time fee/room. Designated rooms, service with restrictions.

🛜 ❎ 🔋 🍴 ⊠

MANCHESTER

▼▼ Weathervane Motel Ⓜ
(802) 362-2444. **Call for rates.** 2212 Main St (Historic SR 7A) 05254. Jct SR 11/30, 2.3 mi s. Ext corridors. **Pets:** Accepted.

🛜 ❎ 🔋 🖵 🏊

MANCHESTER CENTER

▼▼ Casablanca Motel Ⓜ 🐾
(802) 362-2145. **$72-$125, 14 day notice.** 5927 Main St (Rt 7A) 05255. Jct SR 11/30, 1 mi n on Historic SR 7A. Ext corridors. **Pets:** Other species. $15 daily fee/pet. Designated rooms, service with restrictions. ᴱᶜᴼ 🛜 ❎ 🔋 🖵 ⊠

◆◇ ▼▼▼ Manchester View Fine Lodging 🅷 🐾
(802) 362-2739. **$95-$325, 14 day notice.** 77 High Meadows Way 05255. On Historic SR 7A, 2 mi n of jct SR 11/30 N, then just e. Ext/int corridors. **Pets:** Small. $20 daily fee/pet. Designated rooms, service with restrictions, supervision. ⓢⒶⓥⒺ 🛜 ❎ 🔋 🖵 🏊

MANCHESTER VILLAGE

◆◇ ▼▼▼▼ The Equinox, a Luxury Collection Golf Resort & Spa 🅷 🐾
(802) 362-4700. **$199-$569, 21 day notice.** 3567 Main St 05254. 1.3 mi s on Historic SR 7A, from jct SR 11/30. Int corridors. **Pets:** Large, dogs only. $125 one-time fee/pet. Service with restrictions, supervision.
ᴱᶜᴼ ⓢⒶⓥⒺ 🛜 ❎ 🔋 🍴 🏊 ⊠

MIDDLEBURY

▼▼▼ The Middlebury Inn 🅷 🐾
(802) 388-4961. **$129-$299, 3 day notice.** 14 Court Square 05753. On US 7; center. Ext/int corridors. **Pets:** Other species. $25 one-time fee/room. Designated rooms, service with restrictions, supervision.

ᴱᶜᴼ 🛜 ❎ 🔋 🖵 🍴

▼▼▼ Swift House Inn 🅲 🐾
(802) 388-9925. **$129-$299, 7 day notice.** 25 Stewart Ln 05753. 0.3 mi n on US 7 from jct SR 125 W. Ext/int corridors. **Pets:** Medium, dogs only. $50 daily fee/pet. Designated rooms, service with restrictions, supervision. ᴱᶜᴼ 🛜 ❎ 🖵 🍴 ⊠

MONTGOMERY CENTER

▼▼▼ Phineas Swann Bed & Breakfast Inn ᴮᴮ
(802) 326-4306. **$129-$425, 30 day notice.** 195 Main St 05471. Center. Ext/int corridors. **Pets:** Accepted. 🛜 ❎ 🔋 🖵 ⊠

MONTPELIER

▼▼▼ Betsy's B&B ᴮᴮ
(802) 229-0466. **$95-$160, 3 day notice.** 74 E State St 05602. 0.3 mi e of Main St; center. Int corridors. **Pets:** Accepted.
ᴱᶜᴼ 🛜 ❎ 🔋 🖵

MORRISVILLE

◆◇ ▼▼▼ Sunset Motor Inn Ⓜ
(802) 888-4956. **$85-$142, 7 day notice.** 160 SR 15 W 05661. Jct SR 100, just w on SR 15. Ext/int corridors. **Pets:** $50 deposit/pet. Designated rooms, service with restrictions, crate.
ⓢⒶⓥⒺ 🛜 ♿ 🔋 🖵 🍴 🏊

NORTH HERO

▼▼▼ Shore Acres Inn 🅲
(802) 372-8722. **$95-$250, 21 day notice.** 237 Shore Acres Dr 05474. 0.5 mi s on US 2. Ext/int corridors. **Pets:** Dogs only. $20 one-time fee/pet, $5 daily fee/pet. Crate. 🛜 ❎ 🔋 🍴 ⊠ 🍴

PUTNEY

▼▼ The Putney Inn 🅷
(802) 387-5517. **Call for rates.** 57 Putney Landing Rd 05346. I-91 exit 4, just e. Ext corridors. **Pets:** $10 daily fee/pet. Designated rooms, service with restrictions, crate. 🛜 ❎ 🔋 🖵 🍴

RANDOLPH

◆◇ ▼▼▼ Three Stallion Inn 🅲
(802) 728-5575. **$125-$195, 15 day notice.** 665 Stock Farm Rd 05060. I-89 exit 4 (SR 66), 2 mi w; jct SR 12, just e on SR 66, then just s. Ext/int corridors. **Pets:** $400 deposit/room. Designated rooms, service with restrictions, supervision. ⓢⒶⓥⒺ 🛜 ❎ 🖵 🏊 ⊠

RUTLAND

▼▼▼ Comfort Inn at Trolley Square 🅷
(802) 775-2200. **Call for rates.** 19 Allen St 05701. On US 7, 1 mi s from jct US 4 W; 1.5 mi n from US 4 E. Int corridors. **Pets:** Medium. $35 one-time fee/room. Designated rooms, service with restrictions, supervision. 🛜 ❎ ♿ 🔋 🖵 🏊

▼▼▼ Holiday Inn Rutland/Killington 🅷
(802) 775-1911. **$99-$249.** 476 Holiday Dr 05701. 2.4 mi s on US 7 from US 4 W; 0.4 mi n on US 7 from US 4 E. Int corridors. **Pets:** Other species. $25 daily fee/room. Designated rooms, service with restrictions, supervision. 🛜 ♿ 🔋 🖵 🍴 🏊 ⊠

◆◇ ▼▼▼ Red Roof Inn Rutland-Killington 🅷
(802) 775-4303. **$60-$250.** 401 US Hwy 7 S 05701. 0.8 mi s on US 7 and 4. Int corridors. **Pets:** Large, other species. Service with restrictions, supervision. ⓢⒶⓥⒺ 🛜 🔋 🖵 🏊

ST. ALBANS

◆◇ ▼▼ Econo Lodge Ⓜ
(802) 524-5956. **Call for rates.** 287 S Main St (US 7) 05478. I-89 exit 19, 1 mi w on Interstate Access Rd, then 0.5 mi s. Ext/int corridors. **Pets:** Accepted. ⓢⒶⓥⒺ 🛜 🔋 🖵

▼▼ La Quinta Inn & Suites St. Albans 🅷
(802) 524-3300. **$99-$232.** 813 Fairfax Rd 05478. I-89 exit 19, just w on Interstate Access Rd, then just s. Int corridors. **Pets:** Service with restrictions, supervision. 🛜 ♿ 🔋 🖵 🏊

ST. JOHNSBURY

▼▼ Fairbanks Inn Ⓜ
(802) 748-5666. **Call for rates.** 401 Western Ave 05819. I-91 exit 21, 0.8 mi e on US 2. Ext corridors. **Pets:** Dogs only. $25 daily fee/pet. Designated rooms, service with restrictions, crate. 🛜 ❎ 🔋 🏊

SHAFTSBURY

▼▼ **Hillbrook Motel** 🅜
(802) 447-7201. **Call for rates.** 2629 Rt 7A 05262. SR 7 exit 2, 2 mi n. Ext corridors. **Pets:** Accepted.

▼ **Serenity Motel** 🆑
(802) 442-6490. **$70-$90.** 4379 Rt 7A 05262. Jct SR 67, 3.3 mi n on Historic SR 7A. Ext corridors. **Pets:** Other species. Designated rooms, service with restrictions, supervision.

SHELBURNE

🅐🅐🅐 ▼▼ **Quality Inn** 🅜
(802) 985-8037. **$90-$200.** 2572 Shelburne Rd 05482. I-89 exit 13 (I-189/US 7), 2.1 mi s. Ext/int corridors. **Pets:** $10 daily fee/pet. Designated rooms, service with restrictions, supervision.

SOUTH BURLINGTON

🅐🅐🅐 ▼▼▼ **BEST WESTERN PLUS Windjammer Inn &**
Conference Center 🅗 ❀
(802) 863-1125. **$115-$195.** 1076 Williston Rd 05403. I-89 exit 14E, 0.3 mi e on US 2. Int corridors. **Pets:** Large. $10 daily fee/pet. Designated rooms, service with restrictions, supervision.

🅐🅐🅐 ▼▼▼ **DoubleTree by Hilton Hotel Burlington** 🅗
(802) 658-0250. **$129-$299.** 1117 Williston Rd 05403. I-89 exit 14E, just e on US 2. Int corridors. **Pets:** Medium. $75 deposit/room. Designated rooms, service with restrictions, supervision.

▼▼▼ **Green Mountain Suites Hotel** 🅗
(802) 860-1212. **$149-$489, 3 day notice.** 401 Dorset St 05403. I-89 exit 14E, just e on US 2, then 0.8 mi s. Int corridors. **Pets:** Accepted.

▼▼ **La Quinta Inn & Suites South Burlington** 🅗
(802) 865-3400. **$90-$239.** 1285 Williston Rd 05403. I-89 exit 14E, 0.5 mi e on US 2. Int corridors. **Pets:** Service with restrictions, supervision.

🅐🅐🅐 ▼▼▼ **Sheraton Burlington Hotel & Conference**
Center 🅗
(802) 865-6600. **$129-$329.** 870 Williston Rd 05403. I-89 exit 14W, just w on US 2. Int corridors. **Pets:** Accepted.

▼▼▼ **Smart Suites** 🅗
(802) 860-9900. **$99-$199.** 1700 Shelburne Rd 05403. I-89 exit 13 (I-189/US 7) to US 7, 1.5 mi s. Int corridors. **Pets:** Small. $25 one-time fee/pet. Designated rooms, service with restrictions.

SOUTH WOODSTOCK

▼▼▼ **Kedron Valley Inn** 🆑
(802) 457-1473. **$149-$329, 15 day notice.** 4778 South Rd 05071. Jct US 4, 5 mi s. Ext/int corridors. **Pets:** Accepted.

SPRINGFIELD

▼▼▼ **Holiday Inn Express** 🅗
(802) 885-4516. **Call for rates.** 818 Charlestown Rd 05156. I-91 exit 7. Int corridors. **Pets:** Accepted.

STOWE

▼▼▼▼ **1066 Ye Olde England Inne** 🆑
(802) 253-7558. **Call for rates.** 433 Mountain Rd 05672. Jct SR 100, 0.4 mi w on SR 108. Ext/int corridors. **Pets:** Other species. $20 daily fee/pet. Designated rooms, service with restrictions, crate.

🅐🅐🅐 ▼▼▼ **Commodores Inn** 🅗
(802) 253-7131. **$98-$198, 3 day notice.** 823 S Main St 05672. Jct SR 108, 0.8 mi s on SR 100. Int corridors. **Pets:** Other species. $10 daily fee/room.

▼▼▼ **Edson Hill Manor** 🆑
(802) 253-7371. **$139-$239, 15 day notice.** 1500 Edson Hill Rd 05672. Jct SR 100, 3.4 mi w on SR 108, 1.3 mi n. Ext/int corridors. **Pets:** Designated rooms, service with restrictions, supervision.

🅐🅐🅐 ▼▼▼ **Golden Eagle Resort** 🅜 ❀
(802) 253-4811. **$99-$299, 7 day notice.** 511 Mountain Rd 05672. Jct SR 100, 0.5 mi w on SR 108. Ext corridors. **Pets:** Other species. $25 one-time fee/pet. Designated rooms, service with restrictions.

▼▼ **Hob Knob Inn & Restaurant** 🅜
(802) 253-8549. **$90-$300, 14 day notice.** 2364 Mountain Rd 05672. Jct SR 100, 2.5 mi w on SR 108. Ext/int corridors. **Pets:** $20 daily fee/pet.

▼▼▼ **The Mountain Road Resort at Stowe** 🅜
(802) 253-4566. **Call for rates.** 1007 Mountain Rd 05672. Jct SR 100, 1 mi w on SR 108. Ext corridors. **Pets:** Accepted.

▼▼ **The Snowdrift Motel** 🅜
(802) 253-7629. **$90-$160, 7 day notice.** 2135 Mountain Rd 05672. Jct SR 100, 2.1 mi w on SR 108. Designated rooms, service with restrictions, crate. **Pets:** Dogs only. $12 daily fee/pet.

🅐🅐🅐 ▼▼▼ **Stoweflake Mountain Resort &**
Spa 🅗 ❀
(802) 253-7355. **$199-$559, 15 day notice.** 1746 Mountain Rd 05672. Jct SR 100, 1.4 mi w on SR 108. Int corridors. **Pets:** Large, dogs only. $40 daily fee/room. Designated rooms, service with restrictions, supervision.

🅐🅐🅐 ▼▼▼ **The Stowe Inn & Tavern** 🆑
(802) 253-4030. **$99-$379, 3 day notice.** 123 Mountain Rd 05672. Jct SR 100, just n. Ext/int corridors. **Pets:** Accepted.

🅐🅐🅐 ▼▼▼ **Stowe Mountain Lodge** 🅗 ❀
(802) 253-3560. **$199-$829, 14 day notice.** 7412 Mountain Rd 05672. Jct SR 100, 7.3 mi w on SR 108. Int corridors. **Pets:** Large, dogs only. $75 one-time fee/room. Designated rooms, service with restrictions, supervision.

🅐🅐🅐 ▼▼▼ **Sun & Ski Inn and Suites** 🅜
(802) 253-7159. **$79-$199, 15 day notice.** 1613 Mountain Rd 05672. Jct SR 100, 1.7 mi w on SR 108. Ext corridors. **Pets:** Large, other species. $15 daily fee/pet. Service with restrictions, crate.

🅐🅐🅐 ▼▼▼ ▼▼▼ **Topnotch Resort and Spa** 🅗 ❀
(802) 253-8585. **$175-$595, 14 day notice.** 4000 Mountain Rd 05672. Jct SR 100, 4.2 mi w on SR 108. Ext/int corridors. **Pets:** Dogs only. Designated rooms, service with restrictions, supervision.

▼▼▼ **Trapp Family Lodge** 🅗
(802) 253-8511. **$215-$515, 14 day notice.** 700 Trapp Hill Rd 05672. Jct SR 100, 2.1 mi w on SR 108, 1.4 mi s on Luce Hill Rd, follow signs. Int corridors. **Pets:** Accepted.

SWANTON

🅐🅐🅐 ▼▼ **Swanton Motel** 🅜
(802) 868-4284. **$75-$183.** 112 Grand Ave (US 7) 05488. I-89 exit 21, 0.8 mi w on SR 78, then 0.5 mi s. Ext corridors. **Pets:** Medium. $150 deposit/room, $15 daily fee/pet. Designated rooms, service with restrictions, supervision.

VERGENNES

◇◇◇ ▽▽▽▽ Strong House Inn **CI** ✿

(802) 877-3337. **$140-$340, 14 day notice.** 94 W Main St 05491. 0.6 mi s on SR 22A. Int corridors. **Pets:** Large, dogs only. $35 one-time fee/pet. Designated rooms, service with restrictions, supervision.

[SAVE] 📶 ✕ 🏃M 🖥 💻

WARREN

◇◇◇ ▽▽▽▽ The Pitcher Inn **CI**

(802) 496-6350. **$325-$800, 30 day notice.** 275 Main St 05674. Center. Ext/int corridors. **Pets:** Dogs only. $75 daily fee/pet. Designated rooms, service with restrictions, crate. [SAVE] 📶 ✕ 🖥 💻 🍴 ✕

WATERBURY

◇◇◇ ▽▽▽▽ The Old Stagecoach Inn **BB**

(802) 244-5056. **$90-$150, 14 day notice.** 18 N Main St 05676. I-89 exit 10, just s on SR 100, then just e. Ext/int corridors. **Pets:** Other species. $20 daily fee/room. Designated rooms, supervision.

[SAVE] 📶 ✕ 🖥 💻 🍴

WEST BRATTLEBORO

◇ Molly Stark Motel **M**

(802) 254-2440. **$45-$95.** 829 Marlboro Rd 05301. I-91 exit 2, 3.3 mi w on SR 9. Ext corridors. **Pets:** Large, dogs only. $5 daily fee/pet. Supervision. 📶 🖥 💻

WESTMORE

▽▽▽ WilloughVale Inn on Lake Willoughby **CI**

(802) 525-4123. **$79-$329, 30 day notice.** 793 SR 5A 05860. Jct SR 16 and 5A, just s. Ext/int corridors. **Pets:** Medium, dogs only. $32 daily fee/pet. Designated rooms, service with restrictions, supervision.

📶 ✕ 🖥 💻 🍴 ✕

WHITE RIVER JUNCTION

▽▽ ▽ Comfort Inn **H**

(802) 295-3051. **$99-$199.** 56 Ralph Lehman Dr 05001. I-91 exit 11, just e. Int corridors. **Pets:** Service with restrictions, supervision.

📶 🏃M 🖥 💻 🏊

WILLISTON

▽▽▽▽ Residence Inn by Marriott Burlington Williston **H**

(802) 878-2001. **$99-$239.** 35 Hurricane Ln 05495. I-89 exit 12, just s on SR 2A, then just e. Ext corridors. **Pets:** Medium. $75 one-time fee/room. Service with restrictions. 📶 ✕ 🖥 💻 🏊 ✕

WINDSOR

▽▽▽ Juniper Hill Inn **CI**

(802) 674-5273. **Call for rates.** 153 Pembroke Rd 05089. I-91 exit 9, 2.9 mi s on US 5 to Juniper Hill Rd, then 0.5 mi w. Int corridors. **Pets:** Accepted. 📶 ✕ 🍴 ✕ ☎

WOODSTOCK

▽▽ ▽ The Shire Riverview Inn **M**

(802) 457-2211. **$98-$228, 14 day notice.** 46 Pleasant St 05091. 0.4 mi e on US 4; downtown. Ext/int corridors. **Pets:** $25 one-time fee/pet. Designated rooms, service with restrictions, supervision. 📶 ✕ 🖥

VIRGINIA

CITY INDEX

ABINGDON

◆◆◆ ▼▼▼▼ Holiday Inn Express 🄷
(276) 676-2829. **$99-$159.** 940 E Main St 24210. I-81 exit 19 (US 11), just w. Int corridors. **Pets:** Small. $25 daily fee/room. Designated rooms, service with restrictions, supervision. 〔SAVE〕 🛜 🛎 🖥 ⇲

ALTAVISTA

▼▼▼ Comfort Inn 🄷
(434) 369-4000. **$69-$199.** 1558 Main St 24517. US 29 business route, jct US 29. Int corridors. **Pets:** Accepted. 🛜 🛎 🖥 ⇲ 🗙

▼▼▼▼ Days Inn 🄷
(434) 369-4070. **$70-$165.** 1557 Main St 24517. US 29 business route, jct US 29. Int corridors. **Pets:** Other species. $10 daily fee/pet. Designated rooms, service with restrictions, supervision. 🛜 ♿ 🛎 🖥

APPOMATTOX

▼▼▼ Super 8 Ⓜ
(434) 352-2339. **$65-$150.** 7571 Richmond Hwy 24522. US 460, just w of jct US 26. Int corridors. **Pets:** Accepted. 🛜 🛎 🖥

ARRINGTON

▼▼▼▼ Harmony Hill Bed and Breakfast 🄱🄱
(434) 263-7750. **$129-$209.** 929 Wilson Hill Rd 22922. US 29, 0.9 mi e on SR 665. Int corridors. **Pets:** Accepted. 🛜 🗙 🛎 🌲

BEDFORD

▼▼ Super 8 🄷
(540) 587-0100. **$65-$180.** 842 Sword Beach Ln 24523. 1.5 mi w on US 221 and 460. Int corridors. **Pets:** Accepted. 🛜 ♿ 🛎 🖥

BIG STONE GAP

▼ Country Inn Motel Ⓜ
(276) 523-0374. **$46-$57.** 627 Gilley Ave 24219. US 23, 1 mi w on US 23 business route and 58A. Ext corridors. **Pets:** Other species. $3 daily fee/pet. Service with restrictions, supervision. 🛜 🛎

BLACKSBURG

▼▼▼ Comfort Inn 🄷
(540) 951-1500. **$99.** 3705 S Main St 24060. 3.5 mi s on US 460, jct US 460 Bypass. Int corridors. **Pets:** Other species. Service with restrictions, crate. 🛜 🛎 🖥 ⇲

◆◆◆ ▼▼▼ Days Inn Blacksburg 🄷
(540) 951-1330. **$75-$420.** 3503 Holiday Ln 24060. 3.8 mi s on US 460; jct US 460 Bypass. Ext corridors. **Pets:** Accepted.
〔SAVE〕 🛜 🛎 🖥 ⇲

BRISTOL

▼▼▼ Holiday Inn Hotel & Suites 🄷
(276) 466-4100. **Call for rates.** 3005 Linden Dr 24202. I-81 exit 7, just w. Int corridors. **Pets:** Other species. $50 one-time fee/room. Designated rooms, service with restrictions. 〔ECO〕 🛜 ♿ 🛎 🖥 🍴 ⇲

▼▼▼▼ La Quinta Inn Bristol 🄷
(276) 669-9353. **$59-$144.** 1014 Old Airport Rd 24201. I-81 exit 7, just e. Ext corridors. **Pets:** Service with restrictions, supervision.
🛜 ♿ 🛎 🖥 ⇲

▼ Motel 6 #4125 Ⓜ
(276) 466-6060. **$55-$200.** 21561 Clear Creek Rd 24202. I-81 exit 7, 0.3 mi w. Int corridors. **Pets:** Other species. Designated rooms, service with restrictions, supervision. 🛜 ♿ 🛎

BUCHANAN

◆◆◆ ▼▼ Wattstull Inn Ⓜ
(540) 254-1551. **$65-$78, 7 day notice.** 130 Arcadia Rd 24066. I-81 exit 168, just e on SR 614. Ext corridors. **Pets:** $10 daily fee/pet. Designated rooms, service with restrictions, supervision.
〔SAVE〕 🛜 🛎 🖥 🍴 ⇲

CHARLOTTESVILLE

◆◆◆ ▼▼▼ The Cavalier Inn at the University 🄷 🐾
(434) 296-8111. **$75-$350.** 105 N Emmet St 22903. Jct US 29 (Emmet St) and 250 Bypass, 1.3 mi s on US 29 business route. Ext/int corridors. **Pets:** $25 one-time fee/pet. Service with restrictions.
〔ECO〕 〔SAVE〕 🛜 🗙 🛎 🖥 ⇲

◆◆◆ ▼▼▼ Comfort Inn University 🄷
(434) 293-6188. **$89-$149.** 1803 Emmet St 22901. Jct US 250 Bypass, just n on US 29 (Emmet St). Int corridors. **Pets:** Accepted.
〔SAVE〕 🛜 🛎 🖥 ⇲

◆◆◆ ▼▼▼ DoubleTree by Hilton Hotel Charlottesville 🄷 🐾
(434) 973-2121. **$129-$239.** 990 Hilton Heights Rd 22901. I-64 exit 118B (US 29/Emmet St), 4 mi n of jct US 250 Bypass. Int corridors. **Pets:** Small. $25 one-time fee/room. Designated rooms, service with restrictions, supervision. 〔ECO〕 〔SAVE〕 🛜 🛎 🖥 🍴 ⇲

▼▼▼▼ Fairfield Inn by Marriott **H**
(434) 964-9411. **$123-$275.** 577 Branchlands Blvd 22901. US 29 (Emmet St), 1.3 mi n of US 250 Bypass. Int corridors. **Pets:** Medium, dogs only. $50 one-time fee/room. Service with restrictions, crate.
🖥️ ❌ 🛏️ 💻 ⤴️

▼▼▼▼ Holiday Inn-Monticello/Charlottesville **H**
(434) 977-5100. **$89-$160.** 1200 5th St SW 22902. I-64 exit 120, just n on SR 631. Int corridors. **Pets:** Other species. $15 daily fee/pet. Service with restrictions, supervision. 🖥️ 🛏️ 💻 🍴 ⤴️

▼▼▼▼ Omni Charlottesville Hotel **H** 🐾
(434) 971-5500. **$139-$289.** 212 Ridge McIntire Rd 22903. I-64 exit 120, 2.3 mi n on SR 631; downtown. Int corridors. **Pets:** Small, dogs only. $50 one-time fee/room. Service with restrictions.
🌿 🖥️ ❌ 🛏️ 💻 🍴 ⤴️ ❌

🔷〞 ▼▼▼ Red Roof Inn of Charlottesville **H**
(434) 295-4333. **$70-$249.** 1309 W Main St 22903. US 29 (Emmet St), 1 mi e on US 250 (University Ave). Int corridors. **Pets:** Large, other species. Service with restrictions, supervision. 🆂🅰🆅🅴 🖥️ 🛏️ 💻

🔷〞 ▼▼▼▼ Residence Inn by Marriott **H**
(434) 923-0300. **$144-$234.** 1111 Millmont St 22903. I-64 exit 118B (US 29/Emmet St), 2.5 mi n on US 29/250 E, just s on Barracks Rd, then just se. Int corridors. **Pets:** Accepted.
🌿 🆂🅰🆅🅴 🖥️ ❌ 🛏️ 💻 ⤴️ ❌

🔷〞 ▼▼▼▼ Sleep Inn & Suites Monticello **H**
(434) 244-9969. **Call for rates.** 1185 5th St 22902. I-64 exit 120, just n. Int corridors. **Pets:** Accepted. 🆂🅰🆅🅴 🖥️ 🛏️ 💻 ⤴️

CHINCOTEAGUE

🔷〞 ▼▼💎 Americas Best Value Inn & Suites **M**
(757) 336-6562. **$50-$199, 10 day notice.** 6151 Maddox Blvd 23336. Just e on Maddox Blvd. Ext corridors. **Pets:** Medium, dogs only. $10 daily fee/pet. Designated rooms, no service, crate. 🆂🅰🆅🅴 🖥️ 🛏️ 💻 ⤴️

💎▼ Rodeway Inn Chincoteague **H**
(757) 336-6565. **$59-$300.** 6273 Maddox Blvd 23336. Just e on Maddox Blvd. Ext corridors. **Pets:** Medium, dogs only. $15 daily fee/pet. Designated rooms, no service, supervision. 🖥️ &M 🛏️ 💻 ⤴️

CHRISTIANSBURG

🔷〞 ▼▼💎 Econo Lodge **M**
(540) 382-6161. **Call for rates.** 2430 Roanoke St 24073. I-81 exit 118, just w on US 11/460. Ext corridors. **Pets:** Medium. $10 daily fee/pet. Designated rooms, service with restrictions, crate.
🆂🅰🆅🅴 🖥️ &M 🛏️ 💻 ⤴️

▼▼▼▼ Hampton Inn Christiansburg/Blacksburg **H**
(540) 381-5874. **$119-$129.** 380 Arbor Dr 24073. I-81 exit 118B, 4 mi w on US 460 Bypass, just n on Peppers Ferry Rd, then just w. Int corridors. **Pets:** Accepted. 🖥️ 🛏️ 💻 ⤴️

🔷〞 ▼▼▼ Quality Inn **M** 🐾
(540) 382-2055. **$75-$85.** 50 Hampton Blvd 24073. I-81 exit 118C, just e. Ext corridors. **Pets:** Large, other species. $10 daily fee/room. Service with restrictions. 🆂🅰🆅🅴 🖥️ 🛏️ 💻 ⤴️

▼▼ Super 8-Christiansburg West **M**
(540) 382-5813. **$53-$200.** 55 Laurel St NE 24073. I-81 exit 118, 1 mi w on US 11/460, then 3.5 mi nw on US 460 Bypass; jct SR 114. Int corridors. **Pets:** Very small. $10 daily fee/pet. Designated rooms, service with restrictions, supervision. 🖥️ 🛏️

CLARKSVILLE

🔷〞 ▼▼▼▼ BEST WESTERN on the Lake **H**
(434) 374-5023. **Call for rates.** 103 Second St 23927. Just n of US 58 business route; downtown. Int corridors. **Pets:** Other species. $100 deposit/room, $20 daily fee/pet. Designated rooms, service with restrictions, supervision. 🆂🅰🆅🅴 🖥️ &M 🛏️ 💻 ⤴️

COLLINSVILLE

▼▼ Knights Inn **M**
(276) 647-3716. **$55-$60.** 2357 Virginia Ave 24078. Jct US 58, 3 mi n on US 220 business route. Ext corridors. **Pets:** $6 daily fee/room. No service, supervision. 🖥️ 🛏️ ⤴️

▼▼ Quality Inn-Dutch Inn Hotel and Convention Center **H**
(276) 647-3721. **Call for rates.** 2360 Virginia Ave 24078. Jct US 58, 3 mi n on US 220 business route. Ext corridors. **Pets:** Accepted.
🖥️ 🛏️ 💻 🍴 ⤴️

COVINGTON

🔷〞 ▼▼▼ BEST WESTERN Mountain View **H**
(540) 962-4951. **Call for rates.** 820 E Madison St 24426. I-64 exit 16, just n. Ext corridors. **Pets:** $12 daily fee/pet.
🆂🅰🆅🅴 🖥️ 🛏️ 💻 🍴 ⤴️

CULPEPER

▼▼▼ Comfort Inn-Culpeper **M** 🐾
(540) 825-4900. **$89-$129.** 890 Willis Ln 22701. 2 mi s on Main St (US 29 business route); jct US 29, then just e. Ext corridors. **Pets:** Small, other species. $15 daily fee/pet. Service with restrictions, supervision.
🖥️ 🛏️ 💻 ⤴️

DANVILLE

▼▼▼▼ Comfort Inn & Suites **H**
(434) 793-2000. **$79-$100.** 100 Tower Dr 24540. US 58, just w of jct US 29 business route. Int corridors. **Pets:** Small, other species. $15 daily fee/pet. Designated rooms, service with restrictions, supervision.
🖥️ 🛏️ 💻 🍴 ⤴️

▼▼▼▼ Courtyard by Marriott **H**
(434) 791-2661. **$114-$309.** 2136 Riverside Dr 24540. On US 58, just w of jct US 29 business route. Int corridors. **Pets:** Accepted.
🖥️ ❌ &M 🛏️ 💻 🍴 ⤴️

▼▼▼ Innkeeper Danville North **M**
(434) 836-1700. **Call for rates.** 1030 Piney Forest Rd 24540. US 29 N business route, 0.5 mi n of US 58. Ext corridors. **Pets:** Accepted.
🖥️ 🛏️ ⤴️

🔷〞 ▼▼▼ Super 8 **M**
(434) 799-5845. **$65-$177, 3 day notice.** 2385 Riverside Dr 24541. On US 58, just e of jct US 29 business route. Int corridors. **Pets:** Accepted.
🆂🅰🆅🅴 🖥️ 🛏️ 💻

EMPORIA

🔷〞 ▼▼▼ BEST WESTERN Emporia **H**
(434) 634-3200. **$68-$80.** 1100 W Atlantic St 23847. I-95 exit 11B, just w on US 58. Ext corridors. **Pets:** Other species. $10 daily fee/room. Service with restrictions, crate. 🆂🅰🆅🅴 🖥️ 🛏️ 💻 ⤴️

▼▼▼▼ Country Inn & Suites By Carlson Emporia **H**
(434) 336-0001. **$79-$149.** 107 Sadler Ln 23847. I-95 exit 11A, just e on US 58. Int corridors. **Pets:** Large, other species. $15 daily fee/pet. Designated rooms, supervision. 🖥️ ❌ 🛏️ 💻 ⤴️

🔷〞 ▼▼▼ Days Inn-Emporia **H**
(434) 634-9481. **$60-$70.** 921 W Atlantic St 23847. I-95 exit 11B, just w on US 58. Ext corridors. **Pets:** $10 one-time fee/pet. Designated rooms, service with restrictions, supervision. 🆂🅰🆅🅴 🖥️ 🛏️ 💻 🍴 ⤴️

🔷〞 ▼▼▼ Hampton Inn **H** 🐾
(434) 634-9200. **$99-$140.** 898 Wiggins Rd 23847. I-95 exit 11B, just w on US 58. Int corridors. **Pets:** Large, other species. Designated rooms, service with restrictions, supervision.
🌿 🆂🅰🆅🅴 🖥️ &M 🛏️ 💻 ⤴️

◬ ▼▼▼▼ Sleep Inn 🅷

(434) 348-3900. **$79-$120.** 899 Wiggins Rd 23847. I-95 exit 11B, just e on US 58, then just s. Int corridors. **Pets:** $15 one-time fee/pet. Designated rooms, service with restrictions, supervision.

[SAVE] 🛜 🕹M 🔋 💻

EXMORE

◬ ▼▼▼ BEST WESTERN Eastern Shore 🅷

(757) 442-7378. **$99-$140.** 2543 Lankford Hwy 23350. US 13, just n of SR 178. Ext/int corridors. **Pets:** $10 daily fee/room. Service with restrictions, supervision. [SAVE] 🛜 🕹M 🔋 💻 ⇀

▼▼▼ Holiday Inn Express & Suites 🅷

(757) 442-5522. **$60-$100.** 3446 Lankford Hwy 23350. On US 13. Int corridors. **Pets:** Accepted. 🛜 ✕ 🕹M 🔋 💻 ⇀

FANCY GAP

▼▼▼ Doe Run Lodging at Groundhog Mountain 🆑🅾

(276) 398-4099. **Call for rates.** 27 Buck Hollar Rd 24328. Blue Ridge Parkway at MM 189.2; 10 mi n from US 52. Ext corridors.
Pets: Accepted. 🔋 💻 ✕

FARMVILLE

▼▼ Comfort Inn-Farmville 🅷 ❖

(434) 392-8163. **$69-$149.** 2108 S Main St 23901. Jct US 460 Bypass and US 15. Int corridors. **Pets:** Small, dogs only. $30 daily fee/pet. Designated rooms, service with restrictions, supervision. 🛜 🔋 💻 ⇀

FLOYD

▼▼ Hotel Floyd 🇲 ❖

(540) 745-6080. **$79-$109.** 120 Wilson St 24091. Just e; center. Ext corridors. **Pets:** Medium. Designated rooms, service with restrictions, crate.

🔲 🛜 ✕ 🔋 💻

FRANKLIN

▼▼ Super 8 🇲

(757) 562-2888. **$62-$89.** 1599 Armory Dr 23851. Jct US 58 Bypass and SR 671. Int corridors. **Pets:** Accepted. 🛜 🔋 💻

FREDERICKSBURG

◬ ▼▼▼ BEST WESTERN Central Plaza 🇲

(540) 786-7404. **$60-$89.** 3000 Plank Rd 22401. I-95 exit 130B (SR 3). Ext corridors. **Pets:** Other species. $10 daily fee/pet. Service with restrictions, supervision. 🅴🅲🅾 [SAVE] 🛜 🕹M 🔋 💻

◬ ▼▼▼ BEST WESTERN Fredericksburg 🅷 ❖

(540) 371-5050. **$69-$109.** 2205 Plank Rd 22401. I-95 exit 130A (SR 3), 0.3 mi e. Ext corridors. **Pets:** $10 daily fee/pet. Service with restrictions, supervision. 🅴🅲🅾 [SAVE] 🛜 🕹M 🔋 💻 ⇌

◬ ▼▼▼ Clarion Inn Fredericksburg 🅷

(540) 371-5550. **$67-$76.** 564 Warrenton Rd 22406. I-95 exit 133, just nw on US 17. Ext corridors. **Pets:** Small. Designated rooms, service with restrictions, crate. [SAVE] 🛜 🔋 💻 🍴 ⇀ ✕

◬ ▼▼▼ Country Inn & Suites By Carlson, South 🅷

(540) 898-1800. **$99-$159.** 5327 Jefferson Davis Hwy 22408. I-95 exit 126 southbound; exit 126A northbound; just n on US 1. Int corridors. **Pets:** $10 daily fee/pet. Service with restrictions, crate.

[SAVE] 🛜 ✕ 🔋 💻 ⇀

◬ ▼▼▼ Fredericksburg Hospitality House Hotel & Conference Center 🅷 ❖

(540) 786-8321. **$89-$169.** 2801 Plank Rd 22401. I-95 exit 130B (SR 3). Int corridors. **Pets:** Small, dogs only. $25 one-time fee/pet. Designated rooms, service with restrictions, supervision.

[SAVE] 🛜 ✕ 🕹M 🔋 💻 🍴 ⇀

▼▼ Quality Inn Fredericksburg 🇲

(540) 373-0000. **$50-$90.** 543 Warrenton Rd 22406. I-95 exit 133, just n on US 17. Ext corridors. **Pets:** Other species. $25 daily fee/pet. Designated rooms, service with restrictions, crate. 🛜 ✕ 🔋 💻

▼▼ Residence Inn by Marriott 🅷

(540) 786-9222. **$160-$170.** 60 Town Centre Blvd 22407. I-95 exit 130B (SR 3), just w to Mall Dr, then just s. Int corridors. **Pets:** Medium, other species. $100 one-time fee/room. Service with restrictions, supervision.

🛜 ✕ 🕹M 🔋 💻 ⇀ ✕

▼▼▼▼ TownePlace Suites by Marriott 🅷 ❖

(540) 891-0775. **$89-$129.** 4700 Market St 22408. I-95 exit 126 southbound; exit 126A northbound, just n on US 1 (Jefferson Davis Hwy), then just e. Int corridors. **Pets:** Other species. $10 daily fee/pet. Service with restrictions. 🛜 ✕ 🔋 💻 ⇀

FRONT ROYAL

▼▼ Budget Inn 🇲

(540) 635-2196. **Call for rates.** 1122 N Royal Ave 22630. I-66 exit 6, 2.2 mi s on US 340/522 and SR 55. Ext corridors. **Pets:** Accepted. 🔋

GLADE SPRING

▼▼ Econo Lodge Glade Spring 🇲

(276) 429-5191. **Call for rates.** 33361 Lee Hwy 24340. I-81 exit 29, just e. Ext corridors. **Pets:** Accepted. 🛜 🔋

GRETNA

▼▼▼ Hampton Inn Altavista/Chatham 🅷

(434) 656-9000. **$99-$175.** 200 McBride Ln 24557. US 29, just e on SR 40. Int corridors. **Pets:** Accepted. 🛜 🕹M 🔋 💻 ⇀

GRUNDY

▼▼▼ Comfort Inn 🅷

(276) 935-5050. **$99-$129.** 22006 Riverside Dr 24614. On US 460, 0.5 mi e. Int corridors. **Pets:** Accepted. 🛜 🕹M 🔋 💻

HAMPTON ROADS AREA

CHESAPEAKE

◬ ▼▼▼ Aloft Chesapeake 🅷 ❖

(757) 410-9562. **$89-$135, 3 day notice.** 1454 Crossways Blvd 23320. I-64 exit 289B (Greenbrier Pkwy), just s to Jarman Rd (at Crossways Center) to Crossways Blvd, then 0.7 mi n. Int corridors. **Pets:** Medium, dogs only. Designated rooms, service with restrictions.

🅴🅲🅾 [SAVE] 🛜 ✕ 🔋 💻 ⇀

▼▼▼ Candlewood Suites 🅷

(757) 405-3030. **$79-$89.** 4809 Market Pl 23321. I-664 exit 11A (E Portsmouth Blvd/SR 337). Int corridors. **Pets:** Large. $75 one-time fee/pet. Designated rooms, service with restrictions, supervision.

🅴🅲🅾 🛜 🕹M 🔋 💻

▼▼▼ **Comfort Inn & Suites** H
(757) 673-8585. **$69-$169.** 3355 S Military Hwy 23323. I-64 exit 296A, just n on George Washington Memorial Hwy N (US 17 Bypass), then just e on US 460 and 13. Int corridors. **Pets:** Dogs only. $35 daily fee/pet. Service with restrictions, crate. 🛜 ✕ 🚹 🛗 🕭

▼▼ **Extended StayAmerica Chesapeake-Greenbrier Circle** H
(757) 523-7377. **$55-$65.** 809 Greenbrier Cir 23320. I-64 exit 289A (Greenbrier Pkwy), just n. Int corridors. **Pets:** $25 daily fee/pet. Designated rooms, service with restrictions. 🛜 🛗 🚹 🕭

▼▼▼ **Hampton Inn & Suites** H ❈
(757) 819-5230. **$79-$199.** 1421 N Battlefield Blvd 23320. I-64 exit 290B, just s; jct Coastal Way. Int corridors. **Pets:** Service with restrictions, supervision. 🛜 ✕ 🛗 🚹 🕭 🕭

𝄪 ▼▼▼ **Hampton Inn Chesapeake/Greenbrier** H
(757) 420-1550. **$89-$159.** 701A Woodlake Dr 23320. I-64 exit 289A (Greenbrier Pkwy), just n to Woodlake Dr. Int corridors. **Pets:** Dogs only. Designated rooms, service with restrictions, crate.
🕭 🛜 🚹 🕭 🕭

▼▼▼ **Residence Inn by Marriott, Chesapeake-Greenbrier** H
(757) 502-7300. **$109-$209.** 1500 Crossways Blvd 23320. I-64 exit 289B (Greenbrier Pkwy), just s to Jarman Rd (at Crossways Center) to Crossways Blvd, then 0.6 mi n. Int corridors. **Pets:** Accepted.
🕭 🛜 ✕ 🚹 🕭 🕭 ✕

▼▼▼ **Staybridge Suites Greenbrier** H
(757) 420-2525. **$99-$169.** 709 Woodlake Dr 23320. I-64 exit 289A (Greenbrier Pkwy), just n. Int corridors. **Pets:** Other species. $75 one-time fee/pet. Service with restrictions, crate. 🛜 🛗 🚹 🕭 🕭

▼ **Super 8** M
(757) 686-8888. **$56-$73.** 3216 Churchland Blvd 23321. I-664 exit 9B, 1 mi s on SR 17. Int corridors. **Pets:** Accepted. 🛜 🚹 🕭

GLOUCESTER
▼▼▼ **Comfort Inn Gloucester** H
(804) 695-1900. **$89-$109.** 6639 Forest Hill Ave 23061. US 17, just s. Int corridors. **Pets:** Other species. $15 daily fee/pet. Service with restrictions.
🛜 🚹 🕭 🕭

HAMPTON
▼▼▼ **Candlewood Suites** H
(757) 766-8976. **$74-$99.** 401 Butler Farm Rd 23666. I-64 exit 261B (Hampton Roads Center Pkwy) eastbound; exit 262B (Magruder Blvd) westbound, then n. Int corridors. **Pets:** Accepted.
🕭 🛜 🛗 🚹 🕭

▼▼ **Extended StayAmerica-Hampton Coliseum** M
(757) 896-3600. **$59-$69.** 1915 Commerce Dr 23666. I-64 exit 263 (Mercury Blvd), just n, then just e. Int corridors. **Pets:** $25 daily fee/pet. Designated rooms, service with restrictions. 🛜 🛗 🚹 🕭

NEWPORT NEWS
▼▼▼ **Comfort Inn** H
(757) 249-0200. **$89-$129.** 12330 Jefferson Ave 23602. I-64 exit 255A, just s on Clarie Ln. Int corridors. **Pets:** $15 daily fee/pet. Designated rooms, service with restrictions, crate. 🛜 🛗 🚹 🕭 🕭

▼▼▼ **Crestwood Suites** M
(757) 951-1017. **$55-$75.** 11 Old Oyster Point Rd 23602. I-64 exit 256A, just s on Oyster Point Rd to Canon Blvd, just e, then just n. Int corridors. **Pets:** Accepted. 🛜 🚹 🕭

▼▼▼ **Jameson Inn & Suites Newport News** H
(757) 951-1177. **$60-$110.** 21 Old Oyster Point Rd 23602. I-64 exit 256A, just s on Oyster Point Rd to Canon Blvd, just e, then just n. Int corridors. **Pets:** Accepted. 🛜 🛗 🚹 🕭 🕭

𝄪 ▼▼▼ **Mulberry Inn** H
(757) 887-3000. **$79-$139.** 16890 Warwick Blvd 23603. I-64 exit 250A (SR 105/Ft Eustis Blvd S), s to US 60, then 0.3 mi w. Ext/int corridors. **Pets:** $50 one-time fee/room. Designated rooms, service with restrictions, crate. 🕭 🛗 🚹 🕭

▼▼▼ **Omni Newport News Hotel** H
(757) 873-6664. **$79-$164, 3 day notice.** 1000 Omni Blvd 23606. I-64 exit 258A (US 17), just s to Oyster Point Rd. Int corridors.
Pets: Accepted. 🛜 ✕ 🛗 🚹 🕭 🍽 🕭

𝄪 ▼▼▼ **Point Plaza-Suites at City Center** H ❈
(757) 599-4460. **$69-$159.** 950 J Clyde Morris Blvd 23601. I-64 exit 258B (US 17), just n. Ext/int corridors. **Pets:** $50 one-time fee/room. Designated rooms, service with restrictions, crate.
🕭 🕭 🛜 🚹 🕭 🕭

▼▼▼ **Residence Inn by Marriott Newport News Airport** H
(757) 842-6214. **$89-$229.** 531 St Johns Rd 23602. I-64 exit 255A, just s on Jefferson Ave to Freedom Way, then just nw. Int corridors.
Pets: Accepted. 🛜 ✕ 🛗 🚹 🕭 🕭

▼▼ **StudioPLUS-Newport News - I-64 - Jefferson Ave** H
(757) 882-8847. **$65-$75.** 12359 Hornsby Ln 23602. I-64 exit 255A, just s on Jefferson Ave. Int corridors. **Pets:** $25 daily fee/pet. Designated rooms, service with restrictions. 🛜 🚹 🕭 🕭

NORFOLK
▼▼▼ **Candlewood Suites Norfolk Airport** H
(757) 605-4001. **Call for rates.** 5600 Lowery Rd 23502. I-264 exit 13B (US 13/Military Hwy), 1.3 mi n, then just w. Int corridors. **Pets:** Accepted.
🛜 🛗 🚹 🕭

𝄪 ▼▼▼ **Hilton Norfolk Airport** H ❈
(757) 466-8000. **$89-$169.** 1500 N Military Hwy 23502. I-64 exit 281 (Military Hwy), just s; jct US 13 and SR 165. Int corridors. **Pets:** Large, dogs only. $50 one-time fee/room. Designated rooms, supervision.
🕭 🕭 🛜 🛗 🚹 🕭 🍽 🕭

𝄪 ▼▼▼ **La Quinta Inn & Suites Norfolk Airport** H
(757) 466-7001. **$83-$199.** 1387 N Military Hwy 23502. I-64 exit 281 (Military Hwy), just s. Int corridors. **Pets:** Service with restrictions, supervision. 🕭 🛜 ✕ 🚹 🕭 🕭

▼▼▼ **Norfolk Plaza Downtown** H
(757) 627-5555. **$79-$259.** 700 Monticello Ave 23510. Jct Brambleton Ave and St Pauls Blvd; downtown. Int corridors. **Pets:** Medium, other species. $50 one-time fee/room. Service with restrictions, supervision.
🛜 ✕ 🛗 🚹 🕭 🍽 🕭

𝄪 ▼▼▼ **Page House Inn Bed & Breakfast** BB
(757) 625-5033. **$150-$230, 7 day notice.** 323 Fairfax Ave 23507. I-264 exit 9, 1.4 mi n on Waterside Dr to Olney Rd, just w to Mowbray Arch, then just s; in Ghent historic district. Int corridors. **Pets:** Accepted.
🕭 🛜 ✕ 🚹 ✕

▼▼▼ **Quality Suites Lake Wright** H
(757) 461-6251. **$89-$129.** 6280 Northampton Blvd 23502. I-64 exit 282, just w on US 13. Int corridors. **Pets:** Medium, dogs only. $35 one-time fee/room. Designated rooms, service with restrictions, supervision.
🕭 🛜 🛗 🚹 🕭 🍽 🕭

▼▼▼ **Residence Inn by Marriott Downtown** H
(757) 842-6216. **$109-$209.** 227 W Brambleton Ave 23510. Jct Duke St; downtown. Int corridors. **Pets:** Medium. $100 one-time fee/room. Designated rooms, service with restrictions, crate.
🕭 🛜 ✕ 🛗 🚹 🕭 🕭

▼▼▼ **Residence Inn by Marriott Norfolk Airport** H
(757) 333-3000. **$109-$209.** 1590 N Military Hwy 23502. I-64 exit 281B (Military Hwy). Int corridors. **Pets:** Accepted.
🕭 🛜 ✕ 🛗 🚹 🕭 🕭 ✕

Sheraton Norfolk Waterside Hotel 🅷
(757) 622-6664. **$99-$399.** 777 Waterside Dr 23510. I-264 exit 9 (Waterside Dr); downtown. Int corridors. **Pets:** Accepted.

Sleep Inn Lake Wright 🅷
(757) 461-1133. **$69-$109.** 6280 Northampton Blvd 23502. I-64 exit 282, just w on US 13. Int corridors. **Pets:** Medium, dogs only. $25 one-time fee/room. Service with restrictions, supervision.

The Tazewell Hotel, Downtown Norfolk, an Ascend Collection hotel 🅷
(757) 623-6200. **$79-$169.** 245 Granby St 23510. Jct Tazewell St; downtown. Int corridors. **Pets:** Medium. $25 daily fee/pet. Service with restrictions, supervision.

PORTSMOUTH

Governor Dinwiddie Hotel & Suites, an Ascend Collection hotel 🅷
(757) 392-1330. **$99-$159.** 506 Dinwiddie St 23704. Jct High St; in Olde Towne. Int corridors. **Pets:** Medium, other species. $25 daily fee/pet. Designated rooms, service with restrictions, supervision.

SUFFOLK

TownePlace Suites by Marriott 🅷
(757) 483-5177. **$89-$209.** 8050 Harbour View Blvd 23435. I-664 exit 8A (College Dr), just n. Int corridors. **Pets:** Accepted.

VIRGINIA BEACH

Alamar Resort Inn 🅜
(757) 428-7582. **$49-$328, 3 day notice.** 311 16th St 23451. I-264 terminus to Pacific Ave, just s. Ext corridors. **Pets:** Accepted.

Candlewood Suites 🅷
(757) 213-1500. **$79-$199.** 4437 Bonney Rd 23462. I-264 exit 17B (Independence Blvd/Pembroke Area), just n to Bonney Rd, then just e. Int corridors. **Pets:** Accepted.

DoubleTree by Hilton Hotel Virginia Beach 🅷 🐾
(757) 422-8900. **$110-$239.** 1900 Pavilion Dr 23451. I-264 exit 22 (Birdneck Rd), just e. Int corridors. **Pets:** Large. $25 one-time fee/room. Designated rooms, service with restrictions, supervision.

The Founders Inn and Spa 🅷
(757) 424-5511. **$99-$259.** 5641 Indian River Rd 23464. I-64 exit 286B, just e; on campus of Christian Broadcasting Network & Regent University. Int corridors. **Pets:** Accepted.

Homewood Suites by Hilton 🅷 🐾
(757) 552-0080. **$109-$209.** 5733 Cleveland St 23462. I-264 exit 15 (Newtown Rd N), just n. Int corridors. **Pets:** Other species. $75 one-time fee/room. Service with restrictions, crate.

La Quinta Inn & Suites Virginia Beach 🅷
(757) 428-2203. **$75-$320.** 2800 Pacific Ave 23451. I-264 0.5 mi n of terminus. Int corridors. **Pets:** Service with restrictions, supervision.

La Quinta Inn Norfolk/Town Center 🅷
(757) 497-6620. **$59-$166.** 192 Newtown Rd 23462. I-264 exit 284B to I-264 exit Newtown Rd S. Int corridors. **Pets:** Service with restrictions, supervision.

Red Roof Inn VA Beach (Norfolk Airport) 🅜
(757) 460-6700. **$50-$170.** 5745 Northampton Blvd 23455. I-64 exit 282, 1 mi n on US 13 (Northampton Blvd). Ext corridors. **Pets:** Large, other species. Service with restrictions, supervision.

Residence Inn by Marriott Virginia Beach Oceanfront 🅷
(757) 425-1141. **Call for rates.** 3217 Atlantic Ave 23451. I-264 1.5 mi n of terminus; jct 33rd St. Int corridors. **Pets:** Other species. $100 one-time fee/room. Designated rooms, service with restrictions, supervision.

Sheraton Virginia Beach Oceanfront Hotel 🅷
(757) 425-9000. **$259-$329, 3 day notice.** 3501 Atlantic Ave 23451. I-264 1 mi n of terminus; jct 36th St. Int corridors. **Pets:** Accepted.

TownePlace Suites by Marriott 🅷
(757) 490-9367. **$89-$189.** 5757 Cleveland St 23462. I-64 exit 284B to I-264 exit Newtown Rd N. Int corridors. **Pets:** Large, other species. $100 one-time fee/room. Service with restrictions, crate.

The Westin Virginia Beach Town Center 🅷 🐾
(757) 557-0550. **$99-$299, 3 day notice.** 4535 Commerce St 23462. I-264 exit 17B (Independence Blvd), just n, then just e. Int corridors. **Pets:** Medium, dogs only. Designated rooms, service with restrictions, supervision.

Wyndham Virginia Beach Oceanfront 🅷
(757) 428-7025. **$79-$300, 3 day notice.** 5700 Atlantic Ave 23451. I-264 2.2 mi n of terminus. Int corridors. **Pets:** Medium, dogs only. $25 daily fee/pet. Service with restrictions, crate.

END AREA

HARRISONBURG

Candlewood Suites Harrisonburg 🅷
(540) 437-1400. **$99-$299.** 1560 Country Club Rd 22802. I-81 exit 247, just e. Int corridors. **Pets:** Accepted.

Comfort Inn 🅷
(540) 433-6066. **$84-$129.** 1440 E Market St 22801. I-81 exit 247A, just e. Int corridors. **Pets:** Other species. $15 daily fee/room. Service with restrictions, supervision.

Days Inn Harrisonburg 🅜
(540) 433-9353. **$68-$235.** 1131 Forest Hill Rd 22801. I-81 exit 245, just e. Int corridors. **Pets:** Accepted.

Harrisonburg Econo Lodge 🅜
(540) 433-2576. **$60-$147.** 1703 E Market St 22801. I-81 exit 247A, 0.5 mi e on US 33. Ext/int corridors. **Pets:** Accepted.

Microtel Inn & Suites by Wyndham 🅷
(540) 437-3777. **$69-$250.** 85 Pleasant Valley Rd 22801. I-81 exit 243, just w. Int corridors. **Pets:** Other species. $25 deposit/room, $15 daily fee/pet. Designated rooms, service with restrictions.

Ramada 🅷
(540) 434-9981. **$66-$229.** 91 Pleasant Valley Rd 22801. I-81 exit 243, just w, then just n on US 11. Ext corridors. **Pets:** Accepted.

Residence Inn by Marriott Harrisonburg H
(540) 437-7426. **$143-$170.** 1945 Deyerle Ave 22801. I-81 exit 245, just
e. Int corridors. **Pets:** Other species. $100 one-time fee/room. Service
with restrictions.

Sleep Inn & Suites H
(540) 433-7100. **$75-$249.** 1891 Evelyn Byrd Ave 22801. I-81 exit 247A,
0.5 mi e on US 33 to University Blvd, 0.3 mi s to Evelyn Byrd Ave, then
just w. Int corridors. **Pets:** Medium. $15 daily fee/pet. Service with restric-
tions, supervision.

Super 8 M
(540) 433-8888. **$60-$155, 3 day notice.** 3330 S Main St 22801. I-81
exit 243, just e, then just s on US 11. Int corridors. **Pets:** Very small. $10
daily fee/pet. Designated rooms, no service, supervision.

The Village Inn H
(540) 434-7355. **$79-$89.** 4979 S Valley Pike 22801. I-81 exit 240 southbound, 0.6 mi w on SR 257, then 1.5 mi n on US 11; exit 243 northbound, just w to US 11, then 1.7 mi s. Ext corridors. **Pets:** Other species.
$10 daily fee/pet. Service with restrictions, crate.

HILLSVILLE
**BEST WESTERN Four Seasons
South** M
(276) 728-4136. **$65-$99.** 57 Airport Rd 24343. I-77 exit 14, just w on
US 58 and 221. Ext corridors. **Pets:** Other species. $13 deposit/room.
Designated rooms.

Quality Inn H
(276) 728-2120. **$89-$169.** 85 Airport Rd 24343. I-77 exit 14, just w on
US 58 and 221. Ext corridors. **Pets:** Large, other species. $10 daily fee/
pet. Designated rooms, service with restrictions, supervision.

HOPEWELL
Candlewood Suites H
(804) 541-0200. **Call for rates.** 5113 Plaza Dr 23860. I-295 exit 9B (SR
36), just w. Int corridors. **Pets:** $25 daily fee/pet. Designated rooms, ser-
vice with restrictions, supervision.

Fairfield Inn & Suites by Marriott H
(804) 458-2600. **$94-$114.** 3952 Courthouse Rd 23860. I-295 exit 9A
(SR 36), just e. Int corridors. **Pets:** Medium. $50 one-time fee/room. Des-
ignated rooms, service with restrictions, crate.

HOT SPRINGS
The Homestead H
(540) 839-1766. **$175-$400, 7 day notice.** 1766 Homestead Dr 24445.
Center. Int corridors. **Pets:** Accepted.

HUDDLESTON
Mariners Landing CO
(540) 297-4900. **$99-$289, 7 day notice.** 1217 Graves Harbor Tr
24104. On SR 626; on Smith Mountain Lake. Ext/int corridors.
Pets: Medium, dogs only. $15 daily fee/pet. Designated rooms, service
with restrictions, crate.

IRVINGTON
The Tides Inn H
(804) 438-5000. **$210-$395, 7 day notice.** 480 King Carter Dr 22480.
0.3 mi w of SR 200. Ext/int corridors. **Pets:** Large, other species. $35
daily fee/pet. Designated rooms, service with restrictions, supervision.

KESWICK
Keswick Hall at Monticello H
(434) 979-3440. **$195-$995, 7 day notice.** 701 Club Dr 22947. I-64 exit
129, just n. Int corridors. **Pets:** Medium. $75 one-time fee/pet. Service
with restrictions, supervision.

KILMARNOCK
Kilmarnock Inn CI
(804) 435-0034. **$150-$265, 14 day notice.** 34 E Church St 22482. SR
3 to town. Ext/int corridors. **Pets:** $45 deposit/room, $45 one-time fee/
room. Designated rooms, service with restrictions.

LEBANON
Lebanon Super 8 M
(276) 889-1800. **$64-$185.** 71 Townview Dr 24266. Just e on SR 654
from US 19 Bypass. Int corridors. **Pets:** Medium, dogs only. $10 daily
fee/pet. Service with restrictions, supervision.

LEXINGTON
BEST WESTERN Lexington Inn M
(540) 458-3020. **$60-$210.** 850 N Lee Hwy 24450. I-64 exit 55, just s on
US 11; I-81 exit 191, 1.6 mi w. Ext corridors. **Pets:** Large, other species.
$25 one-time fee/room. Service with restrictions, supervision.

**BEST WESTERN PLUS Inn at Hunt
Ridge** H
(540) 464-1500. **$90-$210.** 25 Willow Spring Rd 24450. I-64 exit 55, just
n on US 11 to SR 39; I-81 exit 191, 0.6 mi w. Int corridors. **Pets:** Other
species. $20 one-time fee/room. Service with restrictions, supervision.

Comfort Inn-Virginia Horse Center H
(540) 463-7311. **$99-$109.** 62 Comfort Way 24450. I-64 exit 55, just s on
US 11; I-81 exit 191, 0.6 mi w. Int corridors. **Pets:** Medium, other species.
$25 one-time fee/room. Designated rooms, service with restrictions, super-
vision.

Holiday Inn Express H
(540) 463-7351. **$99-$149.** 880 N Lee Hwy 24450. I-64 exit 55, just s on
US 11; I-81 exit 191, 1 mi w. Int corridors. **Pets:** Large, other species.
$25 one-time fee/room. Service with restrictions, supervision.

Howard Johnson Inn H
(540) 463-9181. **$73-$100.** 2836 N Lee Hwy 24450. I-81 exit 195, just s
on US 11. Int corridors. **Pets:** $12 daily fee/pet. Designated rooms, ser-
vice with restrictions, supervision.

Motel 6 M
(540) 463-7371. **$40-$120.** 65 Econo Ln 24450. I-81 exit 191, just s on
US 11. Ext corridors. **Pets:** Other species. Service with restrictions, supervision.

Quality Inn & Suites H
(540) 463-6400. **Call for rates.** 2814 N Lee Hwy 24450. I-81 exit 195,
just sw on US 11. Int corridors. **Pets:** Medium. $10 daily fee/pet. Desig-
nated rooms, service with restrictions, supervision.

Sleep Inn & Suites H
(540) 463-6000. **$60-$199.** 95 Maury River Rd 24450. I-64 exit 55, just
n. Int corridors. **Pets:** Medium. $15 daily fee/pet. Service with restrictions,
crate.

Super 8 Lexington M
(540) 463-7858. **$75-$149.** 1139 N Lee Hwy 24450. I-64 exit 55, just n.
Int corridors. **Pets:** Medium. $10 daily fee/pet. Designated rooms, service
with restrictions, supervision.

LOW MOOR
Oak Tree Inn M
(540) 965-0090. **$79-$89.** 123 Westvaco Rd 24457. I-64 exit 21, just s.
Int corridors. **Pets:** $10 daily fee/pet. Service with restrictions, supervision.

LURAY

▼▼▼ Days Inn-Luray M
(540) 743-4521. **$80-$170.** 138 Whispering Hill Rd 22835. US 211 Bypass, 1.7 mi e of jct US 340. Ext/int corridors. **Pets:** Medium. $16 daily fee/pet. Designated rooms, service with restrictions, crate.
📶 🛗 ▣ 🏊 ⊠

LYNCHBURG

▲▲▲ ▼▼▼ BEST WESTERN Lynchburg M
(434) 237-2986. **$85-$95.** 2815 Candlers Mountain Rd 24502. Jct US 29 and 460. Ext corridors. **Pets:** Accepted. SAVE 📶 🛗 ▣ 🏊

▲▲▲ ▼▼▼▼ The Craddock Terry Hotel and Event Center H
(434) 455-1500. **$179-$299.** 1312 Commerce St 24504. US 29 business route exit 1 (Main St), just w. Int corridors. **Pets:** $50 one-time fee/room. Service with restrictions, crate. ECO SAVE 📶 ⊠ 🛗 ▣

▼▼ Extended StayAmerica - Lynchburg - University Blvd M
(434) 239-8863. **$62-$75.** 1910 University Blvd 24502. US 460 exit Candlers Mountain Rd/University Blvd. Int corridors. **Pets:** $25 daily fee/pet. Designated rooms, service with restrictions. 📶 ♿M 🛗 ▣

▼▼▼ Hampton Inn H
(434) 237-2704. **$99-$109.** 5604 Seminole Ave 24502. US 460 exit Candlers Mountain Rd, 0.3 mi w; US 29 exit Candlers Mountain Rd. Ext/int corridors. **Pets:** Accepted. 📶 ♿M 🛗 ▣

▼▼▼ Holiday Inn Downtown Lynchburg H
(434) 528-2500. **$89-$139.** 601 Main St 24504. US 29 business route exit 1 (Main St), 0.7 mi w. Int corridors. **Pets:** Accepted.
📶 ⊠ ♿M 🛗 ▣ 🍴 🏊

▼▼▼ Holiday Inn Express H
(434) 237-7771. **$99-$139.** 5600 Seminole Ave 24502. US 460 exit Candlers Mountain Rd, 0.3 mi w; US 29 business route exit Candlers Mountain Rd. Int corridors. **Pets:** Medium, dogs only. $50 one-time fee/room. Service with restrictions, crate. 📶 ⊠ 🛗 ▣ 🏊

▼▼▼ Kirkley Hotel & Conference Center H
(434) 237-6333. **$89-$199.** 2900 Candlers Mountain Rd 24502. US 29 business route exit 8A, just w. Int corridors. **Pets:** Small, dogs only. $50 one-time fee/pet. Designated rooms, service with restrictions, crate.
ECO 📶 🛗 ▣ 🍴 🏊

MARTINSVILLE

▼▼▼ Comfort Inn Martinsville H
(276) 666-6835. **$89-$94.** 1895 Virginia Ave 24112. Jct US 58, 2.4 mi n on US 220 business route. Int corridors. **Pets:** Accepted.
📶 🛗 ▣ 🏊

▼▼ Econo Lodge H
(276) 632-5611. **Call for rates.** US 220 Business Rt S 24112. Jct US 58, 2.3 mi n. Ext corridors. **Pets:** Accepted. 📶 🛗 ▣ 🍴 🏊

▼▼▼ Hampton Inn H
(276) 647-4700. **Call for rates.** 50 Hampton Dr 24112. Jct US 58, 2.5 mi n on US 220 business route. Int corridors. **Pets:** Accepted.
📶 🛗 ▣

MAX MEADOWS

▼▼ Super 8 M
(276) 637-4141. **$65-$130.** 194 Ft Chiswell Rd 24360. I-77/81 exit 80, just e. Ext corridors. **Pets:** Accepted. 📶 🛗 ▣

MIDDLETOWN

▼▼ Super 8 H
(540) 868-1800. **$59-$80.** 91 Reliance Rd 22645. I-81 exit 302. Int corridors. **Pets:** Accepted. 📶 🛗 ▣ 🏊

MINT SPRING

▼▼ Days Inn-Staunton M
(540) 337-3031. **$70-$140.** 372 White Hill Rd 24401. I-81 exit 217, just e on SR 654. Ext corridors. **Pets:** Accepted. 📶 🛗 ▣ 🏊

MOUNT JACKSON

▲▲▲ ▼▼▼ Super 8 - Mt. Jackson M
(540) 477-2911. **$66-$76.** 250 Conicville Blvd 22842. I-81 exit 273, just e. Ext corridors. **Pets:** Large, other species. $15 daily fee/pet. Designated rooms, service with restrictions, supervision. SAVE 📶 🛗 ▣ 🏊

▼▼▼ The Widow Kip's BB 🐾
(540) 477-2400. **$120-$145, 5 day notice.** 355 Orchard Dr 22842. I-81 exit 273, 1.5 mi s on US 11, just w on SR 263, then just sw on SR 698. Int corridors. **Pets:** Large, other species. $20 daily fee/pet. Designated rooms, no service, crate. ECO 📶 ⊠ 🛗 ▣ 🏊

NEW CHURCH

▼▼▼ The Garden & The Sea Inn BB 🐾
(757) 894-9097. **$110-$235, 10 day notice.** 4188 Nelson Rd 23415. US 13, 0.3 mi n, then just w on CR 710 (Nelson Rd). Int corridors. **Pets:** $25 one-time fee/pet. ECO 📶 ⊠ 🛗 ▣ 🏊 ⊠

NORTON

▼ Super 8-Norton M
(276) 679-0893. **$57-$118.** 425 Wharton Ln 24273. Jct US 58 and 23. Int corridors. **Pets:** Accepted. 📶 🛗 ▣

ONANCOCK

▲▲▲ ▼▼▼ 1890 Spinning Wheel Bed & Breakfast BB 🐾
(757) 787-7311. **$99-$125, 5 day notice.** 31 North St 23417. Just n of jct Market (SR 179) and North sts. Int corridors. **Pets:** Large, other species. $10 daily fee/pet. Designated rooms, supervision.
ECO SAVE 📶 ⊠ 📺 ⊠

ORANGE

▼▼▼ Mayhurst Inn BB 🐾
(540) 672-5597. **$179-$245, 10 day notice.** 12460 Mayhurst Ln 22960. On US 15, 0.5 mi s of town from SR 20 at the divided highway. Int corridors. **Pets:** $25 one-time fee/room. Designated rooms.
ECO 📶 ⊠ 🛗 ▣

PETERSBURG

▼▼ Comfort Inn-Petersburg South H 🐾
(804) 732-2000. **$68-$80.** 12001 S Crater Rd 23805. I-95 exit 45, jct US 301. Int corridors. **Pets:** Medium, other species. $25 daily fee/pet. Designated rooms, service with restrictions, supervision.
📶 ♿M 🛗 ▣ 🏊

▼▼ Super 8 M
(804) 732-6020. **$67-$99.** 3138 S Crater Rd 23805. I-95 exit 48B, just w on Wagner Rd, then just n. Ext corridors. **Pets:** Medium. $10 daily fee/pet. Designated rooms, service with restrictions, supervision.
📶 🛗 ▣

POUNDING MILL

▼▼▼ Claypool Hill Holiday Inn Express Hotel & Suites H
(276) 596-9880. **$105-$155.** 180 Clay Dr 24637. 0.5 mi e of US 19/460. Int corridors. **Pets:** Accepted. 📶 🛗 ▣ 🏊

▼ Claypool Hill Super 8 M
(276) 964-9888. **$63-$112.** 12367 Governor GC Peery Hwy 24637. 0.3 mi w on US 19/460. Int corridors. **Pets:** Medium. $10 daily fee/pet. Designated rooms, service with restrictions, supervision. 📶 🛗 ▣

RADFORD

AAA◇ ▼▼▼ BEST WESTERN Radford Inn **H**
(540) 639-3000. **$79-$119.** 1501 Tyler Ave 24141. I-81 exit 109, 2.7 mi nw on SR 177. Int corridors. **Pets:** Accepted.
[SAVE] 🛰 🛏 💻 🍴 ➵ 🚫

AAA◇ ▼▼▼ La Quinta Inn Radford **M**
(540) 633-6800. **$66-$144.** 1450 Tyler Ave 24141. I-81 exit 109, 2.6 mi w on SR 177. Int corridors. **Pets:** Service with restrictions, supervision.
[SAVE] 🛰 🚫 🛏 💻 🍴

▼▼ Super 8-Radford **M**
(540) 731-9355. **$59-$90.** 1600 Tyler Ave 24141. I-81 exit 109, just w. Int corridors. **Pets:** Accepted. 🛰 🛏 💻

RAPHINE

AAA◇ ▼▼◇ Days Inn-Shenandoah Valley **M**
(540) 377-2604. **$75-$130.** 584 Oakland Cir 24472. I-81 exit 205, just sw. Int corridors. **Pets:** Medium. $10 daily fee/pet. Designated rooms, service with restrictions, supervision. [SAVE] 🛰 🛏 ➵

RICHMOND METROPOLITAN AREA

CHESTER

AAA◇ ▼▼▼▼ Fairfield Inn by Marriott **H**
(804) 778-7500. **$94-$114.** 12400 Redwater Creek Rd 23831. I-95 exit 61B, just w of jct SR 10. Int corridors. **Pets:** Medium. $25 one-time fee/ pet. Designated rooms, service with restrictions, crate.
[SAVE] 🛰 🚫 ♿ 🛏 💻 ➵

▼▼▼ Residence Inn by Marriott **H** 🌸
(804) 530-5501. **$139-$189.** 800 Bermuda Hundred Rd 23836. I-295 exit 15, just w; in River's Bend. Int corridors. **Pets:** Other species. $100 deposit/room. Service with restrictions.
[ECO] 🛰 🚫 🛏 💻 ➵ 🚫

CHESTERFIELD

AAA◇ ▼▼▼ La Quinta Inn Richmond South **H**
(804) 743-0770. **$69-$155.** 9040 Pams Ave 23237. I-95 exit 64, just w. Int corridors. **Pets:** Service with restrictions, supervision.
[SAVE] 🛰 ♿ 🛏 💻

COLONIAL HEIGHTS

▼▼▼◇ Candlewood Suites **H**
(804) 526-0111. **$99-$129.** 15820 Woods Edge Rd 23834. I-95 exit 58 northbound; exit 58B southbound, just w. Int corridors. **Pets:** Large. $35 one-time fee/pet. Service with restrictions, crate. 🛰 ♿ 🛏 💻

DOSWELL

AAA◇ ▼▼◇ BEST WESTERN Kings Quarters **H** 🌸
(804) 876-3321. **$70-$140, 3 day notice.** 16102 Theme Park Way 23047. I-95 exit 98, just e on SR 30; entrance to theme park. Ext corridors. **Pets:** Medium, other species. Designated rooms, service with restrictions. [SAVE] 🛰 🛏 💻 🍴 ➵ 🚫

AAA◇ ▼▼◇ Days Inn Kings Dominion **H**
(804) 612-8680. **$50-$100.** 16220 International St 23047. I-95 exit 98, just e on SR 30. Int corridors. **Pets:** Accepted. [SAVE] 🛰 🛏 💻 ➵

AAA◇ ▼▼◇ La Quinta Inn & Suites Doswell - Kings Dominion **H**
(804) 876-6900. **$59-$199.** 16280 International St 23047. I-95 exit 98, just e on SR 30. Int corridors. **Pets:** Service with restrictions, supervision.
[SAVE] 🛰 🚫 ♿ 🛏 💻 ➵

GLEN ALLEN

AAA◇ ▼▼◇ Aloft Richmond West **H** 🌸
(804) 433-1888. **$109-$250.** 3939 Duckling Dr 23060. I-64 exit 178B, just w on W Broad St. Int corridors. **Pets:** Medium, dogs only. Service with restrictions, crate. [SAVE] 🛰 🚫 🛏 💻 ➵

AAA◇ ▼▼▼ BEST WESTERN PLUS Glen Allen Inn **H**
(804) 266-3500. **$70-$140.** 8507 Brook Rd 23060. I-95 exit 83B, 0.5 mi w to Brook Rd, then just n. Int corridors. **Pets:** Medium, dogs only. $25 daily fee/pet. Designated rooms, service with restrictions, supervision.
[SAVE] 🛰 ♿ 🛏 💻 ➵

▼▼▼ Candlewood Suites **H**
(804) 262-2240. **$85-$129.** 10609 Telegraph Rd 23059. I-295 exit 43C, 1.7 mi n to JEB Stuart Pkwy, just w to Telegraph Rd; I-95 exit 86B (SR 656/Elmont), just w, then 1 mi s. Int corridors. **Pets:** Medium. $25 deposit/ pet. Designated rooms, service with restrictions, supervision.
🛰 ♿ 🛏 💻

▼▼▼ Candlewood Suites Richmond-West **H**
(804) 364-2000. **Call for rates.** 4120 Brookriver Dr 23060. I-64 exit 178, just w on W Broad St. Int corridors. **Pets:** Accepted. 🛰 ♿ 🛏 💻

AAA◇ ▼▼▼ TownePlace Suites by Marriott **H**
(804) 747-5253. **$46-$98.** 4231 Park Place Ct 23060. I-64 exit 178B, just e on W Broad St to Cox Rd, then just n to Innslake Dr. Int corridors. **Pets:** Other species. $75 one-time fee/room. Service with restrictions.
[ECO] [SAVE] 🛰 🚫 ♿ 🛏 💻 ➵

MECHANICSVILLE

▼▼▼ Hampton Inn **H**
(804) 559-0559. **$119-$229.** 7433 Bell Creek Rd 23111. I-295 exit 37A (US 360 E) to Bell Creek Rd, just n. Int corridors. **Pets:** Accepted.
🛰 ♿ 🛏 ➵

RICHMOND

AAA◇ ▼▼▼▼ The Berkeley Hotel **H**
(804) 780-1300. **$150-$289.** 1200 E Cary St 23219. Just s of State Capitol; jct 12th St. Int corridors. **Pets:** Small, dogs only. $50 one-time fee/pet. Service with restrictions, supervision. [SAVE] 🛰 🚫 🛏 💻 🍴

▼▼▼ Candlewood Suites **H**
(804) 271-0016. **$80-$110.** 4301 Commerce Rd 23234. I-95 exit 69, just n. Int corridors. **Pets:** $50 one-time fee/room. Service with restrictions, crate. 🛰 ♿ 🛏 💻

AAA◇ ▼▼▼▼ Comfort Inn Midlothian Turnpike **H** 🌸
(804) 320-8900. **$89-$129.** 8710 Midlothian Tpke 23235. Jct Powhite Pkwy (SR 76) and Midlothian Tpke (US 60), just e. Int corridors. **Pets:** Small. $10 daily fee/pet. Designated rooms, service with restrictions, supervision. [SAVE] 🛰 ♿ 🛏 💻 ➵

AAA◇ ▼▼▼▼ Commonwealth Park Suites **H**
(804) 343-7300. **$139-$159.** 901 Bank St 23219. Jct 9th and Bank sts. Int corridors. **Pets:** $50 daily fee/pet. Designated rooms, service with restrictions, crate. [ECO] [SAVE] 🛰 🛏 💻 🍴 🚫

▼▼▼ Extended Stay Deluxe Richmond- I-64 - W Broad St **H**
(804) 285-7050. **$75-$90.** 6807 Paragon Pl 23230. I-64 exit 183C (W Broad St), just w to Glenside Dr, then just n. Int corridors. **Pets:** $25 daily fee/pet. Designated rooms, service with restrictions.
🛰 ♿ 🛏 💻 ➵

▼▼▼ Fairfield Inn & Suites by Marriott Northwest **H**
(804) 545-4200. **$94-$113.** 9937 Mayland Dr 23233. I-64 exit 180B, just n on Gaskins Rd. Int corridors. **Pets:** Medium. $50 one-time fee/room. Designated rooms, service with restrictions, crate.
🛰 🚫 ♿ 🛏 💻 ➵

Hilton Richmond Hotel & Spa/Short Pump H

(804) 364-3600. **$129-$289.** 12042 W Broad St 23233. I-64 exit 178, 2 mi w. Int corridors. **Pets:** Accepted.

Holiday Inn Express H

(804) 934-9300. **$89-$109.** 9933 Mayland Dr 23233. I-64 exit 180B, just n to Mayland Dr, then just w. Int corridors. **Pets:** Small. $25 daily fee/pet. Designated rooms, service with restrictions, supervision.

Holiday Inn South - Bells Road H

(804) 592-2900. **$79-$150.** 4303 Commerce Rd 23234. I-95 exit 69 (Bells Rd), just n. Int corridors. **Pets:** Accepted.

Homestead Studio Suites Hotel-Richmond/Midlothian H

(804) 272-1800. **$60-$70.** 241 Arboretum Pl 23236. Jct Powhite Pkwy (SR 76) and Midlothian Tpke (US 60), just w. Int corridors. **Pets:** $25 daily fee/pet. Designated rooms, service with restrictions.

The Jefferson Hotel H

(804) 788-8000. **$245-$415.** 101 W Franklin St 23220. Jct Franklin and Adams sts; center. Int corridors. **Pets:** Dogs only. $50 daily fee/pet. Designated rooms, service with restrictions, supervision.

Omni Richmond Hotel H

(804) 344-7000. **$139-$309.** 100 S 12th St 23219. I-95 exit 74A (downtown expwy I-195) exit Canal St; in James Center. Int corridors. **Pets:** Accepted.

Quality Inn West End H

(804) 346-0000. **Call for rates.** 8008 W Broad St 23294. I-64 exit 183C (W Broad St) westbound; exit 183 eastbound, 1.5 mi w. Int corridors. **Pets:** Accepted.

Red Roof Inn-Richmond South M

(804) 271-7240. **$50-$100.** 4350 Commerce Rd 23234. I-95 exit 69. Ext corridors. **Pets:** Large, other species. Service with restrictions, supervision.

Residence Inn by Marriott H

(804) 762-9852. **$95-$139.** 3940 Westerre Pkwy 23233. I-64 exit 180, n on Gaskins Rd to W Broad St. Int corridors. **Pets:** $75 one-time fee/room. Designated rooms, service with restrictions.

Sheraton Richmond Park South Hotel H

(804) 323-1144. **$89-$309.** 9901 Midlothian Tpke 23235. Midlothian Tpke (US 60), 1 mi w of Powhite Pkwy (SR 76). Int corridors. **Pets:** Large, other species. Designated rooms, service with restrictions, supervision.

Super 8 M

(804) 262-8880. **$44-$129.** 5615 Chamberlayne Rd 23227. I-95 exit 82. Int corridors. **Pets:** Dogs only. $10 daily fee/pet. Designated rooms, service with restrictions, supervision.

The Westin Richmond H

(804) 282-8444. **$136-$187.** 6631 W Broad St 23230. I-64 exit 183 eastbound; exit 183B westbound; in Reynolds Crossing. Int corridors. **Pets:** Small, dogs only. Designated rooms, service with restrictions, supervision.

SANDSTON

Candlewood Suites Richmond Airport H

(804) 652-1888. **$72-$90.** 5400 Audubon Dr 23231. I-64 exit 197A (Sandston-RIC Airport), 1 mi w. Int corridors. **Pets:** Medium. $75 one-time fee/room.

Comfort Inn Richmond Airport H

(804) 226-1800. **$67-$72.** 5240 Airport Square Ln 23150. I-64 exit 197A (Sandston-RIC Airport), 0.3 mi s to Williamsburg Rd, then 1 mi w. Int corridors. **Pets:** Accepted.

Holiday Inn Express H

(804) 222-1499. **Call for rates.** 491 International Center Dr 23150. I-64 exit 197A (Sandston-RIC Airport), just s to Audubon Dr, then just n. Int corridors. **Pets:** Accepted.

END METROPOLITAN AREA

ROANOKE

BEST WESTERN PLUS Inn at Valley View H

(540) 362-2400. **Call for rates.** 5050 Valley View Blvd 24012. I-581 exit 3E, just e, then just s via shopping center exit. Int corridors. **Pets:** Large, dogs only. $25 one-time fee/room. Designated rooms, no service, crate.

Comfort Inn Airport H

(540) 527-2020. **$99-$129.** 5070 Valley View Blvd 24012. I-81 exit 143 to I-581 exit 3, e to Hershberger Rd. Int corridors. **Pets:** Accepted.

Days Inn M

(540) 366-0341. **$70-$160.** 8118 Plantation Rd 24019. I-81 exit 146, just e on SR 115. Ext/int corridors. **Pets:** Medium, other species. $15 one-time fee/room. Designated rooms, service with restrictions, supervision.

Holiday Inn Roanoke Valley View H

(540) 362-4500. **$89-$149.** 3315 Ordway Dr 24017. I-581 exit 3W, just w to Ordway Dr, then 0.6 mi n via service road. Int corridors. **Pets:** $25 one-time fee/room, $10 daily fee/room. Service with restrictions, crate.

Holiday Inn Tanglewood/Roanoke H

(540) 774-4400. **$99-$149.** 4468 Starkey Rd 24018. I-581 exit US 220 (Franklin Rd/Salem), 0.8 mi s on SR 419 (Electric Rd). Int corridors. **Pets:** Medium. $35 one-time fee/room. Designated rooms, service with restrictions, crate.

MainStay Suites Roanoke Airport H

(540) 527-3030. **$99-$130.** 5080 Valley View Blvd 24012. I-581 exit 3E, just n. Int corridors. **Pets:** Medium, dogs only. $40 one-time fee/pet. Service with restrictions, supervision.

Quality Inn Roanoke-Airport M

(540) 366-8861. **$49-$90.** 6626 Thirlane Rd 24019. I-581 exit 2S, just s on SR 117 (Peters Creek Rd), then just w. Ext corridors. **Pets:** Small, dogs only. $25 daily fee/pet. Designated rooms, service with restrictions, supervision.

Quality Inn/Tanglewood M

(540) 989-4000. **$60-$125.** 3816 Franklin Rd SW 24014. I-581 exit US 220 (Franklin Rd/Salem), just n on US 220 business route, then w on Frontage Rd. Ext corridors. **Pets:** Large, dogs only. $15 daily fee/pet. Service with restrictions, supervision.

Residence Inn by Marriott Roanoke Airport H

(540) 265-1119. **$159-$229.** 3305 Ordway Dr NW 24017. I-581 exit 3W, just s. Int corridors. **Pets:** Medium. $100 one-time fee/pet. Service with restrictions, supervision.

Sheraton Roanoke Hotel & Conference Center H

(540) 563-9300. **$99-$189.** 2801 Hershberger Rd 24017. I-581 exit 3W, just w to Ordway Dr, then just n via service road. Int corridors.
Pets: Accepted. [ECO] [SAVE] 🛜 ✕ &M 🛏 📺 ❌ 🍴 🏊 ❌

Sleep Inn Tanglewood H

(540) 772-1500. **$75-$95.** 4045 Electric Rd 24018. I-581 exit US 220 (Franklin Rd/Salem), 0.7 mi n on SR 419. Int corridors. **Pets:** Small, dogs only. $25 daily fee/pet. Service with restrictions, supervision.

[SAVE] 🛜 🛏 📺

Super 8 M

(540) 563-8888. **$58-$77, 3 day notice.** 6616 Thirlane Rd 24019. I-581 exit 25, s on SR 117 (Peters Creek Rd), then just w. Int corridors. **Pets:** Other species. $10 daily fee/pet. Service with restrictions, crate.

🛜 🛏 📺

ROCKY MOUNT

Comfort Inn-Rocky Mount H

(540) 489-4000. **$65-$95.** 1730 N Main St 24151. 1.5 mi n on US 220 business route. Int corridors. **Pets:** Accepted. 🛜 🛏 📺 🏊

Holiday Inn Express Hotel & Suites H

(540) 489-5001. **$95-$145.** 395 Old Franklin Tpke 24151. US 220 S, just e on SR 40. Int corridors. **Pets:** $25 daily fee/pet. Service with restrictions, supervision. 🛜 🛏 📺 🏊

SALEM

Comfort Suites Inn at Ridgewood Farm H

(540) 375-4800. **$72-$109.** 2898 Keagy Rd 24153. I-81 exit 141, 4.7 mi s on SR 419, then just w. Int corridors. **Pets:** Large, other species. $25 daily fee/room. Designated rooms, service with restrictions.

🛜 ✕ 🛏 📺 🏊

Days Inn M

(540) 986-1000. **$65-$190.** 1535 E Main St 24153. I-81 exit 141, 2 mi s on SR 419, then just w on US 460. Ext/int corridors. **Pets:** $15 daily fee/room. Designated rooms, service with restrictions, supervision.

[SAVE] 🛜 🛏 📺

La Quinta Inn Roanoke Salem H

(540) 562-2717. **$83-$166.** 140 Sheraton Dr 24153. I-81 exit 141, 0.5 mi se on SR 419. Int corridors. **Pets:** Service with restrictions, supervision.

🛜 🛏 📺 🏊

Quality Inn M

(540) 387-1600. **$85-$99.** 151 Wildwood Rd 24153. I-81 exit 137, 0.3 mi e on SR 112. Ext corridors. **Pets:** Other species. $25 one-time fee/room. Service with restrictions, crate. [SAVE] 🛜 🛏 📺 🏊

SOUTH BOSTON

The Berry Hill Resort and Conference Center H

(434) 517-7000. **$149-$279.** 3105 River Rd S 24592. From US 501, 2.1 mi w on Greens Folly Rd (SR 654), then 0.9 mi s. Ext/int corridors. **Pets:** Very small, dogs only. $35 daily fee/room. Designated rooms, service with restrictions, supervision.

🛜 ✕ &M 🛏 📺 🍴 🏊 ❌

Holiday Inn Express H

(434) 575-4000. **$82-$86.** 1074 Bill Tuck Hwy 24592. Just e on US 58, from jct US 501. Int corridors. **Pets:** Accepted. 🛜 &M 🛏 📺 🏊

Super 8 M

(434) 572-8868. **$56-$85, 3 day notice.** 1040 Bill Tuck Hwy 24592. Just e on US 58, from jct US 501. Int corridors. **Pets:** Medium. $11 daily fee/pet. Designated rooms, service with restrictions, supervision.

🛜 🛏 📺

SOUTH HILL

Comfort Inn & Suites H

(434) 447-2200. **$72-$95.** 250 Thompson St 23970. I-85 exit 12A, just n. Int corridors. **Pets:** Other species. $20 deposit/pet, $20 daily fee/pet. No service. [SAVE] 🛜 &M 🛏 📺

Fairfield Inn & Suites by Marriott South Hill I-85 H

(434) 447-6800. **$76-$120.** 150 Arnold Dr 23970. I-85 exit 12A, just e on US 58. Int corridors. **Pets:** Other species. $75 one-time fee/room. Service with restrictions, crate. [ECO] 🛜 ✕ &M 🛏 📺 🏊

Quality Inn H

(434) 447-2600. **$49-$70.** 918 E Atlantic St 23970. I-85 exit 12B, just w. Ext corridors. **Pets:** Other species. $10 daily fee/pet. No service. [SAVE] 🛜 🛏 📺

STAFFORD

BEST WESTERN PLUS Aquia/Quantico Inn H

(540) 659-0022. **$109.** 2868 Jefferson Davis Hwy 22554. I-95 exit 143A, jct US 1 and SR 610. Ext corridors. **Pets:** Medium, other species. $20 daily fee/room. Designated rooms, service with restrictions, crate.

[SAVE] 🛜 🛏 📺 🏊

Country Inn By Carlson H

(540) 659-4330. **$89-$179.** 153 Garrisonville Rd 22554. I-95 exit 143B, just w. Int corridors. **Pets:** $25 daily fee/room. Designated rooms, service with restrictions. [SAVE] 🛜 &M 🛏 📺

Quality Inn & Suites H ❄

(540) 657-5566. **$89-$130.** 28 Greenspring Dr 22554. I-95 exit 143B, just w on Garrisonville Rd. Int corridors. **Pets:** Medium. $20 daily fee/pet. Service with restrictions, crate. 🛜 🛏 📺

Staybridge Suites Stafford/Quantico H ❄

(540) 720-2111. **$90-$169, 3 day notice.** 2996 Jefferson Davis Hwy 22554. I-95 exit 143A, just n on US 1. Int corridors. **Pets:** Large. $75 one-time fee/room. Service with restrictions, supervision.

🛜 ✕ &M 🛏 📺 🏊

TownePlace Suites by Marriott Stafford/Quantico H ❄

(540) 657-1990. **$114-$189.** 2772 Jefferson Davis Hwy 22554. I-95 exit 143A, just s on US 1. Int corridors. **Pets:** Other species. $10 daily fee/pet. Service with restrictions. [SAVE] 🛜 ✕ &M 🛏 📺 🏊

STAUNTON

BEST WESTERN Staunton Inn H ❄

(540) 885-1112. **$84-$135.** 92 Rowe Rd 24401. I-81 exit 222, just e on US 250. Int corridors. **Pets:** Large, other species. Designated rooms, service with restrictions, supervision.

[ECO] [SAVE] 🛜 ✕ 🛏 📺 🏊

Comfort Inn H

(540) 886-5000. **$89-$149.** 1302 Richmond Ave 24401. I-81 exit 222, just w on US 250. Int corridors. **Pets:** Accepted. [SAVE] 🛜 🛏 📺 🏊

Econo Lodge Staunton M

(540) 885-5158. **$55-$129, 3 day notice.** 1031 Richmond Ave 24401. I-81 exit 222, 0.7 mi w on US 250. Ext/int corridors. **Pets:** Medium. $10 daily fee/pet. Service with restrictions, supervision. [SAVE] 🛜 🛏 📺

Holiday Inn Conference Center H

(540) 248-6020. **$99-$299.** 152 Fairway Ln 24401. I-81 exit 225, 0.3 mi w on SR 275 (Woodrow Wilson Pkwy). Int corridors. **Pets:** Other species. $25 one-time fee/pet. Designated rooms, service with restrictions, supervision. [SAVE] 🛜 🛏 📺 🍴 🏊

▼▼ Red Roof Inn #706 M
(540) 885-3117. **$50-$110.** 42 Sangers Ln 24401. I-81 exit 222, just e on US 250. Ext corridors. **Pets:** Large, other species. Service with restrictions, supervision. 🛰 🛇 📠 💻

▼ ▼ Sleep Inn H 🐾
(540) 887-6500. **$89-$119.** 222 Jefferson Hwy 24401. I-81 exit 222, just e on US 250. Int corridors. **Pets:** Large, other species. Service with restrictions, supervision. 🛰 🛇 📠 💻

Ⓐ ▼▼▼ Stonewall Jackson Hotel & Conference Center H 🐾
(540) 885-4848. **$99-$199.** 24 S Market St 24401. Between Beverly and Johnson sts; downtown. Int corridors. **Pets:** $50 one-time fee/pet. Designated rooms, service with restrictions, supervision.
ECO SAVE 🛰 🛇 💻 🍴 🏊 🛇

STEPHENS CITY
Ⓐ ▼ ▼ Comfort Inn-Stephens City H
(540) 869-6500. **$70-$120.** 167 Town Run Ln 22655. I-81 exit 307, just se. Int corridors. **Pets:** Medium, other species. $10 daily fee/pet. Service with restrictions, supervision. SAVE 🛰 📠 💻 🏊

STONY CREEK
▼▼▼ Hampton Inn-Stony Creek H
(434) 246-5500. **$89-$149.** 10476 Blue Star Hwy 23882. I-95 exit 33, 0.3 mi s on SR 301. Int corridors. **Pets:** Medium. Designated rooms, service with restrictions, supervision. 🛰 📶 📠 💻 🏊

▼▼▼ Sleep Inn & Suites H
(434) 246-5100. **Call for rates.** 11019 Blue Star Hwy 23882. I-95 exit 33, 0.3 mi s on SR 301. Int corridors. **Pets:** Accepted.
🛰 📠 💻 🏊

STRASBURG
▼▼▼ Hotel Strasburg CI
(540) 465-9191. **Call for rates.** 213 S Holliday St 22657. I-81 exit 298, 2.2 mi s on US 11, then just s. Int corridors. **Pets:** Accepted. 🛰 🍴

▼▼▼ Ramada H
(540) 465-2444. **$69-$109.** 21 Signal Knob Dr 22657. I-81 exit 298, just e. Int corridors. **Pets:** Small. $10 daily fee/pet. Designated rooms, service with restrictions, crate. 🔌 🛰 📠 💻 🍴 🏊 🛇

TAPPAHANNOCK
▼▼▼ The Essex Inn BB
(804) 443-9900. **$175-$205, 7 day notice.** 203 Duke St 22560. 0.3 mi s on US 17, then just e. Ext/int corridors. **Pets:** Medium. $12 daily fee/pet. Designated rooms, service with restrictions, crate.
ECO 🛰 🛇 📠 💻

▼ Super 8 M
(804) 443-3888. **$63-$75.** 1800 Tappahannock Blvd 22560. US 17 and 360. Int corridors. **Pets:** Accepted. 🛰 📠 💻

TROUTVILLE
ⒶⒶ ▼ ▼ Comfort Inn H
(540) 992-5600. **$89-$119.** 2545 Lee Hwy S 24175. I-81 exit 150A, just s on US 11. Int corridors. **Pets:** Medium. $25 one-time fee/room. Service with restrictions, crate. SAVE 🛰 📠 💻 🏊

WARRENTON
ⒶⒶ ▼▼▼ Holiday Inn Express Hotel & Suites H
(540) 341-3461. **$99-$179.** 410 Holiday Ct 20186. US 15/29 and 17 exit Meetze Rd (SR 643), just w, then 0.8 mi n on Walker Rd. Int corridors. **Pets:** Medium, other species. $25 daily fee/pet. Designated rooms, service with restrictions, crate. SAVE 🛰 🛇 📶 📠 💻 🏊

WARSAW
ⒶⒶ ▼▼▼ Northern Neck Inn Warsaw H
(804) 333-1700. **$90-$103.** 4522 Richmond Rd 22572. US 360, just w of town. Int corridors. **Pets:** Medium, other species. $10 daily fee/pet. Designated rooms, service with restrictions, supervision.
SAVE 🛰 📠 💻 🏊

WASHINGTON
ⒶⒶ ▼▼▼▼ Middleton Inn BB 🐾
(540) 675-2020. **$295-$850, 14 day notice.** 176 Main St 22747. 0.5 mi w on US 211 business route. Ext/int corridors. **Pets:** Dogs only. $60 one-time fee/pet. Designated rooms, service with restrictions, crate.
SAVE 🛰 🛇 📠 💻

WASHINGTON, D.C. METROPOLITAN AREA

ALEXANDRIA
▼▼ Candlewood Suites Alexandria-Ft. Belvoir H
(703) 780-1111. **Call for rates.** 8847 Richmond Hwy 22309. I-95/495 exit 177A, 7.2 mi s on US 1. Int corridors. **Pets:** Accepted.
🛰 🛇 📶 📠 💻

ⒶⒶ ▼ ▼ Comfort Inn & Suites Alexandria H 🐾
(703) 922-9200. **$109-$199.** 5716 S Van Dorn St 22310. I-95/495 exit 173, 2 mi e of jct I-395 and 495. Int corridors. **Pets:** Small. $30 daily fee/pet. Service with restrictions, supervision. SAVE 🛰 📠 💻 🏊

▼▼ Extended StayAmerica-Washington DC-Alexandria-Eisenhower Ave H
(703) 329-3399. **$124-$344.** 200 Bluestone Rd 22304. I-95/495 exit 174 (Eisenhower Ave Connector), just n, then 1.2 mi e. Int corridors. **Pets:** $25 daily fee/pet. Designated rooms, service with restrictions.
🛰 📶 📠 💻

▼▼ Extended StayAmerica-Washington, DC-Alexandria-Landmark H
(703) 941-9440. **$114-$329.** 205 N Breckinridge Pl 22312. I-395 exit 3B, 0.3 mi w on SR 236, 0.4 mi ne on Beauregard St, just e on Gloucester Rd, then just s. Int corridors. **Pets:** $25 daily fee/pet. Designated rooms, service with restrictions. 🛰 📶 📠 💻

ⒶⒶ ▼▼▼ Hawthorn Suites by Wyndham Alexandria H
(703) 370-1000. **$150-$205.** 420 N Van Dorn St 22304. I-395 exit 3A, 0.3 mi e on SR 236 to S Van Dorn St, then 0.5 mi n. Int corridors. **Pets:** $100 one-time fee/pet. Service with restrictions, crate.
SAVE 🛰 🛇 📠 💻 🏊

▼▼▼ Hilton Alexandria Mark Center H
(703) 845-1010. **$99-$399.** 5000 Seminary Rd 22311. I-395 exit 4, just w. Int corridors. **Pets:** Accepted. 🛰 📶 📠 💻 🍴 🏊 🛇

ⒶⒶ ▼▼▼ Holiday Inn Hotel & Suites-Historic District Alexandria H
(703) 548-6300. **$89-$229.** 625 First St 22314. George Washington Memorial Pkwy, just e of jct 1st and Washington sts. Int corridors. **Pets:** Accepted. ECO SAVE 🛰 🛇 📠 💻 🍴 🏊

ⒶⒶ ▼▼▼ Hotel Monaco Alexandria-A Kimpton Hotel H 🐾
(703) 549-6080. **$149-$299.** 480 King St 22314. On SR 7; between S Pitt and S Royal sts; just sw of City Hall. Int corridors. **Pets:** Designated rooms, service with restrictions.
ECO SAVE 🛰 🛇 📠 💻 🍴 🏊 🛇

Ⓐ ▼▼▼▼ Lorien Hotel & Spa-A Kimpton Hotel 🅷 ☙

(703) 894-3434. **$149-$339.** 1600 King St 22314. Between Harvard and Peyton sts. Int corridors. **Pets:** Other species. Designated rooms, service with restrictions, crate. 🅔🅒🅞 ⏏ 🆂🅰🆅🅴 🛜 ☒ ♿ 🛏 🖥 🍴 ☒

Ⓐ ▼▼▼▼ Morrison House-A Kimpton Hotel 🅷 ☙

(703) 838-8000. **$125-$500.** 116 S Alfred St 22314. Jct King and S Alfred sts, just s. Int corridors. **Pets:** Other species. Designated rooms, service with restrictions, crate. 🅔🅒🅞 🆂🅰🆅🅴 🛜 ☒ 🛏 🖥 🍴

▼▼▼▼ Residence Inn by Marriott Alexandria-Old Town/Duke St. 🅷

(703) 548-5474. **$109-$359.** 1456 Duke St 22314. I-95/495 exit 176B, 0.5 mi n on SR 241, then 0.7 mi e on SR 236. Int corridors. **Pets:** Accepted. 🛜 ☒ ♿ 🛏 🖥 🏊

▼▼▼▼ Residence Inn by Marriott Alexandria Old Town South at Carlyle 🅷 ☙

(703) 549-1155. **$99-$339.** 2345 Mill Rd 22314. I-95/495 exit 176B, just n on Telegraph Rd (SR 241 N), just e on Pershing Ave and Stovall St, then just n; in Carlyle area. Int corridors. **Pets:** $150 one-time fee/room, $15 daily fee/room. Service with restrictions, crate. 🛜 ☒ ♿ 🛏 🖥

Ⓐ ▼▼▼▼ Sheraton Suites Old Town Alexandria 🅷

(703) 836-4700. **$109-$529.** 801 N St. Asaph St 22314. Just e of Washington St. Int corridors. **Pets:** Accepted.
🅔🅒🅞 🆂🅰🆅🅴 🛜 ☒ 🛏 🖥 🍴 🏊 ☒

Ⓐ ▼▼▼▼ Washington Suites-Alexandria 🅷

(703) 370-9600. **$99-$409.** 100 S Reynolds St 22304. I-395 exit 3A, 0.8 mi e on SR 236 E (Duke St), then just s. Int corridors. **Pets:** Accepted.
🆂🅰🆅🅴 🛜 ♿ 🛏 🖥 🍴 🏊 ☒

Ⓐ ▼▼▼▼ The Westin Alexandria 🅷 ☙

(703) 253-8600. **$79-$475, 3 day notice.** 400 Courthouse Square 22314. I-95/495 exit 176B, just n on Telegraph Rd (SR 241 N), 0.4 mi e on SR 236, then just s on Dulany St. Int corridors. **Pets:** Medium, dogs only. Designated rooms, service with restrictions, supervision.
🆂🅰🆅🅴 🛜 ☒ ♿ 🛏 🖥 🍴 🏊 ☒

ARLINGTON

Ⓐ ▼▼▼▼ Arlington Court Suites Hotel, A Clarion Collection 🅷

(703) 524-4000. **$109-$399.** 1200 N Courthouse Rd 22201. 1.5 mi sw of Theodore Roosevelt Bridge on US 50. Int corridors. **Pets:** Medium, other species. $75 one-time fee/room, $10 daily fee/pet. Designated rooms, service with restrictions, crate. 🆂🅰🆅🅴 🛜 ☒ ♿ 🛏 🖥

Ⓐ ▼▼▼▼ Hyatt Regency Crystal City at Reagan National Airport 🅷

(703) 418-1234. **$79-$396.** 2799 Jefferson Davis Hwy 22202. 2 mi s of 14th St Bridge on US 1, jct SR 233; entrance just e of US 1 on Clark St. Int corridors. **Pets:** Accepted. 🆂🅰🆅🅴 🛜 ☒ 🛏 🖥 🍴 🏊 ☒

Ⓐ ▼▼▼▼ Le Méridien Arlington 🅷

(703) 351-9170. **$115-$399.** 1121 N 19th St 22209. I-66 exit 73, just sw of Key Bridge. Int corridors. **Pets:** Accepted.
🆂🅰🆅🅴 🛜 ☒ ♿ 🛏 🖥 🍴

▼▼▼▼ Residence Inn by Marriott Arlington Capital View 🅷

(703) 415-1300. **$109-$379.** 2850 S Potomac Ave 22202. 2 mi s of 14th St Bridge on US 1; just s of jct SR 233. Int corridors. **Pets:** Accepted.
🛜 ☒ ♿ 🛏 🖥 🍴 🏊 ☒

▼▼▼▼ Residence Inn by Marriott Arlington Courthouse 🅷 ☙

(703) 312-2100. **$129-$339.** 1401 N Adams St 22201. Jct Clarendon Blvd and N Adams St. Int corridors. **Pets:** Medium, other species. $100 one-time fee/room. Service with restrictions, crate.
🅔🅒🅞 🛜 ☒ ♿ 🛏 🖥 🏊 ☒

▼▼▼▼ Residence Inn by Marriott Arlington Rosslyn 🅷

(703) 812-8400. **$189-$359.** 1651 N Oak St 22209. I-66 exit 73, 0.3 mi s on Fort Myer Dr, 0.3 mi w on Wilson Blvd to N Pierce St, then 2 blks e on Clarendon Blvd. Int corridors. **Pets:** Medium, other species. $100 one-time fee/pet. 🛜 ☒ 🛏 🖥

▼▼▼▼ Residence Inn by Marriott-Pentagon City 🅷

(703) 413-6630. **$109-$379.** 550 Army Navy Dr 22202. I-395 exit 8C, 1 mi s of 14th St Bridge. Int corridors. **Pets:** Accepted.
🅔🅒🅞 🛜 ☒ ♿ 🛏 🖥 🏊 ☒

▼▼▼▼ The Ritz-Carlton, Pentagon City 🅷

(703) 415-5000. **$159-$459.** 1250 S Hayes St 22202. 1 mi s of 14th St Bridge. Int corridors. **Pets:** Accepted.
🅔🅒🅞 🛜 ☒ ♿ 🛏 🖥 🍴 🏊 ☒

Ⓐ ▼▼▼▼ Sheraton Crystal City Hotel 🅷

(703) 486-1111. **$89-$289.** 1800 Jefferson Davis Hwy 22202. I-395 exit 8C, 1.4 mi s of 14th St Bridge on US 1; entrance corner of Eads St. Int corridors. **Pets:** Accepted. 🆂🅰🆅🅴 🛜 ☒ 🛏 🖥 🍴

Ⓐ ▼▼▼▼ Sheraton Pentagon City Hotel 🅷

(703) 521-1900. **$409.** 900 S Orme St 22204. I-395 exit 8A, at SR 27 and 244; 1.3 mi s of 14th St Bridge. Int corridors. **Pets:** Service with restrictions. 🆂🅰🆅🅴 🛜 ☒ 🛏 🖥 🍴 🏊

Ⓐ ▼▼▼ The Virginian Suites, an Ascend Collection Hotel 🅷

(703) 522-9600. **$226-$499.** 1500 Arlington Blvd 22209. 1 mi w of Theodore Roosevelt Bridge on US 50. Int corridors. **Pets:** Accepted.
🆂🅰🆅🅴 🛜 ☒ 🛏 🖥 🏊 ☒

Ⓐ ▼▼▼▼ The Westin Arlington Gateway 🅷 ☙

(703) 717-6200. **$139-$559.** 801 N Glebe Rd 22203. I-66 exit 71, just e on Fairfax Dr to Vermont Ave; just n of jct SR 120 and Wilson Blvd. Int corridors. **Pets:** Medium, dogs only. Supervision.
🅔🅒🅞 🆂🅰🆅🅴 🛜 ☒ ♿ 🛏 🖥 🏊 ☒

ASHBURN

Ⓐ ▼▼▼▼ Aloft Dulles Airport North 🅷

(703) 723-6969. **$69-$215.** 22390 Flagstaff Plaza 20148. On Loudoun County Pkwy (CR 607), just s of jct SR 267 (Toll Rd) exit 7. Int corridors. **Pets:** Accepted. 🅔🅒🅞 🆂🅰🆅🅴 🛜 ☒ ♿ 🛏 🖥 🏊

Ⓐ ▼▼▼▼ Homewood Suites by Hilton/Dulles North 🅷

(703) 723-7500. **$71-$199.** 44620 Waxpool Rd 20147. 1.7 mi w of jct SR 28 and Waxpool Rd (CR 625); SR 7, 3.4 mi s on Loudoun County Pkwy (CR 607), then 0.3 mi w. Int corridors. **Pets:** Accepted.
🆂🅰🆅🅴 🛜 ♿ 🛏 🖥 🏊

CENTREVILLE

▼▼ Extended StayAmerica-Washington DC-Centreville/Manassas 🅷

(703) 988-9955. **$89-$289.** 5920 Fort Dr 20121. I-66 exit 53, 0.9 mi s on SR 28; off SR 28, 0.3 mi s of jct US 29. Int corridors. **Pets:** $25 daily fee/pet. Designated rooms, service with restrictions. 🛜 🛏 🖥

CHANTILLY

▼▼ Extended StayAmerica Washington DC-Chantilly-Airport 🅷

(703) 263-7200. **$99-$299.** 4506 Brookfield Corporate Dr 20151. I-66 exit 53, 3 mi n on SR 28; 1 mi s of jct SR 28 and US 50. Int corridors. **Pets:** $25 daily fee/pet. Designated rooms, service with restrictions.
🛜 ♿ 🛏 🖥 🏊

▼▼▼▼ Hampton Inn Washington Dulles International Airport South 🅷 ☙

(703) 818-8200. **$69-$229.** 4050 Westfax Dr 20151. 1 mi w on US 50 from jct SR 28. Int corridors. **Pets:** Designated rooms, service with restrictions, supervision. 🅔🅒🅞 🛜 ☒ ♿ 🛏 🖥 🏊 ☒

▼▼▼ Holiday Inn Chantilly-Dulles Expo Center **H**
(703) 815-6060. **$69-$189.** 4335 Chantilly Shopping Center 20151. I-66
exit 53, 3 mi n on SR 28; 1 mi s of jct US 50 and SR 28. Int corridors.
Pets: Accepted. 📶 ✖ ♿M 🛏 🖥 🍴 ➴ ⊠

▼▼▼ Residence Inn by Marriott Chantilly Dulles
South **H**
(703) 263-7900. **$79-$229.** 14440 Chantilly Crossing Ln 20151. I-66 exit
57B, on US 50, just w of jct SR 28. Int corridors. **Pets:** Accepted.
🌿 📶 ✖ ♿M 🛏 🖥 ➴ ⊠

▼▼▼ Staybridge Suites Hotel Chantilly/Dulles International
Airport **H**
(703) 435-8090. **$99-$299.** 3860 Centerview Dr 20151. Jct SR 28, just e
on US 50. Int corridors. **Pets:** Large, other species. $75 one-time fee/
room. 🌿 📶 ♿M 🛏 🖥

▼▼ TownePlace Suites by Marriott-Chantilly Dulles
South **H**
(703) 709-0453. **$89-$169.** 14036 Thunderbolt Pl 20151. Jct SR 28, just
e on US 50. Int corridors. **Pets:** Accepted.
🌿 📶 ✖ 🛏 🖥 ➴ ⊠

▼▼ Wingate by Wyndham Dulles Airport-Chantilly **H**
(571) 203-0999. **$79-$259.** 3940 Centerview Dr 20151. Jct SR 28, just e
on US 50. Int corridors. **Pets:** Medium. $75 one-time fee/room. Service
with restrictions, supervision. 📶 ✖ ♿M 🛏 🖥 ➴ ⊠

FAIRFAX

▼▼ Candlewood Suites Fairfax-Washington, D.C. **H**
(703) 359-4490. **Call for rates.** 11400 Random Hills Rd 22030. I-66 exit
57A, 0.5 mi e on US 50, just s on Waples Mill Rd, then 0.4 mi w. Int
corridors. **Pets:** Accepted. 📶 ♿M 🛏 🖥

AAA **▼▼** Comfort Inn University Center **H** 🐾
(703) 591-5900. **$70-$170.** 11180 Fairfax Blvd 22030. I-66 exit 57A, 0.8
mi se on US 50; 0.5 mi nw of jct US 29 and US 50. Int corridors.
Pets: Medium, other species. $25 daily fee/pet. Service with restrictions,
crate. 🌿 🆂🅰🆅🅴 📶 ✖ 🛏 🖥 🍴 ➴ ⊠

▼▼ Extended StayAmerica Washington DC-Fairfax **H**
(703) 359-5000. **$99-$309.** 3997 Fair Ridge Dr 22033. I-66 exit 57B, 1.2
mi w on US 50. Int corridors. **Pets:** $25 daily fee/pet. Designated rooms,
service with restrictions. 📶 ♿M 🛏 🖥

▼▼ Homestead Studio Suites Hotel-Washington
DC-Fairfax-Fair Oaks **M**
(703) 273-3444. **$94-$299.** 12104 Monument Dr 22033. I-66 exit 57B,
0.8 mi w on US 50, 0.3 mi s on SR 620 (W Ox Rd), then just se. Ext
corridors. **Pets:** $25 daily fee/pet. Designated rooms, service with restric-
tions. 📶 ♿M 🛏 🖥

▼▼ Homestead Studio Suites Washington DC-Falls
Church-Merrifield **H**
(703) 204-0088. **$114-$329.** 8281 Willow Oaks Corporate Dr 22031.
I-495 exit 50A, just w on US 50 to Gallows Rd, then just s. Ext corridors.
Pets: $25 daily fee/pet. Designated rooms, service with restrictions.
📶 ♿M 🛏 🖥

AAA **▼▼▼** Hyatt Fairfax at Fair Lakes **H**
(703) 818-1234. **$69-$239.** 12777 Fair Lakes Cir 22033. I-66 exit 55
(Fairfax County Pkwy N), just w, then just s. Int corridors. **Pets:** Accepted.
🌿 🆂🅰🆅🅴 📶 🛏 🖥 🍴 ➴ ⊠

▼▼▼ Residence Inn by Marriott Fairfax City **H**
(703) 267-2525. **$79-$219.** 3565 Chain Bridge Rd 22030. I-66 exit 60,
0.5 mi s on SR 123; jct US 29/50. Int corridors. **Pets:** Accepted.
📶 ✖ ♿M 🛏 🖥 ➴

▼▼▼ Residence Inn by Marriott-Fair Lakes **H**
(703) 266-4900. **$79-$229.** 12815 Fair Lakes Pkwy 22033. I-66 exit 55
(Fairfax County Pkwy N), just w. Int corridors. **Pets:** Large, other species.
$150 one-time fee/room. Service with restrictions, supervision.
🌿 📶 ✖ ♿M 🛏 🖥 ➴ ⊠

FALLS CHURCH

▼▼▼ Homewood Suites by Hilton-Falls Church **H**
(703) 560-6644. **$129-$269.** 8130 Porter Rd 22042. I-495 exit 50A, just
w to SR 650; 0.4 mi n of SR 650. Int corridors. **Pets:** Accepted.
📶 ♿M 🛏 🖥 ➴ ⊠

▼▼▼ Residence Inn by Marriott Fairfax-Merrifield **H**
(703) 573-5200. **$85-$259.** 8125 Gatehouse Rd 22042. I-495 exit 50A,
just w to SR 650 N. Int corridors. **Pets:** Accepted.
📶 ✖ ♿M 🛏 🖥 ➴ ⊠

▼▼ TownePlace Suites by Marriott-Falls Church **H**
(703) 237-6172. **$69-$249.** 205 Hillwood Ave 22046. I-495 exit 50B, 2.5
mi e on US 50, 0.6 mi n on Annandale Rd, then e; just s of
US 29. Int corridors. **Pets:** $100 one-time fee/room. Service with restric-
tions, supervision. 🌿 📶 ✖ ♿M 🛏 🖥 ➴

AAA **▼▼▼** The Westin Tysons Corner **H**
(703) 893-1340. **$79-$389.** 7801 Leesburg Pike 22043. I-495 exit 47B,
just e on SR 7. Int corridors. **Pets:** Accepted.
🌿 🆂🅰🆅🅴 📶 ✖ 🛏 🖥 🍴 ➴ ⊠

HERNDON

▼▼ Candlewood Suites Washington Dulles-Herndon **H**
(703) 793-7100. **Call for rates.** 13845 Sunrise Valley Dr 20171. SR 28,
0.4 mi e on Frying Pan Rd, then 0.7 mi nw. Int corridors. **Pets:** Accepted.
📶 ♿M

AAA **▼▼** Comfort Inn Dulles International Airport **H**
(703) 437-7555. **Call for rates.** 200 Elden St 20170. Just w on CR 606
from jct CR 7100 (Fairfax County Pkwy). Int corridors. **Pets:** Small. $25
daily fee/pet. Designated rooms, service with restrictions, crate.
🆂🅰🆅🅴 📶 ✖ 🛏 🖥

AAA **▼▼** Hilton Washington Dulles Airport **H**
(703) 478-2900. **$89-$209.** 13869 Park Center Rd 20171. SR 267
(Dulles Toll Rd) exit 9, 3 mi s on SR 28; at McLearen Blvd (SR 668). Int
corridors. **Pets:** Accepted.
🌿 🆂🅰🆅🅴 📶 ♿M 🛏 🖥 🍴 ➴ ⊠

AAA **▼▼▼** Hyatt house Herndon **H**
(703) 437-5000. **$89-$259.** 467 Herndon Pkwy 20170. SR 267 (Dulles
Toll Rd) exit 11 CR 7100 (Fairfax County Pkwy), just n to Spring St exit,
just s to Herndon Pkwy (CR 606), then just w on CR 606. Int corridors.
Pets: Medium. $150 one-time fee/pet. Service with restrictions, supervi-
sion. 🆂🅰🆅🅴 📶 ✖ 🛏 🖥 ➴ ⊠

▼▼▼ Residence Inn by
Marriott-Herndon/Reston **H** 🐾
(703) 435-0044. **$79-$249.** 315 Elden St 20170. 0.4 mi w on CR 606
from jct CR 7100 (Fairfax County Pkwy). Int corridors. **Pets:** Other species. $75 one-time fee/room. Service with restrictions, crate.
📶 ✖ ♿M 🛏 🖥 ➴ ⊠

AAA **▼▼▼▼** Sheraton Herndon Dulles Airport Hotel **H**
(571) 643-0950. **$89-$299.** 13715 Sayward Blvd 20171. Jct SR 657 and
267 (Dulles Toll Rd) exit 10, 0.5 mi s on Centreville Rd (SR 657), then
1.1 mi w on Sunrise Valley Dr. Int corridors. **Pets:** Accepted.
🆂🅰🆅🅴 📶 ✖ ♿M 🛏 🖥 🍴 ➴ ⊠

▼▼▼ Staybridge Suites Herndon Dulles **H**
(703) 713-6800. **$69-$199.** 13700 Coppermine Rd 20171. SR 267
(Dulles Toll Rd) exit 10, 0.7 mi s on Centreville Rd (SR 657), then 0.4 mi
w. Ext corridors. **Pets:** Medium. $150 one-time fee/pet. Designated rooms,
service with restrictions, crate. 📶 🛏 🖥 ➴ ⊠

AAA **▼▼▼** The Westin Washington Dulles
Airport **H** 🐾
(703) 793-3366. **$79-$269.** 2520 Wasser Terrace 20171. SR 28, 0.4 mi e
on Frying Pan Rd, then 0.8 mi nw. Int corridors. **Pets:** Medium, dogs
only. Designated rooms, service with restrictions, crate.
🌿 🆂🅰🆅🅴 📶 ✖ ♿M 🛏 🖥 🍴 ➴ ⊠

LEESBURG

◆◆◆ ▼▼▼ BEST WESTERN Leesburg Hotel & Conference Center 🅷 ❀

(703) 777-9400. **$99-$149.** 726 E Market St 20176. Off SR 7 business route, just w of jct US 15. Int corridors. **Pets:** Medium, dogs only. $10 daily fee/pet. Service with restrictions, crate. SAVE 🛜 ❚ 💻 🏊

LORTON

▼▼ Comfort Inn Gunston Corner 🅷

(703) 643-3100. **$89-$149.** 8180 Silverbrook Rd 22079. I-95 exit 163, just w. Int corridors. **Pets:** Medium. $25 one-time fee/pet. Designated rooms, service with restrictions, crate. 🛜 ✕ ❚ 💻 🏊 ✕

MANASSAS

◆◆◆ ▼▼▼ BEST WESTERN Battlefield Inn 🅷 ❀

(703) 361-8000. **$109-$300.** 10820 Balls Ford Rd 20109. I-66 exit 47A westbound; exit 47 eastbound, just s on SR 234 business route. Ext corridors. **Pets:** Other species. $10 daily fee/pet. Service with restrictions.
SAVE 🛜 ✕ ❚ 🍴 🏊

▼▼▼ Candlewood Suites Manassas 🅷

(703) 530-0550. **$99-$129.** 11220 Balls Ford Rd 20109. I-66 exit 47A westbound; exit 47 eastbound, just s on SR 234 business route, then 0.7 mi w. Int corridors. **Pets:** Accepted. 🛜 ⓜ ❚ 💻

▼▼▼ Comfort Suites Manassas 🅷

(703) 686-1100. **$99-$129.** 7350 Williamson Blvd 20109. I-66 exit 47A westbound; exit 47 eastbound, 0.5 mi s on SR 234 business route, then just e. Int corridors. **Pets:** Other species. $50 one-time fee/room. Designated rooms, service with restrictions, supervision.
🛜 ✕ ❚ 💻 🏊 ✕

◆◆◆ ▼▼▼ Red Roof Inn-Manassas Ⓜ

(703) 335-9333. **$59-$99.** 10610 Automotive Dr 20109. I-66 exit 47 eastbound; exit 47A westbound, just s on SR 234 business route, then just e on Balls Ford Rd. Ext corridors. **Pets:** Large, other species. Service with restrictions, supervision. SAVE 🛜 ⓜ ❚

▼▼▼▼ Residence Inn by Marriott Manassas Battlefield Park 🅷

(703) 330-8808. **$100-$160.** 7345 Williamson Blvd 20109. I-66 exit 47A westbound; exit 47 eastbound, 0.5 mi s on SR 234 business route, then just e. Int corridors. **Pets:** Other species. $100 one-time fee/room. Service with restrictions, crate. 🛜 ✕ ⓜ ❚ 💻 🏊 ✕

MCLEAN

◆◆◆ ▼▼▼ BEST WESTERN Tysons Westpark 🅷

(703) 734-2800. **$160.** 8401 Westpark Dr 22102. I-495 exit 47A, 1.3 mi w on SR 7. Int corridors. **Pets:** Other species. $11 daily fee/room. Service with restrictions. SAVE 🛜 ✕ ⓜ ❚ 💻 🏊

▼▼▼▼ Crowne Plaza Tysons Corner 🅷

(703) 893-2100. **$89-$299.** 1960 Chain Bridge Rd 22102. I-495 exit 46A, 0.5 mi s on SR 123, just nw on International Dr, then just sw on Greensboro Dr. Int corridors. **Pets:** Accepted.
ECO 🛜 ✕ ⓜ ❚ 💻 🍴 🏊 ✕

◆◆◆ ▼▼▼▼ The Ritz-Carlton, Tysons Corner 🅷 ❀

(703) 506-4300. **Call for rates.** 1700 Tysons Blvd 22102. I-495 exit 46A, 0.3 mi sw on SR 123, then just nw. Int corridors. **Pets:** Medium, dogs only. $250 one-time fee/pet. Service with restrictions.
ECO SAVE 🛜 ✕ ⓜ ❚ 💻 🍴 🏊 ✕

◆◆◆ ▼▼▼▼ Staybridge Suites-McLean-Tysons Corner (Washington, DC area) 🅷 ❀

(703) 448-5400. **$109-$329.** 6845 Old Dominion Dr 22101. I-495 exit 46B, 2 mi n on SR 123, then 0.3 mi e on SR 309. Int corridors. **Pets:** Medium, other species. $75 one-time fee/room. Service with restrictions, crate. SAVE 🛜 ✕ ⓜ ❚ 💻 🏊 ✕

RESTON

▼▼▼▼ Homestead Studio Suites Washington DC-Reston Ⓜ

(703) 707-9700. **$119-$339.** 12190 Sunset Hills Rd 20190. SR 267 (Dulles Toll Rd) exit 12 (Reston Pkwy), just n, then just w. Ext corridors. **Pets:** $25 daily fee/pet. Designated rooms, service with restrictions.
🛜 ❚ 💻

◆◆◆ ▼▼▼▼ Sheraton Reston Hotel 🅷

(703) 620-9000. **$99-$429.** 11810 Sunrise Valley Dr 20191. SR 267 (Dulles Toll Rd) exit 12 (Reston Pkwy), just s. Int corridors.
Pets: Accepted. SAVE 🛜 ✕ ⓜ ❚ 💻 🍴 🏊 ✕

◆◆◆ ▼▼▼▼ The Westin Reston Heights 🅷

(703) 391-9000. **$129-$489.** 11750 Sunrise Valley Dr 20191. SR 267 (Dulles Toll Rd) exit 12 (Reston Pkwy), just s. Int corridors.
Pets: Accepted. ⧉ SAVE 🛜 ✕ ⓜ ❚ 💻 🍴 🏊 ✕

SPRINGFIELD

▼▼▼ Comfort Inn Washington DC/Springfield 🅷

(703) 922-9000. **$89-$159.** 6560 Loisdale Ct 22150. I-95 exit 169A, just e on SR 644 E; jct I-395 and 495, 0.8 mi s. Int corridors. **Pets:** Accepted.
🛜 ❚ 💻

▼▼▼ Hampton Inn Washington DC/Springfield 🅷 ❀

(703) 924-9444. **$69-$89.** 6550 Loisdale Ct 22150. I-95 exit 169A, just e on SR 644 E; jct I-395 and 495, 0.8 mi s. Int corridors. **Pets:** Medium. Service with restrictions, crate. 🛜 ⓜ ❚ 💻 🏊

▼▼▼ Residence Inn by Marriott Springfield Old Keene Mill 🅷

(703) 644-0020. **$69-$259.** 6412 Backlick Rd 22150. I-95 exit 169A, just nw of SR 644; jct I-395 and 495, 0.8 mi s. Int corridors. **Pets:** Medium. $150 one-time fee/room. Service with restrictions, crate.
🛜 ✕ ⓜ ❚ 💻 🏊 ✕

▼▼▼ TownePlace Suites by Marriott Springfield 🅷

(703) 569-8060. **$98-$224.** 6245 Brandon Ave 22150. I-95 exit 169B, just nw of SR 644; jct I-395 and 495, 0.8 mi s. Int corridors. **Pets:** Accepted.
🛜 ✕ ⓜ ❚ 💻 🏊

STERLING

◆◆◆ ▼▼▼ BEST WESTERN Dulles Airport Inn Ⓜ ❀

(703) 471-8300. **$74-$130.** 45440 Holiday Dr 20166. 1.7 mi n on SR 28 from jct SR 267 (Dulles Toll Rd), just e on CR 846, then just s on Shaw Rd. Ext corridors. **Pets:** Medium. $20 daily fee/room. Service with restrictions, supervision. ECO SAVE 🛜 ❚ 💻

▼▼▼ Candlewood Suites Washington Dulles/Sterling 🅷

(703) 674-2288. **Call for rates.** 44520 Severn Way 20166. 1.3 mi s on SR 28 from jct SR 7, 0.3 mi e on Nokes Blvd, then 0.4 mi s on Atlantic Blvd. Int corridors. **Pets:** Accepted. 🛜 ⓜ ❚ 💻

▼▼▼ Hampton Inn-Dulles/Cascades 🅷

(703) 450-9595. **$89-$189.** 46331 McClellan Way 20165. 1.7 mi e on SR 7 from jct SR 28, 0.5 mi n on CR 1794 (Cascades Pkwy) to Palisade Pkwy, just e, then 0.4 mi s on Whitfield Pl. Int corridors. **Pets:** Accepted.
ECO 🛜 ⓜ ❚ 💻 🏊 ✕

▼▼▼ Holiday Inn Washington Dulles International Airport 🅷

(703) 471-7411. **$79-$189.** 45425 Holiday Dr 20166. 1.7 mi n on SR 28 from jct SR 267 (Dulles Toll Rd), just e on CR 846, then just s on Shaw Rd. Int corridors. **Pets:** Accepted.
ECO 🛜 ⓜ ❚ 💻 🍴 🏊 ✕

▼▼▼ Residence Inn by Marriott Dulles Airport @ Dulles 28 Centre 🅷

(703) 421-2000. **$79-$229.** 45250 Monterey Pl 20166. SR 28 exit CR 625 (Waxpool Rd), just w, just n on Pacific Blvd, then just e on Commercial Dr. Int corridors. **Pets:** Medium, other species. $150 one-time fee/room. Service with restrictions. 🛜 ✕ ⓜ ❚ 💻 🏊 ✕

▼▼ Suburban Extended Stay Hotel
Washington-Dulles/Sterling **H**
(703) 674-2299. **$79-$99.** 45510 E Severn Way 20166. 1.3 mi s on SR 28 from jct SR 7, 0.3 mi e on Nokes Blvd, then 0.4 mi s on Atlantic Blvd. Int corridors. **Pets:** Accepted. 🛜 🛠 💻

▼▼ TownePlace Suites by Marriott at Dulles Airport **H**
(703) 707-2017. **$79-$229.** 22744 Holiday Park Dr 20166. 1.7 mi n on SR 28 from jct SR 267 (Dulles Toll Rd), just e on CR 846, then just s on Shaw Rd. Int corridors. **Pets:** Accepted. 🌐 🛜 🗙 🛠 💻

▼▼ TownePlace Suites by Marriott Dulles North **H**
(703) 421-1090. **$89-$149.** 21123 Whitfield Pl 20165. 1.7 mi e on SR 7 from jct SR 28, 0.5 mi n on SR 1794 (Cascades Pkwy) to Palisades Pkwy, just e, then just s. Int corridors. **Pets:** Accepted.
🛜 🗙 🛠 💻 ≈

VIENNA
AAA ▼▼ Comfort Inn Tysons Corner **M**
(703) 448-8020. **$79-$179.** 1587 Spring Hill Rd 22182. I-495 exit 47A, 1.8 mi w on SR 7, then just s; just e of jct SR 267 (Dulles Toll Rd). Ext corridors. **Pets:** Accepted. 🆂🅰🆅🅴 🛜 🛠 💻 ≈

▼▼ Extended StayAmerica-Washington, DC-Tysons
Corner **H**
(703) 356-6300. **$124-$344.** 8201 Old Courthouse Rd 22182. I-495 exit 47A, 0.6 mi w on SR 7, then just s on Gallows Rd. Int corridors. **Pets:** $25 daily fee/pet. Designated rooms, service with restrictions.
🛜 🅼 🛠 💻

AAA ▼▼▼ Residence Inn by Marriott-Tysons
Corner **H**
(703) 893-0120. **$79-$279.** 8616 Westwood Center Dr 22182. I-495 exit 47A, 1.9 mi w on SR 7, then just s. Ext corridors. **Pets:** Accepted.
🆂🅰🆅🅴 🛜 🗙 🛠 💻 ≈ 🗙

▼▼▼ Residence Inn by Marriott Tysons Corner
Mall **H** 🐾
(703) 917-0800. **$129-$269.** 8400 Old Courthouse Rd 22182. I-495 exit 46A, 1.1 mi s on SR 123; 0.3 mi s of jct SR 7 and 123. Int corridors. **Pets:** Other species. $100 one-time fee/room. Service with restrictions.
🛜 🗙 🅼 🛠 💻 ≈ 🗙

AAA ▼▼▼ Sheraton Premiere At Tysons Corner **H**
(703) 448-1234. **$99-$349.** 8661 Leesburg Pike 22182. SR 7, just e of jct SR 267 (Dulles Toll Rd). Int corridors. **Pets:** Accepted.
🌐 🆂🅰🆅🅴 🛜 🗙 🅼 🛠 💻 🍴 ≈ 🗙

WOODBRIDGE
▼▼▼ Residence Inn by Marriott Potomac Mills **H**
(703) 490-4020. **$129-$409.** 14301 Crossing Pl 22192. I-95 exit 158B (Prince William Pkwy), 0.5 mi sw. Int corridors. **Pets:** $100 one-time fee/room. Designated rooms, service with restrictions.
🛜 🗙 🅼 🛠 💻 ≈ 🗙

END METROPOLITAN AREA

WAYNESBORO
AAA ▼▼▼ BEST WESTERN PLUS Waynesboro Inn &
Suites Conf Ctr **H** 🐾
(540) 942-1100. **$95-$160.** 109 Apple Tree Ln 22980. I-64 exit 94, just n. Int corridors. **Pets:** Large, other species. $10 daily fee/room. Designated rooms, service with restrictions, supervision.
🌐 🆂🅰🆅🅴 🛜 🗙 🛠 💻 ≈

▼▼▼ Comfort Inn Waynesboro **H**
(540) 932-3060. **Call for rates.** 15 Windigrove Dr 22980. I-64 exit 94, 0.5 mi n on US 340, then just e. Int corridors. **Pets:** Small, dogs only. $10 daily fee/pet. Designated rooms, service with restrictions, supervision.
🛜 🛠 💻 ≈

AAA ▼▼ Days Inn Waynesboro **M**
(540) 943-1101. **$70-$105.** 2060 Rosser Ave 22980. I-64 exit 94, 0.5 mi n on US 340. Ext corridors. **Pets:** Other species. $10 daily fee/room. Service with restrictions, supervision. 🆂🅰🆅🅴 🛜 🛠 💻 ≈

AAA ▼▼ Quality Inn Waynesboro **M**
(540) 942-1171. **$61-$136.** 640 W Broad St 22980. I-64 exit 96, 3 mi w on SR 624; jct US 250 and 340. Ext/int corridors. **Pets:** $10 daily fee/pet. Service with restrictions. 🆂🅰🆅🅴 🛜 🛠 💻 ≈

▼▼▼ Residence Inn by Marriott Waynesboro **H** 🐾
(540) 943-7426. **$149-$219.** 44 Windigrove Dr 22980. I-64 exit 94, 0.5 mi n on US 340, then just e. Int corridors. **Pets:** Small, other species. $100 one-time fee/room. Service with restrictions, supervision.
🛜 🗙 🛠 💻 ≈ 🗙

▼▼ Super 8 Waynesboro **M**
(540) 943-3888. **$54-$90.** 2045 Rosser Ave 22980. I-64 exit 94, n on US 340 to Lew Dewitt Blvd, then just w to Apple Tree Ln. Int corridors. **Pets:** $5 daily fee/pet. Designated rooms, service with restrictions, supervision. 🛜 🛠 💻

WILLIAMSBURG, JAMESTOWN & YORKTOWN AREA

CHARLES CITY
▼▼▼ Edgewood Plantation Bed & Breakfast **BB**
(804) 829-2962. **$139-$198, 15 day notice.** 4800 John Tyler Memorial Hwy 23030. Jct SR 609, just e on SR 5. Ext/int corridors. **Pets:** Small. $35 one-time fee/pet. Designated rooms, crate.
🛜 🗙 🛠 💻 ≈ 🗙

WILLIAMSBURG
AAA ▼▼▼ Clarion Hotel Historic District **H** 🐾
(757) 229-4100. **$49-$149.** 351 York St 23185. US 60 E, 0.3 mi se of jct SR 5 and 31. Int corridors. **Pets:** Large, other species. $25 one-time fee/pet. Designated rooms, service with restrictions, crate.
🆂🅰🆅🅴 🛜 🗙 🅼 🛠 💻 🍴 ≈ 🗙

AAA ▼▼▼ Crowne Plaza Williamsburg **H**
(757) 220-2250. **$69-$189.** 6945 Pocahontas Tr 23185. US 60, 0.8 mi e of jct SR 5 and 31. Int corridors. **Pets:** Medium. $45 one-time fee/room. Designated rooms, service with restrictions, crate.
🌐 🆂🅰🆅🅴 🛜 🗙 🛠 💻 🍴 ≈ 🗙

AAA ▼▼▼ Days Hotel Busch Gardens Area **H**
(757) 253-6444. **$60-$130.** 201 Water Country Pkwy 23185. I-64 exit 242B, just w on SR 199; facing Water Country. Int corridors. **Pets:** Dogs only. $50 one-time fee/pet. Designated rooms, service with restrictions, crate. 🆂🅰🆅🅴 🛜 🗙 🅼 🛠 💻 🍴 ≈ 🗙

▼▼▼ Holiday Inn Patriot-Williamsburg 🅷

(757) 565-2600. **Call for rates.** 3032 Richmond Rd 23185. I-64 exit 234 (SR 199 E) to US 60, 2.5 mi e. Int corridors. **Pets:** Small. $25 daily fee/pet. Designated rooms, service with restrictions, supervision.

🛜 🛗 🖥 🍴 ♒

⨀ ▼▼▼▼ Residence Inn by Marriott Williamsburg 🅷

(757) 941-2000. **$98-$310.** 1648 Richmond Rd 23185. US 60, just w of jct Bypass Rd. Int corridors. **Pets:** Large, other species. $25 one-time fee/room. Service with restrictions, crate.

🆂🅰🆅🅴 🛜 ✖ 🛗 🖥 ♒ ✖

⨀ ▼▼▼ Super 8-Williamsburg/Historic Area 🅼

(757) 229-0500. **$40-$100.** 304 2nd St 23185. I-64 exit 242 (SR 199 W), 0.6 mi w to SR 143, 1.6 mi w to SR 162, then just w. Ext corridors. **Pets:** Medium, dogs only. $10 daily fee/pet. No service, supervision.

🆂🅰🆅🅴 🛜 🛗 🖥 ♒

▼▼ ▼▼▼ Williamsburg Inn 🅷 🐾

(757) 220-7978. **$299-$799, 3 day notice.** 136 E Francis St 23185. In Colonial Williamsburg restored area. Int corridors. **Pets:** Medium, dogs only. $500 deposit/room, $50 daily fee/pet. Designated rooms, service with restrictions, crate. 🛜 ✖ 🛗 🍴 ♒ ✖

YORKTOWN

▼▼ ▼▼ Candlewood Suites-Yorktown 🅷

(757) 952-1120. **$59-$169.** 329 Commonwealth Dr 23693. I-64 exit 256B, just n, then just e. Int corridors. **Pets:** Accepted.

🛜 🛗 🖥 ♒

▼▼ Days Inn 🅷

(757) 283-1111. **$56-$120.** 4531 George Washington Memorial Hwy 23692. I-64 exit 256B, 0.8 mi ne on Victory Blvd (SR 171), then 2.4 mi n on US 17. Int corridors. **Pets:** Other species. $20 one-time fee/room. Service with restrictions, supervision. 🛜 🛗 🖥 ♒

▼▼▼ Staybridge Suites 🅷

(757) 251-6644. **$100-$160, 3 day notice.** 401 Commonwealth Dr 23693. I-64 exit 256B, just n, then just e. Int corridors. **Pets:** Accepted.

🅴🅲🅾 🛜 🛗 🖥 ♒

⨀ ▼▼▼ TownePlace Suites by Marriott 🅷

(757) 874-8884. **$119-$129.** 200 Cybernetics Way 23693. I-64 exit 256B, e to Kiln Creek Pkwy. Int corridors. **Pets:** Accepted.

🅴🅲🅾 🆂🅰🆅🅴 🛜 ✖ 🛗 🖥 ♒

END AREA

WINCHESTER

⨀ ▼▼▼ BEST WESTERN Lee-Jackson Inn & Conference Center 🅷

(540) 662-4154. **$64-$72.** 711 Millwood Ave 22601. I-81 exit 313B, just nw on US 50/522/17. Ext corridors. **Pets:** Large, other species. $5 daily fee/pet. Designated rooms, service with restrictions, crate.

🆂🅰🆅🅴 🛜 🛗 🖥 🍴 ♒

▼▼▼ Candlewood Suites 🅷

(540) 667-8323. **$89-$109.** 1135 Millwood Pike 22602. I-81 exit 313 northbound; exit 313A southbound, just se. Int corridors. **Pets:** Accepted.

🅴🅲🅾 🛜 🛗 🖥

▼▼▼ Country Inn & Suites By Carlson 🅷

(540) 869-7657. **$79-$129, 30 day notice.** 141 Kernstown Commons Blvd 22602. I-81 exit 310. Int corridors. **Pets:** Medium. $20 daily fee/pet. Designated rooms, service with restrictions, supervision.

🛜 ✖ 🛗 🖥 ♒

⨀ ▼▼▼ Econo Lodge North 🅼 🐾

(540) 662-4700. **$54-$99.** 1593 Martinsburg Pike 22603. I-81 exit 317, 0.3 mi sw on US 11. Int corridors. **Pets:** Medium, other species. $10 daily fee/pet. Designated rooms, no service, supervision. 🆂🅰🆅🅴 🛜 🛗 🖥

⨀ ▼▼ Red Roof Inn 🅼

(540) 667-5000. **$50-$80.** 991 Millwood Pike 22602. I-81 exit 313 northbound; exit 313A southbound, just se on US 50/17. Ext corridors. **Pets:** Large, other species. Service with restrictions, supervision.

🆂🅰🆅🅴 🛜 🛗

⨀ ▼▼ Super 8 Winchester 🅼

(540) 665-4450. **$46-$60.** 1077 Millwood Pike 22602. I-81 exit 313 northbound; exit 313A southbound, 0.3 mi se on US 50/17. Int corridors. **Pets:** Accepted. 🆂🅰🆅🅴 🛜 🛗 🖥

▼▼▼ TownePlace Suites by Marriott Winchester 🅷 🐾

(540) 722-2722. **$80-$144.** 170 Getty Ln 22602. I-81 exit 315, just e. Int corridors. **Pets:** Other species. $75 deposit/room.

🛜 ✖ 🛗 🖥 ♒

WOODSTOCK

⨀ ▼▼▼ Comfort Inn Woodstock 🅷 🐾

(540) 459-7600. **$85-$135.** 1011 Motel Dr 22664. I-81 exit 283, just e. Int corridors. **Pets:** $10 daily fee/pet. Supervision. 🆂🅰🆅🅴 🛜 🛗 🖥 ♒

WYTHEVILLE

⨀ ▼▼▼ BEST WESTERN Wytheville Inn 🅷 🐾

(276) 228-7300. **$70-$190.** 355 Nye Rd 24382. I-77 exit 41, just e. Int corridors. **Pets:** Other species. $10 daily fee/pet. Designated rooms, service with restrictions, supervision. 🆂🅰🆅🅴 🛜 🛗 🖥 ♒

▼▼▼ Budget Host Inn/Interstate Inn 🅼

(276) 228-8618. **$45-$145.** 705 Chapman Rd 24382. I-77/81 exit 73, just w. Ext corridors. **Pets:** Very small, dogs only. $15 daily fee/pet. Designated rooms, service with restrictions, supervision. 🛜 🛗

▼▼▼ Comfort Inn 🅷

(276) 637-4281. **Call for rates.** 2594 E Lee Hwy 24382. I-77/81 exit 80, just w. Int corridors. **Pets:** Accepted. 🛜 🛗 🖥 ♒

▼▼ Days Inn 🅼

(276) 228-5500. **$58-$145.** 150 Malin Dr 24382. I-77/81 exit 73, just w. Ext corridors. **Pets:** Medium. $10 daily fee/room. Service with restrictions, supervision. 🛜 🛗 🖥

▼▼▼ Econo Lodge 🅼

(276) 228-5525. **Call for rates.** 280 Lithia Rd 24382. I-77/81 exit 73, just w. Ext corridors. **Pets:** Medium, other species. $10 daily fee/pet. Service with restrictions, supervision. 🛜 🛗

⨀ ▼▼▼ La Quinta Inn Wytheville 🅷

(276) 228-7400. **$93-$188.** 1800 E Main 24382. I-77/81 exit 73, just w. Int corridors. **Pets:** Service with restrictions, supervision.

🆂🅰🆅🅴 🛜 ✖ 🛗 🖥 ♒

⨀ ▼▼▼ Red Roof Inn & Suites 🅼

(276) 223-1700. **$59-$149.** 1900 E Main St 24382. I-77/81 exit 73, just w. Ext corridors. **Pets:** Large, other species. Service with restrictions, supervision. 🆂🅰🆅🅴 🛜 🛗 🖥 ♒

▼▼ Super 8 🅼

(276) 228-6620. **$54-$170.** 130 Nye Cir 24382. I-77 exit 41, just e. Ext corridors. **Pets:** Large, other species. $10 one-time fee/room. Service with restrictions. 🛜 🛗 🖥

ZION CROSSROADS

⨀ ▼▼▼ BEST WESTERN PLUS Crossroads Inn & Suites 🅷

(540) 832-1700. **$100-$220.** 135 Wood Ridge Terr 22942. I-64 exit 136, just n. Int corridors. **Pets:** Other species. $20 daily fee/room. Designated rooms, service with restrictions, crate.

🅴🅲🅾 🆂🅰🆅🅴 🛜 ✖ 🛗 🖥 ♒

WASHINGTON

AIRWAY HEIGHTS

▼▼▼ Days Inn & Suites H

(509) 244-0222. **$68-$140.** 1215 S Garfield Rd 99001. I-90/US 2 exit 277 to US 2, 4 mi w. Int corridors. **Pets:** Small, dogs only. $10 daily fee/pet. Designated rooms, service with restrictions, supervision. 🛜 📶 💻

ANACORTES

AAA ▼▼▼ Anacortes Inn M

(360) 293-3153. **$72-$128.** 3006 Commercial Ave 98221. Just s of downtown. Ext corridors. **Pets:** Dogs only. $10 daily fee/pet. Service with restrictions, supervision. SAVE 🛜 📶 💻 🏊

▼▼ Anacortes Ship Harbor Inn M ❖

(360) 293-5177. **$79-$179, 3 day notice.** 5316 Ferry Terminal Rd 98221. 0.3 mi s of ferry landing. Ext corridors. **Pets:** Other species. $25 one-time fee/room. Service with restrictions, supervision.
🛜 ✕ 📶 💻 🐾

AAA ▼▼▼ Cap Sante Inn M ❖

(360) 293-0602. **$69-$99.** 906 9th St 98221. On 9th St, just e. Ext corridors. **Pets:** Dogs only. $10 daily fee/pet. Designated rooms, service with restrictions, supervision. SAVE 🛜 ✕ 📶 🐾

▼▼ Fidalgo Country Inn H

(360) 293-3494. **$88-$143.** 7645 SR 20 98221. Jct Fidalgo Bay Rd. Ext/int corridors. **Pets:** Medium. $20 one-time fee/room. Designated rooms, service with restrictions, supervision. 🛜 📶 📶 💻 🏊

▼▼ Islands Inn M

(360) 293-4644. **$69-$149.** 3401 Commercial Ave 98221. Just s of downtown. Ext corridors. **Pets:** Dogs only. $10 daily fee/room. Supervision.
🛜 📶 💻 🍴 🏊

AAA ▼▼▼ Majestic Inn & Spa H

(360) 299-1400. **Call for rates.** 419 Commercial Ave 98221. At 5th Ave; downtown. Int corridors. **Pets:** Accepted.
SAVE 🛜 ✕ 📶 💻 🍴 🐾

ASHFORD

▼▼ Mountain Meadows Inn Bed & Breakfast BB

(360) 569-2788. **$119-$195, 14 day notice.** 28912 SR 706 E 98304. West end of town. Ext/int corridors. **Pets:** Medium, other species. $25 daily fee/pet. Designated rooms, supervision.
🛜 ✕ 📶 💻 🐾 🐾 🐾

BELLINGHAM

AAA ▼▼▼ Baymont Inn & Suites H ❖

(360) 671-6200. **$79-$130.** 125 E Kellogg Rd 98226. I-5 exit 256A, 1 mi ne via Meridian St. Int corridors. **Pets:** Service with restrictions, supervision. SAVE 🛜 ✕ 📶 📶 💻

▼▼▼ Bellingham GuestHouse Intl Inn H

(360) 671-9600. **Call for rates.** 805 Lakeway Dr 98229. I-5 exit 253 (Lakeway Dr), just ne. Int corridors. **Pets:** Accepted.
🛜 ✕ 📶 📶 💻

AAA ▼▼▼ BEST WESTERN PLUS Heritage Inn H ❖

(360) 647-1912. **Call for rates.** 151 E McLeod Rd 98226. I-5 exit 256A, just e. Int corridors. **Pets:** Medium. $20 daily fee/room. Designated rooms, service with restrictions, supervision.
SAVE 🛜 ✕ 📶 📶 💻 🐾 🐾

AAA ▼▼▼ BEST WESTERN PLUS Lakeway Inn H ❖

(360) 671-1011. **$119-$239.** 714 Lakeway Dr 98229. I-5 exit 253 (Lakeway Dr), just se. Int corridors. **Pets:** Large, dogs only. $20 daily fee/room. Designated rooms, service with restrictions, supervision.
SAVE 🛜 ✕ 📶 📶 💻 🍴 🐾 🐾

AAA ▼▼▼ Econo Lodge Inn & Suites H ❖

(360) 671-4600. **$59-$199.** 3750 Meridian St 98225. I-5 exit 256A, just w. Ext corridors. **Pets:** Dogs only. $10 daily fee/pet. Designated rooms, service with restrictions, supervision. SAVE 🛜 📶 📶 💻 🐾

AAA ▼▼▼ Holiday Inn Express-Bellingham H ❖

(360) 671-4800. **$98-$168.** 4160 Meridian St 98226. I-5 exit 256A, 0.7 mi e. Int corridors. **Pets:** Medium. $20 one-time fee/room. Service with restrictions, supervision. SAVE 🛜 📶 📶 💻 🐾

▼▼▼ Hotel Bellwether H ❖

(360) 392-3100. **$170-$599, 3 day notice.** One Bellwether Way 98225. I-5 exit 253 (Lakeway Dr), 0.9 mi nw via Lakeway Dr and E Holly St, just w on Bay St, 0.6 mi n via W Chestnut St and Roeder Ave, then just w. Int corridors. **Pets:** Large. $25 daily fee/pet. Designated rooms, service with restrictions, crate. 🛜 ✕ 📶 📶 💻 🍴 🐾

AAA ▼▼▼ Quality Inn Grand Suites H ❖

(360) 647-8000. **$89-$149.** 100 E Kellogg Rd 98226. I-5 exit 256A, 1 mi ne via Meridian St. Ext/int corridors. **Pets:** Service with restrictions, supervision. SAVE 🛜 ✕ 📶 📶 💻 🐾 🐾

CASHMERE

Village Inn Motel M
(509) 782-3522. **$59-$94, 7 day notice.** 229 Cottage Ave 98815. On Business Rt US 2 and 97; downtown. Ext corridors. **Pets:** $20 one-time fee/pet. Service with restrictions, crate.

CASTLE ROCK

Timberland Inn & Suites M
(360) 274-6002. **$60-$200.** 1271 Mount St. Helens Way 98611. I-5 exit 49, just ne. Ext corridors. **Pets:** Small, dogs only. $15 daily fee/pet. Designated rooms, service with restrictions, supervision.

CENTRALIA

Motel 6 - #394 M
(360) 330-2057. **$45-$55.** 1310 Belmont Ave 98531. I-5 exit 82, just w on Harrison Ave, then just n. Ext corridors. **Pets:** Other species. Service with restrictions, supervision.

CHEHALIS

BEST WESTERN PLUS Park Place Inn & Suites
(360) 748-4040. **$98-$123.** 201 SW Interstate Ave 98532. I-5 exit 76, just se. Int corridors. **Pets:** Large, dogs only. $20 daily fee/pet. Designated rooms, service with restrictions, supervision.

CHELAN

Lakeside Lodge & Suites
(509) 682-4396. **$99-$249, 7 day notice.** 2312 W Woodin Ave 98816. West end of town. Ext corridors. **Pets:** Accepted.

CHEWELAH

Nordlig Motel M
(509) 935-6704. **$59-$66.** 101 W Grant Ave 99109. North edge of town on US 395. Ext corridors. **Pets:** Dogs only. $5 one-time fee/pet. Designated rooms, service with restrictions, supervision.

CLARKSTON

BEST WESTERN RiverTree Inn
(509) 758-9551. **$101-$129.** 1257 Bridge St 99403. 0.9 mi w of Snake River Bridge on US 12. Ext corridors. **Pets:** Medium. $20 one-time fee/room. Designated rooms, service with restrictions, supervision.

Motel 6 Clarkston #4256 M
(509) 758-1631. **$29-$54.** 222 Bridge St 99403. Just w of Snake River Bridge (on US 12). Ext corridors. **Pets:** Other species. Service with restrictions, supervision.

Quality Inn & Suites Conference Center
(509) 758-9500. **$90-$200.** 700 Port Dr 99403. Just w of Snake River Bridge on US 12, then 0.3 mi n via 5th St. Int corridors. **Pets:** $10 daily fee/pet. Designated rooms, service with restrictions, supervision.

CLE ELUM

Lodge at Suncadia
(509) 649-6460. **Call for rates.** 3600 Suncadia Tr 98922. I-90 exit 80, 2 mi n, then 0.3 mi w. Int corridors. **Pets:** Accepted.

Stewart Lodge M
(509) 674-4548. **$65-$94.** 805 W 1st St 98922. I-90 exit 84 eastbound, just n; exit 85 westbound, 0.6 mi w. Ext corridors. **Pets:** Other species. $10 one-time fee/room. Designated rooms, service with restrictions, supervision.

Timber Lodge Inn M
(509) 674-5966. **Call for rates.** 301 W 1st St 98922. I-90 exit 84 eastbound, 1 mi ne; exit westbound, just w; downtown. Int corridors. **Pets:** Accepted.

COLFAX

BEST WESTERN PLUS Wheatland Inn
(509) 397-0397. **Call for rates.** 701 N Main St 99111. Downtown. Int corridors. **Pets:** Medium, dogs only. $15 daily fee/pet. Service with restrictions, supervision.

DAYTON

The Weinhard Hotel
(509) 382-4032. **$125-$180, 7 day notice.** 235 E Main St 99328. Downtown. Int corridors. **Pets:** Dogs only. $20 one-time fee/pet. Service with restrictions, supervision.

EAST WENATCHEE

Cedars Inn, East Wenatchee
(509) 886-8000. **$59-$179.** 80 9th St NE 98802. Just e of SR 28. Int corridors. **Pets:** Accepted.

EATONVILLE

Mill Village Motel M
(360) 832-3200. **$90-$110.** 210 Center St E 98328. Just e of jct SR 161. Ext corridors. **Pets:** Accepted.

ELLENSBURG

BEST WESTERN PLUS Lincoln Inn & Suites
(509) 925-4244. **$89-$249.** 211 W Umptanum Rd 98926. I-90 exit 109, just n, then just w. Int corridors. **Pets:** Medium, dogs only. $15 daily fee/pet. Designated rooms, service with restrictions, supervision.

Cedars Inn Ellensburg M
(509) 925-9844. **$64-$84.** 1390 N Dollarway Rd 98926. I-90 exit 106, just n. Ext corridors. **Pets:** Medium, dogs only. $20 daily fee/pet. Designated rooms, service with restrictions, supervision.

Days Inn
(509) 933-1500. **$65-$165.** 901 Berry Rd 98926. I-90 exit 109, just s. Int corridors. **Pets:** Medium. $15 daily fee/pet. Designated rooms, service with restrictions, supervision.

Ellensburg Comfort Inn
(509) 925-7037. **Call for rates.** 1722 Canyon Rd 98926. I-90 exit 109. Int corridors. **Pets:** Accepted.

Holiday Inn Express
(509) 962-9400. **$89-$179.** 1620 Canyon Rd 98926. I-90 exit 109, just n. Int corridors. **Pets:** Other species. $15 daily fee/pet. Designated rooms, service with restrictions, supervision.

ELMA

GuestHouse Inn & Suites
(360) 482-6868. **$80-$110.** 800 E Main St 98541. Just ne of jct US 12 and SR 8. Int corridors. **Pets:** Other species. $10 daily fee/room. Service with restrictions, crate.

EPHRATA

BEST WESTERN Rama Inn
(509) 754-7111. **$105-$125.** 1818 Basin St SW 98823. On SR 28; west end of town. Int corridors. **Pets:** Large, other species. $20 deposit/room. Service with restrictions, supervision.

FERNDALE

▼▼ Ferndale Super 8 H
(360) 384-8881. **$75-$160.** 5788 Barrett Rd 98248. I-5 exit 262, just ne. Int corridors. **Pets:** Medium. $20 one-time fee/pet. Designated rooms, service with restrictions, supervision.

◈ ▼▼▼ Silver Reef Hotel Casino & Spa H
(360) 383-0777. **Call for rates.** 4876 Haxton Way 98248. I-5 exit 260, 3.6 mi w on Slater Rd. Int corridors. **Pets:** Small, other species. $15 one-time fee/pet. Designated rooms, service with restrictions.

[SAVE] 🛜 ⑤M 🗎 🖵 🍴 🏊 ⊠

FORKS

◈ ▼▼ Forks Motel M
(360) 374-6243. **$58-$199.** 351 S Forks Ave 98331. On US 101 (S Forks Ave), just s of Division St. Ext corridors. **Pets:** Small. $15 daily fee/pet. Designated rooms, service with restrictions.

[SAVE] 🛜 🗎 🖵 🏊

▼▼ Manitou Lodge BB ✿
(360) 374-6295. **Call for rates.** 813 Kilmer Rd 98331. 7.7 mi sw on SR 110 (LaPush Rd), 0.7 mi w on Mora Rd, then 0.8 mi n. Ext/int corridors. **Pets:** Other species. $10 daily fee/room. Designated rooms, supervision.

🛜 ⊠ 🗎 🖵 🛗 🐾 🎣

▼▼ Miller Tree Inn Bed & Breakfast BB
(360) 374-6806. **$100-$235, 7 day notice.** 654 E Division St 98331. 0.3 mi e of US 101 (S Forks Ave). Ext/int corridors. **Pets:** Other species. $10 daily fee/room. Designated rooms, service with restrictions, crate.

🛜 ⊠ 🗎 🖵 🎣

◈ ▼▼ Olympic Suites Inn M
(360) 374-5400. **$49-$139.** 800 Olympic Dr 98331. North end of town; just ne off US 101 (S Forks Ave). Ext corridors. **Pets:** Dogs only. $10 daily fee/pet. Designated rooms, service with restrictions, supervision.

[SAVE] 🛜 ⊠ 🗎 🖵 🛗

GOLDENDALE

▼▼ Quality Inn & Suites H
(509) 773-5881. **Call for rates.** 808 E Simcoe Dr 98620. US 97 exit Simcoe Dr, just sw. Ext corridors. **Pets:** Accepted. 🛜 🗎 🖵 🏊

HOODSPORT

▼▼ Glen Ayr Hood Canal Waterfront Resort H
(360) 877-9522. **$79-$219, 7 day notice.** 25381 N US 101 98548. 1.5 mi n. Ext corridors. **Pets:** Medium. $15 daily fee/pet. Designated rooms, service with restrictions, supervision.

🛜 ⊠ 🗎 🖵 ⊠ 🛗 🎣

ILWACO

◈ ▼ Heidi's Inn M
(360) 642-2387. **$59-$89, 7 day notice.** 126 E Spruce St 98624. Downtown. Ext corridors. **Pets:** Small, dogs only. $8 daily fee/pet. Designated rooms, service with restrictions, supervision. [SAVE] 🛜 🗎 🖵 🛗

KALALOCH

◈ ▼▼▼ Kalaloch Lodge CA
(360) 962-2271. **$159-$230, 3 day notice.** 157151 Hwy 101 98331. In Kalaloch; at MM 157. Ext/int corridors. **Pets:** Accepted.

[SAVE] 🗎 🖵 🍴 🛗 🎣

KELSO

◈ ▼▼▼ BEST WESTERN Aladdin - Kelso H
(360) 425-9660. **$80-$150.** 310 Long Ave 98626. I-5 exit 39, 1.1 mi w via Allen and W Main sts, then just n on 5th Ave NW. Int corridors. **Pets:** Accepted. [SAVE] 🛜 ⊠ 🗎 🖵 🏊

▼▼ GuestHouse Inn & Suites H
(360) 414-5953. **Call for rates.** 501 Three Rivers Dr 98626. I-5 exit 39, 0.3 mi w on Allen St, then 0.3 mi s. Int corridors. **Pets:** Accepted.

🛜 🗎 🖵 🏊

▼▼ Motel 6 - #43 M
(360) 425-3229. **$49-$85.** 106 Minor Rd 98626. I-5 exit 39, just ne. Ext corridors. **Pets:** Other species. Service with restrictions, supervision.

🛜 🗎 🏊

▼▼▼ Red Lion Hotel & Conference Center Kelso/Longview H
(360) 636-4400. **$153-$265.** 510 Kelso Dr 98626. I-5 exit 39, 0.3 mi se. Int corridors. **Pets:** Other species. $15 one-time fee/room. Service with restrictions, crate. 🛜 ⊠ 🗎 🖵 🍴 🏊

▼▼ Super 8 H
(360) 423-8880. **$69-$155.** 250 Kelso Dr 98626. I-5 exit 39, just se. Int corridors. **Pets:** $15 daily fee/pet. Service with restrictions, supervision.

🛜 ⑤M 🗎 🖵 🏊

KENNEWICK

▼▼ Baymont Inn & Suites H
(509) 736-3326. **$69-$99.** 4220 W 27th Pl 99337. I-82 exit 113 (US 395), 0.8 mi n. Int corridors. **Pets:** Other species. $10 one-time fee/pet. Service with restrictions, supervision. 🛜 ⊠ ⑤M 🗎 🖵 🏊 ⊠

◈ ▼▼▼ BEST WESTERN PLUS Kennewick Inn H ✿
(509) 586-1332. **$105-$150.** 4001 W 27th Ave 99337. I-82 exit 113 (US 395), 0.8 mi n. Int corridors. **Pets:** $10 one-time fee/room. Crate.

[SAVE] 🛜 ⊠ ⑤M 🗎 🖵 🏊 ⊠

◈ ▼▼▼ Cedars Inn & Suites Kennewick H
(509) 396-9979. **$85-$199, 3 day notice.** 602 N Young St 99336. 1 mi s of SR 240 on N Columbia Center Blvd, then just e. Int corridors. **Pets:** Large, dogs only. $15 daily fee/pet. Service with restrictions, supervision. [SAVE] 🛜 ⊠ ⑤M 🗎 🖵 🏊

▼▼ Clover Island Inn H
(509) 586-0541. **$89-$349.** 435 Clover Island Dr 99336. US 395 exit Port of Kennewick, 1 mi e on Columbia Dr, then 0.7 mi n. Int corridors. **Pets:** Other species. $10 one-time fee/room. Designated rooms, service with restrictions. 🛜 🗎 🖵 🍴 🏊 ⊠

▼▼ Comfort Inn M
(509) 783-8396. **$89-$139.** 7801 W Quinault Ave 99336. 0.5 mi s on Columbia Center Blvd from SR 240. Int corridors. **Pets:** Medium, dogs only. $15 daily fee/pet. Designated rooms, service with restrictions, supervision. 🛜 ⑤M 🗎 🖵 🏊

▼▼▼ Fairfield Inn by Marriott H
(509) 783-2164. **$119-$159.** 7809 W Quinault Ave 99336. 0.5 mi s on Columbia Center Blvd from SR 240. Int corridors. **Pets:** Accepted.

🛜 ⊠ ⑤M 🗎 🖵 🏊

◈ ▼▼▼ GuestHouse International Suites H
(509) 735-2242. **Call for rates.** 5616 W Clearwater Ave 99336. US 395, 1.9 mi w. Int corridors. **Pets:** Accepted. [SAVE] 🛜 ⑤M 🗎 🖵

◈ ▼▼▼ Kennewick Super 8 H
(509) 736-6888. **$65-$95, 3 day notice.** 626 N Columbia Center Blvd 99336. 1.1 mi s of SR 240. Int corridors. **Pets:** Other species. $10 daily fee/room. Designated rooms, service with restrictions, supervision.

[SAVE] 🛜 ⑤M 🗎 🖵 🏊

▼▼▼ La Quinta Inn & Suites Kennewick H
(509) 736-3656. **$101-$177.** 2600 S Quillan Pl 99338. I-82 exit 113 (US 395), 0.8 mi n. Int corridors. **Pets:** Service with restrictions, supervision.

🛜 ⊠ 🗎 🖵 🏊

▼▼ Quality Inn Kennewick H
(509) 735-6100. **$74-$104, 14 day notice.** 7901 W Quinault Ave 99336. 0.5 mi s on Columbia Center Blvd from SR 240. Int corridors. **Pets:** Medium. $15 daily fee/pet. Designated rooms, service with restrictions, supervision. 🛜 ⊠ ⑤M 🗎 🖵 🏊

▼▼▼ **Red Lion Hotel Columbia Center-Kennewick** H
(509) 783-0611. **Call for rates.** 1101 N Columbia Center Blvd 99336. SR 240, 0.5 mi s. Int corridors. **Pets:** Other species. $15 one-time fee/room. Service with restrictions, crate.

LACEY

◢◢◢ ▼▼▼ **BEST WESTERN PLUS Lacey Inn &**
Suites H
(360) 456-5655. **$110-$186.** 8326 Quinault Dr NE 98516. I-5 exit 111 (Marvin Rd), just ne. Int corridors. **Pets:** Accepted.
[SAVE]

▼▼▼ **Candlewood Suites** H
(360) 491-1698. **$140-$176.** 4440 3rd Ave SE 98503. I-5 exit 108 northbound, just n; exit 109 southbound, just s on Martin Ave E, just e on College Way, then just s. Int corridors. **Pets:** Large, other species. $75 one-time fee/room. Service with restrictions.

LA CONNER

▼▼ ▼ **La Conner Country Inn** H ❀
(360) 466-3101. **$89-$239.** 107 S 2nd St 98257. Jct 2nd and Morris sts; downtown. Ext/int corridors. **Pets:** Dogs only. $25 one-time fee/room. Designated rooms, service with restrictions, supervision.

LANGLEY

▼▼▼ **Boat Yard Inn** H
(360) 221-5120. **Call for rates.** 200 Wharf St 98260. Corner of Cascade Ave and 1st St. Ext corridors. **Pets:** Accepted.

▼▼▼ **The Inn at Langley** H
(360) 221-3033. **$290-$595, 7 day notice.** 400 1st St 98260. Between Anthes and Park aves. Ext corridors. **Pets:** Accepted.

LEAVENWORTH

▼▼ ▼ **Alpine Rivers Inn** H
(509) 548-8888. **$99-$129, 7 day notice.** 1505 Alpensee Strasse 98826. East edge of town. Ext corridors. **Pets:** Accepted.

◢◢◢ ▼▼ ▼ **Bavarian Ritz Hotel** H
(509) 548-5455. **$89-$269, 3 day notice.** 633 Front St 98826. Center. Int corridors. **Pets:** Dogs only. Service with restrictions, supervision.
[SAVE]

◢◢◢ ▼▼▼ **BEST WESTERN PLUS Icicle Inn** H
(509) 548-7000. **$109-$329.** 505 W US 2 98826. West side of town. Int corridors. **Pets:** Large, dogs only. $20 daily fee/room. Designated rooms, service with restrictions, supervision.
[SAVE]

◢◢◢ ▼▼ ▼ **Der Ritterhof Motor Inn** H ❀
(509) 548-5845. **$95-$195.** 190 US 2 98826. 0.3 mi w. Ext corridors. **Pets:** Dogs only. $20 daily fee/pet. Designated rooms, service with restrictions, supervision. [SAVE]

▼▼ ▼ **Obertal Inn** M ❀
(509) 548-5204. **$89-$299, 3 day notice.** 922 Commercial St 98826. Off US 2; center. Ext corridors. **Pets:** Other species. $15 daily fee/pet. Service with restrictions.

LIBERTY LAKE

◢◢◢ ▼▼▼ **BEST WESTERN PLUS Peppertree Liberty**
Lake Inn H ❀
(509) 755-1111. **$90-$200.** 1816 N Pepper Ln 99019. I-90 exit 296 (Liberty Lake), just n. Int corridors. **Pets:** Dogs only. Service with restrictions, supervision. [SAVE]

LONG BEACH

▼▼ ▼ **Anchorage Cottages** CA ❀
(360) 642-2351. **$80-$138, 14 day notice.** 2209 Boulevard N 98631. Just w of SR 103; just n of downtown. Ext corridors. **Pets:** $10 daily fee/pet. No service, supervision.

◢◢◢ ▼▼ ▼ **The Breakers** CO
(360) 642-4414. **$78-$328, 20 day notice.** 210 26th St NW 98631. North end of downtown. Ext corridors. **Pets:** Dogs only. $15 daily fee/room. Supervision. [SAVE]

▼▼▼ **Our Place at the Beach** H
(360) 642-3793. **$75-$170, 3 day notice.** 1309 Ocean Beach Blvd S 98631. Just w of SR 103; south end of town. Ext corridors. **Pets:** Other species. $8 daily fee/pet. Service with restrictions, supervision.

▼▼ ▼ **Rodeway Inn & Suites** M ❀
(360) 642-3714. **$60-$150.** 115 3rd St SW 98631. Downtown. Ext corridors. **Pets:** Other species. $7 daily fee/pet. Service with restrictions, supervision.

◢◢◢ ▼▼ ▼ **Super 8** H
(360) 642-8988. **$99-$199.** 500 Ocean Beach Blvd 98631. On SR 103; downtown. Int corridors. **Pets:** Accepted.
[SAVE]

LONGVIEW

▼▼ ▼ **Hudson Manor Inn & Suites** M
(360) 425-1100. **Call for rates.** 1616 Hudson St 98632. Downtown. Ext corridors. **Pets:** Accepted.

◢◢◢ ▼▼ ▼ **Longview Travelodge** M
(360) 423-6460. **$60-$155.** 838 15th Ave 98632. Downtown. Ext corridors. **Pets:** Large, other species. $15 daily fee/room. Supervision.
[SAVE]

◢◢◢ ▼ **The Townhouse Motel** M
(360) 423-7200. **$65-$99, 3 day notice.** 744 Washington Way 98632. Downtown. Ext corridors. **Pets:** Large, other species. $5 daily fee/pet. Supervision. [SAVE]

MOCLIPS

◢◢◢ ▼▼ ▼ **Ocean Crest Resort** H
(360) 276-4465. **Call for rates.** 4651 SR 109 98562. South edge of town on SR 109. Ext corridors. **Pets:** Large, other species. $18 daily fee/pet. Designated rooms, service with restrictions, supervision.
[SAVE]

MORTON

◢◢◢ ▼▼ ▼ **Seasons Motel** M
(360) 496-6835. **$90-$110.** 200 Westlake Ave 98356. Corner of US 12 and SR 7. Ext corridors. **Pets:** Small. $10 daily fee/pet. No service, supervision. [SAVE]

MOSES LAKE

▼▼ ▼ **AmeriStay Inn & Suites** H
(509) 764-7500. **$89-$259.** 1157 N Stratford Rd 98837. I-90 exit 179, 1 mi n to SR 17, 2.8 mi nw, exit Stratford Rd, just n, then just e. Int corridors. **Pets:** Accepted.

◢◢◢ ▼▼ ▼ **BEST WESTERN PLUS Lake Front Hotel** H
(509) 765-9211. **$89-$149.** 3000 Marina Dr 98837. I-90 exit 176, just nw. Int corridors. **Pets:** Accepted.
[SAVE]

◢◢◢ ▼▼ ▼ **Comfort Suites Moses Lake** H
(509) 765-3731. **$89-$249.** 1700 E Kittleson Rd 98837. I-90 exit 179, just nw. Int corridors. **Pets:** Small, dogs only. $25 daily fee/pet. Designated rooms, service with restrictions, crate.
[SAVE]

▼▼ Inn at Moses Lake ⛞
(509) 766-7000. **$80-$120.** 1741 E Kittleson Rd 98837. I-90 exit 179, just n. Int corridors. **Pets:** $10 one-time fee/pet. Designated rooms, service with restrictions, crate. 🛰 ✕ 🛢 ▣

〰️ ▼▼ Moses Lake Super 8 ⛞
(509) 765-8886. **$61-$230.** 449 Melva Ln 98837. I-90 exit 176, just n. Int corridors. **Pets:** Accepted. (SAVE) 🛰 🛢 ▣ ➥

▼▼ Shilo Inn Suites-Moses Lake ⛞
(509) 765-9317. **$72-$123.** 1819 E Kittleson Rd 98837. I-90 exit 179, just n. Int corridors. **Pets:** Dogs only. $25 one-time fee/room. Designated rooms, service with restrictions, supervision.
🛰 ✕ 🄼 🛢 ▣ ➥ 🗙

MOUNT RAINIER NATIONAL PARK
〰️ ▼▼▼ Alta Crystal Resort at Mt Rainier ⛞ ❀
(360) 663-2500. **$159-$309, 30 day notice.** 68317 SR 410 E 98022. 2 mi outside northeast entrance. Ext corridors. **Pets:** Dogs only. $50 one-time fee/pet. Designated rooms, service with restrictions, crate.
(SAVE) 🛰 ✕ 🛢 ▣ ➥ 🗙 🄼

MOUNT VERNON
〰️ ▼▼ BEST WESTERN College Way Inn ⛞
(360) 424-4287. **Call for rates.** 300 W College Way 98273. I-5 exit 227, just w. Ext corridors. **Pets:** $20 daily fee/room. Designated rooms, service with restrictions, supervision. (SAVE) 🛰 ✕ 🄼 🛢 ▣ ➥

〰️ ▼▼▼ BEST WESTERN PLUS CottonTree Inn ⛞
(360) 428-5678. **$115-$180.** 2300 Market St 98273. I-5 exit 227, 0.3 mi e on College Way, then 0.5 mi n on Riverside Dr. Int corridors. **Pets:** Dogs only. $25 deposit/room. Designated rooms, service with restrictions, supervision. (SAVE) 🛰 ✕ 🄼 🛢 ▣ ➥

〰️ ▼▼ Quality Inn-Mount Vernon ⛞
(360) 428-7020. **Call for rates.** 1910 Freeway Dr 98273. I-5 exit 227, just w on College Way, then just n. Ext corridors. **Pets:** Medium. $10 daily fee/pet. Designated rooms, service with restrictions, crate.
(SAVE) 🛰 🄼 🛢 ▣ ➥

〰️ ▼▼ Tulip Inn Ⓜ
(360) 428-5969. **$65-$99.** 2200 Freeway Dr 98273. I-5 exit 227, just w on College Way, then just n. Ext corridors. **Pets:** $10 daily fee/room. Designated rooms, service with restrictions. (SAVE) 🛰 ✕ 🄼 🛢 ▣

OAK HARBOR
〰️ ▼▼▼ Candlewood Suites ⛞ ❀
(360) 279-2222. **$119-$169.** 33221 SR 20 98277. Just n of town. Int corridors. **Pets:** Large. $75 deposit/room, $10 daily fee/pet. Service with restrictions, crate. (SAVE) 🛰 ✕ 🄼 🛢 ▣

〰️ ▼▼▼ Coachman Inn ⛞
(360) 675-0727. **$94-$209.** 32959 SR 20 98277. Jct Goldie Rd and Midway Blvd. Ext corridors. **Pets:** $8 daily fee/pet. Designated rooms, service with restrictions, supervision. (SAVE) 🛰 🛢 ▣ ➥ 🗙

OCEAN PARK
▼ Ocean Park Resort Ⓜ
(360) 665-4585. **$70-$195, 10 day notice.** 25904 R St 98640. Just e of SR 103; downtown. Ext corridors. **Pets:** Small, other species. $7 daily fee/pet. Service with restrictions, supervision.
🛰 ✕ 🛢 ▣ ➥ 🗙 🄼 🗷

OCEAN SHORES
〰️ ▼▼ BEST WESTERN PLUS Lighthouse Suites Inn ⛞ ❀
(360) 289-2311. **$109-$239.** 491 Damon Rd NW 98569. 2.5 mi w on SR 115 (Damon Rd). Int corridors. **Pets:** Large, dogs only. $20 daily fee/room. Designated rooms, service with restrictions, supervision.
(SAVE) 🛰 ✕ 🛢 ▣ 🍴 ➥ 🗙 🄼

▼▼ The Canterbury Inn 🄲🄾
(360) 289-3317. **$84-$210.** 643 Ocean Shores Blvd NW 98569. 0.3 mi s of Chance A La Mer Blvd. Int corridors. **Pets:** Large, dogs only. $150 deposit/room, $15 daily fee/pet. Designated rooms, service with restrictions, supervision. 🛰 ✕ 🛢 ▣ ➥ 🄼

〰️ ▼▼▼ The Polynesian Condominium Resort 🄲🄾
(360) 289-3361. **Call for rates.** 615 Ocean Shores Blvd NW 98569. 0.3 mi s of Chance A La Mer Blvd. Ext/int corridors. **Pets:** Accepted.
(SAVE) 🛰 🛢 ▣ 🍴 ➥ ✕ 🄼

▼▼▼ Shilo Inn Suites Hotel - Ocean Shores ⛞
(360) 289-4600. **$108-$270.** 707 Ocean Shores Blvd NW 98569. Northwest corner of Chance A La Mer and Ocean Shores blvds NW. Int corridors. **Pets:** Dogs only. $25 one-time fee/room. Designated rooms, service with restrictions, supervision. 🛰 ✕ 🄼 🛢 ▣ 🍴 ➥ 🗙

OLYMPIA
〰️ ▼▼▼ Red Lion Hotel Olympia ⛞
(360) 943-4000. **Call for rates.** 2300 Evergreen Park Dr SW 98502. I-5 exit 104, 0.7 mi w on US 101, just n on Cooper Point Rd N, 0.7 mi e on S Evergreen Park Dr SW, then just n on Lakeridge Way SW. Int corridors. **Pets:** Other species. $15 one-time fee/room. Service with restrictions, crate. (SAVE) 🛰 ✕ 🄼 🛢 ▣ 🍴 ➥

OLYMPIC NATIONAL PARK
〰️ ▼▼ Lake Crescent Lodge ⛞
(360) 928-3211. **$115-$287, 3 day notice.** 416 Lake Crescent Rd 98363. 22 mi w of Port Angeles on US 101. Ext/int corridors.
Pets: Accepted. (SAVE) 🛰 ✕ 🛢 ▣ 🍴 🗙 🄼 🐾 🗷

▼ Log Cabin Resort 🄲🄰
(360) 928-3325. **Call for rates.** 3183 E Beach Rd 98363. 3.3 mi nw of US 101 (MM 232). Ext corridors. **Pets:** Accepted.
✕ 🛢 ▣ 🍴 🗙 🄼 🐾 🗷

OMAK
〰️ ▼▼▼ BEST WESTERN PLUS Peppertree Inn at Omak ⛞
(509) 422-2088. **$90-$200.** 820 Koala Dr 98841. US 97, just n of Riverside Dr. Int corridors. **Pets:** Accepted.
(SAVE) 🛰 ✕ 🄼 🛢 ▣ ➥

〰️ ▼▼▼ Omak Inn LLC ⛞
(509) 826-3822. **$75-$130.** 912 Koala Dr 98841. On US 97, just n of Riverside Dr. Int corridors. **Pets:** Other species. $25 one-time fee/room. Designated rooms, supervision. (SAVE) 🛰 ✕ 🛢 ▣ ➥

OTHELLO
〰️ ▼▼ BEST WESTERN Othello Inn ⛞
(509) 488-5671. **$100-$110.** 1020 E Cedar St 99344. Just off Main St; jct 10th St. Int corridors. **Pets:** Accepted. (SAVE) 🛰 🛢 ▣ ➥

PACKWOOD
▼▼ Cowlitz River Lodge Ⓜ
(360) 494-4444. **$60-$100, 3 day notice.** 13069 US 12 98361. East end of town. Ext corridors. **Pets:** Dogs only. $20 one-time fee/pet. Designated rooms, service with restrictions, supervision. 🛰 ✕ 🛢

〰️ ▼▼ Crest Trail Lodge ⛞
(360) 494-4944. **$90-$110.** 12729 US 12 98361. West end of town. Int corridors. **Pets:** Small. $10 daily fee/pet. No service, supervision.
(SAVE) 🛰 ✕ 🛢 ▣

PASCO
〰️ ▼▼▼ BEST WESTERN PLUS Pasco Inn & Suites ⛞ ❀
(509) 543-7722. **$120-$170.** 2811 N 20th Ave 99301. I-182 exit 12B, just n. Int corridors. **Pets:** $10 one-time fee/room. Service with restrictions, supervision. (SAVE) 🛰 ✕ 🄼 🛢 ▣ ➥

WWW Holiday Inn Express Pasco at TRAC 🅷
(509) 543-7000. **$139-$219.** 4525 Convention Pl 99301. I-182 exit 9 (Rd 68), just n, then just e. Int corridors. **Pets:** Medium, dogs only. $20 daily fee/pet. Designated rooms, service with restrictions, supervision.
🛜 ✕ ᵫM 🛏 💻 ⇨

WWW Red Lion Hotel Pasco 🅷
(509) 547-0701. **$89-$139.** 2525 N 20th Ave 99301. I-182 exit 12B, just n. Int corridors. **Pets:** Other species. $15 one-time fee/room. Service with restrictions, crate. 🛜 ✕ ᵫM 🛏 💻 ⑪ ⇨

WW Sleep Inn 🅷
(509) 545-9554. **$85-$140.** 9930 Bedford St 99301. I-182 exit 7, just ne. Int corridors. **Pets:** Small. $15 one-time fee/room. Designated rooms, service with restrictions, supervision. 🛜 ✕ ᵫM 🛏 💻 ⇨

PORT ANGELES

WWWW A Hidden Haven & Water Garden Cottages 🅲🅰
(360) 452-2719. **$189-$279, 21 day notice.** 1428 Dan Kelly Rd 98363. 5.5 mi s of downtown on US 101, 2.2 mi sw on SR 112, then 1.4 mi e. Ext corridors. **Pets:** Small, dogs only. $30 daily fee/pet. Designated rooms, service with restrictions, supervision.
🛜 ✕ 🛏 💻 🐾 🖉

AAA WWW Days Inn 🅷
(360) 452-4015. **$55-$159.** 1510 E Front St 98362. Jct Alder St; on east side. Ext corridors. **Pets:** Medium. $25 one-time fee/pet. Designated rooms, service with restrictions, supervision. SAVE 🛜 🛏 💻 ⇨

WWWW Red Lion Hotel Port Angeles 🅷
(360) 452-9215. **$119-$299.** 221 N Lincoln St 98362. On US 101 westbound; at ferry landing. Ext/int corridors. **Pets:** Other species. $15 one-time fee/room. Service with restrictions, crate.
🛜 ✕ 🛏 💻 ⑪ ⇨

WW Super 8 🅼
(360) 452-8401. **$59-$140.** 2104 E 1st St 98362. 1.8 mi e of downtown, just s of US 101. Int corridors. **Pets:** Medium, other species. $10 daily fee/pet. Designated rooms, supervision. 🛜 ᵫM 🛏 💻

PORTLAND METROPOLITAN AREA (NEARBY OREGON)

VANCOUVER

AAA WWW Choice Inn & Suites 🅷
(360) 574-6000. **$55-$100.** 13207 NE 20th Ave 98686. I-5 exit 7. Int corridors. **Pets:** Dogs only. $15 daily fee/pet. Service with restrictions, supervision. SAVE 🛜 ✕ 🛏 💻 ⇨

WW Comfort Inn & Suites Downtown Vancouver 🅷
(360) 696-0411. **$69-$115.** 401 E 13th St 98660. I-5 exit 1C (E Mill Plain Blvd), just w, just s on C St, then just e. Int corridors. **Pets:** Small. $20 one-time fee/room. Designated rooms, service with restrictions, supervision. 🛜 ✕ ᵫM 🛏 💻 ⇨ ⊠

WW Comfort Suites 🅷
(360) 253-3100. **$83-$108.** 4714 NE 94th Ave 98662. I-205 exit 30 (SR 500 W), 0.6 mi w to Thurston Way, just n to Vancouver Mall Dr, then 0.5 mi e; southeast edge of Westfield Shopping Center. Int corridors. **Pets:** Small, dogs only. $20 daily fee/pet. Service with restrictions, supervision. 🛜 ✕ 🛏 💻 ⇨

WW Days Inn & Suites 🅷
(360) 253-5000. **$59-$110.** 9107 NE Vancouver Mall Dr 98662. I-205 exit 30 (SR 500 W), 0.6 mi w to Thurston Way, just n to Vancouver Mall Dr, then 0.5 mi e; southeast edge of Westfield Shopping Center. Int corridors. **Pets:** Accepted. 🛜 🛏 💻 ⇨

WWW Gateway Inn Express Hotel & Suites 🅷
(360) 576-1040. **Call for rates.** 13101 NE 27th Ave 98686. I-205 exit 36, just e on NE 134th St-WSU; I-5 exit 7 (I-205) to exit 36 southbound, just e; exit 7 northbound, 0.5 mi n on NE 134th St-WSU. Int corridors. **Pets:** Accepted. 🛜 ᵫM 🛏 💻 ⇨

AAA WWW Hilton Vancouver Washington 🅷 🐾
(360) 993-4500. **$75-$179.** 301 W 6th St 98660. I-5 exit 1C (E Mill Plain Blvd) southbound, 0.3 mi w, then 0.3 mi s on W Columbia St; exit 1B northbound, 0.5 mi sw, follow signs to City Center/6th St. Int corridors. **Pets:** Large. $35 one-time fee/room. Service with restrictions.
ECO SAVE 🛜 ✕ ᵫM 🛏 💻 ⑪ ⇨ ⊠

WWWW Homewood Suites by Hilton 🅷
(360) 750-1100. **$109-$299.** 701 SE Columbia Shores Blvd 98661. SR 14 exit 1, just s. Ext/int corridors. **Pets:** Other species. $25 daily fee/pet. Designated rooms, service with restrictions, supervision.
🛜 🛏 💻 ⇨ ⊠

AAA WWW Phoenix Inn Suites-Vancouver 🅷
(360) 891-9777. **Call for rates.** 12712 SE 2nd Cir 98684. I-205 exit 28 (E Mill Plain Blvd), 0.8 mi e, then just n on SE 126th Ave. Int corridors. **Pets:** Accepted. SAVE 🛜 ✕ 🛏 💻 ⇨

AAA WWW Quality Inn & Suites 🅷 🐾
(360) 696-0516. **$62-$102.** 7001 NE Hwy 99 98665. I-5 exit 4, 0.5 mi se. Int corridors. **Pets:** Other species. $10 daily fee/room. Service with restrictions, supervision. SAVE 🛜 ✕ 🛏 💻 ⇨

WWW Red Lion Hotel Vancouver at the Quay 🅷
(360) 694-8341. **$89-$149.** 100 Columbia St 98660. 0.5 mi s of dock at foot of Columbia St. Int corridors. **Pets:** Other species. $15 one-time fee/room. Service with restrictions, crate.
🛜 ✕ ᵫM 🛏 💻 ⑪ ⇨ ⊠

WWW Residence Inn by Marriott Portland-North Vancouver 🅷 🐾
(360) 253-4800. **$89-$199.** 8005 NE Parkway Dr 98662. I-205 exit 30 (SR 500 W), 0.5 mi w to Thurston Way, just n to NE Parkway Dr, then just w. Ext corridors. **Pets:** Other species. $75 one-time fee/room. Service with restrictions. 🛜 ✕ ᵫM 🛏 💻 ⇨ ⊠

WWW Shilo Inn & Suites-Salmon Creek 🅷
(360) 573-0511. **$69-$159.** 13206 Hwy 99 98686. I-5 exit 7, just e; I-205 exit 36, just w. Int corridors. **Pets:** Dogs only. $25 one-time fee/room. Designated rooms, service with restrictions, supervision.
🛜 ✕ 🛏 💻 ⇨ ⊠

WWWW Staybridge Suites Vancouver-Portland 🅷
(360) 891-8282. **$99-$219.** 7301 NE 41st St 98662. I-205 exit 30 (SR 500 W), 1.5 mi w to NE Andresen Rd, just n to NE 40th St, just e to NE 72nd St, just n to NE 41st St, then just e. Int corridors. **Pets:** Medium. $20 one-time fee/room, $10 daily fee/pet. Designated rooms, service with restrictions, supervision. 🛜 ᵫM 🛏 💻 ⇨ ⊠

CAMAS

AAA WWW Camas Hotel 🅷 🐾
(360) 834-5722. **$84-$145, 7 day notice.** 405 NE 4th Ave 98607. Jct NE Cedar St; downtown. Int corridors. **Pets:** Dogs only. $20 one-time fee/pet. Designated rooms, crate. SAVE 🛜 ✕ 🛏 💻 ⑪

END METROPOLITAN AREA

PORT LUDLOW

AAA **WWWW** The Resort at Port Ludlow **H**
(360) 437-7000. **$139-$299, 7 day notice.** 1 Heron Rd 98365. 8 mi n of Hood Canal Floating Bridge; in town. Int corridors. **Pets:** Accepted.
[SAVE] 🛰 ✕ 🛏 💻 🍴 ⊠ [AC]

PORT TOWNSEND

WWWW Ann Starrett Mansion **H**
(360) 385-3205. **$98-$150, 14 day notice.** 744 Clay St 98368. On the bluff; corner of Adams St. Ext/int corridors. **Pets:** Dogs only. $20 one-time fee/room. Designated rooms, service with restrictions, supervision.
🛰 ✕ 💻 [AC] [Z]

AAA **WWWW** Bishop Victorian Hotel **H** 🐾
(360) 385-6122. **$120-$275, 3 day notice.** 714 Washington St 98368. Corner of Washington and Quincy sts. Int corridors. **Pets:** Dogs only. $20 daily fee/pet. Designated rooms, service with restrictions, supervision.
[SAVE] 🛰 ✕ 🛏 💻 [AC]

WW Harborside Inn **H**
(360) 385-7909. **Call for rates.** 330 Benedict St 98368. Just s of SR 20, between Jefferson and Washington sts. Ext corridors. **Pets:** Small, dogs only. $15 daily fee/pet. Designated rooms, service with restrictions, supervision. 🛰 ✕ 🛏 💻 ⊳ [AC]

WWW Old Consulate Inn **BB** 🐾
(360) 385-6753. **$99-$220, 7 day notice.** 313 Walker St 98368. Jct Washington St; on the bluff. Int corridors. **Pets:** Dogs only. $25 one-time fee/pet. Designated rooms, supervision. 🛰 ✕ [AC] [W] [Z]

WW Palace Hotel **H**
(360) 385-0773. **Call for rates.** 1004 Water St 98368. Downtown. Int corridors. **Pets:** Accepted. 🛰 ✕ 🛏 💻 [AC]

AAA **WWW** The Swan Hotel **M** 🐾
(360) 385-1718. **$100-$325, 3 day notice.** 216 Monroe St 98368. Downtown. Ext corridors. **Pets:** Dogs only. $20 daily fee/pet. Designated rooms, service with restrictions, supervision.
[SAVE] 🛰 ✕ 🛏 💻 [AC]

PROSSER

AAA **WWWW** BEST WESTERN PLUS The Inn at Horse Heaven **H**
(509) 786-7977. **$80-$160.** 259 Merlot Dr 99350. I-82 exit 80, just s. Int corridors. **Pets:** Dogs only. $10 daily fee/pet. Designated rooms, service with restrictions, supervision. [SAVE] 🛰 ✕ [&M] 🛏 💻 ⊳

PULLMAN

AAA **WWW** Hilltop Inn **H** 🐾
(509) 332-0928. **$70-$249, 3 day notice.** 928 NW Olsen St 99163. 1.6 mi e on SR 270 from US 195. Int corridors. **Pets:** Large, dogs only. $15 daily fee/pet. Designated rooms, service with restrictions, crate.
[SAVE] 🛰 ✕ [&M] 🛏 💻 ⊳ ⊠

WWWW Holiday Inn Express Hotel & Suites **H** 🐾
(509) 334-4437. **$109-$169.** 1190 SE Bishop Blvd 99163. Jct US 195 business route, 0.5 mi s, 1 mi e on SR 270. Int corridors. **Pets:** Large, dogs only. $20 daily fee/pet. Designated rooms, service with restrictions, crate. 🛰 ✕ [&M] 🛏 💻 ⊳ ⊠

AAA **WWW** Quality Inn Paradise Creek **H**
(509) 332-0500. **Call for rates.** 1400 SE Bishop Blvd 99163. Jct US 195 business route, just s, 1 mi e on SR 270. Int corridors. **Pets:** Accepted.
[SAVE] 🛰 ✕ 🛏 💻 ⊳ ⊠

QUINAULT

AAA **WWW** Lake Quinault Lodge **H**
(360) 288-2900. **$99-$350, 3 day notice.** 345 S Shore Rd 98575. 2.2 mi ne of US 101 and S Shore Rd. Ext/int corridors. **Pets:** Accepted.
[SAVE] 🛰 ✕ 💻 🍴 ⊳ ⊠ [AC] [Z]

REPUBLIC

AAA **WWW** Prospector Inn **H**
(509) 775-3361. **$51-$150.** 979 S Clark Ave 99166. Downtown. Int corridors. **Pets:** $12 daily fee/pet. No service, supervision.
[SAVE] 🛰 ✕ 🛏 💻 ⊠

RICHLAND

AAA **WWW** Days Inn **M**
(509) 943-4611. **$59-$99.** 615 Jadwin Ave 99352. I-182 exit 5B, 0.9 mi n; just w of SR 240 business route; downtown. Ext corridors. **Pets:** Dogs only. $15 daily fee/pet. Designated rooms, service with restrictions, crate.
[SAVE] 🛰 🛏 💻 ⊳

WWWW Holiday Inn Express Hotel & Suites **H**
(509) 737-8000. **$119-$179.** 1970 Center Pkwy 99352. Just s on Columbia Center Blvd from SR 240, just w. Int corridors. **Pets:** Accepted.
🛰 ✕ [&M] 🛏 💻 ⊳ ⊠

WWWW Red Lion Hotel Richland Hanford House **H**
(509) 946-7611. **Call for rates.** 802 George Washington Way 99352. I-182 exit 5B, 1.3 mi n on SR 240 business route. Ext/int corridors. **Pets:** Other species. $15 one-time fee/room. Service with restrictions, crate. 🛰 ✕ [&M] 🛏 💻 🍴 ⊳ ⊠

WWW Shilo Inn Suites Hotel - Richland **H**
(509) 946-4661. **$65-$209.** 50 Comstock St 99352. I-182 exit 5B, 0.5 mi n. Ext corridors. **Pets:** Dogs only. $25 one-time fee/room. Designated rooms, service with restrictions, supervision.
🛰 ✕ 🛏 💻 🍴 ⊳ ⊠

RITZVILLE

AAA **WWWW** BEST WESTERN PLUS Bronco Inn **H**
(509) 659-5000. **$80-$200.** 105 W Galbreath Way 99169. I-90 exit 221, cross overpass, then second left. Int corridors. **Pets:** Other species. $20 one-time fee/room. Service with restrictions, supervision.
[SAVE] 🛰 🛏 💻 ⊳

AAA **WWW** Cedars Inn & Suites Ritzville **H**
(509) 659-1007. **$49-$149.** 1513 Smitty's Blvd 99169. I-90 exit 221, just n. Int corridors. **Pets:** Medium, other species. $10 one-time fee/room. Service with restrictions, supervision. [SAVE] 🛰 [&M] 🛏 💻 ⊳

WWW Top Hat Motel **M**
(509) 659-1100. **$44-$68.** 210 E 1st Ave 99169. I-90 exit 221, 1 mi ne via Division St. Ext corridors. **Pets:** Medium, dogs only. $4 one-time fee/room. Service with restrictions, supervision. 🛰 🛏

SAN JUAN ISLANDS AREA

DEER HARBOR

▼▼ Deer Harbor Inn ◨

(360) 376-4110. **Call for rates.** 33 Inn Ln 98243. In Deer Harbor; 7 mi sw of ferry landing; 3.5 mi sw of Westsound. Ext/int corridors.
Pets: Accepted. 🛜 ⊠ 🛏 🖵 🍴 🐾 🏊

EASTSOUND

◈ ▼▼▼ Eastsound Landmark Inn ◧ ❀

(360) 376-2423. **$99-$254, 7 day notice.** 67 Main St 98245. In Eastsound; between N Beach and Orcas rds; downtown. Ext corridors.
Pets: $25 daily fee/room. Designated rooms, supervision.
🆂🅰🆅 🛜 ⊠ 🛏 🖵 🐾

◈ ▼▼▼ Turtleback Farm Inn ⒷⒷ

(360) 376-4914. **$125-$260, 15 day notice.** 1981 Crow Valley Rd 98245. 4 mi sw of Eastsound on Orcas Rd. Int corridors. **Pets:** Dogs only. $25 one-time fee/pet. Designated rooms, service with restrictions, supervision. 🆂🅰🆅 🛜 ⊠ 🛏 🖵 🐾 ⓦ 🏊

FRIDAY HARBOR

▼▼ Argyle House Bed & Breakfast ⒷⒷ 🐾

(360) 378-4084. **$110-$280, 14 day notice.** 685 Argyle Ave 98250. In Friday Harbor; 0.3 mi e of jct Spring St. Ext/int corridors. **Pets:** Dogs only. $25 one-time fee/room. Supervision. 🛜 ⊠ 🛏 🖵 🐾 🏊

◈ ▼▼▼▼ BEST WESTERN PLUS Friday Harbor Suites Ⓗ

(360) 378-3031. **$165-$395, 7 day notice.** 680 Spring St 98250. In Friday Harbor; 0.7 mi w of ferry dock. Int corridors. **Pets:** Designated rooms, service with restrictions, supervision.
🆂🅰🆅 🛜 ⊠ ♿ 🛏 🖵 🍴 🐾 🐾

▼▼ ▼▼ Earthbox Inn & Spa Ⓗ ❀

(360) 378-4000. **$157-$407, 10 day notice.** 410 Spring St 98250. In Friday Harbor; 0.5 mi w of ferry dock. Ext corridors. **Pets:** $15 one-time fee/pet. Designated rooms, service with restrictions, crate.
🛜 ⊠ 🛏 🖵 ➰ 🐾

▼▼▼▼ Friday Harbor House Ⓗ

(360) 378-8455. **Call for rates.** 130 West St 98250. In Friday Harbor; just w of Spring St. Ext/int corridors. **Pets:** Accepted.
🛜 ⊠ 🛏 🖵 🍴 🐾

▼▼▼▼ Lakedale Resort at Three Lakes Ⓗ

(360) 378-2350. **Call for rates.** 4313 Roche Harbor Rd 98250. 4 mi n of Friday Harbor via Tucker Ave. Ext/int corridors. **Pets:** Accepted.
🛜 ⊠ 🛏 🖵 🐾 🐾

▼▼ ▼▼ States Inn & Ranch ⒷⒷ

(360) 378-6240. **Call for rates.** 2687 W Valley Rd 98250. 7 mi nw of Friday Harbor via 2nd St, Guard St and Beaverton Valley Rd. Int corridors. **Pets:** Accepted. 🛜 ⊠ 🛏 🐾 ⓦ 🏊

◈ ▼▼▼▼ Trumpeter Inn Bed & Breakfast ⒷⒷ

(360) 378-3884. **Call for rates.** 318 Trumpeter Way 98250. 1.5 mi w of Friday Harbor via Spring St and San Juan Valley Rd. Int corridors. **Pets:** Dogs only. $100 deposit/pet, $25 one-time fee/pet. Designated rooms, supervision. 🆂🅰🆅 🛜 ⊠ 🐾 ⓦ 🏊

END AREA

SEATTLE METROPOLITAN AREA

ARLINGTON

◈ ▼▼▼▼ Medallion Hotel Ⓗ

(360) 657-0500. **$109-$119.** 16710 Smokey Point Blvd 98223. I-5 exit 206, just e on 172nd St NE, then just s. Int corridors. **Pets:** Medium, dogs only. $25 daily fee/room. Designated rooms, crate.
🆂🅰🆅 🛜 ⊠ ♿ 🛏 🖵 🍴 ➰ 🐾

AUBURN

▼▼ ▼▼ Auburn GuestHouse Inn Ⓗ

(253) 735-9600. **$89-$99.** 9 14th St NW 98001. SR 167 exit 15th St NW, 0.8 mi e, just s on A St NE, then just w. Int corridors. **Pets:** Dogs only. $10 one-time fee/pet. Designated rooms, service with restrictions, supervision. 🛜 🛏 🖵

◈ ▼▼▼▼ BEST WESTERN PLUS Peppertree Auburn Inn Ⓗ ❀

(253) 887-7600. **$100-$200.** 401 8th St SW 98001. SR 18 exit C St, just s, then just w. Int corridors. **Pets:** Dogs only. Designated rooms, supervision. 🆂🅰🆅 🛜 ⊠ 🛏 🖵 ➰ 🐾

▼▼ Cedars Inn Auburn Ⓗ

(253) 833-8007. **$50-$70.** 102 15th St NE 98002. SR 167 exit 15th St NW, 0.8 mi e. Int corridors. **Pets:** Medium, dogs only. $20 daily fee/room. Designated rooms, supervision. 🛜 ⊠ 🛏

▼▼▼▼ La Quinta Inn & Suites Ⓗ

(253) 804-9999. **$102-$232.** 225 6th St SE 98002. SR 18 exit Auburn Way N. Int corridors. **Pets:** Service with restrictions, supervision.
🛜 ⊠ 🛏 🖵 ➰

▼▼ Travelodge Inn & Suites Ⓗ

(253) 833-7171. **$70-$129.** 9 16th St NW 98001. SR 167 exit 15th St NW, 0.8 mi e, then just n on A St NE. Int corridors. **Pets:** Medium. $10 daily fee/pet. Supervision. 🛜 ♿ 🛏 🖵

BAINBRIDGE ISLAND

◈ ▼▼▼▼ BEST WESTERN PLUS Bainbridge Island Suites Ⓗ ❀

(206) 855-9666. **$130-$140.** 350 NE High School Rd 98110. 0.8 mi n of ferry dock on SR 305, then just w. Int corridors. **Pets:** Medium, other species. $20 daily fee/pet. Designated rooms, service with restrictions, crate. 🆂🅰🆅 🛜 ⊠ 🛏 🖵

BELLEVUE

◈ ▼▼▼▼ Embassy Suites Hotel Bellevue Ⓗ

(425) 644-2500. **$99-$209.** 3225 158th Ave SE 98008. I-90 exit 11 westbound; exit 11A (156th Ave SE) eastbound, just ne. Int corridors. **Pets:** Small, other species. $50 one-time fee/pet. Service with restrictions, supervision. 🆂🅰🆅 🛜 ♿ 🛏 🖵 🍴 ➰ 🐾

▼▼ **Extended**
StayAmerica-Seattle-Bellevue-Downtown H
(425) 453-8186. **$90-$105.** 11400 Main St 98004. I-405 exit 13A, just se. Int corridors. **Pets:** $25 daily fee/pet. Designated rooms, service with restrictions. 🛜 ᴴᴹ 🔌 🖥

▼▼▼ **Fairfield Inn by Marriott Seattle Bellevue** H
(425) 869-6548. **$109-$229.** 14595 NE 29th Pl 98007. I-405 exit 14 (SR 520), 2.3 mi e to 148th Ave NE (north exit), then just nw. Int corridors. **Pets:** $50 one-time fee/room. Designated rooms, service with restrictions, supervision. 🛜 ✕ ᴴᴹ 🔌 🖥

🅰🅰🅰 ▼▼▼ **Hotel Bellevue** H ❀
(425) 454-4424. **$199-$2000.** 11200 SE 6th St 98004. I-405 exit 12, 0.4 mi nw. Int corridors. **Pets:** Medium, dogs only. $30 daily fee/room. Service with restrictions, supervision. SAVE 🛜 ✕ ᴴᴹ 🍽 ➤ ✕

🅰🅰🅰 ▼▼▼ **Hyatt house Seattle/Bellevue** H
(425) 747-2705. **$99-$309.** 3244 139th Ave SE 98005. I-90 exit 11 westbound, 0.9 mi w, just n; exit 10B eastbound, just n, 0.7 mi e, then just n. Int corridors. **Pets:** Medium. $200 one-time fee/room. Service with restrictions, crate. SAVE 🛜 ✕ ᴴᴹ 🔌 🖥 🍽 ➤

🅰🅰🅰 ▼▼▼ **Hyatt Regency Bellevue** H ❀
(425) 462-1234. **$119-$379.** 900 Bellevue Way NE 98004. I-405 exit 13B, 1.5 mi w on NE 8th St. Int corridors. **Pets:** Medium, dogs only. $30 daily fee/room. Designated rooms, service with restrictions, supervision. ECO SAVE 🛜 ᴴᴹ 🔌 🖥 🍽 ➤

🅰🅰🅰 ▼▼▼ **La Residence Suite Hotel** H
(425) 455-1475. **$129-$199.** 475 100th Ave NE 98004. I-405 exit 13B, 0.9 mi w on NE 8th St, then just s. Int corridors. **Pets:** Other species. $15 daily fee/pet. Designated rooms, service with restrictions. SAVE 🛜 ✕ 🔌 🖥

▼▼▼ **Larkspur Landing Bellevue/Seattle** H
(425) 373-1212. **Call for rates.** 15805 SE 37th St 98006. I-90 exit 11 westbound; exit 11A (156th Ave SE) eastbound, 0.9 mi se on south frontage road. Int corridors. **Pets:** Accepted. 🛜 ᴴᴹ 🔌 🖥

🅰🅰🅰 ▼▼▼ **Red Lion Hotel Bellevue** H
(425) 455-5240. **$69-$189.** 11211 Main St 98004. I-405 exit 12, 0.4 mi n on 114th St. Int corridors. **Pets:** Other species. $15 one-time fee/room. Service with restrictions, crate. SAVE 🛜 ✕ 🔌 🖥 🍽 ➤

▼▼▼ **Residence Inn by Marriott Seattle Bellevue** H
(425) 882-1222. **$129-$219.** 14455 NE 29th Pl 98007. I-405 exit 14 (SR 520), 2.3 mi e to 148th Ave NE (north exit), then just nw. Ext corridors. **Pets:** Accepted. 🛜 ✕ ᴴᴹ 🔌 🖥 ➤

▼▼▼ **Residence Inn by Marriott Seattle Bellevue/Downtown** H
(425) 637-8500. **$99-$219.** 605 114th Ave SE 98004. I-405 exit 12, just sw. Int corridors. **Pets:** Accepted. 🛜 ✕ ᴴᴹ 🔌 🖥 ➤

🅰🅰🅰 ▼▼▼ **Sheraton Bellevue Hotel** H
(425) 455-3330. **$109-$359.** 100 112th Ave NE 98004. I-405 exit 12 northbound; exit 13 southbound, just s. Int corridors. **Pets:** Accepted. SAVE 🛜 ✕ ᴴᴹ 🔌 🍽

🅰🅰🅰 ▼▼▼ **The Westin Bellevue** H
(425) 638-1000. **$159-$429, 3 day notice.** 600 Bellevue Way NE 98004. I-405 exit 13B, 1.5 mi w on NE 8th St. Int corridors. **Pets:** Accepted. SAVE 🛜 ✕ ᴴᴹ 🖥 🍽 ➤ ✕

BOTHELL
▼▼▼ **Country Inn & Suites By Carlson** H
(425) 485-5557. **Call for rates.** 19333 N Creek Pkwy 98011. I-405 exit 24, just e. Int corridors. **Pets:** Accepted. ECO 🛜 ᴴᴹ 🔌 🖥 🍽 ➤ ✕

▼▼ **Extended StayAmerica-Seattle-Bothell** H
(425) 402-4252. **$75-$95.** 923 228th St SE 98021. I-405 exit 26, just sw. Int corridors. **Pets:** $25 daily fee/pet. Designated rooms, service with restrictions. 🛜 ᴴᴹ 🔌 🖥

▼▼▼ **Residence Inn by Marriott Seattle NE** H
(425) 485-3030. **$89-$199.** 11920 NE 195th St 98011. I-405 exit 24, 0.4 mi ne. Ext corridors. **Pets:** Other species. $75 one-time fee/room. Service with restrictions. 🛜 ✕ ᴴᴹ 🔌 🖥 ➤ ✕

BREMERTON
🅰🅰🅰 ▼▼ **Flagship Inn** H
(360) 479-6566. **$79-$150.** 4320 Kitsap Way 98312. 3.5 mi w of ferry terminal; SR 3 exit Kitsap Way, 0.5 mi e. Int corridors. **Pets:** Small, dogs only. $6 daily fee/pet. Supervision. SAVE 🛜 🔌 🖥 ➤

▼▼ **Midway Inn** H
(360) 479-2909. **$84-$160.** 2909 Wheaton Way 98310. SR 303, 2 mi n. Int corridors. **Pets:** Dogs only. $50 one-time fee/pet. Designated rooms, service with restrictions, supervision. 🛜 🔌 🖥

▼▼ **Super 8** H
(360) 377-8881. **$70-$80.** 5068 Kitsap Way 98312. 4.2 mi w of ferry terminal; SR 3 exit Kitsap Way, just ne. Int corridors. **Pets:** $10 daily fee/pet. Designated rooms, no service, supervision. 🛜 ᴴᴹ 🔌 🖥

DUPONT
▼▼ **GuestHouse Inn & Suites** H
(253) 912-8900. **$99-$179.** 1609 McNeil St 98327. I-5 exit 118, just nw on Center Dr, then just w. Int corridors. **Pets:** Other species. $25 daily fee/room. Designated rooms, service with restrictions, supervision. 🛜 ✕ 🔌 🖥 ➤ ✕

EDMONDS
🅰🅰🅰 ▼▼▼ **BEST WESTERN PLUS Edmonds Harbor Inn** H ❀
(425) 771-5021. **$110-$136.** 130 W Dayton St 98020. Just s at Port of Edmonds. Ext/int corridors. **Pets:** Medium. $20 daily fee/room. Designated rooms, service with restrictions, supervision. SAVE 🛜 ✕ ᴴᴹ 🔌 🖥 ➤ ✕

EVERETT
🅰🅰🅰 ▼▼ **BEST WESTERN Cascadia Inn** H
(425) 258-4141. **$99-$149.** 2800 Pacific Ave 98201. I-5 exit 193 northbound; exit 194 southbound, just w. Int corridors. **Pets:** Medium, other species. $20 one-time fee/room. Designated rooms, service with restrictions, crate. SAVE 🛜 ᴴᴹ 🔌 🖥 ➤

🅰🅰🅰 ▼▼▼ **BEST WESTERN PLUS Navigator Inn & Suites** H ❀
(425) 347-2555. **$129-$159.** 10210 Evergreen Way 98204. I-5 exit 189, 1 mi w on SR 526 to Evergreen Way, then 1.6 mi s. Int corridors. **Pets:** Large, dogs only. $20 daily fee/room. Designated rooms, service with restrictions, supervision. SAVE 🛜 ✕ ᴴᴹ 🔌 🖥 ➤

▼▼ **Extended StayAmerica-Seattle-Everett** H
(425) 355-1923. **$65-$85.** 8410 Broadway 98208. I-5 exit 189, follow signs to Broadway, just nw. Int corridors. **Pets:** $25 daily fee/pet. Designated rooms, service with restrictions. 🛜 ᴴᴹ 🔌 🖥

▼▼ **Extended StayAmerica-Seattle-Everett-Silverlake** H
(425) 337-1341. **$85-$105.** 1431 112th St SE 98208. I-5 exit 189, 1.5 mi se on 19th Ave SE, then 0.3 mi w. Int corridors. **Pets:** $25 daily fee/pet. Designated rooms, service with restrictions. 🛜 ᴴᴹ 🔌 🖥

▼▼▼ **Holiday Inn Downtown Everett** H
(425) 339-2000. **$99-$169.** 3105 Pine St 98201. I-5 exit 193 northbound; exit 194 southbound, just sw. Int corridors. **Pets:** Accepted.

Inn at Port Gardner H
(425) 252-6779. **$109-$249.** 1700 W Marine View Dr 98201. I-5 exit 193 northbound, 1.2 mi w on Pacific Ave, then 1.2 mi n; exit 194 southbound, 1.2 mi w on Everett Ave, then 1 mi n; in Everett Marina Village. Int corridors. **Pets:** Medium, dogs only. $25 one-time fee/room. Service with restrictions, supervision. SAVE 🛰 ✕ 🛇M 🔋 💻

La Quinta Inn Everett H
(425) 347-9099. **$83-$161.** 12619 4th Ave W 98204. I-5 exit 186, just w. Int corridors. **Pets:** Service with restrictions, supervision.
SAVE 🛰 ✕ 🛇M 🔋 💻 🏊

FEDERAL WAY
Clarion Hotel Federal Way H
(253) 941-6000. **$89-$179.** 31611 20th Ave S 98003. I-5 exit 143, 0.5 mi w on 320th St, then just n. Int corridors. **Pets:** Small, dogs only. $15 daily fee/pet. Designated rooms, service with restrictions, crate.
SAVE 🛰 ✕ 🔋 💻 🍴 🏊

FIFE
Emerald Queen Hotel & Casino H
(253) 922-2000. **$89-$129.** 5700 Pacific Hwy E 98424. I-5 exit 137, just ne. Int corridors. **Pets:** Medium. $25 one-time fee/room. Designated rooms, service with restrictions, supervision.
SAVE 🛰 🛇M 🔋 💻 🍴 🏊

Extended StayAmerica-Tacoma-Fife H
(253) 926-6316. **$81-$91.** 2820 Pacific Hwy E 98424. I-5 exit 136B northbound; exit 136 southbound, just nw. Int corridors. **Pets:** $25 daily fee/pet. Designated rooms, service with restrictions. 🛰 🔋 💻

GIG HARBOR
BEST WESTERN PLUS Wesley Inn & Suites H ❧
(253) 858-9690. **$159-$189.** 6575 Kimball Dr 98335. SR 16 exit City Center, just e on Pioneer Way, then 0.3 mi s. Int corridors. **Pets:** Other species. $20 daily fee/pet. Designated rooms, supervision.
SAVE 🛰 ✕ 🛇M 🔋 💻 🏊

The Inn at Gig Harbor H ❧
(253) 858-1111. **$119-$232, 3 day notice.** 3211 56th St NW 98335. SR 16 exit Olympic Dr, just w, then 0.4 mi n. Int corridors. **Pets:** Other species. $25 one-time fee/room, $10 daily fee/room. Designated rooms, service with restrictions, supervision.
SAVE 🛰 ✕ 🛇M 🔋 💻 🍴 🏊

KENT
Comfort Inn Kent H
(253) 872-2211. **$75-$130.** 22311 84th Ave S 98032. SR 167 exit 84th Ave S, just n. Int corridors. **Pets:** Small. $20 daily fee/pet. Designated rooms, service with restrictions, crate. 🛰 🔋 💻 🏊

Hawthorn Suites by Wyndham H ❧
(253) 395-3800. **$129-$219.** 6329 S 212th St 98032. I-5 exit 152, 2.6 mi se via Orilla Rd and 212th St. Ext corridors. **Pets:** $25 daily fee/pet. Designated rooms, service with restrictions, crate. 🛰 🔋 💻 🏊 ✕

TownePlace Suites by Marriott-Seattle Southcenter H ❧
(253) 796-6000. **$89-$179.** 18123 72nd Ave S 98032. I-405 exit 1 (SR 181), 1.6 mi s on W Valley Hwy, just e on S 180th St, then just s. Ext corridors. **Pets:** Other species. $10 daily fee/pet.
🛰 ✕ 🛇M 🔋 💻 🏊 ✕

KIRKLAND
Baymont Inn & Suites H
(425) 822-2300. **$79-$115.** 12223 NE 116th St 98034. I-405 exit 20A northbound; exit 20 southbound, just e; in Totem Lake area. Ext corridors. **Pets:** Medium, dogs only. $25 one-time fee/pet. Designated rooms, service with restrictions, crate. 🛰 ✕ 🛇M 🔋 💻 🏊

The Heathman Hotel H ❧
(425) 284-5800. **$199-$349.** 220 Kirkland Ave 98033. I-405 exit 18 (NE 85th St), 1 mi w, then just s on 3rd St. Int corridors. **Pets:** Other species. Designated rooms, service with restrictions.
SAVE 🛰 ✕ 🛇M 🔋 💻 🍴 ✕

La Quinta Inn & Suites Seattle Bellevue/Kirkland H
(425) 828-6585. **$83-$173.** 10530 NE Northup Way 98033. I-405 exit 14 (SR 520) via 108th Ave exit, 1 mi n on 108th Ave, then just w. Int corridors. **Pets:** Service with restrictions, supervision.
🛰 🛇M 🔋 💻 🏊

Woodmark Hotel, Yacht Club & Spa H ❧
(425) 822-3700. **Call for rates.** 1200 Carillon Point 98033. On Lake Washington Blvd, 1 mi n of SR 520. Int corridors. **Pets:** Dogs only. Designated rooms, service with restrictions, supervision.
SAVE 🛰 ✕ 🛇M 💻 🍴 ✕

LAKEWOOD
Candlewood Suites H
(253) 584-0868. **Call for rates.** 10720 Pacific Hwy SW 98499. I-5 exit 127 (SR 512), 0.3 mi s. Int corridors. **Pets:** Accepted. 🛰 🔋 💻

La Quinta Inn & Suites Lakewood H
(253) 582-7000. **$131-$221.** 11751 Pacific Hwy SW 98499. I-5 exit 125, just nw. Int corridors. **Pets:** Service with restrictions, supervision.
🛰 ✕ 🛇M 🔋 💻 🏊

LYNNWOOD
BEST WESTERN Alderwood H
(425) 775-7600. **$79-$99.** 19332 36th Ave W 98036. I-5 exit 181B northbound, just n on Poplar Way, just w on 196th St SW, then just n; exit 181 (SR 524 W) southbound, just nw. Int corridors. **Pets:** Medium. $25 one-time fee/pet. Designated rooms, service with restrictions, supervision.
SAVE 🛰 🛇M 🔋 💻 🏊

Courtyard by Marriott Seattle North-Lynnwood-Everett H
(425) 670-0500. **$129-$189.** 4220 Alderwood Mall Blvd 98036. I-5 exit 181A northbound, just w on 44th Ave W, then just n; exit 181 (SR 524 W) southbound, 0.5 mi w on 196th SW, just s on 44th Ave W, then just e. Int corridors. **Pets:** Accepted.
SAVE 🛰 ✕ 🛇M 🔋 💻 🍴 🏊

Embassy Suites Hotel Seattle North/Lynnwood H
(425) 775-2500. **$129-$229.** 20610 44th Ave W 98036. I-5 exit 181A northbound, just se; exit 181 (SR 524 W) southbound, 0.5 w on 196th St SW, then 0.6 mi s. Int corridors. **Pets:** Accepted.
🛰 🛇M 🔋 🍴 🏊 ✕

La Quinta Inn Lynnwood H
(425) 775-7447. **$78-$199.** 4300 Alderwood Mall Blvd 98036. I-5 exit 181A northbound, just w; exit 181 (SR 524 W) southbound, 0.5 mi w on 196th St SW, just s on 44th Ave SW, then just e. Int corridors. **Pets:** Service with restrictions, supervision. SAVE 🛰 ✕ 🔋 💻 🏊

Residence Inn by Marriott-Seattle North/Lynnwood H
(425) 771-1100. **$99-$259.** 18200 Alderwood Mall Pkwy 98037. I-5 exit 183 southbound, just w on 164th St SW, then 1.5 mi se on 28th St W; exit 182 northbound on SR 525 exit 1, then just s; just n of Alderwood Mall. Ext corridors. **Pets:** Medium, other species. $15 daily fee/room. Service with restrictions, crate. 🛰 ✕ 🛇M 🔋 💻 🏊

MARYSVILLE
Holiday Inn Express Hotel & Suites-Marysville H
(360) 530-1234. **$99-$209.** 8606 36th Ave NE 98270. I-5 exit 200, just se. Int corridors. **Pets:** Other species. $40 one-time fee/room. Service with restrictions, crate. 🛰 ✕ 🛇M 🔋 💻 🏊

MONROE

AAA ▼▼ **BEST WESTERN Sky Valley Inn** H
(360) 794-3111. **$89-$139.** 19233 SR 2 98272. West end of town. Int corridors. **Pets:** Dogs only. $20 daily fee/pet. Service with restrictions, supervision. [SAVE] 🛜 ✖ 👫M 🔌 🖥 🏊

AAA ▼▼▼ **GuestHouse International Inn & Suites** H
(360) 863-1900. **$114-$144.** 19103 SR 2 98272. West end of town. Int corridors. **Pets:** Dogs only. $20 daily fee/room. Service with restrictions, supervision. [SAVE] 🛜 ✖ 👫M 🔌 🖥 🏊

MUKILTEO

AAA ▼▼▼ **Staybridge Suites Seattle North-Everett** H 🐾
(425) 493-9500. **$129-$189.** 9600 Harbour Pl 98275. Jct Paine Field Blvd and SR 525 (Mukilteo Speedway). Int corridors. **Pets:** Large. $75 one-time fee/room. Designated rooms, service with restrictions, crate.
[SAVE] 🛜 ✖ 👫M 🔌 🖥 🏊 ✖

AAA ▼▼▼ **TownePlace Suites by Marriott-Mukilteo** H 🐾
(425) 551-5900. **$89-$159.** 8521 Mukilteo Speedway 98275. Just se of jct 84th St SW and SR 525 (Mukilteo Speedway). Ext corridors. **Pets:** Other species. $10 daily fee/pet. Service with restrictions.
🛜 ✖ 👫M 🔌 🖥 🏊 ✖

PORT ORCHARD

AAA ▼▼▼ **Comfort Inn Port Orchard** M
(360) 895-2666. **$79-$115.** 1121 Bay St 98366. SR 16 exit Tremont St, 0.9 mi e to Sidney Ave, 1.2 mi n to Bay St, then just e. Ext corridors. **Pets:** Dogs only. $15 daily fee/pet. Designated rooms, service with restrictions, supervision. [SAVE] 🛜 ✖ 👫M 🔌 🖥

▼▼ **Days Inn Port Orchard** H
(360) 895-7818. **$100-$105.** 220 Bravo Terrace 98366. SR 16 exit SR 160 E (Sedgwick Rd), just se. Int corridors. **Pets:** Accepted.
🛜 👫M 🔌 🖥 🏊

POULSBO

▼▼ **GuestHouse International Inn & Suites** H 🐾
(360) 697-4400. **$109-$179.** 19801 7th Ave NE 98370. On SR 305. Int corridors. **Pets:** $30 daily fee/pet. Service with restrictions, supervision.
🛜 👫M 🔌 🖥

AAA ▼▼▼ **Poulsbo Inn & Suites** M
(360) 779-3921. **$99-$130, 7 day notice.** 18680 SR 305 NE 98370. SR 3, 2.3 mi e. Ext corridors. **Pets:** Medium. $15 daily fee/pet. Designated rooms, service with restrictions, supervision.
[SAVE] 🛜 👫M 🔌 🖥 🏊 ✖

PUYALLUP

AAA ▼▼▼ **BEST WESTERN PREMIER Plaza Hotel & Conference Center** H 🐾
(253) 848-1500. **$129-$169.** 620 S Hill Park Dr 98373. SR 512 exit S Hill Park Dr southbound, just w; exit 9th St SW northbound, just w. Int corridors. **Pets:** Dogs only. $3 daily fee/room. Service with restrictions, supervision. [SAVE] 🛜 ✖ 👫M 🔌 🖥 🍴 🏊

▼▼▼ **Holiday Inn Express Hotel & Suites** H
(253) 848-4900. **$149-$189.** 812 S Hill Park Dr 98373. SR 512 exit S Hill Park Dr southbound, just w; exit 9th St SW northbound, just w. Int corridors. **Pets:** Dogs only. $25 one-time fee/room. Service with restrictions, supervision. 🛜 ✖ 🔌 🖥 🏊

REDMOND

AAA ▼▼▼ **Hyatt house Seattle/Redmond** H
(425) 497-2000. **$99-$329.** 15785 Bear Creek Pkwy NE 98052. I-405 exit 14 (SR 520), 4.5 mi e to W Lake Sammamish Pkwy, just n to Leary Way, just e to Bear Creek Pkwy, then just n. Int corridors. **Pets:** Medium. $150 one-time fee/pet. Service with restrictions.
[SAVE] 🛜 ✖ 👫M 🔌 🖥 🍴 🏊 ✖

AAA ▼▼▼▼ **Redmond Marriott Town Center** H
(425) 498-4000. **$119-$269.** 7401 164th Ave NE 98052. I-405 exit 14 (SR 520), 4.5 mi e to W Lake Sammamish Pkwy, just n to Leary Way, just e to Bear Creek Pkwy, just s to NE 74th Ave, then just w. Int corridors. **Pets:** Medium, other species. $150 one-time fee/pet. Service with restrictions, supervision.
[ECO] [SAVE] 🛜 ✖ 👫M 🔌 🖥 🍴 🏊 ✖

▼▼▼ **Residence Inn by Marriott Seattle East / Redmond** H 🐾
(425) 497-9226. **$109-$259.** 7575 164th Ave NE 98052. I-405 exit 14 (SR 520), 4.5 mi e to W Lake Sammamish Pkwy, just n to Leary Way, just e to Bear Creek Pkwy, just s to NE 74th Ave, just w to 164th Ave NE, then just n; center. Int corridors. **Pets:** Medium, other species. $100 one-time fee/room. Service with restrictions, crate.
[ECO] 🛜 ✖ 👫M 🔌 🖥 🏊

RENTON

▼▼▼ **Holiday Inn-Renton** H
(425) 226-7700. **$79-$119.** One S Grady Way 98057. I-405 exit 2 (SR 167/Rainier Ave), 0.4 mi n, then just e. Int corridors. **Pets:** Accepted.
🛜 🔌 🖥 🍴 🏊

▼▼▼ **Larkspur Landing Renton/Seattle** H
(425) 235-1212. **$159-$179.** 1701 E Valley Rd 98057. SR 167 exit E Valley Rd, 1 mi nw. Int corridors. **Pets:** Accepted. 🛜 🔌 🖥

▼▼ **Quality Inn Renton** H
(425) 226-7600. **$99-$149.** 1850 SE Maple Valley Hwy 98057. I-405 exit 4 (Bronson Way) northbound, follow Maple Valley Hwy; exit southbound, 0.6 mi s to 2nd light, then just e. Int corridors. **Pets:** Small, dogs only. $25 one-time fee/room, $10 daily fee/room. Designated rooms, service with restrictions, supervision. 🛜 🔌 🖥

▼▼▼ **TownePlace Suites by Marriott Seattle South/Renton** H
(425) 917-2000. **$80-$189.** 300 SW 19th St 98057. SR 167 exit E Valley Rd, 1 mi nw, then just w. Int corridors. **Pets:** Accepted.
🛜 ✖ 👫M 🔌 🖥 🏊

SEATAC

AAA ▼▼▼▼ **Cedarbrook Lodge** H
(206) 901-9268. **$129-$349.** 18525 36th Ave S 98188. SR 99, just e on 188th St, then just n. Int corridors. **Pets:** Accepted.
🍽 [SAVE] 🛜 ✖ 👫M 🔌 🖥 🍴

▼▼▼ **Clarion Hotel** H
(206) 242-0200. **$107-$117.** 3000 S 176th St 98188. Just e of SR 99. Int corridors. **Pets:** Accepted. 🛜 ✖ 👫M 🔌 🖥 🍴 🏊

▼▼▼ **DoubleTree by Hilton Hotel Seattle Airport** H
(206) 246-8600. **$109-$209.** 18740 International Blvd 98188. On SR 99. Int corridors. **Pets:** Accepted. 🛜 🔌 🖥 🍴 🏊

▼▼▼ **Hilton Seattle Airport & Conference Center** H 🐾
(206) 244-4800. **$129-$249.** 17620 International Blvd 98188. On SR 99. Int corridors. **Pets:** Large. $50 one-time fee/room. Service with restrictions, crate. 🍽 🛜 ✖ 🖥 🍴 🏊

▼▼▼ **Holiday Inn Express Hotel & Suites-Seattle Sea-Tac Airport** H
(206) 824-3200. **$90-$199.** 19621 International Blvd 98188. On SR 99. Int corridors. **Pets:** Medium. $50 one-time fee/room. Service with restrictions, crate. 🛜 🔌 🖥

AAA ▼▼▼ **Holiday Inn Seattle SeaTac International Airport** H
(206) 248-1000. **Call for rates.** 17338 International Blvd 98188. On SR 99. Int corridors. **Pets:** Accepted.
[SAVE] 🛜 ✖ 👫M 🔌 🖥 🍴 🏊

▼▼▼ Radisson Hotel Seattle Airport 🅷
(206) 244-6666. **$99-$259.** 18118 International Blvd 98188. On SR 99.
Int corridors. **Pets:** Accepted. 🄴🄲🄾 🛜 ✕ 🅖🅜 💻 🍽 🏊

AAA ▼▼▼▼ Red Lion Hotel Seattle Airport 🅷
(206) 246-5535. **$89-$239.** 18220 International Blvd 98188. On SR 99.
Int corridors. **Pets:** Other species. $15 one-time fee/room. Service with
restrictions, crate. SAVE 🛜 🅗 💻 🍽 🏊

▼▼ Super 8 Sea-Tac 🅷
(206) 433-8188. **$65-$95.** 3100 S 192nd St 98188. Just e of SR 99. Int
corridors. **Pets:** Large. $10 daily fee/pet. Designated rooms, service with
restrictions, crate. 🛜 🅗 💻

SEATTLE

AAA ▼▼▼ ▼▼▼ Alexis Hotel - A Kimpton Hotel 🅷
(206) 624-4844. **Call for rates.** 1007 1st Ave 98104. Corner of Madison
St and 1st Ave. Int corridors. **Pets:** Accepted.
🄴🄲🄾 🄲🄳 SAVE 🛜 ✕ 🅗 💻 🍽 🏊

AAA ▼▼▼ Comfort Inn & Suites Seattle 🅷
(206) 361-3700. **$75-$180.** 13700 Aurora Ave N 98133. I-5 exit 175, 1.1
mi w on NE 145th St, then 0.3 mi s. Int corridors. **Pets:** Small, dogs only.
$25 daily fee/pet. Designated rooms, supervision.
SAVE 🛜 ✕ 🅗 💻

▼▼▼▼ Crowne Plaza Seattle-Downtown 🅷
(206) 464-1980. **$99-$259, 3 day notice.** 1113 6th Ave 98101. Corner
of 6th Ave and Seneca St. Int corridors. **Pets:** Accepted.
🛜 ✕ 🅖🅜 🅗 💻 🍽

AAA ▼▼▼ ▼▼▼ The Edgewater 🅷 🐾
(206) 728-7000. **$229-$729.** 2411 Alaskan Way, Pier 67 98121. On
waterfront at Pier 67; at base of Wall St. Int corridors. **Pets:** Service with
restrictions, supervision. SAVE 🛜 ✕ 🅗 💻 🍽

▼▼ ▼▼ Executive Hotel Pacific 🅷 🐾
(206) 623-3900. **Call for rates.** 400 Spring St 98104. Between 4th and
5th aves. Int corridors. **Pets:** Medium. $50 deposit/pet. Designated rooms,
service with restrictions, supervision. 🛜 ✕ 💻

AAA ▼▼▼ ▼▼▼ The Fairmont Olympic Hotel 🅷
(206) 621-1700. **$199-$429.** 411 University St 98101. Corner of 4th Ave
and University St. Int corridors. **Pets:** Accepted.
🄴🄲🄾 SAVE 🛜 🅗 💻 🍽 🏊 ✕

AAA ▼▼▼ ▼▼▼ Four Seasons Hotel Seattle 🅷
(206) 749-7000. **$295-$525.** 99 Union St 98101. Southwest corner of 1st
Ave and Union St. Int corridors. **Pets:** Accepted.
SAVE 🛜 ✕ 🅖🅜 🍽 🏊 ✕

AAA ▼▼▼ ▼▼▼ Grand Hyatt Seattle 🅷 🐾
(206) 774-1234. **$169-$379, 3 day notice.** 721 Pine St 98101. Corner
of 7th Ave and Pine St. Int corridors. **Pets:** Medium, dogs only. $50 daily
fee/room. Designated rooms, service with restrictions, supervision.
🄴🄲🄾 SAVE 🛜 🅗 💻 🍽 ✕

▼▼▼ ▼▼▼ Homewood Suites by Hilton-Seattle Downtown 🅷
(206) 281-9393. **Call for rates.** 206 Western Ave W 98119. I-5 exit 167
(Mercer St), 0.3 mi w, 0.5 mi s on Fairview Ave, 1.2 mi w on Denny Way,
then just n. Int corridors. **Pets:** Accepted. 🛜 🅗 💻

▼▼▼ ▼▼▼ Hotel 1000 🅷
(206) 957-1000. **$209-$429.** 1000 1st Ave 98104. Northeast corner of 1st
Ave and Madison St. Int corridors. **Pets:** Accepted. 🛜 ✕ 💻 🍽

▼▼▼ ▼▼▼ Hotel Five 🅷
(206) 441-9785. **$105-$215.** 2200 5th Ave 98121. Corner of Blanchard St
and 5th Ave. Int corridors. **Pets:** Accepted. 🛜 ✕ 🅖🅜 💻 🍽

AAA ▼▼▼▼ Hotel Max 🅷
(206) 728-6299. **$119-$299.** 620 Stewart St 98101. Corner of 7th Ave
and Stewart St. Int corridors. **Pets:** Accepted.
SAVE 🛜 ✕ 🅖🅜 🅗 💻 🍽

AAA ▼▼▼ ▼▼▼ Hotel Monaco Seattle-A Kimpton Hotel 🅷
(206) 621-1770. **$139-$349.** 1101 4th Ave 98101. Corner of 4th Ave and
Spring St. Int corridors. **Pets:** Accepted.
🄴🄲🄾 🄲🄳 SAVE 🛜 ✕ 🍽 ✕

AAA ▼▼ ▼▼ Hotel Nexus Seattle 🅷 🐾
(206) 365-0700. **$109-$209.** 2140 N Northgate Way 98133. I-5 exit 173,
just nw. Ext corridors. **Pets:** $15 daily fee/room. Designated rooms, ser-
vice with restrictions, crate. SAVE 🛜 ✕ 🅖🅜 🅗 💻 🏊

AAA ▼▼▼ ▼▼▼ Hotel Vintage Park-A Kimpton Hotel 🅷 🐾
(206) 624-8000. **Call for rates.** 1100 5th Ave 98101. Corner of Spring St
and 5th Ave. Int corridors. **Pets:** Designated rooms.
🄴🄲🄾 🄲🄳 SAVE 🛜 ✕ 🍽 ✕

▼▼▼▼ Inn at Harbor Steps 🅷
(206) 748-0973. **$225-$375, 3 day notice.** 1221 1st Ave 98101. Corner
of Seneca St and 1st Ave. Int corridors. **Pets:** Accepted.
🛜 ✕ 🅗 💻 🏊 ✕

▼▼▼▼ La Quinta Inn & Suites Seattle Downtown 🅷
(206) 624-6820. **$90-$271.** 2224 8th Ave 98121. Corner of 8th Ave and
Blanchard St. Int corridors. **Pets:** Service with restrictions, supervision.
🛜 ✕ 🅗 💻

▼▼▼▼ The Maxwell Hotel 🅷
(206) 286-0629. **$139-$359.** 300 Roy St 98109. Corner of Roy St and
3rd Ave N. Int corridors. **Pets:** Accepted.
🛜 ✕ 🅖🅜 🅗 💻 🍽 🏊

AAA ▼▼▼ ▼▼▼ Pan Pacific Hotel Seattle 🅷
(206) 264-8111. **$179-$550.** 2125 Terry Ave 98121. Just s of jct E Denny
Way. Int corridors. **Pets:** Accepted. SAVE 🛜 ✕ 💻 🍽 ✕

▼▼▼ ▼▼▼ Red Lion Hotel on Fifth Avenue-Seattle 🅷
(206) 971-8000. **$149-$350.** 1415 5th Ave 98101. Between Pike and
Union sts. Int corridors. **Pets:** Other species. $15 one-time fee/room. Ser-
vice with restrictions, crate. 🛜 ✕ 🅗 💻 🍽

AAA ▼▼▼ ▼▼▼ Renaissance Seattle Hotel 🅷
(206) 583-0300. **$160-$246.** 515 Madison St 98104. Corner of Madison
St and 6th Ave. Int corridors. **Pets:** Other species. $100 one-time fee/
room. No service, crate. SAVE 🛜 ✕ 🅖🅜 💻 ✕

▼▼▼ ▼▼▼ Residence Inn by Marriott Seattle Downtown/Lake Union 🅷 🐾
(206) 624-6000. **$139-$309.** 800 Fairview Ave N 98109. I-5 exit 167
(Mercer St), just ne; south end of Lake Union. Int corridors. **Pets:** Other
species. $10 daily fee/pet. Service with restrictions.
🛜 ✕ 🅗 💻 🏊 ✕

AAA ▼▼▼ The Roosevelt, A Coast Hotel 🅷
(206) 621-1200. **$139-$289.** 1531 7th Ave 98101. Corner of 7th Ave and
Pine St. Int corridors. **Pets:** Accepted. SAVE 🛜 ✕ 🅗 💻 🍽

AAA ▼▼▼ ▼▼▼ Sheraton Seattle Hotel 🅷
(206) 621-9000. **$149-$249.** 1400 6th Ave 98101. Between Pike and
Union sts. Int corridors. **Pets:** Accepted.
SAVE 🛜 ✕ 🅖🅜 💻 🍽 🏊 ✕

AAA ▼▼▼ ▼▼▼ Sorrento Hotel 🅷 🐾
(206) 622-6400. **$145-$345.** 900 Madison St 98104. I-5 exit Madison St,
just e; jct 9th Ave. Int corridors. **Pets:** $60 one-time fee/room. Service
with restrictions, crate. SAVE 🛜 ✕ 🅖🅜 💻 🍽

▼▼ ▼▼ University Inn 🅷

(206) 632-5055. **$125-$239.** 4140 Roosevelt Way NE 98105. I-5 exit 169, 0.5 mi e, then just s. Int corridors. **Pets:** Accepted.

🛜 ⊠ 🛆 📖 🍴 ➰

▼▼▼▼ Watertown 🅷

(206) 826-4242. **$139-$239.** 4242 Roosevelt Way NE 98105. I-5 exit 169, just e, then just s. Int corridors. **Pets:** Accepted.

🛜 ⊠ 🄼 🛆 📖

🅰🅰🅰⬧ ▼▼▼▼ The Westin Seattle 🅷

(206) 728-1000. **$169-$399, 3 day notice.** 1900 5th Ave 98101. Corner of 5th Ave and Stewart St. Int corridors. **Pets:** Accepted.

🄴🄲🄾 🅂🄰🅅🄴 🛜 ⊠ 🄼 📖 ➰

🅰🅰🅰⬧ ▼▼▼▼ W Seattle 🅷 🐾

(206) 264-6000. **$199-$559.** 1112 4th Ave 98101. Corner of 4th Ave and Seneca St. Int corridors. **Pets:** Large. $25 daily fee/pet. Service with restrictions, supervision. 🅂🄰🅅🄴 🛜 ⊠ 🄼 🍴

SILVERDALE

🅰🅰🅰⬧ ▼▼▼ Oxford Inn 🅷

(360) 692-7777. **$84-$103.** 9734 NW Silverdale Way 98383. SR 3 exit Newberry Hill Rd, just e, then 1.2 mi n. Int corridors. **Pets:** Accepted.

🅂🄰🅅🄴 🛜 🛆 📖

🅰🅰🅰⬧ ▼▼▼▼ Oxford Suites Silverdale 🅷 🐾

(360) 698-9550. **$116-$170.** 9550 NW Silverdale Way 98383. SR 3 exit Newberry Hill Rd, 1.5 mi e. Int corridors. **Pets:** Medium. $4 daily fee/pet. Service with restrictions, supervision.

🅂🄰🅅🄴 🛜 ⊠ 🄼 🛆 📖 🍴 ➰ ⊠

🅰🅰🅰⬧ ▼▼▼▼ Silverdale Beach Hotel 🅷

(360) 698-1000. **$115-$199.** 3073 NW Bucklin Hill Rd 98383. SR 3 exit Newberry Hill Rd, just e, 1 mi n on Silverdale Way, then just e. Int corridors. **Pets:** Medium. $20 daily fee/pet. Designated rooms, service with restrictions, crate. 🅂🄰🅅🄴 🛜 ⊠ 🛆 📖 🍴 ➰ ⊠

SNOHOMISH

🅰🅰🅰⬧ ▼▼▼ Inn At Snohomish 🅼

(360) 568-2208. **$75-$135.** 323 2nd St 98290. Just e, corner of Pine St. Ext corridors. **Pets:** Other species. $50 deposit/room. Service with restrictions, supervision. 🅂🄰🅅🄴 🛜 🄼 🛆 📖

SNOQUALMIE

▼▼▼▼ Salish Lodge & Spa 🅷 🐾

(425) 888-2556. **$209-$999, 7 day notice.** 6501 Railroad Ave SE 98065. I-90 exit 27 eastbound, 5 mi ne via North Bend Way, Meadowbrook Way and SR 202; exit 31 westbound, 7 mi nw via SR 202. Int corridors. **Pets:** Dogs only. $50 one-time fee/room. Designated rooms, service with restrictions, supervision. 🛜 ⊠ 🛆 📖 🍴 ⊠

SUQUAMISH

▼▼▼▼ Suquamish Clearwater Casino Resort 🅷 🐾

(360) 598-8700. **$79-$249.** 15347 Suquamish Way 98392. SR 3 exit SR 305, 6.2 mi se. Ext/int corridors. **Pets:** $200 deposit/room, $20 daily fee/pet. Service with restrictions, supervision. 🛜 🛆 📖 🍴 ➰ ⊠

TACOMA

🅰🅰🅰⬧ ▼▼▼▼ Hotel Murano 🅷

(253) 238-8000. **$159-$229.** 1320 Broadway Plaza 98402. I-5 exit 133 (City Center) to I-705 N exit A St, just w on 11th St, then just s; downtown. Int corridors. **Pets:** Accepted. 🅂🄰🅅🄴 🛜 ⊠ 🛆 📖 🍴 ⊠

▼▼▼▼ La Quinta Inn & Suites Tacoma Seattle 🅷

(253) 383-0146. **$83-$184.** 1425 E 27th St 98421. I-5 exit 135 southbound; exit 134 northbound, just n. Int corridors. **Pets:** Service with restrictions, supervision. 🛜 🛆 📖 🍴 ➰

▼▼▼▼ Red Lion Hotel Tacoma 🅷

(253) 548-1212. **$109-$149.** 8402 S Hosmer St 98444. I-5 exit 128 northbound, just ne; exit 129 southbound, just e on 72nd St, then 1 mi s. Int corridors. **Pets:** Other species. $15 one-time fee/room. Service with restrictions, crate. 🛜 ⊠ 🛆 📖 ➰

▼▼ ▼▼ Shilo Inn & Suites - Tacoma 🅷

(253) 475-4020. **$89-$209.** 7414 S Hosmer St 98408. I-5 exit 129, just se. Int corridors. **Pets:** Dogs only. $25 one-time fee/room. Designated rooms, service with restrictions, supervision.

🛜 ⊠ 🛆 📖 ➰ ⊠

TUKWILA

▼▼▼▼ Embassy Suites Hotel 🅷

(425) 227-8844. **$129-$219.** 15920 W Valley Hwy 98188. I-405 exit 1 (SR 181), just s. Int corridors. **Pets:** Accepted.

🛜 🛆 📖 🍴 ➰ ⊠

▼▼ ▼▼ Extended StayAmerica-Seattle-Tukwila 🅷

(206) 244-2537. **$65-$80.** 15451 53rd Ave S 98188. I-5 exit 153 northbound, just n on Southcenter Pkwy, just n on 61st St, just w on Southcenter Blvd, then just sw; exit 154B (Southcenter Mall) southbound, just sw. Ext corridors. **Pets:** $25 daily fee/pet. Designated rooms, service with restrictions. 🛜 🛆 📖

🅰🅰🅰⬧ ▼▼▼▼ Homewood Suites by Hilton Seattle Airport - Tukwila 🅷

(206) 433-8000. **$129-$199.** 6955 Fort Dent Way 98188. I-405 exit 1 (SR 181), just ne. Ext/int corridors. **Pets:** Large. $75 one-time fee/room. Service with restrictions. 🅂🄰🅅🄴 🛜 🛆 📖 ➰ ⊠

▼▼ ▼▼ Ramada Limited Sea-Tac Airport 🅷

(206) 244-8800. **$55-$90.** 13900 Tukwila International Blvd 98168. I-5 exit 158 southbound, 2 mi s; exit 154A (SR 518 W) northbound, 1 mi n on SR 99. Int corridors. **Pets:** Accepted. 🛜 🛆 📖

▼▼ ▼▼ Residence Inn by Marriott-Seattle South 🅷

(425) 226-5500. **$109-$209.** 16201 W Valley Hwy 98188. I-405 exit 1 (SR 181), just s. Ext corridors. **Pets:** Accepted.

🛜 ⊠ 🄼 🛆 📖 ➰

VASHON

▼▼ The Swallow's Nest Guest Cottages 🅲🅰 🐾

(206) 463-2646. **$105-$280.** 6030 SW 248th St 98070. North end Ferry Landing, 7.8 mi s on Vashon Hwy; south end (Tahlequah) Ferry Landing, 5.8 mi n on Vashon Hwy, 1.4 mi e on Quartermaster Dr, 1.5 mi s on Dockton Rd, 0.4 mi s on 75th Ave, then 1 mi e. Ext corridors. **Pets:** Other species. $15 daily fee/pet. Designated rooms, service with restrictions, crate. 🛜 ⊠ 🛆 📖 🄶

WOODINVILLE

▼▼▼▼ Willows Lodge 🅷 🐾

(425) 424-3900. **$199-$599, 3 day notice.** 14580 NE 145th St 98072. I-405 exit 20B (NE 124th St), 0.9 mi e, 1.3 mi n on 132nd Ave NE, 0.6 mi e on NE 143rd Pl, then just e. Int corridors. **Pets:** Dogs only. $35 one-time fee/room. Designated rooms, service with restrictions.

🄴 🛜 ⊠ 📖 🍴 ⊠

END METROPOLITAN AREA

SEQUIM

▼▼▼▼ Juan de Fuca Cottages
(360) 683-4433. **$110-$260, 14 day notice.** 182 Marine Dr 98382. 7 mi
n via Sequim Ave and E Anderson Rd; downtown. Ext corridors.
Pets: Medium, dogs only. $20 daily fee/pet. Designated rooms, service
with restrictions, supervision. 🚫 ❌ 🛏 🖥 🧺 💾

▼▼ Quality Inn & Suites - Sequim 🅷
(360) 683-2800. **Call for rates.** 134 River Rd 98382. US 101 exit River
Rd, just nw. Int corridors. **Pets:** Dogs only. $20 daily fee/room. Desig-
nated rooms, service with restrictions, supervision.
Ⓔ🖲 🚫 ❌ 🛏 🖥 🏊

ⒶⒶⒶ ▼▼▼ Sequim West Inn Ⓜ
(360) 683-4144. **$54-$125.** 740 W Washington St 98382. US 101 exit
River Rd, 0.9 mi ne via River Rd and W Washington St. Ext corridors.
Pets: Small. $10 daily fee/pet. Designated rooms, service with restrictions,
supervision. 🆂🅰🆅🅴 🚫 🛏 🖥

SHELTON

ⒶⒶⒶ ▼▼▼▼ Little Creek Casino Resort 🅷 ✿
(360) 427-7711. **$89-$439.** 91 W SR 108 98584. Jct US 101 and SR
108. Int corridors. **Pets:** Small. $50 one-time fee/pet. Designated rooms,
service with restrictions, supervision.
🆂🅰🆅🅴 🚫 🅼 🛏 🖥 🍴 🏊 ❌

▼▼ Super 8 of Shelton 🅷 ✿
(360) 426-1654. **$61-$89.** 2943 Northview Cir 98584. US 101 exit
Wallace-Kneeland Blvd, just se. Int corridors. **Pets:** Dogs only. $15 daily
fee/pet. Designated rooms, supervision. 🚫 🛏 🖥

SNOQUALMIE PASS

▼▼ Summit Inn 🅷
(425) 434-6300. **$89-$159, 3 day notice.** 603 SR 906 98068. I-90 exit
52 eastbound, 0.3 mi e; exit 53 westbound, 0.3 mi w. Int corridors.
Pets: Small. $25 one-time fee/pet. Designated rooms, no service, supervi-
sion. 🚫 ❌ 🛏 🖥 🍴 🏊 ❌

SOAP LAKE

▼▼ Inn at Soap Lake Ⓜ
(509) 246-1132. **$59-$135.** 226 E Main Ave 98851. Just w of SR 17.
Ext/int corridors. **Pets:** Other species. $5 daily fee/pet. Designated rooms,
service with restrictions, supervision. 🚫 ❌ 🛏 🖥 ❌

▼▼ Notaras Lodge Ⓜ
(509) 246-0462. **$85-$145.** 236 E Main Ave 98851. Just w of SR 17. Ext
corridors. **Pets:** Accepted. 🚫 ❌ 🛏 🖥

SPOKANE

ⒶⒶⒶ ▼▼▼ Apple Tree Inn Ⓜ
(509) 466-3020. **$44-$79.** 9508 N Division St 99218. Jct US 2 and 395,
just n. Ext/int corridors. **Pets:** Small, dogs only. $10 daily fee/pet. Desig-
nated rooms, supervision. 🆂🅰🆅🅴 🚫 🛏 🏊

**ⒶⒶⒶ ▼▼▼▼ BEST WESTERN PLUS Peppertree Airport
Inn** 🅷 ✿
(509) 624-4655. **$90-$200.** 3711 S Geiger Blvd 99224. I-90 exit 276
(Geiger Field), 1.3 mi n, 0.8 mi s, 0.4 mi e, then just s. Int corridors.
Pets: Dogs only. Supervision. 🆂🅰🆅🅴 🚫 ❌ 🅼 🛏 🖥 🏊 ❌

▼▼▼ Comfort Inn North 🅷
(509) 467-7111. **Call for rates.** 7111 N Division St 99208. I-90 exit 281
(Division St), 4.6 mi n. Int corridors. **Pets:** Accepted.
🚫 🛏 🖥 🏊 ❌

**ⒶⒶⒶ ▼▼▼ ▼▼ The Davenport Hotel and
Tower** 🅷 ✿
(509) 455-8888. **$126-$300.** 10 S Post St 99201. Downtown. Int corridors. **Pets:** Dogs only. $30 daily fee/pet. Designated rooms, supervision.
ⒺⒸⓄ 🆂🅰🆅🅴 🚫 ❌ 🅼 🛏 🖥 🍴 🏊 ❌

**ⒶⒶⒶ ▼▼▼ ▼▼ DoubleTree by Hilton Spokane City
Center** 🅷 ✿
(509) 455-9600. **$114-$236.** 322 N Spokane Falls Ct 99201. I-90 exit
281 (Division St), just n; downtown. Int corridors. **Pets:** Large, other species. $50 one-time fee/room. Service with restrictions, supervision.
🆂🅰🆅🅴 🚫 ❌ 🛏 🖥 🍴 🏊 ❌

▼▼▼ Fairbridge Inn Express 🅷
(509) 838-6630. **$70-$100.** 211 S Division St 99202. I-90 exit 281 (Division St), just n. Int corridors. **Pets:** Medium, other species. $25 one-time
fee/pet. Service with restrictions, crate. 🚫 🛏 🖥

▼▼▼ Holiday Inn Express-Downtown 🅷
(509) 328-8505. **$140-$195.** 801 N Division St 99202. I-90 exit 281 (Division St), 0.8 mi n. Ext/int corridors. **Pets:** Dogs only. Designated rooms,
service with restrictions, supervision. 🚫 ❌ 🅼 🛏 🖥

▼▼▼ Holiday Inn Spokane Airport 🅷
(509) 838-1170. **Call for rates.** 1616 S Windsor Dr 99224. I-90 exit 277
westbound; exit 277B eastbound, just w on US 2, then just s. Int corridors. **Pets:** Medium. $50 deposit/pet. Service with restrictions, supervision.
🚫 ❌ 🅼 🛏 🖥 🍴 🏊

▼▼▼ Howard Johnson Inn North Ⓜ
(509) 326-5500. **$49-$159.** 3033 N Division St 99207. I-90 exit 281 (Division St), 2.3 mi n on US 2 and 395. Int corridors. **Pets:** Medium. $150
deposit/room. Designated rooms, service with restrictions, supervision.
🚫 ❌ 🛏 🖥 🏊

ⒶⒶⒶ ▼▼▼ ▼▼ The Madison Inn by Riversage 🅷
(509) 474-4200. **$78-$95.** 15 W Rockwood Blvd 99204. I-90 exit 281
(Division St) eastbound, just e to Cowley St, 0.4 mi s, then just w; exit
westbound, just n to 2nd Ave, just w to Browne St, 0.5 mi s to 9th Ave,
then just e. Int corridors. **Pets:** Other species. $10 daily fee/pet. Desig-
nated rooms, service with restrictions, supervision.
🆂🅰🆅🅴 🚫 ❌ 🛏 🖥

ⒶⒶⒶ ▼▼▼ ▼▼ Montvale Hotel 🅷
(509) 747-1919. **$119-$180.** 1005 W First Ave 99201. At Monroe St;
downtown. Int corridors. **Pets:** Accepted. 🆂🅰🆅🅴 🚫 ❌ 🅼 🍴

ⒶⒶⒶ ▼▼▼ ▼▼ Oxford Suites-Downtown Spokane 🅷
(509) 353-9000. **$117-$158.** 115 W North River Dr 99201. I-90 exit 281
(Division St), 1 mi n, then just n. Int corridors. **Pets:** Accepted.
🆂🅰🆅🅴 🚫 ❌ 🛏 🖥 🍴 🏊 ❌

ⒶⒶⒶ ▼▼ Quality Inn Oakwood 🅷 ✿
(509) 467-4900. **$79-$94.** 7919 N Division St 99208. I-90 exit 281 (Division St), 6.5 mi n. Int corridors. **Pets:** Medium. $30 one-time fee/room.
Designated rooms, service with restrictions, crate.
🆂🅰🆅🅴 🚫 🅼 🛏 🖥 🏊

**▼▼▼ Ramada Spokane Airport & Indoor
Waterpark** 🅷 ✿
(509) 838-5211. **$120-$155.** 8909 Airport Dr 99224. I-90 exit 277B eastbound; exit 277 westbound, 3.4 mi n. Int corridors. **Pets:** $10 daily fee/
pet. Service with restrictions, supervision.
🚫 ❌ 🛏 🖥 🍴 🏊 ❌

▼▼▼ Red Lion Hotel at the Park-Spokane 🅷
(509) 326-8000. **$99-$249.** 303 W North River Dr 99201. I-90 exit 281
(Division St), 1.5 mi n on US 195, then just w. Int corridors. **Pets:** Other
species. $15 one-time fee/room. Service with restrictions, crate.
🚫 ❌ 🛏 🖥 🍴 🏊 ❌

WWW Red Lion River Inn-Spokane H
(509) 326-5577. **Call for rates.** 700 N Division St 99202. I-90 exit 281 (Division St), 0.8 mi n; downtown. Int corridors. **Pets:** Other species. $15 one-time fee/room. Service with restrictions, crate.
🛜 ✕ ᗜᴹ 🛏 🖥 🍽 ➳ ✕

AAA WWW Super 8 Airport West M
(509) 838-8800. **$65-$155.** 11102 W Westbow Blvd 99224. I-90 exit 272 (Medical Lake Rd), just s. Int corridors. **Pets:** Other species. $15 one-time fee/room. Designated rooms, service with restrictions, crate.
SAVE 🛜 ᗜᴹ 🛏 🖥 ➳

WWW Travelodge Spokane at the Convention Center H ❀
(509) 623-9727. **$89-$180.** W 33 Spokane Falls Blvd 99201. I-90 exit 281 (Division St), 0.5 mi n, then just w. Int corridors. **Pets:** Dogs only. $12 daily fee/room. Designated rooms, service with restrictions.
🛜 ✕ ᗜᴹ 🛏 🖥

WWW Wingate by Wyndham Spokane Airport H
(509) 838-3226. **$127-$140.** 2726 S Flint Rd 99201. I-90 exit 277B eastbound; exit 277 westbound, 3 mi w, then just s. Int corridors. **Pets:** $10 one-time fee/room. Designated rooms, service with restrictions, supervision. 🛜 ✕ ᗜᴹ 🛏 🖥 ➳ ✕

SPOKANE VALLEY

AAA WWW Comfort Inn & Suites at Pheasant Hill H ❀
(509) 926-7432. **$80-$190.** 12415 E Mission Ave 99216. I-90 exit 289 (N Pines Rd), just se. Int corridors. **Pets:** Other species. $20 one-time fee/room. Designated rooms, supervision.
SAVE 🛜 ✕ ᗜᴹ 🛏 🖥 ➳

WWWW Holiday Inn Express-Valley H ❀
(509) 927-7100. **$119-$189.** 9220 E Mission Ave 99206. I-90 exit 287, just s. Ext/int corridors. **Pets:** Other species. Designated rooms, service with restrictions, supervision. 🛜 ᗜᴹ 🛏 🖥 ➳

WWWW La Quinta Inn & Suites Spokane H
(509) 893-0955. **$71-$162.** 3808 N Sullivan Rd 99216. I-90 exit 291B, 1.3 mi n. Int corridors. **Pets:** Service with restrictions, supervision.
🛜 ✕ ᗜᴹ 🛏 🖥 ➳

WWWW Mirabeau Park Hotel & Convention Center H
(509) 924-9000. **$90-$150.** 1100 N Sullivan Rd 99037. I-90 exit 291B, just s. Int corridors. **Pets:** $25 one-time fee/room. Designated rooms, service with restrictions, supervision. 🛜 🛏 🖥 ➳ ✕

AAA WWWW Oxford Suites Spokane Valley H ❀
(509) 847-1000. **$115-$199.** 15015 E Indiana Ave 99216. I-90 exit 291A eastbound; exit 291B westbound, just nw. Int corridors. **Pets:** Medium. $25 one-time fee/room. Designated rooms, service with restrictions, supervision. SAVE 🛜 ᗜᴹ 🛏 🖥 🍽 ➳ ✕

WWWW Quality Inn Valley Suites H
(509) 928-5218. **$110-$190.** 8923 E Mission Ave 99212. I-90 exit 287. Int corridors. **Pets:** Accepted. 🛜 ✕ ᗜᴹ 🛏 🖥 ➳ ✕

AAA WWWW Residence Inn by Marriott H
(509) 892-9300. **$149-$199.** 15915 E Indiana Ave 99216. I-90 exit 291 westbound, just e; exit 291B eastbound, just n, then just e. Int corridors. **Pets:** Medium, other species. $25 daily fee/room. Designated rooms, service with restrictions, supervision.
SAVE 🛜 ✕ ᗜᴹ 🛏 🖥 ➳ ✕

WWW Rodeway Inn & Suites H
(509) 535-7185. **$50-$80, 7 day notice.** 6309 E Broadway 99212. I-90 exit 286, just w. Ext/int corridors. **Pets:** Medium. $10 daily fee/pet. Designated rooms, service with restrictions, supervision. 🛜 🛏 🖥 ➳

AAA WWW Super 8 M
(509) 928-4888. **$55-$136.** 2020 N Argonne Rd 99212. I-90 exit 287, just n. Int corridors. **Pets:** Other species. $25 deposit/room, $15 one-time fee/room. Designated rooms, service with restrictions, supervision.
SAVE 🛜 🛏 🖥 ➳

STEVENSON

AAA WWW Skamania Lodge H
(509) 427-7700. **$159-$299, 5 day notice.** 1131 SW Skamania Lodge Way 98648. 1 mi w on SR 14, just n on Rock Creek Dr, then just w. Int corridors. **Pets:** Accepted. SAVE 🛜 ✕ 🛏 🖥 🍽 ➳ ✕

SULTAN

AAA W Dutch Cup Motel M
(360) 793-2215. **$74-$90, 3 day notice.** 819 Main St 98294. Jct US 2 and Main St. Ext corridors. **Pets:** Large, other species. $9 daily fee/room. Designated rooms, service with restrictions, supervision.
SAVE 🛜 🛏 🖥

SUNNYSIDE

AAA WWWW BEST WESTERN PLUS Grapevine Inn H ❀
(509) 839-6070. **$100-$150.** 1849 Quail Ln 98944. I-82 exit 69, just n, then just w. Int corridors. **Pets:** Dogs only. $20 one-time fee/room. Designated rooms, supervision. SAVE 🛜 ✕ ᗜᴹ 🛏 🖥 ➳

TOPPENISH

AAA WWW Quality Inn & Suites H
(509) 865-5800. **$80-$85.** 511 S Elm St 98948. I-82 exit 50, 3.2 mi e. Int corridors. **Pets:** Dogs only. $10 daily fee/pet. Designated rooms, service with restrictions, supervision. SAVE 🛜 ᗜᴹ 🛏 🖥

TUMWATER

WWW Comfort Inn Conference Center H ❀
(360) 352-0691. **$79-$149.** 1620 74th Ave SW 98501. I-5 exit 101, just se. Int corridors. **Pets:** Large, other species. $15 daily fee/pet. Service with restrictions, crate. 🛜 ✕ 🛏 🖥 ➳

WWW Extended StayAmerica - Olympia/Tumwater H
(360) 754-6063. **$80-$90.** 1675 Mottman Rd SW 98512. I-5 exit 104, 0.4 mi nw on US 101, just s on Crosby Blvd, then just se. Int corridors. **Pets:** $25 daily fee/pet. Designated rooms, service with restrictions.
🛜 🛏 🖥

WWW GuestHouse Inn & Suites H ❀
(360) 943-5040. **$79-$139.** 1600 74th Ave SW 98501. I-5 exit 101, just se. Int corridors. **Pets:** Other species. $15 daily fee/pet. Service with restrictions, crate. 🛜 ᗜᴹ 🛏 🖥 ➳

UNION

WWWW Alderbrook Resort & Spa H
(360) 898-2200. **$149-$629, 7 day notice.** 7101 E SR 106 98592. Just e of town. Ext/int corridors. **Pets:** Accepted.
🛜 ✕ 🛏 🖥 🍽 ➳ ✕

UNION GAP

AAA WWWW BEST WESTERN PLUS Ahtanum Inn H
(509) 248-9700. **$80-$140.** 2408 Rudkin Rd 98903. I-82 exit 36, just n. Int corridors. **Pets:** Medium, dogs only. $10 daily fee/pet. Supervision.
SAVE 🛜 ᗜᴹ 🛏 🖥 ✕

WWW Quality Inn-Yakima Valley M
(509) 248-6924. **Call for rates.** 12 E Valley Mall Blvd 98903. I-82 exit 36, just s. Ext corridors. **Pets:** Accepted. 🛜 ᗜᴹ 🛏 🖥 ➳

▼▼ ◊ Super 8 Yakima 🄷
(509) 248-8880. **$71-$86.** 2605 Rudkin Rd 98903. I-82 exit 36, just s. Int corridors. **Pets:** Other species. $10 daily fee/room. Service with restrictions, supervision. 🛜 ⅏ 🛗 📺 ⊳

WALLA WALLA
◊◊◊ ▼ Americas Best Value Inn Ⓜ
(509) 529-4410. **$56-$141.** 305 N 2nd Ave 99362. US 12 exit 2nd Ave, 0.3 mi s. Ext corridors. **Pets:** Medium. $10 daily fee/pet. Designated rooms, service with restrictions, supervision. 🆂🅰🆅🅴 🛜 ✕ ⅏ 🛗

◊◊◊ ▼▼▼ BEST WESTERN PLUS Walla Walla Suites Inn 🄷
(509) 525-4700. **$95-$149.** 7 E Oak St 99362. US 12 exit 2nd Ave, just s. Int corridors. **Pets:** Dogs only. $10 daily fee/pet. Service with restrictions. 🆂🅰🆅🅴 🛜 ✕ ⅏ 🛗 📺 ⊳

▼▼▼▼ Comfort Inn & Suites 🄷
(509) 522-3500. **Call for rates.** 1419 W Pine St 99362. US 12 exit Pendleton/Prescott. Int corridors. **Pets:** Small, dogs only. $15 daily fee/pet. Designated rooms, service with restrictions, supervision. 🛜 ✕ 🛗 📺 🍴 ⊳

▼▼▼▼ Holiday Inn Express 🄷
(509) 525-6200. **$99-$139, 3 day notice.** 1433 W Pine St 99362. US 12 exit Pendleton/Prescott. Int corridors. **Pets:** Other species. $20 daily fee/pet. Designated rooms, crate. 🛜 ✕ 🛗 📺 ⊳ ✕

▼▼ ▼▼ La Quinta Inn Walla Walla 🄷
(509) 525-2522. **$66-$199.** 520 N 2nd Ave 99362. US 12 exit 2nd Ave, 0.3 mi s. Int corridors. **Pets:** Service with restrictions, supervision. 🛜 ✕ 🛗 📺 ⊳

◊◊◊ ▼▼▼▼ Marcus Whitman Hotel & Conference Center 🄷
(509) 525-2200. **$119-$299.** 6 W Rose St 99362. Corner of N 2nd Ave and W Rose St. Int corridors. **Pets:** $25 daily fee/room. Designated rooms, supervision. 🆂🅰🆅🅴 🛜 ✕ 🛗 📺 🍴

▼▼ ▼▼ Super 8 Walla Walla 🄷
(509) 525-8800. **$70-$85.** 2315 Eastgate St N 99362. US 12 exit Wilbur Ave, just se. Int corridors. **Pets:** Accepted. 🛜 ⅏ 🛗 ⊳

WENATCHEE
◊◊◊ ▼ Avenue Motel Ⓜ
(509) 663-7161. **$45-$125.** 720 N Wenatchee Ave 98801. On US 2 business loop; just nw of downtown. Ext/int corridors. **Pets:** Accepted. 🆂🅰🆅🅴 🛜 🛗 📺 ⊳

◊◊◊ ▼▼▼ Coast Wenatchee Center Hotel 🄷 ❀
(509) 662-1234. **$79-$165.** 201 N Wenatchee Ave 98801. Jct 2nd St; downtown. Int corridors. **Pets:** Other species. $10 one-time fee/room. Designated rooms, service with restrictions, supervision. 🆂🅰🆅🅴 🛜 🛗 📺 🍴 ⊳

◊◊◊ ▼▼▼ Comfort Inn Downtown 🄷
(509) 662-1700. **Call for rates.** 815 N Wenatchee Ave 98801. Downtown. Int corridors. **Pets:** Large, other species. $20 daily fee/pet. Designated rooms, service with restrictions, supervision. 🆂🅰🆅🅴 🛜 🛗 📺 ⊳ ✕

▼ Econo Lodge Ⓜ
(509) 663-7121. **Call for rates.** 232 N Wenatchee Ave 98801. Downtown. Ext corridors. **Pets:** Medium, dogs only. $10 daily fee/pet. Service with restrictions, supervision. 🛜 🛗 📺 ⊳

▼▼▼ Holiday Inn Express 🄷
(509) 663-6355. **$109-$169.** 1921 N Wenatchee Ave 98801. Northwest side of town. Int corridors. **Pets:** Medium, other species. Service with restrictions, supervision. 🛜 ✕ ⅏ 🛗 📺 ⊳

▼▼▼ La Quinta Inn & Suites Wenatchee 🄷
(509) 664-6565. **$65-$188.** 1905 N Wenatchee Ave 98801. Northwest side of town. Int corridors. **Pets:** Service with restrictions, supervision. 🛜 ✕ ⅏ 🛗 📺 ⊳ ✕

◊◊◊ ▼▼▼ Red Lion Hotel Wenatchee 🄷
(509) 663-0711. **$89-$199.** 1225 N Wenatchee Ave 98801. Just nw of downtown. Int corridors. **Pets:** Other species. $15 one-time fee/room. Service with restrictions, crate. 🆂🅰🆅🅴 🛜 ✕ 🛗 📺 🍴 ⊳

◊◊◊ ▼▼▼ Super 8 Wenatchee 🄷
(509) 662-3443. **$55-$125.** 1401 N Miller St 98801. 1.5 mi n on US 2. Int corridors. **Pets:** Dogs only. $50 deposit/pet, $10 daily fee/pet. Designated rooms, service with restrictions, supervision. 🆂🅰🆅🅴 🛜 🛗 📺 ⊳

◊◊◊ ▼▼▼ Travelodge-Wenatchee Ⓜ
(509) 662-8165. **$53-$110.** 1004 N Wenatchee Ave 98801. Downtown. Ext corridors. **Pets:** Accepted. 🆂🅰🆅🅴 🛜 ⅏ 🛗 📺 ⊳

WESTPORT
◊◊◊ ▼▼▼ Chateau Westport Resort 🄷 ❀
(360) 268-9101. **$99-$299.** 710 W Hancock St 98595. Just w of SR 105 Spur N; 1.5 mi n of Twin Harbors State Park. Int corridors. **Pets:** Medium, dogs only. $20 daily fee/pet. Designated rooms, service with restrictions, supervision. 🆂🅰🆅🅴 🛜 ✕ 🛗 📺 ⊳ ✕ 🄰🄲

WINTHROP
▼▼ River Run Inn Ⓜ
(509) 996-2173. **$75-$165, 10 day notice.** 27 Rader Rd 98862. 0.5 mi w on SR 20. Ext corridors. **Pets:** $15 daily fee/pet. Designated rooms, service with restrictions, supervision. 🛜 ✕ ⅏ 🛗 📺 ⊳ ✕

◊◊◊ ▼▼ Winthrop Inn Ⓜ ❀
(509) 996-2217. **$70-$135, 7 day notice.** 960 Hwy 20 98862. 0.9 mi e. Int corridors. **Pets:** Large, dogs only. Supervision. 🆂🅰🆅🅴 🛜 ✕ 🛗 ⊳ ✕

WOODLAND
◊◊◊ ▼▼ Lewis River Inn Ⓜ
(360) 225-6257. **$73-$110.** 1100 Lewis River Rd 98674. I-5 exit 21, just e. Ext corridors. **Pets:** $20 daily fee/pet. Designated rooms, no service, supervision. 🆂🅰🆅🅴 🛜 🛗 📺

YAKIMA
◊◊◊ ▼▼▼ BEST WESTERN PLUS Lincoln Inn 🄷 ❀
(509) 453-8898. **$89-$199.** 1614 N 1st St 98901. I-82 exit 31, just s. Int corridors. **Pets:** Large, dogs only. $20 daily fee/room. Designated rooms, service with restrictions, supervision. 🆂🅰🆅🅴 🛜 ✕ ⅏ 🛗 📺 ⊳

▼▼▼ Birchfield Manor Country Inn 🄲🄸
(509) 452-1960. **$119-$219, 14 day notice.** 2018 Birchfield Rd 98901. I-82 exit 34, 2 mi e to Birchfield Rd, then just s. Int corridors. **Pets:** Designated rooms, service with restrictions, crate. 🛜 ✕ ⅏ 🛗 📺 🍴 ⊳ 🄕

◊◊◊ ▼▼▼ Comfort Suites 🄷
(509) 249-1900. **$89-$199.** 3702 Fruitvale Blvd 98902. US 12 exit 40th Ave, just s. Int corridors. **Pets:** Small, dogs only. $20 daily fee/pet. Designated rooms, service with restrictions, supervision. 🆂🅰🆅🅴 🛜 ✕ ⅏ 🛗 📺 ⊳

◊◊◊ ▼▼▼▼ Fairfield Inn & Suites by Marriott 🄷
(509) 452-3100. **$115-$159.** 137 N Fair Ave 98901. I-82 exit 33A eastbound, just s; exit 33 westbound, just w to 9th St, just n to B St, then just e. Int corridors. **Pets:** Accepted. 🆂🅰🆅🅴 🛜 ✕ ⅏ 🛗 📺 ⊳

♦♦♦ ♦♦♦ GuestHouse Inn Yakima M
(509) 452-8101. **$59-$109.** 1010 E A St 98901. I-82 exit 33B eastbound; exit 33 westbound, just w to 9th St, just n to A St, then just e. Ext corridors. **Pets:** Dogs only. $10 daily fee/pet. Designated rooms, service with restrictions, supervision. [SAVE] 📶 🛁

♦♦♦♦ Holiday Inn Downtown Yakima H ❄
(509) 494-7000. **$115-$139.** 802 E Yakima Ave 98901. I-82 exit 33 westbound; exit 33B eastbound, 0.7 mi w. Int corridors. **Pets:** Other species. $20 one-time fee/room. Designated rooms, service with restrictions, supervision. 📶 ✕ ⓜ 🛁 💻 🍴 🏊

♦♦♦ ♦♦♦♦ Holiday Inn Express Yakima H
(509) 249-1000. **$119-$169.** 1001 East A St 98901. I-82 exit 33B eastbound; exit 33 westbound, just w to 9th St, just n to A St, then just e. Int corridors. **Pets:** Medium. $20 daily fee/room. Designated rooms, service with restrictions, crate. [SAVE] 📶 ✕ ⓜ 🛁 💻 🏊

♦♦♦♦ Howard Johnson Plaza Yakima H
(509) 452-6511. **$79-$149.** 9 N 9th St 98901. I-82 exit 33 westbound; exit 33B eastbound, just s. Int corridors. **Pets:** Accepted.
📶 ✕ ⓜ 🛁 💻 🏊

♦♦♦ ♦♦♦ Oxford Inn H ❄
(509) 457-4444. **$79-$99.** 1603 E Yakima Ave 98901. I-82 exit 33 westbound, just e; exit 33B eastbound. Int corridors. **Pets:** Medium. $25 one-time fee/pet. Designated rooms, service with restrictions, supervision.
[SAVE] 📶 ⓜ 🛁 💻 🏊 ✕

♦♦♦ ♦♦♦ Oxford Suites H ❄
(509) 457-9000. **$99-$129.** 1701 E Yakima Ave 98901. I-82 exit 33 westbound; exit 33B eastbound. Int corridors. **Pets:** Medium. $25 one-time fee/room. Service with restrictions, supervision.
[SAVE] 📶 ⓜ 🛁 💻 🏊 ✕

♦♦♦ ♦♦♦♦ Red Lion Hotel Yakima Center H
(509) 248-5900. **$94-$123, 3 day notice.** 607 E Yakima Ave 98901. I-82 exit 33 westbound; exit 33B eastbound, 0.8 mi w. Ext/int corridors. **Pets:** Other species. $15 one-time fee/room. Service with restrictions, crate. [SAVE] 📶 ✕ 🛁 💻 🍴 🏊

ZILLAH

♦♦♦ ♦♦♦ Comfort Inn H ❄
(509) 829-3399. **$94-$125.** 911 Vintage Valley Pkwy 98953. I-82 exit 52, just n. Int corridors. **Pets:** Other species. $10 daily fee/pet. Service with restrictions, crate. 📶 ✕ ⓜ 🛁 💻 🏊 ✕

WEST VIRGINIA

CITY INDEX

BARBOURSVILLE

♦♦♦ ♦♦♦ BEST WESTERN Huntington Mall Inn M
(304) 736-9772. **$79-$99.** 3441 US 60 E 25504. I-64 exit 20A eastbound; exit 20 westbound, 0.3 mi s. Int corridors. **Pets:** Medium. $25 one-time fee/room. Designated rooms, service with restrictions, supervision.
[SAVE] 📶 🛁 💻 🏊

♦♦♦♦ Comfort Inn by Choice Hotels H
(304) 733-2122. **$84-$120.** 249 Mall Rd 25504. I-64 exit 20, 0.4 mi n. Int corridors. **Pets:** Accepted. 📶 ⓜ 🛁 💻 🏊

BECKLEY

♦♦♦ ♦♦♦ Americas Best Value Inn M
(304) 252-0671. **$59-$110.** 1939 Harper Rd 25801. I-64/77 exit 44, just e on SR 3. Ext/int corridors. **Pets:** Other species. $7 daily fee/pet. Service with restrictions, supervision. [SAVE] 📶 💻

♦♦♦♦ Country Inn & Suites By Carlson H
(304) 252-5100. **$99-$199.** 2120 Harper Rd 25801. I-64/77 exit 44, just w on SR 3. Int corridors. **Pets:** Other species. $30 one-time fee/room. Designated rooms, service with restrictions, supervision.
📶 ⓜ 🛁 💻 🏊 ✕

♦♦♦ ♦♦♦ Econo Lodge M ❄
(304) 255-2161. **$59-$129.** 1909 Harper Rd 25801. I-64/77 exit 44, 0.3 mi e on SR 3. Ext/int corridors. **Pets:** Other species. Service with restrictions. [SAVE] 📶 🛁 💻

♦♦♦ ♦♦♦♦ Fairfield Inn & Suites by Marriott H
(304) 252-8661. **$89-$199.** 125 Hylton Ln 25801. I-64/77 exit 44, just e. Int corridors. **Pets:** Medium. $30 one-time fee/room. Designated rooms, service with restrictions, supervision. [SAVE] 📶 ✕ 🛁 💻 🏊

♦♦♦ ♦♦♦ Microtel Inn by Wyndham Beckley M
(304) 256-2000. **$70-$105, 3 day notice.** 2130 Harper Rd 25801. I-64/77 exit 44, just w. Int corridors. **Pets:** Small. $10 daily fee/pet. Designated rooms, service with restrictions, supervision. [SAVE] 📶 🛁 💻

♦♦♦ ♦♦♦ Super 8 M
(304) 253-0802. **$63-$105.** 2014 Harper Rd 25801. I-64/77 exit 44, just e. Int corridors. **Pets:** Medium. $15 one-time fee/room. Designated rooms, service with restrictions, crate. [SAVE] 📶 🛁 💻

BRADLEY

♦♦♦ ♦♦♦ Days Inn M
(304) 877-6455. **$69-$79.** 127 Ontario Dr 25880. I-64/77 exit 48, 1 mi ne on US 19. Int corridors. **Pets:** Small, dogs only. $15 one-time fee/pet. Designated rooms, service with restrictions, supervision.
[SAVE] 📶 🛁 💻 🏊

BRIDGEPORT

♦♦♦ ♦♦♦♦ BEST WESTERN Bridgeport Inn H
(304) 842-5411. **$120-$169.** 100 Lodgeville Rd 26330. I-79 exit 119, just e on US 50. Int corridors. **Pets:** Other species. $25 daily fee/pet. Service with restrictions, crate. [SAVE] 📶 🛁 💻 🍴 🏊

♦♦♦♦ Sleep Inn M
(304) 842-1919. **$80-$89.** 115 Tolley Dr 26330. I-79 exit 119, just e on US 50. Int corridors. **Pets:** Accepted. 📶 ✕ 🛁 💻

♦♦♦♦ TownePlace Suites by Marriott - Bridgeport Clarksburg H
(304) 842-3600. **$143-$229.** 101 Platinum Dr 26330. I-79 exit 119, just w on US 50. Int corridors. **Pets:** Medium. $100 one-time fee/room. Service with restrictions, supervision. 📶 ✕ ⓜ 🛁 💻 🏊

BRUCETON MILLS

▼▼ Microtel Inn & Suites by Wyndham Hazelton **M**
(304) 379-7900. **$74-$125.** 886 Casteel Rd 26525. I-68 exit 29 (Hazelton), just n. Int corridors. **Pets:** Accepted. 📶 ✕ 🛏 💻

CHARLESTON

🔷 ▼▼▼ BEST WESTERN Charleston Plaza
     Hotel **H**
(304) 345-9779. **Call for rates.** 1010 Washington St E 25301. I-64/77 exit 100, 0.3 mi w. Int corridors. **Pets:** $25 daily fee/room. Designated rooms, service with restrictions. SAVE 📶 🛏 💻 ➿

🔷 ▼▼▼ Charleston Residence Inn by Marriott **H**
(304) 345-4200. **$107-$134.** 200 Hotel Cir 25311. I-64/77 exit 99, just e. Int corridors. **Pets:** $75 one-time fee/room. Service with restrictions.
SAVE 📶 ✕ 🛏 💻 ➿ ✕

▼▼▼ Holiday Inn Express Charleston-Kanawha City **H**
(304) 925-1171. **Call for rates.** 107 Alex Ln 25304. I-77 exit 95, just s on SR 61. Int corridors. **Pets:** Accepted. 📶 ✕ 🛏 💻 ➿

🔷 ▼▼▼ Red Roof Inn-Kanawha City **M**
(304) 925-6953. **$56-$89.** 6305 SE MacCorkle Ave 25304. I-77 exit 95, just s on SR 61. Ext corridors. **Pets:** Large, other species. Service with restrictions, supervision. SAVE 📶 🛏

COMFORT

▼▼ Oak Tree Inn **M**
(304) 837-3377. **$70-$80.** 129 Deanna Ave 25049. 1 mi s on SR 3; entrance at V-Mart. Int corridors. **Pets:** Accepted.
📶 ✕ 🛏 💻 🎿 🐾 🐕

CROSS LANES

▼▼ Comfort Inn Charleston West **M**
(304) 776-8070. **$99-$119.** 102 Racer Dr 25313. I-64 exit 47, just s. Int corridors. **Pets:** Accepted. 📶 🛏 💻 ➿

DANIELS

🔷 ▼▼▼ The Resort at Glade Springs **H**
(304) 763-2000. **$152-$442, 7 day notice.** 255 Resort Dr 25832. I-64 exit 125, 1.5 mi w on SR 307, then 2.8 mi w on US 19. Ext/int corridors.
Pets: Accepted. SAVE 📶 🛏 💻 🍴 ➿ ✕

DAVIS

▼▼▼ Black Bear Resort **CA**
(304) 866-4391. **$100-$560.** Cortland Rd, Canaan Valley 26260. 4.5 mi s on SR 32. Ext corridors. **Pets:** $50 one-time fee/pet. Designated rooms, no service, supervision. 📶 🛏 💻 ➿ ✕

DUNBAR

▼ Dunbar Super 8 **M**
(304) 768-6888. **$64-$76.** 911 Dunbar Ave 25064. I-64 exit 53, just w. Int corridors. **Pets:** Medium. $10 daily fee/pet. Service with restrictions, supervision. 📶 🛏 💻

EDRAY

🔷 ▼▼ Marlinton Motor Inn **M**
(304) 799-4711. **$65-$140, 3 day notice.** US 219 N 24954. Center. Ext corridors. **Pets:** Small, dogs only. $15 daily fee/pet. Designated rooms, service with restrictions, supervision. SAVE 📶 🛏 💻 🍴 ➿

ELKVIEW

▼▼▼ Country Inn & Suites By Carlson, Charleston
     North **H**
(304) 965-9200. **Call for rates.** 101 The Crossings Shopping Center 25071. I-79 exit 9, just e. Int corridors. **Pets:** Accepted.
📶 🛏 💻 ➿

FAIRMONT

🔷 ▼▼▼ Clarion Inn Fairmont **H**
(304) 366-5500. **$120-$225.** 930 E Grafton Rd 26554. I-79 exit 137, just e. Int corridors. **Pets:** Medium, other species. $10 one-time fee/room, $5 daily fee/room. Service with restrictions, crate.
SAVE 📶 ♿ 🛏 💻 🍴 ➿

▼▼ Super 8 **M**
(304) 363-1488. **$64-$125.** 2208 Pleasant Valley Rd 26554. I-79 exit 133, just e. Int corridors. **Pets:** Accepted. 📶 ♿ 🛏 💻

FALLING WATERS

▼▼▼ Holiday Inn Express Martinsburg North **H**
(304) 274-6100. **Call for rates.** 1220 TJ Jackson Dr 25419. I-81 exit 20, just w. Int corridors. **Pets:** Accepted. 📶 🛏 💻 ➿

FROST

▼▼▼ The Inn at Mountain Quest **CI**
(304) 799-7267. **Call for rates.** Rt 92 Frost 24954. On SR 92, 0.4 mi n. Ext corridors. **Pets:** Other species. $20 daily fee/pet. 📶 ✕ ✕

GASSAWAY

▼▼ Microtel Inn & Suites by Wyndham
     Gassaway/Sutton **M**
(304) 364-6100. **$66-$87.** 115 Reston Pl 26624. I-79 exit 62, just w. Int corridors. **Pets:** Dogs only. $20 daily fee/pet. Designated rooms, service with restrictions, supervision. 📶 🛏 💻

HARPERS FERRY

▼▼ Quality Hotel Conference Center **H**
(304) 535-6302. **$89-$105.** 4328 William L Wilson Frwy 25425. Just w on US 340. Int corridors. **Pets:** Accepted. 📶 🛏 💻 🍴 ➿

HUNTINGTON

▼▼▼ Ramada Limited and Conference Center **H**
(304) 523-4242. **$97-$150.** 3094 16th Street Rd 25701. I-64 exit 11, just n. Int corridors. **Pets:** Accepted. 📶 🛏 💻 ➿ ✕

▼▼ Super 8 **H**
(304) 525-1410. **$83-$120.** 3090 16th Street Rd 25701. I-64 exit 11, just n. Int corridors. **Pets:** Other species. $20 daily fee/room. Designated rooms, service with restrictions, crate. 📶 🛏 💻 ➿ ✕

▼▼▼ TownePlace Suites by Marriott Huntington **H**
(304) 525-4877. **$76-$149.** 157 Kinetic Dr 25701. I-64 exit 11, just n. Int corridors. **Pets:** Other species. $25 one-time fee/pet. Service with restrictions, crate. 📶 ✕ 🛏 💻 ➿

JANE LEW

🔷 ▼▼ Plantation Inn & Suites **M**
(304) 884-7806. **$65-$100.** 1322 Hackers Creek Rd 26378. I-79 exit 105, just e. Ext corridors. **Pets:** Very small. $10 one-time fee/room. Service with restrictions, supervision. SAVE 📶 🛏 💻

KEYSER

🔷 ▼▼ Keyser Inn **M**
(304) 788-0913. **$58-$72.** 51 Josie Dr 26726. On US 220, 2.3 mi s. Int corridors. **Pets:** Small. $27 one-time fee/room. Designated rooms, service with restrictions, supervision. SAVE 📶 🛏 💻

▼▼ Microtel Inn & Suites by Wyndham Keyser **H**
(304) 597-1400. **$90-$120, 3 day notice.** 70 N Tornado Way 26726. On US 220, 2.1 mi s. Int corridors. **Pets:** Dogs only. $25 daily fee/pet. Designated rooms, service with restrictions, supervision. 📶 🛏 💻

LEWISBURG

▼▼▼ Lewisburg Holiday Inn Express Hotel & Suites **H**
(304) 645-5750. **Call for rates.** 222 Hunter Ln 24901. I-64 exit 169, just s. Int corridors. **Pets:** Accepted. 📶 ✕ 🛏 💻 ➿

AAA **WWW** Quality Inn Lewisburg Conference Center **H**
(304) 645-7722. **Call for rates.** 540 N Jefferson St 24901. I-64 exit 169, just s on US 219. Ext corridors. **Pets:** Accepted.
[SAVE] 🛜 🛗 🖵 ❙❙ 🏊

WWW Super 8 **M**
(304) 647-3188. **$68-$135.** 550 N Jefferson St 24901. I-64 exit 169, just s on US 219. Int corridors. **Pets:** Medium. $10 daily fee/pet. Designated rooms, service with restrictions, supervision. 🛜 🛗 🖵

MARTINSBURG

WWWW Holiday Inn Martinsburg **H**
(304) 267-5500. **$109-$169.** 301 Foxcroft Ave 25401. I-81 exit 13, just e on W King St (CR 15). Int corridors. **Pets:** Other species. $25 one-time fee/room. Designated rooms, service with restrictions, supervision.
🛜 🖵 ❙❙ 🏊

WWW Knights Inn-Martinsburg **M**
(304) 267-2211. **$46-$55.** 1997 Edwin Miller Blvd 25404. I-81 exit 16E, 0.4 mi e on SR 9. Ext corridors. **Pets:** Small. $10 deposit/pet, $10 daily fee/pet. Designated rooms, service with restrictions, supervision.
🛜 🛗

AAA **WWW** Motel 6 **M**
(304) 274-2181. **Call for rates.** 5595 Hammonds Mill Rd 25404. I-81 exit 20, just e. Ext/int corridors. **Pets:** Other species. Service with restrictions, supervision. [SAVE] 🛜 🛗 🖵

WWW Super 8-Martinsburg **M**
(304) 263-0801. **$55-$60.** 2048 Edwin Miller Blvd 25404. I-81 exit 16E, just e on SR 9. Int corridors. **Pets:** Accepted. 🛜 🛗 🖵

MINERAL WELLS

AAA **WWWW** Comfort Suites Parkersburg South **H** 🐾
(304) 489-9600. **$89-$139.** 167 Elizabeth Pike 26150. I-77 exit 170, 0.3 mi se. Ext/int corridors. **Pets:** $10 daily fee/pet. Service with restrictions, supervision. [SAVE] 🛜 ✕ 🛗 🖵 🏊

WWWW Holiday Inn Express Hotel & Suites Parkersburg/ Mineral Wells **H**
(304) 489-4111. **Call for rates.** 80 Old Nicholette Rd 26150. I-77 exit 170. Int corridors. **Pets:** Accepted. 🛜 🛗 🖵 🏊 ✕

MORGANTOWN

WWW Comfort Inn-Morgantown **M** 🐾
(304) 296-9364. **Call for rates.** 225 Comfort Inn Dr 26508. I-68 exit 1, 0.3 mi n on US 119. Int corridors. **Pets:** Medium, dogs only. $10 daily fee/pet. Designated rooms, service with restrictions, supervision.
🛜 ✕ 🛗 🖵 🏊

WWWW Ramada Conference Center **H**
(304) 296-3431. **$89-$165.** 20 Scott Ave 26508. I-68 exit 1, 0.3 mi n. Int corridors. **Pets:** Other species. Designated rooms, service with restrictions, supervision. 🛜 ✕ 🔥M 🛗 🖵 ❙❙ 🏊

WWWW Residence Inn by Marriott Morgantown **H**
(304) 599-0237. **$151-$166.** 1046 Willowdale Rd 26505. I-79 exit 155, 2 mi s on US 19, then 0.9 mi e on SR 705. Int corridors. **Pets:** Accepted.
🛜 ✕ 🔥M 🛗 🖵 🏊 ✕

OAK HILL

AAA **WWWW** Holiday Lodge Hotel and Conference Center **H**
(304) 465-0571. **$70-$165.** 340 Oyler Ave 25901. US 19 exit Oyler Ave, just w. Int corridors. **Pets:** Medium, dogs only. $25 daily fee/room. Designated rooms, no service, supervision.
[SAVE] 🛜 🔥M 🖵 ❙❙ 🏊 ✕

PARKERSBURG

WWWW The Blennerhassett **H**
(304) 422-3131. **$139-$279.** 320 Market St 26101. Between 4th and 5th sts; downtown. Int corridors. **Pets:** Accepted. 🛜 🛗 🖵 ❙❙

WW Red Roof Inn **M**
(304) 485-1741. **$49-$72.** 3714 E 7th St 26104. I-77 exit 176, just w on US 50. Ext corridors. **Pets:** Large, other species. Service with restrictions, supervision. 🛜 🛗 🖵

PHILIPPI

AAA **WW** Mountaineer Inn **M**
(304) 457-5888. **$49-$85, 7 day notice.** Rt 4, Box 155 26416. 2.5 mi s on US 250. Int corridors. **Pets:** Accepted. [SAVE] 🛜 🔥M 🛗

PRINCETON

WWW Comfort Inn-Princeton **M**
(304) 487-6101. **$79-$109.** 136 Ambrose Ln 24740. I-77 exit 9, 0.3 mi w on US 460. Int corridors. **Pets:** Accepted. 🛜 🛗 🖵

AAA **WWW** Days Inn **M**
(304) 425-8100. **$65-$75, 3 day notice.** 347 Meadowfield Ln 24740. I-77 exit 9, 0.3 mi w on US 460, just s on Ambrose Ln, then just e. Ext corridors. **Pets:** Small. $20 daily fee/room. Designated rooms, supervision. [SAVE] 🛜 🛗 🖵 🏊

AAA **WWW** Holiday Inn Express Princeton **H** 🐾
(304) 425-8156. **$85-$180.** 805 Oakvale Rd 24740. I-77 exit 9, just w. Int corridors. **Pets:** Small. $20 daily fee/room. Designated rooms, service with restrictions, supervision. [SAVE] 🛜 🛗 🖵 🏊

AAA **WWW** Microtel Inn & Suites by Wyndham Princeton **M**
(304) 487-3885. **$70-$160.** 250 Ambrose Ln 24740. I-77 exit 9, just w. Int corridors. **Pets:** $20 daily fee/room. Designated rooms, service with restrictions, supervision. [SAVE] 🛜 ✕ 🛗 🖵 🏊

WWW Sleep Inn & Suites **H** 🐾
(304) 431-2800. **$74-$130.** 1015 Oakvale Rd 24740. I-77 exit 9, just w on US 460, then just n via service road. Int corridors. **Pets:** Service with restrictions, crate. 🛜 🛗 🖵 🏊

RIPLEY

WWWW Holiday Inn Express & Suites Ripley **H**
(304) 372-4444. **$125-$250.** 110 Memorial Dr 25271. I-77 exit 138, e on US 33, then s on New Stone Ridge Rd. Int corridors. **Pets:** Other species. $25 daily fee/pet. Service with restrictions, supervision.
🛜 🛗 🖵 🏊

AAA **WWWW** Quality Inn **H**
(304) 372-5000. **Call for rates.** 1 Hospitality Dr 25271. I-77 exit 138, just w on US 33, then 0.3 mi n. Ext/int corridors. **Pets:** Medium, dogs only. $20 daily fee/pet. Designated rooms, service with restrictions, crate.
[SAVE] 🛜 🛗 🖵

WWW Ripley Super 8 **M**
(304) 372-8880. **$62-$70.** 102 Duke Dr 25271. I-77 exit 138, just e on US 33. Int corridors. **Pets:** Accepted. 🛜 🛗 🖵

ROANOKE

AAA **WWWW** Stonewall Resort **H**
(304) 269-7400. **$159-$219, 3 day notice.** 940 Resort Dr 26447. I-79 exit 91, just e. Ext/int corridors. **Pets:** Accepted.
[SAVE] 🛜 🛗 🖵 ❙❙ 🏊 ✕

SHEPHERDSTOWN

WWW Comfort Inn Shepherdstown **M**
(304) 876-3160. **Call for rates.** 70 Maddex Square Dr 25443. Just w on SR 45; center. Int corridors. **Pets:** Accepted. 🛜 🛗 🖵

SOUTH CHARLESTON

AAA **WWWW** Holiday Inn & Suites Charleston West **H**
(304) 744-4641. **Call for rates.** 400 2nd Ave SW 25303. I-64 exit 56, just nw. Int corridors. **Pets:** Accepted. [SAVE] 🛜 🛗 🖵 ❙❙ 🏊

SUMMERSVILLE

Baymont Inn & Suites M
(304) 872-6500. **$75-$90.** 903 Industrial Dr N 26651. US 19, 1.9 mi n of jct SR 39. Int corridors. **Pets:** Accepted. [SAVE] 🛰 🔓 🖥 🏊 ✗

BEST WESTERN Summersville Lake Motor Lodge H
(304) 872-6900. **Call for rates.** 1203 S Broad St 26651. US 19 and Broad St; 0.6 mi s of jct SR 39. Ext corridors. **Pets:** Other species. $15 daily fee/pet. Service with restrictions. [SAVE] 🛰 🔓 🖥

Hampton Inn H
(304) 872-7100. **$80-$100.** 5400 Webster Rd 26651. Just s on SR 41 from US 19. Int corridors. **Pets:** Small, other species. Service with restrictions, supervision. 🛰 ⅏ 🖥 🏊 ✗

Sleep Inn of Summersville M
(304) 872-4500. **Call for rates.** 701 Professional Park Dr 26651. US 19, 1.7 mi n of jct SR 39. Int corridors. **Pets:** Accepted. 🛰 🔓 🖥 🏊

Summersville Inn & Suites H
(304) 872-0555. **$89-$150.** 106 Merchants Walk 26651. US 19, just w. Int corridors. **Pets:** Small. $20 one-time fee/pet. Designated rooms, service with restrictions, crate. 🔓 🖥 🏊

Super 8-Summersville M
(304) 872-4888. **$65-$79.** 306 Merchants Walk 26651. US 19, just n. Int corridors. **Pets:** Accepted. 🛰 🔓

TRIADELPHIA

Econo Lodge Inn Suites Conference Center Wheeling East M
(304) 547-1380. **$99-$149.** 87 Jenkins Ln 26059. I-70 exit 11, 0.3 mi w on CR 41. Int corridors. **Pets:** Small. $25 daily fee/pet. Designated rooms, service with restrictions, supervision. 🛰 🔓 🖥 🏊

VIENNA

Wingate by Wyndham H
(304) 295-5501. **$124.** 1502 Grand Central Ave 26105. I-77 exit 179, 3.9 mi w on SR 68. Int corridors. **Pets:** Other species. $40 daily fee/pet. Crate. 🛰 ✗ 🔓 🖥 🏊 ✗

WEIRTON

Holiday Inn H
(304) 723-5522. **$119-$159, 3 day notice.** 350 Three Springs Dr 26062. I-79 US 22 exit Three Springs Dr. Int corridors. **Pets:** $50 one-time fee/room. Service with restrictions, supervision.
🛰 ⅏ 🔓 🖥 🍴 🏊 ✗

WESTON

Comfort Inn H
(304) 269-7000. **Call for rates.** 2906 US Hwy 33 E 26452. I-79 exit 99, just e. Ext corridors. **Pets:** Medium. $15 daily fee/room. Designated rooms, service with restrictions, supervision. [SAVE] 🛰 🔓 🖥 🏊

Holiday Inn Express Hotel & Suites H
(304) 269-3550. **Call for rates.** 215 Staunton Dr 26452. I-79 exit 99, just e. Int corridors. **Pets:** Accepted. 🛰 🔓 🖥 🏊

WHEELING

Wheeling Super 8 M
(304) 243-9400. **$79-$89.** 2400 National Rd 26003. I-70 exit 5, just e. Int corridors. **Pets:** Small. $11 daily fee/pet. Designated rooms, service with restrictions, supervision. 🛰 🔓 🖥

WHITE SULPHUR SPRINGS

The Greenbrier H 🐾
(304) 536-1110. **Call for rates.** 300 W Main St 24986. I-64 exit 181 westbound, 1.8 mi w on US 60; exit 175 eastbound, just n, then 3.2 mi e on US 60. Ext/int corridors. **Pets:** Small, dogs only. $150 one-time fee/room. Designated rooms, service with restrictions, supervision.
[SAVE] 🛰 ✗ ⅏ 🔓 🍴 🏊 ✗

ABBOTSFORD

▼▼▼ Rodeway Inn 🅷

(715) 223-3337. **$85-$95.** 300 E Elderberry Rd 54405. SR 29 exit 132 (SR 13), just se. Int corridors. **Pets:** $100 deposit/room, $10 daily fee/pet. Designated rooms, service with restrictions.

🛜 ✕ ♿ 🛏 🖵 🏊

ADAMS

🅐🅐🅐 ▼▼▼ Adams Super 8 🅷

(608) 339-6088. **$67-$145.** 2188 SR 13 53910. Just s. Int corridors.
Pets: Accepted. SAVE 🛜 ✕ 🛏

ALGOMA

🅐🅐🅐 ▼ Algoma Beach Motel Ⓜ

(920) 487-2828. **$59-$199, 3 day notice.** 1500 Lake St 54201. Jct SR 54, 0.4 mi s on SR 42. Ext/int corridors. **Pets:** Small, dogs only. $15 daily fee/pet. Designated rooms, service with restrictions, supervision.

SAVE 🛜 ✕ ♿ 🛏

▼ Scenic Shore Inn Ⓜ

(920) 487-3214. **$55-$75, 3 day notice.** 2221 Lake St 54201. Jct SR 54, 0.8 mi s on SR 42. Ext corridors. **Pets:** Accepted. 🛜 ✕ 🛏

ANTIGO

▼▼ America's Best Inn & Suites 🅷

(715) 623-0506. **$55-$91.** 525 Memory Ln 54409. 0.4 mi n of jct SR 64 E and US 45, just w. Int corridors. **Pets:** Other species. $10 daily fee/pet. Service with restrictions, supervision. 🛜 ✕ 🛏 🖵 🏊

▼▼▼ Holiday Inn Express & Suites Antigo 🅷

(715) 627-7500. **$79-$99.** 2407 Neva Rd 54409. Just n of jct SR 64 E and US 45, just e. Int corridors. **Pets:** Dogs only. $15 daily fee/pet. Service with restrictions, supervision. 🛜 ✕ ♿ 🛏 🖵 🏊 🔀

▼▼ Super 8-Antigo 🅷 ❀

(715) 623-4188. **$74-$112.** 535 Century Ave 54409. On US 45 at SR 64 E. Int corridors. **Pets:** Dogs only. $16 daily fee/pet. Designated rooms, service with restrictions, crate. 🛜 ✕ ♿ 🛏 🖵 🏊 🔀

APPLETON

🅐🅐🅐 ▼▼▼ BEST WESTERN Fox Valley Inn 🅷

(920) 731-4141. **$59-$199.** 3033 W College Ave 54914. US 41 exit 137 (SR 125), 0.5 mi e. Int corridors. **Pets:** Medium, dogs only. $20 daily fee/pet. Designated rooms, supervision. SAVE 🛜 ✕ 🛏 🖵 🏊

▼▼ Candlewood Suites 🅷 🐾

(920) 739-8000. **$59-$119.** 4525 W College Ave 54914. US 41 exit 137 (SR 125), just w. Int corridors. **Pets:** Large, other species. $15 daily fee/ pet. Service with restrictions, crate. 🛜 ✕ ♿ 🛏 🖵

🅐🅐🅐 ▼▼◆ Country Inn & Suites By Carlson 🅷

(920) 830-3240. **$99-$170, 3 day notice.** 355 Fox River Dr 54913. US 41 exit 137 (SR 125), just nw. Int corridors. **Pets:** $35 one-time fee/pet. Designated rooms, service with restrictions, supervision.

SAVE 🛜 ✕ 🛏 🖵 🏊 🔀

▼ Days Inn 🅷

(920) 733-5551. **$50-$199.** 210 Westhill Blvd 54914. US 41 exit 137 (SR 125), just e. Int corridors. **Pets:** Other species. $10 daily fee/pet. Service with restrictions. 🛜 ✕ 🛏 🖵

▼▼ Extended StayAmerica-Appleton-Fox Cities 🅷

(920) 830-9596. **$50-$80.** 4141 Boardwalk Ct 54915. US 41 exit 137 (SR 125), just w on College Ave, then just s on Nicolet Rd. Int corridors. **Pets:** $25 daily fee/pet. Designated rooms, service with restrictions.

🛜 ✕ ♿ 🛏 🖵

▼▼ Fairfield Inn by Marriott 🅷

(920) 954-0202. **$99-$149.** 132 N Mall Dr 54913. US 41 exit 137 (SR 125), just nw. Int corridors. **Pets:** Other species. $30 one-time fee/room. Designated rooms, service with restrictions. 🛜 ✕ 🛏 🖵 🏊

▼▼▼ La Quinta Inn & Suites Appleton College Avenue 🅷

(920) 734-7777. **$90-$177.** 3730 W College Ave 54914. US 41 exit 137 (SR 125), just e. Int corridors. **Pets:** Service with restrictions, supervision.

🛜 ✕ ♿ 🛏 🖵 🏊 🔀

▼▼ La Quinta Inn Appleton Fox River Mall Area Ⓜ

(920) 734-6070. **$59-$133.** 3920 W College Ave 54914. US 41 exit 137 (SR 125), just e. Ext/int corridors. **Pets:** Service with restrictions, supervision. 🛜 ✕ 🛏 🖵

▼▼ Microtel Inn & Suites by Wyndham Appleton 🅷

(920) 997-3121. **$60-$200.** 321 Metro Dr 54913. US 41 exit 137 (SR 125), just nw. Int corridors. **Pets:** $10 daily fee/pet. Designated rooms, service with restrictions, supervision. 🛜 ✕ 🛏 🖵

▼▼▼ Residence Inn by Marriott 🅷

(920) 954-0570. **$150-$220.** 310 Metro Dr 54913. US 41 exit 137 (SR 125), just nw on Mall Dr. Int corridors. **Pets:** Other species. $100 one-time fee/room. Service with restrictions, crate.

🛜 ✕ 🛏 🖵 🏊 🔀

ARKDALE

WWW Northern Bay Resort & Castle Course [CO]
(608) 339-2090. **$190-$429, 14 day notice.** 1844 20th Ave 54613. 2.9 mi w on SR 21, 3 mi s on CR Z, 0.9 mi w on Czech Ave, then 0.4 mi se. Int corridors. **Pets:** Medium. $25 daily fee/room. Designated rooms, no service.

ASHLAND

WWW AmericInn of Ashland [H]
(715) 682-9950. **Call for rates.** 3009 Lake Shore Dr E 54806. On US 2, 2.1 mi e of jct SR 13 S. Int corridors. **Pets:** Accepted.

WWW Ashland Lake Superior Lodge [H]
(715) 682-5235. **$70-$190.** 30600 US Hwy 2 54806. 2.5 mi w. Ext/int corridors. **Pets:** Other species. $15 daily fee/room. Designated rooms, service with restrictions, supervision.

BALDWIN

WWW AmericInn Lodge & Suites of Baldwin [H]
(715) 684-5888. **$70-$185.** 500 Baldwin Plaza Dr 54002. I-94 exit 19 (US 63), just ne. Int corridors. **Pets:** Small, dogs only. $15 daily fee/room. Designated rooms, service with restrictions, supervision.

WWW Super 8 [H]
(715) 684-2700. **$64-$109.** 805 Energy Dr 54002. I-94 exit 19 (US 63), just se. Int corridors. **Pets:** $10 daily fee/pet. Designated rooms, service with restrictions, supervision.

BARABOO

WWW Clarion Hotel & Convention Center [H]
(608) 356-6422. **$69-$148.** 626 W Pine St 53913. On US 12, 0.3 mi n of SR 33. Int corridors. **Pets:** Medium, other species. $25 daily fee/room. Designated rooms, service with restrictions, supervision.

BEAVER DAM

WWW Beaver Dam AmericInn [H]
(920) 356-9000. **$85-$140.** 325 Seippel Blvd 53916. US 151 exit 134 (CR B/Industrial Dr). Int corridors. **Pets:** Dogs only. $10 daily fee/pet. Designated rooms, service with restrictions, supervision.

WWW Super 8 [H]
(920) 887-8880. **$64-$91.** 711 Park Ave 53916. US 151 exit 132 (SR 33), just w. Int corridors. **Pets:** Large, other species. $10 one-time fee/pet. Designated rooms, service with restrictions, supervision.

BELOIT

WWW Beloit Inn [H] ❀
(608) 362-5500. **$109-$219.** 500 Pleasant St 53511. Downtown. Int corridors. **Pets:** $100 deposit/room, $10 daily fee/room. Service with restrictions, crate.

WWWW Fairfield Inn & Suites by Marriott [H]
(608) 365-2200. **$89-$159.** 2784 Milwaukee Rd 53511. I-90 exit 185A, just sw; at I-43 and SR 81. Int corridors. **Pets:** Accepted.

WWW Quality Inn of Beloit [H]
(608) 362-2666. **Call for rates.** 2786 Milwaukee Rd 53511. I-90 exit 185A, just w; at I-43 and SR 81. Int corridors. **Pets:** Accepted.

WWW Rodeway Inn [M]
(608) 364-4000. **$56-$60.** 2956 Milwaukee Rd 53511. I-90 exit 185A, 0.3 mi w. Ext/int corridors. **Pets:** Dogs only. $10 daily fee/pet. Designated rooms, service with restrictions, supervision.

BERLIN

WWW Countryside Lodge [M]
(920) 361-4411. **$74-$125.** 227 Ripon Rd 54923. On SR 49, at CR F. Int corridors. **Pets:** Small, dogs only. $10 daily fee/pet. Designated rooms, service with restrictions, supervision.

BIRCHWOOD

WWW Cobblestone Bed & Breakfast [BB] ❀
(715) 354-3494. **$87-$135, 8 day notice.** 319 S Main St 54817. 0.8 mi e of jct SR 48 and Main St; center. Int corridors. **Pets:** Other species.

BLACK RIVER FALLS

WWW BEST WESTERN Arrowhead Lodge & Suites [H]
(715) 284-9471. **$70-$120.** 600 Oasis Rd 54615. I-94 exit 116 (SR 54), just ne. Int corridors. **Pets:** Medium. $20 daily fee/room. Designated rooms, service with restrictions, supervision.

WWW Days Inn [H]
(715) 284-4333. **$60-$136.** 919 Hwy 54 E 54615. I-94 exit 116 (SR 54), just w. Int corridors. **Pets:** $15 deposit/room. Designated rooms, service with restrictions, supervision.

BURLINGTON

WWW AmericInn Lodge & Suites Burlington [H] ❀
(262) 534-2125. **$82-$112.** 2709 Browns Lake Dr 53105. 3 mi n on SR 36 and 83, jct CR W. Int corridors. **Pets:** Medium, dogs only. $25 one-time fee/pet. Designated rooms, service with restrictions, supervision.

CADOTT

WWW Countryside Motel [M]
(715) 289-4000. **$60-$100.** 545 Lavorata Rd 54727. SR 29 exit 91 (SR 27), just s. Int corridors. **Pets:** Small, dogs only. $5 daily fee/pet. Designated rooms, service with restrictions, supervision.

CHIPPEWA FALLS

WWW AmericInn Motel & Suites of Chippewa Falls [H]
(715) 723-5711. **Call for rates.** 11 W South Ave 54729. 2 mi s on SR 124, access via CR J. Int corridors. **Pets:** Accepted.

CLINTONVILLE

WWW Cobblestone Inn & Suites [H]
(715) 823-2000. **$80-$110.** 175 Waupaca St 54929. Jct US 45 and CR C. Int corridors. **Pets:** Other species. $15 one-time fee/room. Service with restrictions.

COLUMBUS

WWW Super 8-Columbus [H]
(920) 623-8800. **$68-$118.** 219 Industrial Dr 53925. US 151 exit 118 (SR 16/60), just ne. Int corridors. **Pets:** Medium. $10 one-time fee/room. Designated rooms, service with restrictions, supervision.

CRANDON

WWW BEST WESTERN Crandon Inn & Suites [H]
(715) 478-4000. **Call for rates.** 9075 E Pioneer St 54520. 0.5 mi e on US 8 and SR 32. Int corridors. **Pets:** Accepted.

WWW Four Seasons Motel [M]
(715) 478-3377. **$55-$80.** 304 W Glen St 54520. 0.5 mi w on US 8. Ext/int corridors. **Pets:** Accepted.

DE FOREST

▼▼▼ Comfort Inn & Suites 🅗
(608) 846-9100. **Call for rates.** 5025 County Hwy V 53532. I-90/94 exit 126 (CR V), just w. Int corridors. **Pets:** Dogs only. $20 deposit/pet. Designated rooms, service with restrictions, crate.

📶 ✕ &M 🛏 💻 🏊 ☒

▼▼▼ Holiday Inn Express 🅗
(608) 846-8686. **Call for rates.** 7184 Morrisonville Rd 53532. I-90/94 exit 126 (CR V), just e. Int corridors. **Pets:** Other species. $20 one-time fee/room. Designated rooms. 🌱 📶 ✕ &M 🛏 💻 🏊

DELAVAN

▼▼ Super 8-Delavan 🅗
(262) 728-1700. **$63-$130.** 518 Borg Rd 53115. I-43 exit 21 (SR 50), just w. Int corridors. **Pets:** Accepted. 📶 ✕ &M 🛏 💻

DE PERE

▼▼▼ Kress Inn, an Ascend Collection hotel 🅗
(920) 403-5100. **$80-$140.** 300 Grant St 54115. US 41 exit 163 (Main Ave), 1 mi e, then just s on 3rd St. Int corridors. **Pets:** Large, dogs only. $15 daily fee/room. Designated rooms, service with restrictions, crate.

📶 ✕ &M 🛏 💻

DODGEVILLE

▼▼▼ BEST WESTERN Quiet House & Suites 🅗
(608) 935-7739. **$99-$119.** 1130 N Johns St 53533. On US 18, just e of jct SR 23. Int corridors. **Pets:** Large. $15 daily fee/pet. Designated rooms, supervision. 💾 📶 ✕ 🛏 💻 🏊

▼▼ Pine Ridge Motel 🅜
(608) 935-3386. **$45-$85, 3 day notice.** 405 CR YZ 53533. 0.5 mi e of jct SR 23. Ext corridors. **Pets:** Very small, dogs only. $10 daily fee/pet. Designated rooms, service with restrictions, supervision.

💾 📶 ✕ 🛏 💻

▼▼ Super 8 of Dodgeville 🅗
(608) 935-3888. **$59-$129, 3 day notice.** 1308 Johns St 53533. Just n of US 18. Int corridors. **Pets:** Dogs only. $50 deposit/pet. Service with restrictions, supervision. 🌱 📶 ✕ &M 🛏 💻

DOOR COUNTY AREA

EGG HARBOR

▼▼▼ The Shallows 🅜
(920) 868-3458. **$75-$425, 30 day notice.** 7353 Horseshoe Bay Rd, Hwy G 54209. On CR G, 2.5 mi s. Ext corridors. **Pets:** Small, dogs only. $40 daily fee/pet. Service with restrictions, supervision.

💾 📶 ✕ 🛏 💻 🏊 ☒

EPHRAIM

▼▼▼ Trollhaugen Lodge, B&B Inn, Motel & Log Cabin 🅜
(920) 854-2713. **$79-$169.** 10176 Hwy 42 54211. 0.6 mi n of Village Hall. Ext/int corridors. **Pets:** Medium, dogs only. $25 one-time fee/room. Designated rooms, supervision. 💾 📶 ✕ 🛏 💻

FISH CREEK

▼ Julie's Park Cafe & Motel 🅜
(920) 868-2999. **Call for rates.** 4020 Hwy 42 54212. On SR 42, 0.3 mi n. Ext corridors. **Pets:** Accepted. 📶 ✕ 🛏 🍴

GILLS ROCK

▼ Maple Grove Motel 🅜
(920) 854-2587. **$80-$100, 15 day notice.** 809 SR 42 54210. On SR 42, 0.3 mi e; 1.5 mi w of car ferry. Ext corridors. **Pets:** Accepted.

✕ 🛏 💻 ☒

SISTER BAY

▼▼▼ Country House Resort 🅜 ❀
(920) 854-4551. **$76-$181, 14 day notice.** 2468 Sunnyside Rd 54234. Jct SR 42 and 57, 0.3 mi s on SR 42 to Highland Ave, just w. Ext corridors. **Pets:** Large, dogs only. $20 daily fee/pet. Designated rooms, service with restrictions, supervision. 🌱 💾 📶 ✕ 🛏 💻 🏊 ☒

STURGEON BAY

▼▼▼ BEST WESTERN Maritime Inn 🅗
(920) 743-7231. **$70-$130.** 1001 N 14th Ave 54235. 1 mi n on Business Rt SR 42/57 at jct N 14th Ave. Int corridors. **Pets:** Other species. $15 daily fee/room. Designated rooms, service with restrictions.

💾 📶 ✕ &M 🛏 💻 🏊

END AREA

EAGLE RIVER

▼▼ Days Inn 🅗
(715) 479-5151. **$72-$152.** 844 Railroad St N 54521. On US 45, 0.5 mi n. Int corridors. **Pets:** Medium, dogs only. $15 daily fee/pet. Designated rooms, service with restrictions, supervision.

📶 ✕ 🛏 💻 🏊 ☒

▼▼ Super 8 🅗
(715) 477-0888. **$68-$150.** 200 W Pine St 54521. On SR 70; center. Int corridors. **Pets:** Medium, dogs only. $10 daily fee/pet. Designated rooms, service with restrictions, supervision.

📶 ✕ &M 🛏 💻 🏊 ☒

EAU CLAIRE

▼▼▼ AmericInn Motel & Suites of Eau Claire 🅗
(715) 874-4900. **$75-$175.** 6200 Texaco Dr 54703. I-94 exit 59, jct US 12. Int corridors. **Pets:** Accepted. 📶 ✕ &M 🛏 💻 🏊

▼▼▼ BEST WESTERN PLUS Trail Lodge Hotel & Suites 🅗
(715) 838-9989. **$100-$110.** 3340 Mondovi Rd 54701. I-94 exit 65, just n. Int corridors. **Pets:** Medium, dogs only. $20 daily fee/pet. Designated rooms, service with restrictions, supervision.

💾 📶 ✕ &M 🛏 💻 🏊 ☒

▼▼ Days Inn 🅗
(715) 834-3193. **$56-$99.** 2305 Craig Rd 54701. I-94 exit 65, 1.3 mi n on SR 37; just w of jct US 12. Int corridors. **Pets:** Accepted.

📶 ✕ &M 🛏 💻

▼▼ Econo Lodge 🅗
(715) 833-8818. **Call for rates.** 4608 Royal Dr 54701. I-94 exit 68, just n on SR 93, just w on Golf Rd, then just s. Int corridors. **Pets:** Accepted.

📶 ✕ &M 🛏 💻

Holiday Inn Campus Area
(715) 835-2211. **$70-$159.** 2703 Craig Rd 54701. I-94 exit 65, 1.3 mi n
on SR 37; just w of jct US 12. Int corridors. **Pets:** Medium. $15 daily
fee/room. Service with restrictions, supervision.

Ramada Convention Center
(715) 835-6121. **$72-$119.** 205 S Barstow St 54701. Jct S Barstow and
Gibson sts; downtown. Int corridors. **Pets:** $15 one-time fee/room. Desig-
nated rooms, service with restrictions, crate.

Sleep Inn & Suites Conference Center
(715) 874-2900. **$79-$129.** 5872 N 33rd Ave 54703. SR 29 exit 69 (CR
T), just sw. Int corridors. **Pets:** Other species. $10 daily fee/room. Desig-
nated rooms, service with restrictions, crate.

ELKHORN

AmericInn Lodge & Suites of Elkhorn
(262) 723-7799. **$82-$112.** 210 E Commerce Ct 53121. I-43 exit 25, just
s. Int corridors. **Pets:** Medium, dogs only. $25 daily fee/pet. Service with
restrictions, supervision.

FITCHBURG

Candlewood Suites
(608) 271-3400. **Call for rates.** 5421 Caddis Bend 53711. US 12/18 exit
260 (Fish Hatchery/CR D), 1.5 mi s. Int corridors. **Pets:** Other species.
$10 daily fee/pet. Service with restrictions, supervision.

Quality Inn & Suites
(608) 274-7200. **Call for rates.** 2969 Cahill Main 53711. US 12/18 exit
260 (Fish Hatchery/CR D), 1.5 mi s at CR PD (McKee Rd). Int corridors.
Pets: Medium. $10 daily fee/room. No service, crate.

FOND DU LAC

Comfort Inn by Choice Hotels Fond du Lac
(920) 921-4000. **$70-$250.** 77 Holiday Ln 54937. US 41 exit 97 (Military
Rd), just sw. Int corridors. **Pets:** Accepted.

Executive Lodge Fond du Lac
(920) 923-2020. **$49-$89.** 649 W Johnson St 54935. US 41 exit 99 (SR
23/Johnson St), 0.3 mi e. Int corridors. **Pets:** Other species. $5 daily fee/
pet. Designated rooms, service with restrictions, crate.

Holiday Inn
(920) 923-1440. **Call for rates.** 625 W Rolling Meadows Dr 54937. US
41 exit 97 (Military Rd), just sw. Int corridors. **Pets:** Service with restrictions, crate.

Microtel Inn & Suites by Wyndham Fond Du Lac
(920) 929-4000. **$50-$200.** 920 S Military Rd 54935. US 41 exit 97 (Military Rd). Int corridors. **Pets:** Accepted.

Super 8-FOND DU LAC
(920) 922-1088. **$55-$185, 3 day notice.** 391 N Pioneer Rd 54935. US
41 exit 99 (SR 23/Johnson St), just n on east frontage road (CR VV). Int
corridors. **Pets:** Accepted.

FORT ATKINSON

Holiday Inn Express Hotel & Suites
(920) 563-3600. **$114-$199.** 1680 Madison Ave 53538. Jct SR 26
Bypass and US 12. Int corridors. **Pets:** Small. $30 one-time fee/room.
Designated rooms, service with restrictions, supervision.

GREEN BAY

Aloft Green Bay
(920) 884-0800. **$99-$299.** 465 Pilgrim Way 54304. US 41 exit 163B,
just e. Int corridors. **Pets:** Small, dogs only. Designated rooms, service
with restrictions, supervision.

**AmericInn Lodge & Suites Green Bay
East**
(920) 964-0177. **$75-$155.** 2628 Manitowoc Rd 54311. I-43 exit 181, just
w. Int corridors. **Pets:** Dogs only. $20 one-time fee/room. Designated
rooms, service with restrictions, supervision.

AmericInn Lodge of Green Bay West
(920) 434-9790. **Call for rates.** 2032 Velp Ave 54303. US 41 exit 170,
0.3 mi w. Int corridors. **Pets:** Accepted.

Baymont Inn-Green Bay
(920) 494-7887. **$59-$229.** 2840 S Oneida St 54304. US 41 exit 164
(Oneida St), just e. Int corridors. **Pets:** Small. $10 daily fee/pet. Desig-
nated rooms, service with restrictions.

Bay Motel
(920) 494-3441. **$49-$75.** 1301 S Military Ave 54304. US 41 exit 167
(Lombardi Ave), 0.4 mi e to Marlee Ln, then 0.6 mi n. Ext corridors.
Pets: Accepted.

**BEST WESTERN Green Bay Inn Conference
Center**
(920) 499-3161. **Call for rates.** 780 Armed Forces Dr 54304. US 41 exit
167 (Lombardi Ave), 1.4 mi e to Holmgren Way, then just s. Int corridors.
Pets: Medium, dogs only. $25 deposit/pet, $25 daily fee/pet. Designated
rooms, service with restrictions, supervision.

Country Inn & Suites By Carlson
(920) 336-6600. **$99-$150, 3 day notice.** 2945 Allied St 54304. US 41
exit 164 (Oneida St), just nw. Int corridors. **Pets:** Small. $15 daily fee/
room. Service with restrictions, supervision.

Extended Stay Airport
(920) 499-3600. **$70-$80, 10 day notice.** 1639 Commanche Ave 54313.
US 41 exit 165, 1 mi w on SR 172, then just s. Int corridors.
Pets: Accepted.

Quality Inn & Suites
(920) 437-8771. **$59-$149.** 321 S Washington St 54301-4214. On east
side of Fox River, just s of Walnut St (SR 29); downtown. Int corridors.
Pets: Medium. $10 one-time fee/room. Designated rooms, service with
restrictions.

**Ramada Plaza Hotel & Conference
Center**
(920) 499-0631. **$69-$349.** 2750 Ramada Way 54304. US 41 exit 164
(Oneida St), just e. Int corridors. **Pets:** Small. $20 daily fee/pet. Desig-
nated rooms, service with restrictions, supervision.

Residence Inn by Marriott
(920) 435-2222. **$85-$151.** 335 W St. Joseph St 54301. SR 172 exit
Riverside Dr, 1.1 mi n on SR 57, then just e. Ext corridors. **Pets:** Other
species. $100 one-time fee/room. Service with restrictions.

Super 8-Airport
(920) 494-2042. **$64-$260.** 2868 S Oneida St 54304. US 41 exit 164
(Oneida St), just e. Int corridors. **Pets:** Accepted.

▼▼ Super 8 East Green Bay I-43 🅗
(920) 406-8200. **$59-$229, 3 day notice.** 2911 Voyager Dr 54311. I-43 exit 183 (Mason St), just e. Int corridors. **Pets:** Small. $15 daily fee/pet. Designated rooms, service with restrictions, supervision.
🛜 ❌ 🕭M 🛏 💻 ➰ 🏊

▼▼ Travelodge Green Bay/Lambeau 🅗
(920) 499-3599. **$59-$299.** 2870 Ramada Way 54304. US 41 exit 164 (Oneida St), just e. Int corridors. **Pets:** Small. Service with restrictions, supervision. 🛜 ❌ 🛏 💻

HAYWARD
▼▼ AmericInn of Hayward 🅗
(715) 634-2700. **$88-$195, 3 day notice.** 15601 US Hwy 63 54843. Just n of jct SR 77. Int corridors. **Pets:** $15 daily fee/pet. Designated rooms, service with restrictions, supervision.
🛜 ❌ 🕭M 🛏 💻 ➰

▼◆▼ Comfort Suites 🅗
(715) 634-0700. **$109-$149.** 15586 CR B 54843. 0.5 mi s of jct SR 27. Int corridors. **Pets:** Other species. $13 daily fee/room. Designated rooms, service with restrictions, supervision.
🛜 ❌ 🕭M 🛏 💻 ➰ 🍽❌

🄰🄰🄰 ▼◆▼ The Flat Creek Inn & Suites 🅗
(715) 634-4100. **$85-$165.** 10290 Hwy 27 S 54843. On SR 27 S, 0.7 mi s of jct US 63. Int corridors. **Pets:** Accepted.
[SAVE] 🛜 ❌ 🕭M 🛏 💻 🍴 🏊 🍽❌

▼▼ Ross' Teal Lake Lodge and Teal Wing Golf Club 🅒🄰 🐾
(715) 462-3631. **Call for rates.** 12425 N Ross Rd 54843. On SR 77, 20 mi ne of jct US 63. Ext corridors. **Pets:** Other species. $10 daily fee/pet. Service with restrictions, supervision.
🛜 ❌ 🛏 💻 🍴 ➰ 🍽❌ 🗋

HILLSBORO
🄰🄰🄰 ▼◆▼ Hotel Hillsboro 🅗
(608) 489-3000. **$75-$125.** 1235 Water Ave (SR 33) 54634. Jct SR 80/82 and 33, just n. Int corridors. **Pets:** $15 one-time fee/room. Designated rooms, service with restrictions, crate.
[SAVE] 🛜 ❌ 🕭M 🛏 💻 🍴 ➰

HUDSON
▼▼ Fairfield Inn by Marriott 🅗
(715) 386-6688. **$77-$105.** 2400 Center Dr 54016. I-94 exit 2 (CR F), 0.3 mi s. Int corridors. **Pets:** Accepted. 🛜 ❌ 🕭M 🛏 💻 ➰

🄰🄰🄰 ▼◆▼ Hudson House Grand Hotel 🅗 🐾
(715) 386-2394. **Call for rates.** 1616 Crest View Dr 54016. I-94 exit 2 (CR F), 0.7 mi w on south frontage road (Crest View Dr). Int corridors. **Pets:** Other species. $15 one-time fee/room. Designated rooms, supervision. [SAVE] 🛜 ❌ 🛏 💻 🍴 ➰ 🍽❌

▼▼ Quality Inn 🅗
(715) 386-6355. **Call for rates.** 811 Dominion Dr 54016. I-94 exit 2 (CR F), 1 mi w on south frontage road (Crestview Dr). Int corridors. **Pets:** Accepted. 🛜 ❌ 🛏 💻 🏊

🄰🄰🄰 ▼◆▼ Super 8 of Hudson 🅗
(715) 386-8800. **$65-$85.** 808 Dominion Dr 54016. I-94 exit 2 (CR F), 1 mi w on south frontage road (Crestview Dr). Int corridors. **Pets:** Medium, dogs only. $15 daily fee/pet. Designated rooms, service with restrictions, supervision. [SAVE] 🛜 ❌ 🛏 💻 ➰

HURLEY
🄰🄰🄰 ▼◆▼ Days Inn of Hurley 🅗
(715) 561-3500. **$78-$140.** 13355 N US Hwy 51 54534. Jct US 2 and 51, 0.4 mi s on US 51. Int corridors. **Pets:** Accepted.
[SAVE] 🛜 ❌ 🛏 💻 ➰ 🍽❌

JANESVILLE
▼▼ Baymont Inn & Suites 🅗 🐾
(608) 758-4545. **$74-$200.** 616 Midland Rd 53546. I-90 exit 175B (SR 11), just ne. Int corridors. **Pets:** Other species. $10 daily fee/pet. Designated rooms, service with restrictions. 🛜 ❌ 🛏 💻 🏊

▼▼ Econo Lodge-Janesville 🅗
(608) 754-0251. **$55-$70.** 3520 Milton Ave 53545. I-90/39 exit 171A, just sw via Frontage Rd. Int corridors. **Pets:** Accepted. 🛜 ❌ 🛏 💻

JOHNSON CREEK
▼◆▼ Comfort Suites by Choice Hotels-Johnson Creek 🅗
(920) 699-2800. **$80-$220.** 725 Paradise Ln 53038. I-94 exit 267 (SR 26), 1.4 mi n, 1.6 mi w on River Dr, 0.8 mi s on CR Y, then just w. Int corridors. **Pets:** Medium, dogs only. $15 one-time fee/pet. Designated rooms, service with restrictions, supervision.
🛜 ❌ 🕭M 🛏 💻 ➰ 🍽❌

▼▼ Days Inn-Johnson Creek 🅗
(920) 699-8000. **$64-$130.** W4545 Linmar Ln 53038. I-94 exit 267 (SR 26), just ne. Int corridors. **Pets:** Accepted.
🛜 ❌ 🛏 💻 ➰ 🍽❌

KENOSHA
🄰🄰🄰 ▼◆▼ BEST WESTERN Harborside Inn & Kenosha Conference Center 🅗
(262) 658-3281. **$80-$160.** 5125 6th Ave 53140. Just ne of jct SR 32 and 158; downtown. Int corridors. **Pets:** Large. $50 deposit/room, $20 daily fee/room. Service with restrictions, crate.
[SAVE] 🛜 ❌ 🕭M 🛏 💻 ➰ 🍽❌

🄰🄰🄰 ▼▼ Candlewood Suites 🅗
(262) 842-5000. **Call for rates.** 10200 74th St 53142. SR 50 exit 104th Ave, just n. Int corridors. **Pets:** Accepted. [SAVE] 🛜 ❌ 🕭M 🛏 💻

KOHLER
🄰🄰🄰 ▼◆▼ Inn on Woodlake 🅗
(920) 452-7800. **$149-$299, 7 day notice.** 705 Woodlake Rd 53044. I-43 exit 126, 0.5 mi w on SR 23, 0.5 mi s on CR Y and Highland Dr; in Woodlake Shopping Center. Int corridors. **Pets:** Large, dogs only. $10 one-time fee/room. Designated rooms, service with restrictions, supervision. [SAVE] 🛜 ❌ 💻 🍽❌

LA CROSSE
🄰🄰🄰 ▼◆▼ BEST WESTERN PLUS Riverfront Hotel 🅗
(608) 781-7000. **$100-$200.** 1835 Rose St 54603. I-90 exit 3, 1 mi s on US 53. Int corridors. **Pets:** Medium, dogs only. $15 daily fee/pet. Designated rooms, service with restrictions.
[SAVE] 🛜 ❌ 🕭M 🛏 💻 🍴 ➰ 🍽❌

🄰🄰🄰 ▼◆▼ Candlewood Suites 🅗 🐾
(608) 785-1110. **$99-$149.** 56 Copeland Ave 54603. I-90 exit 3, 2 mi s on US 53. Int corridors. **Pets:** Other species. $75 one-time fee/room. Service with restrictions. [SAVE] 🛜 ❌ 🕭M 🛏 💻

▼▼ Days Hotel & Conference Center 🅗
(608) 783-1000. **$67-$169.** 101 Sky Harbour Dr 54603. I-90 exit 2, just sw; on French Island. Int corridors. **Pets:** Other species. $15 daily fee/room. Designated rooms, service with restrictions, supervision.
🛜 ❌ 🕭M 🛏 💻 🍴 ➰ 🍽❌

🄰🄰🄰 ▼ Econo Lodge 🅗
(608) 781-0200. **$49-$70.** 1906 Rose St 54603. I-90 exit 3, 0.9 mi s on US 53. Int corridors. **Pets:** Small, dogs only. $10 deposit/pet. Designated rooms, service with restrictions, supervision.
[SAVE] 🛜 ❌ 🕭M 🛏 💻

GrandStay Residential Suites Hotel of La Crosse H

(608) 796-1615. **$89-$209.** 525 Front St N 54601. I-90 exit 3; downtown. Int corridors. **Pets:** Very small, other species. $200 deposit/room, $10 daily fee/pet. Designated rooms, service with restrictions, crate.

Holiday Inn Hotel & Suites H

(608) 784-4444. **$99-$209, 3 day notice.** 200 Pearl St 54601. Downtown. Int corridors. **Pets:** Medium, dogs only. $50 one-time fee/pet. Designated rooms, service with restrictions, supervision.

Howard Johnson Hotel La Crosse H

(608) 781-0400. **$49-$215.** 2150 Rose St 54603. I-90 exit 3, 0.8 mi s on US 53. Int corridors. **Pets:** Accepted.

Settle Inn H

(608) 781-5100. **$60-$120.** 2110 Rose St 54603. I-90 exit 3, 0.9 mi s on US 53. Int corridors. **Pets:** Small, dogs only. $15 daily fee/room. Service with restrictions, supervision.

LADYSMITH

FairBridge Inn Express H

(715) 532-6650. **Call for rates.** 800 W College Ave 54848. On SR 27, 0.5 mi s of US 8. Int corridors. **Pets:** Accepted.

LAKE GENEVA

 Grand Geneva Resort & Spa H ❀

(262) 248-8811. **$159-$449, 3 day notice.** 7036 Grand Geneva Way 53147. On SR 50, just e of jct US 12. Int corridors. **Pets:** Small, dogs only. $35 daily fee/pet. Service with restrictions, supervision.

LAKE MILLS

Americas Best Value Inn H

(920) 648-3800. **$60-$120.** W 7614 Oasis Ln 53551. I-94 exit 259 (SR 89), just n. Int corridors. **Pets:** Large. $15 one-time fee/pet. Service with restrictions, supervision.

LAND O'LAKES

Sunrise Lodge CA

(715) 547-3684. **$89-$235, 21 day notice.** 5894 W Shore Dr 54540. 2 mi s on US 45, 2.8 mi e on CR E, then 1 mi n. Ext corridors. **Pets:** Other species. Service with restrictions.

LODI

Quality Inn & Suites H

(608) 592-1450. **$80-$150.** W 9250 Prospect Dr 53555. I-90/94 exit 119, just w. Int corridors. **Pets:** Medium. $20 one-time fee/pet. Service with restrictions, crate.

MADISON

AmericInn Madison West H

(608) 662-1990. **$82-$149.** 516 Grand Canyon Dr 53719. US 12 and 14 exit 255 (Gammon Rd), just n, then 0.5 mi e on Odana Rd. Int corridors. **Pets:** Large, other species. $20 daily fee/pet. Service with restrictions, crate.

Baymont Inn & Suites H

(608) 241-3861. **$54-$139.** 4202 E Towne Blvd 53704. I-90/94 exit 135A (US 151), 0.5 mi w. Int corridors. **Pets:** Medium. $10 daily fee/pet. Service with restrictions, crate.

 BEST WESTERN PLUS East Towne Suites H

(608) 244-2020. **$90-$380.** 4801 Annamark Dr 53704. I-90/94 exit 135A (US 151) southbound; exit 135C (US 151/High Crossing Blvd) northbound, just sw. Int corridors. **Pets:** Other species. $20 daily fee/pet. Service with restrictions, crate.

BEST WESTERN West Towne Suites H ❀

(608) 833-4200. **$80-$140.** 650 Grand Canyon Dr 53719. US 12 and 14 exit 255 (Gammon Rd), just e on Odana Rd, then just sw. Int corridors. **Pets:** Large. $25 deposit/room, $15 daily fee/room. Designated rooms, service with restrictions, supervision.

Clarion Suites Madison at the Alliant Energy Center H

(608) 284-1234. **$89-$259.** 2110 Rimrock Rd 53713. US 12 and 18 exit 262 (Rimrock Rd), just nw. Int corridors. **Pets:** $25 daily fee/pet. Designated rooms, service with restrictions, supervision.

Comfort Inn & Suites-Airport H

(608) 244-6265. **$69-$200.** 4822 E Washington Ave 53704. I-90/94 exit 135A (US 151), just w. Int corridors. **Pets:** $15 daily fee/pet. Service with restrictions, crate.

Comfort Suites-Madison H

(608) 836-3033. **$79-$209.** 1253 John Q Hammons Dr 53717. US 12 and 14 exit 252 (Greenway Blvd), just sw. Int corridors. **Pets:** Large. $10 daily fee/room. Service with restrictions, crate.

Crowne Plaza Hotel Madison H ❀

(608) 244-4703. **$99-$179.** 4402 E Washington Ave 53704. I-90/94 exit 135A (US 151), 0.4 mi w. Int corridors. **Pets:** $25 one-time fee/pet. Designated rooms, service with restrictions, crate.

Days Inn of Madison H

(608) 223-1800. **$72-$159.** 4402 E Broadway Service Rd 53716. US 12 and 18 exit 266 (US 51), just ne. Int corridors. **Pets:** Medium, dogs only. $10 daily fee/pet. Service with restrictions, supervision.

Econo Lodge of Madison H

(608) 241-4171. **$65-$150.** 4726 E Washington Ave 53704. I-90/94 exit 135A (US 151), just w. Int corridors. **Pets:** Medium. $10 daily fee/pet. Designated rooms, service with restrictions, supervision.

Extended Stay Deluxe Madison West H

(608) 833-2121. **$57-$115.** 45 Junction Ct 53717. US 12 exit 253 (Old Sauk Rd), just w. Int corridors. **Pets:** $25 daily fee/pet. Designated rooms, service with restrictions.

GrandStay Residential Suites Hotel H

(608) 241-2500. **$90-$150.** 5317 High Crossing Blvd 53718. I-90/94 exit 135C (US 151/High Crossing Blvd), 0.5 mi e. Int corridors. **Pets:** Other species. $200 deposit/room, $10 daily fee/pet. Service with restrictions.

Hilton Madison Monona Terrace H

(608) 255-5100. **$149-$450.** 9 E Wilson St 53703. 2 blks e of Capitol Square; downtown. Int corridors. **Pets:** Accepted.

Homewood Suites by Hilton Madison West H

(608) 271-0600. **$109-$399.** 479 Commerce Dr 53719. US 12 exit 254 (Mineral Point Rd), just se. Int corridors. **Pets:** Accepted.

ΔΔΔ ▼▼▼ Hotel Red 🅷 ❖
(608) 819-8228. **$149-$399.** 1501 Monroe St 53711. Downtown. Int corridors. **Pets:** Other species. $50 one-time fee/room. Designated rooms, service with restrictions, supervision.
🆂🅰🆅🅴 📶 ☒ 🅭🅼 🛏 🖥 🍴

▼▼▼ La Quinta Inn & Suites Madison American Center 🅷
(608) 245-0123. **$71-$195.** 5217 E Terrace Dr 53718. US 151 exit 98B (American Pkwy), just sw. Int corridors. **Pets:** Service with restrictions, supervision. 📶 ☒ 🅭🅼 🛏 🖥 ➿

ΔΔΔ ▼▼▼ Magnuson Grand Hotel Madison 🅷 ❖
(608) 224-1500. **$67-$159.** 3510 Mill Pond Rd 53718. I-90 exit 142B, just e on US 12 and 18, then w on south frontage road. Int corridors. **Pets:** Other species. $15 one-time fee/room. Service with restrictions, crate. 🆂🅰🆅🅴 📶 ☒ 🅭🅼 🛏 🖥 ➿

▼▼ Microtel Inn & Suites by Wyndham Madison East 🅷
(608) 242-9000. **$55-$133.** 2139 E Springs Dr 53704. I-90/94 exit 135A (US 151), just s, then 0.5 mi e. Int corridors. **Pets:** Small, dogs only. $10 daily fee/pet. Designated rooms, service with restrictions, supervision. 📶 ☒ 🅭🅼 🛏 🖥

ΔΔΔ ▼▼ Red Roof Inn-Madison #7052 🅼
(608) 241-1787. **$55-$94.** 4830 Hayes Rd 53704. I-90/94 exit 135A (US 151), just sw. Ext corridors. **Pets:** Large, other species. Service with restrictions, supervision. 🆂🅰🆅🅴 📶 ☒ 🅭🅼 🛏 🖥

▼▼▼ Residence Inn by Marriott 🅷
(608) 244-5047. **$139-$169.** 4862 Hayes Rd 53704. I-90/94 exit 135A (US 151), just sw to Hayes Rd, then just ne. Int corridors.
Pets: Accepted. 📶 ☒ 🅭🅼 🛏 🖥 ➿ ☒

ΔΔΔ ▼▼▼ Sheraton Madison Hotel 🅷 ❖
(608) 251-2300. **$89-$209.** 706 John Nolen Dr 53713. US 12 and 18 exit 263 (John Nolen Dr), just n. Int corridors. **Pets:** Large. $25 one-time fee/room. Service with restrictions, supervision.
🅴🅲🅾 🆂🅰🆅🅴 📶 ☒ 🅭🅼 🛏 🖥 🍴 ➿

▼▼▼ Sleep Inn & Suites 🅷
(608) 221-8100. **$79-$129.** 4802 Tradewinds Pkwy 53718. US 12/14/18/ 151 exit 266, 0.5 mi se, then 0.6 mi on Dutch Mill Rd. Int corridors. **Pets:** $5 daily fee/room. Designated rooms, service with restrictions, crate. 📶 ☒ 🅭🅼 🛏 🖥 ➿ ☒

▼▼▼ Staybridge Suites 🅷 ❖
(608) 241-2300. **$89-$199, 3 day notice.** 3301 City View Dr 53718. I-90/94 exit 135C (US 151/High Crossing Blvd), just e. Int corridors. **Pets:** Large. $150 one-time fee/room. Designated rooms, service with restrictions. 📶 ☒ 🅭🅼 🛏 🖥 ➿ ☒

▼▼ Super 8-Madison 🅷
(608) 258-8882. **$60-$150.** 1602 W Beltline Hwy 53713. US 12 and 18 exit 260B (CR D), just w on N Frontage Rd. Int corridors. **Pets:** Medium, other species. $10 one-time fee/pet. Designated rooms, service with restrictions, crate. 📶 ☒ 🛏 🖥 ➿

MANITOWOC

▼▼ AmericInn Lodge & Suites of Manitowoc 🅷
(920) 684-3344. **Call for rates.** 5020 Hecker Rd 54220. I-43 exit 149, just sw. Int corridors. **Pets:** Accepted. 📶 ☒ 🛏 🖥 ➿ ☒

ΔΔΔ ▼▼▼ BEST WESTERN Lakefront Hotel 🅷 ❖
(920) 682-7000. **$79-$99.** 101 Maritime Dr 54220. I-43 exit 152, 4.2 mi e on SR 42 N, then 1 mi s. Int corridors. **Pets:** Other species. $20 one-time fee/room. Designated rooms, service with restrictions, crate.
🆂🅰🆅🅴 📶 ☒ 🛏 🖥 🍴 ➿ ☒

▼▼ Comfort Inn by Choice Hotels 🅷
(920) 683-0220. **$69-$109.** 2200 S 44th St 54220. I-43 exit 149, just e. Int corridors. **Pets:** Large, other species. $25 one-time fee/room. Designated rooms, service with restrictions. 📶 ☒ 🅭🅼 🛏 🖥

▼ Econo Lodge 🅷
(920) 682-8271. **Call for rates.** 908 Washington St 54220. On US 151 business route; downtown. Int corridors. **Pets:** Dogs only. $10 daily fee/ pet. Designated rooms, no service, supervision.
📶 ☒ 🛏 🖥 🍴

▼▼▼ Holiday Inn Manitowoc 🅷
(920) 682-6000. **$129-$169.** 4601 Calumet Ave 54220. I-43 exit 149, just e. Int corridors. **Pets:** Dogs only. $250 deposit/room. Service with restrictions, supervision. 📶 ☒ 🅭🅼 🛏 🖥 🍴 ➿ ☒

MARSHFIELD

▼▼▼ Baymont Inn & Suites-Marshfield 🅷
(715) 384-5240. **$79-$129.** 2107 N Central Ave 54449. On SR 97; 1.6 mi n of SR 13. Int corridors. **Pets:** Dogs only. $10 daily fee/pet. Designated rooms, service with restrictions, supervision.
📶 ☒ 🅭🅼 🛏 🖥 ➿ ☒

▼▼▼ Quality Inn 🅷
(715) 387-8691. **$99-$109.** 114 E Upham St 54449. On SR 97; 0.8 mi n of jct SR 13. Int corridors. **Pets:** Accepted.
📶 ☒ 🅭🅼 🛏 🖥 ➿

MAUSTON

ΔΔΔ ▼▼▼ BEST WESTERN Park Oasis Inn 🅷
(608) 847-6255. **$84-$130.** W5641 Hwy 82 E 53948. I-90/94 exit 69, just se. Int corridors. **Pets:** Other species. $5 daily fee/pet. Designated rooms, service with restrictions, supervision.
🆂🅰🆅🅴 📶 ☒ 🛏 🖥 🍴 ➿

▼▼ Quality Inn 🅷
(608) 847-5959. **Call for rates.** 1001 SR 82 53948. I-90/94 exit 69, just ne. Int corridors. **Pets:** Accepted. 📶 ☒ 🛏 🖥 ➿

▼▼ Super 8 🅼
(608) 847-2300. **$66-$135.** 1001A Hwy 82 E 53948. I-90/94 exit 69, just ne. Int corridors. **Pets:** $10 daily fee/pet. Service with restrictions, supervision. 📶 ☒ 🛏 🖥 ➿

MEDFORD

▼▼ AmericInn Motel of Medford 🅷
(715) 748-2330. **$74-$120.** 435 S 8th St 54451. On SR 13, 0.5 mi s of jct SR 64. Int corridors. **Pets:** $30 one-time fee/pet. Service with restrictions, supervision. 📶 ☒ 🅭🅼 🛏 🖥 ➿ ☒

▼▼ Woodlands Inn & Suites 🅼
(715) 748-3995. **$65-$124.** 854 N 8th St 54451. On SR 13, 0.6 mi n of jct SR 64. Int corridors. **Pets:** $30 one-time fee/room. Designated rooms, service with restrictions, supervision. 📶 ☒ 🛏 🖥 ➿

MENOMONIE

▼ Menomonie Motel 6 #4109 🅷
(715) 235-6901. **$48-$69.** 2100 Stout St 54751. I-94 exit 41 (SR 25), just se. Int corridors. **Pets:** Other species. Service with restrictions, supervision. 📶 ☒ 🛏

ΔΔΔ ▼▼▼ Quality Inn & Suites 🅷
(715) 233-1500. **Call for rates.** 1721 Plaza Dr NE 54751. I-94 exit 45 (CR B), just sw. Int corridors. **Pets:** Other species. $15 one-time fee/pet. 🆂🅰🆅🅴 📶 ☒ 🅭🅼 🛏 🖥 ➿

▼▼ Super 8-Menomonie 🅷
(715) 235-8889. **$69-$105.** 1622 N Broadway 54751. I-94 exit 41 (SR 25), just s. Int corridors. **Pets:** Other species. $10 one-time fee/room. Service with restrictions, crate. 📶 ☒ 🛏 🖥 ➿

MERRILL

▼▼ ◆◆ **America's Best Inn Merrill** 🅷

(715) 536-6880. **$50-$135.** 3209 E Main St 54452. US 51 exit 208, 0.5 mi w on SR 64. Int corridors. **Pets:** Accepted.

🛜 ❌ 🄼 🛏 💻 ➥ ⊠

▼▼ ▼▼ **Americlnn Lodge & Suites of Merrill** 🅷

(715) 536-7979. **$89-$149.** 3300 E Main St 54452. US 51 exit 208, 0.5 mi w on SR 64. Int corridors. **Pets:** Large, other species. $20 daily fee/ pet. Service with restrictions, supervision.

🛜 ❌ 🄼 🛏 💻 ➥ ⊠

🆖 ▼ **Econo Lodge Inn** 🅼

(715) 536-9526. **Call for rates.** 200 S Pineridge Ave 54452. US 51 exit 208, 0.5 mi w on SR 64. Int corridors. **Pets:** Small. $10 daily fee/pet. Designated rooms, service with restrictions, supervision.

[SAVE] 🛜 ❌ 🛏 💻 ➥

MIDDLETON

🆖 ▼▼▼ **Country Inn & Suites By Carlson, Madison West** 🅷

(608) 831-6970. **$114-$169.** 2212 Deming Way 53562. US 12/14 exit 251A, 0.3 mi w on University Ave, then just n. Int corridors. **Pets:** Medium, dogs only. $35 daily fee/pet. Designated rooms, no service, supervision. [SAVE] 🛜 ❌ 🄼 🛏 💻 ➥ ⊠

▼▼▼ **Marriott Madison West** 🅷

(608) 831-2000. **$89-$233.** 1313 John Q Hammons Dr 53562. US 12/14 exit 252 (Greenway Blvd), just w. Int corridors. **Pets:** Accepted.

🛜 ❌ 🄼 🛏 💻 🍴 ➥

▼▼▼ **Residence Inn by Marriott-Madison West/Middleton** 🅷

(608) 662-1100. **$109-$399.** 8400 Market St 53562. US 12/14 exit 252 (Greenway Blvd), just w, then just n; in Greenway Station. Int corridors. **Pets:** Large, other species. $75 one-time fee/room. Designated rooms, service with restrictions. 🛜 ❌ 🄼 🛏 💻 ➥ ⊠

▼▼▼ **Staybridge Suites** 🅷

(608) 664-5888. **$92-$239, 3 day notice.** 7790 Elmwood Ave 53562. US 12/14 exit 251 (University Ave), just nw. Int corridors. **Pets:** Medium, other species. $75 one-time fee/room.

🛜 ❌ 🄼 🛏 💻 ➥ ⊠

MILWAUKEE METROPOLITAN AREA

BROOKFIELD

🆖 ▼▼▼ **BEST WESTERN PLUS Midway Hotel & Suites-Brookfield** 🅷

(262) 786-9540. **$99-$139.** 1005 S Moorland Rd 53005. I-94 exit 301A (Moorland Rd), just s. Int corridors. **Pets:** Small. $15 one-time fee/room. Designated rooms, service with restrictions, supervision.

[SAVE] 🛜 ❌ 🛏 💻 🍴 ➥ ⊠

🆖 ▼▼▼ **Brookfield Suites Hotel & Convention Center** 🅷 ❀

(262) 782-2900. **$99-$395.** 1200 S Moorland Rd 53005. I-94 exit 301A (Moorland Rd), just s. Int corridors. **Pets:** Medium, dogs only. $25 one-time fee/pet. Designated rooms, service with restrictions, crate.

[SAVE] 🛜 ❌ 🄼 🛏 💻 🍴 ➥ ⊠

🆖 ▼▼▼ **Country Inn & Suites By Carlson, Milwaukee-West** 🅷

(262) 782-1400. **$99-$269.** 1250 S Moorland Rd 53005. I-94 exit 301A (Moorland Rd), just se. Int corridors. **Pets:** Accepted.

[SAVE] 🛜 ❌ 🄼 🛏 💻 🍴 ➥ ⊠

▼▼ ▼▼ **Homestead Studio Suites Hotel-Milwaukee/Brookfield** 🅷

(262) 782-9300. **$55-$95.** 325 N Brookfield Rd 53045. I-94 exit 297, 1.1 mi e on US 18, then just e. Int corridors. **Pets:** Medium, dogs only. $25 daily fee/pet. Designated rooms, service with restrictions. 🛜 ❌ 🄼 🛏 💻

▼▼ ▼▼ **La Quinta Inn Milwaukee West Brookfield** 🅷

(262) 782-9100. **$63-$151.** 20391 W Bluemound Rd 53045. I-94 exit 297, just e on US 18. Int corridors. **Pets:** Service with restrictions, supervision. 🛜 ❌ 🄼 🛏 💻

🆖 ▼▼ ▼▼ **Quality Inn-Milwaukee/Brookfield** 🅷

(262) 785-0500. **$69-$150.** 20150 W Bluemound Rd 53045. I-94 exit 297, just e on US 18. Ext/int corridors. **Pets:** $10 one-time fee/room. Designated rooms, service with restrictions, supervision.

[SAVE] 🛜 ❌ 🛏 💻 ➥

🆖 ▼▼▼ **Residence Inn by Marriott Milwaukee-Brookfield** 🅷 ❀

(262) 782-5990. **$99-$399.** 950 S Pinehurst Ct 53005. I-94 exit 301A (Moorland Rd), just s. Ext corridors. **Pets:** Other species. $100 one-time fee/room. Service with restrictions, crate.

[SAVE] 🛜 ❌ 🄼 🛏 💻 ➥ ⊠

🆖 ▼▼▼ **Sheraton Milwaukee Brookfield** 🅷 ❀

(262) 364-1100. **$89-$269.** 375 S Moorland Rd 53005. I-94 exit 301B (Moorland Rd), just n. Int corridors. **Pets:** Medium, dogs only. Service with restrictions, supervision. [SAVE] 🛜 ❌ 🄼 🛏 💻 🍴 ➥

▼▼ ▼▼ **TownePlace Suites by Marriott** 🅷 ❀

(262) 784-8450. **$128-$196.** 600 N Calhoun Rd 53005. I-94 exit 297 eastbound, 2.1 mi e on US 18; exit 301B (Moorland Rd) westbound, 1.5 mi n, then 0.4 mi w on US 18. Int corridors. **Pets:** Large. $100 one-time fee/room. Service with restrictions. 🛜 ❌ 🛏 💻 ➥

BROWN DEER

▼▼ ▼▼ **Candlewood Suites Milwaukee North** 🅷

(414) 355-3939. **$95-$144.** 4483 W Schroeder Dr 53223. Just nw of jct SR 100 and 57. Int corridors. **Pets:** Small. $5 daily fee/pet. Service with restrictions, crate. 🛜 ❌ 🄼 🛏 💻

DELAFIELD

🆖 ▼▼▼ **The Delafield Hotel** 🅷 ❀

(262) 646-1600. **Call for rates.** 415 Genesee St 53018. I-94 exit 285, 0.4 mi n on CR C (Genesee St). Int corridors. **Pets:** Medium, dogs only. $50 one-time fee/pet. Designated rooms, service with restrictions, crate.

[SAVE] 🛜 ❌ 💻 🍴

▼▼ ▼▼ **La Quinta Inn & Suites Milwaukee Delafield** 🅷

(262) 395-1162. **$75-$173.** 2801 Hillside Dr 53018. I-94 exit 287, just s on SR 83, then just e. Int corridors. **Pets:** Service with restrictions, supervision. 🛜 ❌ 🄼 🛏 💻 ➥

FRANKLIN

🆖 ▼▼▼ **Staybridge Suites Milwaukee Airport South** 🅷

(414) 761-3800. **$99-$159, 3 day notice.** 9575 S 27th St 53132. I-94 exit 322 (Ryan Rd), 0.6 mi w at jct 27th St. Int corridors. **Pets:** Medium, dogs only. $50 daily fee/pet. Designated rooms, service with restrictions, supervision. [ECO] [SAVE] 🛜 ❌ 🄼 🛏 💻 ➥ ⊠

GERMANTOWN

▼▼ ▼▼ **Holiday Inn Express Milwaukee NW-Germantown** 🅷

(262) 255-1100. **Call for rates.** W177 N9675 Riversbend Ln 53022. US 41 and 45 exit CR Q (County Line Rd), just w. Int corridors.

Pets: Accepted. 🛜 ❌ 🄼 🛏 💻 ➥

Super 8-Germantown/Milwaukee ⛊
(262) 255-0880. **$68-$95.** N96 W17490 County Line Rd 53022. US 41 and 45 exit CR Q (County Line Rd), just w. Int corridors. **Pets:** Medium, dogs only. $10 daily fee/pet. Service with restrictions, supervision.

GLENDALE

Baymont Inn & Suites Glendale/Milwaukee Northeast ⛊
(414) 961-7272. **$59-$89.** 5485 N Port Washington Rd 53217. I-43 exit 78A (Silver Spring Dr), just se. Int corridors. **Pets:** Medium, other species. $25 daily fee/pet. Crate.

La Quinta Inn & Suites Milwaukee Bayshore Area ⛊
(414) 962-6767. **$90-$188.** 5423 N Port Washington Rd 53217. I-43 exit 78A (Silver Spring Dr), just se. Int corridors. **Pets:** Service with restrictions, supervision.

La Quinta Inn Milwaukee Glendale Hampton Ave ⛊
(414) 964-8484. **$63-$140.** 5110 N Port Washington Rd 53217. I-43 exit 78A (Silver Spring Dr), 0.4 mi se. Int corridors. **Pets:** Service with restrictions, supervision.

Residence Inn by Marriott Milwaukee/Glendale ⛊
(414) 352-0070. **$109-$499.** 7275 N Port Washington Rd 53217. I-43 exit 80 (Good Hope Rd), just e. Ext corridors. **Pets:** Other species. $100 one-time fee/room. Service with restrictions.

GRAFTON

Baymont Inn & Suites Milwaukee-Grafton ⛊
(262) 387-1180. **$84-$139.** 1415 Port Washington Rd 53024. I-43 exit 92 (SR 60), just w, then just s. Int corridors. **Pets:** Accepted.

JACKSON

Comfort Inn & Suites of Jackson ⛊
(262) 677-1133. **$79-$159.** W227 N 16890 Tillie Lake Ct 53037. US 41 exit 64 (SR 60), 2.9 mi e, jct US 45. Int corridors. **Pets:** Medium, dogs only. $15 daily fee/pet. Designated rooms, service with restrictions, supervision.

MEQUON

BEST WESTERN Quiet House & Suites ⛊
(262) 241-3677. **$90-$210.** 10330 N Port Washington Rd 53092. I-43 exit 85 (Mequon Rd), just w on SR 167, then 1 mi s. Int corridors. **Pets:** $15 daily fee/pet. Designated rooms, service with restrictions, supervision.

The Chalet Motel of Mequon Ⓜ
(262) 241-4510. **$59-$159.** 10401 N Port Washington Rd 53092. I-43 exit 85 (Mequon Rd), just w on SR 167, then 1 mi s. Ext corridors. **Pets:** Other species. $10 daily fee/room. Designated rooms, service with restrictions, crate.

MILWAUKEE

Aloft Milwaukee Downtown ⛊ ☘
(414) 226-0122. **$99-$229.** 1230 N Old World 3rd St 53212. I-43 exit 73A, just se. Int corridors. **Pets:** Medium, dogs only. Designated rooms, service with restrictions, supervision.

Ambassador Hotel ⛊
(414) 345-5000. **$119-$399.** 2308 W Wisconsin Ave 53233. I-94 exit 308 (US 41), just n to Wisconsin Ave (US 18) exit, then 1.5 mi e; jct N 24th St. Int corridors. **Pets:** Small, dogs only. $50 one-time fee/room. Designated rooms, service with restrictions, crate.

Comfort Suites at Park Place ⛊
(414) 979-0250. **$89-$149.** 10831 W Park Pl 53224. US 41/45 exit 47B (Good Hope Rd), just e. Int corridors. **Pets:** Medium. $15 daily fee/pet. Designated rooms, service with restrictions, supervision.

Country Inn & Suites By Carlson, Milwaukee Airport ⛊
(414) 762-6018. **Call for rates.** 6200 S 13th St 53221. I-94 exit 319 (College Ave/CR ZZ), just e. Int corridors. **Pets:** Accepted.

Fairfield Inn & Suites by Marriott-Milwaukee Downtown ⛊
(414) 224-8400. **Call for rates.** 710 N Old World 3rd St 53203. Corner of Wisconsin Ave and N Old World 3rd St. Int corridors. **Pets:** Accepted.

Hilton Milwaukee City Center ⛊ ☘
(414) 271-7250. **Call for rates.** 509 W Wisconsin Ave 53203. Corner of W Wisconsin Ave and 5th St. Int corridors. **Pets:** Medium, dogs only. $50 one-time fee/room. Service with restrictions, supervision.

Holiday Inn & Suites Milwaukee Airport ⛊ ☘
(414) 482-4444. **$99-$149, 3 day notice.** 545 W Layton Ave 53207. I-94 exit 317, 1.3 mi e. Int corridors. **Pets:** Other species. $25 one-time fee/room. Designated rooms, service with restrictions, supervision.

Holiday Inn Express & Suites Milwaukee Airport ⛊
(414) 563-4000. **$89-$109.** 1400 W Zellman Ct 53221. I-94 exit 319 (College Ave/CR ZZ), 0.4 mi e to S 13th St, then just s. Int corridors. **Pets:** Service with restrictions, supervision.

Hotel Metro ⛊ ☘
(414) 272-1937. **$159-$389, 3 day notice.** 411 E Mason St 53202. Corner of Mason and Milwaukee sts. Int corridors. **Pets:** Medium, dogs only. $25 daily fee/pet. No service, supervision.

The Iron Horse Hotel ⛊
(414) 374-4766. **$169-$369.** 500 W Florida St 53204. Jct 6th St. Int corridors. **Pets:** Accepted.

La Quinta Inn Milwaukee Northwest ⛊
(414) 535-1300. **$59-$133.** 5442 N Lovers Lane Rd 53225. US 45 exit 46 (Silver Spring Dr), just se. Int corridors. **Pets:** Service with restrictions, supervision.

The Pfister Hotel ⛊
(414) 273-8222. **$139-$2000, 3 day notice.** 424 E Wisconsin Ave 53202. Corner of E Wisconsin Ave and Jefferson St. Int corridors. **Pets:** Accepted.

Sleep Inn & Suites Milwaukee Airport ⛊
(414) 831-2000. **$79-$219.** 4600 S 6th St 53221. I-94/US 41 exit 317 (Layton Ave), 1.5 mi e. Int corridors. **Pets:** Medium, dogs only. $25 daily fee/pet. Designated rooms, service with restrictions.

NEW BERLIN

La Quinta Inn & Suites Milwaukee SW New Berlin ⛊
(262) 717-0900. **$78-$188.** 15300 W Rock Ridge Rd 53151. I-43 exit 57 (Moorland Rd), just se. Int corridors. **Pets:** Service with restrictions, supervision.

OAK CREEK

Candlewood Suites-Milwaukee ⛊ ☘
(414) 570-9999. **Call for rates.** 6440 S 13th St 53154. I-94 exit 319 (College Ave), just e on CR 22, then just s. Int corridors. **Pets:** Medium, other species. $25 daily fee/pet. Service with restrictions, crate.

▼▼▼ Comfort Suites Milwaukee Airport 🅷
(414) 570-1111. **Call for rates.** 6362 S 13th St 53154. I-94 exit 319 (College Ave), just e on CR 22, then just s. Int corridors. **Pets:** Accepted.
🅴🅲🅾 📶 ✖ 🔥M 🔋 💷 🐾 ✖

▼ Days Inn Milwaukee Airport 🅷
(414) 764-1776. **$54-$89.** 1201 W College Ave 53154. I-94 exit 319 (College Ave), just e. Int corridors. **Pets:** Medium, dogs only. $5 daily fee/room. Designated rooms, service with restrictions.
📶 ✖ 🔥M 🔋 💷

▼▼ La Quinta Inn Milwaukee Airport / Oak Creek 🅷
(414) 762-2266. **$63-$144.** 7141 S 13th St 53154. I-94 exit 320 (Rawson Ave), just se. Int corridors. **Pets:** Service with restrictions, supervision.
📶 ✖ 🔥M 🔋 💷

▼▼ MainStay Suites Oak Creek 🅷
(414) 571-8800. **Call for rates.** 1001 W College Ave 53154. I-94 exit 319 (College Ave), just e. Int corridors. **Pets:** Large. $25 one-time fee/room. Service with restrictions, crate. 📶 ✖ 🔥M 🔋 💷

OCONOMOWOC

▼▼ Olympia Resort, Spa & Conference Center 🅷
(262) 369-4999. **$69-$199.** 1350 Royale Mile Rd 53066. I-94 exit 282 (SR 67), 1 mi n. Int corridors. **Pets:** Accepted.
🅴🅲🅾 📶 ✖ 🔥M 🔋 💷 🍴 🐾 ✖

AAA⁀ ▼▼▼ Staybridge Suites Milwaukee West 🅷
(262) 200-2900. **$99-$139, 3 day notice.** 1141 Blue Ribbon Dr 53066. I-94 exit 282 (SR 67), just s. Int corridors. **Pets:** $10 daily fee/pet. Service with restrictions, crate. 🆂🅰🆅🅴 📶 ✖ 🔥M 🔋 💷 🐾 ✖

PEWAUKEE

▼▼▼ Holiday Inn Pewaukee/Milwaukee West 🅷
(262) 506-6300. **Call for rates.** N14 24140 W Tower Pl 53072. I-94 exit 294 (SR 164 N/CR J), just nw. Int corridors. **Pets:** Medium, dogs only. $25 one-time fee/room. Designated rooms, service with restrictions, supervision. 📶 ✖ 🔥M 🔋 💷 🍴 🐾 ✖

PORT WASHINGTON

▼▼ Holiday Inn Harborview 🅷 ✿
(262) 284-9461. **$109-$259, 7 day notice.** 135 E Grand Ave 53074. On SR 33; waterfront of Lake Michigan; downtown. Int corridors. **Pets:** Small. $25 one-time fee/room. Designated rooms, service with restrictions, supervision. 📶 ✖ 🔥M 🔋 💷 🍴 🐾 ✖

SAUKVILLE

AAA⁀ ▼▼ Super 8-Saukville 🅷
(262) 284-9399. **$68-$94.** 180 S Foster Rd 53080. I-43 exit 96, just s. Int corridors. **Pets:** $15 daily fee/pet. Designated rooms, service with restrictions, crate. 🆂🅰🆅🅴 📶 ✖ 🔥M 🔋 💷

WAUKESHA

AAA⁀ ▼▼▼ BEST WESTERN Waukesha Grand 🅷
(262) 524-9300. **Call for rates.** 2840 N Grandview Blvd 53072. I-94 exit 293, just s on CR T. Int corridors. **Pets:** Small, dogs only. $20 one-time fee/room. Designated rooms, supervision.
🆂🅰🆅🅴 📶 ✖ 🔥M 🔋 💷 🐾

▼▼ Extended StayAmerica-Milwaukee-Waukesha 🅷
(262) 798-0217. **$45-$90.** 2520 Plaza Ct 53186. I-94 exit 297, just w on CR JJ (Bluemound Rd). Int corridors. **Pets:** $25 daily fee/pet. Designated rooms, service with restrictions. 📶 ✖ 🔥M 🔋 💷

AAA⁀ ▼▼▼ Ramada Waukesha 🅷
(262) 547-7770. **$50-$105.** 2111 E Moreland Blvd 53186. I-94 exit 297, 0.9 mi sw on US 18 (E Moreland Ave). Int corridors. **Pets:** Small. $10 daily fee/pet. Designated rooms, service with restrictions, supervision.
🆂🅰🆅🅴 📶 ✖ 🔋 💷 🐾 ✖

▼▼ Super 8-Waukesha 🅷
(262) 786-6015. **$54-$95.** 2510 Plaza Ct 53186. I-94 exit 297, just w on CR JJ (Bluemound Rd). Int corridors. **Pets:** Medium. $10 daily fee/pet. Designated rooms, service with restrictions.
📶 ✖ 🔥M 🔋 💷

WAUWATOSA

▼▼ Extended StayAmerica-Milwaukee-Wauwatosa 🅷
(414) 443-1909. **$58-$100.** 11121 W North Ave 53226. US 45 exit 42A, just n. Int corridors. **Pets:** $25 daily fee/pet. Designated rooms, service with restrictions. 📶 ✖ 🔥M 🔋 💷

▼▼ Holiday Inn Express Milwaukee West-Medical Center 🅷
(414) 778-0333. **$79-$159.** 11111 W North Ave 53226. US 45 exit 42A, just n on SR 100, then just w. Int corridors. **Pets:** Medium. $66 one-time fee/room. Service with restrictions, crate. 📶 ✖ 🔥M 🔋 💷

▼▼ Super 8 of Milwaukee West 🅷
(414) 257-0140. **$59-$99.** 115 N Mayfair Rd 53226. I-94 exit 304B, just n on SR 100. Int corridors. **Pets:** Accepted. 📶 ✖ 🔥M 🔋 💷

WEST BEND

▼▼ AmericInn of West Bend 🅷
(262) 334-0307. **$75-$90.** 2424 W Washington St 53095. US 45 exit Washington St/SR 33, just w. Int corridors. **Pets:** Small, dogs only. $30 daily fee/room. Designated rooms, service with restrictions, crate.
📶 ✖ 🔋 💷

END METROPOLITAN AREA

MINOCQUA

▼▼ AmericInn of Minocqua 🅷
(715) 356-3730. **Call for rates.** 700 Hwy 51 54548. On US 51; downtown. Int corridors. **Pets:** Accepted.
🅴🅲🅾 📶 ✖ 🔥M 🔋 💷 🐾 ✖

AAA⁀ ▼▼▼ BEST WESTERN PLUS Concord Inn 🅷 ✿
(715) 356-1800. **$135-$150.** 320 Front St 54548. On US 51; downtown. Int corridors. **Pets:** Medium, dogs only. $10 daily fee/pet. Designated rooms, service with restrictions, supervision.
🆂🅰🆅🅴 📶 ✖ 🔥M 🔋 💷 🐾 ✖

AAA⁀ ▼▼▼ Quality Inn 🅷
(715) 358-2588. **Call for rates.** 8729 Hwy 51 N 54548. On US 51 at SR 70 W. Int corridors. **Pets:** Accepted. 🆂🅰🆅🅴 📶 ✖ 🔋 💷 🐾

▼▼ The Waters of Minocqua 🅷
(715) 358-4000. **$69-$406, 5 day notice.** 8116 Hwy 51 S 54548. On US 51, 1 mi s. Int corridors. **Pets:** Other species. $20 daily fee/pet. No service, supervision. 🅴🅲🅾 📶 ✖ 🔥M 🔋 💷 🍴 🐾 ✖

MONONA

▼▼ AmericInn of Madison South/Monona 🅷
(608) 222-8601. **$90-$140.** 101 W Broadway 53716. US 12/18 exit 265 (Monona Dr), just nw. Int corridors. **Pets:** Other species. $10 daily fee/pet. Designated rooms, no service. 📶 ✖ 🔥M 🔋 💷 🐾 ✖

MONROE

▼▼ Super 8 of Monroe 🅷
(608) 325-1500. **$73-$129.** 500 6th St 53566. On SR 69 S, 0.5 mi s of jct SR 81/11. Int corridors. **Pets:** Accepted.
🅴🅲🅾 📶 ✖ 🔥M 🔋 💷 🐾

NEILLSVILLE

▼▼ Super 8-Neillsville H

(715) 743-8080. **$66-$90.** 1000 E Division St 54456. US 10, jct Boon Blvd and Division St. Int corridors. **Pets:** Accepted.

🛜 ✕ 👤M 🛏 💻 ⌁

NEW GLARUS

◢◣◤ ▼▼▼ Chalet Landhaus Inn H

(608) 527-5234. **$85-$225.** 801 SR 69 53574. On SR 69. Int corridors. **Pets:** Dogs only. $35 daily fee/pet. Service with restrictions, supervision.

SAVE 🛜 ✕ 👤M 🛏 ❙❙ ⌁ ✕

▼▼ Swiss Aire Motel H

(608) 527-2138. **$70-$110.** 1200 SR 69 53574. Just s of jct SR 39/69. Ext/int corridors. **Pets:** Accepted. 🛜 ✕ 🛏 💻

NEW LONDON

▼▼ AmericInn Lodge & Suites of New London H

(920) 982-5700. **$59-$189.** 1404 N Shawano St 54961. US 45 exit US 54, just n. Int corridors. **Pets:** Medium, other species. $10 one-time fee/pet. Designated rooms, service with restrictions, supervision.

🛜 ✕ 👤M 🛏 💻 ⌁

ONALASKA

▼▼ Baymont Inn & Suites LaCrosse-Onalaska H

(608) 783-7191. **$74-$179.** 3300 Kinney Coulee Rd N 54650. I-90 exit 5, just ne. Int corridors. **Pets:** Accepted. 🛜 ✕ 👤M 🛏 💻 ⌁

▼▼▼ Holiday Inn Express H

(608) 783-6555. **Call for rates.** 9409 Hwy 16 54650. I-90 exit 5, 1 mi e. Int corridors. **Pets:** Service with restrictions, supervision.

🛜 ✕ 👤M 🛏 💻 ⌁

▼▼▼ Microtel Inn by Wyndham Onalaska/La Crosse H

(608) 783-0833. **$55-$160.** 3240 N Kinney Coulee Rd 54650. I-90 exit 5, just ne. Int corridors. **Pets:** Accepted. 🛜 ✕ 🛏 💻

▼▼▼ Stoney Creek Inn H

(608) 781-3060. **$89-$117.** 3060 S Kinney Coulee Rd 54650. I-90 exit 5, just se. Int corridors. **Pets:** Accepted.

🛜 ✕ 👤M 🛏 💻 ⌁ ✕

OSCEOLA

▼▼ River Valley Inn & Suites H

(715) 294-4060. **Call for rates.** 1030 Cascade St 54020. Just n on SR 35. Int corridors. **Pets:** Accepted. 🛜 ✕ 🛏 💻 ⌁

OSHKOSH

▼▼▼ Comfort Suites at Oshkosh H

(920) 230-7378. **$70-$170.** 400 S Koeller St 54902. US 41 exit 117 (9th Ave), just e. Int corridors. **Pets:** Medium, dogs only. $15 daily fee/room. Designated rooms, service with restrictions, supervision.

🛜 ✕ 👤M 🛏 💻 ⌁ ✕

▼▼ Fairfield Inn by Marriott H

(920) 233-8504. **$109-$159.** 1800 S Koeller St 54902. US 41 exit 117 (9th Ave), 0.8 mi s on east frontage road. Int corridors. **Pets:** Accepted.

🛜 ✕ 👤M 🛏 💻 ⌁

▼▼▼ Hawthorn Suites by Wyndham H

(920) 303-1133. **$100-$210.** 3105 S Washburn St 54904. US 41 exit 116 (SR 44), just w, then just s. Int corridors. **Pets:** Small, dogs only. $15 daily fee/room. Designated rooms, service with restrictions, supervision.

🛜 ✕ 👤M 🛏 💻 ❙❙ ⌁ ✕

▼▼▼ Holiday Inn Express & Suites H

(920) 303-1300. **Call for rates.** 2251 Westowne Ave 54904. US 41 exit 119, 0.4 mi w of jct SR 21. Int corridors. **Pets:** Accepted.

ECO 🛜 ✕ 👤M 🛏 💻 ⌁

▼▼ La Quinta Inn Oshkosh H

(920) 233-4190. **$59-$133.** 1886 Rath Ln 54902. US 41 exit 119, jct SR 21. Int corridors. **Pets:** Service with restrictions, supervision.

🛜 ✕ 👤M 💻

PLATTEVILLE

▼▼ Mound View Inn H

(608) 348-9518. **$65-$150, 3 day notice.** 1755 E Business Hwy 151 53818. On US 151 exit 21, just w. Int corridors. **Pets:** Accepted.

🛜 ✕ 🛏 ✕

◢◣◤ ▼▼▼ Super 8 H

(608) 348-8800. **$62-$91.** 100 Hwy 80/81 S 53818. Jct US 151 and SR 80. Int corridors. **Pets:** Other species. $10 daily fee/pet. Service with restrictions. SAVE 🛜 ✕ 👤M 🛏 💻

PLEASANT PRAIRIE

▼▼ La Quinta Inn Pleasant Prairie Kenosha H

(262) 857-7911. **$59-$155.** 7540 118th Ave 53158. I-94 exit 344 (SR 50), just e. Int corridors. **Pets:** Service with restrictions, supervision.

🛜 ✕ 👤M 🛏 💻

PLOVER

▼▼ AmericInn of Plover H

(715) 342-1244. **Call for rates.** 1501 American Dr 54467. I-39 exit 153 (CR B), just nw. Int corridors. **Pets:** Medium, other species. $15 daily fee/room. Designated rooms, service with restrictions, crate.

🛜 ✕ 👤M 🛏 💻 ⌁ ✕

▼▼▼ Comfort Inn H

(715) 342-0400. **Call for rates.** 1560 American Dr 54467. I-39 exit 153 (CR B), just w. Int corridors. **Pets:** Accepted.

🛜 ✕ 👤M 🛏 ⌁

PORTAGE

◢◣◤ ▼▼▼ Comfort Suites H

(608) 745-4717. **$74-$199.** N5780 Kinney Rd 53901. I-90/94 exit 108A (SR 78). Int corridors. **Pets:** Medium, dogs only. $20 daily fee/pet. Service with restrictions, supervision. SAVE 🛜 ✕ 👤M 🛏 💻 ⌁ ✕

◢◣◤ ▼▼▼ Days Inn H

(608) 742-1554. **$50-$130.** N 5781 Kinney Rd 53901. I-90/94 exit 108 (SR 78), just s. Int corridors. **Pets:** Dogs only. $10 daily fee/pet. Designated rooms, service with restrictions, crate.

SAVE 🛜 ✕ 🛏 💻 ⌁

▼▼ Super 8-Portage H ✿

(608) 742-8330. **$50-$92.** 3000 New Pinery Rd 53901. I-39 exit 92, just s. Int corridors. **Pets:** Other species. $11 daily fee/room. Service with restrictions, supervision. 🛜 ✕ 🛏 💻

PRAIRIE DU CHIEN

▼▼▼ Country Inn & Suites By Carlson H

(608) 326-5700. **$89-$199.** 1801 Cabela's Ln 53821. On SR 35, 2 mi n of jct US 18/SR 35 S and 27 N. Int corridors. **Pets:** Accepted.

🛜 ✕ 👤M 🛏 💻 ❙❙ ⌁ ✕

▼▼ Super 8-Prairie Du Chien H

(608) 326-8777. **$50-$130.** 1930 S Marquette Rd 53821. On US 18, 1.9 mi e of jct SR 27 N. Ext/int corridors. **Pets:** Accepted.

🛜 ✕ 👤M 🛏 💻

RACINE

▼▼▼ Racine Marriott Hotel H

(262) 886-6100. **$99-$179.** 7111 Washington Ave 53406. I-94 exit 333, 4 mi e on SR 20. Int corridors. **Pets:** Accepted.

🛜 ✕ 👤M 🛏 💻 ❙❙ ⌁ ✕

REEDSBURG

▼▼ Quality Inn **H**

(608) 524-8535. **Call for rates.** 2115 E Main St 53959. Jct SR 23 and 33, then 2 mi e. Int corridors. **Pets:** $10 daily fee/room. Designated rooms, service with restrictions, crate.

RHINELANDER

▼ ▼ Comfort Inn **H**

(715) 369-1100. **$89-$99.** 1490 Lincoln St 54501. On Business Rt US 8, 2.6 mi e of jct SR 47. Int corridors. **Pets:** Dogs only. $25 deposit/pet, $10 daily fee/pet. Designated rooms, service with restrictions, supervision.

(AAA) ▼ ▼ Days Inn & Suites **H**

(715) 362-7100. **$89-$139.** 70 N Stevens St 54501. Between Davenport and Rives sts; downtown. Int corridors. **Pets:** Other species. $10 daily fee/pet. Designated rooms, service with restrictions, supervision.

RICE LAKE

▼ ▼ Microtel Inn & Suites by Wyndham Rice Lake **H**

(715) 736-2010. **$70-$93.** 2771 Decker Dr 54868. US 53 exit 140 (CR O), just ne. Int corridors. **Pets:** $10 one-time fee/pet. Service with restrictions, supervision.

RICHLAND CENTER

▼ ▼ The Center Lodge **H**

(608) 647-8988. **$70-$90, 10 day notice.** 100 Foundry Dr 53581. 0.9 mi e on US 14. Int corridors. **Pets:** Other species. $50 deposit/pet. Service with restrictions, supervision.

RIVER FALLS

▼ ▼ Country Inn River Falls **H**

(715) 425-9500. **$70-$135.** 1525 Commerce Ct 54022. Just n of jct SR 65 and 35. Int corridors. **Pets:** Medium. $10 daily fee/pet. Designated rooms, service with restrictions, crate.

▼▼▼ Riverview Hotel & Suites **H**

(715) 425-1045. **$100-$110.** 100 Spring St 54022. Downtown. Int corridors. **Pets:** Accepted.

ROTHSCHILD

▼ ▼ Candlewood Suites-Wausau **H** 🐾

(715) 355-8900. **Call for rates.** 803 Industrial Park Dr 54474. I-39 exit 185 (Business Rt US 51), just se. Int corridors. **Pets:** Other species. $25 one-time fee/pet. Service with restrictions, crate.

▼▼▼ Holiday Inn Hotel & Suites **H**

(715) 355-1111. **$94-$149, 3 day notice.** 1000 Imperial Ave 54474. I-39 exit 185 (Business Rt US 51), just se. Int corridors. **Pets:** Medium. $35 one-time fee/room. Service with restrictions, supervision.

▼ ▼ Stoney Creek Inn **H** 🐾

(715) 355-6858. **$79-$180.** 1100 Imperial Ave 54474. I-39 exit 185 (Business Rt US 51), just e. Int corridors. **Pets:** Medium, dogs only. $25 daily fee/pet. Designated rooms, service with restrictions, crate.

SHAWANO

▼▼▼ Comfort Inn & Suites **H**

(715) 524-9090. **$89-$93.** W7393 River Bend Rd 54166. SR 29 exit 225, just n on SR 22. Int corridors. **Pets:** Small, dogs only. $25 daily fee/pet. Designated rooms, service with restrictions, supervision.

▼ ▼ Super 8-Shawano **M**

(715) 526-6688. **$65-$109.** 211 Waukechon St 54166. 1.2 mi e on SR 29 business route; SR 29 exit 227, 1.8 mi n, then 1.1 mi w. Int corridors. **Pets:** Other species. $10 daily fee/pet. Service with restrictions, supervision.

SHEBOYGAN

(AAA) ▼▼▼ GrandStay Residential Suites Hotel **H**

(920) 208-8000. **$90-$170.** 708 Niagara Ave 53081. Jct N 7th St; downtown. Int corridors. **Pets:** Other species. $10 daily fee/room. Service with restrictions. (SAVE)

▼ ▼ La Quinta Inn Sheboygan **H**

(920) 457-2321. **$75-$195.** 2932 Kohler Memorial Dr 53081. I-43 exit 126, 1 mi e on SR 23. Int corridors. **Pets:** Service with restrictions, supervision.

(AAA) ▼ ▼ Quality Inn **H**

(920) 457-7724. **$71-$119.** 4332 N 40th St 53083. I-43 exit 128, 0.3 mi e on Business Rt SR 42. Int corridors. **Pets:** Other species. $10 daily fee/pet. Designated rooms, service with restrictions, crate. (SAVE)

SHEBOYGAN FALLS

▼▼▼ The Rochester Inn, A Historic Hotel **BB**

(920) 467-3123. **$110-$170, 21 day notice.** 504 Water St 53085. Just e of downtown via CR PP. Int corridors. **Pets:** Accepted.

SIREN

(AAA) ▼▼▼ The Lodge at Crooked Lake **H**

(715) 349-2500. **$89-$275.** 24271 SR 35 N 54872. On SR 35, 0.5 mi n of jct SR 70. Int corridors. **Pets:** Accepted. (SAVE)

SPARTA

(AAA) ▼▼▼ BEST WESTERN PLUS Sparta Trail Lodge **H**

(608) 269-2664. **Call for rates.** 4445 Theatre Rd 54656. I-90 exit 28 (SR 16), just w. Int corridors. **Pets:** Large. $20 daily fee/pet. Designated rooms, supervision. (SAVE)

▼ ▼ Country Inn & Suites By Carlson **H**

(608) 269-3110. **$89-$150.** 737 Avon Rd 54656. I-90 exit 25 (SR 27), just n. Int corridors. **Pets:** $10 daily fee/pet. Service with restrictions, supervision.

▼ ▼ Super 8 Sparta **H**

(608) 269-8489. **$79-$135.** 716 Avon Rd 54656. I-90 exit 25 (SR 27), just n. Int corridors. **Pets:** Other species. $10 daily fee/pet. Service with restrictions, crate.

SPOONER

(AAA) ▼ ▼ BEST WESTERN American Heritage Inn **H**

(715) 635-9770. **$90-$170.** 101 W Maple St 54801. On SR 70, just e of US 63, 1 mi w of US 53. Int corridors. **Pets:** Accepted. (SAVE)

(AAA) ▼ ▼ Country House Motel & RV Park **M**

(715) 635-8721. **Call for rates.** 717 S River St 54801. On US 63, 0.5 mi s of jct SR 70. Ext/int corridors. **Pets:** Medium, dogs only. $10 daily fee/pet. Designated rooms, service with restrictions, supervision. (SAVE)

▼ Inn Town Motel **M** 🐾

(715) 635-3529. **$40-$70, 3 day notice.** 801 River St 54801. 0.8 mi n of jct US 63 and SR 70. Ext corridors. **Pets:** Dogs only. $10 daily fee/pet. Supervision.

STEVENS POINT

▼▼▼ Country Inn & Suites By Carlson **H**

(715) 345-7000. **$81-$144.** 301 Division St N 54481. I-39 exit 161 (US 51 business route), 0.6 mi s. Int corridors. **Pets:** Other species. $25 one-time fee/room. No service, supervision.

▼▼▼▼ Fairfield Inn by Marriott 🅷
(715) 342-9300. **$90-$180.** 5317 Hwy 10 E 54481. I-39 exit 158A (US 10), just se. Int corridors. **Pets:** Accepted. 📶 ❌ 🛅 💻 🏊

▼▼▼▼ Holiday Inn Express 🅷
(715) 344-0000. **Call for rates.** 1100 Amber Ave 54481. I-39 exit 158 (US 10), 1 mi e, then just n. Int corridors. **Pets:** Large. $25 daily fee/room. Service with restrictions, supervision.
📶 ❌ 🏋 🛅 💻 🏊

▼▼▼ La Quinta Inn & Suites Stevens Point 🅷
(715) 344-1900. **$71-$162.** 4917 Main St 54481. I-39 exit 158B (US 10), just sw. Int corridors. **Pets:** Service with restrictions, supervision.
📶 ❌ 🛅 💻 🏊

SUN PRAIRIE

▲▲▲ ▼▼▼ Quality Inn & Suites-Sun Prairie 🅷
(608) 834-9889. **$69-$179.** 105 Business Park Dr 53590. US 151 exit 103 (CR N), just n. Int corridors. **Pets:** Small, dogs only. $10 daily fee/pet. Service with restrictions, supervision.
[SAVE] 📶 ❌ 🏋 🛅 💻 🏊

SUPERIOR

▲▲▲ ▼▼▼ Barkers Island Inn 🅷
(715) 392-7152. **$79-$189.** 300 Marina Dr 54880. Just ne of US 2/53; on Barkers Island. Int corridors. **Pets:** Large, other species. $10 daily fee/room. Designated rooms, service with restrictions, crate.
[SAVE] 📶 ❌ 🏋 🛅 💻 🍴 🏊 ❎

▲▲▲ ▼▼▼ BEST WESTERN Bay Walk Inn 🅷
(715) 392-7600. **$70-$170.** 1405 Susquehanna Ave 54880. Just e of US 2 on Belknap St. Int corridors. **Pets:** Accepted.
[SAVE] 📶 ❌ 🏋 🛅 💻 🏊 ❎

▲▲▲ ▼▼▼ BEST WESTERN Bridgeview Motor Inn 🅷
(715) 392-8174. **$60-$189.** 415 Hammond Ave 54880. 0.8 mi n at south end of Blatnik Bridge. Int corridors. **Pets:** Accepted.
[SAVE] 📶 ❌ 🏋 🛅 💻 🏊 ❎

THORP

▼▼▼ Fairbridge Inn 🅷
(715) 669-5959. **Call for rates.** 203 1/2 W Hill St 54771. US 29 exit 108 (SR 73), just nw. Int corridors. **Pets:** Accepted.
📶 ❌ 🏋 🛅 💻 🏊 ❎

TOMAH

▼▼▼ AmericInn Lodge & Suites of Tomah 🅷 🐾
(608) 372-4100. **$79-$159.** 750 Vandervort St 54660. I-94 exit 143 (SR 21), just e. Int corridors. **Pets:** Medium. $10 daily fee/room. Designated rooms, service with restrictions, crate. 📶 ❌ 🏋 🛅 💻 🏊

▲▲▲ ▼▼▼ BEST WESTERN Tomah Hotel 🅷
(608) 372-3211. **$70-$120.** 1017 E McCoy Blvd 54660. I-94 exit 143 (SR 21), just e. Int corridors. **Pets:** Accepted.
[SAVE] 📶 ❌ 🛅 💻 🍴 🏊 ❎

▼▼▼ Econo Lodge 🅷
(608) 372-9100. **$50-$200.** 2005 N Superior Ave 54660. I-94 exit 143 (SR 21), just w. Ext/int corridors. **Pets:** Other species. $10 daily fee/pet. Service with restrictions. 📶 ❌ 🛅 💻 🏊

▲▲▲ ▼▼▼ Lark Inn Ⓜ
(608) 372-5981. **$55-$129.** 229 N Superior Ave 54660. I-94 exit 143 (SR 21), 1.5 mi s on US 12; I-90 exit 41, 2 mi n on US 12. Ext/int corridors. **Pets:** Accepted. [SAVE] 📶 ❌ 🏋 🛅 💻

▼▼▼ Quality Inn Tomah 🅷
(608) 372-6600. **Call for rates.** 305 Wittig Rd 54660. I-94 exit 143 (SR 21), just w. Int corridors. **Pets:** Medium. $10 deposit/pet, $10 daily fee/pet. Designated rooms, supervision. 📶 ❌ 🛅 💻 🏊

▲▲▲ ▼▼▼ Super 8-Tomah 🅷
(608) 372-3901. **$66-$139.** 1008 E McCoy Blvd 54660. I-94 exit 143 (SR 21), just e. Int corridors. **Pets:** Other species. $10 daily fee/room. Service with restrictions, crate. [SAVE] 📶 ❌ 🛅 💻

TOMAHAWK

▼▼▼ Rodeway Inn & Suites 🅷
(715) 453-8900. **$69-$130.** 1738 Comfort Dr 54487. US 51 exit 229, just nw. Int corridors. **Pets:** $50 one-time fee/room. Service with restrictions, supervision. 📶 ❌ 🏋 🛅 💻 🏊 ❎

▼▼▼ Super 8-Tomahawk 🅷
(715) 453-5210. **$65-$180.** 108 W Mohawk Dr 54487. US 51 exit 231, 1.4 mi w, then 0.6 mi s on 4th St. Int corridors. **Pets:** $10 daily fee/pet. Designated rooms, service with restrictions, supervision.
📶 ❌ 🏋 🛅 💻 🏊 ❎

TWO RIVERS

▼▼▼ Lighthouse Inn on Lake Michigan 🅷
(920) 793-4524. **$89-$150.** 1515 Memorial Dr 54241. 0.3 mi s on SR 42. Int corridors. **Pets:** Accepted. 📶 ❌ 🏋 🛅 💻 🍴 🏊 ❎

VERONA

▼▼▼ Holiday Inn Express Hotel & Suites Madison-Verona 🅷
(608) 497-4500. **$130-$200.** 515 W Verona Ave 53593. US 18 and 151 exit 76, 0.6 mi ne. Int corridors. **Pets:** Medium. $25 daily fee/pet. Designated rooms, service with restrictions, supervision.
📶 ❌ 🏋 🛅 💻 🏊

VIROQUA

▼▼ Hickory Hill Motel Ⓜ
(608) 637-3104. **Call for rates.** S 5539 US 14 54665. 2.1 mi se of downtown, on US 61/US 14/SR 27/SR 82. Ext corridors. **Pets:** Accepted.
📶 ❌ 🛅 🏊

WATERFORD

▼▼▼ Baymont Inn & Suites-Waterford 🅷
(262) 534-4100. **$89-$209.** 750 Fox Ln 53185. On SR 36, 1 mi s of jct SR 164. Int corridors. **Pets:** Accepted.
📶 ❌ 🏋 🛅 💻 🏊 ❎

WATERTOWN

▼▼▼ Super 8 🅷
(920) 261-1188. **$71-$96.** 1730 S Church St 53094. On SR 26, 1.5 mi s of jct SR 19. Int corridors. **Pets:** Dogs only. $100 deposit/room, $10 daily fee/pet. Service with restrictions, supervision.
📶 ❌ 🏋 🛅 💻 🏊

WAUPACA

▲▲▲ ▼▼▼▼ BEST WESTERN PLUS Grand Seasons Hotel 🅷
(715) 258-9212. **$100-$150.** 110 Grand Seasons Dr 54981. Jct US 10/SR 49/54 and CR QQ, just w. Int corridors. **Pets:** Accepted.
[SAVE] 📶 ❌ 🏋 🛅 💻 🍴 🏊 ❎

▼▼▼ Comfort Suites at Foxfire 🅷
(715) 942-0500. **Call for rates.** 199 Foxfire Dr 54981. Jct US 10/SR 49/54 and CR QQ, 0.7 mi sw. Int corridors. **Pets:** $15 daily fee/room. Service with restrictions, supervision. 📶 ❌ 🏋 🛅 💻 🏊

WAUPUN

▼▼ Inn Town Motel Ⓜ
(920) 324-4211. **$54-$120.** 27 S State St 53963. US 151 exit 146 (SR 49), 1 mi w on Main St, then just s. Ext corridors. **Pets:** Dogs only. $10 daily fee/pet. Designated rooms, service with restrictions, supervision.
📶 ❌ 🏋 🛅 💻

WAUSAU

BEST WESTERN Midway Hotel 🅷 🐾
(715) 842-1616. **$70-$115.** 2901 Hummingbird Rd 54401. I-39 exit 190 (CR NN), just sw. Int corridors. **Pets:** Medium. $20 daily fee/room. Designated rooms, service with restrictions, supervision.
⬛ 🛜 ✖ ♿ 🍴 💻 🍴 🏊 ✖

Days Inn 🅼
(715) 842-0641. **$49-$99.** 116 S 17th Ave 54401. I-39 exit 192, just ne. Int corridors. **Pets:** Accepted. 🛜 ✖ 🍴 💻

Jefferson Street Inn 🅷 🐾
(715) 845-6500. **$109-$325, 3 day notice.** 201 Jefferson St 54403. Just w of jct 2nd St; center. Int corridors. **Pets:** $30 daily fee/room. Designated rooms, service with restrictions, crate.
🌿 ⬛ 🛜 ✖ ♿ 🍴 💻 🍴 🏊 ✖

La Quinta Inn Wausau 🅷
(715) 842-0421. **$59-$133.** 1910 Stewart Ave 54401. I-39 exit 192, just se. Int corridors. **Pets:** Service with restrictions, supervision.
🛜 ✖ 🍴 💻 🏊

Rib Mountain Inn 🅷
(715) 848-2802. **$69-$499, 3 day notice.** 2900 Rib Mountain Way 54401. I-39 exit 190 (CR NN), 1.2 mi w on N Mountain Rd (CR NN), then just s. Ext/int corridors. **Pets:** Accepted. 🛜 ✖ 🍴 💻 ✖

Super 8 Wausau 🅷
(715) 848-2888. **$47-$85.** 2006 Stewart Ave W 54401. I-39 exit 192, just se. Int corridors. **Pets:** Dogs only. $10 daily fee/pet. Designated rooms, service with restrictions, supervision. ⬛ 🛜 ✖ 🍴 💻 🏊

WAUTOMA

Boarders Inn & Suites 🅷
(920) 787-5050. **Call for rates.** W7696 SR 21/73 54982. On SR 21 and 73, 1.2 mi e. Int corridors. **Pets:** Accepted.
🛜 ✖ ♿ 🍴 💻 🏊 ✖

Super 8-Wautoma 🅷
(920) 787-4811. **$73-$136.** W7607 SR 21/73 54982. On SR 21 and 73, 1.5 mi e. Int corridors. **Pets:** Large, other species. $10 one-time fee/pet. Designated rooms, service with restrictions, supervision.
🛜 ✖ ♿ 🍴 💻 🏊

WEST SALEM

AmericInn Motel & Suites of West Salem 🅷
(608) 786-3340. **$83-$153.** 125 Buol Rd 54669. I-90 exit 12, just sw on CR C. Int corridors. **Pets:** Designated rooms, supervision.
🛜 ✖ ♿ 🍴 💻 🏊 ✖

WISCONSIN DELLS

Americas Best Value Day's End Motel 🅼
(608) 254-8171. **$50-$110, 3 day notice.** N 604 Hwy 12-16 53965. I-90/94 exit 85 (US 12), 0.8 mi nw. Ext corridors. **Pets:** Large, other species. $10 daily fee/pet. Designated rooms.
⬛ 🛜 ✖ 🍴 💻 🏊 ✖

Baker's Sunset Bay Resort 🅷 🐾
(608) 254-8406. **$78-$169, 14 day notice.** 921 Canyon Rd 53965. I-90/94 exit 92 (US 12), 0.5 mi w, just e on Adams St, then 0.8 mi n. Ext/int species. $10 daily fee/pet. Service with restrictions, crate. ⬛ 🛜 ✖ 🍴 💻 🏊 ✖

Super 8-Wisconsin Dells 🅷
(608) 254-6464. **$48-$140.** 800 CR H 53965. I-90/94 exit 87 (SR 13), just e. Int corridors. **Pets:** Accepted. 🛜 ✖ 🍴 💻 🏊

WISCONSIN RAPIDS

Hotel Mead 🅷 🐾
(715) 423-1500. **$89-$199.** 451 E Grand Ave 54494. Just e of downtown. Int corridors. **Pets:** Other species. $100 deposit/room, $15 daily fee/room. Designated rooms, no service, supervision.
🛜 ✖ ♿ 🍴 💻 🍴 🏊 ✖

Quality Inn 🅷
(715) 423-5506. **$80-$85.** 3120 8th St S 54494. 1.5 mi s on SR 13. Int corridors. **Pets:** Dogs only. $10 one-time fee/room. Service with restrictions, supervision. 🛜 ✖ 🍴 💻 🏊

Sleep Inn & Suites 🅷
(715) 424-6800. **$64-$120.** 4221 8th St S 54494. 1.3 mi s on SR 13 from jct SR 54. Int corridors. **Pets:** Medium, dogs only. $15 daily fee/room. Designated rooms, service with restrictions, supervision.
🛜 ✖ ♿ 🍴 💻 🏊

WITTENBERG

BEST WESTERN Wittenberg Inn 🅷
(715) 253-3755. **$80-$90.** W17267 Red Oak Ln 54499. US 29 exit 198, just se. Int corridors. **Pets:** $20 one-time fee/room. Designated rooms, service with restrictions, supervision.
⬛ 🛜 ✖ ♿ 🍴 💻 🏊 ✖

WYOMING

AFTON

◈◈◈ ▼ Lazy B Motel
(307) 885-3187. **$82-$110.** 219 Washington St (US 89) 83110. On US 89; center. Ext corridors. **Pets:** Large, dogs only. Service with restrictions, supervision. ⟨SAVE⟩ 🛜 ⊠ 🛏 🖥 🏊

BUFFALO

◈◈◈ ▼▼▼ BEST WESTERN Crossroads Inn H
(307) 684-2256. **Call for rates.** 75 N Bypass Rd 82834. I-25 exit 299 (US 16), just w. Ext/int corridors. **Pets:** Other species. $10 daily fee/pet. Designated rooms, service with restrictions, supervision.
⟨SAVE⟩ 🛜 🛏 🖥 🍴 🏊

◈◈◈ ▼▼▼ Comfort Inn H
(307) 684-9564. **$74-$130.** 65 US Hwy 16 E 82834. I-25 exit 299 (US 16 E), just e; I-90 exit 58, 1.3 mi w. Ext/int corridors. **Pets:** Medium, other species. $10 daily fee/pet. Designated rooms, service with restrictions, supervision. ⟨SAVE⟩ 🛜 ⊠ ⟨&M⟩ 🛏 🖥 🏊

◈◈◈ ▼▼▼ The Occidental Hotel H ❀
(307) 684-0451. **$75-$285, 14 day notice.** 10 N Main St 82834. Center. Int corridors. **Pets:** $10 one-time fee/room. Designated rooms, service with restrictions, supervision. ⟨SAVE⟩ 🛜 ⊠ 🍴 ⟨🄲⟩

◈◈◈ ▼▼ Super 8 of Buffalo H
(307) 684-2531. **$65-$105.** 655 E Hart St 82834. I-25 exit 299 (US 16), just w; I-90 exit 58, 1.3 mi w. Int corridors. **Pets:** Other species. $10 daily fee/pet. Designated rooms, service with restrictions, supervision.
⟨SAVE⟩ 🛜 🛏 🖥

▼ WYO Motel
(307) 684-5505. **$49-$129.** 610 E Hart St 82834. I-25 exit 299 (US 16), just w; I-90 exit 58, 1.3 mi w. Ext corridors. **Pets:** Accepted.
🛜 🛏 🖥 🏊

CASPER

◈◈◈ ▼▼▼ BEST WESTERN Ramkota Hotel H ❀
(307) 266-6000. **Call for rates.** 800 N Poplar St 82601. I-25 exit 188B (N Poplar St), just ne. Int corridors. **Pets:** Large, dogs only. $20 daily fee/room. Designated rooms, service with restrictions, crate.
⟨SAVE⟩ 🛜 ⟨&M⟩ 🛏 🖥 🍴 🏊 ⊠

▼▼ Days Inn Casper H
(307) 234-1159. **$80-$115, 3 day notice.** 301 E 'E' St 82601. I-25 exit 188A (Center St), just s, then just e. Int corridors. **Pets:** Accepted.
🛜 🛏 🖥

▼▼ Quality Inn & Suites Casper H
(307) 266-2400. **$109-$189.** 821 N Poplar St 82601. I-25 exit 188B (N Poplar St), just e. Int corridors. **Pets:** Accepted. 🛜 ⊠ 🛏 🖥

▼▼ Super 8 Casper West M
(307) 266-3480. **$95-$145.** 3838 CY Ave 82604. I-25 exit 188B (N Poplar St), 1.5 mi s to CY Ave, then 1.7 mi w. Int corridors. **Pets:** Accepted.
🛜 🛏 🖥

CHEYENNE

▼▼ Cheyenne Super 8 M
(307) 635-8741. **$69-$179.** 1900 W Lincolnway 82001. I-25 exit 9, 0.7 mi e. Int corridors. **Pets:** Other species. $11 daily fee/pet. Service with restrictions, crate. 🛜 ⟨&M⟩ 🛏 🖥

▼▼ Comfort Inn of Cheyenne H ❀
(307) 638-7202. **$89-$139.** 2245 Etchepare Dr 82007. I-25 exit 7, just w. Int corridors. **Pets:** Large, other species. $15 one-time fee/room. Designated rooms, service with restrictions, supervision.
🛜 ⊠ ⟨&M⟩ 🛏 🖥 🏊

▼▼▼ Days Inn Cheyenne H
(307) 778-8877. **$120-$330.** 2360 W Lincolnway 82001. I-25 exit 9, just e. Int corridors. **Pets:** Dogs only. $5 daily fee/pet. Designated rooms, supervision. 🛜 🛏 🖥 🏊

◈◈◈ ▼▼▼ Historic Plains Hotel H
(307) 638-3311. **$109-$299.** 1600 Central Ave 82001. I-80 exit 362, 1 mi n on I-180/I-25 business loop/US 85/87 business route, then just w on I-80 business loop/US 30; downtown. Int corridors. **Pets:** Other species. $25 one-time fee/room. Service with restrictions, crate.
⟨SAVE⟩ 🛜 🛏 🖥 🍴

▼▼ La Quinta Inn Cheyenne H
(307) 632-7117. **$71-$155.** 2410 W Lincolnway 82009. I-25 exit 9, just e. Int corridors. **Pets:** Service with restrictions, supervision.
🛜 🛏 🖥 🏊

◈◈◈ ▼▼▼▼ Nagle Warren Mansion B & B BB ❀
(307) 637-3333. **$158-$192, 3 day notice.** 222 E 17th St 82001. I-80 exit 362, 1 mi n on I-25 business loop/US 85/87 business route, then just e; jct House St; downtown. Int corridors. **Pets:** Medium, other species. $25 one-time fee/pet. Designated rooms, service with restrictions, supervision. ⟨SAVE⟩ 🛜 ⊠ ⟨&M⟩ ⊠

▼▼ Oak Tree Inn-Cheyenne H
(307) 778-6620. **Call for rates.** 1625 Stillwater Ave 82009. I-25 exit 12, 0.8 mi se to Yellowstone Rd, 0.3 mi n to Dell Range Blvd, 1.2 mi e, then just se. Ext/int corridors. **Pets:** Accepted. 🛜 ⊠ 🛏 🖥 🍴

▼▼▼ Windy Hills Guest House BB ❀
(307) 632-6423. **$159-$310, 3 day notice.** 393 Happy Jack Rd 82009. I-25 exit 10B, 22 mi w on SR 210 (Happy Jack Rd), then 1 mi s on private gravel road. Ext corridors. **Pets:** $35 one-time fee/room. Designated rooms, service with restrictions, crate. 🛜 ⊠ 🛏 🖥 ⊠ ⟨🄹⟩

CODY

◈◈◈ ▼▼▼ BEST WESTERN Sunset Motor Inn M
(307) 587-4265. **$139-$200.** 1601 8th St 82414. 0.8 mi w on US 14/16/20. Ext corridors. **Pets:** Small, other species. $25 one-time fee/pet. Designated rooms, service with restrictions, crate.
⟨SAVE⟩ 🛜 ⊠ 🛏 🖥 🍴 🏊 ⊠

◈◈◈ ▼▼▼ The Cody H ❀
(307) 587-5915. **$110-$285.** 232 W Yellowstone Ave 82414. 2 mi w on US 14/16/20. Int corridors. **Pets:** Dogs only. $18 daily fee/pet. Designated rooms, service with restrictions, supervision.
⟨SAVE⟩ 🛜 ⊠ ⟨&M⟩ 🛏 🖥 🏊 ⊠

(AAA) ◊ Cody Motor Lodge M
(307) 527-6291. **$120-$150.** 1455 Sheridan Ave 82414. Just w on US 14/16/20 and SR 120. Int corridors. **Pets:** Large, other species. Designated rooms, supervision. (SAVE) 🖩 🛅 🖵

DOUGLAS

◊◊ Clarion Inn & Conference Center H
(307) 358-9790. **$105-$190.** 1450 Riverbend Dr 82633. I-25 exit 140, 0.8 mi e. Int corridors. **Pets:** Large. $100 deposit/room, $10 daily fee/room. Designated rooms, supervision. 🖩 ⒣ 🛅 🖵 🍴 ⇌ ⊠

DUBOIS

(AAA) ◊◊ The Longhorn Ranch Lodge and RV Resort M ✿
(307) 455-2337. **$50-$109, 3 day notice.** 5810 US Hwy 26 82513. 3 mi e on US 26 and 287. Ext corridors. **Pets:** Other species. $10 daily fee/room. Supervision. (SAVE) 🖩 ⊠ ⒣ 🛅 🖵 ⊠ ⓩ

◊ Rocky Mountain Lodge M
(307) 455-2844. **$60-$115, 3 day notice.** 1349 W Ramshorn St 82513. 1.6 mi w on US 26 and 287. Ext corridors. **Pets:** $5 daily fee/pet. Designated rooms, service with restrictions, supervision.
🖩 ⊠ ⒣ 🛅 🖵 ⓚ

(AAA) ◊◊ Stagecoach Motor Inn M ✿
(307) 455-2303. **$58-$98.** 103 Ramshorn St 82513. On US 26 and 287; center. Ext corridors. **Pets:** Small, dogs only. $10 daily fee/pet. Designated rooms, service with restrictions, supervision.
(SAVE) 🖩 ⒣ 🛅 🖵 ⇌ ⊠ ⓚ

EVANSTON

(AAA) ◊◊ BEST WESTERN Dunmar Inn M
(307) 789-3770. **$90-$130.** 1601 Harrison Dr 82930. I-80 exit 3 (Harrison Dr), just n. Ext corridors. **Pets:** Small. $10 daily fee/room. Designated rooms, service with restrictions, supervision.
(SAVE) 🖩 ⒣ 🛅 🖵 🍴 ⇌ ⊠

◊◊ Comfort Inn H
(307) 789-7799. **Call for rates.** 1931 Harrison Dr 82930. I-80 exit 3 (Harrison Dr), just n. Int corridors. **Pets:** Other species. $10 daily fee/pet. Service with restrictions, supervision. 🖩 ⒣ 🖵 ⇌ ⊠

(AAA) ◊ Prairie Inn M
(307) 789-2920. **$58-$64.** 264 Bear River Dr 82930. I-80 exit 6, 0.3 mi n. Ext/int corridors. **Pets:** Other species. $10 daily fee/room. Designated rooms, service with restrictions, supervision. (SAVE) 🖩 ⒣

EVANSVILLE

◊◊◊ Sleep Inn & Suites Casper East-Evansville H
(307) 235-3100. **Call for rates.** 6733 Bonanza Rd 82636. I-25 exit 182, just n on Hat Six Rd. Int corridors. **Pets:** Accepted.
🖩 ⊠ ⒣ 🖵 ⇌

◊◊ Super 8 Casper East-Evansville H
(307) 237-8100. **$100-$134.** 269 Miracle St 82636. I-25 exit 185, just n to Lathrop Rd, then just e. Int corridors. **Pets:** Large. $10 daily fee/room. Service with restrictions, supervision. 🖩 ⓜ ⒣ 🖵 ⇌

GILLETTE

(AAA) ◊◊◊ BEST WESTERN Tower West Lodge H
(307) 686-2210. **$80-$180.** 109 N US Hwy 14-16 82716. I-90 exit 124, just n. Int corridors. **Pets:** Other species. $20 daily fee/pet. Designated rooms, service with restrictions, supervision.
(SAVE) 🖩 ⒣ 🖵 🍴 ⇌

(AAA) ◊◊ Budget Inn Express M
(307) 686-1989. **$49-$199.** 2011 Rodgers Dr 82716. I-90 exit 124, just n. Int corridors. **Pets:** Small. $15 daily fee/pet. Designated rooms, supervision. (SAVE) 🖩 ⒣ ⇌

◊◊ Candlewood Suites H
(307) 682-6100. **Call for rates.** 904 Country Club Rd 82718. I-90 exit 126, 0.5 mi s, then just e. Int corridors. **Pets:** Accepted.
🖩 ⊠ ⒣ 🖵

(AAA) ◊◊◊ Comfort Inn & Suites of Gillette H
(307) 685-2223. **$89-$110.** 1607 W 2nd Ave 82716. I-90 exit 124, 0.3 mi ne, then just se. Int corridors. **Pets:** Small, other species. $15 deposit/pet. Designated rooms, service with restrictions, supervision.
(SAVE) 🖩 ⊠ ⓜ ⒣ 🖵 ⇌

◊◊◊ Holiday Inn Express & Suites H
(307) 686-9576. **Call for rates.** 1908 Cliff Davis Dr 82718. I-90 exit 126, just s to Boxelder Rd, then just e to Cliff Davis Dr. Int corridors. **Pets:** Medium, other species. $25 one-time fee/pet. Designated rooms, service with restrictions, supervision. 🖩 ⒣ 🖵 ⇌

GREEN RIVER

◊◊◊ Hampton Inn & Suites H
(307) 875-5300. **$89-$189.** 1055 Wild Horse Canyon Rd 82935. I-80 exit 89, 0.4 mi s to Wild Horse Canyon Rd, then 0.5 mi n. Int corridors. **Pets:** Medium, other species. Service with restrictions, supervision.
🖩 ⓜ ⒣ 🖵 ⇌

◊◊ Oak Tree Inn - Green River M
(307) 875-3500. **Call for rates.** 1170 W Flaming Gorge Way 82935. I-80 exit 89, 0.3 mi s. Ext/int corridors. **Pets:** Accepted.
🖩 ⊠ ⒣ 🖵 🍴

GUERNSEY

(AAA) ◊ Bunkhouse Motel M
(307) 836-2356. **$77-$139, 5 day notice.** 350 W Whalen St 82214. On US 26; center. Ext corridors. **Pets:** Dogs only. $10 daily fee/pet. Designated rooms, service with restrictions, supervision. (SAVE) 🖩 ⒣ 🖵

HULETT

(AAA) ◊◊◊ BEST WESTERN Devils Tower Inn H
(307) 467-5747. **Call for rates.** 229 Hwy 24 82720. Center. Int corridors. **Pets:** Large, dogs only. $20 daily fee/room. Designated rooms, service with restrictions, supervision. (SAVE) 🖩 ⊠ ⒣ 🖵 ⇌

(AAA) ◊ Hulett Motel M
(307) 467-5220. **$88-$118.** 202 Main St 82720. On SR 24 (Main St), north end of town. Ext corridors. **Pets:** Large, dogs only. $20 one-time fee/room. Designated rooms, service with restrictions, supervision.
(SAVE) 🖩 ⊠ ⒣ 🖵

JACKSON HOLE AREA

ALPINE

(AAA) ◊◊ Alpen Haus Hotel Resort H
(307) 654-7545. **$55-$150.** 46 W Hwy 26 83128. Jct US 26 and 89. Int corridors. **Pets:** Medium. $10 daily fee/room. Designated rooms, service with restrictions, crate. (SAVE) 🖩 ⒣ 🍴

GRAND TETON NATIONAL PARK

◊◊ Headwaters Lodge & Cabins at Flagg Ranch H
(307) 543-2861. **Call for rates.** Hwy 89 83013. US 89 and 191; 2 mi s of Yellowstone National Park south entrance; 5 mi n of Grand Teton National Park north entrance. Ext corridors. **Pets:** Accepted.
🖩 ⓜ ⒣ 🖵 🍴 ⊠ ⓚ ⓦ

◊◊◊ Jackson Lake Lodge H
(307) 543-2811. **Call for rates.** US Hwy 89 83013. 5 mi nw of Moran. Ext/int corridors. **Pets:** Accepted.
(ECO) 🖩 ⊠ ⓜ ⒣ 🖵 🍴 ⇌ ⊠ ⓚ ⓦ

⟨AAA⟩ ▼▼▼ Signal Mountain Lodge 🄷
(307) 543-2831. **$143-$328, 7 day notice.** 1 Inner Park Rd 83013. Teton Park Rd, 2 mi s of US 89, 191 and 287. Ext corridors. **Pets:** Other species. $20 daily fee/room. Designated rooms, service with restrictions, crate. 🄴🄲🄾 🆂🄰🅅🄴 🛜 ⊠ 🖥 🛏 💼 ⊠ 🄺 🅆

⟨AAA⟩ ▼▼▼ Togwotee Mountain Lodge 🄲🄰
(307) 543-2847. **Call for rates.** 27655 Hwy US 26 & 287 83013. 16.5 mi e of Moran, jct US 26 and 287. Ext/int corridors. **Pets:** Other species. $20 one-time fee/pet. Designated rooms, service with restrictions, crate.
🆂🄰🅅🄴 🛜 ⊠ 🖥 💼 🍴 ⊠

JACKSON

⟨AAA⟩ ▼▼▼ 49'er Inn and Suites (Quality Inn and Suites) 🄷
(307) 733-7550. **$79-$339.** 330 W Pearl St 83001. Just w, just s of town square. Ext/int corridors. **Pets:** Service with restrictions, supervision.
🆂🄰🅅🄴 🛜 🖥 💼 ⊠

⟨AAA⟩ ▼▼▼ Antler Inn 🄷
(307) 733-2535. **$86-$275, 4 day notice.** 43 W Pearl St 83001. Just s of town square. Ext/int corridors. **Pets:** Dogs only. Supervision.
🆂🄰🅅🄴 🛜 🖥 💼 ⊠

⟨AAA⟩ ▼▼▼ Cowboy Village Resort 🄲🄰
(307) 733-3121. **$86-$284.** 120 S Flat Creek Dr 83002. 0.3 mi w on Broadway to Flat Creek Dr, just s; downtown. Ext corridors. **Pets:** Service with restrictions, supervision. 🆂🄰🅅🄴 🛜 ⊠ 🖥 💼 🏊

⟨AAA⟩ ▼▼▼ Elk Country Inn 🄼 🐾
(307) 733-2364. **$76-$230, 7 day notice.** 480 W Pearl St 83001. Just w, then just s of town square. Ext/int corridors. **Pets:** Other species. Designated rooms, supervision. 🆂🄰🅅🄴 🛜 ⊠ 🖥 💼 ⊠

▼▼▼ Homewood Suites by Hilton 🄷
(307) 739-0808. **$139-$359.** 260 N Millward St 83001. Just nw of town square, n on Millward St or w on Mercill Ave, from US 26/89/191 (Broadway). Int corridors. **Pets:** Accepted. 🛜 🄼 🖥 💼 ⊠

⟨AAA⟩ ▼▼▼ Jackson Hole Lodge 🄷
(307) 733-2992. **$89-$339, 15 day notice.** 420 W Broadway 83001. 0.3 mi w on US 26/89/191 (Broadway). Ext corridors. **Pets:** Large, other species. $10 daily fee/room. Designated rooms, service with restrictions, crate. 🆂🄰🅅🄴 🛜 🖥 💼 🏊 ⊠

⟨AAA⟩ ▼▼▼ Painted Buffalo Inn 🄼 🐾
(307) 733-4340. **$90-$225.** 400 W Broadway 83001. Just w of town square. Ext corridors. **Pets:** Other species. $20 one-time fee/pet. Service with restrictions, supervision. 🆂🄰🅅🄴 🛜 🄼 🖥 💼 🏊

▼▼▼ Snow King Resort 🄷
(307) 733-5200. **Call for rates.** 400 E Snow King Ave 83001. Just se of town square. Ext/int corridors. **Pets:** Dogs only. $50 one-time fee/room. Designated rooms, no service, supervision.
🛜 ⊠ 🖥 💼 🍴 🏊 ⊠

TETON VILLAGE

⟨AAA⟩ ▼▼▼▼ Four Seasons Resort Jackson Hole 🄷 🐾
(307) 732-5000. **$375-$6750, 30 day notice.** 7680 Granite Loop Rd 83025. At base of Jackson Hole Mountain Resort. Int corridors. **Pets:** Small, dogs only. Service with restrictions, supervision.
🆂🄰🅅🄴 🛜 ⊠ 🄼 🖥 💼 🍴 🏊 ⊠

▼▼▼ Inn at Jackson Hole 🄷
(307) 733-2311. **$79-$489, 14 day notice.** 3345 W Village Dr 83025. Center. Ext corridors. **Pets:** Dogs only. $10 daily fee/pet. Crate.
🛜 ⊠ 🖥 💼 🍴 🏊 ⊠

⟨AAA⟩ ▼▼▼ ▼▼▼ Teton Mountain Lodge & Spa 🄷
(307) 734-7111. **$119-$2500, 14 day notice.** 3385 W Cody Ln 83025. Center. Int corridors. **Pets:** Dogs only. $25 daily fee/pet. Designated rooms, supervision. 🆂🄰🅅🄴 🛜 ⊠ 🄼 🖥 💼 🍴 🏊 ⊠

END AREA

KEMMERER

⟨AAA⟩ ▼▼▼ BEST WESTERN PLUS Fossil Country Inn & Suites 🄷
(307) 877-3388. **$98-$118.** 760 US 30/189 83101. Jct US 30 and 189. Int corridors. **Pets:** Medium, other species. $10 daily fee/room. Designated rooms, service with restrictions, supervision.
🆂🄰🅅🄴 🛜 ⊠ 🄼 🖥 💼 🏊

LANDER

⟨AAA⟩ ▼▼▼ BEST WESTERN The Inn at Lander 🄷
(307) 332-2847. **$90-$125.** 260 Grand View Dr 82520. Jct US 287 and SR 789. Int corridors. **Pets:** $25 daily fee/pet. Designated rooms, supervision. 🆂🄰🅅🄴 🛜 ⊠ 🖥 💼 🍴 🏊

▼▼▼ Holiday Inn Express & Suites Lander 🄷
(307) 332-4005. **$89-$139.** 1002 11th St 82520. 1 mi w on US 287, just w on Lincoln St. Int corridors. **Pets:** Dogs only. $25 one-time fee/room. Designated rooms, service with restrictions, supervision.
🛜 🄼 🖥 💼 🏊

⟨AAA⟩ ▼▼ Holiday Lodge 🄼
(307) 332-2511. **$65-$75.** 210 McFarlane Dr 82520. Just e of jct US 287 and SR 789. Ext corridors. **Pets:** $10 daily fee/pet. Designated rooms, service with restrictions, crate. 🆂🄰🅅🄴 🛜 🖥

⟨AAA⟩ ▼▼▼ Rodeway Inn & Suites/Pronghorn Lodge 🄼 🐾
(307) 332-3940. **Call for rates.** 150 E Main St 82520. Just n of jct US 287 and SR 789. Ext corridors. **Pets:** Small. $10 daily fee/pet. Designated rooms, supervision. 🆂🄰🅅🄴 🛜 🖥 💼

LARAMIE

⟨AAA⟩ ▼▼▼ AmericInn Lodge & Suites of Laramie 🄷
(307) 745-0777. **$90-$160.** 4712 E Grand Ave 82070. I-80 exit 316 (Grand Ave), just n. Int corridors. **Pets:** Accepted.
🆂🄰🅅🄴 🛜 ⊠ 🄼 🖥 💼 🏊 ⊠

⟨AAA⟩ ▼▼▼ BEST WESTERN Laramie Inn & Suites 🄷
(307) 745-5700. **$89-$149.** 1767 N Banner Rd 82072. I-80 exit 310 (Curtis St), just n. Int corridors. **Pets:** Medium. $20 daily fee/pet. Service with restrictions, supervision. 🆂🄰🅅🄴 🛜 ⊠ 🖥 💼 🏊

▼▼ Days Inn 🄷
(307) 745-5678. **$69-$129.** 1368 N McCue St 82072. I-80 exit 310 (Curtis St), 0.3 mi e, then just s. Int corridors. **Pets:** Accepted.
🛜 🖥 💼 🏊

▼▼▼ Holiday Inn 🄷
(307) 721-9000. **$139-$199.** 204 S 30th St 82070. I-80 exit 316 (Grand Ave), 2.5 mi w to 30th St. Int corridors. **Pets:** Other species. $25 one-time fee/pet. Service with restrictions.
🛜 ⊠ 🄼 🖥 💼 🍴 🏊

◆◆◆◆ Quality Inn & Suites **H**
(307) 742-6665. **$75-$139.** 1655 Centennial Dr 82070. I-80 exit 310 (Curtis St), just w, then just s. Int corridors. **Pets:** Accepted.

◆ Royal Super 8 **M**
(307) 745-8901. **$60-$85.** 1987 Banner Rd 82072. I-80 exit 310 (Curtis St), just n. Int corridors. **Pets:** Accepted.

LITTLE AMERICA
◆◆◆ ◆◆ Little America Hotel **M**
(307) 875-2400. **$69-$124.** I-80, exit 68 82929. I-80 exit 68, just n. Ext/int corridors. **Pets:** Other species. $20 one-time fee/pet. Designated rooms, crate.

LUSK
◆◆◆ ◆◆ Americas Best Value Inn Covered Wagon **M**
(307) 334-2836. **$72-$155.** 730 S Main St 82225. Just n of jct US 20/85. Ext/int corridors. **Pets:** Small, dogs only. $20 daily fee/room. Designated rooms, service with restrictions, supervision.

◆◆◆ ◆◆ BEST WESTERN Pioneer **M**
(307) 334-2640. **$105-$120.** 731 S Main St 82225. Just n of jct US 20/85. Ext corridors. **Pets:** $20 one-time fee/pet, $20 daily fee/pet. Designated rooms, service with restrictions.

NEWCASTLE
◆◆◆ ◆ Auto Inn Motel **M**
(307) 746-2734. **$59-$195.** 2503 W Main St 82701. 1.5 mi w of center on US 16. Ext corridors. **Pets:** Medium. $6 daily fee/pet. Designated rooms, no service, supervision.

PAINTER
◆ Hunter Peak Ranch **RA**
(307) 587-3711. **$150-$220, 91 day notice.** 4027 Crandall Rd 82414. SR 296, 5 mi s of US 212; 40 mi n of SR 120. Ext corridors. **Pets:** Dogs only. $20 daily fee/pet. No service, supervision.

PINEDALE
◆◆ Baymont Inn & Suites **H**
(307) 367-8300. **$99-$144.** 1624 W Pine St 82941. 1 mi n on US 191. Int corridors. **Pets:** Accepted.

◆◆◆ ◆◆ BEST WESTERN Pinedale Inn **H**
(307) 367-6869. **$80-$150.** 850 W Pine St 82941. 0.5 mi n on US 191. Int corridors. **Pets:** Other species. Designated rooms, service with restrictions, supervision.

◆◆◆ ◆◆ The Lodge at Pinedale **H**
(307) 367-8800. **$70-$110.** 1054 W Pine St 82941. 0.7 mi n on US 191. Int corridors. **Pets:** Other species. $10 daily fee/room. Designated rooms, service with restrictions, supervision.

POWELL
◆◆◆ ◆◆ Americas Best Value Inn **M**
(307) 754-5117. **$80-$175.** 777 E 2nd St 82435. 0.3 mi e on US 14A. Ext corridors. **Pets:** $10 daily fee/pet. Designated rooms, service with restrictions, crate.

RAWLINS
◆◆◆ ◆◆ BEST WESTERN CottonTree Inn **M**
(307) 324-2737. **$99-$209.** 2221 W Spruce St 82301. I-80 exit 211, just n. Ext/int corridors. **Pets:** Small, dogs only. $10 daily fee/room. Crate.

◆◆◆ ◆◆ Comfort Inn & Suites **H**
(307) 324-3663. **$89-$179.** 2366 Cedar St 82301. I-80 exit 215 (Cedar St), 0.3 mi w. Int corridors. **Pets:** Accepted.

◆◆◆ Hampton Inn **H**
(307) 324-2320. **$129-$189.** 406 Airport Rd 82301. I-80 exit 215 (Cedar St), 0.8 mi nw. Int corridors. **Pets:** Accepted.

◆◆◆ Holiday Inn Express **H**
(307) 324-3760. **$119-$189.** 201 Airport Rd 82301. I-80 exit 215 (Cedar St), 0.8 mi nw. Int corridors. **Pets:** Accepted.

◆◆◆ Pronghorn Inn & Suites **H**
(307) 324-5588. **$100-$175.** 812 Locust St 82301. I-80 exit 214, 0.4 mi n on Higley Blvd, then just e. Int corridors. **Pets:** Other species. $15 daily fee/pet. Service with restrictions, supervision.

RIVERTON
◆◆◆ Comfort Inn & Suites **H**
(307) 856-8900. **$89-$127.** 2020 N Federal Blvd 82501. 1.5 mi ne on US 26/SR 789. Int corridors. **Pets:** Accepted.

◆◆◆ Days Inn **M**
(307) 856-9677. **$70-$135.** 909 W Main St 82501. 0.5 mi nw on US 26. Ext corridors. **Pets:** Accepted.

◆◆◆◆ Hampton Inn & Suites-Riverton **H** ✿
(307) 856-3500. **$114-$134.** 2500 N Federal Blvd (US 26) 82501. 2 mi ne on US 26/SR 789. Int corridors. **Pets:** Large. Service with restrictions, supervision.

◆ Super 8 **M**
(307) 857-2400. **$65-$99, 3 day notice.** 1040 N Federal Blvd 82501. 1 mi ne on US 26/SR 789. Int corridors. **Pets:** Accepted.

◆◆◆ ◆◆◆◆ Wind River Hotel & Casino **H**
(307) 856-3964. **$80-$149.** 10269 Hwy 789 82501. 2 mi s from jct US 26. Int corridors. **Pets:** Dogs only. $25 daily fee/room. Designated rooms, service with restrictions, crate.

ROCK SPRINGS
◆◆◆ Hampton Inn **H**
(307) 382-9222. **Call for rates.** 1901 Dewar Dr 82901. I-80 exit 102 (Dewar Dr), 0.5 mi se. Int corridors. **Pets:** Other species. Service with restrictions, supervision.

◆◆◆ Holiday Inn **H** 🐾
(307) 382-9200. **$109-$149.** 1675 Sunset Dr 82901. I-80 exit 102 (Dewar Dr), just e, then 0.7 mi sw. Ext/int corridors. **Pets:** Other species. $10 daily fee/pet. Designated rooms, service with restrictions, crate.

◆◆◆◆ Holiday Inn Express & Suites **H**
(307) 362-9200. **$130-$200.** 1660 Sunset Dr 82901. I-80 exit 102 (Dewar Dr), just e on Dewar Dr, then 0.5 mi sw. Int corridors. **Pets:** Accepted.

◆◆◆ La Quinta Inn Rock Springs **H**
(307) 362-1770. **$71-$199.** 2717 Dewar Dr 82901. I-80 exit 102 (Dewar Dr), just n. Int corridors. **Pets:** Service with restrictions, supervision.

◆◆◆ Quality Inn **M**
(307) 382-9490. **$79-$130.** 1670 Sunset Dr 82901. I-80 exit 102 (Dewar Dr), just e on Dewar Dr, then 0.5 mi sw. Ext corridors. **Pets:** Accepted.

SARATOGA

Hacienda Motel Ⓜ
(307) 326-5751. **Call for rates.** 1500 S First St 82331. On SR 130, 0.4 mi s of center. Int corridors. **Pets:** Accepted. 🛜 📧

SHERIDAN

Americas Best Value Inn Ⓜ
(307) 672-9757. **$59-$99.** 580 E 5th St 82801. I-90 exit 23 (5th St), 0.4 mi w. Ext corridors. **Pets:** Other species. Designated rooms, service with restrictions, supervision. 🅂🅰🆅🅴 🛜 📧 🖵

BEST WESTERN Sheridan Center Ⓗ
(307) 674-7421. **$80-$150.** 612 N Main St 82801. I-90 exit 23 (5th St), 1 mi w, then just s. Ext/int corridors. **Pets:** $25 one-time fee/room. Designated rooms, service with restrictions. 🅂🅰🆅🅴 🛜 📧 🖵 🍽 🔜

Budget Host Inn Ⓜ
(307) 674-7496. **$70-$129.** 2007 N Main St 82801. I-90 exit 20, 0.7 mi s. Ext corridors. **Pets:** $10 daily fee/room. Designated rooms, service with restrictions, crate. 🅂🅰🆅🅴 🛜 📧 🖵

Candlewood Suites Ⓗ
(307) 675-2100. **Call for rates.** 1709 Sugarland Dr 82801. I-90 exit 25, just w, then just n. Int corridors. **Pets:** Accepted. 🛜 🅶🅼 📧 🖵

Holiday Inn Atrium & Convention Center Ⓗ
(307) 672-8931. **$109-$159.** 1809 Sugarland Dr 82801. I-90 exit 25, 0.3 mi nw. Int corridors. **Pets:** Accepted.
🅂🅰🆅🅴 🛜 📧 🖵 🍽 🔜 ✖

Mill Inn Ⓜ
(307) 672-6401. **$65-$130.** 2161 Coffeen Ave 82801. I-90 exit 25, 0.3 mi w. Ext/int corridors. **Pets:** $15 one-time fee/pet. Designated rooms, service with restrictions, crate. 🅂🅰🆅🅴 🛜 📧 🖵

SUNDANCE

BEST WESTERN Inn at Sundance Ⓗ ❀
(307) 283-2800. **Call for rates.** 2719 E Cleveland St 82729. I-90 exit 189, just n, then just w; 1.5 mi ne of SR 585. Int corridors.
Pets: Medium, other species. $10 daily fee/pet. Service with restrictions, supervision. 🅂🅰🆅🅴 🛜 📧 🅶🅼 📧 🖵 🔜

THERMOPOLIS

Days Inn Hot Springs Convention Center Ⓗ
(307) 864-3131. **$77-$149.** 115 E Park St 82443. In Hot Springs State Park. Ext/int corridors. **Pets:** $15 daily fee/pet. Service with restrictions.
🛜 🖵 🍽 🔜 ✖

Hot Springs Super 8 Ⓗ
(307) 864-5515. **$68-$125.** Lane 5 Hwy 20 S 82443. On US 20, just se. Int corridors. **Pets:** Accepted. 🛜 🅶🅼 📧 🖵 🔜 ✖

TORRINGTON

Holiday Inn Express & Suites Ⓗ
(307) 532-7600. **Call for rates.** 1700 E Valley Rd 82240. On E Valley Rd (US 26), 0.4 mi e of Main St (US 85). Int corridors. **Pets:** Accepted.
🛜 ✖ 🅶🅼 📧 🖵 🏊

UCROSS

The Ranch at Ucross 🆁🅰
(307) 737-2281. **$94-$150, 3 day notice.** 2673 US Hwy 14 E 82835. Jct US 14/16, 0.5 mi w. Ext/int corridors. **Pets:** Dogs only. $100 deposit/room. Service with restrictions, supervision.
🅂🅰🆅🅴 🛜 ✖ 🍽 🔜 ✖ 🐾

WAPITI

Green Creek Inn Ⓜ ❀
(307) 587-5004. **$65-$180, 7 day notice.** 2908 Northfork Hwy 82414. 2.8 mi w on US 14/16/20; between Cody and Yellowstone National Park. Ext corridors. **Pets:** $10 daily fee/pet. Service with restrictions, supervision. 🛜 ✖ 📧 🖊

Yellowstone Valley Inn Ⓜ
(307) 587-3961. **$99-$169, 14 day notice.** 3324 Yellowstone Park Hwy 82450. 3.3 mi w on US 14/16/20; halfway between Cody and Yellowstone National Park. Ext corridors. **Pets:** Accepted.
🛜 ✖ 📧 🖵 🍽 🔜 ✖ 🖊

WHEATLAND

BEST WESTERN Torchlite Motor Inn Ⓜ ❀
(307) 322-4070. **Call for rates.** 1809 16th St 82201. I-25 exit 80, just e, then 0.6 mi s. Ext corridors. **Pets:** Large, other species. $10 daily fee/pet. Designated rooms, service with restrictions, supervision.
🅂🅰🆅🅴 🛜 📧 🖵 🔜

WRIGHT

Wright Hotel Ⓗ
(307) 464-6060. **$129-$139, 3 day notice.** 300 Reata Dr 82732. Just w of jct SR 59 and 387. Int corridors. **Pets:** $25 daily fee/pet. Designated rooms, service with restrictions, supervision.
🛜 ✖ 🅶🅼 📧 🖵 🍽

YELLOWSTONE NATIONAL PARK

Elephant Head Lodge 🅲🅰
(307) 587-3980. **$150-$350, 30 day notice.** 1170 Yellowstone Hwy 82414. 11.7 mi e of Yellowstone National Park on US 14/16/20. Ext corridors. **Pets:** Other species. $20 one-time fee/pet. Service with restrictions, crate. 🅂🅰🆅🅴 ✖ 📧 🖵 🍽 ✖ 🎾 🖊 🖊

Shoshone Lodge 🅲🅰
(307) 587-4044. **Call for rates.** 349 North Fork Hwy 82190. 3.5 mi e of Yellowstone National Park East Gate on US 14/16/20. Ext corridors.
Pets: Accepted. 🛜 📧 🖵 🍽 ✖ 🎾 🖊

Canadian Lodgings

ALBERTA

ATHABASCA

 Days Inn Athabasca ☐
(780) 675-7020. **$139-$149.** 2805 48th Ave T9S 0A4. Jct Hwy 2 and 55, 1.6 mi (2.7 km) e; east end of town. Int corridors. **Pets:** Accepted.
🛜 ☒ 🛏 💻

BANFF

▽▽▽ **Banff International Hotel** ☐
(403) 762-5666. **$145-$245.** 333 Banff Ave T1L 1B1. Corner of Elk St; center. Int corridors. **Pets:** Accepted.
🛜 ☒ 🛏 💻 🍴 ☒ 🐾

▽▽ **Banff Ptarmigan Inn** ☐
(403) 762-2207. **Call for rates.** 337 Banff Ave T1L 1B1. Between Moose and Elk sts. Int corridors. **Pets:** Accepted.
🛜 ☒ 🛏 💻 🍴 ☒ 🐾

▽▽▽ **Banff Rocky Mountain Resort** CO
(403) 762-5531. **$99-$219, 3 day notice.** 1029 Banff Ave T1L 1A2. Banff Ave and Tunnel Mountain Rd; just s of Trans-Canada Hwy 1. Ext corridors. **Pets:** Accepted. 🛜 ☒ 🛏 💻 🍴 ☒ 🐾

CAA ▽▽▽ **BEST WESTERN PLUS Siding 29 Lodge** ☐
(403) 762-5575. **$100-$221.** 453 Marten St T1L 1B3. 0.6 mi (1 km) ne, just off Banff Ave. Int corridors. **Pets:** Other species. $15 daily fee/pet. Service with restrictions, supervision. SAVE 🛜 ☒ 🛏 💻 ☒

▽▽▽ **Castle Mountain Chalets** CA 🐾
(403) 762-3868. **$149-$349, 14 day notice.** Bow Valley Pkwy (Hwy 1A) & Hwy 93 S T1L 1B5. 20 mi (32 km) w on Trans-Canada Hwy 1, jct Castle, 0.6 mi (1 km) ne on Hwy 1A (Bow Valley Pkwy). Ext corridors. **Pets:** Dogs only. $25 daily fee/pet. Designated rooms, service with restrictions, supervision. 🛜 ☒ 🛏 💻 ☒ 🐾 🅩

CAA ▽▽▽ **Douglas Fir Resort & Chalets** CO
(403) 762-5591. **$125-$475.** 525 Tunnel Mountain Rd T1L 1B2. Jct Banff Ave and Wolf St, 1 mi (1.6 km) ne. Ext/int corridors. **Pets:** Accepted.
SAVE 🛜 ☒ 🛏 💻 ☒

CAA ▽▽▽▽ **The Fairmont Banff Springs** ☐ 🐾
(403) 762-2211. **$250-$593, 3 day notice.** 405 Spray Ave T1L 1J4. Just s on Banff Ave over the bridge, 0.3 mi (0.5 km) e. Int corridors. **Pets:** $25 daily fee/room. Designated rooms, service with restrictions, crate.
ECO SAVE 🛜 ☒ 🛏 💻 🍴 ☒ 🐾

▽▽▽ **Hidden Ridge Resort** CO
(403) 762-3544. **$129-$249, 3 day notice.** 901 Hidden Ridge Way T1L 1B7. 1.5 mi (2.4 km) ne at Tunnel Mountain Rd. Ext corridors.
Pets: Accepted. 🛜 ☒ 🛏 💻 ☒

▽ **Homestead Inn** M 🐾
(403) 762-4471. **$99-$149, 3 day notice.** 217 Lynx St T1L 1A7. Banff Ave, just w on Caribou St, then just n; downtown. Ext corridors.
Pets: Dogs only. $25 daily fee/pet. Designated rooms, service with restrictions, crate. 🛜 ☒ 🛏 💻 🐾

CAA ▽▽▽ **Irwin's Mountain Inn** ☐
(403) 762-4566. **$119-$219.** 429 Banff Ave T1L 1B2. North of Rabbit St. Int corridors. **Pets:** $10 daily fee/pet. Designated rooms, service with restrictions, crate. SAVE 🛜 ☒ 🛏 💻 🍴 ☒

CAA ▽▽▽ **Johnston Canyon Resort** CA
(403) 762-2971. **$149-$314.** Hwy 1A T1L 1A9. 15 mi (24 km) nw on Hwy 1A (Bow Valley Pkwy). Ext corridors. **Pets:** Accepted.
ECO SAVE ☒ 🛏 💻 🍴 🅩 🅩

▽▽▽ **The Juniper** ☐
(403) 762-2281. **Call for rates.** 1 Mt. Norquay Rd T1L 1E1. Trans-Canada Hwy 1 exit Mt. Norquay Rd, just n. Int corridors. **Pets:** Accepted.
ECO 🛜 ☒ 🛏 💻 🍴

CAA ▽▽▽ **Red Carpet Inn** ☐
(403) 762-4184. **$89-$189.** 425 Banff Ave T1L 1B6. Between Beaver and Rabbit sts. Ext/int corridors. **Pets:** $15 daily fee/room. Designated rooms, service with restrictions, crate. SAVE 🛜 ☒ 🛏 💻

CAA ▽▽▽▽ **The Rimrock Resort Hotel** ☐ 🐾
(403) 762-3356. **$218-$395, 3 day notice.** 300 Mountain Ave T1L 1J2. 2.4 mi (4 km) s via Sulphur Mountain Rd; adjacent to Upper Hot Springs Pool. Int corridors. **Pets:** Other species. $40 daily fee/pet. Designated rooms, service with restrictions, supervision.
SAVE 🛜 ☒ 🔊M 🛏 💻 🍴 ☒ 🐾

BONNYVILLE

CAA ▽▽▽▽ **BEST WESTERN Bonnyville Inn & Suites** ☐
(780) 826-6226. **$145-$150.** 5401 43rd St T9N 0H3. Hwy 28, just n at 44th St. Int corridors. **Pets:** Accepted. SAVE 🛜 ☒ 🔊M 🛏 💻

BROOKS

▽▽ **Heritage Inn Hotel & Convention Centre** ☐
(403) 362-6666. **$116-$177.** 1217 2nd St W T1R 1P7. Trans-Canada Hwy 1 exit Hwy 873, 0.5 mi (0.8 km) s. Int corridors. **Pets:** Medium, dogs only. $20 daily fee/pet. Designated rooms, service with restrictions, crate.
🛜 🛏 💻 🍴

CAA ▽▽▽ **Lakeview Inns & Suites** ☐
(403) 362-7440. **Call for rates.** 1307 2nd St W T1R 1P7. Trans-Canada Hwy 1 exit Hwy 873, 0.5 mi (0.8 km) s. Int corridors. **Pets:** Accepted.
SAVE 🛜 🛏 💻 ☒

▽▽▽ **Ramada Brooks** ☐ 🐾
(403) 362-6440. **$140-$219.** 1319 2nd St W T1R 1P7. Trans-Canada Hwy 1 exit Hwy 873, 0.5 mi (0.8 km) s. Ext/int corridors. **Pets:** Other species. $15 daily fee/pet. Service with restrictions, crate.
ECO 🛜 ☒ 🛏 💻 ☒ 🐾

CAA ▽▽▽ **Super 8 Brooks** ☐
(403) 363-0080. **$120-$130.** 115 15th Ave W T1R 1C4. Just s off Trans-Canada Hwy 1. Ext/int corridors. **Pets:** Accepted.
ECO SAVE 🛜 ☒ 🛏 💻 🍴 ☒ 🐾

CALGARY METROPOLITAN AREA

AIRDRIE

ⓐ ▼▼ BEST WESTERN Regency Inn ⊞
(403) 948-3838. **$130-$200.** 121 Edmonton Tr SE T4B 1S2. Hwy 2 exit Airdrie/Irricana, just w, then 0.5 mi (0.9 km) s. Ext/int corridors. **Pets:** Medium, other species. $20 daily fee/pet. Designated rooms, supervision. ⓢⓐⓥⓔ 🛜 ✖ 🛏 💻 🍴

ⓐ ▼▼▼ Comfort Inn & Suites Airdrie ⊞
(403) 948-3411. **$129-$149.** 133 Sierra Springs Dr SE T4B 3G6. Hwy 2 exit 282 (Yankee Valley Blvd), just w. Int corridors. **Pets:** Medium, dogs only. $20 daily fee/pet. Supervision. ⓢⓐⓥⓔ 🛜 ✖ 🛏 💻 ⇌

▼▼▼▼ Holiday Inn Express & Suites Airdrie-Calgary North ⊞ 🐾
(403) 912-1952. **$129-$169.** 64 E Lake Ave NE T4A 2G8. Hwy 2 exit E Airdrie, 0.6 mi (1 km) n. Int corridors. **Pets:** Large. $10 daily fee/pet. Designated rooms, service with restrictions, supervision. 🄴🄲🄾 🛜 ✖ 🛏 💻 ⇌ ✖

▼▼ Ramada Inn & Suites ⊞
(403) 945-1288. **$140-$220.** 191 E Lake Crescent T4A 2H7. Hwy 2 exit E Airdrie. Int corridors. **Pets:** Accepted. 🄴🄲🄾 🛜 ✖ 🛏 💻 🍴 ⇌ ✖

▼▼ Super 8 Airdrie ⊞
(403) 948-4188. **$125-$140.** 815 E Lake Blvd T4A 2G4. Hwy 2 exit E Airdrie, just e. Int corridors. **Pets:** Other species. $15 one-time fee/pet. Designated rooms, service with restrictions, supervision. 🛜 ✖ 🛏 💻

CALGARY

ⓐ ▼▼▼ BEST WESTERN PLUS Port O'Call Hotel ⊞
(403) 291-4600. **$129-$199.** 1935 McKnight Blvd NE T2E 6V4. 1.6 mi (2.5 km) ne of jct Hwy 2 (Deerfoot Tr); at 19th St NE. Int corridors. **Pets:** Accepted. 🄴🄲🄾 ⓢⓐⓥⓔ 🛜 ✖ 🛏 💻 🍴 ⇌ ✖

ⓐ ▼▼▼▼ Calgary Marriott Downtown ⊞
(403) 266-7331. **$139-$599.** 110 9th Ave SE T2G 5A6. Jct 9th Ave and Centre St; adjacent to TELUS Convention Centre. Int corridors. **Pets:** Medium, other species. Service with restrictions. 🄴🄲🄾 ⓢⓐⓥⓔ 🛜 ✖ 🛏 💻 🍴 ⇌

▼▼▼ Calgary Westways Guest House ⒷⒷ 🐾
(403) 229-1758. **$109-$180, 4 day notice.** 216 25th Ave SW T2S 0L1. 1.1 mi (1.7 km) s on Hwy 2A (Macleod Tr S), just w. Int corridors. **Pets:** Other species. $8 daily fee/pet. 🛜 ✖

ⓐ ▼▼▼ Carriage House Inn ⊞ 🐾
(403) 253-1101. **$135-$249.** 9030 Macleod Tr S T2H 0M4. On Hwy 2A (Macleod Tr); corner of 90th Ave SW. Int corridors. **Pets:** $20 daily fee/pet. Designated rooms, service with restrictions, crate. 🄴🄲🄾 ⓢⓐⓥⓔ 🛜 ✖ 🛏 💻 🍴 ⇌ ✖

▼▼▼ Coast Plaza Hotel & Conference Centre ⊞ 🐾
(403) 248-8888. **$99-$399.** 1316 33rd St NE T2A 6B6. Just s of jct 16th Ave (Trans-Canada Hwy 1) and 36th St NE, just w on 12th Ave NE. Int corridors. **Pets:** $20 daily fee/room. Designated rooms, service with restrictions, crate. 🄴🄲🄾 🛜 🛏 💻 🍴 ⇌ ✖

▼▼▼ Delta Bow Valley ⊞
(403) 266-1980. **$109-$409, 3 day notice.** 209 4th Ave SE T2G 0C6. 1st St SE and 4th Ave SE. Int corridors. **Pets:** Accepted. 🄴🄲🄾 🛜 ✖ 🛏 💻 🍴 ⇌ ✖

▼▼▼ Delta Calgary Airport ⊞
(403) 291-2600. **$149-$409.** 2001 Airport Rd NE T2E 6Z8. At Calgary International Airport. Int corridors. **Pets:** Medium, other species. $35 one-time fee/room. Service with restrictions, supervision. 🄴🄲🄾 🛜 ✖ 🛏 🛏 💻 🍴 ⇌

▼▼▼ Delta Calgary South ⊞ 🐾
(403) 278-5050. **$109-$429.** 135 Southland Dr SE T2J 5X5. On Hwy 2A (Macleod Tr); corner of Southland Dr. Int corridors. **Pets:** Medium. $35 one-time fee/room. Designated rooms, service with restrictions, supervision. 🄴🄲🄾 🛜 ✖ 🛏 🛏 💻 🍴 ⇌ ✖

ⓐ ▼▼ Econo Lodge Motel Village Ⓜ 🐾
(403) 289-2561. **$70-$109.** 2440 16th Ave NW T2M 0M5. Jct 16th Ave NW (Trans-Canada Hwy 1) and Banff Tr NW. Ext/int corridors. **Pets:** Medium. $10 daily fee/pet. Designated rooms, crate. ⓢⓐⓥⓔ 🛜 🛏 💻

ⓐ ▼▼ Econo Lodge South Ⓜ
(403) 252-4401. **$90-$130.** 7505 Macleod Tr SW T2H 0L8. Corner of Hwy 2A (Macleod Tr) and 75th Ave. Ext/int corridors. **Pets:** Medium. $10 daily fee/pet. Designated rooms, service with restrictions. 🄴🄲🄾 ⓢⓐⓥⓔ 🛜 🛏 💻 ⇌

▼▼▼ Executive Royal Hotel North Calgary ⊞ 🐾
(403) 291-2003. **$104-$220.** 2828 23rd St NE T2E 8T4. Barlow Tr NE, just w; at 27th Ave NE. Int corridors. **Pets:** Other species. $25 one-time fee/room. Service with restrictions, crate. 🄴🄲🄾 🛜 ✖ 🛏 💻 🍴 ✖

▼▼▼▼ The Fairmont Palliser ⊞
(403) 262-1234. **$179-$709.** 133 9th Ave SW T2P 2M3. 9th Ave SW and 1st St SW. Int corridors. **Pets:** Accepted. 🄴🄲🄾 🛜 🛏 💻 🍴 ⇌ ✖

▼▼▼ Holiday Inn Calgary-Airport ⊞
(403) 230-1999. **$120-$160.** 1250 McKinnon Dr NE T2E 7T7. 0.6 mi (1 km) e of jct Hwy 2 (Deerfoot Tr) and 16th Ave NE (Trans-Canada Hwy 1). Int corridors. **Pets:** Accepted. 🛜 ✖ 🛏 💻 🍴 ⇌

ⓐ ▼▼▼ Holiday Inn Calgary-Macleod Trail South ⊞
(403) 287-2700. **$119-$269.** 4206 Macleod Tr S T2G 2R7. Corner of 42nd Ave SW and Macleod Tr S. Int corridors. **Pets:** Small. $20 one-time fee/room. Designated rooms, service with restrictions, supervision. 🄴🄲🄾 ⓢⓐⓥⓔ 🛜 ✖ 💻 🍴 ⇌

▼▼▼ Holiday Inn Express Hotel & Suites Calgary Downtown ⊞
(403) 269-8262. **Call for rates.** 1020 8th Ave SW T2P 1J2. At 10th St SW. Int corridors. **Pets:** Accepted. 🛜 🛏 💻

▼▼▼ Holiday Inn Express Hotel & Suites Calgary-South ⊞
(403) 225-3000. **$139-$259.** 12025 Lake Fraser Dr SE (Macleod Tr S) T2J 7G5. Hwy 2 (Deerfoot Tr) exit Anderson Rd W, just s on Macleod Tr, just e on Lake Fraser Gate, then 0.4 mi (0.7 km) n. Int corridors. **Pets:** $3 daily fee/pet. Designated rooms, supervision. 🛜 🛏 💻 ⇌ ✖

▼▼▼ Hotel Arts ⊞
(403) 266-4611. **$139-$299.** 119 12th Ave SW T2R 0G8. At 1st St SW; center. Int corridors. **Pets:** $30 daily fee/pet. Designated rooms, service with restrictions, supervision. 🛜 ✖ 🛏 🛏 💻 🍴 ⇌

▼▼▼ Hotel Blackfoot ⊞
(403) 252-2253. **$119-$289.** 5940 Blackfoot Tr SE T2H 2B5. At 58th Ave SE. Int corridors. **Pets:** Other species. $10 daily fee/room. Service with restrictions, crate. 🄴🄲🄾 🛜 🛏 🛏 💻 🍴 ⇌ ✖

ⓐ ▼▼▼▼ Hotel Le Germain Calgary ⊞ 🐾
(403) 264-8990. **$199-$539.** 899 Centre St SW T2G 1B8. Corner of 1st St SW and 9th Ave SW; center. Int corridors. **Pets:** Dogs only. $30 daily fee/pet. Service with restrictions, supervision. ⓢⓐⓥⓔ 🛜 ✖ 💻 🍴 ✖

◇◇ ▽▽▽▽ Hyatt Regency Calgary 🅷 ❀
(403) 717-1234. **$129-$549.** 700 Centre St SE T2G 5P6. Corner of Centre St and 7th Ave SW. Int corridors. **Pets:** Medium. $50 one-time fee/room. Designated rooms, service with restrictions, supervision.
[SAVE] [📶] [📱] [🍽] [🏊] [✕]

◇◇ ▽▽▽▽ Lakeview Signature Inn 🅷
(403) 735-3336. **$140-$310.** 2622 39th Ave NE T1Y 7J9. Barlow Tr NE, just e. Int corridors. **Pets:** Accepted.
[ECO] [SAVE] [📶] [✕] [⅃M] [📱] [📱] [🏊] [✕]

◇◇ ▽▽▽▽ Radisson Hotel Calgary Airport 🅷
(403) 291-4666. **$129-$299.** 2120 16th Ave NE T2E 1L4. Just e of jct 16th Ave NE (Trans-Canada Hwy 1) and Hwy 2 (Deerfoot Tr). Int corridors. **Pets:** Very small. $25 one-time fee/room. Designated rooms, supervision. [ECO] [SAVE] [📶] [✕] [⅃M] [📱] [📱] [🍽] [🏊]

◇◇ ▽▽▽▽ Residence Inn by Marriott Calgary Airport 🅷
(403) 278-1000. **$139-$419.** 2530 48th Ave NE T3J 4V8. Just n of jct Barlow Tr NE and McKnight Blvd NE. Int corridors. **Pets:** $100 one-time fee/room. Designated rooms, service with restrictions, supervision.
[SAVE] [📶] [✕] [⅃M] [📱] [📱] [🍽] [🏊]

▽▽▽▽ Sandman Hotel Downtown Calgary 🅷
(403) 237-8626. **Call for rates.** 888 7th Ave SW T2P 3J3. Corner of 7th Ave SW and 8th St SW. Int corridors. **Pets:** Accepted.
[ECO] [📶] [📱] [📱] [🍽] [🏊]

▽▽▽▽ Sandman Hotel Suites & Spa Calgary Airport 🅷
(403) 219-2475. **$129-$219.** 25 Hopewell Way NE T3J 4V7. Just n of jct Barlow Tr and McKnight Blvd. Int corridors. **Pets:** Accepted.
[ECO] [📶] [⅃M] [📱] [📱] [🍽] [🏊]

◇◇ ▽▽▽ Service Plus Inn & Suites Calgary 🅷
(403) 256-5352. **$129-$149.** 3503 114th Ave SE T2Z 3X2. South end of Barlow Tr, just w. Int corridors. **Pets:** $15 daily fee/room. Designated rooms, service with restrictions, supervision.
[SAVE] [📶] [✕] [⅃M] [📱] [📱] [🏊] [✕]

◇◇ ▽▽▽▽ Sheraton Cavalier Hotel 🅷 ❀
(403) 291-0107. **$139-$469.** 2620 32nd Ave NE T1Y 6B8. Barlow Tr at 32nd Ave NE. Int corridors. **Pets:** Large. Service with restrictions, supervision. [ECO] [SAVE] [📶] [✕] [📱] [🍽] [🏊] [✕]

◇◇ ▽▽▽▽ Sheraton Suites Calgary Eau Claire 🅷 ❀
(403) 266-7200. **$149-$549.** 255 Barclay Parade SW T2P 5C2. At 3rd St SW and 2nd Ave SW. Int corridors. **Pets:** Medium, dogs only. Designated rooms, service with restrictions, supervision.
[ECO] [SAVE] [📶] [✕] [📱] [📱] [🍽] [🏊] [✕]

◇◇ ▽▽▽ Staybridge Suites Calgary Airport 🅷
(403) 204-7829. **$169-$269.** 2825 Sunridge Way NE T1Y 7K7. Trans-Canada Hwy 1 exit Barlow Tr NE, just n, then just e. Int corridors. **Pets:** Small. $75 one-time fee/pet. Designated rooms, crate.
[SAVE] [📶] [✕] [⅃M] [📱] [📱] [🏊] [✕]

◇◇ ▽▽ ▽▽ Travelodge Calgary University 🅷 🐾
(403) 289-6600. **$109-$199.** 2227 Banff Tr NW T2M 4L2. 16th Ave NW (Trans-Canada Hwy 1) and Banff Tr NW. Int corridors. **Pets:** Large, other species. $10 one-time fee/pet. Designated rooms, service with restrictions, supervision. [ECO] [SAVE] [📶] [📱] [📱] [🏊]

◇◇ ▽▽▽▽ Travelodge Hotel Calgary Airport 🅷
(403) 291-1260. **$113-$300.** 2750 Sunridge Blvd NE T1Y 3C2. Just se of jct 32nd Ave NE and Barlow Tr NE. Int corridors. **Pets:** Accepted.
[ECO] [SAVE] [📶] [📱] [📱] [🍽] [🏊]

◇◇ ▽▽▽▽ The Westin Calgary 🅷
(403) 266-1611. **$139-$519.** 320 4th Ave SW T2P 2S6. Corner of 4th Ave SW and 3rd St. Int corridors. **Pets:** Accepted.
[ECO] [SAVE] [📶] [✕] [⅃M] [📱] [📱] [🍽] [🏊] [✕]

▽▽▽▽ Wingate by Wyndham Calgary 🅷
(403) 514-0099. **$129-$309.** 400 Midpark Way SE T2X 3S4. Hwy 2A (Macleod Tr), 0.3 mi (0.5 km) e on Sun Valley Blvd SE, just n on Midpark Blvd SE, then just s. Int corridors. **Pets:** Accepted.
[ECO] [📶] [✕] [⅃M] [📱] [📱] [🏊] [✕]

COCHRANE

▽▽▽▽ Days Inn & Suites Cochrane 🅷
(403) 932-5588. **$99-$180.** 5 West Side Dr T4C 1M1. Jct Hwy 1A, 0.3 mi (0.5 km) s on Hwy 22, just e on Quigley Dr, then just s. Int corridors. **Pets:** Dogs only. $10 daily fee/pet. Service with restrictions, supervision.
[📶] [📱] [📱]

▽▽▽▽ Ramada Cochrane 🅷
(403) 932-6355. **$115-$165.** 10 West Side Dr T4C 1M1. Jct Hwy 1A, 0.3 mi (0.5 km) s on Hwy 22, just e on Quigley Dr, then just s. Int corridors. **Pets:** Accepted. [ECO] [📶] [✕] [📱] [📱] [🏊] [✕]

▽▽ ▽▽ Super 8 Cochrane 🅷
(403) 932-1410. **$120-$150.** 11 West Side Dr T4C 1M1. Jct Hwy 1A, 0.3 mi (0.5 km) s on Hwy 22, just e on Quigley Dr, then just s. Ext/int corridors. **Pets:** Other species. $10 daily fee/pet. Designated rooms, service with restrictions, crate. [📶] [✕] [📱] [📱] [✕]

OKOTOKS

◇◇ ▽▽ ▽▽ Lakeview Inns & Suites 🅷 ❀
(403) 938-7400. **$125-$130, 14 day notice.** 22 Southridge Dr T1S 1N1. Hwy 2 exit 2A, 2.4 mi (4 km) s to Southridge Dr. Int corridors. **Pets:** Other species. $10 daily fee/pet. Designated rooms, service with restrictions, supervision. [ECO] [SAVE] [📶] [📱] [📱]

STRATHMORE

◇◇ ▽▽▽▽ BEST WESTERN Strathmore Inn 🅷
(403) 934-5777. **Call for rates.** 550 Hwy 1 T1P 1M6. Trans-Canada Hwy 1, jct Hwy 817; center. Int corridors. **Pets:** $10 daily fee/room. Designated rooms, service with restrictions, supervision.
[SAVE] [📶] [✕] [📱] [📱] [🏊]

◇◇ ▽▽▽▽ Days Inn & Suites 🅷
(403) 934-1134. **$130-$150.** 400 Ranch Market T1P 0B2. Trans-Canada Hwy 1, just n at Lakeside Blvd (Centre St). Int corridors. **Pets:** Large. $15 daily fee/pet. Designated rooms, service with restrictions, supervision.
[SAVE] [📶] [✕] [⅃M] [📱] [📱] [🏊] [✕]

▽▽▽▽ Travelodge Strathmore 🅷 🐾
(403) 901-0000. **$129-$144.** 350 Ridge Rd T1P 1B5. Just n of Trans-Canada Hwy 1; at Ridge Rd. Int corridors. **Pets:** Dogs only. $15 daily fee/room. Designated rooms, service with restrictions, supervision.
[📶] [📱] [📱] [🏊] [✕]

END METROPOLITAN AREA

CAMROSE

(CAA) ▼▼▼▼ BEST WESTERN PLUS Camrose Resort Casino 🅷

(780) 679-2376. **Call for rates.** 3201 48 Ave T4V 0K9. Hwy 13 (48th Ave), just s of Correction Line Rd; eastern approach to city. Int corridors. **Pets:** Accepted. [SAVE] 🛜 ✕ 🖨 🅼 🔒 💻 ｜｜ 🌊 ✕

▼▼▼ Norsemen Inn 🅷

(780) 672-9171. **$105-$199.** 6505 48th Ave T4V 3K3. Hwy 13 (48th Ave) at 65th St; west end of town. Int corridors. **Pets:** Other species. $20 one-time fee/room. Designated rooms, service with restrictions. 🛜 ✕ 🔒 🖨 ｜｜

▼▼▼ Ramada Inn & Suites Camrose 🅷

(780) 672-5220. **$145-$220.** 4702 73rd St T4V 0E5. Hwy 13 (48th Ave), just s. Int corridors. **Pets:** Accepted. 🛜 ✕ 🔒 🖨 💻 🌊 ✕

▼▼▼ Super 8 Camrose 🅷

(780) 672-7303. **$135-$200.** 4710 73rd St T4V 0E5. Hwy 13 (48th Ave), just s. Int corridors. **Pets:** Other species. $15 daily fee/pet. Designated rooms, service with restrictions, crate. 🛜 ✕ 🔒 🖨 💻 🌊 ✕

CANMORE

(CAA) ▼▼▼ Banff Boundary Lodge 🅒🅞

(403) 678-9555. **$84-$189, 3 day notice.** 1000 Harvie Heights Rd T1W 2W2. Trans-Canada Hwy 1 exit 86, just n. Ext corridors. **Pets:** Large. $15 daily fee/pet. Designated rooms, no service, supervision. [SAVE] 🛜 ✕ 🔒 🖨 💻 🄰🄲

(CAA) ▼▼▼▼ BEST WESTERN PLUS Pocaterra Inn 🅷

(403) 678-4334. **$110-$210.** 1725 Mountain Ave T1W 2W1. Trans-Canada Hwy 1 exit 86, 1.3 mi (2.1 km) e. Int corridors. **Pets:** Large, other species. $10 daily fee/pet. Designated rooms, service with restrictions, crate. [SAVE] 🛜 ✕ 🅼 🔒 🖨 💻 🌊 ✕

▼▼▼ Blackstone Mountain Lodge 🅷

(403) 609-8098. **$139-$249.** 170 Kananaskis Way T1W 0A8. Trans-Canada Hwy 1 exit 89, 1.2 mi (2 km) s. Int corridors. **Pets:** Accepted. 🄴🄲🄾 🛜 ✕ 🔒 🖨 💻 🌊 ✕

▼▼▼ Bow Valley Motel 🅜

(403) 678-5085. **$75-$110.** 610 8th St T1W 2B5. Trans-Canada Hwy 1 exit 89, 1.1 mi (1.8 km) se. Ext corridors. **Pets:** Dogs only. $10 daily fee/room. Designated rooms, supervision. 🛜 ✕ 🔒 💻

(CAA) ▼▼▼ Canadian Rockies Chalets 🅒🅞

(403) 678-3799. **$89-$249, 3 day notice.** 1206 Bow Valley Tr T1W 1N6. Trans-Canada Hwy 1 exit 89, 0.9 mi (1.5 km) se. Ext corridors. **Pets:** Large. $15 daily fee/pet. Designated rooms, supervision. [SAVE] 🛜 ✕ 🔒 💻 🄰🄲

(CAA) ▼▼▼ Econo Lodge Canmore 🅷

(403) 678-5488. **$94-$150.** 1602 2nd Ave T1W 1M8. Trans-Canada Hwy 1 exit 89, 1.3 mi (2.1 km) e. Int corridors. **Pets:** Accepted. [SAVE] 🛜 ✕ 🔒 🖨 💻 ｜｜

▼▼▼▼ Fire Mountain Lodge 🅒🅞

(403) 609-9949. **$154-$319, 7 day notice.** 121 Kananaskis Way T1W 2X2. Trans-Canada Hwy 1 exit 89, 1 mi (1.6 km) e. Ext corridors. **Pets:** Accepted. 🛜 ✕ 🔒 💻

▼▼▼▼ Mystic Springs Chalets & Hot Pools 🅒🅞 🐾

(403) 609-0333. **Call for rates.** 140 Kananaskis Way T1W 2X2. Trans-Canada Hwy 1 exit 89, 1.1 mi (1.8 km) s. Ext corridors. **Pets:** Medium. $25 daily fee/room. Service with restrictions, crate. 🄴🄲🄾 🛜 ✕ 🔒 🖨 💻 🌊 ✕

(CAA) ▼▼▼▼ Quality Resort-Chateau Canmore 🅷 🐾

(403) 678-6699. **$89-$119.** 1720 Bow Valley Tr T1W 2X3. Trans-Canada Hwy 1 exit 86, 0.5 mi (0.8 km) s. Int corridors. **Pets:** $45 deposit/pet. Service with restrictions, supervision. [SAVE] 🛜 ✕ 🔒 🖨 💻 ｜｜ 🌊 ✕

(CAA) ▼▼▼▼ Radisson Hotel & Conference Centre 🅷 🐾

(403) 678-3625. **$99-$249, 3 day notice.** 511 Bow Valley Tr T1W 1N7. Trans-Canada Hwy 1 exit 89, 1.4 mi (2.2 km) s. Ext/int corridors. **Pets:** Other species. $25 daily fee/room. Service with restrictions, crate. 🄴🄲🄾 [SAVE] 🛜 ✕ 🅼 🔒 🖨 💻 ｜｜ 🌊 ✕

▼▼▼▼ Ramada Inn & Suites Canmore 🅷

(403) 609-4656. **$79-$179.** 1402 Bow Valley Tr T1W 1N5. Trans-Canada Hwy 1 exit 89, 1 mi (1.6 km) se. Int corridors. **Pets:** Accepted. 🛜 ✕ 🅼 🔒 🖨 💻 🌊 ✕

(CAA) ▼▼▼ Rocky Mountain Ski Lodge 🅜

(403) 678-5445. **$119-$209.** 1711 Bow Valley Tr T1W 2T8. Trans-Canada Hwy 1 exit 86, 0.5 mi (0.8 km) s. Ext corridors. **Pets:** Medium. $10 daily fee/pet. Designated rooms, service with restrictions, supervision. 🄴🄲🄾 [SAVE] 🛜 ✕ 🔒 🖨 💻 ✕

▼▼▼▼ Solara Resort & Spa 🅒🅞

(403) 609-3600. **$159-$299.** 187 Kananaskis Way T1W 0A3. Trans-Canada Hwy 1 exit 89, 1.2 mi (2 km) s. Int corridors. **Pets:** Accepted. 🛜 ✕ 🔒 🖨 💻 ✕

▼▼▼ Windtower Lodge & Suites 🅒🅞

(403) 609-6600. **$119-$289.** 160 Kananaskis Way T1W 3E2. Trans-Canada Hwy 1 exit 89, 1.1 mi (1.8 km) s. Int corridors. **Pets:** Accepted. 🛜 ✕ 🔒 🖨 💻 ✕ 🄰🄲

CLARESHOLM

▼▼▼ Bluebird Motel 🅜

(403) 625-3395. **Call for rates.** 5505 1st St W T0L 0T0. 0.3 mi (0.5 km) n on Hwy 2. Ext corridors. **Pets:** Accepted. 🛜 ✕ 🔒 💻

▼▼▼ Motel 6 Claresholm 🅷

(403) 625-4646. **$86-$96.** 11 Alberta Rd (Hwy 2) T0L 0T0. North end of town. Int corridors. **Pets:** Other species. Service with restrictions, supervision. 🛜 🅼 🔒

COLD LAKE

(CAA) ▼▼▼▼ BEST WESTERN Cold Lake Inn 🅷

(780) 594-4888. **Call for rates.** 4815 52nd St T9M 1P1. Corner of 55th Ave (Hwy 26 and 55) and 52nd St; south end of city. Ext/int corridors. **Pets:** Accepted. [SAVE] 🛜 ✕ 🅼 🔒 🖨 💻 ｜｜ 🌊 ✕

DEAD MAN'S FLATS

(CAA) ▼▼▼▼ Copperstone Resort Hotel 🅒🅞 🐾

(403) 678-0303. **$129-$299.** 250 2nd Ave T1W 2W4. Trans-Canada Hwy 1 exit 98, just n on 2nd St, then just e. Int corridors. **Pets:** Other species. $20 daily fee/room. Service with restrictions. [SAVE] 🛜 ✕ 🔒 💻

DRAYTON VALLEY

(CAA) ▼▼▼ Lakeview Inns & Suites 🅷

(780) 542-3200. **Call for rates.** 4302 50th St T7A 1M4. Hwy 22 exit Drayton Valley, 1.5 mi (2.4 km) n. Int corridors. **Pets:** Accepted. [SAVE] 🛜 🔒 💻 ｜｜

▼▼▼▼ Ramada Inn Drayton Valley 🅷

(780) 514-7861. **$140-$220.** 2051 50th St T7A 1S5. Just n on Hwy 39; south end of town. Ext/int corridors. **Pets:** Accepted. 🄴🄲🄾 🛜 ✕ 🅼 🔒 🖨 💻 🌊 ✕

DRUMHELLER

▼▼▼▼ Canalta Jurassic Hotel 🅷

(403) 823-7700. **Call for rates.** 1103 Hwy 9 S T0J 0Y0. Hwy 9, south-east access to town. Ext/int corridors. **Pets:** Accepted. 🄴🄲🄾 🛜 ✕ 🔒 🖨 💻 ✕

▼▼▼▼ Inn and Spa at Heartwood 🅷 🐾

(403) 823-6495. **$105-$315, 3 day notice.** 320 N Railway Ave E T0J 0Y4. Jct Hwy 9 and 575 (S Railway Ave SE), just n, then just e. Ext/int corridors. **Pets:** Other species. $25 one-time fee/room. Designated rooms, service with restrictions, supervision. 🛜 ✕ 🔒 🖨 💻

▼▼▼ Ramada Inn & Suites 🅷

(403) 823-2028. **$150-$220.** 680 2nd St SE T0J 0Y0. Jct Hwy 9 and 575 (S Railway Ave SE), just ne. Ext/int corridors. **Pets:** $15 daily fee/pet. Designated rooms, service with restrictions, supervision.

ECO 🛜 ✕ 🐾M 🛏 💷 ⤳ ✕

▼▼ Super 8 🅷

(403) 823-8887. **$140-$180.** 600-680 2nd St SE T0J 0Y0. Jct Hwy 9 and 575 (S Railway Ave SE), just ne. Ext/int corridors. **Pets:** Accepted.

ECO 🛜 ✕ 🛏 💷 ⤳ ✕

EDMONTON METROPOLITAN AREA

EDMONTON

🅐 ▼▼▼ BEST WESTERN Cedar Park Inn 🅷

(780) 434-7411. **$130-$160, 7 day notice.** 5116 Gateway Blvd T6H 2H4. Hwy 2 (Gateway Blvd) at 51st Ave. Int corridors. **Pets:** Medium. $20 daily fee/room. Designated rooms, service with restrictions, crate.

SAVE 🛜 ✕ 🐾M 🛏 💷 🍴 ⤳

🅐 ▼▼▼▼ BEST WESTERN PLUS Westwood Inn 🅷

(780) 483-7770. **$140, 7 day notice.** 18035 Stony Plain Rd T5S 1B2. Hwy 16A (Stony Plain Rd) at 180th St. Int corridors. **Pets:** Other species. $20 daily fee/pet. Designated rooms, service with restrictions, supervision.

SAVE 🛜 🛏 🍴 ⤳

▼▼▼▼ Coast Edmonton House CO

(780) 420-4000. **$129-$300.** 10205 100th Ave T5J 4B5. Just se of jct 102nd St and 100th Ave. Int corridors. **Pets:** Accepted.

ECO 🛜 🛏 💷 🍴 ⤳

🅐 ▼▼ Comfort Inn West 🅷

(780) 484-4415. **$99-$139.** 17610 100th Ave T5S 1S9. At 176th St. Int corridors. **Pets:** Medium, other species. $10 daily fee/pet. Service with restrictions, supervision. ECO SAVE 🛜 🐾M 🛏 💷 🍴

🅐 ▼▼ ▼ Continental Inn 🅷

(780) 484-7751. **$110-$145, 6 day notice.** 16625 Stony Plain Rd T5P 4A8. On Hwy 16A (Stony Plain Rd) at 166th St. Int corridors. **Pets:** Small, dogs only. $50 deposit/pet, $50 one-time fee/pet. Designated rooms, service with restrictions, supervision. SAVE 🛜 🛏 💷 🍴

▼▼▼ Courtyard by Marriott Edmonton Downtown 🅷

(780) 423-9999. **$155-$171.** 1 Thornton Ct T5J 2E7. Just off Jasper Ave; between 99th and 97th sts. Int corridors. **Pets:** Accepted.

🛜 ✕ 🐾M 🛏 💷 🍴

🅐 ▼▼▼ Delta Edmonton Centre Suite Hotel 🅷

(780) 429-3900. **$109-$339.** 10222 102nd St NW T5J 4C5. At 102nd St NW and 103rd Ave NW. Int corridors. **Pets:** Medium, other species. $35 daily fee/room. Service with restrictions, crate.

ECO SAVE 🛜 ✕ 🐾M 🛏 💷 🍴 ✕

🅐 ▼▼▼ Delta Edmonton South Hotel and Conference Centre 🅷 ❀

(780) 434-6415. **$100-$350.** 4404 Gateway Blvd T6H 5C2. Jct Calgary Tr (Hwy 2) and Whitemud Dr. Int corridors. **Pets:** Medium, other species. $35 one-time fee/pet. Service with restrictions, crate.

ECO SAVE 🛜 ✕ 🛏 💷 🍴 ⤳

🅐 ▼▼▼ Edmonton Hotel and Convention Centre 🅷

(780) 468-5400. **$139-$299.** 4520 76th Ave T6B 0A5. Hwy 14, just s via 50th St exit, then just e. Int corridors. **Pets:** Accepted.

SAVE 🛜 🛏 💷 🍴 ⤳ ✕

▼▼▼▼ Executive Royal Inn West Edmonton 🅷

(780) 484-6000. **$120.** 10010 178th St T5S 1T3. Corner of 178th St and 100th Ave. Int corridors. **Pets:** Accepted. ECO 🛜 ✕ 🛏 💷 🍴

🅐 ▼▼▼▼ The Fairmont Hotel Macdonald 🅷

(780) 424-5181. **$189-$399, 3 day notice.** 10065 100th St T5J 0N6. Just s of Jasper Ave. Int corridors. **Pets:** Accepted.

ECO SAVE 🛜 🐾M 💷 🍴 ⤳ ✕

🅐 ▼▼▼ Four Points by Sheraton Edmonton South 🅷 ❀

(780) 465-7931. **$125, 7 day notice.** 7230 Argyll Rd T6C 4A6. Hwy 2 (Gateway Blvd), 2.3 mi (3.7 km) e at 63rd Ave (which becomes Argyll Rd); at 75th St. Int corridors. **Pets:** $25 daily fee/pet. Designated rooms, crate. SAVE 🛜 ✕ 🐾M 🛏 💷 🍴 ⤳ ✕

▼▼▼ Holiday Inn Express & Suites Edmonton South 🅷

(780) 440-5000. **$129-$159.** 2440 Calgary Tr T6J 5J6. Hwy 2, just w at 31st Ave, then 0.5 mi (0.8 km) s on 104th St; Hwy 2 northbound, just w at 23 Ave, then just n. Int corridors. **Pets:** Medium. $25 one-time fee/room. Designated rooms, service with restrictions, supervision.

🛜 ✕ 🐾M 🛏 💷 ⤳

🅐 ▼▼▼ Holiday Inn Express Edmonton Downtown 🅷 ❀

(780) 423-2450. **$149-$199.** 10010 104th St T5J 0Z1. Corner of 100th Ave; center. Int corridors. **Pets:** Medium. $30 one-time fee/pet. Designated rooms, service with restrictions, supervision.

ECO SAVE 🛜 ✕ 🐾M 🛏 💷 ⤳ ✕

▼▼▼ Mayfield Inn & Suites at West Edmonton 🅷

(780) 484-0821. **Call for rates.** 16615 109th Ave T5P 4K8. 1 mi (1.6 km) n of jct Hwy 2 (170th St) and 16A (Stony Plain Rd). Int corridors. **Pets:** Accepted. ECO 🛜 ✕ 🛏 💷 🍴 ⤳ ✕

▼▼▼ Metterra Hotel on Whyte 🅷 ❀

(780) 465-8150. **$130-$200.** 10454 82nd Ave (Whyte Ave) T6E 4Z7. Just e of 105th St. Int corridors. **Pets:** Dogs only. $25 daily fee/pet. Designated rooms, service with restrictions, supervision.

🛜 ✕ 🐾M 🛏 💷

▼▼▼ Quality Inn West Harvest 🅷 ❀

(780) 484-8000. **$115-$135.** 17803 Stony Plain Rd NW T5S 1B4. Jct Hwy 16A (Stony Plain Rd) and 178th St. Int corridors. **Pets:** Medium, other species. $20 daily fee/pet. Designated rooms, service with restrictions, supervision. 🛜 ✕ 🛏 💷 🍴

🅐 ▼▼▼ Radisson Hotel Edmonton South 🅷

(780) 437-6010. **$175-$300.** 4440 Gateway Blvd NW T6H 5C2. Between Whitemud Dr and 45th Ave. Int corridors. **Pets:** Small. $10 daily fee/pet. Designated rooms, service with restrictions, supervision.

ECO SAVE 🛜 🛏 💷 🍴 ⤳ ✕

▼▼▼ Sawridge Inn Edmonton South 🅷

(780) 438-1222. **$109-$189.** 4235 Gateway Blvd T6J 5H2. Just s of Whitemud Dr. Int corridors. **Pets:** Accepted.

ECO 🛜 ✕ 🛏 💷 🍴

▼▼ Super 8 Edmonton South 🅷

(780) 433-8688. **$120-$140.** 3610 Gateway Blvd T6J 7H8. Jct 36th Ave. Int corridors. **Pets:** Accepted. 🛜 ✕ 🐾M 🛏 💷 ⤳ ✕

▼▼▼ The Sutton Place Hotel Edmonton 🅷

(780) 428-7111. **$259-$450.** 10235 101st St T5J 3E9. 102nd Ave at 101st St. Int corridors. **Pets:** Small. $35 one-time fee/pet. Designated rooms, service with restrictions, crate.

ECO 🛜 ✕ 🛏 💷 🍴 ⤳ ✕

🅐 ▼▼▼ Travelodge Edmonton East 🅷

(780) 474-0456. **$89-$99.** 3414 118th Ave T5W 0Z4. 5 mi (8 km) e of Capilano Dr, 0.6 mi (1 km) s from W Hwy 16 (Yellowhead Tr) exit Victoria Tr. Int corridors. **Pets:** Accepted. ECO SAVE 🛜 🛏 💷 🍴

Ⓐ ▽▼▽ **Travelodge Edmonton South** 🅷
(780) 436-9770. **$105-$135.** 10320 45th Ave S T6H 5K3. Jct Calgary Tr (Hwy 2) and 45th Ave, just n of Whitemud Dr. Int corridors.
Pets: Accepted. 🄴🄲🄾 🅂🄰🅅 📶 🛏 💻 〰

▽▼▽▼ **Varscona Hotel on Whyte** 🅷
(780) 434-6111. **$125-$400.** 8208 106th St T6E 6R9. Corner of 82nd Ave (Whyte Ave) and 106th St. Int corridors. **Pets:** Accepted.
🄴🄲🄾 📶 ✕ 🛏 💻 🍴

Ⓐ ▽▼▽ **West Edmonton Mall Inn** 🅷
(780) 444-9378. **$119-$194.** 17504 90th Ave T5T 6L6. From Whitemud Dr exit 170th St N, just w. Int corridors. **Pets:** Accepted.
🅂🄰🅅 📶 ✕ 🄼 🛏 💻

Ⓐ ▽▼▽ ▽▼ **The Westin Edmonton** 🅷
(780) 426-3636. **$119-$489.** 10135 100th St T5J 0N7. 101st Ave at 100th St. Int corridors. **Pets:** Accepted.
🄴🄲🄾 🅂🄰🅅 📶 ✕ 🛏 💻 🍴 〰 ✕

▽▼▽▼ **Wingate Inn Edmonton West** 🅷
(780) 443-1000. **$125-$225.** 18220 100th Ave T5S 2V2. From Anthony Henday Dr, 0.9 mi (1.5 km) e at 182nd St. Int corridors. **Pets:** Accepted.
📶 ✕ 🛏 💻 🍴 〰 ✕

FORT SASKATCHEWAN

Ⓐ ▽▼▽ **Lakeview Inns & Suites** 🅷
(780) 998-7888. **Call for rates.** 10115 88th Ave T8L 2T1. Just w of Hwy 15/21 and 101st St. Int corridors. **Pets:** Accepted.
🄴🄲🄾 🅂🄰🅅 📶 🛏 💻 🍴

Ⓐ ▽▼▽ **Musgrave's Hospitality Inns & Suites** 🅷
(780) 998-2770. **$139-$199.** 9820 86th Ave T8L 4P4. Just sw of Hwy 15/21 and 101st St. Int corridors. **Pets:** Accepted.
🅂🄰🅅 📶 ✕ 🄼 🛏 💻 🍴

ST. ALBERT

Ⓐ ▽▼▽ **BEST WESTERN PLUS The Inn at St. Albert** 🅷
(780) 470-3800. **$145-$160.** 460 St. Albert Tr T8N 5J9. Hwy 2 (St. Albert Tr), just w at Lennox Dr. Int corridors. **Pets:** Medium. $20 daily fee/room. Designated rooms, service with restrictions, crate.
🅂🄰🅅 📶 ✕ 🛏 💻 〰

SHERWOOD PARK

▽▼▽▼ **Coast Edmonton East Hotel** 🅷
(780) 464-4900. **$139-$159.** 2100 Premier Way T8H 2G4. Hwy 16 exit Broadmoor Blvd, 0.6 mi (1 km) sw. Int corridors. **Pets:** Accepted.
📶 ✕ 🛏 💻 🍴

Ⓐ ▽▼▽ **Franklin's Inn** 🅷
(780) 467-1234. **$129-$169, 3 day notice.** 2016 Sherwood Dr T8A 3X3. At Granada Blvd. Int corridors. **Pets:** Other species. $10 daily fee/room. Designated rooms, service with restrictions, crate.
🅂🄰🅅 📶 🛏 💻 🍴 🄶

Ⓐ ▽▼▽ **MainStay Suites East Edmonton/Sherwood Park** 🅷
(780) 570-8080. **$149-$169.** 201 Palisades Way T8H 0N3. Hwy 16 exit 403 (Sherwood Dr), 0.9 mi (1.5 km) s. Int corridors. **Pets:** Accepted.
🅂🄰🅅 📶 🄼 🛏 💻

▽▼▽ **Ramada Limited-Edmonton East/Sherwood Park** 🅷
(780) 467-6727. **$120-$150.** 30 Broadway Blvd T8H 2A2. Hwy 16 exit Broadmoor Blvd, 1.2 mi (2 km) s. Int corridors. **Pets:** Accepted.
📶 ✕ 🛏 💻

▽▼▽ **Super 8 Sherwood Park/Edmonton Area** 🅷
(780) 464-1000. **$129-$144.** 26 Strathmoor Dr T8H 2B6. Hwy 16 exit Broadmoor Blvd, just sw. Int corridors. **Pets:** Accepted.
📶 🛏 💻 🍴

STONY PLAIN

Ⓐ ▽▼▽▼ **BEST WESTERN Sunrise Inn & Suites** 🅷
(780) 968-1716. **$151-$221.** 3101 43rd Ave T7Z 1L1. Hwy 16A (Township Rd 530), just s at S Park Dr, then just e. Int corridors.
Pets: Accepted. 🅂🄰🅅 📶 ✕ 🛏 💻 〰 ✕

▽▼▽ **Motel 6 Stony Plain** 🅷
(780) 968-5123. **Call for rates.** 66 Boulder Blvd T7Z 1V7. Just off Hwy 16A (Township Rd 530). Int corridors. **Pets:** Other species. Service with restrictions, supervision. 🄴🄲🄾 📶 ✕ 🛏

▽▼▽ **Ramada Inn & Suites** 🅷
(780) 963-0222. **$111-$139.** 3301 43rd Ave T7Z 1L1. Hwy 16A (Township Rd 530), just s on S Park Dr, then just e. Ext/int corridors.
Pets: Accepted. 📶 🛏 💻 🍴 〰

END METROPOLITAN AREA

EDSON

Ⓐ ▽▼▽ **BEST WESTERN High Road Inn** 🅷
(780) 712-2378. **$139-$149.** 300 52nd St T7E 1V8. On 2nd Ave; center. Int corridors. **Pets:** Accepted. 🅂🄰🅅 📶 🄼 🛏 💻 🍴 〰 ✕

▽▼ **Guest House Inn & Suites** 🄼
(780) 723-4486. **Call for rates.** 4411 4th Ave T7E 1B8. 0.6 mi (1 km) e on Hwy 16. Ext/int corridors. **Pets:** Accepted. 📶 🛏 💻 🍴 ✕

Ⓐ ▽▼▽ **Lakeview Inn & Suites Edson Airport West** 🅷
(780) 723-7508. **Call for rates.** 528 63rd St T7E 1M1. Hwy 16, west end of town. Int corridors. **Pets:** Accepted.
🄴🄲🄾 🅂🄰🅅 📶 🄼 🛏 💻

Ⓐ ▽▼▽ **Lakeview Inns & Suites East** 🅷
(780) 723-2500. **$94-$114.** 4300 2nd Ave T7E 1B8. 0.6 mi (1 km) e on Hwy 16. Int corridors. **Pets:** Accepted. 🄴🄲🄾 🅂🄰🅅 📶 🛏 💻

FORT MACLEOD

Ⓐ ▽▼ **Sunset Motel** 🄼
(403) 553-4448. **$80-$88.** 104 Hwy 3 W T0L 0Z0. 0.6 mi (1 km) w on Hwy 2 and 3. Ext corridors. **Pets:** Other species. Service with restrictions, supervision. 🅂🄰🅅 📶 🛏 💻

FORT MCMURRAY

▽▼▽▼ **Clearwater Suite Hotel** 🅷
(780) 799-7676. **Call for rates.** 4 Haineault St T9H 1L6. Hwy 63 (Sakitawaw Tr), just n on Hardin St, just e on Franklin Ave, then just s. Int corridors. **Pets:** Accepted. 🄴🄲🄾 📶 ✕ 🛏 💻 ✕

▽▼▽ **Vantage Inn & Suites** 🅷
(780) 713-4111. **Call for rates.** 200 Parent Way T9H 5E6. 3.1 mi (5 km) s on Hwy 63 (Sakitawaw Tr). Int corridors. **Pets:** Other species. $20 daily fee/pet. Service with restrictions. 🄴🄲🄾 🛏 💻

GRANDE PRAIRIE

ⒶⒶ ▼▼▼▼ BEST WESTERN Grande Prairie Hotel & Suites H ❖

(780) 402-2378. **$169-$174.** 10745 117th Ave T8V 7N6. Corner of Hwy 43 (100th Ave) and 117th Ave. Int corridors. **Pets:** Large. $35 one-time fee/room. Designated rooms, service with restrictions, crate.

ECO SAVE 🛜 🛗 🖼️ ⊪ ⤳

▼▼▼ Days Inn Grande Prairie H

(780) 532-2773. **$110-$145.** 10218 162nd Ave T8V 0P2. Jct Hwy 2 and 43 (100th Ave), just s. Int corridors. **Pets:** $20 daily fee/pet. Designated rooms. 🛜 🛗 🖼️

ⒶⒶ ▼▼▼▼ Holiday Inn Hotel & Suites H ❖

(780) 402-6886. **$150-$180.** 9816 107th St T8V 8E7. Jct Hwy 43 (100th Ave) and 40 (108th St). Int corridors. **Pets:** Other species. $25 daily fee/room. Designated rooms, service with restrictions, supervision.

ECO SAVE 🛜 ♿M 🛗 🖼️ ⊪ ⤳ ✕

▼▼▼ Motel 6 Grande Prairie #5709 H

(780) 830-7744. **$76-$81.** 15402 101st St T8V 0P7. Jct Hwy 2 and 43 (100th Ave), just s. Int corridors. **Pets:** Other species. Service with restrictions, supervision. ECO ♿M 🖼️

▼▼▼ Podollan Inn & Spa H

(780) 830-2000. **$149-$169, 3 day notice.** 10612 99th Ave T8V 8E8. Jct Hwy 43 (100th Ave) and 40 (108th St), just e. Int corridors. **Pets:** Accepted. 🛜 🛗 🖼️ ⊪

▼▼▼ Pomeroy Hotel H

(780) 532-5221. **$119-$299.** 11633 100th St T8V 3Y4. Jct Hwy 43 (100th Ave) and 116th Ave. Int corridors. **Pets:** Accepted.

ECO 🛜 🛗 🖼️ ⊪ ⤳ ✕

ⒶⒶ ▼▼▼▼ Pomeroy Inn & Suites, Grande Prairie H ❖

(780) 831-2999. **$150-$160. Call for rates.** 11710 102nd St T8V 7S7. 102nd St at 117th Ave. Int corridors. **Pets:** Other species. $50 one-time fee/room. Supervision. ECO SAVE 🛜 🛗 🖼️ ⤳ ✕

ⒶⒶ ▼▼ Quality Hotel & Conference Centre Grande Prairie H

(780) 539-6000. **$129-$169.** 11201 100th Ave T8V 5M6. 1.8 mi (2.9 km) w on Hwy 2. Int corridors. **Pets:** Accepted.

ECO SAVE 🛜 🛗 🖼️ ⊪

▼▼▼ Service Plus Inns and Suites H

(780) 538-3900. **Call for rates.** 10810 107A Ave T8V 7A9. 1.4 mi (2.2 km) w on Hwy 2, just n. Int corridors. **Pets:** Accepted.

🛜 🛗 🖼️ ⤳ ✕

▼▼ Stanford Inn H ❖

(780) 539-5678. **$99-$120.** 11401 100th Ave T8V 5M6. Hwy 2 and 43 (100th Ave), just e of 116 St. Ext/int corridors. **Pets:** Other species. $8 daily fee/pet. Service with restrictions, supervision.

ECO 🛜 🛗 🖼️ ⊪

▼▼ Stonebridge Hotel H

(780) 539-5561. **$129-$189.** 12102 100th St T8V 5P1. 100th St at 121st Ave. Int corridors. **Pets:** Large. $25 one-time fee/pet. Service with restrictions, supervision. 🛜 🛗 🖼️ ⊪

▼▼ Super 8 H ❖

(780) 532-8288. **$110-$170.** 10050 116th Ave T8V 4K5. 102nd St at 117th Ave. Int corridors. **Pets:** Medium, other species. $25 daily fee/pet. Designated rooms, service with restrictions, supervision.

ECO 🛜 🛗 🖼️ ⤳ ✕

GRIMSHAW

▼▼▼ Pomeroy Inn & Suites H

(780) 332-2000. **Call for rates.** 4311 51st St T0H 1W0. On Hwy 2; south end of town. Int corridors. **Pets:** Accepted.

ECO 🛜 🛗 🖼️ ⤳ ✕

HANNA

▼▼ Super 8 Hanna H

(403) 854-2400. **$130-$140.** 113 Palliser Tr T0J 1P0. Hwy 9, just n. Ext/int corridors. **Pets:** Accepted. ECO 🛜 🛗 🖼️

HIGH LEVEL

ⒶⒶ ▼▼▼▼ BEST WESTERN PLUS Mirage Hotel & Resort H

(780) 821-1000. **$177-$197.** 9616 Hwy 58 T0H 1Z0. Jct Hwy 35 and 58; north end of town. Ext/int corridors. **Pets:** Medium, dogs only. $20 daily fee/pet. Designated rooms, service with restrictions, supervision.

SAVE 🛜 🛗 🖼️ ⊪ ⤳ ✕

ⒶⒶ ▼▼▼ Super 8 High Level H ❖

(780) 841-3448. **$135.** 9502 114th Ave T0H 1Z0. Hwy 35, just se; south end of town. Ext/int corridors. **Pets:** Medium, other species. $25 one-time fee/pet. Designated rooms, service with restrictions, supervision.

ECO SAVE 🛜 ♿M 🛗 🖼️ ⤳ ✕

HIGH PRAIRIE

▼▼▼ Peavine Inn & Suites H

(780) 523-2398. **$129-$169.** 3905 51st Ave T0G 1E0. Hwy 2, just n; east end of town. Ext/int corridors. **Pets:** Medium. $25 daily fee/room. Designated rooms, service with restrictions, supervision.

🛜 🛗 🖼️ ⊪ ⤳ ✕

HIGH RIVER

▼▼ Heritage Inn Hotel & Convention Centre H

(403) 652-3834. **$129-$185.** 1104 11th Ave SE T1V 1M4. Trans-Canada Hwy 2 exit 23, 0.5 mi (0.8 km) w. Int corridors. **Pets:** Medium, dogs only. $20 daily fee/pet. Designated rooms, service with restrictions, crate.

🛜 🛗 🖼️ ⊪

▼▼ Super 8 H

(403) 652-4448. **$120-$140.** 1601 13th Ave SE T1V 2B1. Trans-Canada Hwy 2 exit High River, just w. Int corridors. **Pets:** Accepted.

ECO 🛜 ✕ 🛗 🖼️ ⤳ ✕

HINTON

ⒶⒶ ▼▼ BEST WESTERN White Wolf Inn H ❖

(780) 865-7777. **$150-$160.** 828 Carmichael Ln T7V 1T1. At west end of town; just off Hwy 16. Ext corridors. **Pets:** Large, other species. $100 deposit/room. Designated rooms, service with restrictions, crate.

SAVE 🛜 🛗 🖼️

▼▼▼ Holiday Inn Hinton H

(780) 865-3321. **$139-$159.** 393 Gregg Ave T7V 1N1. 0.3 mi (0.5 km) w on Hwy 16. Int corridors. **Pets:** Accepted.

ECO 🛜 ♿M 🛗 🖼️ ⊪ ⤳ ✕

ⒶⒶ ▼▼▼▼ Lakeview Inns & Suites H

(780) 865-2575. **Call for rates.** 500 Smith St T7V 2A1. 1.1 mi (1.7 km) e on Hwy 16. Ext/int corridors. **Pets:** Accepted.

ECO SAVE 🛜 🛗 🖼️

▼▼ Overlander Mountain Lodge CI

(780) 866-2330. **$139-$249, 3 day notice.** Hwy 16 T7V 1X5. Hwy 16, 15 mi (24 km) w; just outside Jasper National Park gates. Ext/int corridors. **Pets:** Accepted. 🛜 ✕ 🛗 🖼️ ⊪ ⊟

▼▼ ▼▼ Super 8 🅷
(780) 817-2228. **$100-$200.** 284 Smith St T7V 2A1. 1 mi (1.6 km) e on Hwy 16. Int corridors. **Pets:** Accepted. 🛜 🗄 💻 🏊

JASPER

🅰 ▼▼ ▼▼ Amethyst Lodge 🅷 🐾
(780) 852-3394. **$85-$285.** 200 Connaught Dr T0E 1E0. 0.3 mi (0.5 km) e. Ext/int corridors. **Pets:** $15 daily fee/room. Designated rooms, service with restrictions, crate. 🄴🄲🄾 🅂🄰🅅🄴 🛜 ✖ 🗄 💻 🍴

🅰 ▼▼▼▼ BEST WESTERN Jasper Inn & Suites 🅷 🐾
(780) 852-4461. **$150-$240, 3 day notice.** 98 Geikie St T0E 1E0. Corner of Geikie and Bonhomme sts. Ext/int corridors. **Pets:** Other species. $20 daily fee/room. Designated rooms, service with restrictions, supervision. 🅂🄰🅅🄴 🛜 ✖ 🗄 💻 🍴 🏊 ✖ 🄰🄲

🅰 ▼▼▼▼ Chateau Jasper 🅷 🐾
(780) 852-5644. **$109-$295.** 96 Geikie St T0E 1E0. Corner of Juniper and Geikie sts. Int corridors. **Pets:** $15 daily fee/room. Designated rooms, service with restrictions, crate. 🄴🄲🄾 🅂🄰🅅🄴 🛜 ✖ 🗄 💻 🍴 🏊

🅰 ▼▼▼▼ The Fairmont Jasper Park Lodge 🅷 🐾
(780) 852-3301. **Call for rates.** 1 Old Lodge Rd T0E 1E0. 3 mi (4.8 km) ne via Hwy 16, 2 mi (3.2 km) se off highway via Maligne Rd, follow signs. Ext corridors. **Pets:** Other species. $50 one-time fee/room. Service with restrictions, supervision.
🄴🄲🄾 🅂🄰🅅🄴 🛜 ✖ ♿ 🗄 💻 🍴 🏊 ✖ 🄰🄲

🅰 ▼▼▼▼ Lobstick Lodge 🅷 🐾
(780) 852-4431. **$99-$255.** 94 Geikie St T0E 1E0. Corner of Geikie and Juniper sts. Int corridors. **Pets:** $15 daily fee/room. Designated rooms, service with restrictions, supervision.
🄴🄲🄾 🅂🄰🅅🄴 🛜 ✖ 🗄 💻 🍴 🏊 ✖ 🄰🄲

🅰 ▼▼ ▼▼ Marmot Lodge 🅼 🐾
(780) 852-4471. **$89-$255.** 86 Connaught Dr T0E 1E0. 1 mi (1.6 km) ne. Ext corridors. **Pets:** $15 daily fee/room. Designated rooms, service with restrictions, crate. 🄴🄲🄾 🅂🄰🅅🄴 🛜 ✖ ♿ 🗄 💻 🍴 🏊

▼▼ ▼▼ Patricia Lake Bungalows 🄲🄰
(780) 852-3560. **$87-$325, 7 day notice.** Pyramid Lake Rd T0E 1E0. 3 mi (4.8 km) nw via Pyramid Lake Rd. Ext corridors. **Pets:** Medium, dogs only. $10 daily fee/room. Designated rooms, service with restrictions, supervision. 🛜 ✖ 🗄 💻 ✖ 🄯

🅰 ▼▼ ▼▼ Pyramid Lake Resort 🅷 🐾
(780) 852-4900. **$161-$368.** Pyramid Lake Rd T0E 1E0. Jct Connaught Dr and Cedar St, 3.8 mi (6 km) nw via Pyramid Lake Rd. Ext corridors. **Pets:** $15 daily fee/room. Designated rooms, service with restrictions, crate. 🄴🄲🄾 🅂🄰🅅🄴 🛜 ✖ 🗄 💻 🍴 ✖ 🄰🄲

🅰 ▼▼▼▼ Sawridge Inn & Conference Centre Jasper 🅷
(780) 852-5111. **$92-$284, 3 day notice.** 76 Connaught Dr T0E 1E0. 1.1 mi (1.7 km) e. Int corridors. **Pets:** Dogs only. $20 daily fee/room. Designated rooms, service with restrictions, supervision.
🄴🄲🄾 🅂🄰🅅🄴 🛜 ✖ ♿ 🗄 💻 🍴 ✖

🅰 ▼▼ ▼▼ Sunwapta Falls Rocky Mountain Lodge 🄲🄰
(780) 852-4852. **$99-$409.** Hwy 93 T0E 1E0. 34.7 mi (55 km) s on Icefields Pkwy (Hwy 93). Ext corridors. **Pets:** Accepted.
🅂🄰🅅🄴 🛜 ✖ 🗄 💻 🍴 ✖ 🄰🄲 🄯

▼▼ ▼▼ Tonquin Inn 🅼 🐾
(780) 852-4987. **$135-$400.** 100 Juniper St T0E 1E0. Corner of Juniper and Geikie sts. Ext corridors. **Pets:** Medium. $25 one-time fee/pet. Designated rooms, service with restrictions, crate.
🛜 ✖ 🗄 💻 🍴 🏊 ✖

KANANASKIS

▼▼▼▼ Delta Lodge at Kananaskis 🅷 🐾
(403) 591-7711. **$159-$309, 3 day notice.** Kananaskis Village T0L 2H0. Trans-Canada Hwy 1, 14.7 mi (23.5 km) s on Hwy 40 (Kananaskis Tr), then 1.8 mi (3 km) on Kananaskis Village access road, follow signs. Int corridors. **Pets:** Other species. $35 one-time fee/room. Service with restrictions. 🄴🄲🄾 🛜 ✖ 🗄 💻 🍴 🏊 ✖

LAKE LOUISE

🅰 ▼▼▼▼ The Fairmont Chateau Lake Louise 🅷 🐾
(403) 522-3511. **Call for rates.** 111 Lake Louise Dr T0L 1E0. 1.8 mi (3 km) up the hill from the village. Int corridors. **Pets:** $25 daily fee/pet. Designated rooms, service with restrictions, supervision.
🄴🄲🄾 🅂🄰🅅🄴 🛜 ✖ 🗄 💻 🍴 🏊 ✖

▼▼ ▼▼ Lake Louise Inn 🅷
(403) 522-3791. **Call for rates.** 210 Village Rd T0L 1E0. Just w of 4-way stop. Ext/int corridors. **Pets:** Other species. $50 one-time fee/room. Designated rooms, service with restrictions.
🛜 ✖ 🗄 💻 🍴 🏊 ✖

LETHBRIDGE

▼▼ ▼▼ Comfort Inn 🅷
(403) 320-8874. **$107-$179.** 3226 Fairway Plaza Rd S T1K 7T5. Hwy 3 (Crowsnest Tr) exit Mayor Magrath Dr S, 1.8 mi (3 km) s, then just e on 24th Ave. Int corridors. **Pets:** Accepted. 🛜 🗄 💻 🏊

▼▼ ▼▼ Days Inn Lethbridge 🅷
(403) 327-6000. **$99-$120.** 100 3rd Ave S T1J 4L2. Corner of 3rd Ave and Scenic Dr; center. Ext/int corridors. **Pets:** $10 daily fee/pet. Designated rooms, service with restrictions, crate. 🄴🄲🄾 🛜 🗄 💻 🏊

▼▼ ▼▼ Holiday Inn Express Hotel & Suites Lethbridge 🅷
(403) 394-9292. **Call for rates.** 120 Stafford Dr S T1J 4W4. Hwy 3 (Crowsnest Tr) exit Stafford Dr, just s; downtown. Int corridors. **Pets:** Large. $25 one-time fee/room. Designated rooms, service with restrictions, crate. 🛜 ✖ 🗄 💻 ✖

▼▼ ▼▼ Holiday Inn Hotel Lethbridge 🅷
(403) 380-5050. **$139-$199.** 2375 Mayor Magrath Dr S T1K 7M1. Hwy 3 (Crowsnest Tr) exit Mayor Magrath Dr S, 1.8 mi (3 km) s, then just e on 22nd St. Int corridors. **Pets:** $10 daily fee/pet. Designated rooms, service with restrictions, supervision. 🄴🄲🄾 🛜 ✖ 🗄 💻 🍴 🏊 ✖

🅰 ▼▼ ▼▼ Lethbridge Lodge Hotel and Conference Centre 🅷
(403) 328-1123. **$109-$199.** 320 Scenic Dr T1J 4B4. Scenic Dr at 4th Ave S; center. Int corridors. **Pets:** Other species. $15 daily fee/pet. Designated rooms, service with restrictions, crate.
🄴🄲🄾 🅂🄰🅅🄴 🛜 ✖ 🗄 💻 🍴 🏊

🅰 ▼▼ ▼▼ Quality Inn & Suites 🅷
(403) 331-6440. **$105-$195.** 4070 2nd Ave S T1J 3Z2. Hwy 3 (Crowsnest Tr), just s on WT Hill Blvd, then just e. Int corridors. **Pets:** Dogs only. $10 daily fee/pet. Designated rooms, supervision.
🅂🄰🅅🄴 🛜 ♿ 🗄 💻 🏊 ✖

▼▼ ▼▼ Sandman Hotel Lethbridge 🅷
(403) 328-1111. **$114-$199.** 421 Mayor Magrath Dr S T1J 3L8. Hwy 3 (Crowsnest Tr) exit Mayor Magrath Dr S, just s. Int corridors. **Pets:** $11 daily fee/pet. Designated rooms, service with restrictions, crate.
🄴🄲🄾 🛜 ✖ 🗄 💻 🍴 🏊

MEDICINE HAT

🅰 ▼▼▼▼ BEST WESTERN PLUS Sun Country 🅷
(403) 527-3700. **$116-$150, 30 day notice.** 722 Redcliff Dr T1A 5E3. On Trans-Canada Hwy 1, 0.3 mi (0.4 km) w of jct Hwy 3, access 7th St SW. Ext/int corridors. **Pets:** Accepted.
🄴🄲🄾 🅂🄰🅅🄴 🛜 ✖ ♿ 🗄 💻 🏊 ✖

ⒸⒶ ▼▼▼ **Comfort Inn & Suites** 🏠 🐾

(403) 504-1700. **$93-$210.** 2317 Trans-Canada Way SE T1B 4E9. Trans-Canada Hwy 1, just n on Dunmore Rd, then just w. Int corridors. **Pets:** Medium. $25 daily fee/pet. Designated rooms, service with restrictions, supervision. 🅴🅲🅾 🆂🅰🆅🅴 📶 🔋 💻 🏊

▼▼▼ **Holiday Inn Express Hotel & Suites** 🏠

(403) 504-5151. **$159-$189.** 9 Strachan Bay SE T1B 4Y2. Trans-Canada Hwy 1, just s on Dunmore Rd, then just e; east end of city. Int corridors. **Pets:** Other species. Designated rooms, service with restrictions, supervision. 🅴🅲🅾 📶 🔋 💻 🏊 ✕

▼▼▼ **Medicine Hat Lodge Resort, Casino & Spa** 🏠

(403) 529-2222. **$114-$194.** 1051 Ross Glen Dr SE T1B 3T8. Trans-Canada Hwy 1, just n on Dunmore Rd. Int corridors. **Pets:** $10 daily fee/room. Designated rooms, service with restrictions, supervision.

📶 ✕ 🅼 🔋 💻 🍴 🏊 ✕

▼ **Motel 6 Medicine Hat** 🏠

(403) 527-1444. **$85-$95.** 20 Strachan Ct SE T1B 4R7. Trans-Canada Hwy 1, just s on Dunmore Rd, then just w; southeast end of city. Int corridors. **Pets:** Other species. Service with restrictions, supervision.

🅴🅲🅾 📶 🅼 🔋 💻

▼▼ **Super 8** 🏠

(403) 528-8888. **$96-$110.** 1280 Trans-Canada Way SE T1B 1J5. Trans-Canada Hwy 1 at 13th Ave SE; just n off Trans-Canada Hwy 1. Ext/int corridors. **Pets:** Other species. $10 one-time fee/room. Service with restrictions, supervision. 📶 🔋 💻 🏊

MORLEY

▼▼▼ **Stoney Nakoda Resort** 🏠 🐾

(403) 881-2830. **$99-$169.** Jct Trans-Canada Hwy 1 and Hwy 40 T0L 1N0. Jct Hwy 40, just s. Int corridors. **Pets:** Large. $20 daily fee/room. Service with restrictions. 📶 🔋 💻 🍴 🏊 ✕

PINCHER CREEK

▼▼ **Heritage Inn & Hotel Convention Centre Pincher Creek** 🏠

(403) 627-5000. **$125-$269.** 919 Waterton Ave (Hwy 6) T0K 1W0. Jct Hwy 785, just s. Int corridors. **Pets:** Medium, dogs only. $20 daily fee/pet. Designated rooms, service with restrictions, crate.

📶 🔋 💻 🍴 🏊

▼▼▼ **Ramada Inn & Suites** 🏠

(403) 627-3777. **$140-$219.** 1132 Table Mountain St T0K 1W0. Hwy 3 (Crowsnest Tr), 1.3 mi (2.1 km) s on Hwy 6. Ext/int corridors. **Pets:** Accepted. 🅴🅲🅾 📶 ✕ 🔋 🔋 💻 🏊 ✕

RED DEER

ⒸⒶ ▼▼▼ **BEST WESTERN PLUS Red Deer Inn & Suites** 🏠

(403) 346-3555. **$135-$145.** 6839 66th St T4P 3T5. Hwy 2 exit 67th St, just e. Int corridors. **Pets:** Accepted.

🅴🅲🅾 🆂🅰🆅🅴 📶 🅼 🔋 💻 🏊

▼▼▼ **Comfort Inn & Suites** 🏠

(403) 348-0025. **$130-$170.** 6846 66th St T4P 3T5. Hwy 2 exit 67th St, just e. Int corridors. **Pets:** Accepted. 📶 🔋 💻 🏊 ✕

◆◆ **Motel 6-Red Deer** 🏠

(403) 340-1749. **$75-$109.** 900-5001 19th St T4R 3R1. Hwy 2 exit 394 (Gaetz Ave), just w; in Southpointe Common Shopping District. Int corridors. **Pets:** Other species. Service with restrictions, supervision. 🅴🅲🅾 🔋

ⒸⒶ ▼▼▼▼ **Quality Inn North Hill** 🏠

(403) 343-8800. **$129-$199.** 7150 50th Ave T4N 6A5. Hwy 2 exit 401 (67th St), 1.7 mi (2.9 km) e, then 0.5 mi (0.8 km) n. Int corridors. **Pets:** $10 daily fee/pet. Designated rooms, service with restrictions, supervision. 🆂🅰🆅🅴 📶 🔋 💻 🍴 🏊

ⒸⒶ ▼▼▼ **Red Deer Lodge Hotel and Conference Centre** 🏠

(403) 346-8841. **Call for rates.** 4311 49th Ave T4N 5Y7. Hwy 2 exit 394 (Gaetz Ave), 2.6 mi (4.2 km) n. Int corridors. **Pets:** Other species. Designated rooms, service with restrictions, supervision.

🅴🅲🅾 🆂🅰🆅🅴 📶 🔋 💻 🍴 🏊 ✕

▼▼▼ **Sandman Hotel Red Deer** 🏠

(403) 343-7400. **$129-$149.** 2818 Gaetz Ave T4R 1M4. 1 mi (1.6 km) n on Hwy 2A (Gaetz Ave). Int corridors. **Pets:** Accepted.

🅴🅲🅾 📶 🔋 💻 🍴 🏊

ⒸⒶ ▼▼▼▼ **Sheraton Red Deer Hotel** 🏠 🐾

(403) 346-2091. **$119-$299.** 3310 50th Ave T4N 3X9. 1.3 mi (2 km) n on Hwy 2A (Gaetz Ave). Int corridors. **Pets:** Other species. Service with restrictions, supervision. 🆂🅰🆅🅴 📶 ✕ 🔋 💻 🍴 🏊

RIMBEY

ⒸⒶ ▼▼▼▼ **BEST WESTERN Rimstone Ridge Hotel** 🏠 🐾

(403) 843-2999. **$135-$160.** 5501 50th Ave T0C 2J0. Hwy 20, 1.2 mi (2 km) e. Int corridors. **Pets:** Large, dogs only. $20 daily fee/room. Service with restrictions, supervision. 🆂🅰🆅🅴 📶 ✕ 🔋 💻 🍴 🏊 ✕

ROCKY MOUNTAIN HOUSE

ⒸⒶ ▼▼▼▼ **BEST WESTERN Rocky Mountain House Inn & Suites** 🏠 🐾

(403) 844-3100. **Call for rates.** 4407 41st Ave T4T 1A5. Hwy 11 and 22, just w on 42nd Ave, then just s; east end of town. Int corridors. **Pets:** $20 daily fee/pet. Service with restrictions, crate.

🅴🅲🅾 🆂🅰🆅🅴 📶 🔋 💻 🏊 ✕

▼▼ **Rocky Inn Express** 🏠

(403) 845-2871. **Call for rates.** 4715 45th St T4T 1B1. Hwy 11 and 22, just e on 47th Ave, then just n. Int corridors. **Pets:** Accepted.

🅴🅲🅾 📶 🅼 🔋 💻

▼▼▼ **Super 8** 🏠

(403) 846-0088. **$135-$155.** 4406 41st Ave T4T 1J6. Hwy 11 and 22, just w on 42nd Ave, then just s; east end of town. Ext/int corridors. **Pets:** Accepted. 🅴🅲🅾 📶 ✕ 🅼 🔋 💻 🏊 ✕

SLAVE LAKE

ⒸⒶ ▼▼▼▼ **Lakeview Inns & Suites** 🏠

(780) 849-9500. **$121-$190.** 1550 Holmes Tr SE T0G 2A3. Hwy 2, just n; east end of town. Int corridors. **Pets:** Accepted.

🅴🅲🅾 🆂🅰🆅🅴 📶 🔋 💻

SYLVAN LAKE

ⒸⒶ ▼▼▼▼ **BEST WESTERN PLUS Chateau Inn** 🏠 🐾

(403) 887-7788. **$150-$190.** 5027 Lakeshore Dr T4S 1R3. Jct Hwy 11 and 781 (50th St), 1.9 mi (3.1 km) n, just e. Int corridors. **Pets:** Large, other species. $20 daily fee/pet. Designated rooms, service with restrictions, supervision. 🆂🅰🆅🅴 📶 ✕ 🔋 💻 🏊

▼▼▼ **Chateau Suites at Sylvan Bay** 🅒🅞

(403) 887-6699. **$169-$310.** 5100 Lakeshore Dr, #1 T4S 2L7. Jct Hwy 11 and 781 (50th St), 1.9 mi (3.1 km) n. Ext corridors. **Pets:** Accepted.

🔋 💻

TABER

▼▼▼ **Heritage Inn Hotel & Convention Centre Taber** 🏠

(403) 223-4424. **$100-$160.** 4830 46th Ave T1G 2A4. Jct Hwy 3 and 36 S, 1.5 mi (2.5 km) se. Int corridors. **Pets:** Medium, dogs only. $20 daily fee/pet. Designated rooms, service with restrictions, crate.

📶 🔋 💻 🍴 ✕

◇◇ Super 8 Taber ⛨
(403) 223-8181. **$96-$107.** 5700 46th Ave T1G 2B1. Jct Hwy 3 and 36 S, 0.5 mi (0.9 km) se. Ext/int corridors. **Pets:** Medium. $10 daily fee/pet. Service with restrictions, supervision. 🛜 📶 💻

THREE HILLS

🅐 ◇◇◇ BEST WESTERN Diamond Inn ⛨
(403) 443-7889. **$120-$125.** 351 7th Ave N T0M 2A0. Hwy 21 and 27, 1.1 mi (1.9 km) w. Int corridors. **Pets:** Accepted. (SAVE) 🛜 📶 💻

VALLEYVIEW

🅐 ◇◇◇ Western Valley Inn Ⓜ
(780) 524-4000. **$79-$139.** 5402 Highway St T0H 3N0. Just w of jct Hwy 43 and 49. Ext corridors. **Pets:** Dogs only. $20 one-time fee/pet. Supervision. (SAVE) 🛜 📶 💻 ⏍

WAINWRIGHT

🅐 ◇◇◇◇ BEST WESTERN Wainwright Inn & Suites ⛨
(780) 845-9934. **$140.** 1209 27th St T9W 0A2. Jct Hwy 14 and 41, just e. Int corridors. **Pets:** Medium. $20 daily fee/pet. Designated rooms, service with restrictions, supervision. (SAVE) 🛜 📶 💻 🏊

WATERTON PARK

🅐 ◇◇◇ Aspen Village Inn Ⓜ
(403) 859-2255. **$89-$259.** 111 Windflower Ave T0K 2M0. Center. Ext corridors. **Pets:** Accepted. (SAVE) 🛜 ✖ 📶 💻 ⏍

🅐 ◇◇◇ Bayshore Inn Resort & Spa Ⓜ
(403) 859-2211. **$122-$282, 3 day notice.** 111 Waterton Ave T0K 2M0. Center. Ext/int corridors. **Pets:** $20 daily fee/pet. Designated rooms.
(SAVE) 🛜 ✖ 📶 📶 💻 ⏍

🅐 ◇◇◇◇ Waterton Lakes Resort ⛨
(403) 859-2150. **$149-$289.** 101 Clematis Ave T0K 2M0. Center. Ext/int corridors. **Pets:** Accepted. (SAVE) 🛜 ✖ 📶 💻 ⏍ 🐾 ✖

WESTEROSE

◇◇ Village Creek Country Inn ⛨
(780) 586-0006. **$129-$199, 3 day notice.** 15 Village Dr, RR 2 T0C 2V0. Hwy 2 exit 482, 17.5 mi (28 km) w on Hwy 13; in Village at Pigeon Lake. Ext/int corridors. **Pets:** Accepted. 🛜 📶 💻 ⏍

WESTLOCK

🅐 ◇◇◇ BEST WESTERN Westlock ⛨
(780) 349-4102. **Call for rates.** 10520 100th St T7P 2C6. Jct Hwy 18 and 44, just e. Ext/int corridors. **Pets:** Accepted.
(SAVE) 🛜 📶 💻 ⏍

WETASKIWIN

🅐 ◇◇◇ BEST WESTERN Wayside Inn ⛨ 🐾
(780) 312-7300. **$125-$140.** 4103 56th St T9A 1V2. On Hwy 2A, just n of jct Hwy 13 W. Int corridors. **Pets:** Medium, other species. $50 deposit/room, $5 daily fee/pet. Designated rooms, service with restrictions, crate.
(SAVE) 🛜 ✖ 📶 💻 ⏍

◇◇ Super 8 ⛨
(780) 361-3808. **$120-$130.** 3820 56th St T9A 2B2. On Hwy 2A, just s of jct Hwy 13 W. Ext/int corridors. **Pets:** Accepted. 🛜 📶 💻

WHITECOURT

◇◇◇ Holiday Inn Express & Suites Whitecourt ⛨
(780) 778-2512. **$149-$159.** 4721 49th St T7S 1N5. Hwy 43, just n on 51st St, just e. Int corridors. **Pets:** Very small. $40 deposit/room. Designated rooms, service with restrictions, supervision. 🛜 📶 📶 💻

🅐 ◇◇◇ Super 8 ⛨
(780) 778-8908. **$135-$145.** 4121 Kepler St T7S 0A3. On Hwy 43, just e of Hwy 32. Int corridors. **Pets:** $25 one-time fee/pet. Designated rooms, service with restrictions, supervision. (ECO) (SAVE) 🛜 📶 💻

BRITISH COLUMBIA

CITY INDEX

100 MILE HOUSE

▼▼ 100 Mile House Super 8 Ⓜ

(250) 395-8888. **$79-$149.** 989 Alder Ave V0K 2E0. 0.6 mi (1 km) s on Hwy 97. Ext corridors. **Pets:** Accepted. 🛜 ⊠ Ⓜ 🛢 🖵

ABBOTSFORD

Ⓐ ▼▼▼ BEST WESTERN Bakerview Inn Ⓜ ❀

(604) 859-1341. **$110-$140, 3 day notice.** 1821 Sumas Way V2S 4L5. Trans-Canada Hwy 1 exit 92 (Town Centre), just n on Hwy 11. Ext corridors. **Pets:** Dogs only. Service with restrictions, supervision.
🌿 SAVE 🛜 🛢 🖵 ⤳

BARRIERE

▼▼ Mountain Springs Motel & RV Park Ⓜ

(250) 672-0090. **$70-$80.** 4253 Yellowhead Hwy V0E 1E0. 0.6 mi (1 km) s on Hwy 5 (Yellowhead Hwy). Ext corridors. **Pets:** Accepted.
🛜 ⊠ Ⓜ 🛢 🖵

BLUE RIVER

▼▼ Glacier Mountain Lodge Ⓗ

(250) 673-2393. **$99-$209.** 869 Shell Rd V0E 1J0. On Hwy 5 (Yellowhead Hwy); at Shell Rd, follow signs. Int corridors. **Pets:** Accepted.
🛜 ⊠ 🛢

CACHE CREEK

Ⓐ ▼▼ Bonaparte Motel Ⓜ

(250) 457-9693. **$59-$129.** 1395 Hwy 97 N V0K 1H0. Just n of jct Trans-Canada Hwy 1. Ext corridors. **Pets:** Accepted.
SAVE 🛜 ⊠ 🛢 🖵 ⤳

CAMPBELL RIVER

▼▼ Anchor Inn & Suites Ⓗ

(250) 286-1131. **$99-$149.** 261 Island Hwy V9W 2B3. On Island Hwy 19A, 1.3 mi (2 km) s. Int corridors. **Pets:** Accepted.
🛜 Ⓜ 🛢 🖵 🍴 ⤳ Ⓐ

Ⓐ ▼▼▼▼ BEST WESTERN PLUS Austrian Chalet Ⓜ

(250) 923-4231. **$119-$299.** 462 S Island Hwy V9W 1A5. 2 mi (3.2 km) s on Island Hwy 19A. Ext/int corridors. **Pets:** Small. $20 one-time fee/room. Designated rooms, service with restrictions, supervision.
SAVE 🛜 ⊠ Ⓜ 🛢 🖵 ⤳ ⊠

▼▼ Ocean Resort Ⓜ

(250) 923-4281. **$125-$145.** 4834 S Island Hwy V9H 1E8. 11 mi (18 km) s on Island Hwy 19A. Int corridors. **Pets:** $20 daily fee/pet. Designated rooms, service with restrictions, supervision. 🛜 ⊠ 🛢 ⊠ Ⓐ

▼▼ Town Centre Inn Ⓜ

(250) 287-8866. **$79-$94.** 1500 Dogwood St V9W 3A6. Follow Island Hwy 19A through town, follow signs, just e; corner of 16th Ave. Ext corridors. **Pets:** Small, dogs only. $5 daily fee/pet. Designated rooms, service with restrictions, supervision. 🛜 🛢 🖵 Ⓐ

▼▼ Travelodge Campbell River Ⓜ

(250) 286-6622. **$72-$140.** 340 S Island Hwy V9W 1A5. 1.9 mi (3 km) s on Island Hwy 19A. Int corridors. **Pets:** Other species. $10 daily fee/pet. Designated rooms, service with restrictions, supervision.
🌿 🛜 ⊠ Ⓜ 🛢 🖵 ⤳

CASTLEGAR

▼▼ Quality Inn Castlegar Ⓗ

(250) 365-2177. **$90-$130.** 1935 Columbia Ave V1N 2W8. Jct Hwy 3A and 3B, just s. Int corridors. **Pets:** Medium. $10 daily fee/pet. Designated rooms, service with restrictions. 🛜 ⊠ 🛢 🖵 🍴

▼▼ Super 8-Castlegar Ⓗ

(250) 365-2700. **$125-$150.** 651 18th St V1N 2N1. Jct Hwy 3, just n on Hwy 22. Int corridors. **Pets:** Other species. $10 daily fee/pet. Designated rooms, service with restrictions, supervision.
🌿 🛜 ⊠ 🛢 🖵 🍴 ⤳

CHASE

▼▼ Chase Country Inn Motel Ⓜ

(250) 679-3333. **$69-$99.** 576 Coburn St V0E 1M0. Trans-Canada Hwy 1 and Coburn St. Ext corridors. **Pets:** $5 daily fee/room.
🛜 Ⓜ 🛢 🖵 🍴

Ⓐ ▼▼▼ Quaaout Lodge & Spa, Talking Rock Golf Ⓗ

(250) 679-3090. **$100-$350, 3 day notice.** 1663 Little Shuswap Lake Rd W V0E 1M0. Trans-Canada Hwy 1 exit Squilax Bridge, 1.5 mi (2.5 km) w on Little Shuswap Rd. Int corridors. **Pets:** Medium. $15 daily fee/pet. Designated rooms, service with restrictions.
SAVE 🛜 ⊠ Ⓜ 🛢 🖵 🍴 ⤳ ⊠

CHEMAINUS

Ⓐ ▼▼▼ BEST WESTERN PLUS Chemainus Inn Ⓗ ❀

(250) 246-4181. **$137-$199.** 9573 Chemainus Rd V0R 1K5. Trans-Canada Hwy 1 exit Henry Rd, 0.9 mi (1.4 km) e. Int corridors. **Pets:** Medium, other species. $20 daily fee/room. Designated rooms, service with restrictions, supervision.
🌿 SAVE 🛜 ⊠ Ⓜ 🛢 🖵 ⤳ ⊠

CHETWYND

♦♦♦♦ Lakeview Inns & Suites 🅷 ❄

(250) 788-3000. **$129.** 4820 N Access Rd V0C 1J0. Hwy 29 and 97, just n on 48th St, then just e. Int corridors. **Pets:** $25 one-time fee/room. Designated rooms, service with restrictions, supervision.

♦♦♦♦ Pomeroy Inn & Suites 🅷 ❄

(250) 788-4800. **$161.** 5200 N Access Rd V0C 1J0. Hwy 29 and 97, just n on 52nd St. Int corridors. **Pets:** Other species. Service with restrictions, supervision.

CHILLIWACK

♦♦♦ BEST WESTERN Rainbow Country Inn 🅷

(604) 795-3828. **$105-$140, 7 day notice.** 43971 Industrial Way V2R 3A4. Trans-Canada Hwy 1 exit 116 (Lickman Rd). Int corridors. **Pets:** Small. $10 daily fee/pet. Designated rooms, service with restrictions, supervision.

♦♦♦ The Coast Chilliwack Hotel 🅷 ❄

(604) 792-5552. **$109-$164.** 45920 First Ave V2P 7K1. Trans-Canada Hwy 1 exit 119, 1.8 mi (2.9 km) n on Vedder Rd, then just e. Int corridors. **Pets:** $15 daily fee/pet. Designated rooms, service with restrictions.

♦♦ Comfort Inn Ⓜ ❄

(604) 858-0636. **$97-$135.** 45405 Luckakuck Way V2R 3C7. Trans-Canada Hwy 1 exit 119, s on Vedder Rd, then 0.6 mi (1 km) w. Int corridors. **Pets:** Medium, other species. $5 daily fee/room. Designated rooms, service with restrictions, supervision.

♦♦♦ Travelodge Hotel, Chilliwack 🅷

(604) 792-4240. **$96-$130, 3 day notice.** 45466 Yale Rd W V2R 3Z8. Trans-Canada Hwy 1 exit 119, just n. Int corridors. **Pets:** $10 daily fee/pet. Designated rooms, service with restrictions, supervision.

CHRISTINA LAKE

♦♦ New Horizon Motel Ⓜ ❄

(250) 447-9312. **$85-$175, 14 day notice.** 2037 Hunter Frontage Rd (Hwy 3) V0H 1E2. Just e on Hwy 3. Ext corridors. **Pets:** Medium. $10 daily fee/pet. Designated rooms, service with restrictions, supervision.

CLEARWATER

♦♦♦ Clearwater Valley Resort & KOA Kampground 🅲🅰

(250) 674-3909. **$110-$170.** 373 Clearwater Valley Rd V0E 1N1. Jct Hwy 5 (Yellowhead Hwy) and Clearwater Valley Rd. Ext corridors. **Pets:** Small. $10 daily fee/pet. Designated rooms, service with restrictions, supervision.

COMOX

♦♦♦ Port Augusta Inn & Suites Ⓜ

(250) 339-2277. **$65-$150.** 2082 Comox Ave V9M 1P8. Hwy 19A (Cliffe Ave), follow signs to Comox Ave, then 2.5 mi (4 km) e. Ext/int corridors. **Pets:** $5 daily fee/pet. Designated rooms, service with restrictions, supervision.

COURTENAY

♦♦♦♦ BEST WESTERN PLUS The Westerly Hotel & Convention Centre 🅷

(250) 338-7741. **$110-$200.** 1590 Cliffe Ave and Island Hwy 19A N. Int corridors. **Pets:** Large. $15 daily fee/pet. Designated rooms, service with restrictions, supervision.

♦♦♦♦ Crown Isle Resort & Golf Community 🅷

(250) 703-5050. **$139-$279.** 399 Clubhouse Dr V9N 9G3. Island Hwy 19A N, 0.9 mi (1.5 km) n on Comox Ave, then 1.6 mi (2.5 km) ne on Ryan Rd, follow signs. Ext corridors. **Pets:** Accepted.

♦♦♦ Holiday Inn Express & Suites Comox Valley 🅷 ❄

(778) 225-0010. **$130-$150.** 2200 Cliffe Ave V9N 2L4. 0.6 mi (1.1 km) s on Island Hwy 19A S. Int corridors. **Pets:** Large, other species. $15 daily fee/room. Designated rooms, service with restrictions, supervision.

♦♦♦♦ Kingfisher Oceanside Resort & Spa 🅷 ❄

(250) 338-1323. **$115-$415.** 4330 S Island Hwy V9N 9R9. 3.8 mi (6 km) s on Island Hwy 19A S, follow signs. Ext corridors. **Pets:** Other species. $25 daily fee/room. Designated rooms, service with restrictions.

♦♦♦ Travelodge Courtenay Ⓜ

(250) 334-4491. **$85-$102.** 2605 Cliffe Ave V9N 2L8. 0.8 mi (1.2 km) s on Island Hwy 19A S. Ext corridors. **Pets:** Accepted.

CRANBROOK

♦♦♦ BEST WESTERN Cranbrook Hotel 🅷

(250) 417-4002. **Call for rates.** 1019 Cranbrook St N V1C 3S4. Hwy 3 and 95; center. Int corridors. **Pets:** Accepted.

♦♦ Days Inn Cranbrook 🅷

(250) 426-6683. **$95-$124.** 600 Cranbrook St N V1C 3R7. Corner of 6th St and Cranbrook St N. Int corridors. **Pets:** Accepted.

♦♦ Heritage Inn Hotel & Convention Centre Cranbrook 🅷

(250) 489-4301. **$112-$220.** 803 Cranbrook St N V1C 3S2. Hwy 3 and 95; center. Int corridors. **Pets:** Medium, dogs only. $20 daily fee/pet. Designated rooms, service with restrictions, crate.

♦♦♦ St. Eugene Golf Resort & Casino 🅷

(250) 420-2000. **$129-$189.** 7731 Mission Rd V1C 7E5. Hwy 3 exit Kimberley/Airport (Hwy 95A) to Mission Rd, 2.8 mi (4.5 km) n. Int corridors. **Pets:** $25 daily fee/room. Designated rooms, service with restrictions, supervision.

CRESTON

♦♦♦ Skimmerhorn Inn Ⓜ ❄

(250) 428-4009. **$65-$155.** 2711 Hwy 3 V0B 1G0. Hwy 3, 0.8 mi (1.3 km) e. Ext corridors. **Pets:** Dogs only. $5 daily fee/pet. Designated rooms, service with restrictions, supervision.

♦♦♦ Sunset Motel Ⓜ ❄

(250) 428-2229. **$79-$109.** 2705 Canyon St (Hwy 3 E) V0B 1G0. Hwy 3, 0.8 mi (1.3 km) e. Ext corridors. **Pets:** Other species. $10 daily fee/room. Service with restrictions.

DAWSON CREEK

♦♦♦ BEST WESTERN Dawson Creek Inn 🅷

(250) 782-6226. **Call for rates.** 500 Hwy 2 V1G 0A4. Jct Hwy 49, 1.6 mi (2.6 km) s on 8th St (Hwy 2), then just e; south end of town. Int corridors. **Pets:** Accepted.

♦♦♦ Dawson Creek Super 8 🅷

(250) 782-8899. **$146-$337.** 1440 Alaska Ave V1G 1Z5. Jct Hwy 2 and 49, 0.5 mi (0.8 km) ne. Int corridors. **Pets:** Medium, other species. $10 one-time fee/room. Designated rooms, service with restrictions, supervision.

♦♦♦ Pomeroy Inn & Suites 🅷

(250) 782-3700. **$170-$329.** 540 Hwy 2 V1G 0A4. Jct Hwy 49, 1.6 mi (2.6 km) s on 8th St (Hwy 2), then just e; south end of town. Int corridors. **Pets:** Other species. $25 one-time fee/room. Service with restrictions, supervision.

DUNCAN

(CAA) ♥♥♥ BEST WESTERN Cowichan Valley Inn [H]
(250) 748-2722. **$119-$169.** 6474 Trans-Canada Hwy 1 V9L 6C6. 1.8 mi (3 km) n. Int corridors. **Pets:** Medium, dogs only. $20 one-time fee/room. Designated rooms, service with restrictions, supervision.
[SAVE] 🛜 ⊠ 🔲 💻 ⑪ ⇌

♥♥ Super 8 Hotel [H]
(250) 748-0661. **$89-$139.** 5325 Trans-Canada Hwy V9L 5J2. 1 mi (1.6 km) s at Chaster Rd. Int corridors. **Pets:** Accepted.
🛜 ⊠ 🔲 💻 ⑪

♥♥ Travelodge Duncan [H]
(250) 748-4311. **$109-$200.** 140 Trans-Canada Hwy V9L 3P7. Just n of Silver Bridge. Ext corridors. **Pets:** Accepted. [ECO] 🛜 🔲 💻 ⑪

FAIRMONT HOT SPRINGS

(CAA) ♥♥♥♥ Fairmont Hot Springs Resort [H]
(250) 345-6070. **$105-$355, 7 day notice.** 5225 Fairmont Resort Rd V0B 1L1. 1 mi (1.6 km) e off Hwy 93 and 95. Ext/int corridors. **Pets:** Dogs only. $20 daily fee/pet. Designated rooms, service with restrictions, crate. [ECO] [SAVE] 🛜 ⊠ 🔲 💻 ⑪ ⇌ ⊠

FERNIE

(CAA) ♥♥♥♥ BEST WESTERN PLUS Fernie Mountain Lodge [H] ✿
(250) 423-5500. **$150-$210.** 1622 7th Ave V0B 1M0. Jct Hwy 3 and 7th Ave; east end of town. Int corridors. **Pets:** $20 daily fee/pet. Designated rooms, service with restrictions, supervision.
[ECO] [SAVE] 🛜 ⊠ 🔲 💻 ⑪ ⇌ ⊠

(CAA) ♥♥♥♥ Park Place Lodge [H]
(250) 423-6871. **$132-$272.** 742 Hwy 3 V0B 1M0. At 7th St. Int corridors. **Pets:** Other species. Designated rooms, service with restrictions, supervision. [SAVE] 🛜 🔲 💻 ⑪ ⇌ ⊠

FORT NELSON

(CAA) ♥♥ Lakeview Inn & Suites [H]
(250) 233-5001. **$130-$140.** 4507 50th Ave S V0C 1R0. Just off Hwy 97 (Alaska Hwy); at 44th St. Int corridors. **Pets:** Medium, other species. $25 daily fee/room. Service with restrictions, supervision.
[ECO] [SAVE] 🛜 🔲 💻 ⊠

FORT ST. JOHN

(CAA) ♥♥♥ Lakeview Inns & Suites [H]
(250) 787-0779. **$116-$143.** 10103 98th Ave V1J 1P8. Corner of 100th Ave; center of downtown. Int corridors. **Pets:** Accepted.
[ECO] [SAVE] 🛜 🔲 💻 ⑪

(CAA) ♥♥♥ Pomeroy Hotel [H]
(250) 262-3233. **$179-$249, 14 day notice.** 11308 Alaska Rd V1J 5T5. Just w on Hwy 97 (Alaska Hwy). Int corridors. **Pets:** Medium, dogs only. $25 daily fee/pet. Service with restrictions, supervision.
[SAVE] 🛜 ⊠ [&M] 🔲 💻 ⑪ ⇌ ⊠

(CAA) ♥♥♥ Pomeroy Inn & Suites [H]
(250) 262-3030. **$129-$159.** 9320 Alaska Rd V1J 6L5. Just s on Hwy 97 (Alaska Hwy). Int corridors. **Pets:** Accepted. [SAVE] 🛜 🔲 💻

♥♥♥ Quality Inn Northern Grand [H] ✿
(250) 787-0521. **$179-$189.** 9830 100th Ave V1J 1Y5. Center. Int corridors. **Pets:** Other species. $25 daily fee/pet. Designated rooms, service with restrictions, crate. [ECO] 🛜 🔲 💻 ⑪ ⇌ ⊠

(CAA) ♥♥♥ Super 8-Fort St. John [H]
(250) 785-7588. **$150.** 9500 W Alaska Rd V1J 6L5. Just s on Hwy 97 (Alaska Hwy). Int corridors. **Pets:** Medium. $25 daily fee/pet. Designated rooms, service with restrictions, supervision.
[ECO] [SAVE] 🛜 [&M] 🔲 💻 ⑪ ⇌ ⊠

FORT STEELE

♥♥♥♥ Bull River Guest Ranch [RA]
(250) 429-3760. **Call for rates.** 2975 Bull River Rd V1C 4H7. Hwy 95, 12.9 mi (21.4 km) se of town on Ft Steele-Wardner Rd, 7.2 mi (12 km) ne on gravel road; Hwy 3 W, 24.6 mi (41 km) e of Cranbrook, 5 mi (8.2 km) n on Ft Steele-Wardner Rd, 7.2 mi (12 km) ne on gravel road. Ext corridors. **Pets:** Accepted. 🛜 ⊠ 🔲 💻 ⊠ [AC] [W] ⊘

GIBSONS

♥♥♥♥ Bonniebrook Lodge Oceanfront Inn [CI]
(604) 886-2887. **$159-$328, 7 day notice.** 1532 Ocean Beach Esplanade V0N 1V5. Hwy 101, 3.8 mi (6 km) s on Veterans Rd to Ratcliff Rd, just sw to King Rd, 0.6 mi (1 km) sw to Chaster Rd, then 5 mi (8 km) sw to Gower Pt Rd, follow signs. Ext/int corridors. **Pets:** $25 daily fee/pet. Designated rooms, service with restrictions, supervision.
🛜 ⊠ 🔲 💻 ⑪ [AC]

GOLD BRIDGE

♥♥♥♥ Tyax Wilderness Resort & Spa [H]
(250) 238-2221. **$199-$289, 30 day notice.** 1 Tyaughton Lake Rd V0K 1P0. 5 mi (8 km) n from the Tyaughton Lake turnoff, follow signs. Int corridors. **Pets:** Accepted. 🛜 ⊠ [&M] 💻 ⑪ ⊠ [AC]

GOLDEN

(CAA) ♥♥♥♥ BEST WESTERN Mountainview Inn [H]
(250) 344-2333. **$120-$200.** 1024 11th St N V0A 1H2. Just w of jct Hwy 95 and Trans-Canada Hwy 1; on S Service Rd. Int corridors. **Pets:** Other species. $20 daily fee/room. Designated rooms, service with restrictions, supervision. [SAVE] 🛜 ⊠ 🔲 💻 ⇌

♥♥ Days Inn Golden [M]
(250) 344-2216. **$150-$205.** 1416 Golden View Rd V0A 1H1. On Trans-Canada Hwy 1, 1 mi (1.6 km) e of jct Hwy 95. Ext corridors. **Pets:** Medium, other species. $15 deposit/pet. Designated rooms, service with restrictions, supervision. 🛜 🔲 💻 ⑪ ⇌ ⊠

GRAND FORKS

(CAA) ♥♥♥ Western Traveller Motel [M]
(250) 442-5566. **$69-$139.** 1591 Central Ave V0H 1H0. West end of town on Hwy 3. Ext corridors. **Pets:** Medium, dogs only. $10 daily fee/pet. Designated rooms, no service, supervision. [SAVE] 🛜 [&M] 🔲 💻

GULF ISLANDS AREA

GALIANO ISLAND

♥♥♥♥ Galiano Inn & Spa [H] ✿
(250) 539-3388. **$199-$425, 7 day notice.** 134 Madrona Dr V0N 1P0. From Sturdies Bay Ferry Terminal, just ne on Sturdies Bay Rd. Ext/int corridors. **Pets:** Other species. $50 one-time fee/room. Designated rooms, service with restrictions, supervision.
🛜 ⊠ [&M] 🔲 💻 ⑪ [AC]

PENDER ISLANDS

♥♥♥ Poets Cove Resort & Spa [H]
(250) 629-2100. **$199-$309, 3 day notice.** 9801 Spalding Rd V0N 2M3. From Otter Bay Ferry Terminal, follow signs to South Pender Island, then 10 mi (16 km) s; Otter Bay Rd to Bidwell Harbour Rd to Canal Rd. Ext/int corridors. **Pets:** Medium. $50 one-time fee/pet. Designated rooms, service with restrictions, supervision. 🛜 ⊠ 🔲 💻 ⑪ ⇌ ⊠ [AC]

QUADRA ISLAND

▼▼ ▼▼ Taku Resort & Marina Ⓜ ✥
(250) 285-3031. **$99-$325, 30 day notice.** 616 Taku Rd V0P 1H0. From Campbell River Ferry Terminal, 4.1 mi (6.6 km) n on West Rd, then just e on Heriot Bay Rd, follow signs to Heriot Bay. Ext corridors. **Pets:** $15 daily fee/pet. Designated rooms, service with restrictions, supervision. 🛰 ☒ 🛏 💻 ⊠ 🐾 🏊

▼▼ ▼▼ Tsa-Kwa-Luten Lodge Ⓗ
(250) 285-2042. **$105-$380, 3 day notice.** 1 Lighthouse Rd V0P 1N0. From Campbell River Ferry Terminal, just se on Green Rd, 0.6 mi (1 km) e on Noble Rd, 1.8 mi (2.9 km) se on Cape Mudge Rd to Joyce Rd, 0.6 mi (1 km) sw, then 1.4 mi (2.2 km) s. Ext/int corridors. **Pets:** Designated rooms, supervision.
🅴🅲🅾 🛰 ☒ ⓜ 🛏 💻 🍴 ⊠ 🐾 🏊

SALT SPRING ISLAND

▼▼ ▼▼ Harbour House Hotel Ⓗ
(250) 537-5571. **Call for rates.** 121 Upper Ganges Rd V8K 2S2. 0.6 mi (1 km) n on Lower Ganges Rd, then just e, towards Long Harbour Ferry Terminal. Ext/int corridors. **Pets:** Accepted.
🅴🅲🅾 🛰 ☒ ⓜ 🛏 💻 🍴

▼▼ ▼▼ Salt Springs Spa Resort 🅲🅰
(250) 537-4111. **Call for rates.** 1460 N Beach Rd V8K 1J4. From Ganges Township, 4.9 mi (8 km) n on North End Rd, 0.6 mi (1 km) ne on Fernwood Rd, then 6.8 mi (10.8 km) nw. Ext corridors. **Pets:** $20 daily fee/pet. Designated rooms, no service, supervision.
🛰 ☒ 🛏 💻 🐾 🏊

END AREA

HARRISON HOT SPRINGS

Ⓐ ▼▼▼▼ Harrison Beach Hotel Ⓗ ✥
(604) 796-1111. **$99-$269, 3 day notice.** 160 Esplanade Ave V0M 1K0. Just w; on lakefront. Int corridors. **Pets:** Other species. $15 daily fee/room. Designated rooms, service with restrictions, supervision.
🆂🅰🆅🅴 🛰 ☒ ⓜ 🛏 💻 🍴 ⇌

Ⓐ ▼▼▼▼ Harrison Hot Springs Resort & Spa Ⓗ ✥
(604) 796-2244. **$119-$289, 3 day notice.** 100 Esplanade Ave V0M 1K0. Just w; on lakefront. Int corridors. **Pets:** Large. Designated rooms, service with restrictions, crate.
🅴🅲🅾 🆂🅰🆅🅴 🛰 ☒ ⓜ 🛏 💻 🍴 ⇌ ⊠

HOPE

Ⓐ ▼▼ ▼▼ Alpine Motel Ⓜ
(604) 869-9931. **$72-$115.** 505 Old Hope-Princeton Way V0X 1L0. Trans-Canada Hwy 1 exit 173 westbound; exit 170 eastbound, just n from lights. Ext corridors. **Pets:** Small. $50 deposit/room, $10 daily fee/room. No service, supervision. 🆂🅰🆅🅴 🛰 🛏 💻

Ⓐ ▼▼ Best Continental Motel Ⓜ
(604) 869-9726. **$69-$115.** 860 Fraser Ave V0X 1L0. Trans-Canada Hwy 1 exit 170 to downtown; at Fort St. Ext corridors. **Pets:** Small, dogs only. $7 daily fee/pet. No service, supervision. 🆂🅰🆅🅴 🛰 🛏 💻

Ⓐ ▼▼ ▼▼ Heritage Inn Ⓜ
(604) 869-7166. **$78-$116.** 570 Old Hope-Princeton Way V0X 1L0. Trans-Canada Hwy 1 exit 173 westbound; exit 170 eastbound, just n from lights. Ext corridors. **Pets:** Dogs only. $10 daily fee/pet. Designated rooms, supervision. 🆂🅰🆅🅴 🛰 ☒ ⓜ 🛏 💻

Ⓐ ▼▼ ▼▼ Skagit Motor Inn Ⓜ
(604) 869-5220. **$83-$190, 3 day notice.** 655 3rd Ave V0X 1L0. Trans-Canada Hwy 1 exit 170 to downtown, just e of Water Ave. Ext corridors. **Pets:** Accepted. 🆂🅰🆅🅴 🛰 ⓜ 🛏 💻

Ⓐ ▼▼ ▼▼ Travelodge Ⓜ
(604) 869-9951. **$90-$115.** 350 Old Hope-Princeton Way V0X 1L0. Trans-Canada Hwy 1 exit 173 westbound; exit 170 eastbound, just n from lights. Int corridors. **Pets:** Small. Service with restrictions, supervision.
🆂🅰🆅🅴 🛰 ⓜ 🛏 💻 ⇌

HUDSON'S HOPE

Ⓐ ▼▼▼▼ BEST WESTERN Hudson's Hope Inn & Suites Ⓗ
(250) 783-2300. **Call for rates.** 9006 Clark Ave V0C 1V0. Hwy 29, north end of town. Int corridors. **Pets:** Accepted.
🆂🅰🆅🅴 🛰 ⓜ 🛏 💻 🍴

INVERMERE

Ⓐ ▼▼ ▼▼ BEST WESTERN Invermere Inn Ⓗ
(250) 342-9246. **$119-$199.** 1310 7th Ave V0A 1K0. Hwy 93 and 95 exit Invermere, 1.8 mi (3 km) w; center. Int corridors. **Pets:** Small. $15 daily fee/pet. Service with restrictions, supervision.
🆂🅰🆅🅴 🛰 ☒ 🛏 💻 🍴

▼▼ ▼▼ Copperpoint Resort Ⓗ
(250) 341-4000. **Call for rates.** 760 Cooper Rd V0A 1K2. Hwy 93 and 95, just w. Int corridors. **Pets:** Dogs only. $25 daily fee/pet. Designated rooms, service with restrictions, supervision.
🛰 ☒ 🛏 💻 🍴 ⇌ ⊠

KAMLOOPS

Ⓐ ▼▼ ▼▼ Accent Inns Ⓜ ✥
(250) 374-8877. **$99-$179.** 1325 Columbia St W V2C 6P4. Trans-Canada Hwy 1 exit 369 (Columbia St) eastbound, at Notre Dame Dr; exit 370 (Summit Dr) westbound. Ext corridors. **Pets:** Medium. $20 daily fee/pet. Designated rooms, service with restrictions, supervision.
🅴🅲🅾 🆂🅰🆅🅴 🛰 ☒ ⓜ 🛏 💻 ⇌ ⊠

Ⓐ ▼▼▼▼ BEST WESTERN PLUS Kamloops Hotel Ⓗ ✥
(250) 374-7878. **$125-$225.** 660 Columbia St W V2C 1L1. Trans-Canada Hwy 1 exit 369 (Columbia St) eastbound, 1.3 mi (2 km) n; exit 370 (Summit Dr) westbound to Columbia St via City Centre, then just n. Int corridors. **Pets:** $20 one-time fee/room. Designated rooms, service with restrictions, supervision. 🅴🅲🅾 🆂🅰🆅🅴 🛰 ☒ ⓜ 🛏 💻 ⇌

Ⓐ ▼▼ Canadas Best Value Inn and Suites Ⓜ
(250) 374-8100. **$69-$199.** 1200 Rogers Way V1S 1N5. Trans-Canada Hwy 1 exit 368 (Hillside Ave), just s. Ext corridors. **Pets:** Medium. $20 daily fee/room. Designated rooms, service with restrictions, supervision.
🆂🅰🆅🅴 🛰 🛏 💻 ⇌

▼▼ ▼▼ The Coast Kamloops Hotel & Conference Centre Ⓗ
(250) 828-6660. **$130-$185.** 1250 Rogers Way V1S 1N5. Trans-Canada Hwy 1 exit 368 (Hillside Ave), just s. Int corridors. **Pets:** Large, other species. $20 daily fee/room. Designated rooms, service with restrictions, supervision. 🅴🅲🅾 🛰 ☒ ⓜ 🛏 💻 🍴 ⇌ ⊠

Ⓐ ▼▼▼▼ Four Points by Sheraton Kamloops Ⓗ ✥
(250) 374-4144. **$105-$225.** 1175 Rogers Way V1S 1R5. Trans-Canada Hwy 1 exit 368 (Hillside Ave), just s. Int corridors. **Pets:** Dogs only. $50 one-time fee/pet. Designated rooms, service with restrictions, supervision.
🅴🅲🅾 🆂🅰🆅🅴 🛰 ☒ ⓜ 🛏 💻 🍴 ⇌ ⊠

Ⓐ ▼▼▼▼ Hampton Inn by Hilton Ⓗ ✥
(250) 571-7897. **$129-$209.** 1245 Rogers Way V1S 1R9. Trans-Canada Hwy 1 exit 368 (Hillside Ave), just s via Hillside Way. Int corridors. **Pets:** Dogs only. $20 daily fee/pet. Designated rooms, service with restrictions, supervision. 🅴🅲🅾 🆂🅰🆅🅴 🛰 ☒ ⓜ 🛏 💻 ⇌ ⊠

ⒶⒶ ◈◈◈◈ Holiday Inn & Suites 🅷 🐾
(250) 376-8288. **$129-$199.** 675 Tranquille Rd V2B 3H7. Trans-Canada Hwy 1 exit 374 (Jasper Ave), 2.5 mi (4 km) w on Halston Connector Rd, 1.8 mi (3 km) s on 8th St to Fortune Dr, then just s. Int corridors. **Pets:** Dogs only. $20 daily fee/pet. Designated rooms, service with restrictions, supervision. 🆂🅰🆅🅴 📶 ✖ 🅴&M 🖥 💻 🍴 ⇌

◈◈◈◈ Holiday Inn Express Kamloops 🅷
(250) 372-3474. **$130-$165.** 1550 Versatile Dr V1S 1X4. Trans-Canada Hwy 1 exit 367 (Pacific Way), just w. Int corridors. **Pets:** Other species. $30 one-time fee/room. Designated rooms, service with restrictions, crate.
🅴🅲🅾 📶 ✖ 🅴&M 🖥 💻 ⇌

◈◈◈◈ Kamloops Super 8 🅼
(250) 374-8688. **$70-$120.** 1521 Hugh Allan Dr V1S 1P4. Trans-Canada Hwy 1 exit 367 (Pacific Way). Int corridors. **Pets:** Dogs only. $15 daily fee/pet. Designated rooms, service with restrictions, supervision.
📶 🅴&M 🖥 💻

◈◈◈◈ Pacific Host Inn & Suites 🅷
(250) 372-0952. **$120-$170.** 1820 Rogers Pl V1S 1T7. Trans-Canada Hwy 1 exit 368 (Hillside Ave), just w. Int corridors. **Pets:** Accepted.
📶 ✖ 🅴&M 🖥 💻 🍴 ⇌

ⒶⒶ ◈◈◈ Quality Inn 🅼
(250) 851-0111. **$79-$129.** 1860 Rogers Pl V1S 1T7. Trans-Canada Hwy 1 exit 368 (Hillside Ave). Int corridors. **Pets:** Accepted.
🆂🅰🆅🅴 📶 🖥 💻 ⇌

◈◈◈ Ranchland Motel 🅼
(250) 828-8787. **$79-$125.** 2357 Trans-Canada Hwy 1 E V2C 4A8. 2.8 mi (4.5 km) e on Trans-Canada Hwy 1 exit River Rd, then just w along service access road. Ext corridors. **Pets:** Medium. $10 daily fee/pet. Designated rooms, service with restrictions, supervision. 📶 🅴&M 🖥 💻

ⒶⒶ ◈◈◈ Scott's Inn & Restaurant 🅼 🐾
(250) 372-8221. **$80-$130.** 551 11th Ave V2C 3Y1. Trans-Canada Hwy 1 exit 369 (Columbia St) eastbound, 3.1 mi (5 km) n; exit City Centre westbound, 1 mi (1.6 km) s on Columbia St. Ext corridors. **Pets:** $10 daily fee/pet. Designated rooms, crate.
🆂🅰🆅🅴 📶 ✖ 🅴&M 🖥 💻 🍴 ⇌

KIMBERLEY

ⒶⒶ ◈◈◈◈ Trickle Creek Lodge 🅷
(250) 427-5175. **$163-$272, 7 day notice.** 500 Stemwinder Dr V1A 2Y6. From Gerry Sorensen Way, follow signs. Int corridors.
Pets: Accepted. 🆂🅰🆅🅴 📶 ✖ 🖥 💻 ⇌ ✖

MADEIRA PARK

◈◈◈◈ Painted Boat Resort Spa & Marina 🅲🅾
(604) 883-2456. **$175-$390, 3 day notice.** 12849 Lagoon Rd V0N 2H0. Hwy 101, just w on Gonzales Rd, then just s, follow signs. Ext corridors. **Pets:** Dogs only. $25 daily fee/pet. Designated rooms, service with restrictions, crate. 📶 ✖ 🖥 💻 🍴 ⇌ ✖ 🏌

◈◈◈◈ Sunshine Coast Resort & Marina 🅲🅾 🐾
(604) 883-9177. **$99-$215, 21 day notice.** 12695 Sunshine Coast Hwy V0N 2H0. Just n of Madeira Park Rd, follow signs. Ext/int corridors. **Pets:** Other species. $20 daily fee/room. Supervision.
📶 🅴&M 🖥 💻 ✖

MCBRIDE

ⒶⒶ ◈◈◈ North Country Lodge 🅼
(250) 569-0001. **$85-$90.** 868 N Frontage Rd V0J 2E0. Just w of village main exit, on Hwy 16 north service road. Ext corridors. **Pets:** Other species. $15 daily fee/pet. Designated rooms, service with restrictions, crate.
🆂🅰🆅🅴 📶 🖥 💻 🍴

MERRITT

ⒶⒶ ◈◈◈◈ Quality Inn 🅷
(250) 378-4253. **$90-$135.** 4025 Walters St V1K 1K1. Hwy 5 exit 290, 0.6 mi (1 km) w. Ext corridors. **Pets:** Small. $10 daily fee/pet. Designated rooms, service with restrictions, supervision.
🆂🅰🆅🅴 📶 🅴&M 🖥 💻 🍴 ⇌

ⒶⒶ ◈◈◈ Ramada 🅼
(250) 378-3567. **$80-$135.** 3571 Voght St V1K 1C5. Hwy 5 exit 290, just w. Ext corridors. **Pets:** Accepted. 🆂🅰🆅🅴 📶 🖥 💻 ⇌ ✖

◈◈◈ Super 8 Merritt 🅼
(250) 378-9422. **$75-$185.** 3561 Voght St V1K 1C5. Hwy 5 exit 290, just w. Ext corridors. **Pets:** Accepted. 📶 🅴&M 🖥 💻 🍴 ⇌

NAKUSP

ⒶⒶ ◈◈◈ The Selkirk Inn 🅼
(250) 265-3666. **$65-$105.** 210 W 6th Ave NW V0G 1R0. Center. Int corridors. **Pets:** Medium, dogs only. $10 deposit/pet, $10 daily fee/pet. Designated rooms, supervision. 🆂🅰🆅🅴 📶 ✖ 🅴&M 🖥 💻

NANAIMO

ⒶⒶ ◈◈◈◈ BEST WESTERN Northgate Inn 🅷 🐾
(250) 390-2222. **$130-$200.** 6450 Metral Dr V9T 2L8. Hwy 19A (Island Hwy), just w on Aulds Rd, then just s. Int corridors. **Pets:** Large. $20 daily fee/pet. Designated rooms, service with restrictions, supervision. 🆂🅰🆅🅴 📶 ✖ 🖥 💻 🍴 ✖

ⒶⒶ ◈◈◈◈ BEST WESTERN PLUS Dorchester Hotel 🅷 🐾
(250) 754-6835. **$99-$189.** 70 Church St V9R 5H4. Hwy 19A (Island Hwy) to Comox Rd; downtown. Int corridors. **Pets:** Medium, dogs only. $20 daily fee/pet. Designated rooms, service with restrictions, supervision. 🅴🅲🅾 🆂🅰🆅🅴 📶 ✖ 🖥 💻 🍴

◈◈◈ Days Inn Nanaimo Harbourview 🅷
(250) 754-8171. **$90-$120.** 809 Island Hwy S V9R 5K1. On Island Hwy 1, 1.3 mi (2 km) s. Int corridors. **Pets:** Medium. $15 daily fee/pet. Designated rooms, service with restrictions, supervision.
🅴🅲🅾 📶 ✖ 🅴&M 🖥 💻 🍴 ⇌

◈◈◈◈ The Grand Hotel Nanaimo 🅷 🐾
(250) 758-3000. **$119-$320.** 4898 Rutherford Rd V9T 4Z4. 3.8 mi (6 km) n on Hwy 19A (Island Hwy) from Departure Bay Ferry Terminal, then just e. Int corridors. **Pets:** $20 daily fee/pet. Designated rooms, service with restrictions. 📶 ✖ 🅴&M 🖥 💻 🍴 ⇌

ⒶⒶ ◈◈◈◈ Inn on Long Lake 🅷 🐾
(250) 758-1144. **$109-$299.** 4700 Island Hwy N Hwy N V9T 1W6. 3.1 mi (5 km) n on Hwy 19A (Island Hwy) from Departure Bay Ferry Terminal. Ext corridors. **Pets:** $20 one-time fee/room. Designated rooms, service with restrictions, supervision. 🅴🅲🅾 🆂🅰🆅🅴 📶 🅴&M 🖥 💻 ✖

ⒶⒶ ◈◈◈ Travelodge Nanaimo 🅷
(250) 754-6355. **$94-$199.** 96 Terminal Ave N V9S 4J2. Jct Terminal Ave and Hwy 19A (Island Hwy). Int corridors. **Pets:** Other species. $15 daily fee/pet. Designated rooms, service with restrictions, supervision.
🅴🅲🅾 🆂🅰🆅🅴 📶 ✖ 🖥 💻

NELSON

ⒶⒶ ◈◈◈◈ BEST WESTERN PLUS Baker Street Inn & Convention Centre 🅷
(250) 352-3525. **$130-$175.** 153 Baker St V1L 4H1. Jct Hwy 6 and 3A. Int corridors. **Pets:** Medium. $20 daily fee/pet. Designated rooms, service with restrictions, supervision. 🅴🅲🅾 🆂🅰🆅🅴 📶 ✖ 🅴&M 🖥 💻 🍴

◈◈◈ North Shore Inn 🅼 🐾
(250) 352-6606. **$62-$85.** 687 Hwy 3A V1L 5P7. 1.9 mi (3 km) n on Hwy 3A via Nelson Bridge. Int corridors. **Pets:** Dogs only. $7 daily fee/room. Designated rooms, supervision. 📶 ✖ 🖥

NEW DENVER

◈◈◈ Sweet Dreams Guesthouse 🅲🅸
(250) 358-2415. **Call for rates.** 702 Eldorado St V0G 1S0. Just w of Hwy 6 on Slocan Ave. Int corridors. **Pets:** Accepted.
📶 ✖ 🏌 🏌 ✖

OKANAGAN VALLEY AREA

KELOWNA

ⓐ ▼▼▼ Accent Inns ⊞

(250) 862-8888. **$89-$189.** 1140 Harvey Ave V1Y 6E7. Corner of Hwy 97 N (Harvey Ave) and Gordon Dr. Ext corridors. **Pets:** Accepted.

ECO SAVE 🛜 ☒ ♿M 🛋 💻 ➴ ☒

ⓐ ▼▼▼▼ BEST WESTERN PLUS Kelowna Hotel & Suites ⊞ ❖

(250) 860-1212. **$139-$219.** 2402 Hwy 97 N V1X 4J1. 0.6 mi (1 km) s of jct Hwy 33 and 97 N (Harvey Ave); corner of Leckie Rd. Int corridors. **Pets:** $20 daily fee/pet. Designated rooms, service with restrictions, supervision. ECO ⊟ SAVE 🛜 ☒ ♿M 🛋 💻 🍴 ➴ ☒

ⓐ ▼▼▼▼ Comfort Suites ⊞ ❖

(250) 861-1110. **$115-$289.** 2656 Hwy 97 N V1X 4J4. Jct Hwy 97 N and 33, 0.5 mi (0.9 km) n. Int corridors. **Pets:** Large. $25 daily fee/pet. Designated rooms, service with restrictions, supervision.

ECO SAVE 🛜 ☒ ♿M 🛋 💻 ➴ ☒

▼▼▼▼ Delta Grand Okanagan Resort & Conference Centre ⊞ ❖

(250) 763-4500. **$119-$399, 3 day notice.** 1310 Water St V1Y 9P3. Hwy 97 (Harvey Ave), 0.6 mi (1 km) w along Water St. Int corridors. **Pets:** Medium. $35 one-time fee/room. Designated rooms, supervision.

ECO 🛜 ☒ ♿M 🛋 💻 🍴 ➴ ☒

ⓐ ▼▼▼ Econo Lodge Ⓜ

(250) 762-3221. **$89-$134.** 1780 Gordon Dr V1Y 3H2. Hwy 97 N (Harvey Ave), just s. Ext corridors. **Pets:** Small, other species. $10 daily fee/pet. Supervision. SAVE 🛜 ☒ 🛋 💻 ➴

▼▼▼▼ Fairfield Inn & Suites by Marriott Kelowna ⊞ ❖

(250) 763-2800. **$125-$195.** 1655 Powick Rd V1X 4L1. Just s of jct Hwy 97 N (Harvey Ave) and 33. Int corridors. **Pets:** Other species. $15 daily fee/pet. Designated rooms, service with restrictions, crate.

ECO 🛜 ☒ ♿M 🛋 💻 ➴ ☒

▼▼▼ Kelowna Inn & Suites Ⓜ

(250) 762-2533. **$95-$195.** 1070 Harvey Ave V1Y 8S4. Corner of Hwy 97 N (Harvey Ave) and Gordon Dr. Ext/int corridors. **Pets:** Small, dogs only. $10 daily fee/room. Designated rooms, service with restrictions, supervision. ECO 🛜 ♿M 🛋 💻 🍴 ➴

▼▼▼ Ramada Hotel & Conference Centre ⊞ ❖

(250) 860-9711. **$129-$239.** 2170 Harvey Ave V1Y 6G8. Hwy 97 N (Harvey Ave) at Dilworth Dr. Ext/int corridors. **Pets:** Other species. Designated rooms, service with restrictions. 🛜 ☒ ♿M 🛋 💻 🍴 ➴

ⓐ ▼▼▼ Recreation Inn & Suites Ⓜ

(250) 860-3982. **$69-$129.** 1891 Parkinson Way V1Y 7V6. Hwy 97 (Harvey Ave), just n on Spall Rd. Ext corridors. **Pets:** Medium. $10 daily fee/pet. Designated rooms, service with restrictions, supervision.

SAVE 🛜 🛋 💻 🍴 ➴

ⓐ ▼▼▼ The Royal Anne Hotel ⊞

(250) 763-2277. **$89-$199.** 348 Bernard Ave V1Y 6N5. Corner of Pandosy St (which becomes Lakeshore Rd) and Bernard Ave; downtown. Int corridors. **Pets:** Medium. $20 daily fee/pet. Designated rooms, service with restrictions, supervision. SAVE 🛜 ☒ 🛋 💻

OSOYOOS

ⓐ ▼▼▼▼ BEST WESTERN PLUS Sunrise Inn ⊞ ❖

(250) 495-4000. **$109-$179.** 5506 Main St V0H 1V0. Jct Hwy 97, 1.9 mi (3 km) on Hwy 3 (Main St). Int corridors. **Pets:** Small, other species. $20 daily fee/pet. Designated rooms, service with restrictions, supervision.

ECO SAVE 🛜 ☒ ♿M 🛋 💻 🍴 ➴

ⓐ ▼▼▼ Holiday Inn & Suites ⊞

(250) 495-7223. **$79-$219, 3 day notice.** 7906 Main St V0H 1V0. Jct Hwy 97, 1 mi (1.6 km) e on Hwy 3 (Main St). Int corridors. **Pets:** $20 daily fee/pet. Designated rooms, service with restrictions, supervision.

ECO SAVE 🛜 ☒ ♿M 🛋 💻 🍴 ➴

▼▼▼ Spirit Ridge Vineyard Resort & Spa CO

(250) 495-5445. **$129-$479.** 1200 Rancher Creek Rd V0H 1V6. Hwy 97 S, e on Hwy 3 (Main St), cross bridge, left on 45th St, then 0.9 mi (1.5 km) e. Ext/int corridors. **Pets:** Accepted.

ECO 🛜 ☒ ♿M 🛋 💻 🍴 ➴ ☒

▼▼▼ Watermark Beach Resort CO ❖

(250) 495-5500. **$99-$699.** 15 Park Pl V0H 1V0. Corner of Park Pl and Main St; downtown. Ext/int corridors. **Pets:** Large. $25 daily fee/room. Service with restrictions, crate.

ECO 🛜 ☒ ♿M 🛋 💻 🍴 ➴ ☒

PENTICTON

ⓐ ▼▼▼▼ BEST WESTERN PLUS Inn at Penticton ⊞

(250) 493-0311. **$89-$199.** 3180 Skaha Lake Rd V2A 6G4. From downtown, 2.5 mi (4 km) s. Ext corridors. **Pets:** Accepted.

ECO SAVE 🛜 ☒ 🛋 💻 ➴ ☒

ⓐ ▼▼▼ Coast Penticton Hotel ⊞

(250) 492-0225. **$79-$269, 7 day notice.** 950 Westminster Ave W V2A 1L2. Hwy 97 (Eckhardt Ave W), just n to Westminster Ave W, then just e. Ext/int corridors. **Pets:** $20 daily fee/pet. Designated rooms, service with restrictions, supervision. SAVE 🛜 ☒ 🛋 💻 🍴 ➴

▼▼▼ Days Inn & Conference Centre Penticton ⊞

(250) 493-6616. **$104-$194.** 152 Riverside Dr V2A 5Y4. Hwy 97, just n. Int corridors. **Pets:** Accepted.

ECO 🛜 ☒ ♿M 🛋 💻 🍴 ➴ ☒

ⓐ ▼▼▼ Penticton Lakeside Resort, Convention Centre & Casino ⊞ ❖

(250) 493-8221. **$120-$246.** 21 Lakeshore Dr W V2A 7M5. Main St at Lakeshore Dr W. Int corridors. **Pets:** Other species. $26 one-time fee/room. Designated rooms, service with restrictions, supervision.

ECO SAVE 🛜 ☒ ♿M 🛋 💻 🍴 ➴ ☒

ⓐ ▼▼▼ Ramada Inn & Suites ⊞ ❖

(250) 492-8926. **$99-$299.** 1050 Eckhardt Ave W V2A 2C3. 0.8 mi (1.2 km) w on Hwy 97. Ext/int corridors. **Pets:** Other species. $15 daily fee/room. Designated rooms, service with restrictions, supervision.

ECO SAVE 🛜 ☒ ♿M 🛋 💻 🍴 ➴ ☒

ⓐ ▼▼ Spanish Villa Resort Ⓜ

(250) 492-2922. **$68-$350, 14 day notice.** 890 Lakeshore Dr W V2A 1C1. Corner of Power St and Lakeshore Dr W. Ext corridors. **Pets:** Medium, dogs only. $10 daily fee/pet. Designated rooms, service with restrictions, supervision. SAVE 🛜 ☒ 🛋 💻 ➴

▼▼▼ Super 8 Penticton Ⓜ

(250) 492-3829. **$95-$320.** 1706 Main St V2A 5G8. Jct Main St and Industrial Ave. Ext/int corridors. **Pets:** Dogs only. $15 daily fee/pet. Designated rooms, service with restrictions, supervision.

🛜 ☒ ♿M 🛋 💻 ➴

SUMMERLAND

▼▼▼ Summerland Motel Ⓜ

(250) 494-4444. **$69-$159, 10 day notice.** 2107 Tait St V0H 1Z4. 3.1 mi (5 km) s on Hwy 97 (32nd St). Ext corridors. **Pets:** $15 daily fee/room. Designated rooms, service with restrictions, crate.

🛜 ☒ ♿M 🛋 💻 ➴

VERNON

(CAA) ▼▼▼ **BEST WESTERN PLUS Vernon Lodge & Conference Centre** H ❖

(250) 545-3385. **$114-$180.** 3914 32nd St V1T 5P1. 1 mi (1.6 km) n on Hwy 97 (32nd St). Int corridors. **Pets:** Other species. $15 daily fee/room. Designated rooms, service with restrictions, crate.

(SAVE) 🛜 ✕ 🔊 🛢 💻 ⍦ ⌇

(CAA) ▼▼▼ **BEST WESTERN Villager Motor Inn** M

(250) 549-2224. **$100-$120.** 5121 26th St V1T 8G4. 1.5 mi (2.5 km) n on 27th St. Ext corridors. **Pets:** Other species. $20 daily fee/room. Service with restrictions, crate. (SAVE) 🛜 🔊 🛢 💻 ⍦

(CAA) ▼▼▼ **Holiday Inn Express Hotel & Suites Vernon** H

(250) 550-7777. **Call for rates.** 4716 34th St V1T 5Y9. Hwy 97 (32nd St) northbound at 48th Ave. Int corridors. **Pets:** $20 one-time fee/room. Designated rooms, service with restrictions, supervision.

(SAVE) 🛜 🔊 🛢 💻 ⍦

(CAA) ▼▼▼ ▼▼▼ **Sparkling Hill Resort** H

(250) 275-1556. **$340-$520, 3 day notice.** 888 Sparkling Pl V1H 2K7. 6 mi (10 km) s on Hwy 97, 1.1 mi (1.9 km) n on Bailey Rd, 2.4 mi (4 km) nw on Commonage Rd, then 1.8 mi (3 km) w on Predator Ridge Dr, follow signs. Int corridors. **Pets:** Accepted.

(SAVE) 🛜 ✕ 🔊 🛢 ⍦ ⌇

WEST KELOWNA

▼▼▼ **The Cove Lakeside Resort** H

(250) 707-1800. **$155-$889, 3 day notice.** 4205 Gellatly Rd V4T 2K2. Hwy 97 (Dobbin Rd), 1 mi (1.6 km) s, follow signs. Int corridors. **Pets:** Small, dogs only. $20 daily fee/pet. Designated rooms, service with restrictions, supervision. (ECO) 🛜 ✕ 🔊 🛢 💻 ⍦ ⌇

(CAA) ▼▼▼ **Super 8 West Kelowna Hotel** H

(250) 769-2355. **$90-$130.** 1655 Westgate Rd V1Z 3P1. Jct Hwy 97 (Harvey Ave) and Bartley Rd, s to Ross Rd. Int corridors. **Pets:** Accepted.

(SAVE) 🛜 ✕ 🔊 🛢 💻 ⍦

END AREA

PARKSVILLE

▼▼ **Arbutus Grove Motel** M

(250) 248-6422. **Call for rates.** 1182 E Island Hwy V9P 1W3. Island Hwy 19 exit 46 (Parksville), 1 mi (1.6 km) n on Hwy 19A. Ext corridors. **Pets:** Accepted. ✕ 🛢 💻

▼▼▼ **Beach Acres Resort** CA ❖

(250) 248-3424. **$99-$414, 3 day notice.** 1051 Resort Dr, Unit 25 V9P 2E4. Island Hwy 19 exit 46 (Parksville), 1.6 mi (2.5 km) n on Hwy 19A. Ext corridors. **Pets:** Medium, dogs only. $35 daily fee/pet. Designated rooms, no service, supervision.

🛜 ✕ 🛢 💻 ⍵ ⍦ ⌇ ⚷

▼▼▼ **Oceanside Village Resort** CA

(250) 248-8961. **$115-$310, 30 day notice.** 1080 Resort Dr V9P 2E3. Island Hwy 19 exit 46 (Parksville), 1.8 mi (2.5 km) n on Hwy 19A. Ext corridors. **Pets:** $20 daily fee/pet. Supervision.

🛜 ✕ 🛢 💻 ⍦ ⚷

(CAA) ▼▼▼ **Quality Resort Bayside** H

(250) 248-8333. **$99-$189.** 240 Dogwood St V9P 2H5. Island Hwy 19 exit 51 (Parksville/Coombs), 1.3 mi (2 km) e, then 0.6 mi (1 km) n on Hwy 19A. Int corridors. **Pets:** Dogs only. $15 daily fee/room. Designated rooms, service with restrictions. (SAVE) 🛜 ✕ 🔊 💻 ⍵ ⍦

(CAA) ▼▼▼ **Tigh-Na-Mara Seaside Spa Resort & Conference Centre** H ❖

(250) 248-2072. **$125-$237, 5 day notice.** 1155 Resort Dr V9P 2E3. Island Hwy 19 exit 46 (Parksville), 1.3 mi (2 km) n on Hwy 19A. Ext corridors. **Pets:** Small. $30 one-time fee/room. Designated rooms, service with restrictions, crate. (SAVE) 🛜 ✕ 🛢 💻 ⍵ ⍦ ⌇ ⚷

▼▼ **Travelodge Parksville** H ❖

(250) 248-2232. **$89-$189.** 424 W Island Hwy V9P 1K8. Island Hwy 19 exit 51 (Parksville/Coombs), 1.3 mi (2 km) e, then just n on Hwy 19A. Int corridors. **Pets:** Other species. $10 daily fee/pet. Designated rooms, service with restrictions, supervision. (ECO) 🛜 ✕ 🔊 🛢 💻 ⍦

(CAA) ▼▼ **V.I.P. Motel** M

(250) 248-3244. **$69-$169.** 414 W Island Hwy V9P 1K8. Island Hwy 19 exit 51 (Parksville/Coombs), 1.3 mi (2 km) e, then just n on Hwy 19A. Ext corridors. **Pets:** Medium. $10 daily fee/pet. Service with restrictions, supervision. (SAVE) 🛜 🛢 💻

PARSON

▼▼ **Alexa Chalets-Timber Inn & Restaurant** CI

(250) 348-2228. **Call for rates.** 3483 Hwy 95 V0A 1L0. Just off Hwy 95; 21.3 mi (34 km) s of Golden. Ext/int corridors. **Pets:** Accepted.

🛜 ✕ 🛢 💻 ⍵ ⌇ ⚷ ⌗

PEMBERTON

▼▼▼ **Pemberton Valley Lodge** H ❖

(604) 894-2000. **$129-$409.** 1490 Sea to Sky Hwy V0N 2L1. Just e on Hwy 99 from Pioneer Junction. Int corridors. **Pets:** Dogs only. $45 one-time fee/room. Designated rooms, service with restrictions, supervision.

(ECO) 🛜 ✕ 🔊 🛢 💻 ⍦ ⌇

PORT ALBERNI

(CAA) ▼▼▼ **BEST WESTERN PLUS Barclay Hotel** H

(250) 724-7171. **$110-$170.** 4277 Stamp Ave V9Y 7X8. Johnston Rd (Hwy 4), just s on Gertrude St. Int corridors. **Pets:** Accepted.

(SAVE) 🛜 ✕ 🔊 🛢 💻 ⍵ ⌇

(CAA) ▼▼▼ **The Hospitality Inn** H ❖

(250) 723-8111. **$85-$135.** 3835 Redford St V9Y 3S2. 2 mi (3.2 km) sw of jct Hwy 4 via City Centre/Port Alberni South Route. Int corridors. **Pets:** Other species. $10 daily fee/pet. Designated rooms, service with restrictions. (ECO) (SAVE) 🛜 🛢 💻 ⍵ ⍦

▼▼ **Riverside Motel** M

(250) 724-9916. **$99-$159.** 5065 Roger St V9Y 3Y9. Johnston Rd (Hwy 4), just s on Gertrude St, then just w. Ext corridors. **Pets:** Accepted.

🛜 ✕ 🛢 💻

▼▼ **Somass Motel** M

(250) 724-3236. **$65-$135.** 5279 River Rd V9Y 6Z3. 2 mi (3.2 km) on River Rd (Hwy 4) from Johnston Rd. Ext corridors. **Pets:** Medium, other species. $10 daily fee/pet. Service with restrictions, supervision.

🛜 ✕ 🛢 💻 ⍦

PORT HARDY

▼▼ **Glen Lyon Inn** H

(250) 949-7115. **$89-$185, 3 day notice.** 6435 Hardy Bay Rd V0N 2P0. Hwy 19, 0.9 mi (1.5 km) n, follow signs. Ext corridors. **Pets:** Accepted.

🛜 ✕ 🔊 🛢 💻 ⍵ ⚷

▼▼ **Quarterdeck Inn & Marina** H ❖

(250) 902-0455. **$125-$145.** 6555 Hardy Bay Rd V0N 2P0. Hwy 19, 0.9 mi (1.5 km) n. Int corridors. **Pets:** Medium, dogs only. $10 daily fee/pet. Designated rooms, service with restrictions, supervision.

✕ 🔊 🛢 💻 ⍵ ⚷

POWELL RIVER

▼▼ **Powell River Town Centre Hotel** H

(604) 485-3000. **$109-$200.** 4660 Joyce Ave V8A 3B6. 0.5 mi (0.8 km) e on Duncan St (Westview-Powell Ferry Terminal), then 0.6 mi (1 km) n. Int corridors. **Pets:** Accepted. 🛜 ✕ 🔊 💻 ⍵

PRINCE GEORGE

City Centre Inn

(250) 563-1267. **Call for rates.** 910 Victoria St V2L 2K8. Just n of Victoria St (Hwy 16) and Patricia Blvd; downtown. Ext corridors. **Pets:** Other species. Service with restrictions, supervision.

PRINCE RUPERT

Aleeda Motel

(250) 627-1367. **$60-$105.** 900 3rd Ave W V8J 1M8. Corner of 3rd Ave W and 8th St. Int corridors. **Pets:** Small, dogs only. $10 deposit/pet. Service with restrictions, supervision.

Inn on the Harbour

(250) 624-9107. **$99-$179.** 720 1st Ave W V8J 3V6. Corner of 6th St. Int corridors. **Pets:** Accepted.

PRINCETON

Canadas Best Value Princeton Inn & Suites

(250) 295-3537. **$110-$150.** 169 Hwy 3 V0X 1W0. Hwy 3, just n on Vermilion Ave. Ext corridors. **Pets:** Medium, dogs only. $15 daily fee/pet. Designated rooms, service with restrictions, supervision.

QUESNEL

Quality Inn & Suites

(250) 992-7247. **$99-$179.** 753 Front St V2J 2L2. Hwy 97, 0.6 mi (1 km) n of Carson Ave. Int corridors. **Pets:** Medium. $10 daily fee/pet. Designated rooms, service with restrictions, supervision.

Travelodge

(250) 992-7071. **$77.** 524 Front St V2J 2K6. Hwy 97, 0.5 mi (0.8 km) n of Carson Ave. Ext corridors. **Pets:** $25 daily fee/pet. Service with restrictions, supervision.

RADIUM HOT SPRINGS

Bighorn Motel

(250) 347-9111. **$70-$80.** 4881 St. Mary's St E V0A 1M0. Jct Hwy 93 and 95, just s along Main St W, then just w. Ext corridors. **Pets:** Dogs only. Designated rooms, service with restrictions, supervision.

Lido Motel

(250) 347-9533. **$65-$95, 7 day notice.** 4876 McKay St V0A 1M0. Jct Hwy 93 and 95, just s along Main St W, then just w. Ext corridors. **Pets:** $10 daily fee/pet. Service with restrictions, crate.

Prestige Radium Hot Springs

(250) 347-2300. **$130-$210.** 7493 Main St W V0A 1M0. Jct Hwy 93 and 95. Int corridors. **Pets:** Accepted.

REVELSTOKE

BEST WESTERN PLUS Revelstoke

(250) 837-2043. **$180-$210.** 1925 Laforme Blvd V0E 2S0. Trans-Canada Hwy 1, just n. Int corridors. **Pets:** Other species. $20 daily fee/pet. Designated rooms, service with restrictions, supervision.

The Hillcrest Hotel a Coast Resort

(250) 837-3322. **$131-$181.** 2100 Oak Dr V0E 2S0. 2.7 mi (4.3 km) e on Trans-Canada Hwy 1, 0.6 mi (1 km) sw. Int corridors. **Pets:** $15 daily fee/room. Designated rooms, service with restrictions, crate.

ROSSLAND

Casa Alpina

(250) 362-7364. **Call for rates.** 1199 Nancy Greene Hwy V0G 1Y0. 0.6 mi (1 km) w on Hwy 3B; jct Hwy 22. Ext corridors. **Pets:** Accepted.

SALMON ARM

BEST WESTERN Salmon Arm Inn

(250) 832-9793. **$109-$249.** 61 10th St SW V1E 1E4. 0.7 mi (1.1 km) w on Trans-Canada Hwy 1. Ext corridors. **Pets:** Medium. $20 daily fee/pet. Designated rooms, service with restrictions, supervision.

Comfort Inn & Suites

(250) 832-7711. **$123-$295.** 1090 22nd St NE V1E 2V5. 0.5 mi (0.8 km) e on Trans-Canada Hwy 1. Int corridors. **Pets:** Other species. $15 daily fee/pet. Designated rooms, service with restrictions, supervision.

Podollan Inn

(250) 832-6025. **$109-$199, 3 day notice.** 1460 Trans-Canada Hwy NE V1E 4N1. Just e on Trans-Canada Hwy 1; at 14th St NE. Ext/int corridors. **Pets:** Other species. $15 daily fee/room. Designated rooms, service with restrictions, supervision.

Super 8

(250) 832-8812. **$80-$230.** 2901 10th Ave NE V1E 2S3. 0.6 mi (1 km) e on Trans-Canada Hwy 1. Int corridors. **Pets:** Other species. $15 daily fee/pet. Designated rooms.

SICAMOUS

BEST WESTERN Sicamous Inn

(250) 836-4117. **$130-$285.** 806 Trans-Canada Hwy 1 V0E 2V0. Jct Trans-Canada Hwy 1 and 97; at east end of town. Ext/int corridors. **Pets:** Dogs only. $20 daily fee/pet. Designated rooms, service with restrictions, supervision.

SMITHERS

Aspen Inn & Suites

(250) 847-4551. **Call for rates.** 4628 Yellowhead Hwy V0J 2N0. 0.9 mi (1.5 km) w on Hwy 16. Ext corridors. **Pets:** Accepted.

SQUAMISH

BEST WESTERN Mountain Retreat Hotel

(604) 815-0883. **$100.** 38922 Progress Way V8B 0K5. 0.9 mi (1.5 km) n on Hwy 99; at Industrial Way. Int corridors. **Pets:** Other species. $20 daily fee/room. Designated rooms, service with restrictions, supervision.

SUN PEAKS

Coast Sundance Lodge

(250) 578-0200. **Call for rates.** 3160 Creekside Way V0E 5N0. Hwy 5, 19.5 mi (31 km) ne on Todd Mountain Rd, follow signs to village. Int corridors. **Pets:** $20 daily fee/room. Service with restrictions, supervision.

Delta Sun Peaks Resort

(250) 578-6000. **$89-$599.** 3240 Village Way V0E 5N0. Hwy 5, 19.4 mi (31 km) ne on Todd Mountain Rd, follow signs to village. Int corridors. **Pets:** Accepted.

Hearthstone Lodge

(250) 578-8588. **$89-$499, 3 day notice.** 3170 Creekside Way V0E 5N0. Hwy 5, 19.4 mi (31 km) ne on Todd Mountain Rd, follow signs to village. Int corridors. **Pets:** Medium. $20 daily fee/room. Designated rooms, service with restrictions, supervision.

TERRACE

BEST WESTERN PLUS Terrace Inn

(250) 635-0083. **Call for rates.** 4553 Greig Ave V8G 1M7. Hwy 16, just e on Greig Ave, follow City Centre signs. Int corridors. **Pets:** Accepted.

▼▼▼　Coast Inn of the West 🅷

(250) 638-8141. **Call for rates.** 4620 Lakelse Ave V8G 1R1. Hwy 16 to City Centre; between Emerson and Kalum sts; downtown. Int corridors. **Pets:** Accepted. 🌐 🛜 ⊠ 🛗 🍽 🍴

TOFINO

Ⓐ ▼▼▼▼　BEST WESTERN Tin Wis Resort

Lodge 🅷 🐾

(250) 725-4445. **$119-$319.** 1119 Pacific Rim Hwy V0R 2Z0. 1.8 mi (3.5 km) s on Hwy 4. Ext corridors. **Pets:** $25 one-time fee/room. Designated rooms, service with restrictions.

🌐 💲 🛜 ⊠ 🛗 🛗 🍽 🍴 ⊠ 🐾

▼▼▼　Long Beach Lodge Resort 🅷 🐾

(250) 725-2442. **$169-$639, 7 day notice.** 1441 Pacific Rim Hwy V0R 2Z0. 4.7 mi (7.5 km) s on Hwy 4. Ext/int corridors. **Pets:** Other species. $50 one-time fee/room. Designated rooms, service with restrictions, crate.

🛜 ⊠ 🛗 🛗 🍽 🍴 ⊠ 🐾

Ⓐ ▼▼▼▼　Pacific Sands Beach Resort 🅷 🐾

(250) 725-3322. **$195-$750, 7 day notice.** 1421 Pacific Rim Hwy V0R 2Z0. 4.7 mi (7.5 km) s on Hwy 4. Ext corridors. **Pets:** $200 deposit/room, $40 one-time fee/pet. Designated rooms, supervision.

💲 🛜 ⊠ 🛗 🛗 🍽 🐾

▼▼▼　Tofino Motel 🅼 🐾

(250) 725-2055. **$75-$185.** 542 Campbell St V0R 2Z0. Campbell and 4th sts; downtown. Ext corridors. **Pets:** Dogs only. $15 one-time fee/pet. Designated rooms, no service, supervision. 🛜 ⊠ 🛗 🛗 🍽 🐾

Ⓐ ▼▼▼ ▼▼▼　Wickaninnish Inn 🅷 🐾

(250) 725-3100. **$300-$580, 14 day notice.** 500 Osprey Ln at Chesterman Beach V0R 2Z0. 2.7 mi (4.3 km) e on Hwy 4. Int corridors. **Pets:** Other species. $40 daily fee/pet. Designated rooms, service with restrictions, crate.

🌐 📶 💲 🛜 ⊠ 🛗 🛗 🍽 🍴 ⊠ 🐾

TUMBLER RIDGE

▼▼▼　Trend Mountain Hotel & Conference Center 🅷

(250) 242-2000. **Call for rates.** 375 Southgate V0C 2W0. Hwy 29, just n on Monkman Way, then 0.5 mi (0.9 km) ne. Int corridors. **Pets:** Accepted.

🛗 🛗 🍽 🍴 🕎

UCLUELET

▼▼▼　Black Rock Oceanfront Resort 🅷 🐾

(250) 726-4800. **$169-$559, 7 day notice.** 596 Marine Dr V0R 3A0. 1 mi (1.6 km) e on Peninsula Rd, just s on Matterson Rd, then just w. Ext/int corridors. **Pets:** $25 daily fee/pet. Designated rooms, service with restrictions, supervision.

🌐 🛜 ⊠ 🛗 🛗 🍽 🍴 🛋 ⊠ 🐾

VALEMOUNT

Ⓐ ▼▼▼▼　BEST WESTERN PLUS Valemount Inn &

Suites 🅷 🐾

(250) 566-0086. **$123-$176.** 1950 Hwy 5 S V0E 2Z0. 0.9 mi (1.5 km) s on Hwy 5 (Yellowhead Hwy). Int corridors. **Pets:** Other species. $20 one-time fee/room. Designated rooms, service with restrictions, crate.

💲 🛜 ⊠ 🛗 🛗 🍽 🍴 🛋 ⊠

VANCOUVER METROPOLITAN AREA

ALDERGROVE

Ⓐ ▼▼▼▼　BEST WESTERN PLUS Country Meadows

Inn 🅷 🐾

(604) 856-9880. **$89-$149.** 3070 264th St V4W 3E1. Trans-Canada Hwy 1 exit 73 (264th St/Aldergrove), 3.1 mi (5 km) s on 264th St (Hwy 13). Int corridors. **Pets:** Medium, dogs only. $15 daily fee/room. Designated rooms, supervision. 🌐 💲 🛜 ⊠ 🛗 🛗 🍽 🍴 🛋

BURNABY

Ⓐ ▼▼▼　Accent Inns 🅷

(604) 473-5000. **$109-$179.** 3777 Henning Dr V5C 6N5. Trans-Canada Hwy 1 exit 28 (Grandview Hwy), just n on Boundary Rd. Ext corridors. **Pets:** $20 daily fee/room. Designated rooms, service with restrictions, supervision. 🌐 💲 🛜 ⊠ 🛗 🛗 🍽 🍴 ⊠

Ⓐ ▼▼▼▼　BEST WESTERN PLUS Kings Inn & Conference

Center 🅷 🐾

(604) 438-1383. **$99-$139.** 5411 Kingsway V5H 2G1. Trans-Canada Hwy 1 exit 29 (Willingdon Ave), 1.9 mi (3 km) s to Kingsway, then 1.2 mi (2 km) e. Ext corridors. **Pets:** Medium. $15 daily fee/pet. Designated rooms, service with restrictions, supervision. 💲 🛜 🛗 🛗 🍽 🛋

Ⓐ ▼▼▼ ▼▼▼　Delta Burnaby Hotel and Conference

Centre 🅷 🐾

(604) 453-0750. **$129-$1300.** 4331 Dominion St V5G 1B2. Trans-Canada Hwy 1 exit 29 (Willingdon Ave), just w on Canada Way, then n on Sumner St. Int corridors. **Pets:** $35 daily fee/room. Service with restrictions, supervision. 🌐 💲 🛜 ⊠ 🛗 🛗 🍽 🍴 ⊠

▼▼▼ ▼▼▼　Hilton Vancouver Metrotown 🅷 🐾

(604) 438-1200. **$116-$197.** 6083 McKay Ave V5H 2W7. Trans-Canada Hwy 1 exit 29 (Willingdon Ave), 1.8 mi (3 km) s to Kingsway, then just e. Int corridors. **Pets:** $29 one-time fee/room. Designated rooms, service with restrictions, crate. 🌐 🛜 🛗 🛗 🍽 🍴 🛋

▼▼▼ ▼▼▼　Holiday Inn Express Metrotown 🅷

(604) 438-1881. **$139-$194.** 4405 Central Blvd V5H 4M3. Trans-Canada Hwy 1 exit 29 (Willingdon Ave), 3.1 mi (5 km) s to Central Blvd, then just e. Int corridors. **Pets:** Small. $25 one-time fee/room. Designated rooms, service with restrictions, crate. 🌐 🛜 ⊠ 🛗 🛗 🍽 🛋

COQUITLAM

▼▼▼　Ramada Coquitlam 🅷

(604) 931-4433. **$99-$139.** 631 Lougheed Hwy V3K 3S5. Trans-Canada Hwy 1 exit 44 (Coquitlam), 1.9 mi (3 km) w on Lougheed Hwy (Hwy 7). Ext/int corridors. **Pets:** Medium. $10 daily fee/pet. Designated rooms, service with restrictions, supervision. 🛜 ⊠ 🛗 🛗 🍽 🍴 🛋

DELTA

Ⓐ ▼▼▼▼　The Coast Tsawwassen Inn 🅷 🐾

(604) 943-8221. **$111-$233.** 1665 56th St V4L 2B2. Hwy 99 exit 28 (Tsawwassen Ferries), 5 mi (8 km) w on Hwy 17; 3.1 mi (5 km) from Tsawwassen Ferry Terminal. Int corridors. **Pets:** Other species. $15 daily fee/pet. Service with restrictions, supervision.

🌐 💲 🛜 ⊠ 🛗 🛗 🍽 🍴 🛋 ⊠

LANGLEY

Ⓐ ▼▼▼▼　BEST WESTERN PLUS Langley Inn 🅷

(604) 530-9311. **$117-$142.** 5978 Glover Rd V3A 4H9. Trans-Canada Hwy 1 exit 66 (232nd St), 3.6 mi (6 km) s, follow signs. Int corridors. **Pets:** Accepted. 💲 🛜 ⊠ 🛗 🛗 🍽 🍴 🛋

▼▼▼　Canadas Best Value Inn Langley 🅼

(604) 534-9238. **$69-$99.** 19682 Fraser Hwy V3A 4C7. Trans-Canada Hwy 1 exit 58 (200th St/Langley City), 3.1 mi (5 km) s on 200th St, 0.6 mi (1 km) w on Hwy 10, then just w. Ext corridors. **Pets:** Medium. $5 daily fee/pet. Service with restrictions, supervision. 🛗 🍽

Ⓐ ▼▼▼ ▼▼▼　Coast Hotel & Convention Centre 🅷 🐾

(604) 530-1500. **$112-$149.** 20393 Fraser Hwy V3A 7N2. Trans-Canada Hwy 1 exit 58 (200th St/Langley City), 3.9 mi (6.3 km) s on 200th St, then just e. Int corridors. **Pets:** Other species. $15 daily fee/room. Designated rooms, service with restrictions, supervision.

🌐 💲 🛜 ⊠ 🛗 🍽 🍴

Ⓐ ▼▼ ▼▼　Days Inn & Suites Langley 🅷

(604) 539-0100. **$75-$119.** 20250 Logan Ave V3A 4L6. Trans-Canada Hwy 1 exit 58 (200th St/Langley City), 3.9 mi (6.3 km) s on 200th St, then just e. Int corridors. **Pets:** $10 daily fee/room. Designated rooms, service with restrictions, supervision. 🌐 💲 🛜 🛗 🛗 🍽

Ⓐ ▼▼▼▼ **Holiday Inn Express Hotel & Suites Langley** 🏨
(604) 882-2000. **$109-$169.** 8750 204th St V1M 2Y5. Trans-Canada Hwy 1 exit 58 (200th St/Langley City), just e on 88th Ave. Int corridors. **Pets:** Small. $10 daily fee/pet. Designated rooms, service with restrictions, supervision. 🌿 SAVE 🛜 ✕ 🛗 🍴 🛏 🎱 ✕

▼▼ **Sandman Hotel Langley** 🏨
(604) 888-7263. **$109-$139.** 8855 202nd St V1M 2N9. Trans-Canada Hwy 1 exit 58 (200th St/Langley City), just e on 88th Ave. Int corridors. **Pets:** Accepted. 🌿 🛜 🛗 🍴

MAPLE RIDGE

Ⓐ ▼▼▼▼ **Quality Inn** 🏨
(604) 463-5111. **$89-$209.** 21735 Lougheed Hwy V2X 2S2. 1.2 mi (2 km) w on Lougheed Hwy (Hwy 7). Ext corridors. **Pets:** Medium, dogs only. $20 daily fee/pet. Designated rooms, service with restrictions, crate. SAVE 🛜 🛗 🍴

MISSION

Ⓐ ▼▼▼ **BEST WESTERN PLUS Mission City Lodge** 🏨 🐾
(604) 820-5500. **$97-$107.** 32281 Lougheed Hwy V2V 1A3. Just w of Hwy 11; corner of Lougheed Hwy (Hwy 7) and Hurd St. Int corridors. **Pets:** Medium, dogs only. $15 daily fee/pet. Designated rooms, service with restrictions, supervision. SAVE ✕ 🛗 🍴 🎱 ✕

NORTH VANCOUVER

Ⓐ ▼▼▼ **Holiday Inn & Suites North Vancouver** 🏨 🐾
(604) 985-3111. **$139-$169.** 700 Old Lillooet Rd V7J 2H5. Trans-Canada Hwy 1 exit 22 (Mt Seymour Pkwy), follow signs. Int corridors. **Pets:** Medium, dogs only. $200 deposit/room, $25 daily fee/pet. Designated rooms, service with restrictions, supervision. 🌿 SAVE 🛜 🛗 🍴 🎱 ✕

▼▼ **Lionsgate Travelodge** 🅼
(604) 985-5311. **$59-$169.** 2060 Marine Dr V7P 1V7. Trans-Canada Hwy 1 exit 14 (Capilano Rd), 0.9 mi (1.5 km) s, then just w; from north end of Lions Gate Bridge, just e. Ext corridors. **Pets:** Medium, other species. 🛜 🛗 🍴

Ⓐ ▼▼ **North Vancouver Hotel** 🅼
(604) 987-4461. **$79-$149.** 1800 Capilano Rd V7P 3B6. Trans-Canada Hwy 1 exit 14 (Capilano Rd), 0.9 mi (1.5 km) s; from north end of Lions Gate Bridge, 0.6 mi (1 km) e on Marine Dr, then just n. Ext corridors. **Pets:** Accepted. SAVE 🛜 ✕ 🛗 🍴

▼▼▼ **Pinnacle Hotel at the Pier** 🏨 🐾
(604) 986-7437. **$129-$259.** 138 Victory Ship Way V7L 0B1. Corner of Esplanade St and Lonsdale Ave. Int corridors. **Pets:** Other species. $25 daily fee/room. Designated rooms, supervision. 🌿 🛜 ✕ 🛗 🍴 🎱 ✕

RICHMOND

Ⓐ ▼▼▼ **Accent Inns** 🏨 🐾
(604) 273-3311. **$89-$179.** 10551 St Edwards Dr V6X 3L8. Hwy 99 exit 39 (Bridgeport Rd/Airport) northbound to St Edwards Dr; exit 39A (Richmond/Airport) southbound to St Edwards Dr. Ext corridors. **Pets:** Medium. $20 daily fee/room. Designated rooms, service with restrictions, crate. 🌿 SAVE 🛜 ✕ 🛗 🍴 ✕

Ⓐ ▼▼▼▼ **BEST WESTERN PLUS Abercorn Inn** 🏨
(604) 270-7576. **$110-$150.** 9260 Bridgeport Rd V6X 1S1. Hwy 99 exit 39 (Bridgeport Rd/Airport) northbound; exit 39A (Richmond/Airport) southbound. Int corridors. **Pets:** Small. $15 daily fee/pet. Designated rooms, service with restrictions, supervision. 🌿 SAVE 🛜 ✕ 🛗 🍴

Ⓐ ▼▼▼▼ **Delta Vancouver Airport** 🏨
(604) 278-1241. **$149-$329.** 3500 Cessna Dr V7B 1C7. Corner of Russ Baker Way and Cessna Dr; near Moray Bridge. Int corridors. **Pets:** Accepted. 🌿 SAVE 🛜 ✕ 🛗 🎱

Ⓐ ▼▼▼▼ **The Fairmont Vancouver Airport** 🏨
(604) 207-5200. **$299-$399.** 3111 Grant McConachie Way V7B 0A6. In Vancouver International Airport. Int corridors. **Pets:** Accepted. 🌿 SAVE 🛜 🛗 🍴 🎱 ✕

Ⓐ ▼▼▼▼ **Hilton Vancouver Airport** 🏨 🐾
(604) 273-6336. **$169-$229.** 5911 Minoru Blvd V6X 4C7. Corner of Minoru Blvd and Westminster Hwy. Int corridors. **Pets:** Medium, other species. $35 one-time fee/room. Designated rooms, service with restrictions, supervision. 🌿 SAVE 🛜 🛗 🍴 🎱 ✕

▼▼▼ **Holiday Inn Express Vancouver-Airport** 🏨 🐾
(604) 273-8080. **$119-$179.** 9351 Bridgeport Rd V6X 1S3. Hwy 99 exit 39 (Bridgeport Rd/Airport) northbound; exit 39A (Richmond/Airport) southbound. Int corridors. **Pets:** Medium. $25 daily fee/room. Designated rooms, service with restrictions, supervision. 🌿 🛜 ✕ 🛗 🍴

▼▼▼ **Holiday Inn Vancouver Airport-Richmond** 🏨 🐾
(604) 821-1818. **$115-$189.** 10720 Cambie Rd V6X 1K8. Hwy 99 exit 39A (Bridgeport Rd/Airport) northbound to St. Edwards Dr, then 0.6 mi (1 km) n; exit 39B (No 4 Rd) southbound, just e. Int corridors. **Pets:** Medium. $25 daily fee/room. Designated rooms, service with restrictions, supervision. 🌿 🛜 ✕ 🛗 🍴

▼▼▼ **Hotel at River Rock** 🏨 🐾
(604) 247-8900. **Call for rates.** 8888 River Rd V6X 3P8. Hwy 99 exit 39 (Bridgeport Rd/Airport) northbound; exit 39A (Richmond/Airport) southbound, just w on Bridgeport Rd, then just n on Great Canadian Way. Int corridors. **Pets:** Large, other species. $25 daily fee/room. Service with restrictions, crate. 🛜 ✕ 🛗 🍴

Ⓐ ▼▼▼ ▼▼▼ **River Rock Casino Resort** 🏨
(604) 247-8900. **$139-$189.** 8811 River Rd V6X 3P8. Hwy 99 exit 39 (Bridgeport Rd/Airport) northbound; exit 39A (Richmond/Airport) southbound, just w on Bridgeport Rd, then just n on Great Canadian Way. Int corridors. **Pets:** Accepted. SAVE 🛜 ✕ 🛗 🍴 🎱 ✕

▼▼▼ **Sandman Hotel Vancouver Airport** 🏨
(604) 303-8888. **$99-$169.** 3233 St Edwards Dr V6X 3K4. Hwy 99 exit 39 (Bridgeport Rd/Airport) northbound to St Edwards Dr; exit 39A (Richmond/Airport) southbound. Int corridors. **Pets:** Accepted. 🌿 🛜 🛗 🍴 🎱

Ⓐ ▼▼▼▼ **Sheraton Vancouver Airport Hotel** 🏨 🐾
(604) 273-7878. **$139-$359.** 7551 Westminster Hwy V6X 1A3. Corner of Minoru Blvd and Westminster Hwy. Int corridors. **Pets:** Other species. $20 one-time fee/room. Service with restrictions, supervision. 🌿 SAVE 🛜 ✕ 🛗 🍴 🎱

▼▼▼▼ **Vancouver Airport Marriott** 🏨
(604) 276-2112. **$169-$259.** 7571 Westminster Hwy V6X 1A3. Corner of Minoru Blvd and Westminster Hwy. Int corridors. **Pets:** Other species. $20 daily fee/room. Designated rooms, service with restrictions, supervision. 🛜 ✕ 🛗 🍴 🎱

Ⓐ ▼▼▼▼ **The Westin Wall Centre Vancouver Airport** 🏨
(604) 303-6565. **$149-$409.** 3099 Corvette Way V6X 4K3. Hwy 99 exit 39 (Bridgeport Rd/Airport) northbound; exit 39A (Richmond/Airport) southbound, just w to No 3 Rd. Int corridors. **Pets:** Accepted. SAVE 🛜 ✕ 🛗 🍴 🎱 ✕

SURREY

▼▼ **Coast Surrey Guildford Hotel** 🏨
(604) 930-4700. **Call for rates.** 10410 158th St V4N 5C2. Trans-Canada Hwy 1 exit 50 (160th St), just w on 104th Ave. Int corridors. **Pets:** Accepted. 🛜 ✕ 🛗 🍴 🎱

▼▼▼ **Comfort Inn & Suites Surrey** 🏨
(604) 576-8888. **$99-$149.** 8255 166th St V4N 5R8. Trans-Canada Hwy 1 exit 53 (176th St/Hwy 15), 2.9 mi (4.8 km) s to Fraser Hwy (Hwy 1A), then 1.6 mi (2.6 km) nw. Int corridors. **Pets:** Medium, dogs only. $10 daily fee/pet. Designated rooms, service with restrictions, crate. 🛜 ✕ 🛗

▼▼ Compass Point Inn H

(604) 588-9511. **$99-$129, 3 day notice.** 9850 King George Blvd V3T 4Y3. Jct Hwy 1A (Fraser Hwy) and 99A (King George Hwy). Int corridors. **Pets:** Accepted. 🛰 ✖ 🗄 🛏 💻 ⁑ ⊠

CAA ▼▼▼ Ramada Langley-Surrey H ❀

(604) 576-8388. **$99-$149.** 19225 Hwy 10 (56 Ave) V3S 8V9. Trans-Canada Hwy 1 exit 58 (200th St/Langley City), 3.1 mi (5 km) s on 200th St, then 1.2 mi (2 km) w on Rt 10 (56 Ave); corner of 192nd St and Rt 10. Int corridors. **Pets:** Medium, dogs only. $15 daily fee/pet. Designated rooms, service with restrictions, crate.
SAVE 🛰 ✖ 🗄 🛏 💻 ⁑ ⊠

CAA ▼▼▼▼ Sheraton Vancouver Guildford Hotel H ❀

(604) 582-9288. **$105-$165.** 15269 104th Ave V3R 1N5. Trans-Canada Hwy 1 exit 48 eastbound, 0.6 mi (1 km) s on 152nd St, then just e; exit 50 westbound, then just w. Int corridors. **Pets:** Medium, dogs only. Service with restrictions, crate.
ECO SAVE 🛰 ✖ 🗄 🛏 💻 ⁑ ⊠ ✖

VANCOUVER

CAA ▼ 2400 Motel M ❀

(604) 434-2464. **$89-$189.** 2400 Kingsway V5R 5G9. 4.5 mi (7.2 km) se on Hwy 1A and 99A (Kingsway and 33rd Ave). Ext corridors. **Pets:** Small. $15 daily fee/pet. Designated rooms, service with restrictions, crate.
SAVE 🛰 💻 ✖

CAA ▼▼▼ BEST WESTERN PLUS Downtown Vancouver H ❀

(604) 669-9888. **$99-$199.** 718 Drake St V6Z 2W6. Between Howe and Granville sts. Int corridors. **Pets:** Small, dogs only. $20 daily fee/pet. Designated rooms, supervision.
ECO SAVE 🛰 ✖ 🗄 🛏 💻 ⁑ ⊠

CAA ▼▼▼▼ BEST WESTERN PLUS Sands Hotel H ❀

(604) 682-1831. **$109-$260.** 1755 Davie St V6G 1W5. Between Bidwell and Denman sts. Int corridors. **Pets:** $14 daily fee/pet. Designated rooms, service with restrictions, supervision.
ECO SAVE 🛰 ✖ 🗄 🛏 💻

▼▼ The Burrard H ❀

(604) 681-2331. **$129-$209.** 1100 Burrard St V6Z 1Y7. Between Helmcken and Davie sts. Ext corridors. **Pets:** $30 daily fee/room. Designated rooms, supervision. 🛰 ✖ 🛏 💻 ✖

CAA ▼▼▼ Delta Vancouver Suites H

(604) 689-8188. **$159-$299.** 550 W Hastings St V6B 1L6. Between Seymour and Richards sts; entrance in alley way. Int corridors.
Pets: Accepted. ECO SAVE 🛰 ✖ 🗄 🛏 💻 ⁑

CAA ▼▼▼▼ Executive Hotel Le Soleil H ❀

(604) 632-3000. **$199-$399.** 567 Hornby St V6C 2E8. Between Dunsmuir and Pender sts. Int corridors. **Pets:** Large. $75 one-time fee/room. Service with restrictions, supervision. ECO SAVE 🛰 🗄 🛏 💻 ✖

CAA ▼▼▼▼ The Fairmont Hotel Vancouver H

(604) 684-3131. **$179-$449.** 900 W Georgia St V6C 2W6. Corner of Burrard at W Georgia St; enter from Hornby St. Int corridors.
Pets: Accepted. ECO ⊟ SAVE 🛰 🗄 💻 ⁑ ⊠ ✖

CAA ▼▼▼▼ Fairmont Pacific Rim H ❀

(604) 695-5300. **$269-$599.** 1038 Canada Place V6C 0B9. Between Burrard and Thurlow sts. Int corridors. **Pets:** Medium. $30 daily fee/room. Service with restrictions, supervision.
ECO SAVE 🛰 ✖ 🗄 💻 ⁑ ⊠

CAA ▼▼▼▼ The Fairmont Waterfront H

(604) 691-1991. **$199-$449.** 900 Canada Place Way V6C 3L5. Between Howe and Burrard sts. Int corridors. **Pets:** Accepted.
ECO ⊟ SAVE 🛰 ✖ 🗄 💻 ⁑ ⊠ ✖

CAA ▼▼▼▼ Four Seasons Hotel Vancouver H

(604) 689-9333. **$225-$2950.** 791 W Georgia St V6C 2T4. Between Howe and Granville sts. Int corridors. **Pets:** Accepted.
ECO SAVE 🛰 ✖ 🗄 🛏 ⁑ ⊠ ✖

CAA ▼▼▼ Georgian Court Hotel H ❀

(604) 682-5555. **$159-$399.** 773 Beatty St V6B 2M4. Between Georgia and Robson sts. Int corridors. **Pets:** Other species. $20 daily fee/pet. Service with restrictions, supervision.
SAVE 🛰 🗄 🛏 💻 ⁑ ⊠

CAA ▼▼▼ Granville Island Hotel H ❀

(604) 683-7373. **$189-$550.** 1253 Johnston St V6H 3R9. Granville Island; below the bridge, follow signs. Int corridors. **Pets:** Other species. $25 daily fee/room. Designated rooms, service with restrictions.
SAVE 🛰 ✖ 🗄 🛏 💻 ⁑ ⊠

▼▼ Holiday Inn Express Vancouver H

(604) 254-1000. **$119-$309.** 2889 E Hastings St V5K 2A1. Between Renfrew and Kaslo sts. Int corridors. **Pets:** Medium. $15 daily fee/pet. Designated rooms, service with restrictions, supervision.
ECO 🛰 ✖ 🗄 🛏 💻

▼▼ Howard Johnson Hotel Downtown Vancouver H

(604) 688-8701. **$79-$259.** 1176 Granville St V6Z 1L8. Between Davie and Helmcken sts. Int corridors. **Pets:** Accepted.
ECO 🛰 ✖ 🗄 🛏 💻 ⁑

CAA ▼▼▼▼ Hyatt Regency Vancouver H

(604) 683-1234. **$125-$396.** 655 Burrard St V6C 2R7. Between W Georgia and Melville sts. Int corridors. **Pets:** Accepted.
ECO SAVE 🛰 ✖ 🗄 🛏 💻 ⁑ ⊠

▼▼▼▼ L'Hermitage Hotel H

(778) 327-4100. **$190-$595.** 788 Richards St V6B 3A4. Between Robson and W Georgia sts. Int corridors. **Pets:** Accepted.
🛰 ✖ 🗄 🛏 💻 ⁑ ⊠

CAA ▼▼▼▼ Pan Pacific Vancouver H ❀

(604) 662-8111. **$179-$439.** 300-999 Canada Pl V6C 3B5. Between Howe and Burrard sts. Int corridors. **Pets:** Other species. $30 daily fee/pet. Service with restrictions, supervision.
ECO SAVE 🛰 ✖ 🗄 💻 ⁑ ⊠

▼▼ Quality Hotel Downtown-The Inn at False Creek H

(604) 682-0229. **$79-$229.** 1335 Howe St V6Z 1R7. Between Drake and Pacific sts. Int corridors. **Pets:** Medium. $15 daily fee/pet.
ECO 🛰 🗄 🛏 💻 ⁑

CAA ▼▼▼ Ramada Inn & Suites Downtown Vancouver H

(604) 685-1111. **$99-$299.** 1221 Granville St V6Z 1M6. Between Davie and Drake sts. Int corridors. **Pets:** Large, other species. $20 daily fee/room. Service with restrictions, crate.
ECO SAVE 🛰 ✖ 🗄 🛏 💻 ⁑

▼▼▼ Renaissance Vancouver Harbourside Hotel H

(604) 689-9211. **$169-$329.** 1133 W Hastings St V6E 3T3. Between Bute and Thurlow sts. Int corridors. **Pets:** Accepted.
ECO 🛰 ✖ 🗄 🛏 💻 ⁑ ⊠

CAA ▼▼▼ Residence Inn by Marriott Vancouver Downtown H ❀

(604) 688-1234. **Call for rates.** 1234 Hornby St V6Z 1W2. Between Drake and Davie sts. Int corridors. **Pets:** Medium. $75 one-time fee/room. Designated rooms, service with restrictions.
ECO SAVE 🛰 ✖ 🗄 🛏 💻 ⁑ ⊠

CAA ▼▼▼▼ Rosewood Hotel Georgia H ❀

(604) 682-5566. **$215-$410.** 801 W Georgia St V6C 1P7. Between Hornby and Howe sts, entrance on Howe St. Int corridors. **Pets:** Small. $51 one-time fee/room. Service with restrictions, supervision.
SAVE 🛰 🗄 💻 ⁑ ⊠

▼▼ Sandman Hotel Vancouver City Centre H

(604) 681-2211. **$89-$179.** 180 W Georgia St V6B 4P4. Between Cambie and Beatty sts. Int corridors. **Pets:** Accepted.
ECO 🛰 ✖ 🗄 🛏 💻 ⁑ ⊠

(CAA) ▼▼▼▼▼ **Shangri-La Hotel Vancouver** 🅷 ❖
(604) 689-1120. **Call for rates.** 1128 W Georgia St V6E 0A8. Between Thurlow and Bute sts. Int corridors. **Pets:** Medium. $50 one-time fee/room. Service with restrictions, supervision.
ECO SAVE 🛜 ✕ ♿M 🖥 💻 🍴 🏊 ⊠

(CAA) ▼▼▼▼ **Sheraton Vancouver Wall Centre Hotel** 🅷
(604) 331-1000. **$159-$509.** 1088 Burrard St V6Z 2R9. Between Helmcken and Nelson sts. Int corridors. **Pets:** Accepted.
ECO SAVE 🛜 ✕ ♿M 🖥 💻 🍴 🏊 ⊠

(CAA) ▼▼▼▼ **The Sutton Place Hotel** 🅷 ❖
(604) 682-5511. **Call for rates.** 845 Burrard St V6Z 2K6. Between Smithe and Robson sts. Int corridors. **Pets:** Medium. $40 one-time fee/room. Supervision. ECO SAVE 🛜 ✕ ♿M 💻 🍴 🏊 ⊠

▼▼ ▼▼ **Sylvia Hotel** 🅷 ❖
(604) 681-9321. **$100-$400.** 1154 Gilford St V6G 2P6. Between Pendrell St and Beach Ave. Int corridors. **Pets:** Other species. Service with restrictions, supervision. 🛜 ✕ 🖥 💻 🍴 🄰

(CAA) ▼▼▼▼ **Vancouver Marriott Pinnacle Downtown** 🅷
(604) 684-1128. **$169-$329.** 1128 W Hastings St V6E 4R5. Between Thurlow and Bute sts. Int corridors. **Pets:** Accepted.
ECO SAVE 🛜 ✕ ♿M 🖥 💻 🍴 🏊 ⊠

(CAA) ▼▼▼ ▼▼▼ **The Westin Bayshore Vancouver** 🅷 ❖
(604) 682-3377. **$189-$460.** 1601 Bayshore Dr V6G 2V4. Jct W Georgia and Cardero sts. Int corridors. **Pets:** Large, dogs only. Service with restrictions, supervision.
ECO SAVE 🛜 ✕ ♿M 🖥 💻 🍴 🏊 ⊠

(CAA) ▼▼▼ ▼▼ **The Westin Grand, Vancouver** 🅷
(604) 602-1999. **$169-$679.** 433 Robson St V6B 6L9. Between Homer and Richards sts. Int corridors. **Pets:** Accepted.
ECO SAVE 🛜 ✕ ♿M 🖥 💻 🍴 🏊 ⊠

WHITE ROCK

▼▼▼▼ **Ocean Promenade Hotel** 🅷
(604) 542-0102. **Call for rates.** 15611 Marine Dr V4B 1E1. Hwy 99 exit 2B southbound; exit 2 (White Rock/8th Ave) northbound, 1.3 mi (2 km) w. Ext/int corridors. **Pets:** Accepted. 🛜 ✕ ♿M 🖥 💻

END METROPOLITAN AREA

VICTORIA METROPOLITAN AREA

SAANICH

▼▼ ▼▼ **Howard Johnson Hotel & Suites** 🅷 ❖
(250) 704-4656. **$99-$169.** 4670 Elk Lake Dr V8Z 5M2. Blanshard St (Hwy 17), just w on Royal Oak Dr, then just n. Ext/int corridors. **Pets:** Medium, other species. $15 daily fee/room. Designated rooms, service with restrictions, supervision.
ECO 🛜 ✕ ♿M 🖥 💻 🍴 🏊

SAANICHTON

(CAA) ▼▼ ▼▼ **Quality Inn Waddling Dog** 🅷
(250) 652-1146. **$89-$139.** 2476 Mt Newton Crossroad V8M 2B8. Corner of Blanshard St (Hwy 17) and Mt Newton Crossroad. Int corridors. **Pets:** Dogs only. $15 daily fee/pet. Service with restrictions, crate.
SAVE 🛜 ✕ 💻 🍴

SIDNEY

(CAA) ▼▼▼▼ **BEST WESTERN PLUS Emerald Isle Motor Inn** 🅷 ❖
(250) 656-4441. **$140-$200.** 2306 Beacon Ave V8L 1X2. Hwy 17 exit 28 (Sidney), just e. Int corridors. **Pets:** Other species. $15 daily fee/room. Service with restrictions, crate.
ECO SAVE 🛜 ✕ ♿M 🖥 💻 🍴 ⊠

(CAA) ▼▼▼▼ **The Cedarwood Inn & Suites** 🅷
(250) 656-5551. **$95-$255, 3 day notice.** 9522 Lochside Dr V8L 1N8. Hwy 17 exit 26, just e on McTavish Rd, then 0.8 mi (1.4 km) n. Ext corridors. **Pets:** Other species. $15 daily fee/pet. Designated rooms, service with restrictions, supervision. SAVE 🛜 ✕ ♿M 🖥 💻 🄰

(CAA) ▼▼▼▼ **The Sidney Pier Hotel & Spa** 🅷 ❖
(250) 655-9445. **$139-$369.** 9805 Seaport Pl V8L 4X3. Hwy 17 exit 28 (Beacon Ave), 0.6 mi (1 km) e. Int corridors. **Pets:** Small, dogs only. $30 daily fee/pet. Designated rooms, supervision.
ECO SAVE 🛜 ✕ ♿M 🖥 💻 🍴 ⊠

(CAA) ▼▼▼ ▼▼ **Victoria Airport Travelodge Sidney** 🅷 ❖
(250) 656-1176. **$90-$160.** 2280 Beacon Ave V8L 1X1. Hwy 17 exit 28 (Beacon Ave), just e. Int corridors. **Pets:** Large, other species. $15 daily fee/room. Designated rooms, service with restrictions, supervision.
SAVE 🛜 ♿M 🖥 💻 🏊

SOOKE

▼▼ ▼▼ **Ocean Wilderness Inn** BB
(250) 646-2116. **$130-$220, 7 day notice.** 9171 W Coast Rd V9Z 1G3. 8.6 mi (14 km) w on Hwy 14. Ext/int corridors. **Pets:** $25 daily fee/pet. Designated rooms, no service, supervision.
🛜 ✕ 🖥 🄰 🅆 🏊

(CAA) ▼▼▼▼ **Sooke Harbour House** 🄲🄸 ❖
(250) 642-3421. **$230-$699, 7 day notice.** 1528 Whiffen Spit Rd V9Z 0T4. 1.2 mi (2 km) w on Hwy 14. Ext/int corridors. **Pets:** Other species. $40 daily fee/pet. ECO SAVE 🛜 ✕ ♿M 🖥 💻 🍴 🄰 🅆

(CAA) ▼▼▼▼ **Sooke Harbour Resort and Marina** 🄲🄾
(250) 642-3236. **Call for rates.** 6971 W Coast Rd V9Z 0V1. 1 mi (1.6 km) w on Hwy 14. Ext corridors. **Pets:** Dogs only. $40 one-time fee/pet. Designated rooms, no service. SAVE 🛜 ✕ 🖥 💻 🄰

VICTORIA

▼▼ ▼▼ **Abigail's Hotel** 🅷
(250) 388-5363. **$159-$359, 14 day notice.** 906 McClure St V8V 3E7. Blanshard St (Hwy 17), just e on Fairfield Rd, then just n on Vancouver St. Int corridors. **Pets:** Accepted. 🛜 ✕ 🖥 💻

(CAA) ▼▼ ▼▼ **Accent Inns** 🅷
(250) 475-7500. **$79-$179.** 3233 Maple St V8X 4Y9. 1.9 mi (3 km) n on Blanshard St (Hwy 17); corner of Blanshard St and Cloverdale Ave. Ext corridors. **Pets:** Accepted. ECO SAVE 🛜 ✕ ♿M 🖥 💻 🍴

(CAA) ▼▼▼▼ **BEST WESTERN PLUS Carlton Plaza Hotel** 🅷 ❖
(250) 388-5513. **$89-$259.** 642 Johnson St V8W 1M6. Between Douglas and Broad sts. Int corridors. **Pets:** Medium. $10 one-time fee/pet. Designated rooms, service with restrictions, supervision.
ECO SAVE 🛜 ✕ ♿M 🖥 💻 🍴

(CAA) ▼▼▼▼ **Blue Ridge Inns** 🄼
(250) 388-4345. **$59-$149.** 3110 Douglas St V8Z 3K4. Between Finlayson St and Speed Ave. Ext corridors. **Pets:** Medium. $15 daily fee/room. Designated rooms, service with restrictions, supervision.
ECO SAVE 🛜 🖥 💻 🍴 🏊 🄰

Chateau Victoria Hotel and Suites H ❀
(250) 382-4221. **$89-$249.** 740 Burdett Ave V8W 1B2. Between Douglas and Blanshard (Hwy 17) sts. Int corridors. **Pets:** Dogs only. $15 daily fee/pet. Designated rooms, service with restrictions, crate.
ECO SAVE 📶 ✕ 🔌 💻 🍴 ⚓

Days Inn Victoria on the Harbour H ❀
(250) 386-3451. **$93-$173.** 427 Belleville St V8V 1X3. Between Oswego and Menzies sts. Int corridors. **Pets:** Other species. $15 daily fee/room. Designated rooms, service with restrictions, crate.
ECO SAVE 📶 ✕ 🔌 💻 🍴 ⚓ 🐾

Delta Victoria Ocean Pointe Resort and Spa H ❀
(250) 360-2999. **$129-$328.** 45 Songhees Rd V9A 6T3. Just w of Johnson St Bridge; Esquimalt at Tyee Rd. Int corridors. **Pets:** Large, other species. $35 one-time fee/room. Designated rooms, service with restrictions, supervision. ECO SAVE 📶 ✕ 🔌 💻 🍴 ⚓ 🐾

Econo Lodge Inn & Suites M
(250) 388-7861. **$109-$189.** 101 Island Hwy V9B 1E8. Douglas St, 3.1 mi (5 km) w on Gorge Rd, then just s on Admirals Rd. Ext/int corridors. **Pets:** Medium, dogs only. $15 daily fee/pet. Designated rooms, service with restrictions, supervision. SAVE 📶 🔌 💻 ⚓

Executive House Hotel H
(250) 388-5111. **$99-$215.** 777 Douglas St V8W 2B5. Between Blanshard (Hwy 17) and Douglas sts; downtown. Int corridors. **Pets:** $25 daily fee/pet. Service with restrictions. SAVE 📶 ✕ 🔌 💻 🍴 🐾

The Fairmont Empress H
(250) 384-8111. **$199-$499, 3 day notice.** 721 Government St V8W 1W5. Between Belleville and Humboldt sts. Int corridors. **Pets:** Accepted.
ECO 📶 ✕ 🔌 💻 🍴 ⚓ 🐾

Harbour Towers Hotel & Suites H
(250) 385-2405. **$94-$450.** 345 Quebec St V8V 1W4. Between Oswego and Pendray sts. Int corridors. **Pets:** Small. $20 daily fee/pet. Service with restrictions, crate.
ECO SAVE 📶 ✕ 🔌 💻 🍴 ⚓ 🐾

Howard Johnson Hotel-City of Victoria H
(250) 382-2151. **$59-$124.** 310 Gorge Rd E V8T 2W2. From Douglas St, 0.6 mi (1.4 km) w; between Jutland St and Washington Ave. Int corridors. **Pets:** Accepted. ECO SAVE 📶 ✕ 🔌 💻 🍴 ⚓

Huntingdon Hotel & Suites H
(250) 381-3456. **$79-$389.** 330 Quebec St V8V 1W3. Between Oswego and Pendray sts. Int corridors. **Pets:** Accepted.
SAVE 📶 ✕ 🔌 💻 🍴

The Magnolia Hotel & Spa H
(250) 381-0999. **$189-$369.** 623 Courtney St V8W 1B8. Corner of Courtney and Gordon sts. Int corridors. **Pets:** Accepted.
ECO SAVE 📶 ✕ 🔌 💻 🍴 🐾

Quality Inn Downtown Inner Harbour Victoria H
(250) 385-6787. **$79-$159.** 850 Blanshard St V8W 2H2. Between Courtney St and Burnett Ave. Int corridors. **Pets:** Accepted.
ECO SAVE 📶 ✕ 🔌 💻 🍴 ⚓ 🐾

Ramada Victoria H ❀
(250) 386-1422. **$65-$150.** 123 Gorge Rd E V9A 1L1. From Douglas St, 1.2 mi (2.4 km) w. Int corridors. **Pets:** Small, dogs only. $10 daily fee/pet. Designated rooms, service with restrictions, crate.
ECO 📶 ✕ 🔌 💻 🍴 ⚓

Robin Hood Motel M
(250) 388-4302. **$54-$99.** 136 Gorge Rd E Rd V9A 1L4. From Douglas St, 1.2 mi (2.4 km) w. Ext corridors. **Pets:** Dogs only. $5 daily fee/pet. Designated rooms, service with restrictions, supervision.
SAVE 📶 🔌 💻

Royal Scot Hotel & Suites H
(250) 388-5463. **$120-$299.** 425 Quebec St V8V 1W7. Between Menzies and Oswego sts. Int corridors. **Pets:** Medium, dogs only. $50 one-time fee/pet. Designated rooms, crate.
ECO SAVE 📶 ✕ 🔌 💻 🍴 ⚓ 🐾

Spinnakers Gastro Brewpub and Guesthouses BB
(250) 386-2739. **$149-$299, 7 day notice.** 308 Catherine St V9A 3S8. 1.3 mi (2 km) nw over Johnson St Bridge, then just s. Ext/int corridors. **Pets:** Accepted. 📶 ✕ 🔌 💻 🍴

Swans Suite Hotel H
(250) 361-3310. **$149-$359.** 506 Pandora Ave V8W 1N6. Corner of Pandora Ave and Store St. Int corridors. **Pets:** Accepted.
📶 ✕ 🔌 💻 🍴

Travelodge Victoria H ❀
(250) 388-6611. **$80-$130.** 229 Gorge Rd E V9A 1L1. From Douglas St, 1.2 mi (2 km) w at Washington Ave. Ext corridors. **Pets:** $10 daily fee/pet. Service with restrictions, crate. ECO SAVE 📶 🔌 💻 🍴 ⚓

Victoria Marriott Inner Harbour H ❀
(250) 480-3800. **$209-$309.** 728 Humboldt St V8W 3Z5. Between Blanshard (Hwy 17) and Douglas sts. Int corridors. **Pets:** Medium. $50 one-time fee/room. Designated rooms, service with restrictions, supervision.
ECO SAVE 📶 ✕ 🔌 💻 🍴 ⚓

Westin Bear Mountain Golf Resort & Spa H ❀
(250) 391-7160. **$139-$599.** 1999 Country Club Way V9B 6R3. Trans-Canada Hwy 1 exit 14 (Langford/Highlands), 1.1 mi (1.7 km) n on Millstream Rd, then 1.9 mi (3 km) ne on Bear Mountain Pkwy, follow signs. Int corridors. **Pets:** Medium, dogs only. $20 daily fee/room. Designated rooms, service with restrictions, supervision.
ECO SAVE 📶 ✕ 🔌 💻 🍴 ⚓

END METROPOLITAN AREA

WHISTLER

Aava Whistler H ❀
(604) 932-2522. **$101-$450, 14 day notice.** 4005 Whistler Way V0N 1B4. Hwy 99, just e on Village Gate Blvd. Int corridors. **Pets:** $25 one-time fee/room. Designated rooms, service with restrictions, supervision.
📶 ✕ 🔌 💻 🍴 ⚓

The Coast Blackcomb Suites at Whistler CO
(604) 905-3400. **$125-$799, 60 day notice.** 4899 Painted Cliff Rd V0N 1B4. Hwy 99, 0.6 mi (1 km) e on Lorimer Rd (Upper Village), just se on Blackcomb Way, then just w, follow road all the way to the end. Int corridors. **Pets:** Accepted. ECO 📶 ✕ 🔌 💻 ⚓

Crystal Lodge & Suites H ❀
(604) 932-2221. **$99-$339, 30 day notice.** 4154 Village Green V0N 1B4. Hwy 99, just e on Village Gate Blvd, then follow road to Whistler Way. Int corridors. **Pets:** Dogs only. $20 daily fee/pet. Service with restrictions. ECO 📶 ✕ 🔌 💻 🍴 ⚓

Delta Whistler Village Suites H ❀
(604) 905-3987. **$109-$409, 30 day notice.** 4308 Main St V0N 1B4. Hwy 99, just e on Village Gate Blvd, just n on Northlands Blvd, then just e. Int corridors. **Pets:** $35 one-time fee/room. Designated rooms, service with restrictions. ECO SAVE 📶 ✕ 🔌 💻 🍴 ⚓

(CAA) ▼▼▼ Edgewater Lodge [H]
(604) 932-0688. **$135-$339, 14 day notice.** 8020 Alpine Way V0N 1B0. 2.5 mi (4 km) n of Whistler Village via Hwy 99, then just e. Ext corridors. **Pets:** Accepted. [SAVE] [📶] [✕] [🛗] [🍴] [♿]

(CAA) ▼▼▼▼▼▼ The Fairmont Chateau Whistler [H] ❖
(604) 938-8000. **$179-$900, 3 day notice.** 4599 Chateau Blvd V0N 1B4. Hwy 99, 0.6 mi (1 km) e on Lorimer Rd (Upper Village), just w on Blackcomb Way. Int corridors. **Pets:** Other species. $25 daily fee/pet. Supervision. [ECO] [SAVE] [📶] [✕] [🛗M] [🛗] [💻] [🍴] [🐾] [✕]

(CAA) ▼▼▼▼▼▼ Four Seasons Resort Whistler [H]
(604) 935-3400. **$305-$920, 30 day notice.** 4591 Blackcomb Way V0N 1B4. Hwy 99, 0.6 mi (1 km) e on Lorimer Rd (Upper Village). Int corridors. **Pets:** Accepted. [SAVE] [📶] [✕] [🛗M] [🛗] [💻] [🍴] [🐾] [✕]

(CAA) ▼▼▼▼▼▼ Hilton Whistler Resort & Spa [H]
(604) 932-1982. **Call for rates.** 4050 Whistler Way V0N 1B4. Hwy 99, just e on Village Gate Blvd, then follow Whistler Way. Int corridors. **Pets:** Accepted. [ECO] [SAVE] [📶] [✕] [🛗M] [🛗] [💻] [🍴] [🐾] [✕]

▼▼▼▼ The Listel Hotel Whistler [H]
(604) 932-1133. **Call for rates.** 4121 Village Green V0N 1B4. Hwy 99, just e on Village Gate Blvd, then follow Whistler Way. Int corridors. **Pets:** Accepted. [📶] [✕] [🛗M] [🛗] [💻] [🍴]

▼▼▼▼▼ Nita Lake Lodge [H]
(604) 966-5700. **$150-$500.** 2131 Lake Placid Rd V0N 1B2. 1.8 mi (3 km) s on Hwy 99, just w. Int corridors. **Pets:** Accepted. [ECO] [📶] [✕] [🛗M] [🛗] [💻] [🍴] [🐾] [✕]

▼▼▼▼▼ Pan Pacific Whistler Village Centre [H]
(604) 966-5500. **Call for rates.** 4299 Blackcomb Way V0N 1B4. Hwy 99, just e on Village Gate Blvd. Int corridors. **Pets:** Accepted. [ECO] [📶] [✕] [🛗M] [🛗] [💻] [🍴] [🐾] [✕]

▼▼▼▼ Summit Lodge & Spa [H]
(604) 932-2778. **Call for rates.** 4359 Main St V0N 1B4. Hwy 99, just n on Village Gate Blvd, then just w on Northlands Blvd. Int corridors. **Pets:** Accepted. [ECO] [📶] [✕] [🛗M] [🛗] [💻] [🍴] [🐾] [✕]

▼▼▼ Tantalus Resort Lodge [CO]
(604) 932-4146. **$139-$599.** 4200 Whistler Way V0N 1B4. Hwy 99, just e on Village Gate Blvd, then follow Whistler Way to the end. Int corridors. **Pets:** Accepted. [ECO] [📶] [✕] [🛗] [🛗] [💻] [🐾] [✕] [♿]

(CAA) ▼▼▼▼▼▼ The Westin Resort & Spa, Whistler [H] ❖
(604) 905-5000. **$149-$949, 21 day notice.** 4090 Whistler Way V0N 1B4. Hwy 99, just e on Village Gate Blvd, then s. Int corridors. **Pets:** Dogs only. Service with restrictions, supervision. [ECO] [SAVE] [📶] [✕] [🛗M] [🛗] [💻] [🍴] [🐾] [✕]

▼▼▼ Whistler Pinnacle Hotel [H]
(604) 938-3218. **$129-$348, 30 day notice.** 4319 Main St V0N 1B4. Hwy 99, just e on Village Gate Blvd, just n on Northlands Blvd, then just e. Int corridors. **Pets:** Accepted. [📶] [✕] [🛗M] [🛗] [💻] [🐾]

WILLIAMS LAKE

▼▼▼ Drummond Lodge Motel [M]
(250) 392-5334. **$82-$145.** 1405 Cariboo Hwy V2G 2W3. 0.6 mi (1 km) s on Hwy 97. Ext corridors. **Pets:** Accepted. [📶] [🛗] [💻]

(CAA) ▼▼▼ Williams Lake Super 8 [M]
(250) 398-8884. **$100-$107.** 1712 Broadway Ave S V2G 2W4. 1.2 mi (2 km) s on Hwy 97. Int corridors. **Pets:** Accepted. [SAVE] [📶] [✕] [🛗M] [🛗] [💻]

MANITOBA

CITY INDEX

BEAUSEJOUR

▼▼▼ Superior Inn [H]
(204) 268-9050. **Call for rates.** 1055 Park Ave R0E 0C0. On Hwy 215; jct Hwy 12/44/302. Int corridors. **Pets:** Accepted. [📶] [🛗M] [🛗] [💻] [🐾]

BRANDON

(CAA) ▼▼▼▼ Canad Inns-Destination Centre Brandon [H]
(204) 727-1422. **$120-$250.** 1125 18th St R7A 7C5. On Hwy 10 (18th St); jct Brandon Ave. Int corridors. **Pets:** Accepted. [ECO] [SAVE] [📶] [✕] [🛗M] [🛗] [💻] [🍴] [🐾] [✕]

▼▼▼ Comfort Inn Brandon [M] ❖
(204) 727-6232. **$101-$128.** 925 Middleton Ave R7C 1A8. Trans-Canada Hwy 1; between Hwy 10 (18th St) N and 10 S; on northside of service road. Int corridors. **Pets:** Other species. $10 daily fee/room. Service with restrictions, supervision. [ECO] [📶] [🛗M] [🛗] [💻]

▼▼▼ Days Inn Brandon [H]
(204) 727-3600. **$89-$170.** 2130 Currie Blvd R7B 4E7. Jct Trans-Canada Hwy 1, 4.9 mi (7.9 km) s on Hwy 10 (18th St). Int corridors. **Pets:** $15 daily fee/pet. Designated rooms, service with restrictions, crate. [ECO] [📶] [✕] [🛗M] [🛗] [💻]

▼▼▼ Victoria Inn [H]
(204) 725-1532. **$116-$199.** 3550 Victoria Ave R7B 2R4. Jct Trans-Canada Hwy 1 and 10 (18 St), 3.1 mi (5 km) s, then 0.9 mi (1.4 km) w. Int corridors. **Pets:** Accepted. [ECO] [📶] [✕] [🛗M] [🛗] [💻] [🍴] [🐾]

FLIN FLON

▼▼▼ Victoria Inn North [H]
(204) 687-7555. **$140-$190.** 160 Hwy 10A N R8A 0C6. Jct Hwy 10 and 10A, 0.6 mi (1 km) nw (eastern approach to city). Int corridors. **Pets:** Accepted. [📶] [✕] [🛗M] [🛗] [💻] [🍴] [🐾]

PORTAGE LA PRAIRIE

▼▼▼ Super 8 [H]
(204) 857-8883. **$99-$104.** 2668 Hwy 1A W R1N 3B2. On Hwy 1A, 0.9 mi (1.5 km) w. Int corridors. **Pets:** Other species. $10 daily fee/pet. Designated rooms, service with restrictions, supervision. [📶] [✕] [🛗M] [🛗] [💻] [🐾]

RUSSELL

▼▼▼ The Russell Inn Hotel & Conference Centre [H] ❖
(204) 773-2186. **$100-$196, 14 day notice.** Hwy 16 R0J 1W0. 0.8 mi (1.2 km) se on Hwy 16 and 83. Ext/int corridors. **Pets:** Small. Service with restrictions, supervision. [📶] [✕] [🛗] [💻] [🍴] [🐾] [✕]

STEINBACH

▼▼▼ Days Inn [H]
(204) 320-9200. **$110-$120.** 75 Hwy 12 N R5G 1T3. 0.5 mi (0.8 km) n of jct Hwy 52. Int corridors. **Pets:** Accepted. [📶] [✕] [🛗M] [🛗] [💻] [🐾] [✕]

SWAN RIVER

▼▼ Swan Valley Super 8 🄷

(204) 734-7888. **$109-$154.** 115 Kelsey Tr R0L 1Z0. Corner of Hwy 10 and 83. Int corridors. **Pets:** Other species. $10 daily fee/pet. Designated rooms, service with restrictions, supervision. 🄴🄲🄾 🛜 👤Ⓜ 🛏 🖥 🏊

THE PAS

▼▼ Kikiwak Inn 🄷

(204) 623-1800. **Call for rates.** Hwy 10 N R0B 2J0. On Hwy 10, 0.4 mi (0.6 km) n. Int corridors. **Pets:** Accepted. 🛜 👤Ⓜ 🛏 🖥 🍽 🏊

▼▼ Super 8 🄷

(204) 623-1888. **$115-$135.** 1717 Gordon Ave R9A 1K3. At southern approach to town. Int corridors. **Pets:** Accepted.

🛜 ✕ 👤Ⓜ 🛏 🖥 🏊

THOMPSON

🄰🄰 ▼▼ Lakeview Inn & Suites 🄷 🐾

(204) 778-8879. **$120.** 70 Thompson Dr N R8N 1Y8. Just w of Hwy 6. Int corridors. **Pets:** Other species. Designated rooms, service with restrictions, supervision. 🄴🄲🄾 🅂🅰🅅🅴 🛜 👤Ⓜ 🛏 🖥 ✕

WINNIPEG METROPOLITAN AREA

WINNIPEG

🄰🄰 ▼▼▼▼ BEST WESTERN PLUS Pembina Inn & Suites 🄷 🐾

(204) 269-8888. **$120-$299.** 1714 Pembina Hwy R3T 2G2. 0.6 mi (1 km) n of jct Bishop Grandin Blvd. Int corridors. **Pets:** Other species. $12 daily fee/pet. Designated rooms, service with restrictions, supervision.

🄴🄲🄾 🅂🅰🅅🅴 🛜 ✕ 👤Ⓜ 🛏 🖥 🏊 ✕

▼▼▼▼ Canad Inns Destination Centre Polo Park 🄷

(204) 775-8791. **$115-$259.** 1405 St. Matthews Ave R3G 0K5. Just e of St James St. Int corridors. **Pets:** Accepted.

🄴🄲🄾 🅂🅰🅅🅴 🛜 ✕ 👤Ⓜ 🛏 🖥 🍽 🏊 ✕

▼▼▼▼ Clarion Hotel & Suites 🄷 🐾

(204) 774-5110. **$143-$250.** 1445 Portage Ave R3G 3P4. Jct Empress St. Int corridors. **Pets:** Other species. $15 daily fee/pet. Designated rooms, service with restrictions, crate.

🄴🄲🄾 🛜 👤Ⓜ 🛏 🖥 🍽 🏊 ✕

🄰🄰 ▼▼▼ Comfort Inn Airport 🄼

(204) 783-5627. **$99-$138.** 1770 Sargent Ave R3H 0C8. At King Edward St. Int corridors. **Pets:** Accepted. 🄴🄲🄾 🅂🅰🅅🅴 👤Ⓜ 🛏 🖥

🄰🄰 ▼▼▼ Comfort Inn South 🄼

(204) 269-7390. **$117-$138.** 3109 Pembina Hwy R3T 4R6. Just n of jct Perimeter Hwy 100 and 75. Int corridors. **Pets:** Medium, other species. $10 daily fee/room. Designated rooms, service with restrictions, supervision. 🄴🄲🄾 🅂🅰🅅🅴 🛜 👤Ⓜ 🛏 🖥

▼▼ Country Inn & Suites By Carlson 🄷

(204) 783-6900. **$110-$140, 4 day notice.** 730 King Edward St R3H 1B4. Just s of Wellington Ave. Int corridors. **Pets:** $25 one-time fee/pet. Service with restrictions. 🄴🄲🄾 🛜 ✕ 👤Ⓜ 🛏 🖥

▼▼▼ Delta Winnipeg 🄷 🐾

(204) 942-0551. **$99-$399, 7 day notice.** 350 St. Mary Ave R3C 3J2. At Hargrave St. Int corridors. **Pets:** Medium. $35 one-time fee/pet. Service with restrictions, crate. 🄴🄲🄾 🛜 ✕ 👤Ⓜ 🛏 🖥 🍽 🏊 ✕

▼▼▼ Fairfield Inn & Suites by Marriott 🄷 🐾

(204) 783-7900. **$129-$169.** 1301 Ellice Ave R3G 1T7. Between Empress and Strathcona sts. Int corridors. **Pets:** Medium. $100 deposit/room, $25 one-time fee/room. Designated rooms, service with restrictions, supervision. 🛜 ✕ 🛏 🖥 🏊

▼▼▼ The Fairmont Winnipeg 🄷

(204) 957-1350. **$159-$299.** 2 Lombard Pl R3B 0Y3. Just e of Portage Ave and Main St. Int corridors. **Pets:** Accepted.

🄴🄲🄾 🛜 👤Ⓜ 🖥 🍽 🏊 ✕

▼▼▼ Greenwood Inn & Suites 🄷

(204) 775-9889. **$109-$159.** 1715 Wellington Ave R3H 0G1. At Century St. Int corridors. **Pets:** Accepted.

🄴🄲🄾 🛜 👤Ⓜ 🛏 🖥 🍽 🏊 ✕

▼▼▼▼ Hilton Suites Winnipeg Airport 🄷 🐾

(204) 783-1700. **$119-$239.** 1800 Wellington Ave R3H 1B2. At Berry St. Int corridors. **Pets:** Large. Designated rooms, service with restrictions, crate. 🄴🄲🄾 🛜 ✕ 👤Ⓜ 🛏 🖥 🍽 🏊 ✕

▼▼▼ Holiday Inn Winnipeg South 🄷

(204) 452-4747. **$139-$179.** 1330 Pembina Hwy R3T 2B4. At McGillivray Blvd. Int corridors. **Pets:** Other species. $15 daily fee/room. Service with restrictions, supervision. 🄴🄲🄾 🛜 👤Ⓜ 🛏 🖥 🏊

🄰🄰 ▼▼▼▼ MainStay Suites Winnipeg 🄷 🐾

(204) 594-0500. **$94-$160.** 670 King Edward St R3H 0P2. Between Sargent and Ellice aves. Int corridors. **Pets:** Medium. $10 daily fee/pet. Designated rooms, service with restrictions, crate.

🅂🅰🅅🅴 🛜 ✕ 👤Ⓜ 🛏 🖥 ✕

🄰🄰 ▼▼▼▼ Place Louis Riel Suite Hotel 🄷

(204) 947-6961. **$120-$300.** 190 Smith St R3C 1J8. At St. Mary Ave. Int corridors. **Pets:** Medium. $10 daily fee/pet. Service with restrictions, supervision. 🄴🄲🄾 🅂🅰🅅🅴 🛜 ✕ 👤Ⓜ 🛏 🖥 🍽

🄰🄰 ▼▼▼ Quality Inn & Suites 🄷

(204) 453-8247. **$90-$300.** 635 Pembina Hwy R3M 2L4. Jct s of Grant Ave. Int corridors. **Pets:** Accepted. 🅂🅰🅅🅴 🛜 🛏 🖥 🍽

🄰🄰 ▼▼▼▼ Radisson Hotel Winnipeg Downtown 🄷

(204) 956-0410. **$171-$265.** 288 Portage Ave R3C 0B8. At Smith St. Int corridors. **Pets:** Accepted. 🄴🄲🄾 🅂🅰🅅🅴 🛜 ✕ 👤Ⓜ 🛏 🖥 🍽

🄰🄰 ▼▼▼▼ Ramada Viscount Gort Hotel 🄷 🐾

(204) 775-0451. **$120-$170.** 1670 Portage Ave R3J 0C9. Jct Rt 90. Int corridors. **Pets:** Medium. $25 deposit/room, $10 daily fee/room. Designated rooms, service with restrictions, crate.

🅂🅰🅅🅴 🛜 ✕ 👤Ⓜ 🛏 🖥 🍽 🏊 ✕

▼▼▼ Sandman Hotel & Suites Winnipeg Airport 🄷

(204) 775-7263. **Call for rates.** 1750 Sargent Ave R3H 0C7. Between King Edward and Century sts. Int corridors. **Pets:** Accepted.

🄴🄲🄾 🛜 👤Ⓜ 🛏 🖥 🍽 🏊

🄰🄰 ▼▼▼ Travelodge Winnipeg 🄷 🐾

(204) 255-6000. **$116-$130.** 20 Alpine Ave R2M 0Y5. Just e of jct Fermor Ave and St. Anne's Rd. Int corridors. **Pets:** Other species. $10 daily fee/pet. Designated rooms, service with restrictions, supervision.

🄴🄲🄾 🅂🅰🅅🅴 🛜 ✕ 👤Ⓜ 🛏 🖥 🍽 🏊 ✕

🄰🄰 ▼▼▼▼ Victoria Inn Hotel & Convention Centre 🄷

(204) 786-4801. **$134-$174.** 1808 Wellington Ave R3H 0G3. At Berry St. Int corridors. **Pets:** Accepted.

🄴🄲🄾 🅂🅰🅅🅴 🛜 ✕ 👤Ⓜ 🛏 🖥 🍽 🏊 ✕

END METROPOLITAN AREA

NEW BRUNSWICK

BATHURST

▼▼ ▼▼ Atlantic Host Hotel 🅷
(506) 548-3335. **$120-$195.** 1450 Vanier Blvd E2A 4H7. Rt 11 exit 310 (Vanier Blvd). Int corridors. **Pets:** Accepted. 🛜 💻 🍽 🏊 ✕

▼▼ ▼▼ Comfort Inn 🅷
(506) 547-8000. **$89-$125.** 1170 St. Peter Ave E2A 2Z9. 2.1 mi (3.4 km) n on Rt 134 (St. Peter Ave). Int corridors. **Pets:** $15 daily fee/room. Designated rooms, service with restrictions, supervision. 🛜 🔌 💻

▼▼ ▼▼ Danny's Inn & Conference Centre 🅷 🐾
(506) 546-6621. **$91-$159.** Rt 134 E2A 3Z2. Rt 11 exit 310 (Vanier Blvd) northbound to Rt 134 (St. Peter Ave), 2.5 mi (4 km) n; exit 318 southbound to Rt 134 (St. Peter Ave), 2.3 mi (3.8 km) s. Ext/int corridors. **Pets:** Other species. Designated rooms, service with restrictions, crate. 🛜 ✕ 🔌 💻 🍽 🏊 ✕

BLOOMFIELD

▼▼ ▼▼ Evelyn's Bed & Breakfast 🅱🅱
(506) 832-7788. **$99-$119, 7 day notice.** 374 Rt 121 E5N 4T4. Hwy 1 exit 166, follow signs. Int corridors. **Pets:** Accepted. 🛜 ✕ 🏊 🅐

BOUCTOUCHE

▼▼ ▼▼ Auberge Bouctouche Inn & Suites 🅷
(506) 743-5003. **$85-$165.** 50 Industrielle St E4S 3H9. Rt 11 exit 32A/B. Int corridors. **Pets:** Dogs only. $10 daily fee/pet. Designated rooms, service with restrictions, supervision. 🛜 ✕ ᴍ 🔌 💻

CAMPBELLTON

▼▼ ▼▼ Comfort Inn 🅷
(506) 753-4121. **$120-$200.** 111 chemin Val D'Amour Rd E3N 5B9. Hwy 11 exit 415, 0.6 mi (1 km) e on Sugarloaf St W. Ext/int corridors.
Pets: Accepted. 🄴🄲🄾 🛜 🔌 💻

Ⓐ ▼▼ ▼▼ Quality Hotel & Conference Centre 🅷
(506) 753-4133. **$97-$139.** 157 Water St E3N 3H2. Hwy 134; in City Centre Complex. Int corridors. **Pets:** Accepted. 🆂🅰🆅🅴 🛜 🔌 💻 🍽

▼▼ ▼▼ Super 8-Campbellton 🅷
(506) 753-8080. **$100-$140.** 26 Duke St E3N 2K3. Just s of Roseberry St; jct George and Duke sts; downtown. Ext/int corridors **Pets:** Accepted. 🄴🄲🄾 🛜 ✕ ᴍ 🔌 💻 🏊 ✕

CARAQUET

▼▼ ▼▼ Super 8 🅷
(506) 727-0888. **$99-$169.** 9 Carrefour Ave E1W 1B6. Just e of jct Rt 11 and St. Pierre Blvd E. Int corridors. **Pets:** Accepted.
🛜 ✕ ᴍ 🔌 💻 🏊 ✕

CHARLO

▼▼ ▼▼ Heron's Nest Cottages 🅲🅰
(506) 684-3766. **Call for rates.** 6 Heron Rd E8E 2L1. Hwy 11 exit 388, 1.2 mi (2 km) n on Rt 288 to Rt 134. Ext corridors. **Pets:** Accepted.
🛜 ✕ 🔌 💻 🅐

DALHOUSIE

Ⓐ ▼▼ ▼▼ BEST WESTERN PLUS Manoir Adelaide 🅷
(506) 684-5681. **$90-$110.** 385 Adelaide St E8C 1B4. At Brunswick St; center. Int corridors. **Pets:** Other species. $10 daily fee/room. Designated rooms, service with restrictions, crate. 🆂🅰🆅🅴 🛜 ✕ 🔌 💻 🍽

DIEPPE

Ⓐ ▼▼▼▼ Ramada Plaza Crystal Palace & Convention Centre 🅷
(506) 858-8584. 499 Paul St E1A 6S5. Trans-Canada Hwy 2 exit 459A eastbound, s on Rt 115 to Lewisville Rd, then left; exit 467A westbound, 4.8 mi (8 km) w on Rt 15 to rotary. Int corridors.
Pets: Accepted. 🄴🄲🄾 🆂🅰🆅🅴 🛜 ✕ 🔌 💻 🍽 🏊 ✕

Ⓐ ▼▼▼▼ Super 8 Moncton/Dieppe 🅷
(506) 858-8880. **$110-$200.** 370 Dieppe Blvd E1A 8H4. Hwy 15 exit 16, 0.6 mi (1 km) s. Int corridors. **Pets:** Medium. Service with restrictions, crate. 🄴🄲🄾 🆂🅰🆅🅴 🛜 ✕ ᴍ 🔌 💻 🏊 ✕

DOAKTOWN

▼▼▼▼ The Ledges Inn 🅲🅸
(506) 365-1820. **$100-$150, 7 day notice.** 30 Ledges Inn Ln E9C 1A7. On Rt 8; center. Int corridors. **Pets:** Dogs only. $50 deposit/room. Supervision. 🛜 ✕ 🍽

EDMUNDSTON

▼▼ ▼▼ Auberge Les Jardins Inn 🅷
(506) 739-5514. **$89-$179.** 60 Principale St E7B 1V7. Trans-Canada Hwy 2 exit 8. Ext/int corridors. **Pets:** Accepted. 🛜 🔌 💻 🍽 🏊

Ⓐ ▼▼ ▼▼ BEST WESTERN PLUS Edmundston Hotel 🅷
(506) 739-0000. **$109-$163.** 280 Hebert Blvd E3V 0A3. Trans-Canada Hwy 2 exit 18 (Hebert Blvd). Int corridors. **Pets:** Medium, other species. Designated rooms, service with restrictions, supervision.
🄴🄲🄾 🆂🅰🆅🅴 🛜 ✕ 🔌 💻 🏊 ✕

▼▼▼▼ Chateau Edmundston 🅷
(506) 739-7321. **Call for rates.** 100 rue Rice E3V 1T4. Trans-Canada Hwy 2 exit 18 (Hebert Blvd), 1 mi (1.6 km) sw, then just w on Church Rd. Int corridors. **Pets:** Designated rooms, service with restrictions, crate.
🛜 🔌 💻 🍽 🏊

Ⓐ ▼▼ ▼▼ Comfort Inn 🅷
(506) 739-8361. **$105-$195.** 5 Bateman Ave E3V 3L1. Trans-Canada Hwy 2 exit 18 (Hebert Blvd). Int corridors. **Pets:** Other species. Service with restrictions, crate. 🄴🄲🄾 🆂🅰🆅🅴 🛜 🔌 💻

▼▼▼▼ Days Inn Edmundston 🅷
(506) 263-0000. **$86-$146.** 10 rue Mathieu E7C 3E1. Trans-Canada Hwy 2 exit 26. Int corridors. **Pets:** Other species. $10 daily fee/room. Designated rooms, service with restrictions. 🄴🄲🄾 🛜 🔌 💻

▼▼ ▼▼ Quality Inn 🅷
(506) 735-5525. **Call for rates.** 919 Canada Rd E3V 3X2. Trans-Canada Hwy 2 exit 13B eastbound; exit 13BA westbound. Ext/int corridors. **Pets:** Designated rooms, service with restrictions, supervision.
🛜 ᴍ 🔌 💻 🍽 🏊 ✕

FREDERICTON

(CAA) ◆◆◆◆ BEST WESTERN PLUS Fredericton Hotel & Suites **H** ✿

(506) 455-8448. **$135-$250.** 333 Bishop Dr E3C 2M6. Rt 8 exit 6A eastbound; exit 6B westbound, just w of Regent Mall. Int corridors. **Pets:** Medium. $20 daily fee/room. Designated rooms, service with restrictions, supervision. ECO SAVE 🛜 ✕ &M ▤ 💻 ➰

◆◆ City Motel **H**

(506) 450-9900. **$85-$135.** 1216 Regent St E3B 3Z4. Trans-Canada Hwy 2 exit 285A eastbound; exit 285B westbound, 2 mi (3.3 km) n on Rt 101 (Regent St). Int corridors. **Pets:** $200 deposit/room. Designated rooms, service with restrictions, supervision. 🛜 ▤ 💻 ⑪

(CAA) ◆◆◆ Comfort Inn **H** ✿

(506) 453-0800. **$125-$143.** 797 Prospect St E3B 5Y4. Trans-Canada Hwy 2 exit 281, 2.5 mi (4 km) ne on Rt 640 (Hanwell Rd). Int corridors. **Pets:** Other species. ECO SAVE 🛜 ▤ 💻

(CAA) ◆◆◆◆ Crowne Plaza Fredericton Lord Beaverbrook **H** ✿

(506) 455-3371. **$140-$260.** 659 Queen St E3B 5A6. Corner of Regent St. Int corridors. **Pets:** Designated rooms, service with restrictions, supervision. ECO SAVE 🛜 ✕ ▤ 💻 ⑪ ➰ ✕

(CAA) ◆◆◆◆ Delta Fredericton **H** ✿

(506) 457-7000. **$129-$210.** 225 Woodstock Rd E3B 2H8. 1 mi (1.6 km) n on Rt 102; downtown. Int corridors. **Pets:** Other species. Designated rooms, service with restrictions.
ECO SAVE 🛜 ✕ &M ▤ 💻 ⑪ ➰ ✕

◆◆ Howard Johnson Plaza Hotel Fredericton **H**

(506) 462-4444. **$80-$119.** 958 Prospect St E3B 2T8. Rt 8 exit 3 (Hanwell Rd) eastbound; exit 5 (Smythe St) westbound. Ext/int corridors. **Pets:** Accepted. 🛜 ▤ 💻 ⑪ ➰ ✕

(CAA) ◆◆◆ Lakeview Inns & Suites-Fredericton **H** ✿

(506) 459-0035. **$107-$140.** 665 Prospect St E3B 6B8. Rt 8 exit 3 (Hanwell Rd) eastbound; exit 5 (Smythe St) westbound. Int corridors. **Pets:** Small. $10 daily fee/pet. Service with restrictions, supervision.
ECO SAVE 🛜 ✕ ▤ 💻

◆◆◆ Ramada Hotel Fredericton **H**

(506) 460-5500. **$119-$199.** 480 Riverside Dr E3A 8C2. On Rt 105; at north of Princess Margaret Bridge. Int corridors. **Pets:** Accepted.
ECO 🛜 ✕ ▤ 💻 ➰ ✕

GRAND FALLS

(CAA) ◆◆◆ BEST WESTERN PLUS Grand Sault Hotel & Suites **H** ✿

(506) 473-6200. **$135-$250.** 187 Ouellette St E3Z 3E8. Trans-Canada Hwy 2 exit 79. Int corridors. **Pets:** Medium. $20 daily fee/room. Designated rooms, service with restrictions, supervision.
ECO SAVE 🛜 ✕ &M ▤ 💻 ➰

◆◆ Quality Inn Grand Falls **H**

(506) 473-1300. **$125-$190.** 10039 Rt 144 E3Y 3H5. Trans-Canada Hwy 2 exit 75, just w. Ext/int corridors. **Pets:** Very small. $15 one-time fee/room. Designated rooms, service with restrictions, supervision.
🛜 &M ▤ 💻 ⑪ ➰ ✕

MIRAMICHI

◆◆ Days Inn **H**

(506) 622-1215. **$89-$149.** 201 Edward St E1V 2Y7. 0.6 mi (1 km) w on Rt 8. Int corridors. **Pets:** Dogs only. $10 daily fee/pet. Designated rooms, service with restrictions, supervision. ECO 🛜 ▤ 💻

◆◆ Howard Johnson Inn & Suites Miramichi **H**

(506) 622-0302. **$84-$104.** 1 Jane St E1V 2S6. Just s off King George Hwy. Int corridors. **Pets:** Accepted. 🛜 ✕ ▤ 💻 ⑪ ➰

(CAA) ◆◆◆ Lakeview Inns & Suites **H**

(506) 627-1999. **Call for rates.** 333 King George Hwy E1V 1L2. 1.1 mi (1.8 km) w on Rt 8. Int corridors. **Pets:** Accepted.
ECO SAVE 🛜 ▤ 💻

◆◆◆◆ Rodd Miramichi River-A Rodd Signature Hotel **H**

(506) 773-3111. **$112-$175.** 1809 Water St E1N 1B2. Hwy 11 exit 120, 0.4 mi (0.6 km) e. Int corridors. **Pets:** Accepted.
ECO 🛜 ✕ &M ▤ 💻 ⑪ ➰ ✕

MONCTON

(CAA) ◆◆◆◆ Casino New Brunswick **H** ✿

(506) 861-4661. **$149-$999.** 21 Casino Dr E1G 0R7. Trans-Canada Hwy 2 exit 450. Int corridors. **Pets:** Small. $30 one-time fee/room. Service with restrictions, supervision. SAVE 🛜 ✕ &M ▤ 💻 ⑪ ➰ ✕

(CAA) ◆◆◆ Coastal Inn **H**

(506) 857-9686. **$99-$154.** 502 Kennedy St E1A 5Y7. At Paul St. Ext/int corridors. **Pets:** Small. Designated rooms, service with restrictions, supervision. ECO SAVE 🛜 ▤ 💻 ➰

◆◆◆ Colonial Hotel and Suites **H**

(506) 382-3395. **$100-$127.** 42 Highfield St E1C 8T6. 1 blk n of Main St; center. Ext/int corridors. **Pets:** Medium. $25 one-time fee/room. Designated rooms, service with restrictions, supervision. 🛜 ▤ ⑪ ➰

◆◆◆ Comfort Inn **H**

(506) 384-3175. **$107-$170.** 2495 Mountain Rd E1G 2W4. Trans-Canada Hwy 2 exit 450. Int corridors. **Pets:** Large, other species. Designated rooms, service with restrictions, crate. ECO 🛜 ▤ 💻

(CAA) ◆◆◆ Comfort Inn **H**

(506) 859-6868. **$99-$229.** 20 Maplewood Dr E1A 6P9. Trans-Canada Hwy 2 exit 459A on Hwy 115 S, left on Rt 134 E (Lewisville Rd). Int corridors. **Pets:** Service with restrictions, crate. ECO SAVE 🛜 ▤ 💻

(CAA) ◆◆◆◆ Crowne Plaza Moncton Downtown **H** ✿

(506) 854-6340. **$99-$139.** 1005 Main St E1C 1G9. At Highfield and Main sts; downtown. Int corridors. **Pets:** Medium, other species. Service with restrictions, supervision.
ECO SAVE 🛜 ✕ ▤ 💻 ⑪ ➰ ✕

◆◆◆◆ Delta Beausejour **H**

(506) 854-4344. **$209-$329.** 750 Main St E1C 1E6. Jct Main St and Sommet Ln; downtown. Int corridors. **Pets:** Accepted.
ECO 🛜 ✕ ▤ 💻 ⑪ ➰ ✕

◆◆◆ Future Inns Moncton Hotel & Conference Centre **H** ✿

(506) 852-9600. **$119-$189.** 40 Lady Ada Blvd E1G 0E3. Trans-Canada Hwy 2 exit 454. Int corridors. **Pets:** Other species. Designated rooms, service with restrictions, supervision. 🛜 ✕ &M ▤ 💻 ⑪

(CAA) ◆◆◆ Hampton Inn & Suites Moncton **H** ✿

(506) 855-4819. **$129-$359.** 700 Mapleton Rd E1G 0L7. Trans-Canada Hwy 2 exit 454. Int corridors. **Pets:** Other species. Designated rooms, service with restrictions, crate. SAVE 🛜 ✕ &M ▤ 💻 ➰

(CAA) ◆◆◆ Holiday Inn Express Hotel & Suites Moncton **H** ✿

(506) 384-1050. **$109-$159.** 2515 Mountain Rd E1G 2W4. Trans-Canada Hwy 2 exit 450. Ext/int corridors. **Pets:** Medium. $20 one-time fee/pet. Designated rooms, service with restrictions, supervision.
ECO SAVE 🛜 ✕ &M ▤ 💻 ✕

◆◆◆ Hotel St. James **H**

(506) 388-4283. **$159-$289.** 14 Church St E1C 4Y9. Corner of Main and Church sts. Int corridors. **Pets:** $15 daily fee/pet. Service with restrictions, supervision. 🛜 ✕ ⑪

▼▼ Howard Johnson Inn Moncton Ⓜ
(506) 384-1734. **$85-$115.** 1062 Mountain Rd E1C 2T1. Trans-Canada Hwy 2 exit 454 (Mapleton Rd), 1.7 mi (2.8 km) s to Rt 126 (Mountain Rd), then just se. Ext/int corridors. **Pets:** Medium. $10 deposit/pet. Service with restrictions, supervision. 🛜 ✖ 🖥 💻 🏊

Ⓐ ▼▼ Motel 6 Moncton Ⓗ
(506) 386-6749. **$69-$129.** 2530 Mountain Rd E1G 1B4. Trans-Canada Hwy 2 exit 450. Int corridors. **Pets:** Other species. Service with restrictions, supervision. (SAVE) 🛜 ✖ ♿ 🖥 🏊

Ⓐ ▼▼▼ Residence Inn by Marriott Moncton Ⓗ
(506) 854-7100. **$134-$199.** 600 Main St E1C 0M6. At Assomption Blvd. Int corridors. **Pets:** Accepted.
(ECO) (SAVE) 🛜 ✖ ♿ 🖥 💻 🍽 🏊

Ⓐ ▼▼▼ Rodd Moncton Ⓗ
(506) 382-1664. **$99-$159.** 434 Main St E1C 1B9. On Rt 106 (Main St) at King St. Ext/int corridors. **Pets:** Medium. Service with restrictions, crate. (ECO) (SAVE) 🛜 ✖ 💻 🏊

Ⓐ ▼▼▼ Travelodge Suites Moncton Ⓗ 🐾
(506) 852-7000. **$79-$300.** 2475 Mountain Rd E1G 2J5. Trans-Canada Hwy 2 exit 450. Int corridors. **Pets:** $25 one-time fee/room. Service with restrictions, supervision. (ECO) (SAVE) 🛜 🖥 💻

OROMOCTO

Ⓐ ▼▼▼ Days Inn Oromocto Ⓗ
(506) 357-5657. **$110-$130.** 60 Brayson Blvd E2V 4T9. Trans-Canada Hwy 2 exit 301 eastbound; exit 303 westbound, just s to Pioneer Ave, then 1 mi (1.6 km) w. Int corridors. **Pets:** Medium, other species. $15 daily fee/pet. Designated rooms, service with restrictions, supervision.
(ECO) (SAVE) 🛜 ♿ 🖥 💻 🍽 🏊

PERTH-ANDOVER

Ⓐ ▼▼▼ The Castle Inn Ⓒⓘ
(506) 273-9495. **$119-$229.** 21 Brentwood Dr E7H 1P1. Trans-Canada Hwy 2 exit 115, follow signs over St. John River. Int corridors. **Pets:** No service, crate. (SAVE) 🛜 ✖ 💻 🍽 🏊 ✖

SACKVILLE

▼▼ Coastal Inn Sackville Ⓗ
(506) 536-0000. **$99-$155.** 15 Wright St E4L 4P8. Trans-Canada Hwy 2 exit 504. Int corridors. **Pets:** Designated rooms, service with restrictions, supervision. (ECO) 🛜 ✖ 🖥

Ⓐ ▼▼▼ Marshlands Inn Ⓒⓘ
(506) 536-0170. **$94-$225.** 55 Bridge St E4L 3N8. On Hwy 106; center. Int corridors. **Pets:** Medium, other species. Designated rooms, service with restrictions. (SAVE) 🛜 ✖ 🍽

ST. ANDREWS

▼▼▼▼ The Algonquin Resort Ⓗ
(506) 529-8823. **Call for rates.** 184 Adolphus St E5B 1T7. Off Hwy 127. Int corridors. **Pets:** Accepted. (ECO) 🛜 ✖ 🖥 💻 🍽 🏊 ✖

Ⓐ ▼▼▼▼ Tara Manor Inn ⒷⒷ
(506) 529-3304. **$99-$149, 7 day notice.** 559 Mowat Dr E5B 2P2. 1.7 mi (2.8 km) n on Hwy 127. Ext corridors. **Pets:** Accepted.
(SAVE) 🛜 ✖ 🖥 🏊

SAINT JOHN

Ⓐ ▼▼▼▼ BEST WESTERN PLUS Saint John Hotel & Suites Ⓗ 🐾
(506) 657-9966. **$99-$199.** 55 Majors Brook Dr E2J 0B2. Hwy 1 exit 129 westbound, 1 mi (1.6 km) s on Rt 100 (Rothesay Ave) to McAllister Dr, then just e; exit 128 eastbound, 1 mi (1.6 km) n on Rt 100 (Rothesay Ave), just n to McAllister Dr, then just e. Int corridors. **Pets:** Large. $15 daily fee/room. Designated rooms, service with restrictions, supervision.
(SAVE) 🛜 ✖ ♿ 🖥 💻 🏊

Ⓐ ▼▼ Colonial Inn Saint John Ⓗ
(506) 652-3000. **$114-$130.** 175 City Rd E2L 3M9. Hwy 1 exit 123. Ext/int corridors. **Pets:** Medium. $10 daily fee/pet. Designated rooms, service with restrictions, crate. (SAVE) 🛜 🖥 🍽 🏊 ✖

Ⓐ ▼▼ Comfort Inn Ⓗ
(506) 674-1873. **$128-$138.** 1155 Fairville Blvd E2M 5T9. Hwy 1 exit 117 westbound; exit 119 eastbound, then left. Int corridors. **Pets:** Accepted.
(ECO) (SAVE) 🛜 🖥 💻

▼▼▼▼ Delta Brunswick Ⓗ
(506) 648-1981. **$99-$199.** 39 King St E2L 4W3. Center of downtown; in Brunswick Square Mall. Int corridors. **Pets:** Accepted.
(ECO) 🛜 🖥 💻 🍽 🏊

Ⓐ ▼▼▼▼ Hampton Inn & Suites Ⓗ
(506) 657-4600. **$104-$142.** 51 Fashion Dr E2J 0A7. Hwy 1 exit 129, 1.5 mi (2.4 km) s on Rothesay Ave to Retail Dr; behind Home Depot. Int corridors. **Pets:** Accepted. (SAVE) 🛜 ✖ ♿ 🖥 💻 🏊 ✖

Ⓐ ▼▼▼▼ Hilton Saint John Ⓗ 🐾
(506) 693-8484. **$99-$199.** 1 Market Square E2L 4Z6. Hwy 1 exit 122; at Market Square. Int corridors. **Pets:** Medium, other species. Service with restrictions, supervision. (ECO) (SAVE) 🛜 🖥 💻 🍽 🏊

Ⓐ ▼▼▼▼ Holiday Inn Express & Suites Ⓗ
(506) 642-2622. **$119-$159.** 400 Main St/Chesley Dr E2K 4N5. 0.6 mi (1 km) w on Hwy 1; north end of Chesley Dr exit 121; off Harbour Bridge. Int corridors. **Pets:** Other species. Service with restrictions.
(ECO) (SAVE) 🛜 ✖ 🖥 💻 🏊

▼▼▼ Homeport Historic Inn Circa 1858 ⒷⒷ 🐾
(506) 672-7255. **$109-$175, 4 day notice.** 80 Douglas Ave E2K 1E4. Hwy 1 exit 121 eastbound; exit 123 westbound. Int corridors. **Pets:** Dogs only. Supervision. 🛜 ✖ 🖥

▼▼ Howard Johnson Fort Howe Plaza & Convention Center Ⓗ
(506) 657-7320. **$99-$149.** 10 Portland St E2K 4H8. Hwy 1 exit 121 eastbound off Harbour Bridge; exit 123 westbound. Int corridors.
Pets: Accepted. (ECO) 🛜 🖥 💻 🍽 🏊

Ⓐ ▼▼ Travelodge Suites Saint John Ⓗ
(506) 635-0400. **$119-$139.** 1011 Fairville Blvd E2M 5T9. Hwy 1 exit 119B eastbound, left on Catherwood Dr, left at lights; exit 119A westbound. Int corridors. **Pets:** Accepted. (ECO) (SAVE) 🛜 🖥 💻

ST-LEONARD

Ⓐ ▼▼ Daigle's Motel Ⓗ
(506) 423-6351. **$85-$109.** 68 rue DuPont E7E 1Y1. Hwy 17, 0.6 mi (1 km) s of Trans-Canada Hwy 2 exit 58. Ext corridors. **Pets:** Small. $10 daily fee/pet. Designated rooms, no service, supervision.
(SAVE) 🛜 🍽 🏊

SAINT-QUENTIN

▼▼ Auberge Evasion de Reves Inn Ⓜ
(506) 235-3551. **Call for rates.** 11 Canada St E8A 1J2. 1 mi (1.6 km) w on Rt 17. Int corridors. **Pets:** Accepted. 🛜 ✖ 🖥 💻 🏊

ST. STEPHEN

▼▼ St. Stephen Inn Ⓜ
(506) 466-1814. **$55-$130.** 99 King St E3L 2C6. Just n of Prince William St; center. Ext/int corridors. **Pets:** Accepted. 🛜 🖥

Ⓐ ▼▼ Winsome Inn Ⓜ
(506) 466-2130. **$92-$129.** 198 King St E3L 2E2. Hwy 1 exit King St, just s on Rt 3. Ext corridors. **Pets:** $10 daily fee/room. Designated rooms, service with restrictions, supervision. (SAVE) 🛜 ✖ 🖥 🏊

SHEDIAC

Gaudet Chalets & Motel M

(506) 533-8877. **Call for rates.** 14 Bellevue Heights E4P 1H2. On Rt 133, 1.4 mi (2.4 km) w of Rt 15 exit 37. Ext corridors. **Pets:** Accepted.

Seely's Motel M

(506) 532-6193. **$79-$179, 3 day notice.** 21 Bellevue Heights E4P 1G9. On Rt 133, 1.5 mi (2.4 km) w of Rt 15 exit 37. Ext corridors. **Pets:** Medium, dogs only. $15 daily fee/pet. Designated rooms, service with restrictions, supervision.

SUSSEX

All Seasons Inn M

(506) 433-2220. **$69-$139, 3 day notice.** 1015 Main St E4E 2M6. Hwy 1 exit 192 eastbound; exit 198 westbound, left towards Sussex Corner; center. Ext corridors. **Pets:** Medium. $12 daily fee/room. Service with restrictions, supervision.

Fairway Inn H

(506) 433-3470. **$125-$175.** 216 Roachville Rd E4E 5L6. Hwy 1 exit 193. Ext/int corridors. **Pets:** Medium. $10 daily fee/pet. Designated rooms, service with restrictions, supervision.

Pine Cone Motel M

(506) 433-3958. **Call for rates.** 12808 Rt 114 E4E 5L9. Hwy 1 exit 198, 1.2 mi (2 km) e on Rt 114 towards Penobsquis. Ext corridors. **Pets:** Accepted.

WOODSTOCK

BEST WESTERN PLUS Woodstock Hotel and Conference Centre H

(506) 328-2378. **$135-$170.** 123 Gallop Ct E7M 3P7. Trans-Canada Hwy 2 exit 185. Int corridors. **Pets:** Medium. $20 one-time fee/room. Designated rooms, service with restrictions, supervision.

Canadas Best Value Inn & Suites H

(506) 328-8876. **$70-$120.** 168 Rt 555 E7M 6B5. Trans-Canada Hwy 2 exit 188 (Houlton Rd). Ext/int corridors. **Pets:** Small. $10 daily fee/pet. Designated rooms, service with restrictions, supervision.

Howard Johnson Inn H

(506) 328-3315. **$75-$139.** 159 Rt 555 exit 188 TCH E7M 6B5. Trans-Canada Hwy 2 exit 188 (Houlton Rd). Ext/int corridors. **Pets:** Accepted.

YOUNGS COVE

McCready's Motel M

(506) 362-2916. **Call for rates.** 10995 Rt 10 E4C 2G5. Trans-Canada Hwy 2 exit 365, just w at Irving One Stop. Ext corridors. **Pets:** Accepted.

NEWFOUNDLAND AND LABRADOR

CITY INDEX

CHANNEL-PORT AUX BASQUES

Hotel Port Aux Basques H

(709) 695-2171. **$115.** 1 Grand Bay Rd A0M 1C0. Jct Trans-Canada Hwy 1. Int corridors. **Pets:** $10 daily fee/room. Designated rooms, service with restrictions, supervision.

St. Christopher's Hotel H

(709) 695-7034. **Call for rates.** 146 Caribou Rd A0M 1C0. Trans-Canada Hwy 1 exit Port aux Basques, follow signs 1.2 mi (2 km); downtown. Int corridors. **Pets:** Accepted.

CLARENVILLE

Restland Motel H

(709) 466-7636. **$124-$144.** 262 Memorial Dr A5A 1N9. Center. Ext/int corridors. **Pets:** Accepted.

St. Jude Hotel H

(709) 466-1717. **$113-$134.** 247 Trans-Canada Hwy A5A 1Y4. On Trans-Canada Hwy 1; center. Int corridors. **Pets:** Medium. $15 one-time fee/room. Designated rooms, service with restrictions, supervision.

CORNER BROOK

Comfort Inn H

(709) 639-1980. **$130-$145.** 41 Maple Valley Rd A2H 6T2. Trans-Canada Hwy 1 exit 5 eastbound; exit 6 westbound, via Confederation Ave. Int corridors. **Pets:** Other species. Designated rooms, service with restrictions, supervision.

Glynmill Inn H

(709) 634-5181. **$118-$190.** 1B Cobb Ln A2H 2V3. Just w of W Valley Rd; center. Int corridors. **Pets:** Designated rooms, service with restrictions, supervision.

Greenwood Inn & Suites-Corner Brook H

(709) 634-5381. **Call for rates.** 48 West St A2H 2Z2. At Chestnut St; center. Int corridors. **Pets:** Accepted.

Mamateek Inn H

(709) 639-8901. **Call for rates.** 64 Maple Valley Rd A2H 6G7. Trans-Canada Hwy 1 exit 5 eastbound; exit 6 westbound, via Confederation Ave. Int corridors. **Pets:** Accepted.

COW HEAD

Shallow Bay Motel & Cabins H

(709) 243-2471. **$105-$135.** Rt 430, The Viking Tr A0K 2A0. Hwy 430, 2.5 mi (4 km) w towards the ocean, follow signs. Ext/int corridors. **Pets:** Medium, other species. $15 daily fee/room. Designated rooms, service with restrictions, supervision.

GANDER

Albatross Hotel H

(709) 256-3956. **Call for rates.** Trans-Canada Hwy A1V 1W8. On Trans-Canada Hwy 1. Ext/int corridors. **Pets:** Accepted.

Comfort Inn H

(709) 256-3535. **$144-$154.** 112 Trans-Canada Hwy 1 A1V 1P8. Center. Ext/int corridors. **Pets:** Accepted.

Sinbad's Hotel & Suites H

(709) 651-2678. **$115-$290.** 133 Bennett Dr A1V 1W8. Center; opposite Gander Mall. Ext corridors. **Pets:** Medium, other species. Designated rooms, service with restrictions, supervision.

GRAND FALLS-WINDSOR

▼▼ Mount Peyton Hotel H

(709) 489-2251. **$118-$137.** 214 Lincoln Rd A2A 1P8. 0.6 mi (1 km) ne on Trans-Canada Hwy 1. Ext/int corridors. **Pets:** Accepted.

ⒺⒸⓄ 🛜 📶 💻 🍴

LABRADOR CITY

▼▼ Carol Inn H

(709) 944-7736. **Call for rates.** 215 Drake Ave A2V 2B6. Center. Int corridors. **Pets:** Accepted. 🛜 📶 💻 🍴

L'ANSE AU CLAIR

▼▼ Northern Light Inn H

(709) 931-2332. **$109-$159.** Rt 510 A0K 3K0. Center. Int corridors. **Pets:** Accepted. 🛜 📶 💻 🍴

PORT BLANDFORD

▼▼ Terra Nova Golf Resort H

(709) 543-2525. **Call for rates.** Trans-Canada Hwy 1 A0C 2G0. Center. Int corridors. **Pets:** Accepted. 🛜 📶 💻 🍴 ⚓ ⊠

ST. JOHN'S

▼▼ Comfort Inn Airport H

(709) 753-3500. **Call for rates.** 106 Airport Rd A1A 4Y3. Trans-Canada Hwy 1 exit 47A, 0.6 mi (1 km) n on Rt 40 (Portugal Cove Rd). Int corridors. **Pets:** Accepted. 🛜 📶 💻 🍴

▼▼▼ Delta St. John's Hotel and Conference Centre H

(709) 739-6404. **$179-$269.** 120 New Gower St A1C 6K4. At Barter's Hill Rd; center. Int corridors. **Pets:** Accepted.

ⒺⒸⓄ 🛜 ⊠ 📶 📶 💻 🍴 ⚓ ⊠

▼▼ Extended Stay Deluxe St. John's - Downtown H

(709) 754-7888. **$144-$165.** 222 LeMarchant Rd A1C 2H9. Corner of Pleasant St. Int corridors. **Pets:** daily fee/pet. Designated rooms, service with restrictions. 🛜 ⊠ 📶 📶 💻

▼▼ The Guv'nor Inn H

(709) 726-0092. **$120-$230.** 389 Elizabeth Ave A1B 1V1. 2 blks n of Freshwater Rd. Ext/int corridors. **Pets:** Small. Designated rooms, service with restrictions, supervision. 🛜 📶 💻 🍴

▼▼▼ Holiday Inn St. John's-Govt Centre H 🐾

(709) 722-0506. **$159-$219.** 180 Portugal Cove Rd A1B 2N2. Trans-Canada Hwy 1 exit 47A, 0.9 mi (1.4 km) s. Ext/int corridors. **Pets:** Other species. $25 deposit/room. Designated rooms, service with restrictions, supervision. ⒺⒸⓄ 🛜 📶 📶 💻 🍴 ⚓

Ⓐ ▼▼▼ Sheraton Hotel Newfoundland H 🐾

(709) 726-4980. **$129-$330.** 115 Cavendish Square A1C 3K2. At Duckworth and Ordnance sts. Int corridors. **Pets:** Other species. Service with restrictions, supervision. ⒺⒸⓄ Ⓢ 🛜 ⊠ 📶 💻 🍴 ⚓ ⊠

▼▼ Super 8 H 🐾

(709) 739-8888. **$126-$180.** 175 Higgins Line A1B 4N4. Trans-Canada Hwy 1 exit 47A, just s on Rt 40 (Portugal Cove Rd). Int corridors. **Pets:** Designated rooms, service with restrictions, supervision.

ⒺⒸⓄ 🛜 ⊠ 📶 📶 💻 ⚓

STEPHENVILLE

▼▼ Holiday Inn Stephenville H 🐾

(709) 643-6666. **Call for rates.** 44 Queen St A2N 2M5. Center. Int corridors. **Pets:** Service with restrictions, supervision.

ⒺⒸⓄ 🛜 ⊠ 📶 💻 🍴

NORTHWEST TERRITORIES

YELLOWKNIFE

Ⓐ ▼▼▼ Chateau Nova Hotel & Suites H

(867) 873-9700. **$149-$199.** 4401 50th Ave X1A 2N2. Downtown. Int corridors. **Pets:** Medium, other species. $25 daily fee/room. Designated rooms, service with restrictions, supervision.

Ⓢ 🛜 ⊠ 📶 💻 🍴

▼▼▼ Coast Fraser Tower H

(867) 873-8700. **Call for rates.** 5303 52nd St X1A 1V1. Corner of 52nd St and 53rd Ave. Int corridors. **Pets:** $15 daily fee/pet. Designated rooms, service with restrictions, crate. ⒺⒸⓄ 🛜 📶 💻 Ⓚ

▼▼▼ The Explorer Hotel H

(867) 873-3531. **$149-$199.** 4825 49th Ave X1A 2R3. Downtown. Int corridors. **Pets:** Accepted. 🛜 📶 💻 🍴

▼▼ Super 8 Yellowknife M 🐾

(867) 669-8888. **$179-$182.** 308 Old Airport Rd X1A 3G3. 1.2 mi (2 km) s on Franklin Ave, 0.6 mi (1 km) w; in Wal-Mart Plaza. Int corridors. **Pets:** Large, other species. $25 one-time fee/room. Designated rooms, service with restrictions, crate. ⒺⒸⓄ 🛜 ⊠ 📶 💻

NOVA SCOTIA

CITY INDEX

AMHERST

Amherst Wandlyn Meeting & Convention Hotel

(902) 667-3331. **Call for rates.** 1539 Southampton Rd B4H 3Z2. Trans-Canada Hwy 104 exit 3, 0.6 mi (1 km) w. Ext/int corridors. **Pets:** $15 one-time fee/pet. Designated rooms, service with restrictions, crate.

Comfort Inn

(902) 667-0404. **$110-$135.** 143 Albion St S B4H 2X2. Trans-Canada Hwy 104 exit 4, 1 mi (1.6 km) n on Rt 2. Int corridors. **Pets:** Medium, other species. Service with restrictions, crate.

Super 8

(902) 660-8888. **$101-$164.** 40 Lord Amherst Dr B4H 4W6. Trans-Canada Hwy 104 exit 4. Int corridors. **Pets:** Medium, other species. $10 daily fee/pet. Service with restrictions, supervision.

ANNAPOLIS ROYAL

Annapolis Royal Inn

(902) 532-2323. **$89-$150, 30 day notice.** 3924 Hwy 1 B0S 1A0. 0.6 mi (1 km) w. Ext corridors. **Pets:** Accepted.

Hillsdale House Inn

(902) 532-2345. **$87-$167.** 519 St. George St B0S 1A0. Just e of Rt 1; center. Int corridors. **Pets:** Accepted.

The King George Inn

(902) 532-5286. **$80-$160.** 548 Upper St. George St B0S 1A0. Jct Rt 1 and 8, just e on Rt 8. Int corridors. **Pets:** Supervision.

ANTIGONISH

Maritime Inn Antigonish

(902) 863-4001. **$119-$195.** 158 Main St B2G 2B7. Between St. Mary's and Court sts; center. Ext/int corridors. **Pets:** Other species. Service with restrictions, supervision.

AULD'S COVE

Cove Motel & Restaurant/Gift Shop

(902) 747-2700. **$105-$130.** 227 Auld's Cove Rd B0H 1P0. 0.6 mi (1 km) n off Trans-Canada Hwy 104; 1.9 mi (3 km) w of Canso Cswy. Ext corridors. **Pets:** Dogs only. Designated rooms, service with restrictions, supervision.

BADDECK

Hunter's Mountain Chalets

(902) 295-3392. **$88-$138, 4 day notice.** 562 Cabot Tr B0E 1B0. Trans-Canada Hwy 105 exit 7, 1.6 mi (2.6 km) n. Ext corridors. **Pets:** Dogs only. $5 daily fee/pet. No service, supervision.

Inverary on Baddeck Bay

(902) 295-3500. **$99-$159, 3 day notice.** 368 Shore Rd B0E 1B0. Trans-Canada Hwy 105 exit 8, 1 mi (1.6 km) e on Rt 205 (Shore Rd). Ext/int corridors. **Pets:** Accepted.

McIntyre's Housekeeping Cottages

(902) 295-1133. **$80-$350, 4 day notice.** 8908 Hwy 105 B0E 1B0. Trans-Canada Hwy 105, 3 mi (5 km) w. Ext corridors. **Pets:** Other species. $20 daily fee/pet. Designated rooms, service with restrictions, crate.

Silver Dart Lodge & MacNeil House

(902) 295-2340. **$99-$240.** 257 Shore Rd B0E 1B0. Trans-Canada Hwy 105 exit 8, 0.6 mi (1 km) e on Rt 205 (Shore Rd). Ext/int corridors. **Pets:** Other species. Designated rooms, service with restrictions, crate.

BAYFIELD

Sea'Scape Cottages

(902) 386-2825. **$115-$145, 30 day notice.** 6 Sea Scape Cottage Ln B0H 1R0. Trans-Canada Hwy 104 exit 36, 3.2 mi (5.3 km) n on Sunrise Tr, then 1.1 mi (1.8 km) w on Ferry Rd. Ext corridors. **Pets:** Dogs only. $50 deposit/pet. Designated rooms, service with restrictions, supervision.

BRIDGETOWN

Bridgetown Motor Inn

(902) 665-4403. **Call for rates.** 396 Granville St B0S 1C0. Hwy 101 exit 20, 0.6 mi (1 km) w on Rt 1. Ext corridors. **Pets:** Accepted.

BRIDGEWATER

BEST WESTERN PLUS Bridgewater Hotel & Convention Centre

(902) 530-0101. **$110-$170.** 527 Hwy 10 B4V 7P4. Hwy 103 exit 12, just n. Int corridors. **Pets:** Large, dogs only. $20 daily fee/pet. Designated rooms, service with restrictions, supervision.

The Bridgewater Hotel

(902) 543-8171. **Call for rates.** 35 High St B4V 1V8. Hwy 103 exit 13, just e. Int corridors. **Pets:** Accepted.

Comfort Inn

(902) 543-1498. **$101-$126.** 49 North St B4V 2V7. Hwy 103 exit 12, 1.1 mi (1.7 km) s on Rt 10. Int corridors. **Pets:** Other species. Designated rooms, service with restrictions, supervision.

Days Inn & Conference Centre Bridgewater

(902) 543-7131. **$86-$118.** 50 North St B4V 2V6. Hwy 103 exit 12, 1.1 mi (1.7 km) s on Rt 10. Int corridors. **Pets:** Accepted.

CHARLOS COVE

▼▼▼▼ Seawind Landing Country Inn **CI** ❖
(902) 525-2108. **$99-$169.** 159 Wharf Rd B0H 1T0. Rt 316, 0.5 mi (0.8 km) se on gravel road. Ext/int corridors. **Pets:** Other species. Designated rooms. 📶 ✕ 🏋 ❗ 🍴 🎿

CHESTER

▼▼ Windjammer Motel **M**
(902) 275-3567. **$75-$85.** 4070 Rt 3 B0J 1J0. 0.6 mi (1 km) w. Ext corridors. **Pets:** Medium, other species. Designated rooms, service with restrictions, supervision. 📶 ❗

CHESTER BASIN

▼▼ The Sword & Anchor Bed & Breakfast **BB**
(902) 275-2418. **Call for rates.** 5306 Hwy 3 B0J 1K0. Center. Int corridors. **Pets:** Accepted. 📶 ✕ ❗ 🍴 ☎

CHÉTICAMP

▼▼ Cabot Trail Sea & Golf Chalets **CA**
(902) 224-1777. **$139-$179, 7 day notice.** 71 Fraser Doucet Ln B0E 1H0. Center. Ext corridors. **Pets:** Accepted. 📶 ✕ 🏋 ❗ 🍴 ✕ 🎿 ☎

ⒶⒶ ▼▼ Laurie's Motor Inn **H**
(902) 224-2400. **$99-$249.** 15456 Laurie Rd B0E 1H0. Center. Ext/int corridors. **Pets:** Large. Designated rooms, service with restrictions, crate. SAVE 📶 ✕ ❗ 🍴 🍴

CHURCH POINT

▼▼ Le Manoir Samson **M**
(902) 769-2526. **$80-$110.** 1768 Rt 1 B0W 1M0. Center. Ext corridors. **Pets:** Accepted. 📶 ✕ ❗ 🍴

DARTMOUTH

ⒶⒶ ▼▼ Comfort Inn **H** ❖
(902) 463-9900. **$120-$140.** 456 Windmill Rd B3A 1J7. Hwy 111 exit Shannon Park. Int corridors. **Pets:** Service with restrictions, supervision. ECO SAVE 📶 ❗ 🍴

ⒶⒶ ▼▼ Days Inn Dartmouth **H**
(902) 465-6555. **$99-$139.** 20 Highfield Park Dr B3A 4S8. From A. Murray MacKay Bridge, 0.8 mi (1.2 km) n on Hwy 111 exit 3 (Burnside Dr). Ext/int corridors. **Pets:** Designated rooms, service with restrictions, supervision. ECO SAVE 📶 🏋 ❗ 🍴 🍴 🎿

ⒶⒶ ▼▼▼ Hampton Inn & Suites by Hilton-Halifax/Dartmouth **H**
(902) 406-7700. **$119-$169.** 65 Cromarty Dr B3B 0G2. Hwy 118 (Lakeview Dr) exit Wright Ave; in Dartmouth Crossing Outlet Mall. Int corridors. **Pets:** Other species. Designated rooms, service with restrictions, supervision. ECO SAVE 📶 ✕ 🏋 ❗ 🍴 🎿 ✕

ⒶⒶ ▼▼▼ Holiday Inn Halifax-Harbourview **H** ❖
(902) 463-1100. **$109-$159.** 101 Wyse Rd B3A 1L9. Adjacent to Angus L MacDonald Bridge. Int corridors. **Pets:** Medium. $25 one-time fee/room. Designated rooms, no service, supervision. ECO SAVE 📶 ✕ 🏋 ❗ 🍴 🍴 🎿

ⒶⒶ ▼▼▼ Park Place Hotel & Conference Centre Ramada Plaza **H** ❖
(902) 468-8888. **$120-$160.** 240 Brownlow Ave B3B 1X6. From A. Murray MacKay Bridge, 0.7 mi (1.2 km) n on Hwy 111 exit 3 (Burnside Dr). Int corridors. **Pets:** Small. $50 deposit/pet. Designated rooms, service with restrictions, supervision. ECO SAVE 📶 🏋 ❗ 🍴 🍴 🎿 ✕

ⒶⒶ ▼▼ Quality Inn Halifax/Dartmouth **H** ❖
(902) 469-5850. **$120-$130.** 313 Prince Albert Rd B2Y 1N3. Hwy 111 exit 6A, 1 blk s. Int corridors. **Pets:** Medium, other species. Designated rooms, service with restrictions, supervision. SAVE 📶 ✕ ❗ 🍴 🍴

▼▼ Super 8 Hotel-Dartmouth **H**
(902) 463-9520. **$90-$149.** 65 King St B2Y 4C2. Corner of King and Queen sts; center of downtown. Int corridors. **Pets:** Accepted. ECO 📶 ❗ 🍴

ⒶⒶ ▼▼▼ Travelodge Suites Dartmouth **H** ❖
(902) 465-4000. **$105-$135.** 101 Yorkshire Ave Ext B3A 0C5. Hwy 111 exit Princess Margaret Blvd; at toll booth for A. Murray MacKay Bridge. Int corridors. **Pets:** Medium. $150 deposit/pet, $25 one-time fee/pet. Designated rooms, service with restrictions, supervision. ECO SAVE 📶 ✕ ❗ 🍴

DIGBY

ⒶⒶ ▼▼▼ Admiral Digby Inn & Cottages **H**
(902) 245-2531. **$99-$129.** 441 Shore Rd B0V 1A0. Hwy 101 exit 26, 1.5 mi (2.5 km) n, follow Saint John Ferry signs, then 3 mi (5 km) w on Victoria Rd; just e of ferry terminal. Ext corridors. **Pets:** $20 daily fee/room. Designated rooms, service with restrictions, supervision. SAVE 📶 ✕ ❗ 🍴 🍴 🎿

ⒶⒶ ▼▼▼ Digby Pines Golf Resort and Spa **H** ❖
(902) 245-2511. **$182-$338, 3 day notice.** 103 Shore Rd B0V 1A0. Hwy 101 exit 26, 1.5 mi (2.5 km) n, follow Saint John Ferry signs, 1.5 mi (2.5 km) w on Victoria Rd, follow signs; 1.2 mi (2 km) e of ferry terminal. Ext/int corridors. **Pets:** $25 daily fee/room. Designated rooms, service with restrictions. ECO SAVE 📶 ✕ 🏋 ❗ 🍴 🍴 🎿 ✕

▼▼▼▼ Dockside Suites **H**
(902) 245-4950. **$89-$159.** 34 Water St B0V 1A0. Center; in Fundy Complex. Ext/int corridors. **Pets:** $10 daily fee/pet. Service with restrictions. 📶 ✕ ❗ 🍴 🍴

HALIFAX

ⒶⒶ ▼▼▼▼ Atlantica Hotel Halifax **H**
(902) 423-1161. **$119-$260.** 1980 Robie St B3H 3G5. Jct Quinpool St. Int corridors. **Pets:** Medium. Service with restrictions, supervision. ECO SAVE 📶 ✕ ❗ 🍴 🍴 🎿 ✕

ⒶⒶ ▼▼▼▼ BEST WESTERN PLUS Chocolate Lake Hotel **H** ❖
(902) 477-5611. **$119-$129, 30 day notice.** 20 St. Margaret's Bay Rd B3N 1J4. 0.4 mi (0.7 km) e of Armdale Rotary. Ext/int corridors. **Pets:** Large, other species. Designated rooms, service with restrictions, supervision. ECO SAVE 📶 ✕ 🏋 ❗ 🍴 🍴 ❖ ✕

ⒶⒶ ▼▼▼ Cambridge Suites Hotel **H** ❖
(902) 420-0555. **$129-$229.** 1583 Brunswick St B3J 3P5. Corner of Brunswick and Sackville sts. Int corridors. **Pets:** Other species. $25 one-time fee/room. Supervision. ECO SAVE 📶 ✕ 🏋 ❗ 🍴 🍴 ✕

▼▼ Chebucto Inn **H**
(902) 453-4330. **$85.** 6151 Lady Hammond Rd B3K 2R9. Jct Hwy 111 and Rt 2 (Bedford Hwy), 0.4 mi (0.7 km) e. Ext corridors. **Pets:** Accepted. 📶 🍴

ⒶⒶ ▼▼▼ Comfort Inn Halifax **H**
(902) 443-0303. **$99-$169.** 560 Bedford Hwy B3M 2L8. On Rt 2 (Bedford Hwy), 6 mi (9.6 km) w. Int corridors. **Pets:** $10 one-time fee/pet. Service with restrictions, supervision. SAVE 📶 🏋 ❗ 🍴 🍴

▼▼▼ Delta Barrington **H** ❖
(902) 429-7410. **$139-$239.** 1875 Barrington St B3J 3L6. Between Cogswell and Duke sts. Int corridors. **Pets:** Other species. $35 one-time fee/room. Service with restrictions, supervision. ECO 📶 ✕ ❗ 🍴 🍴 🎿 ✕

▼▼▼▼ Delta Halifax **H** ❖
(902) 425-6700. **$115-$209.** 1990 Barrington St B3J 1P2. Corner of Cogswell and Barrington sts. Int corridors. **Pets:** Other species. $35 one-time fee/room. Service with restrictions, supervision. ECO 📶 🏋 ❗ 🍴 🍴 🎿 ✕

ⒶⒶ ▼▼▼ Esquire Motel Ⓜ

(902) 835-3367. **$79-$145.** 771 Bedford Hwy B4A 1A1. Hwy 102 exit 4A, 3.3 mi (5.3 km) e on Rt 2 (Bedford Hwy). Ext corridors. **Pets:** $10 daily fee/room. Service with restrictions, supervision.

🆂🅰🆅🅴 📶 📵 🔌 🛏 🏊 🅰🅲

ⒶⒶ ▼▼▼▼ Four Points by Sheraton Halifax Ⓗ ❀

(902) 423-4444. **$100-$220.** 1496 Hollis St B3J 3Z1. Between Salter and Bishop sts. Int corridors. **Pets:** Medium, dogs only. Designated rooms, service with restrictions, supervision.

🅴🅲🅾 🆂🅰🆅🅴 📶 ❌ 🔌 🛏 🖥 🍽

▼▼▼▼ Future Inns Halifax Ⓗ

(902) 443-4333. **$119-$179.** 30 Fairfax Dr B3S 1P1. Hwy 102 exit 2A. Int corridors. **Pets:** Accepted. 📶 ❌ 🔌 🛏 🖥 🍽

ⒶⒶ ▼▼▼▼ ▼▼▼▼ Halifax Marriott Harbourfront Ⓗ

(902) 421-1700. **$169-$339.** 1919 Upper Water St B3J 3J5. Adjacent to historic properties and Casino Nova Scotia. Int corridors. **Pets:** $50 one-time fee/room. Supervision.

🅴🅲🅾 🆂🅰🆅🅴 📶 ❌ 🔌 🛏 🖥 🍽 🏊 ❌

▼▼▼ Holiday Inn Express Halifax Airport Ⓗ ❀

(902) 576-7600. **$139-$199.** 180 Pratt & Whitney Dr B2T 0A2. Hwy 102 exit 5A, 0.8 mi (1.2 km) e, then just n. Int corridors. **Pets:** Designated rooms, service with restrictions, supervision.

📶 ❌ 🔌 🛏 🖥 🏊

ⒶⒶ ▼▼▼▼ Holiday Inn Express Halifax/Bedford Ⓗ ❀

(902) 445-1100. **$99-$149.** 133 Kearney Lake Rd B3M 4P3. Hwy 102 exit 2. Int corridors. **Pets:** Medium. $25 one-time fee/room. Designated rooms, service with restrictions, supervision.

🅴🅲🅾 🆂🅰🆅🅴 📶 ❌ 🔌 🛏 🖥 🏊

ⒶⒶ ▼▼▼ Lakeview Inns & Suites Ⓗ ❀

(902) 450-3020. **$139-$299.** 98 Chain Lake Dr B3S 1A2. Hwy 102 exit 2A eastbound; Hwy 103 exit 2. Int corridors. **Pets:** Medium. $10 daily fee/pet. Service with restrictions, crate.

🅴🅲🅾 🆂🅰🆅🅴 📶 ❌ 🔌 🛏 🖥 🏊

ⒶⒶ ▼▼▼ The Lord Nelson Hotel & Suites Ⓗ

(902) 423-6331. **$189.** 1515 S Park St B3J 2L2. Corner of Park St and Spring Garden Rd. Int corridors. **Pets:** $25 deposit/room. Designated rooms, service with restrictions, supervision.

🅴🅲🅾 🆂🅰🆅🅴 📶 ❌ 🔌 🛏 🖥 🍽

ⒶⒶ ▼▼▼▼ ▼▼▼▼ The Prince George Hotel Ⓗ

(902) 425-1986. **$149-$279.** 1725 Market St B3J 3N9. Between Prince and Carmichael sts. Int corridors. **Pets:** Accepted.

🅴🅲🅾 🆂🅰🆅🅴 📶 ❌ 🔌 🛏 🖥 🍽 🏊 ❌

▼▼▼ Quality Inn & Suites Halifax Ⓗ ❀

(902) 444-6700. **$110-$160.** 980 Parkland Dr B3M 4Y7. Hwy 102 exit 2. Int corridors. **Pets:** Medium. Service with restrictions, supervision.

🅴🅲🅾 📶 ❌ 🔌 🛏 🖥 🏊 ❌

▼▼▼ Quality Inn Halifax Airport Ⓗ

(902) 873-3000. **$120-$170.** 60 Sky Blvd B2T 1K3. Hwy 102 exit 6. Int corridors. **Pets:** Medium. Service with restrictions, supervision.

🅴🅲🅾 📶 ❌ 🔌 🛏 🖥 🍽 🏊 ❌

ⒶⒶ ▼▼▼▼ Residence Inn by Marriott Halifax Downtown Ⓗ

(902) 422-0493. **$119-$229.** 1599 Grafton St B3J 2C3. Corner of Sackville St. Int corridors. **Pets:** Accepted.

🅴🅲🅾 🆂🅰🆅🅴 📶 ❌ 🔌 🛏 🖥

ⒶⒶ ▼▼▼▼ ▼▼▼▼ The Westin Nova Scotian Ⓗ

(902) 421-1000. **$139-$395.** 1181 Hollis St B3H 2P6. Between Barrington and Lower Water sts. Int corridors. **Pets:** Accepted.

🅴🅲🅾 🆂🅰🆅🅴 📶 ❌ 🔌 🖥 🍽 🏊 ❌

INGONISH BEACH

ⒶⒶ ▼▼▼▼ Keltic Lodge Resort & Spa Ⓗ ❀

(902) 285-2880. **$155-$345, 3 day notice.** Middle Head Peninsula B0C 1L0. In Cape Breton Highlands National Park; off Cabot Tr. Ext/int corridors. **Pets:** $25 one-time fee/room. Designated rooms, service with restrictions, crate. 🆂🅰🆅🅴 📶 ❌ 🔌 🛏 🖥 🍽 🏊 ❌

KEMPTVILLE

▼▼▼ Trout Point Lodge Ⓒ🅸

(902) 761-2142. **$139-$459, 21 day notice.** 189 Trout Point Rd B0W 1Y0. 6.6 mi (11 km) e on Rt 203, 2.1 mi (3.5 km) n on gravel entry road. Ext corridors. **Pets:** Accepted. 📶 ❌ 🔌 🛏 🍽 ❌ 🅰🅲

KENTVILLE

▼▼▼ Sun Valley Motel Ⓜ

(902) 678-7368. **$78-$98.** 843 Park St B4N 3V7. Hwy 101 exit 14, 0.5 mi (0.8 km) e on Rt 1. Ext corridors. **Pets:** Medium, dogs only. $5 deposit/pet. Designated rooms, service with restrictions, supervision.

📶 🔌 🛏 🅰🅲 ❌

KINGSTON

ⒶⒶ ▼▼▼ BEST WESTERN Aurora Inn Ⓗ

(902) 765-3306. **$140-$150.** 831 Main St B0P 1R0. Hwy 101 exit 17 to Rt 1, follow signs. Ext corridors. **Pets:** $10 one-time fee/pet. Supervision.

🆂🅰🆅🅴 📶 ❌ 🔌 🖥 🍽

LISCOMB

ⒶⒶ ▼▼▼ Liscombe Lodge Resort & Conference Centre Ⓗ

(902) 779-2307. **$140-$210, 3 day notice.** 2884 Hwy 7 (RR 1) B0J 2A0. On Hwy 7. Ext/int corridors. **Pets:** Designated rooms, service with restrictions, crate. 🆂🅰🆅🅴 📶 ❌ 🔌 🛏 🖥 🍽 🏊 ❌

LIVERPOOL

ⒶⒶ ▼▼▼▼ BEST WESTERN PLUS Liverpool Hotel & Conference Centre Ⓗ

(902) 354-2377. **$130-$140.** 63 Queens Place Dr B0T 1K0. Hwy 103 exit 19, just e. Int corridors. **Pets:** $20 one-time fee/room. Designated rooms, service with restrictions, crate. 🅴🅲🅾 🆂🅰🆅🅴 📶 ❌ 🔌 🛏 🖥 🏊

ⒶⒶ ▼▼▼ Lane's Privateer Inn Ⓗ

(902) 354-3456. **$85-$142.** 27 Bristol Ave B0T 1K0. Hwy 103 exit 19, 1.2 mi (2 km) se on Rt 8 and 3. Ext/int corridors. **Pets:** Accepted.

🆂🅰🆅🅴 📶 ❌ 🍽

LOWER ARGYLE

ⒶⒶ ▼▼▼▼ Ye Olde Argyler Lodge Ⓒ🅸

(902) 643-2500. **$100-$215, 3 day notice.** Rt 3 B0W 1W0. Hwy 103 exit 32, 4.5 mi (7.5 km) e. Int corridors. **Pets:** Other species. $25 one-time fee/pet. Designated rooms, service with restrictions.

🆂🅰🆅🅴 📶 ❌ 🍽

LUNENBURG

▼▼▼ The Homeport Motel Ⓜ

(902) 634-8234. **$89-$175.** 167 Victoria Rd B0J 2C0. 0.6 mi (1 km) w on Rt 3. Ext corridors. **Pets:** Accepted. 📶 ❌ 🔌 🖥

▼▼▼ Lunenburg Arms Hotel & Spa Ⓗ

(902) 640-4040. **$129-$299.** 94 Pelham St B0J 2C0. Corner of Pelham and Duke sts; center. Int corridors. **Pets:** $25 one-time fee/room. Service with restrictions, supervision. 📶 ❌ 🔌 🛏 🖥 🍽

MAHONE BAY

▼▼▼ Bayview Pines Country Inn Ⓑ🅱

(902) 624-9970. **$100-$135, 5 day notice.** 678 Oakland Rd B0J 2E0. Hwy 103 exit 10, 1.2 mi (2 km) w on Rt 3 to Kedy's Landing, then 3.6 mi (6 km) e of Mahone Bay. Ext/int corridors. **Pets:** Accepted.

📶 ❌ 🔌 🛏 🖥 🅰🅲 ❌

MAVILLETTE

◈ **Cape View Motel & Cottages** Ⓜ
(902) 645-2258. **Call for rates.** 124 John Doucette Rd B0W 2Y0. Rt 1, 19.2 mi (32 km) ne of Yarmouth; center. Ext corridors. **Pets:** Accepted.
🛜 ✕ 🛏 💻 🐾 ☎

MIDDLETON

◈◈ **Mid-Valley Motel** Ⓜ
(902) 825-3433. **Call for rates.** 121 Main St B0S 1P0. Hwy 101 exit 18, 0.6 mi (1 km) w on Rt 1. Ext corridors. **Pets:** Accepted. 🛜 🛏 ≋

NEW GLASGOW

◈◈ **Comfort Inn** Ⓗ ❖
(902) 755-6450. **$110-$160.** 740 Westville Rd B2H 2J8. On Hwy 289, just e of jct Trans-Canada Hwy 104 exit 23. Int corridors. **Pets:** Large. Designated rooms, service with restrictions, supervision.
Ⓔ🛜 🛏 💻

◈◈ **Travelodge Suites** Ⓗ ❖
(902) 928-1333. **$124-$137.** 700 Westville Rd B2H 2J8. On Hwy 289, just e of jct Trans-Canada Hwy 104 exit 23. Int corridors. **Pets:** Large. $25 one-time fee/pet. Designated rooms, service with restrictions, crate.
Ⓔ🛜 ✕ 🛏 💻

NEW HARBOUR

◈◈◈ **Lonely Rock Seaside Bungalows** Ⓒᴬ
(902) 387-2668. **$90-$230, 14 day notice.** 150 New Harbour Rd B0H 1T0. Rt 316, 0.4 mi (0.7 km) s. Ext corridors. **Pets:** Dogs only. $10 daily fee/pet. Designated rooms, supervision. 🛜 ✕ ♿ 🛏 💻 🐾

NORTH SYDNEY

Ⓒᴬᴬ ◈◈ **Clansman Motel** Ⓜ
(902) 794-7226. **$89-$125.** 9 Baird St B2A 0A9. Hwy 125 exit 2, just e on King St. Ext/int corridors. **Pets:** Other species. Designated rooms, service with restrictions. 🅢🅐🅥🅔 🛜 ♿ 🛏 💻 🍽 ≋

PARRSBORO

◈◈◈ **Gillespie House Inn** ᴮᴮ
(902) 254-3196. **Call for rates.** 358 Main St B0M 1S0. On Rt 2; center. Int corridors. **Pets:** Designated rooms, service with restrictions, supervision. 🛜 ✕ ♿ 🐾 🐾 ☎

◈◈◈ **The Sunshine Inn** Ⓜ
(902) 254-3135. **$89-$175.** Rt 2 B0M 1S0. 2 mi (3.2 km) n. Ext corridors. **Pets:** Accepted. 🛜 🛏 ✕ ☎

PICTOU

◈◈◈ **Caribou River Cottage** Ⓒᴬ
(902) 485-6352. **$80-$140, 7 day notice.** 1308 Shore Rd B0K 1H0. From PEI ferry terminal, 2.7 mi (4.5 km) w on Three Brooks Rd to Shore Rd. Ext corridors. **Pets:** Accepted. 🛜 ✕ 🛏 ✕ 🐾 ☎

Ⓒᴬᴬ ◈◈ **Pictou Lodge Beach Resort** Ⓗ ❖
(902) 485-4322. **$109-$425, 3 day notice.** 172 Lodge Rd B0K 1H0. 4.3 mi (7 km) nw on Braeshore Rd; midway between Pictou and PEI ferry terminal at Caribou. Ext corridors. **Pets:** Dogs only. $30 one-time fee/room. Designated rooms, service with restrictions, crate.
🅢🅐🅥🅔 🛜 ✕ 🛏 🍽 ≋ ✕

◈◈ **Willow House Inn** ᴮᴮ
(902) 485-5740. **Call for rates.** 11 Willow St B0K 1H0. Corner of Willow and Church sts; center. Int corridors. **Pets:** Dogs only. 🛜 ✕

PORT DUFFERIN

Ⓒᴬᴬ ◈◈ **Marquis of Dufferin Seaside Inn** Ⓜ
(902) 654-2696. **$94.** 25658 Hwy 7, RR 1 B0J 2R0. On Hwy 7. Ext corridors. **Pets:** Other species. Service with restrictions.
🅢🅐🅥🅔 🛜 ✕ 💻 ✕ 🐾 ☎

PORT HASTINGS

◈◈ **Canadas Best Value Inn - Port Hawkesbury/ Port Hastings** Ⓜ
(902) 625-0621. **Call for rates.** 373 Hwy 4 B9A 1M8. 1 mi (1.6 km) n; 1 mi (1.6 km) s of Canso Cswy. Ext corridors. **Pets:** Large, other species. Designated rooms, service with restrictions.
🛜 ✕ ♿ 🛏 💻 ≋

PORT HAWKESBURY

Ⓒᴬᴬ ◈◈ **Maritime Inn Port Hawkesbury** Ⓗ
(902) 625-0320. **$117-$199.** 717 Reeves St B9A 2S2. 4.2 mi (6.4 km) e of Canso Cswy on Hwy 4; opposite shopping center. Ext/int corridors.
Pets: Accepted. 🅢🅐🅥🅔 🛜 ✕ 🛏 💻 🍽 ≋

PORT HOOD

◈◈ **Haus Treuburg Country Inn & Cottages** Ⓒᴵ
(902) 787-2116. **$105-$210, 7 day notice.** 175 Main St B0E 2W0. Center. Ext/int corridors. **Pets:** Other species. Designated rooms, no service, supervision. 🛜 ✕ 🛏 💻 🍽 🐾

SCOTSBURN

◈◈◈ **Stonehame Lodge & Chalets** Ⓒᴬ
(902) 485-3468. **$85-$240, 14 day notice.** 310 Fitzpatrick Mountain Rd B0K 1R0. Rt 256, 7.5 mi (12 km) w of Pictou via Rt 376, last 1.2 mi (2 km) on gravel entry road. Ext corridors. **Pets:** Accepted.
🛜 ✕ ♿ 🛏 💻 ≋ ✕

SMITHS COVE

Ⓒᴬᴬ ◈◈ **Harbourview Inn** ᴮᴮ
(902) 245-5686. **$119-$179, 7 day notice.** 25 Harbourview Rd B0S 1S0. Hwy 101 exit 25 eastbound; exit 24 westbound. Ext/int corridors.
Pets: Medium, dogs only. $10 one-time fee/room. Service with restrictions, supervision. 🅢🅐🅥🅔 🛜 ✕ 🛏 💻 ≋ ✕

◈◈ **Hedley House Inn By The Sea** Ⓜ
(902) 245-2500. **$85-$135.** RR 1 B0S 1S0. Hwy 101 exit 25 eastbound; exit 24 westbound. Ext corridors. **Pets:** Accepted.
🛜 ✕ 🛏 💻 🐾 ☎

STELLARTON

Ⓒᴬᴬ ◈◈◈ **Holiday Inn Express Stellarton-New Glasgow** Ⓗ ❖
(902) 755-1020. **$129-$149.** 86 Lawrence Blvd B0K 1S0. Hwy 104 exit 24, just s, then 0.6 mi (1 km) w. Int corridors. **Pets:** Other species. $25 one-time fee/room. Designated rooms, service with restrictions, supervision. 🅢🅐🅥🅔 🛜 ✕ ♿ 🛏 💻 ≋ ✕

SYDNEY

Ⓒᴬᴬ ◈◈◈ **Cambridge Suites Hotel** Ⓗ ❖
(902) 562-6500. **$139-$239, 30 day notice.** 380 Esplanade B1P 1B1. Hwy 4, 3.1 mi (5 km) e of jct Hwy 125 exit 6E; downtown. Int corridors.
Pets: Other species. $25 one-time fee/pet. Service with restrictions, supervision. Ⓔ 🅢🅐🅥🅔 🛜 ✕ 🛏 💻 🍽 ✕

◈◈ **Comfort Inn** Ⓗ ❖
(902) 562-0200. **$107-$153.** 368 Kings Rd B1S 1A8. Hwy 4, 2.1 mi (3.5 km) e of jct Hwy 125 exit 6E. Int corridors. **Pets:** Service with restrictions, supervision. Ⓔ 🛜 🛏 💻

Ⓒᴬᴬ ◈◈◈ **Days Inn Sydney** Ⓗ
(902) 539-6750. **$105-$145.** 480 Kings Rd B1S 1A8. Hwy 4, 1.7 mi (2.8 km) e of jct Hwy 125 exit 6E. Int corridors. **Pets:** Other species. Service with restrictions. 🅢🅐🅥🅔 🛏 💻 🍽 ≋ ✕

◈◈◈ **Hampton by Hilton Sydney** Ⓗ
(902) 564-6555. **$129-$219.** 60 Maillard St B1S 3W3. Hwy 125 exit 7, 1.2 mi (2 km) n on Rt 327 to Membertou St, then just s. Int corridors.
Pets: Accepted. 🛜 ✕ ♿ 🛏 💻 ≋

▼▼▼ Holiday Inn Sydney - Waterfront H

(902) 562-7500. **Call for rates.** 300 Esplanade B1P 1A7. At Prince St; center. Int corridors. **Pets:** Accepted.

ECO 🛰 ✕ 🛏 🖵 🍴 ⇌ ✕

Ⓐ ▼▼ Quality Inn Sydney H

(902) 539-8101. **$100-$120.** 560 Kings Rd B1S 1B8. Hwy 4, 2 mi (3.3 km) e of jct Hwy 125. Int corridors. **Pets:** Accepted.

SAVE 🛰 ✕ 🛏 🖵 🍴 ⇌

TRURO

▼▼ Comfort Inn H

(902) 893-0330. **$100-$130.** 12 Meadow Dr B2N 5V4. Hwy 102 exit 14. Int corridors. **Pets:** Accepted. ECO 🛰 🛏 🖵

▼▼▼ Holiday Inn Hotel & Conference Centre
        Truro H 🐾

(902) 895-1651. **$129-$139.** 437 Prince St B2N 1E6. Just e of Willow St; center. Int corridors. **Pets:** Other species. $25 one-time fee/room. Designated rooms, service with restrictions, supervision.

ECO 🛰 ✕ 🛗M 🛏 🖵 🍴 ⇌

▼▼ Super 8 H 🐾

(902) 895-8884. **$89-$131.** 85 Treaty Tr B2N 5A9. Hwy 102 exit 13A. Int corridors. **Pets:** Medium. $10 daily fee/pet. Designated rooms, service with restrictions, supervision. ECO 🛰 🛗M 🛏 🖵 ⇌

WESTERN SHORE

Ⓐ ▼▼▼ Atlantica Hotel & Marina Oak Island H

(902) 627-2600. **$99-$189, 3 day notice.** 36 Treasure Dr B0J 3M0. Hwy 103 exit 9 or 10, follow signs on Rt 3; 6 mi (10 km) e of Mahone Bay. Int corridors. **Pets:** Accepted.

ECO SAVE 🛰 ✕ 🛗M 🛏 🖵 🍴 ⇌ ✕

WHITE POINT

▼▼▼ White Point Beach Resort H

(902) 354-2711. **$125-$325, 3 day notice.** 75 White Point Rd 2 B0T 1G0. Hwy 103 exit 20A westbound, 5 mi (8 km) w on Rt 3; exit 20 eastbound, 6 mi (10 km) e on Rt 3. Ext/int corridors. **Pets:** Other species. $25 one-time fee/room. ECO 🛰 ✕ 🛏 🖵 🍴 ⇌ ✕

WHYCOCOMAGH

▼▼▼ Keltic Quay Bayfront Lodge & Cottages Ⓒ🅐

(902) 756-1122. **$149-$299, 3 day notice.** 90 Main St B0E 3M0. Just se off Trans-Canada Hwy 105; center. Ext corridors. **Pets:** Dogs only. No service, supervision. 🛰 ✕ 🛗M 🛏 🖵 ✕ 🐾

WINDSOR

▼▼ Super 8 H

(902) 792-8888. **$120-$130.** 63 Cole Dr B0N 2T0. Hwy 101 exit 5A, just s. Int corridors. **Pets:** Medium, other species. $20 one-time fee/room. Designated rooms, service with restrictions.

ECO 🛰 ✕ 🛗M 🛏 🖵 ⇌

WOLFVILLE

Ⓐ ▼▼▼ Tattingstone Inn ⒷⒷ

(902) 542-7696. **$108-$188.** 620 Main St B4P 1E8. 0.4 mi (0.6 km) w on Rt 1. Ext/int corridors. **Pets:** Designated rooms, service with restrictions, supervision. SAVE 🛰 ✕ ⇌

YARMOUTH

Ⓐ ▼▼ BEST WESTERN Mermaid M

(902) 742-7821. **$116-$141.** 545 Main St B5A 1J6. Corner of Main St and Starrs Rd. Ext corridors. **Pets:** $10 daily fee/room. Designated rooms, service with restrictions, supervision. SAVE 🛰 🛏 🖵 ⇌ 🐾

▼▼ Comfort Inn H

(902) 742-1119. **$98-$170.** 96 Starrs Rd B5A 2T5. Jct Hwy 101 E and 3. Int corridors. **Pets:** Accepted. ECO 🛰 🛏 🖵

▼ Lakelawn Motel M

(902) 742-3588. **$59-$79.** 641 Main St B5A 1K2. 0.6 mi (1 km) n on Hwy 1. Ext/int corridors. **Pets:** $5 daily fee/pet. Service with restrictions, supervision. 🛰 ✕ 🛏 🍴 🐾 🎞

▼▼ Rodd Grand Yarmouth H

(902) 742-2446. **$95-$121.** 417 Main St B5A 4B2. Corner of Grand St. Int corridors. **Pets:** Accepted. ECO 🛰 ✕ 🛏 🖵 🍴 ⇌ ✕

▼▼ Voyageur Motel M

(902) 742-7157. **$79-$189, 3 day notice.** RR 1 B5A 4A5. 3 mi (4.8 km) ne on Hwy 1. Ext corridors. **Pets:** Accepted. 🛰 🛏 🐾

ONTARIO

CITY INDEX

AJAX

Super 8-Ajax

(905) 428-6884. **$99-$124.** 210 Westney Rd S L1S 7P9. Hwy 401 exit Westney Rd, 0.6 mi (1 km) s; jct Bayly St. Int corridors. **Pets:** Other species. $20 daily fee/pet. Designated rooms, service with restrictions.

ALGONQUIN PROVINCIAL PARK

Killarney Lodge

(705) 633-5551. **$358-$718, 3 day notice.** Hwy 60-Lake of Two Rivers-Algonquin P1H 2G9. 21 mi (33 km) into park from west gate; 14 mi (23 km) from east gate. Ext corridors. **Pets:** Large, dogs only. $25 daily fee/pet. Designated rooms, service with restrictions, crate.

ALLISTON

Red Pine Inn & Conference Centre

(705) 435-4381. **$125.** 497 Victoria St E L9R 1T9. 1.8 mi (3 km) e of King St. Ext/int corridors. **Pets:** Medium. $10 daily fee/pet. Designated rooms, service with restrictions, supervision.

ALTON

Millcroft Inn & Spa

(519) 941-8111. **$159-$299, 5 day notice.** 55 John St L7K 0C4. 2.5 mi (4 km) n off Hwy 136 from Hwy 24, 0.6 mi (1 km) w on Queen St E, then just n. Ext/int corridors. **Pets:** Accepted.

ARNPRIOR

Country Squire Motel

(613) 623-6556. **$59-$135, 3 day notice.** 111 Staye Court Dr K7S 0E8. Hwy 17 exit White Lake Rd, just n to Staye Court Dr, then just w. Ext corridors. **Pets:** Small, dogs only. $15 daily fee/pet. Service with restrictions, supervision.

Quality Inn

(613) 623-7991. **Call for rates.** 70 Madawaska Blvd K7S 1S5. Hwy 417 exit 180, 0.4 mi (0.7 km) n on CR 29, then 1.4 mi (2.3 km) w. Int corridors. **Pets:** $10 daily fee/pet. Service with restrictions, crate.

BANCROFT

BEST WESTERN Sword Motor Inn

(613) 332-2474. **$130-$136.** 146 Hastings St K0L 1C0. On Hwy 62 N; center. Ext/int corridors. **Pets:** Large, dogs only. $10 one-time fee/pet. Designated rooms, supervision.

BARRIE

Comfort Inn

(705) 722-3600. **$85-$130.** 75 Hart Dr L4N 5M3. Hwy 400 exit 96A E (Dunlop St). Int corridors. **Pets:** $100 deposit/room, $6 daily fee/pet. Designated rooms, service with restrictions, supervision.

Comfort Inn & Suites

(705) 721-1122. **$92-$113.** 210 Essa Rd L4N 3L1. Hwy 400 exit 94 (Essa Rd), just e. Int corridors. **Pets:** Other species. $50 deposit/room. Designated rooms, service with restrictions, crate.

Days Inn Barrie

(705) 733-8989. **$106-$153.** 60 Bryne Dr L4N 9Y4. Hwy 400 exit 94 (Essa Rd), just s, then just e. Int corridors. **Pets:** Accepted.

Holiday Inn Barrie-Hotel & Conference Centre

(705) 728-6191. **$99-$149.** 20 Fairview Rd L4N 4P3. Hwy 400 exit 94 (Essa Rd), just e. Int corridors. **Pets:** Small, other species. Designated rooms, service with restrictions, supervision.

Holiday Inn Express Hotel & Suites Barrie

(705) 725-1002. **$115-$149.** 506 Bryne Dr L4N 9P6. Hwy 400 exit 90 (Mapleview Dr), just sw. Int corridors. **Pets:** Medium. $15 one-time fee/room. Designated rooms, service with restrictions, supervision.

Horseshoe Resort

(705) 835-2790. **$99-$349, 8 day notice.** 1101 Horseshoe Valley Rd W L4M 4Y8. Hwy 400 exit 117 (Horseshoe Valley Rd), 3.8 mi (6 km) e. Int corridors. **Pets:** Other species. $15 daily fee/room. Designated rooms, service with restrictions, supervision.

Super 8 Barrie

(705) 814-8888. **$100-$130.** 441 Bryne Dr L4N 6C8. Hwy 400 exit 90 (Mapleview Dr), just nw. Int corridors. **Pets:** $15 one-time fee/pet. Designated rooms, service with restrictions, supervision.

Travelodge Barrie

(705) 734-9500. **$90.** 55 Hart Dr L4N 5M3. Hwy 400 exit 96A E (Dunlop St). Int corridors. **Pets:** Other species. $100 deposit/room. Designated rooms, service with restrictions, supervision.

BARRY'S BAY

Mountain View Motel M

(613) 756-2757. **$75-$190, 7 day notice.** 18508 Hwy 60 E K0J 1B0. 2.5 mi (4 km) e of town. Ext corridors. **Pets:** Other species. Supervision.

BAYFIELD

The Little Inn of Bayfield CI

(519) 565-2611. **$202-$405, 3 day notice.** 26 Main St N0M 1G0. Hwy 21 exit Main St; jct Catherine St. Int corridors. **Pets:** Dogs only. $50 one-time fee/pet. Designated rooms, service with restrictions, supervision.

BELLEVILLE

BEST WESTERN Belleville H

(613) 969-1112. **$129-$200.** 387 N Front St K8P 3C8. Hwy 401 exit 543A, 0.3 mi (0.5 km) s on Hwy 62. Int corridors. **Pets:** Accepted.

Comfort Inn H

(613) 966-7703. **Call for rates.** 200 N Park St K8P 2Y9. Hwy 401 exit 543A, 0.6 mi (1 km) s on Hwy 62. Int corridors. **Pets:** Accepted.

Travelodge Hotel Belleville H

(613) 968-3411. **$121-$163.** 11 Bay Bridge Rd K8P 3P6. 0.3 mi (0.5 km) s of Hwy 2 (Dundas St). Int corridors. **Pets:** Large, other species. $15 daily fee/pet. Service with restrictions.

BLIND RIVER

Lakeview Inn M

(705) 356-0800. **$89-$110, 3 day notice.** 143 Causley St P0R 1B0. On Hwy 17, just e of Hwy 557. Ext corridors. **Pets:** Small. $10 daily fee/pet. Designated rooms, service with restrictions, supervision.

BLUE MOUNTAINS

The Westin Trillium House, Blue Mountain H

(705) 443-8080. **$149-$389, 7 day notice.** 220 Gord Canning Dr L9Y 0V9. Jct Hwy 26 and Mountain Rd, 6.3 mi (10 km) w on Mountain Rd, just w on Jozo Weider Blvd, then just w. Int corridors. **Pets:** Medium, dogs only. Designated rooms, service with restrictions, supervision.

BOWMANVILLE

Holiday Inn Express & Suites Bowmanville H

(905) 697-8089. **$129-$159.** 37 Spicer Square L1C 5M2. Jct Hwy 401 and Waverly Rd N. Int corridors. **Pets:** Large, other species. $25 daily fee/pet. Service with restrictions, crate.

Howard Johnson Bowmanville H

(905) 623-8500. **$70-$150.** 160 Liberty St S L1C 2W4. Hwy 401 exit 432 (Liberty St), just n. Int corridors. **Pets:** Accepted.

BRACEBRIDGE

Travelodge Bracebridge M

(705) 645-2235. **$79-$189.** 320 Taylor Rd P1L 1K1. Hwy 11 exit 189 (Hwy 42/Taylor Rd), 0.6 mi (1 km) w. Ext corridors. **Pets:** Accepted.

BRAMPTON

Motel 6 Brampton #1902 H

(905) 451-3313. **$65-$75.** 160 Steelwell Rd L6T 5T3. Hwy 410 exit Steeles Ave E, s on Tomken Rd, then just w. Int corridors. **Pets:** Other species. Service with restrictions, supervision.

BRANTFORD

BEST WESTERN PLUS Brant Park Inn & Conference Centre H

(519) 753-8651. **$125-$144.** 19 Holiday Dr N3R 7J4. Jct Hwy 403 and Wayne Gretzky Pkwy. Int corridors. **Pets:** Medium, other species. $20 deposit/room. Designated rooms, service with restrictions, crate.

Comfort Inn H

(519) 753-3100. **$90-$130.** 58 King George Rd N3R 5K4. Just s of jct Hwy 403 and 24. Int corridors. **Pets:** Medium. Service with restrictions, supervision.

Days Inn H

(519) 759-2700. **$80-$159.** 460 Fairview Dr N3R 7A9. Hwy 403 exit Wayne Gretzky Pkwy, 0.5 mi (0.8 km) n. Int corridors. **Pets:** Other species. $15 one-time fee/room. Designated rooms, service with restrictions.

BRIGHTON

Timber House Country Inn CI

(613) 475-3304. **$95-$165.** 116 Cedardale Rd K0K 1H0. Jct 2 and 64, just w over swing bridge, follow signs. Int corridors. **Pets:** Accepted.

BROCKVILLE

BEST WESTERN White House Inn M

(613) 345-1622. **Call for rates.** 1843 Hwy 2 E K6V 5T1. Hwy 401 exit 698, 1.2 mi (1.9 km) s on N Augusta Rd, then 0.9 mi (1.5 km) e. Ext corridors. **Pets:** Accepted.

Comfort Inn H

(613) 345-0042. **$130-$200.** 7777 Kent Blvd K6V 6N7. Hwy 401 exit 696, just nw. Int corridors. **Pets:** $15 daily fee/pet. Designated rooms, service with restrictions, crate.

BURLINGTON

Admiral Inn H

(905) 639-4780. **$95-$105.** 3500 Billings Ct L7N 3N6. QEW exit Walkers Line westbound, just s to Harvester Rd, then just w to S Service Rd; exit Guelph Line Rd eastbound, just s to Harvester Rd, then just e to S Service Rd. Int corridors. **Pets:** Accepted.

Comfort Inn H

(905) 639-1700. **Call for rates.** 3290 S Service Rd L7N 3M6. QEW exit Walkers Line westbound, just s to Harvester Rd, then just w; exit Guelph Line Rd eastbound, just s to Harvester Rd, then just e. Int corridors. **Pets:** Designated rooms, service with restrictions, supervision.

Homewood Suites by Hilton H

(905) 631-8300. **$134-$251.** 975 Syscon Rd L7L 5S3. QEW exit Burloak Dr, s to Harvester Rd, then w. Int corridors. **Pets:** Accepted.

Motel 6 Burlington #1900 H

(905) 331-1955. **$65-$75.** 4345 N Service Rd L7L 4X7. QEW exit Walker's Line N to N Service Rd, 0.9 mi (1.4 km) e. Int corridors. **Pets:** Other species. Service with restrictions, supervision.

Quality Hotel Burlington H

(905) 639-9290. **$100-$180.** 950 Walker's Line L7N 2G2. QEW exit Walker's Line, just s. Int corridors. **Pets:** Small. $25 deposit/room. Designated rooms, service with restrictions, supervision.

Waterfront Hotel - Downtown Burlington H

(905) 681-5400. **$149-$199.** 2020 Lakeshore Rd L7R 4G8. Corner of Brant St; downtown. Int corridors. **Pets:** $10 daily fee/room. Designated rooms, service with restrictions.

CAMBRIDGE

CAA ◆◆◆◆ **Cambridge Hotel Conference Centre H**
(519) 622-1505. **$105-$140, 30 day notice.** 700 Hespeler Rd N3H 5L8. Hwy 401 exit 282, just s. Int corridors. **Pets:** Accepted.

CAA ◆◆◆ **Comfort Inn H**
(519) 658-1100. **$95-$130.** 220 Holiday Inn Dr N3C 1Z4. Hwy 401 exit 282, just n to Groh Ave. Int corridors. **Pets:** Accepted.

◆◆◆◆ **Homewood Suites by Hilton Cambridge/Waterloo H** ✿
(519) 651-2888. **$174-$204.** 800 Jamieson Pkwy N3C 4N6. Hwy 401 exit 286 (Townline Rd), just n. Int corridors. **Pets:** Medium. $75 one-time fee/room. Service with restrictions, crate.

CAA ◆◆◆◆◆ **Langdon Hall Country House Hotel & Spa CI** ✿
(519) 740-2100. **$289-$659, 3 day notice.** 1 Langdon Dr N3H 4R8. Hwy 401 exit 275, 0.8 mi (1.3 km) se on Fountain St, then 0.6 mi (1 km) s on Blair Rd, follow signs. Ext/int corridors. **Pets:** Other species. Designated rooms, service with restrictions.

◆◆◆ **Super 8 Cambridge H**
(519) 622-1070. **$90-$115.** 650 Hespeler Rd N1R 6J8. Hwy 401 exit 282, 0.6 mi (1 km) s. Int corridors. **Pets:** Dogs only. $10 daily fee/pet. Service with restrictions, supervision.

CHATHAM

◆◆◆ **Comfort Inn H**
(519) 352-5500. **$92-$120.** 1100 Richmond St N7M 5J5. Hwy 401 exit 81 (Bloomfield Rd), 3.1 mi (5 km) n. Int corridors. **Pets:** Other species. Service with restrictions, supervision.

◆◆◆◆ **Holiday Inn Express & Suites H**
(519) 351-1100. **$139-$179.** 575 Richmond St N7M 1R2. Hwy 401 exit 81 (Bloomfield Rd) to jct Hwy 2, 0.9 mi (1.5 km) e, then 0.9 mi (1.5 km) w. Int corridors. **Pets:** Accepted.

CHATSWORTH

◆◆◆ **Key Motel M**
(519) 794-2350. **$75-$85.** 317051 Hwy 6/10 N0H 1G0. On SR 6 and 10. Ext/int corridors. **Pets:** Accepted.

COBOURG

CAA ◆◆◆◆ **BEST WESTERN PLUS Cobourg Inn & Convention Centre H** ✿
(905) 372-2105. **$157-$169, 3 day notice.** 930 Burnham St K9A 2X9. Hwy 401 exit 472 (Burnham St S). Int corridors. **Pets:** Other species. Service with restrictions, supervision.

◆◆◆ **Comfort Inn H**
(905) 372-7007. **$100-$130.** 121 Densmore Rd K9A 4J9. Hwy 401 exit 474, just se. Int corridors. **Pets:** Accepted.

CORNWALL

CAA ◆◆◆◆ **BEST WESTERN PLUS Parkway Inn & Conference Centre H**
(613) 932-0451. **$140-$170.** 1515 Vincent Massey Dr K6H 5R6. Hwy 401 exit 789 (Brookdale Ave), 1.8 mi (2.8 km) s, then just w. Int corridors. **Pets:** Medium. $10 daily fee/room. Designated rooms, service with restrictions, supervision.

◆◆◆ **Comfort Inn-Cornwall H**
(613) 937-0111. **$114-$169.** 1625 Vincent Massey Dr K6H 5R6. Hwy 401 exit 789 (Brookdale Ave), 1.8 mi (2.8 km) s, then 0.4 mi (0.7 km) w. Int corridors. **Pets:** $20 one-time fee/room. Designated rooms, supervision.

DRYDEN

CAA ◆◆◆◆ **BEST WESTERN PLUS Dryden Hotel & Conference Centre H**
(807) 223-3201. **$146-$156.** 349 Government St P8N 2P4. On Hwy 17. Int corridors. **Pets:** Other species. $10 daily fee/room. Designated rooms, service with restrictions, supervision.

◆◆ **Comfort Inn M**
(807) 223-3893. **$120-$129.** 522 Government St P8N 2P7. On Hwy 17. Int corridors. **Pets:** Accepted.

FONTHILL

◆ **Hipwell's Motel M**
(905) 892-3588. **$45-$75.** 299 Reg Rd 20 W L0S 1E0. 1 mi (1.6 km) w; center. Ext corridors. **Pets:** Dogs only. $5 daily fee/pet. Designated rooms, service with restrictions, supervision.

FORT FRANCES

CAA ◆◆◆ **La Place Rendez-Vous H**
(807) 274-9811. **$104-$114.** 1201 Idylwild Dr, B2-RR 2 P9A 3M3. Hwy 11, just e on Lake Rd; east end of town. Int corridors. **Pets:** Medium. $10 one-time fee/room. Designated rooms, service with restrictions, supervision.

◆◆ **Super 8 H**
(807) 274-4945. **$106-$179.** 810 Kings Hwy P9A 2X4. On Hwy 11. Int corridors. **Pets:** Other species. $10 one-time fee/pet. Designated rooms, service with restrictions, crate.

FRENCH RIVER

CAA ◆ **French River Trading Post Motel M**
(705) 857-2115. **$81-$95, 3 day notice.** 20112 Hwy 69 P0M 1A0. Trans-Canada Hwy 69, 0.6 mi (1 km) n of French River Bridge. Ext corridors. **Pets:** $10 daily fee/pet. Designated rooms, service with restrictions, supervision.

GANANOQUE

CAA ◆◆◆◆ **BEST WESTERN Country Squire Resort H**
(613) 382-3511. **$70-$190.** 715 King St E K7G 1H4. Hwy 401 exit 647 eastbound; exit 648 westbound, 0.6 mi (1 km) w on Hwy 2 (King St). Ext/int corridors. **Pets:** Accepted.

CAA ◆◆◆ **Comfort Inn 1000 Islands M**
(613) 382-4728. **Call for rates.** 785 King St E K7G 1H4. Hwy 401 exit 647 eastbound; exit 648 westbound, 0.3 mi (0.5 km) w on Hwy 2 (King St). Ext/int corridors. **Pets:** $15 daily fee/room. Designated rooms, service with restrictions.

CAA ◆◆◆ **Holiday Inn Express & Suites 1000 Islands H**
(613) 382-8338. **$99-$269.** 777 King St E K7G 1H4. Just w of jct Hwy 2 (King St), 401 and 1000 Islands Pkwy. Int corridors. **Pets:** $15 daily fee/room. Designated rooms, service with restrictions, supervision.

◆◆◆ **Quality Inn & Suites 1000 Islands M**
(613) 382-1453. **Call for rates.** 650 King St E K7G 1H3. Hwy 401 exit 647 eastbound; exit 648 westbound, 0.6 mi (1 km) w on Hwy 2 (King St). Ext corridors. **Pets:** Accepted.

◆◆ **Ramada Provincial Inn M**
(613) 382-2038. **$89-$229.** 846 King St E K7G 1H3. Hwy 401 exit 647 eastbound; exit 648 westbound, 0.3 mi (0.5 km) w on Hwy 2 (King St). Ext corridors. **Pets:** Accepted.

◆◆◆ **Trinity House Inn CI**
(613) 382-8383. **$99-$250, 7 day notice.** 90 Stone St S K7G 1Z8. Corner of Pine St; center. Int corridors. **Pets:** Designated rooms, service with restrictions, crate.

GEORGETOWN

(AA) ▼▼▼ BEST WESTERN Inn On The Hill **H**
(905) 877-6986. **$99-$149.** 365 Guelph St (Hwy 7) L7G 4B6. At Delrex Blvd. Ext corridors. **Pets:** Medium. $20 daily fee/room. Designated rooms, service with restrictions, supervision. (SAVE) 📶 🛎 💻

GRAVENHURST

▼▼▼ Residence Inn by Marriott Gravenhurst Muskoka Wharf **H** 🐾
(705) 687-6600. **$129-$279.** 285 Steamship Bay Rd P1P 1Z9. Hwy 11 exit 169 (Bethune Dr), follow signs. Int corridors. **Pets:** Medium. $100 one-time fee/room. Service with restrictions, supervision.
📶 ✕ 🛗 🛎 💻 ⇌

GRIMSBY

(AA) ▼▼▼ Super 8-Grimsby **H**
(905) 309-8800. **$106-$126.** 11 Windward Dr L3M 4E9. QEW exit 74 (Casablanca Blvd N). **Pets:** Medium, other species. $10 daily fee/pet. Service with restrictions, crate.
(SAVE) 📶 ✕ 🛎 💻 ⇌

GUELPH

(AA) ▼▼▼ BEST WESTERN PLUS Royal Brock Hotel & Conference Centre **H**
(519) 836-1240. **$110-$112.** 716 Gordon St N1G 1Y6. Jct Stone Rd; 5 mi (8 km) n of Hwy 401 via Brock Rd. Int corridors. **Pets:** Accepted.
(SAVE) 📶 ✕ 🛎 💻 ⫪ ⇌

(AA) ▼▼▼ Comfort Inn Guelph **H**
(519) 763-1900. **$90-$110.** 480 Silvercreek Pkwy N1H 7R5. Jct Hwy 6 and 7. Int corridors. **Pets:** Accepted. (ECO) (SAVE) 📶 🛎 💻

(AA) ▼▼▼ Days Inn-Guelph **H**
(519) 822-9112. **$92-$160.** 785 Gordon St N1G 1Y8. Hwy 401 exit 299 (Brock Rd), 7 mi (11.5 km) n. Int corridors. **Pets:** Service with restrictions, supervision. (ECO) (SAVE) 📶 ✕ 🛎 💻

(AA) ▼▼▼ Delta Guelph Hotel and Conference Centre **H** 🐾
(519) 780-3700. **$129-$219.** 50 Stone Rd W N1G 0A9. Jct Gordon St. Int corridors. **Pets:** $35 one-time fee/room. Designated rooms, service with restrictions, supervision. (ECO) 📶 ✕ 🛗 🛎 💻 ⫪

(AA) ▼▼▼ Holiday Inn Guelph Hotel & Conference Centre **H** 🐾
(519) 836-0231. **$99-$169.** 601 Scottsdale Dr N1G 3E7. Jct Hwy 6 N and Stone Rd E; 5 mi (8 km) n of jct Hwy 401. Int corridors. **Pets:** Medium, other species. $35 one-time fee/room. Designated rooms, service with restrictions, crate. (ECO) (SAVE) 📶 🛎 💻 ⫪ ⇌ ✕

(AA) ▼▼▼ Staybridge Suites **H**
(519) 767-3300. **$115-$150.** 11 Corporate Ct N1G 5G5. Jct Hwy 6 and Laird St, just e. Int corridors. **Pets:** Accepted.
(ECO) (SAVE) 📶 🛗 🛎 💻 ⇌

(AA) ▼▼▼ Super 8-Guelph **M**
(519) 836-5850. **$90-$116.** 281 Woodlawn Rd W N1H 7K7. Jct Hwy 6 and 7. Ext/int corridors. **Pets:** Small. $10 daily fee/pet. Designated rooms, service with restrictions, supervision. (SAVE) 📶 🛎 💻 ⫪

HALIBURTON

▼▼ Lakeview Motel **M**
(705) 457-1027. **$124-$260, 5 day notice.** 4951 CR 21 K0M 1S0. Jct Hwy 118, 1.6 mi (2.5 km) w. Ext corridors. **Pets:** Accepted.
📶 ✕ 🛎 💻 ⫪ ⇌

(AA) ▼▼▼ Pinestone Resort, Conference Centre, Spa & Golf Course **H**
(705) 457-1800. **$129-$259, 3 day notice.** 4252 County Rd 21 K0M 1S0. 3.8 mi (6 km) s of town. Ext/int corridors. **Pets:** Accepted.
(ECO) (SAVE) 📶 ✕ 🛎 💻 ⫪ ⇌ ✕

HAMILTON

(AA) ▼▼▼▼ Sheraton Hamilton Hotel **H**
(905) 529-5515. **$127-$359.** 116 King St W L8P 4V3. Between Bay and James sts; downtown. Int corridors. **Pets:** Accepted.
(SAVE) 📶 ✕ 🛗 🛎 💻 ⫪ ⇌

(AA) ▼▼▼▼ Staybridge Suites - Hamilton Downtown **H**
(905) 527-1001. **Call for rates.** 20 Caroline St S L8P 0B1. Between Main and King sts. Int corridors. **Pets:** Accepted.
(SAVE) 📶 ✕ 🛎 💻 ⇌

▼▼ Super 8-Hamilton Airport/Mount Hope **H**
(905) 679-3355. **$90-$105.** 2975 Homestead Dr L0R 1W0. Jct Hwy 6 S (Upper James St) and Homestead Dr. Int corridors. **Pets:** $10 daily fee/pet. Designated rooms, service with restrictions, supervision.
📶 🛎 💻

HUNTSVILLE

▼▼ Comfort Inn **H** 🐾
(705) 789-1701. **$94-$164.** 86 King William St P1H 1E4. Int corridors. **Pets:** Other species. Designated rooms, service with restrictions, supervision. (ECO) 📶 🛎 💻

(AA) ▼▼▼ Deerhurst Resort **H**
(705) 789-6411. **$119-$339, 7 day notice.** 1235 Deerhurst Dr P1H 2E8. Jct Hwy 11, 4.3 mi (7 km) e on Hwy 60 to Deerhurst Canal Rd (CR 23), then 1.2 mi (2 km), follow signs. Ext/int corridors. **Pets:** $50 one-time fee/room. Designated rooms, supervision.
(ECO) (SAVE) 📶 ✕ 🛎 💻 ⫪ ⇌ ✕

▼▼▼ Hidden Valley Resort, an Ascend Collection hotel **H**
(705) 789-2301. **$89-$179, 3 day notice.** 1755 Valley Rd P1H 1Z8. Jct Hwy 11, 4 mi (6.5 km) e on Hwy 60 to Canal Rd, follow signs. Int corridors. **Pets:** Medium. $35 one-time fee/room. Designated rooms, service with restrictions, supervision. 📶 ✕ 🛎 💻 ⫪ ⇌ ✕

▼▼▼ Holiday Inn Express Hotel & Suites **H** 🐾
(705) 788-9500. **$110-$200.** 100 Howland Dr P1H 2P9. Jct Hwy 11 and 60, just se. Int corridors. **Pets:** $25 one-time fee/room. Designated rooms, supervision. 📶 ✕ 🛎 💻 ⇌

▼▼ Motel 6-Huntsville **H**
(705) 787-0118. **Call for rates.** 70 Howland Dr P1H 2P9. Jct Hwy 11 and 60, just se. Int corridors. **Pets:** Other species. Service with restrictions, supervision. (ECO) 📶 🛎 ⇌

▼▼ Travelodge **H**
(705) 789-5504. **$80-$120.** 225 Main St W P1H 1Y1. Hwy 11 exit 219 (Muskoka Rd 3), just e. Int corridors. **Pets:** Accepted.
📶 ✕ 🛎 💻

▼ Tulip Inn **M**
(705) 789-4001. **$69-$140, 3 day notice.** 211 Arrowhead Park Rd P1H 2J4. Hwy 11 exit 226 (Muskoka Rd 3), follow signs for Arrowhead Park. Ext corridors. **Pets:** Other species. Service with restrictions, supervision.
📶 🛎 💻

IGNACE

(AA) ▼ Trading Post Motel **M**
(807) 934-2386. **$65-$79.** 1001 Main St, Hwy 17 E P0T 1T0. On Hwy 17, east end of town. Ext corridors. **Pets:** Other species. Supervision.
(SAVE) 📶 🛎 💻

INGERSOLL

▼▼▼ Comfort Inn & Suites **H**
(519) 425-1100. **$90-$140.** 20 Samnah Cres N5C 3J7. Hwy 401 exit 216 (Culloden Rd). Int corridors. **Pets:** Accepted. 📶 🛎 💻 ⇌

JACKSONS POINT

◆◆◆◆ The Briars Resort and Spa 🄷

(905) 722-3271. **$159-$450, 21 day notice.** 55 Hedge Rd, RR 1 L0E 1L0. Hwy 48, through Sutton to Jacksons Point, 0.6 mi (1 km) e. Ext/int corridors. **Pets:** Accepted.

KAPUSKASING

◆◆ Comfort Inn 🄷

(705) 335-8583. **$109-$119.** 172 Government Rd E P5N 2W9. Hwy 11; corner of Brunelle Rd. Int corridors. **Pets:** Accepted. 🄴🄲🄾 📶 🔋 💻

◆◆◆◆ Super 8 🄷 🐾

(705) 335-8887. **$110-$145.** 430 Government Rd P5N 2X7. Hwy 11. Int corridors. **Pets:** Other species. $10 one-time fee/room. Designated rooms, service with restrictions, supervision.
🅂🄰🅅🄴 📶 ✕ 🔋 💻 ➷ ✕

KENORA

◆◆ BEST WESTERN Lakeside Inn & Conference Centre 🄷 🐾

(807) 468-5521. **$122-$165.** 470 1st Ave S P9N 1W5. Just s on 4th Ave S from jct Hwy 17. Int corridors. **Pets:** Other species. $100 deposit/room, $15 daily fee/room. Designated rooms, service with restrictions, supervision. 🄴🄲🄾 🅂🄰🅅🄴 📶 ✕ 🔋 💻 🍴 ➷

◆◆ Comfort Inn 🄼

(807) 468-8845. **$101-$152.** 1230 Hwy 17 E P9N 1L9. 0.9 mi (1.5 km) e of town. Int corridors. **Pets:** Accepted. 📶 🔋 💻

KILLALOE

◆◆◆◆ Annie's Inn Bed & Breakfast 🄱🄱

(613) 757-0950. **$75-$200, 7 day notice.** 67 Roche St K0J 2A0. Hwy 60 exit Maple St, 1 blk to Roche St, then w; driveway entrance is at the end of the street. Int corridors. **Pets:** Accepted. ✕ 🔋 💻 ✓

KINCARDINE

◆◆◆◆ BEST WESTERN PLUS Governor's Inn 🄷

(519) 396-8242. **$149-$165.** 791 Durham St N2Z 1M4. Jct Hwy 21. Int corridors. **Pets:** Medium, dogs only. $20 daily fee/room. Designated rooms, service with restrictions, supervision.
🅂🄰🅅🄴 📶 ✕ 🔋 💻 🍴 ✕

◆◆◆◆ Holiday Inn Express and Suites-Kincardine 🄷

(519) 395-3545. **Call for rates.** 2 Millenium Way N2Z 0B5. Jct Hwy 21. Int corridors. **Pets:** Accepted. 📶 ✕ 🄼 🔋 💻 ➷

KINGSTON

◆◆◆◆ BEST WESTERN PLUS Fireside Inn 🄷

(613) 549-2211. **$139-$179.** 1217 Princess St K7M 3E1. Hwy 401 exit 615 (Sir John A MacDonald Blvd), 2.5 mi (4 km) sw. Int corridors. **Pets:** Medium, dogs only. $10 deposit/pet. Designated rooms, service with restrictions, supervision. 🅂🄰🅅🄴 📶 ✕ 🔋 💻 🍴 ✕

◆◆◆ Comfort Inn Hwy 401 🄷 🐾

(613) 546-9500. **Call for rates.** 55 Warne Cres K7K 6Z5. Hwy 401 exit 617 (Division St), just s to Dalton Ave. Int corridors. **Pets:** Service with restrictions, crate. 🄴🄲🄾 🅂🄰🅅🄴 📶 🔋 💻

◆◆ Comfort Inn Midtown 🄷

(613) 549-5550. **$104-$129.** 1454 Princess St K7M 3E5. Hwy 401 exit 613 (Sydenham Rd), 2.5 mi (4 km) se. Int corridors. **Pets:** Accepted.
🄴🄲🄾 📶 🔋 💻

◆◆ Confederation Place Hotel 🄷 🐾

(613) 549-6300. **$89-$189.** 237 Ontario St K7L 2Z4. Center of downtown. Int corridors. **Pets:** $15 daily fee/pet. Designated rooms, service with restrictions, supervision. 📶 🔋 💻 ➷

◆◆◆ The Executive Inn & Suites 🄼

(613) 549-1620. **$99-$149, 3 day notice.** 794 Hwy 2 E K7L 4V1. Hwy 401 exit 623, 5 mi (8 km) s, then 1.3 mi (2 km) e. Ext corridors.
Pets: Accepted. 📶 ✕ 🔋 💻 ➷

◆◆◆◆ Holiday Inn Kingston-Waterfront 🄷

(613) 549-8400. **$129-$249.** 2 Princess St K7L 1A2. Corner of Ontario St; center of downtown. Int corridors. **Pets:** Other species. $35 daily fee/room. Designated rooms, service with restrictions, supervision.
🄴🄲🄾 🅂🄰🅅🄴 📶 ✕ 🄼 🔋 💻 🍴 ➷ ✕

◆◆◆ Motel 6 Kingston 🄷

(613) 507-6666. **$59-$129.** 1542 Robinson Ct K7L 4V2. Hwy 401 exit 611, just s. Int corridors. **Pets:** Other species. Service with restrictions, supervision. 🄴🄲🄾 📶 ✕ 🄼 🔋

◆◆◆ Peachtree Inn 🄷 🐾

(613) 546-4411. **Call for rates.** 1187 Princess St K7M 3E1. Hwy 401 exit 615 (Sir John A MacDonald Blvd), 2.5 mi (4 km) sw. Int corridors. **Pets:** Other species. $20 one-time fee/pet. 🅂🄰🅅🄴 📶 ✕ 🔋 💻

◆◆◆◆ Residence Inn by Marriott Kingston Water's Edge 🄷

(613) 544-4888. **$152-$227.** 7 Earl St K7L 0A4. Hwy 401 exit 617 (Division St) to Princess St, right on King St, then left, 2 blks w of city hall. Int corridors. **Pets:** Other species. $100 one-time fee/room. Service with restrictions. 📶 ✕ 🄼 🔋 💻 🍴 ➷ ✕

KIRKLAND LAKE

◆◆ Comfort Inn 🄷 🐾

(705) 567-4909. **$150-$185.** 455 Government Rd W P0K 1A0. On Hwy 66. Int corridors. **Pets:** Other species. Service with restrictions.
🄴🄲🄾 📶 🔋 💻

KITCHENER

◆◆◆ Delta Kitchener-Waterloo 🄷

(519) 744-4141. **Call for rates.** 105 King St E N2G 2K8. Corner of King and Benton sts; downtown. Int corridors. **Pets:** Accepted.
🄴🄲🄾 📶 ✕ 🔋 💻 🍴 ➷ ✕

◆◆◆◆ Radisson Hotel Kitchener-Waterloo 🄷 🐾

(519) 894-9500. **Call for rates.** 2960 King St E N2A 1A9. Hwy 401 exit 278, 3.8 mi (6 km) w on Hwy 8 exit Weber St. Int corridors. **Pets:** Designated rooms, service with restrictions, crate.
🄴🄲🄾 🅂🄰🅅🄴 📶 🔋 💻 🍴 ➷

◆◆◆◆ The Walper Hotel 🄷

(519) 745-4321. **$139-$199.** 20 Queen St S N2G 1V6. Corner of King and Queen sts; downtown. Int corridors. **Pets:** $100 deposit/room, $35 one-time fee/room. Service with restrictions.
🅂🄰🅅🄴 📶 ✕ 🔋 💻 🍴

LEAMINGTON

◆◆ Comfort Inn 🄷 🐾

(519) 326-9071. **$94-$162.** 279 Erie St S N8H 3C4. 0.6 mi (1 km) s of jct Talbot and Erie sts; on direct route to Point Pelee National Park. Int corridors. **Pets:** Medium. $10 daily fee/room. Designated rooms, service with restrictions, supervision. 🄴🄲🄾 📶 ✕ 🔋 💻

◆◆ Howard Johnson Inn Leamington 🄷

(519) 325-0260. **$100-$190, 3 day notice.** 201 Erie St N N8H 3A5. 0.6 mi (1 km) n of Talbot St. Int corridors. **Pets:** Other species. $150 deposit/room, $15 daily fee/pet. Designated rooms, service with restrictions, crate.
🄴🄲🄾 📶 🔋 💻 ➷ ✕

LIVELY

◆◆ Red Carpet Inn & Suites 🄼

(705) 692-3632. **Call for rates.** 450 Regional Rd 55 P3Y 1C4. Jct RR 24. Int corridors. **Pets:** Accepted. 📶 🔋 💻 🍴

LONDON

▼▼ ◆◆ Airport Inn & Suites H
(519) 457-1200. **$96-$103, 7 day notice.** 2230 Dundas St E N5V 1R5. Hwy 401 exit Veteran's Memorial Pkwy, 4.8 mi (7.7 km) n; corner of Airport Rd and Dundas St E. Int corridors. **Pets:** $15 daily fee/pet. Designated rooms, service with restrictions, crate. 🛰 🎁 💻

Ⓐ ▼▼▼▼ BEST WESTERN PLUS Lamplighter Inn & Conference Centre H ❀
(519) 681-7151. **$129-$179.** 591 Wellington Rd S N6C 4R3. Hwy 401 exit 186 (Wellington Rd), 2.3 mi (3.7 km) n. Int corridors. **Pets:** Medium, other species. $10 daily fee/pet. Designated rooms, service with restrictions, supervision. 🅴🅲🅾 🆂🅰🆅🅴 🛰 🗙 🎁 💻 🍽 ➰ 🗙

Ⓐ ▼▼ Comfort Inn H
(519) 685-9300. **$92-$104.** 1156 Wellington Rd N6E 1M3. Hwy 401 exit 186B (Wellington Rd), just n. Int corridors. **Pets:** Accepted. 🅴🅲🅾 🆂🅰🆅🅴 🛰 🎁 💻

▼▼▼▼ Courtyard by Marriott London H
(519) 680-0077. **$123-$149.** 864 Exeter Rd N6E 1L5. Hwy 401 exit 186B (Wellington Rd), just n. Int corridors. **Pets:** Accepted. 🛰 🗙 🎁 💻 🍽 💻

Ⓐ ▼▼▼ Days Inn London H
(519) 681-1240. **$65-$209.** 1100 Wellington Rd S N6E 1M2. Hwy 401 exit 186B (Wellington Rd), 0.9 mi (1.5 km) n. Int corridors. **Pets:** Medium. $50 deposit/room, no service, supervision. 🅴🅲🅾 🆂🅰🆅🅴 🛰 🎁 💻 🍽 ➰

Ⓐ ▼▼▼▼ Delta London Armouries H
(519) 679-6111. **Call for rates.** 325 Dundas St N6B 1T9. Between Wellington and Waterloo sts. Int corridors. **Pets:** Medium, other species. $35 one-time fee/room. Service with restrictions, crate. 🅴🅲🅾 🆂🅰🆅🅴 🛰 🗙 🎁 💻 🍽 ➰ 🗙

Ⓐ ▼▼▼▼ Hilton London Ontario H ❀
(519) 439-1661. **Call for rates.** 300 King St N6B 1S2. Jct King St and Wellington Rd. Int corridors. **Pets:** Large, other species. $50 one-time fee/room. Designated rooms, service with restrictions, supervision. 🅴🅲🅾 🆂🅰🆅🅴 🛰 🗙 💪M 🎁 💻 🍽 ➰ 🗙

▼▼▼ Homewood Suites by Hilton London H
(519) 686-7700. **$118-$174.** 45 Bessemer Rd N6E 0A2. Hwy 401 exit 186B (Wellington Rd), just n. Int corridors. **Pets:** Medium, other species. $40 daily fee/room. Designated rooms, service with restrictions, supervision. 🛰 💪M 🎁 💻 ➰

▼▼▼▼ Hotel Metro-London H
(519) 518-9000. **$129-$189.** 32 Covent Market Pl N6A 1E8. Jct Talbot St. Int corridors. **Pets:** Small. $65 one-time fee/room. Service with restrictions. 🛰 🗙 🎁 💻

Ⓐ ▼▼▼▼ London Hotel and Suites H
(519) 668-7900. **Call for rates.** 855 Wellington Rd S N6E 3N5. Jct Wellington and Southdale rds. Int corridors. **Pets:** Medium. $40 daily fee/room. Service with restrictions, crate. 🅴🅲🅾 🆂🅰🆅🅴 🛰 🎁 💻 🍽 ➰

▼▼ Motel 6 London #5703 H
(519) 680-0900. **Call for rates.** 810 Exeter Rd N6E 1L5. Hwy 401 exit 186 (Wellington Rd), just n. Int corridors. **Pets:** Other species. Service with restrictions, supervision. 🅴🅲🅾 🛰 💪M 🎁 ➰

Ⓐ ▼▼▼▼ Quality Suites H
(519) 680-1024. **$90-$130.** 1120 Dearness Dr N6E 1N9. Hwy 401 exit 186B (Wellington Rd), 1 mi (1.6 km) n. Int corridors. **Pets:** Accepted. 🅴🅲🅾 🆂🅰🆅🅴 🛰 🎁 💻

Ⓐ ▼▼ Ramada London H
(519) 681-4900. **$79-$159.** 817 Exeter Rd N6E 1W1. Hwy 401 exit 186B (Wellington Rd), just n. Int corridors. **Pets:** Accepted. 🆂🅰🆅🅴 🛰 🎁 💻 🍽 ➰

▼▼▼▼ Residence Inn by Marriott London H ❀
(519) 433-7222. **$144-$229.** 383 Colborne St N6B 3P5. Jct King St. Int corridors. **Pets:** Other species. $75 one-time fee/room. Designated rooms, service with restrictions, crate. 🅴🅲🅾 🛰 🗙 🎁 💻 ➰

Ⓐ ▼▼▼▼ StationPark All Suite Hotel H ❀
(519) 642-4444. **$129-$204.** 242 Pall Mall St N6A 5P6. Hwy 401 exit 186B (Wellington Rd), 5.6 mi (9 km) n. Int corridors. **Pets:** Designated rooms, crate. 🆂🅰🆅🅴 🛰 🗙 🎁 💻 🍽 🗙

Ⓐ ▼▼▼▼ Staybridge Suites H ❀
(519) 649-4500. **Call for rates.** 824 Exeter Rd N6E 1L5. Hwy 401 exit 186B (Wellington Rd), just n. Int corridors. **Pets:** $40 one-time fee/room. Service with restrictions, crate. 🅴🅲🅾 🆂🅰🆅🅴 🛰 💪M 🎁 💻 ➰

Ⓐ ▼▼ ▼ Travelodge London South H
(519) 681-1200. **$65-$150.** 800 Exeter Rd N6E 1L5. Hwy 401 exit 186B (Wellington Rd), just n. Int corridors. **Pets:** Medium, other species. $15 daily fee/room. Service with restrictions, crate. 🅴🅲🅾 🆂🅰🆅🅴 🛰 🎁 💻

MARATHON

▼▼ ▼ Travelodge Marathon H
(807) 229-1213. **$97-$109.** Hwy 17 P0T 2E0. On Hwy 17, jct Peninsula Rd. Int corridors. **Pets:** Accepted. 🛰 🎁 💻

MASSEY

▼▼ Mohawk Motel Inc M
(705) 865-2722. **$82-$155.** 335 Sable St P0P 1P0. Center. Ext/int corridors. **Pets:** Medium, dogs only. $100 deposit/room, $10 daily fee/pet. Designated rooms, service with restrictions, supervision. 🛰 🗙 🎁 💻

MIDLAND

▼▼ Comfort Inn H ❀
(705) 526-2090. **$90-$130.** 980 King St L4R 4K3. Jct Hwy 12 and King St. Int corridors. **Pets:** Medium, other species. $10 one-time fee/room. Designated rooms, service with restrictions, supervision. 🅴🅲🅾 🛰 🎁 💻

Ⓐ ▼▼ ▼ Super 8 Midland H ❀
(705) 526-8288. **$90-$126.** 1144 Hugel Ave L4R 0B1. Jct Hwy 93 N. Int corridors. **Pets:** Other species. $8 daily fee/room. Designated rooms, service with restrictions, crate. 🅴🅲🅾 🆂🅰🆅🅴 🛰 🗙 🎁 💻 ➰

MILTON

Ⓐ ▼▼▼▼ BEST WESTERN PLUS Milton H
(905) 875-3818. **$120-$180.** 161 Chisholm Dr L9T 4A6. Jct Hwy 401 and 25 S. Int corridors. **Pets:** Accepted. 🆂🅰🆅🅴 🛰 🎁 💻 🍽 ➰

MINDEMOYA

▼▼ Mindemoya Motel M
(705) 377-4779. **$89-$129, 3 day notice.** 6375 Hwy 542 P0P 1S0. In Mindemoya; 0.6 mi (1 km) w of jct Hwy 551 and 542. Ext corridors. **Pets:** Accepted. 🛰 🎁 💻

MISSISSAUGA

▼▼ Comfort Inn Airport West H
(905) 624-6900. **$75-$200.** 1500 Matheson Blvd L4W 3Z4. Hwy 401 exit Dixie Rd, then s. Int corridors. **Pets:** Accepted. 🅴🅲🅾 🛰 🎁 💻 🍽

Ⓐ ▼▼ ▼ Comfort Inn Toronto Airport H
(905) 677-7331. **$100-$130.** 6355 Airport Rd L4V 1E4. 1.3 mi (2 km) s of Derry Rd. Int corridors. **Pets:** Other species. $10 daily fee/pet. Service with restrictions, crate. 🆂🅰🆅🅴 🛰 🗙 🎁 💻 🍽

Ⓐ ▼▼▼▼ **Delta Meadowvale Hotel and Conference Centre** Ⓗ ❀

(905) 821-1981. **$99-$229.** 6750 Mississauga Rd L5N 2L3. Hwy 401 W exit 336 (Mississauga Rd), just s. Int corridors. **Pets:** Medium. $35 one-time fee/room. Designated rooms, service with restrictions, supervision.

ECO SAVE 📶 ✖ 🔓M 🛄 💻 🍴 ↪ ✖

Ⓐ ▼▼▼ **Delta Toronto Airport West** Ⓗ

(905) 624-1144. **$99-$219.** 5444 Dixie Rd L4W 2L2. 0.6 mi (1 km) s of jct Hwy 401 and Dixie Rd. Int corridors. **Pets:** Accepted.

ECO SAVE 📶 ✖ 🛄 💻 🍴 ↪ ✖

Ⓐ ▼▼▼ **Four Points by Sheraton Mississauga Meadowvale** Ⓗ

(905) 858-2424. **$99-$220.** 2501 Argentia Rd L5N 4G8. Hwy 401 exit 336 (Mississauga Rd), just s on Erin Mills Pkwy, then 1 mi (1.6 km) w. Int corridors. **Pets:** Accepted.

ECO SAVE 📶 ✖ 🔓M 🛄 💻 🍴 ↪

Ⓐ ▼▼▼▼ **Holiday Inn Mississauga Toronto West** Ⓗ

(905) 890-5700. **$89-$199.** 100 Britannia Rd E L4Z 2G1. Hwy 401 exit Hwy 10 S (Hurontario St). Int corridors. **Pets:** Medium. $25 daily fee/room. Designated rooms, service with restrictions, supervision.

ECO SAVE 📶 🛄 💻 🍴 ↪

▼▼▼ **Holiday Inn Toronto-Mississauga** Ⓗ

(905) 855-2000. **$89-$159.** 2125 N Sheridan Way L5K 1A3. QEW exit Erin Mills Pkwy. Int corridors. **Pets:** Medium, dogs only. $35 one-time fee/room. Designated rooms, service with restrictions, supervision.

📶 🔓M 🛄 💻 🍴 ↪

▼▼▼ **Motel 6 Mississauga #1910** Ⓗ

(905) 814-1664. **$75-$81.** 2935 Argentia Rd L5N 8G6. Hwy 401 exit 333 (Winston Churchill Blvd), just s. Int corridors. **Pets:** Other species. Service with restrictions, supervision. ECO 📶 🔓M 🛄

Ⓐ ▼▼▼▼ **Novotel Toronto Mississauga Centre** Ⓗ

(905) 896-1000. **$149-$249.** 3670 Hurontario St L5B 1P3. Hwy 403 exit 344, 0.8 mi (1.2 km) s on Hwy 10 (Hurontario St); at Burnhamthorpe Rd. Int corridors. **Pets:** Accepted. ECO SAVE 📶 🛄 💻 🍴 ↪ ✖

▼▼▼▼ **Residence Inn by Marriott Mississauga Airport Corporate Centre West** Ⓗ

(905) 602-7777. **$101-$199.** 5070 Creekbank Rd L4W 5R2. Hwy 401 W exit Dixie Rd S, 0.9 mi (1.5 km) e to Eglinton Ave, then 0.6 mi (1 km). Int corridors. **Pets:** $100 one-time fee/room. Service with restrictions, supervision. 📶 ✖ 🛄 💻 ↪ ✖

▼▼▼▼ **Residence Inn by Marriott Toronto-Mississauga/Meadowvale** Ⓗ

(905) 567-2577. **$107-$209.** 7005 Century Ave L5N 7K2. Hwy 401 exit Erin Mills Pkwy/Mississauga Rd, s to Argentia Rd. Int corridors.
Pets: Accepted. 📶 ✖ 🔓M 🛄 💻 ↪ ✖

Ⓐ ▼▼▼▼ **Sheraton Gateway Hotel in Toronto International Airport** Ⓗ ❀

(905) 672-7000. **$139-$309.** Terminal 3, Toronto AMF L5P 1C4. In Toronto Pearson International Airport. Int corridors. **Pets:** Small. Service with restrictions, supervision.

SAVE 📶 ✖ 🔓M 🛄 💻 🍴 ↪ ✖

▼▼▼ **Staybridge Suites Mississauga** Ⓗ

(905) 564-6892. **$149-$169.** 6791 Hurontario St L5T 2W1. Hwy 401 W exit Hwy 10 (Hurontario St), 0.9 mi (1.5 km) n; just s of Derry Rd. Int corridors. **Pets:** Accepted. 📶 🛄 💻 🍴 ↪

▼▼▼ **Studio 6 Mississauga #1908** Ⓜ

(905) 502-8897. **$83-$93.** 60 Britannia Rd E L4Z 2T2. Hwy 401 exit Hwy 10 (Hurontario St). Int corridors. **Pets:** Other species. $10 daily fee/room. Service with restrictions, supervision. ECO 📶 🛄 💻

Ⓐ ▼▼▼▼ **TownePlace Suites by Marriott Mississauga - Airport Corporate Centre** Ⓗ

(905) 238-9600. **$149-$169.** 5050 Orbitor Dr L4W 4X2. Jct Eglinton Ave and Renforth Dr, 1.4 mi (2.3 km) w on Eglinton Ave. Int corridors.
Pets: Accepted. ECO SAVE 📶 ✖ 🛄 💻 ↪

MONETVILLE

▼▼▼ **Memquisit Lodge** Ⓒ

(705) 898-2355. **Call for rates.** 506 Memquisit Rd P0M 2K0. 13 mi (20.8 km) ne on west arm of Lake Nipissing, on Hwy 64 and Memquisit Lodge Rd; 23 mi (36.8 km) sw off Hwy 17, on Hwy 64. Ext corridors.
Pets: Accepted. 📶 🛄 💻 🍴 ✖ Ⓚ Ⓟ ✖

MORRISBURG

Ⓐ ▼▼▼ **The McIntosh Country Inn & Conference Centre** Ⓗ

(613) 543-3788. **$99-$209.** 12495 Hwy 2 E K0C 1X0. Hwy 401 exit 750, 1.2 mi (2 km) s on Rt 31, then 0.6 mi (1 km) e. Int corridors. **Pets:** $10 daily fee/pet. Service with restrictions, supervision.

SAVE 📶 🛄 💻 🍴 ↪ ✖

NEWMARKET

▼▼▼ **Comfort Inn** Ⓗ

(905) 895-3355. **$110-$140.** 1230 Journey's End Cir L3Y 8Z6. Hwy 404 exit 51 (Davis Dr), just w, then just n on Harry Walker Pkwy. Int corridors. **Pets:** Other species. $10 daily fee/room. Designated rooms, service with restrictions, supervision. ECO 📶 🛄 💻

NIAGARA FALLS METROPOLITAN AREA

FORT ERIE

Ⓐ ▼▼▼▼ **Clarion Hotel & Conference Centre** Ⓗ

(905) 871-8333. **Call for rates.** 1485 Garrison Rd L2A 1P8. QEW exit Gilmore Rd. Int corridors. **Pets:** Medium. $30 daily fee/room. Designated rooms, service with restrictions, supervision.

ECO SAVE 📶 ✖ 🛄 💻 🍴 ↪ ✖

LINCOLN

Ⓐ ▼▼▼ **BEST WESTERN Beacon Harbourside Inn & Suites Conference Centre** Ⓗ

(905) 562-4155. **Call for rates.** 2793 Beacon Blvd L0R 1S0. QEW exit 55. Int corridors. **Pets:** Accepted.

SAVE 📶 ✖ 🛄 💻 🍴 ↪ ✖

▼▼▼ ▼▼▼ **Inn on the Twenty** Ⓒ

(905) 562-5336. **$159-$389, 7 day notice.** 3845 Main St L0R 1S0. QEW exit 57 (Victoria Ave/Reg Rd 24), 1.9 mi (3 km) s, 1.9 mi (3 km) e on Reg Rd 81, then just n. Ext/int corridors. **Pets:** Accepted.

📶 ✖ 🛄 💻

NIAGARA FALLS

Ⓐ ▼▼▼ **BEST WESTERN Fallsview** Ⓗ ❀

(905) 356-0551. **$60-$400, 3 day notice.** 6289 Fallsview Blvd L2G 3V7. Jct Niagara River Pkwy, just n on Murray St. Ext/int corridors. **Pets:** $25 daily fee/pet. Designated rooms, service with restrictions, crate.

ECO SAVE 📶 ✖ 💻 🍴 ↪

▼▼▼ **Days Inn Clifton Hill Casino** Ⓗ

(905) 356-2461. **$59-$379.** 5657 Victoria Ave L2G 3L5. Just e on Hwy 20. Ext/int corridors. **Pets:** Accepted. 📶 🛄 💻 🍴 ↪ ✖

Ⓐ ▼▼ ▼▼ **Days Inn Fallsview** Ⓗ
(905) 356-1722. **$49-$999.** 6519 Stanley Ave L2G 7L2. Corner of Dixon Ave; 2 blks from Konica Minolta Tower. Int corridors. **Pets:** Accepted.
SAVE 🕿 ✕ 🛢 💻 ⑪ ⤰

Ⓐ ▼▼ ▼▼ **Falls Manor Resort & Restaurant** Ⓜ
(905) 358-3211. **$49-$149.** 7104 Lundy's Ln L2G 1W2. On Hwy 20, 2.1 mi (3.4 km) w. Ext corridors. **Pets:** Large. $20 daily fee/pet. Designated rooms, service with restrictions, crate. SAVE 🕿 🛢 ⑪ ⤰

Ⓐ ▼▼ ▼▼ **Howard Johnson Express Inn** Ⓜ
(905) 358-9777. **$45-$220.** 8100 Lundy's Ln L2H 1H1. QEW exit Hwy 20, 3.1 mi (5 km) w. Ext corridors. **Pets:** Accepted.
SAVE 🕿 🛢 💻 ⤰

Ⓐ ▼▼ ▼▼ **Howard Johnson Hotel by the Falls** Ⓗ
(905) 357-4040. **$55-$335.** 5905 Victoria Ave L2G 3L8. On Hwy 20; 0.4 mi (0.6 km) from the falls. Int corridors. **Pets:** Small. $20 daily fee/pet. Designated rooms, service with restrictions, supervision.
ECO SAVE 🕿 ✕ 🔆M 🛢 💻 ⑪ ⤰ ✕

▼▼ ▼▼ **Imperial Hotel & Suites** Ⓗ
(905) 356-2648. **$49-$299.** 5851 Victoria Ave L2G 3L6. On Hwy 20, 0.3 mi (0.5 km) from the falls. Int corridors. **Pets:** Accepted.
🕿 🛢 💻 ⑪ ⤰ ✕

▼▼ **Niagara Parkway Court Motel** Ⓜ
(905) 295-3331. **$39-$149.** 3708 Main St (Niagara Pkwy S) L2G 6B1. 1.6 mi (2.5 km) s of the falls. Ext corridors. **Pets:** $15 daily fee/pet. Designated rooms, no service, crate. 🕿 🛢 💻

Ⓐ ▼▼ ▼▼ **Peninsula Inn & Resort** Ⓗ
(905) 354-8812. **$59-$339.** 7373 Niagara Square Dr L2E 6S5. QEW exit McLeod Rd, just w. Int corridors. **Pets:** Small. $10 daily fee/pet. Designated rooms, service with restrictions, crate.
SAVE 🕿 🔆M 🛢 💻 ⑪ ⤰ ✕

NIAGARA-ON-THE-LAKE

▼▼ ▼▼ **Harbour House Hotel** Ⓗ ❖
(905) 468-4683. **$199-$475, 10 day notice.** 85 Melville St L0S 1J0. Jct Ricardo St. Int corridors. **Pets:** Dogs only. $25 daily fee/room. Designated rooms, service with restrictions, supervision. 🕿 ✕ 🛢 💻

Ⓐ ▼▼ ▼▼ **The Oban Inn, Spa and Restaurant** Ⓗ
(905) 468-2165. **$150-$495, 7 day notice.** 160 Front St L0S 1J0. Jct Gate St. Ext/int corridors. **Pets:** Very small, dogs only. $50 daily fee/pet. Designated rooms, service with restrictions, crate.
SAVE 🕿 ✕ 💻 ⑪ ⤰ ✕

Ⓐ ▼▼ ▼▼ **Pillar and Post Hotel** Ⓒⓘ
(905) 468-2123. **$179-$409.** 48 John St L0S 1J0. Just n on Hwy 55 (Mississauga St), just e; 13 mi (20.8 km) from QEW. Ext/int corridors.
Pets: Accepted. SAVE 🕿 ✕ 🛢 💻 ⑪ ⤰ ✕

Ⓐ ▼▼ ▼▼ **Prince of Wales Hotel & Spa** Ⓗ
(905) 468-3246. **$189-$429.** 6 Picton St L0S 1J0. Jct Picton and King sts; 9 mi (14.4 km) e of jct QEW and Hwy 55, via Hwy 55. Ext/int corridors. **Pets:** Accepted. SAVE 🕿 ✕ 🛢 💻 ⑪ ⤰ ✕

▼▼ ▼▼ **Shaw Club Hotel and Spa** Ⓗ ❖
(905) 468-5711. **$99-$510, 10 day notice.** 92 Picton St L0S 1J0. Jct Wellington St. Int corridors. **Pets:** Dogs only. $25 daily fee/pet. Designated rooms, service with restrictions, supervision.
🕿 ✕ 🛢 💻 ⑪ ✕

ST. CATHARINES

Ⓐ ▼▼ ▼▼ **BEST WESTERN St. Catharines Hotel & Conference Centre** Ⓗ
(905) 934-8000. **$119-$299.** 2 N Service Rd L2N 4G9. QEW exit 46 (Lake St), just e. Int corridors. **Pets:** Accepted.
ECO SAVE 🕿 ✕ 🛢 💻 ⑪ ⤰ ✕

Ⓐ ▼▼ ▼▼ **Comfort Inn** Ⓗ ❖
(905) 687-8890. **$100-$150.** 2 Dunlop Dr L2R 1A2. QEW exit 46 (Lake St); between Lake and Geneva sts. Int corridors. **Pets:** Designated rooms, service with restrictions, supervision.
ECO SAVE 🕿 🔆M 🛢 💻

Ⓐ ▼▼ ▼▼ **Days Inn St. Catharines Niagara** Ⓗ
(905) 934-5400. **$99-$209.** 89 Meadowvale Dr L2N 3Z8. QEW exit 46 (Lake St). Int corridors. **Pets:** $15 daily fee/pet. Designated rooms, service with restrictions, crate. SAVE 🕿 🛢 💻 ⑪ ⤰ ✕

Ⓐ ▼▼ ▼▼ **Holiday Inn & Suites Parkway Conference Center** Ⓗ ❖
(905) 688-2324. **Call for rates.** 327 Ontario St L2R 5L3. QEW exit 47 (Ontario St), 0.5 mi (0.8 km) s. **Pets:** $15 daily fee/room. Designated rooms, service with restrictions, crate.
SAVE 🕿 ✕ 🔆M 🛢 💻 ⑪ ⤰ ✕

THOROLD

Ⓐ ▼▼ ▼▼ **Four Points by Sheraton St. Catharines Niagara Suites** Ⓗ
(905) 984-8484. **$125-$225.** 3530 Schmon Pkwy L2V 4Y6. Hwy 406 exit St. David's Rd W; just s of Brock University. Int corridors. **Pets:** $20 daily fee/room. Designated rooms, service with restrictions, crate.
SAVE 🕿 ✕ 🛢 💻 ⤰ ✕

WELLAND

▼▼ ▼▼ **Comfort Inn-Niagara Falls/Welland** Ⓗ
(905) 732-4811. **$80-$90.** 870 Niagara St L3C 1M3. 1.5 mi (2.5 km) n. Int corridors. **Pets:** Other species. $15 deposit/pet. Designated rooms, crate. 🕿 🛢 💻

END METROPOLITAN AREA

NORTH BAY

Ⓐ ▼▼ ▼▼ **BEST WESTERN North Bay Hotel and Conference Centre** Ⓗ ❖
(705) 474-5800. **$130-$190.** 700 Lakeshore Dr P1A 2G4. Hwy 11 exit 338, 2.5 mi (4 km) w. Int corridors. **Pets:** Other species. Service with restrictions, crate. ECO SAVE 🕿 🛢 💻 ⑪ ⤰ ✕

Ⓐ ▼▼ ▼▼ **Clarion Resort Pinewood Park** Ⓗ ❖
(705) 472-0810. **$79-$148.** 201 Pinewood Park Dr P1B 8Z4. Hwy 11 exit 338, just w on Lakeshore Dr, then 0.4 mi (0.7 km) s. Int corridors.
Pets: Other species. Service with restrictions, crate.
SAVE 🕿 ✕ 🛢 💻 ⑪ ⤰ ✕

Ⓐ ▼▼ ▼▼ **Comfort Inn-Airport** Ⓗ
(705) 476-5400. **$130-$155.** 1200 O'Brien St P1B 9B3. On Hwy 11/17; jct O'Brien St. Int corridors. **Pets:** Accepted. SAVE 🕿 🛢 💻

Ⓐ ▼▼ ▼▼ **Holiday Inn Express Hotel & Suites** Ⓗ
(705) 476-7700. **$129-$189.** 1325 Seymour St P1B 9V6. Jct Hwy 11/17. Int corridors. **Pets:** Designated rooms, service with restrictions, supervision. ECO SAVE 🕿 ✕ 🛢 💻

Ⓐ ▼▼ ▼▼ **Super 8 North Bay** Ⓗ
(705) 495-4551. **$90-$110.** 570 Lakeshore Dr P1A 2E6. Hwy 11 exit 338, 2.8 mi (4.5 km) w. Int corridors. **Pets:** Designated rooms, service with restrictions, supervision. SAVE 🕿 🛢 💻

ⓒⒶ ▼▼▼ **Travelodge Airport North Bay** 🅗
(705) 495-1133. **$120-$190.** 1525 Seymour St P1B 8G4. Jct Hwy 11/17. Int corridors. **Pets:** Large. Service with restrictions, supervision.
🅔🅒🅞 [SAVE] 🛜 🛏 💻 ⊷

ⓒⒶ ▼▼▼ **Travelodge Lakeshore** 🅗
(705) 472-7171. **$99-$130.** 718 Lakeshore Dr P1A 2G4. Hwy 11 exit 338, 2.5 mi (4 km) w. Int corridors. **Pets:** Accepted. 🅔🅒🅞 [SAVE] 🛜 🛏 💻

OAKVILLE

ⓒⒶ ▼▼▼▼ **Holiday Inn Oakville Centre** 🅗
(905) 842-5000. **$99-$140.** 590 Argus Rd L6J 3J3. QEW exit 118 (Trafalgar Rd), just s. Int corridors. **Pets:** Other species. $25 one-time fee/room. Service with restrictions, supervision.
🅔🅒🅞 [SAVE] 🛜 ⊠ 🏋 🛏 💻 ⊷

ⓒⒶ ▼▼▼ **Staybridge Suites Oakville Burlington** 🅗
(905) 847-2600. **$119-$184.** 2511 Wyecroft Rd L6L 6P8. QEW exit 111 (Bronte Rd/Hwy 25), 0.3 mi (0.5 km) s, then just e. Int corridors. **Pets:** Large. $75 one-time fee/pet. Designated rooms, service with restrictions, crate. [SAVE] 🛜 🏋 🛏 💻 ⊷

ORILLIA

ⓒⒶ ▼▼▼▼ **BEST WESTERN PLUS Couchiching Inn** 🅗 🐾
(705) 325-6505. **Call for rates.** 440 Couchiching Point Rd L3V 6P8. Jct Hwy 12 S and Couchiching Point Rd. Int corridors. **Pets:** Medium, dogs only. $10 daily fee/pet. Designated rooms, service with restrictions, supervision. 🅔🅒🅞 [SAVE] 🛜 🛏 💻 🍴 ⊠

ⓒⒶ ▼▼▼▼ **BEST WESTERN PLUS Mariposa Inn & Conference Centre** 🅗 🐾
(705) 325-9511. **$119-$209.** 400 Memorial Ave L3V 6J3. Jct Hwy 12 and Memorial Ave, just s. Int corridors. **Pets:** Medium, dogs only. $10 daily fee/pet. Designated rooms, service with restrictions, supervision.
🅔🅒🅞 [SAVE] 🛜 🛏 💻 🍴 ⊷ ⊠

ⓒⒶ ▼▼▼ **Comfort Inn** 🅗 🐾
(705) 327-7744. **$90-$130.** 75 Progress Dr L3V 6H1. Hwy 11 N exit Hwy 12, s on Memorial Ave; corner of Progress Dr and Memorial Ave. Int corridors. **Pets:** Other species. $10 daily fee/room. Service with restrictions.
🅔🅒🅞 [SAVE] 🛜 🛏 💻

ⓒⒶ ▼▼▼ **Highwayman Inn & Conference Centre** 🅗
(705) 326-7343. **$99-$126.** 201 Woodside Dr L3V 6T4. Hwy 11 exit Hwy 12 (Coldwater Rd), just e, then just s. Int corridors. **Pets:** Dogs only. $15 daily fee/room. Service with restrictions, supervision.
[SAVE] 🛜 🛏 💻 🍴 ⊷ ⊠

▼▼ **Quality Champlain Hotel Orillia** 🅗
(705) 325-0770. **Call for rates.** 2 Front St N L3V 4R5. Jct Mississaga St; downtown. Int corridors. **Pets:** Accepted. 🛜 🛏 💻

OSHAWA

▼▼ **Comfort Inn** 🅗
(905) 434-5000. **$85-$179.** 605 Bloor St W L1J 5Y6. Hwy 401 exit 415 (Stevenson Rd), s to Bloor St, then 0.5 mi (0.8 km) w. Int corridors. **Pets:** Other species. Service with restrictions, crate. 🅔🅒🅞 🛜 🛏 💻

ⓒⒶ ▼▼▼ **Quality Hotel & Conference Centre** 🅗
(905) 576-5101. **$115-$140.** 1011 Bloor St E L1H 7K6. Hwy 401 exit 419 (Harmony Rd). Int corridors. **Pets:** Small. $15 daily fee/pet. Designated rooms, service with restrictions, supervision.
[SAVE] 🛜 🛏 💻 🍴 ⊷ ⊠

▼▼ **Travelodge Oshawa** 🅗 🐾
(905) 436-9500. **$79-$209.** 940 Champlain Ave L1J 7A6. Hwy 401 exit 412 (Thickson Rd N). Int corridors. **Pets:** $25 one-time fee/room. Designated rooms, service with restrictions, crate.
🅔🅒🅞 🛜 🛏 💻 ⊷ ⊠

OTTAWA METROPOLITAN AREA

KANATA

ⓒⒶ ▼▼▼▼ **Brookstreet Hotel** 🅗 🐾
(613) 271-1800. **$129-$499.** 525 Legget Dr K2K 2W2. Hwy 417 exit 138 (March Rd), 2.3 mi (3.7 km) n, just e on Solandt Dr to Legget Dr, then just n. Int corridors. **Pets:** $250 deposit/pet, $25 daily fee/pet. Designated rooms, service with restrictions, supervision.
🅔🅒🅞 [SAVE] 🛜 💻 🍴 ⊷ ⊠

ⓒⒶ ▼▼▼ **Comfort Inn Ottawa West Kanata** 🅗
(613) 592-2200. **$110-$161.** 222 Hearst Way K2L 3A2. Hwy 417 exit 138 (Eagleson Rd), 0.4 mi (0.6 km) s, just w on Katimavik Rd, then 0.5 mi (0.8 km) n. Int corridors. **Pets:** Other species. Designated rooms, service with restrictions, crate. 🅔🅒🅞 [SAVE] 🛜 🛏 💻

OTTAWA

ⓒⒶ ▼▼▼▼ **ARC The.Hotel** 🅗
(613) 238-2888. **Call for rates.** 140 Slater St K1P 5H6. Between Metcalfe and O'Connor sts. Int corridors. **Pets:** Accepted.
🅔🅒🅞 [SAVE] 🛜 🛏 💻 🍴

ⓒⒶ ▼▼▼▼ **BEST WESTERN PLUS Ottawa/Kanata Hotel & Conference Centre** 🅗
(613) 828-2741. **$119-$169.** 1876 Robertson Rd K2H 5B8. Hwy 417 exit 130, 1.8 mi (2.9 km) s. Int corridors. **Pets:** Medium, other species. $20 daily fee/room. [SAVE] 🛜 ⊠ 🛏 💻 🍴 ⊷ ⊠

▼▼ **Cartier Place Suite Hotel** 🅗
(613) 236-5000. **$159-$199.** 180 Cooper St K2P 2L5. Between Elgin and Cartier sts. Int corridors. **Pets:** Other species. $35 daily fee/pet.
🛜 🛏 💻 🍴 ⊷ ⊠

ⓒⒶ ▼▼▼ **Comfort Inn** 🅗
(613) 744-2900. **$100-$140.** 1252 Michael St K1J 7T1. Hwy 417 exit 115 (St. Laurent Blvd), just ne. Int corridors. **Pets:** Accepted.
🅔🅒🅞 [SAVE] 🛜 🛏 💻

ⓒⒶ ▼▼▼ **Days Inn-Downtown Ottawa** 🅗
(613) 789-5555. **$100-$205.** 319 Rideau St K1N 5Y4. Between Nelson St and King Edward Ave. Ext/int corridors. **Pets:** Accepted.
🅔🅒🅞 [SAVE] 🛜 🛏 💻 🍴

ⓒⒶ ▼▼▼ **The Days Inn Ottawa West** 🅗
(613) 726-1717. **$100-$160.** 350 Moodie Dr K2H 8G3. Hwy 417 exit 134, 0.9 mi (1.5 km) s. Int corridors. **Pets:** $20 daily fee/room. Designated rooms, service with restrictions, supervision.
🅔🅒🅞 [SAVE] 🛜 ⊠ 🛏 💻 🍴

ⓒⒶ ▼▼▼▼ **Delta Ottawa City Centre** 🅗
(613) 237-3600. **$149-$289.** 101 Lyon St K1R 5T9. Entrance at corner of Albert St. Int corridors. **Pets:** Accepted.
🅔🅒🅞 [SAVE] 🛜 ⊠ 🛏 💻 🍴 ⊷ ⊠

▼▼ **Extended Stay Deluxe Ottawa Downtown** 🅗
(613) 236-7500. **$121-$131.** 141 Cooper St K2P 0E8. Between Elgin and Cartier sts. Int corridors. **Pets:** $25 daily fee/pet. Designated rooms, service with restrictions. 🛜 🛏 💻 🍴 ⊠

ⓒⒶ ▼▼▼▼ **Fairmont Château Laurier** 🅗
(613) 241-1414. **$189-$369.** 1 Rideau St K1N 8S7. Just e of Parliament buildings. Int corridors. **Pets:** Accepted.
🅔🅒🅞 [SAVE] 🛜 🏋 🛏 💻 🍴 ⊠

▼▼▼▼ Holiday Inn & Suites Ottawa Downtown H
(613) 238-1331. **Call for rates.** 111 Cooper St K2P 2E3. Corner of Cartier St. Int corridors. **Pets:** Large. Designated rooms.
ECO 🛜 ✖ 🛏 💻 🍴

▼▼▼▼ Hotel Indigo Ottawa H
(613) 231-6555. **$139-$299.** 123 Metcalfe St K1P 5L9. Corner of Laurier Ave W. Int corridors. **Pets:** Accepted.
ECO 🛜 ✖ 🛏 💻 🍴 ≈ ✖

Ⓐ ▼▼▼▼ Les Suites Hotel Ottawa H
(613) 232-2000. **Call for rates.** 130 Besserer St K1N 9M9. Between Nicholas and Waller sts. Int corridors. **Pets:** Accepted.
ECO SAVE 🛜 ✖ 🔧 🛏 💻 🍴 ≈ ✖

▼▼◆ Lord Elgin Hotel H
(613) 235-3333. **$109-$329.** 100 Elgin St K1P 5K8. Between Laurier Ave and Slater St. Int corridors. **Pets:** Accepted.
ECO ✖ 🛏 💻 🍴 ≈ ✖

Ⓐ ▼▼▼▼ Marriott Ottawa Hotel H
(613) 238-1122. **$129-$299.** 100 Kent St K1P 5R7. Corner of Queen St. Int corridors. **Pets:** Accepted.
ECO SAVE 🛜 ✖ 🛏 💻 🍴 ≈ ✖

Ⓐ ▼▼◆ The Monterey Hotel H ❀
(613) 288-3500. **$109-$139.** 2259 Prince of Wales Dr K2E 6Z8. 0.5 mi (0.8 km) s of Hunt Club Rd. Ext corridors. **Pets:** Medium. $10 daily fee/pet. Designated rooms, service with restrictions, supervision.
ECO SAVE 🛜 🛏 💻 🍴 ≈ ✖

Ⓐ ▼▼▼ The National Hotel and Suites Ottawa, an Ascend Collection hotel H
(613) 238-6000. **Call for rates.** 361 Queen St K1R 7S9. Corner of Lyon St. Int corridors. **Pets:** Medium, other species. $35 daily fee/room. Service with restrictions, crate. ECO SAVE 🛜 ✖ 🛏 💻 🍴 ≈ ✖

Ⓐ ▼▼▼ Novotel Ottawa Hotel H
(613) 230-3033. **$129-$299.** 33 Nicholas St K1N 9M7. Corner of Daly Ave. Int corridors. **Pets:** Accepted.
ECO SAVE 🛜 🛏 💻 🍴 ≈ ✖

Ⓐ ▼▼▼ Quality Hotel Downtown Ottawa H
(613) 789-7511. **$99-$199.** 290 Rideau St K1N 5Y3. Corner of King Edward Ave. Int corridors. **Pets:** Accepted.
ECO SAVE 🛜 ✖ 🛏 💻 🍴

Ⓐ ▼▼▼▼ Radisson Hotel Ottawa Parliament Hill H
(613) 236-1133. **Call for rates.** 402 Queen St K1R 5A7. Corner of Bay and Queen sts. Int corridors. **Pets:** Medium. Designated rooms, service with restrictions, crate. ECO SAVE 🛜 ✖ 🛏 💻 🍴

▼▼▼▼ Residence Inn by Marriott Ottawa H
(613) 231-2020. **$149-$299.** 161 Laurier Ave W K1P 5J2. Corner of Elgin St. Int corridors. **Pets:** $85 one-time fee/pet. Service with restrictions.
ECO 🛜 ✖ 🛏 💻 ≈ ✖

Ⓐ ▼▼▼ Rideau Heights Inn M
(613) 226-4152. **$99-$129.** 72 Rideau Heights Dr K2E 7A6. Hwy 16 (Prince of Wales Dr), 0.3 mi (0.5 km) n of Hunt Club Rd. Ext corridors. **Pets:** Small. $10 daily fee/pet. Designated rooms, service with restrictions, supervision. SAVE 🛜 ✖ 🛏 💻

Ⓐ ▼▼▼▼ Sheraton Ottawa Hotel H ❀
(613) 238-1500. **$139-$450.** 150 Albert St K1P 5G2. Corner of O'Connor St. Int corridors. **Pets:** Other species. Supervision.
ECO SAVE 🛜 ✖ 🛏 💻 🍴 ≈

Ⓐ ▼▼▼ Southway Hotel H
(613) 737-0811. **$109-$225.** 2431 Bank St K1V 8R9. On Hwy 31; jct Hunt Club Rd. Int corridors. **Pets:** Accepted.
SAVE 🛜 ✖ 🛏 💻 🍴 ≈ ✖

Ⓐ ▼▼▼ Travelodge Ottawa East H
(613) 745-1133. **$120-$160.** 1486 Innes Rd K1B 3V5. Hwy 417 exit 112 (Innes Rd), just e. Int corridors. **Pets:** Other species. Designated rooms, service with restrictions. ECO SAVE 🛜 🛏 💻 🍴 ≈

Ⓐ ▼▼▼▼ Travelodge Ottawa Hotel & Conference Centre H
(613) 722-7600. **$110-$179.** 1376 Carling Ave K1Z 7L5. Hwy 417 exit 124, just s. Int corridors. **Pets:** Accepted.
ECO SAVE 🛜 ✖ 🛏 💻 🍴 ≈ ✖

Ⓐ ▼▼▼ Webb's Motel M
(613) 728-1881. **$85-$125.** 1705 Carling Ave K2A 1C8. Hwy 417 exit 126, 0.3 mi (0.5 km) n on Maitland Ave, then 0.3 mi (0.5 km) e. Ext/int corridors. **Pets:** Very small. Designated rooms, service with restrictions, supervision. SAVE 🛜 🛏 💻 🍴

Ⓐ ▼▼▼ WelcomINNS H
(613) 748-7800. **$110-$140.** 1220 Michael St K1J 7T1. Hwy 417 exit 115 (St. Laurent Blvd), just ne. Int corridors. **Pets:** Small. $20 daily fee/pet. Service with restrictions, crate. ECO SAVE 🛜 ✖ 🛏 💻

Ⓐ ▼▼▼ ▼▼▼ The Westin Ottawa H ❀
(613) 560-7000. **$189-$650.** 11 Colonel By Dr K1N 9H4. Corner of Rideau St. Int corridors. **Pets:** Large. Service with restrictions, supervision.
ECO SAVE 🛜 ✖ 🛏 💻 🍴 ≈ ✖

END METROPOLITAN AREA

OWEN SOUND

▼▼ Comfort Inn H
(519) 371-5500. **Call for rates.** 955 9th Ave E N4K 6N4. Jct Hwy 6, 10, 21 and 26. Int corridors. **Pets:** Accepted. ECO 🛜 🛏 💻

Ⓐ ▼▼▼▼ Days Inn and Conference Centre H
(519) 376-1551. **$109-$189.** 950 6th St E N4K 1H1. Just off Hwy 6 and 10. Int corridors. **Pets:** $20 daily fee/pet. Designated rooms, service with restrictions, supervision. ECO SAVE 🛜 🛏 💻 🍴 ≈ ✖

PARRY SOUND

▼▼ Comfort Inn H
(705) 746-6221. **$130-$160.** 120 Bowes St P2A 2L7. Hwy 69 exit 224 (Bowes St), just w. Int corridors. **Pets:** Accepted. ECO 🛜 🛏 💻

▼▼ Microtel Inn by Wyndham Parry Sound H
(705) 746-2700. **$94-$137.** 292 Louisa St P2A 0A1. Hwy 69 exit 224 (Bowes St), just w. Int corridors. **Pets:** Accepted. 🛜 ✖ 🛏 💻

PEMBROKE

▼▼ Colonial Fireside Inn M
(613) 732-3623. **$59-$120.** 1350 Pembroke St W K8A 7A3. 2.7 mi (4.3 km) n on Forest Lea Rd (CR 42) from jct Hwy 17, just e. Ext corridors. **Pets:** Very small, dogs only. $5 daily fee/pet. Designated rooms, no service, supervision. 🛜 🛏 💻

Ⓐ ▼▼ Comfort Inn H ❀
(613) 735-1057. **$130-$150.** 959 Pembroke St E K8A 3M3. 1 mi (1.6 km) e of town center. Int corridors. **Pets:** Other species. $10 daily fee/room. Designated rooms, service with restrictions, supervision.
ECO SAVE 🛜 🛏 💻

PETAWAWA

CAA ▼▼▼ **Petawawa River Inn & Suites** 🏠
(613) 687-4686. **$115-$200.** 3520 Petawawa Blvd K8H 1W9. Hwy 17 exit Paquette Rd, 1.5 mi (2.4 km) e, then just s. Int corridors. **Pets:** Other species. $10 daily fee/pet. Designated rooms, service with restrictions, supervision. 🅔🅒🅞 ⟨SAVE⟩ 🛜 🛇 🎒 💻 🍽

CAA ▼▼▼ **Quality Inn & Suites Petawawa** 🏠
(613) 687-2855. **Call for rates.** 3119-B Petawawa Blvd K8H 1X9. Hwy 17 exit Murphy Rd (Hwy 37), 1.8 mi (3 km) ne. Int corridors. **Pets:** Medium. $10 daily fee/pet. Designated rooms, service with restrictions, supervision. ⟨SAVE⟩ 🛜 🛇 ⟨&M⟩ 🎒 💻 🏊 🛇

PETERBOROUGH

CAA ▼▼▼ **Comfort Hotel & Suites** 🏠
(705) 740-7000. **$89-$119.** 1209 Lansdowne St W K9J 7M2. 0.4 mi (0.6 km) w of jct Hwy 28. Int corridors. **Pets:** Medium. Designated rooms, no service, supervision. 🅔🅒🅞 ⟨SAVE⟩ 🛜 🎒 💻 🍽 🏊

▼▼ **King Bethune House, Guest House & Spa** 🅱🅱 ❖
(705) 743-4101. **$139-$399, 14 day notice.** 270 King St K9J 2S2. From Charlotte and George sts (clock tower), 1 blk s on George St to King St, then just w. Int corridors. **Pets:** Other species. $25 daily fee/pet. Service with restrictions, supervision. 🛜 🛇 🎒 💻

CAA ▼▼▼ **Motel 6 - Peterborough** 🏠
(705) 748-0550. **$69-$109.** 133 Landsdowne St E K9J 7P7. 1.6 mi (2.6 km) e of The Parkway. Int corridors. **Pets:** Other species. Service with restrictions, supervision. 🅔🅒🅞 ⟨SAVE⟩ 🛜 🎒

CAA ▼▼▼ **Quality Inn** 🏠 ❖
(705) 748-6801. **$80-$129.** 1074 Lansdowne St W K9J 1Z9. 1.9 mi (3 km) from jct Hwy 115. Int corridors. **Pets:** Medium. Service with restrictions. 🅔🅒🅞 ⟨SAVE⟩ 🛜 🎒 💻

CAA ▼▼▼▼ **Super 8 Peterborough** 🏠 🐾
(705) 876-8898. **$89-$129.** 1257 Lansdowne St W K9J 7M2. 0.3 mi (0.5 km) e from jct Hwy 28. Int corridors. **Pets:** Other species. $25 one-time fee/room. Designated rooms, service with restrictions. 🅔🅒🅞 ⟨SAVE⟩ 🛜 🛇 🎒 💻 🏊

PICKERING

CAA ▼▼ **Comfort Inn** 🏠 🐾
(905) 831-6200. **$100-$140.** 533 Kingston Rd L1V 3N7. Hwy 401 exit 394N (White's Rd) to Hwy 2, 0.3 mi (0.5 km) w. Int corridors. **Pets:** $10 one-time fee/room. Designated rooms, service with restrictions. 🅔🅒🅞 ⟨SAVE⟩ 🛜 🎒 💻

PLANTAGENET

▼▼ **Motel de Champlain** 🅜
(613) 673-5220. **$65-$111.** 5999 Hwy 17 K0B 1L0. Jct CR 9. Ext/int corridors. **Pets:** Other species. $20 daily fee/room. Service with restrictions. 🛜 🛇 🎒 🍽

PORT HOPE

▼▼ **Comfort Inn** 🏠
(905) 885-7000. **$100-$110.** 2211 County Rd 28 L1A 3V6. Hwy 401 exit 464 (Hwy 28), just n. Int corridors. **Pets:** Accepted. 🛜 🎒 💻

PROVIDENCE BAY

CAA ▼ **Aux Huron Sands Motel** 🅜
(705) 377-4616. **$80-$160, 3 day notice.** 5216 Hwy 551 P0P 1T0. In Providence Bay; center. Ext corridors. **Pets:** Accepted. ⟨SAVE⟩ 🛜 🎒 🅩

RENFREW

CAA ▼▼▼ **BEST WESTERN Renfrew Inn & Conference Centre** 🏠
(613) 432-8109. **$109-$119.** 760 Gibbons Rd K7V 3Z4. Hwy 17 exit O'Brien Rd, just s to Wrangler Rd, then just w. Int corridors. **Pets:** Medium, dogs only. $20 daily fee/pet. Service with restrictions, supervision. ⟨SAVE⟩ 🛜 🛇 🎒 💻 🍽 🏊

▼ **The Rocky Mountain Lodge** 🅜
(613) 432-5801. **Call for rates.** 409 Stewart St N K7V 1Y4. Hwy 17 exit Bruce St, 1.9 mi (3.1 km) s, then just w. Ext corridors. **Pets:** Accepted. 🛜 🎒 💻 🍽

ST. THOMAS

CAA ▼▼▼ **Cardinal Court Motel** 🅜
(519) 633-0740. **$69-$91.** 10401 Sunset Rd, RR 7 N5P 3T2. Hwy 4, 4.1 mi (6.5 km) s of jct Hwy 4 and 401 exit 177A. Ext corridors. **Pets:** Small, dogs only. $10 one-time fee/pet. Service with restrictions, supervision. ⟨SAVE⟩ 🛜 🎒 💻

▼▼ **Comfort Inn** 🏠
(519) 633-4082. **$84-$130.** 100 Centennial Ave N5R 5B2. On Hwy 3, 4.1 mi (6.5 km) e. Int corridors. **Pets:** Accepted. 🛜 🎒 💻

SARNIA

CAA ▼▼▼▼ **BEST WESTERN PLUS Guildwood Inn** 🏠 ❖
(519) 337-7577. **$124-$134.** 1400 Venetian Blvd N7T 7W6. 0.6 mi (1 km) e of Bluewater Bridge. Ext/int corridors. **Pets:** Small. $10 daily fee/pet. Designated rooms, service with restrictions, supervision. ⟨SAVE⟩ 🛜 🛇 🎒 💻 🍽 🏊

▼▼▼ **Comfort Inn** 🏠 ❖
(519) 383-6767. **$90-$170.** 815 Mara St N7V 1X4. Jct Church St. Int corridors. **Pets:** Medium. $20 one-time fee/pet. Designated rooms, no service, crate. 🛜 🎒 💻

▼▼ **Super 8-Sarnia** 🏠
(519) 337-3767. **$80-$180.** 420 Christina St N N7T 5W1. Between Exmouth St and London Rd. Ext/int corridors. **Pets:** Other species. $25 one-time fee/room. Service with restrictions, supervision. 🛜 ⟨&M⟩ 🎒 💻 🍽

SAULT STE. MARIE

▼ **Adams Motel** 🅜
(705) 254-4345. **$69-$99.** 647 Great Northern Rd (Hwy 17) P6B 5A1. Hwy 17, 2.8 mi (4.4 km) n. Ext corridors. **Pets:** Accepted. 🛜 🎒 💻

CAA ▼▼▼▼ **Algoma's Water Tower Inn & Suites** 🏠
(705) 949-8111. **$129-$189, 7 day notice.** 360 Great Northern Rd P6B 4Z7. Jct Hwy 17 and Second Line. Int corridors. **Pets:** Accepted. 🅔🅒🅞 ⟨SAVE⟩ 🛜 🛇 🎒 💻 🍽 🏊 🛇

▼ **Ambassador Motel** 🅜
(705) 759-6199. **$59-$99.** 1275 Great Northern Rd P6A 5K7. 4 mi (6.4 km) n on Hwy 17. Ext corridors. **Pets:** Accepted. 🛜 🎒 💻 🏊 🛇

CAA ▼ **Bel-Air Motel** 🅜
(705) 945-7950. **$55-$99.** 398 Pim St P6B 2V1. 1.3 mi (2 km) n on Hwy 17B. Ext corridors. **Pets:** Medium, dogs only. $10 daily fee/pet. Designated rooms, service with restrictions. ⟨SAVE⟩ 🛜 🎒 💻

CAA ▼ **Catalina Motel** 🅜 ❖
(705) 945-9260. **$99-$125.** 259 Great Northern Rd P6B 4Z2. 2 mi (3.2 km) n on Hwy 17B. Ext corridors. **Pets:** Service with restrictions, crate. ⟨SAVE⟩ 🛜 🛇 🎒 💻

Ⓐ 🛥🛥🛥 **City Centre Travelodge Inn & Suites** 🄷
(705) 759-1400. **$107-$200.** 332 Bay St P6A 1X1. Between Elgin and
Bruce sts; downtown; opposite Station Mall. Int corridors. **Pets:** Other
species. $100 deposit/room. Designated rooms, service with restrictions,
crate. 🄴🄲🄾 🆂🄰🆅🄴 📶 🛢 💻 🍴

Ⓐ 🛥🛥 **Comfort Inn** 🄷
(705) 759-8000. **$95-$175.** 333 Great Northern Rd P6B 4Z8. 2.3 mi (3.6
km) n on Hwy 17B. Int corridors. **Pets:** Medium, dogs only. $10 daily
fee/pet. Designated rooms, service with restrictions, supervision.
🄴🄲🄾 🆂🄰🆅🄴 📶 🛢 💻

🛥🛥🛥 **Delta Sault Ste. Marie Waterfront Hotel and**
          Conference Centre 🄷
(705) 949-0611. **$129-$179.** 208 St. Marys River Dr P6A 5V4. On the
waterfront. Int corridors. **Pets:** $35 one-time fee/pet. Service with restric-
tions, supervision. 🄴🄲🄾 📶 ❌ 🛢 💻 🍴 🏊 ⊠

🛥🛥 **Glenview Cottages** 🄲🄰 🐾
(705) 759-3436. **$125-$195.** 2611 Great Northern Rd P6A 5K7. 6 mi (9.6
km) n on Hwy 17. Ext corridors. **Pets:** Medium, dogs only. $10 daily fee/
room. Designated rooms, service with restrictions, crate.
🄴🄲🄾 📶 🛢 💻 🏊 ⊠

🛥 **Holiday Motel** 🄼
(705) 759-8608. **$60-$90.** 435 Trunk Rd P6A 3T1. On Hwy 17, just e of
jct Hwy 17B. Ext corridors. **Pets:** Accepted. 📶 🛢 💻

🛥 **Northlander Motel** 🄼
(705) 254-6452. **$60-$100.** 243 Great Northern Rd P6B 4Z2. 1.9 mi (3
km) n on Hwy 17B. Ext corridors. **Pets:** Accepted. 📶 🛢 💻

🛥 **Satelite Motel** 🄼
(705) 759-2897. **$55-$95, 5 day notice.** 248 Great Northern Rd P6B
4Z6. 1.9 mi (3 km) n on Hwy 17B. Ext corridors. **Pets:** Accepted.
📶 🛢 💻

Ⓐ 🛥 **Skyline Motel** 🄼
(705) 942-1240. **$65-$85, 5 day notice.** 232 Great Northern Rd P6B
4Z5. 1.9 mi (3 km) n on Hwy 17B. Ext corridors. **Pets:** $5 daily fee/pet.
Designated rooms, service with restrictions, supervision.
🆂🄰🆅🄴 📶 🛢 💻

🛥🛥 **Sleep Inn** 🄷
(705) 253-7533. **Call for rates.** 727 Bay St P6A 6Y3. Between East and
Church sts; downtown. Int corridors. **Pets:** Other species. $10 daily fee/
pet. Service with restrictions, supervision. 📶 ❌ 🛢 💻

Ⓐ 🛥🛥 **Super 8** 🄷
(705) 254-6441. **$88-$110.** 184 Great Northern Rd P6B 4Z3. 1.3 mi (2
km) n on Hwy 17B. Int corridors. **Pets:** Accepted. 🆂🄰🆅🄴 📶 🛢 💻

🛥 **Villa Inn Motel** 🄼
(705) 942-2424. **Call for rates.** 724 Great Northern Rd P6B 5A3. 2.9 mi
(4.6 km) n on Hwy 17B. Ext corridors. **Pets:** Accepted. 📶 🛢 💻

SIMCOE

Ⓐ 🛥🛥 **BEST WESTERN Little River Inn** 🄷
(519) 426-2125. **$112-$260.** 203 Queensway W N3Y 2M9. Jct Hwy 24,
just w on Hwy 3. Int corridors. **Pets:** Medium. Designated rooms, service
with restrictions, supervision. 🆂🄰🆅🄴 📶 🛢 💻 🍴 🏊

🛥🛥 **Comfort Inn** 🄷 🐾
(519) 426-2611. **$99-$180.** 85 Queensway E N3Y 4M5. 0.3 mi (0.5 km)
e on Hwy 3. Int corridors. **Pets:** Other species. Designated rooms, service
with restrictions, supervision. 🄴🄲🄾 📶 🛢 💻

🛥🛥 **Travelodge Simcoe** 🄷
(519) 426-4751. **$114-$134.** 385 Queensway W (Hwy 3) N3Y 2M9. 0.6
mi (1 km) w. Ext/int corridors. **Pets:** Accepted.
🄴🄲🄾 📶 🅶🄼 🛢 💻 🏊 ⊠

SMITHS FALLS

Ⓐ 🛥🛥 **BEST WESTERN Colonel By Inn** 🄷
(613) 284-0001. **$100-$160.** 88 Lombard St K7A 4G5. On Hwy 15, just
w of jct Hwy 29. Int corridors. **Pets:** Small, dogs only. $10 daily fee/pet.
Designated rooms, service with restrictions, supervision.
🆂🄰🆅🄴 📶 ❌ 🛢 💻 🏊

SOUTH BAYMOUTH

Ⓐ 🛥 **Huron Motor Lodge** 🄼
(705) 859-3131. **$112-$185.** 24 Water St N P0P 1Z0. In South Bay-
mouth; center. Ext corridors. **Pets:** $10 daily fee/pet. Designated rooms,
supervision. 🆂🄰🆅🄴 ❌ 🛢 🏊 🄰🄲 ☎

STRATFORD

🛥🛥🛥 **Arden Park Hotel** 🄷
(519) 275-2936. **$99-$199.** 552 Ontario St (Hwy 7 & 8) N5A 3J3. Jct
Romeo St. Int corridors. **Pets:** Accepted.
📶 ❌ 🅶🄼 🛢 💻 🍴 🏊

STURGEON FALLS

🛥🛥🛥 **Comfort Inn** 🄷
(705) 753-5665. **$99-$120.** 11 Front St P2B 3L3. On Hwy 17 at western
approach to town. Int corridors. **Pets:** Accepted.
📶 ❌ 🛢 💻 🏊

SUDBURY

Ⓐ 🛥🛥 **BEST WESTERN Downtown Sudbury**
          Centreville 🄷
(705) 673-7801. **$99-$108.** 151 Larch St P3E 1C3. Just w of Paris St;
center. Int corridors. **Pets:** $20 daily fee/room. Designated rooms, service
with restrictions, supervision. 🆂🄰🆅🄴 📶 ❌ 🛢 💻 🍴

Ⓐ 🛥🛥 **Comfort Inn** 🄷 🐾
(705) 522-1101. **Call for rates.** 2171 Regent St P3E 5V3. Trans-Canada
Hwy 17 exit Hwy 69/RR 46, 1.8 mi (2.8 km) n. Int corridors. **Pets:** Other
species. Designated rooms, service with restrictions, crate.
🄴🄲🄾 🆂🄰🆅🄴 📶 🛢 💻

Ⓐ 🛥🛥 **Comfort Inn East** 🄷
(705) 560-4502. **$120-$154.** 440 2nd Ave N P3B 4A4. Just s of Kingsway Rd. Int corridors. **Pets:** Other species. $15 one-time fee/room. Ser-
vice with restrictions, crate. 🄴🄲🄾 🆂🄰🆅🄴 📶 🅶🄼 🛢 💻

🛥🛥 **Days Inn-Sudbury** 🄷 🐾
(705) 674-7517. **$110-$140.** 117 Elm St P3C 1T3. Corner of Lorne St;
downtown. Int corridors. **Pets:** Medium, other species. $20 daily fee/room.
Designated rooms, service with restrictions, supervision.
🄴🄲🄾 📶 ❌ 🛢 💻 🍴 🏊 ⊠

Ⓐ 🛥🛥🛥 **Holiday Inn Hotel Sudbury** 🄷
(705) 522-3000. **$124-$129.** 1696 Regent St P3E 3Z8. Trans-Canada
Hwy 17 exit Hwy 69/RR 46, 2.4 mi (3.9 km) n. Int corridors. **Pets:** $20
daily fee/pet. Designated rooms, service with restrictions, supervision.
🆂🄰🆅🄴 📶 🛢 💻 🍴 🏊 ⊠

Ⓐ 🛥🛥🛥 **Homewood Suites by Hilton Sudbury** 🄷
(705) 523-8100. **$139-$269.** 2270 Regent St P3E 0B4. Trans-Canada
Hwy 17 exit Hwy 69/RR 46, 1.6 mi (2.5 km) n. Int corridors.
Pets: Accepted. 🆂🄰🆅🄴 📶 🅶🄼 🛢 💻 🏊

🛥🛥 **Quality Inn & Conference Centre** 🄷
(705) 675-1273. **$109-$249.** 390 Elgin St S P3B 1B1. 0.6 mi (0.9 km) s
on Paris St from jct Kingsway Rd and Elm St. Int corridors.
Pets: Medium, other species. $10 daily fee/room. Designated rooms,
supervision. 🄴🄲🄾 📶 ❌ 🛢 💻 🍴 🏊

Ⓐ 🛥🛥🛥 **Radisson Hotel Sudbury Downtown** 🄷
(705) 675-1123. **$109-$299.** 85 Ste. Anne Rd P3E 4S4. Jct Notre Dame
Ave; downtown. Int corridors. **Pets:** Large. $35 one-time fee/room. Desig-
nated rooms, service with restrictions, supervision.
🆂🄰🆅🄴 📶 🛢 💻 🍴 🏊 ⊠

(CAA) ▼▼▼ **TownePlace Suites by Marriott Sudbury** 🅷 ❀

(705) 525-7700. **$149-$175.** 1710 The Kingsway Ave P3B 0E4. Just e of jct Falconbridge Rd. Int corridors. **Pets:** Other species. $50 one-time fee/room. Designated rooms, service with restrictions, crate.

SAVE 🛜 ✕ 👤M 🛏 💻 🏊 ✕

(CAA) ▼▼▼ **Travelodge Hotel Sudbury** 🅷 ❀

(705) 522-1100. **$115-$185.** 1401 Paris St P3E 3B6. Trans-Canada Hwy 17 exit Hwy 69/RR 46, 2 mi (3.2 km) n on Regent St, then 0.9 mi (1.5 km) e. Int corridors. **Pets:** Other species. $25 one-time fee/pet. Designated rooms, service with restrictions, crate.

ECO SAVE 🛜 ✕ 🛏 💻 🍴 🏊

THESSALON

(CAA) ▼ **Carolyn Beach Motor Inn** 🅼

(705) 842-3330. **$97-$140.** 1 Lakeside Dr P0R 1L0. On Hwy 17B, just s of jct Hwy 17. Ext corridors. **Pets:** $12 daily fee/pet. Service with restrictions, supervision. SAVE 🛜 ✕ 🛏 💻 🍴 ✕

THUNDER BAY

(CAA) ▼▼▼ **BEST WESTERN Crossroads Motor Inn** 🅷

(807) 577-4241. **$117-$142.** 655 W Arthur St P7E 5R6. Just e of jct Hwy 61. Int corridors. **Pets:** Small. $15 daily fee/room. Designated rooms, service with restrictions, supervision. SAVE 🛜 ✕ 🛏 💻

(CAA) ▼▼▼ **BEST WESTERN PLUS Nor'Wester Hotel & Conference Centre** 🅷

(807) 473-9123. **$130-$153.** 2080 Hwy 61 P7J 1B8. On Hwy 61 at Loch Lomond Rd. Int corridors. **Pets:** Dogs only. $20 one-time fee/room. Designated rooms, service with restrictions, crate.

SAVE 🛜 ✕ 👤M 🛏 💻 🍴 🏊 ✕

(CAA) ▼▼ **Comfort Inn** 🅼

(807) 475-3155. **$122-$155.** 660 W Arthur St P7E 5R8. Just e of jct Hwy 61. Int corridors. **Pets:** Other species. Service with restrictions, supervision. ECO SAVE 🛜 🛏 💻

(CAA) ▼▼▼ **Econo Lodge** 🅷

(807) 344-6688. **$85-$160.** 686 Memorial Ave P7B 3Z5. 0.6 mi (1 km) e of jct Harbour Expwy. Int corridors. **Pets:** Medium. $20 one-time fee/room. Designated rooms, service with restrictions, supervision.

SAVE 🛜 ✕ 🛏 💻

(CAA) ▼▼▼ **Super 8** 🅷

(807) 344-2612. **$88-$108.** 439 Memorial Ave P7B 3Y6. Jct Hwy 11, 17 and Harbour Expwy, 1.9 mi (3 km) e on Harbour Expwy, 1.3 mi (2 km) n. Int corridors. **Pets:** Accepted. SAVE 🛜 ✕ 🛏 💻

▼▼ **Victoria Inn Hotel & Convention Centre** 🅷

(807) 577-8481. **$125-$150.** 555 W Arthur St P7E 5R5. 0.5 mi (0.8 km) e of jct Hwy 11B, 17B and 61 (western access to town). Int corridors. **Pets:** Accepted. 🛜 ✕ 🛏 💻 🍴 🏊 ✕

TILLSONBURG

▼▼ **Howard Johnson/Tillsonburg** 🅷

(519) 842-7366. **$99-$120.** 92 Simcoe St N4G 2J1. Hwy 19, just e. Int corridors. **Pets:** $10 daily fee/pet. Service with restrictions, supervision. ECO 🛜 ✕ 🛏 💻 🍴

TIMMINS

(CAA) ▼▼ **Comfort Inn** 🅷

(705) 264-9474. **$115-$139.** 939 Algonquin Blvd E P4N 7J5. Hwy 101, 0.3 mi (0.5 km) e of Hwy 655. Int corridors. **Pets:** Designated rooms, service with restrictions, crate. ECO SAVE 🛜 🛏 💻

▼▼ **Travelodge** 🅷

(705) 360-1122. **$125-$165.** 1136 Riverside Dr P4R 1A2. Hwy 101, 2.8 mi (4.4 km) w of Hwy 655. Int corridors. **Pets:** Accepted. ECO 🛜 🛏 💻

TOBERMORY

▼ **Coach House Inn** 🅼

(519) 596-2361. **$59-$129.** 7189 Hwy 6 N0H 2R0. Hwy 6, 1.2 mi (2 km) s of ferry docks. Ext corridors. **Pets:** Accepted.

🛜 ✕ 🛏 🏊 ✕ ✒

TORONTO METROPOLITAN AREA

MARKHAM

▼▼▼ **Comfort Inn** 🅷

(905) 477-6077. **$94-$129.** 8330 Woodbine Ave L3R 2N8. Hwy 401 exit 375, 5.6 mi (9 km) n; Hwy 404 exit Hwy 7, just e, then s. Int corridors. **Pets:** Accepted. 🛜 🛏 💻 🏊 ✕

▼▼▼ **Delta Markham** 🅷

(905) 477-2010. **$99-$179.** 50 E Valhalla Dr L3R 0A3. Hwy 404 exit Hwy 7, just e. Int corridors. **Pets:** Medium, other species. $35 one-time fee/room. Service with restrictions, crate.

ECO 🛜 🛏 💻 🍴 🏊 ✕

(CAA) ▼▼▼▼ **Hilton Toronto/Markham Suites Conference Centre & Spa** 🅷

(905) 470-8500. **Call for rates.** 8500 Warden Ave L6G 1A5. Hwy 404 exit Hwy 7, 2 mi (3.2 km) e. Int corridors. **Pets:** Small. $15 one-time fee/pet. Service with restrictions, supervision.

ECO SAVE 🛜 🛏 💻 🍴 🏊 ✕

(CAA) ▼▼▼ **Holiday Inn Hotel & Suites Toronto-Markham** 🅷

(905) 474-0444. **$95-$139.** 7095 Woodbine Ave L3R 1A3. Just n of Steeles Ave. Int corridors. **Pets:** Accepted.

SAVE 🛜 ✕ 🛏 💻 🍴 🏊 ✕

▼▼▼ **Homewood Suites by Hilton Toronto/Markham** 🅷

(905) 477-4663. **$109-$189.** 50 Bodrington Ct L6G 0A9. Hwy 407 exit 84 (Woodbine Ave), just ne. Int corridors. **Pets:** Accepted.

🛜 👤M 🛏 💻 🏊

▼▼▼ **Howard Johnson Hotel Toronto-Markham** 🅷

(905) 479-5000. **$80-$129.** 555 Cochrane Dr L3R 8E3. Hwy 404 N exit Hwy 7 E to E Valhalla Dr. Int corridors. **Pets:** Accepted.

ECO 🛜 🛏 💻 🍴 🏊 ✕

▼▼▼ **Residence Inn by Marriott Toronto-Markham** 🅷

(905) 707-7933. **$125-$179.** 55 Minthorn Blvd L3T 7N5. Hwy 404 exit Hwy 7, 0.7 mi (1.1 km) w. Int corridors. **Pets:** Accepted.

🛜 ✕ 🛏 💻 🏊 ✕

▼▼▼ **Staybridge Suites Toronto-Markham** 🅷

(905) 771-9333. **$119-$160.** 355 S Park Rd L3T 7W2. Hwy 404 exit Hwy 7, 0.9 mi (1.4 km) w, 0.3 mi (0.5 km) s on Commerce Valley Dr W, then just e. Int corridors. **Pets:** Accepted. 🛜 🛏 💻 🏊

RICHMOND HILL

(CAA) ▼▼▼ **Holiday Inn Express & Suites Toronto-Markham** 🅷

(905) 695-5990. **$115-$179.** 10 E Pearce St L4B 0A8. Just n of jct Leslie St and Hwy 7. Int corridors. **Pets:** Medium. $50 one-time fee/pet. Supervision. ECO SAVE 🛜 ✕ 👤M 🛏 💻 🏊

(CAA) ▼▼▼▼ **Sheraton Parkway Toronto North Hotel and Suites** 🅷 ❀

(905) 881-2121. **$119-$179.** 600 Hwy 7 E L4B 1B2. Hwy 404 exit 27, 0.6 mi (1 km) w. Int corridors. **Pets:** Small. $100 one-time fee/room. Designated rooms, service with restrictions, supervision.

ECO SAVE 🛜 ✕ 💻 🍴 🏊 ✕

TORONTO

BEST WESTERN PLUS Roehampton Hotel & Suites 🄷
(416) 487-5101. **$145-$250.** 808 Mt. Pleasant Rd M4P 2L2. Just n of Eglinton Ave. Int corridors. **Pets:** Accepted.

Comfort Inn 🄷
(416) 967-6781. **Call for rates.** 321 Jarvis St M5B 2C2. Just s of Gerrard St. Int corridors. **Pets:** Accepted.

Comfort Inn 🄷
(416) 736-4700. **$90-$125.** 66 Norfinch Dr M3N 1X1. Hwy 400 exit Finch Ave E, just n. Int corridors. **Pets:** Medium. $15 daily fee/pet. Service with restrictions, supervision.

Comfort Inn Toronto East 🄷
(416) 269-7400. **$90-$120.** 3306 Kingston Rd M1M 1P8. Hwy 401 exit 383 (Markham Rd), 3.1 mi (5 km) s to Hwy 2 (Kingston Rd), then 0.6 mi (1 km) w. Int corridors. **Pets:** Small. $20 daily fee/pet. Designated rooms, service with restrictions, supervision.

Cosmopolitan Hotel & Residences 🄷
(416) 350-2000. **Call for rates.** 8 Colborne St M5E 1E1. Between King and Wellington sts. Int corridors. **Pets:** Accepted.

Crowne Plaza Toronto Airport 🄷
(416) 675-1234. **$119-$229.** 33 Carlson Ct M9W 6H5. Just w of jct Hwy 27, n of Dixon Rd. Int corridors. **Pets:** Accepted.

Days Hotel & Conference Centre Toronto Don Valley 🄷
(416) 493-9000. **$109-$129.** 185 Yorkland Blvd M2J 4R2. Just s of Sheppard Ave. Int corridors. **Pets:** Accepted.

Delta Chelsea Hotel 🄷
(416) 595-1975. **$119-$369.** 33 Gerrard St W M5G 1Z4. Just w of Yonge St; just s of College St. Int corridors. **Pets:** Small. $35 one-time fee/room. Service with restrictions, crate.

Delta Toronto East 🄷 ❀
(416) 299-1500. **Call for rates.** 2035 Kennedy Rd M1T 3G2. Hwy 401 exit 379 (Kennedy Rd), just ne. Int corridors. **Pets:** Medium. $35 one-time fee/room. Designated rooms, service with restrictions, supervision.

DoubleTree by Hilton Hotel Toronto Airport 🄷
(416) 244-1711. **$109-$169.** 655 Dixon Rd M9W 1J3. Jct Hwy 27 N, just w of jct Hwy 401. Int corridors. **Pets:** Small. Service with restrictions, supervision.

The Fairmont Royal York 🄷
(416) 368-2511. **Call for rates.** 100 Front St W M5J 1E3. QEW/Gardiner Expwy, exit n on York or Bay sts; entrance on Wellington St. Int corridors. **Pets:** Accepted.

The Grand Hotel & Suites Toronto 🄷
(416) 863-9000. **$189-$1299.** 225 Jarvis St M5B 2C1. Jct Dundas St. Int corridors. **Pets:** Accepted.

Holiday Inn Express Toronto Downtown 🄷 ❀
(416) 367-5555. **$129-$159.** 111 Lombard St M5C 2T9. Gardiner Expwy exit Jarvis St, 0.6 mi (1 km) n, then just w; between Adelaide and Richmond sts. Int corridors. **Pets:** Medium. Service with restrictions, supervision.

Holiday Inn Express Toronto-North York 🄷
(416) 665-3500. **$105-$134.** 30 Norfinch Dr M3N 1X1. Hwy 400 exit Finch Ave E. Int corridors. **Pets:** Accepted.

Holiday Inn Toronto Airport East 🄷
(416) 240-7511. **Call for rates.** 600 Dixon Rd M9W 1J1. E of jct Hwy 27 N and Dixon Rd; w of jct Hwy 401 and Dixon Rd. Int corridors. **Pets:** Accepted.

Holiday Inn Toronto Downtown Centre 🄷
(416) 977-6655. **Call for rates.** 30 Carlton St M5B 2E9. Adjacent to Maple Leaf Gardens. Int corridors. **Pets:** Medium. $25 one-time fee/room, $10 daily fee/room. Service with restrictions, crate.

Hotel Carlingview Toronto Airport 🄷
(416) 675-3303. **Call for rates.** 221 Carlingview Dr M9W 5E8. QEW exit Hwy 427 N to Dixon Rd E, 0.6 mi (1 km) to Carlingview Dr, then just s. Ext/int corridors. **Pets:** $45 one-time fee/room. Designated rooms, service with restrictions, crate.

Hotel Indigo Toronto Airport 🄷
(416) 637-7000. **$89-$149.** 135 Carlingview Dr M9W 5E7. Just n of Dixon Rd. Int corridors. **Pets:** Accepted.

Hotel Le Germain Maple Leaf Square 🄷 ❀
(416) 649-7575. **$264-$584.** 75 Bremner Blvd M5J 0A1. Jct York St, just w of Air Canada Centre. Int corridors. **Pets:** Other species. $35 daily fee/room. Service with restrictions, supervision.

Hotel Le Germain Toronto 🄷
(416) 345-9500. **$235-$2900.** 30 Mercer St M5V 1H3. Between John St and Blue Jays Way. Int corridors. **Pets:** Accepted.

Hyatt Regency Toronto on King 🄷 ❀
(416) 343-1234. **$99-$429.** 370 King St W M5V 1J9. Between Spadina Ave and Peter St. Int corridors. **Pets:** Medium, dogs only. $30 daily fee/room. Designated rooms, service with restrictions.

InterContinental Toronto Centre 🄷 ❀
(416) 597-1400. **$189-$309.** 225 Front St W M5V 2X3. Between Spadina and University aves. Int corridors. **Pets:** Medium, other species. $50 one-time fee/room. Designated rooms, service with restrictions, crate.

InterContinental Toronto Yorkville 🄷
(416) 960-5200. **$195-$405.** 220 Bloor St W M5S 1T8. Just w of Avenue Rd. Int corridors. **Pets:** Accepted.

The King Edward Hotel 🄷
(416) 863-9700. **$159-$725.** 37 King St E M5C 1E9. Just e of Yonge St. Int corridors. **Pets:** Accepted.

Metropolitan Hotel 🄷
(416) 977-5000. **$119-$500.** 108 Chestnut St M5G 1R3. Just s of Dundas St. Int corridors. **Pets:** Medium. $25 daily fee/pet. Service with restrictions, crate.

Montecassino Hotel & Event Venue 🄷
(416) 630-8100. **$119-$139.** 3710 Chesswood Dr M3J 2W4. Jct Sheppard Ave. Int corridors. **Pets:** Small. $15 one-time fee/pet. Service with restrictions, supervision.

Novotel Toronto Centre 🄷
(416) 367-8900. **$159-$295.** 45 The Esplanade M5E 1W2. Just ne of Gardiner Expwy via Yonge St. Int corridors. **Pets:** Accepted.

ⓐ ♦♦♦ **Novotel Toronto North York** 🏨
(416) 733-2929. **$145-$335.** 3 Park Home Ave M2N 6L3. Hwy 401 exit Yonge St, 1.1 mi (1.7 km) n, then just w. Int corridors. **Pets:** Accepted.
[ECO] [SAVE] 🛜 ✕ 🛏 🖥 🍴 ⇌

ⓐ ♦♦♦ **Pantages Hotel Toronto Centre** 🏨 🐾
(416) 362-1777. **Call for rates.** 200 Victoria St M5B 1V8. Jct Shuter St. Int corridors. **Pets:** Small. $50 one-time fee/pet. Service with restrictions, supervision. [ECO] [SAVE] 🛜 🛏 🖥 🍴 ⇌ ✕

ⓐ ♦♦♦ **Park Hyatt Toronto** 🏨
(416) 925-1234. **$225-$799, 3 day notice.** 4 Avenue Rd M5R 2E8. Corner of Bloor St W. Int corridors. **Pets:** Accepted.
[SAVE] 🛜 ♿ 🍴 ✕

ⓐ ♦♦♦♦ **Quality Hotel & Suites Toronto Airport East** 🏨
(416) 240-9090. **$119-$219.** 2180 Islington Ave M9P 3P1. Hwy 401 exit 356, just s. Int corridors. **Pets:** Accepted.
[ECO] [SAVE] 🛜 ✕ 🛏 🖥 🍴

ⓐ ♦♦♦ **Quality Suites Toronto Airport** 🏨
(416) 674-8442. **$100-$125.** 262 Carlingview Dr M9W 5G1. 0.6 mi (1 km) w of jct Hwy 27 N and Dixon Rd. Int corridors. **Pets:** Accepted.
[ECO] [SAVE] 🛜 🛏 🖥 🍴

ⓐ ♦♦♦ **Radisson Hotel Toronto East** 🏨
(416) 493-7000. **Call for rates.** 55 Hallcrown Pl M2J 4R1. Hwy 401 exit Victoria Park N to Consumers Rd, then w. Int corridors. **Pets:** $25 daily fee/pet. Service with restrictions, supervision.
[ECO] [SAVE] 🛜 ♿ 🖥 ⇌

ⓐ ♦♦♦ **Radisson Suite Hotel Toronto Airport** 🏨
(416) 242-7400. **Call for rates.** 640 Dixon Rd M9W 1J1. Just e of jct Hwy 27; just w of jct Hwy 401. Int corridors. **Pets:** Other species. $50 one-time fee/room. Service with restrictions, crate.
[ECO] [SAVE] 🛜 🛏 🖥 🍴

ⓐ ♦♦♦♦ **Renaissance Toronto Downtown Hotel** 🏨 🐾
(416) 341-7100. **$189-$289.** 1 Blue Jays Way M5V 1J4. Jct Front St. Int corridors. **Pets:** Dogs only. $50 one-time fee/room. Service with restrictions, crate. [ECO] [SAVE] 🛜 ✕ 🛏 🖥 🍴 ⇌ ✕

♦♦♦♦ **Residence Inn by Marriott Toronto Airport** 🏨
(416) 798-2900. **$109-$299.** 17 Reading Ct M9W 7K7. Just w of jct Hwy 27 and Dixon Rd. Int corridors. **Pets:** Other species. $100 one-time fee/room. Designated rooms, service with restrictions.
[ECO] 🛜 ✕ ♿ 🛏 🖥 ⇌ ✕

ⓐ ♦♦♦♦ **Residence Inn by Marriott Toronto Downtown/ Entertainment District** 🏨
(416) 581-1800. **$189-$349.** 255 Wellington St W M5V 3P9. Jct Blue Jays Way. Int corridors. **Pets:** Accepted.
[ECO] [SAVE] 🛜 ✕ 🛏 🖥 ⇌

ⓐ ♦♦♦♦♦ **The Ritz-Carlton, Toronto** 🏨 🐾
(416) 585-2500. **$360-$600.** 181 Wellington St W M5V 3G7. Between Simcoe and John sts. Int corridors. **Pets:** Small, dogs only. $150 one-time fee/room. Service with restrictions.
[SAVE] 🛜 ✕ ♿ 🖥 🍴 ⇌ ✕

ⓐ ♦♦♦♦ **Sheraton Centre Toronto Hotel** 🏨
(416) 361-1000. **$159-$629.** 123 Queen St W M5H 2M9. Opposite Toronto Civic Centre and City Hall. Int corridors. **Pets:** Accepted.
[ECO] ⊟ [SAVE] 🛜 ✕ ♿ 🛏 🖥 🍴 ⇌ ✕

ⓐ ♦♦♦♦ **Sheraton Toronto Airport Hotel & Conference Centre** 🏨 🐾
(416) 675-6100. **$109-$259.** 801 Dixon Rd M9W 1J5. Jct Hwy 27 N and Dixon Rd. Int corridors. **Pets:** Dogs only. Service with restrictions, crate.
[ECO] [SAVE] 🛜 ✕ ♿ 🛏 🖥 🍴 ⇌

ⓐ ♦♦♦ **SoHo Metropolitan Hotel** 🏨 🐾
(416) 599-8800. **$250-$895.** 318 Wellington St W M5V 3T4. Jct Blue Jays Way. Int corridors. **Pets:** Medium. $50 one-time fee/room. Service with restrictions, crate. [SAVE] 🛜 🛏 🖥 🍴 ⇌ ✕

ⓐ ♦♦♦ **Super 8 Downtown Toronto** 🏨
(647) 426-8118. **$88-$201.** 222 Spadina Ave M5T 2C2. At Dundas St; at Chinatown Centre. Int corridors. **Pets:** Accepted.
[ECO] [SAVE] 🛜 ✕ 🛏

ⓐ ♦♦♦ **Toronto Don Valley Hotel & Suites** 🏨 🐾
(416) 449-4111. **$119-$159.** 175 Wynford Dr M3C 1J3. Don Valley Pkwy exit 375 (Wynford Dr); jct Don Valley Pkwy and Eglinton Ave E. Int corridors. **Pets:** Very small, other species. $25 daily fee/pet. Designated rooms, service with restrictions, supervision.
[ECO] [SAVE] 🛜 ✕ 🛏 🖥 🍴 ⇌ ✕

ⓐ ♦♦♦ **Toronto Marriott Bloor Yorkville** 🏨
(416) 961-8000. **$189-$289.** 90 Bloor St E M4W 1A7. Just e of Yonge St. Int corridors. **Pets:** Medium. $50 one-time fee/room. Service with restrictions. [ECO] [SAVE] 🛜 ✕ ♿ 🛏 🖥 🍴

ⓐ ♦♦♦ **Travelodge Toronto Airport (Dixon Road)** 🏨
(416) 674-2222. **$99-$129.** 925 Dixon Rd M9W 1J8. Corner of Carlingview Dr. Int corridors. **Pets:** $25 one-time fee/pet. Designated rooms, service with restrictions, supervision.
[ECO] [SAVE] 🛜 🛏 🖥 🍴 ⇌

♦♦ **Travelodge Toronto East** 🏨
(416) 299-9500. **$109-$125.** 20 Milner Business Ct M1B 3C6. Jct Hwy 401 exit 383 (Markham Rd), just n. Int corridors. **Pets:** Accepted.
[ECO] 🛜 🛏 🖥 🍴 ⇌

♦♦ **Travelodge Toronto North (North York)** 🏨
(416) 663-9500. **$100-$130.** 50 Norfinch Dr M3N 1X1. Hwy 400 exit 25 (Finch Ave E). Int corridors. **Pets:** Accepted.
[ECO] 🛜 🛏 🖥 🍴 ⇌

ⓐ ♦♦♦♦ **Trump International Hotel and Tower Toronto®** 🏨 🐾
(416) 306-5800. **$395-$950.** 325 Bay St M5H 4G3. Jct Adelaide St. Int corridors. **Pets:** Other species. Supervision.
[SAVE] 🛜 ✕ ♿ 🖥 🍴 ⇌ ✕

ⓐ ♦♦♦♦ **The Westin Bristol Place Toronto Airport** 🏨
(416) 675-9444. **$109-$229.** 950 Dixon Rd M9W 5N4. 1.6 mi (2.6 km) w of jct Hwy 401. Int corridors. **Pets:** Accepted.
[SAVE] 🛜 ✕ 🛏 🖥 🍴 ⇌

ⓐ ♦♦♦♦ **The Westin Harbour Castle** 🏨 🐾
(416) 869-1600. **$159-$549.** One Harbour Sq M5J 1A6. At the foot of Bay St. Int corridors. **Pets:** Small, dogs only. Designated rooms, service with restrictions, supervision.
[ECO] [SAVE] 🛜 ✕ 🛏 🖥 🍴 ⇌ ✕

ⓐ ♦♦♦♦ **The Westin Prince Toronto** 🏨
(416) 444-2511. **$139-$389.** 900 York Mills Rd M3B 3H2. Just s of Hwy 401 via Leslie St exit to York Mills Rd E. Int corridors. **Pets:** Accepted.
[SAVE] 🛜 ✕ ♿ 🛏 🖥 🍴 ⇌ ✕

♦♦♦♦ **Windsor Arms Hotel** 🏨 🐾
(416) 971-9666. **$395-$1750.** 18 St. Thomas St M5S 3E7. Just s of Bloor St. Int corridors. **Pets:** Medium. $200 deposit/pet, $50 one-time fee/pet. Service with restrictions, supervision.
🛜 ✕ 🖥 🍴 ⇌ ✕

VAUGHAN

ⓐ ♦♦♦ **Aloft Vaughan Mills** 🏨
(905) 695-0500. **$109-$219.** 151 Bass Pro Mills Dr L4K 0E6. Hwy 400 exit 33 (Rutherford Rd) southbound; exit 32 (Bass Pro Mills Dr) northbound. Int corridors. **Pets:** Accepted.
[SAVE] 🛜 ✕ ♿ 🛏 🖥 ⇌

▼▼▼ Holiday Inn Express & Suites Vaughan-Southwest H

(905) 851-1510. **$128-$156.** 6100 Hwy 7 L4H 0R2. Jct Hwy 27. Int corridors. **Pets:** Large, other species. $25 one-time fee/room. Service with restrictions, crate. ECO 🛰 ✕ 🛏 🖳

Ⓐ ▼▼▼ Novotel Toronto Vaughan Centre H ✿

(905) 660-0212. **$99-$249.** 200 Bass Pro Mills Dr L4K 0B9. Hwy 400 S exit 33 Rutherford Rd; Hwy 400 N exit 32 Bass Pro Mills Dr. Int corridors. **Pets:** Large, other species. Designated rooms, service with restrictions. ECO SAVE 🛰 ✕ 🛏 🖳 ⑪ ⛱

▼▼▼ Residence Inn by Marriott Toronto/Vaughan H

(905) 695-4002. **$129-$189.** 11 Interchange Way L4K 5W3. Hwy 400 exit 29 (Hwy 7), 0.6 mi (1 km) e. Int corridors. **Pets:** $100 one-time fee/room. Service with restrictions, crate. 🛰 ✕ 🛏 🖳 ⛱ ✕

END METROPOLITAN AREA

TRENTON

▼▼ Comfort Inn H

(613) 965-6660. **$100-$125.** 68 Monogram Pl K8V 6S3. Hwy 401 exit 526 (Glen Miller Rd), just s, then just e. Int corridors. **Pets:** Accepted. ECO 🛰 🛏 🖳

Ⓐ ▼▼▼ Ramada Trenton Hotel H

(613) 394-4855. **$120-$200.** 99 Glen Miller Rd K8V 5P8. Hwy 401 exit 526 (Glen Miller Rd), just s. Int corridors. **Pets:** Other species. $15 daily fee/room. Service with restrictions, supervision. ECO SAVE 🛰 ✕ 🛏 🖳 ⑪ ⛱

Ⓐ ▼▼ Travelodge Trenton H

(613) 965-6789. **$110-$121.** 598 Old Hwy 2 K8V 5P5. Hwy 401 exit 538, 1.3 mi (2 km) s to Old Hwy 2, then 3.8 mi (6 km) w; 3.1 mi (4.9 km) e of jct Hwy 33. Int corridors. **Pets:** Accepted. ECO SAVE 🛰 ✕ 🛏 🖳

TWEED

▼ Park Place Motel M

(613) 478-3134. **$90-$115, 4 day notice.** 43 Victoria St S K0K 3J0. Hwy 37, 0.3 mi (0.5 km) s of center. Ext corridors. **Pets:** Medium, dogs only. $10 daily fee/pet. Service with restrictions, supervision. 🛰 🛏

WALLACEBURG

▼▼ Days Inn Wallaceburg H

(519) 627-0781. **$100-$105.** 76 McNaughton Ave N8A 1R9. On Hwy 40 (McNaughton Ave); south side of town. Int corridors. **Pets:** Accepted. 🛰 🛏 🖳

WATERLOO

Ⓐ ▼▼ Comfort Inn H

(519) 747-9400. **$125-$139.** 190 Weber St N N2J 3H4. Jct University Ave, just s. Int corridors. **Pets:** Other species. Service with restrictions, crate. ECO SAVE 🛰 🛏 🖳 ⑪

▼▼▼ Les Diplomates B & B (Executive Guest House) BB

(519) 725-3184. **$138-$156, 3 day notice.** 100 Blythwood Rd N2L 4A2. Hwy 85 N exit King St, s to Columbia St, w to Hazel St, then just n. Ext/int corridors. **Pets:** Accepted. 🛰 ✕ 🛏 🖳

▼▼▼ The Waterloo Inn Conference Hotel H

(519) 884-0220. **$149-$209.** 475 King St N N2J 2Z5. 1.9 mi (3 km) n on King St, jct Hwy 85. Int corridors. **Pets:** Large, other species. $15 daily fee/pet. Designated rooms, service with restrictions. 🛰 ✕ 🛏 🖳 ⑪ ⛱ ✕

WAWA

▼▼ Best Northern Motel & Restaurant M

(705) 856-7302. **$89-$135.** 150 Hwy 17 S P0S 1K0. On Hwy 17, 3.3 mi (5.3 km) s of jct Hwy 101. Ext corridors. **Pets:** Medium, other species. $8 daily fee/pet. Designated rooms, service with restrictions, supervision. 🛰 ✕ 🛏 🖳 ⑪ ✕ 🐾

▼ Northern Lights Motel & Breakfast M

(705) 856-1900. **Call for rates.** 1014 Hwy 17 P0S 1K0. On Hwy 17, 5 mi (8 km) n of jct Hwy 101. Ext corridors. **Pets:** Accepted. 🛰 ✕ 🛏 🖳 🐾

Ⓐ ▼▼ Parkway Motel M

(705) 856-7020. **$89-$129.** 232 Hwy 17 S P0S 1K0. On Hwy 17, 2.5 mi (4 km) s of jct Hwy 101. Ext corridors. **Pets:** Other species. $10 daily fee/pet. Service with restrictions, supervision. SAVE 🛰 ✕ 🛏 🖳 ✕ 🐾

▼ Sportsman's Motel M

(705) 856-2272. **Call for rates.** 171 Mission Rd P0S 1K0. On Hwy 101, 1.5 mi (2.4 km) e of jct Hwy 17. Ext corridors. **Pets:** Dogs only. $10 daily fee/pet. Service with restrictions. 🛰 🛏 🖳

WHITBY

▼▼ Canadiana Inn M

(905) 668-3686. **Call for rates.** 732 Dundas St E (Hwy 2) L1N 2J7. Hwy 401 exit 410 (Brock St/Hwy 12), 1 mi (1.6 km) n to Dundas St, then 0.6 mi (1 km) e. Ext corridors. **Pets:** Accepted. 🛰 🛏 🖳 ⛱

▼▼ Motel 6 Whitby #1907 H

(905) 665-8883. **$69-$79.** 165 Consumers Dr L1N 1C4. Hwy 401 exit 410 (Brock St/Hwy 12), just ne. Int corridors. **Pets:** Other species. Service with restrictions, supervision. ECO 🛰 🛏

Ⓐ ▼▼▼ Quality Suites H

(905) 432-8800. **$99-$169.** 1700 Champlain Ave L1N 6A7. Hwy 401 exit 412 (Thickson Rd), 0.3 mi (0.5 km) n to Champlain Ave, then 0.6 mi (1 km) e. Int corridors. **Pets:** Accepted. ECO SAVE 🛰 🛏 🖳

▼▼▼▼ Residence Inn by Marriott Whitby H

(905) 444-9756. **$139-$199.** 160 Consumers Dr L1N 9S3. Hwy 401 exit 410 (Brock St/Hwy 12). Int corridors. **Pets:** Other species. $75 one-time fee/room. Service with restrictions, crate. 🛰 ✕ 🛏 🖳 ⛱ ✕

WIARTON

▼▼ Glen Miller Motel M

(519) 534-0175. **Call for rates.** 143 Hwy 6 N0H 2T0. 1.6 mi (2.5 km) n of town; center. Ext corridors. **Pets:** Accepted. 🛰 ✕ 🛏 🖳 ✕

WINDSOR

▼▼ Cadillac Inn M

(519) 969-9340. **$79-$109, 7 day notice.** 2498 Dougall Ave N8X 1T2. 2.5 mi (4 km) s on Hwy 3B from Detroit-Windsor Tunnel, just w on Eugenie St, then just n. Ext corridors. **Pets:** Accepted. 🛰 🛏 🐾

Ⓐ ▼▼ Comfort Inn H

(519) 966-7800. **Call for rates.** 2955 Dougall Ave N9E 1S1. 3.3 mi (5.3 km) s on Hwy 3B, off Hwy 401 via Detroit-Windsor Tunnel exit. Int corridors. **Pets:** Accepted. ECO SAVE 🛰 🛏 🖳

ⒶⒶ ▼▼▼ Comfort Inn & Suites Ambassador
Bridge 🅷 ❀

(519) 972-1100. **$105-$129.** 2330 Huron Church Rd N9E 3S6. N of EC Row Expwy. Int corridors. **Pets:** Very small. $20 one-time fee/room. Designated rooms, service with restrictions, supervision.

🆂🅰🆅🅴 📶 ✕ 🅷 🖳 🏊

▼▼▼ Hampton Inn & Suites by Hilton 🅷

(519) 972-0770. **$139-$158.** 1840 Huron Church Rd N9C 2L5. 0.9 mi (1.5 km) n of EC Row Expwy. Int corridors. **Pets:** Accepted.

📶 🅼 🅷 🖳 🏊

ⒶⒶ ▼▼▼ Hilton Windsor 🅷

(519) 973-5555. **$105-$164.** 277 Riverside Dr W N9A 5K4. 0.6 mi (1 km) w of Detroit-Windsor Tunnel; 0.6 mi (1 km) e of Ambassador Bridge; downtown. Int corridors. **Pets:** Accepted.

🅴🅲🅾 🆂🅰🆅🅴 📶 🅷 🖳 🍴 🏊 ✕

▼▼▼ Holiday Inn & Suites Windsor (Ambassador
Bridge) 🅷 ❀

(519) 966-1200. **$129-$143.** 1855 Huron Church Rd N9C 2L6. Jct Huron Church and Malden rds; 0.9 mi (1.5 km) n of EC Row Expwy. Int corridors. **Pets:** Service with restrictions, supervision.

🅴🅲🅾 📶 🅷 🖳 🍴 🏊 ✕

ⒶⒶ ▼▼▼ Holiday Inn Downtown Windsor 🅷 ❀

(519) 256-4656. **$129-$249.** 430 Ouellette Ave N9A 1B2. 0.3 mi (0.5 km) s of Riverside Dr at Park St W. Int corridors. **Pets:** $30 one-time fee/room. Designated rooms, service with restrictions, crate.

🆂🅰🆅🅴 📶 🅼 🅷 🖳 🍴 🏊

ⒶⒶ ▼▼▼ Howard Johnson Plaza Hotel - Windsor
Central 🅷 ❀

(519) 966-1860. **$60-$140.** 2530 Ouellette Ave N8X 1L7. Jct Eugenie St. Int corridors. **Pets:** $10 daily fee/pet. Service with restrictions, crate.

🆂🅰🆅🅴 📶 🅷 🖳 🍴

ⒶⒶ ▼▼▼ Ivy Rose Motor Inn Ⓜ

(519) 966-1700. **$74-$99.** 2885 Howard Ave N8X 3Y4. 3 mi (4.8 km) s of downtown; just n of Devonshire Mall. Ext corridors. **Pets:** Accepted.

🆂🅰🆅🅴 📶 🅷 🍴 🏊

ⒶⒶ ▼▼▼ Quality Suites Windsor 🅷

(519) 977-9707. **$100-$120.** 250 Dougall Ave N9A 7C6. Jct Chatham St; downtown. Int corridors. **Pets:** $25 one-time fee/room. Service with restrictions, supervision. 🅴🅲🅾 🆂🅰🆅🅴 📶 🅼 🅷 🖳 🍴

▼▼ Stonecroft Inn 🅷

(519) 969-7600. **$85-$95.** 3032 Dougall Ave N9E 1S4. 0.3 mi (0.5 km) s of EC Row Expwy. Int corridors. **Pets:** Accepted. 📶 🅷 🖳 🍴

ⒶⒶ ▼▼▼ Travelodge Hotel Downtown Windsor 🅷

(519) 258-7774. **$90-$220.** 33 Riverside Dr E N9A 2S4. Jct Ouellette Ave; downtown. Int corridors. **Pets:** Accepted.

🅴🅲🅾 🆂🅰🆅🅴 📶 🅷 🖳 🏊

ⒶⒶ ▼▼▼ Windsor Riverside Inn 🅷 ❀

(519) 977-9777. **Call for rates.** 333 Riverside Dr W N9A 5K4. 0.6 mi (1 km) w of Detroit-Windsor Tunnel; 0.6 mi (1 km) e of Ambassador Bridge; downtown. Int corridors. **Pets:** Medium, other species. Supervision.

🅴🅲🅾 🆂🅰🆅🅴 📶 🅷 🖳 🍴 🏊 ✕

WOODSTOCK

ⒶⒶ ▼▼▼ Econo Lodge Hotel 🅷

(519) 533-6066. **$80-$103.** 15 Graham St N4S 6J5. At Dundas St. Int corridors. **Pets:** Small. $20 one-time fee/room. Service with restrictions, supervision. 🆂🅰🆅🅴 📶 🅷 🖳

▼▼▼ Microtel Inn & Suites by Wyndham Woodstock 🅷

(519) 537-2320. **$79-$124.** 811 Athlone Ave N4V 0B6. Hwy 401 exit 232, just n, then just w on Juliana Ave. Int corridors. **Pets:** Accepted.

📶 ✕ 🅼 🅷 🖳 🏊

ⒶⒶ ▼▼▼ Quality Hotel and Suites 🅷 ❀

(519) 537-5586. **$105-$130.** 580 Bruin Blvd N4V 1E5. Hwy 401 exit 232, just n; w of Hwy 59. Int corridors. **Pets:** Designated rooms, service with restrictions, crate. 🅴🅲🅾 🆂🅰🆅🅴 📶 🅷 🖳 🍴 🏊 ✕

▼▼▼ Super 8 🅷

(519) 421-4588. **$89-$120.** 560 Norwich Ave N4V 1C6. Hwy 401 exit 232, just n; w of Hwy 59. Int corridors. **Pets:** Accepted. 📶 🅷 🖳

PRINCE EDWARD ISLAND

CITY INDEX

ALBERTON

▼▼▼ Briarwood Inn, Cottages & Lodge Ⓜ

(902) 853-2518. **$60-$125, 30 day notice.** 253 Matthews Ln C0B 1B0. 1.9 mi (3 km) e on Rt 12. Ext/int corridors. **Pets:** Accepted.

📶 ✕ 🅷 🖳 🖋

CAVENDISH

▼▼▼ Bay Vista Motel Ⓜ

(902) 963-2225. **$59-$135.** 9517 Cavendish Rd C0A 1E0. Jct Rt 13, 2.8 mi (4.8 km) w on Rt 6. Ext corridors. **Pets:** Medium. Designated rooms, service with restrictions, crate. 📶 ✕ 🅷 🏊

▼▼▼ Cavendish Bosom Buddies Cottages & Suites ᴄᴀ

(902) 963-3449. **$90-$300, 14 day notice.** RR 1 C0A 1N0. Jct Rt 6 and 13, 0.4 mi (0.7 km) e on Rt 6. Ext corridors. **Pets:** Large, other species. $10 daily fee/pet. Designated rooms, service with restrictions, supervision.

📶 ✕ 🅷 🖳 🖋

ⒶⒶ ▼▼▼ Cavendish Maples Cottages ᴄᴀ

(902) 963-2818. **$79-$319, 30 day notice.** 73 Avonlea Blvd C0A 1M0. Jct Rt 6 and 13, 1.5 mi (2.5 km) w on Rt 6. Ext corridors.
Pets: Accepted. 🆂🅰🆅🅴 📶 ✕ 🅷 🖳 🏊 ✕

ⒶⒶ ▼▼▼ Sundance Cottages ᴄᴀ

(902) 963-2149. **$85-$350, 14 day notice.** 34 MacCoubrey Ln C0A 1N0. Jct Rt 13, 0.4 mi (0.6 km) e on Rt 6. Ext corridors. **Pets:** Other species. $10 daily fee/pet. Service with restrictions, crate.

🆂🅰🆅🅴 📶 ✕ 🅷 🏊 ✕

CHARLOTTETOWN

ⒶⒶ ▼▼▼ BEST WESTERN Charlottetown 🅷

(902) 892-2461. **$109-$209.** 238 Grafton St C1A 1L5. Between Hillsborough and Weymouth sts; center. Int corridors. **Pets:** Large. Service with restrictions, supervision. 🅴🅲🅾 🆂🅰🆅🅴 📶 ✕ 🅼 🅷 🖳 🏊

ⓐⒶ ▼▼▼ Comfort Inn 🏨 🐾

(902) 566-4424. **$96-$153.** 112 Capital Dr C1E 1E7. Trans-Canada Hwy 1, 2.8 mi (4.5 km) w. Int corridors. **Pets:** Service with restrictions, supervision. 🅔🅒🅞 🆂🅰🆅🅴 🛜 🛏 🖳 🖵

ⓐⒶ ▼▼▼▼ Delta Prince Edward 🏨 🐾

(902) 566-2222. **$126-$349.** 18 Queen St C1A 8B9. At Water and Queen sts. Int corridors. **Pets:** Medium. $35 one-time fee/room. Service with restrictions, supervision. 🅔🅒🅞 🆂🅰🆅🅴 🛜 🛏 🖳 🍽 🏊 ⊠

▼▼ Econo Lodge Ⓜ

(902) 368-1110. **Call for rates.** 20 Lower Malpeque Rd C1A 7J9. Jct Trans-Canada Hwy 1 and Lower Malpeque Rd, 2.8 mi (4.5 km) w. Ext/int corridors. **Pets:** Medium, other species. Designated rooms, service with restrictions. 🛜 🛏 🖳 🏊

ⓐⒶ ▼▼▼▼ Holiday Inn Express & Suites Charlottetown 🏨

(902) 892-1201. **Call for rates.** 200 Capital Dr C1E 2E8. On Trans-Canada Hwy 1, 3 mi (5 km) w. Int corridors. **Pets:** Service with restrictions, supervision. 🅔🅒🅞 🆂🅰🆅🅴 🛜 ⊠ 🖥 🛏 🖳 🏊

ⓐⒶ ▼▼▼ ▼▼▼ The Holman Grand Hotel 🏨

(902) 367-7777. **$164-$264.** 123 Grafton St C1A 1K9. Between University Ave and Queen St. Int corridors. **Pets:** Accepted.
🆂🅰🆅🅴 🛜 ⊠ 🖥 🛏 🖳 🍽 🏊 ⊠

▼▼ ▼▼ Quality Inn & Suites Downtown 🏨 🐾

(902) 894-8572. **$90-$200.** 150 Euston St C1A 1W5. Just e of University Ave. Int corridors. **Pets:** Other species. Designated rooms, service with restrictions, crate. 🛜 ⊠ 🛏 🖳 🍽

▼▼▼ Rodd Charlottetown-A Rodd Signature Hotel 🏨

(902) 894-7371. **$125-$247.** 75 Kent St C1A 7K4. Corner of Kent and Pownal sts. Int corridors. **Pets:** Accepted.
🅔🅒🅞 🛜 ⊠ 🛏 🖳 🍽 🏊 ⊠

▼▼ Rodd Royalty 🏨

(902) 894-8566. **$99-$195.** Intersection Hwy 1 & 2 C1A 8C2. 2.5 mi (4 km) w on Trans-Canada Hwy 1. Ext/int corridors. **Pets:** Other species. Service with restrictions, supervision. 🅔🅒🅞 🛜 🛏 🖳 🍽 🏊

CORNWALL

▼▼ Howard Johnson Hotel 🏨

(902) 566-2211. **$79-$155.** 100 Trans-Canada Hwy C0A 1H0. On Hwy 1, 4.3 mi (7 km) w of Charlottetown. Ext/int corridors. **Pets:** Dogs only. $10 daily fee/pet. Designated rooms, service with restrictions, crate.
🅔🅒🅞 🛜 ⊠ 🛏 🖳 🍽 🏊

▼ Sunny King Motel Ⓜ

(902) 566-2209. **$54-$116, 3 day notice.** 3 Centennial Dr C0A 1H0. On Hwy 1; center. Ext corridors. **Pets:** Accepted. 🛜 🛏 🖳 🏊 🅐🅒

▼▼ Super 8 🏨 🐾

(902) 892-7900. **$90-$141.** 15 York Point Rd C0A 1H0. On Hwy 1, 3.7 mi (6 km) w of Charlottetown. Int corridors. **Pets:** Medium. $15 one-time fee/pet. Designated rooms, service with restrictions, supervision.
🛜 ⊠ 🛏 🖳 🏊

DALVAY BEACH

▼▼▼ Dalvay by-the-Sea Heritage Inn 🅒🅘

(902) 672-2048. **$179-$399, 15 day notice.** 16 Cottage Cres PEI National Pkwy C0A 1P0. Off Rt 6; at east end of PEI National Park. Ext/int corridors. **Pets:** Accepted.
🅔🅒🅞 🛜 ⊠ 🖥 🛏 🖳 🍽 ⊠ 🅐🅒 🎦 🎵

FRENCH RIVER

▼▼▼▼ The Beach House Inn 🅑🅑 🐾

(902) 886-2145. **$79-$189, 14 day notice.** Cape Rd C0B 1M0. Just off Rt 20; center. Ext/int corridors. **Pets:** $10 daily fee/room. Designated rooms, service with restrictions, crate. 🛜 ⊠ 🛏 🖳 🅐🅒

MAYFIELD

▼▼ ▼▼ Cavendish Gateway Resort 🏨

(902) 963-2213. **$100-$170.** 6596 Rt 13 C0A 1N0. On Rt 13, 3.6 mi (6 km) w of Cavendish; center. Ext/int corridors. **Pets:** Medium. $10 daily fee/pet. Designated rooms, service with restrictions, supervision.
🛜 ⊠ 🛏 🖳 🏊

MORELL

▼▼▼ Rodd Crowbush Golf & Beach Resort 🏨

(902) 961-5600. **$139-$246, 3 day notice.** Rt 350 Lakeside C0A 1S0. 3 mi (5 km) w on Rt 2, follow signs. Ext/int corridors. **Pets:** Accepted.
🛜 ⊠ 🖥 🛏 🖳 🍽 🏊 ⊠

ROSENEATH

▼▼▼▼ Brudenell Chalets 🅒🅐

(902) 652-2900. **$150-$225, 30 day notice.** 1068 Georgetown Rd C0A 1L0. Jct Rt 4 and 3, 4 mi (6.4 km) e on Rt 3. Ext corridors.
Pets: Accepted. 🛜 ⊠ 🛏 🖳 🏊 ⊠

▼▼▼▼ Rodd Brudenell River-A Rodd Signature Resort 🏨

(902) 652-2332. **$119-$208, 3 day notice.** 86 Dewars Ln, Rt 3 C0A 1L0. Jct Rt 4, 3.3 mi (5.5 km) e. Ext/int corridors. **Pets:** Accepted.
🛜 ⊠ 🖥 🛏 🖳 🍽 🏊 ⊠

ST. PETERS

▼▼▼ The Inn at St. Peters 🅒🅘

(902) 961-2135. **$175-$270, 7 day notice.** 1668 Greenwich Rd C0A 2A0. Jct Rt 16 and 313, 0.6 mi (1 km) w on Rt 313. Ext corridors.
Pets: Service with restrictions. 🛜 ⊠ 🖥 🛏 🖳 🍽

STANLEY BRIDGE

▼▼▼ Inn at the Pier 🅒🅘

(902) 886-3126. **$109-$249, 14 day notice.** 9796 Cavendish Rd C0A 1E0. Rt 6, 3.6 mi (6 km) w of Cavendish; center. Ext/int corridors.
Pets: Accepted. 🛜 ⊠ 🛏 🖳 🍽 🏊

SUMMERSIDE

ⓐⒶ ▼▼▼ Quality Inn & Suites 🏨 🐾

(902) 436-2295. **$114-$329.** 618 Water St C1N 2V5. 1 mi (1.6 km) e on Hwy 11. Ext/int corridors. **Pets:** Medium. $10 one-time fee/room. Designated rooms, service with restrictions, supervision.
🆂🅰🆅🅴 🛜 ⊠ 🛏 🖳 🏊 ⊠

ⓐⒶ ▼▼▼ Slemon Park Hotel & Conference Centre 🏨

(902) 432-1780. **$113-$133.** 12 Redwood Ave C0B 1T0. On Rt 2, 3 mi (5 km) w at Summerside Airport. Int corridors. **Pets:** Small. $200 deposit/room. Designated rooms, service with restrictions, supervision.
🆂🅰🆅🅴 🛜 ⊠ 🖥 🛏 🖳 🍽 ⊠

▼▼ Econo Lodge 🏨

(902) 436-9100. **Call for rates.** 80 All Weather Hwy C1N 4P3. Jct Hwy 1A and 2, 3.1 mi (5 km) w on Hwy 2. Int corridors. **Pets:** Accepted.
🛜 ⊠ 🛏 🖳 🍽 🏊

WOODSTOCK

▼▼ ▼▼ Rodd Mill River 🏨

(902) 859-3555. **$95-$156, 3 day notice.** Rt 136 C0B 1V0. On Rt 136, just e of jct Rt 2. Int corridors. **Pets:** Accepted.
🛜 ⊠ 🛏 🖳 🍽 🏊 ⊠

QUEBEC

ALMA

▽▽▽ Comfort Inn H

(418) 668-9221. **$120-$130.** 870 ave du Pont S G8B 2V8. On Hwy 169; center. Int corridors. **Pets:** Accepted. 🛜 📶 💻

AMOS

▽▽ Amosphere Complexe Hotelier H

(819) 732-7777. **$93-$130.** 1031 Rt 111 est J9T 1N2. Center. Ext/int corridors. **Pets:** Accepted. 🛜 📶 💻 🍽 ✕

AYER'S CLIFF

Ⓐ ▽▽▽▽ Ripplecove Lakefront Hotel ⒞

(819) 838-4296. **$155-$558, 7 day notice.** 700 Ripplecove Rd J0B 1C0. Hwy 55 exit 21, 5 mi (8 km) s on Rt 141. Int corridors. **Pets:** Small, cats only. $200 deposit/pet, $40 daily fee/pet. Designated rooms, service with restrictions. (SAVE) 🛜 ✕ 📶 💻 🍽 🏊 ✕

BAIE-COMEAU

▽▽ Comfort Inn H

(418) 589-8252. **$123-$155.** 745 boul Lafleche G5C 1C6. On Rt 138. Int corridors. **Pets:** $25 one-time fee/room. Service with restrictions, supervision. 🔲 🛜 ✕ 📶 💻

▽▽▽ Hotel Le Manoir H

(418) 296-3391. **$125-$135, 30 day notice.** 8 ave Cabot G4Z 1L8. Jct Rt 138 and boul Lasalle, 2.6 mi (4.4 km) e, follow signs. Int corridors. **Pets:** Accepted. 🛜 ✕ 📶 💻 ✕

BAIE-ST-PAUL

Ⓐ ▽▽▽ Hotel Baie-Saint-Paul H

(418) 435-3683. **$69-$139, 5 day notice.** 911 boul Mgr-de-Laval G3Z 1A1. On Rt 138, 0.3 mi (0.5 km) e of Rt 362. Int corridors. **Pets:** Small. $10 daily fee/pet. Designated rooms, service with restrictions, supervision. (SAVE) 🛜 📶 💻 🍽 ✕

BROMONT

▽▽▽▽ Le St-Martin Bromont Hotel & Suites H

(450) 534-0044. **Call for rates.** 111 boul du Carrefour J2L 3L1. Hwy 10 exit 78. Int corridors. **Pets:** Accepted. 🛜 ✕ 📶 💻 🏊

COWANSVILLE

▽▽ Auberge des Carrefours H

(450) 263-7331. **$108-$125.** 111 Place Jean-Jacques Bertrand J2K 3R5. Hwy 10 exit 68, 9.9 mi (15.9 km) s on Rt 139. Int corridors. **Pets:** Accepted. 🛜 ✕ 📶 💻 🍽

DRUMMONDVILLE

Ⓐ ▽▽▽▽ BEST WESTERN PLUS Hotel Universel H

(819) 478-4971. **$99-$299.** 915 rue Hains J2C 3A1. Hwy 20 exit 177, just s on boul St-Joseph, then just e. Int corridors. **Pets:** Medium. Designated rooms, no service, supervision. (SAVE) 🛜 📶 💻 🍽 🏊

▽▽▽ Comfort Inn H

(819) 477-4000. **$79-$125.** 1055 rue Hains J2C 6G6. Hwy 20 exit 177, 0.3 mi (0.5 km) s on boul St-Joseph, then just w. Int corridors. **Pets:** Medium. $25 one-time fee/pet. Designated rooms, service with restrictions, supervision. 🔲 🛜 📶 💻

▽▽▽ Hotel & Suites Le Dauphin H

(819) 478-4141. **$99-$150, 30 day notice.** 600 boul St-Joseph J2C 2C1. Hwy 20 exit 177, 0.8 mi (1.3 km) s. Ext/int corridors. **Pets:** Medium. $15 daily fee/pet. Service with restrictions, supervision. 🔲 🛜 ✕ 📶 💻 🍽 🏊

Ⓐ ▽▽▽ Hotel-Motel Drummond M

(819) 478-4614. **$85-$135.** 1055 boul St-Joseph ouest J2E 1A4. Hwy 20 exit 177, just n on boul St-Joseph, then just w on rue St-Roch. Ext corridors. **Pets:** Small, other species. $12 daily fee/room. Designated rooms, supervision. (SAVE) 🛜 📶 💻 🍽

▽▽▽ Quality Suites H 🐾

(819) 472-2700. **$99-$155.** 2125 rue Canadien J2C 7V8. Hwy 20 exit 175, just s. Int corridors. **Pets:** Other species. $25 one-time fee/room. Designated rooms, service with restrictions, supervision. 🔲 🛜 ✕ 📶 💻 🏊

FORESTVILLE

▽▽▽ Econo Lodge M

(418) 587-2278. **$95-$135, 7 day notice.** 5 Rt 138 est G0T 1E0. Center. Ext/int corridors. **Pets:** Accepted. 🛜 📶 💻 🍽

GATINEAU

Ⓐ ▽▽▽ Comfort Inn Gatineau H

(819) 243-6010. **$93-$136.** 630 boul La Gappe J8T 7S8. Hwy 50 exit 140, 1.1 mi (1.9 km) e; in Hull Sector. Int corridors. **Pets:** Large, other species. $25 one-time fee/room. Designated rooms, service with restrictions, supervision. 🔲 (SAVE) 🛜 ✕ 📶 💻

Ⓐ ▽▽▽ Crowne Plaza Gatineau-Ottawa H

(819) 778-3880. **$120-$180.** 2 rue Montcalm J8X 4B4. 0.5 mi (0.8 km) w of Portage Bridge at Rt 148 and rue Montcalm; in Hull sector. Int corridors. **Pets:** Large. $50 one-time fee/room. Designated rooms, service with restrictions, supervision. (SAVE) 🛜 ✕ 📶 💻 🍽 🏊 ✕

Ⓐ ▽▽▽ Four Points by Sheraton Hotel & Conference Centre Gatineau-Ottawa H 🐾

(819) 778-6111. **$110-$239.** 35 rue Laurier J8X 4E9. Corner of rue Victoria; across from Canadian Museum of Civilization; in Hull sector. Int corridors. **Pets:** Other species. Service with restrictions, supervision. 🔲 (SAVE) 🛜 ✕ 📶 💻 🍽 🏊

Ⓐ ▽▽▽▽ Hilton Lac-Leamy H

(819) 790-6444. **$189-$389.** 3 boul du Casino J8Y 6X4. In Casino du Lac Leamy; in Hull sector. Int corridors. **Pets:** Accepted. 🔲 (SAVE) 🛜 ✕📶 📶 💻 🍽 🏊 ✕

ISLE-AUX-COUDRES

▼▼ ▼▼ Hotel Motel La Roche Pleureuse 🅷

(418) 438-2734. **$80-$118, 3 day notice.** 2901 chemin des Coudriers G0A 2A0. On Ile aux Coudres, 4.8 mi (8 km) e of ferry dock, follow signs; in la Baleine sector; access by ferry boat. Ext/int corridors.
Pets: Accepted. 🛜 ⊠ 🍴 ⊇ ⊠

JONQUIÈRE

▼▼ ▼▼ Delta Saguenay Hotel 🅷 ❀

(418) 548-3124. **Call for rates.** 2675 boul du Royaume G7S 5B8. Hwy 70 exit 39, just ne, follow signs. Int corridors. **Pets:** Small. $35 one-time fee/room. Service with restrictions, supervision.

🛜 ⊠ 🖥 ⊇ 🍴 ⊇ ⊠

LAC-BROME (KNOWLTON)

▼▼ ▼▼ Auberge Knowlton 🅲🅸

(450) 242-6886. **$125-$150.** 286 chemin Knowlton J0E 1V0. Corner of Hwy 104 and Rt 243; center. Int corridors. **Pets:** Accepted.

🛜 ⊠ 🍴

⨿ ▼▼ ▼▼ Auberge Quilliams Inn 🅲🅸

(450) 243-0404. **$159-$350, 3 day notice.** 572 chemin Lakeside J0E 1R0. Hwy 10 exit 90, 3.1 mi (4.9 km) s on Rt 243. Int corridors. **Pets:** $10 daily fee/pet. Service with restrictions, supervision.

🆂🅰🆅🅴 🛜 ⊠ 🖥 ⊇ 🍴 ⊇ ⊠

LA MALBAIE

⨿ ▼▼ ▼▼ Fairmont Le Manoir Richelieu 🅷 ❀

(418) 665-3703. **$129-$299.** 181 rue Richelieu G5A 1X7. On Rt 362, 2.6 mi (4.1 km) w of jct Rt 138. Int corridors. **Pets:** $25 daily fee/room. Supervision. 🅴🅲🅾 🆂🅰🆅🅴 🛜 🖥 ⊇ 🍴 ⊇ ⊠

▼▼ ▼▼ La Pinsonnière 🅲🅸 ❀

(418) 665-4431. **$275-$495, 15 day notice.** 124 rue St-Raphael G5A 1X9. Just off Rt 138, follow signs; in Cap-a-L'Aigle sector. Int corridors. **Pets:** Medium. $20 one-time fee/pet. Designated rooms, supervision.

🛜 ⊠ ⊇ 🍴 ⊇ ⊠

LA POCATIÈRE

▼▼ ▼▼ Motel Le Pocatois 🅼

(418) 856-1688. **Call for rates.** 235 Rt 132 G0R 1Z0. Hwy 20 exit 439, 0.5 mi (0.8 km) s. Ext/int corridors. **Pets:** Accepted. 🛜 🖥 ⊇ 🍴

LOUISEVILLE

▼▼ ▼▼ Gite du Carrefour et Maison historique J.L.L. Hamelin 🅱🅱

(819) 228-4932. **$65-$95, 15 day notice.** 11 ave St-Laurent ouest J5V 1J3. On Rt 138; Hwy 40 exit 174 westbound; exit 166 eastbound; center. Int corridors. **Pets:** Designated rooms, no service, supervision.

🄺 🅦 🅩

MONTEBELLO

⨿ ▼▼ ▼▼▼ Fairmont Le Château Montebello 🅷 ❀

(819) 423-6341. **$179-$439, 3 day notice.** 392 rue Notre-Dame J0V 1L0. On Rt 148. Int corridors. **Pets:** Dogs only. $35 daily fee/pet. Designated rooms, service with restrictions.

🅴🅲🅾 🆂🅰🆅🅴 🛜 ⊠ 🖥 ⊇ 🍴 ⊇ ⊠

MONT-LAURIER

⨿ ▼▼ ▼▼ BEST WESTERN PLUS Mont-Laurier 🅷

(819) 623-5252. **$116-$119.** 1231 boul Albiny-Paquette J9L 1M6. On Rt 117; center. Ext/int corridors. **Pets:** Other species. $25 one-time fee/room. Designated rooms, service with restrictions, supervision.

🆂🅰🆅🅴 🛜 🖥 ⊇

▼▼ ▼▼ Comfort Inn 🅷

(819) 623-6465. **$116-$131.** 700 boul Albiny-Paquette J9L 1L4. On Hwy 117; center. Ext/int corridors. **Pets:** Accepted. 🛜 🖥 ⊇ 🍴 ⊠

⨿ ▼▼ ▼▼ Quality Inn Mont-Laurier 🅷

(819) 623-3555. **Call for rates.** 111 boul Albiny-Paquette J9L 1J2. On Rt 117; center. Ext/int corridors. **Pets:** Accepted.

🆂🅰🆅🅴 🛜 🖥 ⊇ 🍴 ⊇ ⊠

MONTRÉAL METROPOLITAN AREA

ANJOU

⨿ ▼▼ ▼▼ Quality Hotel East 🅷

(514) 493-6363. **$90-$220.** 8100 ave Neuville H1J 2T2. Hwy 40 exit 78, just n on boul Langelier, 0.4 mi (0.7 km) e on rue Jarry, then s. Int corridors. **Pets:** Other species. $25 one-time fee/room. Service with restrictions, crate. 🅴🅲🅾 🆂🅰🆅🅴 🛜 🖥 ⊇ 🍴

BELOEIL

⨿ ▼▼ ▼▼ Hostellerie Rive Gauche 🅷

(450) 467-4477. **$130.** 1810 boul Richelieu J3G 4S4. Hwy 20 exit 112, 0.6 mi (1 km) s on rue Serge-Pepin, then just sw on Rt 223, follow signs. Int corridors. **Pets:** Accepted. 🆂🅰🆅🅴 🛜 ⊠ 🖥 ⊇ 🍴

BROSSARD

▼▼▼ ▼▼ Alt Hotel Quartier Dix 30 🅷

(450) 443-1030. **$144-$184.** 6500 boul de Rome J4Y 0B6. Jct Hwy 10 and 30, just w on Hwy 30 exit boul de Rome; in Quartier Dix 30 Mall. Int corridors. **Pets:** $30 one-time fee/room. Designated rooms, service with restrictions, supervision. 🅴🅲🅾 🛜 ⊠ 🖥 ⊇ ⊠

⨿ ▼▼▼▼ BEST WESTERN PLUS Brossard 🅷

(450) 466-6756. **$142-$166.** 7746 boul Taschereau J4X 1C2. Rt 134 0.8 mi (1.3 km) w of Hwy 10 exit boul Taschereau ouest. Int corridors. **Pets:** Medium. $35 daily fee/pet. Supervision.

🅴🅲🅾 🆂🅰🆅🅴 🛜 🖥 ⊇

▼▼ ▼▼ Comfort Inn 🅷

(450) 678-9350. **$100-$127.** 7863 boul Taschereau J4Y 1A4. Rt 134, 0.9 mi (1.5 km) w of Hwy 10 exit boul Taschereau ouest. Int corridors. **Pets:** Accepted. 🅴🅲🅾 🛜 🖥 ⊇

⨿ ▼▼ ▼▼ Econo Lodge Montreal - Brossard 🅼

(450) 466-2186. **$87-$200.** 8350 boul Taschereau J4X 1C2. Rt 134, 1.4 mi (2.3 km) w of Hwy 10 exit boul Taschereau ouest. Ext/int corridors. **Pets:** Very small. $10 daily fee/pet. Service with restrictions, supervision.

🆂🅰🆅🅴 🛜 🖥 ⊇

DORVAL

⨿ ▼▼ ▼▼ Aloft Montreal Airport 🅷 ❀

(514) 633-0900. **$99-$229.** 500 ave McMillan H9P 0A2. Just n of Hwy 520 on north side service road at airport entrance. Int corridors. **Pets:** Medium, other species. Designated rooms, service with restrictions, crate. 🆂🅰🆅🅴 🛜 ⊠ 🅼 🖥 ⊇ 🍴 ⊇

⨿ ▼▼ ▼▼ Comfort Inn Dorval 🅷

(514) 636-3391. **$95-$145.** 340 ave Michel-Jasmin H9P 1C1. Hwy 520 exit 2 eastbound; exit 1 westbound, just e along service road to ave Marshall, follow to ave Michel-Jasmin. Int corridors. **Pets:** Accepted.

🅴🅲🅾 🆂🅰🆅🅴 🛜 🖥 ⊇

⨿ ▼▼ ▼▼ Hampton Inn & Suites by Hilton Montreal (Dorval) 🅷

(514) 633-8243. **$119-$230.** 1900 Rt Transcanadienne (Hwy 40) H9P 2N4. Hwy 40 exit 55, 0.5 mi (0.8 km) e of boul des Sources on south side service road. Int corridors. **Pets:** Medium. $50 one-time fee/room. Designated rooms, service with restrictions, supervision.

🆂🅰🆅🅴 🛜 🅼 🖥 ⊇ ⊇

(CAA) ▼▼ ▼▼ **The Sheraton Montreal Airport Hotel** 🏨 ❖

(514) 631-2411. **$139-$259.** 555 McMillan Ave H9P 1B7. Just n of Hwy 520 on north side service road; at airport entrance. Int corridors. **Pets:** Small. $25 deposit/pet. Designated rooms, service with restrictions, supervision. [SAVE] 🛜 ✕ 👤M 🖥 💻 🍴 ⋙ ✕

LAVAL

(CAA) ▼▼ ▼▼ **BEST WESTERN PLUS Laval-Montreal** 🏨

(450) 681-9000. **Call for rates.** 3655 Autoroute des Laurentides H7L 3H7. Hwy 15 exit 10, just n on east side service road. Int corridors. **Pets:** Accepted. [SAVE] 🛜 ✕ 🖥 💻 ⋙

(CAA) ▼▼ ▼▼ **Comfort Inn** 🏨

(450) 686-0600. **$121-$173.** 2055 Autoroute des Laurentides H7S 1Z6. Hwy 15 exit 8 (boul St-Martin), e on boul St-Martin, 0.4 mi (0.7 km) n on boul Le Corbusier, then just w on boul Tessier. Int corridors. **Pets:** Medium. $10 daily fee/room. Designated rooms, supervision. [ECO] [SAVE] 🛜 🖥 💻 🍴

▼▼ ▼▼ **Econo Lodge** 🏨

(450) 682-2001. **$93-$124.** 1981 boul Cure-Labelle H7T 1L4. Hwy 15 exit 8 (boul St-Martin) northbound; exit 10 southbound 1.3 mi (2 km) w on boul St-Martin ouest, then 0.3 mi (0.5 km) n. Ext/int corridors. **Pets:** Medium. Service with restrictions, supervision. 🛜 🖥 💻 ⋙

(CAA) ▼▼ ▼▼ **Quality Suites Laval** 🏨

(450) 686-6777. **$131-$193.** 2035 Autoroute des Laurentides H7S 1Z6. Hwy 15 exit 8 (boul St-Martin), 0.4 mi (0.7 km) n on boul Le Corbusier, then just w on boul Tessier. Int corridors. **Pets:** Medium. $10 daily fee/room. Designated rooms, supervision. [ECO] [SAVE] 🛜 🖥 💻

(CAA) ▼▼ ▼▼ ▼▼ **Sheraton Laval Hotel** 🏨 ❖

(450) 687-2440. **$129-$269.** 2440 Autoroute des Laurentides H7T 1X5. Hwy 15 exit 10. Int corridors. **Pets:** Medium, dogs only. Designated rooms, service with restrictions, supervision. [ECO] [SAVE] 🛜 ✕ 🖥 💻 🍴 ⋙ ✕

MONTRÉAL

(CAA) ▼▼ ▼▼ ▼▼ **Candlewood Suites Montreal** 🏨 ❖

(514) 667-5002. **$99-$169.** 191 boul Rene-Levesque est H2X 3Z9. Corner of rue Hotel-de-ville. Int corridors. **Pets:** Other species. $35 one-time fee/room. Service with restrictions, crate. [ECO] [SAVE] 🛜 👤M 🖥 💻

(CAA) ▼▼ ▼▼ ▼▼ **Château Versailles Hotel** 🏨 ❖

(514) 933-3611. **$155-$465.** 1659 rue Sherbrooke ouest H3H 1E3. Corner of rue St-Mathieu. Int corridors. **Pets:** Small. $20 daily fee/pet. Designated rooms, service with restrictions, crate. [SAVE] 🛜 ✕

▼▼ ▼▼ ▼▼ **Crowne Plaza Montreal Airport** 🏨

(514) 344-1999. **$99-$250.** 6600 Cote-de-Liesse H4T 1E3. Hwy 520 exit 5 eastbound on south side service road; exit westbound to rue Ness, follow signs for rue Hickmore and Hwy 520 E. Int corridors. **Pets:** Medium. $50 one-time fee/room. Service with restrictions, supervision. 🛜 ✕ 🖥 💻 🍴 ⋙ ✕

(CAA) ▼▼ ▼▼ ▼▼ **Delta Centre-Ville** 🏨

(514) 879-1370. **$149-$249.** 777 rue University H3C 3Z7. Corner of rue St-Antoine. Int corridors. **Pets:** $35 one-time fee/room. Service with restrictions, supervision. [ECO] [SAVE] 🛜 ✕ 👤M 🖥 💻 🍴 ⋙ ✕

(CAA) ▼▼ ▼▼ ▼▼ **Delta Montreal** 🏨

(514) 286-1986. **$145-$322.** 475 ave President-Kennedy H3A 1J7. Corner of rue City Councillors. Int corridors. **Pets:** Accepted. [ECO] [SAVE] 🛜 ✕ 🖥 💻 🍴 ⋙ ✕

(CAA) ▼▼ ▼▼ ▼▼ **Embassy Suites by Hilton Montreal** 🏨 ❖

(514) 288-8886. **$149-$579.** 208 rue St-Antoine ouest H2Y 0A6. Corner of rue St-Francois-Xavier. Int corridors. **Pets:** Small, other species. $35 one-time fee/room. Service with restrictions, supervision. [ECO] [SAVE] 🛜 🖥 💻 🍴

(CAA) ▼▼ ▼▼ ▼▼ **Fairmont The Queen Elizabeth** 🏨 ❖

(514) 861-3511. **$169-$359.** 900 boul Rene-Levesque ouest H3B 4A5. Between rue University and Mansfield. Int corridors. **Pets:** Small, other species. $25 daily fee/pet. Supervision. [ECO] [SAVE] 🛜 👤M 🖥 💻 🍴 ⋙ ✕

(CAA) ▼▼ ▼▼ ▼▼ **Hilton Montréal Bonaventure** 🏨

(514) 878-2332. **$199-$399.** 900 rue de la Gauchetiere ouest H5A 1E4. Corner of Mansfield. Int corridors. **Pets:** Medium. $50 one-time fee/room. Designated rooms, service with restrictions, supervision. [ECO] [SAVE] 🛜 👤M 🖥 💻 🍴 ⋙

(CAA) ▼▼ ▼▼ **Holiday Inn Express Hotel & Suites Montreal Centre-Ville** 🏨 ❖

(514) 448-7100. **$107-$199.** 155 boul Rene-Levesque est H2X 3Z8. Corner of rue de Bullion. Int corridors. **Pets:** Other species. $50 one-time fee/room. Service with restrictions, crate. [ECO] [SAVE] 🛜 🖥 💻

(CAA) ▼▼ ▼▼ ▼▼ **Holiday Inn Montreal-Midtown** 🏨

(514) 842-6111. **$109-$149, 3 day notice.** 420 rue Sherbrooke ouest H3A 1B4. Between rue de Bleury and Aylmer. Int corridors. **Pets:** Accepted. [ECO] [SAVE] 🛜 🖥 💻 🍴 ⋙ ✕

▼▼ ▼▼ ▼▼ **Hotel 10 Montreal** 🏨

(514) 843-6000. **$149-$549.** 10 rue Sherbrooke ouest H2X 4C9. Corner of boul St-Laurent. Int corridors. **Pets:** Large. $50 one-time fee/room. Supervision. 🛜 ✕ 🖥 💻 🍴

▼▼ ▼▼ ▼▼ **Hôtel Espresso Montréal Centre-Ville/Downtown** 🏨

(514) 938-4611. **$99-$399.** 1005 rue Guy H3H 2K4. Just s of boul Rene-Levesque. Int corridors. **Pets:** Accepted. 🛜 ✕ 🖥 💻 🍴 ⋙ ✕

(CAA) ▼▼ ▼▼ ▼▼ **Hotel Gault** 🏨 ❖

(514) 904-1616. **$240-$720.** 449 rue Ste-Helene H2Y 2K9. Just s of rue Notre-Dame. Int corridors. **Pets:** $50 daily fee/pet. Supervision. [SAVE] 🛜 ✕ 🖥 💻 🍴

(CAA) ▼▼ ▼▼ ▼▼ **Hotel Gouverneur Place Dupuis** 🏨

(514) 842-4881. **$109-$399.** 1415 rue St-Hubert H2L 3Y9. Between boul de Maisonneuve and rue Ste-Catherine. Int corridors. **Pets:** Medium. $30 one-time fee/room. Service with restrictions, supervision. [ECO] [SAVE] 🛜 🖥 💻 🍴 ⋙

(CAA) ▼▼ ▼▼ ▼▼ **Hôtel Le Crystal** 🏨

(514) 861-5550. **Call for rates.** 1100 rue de la Montagne H3G 0A1. Corner of boul Rene-Levesque. Int corridors. **Pets:** Accepted. [ECO] [SAVE] 🛜 ✕ 👤M 🖥 💻 🍴 ⋙ ✕

▼▼ ▼▼ ▼▼ **Hôtel Le Germain Montréal** 🏨

(514) 849-2050. **$214-$260.** 2050 rue Mansfield H3A 1Y9. Corner of ave President-Kennedy. Int corridors. **Pets:** Accepted. 🛜 ✕ 🖥 🍴

▼▼ ▼▼ **Hotel Le Prestige** 🏨

(514) 640-5500. **$96-$150.** 12555 rue Sherbrooke est H1B 1C8. Hwy 40 exit 87, 0.6 mi (1 km) s on boul du Tricentenaire, then just w. Int corridors. **Pets:** Medium. $10 deposit/pet. Service with restrictions, crate. 🛜 🖥 💻 ⋙

▼▼ ▼▼ **Hotel Le Roberval** 🏨

(514) 286-5215. **$90-$169.** 505 boul Rene-Levesque est H2L 5B6. Corner of rue Berri. Int corridors. **Pets:** Accepted. 🛜 ✕ 🖥 💻

(CAA) ▼▼ ▼▼ ▼▼ **Hôtel Le St-James** 🏨 ❖

(514) 841-3111. **Call for rates.** 355 rue St-Jacques ouest H2Y 1N9. Corner of rue St-Pierre. Int corridors. **Pets:** Other species. $40 daily fee/pet. Service with restrictions, crate. [SAVE] 🛜 💻 🍴 ✕

(CAA) ▼▼ ▼▼ ▼▼ **Hôtel Omni Mont-Royal** 🏨 ❖

(514) 284-1110. **$179-$279.** 1050 rue Sherbrooke ouest H3A 2R6. Corner of rue Peel. Int corridors. **Pets:** Small, dogs only. $50 one-time fee/room. Designated rooms, service with restrictions, supervision. [SAVE] 🛜 ✕ 🖥 💻 🍴 ⋙ ✕

ⓐⓐ ▼▼ ▼▼ **Hotel Travelodge Montreal Centre** 🅷 ☙
(514) 874-9090. **$89-$300.** 50 boul Rene-Levesque ouest H2Z 1A2. Between rue Clark and St-Urbain. Int corridors. **Pets:** Medium. $10 daily fee/pet. Designated rooms, service with restrictions, supervision.
ⓔⓒⓞ ⓢⓐⓥⓔ 🛜 ✕ 🛏 💻

ⓐⓐ ▼▼▼ ▼▼▼ **Hyatt Regency Montreal** 🅷 ☙
(514) 982-1234. **$89-$529.** 1255 Jeanne-Mance H5B 1E5. Corner of rue Ste-Catherine. Int corridors. **Pets:** Small, other species. $35 one-time fee/room. Supervision. ⓢⓐⓥⓔ 🛜 ♿ 🛏 💻 🍴 ≈ ✕

ⓐⓐ ▼▼▼ ▼▼▼ **InterContinental Montréal** 🅷 ☙
(514) 987-9900. **$159-$289.** 360 rue St-Antoine ouest H2Y 3X4. Corner of rue St-Pierre. Int corridors. **Pets:** Small. $45 one-time fee/room. Designated rooms, service with restrictions, supervision.
ⓔⓒⓞ ⓢⓐⓥⓔ 🛜 ✕ 🛏 💻 🍴 ≈ ✕

ⓐⓐ ▼▼ ▼▼ **L'Appartement Hotel** 🅷
(514) 284-3634. **$115-$245.** 455 rue Sherbrooke ouest H3A 1B7. Corner of rue Durocher. Int corridors. **Pets:** Accepted.
ⓔⓒⓞ ⓢⓐⓥⓔ 🛜 🛏 💻 ≈

ⓐⓐ ▼▼▼ ▼▼▼ **Le Centre Sheraton** 🅷
(514) 878-2000. **$144-$719.** 1201 boul Rene-Levesque ouest H3B 2L7. Between rue Drummond and rue Stanley. Int corridors. **Pets:** Accepted.
ⓔⓒⓞ ⓢⓐⓥⓔ 🛜 ✕ 🛏 💻 🍴 ≈ ✕

ⓐⓐ ▼▼▼ ▼▼▼ **Le Meridien Versailles-Montreal** 🅷 ☙
(514) 933-8111. **$119-$509.** 1808 rue Sherbrooke ouest H3H 1E5. Corner of rue St-Mathieu. Int corridors. **Pets:** Medium, other species. $20 daily fee/pet. Designated rooms, service with restrictions, crate.
ⓢⓐⓥⓔ 🛜 🛏 💻 🍴

ⓐⓐ ▼▼▼ ▼▼▼ **Le Saint-Sulpice Hôtel Montréal** 🅷
(514) 288-1000. **$189-$539.** 414 rue St-Sulpice H2Y 2V5. Just n of rue St-Paul. Int corridors. **Pets:** Accepted. ⓢⓐⓥⓔ 🛜 ✕ 🛏 💻 🍴

ⓐⓐ ▼▼▼ ▼▼▼ **Le Square Phillips Hotel & Suites** 🅷
(514) 393-1193. **$145-$369.** 1193 Place Phillips H3B 3C9. Between rue Ste-Catherine and boul Rene-Levesque. Int corridors. **Pets:** Service with restrictions, supervision. ⓔⓒⓞ ⓢⓐⓥⓔ 🛜 ✕ 🛏 💻 🍴 ≈

ⓐⓐ ▼▼▼ ▼▼▼ **Loews Hôtel Vogue** 🅷 ☙
(514) 285-5555. **$152-$809.** 1425 rue de la Montagne H3G 1Z3. Between rue Ste-Catherine and boul de Maisonneuve. Int corridors. **Pets:** Large. $25 one-time fee/room. Service with restrictions, supervision.
ⓢⓐⓥⓔ 🛜 🛏 💻 🍴 ✕

▼▼▼ ▼▼ **Novotel Montreal Centre** 🅷
(514) 861-6000. **$119-$499.** 1180 rue de la Montagne H3G 1Z1. Between rue Ste-Catherine and boul Rene-Levesque. Int corridors. **Pets:** Accepted. ⓔⓒⓞ 🛜 💻 🍴

▼▼▼ **Parc Suites Hotel** 🅷
(514) 985-5656. **$99-$199, 3 day notice.** 3463 ave du Parc H2X 2H6. Between rue Sherbrooke and Milton. Int corridors. **Pets:** Accepted.
🛜 ✕ 🛏 💻

ⓐⓐ ▼▼ ▼▼ **Quality Hotel Downtown Montreal** 🅷
(514) 849-1413. **$98-$179.** 3440 ave du Parc H2X 2H5. Between rue Sherbrooke and Milton. Int corridors. **Pets:** Medium. $40 one-time fee/room. Service with restrictions, crate. ⓔⓒⓞ ⓢⓐⓥⓔ 🛜 🛏 💻 🍴

▼▼▼ ▼▼▼ **Residence Inn by Marriott Montreal Airport** 🅷
(514) 336-9333. **$129-$249.** 6500 Place Robert-Joncas H4M 2Z5. Hwy 40 exit 64 (boul Cavendish), 0.3 mi (0.5 km) w on north side service road, then just n on rue Beaulac. Int corridors. **Pets:** Accepted.
ⓔⓒⓞ 🛜 ✕ ♿ 🛏 💻 🍴 ≈ ✕

ⓐⓐ ▼▼▼ ▼▼▼ **Residence Inn by Marriott Montreal-Downtown** 🅷
(514) 982-6064. **$169-$595.** 2045 rue Peel H3A 1T6. Between rue Sherbrooke and boul de Maisonneuve. Int corridors. **Pets:** Other species. $100 one-time fee/room. Service with restrictions.
ⓔⓒⓞ ⓢⓐⓥⓔ 🛜 ✕ 🛏 💻

ⓐⓐ ▼▼▼ ▼▼▼ **Residence Inn by Marriott Montreal Westmount** 🅷
(514) 935-9224. **$145-$201.** 2170 ave Lincoln H3H 2N5. Just e of rue Atwater. Int corridors. **Pets:** Medium. $75 one-time fee/room. Service with restrictions, supervision. ⓔⓒⓞ ⓢⓐⓥⓔ 🛜 ✕ ♿ 🛏 💻 ≈

ⓐⓐ ▼▼▼ ▼▼▼ **The Ritz-Carlton Montréal** 🅷
(514) 842-4212. **$380-$425.** 1228 rue Sherbrooke ouest H3G 1H6. Corner of rue de la Montagne. Int corridors. **Pets:** Accepted.
ⓢⓐⓥⓔ 🛜 ✕ 💻 🍴 ≈

ⓐⓐ ▼▼▼ ▼▼▼ **Sofitel Montréal Le Carré Doré** 🅷
(514) 285-9000. **$180-$350, 3 day notice.** 1155 rue Sherbrooke ouest H3A 2N3. Corner of rue Stanley. Int corridors. **Pets:** Accepted.
ⓔⓒⓞ ⓢⓐⓥⓔ 🛜 ✕ 🛏 🍴

ⓐⓐ ▼▼▼ ▼▼▼ **W Montréal** 🅷 ☙
(514) 395-3100. **$169-$799.** 901 Square Victoria H2Z 1R1. Corner of rue St-Antoine. Int corridors. **Pets:** Large, other species. $100 one-time fee/room, $25 daily fee/room. Supervision. ⓢⓐⓥⓔ 🛜 ✕ ♿ 💻 🍴

POINTE-CLAIRE

ⓐⓐ ▼▼ ▼▼ **Comfort Inn** 🅷
(514) 697-6210. **$100-$143.** 700 boul St-Jean H9R 3K2. Hwy 40 exit 52, just s. Int corridors. **Pets:** Other species. $25 one-time fee/room. Service with restrictions, supervision. ⓔⓒⓞ ⓢⓐⓥⓔ 🛜 🛏 💻

ⓐⓐ ▼▼▼ ▼▼▼ **Quality Suites Montreal Aeroport, Pointe-Claire** 🅷
(514) 426-5060. **$120-$170.** 6300 Rt Transcanadienne H9R 1B9. Hwy 40 exit 52 eastbound, south side service road; exit westbound, follow signs for boul St-Jean sud and Hwy 40 est to access south side service road. Int corridors. **Pets:** Accepted. ⓔⓒⓞ ⓢⓐⓥⓔ 🛜 ♿ 🛏 💻 🍴

ST-JÉRÔME

▼▼▼ **Super 8 St-Jerome** 🅷
(450) 438-4388. **$99-$129.** 3 boul J. F. Kennedy J7Y 4B4. Hwy 15 exit 41 southbound, just n; on west side of autoroute. Int corridors.
Pets: Accepted. ⓔⓒⓞ 🛜 ✕ ♿ 🛏 💻 ≈ ✕

ST-LAURENT

ⓐⓐ ▼▼▼ ▼▼▼ **Holiday Inn Montreal-Airport** 🅷 ☙
(514) 739-3391. **$95-$189.** 6500 Cote-de-Liesse H4T 1E3. Hwy 520 exit 5 eastbound on south side service road; exit westbound to rue Ness, follow signs for rue Hickmore and Hwy 520 E. Ext/int corridors.
Pets: Medium. $50 daily fee/pet. Designated rooms, service with restrictions, supervision. ⓢⓐⓥⓔ 🛜 ✕ ♿ 🛏 💻 🍴 ≈ ✕

ⓐⓐ ▼▼▼ ▼▼▼ **Novotel Montreal Airport** 🅷 ☙
(514) 337-3222. **$129-$329.** 2599 boul Alfred-Nobel H4S 2G1. Hwy 40 exit 60 (boul Alfred-Nobel); in St-Laurent Technoparc, just s of south side service road. Int corridors. **Pets:** Medium, other species. $25 deposit/room. Designated rooms, service with restrictions, crate.
ⓔⓒⓞ ⓢⓐⓥⓔ 🛜 ✕ 🛏 💻 🍴 ≈

▼▼▼ ▼▼▼ **Travelodge Hotel Montreal Airport** 🅷
(514) 733-8818. **$79-$249.** 7300 Cote-de-Liesse H4T 1E7. Hwy 520 exit 4 eastbound on south side service road; exit 4 (Montee-de-Liesse) westbound. Int corridors. **Pets:** Accepted. 🛜 🛏 💻 🍴 ≈

TERREBONNE

💎💎💎 Super 8 Hotel Lachenaie Terrebonne 🏨

(450) 582-8288. **$116-$200.** 1155 ave Yves-Blais J6V 0A9. Hwy 640 exit 50, just s on Montee des Pionniers, then just e; in Lachenaie sector. Int corridors. **Pets:** Medium. $20 daily fee/pet. Service with restrictions, supervision. 🔢 🛜 ✖ 🔧 🍴 💻 🌊 ⊠
eb

VAUDREUIL-DORION

💎💎 Super 8 🏨

(450) 424-8898. **$94-$150.** 3200 boul de la Gare J7V 8W5. Hwy 40 exit 35, just s on ave St-Charles, 0.3 mi (0.4 km) w on boul de la Cite-des-Jeunes, then just w. Int corridors. **Pets:** Accepted.
🔢 🛜 ✖ 🔧 💻 🌊

END METROPOLITAN AREA

MONT-TREMBLANT

Ⓐ 💎💎💎💎 Fairmont Tremblant 🏨 🐾

(819) 681-7000. **$199-$599, 7 day notice.** 3045 chemin de la Chapelle J8E 1E1. In Mont-Tremblant Resort Centre. Int corridors. **Pets:** Dogs only. $35 daily fee/pet. Supervision. 🔢 🔲 🛜 🍴 💻 🍴 🌊 ⊠

Ⓐ 💎💎💎 Le Grand Lodge Mont-Tremblant 🏨

(819) 425-2734. **$134-$384, 8 day notice.** 2396 rue Labelle J8E 1T8. On Rt 327, 0.3 mi (0.4 km) s of Montee Ryan. Int corridors. **Pets:** Accepted. 🔲 🛜 ✖ 🔧 💻 🍴 🌊 ⊠

Ⓐ 💎💎💎💎 Le Westin Resort & Spa, Tremblant 🏨 🐾

(819) 681-8000. **$199-$559.** 100 chemin Kandahar J8E 1E2. Hwy 117 N exit 119 (Montee Ryan), 6 mi (10 km) e, follow signs. Int corridors. **Pets:** Small, dogs only. $75 one-time fee/room. Designated rooms, service with restrictions, supervision.
🔲 🛜 ✖ 🔧 💻 🍴 🌊 ⊠

ORFORD

💎💎💎 Hotel Cheribourg 🏨

(819) 843-3308. **$130-$260.** 2603 chemin du Parc J1X 8C8. Hwy 10 exit 118, 1.9 mi (3 km) n on Hwy 141. Ext/int corridors. **Pets:** $30 one-time fee/room. Designated rooms, service with restrictions, supervision.
🛜 ✖ 🔧 💻 🍴 🌊 ⊠

PERCÉ

💎 Au Pic de l'Aurore Ⓒ

(418) 782-2151. **$76-$239, 3 day notice.** 1 Rt 132 W G0C 2L0. 1.2 mi (2 km) w from village. Ext corridors. **Pets:** Medium, dogs only. $25 one-time fee/pet. Designated rooms, service with restrictions, supervision.
🛜 ✖ 🔧 💻

💎💎 Hotel La Normandie 🏨

(418) 782-2112. **$79-$259.** 221 Rt 132 ouest G0C 2L0. Center. Int corridors. **Pets:** Small. $30 one-time fee/pet. Designated rooms, service with restrictions, crate. 🛜 ✖ 🔧 🍴 🎬

💎💎 Hotel/Motel Le Mirage Ⓜ

(418) 782-5151. **$82-$198.** 288 Rt 132 ouest G0C 2L0. On Rt 132. Ext corridors. **Pets:** Small. $20 daily fee/pet. Designated rooms, supervision.
🛜 ✖ 🔧 🍴

💎💎 Hotel Motel Manoir de Percé 🏨

(418) 782-2022. **$68-$178.** 212 Rt 132 G0C 2L0. Center. Ext/int corridors. **Pets:** Other species. $25 one-time fee/room. Service with restrictions, supervision. 🛜 ✖ 🔧 🍴

QUÉBEC METROPOLITAN AREA

BOISCHATEL

Ⓐ 💎💎 Econo Lodge Montmorency 🏨

(418) 822-4777. **$75-$145.** 5490 boul Ste-Anne G0A 1H0. On Hwy 138. Int corridors. **Pets:** Medium. $15 daily fee/pet. Designated rooms, service with restrictions, supervision. 🔲 🛜 🔧

L'ANCIENNE-LORETTE

💎💎 Comfort Inn 🏨

(418) 872-5900. **$95-$129.** 1255 boul Duplessis G2G 2B4. Jct boul Duplessis and Wilfrid-Hamel (Hwy 138). Int corridors. **Pets:** Medium, other species. $25 one-time fee/room. Service with restrictions, crate.
🔢 🛜 🔧 💻

LÉVIS

Ⓐ 💎💎 Comfort Inn 🏨

(418) 835-5605. **$92-$147.** 10 du Vallon est G6V 9J3. Hwy 20 exit 325S eastbound; exit 325 westbound. Int corridors. **Pets:** Accepted.
🔢 🔲 🛜 🔧 💻

Ⓐ 💎💎💎 Comfort Inn & Suites Rive-Sud Quebec 🏨

(418) 836-3336. **Call for rates.** 495 Rt-du-Pont G7A 2N9. Hwy 20 exit 311, just ne on Rt 116; in St-Nicolas sector. Int corridors. **Pets:** Very small. $20 one-time fee/pet. Designated rooms, service with restrictions, supervision. 🔲 🛜 ✖ 🔧 💻 🌊

💎💎 Hotel Kennedy 🏨

(418) 837-0233. **Call for rates.** 129 Rt du President-Kennedy G6V 6C8. Hwy 20 exit 325N, just n. Ext/int corridors. **Pets:** Accepted.
🛜 🍴 🔧 💻

QUÉBEC

💎💎💎 ALT Hotel-Quebec 🏨

(418) 658-1224. **$139-$149.** 1200 ave Germain-des-Pres G1V 3M7. Just n of boul Laurier; facing Place Laurier mall. Int corridors. **Pets:** Accepted.
🛜 ✖ 🔧 🍴

💎💎 Appartements La Pergola Ⓒ

(418) 681-1428. **Call for rates.** 405 boul Rene-Levesque ouest G1S 1S2. Between aves Moncton and des Erables. Int corridors.
Pets: Accepted. 🛜 ✖ 🔧 💻

Ⓐ 💎💎💎 Auberge Place d'Armes 🏨

(418) 694-9485. **$139-$329.** 24 rue Ste-Anne G1R 3X3. Just w of rue du Trésor. Int corridors. **Pets:** Accepted. 🔲 🛜 ✖ 🔧 🍴

Ⓐ 💎💎💎 BEST WESTERN PLUS City Centre/Centre-Ville 🏨 🐾

(418) 649-1919. **$120-$600.** 330 rue de la Couronne G1K 6E6. Corner of rue du Roi. Int corridors. **Pets:** Large. $15 daily fee/room. Service with restrictions, supervision. 🔲 🛜 ✖ 🔧 💻 🍴 🌊

💎💎💎 Delta Quebec 🏨 🐾

(418) 647-1717. **$110-$299.** 690 boul Rene-Levesque est G1R 5A8. Just w of boul Honore-Mercier. Int corridors. **Pets:** Medium. $35 one-time fee/room. Designated rooms, supervision.
🔢 🛜 ✖ 🔧 💻 🍴 🌊 ⊠

Ⓐ 💎💎💎💎 Fairmont Le Château Frontenac 🏨 🐾

(418) 692-3861. **$199-$459.** 1 rue des Carrieres G1R 4P5. In Old Quebec. Int corridors. **Pets:** $35 daily fee/pet. Service with restrictions, supervision. 🔢 🔲 🛜 🔧 💻 🍴 🌊 ⊠

◯ ▼▼▼ ▼▼▼ Hilton Québec 🅗 ✿
(418) 647-2411. **$159-$359.** 1100 boul Rene-Levesque est G1R 4P3.
Corner of ave Honore-Mercier. Int corridors. **Pets:** $25 one-time fee/room.
Supervision. 🅔🅒🅞 🆂🅰🆅🅴 🛜 📶 🚫 📺 🛏 ⛱ 🚫

▼▼▼▼ Hotel & Suites Normandin 🅗
(418) 622-1611. **$116-$249.** 4700 boul Pierre-Bertrand G2J 1A4. Hwy 40
exit 312N eastbound to boul Pierre-Bertrand, then n to rue Bouvier; exit
312N westbound, just w. Int corridors. **Pets:** Accepted.
🛜 🚫 🅼 📶 📺 🍴

◯ ▼▼▼▼ Hotel Champlain Vieux-Quebec 🅗
(418) 694-0106. **$119-$279.** 115 rue Ste-Anne G1R 3X6. Between rue
Ste-Angele and St-Stanislas. Int corridors. **Pets:** Accepted.
🆂🅰🆅🅴 🛜 🚫 📶

▼▼▼ Hôtel Citadelle 🅗
(418) 871-3938. **Call for rates.** 4800 boul Wilfrid-Hamel G1P 2J9. Just e
of Hwy 73. Ext/int corridors. **Pets:** Accepted. 🛜 📶 📺

◯ ▼▼▼▼ Hotel Clarion Quebec 🅗
(418) 653-4901. **$99-$149.** 3125 boul Hochelaga G1V 4A8. Hwy 73 exit
136 (Hochelaga ouest). Int corridors. **Pets:** Other species. $20 one-time
fee/room. Service with restrictions, crate.
🆂🅰🆅🅴 🛜 🚫 📶 📺 🍴 ⛱ 🚫

▼▼▼▼ Hotel Dauphin Quebec City 🅗 ✿
(418) 688-3888. **$87-$170.** 400 rue du Marais G1M 3R1. Hwy 40 exit
312S (Pierre-Bertrand sud), just w of Rt 358. Int corridors. **Pets:** Other
species. $15 daily fee/room. Designated rooms, service with restrictions,
supervision. 🅔🅒🅞 🛜 🚫 🅼 📶 📺

▼▼▼▼ Hôtel Le Germain Dominion 🅗
(418) 692-2224. **$189-$415.** 126 rue St-Pierre G1K 4A8. Corner of rue
St-Paul. Int corridors. **Pets:** Accepted. 🛜 🚫 📺

◯ ▼▼▼ Hotel Quality Suites Quebec 🅗
(418) 622-4244. **$115-$195.** 1600 rue Bouvier G2K 1N8. Hwy 40 exit
312N (Pierre-Bertrand nord), 1.3 mi (2 km) w of jct Rt 358. Int corridors.
Pets: Other species. $25 one-time fee/room. Designated rooms, supervi-
sion. 🅔🅒🅞 🆂🅰🆅🅴 🛜 📶 📺

▼▼▼▼ Hotel Super 8 Quebec Ste-Foy 🅗
(418) 877-6888. **$80-$170.** 7286 boul Wilfred Hamel G2G 1C1. Hwy 138,
0.7 mi (1.1 km) w of boul Duplessis. Int corridors. **Pets:** Accepted.
🅔🅒🅞 🛜 📶 📺 ⛱ 🚫

◯ ▼▼▼ ▼▼▼ Le Château Bonne Entente 🅗 ✿
(418) 653-5221. **$159-$499.** 3400 chemin Ste-Foy G1X 1S6. Hwy 540
(Autoroute Duplessis) exit chemin Ste-Foy, just w. Int corridors.
Pets: Large. $35 one-time fee/room. Service with restrictions, supervision.
🆂🅰🆅🅴 🛜 🚫 🅼 📺 🍴 ⛱ 🚫

◯ ▼▼▼▼ L'Hôtel du Vieux-Quebec 🅗
(418) 692-1850. **$128-$328.** 1190 rue St-Jean G1R 1S6. Corner of rue
de l'Hotel-Dieu. Int corridors. **Pets:** Other species. $25 daily fee/pet. Des-
ignated rooms, service with restrictions, supervision.
🅔🅒🅞 🆂🅰🆅🅴 🛜 🚫 📶 📺 🍴

◯ ▼▼▼ ▼▼▼ Loews Hôtel Le Concorde 🅗 ✿
(418) 647-2222. **$129-$299.** 1225 Cours du General-de-Montcalm G1R
4W6. Corner of Grande Allee est. Int corridors. **Pets:** $25 one-time fee/
room. Service with restrictions, supervision.
🅔🅒🅞 🆂🅰🆅🅴 🛜 🚫 📶 📺 🍴 ⛱ 🚫

▼▼▼ N Hôtel 🅗 ✿
(418) 666-1226. **Call for rates.** 3390 boul Ste-Anne G1E 3L7. Hwy 440
exit Francois-de-Laval. Int corridors. **Pets:** Medium. $15 daily fee/room.
Designated rooms, service with restrictions, supervision.
🅔🅒🅞 🛜 📶 📺

◯ ▼▼▼ ▼▼▼ Relais & Chateaux Auberge
Saint-Antoine 🅗
(418) 692-2211. **$189-$1500, 3 day notice.** 8 rue St-Antoine G1K 4C9.
Corner of rue Dalhousie. Int corridors. **Pets:** Medium. $150 one-time fee/
room. Service with restrictions, crate.
🆂🅰🆅🅴 🛜 🚫 📶 📺 🍴 🚫

◯ ▼▼▼▼ TRYP Quebec Hotel PUR 🅗
(418) 647-2611. **$98-$269.** 395 rue de la Couronne G1K 7X4. Corner of
rue St-Joseph est. Int corridors. **Pets:** Dogs only. Service with restrictions,
supervision. 🆂🅰🆅🅴 🛜 🅼 📶 📺 🍴 ⛱ 🚫

ST-FERRÉOL-LES-NEIGES

▼▼▼ Chalets Montmorency Condominiums
Mont-Sainte-Anne Quebec 🅒🅞
(418) 826-2600. **$89-$159, 30 day notice.** 1768 ave Royale G0A 3R0.
On Hwy 360. Ext corridors. **Pets:** Dogs only. $25 daily fee/pet. No ser-
vice, supervision. 🛜 🚫 📶 📺 ⛱ 🚫

STE-ANNE-DE-BEAUPRÉ

◯ ▼▼▼ Quality Suites Mont Sainte-Anne 🅗
(418) 827-1570. **Call for rates.** 9800 boul Ste-Anne G0A 3C0. On Hwy
138. Int corridors. **Pets:** Small, other species. $20 daily fee/pet. Desig-
nated rooms, service with restrictions, supervision.
🆂🅰🆅🅴 🛜 🚫 📶 📺

END METROPOLITAN AREA

RIGAUD

▼▼▼ Howard Johnson 🅗
(450) 458-7779. **$84-$151.** 93 Montee Lavigne (Rt 201) J0P 1P0. Hwy
40 exit 17, just ne. Int corridors. **Pets:** Accepted.
🛜 🚫 📶 📺 🍴

RIMOUSKI

▼▼▼ Comfort Inn 🅗
(418) 724-2500. **$109-$139.** 455 boul St-Germain ouest G5L 3P2. On Rt
132. Int corridors. **Pets:** $25 one-time fee/room. Designated rooms, ser-
vice with restrictions, supervision. 🅔🅒🅞 🛜 🚫 📶 📺

◯ ▼▼▼ Hotel Gouverneur Rimouski 🅗
(418) 723-4422. **$95-$159, 5 day notice.** 155 boul Rene-Lepage E G5L
1P2. On Rt 132. Int corridors. **Pets:** Small. $25 one-time fee/pet. Desig-
nated rooms, service with restrictions, supervision.
🆂🅰🆅🅴 🛜 📶 📺 🍴 ⛱

RIVIÈRE-DU-LOUP

▼▼▼ Comfort Inn 🅗
(418) 867-4162. **$113-$175.** 85 boul Cartier G5R 4X4. Hwy 20 exit 507,
just se; Hwy 85 exit 96 (Fraserville), follow signs. Int corridors.
Pets: Accepted. 🅔🅒🅞 🛜 📶 📺

▼▼▼ Days Inn Riviere-du-Loup 🅗
(418) 862-6354. **$95-$194.** 182 rue Fraser G5R 1C8. Hwy 20 exit 503,
0.6 mi (1 km) e on Rt 132. Ext/int corridors. **Pets:** Accepted.
🅔🅒🅞 🛜 🚫 📶 📺 ⛱

ROUYN-NORANDA

◯ ▼▼▼▼ BEST WESTERN PLUS Albert Centre-Ville 🅗
(819) 762-3545. **$118-$132.** 84 Ave Principale J9X 4P2. Center. Int corridors. **Pets:** Other species. $25 daily fee/room.
🆂🅰🆅🅴 🛜 🚫 📶 📺 🍴 🚫

◈◈ **Comfort Inn** 🅷
(819) 797-1313. **$106-$146.** 1295 ave Lariviere J9X 6M6. On Rt 117, 2.5 mi (4 km) s from town center. Int corridors. **Pets:** Accepted.
🅴🅲🅾 📶 🛠 💻

◈◈◈ **Hôtel Gouverneur le Noranda** 🅷
(819) 762-2341. **$112-$132.** 41 6ieme rue J9X 1Y8. Corner of rue Murdoch; center. Ext/int corridors. **Pets:** Other species. $25 daily fee/room. Designated rooms, service with restrictions, crate.
📶 ✖ 🛠 💻 🍴 ⊠

ST-APOLLINAIRE
🅲🅰🅰 ◈◈◈ **Hotel Econo Lodge** 🅷
(418) 881-3335. **$85-$120.** 372 rue Laurier G0S 2E0. Hwy 20 exit 291, just ne. Ext/int corridors. **Pets:** Small. $15 daily fee/pet. Designated rooms, service with restrictions, supervision. 🆂🅰🆅🅴 📶 🛠 💻

ST-FAUSTIN-LAC-CARRÉ
◈ **Motel Tremblant sur la Colline** 🅼
(819) 688-2102. **$69-$119, 7 day notice.** 357 Rt 117 J0T 1J2. On Rt 117, 2.5 mi (4 km) n of exit for city. Ext/int corridors. **Pets:** Accepted.
📶 ✖ 🛠 💻 ⊅

ST-HYACINTHE
◈◈◈ **Holiday Inn Express & Suites** 🅷
(450) 251-1111. **$119-$250.** 1500 rue Johnson est J2S 8W5. Hwy 20 exit 133, just sw on boul Casavant est. Int corridors. **Pets:** Medium. $30 one-time fee/room. Service with restrictions, supervision.
📶 ✖ 🅶🅼 🛠 💻 ⊅

🅲🅰🅰 ◈◈◈ **Hotel des Seigneurs Saint-Hyacinthe** 🅷 🐾
(450) 774-3810. **$120-$240.** 1200 rue Johnson J2S 7K7. Hwy 20 exit 130S, just e on rue Gauvin from boul Laframboise. Int corridors. **Pets:** $25 one-time fee/pet. Designated rooms, service with restrictions, crate. 🅴🅲🅾 🆂🅰🆅🅴 📶 ✖ 🅶🅼 🛠 💻 🍴 ⊅ ⊠

ST-JEAN-PORT-JOLI
◈◈ **Auberge Du Faubourg** 🅼
(418) 598-6455. **$80-$275, 10 day notice.** 280 ave de Gaspe ouest (Rt 132) G0R 3G0. 1.4 mi (2.4 km) w from jct Rt 204; Hwy 20 exit 414. Ext corridors. **Pets:** Accepted. 📶 ✖ 🛠 💻 🍴 ⊅ 🅰🅲

ST-JEAN-SUR-RICHELIEU
◈◈◈ **Holiday Inn Express** 🅷
(450) 359-4466. **Call for rates.** 700 rue Gadbois J3A 1V1. Hwy 35 exit 45, e on rue Pierre-Caisse. Int corridors. **Pets:** Accepted.
📶 ✖ 🅶🅼 🛠 💻 ⊅

STE-AGATHE-DES-MONTS
◈◈◈ **Super 8 Ste-Agathe** 🅷
(819) 324-8880. **$77-$125.** 500 rue Leonard J8C 0A3. Hwy 15 exit 86, just w on Rt 117 to rue Leonard, then 0.3 mi (0.5 km) s. Int corridors. **Pets:** Accepted. 🅴🅲🅾 📶 🛠 💻 ⊅ ⊠

STE-EULALIE
◈◈ **Motel Marie-Dan** 🅼
(819) 225-4604. **$50-$85.** 311 rue des Bouleaux (Rt 161) G0Z 1E0. Hwy 20 exit 210, follow signs to Rt 161, then just s. Ext corridors. **Pets:** Small. $10 one-time fee/room. Supervision. 📶 🛠 ⊅

SHAWINIGAN
◈◈ **Auberge Escapade Inn** 🅷
(819) 539-6911. **Call for rates.** 3383 rue Garnier G9N 6R4. Hwy 55 exit 217, 0.3 mi (0.5 km) n on Rt 351. Ext/int corridors. **Pets:** Accepted.
📶 ✖ 🛠 🍴

◈◈◈ **Auberge Gouverneur & Centre de Congrès Shawinigan** 🅷
(819) 537-6000. **$82-$279.** 1100 Promenade-du-St-Maurice G9N 1L8. Hwy 55 N exit 211, 2.8 mi (4.4 km) n on Hwy 153, follow signs. Int corridors. **Pets:** Accepted. 📶 ✖ 🛠 💻 🍴 ⊅ ⊠

◈◈◈ **Comfort Inn & Suites** 🅷
(819) 536-2000. **$89-$139.** 500 boul du Capitaine G9P 5J6. Hwy 55 N exit 211, 2.8 mi (4.4 km) n on Hwy 153, then 1.3 mi (2 km) s on Rt 157. Int corridors. **Pets:** Accepted. 🅴🅲🅾 📶 🛠 💻

SHERBROOKE
◈◈ **Comfort Inn** 🅷
(819) 564-4400. **$103-$131.** 4295 boul Bourque J1N 1S4. Hwy 410 exit 4W, 0.9 mi (1.5 km) w on Rt 112. Ext/int corridors. **Pets:** Medium, dogs only. $25 one-time fee/pet. Designated rooms, service with restrictions, supervision. 🅴🅲🅾 📶 🛠 💻

◈◈◈ **Delta Sherbrooke Hotel and Conference Centre** 🅷 🐾
(819) 822-1989. **$104-$279.** 2685 rue King ouest J1L 1C1. Hwy 410 exit 4W, 0.6 mi (1 km) e on Rt 112. Int corridors. **Pets:** $35 one-time fee/room. Supervision. 🅴🅲🅾 📶 ✖ 🛠 💻 🍴 ⊅ ⊠

THETFORD MINES
◈◈ **Comfort Inn** 🅷
(418) 338-0171. **$122-$140.** 123 boul Frontenac ouest G6G 7S7. On Rt 112. Int corridors. **Pets:** Accepted. 🅴🅲🅾 📶 🛠 💻

TROIS-RIVIÈRES
🅲🅰🅰 ◈◈◈ **Comfort Inn** 🅷
(819) 371-3566. **$105-$135.** 6255 rue Corbeil G8Z 4P9. Hwy 55 exit 183 (boul Jean XXIII); 1.3 mi (2 km) n of Laviolette Bridge, then 0.3 mi (0.5 km) e. Int corridors. **Pets:** Accepted. 🅴🅲🅾 🆂🅰🆅🅴 📶 🛠 💻

🅲🅰🅰 ◈◈◈ **Delta Trois-Rivieres Hotel and Conference Centre** 🅷
(819) 376-1991. **$114-$275, 3 day notice.** 1620 rue Notre-Dame Centre G9A 6E5. Corner of rue St-Roch; center. Int corridors. **Pets:** Accepted.
🅴🅲🅾 🆂🅰🆅🅴 📶 ✖ 🛠 💻 🍴 ⊅ ⊠

◈◈◈ **Super 8 Trois-Rivieres** 🅷
(819) 377-5881. **$110-$150.** 3185 boul St-Jean G9B 2M4. Hwy 55 exit 183 (boul Jean XXIII), just nw. Int corridors. **Pets:** Accepted.
🅴🅲🅾 📶 ✖ 🛠 💻 ⊠

VAL-D'OR
◈◈ **Comfort Inn** 🅷
(819) 825-9360. **$126-$156.** 1665 3ieme Ave J9P 1V9. In town center. Int corridors. **Pets:** Accepted. 🅴🅲🅾 📶 🛠 💻

◈◈ **L'Escale Hotel Motel Suite** 🅷
(819) 824-2711. **$124-$145.** 1100 rue L'Escale J9P 4G8. In town center. Ext/int corridors. **Pets:** Service with restrictions, supervision.
📶 ✖ 🛠 💻 🍴

VICTORIAVILLE
◈◈◈ **Quality Inn & Suites Victoriaville** 🅷
(819) 330-8888. **$102-$180.** 1 boul Arthabaska est G6P 4B8. Corner of Notre-Dame est; in east downtown sector; near industrial park. Int corridors. **Pets:** Accepted. 📶 ✖ 🛠 💻 ⊠

WAKEFIELD
◈◈◈ **Moulin Wakefield Mill Hotel & Spa** 🅷
(819) 459-1838. **$179-$219, 7 day notice.** 60 chemin Mill J0X 3G0. 0.6 mi (1 km) w of Riverside Dr; center. Int corridors. **Pets:** Medium, dogs only. $35 one-time fee/room. Designated rooms, service with restrictions, crate. 🅴🅲🅾 ⊟ 📶 ✖ 💻 🍴 ⊅ ⊠

SASKATCHEWAN

ESTEVAN

BEST WESTERN PLUS Estevan Inn & Suites

(306) 634-7447. **$153-$170.** 92 King St S4A 2T5. Hwy 39, 1 mi (1.6 km) n at Kensington Ave. Int corridors. **Pets:** Medium. $10 daily fee/pet. Designated rooms, no service, supervision.

Motel 6 Estevan

(306) 634-8666. **Call for rates.** 88 King St E S4A 2A4. Hwy 39, 1 mi (1.7 km) n at Kensington Ave,then just e. Int corridors. **Pets:** Other species. Service with restrictions, supervision.

KINDERSLEY

Nova Inn

(306) 463-4687. **Call for rates.** 100 12th Ave NW S0L 1S0. Jct of Hwy 7 and 21. Ext/int corridors. **Pets:** Accepted.

MOOSE JAW

Comfort Inn

(306) 692-2100. **$120-$145.** 155 Thatcher Dr W S6J 1M1. 0.8 mi (1.2 km) s on Hwy 2 from jct Trans-Canada Hwy 1, then just w. Int corridors. **Pets:** Other species. $15 one-time fee/room. Designated rooms, service with restrictions, crate.

Heritage Inn Moose Jaw

(306) 693-7550. **$127-$252.** 1590 Main St N S6J 1L3. On Hwy 2, 0.9 mi (1.4 km) s of jct Trans-Canada Hwy 1. Int corridors. **Pets:** Medium, dogs only. $20 daily fee/pet. Designated rooms, service with restrictions, crate.

Prairie Oasis Motel

(306) 692-4894. **$89-$99.** 955 Thatcher Dr E S6H 4N9. Just s of jct Trans-Canada Hwy 1. Ext corridors. **Pets:** Medium, dogs only. Designated rooms, crate.

Super 8-Moose Jaw

(306) 692-8888. **$115-$135.** 1706 Main St N S6J 1L4. On Hwy 2, 0.7 mi (1.1 km) s of jct Trans-Canada Hwy 1. Int corridors. **Pets:** Other species. $15 daily fee/room. Designated rooms, service with restrictions, crate.

NORTH BATTLEFORD

Super 8

(306) 446-8888. **$95-$125.** 1006 Hwy 16 S9A 3W2. 0.3 mi (0.5 km) nw of jct Hwy 16 (Yellowhead Hwy). Int corridors. **Pets:** Other species. $25 one-time fee/room. Designated rooms, supervision.

Tropical Inn

(306) 446-4700. **Call for rates.** 1001 Hwy 16 Bypass S9A 3W2. Corner of Battleford Rd. Int corridors. **Pets:** Accepted.

PRINCE ALBERT

BEST WESTERN Marquis Inn & Suites

(306) 922-9595. **$115.** 602 36th St E S6V 7P2. Jct Hwy 3 (6th Ave E) and Marquis Rd. Int corridors. **Pets:** Other species. Designated rooms, supervision.

Comfort Inn

(306) 763-4466. **$144-$188.** 3863 2nd Ave W S6W 1A1. 1.6 mi (2.6 km) s on Hwy 2. Int corridors. **Pets:** Other species. Service with restrictions, crate.

Ramada Prince Albert

(306) 922-1333. **$120-$150.** 3245 2nd Ave W S6V 5G1. 1.2 mi (2 km) s on Hwy 2. Int corridors. **Pets:** Other species. $20 one-time fee/room. Designated rooms, supervision.

Super 8

(306) 953-0088. **$124-$129.** 4444 2nd Ave W S6V 5R7. 1.7 mi (2.7 km) s on Hwy 2. Int corridors. **Pets:** Small. $10 daily fee/room. Designated rooms, service with restrictions, supervision.

Travelodge Prince Albert

(306) 764-6441. **$116-$140.** 3551 2nd Ave W S6V 5G1. 1.4 mi (2.2 km) s on Hwy 2. Int corridors. **Pets:** Other species. Service with restrictions, crate.

REGINA

BEST WESTERN Seven Oaks Inn

(306) 757-0121. **$150.** 777 Albert St S4R 2P6. On Hwy 6; jct 2nd Ave. Int corridors. **Pets:** Small. $10 daily fee/pet. Designated rooms, service with restrictions, supervision.

Comfort Inn

(306) 789-5522. **$136-$148.** 3221 E Eastgate Dr S4Z 1A4. Trans-Canada Hwy 1, 1.3 mi (2 km) e of Ring Rd; at eastern approach to city. Int corridors. **Pets:** Accepted.

Country Inn & Suites By Carlson

(306) 789-9117. **$115-$199, 3 day notice.** 3321 Eastgate Bay S4Z 1A4. Trans-Canada Hwy 1, 1.2 mi (2 km) e of Ring Rd; at eastern approach to city. Int corridors. **Pets:** Accepted.

Delta Regina

(306) 525-5255. **$165-$230.** 1919 Saskatchewan Dr S4P 4H2. At Rose St; center. Int corridors. **Pets:** Other species. $35 one-time fee/room. Designated rooms, service with restrictions, crate.

Executive Royal Hotel Regina

(306) 586-6755. **$122.** 4025 Albert St S S4S 3R6. On Hwy 6, 1.2 mi (2 km) n of jct Trans-Canada Hwy 1. Int corridors. **Pets:** $25 daily fee/room. Designated rooms, service with restrictions.

Quality Hotel

(306) 569-4656. **$119-$159.** 1717 Victoria Ave S4P 0P9. Just e of Broad St; downtown. Int corridors. **Pets:** Accepted.

Radisson Plaza Hotel Saskatchewan

(306) 522-7691. **$140-$290.** 2125 Victoria Ave S4P 0S3. At Scarth St; center. Int corridors. **Pets:** Medium. $50 one-time fee/pet. Service with restrictions.

Sandman Hotel Suites & Spa Regina

(306) 757-2444. **Call for rates.** 1800 Victoria Ave E S4N 7K3. On Trans-Canada Hwy 1, just e of Ring Rd; at eastern approach to city. Int corridors. **Pets:** Accepted.

Super 8 Regina

(306) 789-8833. **$115-$125.** 2730 Victoria Ave E S4N 6M5. On Trans-Canada Hwy 1, 1 mi (1.6 km) e of Ring Rd; at eastern approach to city. Int corridors. **Pets:** Other species. $10 daily fee/pet. Designated rooms, service with restrictions.

▼▼▼ **Wingate by Wyndham** 🏨
(306) 584-7400. **$119-$199.** 1700 Broad St S4P 1X4. Corner of Saskatchewan Dr; center. Int corridors. **Pets:** Accepted.
ECO 📶 ✕ 🖥 🍴

SASKATOON

CAA ▼▼▼▼ **BEST WESTERN Harvest Inn** 🏨
(306) 244-5552. **$129-$138.** 1715 Idylwyld Dr N S7L 1B4. On Hwy 11 (Idylwyld Dr), 0.4 mi (0.7 km) s of jct Circle Dr. Int corridors.
Pets: Accepted. ECO SAVE 📶 ✕ 🖥 🍴

CAA ▼▼▼▼ **BEST WESTERN PLUS Blairmore** 🏨
(306) 242-2299. **$152-$162.** 306 Shillington Crescent S7M 1L7. Jct Hwy 7 and 14. Int corridors. **Pets:** Medium. $20 daily fee/room. Designated rooms, service with restrictions, supervision.
SAVE 📶 ✕ 🖥 ⊷ ✕

CAA ▼▼▼ **Colonial Square Inn & Suites** 🏨
(306) 343-1676. **$114-$149.** 1301 8th St E S7H 0S7. 1.5 mi (2.4 km) e of jct Hwy 11 (Idylwyld Dr); 1.4 mi (2.3 km) w of jct Circle Dr. Int corridors. **Pets:** Small, dogs only. $20 daily fee/pet. Designated rooms, service with restrictions, supervision. SAVE 📶 ✕ 🖥

CAA ▼▼▼ **Comfort Inn** 🏨
(306) 934-1122. **$124-$180.** 2155 Northridge Dr S7L 6X6. Just ne of Hwy 11 (Idlwyld Dr) and Circle Dr. Int corridors. **Pets:** Large. $15 daily fee/pet. Designated rooms, service, crate.
ECO SAVE 📶 🖥

▼▼▼ **Country Inn & Suites By Carlson** 🏨 🐾
(306) 934-3900. **$120-$160.** 617 Cynthia St S7L 6B7. Just w on Circle Dr from jct Hwy 11 (Idylwyld Dr), then just n on Ave CN. Int corridors. **Pets:** $25 one-time fee/room. Designated rooms, service with restrictions, supervision. ECO 📶 🖥

CAA ▼▼▼▼ **Delta Bessborough** 🏨 🐾
(306) 244-5521. **$139-$399.** 601 Spadina Crescent E S7K 3G8. At 21st St E; center. Int corridors. **Pets:** Medium. $35 one-time fee/room. Service with restrictions. ECO SAVE 📶 ✕ 🖥 🍴 ⊷ ✕

▼▼▼ **Holiday Inn Express Hotel & Suites** 🏨
(306) 384-8844. **$144-$171.** 315 Idylwyld Dr N S7L 0Z1. On Hwy 11 (Idylwyld Dr), just n of 23rd St. Int corridors. **Pets:** Accepted.
ECO 📶 ✕ 🖥 ⊷

▼▼▼ **Motel 6 Saskatoon** 🏨
(306) 665-6688. **Call for rates.** 231 Marquis Dr S7R 1B7. E of jct Trans-Canada Hwy 16; 0.4 mi (0.7 km) w of Hwy 11 (Idylwyld Dr). Int corridors. **Pets:** Other species. Service with restrictions, supervision.
📶 ✕ 🖥 ⊷

CAA ▼▼▼▼ **Radisson Hotel Saskatoon** 🏨
(306) 665-3322. **$169-$249, 3 day notice.** 405 20th St E S7K 6X6. At 4th Ave S; center. Int corridors. **Pets:** Accepted.
ECO SAVE 📶 ✕ 🖥 🍴 ⊷ ✕

▼▼▼ **Ramada Hotel & Golf Dome** 🏨
(306) 665-6500. **$109-$179.** 806 Idylwyld Dr N S7L 0Z6. On Hwy 11 (Idylwyld Dr), 2.5 mi (4 km) s of jct Circle Dr. Int corridors.
Pets: Accepted. ECO 📶 🖥 🍴 ⊷ ✕

▼▼▼ **Sandman Hotel** 🏨
(306) 477-4844. **Call for rates.** 310 Circle Dr W S7L 2Y5. Just w of Hwy 11 (Idylwyld Dr). Int corridors. **Pets:** Accepted.
ECO 📶 ✕ 🖥 🍴 ⊷

CAA ▼▼▼ **Saskatoon Inn Hotel and Conference Centre** 🏨
(306) 242-1440. **$139-$199.** 2002 Airport Dr S7L 6M4. Jct Hwy 16 (Circle Dr) and 11 (Idylwyld Dr N), 0.6 mi (1 km) sw, then just nw. Int corridors. **Pets:** Medium. $30 daily fee/room. Designated rooms, service with restrictions, supervision. ECO SAVE 📶 ✕ 🖥 🍴 ⊷

CAA ▼▼▼▼ **Sheraton Cavalier Saskatoon Hotel** 🏨
(306) 652-6770. **$159-$289.** 612 Spadina Crescent E S7K 3G9. At 21st St E; center. Int corridors. **Pets:** Accepted.
ECO SAVE 📶 ✕ 🖥 🍴 ⊷ ✕

▼▼ **Super 8** 🏨
(306) 384-8989. **$127-$132.** 706 Circle Dr E S7K 3T7. 1.3 mi (2 km) e of jct Hwy 11 (Idylwyld Dr). Int corridors. **Pets:** Medium. $15 daily fee/room. Designated rooms, service with restrictions, supervision.
📶 ✕ 🖥 🖥

SWIFT CURRENT

▼▼ **Comfort Inn** 🏨
(306) 778-3994. **$112-$126.** 1510 S Service Rd E S9H 3X6. On south side service road of Trans-Canada Hwy 1, just w of 22nd Ave NE. Int corridors. **Pets:** Accepted. ECO 📶 ✕ 🖥 🖥

▼▼ **Motel 6 Swift Current** 🏨
(306) 778-6060. **$100-$111.** 1185 5th Ave NE S9H 5N7. Trans-Canada Hwy 1, just e of Central Ave N, then just n; just n of N Service Rd. Int corridors. **Pets:** Other species. Service with restrictions, supervision.
📶 ✕ 🖥

UNITY

▼▼▼ **Prairie Moon Inn & Suites** 🏨
(306) 228-3333. **$116-$152.** 103 2nd Ave S S0K 4L0. Hwy 14, west end of town. Int corridors. **Pets:** Accepted. 📶 ✕ 🖥 🖥

WEYBURN

▼▼▼ **Canalta Hotel** 🏨
(306) 842-8000. **Call for rates.** 1360 Sims Ave S4H 3N9. On Hwy 39, just w of Hwy 35. Ext/int corridors. **Pets:** Accepted.
ECO 📶 ✕ 🖥 🖥 ✕

CAA ▼▼▼ **Perfect Inns & Suites** Ⓜ
(306) 842-2691. **$95-$250.** 238 Sims Ave S4H 2J8. 0.3 mi (0.5 km) w of jct Hwy 35 and 39. Ext/int corridors. **Pets:** Accepted.
SAVE 📶 🖥 🖥

▼▼▼ **Ramada Inn & Suites** 🏨
(306) 842-4994. **$139-$219.** 1420 Sims Ave S4H 3N9. On Hwy 39, just w of Hwy 35. Ext/int corridors. **Pets:** $15 daily fee/room. Designated rooms, service with restrictions, crate. ECO 📶 ✕ 🖥 🖥 ⊷

YORKTON

▼▼ **Ramada Yorkton** 🏨
(306) 783-9781. **$119-$149.** 100 Broadway St E S3N 0K9. On Hwy 9, 10, and 16 (Yellowhead Hwy); downtown. Int corridors. **Pets:** $20 daily fee/room. Designated rooms, service with restrictions, supervision.
📶 🖥 🖥 🍴 ⊷ ✕

YUKON

DAWSON CITY

◆◆ Klondike Kate's Cabins 🄲🄰
(867) 993-6527. **$145-$195.** 1102 3rd Ave Y0B 1G0. Corner of 3rd Ave and King St. Ext corridors. **Pets:** Other species. $50 one-time fee/room. Service with restrictions. 🛜 ⊠ ⅏ 🖥 💻 🍴 🄰🄲

◆◆ Westmark Inn Dawson City 🄷
(867) 993-5542. **$119-$189.** 813 5th Ave Y0B 1G0. At Harper St. Int corridors. **Pets:** Accepted. 🛜 ⊠ ⅏ 🖥 💻 🍴

WHITEHORSE

ⒸⒶⒶ ◆◆◆ BEST WESTERN Gold Rush Inn 🄷
(867) 668-4500. **$140-$175.** 411 Main St Y1A 2B6. Between 4th and 5th aves; center. Int corridors. **Pets:** $20 daily fee/pet. Designated rooms, service with restrictions, crate. 🄴🄲🄾 🆂🄰🆅🄴 🛜 ⊠ 🖥 💻

ⒸⒶⒶ ◆◆ High Country Inn 🄷
(867) 667-4471. **$140-$175, 3 day notice.** 4051 4th Ave Y1A 1H1. 0.4 mi (0.6 km) e of Main St. Int corridors. **Pets:** $15 daily fee/pet. Designated rooms, service with restrictions, crate. 🄴🄲🄾 🆂🄰🆅🄴 🛜 ⊠ 🖥 💻 🍴

◆◆◆ Westmark Whitehorse Hotel & Conference Center 🄷
(867) 393-9700. **$119-$249.** 201 Wood St Y1A 2E4. At 2nd Ave; center. Int corridors. **Pets:** Designated rooms, service with restrictions, supervision. 🛜 ⊠ ⅏ 🖥 💻 🍴 🄰🄲

Pet-Friendly Campgrounds

United States
Canada

United States

Camping information provided by Woodall's®

Alabama

ELBERTA — LAKE OSPREY RV COUNTRY CLUB. (251) 986-3800. **$35-$45.** 12054 Gateway Dr 36530. From Jct of I-10 & Exit 44 (SR-59), S 18.7 mi to US 98, E 8.2 mi to CR-95, S 1.2 mi (R). 🏕️ �'' 💲 🖑ᴹ

FOLEY — ANCHORS AWEIGH RV RESORT. (251) 971-6644. **$32-$36.** 19814 County Rd 20 S 36535. From Jct of SR-59 & CR-20 South, W 0.25 mi on CR-20 South (L) Note: S-bnd on SR-59 2nd CR20S after Cracker Barrel 🏕️ �'' 💲 🖑ᴹ

FOLEY — BELLA TERRA OF GULF SHORES. (866) 417-2416. **$50-$65.** 101 Via Bella Terra 36535. From Jct of I-10 & Hwy 59 (Exit 44) S 15 mi on SR-59 to Foley Beach Expressway SE 10 mi to Brinks Willis Rd, W 0.25 mi (L) 🏕️ �'' 💲 🖑ᴹ

GULF SHORES — GULF BREEZE RV RESORT. (251) 968-8462. **$32.** 19800 Oak Rd W 36542. From Jct of SR-59 & CR-6, W 0.2 mi on CR-6 (L) 🏕️ �'' 💲 🖑ᴹ

GULF SHORES — ISLAND RETREAT RV PARK. (251) 967-1666. **$32-$35.** 18201 State Hwy 180 (Ft Morgan Rd) 36542. From Jct of SR-59 & SR-180 (Fort Morgan Rd), W 1.6 mi on SR-180 (R) 🏕️ �'' 💲 🖑ᴹ

GUNTERSVILLE — BLUE HERON RV RESORT. (256) 571-7527. **$30-$50.** 1727 Convict Camp Rd 35976. From Jct of large river bridge (Guntersville) & Hwy 431, N 3 mi on Hwy 431 to Hwy 79, N on Hwy 79 2.5 mi (L) 🏕️ �'' 💲 🖑ᴹ

LANGSTON — WINDEMERE COVE RV RESORT. (256) 228-3010. **$24-$49.** 10174 County Rd 67 35755. From Jct of US 431 & Hwy 227 (Guntersville), go 12 mi E on Hwy 227, then at Jct of Hwy 227 & S. Sauty Rd (CR-67) continue going E 8 mi on CR-67 (R) 🏕️ �'' 💲 🖑ᴹ

ORANGE BEACH — HERITAGE MOTORCOACH RESORT & MARINA. (888) 743-7256. **$60-$105.** 28888 Canal Rd. 36561. From Jct of I-10 & AL 59 (Exit 44), S 15.3 mi on AL 59 to Foley Beach Expy, E 14 mi on Foley Beach Expy to AL 180 (Canal Rd), E 5.8 mi on AL 180 (Canal Rd) (R) 🏕️ 💲 🖑ᴹ

OZARK — OZARK FORT RUCKER KOA. (800) 359-3218. **$35.** 2414 N US Hwy 231 36360. N-Bnd: North of Dothan, From Jct of 231 Bypass (Ross Clark Cir.) & N US-231, N 20 mi on US-231, MP 47 (R); or S-Bnd: In Troy, Jct US 29 & US 231, S 30.4 mi on US 231 MP47 (L) �'' 💲

TROY — DEER RUN RV PARK. (800) 552-3036. **$29.** 25629 US Hwy 231 36081. From Jct of US-29 (N end of Troy) & US-231, N 6.5 mi on US-231 (L) or From Jct of Hwy 271 (Taylor Rd) (Montgomery) & Hwy 231, S 31 mi to CR 1124 (MP 83.5) (R) 🏕️ �'' 💲 🖑ᴹ

Arizona

AMADO — DE ANZA RV RESORT. (520) 398-8628. **$36.** 2869 E Frontage Rd 85645. S-bnd: From Jct of I-19 & Arivaca Rd (Exit 48), S 1.5 mi on East Frontage Rd (L); N-bnd: From Jct of I-19 & Agualinda Rd (Exit 42), N 2 mi on East Frontage Rd (R) 🏕️ 🚑 💲 🖑ᴹ

APACHE JUNCTION — GOLDEN SUN RV RESORT/PMP. (866) 226-6180. **$40.** 999 W Broadway Ave 85120. E-bnd: From Jct of Hwy 60 & Ironwood Dr (Exit 195), N 1.4 mi on Ironwood Dr to Broadway, E 0.4 mi (R); or W-bnd: From Jct of Hwy 60 & AZ 202 N (Exit 190A), N 1.2 mi on AZ 202 N to Broadway (Exit 28), E 4.8 mi (R) 🏕️ 🚑 💲 🖑ᴹ

APACHE JUNCTION — LA HACIENDA RV RESORT/PMP. (480) 982-2808. **$42.** 1797 W 28th Ave 85120. From Jct of US Hwy 60 & Ironwood Dr (exit 195), N 200 yds on Ironwood Dr to 28th, W 250 ft (L) 🏕️ 🚑 💲 🖑ᴹ

APACHE JUNCTION — MERIDIAN RV RESORT. (866) 770-0080. **$42.** 1901 S Meridian 85120. From Jct of US-60 & Signal Butte Rd, (exit 193), N 0.5 mi on Signal Butte Rd to Southern Ave, E 1 mi to Meridian, N 0.2 mi (R) 🏕️ 🚑 💲

APACHE JUNCTION — SHIPROCK RV RESORT ARIZONA. (480) 505-1300. **$38-$50.** 1700 W Shiprock St 85120. From jct Fwy 202 Loop & US 60 (Superstition Fwy): Go 5 mi E on US 60 (exit 195/Ironwood Dr), then 2-3/4 mi N on Ironwood Dr, then 300 ft W on Shiprock St. 🏕️ 🚑 💲 🖑ᴹ

APACHE JUNCTION — SUNRISE RV RESORT/PMP. (480) 983-2500. **$39. (no credit cards).** 1403 W Broadway Ave 85120. From Jct of US Hwy 60 & Ironwood Dr (exit 195), N 1.4 mi on Ironwood Dr to Broadway, E 0.1 mi (R) 🏕️ 🚑 💲 🖑ᴹ

APACHE JUNCTION — SUPERSTITION LOOKOUT TRAVEL TRAILER RESORT/PMP. (480) 982-2008. **$35.** 1371 E 4th Ave 85119. From Jct of US Hwy 60 & Tomahawk Rd (exit 197), N 1.6 mi on Tomahawk Rd to 4th Ave, W 600 ft (L) 🏕️ 🚑 💲 🖑ᴹ

APACHE JUNCTION — SUPERSTITION SUNRISE RV RESORT/PMP. (800) 624-7027. **$30-$50. (no credit cards).** 702 S Meridian Rd 85120. From Jct of US Hwy 60 & Ironwood Dr (exit 195), N 0.5 mi on Ironwood Dr to Southern Ave, W 1 mi to Meridian Rd, N 0.6 mi (L) 🏕️ 🚑 💲 🖑ᴹ

APACHE JUNCTION — WEAVER'S NEEDLE TRAVEL TRAILER RESORT/PMP. (480) 982-3683. **$36.** 250 SO Tomahawk Rd 85119. From Jct of US Hwy 60 & Tomahawk Rd (exit 197), N 1.7 mi on Tomahawk Rd (L) 🏕️ 🚑 💲

ARIZONA CITY — QUAIL RUN RV RESORT. (800) 301-8114. **$40-$45.** 14010 S Amado Blvd 85123. From Jct of I-10 & Sunland Gin Rd (exit 200): Go south 3.6 mi on Sunland Gin Rd to Santa Cruz Blvd, W 0.7 mi to Park (R) Santa Cruz changes to Amado Blvd. Call for GPS directions 🏕️ 🚑 💲 🖑ᴹ

BENSON — BUTTERFIELD RV RESORT. (800) 863-8160. **$37.** 251 S Ocotillo Ave 85602. From Jct of I-10 & Ocotillo Ave (exit 304), go S 0.6 mi on Ocotillo Ave/past Safeway shopping center to 3rd entrance on (L)

BENSON — COCHISE TERRACE RV RESORT. (520) 720-0911. **$30.** 1030 S Barrel Cactus Ridge 85602. From Jct of I-10 & Hwy 90 (exit 302), S 0.9 mi on Hwy 90 (R)

BENSON — SAN PEDRO RESORT COMMUNITY. (520) 586-9546. **$30.** 1110 South Hwy 80 Box 1 85602. From Jct of I-10 & Ocotillo St (exit 304), S 0.5 mi on Ocotillo St to Bus 10, E 0.9 mi to SR-80, S 1.3 mi (R)

BUCKEYE — LEAF VERDE RV RESORT. (623) 386-3132. **$34.** 1500 S Apache Rd 85326. E-bnd: From Jct of I-10 & Miller Rd-Buckeye (Exit 114), S 50 ft on Miller Rd to Yuma Rd, E 1.1 mi to Apache Rd, S 0.2 mi (R); or W-bnd: From Jct of I-10 & Watson Rd (Exit 117), S 0.6 mi on Watson Rd to Yuma Rd, W 1 mi to Apache Rd, S 0.3 mi (R)

BULLHEAD CITY — COLORADO RIVER OASIS RV PARK. (928) 763-4385. **$35.** 1641 Highway 95 86442. From Jct of Hwy 95 & Bullhead City Pkwy (Laughlin Bridge), S 3.4 mi on Hwy 95 (R)

BULLHEAD CITY — SILVERVIEW RV RESORT/PMP. (928) 763-5500. **$30-$35.** 1501 Gold Rush Rd 86442. From Jct of Hwy 95 & Bullhead City Pkwy (Laughlin Bridge), S 4.5 mi on Hwy 95 to Silver Creek Rd, E 0.7 mi to Gold Rush Rd, S 60 ft. (R)

CAMP VERDE — DISTANT DRUMS RV RESORT. (928) 554-8000. **$25-$39.** 583 W Middle Verde Rd 86322. From Jct of I-17 & exit 289 (Montezuma Castle), NW 200 yards on Montezuma Castle Rd (L)

CASA GRANDE — CASITA VERDE RV RESORT/PMP. (520) 836-9031. **$38.** 2200 N Trekell Rd 85122. From Jct of I-10 & McCartney Rd (exit 190), W 2.1 mi on McCartney Rd to Trekell Rd, S 1.5 mi (L)

CASA GRANDE — FIESTA GRANDE RV RESORT/PMP. (888) 934-3782. **$40.** 1511 E Florence Blvd 85122. From Jct of I-10 & Hwy 287 (exit 194), W 2 mi on Hwy 287/Florence Blvd (L)

CASA GRANDE — PALM CREEK GOLF & RV RESORT/PMP. (800) 421-7004. **$33-$54.** 1110 N Henness Rd 85122. From Jct of I-10 & Florence Blvd (exit 194), W 0.5 mi on Florence Blvd to Henness Rd, N 0.2 mi (R)

CASA GRANDE — SUNDANCE 1 RV RESORT/PMP. (520) 426-9662. **$25-$38.** 1703 N Thornton Rd 85122. From Jct of I-10 & Pinal Ave (exit 185), S 7.3 mi on Pinal Ave to Cottonwood, W 1 mi to Thornton Rd, N 0.2 mi (L); or From Jct of I-8 & Thornton Rd (Exit 172), N 5 mi on Thornton Rd (L)

CASA GRANDE — VAL VISTA RV PARK. (520) 836-7800. **$37.** 16680 W Val Vista Blvd 85122. From Jct of I-10 & Pinal Ave (Exit 185, SR-387), S 2.5 mi on Pinal Ave to Val Vista Blvd, E 0.6 mi (L)

DEWEY-HUMBOLDT — ORCHARD RANCH RV RESORT/PMP. (928) 772-8266. **$35.** 11250 E Hwy 69 86327. From Jct of I-17 & Hwy 169 (Exit 278), W 15.1 mi on Hwy 169 to SR 69 (in Dewey), NW 3.2 mi (R)

EHRENBERG — COLORADO RIVER OASIS RESORT. (928) 923-8230. **$40.** 50238 Ehrenberg/Parker Hwy 85334. From Jct of I-10 & Exit 1 (Parker/Ehrenberg), N 0.25 mi on Poston Rd to Ehrenberg/Parker Hwy, W 0.3 mi (R)

EHRENBERG — RIVER BREEZE RV PARK & OHV RESORT. (928) 923-7483. **$36-$47.** 50202 Ehrenberg Parker Hwy 85334. From Jct of I-10 & Exit 1, N 0.25 mi on Access Rd to Ehrenberg/Parker Hwy, W 600 ft (R)

EL MIRAGE — PUEBLO EL MIRAGE GOLF & RV RESORT. (800) 445-4115. **$49.** 11201 N El Mirage Rd 85335. From Jct of I-10 & Dysart Rd (Exit 129), N 6.9 mi on Dysart Rd to Olive Ave, E 1 mi to El Mirage Rd, N 1.5 mi (R); or From Jct of I-10 & Loop 101 (Exit 133), N 9 mi on Loop 101 to Olive Ave (Exit 9), W 3.8 mi to El Mirage Rd, N 1.5 mi (R).

ELOY — DESERT VALLEY RV PARK. (866) 502-4700. **$34.** 4555 W Tonto Rd 85131. From Jct of I-10 & Toltec Rd (exit 203): Go N for .5 mi on Toltec Rd, turn W on Tonto Rd for .5 mi in to Park

ELOY — LAS COLINAS RV PARK. (520) 836-5050. **$36. (no credit cards).** 7136 Sunland Gin Rd 85131. From Jct of I-10 & Exit 200 (Sunland Gin Rd): Go N on Sunland Gin Rd for .5 mi to Redd Rd (First St), turn W on Redd Rd, go 300 ft (L)

FLORENCE — DESERT GARDENS RV PARK. (520) 868-3800. **$36-$40. (no credit cards).** 9668 N Hwy 79 85132. From Jct of Hwy 79 & SR-287, S 4.2 mi on Hwy 79 (R)

FORT MCDOWELL — EAGLE VIEW RV RESORT AT FORT MCDOWELL. (800) 843-3678. **$42-$47.** 9605 N Fort McDowell Rd 85264. From Jct of SR-87 (Beeline Hwy) & N Fort McDowell Rd, S 0.4 mi on N Fort McDowell Rd (E)

GOLD CANYON — CANYON VISTAS RV RESORT & SUPERSTITION VIEWS RESORT. (888) 940-8989. **$40.** 6601 E US Hwy 60 85118. From Jct Hwy 88 & US 60: Go E 4.9 mi on US 60 for 4.9 mi.

GOLD CANYON — GOLD CANYON RV & GOLF RESORT. (877) 465-3226. **$32-$45. (no credit cards).** 7151 E US Hwy 60 85118. From Jct of E US Hwy 60 & Goldfield exit (end of freeway), E 3.4 mi on Hwy 60 at mm 202 (R)

GOODYEAR — COTTON LANE RV & GOLF RESORT/PMP. (888) 907-7223. **$34.** 17506 W. Van Buren 85338. From Jct of I-10 & Cotton Ln (exit 124), S 0.7 mi on Cotton Ln to Van Buren St, W 0.5 mi (R)

GOODYEAR — DESTINY PHOENIX RV RESORTS. (888) 667-2454. **$26-$40.** 416 N Citrus Rd 85338. Beginning Sept 2012, Cotton Lane/I-10 ramps will be closed. Call for directions.

GREEN VALLEY — **GREEN VALLEY RV RESORT/PMP.**
(520) 625-3900. **$40. (no credit cards).** 19001 S Richfield Ave
85614. From Jct of I-19 & Duval Mine Rd (exit 69), W 0.25 mi on
Duval Mine Rd (R) 🏕️ 🛶 🗶 ♿M

HUACHUCA CITY — **TOMBSTONE TERRITORIES RV
PARK.** ⒶⒶⒶ (520) 457-2584. **$30-$34.** 2111 E Hwy 82 85616.
From Jct of I-10 & AZ Hwy 90 (Exit 302), go S on AZ-90 for 19 mi
to AZ-82, turn E on to AZ-82, go 7.8 mi (L) 🏕️ 🛶 🗶 ♿M

LAKE HAVASU CITY — **HAVASU RV RESORT.** (928)
764-2020. **$50.** 1905 Victoria Farms Rd 86404. From Jct of Hwy
95 & Chenoweth Rd (N of town), E 0.2 mi on Chenoweth Rd to
Victoria Farms Rd, N 0.2 mi (L) 🏕️ 🛶 🗶

LAKE HAVASU CITY — **ISLANDER RV RESORT.** (928)
680-2000. **$46-$89.** 751 Beachcomber Blvd 86403. From Jct of
Hwy 95 & Mesquite Ave, E 0.1 mi on Mesquite Ave to Lake
Havasu Ave, S 0.1 mi to McCulloch Blvd (becomes Beachcomber),
W 1.8 mi across London Bridge (L) 🏕️ 🛶 🗶 ♿M

MARANA — **VALLEY OF THE SUN MH/RV PARK.** (520)
682-3434. **$30.** 13377 N Sandario Rd 85653. From Jct of I-10 &
Marana Rd (exit 236), S 0.7 mi on Sandario Rd (R) 🏕️ 🛶 🗶

MESA — **APACHE WELLS RV RESORT.** (888) 940-8989. **$22-
$43.** 2656 N 56th St 85215. From Jct of Loop 202 & Higley Rd, S
1 mi on Higley Rd to McDowell Rd, E 0.5 mi to N 56th St, S 200
ft (R) 🏕️ 🛶 🗶

MESA — **GOOD LIFE RV RESORT/PMP.** (888) 940-8989. **$22-
$43.** 3403 E Main St 85213. From Jct of US Hwy 60 & Val Vista
Rd (exit 184), N 2 mi on Val Vista Rd to Main St, W 0.2 mi (L)
🏕️ 🛶 🗶 ♿M

MESA — **MONTE VISTA VILLAGE/MHP-ENCORE.** (800) 435-
7128. **$51.** 8865 E Baseline Rd 85209. From Jct of US-60 & Ells-
worth Rd (Exit 191), S 0.5 mi on Ellsworth Rd to Baseline Rd, W
0.25 mi (L) 🏕️ 🛶 🗶

MESA — **MESA REGAL RV RESORT/PMP.** (800) 845-4752.
$20-$39. 4700 E Main 85205. From Jct of US Hwy 60 (Superstition Fwy) & Greenfield Rd (exit 185), N 2 mi on Greenfield Rd to
Main St, E 0.4 mi (L) 🏕️ 🛶 🗶

MESA — **MESA SPIRIT RV RESORT/PMP.** ⒶⒶⒶ (877) 924-
6709. **$29-$60.** 3020 E Main St 85213. From Jct of Superstition
Fwy (US Hwy 60) & Gilbert Rd (182), N 2 mi on Gilbert Rd to Main
St, E 1.25 mi (L) 🏕️ 🛶 🗶 ♿M

MESA — **PALM GARDENS MHC & RV PARK.** (480) 832-0290.
$35. (no credit cards). 2929 E. Main St 85213. From Jct of US-60
& Gilbert St (Exit 132): Go N on Gilbert St for 2 mi, turn E onto E.
Main for 1.1 mi to Park on right 🏕️ 🛶 🗶

MESA — **SILVERIDGE RV RESORT/PMP.** (800) 354-0054.
$50. 8265 E Southern Ave 85209. From Jct of US Hwy 60 & Ells-
worth (Exit 191), N 0.4 mi on Ellsworth Rd to Southern Ave, W 1.1
mi (L) 🏕️ 🛶 🗶 ♿M

MESA — **SUN LIFE RV RESORT/PMP.** (888) 940-8989. **$23-
$45.** 5055 E University Dr 85205. From Jct of Hwy 60 & Higley Rd
(exit 186), N 2.5 mi on Higley Rd to University Dr, W 0.2 mi (L)
🏕️ 🛶 🗶 ♿M

MESA — **THE RESORT.** (866) 386-1101. **$50.** 1101 S Ellsworth
Rd 85208. From Jct of US Hwy 60 & Ellsworth Rd (Exit 191), N
0.6 mi on Ellsworth Rd (R) 🏕️ 🛶 🗶 ♿M

MESA — **TOWERPOINT RESORT/PMP.** ⒶⒶⒶ (888) 940-8989.
$20-$40. 4860 E Main St 85205. From Jct of US Hwy 60 & Higley Rd (exit 186), N 2 mi on Higley Rd to Main St, W 0.4 mi (R)
🏕️ 🛶 🗶 ♿M

MESA — **VALLE DEL ORO RV RESORT/PMP.** (888) 940-8989.
$28-$45. 1452 S Ellsworth Rd 85209. From Jct of US Hwy 60 &
Ellsworth Rd (exit 191), N 0.1 mi on Ellsworth Rd (L)
🏕️ 🛶 🗶 ♿M

MESA — **VIEWPOINT RV & GOLF RESORT.** (480) 373-8700.
$33-$62. 8700 E University Dr 85207. From Jct of US Hwy 60 &
AZ 202N (Exit 190A), N 2.5 mi on AZ 202N to University Dr, W
0.4 mi (R) 🏕️ 🛶 🗶 ♿M

MOHAVE VALLEY — **MOON RIVER RESORT.** (928) 788-
6666. **$33-$36.** 1325 Boundary Cone Rd 86440. From Jct of Hwy
95 & Boundary Cone Rd, W 200 yds on Boundary Cone Rd (R);
or From SR 68 & Hwy 95, (Laughlin Bridge), S 15.2 mi on Hwy 95
to Boundary Cone Rd, W 200 yds (R). Note: GPS users please call
🏕️ 🛶 🗶

PAGE — **WAHWEAP LODGE & MARINA/RV PARK (LAKE
POWELL).** (800) 528-6154. **$48.** 100 Lake Shore Dr 86040. From
Jct of US-89 & SR-98 (on S side of Page), go N 4.3 mi on US-89
(crossing over dam) to Wahweap S entrance, E 4.3 mi, follow
signs (L) 🛶 🗶 ♿M

PAYSON — **PAYSON CAMPGROUND AND RV RESORT.**
ⒶⒶⒶ (928) 472-2267. **$35-$40.** 808 E Hwy 260 85541. From Jct of
Hwy 87 & Hwy 260, go E 0.7 mi on Hwy 260 (L) 🛶 🗶

PEORIA — **PLEASANT HARBOR RV RESORT.** (800) 475-
3272. **$25-$39.** 8708 W Harbor Blvd 85383. From Jct of I-17 &
Carefree Hwy (Exit 223B), W 8 mi on Carefree Hwy to 87th Ave,
N 1.8 mi (L) 🛶 🗶 ♿M

PHOENIX — **DESERT SHADOWS RV RESORT/PMP.** ⒶⒶⒶ
(800) 595-7290. **$37-$41.** 19203 N 29th Ave 85027. N-bnd: From
Jct of I-17 & Union Hills Dr (Exit 214 A & B), W 0.4 mi on Union
Hills Dr to 29th Ave, N 0.4 mi (R); or S-bnd: From Jct of I-17 &
Union Hills Dr/Yorkshire (Exit 214 A & B), S 0.6 mi on N Black
Canyon Hwy/Frontage Rt to Union Hills Dr, W 0.4 mi to 29th Ave,
N 0.4 mi (R) 🏕️ 🛶 🗶 ♿M

PHOENIX — **DESERT'S EDGE RV-THE PURPLE PARK.**
(623) 587-0940. **$46.** 22623 N Black Canyon Hwy 85027. S-bnd:
From Jct of I-17 & Deer Valley Rd/Exit 215B (N side of Phoenix),
E 0.1 mi on Deer Valley to 23rd Ave, N 0.4 mi on 23rd Ave to Wil-
liams Dr, W 0.1 mi (R); or N-bnd: I-17 & Deer Valley/Rose Garden
(Exit 215A), E 0.1 mi on Rose Garden to 23rd Ave, N 0.9 mi to
Williams Dr, W 0.1 mi (R) 🏕️ 🛶 🗶

PHOENIX — **PHOENIX METRO RV PARK.** (877) 582-0390.
$30. 22701 N. Black Canyon Hwy 85027. From Jct of 101 & I-17,
N 1 mi on I-17 to Deer Valley Rd/Rose Garden (Exit 215), N 0.7
mi on N Black Canyon Hwy/E Frontage Rd (R). If using GPS, call
🏕️ 🛶 🗶 ♿M

PHOENIX — **ROYAL PALM RV RESORT/MHC.** (602) 943-5833. **$32-$36.** 2050 West Dunlap Ave 85021. From Jct of I-10 & I-17, N 6.5 mi on I-17 (Exit 207) to Dunlap Ave, E 0.8 mi (L)

QUEEN VALLEY — **QUEEN VALLEY RV RESORT/PMP.** (877) 337-2757. **$35.** 50 West Oro Viejo Dr 85118. From Jct of US Hwy 60 & Idaho Rd (in Apache Jct), E 17.6 mi on US-60, past Hwy 60/79 Jct, to Queen Valley Rd (M 214), NW 5.4 mi, follow signs (R) or From Jct of US 60 & Hwy 79 (Florence Jct), E 2 mi on US 60 to Queen Valley Rd (M 214), NW 5.4 mi (follow signs) (R)

SALOME — **BLACK ROCK RV VILLAGE/PMP.** (928) 927-4206. **$31-$39.** 46751 E Hwy 60 85348. From Jct of I-10 & Hwy 60 (exit 31), NE 4 mi on Hwy 60 (L)

SALOME — **DESERT GOLD RV RESORT/PMP.** (800) 927-2101. **$30.** 46628 E Hwy 60 85348. From Jct of I-10 & Hwy 60 E (exit 31), NE 4 mi on Hwy 60 E (R); or W-bnd: From Jct of I-10 & Exit 45 (Vicksburg Rd), N 7 mi on Vicksburg Rd to Hwy 60, SW 10 mi (L)

SNOWFLAKE — **PUTTER'S PARADISE RV PARK.** (928) 536-2127. **$30.** 2085 W. Hwy 277 85937. From jct Hwy 77 & Hwy 277 (Snowflake Blvd): Go 2 mi W on Hwy 277 (Snowflake Blvd) (L)

SUN CITY — **PARADISE RV RESORT - ENCORE.** (800) 405-6188. **$27-$45.** 10950 W Union Hills Dr 85373. S-bnd: From Jct of I-17 & 101 Loop (Exit 215A), W 7 mi on 101 Loop to Union Hills Dr (Exit 15), W 3.5 mi (R); or N-bnd: From Jct of I-10 (E or W) & 101 Loop (Exit 133), N 14 mi on 101 Loop to Union Hills Dr (Exit 15), W 3.5 mi (R)

SURPRISE — **SUNFLOWER RV RESORT/PMP.** (623) 583-0100. **$25-$55.** 16501 N. El Mirage Rd 85378. N-bnd: From Jct of I-10 & 101 Loop (Exit 133), N 12.5 mi on the 101 Loop to Bell Rd (Exit 14), W 5.6 mi on Bell Rd to N El Mirage Rd, S 0.3 mi (L); or S-bnd: From Jct of I-17 & 101 Loop (Exit 285), W 8 mi on 101 Loop to Bell Rd (Exit 14), W 5.6 mi on to El Mirage Rd, S 0.3 mi (L).

TONOPAH — **SADDLE MOUNTAIN RV PARK.** (623) 386-3892. **$30.** 40902 W Osborn Rd 85354. From Jct of I-10 & Exit 94 (Tonopah), S 0.7 mi on N 411th Ave to Osborn, E 0.2 mi (L)

TUCSON — **FAR HORIZONS TUCSON VILLAGE RV RESORT.** (800) 480-3488. **$26-$44.** 555 N Pantano Rd 85710. From Jct of I-10 & Kolb Rd (Exit 270), N 9 mi on Kolb Rd to Speedway, E 1 mi to Pantano Rd, S 0.5 mi (R)

TUCSON — **MISSION VIEW RV RESORT.** (800) 444-8439. **$25-$36. (no credit cards).** 31 West Los Reales 85756. From Jct of I-10 & I-19 (Exit 260), S 8.5 mi on I-19 to San Xavier Loop Rd (Exit 92), E 1.4 mi on San Xavier Loop Rd (L).

TUCSON — **PRINCE OF TUCSON RV PARK.** (800) 955-3501. **$26.** 3501 N Freeway 85705. E-bnd: From Jct of I-10 & Prince Rd (exit 254), continue 0.5 mi on exit to Prince Rd, cross intersection, S 100 ft (R) Some construction on I-10, call for directions. Do not use GPS.

TUCSON — **RINCON COUNTRY EAST RV RESORT.** (520) 886-8431. **$38-$40.** 8989 E Escalante Rd 85730. From Jct of I-10 & Kolb Rd (exit 270), N 5 mi on Kolb Rd to Escalante Rd, E 2.5 mi (L)

TUCSON — **RINCON COUNTRY WEST RV RESORT.** (520) 294-5608. **$40-$46.** 4555 S Mission Rd 85746. From Jct of I-10 & I-19 (exit 260), S 1.5 mi on I-19 to Ajo Way (exit 99), W 1 mi to Mission Rd, S 0.5 mi (L)

TUCSON — **VOYAGER RV RESORT/PMP.** (AAA) (800) 424-9191. **$28-$49.** 8701 S Kolb Rd 85756. From Jct of I-10 & Kolb Rd (exit 270), S 0.5 mi on Kolb Rd (L)

TUCSON — **WESTERN WAY RV RESORT.** (800) 292-8616. **$52.** 3100 S Kinney Rd 85713. From Jct of I-19 & I-10 (Exit 260), S 1.5 mi on I-19 to Ajo Way (Exit 99), W 5 mi on Ajo Way to Kinney Rd, N 1.5 mi to Western Way Cir, SW 500 ft (R)

WILLOW BEACH — **WILLOW BEACH RV & CAMPGROUND.** (928) 767-4747. **$35.** 25804 N Willow Beach Rd 86445. From Jct of US 93 & Willow Beach Rd (between Mile Marker 14 & 15), NW 4.2 mi on Willow Beach Rd (E)

YUMA — **ARABY ACRES RV RESORT/PMP.** (800) 833-6046. **$49.** 6649 E 32nd St 85365. From Jct of I-8 & Araby Rd (exit 7), S 0.5 mi on Araby Rd to 32nd St (Bus 8), E 500 ft (R)

YUMA — **COCOPAH BEND RV & GOLF RESORT.** (800) 537-7901. **$43.** 6800 Strand Ave 85364. From Jct of I-8 & Winterhaven/4th Ave (CA Exit 172), S 0.4 mi on 4th Ave (I-8 Bus Loop) to 1st St, W 2.3 mi to Ave C, S 0.3 mi to Riverside Dr, W 1.4 mi to Strand Ave, N 0.9 mi (E)

YUMA — **DEL PUEBLO RV PARK AND TENNIS RESORT/PMP.** (928) 341-2100. **$48.** 14794 Ave 3E 85365. Jct of I-8 & Ave 3E (exit 3), S 5.2 mi on Ave 3E (R)

YUMA — **DESERT HOLIDAY RV RESORT.** (928) 344-4680. **$30-$39.** 3601 S 4th Ave 85365. From Jct of I-8 & 4th Ave (Exit 172 in CA), S 4 mi on 4th Ave to 4th Ave Extension, S 0.6 mi (L)

YUMA — **FRIENDLY ACRES RV PARK.** (928) 783-8414. **$25.** 2779 W 8th St 85364. From Jct of I-8 & 4th Ave (Exit 172 in CA), S 1.3 mi on 4th Ave to 8th St, W 1.5 mi (L)

YUMA — **LAS QUINTAS OASIS RV RESORT.** (928) 305-9005. **$40.** 10442 N Frontage Rd 85365. From Jct of I-8 & Exit 12 (Fortuna Rd), N on Fortuna Rd to Frntg Rd, W 0.6 mi (R)

YUMA — **SHANGRI-LA RV RESORT.** (928) 342-9123. **$33-$43.** 10498 N Frontage Rd 85365. From Jct of I-8 & Exit 12 (Fortuna Rd), N on Fortuna Rd to frntg rd, W 0.4 mi (R). Note: Do not use GPS

YUMA — **SUN VISTA RV RESORT.** (AAA) (800) 423-8382. **$47.** 7201 E 32nd St 85365. W-bnd: From Jct of I-8 & Exit 9 (Ave 8 1/2 E), W 0.7 mi on N Frontage Rd to 32nd St (Bus 8), W 0.9 mi (L); or E-bnd: From Jct of I-8 & Araby Rd (exit 7), S 0.5 mi on Araby Rd to 32nd St (Bus 8), E 0.6 mi (R)

YUMA — **THE PALMS RV RESORT.** (928) 341-4646. **$49.** 3400 S Ave 7E 85365. From Jct of I-8 & Araby Rd (Exit 7), S 0.5 mi on Araby Rd to 32nd St, E 0.5 mi on 32nd St to Ave 7E, S 0.2 mi (R) 🏕 🛶 ⊠

YUMA — **VILLA ALAMEDA RV RESORT.** (928) 344-8081. **$33. (no credit cards).** 3547 S Ave 5 E 85365. From Jct of I-8 & Ave 3E (exit 3), S 1.2 mi on Ave 3E to 32nd St (Bus 8), E 2 mi to Ave 5E, S 0.4 mi (L) or From Jct of I-8 & Araby Rd (Exit 7), S 0.5 mi on Araby Rd to 32nd St (Bus 8), W 1.5 mi to Ave 5E, S 0.4 mi (L) 🏕 🛶 ⊠ ⑤M

YUMA — **WESTWIND RV & GOLF RESORT.** ⒶⒶⒶ (928) 342-2992. **$32-$50.** 9797 E 32nd St 85365. From Jct of I-8 & Fortuna Rd (exit 12), S 50 ft on Fortuna Rd to S Frontage Rd, W 1 mi (L) Do not use GPS 🏕 🛶 ⊠

Arkansas

HOT SPRINGS — **CATHERINE'S LANDING AT HOT SPRINGS.** (501) 262-2550. **$29-$42.** 1700 Shady Grove Rd 71901. From Jct of US 270 & AR 128 (Exit 7), W 0.3 mi on AR 128 (Carpenter Dam Rd) to Shady Grove Rd, SE 1.7 mi (R) 🏕 🛶 ⊠ ⑤M

HOT SPRINGS NATIONAL PARK — **HOT SPRINGS NATIONAL PARK KOA.** (501) 624-5912. **$35-$75.** 838 McClendon Rd 71901. W-bnd: From Jct of I-30 & US-70, W 20 mi on US-70 to Ex 4, W 0.7 mi on Svs Rd (R); N or E-bnd: From Jct of US-270/70 & SR 7, E 6.8 mi to Hot Springs Ex, (L) on US-70B 1.3 mi to Ex 4, W 0.7 mi on Svs Rd (R); S-bnd: From Jct of SR 7 & 7S, SE1 🛶 ⊠ ⑤M

OAK GROVE — **OUTDOOR RESORTS/OZARK RV RESORT.** (888) 749-7396. **$55.** 1229 CR-663 72660. From Jct of US-65 & SR-86, W 11.6 mi on SR-86 to SR-13/21, S 1.1 mi to SR-311 (straight thru Blue Eye), E 4.9 mi to entrance sign, E 1.2 mi (R) 🏕 🛶 ⊠ ⑤M

California

AGUANGA — **OUTDOOR RESORTS RANCHO CALIFORNIA.** (888) 767-0848. **$75.** 45525 Hwy 79 S 92536. From Jct of Hwy 79 S & Hwy 371, E 0.3 mi on Hwy 79 S (R); or From Jct of I-15 & Hwy 79, S 18.5 mi on Hwy 79 (R) 🏕 🛶 ⊠ ⑤M

ARCATA — **MAD RIVER RAPIDS RV PARK.** ⒶⒶⒶ (800) 822-7776. **$38-$45.** 3501 Janes Rd 95521. From Jct of US-101 & SR-299, N 0.2 mi on US-101 to Giuntoli Ln/Janes Rd Exit 716B, W 0.3 mi on Janes Rd (L) 🏕 🛶 ⊠ ⑤M

AUBURN — **AUBURN GOLD COUNTRY RV PARK.** (530) 885-0990. **$42-$49.** 3550 KOA Way 95602. From Jct of I-80 & (Bell Rd) Exit 123, NW 2.9 mi on Bell Rd to SR-49, N 0.2 mi to Rock Creek Rd, E 0.1 mi to KOA Way, N 0.1 mi (R) 🛶 ⊠

BAKERSFIELD — **A COUNTRY RV PARK.** (866) 787-2750. **$35.** 622 S Fairfax Rd 93307. From Jct of Hwy 99 & Hwy 58, E 6 mi on Hwy 58 to Fairfax Rd, S 0.1 mi (R) 🏕 🛶 ⊠ ⑤M

BAKERSFIELD — **BAKERSFIELD RIVER RUN RV PARK.** ⒶⒶⒶ (888) 748-7786. **$35-$59.** 3715 Burr St 93308. From Jct of Hwy 99 & Hwy 58 W/Rosedale Hwy (Exit 26), W 0.4 mi on Hwy 58 to Gibson St, S 0.3 mi to Burr St, E 0.2 mi (E) 🏕 🛶 ⊠ ⑤M

BAKERSFIELD — **BAKERSFIELD RV RESORT.** (661) 833-9998. **$39-$55.** 5025 Wible Rd 93313. From Jct of Hwy 99 & White Lane (exit 21), W 100 ft on White Lane to Wible Road, S 0.5 mi (R) 🏕 🛶 ⊠ ⑤M

BAKERSFIELD — **ORANGE GROVE RV PARK.** ⒶⒶⒶ (661) 366-4662. **$27-$39.** 1452 S Edison Rd 93307. E-bnd: From Jct of Hwys 99 & 58E (exit 24), E 8 mi on Hwy 58 to exit 119 (S Edison Rd), S 500 ft (R) 🏕 🛶 ⊠ ⑤M

BORREGO SPRINGS — **THE SPRINGS AT BORREGO RV RESORT & GOLF COURSE.** (866) 330-0003. **$29-$102.** 2255 DiGiorgio Road 92004. From Jct of Hwys S-3 & S-22 (in town), E 0.5 mi on Hwy S-22 to Di Giorgio Rd, N 0.6 mi (R) 🏕 🛶 ⊠ ⑤M

BUELLTON — **FLYING FLAGS RV RESORT & CAMP-GROUND.** ⒶⒶⒶ (877) 783-5247. **$32-$98.** 180 Avenue Of Flags 93427. From Jct of Hwy 101 & Rte 246 (Exit 140), W 0.25 mi on Rte 246 to Ave of the Flags, S 0.2 mi (L) 🛶 ⊠ ⑤M

CATHEDRAL CITY — **OUTDOOR RESORT PALM SPRINGS RV COUNTRY CLUB.** (800) 843-3131. **$41-$84.** 69-411 Ramon Rd 92234. From Jct of I-10 & Date Palm Dr (Exit 126), S 2 mi on Date Palm Dr to Ramon Rd, E 0.5 mi (R) 🏕 🛶 ⊠ ⑤M

CHICO — **ALMOND TREE RV PARK.** ⒶⒶⒶ (530) 899-1271. **$39.** 3124 Esplanade 95973. From Jct of SR-99 & SR-32 (SE of town/Exit 389), N 3.7 mi on SR-99 to Eaton Rd, SW 0.2 mi to Esplanade, SE 0.4 mi (L) 🏕 🛶 ⊠ ⑤M

CHOWCHILLA — **THE LAKES RV & GOLF RESORT.** (866) 665-6980. **$45-$55.** 5001 E Robertson 93610. From Jct of Hwy 99 E Robertson Blvd/Exit 170, E 1.3 mi on Robertson Blvd (R) 🏕 🛶 ⊠ ⑤M

CHULA VISTA — **CHULA VISTA RV RESORT AND MARINA.** ⒶⒶⒶ (800) 770-2878. **$50-$66.** 460 Sandpiper Way 91910. From Jct of I-5 & J St (exit 7B), W 500 ft on J St (becomes Marina Pkwy), continue 0.5 mi on Marina Pkwy to Sandpiper Way, W 0.2 mi (L) 🏕 🛶 ⊠ ⑤M

COLEVILLE — **MEADOWCLIFF LODGE & RV RESORT.** (530) 495-2255. **$35-$45.** 110437 US Hwy 395 96107. S-bnd: From Jct of Hwy 89 & Hwy 395, S 6 mi on Hwy 395 (1 mile S of Coleville) (R); or N-bnd: From Jct of Hwy 108 & Hwy 395, N 18 mi on Hwy 395 (3 miles N of Walker) (L) 🏕 🛶 ⊠ ⑤M

DESERT HOT SPRINGS — **SANDS RV & GOLF RESORT.** (760) 251-1030. **$38-$46.** 16400 Bubbling Wells Rd 92240. From Jct of I-10 & Palm Dr (Exit 123), N 3 mi on Palm Dr to Dillon Rd, E 1 mi to Bubbling Wells Rd, N 0.2 mi (R) 🏕 🛶 ⊠ ⑤M

EL CENTRO — **RIO BEND RV & GOLF RESORT.** ⒶⒶⒶ (760) 352-7061. **$38-$70.** 1589 Drew Rd 92243. From Jct of I-8 & Hwy 86 (Imperial Ave), W 8 mi on I-8 to Drew Rd (Exit 107), S 0.4 mi (R) 🏕 🛶 ⊠ ⑤M

FORTUNA — RIVERWALK RV PARK & CAMPGROUND. (707) 725-3359. **$38-$47.** 2189 Riverwalk Dr 95540. From Jct of US-101 & Kenmar Rd/Riverwalk Dr (Exit 687), W 0.2 mi on Riverwalk Dr (R) 🚐 ⊠ 🅜

GOLETA — OCEAN MESA AT EL CAPITAN. ⓐⓐⓐ (866) 410-5783. **$70-$90.** 100 El Capitan Terrace Lane 93117. S-bnd: From Jct of Hwy 101 & El Capitan State Beach Rd (Exit 117), N 0.2 mi on El Capitan State Beach Rd (under freeway) to Calle Real, S 0.4 mi (R); or N-bnd: From Jct of Hwy 101 & El Capitan State Beach Rd (Exit 117), S 0.6 mi on Calle Real (R) 🚐 ⊠ 🅜

HEMET — GOLDEN VILLAGE PALMS RV RESORT - SUN-LAND. ⓐⓐⓐ (866) 225-6320. **$42-$70.** 3600 W Florida Ave 92545. From Jct of Hwys 74/79 (Florida Ave) & Sanderson Ave, W 0.2 mi on Florida Ave (R) 🏕 🚐 ⊠ 🅜

INDIO — INDIAN WATERS RV RESORT. (760) 342-8100. **$36-$51.** 47-202 Jackson St. 92201. From Jct of I-10 & Golf Center Pky (Exit 144): Go SW 0.9 mi on Gold Center Pkwy to Hwy 111, then W 0.3 mi to Jackson St, then S 0.7 mi (L) 🏕 🚐 ⊠ 🅜

INDIO — INDIAN WELLS CAREFREE RV RESORTS. (508) 398-2811. **$45-$75.** 47-340 Jefferson St 92201. From Jct of I-10 & Jefferson St (Exit 139), S 2.7 mi on Jefferson St (L) 🏕 🚐 ⊠

INDIO — MOTORCOACH COUNTRY CLUB. (888) 277-0789. **$69-$168.** 80-501 Avenue 48 92201. From Jct of I-10 & Jefferson St (Exit 139), S 3 mi on Jefferson St to Ave 48, E 0.5 mi (R). 🏕 🚐 ⊠ 🅜

INDIO — OUTDOOR RESORT INDIO. (800) 892-2992. **$57-$104.** 80-394 Avenue 48 92201. From Jct of I-10 & Jefferson St (Exit 139), S 3 mi on Jefferson St to Ave 48, E 0.3 mi (L). 🏕 🚐 ⊠ 🅜

INDIO — SHADOW HILLS RV RESORT. (760) 360-4040. **$32-$60.** 40 655 Jefferson Street 92203. From Jct of I-10 & Jefferson St (Exit 139), N 0.25 mi on Jefferson St (L) 🚐 ⊠ 🅜

JACKSON — JACKSON RANCHERIA RV PARK. (800) 822-WINN. **$40-$50.** 12222 New York Ranch Rd. 95642. From Jct of Hwy 49 & Hwy 88 (in Jackson), E 2.5 mi on Hwy 88 to Dalton Rd, N 0.9 mi (L) 🏕 🚐 ⊠ 🅜

KINGSBURG — CLUB ROYAL OAK. (559) 897-0351. **$30-$60.** 39700 Road 28 93631. From Jct of Hwy 99 & Sierra St (E 201) Exit 112: E 2.7 mi on Sierra St (Ave 400) to Road 28, S on Road 28 (E) 🏕 ⊠ 🅜

LAKESIDE — RANCHO LOS COCHES RV PARK. (800) 630-0448. **$36-$45.** 13468 Hwy 8 Bus 92040. From Jct of I-8 & Los Coches Rd (Exit 22), N 0.5 mi on Los Coches Rd to Hwy 8 Bus, E 0.4 mi (L) 🚐 ⊠ 🅜

LODI — FLAG CITY RV RESORT. ⓐⓐⓐ (866) 371-4855. **$54.** 6120 W Banner Rd 95242. From Jct of I-5 & SR 12, E 0.2 mi on SR 12 to Star St, S 500 ft to Banner St, E 0.1 mi (R) 🏕 🚐 🅜

LONE PINE — BOULDER CREEK RV RESORT. ⓐⓐⓐ (760) 876-4243. **$35-$39.** 2550 S Hwy 395 93545. From Jct of US-395 & SR-136, S 2.6 mi on US-395 (L) 🚐 ⊠ 🅜

MORGAN HILL — COYOTE VALLEY RV RESORT. ⓐⓐⓐ (866) 376-5500. **$55-$70.** 9750 Monterey Rd 95037. From Jct of Hwy 101 & exit 367/Cochrane Rd, W 0.8 mi on Cochrane Rd to Monterey Rd., N 4.1 mi (R) 🏕 🚐 ⊠ 🅜

NEWPORT BEACH — NEWPORT DUNES WATERFRONT RESORT & MARINA. (800) 765-7661. **$60-$399.** 1131 Back Bay Dr 92660. From Jct of Pacific Coast Hwy (Hwy 1) & Jamboree Rd exit, N 0.2 mi on Jamboree Rd to Back Bay Dr, W 0.1 mi (L); or From Jct of I-405 & Jamboree Rd exit (in Irvine), S 5 mi on Jamboree Rd to Back Bay Dr, W 0.1 mi (L) 🚐 ⊠ 🅜

NILAND — FOUNTAIN OF YOUTH SPA RV RESORT. (760) 354-1340. **$35-$48.** 1500 Spa Rd 92257. From Jct of Hwy 111 & Hot Mineral Spa Rd (14 mi N of Niland), E 1.5 mi to Spa Rd, SE 1 mi (L) 🚐 ⊠ 🅜

NOVATO — NOVATO RV PARK. (800) 733-6787. **$60.** 1530 Armstrong Ave 94945. From Jct of US-101 & Atherton Ave/San Marin Dr exit, E 300 ft on Atherton Ave to Armstrong Ave, S 0.1 mi (L) 🏕 🚐 🅜

ORLAND — THE PARKWAY RV RESORT & CAMPGROUND. (530) 865-9188. **$34-$37.** 6330 County Road 200 95963. From Jct of I-5 & SR-32, Exit 619 (Orland/Chico), W 0.5 mi on Rd 200 (R) 🚐 ⊠

OROVILLE — FEATHER FALLS KOA & CASINO. (800) 562-5079. **$37-$75.** #1 Feather Falls Blvd. 95966. From Jct of Hwy 70 & Ophir Rd, E 3.3 mi on Ophir Rd (L) 🏕 🚐 ⊠ 🅜

PALM DESERT — EMERALD DESERT RV RESORT - SUN-LAND. ⓐⓐⓐ (866) 226-9001. **$55-$95.** 76-000 Frank Sinatra Dr 92211. From Jct of I-10 & Cook St (Exit 134), S 0.9 mi on Cook St to Frank Sinatra Dr, E 1 mi to El Dorado (L) 🏕 🚐 ⊠ 🅜

PASO ROBLES — WINE COUNTRY RV RESORT. (805) 238-4560. **$39-$85.** 2500 Airport Rd 93446. From Jct of Hwy 101 & Hwy 46E, E 2.2 mi on Hwy 46E to Airport Rd, N 0.2 mi (R) 🏕 🚐 ⊠ 🅜

PETALUMA — SAN FRANCISCO NORTH/PETALUMA KOA. ⓐⓐⓐ (800) 992-2267. **$30-$77.** 20 Rainsville Rd 94952. From Jct of US-101 & SR-116E, N 3.8 mi on US-101 to Old Redwood Hwy/Penngrove exit (34 mi N of Golden Gate Bridge), exit to W side of fwy, W 300 ft to Stony Point Rd, N 0.4 mi to Rainsville Rd, W 300 ft (R) 🚐 ⊠ 🅜

PISMO BEACH — PISMO COAST VILLAGE RV RESORT. (888) 782-3224. **$44-$60.** 165 S Dolliver St 93449. N-bnd: From Jct of US-101 & Price St, N 75 ft on Price St to Ocean View Rd, W 0.1 mi to Dolliver St (SR-1), S 0.5 mi (R); or S-bnd: From Jct of US-101 & Pismo Beach exit (Hwy 1 Dolliver St), S 0.9 mi on Dolliver St (R) 🏕 🚐 ⊠ 🅜

PLYMOUTH — FAR HORIZONS 49ER VILLAGE RV RESORT. (209) 245-6981. **$39-$76.** 18265 Hwy 49 95669. From Sacramento: From Jct of Hwy 50 & Latrobe Rd (Exit 31A), S 16.8 mi on Latrobe Rd to Hwy 16, E 2.8 mi on Hwy 16 (which turns into Hwy 49) continue E 1.8 mi on Hwy 49 (L) 🏕 🚐 ⊠ 🅜

QUINCY — PIONEER RV PARK. (530) 283-0769. **$35.** 1326 Pioneer Rd 95971. E-bnd: From Jct SR-70/SR-89 & Fairground Rd (in town), N 0.1 mi on Fairground Rd to Pioneer Rd, E 0.1 mi (E) 🏕 ⊠

RED BLUFF — DURANGO RV RESORT. (530) 527-5300. **$35-$58.** 100 Lake Ave 96080. From Jct of I-5 & Antelope Blvd (Exit 649), W 0.1 mi on Antelope Blvd to Belle Mill Rd, N 0.1 mi to East Ave, NE 0.1 mi (L) 🅐 ⤵ ⊠ ♿M

REDDING — JGW RV PARK. (530) 365-7965. **$35-$47.** 6612 Riverland Dr. 96002. From Jct of I-5 & Knighton Rd exit 673 (6 mi S of town), exit to W side of I-5 to Riverland Dr (Frntg Rd), S 2 mi (R) 🅐 ⤵ ⊠ ♿M

REDDING — MOUNTAIN GATE RV PARK. (800) 404-6040. **$28-$37.** 14161 Holiday Rd 96003. From Jct of I-5 & SR-44/SR-299E, N 6.5 mi on I-5 to Mountain Gate/Wonderland Blvd (Old Oregon Trail) exit 687, E 100 ft on Old Oregon Trail (unmarked rd) to Holiday Rd, S 0.4 mi (L) 🅐 ⤵ ⊠ ♿M

REDDING — PREMIER RV RESORTS-REDDING. (888) 710-8450. **$36-$45.** 280 N Boulder Dr 96003. From Jct of I-5 & Exit 680 (SR-299E/Lake Blvd/Burney-Alturas), W 0.2 mi on Lake Blvd to N Boulder Dr, N 0.1 mi (L) ⤵ ⊠ ♿M

REDDING — REDDING RV PARK. (530) 241-0707. **$26-$33.** 11075 Campers Ct 96003. From Jct of I-5 & SR-299E (Exit 680), W 0.2 mi on Lake Blvd to Black Marble/Boulder (second stoplight W of I-5, get in inside lane), S 50 ft to Boulder Dr, SE 0.2 mi on Frontage Rd (Boulder Dr) to Campers Ct, S 0.2 mi (L) 🅐 ⤵ ⊠ ♿M

SAN JUAN BAUTISTA — BETABEL RV PARK. (800) 278-7275. **$40.** 9664 Betabel Rd 95045. N-bnd: From Jct of US-101 & Hwy 156 E, N 3 mi on US-101 to Betabel Rd (Go over freeway), S 0.2 mi (R); or S-bnd: From Jct of US-101 & Hwy 152, S 10 mi on US-101 to Betabel Rd Exit, S 0.2 mi (R) 🅐 ⤵ ⊠ ♿M

SUSANVILLE — SUSANVILLE RV PARK. ⒶⒶⒶ (877) 686-7878. **$42.** 3075 Johnstonville Rd 96130. E-bnd: From Jct of SR-36 & SR-139, SE 1.1 mi on SR-36 to E Riverside Dr, NE (left turn) 0.1 mi to Johnstonville Rd (1st left turn), NW 0.1 mi (R); or W-bnd: From Jct of SR-36 & US-395, NW 2.9 mi on SR-36 to E Riverside Dr, NE (right turn) 0.1 mi to Johnstonville Rd (1st left turn), NW 0.1 mi (R) 🅐 ⤵ ♿M

TEMECULA — PECHANGA RV RESORT. ⒶⒶⒶ (951) 770-2656. **$45-$99.** 45000 Pechanga Pkwy 92592. From Jct of I-15 & Hwy 79S/Temecula Pkwy), E 0.8 mi on Hwy 79S/Temecula Pkwy) to Pechanga Pkwy, SE 2.1 mi to Pechanga Resort Dr, S 0.25 mi (L) 🅐 ⤵ ⊠ ♿M

VACAVILLE — VINEYARD RV PARK. (866) 447-8797. **$44-$48.** 4985 Midway Rd 95688. From Jct of I-80 & I-505, N 3.3 mi to Midway Rd, E 0.4 mi (L) or From Jct of I-80 & Midway Rd exit, W 0.1 mi to Midway Rd, W 3 mi (R) ⤵ ⊠

WATSONVILLE — SANTA CRUZ/MONTEREY BAY KOA. (831) 722-0551. **$82-$96.** 1186 San Andreas Rd 95076. From Jct of Hwy 1 & Larkin Valley/San Andreas exit, W 3 mi on San Andreas Rd (L) ⤵ ⊠ ♿M

WILLITS — WILLITS KOA. (800) 562-8542. **$45-$75.** 1600 Hwy 20 95490. From Jct of US-101 & SR-20, W 1.5 mi on SR-20 (R) ⤵ ⊠ ♿M

Colorado

BRECKENRIDGE — TIGER RUN RV RESORT. (800) 895-9594. **$40-$80.** 85 Tiger Run Rd 80424. From Jct of I-70 & SR-9 (Exit 203), S 6.3 mi on SR-9 (L) 🅐 ⤵ ⊠

CAÑON CITY — ROYAL VIEW @ ROYAL GORGE CAMP-GROUND. (719) 275-1900. **$31-$55.** 43590 US Hwy 50 W 81212. E-bnd: From Jct of US-50 & SR-9, E 500 ft on US-50, between MP-269 & 270 (R); or W-bnd: From Jct of US-50 & Royal Gorge Rd, W 1 mi on US-50 (L) ⤵ ⊠

FORT COLLINS — FORT COLLINS KOA LAKESIDE. (800) 562-9168. **$37-$91.** 1910 Lakeside Resort Ln. 80524. From Jct of I-25 & SR-14, W 3.3 mi on SR-14 to Riverside Ave, NW 1 mi to College Ave(US-287), N 4.1 mi to CR 54G (toward LaPorte) to Taft Hill Rd (CR 19), S 0.08 mi (L) ⤵ ⊠ ♿M

GOLDEN — DAKOTA RIDGE RV RESORT. (800) 398-1625. **$39-$52.** 17800 W Colfax Ave 80401. E-bnd: From Jct of I-70 & US-40 (exit 259), NE 1.5 mi on US-40/Colfax Ave (R); or W-bnd: From Jct of I-70 & US-40 (exit 262), W 1.7 mi on US-40/Colfax Ave (L) 🅐 ⤵ ⊠ ♿M

IGNACIO — SKY UTE CASINO RV PARK. (888) 842-4150. **$30.** 14324 Hwy 172N 81137. From Jct of US 160 & US 550 (E edge of Durango), E 2 mi on US 160 to SR-172, S 17 mi (L) 🅐 ⤵ ♿M

MANCOS — MESA VERDE RV RESORT. ⒶⒶⒶ (800) 776-7421. **$36-$45.** 35303 US Hwy 160 81328. From Jct of US-160 & SR-184 (in Mancos), W 6.5 mi on US-160 (R); or From Jct of US-160 & Mesa Verde Nat'l Park exit, E 0.75 mi on US-160 (L) ⤵ ⊠ ♿M

PAGOSA SPRINGS — WOLF CREEK RUN MOTOR COACH RESORT. (970) 264-0365. **$52-$62.** 1742 E Hwy 160 81147. From Jct of US 160 & Hwy 84, E 0.4 mi on US 160 (L) 🅐 ⊠ ♿M

PUEBLO — PUEBLO SOUTH/COLORADO CITY KOA. (888) 676-3370. **$38-$43.** 9040 I-25 S Exit 74 81004. From Jct of I-25 & (Exit 74), E .01 mi on exit rd to frntg rd, S 0.25 mi (L) ⤵ ⊠ ♿M

Connecticut

EAST CANAAN — LONE OAK CAMPSITES. (800) 422-2267. **$44-$84.** 360 Norfolk Rd 06024. From Jct of Hwys 7 & 44, E 3.5 mi on Hwy 44 (R) ⤵ ⊠ ♿M

EAST LYME — ACES HIGH RV PARK. (877) 785-8478. **$54-$59.** 301 Chesterfield Road 06333. From Jct of I-95 & SR-161 (exit 74), N 3 mi on SR-161 (R) 🅐 ⤵ ⊠ ♿M

NORWICH — STRAWBERRY PARK RV RESORT. (860) 886-1944. **$40-$99.** P.O. Box 830 06365. From Jct of Hwy 164 & Hwy 165, E 1 mi on Hwy 165 to Pierce Rd, N 0.5 mi (R) ⤵ ⊠ ♿M

PRESTON — HIDDEN ACRES FAMILY CAMPGROUND. (860) 887-9633. **$35-$50.** 47 River Rd 06365. From Jct of I-395 & Hwy 164 (Exit 85), S 0.9 mi on Hwy 164 (rt turn) to Palmer Rd (River Ridge Golf Course), SW 1.6 mi to River Rd, W 1.4 mi (R). ⤵ ⊠ ♿M

Delaware

LINCOLN — YOGI BEAR'S JELLYSTONE PARK AT DELA-
WARE BEACH. (302) 491-6614. **$55-$80.** 8295 Brick Granary Rd
19960. From Jct of US 113 & SR-1 (E of Lincoln), S 6.5 mi on
SR-1 (towards beaches) to Brick Granary Rd, Right 0.2 mi (L)
⊇ ⊠ ⑤M

MILLSBORO — LEISURE POINT RESORT. (302) 945-2000.
$60. 25491 Dogwood Ln 19966. From Jct of RT-113 & RT-24, E
8 mi on RT-24 to Longneck Rd, S 2 mi on Longneck Rd to Dogwood Lane (L) ⚔ ⊇ ⊠

REHOBOTH BEACH — BIG OAKS FAMILY CAMP-
GROUND. (302) 645-6838. **$56-$65. (no credit cards).** 35567 Big
Oaks Lane 19971. S-bnd: From Jct of SR-1 & SR-24 (John Wil-
liams Hwy), S 0.7 mi on SR-1 to Munchy Branch Rd (CR 270A),
E 1.1 mi to Wolf Neck Rd, N 0.1 mi (L); or N-bnd: From Jct of
SR-1 & CR-270 (Wolf Neck Rd), E 0.5 mi on CR-270 (L) ⊇ ⊠

Florida

ARCADIA — CROSS CREEK RV RESORT. (863) 494-7300.
$53. 6837 NE Cubitis Ave 34266. From Jct of SR-70 & US-17, N
4.9 mi on US-17 to CR-660, W (L) 100 yds to NE Cubitis Ave, N
(R) 0.9 mi (L) ⚔ ⊇ ⊠ ⑤M

ARCADIA — RIVERSIDE RV RESORT & CAMPGROUND.
🆎 (800) 795-9733. **$40-$55.** 9770 SW CR-769 Kings Hwy
34269. From Jct of I-75 & CR-769 (Exit 170), NE 4.5 mi on
CR-769/Kings Hwy (R) ⊇ ⊠ ⑤M

BEVERLY HILLS — SANDY OAKS RV RESORT. (352) 465-
7233. **$34-$40.** 6760 N Lecanto Hwy (CR-491) 34465. From Jct of
US 41 & CR 491, S 0.7 mi on CR 491 (R) ⊇ ⊠

BOWLING GREEN — TORREY OAKS RV & GOLF
RESORT. (863) 773-3157. **$30-$40.** 2908 Country Club Dr 33834.
Hwy 62 & US-17, N 0.5 mi on US-17 to Bostick Rd, W 0.3 mi (R).
⚔ ⊇ ⊠ ⑤M

BROOKSVILLE — BELLE PARC RV RESORT. (352) 796-
5760. **$35-$55.** 11089 Ancient Trail 34601. From Jct of I-75 &
US-98 (Exit 301), W 9.6 mi on US-98 to US-41, N 2.3 mi on US-41
(L) ⚔ ⊇ ⊠ ⑤M

CARRABELLE BEACH — CARRABELLE BEACH RV
RESORT. (850) 697-2638. **$43.** 1843 Hwy 98 W 32322. From
town Bus Dist, W 1.5 mi on US-98 (R) ⚔ ⊇ ⊠

CEDAR KEY — CEDAR KEY RV RESORT. (352) 543-5097.
$30. 11980 SW Shiloh Rd 32625. From Jct of Hwy 19/98 & SR-24
(Otter Creek), W 15 mi on Hwy 24 to Shiloh Rd, N .01 mi (L)
⚔ ⊇ ⑤M

CHOKOLOSKEE — OUTDOOR RESORTS/CHOKOLOSKEE
ISLAND. (239) 695-3788. **$69-$89.** 150 Smallwood Dr, Hwy 29 S
34138. From jct US-41 & Hwy-29 (CR 29): Go 8 mi S on CR 29
(L) ⚔ ⊇ ⊠ ⑤M

CLERMONT — OUTDOOR RESORTS AT ORLANDO, INC.
(863) 424-1407. **$30.** 9000 US Hwy 192 #1000 34714. From Jct of
US-27 & US-192, E 0.8 mi on US-192 (R) ⚔ ⊇ ⊠ ⑤M

CORTEZ — HOLIDAY COVE RV RESORT. (941) 792-1111.
$69-$115. P.O. Box 713 34215. From Jct of I-75 & SR-70 (Exit
217), W 13 mi on SR-70 to Cortez Rd (SR-684), W 2.8 mi (R)
⚔ ⊇ ⊠ ⑤M

CRYSTAL RIVER — ROCK CRUSHER CANYON RV PARK
LLC. (352) 564-9350. **$34-$42.** 237 S Rock Crusher Rd 34429.
From Jct of US-19 & SR-44, E 3.4 mi on SR-44 to Rock Crusher
Rd, S 1.6 mi (L); or From Jct of I-75 & SR-44 (exit 329), W 22 mi
to CR-490, SW 3.5 mi to Rock Crusher Rd, N 2.1 mi (R)
⚔ ⊇ ⊠ ⑤M

DE FUNIAK SPRINGS — SUNSET KING LAKE RESORT.
(850) 892-7229. **$36.** 366 Paradise Island Dr 32433. From Jct of
I-10 & Hwy 331 (exit 85), N 2 mi on Hwy 331 to Hwy 90/331, W
2 mi to Hwy 331 N, N 5.3 mi to Kings Lake Rd, S.W. 0.8 mi to
Paradise Island Dr, S.E. 0.3 mi (R) ⊇ ⊠ ⑤M

DESTIN — CAMP GULF. (877) 226-7485. **$55-$165.** 10005 W
Emerald Coast Pkwy 32550. From Jct of Mid Bay Bridge (SR-293)
& US-98, E 5 mi on US-98 (R); or From Jct of Hwy 331 & Hwy 98,
W 9 mi on Hwy 98 (L) ⊇ ⊠ ⑤M

DUNEDIN — DUNEDIN CAREFREE RV RESORT & THE
BLUE MOON INN. (727) 784-3719. **$40-$66.** 2920 Alt 19 N 34698.
From Jct of Alt US-19 & SR-586 (Curlew Rd), N 0.5 mi on Alt
US-19 (R) ⚔ ⊇ ⊠ ⑤M

EVERGLADES CITY — EVERGLADES ISLE MOTOR-
COACH RETREAT & MARINA. (239) 695-2600. **$79-$99.** 803 N.
Collier Ave 34139. From Jct of US 41 & SR-29, S 3 mi on SR-29
(R) ⚔ ⊇ ⊠ ⑤M

FORT MYERS — CYPRESS WOODS RV RESORT. (888)
299-6637. **$40-$80.** 5551 Luckett Rd 33905. From jct Hwy 82 &
I-75: Go 1-1/2 mi N on I-75 (exit 139), then 1/2 mi E on Luckett
Rd. (L) ⚔ ⊇ ⊠ ⑤M

FORT MYERS — WOODSMOKE CAMPING RESORT. 🆎
(800) 231-5053. **$48-$77.** 19551 S Tamiami Trail (US 415) 33908.
From Jct of I-75 & Corkscrew Rd (exit 123), W 2 mi on Corkscrew
Rd to US-41, N 2 mi (R) ⊇ ⊠ ⑤M

FORT MYERS BEACH — GULF WATERS RV RESORT.
🆎 (239) 437-5888. **$42-$72.** 11301 Summerlin Sq. Dr 33931.
From Hwy 82 & I-75: Go 6 mi S on I-75 (exit 131), then 5-3/4 mi
W on Daniels Rd/Cypress Lake Dr, then 5-1/2 mi S on Summerlin
Rd, then 100 feet E on Pine Ridge Rd, then 500 feet S on Sum-
merlin Sq Dr (L) ⚔ ⊇ ⊠ ⑤M

FORT MYERS BEACH — INDIAN CREEK RV RESORT.
🆎 (888) 239-2113. **$36-$51.** 17340 San Carlos Blvd 33931.
From Jct of I-75 & Daniels Pkwy (exit 131), W 5.5 mi on Daniels
Pkwy/Cypress Lake Dr to Summerlin Rd, SW 5.6 mi to San Carlos Blvd, SW 0.25 mi (R) ⚔ ⊇ ⊠ ⑤M

FORT PIERCE — ROAD RUNNER TRAVEL RESORT. 🆎
(800) 833-7108. **$40-$42.** 5500 St Lucie Blvd 34946. From Jct of
FL Tpke & SR-713 (exit 152), N 5 mi on SR-713 to CR-608, E 1.2
mi (L); or From Jct of I-95 & Indrio Rd (exit 138), E 3.2 mi on Indrio
Rd to SR-713, S 2.5 mi to CR-608 (St Lucie Blvd), E 1.2 mi (L)
⊇ ⊠ ⑤M

FORT PIERCE — TREASURE COAST RV RESORT. (772) 468-2099. **$39-$46.** 2550 Crossroads Parkway 34945. From Jct of I-95 & exit 129 (Okeechobee Rd/SR 70), W 0.1 mi on Okeechobee Rd/SR 70 to Peters Rd/Crossroads Pkwy, N 0.25 mi (R); or From Jct of FL Tpke & exit 152 (Okeechobee Rd/SR 70), E 0.2 mi on Okeechobee Rd/SR 70 to Peters Rd/Crossroads Pkwy, N 0.25 mi (R) 🏕 ⇌ 🍽 ♿M

FORT WALTON BEACH — DESTIN WEST RV RESORT. (850) 200-4533. **$97.** 1310 Miracle Strip Pkwy SE 32548. From Jct of US 98 & Santa Rosa Blvd, E 0.3 mi on US 98 (L) 🏕 ⇌ 🍽

FREEPORT — LIVE OAK LANDING. ⨁ (877) 436-5063. **$40-$45.** 229 Pitts Ave 32439. From Jct of US 331 & CR-3280, E 1.2 mi on CR-3280 to McDaniels Fish Camp Rd, S 0.8 mi (L) 🏕 ⇌ 🍽

FROSTPROOF — RAINBOW RESORT. (863) 635-7541. **$35. (no credit cards).** 700 CR-630A 33843. From Jct of US 27 & SR-60, go S 10.2 mi on US 27 to CR-630A, then E 0.8 mi (L) 🏕 ⇌ 🍽 ♿M

JACKSONVILLE — FLAMINGO LAKE RV RESORT. ⨁ (800) 782-4323. **$42.** 3640 Newcomb Rd 32218. From Jct of I-295 & Lem Turner Rd exit 32, W 0.1 mi on Lem Turner Rd to Newcomb Rd, S 100 yds (E) 🏕 ⇌ 🍽 ♿M

JACKSONVILLE — PECAN PARK RV RESORT. (904) 751-6770. **$42.** 650 Pecan Park Rd 32218. From Jct of I-95 & Pecan Park Rd Exit 366, W 0.1 mi on Pecan Park Rd (L) 🏕 ⇌ 🍽 ♿M

JASPER — FLORIDA GATEWAY RESORT. (386) 792-2692. **$40-$80.** 7516 SE 113th Blvd 32052. From Jct of I-75 & US 129 (Exit 451), SW 0.6 mi on US 129 to SW 113 Blvd, S (left) 1.3 mi (L) ⇌ 🍽 ♿M

JUNO BEACH — JUNO OCEAN WALK RV RESORT. (561) 622-7500. **$24-$75.** 900 Juno Ocean Walk 33408. From Jct of I-95 & Exit 83, Donald Ross Rd, E 4.4 mi on Donald Ross Rd to US 1, N 0.8 mi to Juno Ocean Walk, W 0.2 mi (R) 🏕 ⇌ 🍽 ♿M

KEY WEST — BLUEWATER KEY RV RESORT. ⨁ (305) 745-2494. **$63-$150.** 2950 US-1 33040. S-bnd: On US-1 at MP-14.5 (L) 🏕 ⇌ 🍽 ♿M

KISSIMMEE — TROPICAL PALMS RESORT & CAMPGROUND. (800) 647-2567. **$30-$85.** 2650 Holiday Trail 34746. From Jct of I-4 (exit 64A) & US-192, go E 1 mi on US-192, then S 0.25 mi on Holiday Trail (E) ⇌ 🍽 ♿M

LABELLE — RIVER BEND MOTORCOACH RESORT. (866) 787-4837. **$45-$105.** 5800 West SR-80 33935. From Jct of I-75 & SR-80 (exit 141 in Ft Myers), E 16.5 mi on SR-80 (L) 🏕 ⇌ 🍽 ♿M

LABELLE — WHISPER CREEK RV RESORT. ⨁ (855) 675-6888. **$40.** 1887 North State Rd 29 33935. From Jct of SR-80 & SR-29, N 1.8 mi on SR-29 (L) 🏕 ⇌ 🍽 ♿M

LAKE BUENA VISTA — DISNEY'S FORT WILDERNESS RESORT & CAMPGROUND. ⨁ (407) 939-2267. **$48-$126.** 4510 N. Fort Wilderness Trail 32830. From Jct I-4 (exit 64) & US-192: Go w 0.75 mi on US-192, then N 1 mi on World Dr. (R) ⇌ 🍽 ♿M

MALABAR — CAMELOT RV PARK, INC. (321) 724-5396. **$34-$39.** 1600 US-1 32950. From Jct of I-95 (exit 173) & SR-514 (Malabar Rd): Go E 4.2 mi on Malabar Rd, then S 0.3 mi on US-1 (R) 🏕 ⇌ 🍽 ♿M

MARGATE — AZTEC RV RESORT. (954) 975-6411. **$67.** 1 A Sundial Circle (Aztec Blvd.) 33068. From Jct of I-95 & Exit 36 (SR-814, W. Atlantic Blvd), W 5 mi on SR-814 (W. Atlantic Blvd) to US 441 (SR-7), S 0.6 mi to Aztec Blvd, E 0.4 mi (E); or From Jct of Florida Turnpike & Exit 62 (SR-870, NW 56th St), E 0.5 mi on SR-870 (NW 56th St) to US 441 (SR-7), N 2.7 mi to Aztec Blvd, E 0.4 mi (E) 🏕 ⇌ 🍽 ♿M

MELBOURNE BEACH — OUTDOOR RESORTS/MELBOURNE BEACH. (321) 724-2600. **Call for rates.** 214 Horizon Ln 32951. From jct US 192 & Hwy A1A: Go 4 mi S on Hwy A1A. 🏕 ⇌ 🍽

MIAMI — MIAMI EVERGLADES RESORT. ⨁ (800) 917-4923. **$35-$65.** 20675 SW 162 Ave 33187. From Jct of US-1 & Quail Roost, W 6.5 mi on Quail Roost to 162nd Ave, S (left) 0.5 mi (L); or From Jct of SR-997 (Krome Ave) & Quail Roost, E 2 mi on Quail Roost to SW 162 Ave, S (right) 0.5 mi (L); or From FL Tpke S-bnd exit 13, go past Eureka to Quail Roost, W 5.5 mi to 162 Ave, S (left) 0.5 mi (L) ⇌ 🍽 ♿M

NAPLES — CRYSTAL LAKE RV RESORT. (239) 348-0017. **$35-$80.** 14960 Collier Blvd 34119. From Jct of I-75 & CR-846 (exit 111/Immokalee Rd), E 3.2 mi on CR-846 to CR-951/Collier Blvd, S 0.5 mi (L) 🏕 ⇌ 🍽 ♿M

NAPLES — PELICAN LAKE MOTORCOACH RESORT. ⨁ (800) 835-4389. **$60-$125.** 4555 Southern Breeze Dr 34114. From Jct of I-75 & Collier Blvd (exit 101), S 9.2 mi on Collier Blvd (CR-951) (L) 🏕 ⇌ 🍽 ♿M

NAPLES — SIGNATURE MOTORCOACH RESORT AT NAPLES. (866) 942-2942. **$39-$99.** 13300 Tamiami Trail E 34114. From Jct of I-75 & Collier Blvd (CR-951/Exit 101), S 7 mi on Collier Blvd/CR-951 to US 41, SE 0.7 mi (R) 🏕 ⇌ 🍽 ♿M

NAPLES — SILVER LAKES RV RESORT & GOLF CLUB. (800) 843-2836. **$45-$79.** 1001 Silver Lakes Blvd 34114. From Jct of I-75 & Collier Blvd (CR-951/Exit 101), S 9 mi on Collier Blvd (CR-951) (L) 🏕 ⇌ 🍽 ♿M

NAVARRE — EMERALD BEACH RV PARK. (866) 939-3431. **$42-$68.** 8885 Navarre Pkwy 32566. E-bnd: From the Jct of US 87 & US 98, E 1 mi on US 98 (R); W-bnd: From entrance to Hurlburt Field (US Army Installation) & US 98, W 9 mi on US 98 (past park entrance) to Navarre Sound Circle, U-turn if possible or S onto Navarre Sound Circle & back to Hwy 98, E 0.1 mi (R) 🏕 ⇌ 🍽

NAVARRE — NAVARRE BEACH CAMPGROUND. ⨁ (888) 639-2188. **$49-$85.** 9201 Navarre Pkwy 32566. From Jct of Hwy 87 & US-98, E 2 mi on US-98 (R) ⇌ 🍽 ♿M

NAVARRE — ST ROSA SOUND RV RESORT. (888) 936-4791. **$45-$95. (no credit cards).** 8315 Navarre Pkwy 32566. From the Jct of IH & SR-87, go S 16 mi on SR-87 to dead end at Hwy 98, W 0.1 mi (L) 🏕 ⇌ 🍽

NOKOMIS — ROYAL COACHMAN RV RESORT. (800) 548-8678. **$40-$85.** 1070 Laurel Rd E 34275. From Jct of I-75 & Laurel Rd (Exit 195), W 2 mi on Laurel Rd to Terra Cove Rd, S 0.25 mi (E) 🏕️ 🛶 ❌ ♿M

NORTH FORT MYERS — RAINTREE RV RESORT. (239) 731-1441. **$55-$70.** 19250 N Tamiami Tr 33903. S-bnd: From Jct of I-75 & Tuckers Grade Rd (exit 158), W 1 mi on Tuckers Grade Rd to US-41, S 9 mi (L); or N-bnd: From Jct of I-75 & SR-78 (exit 143), W 5.3 mi on SR-78 to Bus US-41, N 2.4 mi to US-41, NW 2.3 mi (R) 🏕️ 🛶 ❌ ♿M

NORTH FORT MYERS — UPRIVER RV RESORT. 🅰🅰🅰 (800) 848-1652. **$42-$72.** 17021 Upriver Dr 33917. From Jct of I-75 & SR-78 (exit 143/Bayshore Rd), E 1.6 mi on SR-78 (R) 🏕️ 🛶 ❌ ♿M

OCALA — OCALA SUN RV RESORT. (352) 307-1100. **$28-$38.** 2559 SW Hwy 484 34473. From Jct of I-75 & SR-484 (Exit 341), W 0.5 mi on SR-484 (R) 🏕️ 🛶 ❌ ♿M

OKEECHOBEE — SILVER PALMS RV VILLAGE/PMP. (863) 467-5800. **$50-$85.** 4143 Hwy 441 S 34974. From Jct of US-441 & SR 70, S 4 mi on US-441 (R) 🏕️ 🛶 ❌

OLD TOWN — YELLOW JACKET RESORT. (352) 542-8365. **$34-$49.** 55 SE 503 Ave 32680. From Jct of US 19/98 & SR 349, S 10 mi on SR 349 to Yellow Jacket Rd, E 0.8 mi to SE 477 Ave, E 0.3 mi (R) 🛶 ❌

ORANGE LAKE — GRAND LAKE RV & GOLF RESORT. 🅰🅰🅰 (888) 239-2113. **$25-$35.** 18545 N.W. 45th Ave Rd 32681. From Jct of I-75 (exit 368) & Hwy 318, E 2.9 mi on Hwy 318, cross over Hwy 441 (L) 🏕️ 🛶 ❌ ♿M

PANAMA CITY BEACH — EMERALD COAST RV BEACH RESORT. (800) 232-2478. **$58-$82.** 1957 Allison Ave 32407. From Hathaway Bridge, W 1.5 mi on US-98 (Panama City Beach Pkwy) to Alison Ave, S 0.25 mi (R) 🏕️ 🛶 ❌ ♿M

PANAMA CITY BEACH — PANAMA CITY BEACH RV RESORT. (866) 637-3529. **$54-$72.** 4702 Thomas Dr. 32408. From Jct of US 98 & Thomas Rd, S 3.5 mi on Thomas Rd to CR 392, E 0.3 mi (L) 🏕️ 🛶

PENSACOLA — PERDIDO COVE RV RESORT & MARINA. 🅰🅰🅰 (877) 402-7873. **$57-$110.** 13770 River Rd. 32507. From Jct of IH 10 & Pine Forest Rd (Exit 7A), S 2.5 mi on Pine Forest to Blue Angel Pkwy, S 10.5 mi to Sorrento Rd (SR 292), W 6 mi across the Theo Barrs Bridge to Gongora Rd, E 100 ft to Don Carlos Dr, N 0.1 mi to River Rd, W 0.1 mi (R) 🏕️ 🛶 ❌ ♿M

PENSACOLA BEACH — PENSACOLA BEACH RV RESORT. (850) 438-1266. **Call for rates.** 17 Via De Luna Dr. 32561. From Jct of US 98 & Pensacola Beach Blvd, E 2.2 mi on Pensacola Beach Blvd (becomes Via De Luna Dr at Fort Pickens Rd) (L) 🛶 ❌ ♿M

PORT CHARLOTTE — HARBOR LAKES RV RESORT. (800) 468-5022. **$33-$63.** 3737 El Jobean Rd 33953. From Jct of I-75 & North Port/Toledo Blade Blvd (Exit 179), S 6.3 mi on Toledo Blade Blvd to SR-776, W 3.5 mi (R) 🏕️ 🛶 ❌

PORT ST. LUCIE — OUTDOOR RESORTS AT ST LUCIE WEST. (866) 456-2303. **$65.** 800 NW Peacock Blvd 34986. From Jct of I-95 & St Lucie Blvd (Exit 121), E 0.3 mi on St Lucie Blvd to NW Peacock Blvd, N 1.3 mi (L) 🏕️ 🛶 ❌ ♿M

SARASOTA — SUN-N-FUN RV RESORT. 🅰🅰🅰 (941) 371-2505. **$38-$75.** 7125 Fruitville Rd 34240. From Jct of I-75 & SR-780 (exit 210), E 1.1 mi on SR-780/Fruitville Rd (L) 🛶 ❌ ♿M

SEBASTIAN — VERO BEACH KAMP, INC. (877) 589-5643. **$38-$50.** 8850 N US Hwy-1 32958. From Jct of I-95 (Exit 156) & CR-512: Go E 2.4 mi on CR-512, then S 5.8 mi on CR-510, then N 0.4 mi on US-1 (R) 🛶 ❌ ♿M

SEBRING — THE OUTBACK RV RESORT AT TANGLE-WOOD. (863) 402-1500. **$38-$54.** 3000 Tanglewood Pkwy 33872. From Jct of US-27 & CR-634A, N 0.7 mi on US-27 (L) 🏕️ 🛶 ❌ ♿M

SILVER SPRINGS — WILDERNESS RV RESORT AT SILVER SPRINGS. (352) 625-1122. **$37-$40.** 2771 NE 102nd Ave Rd 34488. From jct I-75 & Hwy 326 (Exit 358): Go E 9 mi on Hwy 326 to US 40, then E 3 mi (L) 🏕️ 🛶 ❌

TAMPA — BAY BAYOU RV RESORT. 🅰🅰🅰 (813) 855-1000. **$42-$62.** 8492 Manatee Bay Dr 33635. From Jct of I-275 (exit 47) & SR-580/Hillsborough Ave: Go W 10.8 m, then N 0.5 mi on Country Way Blvd, then W 0.75 mi on Memorial Hwy (L) 🏕️ 🛶 ❌ ♿M

TITUSVILLE — SEASONS IN THE SUN RV RESORT. (877) 687-7275. **$33-$45.** 2400 Seasons In The Sun Blvd 32754. From Jct of I-95 (exit 223) & SR-46: Go W 0.4 mi on SR-46 (L) 🏕️ 🛶 ♿M

TITUSVILLE — THE GREAT OUTDOORS RV, NATURE & GOLF RESORT. (321) 269-5004. **$40-$55.** 125 Plantation Drive 32780. From Jct of I-95 (exit 215) & SR-50: Go W 0.5 mi on SR-50 (Cheney Hwy) to entrance rd (L) 🏕️ 🛶 ❌ ♿M

WEBSTER — FLORIDA GRANDE MOTORCOACH RESORT. (352) 568-2763. **$35.** 9675 SE 47th Way 33597. From Jct of CR-478 & CR-471, E 2 mi on CR-478 (L) 🏕️ 🛶 ❌ ♿M

WESLEY CHAPEL — QUAIL RUN RESORT. (800) 582-7084. **$38-$44.** 6946 Old Pasco Rd 33544. From Jct of I-75 & SR-54 (exit 279), W 0.5 mi on SR-54 to Old Pasco Rd, N 2 mi (R) 🏕️ 🛶 ❌ ♿M

WEST PALM BEACH — VACATION INN RESORT OF THE PALM BEACHES. (561) 848-6170. **$35-$67.** 6500 N Military Tr 33407. From Jct of US 98/80 (Southern Blvd) & I-95: Go 8 mi N on I-95 (Exit 76), then 1/2 mi W on Hwy 708 (Blue Heron Blvd), then 3/4 mi S on Hwy 809 (Military Rd) (L) 🏕️ 🛶 ❌ ♿M

WILLISTON — WILLISTON CROSSINGS RV RESORT. 🅰🅰🅰 (877) 785-4405. **$34-$39.** 410 N.E. 5th St 32696. S-bnd: From Jct of I-75 & CR-121/Williston Rd (Exit 382), SW 15 mi on CR-121/Williston Rd to US 27/41, S 0.3 mi to US 27/Alt 27, SE 0.4 mi to NE 5th St, N 0.2 mi (R); or N-bnd: From Jct of I-75 & US 27 (Exit 354) NW 21 mi on US 27 to NE 5th St, N 0.2 mi (R) 🏕️ 🛶 ❌ ♿M

ZEPHYRHILLS — MAJESTIC OAKS CAREFREE RV RESORT. (813) 783-7518. **$32.** 3751 Laurel Valley Blvd 33542. From Jct of US-301 & SR-54, S 2 mi on US-301 to Chancey Rd, E 1.5 mi (L) 🏕️ 🛶 ☒ ♿

Georgia

BREMEN — YOGI BEARS JELLYSTONE PARK-CAMP RESORT. (770) 537-3140. **$30-$36.** 106 King St 30110. From Jct of I-20 (Exit 9) & Waco Rd, N 1.1 mi on Waco Rd to US-78/SR-8, W 0.7 mi to King St, SW 0.3 mi (L) 🛶 ☒ ♿

BRUNSWICK — COASTAL GEORGIA GA RV RESORT. (912) 264-3869. **$40.** 287 South Port Parkway 31523. From the Jct of I-95 (Exit 29) & US 17/US 82: W on US 17/US-82 0.6 mi to US 17 South, S 0.3 mi to Martin Palmer Dr, SE 0.6 mi on South Port Parkway (E) 🏕️ 🛶 ☒ ♿

DILLARD — RIVER VISTA MOUNTAIN VILLAGE. (888) 850-7275. **$25-$60.** 20 River Vista Dr. 30537. From Jct of US-441 & SR-246, E 1 mi on SR-246 (R) 🏕️ 🛶 ☒ ♿

HIAWASSEE — BALD MOUNTAIN CAMPING RESORT. (706) 896-8896. **$35.** 751 Gander Gap Rd 30546. From E Jct of US-76 & SR-288, SW 0.2 mi on SR-288 to Fodder Creek Rd, S 3.6 mi (L) 🛶 ☒ ♿

Idaho

COEUR D'ALENE — BLACKWELL ISLAND RV RESORT. (888) 571-2900. **$40-$57.** 800 S Marina Dr 83814. From Jct of I-90 (exit 12) & Hwy 95, S 1.5 mi on Hwy 95 to Marina Dr (L) (Follow 95 thru traffic signs) 🏕️ ☒ ♿

DECLO — VILLAGE OF TREES RV RESORT. 🅰🅰🅰 (800) 777-9121. **$32.** 274 Hwy 25 83323. From Jct of I-84 & Rupert-Declo Rd (exit 216), N 200 yds on Rupert-Declo Rd (L) 🛶 ☒ ♿

MCCALL — MCCALL RV RESORT. 🅰🅰🅰 (855) 634-5648. **$38-$44.** 200 Scott Street 83638. From Jct of Hwy 55 & Deinhard, W 0.5 mi on Deinhard to Mission, S 0.2 mi to Scott St, W 100 yrds (E) 🏕️ 🛶 ☒ ♿

MOUNTAIN HOME — MOUNTAIN HOME RV PARK. (208) 580-1211. **$35.** 2295 American Legion Blvd 83647. From Jct of I-84 & Hwy 51/American Legion Blvd (Exit 95), S 0.5 mi on Hwy 51/American Legion Blvd (L) ☒ ♿

POST FALLS — COEUR D'ALENE RV PARK. (208) 773-3527. **$38-$41.** 2652 E Mullan Ave 83854. From Jct of I-90 & Exit 7, onto Hwy 41, N 0.3 mi to Mullan Ave, W 0.8 mi (L) 🏕️ 🛶 ☒ ♿

Illinois

AMBOY — O'CONNELL'S YOGI BEAR JELLYSTONE PARK CAMP RESORT. (815) 857-3860. **$38-$59.** 970 Green Wing Rd. 61310. From Jct of I-39 & US-30, W 13 mi on US-30 to Pine Hill Rd, S 1 mi to Inlet Rd, W 0.7 mi to Green Wing Rd, S 1.5 mi (L); or From Jct of US-30 & US-52, S 2 mi on US-52 to Main St, E 1.2 mi to Shaw Rd, SE 2.5 mi to Green Wing Rd, N 1.2 mi (R) 🛶 ☒ ♿

CHATHAM — DOUBLE J CAMPGROUND & RV PARK. (217) 483-9998. **$39.** 9683 Palm Rd 62629. S-bnd: From Jct of I-55 & Exit 88, SW 2 mi on Frntg Rd (Palm Rd) (R); or N-bnd: From Jct of I-55 & Exit 83 (to stop sign), W 0.3 mi to Frntg Rd, N 2.5 mi (L) 🛶 ☒

EAST ST. LOUIS — CASINO QUEEN RV PARK. (800) 777-0777. **$26-$37.** 200 S. Front St. 62201. W-bnd: From Jct of I-55/70 & Exit 2A (3rd St), S 0.3 mi on 3rd St to River Park Dr, W 0.4 mi (L); or E-bnd: From Jct of I-55/64/70 (at bridge, on MO side), E 1.5 mi on I-55/64/70 over bridge to 4th St (bus exit), NE 0.4 mi on exit rd to River Park Dr, W 0.5 mi (L) 🏕️ 🛶 ♿

GRANITE CITY — GRANITE CITY KOA. (618) 931-5160. **$38-$42.** 3157 W Chain Of Rocks Rd 62040. From Jct of I-270 & SR-3 (exit 3), S 0.2 mi on SR-3 to Chain of Rocks Rd, E 0.5 mi to Dial Rd, S 0.2 mi (R) 🛶 ☒

JOLIET — LEISURE LAKE RESORT. (815) 741-9405. **$50.** 21900 SW Frontage Rd 60404. S-bnd: From Jct of I-55 & IL-59 (Exit 251), W 0.1 mi on Seil Rd to Frontage Rd, S 1.3 mi (R); or N-bnd: From Jct of I-55 & US 52, W 0.5 mi on US 52 (Jefferson St) to IL-59, S 1 mi on IL-59 (Cottage St) to Seil Rd, W 0.1 mi on Seil Rd to Frontage Rd, S 1.3 mi (R) 🏕️ 🛶 ☒ ♿

KNOXVILLE — GALESBURG EAST BEST HOLIDAY TRAV-L-PARK. (309) 289-2267. **$30-$35.** 1081 US Hwy 150 E 61448. From Jct of I-74 & US-150 (exit 54), E 0.5 mi on US-150 (L) 🛶 ☒

UTICA — HICKORY HOLLOW CAMPGROUND. (815) 667-4996. **$35-$37.** 757 N 3029 Rd 61373. From Jct of I-80 (Utica exit 81) & Hwy 178, N 20 ft on Hwy 178 to Service Rd, W 0.5 mi (R) 🛶 ☒ ♿

WHITTINGTON — WHITTINGTON WOODS CAMP-GROUND AT BENTON. (618) 435-3401. **$32-$36.** 14297 State Highway 37 62897. From Jct of I-57 & SR-154 (exit 77), E 0.25 mi on SR-154 to SR-37, S 0.25 mi (R) 🛶 ☒ ♿

Indiana

BLOOMINGTON — JELLYSTONE PARK AT LAKE MON-ROE. (812) 824-3322. **$35-$56.** 9396 S Strain Ridge Rd 47401. From Jct of Hwy 37 & Harrodsburg/Lake Monroe exit, E 0.1 mi to East Monroe Dam Rd, E 0.8 mi to South Strain Ridge Rd, N 0.5 mi (L) 🛶 ☒ ♿

BLOOMINGTON — LAKE MONROE VILLAGE. (812) 824-2267. **$45-$60.** 8107 S Fairfax Rd 47401. From Jct of SR-45/46 & SR-37, S 9 mi on SR-37 to Smithville Rd, E 1.8 mi on Smithville Rd to Fairfax Rd (unmarked) 2nd stop sign, S 1.8 mi (L) 🛶 ☒ ♿

FLORENCE — FOLLOW THE RIVER RV RESORT. (812) 427-3330. **$34-$49.** 12273 Markland Town Rd 47020. From Jct of I-71 & (Kentucky SR 1039) Exit 55, N 6 mi on SR 1039, W 1 mi on (Indiana SR 156) (R) 🏕️ 🛶 ☒ ♿

NASHVILLE — THE LAST RESORT RV PARK & CAMP-GROUND. 🅰🅰🅰 (812) 988-4675. **$27-$39.** 2248 SR-46 East 47448. From Jct of I-65 & SR-46 (exit 68), W 14 mi on SR-46 (R) 🛶 ☒ ♿

RISING SUN — LITTLE FARM ON THE RIVER RV PARK CAMPING RESORT, LLC. (812) 438-4500. **$29-$40.** 1343 E Bellview Ln 47040. From Jct of I 275 & US 50, W 7.9 mi on US 50 to SR 56, S 8 mi to E Bellview Lane, E 0.2 mi (R) 🛒 ✕ ♿

SANTA CLAUS — LAKE RUDOLPH CAMPGROUND & RV RESORT. (877) 478-3657. **$30-$60.** PO Box 98-78 North Holiday Blvd. 47579. From Jct of I-64 & SR-162 (exit 63), S 7.2 mi on SR-162 to SR 245 (Holiday Blvd.), N 0.2 mi (R) 🛒 ✕ ♿

Iowa

WAUKEE — TIMBERLINE CAMPGROUND. (515) 987-1714. **$35-$36.** 31635 Ashworth Rd 50263. From Jct of I-35 & I-80 (West Jct), W 5 mi on I-80 to CR-R22 (Exit 117), N 0.9 mi to CR-F64 (Ashworth Rd), E 0.4 mi (L). Don't rely on GPS. Call to verify GPS directions 🛒 ✕

Kansas

DODGE CITY — GUNSMOKE TRAV-L-PARK. (620) 227-8247. **$32-$34.** 11070 108 Rd 67801. E-bnd: (W of town) 0.1 mi BEFORE Jct of US-50 & Bus US-50 (L); or W-bnd: From Jct of US-400 & US 56/283, N 0.4 mi on US-283 to W Business 50, W 4.9 mi (R). Note: At Jct of US-50 & Bypass 50 W of town; or N-bnd: From Jct of US-56 & US-283, N 2 mi on 2nd Ave, W 3 mi on Bus US-50 (R) 🛒 ✕ ♿

LAWRENCE — YOGI BEAR'S JELLYSTONE PARK KANSAS CITY. (888) 703-3281. **$37-$48.** 1473 N. 1800 Rd/Hwy 24/40 66044. From Jct of I-70 & US-59 (exit 204), N 0.5 mi on US-59 to US-24, E 0.25 mi (R) 🛒 ✕

MAYETTA — PRAIRIE BAND CASINO RESORT RV PARK. (877) 278-7275. **$21-$32.** 12305 150th Rd 66509. From Jct of I-70 & US-75 (Exit 358A), N 17.3 mi on US-75 to 150th RD, W 1.7 mi (L) 🏊 ♿

TOPEKA — DEER CREEK VALLEY RV PARK LLC. (785) 357-8555. **$40.** 3140 S.E. 21st Street 66607. From Jct of I-70 & Carnahan (Exit 364B), S 0.25 mi on Carnahan to 21st St, E 0.25 mi (L) 🏊 🛒 ✕ ♿

Louisiana

BREAUX BRIDGE — CAJUN PALMS RV RESORT. (337) 667-7772. **$32-$74.** 1055 N Barn Road 70517. From Jct of I-10 & Exit 115 (Henderson), NE 0.6 mi on LA 347 (Grand Point Hwy) to N Barn Rd, E 0.3 mi (L) 🏊 🛒 ✕ ♿

CARENCRO — BAYOU WILDERNESS RV RESORT. (337) 896-0598. **$39-$42.** 201 St Clair 70520. From Jct of I-10 & I-49/US 167 (Exit 103-B), N 2.5 mi on I-49/US 167 to Gloria Switch Rd (Exit 2), E 2.3 mi to N Wilderness Trail, N 0.7 mi (R). Note: Left turn 25 ft past bridge 🛒 ✕ ♿

DUSON — FROG CITY RV PARK. (337) 873-9085. **$35.** 3003 Daulat Dr. 70529. From Jct of I-10 & Exit 92 (LA95), S 0.4 mi on LA-95 to Service Rd (Daulat Dr), W 1000 ft (E) or From Jct of US 90 & LA 95, N 0.5 mi on LA 95 to Service Rd, W 1000 ft (E) 🛒 ✕ ♿

KINDER — COUSHATTA CASINO LUXURY RV RESORT AT RED SHOES PARK. (800) 584-7263. **$20-$25.** 711 Pow Wow Parkway 70648. From Jct of I-10 & US-165 (exit 44), N 22.6 mi on US-165 (L); or From Alexandria Jct of I-49 & US-165 (exit 86), S 55 mi on US-165 (R) 🏊 🛒 ✕ ♿

LIVINGSTON — LAKESIDE RV PARK. (225) 686-7676. **$30-$37.** 28370 S Frost Rd 70754. From Jct of I-12 & LA 63/Frost Rd (exit 22), S 1 mi on Frost Rd (L) 🏊 🛒 ✕ ♿

MARKSVILLE — PARAGON CASINO RV RESORT. (800) 946-1946. **$17-$32.** 124 Earl J Barbry Sr Blvd 71351. From Jct of SR 1 & SR-115/107 (in town), S 1.4 mi on SR-1 (L) 🏊 🛒 ✕ ♿

NEW ORLEANS — PONTCHARTRAIN LANDING. (877) 376-7850. **$49-$149.** 6001 France Road 70126. E-bnd: From Jct of I-10 exit 239B, exit to Louisa St N, N 0.2 mi (lt) to Chef Menteur, E 0.4 mi (rt) to France Rd, N 1.1 mi (R) or W-bnd: From Jct of I-10 & exit 239, exit to Old Gentilly Hwy, E 200 ft (rt) to Desire, N 500 ft (lt) to Chef Menteur, E 0.3 mi (rt) to France Rd, N 1.1 mi (R) 🛒 ✕ ♿

SULPHUR — A+ MOTEL & RV PARK. (337) 583-2631. **$28-$33.** 4631 Hwy 27 South 70665. From Jct of I-10 & Exit 20 (LA 27S), S 2.1 mi on LA 27S (L) 🏊 🛒 ✕ ♿

VIDALIA — RIVER VIEW RV PARK AND RESORT. (888) 628-2430. **$30-$39.** 100 River View Parkway 71373. From Jct of US-65/US-84 & LA-131 (on the West side of Mississippi River Bridge), S 0.8 mi on LA-131 (also Martin Luther King Ave) (L). 🛒 ✕ ♿

Maine

DURHAM — FREEPORT DURHAM KOA. (207) 688-4288. **$35-$48.** 82 Big Sky Ln 04222. From Jct of I-295 & Rte 136 (exit 22/old exit 20), N 3 mi on Rte 136 to Brown Rd, NW 2.6 mi to Rte 9, N 0.3 mi (R) 🛒 ✕ ♿

KENNEBUNKPORT — RED APPLE CAMPGROUND. (207) 967-4927. **$40-$54. (no credit cards).** 111 Sinnott Rd 04046. From Jct of ME Tpke & Rte 35 (exit 25), SE 1.8 mi on Rte 35 to US-1, N 1.5 mi to Old Post Rd, E (right) 0.7 mi to Sinnott Rd, E (continue straight) 1.5 mi (L) ✕ ♿

OLD ORCHARD BEACH — HID'N PINES FAMILY CAMPGROUND. 🆔 (207) 934-2352. **$30-$60.** 8 Cascade Rd 04064. From Jct of ME Tpke & I-195 (exit 36), E 1.2 mi on I-195 to Rte 1, NE 3 mi to Rte 98, S 2 mi (L) 🛒 ✕ ♿

OLD ORCHARD BEACH — POWDER HORN FAMILY CAMPING RESORT. 🆔 (207) 934-4733. **$30-$70.** 48 Cascade Rd 04064. From Jct of ME Tpke & I-195 (exit 36), E 1.2 mi on I-195 to US-1, N 3 mi to Rte 98, S 1.8 mi (L) 🛒 ✕ ♿

SCARBOROUGH — BAYLEY'S CAMPING RESORT. 🆔 (207) 883-6043. **$30-$87.** 275 Pine Point Rd 04074. From Jct I-95 Maine Tpk (exit 42) & Scarborough (US-1): Go 1-1/2 mi S on US-1, then 3 mi E on Hwy 9 West to Pine Point. (R) 🛒 ✕

WELLS — SEA-VU CAMPGROUND. 🆔 (207) 646-7732. **$45-$65.** 1733 Post Rd. 04090. From Jct of ME Tpke & Rte 109 (exit 19 Wells-Sanford), E 1.5 mi on Rte 109 to US-1, N 0.4 mi (R) 🛒 ✕

WELLS — **WELLS BEACH RESORT.** ◬ (207) 646-7570. **$49-$83.** 1000 Post Rd - US Rte 1 04090. From Jct of ME Tpke (I-95) & Rte 109 (exit 19, Wells-Sanford), E 1.5 mi on Rte 109 to US-1, S 1.4 mi (R) ⊇ ⊠

Maryland

ABINGDON — **BAR HARBOR RV PARK & MARINA.** ◬ (800) 351-2267. **$51-$54.** 4228 Birch Ave 21009. From Jct of I-95 & SR-543 (exit 80), S 1.4 mi on SR-543 to US-40, W 1.4 mi to Long Bar Harbor Rd, SE 0.7 mi to Baker Ave, E 0.5 mi (E) ⍓ ⊇ ⊠

BERLIN — **CASTAWAYS RV RESORT & CAMPGROUND.** (410) 213-0097. **$49-$105.** 12550 Eagles Nest Rd 21811. From Jct of US-50 & SR-611, right (SW) 2.2 mi on SR-611 to Eagles Nest Rd, E (left) 1.5 mi at Y in Rd, stay left (R) ⊇ ⊠

CALLAWAY — **TAKE-IT-EASY CAMPGROUND.** (301) 994-0494. **$45-$64.** 45285 Take-It-Easy Ranch Rd. 20620. From Jct of SR 4 & SR 5, S 7 mi on SR 5 to Piney Point Rd (SR-249), W 0.8 mi to Take It Easy Ranch Rd, S 0.5 mi (R) ⊇ ⊠ ⛓ᴹ

COLLEGE PARK — **CHERRY HILL PARK.** ◬ (301) 937-7116. **$60-$70.** 9800 Cherry Hill Rd 20740. S-bnd: From Jct of I-95 & SR-212/Powder Mill Rd (exit 29B Calverton), W 1.2 mi on SR-212/Powder Mill Rd to Cherry Hill Rd, S (Lt turn) 1.1 mi (R); or From Beltway I-495/95 & US-1/ Baltimore Ave (exit 25), S 0.4 mi on US-1/Baltimore Ave to Cherry Hill Rd (Rt Turn) 1 mi (L) ⊇ ⊠ ⛓ᴹ

LOTHIAN — **DUNCAN'S FAMILY CAMPGROUND.** ◬ (410) 741-9558. **$45-$61.** 5381 Sands Rd 20711. From Jct of I-95/I-495 & SR-4 (exit 11A), E 9.6 mi on SR-4 to SR-408 (Lt turn at off ramp end), E 0.5 mi to Sands Rd (Lt turn), N 0.3 mi (R) ⊇ ⊠ ⛓ᴹ

OCEAN CITY — **FRONTIER TOWN CAMPGROUND.** (800) 228-5590. **$39-$101.** 8428 Stephen Decatur Hwy. 21843. From Jct of US-50 & SR-611, SW 3.7 mi on SR-611 (L) ⊇ ⊠ ⛓ᴹ

WHALEYVILLE — **FORT WHALEY CAMPGROUND.** (888) 322-7717. **$35-$81.** 11224 Dale Road 21872. From Jct of US-50 & SR-528 (at S end of Ocean City), W 13.8 mi on US-50 to SR-610 (Whaleyville), entrance is on SE corner of intersection (L) ⊇ ⊠

WILLIAMSPORT — **YOGI BEAR'S JELLYSTONE PARK CAMP-RESORT/HAGERSTOWN.** (301) 223-7117. **$36-$76.** 16519 Lappans Rd 21795. From Jct of I-81 & SR-68 (exit 1), E 1.3 mi on SR-68 (R); or From Jct of I-70 and SR-632 (exit 28), SW 2.7 mi on SR-632 to SR-68W, W 0.8 mi (L) ⊇ ⊠

WOODBINE — **RAMBLIN' PINES FAMILY CAMPGROUND & RV PARK.** ◬ (800) 550-8733. **$53.** 801 Hoods Mill Rd 21797. E-bnd: From Jct of I-70 & SR-94 (exit 73), N 3.4 mi on SR-94 to Hoods Mill Rd, E 2.3 mi (R); or W-bnd: From Jct of I-70 & SR-97 (exit 76), N 2.7 mi on SR-97 (left turn) onto Hoods Mill Rd, W 0.6 mi (L) ⊇ ⊠ ⛓ᴹ

Massachusetts

BELLINGHAM — **CIRCLE CG FARM CAMPGROUND.** ◬ (508) 966-1136. **$45-$55.** 131 N Main St 02019. From Jct of MA Pike & I-495, S 12 mi on I-495 to Hwy 126 (exit 18), S 1 mi (L); or From Jct of I-95 & I-495, N 13 mi on I-495 to Hwy 126 (exit 18), S 1 mi (L) ⊇ ⊠

BOURNE — **BAY VIEW CAMPGROUNDS.** (508) 759-7610. **$45-$57.** 260 MacArthur Blvd 02532. From Jct of I-195 & I-495/Rte 25, SE 9 mi on Rte 25 to Bourne bridge (over bridge to Rotary) to Rte 28S, S 1.2 mi (R) ⊇ ⊠ ⛓ᴹ

DENNIS PORT — **CAMPERS HAVEN RV RESORT.** (508) 398-2811. **$45-$70.** 184 Old Wharf Rd 02639. From Jct of US 6 & Hwy 134 (Exit 9A), S 2 mi on Hwy 134 (then cross Rte 28) to Swan River Rd, S 1 mi to Lower County Rd, E 0.3 mi to Old Wharf Rd, SE 0.75 mi (L) ⊠ ⛓ᴹ

EAST FALMOUTH — **CAPE COD CAMPRESORT & CABINS.** (508) 548-1458. **$39-$95.** 176 Thomas B Landers Rd 02536. From Jct of Rte 28S & Thomas B Landers Rd, E 2.5 mi on Thomas B Landers Rd (R) ⊇ ⊠ ⛓ᴹ

FOXBORO — **NORMANDY FARMS FAMILY CAMPING RESORT.** (866) 673-2767. **$49-$79.** 72 West St 02035. From Jct of I-95 & Rte 1 (exit 9), S 6.7 mi on Rte 1 to Thurston St, E 1.3 mi (R); or From Jct of I-495 & Rte 1 (exit 14A), N 1 mi on Rte 1 to Thurston St (2nd traffic light), E 1.3 mi (R) ⊇ ⊠ ⛓ᴹ

LITTLETON — **BOSTON MINUTEMAN CAMPGROUND.** ◬ (978) 772-0042. **$44-$55.** 264 Ayer Rd 01460. From Jct of I-495 & Rte 2A (exit 30), W 3 mi on Rte 2A (L) ⊇ ⊠ ⛓ᴹ

MONSON — **SUNSETVIEW FARM CAMPING AREA, INC.** ◬ (413) 267-9269. **$34-$52.** 57 Town Farm Rd 01057. E-bnd: From Jct of MA Pike & Rte 32 (exit 8), S 2.5 mi on Rte 32 to Fenton Rd, E 0.5 mi to Town Farm Rd, S 1.5 mi (L); or N-bnd: From CT: From Jct of I-84 & Rte 32 (exit 70), N 17 mi on Rte 32 to Brimfield Rd (in town), E 2 mi to Town Farm Rd, N 0.5 mi (R) ⊇ ⊠ ⛓ᴹ

OAKHAM — **PINE ACRES FAMILY CAMPING RESORT.** (508) 882-9509. **$38-$75.** 203 Bechan Rd 01068. From Jct of Hwy 122 & Hwy 148, SW 2 mi on Rte 148 to Spencer Rd, S 0.1 mi to Bechan Rd, E 0.4 mi (L) ⊇ ⊠ ⛓ᴹ

PHILLIPSTON — **LAMB CITY CAMPGROUND.** (800) 292-5262. **$31-$48.** 85 Royalston Rd 01331. E-bnd: From Jct of Rtes 2 & 2A (Exit 19), N 0.1 mi on Rte 2A to Royalston Rd, W 0.5 mi (L); or W-bnd: From Jct of Rtes 2 & 2A (Exit 19), W 300 ft on Rte 2A to Royalston Rd, W 0.5 mi (L) ⊇ ⊠

SALISBURY — **BEACH ROSE RV PARK.** (800) 382-2230. **$37-$60.** 147 Beach Rd 01952. N-Bnd: From Jct of I-495 & Rte 110/exit 55, E 3.5 mi on Rte 110 to Rte 1, N 500 ft to Rte 1A, E 1.3 mi (L); OR S-Bnd: From Jct of I-95 & Rte 110/exit 58, E 2.4 mi on Rte 110 to Rte 1, N 500 ft to Rte 1A, E 1.3 mi (L) ⍓ ⊇ ⊠ ⛓ᴹ

SALISBURY — **BLACK BEAR CAMPGROUND.** (978) 462-3183. **$42-$50.** 54 Main St 01952. N-bnd: From Jct of I-495 & I-95, N 0.5 mi on I-95 to Exit 60 to 1st set of lights (Main St), E 0.1 mi (L); or S-bnd: From Jct of I-95 & Exit 60, exit rd to 1st set of lights (Main St), E 0.1 mi (L) ⊇ ⊠ ⛓ᴹ

SHELBURNE FALLS — COUNTRY AIRE CAMPGROUND. (413) 625-2996. **$25-$35.** 1753 Mohawk Trail 01370. From Jct of I-91 & Rte 2 (exit 26), W 13 mi on Rte 2 (R) 🚐 🗶

WESTHAMPTON — NORTHAMPTON - SPRINGFIELD **KOA.** (413) 527-9862. **$31-$47.** 139 South Rd 01027. S-bnd: From Jct of I-91 & Rte 5 (exit 18), NW 0.8 mi on Rte 5 to Rte 66, W (left turn) 8 mi to South Rd, N 0.1 mi (L); or N-bnd: From Jct of I-90 & I-91, N 4 mi on I-91 (exit 17B) to Hwy 141, W 4.7 mi to Rte 10, SW 0.5 mi (first right) to Glendale, N 4 mi to Rte 66, W 2 mi to South Rd, N 0.2 mi (L) 🚐 🗶

Michigan

BALDWIN — PERE MARQUETTE OAKS CONDOMINIUM **RV PARK.** (231) 898-2665. **$40. (no credit cards).** 6150 W 76th St. 49304. From South Jct of M-37 & US-10, S 3.6 mi on M-37 to 76th St, W 3.5 mi (R) 🏕 🚐 🗶 ⅏M

BAY HARBOR — SIGNATURE MOTORCOACH RESORT **AT BAY HARBOR.** (877) 348-2401. **$59-$79.** 5505 US 31 South 49770. From Jct of US 131 & US 31, S 5 mi on US 31 (L) 🏕 🚐 🗶 ⅏M

BUCKLEY — TRAVERSE CITY KOA. (800) 249-3203. **$25-$54.** 9700 S M 37 49620. S-bnd: From Jct of US 31 & M-37 (S of Traverse City), S 9.6 mi on M-37 (R); or N-bnd: From Buckley, N 3 mi on M-37 (L) 🚐 🗶 ⅏M

CARSONVILLE — LAKE HURON CAMPGROUND. (866) 360-2267. **$27-$69.** 2353 N Lakeshore Rd 48419. From Jct of M-25 & M 46 in Port Sanilac, N 4.5 mi on M-25 (L) 🚐 🗶 ⅏M

CEDAR SPRINGS — LAKESIDE CAMP PARK. (616) 696-1735. **$29-$32.** 13677 White Creek Ave 49319. From Jct of US-131 & M-46 (17 Mile Rd exit 104), E 0.1 mi on 17 Mile Rd to White Creek Ave, S 0.25 mi (R) 🗶 ⅏M

COVERT — COVERT/SOUTH HAVEN KOA RV RESORT. (269) 764-0818. **$30-$50.** 39397 M-140 Highway 49043. From Jct of I-196 & M-140 (Exit 18) S 6.2 mi on M-140 (L) From Jct of I 94 & M-140 (Exit 41), N 7.3 mi on M-140 (R) 🚐 🗶 ⅏M

FRANKENMUTH — YOGI BEAR'S JELLYSTONE PARK **CAMP-RESORT.** (989) 652-6668. **$38-$69.** 1339 Weiss St 48734. N-bnd: From Jct of I-75 & M-83 (Exit 136), E 2 mi on M-83 (Birch Run Rd) to M-83 (Gera Rd), N 5 mi to Weiss St, NE .01 mi (R) 🚐 🗶 ⅏M

GAYLORD — GAYLORD KOA RESORT. (800) 562-4146. **$26-$50.** 5101 Campfires Parkway 49735. From Jct of I-75 & Old US-27 (exit 279), S 2 mi on Old US-27 to Charles Brink Rd, E 1.0 mi (R) 🚐 🗶

HILLSDALE — GATEWAY PARK CAMPGROUND. (517) 437-7005. **$39-$53.** 4111 W Hallett Rd 49242. From Jct of US-12 & M-99S (in Jonesville), S 1.4 mi on M-99S to Lake Wilson Rd, SW 3.4 mi to Hallett Rd, W 1.1 mi (L) 🏕 🚐 🗶

HOLLAND — OAK GROVE RESORT. (616) 399-9230. **$38-$50.** 2011 Ottawa Beach Rd 49424. From Jct of US-31 & Lakewood Blvd, W 1.2 mi on Lakewood Blvd to Douglas Ave/Ottawa Beach Rd, SW 4.8 mi (R) 🏕 🚐 🗶 ⅏M

HOPKINS — HIDDEN RIDGE AN RV COMMUNITY. (888) 794-8792. **$39-$49.** 2306 12th St 49328. From Jct of US 131 & 124th Ave (exit 59), W 0.1 mi on 124th Ave to 12th St, S 0.3 mi (R) 🏕 🚐 🗶 ⅏M

HOWELL — LAKE CHEMUNG OUTDOOR RESORT. (517) 546-6361. **$30-$38. (no credit cards).** 320 S Hughes Rd 48843. From Jct of I-96 & Exit 145 (Grand River Ave), NW on Grand River Ave, 3 mi to Hugh Rd, N .2 mi (R) 🏕 🚐 🗶 ⅏M

INDIAN RIVER — INDIAN RIVER RV RESORT & CAMP-**GROUND.** (231) 238-0035. **$28-$42.** 561 N Straits Hwy 49749. From Jct of I-75 & M-27 (exit 313), N 1.5 mi on M-27 (L) 🚐 🗶 ⅏M

IRONS — IRONS RV PARK AND CAMPGROUND. (231) 266-2070. **$25-$35.** 4623 West 10 1/2 Mile Road 49644. From Jct of M-37 & M-55, S 6.4 mi on M-37 to 10 Mile Rd, W 5 mi on 10 Mile Rd, changes to Merryville Rd, then to 10 1/2 Mile Rd (L) 🚐 🗶 ⅏M

JACKSON — GREENWOOD ACRES FAMILY CAMP-**GROUND.** 🆎 (517) 522-8600. **$38-$44.** 2401 Hilton Rd 49201. From Jct of I-94 & Race Rd (exit 147), S 0.2 mi on Race Rd to Ann Arbor Rd, W 0.8 mi to Portage Rd, S 1.25 mi to Greenwood Rd, E 0.4 mi to Hilton Rd (L) 🚐 🗶 ⅏M

LAKE LEELANAU — LAKE LEELANAU RV PARK. (231) 256-7236. **$54-$69.** 3101 Lake Shore Dr 49653. From Jct of M-204 & CR-643 (in Lake Leelanau), S 3.5 mi on CR-643 (L) 🗶 ⅏M

LUDINGTON — PONCHO'S POND. (888) 308-6602. **$48-$51.** 5335 W Wallace Lane 49431. From W Jct of US-31 & US-10, W 1.5 mi on US-10 to Pere Marquette Rd, S 0.1 mi (L) 🚐 🗶 ⅏M

LUDINGTON — VACATION STATION RV RESORT. 🆎 (800) 499-1060. **$20-$50.** 4895 W US-10 49431. From W Jct of US 31 & US 10, W 1 mi on US 10 (L) 🚐 🗶 ⅏M

MANISTEE — LITTLE RIVER CASINO RV PARK. (866) 572-4386. **$20-$38.** 2700 Orchard Hwy 49660. From Jct of US 31 & M-55, N 3.1 mi on US 31 to M-22, W 0.1 mi (L). Follow signs to RV Park 🏕 🚐 🗶 ⅏M

MARSHALL — CAMP TURKEYVILLE RV RESORT. (269) 781-4293. **$40.** 18935 15 1/2 Mile Rd 49068. From Jct of I-69 & Exit 42 (N Dr & Turkeyville Rd), W 0.9 mi on Turkeyville Rd to 15 1/2 Mile Rd (L) 🏕 🚐 🗶 ⅏M

MARSHALL — QUALITY CAMPING INC. (517) 767-4161. **$25-$30.** 5775 Old US 27 S 49068. From Jct of I-69 & M-60 (Exit 25), E 0.4 mi on M-60 to Old US 27, N 3.6 mi (L) 🚐 🗶 ⅏M

MONROE — HARBORTOWN RV RESORT. (734) 384-4700. **$38-$50.** 14931 Laplaisance Rd 48161. From Jct of I-75 & La Plaisance Rd (exit 11), W 0.6 mi on La Plaisance Rd (L) 🏕 🚐 🗶 ⅏M

MOUNT PLEASANT — SOARING EAGLE HIDEAWAY **RV PARK.** (989) 817-4800. **$32-$53.** 5050 E Airport Rd 48858. From the Jct of US-127 & Exit 143 (Pickard Rd), E .2 mi on Pickard Rd (L) 🏕 🚐 🗶 ⅏M

MUSKEGON — DUCK CREEK RV RESORT. (231) 766-3646. **$40-$60.** 1155 W Riley Thompson Rd 49445. From Jct of US-31 & Russell Rd (Exit 121), N 1 mi to Riley Thompson Rd, W 1.5 mi (L) 🏕 🛶 ⊠ ⅏M

PETOSKEY — HEARTHSIDE GROVE MOTORCOACH RESORT. (888) 476-8388. **$35-$169.** 2400 US 31 North 49770. From Jct of US 31 N & M119 (E of town), NE 2.5 mi on US 31 N (R) 🏕 🛶 ⊠ ⅏M

PETOSKEY — PETOSKEY KOA RV & CABIN RESORT. (800) 933-1574. **$39-$65.** 1800 US-31 North 49770. From Jct of US-31N & M-119 (E of town), N 1 mi on US-31N (R) 🛶 ⊠ ⅏M

SILVER LAKE — SILVER CREEK RV RESORT. ⒶⒶⒶ (866) 832-7601. **$25-$60.** 1441 N. 34th Ave 49436. From Jct of US-31 & Polk Rd (Hart/Mears exit), W 1.2 mi on Polk Rd to 56th St, S 0.5 mi to Fox Rd, W 2.7 mi to 34th Ave, S 0.7 mi (R) 🏕 🛶 ⊠ ⅏M

SILVER LAKE — SILVER LAKE RESORT AND CAMP-GROUND. (231) 873-7199. **$25-$65.** 1786 N 34th Ave 49436. From Jct of US-31 & Polk Rd (Hart/Mears exit), W 1.2 mi on Polk Rd to 56th St, S 0.5 mi to Fox Rd, W 2.7 mi to 34th Ave, S 0.4 mi (L) 🛶 ⊠ ⅏M

SOUTH HAVEN — SOUTH HAVEN FAMILY CAMP-GROUND. (269) 637-6153. **$22-$45.** 03403 64th Street 49090. From Jct of I-196 & CR 388, Exit 20 (Phoenix Rd), E 4.2 mi to 64th St, N 0.4 mi (R) 🛶 ⊠ ⅏M

SOUTH HAVEN — SOUTH HAVEN SUNNY BROOK RV RESORT. (888) 499-5253. **$43-$58.** 68300 CR 388 Phoenix Rd 49090. From Jct of I-196 & CR 388 (Phoenix Rd Exit 20), E 2.2 mi on CR 388/ Phoenix Rd (L) 🏕 🛶 ⊠ ⅏M

STANWOOD — RIVER RIDGE RV RESORT & MARINA. (877) 287-4837. **$48-$55.** 22265 8 Mile Rd 49346. From Jct of US 131 & M-20 (Exit 131), W 2 mi on M-20 (8 Mile Road) to Elder Rd, S 0.2 mi (L) 🏕 🛶 ⊠ ⅏M

WILLIAMSBURG — TRAVERSE BAY RV RESORT. (231) 938-5800. **$45-$79.** 5555 M-72 East 49690. From N Jct of US 31N & Hwy 72, E 1.5 mi on Hwy 72 (L) 🏕 🛶 ⊠ ⅏M

Minnesota

DETROIT LAKES — FOREST HILLS RV & GOLF RESORT. (800) 482-3441. **$60.** 22931 185th St 56501. From Jct of US-59 & US-10, W 3.3 mi on US-10 (L) 🏕 🛶 ⊠

FARIBAULT — CAMP FARIBO. (507) 332-8453. **$36-$38.** 21851 Bagley Ave 55021. From Jct of I-35 & SR-60 (exit 56), E 0.3 mi on SR-60 to Western/Bagley Ave, S 1.5 mi (L) 🛶 ⊠

GRANITE FALLS — PRAIRIE VIEW RV PARK & CAMP-GROUND. (866) 293-2121. **$16-$24.** 5616 Prairies Edge Lane 56241. From Jct of Hwy 23 & Hwy 212 (in town) S. 2.2 mi on Hwy 23 to Hwy 274, S 0.4 mi on Hwy 274 to Prairies Edge Lane E 0.8 mi (L). Note: Don't use GPS coordinates 🛶 ⊠ ⅏M

HINCKLEY — GRAND CASINO HINCKLEY RV RESORT. ⒶⒶⒶ (800) 472-6321. **$23-$28.** 1326 Fire Monument Rd 55037. From Jct of I-35 & SR-48 (Exit 183), E 1 mi on SR-48 (R) 🏕 🛶 ⊠ ⅏M

HOWARD LAKE — CODGER'S COVE RV RESORT. (320) 543-2218. **$39-$45.** 5912 County Rd 6 SW 55349. From Jct of US-12 & CR-6, N 0.4 mi on CR-6 (R). CAUTION: 11 ft 6″ low clearance RR overpass on CR-6; Detour W 0.2 mi on 4th St, N 0.1 mi on 13th Ave (cross tracks), E 0.2 mi on 1st St, N 0.1 mi on CR-6 (R). Call if uncertain. 🏕 ⊠ ⅏M

PEQUOT LAKES — RV RESORT VILLAGE AT THE PRE-SERVE. (218) 568-8009. **$39-$49.** 28668 Hurtig Rd 56472. From the center of Nisswa, N 4 mi on Hwy 371 to CR-168, W 0.2 mi to Hurtig Rd, S 0.2 mi (L) 🏕 🛶 ⊠ ⅏M

PRIOR LAKE — DAKOTAH MEADOWS RV PARK. (800) 653-2267. **$23-$33.** 2341 Park Place N.W. 55372. From Jct of I-35 & 185th St. W (Exit 84), W 1.2 mi on SR-23 to 185th St (185th St becomes CR-21) to CR-21, then NW 7.2 mi on CR-21 to CR-82/154th St, W 1.8 mi to Mystic Lake Blvd, N 0.2 mi (R) 🏕 🛶 ⊠ ⅏M

ROCHESTER — KOA ROCHESTER/MARION. (507) 288-0785. **$26-$40.** 5232 65th Ave SE 55904. From Jct of I-90 & US-52, S 0.6 mi on US-52 to 54 SE St, E 0.1 mi to 65th Ave SE, (L). 🛶 ⊠

ST. CLOUD — ST CLOUD CAMPGROUND & RV PARK. (320) 251-4463. **$33-$37.** 2491 2nd St SE 56304. From Jct of US-10 & SR-23, E 0.1 mi on SR-23 to CR-8 (14th Ave SE), S 0.1 mi on CR-8, E 1 mi on CR-8 (L) S-bnd: From Jct of SR-23 & CR-8, E 1 mi on CR-8 to 2nd St SE, S 1 mi on 2nd St SE (R) 🛶 ⊠ ⅏M

SPRING GROVE — HIDDEN BLUFFS RESORT. ⒶⒶⒶ (866) 936-2267. **Call for rates.** 22885 Cty 19 55974. From Int SR-44 & CR-4, N 3.3 mi on CR-4 to CR-19, L 2.6 mi on CR-19 (L) 🛶 ⊠

TENSTRIKE — SUMMER HAVEN R.V. RESORT. (218) 586-2842. **$49-$54.** 21588 Gull Lake Loop Road N.E. 56683. From Jct of US-71 & CR-23 (North of Bemidji), N 6 mi on CR-23 (R). Caution: Use GPS - lon & lat not address 🏕 🛶 ⊠

WALKER — TRAILS RV PARK. (877) 280-0322. **$36-$43.** 9424 State 371 NW 56484. From Jct of SR 200/371 & SR 34 (in Walker), N 4.1 mi on SR 371 (R). 🛶 ⊠ ⅏M

WASECA — KIESLER'S CAMPGROUND AND RV RESORT. (507) 835-3179. **$43-$70.** 14360 Hwy 14 East 56093. From Jct of SR-13 & US-14, E 1.5 mi on US-14 (R) 🛶 ⊠

WATERVILLE — KAMP DELS. (507) 362-8616. **$42-$66.** 14842 Sakatah Lake Rd 56096. From Jct of US-60 & SR 13, N 0.9 mi on SR 13 to CR-131, E 0.5 mi (L) 🛶 ⊠ ⅏M

Mississippi

BAY ST. LOUIS — BAY HIDE AWAY RV PARK & CAMP-GROUND. (228) 466-0959. **$25-$50.** 8360 Lakeshore Rd 39520. E-bnd: From Jct of I-10 (exit 2 Welcome Center) & Hwy 607/US-90, SE 8.6 mi on Hwy 607/US-90 to Lakeshore Rd, S 0.5 mi (L); or W-bnd: From Jct of I-10 (exit 13) & Hwys 43/603, S 6 mi on Hwys 43/603 to US-90, W 4.7 mi to Lakeshore Rd, S 0.5 mi (L) 🏕 🛶 ⊠

BAY ST. LOUIS — HOLLYWOOD CASINO RV PARK. (866) 758-2591. **$35-$45.** 711 Hollywood Blvd 39520. E-Bnd: From Jct of I-10 & SR-607 (exit 2), SE 7 mi on SR-607 to US-90, E 9 mi to Blue Meadow Rd, N 0.6 mi to Hollywood Blvd, E 1.3 mi (E); or W-Bnd: From Jct of I-10 & SR-603 (exit 13), SE 5.2 mi on SR-603 to US-90, E 3.5 mi to Blue Meadow Rd, N 0.6 mi to Hollywood Blvd, E 1.3 mi (E) 🅰 🌰 🗙 ⛐M

BILOXI — MAJESTIC OAKS RV RESORT. (228) 436-4200. **$39-$44.** 1750 Pass Road 39531. From Jct of I-10 & I-110 (Exit 46A), S 4.2 mi on I-110 to US-90, W 3.1 mi to Rodenberg Ave, N 0.6 mi to Pass Rd, W 0.2 mi (R) 🅰 🌰 ⛐M

BILOXI — PARKER'S LANDING RV PARK. (228) 392-7717. **$28-$32.** 7577 E Oaklawn Rd 39532. From Jct of I-10 & Hwy 67 (exit 41), S 0.3 mi on SR-67 to E Oaklawn Rd, E 0.2 mi (R) 🌰 🗙

CLINTON — SPRINGRIDGE RV PARK/MOBILE HOME ESTATES. (800) 513-0728. **$30.** 499 Springridge Rd 39056. From Jct of I-20 & Springridge Rd (exit 36), S 0.4 mi on Springridge Rd (L) 🌰 🗙

HORN LAKE — MEMPHIS JELLYSTONE CAMP RESORT. (662) 280-8282. **$45-$55.** 1400 Audubon Point Drive 38637. From Jct of I-55 & Church Rd (exit 287), W 1.0 mi on Church Rd to US-51, N 0.8 mi to Audubon Point Dr, E 500 ft (E) 🌰 🗙 ⛐M

PELAHATCHIE — YOGI ON THE LAKE. 🅰🅰🅰 (601) 854-6859. **$24-$55.** 143 Campground Rd 39145. From Jct of I 20 (exit 68) & Hwy 43, N 2.2 mi on Hwy 43 to Lake Rd, W 1.1 mi to Campground Rd, N 0.2 mi (E) 🌰 🗙

ROBINSONVILLE — HARRAH'S MID-SOUTH RV PARK. (800) 946-4946. **$14-$16.** 111 Resort Village Rd. 38664. N-bnd: From South Jct of US 61 & SR 304, N 2.1 mi on US 61 to Harrah's Pkwy S, NW 1.2 mi (L); or S-bnd: From Jct of I-69 & US 61, S 0.8 mi on US 61/SR 304 to Harrah's Pkwy N, SW 3.3 mi (R) 🅰 🌰 🗙 ⛐M

SOUTHAVEN — EZ DAZE RV PARK. (662) 342-7720. **$33.** 536 W.E. Ross Pkwy 38671. From Jct of I-55 & Church Rd (Exit 287), W 0.2 mi on Church Rd to Pepper Chase Dr, N 0.5 mi to W E Ross Pkwy, W 0.2 mi (R) 🅰 🌰 🗙 ⛐M

VICKSBURG — AMERISTAR RV PARK. (800) 700-7770. **$25-$30.** 725 Lucy Bryson St 39180. From Jct of I-20 & Washington St (exit 1A), N 0.3 mi on Washington St (R) 🅰 🌰

Missouri

BRANSON — AMERICA'S BEST CAMPGROUND. (800) 671-4399. **$37.** 499 Buena Vista Rd 65616. From Jct of US 65 & SR-248, W 1.7 mi on SR-248 (move to right turning lane), continue N 1.3 mi on SR-248 to Buena Vista Rd, W 0.3 mi (L). Use these directions, do not use GPS 🌰 🗙 ⛐M

BRANSON — BRANSON KOA & CONVENTION CENTER. (800) 562-4177. **$32-$50.** 397 Animal Safari Rd 65616. From Jct of US-65 & SR-76, W 3.3 mi on SR-76 to SR-165 (Gretna Rd), S 0.7 mi to Animal Safari Rd, W 0.1 mi (L) 🌰 🗙 ⛐M

BRANSON — COMPTON RIDGE CAMPGROUND. (800) 233-8648. **$33-$43.** 5040 State Hwy 265 65616. S-Bnd: From Jct of Hwy 65 & Hwy 465/Ozark Mtn Highroad, S 7 mi on Hwy 465 to Hwy 76, W 0.5 mi to Hwy 265, S 0.6 mi (L) 🌰 🗙

BRANSON — COOPER CREEK CAMPGROUND & RESORT. (800) 261-8398. **$29-$35.** 471 Cooper Creek Rd 65616. From Jct of US-65 & SR-76, W 1 mi on SR-76 to Fall Creek Rd, 2 mi on Fall Creek Rd, L on River Ln, then .1 mi to L on Cooper Creek Rd. 🌰 🗙

BRANSON — MUSICLAND KAMPGROUND, LLC. (888) 248-9080. **$27-$39.** 116 Gretna Rd 65616. From Jct of US-65 & Hwy-248, W 1.9 mi on Hwy-248 to Gretna Rd. (stay in left lane, continue straight ahead) 3.1 mi (L) 🌰 🗙

BRANSON WEST — ACORN ACRES RV PARK & VILLAS. (800) 338-2504. **$24-$58.** 159 Acorn Acres Lane 65737. S-bnd: From Jct of US-65 & State Hwy 465/Ozark Mountain Highroad (North of Branson), S 7 mi on State Hwy 465 to Hwy 76, W 2.5 mi (L); or N-bnd: From Jct of US-65 & State Hwy 465/Ozark Mountain Highroad, S 7 mi on State Hwy 465 to Hwy 76, W 2.5 mi on Hwy 76 (L) 🌰 🗙

CAPE GIRARDEAU — THE LANDING POINT RV PARK. (573) 334-7878. **$30.** 3020 Boutin Dr 63701. From Jct of I-55 and LaSalle Ave (Exit 102), E 2.2 mi on LaSalle Ave to Route W, S 1.8 mi on Route W, continue S on Route W 0.2 mi (L)

COLUMBIA — COTTONWOODS RV PARK. 🅰🅰🅰 (573) 474-2747. **$22-$33.** 5170 Oakland Gravel Rd 65202. From Jct of I-70 & US-63 (exit 128A), N 3 mi on US-63 to Oakland Gravel Rd (paved), NE 0.25 mi (R); or S-bnd: From Jct of US-63 & Prathersville Rd, E 0.2 mi to Oakland Gravel Rd (paved), S 0.25 mi (L) 🌰 🗙 ⛐M

FORSYTH — JELLYSTONE CAMP RESORT. (417) 546-3000. **$43-$55.** 11020 E State Hwy 76 65653. From Jct of US 65 & US 160, E 12 mi (thru Forsyth) to St Hwy 76, S 1.2 mi on US 160 (L) 🌰 🗙 ⛐M

KANSAS CITY — WORLDS OF FUN VILLAGE. (816) 454-4545. **$39-$42.** 4545 Worlds Of Fun Ave 64161. From Jct of I-435 & Exit 54, E 0.4 mi on Parvin Rd (L) 🅰 🌰 ⛐M

MONROE CITY — MARK TWAIN LANDING RESORT. 🅰🅰🅰 (573) 735-9422. **$39-$48.** 42819 Landing Ln 63456. From Jct of US-36 & CR-J, S 7.7 mi on CR-J (R) 🗙 ⛐M

OSAGE BEACH — OSAGE BEACH RV PARK. (573) 348-3445. **$29-$32.** 3949 Campground Ln 65065. From Jct of US 54 Expressway & SR-42/Osage Beach Parkway North Exit, N 0.5 mi to SR-42, E 0.25 mi on SR-42 (watch for sign on right) to Access Road, S 0.1 mi to office (R) 🌰 🗙

PLATTE CITY — BASSWOOD RESORT. 🅰🅰🅰 (800) 242-2775. **$37-$50.** 15880 Interurban Rd 64079. From Jct of I-29 & SR-92 (exit 18), E 3.4 mi on SR-92 to N Winan Rd, N 1.7 mi to Interurban Rd, NW 0.3 mi (L) 🌰 🗙 ⛐M

Montana

BILLINGS — BILLINGS KOA. (406) 252-3104. **$30-$79.** 547 Garden Ave 59101. From Jct of I-90 & 27th St (exit 450), E 200 yds on 27th St to Garden Ave, S 0.6 mi (L) 🌰 🗙 ⛐M

BILLINGS — YELLOWSTONE RIVER RV PARK & CAMPGROUND. (800) 654-0878. $34-$65. 309 Garden Ave. 59101. W-bnd: From Jct I-90 (Exit 450) & Hwy 3/27th St: Go 1 block S on 27th St, then 1/4 mi SW on Garden Ave (L) E-bnd: From Jct I-90 & S Billings Blvd (Exit 447): Go 1/4 mi S on S Billings Blvd, then 3 mi E on S Frontage Rd/Garden Ave (R) 🖾 🗙 🕹M

MISSOULA — JELLYSTONE RV PARK. (800) 318-9644. $29-$39. 9900 Jellystone Dr 59808. From Jct of I-90 & US-93 (exit 96, W of town), N 1/2 mi on US-93 (L) 🖾 🗙 🕹M

POLSON — EAGLE NEST RV RESORT. (406) 883-5904. $25-$44. 35800 Eagle Nest Dr (Mt 35) 59860. From Jct of US-93 & SR-35, E 0.3 mi on SR-35 (L) 🖾 🗙

POLSON — POLSON MOTORCOACH & RV RESORT. (800) 985-0421. $45-$77. 200 Irvine Flats Rd 59860. From Jct of US-93 & SR-35 (S edge of town), NW 3 mi on US-93 to Irvine Flats Rd (MP-62 1/4), S 0.3 mi (R) 🖾 🖾 🗙 🕹M

POLSON — POLSON/FLATHEAD LAKE KOA. (888) 883-2151. $27-$57. 200 Irvine Flats Rd 59860. From Jct of US-93 & SR-35 (S edge of town), NW 3 mi on US-93 to Irvine Flats Rd (MP-62 1/4), S 0.3 mi (R) 🖾 🖾 🗙 🕹M

ST. REGIS — NUGGET RV PARK. (888) 800-0125. $30-$36. 1037 Old Highway 10 East 59866. From Jct of I-90 & SR-135 (exit 33), N 300 ft on SR-135 to Mullan Rd (flashing red light), E (R) 1 mi (L) 🖾 🗙

WEST YELLOWSTONE — YELLOWSTONE PARK KOA. 🆀🆀🆀 (800) 562-7591. $44-$74. 3305 Targhee Pass/US 20 59758. From Jct of US-20/191 & 287, W 6 mi on US-20 (R) 🖾 🗙 🕹M

Nebraska

GREENWOOD — PINE GROVE RV PARK. (402) 944-3550. $32-$36. 23403 Mynard Rd 68366. From Jct of I-80 & SR-63 (exit 420), N 0.1 mi on SR-63 to Mynard Rd, W 0.4 mi (L) 🖾 🗙

LINCOLN — CAMP-A-WAY. 🆀🆀🆀 (402) 476-2282. $36-$47. 200 Campers Circle 68521. From Jct of I-80 Downtown (Exit 401/401A) & Hwy 34 East, go S 1/4 mi to Superior St (exit 1), then go W on Superior 1/4 mi to Campers Circle, then go N 1/4 mi to entrance. 🖾 🗙

Nevada

CARSON CITY — COMSTOCK COUNTRY RV RESORT. 🆀🆀🆀 (775) 882-2445. $30-$39. 5400 S Carson St 89701. N-bnd: From Jct of US-395 & Jacks Valley Rd/N Sunridge Dr (Hwy 206), N 1 mi to Old Clear Creek Rd, W 750 ft (R) or From (In town) Jct of US-395 & US-50, S 3.4 mi on US 395 (Carson St) to Jct US-395/US-50 West, S 1600 ft on US 395 to Old Clear Creek Rd, W 720 ft (R) 🖾 🗙 🕹M

ELKO — IRON HORSE RV RESORT. (800) 782-3556. $30-$45. 3400 East Idaho St 89801. From Jct of I-80 & Exit 303 (Jennings Way), E 0.1 mi on Jennings Way (not marked) to Idaho St, N 0.3 mi (R) 🖾 🖾 🗙

LAS VEGAS — ARIZONA CHARLIE'S BOULDER RV PARK. (800) 970-7280. $32. 4445 Boulder Hwy 89121. From Jct of I-515/93/95 & Boulder Hwy (exit 70), S 1.1 mi on Boulder Hwy (L) 🖾 🖾 🗙 🕹M

LAS VEGAS — HITCHIN' POST RV PARK. 🆀🆀🆀 (888) 433-8402. $29. 3640 Las Vegas Blvd North 89115. S-bnd: From Jct of I-15 & Exit 50 (Lamb), S 2 mi on Lamb to Las Vegas Blvd, S 0.1 mi (L) or N-bnd: From Jct of I-15 & Craig Rd (exit 48), E 1.2 mi on Craig Rd to Lamb Blvd, SE 1 mi to Las Vegas Blvd, SW 0.1 mi (L) 🖾 🖾 🗙 🕹M

LAS VEGAS — LAS VEGAS RV RESORT. (702) 451-8005. $29-$45. 3890 S Nellis Blvd 89121. From Jct of Boulder Hwy & Nellis Blvd, N 0.3 mi on Nellis Blvd (R) 🖾 🖾 🗙 🕹M

LAS VEGAS — LVM RESORT. 🆀🆀🆀 (866) 897-9300. $69-$99. 8175 Arville St 89139. From Jct of I-15 & I-215, S 0.8 mi on I-15 to Exit 33 (Blue Diamond Rd), SW 1.1 mi on Blue Diamond Rd (SR-106) to Arville St., N 580 yds (L) 🖾 🖾 🗙 🕹M

MINDEN — SILVER CITY RV RESORT. 🆀🆀🆀 (800) 997-6393. $35. 3165 Hwy 395 N 89423. N-Bnd: From Jct of US-395 & SR-88, N 7.3 mi on US-395 (R); or S-Bnd: From Jct of US-395 S & US-50 W in Carson City, S 3.2 mi on US-395 S (L) 🖾 🗙 🕹M

PAHRUMP — LAKESIDE CASINO & RV RESORT. (888) 558-5253. $29-$49. 5870 S Homestead Rd 89048. From Jct of Hwy 160 & Homestead Rd (at S end of town), S 3.8 mi on Homestead Rd to Thousandaire Rd, W 100 ft (R) 🖾 🖾 🗙 🕹M

PAHRUMP — NEVADA TREASURE RV RESORT. 🆀🆀🆀 (800) 429-6665. $40-$60. 301 West Leslie St. 89060. From Jct of SR-160 & SR-372 (in town), N 7.6 mi on SR-160 to Leslie St, S 0.1 mi (L) 🖾 🖾 🗙 🕹M

PAHRUMP — WINE RIDGE RV RESORT. (775) 751-7805. $20-$26. 3810 Winery Road #2 89048. From Jct of SR-160 & Winery Rd, N 0.8 mi on Winery Rd (L) 🖾 🖾 🗙

RENO — BORDERTOWN CASINO & RV RESORT. (800) 218-9339. $29-$43. 19575 Hwy 395 N 89508. N-bnd: From Jct of US-395 & Exit 83 (N of Reno at NV/CA border), SW 500 ft to Scott Rd (Frontage Rd), NW 0.2 mi (right turn) (L); or S-bnd: From Jct of US-395 & Exit 83 (1st exit S of NV/CA border), SW 150 ft to Scott Rd (Frontage Rd), NW 0.2 mi (L) 🖾 🗙 🕹M

RENO — SHAMROCK RV PARK. (775) 329-5222. $31-$35. 260 Parr Blvd 89512. From Jct of I-80 & Exit 15/US-395, N 3 mi on US-395 to Exit 71/Parr Blvd, W 1 mi (L) 🖾 🖾 🕹M

SPARKS — SPARKS MARINA RV PARK. 🆀🆀🆀 (775) 851-8888. $23-$43. 1200 E Lincoln Way 89434. From Jct of I-80 & Exit 20 (Sparks Blvd), N 0.3 mi on Sparks Blvd to Lincoln Way, W 0.5 mi (R) 🖾 🖾 🗙 🕹M

VERDI — GOLD RANCH CASINO & RV RESORT. (877) 914-6789. $29-$32. 320 Gold Ranch Road 89439. E-bnd: From Jct of I-80 & Exit 2, continue North on exit ramp to SR 40, SW 0.4 mi (L-Turn) to Park Entrance Rd (R) or W-bnd: From Jct of I-80 & Exit 2, exit to SR 40 (Gold Ranch Rd), S 520 ft (L-Turn) (R) 🖾 🖾

WINNEMUCCA — HI-DESERT RV. ⬢ (775) 623-4513. **$19-$35.** 5575 E Winnemucca Blvd 89445. From Jct of I-80 & Exit 180, S 0.8 mi on East Winnemucca Blvd (R); or S-bnd US 95: From Jct of US 95 & Winnemucca Blvd, NE 0.6 mi on Winnemucca Blvd to I-80E, I-80E 1.5 mi to Exit 180 (E Winnemucca Blvd), S 0.8 mi (R) ⊶ ⊠ ⬢M

New Hampshire

ASHLAND — AMES BROOK CAMPGROUND. (603) 968-7998. **$34-$38.** 104 Winona Rd 03217. From Jct of I-93 & Exit 24 (Rtes 3 & 25), S 0.75 mi on Rte 3 & 25 to Rte 132, S 0.25 mi to Winona Rd, S 0.5 mi (R) (Avoid S end of Winona Rd, low bridge) ⊶ ⊠

FREEDOM — DANFORTH BAY CAMPING & RV RESORT. (603) 539-2069. **$44-$76.** 196 Shawtown Rd 03836. From Jct of Rte 16 & Rte 41 (in West Ossipee), E 0.5 mi on Rte 41 to Ossipee Lake Rd, SE 4.8 mi to Shawtown Rd, NE 1 mi (R) ⊶ ⊠ ⬢M

FREEDOM — THE BLUFFS RV RESORT. (603) 539-2069. **$44-$48.** 196 Shawtown Rd 03836. From Jct of Rte 16 & Rte 41 (in West Ossipee), E 0.5 mi on Rte 41 to Ossipee Lake Rd, SE 4.8 mi to Shawtown Rd, NE 1 mi (R) ⬟ ⊶ ⊠ ⬢M

LANCASTER — MOUNTAIN LAKE. (603) 788-4509. **$43-$55.** 485 Prospect St 03584. From Jct of US-3 & US-2 (in town), S 4.5 mi on US-3 (R) ⊶ ⊠

NEW BOSTON — FRIENDLY BEAVER CAMPGROUND. (603) 487-5570. **$38-$42.** 98 Cochran Hill Rd 03070. From Jct of Rtes 77 & 136 & 13 (in town), S 100 ft on Rte 13 to Old Coach Rd, W 2 mi (R) ⊶ ⊠ ⬢M

NEW HAMPTON — TWIN TAMARACK FAMILY CAMPING & RV RESORT. ⬢ (603) 279-4387. **$40-$48.** 41 Twin Tamarack Rd 03256. From Jct of I-93 & Rte 104 (exit 23), E 2.5 mi on Rte 104 (L) ⊶ ⊠

STRAFFORD — CROWN POINT CAMPGROUND. ⬢ (603) 332-0405. **$30-$42.** 79 First Crown Point Rd 03884. From Jct of Spaulding Tpke exit 14 & Ten Rod Road, S 0.2 mi to Rte 11/Main St, E 0.1 mi to Twombly St, SW 0.3 mi to Rte 202A, W 4 mi to First Crown Point Rd, N 0.3 mi (L) ⊶ ⊠

TAMWORTH — CHOCORUA CAMPING VILLAGE KOA. ⬢ (888) 237-8642. **$39-$76.** 893 White Mountain Hwy 03817. From N Jct of Hwy 16 & Rte 25W, N 3 mi on Hwy 16 (R). Do not use GPS. Call for directions ⊶ ⊠ ⬢M

WEARE — COLD SPRINGS CAMP RESORT. (603) 529-2528. **$54-$58.** 62 Barnard Hill Rd 03281. From S Jct of I-93 & I-293, W 3 mi on I-293 to Rte 101, W 1.5 mi to Rte 114, NW 12 mi to Barnard Hill Rd, N 0.2 mi (R) ⊶ ⊠

New Jersey

CAPE MAY — HOLLY SHORES CAMPGROUND & RV RESORT. ⬢ (877) 494-6559. **$35-$71.** 491 Rte 9 08204. From Jct of Garden State Pkwy & SR-47 (exit 4A), W 0.5 mi on SR-47 to US-9, S 1 mi (L) ⊶ ⊠

CAPE MAY — SEASHORE CAMPSITES. ⬢ (800) 313-2267. **$25-$67.** 720 Seashore Rd 08204. From Jct of Garden State Pkwy & SR-47 (exit 4A), N 0.9 mi on SR-47 to SR-626 (Railroad Ave), S 2.7 mi (R); or From Cape May-Lewes Ferry, E 1.9 mi on US-9N to SR-626 N (Seashore Rd), N 1.2 mi (L) ⊶ ⊠ ⬢M

CAPE MAY COURT HOUSE — BIG TIMBER LAKE CAMPING RESORT. (800) 542-2267. **$44-$74.** 116 Swainton-Goshen Rd 08210. From Jct of Garden State Pkwy & Rte 601 (exit 13), W 0.5 mi on Rte 601 to US-9, S 0.8 mi to CR-646, W 1 mi (R); or From Dennisville, S 1.7 mi on SR-47 to Rte 657, S 3 mi to Rte 646, E 0.8 mi (L) ⊶ ⊠ ⬢M

CAPE MAY COURT HOUSE — DRIFTWOOD TOO CAMPING RESORT. (609) 624-9015. **$62.** 1142 Rte 83 08210. From Jct of Garden State Pkwy & CR-625 (exit 17), W 0.25 mi on CR-625 to US-9, S 3 mi to SR-83, W 0.5 mi (R) ⊶ ⊠ ⬢M

CLARKSBORO — TIMBERLANE CAMPGROUND. ⬢ (856) 423-6677. **$45-$48.** 117 Timber Ln Rd 08020. S-bnd: From Jct of I-295 & Rte 667 (Exit 18), SE 1 mi on Rte 667 to Friendship Rd, W 0.3 mi to Timber Ln, N 200 ft (L); or N-bnd: From Jct of I-295 & Timber Lane Rd (Exit 18), E 0.8 (R) ⊶ ⊠ ⬢M

CLERMONT — AVALON CAMPGROUND. ⬢ (609) 624-0075. **$42-$62.** 1917 N Rte 9 08210. From Jct of Garden State Pkwy & Rte 601 (exit 13), W 0.4 mi on Rte 601 to US-9, N 1.5 mi (L) ⊶ ⊠

CLERMONT — DRIFTWOOD CAMPING RESORT. (609) 624-1899. **$62.** 1955 Rte 9 08210. From Jct of US 9 & SR-83, S 0.1 mi on US 9 (R) ⊶ ⊠ ⬢M

DOROTHY — COUNTRY OAKS CAMPGROUND. (609) 476-2143. **$48-$52.** 13 S Jersey Ave 08317. From Jct of Rte 50 & Rte 40 (in May's Landing), S 1.1 mi on Rte 50 to Rte 669 (11th Ave), SW 5.5 mi to S Jersey (turn before RR tracks), NW 1.2 mi (R) ⊶ ⊠

GALLOWAY — POMONA RV PARK. (609) 965-2123. **$48-$53.** 536 S Pomona Rd 08201. S-bnd: From Jct of Garden State Pkwy & CR-575 (exit 44), S 5 mi on CR-575 (L) E-bnd: From Jct of Atlantic City Expressway & CR-575 (exit 12), N 3 mi on CR 575 (R) ⊶ ⊠

MARMORA — WHIPPOORWILL CAMPGROUND. (609) 390-3458. **$58.** 810 S Shore Rd 08223. From Jct of Garden State Pkwy & CR-623 (Exit 25), W 0.25 mi on CR-623 to US 9, S 1.5 mi (R) ⊶ ⊠ ⬢M

OCEAN VIEW — OCEAN VIEW RESORT CAMPGROUND. ⬢ (609) 624-1675. **$39-$84.** 2555 Rte 9 08230. From Jct of Garden State Pkwy & CR-625 (exit 17), W 0.4 mi on CR-625 to US-9, N 0.3 mi (L) ⊶ ⊠ ⬢M

WEST CREEK — SEA PIRATE CAMPGROUND. ⬢ (609) 296-7400. **$45-$62.** 148 Main St 08092. From Jct of Garden State Pkwy & SR-72 (exit 63), SE 1 mi on SR-72 to US-9, S 4.9 mi (L) ⊶ ⊠ ⬢M

WILLIAMSTOWN — HOSPITALITY CREEK CAMPGROUND. (856) 629-5140. **$55-$69.** 117 Coles Mill Rd 08094. From Jct of Atlantic City Expwy & Rte 54 (exit 28), S 1.9 mi on Rte 54 to Rte 332, NW 4.5 mi to Rte 538 (Coles Mill Rd), W 0.2 mi (R) ⊶ ⊠ ⬢M

New Mexico

CARLSBAD — CARLSBAD KOA. (575) 457-2000. **$40-$57.** #
2 Manthei Rd 88220. From Carlsbad, N 15 mi on Hwy 285 to Sky-
ward Dr, (between MM 51 & MM 52) on Hwy 285, E 0.3 mi (R)
🏊 ⊠ &M

GALLUP — USA RV PARK. (505) 863-5021. **$29-$35.** 2925 W
Hwy 66 87301. From Jct of I-40 & Exit 16 (Historic Route 66/W US
Hwy 66/Hwy 118/Bus Loop 40), E 1.1 mi on W US Hwy 66/Hwy
118/Bus Loop 40 (R) 🏊 ⊠

RIO RANCHO — STAGECOACH STOP RV PARK. (505)
867-1000. **$39-$45.** 3650 State Hwy 528 NE 87144. From Jct of
I-25 & Exit 242 (Hwy 550), W 2.2 mi on Hwy 550 to Hwy 528, S
0.5 mi (L) 🏕 🏊 ⊠ &M

**SANTA FE — THE TRAILER RANCH RV RESORT & 55+
COMMUNITY.** (505) 471-9970. **$37-$45.** 3471 Cerrillos Rd 87507.
From Jct of I-25 & Cerrillos Rd (exit 278 or 278B), NE 3.5 mi on
Cerrillos Rd (L) or (S bnd) From (North of Santa Fe) US-285/St
Francis Dr to Cerrillos Rd, SW 3.5 mi (R) 🏕 🏊

New York

**CANANDAIGUA — KOA CANANDAIGUA/ROCHESTER
KAMPGROUND.** (585) 398-3582. **$34-$49.** 5374 Canandaigua
Farmington Townline Rd 14425. From Jct of I-90 & SR-332 (exit
44), SE 3 mi on SR-332 to Canandaigua/Farmington Townline Rd,
E 1.3 mi (L); or From Jct of I-90 & SR-21 (exit 43) S on SR 21,
0.2 mi, NW 2.5 mi on SR-96 to CR-28, S 1.5 mi to Townline Rd,
W 1.5 mi (R) 🏊 ⊠

**CLAYTON — MERRY KNOLL 1000 ISLANDS CAMP-
GROUND.** (315) 686-3055. **$33-$38. (no credit cards).** 38115 Rt
12E 13624. From Jct of SR-12 & SR-12E, S 2.5 mi on SR-12E (R)
🏊 ⊠

**CUDDEBACKVILLE — DEERPARK/NEW YORK CITY NW
KOA.** (845) 754-8388. **$48-$76.** 108 Guymard Turnpike 12729.
From Jct of I-84 & US-6 (exit 1), NW 1.4 mi on US-6 to US-209,
NE 6 mi to Guymard Tpke, E 0.5 mi (R) 🏊 ⊠ &M

DEWITTVILLE — CHAUTAUQUA LAKE KOA. (716) 386-
3804. **$42-$59.** 5652 Thumb Rd 14728. From Jct of I-86/SR-17 &
SR-430 (exit 10), W 5 mi on SR-430 to Thumb Rd, E 0.5 mi (L)
🏊 ⊠ &M

**DIAMOND POINT — LAKE GEORGE ESCAPE CAMPING
RESORT.** (800) 327-3188. **$55-$77.** 175 E Schroon River Rd
12824. From Jct of I-87 (Northway) & Diamond Point Rd (exit 23),
E 0.5 mi on Diamond Point Rd to E Schroon River Rd, N 0.8 mi
(L) 🏊 ⊠ &M

FLORIDA — BLACK BEAR CAMPGROUND INC. (845) 651-
7717. **$50-$60.** 197 Wheeler Rd 10921. From Jct of SR-17 &
SR-94 (exit 126), SW 4.7 mi on SR-94 to Bridge St, W 2 blks to
CR 41, 1.5 mi (L) 🏕 🏊 ⊠ &M

**FRANKLINVILLE — TRIPLE R CAMPING RESORT &
TRAILER SALES.** (716) 676-3856. **$39.** 3491 Bryant Hill Rd
14737. S-bnd: From Jct of SR-98 & SR-16, S 1.9 mi on SR-16 to
Elm St (traffic light), W 1.5 mi to Bryant Hill Rd, W 0.3 mi (L); or
N-bnd: From Jct of I-86 (SR-17) & SR-16 (Exit 27), N 12 mi on
SR-16 to Elm St (traffic light), W 1.5 mi to Bryant Hill Rd, W 0.3
mi (L) 🏊 ⊠ &M

**GARDINER — YOGI BEAR'S JELLYSTONE PARK AT LAZY
RIVER.** (845) 255-5193. **$42-$70.** 50 Bevier Rd 12525. From Jct
of US-44/55 & SR-32, W 4 mi on US-44/55 to Albany Post Rd, S
0.2 mi (across bridge) to Bevier Rd, E 0.5 mi (L) 🏊 ⊠ &M

**GREENFIELD PARK — SKYWAY CAMPING RESORT
INC.** (800) 447-5992. **$65.** 99 Mountaindale Rd. 12435. From Jct
of SR-52 & US-209 (in Ellenville), W 5 mi on SR-52 to Mountain-
dale Rd., SW 1.2 mi (L) 🏊 ⊠ &M

**HENDERSON — KOA 1000 ISLANDS AT ASSOCIATION
ISLAND.** (800) 393-4189. **$35-$75.** 15530 Snowshoe Rd 13650.
From Jct of I-81 & Rt 178 (Exit 41), W 9 mi on Rt 178 to Snow-
shoe Rd, NW 2.5 mi to end, cross causeway to island (E) CAU-
TION: Registration and security gate closed at 8:30pm.
🏊 ⊠ &M

LAKE GEORGE — LAKE GEORGE RV PARK. 🆎 (518)
792-3775. **$55-$77.** 74 SR-149 12845. From Jct of I-87 & US-9
(exit 20), N 0.5 mi on US-9 to SR-149, E 0.5 mi (R)
🏕 🏊 ⊠ &M

LOCKPORT — NIAGARA'S LAZY LAKES. (800) 874-2957.
$55. 4312 Church Road 14094. From Jct of SR-104 & SR-425, W
2 mi on SR-104 to Church Rd, N 1000 ft (L). 🏕 🏊 ⊠ &M

**NORTH HUDSON — YOGI BEAR'S JELLYSTONE PARK
AT PARADISE PINES CAMPING RESORT.** (518) 532-7493. **$57-
$59.** 4035 Blue Ridge Rd 12855. From Jct of I-87 & Blue Ridge
Rd (exit 29), E 0.1 mi on Blue Ridge Rd (L) 🏊 ⊠

RHINEBECK — INTERLAKE RV PARK & SALES. (845) 266-
5387. **$47-$55.** 428 Lake Dr 12572. From Jct of US 9 & SR-9G (N
of town), S 3.5 mi on SR-9G to Slate Quarry Rd (CR-19), E 3.5 mi
on CR-19 to Lake Dr, S 0.3 mi (L) 🏊 ⊠

STOW — CAMP CHAUTAUQUA CAMPING RESORT. (716)
789-3435. **$35-$65.** 3900 W. Lake Rd 14785. From Jct of I-86/
SR-17 & SR-394 (exit 8), N 2 mi on SR-394 (R) 🏊 ⊠ &M

VERONA — THE VILLAGES AT TURNING STONE. (315)
361-7275. **$40-$55.** 5065 SR 65 13478. From Jct of I-90 (exit 33)
& SR-365, W 1 mi on SR-365 (R) 🏕 🏊 ⊠ &M

WILMINGTON — NORTH POLE CAMPGROUND & INN.
🆎 (518) 946-7733. **$44.** 5644 Rte 86 12997. N-bnd: From Jct of
I-87 & SR-73 (Exit 30), NW 16 mi on SR-73 to SR-9N, 10 mi N on
SR-9N to SR-86, W 5 mi on SR-86 to Jct 431, continue on SR-86
W 0.2 mi (L); or S-bnd: From Jct of I-87 & SR-9N (Exit 34), S 16
mi on SR-9N to SR-86, W 5 mi on SR-86 to Jct 431, continue on
SR-86 W 0.2 mi (L) 🏊 ⊠

North Carolina

ASHEBORO — ZOOLAND FAMILY CAMPGROUND, LLC. (336) 381-3422. **$31-$34.** 3671 Pisgah Covered Bridge Rd 27205. From Jct of US 64 & US 220 (Bypass), S 4.7 mi on US 220 (Bypass) to exit 51 (Ulah-Troy), W 1.2 mi on Dawson-Miller Rd to Pisgah Covered Bridge Rd, SW 1.4 mi (L) 〰️ ⊠ 🅼

ASHEVILLE — ASHEVILLE BEAR CREEK RV PARK. ⓐⓐⓐ (800) 833-0798. **$40-$48.** 81 S Bear Creek Rd 28806. W-bnd: From Jct of I-40 & NC-191 (exit 47), cross NC-191 to S Bear Creek Rd, W 0.6 mi (L); or E-bnd: From Jct of I-40 & NC-191 (exit 47), N 0.1 mi on NC-191 to S Bear Creek Rd, W 0.6 mi (L); or From Jct of I-26 & NC-191 (exit 33), N 2.1 mi on NC-191 to S Bear Creek Rd, W 0.6 mi (L) 🅰️ 〰️ ⊠

CANDLER — ASHEVILLE-WEST KOA. (800) 562-9015. **$35-$43.** 309 Wiggins Rd 28715. From Jct of I-40 & US-19/23 (exit 37), S 200 ft on unmarked rd to US-19/23, W 0.4 mi to Wiggins Rd, N 0.2 mi (R) 〰️ ⊠ 🅼

CEDAR MOUNTAIN — BLACK FOREST FAMILY CAMPING RESORT. (828) 884-2267. **$32-$41.** 100 Summer Rd 28718. N-bnd: From Jct of I-85 & Exit 48/Hwy 276, NW 36.3 mi on Hwy 276 to Caesars Head St Pk, con't 3 mi to Summer Rd, E 0.4 mi (R); or S-bnd: From Jct of US-64 & US-276 (in downtown Brevard), SE 12.6 mi on US-276 to Summer Rd, E 0.4 mi (R) 〰️ ⊠ 🅼

CHARLOTTE — CAROWINDS CAMP WILDERNESS RESORT. (704) 587-9116. **$40-$60.** 14523 Carowinds Blvd 28273. From Jct of I-77 & Exit 90 (NC/SC Border), W 1 mi to Catawba Trace, N 0.1 mi (L) 〰️ ⊠ 🅼

CHEROKEE — HAPPY HOLIDAY CAMPGROUND. (828) 497-9204. **$37-$47.** 1553 Wolfetown Rd (US-19) 28719. From W Jct of US 74 & US 441N, N 3.8 mi on US 441N to Bus-441N, NE 0.8 mi to US 19N, N 3.3 mi (L); or From Jct of Blue Ridge Pkwy (MP-455.5) & US 19, SW 7.6 mi on US 19S (R) 〰️ ⊠ 🅼

CHEROKEE — YOGI IN THE SMOKIES. ⓐⓐⓐ (828) 497-9151. **$43-$64.** 317 Galamore Bridge Rd 28719. From W Jct of US-19 & US-441, N 2.2 mi on US-441 to Big Cove Rd, NE 7.7 mi (R) 〰️ ⊠

EMERALD ISLE — HOLIDAY TRAV-L-PARK RESORT FOR CAMPERS. (252) 354-2250. **$50-$100.** 9102 Coast Guard Rd 28594. From Jct of NC-24 & NC-58, S 2 mi on NC-58 to Coast Guard Rd (traffic light), S 200 ft (L) 〰️ ⊠ 🅼

FLAT ROCK — LAKEWOOD RV RESORT. (888) 819-4200. **$35-$39.** 15 Timmie Lane 28731. From Jct of I-26 & Upward Rd (exit 53), E 0.2 mi on Upward Rd (unmarked) to Ballenger Rd, NE 0.2 mi (R) 🅰️ 〰️ ⊠

FLETCHER — RUTLEDGE LAKE RV RESORT. (828) 654-7873. **$39-$60.** 170 Rutledge Rd 28732. From Jct of I-26 & NC-280 (exit 40), E 1 mi on NC-280 (Airport Rd) to Rutledge Rd, S 1 mi (L) 〰️ ⊠ 🅼

FRANKLIN — THE GREAT OUTDOORS RV RESORT. (828) 349-0412. **$37-$40.** 321 Thumpers Trail 28734. N-bnd: From Jct of US 64 & US 441/23, N 6.2 mi on US 441 to Echo Valley Rd, W 200 ft (R); or S-bnd: From Jct of US 74 & US 23/441 (Exit 81A), S 13.8 mi on US 23/441 to Echo Valley Rd, W 200 ft (R) 🅰️ 〰️ ⊠ 🅼

HENDERSONVILLE — JAYMAR TRAVEL PARK. (828) 685-3771. **$28-$33. (no credit cards).** 140 Jaymar Park Dr 28792. From Jct of I-26 & US-64 (exit 49A), E 2.7 mi on US-64 (L) 🅰️ ⊠

LAKE TOXAWAY — BLUERIDGE MOUNTAINS MOTOR COACH RESORT. (828) 966-9350. **$50-$65.** 20 Resorts Blvd 28747. E-bnd: From Jct of US-64 & NC-281 (S), E 1.9 mi on US-64 (R); or W-bnd: From Jct of US-64 & NC-281, W 0.8 mi on US-64 (L) 🅰️ 〰️ ⊠ 🅼

LUMBERTON — SLEEPY BEAR'S RV PARK. (910) 739-4372. **$33-$35.** 465 Kenric Rd 28360. From Jct of I-95 & US-72 (Exit 17) W 0.3 mi on US-72 to Kenric Dr. S 3 mi (R) 〰️ ⊠ 🅼

NEW BERN — NEW BERN KOA. (800) 562-3341. **$40-$75.** 1565 B St 28560. N-bnd: From SE Jct of US 70 & US 17 (exit 417), N 4.8 mi on US 17 (toward Washington) (L) 〰️ ⊠ 🅼

NEWPORT — GOOSE CREEK RESORT. (252) 393-2628. **$57-$67.** 350 Red Barn Rd 28570. From Jct of NC-58 & NC-24, E 4 mi on NC-24 to Red Barn Rd, S 0.6 mi (R) 〰️ ⊠ 🅼

NEWPORT — WHISPERING PINES RV PARK. (252) 726-4902. **$50.** 25 Whispering Pines 28570. From jct US 70 & Hwy 24: Go 8 mi W on Hwy 24. 🅰️ 〰️ ⊠ 🅼

ROANOKE RAPIDS — THE RV RESORT AT CAROLINA CROSSROADS. (252) 538-9776. **$25-$43.** 415 Wallace Fork Road 27870. From Jct of I-95 & Hwy 125 (exit 171), S 0.2 mi on Hwy 125 to Carolina Crossroads Blvd, (main entrance to Carolina Crossroads), N 0.9 mi (R) 🅰️ 〰️ ⊠ 🅼

RODANTHE — OCEAN WAVES CAMPGROUND. (252) 987-2556. **$40-$44.** 25313 Hwy 12 27982. S-bnd: From Jct of US-158/164/264 & NC-12, S 25.3 mi on NC-12, in Waves (L); or N-bnd: From Ocracoke/Hatteras Ferry, N 33.8 mi on NC-12 (R) 〰️ ⊠ 🅼

SHAWBORO — NORTH RIVER CAMPGROUND. (252) 336-4414. **$40.** 256 Garrington Island Rd 27973. From Jct of NC 168 & NC 34, SW 3.5 mi on SC 34 to Indian Town Rd, S 8.2 to Garrington Island Rd, E 1.5 mi (R) 〰️ ⊠ 🅼

SHERRILLS FORD — LAKE NORMAN RV RESORT. (877) 489-6033. **$40-$65.** 6738 East NC Hwy 150 28673. E-bnd: From Jct of I-85 & US 321 (Exit 17), N 14 mi on US 321 to NC 150 (Exit 24 Lincolnton), E 14 mi on NC 150 (L); or W-bnd: From Jct of I-77 & NC-150 (exit 36) W 10.3 mi on NC-150 (R) 🅰️ ⊠ 🅼

STATESVILLE — STATESVILLE EAST/I-40/WINSTON-SALEM KOA. (800) 562-8651. **$39-$49.** 114 Midway Dr 28625. E-bnd: From Jct of I-77 & I-40, E 9.6 mi on I-40 to Exit 162/Cool Springs/ US-64, W (right) 0.1 mi on US-64 to Campground Rd, E (left) 0.2 mi (L); or W-bnd: From Jct of I-40 & Exit 162/Cool Springs/US-64, W (left) 0.2 mi on US-64 to Campground Rd, E (left) 0.2 mi (L) 〰️ ⊠

STELLA — WHITE OAK SHORES CAMPING & RV RESORT. (252) 393-3244. **$50-$70.** 400 Wetherington Landing Rd 28582. From Jct of NC 24 & NC 58, NW 8.5 mi on NC 58 to Morristown Rd, S 1 mi to Wetherington Landing Rd, N 0.7 mi (L) 〰️ ⊠ 🅼

SUNSET BEACH — BRUNSWICK BEACHES CAMPING RESORT. (888) 562-4240. **$45-$60.** 7200 KOA Dr 28468. From Jct of NC 17 & NC 904, E 0.7 mi on NC 904 (R) 🛶 ⊠ 🔥M

TABOR CITY — YOGI BEARS JELLYSTONE PARK AT DADDY JOE'S. (877) 668-8586. **$28-$65.** 626 Richard Wright Rd 28463. From Jct of SC-9 & US 701, N 5.8 mi on US 701 (Bypass) to Richard Wright Rd, E 0.3 mi (R); or S-bnd: From Jct of I-95 & NC-74 (exit 14), E 26 mi on NC-74 to NC-410, SE 15 mi to NC-701, S 0.5 mi to Richard Wright Rd, E 0.3 mi (R) 🛶 ⊠ 🔥M

WADE — FAYETTEVILLE RV RESORT. (910) 484-5500. **$46-$54.** 6250 Wade-Stedman Rd 28395. From Jct of I-95 & Exit 61 (Wade-Stedman Rd), E 0.3 mi on Wade-Stedman Rd (L) 🛶 ⊠ 🔥M

WAVES — CAMP HATTERAS. (252) 987-2777. **$43-$98.** 24798 Hwy 12, Mile Post 40.5 27968. S-bnd: From Jct of US-158/64/264 & NC-12, S 24.7 mi on NC-12 (L); or N-bnd: From Jct of Ocracoke/Hatteras Ferry & NC-12, N 34.3 mi on NC-12 (R) (Mile Post 40.5) 🛶 ⊠ 🔥M

WILMINGTON — WILMINGTON KOA. (888) 562-5699. **$49-$95.** 7415 Market St 28411. From Jct of I-40 & Hwy 17 (exit 416B), E 4.8 mi on Hwy 17 to 17 Bus South, S 2.3 mi (R) 🛶 ⊠

North Dakota

BISMARCK — BISMARCK KOA KAMPGROUND. (701) 222-2662. **$39-$49.** 3720 Centennial Rd 58503. From Jct of I-94 & Bismarck Expressway (exit 161): Go 1 mi N on Centennial Rd (L) 🛶 ⊠

Ohio

BROOKVILLE — DAYTON TALL TIMBERS RESORT KOA. (800) 562-3317. **$45-$58.** 7796 Wellbaum Rd 45309. W-bnd: From W Jct of I-70 & SR-49 (Exit 24), N 0.5 mi on SR-49 to Pleasant Plain Rd, W 0.6 mi to Welbaum Rd, S 0.2 mi (L); or E-bnd: From Jct of I-70 & Brookville/Salem Rd (Exit 24), SW 0.3 mi on Brookville/Salem Rd to Welbaum Rd, N 0.3 mi (R) 🛶 ⊠

DELAWARE — CROSS CREEK CAMPING RESORT. ⓐⓐⓐ (740) 549-2267. **$31-$60.** 3190 S Old State Rd 43015. From Jct of I-71 (Exit 131) & SR-36/37: Go 3 mi W on SR-36/37, then 3 mi S on Lackey (Old State Rd). 🛶 ⊠ 🔥M

DUNDEE — EVERGREEN PARK R.V. RESORT. (888) 359-6429. **$50.** 16359 Dover Rd 44624. E-bnd: From Jct of US-250 & SR 241, S 0.4 mi on US-250 (R); or From Jct of I-77 & US-250, NW 12.6 mi on US-250 (L) 🛶 ⊠ 🔥M

EAST SPARTA — BEAR CREEK RESORT RANCH KOA. (330) 484-3901. **$37-$53.** 3232 Downing St SW 44626. S-bnd: From Jct of I-77 & Fohl Rd (Exit 99), W 0.5 mi on Fohl Rd to Sherman Church Ave SW, S 2.4 mi to Haut St, E 1.2 mi (R); or N-bnd: From Jct of I-77 & Zoar Bolivar Rd (Exit 93), W 0.1 mi to CR-102, N 3 mi to Haut St, E 1 mi (R) 🛶 ⊠ 🔥M

GRANVILLE — LAZY RIVER AT GRANVILLE. ⓐⓐⓐ (740) 366-4385. **$28-$51.** 2340 Dry Creek Rd NE 43023. From Jct of I-70 & SR-37 (exit 126), N 8 mi on SR-37 to SR-661 (Granville), N 4.5 mi to Dry Creek Rd, E 1.2 mi (R) 🛶 ⊠ 🔥M

LISBON — LOCK 30 WOODLANDS RV RESORT CAMPGROUND. (877) 856-2530. **$28-$45.** 45529 Middle Beaver Rd 44432. From Jct of Hwy 11 & Hwy 154, E 1.5 mi on Hwy 154 to CR-419, E 3.5 mi (R) 🛶 ⊠ 🔥M

LOUISVILLE — CUTTY'S SUNSET CAMPING RESORT. (800) 533-7965. **$31-$38.** 8050 Edison St NE 44641. From Jct of I-77 & US-62 (exit 107B), E 7.4 mi on US-62 to SR-44, N 6.4 mi to SR-619, E 0.3 mi (R) 🛶 ⊠ 🔥M

SANDUSKY — SANDUSKY/BAYSHORE ESTATES KOA. (800) 962-3786. **$29-$67.** 2311 Cleveland Rd E 44870. From Jct of I-80/I-90 & US-250 (exit 7), N 10 mi on US-250 to US-6, E 1.8 mi to Shoreway Rd, N 0.1 mi (R) 🛶 ⊠ 🔥M

SEVILLE — MAPLE LAKES RECREATIONAL PARK. (330) 336-2251. **$41.** 4275 Blake Rd 44273. From Jct of I-76 & SR-3 (exit 2), N 0.9 mi on SR-3 to Blake Rd, E 1 mi (L) 🛶 ⊠

SHELBY — SHELBY-MANSFIELD KOA. (888) 562-5607. **$35-$77.** 6787 Baker 47 44875. From Jct of SR-96 & SR-39 (on west side of town), W 2 mi on SR-39 to Baker 47, N 4.5 mi (R) 🛶 ⊠ 🔥M

WAPAKONETA — WAPAKONETA KOA. (419) 738-6016. **$40-$60.** 14719 Cemetery Rd 45895. S-Bnd: From Jct of I-75 & Bellefontaine Rd (Exit 111), E 0.3 mi on Bellefontaine Rd to CR-161 (Cemetery Rd), N 0.5 mi (L); N-Bnd: From Jct of I-75 & US 33 (Exit 110), E 0.1 mi on US 33 to CR-161 (Cemetery Rd), N 0.8 mi (L) 🛶 ⊠ 🔥M

ZANESVILLE — WOLFIES CAMPGROUND. ⓐⓐⓐ (740) 454-0925. **$29-$35.** 101 Buckeye Dr 43701. From Jct of I-70 & SR-146 W (Exit 155, Eastbound must turn east at bottom of the ramp onto Elberon), W 0.25 mi on SR-146, N 0.75 mi on OH-666, N 0.75 mi on Lewis Dr (OH-666), first right past "Riverside Park," (Buckeye Dr), E 0.2 mi on Buckeye Dr (L) 🛶 ⊠

Oklahoma

CHOCTAW — OKLAHOMA CITY EAST KOA. (800) 562-5076. **$35-$45.** 6200 S Choctaw Rd 73020. From Jct of I-40 & Choctaw Rd (exit 166), N 0.5 mi on Choctaw Rd (R) 🛶 ⊠ 🔥M

DURANT — CHOCTAW KOA RV PARK. (800) 562-6073. **$30-$50.** 3650 Enterprise Blvd. 74701. From Jct of US-70 & US-69, S 3.5 mi on US-69 to Choctaw Road, E 0.2 mi to Enterprise Dr, N 0.1 mi (R) 🏕 🛶 ⊠ 🔥M

THACKERVILLE — WINSTAR RV PARK. (580) 276-8900. **$25.** 21902 Merle Wolfe Rd 73459. From Jct of I-35 & Exit 1 to Casino Blvd, E 1.2 mi on Casino Blvd to Merle Wolfe Rd, E 0.5 mi (L) 🛶 ⊠ 🔥M

Oregon

ALBANY — BLUE OX RV PARK. (541) 926-2886. **$34-$37.** 4000 Blue Ox Dr SE 97322. From Jct of I-5 & Hwy 20 (exit 233), E 0.2 mi on Hwy 20 to Price Rd, N 0.1 mi (R) (Note: Use address for GPS units) 🏕 🛶 🔥M

BEND — BEND/SISTERS GARDEN RV RESORT. (888) 503-3588. **$40-$60.** 67667 Hwy 20 97701. From Jct of US-20 & Hwy 126 (E edge of Sisters), SE 4 mi on US-20 (R) 🏕 🛶 ⊠ 🔥M

BEND — **CROWN VILLA RV RESORT.** (541) 388-1131. **$35-$70.** 60801 Brosterhous Rd 97702. N-bnd & S-bnd: From Jct of Business-97/3rd St & Murphy Rd (S of town), E 1.2 mi on Murphy Rd to Brosterhous Rd, S 0.1 mi (R) 🅰 ⊠ 🅼

CANYONVILLE — **SEVEN FEATHERS RV RESORT.** ⒶⒶⒶ (877) 839-3599. **$39-$47.** 325 Quintioosa Blvd 97417. S-Bnd: From Jct of I-5 (exit 99) to Quintioosa Blvd (R); N-Bnd: From Jct of I-5 & exit 99, N on Frontage Rd, under freeway 0.2 mi to Quintioosa Blvd (L) 🅰 ⇴ ⊠ 🅼

COBURG — **PREMIER RV RESORT - EUGENE.** (888) 710-8451. **$40-$45.** 33022 Van Duyn Rd 97408. From Jct of I-5 & Van Duyn Rd (Coburg exit 199), E 300 ft on Van Duyn Rd (R) 🅰 ⇴ ⊠ 🅼

COOS BAY — **AAA MIDWAY RV PARK.** (541) 888-9300. **$30-$60.** 92478 Cape Arago Hwy 97420. From Jct of US 101 & Newmark (at casino), W 2.9 mi on Newmark to Empire (Cape Arago Hwy), S 1.2 mi (L) 🅰 ⊠ 🅼

DAYTON — **WILLAMETTE WINE COUNTRY RV PARK.** (503) 864-2233. **$32.** 16205 SE Kreder Rd 97114. From Jct of US-99W & Hwy 18/SE Dayton Bypass, SW 0.9 mi on Hwy 18 (L) 🅰 ⇴ ⊠ 🅼

FAIRVIEW — **PORTLAND FAIRVIEW RV PARK.** (877) 777-1047. **$40.** 21401 NE Sandy Blvd 97024. From Jct of I-84 & 207th Ave N (exit 14), N 0.1 mi on 207th Ave to NE Sandy Blvd, E 0.3 mi (L) 🅰 ⇴ ⊠

FLORENCE — **PACIFIC PINES RV PARK.** (541) 997-1434. **$30-$33.** 4044 Hwy 101-At 42nd St 97439. From Jct of US-101 & Hwy 126 (in town), N 2 mi on US-101 to 42nd St, E 0.1 mi (R) 🅰 ⊠ 🅼

GRANTS PASS — **BRIDGEVIEW RV RESORT.** ⒶⒶⒶ (541) 582-5980. **$34-$40.** 8880 Rogue River Hwy 97527. From Jct of I-5 & exit 48, SW across river, 0.2 mi to Hwy 99, NW 500 ft (R) 🅰 ⊠ 🅼

GRANTS PASS — **RIVERPARK RV RESORT.** ⒶⒶⒶ (541) 479-0046. **$33-$40.** 2956 Rogue River Hwy 97527. From Jct of I-5 & US-199 (Grants Pass exit 55), W 1.8 mi on US-199 to Parkdale Dr, S (left) 0.3 mi to Rogue River Hwy, E 1.9 mi (L); or E-bnd: From Jct of Hwys 199 & 99 (Rogue River Hwy/Medford South), E 2.5 mi on Rogue River Hwy (L)

HARRISBURG — **RIVER BEND RESORT.** (541) 995-9995. **$29-$35.** 23650 Peoria Rd 97446. From Jct of Hwy 99 & Peoria Rd (N of town), N 0.5 mi on Peoria Rd (L) 🅰 ⇴

LA GRANDE — **EAGLES HOT LAKE RV PARK.** ⒶⒶⒶ (541) 963-5253. **$34.** 65182 Hot Lake Ln 97850. From Jct of I-84 & Hwy 203 (exit 265), SE 4.5 mi on Hwy 203 to Hot Lake Ln, W 0.3 mi (L) ⇴ ⊠ 🅼

LEBANON — **MALLARD CREEK GOLF & RV RESORT.** (866) 632-9133. **$43.** 31958 Bellinger Scale Rd 97355. From the Jct of Hwy 20 & Waterloo Rd 4.5 mi E (SW of Lebanon), NE 2.3 mi on Waterloo Rd to Berlin Rd, E 0.3 mi to Bellinger Scale Rd, N 0.4 mi (L) 🅰 ⊠ 🅼

LINCOLN CITY — **DEVILS LAKE RV PARK.** ⒶⒶⒶ (541) 994-3400. **$35-$38.** 4041 NE West Devils Lake Rd 97367. N-bnd: From Jct of Hwy 101 & W Devils Lake Rd (N of town), E (R) 0.2 mi on W Devils Lake Rd (R); or S-bnd: From Jct of Hwy 101 & W Devils Lake Rd (1st light in town), E (L) 0.2 mi on W Devils Lake Rd (R) ⊠ 🅼

LINCOLN CITY — **PREMIER RV RESORTS-LINCOLN CITY.** (877) 871-0663. **$42-$44.** 4100 SE Hwy 101 97367. N-Bnd: From Jct of Hwy 101 & 51st St (S of town), N 0.2 mi on Hwy 101 (R); or S-Bnd: From Jct of Hwy 101 & E Devils Lake Rd (outlet mall), S 2.5 mi on Hwy 101 (L) 🅰 ⊠ 🅼

MCMINNVILLE — **OLDE STONE VILLAGE RV PARK.** (877) 472-4315. **$31.** 4155 NE Three Mile Ln 97128. From Jct of Hwy 99W & E Hwy 18 bypass (S of McMinnville), NE 4.2 mi on Hwy 18 bypass to MP-48.25 (L) 🅰 ⇴ ⊠ 🅼

PACIFIC CITY — **CAPE KIWANDA RV RESORT & MARKET PLACE.** (503) 965-6230. **$35-$47.** 33305 Cape Kiwanda Dr 97135. From Jct of US-101 & Brooten Rd Pacific City Jct (MP-90.3 N of Lincoln City), NW 3 mi on Brooten Rd to Pacific Ave (blinking light in town), W 0.2 mi to Kiwanda Dr, N 1 mi (R). Note: Some GPS require Cloverdale, OR as city ⇴ ⊠ 🅼

SALEM — **HEE HEE ILLAHEE RV RESORT.** (877) 564-7295. **$34-$36.** 4751 Astoria Street N.E. 97305. From Jct of I-5 (Exit 258) & Hwy 99E (Portland Rd), N 0.25 mi on Hwy 99E (Portland Rd) to Astoria St, NW 0.25 mi (L) 🅰 ⇴ ⊠

SALEM — **PHOENIX RV PARK.** ⒶⒶⒶ (503) 581-2497. **$36-$40.** 4130 Silverton Rd NE 97305. S-bnd: From Jct of I-5 & Market St (Exit 256), N 0.1 mi on off ramp to Market St, E 0.3 mi to Lancaster Dr, N 1.5 mi to Silverton Rd, E 0.1 mi (R); or N-bnd: From Jct of I-5 & Market St (exit 256), E 0.3 mi on Market to Landcaster, N 1.5 mi, to Silverton Rd, E 0.1 mi (R) 🅰 ⊠ 🅼

SALEM — **PREMIER RV RESORTS SALEM.** (877) 364-9990. **$38-$48.** 4700 Salem-Dallas Hwy 22 97304. S-bnd: From Jct of I-5 & Exit 260 A/Salem Pkwy, SW 4.7 mi on Salem Pkwy to Hwy 22W (Marion St Bridge), W 4.7 mi (L); N-bnd: From Jct I-5 & Commercial St (Exit 249), NW 6.4 mi on Commercial to Front/Ferry St bypass, W .4 mi to onramp (Marion St Bridge) Hwy 22W, W 4.7 mi on Hwy 22W (L) ⇴ ⊠ 🅼

TROUTDALE — **SANDY RIVERFRONT RV RESORT, LLC.** (503) 665-6722. **$33-$37.** 1097 E Historic Columbia River Hwy 97060. From Jct of I-84 & Exit 17, E 0.3 mi on Frontage Rd to Graham (Loves), S 0.3 mi to Historic Columbia River Hwy, E & S 0.6 mi (L) 🅰 ⊠ 🅼

WESTFIR — **CASEY'S RIVERSIDE RV PARK.** (541) 782-1906. **$38.** 46443 Westfir Rd 97492. E-bnd: From Jct of I-5 & Hwy 58 (exit 188A), E 31.3 mi on Hwy 58 to Westfir Rd (Old Willamette Hwy), SE (left turn) 0.4 mi (L); or W-bnd: From Jct of Hwy 97 & Hwy 58, W 55 mi on Hwy 58 to Westfir Rd, at MP-31 1/4, NE 0.4 mi (L) 🅰 ⇴ ⊠ 🅼

WILSONVILLE — **PHEASANT RIDGE RV RESORT.** ⒶⒶⒶ (503) 682-7829. **$39-$43.** 8275 SW Elligsen Rd 97070. From Jct of I-5 & SW Elligsen Rd/N Wilsonville (exit 286), E 0.5 mi on SW Elligsen Rd (L) 🅰 ⇴ ⊠ 🅼

YACHATS — SEA PERCH RV RESORT. (541) 547-3505. **$50-$80.** 95480 Hwy 101 S - MP 171 97498. From Jct of US 101 & Hwy 126 (in Florence), N 17 mi on US 101 at MP-171, 8 mi N of Sea Lion Caves (L) 🏕️ 🚫 ⑤M

Pennsylvania

BEDFORD — FRIENDSHIP VILLAGE CAMPGROUND & RV PARK. 🅐🅐🅐 (814) 623-1677. **$30-$43.** 348 Friendship Village Rd 15522. From Jct I-76 & US-220 (exit 146): Go N 300 yds on Bus. US-220, then S 1-1/2 mi on US-220, then NW 1-1/2 mi on US-30, then NE 1/2 mi on Friendship Village Rd. (E) �'sup' 🚫 ⑤M

BELLEFONTE — BELLEFONTE/STATE COLLEGE KOA. (800) 562-8127. **$30-$65.** 2481 Jacksonville Rd 16823. From Jct of I-80 & SR-26 (exit 161), N 2.4 mi on SR-26 (L) �'sup' 🚫

CHARLEROI — PINE COVE BEACH CLUB & RV RESORT. (724) 239-2900. **$40-$50.** 1495 State Rte 481 15022. From Jct of I-70 & Rte 481 (Exit 35): Go N 1/4 mi on Rte 481 (L) 🏕️ �'sup' 🚫 ⑤M

CORRY — HARECREEK CAMPGROUND. (814) 664-9684. **$30.** 375 Sciota St 16407. From Jct of US-6 & SR-426, E 0.6 mi on US-6 to Sciota St, S 0.3 mi (R) �'sup' 🚫

EAST STROUDSBURG — MOUNTAIN VISTA CAMP-GROUND. (570) 223-0111. **$40-$58.** 415 Taylor Drive 18301. From I-80 & US-209 (Exit 309), Go N 3 mi on US-209/Seven Bridges Rd N, then enter roundabout, take 2nd exit (follow signs for Bus US-209 to Marshalls Creek), then N 1/2 mi on SR-1019/Seven Bridges Rd N, then W 1/2 mi on Bus US-209, then N 1 mi on Craigs Meadow Rd, then W 1/2 block on Taylor Dr (R) �'sup' 🚫

EAST STROUDSBURG — OTTER LAKE CAMP-RESORT. 🅐🅐🅐 (570) 223-0123. **$36-$68.** 1639 Marshalls Creek Rd 18302. From Jct of I-80 & US-209 (Exit 309), NE 3.9 mi on US-209 to SR-402, N 300 ft to Marshalls Creek Rd, NW 7.4 mi (L) �'sup' 🚫

ELIZABETHTOWN — ELIZABETHTOWN/HERSHEY KOA. 🅐🅐🅐 (800) 562-4774. **$46-$74.** 1980 Turnpike Rd 17022. From Jct SR-283 & SR-743 (Elizabethtown/Hershey exit), go S 1 1/2 mi on SR-743 to SR-230 (Market St), then E 1/2 mi to High St W, then W 1/2 mi to Turnpike Rd, right 2.3 mi (L) �'sup' 🚫 ⑤M

EMLENTON — GASLIGHT CAMPGROUND. (724) 867-6981. **$34-$40.** 6297 Emlenton Clintonville Rd 16373. From Jct of I-80 & SR-38 (exit 42), N 0.1 mi on SR-38 to SR-208, W 0.3 mi (R). �'sup' 🚫

GETTYSBURG — DRUMMER BOY CAMPING RESORT. (800) 293-2808. **$49-$66.** 1300 Hanover Rd 17325. From Jct of US-15 bypass & SR-116, E 150 ft on SR-116 (L) �'sup' 🚫 ⑤M

GETTYSBURG — GETTYSBURG CAMPGROUND. 🅐🅐🅐 (717) 334-3304. **$37-$56.** 2030 Fairfield Rd 17325. From Jct of US-30 & Bus US-15 S (Lincoln Square) (in town), S 1 blk on Bus US-15 to SR-116 (Middle St), go W 3 mi (L) �'sup' 🚫

HARRISVILLE — JELLYSTONE PARK AT KOZY REST. (724) 735-2417. **$35-$57.** 449 Campground Rd 16038. From Jct of I-80 & SR-8 (exit 29), S 5 mi on SR-8 to SR-58, E 0.4 mi to Campground Rd, N 2 mi (L); or From Jct of I-79 & SR-208 (exit 113), E 3.9 mi on SR-208 to SR-58, SE 4.8 mi to Campground Rd, N 2 mi (L) �'sup' 🚫 ⑤M

HUMMELSTOWN — HERSHEY HIGHMEADOW CAMP-GROUND. (800) 437-7439. **$33-$57.** 1200 Matlack Rd 17036. E-bnd: From Jct of US-322/422 & SR-39W (Hershey Park Dr), N 0.5 mi on SR-39W (Hershey Park Dr) (L); or W-bnd: From Jct of I-81 & SR-39E (exit 77), W 6.1 mi on SR-39E to Hershey Park Dr, W 1 mi (R) �'sup' 🚫 ⑤M

LEBANON (LEBANON COUNTY) — HERSHEY - THOUSAND TRAILS PRESERVE. (800) 405-6188. **$53.** 493 South Mt. Pleasant Rd 17042. From jct of I-76 (PA turnpike) & Exit 266 (Route 72): Go N on Route 72 to Route 322 West, then turn left on Mount Pleasant Road. �'sup' 🚫 ⑤M

LEHIGHTON — STONEYBROOK CAMPGROUND. (570) 386-4088. **$40-$45.** 1435 Germans Rd 18235. From Jct of SR-309 & SR-895 (in Snyders, SW of Lehighton), NE 7.1 mi on SR-895 to Lauchnor Rd, S 1.5 mi to Germans Rd, NE 0.1 mi (R) 🏕️ �'sup' 🚫

LEWISTOWN — WATERSIDE CAMPGROUND & RV PARK. (717) 248-3974. **$36-$47.** 475 Locust Rd 17044. From Jct of US 22 & SR-103 (in Lewistown), WSW 2.4 mi on US 22/W 4th St to Loop Rd, ESE 1.9 mi on Loop Rd to Locust Rd, S 0.4 mi on Locust Rd (E) �'sup' 🚫 ⑤M

LOYSVILLE — PARADISE STREAM FAMILY CAMP-GROUND. (717) 789-2117. **$38-$47.** 693 Paradise Stream Rd 17047. From Jct of SR-850 & SR-274 (in Loysville), W 4.7 mi on SR-274 to Rte 3008 (Couchtown Rd), S 0.3 mi to Paradise Stream Rd, SW 0.5 mi (R). No GPS after Loysville �'sup' 🚫

MANHEIM — PINCH POND FAMILY CAMPGROUND. 🅐🅐🅐 (800) 659-7640. **$40-$45.** 3075 Pinch Rd 17545. From Jct of PA Tpke I-76 & SR-72 (Exit 266), S 1 mi on SR-72 to Cider Press Rd, W 0.5 mi to Pinch Rd, N 1 mi (R) �'sup' 🚫 ⑤M

MCKEAN — ERIE KOA KAMPGROUNDS. (800) 562-7610. **$40-$75.** 6645 West Rd 16426. From Jct of I-90 & SR-832 (Presque Isle Exit 18), S 1 mi on SR-832 to West Rd, E 0.5 mi (R); or From Jct of I-79 & West Rd (McKean Exit 174), W 1.5 mi on West Rd (L) �'sup' 🚫 ⑤M

MEADVILLE — MEADVILLE KOA. (814) 789-3251. **$33-$54.** 25164 Hwy 27 16335. From Jct of I-79 & US-6/19 (exit 147A), NE 1.6 mi on US 6/19 to Park Ave, N 0.6 mi on Park Ave to North St (SR 27), E 6 mi on SR 27 (L) �'sup' 🚫 ⑤M

MEXICO — BUTTONWOOD CAMPGROUND. (717) 436-8334. **$40-$57.** PO Box 223 17056. From Jct of US-22/322 & SR-75 (Port Royal exit), S 0.8 mi on SR-75 to Old US-22, E (left) 0.9 mi to Foster Rd, (bear right), 0.3 mi to River Rd., right 0.1 mi (R) �'sup' 🚫 ⑤M

MUNCY VALLEY — PIONEER CAMPGROUND. 🅐🅐🅐 (570) 946-9971. **$36-$44.** 307 Pioneer Trail 17758. From Jct of US 220 & SR-42 (in La Porte), S 2 mi on US 220 (R) �'sup' 🚫

NARVON — LAKE-IN-WOOD RESORT. (717) 445-5525. **$52-$65.** 576 Yellow Hill Rd 17555. From Jct of SR-23 & SR-625, N 4 1/2 mi on SR-625 to Oaklyn Dr, E 1 1/2 mi to Yellow Hill Rd, NE 1 1/2 mi (R) �'sup' 🚫 ⑤M

NEW TRIPOLI — ALLENTOWN-LEHIGH VALLEY KOA. (610) 298-2160. **$42-$53.** 6750 KOA Dr 18066. From Jct of PA Turnpike/I-476 & I-78/US-22, W 3 mi on I-78/US-22 to SR-100 (Exit 49B), N 6.5 mi on SR-100 to Narris Rd, W 0.5 mi (L) Do not use GPS. 🐾 ⊠ 🅰M

PINE GROVE — TWIN GROVE RESORT & CAMPGROUND. (800) 562-5471. **$35-$70.** 1445 Suedberg Rd 17963. From Jct of I-81 & SR-443 (Exit 100): Go W 4.9 mi on SR-443 (R) 🐾 ⊠ 🅰M

PORTERSVILLE — BEAR RUN CAMPGROUND. 🆔 (724) 368-3564. **$35-$57.** 184 Badger Hill Rd 16051. From Jct I-79 & SR-488 (exit 96): Go E 50 yds on SR-488, then N 1/2 mi on Badge Hill Rd. 🐾 ⊠

QUARRYVILLE — YOGI BEAR'S JELLYSTONE PARK/ LANCASTER SOUTH/QUARRYVILLE. (717) 786-3458. **$39-$113.** 340 Blackburn Rd 17566. From Jct of US-222 & SR-372, S 2.6 mi on US-222 to Blackburn Rd, E 1.5 mi (L) 🐾 ⊠ 🅰M

SOMERSET — PIONEER PARK CAMPGROUND. (814) 445-6348. **$37-$51.** 273 Trent Rd 15501. E-bnd: From Jct of PA Tpke I-70/76 Tpke exit Rd (Exit 110), E 0.3 mi on PA Tpke exit rd to SR-601, S 0.5 mi to SR-31, W 7 mi to Trent Rd, S 0.3 mi (R). W-bnd: From Jct of PA Tpke I-70/76 (Exit 91), E 12 mi SR-31, then 1/4 mi on Trent Rd (R) 🐾 ⊠ 🅰M

TOBYHANNA — HEMLOCK CAMPGROUND & COT-TAGES. (570) 894-4388. **$41-$46.** 559 Hemlock Dr 18466. From Jct of I-380 & SR-940 (Exit 3), NE 2.5 mi on SR-940 to SR-611, N 1.8 mi to Hemlock Dr, NE 0.2 mi (R) 🐾 ⊠

TRANSFER — SHENANGO VALLEY RV PARK. (724) 962-9800. **$42-$50.** 559 E Crestview Drive 16154. From Jct of I-80 & SR-18 (Exit 4B), N 13 mi on SR-18 to Reynolds Industrial Rd, E 1/2 mi to Crestview Dr, SE 1 mi on Crestview Dr, then stay left at Y on E Crestview for 1 mi to park entrance (L) 🐾 ⊠ 🅰M

WAYMART — KEEN LAKE CAMPING & COTTAGE RESORT. (800) 443-0412. **$40-$59.** 155 Keen Lake Rd 18472. From Jct of US-6 & SR-296, E 1.7 mi on US-6 (R) 🐾 ⊠ 🅰M

South Carolina

CHARLESTON — OAK PLANTATION CAMPGROUND, LP. (843) 766-5936. **$29-$36.** 3540 Savannah Hwy 29455. From W Jct of I-526 & US-17, S 4.4 mi on US-17 (R) or From Jct of I-95 & Hwy 17, N on Hwy 17 (N) 53 mi (L) (Do not take 17A) 🏊 🐾 ⊠ 🅰M

CROSS HILL — LAKE GREENWOOD RV RESORT & MARINA. (864) 992-4700. **$49-$59.** 463 Cane Creek Rd 29332. From Jct of SC-72 & SC-39, S 1.9 mi on SC-39 to Watts Bridge Rd, W 1.7 mi to Whiteford Rd, N 1.9 mi to Cane Creek Camp Rd, NW 0.4 mi (R). 🏊 🐾 ⊠

GAFFNEY — SPARTANBURG NORTHEAST/GAFFNEY KOA. (800) 562-0362. **$29-$44.** 160 Sarratt School Rd 29341. From Jct I-85 (exit 87) & Hwy 39: Go to I-85 N-Bnd on-ramp, take ramp 250 ft to Overbrook Dr, then E 1 mi on Overbrook Dr, then S 1/4 mi on Sarratt School Rd (R) 🐾 ⊠

HAMER — CAMP PEDRO. 🆔 (843) 774-2411. **$25.** 3346 Hwy 301N 29547. From Jct of I-95 & US 301 (Exit 1A in NC), S 0.1 mi on US 301 (L). Behind Rocket City 🏊 🐾 ⊠

HILTON HEAD ISLAND — HILTON HEAD HARBOR RV RESORT & MARINA. (843) 681-3256. **$49-$64.** 43-A Jenkins Rd 29926. From Jct of I-95 & US-278 (exit 8), E 19 mi on US-278 to Jenkins Rd, N 0.4 mi (L) 🏊 🐾 ⊠ 🅰M

HILTON HEAD ISLAND — HILTON HEAD ISLAND MOTORCOACH RESORT/OUTDOOR RESORTS. (800) 722-2365. **$60-$80.** 133 Arrow Rd 29928. From Jct of I-95 & US-278 (exit 8), E 20.4 mi on US-278 to Cross Island Expwy (toll road - becomes Palmetto Bay Rd), S 5.4 mi on Expwy to Target Rd, N 0.1 mi to Arrow Rd, E 500 ft (L) 🏊 🐾 ⊠ 🅰M

LONGS — WILLOWTREE RV RESORT & CAMPGROUND. (866) 207-2267. **$31-$93.** 520 Southern Sights Drive 29568. From Jct of SC-9 & SC-905, N 1.8 mi on SC-905 to Old Buck Creek Rd, N 1.5 mi (R) 🏊 🐾 ⊠ 🅰M

MOUNT PLEASANT — MT PLEASANT/CHARLESTON KOA. (800) 562-5796. **$40-$59.** 3157 Hwy 17 29466. From E Jct of I-526 & US-17 Exit 29 (N-bnd), NE 5 mi on US-17 (R) 🐾 ⊠ 🅰M

MYRTLE BEACH — BRIARCLIFFE RV RESORT. (843) 272-2730. **$47.** 10495 N Kings Hwy 29572. From Jct of US 501 & SC 22, E 28 mi on SC 22 to North Myrtle Beach Exit (US 17/N. Kings Hwy) N 1.2 mi (L) 🏊 🐾 ⊠

MYRTLE BEACH — CYPRESS CAMPING RESORT. (843) 293-0300. **$30-$58.** 101 Waterway Lane 29588. From the Jct of US-31 & US-544: Go 1 mi E on US-544, then 1/4 mi N on US-707, then 1/4 mi W on River Rd (L) 🐾 ⊠ 🅰M

MYRTLE BEACH — LAKEWOOD CAMPING RESORT. 🆔 (877) 525-3966. **$27-$75.** 5901 S Kings Hwy 29575. From Jct of US-501 & SC 544, SE 14.5 mi to Bus US-17, NE 0.4 mi (R) 🐾 ⊠ 🅰M

MYRTLE BEACH — MYRTLE BEACH TRAVEL PARK. 🆔 (800) 255-3568. **$37-$69.** 10108 Kings Rd 29572. From Jct of US-501 & SC 22, E 28 mi on SC 22 to Kings Rd Exit, E 0.6 mi (L) 🐾 ⊠ 🅰M

MYRTLE BEACH — MYRTLE BEACH KOA. (800) 562-7790. **$29-$76.** 613 5th Ave S 29577. From Jct of US-501 & US-17, E 1 mi on US-501 to 3rd Ave S, SE 1 mi to Bus US-17 (Kings Hwy), S 0.2 mi to 5th Ave S, NW 0.2 mi (L) 🐾 ⊠ 🅰M

MYRTLE BEACH — OCEAN LAKES FAMILY CAMP-GROUND. 🆔 (800) 341-6659. **$28-$71.** 6001 S Kings Hwy 29575. From Jct of US-501 & SC 544, SE 14.5 mi to Kings Hwy US 17 Bus (E) 🐾 ⊠ 🅰M

ROEBUCK — PINE RIDGE CAMPGROUND. (866) 576-0302. **$28.** 199 Pine Ridge Campground Rd 29376. From Jct of I-85 & I-26, SE 9.2 mi on I-26 to US 221 (exit 28), NE 0.2 mi to Stillhouse Rd., E 1 mi to Otts Shoals Rd (end of Stillhouse Rd), N (left) 1.5 mi on Otts Shoals Rd to Pine Ridge Campground Rd. (R) 🏊 🐾 ⊠

SWANSEA — YOGI BEAR'S JELLYSTONE PARK AT RIVER BOTTOM FARMS. (803) 568-4182. **$34.** 357 Cedar Creek Rd 29160. S-bnd: From Jct of I-77 & US 321 S (Exit 71), S 15 mi on US 321 to SC3, SW 6.5 mi on SC-3 to SC-178, NW 0.5 mi on 178 to Cedar Creek Rd, W 0.7 mi (L); N-bnd: From Jct of US-321 & SC 178 (S of Swansea), W 6.3 mi on SC 178 to Cedar Creek Rd, W 0.7 mi (L) 🛶 ✕ ⛽ᴹ

TOWNVILLE — LAKE HARTWELL CAMPING & CABINS. (888) 427-8935. **$27-$35.** 400 Ponderosa Point 29689. From Jct of I-85 & SC-24 (exit 11), NW 2.6 mi on SC-24 to O'Neal Ferry Rd, NE 0.3 mi to Ponderosa Point Rd, E 0.5 mi (E) 🛶 ✕

WEST UNION — CROOKED CREEK RV PARK. (864) 882-5040. **$30-$40.** 777 Arvee Ln 29696. S-bnd: From Jct of I-85/US 76/US 28 (exit 19B), W 21.4 mi on SC 28 to SC 188, NE 3.3 mi to Ebenezer Rd, NW 1.6 mi to Arvee Ln (R). Call for directions 🛶 ✕ ⛽ᴹ

South Dakota

ABERDEEN — WYLIE PARK & STORYBOOK LAND. (888) 326-9693. **$28-$29.** 2301 24th Ave NW 57401. From Jct US-12 & US-281: Go 2 1/4 mi N on US-281, then 1/4 mi W on Seratoma Pkwy (L) Don't rely on GPS - Call for directions ✕ ⛽ᴹ

BRANDON — SIOUX FALLS YOGI BEAR. (605) 332-2233. **$25-$51.** 26014 478th Ave 57005. From Jct of I-29 & I-90: Go 6 mi E on I-90 (Exit 402), then 1 block N on CR-121. (R) 🛶 ✕ ⛽ᴹ

CUSTER CITY — BEAVER LAKE CAMPGROUND. ⒶⒶⒶ (800) 346-4383. **$34-$38.** 12005 W Hwy 16 57730. From Jct of US 385 & US 16 (in town): Go 3.5 mi W on US 16 (L). Note: Call for directions 🛶 ✕ ⛽ᴹ

DEADWOOD — WHISTLER GULCH RV PARK & CAMP-GROUND. (800) 704-7139. **$35-$47.** 235 Cliff St (Hwy 85 S) 57732. From Jct of US 85 & US 14A, S 3 mi on US 85 (L); or From Jct of US 385 & US 85, E 0.5 mi on US 85 (R). Note: Don't use GPS - Call for directions 🛶 ✕ ⛽ᴹ

HILL CITY — CROOKED CREEK RESORT INC. ⒶⒶⒶ (800) 252-8486. **$27-$48.** 24184 Hwy 16 57745. From south city limit of Hill City: Go 2 mi S on US-16/385 (L) 🛶 ✕

HILL CITY — MT RUSHMORE KOA. (800) 562-8503. **$44-$67.** 12620 Hwy 244 57745. From south city limits of Hill City: Go 2 1/2 mi S on US-16/385, then 3 mi E on SR-244 (L) 🛶 ✕ ⛽ᴹ

HILL CITY — RAFTER J BAR RANCH CAMPING RESORT. (605) 574-2527. **$33-$52.** 12325 Rafter J Rd 57745. From south city limits of Hill City: Go 2 1/4 mi S on US-16/385 (R) 🛶 ✕ ⛽ᴹ

INTERIOR — BADLANDS/WHITE RIVER KOA. (800) 562-3897. **$31-$43.** 20720 SD Hwy 44 57750. From Jct I-90 (Exit 131) & SR-240: go 8 1/4 mi S on SR-240, then 2 1/4 mi S on SR-377 (towards interior), then 4 mi E on SR-44 (L) 🛶 ✕

NORTH SIOUX CITY — SIOUX CITY NORTH KOA. (605) 232-4519. **$35-$46.** 675 Streeter Dr 57049. From Jct of I-90 (Exit 2) & River Dr: Go 500 ft W on River Dr, then 3/4 mi N on Streeter Dr/W Service Rd (L) 🛶 ✕ ⛽ᴹ

RAPID CITY — MYSTERY MOUNTAIN RESORT. (605) 342-5368. **$32-$38.** 13752 S Hwy 16 West 57702. From Jct of I-90 & US-16W (Exit 61), S 13.5 mi on US-16W (R) 🛶 ✕ ⛽ᴹ

RAPID CITY — RUSHMORE SHADOWS RESORT. ⒶⒶⒶ (800) 231-0425. **$33-$55.** 23680 Busted Five Court 57702. From Jct I-90 (Exit 61) & US-16 Truck/Hwy 79: Go 9 mi S & W on US-16 Truck, then 6-1/2 mi W on US-16 W (R) 🛶 ✕ ⛽ᴹ

SALEM — CAMP AMERICA CAMPGROUND. (605) 425-9085. **$27-$35.** 25495 US-81 57058. From Jct of I-90 (Exit 364) & US-81: Go 1.25 mi N on US-81 (L) 🛶 ✕

SPEARFISH — CHRIS' CAMP. ⒶⒶⒶ (800) 350-2239. **$30-$33. (no credit cards).** 701 Christensen Dr 57783. From Jct of US-85 N & I-90: Go 4 mi E on I-90 (Exit 14), then 1/2 mi W on Bus I-90, then 3/4 mi S on Christensen Dr (R) 🛶 ✕ ⛽ᴹ

SPEARFISH — ELKHORN RIDGE RV RESORT & GOLF CLUB. ⒶⒶⒶ (877) 722-1800. **$50.** 20189 US Hwy 85 57783. From Jct of I-90 & US 85 (Exit 17): Go SE 0.6 mi on US 85 (R) 🛶 ✕ ⛽ᴹ

STURGIS — RUSH NO MORE RV RESORT & CAMP-GROUND. (605) 347-2916. **$30-$52.** 21137 Brimstone Pl 57785. From Jct US-14A & I-90: Go 5 mi SE on I-90 (Exit 37), then 3/4 mi W on Pleasant Valley Rd, then 1/4 mi S on Brimstone Pl (R) 🛶 ✕ ⛽ᴹ

Tennessee

CHATTANOOGA — BEST HOLIDAY TRAV-L-PARK. (800) 693-2877. **$37-$39.** 1709 Mack Smith Rd 37412. N-bnd: From Jct of I-75 & US-41N (exit 1B, North US-41), W 0.5 mi on US-41N to Mack Smith Rd, S 0.7 mi (R); or S-bnd: From Jct of I-75 & US-41N (exit 1), W 0.25 mi on US-41N to Mack Smith Rd, S 0.7 mi (R) 🛶 ✕ ⛽ᴹ

CROSSVILLE — DEER RUN RV RESORT. (931) 484-3333. **$34.** 3609 Peavine Firetower Rd 38571. From Jct of I 40 & Hwy 101 (Exit 322), NE 1.9 mi on Hwy 101 to Peavine Firetower Rd, N 3.6 mi (L) 🛶 ✕ ⛽ᴹ

GATLINBURG — GREAT SMOKY JELLYSTONE CAMP-RESORT. (800) 210-2119. **$25-$59.** 4946 Hooper Hwy 37722. E-bnd: From Jct of I-40 & US-321S (exit 435), S 14 mi on US-321S (L); or W-bnd on I-40: From Jct of I-40 & Hwy 73 (exit 440), W 2 mi on Hwy 73 to US-321S, S 10 mi (L); or E-bnd From Gatlinburg: From Jct of US-441 & US-321N, E 15 mi on US-321N (R) 🛶 ✕ ⛽ᴹ

GATLINBURG — SMOKY BEAR CAMPGROUND. (800) 850-8372. **$33-$45.** 4857 E Parkway 37738. E-bnd: From Jct of I-40 & US 321 (exit 435), S 17.2 mi on US 321 (R); or W-bnd: From Jct of I-40 & US 73 (Exit 440), S 2.3 mi on US 73 to US 321, S 11.6 mi (R) 🛶 ⛽ᴹ

GATLINBURG — TWIN CREEK RV RESORT. (800) 252-8077. **$50-$54.** 1202 E Parkway 37738. From Jct of US-441 & US-321N (traffic light #3 in downtown Gatlinburg), E 2 mi on US-321N/East Parkway (R) 🏕 🛶 ✕

HARRIMAN — **CANEY CREEK RV RESORT & MARINA.** (865) 882-4042. **$49-$65.** 3615 Roane State Hwy 37748. From Jct of I-40 & SR 29 (Exit 350), S 0.5 mi on SR 29 to US-70, W 3 mi (L) Entrance just past county park 🏕 🛶 ✕ 🚿

HERMITAGE — **NASHVILLE SHORES RV PARK.** (615) 889-7050. **$45-$55.** 4001 Bell Rd 37076. From Jct of I-40 & Old Hickory Blvd (Exit 221 & 221B), S 0.5 mi on Old Hickory Blvd to Bell Rd, W 0.5 mi (L) ✕

MANCHESTER — **MANCHESTER KOA.** (800) 562-7785. **$32-$65.** 586 Campground Rd 37355. From Jct of I-24 & US-41 (exit 114), SE 300 ft on US-41 to Campground Rd, N 0.5 mi (R) 🛶 ✕

SEVIERVILLE — **RIVERSIDE RV PARK & RESORT.** (800) 341-7534. **$32-$35.** 4280 Boyds Creek Hwy 37876. From Jct of I-40 & Hwy 66 (exit 407), S 4 mi on Hwy 66 to Boyds Creek Rd, W 500 ft (R) 🏕 🛶 ✕ 🚿

SEVIERVILLE — **TWO RIVERS LANDING RV RESORT.** (866) 727-5781. **$45-$65.** 2328 Business Center Circle 37876. From Jct of I 40 & Hwy 66 (Exit 407), S 3 mi on Hwy 66 to Knife Works Ln, W 0.1 mi to Business Center Circle (R) 🏕 🛶 ✕ 🚿

SWEETWATER — **SWEETWATER VALLEY KOA.** (800) 562-9224. **$30-$58.** 269 Murrays Chapel Rd 37874. From Jct of I-75 & Hwy 322 (exit 62), W 0.8 mi on Hwy 322 to Murray's Chapel Rd, S 0.4 mi (L) 🛶 ✕ 🚿

TOWNSEND — **BIG MEADOW FAMILY CAMPGROUND.** (888) 497-0625. **$40-$50.** 8215 Cedar Creek Road 37882. From Jct of US-321 & Hwy 73, NE 0.2 mi on US-321 to Cedar Creek Rd, W 300 ft (R) 🏕 ✕ 🚿

WALLAND — **MISTY RIVER CABINS & RV RESORT.** (877) 981-4300. **$45-$47.** 5050 Old Walland Hwy 37886. In Townsend, Jct US-321 & SR-337, NW 8.3 mi on US 321, SE 0.1 mi on Millers Cove Rd, N 0.7 mi on Old Walland Hwy (L) 🏕 🛶 ✕ 🚿

Texas

ALEDO — **COWTOWN RV PARK.** (817) 441-7878. **$33.** 7000 East I-20 76008. From Jct I-20 (exit 418) & Ranch House Rd: Go 1 mi E on S Frontage Rd. (R) 🏕 🛶 ✕

ALPINE — **LOST ALASKAN RV RESORT.** (800) 837-3604. **$32-$51.** 2401 N Hwy 118 79830. From Jct of US-90 & Hwy 118: Go 1-1/2 mi N on Hwy 118. (L) 🛶 🚿

AMARILLO — **AMARILLO RANCH RV PARK.** (806) 373-4962. **$33.** 1414 Sunrise Dr 79104. From Jct of I-40 (exit 74) & Whitaker Rd: Go 1/2 mi W on N Service Rd (R) 🛶 ✕

AMARILLO — **FORT AMARILLO RV RESORT.** (806) 331-1700. **$34-$45.** 10101 Amarillo Blvd W 79124. From jct I-40 (exit 64) & Loop 335: Go 1/4 mi N on W Loop 335, then 1-1/4 W on Rt 66/Amarillo Blvd W (L) 🏕 🛶 ✕ 🚿

ARANSAS PASS — **RANSOM ROAD RV PARK.** (361) 758-2715. **$32.** 240 Ransom Road 78336. From Jct of Bus 35 & Commercial St (S Loop 90), SW 1.6 mi on Commercial St to Ransom Rd, E 0.1 mi (L) 🏕 ✕

AUSTIN — **LA HACIENDA RV RESORT.** (512) 266-8001. **$48-$52.** 5220 Hudson Bend Rd 78734. S-Bnd: From Jct of I-35 & FM-620, S 18.7 mi on FM-620 to Hudson Bend Rd, W 1.5 mi (L); N-Bnd: From Jct of I-35 & (Exit 230) Hwy 290/71, W 7.7 mi on US 290 to TX 71, NW 7.1 mi to Ranch Road 620, N 7.9 mi to Hudson Bend Rd, NW 1.4 mi (L) 🏕 🛶 ✕ 🚿

AUSTIN — **OAK FOREST RV PARK.** (512) 926-8984. **$44.** 8207 Canoga Ave 78724. From Jct of I-35 (Exit 238B) & Hwy 290: Go E 6.5 mi E on Hwy 290, then 4 mi S on Decker Ln (FM 3177), then 500 ft W on Canoga (L) 🏕 🛶 ✕ 🚿

BACLIFF — **KEMAH RV RESORT.** (281) 559-2362. **$35-$39.** 675 Miles Rd 77518. From Jct of I-45 & FM 518 (exit 23), E 6.5 mi on FM-518 to Hwy 146, SE 1.8 mi to Miles Rd, NE 0.3 mi (R) 🏕 🛶 ✕ 🚿

BAYTOWN — **HOUSTON EAST RV RESORT.** (888) 383-3618. **$38.** 11810 I-10 E 77523. W-bnd: From Jct of I-10 & Hwy 146 (Exit 798), E 1.4 mi on S Frntg Rd (R); or E-bnd: From Jct of I-10 & Exit 797, E 1.5 mi on S. Frntg Rd (R) 🏕 🛶 ✕

BULLARD — **K.E. BUSHMAN'S CAMP.** (903) 894-8221. **$21-$32.** 51152 S US Hwy 69 N 75757. From Jct of FM 344 & US 69: Go 1-1/2 mi S on US 69. (L) 🛶 ✕ 🚿

CANTON — **MILL CREEK RANCH RESORT.** (866) 599-7275. **$35-$64.** 2102 N. Trade Days Blvd 75103. From Jct I-20 (Exit 527) & Hwy 19 (Trade Days Blvd): Go 1/4 mi S on Hwy 19 (L) 🏕 🛶 ✕ 🚿

CANYON LAKE — **YOGI BEAR'S JELLYSTONE PARK HILL COUNTRY.** (877) 964-3731. **$36-$47.** 12915 Hwy 306 78133. From Jct FM 2673 & FM 306: Go 3/4 mi NW on FM 306 (L) 🛶 ✕ 🚿

CORPUS CHRISTI — **COLONIA DEL REY RV PARK.** (361) 937-2435. **$32-$40.** 1717 Waldron Rd 78418. From Jct of I-37 & Hwy 358 (Padre Island Dr), SE 15.7 mi on Hwy 358 to Waldron Rd exit, S 0.8 mi (L) 🛶 ✕

DALE — **LAKE FALLING STAR RV RESORT.** (512) 398-7827. **$29-$37.** 7655 FM 713 78616. From Jct of FM 713 & TX 86 (in McMahan), NE 1 mi on FM 713 (L) 🏕 🛶 ✕

DENTON — **DESTINY RV RESORTS-DALLAS.** 🅰🅰🅰 (888) 238-1532. **$32-$41.** 7100 S I-35E 76210. From Jct of I-35E & Exit 460: Go 1 mi S on W Service Rd. (R) 🏕 🛶 ✕ 🚿

GALVESTON — **JAMAICA BEACH RV PARK.** 🅰🅰🅰 (866) 725-5511. **$38-$52.** 17200 FM 3005 77554. From Jct of I-45 & 61st St. exit, S 1.7 mi to Seawall Blvd (FM-3005), W 11.2 mi (R) 🏕 🛶 ✕

GALVESTON — **SANDPIPER RV RESORT.** (409) 765-9431. **$40-$50.** 201 Seawall Blvd 77550. From I-45 in Galveston (Broadway St), continue S .5 mi on Broadway St to Seawall Blvd (curve left), E 0.3 mi on Seawall Blvd (R) 🏕 🛶 ✕

GEORGETOWN — **NEW LIFE RV PARK.** (512) 931-2073. **$28-$32. (no credit cards).** 1200 County Rd 152 78626. S: Jct of I-35 & exit 264, cross over to Austin Ave, N 0.8 mi on Austin Ave (keep rt) to Frntg Rd for S130 Toll Rd (stay on Frntg Rd), SE 0.7 mi to CR 152, NE 0.3 mi (R); N: Jct of I-35 & exit 265/Austin Ave (keep rt) to Frntg Rd for S130 Toll Rd (stay on Frntg Rd), SE 0.7 mi to CR 152, NE 0.3 mi (R) 🏕️ 🛶

GILMER — **WATTS RV PARK.** (903) 734-3380. **$27-$30.** 2212 Chinaberry Rd 75645. From S Jct of US 271 & SH 155: Go 3-1/4 mi SW on SH 155, then 1 mi S on Chinaberry Rd. (R) 🛶 ⊠

GLADEWATER — **SHALLOW CREEK RV RESORT.** (888) 984-4513. **$33.** 5261 Hwy 135 N 75647. From Jct of I-20 (exit 583) & SR 135: Go 1-1/2 mi N on SR 135. (R) 🏕️ 🛶 ⊠

HIGHLANDS — **SAN JACINTO RIVERFRONT RV PARK.** (281) 426-6919. **$39.** 540 S. Main 77562. From Jct of I-10 & Exit 787 Highlands/Crosby-Lynchburg Rd (S. Main), N 1 mi on Crosby-Lynchburg/S. Main (L) 🏕️ 🛶 ⊠

HOUSTON — **ADVANCED RV RESORT.** (888) 515-6950. **$44-$49.** 2850 S Sam Houston Pkwy East 77047. From Jct of I-610 & Hwy 288, S 5.5 mi on US 288 to Beltway 8 exit, SE 0.5 mi on Beltway 8 Frontage Rd (R) 🏕️ 🛶 ⊠ ♿M

HOUSTON — **LAKE VIEW RV RESORT.** (AAA) (800) 385-9122. **$34-$49.** 11991 South Main St 77035. From S Jct of I-610 & US-90A (South Main St), SW 1.9 mi on S Main St to Holmes Rd/Hiram Clark exit, E under bridge to frontage rd, NE .01 (R) 🏕️ 🛶 ⊠ ♿M

HOUSTON — **TRADERS VILLAGE RV PARK.** (281) 890-5500. **$30-$33.** 7979 N Eldridge Rd 77041. From Jct of I-10 & Eldridge Rd (exit 753A), N 7.8 mi on Eldridge Rd (L); or From N Jct of I-45 & Beltway 8/Sam Houston Tollway (exit 60), W 12.6 mi on Beltway 8/Sam Houston Tollway to US-290, NW 2.2 mi to Eldridge Rd, S 0.6 mi (R) 🛶 ⊠ ♿M

KEMAH — **MARINA BAY RV RESORT.** (281) 334-9944. **$49-$53.** 925 FM 2094 77565. From Jct of I-45 & exit 23 (FM-518), E 2.7 mi to FM-518 to FM-2094, E 3.5 mi (R) 🏕️ 🛶 ⊠

KERRVILLE — **BUCKHORN LAKE RESORT.** (830) 895-0007. **$42-$52.** 2885 Goat Creek Rd 78028. From Jct of I-10 & Exit 501 (FM-1338/Goat Creek Rd) - on the NW corner of N access rd & Goat Creek Rd, N 50 yds on Goat Creek Rd (L) 🏕️ 🛶 ⊠

KERRVILLE — **GUADALUPE RIVER RV RESORT.** (830) 367-5676. **$35-$50.** 2605 Junction Hwy 27 78028. From Jct of I-10 & exit 505 (Harper Rd), S 2.4 mi on Harper Rd to Hwy 27, W 2.6 mi (L) 🏕️ 🛶 ⊠ ♿M

LONGVIEW — **FERNBROOK PARK.** (903) 643-8888. **$33-$38.** 2073 FM 2011 75603. From Jct of I-20 (exit 591) & FM 2011: Go 2 mi SE on FM 2011. (L) 🏕️ 🛶 ⊠ ♿M

MANSFIELD — **TEXAN RV RANCH.** (817) 473-1666. **$32.** 1961 Lone Star Rd 76063. From Jct of I-20 & US-287: Go 10 1/2 mi S on US-287, then 1/4 mi SW on Lone Star Rd (FM 157) (R) 🏕️ 🛶 ⊠ ♿M

MARBLE FALLS — **SUNSET POINT ON LAKE LBJ.** (830) 798-8199. **$43-$75.** 2322 N Wirtz Dam Rd 78654. From Jct of US 281 & FM 1431 (in Marble Falls): Go 3 1/4 mi W on FM 1431, then 2 1/4 mi S on Wirtz Dam Rd (R) 🏕️ ⊠ ♿M

MERCEDES — **LLANO GRANDE LAKE PARK RESORT & COUNTRY CLUB MHP.** (956) 565-2638. **$30-$50.** 2215 East W. Blvd 78570. From Jct of Expwy 83 & Mile 2 W Rd exit, S 1.5 mi on Mile 2 W Rd (E) 🏕️ 🛶 ⊠

MISSION — **BENTSEN PALM VILLAGE RV RESORT.** (877) 247-3727. **$40-$51.** 2500 S Bentsen Palm Dr 78572. E-bnd: From Jct of US-83 Expwy & Bentsen Palm Dr, S 3.1 mi on Bentsen Palm Dr (L); W-bnd: From Jct of US-83 Expwy & Hwy 364/La Homa/Bentsen Palm Dr exit, W 1.5 mi on N Frntg Rd to Bentsen Palm Dr (second light), S 3.1 mi on Bentsen Palm Dr (L) 🏕️ 🛶 ⊠ ♿M

MISSION — **BENTSEN GROVE RESORT MHP.** (956) 585-7011. **$27-$37. (no credit cards).** 810 Bentsen Palm Drive 78572. W-bnd: From Jct of US-83 (Expwy) & Hwy 364/La Homa Rd/Bentsen Palm Dr exit, W 1.5 mi on N Frntg Rd to Bentsen Palm Dr (second light), S 0.9 mi on Bentsen Palm Dr (L); E-bnd: From Jct of US Expwy 83 & Bentsen Palm Dr, S 0.9 mi on Bentsen Palm Dr (L) 🏕️ 🛶 ⊠

MISSION — **SPLIT RAIL RV PARK.** (956) 585-8135. **$38. (no credit cards).** 513 N Los Ebanos 78572. E-bnd: From Jct of US-83 (Expwy) & Los Ebanos Rd exit, N 0.1 mi on Los Ebanos (L); or W-bnd: From Jct of US 8 & Expwy & Los Ebanos Rd exit, W 1 mi on N frntg Rd to Los Ebanos Rd, N 0.1 mi (L) 🏕️ 🛶 ⊠

NEW CANEY — **FOREST RETREAT RV PARK.** (888) 354-9888. **$37-$47.** 21711 McCleskey Rd 77357. From Jct of Hwy 59 & FM 1485 (New Caney exit), S 1 mi on Frontage Rd to McCleskey Rd, W 0.75 mi (R) 🏕️ 🛶 ⊠

ONALASKA — **NORTH SHORE RV RESORT.** (936) 646-3124. **$35-$50.** 168 Butler 77360. E-bnd: From Jct of US 190 & FM 356 (in Onalaska), E 1.5 mi on US-190 (R); W-bnd: From Jct of US 59 & US 190 (West of Livingston), W 11.4 mi on US-190 (L) 🏕️ 🛶 ⊠

PORT ARANSAS — **PIONEER BEACH RESORT.** (361) 749-6248. **$39-$45.** 120 Gulfwind Dr 78373. From Jct of ferry landing & Hwy 361 (Cutoff Rd), SE 1 mi on Hwy 361 to first light, SW 3.4 mi on Hwy 361 (L); or From Jct of Park Rd 22 (Hwy 358) & Hwy 361, N 13.7 mi on Hwy 361 (R) 🏕️ 🛶 ⊠

PORTLAND — **SEA BREEZE RV PARK.** (AAA) (361) 643-0744. **$35-$40.** 1026 Seabreeze Ln 78374. From Jct of US-181 & FM-893/Moore Ave exit, NW 1 mi on FM-893/Moore Ave to Marriott St, SW 0.5 mi to CR 3671, S 0.2 mi (R) 🏕️ 🛶 ⊠

RUSK — **RUSK KOA KAMPGROUND.** (903) 683-6641. **$36-$40.** 745 FM 343 East 75785. From Jct of US 69 & FM 343, E 0.6 mi on FM 343 (L) 🛶 ⊠ ♿M

SAN ANTONIO — **ADMIRALTY RV RESORT.** (210) 647-7878. **$36-$60.** 1485 N Ellison Dr 78251. From Jct of Loop 410 & Hwy 151, Sea World (Exit 9A), NW 2.7 mi on Hwy 151 to W. Military Dr, W 0.3 mi to Ellison S .02 mi (R) 🏕️ 🛶 ⊠

SAN ANTONIO — BLAZING STAR LUXURY RV RESORT. (888) 239-2113. **$42-$60.** 1120 W Loop 1604 N 78251. (W Bnd from Houston) East Jct of I-10 & Loop 410, W 8.3 mi on I-10 to Hwy 90, W 11.7 mi on Hwy 90 to Loop 1604, N 4.5 mi (R) Located between Potranco Rd & Military Dr W (E Bnd from El Paso) W Jct of I-10 & Loop 1604, SW 14 mi on Loop 1604 to Potranco Rd. Turn around & go back 0.6 mi on Loop 1604 (R)

🏕️ �m� 📷 ♿

SAN ANTONIO — TRAVELER'S WORLD RV RESORT. (210) 532-8310. **$41-$44.** 2617 Roosevelt Ave 78214. From Jct of I-37S & Military Dr W (exit 135), W 3.1 mi on Military Dr to Roosevelt, N 1.3 mi (L); or From Jct of I-35S & Military Dr (exit 150B), E 2.7 mi on Military Dr to Roosevelt, N 1.3 mi (L) 🚐 📷

SAN MARCOS — PECAN PARK RIVERSIDE RV & CABINS. (512) 396-0070. **$35-$50.** 50 Squirrel Run 78666. From Jct I-35 (exit 205) & Hwy 80: Go 2 mi SE on Hwy 80 (1 mi past Blanco River Bridge), then 1 block S on Old Bastrop Hwy, then 1/2 mi E on Martindale Rd. (R) 🏕️ 🚐 📷

SANTO — COFFEE CREEK RV RESORT & CABINS. (940) 769-2277. **$30-$38.** P.O. Box 37 76472. From Jct of I-20 & Exit 386 (US 281): Go 1/2 mi N on US 281 (R) 🏕️ 🚐 📷 ♿

SOUTH PADRE ISLAND — SOUTH PADRE KOA. (800) 562-9724. **$46-$68.** 1 Padre Blvd 78597. From Jct of Queen Isabella Causeway & Padre Blvd (Park Rd 100), S 0.3 mi on Padre Blvd (R) 🏕️ 🚐 📷 ♿

SPRING — RAYFORD CROSSING RV RESORT. (281) 298-8008. **$39-$52.** 29321 S. Plum Creek Dr 77386. From Jct of I-45 & Rayford Rd (Exit 73), E 1.5 mi on Rayford Rd to Geneva Rd, S 0.6 mi on Geneva to dead end, E 0.2 mi on N Plum Creek Dr (L)

🏕️ 🚐 📷 ♿

TERRELL — BLUEBONNET RIDGE RV PARK. (866) 419-0100. **$35.** 16543 FM 429 75161. From Jct of I-20 (exit 506) & FM-429: Go 1/2 mi N on FM-429. (L) 🏕️ 🚐 📷 ♿

TEXARKANA — SHADY PINES RV PARK. (903) 832-1268. **$30.** 10010 W 7th St 75501. From Jct of US 59 & US 67 (W side of Texarkana): Go 6 mi W on US 67. (R) 🏕️ 📷

VICTORIA — LAZY LONGHORN RV PARK. (361) 485-1598. **$28-$31. (no credit cards).** 1402 S Laurent 77901. From Jct of US-59 & Hwy 185, NW 1 mi on Hwy 185 (Laurent St) (R) or From Jct of Bus Hwy 59 & Laurent St (Hwy 185), SE 2 mi on Laurent St (L) 🏕️ 🚐 📷 ♿

WALLER — YOGI BEAR JELLYSTONE PARK/LONESTAR. 🅰🅰🅰 (979) 826-4111. **$34-$63.** 34843 Betka Rd 77484. From Jct of US 290 & FM-1098 (E of Hempstead), S 4.1 mi on FM-1098 (E) 🚐 📷 ♿

WEATHERFORD — OAK CREEK RV PARK. (817) 594-0200. **$35.** 7652 W I-20 76088. From Jct FM 1189 & I-20 (Exit 397): Go 1/2 mi W on N Service Rd (R) 🏕️ 🚐 📷

WICHITA FALLS — COYOTE RANCH RESORT. (940) 767-6700. **$35-$50.** 14145 US Hwy 287 N 76310. From jct US 82/287 & Stephens Ranch Rd: Go 1-1/2 mi E on Stephens Ranch Rd. (R) 🚐 📷 ♿

WICHITA FALLS — WICHITA FALLS RV PARK. 🅰🅰🅰 (800) 252-1532. **$25-$28.** 2944 Seymour Hwy 76301. N-bnd: From Jct of US 287 & Broad St exit: Go 3/4 mi N (stay right at split), then 1-1/4 mi W on 5th St/Seymour Hwy. (R) S-bnd: From Jct of US 287 & exit 1A: Go 1-1/4 mi SW on Bus 277 (5th/Seymour Hwy). (R)

🏕️ 🚐 📷

Utah

MONUMENT VALLEY — GOULDING'S MONUMENT VALLEY & RV PARK CAMPGROUND. 🅰🅰🅰 (435) 727-3235. **$44.** 2000 Main St 84536. From Kayenta, AZ, N 22 mi on US-163 to Monument Valley Rd, W 2 mi (R); or From Mexican Hat town center, SW 21 mi on US-163 to Monument Valley Rd, W 2 mi (R) 🚐 📷 ♿

PROVO — LAKESIDE RV CAMPGROUND. (801) 373-5267. **$30-$33.** 4000 West Center St 84601. S-bnd: From Jct of I-15 & Center St (exit 265), W 2 mi on Center St (R); or N-bnd: From Jct of I-15 & Center St (exit 265B), W 2 mi on Center St (R) 🚐 📷

ST. GEORGE — MCARTHUR'S TEMPLE VIEW RV RESORT. 🅰🅰🅰 (800) 510-6765. **$42.** 975 S Main St 84770. From Jct of I-15 & Bluff St (exit 6), N 0.2 mi on Bluff St to Main St, NE 0.3 mi (R) 🚐 📷 ♿

VIRGIN — ZION RIVER RESORT. (888) 466-8594. **$48-$59.** 551 E Hwy 9 84779. N-bnd: From Jct of I-15 & Hwy 9 (exit 16), E 18.9 mi on Hwy 9 to MP 19 (R); or S-bnd: From Jct of I-15 & Hwy 17 (exit 27), S 6 mi on Hwy 17 to Hwy 9, E 6.3 mi to MP 19 (R) 🚐 📷 ♿

Vermont

COLCHESTER — LONE PINE CAMPSITES. (802) 878-5447. **$34-$55.** 52 Sunset View Rd 05446. N-bnd: From Jct of I-89 & US 7 (Exit 16), NW 3.2 mi on US 7 to Jct of Rte 2A & Bay Rd, W 1 mi on Bay Rd (R); or S-bnd: From Jct of I-89 & US 7 (Exit 17), S 3.2 mi on US 7 to Bay Rd, S 1 mi (R) 🚐 📷

DANVILLE — SUGAR RIDGE RV VILLAGE & CAMPGROUND INC. (802) 684-2550. **$40-$42.** 24 Old Stagecoach Rd 05828. From Jct of I-91 & Rte 2 (exit 21), W 4.5 mi on Rte 2 (L) 🚐 📷 ♿

Virginia

FREDERICKSBURG — FREDERICKSBURG-WASH, DC KOA. (800) 562-1889. **$33-$51.** 7400 Brookside Ln 22408. S-bnd: Jct I-95 & US-1 (exit 126/Massaponax), S 4 mi on US-1 to SR-607, E 2.5 mi (R); or N-bnd: Jct I-95 & Rte 606 (exit 118/Thornburg), W 0.2 mi on Rte 606 to US-1, N 4 mi to SR-607, E 2.5 mi (R) 🚐 📷 ♿

GREENWOOD — MISTY MOUNTAIN RV & CAMP RESORT. 🅰🅰🅰 (888) 647-8900. **$27-$46.** 56 Misty Mountain Rd 22943. From Jct of I-64 (exit 107/Crozet) & US-250 (13 mi W of Charlottesville), W 0.7 mi on US-250 (L) 🚐 📷

HILLSVILLE — LAKE RIDGE RV RESORT. 🅰🅰🅰 (866) 513-1773. **$34-$49.** 8736 Double Cabin Rd 24343. From Jct of I-77 & US 58/221 (Exit 14), E 4.5 mi on US 221 to SR 100, N 4 mi on SR 100 to SR 783, SE 0.5 to SR 753 (Double Cabin Rd), E 0.5 mi (L) Note: Follow signs. 🚐 📷 ♿

LURAY — **LURAY KOA.** (800) 562-2790. **$49.** 3402 Kimball Rd 22835. From Jct of US 211 & US 340 (in Luray), N 2.3 mi on US 340 to SR-658/Kimball Rd, E 0.25 mi (L); or From Jct of I-66 & US 340 (Exit 6), S 23 mi on US 340 to SR-658/Kimball Rd, E 0.25 mi (L) 🛒 🗙

STAUNTON — **STAUNTON / WALNUT HILLS KOA.** (800) 699-2568. **$33-$61.** 484 Walnut Hills Rd 24401. N-bnd: From Jct of I-81 & US-11 (Exit 213), S (R) 0.2 mi on US-11 to US-340/ Stuarts Draft Hwy, NE (L) 2.5 mi to SR-655/Walnut Hills Rd, N (L) 03. mi; or S-bnd: From Jct of I-81 & White Hill Rd (Exit 217), W (R) 0.4 mi on White Hill Rd to US-11, S (L) 1.5 mi to SR-655/ Walnut Hills Rd, E (L) 1 mi (L) 🛒 🗙

TEMPERANCEVILLE — **TALL PINES HARBOR WATER-FRONT CAMPGROUND.** (757) 824-0777. **$30-$71.** 8107 Tall Pines Ln 23442. From Jct of SR-695 and US-13 in Temperanceville, W 6.5 mi on SR-695 to Entrance Rd (R) 🛒 🗙

TOPPING — **GREY'S POINT CAMP.** (804) 758-2485. **$40-$75.** 3601 Greys Point Rd 23169. From Jct of US 17 & SR-33 (in Saluda), E 8 mi on SR-33 to SR-3, NW approx 4 mi (L) 🏊 🛒 🗙

URBANNA — **BETHPAGE CAMP RESORT.** (804) 758-4349. **$40-$75.** 679 Browns Lane 23175. From Jct of US-17 & SR-33 (in Saluda), NW 1 mi on US-17 to Rte 616, E 2 mi to Rte 602, NW 0.1 mi to Rte 684, N 0.5 mi to entrance rd (R) 🏊 🛒 🗙

WILLIAMSBURG — **AMERICAN HERITAGE RV PARK.** ⓐⓐ (888) 530-2267. **$46-$50.** 146 Maxton Lane 23188. From Jct of I-64 & Rte 607 (exit 231A), SW 0.5 mi on Rte 607 to Maxton Ln on left, S 0.2 mi (L) 🛒 🗙 ⓜ

WILLIAMSBURG — **COLONIAL CENTRAL KOA.** (800) 562-1733. **$35-$68.** 4000 Newman Rd 23188. E-bnd: From Jct of I-64 (exit 234) & Rte 646 (Newman Rd), NE 1 mi on Rte 646 (R); or W-bnd: From Jct of I-64 (exit 234B) & Rte 646 (Newman Rd), NE 1 mi on Rte 646 (R) 🛒 🗙

WILLIAMSBURG — **WILLIAMSBURG KOA.** ⓐⓐ (800) 562-1733. **$35-$68.** 5210 Newman Road 23188. E-bnd: From Jct of I-64 & Rte 646 (exit 234/Newman Rd)lt turn, NE 1.5 mi on Rte 646 (R); or W-bnd: From Jct of I-64 & Rte 646 (exit 234B), NE 1.5 mi on Rte 646 (R) 🛒 🗙

Washington

CASTLE ROCK — **TOUTLE RIVER RV RESORT.** (360) 274-8373. **$30-$42.** 150 Happy Trails 98611. From Jct of I-5 (Exit 52) & Barnes Rd, W 0.1 mi on Barnes Rd (L) 🛒 🗙 ⓜ

CLARKSTON — **GRANITE LAKE PREMIER RV RESORT.** (800) 989-4578. **$35-$45.** 306 Granite Lake Dr 99403. From Jct of Hwy 12 & 5th St (in town), N 0.3 mi on 5th St (E) 🏊 🗙 ⓜ

CLARKSTON — **HELLS CANYON RV RESORT & MARINA.** (509) 758-6963. **$27-$40.** 1550 Port Drive 99403. From Jct of SR-12 & SR 193 (15th St, W-side of town), N 600 ft on SR-193 to Port Dr, W 100 ft (L) 🛒 🗙 ⓜ

DEER PARK — **SPOKANE RV RESORT AT DEER PARK GOLF CLUB.** ⓐⓐ (877) 276-1555. **$36.** 1205 Country Club Dr 99006. From Jct of US-395 & Crawford St (between MP 180 & 181): Go E 1.8 mi on W Crawford St to N. Country Club Dr, then N 0.9 mi (E) or From Jct of US-2 & E Deer Park/Milan Rd: Go W 5 mi on E Deer Park/Milan Rd to N. Country Club Dr, then N .09 mi (E) 🏊 🛒 🗙 ⓜ

FERNDALE — **THE CEDARS RV RESORT.** (360) 384-2622. **$38-$41.** 6335 Portal Way 98248. From Jct of I-5 & Portal Way (exit 263), N 1 mi on Portal Way (L) 🛒 🗙 ⓜ

GIG HARBOR — **GIG HARBOR RV RESORT.** ⓐⓐ (253) 858-8138. **$34.** 9515 Burnham Dr NW 98332. From Jct of I-5 & SR-16 (exit 132), W 12.4 mi on SR-16 to Burnham Dr exit (btwn MP 14-15), go to traffic circle east of freeway, take first exit (Burnham Dr), E 1.2 mi (L) 🛒 🗙 ⓜ

KELSO — **BROOKHOLLOW RV PARK.** (800) 867-0453. **$35.** 2506 Allen St 98626. From Jct of I-5 & Allen St (exit 39), E 1 mi on Allen St/just past mobile home park (Look for white RV park sign) (R) 🏊 🗙 ⓜ

MEAD — **ALDERWOOD RV RESORT.** (888) 847-0500. **$30-$42.** 14007 N Newport Hwy 99021. From Jct of I-90 & Argonne Rd. (Exit 287): Go N 8.4 mi on Argonne Rd to US-206, then W 2.3 mi to US-2, then S 0.1 mi (R), or S-Bnd: From Jct of US-2 & US-206: Go S 0.1 mi on US-2 (R) 🛒 🗙 ⓜ

PROSSER — **WINE COUNTRY RV PARK.** (800) 726-4969. **$26-$39.** 330 Merlot Dr 99350. From Jct of I-82 & Wine Country Rd (exit 80), SE 100 ft on Wine Country Rd to Merlot Dr, E 0.3 mi (R) 🛒 🗙 ⓜ

RICHLAND — **HORN RAPIDS RV RESORT.** (866) 557-9637. **$36.** 2640 Kingsgate Way 99354. From Jct of I-182 & Hwy 240W (exit 4), NW 6 mi on Hwy 240W to Kingsgate Wy, W 0.1 mi on Kingsgate Wy (R) 🏊 🛒 🗙 ⓜ

WOODLAND — **COLUMBIA RIVERFRONT RV PARK.** ⓐⓐ (800) 845-9842. **$30-$42.** 1881 Dike Rd 98674. From Jct of I-5 & Exit 22, W 1.6 mi on Dike Access Rd to Dike Rd, S 1 mi (R) 🏊 🛒 🗙 ⓜ

Wisconsin

BAILEYS HARBOR — **BAILEYS GROVE CAMPGROUND.** (920) 839-2559. **$35-$39.** 2552 County Road F 54202. From Jct of Hwy 57 & CR-F & EE, W 0.7 mi on CR-F & EE (R) 🛒 🗙

CALEDONIA — **YOGI BEAR'S JELLYSTONE PARK CAMP-RESORT.** (262) 835-2565. **$23-$66.** 8425 State Hwy 38 53108. From Jct of I-94 & Seven Mile Rd (exit 326), E 2 mi on Seven Mile Rd to Hwy 38, N 0.4 mi (R) 🛒 🗙 ⓜ

DE FOREST — **MADISON KOA.** (800) 562-5784. **$32-$48.** 4859 County Road V 53532. From Jct of I-90/94 & CR-V (exit 126), E 0.25 mi on CR-V (R) 🛒 🗙

FORT ATKINSON — **YOGI BEAR'S JELLYSTONE PARK OF FORT ATKINSON.** (877) 232-7386. **$45.** N551 Wishing Well Dr 53538. From Jct of US-12 & Hwy 26, S 5 mi on Hwy 26 to Koshkonong Rd, W 0.7 mi to Wishing Well Dr, S 0.2 mi (E) 🛒 🗙 ⓜ

GLENBEULAH — NASCAR RV RESORTS AT WESTWARD HO. (920) 526-3407. **$28-$50.** N5456 Division Rd 53023. From Jct US-41 & Hwy 23: Go 16 mi E on Hwy 23, then 3 mi S on CR-G, then 1/2 mi E on CR-T & follow signs. 🚐 ⊠ ♿ᴹ

MILTON — HIDDEN VALLEY RV RESORT & CAMP-GROUND. (800) 469-5515. **$38-$78.** 872 E Hwy 59 53563. From Jct of I-90 & Hwy 59E (exit 163), E 0.5 mi on Hwy 59E (R) 🚐 ⊠

MONTELLO — BUFFALO LAKE CAMPING RESORT. (608) 297-2915. **$34-$45.** 555 Lake Ave 53949. From Jct of SR-23 & W Jct of SR 22 (in town), W 0.1 mi on SR-23 to CR-C (left turn), W 0.7 mi on CR-C (R) 🚐 ⊠ ♿ᴹ

OSSEO — STONEY CREEK RV RESORT. (888) 349-6399. **$35-$50.** 50483 Oak Grove Rd 54758. From Jct of Hwy 10 & I-94 (exit 88), E 0.1 mi on Hwy 10 to Oak Grove Rd, S 0.4 mi (R) 🚐 ⊠ ♿ᴹ

RIO — SILVER SPRINGS CAMPSITES. (877) 992-3538. **$38-$49.** N 5048 Ludwig Rd 53960. From Jct of Hwy 16 & CR-B, N 0.5 mi on CR-B into RIO, E 3.3 mi on Cty B to Ludwig Rd, N 1 mi (R) 🚐 ⊠ ♿ᴹ

SPRING GREEN — WISCONSIN RIVERSIDE RESORT. (608) 588-2826. **$36-$55.** S13220 Shifflet Rd 53588. From Jct of Hwy 23 & Hwy 14, S 0.8 mi on Hwy 23 to Madison St, W 0.7 mi on Madison St to Shifflet Rd, S 0.75 mi (L) 🚐 ⊠ ♿ᴹ

WARRENS — YOGI BEAR'S JELLYSTONE PARK CAMP-RESORT. 🅐🅐🅐 (888) 386-9644. **$30-$65.** 1500 Jellystone Park Dr. 54666. From Jct of I-94 & CR-EW (Warren exit 135), E 0.4 mi on CR-EW(L) 🚐 ⊠ ♿ᴹ

WEST SALEM — NESHONOC LAKESIDE CAMP-RESORT. (608) 786-1792. **$48-$59.** N 5334 Neshonoc Rd 54669. From Jct of I-90 & C (West Salem Exit 12), N 1 mi on C to Hwy 16, E 1.5 mi (R) 🚐 ⊠

WILD ROSE — EVERGREEN CAMPSITES & RESORT. 🅐🅐🅐 (866) 450-2267. **$49.** W 5449 Archer Lane 54984. From Jct of SR-22 & CRs-G & H, E 3 mi on CR-H to Archer Ln, E 1.75 mi (R) 🚐 ⊠ ♿ᴹ

WISCONSIN DELLS — DELL BOO. (608) 356-5898. **$40-$48.** E 10562 Shady Lane Rd 53913. From Jct of I-90/94 & US-12 (exit 92), SE 1.5 mi on US-12 to Shady Lane Rd, W 0.8 mi (R) 🚐 ⊠ ♿ᴹ

WISCONSIN DELLS — SHERWOOD FOREST CAMPING & RV PARK. 🅐🅐🅐 (877) 474-3796. **$35-$55.** S 352 Hwy 12 & 16 53965. From Jct of I-90/94 & SR-13 (exit 87), E 0.25 mi on SR-13 to US-12/SR-16, NW 0.4 mi (R) 🚐 ⊠

WISCONSIN DELLS — STAND ROCK CAMPGROUND. 🅐🅐🅐 (608) 253-2169. **$42-$45.** N 570 Hwy N 53965. From Jct of I-90/94 & US-12/16 (exit 85), E 600 ft on US-12/16 to 60th, NE 1 mi to Standrock Rd (Hwy N), N 0.25 mi (R) 🚐 ⊠

WISCONSIN DELLS — WISCONSIN DELLS KOA. (800) 254-4177. **$36-$65.** S 235 A Stand Rock Rd 53965. From Jct of I-90/94 & Hwy 13N (Exit 87), E 1 mi on Hwy 13N to Standrock Rd (3rd stoplight), N 0.75 mi (L); or From Jct of I-90/94 & Hwy 12/16 (Exit 85), E 0.2 mi on Hwy 12/16 to Hwy A, N 0.5 mi on Hwy A to Stand Rock Rd, S 0.3 mi (R) 🚐 ⊠ ♿ᴹ

WISCONSIN DELLS — YOGI BEAR'S JELLYSTONE PARK CAMP-RESORT. 🅐🅐🅐 (800) 462-9644. **$25-$115.** S1915 Ishnala Rd 53965. From Jct of I-90/94 & US-12 (exit 92), NW 0.5 mi on US-12 to Gasser Rd, W 1 mi to Ishnala Rd, S 100 ft (R) 🚐 ⊠ ♿ᴹ

WOODRUFF — HIAWATHA TRAILER RESORT. (888) 429-2842. **$39-$42.** 1077 Old Hwy 51S 54568. From Jct of Hwys 51 & 47, E 0.3 mi on Hwy 47 to Old Hwy 51 (Balsam St), N 0.5 mi (L) 🏕 ⊠

Wyoming

BUFFALO — BUFFALO KOA. 🅐🅐🅐 (307) 684-5423. **$33-$44.** 87 US Hwy 16E 82834. From Jct of I-90 & US-16 (exit 58), W 1 mi on US-16 (L); or From Jct of I-25 & US-16 (exit 299), E 0.3 mi on US-16 (R) 🚐 ⊠

BUFFALO — DEER PARK. 🅐🅐🅐 (307) 684-5722. **$30-$40.** 146 US Hwy 16E Deer Park Rd 82834. From Jct of I-90 & US-16 (exit 58), W 0.7 mi on US-16 (R); or From Jct of I-25 & US-16 (exit 299), E 0.7 mi on US-16 (L) 🚐

Canada

Camping information provided by Woodall's®

Alberta

COCHRANE — SPRINGHILL RV PARK. 🅐🅐 (403) 932-2010. **$36-$44.** 41216 Big Hill Springs Rd T4C 1A1. From Jct of Hwy 22 & Hwy 567, E 0.1 mi on Hwy 567 (L) ⊠ ♿ᴹ

British Columbia

ALDERGROVE — EAGLE WIND RV PARK. (604) 856-6674. **$37-$52.** 26920 52nd Ave V4W 1N6. From Hwy 1 (TCH) & 264th St (Exit 73) S 0.1 mi to 52nd Ave, E 0.6 mi (R) 🚐 ♿ᴹ

BLACK CREEK — PACIFIC PLAYGROUNDS RV PARK COTTAGES MARINA. (877) 239-5600. **$37-$46.** 9082 Clarkson Ave V9J 1B3. From Jct of Hwy 19 & Hamm Rd (exit 144), E 3.2 mi (5 km) on Hamm Rd to Hwy 19A, N 1 mi (1.6 km) to Regent Rd, E 0.3 mi (0.4 km) to Saratoga Rd (which becomes Henderson Ave.), S 0.4 mi (.6 km) to Eyre St, E 0.1 mi to Clarkson Dr, N 0.4 mi (.6 km) (E) 🚐 ⊠ ♿ᴹ

BURNABY — BURNABY CARIBOO RV PARK AND CAMP-GROUND. 🅐🅐 (604) 420-1722. **$62-$68.** 8765 Cariboo Place V3N 4T2. From Jct of Hwy 1 & Gaglardi Way (exit 37) (W 6 mi (9.6 km) of Port Mann Bridge), N 300 ft (90 m) to traffic light, E 300 ft (90 m) on Cariboo Rd, N 0.2 mi on Cariboo Rd (under overpass) to Cariboo Pl (E) 🚐 ⊠ ♿ᴹ

CAMPBELL RIVER — RIPPLE ROCK RV PARK. (250) 287-7108. **$26-$46.** 15021 Brown's Bay Rd V9H 1N9. From Jct of Hwy 19 & Hwy 28, N 12 mi on Hwy 19 to park sign at Brown's Bay Rd, E 3.2 mi (R) ⟨ⅹ⟩ ⟨&M⟩

CAMPBELL RIVER — SALMON POINT RESORT RV PARK & MARINA. (866) 246-6605. **$30-$46.** 2176 Salmon Point Rd V9H 1E5. N-bnd: From Jct of Hwy 19 & Hamm Rd (exit 144), E 3.2 mi on Hamm Rd to Hwy 19A, N 2.6 mi to Salmon Pt Rd, E 0.4 mi (L); or S-bnd: From Jct of Hwy 19 & Jubilee Pkwy (exit 161), E 2.5 mi on Jubilee Pkwy to Hwy 19A, S 6.5 mi (L) ⟨➤⟩ ⟨ⅹ⟩ ⟨&M⟩

CHEMAINUS — COUNTRY MAPLES RV RESORT. (250) 246-2078. **$32-$53.** 9010 Trans Canada Hwy V0R 1K4. From Jct of Hwy 1 & Mt Sicker Rd, N 1.9 mi on Hwy 1 to U-turn route (Henry Rd), follow signs to Hwy 1, S 1.1 mi on Hwy 1 (R) ⟨➤⟩ ⟨ⅹ⟩ ⟨&M⟩

FAIRMONT HOT SPRINGS — FAIRMONT HOT SPRINGS RESORT LTD. ⟨AA⟩ (250) 345-6033. 5225 Fairmont Resort Rd. V0B 1L1. From Jct of Hwy 93/95 & Fairmont Resort Rd, E 0.5 mi on Fairmont Resort Rd (E) ⟨Ⓚ⟩ ⟨➤⟩ ⟨ⅹ⟩ ⟨&M⟩

HIXON — CANYON CREEK CAMPGROUND & RV PARK. (250) 998-4384. **$21-$28.** 39035 Hwy 97S V0K 1S0. From Jct of Hwy 97 & Thorley Rd, N 0.6 mi (1 km) on Hwy 97 (L) ⟨ⅹ⟩

HOPE — SUNSHINE VALLEY RV RESORT & CAMPING CABINS. (604) 869-0066. **$40-$54.** 14850 Alpine Blvd V0X 1L5. From Jct of Hwy 1 (Exit 170) & Hwy 3, E 12.9 mi on Hwy 3 to Branch Bend, S 100 ft to Cedar Blvd (becomes Alpine Blvd), E 0.2 mi on Cedar Blvd/Alpine Blvd 0.2 mi (L) ⟨≋⟩ ⟨ⅹ⟩ ⟨&M⟩

KELOWNA — HOLIDAY PARK RESORT. (250) 766-4255. **$40-$63.** I-415 Commonwealth Rd V4V 1P4. From Jct Hwy 97 & Commonwealth Rd, 0.4 mi on Commonwealth Rd (L) ⟨Ⓚ⟩ ⟨➤⟩ ⟨ⅹ⟩ ⟨&M⟩

OSOYOOS — NK'MIP CAMPGROUND & RV PARK. (250) 495-7279. **$40-$52.** 8000 45th St V0H 1V6. From Jct of Hwy 3 & 45th St, N 0.8 mi on 45th St (E) ⟨➤⟩ ⟨ⅹ⟩ ⟨&M⟩

OSOYOOS — WALTON'S LAKEFRONT RESORT. (800) 964-1148. **$35-$80.** 3207 Lakeshore Drive V0H 1V6. From Jct of Hwy 3 & Lakeshore Dr, S 0.5 mi on Lakeshore Dr (L) ⟨Ⓚ⟩ ⟨➤⟩ ⟨ⅹ⟩ ⟨&M⟩

PARKSVILLE — SURFSIDE RV RESORT. (866) 642-2001. **$35-$63.** 200 N Corfield St V9P 2H5. From Jct of Hwy 19 & Hwy 4A (Parksville/Coombs exit 51), E 1.2 mi (2 km) on Hwy 4A to Hwy 19A, S 0.3 mi (.5 km) to N Corfield St, E 0.1 mi (.2 km) (E) ⟨Ⓚ⟩ ⟨➤⟩ ⟨ⅹ⟩ ⟨&M⟩

RADIUM HOT SPRINGS — RADIUM VALLEY VACATION RESORT. (250) 347-9715. **$55-$65.** 7274 Radium Valley Rd V0A 1M0. From Jct of Hwy 93 & Hwy 95, N 0.7 mi on Hwy 95 to Radium Valley Vacation Resort Rd (L) ⟨Ⓚ⟩ ⟨➤⟩ ⟨ⅹ⟩

ROSEDALE — CAMPERLAND BRIDAL FALLS. (604) 794-7361. **$48-$54.** 53730 Bridal Falls Rd V0X 1X1. From Jct of Hwy 1 & Hwy 9 (exit 135), S 0.1 mi on Hwy 9 to Bridal Falls Rd, E 1 mi on Bridal Falls Rd (R) ⟨➤⟩ ⟨ⅹ⟩ ⟨&M⟩

SAANICHTON — OCEANSIDE RV RESORT. ⟨AA⟩ (250) 544-0508. **$33-$50.** 3000 Stautw Rd V8M 2K5. From Jct of Hwy 17 & Mt Newton X Rd, E 0.3 mi on Mt Newton X Rd to Stautw Rd, E 0.7 mi (R) ⟨ⅹ⟩ ⟨&M⟩

SURREY — HAZELMERE RV PARK & CAMPGROUND. ⟨AA⟩ (604) 538-1167. **$36-$40.** 18843-8th Ave V3S 9R9. From Jct Pacific Hwy (Hwy 15) & 8th Ave, E 1-1/2 mi (2.6 km) on 8th Ave (L) ⟨➤⟩ ⟨ⅹ⟩ ⟨&M⟩

VANDERHOOF — DAVE'S RV PARK. (250) 567-3161. **$28-$35.** 1048 Derksen Rd V0J 3A0. From town, E 1 mi on Hwy 16 to Derksen Rd, N 0.5 mi (R) ⟨ⅹ⟩

VICTORIA — PEDDER BAY RV RESORT & MARINA. (250) 478-1771. **$36-$66.** 925 Pedder Bay Dr V9C 4H1. From Jct of Hwy 1 & Hwy 14 (Exit 14), S 5.8 km (4 mi) on Hwy 14 (Millstream Rd/Veterans Memorial Pkwy) to Latoria, W 2 km (1.2 mi) to Happy Valley Rd, SW 4.9 km (3 mi) to Rocky Point Rd, S 5.1 km (3.2 mi) to Pedder Bay Dr, S 150 meters (0.1 mi) (L) ⟨ⅹ⟩

WHISTLER — RIVERSIDE RESORT. ⟨AA⟩ (604) 905-5533. **$35-$57.** 8018 Mons Rd V0N 1B8. From Jct of Hwy 99 & Blackcomb Way, E 100 ft (30 meters) to Mons Rd, N 0.3 mi (.4 km) (R) ⟨ⅹ⟩ ⟨&M⟩

New Brunswick

CARAQUET — CAMPING COLIBRI. (506) 727-2222. **$32-$45.** CP 5526 E1W 1B7. At W-end of town on Rte 11 (L) ⟨➤⟩ ⟨ⅹ⟩

FREDERICTON — HARTT ISLAND RV RESORT. (506) 462-9400. **$39-$59.** 2475 Woodstock Rd Rte 102 E3C 1P6. W-bnd:From Jct of TCH-2 & Exit 294 (Hwy 7 to Hwy 8), N 6 mi on Hwy 7 to Edmundston-Mactaquac exit (Hwy 8-S), S 2 mi to exit 3 (Hanwell/Rte 102), N 3 mi (R); or E-bnd:From Jct of TCH-2 & Exit 280 (Hwy 8), N 2 mi on Hwy 8 to Exit 3, (Fredericton Centre), N 0.2 mi to Prospect St/Rte 102, N 3 mi (R) ⟨➤⟩ ⟨ⅹ⟩

MONCTON — CAMPER'S CITY RV RESORT. (877) 512-7868. **$18-$44.** 138 Queensway Dr E1G 2L2. From Jct of TCH-2 & Exit 454 (Mapleton Rd), N 500 ft on Mapleton Rd to Queensway Dr, E 0.25 mi (L) ⟨➤⟩ ⟨ⅹ⟩

SHIPPAGAN — CAMPING KOA POKEMOUCHE. (506) 727-6090. **$32-$45.** 11220 Hwy 11 E8S 1T1. From Jct of Hwy 11 & 113, S 1.5 mi (L) ⟨➤⟩ ⟨ⅹ⟩ ⟨&M⟩

WOODSTOCK — YOGI BEAR'S JELLYSTONE PARK. (506) 328-6287. **$42-$45.** PO Box 9004 E7M 6B5. From Jct of TCH-2 & Exit 191 (Beardsley Rd/Woodstock Direction), N 0.25 mi on Beardsley Rd to Hemlock St, W 0.25 mi, follow signs (E) ⟨➤⟩ ⟨ⅹ⟩ ⟨&M⟩

Nova Scotia

AMHERST — LOCH LOMOND TENT & TRAILER PARK. (902) 667-3890. **$25-$33.** RR 6 B4H 3Y4. From Jct of TCH-104 & Exit 4 (Rte 2), S 0.25 mi on Rte 2 to Blair Lake Rd, W 500 ft (L) ⟨➤⟩ ⟨ⅹ⟩

BADDECK — BADDECK CABOT TRAIL CAMPGROUND. (AA) (902) 295-2288. **$28-$44.** 9584 Hwy 105 B0E 1B0. W-bnd: From town, W 5 mi on TCH-105 (R); or E-bnd: From Jct of TCH-105 & Exit 7 (Cabot Trail Entrance), E 0.5 mi on TCH-105 (L) ⛺ ⊠

BADDECK — BRAS D'OR LAKES CAMPGROUND. (AA) (902) 295-2329. **$28-$44.** Box 595, 8885 Hwy 105 B0E 1B0. From town, W 3 mi on TCH-105 (L). Between Exit 7 & 8, MM 80 ⛺ ⊠

DEBERT — ELM RIVER RV PARK LTD. (AA) (888) 356-4356. **$30-$42.** RR 1, 85 Elm River Parkway B0M 1G0. E-bnd: From Jct of Hwy 104 & Exit 11 (Rtes 2 & 4), E 1 mi on Rte 4 (L); or W-bnd: From Jct of Hwy 104 & Exit 12 (Rtes 2 & 4), W 0.6 mi on Rte 4 (R) ⛺ ⊠ ⛾ᴹ

GRANVILLE FERRY — DUNROMIN CAMPSITE. (902) 532-2808. **$32-$45.** 4618 Hwy 1 B0S 1K0. From Jct of Hwy 101 & Exit 22 (Rtes 8 & 1), N 3.8 mi on Rte 8 to Rte 1, E 1.4 mi (R) ⛺ ⊠ ⛾ᴹ

HILDEN — SCOTIA PINE CAMPGROUND. (877) 893-3666. **$28-$40.** 1911 Hwy 2 B0N 1C0. From Jct of Hwy 102 & Exit 12 (Rte 289), E 0.6 mi on Rte 289 to Rte 2, N 2.4 mi (R) ⛺ ⊠ ⛾ᴹ

KINGSTON — YOGI BEAR'S JELLYSTONE PARK CAMP RESORT. (888) 225-7773. **$31-$54.** RR 1-43 Boo Boo Blvd. B0P 1R0. E-Bnd: From Jct of Hwy 101 & Exit 17, N 0.8 mi on exit rd (Marshall Rd) to Brooklyn St, W 300 ft, Follow signs (R); or W-bnd: From Jct of Hwy 101 & Exit 17, N 0.75 mi on Exit Rd to Brooklyn St, W 1 mi (R) ⛺ ⊠ ⛾ᴹ

MAHONE BAY — RAYPORT CAMPGROUND. (AA) (902) 627-2678. **$27-$34.** 165 Shingle Mill Rd B0J 2E0. From Jct of Hwy 103 & Exit 10 (Rte 3), S. 0.5 mi on access rd to Rte 3, E 2 mi, Follow signs (L). ⛺ ⊠

UPPER SACKVILLE — HALIFAX WEST KOA. (888) 562-4705. **$30-$47.** 3070 Sackville Dr. B4E 3C9. From Jct of Hwy 101 & Exit 3 (Rte 1), SE 1.25 mi on Rte 1 (R) ⛺ ⊠ ⛾ᴹ

Ontario

BARRIE — BARRIE KOA. (AA) (800) 562-7397. **$43-$82.** 3138 Penetanguishene Rd, RR 1 L4M 4Y8. From Jct of Hwys 400 & 22 (Exit 117), E 1.2 km (0.7 mi) on CR-22 (Horseshoe Valley Rd) to CR-93, (Penetanguishene Rd) S 1.6 km (1 mi) (R) ⛺ ⊠ ⛾ᴹ

CHERRY VALLEY — QUINTE'S ISLE CAMPARK. (AA) (613) 476-6310. **$50-$55.** RR 1, 237 Salmon Pt Rd K0K 1P0. From Jct of Hwys 401 & 62 (Exit 543A), S 46.6 mi (29 mi) on Hwy 62 to Hwy 33, E 9.6 km (6 mi) to CR-10 (Lake St, in Picton), S 8 km (5 mi) to CR-18, SW 8 km (5 mi) to Salmon Pt Rd, S 2 km (1.25 mi) (L). ⛺ ⊠ ⛾ᴹ

KINCARDINE — FISHERMAN'S COVE TENT & TRAILER PARK. (519) 395-2757. **$47-$52.** 13 Southline Ave, RR4 N2Z 2X5. From Jct of Hwys 21 & 9, E 18 km (11.25 mi) on Hwy 9 to Bruce CR-1, S 2 km (1.3 mi) to Southline, SE 0.8 km (0.5 mi) (E) ⛺ ⊠ ⛾ᴹ

MCGREGOR — WILDWOOD GOLF & RV RESORT. (866) 994-9699. **$44.** RR 1 N0R 1J0. From Jct of Hwy 401 & CR-19 (Manning Rd) Exit 21, S 4.7 km (2.9 mi) on CR-19 to Hwy 3, SE 4.8 km (3 mi) to N. Malden Rd, SW 9.2 km (5.7 mi) to 11th Conc Rd, W 0.6 km (0.4 mi) (R) 🎣 ⛺ ⛾ᴹ

SAUBLE BEACH — CARSONS' CAMP LIMITED. (519) 422-1143. **$42-$54.** RR 1, 110 Southampton Pkwy N0H 2G0. From Jct of CR-8 & CR-13 (Southampton Pkwy), S 0.8 km (0.5 mi) on CR-13 (Southampton Pkwy) (R). ⛺ ⊠ ⛾ᴹ

SAUBLE BEACH — WOODLAND PARK. (519) 422-1161. **$32-$53.** RR 1 N0H 2G0. From Jct of CR-8 & CR-13 (Sauble Falls Pkwy), N 0.4 km (0.25 mi) on CR-13/Sauble Falls Pkwy (R) ⛺ ⊠ ⛾ᴹ

SHERKSTON — SHERKSTON SHORES. (877) 482-3224. **$25-$99.** RR1 490 Empire Rd L0S 1R0. From Jct of Hwy 140 (Elizabeth St) & Hwy 3, E 8.2 km (5.1 mi) on Hwy 3 to Empire Rd, S 2.4 km (1.5 mi) (R). ⛺ ⊠ ⛾ᴹ

VINELAND — N.E.T. CAMPING RESORT. (866) 490-4745. **$36-$55.** Box 541, 2325 RR 24 L0R 2C0. W-bnd: From Jct of QEW & N Service Rd, NW 0.16 km (0.1 mi) on N Service Rd to Victoria Ave (RR24), S 11.6 km (7.2 mi) (L); or E-bnd: From Jct of QEW & S Service Rd (Exit 57), W 0.16 km (0.1 mi) on S Service Rd to Victoria Ave (RR 24) S 11.3 km (7 mi) (L). ⛺ ⊠ ⛾ᴹ

Prince Edward Island

BRACKLEY BEACH — VACATIONLAND RV PARK. (902) 672-2317. **$36-$48.** 29 Brittain Shore Rd C1E 1Z3. In Charlottetown: From Jct of TCH-1 (Arterial Hwy) & Rte 15, N 9 mi on Rte 15 to Britain Shore Rd, E 1 mi (R) ⛺ ⊠

CAVENDISH — CAVENDISH SUNSET CAMPGROUND. (AA) (902) 963-2440. **$37-$42.** 9115 Rte 6 C0A 1M0. From Jct of Rtes 6 & 13, W 1.6 mi on Rte 6 (L) ⛺ ⊠ ⛾ᴹ

CHARLOTTETOWN — PINE HILLS RV PARK. (877) 226-2267. **$39-$49.** 1531 Brackley Pt Rd (Harrington) C1E 1Z3. In Charlottetown: From Jct of TCH 1 (Arterial Hwy) & Rte 15, N 6 mi on Rte 15 (L); or W-bnd: From Wood Island, W 32 mi on TCH-1 to Hillsborough Bridge, cross bridge, take first right (Riverside Dr), NE 4 mi to Rte 15, N 6 mi (L) 🎣 ⛺ ⊠

CORNWALL — CORNWALL KOA. (902) 566-2421. **$34-$55.** 208 Ferry Rd. C0A 1H0. E-bnd: From Jct of TCH-1 & Rte 248 (Ferry Rd), E 1 mi on Rte 248 to park entrance (R); or W-bnd: From Jct of TCH-1 & Rte 248 (York Point Rd), S 2.2 mi on Rte 248 to Ferry Rd, W 1.3 mi to park entrance (L) ⛺ ⊠ ⛾ᴹ

HUNTER RIVER — CAVENDISH KOA. (AA) (800) 562-1879. **$28-$45.** 198 Forest Hill Lane C0A 1N0. From Jct of Rtes 6 & 13, W 0.8 mi on Rte 6 (L) ⛺ ⊠ ⛾ᴹ

HUNTER RIVER — MARCO POLO LAND INC. (AA) (902) 963-2352. **$38-$44.** Route 13 C0A 1N0. From Jct of Rtes 6 & 13, S 0.5 mi on Rte 13 (L) ⛺ ⊠ ⛾ᴹ

HUNTER RIVER — NEW GLASGOW HIGHLANDS. (902) 964-3232. **$32-$42.** RR3 2497 Hwy 224 C0A 1N0. From jct Hwy 13 & Hwy 224: Go 1.9 km/1-1/4 mi E on Hwy 224. ⛺ ⊠

MONTAGUE — SEAL COVE CAMPGROUND. (902) 962-2745. **$20-$35**. RR 4, Murray Harbour N C0A 1R0. From Jct of Rtes 4 & 17 in Murray River, N 6 mi on Rte 17 to Mink River Rd, S 0.25 mi (L) 🛶 ⊠

Québec

BROMONT — DU VILLAGE BROMONT RV RESORT. ⒶⒶ (450) 534-2404. **$29-$47**. 1699 Shefford J2L 3N8. From Jct of Hwy 10 & Exit 74 (Rte Pierre Laporte), S 3.5 mi on Rte Pierre Laporte to Shefford Rd, E 100 ft (R) 🛶 ⊠

COMPTON — CAMPING DE COMPTON. (800) 563-5277. **$35-$44**. 24 Chemin De La Station J0B 1L0. From jct Hwy 208 W & Hwy 147: Go 65 meters/215 ft N on Hwy 147, then 0.3 km/1/4 mi W on Rue de la Station. 🛶 ⊠

ÎLE D'ORLÉANS — CAMPING ILE D'ORLEANS. (418) 829-2953. **$39-$54**. 357 Chemin Royal G0A 3S0. From Jct of Hwy 40 & Exit 325 (Ile D'Orleans Rte 368), S 2.5 mi on Orleans Bridge to Rte 368, E 20 mi (L) 🛶 ⊠ ♿M

LA BAIE — CAMPING AU JARDIN DE MON PERE. (418) 544-6486. **$20-$40**. 3736 Chemin St Louis G7B 4M8. From Jct of Rtes 170 & 381 (in town), S 1 mi on Rte 381, follow signs (R) 🛶 ⊠ ♿M

L'ACADIE — CAMPING LES CEDRES. (450) 346-9276. **$36-$42**. 658 219 Rte J2Y 1C4. 🛶 ⊠

LAC-A-LA-TORTUE — CAMPING OTAMAC. (819) 538-9697. **$48-$50**. 5431 Av Tour Du Lac G0X 1L0. From Jct of N-end of Hwy 55 & Exit Rd (Route 153), E 0.7 mi on Exit Rd to Rte 153, S 1.5 mi to Route 359, S 1.5 mi to 49 Ieme Ave, E 0.8 mi (R) 🛶 ⊠ ♿M

LÉVIS — CAMPING TRANSIT. (418) 838-0948. **$40-$55**. 600 Chemin St. Roch G6V 6N4. E-bnd: From Jct of Hwy 20 & Exit 330 (Rte Lallemand/Chemin St-Roch), E 2.5 mi on Chemin St-Roch, follow signs (L); or W-bnd: From Jct of Hwy 20 & Exit 337 (Rte 279), S 0.5 mi on Rte 279 to Chemin St-Roch Rd, W 2 mi (R) 🛶 ⊠ ♿M

ST-APOLLINAIRE — DOMAINE DE LA CHUTE. (418) 831-1311. **$40**. 74 Chemin De La Chute G0S 2E0. E-bnd: From Jct of Hwy 20 & Exit 296 (Rte Du Cap), S 0.7 mi on Rte Du Cap to Chemin de la Chute, E 1.5 mi, follow signs (E) 🛶 ⊠ ♿M

ST-AUGUSTIN-DE-DESMAURES — CAMPING JUNEAU CHALETS. (866) 871-9090. **$26-$35**. 155 Ch Du Lac RR 1 G3A 1W7. From Jct of Hwy 40 & Exit 300 (Chemin du Lac), S 0.5 mi on Chemin du Lac (L) ⊠ ♿M

ST-MATHIEU-DE-BELOEIL — CAMPING ALOUETTE. ⒶⒶ (450) 464-1661. **$39-$50**. 3449 De L'Industrie J3G 4S5. From Jct of TCH 20 & Exit 105, E 1 mi on N service rd (De L'Industrie St) (L) 🛶 ⊠

ST-NICOLAS — KOA QUEBEC CITY. ⒶⒶ (418) 831-1813. **$35-$63**. 684 Chemin Olivier G7A 2N6. E-bnd: From Jct of Hwy 20 & Exit 311 (Rte 116), SE 0.1 mi on Arena St to Rte 116, E 0.4 mi to Chemin Olivier (N Service Rd), W 1 mi (R); or W-bnd: From Jct of Hwy 20 & exit 311, N 200 ft on exit rd to Chemin Olivier, W 1 mi (R) 🛶 ⊠ ♿M

ST-PHILIPPE — CAMPING LA CLE DES CHAMPS RV RESORT. (450) 659-3389. **$42-$48**. 415 Montee St-Claude J0L 2K0. From Jct of Hwy 30 & Exit 104 (Rte 104), E 1.7 mi on Rte 104 to Rang St-Raphael, S 2 mi to Montee St-Claude, W 0.5 mi (R) 🏕 🛶 ⊠ ♿M

VALCARTIER — CAMPING VALCARTIER. (418) 844-2200. **$35-$65**. 1860 Boul, Valcartier G0A 4S0. From Jct of Hwy 573 & 40, N 7 mi on Hwy 573 to Rue De Montolieu, E 2 mi to Rte 371, N 6 mi. Follow signs (R) 🏕 🛶 ⊠ ♿M

Saskatchewan

INDIAN HEAD — INDIAN HEAD CAMPGROUND. (855) 695-3635. **$36-$39**. 1100 McKay St S0G 2K0. From Jct of Hwy 1 & Entrance Rd (East Indian Head Access), N 0.2 mi on Entrance Rd (L) 🛶 ⊠

MAPLE CREEK — EAGLE VALLEY PARK CAMPGROUND. (306) 662-2788. **$20-$34**. 4 KM West Jct Of 1 & 21 On Hwy 1 S0N 1N0. From Jct of Trans Cda Hwy 1 & Hwy 21, W 3 mi (4 km) on Tran Cda Hwy 1 (L) 🛶 ⊠

AAA PetBook Reader Questionnaire

We "paws-itively" want to hear from you! Your comments, opinions and suggestions are important to AAA. Please help us to improve the AAA PetBook® by taking a few minutes to complete this simple questionnaire.

> Please mail your completed questionnaire to: AAA PetBook, Mail Stop 64, 1000 AAA Drive, Heathrow, FL 32746-5063
>
> Or, email us your comments at PetBookFeedback@national.aaa.com

1. Where did you purchase the AAA PetBook®?
   ☐ AAA Club _____ (club name)
   ☐ Bookstore _____ (name of bookstore)
   ☐ Online _____ (web site)

2. What specific pet-related information contained in the AAA PetBook is important to you when planning to travel with your pet? (Please check all that apply)
   ☐ Lodgings
   ☐ Campgrounds
   ☐ National Public Lands
   ☐ Attractions
   ☐ Dog Parks
   ☐ Emergency Animal Clinics
   ☐ U.S. / Canada Border Crossing Procedures
   ☐ Traveling by Car
   ☐ Traveling by Air
   ☐ Traveling with Disabilities

3. When traveling with your pet, what additional information would be helpful?
   _____

4. How well does the AAA PetBook® meet your expectations?
   ☐ Exceeds
   ☐ Meets all
   ☐ Meets most
   ☐ Falls below

5. Are you familiar with the annual photo contest at AAA.com/PetBook? ☐ Yes ☐ No

Additional feedback or comments about the AAA PetBook:
   _____
   _____

Which age group are you in?   ☐ Under 25   ☐ 25-34   ☐ 35-44   ☐ 45-54   ☐ 55-64   ☐ 65 +

On average, how many overnight leisure trips do you take a year?
   ☐ None   ☐ One   ☐ Two   ☐ Three or more

How many trips/outings a year include traveling with your pet? _____

What is the average distance traveled? _____

In addition to the AAA PetBook, did you buy any other pet-travel or general travel guides for your trip?   ☐ Yes   ☐ No

If yes, which ones?
   _____
   _____

Optional:
Name (Mr/Mrs/Ms) _____
Address _____
City _____ State _____ Zip _____

Are you a AAA member?   ☐ Yes   ☐ No, If yes, name of AAA club: _____

Thank you for taking the time to complete this questionnaire. We appreciate your feedback.

All information including name and address is for AAA internal use only and will NOT be distributed outside the organization to any third parties.

❀ Pet-Friendly Travel Notes ❀